Historical Common Names

of Great Plains Plants,

with Scientific Names Index

Volume II: Scientific Names Index

Compiled by Elaine Nowick

Zea Books
Lincoln, Nebraska
2015

Title page: *Acorus calamus* L. (Calamus), 1778, by P. J. Buchoz

Historical Common Names of Great Plains Plants, with Scientific Names Index:
Volume II: Scientific Names Index

ISBN 978-1-60962-063-9   hardcover
ISBN 978-1-60962-060-8   paperback
ISBN 978-1-60962-061-5   e-book

Set in Times New Roman types.
Design and composition by Paul Royster.
Illustrations are based on published originals
found online at www.plantillustrations.org

Zea Books are published by the
University of Nebraska–Lincoln Libraries.

Electronic edition (pdf) available online at http://digitalcommons.unl.edu/zeabook/
Print edition can be ordered from http://www.lulu.com/spotlight/unllib

Contents

Eupatorium perfoliatum (Joe Pye weed)
[C.F. Millspaugh, 1892]

Preface

Although the term "common names" occurs in the title of this book, there are relatively few plants known to the majority of people. Many individuals today suffer from "plant blindness" and don't really notice the plant life around them. Some environmentalists look to a past golden age when people were more in tune with the natural world. In the millennia before agriculture, our species and our hominid ancestors survived by hunting and gathering. Being able to recognize edible and poisonous plants would have been a vital skill for them, as it is for all animal species except strict carnivores. It is not known when speech first evolved, but plant names were most likely among the earliest words. As Gilmore (1932) states, "Indigenous peoples always have names for the plants they use and even the ones they don't use but are aware of." Most of these ancient names have been lost in the sands of time.

From the onset of agriculture about 10,000 years ago until the mid-twentieth century, most of the human species survived by farming. Survival came to depend on the few cultivated species, and humankind's attention shifted to those species and their weedy pests. The exceptions were often the herbal practitioners. Among Europeans up until the Middle Ages, and among other peoples around the world, healers were often the most knowledgeable about botany. Even among formally trained medical doctors until quite recently, botany was an integral part of their training. Writers of herbals and pharmacopeias were very concerned that herbal practitioners and herb gatherers be able to identify accurately the correct plant species to be used to treat a specific ailment, and modern editors of ancient herbals can often reliably assign a contemporary scientific name to plants from their descriptions.

The age of exploration greatly accelerated the movement of plant species around the world. The earliest Europeans to arrive in the New World were very interested in the plant species used by the indigenous peoples. Plant species from the Americas began appearing in herbals around the 1600's. Early European settlers often adopted the native names, sometimes in garbled form. The Joe Pye weed (*Eupatorium perfoliatum* L. or *Eupatorium purpureum* L.) is an example. The original Native American name was said to be "jopi." Homesickness may have led some Europeans to give names familiar to them to similar but unrelated plants, such as the Evening-primrose (*Oenothera*) which is not related to the European primrose (*Primula*). Europeans also invented names for the new plants they observed. Some of the earliest botanical explorers in the Americas were sponsored by wealthy Europeans wanting the distinction of owning rare or unusual plants for their gardens and conservatories. Collectors such as John Banister, John and William Bartram, Frederick Pursh, André and François Michaux, and Peer Kalm sent herbarium samples, plants, seeds, and cuttings to nurseries, gardens, and institutions throughout Europe. The proliferation of known types of plants and also of names for them created an awareness of the need for proper identification and a uniform terminology. Common names were often confusing. The same name could be used for several different species and several names could be used for the same species. Plant names for the same species often differed by locality or dialect. Educated people of the time used Latin as their common language and in communicating about plants they used lengthy Latin descriptions. Tournefort, the Bauhins, and others provided detailed but cumbersome descriptions of the new plants species they were cataloging. Linnaeus is generally credited with creating the Latin binomial system. His "Genera Plantarum" published in 1737 and "Species Plantarum" in 1753 serve as the basis for scientific plant names now in use. One of the beauties of the Latin binomial system is that it not only simplifies the Latin descriptions, but also reflects relationships among plant species. All species in the given genus have a close morphological similarity and later research has often revealed genetic similarities that for the most part support these relationships. Often, Linnaeus' scientific names were adapted from the classical Greek or Latin name for the species or a closely related plant, but often were quite arbitrary and may have said little about the named species itself.

For many Great Plains and Western species, scientific names predate common names, at least in European languages, unlike plant species from Europe and eastern North America. The first Europeans to arrive in the Great Plains and the West were the Spanish in the southern range and the French trappers arriving from the north. But even before the Europeans arrived, their influence on the region was being felt. The arrival of the first horses, the descendants of horses escaped from the early Spanish explorers, brought huge cultural changes. Displacements of indigenous people from the East caused waves of war and social disruption to radiate into the Plains and Rocky Mountains. European diseases preceded movement of people and devastated the native tribes. These changes surely would have been accompanied by changes in language referring to plants, disruptions in the passing of knowledge about the uses of plants, and unfortunately loss of knowledge of plant life as long-term residents of the environment were pushed out. Works on ethnobotany and journals of early botanical explorers often recorded native names when they were aware of them. The explorers' journals also sometimes provided Spanish, French, or German names for Great Plains and Western flora. The spelling and tribal designations in this book are as reported in the original work. Later works by anthropologists and ethnobotanists were also consulted for current plant names of Native Americans.

The Lewis and Clark Expedition to explore the northern limits of the Louisiana Purchase ushered in a fifty-year period of government-sponsored scientific surveys of botany, geology, zoology and general natural history in the western territories, inspired by the visionary Thomas Jefferson. Lewis, Clark, and the other journal keepers of the Corps of Discovery recorded native plant names and noted plants they recognized on the way. Closely following Lewis and Clark, were collectors such as Thomas Nuttall, Constantine Rafinesque, and John Bradbury. Travelers such as Josiah Gregg, Henry Marie Brackenridge, and Prince Maximilian were broadly educated and took great interest in natural history and anthropology, noting the plant species they observed and their native uses. Many of Lewis and Clark's species were described after much delay by Frederich Pursh, who also collected botanical samples in the eastern United States. The Lewis and Clark expedition was succeeded by a series of military-led scientific explorations following the courses of the major rivers in the Great Plains and then by the railroad surveys attempting to find the best route to the Pacific by rail. These surveys included botanists, zoologists, and geologists, as well as surveyors.

The Civil War put an end to these surveys, but the Hatch Act passed by Congress in 1862 set in motion an entirely new phase in plant research. The founding of the "People's Universities" put science at the service of the common person. The land grant universities were given a mission not only to perform serious scientific research, but also to translate that research into a form that ordinary farmers could use to improve their lives. The publications of the land grant universities and the cooperative extension services in the Plains states were rich sources of information for this dictionary. The extension agents and university professors were anxious both to identify accurately the species mentioned and to enable the common people to recognize them by using local names for the species.

In the 1800's a number of periodicals dealing with botany were published in the United States, and these were also used as sources of names. In the late 1800's quite a few popular guides to wildflowers were published. As settlers became established in the western United States, some of them became better educated and had more time to spend on activities beyond the basics of life. The appearance of these

botanical guides may also reflect an increasing alienation from the natural world—there is an underlying assumption in these works that the readers would not be familiar with the wildflowers and not have either common or scientific names for them.

It is a myth that each species has one and only one, permanent and unique scientific name. For example, the USDA Plants Database (http://plants.usda.gov/) lists 21 scientific synonyms for *Calamagrostis stricta* ssp. *inexpansa* (northern reedgrass). Linnaeus and his contemporaries believed that species were static and permanently distinct, although the differences might be subtle. Darwin's *On the Origin of Species* was published in 1859; his revolutionary idea was that species changed through time. We now know that species do evolve, and that populations within a species can diverge, and that there are degrees of plant-to-plant variation within a species arising from genetic differences and environmental effects. During the 1700s, when new plants were arriving in Europe at a very fast rate, communications were slow and unreliable, so it is not surprising that some species designations have needed revision. New techniques such as chromosome karyotyping, biochemical analysis, and DNA sequencing have shed further light on taxonomic relations.

One of the great strengths of the binomial system is that there is a mechanism for determining the "correct" name for each species and publishing the accepted name as well as its Latin synonyms. The *International Code of Botanical Nomenclature* as adopted by the International Botanical Congress is updated periodically. Names of new or revised species are created and disseminated in accord with the code. For this work the references used for contemporary Latin names and synonyms unless otherwise noted were: The Plants Database (http://plants.usda.gov) published by the USDA; W3Tropicos (http://www.tropicos.org/) from the Missouri Botanic Gardens; and the International Plant Names Index (http://www.ipni.org/), a joint project of the Royal Botanic Gardens, Kew Gardens, the Harvard University Herbaria, and the Australian National Herbarium.

While scientists were adopting the system of Latin binomials, common names continued to be created and are still invented even today. Latin binomials are the best way for scientists to communicate with one another about plant species, but common names have both interest and value, and there is a great deal of information embedded within common names. They record the relation of humans to a particular plant species, and they are accessible to people who are not formally trained in botany. Some academic researchers had mixed feelings or even hostility towards common names. John Torrey and Asa Gray are considered to be the joint parents of American botany. In one of his botanical reports attached to the railroad surveys, Torrey condescendingly states, "There is, however, little dependence to be placed on the common names of plants, especially among rude and ignorant people." Nathaniel Britton and Addison Brown, on the other hand, saw no antagonism between common and scientific names and felt that, "they [popular names] are invaluable; not for science, but for the common intelligence, and the appreciation and enjoyment of the plant world."

There have been occasional efforts to standardize common names. The Pharmacopeias and Dispensatories used conventionalized vocabularies usually in English for the plant species used as medicinals. Several associations representing the nursery industry, landscape architects, florists and other horticulturists formed the American Joint Committee on Horticultural Nomenclature. This committee issued several editions of standardized plant names. In the second edition of *Standardized Plant Names*, Harlan Kelsey, Secretary of the American Joint Committee on Horticultural Nomenclature recognizes the value of common names while acknowledging their limitations.

> "In this 1942 edition of STANDARDIZED PLANT NAMES the editors have adopted what seemed the best common names for plants and plant products so far as was feasible at this time. Many thousands of new names were supplied for plants that had no common names, or with common names wholly unsuitable or more properly belonging to other plants.
>
> "In thousands of other cases, especially of plants new or little known, common names are missing, for an appropriate name suggests itself usually only on intimate acquaintance with the particular plant or with its history."

Some botanists have included English names in their works, more rightly called vernacular names than common names, since they are often direct translations of the Latin scientific name. Britton and Brown, Thomas Meehan, and others admit that they made up likely common names for species when they didn't know of one. As Liberty Hyde Bailey states, "One cannot 'make' common names, although one may coin an English name. A name is not common until it comes into general use. Most plants do not possess true common names."[1] Nevertheless, in this work there has been no attempt to distinguish between vernacular and true common names.

What's in a common name? Why bother with names that may be confusing or misleading and in some cases racist,

sexist, or otherwise insensitive? As John Smith (1882) says "With regard to the adoption of common, or what are termed popular, names, it is unfortunate that many of them are vulgar and undignified, and derogatory to the useful, pretty, and curious plants which they designate…" In their defense, common names often reflect knowledge of a plant species' ecology. Common names may also refer to the appearance of the plant, its taste, or its use. While common names may refer to the function of a plant in relation to humans, rather than to anything about the plant itself, this still may be more telling than a scientific name given as a tribute to a person who may have had no relation either to the named species or the region. Scientific names have also rather arbitrarily been given for a species' resemblance to another species more familiar to the namer. Yet other scientific names are based on classical names for either different plant species or unknown species. No one would argue for a preference for common names in the scientific literature, but in a time when humans are becoming increasingly "plant-blind" and detached from the natural world, encouraging the use of current common names and even creation of new ones may encourage humans to look again at the ultimate source of all their nourishment and of even the air they breathe.

It is hoped that this reference work will be of use to historians, writers of historical fiction or natural history, restorationists, and the general public. This dictionary was compiled from first person accounts of early explorers and plant collectors. When they were available or when the original writer did not include a scientific name, later editions with appropriate footnotes were used. Other sources include floras, extension publications, government reports, botanical periodicals, earlier common name compilations, wildflower guides, and other publications. Dates and locations are included when appropriate. The dates are the reporting dates since it would not be possible to accurately determine when a name came into existence or became archaic. Explanations for the common names are included if they are known. Common name spellings are according to Kartesz and Thieret (1991). Alternate spelling are enclosed in parentheses. Readers are encouraged to send additions to these names if they are aware of them to the author for inclusion in later editions. Please include as much information as possible.

Elaine Nowick
Cañon City, Colorado
April 2014

1. Bailey, L.H. 1933. *How plants get their names* New York: MacMillan Co.

Echinacea purpurea [Rudbeckia purpurea] (Purple coneflower, Red sunflower)
[W.P.C. Barton, 1823]

Acknowledgments

This work would not have been possible without the online availability of many sources consulted, including the Biological Heritage Library and several taxonomic databases among others. In the past, consulting many of these sources would have involved traveling to archives where they are housed. Now they are available to everyone. I also am especially grateful to the Wyoming Heritage Center and the University of Nebraska Library Archives for access to their materials.

Sue Ann Gardner, Linnea Fredrickson, and Paul Royster of University of Nebraska Libraries Office of Scholarly Communications have provided patient editing and generous preparation of the online and print editions. This work was begun as a sabbatical project funded by the University of Nebraska and I am grateful for continuing support in hosting the electronic version.

Taraxacum officinale (Aphaka, Blow-ball, Cankerwort, Caput monach, Couronne de moine, Dandelion, Doonhead, Grunsel, Irish daisy, Lion's tooth, Milk gowan, Monk's head, One-o'clock, Papencruitz, Pissabed, Puffball, Swine's snout, Wild endive, Witch gowan) [Martin Cilenšek, 1892]

References

1. Rydberg, Per Axel. 1932. *Flora of the Prairie and Plains of Central North America*. Lancaster, Pa: Science Press Printing Co.

2. Gray, Asa, revised and extended by L.H. Bailey. 1895. *Field, Forest, and Garden Botany: A Simple introduction to the common plants of the United States East of the 100th Meridian, both wild and cultivated*. New York: American Book Company.

3. Great Plains Flora Association. 1977. *Atlas of the Flora of the Great Plains*. Coordinator, R.L. McGregor; Editor, T.M. Barkley. Ames: Iowa State University Press.

4. Macgregor, Ronald L., T.M. Barkley, and the Great Plains Flora Association. 1986. *Flora of the Great Plains*. University Press of Kansas.

5. Britton, N., and Addison Brown. 1913. *An Illustrated Flora of the Northern United States and Canada from Newfoundland to the Parallel of the Southern Boundary of Virginia and from the Atlantic Ocean Westward to the 102d Meridian*. New York: Dover Publications, 1970.

6. Millspaugh, Charles F. 1974. *American Medicinal Plants; An Illustrated and Descriptive Guide to Plants Indigenous to and Naturalized in the United States which are Used in Medicine*. New York: Dover Publ.

7. Rafinesque, C.S. 1828. *Medical Flora or Manual of the Medical Botany of the United States of North America. Containing a selection of above 100 figures and descriptions of medical plants, with their names, qualities, properties, history, &c.: and notes or remarks on nearly 500 equivalent substitutes*. Philadelphia: Atkinson & Alexander.

8. Marshall, Humphry. 1785. *Arbustum Americanum: The American Grove or, and Alphabetical Catalogue of Forest Trees and Shrubs, Native of the American United States, Arranged According to the Linnaean System*. Containing, the particular distinguishing Characters of each Genus, with plain simple and familiar Descriptions of the Manner of Growth, Appearance, etc. of their several Species and Varieties. Also some hints of their uses in Medicine, Dyes, and Domestic Oeconomy (Facsimile of the edition of 1785), and *Catalogue Alphabetique des Arbres et Arbrisseaux* (Facsimile of the edition of 1788). New York: Hafner Publishing Co. 1967.

9. Charles E. Bessey. Papers (1865-1915). University of Nebraska-Lincoln.

10. Nuttall, Thomas. 1818. *The Genera of North American Plants and a Catalogue of the Species to the Year 1817*. Philadelphia: D. Heart.

11. Bessey, Charles E. 1888. *The Grasses and Forage Plants of Nebraska*. Annual Report of the State Board of Agriculture for the year 1887, pages 140-172. Prepared by Robert W. Furnas, Secretary Nebraska State Board of Agriculture Lincoln Neb: State Journal Company Printers.

12. Nuttall, Thomas. 1821. *Journal of the Travels into the Arkansa Territory during the Year 1819 with Occasional Observations on the Manners of the Aborigines*. Philadelphia: Thos. H. Palmer.

13. Gray, Asa. 1849. *The Genera of the Plants of the United States*, illustrated by figures and analyses from nature by Isaac Sprague. New York: George P. Putnam.

14. Smith, John. 1882. *Dictionary of Popular Names of the Plants which Furnish the Natural and Acquired Wants of Man, in All Matters of Domestic and General Economy: Their History, Products, & Uses*. London: Macmillan and Co.

15. Gray, Asa, Sereno Watson continued, and edited by Benjamin Lincoln Robinson. 1895. *Synoptical Flora of North America*. New York: American Book Co.

16. Nuttall, Thomas. 1837. Collections towards a Flora of the Territory of Arkansas. *Transactions of the American Philosophical Society*, new series. Volume 5, part 6, pages 139-203.

17. *Journal of André Michaux, 1793-1796*. 1889. Source: Englished from the original French, appearing in American Philosophical Society, *Proceedings*, 1889, pages 91-101, 114-140, from Reuben Gold Thwaites. 1904. Early Western Travels 1748-1846.

18. Michaux, François André. 1904. *Travels to the West of the Alleghany Mountains*. Reprint from London edition 1805 from Reuben Gold Thwaites. Early Western Travels 1748-1846.

19. Eaton, Amos, and John Wright. 1840. *North American Botany Comprising the Native and Common Cultivated Plants North of Mexico: Genera Arranged According*

to the Artificial and Natural Methods. Troy, New York: Elias Gates.

20. Michaux, François André. 1857. *North American Sylva or a Description of the Forest Trees of the United States, Canada, and Nova Scotia Considered Particularly with Respect to Their Use in the Arts and Their Introduction to Commerce to which is Added a Description of the Most Useful of the European Forest Trees.* Translated from the French of François André Michaux. Philadelphia: D. Rice & A. N. Hart.

21. Edith S. and Frederic E. Clements papers, 1893-1967. Accession Number 1678, Box Number 36, Folder Number 13, American Heritage Center, University of Wyoming Laramie, Wyoming.

22. Edith S. and Frederic E. Clements papers, 1893-1967. Accession Number 1678, Box Number 48, Folder Number 1, American Heritage Center, University of Wyoming Laramie, Wyoming.

23. Graustein, Jeannette E. (editor). 1950/51. Nuttall's travels into the Old Northwest: An unpublished 1810 diary. *Cronica Botanic*, Volume 14(1/2).

24. Nuttall, Thomas. 1817. Observation on the genus Eriogonum, and the natural order Polygonae of Jussieu. *Journal of the Academy of Natural Sciences of Philadelphia*, Volume 1, number 3: 24-37.

25. Nuttall, Thomas, and Nathaniel J. Wyeth. 1834. A catalogue of a collection of plants made chiefly in the valleys of the Rocky Mountains or Northern Andes, towards the sources of the Columbia River, by Mr. Nathaniel B. Wyeth. *Journal of the Academy of Natural Sciences Philadelphia*, Volume 7: [5]-60, 8 leaves of plates.

26. Torrey, John. 1826. *A compendium of the Flora of the Northern and Middle States.* New York: S.B. Collins, Selected Americana from Sabin.

27. Bradbury, John. 1986. *Travels in the Interior of America in the Years 1809, 1810, and 1811.* Bison book reprint. Originally published London: Sherwood, Neely, and Jones, 1819.

28. Fremont, J.C. Brevet, Col. 1850. *The Exploring Expedition to the Rocky Mountains, Oregon, and California to which is Added a Description of the Physical Geography of California with Recent Notices of the Gold Region from the Latest and most Authentic Sources.*

29. Pursh, Frederick. 1869. *Journal of a Botanical Excursion in the Northeastern Parts of the States of Pennsylvania and New York during the Year 1807.* Reprinted in 1969 by Ira J. Friedman, Inc. Port Washington, Long Island, New York, Empire State Historical Publications Series, number 73.

30. Josiah, Gregg. 1954. *Commerce of the Prairies*, edited by Max L. Moorhead. Norman, Oklahoma: University of Oklahoma Press. Originally published in 1844.

31. *Diary & Letters of Josiah Gregg: Southwestern Enterprises, 1840-1847.* Edited by Maurice Garland Fulton. Norman, Oklahoma: University of Oklahoma Press, 1941.

32. Rydberg, Per Axel. 1895. *Botanical Exploration of Central Nebraska.* Thesis presented by Per Axel Rydberg for the degree of Master of Arts, University of Nebraska, 1895.

33. Royal Horticultural Society. 1914. *Journal Kept by David Douglas during his Travels in North America, 1823-1827, Together with a Particular Description of Thirty-Three Species of American Oaks and Eighteen Species of Pinus.* London: William Wesley & Son.

34. Maximilian, Alexander Philipp, Prince. 1843. *Travels in the Interior of North America in the Years 1832, 1833, and 1834.* London: [s.n.], 1844.

35. Moulton, Gary E. (editor). 1986. *The Journals of the Lewis & Clark Expedition.* Lincoln: University of Nebraska Press.

36. Wislizenus, F.A. 1912. *A Journey to the Rocky Mountains in the Year 1830.* St. Louis: Missouri Historical Society.

37. Gilmore, Melvin R. *Uses of Plants by the Indians of the Missouri River Region.* Reprint of the 1919 edition. Lincoln: University of Nebraska Press.

38. James, Edwin (compiler). 1823. *Account of an Expedition from Pittsburgh to the Rocky Mountains Performed in the Years 1819 and '20* by order of the Hon. J.C. Calhoun, Sec'y of War, under the command of Major Stephen H. Long, from the notes of Major Long, Mr. T. Say, and other gentlemen of the exploring party. Philadelphia: H.C. Carey and I. Lea.

39. Brackenridge, Henri Marie. 1814. *Views of Louisiana, Together with a Journal of a Voyage up the Missouri River in 1811.* Chicago: Quadrangle Books, [1962].

40. Densmore, Frances. 1928. *Uses of Plants by the Chippewa*, pages 275-397 in *Forty-fourth Annual Report of the Bureau of Ethnology to the Secretary of the Smithsonian Institution*, 1926-1927. Washington: U.S. Government Printing Office.

41. *The America of 1750: Peters Kalm's Travels in North America*, the English edition of 1770. New York: Dover Publications, Inc. 1937, 1964.

42. Green, Jacob. 1814. *An Address on the Botany of the United States*, delivered before the Society for the Promotion of Useful Arts. To which is added *A Catalogue of Plants Indigenous to the State of New York*. Albany: Websters and Skinners.

43. Williams, Mentor L. (editor). 1992. *Schoolcraft's Narrative Journal of Travels through the Northwestern Regions of the United States extending from Detroit through the Great Chain of American Lakes to the Sources of the Mississippi River in the Year 1820.* East Lansing: Michigan State University Press.

44. Carroll, H. Bailey (editor). 1941. *Gúadal p'a: The Journal of J.W. Abert, from Bent's Fort to St. Louis in 1845.* Canyon, Texas: The Panhandle-Plains Historical Society.

45. Beal, W.J. 1896. *Grasses of North America.* New York: Henry Holt and Co.

46. Pickering, Charles. 1879. *Chronological History of Plants: Man's Record of his Own Existence Illustrated through their Names, Uses, and Companionship.* Boston: Little, Brown & Co.

47. Owen, Daid Dale, et al. 1852. *Report of a Geological Survey of Wisconsin, Iowa, and Minnesota; and Incidentally of a Portion of Nebraska Territory.* Philadelphia: Lippincott, Grambo & Co.

48. Welch, J. Milton. 1882/92. The Medical Flora of Kansas or, the Medical Plants Indigenous in That State. *Transactions of the National Eclectic Medical Association.* http://www.henriettesherbal.com/eclectic/journals/net-1882-kansas.html (Mar. 10, 2006).

49. Felter, Harvey Wickes, and John Uri Lloyd. 1898. *King's American Dispensatory.* Scanned version, 1999-2005. Henriette Kress, copyright. http://www.ibiblio.org/herbmed/eclectic/kings/main.html (August 9, 2005).

50. USDA, NRCS. 2014. The PLANTS Database. http://plants.usda.gov (March 31, 2014). Greensboro, North Carolina: National Plant Data Team.

51. *Selected North Dakota and Minnesota Range Plants.* http://www.ext.nodak.edu/extpubs/ansci/range/eb69-1.htm#North (January 16, 2004).

52. Ellingwood, Finley. 1919. *American Materia Medica.* Scanned version copyright 2001-2004, Michael Moore. http://www.ibiblio.org/herbmed/eclectic/ellingwood/main.html (June 2, 2004).

53. Felter, Harvey Wickes. 1922. *The Eclectic Materia Medica, Pharmacology and Therapeutics.* http://www.ibiblio.org/herbmed/eclectic/felter/main.html (June 7, 2004).

54. Petersen, Fred J. 1905. *Materia Medica and Clinical Therapeutics.* http://www.ibiblio.org/herbmed/eclectic/petersen/main.html (June 9, 2004).

55. Council of the Pharmaceutical Society of Great Britain. 1911. *British Pharmaceutical Codex.* http://www.ibiblio.org/herbmed/eclectic/bpc1911/main.html (June 10, 2004).

56. Pammel, L.H., and J.B. Weems. 1901. *Grasses of Iowa.* Ames, Iowa: Iowa Geological Survey, *Bulletin* No. 1.

57. Sayre, Lucius E. 1917. *A Manual of Organic Materia Medica and Pharmacognosy.* http://www.ibiblio.org/herbmed/eclectic/sayre/main.html (June 22, 2004).

58. Cook, William, 1869. *Physiomedical Dispensatory.* http://www.ibiblio.org/herbmed/eclectic/cook/cook.htm (June 23, 2004).

59. Lloyd, John Uri. 1911. *History of the Vegetable Drugs of the Pharmacopoeia of the United States.* http://www.ibiblio.org/herbmed/eclectic/lloyd-hist/main.html (June 27, 2004).

60. Potter, Samuel O.L. 1902. *Compendium of Materia Medica, Therapeutics, and Prescription Writing.* Scanned version, copyright 2000-2004, Henriette Kress. http://www.ibiblio.org/herbmed/eclectic/potter-comp/main.html (June 29, 2004).

61. Scudder, John M. 1870. *Specific Medication and Specific Medicines.* Scanned version copyright, 1999-2004, Henriette Kress. http://www.ibiblio.org/herbmed/eclectic/spec-med/main.html (June 30, 2004).

62. Blatchley, W.S. 1912. *Indiana Weed Book.* Indianapolis, Indiana: Nature Publishing Co.

63. Fitzpatrick, T.J. 1899. *Manual of the Flowering Plants of Iowa.* Privately published.

64. Harding, A.R. 1908. *Ginseng and Other Medicinal Plants: A Book of Valuable Information for Growers as well as Collectors of Medicinal Roots, Barks, Leaves, etc.* Columbus, Ohio: A. R. Harding.

65. Bruner, W.E. 1931. Vegetation of Oklahoma. *Ecological Monographs*, Volume 1, number 2: 98-188.

66. Flint, Charles L. 1903. *Grasses and Forage Plants: A Practical Treatise.* Revised edition. Boston: Lee and Shepard Publishers.

67. Hackel, Eduard. 1890. *The True Grasses.* Translated from *Die naturlichen pflanzenfamilies* by F. Lamson-Scribner and Effie A. Southworth. New York: Henry Holt and Co.

68. Clarke, Geo. H., and M. Oscar Malte. 1913. *Fodder and Pasture Plants.* Published by direction of The Honourable Martin Burrell, Minister of Agriculture. Ottawa: Government Printing Bureau.

69. Henkel, Alice. 1904. *Weeds Used in Medicine. Farmers' Bulletin,* number 188. U.S. Department of Agriculture. Washington: Government Printing Office.

70. Dewey, Lyster H. 1895. *Weeds, and How to Kill Them. Farmers' Bulletin,* number 28. U.S. Department of Agriculture. Washington: Government Printing Office.

71. Chesnut, V.K. 1898. *Thirty Poisonous Plants of the United States. Farmers' Bulletin*, number 86. U.S. Department of Agriculture. Washington: Government Printing Office.

72. Greene, Wesley. 1907. Plants of Iowa: A Preliminary List of the Native and Introduced Plants of the State, Not under Cultivation. *Bulletin of the State Horticultural Society*. Des Moines: Bishard Brothers Printers.

73. Bergen, Francis D. 1892. Popular American Plant Names. *Botanical Gazette*, Volume 17, number 6: 361-380.

74. Bergen, Francis D. 1893. Popular American Plant Names II. *Botanical Gazette*, Volume 18, number 11: 20-427.

75. Bergen, Fannie D. 1894. Popular American Plant Names III. *Botanical Gazette*, Volume 19, number 11: 429-444. Informant for grass is Charles Bessey.

76. Bergen, Fannie D. 1896. Popular American Plant Names IV. *Botanical Gazette*, Volume 22, number 6: 473-487. Names marked with (W) come from Williamson's *History of Maine*.

77. Bergen, Fannie D. 1898. Popular American plant names V. *Botanical Gazette*, Volume 26, number 4: 247-252.

78. Bergen, Fannie D. 1898. Popular American Plant Names VI. *Botanical Gazette*, Volume 26, number 4: 253-258.

79. Hayward, Sylvanus. 1891. Popular Names of American Plants. *Journal of American Folklore*, Volume 4, number 13: 147-150.

80. Kay, George F., and James H. Lees. 1913. *The Weed Flora of Iowa*. Iowa Geologic Survey, *Bulletin*, number 4. Des Moines: Iowa Geological Survey.

81. Hitchcock, A.S. 1951. *Manual of the grasses of the United States*. Second edition, revised by Agnes Chase. New York: Dover, reprinted in 1971. Originally published as USDA *Miscellaneous Publication*, number 200.

82. Pammel, L.H., and Charlotte M. King. 1930. *Honey plants of Iowa*. Iowa Geological Survey, *Bulletin*, number 7. Des Moines: Iowa Geological Survey.

83. Kurz, Rudolph Freidrich. 1937. *Journal of Rudolph Friedrich Kurz: An Account of His Experiences among Fur Traders and American Indians on the Mississippi and the Upper Missouri Rivers during the Years 1846-1852*. Translated by Myrtis Jarrell, edited by J.N.B. Hewitt. Lincoln, Nebraska: Bison Books, University of Nebraska.

84. Meehan, Thomas. 1880. *Native Ferns and Flowers of the United States*. Philadelphia: American Natural History Publications Co. Ltd.

85. Over, William H. 1932. *Flora of South Dakota: An Illustrated Check-List of Flowering Plants, Shrubs, and Trees of South Dakota*. Vermillion, South Dakota: University of South Dakota.

86. Meehan, Thomas. 1878. *Native Flowers and Ferns of the United States in Their Botanical, Horticultural, and Popular Aspects*. Boston: L. Prang and Co.

87. Vasey, George. 1884. *Agricultural Grasses of the United States*. Washington: Government Printing Office.

88. Vasey, George. 1885. *A Descriptive Catalogue of the Grasses of the United States, including Especially the Grass Collections at the New Orleans Exposition Made by the U.S. Department of Agriculture, and the State Exhibit of Grasses*, with notes on such species as are more or less employed in agriculture, or deserving of trial for cultivation. Washington: Gibson Bros., Printers and Bookbinders.

89. Tabeau, Pierre Antoine, 1755-1820. 1939. *Tabeau's Narrative of Loisel's Expedition to the Upper Missouri*, edited by Annie Heloise Abel, translated from the French by Rose Abel Wright. Norman: University of Oklahoma Press.

90. Fernald, C.H. 1885. *Grasses of Maine*. Augusta: Sprague & Son, Printer to the State.

91. Pammel, L.H. 1911. *A Manual of Poisonous Plant: Chiefly of Eastern North America*, with brief notes on economic and medicinal plants, and numerous illustrations. Cedar Rapids, Iowa: Torch Press.

92. Hobbs, Charles E. 1876. *C.E. Hobbs' Botanical Hand-Book of Common Local, English, Botanical and Pharmacopoeial Names Arranged in Alphabetical Order, of Most of the Crude Vegetable Drugs, etc. in Common Use*. Boston: Chas. C. Roberts.

93. Winter, John Mack. 1936. *An Analysis of the Flowering Plants of Nebraska with Keys to the Families, Genera, and Species, and with Notes Concerning Their Occurrence, Range, and Frequency within the State*. Conservation and Survey Division, University of Nebraska, contribution from the Botanical Survey of Nebraska, New Series, number X. Printed by the authority of the State of Nebraska.

94. Lamson-Scribner, F. 1897-1901. *American Grasses*. Washington: U.S. Government Printing Office.

95. Petersen, N.F. 1911. *Flora of Nebraska: A List of the Conifers and Flowering Plants of the State with Keys for their Determination*. 2nd edition. Plainview, Nebraska: Published by the author.

96. Carleton, M.A. 1891. Observations on the Native Plants of Oklahoma Territory and Adjacent Districts. *Contributions from the U.S. National Herbarium*, Volume 1: 220-232.

97. Stemen, Thomas R., and W. Stanley Myers. 1937. *Oklahoma Flora*. Oklahoma City, Oklahoma: Harlow Publishing Co. 706 pgs.

98. Sandoz, Flora. 1926. Flora Sandoz collection. Manuscript & archival materials. Chadron State University Herbarium.

99. Prier, C.W. 1923. Systematic List of the Grasses Collected near Norman in the Fall of 1922. *Proceedings of the Oklahoma Academy of Science* Volume 3: 85-87.

100. Goyne, Minetta Altgelt. 1991. *A Life among the Texas Flora: Ferdinand Lindheimer's Letters to George Engelmann*. College Station: Texas A&M University Press, 236 pages.

101. Blankenship, J. W. 1905. *Native Economic Plants of Montana*. Montana Agricultural College Experiment Station, *Bulletin*, Volume 56, 38 pages.

102. Mooney, James. 1981. *Sacred Formulas of the Cherokees*. Smithsonian Institution, Bureau of American Ethnology, *Seventh Annual Report for 1885-1886*, pages 301-397.

103. Palmer, Edward. 1871. *Food Products of the North American Indians*. U.S. Department of Agriculture, *Report of the Commission for 1870*, pages 404-428.

104. Havard, V. 1896. Drink Plants of the North American Indians. *Bulletin of the Torrey Botanical Club*, Volume 23, number 2: 33-46.

105. Gilmore, Melvin R. 1932. Some Chippewa Uses of Plants. *Papers of the Michigan Academy of Science, Arts, and Letters*, Volume 17: 119-143.

106. Pellet, Frank C. 1930. *American Honey Plants: Together with Those which Are of Special Value to the Beekeeper as Sources of Pollen*. 3rd edition. Hamilton, Illinois: *American Bee Journal*, 419 pages.

107. Hedrick, U.P. 1919. *Sturtevant's Notes on Edible Plants. Report of the New York Agricultural Experiment Station for the Year 1919*, Part 2. Albany: J.B. Lyon, State Printers.

108. Havard, V. 1878. *Botanical Outlines of the Country Marched over by the Seventh United States Cavalry, during the Summer of 1877*. Report of the chief of Engineers App. QQ, pages 1,681-1,687.

109. Bailey, L.H. 1949. *Manual of Cultivated Plants, Most Commonly Grown in the Continental United States and Canada*. New York: MacMillan Co.

110. De Candolle, Alphonse. 1964. *Origin of Cultivated Plants*. Reprint of 2nd edition, 1886. New York: Hafner Publishing Co.

111. Wilcox, E. Mead, George K.K. Link, and Venus W. Pool. 1915. *Handbook of Nebraska Grasses, with Illustrated Keys for Their Identification, Together with a General Account of Their Structure and Economic Importance. Bulletin of the Agricultural Experiment Station of Nebraska* V, XXVII, Article V.

112. McComb, H.A. 1937. *Trees, Shrubs, and Vines at the North Platte Experimental Substation. Bulletin of the Agricultural Experiment Station of Nebraska*, number 310, *Bulletin*, number 42 of the North Platte Experimental Substation.

113. Bessey, Charles E. 1890. *Preliminary Report on the Native Trees and Shrubs of Nebraska. Bulletin of the Agricultural Experiment Station of Nebraska*, number 18, Volume IV, article 4. Lincoln, Nebraska: University of Nebraska.

114. Bessey, Charles E. 1894. *Preliminary List of the Honey-Producing Plants of Nebraska. Bulletin of the Agricultural Experiment Station of Nebraska*, number 40, Volume VII, article IV. Lincoln, Nebraska: State Journal Company Printers.

115. Keim, F.D., G.W. Beadle, and A.L. Frolik. 1932. *Identification of the More Important Prairie Hay Grasses of Nebraska by Their Vegetative Characters*. Agricultural Experiment Station, *Research Bulletin*, number 65.

116. Frolik, A.L., and F.D. Keim. 1958. *Common Native Grasses of Nebraska*. Nebraska Agricultural Experiment Station, *Circular*, number 59.

117. Sanborn, C.E., and E.E. Scholl. 1908. *Texas Honey Plants*. Texas Agricultural Experiment Stations, *Bulletin* number 102.

118. Pittuck, B.C. 1898. *Grasses and Forage Plants*. Texas Agricultural Experiment Station *Bulletin*, number 46.

119. Featherly, Henry Ira. 1938. *Grasses of Oklahoma. Technical Bulletin*, Oklahoma Agricultural Experiment Station, number 3.

120. Gruchy, James H. B. 1938. *A preliminary Study of the Larger Aquatic Plants of Oklahoma with Special Reference to Their Value in Fish Culture*. Oklahoma Agricultural and Mechanical College, *Technical Bulletin*, number 4.

121. Munson, Patrick J. 1981. Contributions to Osage and Lakota Ethnobotany. *Plains Anthropologist*, Volume 93: 229-240.

122. Cory, V.L., and H.B. Parks. 1937. *Catalogue of the Flora of the State of Texas*. Texas Agricultural Experiment Station, *Bulletin*, number 550.

123. Torrey, John. 1856. Botanical Report. *Explorations and Surveys for a Railroad Route from the Mississippi River to the Pacific Ocean*. War Department. Routes in California to connect with the route near the thirty-fifth and thirty-second parallels, and route near the thirty-second parallel, between the Rio Grande and Pimas villages,

explored by Lieutenant John G. Parke, Corps of Topographical engineers in 1854 and 1855. Reports of Explorations and to aecertain the most practicable and economical route for a railroad from the Mississippi River to the Pacific Ocean made under the direction of the secretary of War in 1852-1856, according to the Acts of Congress of March 3, 1853, May 31, 1854, and August 6, 1854. Volume VII.

124. Conner, A.B. 1937. *Valuable Plants Native to Texas.* Texas Agricultural Experiment Station, *Bulletin*, number 551.

125. Gates, Frank. 1930. *Principal Poisonous Plants in Kansas.* Kansas State Agricultural Experiment Station, *Technical Bulletin*, number 25.

126. Stevens, O.A. 1933. *Poisonous Plants and Plant Products.* North Dakota Agricultural Experiment Station, *Bulletin*, number 265.

127. Steven, O.A. 1933. *Wild Flowers of North Dakota.* North Dakota Agricultural Experiment Station, *Bulletin*, number 269.

128. Barnett, H.L. 1933. *Some Edible and Poisonous Mushrooms of North Dakota.* North Dakota Agricultural Experiment Station, *Bulletin*, number 270.

129. Departments of Chemistry and Botany. 1894. *Native and Introduced Forage Plants.* South Dakota Agricultural College and Experiment Station, *Bulletin*, number 40.

130. Williams, Thomas A. 1895. *Native Trees and Shrubs of South Dakota.* South Dakota Agricultural College and Experiment Station, *Bulletin*, number 43.

131. Saunders, D.A. 1899. *Ferns and Flowering Plants of South Dakota.* South Dakota Agricultural Experiment Station, *Bulletin*, number 64.

132. Whipple, Lieut. A.W., Thomas Eubank, and Prof. William W. Turner. 1855. Report upon the Indian Tribes. *Explorations and Surveys for a Railroad Route from the Mississippi River to the Pacific Ocean Route Near the Thirty-Fifth Parallel*, under the command of Lieut. A.W. Whipple Topographical Engineers in 1853 and 1854, Volume 3.

133. Van Es, L., and L.R. Waldron. 1903. *Some Stock Poisoning Plants of North Dakota.* North Dakota Agricultural Experiment Station, *Bulletin*, number 58.

134. Copple, R.F., and A.E. Aldous. 1932. *Identification of Certain Native and Naturalized Grasses by Their Vegetative Characters.* Kansas State Agricultural Experiment Station, *Technical Bulletin*, number 32.

135. Fisher, R.W. 1910. *Ornamental Trees and Shrubs for Montana.* Montana Agricultural Experiment Station, *Bulletin*, number 80.

136. Hansen, N.E. 1930. *Evergreens in South Dakota.* South Dakota Agricultural Experiment Station, *Bulletin*, number 254.

137. Hansen, N.E. 1931. *Ornamental Trees of South Dakota.* South Dakota State Agricultural Experiment Station, *Bulletin*, number 260.

138. Olmsted, Frederick Law, Frederick V. Coville, and Harlan P. Kelsey. 1923. *Standardized Plant Names.* Salem, Massachusetts: American Joint Committee on Horticultural Nomenclature.

139. Smith, E.C., and L.W. Durrell. 1944. *Sedges and Rushes of Colorado (Grass-Like Plants).* Colorado Agricultural Experiment Station, *Technical Bulletin*, number 32.

140. Harrington, H.D., and L.W. Durrell. 1944. *Key to Some Colorado Grasses in Vegetative Condition.* Colorado Agricultural Experiment Station, *Technical Bulletin*, number 33.

141. Nelson, Aven. 1899. *Some Native Forage Plants for Alkali Soils.* Wyoming Agricultural Experiment Station, *Bulletin*, number 42.

142. Nelson, Aven. 1902. *Native Vines in Wyoming Homes.* Wyoming Agricultural Experiment Station, *Bulletin*, number 50.

143. Nowosad, F.S., D.E. Newton Swales, and W.G. Dore. 1936. *Identification of Certain Native and Naturalized Hay and Pasture Grasses by Their Vegetative Characters.* MacDonald College, *Technical Bulletin*, number 16.

144. Hitchcock, A.S., and G.L. Clothier. 1899. *Native Agricultural Grasses of Kansas.* Kansas State Agricultural Experiment Station, *Bulletin*, number 87.

145. Hitchcock, A.S., and Geo. L. Clothier. 1897. *Kansas Weeds.* IV. *Fruits and Seeds.* Kansas State Agricultural Experiment Station, *Bulletin*, number 66.

146. Reitz, Louis P., and H.E. Morris. 1939. *Important Grasses and Other Common Plants on Montana Ranges.* Montana State Agricultural Experiment Station, *Bulletin*, number 375.

147. Bigelow, J.M. 1856. Report on the botany of the expedition. *Explorations and Surveys for a Railroad Route from the Mississippi River to the Pacific Ocean.* War Department. Route near the thirty-fifth parallel explored by Lieutenant A. W. Whipple, topographical engineers in 1853 and 1854, Volume 4.

148. Durrell, L.W., and I.E. Newsom. 1939. *Colorado's Poisonous and Injurious plants.* Colorado State Experiment Station, *Bulletin*, number 455.

149. Wooton, E.O. 1904. *Native Ornamental Plants of New Mexico*. New Mexico Agricultural Experiment Station, *Bulletin*, number 51.

150. Wooton, E.O. 1894. *New Mexico Weeds*. New Mexico Agricultural Experiment Station, *Bulletin*, number 13.

151. Wooton, E.O. 1896. *Some New Mexico Forage Plants*. New Mexico Agricultural Experiment Station, *Bulletin*, number 18.

152. Wooton, E.O., and Paul C. Standley. 1912. *Grasses and Grass-Like plants of New Mexico*. New Mexico Agricultural Experiment Station, *Bulletin*, number 81.

153. Wooton, E.O. 1913. *Trees and Shrubs of New Mexico*. New Mexico Agricultural Experiment Station, *Bulletin*, number 87.

154. Torrey, John. 1857. *Descriptions of Plants Collected along the Route, by W.P. Blake, and at the Mouth of the Gila*. Article VII in Lieutenant R.S. Williamson. Report of Explorations in California for Railroad Routes to connect with the routes near the 35th and 32d parallels of north latitude. Volume 5 in *Explorations and Surveys for a Railroad Route from the Mississippi River to the Pacific Ocean*.

155. American Joint Committee on Horticultural Nomenclature. 1942. *Standardized Plant Names*. Second edition. Harlan P. Kelsey and William A. Dayton (editors). Harrisburg, Pennsylvania: J. Horace McFarland Co.

156. Clute, Willard N. 1923. *American Plant Names*. Second edition. Joliet, Illinois: Willard N. Clute & Co.

157. Stuhr, Ernst T. 1929. *Native Drug Plants of Nebraska*. Corvallis, Oregon: School of Pharmacy, Oregon State University.

158. Lyons, A.B. 1900. *Plant Names, Scientific and Popular*. Detroit: Nelson, Baker & Co.

159. *The International Plant Names Index* (2012). Published on the Internet, http://www.ipni.org [accessed April 5, 2014].

160. Cooper, J.G. 1860. *Botanical Report*. In: *Explorations and Surveys for a Railroad Route from the Mississippi River to the Pacific Ocean*. Volume 12, part 2. Route near the forty-seventh and forty-ninth parallels, explored by I.I. Stevens, Governor of Washington Territory in 1853-55. Washington: A.O.P. Nicholson, Printer.

161. Newberry, J.S. 1857. *Botanical Report*. In: *Explorations and Surveys for a Railroad Route from the Mississippi River to the Pacific Ocean*. Volume 6. Routes in California and Oregon explored by Lieut. R.S. Williamson, Corps of Topographical Engineers and Lieut. Henry L. Abbot, Corps of Topographical Engineers in 1855. Washington: A.O.P. Nicholson, Printer.

162. Woodward, Marcus. 1969. *Leaves from Gerard's Herball*. New York: Dover Publications, 305 pages.

163. Silveus, W.A. 1933. *Texas Grasses: Classification and Description of Grasses*. San Antonio, Texas: Clegg Co.

164. Marcy, Randolph B. 1854. *Exploration of the Red River of Louisiana in the Year 1852*. Washington: A.O.P. Nicholson, Public Printer. Including App. G. Botany: Description of the plants collected during the expedition by Dr. John Torrey.

165. Miller, Philip. 1768. *The Gardeners' Dictionary*. Eighth edition. Printed for the author; and sold by John and Francis Rivington.

166. Merrill, Elmer Drew. 1949. *Index Rafinesquianus; the Plant Names Published by C. S. Rafinesque with Reductions, and a Consideration of His Methods, Objectives, and Attainments*. Jamaica Plain, Massachusetts, Arnold Arboretum of Harvard University.

167. Rich, Oliver O. 1814. *A Synopsis of the Genera of American Plants*. Georgetown, District of Columbia: Printed by J.M. Carter.

168. Michaux, André. 1803. *Flora Boreali-Americana*. Facsimile of the 1803 edition with introduction by Joseph Ewan. New York: Hafner Press.

169. Index Fungorum Partnership. 2004. *Index Fungorum*. CABI Bioscience. http://www.indexfungorum.org/Names/Names.asp (October 28, 2005).

170. Lincoff, Gary H. 1995. *National Audubon Society Field Guide to North American Mushrooms*. Alfred A. Knopf: New York.

171. Missouri Botanical Garden. 2005. W3 Most nomenclature. http://mobot.mobot.org/W3T/Search/most.html (November 1, 2005).

172. Goodale, George L. 1882. *Wild Flowers of America*, with fifty-colored plates, from original drawings, by Isaac Sprague. Boston: S.E. Cassino, 1882, c1879.

173. Clarke, Charles Baron. 1909. *Illustrations of Cyperaceae*. London: Williams & Norgate.

174. Linnaeus, Carl. 1753. *Species Plantarum*. A facsimile of the first edition 1753. London: the Ray Society reprinted 1957.

175. Miller, Orson K., Jr. 1972. *Mushrooms of North America*. New York: E. P. Dutton & Co.

176. Huffamn, D.M., L.H. Tiffany, G. Knaphus, and R.A. Healy. 2008. *Mushrooms and Other Fungi of the Midcontinental United States*. Second edition. Iowa City: University of Iowa Press.

177. Gronovius, J.F., and John Clayton. 1762. *Flora virginica. Lugduni Batavorum.* Photolithographed by Murray Printing Co. Cambridge, Massachusetts, for the Arnold Arboretum, 1946.

178. *John Gerard's Grete Herball Catalogue Horti – Modern Scientific Names by Benjamin Daydon Jackson – Cultivated in His Garden, 1596-1599.* 1876, privately printed.

179. Ryden, Mats. 1984. *English Plant Names in the Great Herball* (1526).

180. Gerarde, John. 1633. *The herball or Generall historie of plantes.* Gathered by Iohn Gerarde of London Master in Chirurgerie very much enlarged and amended by Thomas Iohnson citizen and apothecarye of London.

181. Ewan, Joseph, and Nesta Ewan. 1970. *John Banister and His Natural History of Virginia, 1678-1692.* Urbana, Chicago, London: University of Illinois Press.

182. Harper, Francis. 1791. *The Travels of William Bartram.* Francis Harpers Naturalist edition. Athens and London: University of Georgia Press, 1998.

183. Bartram, William. 1968. *Botanical and Zoological Drawings, 1756-1788*; reproduced from the Fothergill album in the British Museum (Natural History). Edited, with an introduction and commentary, by Joseph Ewan.

184. Muhlenberg, Henry. 1793. Index Lancastriensis, Auctore Henrico Muhlenberg, D. D. *Transactions of the American Philosophical Society*, Volume 3: 157-184.

185. Pechanec, Joseph F. 1936. The Identification of Grasses on the Upper Snake River Plains by their Vegetative Characters. *Ecology*, Volume 17, number 3: 479-490.

186. Barton, William. 1814. *Vegetable Materia Medica of the United States, or, Medical Botany: Containing a Botanical, General, and Medical History of Medicinal Plants Indigenous to the United States.* Illustrated by coloured engravings, made after drawings from nature, done by the author. Philadelphia: H.C. Carey and I. Lea, 1825. Biodiversity Heritage Library, http://www.biodiversitylibrary.org/Default.aspx.

187. Barton, William. 1818. *Compendium Florae Philadelphicae: Containing a Description of the Indigenous and Naturalized Plants Found within a Circuit of Ten Miles around Philadelphia.* V, II only. Philadelphia: Carey & Sons. Biodiversity Heritage Library, http://www.biodiversitylibrary.org/item/84268#7 (accessed January 22, 2010).

188. Hooker, William Jackson. 1829. *Flora Boreali-Americana Atlas; or the Botany of the Northern Parts of British America.* London: Henry G. Bohn.

189. Catesby, Mark. 1767. *Hortus Europae americanus, or, A collection of 85 Curious Trees and Shrubs: The Produce of North America, Adapted to the Climates and Soils of Great-Britain, Ireland, and Most Parts of Europe, &c Together with Their Blossoms, Fruits and Seeds, Observations on Their Culture, Growth, Constitution and Virtues, with Directions How to Collect, Pack Up and Secure Them in Their Passage.* London: Printed for J. Millan.

190. Rickett, H.W. 1963. *Jane Colden: Botanic Manuscript.* New York: Chanticleer Press.

Historical Common Names of Great Plains Plants

Volume II:

Scientific Names Index

Abutilon theophrasti
[J.F. Jacquin, 1811]

A

Absynthium officinale **Tourn.** – possibly *Artemisia absinthium* L.

Abutilon (**Tourn.**) **Mill.** – See *Abutilon* Mill.

Abutilon abutilon (**L.**) **Rusby** – See *Abutilon theophrasti* Medik.

Abutilon avicennae **Gaert.** – See *Abutilon theophrasti* Medik.

Abutilon berlandieri **Gray ex S. Wats.** – Berlandier's abutilon [Berlandier abutilon] (155) (1942), Berlandier's Indian mallow (50) (present)

Abutilon californicum **auct. non Benth.** – See *Abutilon berlandieri* Gray ex S. Wats.

Abutilon crispum – See *Herissantia crispa* (L.) Briz.

Abutilon **Gaertn.** – possibly *Abutilon* Mill.

Abutilon incanum (**Link**) **Sweet** – Indian mallow [Indian-mallow, Indian mallows] (122) (1937), Indian mallow abutilon [Indianmallow abutilon] (155) (1942), Pelotazo (50) (present)

Abutilon indicum (**L.**) **Sweet** – Indian abutilon [India abutilon] (155) (1942), Monkey bush [Monkeybush] (50) (present)

Abutilon **Mill.** – Abutilon (138, 155, 158) (1900–1942), Carolina tea (190) (~1759), Flowering maple (109) (1949), Indian mallow [Indian-mallow, Indian mallows] (1, 4, 50, 15, 156) (1895–present), Mountain lily [Mountaine Lillie, Mountaine Lilly] (76) (1896) ME, Velvetleaf [Velvet leaf, Velvet-leaf] (13, 93) (1849–1936)

Abutilon mollicomum (**Willd.**) **Sweet** – Painted abutilon (138, 155) (1931–1942), Sonora abutilon (155) (1942), Sonoran Indian mallow (50) (present)

Abutilon parvulum **Gray** – Dwarf Indian mallow [Dwarf Indian-mallow] (50) (present)

Abutilon pauciflorum **A.St.-Hil.** – See *Abutilon hulseanum* (Torr. & A. Gray) Torr. ex A. Gray

Abutilon sonorae – See *Abutilon mollicomum* (Willd.) Sweet

Abutilon theophrasti **Medik** – Abutilon (177) (1762), American hemp (5, 156, 158) (1900–1923) misapplied, American jute (5, 62, 74, 156, 157, 158) (1895–1929), Butter-print [Butter print] (5, 62, 76, 80, 156, 158) (1896–1923), Butterweed [Butter weed, Butter-weed] (5, 73, 156, 157, 158) (1892–1929) Peoria IL, Buttonweed [Button-weed, Button weed] (5, 73, 156, 157, 158) (1892–1929) Chesterton MD, Changma abutilon (155) (1942), Cottonweed [Cottonweed, Cotton weed] (5, 156, 157, 158) (1900–1929), Indian hemp [Indianhemp] (5, 76, 156, 158) (1896–1923) OH, Indian mallow [Indian-mallow, Indian mallows] (5, 58, 62, 80, 85, 92, 97, 131, 156, 157, 158) (1840–1937), Marshmallow with yellow flowers [Marsh Mallow with yellow flowers] (178) (1526), Mormon weed [Mormon-weed] (5, 73, 156, 158) (1892–1923) Quincy IL, Piemarker [Pie marker, Pie-marker] (5, 76, 155, 156, 158) (1896–1942) used to stamp pie-crust, Pie-print [Pie print] (5, 76, 156, 157, 158) (1896–1929) used to stamp pie-crust, Purple mallow (178) (1526), Round-leaf Indian Mallow [Round-leaved Indian Mallow] (187) (1818), Sheepweed [Sheep weed, Sheep-weed] (5, 73, 156, 157, 158) (1892–1929) Quincy IL, Velvetleaf [Velvet leaf, Velvet-leaf] (1, 3, 4, 5, 15, 50, 62, 72, 80, 92, 95, 145, 156, 157, 158) (1895–present), Velvetweed [Velvet weed, Velvet-weed] (5, 73, 156, 158) (1892–1923) Quincy IL, Wild okra (156) (1923)

Abutilon thurberi **Gray** – Thurber's abutilon [Thurber abutilon] (155) (1942), Thurber's Indian mallow (50) (present)

Acacia **Adans.** – possibly *Acacia* Mill.

Acacia adansoni – See *Acacia nilotica* (L.) Willd. ex Delile subsp. *adstringens* (Schumach. & Thonn.) Roberty

Acacia adansonii **Guill. & Perr.** – See *Acacia nilotica* (L.) Willd. ex Delile subsp. *adstringens* (Schumach. & Thonn.) Roberty

Acacia amentacea **DC.** – See *Acacia rigidula* Benth.

Acacia aneura **F. Muell. ex Benth.** – Mulga (50) (present), Mulga acacia (155) (1942)

Acacia angustissima (**Mill.**) **Kuntze** – Fern-leaf acacia [Fernleaf acacia] (155) (1942), Prairie acacia (3, 4, 5, 50, 97, 155) (1913–present), Prairie guajillo (124) (1937) TX

Acacia angustissima (**Mill.**) **Kuntze var.** *hirta* (**Nutt.**) **B.L. Robins.** – Lemmon's acacia [Lemmons acacia] (155) (1942)

Acacia angustissima (**Mill.**) **Kuntze var.** *shrevei* (**Britton & Rose**) **Isely** – Shreve's acacia [Shreve acacia] (155) (1942), Shreve's prairie acacia (50) (Present)

Acacia arabica (**Lam.**) **Willd.** – See *Acacia nilotica* (L.) Willd. ex Delile

Acacia armata **R. Br.** – See *Acacia paradoxa* DC.

Acacia auriculaeformis – See *Acacia auriculiformis* A. Cunningham ex Benth.

Acacia auriculiformis **A. Cunningham ex Benth.** – Ear-leaf acacia [Earleaf acacia] (155) (1942)

Acacia baileyana **F. Muell.** – Cootamundra wattle (50, 138) (1923–present), Cootamundra-wattle acacia (155) (1942)

Acacia berlandieri **Benth.** – Guajillo (122, 124) (1937) TX, Huajillo (106) (1930) TX

Acacia constricta **Benth.** – Mescat acacia (155) (1942), White-thorn acaia [Whitethorn acaia] (50) (present)

Acacia cornigera (**L.**) **Willd.** – Bull-horn acacia [Bullhorn acacia] (138, 155) (1931–1942), Bull-horn wattle [Bullhorn wattle] (50) (present), Oxhorn acacia (155) (1942)

Acacia cyanophylla – See *Acacia saligna* (Labill.) Wendl. f.

Acacia cyclops **G. Don** – Cyclops acacia (50, 138, 155) (1923–present)

Acacia decurrens dealbata – See *Acacia decurrens* Willd.

Acacia decurrens mollis – See *Acacia mearnsii* De Wild.

Acacia decurrens **var.** *mollis* **Lindl.** – See *Acacia mearnsii* De Wild.

Acacia decurrens **Willd.** – Green wattle (50, 109, 138) (1923–present), Silver wattle (138) (1923), Silver-green wattle acacia [Silvergreen-wattle acacia] (155) (1942)

Acacia decurrens **Willd. var.** *mollis* **Lindl.** – See *Acacia mearnsii* De Wild.

Acacia elata **A. Cunningham ex Benth.** – Cedar acacia (155) (1942), Cedar wattle (50) (present)

Acacia farnesiana (**L.**) **Willd.** – Black thorn [Black-thorn] (19) (1840), Cassia flower [Cassia-flower] (158) (1900), Cassie (92, 109, 156, 158) (1876–1949), Cassie-oil plant (107) (1919), Goldbrier [Goldbriar] (7) (1828), Huisache (106, 107, 109, 122, 124) (1919–1949), Kalú (158) (1900) HI, Matitas (158) (1900) Mexico, Opopanax (107, 109) (1919–1949), Popinac (107, 109) (1919–1949), Popniac (7) (1828), Sponge tree (107, 158) (1900–1919), Sweet acacia (50, 106, 109, 138, 155) (1923–present), West Indian blackthorn (107) (1919)

Acacia farnesiana **Willd.** – See *Acacia farnesiana* (L.) Willd.

Acacia filicioides (**Cavar.**) **Branner & Coville** – See *Acacia angustissima* (Mill.) Kuntze

Acacia greggii **Gray** – Cat-claw acacia [Catclaw acacia] (50, 155) (1942–present), Cat's-claw [Catclaw, Cat-claw, Catsclaw, Cat's-claws, Cat's claws] (76, 106) (1896–1930), Devil's-claw [Devil's claw, Devil's claws, Devilsclaws] (106) (1930), Long-flower catsclaw [Long-flowered catsclaw] (124) (1937), Paradise flower (106) (1930), Texas catsclaw (106, 124) (1930–1937), Tree catsclaw (106, 122) (1930–1937), Wright's acacia [Wright acacia] (155) (1942)

Acacia koa **Gray** – Koa (50) (present), Koa acacia (155) (1942)

Acacia latifolia – See *Acacia longifolia* (Andr.) Willd.

Acacia latisiliqua [(**L.**) **Willd.**] – See *Lysiloma latisiliquum* (L.) Benth.

Acacia lemmoni – See *Acacia angustissima* (Mill.) Kuntze

Acacia longifolia (**Andr.**) **Willd.** – Broad-leaf acacia [Broadleaf acacia]

(138, 155) (1923–1942), Golden wattle (106) (1930), Sydney acacia (155) (1942), Sydney golden wattle (50, 106, 107, 109, 155) (1919–1930), Sydney wattle (138) (1923)

Acacia longifolia **Willd.** – See *Acacia longifolia* (Andr.) Willd.

Acacia lutea **Leavenw.** – See *Neptunia lutea* (Leavenworth) Benth.

Acacia mearnsii **De Wild.** – Acacia (106, 107) (1919–1930), Black green-wattle acacia [Blackgreen-wattle acacia] (155)(1942), Black wattle or Black wattle tree (106, 107, 109, 138, 158) (1900–1949), Green wattle (107) (1919), Green-wattle acacia [Greenwattle acacia] (107, 155) (1919–1942), Silver wattle (107) (1919) naturalized in CA OR

Acacia melanoxylon **R. Br. ex Aiton f.** – Blackwood [Black wood] or Black-wood tree (50, 158) (1900–present), Black-wood acacia [Blackwood acacia] (109, 138, 155) (1923–1949), Lightwood [Light wood] (155) (1942), Mimosa bark (92) (1876)

Acacia **Mill.** – Acacia (1, 50, 138, 155, 158) (1900–present), Cat's-claw [Catclaw, Cat-claw, Catsclaw, Cats-claw, Cat's-claws, Cat's claws] (106) (1930), Wattle (158) (1900) Australia

Acacia minuta **(M.E. Jones) Beauchamp** – See *Acacia farnesiana* (L.) Willd.

Acacia minuta **(M.E. Jones) Beauchamp subsp. *densiflora* (Alexander ex Small) Beauchamp** – See *Acacia farnesiana* (L.) Willd.

Acacia nilotica **(L.) Delile** – See *Acacia nilotica* (L.) Willd. ex Delile introduced

Acacia nilotica **(L.) Willd. ex Delile** – Adanson's acacia [Adanson acacia] (155) (1942), Babul acacia (155) (1942), Babur (158) (1900), Egyptian gum Arabic tree (158) (1900), Egyptian thorn (158) (1900), Fiddleneck acacia (155) (1942), Gum Arabic tree (50) (present), Kikar (158) (1900)

Acacia paradoxa **DC.** – Kangaroo-thorn [Kangaroo thorn] (109, 138) (1923–1949), Kangaroo-thorn acacia (155) (1942), Paradox acacia (50) (present)

Acacia podalyriaefolia **Cunn.** – See *Acacia podalyriifolia* A. Cunningham ex G. Don

Acacia podalyriifolia **A. Cunningham ex G. Don** – Pearl acacia (109, 137, 155) (1923–1949), Pearl wattle (50) (present)

Acacia polyacantha **Willd.** – Catchu tree (50) (present), Suma-catechu acacia (155) (1942)

Acacia pycnantha **Benth.** – Broad-leaf wattle [Broad-leaved wattle] (109) (1949), Golden wattle (50, 109, 138, 158) (1900–present), Golden-wattle acacia [Goldenwattle acacia] (138) (1923)

Acacia retinodes **Schlecht.** – Water wattle (50) (present), Wirilda acacia (155) (1942)

Acacia rigidula **Benth.** – Blackbrush [Black brush] (106, 122, 124) (1930–1937) TX, Black-brush acacia [Blackbrush acacia (50) (present)

Acacia roemeriana **Scheele** – Roemer's acacia [Roemer acacia] (155) (1942), Round-flower cat's-claw [Round-flowered catsclaw, Round-flower catclaw, Roundflower catclaw] (50, 106, 124) (1930–present)

Acacia salicina **Lindl.** – Blue-leaf acacia [Blueleaf acacia] (138, 155) (1923–1942), Gold-wreath acacia [Goldwreath acacia] (155) (1942), Orange wattle (50) (present)

Acacia scorpioides **[W. Wight]** – See *Acacia nilotica* (L.) Willd. ex Delile

Acacia smallii **Isely** – See *Acacia farnesiana* (L.) Willd.

Acacia spadicigera **Schltdl. & Cham.** – See *Acacia cornigera* (L.) Willd.

Acacia suma **(Roxb.) Buch.-Ham. ex Voigt** – See *Acacia polyacantha* Willd.

Acacia tortuosa **(L.) Willd.** – Huisachillo (124) (1937) TX, Poponax (50) (present), Twisted acacia (155) (1942)

Acacia verticillata **(L'Hér.) Willd.** – Prickly Moses (50) (present), Star acacia (109, 138, 155) (1923–1949), Whorl-leaf acacia [Whorl-leaved acacia] (109) (1949)

Acacia verticillata **Willd.** – See *Acacia verticillata* (L'Hér.) Willd.

Acacia verucillata – See *Acacia verticillata* (L'Hér.) Willd.

Acacia wrightii **Benth.** – See *Acacia greggii* Gray var. *wrightii* (Benth.) Isely

Acaciella **Britton & Rose** – See *Acacia* Mill. all US species

Acaciella shrevei **Britton & Rose** – See *Acacia angustissima* (Mill.) Kuntze var. *shrevei* (Britton & Rose) Isely

Acaena **L.** – See *Acaena* Mutis ex L.

Acaena **Mutis ex L.** – Acaena (50, 138) (1923–present), Sheepbur [Sheep burr, Sheep-bur] (155) (1942)

Acaena novae-zelandiae **Kirk** – Biddy-biddy (50) (present), Burnet sheepbur (155) (1942), New Zealand sheepbur (155) (1942)

Acaena pinnatifida **Ruiz & Pavón** – Feather-leaf sheepbur [Feather-leaf sheepbur] (155) (1942), Sheepbur [Sheep burr, Sheep-bur] (50) (present)

Acaena sanguisorbae **auct. non (L. f.) Vahl** – See *Acaena novae-zelandiae* Kirk

Acalypha amentacea **Roxb. subsp. *wilkesiana* (Muell.-Arg.) Fosberg** – Wilkes' acalypha (50) (present)

Acalypha armentacea **Roxb.** – Crimson-sedge copperleaf [Crimsonsedge copperleaf] (138) (1923), Painted copperleaf (138, 155) (1923–1942)

Acalypha californica **Benth.** – California copperleaf (50, 155) (1942–present)

Acalypha caroliniana **Ell.** – See *Acalypha ostryifolia* Riddell

Acalypha gracilens **Gray** – See *Acalypha monococca* (Engelm. ex Gray) L. Mill. & Gandhi*)*

Acalypha hispida **Burm. f.** – Bristly copperleaf (50) (present), Chenille copperleaf (138, 155) (1923–1942), Chenille-plant (109) (1949), Redhot-cattail (109) (1949)

Acalypha **L.** – Copperleaf [Copper-leaf, Copper leaf] (50, 109, 138, 155) (1923–present), Mercury (93) (1936), Three-seed mercury [Three-seeded mercury] (4) (1986)

Acalypha lindheimeri **Muell.** – See *Acalypha phleoides* Cav.

Acalypha monococca **(Engelm. ex Gray) L. Mill. & Gandhi** – Slender copperleaf (155) (1942), Slender three-seed mercury [Slender three-seeded mercury] (5, 50, 72, 97, 122) (1907–present)

Acalypha neomexicana **Müll. Arg.** – New Mexico copperleaf (50, 155) (1942–present)

Acalypha ostryaefolia **Riddell** – See *Acalypha ostryifolia* Riddell

Acalypha ostryifolia **Riddell** – Hop-hornbeam copperleaf [Hophornbeam copperleaf] (155) (1942), Hornbeam three-seed mercury [Hornbeam three-seeded mercury] (5, 97, 122) (1913–1937), Pineland three-seed mercury [Pineland threeseed mercury] (50, 187) (1818–present), Three-seed mercury [Three-seeded mercury] (3, 145) (1897–1977)

Acalypha phleoides **Cav.** – Cardinal-feather [Cardinal feather, Cardinal's feather, Cardinal's feather] (124) (1937) TX, Lindheimer's copperleaf [Lindheimer copperleaf] (155) (1942)

Acalypha poireti – See *Acalypha poiretii* Spreng.

Acalypha poiretii **Spreng.** – Poiret's copperleaf [Poirets copperleaf] (50, 155) (1942–present)

Acalypha radians **Torr.** – Cardinal-feather [Cardinal feather, Cardinal's feather, Cardinal's feather] (50, 124) (1937–present)

Acalypha rhomboidea **Raf.** – Rhombic copperleaf (3, 4) (1977–1986)

Acalypha virginiana – possibly *Acalypha virginica* L.

Acalypha virginica **L.** – Copperleaf [Copper-leaf, Copper leaf] (62, 156) (1912–1923), Mercury-weed [Mercury weed] (5, 7, 92, 156, 157, 158) (1828–1923), Three-seed mercury [Three-seeded mercury] (3, 19, 62, 80, 93, 156) (1840–1977), Virginia acalypha [Virginian acalypha] (165) (1768), Virginia copperleaf (155) (1942), Virginia three-seed mercury [Virginia threeseed mercury, Virginia three-seeded mercury] (5, 50, 97, 156, 157, 158) (1900–present), Wax-ball (62, 156) (1912–1923) IN

Acalypha wilkesiana **Muell.-Arg.** – See *Acalypha amentacea* Roxb. subsp. *wilkesiana* (Muell.-Arg.) Fosberg

Acamptoclados **Nash.** – See *Eragrostis* von Wolf

Acamptoclados sessilispicus **(Buckley) Nash** – See *Eragrostis sessilispica* Buckl.

Acamptopappus **(Gray) Gray** – Goldenhead (50, 155) (1942–present)

Acamptopappus shockleyi **Gray** – Shockley's goldenhead [Shockley goldenhead (50, 155) (1942–present)

Acamptopappus sphaerocephalus (**Harvey & Gray ex Gray**) **Gray** – Rayless goldenhead (50, 155) (1942–present)

Acanthocereus tetragonus (**L.**) **Humm.** – Triangle cactus (50) (present)

Acanthopanax (**Dcne. & Planch.**) **Miq.** – See *Eleutherococcus* Maxim.

Acanthospermum **Schrank** – Amber tree (92) (1876), *B*eakchervil (155) (1942), Starbur [Starburr] (50, 155) (1942–present)

Acanthospermum australe (**Loefl.**) **Kuntze** – Paraguay starbur [Paraguay starburr] (50, 155) (1942–present), Spiny bur (5) (1913)

Acanthoxanthium spinosum (**L.**) **Fourr.** – See *Xanthium spinosum* L.

Acanthus **L.** – Acanthus (50, 138, 155) (1923–present), Bearbreeches [Bear's breeches, Bear's breech] (109) (1949)

Acanthus mollis **L.** – Bearbough [Beares bough] (179) (1526), Bearbreeches [Bear's breeches, Bear's breech] (50) (present), Bearefore (179) (1526), Beartwig [Beares twygge] (179) (1526), Branca ursina (165) (1768) medicinal name, Garden bear's-britches [Garden Beares breech] (178) (1526), Smooth acanthus (165) (1768), Soft acanthus (138, 155) (1931–1942)

Acer (**Tourn.**) **L.** – See *Acer* L.

Acer barbatum **Michx.** – Bearded maple (20) (1857), Florida maple (155) (1942), Hairy Florida maple (155) (1942), Hairy maple (19) (1840), Southern sugar maple (50, 124) (1937–present)

Acer barbatum **Michx. var.** *longii* (**Fern.**) **Fern.** – See *Acer barbatum* Michx.

Acer barbatum **Michx. var.** *villipes* (**Rehd.**) **Ashe** – See *Acer barbatum* Michx.

Acer brachypterum **Wooton & Standl.** – See *Acer saccharum* subsp. *grandidentatum* (Torr. & A.Gray) Desmarais

Acer campestre **L.** – Common maple (165) (1768), Hedge maple (50, 109 137, 138, 155) (1923–present)

Acer canadense [**Duham.**] – See *Acer pensylvanicum* L.

Acer carolinianum **Walt.** – See *Acer rubrum* L. var. *trilobum* Torr. & Gray ex K. Koch)

Acer circinatum **Pursh** – Bois de diable (French) (33) (1827), Erable circiné (French) (20) (1857), Round-leaf maple [Round leaved maple] (20) (1857), Soft maple (35) (1806), Vine maple (2, 15, 50, 106, 109, 138, 155, 160, 161) (1857–present)

Acer coccineum [**Michx.**] – possibly *Acer rubrum* L. *Acer dasycarpum* **Ehrh.** – See *Acer saccharinum* L.

Acer dasycarpum **var.** *weiri* **Schwerin** – See *Acer saccharinum* L.

Acer drummondii **Hook. & Arn.** – See *Acer rubrum* L. var. *drummondii* (Hook. & Arn. ex Nutt.) Sarg.

Acer eriocarpum **Michx.** – See *Acer saccharinum* L.

Acer floridanum (**Chapman**) **Pax** – See *Acer barbatum* Michx.

Acer floridanum (**Chapman**) **Pax var.** *longii* **Fern.** – See *Acer barbatum* Michx.

Acer floridanum (**Chapman**) **Pax var.** *villipes* **Rehd.** – See *Acer barbatum* Michx.

Acer floridanum villipes – See *Acer barbatum* Michx.

Acer ginnala **Maxim.** – Amur maple (50, 109, 112, 137, 138, 155) (1923–present), Manchurian maple (135) (1910), Tatarian maple (82) (1930)

Acer glabrum douglasi – See *Acer glabrum* Torr. var. *douglasii* (Hook.) Dippel

Acer glabrum **Torr.** – Bark maple (5) (1913), Currant-leaf maple [Currant leaved maple] (20) (1857), Dwarf maple (20, 93) (1857–1936), Dwarf mountain maple (5) (1913), Dwarf Rocky Mountain maple (112) (1937), Erable triparti (French) (20) (1857), Mountain maple (4, 95, 101, 130) (1895–1986), Red maple (149) (1904) NM, Rocky Mountain maple (5, 50, 93, 137, 138, 155) (1923–present), Rocky Mountain maple (50) (present), Shrub maple (101) (1905) MT, Shrubby maple (5) (1913), Soft maple (5, 35) (1806–1913), Threeleaf Rocky Mountain maple [ThreeleafRockyountain maple] (155) (1942), White maple (35) (1806)

Acer glabrum **Torr. subsp.** *douglasii* (**Hook.**) **Wesmael** – See *Acer glabrum* Torr. var. *douglasii* (Hook.) Dippel

Acer glabrum **Torr. var.** *douglasii* (**Hook.**) **Dippel** – Douglas' maple [Douglas maple] (50) (present), Douglas' Rocky Mountain maple [Douglas Rocky Mountain maple] (155) (1942)

Acer glabrum tripartitum – See *Acer glabrum* Torr. var. *glabrum*

Acer glaucum – See *Acer rubrum* L.

Acer grandidentatum brachypterum – See *Acer saccharum* subsp. *grandidentatum* (Torr. & A.Gray) Desmarais

Acer grandidentatum **Nutt.** – Balcones Escarpment maple (124) (1937), Big-tooth maple [Bigtooth maple] (50, 138, 155) (1923–present), Erable de montagne (French) (20) (1857), Mountain sugar maple (20) (1857), Rocky Mountain maple (97) (1937), Sugar maple (122) (1937)

Acer grandidentatum **Nutt. var.** *brachypterum* (**Woot. & Standl.**) **Palmer** – See *Acer saccharum* subsp. *grandidentatum* (Torr. & A.Gray) Desmarais

Acer grandidentatum **Nutt. var.** *sinuosum* (**Rehd.**) **Little** – See *Acer saccharum* subsp. *grandidentatum* (Torr. & A.Gray) Desmarais

Acer japonicum **Thunb.** – Fern-leaf maple [Fernleaf maple] (109) (1949), Fullmoon maple (109, 137, 155) (1923–1949), Japanese maple (165) (1768)

Acer japonicum **var.** *aconitifolium* **Meehan** – See *Acer japonicum* Thunb.

Acer **L.** – Ash-leaf maple [Ash-leaved maple] (1, 13, 108) (1849–1932), Box elder [Box-elder, Box elder] (1, 13) (1849–1932), Erable (French) (8, 20) (1785–1857), Maple (1, 4, 8, 10, 13, 15, 50, 82, 93, 106, 109, 156, 167, 184) (1785–present)

Acer leucoderme **Small** – Chalk maple (50, 138, 155) (1923–present)

Acer macrophyllum **Pursh** – Big-leaf maple [Bigleaf maple] (50, 106, 155) (1930–present), California maple (106) (1930), Erable à grandes feuilles (French) (20) (1857), Large-leaf maple [Large-leaved maple] (20, 161) (1857), Oregon maple (106, 109, 138) (1923–1949), Water maple (106) (1930), White maple (106, 160) (1860–1930)

Acer montanum [**Ait.**] – See *Acer spicatum* Lam.

Acer negundo arizonicum – See *Acer negundo* L. var. *arizonicum* Sarg.

Acer negundo californicum – See *Acer negundo* L. var. *californicum* (Torr. & Gray) Sarg.

Acer negundo interius – See *Acer negundo* L. var. *interius* (Britton) Sarg.

Acer negundo **L.** – Ash maple (92, 57) (1876–1900), Ash-leaf maple [Ash-leaved maple] (5, 8, 20, 28, 41, 42, 43, 93, 106, 130, 131, 156, 158, 165, 187, 189) (1767–1936), Black ash (5, 156, 158) (1900–1923), Box elder [Box-elder, Box elder] (3, 4, 5, 9, 12, 15, 20, 28, 35, 37, 38, 42, 43, 50, 65, 72, 82, 92, 93, 95, 97, 106, 109, 112, 114, 122, 124, 130, 131, 135, 138, 153, 155, 156, 157, 95, 138, 155, 158, 187) (1814–present), Chan-shushka (Dakota-Teton) (37) (1919), Cut-leaf maple [Cut-leaved maple] (156, 157, 158) (1900–1923), Erable à feuilles de frêne (French) (8) (1785), Manitoba maple (106, 156) (1923–1930) Western Canada, Maple-ash [Maple ash] (5, 156, 158) (1900–1923), Nahosh (Winnebago) (37) (1919), Ósako (Pawnee) (37) (1919), Red River maple (5, 156, 158) (1900–1923), Sugar maple (5, 157, 158) (1900–1929), Tashkadan (Dakota) (37) (1919), Virginia ash-leaf maple [Virginian ash-leaved maple] (165) (1768), Water-ash [Water ash] (5, 93, 156, 157, 158) (1900–1936), Zhaba-tazhon (Omaha-Ponca, beaver wood) (37) (1919),

Acer negundo **L. var.** *arizonicum* **Sarg.** – Arizona boxelder (50, 155) (1942–present)

Acer negundo **L. var.** *californicum* (**Torr. & Gray**) **Sarg.** – California boxelder [California box-elder, Californian box elder] (20) (1857), Erable de Californie (French) (20) (1857)

Acer negundo **L. var.** *interius* (**Britton**) **Sarg.** – Inland boxelder (155) (1942)

Acer negundo **L. var.** *negundo* – Ash maple (19) (1840), Ash-leaf maple [Ash-leaved maple] (2, 107, 108) (1878–1919), Box elder [Box-elder, Box elder] (2, 20, 19, 50, 101, 107, 149) (1840–present)

Acer negundo **L. var.** *texanum* **Pax** – Texas boxelder (155) (1942)

Acer negundo **L. var.** *violaceum* (**Kirchn.**) **Jaeger** – Box elder [Box-elder, Box elder] (50, 85) (1932–present), Violet boxelder (155) (1942)

Acer negundo texanum – See *Acer negundo* L. var. *texanum* Pax

Acer negundo violaceum – See *Acer negundo* L. var. *violaceum* (Kirchn.) Jaeger

Acer nigrum **Michx.** – See *Acer nigrum* Michx. f.

Acer nigrum **Michx. f. var.** *floridanum* **(Chapman) Fosberg** – See *Acer barbatum* Michx.

Acer nigrum **Michx. f. var.** *palmeri* **Sargent** – See *Acer nigrum* Michx. f.

Acer nikoense **Maximowicz** – See *Parthenocissus tricuspidata* (Sieb. & Zucc.) Planch.

Acer palmatum **Thunb.** – Black maple (3, 4, 5, 15, 19, 50, 82, 138, 155, 158) (1840–present), Black sugar maple (2, 5, 20, 72, 82, 85, 97, 158) (1857–1937), Hand-leaf maple [Hand-leaved maple] (165) (1768), Hard maple (5, 158) (1900), Japanese maple (50, 109 137, 138, 155) (1923–present), Palmer's black maple [Palmer black maple] (155) (1942), Sugar maple (46) (1783), Sweet tree (19) (1840)

Acer pensylvanicum **L.** – American striped maple (8) (1785), Bush maple (156) (1923), Erable de Canada (French) (8) (1785), Erable de Pensylvanie (French) (8) (1785), Erable jaspé (French) (168) (1803), False dogwood (92, 156) (1898–1923), Goose-foot maple [Goose foot maple] (5, 156) (1913–1923), Moosewood [Moose-wood, Moose wood] (2, 5, 15, 76, 109, 156) (1895–1949), Mountain alder (156) (1923), Northern maple (5, 109, 156) (1913–1949), Pennsylvania dwarf mountain maple [Pennsylvanian dwarf mountain maple] (8) (1785), Pennsylvania maple [Pensylvanian maple] (165) (1768), Striped dogwood (92, 156) (1876–1923), Striped maple (2, 15, 50, 92, 109, 138, 155, 156) (1895–present), Whistlewood [Whistle wood, Whistle-wood] (76, 79, 156) (1891–1923) Paris ME, NH

Acer pictum **Thunb.** – See Kalopanax septemlobus (Thunb.) Koidz.

Acer platanoides **L.** – Norway maple (20, 50, 82, 93, 107, 135. 137, 138, 165) (1768–present), Schwedler's maple [Schwedler maple] (137, 138) (1923–1931)

Acer platanoides **L.** *schwedleri* – See *Acer platanoides* L.

Acer pseudoplatanus euchlorum – See *Acer pseudoplatanus* L.

Acer pseudoplatanus **L.** – Big Key plane-tree maple [Bigkey plane-tree maple] (155) (1942), Great maple (165, 178) (1526–1768), Mock plane [Mock-plane] (107, 165) (1768–1919) England, Plane tree [Planetree, Plane-tree] (165) (1768) Scotland, Plane-tree maple [Planetree maple] (155) (1942), Sycamore maple (50, 93, 107, 109, 137, 138) (1923–present), Sycamore or Sycamore tree [Sycamore-tree] (20, 92, 165) (1768–1876) England

Acer pseudo-platanus **L.** – See *Acer pseudoplatanus* L.

Acer rubrum drummondi – See *Acer rubrum* L. var. *drummondii* (Hook. & Arn. ex Nutt.) Sarg.

Acer rubrum **L.** – Erable à feuilles argentées (French) (8) (1785), Erable rouge (8) (1785), Hard maple (5, 76, 156) (1896–1923), Knotty maple [Knottie maple] (46) (1879), Pale-flower red maple [Paleflower red maple] (155) (1942), Plaine (French Canadian) (107) (1919), Red maple (2, 5, 15, 19, 20, 38, 41, 42, 46, 50, 57, 72, 76, 82, 92, 93, 106, 107, 109, 122, 124, 138, 155, 156) (1770–present), Red-flower maple [Red-flowering maple, Red flowering maple] (20, 41, 189) (1767–1857), Scarlet maple (5, 15, 20, 42, 93, 97, 109, 156, 182, 187) (1791–1949), Scarlet-flower maple [Scarlet-flowering maple, Scarlet flowering maple] (8, 165) (1768–1785), Shoe peg maple [Shoe-peg maple (5, 156) (1913–1923), Silver-leaf maple [Silver-leaved maple] (8) (1785), Soft maple (5, 19, 74, 76, 156) (1840–1923), Swamp maple (2, 5, 57, 72, 82, 93, 106, 107, 109, 156, 187) (1818–1949), Thick-leaf maple [Thickleaf maple] (155) (1942), Water maple (5, 156) (1913–1923), Whistlewood [Whistle wood, Whistle-wood] (92) (1876), White maple (5, 42, 76, 156) (1814–1896)

Acer rubrum **L. subsp.** *drummondii* **(Hook. & Arn. ex Nutt.) E. Murr.** – See *Acer rubrum* L. var. *drummondii* (Hook. & Arn. ex Nutt.) Sarg.

Acer rubrum **L. var.** *tridens* **Wood** – See *Acer rubrum* L. var. *trilobum* Torr. & Gray ex K. Koch

Acer rubrum pallidiflorum – See *Acer rubrum* L.

Acer rubrum trilobum – See *Acer rubrum* L. var. *trilobum* Torr. & Gray ex K. Koch

Acer rubrum **var.** *pallidiflorum* **K. Koch ex Pax** – See *Acer rubrum* L.

Acer saccharaum schnecki – See *Acer saccharum* Marsh. var. *schneckii* Rehd.

Acer saccharinum **L.** – American sugar maple (165) (1768), Creek maple (5, 156, 157, 158) (1900–1929), Curled maple (12) (1821), Drummond's maple (5, 20, 50) (1857–present), Drummond's red maple [Drummond red maple] (155) (1942), Erable sucre (French) (8) (1785), Hard maple (19, 65, 74) (1840–1931), Maple-sugar tree [Maple sugar tree] (92) (1876), Red maple (158) (1900), River maple (5, 156, 158) (1900–1923), Rock maple (2, 19, 92, 107) (1840–1919), Šigme-winš (Chippewa) (105) (1932), Silver maple (2, 3, 4, 5, 9, 15, 19, 50, 82, 93, 97, 105, 106, 107, 109, 112, 114, 130, 131, 135, 138, 155, 156, 157, 158) (1840–present), Silver-leaf maple [Silver-leaved maple] (5, 156, 157, 158) (1900–1929), Soft maple (3, 5, 37, 72, 76, 82, 85, 93, 105, 106, 107, 112, 124, 130, 131, 135, 156, 157, 158) (1895–1986), Sugar maple (2, 8, 14, 18, 19, 20, 33, 41, 103, 105, 107, 124) (1770–1937), Sugar tree [Sugartree, Sugar-tree] (35, 37, 43, 76) (1806–1919), Swamp maple (5, 156, 158) (1900–1923), Sweet tree (92) (1876), Tahado (Dakota) (37) (1919), Water maple (5, 156, 157, 158) (1900–1929), Weir's maple [Weir maple] (137) (1931), Wenu-shabethe-he (Omaha-Ponca, tree to dye black) (37) (1919), Wešabeðe (Osage, black-dye tree) (121) (1918?–1970?), White maple (2, 5, 19, 20, 42, 76, 85, 92, 93, 106, 107, 109, 158, 187) (1814–1919), Wier's weeping maple [Wiers weeping maple] (109) (1949), Wissep-hu (Winnebago, tree to dye black) (37) (1919)

Acer saccharinum **L. var.** *floridanum* **Chapman** – See *Acer barbatum* Michx.

Acer saccharinum **L. var.** *laciniatum* **Pax** – See *Acer saccharinum* L.

Acer saccharum **Marsh.** – A'nina'tĭg (Chippewa) (40) (1928), Black maple (5, 156, 158) (1900–1923), Chan-ha san (Dakota, pale bark) (37) (1919), Hard maple (5, 37, 72, 82, 85, 106, 156) (1907–1932), Nan-sank (Winnebago, pure or genuine wood) (37) (1919), Rock maple (5, 15, 109, 131, 135, 156, 158) (1895–1949), Rough maple (156) (1923), Sugar maple (3, 4, 5, 15, 40, 50, 65, 82, 85, 93, 97, 106, 109, 112, 124, 131, 135, 138, 155, 156, 158) (1895–present), Sugar tree [Sugartree, Sugar-tree] (5, 35, 156, 158, 177) (1762–1923), Sweet maple (5, 156) (1913–1923)

Acer saccharum **Marsh. subsp.** *floridanum* **(Chapman) Desmarais** – See *Acer barbatum* Michx.

Acer saccharum **Marsh. var.** *floridanum* **(Chapman) Small & Heller** – See *Acer barbatum* Michx.

Acer saccharum **Marsh. var.** *nigrum* **(Michx. f.) Britton** – See *Acer nigrum* Michx. f.

Acer saccharum **Marsh. var.** *schneckii* **Rehd.** – Rugel's sugar maple [Rugel sugar maple] (138) (1923), Schneck's sugar maple [Schneck sugar maple] (155) (1942)

Acer saccharum **Marsh. var.** *sinuosum* **(Rehd.) Sarg.** – See *Acer grandidentatum* Nutt. var. *grandidentatum*

Acer saccharum rugeli – See *Acer saccharum* Marsh. var. *schneckii* Rehd.

Acer saccharum **subsp.** *grandidentatum* **(Torr. & A.Gray) Desmarais** – Big tooth maple (124) (1937), Maple (122) (1937), Southwestern bigtooth maple (155) (1942)

Acer spicatum **Lam.** – Bois d'orignal (French, elk wood) (41) (1770), Bois noir (French, black wood) (41) (1770), Bush maple (82, 156) (1923–1930), Dock-mockie maple (58) (1869), Elkwood [Elk-wood, Elk wood] (29) (1869), False dogwood (19) (1840), Goose-foot maple [Goose foot maple] (156) (1923), Low maple (5, 156) (1913–1923), Maple bush (43) (1820), Moose maple (5, 156) (1913–1923), Moosewood [Moose-wood, Moose wood] (19, 20, 58, 92) (1840–1876), Mossewood (42) (1814), Mountain maple (2, 5, 15, 20, 41, 42, 50, 82, 109, 138, 155, 156, 165) (1768–present), Mountain maple bush [Mountain maple-bush (19, 156) (1840–1923), Spiked maple (156) (1923), Striped dogwood (58) (1869), Striped maple (19, 42, 58) (1814–1869), Swamp maple (5, 76, 156) (1896–1923) Paris ME, Water maple (5, 156) (1913–1923), Whistlewood [Whistle wood, Whistle-wood] (58) (1869)

Acer stenocarpum **Britton** – See *Acer rubrum* L. var. *rubrum*

Acer striatum – See *Acer spicatum* Lam.

Acer tataricum **L.** – Tartarian maple (135) (1910), Tatarian maple (50, 137, 138, 155) (1923–present)

Acer tomentosum **Hort. paris.** – possibly *Acer saccharinum* L.

Acer tripartitum – See *Acer glabrum* Torr. var. *glabrum*

Acerates angustifolia **(Nutt.) Dcne.** – See *Asclepias stenophylla* Gray

Acerates auriculata **Engelm.** – See *Asclepias engelmanniana* Woods.

Acerates **Ell.** – Mostly *Asclepias* L.

Acerates floridana **(Lam.) A.S. Hitchc.** – See *Asclepias longifolia* Michx.

Acerates lanuginosa **(Nutt.) Dec.** – See *Asclepias lanuginosa* Nutt.

Acerates longifolia **(Michx.) Elliott** – See *Asclepias longifolia* Michx.

Acerates longifolia **Ell.** – See *Asclepias longifolia* Michx.

Acerates viridiflora **(Raf.) Eaton** – See *Asclepias viridiflora* Raf.

Achas sapota **L.** – See *Manilkara zapota* (L.) van Royen

Achillea **(Valliant) L.** – See *Achillea* L.

Achillea ageratum **L.** – Maudleine (178) (1526), Maudlin (92, 165) (1768–1876), Sweet maudlin (165) (1768), Sweet milfoil (165) (1768), Sweet yarrow (50, 109, 138, 155) (1923–present)

Achillea alpina **L.** – Alpine milfoil (165) (1768), Alpine yarrow (155) (1942)

Achillea borealis **Bongard** – See *Achillea millefolium* L. var. *borealis* (Bong.) Farw.

Achillea eupatorium **M. Bieb.** – See *Achillea filipendulina* Lam. introduced

Achillea filipendulina **Lam.** – Fern-leaf yarrow [Fernleaf yarrow] (109, 137, 155) (1923–1949)

Achillea **L.** – Milfoil [Myllefoyle] (1, 10, 156, 158) (1818–1932), Sneezewort [Sneeze-wort, Sneeze woort] (2) (1895), Yarrow [Yarowe] (1, 2, 4, 42, 50, 93, 109, 125, 138, 155, 156, 158, 167, 184) (1793–present)

Achillea lanulosa alpicola – See *Achillea lanulosa* Nutt. var. *alpicola* Rydb.

Achillea lanulosa **Nutt.** – See *Achillea millefolium* L. var. *occidentalis* DC.

Achillea lanulosa **var.** *alpicola* **Rydb.** – See *Achillea millefolium* L.

Achillea ligustica – See *Achillea millefolium* L.

Achillea magna **[L.]** – See *Achillea millefolium* L.

Achillea millefolium **L.** – A'djidamo'wano (Chippewa, squirrel tail) (40, 155, 165) (1768–1942), Blodworte (179) (1526), Bloodwort [Blood wort, Blood-wort] (69, 157, 158) (1526–1900), Camil (158) (1900), Cammock (158) (1900), Carpenter's-grass [Carpenter's grass, Carpenters grasse] (69, 158, 179) (1526–1904), Common milfoil [Common millfoil] (41, 63, 165) (1768–1899), Common yarrow (2, 6, 45, 50, 63, 109, 138, 155, 156, 165, 178) (1596–present), Dog daisy [Dog-daisy] (157, 158) (1900–1929), Feldgarbe (German) (158) (1900), Gachelkraut (German) (158) (1900), Gordaldo (156) (1923), Gordoloba (69, 76, 158) (1896–1904), Gordolobo (69, 76, 158) (1896–1904) CA, Green-arrow [Greenarrow, Green arrow] (69, 156, 158) (1900–1923), Hank-sintsh (Winnebago, woodchuck tail) (37) (1919), Herb-aux-charpentiers [Herbe aux Charpentiers] (French) (156, 158) (1900–1923), Hundredleaf-grass [Hundred-leaf grass, Hundred-leaved grass] (107, 156) (1919–1923), Lovage yarrow (155) (1942), Marjoram-scented milfoil (165) (1768), Milfoil [Myllefoyle] (2, 6, 7, 19, 28, 37, 42, 46, 49, 53, 57, 58, 62, 69, 85, 92, 95, 101, 107, 109, 122, 127, 156, 157, 158, 179, 187) (1526–1937), Millefeuille (French) (6, 158) (1892–1900), Millefoil (148) (1939), Nosebleed [Nose-bleed, Nose bleed, Nose bleede (6, 69, 92, 107, 148, 156, 157, 158, 178) (1596–1929), Nosebleed sanguinary [Nosebleed-sanguinary] (156) (1923), Old-man's-pepper [Old man's pepper] (69, 156, 157, 158) (1900–1929), Palmer's yarrow [Palmer yarrow] (155) (1942), Penerial yarrow (46) (1879), Pink common

yarrow (155) (1942), Red yarrow (178) (1526), Sanguinary (69, 107, 156, 158, 179) (1526–1919), Schafgarbe (German) (6, 158) (1892–1900), Schafgrippe (German) (158) (1900), Schafrippe (German) (6) (1892), Sneezefoil (156) (1923), Soldier's-woundwort [Soldier's woundwort] (69, 156, 157, 158) (1900–1929), Subalpine yarrow (155) (1942), Tansy [Tansey, Tansie] (127, 158) (1900–1933) ND, Taopi pežuta (Lakota, wound medicine) (121) (1918?–1970?), Thousand-leaf [Thousand leaf, Thousandleaf] (49, 53, 69, 156, 158) (1898–1923), Thousand-leaf clover [Thousand-leaved clover] (69, 157, 158)(1900–1929), Thousand-seal [Thousand seal, thousand-seal] (107, 156) (1919–1923), Western yarrow (50, 72, 155) (1907–present), Wetsaθiŋdse egoŋ (Osage, rattlesnake's tail-like) (121) (1918?–1970?), Wild tansy [Wild tansey] (35, 101) (1806–1905), Woolly milfoil (165) (1768), Woolly yarrow (5, 93, 97, 109, 138, 155) (1913–1949), Xaŋte čaŋxloğaŋ (Lakota, cedar wood) (121) (1918?–1970?), Yarrow [Yarowe] (3, 7, 19, 37, 40, 45, 46, 49, 52, 53, 57, 58, 61, 62, 72, 80, 82, 85, 92, 93, 95, 97, 107, 122, 124, 127, 131, 146, 148, 157, 158, 179, 187) (1526–1977), Yarroway (158) (1900), Yerba de San Juan [Yerba-de-San-Juan] (156) (1923), Yerrow (158) (1900)

Achillea millefolium **L. subsp.** *lanulosa* **(Nutt.) Piper** – See *Achillea millefolium* L. var. *occidentalis* DC.

Achillea millefolium **L. var.** *borealis* **(Bong.) Farw.** – Northern yarrow (5) (1913), Wild tansy [Wild tansey] (106, 156) (1923–1930)

Achillea millefolium **lanulosa** – See *Achillea millefolium* L. var. *occidentalis* DC.

Achillea millefolium **roseum** – See *Achillea millefolium* L. var. *occidentalis* DC.

Achillea nobilis **L.** – Noble milfoil (165) (1768), Noble yarrow (50, 92) (1876–present), White yarrow (178) (1526)

Achillea palmeri **Rydb.** – See *Achillea millefolium* L.

Achillea ptarmica **L.** – Bachelor's-button [Bachelor's button, Bachelor's buttons, Batchelor's buttons] (165) (1768) England, Bastard pellitory (5, 92, 165) (1768–1913) England, Double ptarmica (165) (1768) England, Double sneezewort [Double Sneeze woort] (178) (1526), European pellitory (5, 156) (1913–1923), Fair-maid-of-France [Fair maids of France] (5, 156) (1913–1923), Field pellitory (165) (1768) England, German pellitory (92) (1876), Goose-tongue [Goose tongue] (5, 92, 156, 165) (1768–1923) England, Ptarmica (178) (1526), Seven-years'-love [Seven years' love] (156) (1923), Sneezeweed [Sneeze weed, Sneeze-weed] (156) (1923), Sneezewort [Sneeze-wort, Sneeze woort] (5, 10, 92, 109, 138, 156, 165, 178) (1526–1949), Sneezewort milfoil (165) (1768), Sneezewort-tansy (5, 156) (1913–1923), Sneezewort-yarrow (sneezewort yarrow) (5, 155, 156) (1913–1942), White tansy (5, 156) (1913–1923), Wild pellitory [Wilde pellitorie] (5, 156, 178) (1526–1923)

Achillea sibirica **Ledeb.** – Siberian yarrow (50, 138, 155) (1923–present)

Achillea tomentosa **L.** – See *Achillea millefolium* L. var. *occidentalis* DC.

Achlys **DC.** – Vanilla leaf [Vanilla leaf, Vanillaleaf] (155) (1942)

Achlys triphylla **(Sm.) DC.** – Deer-foot vanilla-leaf [Deerfoot vanilla-leaf] (155) (1942), May apple [Mayapple, May-apple] (76) (1896), Sweet-after-death [Sweet after death] (50) (present)

Achnatherum **×*bloomeri*** **(Boland.) Barkworth** [*hymenoides* × *occidentale*] – Bloomer's ricegrass [Bloomers ricegrass] (155) (1942), Bloomer's stipa (94) (1901)

Achnatherum **Beauv.** – Needle grass [Needle-grass, Needlegrass] (50) (present), Woolly grass [Woollygrass, Wooly grass] (92) (1876)

Achnatherum coronatum **(Thurb.) Barkworth** – Crested feather grass [Crested feather-grass] (94) (1901)

Achnatherum eminens **(Cav.) Barkworth** – Beard grass [Beard-grass, Beardgrass] (87) (1884), Feather grass [Feathergrass, Feather-grass] (87) (1884)

Achnatherum hymenoides **(Roemer & J. A. Schultes) Barkworth** – Bunch grass [Bunchgrass, Bunch-grass] (45, 87, 129) (1884–1896),

Indian millet (5, 56, 94, 101, 111, 129, 141) (1886–1915), Indian mountain rice (163) (1852), Indian rice grass [Indian ricegrass] (3, 50, 98, 140, 146, 155, 185) (1926–present), Mountain rice grass [Mountain ricegrass] (146) (1939), Mountain-rice [Mountain rice] (146) (1939), Quincy grass (146) (1939) MT, Sand grass [Sand-grass, Sand-grass] (4, 5, 50, 72, 146) (1907–present), Silk grass [Silkgrass, Silk-grass] (92) (1876), Silky grass [Silky-grass] (5, 163) (1852–1913), Wild millet (5) (1913), Wild rice [Wildrice] (101) (1905)

Achnatherum lemmonii (**Vasey**) **Barkworth** – Columbia needle grass [Columbia needlegrass] (122, 185) (1936–1937)

Achnatherum lettermanii (**Vasey**) **Barkworth** – Letterman's needle-grass [Letterman needlegrass] (140) (1944) TX

Achnatherum occidentale (**Thurb. ex S. Watson**) **Barkworth** – Columbia needle grass [Columbia needlegrass] (3) (1977), Narrow-top feather grass [Narrow-topped feather-grass] (94) (1901), Western needle grass [Western needlegrass, Western needle-grass] (50, 94, 155) (1901–present)

Achnatherum **P. Beauv.** – Indian millet (1, 93) (1932–1936), Sand-rice [Sand rice] (1) (1932), Silk grass [Silkgrass, Silk-grass] (10) (1818), Silky grass [Silky-grass] (93) (1936), Wild rice [Wildrice] (1) (1932)

Achnatherum parishii (**Vasey**) **Barkworth** – Parish's feather grass [Parish's feather-grass] (94) (1901)

Achnatherum richardsonii (**Link**) **Barkworth** – Richardson's feather (66, 90) (1885–1903), Richardson's feather grass [Richardson's feather-grass] (94) (1901), Richardson's needle grass [Richardson's needlegrass, Richardson needlegrass] (3, 50, 155) (1942–present)

Achnatherum robustum (**Vasey**) **Barkworth** – Sleepy grass [Sleepygrass, Sleepy-grass] (122, 140, 148, 152, 155, 163) (1852–1944)

Achnatherum scribneri (**Vasey**) **Barkworth** – Scribner's feather grass [Scribner's feather-grass] (94) (1901), Scribner's needlegrass [Scribner needlegrass] (50, 155) (1942–present)

Achnatherum speciosum (**Trin. & Rupr.**) **Barkworth** – Showy feather-grass (94) (1901)

Achras sapota **L.** – See *Manilkara zapota* (L.) van Royen

Achras zapotilla **Nutt.** – See *Manilkara zapota* (L.) van Royen

Achroanthes unifolia (**Michx.**) **Raf.** – See *Malaxis unifolia* Michx.

Achyrachaena mollis **Schauer** – Blow-wives [Blowwives] (50, 155) (1942–present)

Achyranthes repens **E.** – See *Alternanthera pungens* Kunth

Achyrodes aureum – See *Lamarckia aurea* (L.) Moench

Acinos arvensis (**Lam.**) **Dandy** – Basil (156) (1923), Basil-balm [Basil balm] (5, 156) (1913–1923), Basil-thyme [Basil thyme] (5) (1913), Mother-of-thyme [Mother of thyme] (5, 156) (1913–1923), Polly mountain [Polly-mountain] (5, 156) (1913–1923) no longer in use by 1923

Acleisanthes longiflora **Gray** – Angel's-trumpets [Angel trumpets, Angel-trumpets] (5, 73, 122, 124, 156) (1892–1937)

Acmella oppositifolia (**Lam.**) **R.K. Jansen** – Golden camomile [Golden chamomile] (155) (1942), Spilanthes (5, 97) (1913–1937)

Acmella repens (**Walter**) **Rich.** – See *Acmella oppositifolia* (Lam.) R. K. Jansen var. *repens* (Walt.) R. K. Jansen

Acnida alabamensis – See *Amaranthus australis* (Gray) Sauer

Acnida altissima (**Riddell**) **Moq. ex Standl.** – See *Amaranthus tuberculatus* (Moq.) Sauer

Acnida cannabina **L.** – See *Amaranthus cannabinus* (L.) Sauer

Acnida cannabina **Willd.** – See *Amaranthus cannabinus* (L.) Sauer

Acnida floridana **S. Watson** – Florida waterhemp (155) (1942)

Acnida **L.** – See *Amaranthus* L.

Acnida ruscocarpa **Willd.** – See *Amaranthus cannabinus* (L.) Sauer

Acnida tamarascina tuberculata (**Moq.**) **Uline & Bray** – See *Amaranthus tuberculatus* (Moq.) Sauer

Acnida tamariscina (**Nutt.**) **Wood** – See *Amaranthus rudis* Sauer

Acnida tuberculata **Moq.** – See *Amaranthus tuberculatus* (Moq.) Sauer

Acnistus arborescens (**L.**) **Schlecht.** – Tree wild tobacco [Tree wildto-bacco] (155) (1942)

Acnistus **Schott** – Wild tobacco [Wild-tobacco, Wildtobacco] (155) (1942)

Acoelorraphe wrightii (**Griseb. & H. Wendl.**) **H. Wendl. ex Becc.** – Saw cabbage-palm [Saw-cabbage palm] (106) (1930)

Aconitum bakeri **Greene** – See *Aconitum columbianum* Nutt.

Aconitum columbianum **Nutt.** – Aconite (148) (1939), Baker's monks-hood [Baker monkshood] (155) (1942), Columbia monkshood (155) (1942), Columbian monkshood (50, 155) (1942–present), Howell's monkshood [Howell monkshood] (155) (1942), Leiberg's monks-hood [Leiberg monkshood] (155) (1942), Monkshood [Monk's-hood, Monk's hood] (3, 85, 148) (1932–1977), Yellow monkshood [Yellow monk's-hood] (155) (1942)

Aconitum howellii **A. Nels. & J.F. Macbr.** – See *Aconitum columbianum* Nutt. subsp. *columbianum*

Aconitum **L.** – Aconite (1, 109) (1932–1949), Monkshood [Monk's-hood, Monk's hood] (1, 4, 50, 13, 15, 109, 138, 155, 156, 158, 167) (1814–present), Mouse-bane [Mouse bane] (92) (1876), Wolf's-bane [Wolfbane, Wolf bane, Wolf's bane, Wolfsbane, Wolfs-bane] (1, 10, 13, 15, 109, 158) (1818–1949)

Aconitum leibergii **Greene** – See *Aconitum columbianum* Nutt. subsp. *columbianum*

Aconitum lutescens – See *Aconitum columbianum* Nutt. subsp. *columbianum*

Aconitum lycoctonum **L.** – Great yellow monk's-hood (165) (1768), Great yellow wolf's-bane (165) (1768), Wolf-bane monkshood [Wolfbane monkshood] (155) (1942), Wolf's-bane [Wolfbane, Wolf bane, Wolf's bane, Wolfsbane, Wolfs-bane] (107, 138) (1919–1923), Yellow monkshood [Yellow monk's-hood] (165) (1768), Yellow wolf's-bane [Yellow wolf's bane, Yellow wolfes bane] (92, 165, 178) (1526–1876)

Aconitum lycotonum – See *Aconitum lycoctonum* L.

Aconitum napellus **L.** – Aconite (53, 54, 55, 57, 59, 60, 61, 92, 107, 138, 156) (1870–1923), Aconite monkshood (155) (1942), Aconi-tum (60) (1902), Adam-and-Eve [Adam and Eve] (74) (1893) Washington Co. ME, Adam-and-Eve-in-the-bower (76) (1896) Deering ME, Bear's-foot [Bear's foot, Bearsfoot] (107, 156) (1919–1923), Blue rocket (156) (1923), Common monkshood [Common monk's-hood] (165) (1768), Common wolf's-bane (165) (1768), Cuck-oo's-cap [Cuckoo's cap] (156) (1923), Friar's-cap [Friar's cap, Friars' cap] (92, 107, 156) (1876–1923), Friar's-cowl [Friar's cowl] (92, 156) (1876–1923), Helmet flower [Helmet-flower] (107, 156) (1919–1923), Luckie's mutch (107) (1919), Monkshood [Monk's-hood, Monk's hood] (49, 52, 53, 54, 57, 60, 92, 156) (1898–1923), Mouse-bane [Mouse bane] (156) (1923), Soldier's-cap [Soldier's cap] (107, 156) (1919–1923), Turk's-cap [Turk's cap, Turkscap] (107, 156) (1919–1923), Venus'-chariot [Venus' chariot] (50) (present), Wolf root [Wolf-root] (92, 156) (1898–1923), Wolf's-bane [Wolfbane, Wolf bane, Wolf's bane, Wolfsbane, Wolfs-bane] (7, 19, 49, 53, 54, 92, 156) (1828–1923), Wolf's-bane with the turnip root [Wolfesbane with the turnep roote] (178) (1526)

Aconitum noveboracense **Gray ex Coville** – New York monkshood (5) (1913)

Aconitum ramosum **A. Nels.** – See *Aconitum columbianum* Nutt.

Aconitum reclinatum **Gray** – Trailing monkshood (5) (1913), Trailing wolfsbane (5) (1913)

Aconitum tenue **Rydb.** – See *Aconitum columbianum* Nutt.

Aconitum uncinatum **L.** – American monk's-hood (165) (1768), American wolf's-bane (165) (1768), Clambering monkshood (138, 155) (1931–1942), Manchurian monkshood (50, 138, 155) (1931–present), Monkshood [Monk's-hood, Monk's hood] (19) (1840), Small blue monk's-hood (165) (1768), Variegated monk's-hood (165) (1768), Wild wolfbane (5) (1913), Wold monkhood (5) (1913)

Acorus americanus (**Raf.**) **Raf.** – Sweetflag [Sweet flag, Sweet-flag] (50) (present)

Acorus calamus L. − Acore odorant (French) (7, 186) (1814), Acore vrai (French) (158) (1900), Acoro (Italian) (186) (1814), Acoro calamo (Spanish, Portuguese) (186) (1814), Acorum (186) (1814), Acorus des Indes ou Asiatique (French) (186) (1814), Aromatic calamus (42) (1814), Aromatic sweet-flag [Aromatic sweet flag] (42) (1814), Bamira (186) (1814), Bassombe (186) (1814), Bastard calamus (178) (1596), Bastard calamus aromaticus (46) (1671), Beewort (5, 64, 156, 157, 158) (1900–1929), Bembi (186) (1814), Calami Radix (Official name of Materia Medica) (7) (1828), Calamo aromatico (Spanish, Italian) (158) (1900), Calamo odoranto (Italian) (186) (1814), Calamus (5, 10, 19, 49, 50, 53, 57, 58, 59, 64, 92, 93, 97, 121, 155, 156, 158, 186, 187) (1814–present), Calamus Aromaticus (Official name of Materia Medica) (7, 165, 180) (1633–1828), Calamus-root [Calamus root] (72, 85, 101, 122, 138, 156, 157) (1886–1937), Calmus (75, 158, 186) (1814–1900), Cassabel (186) (1814), Cinnamon sedge (64, 158) (1900–1908), Common calamus aromaticus (165) (1768), Common sweetflag [Common sweet flag] (2, 42) (1814–1895), Common sweet-rush (165) (1768), Drug sweetflag (155) (1942), Flag root [Flag-root] (5, 7, 93, 156, 157) (1828–1936), Gemeine Calamus (German) (186) (1814), Hoxwa (Lakota) (121) (1918–1970), Ir (186) (1814), Kalmus (Danish, Dutch, German) (7, 158, 186) (1814–1900), Kalmusfid (186) (1814), Kalmuss (Swedish, Hungarian) (186) (1814), Kalmuss sakkenes (186) (1814), Karili (186) (1814), Karweles (186) (1814), Kawa subo (Japanese) (186) (1814), Kneh-boschem (186) (1814), Koren (Russia) (186) (1814), Milsean-Mara (Gaelic) (186) (1814), Myrtle flag [Myrtle-flag] (5, 7, 64, 156, 157, 158, 186) (1814–1908), Myrtle-grass [Myrtle grass] (5, 64, 92, 156, 158, 184) (1793–1908), Myrtle-sedge [Myrtle sedge] (5, 64, 156, 158) (1900–1908), Peže bthaΘka (Osage, flat herb) (121) (1918–1970?), Prassworec (186) (1814), Pruskworek (Bohemian) (186) (1814), Sea-sedge [Sea sedge] (5, 156) (1913–1923), Sedge root (5) (1913), Sedge-cane [Sedge cane] (5, 156) (1913–1923), Sedge-rush [Sedge rush] (5, 156) (1913–1923), Sįŋkpe tawote (Lakota, muskrat food) (121) (1918–1970) SD, So ingwer (186) (1814), Šuŋkače (Lakota, dog penis) (121) (1918–1970), Sweet cane (186) (1814), Sweet garden flag (180) (1633), Sweet grass [Sweet-grass, Sweetgrass] (186) (1814), Sweet myrtle-grass (186) (1814), Sweet-cane [Sweet cane] (7, 64, 92, 156, 157, 158) (1828–1929), Sweetflag [Sweet flag, Sweet-flag] (3, 5, 7, 10, 14, 19, 49, 53, 55, 57, 58, 64, 85, 92, 93, 97, 109, 120, 121, 156, 157, 158, 186, 187) (1814–1977), Sweet-grass [Sweet grass] (7, 64, 92, 158) (1828–1908), Sweet-myrtle [Sweet myrtle] (5, 64, 156, 157, 158) (1900–1929), Sweetroot [Sweet root] (7, 64, 92, 156, 158) (1828–1923), Sweet-rush [Sweet rush] (7, 64, 92, 156, 158) (1828–1923), Sweet-sedge [Sweet sedge] (64, 92, 156, 158) (1876–1923), Sweet-segg [Sweet segg] (64, 158) (1900–1908), Sweet-smelling flag (186) (1814), Sweet-smelling reed (180) (1633), Tatarskie ziele (Polish) (186) (1814), Vacha (India) (59) (1911)

Acorus L. − Calamus-root [Calamus root] (1) (1932), Sweetflag [Sweet flag, Sweet-flag] (1, 50, 93, 138, 155, 156, 158, 167) (1814–present)

Acrocomia Mart. − Acrocomia (155) (1942)

Acrolasia Presl. − See *Mentzelia* L.

Acroptilon Cass. − Hardheads [Hard-head] (50) (present)

Acroptilon repens (L.) DC. − Hardheads [Hard-head] (50) (present)

Acrostichum areolatum L. − See *Woodwardia areolata* (L.) T. Moore

Acrostichum aureum L. − Fork fern [Fork-fern, Forkfern] (19) (1840), Forked fern (92) (1876), Golden leatherfern (50) (present)

Acrostichum L. − Acrostichum (158) (1900), Chrysodium (2) (1895), Fork fern [Fork-fern, Forkfern] (167) (1814), Leather fern [Leather-fern] (50) (present), Wall-rue [Wall rue] (167) (1814)

Acrostichum polypodioides L. − See *Pleopeltis polypodioides* (L.) Andrews & Windham subsp. *polypodioides*

Actaea alba (Aiton) Willd. − See *Actaea pachypoda* Ell.

Actaea alba Bigelow − See *Actaea pachypoda* Ell.

Actaea americana [Prantl] − See *Actaea podocarpa* DC.

Actaea americana [Pursh] − See *Actaea rubra* (Aiton) Willd.

Actaea americana Green − possibly *Actaea rubra* (Aiton) Willd.

Actaea americana Green alba − See *Actaea rubra* (Aiton) Willd.

Actaea arguta Nutt. − See *Actaea rubra* (Aiton) Willd.

Actaea L. − Baneberry [Bane berry, Bane-berry, Bane berries] (1, 4, 42, 50, 13, 15, 63, 93, 109, 138, 155, 156, 158) (1814–present), Black cohosh (93) (1936), Cohosh [Co-hosh] (63, 109, 158) (1899–1949), Necklace-weed [Necklace weed] (76) (1896) ME, Rattleweed [Rattle-weed, Rattle weed] (167) (1814), Richweed [Rich-weed, Rich weed] (190) (~1759)

Actaea pachypoda Ell. − American herb Christopher (6) (1892), American herb Christopher with white berries (165) (1768), Baneberry [Bane berry, Bane-berry, Bane berries] (156) (1923), Blue cohosh (76) (1896) Paris ME, Cohush (79) (1891), Doll's-eyes (156) (1923), Herb Christopher [Herb-Christopher] (156, 158) (1900–1923), Herbe de Ste. Christophr blanc (French) (6) (1892), Necklace-weed [Necklace weed] (5, 19, 49, 92, 156, 158) (1840–1923), Rattlesnake herb [Rattlesnake-herb] (156) (1923), Snakeroot [Snake root, Snake-root] (5, 156, 158) (1900–1923), Toadroot [Toad root, Toad-root] (6, 7) (1828–1932), Wapkadak (Chippewa) (105) (1932), Weisses Christophskraut (German) (6) (1892), White baneberry [White bane berry] (2, 6, 7, 49, 50, 53, 63, 72, 85, 92, 97, 105, 131, 138, 155, 158) (1828–present), White cohosh (5, 6, 7, 49, 53, 57, 61, 76, 92, 156, 158) (1828–1923), White grapewort (156, 158) (1900–1923), Whitebeads [White beads, White-beads] (5, 49, 53, 92, 156, 158) (1898–1923), Whiteberry [White berry, White-berry] (5, 156, 158) (1900–1923), White-berry snakeroot [Whiteberry snakeroot, White berry snakeroot] (7, 92) (1828–1876)

Actaea racemosa L. − Black cohosh (5, 6, 7, 15, 49, 52, 53, 54, 55, 57, 58, 92, 156) (1828–1923), Rattlesnake-root [Rattlesnake root, Rattle-Snake-Root, Rattlesnakes' root, Rattlesnakeroot] (5, 6, 7, 53, 64, 92) (1828–1922), Rattleweed [Rattle-weed, Rattle weed] (5, 6, 7, 53, 64, 74, 92, 156) (1876–1923), Schwarz Schlangewurz (German) (7) (1828), Sepentaire noire (French) (7) (1828), Serpentaria nigra (Official name of Materia Medica) (7) (1828), Squawroot [Squaw-root, Squaw root] (7, 49, 58, 64, 92) (1828–1908)

Actaea racemosa Willd. − See *Cimicifuga racemosa* (L.) Nutt.

Actaea rubra (Aiton) Willd. − American baneberry [American bane berry] (42) (1814) SD, American herb Christopher with red berries (165) (1768), Baneberry [Bane berry, Bane-berry, Bane berries] (3, 10, 19, 127, 156) (1818–1977), Black cohosh (5, 156) (1913–1923), Black cohosh (76) (1896), Blue cohosh (158) (1900), Cohosh [Co-hosh] (187) (1818), Coral-and-pearl (157, 158) (1900–1929), Coralberry [Coral-berry, Coral berry] (5, 156) (1913–1923), Grapewort [Grape wort] (5, 156) (1913–1923), Green baneberry (155) (1942), Herb Christopher [Herb-Christopher] (5, 10, 156, 157, 158, 187) (1818–1929), Pearlberry [Pearl berry] (5) (1913), Poison-berry [Poison berry] (5, 92, 156, 157, 158) (1876–1929), Rattlesnake herb [Rattlesnake-herb] (5, 156, 157, 158) (1900–1929), Red baneberry [Red bane-berry, Red bane berry] (5, 40, 42, 50, 63, 72, 85, 92, 93, 131, 138, 155, 157, 158) (1814–present), Red cohosh (7, 92, 156, 157, 158) (1828–1923), Redberry [Red-berry, Red berry] (5, 157, 158) (1900–1929), Red-berry snakeroot [Red berry snake root, Red-berry snakeroot] (7, 92, 57) (1828–1900), Snakeberry [Snake berry, Snake-berry] (5, 156, 157, 158) (1900–1929), Snakeroot [Snake root, Snake-root] (5, 156, 158) (1900–1923), Toadroot [Toad root, Toad-root] (5, 92, 156, 157, 158) (1876–1929), Western baneberry (155) (1942), White baneberry [White bane berry] (42) (1814), Wi'cosidji'bĭk (Chippewa, drawing plant or root) (40) (1928)

Actaea rubra arguta (Nutt.) Greene − See *Actaea rubra* (Aiton) Willd. subsp. *arguta* (Nutt.)

Actaea spicata L. − Baneberry [Bane berry, Bane-berry, Bane berries] (14, 92) (1876–1882), Black baneberry (138, 155) (1931–1942), Common baneberry [Common bane berry] (42) (1814), Coral baneberry [Coral bane berry] (42) (1814), Herb Christopher [Herb-Christopher] (92) (1876), Pearl baneberry [Pearl bane berry] (42) (1814), Rattlesnake herb [Rattlesnake-herb] (92) (1876), Red cohosh (29)

9

(1869) Pursh says berry color differs witihin population, St. Christopher's herb [Saint Christopher herb, St. Christopher's-herb, S. Christophers herbe] (178) (1526), White cohosh (29) (1869) Pursh says berry color differs witihin populations

Actaea spicata L. var. *rubra* Ait – See *Actaea rubra* (Aiton) Willd. subsp. *rubra*

Actaea viridiflora Greene – See *Actaea rubra* (Aiton) Willd.

Actinea acaulis (Pursh) Spreng. – See *Tetraneuris acaulis* (Pursh) Greene var. *acaulis*

Actinea acaulis arizonica – See *Tetraneuris acaulis* (Pursh) Greene var. *arizonica* (Greene) Parker

Actinea acaulis lanigera – See *Tetraneuris acaulis* (Pursh) Greene var. *caespitosa* A. Nelson

Actinea acaulis septentrionalis – See *Tetraneuris acaulis* (Pursh) Greene var. *acaulis*

Actinea acaulis simplex – See *Tetraneuris acaulis* (Pursh) Greene var. *acaulis*

Actinea grandiflora (Torr. & A. Gray) Kuntze – See *Tetraneuris grandiflora* (Torr. & Gray ex Gray) Parker

Actinea herbacea (Greene) B.L. Rob. – See *Tetraneuris herbacea* Greene

Actinea linearifolia (Hook.) Kuntze – See *Tetraneuris linearifolia* (Hook.) Greene var. *linearifolia*

Actinea odorata (DC.) Kuntze – See *Actinella odorata* (DC.) A.Gray

Actinea richardsoni – See *Hymenoxys richardsonii* (Hook.) Cockerell var. *richardsonii*

Actinea scaposa (DC.) Kuntze – See *Tetraneuris scaposa* (DC.) Greene

Actinea texana (Coulter & Rose) Cory – See *Hymenoxys texana* (Coult. & Rose) Cockerell

Actinella acaulis Nutt. – See *Tetraneuris acaulis* (Pursh) Greene var. *acaulis*

Actinella odorata (DC.) A.Gray – Bitterweed actinea (155) (1942), Limonilla (122, 158) (1900–1937), Western bitterweed [Western bitter weed] (122, 124) (1937)

Actinella richardsonii (Hook.) Nutt. var. *floribunda* Gray – See *Hymenoxys richardsonii* (Hook.) Cockerell var. *floribunda* (Gray) Parker

Actinidia arguta (Sieb. & Zucc.) Planch. ex Miq. – Bower actinidia (109, 137, 155) (1923–1949), Girald's actinidia [Girald actinidia] (155) (1942), Tara vine [Tara-vine] (50, 109, 138) (1923–present)

Actinidia arguta Miq. – See *Actinidia arguta* (Sieb. & Zucc.) Planch. ex Miq. introduced

Actinidia giraldi – See *Actinidia arguta* (Sieb. & Zucc.) Planch. ex Miq.

Actinidia giraldii Diels – See *Actinidia arguta* (Sieb. & Zucc.) Planch. ex Miq.

Actinidia Lindl. – Actinidia (138, 155) (1931–1942)

Actinidia polygama (Siebold & Zucc.) Maxim. – Silver vine [Silvervine, Silver-vine] (109, 138) (1923–1949), Silver-vine actinidia [Silvervine actinidia] (155) (1942)

Actinidia polygama Maxim. – See *Actinidia polygama* (Siebold & Zucc.) Maxim. introduced

Actinolepis DC. – possibly Eriophyllum Lag

Actinomeris alternifolia (L.) DC. – See *Verbesina alternifolia* (L.) Britton ex Kearney

Actinomeris helianthoides (Michx.) Nutt. – See *Verbesina helianthoides* Michx.

Actinomeris Nutt. – See *Verbesina* L. all US species

Actinomeris squarrosa Nutt. – See *Verbesina coreopsis* Michx.

Acuan illinoensis (Michx.) Kuntze – See *Desmanthus illinoensis* (Michx.) MacM. ex B.L. Robins. & Fern.

Acuan jamesii (T. & G.) Kuntze – See *Desmanthus cooleyi* (Eaton) Trel.

Acuan leptoloba (Torr. & Gray) Kuntze – See *Desmanthus leptolobus* Torr. & Gray

Acuan Medik. – See *Desmanthus* Willd.

Adansonia digitata L. – Abavo (165) (1768), Baobab (50, 92, 107, 109, 155, 165) (1768–present), Cork or Cork tree [Cork-tree, Corktree] (107) (1919) Florida Keys, Ethiopian sour-gourd (165) (1768), Monkey-bread tree (109) (1949), Sour gourd (107) (1919)

Adelea – possibly *Adelia* L.

Adelia (P. Br.) Michx. – possibly *Adelia* L.

Adelia acuminata Michx. – See *Forestiera acuminata* (Michx.) Poir.

Adelia L. – Adelia (155, 158) (1900–1942), Palo blanco [Paloblanco] (153) (1913) NM, Wild lime or Wild lime tree [Wild lime-tree] (50) (present)

Adelia P. Br. – See *Adelia* L.

Adelia vaseyi (Coult.) Pax & K. Hoffmann – Bead tree [Beade tree] (109, 137, 155) (1923–1949), Vasey's adelia [Vasey adelia] (155) (1942), Vasey's wild lime (50) (present)

Adenanthera pavonina L. – Barbados pride [Barbadoes pride] (107) (1919), Coral pea (107) (1919), False red sandal (92) (1876), Red sandalwood (107) (1919), Redbead (138) (1923), Sandal bead tree [Sandal beadtree] (155) (1942)

Adenocaulon bicolor Hook. – Adenocaulon (5) (1913), American adenocaulon (155) (1942), American trail plant [American trailplant] (50) (present), Silver-green (156) (1923)

Adenocaulon Hook. – Adenocaulon (155, 158) (1900–1942), Trail plant [Trailplant] (1, 50) (1932–present)

Adenorachis arbutifolia – See *Adenorachis arbutifolia* (L.) Nieuwl.

Adenorachis arbutifolia (L.) Nieuwl. – Attitaash (46) (1879), Chokeberry [Choke-berry, Choke berry] (46, 47, 76, 82, 92, 107, 156) (1876–1930)

Adenostoma fasciculatum Hook. & Arn. – Chamisal (106) (1930), Chamise (74, 106) (1893–1930) Santa Barbara CA

Adiantum (Tourn.) L. – See *Adiantum* L.

Adiantum capillus-veneris L. – Australian maidenhair fern (138) (1923), Maidenhair [Maiden-hair, Maiden hair] (49, 92, 158) (1876–1900), Black maidenhair [Black maiden's hair, Blacke maiden haire] (5, 109, 158) (1900–1949), Capillaire de Montpelier (French) (97) (1937), Common maidenhair (50) (present), Culantrillo (Spanish) (158) (1900), Dudder-grass [Dudder grass] (5, 158) (1900–1913), Maidenhair fern [Maiden-hair fern, Maiden hair fern] (49) (1898), Maydin here (178, 179) (1526–1596), European maidenhair (158) (1900), Frauenhaar [Frauen-haar] (German) (158) (1900), Lady's-hair [Lady's hair] (5, 158) (1900–1913), Southern maidenhair (155) (1942), Southern maidenhair fern (138) (1923), True maidenhair [True maiden's hair] (5, 109, 165) (1768–1949), True maidenhair fern [True maiden-hair fern] (86) (1878), Venushaar (German) (158) (1900), Venus'-hair [Venushair, Venus-hair, Venus' hair] (92, 97, 109, 158) (1900–1949), Venus'-hair fern [Venus' hair fern, Venus hair fern, Venus-hair fern, Venus's hair fern] (3, 4, 5, 72, 122, 124, 131) (1899–1986)

Adiantum caudatum L. – Tail-leaf maidenhair [Tail-leaved maidenhair] (165) (1768), Trailing maidenhair fern (138) (1923)

Adiantum cuneatum – See *Adiantum raddianum* K. Presl

Adiantum formosum R. Br. – See *Adiantum capillus-veneris* L.

Adiantum L. – Maidenhair [Maiden-hair, Maiden hair] (138, 155, 158) (1900–1942), Maidenhair fern [Maiden-hair fern, Maiden hair fern] (1, 4, 50, 109, 138) (1923–present), Venus'-hair fern [Venus' hair fern, Venus hair fern, Venus-hair fern, Venus's hair fern] (1) (1932)

Adiantum pedatum L. – Adiantum (57) (1917), American maidenhair (7, 109, 138, 155, 157, 158) (1828–1949), Canadian maidenhair, Canadian maiden hair (42, 46, 165)(1768–1879), Capil Veneris (Official name of Materia Medica) (7) (1828), Capillaire du Canada (French) (7, 158) (1828–1900), Filix Veneris (Official name of Materia Medica) (7) (1828), Frauenhaar [Frauen-haar] (German) (7) (1828), Hair fern (157, 158) (1900–1929), Herba Veneris (Official name of Materia Medica) (7) (1828), Kâ'ga skûntaï (Cherokee, crow shin) (102) (1885), Lock-hair fern (5) (1913), Maidenhair [Maiden-hair, Maiden hair] (7, 19, 46, 49, 57, 157, 158, 184, 187) (1793–1929), Maidenhair fern [Maiden-hair fern, Maiden hair fern] (3, 4, 49, 72, 97, 102) (1886–1986), Mow-hair (187) (1818), Nordamerikanisches Frauenhaar (German) (158) (1900), Northern maidenhair (50) (present), Rock fern (7, 92, 157, 158) (1828–1929), Sweet fern

[Sweetfern, Sweet-fern] (7) (1828), Venus'-hair [Venushair, Venushair, Venus' hair] (46) (1649)

Adiantum raddianum **K. Presl** – Delta maidenhair fern (138) (1923), Wedge-leaf maidenhair [Wedge-leaved maidenhair] (165) (1768)

Adiantum tenerum **Sw.** – Brittle maidenhair (109) (1949), Fan maidenhair fern (138) (1923), Tender maidenhair (165) (1768)

Adiantum trapeziforme **L.** – Diamond maidenhair fern (138) (1923)

Adicea glaberrima **Raf.** – possibly *Pilea pumila* (L.) Gray var. *pumila*

Adicea pumila **(L.) Raf.** – See *Pilea pumila* (L.) Gray var. *pumila*

Adicea **Raf.** – See *Pilea* Lindl.

Adicea **Raf. ex Britton & A. Br.** – See *Pilea* Lindl.

Adlumia cirrhosa **Raf.** – See *Adlumia fungosa* (Aiton) Greene ex B. S. P.

Adlumia fungosa **(Aiton) Greene ex B. S. P.** – Adluma (2) (1895) Madison WI, Allegheny fringe [Alleghany fringe] (5, 92, 156) (1876–1923), Allegheny vine [Alleghany vine, Alleghany-vine] (5, 50, 73, 109, 156) (1892–present), Canary vine [Canary-vine] (5, 76, 156) (1896–1923) Madison WI, Climbing colicweed [Climbing colic weed] (19) (1840), Climbing fumitory (2, 72, 92, 109, 138, 156) (1876–1949), Cypress vine [Cypress-vine, Cypress-vine, Cyprus vine (5, 156) (1913–1923), Fairy creeper (5, 73, 156) (1892–1923) Fredericton, NB, Mountain fringe (5, 48, 73, 76, 92, 109, 155, 156) (1876–1949), Wood fringe (5, 76, 92, 156) (1876–1923) Paris ME

Adlumia fungosa **Greene** – See *Adlumia fungosa* (Aiton) Greene ex B. S. P.

Adlumia **Raf. ex DC.** – Adlumia (50) (present), Allegheny vine [Alleghany vine, Alleghany-vine] (1) (1932), Climbing fumitory (1, 138, 156) (1923–1932), Mountain-fringe [Mountainfringe] (155) (1942)

Adnaria resinosa **Kuntze** – See *Gaylussacia baccata* (Wang.) K. Koch

Adolphia californica **S. Watson** – California adolphia (155) (1942)

Adolphia infesta **(Kunth) Meisn.** – Texas adolphia (155) (1942)

Adolphia **Meisn.** – Adolphia (155) (1942)

Adonis aestivalis **L.** – Summer adonis (109, 137, 155) (1923–1949), Tall adonis (165) (1768)

Adonis annua **L.** – Adonis with red floures (180) (1633), Adonis'-flower [Adonis' flower, Adonis flower, Adonis floure] (5, 178, 180) (1526–1913), Autumn adonis (109) (1949), Autumnal adonis (42) (1814), Bird's-eye [Bird's eye, Bird's-eyes, Birds-eyes] (5, 156, 165) (1768–1923), Camomile [Chamomile, Camomylle] (5, 156) (1913–1923), Common adonis (165) (1768), Flos Adonis (178) (1526), Pheasant's-eye [Pheasantseye, Pheasant's-eye] (2, 5, 15, 19, 42, 92, 138, 156, 165) (1768–1923), Pheasants-eye adonis (155) (1942), Red maithes (165) (1768), Red Morocco (5, 92, 156, 165) (1768–1923) florist name in England

Adonis autumnalis **L.** – See *Adonis annua* L.

Adonis **L.** – Adonis (138, 155) (1923–1942), Pheasant's-eye [Pheasantseye, Pheasant's-eye] (109, 156) (1923–1949)

Adonis vernalis **L.** – Bird's-eye [Bird's eye, Bird's-eyes, Birds-eyes] (92) (1876), False hellebore [False-hellebore] (49, 57, 92) (1876–1917), Ox-eye [Ox eye, Oxeye, Oxe eie] (178) (1526), Perennial adonis [Perrenial adonis] (165) (1768), Pheasant's-eye [Pheasantseye, Pheasant's-eye] (49, 52, 53) (1919–1922), Spring adonis (2, 109, 138, 155, 165) (1768–1949), Spring pheasant's-eye [Spring pheasant's eye] (50) (present)

Adopogon dandelion **(L.) Kuntze** – See *Krigia dandelion* (L.) Nutt.

Adopogon virginicum **(L.) Kuntze** – See *Krigia virginica* (L.) Willd.

Adoxa **L.** – Adoxa (50) (present), Moschatel (158) (1900), Muskroot [Musk-root, Musk root] (155, 158) (1900–1942)

Adoxa moschatellina **L.** – Bulbous fumitory (5, 156, 158, 165) (1768–1923), Gloryless [Glory-less] (5, 158) (1900–1913), Green hollowroot [Greene hollow roote] (178) (1526), Hollowroot [Hollow root, Hollow-root] (5, 158, 165) (1768–1913), Hollow-root musk (156) (1923), Moschatel (3, 4, 5, 63, 92, 131, 156, 158) (1899–1986), Moschatella (174) (1753), Musk (158) (1900), Musk wood-crowfoot (158) (1900), Musk-crowfoot [Musk crowfoot] (5, 156, 158, 165) (1768–1923), Muskroot [Musk-root, Musk root] (4, 50, 63, 72,

131, 155, 156, 158) (1899–present), Tuberous moschatel (19, 165) (1768–1840), Wood-crowfoot [Wood crowfoot] (5) (1913)

Aegilops cylindrica **Host** – Aegilops (119) (1938), Goat grass [Goatgrass] (3) (1977), Jointed goatgrass (50, 119, 155) (1938–present), Wild wheat (119) (1938) OK

Aegilops **L.** – Goat grass [Goatgrass] (50, 155) (1942–present)

Aegopodium **L.** – Goutweed [Gout-weed, Gout weed] (50, 138, 155, 156, 165) (1768–present), Podagraire (French) (165) (1768)

Aegopodium podagraria **L.** – Aiseweed [Aise weed, Aise-weed] (5, 156) (1913–1923), Ashweed [Ash-weed, Ash weed, Ashe weed, Ashe-weed] (5, 107, 156, 165) (1768–1923), Axweed [Ax weed] (5, 92) (1876–1913), Bishop's goutweed [Bishops goutweed] (155) (1942), Bishop's-elder [Bishop's elder] (5, 156) (1913–1923), Bishop's-weed [Bishop's weed, Bishop weed] (5, 107, 109) (1913–1949), Dog-elder [Dog elder] (5, 156) (1913–1923), Dwarf ash (156) (1923), Dwarf elder (5, 156) (1913–1923), English masterwort (5) (1913), Garden plague (5, 156) (1913–1923), Goat's-foot [Goat's foot] (92, 156) (1876–1923), Goutweed [Gout-weed, Gout weed] (5, 92, 107, 109, 138, 156, 165) (1768–1949) used in Germany for pain of gout, Goutwort [Gout-wort, Goutwoort] (5, 156, 178) (1526–1923), Ground-ash [Ground ash] (107, 156) (1919–1923), Herb ax-weed (156) (1923), Herb Gerard [Herb-Gerard, Herbe Gerard] (5, 107, 156, 165, 178) (1526–1923), Jack-jump-about (156) (1923), Silver-edge bishop's goutweed [Silveredge bishops goutweed] (155) (1942), White ash herb (156) (1923), White ashweed [White ash weed] (5) (1913), Wild alder (156) (1923), Wild elder [Wild-elder] (156) (1923), Wild masterwort (5, 156, 165) (1768–1923)

Aegopodium podagraria variegatum – See *Aegopodium podagraria* L.

Aegopogon **Beauv.** – See *Aegopogon* Humb. & Bonpl. ex Willd.

Aegopogon cenchroides **Humb. & Bonpl. ex Willd.** – Goat's-beard grass [Goats' beard grass] (92) (1876)

Aegopogon **Humb. & Bonpl. ex Willd.** – Goat's-beard grass [Goats' beard grass] (45) (1896), Schellingia (45) (1896)

Aegopogon pusillus – See *Aegopogon cenchroides* Humb. & Bonpl. ex Willd.

Aeonium arboreum **(L.) Webb & Berthel.** – House leek tree (92) (1876), Tree houseleek (19) (1840)

Aeonium **Webb & Berth.** – Aeonium (155) (1942)

Aeschynomene americana **L.** – American jointvetch (155) (1942), Hairy aeschynomene (165) (1768), Pois du Duc de Choifeul (French) (165) (1768)

Aeschynomene hispida **Willd.** – See *Aeschynomene virginica* (L.) Britton, Sterns & Poggenb.

Aeschynomene **L.** – Jointvetch (50, 155) (1942–present)

Aeschynomene virginica **(L.) Britton, Sterns & Poggenb.** – Bastard sensitive plant (5) (1913), False sensitive plant (19) (1840), Sensitive joint-vetch [Sensitive jointvetch, Sensitive joint vetch] (2, 5, 155) (1895–1942)

Aeschynomene viscidula – Sticky jointvetch (155) (1942)

Aesculus ×*bushii* **Schneid.** *[glabra × pavia]* – Arkansas buckeye (138) (1923)

Aesculus ×*carnea* **Hayne** *[hippocastanum × pavia]* – Red horse-chestnut (109) (1949)

Aesculus ×*mutabilis* **(Spach) Scheele** *[pavia × sylvatica]* – Harbison's buckeye [Harbison buckeye] (138) (1923)

Aesculus ×*neglecta* **Lindl.** *[flava × sylvatica]* – Painted buckeye (155) (1942)

Aesculus arguta **Buckl.** – See *Aesculus glabra* Willd. var. *arguta* (Buckl.) B.L. Robins.

Aesculus austrina **Small.** – See *Aesculus pavia* L. var. *pavia*

Aesculus bushi – See *Aesculus* ×*bushii* Schneid. *[glabra × pavia]*

Aesculus californica **(Spach) Nutt.** – California buckeye (71, 106, 109, 138, 155) (1898–1949), California horse-chestnut [Californian horse chestnut] (2, 20, 103, 107) (1857–1919), Marronier de Californie (French) (20) (1857)

Aesculus californica **Nutt.** – See *Aesculus californica* (Spach) Nutt.

Aesculus carnea **Hayne** – See *Aesculus ×carnea* Hayne [*hippocastanum × pavia*]

Aesculus discolor flavescens – See *Aesculus pavia* var. *flavescens* (Sarg.) Correll

Aesculus discolor mollis – See *Aesculus pavia* L. var. *pavia*

Aesculus discolor **Pursh** – See *Aesculus pavia* L. var. *pavia*

Aesculus discolor var. *flavescens* **Sargent** – See *Aesculus pavia* var. *flavescens* (Sarg.) Correll

Aesculus flava **Aiton** – Big buckeye (5, 156) (1913–1923), Buck-eye [Buckeye] (23, 35) (1806–1810), Carolina yellow buckeye (155) (1942), Large buckeye (5, 20, 156) (1857–1923), New River horse-chestnut [New River horse chestnut] (8) (1785), Ohio buckeye (2, 58) (1869–1895), Pavia jaune (French) (8) (1785), Sweet buckeye (2, 15, 72, 109, 156) (1895–1949), Tricolor yellow buckeye (155) (1942), Yellow buckeye (2, 20, 109, 138, 155, 156) (1857–1949), Yellow sweet buckeye (5, 97) (1913–1937), Yellow-flower horse-chestnut [Yellow-flowered horse-chestnut] (165) (1768)

Aesculus georgiana – See *Aesculus sylvatica* Bartr.

Aesculus glabra leucodermis – See *Aesculus glabra* Willd.

Aesculus glabra monticola – See *Aesculus glabra* Willd.

Aesculus glabra pallida – See *Aesculus glabra* Willd.

Aesculus glabra sargenti – See *Aesculus glabra* Willd.

Aesculus glabra **Willd.** – American horse-chestnut [American horse chestnut] (5, 20, 156, 157, 158) (1857–1929), Buck-eye [Buckeye] (23, 52, 61, 92, 148) (1810–1939), Fetid buckeye (2, 5, 13, 15, 49, 53, 93, 156, 157, 158) (1849–1936), Horse-chestnut [Horse chestnut, Horsechestnut] or Horse-chestnut tree (124) (1937), Little buckeye (19) (1840), Ohio buckeye (2, 5, 13, 15, 20, 49, 50, 53, 57, 58, 65, 71, 72, 95, 97, 106, 109, 113, 138, 155, 156, 157, 158) (1857–present), Oklahoma buckeye (155) (1942), Pale Ohio buckeye (155) (1942), Shrubby buckeye (5, 97, 125, 156) (1913–1937), Smooth buckeye (49, 53) (1898), Taška hi (Osage, white oak-like? tree) (121) (1918?–1970?), Texas buckeye [Texan buckeye] (124, 138, 155) (1923–1942), Western buckeye (3, 4, 5, 97, 125, 156) (1913–1986), White-bark buckeye [Whitebark buckeye] (138) (1923), White-bark Ohio buckeye [Whitebark Ohio buckeye] (155) (1942)

Aesculus glabra **Willd.** var. *leucodermis* **Sargent** – See *Aesculus glabra* Willd.

Aesculus glabra **Willd.** var. *micrantha* **Sargent** – See *Aesculus glabra* Willd.

Aesculus glabra **Willd.** var. *monticola* **Sargent** – See *Aesculus glabra* Willd.

Aesculus glabra **Willd.** var. *pallida* **(Willd.) Kirchn.** – See *Aesculus glabra* Willd.

Aesculus glabra **Willd.** var. *sargentii* **Rehd.** – See *Aesculus glabra* Willd.

Aesculus harbisoni – See *Aesculus ×mutabilis* (Spach) Scheele [*pavia × sylvatica*]

Aesculus hippocastanum **L.** – Asiatic horse chestnut (6) (1892), Bongay (5, 156) (1913–1923), Buck-eye [Buckeye] (6) (1892), Common horsechestnut [Common horse-chestnut, Common horse chestnut] (6, 71, 82, 109, 155, 165) (1768–1942), Conquerors (156) (1923), Horse-chestnut [Horse chestnut, Horsechestnut] or Horse-chestnut tree (5, 6, 19, 46, 49, 53, 54, 58, 61, 82, 85, 92, 112, 107, 138, 156) (1840–1937), Konker tree [Konker-tree] (156) (1923), Lambs (5, 156) (1913–1923), Marronier d'inde (French) (6) (1892), Rosskastanie (German) (6) (1892)

Aesculus **L.** – Buck-eye [Buckeye] (1, 10, 13, 15, 18, 50, 82, 106, 109, 155) (1805–present), Hippocastanum (165) (1768) used as food for horses & resembles chestnut, Horse-chestnut [Horse chestnut, Horsechestnut] or Horse-chestnut tree (1, 8, 10, 13, 15, 82, 109, 138, 155, 156, 158, 167) (1785–1949), Marronier d'inde (French) (8) (1785), Scarlet-flower horse-chestnut [Scarlet flowering horse-chestnut, Scarlet flowering horse chestnut] (189) (1767)

Aesculus lutea **Michx.** – See *Aesculus flava* Aiton

Aesculus macrostachya **Michx.** – See *Aesculus parviflora* Walt.

Aesculus neglecta – See *Aesculus ×neglecta* Lindl. [*flava × sylvatica*]

Aesculus octandra **Marsh.** – See *Aesculus flava* Aiton

Aesculus octandra vestita – See *Aesculus flava* Aiton

Aesculus octandra virginica – See *Aesculus flava* Aiton

Æsculus octandria – possibly *Aesculus flava* Aiton

Aesculus parviflora **Walt.** – Bottle-brush buckeye [Bottlebrush buckeye] (109, 138, 155) (1923–1949), Buck-eye [Buckeye] (107) (1919), Dwarf horse-chestnut (109) (1949), Long-spike pavia [Long-spiked pavia] (20) (1857), Small buckeye (2) (1895)

Aesculus pavia **L.** – Buck-eye [Buckeye, Buck's Eyes] (71, 177) (1762–1898), Dear's-eye [Dear's eye] (177) (1762), Fish poison (5, 156) (1913–1923), Flame buckeye (155) (1942), Horse-chestnut [Horse chestnut, Horsechestnut] or Horse-chestnut tree (71) (1898), Little buckeye (5, 92, 156) (1876–1923), Pavia rouge (French) (8) (1785), Red buckeye (2, 5, 71, 82, 92, 109, 138, 155, 156) (1876–1949), Red buckeye (97) (1937), Scarlet buckeye (138) (1923), Scarlet horse-chestnut (165) (1768), Scarlet woolly buckeye (155) (1942), Scarlet-flower horse-chestnut [Scarlet flowering horse-chestnut, Scarlet flowering horse chestnut] (8) (1785), Small buckeye (71) (1898), Woolly buckeye (124, 138, 155) (1923–1942), Yellow woolly buckeye (155) (1942), Zamouna (177) (1762)

Æsculus pavia **L.** – See *Aesculus pavia* L.

Aesculus splendens – See *Aesculus pavia* L. var. *pavia*

Aesculus sylvatica **Bartr.** – Georgia buckeye (138) (1923)

Aethionema saxatile – See *Aurinia saxatilis* (L.) Desv.

Aethusa cynapium **L.** – Aethusa (174) (1753), Common fool's-parsley (165) (1768), Dog parsley [Dog's parsley] (6) (1892), Dog poison [Dog-poison] (5, 6, 92, 156) (1876–1923), Dog-parsley [Dog parsley, Dogparsley] (5, 156) (1913–1923), False parsley (5, 156) (1913–1923), Fool's-cicely [Fool's cicely] (5, 156) (1913–1923), Fool's-parsley [Fool's parsley, Fools' parsley] (5, 6, 14, 72, 156) (1882–1923), Fools-parsley aethusa (155) (1942), Garden hemlock (6) (1892), Hundspetersilie (German) (6) (1892), Kleiner Scheilung (German) (6) (1892), La petite cique (French) (6) (1892), Lesser hemlock (5, 6, 156, 165) (1768–1923), Small hemlock (5, 6, 92, 156) (1876–1923)

Aethusa **L.** – Aethusa (155) (1942), Fool's-parsley [Fool's parsley, Fools' parsley] (1, 10) (1818–1932)

Afzelia **Gmel.** – See *Seymeria* Pursh

Afzelia macrophylla **(Nutt.) Kuntze** – See *Dasistoma macrophylla* (Nutt.) Raf.

Agalinis aspera **(Dougl. ex Benth.) Britton** – Gerardia (85) (1932), Rough gerardia (131) (1899), Rough purple agalinis (5) (1913), Rough purple gerardia (72, 97) (1907–1937), Tall false foxglove (50) (present)

Agalinis auriculata **(Michx.) Blake** – Auricled gerardia (5, 72, 97) (1907–1937), Cut-leaf gerardia [Cutleaf gerardia, Cut-leaved gerardia] (5, 97, 122) (1913–1937), Ear-leaf false foxglove [Earleaf false foxglove] (50) (present), Ear-leaf gerardia [Earleaf gerardia] (3, 4) (1977–1986), Fine-leaf gerardia [Fineleaf gerardia] (3, 4) (1977–1986), Osage false foxglove (50) (present)

Agalinis besseyana **Britton** – See *Agalinis tenuifolia* (Vahl) Raf. var. *macrophylla* (Benth.) Blake

Agalinis fasciculata **(Ell.) Raf.** – Beach false foxglove (50) (present), Fascicled agalinis (5) (1913)

Agalinis gattingeri **(Small) Small** – Gattinger's agalinis (5) (1913), Round-stem false foxglove [Roundstem false foxglove] (50) (present)

Agalinis heterophylla **(Nutt.) Small ex Britton** – Prairie agalinis (5) (1913), Prairie false foxglove (50) (present), Prairie gerardia (97, 122, 124) (1937)

Agalinis linifolia **(Nutt.) Britt.** – Flax-leaf agalinis [Flax-leaved agalinis] (5) (1913), Flax-leaf gerardia [Flax-leaved gerardia] (72) (1907)

Agalinis maritima **(Raf.) Raf.** – Saltmarsh agalinis [Salt marsh agalinis] (5) (1913), Seaside agalinis [Sea-side agalinis] (5) (1913)

Agalinis maritima **(Raf.) Raf.** var. *grandiflora* **(Benth.) Shinners** – Saltmarsh gerardia [Salt marsh gerardia] (122, 156) (1923–1937)

Agalinis maritima (Raf.) Raf. var. *maritima* – Seaside gerardia (156) (1923)

Agalinis maritima Raf. – See *Agalinis maritima* (Raf.) Raf.

Agalinis obtusifolia Raf. – Ten-lobe agalinis [Ten-lobed agalinis] (5) (1913)

Agalinis parviflora (Chapman) Small. – possibly *Agalinis obtusifolia* Raf.

Agalinis paupercula (Gray) Britton – Small-flower agalinis [Small-flowered agalinis] (5) (1913)

Agalinis paupercula (Gray) Britton var. *paupercula* – Small-flower gerardia [Small-flowered gerardia] (72, 97) (1907–1937)

Agalinis purpurea (L.) Britton – See *Agalinis purpurea* (L.) Pennell

Agalinis purpurea (L.) Pennell – Large purple agalinis (5, 93) (1913–1936), Large purple gerardia (72, 122, 124) (1907–1937), Purple false foxglove (50) (present), Purple gerardia (155, 156) (1923–1942)

Agalinis Raf. – False foxglove (50) (present), Feverweed [Fever weed, Fever-weed] (48) (1882) IA, Foxglove [Fox glove, Fox-glove, Foxgloves] (48) (1882) KS, Gerardia (1, 4) (1932–1986), Yellow foxglove (156) (1923)

Agalinis setacea (J. Gmelin) Raf. – Thread-leaf agalinis [Thread-leaved agalinis] (5) (1913)

Agalinis setacea (Walt.) Raf. – See *Agalinis setacea* (J. Gmelin) Raf.

Agalinis skinneriana (Wood) Britton – Skinner's agalinis (5) (1913), Skinner's false foxglove (50) (Present), Skinner's gerardia (97) (1937)

Agalinis strictifolia (Benth.) Pennell – Small gerardia (97) (1937) OK

Agalinis tenuifolia (Vahl) Raf. – Gerardia (98) (1926), Purple foxglove [Purple foxe gloues (156) (1923), Slender agalinis (5) (1913), Slender gerardia (72, 98, 156) (1907–1926), Slender-leaf false foxglove [Slenderleaf false foxglove] (50) (present)

Agalinis viridis (Small) Pennell – Green false foxglove (50) (present), Green gerardia (4) (1986)

Agapanthus L'Hér. – African lily (92) (1876), Agapanthus (138, 155) (1923–1942) Greek for love flower, Love flower (92) (1876)

Agaricus arvensis Schaeff. – Horse agaricus (155) (1942), Horse mushroom (92, 170) (1876–1995)

Agaricus bitorquis (Quél.) Sacc. – Rodman's agaricus [Rodmans agaricus] (155) (1942), Spring agaricus (170) (1995), Urban agaric (170) (1995)

Agaricus campestris L. – Agaricus (42) (1814), Champignon (165) (1768), Common mushroom (128, 165) (1768–1933), Common mushroom agaricus (155) (1942), Meadow mushroom (170) (1995)

Agaricus L. – Agaricus (155) (1942), Punk (7, 92) (1828–1876), Tinder (92) (1876), Toadstool (92) (1876)

Agaricus placomyces Peck – Eastern flat-top agaricus [Eastern flat-topped agaricus] (170) (1995), Flat-cup agaricus [Flatcup agaricus] (155) (1942)

Agaricus rodmani – See *Agaricus bitorquis* (Quel.) Sacc.

Agaricus silvicola (Vittad.) Peck – Forest agaricus (155) (1942)

Agarista populifolia (Lam.) W.S. Judd – Pipestem wood [Pipe-stem-wood, Pipe-stem wood] (182) (1791)

Agarum clathratum Dumortier – Sea colander (92) (1876)

Agarum turneri [Rosenvinge] – See *Agarum clathratum* Dumortier

Agastache anethiodora (Nutt.) Britton – See *Agastache foeniculum* (Pursh) Kuntze

Agastache cana (Hook.) Woot. & Standl. – Mosquito plant [Mosquitoplant] (155) (1942)

Agastache Clayton ex Gronov. – Giant hyssop [Gianthyssop] (1, 50, 82, 93, 109, 155, 156, 158) (1900–present)

Agastache foeniculum (Pursh) Kuntze – Anise hyssop (5, 157, 158) (1900–1929), Be'dukadak'igisĭn (Chippewa, it sticks up) (40) (1928), Blue giant hyssop (50) (present), False anise (127) (1933) ND, Fennel giant-hyssop [Fennel gianthyssop] (155) (1942), Fragrant giant hyssop (5, 37, 72, 93, 106, 131, 157, 158) (1899–1936),

Lavender hyssop (3, 4, 98) (1926–1986), Umbrella plant [Umbrella-plant] (40) (1928), Wild anise (37) (1919)

Agastache mexicana (Kunth) Lint & Epling – Mexican cendronellá (138) (1923), Mexican giant-hyssop [Mexican gianthyssop] (155) (1942)

Agastache nepetoides (L.) Kuntze – Calmint hyssop (187) (1818), Catmint [Cat mint, Cat-mint] (156) (1923), Catnip (131) (1899) SD, Catnip giant hyssop [Catnep giant-hyssop] (3, 4, 5, 72, 93, 97, 155) (1907–1986), Giant hyssop [Gianthyssop] (19, 82, 85, 106, 114, 131, 156) (1840–1930), Hyssop [Hysop, Hysope] (106) (1930), Tall hyssop (187) (1818), Yellow giant hyssop (50) (present)

Agastache scrophulariaefolia (Willd.) Kuntze. – See *Agastache scrophulariifolia* (Willd.) Kuntze

Agastache scrophulariifolia (Willd.) Kuntze – Agastache (187) (1818), Figwort giant-hyssop (5) (1913), Giant hyssop [Gianthyssop] (63, 72, 93) (1899–1936), Purple giant hyssop (3, 50) (1977–present)

Agastache urticifolia (Benth.) Kuntze – Nettle-leaf giant-hyssop [Nettleleaf gianthyssop] (155) (1942)

Agathis robusta (C. Moore ex F. Muell.) Bailey – Australian dammar-pine (138) (1923), Big dammarpine (155) (1942), Queensland kauri (109) (1949)

Agathis robusta F. Muell. – See *Agathis robusta* (C. Moore ex F. Muell.) Bailey introduced

Agathis Salisb. – Dammar-pine [Dammarpine] (109, 138, 155) (1923–1949)

Agathotes D. Don – See *Swertia* L.

Agave americana L. – American agave (92) (1876), American aloe (2, 92, 103, 110) (1871–1895), American century plant (50) (present), Century plant [Centuryplant] (61, 92, 109, 122, 124, 138, 147) (1870–1949), Common American agave (165) (1768), Common century plant (2) (1895), Flowering aloe [Flowering aloes] (7, 92) (1828–1876), Great American aloe (165) (1768), Kerrato agave (165) (1768), Maguey (7, 92, 110, 123) (1828–1886) Mexico, Mescal (103) (1871), Metl (110) (1886) Mexico, Pita (7) (1828), Red-spine American agave [Red-spined American agave] (165) (1768), Spiked aloe (92) (1876), Zabara (Cuba) (31) (1847)

Agave heterocantha Zucc. – See *Agave univittata* Haw.

Agave karatto – See *Agave americana* L.

Agave L. – Agave (138, 155) (1923–1942), American aloe (2, 156, 167) (1814–1923), Century plant [Centuryplant] (149) (1904), Indian maguey (75, 147) (1856–1894), Mescal (149) (1904)

Agave lata Shinners – See *Manfreda virginica* (L.) Salisb. ex Rose

Agave lecheguilla Torr. – Lechuguilla (122, 138) (1923–1937) TX

Agave lophantha Schiede – See *Agave univittata* Haw.

Agave parryi Engelm. – Century plant [Centuryplant] (78) (1898) AZ

Agave sisalana Perrine – Sisal (138) (1923)

Agave tigrina (Engelm.) Cory – See *Manfreda virginica* (L.) Salisb. ex Rose

Agave univittata Haw. – Crested agave (138) (1923), Lechuguilla (124) (1937) TX

Agave variegata Jacobi – See *Manfreda variegata* (Jacobi) Rose

Agave virginica L. – See *Manfreda virginica* (L.) Salisb. ex Rose

Ageratina altissima (L.) King & H. E. Robins. – Black-stikweet (177) (1762), Boneset (80) (1913) IA, Deerwort boneset [Deerwort-boneset] (5, 7, 92, 156) (1828–1923), Hemp agrimony (156) (1923), Indian sanicle (5, 92, 156) (1876–1923), Milk-sick-plant (156) (1923), Pool root [Poolroot, Pool-root] (58, 92, 156) (1869–1923), Poolwort [Pool wort, Pool-wort] (156) (1923), Richweed [Rich-weed, Rich weed] (5, 75, 156) (1894–1923) Banner Elk NC, Snow thoroughwort (138, 156) (1923), Squaw-weed [Squawweed, Squaw-weed] (156) (1923), Stevia (5, 76, 156) (1896–1923) Madison WI, White sanicle (5, 62, 72, 92, 156) (1876–1923), White snakeroot [White snake root, White snake-root] (2, 4, 5, 50, 58, 62, 63, 80, 82, 85, 93, 97, 106, 109, 114, 122, 125, 126, 131, 155, 156) (1869–present)

Ageratina aromatica (L.) Spach – Balm-leaf hempweed [Balm-leaved hemp-weed] (187) (1818), Melissa thoroughwort (138) (1923), Pool root [Poolroot, Pool-root] (5, 92, 156) (1876–1923), Poolwort [Pool wort, Pool-wort] (5, 92, 156) (1876–1923), Smaller white snakeroot [Smaller white snakeroot, Smaller white snake-root] (5, 156) (1913–1923), White snakeroot [White snake root, White snake-root] (61, 92) (1870–1876), Wild horehound [Wild hoarhound] (5, 156) (1913–1923)

Ageratina **Spach** – Snakeroot [Snake root, Snake-root] (50) (present)

Ageratum altissimum **L.** – See *Ageratina altissima* (L.) King & H.E. Robins.

Ageratum conyzoides **L.** – Ageratum (174) (1753), Garden ageratum (82) (1930) IA, Hairy ageratum (165) (1768), Little blue-star ageratum [Little bluestar ageratum] (138) (1923), Tropic ageratum (155) (1942)

Ageratum corymbosum **Zuccagni** – Mexican eupatorium (138) (1923), Purple boneset (124) (1937) TX

Ageratum houstonianum **Mill.** – Ageratum (92) (1876), Mexican ageratum (138, 155) (1923–1942)

Ageratum **L.** – Ageratum (82, 138, 155) (1930–1942)

Ageratum latifolium – See *Ageratum conyzoides* L.

Ageratum mexicanum – See *Ageratum houstonianum* Mill.

Aglaonema modestum **Schott ex Engl.** – Chinese evergreen (109) (1949)

Agoseris arizonica **(Greene) Greene** – See *Agoseris glauca* (Pursh) Raf. var. *laciniata* (D.C. Eat.) Smiley

Agoseris aurantiaca **(Hook.) Greene** – Greene's slender agoseris [Greenes slender agoseris] (155) (1942)

Agoseris aurantiaca **(Hook.) Greene** – Orange agoseris (155) (1942)

Agoseris cuspidata **(Pursh) D. Dietr.** – See *Nothocalais cuspidata* (Pursh) Greene

Agoseris glauca **(Pursh) D. Dietr.** – See *Agoseris glauca* (Pursh) Raf.

Agoseris glauca **(Pursh) Greene** – possibly *Agoseris glauca* (Pursh) Raf.

Agoseris glauca **(Pursh) Raf.** – Arizona agoseris (155) (1942), False dandelion (3, 127, 156) (1923–1977), Large-flower agoseris [Large-flowered agoseris] (5) (1913), Little-flower agoseris [Littleflower agoseris] (155) (1942), Pale agoseris (50) (present), Prairie dandelion (127) (1937) TX, Small-flower agoseris [Small-flowered agoseris] (5, 131) (1899–1913)

Agoseris glauca parviflora – See *Agoseris glauca* (Pursh) Raf. var. *laciniata* (D.C. Eat.) Smiley

Agoseris gracilens **var. *greenei* (Gray) Jeps.** – See *Agoseris aurantiaca* (Hook.) Greene var. *aurantiaca*

Agoseris graciliens greenei – See *Agoseris aurantiaca* (Hook.) Greene var. *aurantiaca*

Agoseris heterophylla **(Nutt.) Greene** – Annual agoseris (155) (1942)

Agoseris monticola **Greene** – Goat-chicory [Goat chicory] (85) (1932), Low agoseris (155) (1942), Western agoseris (131) (1899)

Agoseris parviflora **(Nutt.) Greene** – See *Agoseris glauca* (Pursh) Raf. var. *laciniata* (D.C. Eat.) Smiley

Agoseris pumila **(Nutt.) Rydb.** – See *Agoseris monticola* Greene

Agoseris **Raf.** – Agoseris (50, 155) (1942–present), False dandelion (4, 156) (1923–1986), Goat-chicory [Goat chicory] (1) (1932)

Agoseris scorzoneraefolia **(Schrad.) Greene** – See *Agoseris monticola* Greene

Agoseris scorzonerifolia **(Schrad.) Greene** – See *Agoseris monticola* Greene

Agrimonia **(Tourn.) L.** – See *Agrimonia* L.

Agrimonia eupatoria **L.** – Agrimonia (57) (1917), Agrimony (14, 19, 46, 49, 52, 53, 57, 58, 92, 107, 156) (1649–1923), Aigremoine Commune (French) (7) (1828), Beggar's-lice [Beggar lice, Beggar-lice, Beggarlice, Beggarslice] (156) (1923), Beggarticks [Beggar ticks, Beggar's ticks, Beggars' ticks, Beggars-ticks, Beggar-ticks] (74, 156) (1893–1923) WV, Churchsteeples (50) (present), Cocklebur [Cockle bur, Cockle-bur, Cockle-burr, Cockle burr, Cockleburr] (7, 49, 52, 53, 58, 92, 107, 156) (1828–1923), Common agrimony (2, 7, 155, 165) (1768–1942), Egrimony (46, 179) (1526–1671),

Eupatorium (174, 177) (1753–1762), Gemeine Oderminig (German) (7) (1828), Hairy agrimonia (131) (1899) SD, Harvestlice [Harvest lice, Harvest-lice] (156) (1923), Herba agrimonia (Official name of Materia Medica) (7) (1828), Liverwort [Liver-wort, Liver wort] (107) (1919), Rough agrimony (156) (1923), Sticklewort (107, 156) (1919–1923) WV, Stickseed [Stick seed, Stick-seed] (74, 156) (1893–1923), Stickweed [Stick-weed, Stick weed] (156) (1923), Stickwort (7, 49, 52, 53, 58, 92) (1828–1922), Tall hairy agrimony (72) (1907) IA

Agrimonia eupatoris **L.** – possibly *Agrimonia eupatoria* L.

Agrimonia gryposepala **Wallr.** – Agrimony (3, 48) (1882–1977), Beggarticks [Beggar ticks, Beggar's ticks, Beggars' ticks, Beggars-ticks, Beggar-ticks] (5) (1913), Cocklebur [Cockle bur, Cockle-bur, Cockle-burr, Cockle burr, Cockleburr] (5) (1913), Feverfew [Fever few, fever-few] (5) (1913), Hooked agrimony (4) (1986), Stickseed [Stick seed, Stick-seed] (5) (1913), Stickweed [Stick-weed, Stick weed] (5) (1913), Tall hairy agrimony (5, 50, 93) (1913–present)

Agrimonia hirsuta **(Muhl.) Bick.** – See *Agrimonia eupatoria* L.

Agrimonia **L.** – Agrimony (1, 2, 4, 10, 50, 93, 155, 156, 157, 158, 167, 184) (1793–present)

Agrimonia microcarpa **Wallr.** – Small-fruit agrimony [Small-fruited agrimony] (5) (1913)

Agrimonia mollis **(Torr. & Gray) Britton** – See *Agrimonia pubescens* Wallr.

Agrimonia parviflora **Aiton** – Harvestlice [Harvest lice, Harvest-lice] (50) (present), Large agrimony (48) (1882), Many-flower agrimony [Many-flowered agrimony] (3, 4, 5, 72, 97, 131) (1899–1986), Small-flower agrimony [Small-flowered agrimony] (165) (1768), Spotted agrimony (19, 187) (1818–1840)

Agrimonia pubescens **Wallr.** – Agrimony (5, 50) (1913–present), Beaked agrimony (50) (present), Downy agrimony (3, 4) (1977–1986), Soft agrimony (50, 72, 97) (1907–present), Woodland agrimony (3, 4, 5) (1913–1986), Wood-lawn agrimony [Woodlawn agrimony] (97) (1937)

Agrimonia pumila **Muhl.** – See *Agrimonia microcarpa* Wallr.

Agrimonia striata **Michx.** – Agrimony (3) (1977), Britton's agrimony (5) (1913), Roadside agrimony (50, 155) (1942–present), Striate agrimony (4) (1986), Woodland agrimony (97) (1937)

Agropogon littoralis **(Sm.) C.E. Hubbard** *[Agrostis stolonifera × Polypogon monospeliensis]* – Beard grass [Beard-grass, Beardgrass] (94) (1901), Ditch polypogon (122, 155) (1937–1942)

Agropyron albicans **Scribn. & J.G. Sm.** – See *Elymus albicans* (Scribn. & J. G. Sm.) A. Löve

Agropyron arizonicum **Scribn. & Smith** – See *Elymus arizonicus* (Scribn. & J. G. Sm.) Gould

Agropyron biflorum **(Brignoli) R. & S.** – See *Elymus trachycaulus* (Link) Gould ex Shinners subsp. *trachycaulus*

Agropyron caninoides **(Ramaley) Beal.** – See *Elymus trachycaulus* (Link) Gould ex Shinners subsp. *subsecundus* (Link) A. & D. Löve

Agropyron caninum **(L.) Beauv.** – See *Elymus caninus* (L.) L.

Agropyron caninum **(L.) Beauv. subsp. *majus* (Vasey) C. L. Hitchc.** – See *Elymus trachycaulus* (Link) Gould ex Shinners subsp. *trachycaulus*

Agropyron cristatum **(L.) Gaertn.** – Crested wheat grass [Crested wheatgrass, Crested wheat-grass] (3, 50, 140, 143, 146, 155, 185) (1852–present), Vetiver (57, 92) (1876–1917), Vetiveria (57) (1917), Vetivert (92) (1876), Vittievar (92) (1876), Vittivert (92) (1876)

Agropyron dasystachyum **(Hook.) Scribn.** – See *Elymus lanceolatus* (Scribn. & J.G. Sm.) Gould

Agropyron dasystachyum **(Hook.) Vasey** – See *Elymus lanceolatus* (Scribn. & J.G. Sm.) Gould subsp. *lanceolatus*

Agropyron divergens **Nees in Steud.** – See *Pseudoroegneria spicata* (Pursh) Á. Löve

Agropyron elmeri **Scribn.** – See *Elymus lanceolatus* (Scribn. & J.G. Sm.) Gould

Agropyron elongatum (Host) Beauv. – See *Thinopyrum ponticum* (Podp.) Z.-W. Liu & R.-C. Wang

Agropyron Gaertner – Couch grass [Couch-grass] (93) (1936), Quack grass [Quack-grass, Quackgrass] (1, 93) (1932–1936), Quick grass [Quick-grass] (1) (1932), Quitch grass [Quitch-grass] (1) (1932), Wheat grass [Wheat-grass, Wheatgrass] (1, 50, 93, 152, 155, 158) (1900–present)

Agropyron glaucum (Desf.) R. & S. – See *Thinopyrum intermedium* (Host) Barkworth & D.R. Dewey

Agropyron gmelini Scribn. & Smith – See *Elymus sierrae* Gould

Agropyron griffithsii Scribn. – See *Elymus albicans* (Scribn. & J.G. Sm.) A. Löve

Agropyron inerme (Scribn. & J.G. Sm.) Rydb. – See *Pseudoroegneria spicata* (Pursh) A. Löve subsp. *inermis* (Scribn. & J.G. Sm.) A. Löve

Agropyron intermedium (Host) Beauv. – See *Thinopyrum intermedium* (Host) Barkworth & D.R. Dewey

Agropyron intermedium (Host) Beauv. var. *trichophorum* (Link) Halac. – See *Thinopyrum intermedium* (Host) Barkworth & D.R. Dewey

Agropyron littorale auct. non (Host) Dur. – See *Thinopyrum pycnanthum* (Godr.) Barkworth

Agropyron muricatus Retz. – possibly *Agropyron cristatum* (L.) Gaertn.

Agropyron occidentale Scribn. – See *Pascopyrum smithii* (Rydb.) A. Löve

Agropyron occidentale var. *molle* Scribn. & Smith – See *Pascopyrum smithii* (Rydb.) A. Löve

Agropyron parishii Scribn. & J.G. Sm. – See *Elymus stebbinsii* Gould

Agropyron pauciflorum (Schwein.) A.S. Hitchc. – See *Elymus trachycaulus* (Link) Gould ex Shinners subsp. *trachycaulus*

Agropyron petinifore R & S – See *Agropyron cristatum* (L.) Gaertn. subsp. *pectinatum* (Bieb.) Tzvelev

Agropyron pseudorepens Scribn. & Sm. – See *Elymus* ×*pseudorepens* (Scribn. & J.G. Sm.) Barkworth & D.R. Dewey [*lanceolatus* × *trachycaulus*]

Agropyron pseudo-repens Scribn. & Sm. – See *Elymus* ×*pseudorepens* (Scribn. & J.G. Sm.) Barkworth & D.R. Dewey [*lanceolatus* × *trachycaulus*]

Agropyron pungens (Pers.) R. & S. – See *Thinopyrum pycnanthum* (Godr.) Barkworth

Agropyron pycnanthum (Godr.) Godr. & Gren. – See *Thinopyrum pycnanthum* (Godr.) Barkworth

Agropyron repens (L.) Beauv. – See *Elymus repens* (L.) Gould

Agropyron richardsonii Schrad – See *Elymus trachycaulus* (Link) Gould ex Shinners subsp. *subsecundus* (Link) A.& D. Löve

Agropyron riparium Scribner & J. G. Smith – See *Elymus lanceolatus* (Scribn. & J.G. Sm.) Gould

Agropyron scribneri Vasey – See *Elymus scribneri* (Vasey) M.E. Jones

Agropyron smithii Rydb. – See *Pascopyrum smithii* (Rydb.) A. Löve

Agropyron spicatum (Pursh) Scribn. & Sm. – See *Pseudoroegneria spicata* (Pursh) A. Löve subsp. *inermis* (Scribn. & J.G. Sm.) A. Löve

Agropyron trichophorum (Link) Richter – See *Thinopyrum intermedium* (Host) Barkworth & D.R. Dewey

Agropyron vaseyi Scribn. & J.G. Sm. – See *Pseudoroegneria spicata* (Pursh) A. Löve subsp. *inermis* (Scribn. & J.G. Sm.) A. Löve

Agropyron violaceum (Hornem.) Vasey – See *Elymus alaskanus* (Scribn. & Merr.) A. Löve subsp. *latiglumis* (Scribn. & J.G. Sm.) A. Löve

Agropyron vulpinum (Rydb.) A.S. Hitchc. – See *Elymus vulpinus* Rydb.

Agropyrum caninum (L.) Beauv. – See *Elymus caninus* (L.) L.

Agropyrum caninum (L.) R. & S. – See *Elymus caninus* (L.) L.

Agropyrum glaucum occidentale Scribn. (sic) – See *Pascopyrum smithii* (Rydb.) A. Löve

Agropyrum glaucum R. & S. (sic) – See *Thinopyrum intermedium* (Host) Barkworth & D.R. Dewey

Agropyrum repens – See *Elymus repens* (L.) Gould

Agropyrum tenerum Vasey – See *Elymus trachycaulus* (Link) Gould ex Shinners subsp. *trachycaulus*

Agropyrum unilaterale Vasey & Scribn. (sic) – See *Thinopyrum intermedium* (Host) Barkworth & D.R. Dewey

Agropyrum violacescens Beal. (sic) – See *Elymus trachycaulus* (Link) Gould ex Shinners subsp. *trachycaulus*

Agrostemma coronaria – See *Lychnis coronaria* (L.) Desr.

Agrostemma githago L. – Bastard nigelle (71) (1898), Cockle [Cockles, Cokyll] (6, 19, 71, 148, 165, 179, 184, 187) (1768–1939), Cockle-corn [Cockle corn] (92) (1876), Common corncockle (50, 155) (1942–present), Corn campion (1, 5, 85, 156, 157, 158, 165) (1768–1932), Corn pink (5, 156, 157, 158) (1900–1929), Corncockle [Corn-cockle, Corn cockle] (1, 5, 6, 10, 42, 62, 71, 72, 80, 85, 97, 131, 148, 156, 157, 158) (1814–1939), Corn-rose [Corn Rose] (5, 156, 157, 158) (1900–1929), Crown-of-the-field [Crown of the field] (5, 156, 157, 158) (1900–1920), Darnell (179) (1526), Drawke (179) (1526), Gemeine Rade (German) (6) (1892), Korn Rade (German) (6) (1892), La nielle des bles (French) (6) (1892), Licheta (71, 74) (1893–1929) Vermount, L'Ivraie (French) (6) (1892), Mullein pink [Mullen pink] (5, 71, 73, 156, 157, 158) (1892–1929) Nova Scotia, Old-maid's pink [Old maid pink, Old maid's pink] (5, 71, 73, 156, 157, 158) (1892–1929), Purple cockle (62, 148) (1912–1939), Ray (179) (1526), Rode campion (6) (1892), Rose-campion [Rose campion] (71) (1898), Rose-of-heaven [Rose of heaven] (156) (1923), Woolly pink (156) (1923)

Agrostemma L. – Cockle [Cockel, Cokyll] (190) (~1759), Corn campion (1, 93) (1932–1936), Corncockle [Corn-cockle, Corn cockle] (1, 4, 15, 50, 93, 155, 156, 158, 167) (1814–present), Rose campion (42) (1814)

Agrostis alba L. – See *Agrostis gigantea* Roth

Agrostis alba vulgaris (With.) Thurb. – possibly *Agrostis capillaris* L.

Agrostis algida C.J. Phipps – See *Phippsia algida* (C.J. Phipps) R. Br.

Agrostis altissima (Walt.) Tuckerm. – See *Agrostis perennans* (Walt.) Tuckerman

Agrostis asperifolia Trin. – See *Agrostis exarata* Trin.

Agrostis bakeri Rydb. – See *Agrostis mertensii* Trin.

Agrostis borealis Hartm. – See *Agrostis mertensii* Trin.

Agrostis canina L. – Alpine brown bent (66) (1903), Brown bent grass [Brown bent-grass] (2, 5, 19, 66, 90, 165) (1768–1913), Brun-hwen (Swedish) (46) (1879), Dog bent [Dog's bent] (66) (1903), Dog bent grass [Dog's bent grass] (5, 87, 90, 92) (1876–1913), Finetop [Fine-top, Fine top] (5) (1913), Furzetop [Furze top] (5) (1913), Mountain redtop [Mountain red top] (87, 90) (1884–1885), Rhode island bent grass [Rhode Island bent-grass] (2, 5, 56) (1895–1911), Velvet bent (109) (1949), Velvet bent grass [Velvet bentgrass] (50) (present)

Agrostis canina L. subsp. *montana* (Hartman) Hartman – See *Agrostis vinealis* Schreb.

Agrostis canina L. var. *montana* Hartman – See *Agrostis vinealis* Schreb.

Agrostis capillaris L. – Bent grass [Bentgrass, Bent-grass] (56, 87, 88, 90) (1885–1901), Bonnet grass (45) (1896), Borden's grass (87) (1884), Browntop [Brown-top, Brown top] (143) (1936) Quebec, Burden's grass (66, 90) (1885–1903) ME, Colonial bent grass [Colonial bent-grass, Colonial bentgrass] (50, 143) (1936–present), Creeping bent (45) (1896), English grass (66) (1903), Fancy (56) (1901) IA, Fearh grass (46) (1879), Fine bent (66) (1903) England, Fine bent grass [Fine bent-grass] (165) (1768), Finetop [Fine-top, Fine top] (66, 87, 88, 90) (1885–1903), Fiorin (45, 46) (1879–1896), Herd's grass [Herds-grass, Herd's-grass, Herds-grass, Herd grass] (66, 90) (1885–1903), Herd's grass of Pennsylvania [Herds grass of Pennsylvania] (87, 88, 92) (1876–1885), Marsh bent (45) (1896), Redtop [Red-top, Red top] (11, 19, 45, 56, 66, 67, 87, 88, 90, 92, 129, 187) (1818–1912), Redtop grass [Red top grass] (92) (1876), Rhode Island bent (90, 138) (1885–1923), Rhode island bent grass [Rhode Island bent-grass] (143) (1852–1936), Slender bent grass [Slender bent-grass] (94) (1901), White bent (45) (1896), Whitetop [White top, White-top] (45) (1896)

Agrostis densiflora Vasey – Densely-flowered bent (94) (1901)

Agrostis dispar – See *Agrostis gigantea* Roth

Agrostis elata (Pursh) Trin. – See *Agrostis perennans* (Walt.) Tuckerman

Agrostis elliottiana Schultes – Annual tickle grass [Annual ticklegrass] (155) (1942), Elliot's bent grass [Elliot's bent-grass, Elliott bentgrass] (5, 50, 119, 155) (1913–present), Six-weeks bent grass [Six-weeks bentgrass] (155) (1942), Spider bent grass [Spider bent-grass (5, 94, 119) (1901–1938)

Agrostis exarata Trin. – Northern red-top (3, 5, 56, 50, 87, 111, 122, 155) (1884–present)

Agrostis exarata Trin. subsp. minor (Hook.) C.L.Hitchc. – See *Agrostis exarata* Trin.

Agrostis exarata Trin. var. monolepis (Torr.) A.S. Hitchc. – See *Agrostis exarata* Trin.

Agrostis exigua Thurb. – See *Agrostis elliottiana* Schultes

Agrostis filiformis – possibly *Muhlenbergia mexicana* (L.) Trin. current species depends on author

Agrostis geminata Trin. – See *Agrostis scabra* Willd.

Agrostis gigantea Roth – Bent grass [Bentgrass, Bent-grass] (56, 92) (1876–1901), Black bent grass [Black bentgrass] (155) (1942), Black quick-grass (119) (1938), Black quitch (5) (1913), Bonnet grass (5, 19, 66, 92) (1840–1913), Burden's dew grass (5) (1913), Burden's grass (45) (1896), Conch grass (5) (1913), Creeping bent (45) (1896), Creeping bent grass [Creeping bent-grass, Creeping brentgrass] (5, 119) (1913–1938), Dew grass (66) (1903), English bent (66) (1903), English grass (56) (1901) IA, Fine-John [Fine John] (5) (1913), Fine's bent [Fines bent] (56) (1901) IA, Fiorin (5, 45, 56, 109, 119) (1896–1949), Fiorin grass (67, 88, 92) (1885–1890) from Irish name, Herd's grass [Herds-grass, Herd's-grass, Herds-grass, Herd grass] (5, 45, 92, 94, 187) (1818–1901), Marsh bent grass [Marsh bent-grass] (5, 92, 119) (1876–1938), Monkey dew grass [Monkey's dew grass] (5) (1913), Redtop [Red-top, Red top] (5, 45, 50, 56, 93, 94, 109, 111, 115, 119, 122, 140, 143, 152, 155, 163) (1852–present), Southern bent (66) (1903), Summer dew grass (5, 45) (1896–1913), Tussocks (5) (1913), Water twitch (5) (1913), White bent grass [White bentgrass, White bent-grass] (5, 66, 92, 119, 165) (1768–1938), White grass [White-grass, White-grass] (92) (1876), Whitetop [White top, White-top] (5, 19, 66, 119) (1840–1938) White-top grass [White top grass] (92) (1876)

Agrostis hiemalis (Walt.) B.S.P. (sic) – See *Agrostis hyemalis* (Walt.) Britton, Sterns & Poggenb.

Agrostis hyemalis (Walt.) Britton, Sterns & Poggenb. – Fly-away (5) (1913), Fly-away grass [Fly away grass, Fly-away-grass] (119, 143, 163) (1852–1938), Fool hay [Fool-hay] (5, 119) (1913–1938), Hair grass [Hairgrass, Hair-grass] (111, 140, 143) (1915–1944), Hairy grass [Hairy-grass] (93) (1936), Rough bent grass (5) (1913), Rough hair grass [Rough hair-grass] (5, 119, 163) (1852–1938), Rough-leaf bent grass [Rough-leaved bent grass] (5) (1913), Silk grass [Silkgrass, Silk-grass] (5, 119) (1913–1938), Tickle grass [Ticklegrass, Tickle-grass] (3, 5, 50, 85, 122, 129, 140, 143, 163) (1852–present), Winter bent grass [Winter bentgrass] (50, 140, 155) (1942–present)

Agrostis indica L. – See *Sporobolus indicus* (L.) R. Br. var. *indicus*

Agrostis intermedia Balb. – Upland bent grass [Upland bentgrass, Upland bent-grass] (56) (1901)

Agrostis L. – Bent grass [Bentgrass, Bent-grass] (1, 10, 41, 66, 87, 92, 93, 109, 138, 155, 184) (1770–1949), Redtop [Red-top, Red top] (1, 93) (1932–1936), Tickle grass [Ticklegrass, Tickle-grass] (1, 93) (1932–1936), Walter's grass [Walter grass] (7) (1828)

Agrostis longiligula A.S. Hitchc. – See *Agrostis exarata* Trin.

Agrostis maritima Lam. – See *Agrostis stolonifera* L.

Agrostis mertensii Trin. – Marsh bent (94) (1901), Northern bent grass [Northern bentgrass] (50) (present), Red bent (94) (1901), Red bent grass [Red bent-grass] (5, 165) (1768–1913), Rock bent grass (5) (1913)

Agrostis mexicana L. – See *Muhlenbergia mexicana* (L.) Trin.

Agrostis nebulosa Boiss. & Reut. – Cloud grass [Cloudgrass, Cloudgrass] (109, 138) (1923–1949)

Agrostis nigra With. – See *Agrostis gigantea* Roth

Agrostis oreophila Trin. – See *Agrostis perennans* (Walt.) Tuckerman

Agrostis paludosa Scribn. – See *Agrostis mertensii* Trin.

Agrostis palustris Huds. – See *Agrostis stolonifera* L.

Agrostis perennans (Walt.) Tuckerman – Autumn bent grass [Autumn bentgrass] (3, 122, 155) (1937–1977), New England bent grass (5, 50) (1913–present), Northern red-top (5) (1913), Perennial bent (94) (1901), Rough-leaf bent grass [Rough-leaved bent grass] (5) (1913), Tall bentgrass [Tall bent grass] (5) (1913), Tall thin grass [Tall thin-grass] (5) (1913), Taller thin grass (66) (1903), Thin grass [Thingrass, Thin-grass] (5, 45, 56, 66, 90, 94, 111, 163) (1852–1915), Twin grass [Twingrass] (5) (1913), Upland bent grass [Upland bent-grass, Upland bent-grass] (5, 50, 93, 119) (1913–present)

Agrostis rubra L. – See *Agrostis mertensii* Trin.

Agrostis rupestris Allioni – See *Agrostis mertensii* Trin.

Agrostis scabra Willd. – Fly-away grass [Fly away grass, Fly-away-grass] (56, 66, 90) (1885–1903), Hair grass [Hairgrass, Hair-grass] (56, 66, 90, 92) (1885–1903), Loose-flower hair-grass [Loose-flowered hair-grass] (187) (1818), Mountain bent (94) (1901), Rough bent grass (50) (present), Tickle grass [Ticklegrass, Tickle-grass] (3, 11, 66, 90, 92) (1876–1977), Twin bent grass [Twin bentgrass] (5) (1913)

Agrostis schweinitzii Trin. – See *Agrostis perennans* (Walt.) Tuckerman

Agrostis spicaventi W. – See *Apera spica-venti* (L.) Beauv.

Agrostis stolonifera L. – Bastard fiorin grass [Bastard fiorin-grass] (187) (1818), Broad-leaf creeping bent [Broad-leaved creeping bent] (66) (1903), Carpet bent (138) (1923), Carpet bent grass [Carpet bent-grass] (143) (1852–1936), Creeping bent (109, 138, 163) (1852–1949), Creeping bent grass [Creeping bent-grass, Creeping brentgrass] (42, 50, 56, 68, 122, 143, 155, 165) (1768–present), Dense-flower bent grass [Dense flowered bent grass] (5) (1913), Fiorin (66) (1903), Fiorin grass (42, 68, 92) (1814–1890), Redtop [Redtop, Red top] (3, 68, 85, 125, 138) (1913–1977), Redtop grass [Red top grass] (21) (1893), Water bent grass [Water bent-grass, Water bentgrass] (152) (1912) NM, White bent grass [White bentgrass, White bent-grass] (68) (1890)

Agrostis stricta W. – See *Agrostis vinealis* Schreb.

Agrostis sylvatica Huds. – See *Agrostis capillaris* L.

Agrostis tenuiflora Willd. – See *Muhlenbergia tenuiflora* (Willd.) Britton, Sterns & Poggenb.

Agrostis tenuis Sibthorp – See *Agrostis capillaris* L.

Agrostis trinii Turcz. – See *Agrostis vinealis* Schreb.

Agrostis varians Trin. – See *Agrostis capillaris* L.

Agrostis verticillata Vill. – See *Polypogon viridis* (Gouan) Breistr.

Agrostis vinealis Schreb. – Bent grass [Bentgrass, Bent-grass] (19) (1840)

Agrostis virginica L. – See *Sporobolus virginicus* (L.) Kunth

Agrostis vulgaris Withering – See *Agrostis capillaris* L.

Ailanthus altissima (Mill) Swingle – Ailante (6) (1892), Ailanthus (5, 52, 85, 92, 137, 138, 158) (1876–1932), Ailanto (49) (1898), Chinese ailanthus (6) (1892), Chinese sumac [Chinese sumach] (5, 6, 49, 52, 57, 92, 106, 156, 158) (1876–1930), Devil's-walkingstick [Devil's walking-stick, Devil's walking stick, Devil's-walking-stick] (5, 76, 156, 158) (1896–1923) Sulphur Grove OH, False varnish tree [False varnish-tree] (5, 156, 158) (1900–1923), Girald's ailanthus [Girald ailanthus] (155) (1942), Götterbaum (German) (6, 158) (1892–1900), Heavenward tree (5, 156, 158) (1900–1923) no longer in use by 1923, Paradise tree [Paradise-tree] (106) (1930), Smoke tree [Smoke-tree] (4) (1986), Tall ailanthus (165) (1768), Tallow tree [Tallow-tree] (92) (1876), Tillow tree (6) (1892), Tree-of-heaven [Tree of heaven] (3, 4, 5, 6, 49, 50, 52, 54, 57, 85, 92, 97, 106, 107, 109, 112, 124, 135, 137, 138, 153, 156, 158) (1876–present), Tree-of-heaven ailanthus [Treeof-heaven ailanthus] (155) (1942), Tree-of-the-gods (158) (1900), Varnish tree (106, 107) (1919–1930), Vernis des Japon (French) (6, 158) (1892–1900), Vilmorin's ailanthus [Vilmorin ailanthus] (155) (1942)

Ailanthus **Desf.** – Ailanthus (50, 138, 155) (1923–present), Ailantus tree (15) (1895), Chinese sumac [Chinese sumach] (15) (1895), Tree-of-heaven [Tree of heaven] (1, 4, 93, 122, 158) (1900–1986)

Ailanthus giraldi – See *Ailanthus altissima* (Mill) Swingle

Ailanthus giraldii **Dode** – See *Ailanthus altissima* (Mill) Swingle

Ailanthus glandulosa **Desf.** – See *Ailanthus altissima* (Mill) Swingle

Ailanthus vilmoriniana **Dode** – See *Ailanthus altissima* (Mill) Swingle

Aira aquatica **L.** – See *Catabrosa aquatica* (L.) Beauv.

Aira atropurpurea **Wahlenb.** – See *Vahlodea atropurpurea* (Wahlenb.) Fries ex Hartman

Aira caerula **L.** – See *Molinia caerulea* (L.) Moench

Aira caespitosa **L.** – See *Deschampsia caespitosa* (L.) Beauv.

Aira capillaris **Host.** – See *Aira elegans* Willd. ex Kunth

Aira caryophylla **L.** – possibly *Aira caryophyllea* L.

Aira caryophyllea **L.** – Mouse grass (5) (1913), Silver aira grass [Silver aira-grass] (165) (1768), Silver hair grass [Silver hair-grass] (50) (present), Silvery hair grass [Silvery hair-grass] (5, 94) (1897–1913)

Aira coerula **L.** – See *Molinia caerulea* (L.) Moench

Aira elegans **Willd. ex Kunth** – Hair grass [Hairgrass, Hair-grass] (122) (1937)

Aira flexuosa **L.** – See *Deschampsia flexuosa* (L.) Trin. var *flexuosa*

Aira **L.** – Hair grass [Hairgrass, Hair-grass] (10, 66, 92, 155, 164) (1793–1942)

Aira melicoides – See *Trisetum melicoides* (Michx.) Vasey ex Scribn.

Aira obtusata **Michx.** – See *Sphenopholis obtusata* (Michx.) Scribn.

Aira praecox **L.** – Early aira grass [Early aira-grass] (165) (1768), Early hair grass (5) (1913), Early wild oat (66) (1903), Early wild oat grass [Early wild oat-grass] (94) (1901), Early-flowering hair grass [Early flowering hair-grass] (187) (1818), Wartatel (Swedish) (46) (1879), Yellow hair grass [Yellow hairgrass] (50) (present)

Aira triflora **Elliot** – See *Poa cuspidata* Nutt.

Airopsis praecox – See *Aira praecox* L.

Ajuga chamaepithys **W.** – See *Ajuga chamaepitys* (L.) Schreb.

Ajuga chamaepitys **(L.) Schreb.** – Bugle (19, 92) (1840–1876), Field cypress (92) (1876), Groundpine [Ground-pine, Ground pine] (92) (1876), Groundpine bugle (155) (1942), Chamaepitys (178) (1526), Lowe's pine [Lowe pine] (178) (1526)

Ajuga genevensis **L.** – Erect bugle (5) (1913), Geneva bugle (138, 155, 165) (1768–1942)

Ajuga **L.** – Bugle (10, 50, 138, 155, 158, 167) (1814–present), Bugle-weed [Bugle weed, Bugle-weed] (109, 156) (1923–1949), Ground-pine [Ground-pine, Ground pine] (10, 158) (1818–1900)

Ajuga reptans **L.** – Brown bugle (5, 158) (1900–1913), Bugle (5, 156, 158) (1900–1923), Bugle (French) (158) (1900), Bugleweed [Bugle weed, Bugle-weed] (156) (1923), Carpenter's-herb [Carpenter's herb, Carpenter-herb] (5, 156, 158) (1900–1923) no longer in use by 1923, Carpet bugle (138, 155) (1923–1942), Common bugle (50, 92, 165) (1768–present), Dead-men's-bellows (158) (1900), Goldner Günsel (German) (158) (1900), Helfringwort (158) (1900), Middle comfrey [Middle-comfrey (5, 156, 158) (1900–1923), Middle-consound [Middle consound (156, 158, 165) (1768–1923) consolida meant healing, Sicklewort [Sickle wort, Sicklewort] (5, 156, 158) (1900–1923) no longer in use by 1923, White bugle (178) (1526), Wild mint [Wylde mynte] (158) (1900)

Akebia **Dcne.** – Akebia (138, 155) (1931–1942)

Akebia quinata **(Houtt.) Dcne.** – Five-leaf akebia [Fiveleaf akebia] (138, 155) (1931–1942)

Alaria esculenta **(L.) Greville** – Badderlock (107) (1919), Badderlocks wingkelp (155) (1942)

Alaria **Grev.** – Kombu (155) (1942), Murlin (155) (1942), Wingkelp (155) (1942)

Albizia distachya **Macb.** – See *Paraserianthes lophantha* (Willd.) I. Nielsen

Albizia **Durazz.** – Albizzia (138, 155) (1931–1942)

Albizia julibrissin **Durazz.** – Pink siris (5) (1913), Silk tree [Silktree, Silk-tree] (5, 50, 109, 138) (1913–present), Silk-tree albizzia [Silk-tree albizzia] (155) (1942)

Albizia lebbeck **(L.) Benth.** – Lebbeck's tree [Lebbeck-tree] (109) (1949), Lebbek (138) (1923), Siris tree [Siris-tree] (109) (1949), Woman's-tongue tree [Womans-tongue-tree] (109) (1949)

Albizia procera **(Roxb.) Benth.** – Tall albizzia (155) (1942)

Albizzia lebbeck **Benth.** – See *Albizia lebbeck* (L.) Benth.

Albizzia lophanthus – See *Paraserianthes lophantha* (Willd.) I. Nielsen

Alcea **L.** – Hollyhock [Hollyhocks, Hollihocke, Holyhocke] (50) (present)

Alcea rosea **L.** – Althea rose (46) (1879), Common hollyhock (165) (1768), Double red hollyhock [Double red hollyhocke] (178) (1526), Garden malowe (179) (1526), Hock [Hocke] (158, 179) (1526–1900), Hockholler (158) (1900), Hollek (158) (1900), Hollihocke (178) (1526), Hollikocke (158) (1900), Hollyhock [Hollyhocks, Hollihocke, Holyhocke] (3, 4, 46, 50, 57, 58, 82, 85, 92, 106, 107, 109, 114, 138, 155, 156, 158, 179, 184) (1671–present), Holly-oak [Holly oak] (158) (1900), Holy hoke (158) (1900), Passerose (French) (158) (1900), Rose tremière (French) (158) (1900), Scarlet-colored hollyhock [Scarlet coloured hollyhocke] (178) (1526), Stockmalve (German) (158) (1900), Stockrose (German) (158) (1900), Tame mallow [Tame malowe] (179) (1526), Tree mallow [Tree mallows, Tree mallowes] (178) (1526)

Alchemilla alpina **L.** – Alpine ladies'-mantle [Alpine ladies mantle] (165) (1768), Cinquefoil [Cink-foil, Cinque-foil] (165) (1768), Lady's-mantle [Ladies' mantle [Ladies mantle, Ladysmantle, Lady's mantle] (7, 10, 19) (1818–1840), Mountain lady's-mantle [Mountain ladysmantle] (155) (1942)

Alchemilla arvense – See *Aphanes arvensis* L.

Alchemilla arvensis **(sic)** – See *Aphanes arvensis* L.

Alchemilla arvensis **Lam.** – possibly *Aphanes arvensis* L.

Alchemilla **L.** – Lady's-mantle [Ladies' mantle, Ladies mantle, Ladysmantle, Lady's mantle] (50, 155, 156) (1923–present), Lion's-foot [Lion's foot, Lions' foot, Lyons fote] (179) (1526), Pedelyon (179) (1526)

Alchemilla monticola **Opiz** – Common lady's-mantle [Common ladysmantle, Common ladies mantle] (155, 165) (1768–1942)

Alchemilla monticola **Opiz (possibly)** – Bear's-foot [Bear's foot, Bearsfoot] (156, 165) (1768–1923), Dew cup [Dewcup] (5) (1913), Duck's-foot [Duck foot, Duck's foot, Ducks foot, Ducks' foot] (156) (1923), Great sanicle (156) (1923), Lady's-mantle [Ladies' mantle, Ladies mantle, Ladysmantle, Lady's mantle] (5, 92, 156, 178) (1876–1923) from leaf shape, Pedelion (156) (1923)

Alchemilla pratensis **auct. non F. W. Schmidt** – See *Alchemilla monticola* Opiz

Alchemilla pratensis **F. W. Schmidt** – possibly *Alchemilla monticola* Opiz

Alchemilla vulgaris **auct. non L.** – See *Alchemilla monticola* Opiz

Alchornea **Sw.** – Alchornea (50) (present), Christmas bush [Christmas-bush] (155) (1942)

Alcicornium – See *Platycerium* Desv.

Alcicornium bifurcatum **[(Cav.) Underw.]** – See *Platycerium bifurcatum* (Cav.) C. Chr.

Alectoria **Ach.** – Alectoria (155) (1942)

Alectoria jubata **(L.) Ach.** – possibly *Parmelia jubata* (L.) Ach.

Alectorolophus – See *Rhinanthus* L.

Alectryon **Gaertn.** – Alectryon (155) (1942), Titoki (138) (1923)

Aletes **J.M. Coult. & Rose** – Indian parsley (50) (present)

Aletris alba **Michx.** – See *Aletris farinosa* L.

Aletris aurea **Michx.** – possibly *Aletris aurea* Walt.

Aletris aurea **Walt.** – Stud-flower Virginia spiderwort [Studded flowrd Virginia spiderwort] (181) (~1678), Yellow colic-root (97) (1937) OK, Yellow star root (19, 92) (1840–1876) (possibly)

Aletris farinosa **L.** – Ague root (ague-root) (5, 6, 7, 64, 92, 156) (1828–1923), Ague-grass [Ague grass] (7, 64, 92, 156) (1828–1923), Agur-grass [Agur grass] (5, 6) (1892–1913), Aletris (52, 54, 64) (1905–1919), Alétris Farineux (French) (6) (1892), Aletris Meunier

(French) (7) (1828), Aletris radix (Official name of Materia Medica) (7) (1828), Aloe root [Aloe-root] (5, 6, 7, 64, 92, 156) (1828–1923), Alteris (57) (1917), American aletris (165) (1768), Bettie grass (6) (1892), Bitter-grass [Bitter grass] (5, 6, 7, 92, 156) (1828–1923), Bitter-plant [Bitter plant] (5, 156) (1913–1923), Blackroot [Black-root, Black root] (6, 7) (1828–1892), Blazing star [Blazing-star, Blazingstar] (5, 6, 7, 49, 53, 64, 92, 156) (1828–1923), Colic root [Colic-root, Colicroot] (5, 6, 14, 55, 57, 64, 92, 156) (1871–1923), Crow-corn [Crow corn] (5, 6, 64, 156) (1892–1923), Crow-corn root [Crow corn root] (92) (1876), Devil's-bit [Devil's bit, Devilbit] (6, 7, 42, 64, 156) (1814–1923), False aloe [False-aloe] (19) (1840), False star-grass [False star grass] (19, 92) (1840–1876), False unicorn-root [False unicorn root] (6, 49, 52, 53) (1892–1922), False unicorn-wort [False unicorn wort] (49) (1898), Himili (7) (1828), Huskroot [Husk root] (5) (1913), Huskwort (64, 156) (1908–1923), Mealy aletris (42) (1814), Mealy starwort (5, 7, 64, 92, 156) (1828–1923), Mehlige Aletris (German) (6) (1892), Mehlige Sterngrass (German) (7) (1828), Star root (5, 6, 7, 92, 181, 184) (~1678–1913), Star-grass [Star grass, Stargrass] (5, 6, 7, 42, 49, 52, 53, 54, 64, 92, 138, 156, 181, 187) (~1678–1923), Starwort [Star-wort, Star wort] (6, 49, 52, 53, 55, 57, 64) (1892–1922), True unicorn root [True unicorn-root] (64) (1908), Unicorn (92, 156) (1876–1923), Unicorn plant [Unicorn-plant, Unicornplant] (64, 156) (1908–1923), Unicorn root [Unicorn-root] (5, 6, 7, 19, 64, 92) (1828–1913), Unicorn-horn [Unicorn's horn, Unicorns' horn, Unicorn horn] (5, 64) (1908–1913), White colic root (50) (present), White-tube stargrass [Whitetube stargrass] (155) (1942)

Aletris L. – Colic root [Colic-root, Colicroot] (1, 109) (1932–1949), False aloe [False-aloe] (167) (1814), Star-grass [Star grass, Stargrass] (1, 109, 138, 155) (1923–1949)

Aleurites fordi – See *Vernicia fordii* (Hemsl.) Airy Shaw

Aleurites fordii **Hemsl.** – See *Vernicia fordii* (Hemsl.) Airy Shaw

Aleurites **Forst.** – See *Aleurites* J.R. Forst. & G. Forst.

Aleurites **J.R. Forst. & G. Forst.** – Aleurites (50) (present)

Aleurites moliccana **Willd.** – See *Aleurites moluccana* (L.) Willd.

Aleurites moluccana **(L.) Willd.** – Candleberry tree [Candel berry tree, Candle-berry-tree] (92, 109) (1876–1949), Candlenut tree [Candelnut tree, Candle-nut tree, Candlenuttree] (107, 109, 138, 155) (1919–1949), Country walnut (107) (1919), Otaheite walnut (107) (1919)

Aleurites moluccana **Willd.** – See *Aleurites moluccana* (L.) Willd.

Aleurites montana **(Lour.) P. Wilson** – Mu-oil tree [Mu-oiltree] (155) (1942)

Aleurites montanus – See *Aleurites montana* (Lour.) P. Wilson

Aleurites triloba **Forst.** – See *Aleurites moluccana* (L.) Willd.

Algarobia glandulosa **Torr. & Gray** – See *Prosopis glandulosa* Torr.

Alhagi camelorum **Fisch.** – See *Alhagi maurorum* Medik.

Alhagi maurorum **Medik.** – Camel's-thorn [Camel's thorn, Camelsthorn] (92, 107, 155) (1876–1942), False manna (92) (1876), Manna plant [Manna-plant] (107) (1919)

Alhagi pseudalhagi – See *Alhagi maurorum* Medik.

Alisma brevipes **Greene** – See *Alisma triviale* Pursh

Alisma geyeri **Torr.** – See *Alisma gramineum* Lej.

Alisma gramineum **Gmel.** – See *Alisma gramineum* Lej.

Alisma gramineum **Lej.** – Geyer's water-plantain [Geyer waterplantain, Geyer's water plantain] (5, 93, 155) (1913–1942), Narrow-leaf water-plantain [Narrowleaf water plantain] (50) (present)

Alisma **L.** – Water-plantain [Water plantain, Waterplantain] (1, 10, 50, 93, 106, 138, 155, 167) (1814–present)

Alisma odorata **Raf.** – See *Alisma triviale* Pursh

Alisma odoratum **Raf.** – See *Alisma triviale* Pursh

Alisma plantago **L.** – See *Alisma plantago-aquatica* L.

Alisma plantago-aquatica **L.** – American water-plantain [American waterplantain] (155, 156) (1923–1942), Common water plantain (42) (1814), Deil's spoons (156) (1923), Grass water-plantain [Grass waterplantain] (155) (1942), Great thumb-wort (156) (1923), Great water plantain (165) (1768), Mad-dog weed [Mad

dog weed] (19, 58, 92, 156) (1840–1923), Thrumwort [Thrumwort] (184) (1793), Water-plantain [Water plantain, Waterplantain, Water plantane] (7, 19, 44, 46, 48, 58, 72, 92, 120, 131, 138, 156) (1671–1938), Herbe a malo (French) (166) (1807), Sweet plantain (7) (1828) (possibly)

Alisma plantago-aquatica **L. var. americanum R. & S.** – See *Alisma triviale* Pursh

Alisma subcordatum **Raf.** – American water-plantain [American waterplantain] (5, 50, 93, 97) (1913–present), Deil's spoons (5) (1913), Devil's-spoons (157) (1929), Great thrumwort (5, 157) (1900–1913), Mad-dog weed [Mad dog weed] (5, 157) (1913–1929), Water-plantain [Water plantain, Waterplantain, Water plantane] (3, 85, 122, 157) (1932–1977)

Alisma tenellum **Mart.** – See *Echinodorus tenellus* (Mart.) Buch.

Alisma triviale **Pursh** – Northern water-plantain [Northern water plantain] (50) (present), Water-plantain [Water plantain, Waterplantain, Water plantane] (3) (1977), Western water-plantain (5) (1913)

Allamanda blanchetii **A.DC.** – Violet allamanda (155) (1942)

Allamanda cathartica grandiflora – See *Allamanda cathartica* L.

Allamanda cathartica hendersoni – See *Allamanda cathartica* L.

Allamanda cathartica **L.** – Big-flower common allamanda, Bigflower common allamanda] (155) (1942), Common allamanda (138, 155) (1931–1942), Henderson's allamanda [Henderson allamanda] (138) (1923), Henderson's common allamanda [Henderson common allamanda] (155) (1942)

Allamanda cathartica **L. var. grandiflora (Aubl.) Bailey & C.P. Raffill** – See *Allamanda cathartica* L.

Allamanda cathartica schotti – See *Allamanda schottii* Pohl

Allamanda **L.** – Allamanda (138, 155) (1931–1942)

Allamanda neriifolia – See *Allamanda schottii* Pohl

Allamanda schottii **Pohl** – Oleander allamanda (138, 155) (1931–1942), Schott's common allamanda [Schott common allamanda] (155) (1942)

Allamanda violacea **Gardner & Fielding** – See *Allamanda blanchetii* A.DC. introduced

Allenrolfea **Kuntze** – Burro weed [Burroweed] (153) (1913) NM, Pickleweed (155) (1942)

Alliaria **Adans.** – possibly *Alliaria* Heister ex Fabr.

Alliaria alliaria **(L.) Britton** – See *Alliaria petiolata* (Bieb.) Cavara & Grande

Alliaria **Heister ex Fabr.** – Alliaria (50) (present), Garlic mustard [Garlicmustard, Garlicke mustard] (1, 4) (1932–1986) (possibly), Hedge-garlic [Hedge garlic] (1, 158) (1900–1932) (possibly)

Alliaria officinalis **Andrz.** – See *Alliaria petiolata* (Bieb.) Cavara & Grande

Alliaria petiolata **(Bieb.) Cavara & Grande** – Alliaire Commune (French) (158) (1900), Alliaria (178) (1526), Cardiacke (158) (1900), English treacle (158) (1900), Garlic mustard [Garlicmustard, Garlicke mustard] (3, 4, 5, 50, 155, 158) (1900–present), Garlic root [Garlic-root] (5, 156) (1913–1923), Garlicwort [Garlic wort] (107, 158) (1900–1919), Hedge-garlic [Hedge garlic] (5, 92, 156, 158) (1876–1923), Jack-by-the-hedge [Iacke by the hedge] (5, 92, 156, 158, 178) (1526–1923) no longer in use by 1923, Jack-in-the-bush (5) (1913), Knoblauchkraut (German) (158) (1900), Leek cress (156, 158) (1900–1923), Penny-hedge [Penny hedge] (5, 158) (1900–1913), Poor-man's-mustard [Poor man's mustard] (5, 156, 158) (1900–1923), Poor-man's-treacle [Poor-man's treacle] (158) (1900), Sasskraut (German) (107) (1919), Sauce-alone [Sauce alone] (5, 156, 158, 178) (1526–1923), Swarms (158) (1900), Treacle mustard [Treakle mustard] (156) (1923)

Allibertia intermedia **Marion** – See *Manfreda virginica* (L.) Salisb. ex Rose

Alliona carletoni **Standley [Allionia?]** – See *Mirabilis glabra* (S. Wats.) Standl.

Alliona hirsuta – See *Mirabilis hirsuta* (Pursh) MacM.

Alliona linearis **Pursh** – See *Mirabilis linearis* (Pursh) Heimerl

Alliona nyctaginea **Michx** – See *Mirabilis nyctaginea* (Michx.) MacM.

Allionia albida **Walt.** – See *Mirabilis albida* (Walt.) Heimerl

Allionia glabra **(S. Wats.) Kuntze** – See *Mirabilis glabra* (S. Wats.) Standl.

Allionia hirsuta **Pursh** – See *Mirabilis hirsuta* (Pursh) MacM.

Allionia incarnata **L.** – Trailing four-o-clock (4) (1986), Trialing windmills (50) (present)

Allionia **L.** – Trailing four-o-clock (4) (1986), Umbrella-wort [Umbrella wort] (1, 93, 158) (1900–1936), Windmills (50) (present)

Allionia **Loefl.** – See *Allionia* L.

Allionia nyctaginea **Michx.** – See *Mirabilis nyctaginea* (Michx.) MacM.

Allium **(Tourn.) L.** – See *Allium* L.

Allium acuminatum **Hook.** – Taper-tip onion [Tapertip onion] (155) (1942)

Allium alleghaniense **Small.** – See *Allium allegheniense* Small.

Allium allegheniense **Small.** – Allegheny onion [Alleghany onion] (5, 155) (1913–1942)

Allium ampeloprasum **L.** – Garlic leek [Garlicke leke] (178) (1596), Great mountain garlic [Great mountaine Garlicke] (180) (1633), Great round-head garlic [Great round-headed garlick] (165) (1768)

Allium ampeloprasum **L. var.** *atroviolaceum* **(Boiss.) Regel** – See *Allium atroviolaceum* Boiss.

Allium ampeloprasum **L. var.** *porrum* – See *Allium atroviolaceum* Boiss.

Allium arenicola **Small** – See *Allium canadense* L. var. *mobilense* (Regal) Ownbey

Allium atroviolaceum **Boiss.** – Leek [Leeks, Leke, Leekes] (110) (1886)

Allium bisceptrum **S. Wats. var.** *palmeri* **(S. Wats.) Cronq.** – Palmer's onion (86) (1878) for Dr. Palmer, western botanist

Allium bolanderi **S. Wats.** – Bolander's onion [Bolander onion] (155) (1942)

Allium brandegeei **S. Wats.** – Brandegee's onion [Brandegee onion] (155) (1942)

Allium brandegei (sic) – See *Allium brandegeei* S. Wats.

Allium breweri – See *Allium falcifolium* Hook. & Arn.

Allium burdickii **(Hanes) A. G. Jones** – Narrow-leaf wild leek [Narrowleaf wild leek] (50) (present)

Allium canadense **L.** – Allia (46) (1879), American garlic (46) (1879), American onion garlick (42) (1814), Canadian garlic [Canada garlic] (155) (1942), Canadian tree onion [Canada tree onion] (165) (1768), Homer's molley (46) (1671), Meadow garlic (19, 50, 72, 92, 93, 97, 138, 158) (1840–present), Wild garlic (85, 156, 158) (1900–1932), Wild leek [Wild leekes] (46) (1879), Wild onion (23, 80) (1810–1913)

Allium canadense **L. var.** *canadense* – Meadow garlic (50) (present), Wild onion (3) (1977)

Allium canadense **L. var.** *fraseri* **M. Ownbey** – Fraser's meadow garlic [Fraser meadow garlic] (50) (present), Fraser's wild onion (50) (present), Wild onion (3) (1977)

Allium canadense **L. var.** *hyacinthoides* **(Bush) M. Ownbey** – Hyacinth meadow garlic (50) (present), Wild onion (3) (1977)

Allium canadense **L. var.** *lavendulare* **(Bates) M. Ownbey & Aase** – Meadow garlic (50) (present), Wild onion (3) (1977)

Allium canadense **L. var.** *mobilense* **(Regal) Ownbey** – Common wild onion (93) (1936), Manzhonka-mantanaha (Omaha-Ponca) (37) (1830), Meadow garlic (50) (present), Osidiwa (Pawnee) (37) (1830), Osidiwa tsitschiks (Pawnee) (37) (1830), Pshin (Dakota) (37) (1830), Sand onion (97) (1937) OK, Shinhop (Winnebago) (37) (1830), Wild onion (5, 37, 97) (1913–1937)

Allium cepa **L.** – Bolle (German) (158) (1900), Common onion (165) (1768), Cultivated onion (106) (1930), Garden onion (19, 50, 155) (1840–present), Krommunda (Modern Greek) (110) (1886), Krommuon (110) (1886), Multiplier onion (109) (1949), Oignon commun (French) (158) (1900), Onion [Onions] (49, 53, 92, 109, 110, 138, 158, 178, 179) (1526–1949) from union because bulb never throws off any offsets (165), Palandu (India) (110) (1886), Top onion (155) (1942), Xonacatl (Mexico) (110) (1813), Zipolle (German) (158) (1900), Zweibel (German) (158) (1900)

Allium cepa **L. var.** *cepa* – Multiplier onion (155) (1942), Potato onion (109) (1949)

Allium cepa **L. var.** *viviparum* **M.C. Metz** – See *Allium cepa* L. introduced

Allium cepa solanium – See *Allium cepa* L. var. *cepa*

Allium cepa **var.** *aggregatum* **Don** – See *Allium cepa* L. var. *cepa*

Allium cepa viviparum – See *Allium cepa* L.

Allium cernuum **Roth** – Mountain garlic [Mountaine garlicke, Mountain garlick] (42) (1814), Nodding garlic (156) (1923), Nodding onion (50, 138, 155) (1923–present), Nodding wild onion (5, 72, 93, 156) (1907–1936), Wild onion (3, 85) (1932–1977)

Allium cernuum **Roth var.** *cernuum* – Nodding onion (50) (present)

Allium coryi **M.E. Jones** – Cory's onion [Cory onion] (155) (1942), Yellow onion (122) (1937), Yellow-flower onion [Yellow-flowered onion] (124) (1937)

Allium crispum **Greene** – Curled Mexicali onion (155) (1942)

Allium dichlamydeum **Greene** – Two-cloak onion [Twocloak onion] (155) (1942)

Allium douglasi – See *Allium douglasii* Hook.

Allium douglasii **Hook.** – Douglas' onion [Douglas onion] (155) (1942)

Allium drummondii **Regel** – Drummond's onion (50) (present), Heller's wild onion (97) (1937), Nuttall's onion [Nuttall onion] (155) (1942), Nuttall's wild onion (5, 93, 97) (1913–1937), White onion (122) (1937), White-flower onion [White-flowered onion] (124) (1937), Wild onion (3, 85) (1932–1977)

Allium falcifolium **Hook. & Arn.** – Brewer's onion [Brewer onion] (155) (1942), Sickle-leaf onion [Sickleleaf onion] (155) (1942)

Allium fibrillum **M.E. Jones** – Blue Mountain onion [BlueMountain onion] (155) (1942)

Allium fistulosum **L.** – Ciboule (165) (1768), Spring onion (109, 110) (1886–1949), Welsh onion (19, 50, 109, 110, 138, 165) (1768–present)

Allium fragrans **auct. non Vent.** – See *Nothoscordum borbonicum* Kunth

Allium geyeri **Wats.** – Geyer's onion [Geyer onion] (50, 155) (1942–present)

Allium haematochiton **S. Wats.** – Blood-tunic onion [Bloodtunic onion] (155) (1942)

Allium helleri **Small** – See *Allium drummondii* Regel

Allium hyalinum **Curran** – Eldorado onion (155) (1942)

Allium inodorum **auct. non Ait.** – See *Nothoscordum borbonicum* Kunth

Allium **L.** – Ceba (Spanish) (180) (1633), Cebola (Spanish) (180) (1633), Cebolla (Spanish) (180) (1633), Cepe (180) (1633), Cipolla (Italian) (180) (1633), Garlic [Garlick, Garlicke, Garlyke] (101, 156, 184) (1793–1923), Landlauch (7) (1828), Leek [Leeks, Leke, Leekes] (121) (1918–1970), Moly (165) (1768), Moŋžoŋxe (Osage, earth + bury) (121) (1918–1970), Oignon (French) (180) (1633), Onion [Onions] (1, 93, 106, 109, 121, 148, 138, 155, 156, 167, 180) (1633–1970) from union because bulb never throws off any offsets, Onion wibel (German) (180) (1633), Pšiŋ (Lakota) (121) (1918–1970), Ramps (75) (1894), Scoroprasum (165) (1768), Setanie (French) (180) (1633), Wild garlic (7, 121, 148) (1828–1970), Wild leek [Wild leekes] (1) (1932), Wild onion (101, 127) (1905–1933)

Allium lemmoni – See *Allium lemmonii* S. Wats.

Allium lemmonii **S. Wats.** – Lemmon's onion [Lemmons onion] (155) (1942)

Allium multibulbosum **Jacq** – possibly *Allium nigrum* L.

Allium mutabile **Michx.** – See *Allium canadense* L. var. *mobilense* (Regal) Ownbey

Allium nevadense **S. Wats.** – Nevada onion (155) (1942)

Allium nigrum **L.** – Black onion (155, 165) (1768–1942), Serpent's-moly [Serpents moly] (178) (1596)

Allium nuttallii **S. Wats.** – See *Allium drummondii* Regel

Allium oleraceum **L.** – Field garlic (50) (present), Potherb onion (155) (1942), Purple-stripe garlic [Purple-striped garlick] (165) (1768), Striped onion (19) (1840)

Allium palmeri **S. Wats.** – See *Allium bisceptrum* S. Wats. var. *palmeri* (S. Wats.) Cronq. for Dr. Palmer, western botanist

Allium paniculatum **L.** – Mediterranean onion (155) (1942), Panicled garlic [Panicled garlick] (165) (1768)

Allium peninsulare – See *Allium peninsulare* J.G. Lemmon ex Greene

Allium peninsulare crispum – See *Allium crispum* Greene

Allium peninsulare **J.G. Lemmon ex Greene** – Mexicali onion (155) (1942)

Allium perdulce **S. V. Fraser** – Plains onion (50) (present)

Allium perdulce **S.V. Fraser var.** *perdulce* – See *Allium perdulce* S. V. Fraser

Allium perdulce **S.V. Fraser var.** *sperryi* **Ownbey** – Sperry's onion (50) (present)

Allium porrum **L.** – Common leek (165) (1768), French leek (158) (1900), Garden leek (50) (present), Lauch (German) (158, 180) (1633–1900), Leek [Leeks, Leke, Leekes] (3, 19, 92, 109, 138, 155, 158, 178, 179, 180) (1526–1977), Ollick (158) (1900), Porreau (French) (158, 180) (1633–1900), Scallion (158) (1900), Pozreue (Brabanders) (180) (1633) (possibly), Puerro (Spanish) (180) (1633) (possibly)

Allium reticulatum **G. Don** – See *Allium textile* A. Nels. & Macbr.

Allium sativum **L.** – Ail (French) (158) (1900), Allium (52) (1919), Cenhinnen (Welsh) (110) (1886), Churl's treacle [Churles tryacle] (178, 179) (1526–1596), Clove garlic (92) (1876), Clown's treacle (158) (1900), Common garlic (50, 165) (1768–present), Craf (Welsh) (110) (1886), Cultivated garlic (50) (present), Garlic [Garlick, Garlicke, Garlyke] (3, 19, 49, 52, 53, 57, 58, 92, 109, 110, 138, 155, 158, 165, 178, 179) (1526–1977), Garlleg (Welsh) (110) (1886), Gartenlauch (German) (158) (1900), Kiplohkos (Lettons) (110) (1886), Knoblauch (German) (110, 158) (1886–1900), Krunslauk (Esthonian) (110) (1886), Onion [Onions] (52) (1919), Poor-man's-treacle [Poor-man's treacle] (158) (1900) treacle meant antidote to venomous bite, same as theriac, Scordon (Modern Greek) (110) (1886), Scorodon (Ancient Greek) (50) (present)

Allium schoenoprasum **L.** – Biesloack (Dutch) (180) (1633), Brelles (French) (180) (1633), Chiballs (46) (1607), Chives [Chiues] (2, 92, 109, 110, 138, 155, 156, 165, 180) (1633–1949), Ciuet (180) (1633), Cives [Ciues] (19, 92, 156, 165, 178, 180) (1596–1876), Cyuers (178, 179) (1526–1596), Rush garlic (156) (1923), Rush leek [Rush leeke] (180) (1633), Shore onion (75, 156) (1894–1923), Siuves (178) (1596), Sweth (180) (1633), Wild chives (50) (present)

Allium schoenoprasum **L. var.** *sibiricum* **(L.) Hartman** – Siberian chive (155) (1942)

Allium schoenoprasum sibiricum – See *Allium schoenoprasum* L. var. *sibiricum* (L.) Hartman

Allium scorodoprasum **L.** – Eschalote d'Espagne (French) (110) (1886), Giant garlic (155) (1942), Keipe (Sweden) (110) (1886), Mountain garlic [Mountaine garlicke, Mountain garlick] (178) (1596), Rackenboll (Sweden) (110) (1886), Rocambole (110, 165) (1768–1886), Rockenbolle (German) (110) (1886), Skovlög (Denmark) (110) (1886)

Allium stellatum **Ker** – Autumn onion (50) (present), Mûckode'cigaga'wûn (Chippewa, prairie skunk plant) (40) (1928), Pink wild onion (3) (1977), Prairie onion (155) (1942), Prairie wild onion (5, 72, 93, 97) (1907–1937), Wild garlic (108) (1878), Wild onion (40) (1928)

Allium textile **A. Nels. & Macbr.** – Fraser's wild onion (93, 97) (1936–1937), Textile onion (50, 155) (1942–present), White wild onion (3) (1977), Wild garlic (108) (1878), Wild onion (98, 126) (1926–1933)

Allium tolmiei **(Hook.) Baker ex S. Wats.** – Tolmei's onion [Tolmei onion] (155) (1942)

Allium tribracteatum **Torr.** – Three-bract onion [Threebract onion] (155) (1942)

Allium tricoccum **Ait.** – Broad-leaf onion garlick [Broad-leaved onion garlick] (42) (1814), Lance-leaf garlic [Lance-leaved garlic] (156) (1923), Mountain leek [Mountain leak] (19) (1840), Ramps (23, 75, 156) (1810–1923), Siga'gawûnj' (Chippewa, onion) (40) (1928),

Three-seed garlic [Three-seeded garlick] (165) (1768), Three-seed leek [Three seed leek, Three seeded leek, Three-seeded leek] (19, 92, 158) (1840–1900), Three-seed onion garlic [Three-seeded onion garlick] (42) (1814), Wild leek [Wild leekes] (3, 40, 50, 72, 85, 155, 156, 158) (1900–present), Wood leek (138) (1923)

Allium triflorum **Raf.** – See *Allium tricoccum* Ait.

Allium triquetrum **L.** – Three-corner moly [Three-cornered moly] (165) (1768), Triangle onion (155) (1942)

Allium tuberosum **Rottl. ex Spreng.** – Chinese chives (50) (present)

Allium unifolium **Kellogg** – One-leaf onion [Oneleaf onion] (155) (1942)

Allium validum **S. Wats.** – Pacific onion (155) (1942)

Allium victorialis **L.** – First broad-leaf mountain moly [First broad leaued mountaine moly] (180) (1633), Long-root garlic [Long-rooted garlick] (165) (1768), Long-root onion [Longroot onion] (155) (1942), Mountain moly [Mountaine moly] (178) (1596)

Allium vineale **L.** – Cow garlic [Cow-garlic] (156, 158) (1900–1923), Crow garlic [Crow garlick] (5, 155, 156, 158, 165) (1768–1942), Crow onion (156, 158) (1900–1923), Crowfoot garlic [Crow foot garlic] (92) (1876), Field garlic (5, 19, 62, 85, 155, 156, 158) (1840–1942), Garlic [Garlick, Garlicke, Garlyke] (56) (1901), Hart's garlic [Harts garlicke] (178) (1596), Wild garlic (3, 5, 50, 62, 80, 93, 158) (1900–present), Wild onion (62) (1912)

Allium vineale **L. subsp.** *compactum* **(Thuill.) Coss. & Germ.** – Compact onion (50) (present)

Allium vineale **L. subsp.** *vineale* – Wild garlic (50) (present)

Allocarya **Greene** – See *Plagiobothrys* Fisch. & C.A. Mey. all US species

Allocarya scopulorum **Greene** – See *Plagiobothrys scouleri* (Hook. & Arn.) I.M. Johnston var. *hispidulus* (Greene) Dorn

Almutaster pauciflorus **(Nutt.) A. & D. Löve** – Alkali marsh aster (50) (present), Few-flower aster [Fewflower aster, Few-flowered aster] (3, 4) (1977–1986)

Alnus **(Tourn.) Hill.** – See *Alnus* Mill.

Alnus alnobetula **(Ehrh.) K. Koch** – See *Alnus viridis* (Vill.) Lam. & DC.

Alnus alnus **(L.) Britton** – See *Alnus glutinosa* (L.) Gaertn.

Alnus cordata **(Loisel.) Loisel. Or Desf.** – Italian alder (138, 155) (1931–1942)

Alnus crispa – See *Alnus viridis* (Vill.) Lam. & DC.

Alnus crispa mollis – See *Alnus viridis* (Vill.) Lam. & DC.

Alnus **Ehrh.** – possibly *Alnus* Mill.

Alnus fruticosa – See *Alnus viridis* subsp. *fruticosa* (Rupr.) Nyman

Alnus **Gaertn.** – See *Alnus* Mill.

Alnus glauca **Michx.** – See *Alnus incana* (L.) Moench subsp. *rugosa* (DuRoi) Clausen

Alnus glutinosa **(L.) Gaertn.** – Alder or Alder tree [Alder-tree] (5, 41, 187) (1770–1913), Black alder [Blacke aller] or Black alder tree (5, 109, 156) (1913–1949), Common European alder (20) (1857), Eller (5, 156) (1913–1923), European alder (5, 92, 137, 138, 155, 156) (1876–1942), Hollard (5, 156) (1913–1923), Irish mahogany (5, 156) (1913–1923), Ooler (5) (1913), Owler (92) (1876)

Alnus glutinosa **Gaertn.** – See *Alnus glutinosa* (L.) Gaertn.

Alnus incana **(L.) Moench** – Alder or Alder tree [Alder-tree] (40, 95) (1911–1928), Black alder [Blacke aller] or Black alder tree (5, 35, 156) (1806–1923), Eller (46) (1879), European alder (109) (1949), Glaucous alder (42) (1814), Hoary alder (2, 5, 46, 72, 82, 93, 156) (1879–1936), Hoary-leaf alder [Hoary leaved alder] (42) (1814), Oryelle tree (46) (1879), Speckled alder (1, 82, 92, 105, 113, 138, 155, 156) (1876–1942), Tag alder [Tag-alder] (5, 156) (1913–1923), Tōp (Chippewa) (105) (1932), Wadûb (Chippewa) (40) (1928), Spreckled alder (5) (1913) (possibly), White alder (20) (1857) (possibly)

Alnus incana **(L.) Moench subsp.** *rugosa* **(DuRoi) Clausen** – Alder or Alder tree [Alder-tree] (101, 122, 124) (1905–1937), American alder (5, 156, 158) (1900–1923), Aune à feuilles argentées (French) (8) (1785), Aune menu feuillé (French) (20) (1857), Black alder [Blacke aller] or Black alder tree (20) (1857), Common alder (5, 156, 158)

(1900–1923), Green alder (5, 156, 158) (1900–1923), Hazel alder (5, 138, 155, 156) (1913–1942), Mountain alder (138) (1923), Red alder (156, 158) (1900–1923), River alder (1) (1932), Silver-leaf alder [Silver-leaved alder] (8) (1785), Smooth alder (1, 5, 65, 97, 156, 158) (1900–1937), Speckled alder (3, 4, 46, 50, 109, 156, 158) (1879–present), Tag alder [Tag-alder] (5, 156, 158) (1900–1923), Thin-leaf alder [Thin-leaved alder] (20, 155) (1857–1942)

Alnus incana **(L.) Willd.** – possibly *Alnus incana* (L.) Moench

Alnus incana **Willd.** – See *Alnus incana* (L.) Moench

Alnus maritima **(Marsh.) Muhl. ex Nutt.** – Aune maritime (8, 20) (1785–1857), Seaside alder (5, 20, 97, 155, 156) (1857–1942)

Alnus mitchelliana – See *Alnus viridis* (Vill.) Lam. & DC.

Alnus mollis **Fernald.** – See *Alnus viridis* (Vill.) Lam. & DC.

Alnus nepalensis **D. Don** – Nepal alder (155) (1942)

Alnus oblongifolia **Torr.** – New Mexico alder [New Mexican alder] (155) (1942)

Alnus oregona – See *Alnus rubra* Bong.

Alnus oregona **Nutt. var. *pinnatisecta* Starker** – See *Alnus rubra* Bong.

Alnus **Mill.** – Alder or Alder tree [Alder-tree] (1, 4, 8, 10, 50, 82, 106, 109, 138, 155, 158, 167) (1785–present), Aune (French) (8) (1785) (possibly)

Alnus rhombifolia bernardina – See *Alnus rhombifolia* Nutt.

Alnus rhombifolia **Nutt.** – Rhombic-leaf alder [Rhombic-leaved alder] (20) (1857), Santa Ana Sierra alder [SantaAna Sierra alder] (155) (1942), Sierra alder (155) (1942), White alder (50) (present)

Alnus rhombifolia **Nutt. var. *bernardina* Munz & Johnston** – See *Alnus rhombifolia* Nutt.

Alnus rubra **Bong.** – Alnus (52) (1919), Aune de l'Oregon (French) (20) (1857), Common alder (8, 92) (1785–1876), Cut-leaf red alder [Cutleaf red alder] (155) (1942), Oregon alder (20, 160, 161) (1857–1860), Red alder (50, 61, 92, 155) (1870–present), Smooth alder (92) (1876), Smooth swamp alder (92) (1876), Swamp alder (92) (1876), Tag alder [Tag-alder] (52, 92) (1876–1919), Aune commun (French) (8) (1785) (possibly)

Alnus rubra pinnatisecta – See *Alnus rubra* Bong.

Alnus rugosa **(Du Roi) Spreng.** – See *Alnus incana* (L.) Moench subsp. *rugosa* (DuRoi) Clausen

Alnus rugosa **Spreng.** – See *Alnus incana* (L.) Moench subsp. *rugosa* (DuRoi) Clausen

Alnus serrulata **(Aiton) Willd.** – Alder or Alder tree [Alder-tree] (19) (1840), American alder (92) (1876), Black alder [Blacke aller] or Black alder tree (7, 49, 53) (1828–1898), Candle alder (187) (1818), Common alder (3, 20, 49, 53, 187) (1818–1977), Common American alder (42) (1814), Hazel alder (50, 109, 187) (1818–present), Red alder (49, 53) (1898–1922), Smooth alder (2, 4, 46, 49, 53, 58, 109) (1879–1949), Swamp alder (58) (1869), Tag alder [Tag-alder] (49, 53, 57, 58, 92) (1869–1922)

Alnus serrulata **Aiton** – See *Alnus serrulata* (Aiton) Willd.

Alnus serrulata **Willd.** – See *Alnus serrulata* (Aiton) Willd.

Alnus sinuata – See *Alnus viridis* (Vill.) Lam. & DC.

Alnus tenuifolia **Nutt.** – See *Alnus incana* (L.) Moench subsp. *rugosa* (DuRoi) Clausen

Alnus undulata **Willd.** – See *Alnus viridis* subsp. *crispa* (Aiton) Turrill

Alnus viridis **(Vill.) Lam. & DC.** – American green alder (138, 155) (1923–1942), Green alder (2, 5, 156) (1895–1923), Mountain alder (2, 5, 20, 156) (1857–1923), Downy alder (1) (1932), Downy green alder (156) (1923), European green alder (138, 155) (1931–1942), Silky green alder (155) (1942), Sitka alder (155) (1942)

Alnus viridis **DC.** – See *Alnus viridis* (Vill.) Lam. & DC.

Alnus viridis **subsp. *fruticosa* (Rupr.) Nyman** – Manchu alder (155) (1942)

Alnus viridis **subsp. *crispa* (Aiton) Turrill** – Waved alder (19) (1840)

Alnus vulgaris – See *Alnus glutinosa* (L.) Gaertn.

Alnus **Willd.** – possibly *Alnus* Mill.

Alocasia **(Schott) G. Don** – Alocasia (138, 155) (1923–1942)

Alocasia indica – See *Alocasia macrorrhizos* (L.) Schott

Alocasia indica metallica – See *Alocasia plumbea* Van Houtte

Alocasia macrorrhiza **Schott** – See *Alocasia macrorrhizos* (L.) Schott

Alocasia macrorrhizos **(L.) Schott** – Apé (Otahiti) (110) (1886), Giant alocasia (155) (1942), Giant taro (138) (1923), Hawaiian giant taro (138) (1923), Indo-Malayan alocasia [IndoMalayan alocasia] (155) (1942), Large-root alocasia [Large-rooted alocasia] (110) (1886)

Aloe barbadensis **Mill.** – See *Aloe vera* (L.) Burm. f.

Aloe guineensis **L.** – See *Sansevieria hyacinthoides* (L.) Druce

Aloe guinensis **(sic)** – See *Sansevieria hyacinthoides* (L.) Druce

Aloe **L.** – Aloe (109, 178, 179) (1526–1949)

Aloe vera **(L.) Burm. f.** – Aie green (178) (1596), Aloe (178) (1596), Barbados aloe [Barbadoes aloe, Barbadoes alloe] (92, 109, 165) (1768–1949), Bitter aloe (92) (1876), Live-long [Live long] (178) (1596)

Aloe vulgaris – See *Aloe vera* (L.) Burm. f.

Alopecurus aequalis **Sobol.** – Short-awn foxtail [Shortawn foxtail] (3, 50, 140, 155) (1942–present), Water grass [Water-grass] (152) (1912) NM

Alopecurus aequalis **Sobol. var. *aequalis*** – Marsh foxtail [Marsh foxtail] (85) (1932), Short-awn foxtail [Shortawn foxtail, Short-awned foxtail] (5, 50) (1913–present), Water foxtail [Water-fox tail] (88) (1885), Wild water foxtail [Wild water fox-tail] (66, 129) (1894–1903)

Alopecurus agrestis **L.** – See *Alopecurus myosuroides* Huds

Alopecurus agrostis – possibly *Alopecurus myosuroides* Huds

Alopecurus alpinus **Sm.** – Alpine foxtail (5, 45, 94) (1896–1913), Mountain foxtail (94) (1901), Rocky Mountain foxtail (118) (1898)

Alopecurus aristulatus **Michx.** – See *Alopecurus aequalis* Sobol. var. *aequalis*

Alopecurus arundinaceus **Poir** – Creeping foxtail (3, 155) (1942–1977), Creeping meadow foxtail (50) (present)

Alopecurus carolinianus **Walt.** – Carolina foxtail (3, 50, 155) (1942–present), Foxtail [Fox tail, Fox-tail, Fox tails, Foxetaile, Fox-taile] (122) (1937), Marsh foxtail [Marsh fox tail] (119) (1938)

Alopecurus fulvus **Smith.** – See *Alopecurus aequalis* Sobol.

Alopecurus geniculatus **L.** – Black grass [Blac-grass] (165) (1768), Float foxtail grass [Flote fox-tail grass] (165) (1768), Float grass [Flote grass] (5, 46) (1879–1913), Floating foxtail (5, 19, 45, 66, 90, 94) (1840–1912), Kiarr-kafle (Swedish) (46) (1879), Marsh foxtail [Marsh fox tail] (3, 5, 56) (1911–1977), Stakra (46) (1879), Washington foxtail (155) (1942), Water foxtail [Water fox tail] (5, 45, 50, 87, 111, 155) (1884–present), Water foxtail grass (90) (1885)

Alopecurus geniculatus **L. var. *aristulatus* (Michx.) Torr.** – See *Alopecurus aequalis* Sobol. var. *aequalis*

Alopecurus **L.** – Foxtail [Fox tail, Fox-tail, Fox tails, Foxetaile, Fox-taile] (1, 45, 50, 155) (1896–present), Foxtail grass [Fox tail grass, Fox-tail grass, Foxtail-grass] (10, 66, 93) (1818–1936)

Alopecurus monspeliensis **L.** – See *Polypogon monspeliensis* (L.) Desf.

Alopecurus myosuroides **Huds** – Bennet weed (5) (1913), Black bent grass [Black bentgrass] (5) (1913), Black couch grass (5) (1913), Black grass (92) (1876), Field foxtail grass [Field fox-tail grass] (165) (1768), Hunger grass (5) (1913), Mouse foxtail (155) (1942), Mouse-tail [Mousetail, Mouse-tail, Mousetaile] (5) (1913), Slender foxtail (3, 5, 56, 66) (1901–1977), Slender meadow foxtail (50) (present), Mouse-tail grass [Mouse tail gass] (92, 165) (1768, 1876) (possibly)

Alopecurus occidentalis **Scribn.** – See *Alopecurus alpinus* Sm.

Alopecurus occidentalis **Scribn. & Tweedy** – See *Alopecurus alpinus* Sm.

Alopecurus pallescens **Piper** – See *Alopecurus geniculatus* L.

Alopecurus pratensis **L.** – Common foxtail grass (90) (1885), Foxtail [Fox tail, Fox-tail, Fox tails, Foxetaile, Fox-taile] (19, 184) (1793–1840), Foxtail grass [Fox tail grass, Fox-tail grass, Foxtail-grass] (46) (1879), Meadow foxtail [Meadow fox tail, Meadow fox-tail] (3, 5, 45, 50, 56, 66, 67, 68, 87, 88, 90, 92, 94, 109, 129, 138, 143, 155) (1884–present), Meadow fox-tail grass (165) (1768), Meadow grass [Meadow-grass, Medow Grasse] (19) (1840)

Alopecurus pratensis L. subsp. *alpestris* (Wahlenb.) Selander – Mountain timothy (45) (1896)

Alopecurus pratensis var. *alpestris* Wahl. – See *Alopecurus pratensis* L. subsp. *alpestris* (Wahlenb.) Selander

Alopecurus ventricosus [Pers.] – See *Alopecurus arundinaceus* Poir

Aloysia citriodora Palau – See *Aloysia triphylla* (L'Hér.) Britt.

Aloysia gratissima (Gillies & Hook.) Troncoso – White brush (106, 122, 124) (1930–1937)

Aloysia Juss. – See *Aloysia* Palau

Aloysia macrostachya (Torr.) Moldenke – Spatulate-leaf fogfruit [Spatulate-leaved fog-fruit] *(*122) (1937)

Aloysia Ort. – possibly *Aloysia* Palau

Aloysia triphylla (L'Hér.) Britt. – Lemon verbena (92, 109) (1876–1949), Lemon-verbena (138) (1923), Sweet verbena (92) (1876), Thimbleweed [Thimble weed, Thimble-weed] (187) (1818), Verbena (92) (1876)

Aloysia triphylla Britt. – See *Aloysia triphylla* (L'Hér.) Britt.

Alphitonia – See *Alphitonia* Reissek ex Endl.

Alphitonia Reissek ex Endl. – Tree buckthorn [Treebuckthorn] (155) (1942)

Alpinia L. – See *Alpinia* Roxb. for Prosper Alpinius, 1536–1617, Italian botanist

Alpinia mutica Roxb. – Malay galangal (155) (1942)

Alpinia nutans – See *Alpinia zerumbet* (Pers.) Burtt & R.M. Sm.

Alpinia Roxb. – Alpinia (138) (1923), Galangal (155) (1942)

Alpinia speciosa Schum. – See *Alpinia zerumbet* (Pers.) Burtt & R.M. Sm.

Alpinia zerumbet (Pers.) Burtt & R.M. Sm. – Shell flower [Shellflower, Shellflower) (109, 138) (1923–1949), Shell-flower galangal [Shellflower galangal] (155) (1942)

Alsidium helminthochorton (Schwendimann) Kützing – Corsican moss (92) (1876), Worm moss (92) (1876) IN Kansas

Alsine (Tourn.) L. – See *Spergularia* (Pers.) J.& K. Presl

Alsine (Tourn.) Wahlenb. – See *Spergularia* (Pers.) J.& K. Presl

Alsine aquatica (L.) Britton – See *Myosoton aquaticum* (L.) Moench

Alsine borealis (Bigelow) Britton – See *Stellaria borealis* Bigelow subsp. *borealis*

Alsine crassifolia Ehrh. – See *Stellaria crassifolia* Ehrh. var. *crassifolia*

Alsine fontinalis (Short & Peter) Britton – See *Stellaria fontinalis* (Short & Peter) B.L. Robins.

Alsine glauca (With.) Britton – See *Stellaria palustris* (Murr.) Retz.

Alsine graminea (L.) Britton – See *Stellaria graminea* L.

Alsine holostea (L.) Britton – See *Stellaria holostea* L.

Alsine humifusa (Rottb.) Britton – See *Stellaria humifusa* Rottb.

Alsine L. – See *Spergularia* (Pers.) J.& K. Presl

Alsine longifolia (Muhl.) Britton – See *Stellaria longifolia* Muhl. ex Willd. var. *longifolia*

Alsine longipes (Glodie) Coville – See *Stellaria longipes* Goldie

Alsine media L. – See *Stellaria media* (L.) Vill. subsp. *media*

Alsine pubera (Michx.) Britton – See *Stellaria pubera* Michx.

Alsine tennesseensis (C. Mohr.) Small. – See *Stellaria corei* Shinners

Alsine uliginosa (Murray) Britton – See *Stellaria alsine* Grimm

Alsophila R. Br. – Tree fern [Treefern] (138, 155) (1923–1942)

Alstonia macrophylla Wallich ex G. Don – Devil-tree alstonia [Devil-tree alstonia] (155) (1942)

Alstonia R. Br. – Alstonia (155) (1942)

Alstroemeria haemantha Ruiz & Pavón – Purple-spot alstroemeria [Purplespot alstroemeria] (155) (1942)

Alstroemeria L. – Alstroemeria (138, 155) (1923–1942)

Alstroemeria psittacina – See *Alstroemeria pulchella* L. f. introduced

Alstroemeria pulchella L. f. – Parrot alstroemeria (138, 155) (1923–1942)

Alternanthera achyrantha (L.) R. Br. ex Sweet – See *Alternanthera pungens* Kunth

Alternanthera amoena – See *Alternanthera bettzichiana* (Regel) Voss

Alternanthera bettzichiana (Regel) Voss – Copper alternathera (155) (1942), Garden alternthera (138) (1923), Tom-thumb alternathera [Tomthumb alternathera] (155) (1942)

Alternanthera caracasana Kunth – Mat chaff flower (4) (1986), Washerwoman (50) (present)

Alternanthera ficoidea (L.) P. Beauv. – Rabbit-meat alternathera [Rabbitmeat alternathera] (155) (1942)

Alternanthera Forsk. – Alternathera (155) (1942), Joyweed (50) (present)

Alternanthera philoxeroides (Mart.) Griseb. – Alligator alternathera (155) (1942)

Alternanthera pungens Kunth – Khakiweed (50) (present)

Alternanthera tenella Colla – See *Alternanthera ficoidea* (L.) P. Beauv.

Alternanthera versicolor – See *Alternanthera bettzichiana* (Regel) Voss

Althaea cannabina L. – Palm-leaf marshmallow (50) (present) *Althaea* L. – Guimauve (French) (165) (1768), Hollyhock [Hollyhocks, Hollihocke, Holyhocke] (1, 4, 82) (1930–1986), Marshmallow [Marsh mallow, Marsh mallows, Marsh-mallow] (1, 50, 156, 165) (1768–present)

Althaea officinalis L. – Altea (Spanish) (158) (1900), Althee (German) (158) (1900), Common marshmallow (50, 165) (1768–present), Eibisch (German) (158) (1900), French mallowes (46) (1617), Guimauve (French) (55, 158) (1900–1911), Hye malowe (179) (1526), Malvavisco (Spanish) (158) (1900), Marshmallow [Marsh mallow, Marsh mallows, Marsh-mallow] (4, 3, 5, 7, 19, 46, 49, 52, 53, 55, 57, 58, 92, 107, 109, 138, 155, 156, 158, 178) (1596–1986), Mortification root [Mortification-root] (5, 92, 156, 158) (1876–1923), Officinal marshmallow [Officinal marsh-mallow] (165) (1768), Sweatweed [Sweat weed, Sweat-weed] (5, 92, 156, 158) (1876–1923), White mallow (107, 156, 158) (1900–1923), Wild mallow [Wylde malowe] (179) (1526), Wymote (92, 156, 158, 184) (1793–1923) no longer in use by 1923

Althaea rosea (L.) Cavar. – See *Alcea rosea* L.

Althaea rosea Cavar. – See *Alcea rosea* L.

Alvaradoa amorphoides Liebm. – Mexican alvaradoa (155) (1942)

Alvaradoa Liebm. – Alvaradoa (155) (1942)

Alyssum alyssoides (L.) Gouan. – possibly *Alyssum alyssoides* (L.) L.

Alyssum alyssoides (L.) L. – Calycine madwort (165) (1768), Heal-bite [Heal bite] (5, 156, 158) (1900–1923), Heal-dog (158) (1900), Pale alyssum (4, 155) (1942–1986), Pale madwort (50) (present), Small alyssum (5, 158) (1900–1913), Yellow alyssum (5, 158) (1900–1913), Sweet alyssum [Sweet-alyssum] (85) (1932) (possibly)

Alyssum calycinum L. – See *Alyssum alyssoides* (L.) L.

Alyssum desertorum Stapf – Alyssum (4) (1986), Desert madwort (50) (present)

Alyssum desertorum Stapf var. *desertorum* – Desert madwort (50) (present)

Alyssum incanum L. – See *Berteroa incana* (L.) DC.

Alyssum L. – Alyssum (1, 4, 138, 155, 158) (1900–1986), Gold-of-Pleasure [Gold of Pleasure] (10) (1818), Madwort (50, 109 156) (1923–present), Sweet alyssum [Sweet-alyssum] (1, 93) (1932–1936)

Alyssum maritimum [(L.) Lam.] – See *Lobularia maritima* (L.) Desv.

Alyssum minus (L.) Rothm. – Alyssum (50) (present)

Alyssum murale Waldst. & Kit. – Yellow-tuft (109) (1949)

Alyssum saxatile L. – See *Aurinia saxatilis* (L.) Desv.*)* ())

Alyxia Banks ex R. Br. – Alyxia (155) (1942)

Alyxia olivaeformis – See *Alyxia oliviformis* Gaud.

Amanita caesarea (Scop.) Pers. – Caesar's amanita [Caesars amanita] (155) (1942)

Amanita muscaria (L.) Lam. – Amanita (14, 148) (1882–1939)

Amanita muscaria var. *muscaria* (L.) Pers. – Deadly amanita (71) (1898), False orange amanita (71) (1898), Fly agaric (52, 53, 60, 71, 92, 170) (1876–1995), Fly amanita (71, 155) (1898–1942), Fly fungus (71) (1898), Fly-killer [Fly killer] (71) (1898), Anamita (92) (1876)

Amanita Pers. – Amanita (155) (1942)

Amanita phalloides (Fr.) Link – Bulbous amanita (71) (1898), Death cup (71) (1898), Death-cup amanita [Deathcup amanita] (155) (1942), Poison amanita (71) (1898)

Amanita strobiliformis **(Paulet ex Vittad.) Bertill.** – Fir-cone amanita [Fircone amanita] (155) (1942)

Amanita vaginata **var. *vaginata* (Bull.) Fr.** – Sheathed amanitopsis (155) (1942)

Amanita verna **(Bull.) Lam.** – Spring amanita (155) (1942)

Amanitopsis **Roze** – Amanitopsis (155) (1942)

Amaracus **Gleditsch.** – See *Origanum* L.

Amaranthus **(Tourn.) L.** – See *Amaranthus* L.

Amaranthus albus **L.** – White amaranth (165) (1768), White coxscomb (19) (1840), Pigweed [Pig-weed, Pig weed] (92) (1876), Tumble-weed [Tumble weed, Tumble-weed] (3, 4, 5, 62, 70, 72, 77, 80, 85, 93, 95, 97, 122, 131, 145, 156, 158) (1895–1986), Tumbleweed amaranth (155) (1942) (possibly), Tumbling pigweed (80) (1913) (possibly) IA, White pigweed (62) (1912) (possibly)

Amaranthus arenicola **I.M. Johnston** – Sandhill amaranth (50) (present), Sandhills pigweed (4) (1986)

Amaranthus australis **(Gray) Sauer** – Gulf Coast waterhemp [Gulf-coast waterhemp] (155) (1942)

Amaranthus blitoides **S. Wats.** – Calite de agua (Spanish) (150) (1894) NM, Low amaranth (62, 150) (1894–1912), Mat amaranth (50) (present), Pigweed purslane (145) (1897) KS, Prostrate amaranth (93, 97, 122, 131, 155) (1899–1937), Prostrate pigweed (62, 72, 80) (1907–1912), Pursely (101) (1905) MT, Spreading pigweed (156) (1923)

Amaranthus blitum **L.** – All-seed [All seed] (92) (1876), Blite (165) (1768), Lead amaranth (19) (1840), Lead-colored amaranth [Lead coloured amaranth] (42) (1814), Least amaranth (165) (1768), Livid amaranth (165) (1768), Purplish amaranth (5) (1913), Wild amaranth (92) (1876), Wild blite (107) (1919)

Amaranthus californicus **(Moq.) S. Wats.** – California amaranth (50) (present)

Amaranthus cannabinus **(L.) Sauer** – Acnida (174, 177) (1753–1762), Rough-fruit acnida [Rough-fruited acnida] (187) (1818), Saltmarsh water-hemp [Salt marsh water hemp, Salt-marsh water-hemp] (5, 156) (1913–1923), Tide-marsh water hemp [Tidemarsh waterhemp] (155) (1942), Virginia hemp [Virginian hemp] (165) (1768), Water-hemp [Water hemp, Waterhemp] (19, 92, 156) (1840–1923), Waterleaf [Water leaf, Water-leaf] (156) (1923), Willow hemp (7, 92) (1828–1876), Smooth-fruit acnida [Smooth-fruited acnida] (187) (1818) (possibly)

Amaranthus caudatus **L.** – Bloody amaranth (165) (1768), Great flower-gentle [Great flower gentle] (178) (1526), Love-lies-bleeding [Love lies bleeding] (109, 138, 155, 165) (1768–1942), Lovely-bleeding [Lovely bleeding] (7) (1828), Pendulous amaranth (165) (1768), Prince's-feather [Prince's feather, Princes-feather, Princesfeather] (92) (1876), Spreading amaranth (165) (1768), Tassel flower [Tassel-flower, Tasselflower, Tassell flower] (109) (1949)

Amaranthus chlorostachys **Willd.** – See *Amaranthus hybridus* L.

Amaranthus crispus **(Lesp. & Thev.) N. Terracc** – Crisp-leaf amaranth [Crisp-leaved amaranth] (5) (1913)

Amaranthus cruentus **L.** – Prince's-feather [Prince's feather, Princes-feather, Princesfeather] (107) (1919), Purple amaranth (156) (1923), Red amaranth (50, 107) (1919–present), Tassel amaranth (138) (1923), Various-leaf amaranth [Various-leaved amaranth] (165) (1768)

Amaranthus deflexus **L.** – Low amaranth (5) (1913)

Amaranthus gangeticus **L.** – See *Amaranthus tricolor* L.

Amaranthus graecizans **auct. non L.** – See *Amaranthus albus* L. or *Amaranthus blitoides* S. Wats.

Amaranthus graecizans **L.** – Iowa pigweed (80) (1913) IA, Pellitory-leaf amaranth [Pellitory-leaved amaranth] (165) (1768), Pigweed [Pig-weed, Pig weed] (156, 158) (1900–1923), Prostrate amaranth (5) (1913), Prostrate pigweed (4, 50) (1986–present)

Amaranthus hybridus **L.** – Amaranth (157, 158) (1900–1929), Balder-herb [Balder-herb] (156, 158) (1900–1923), Careless (5, 156, 157, 158) (1900–1929), Clustered amaranth (165) (1768), Cluster-flower

amaranth [Cluster-flowered amaranth] (187) (1818), Cockscomb [Cock's comb, Cocks-comb, Cock's-comb] (156) (1923), Floramor [Floramour] (5, 156, 158, 165) (1768–1923), Flower-gentle [Flower gentle] (5, 156, 158) (1900–1923), Flower-velure (165) (1768) obsolete by this time, Green amaranth (156, 157, 158) (1900–1929), Green pigweed [Green pig-weed] (4) (1986), Lovely-bleeding [Lovely bleeding] (158) (1900), Pigweed [Pig-weed, Pig weed] (145, 157, 158) (1897–1929), Pilewort [Pile-wort, Pile wort] (5, 156, 157, 158) (1900–1929), Prince's-feather [Prince's feather, Princes-feather, Princesfeather] (5, 156, 158) (1900–1923), Red amaranth (5, 93, 156, 157, 158) (1900–1936), Red cockscomb [Red coxcomb] (5, 158) (1900–1913), Redroot [Red-root, Red root] (62) (1912), Rough amaranth (150) (1894), Slender pigweed (3, 4, 5, 21, 62, 72, 93, 131, 157, 158) (1893–1986), Slim amaranth (50, 155, 156) (1923–present), Spleen amaranth (5, 93, 97, 122, 156) (1913–1937), Tree amaranth (165) (1768), Velvet flower [Velvet-flower] (165) (1768) Old English name no longer in use by 1768, possibly this species

Amaranthus hybridus **L. subsp. *hypochondriacus* (L.) Thellung** – See *Amaranthus hypochondriacus* L.

Amaranthus hybridus **L. var. *paniculatus* (L.) Thell.** – See *Amaranthus hybridus* L.

Amaranthus hypochondriacus **L.** – Amaranth (49, 58, 92) (1869–1898), Kiery (110) (1886), Lovely-bleeding [Lovely bleeding] (49) (1898), Pilewort [Pile-wort, Pile wort] (92) (1876), Prince-of-Wales feather (50) (present), Prince's-feather [Prince's feather, Princes-feather, Princesfeather] (10, 49, 58, 92, 109, 138) (1818–1949), Prince's-feather amaranth (165) (1768), Red cockscomb [Red coxcomb] (49, 92) (1876–1898), Spleen amaranth (19, 92) (1840–1876)

Amaranthus hypochondriacus **W.** – See *Amaranthus hypochondriacus* L.

Amaranthus **L.** – Amaranth (1, 10, 109, 138, 155) (1818–1949), Carelessweed [Careless-weed, Careless weed] (106) (1930), Green amaranth (92) (1876), Pigweed [Pig-weed, Pig weed] (1, 4, 50, 93, 126) (1932–present), Prince's-feather [Prince's feather, Princes-feather, Princesfeather] (10, 167) (1814–1818), Tumbleweed [Tumble weed, Tumble-weed] (1, 93) (1932–1936), Water-hemp [Water hemp, Waterhemp] (1, 2, 93, 138, 158) (1895–1936)

Amaranthus lividus **L.** – See *Amaranthus blitum* L.

Amaranthus maximus **[Mill.]** – See *Amaranthus caudatus* L.

Amaranthus melancholicus **[L.]** – See *Amaranthus tricolor* L.

Amaranthus palmeri **S. Wats.** – Carelessweed [Careless-weed, Careless weed] (50) (present), Palmer's amaranth (5, 97, 122) (1913–1937), Palmer's pigweed (3, 4) (1977–1986)

Amaranthus paniculatus **L.** – See *Amaranthus cruentus* L.

Amaranthus powellii **S. Wats.** – Powell's amaranth [Powell amaranth] (50, 155) (1942–present), Powell's pigweed (4) (1986)

Amaranthus pumilus **Raf.** – Coast amaranth (5) (1913), Dwarf amaranth (19) (1840)

Amaranthus retroflexus **L.** – Abraham's-cabbage [Abraham's cabbage] (79) (1891) NH, Beetroot [Beet-root] (157, 158) (1900–1929), Calite de agua (Spanish) (150) (1894) NM, Carelessweed [Careless-weed, Careless weed] (122) (1937), Common pigweed (93, 150, 157, 158) (1894–1936), Curls (77) (1898) Sulphur Grove OH, Green amaranth (5, 93, 107, 148, 156) (1913–1939), Hairy amaranth (165) (1768), Lighthouses [Light-houses] (77) (1898) Southold Long Island, from speed with which they tower above crops in the field, Pigweed [Pig-weed, Pig weed] (21, 80, 85, 107, 125, 148) (1893–1932), Redroot [Red-root, Red root] (5, 77, 80, 93, 97, 125, 145, 148, 156, 158)(1897–1937), Red-root amaranth [Redroot amaranth] (50, 155) (1942–present), Rough amaranth (19, 150) (1840–1894), Rough pigweed (3, 4, 62, 72, 93, 131, 156, 157, 158) (1899–1986), Wild beet (77) (1898) Oxford ME

Amaranthus rudis **Sauer** – Acnida (125) (1930) KS, Tall amaranth (50) (present), Water-hemp [Water hemp, Waterhemp] (3, 21, 85, 122, 125) (1893–1986), Western waterhemp [Western water-hemp, Western water hemp] (4, 5, 72, 93, 97, 131) (1907–1986)

Amaranthus salicifolius **Hort. Veitch** – See *Amaranthus tricolor* L.

23

Amaranthus sanguineus **L.** – See *Amaranthus caudatus* L.

Amaranthus spinosus **L.** – Prickly amaranth (165, 187) (1768–1818), Prickly calalue (107) (1774) Jamaica, Red amaranth (5, 93, 156) (1913–1936), Red careless-weed [Red careless weed] (62) (1912) IN, Soldierweed [Soldier-weed] (62) (1912) IN, Spiny amaranth (5, 21, 50, 62, 70, 93, 97, 145, 155, 156) (1893–present), Spiny careless-weed [Spiny careless weed] (62) (1912) IN, Spiny pigweed (3, 4) (1977–1986), Thorny amaranth (5, 93, 107, 122, 156) (1913–1937)

Amaranthus torreyi **(Gray) Benth. ex S. Wats.** – Torrey's amaranth (5, 72, 93, 122) (1907–1937)

Amaranthus tricolor **L.** – Amaranth (110) (1886), Brède de Malabar (110) (1886), Cockscomb [Cock's comb, Cocks-comb, Cock's-comb] (58) (1869), Fountain plant [Fountain-plant] (75) (1894), Ganges amaranth (138) (1923), Joseph's coat amaranth (155) (1942), Joseph's-coat [Joseph's coat] (92) (1876), Love-lies-bleeding [Love lies bleeding] (19, 58, 92) (1840–1892), Nuns' whipping rope (92) (1876), Oval-spike amaranth [Oval-spiked amaranth] (165) (1768), Three-color coxscomb [Three-colored coxscomb] (19) (1840), Tota kura (Telinga) (110) (1886), Two-color amaranth [Two-coloured amaranth] (165) (1768)

Amaranthus tuberculatus **(Moq.) Sauer** – Rough-fruit amaranth [Roughfruit amaranth] (50) (present), Rough-fruit waterhemp [Rough-fruited water hemp] (5, 93) (1913–1936), Tall waterhemp [Tall water hemp] (3, 4, 155) (1977–1986), Tubercled waterhemp [Tubercaled water-hemp] (131) (1899), Water-hemp [Water hemp, Waterhemp] (80, 145) (1897–1913)

Amaranthus viridis **L.** – Green-flower amaranth [Green-flowered amaranth] (187) (1818)

Amaranthus viridis **Willd.** – See *Amaranthus viridis* L.

Amarantus **(sic) blitoides** – See *Amaranthus blitoides* S. Wats.

Amarantus **(sic) blitum** – See *Amaranthus blitum* L.

Amarantus **(sic) frumentaceus [Buch.-Ham. ex Roxb.]** – See *Amaranthus hypochondriacus* L.

Amarantus **(sic) gangeticus L.** – See *Amaranthus tricolor* L.

Amarantus caudatus **(sic)** – See *Amaranthus caudatus* L.

Amarantus chlorostachys – See *Amaranthus hybridus* L.

Amarantus reflexus **L.** – See *Amaranthus retroflexus* L.

Amarella **Gilib.** – See *Gentiana* L.

Amaryllis belladonna **L.** – Belladonna lily [Belladonnalily] (138, 155, 165) (1768–1942)

Amaryllis **L.** – Amaryllis (155) (1942) Greek for splendor, name of sheperdess in Virgil, Atamasco lily [Atamasco-lily] (167) (1814)

Amberboa **(Pers.) Less.** – Amberboa (155) (1942)

Amberboa moschata **(L.) DC.** – Sweet sultan [Sweet-sultan] (82, 92, 138) (1876–1930), Sweet sultana (19) (1840)

Amblyolepis setigera **DC.** – Arnica weed (106) (1930)

Ambrosia **(Tourn.) L.** – See *Ambrosia* L.

Ambrosia acanthicarpa **Hook.** – Annual bursage (3, 4) (1977–1986), Bur ragweed [Bur-ragweed] (93) (1936), Flat-spine burr ragweed [Flatspine burr ragweed] (50) (present), Hooker's gaertneria (5) (1913), Rosetilla (150) (1894), Sand bur [Sand-bur, Sand burr, Sand bur] (5, 75) (1894–1913)

Ambrosia aptera **DC.** – See *Ambrosia trifida* L. var. *texana* Scheele

Ambrosia artemisaefolia **L.** – See *Ambrosia artemisiifolia* L.

Ambrosia artemisifolia **L. [sic]** – See *Ambrosia artemisiifolia* L.

Ambrosia artemisiifolia **L.** – Ambrosia (57, 92) (1876–1917), Ambrosie (6) (1892), Annual ragweed (50) (present), Bastard wormwood (6, 158) (1892–1900), Bitterweed [Bitter weed, Bitter-weed] (6, 58, 75, 76, 156, 158) (1869–1923) from effect on milk when eaten by cattle, Blackweed [Black weed] (76, 156, 158) (1896–1923) Long Island NY, no longer in use by 1923, Čaηxloğaη waštemna (Lakota, odorous weed) (121) (1918?–1970?), Carrotweed [Carrot-weed, Carrot weed] (6, 156, 158) (1892–1923) no longer in use by 1923, Common ragweed (3, 4, 92, 155, 156, 158) (1898–1986), Conotweed [Conot weed] (6) (1892), False wormwood (156) (1923), Hay-fever weed [Hay fever weed] (156) (1923), Hogweed [Hog-weed, Hog weed] (2, 6, 58, 62, 72, 80, 92, 152, 158) (1869–1923), Mugwort-leaf ambrosia [Mugwort-leaved ambrosia] (165) (1768), Oak-of-Cappadocia [Oak of Cappadocia] (46) (1671), Ragweed [Rag-weed, Rag weed] (2, 6, 57, 58, 62, 72, 95, 131, 145, 158) (1869–1917), Roman wormwood (2, 6, 48, 58, 62, 82, 156, 158) (1869–1930), Short ragweed (4) (1986), Small ragweed (80, 82) (1913–1930), Smaller ragweed (80) (1913), Stammerwort [Stammer-wort] (92, 156, 158) (1876–1923) no longer in use by 1923, Stickweed [Stick-weed, Stick weed] (156, 158) (1900–1923) no longer in use by 1923, Tasselweed [Tassel weed, Tassel-weed] (73, 156, 158) (1892–1923), Traubenkraut (German) (6) (1892), Wild tansy [Wild tansey] (156, 158) (1900–1923), Wild wormwood (6) (1892), Wormwood-leaf hogweed [Wormwood-leaved hogweed] (187) (1818)

Ambrosia artemisiifolia **L. var. elatior (L.) Descourtils** – Ambrosia (92) (1876), Bastard wormwood (7, 92, 157) (1828–1929), Bitterweed [Bitter weed, Bitter-weed] (5) (1913), Blackweed [Black weed] (5) (1913), Carrotweed [Carrot-weed, Carrot weed] (5, 7, 92) (1828–1913), Conotweed [Conot weed] (7) (1828), Cut-leaf ragweed [Cut-leaved ragweed] (93) (1936), Hay-fever weed [Hay fever weed] (5) (1913), Hogweed [Hog-weed, Hog weed] (5, 19, 92, 157) (1840–1929), Ragweed [Rag-weed, Rag weed] (5, 37, 85, 92, 125, 157) (1876–1932), Roman wormwood (5, 19, 157) (1840–1929), Short ragweed (21, 97) (1893–1937), Stammerwort [Stammer-wort] (5) (1913), Stickweed [Stick-weed, Stick weed] (5) (1913), Tall ambrosia (165) (1768), Tall hogweed (187) (1818), Tasselweed [Tassel weed, Tassel-weed] (5, 157) (1913–1929), Wild tansy [Wild tansey] (5, 157) (1913–1929)

Ambrosia bidentata **Michx.** – Lance-leaf ragweed [Lanceleaf ragweed, Lance-leaved ragweed] (5, 50, 62, 97, 122, 155) (1912–present), Ragweed [Rag-weed, Rag weed] (3) (1977), Roadweed (21) (1893), Southern ragweed (4) (1986)

Ambrosia confertiflora **DC.** – Slim-leaf bursage [Slimleaf bursage] (155) (1942), Weak-leaf bur ragweed [Weakleaf burr ragweed] (50) (present)

Ambrosia coronopifolia **Torr. & Gray** – See *Ambrosia psilostachya* DC.

Ambrosia elatior **L.** – See *Ambrosia artemisiifolia* L. var. *elatior* (L.) Descourtils

Ambrosia grayi **(A. Nels.) Shinners** – Bur ragweed [Bur-ragweed] (3, 4) (1977–1986), Woolly bursage (155) (1942), Woolly franseria (122) (1937), Woolly-leaf bur ragweed [Woollyleaf burr ragweed] (50) (present)

Ambrosia **L.** – Bitterweed [Bitter weed, Bitter-weed] (1, 10, 12, 93) (1818–1936), Bursage (155) (1942), Hogweed [Hog-weed, Hog weed] (45) (1896), Ragweed [Rag-weed, Rag weed] (1, 2, 4, 45, 50, 82, 93, 155, 156, 158) (1895–present), Roman wormwood (1, 45, 93) (1896–1936)

Ambrosia linearis **(Rydb.) Payne** – Streaked bur ragweed [Streaked burr ragweed] (50) (present)

Ambrosia psilostachya **DC.** – Cuman ragweed (50) (present), Perennial ragweed (80, 145) (1897–1913), Ragweed [Rag-weed, Rag weed] (95, 157) (1900–1929), Western ragweed (3, 4, 5, 21, 72, 82, 85, 93, 97, 98, 125, 131, 155, 157) (1893–1986)

Ambrosia pumila **(Nutt.) Gray** – Dwarf ragweed (155) (1942)

Ambrosia tomentosa **Nutt.** – Perennial bursage (3, 4) (1977–1986), Skeleton-leaf burr ragweed [Skeletonleaf burr ragweed] (50) (Present), Skeleton-leaf bursage [Skeletonleaf bursage] (155) (1942), White-leaf gaertneria [White-leaved gaertneria] (5, 93, 131) (1899–1936), Woolly gaertneria (5, 93) (1913–1936)

Ambrosia trifida **L.** – Bitterweed [Bitter weed, Bitter-weed] (5, 49, 92, 131, 156, 157, 158) (1898–1929), Bloodweed [Blood weed, Bloodweed] (82) (1930), Buffalo-weed [Buffalo weed] (5, 156, 157, 158) (1900–1929), Giant ragweed (3, 4, 21, 62, 82, 97, 125, 155, 157, 158) (1893–1986), Great bitterweed [Great bitter-weed] (19) (1840), Great ragweed (5, 49, 50, 62, 63, 80, 92, 93, 106, 131, 156, 157, 158) (1898–present), Greater ragweed (80, 82) (1913–1930), Hay-fever weed [Hay fever weed] (5, 72, 156) (1907–1923), Horsecane [Horse cane, Horse-cane] (5, 49, 92, 156, 158) (1898–1923), Horseweed

[Horse-weed, Horse weed] (5, 7, 49, 62, 76, 92, 106, 122, 145, 156, 157, 158) (1828–1937), Ironweed [Iron weed, Iron weed] (157) (1929), Kinghead [King-head] (62, 156) (1912–1923), Ragweed [Rag-weed, Rag weed] (85, 106) (1930–1932), Richweed [Rich-weed, Rich weed] (5, 49, 92, 155, 156, 158) (1898–1942), River ragweed (156) (1923), Tall ambrosia (5, 49, 92, 158) (1876–1923), Three-lobe ragweed [Three-lobed ragweed] (156) (1923), Trifid-leaf [Trifid-leaved ambrosia] (165) (1768), Trifid-leaf hogweed [Trifid-leaved hogweed] (187) (1818), Wild hemp [Wylde hempe] (5, 7, 49, 92, 156, 157, 158) (1828–1929)

Ambrosia trifida L. var. *integrifolia* (**Muhl. ex Willd.**) **Torr. & Gray** – See *Ambrosia trifida* L. var. *trifida*

Ambrosia trifida L. var. *texana* **Scheele** – Blood ragweed (155) (1942), Bloodweed [Blood weed, Blood-weed] (122) (1937), Texas tall ragweed [Texan tall ragweed] (50) (present), Wingless-petiole ragweed [Wingless-petioled ragweed] (97) (1937)

Ambrosia trifida L. var. *trifida* – Entire-leaf ragweed [Entire-leaved ragweed] (72) (1907), Great ragweed (50) (present)

Amelanchier ×intermedia Spach [*arborea × canadensis*] – Currant tree [Currant-tree] (5) (1913), Flowering-dogwood [Flowering dog-wood] (5) (1913), May bush (5) (1913), Shad bush [Shadbush, Shad-bush] (5) (1913), Swamp sugar-pear [Swamp sugar pear] (5) (1913), Wild pear tree [Wild pear-tree] (5) (1913)

Amelanchier alnifolia (Nutt.) **Nutt. ex M. Roemer** – Haz shutsh (Winnebago, red fruit) (37) (1919), Juneberry [June-berry, June berry] (3, 37, 130) (1895–1977), Low juneberry [Low june-berry, Low june berry] (114) (1894), Northwestern Juneberry [North-western-juneberry, Northwestern June-berry, Northwestern June berry] (5, 72, 131, 157, 158) (1899–1929), Northwestern service-berry [Northwestern service berry] (5, 157, 158) (1900–1929), Pigeon-berry [Pigeon berry] (5, 157, 158) (1900–1929), Sarvice berry (101) (1905) MT, Saskatoon (37, 106, 138) (1919–1930), Saskatoon serviceberry [Saskatoon service-berry] (4, 50, 155) (1942–present), Serviceberry [Service berry, Service-berry] (35, 146, 160) (1806–1939), Small serviceberry [Small service-berry] (113) (1890), Sugarberry [Sugar-berry, Sugar berry] (130) (1895) SD, Suscutan (130) (1895) SD, Tee-amp (Snake) (101) (1905) MT, Western juneberry [Western june-berry, Western june berry] (85, 93, 157) (1900–1929), Western serviceberry [Western service berry] (107, 135) (1910–1919), Wipazuka (Dakota) (37) (1919), Zhon h'uda (Omaha-Ponca, gray wood) (37) (1919)

Amelanchier alnifolia (Nutt.) **Nutt. ex M. Roemer var.** *cusickii* (**Fern.**) **C.L. Hitchc.** – Cusick's serviceberry [Cusick serviceberry] (155) (1942)

Amelanchier alnifolia (Nutt.) **Nutt. ex M. Roemer var.** *semiintegrifolia* (**Hook.**) **C.L. Hitchc.** – Pacific serviceberry (155) (1942)

Amelanchier alnifolia *pumila* – See *Amelanchier pumila* (Torr. & Gray) Nutt. ex M. Roemer

Amelanchier amabilis – See *Amelanchier sanguinea* (Pursh) DC. var. *sanguinea*

Amelanchier arborea (Michx. f.) **Fern.** – Allegheny service-berry [Allegany serviceberry] (155) (1942), Allegheny shadblow (138) (1923), Common serviceberry (50) (present), Juneberry [June-berry, June berry] (3, 4, 20) (1857–1986), Serviceberry [Service berry, Ser-vice-berry] (4) (1986), Shadberry [Shad berry] (4) (1986), Wild pear [Wylde pere] or Wild pear tree [Wild pear-tree] (20) (1857) North-eastern US

Amelanchier arborea (Michx. f.) **Fern. var.** *arborea* – Thicket service-berry (155) (1942), Thicket shadblow (138) (1923)

Amelanchier barteamiana (Tausch) **Roem.** – See *Amelanchier bartra-miana* (Tausch) M. Roem.

Amelanchier bartramiana (Tausch) **M. Roem.** – Bartram's service-berry [Bartram serviceberry] (155) (1942), Bartram's shadblow [Bartram shadblow] (138) (1923), Oblong-fruit Juneberry [Oblong-fruited June berry] (5) (1913)

Amelanchier botryapium (L.f.) **DC.** – See *Amelanchier canadensis* (L.) Medik.

Amelanchier canadensis (L.) **Medic** – See *Amelanchier canadensis* (L.) Medik.

Amelanchier canadensis (L.) **Medik.** – Bilberry [Bill berry] (5, 156, 158) (1900–1923), Bloody choakberry (19) (1840), Boxwood [Box wood] (5, 76, 156, 158) (1896–1923) Western US, Choke-cherry [Choke cherry, Choke-cherry, Choke cherries, Choke-cher-ries, Choak cherry] (92) (1876), Common dwarf Juneberry [Com-mon dwarf June berry] (135) (1910), Currant tree [Currant-tree] (106, 156) (1923–1930) Southeastern US, no longer in use by 1923, Dogwood [Dog-wood, Dog wood] (76, 158) (1896–1900) West-ern US, Downy saskatoon (137) (1931) SD, Downy serviceberry (155) (1942), Downy shadblow (138) (1923), Dwarf red-fruit med-lar [Dwarf red fruited medlar] (8) (1785), Épine de Canada (French) (8) (1785), Grape-pear (107) (1919), Indian cherry [Indian-cherry] (5, 106, 156, 158) (1895–1930) PA, no longer in use by 1923, Indian pear (5, 156, 158) (1900–1923) no longer in use by 1923, Juice-pear [Juice pear] (5, 73, 158) (1892–1913), Juice-plum (156) (1923) no longer in use by 1923 156, Juicy-pear [Juicy pear] (73) (1892) Prov-incetown MA, June plum (5, 76) (1896–1913) Western US, June-berry [June-berry, June berry] (5, 7, 19, 46, 63, 65, 72, 73, 85, 92, 93, 95, 105, 107, 106, 108, 112, 114, 131, 147, 156, 158) (1828–1937), May cherry [May-cherry] (5, 156, 158) (1900–1923) no longer in use by 1923, May-pear [May pear] (5, 73, 158) (1892–1913) New Brunswick, from time of flowering, Medlar [Medlars] (92) (1876), Medlar bush (19) (1840), Misascutu (Algic tribes) (7) (1828), Negui-min (Chippewa) (105) (1932), Pemmican-berry [Pemmican berry] (108) (1878), Poires (French Canadians) (46, 107) (1879–1919), Sand cherry [Sand-cherry] (5, 74, 93, 156, 158) (1893–1936) MT, Saskatoon (156) (1923), Service tree [Servicetree, Seruice tree] (5, 158) (1900–1913), Serviceberry [Service berry, Ser-vice-berry] (5, 9, 14, 63, 85, 93, 95, 97, 107, 113, 124, 130, 131, 156) (1873–1936), Shad bush [Shadbush, Shad-bush] (2, 5, 19, 40, 46, 72, 92, 106, 130, 156, 158) (1840–1928), Shad or Shad tree (7, 92, 107) (1828–1919), Shadberry [Shad berry] (103) (1870), Shad-blow [Shadblow] (73, 156) (1892–1923) NH, Shadblow service-berry (155) (1942), Shad-flower [Shadflower, Shad flower] (156) (1923), Snowy medlar (74) (1893) NY, Snowy mespilus (14, 156) (1882–1923), Sugar pear (5, 73, 74, 156, 158) (1892–1923), Sugar-berry [Sugar-berry, Sugar berry] (5, 74, 156, 158) (1893–1923) NH, Sugar-plum [Sugar plum, Sugar-plums, Sugar plums] (5, 73, 74, 156, 158) (1892–1923) NH, no longer in use by 1923, Sweet-pear [Sweet pear, Sweet pears] (46, 107) (1879–1919) ME, Tall Juneberry (112) (1937), Wild Indian pear (106) (1930) Newfoundland, Wild pear tree [Wild pear-tree] (76) (1896) Western US, Wipazukaŋ (Lakota) (121) (1918?–1970?), (possibly) European shadblow (138) (1923) (possibly), Guzigwa'komĭnaga'wûnj (Chippewa, thorny wood) (40) (1928) (possibly), Pembina (47) (1852) (possibly), Round-leaf june-berry [Round-leaved june-berry, Round-leaved june berry] (72, 131) (1899–1907) (possibly)

Amelanchier canadensis Medic – See *Amelanchier canadensis* (L.) Medik.

Amelanchier canadensis *obovalis* – See *Amelanchier canadensis* subsp. *obovalis* (Michx.) P. Landry

Amelanchier canadensis **subsp.** *obovalis* (**Michx.**) **P. Landry** – Long-leaf saskatoon (137) (1931)

Amelanchier canadensis **Torr. & Gray.** – possibly *Amelanchier ca-nadensis* (L.) Medik.

Amelanchier canadensis **var.** *oblongifolia* **Torr. & A.Gray** – See *Amelanchier oblongifolia* (Torr. & A. Gray) M. Roem.

Amelanchier cusicki – See *Amelanchier alnifolia* (Nutt.) Nutt. ex M. Roemer var. *cusickii* (Fern.) C.L. Hitchc.

Amelanchier florida – See *Amelanchier alnifolia* (Nutt.) Nutt. ex M. Roemer var. *semiintegrifolia* (Hook.) C.L. Hitchc.

Amelanchier grandiflora – See *Amelanchier sanguinea* (Pursh) DC. var. *grandiflora* (Wieg.) Rehd.

Amelanchier humilis Wiegand – Low juneberry [Low june-berry, Low june berry] (85) (1932), Low serviceberry (4, 50, 155)

(1942–present), Low shadblow (138) (1923), Northern Juneberry [Northern June-berry] (93) (1936)

Amelanchier intermedia Spach. – See *Amelanchier ×intermedia* Spach [*arborea × canadensis*]

Amelanchier laevis Wiegand – See *Amelanchier arborea* (Michx. f.) Fern.

Amelanchier Medik. – Juneberry [June-berry, June berry] (1, 2, 4, 93, 106, 109, 138, 155, 156, 158) (1895–1986), Pigeon-berry [Pigeon berry] (106) (1930), Sarvice (106) (1930), Serviceberry [Service berry, Service-berry] (1, 2, 4, 35, 50, 106, 109, 122, 138, 153, 155) (1895–present) Spelled various ways by Lewis & Clark (35), Shadberry [Shad berry] (1) (1932), Shadblow (138, 155) (1923–1942), Shadbush (4, 109, 138, 155) (1942–1986), Sugar-plum [Sugar plum, Sugar-plums, Sugar plums] (4) (1986)

Amelanchier oblongifolia (Torr. & Gray) M. Roemer – See *Amelanchier arborea* (Michx. f.) Fern. var. *arborea*

Amelanchier oligocarpa – See *Amelanchier bartramiana* (Tausch) M. Roem.

Amelanchier oreophila – See *Amelanchier utahensis* Koehne var. *utahensis*

Amelanchier polycarpa – See *Amelanchier pumila* (Torr. & Gray) Nutt. ex M. Roemer

Amelanchier pumila (Torr. & Gray) Nutt. ex M. Roemer – Cluster serviceberry (155) (1942), Dwarf saskatoon (138) (1923), Dwarf saskatoon service-berry [Dwarf saskatoon serviceberry] (155) (1942)

Amelanchier rotundifolia (Michx.) Roem. – possibly *Amelanchier canadensis* (L.) Medik.

Amelanchier sanguinea (Pursh) DC. – Pigeon-berry [Pigeon berry] (156) (1923), Round-leaf juneberry [Round-leaved june-berry, Round-leaved june berry] (5, 85) (1913–1932), Round-leaf serviceberry [Roundleaf serviceberry] (155) (1942), Round-leaf shadblow [Roundleaf shadblow] (138) (1923), Serviceberry [Service berry, Service-berry] (34) (1834)

Amelanchier sanguinea (Pursh) DC. var. *grandiflora* (Wieg.) Rehd. – Apple serviceberry (155) (1942), Apple shadblow (138) (1923)

Amelanchier sanguinea (Pursh) DC. var. *sanguinea* – Snowy serviceberry (155) (1942), Snowy shadblow (138) (1923)

Amelanchier spicata (Lam.) C. Koch. – See *Amelanchier stolonifera* Wieg.

Amelanchier stolonifera Wieg. – Low juneberry [Low june-berry, Low june berry] (5, 82) (1913–1930), Running serviceberry (155) (1942), Running shadblow (138) (1923), Saskatoon (156) (1923)

Amelanchier utahensis Koehne – Utah serviceberry (155) (1942)

Amelanchier utahensis Koehne var. *utahensis* – Mountain serviceberry (155) (1942)

Amianthecum muscaetoxicum – See *Amianthium muscitoxicum* (Walt.) Gray

Amianthium A. Gray – Crow-poison [Crow poison, Crowpoison] (155) (1942), Fly poison [Fly-poison, Flypoison, Fly Pison] (156) (1923), Redseed [Red-seed, Red seed] (7) (1828)

Amianthium muscaetoxicum (Walt.) Gray – See *Amianthium muscitoxicum* (Walt.) Gray

Amianthium muscaetoxicum Gray. – See *Amianthium muscitoxicum* (Walt.) Gray

Amianthium muscitoxicum (Walt.) Gray – Broad-leaf fly-poison [Broad-leaved fly poison] (2) (1895), Channel-leaf helonias [Channelled-leaved helonias] (187) (1818), Crow-poison [Crow poison, Crowpoison] (5, 75, 138, 155) (1894–1942) Banner Elk NC, Fall poison (92) (1876), Fly poison [Fly-poison, Flypoison, Fly Pison] (2, 5, 50, 92, 97, 183) (1756–present), Hellebore (5, 156) (1913–1923), Unicorn (29) (1869)

Ammannia auriculata Willd. – Eared redstem (50) (present), Ear-leaf ammannia [Earleaf ammannia] (3, 155) (1942–1977), Wright's ammannia (5, 97) (1913–1937)

Ammannia coccinea Rottb. – Long-leaf ammannia [Long-leaved ammannia] (72, 93, 97, 120, 131) (1899–1938), Long-lived ammannia (5) (1913), Loosestrife [Loose strife, Loose-strife] (85) (1932),

Purple ammannia (155) (1942), Tooth-cup [Tooth cup, Tooth-cup] (3) (1977), Valley redstem (50) (present)

Ammannia humilis Michx. – See *Rotala ramosior* (L.) Koehne

Ammannia koehnei Britton – See *Ammannia latifolia* L.

Ammannia L. – Ammania (155, 158) (1900–1942), Redstem [Redstem] (50) (present), Tooth-cup [Tooth cup, Tooth-cup] (4) (1986)

Ammannia latifolia L. – Koehne's ammannia (5, 155) (1913–1942), Tooth-cup [Tooth cup, Tooth-cup] (5, 156) (1913–1923)

Ammannia ramosior Walt. – possibly *Rotala ramosior* (L.) Koehne

Ammannia robusta Heer & Regel – Grand redstem (50) (present)

Ammi copticum – See *Trachyspermum copticum* (L.) Link

Ammi L. – Ammi (155) (1942), Bishop's-weed [Bishop's weed, Bishop weed] (10) (1818)

Ammi majus L. – Bishop's-weed [Bishopsweede] (178) (1526), Greater ammi (155) (1942)

Ammi visnaga (L.) Lam. – Spanish toothpikes (178) (1526), Toothpick ammi (155) (1942)

Ammobium R. Br. – See *Helichrysum* Mill.

Ammobroma sonora – See *Pholisma sonorae* (Torr. ex Gray) Yatskievych

Ammophila arenaria (L.) Link – Beach grass [Beachgrass, Beachgrass] (45, 56, 66, 87, 88, 90, 94, 138) (1885–1923), Common sea reed (90) (1885) ME, European beach grass [European beach-grass] (109) (1949), Marram grass [Marram-grass] (56, 84, 94) (1880–1901), Mat grass [Mat-grass, Matgrass] (66, 87, 90) (1884–1903), Sand grass [Sand-grass, Sandgrass] (45, 88) (1885–1896), Sand reed (41, 67) (1770–1890), Sea mat grass (92) (1876), Sea mat-weed (45) (1896), Sea sand grass (92) (1876), Sea-sand reed (2, 66, 87, 90) (1885–1903)

Ammophila arundinacea Hort. – See *Ammophila arenaria* (L.) Link

Ammophila Host – Beach grass [Beachgrass, Beach-grass] (109, 138) (1923–1949) ME

Ammoselinum butleri (Engelm. ex S. Wats.) Coult. & Rose – Butler's sand-parsley [Butler's sandparsley] (50, 97) (1937–present)

Ammoselinum butleri (S. Wats.) Coult. & Rose – See *Ammoselinum butleri* (Engelm. ex S. Wats.) Coult. & Rose

Ammoselinum popei Torr. & Gray – Plains sand-parsley [Plains sandparsley] (50) (present), Pope's sand-parsley [Pope's sand parsley] (5, 97) (1913–1937)

Ammoselinum Torr. & Gray – Sand-parsley [Sand parsley] (1, 4, 50, 158) (1900–present)

Amorpha californica Nutt. – California amorpha (155) (1942), California false indigo (106) (1930)

Amorpha canescens (Nutt.) Pursh – See *Amorpha canescens* Pursh

Amorpha canescens Pursh – Amorpha (28) (1850), False indigo [False-indigo] (22) (1893), Leadplant [Lead plant, Lead plant] (3, 4, 5, 19, 28, 47, 50, 63, 82, 85, 92, 95, 97, 106, 109, 112, 114, 122, 127, 130, 131, 138, 156, 158) (1850–present), Leadplant amorpha (155) (1942), Leadwort [Lead wort] (156) (1923), Prairie shoestrings [Prairie shoe-strings] (93) (1936), Shoestrings [Shoe strings, Shoe string, Shoestring, Shoe-string, Shoe-strings] (5, 72, 73, 76, 95, 97, 106, 112, 114, 130, 131, 156) (1892–1937) from long tough roots, Wild tea (5, 92, 156, 158) (1876–1923)

Amorpha croceo-lanata P.W. S. Wats. – See *Amorpha fruticosa* L.

Amorpha fragrans nanna – possibly *Amorpha fruticosa* L.

Amorpha fragrans Sweet – See *Amorpha fruticosa* L.

Amorpha fruticosa albiflora – See *Amorpha fruticosa* L.

Amorpha fruticosa angustifolia – See *Amorpha fruticosa* L.

Amorpha fruticosa coerulea – See *Amorpha fruticosa* L.

Amorpha fruticosa humilis – See *Amorpha fruticosa* L.

Amorpha fruticosa L. – Amorpha (174) (1753), Amorpha d'Amerique (French) (8) (1785), Bastard indigo (5, 106, 109, 157, 158, 165) (1768–1949), Cerulean indigo-bush amorpha [Cerulean indigobush amorpha] (155) (1942), Desert false indigo (50) (present), Drooping indigobush amorpha (155) (1942), False indigo [False-indigo] (3, 4, 5, 9, 37, 63, 72, 82, 85, 93, 95, 97, 106, 112, 113, 114, 130, 131, 156, 157, 158) (1873–1986), Fragrant amorpha (155) (1942),

Ground indigo-bush amorpha [Ground indigobush amorpha] (155) (1942), Indigo bush [Indigobush, Indigo-bush] (138, 156) (1923), Indigo plant (112) (1937), Indigo-bush amorpha [Indigobush amorpha] (155) (1942), Leadplant [Lead plant, Lead plant] (131, 156, 157) (1899–1929), Midwest indigo-bush amorpha [Midwest indigo-bush amorpha] (155) (1942), Rabbit bush (156) (1923), River-locust [River locust] (5, 76, 97, 106, 112, 156, 157, 158) (1896–1937), Shrubby bastard indigo (8) (1785), Te-hunton-hi (Omaha-Ponca, buffalo bellow plant) (37) (1919), Tennessee indigo [Tennessee-indigo] (138) (1923), Tennessee indigo-bush amorpha [Tennessee indigobush amorpha] (155) (1942), Water-string [Waterstring, Water string] (37) (1919), White indigo-bush amorpha [White indigobush amorpha] (155) (1942), Wild indigo plant [Wild indigo-plant] (82, 124) (1930–1937), Willow herb [Willow-herb, Willowherb] (63) (1899), Yellow-wool amorpha [Yellowwool amorpha] (155) (1942), Ziŋtkala tačaŋ (Lakota, small bird's perch) (121) (1918?–1970?), Dwarf false indigo (112) (1937) (possibly), Indigo tree [Indigo-tree] (189) (1767) (possibly), Jove's-beard [Jove's beard] (189) (1767) (possibly)

***Amorpha fruticosa* L. var. *angustifolia* Pursh** – See *Amorpha fruticosa* L.

Amorpha fruticosa* L. var. *tennesseensis* (Shuttlw. ex Kunze) Palmer, *Amorpha fruticosa tennessensis – See *Amorpha fruticosa* L.

Amorpha fruticosa pendula – See *Amorpha fruticosa* L.

***Amorpha glabra* Desf. ex Poir.** – Mountain-indigo (138) (1923), Mountain-indigo amorpha [Mountainindigo amorpha] (155) (1942), Smooth amorpha (106) (1930)

***Amorpha herbacea* Walt.** – Cluster-spike amorpha [Clusterspike amorpha] (155) (1942)

***Amorpha* L.** – Amorpha (8, 155) (1785–1942), Bastard indigo (8) (1785), False indigo [False-indigo] (1, 2, 50, 93, 106, 138, 158) (1895–present), Indigo leadplant [Indigo lead plant] (82) (1930) IA, Leadplant [Lead plant, Lead plant] (112) (1937), Shoestrings [Shoe strings, Shoe string, Shoestring, Shoe-string, Shoe-strings] (1, 93) (1932–1936)

***Amorpha microphylla* Pursh** – See *Amorpha nana* Nutt. ex Fraser

***Amorpha nana* Nutt. ex Fraser** – Dwarf false indigo (5, 50, 85, 93, 106, 112, 130) (1895–present), Dwarf indigo [Dwarf-indigo] (138) (1923), Dwarf indigo amorpha [Dwarfindigo amorpha] (155) (1942), Dwarf wild indigo (3, 4) (1977–1986), Dwarf-indigo amorpha [Dwarfindigo amorpha] (155) (1942), Fragrant false indigo (5, 72, 93, 97, 131) (1899–1937), Shoestring [Shoe string] (76) (1896) Burnside SD

***Amorpha nitens* Boynt.** – Georgia amorpha (155) (1942)

***Amorpha paniculata* Torr. & Gray** – Panicled amorpha (155) (1942), Panicled false indigo (50) (present)

***Amorpha pumila* Michx.** – See *Amorpha herbacea* Walter

***Amorpha tennesseensis* Shuttlw. ex Kunze** – See *Amorpha fruticosa* L.

***Ampelanus* Brit.** – possibly *Cynanchum* L.

***Ampelaster carolinianus* (Walt.) Nesom** – Carolina aster (155) (1942)

***Ampelopsis aconitifolia* Bunge** – Monkshood vine [Monkshood-vine, Monkshoodvine] (138, 155) (1923–1942)

***Ampelopsis arborea* (L.) Koehne** – Carolina vine [Carolinian vine] (8) (1785), Cowitch [Cow-itch, Cow itch] (106) (1930), Crossvine [Cross vine, Cross-vine] (106) (1930) GA, Pepper tree [Pepper-tree, Peppertree] (8) (1785), Pepper vine [Pepper-vine, Peppervine] (5, 97, 106, 109, 122, 138, 155, 156) (1913–1949), Pepperidge [Peperidge] (106) (1930), Pinnate-leaf ampelopsis [Pinnate-leaved ampelopsis] (5) (1913), Seven-leaf ivy [Seven-leaved ivy, Seven-leafed ivy] (106) (1930), Snow vine [Snow-vine, Snowvine] (106) (1930) GA, Vigne en arbre (French) (8) (1785), Bird cherry [Bird-cherry, Birdcherry, Birds cherries]] (156) (1923) (possibly), Pepper vine of South Texas (124) (1937) (possibly)

***Ampelopsis arborea* (L.) Rusby** – See *Ampelopsis arborea* (L.) Koehne

***Ampelopsis arborea* Koehne** – See *Ampelopsis arborea* (L.) Koehne

***Ampelopsis bipinnata* [Michx.]** – See *Ampelopsis arborea* (L.) Koehne

***Ampelopsis brevipedunculata* (Maxim.) Trautv.** – Amur ampelopsis (155) (1942), Porcelain ampelopsis (138, 155) (1923–1942)

Ampelopsis brevipedunculata maximowiczi – See *Ampelopsis brevipedunculata* (Maxim.) Trautv.

***Ampelopsis cordata* Michx.** – Coo-grape (156) (1923), Cordate cissus (106) (1930), Heart-leaf ampelopsis [Heartleaf ampelopsis] (138, 155) (1923–1942), Heart-leaf peppervine [Heartleaf peppervine] (50) (present), Marine ivy (156) (1923), Raccoon grape (3, 4, 156) (1923–1986), Simple-leaf ampelopsis [Simple leafed ampelopsis, Simple-leaved ampelopsis] (5, 72, 97, 124) (1907–1937), Swamp-grape [Swamp grape] (156) (1923)

***Ampelopsis hederacea* Michx.** – See *Parthenocissus quinquefolia* (L.) Planch.

Ampelopsis heterophylla – See *Ampelopsis brevipedunculata* (Maxim.) Trautv.

***Ampelopsis* Michx.** – American joy [American-joy] (42) (1814), Ampelopsis (155, 158) (1900–1942), False grape [False grapes] (42) (1814), Pepper vine [Pepper-vine, Peppervine] (50, 106) (1930–present), Snow vine [Snow-vine, Snowvine] (106) (1930)

Ampelopsis quinquefolia hirsuta – See *Parthenocissus quinquefolia* (L.) Planch.

***Ampelopsis quinquefolia* Michx.** – See *Parthenocissus quinquefolia* (L.) Planch.

Ampelopsis quinquefolia murorum – See *Parthenocissus quinquefolia* (L.) Planch.

Ampelopsis quinquefolia saintpauli – possibly *Parthenocissus quinquefolia* (L.) Planch.

***Ampelopsis quinquefolia* var. *hirsuta* (Pursh) Torr. & Gray** – See *Parthenocissus quinquefolia* (L.) Planch.

***Ampelopsis quinquefolia* var. *murorum* Rehder** – See *Parthenocissus quinquefolia* (L.) Planch.

Ampelopsis tricuspidata – See *Parthenocissus tricuspidata* (Sieb. & Zucc.) Planch.

***Amphiachyris* (A. DC.) Nutt.** – Broomweed [Broom-weed, Broom weed] (50) (present)

***Amphiachyris dracunculoides* (DC.) Nutt.** – Amphiachyris (5, 158) (1900–1913), Broomweed [Broom-weed, Broom weed] (3, 4, 106, 155, 156) (1923–1986), Prairie broomweed (50) (present), Small-head broomweed [Small headed broom weed] (124) (1937), Tarragon snakeweed (155) (1942), Yellow-weed [Yellow weed] (21, 156) (1893–1923)

***Amphicarpa* Ell.** – See *Amphicarpaea* Ell. ex Nutt.

***Amphicarpa monoica* Ell.** – See *Amphicarpaea bracteata* (L.) Fern.

***Amphicarpa pitcheri* Torr. & Gray** – See *Amphicarpaea bracteata* (L.) Fern.

***Amphicarpaea bracteata* (L.) Fern.** – American hogpeanut (50) (present), Ground bean (105) (1932), Hog-peanut [Hogpeanut, Hog peanut, Hog pea nut, Hog pea-nut] (3, 4, 107, 121, 156) (1918?–1986), Hoŋbðiŋθu (Osage, cut bean) (121) (1918?–1970?), Licorice [Liquorice] (156) (1923), Makatomniča (Lakota, ground bean) (121) (1918?–1970?), Pea vine [Peavine, Pea-vine] (7, 35) (1806–1828), Pitcher's hog peanut [Pitcher's hog pea nut, Pitchers hogpeanut] (82, 155) (1930–1942), Southern hogpeanut (155) (1942), Wild pea vine [Wild peavine, Wild pea-vine] (156) (1923)

***Amphicarpaea bracteata* (L.) Fern. var. *comosa* (L.) Fern.** – American licorice (5) (1913), Ati-kuraru (Pawnee) (37) (1919), Bûgwûdj'mĭskodi'simĭn (Chippewa, unusual reddish bean) (40) (1928), Hinbthi-abe (Omaha-Ponca, beans) (37) (1919) Hinbthi-abe-hu (bean vine), Hog-peanut [Hogpeanut, Hog peanut, Hog pea nut, Hog pea-nut] (5, 40, 72, 93, 124, 127, 131, 158) (1899–1937), Honink-boije (Winnebago) (37) (1919), Maka ta omnicha or onmni-cha (Dakota) (37) (1919), Pea vine [Peavine, Pea-vine] (5, 158) (1900–1913), Pitcher's hog peanut [Pitcher's hog pea nut, Pitchers hogpeanut] (5, 72, 93, 97, 131) (1899–1937), Wild peanut [Wild pea nut, Wild pea-nut] (5, 85, 93, 95, 97, 156, 158) (1900–1937)

***Amphicarpaea* Ell. ex Nutt.** – Hog-peanut [Hogpeanut, Hog peanut, Hog pea nut, Hog pea-nut] (2, 50, 82, 93, 155, 156, 158) (1900–present)

***Amphicarpaea monoica* Nutt** – See *Amphicarpaea bracteata* (L.) Fern.

Amphicarpon amphicarpon (**Pursh**) **Nash** – See *Amphicarpum purshii* Kunth

Amphicarpon floridanum **Chapm.** – See *Amphicarpum muehlenbergianum* (J.A. Schultes) A.S. Hitchc.

Amphicarpum amphicarpon (**Pursh**) **Nash** – See *Amphicarpum purshii* Kunth

Amphicarpum floridanum **Chapman** – See *Amphicarpum muehlenbergianum* (J.A. Schultes) A.S. Hitchc.

Amphicarpum muehlenbergianum (**J.A. Schultes**) **A.S. Hitchc.** – Florida amphicarpon (94) (1901)

Amphicarpum purshii **Kunth** – Pursh's amphicarpon (5, 94) (1901–1913)

Amphiglottis conopsea (**Ait. f.**) **Small** – See *Epidendrum conopseum* Ait.f.

Amphilophis saccharoides (**Sw.**) **Nash** – See *Bothriochloa saccharoides* (Sw.) Rydb.

Amsinckia douglasiana **A. DC.** – Douglas' fiddleneck [Douglas fiddleneck] (155) (1942)

Amsinckia idahoensis **M.E.Jones** – See *Amsinckia menziesii* (Lehm.) A. Nels. & J.F. Macbr. var. *menziesii*

Amsinckia intermedia **Fisch. & Mey.** – See *Amsinckia menziesii* (Lehm.) A. Nels. & J.F. Macbr. var. *intermedia* (Fisch & C.A. Mey.) Ganders

Amsinckia **Lehm.** – Amsinckia (158) (1900), Buckthorn-weed (1) (1932), Fiddleneck [Fiddle neck] (1, 4, 50, 155) (1932–present), Tarweed [Tar weed, Tar-weed] (77) (1898) CA

Amsinckia lycopsoides **Lehm.** – Amsinckia (5) (1913), Fireweed [Fire weed, Fire-weed] (106) (1930) CA, a skin irritant, Leather-breeches (106) (1930), Tarweed fiddleneck (50, 155) (1942–present), Woolly-breeches (106) (1930)

Amsinckia menziesii (**Lehm.**) **A. Nels. & J.F. Macbr.** – Common fiddleneck (50) (present), Fiddleneck [Fiddle neck] (3) (1977), Fireweed fiddleneck (155) (1942), Menzies' fiddleneck (50) (present)

Amsinckia spectabilis **Fisch. & C.A. Mey.** – Coast fiddleneck (155) (1942)

Amsinckia tessellata **Gray** – Fiddleneck [Fiddle neck] (97) (1937) OK

Amsonia amsonia (**L.**) **Britton** – See *Amsonia tabernaemontana* Walt. var. *tabernaemontana*

Amsonia angustifolia **Michx.** – See *Amsonia ciliata* Walter var. *ciliata*

Amsonia ciliata **Walt.** var. *texana* (**Gray**) **Coult.** – Blue Texas star (124) (1937), Texas amsonia (4, 155) (1942–1986), Texas bluestar (50) (present)

Amsonia eastwoodiana – See *Amsonia tomentosa* Torr. & Frém. var. *stenophylla* Kearney & Peebles

Amsonia illustris **Woods.** – Ozark bluestar (50) (present)

Amsonia palmeri **Gray** – Palmer's amsonia [Palmer amsonia] (155) (1942)

Amsonia salicifolia **Pursh** – See *Amsonia tabernaemontana* Walt. var. *salicifolia* (Pursh) Woods.

Amsonia tabernaemontana **Walt.** – Amsonia (82) (1930), Eastern bluestar (50) (present), Willow amsonia (4, 138, 155) (1923–1986)

Amsonia tabernaemontana **Walt.** var. *salicifolia* (**Pursh**) **Woods.** – Narrow-leaf amsonia [Narrow-leaved amsonia] (97) (1937), Willow amsonia (122) (1937)

Amsonia tabernaemontana **Walt.** var. *tabernaemontana* – Amsonia (5, 97) (1913–1937)

Amsonia texana – See *Amsonia ciliata* Walt. var. *texana* (Gray) Coult.

Amsonia tomentosa **Torr. & Frém.** var. *stenophylla* **Kearney & Peebles** – Eastwood's amsonia [Eastwood amsonia] (155) (1942)

Amsonia **Walt.** – Amsonia (4, 82, 155, 158) (1900–1986), Blue Texas star (122) (1937), Bluestar [Blue star] (4, 50) (1986–present)

Amygdalus communis dulcis – See *Prunus amygdalus* Batsch

Amygdalus communis **L.** – See *Prunus dulcis* (Mill.) D.A. Webber

Amygdalus davidiana **Franch.** – possibly *Prunus persica* (L.) Batsch

Amygdalus **L.** – See *Prunus* L. all US species

Amygdalus persica **L.** – See *Prunus persica* (L.) Batsch

Amyris balsamifera **L.** – Balsam amyris (155) (1942), Candlewood [Candlewood, Candle wood] (92) (1876), Rhodes wood (92) (1876), Sweet amyris (165) (1807), White candlewood [White candle wood] (165) (1807), White rosewood [White rose wood] (165) (1807)

Amyris elemifera **L.** – Balsamier des Florides (French) (20) (1857), Florida balsam (92) (1876), Florida balsam tree (7) (1828), Florida torch wood [Florida torch wood] (20) (1857), Gum elemi tree (165) (1807), Sea amyris (155) (1942)

Amyris floridana **Nutt.** – See *Amyris elemifera* L.

Amyris floridana **Ware ex Nutt.** – See *Amyris elemifera* L.

Amyris **P. Br.** – Amyris (155) (1942), Gum elemi tree (167) (1814), Rosewood [Rose wood] (15) (1895), Torchwood [Torch wood] (15) (1895)

Amyris toxifera – See *Metopium toxiferum* (L.) Krug & Urban

Anacardium excelsum (**Bertero & Balb. ex Kunth**) **Skeels** – Guiana cashew (155) (1942)

Anacardium **L.** – Cashew (155) (1942)

Anacardium occidentale **L.** – Acajou [Acaju] (110, 165) (1807–1886) Brazil, Anacardium (52, 57) (1917–1919), Cachew nut [Cachew nut] (7, 91) (1828–1911), Caschou (165) (1807), Cashew (107, 109, 110, 138) (1886–1923), Cashew nut [Cashew-nut] (52, 57, 92, 165) (1807–1917), Cassu (165) (1807), Cassuvium (165) (1807), Common cashew (155) (1942), Kapa-mava [Kapa mava] (110, 165) (1807–1886), Pommier d'acajou (French, mahogany apple tree) (110) (1886)

Anacardium rhinocarpus – See *Anacardium excelsum* (Bertero & Balb. ex Kunth) Skeels

Anacharis alsinastrum [**Bab. ex Planch.**] – See *Elodea canadensis* Michx.

Anacharis canadensis (**Michx.**) **Planch.** – See *Elodea canadensis* Michx.

Anacharis linearis [(**Rydb.**) **Vict.**] – See *Elodea canadensis* Michx.

Anacharis occidentalis (**Pursh**) **Victorin** – See *Elodea nuttallii* (Planch.) St. John

Anacharis planchonii **Rydb.** – See *Elodea canadensis* Michx.

Anagallis (**Tourn.**) **L.** – See *Anagallis* L.

Anagallis arvensis **L.** – Bird's-eye [Bird's eye, Bird's-eyes, Birds-eyes] (5, 156, 157, 158) (1900–1929), Bird's-tongue [Birds tongue] (5, 156, 157, 158) (1900–1929), Burnet-rose [Burnet rose] (5, 156, 157, 158) (1900–1929), Chickweed [Chick-weed, Chick weed] (42, 157) (1814–1929), Collmarkraut (158) (1900), Common pimpernel (42, 165) (1807–1814), Eyebright [Eye-bright, Eye bright] (5, 156, 158) (1900–1923), Gauchheil (German) (158) (1900), Hühnerdarn (German) (6) (1892), John-go-to-bed-at-noon (158) (1900), Mouron (French) (6) (1892), Mouron rouge (French) (157, 158) (1900–1929), Orange-lily pernel (157) (1929), Pimpernel (4, 10, 107) (1818–1986), Poison chickweed (77) (1898) CA, Poor Mavis (157) (1929), Poor-man's-weatherglass [Poor man's weatherglass, Poor-man's weather-glass, Poor-man's-weather-glass, Poor man's weather glass] (4, 5, 6, 49, 92, 107, 109, 156, 158, 165) (1807–1986) flowers close in bad weather, Red chickenweed (158) (1900), Red chickweed (5, 6, 19, 49, 61, 77, 92, 156, 158, 187) (1818–1923), Red pimpernel (5, 6, 7, 49, 92, 97, 156, 157, 158, 184) (1793–1937), Rothe Miere (German) (158) (1900), Scarlet pimpernel (3, 5, 50, 19, 49, 57, 72, 92, 97, 122, 155, 156, 157, 158, 187) (1818–present), Shepherd's-calender (158) (1900), Shepherd's-clock [Shepherd's clock] (5, 107, 156, 157, 158) (1900–1929), Shepherd's-delight [Shepherd's delight, shepherds delight] (5, 156, 158) (1900–1923), Shepherd's-sundial [Shepherd's sundial] (156, 158) (1900–1923), Shepherd's-warning (158) (1900), Shepherd's-watch (158) (1900), Shepherd's-weatherglass [Shepherd's weather glass, Shepherds' weatherglass or Shepherd's weather-glass] (5, 92, 156, 157, 165) (1876–1929) flowers close in bad weather, Sunflower [Sun-flower] (5, 156, 158) (1900–1923), Tawny pimpernel [Tawnie pimpernell] (178) (1526), Tom pimpermowl (158) (1900), Waywort (156, 158) (1900–1923), Weather-glass [Weatherglass] (92, 157) (1876–1929), Wincopipe (158) (1900), Wink-a-peep (5, 156, 157, 158) (1900–1929)

Anagallis arvensis L. subsp. *arvensis* – Scarlet pimpernel (50) (present)

Anagallis arvensis L. subsp. *foemina* (Mill.) Schinz & Thellung – Blue pimpernel [Blew pimpernell] (178) (1526), Blue scarlet-pimpernel [Blue scarlet pimpernel] (92) (1876)

Anagallis caerulea – See *Anagallis arvensis* L. subsp. *foemina* (Mill.) Schinz & Thellung

Anagallis coerulea – See *Anagallis arvensis* L. subsp. *foemina* (Mill.) Schinz & Thellung

Anagallis L. – Bastard pimpernel (10) (1818), Chaffweed [Chaff weed] (1, 10, 156) (1818–1932), False pimpernel [Falsepimpernel] (1) (1932), Pimpernel (1, 4, 6, 50, 82, 109, 138, 155, 156, 158) (1892–present), Poor-man's-weatherglass [Poor man's weatherglass, Poor-man's weather-glass, Poor-man's-weather-glass, Poor man's weather glass] (1, 4) (1932–1986), Shepherd's-weatherglass [Shepherd's weatherglass] (1, 93) (1932–1936)

Anagallis linifolia L. – See *Anagallis monelli* L.

Anagallis minima (L.) Krause – Bastard pimpernel (5, 19, 92) (1840–1913), Chaffweed [Chaff weed] (4, 5, 50, 85, 92, 93, 131, 156) (1899–present), Common pimpernel (3) (1977), False pimpernel [Falsepimpernel] (5, 97, 122, 156) (1913–1937)

Anagallis monelli L. – Flax-leaf pimpernel [Flaxleaf pimpernel, Flax-leaved pimpernel] (138, 155, 165) (1807–1942), Pimpernel (82) (1930)

Anagallis phenicea Lam. – See *Anagallis arvensis* L.

Anamomis dichotoma Sargent – See *Myrcianthes fragrans* (Sw.) McVaugh

Ananas comosus (L.) Merr. – Pineapple [Pine-apple, Pine apple] (7, 109, 155) (1828–1949)

Ananas comosus (L.) Merr.var. *comosus* – Ananas (Spanish) (110) (1886), Matzatli (Mexican) (110) (1886), Pinas (Spanish) (110) (1886), Pineapple [Pine-apple, Pine apple] (92, 110, 138) (1876–1923)

Ananas comosus Merr. – See *Ananas comosus* (L.) Merr.

Ananas L. – See *Ananas* Mill. from aboriginal (S. American) name

Ananassa sativa Lindl. – See *Ananas comosus* (L.) Merr.var. *comosus*

Anaphalis DC. – Life-everlasting [Life everlasting] (158) (1900), Pearl-everlasting [Pearleverlasting] (155) (1942), Pearly-everlasting [Pearly everlasting] (1, 4, 50, 93) (1932–present)

Anaphalis margaritacea (L.) Benth. – See *Anaphalis margaritacea* (L.) Benth. & Hook

Anaphalis margaritacea (L.) Benth. & Hook – Coffin plant [Coffin-plant] (187) (1818), Common pearl-everlasting [Common pearleverlasting] (155) (1942), Cottonweed [Cotton-weed, Cotton weed] (5, 92, 156, 158) (1876–1923), Cudweed of America [Cudweede of America] (178) (1526), Dead-man's flower (187) (1818), Everlasting (2, 106, 190) (~1759–1930), Everlasting flower (46) (1879), Everwhite [Ever-white] (156, 158) (1900–1923), Indian posy [Indian-posy, Indian posey] (5, 156, 158, 190) (~1759–1923), Lady-never-fade (5, 156, 158) (1900–1923), Lady's-tobacco [Ladies' tobacco] (5, 76, 106, 156, 158) (1896–1923) Eastern US, Large-flower everlasting [Large-flowered everlasting, Large flowered everlasting] (5, 72, 97, 156, 158) (1900–1936), Life-everlasting [Life everlasting] (5, 41, 106, 158, 187) (1770–1930), Life-of-man [Life of man, Life-o'-man] (73) (1892) NH, Live-forever [Liveforever, Live forever] (46) (1879), Live-long [Live long] (156, 158) (1900–1923), Moonshine (5, 106, 156, 158) (1900–1923) Eastern U.S., None-so-pretty [None so pretty] (5, 7, 92, 156, 158) (1828–1923), Old-sow (158) (1900), Pearl-flower life-everlasting [Pearl-flowered life everlasting, Pearl-flowered life everlasting] (19, 49, 92) (1840–1898), Pearly-everlasting [Pearly everlasting] (3, 4, 5, 40, 49, 85, 106, 107, 156, 158) (1900–1986), Poverty-weed [Povertyweed, Poverty weed] (5, 75, 156) (1894–1923) Penobscot ME, Silver-button [Silver button] (5, 106, 156, 158) (1900–1930), Silverleaf [Silver leaf, Silver-leaf] (5, 7, 91, 156, 158) (1828–1923), Silverleaf life-everlasting [Silver-leaved life-everlasting] (156) (1923),

Strawflower [Straw-flower] (106) (1930) WA, Wa'bigwûn (Chipewwa, flowers) (40) (1928), Western common pearl-everlasting [Western common pearleverlasting] (155) (1942), Western pearly-everlasting [Western pearly everlasting] (50) (present)

Anaphalis margaritacea (L.) C. B. Clarke – See *Anaphalis margaritacea* (L.) Benth. & Hook

Anaphalis margaritacea occidentalis – See *Anaphalis margaritacea* (L.) Benth. & Hook

Anaphalis margaritacea subalpina – See *Anaphalis margaritacea* (L.) Benth. & Hook

Anaphalis subalpina (Gray) Rydb. – See *Anaphalis margaritacea* (L.) Benth. & Hook

Anastrophus compressus (Sw.) Schlecht. – See *Axonopus compressus* (Sw.) Beauv.

Anatherum muricatum – See *Vetiveria zizaniodes* (L.) Nash

Anchistea virginica (L.) Prsel. – See *Woodwardia virginica* (L.) Sm.

Anchusa arvensis (L.) Bieb. – Bugloss [Buglos, Buglosse] (93) (1936), Small bugloss (3, 5, 50, 82, 85, 156, 158) (1900–present), Wild bugloss [Wilde bugloss] (19, 156, 158, 178) (1526–1923)

Anchusa azurea Mill. – Buglossum (165) (1768), Italian alkanet (165) (1807), Italian bugloss (50, 138, 155) (1923–present)

Anchusa barrelieri (All.) Vitman – Barrelier's alkanet (165) (1807), Barrelier's bugloss (50) (present), Early bugloss (138, 155) (1931–1942)

Anchusa capensis Thunb. – Cape bugloss (82, 138, 155) (1923–1942)

Anchusa italica – See *Anchusa azurea* Mill.

Anchusa L. – Alkanet (1, 82, 85, 109, 158) (1900–1949), Bugloss [Buglos, Buglosse] (1, 50, 82, 109, 138, 155, 156, 179) (1526–present) SD, Lang-de-beef [Langue-de-beef, Langdebefe] (179) (1526), Ox-tongue [Ox-tongue] (179) (1526), Small bugloss (10) (1818), Wild bourache [Wylde bourache] (179) (1526)

Anchusa officinalis L. – Anchu (107) (1919), Bugloss [Buglos, Buglosse] (19, 46, 107) (1617–1919), Common bugloss (138, 155) (1931–1942), Garden alkanet (165) (1807), Garden bugloss (165) (1807), Officinal alkanet (165) (1807), Officinal bugloss (165) (1807), Oxtongue [Ox-tongue] (92) (1876)

Anchusa sempervirens – See *Pentaglottis sempervirens* (L.) Tausch ex Bailey

Anchusa virginica – possibly *Lithospermum caroliniense* (Walter ex J. F. Gmel.) MacMill. var. *caroliniense*

Andira – See *Andira* Juss.

Andira inermis (W. Wright) Kunth ex DC. – Cabbage angelin or Cabbage angelin tree [Cabbage angelintree] (138, 155) (1923–1942), Cabbage-bark tree [Cabbagebark tree] (50) (present), Partridge wood (92) (1876), Worm-bark (92) (1876)

Andira jamaicensis (W. Wright) Urban – See *Andira inermis* (W. Wright) Kunth ex DC.

Andira Juss. – Angelin (138) (1923), Angelin tree [Angelintree] (155) (1942)

Andredera vescaria (Lam.) Gaertn. f. ex Gaertn. – See *Anredera vesicaria* (Lam.) C. F. Gaertn.

Androcera Nutt. – See *Solanum* L.

Androcera rostrata (Dunal) Rydb. – See *Solanum rostratum* Dunal

Andromeda acuminata Aiton – See *Agarista populifolia* (Lam.) W.S. Judd

Andromeda arborea – possibly *Oxydendrum arboreum* (L.) DC.

Andromeda axillaris Lam. – See *Leucothoe axillaris* (Lam.) D. Don.

Andromeda calyculata – See *Chamaedaphne calyculata* (L.) Moench

Andromeda catesbaei Walt. – possibly *Leucothoe axillaris* (Lam.) D. Don.

Andromeda coriacea Hort. Kew. – possibly *Lyonia lucida* (Lam.) K. Koch

Andromeda ferruginea Walt. – possibly *Lyonia ferruginea* (Walt.) Nutt.

Andromeda floribunda Pursh. – possibly *Pieris floribunda* (Pursh) Benth. & Hook. f.

Andromeda formosissima **Bart.** – possibly *Agarista populifolia* (Lam.) W.S. Judd

Andromeda glaucophylla – See *Andromeda polifolia* L. var. *glaucophylla* (Link) DC.

Andromeda hypnoides **W.** – See *Cassiope hypnoides* (L.) D.Don

Andromeda **L.** – Andromeda (8, 14, 155) (1785–1942), Andromede (French) (8) (1785), Bog rosemary (138) (1923), Redbud [Red-bud, Red bud, Red-budds] or Redbud tree [Red bud tree, Redbud-tree, Redbud tree] (167) (1814)

Andromeda laurina **Michx.** – possibly *Agarista populifolia* (Lam.) W.S. Judd

Andromeda ligustrina **Muhl.** – possibly *Lyonia ligustrina* (L.) DC.

Andromeda lucida **Jacq.** – possibly *Agarista populifolia* (Lam.) W.S. Judd

Andromeda mariana **L.** – See *Lyonia mariana* (L.) D. Don

Andromeda nitida **Bartr.** – See *Lyonia lucida* (Lam.) K. Koch

Andromeda paniculata **Michx.** – possibly *Leucothoe racemosa* (L.) Gray

Andromeda polifera **L.** – possibly *Andromeda polifolia* L.

Andromeda polifolia **L.** – Bog-rosemary [Bog rosemary] (138, 156) (1923), Bog-rosemary andromeda [Bogrosemary andromeda] (155) (1942), Marsh andromeda (165) (1807), Marsh chistus (165) (1807), Marsh holywort (156) (1923) no longer in use by 1923, Marsh-rosemary [Marsh rose-mary, Marsh rosemary] (5, 156) (1913–1923), Moorwort [Moor-wort] (5, 156, 165) (1807–1923), Poley mountain (165) (1807), Rosemary-leaf andromeda [Rosemary leaved andromeda] (42) (1814), Wild rosemary (5, 19, 156, 165) (1807–1923), Marsh holy-rose [Marsh holy rose] (5, 165) (1807–1913) (possibly)

Andromeda polifolia **L. var. *glaucophylla* (Link) DC.** – Bog rosemary (156) (1923), Downy andromeda (155) (1942), Downy bog-rosemary (138) (1923)

Andromeda populifolia **Lam.** – See *Agarista populifolia* (Lam.) W.S. Judd

Andromeda pulverulenta – See *Zenobia pulverulenta* (Bartr. ex Willd.) Pollard

Andromeda racemosa **L.** – possibly *Leucothoe racemosa* (L.) Gray

Andromeda reticulata **Walt.** – possibly *Agarista populifolia* (Lam.) W.S. Judd

Andromeda speciosa **Michx.** – possibly *Zenobia pulverulenta* (Bartr. ex Willd.) Pollard

Andropogon **(Royen) L.** – See *Andropogon* L.

Andropogon argenteus – See *Andropogon ternarius* Michx.

Andropogon argyraeus **Schultes** – See *Andropogon ternarius* Michx.

Andropogon avenaceus **Michx.** – See *Sorghastrum nutans* (L.) Nash

Andropogon barbinodis **Lag.** – See *Bothriochloa barbinodis* (Lag.) Herter

Andropogon bicorne – See *Andropogon bicornis* L.

Andropogon bicornia – See *Andropogon bicornis* L.

Andropogon bicornis **L.** – Foxtail grass [Fox tail grass, Fox-tail grass, Foxtail-grass] (East Indies) (165) (1807), Indian grass [Indian-grass, Indiangrass] (41) (1770), Mountain grass (92) (1876), Wild grass [Wildgrass] (41) (1770)

Andropogon brachystachys **Chapm.** – See *Andropogon brachystachyus* Chapm.

Andropogon brachystachyus **Chapm.** – Short-spike broom-sedge [Short-spiked broom sedge] (94) (1901)

Andropogon cabanisii **Hack.** – See *Andropogon ternarius* Michx. var. *cabanisii* (Hack.) Fern. & Grisc.

Andropogon chrysocomus **Nash.** – See *Andropogon gerardii* Vitman

Andropogon cirratus Hack. – See *Schizachyrium cirratum* (Hack.) Woot. & Standl.

Andropogon citratum – See *Cymbopogon citratus* (DC. ex Nees) Stapf

Andropogon contortum **L.** – See *Heteropogon contortus* (L.) Beauv. ex Roemer & J.A. Schultes

Andropogon contortus **L.** – See *Heteropogon contortus* (L.) Beauv. ex Roemer & J.A. Schultes

Andropogon dissitiflorus **Michx.** – See *Andropogon virginicus* L.

Andropogon elliottii **Chapm.** – See *Andropogon gyrans* Ashe var. *gyrans*

Andropogon furcatus **Muhl.** – See *Andropogon gerardii* Vitman

Andropogon gerardii **Vitman** – Beard grass [Beard-grass, Beardgrass] (108, 119) (1878–1938), Big bluestem [Big blue-stem Big blue stem] (3, 5, 11, 50, 56, 65, 85, 93, 94, 111, 115, 119, 122, 124, 129, 134, 140, 144, 155, 163) (1852–present), Bluejoint [Bluejoint, Blue joint] (5, 45, 75, 119) (1894–1938), Blue-joint grass [Blue joint grass] (56) (1901) IA, Bluestem [Blue-stem, Blue stem] (40, 45, 56, 78, 87, 90, 144) (1885–1928), Broom grass [Broomgrass] (5) (1913), Finger grass [Fingergrass, Finger-grass] (45) (1896), Finger-spike broom grass [Finger-spiked broom grass] (87, 88) (1884–1885), Finger-spike Indian grass [Finger-spiked Indian grass] (144) (1899), Finger-spike wood grass [Finger-spiked wood grass] (66, 90) (1885–1903), Forked beard grass [Forked beardgrass, Forked beardgrass] (5, 99, 131) (1899–1923), Forked spike (19, 92) (1840–1876), H'ade-zhide (Omaha-Ponca, red hay) (37) (1830), Mûckode'kanĕs (Chippewa, small prairie) (40) (1928), Tennessee bluestem [Tennessee blue stem] (56) (1901) IA, Turkey-foot [Turkey foot, Turkeyfoot] (45, 140, 144, 163) (1852–1944), Turkey-foot grass [Turkeyfoot grass, Turkey-foot-grass] (129) (1894), Yellow-hair beard grass [Yellow-haired beard-grass] (5, 93, 99) (1913–1936)

Andropogon glomeratus **(Walt.) B.S.P.** – Brook grass [Brook-grass, Brookgrass] (5, 94) (1901–1913), Cluster-flower beard grass [Cluster-flowered beard grass] (66, 187) (1818–1903), Heavy-top broom grass [Heavy-topped broom grass] (87, 88) (1884–1885), Indian beard grass [Indian beard-grass] (5) (1913), Indian grass [Indiangrass, Indiangrass] (19) (1840)

Andropogon glomeratus **(Walt.) B.S.P. var. *glomeratus*** – Bushy beard grass [Bushy beard-grass, Bushy beardgrass] (3, 5, 119, 122, 155, 163) (1852–1977), Bushy bluestem [Bushy blue-stem, Bushy blue stem] (119) (1938)

Andropogon glomeratus **(Walt.) B.S.P. var. *scabriglumis* C. Campbell** – Rough-glume bushy beard grass [Roughglume bushy beardgrass] (50) (present)

Andropogon gyrans **Ashe var. *gyrans*** – Elliot's beard grass [Elliot's beard-grass, Elliotts beardgrass] (5, 122, 163) (1852–1937), Elliot's bluestem (50) (present), Elliot's broom-sedge [Elliot's broom sedge] (94) (1901)

Andropogon halepensis **(L.) Brot. Fl.** – See *Sorghum halepense* (L.) Pers.

Andropogon hallii **Hack.** – Colorado sand grass (56, 94, 111) (1901–1915), Few-hair beard grass [Few-haired beard-grass] (5) (1913), Hall's beard-grass [Hall's beardgrass] (5, 56, 72, 119, 131, 163) (1852–1938), Hall's bluestem [Hall's blue-stem] (85) (1932), Sand bluestem [Sand blue-stem] (3, 50, 140, 155) (1942–present), Sand grass [Sandgrass, Sand-grass] (144) (1899) KS, Sand-hill bluestem [Sand-hill blue-stem] (93) (1936) Neb, Turkey-foot [Turkey foot, Turkeyfoot] (75, 140) (1894–1944), Turkey-foot grass [Turkeyfoot grass, Turkey-foot-grass] (5, 56, 119, 122, 131) (1899–1938)

Andropogon intermedius **R. Br.** – See *Bothriochloa bladhii* (Retz.) S.T. Blake

Andropogon ischaemum **L. var. *songaricus* Fisch. & Mey.** – See *Bothriochloa ischaemum* (L.) Keng var. *songarica* (Rupr. ex Fisch. & C.A. Mey.) Celarier & Harlan

Andropogon **L.** – Beard grass [Beard-grass, Beardgrass] (1, 10, 56, 138, 155, 158, 184) (1793–1942), Bluestem [Blue-stem, Blue stem] (1, 50, 93, 155) (1932–present), Broom grass [Broom-grass] (1) (1932), Broom-sedge [Broom sedge, Broomsedge] (155) (1942), Sedge grass (7) (1828), Tall sage grass (152) (1912)

Andropogon littoralis **Nash** – See *Schizachyrium littorale* (Nash) Bicknell

Andropogon longiberbis **Hack.** – Long-beard broom sedge [Long-bearded broom sedge] (94) (1901)

Andropogon macrourum **Michx.** – See *Andropogon glomeratus* (Walt.) Britton, Sterns & Poggenb.

Andropogon maritimus **Chapm.** – See *Schizachyrium maritimum* (Chapman) Nash

Andropogon melanocarpus **Ell.** – See *Heteropogon melanocarpus* (Ell.) Ell. ex Benth.

Andropogon mohrii **(Hack.) Hack. ex Vasey** – Mohr's broom sedge (94) (1901)

Andropogon mohrii **Hack.** – See *Andropogon mohrii* (Hack.) Hack. ex Vasey

Andropogon nardus – See *Cymbopogon nardus* (L.) Rendle

Andropogon nutans avenaceus **(Michx.) Hack** – See *Sorghastrum nutans* (L.) Nash

Andropogon nutans **L.** – See *Sorghastrum nutans* (L.) Nash

Andropogon pauciflorus **(Chapm.) Hack.** – See *Chrysopogon pauciflorus* (Chapm.) Benth. ex Vasey

Andropogon paucipilus **Nash.** – See *Andropogon hallii* Hack.

Andropogon perforatus **Trin. ex Fourn.** – See *Bothriochloa barbinodis* (Lag.) Herter

Andropogon provincialis **Lam.** – See *Andropogon gerardii* Vitman

Andropogon saccharoides **Sw.** – See *Bothriochloa saccharoides* (Sw.) Rydb.

Andropogon saccharoides **Sw. var.** *torreyanus* **(Steud.) Hack.** – See *Bothriochloa laguroides* (DC.) Herter subsp. *torreyana* (Steud.) Allred & Gould

Andropogon scoparius **Michx.** – See *Schizachyrium scoparium* (Michx.) Nash var. *scoparium*

Andropogon scoparius **Michx. var.** *divergens* **Hackel** – See *Schizachyrium scoparium* (Michx.) Nash var. *divergens* (Hack.) Gould

Andropogon scoparius **Michx. var.** *littoralis* **(Nash) A.S. Hitchc.** – See *Schizachyrium littorale* (Nash) Bicknell

Andropogon scoparius **Michx. var.** *neomexicanus* **(Nash) A.S. Hitchc.** – See *Schizachyrium scoparium* (Michx.) Nash var. *scoparium*

Andropogon semiberbis **Kunth** – See *Schizachyrium sanguineum* (Retz.) Alston var. *sanguineum*

Andropogon sorghum **Brot. Fl.** – See *Sorghum bicolor* (L.) Moench

Andropogon sorghum **Brot. var.** *halapensis* **Hack.** – See *Sorghum halepense* (L.) Pers.

Andropogon tener **Kunth** – See *Schizachyrium tenerum* Nees

Andropogon tennesseensis **Scribner** – See *Andropogon gerardii* Vitman

Andropogon ternarius **Michx.** – Silver beard grass [Silver beardgrass, Silver beardgrass] (66) (1903), Silver-beard (5, 94) (1901–1913), Silvery beard grass [Silvery beard-grass] (3, 5, 94, 99, 119, 163) (1852–1977), Split-beard bluestem [Splitbeard blue-stem] (50) (present)

Andropogon ternarius **Michx. var.** *cabanisii* **(Hack.) Fern. & Grisc.** – Cabanis beard-grass (5) (1913), Split-beard bluestem [Splitbeard blue-stem] (50) (present)

Andropogon unilateralis **Hack.** – See *Sorghastrum secundum* (Ell.) Nash

Andropogon virginicus **L.** – Bent grass [Bentgrass, Bent-grass] (19) (1840), Broom grass [Broom-grass] (87) (1884), Broom-sedge [Broom sedge, Broomsedge] (3, 5, 62, 67, 87, 94, 119, 122, 124, 163) (1852–1977), Broom-sedge bluestem [Broom sedge bluestem] (5, 50) (1913–present), Common broom grass [Common broomgrass] (187) (1818), Indian grass [Indian-grass, Indiangrass] (187) (1818), Slender-spike beard grass [Slender-spiked beard-grass] (187) (1818), Virginia beard grass [Virginia beard-grass, Virginian beard-grass] (5, 62, 66, 99) (1903–1923), Yellow-sedge bluestem [Yellowsedge bluestem] (155) (1942)

Andropogon virginicus **L. var.** *virginicus* – Many-flower broom-sedge [Many-flowered broom sedge] (94) (1901)

Andropogon virginicus tetrastachys **(Ell.) Hack.** – See *Andropogon virginicus* L. var. *virginicus*

Andropogon virginicus **var.** *corymbosus* **(Chapm.) Fern. & Griscom.** – See *Andropogon glomeratus* (Walt.) Britton, Sterns & Poggenb. var. *glomeratus*

Andropogon wrightii **Hack.** – See *Bothriochloa wrightii* (Hack.) Henr.

Androsace arizonica **(Gray) Derganc** – See *Androsace occidentalis* Pursh

Androsace **L.** – Rock-jasmine [Rockjasmine] (50, 101, 155) (1905–present)

Androsace occidentalis **Pursh** – Dwarf rockjasmine (155) (1942), Western rock-jasmine [Western rock jasmine, Western rockjasmine] (3, 4, 50, 155) (1942–present)

Androsace septentrionalis **L.** – Mountain androsace (131) (1899), Northern rock-jasmine [Northern rock jasmine] (4) (1986), Pygmyflower rock-jasmine [Pygmyflower rockjasmine] (50) (present), Tooth-leaf androsace [Tooth-leaved androsace] (165) (1807)

Androsaemum officinale **All.** – Park leaves [Parke leaues] (92) (1876), Tutsan (92) (1876)

Androstephium caeruleum **(Scheele) Greene** – Androstephium (3, 5, 97) (1913–1977), Baby's-breath [Babies' breath, Baby's breath, Babies'-breath] (158) (1900), Blue funnel-lily [Blue funnel lily, Blue funnellily] (50, 155) (1942–present), Crowned lily (86) (1878)

Androstephium coeruleum **(Scheele) Greene** – See *Androstephium caeruleum* (Scheele) Greene*)* ()

Androstephium **Torr.** – Androstephium (158) (1900) Greek for 'man's crown', the filaments forming a crown, Funnel-lily [Funnellily] (155) (1942)

Androstephium violaceum **Torr.** – See *Androstephium caeruleum* (Scheele) Greene

Andryala integrifolia **L.** – Crooked andryala (42) (1814), Hoary andryala (165) (1807)

Andryala sinuata – See *Andryala integrifolia* L.

Aneilema nudicaule **(Burm. f.) G. Don** – See *Murdannia nudiflora* (L.) Brenan

Aneilema nudiflorum **(L.) Sweet** – See *Murdannia nudiflora* (L.) Brenan

Anemone **(Tourn.) L.** – See *Anemone* L.

Anemone acultiloba **L.** – See *Hepatica nobilis* Schreb. var. *acuta* (Pursh) Steyermark

Anemone berlandieri **Pritz.** – Greek anemone (155) (1942), Spring anemone (124) (1937) TX, Ten-petal anemone [Tenpetal anemone, Ten-petalled anemone] (3, 4, 155, 165) (1807–1986), Ten-petal thimbleweed [Tenpetal thimbleweed] (50) (present)

Anemone blanda **Schott & Kotschy** – Greek anemone (155) (1942), Sapphire anemony (109) (1949)

Anemone canadensis **L.** – Canadian anemone [Canada anemone] (5, 50, 72, 82, 85, 93, 127, 131, 158) (1899–present), Crowfoot [Crowfoot, Crow foot, Crowfote, Crow's foot] (5) (1913) Burnside SD, Drummond's anemone [Drummond anemone] (155) (1942), Heart liverleaf [Heart liver-leaf, Heart liver leaf] (49, 53) (1898–1922), Meadow anemone (3, 4, 138, 155, 165) (1807–1986), Meadow anemony (109) (1949), Pennsylvania anemone [Pennsylvanian anemone, Pensylvania anemone, Pensylvanican anemone] (42, 158, 165) (1807–1900), Round-head anemone [Round-headed anemone] (5, 158) (1900–1913), Round-leaf anemone [Round-leaved anemone] (5, 93, 158) (1900–1936), Te-zhinga-makan (Omaha-Ponca, little buffalo medicine) (37) (1919), Wabesgung (Chippewa, numb-taste) (105) (1932), White-flower anmeone [White-flowered anemone] (158) (1900), White-flower crowfoot [White-flowered crowfoot] (158) (1900), Windflower [Wind flower, Wind-flower, Wind-floures, Winde-floures] (37) (1919), Wolfsbane-leaf anemone [Wolf's bane leaved anemone] (42) (1814)

Anemone caroliniana **Walt.** – Carolina anemone (3, 4, 5, 50, 72, 85, 86, 93, 97, 131, 155) (1878–present), Mayflower [May flower, Mayflower] (76, 156, 158) (1896–1923), Purple anemone (156, 158) (1900–1923), Wood flower [Woodflower, Wood-flower] (156, 158) (1900–1923)

Anemone cylindrica **Gray** – Candle anemone [Candle anemony] (3, 4, 50, 109, 138, 155, 156) (1923–present), Cottonweed [Cotton-weed, Cotton weed] (127, 156) (1923–1933), Long-fruit anemone [Long-fruited anemone] (5, 37, 72, 93, 131) (1899–1936), Nimbleweed [Nimble-weed, Nimble weed] (156) (1923), Tumbleweed [Tumble weed, Tumble-weed] (156) (1923), Wathibaba-makan (Pawnee, playing card medicine) (37) (1919)

Anemone decapetala **Ard.** – See *Anemone berlandieri* Pritz.

Anemone deltoidea **Hook.** – Three-leaf anemone [Threeleaf anemone] (155) (1942)

Anemone drummondi – See *Anemone drummondii* S. Wats.

Anemone drummondii **S. Wats.** – Drummond's anemone [Drummond anemone] (155) (1942)

Anemone globosa **Nutt.** – See *Anemone multifida* Poir. var. *hudsoniana* DC.

Anemone hepatica **L.** – See *Hepatica nobilis* Schreb. var. *obtusa* (Pursh) Steyermark

Anemone hudsonia **Richards** – See *Anemone multifida* Poir. var. *hudsoniana* DC.

Anemone hupehensis **(Lemoine) Lemoine** – Japanese anemone [Japanese anemony] (109, 138) (1923–1949)

Anemone hupehensis **var.** *japonica* **(Thunb.) Bowles & Stearn** – Japanese anemone [Japanese anemony] (138) (1923)

Anemone huphensis **Lemoine** – See *Anemone hupehensis* (Lemoine) Lemoine

Anemone japonica **Zieb. & Zucc.** – See *Anemone hupehensis* var. *japonica* (Thunb.) Bowles & Stearn

Anemone **L.** – American pasqueflower [American pasque-flower] (155) (1942), Anemone (1, 2, 15, 50, 63, 82, 109, 138, 155, 156, 158, 165) (1807–present), Anemoy (15) (1895), Windflower [Wind flower, Wind-flower, Wind-floures, Winde-floures] (1, 2, 4, 13, 15, 63, 82, 93, 109, 156, 162, 165) (1597–1986) Pliny claimed that flower only opened when the wind was blowing

Anemone lancifolia **Pursh** – Lance-leaf anemone [Lanceleaf anemone] (155) (1942), Mountain anemone (5) (1913), Small cut white windflower (178) (1526), possibly Spring-beauty [Spring beauty, Springbeauty] (76) (1896) Oxford Co. ME

Anemone ludoviciana **Nutt.** – See *Pulsatilla patens* (L.) Mill.subsp. *multifida* (Pritz.) Zamels

Anemone lyalli – See *Anemone lyallii* Britt.

Anemone lyallii **Britt.** – Lyall's anemone [Lyall anemone] (155) (1942)

Anemone multifida **Poir.** – Argentine anemone (155) (1942), Cut-leaf anemone [Cutleaf anemone, Cut-leaved anemone] (156, 158) (1900–1923), Pacific anemone (50) (present), Red wind anemone (131) (1899), Red windflower [Red wind-flower, Red wind flower] (156, 158) (1900–1923)

Anemone multifida **Poir. var.** *hudsoniana* **DC.** – Cut-leaf anemone [Cutleaf anemone, Cut-leaved anemone] (5, 93) (1913–1936), Hudsonian anemone (155) (1942), Japanese anemone [Japanese anemony] (109) (1949), Pacific anemone (155) (1942), Red windflower [Red wind-flower, Red wind flower] (5, 93) (1913–1936)

Anemone multifida **Poir. var.** *multifida* – Narcissus anemone (155) (1942)

Anemone multifida **Poir. var.** *nowosadii* **Boivin** – See *Anemone multifida* Poir. var. *multifida*

Anemone narcissiflora **L.** – Narcissus anemone (155) (1942), Narcissus-flower anemone [Narcissus-flowered anemone] (165) (1807)

Anemone nemorosa **L.** – European wood anemone (109, 137, 155) (1923–1949), Low anemone (19) (1840), Mayflower [May flower, May-flower] (73) (1892), Snowdrop [Snowdrops, Snow-drops, Snow drop] (76) (1896) Lynn MA, Wild windflowers [Wilde windflowers] (178) (1526), Wind crowfoot (49) (1898), Windflower [Wind flower, Wind-flower, Wind-floures, Winde-floures] (49, 61, 86, 92) (1870–1898), Wood anemone [Woods anemone] (19, 49, 61, 86, 92, 165) (1807–1898)

Anemone occidentalis – See *Pulsatilla occidentalis* (S. Wats.) Freyn

Anemone oregana **Gray** – Mediterranean anemone (155) (1942), Oregon anemone (155) (1942)

Anemone parviflora **Michx.** – Arctic anemone (155) (1942), Crocus [Crocuses] (106) (1930), Mediterranean anemone (155) (1942), Northern anemone (5) (1913), Small-flower anemone [Small-flowered anemone] (5, 42) (1814–1913)

Anemone patens **L.** – See *Pulsatilla patens* (L.) Mill.subsp. *multifida* (Pritz.) Zamels

Anemone patens **L. var.** *nuttalliana* **(DC.) Gray** – See *Pulsatilla patens* (L.) Mill.subsp. *multifida* (Pritz.) Zamels

Anemone patens **L. var.** *nuttalliana* **Gray** – See *Pulsatilla patens* (L.) Mill. subsp. *multifida* (Pritz.) Zamels

Anemone patens **L. var.** *wolfgangiana* **(Bess. ex Richards) Trauvtr. & Mey ex F. Kurtz** – See *Pulsatilla patens* (L.) Mill. subsp. *multifida* (Pritz.) Zamels

Anemone pennsylvanica **L.** – See *Anemone canadensis* L.

Anemone quinquefolia **L.** – American wood anemony (109, 138) (1923–1949), Anemone (82) (1930), Five-leaf anemone [Five leaved anemone] (42) (1814), Mayflower [May flower, May-flower] (5, 158) (1900–1913), Nightcaps (50, 156) (1923–present), Nimbleweed [Nimble-weed, Nimble weed] (5) (1913), Snowdrop [Snow-drops, Snow-drops, Snow drop] (5, 156, 158) (1900–1923), Strawberry-leaf Virginia crowfoot [Strawberry leaved Virginia crowfoot] (181) (~1678), Thimbleweed [Thimble weed, Thimble-weed] (158) (1900), Wild cucumber [Wild-cucumber, Wilde cucumbers] (5) (1913), Windflower [Wind flower, Wind-flower, Wind-floures, Winde-floures] (5, 156, 158) (1900–1923), Wood anemone [Woods anemone] (3, 4, 5, 72, 82, 85, 156) (1907–1986), Wood flower [Woodflower, Wood-flower] (5) (1913)

Anemone richardsonii **Hook.** – Richardson's anemone (5) (1913)

Anemone riparia **Fern.** – See *Anemone virginiana* L.

Anemone thalictroides **L.** – See *Anemonella thalictroides* (L.) Spach

Anemone trifolia **L.** – See *Anemone lancifolia* Pursh

Anemone trifolium – possibly *Anemone lancifolia* Pursh

Anemone tuberosa **Rydb.** – Tuber anemone (155) (1942)

Anemone virginiana **L.** – Nimbleweed [Nimble-weed, Nimble weed] (156) (1923), Riverbank anemone (155) (1942), Tall anemone (3, 4, 5, 72, 85, 86, 93, 97, 131, 158) (1878–1986), Tall thimbleweed (50) (present), Thimbleweed [Thimble weed, Thimble-weed] (5, 19, 74, 79, 86, 156, 158) (1840–1923), Tumbleweed [Tumble weed, Tumble-weed] (5) (1913), Virginia anemone [Virginian anemone] (155, 156, 158, 165) (1807–1942), Wild flower [Wildflower] (19) (1840), possibly Windbloom [Wind-bloom] (7, 92) (1828–1876)

Anemone virginiana **L. var.** *virginiana* – Tall thimbleweed (50) (present)

Anemone virginica – possibly *Anemone virginiana* L.

Anemonella **Spach.** – See *Thalictrum* L.

Anemonella thalictroides **(L.) Spach** – Meadowrue-leaf anemone [Meadow-rue leaved anemone] (42) (1814), Wild anemone (187) (1818)

Anemonoides ranunculoides **L.** – Yellow wood anemone (155) (1942)

Anemonoides ranunculoides **(L.) Holub** – See *Anemonoides ranunculoides* L.

Anemopsis californica **(Nutt.) Hook. & Arn.** – Yerba del Manza (52, 53) (1919–1922), Yerba mansa [Yerbamansa] (49, 50, 53, 57, 155, 158) (1898–present)

Anemopsis **Hook. & Arn.** – Yerba mansa [Yerbamansa] (4, 50) (1986–present)

Anethum **(Tourn.) L.** – See *Anethum* L.

Anethum feniculum **L** – See *Foeniculum vulgare* Mill.

Anethum foeniculum **L.** – See *Foeniculum vulgare* Mill.

Anethum graveolens **L.** – Anet (158, 179) (1526–1900), Anethon (107) (1919), Anise (of scripture) (158) (1900), Arrise (107) (1919) of New Testament, Common dill (165) (1807), Dill (German) (158) (1900), Dill [Dyll] (1, 3, 4, 5, 19, 50, 58, 82, 85, 107, 109, 138, 155, 156, 158, 165, 179, 184) (1538–present), Dilly (158) (1900), Eneldo (Spanish) (158) (1900), Fenouil puant (French) (158) (1900), Garden dill (158) (1900), possibly Yampah (Shoshone) (28, 103) (1850–1870)

Anethum hortense – See *Anethum graveolens* L.

Anethum **L.** – Archangel (5, 92, 156) (1876–1923), Dill [Dyll] (50, 82, 158) (1900–present), Fennel [Fenell] (7, 19, 165, 184) (1793–1840)

Aneurolepidium condensatum **(J. Presl) Nevski** – See *Leymus condensatus* (J. Presl) A. Löve

Angelica archangelica L. – Angelica or Angelica tree [Angelica-tree] (58) (1869), Archangel (19) (1840), European angelica (57, 64) (1908–1917), Garden angelica (49, 57, 58, 64, 92, 165) (1807–1917), Holy grass [Holygrass] (92) (1876)

Angelica arguta Nutt. – Lyall's angelica [Lyall angelica] (155) (1942)

Angelica atropurpurea L. – American angelica (64) (1907), American archangel (57) (1917), Angelica or Angelica tree [Angelica-tree] (7, 64) (1828–1907), Archangel (5, 92, 156) (1876–1923), Aunt Jerichos (5, 156) (1913–1923), Brewer's angelica [Brewer angelica] (155) (1942), Common angelica (6) (1892), Deadnettle [Dead-nettle, Dead nettle] (92) (1876), Great angelica (46, 49, 64, 107, 156) (1629–1923), Great high angelica (5) (1913), High angelica (6, 49, 92) (1876–1898), High angelicam (64) (1907), Masterwort [Masterwort, Master wort, Masterwoorts] (5, 6, 7, 49, 58, 64, 92, 107, 156) (1828–1923), Purple angelica (7, 49, 64, 92, 165) (1807–1908), Purple-stem angelica [Purplestem angelica, Purple-stemmed angelica] (5, 64, 138, 155, 156) (1907–1942), Purpurfarbige angelica (German) (6) (1892), Wild angelica, majoris (46) (1629)

Angelica breweri Gray – Brewer's angelica [Brewer angelica] (155) (1942), Filmy angelica (155) (1942)

Angelica curtisi – See *Angelica triquinata* Michx.

Angelica curtisii Buckl. – See *Angelica triquinata* Michx.

Angelica gmelinii (DC.) Pimenov – Sea-coast angelica [Sea coast angelica] (5, 156) (1913–1923)

Angelica grayi (Coult. & Rose) Coult. & Rose – Angelica or Angelica tree [Angelica-tree] (64) (1907), Gray's angelica [Grays angelica] (155) (1942)

Angelica hirsuta triquinata – possibly *Angelica triquinata* Michx. [possibly]

Angelica L. – Angelica or Angelica tree [Angelica-tree] (1, 50, 138, 155) (1923–present), Aunt Jerichos (75) (1894) Northeastern US, Nondo (white root) (182) (1791)

Angelica lucida L. – Angelic-root [Angelic root] (7, 124) (1828–1937), Belly-ache root [Bellyache root] (7, 92, 177) (1726–1876), Habascon (46) (1879), Lagonihah (Missouri tribes) (7) (1828), Lyall's angelica [Lyall angelica] (155) (1942), Masterwort [Master-wort, Master wort, Masterwoorts] (10) (1818), Nendo (Virginian Indians) (7) (1828), Shining angelica (165) (1807), White root (Southern tribes) (7) (1828)

Angelica lyalli – See *Angelica arguta* Nutt.

Angelica officinalis Moench – See *Angelica archangelica* L.

Angelica peregrina Nutt. – See *Angelica lucida* L.

Angelica pinnata S. Wats. – Small-leaf angelica (155) (1942)

Angelica sativa Mill. – See *Angelica archangelica* L.

Angelica sylvestris L. – Goutweed [Gout-weed, Gout weed] (92) (1876), Ground-ash [Ground ash] (107) (1919), Holy grass [Holygrass] (107) (1919), Wild angelica [Wilde angelica] (92, 107, 165, 178) (1526–1919), Woodland villosa (155) (1942)

Angelica triquinata Michx. – Curtis' angelica [Curtis angelica] (5) (1913), Filmy angelica (138, 155) (1923–1942), Gray's angelica [Grays angelica] (155) (1942), Wild angelica [Wilde angelica] (187) (1818), Wild angelica minoris (46) (1879), possibly Downy archangel (42) (1814)

Angelica venenosa (Greenway) Fern. – Hairy angelica (5, 138, 155, 156) (1913–1942), Pubescent angelica (5) (1913), Wood angelica (156) (1923)

Angelica villosa (Walt.) B.S.P. – See *Angelica venenosa* (Greenway) Fern.) (())

Angelica wheeleri S. Wats. – Wheeler's angelica [Wheeler angelica] (155) (1942)

Angelonia Humb. & Bonpl. – Angelonia (138, 155) (1931–1942), Peyote (104) (1896)

Angiopteris Hoffmann – Vessel fern [Vesselfern] (155) (1942)

Anhalonium engelmanni Lem. – See *Ariocarpus fissuratus* (Engelm.) K. Schum.

Anhalonium engelmannii Lem. – See *Ariocarpus fissuratus* (Engelm.) K. Schum.

Anhalonium lewini Henning – See *Lophophora lewinii* (Hennings ex Lewin) C.H. Thomps.

Anhalonium lewinii Henninegs – See *Lophophora lewinii* (Hennings ex Lewin) C.H. Thomps.

Anisostichus capreolata (L.) Bureau – See *Bignonia capreolata* L.

Annona cherimola Miller – Cherimoya (109, 137, 155) (1923–1949), possibly Chirimoya (110) (1886)

Annona glabra L. – Alligator-apple [Alligator apple] (92, 165) (1807–1876), Assimnier glabre (French) (8) (1785), Bullock's-heart [Bulock's heart] (110) (1886), Carolina smooth-bark annona [Caroliniana smooth-barked annona] (8) (1785), Cork wood [Cork-wood, Corkwood] (165) (1807) Jamaica, Pond-apple [Pond apple] (109, 138) (1923–1949), Shining-leaf custard-apple [Shining-leaved custard apple] (165) (1807), Smooth custard apple (165) (1807), Water-apples [Water apples] (92) (1876)

Annona grandiflora Bartr. – See *Asimina incana* (W.Bartram) Exell

Annona L. – Custard-apple [Custardapple, Custard apple] (15, 109) (1895–1949), Papaw [Pawpaw, Paw-paw] or Papaw tree [Papaw-tree, Pappaw tree] (167) (1814)

Annona montana Macfad. – Acimine (41) (1770), Mountain soursop (155) (1942)

Annona muricata L. – Acimine (41) (1770), Alligator-apple [Alligator apple] (92, 165) (1807–1876), Araticu porche (177) (1762), Araticu-ponhe (165)

Anoda Cav. – Crested anoda (50) (present)

Anoda cristata (L.) Schlecht. – Anoda (50, 155, 158) (1900–present), Crested anoda (50) (present)

Anoda lanceolata Hook. & Arn. – Prairie evening-primrose [Prairie evening primrose] (5, 131) (1899–1913), Wright's anoda [Wrights anoda] (155) (1942)

Anoda wrighti – See *Anoda lanceolata* Hook. & Arn.

Anogra albicaulis (Pursh) Britton – See *Oenothera albicaulis* Pursh

Anogra coronopifolia (Torr. & Gray) Britton – See *Oenothera coronopifolia* Torr. & Gray

Annona reticulata L. – Bullock-heart custard apple [Bullockheart custardapple] (155) (1942), Bullock's-heart [Bullocks-heart] (109, 110) (1886–1949), Custard-apple [Custardapple, Custard apple] (America) (41, 110) (1770–1886), Guanabana (109, 155) (1942–1949), Papaw [Pawpaw, Paw-paw] or Papaw tree [Papaw-tree, Pappaw tree] (41, 177) (1750–1770), Rough-fruit custard-apple [Rough-fruited custard apple] (165) (1807), Rough-fruit soursop [Rough-fruited sour sop] (165) (1807), Soorstak (177) (1762), Soursop [Sour sop] (92, 109, 110, 137) (1876–1949), Zuursak (177) (1762) Custard apple] (West Indies) (110, 138) (1886–1923), Netted custard-apple [Netted custard apple] (165) (1807)

Annona pygmaea Bart. – possibly *Asimina parviflora* (Michx.) Dunal

Annona squamosa L. – Ahate di Panucho (Mexico) (110) (1886), Assimnier à trois lobes (French) (8) (1785), Atamaran (165) (1678), Ate (Mexico) (110) (1886), Attoa (110) (1886), Custard-apple [Custardapple, Custard apple] (British India) (110, 155) (1886–1942), Sugar-apple [Sugarapple (109, 110, 137, 155) (1886–1949), Sweet-sop [Sweet sop] (92, 109, 110, 155) (1876–1949), Undulated custard-apple [Undulated custard apple] (165) (1807), Undulated soursop [Undulated sour sop] (165) (1807)

Annona triloba L. – See *Asimina triloba* (L.) Dunal

Anoda acerifolia auct. non (Zucc. ex Roemer & J.A. Schultes) Dcne. – See *Anoda cristata* (L.) Schltdl.

Anogra perplexa Rydb. – See *Oenothera albicaulis* Pursh

Anogra Spach. – See *Oenothera* L.

Anona cherimola Lam. – possibly *Annona cherimola* Mill.

Anona muricatus – See *Annona muricata* L.

Anona palustris – See *Annona glabra* L.

Anona squamosa L. – See *Annona squamosa* L.

Anonymos frutescens Walt. – possibly *Wisteria frutescens* (L.) Poir.

Anonymos sempervirens Walt. – See *Gelsemium sempervirens* (L.) J. St.-Hil.

Anoplanthus Endl. – See *Orobanche* L. all US species

Anredera cordifolia (Ten.) Steenis – Madeira vine [Madeira-vine] (109) (1949), Mignonette vine [Mignonette-vine] (109) (1949)

Anredera vesicaria (Lam.) C.F.Gaertn. – Texas Madiera vine (122) (1937) TX

Antennaria alpina (L.) Gaertn. – Alpine everlasting (5) (1913), Alpine pussytoes (155) (1942)

Antennaria ampla Bush – See *Antennaria parlinii* Fern. subsp. *fallax* (Greene) Bayer & Stebbins

Antennaria anaphaloides Rydb. – Anaphalis pussy-toes (3, 4) (1977–1986), Pearly pussy-toes [Pearly pussytoes] (50) (present)

Antennaria angustiarum Lunell – See *Antennaria neglecta* Greene

Antennaria aprica Greene – See *Antennaria parviflora* Nutt.

Antennaria calophylla Greene – See *Antennaria parlinii* Fern. subsp. *fallax* (Greene) Bayer & Stebbins

Antennaria campestris Rydb. – See *Antennaria neglecta* Greene

Antennaria campestris Rydb. var. *athabascensis* (Greene) Boivin – See *Antennaria neglecta* Greene

Antennaria canadensis Greene – See *Antennaria howellii* Greene subsp. *canadensis* (Greene) Bayer

Antennaria caroliniana Rydb. – See *Antennaria plantaginifolia* (L.) Richards

Antennaria decipiens Greene – See *Antennaria plantaginifolia* (L.) Richards

Antennaria denikeana Boivin – See *Antennaria plantaginifolia* (L.) Richards

Antennaria dimorpha (Nutt.) Torr. & Gray – Cat's-foot [Cats foot, Cat's foot, Cat foot] (46) (1879), Low everlasting (5, 93) (1913–1936), Low pussytoes (50, 155) (1942–present)

Antennaria dioica (L.) Gaertn. – Cat's-foot [Cats foot, Cat's foot, Cat foot] (46) (1879), Common everlasting (156) (1923), Common pussytoes (138, 155) (1931–1942), Hasenpfatlin (German) (46) (1879), Meussorlin (German) (46) (1879), Moor-everlasting [Moor everlasting] (156) (1923), Mountain cudweed [Mountain cud-weed, Mountain cudweede] (156, 178) (1526–1923), Mountain everlasting (131) (1899) SD, Plantain-leaf everlasting [Plantain leaf everlasting, Plantain-leaved everlasting] (156) (1923), White plantain (17, 18) (1796–1805)

Antennaria Gaertner – Cat's-paw [Cat's paws, Cat's-paws] (1, 50, 98) (present), Everlasting (1, 2, 4, 109, 127, 158) (1895–1986), Indian tobacco [Indian-tobacco] (93) (1936) Neb, Lady's-tobacco [Ladies' tobacco] (1) (1932), Pussy's-toes [Pussies' toes, Pussy's toes, Pussy-toes, Pussy-toes] (1, 50, 93, 109, 127, 138, 155) (1923–present)

Antennaria howellii Greene – Howell's pussytoes (50) (present)

Antennaria howellii Greene subsp. *canadensis* (Greene) Bayer – Canadian cat's-foot [Canadian cat's foot] (5) (1913), Canadian pussytoes (155) (1942), Cat's-foot [Cats foot, Cat's foot, Cat foot] (156) (1923)

Antennaria howellii Greene subsp. *neodioica* (Greene) Bayer – Smaller cats-foot [Smaller cat's foot] (5, 131) (1899–1913), Smaller pussy-toes [Smaller pussytoes] (155) (1942), Northern pussy-toes (4) (1986) Rattlesnakes' plantain] (7, 85, 92,) (1828–1932), possibly Scinjachu (some Indians) (7) (1828), (possibly) – Squirrel's-ear [Squirrel ear] (7) (1828)

Antennaria lanata (Hook.) Greene – Woolly pussytoes (155) (1942)

Antennaria latisquamea Greene – See *Antennaria parviflora* Nutt.

Antennaria longifolia Greene – See *Antennaria neglecta* Greene

Antennaria lunellii Greene – See *Antennaria neglecta* Greene

Antennaria luzuloides Torr. & Gray – Rush pussytoes (155) (1942)

Antennaria margaritacea Hook. – See *Anaphalis margaritacea* (L.) Benth. & Hook)

Antennaria alpina (L.) Gaertn. – Alpine everlasting (5) (1913), Alpine pussytoes (155) (1942)

Antennaria ampla Bush – See *Antennaria parlinii* Fern. subsp. *fallax* (Greene) Bayer & Stebbins

Antennaria anaphaloides Rydb. – Anaphalis pussy-toes (3, 4) (1977–1986), Pearly pussy-toes [Pearly pussytoes] (50) (present)

Antennaria angustiarum Lunell – See *Antennaria neglecta* Greene

Antennaria aprica Greene – See *Antennaria parviflora* Nutt.

Antennaria calophylla Greene – See *Antennaria parlinii* Fern. subsp. *fallax* (Greene) Bayer & Stebbins

Antennaria campestris Rydb. – See *Antennaria neglecta* Greene

Antennaria campestris Rydb. var. *athabascensis* (Greene) Boivin – See *Antennaria neglecta* Greene

Antennaria canadensis Greene – See *Antennaria howellii* Greene subsp. *canadensis* (Greene) Bayer

Antennaria microphylla Rydb. – Little-leaf pussytoes [Littleleaf pussytoes] (50, 155) (1942–present), Pink pussy-toes (4) (1986), Small-leaf cat's-foot [Small-leaved cat's foot] (5, 93) (1913–1936)

Antennaria nebraskensis Greene – See *Antennaria neglecta* Greene

Antennaria neglecta Greene – Canadian cat's-foot [Canadian cat's foot] (5) (1913), Early everlasting (5) (1913), Field pussytoes (3, 4, 50, 155) (1942–present), Field's cat's-foot [Field's cat's foot] (5) (1913), Prairie cat's-foot [Prairie cat's foot, Prairie cats-foot] (97, 131) (1899–1937), Prairie cat's-paw [Prairie cat's paw] (65) (1931), Pussy's-toes [Pussies' toes, Pussy's toes, Pussytoes, Pussy-toes] (85) (1932), Rush pussytoes (155) (1942)

Antennaria nemoralis Greene – See *Antennaria plantaginifolia* (L.) Richards

Antennaria neodioica Greene – See *Antennaria howellii* Greene subsp. *neodioica* (Greene) Bayer

Antennaria parlinii Fern. – Parlin's pussy-toes [Parlin's pussytoes] (50) (present)

Antennaria parlinii Fern. subsp. *fallax* (Greene) Bayer & Stebbins – Anaphalis pussy-toes (3, 4) (1977–1986), Cat's-foot [Cats foot, Cat's foot, Cat foot] (127) (1933), Parlin's cat's-foot [Parlin's cat's foot] (5) (1913), Prairie cat's-foot [Prairie cat's foot, Prairie cats-foot] (5, 72, 93) (1907–1936)

Antennaria parlinii Fern. var. *farwellii* (Greene) Boivin – See *Antennaria parlinii* Fern. subsp. *fallax* (Greene) Bayer & Stebbins

Antennaria parviflora Nutt. – Cudweed [Cud-weed, Cud weed] (157) (1929), Lion's-foot [Lion's foot, Lions' foot, Lyons fote] (157) (1929), Pussy's-toes [Pussies' toes, Pussy's toes, Pussytoes, Pussy-toes] (3, 4, 97) (1937–1986), Rocky Mountain cudweed [Rocky Mountain cud-weed, Rocky Mountain cud weed] (5, 93) (1913–1936), Rocky Mountain pussytoes (155) (1942), Rose pussytoes (155) (1942), Small-leaf pussy-toes [Small-leaf pussytoes] (50) (present)

Antennaria petiolata Fern. – See *Antennaria plantaginifolia* (L.) Richards

Antennaria pinetorum Greene – See *Antennaria plantaginifolia* (L.) Richards

Antennaria plantagineum – See *Antennaria plantaginifolia* (L.) Richards

Antennaria plantaginifolia (L.) Richards – Cat's-ear [Cat's ear, Cats-ear] (156) (1923), Cat's-foot [Cats foot, Cat's foot, Cat foot] (156) (1923), Cat's-paw [Cat's paws, Cat's-paws] (156) (1923), Cotton-weed [Cotton-weed, Cotton weed] (156) (1923), Cudweed [Cud-weed, Cud weed] (92) (1876), Dog's-toes [Dog toes, Dog-toes, Dog's toes] (5, 73, 75, 76, 156, 158) (1892–1923), Dwarf pussy-toes (3, 4) (1977–1986), Early everlasting (5, 156, 158) (1900–1923), Four-toes [Four toes] (5, 76, 156, 158) (1896–1923) Salem MA, Indian tobacco [Indian-tobacco] (5, 62, 73, 156, 158) (1892–1923), Lady's chewing-tobacco [Ladies chewing tobacco] (73) (1892) WI, Lady's-tobacco [Ladies' tobacco] (5, 156, 158) (1900–1923), Love's-test [Love's test] (5, 76, 156, 158) (1896–1923) IN, game played with leaves supposed to determine strength of love, no longer in use by 1923, Mouse-ear [Mouse ear, Mouse ears, Mouse's ear, Mows eare] (62, 76, 92) (1876–1912), Mouse-ear everlasting (86, 158) (1878–1900), Mouse-ear plantain (156) (1923), Parlin's pussy-toes [Parlin's pussytoes] (155) (1942), Pearly mouse-ear everlasting (5, 156) (1913–1923), Pearly-everlasting [Pearly everlasting] (76, 158) (1896–1900) Salem MA, 1923) Hingham MA, Pincushion [Pincushions, Pin-cushion, Pin cushions] (75, 156, 158) (1894–1923), Plain-leaf pussytoes [Plainleaf pussytoes] (3, 4) (1977–1986),

Plaintain-leaf everlasting (5, 62, 72) (1907–1913), White plantain (17, 18)(1796–1805)

Antennaria plantaginifolia **Hook.** – See *Antennaria plantaginifolia* (L.) Richards.

Antennaria pulcherrima (**Hook.**) **Green** – Showy pussytoes (155) (1942)

Antennaria racemosa **Hook.** – Raceme pussytoes (155) (1942)

Antennaria rhodanthus **Suksdorf** – See *Antennaria parviflora* Nutt.

Antennaria rosea **Greene** – See *Antennaria microphylla* Rydb.

Antennaria solitaria **Rydb.** – Single-head cat's-foot [Single-headed cat's foot] (5) (1913)

Antennaria wilsonii **Greene** – See *Antennaria neglecta* Greene

Antenoron virginianum (**L.**) **Roberty & Vautier** – See *Polygonum virginianum* L.

Anthaenantia **Beauv.** – Silky-scale [Silkyscale] (155) (1942)

Anthaenantia rufa (**Nutt.**) **J.A. Schultes** – Red-hair anthenantia [Red-haired anthenantia] (94) (1901)

Anthemis (**Michx.**) **L.** – See *Anthemis* L.

Anthemis altissima **L.** – Chamomile Romaine (French) (6) (1892), Tall camomile (155, 165) (1807–1942)

Anthemis arvensis **L.** – Corn camomile [Corn chamomile] (3, 4, 5, 19, 50, 63, 92, 156, 158, 165) (1807–present), Corn feverfew (6) (1892), Corn-field camomile [Cornfield camomile] (155) (1942), Field camomile (5, 72, 155, 156, 158) (1900–1942), Garden camomile [Garden chamomile] (6) (1892), Römische Kamillen (German) (6) (1892), True camomile [True chamomile] (6) (1892)

Anthemis arvensis **L. var.** *agrestis* (**Wallr.**) **DC.** – See *Anthemis arvensis* L.

Anthemis arvensis **Pursh** – See *Anthemis cotula* L.

Anthemis cotula **L.** – Bakerblom (186) (1814), Balderbrae (158) (1900), Balderbraw (157) (1929), Balders (5, 76, 156, 157, 158) (1896–1929), Baldersbraa (186) (1814), Bald-eyebrow [Bald-eyebrow] (157, 158) (1900–1929), Ballensbro (186) (1814), Büdöskey ar (186) (1814), Camomile [Chamomile, Camomylle] (138, 155, 158, 167) (1814–1942), Camomile puante (French) (7, 186) (1814–1828), Camomilla fetida (Italian) (186) (1814), Chiggerweed [Chigger-weed, Chigger weed] (5, 76, 156, 157, 158) (1896–1929) said to harbor chigger mites, Common dog-fennel [Common dog fennel] (62) (1912), Common mayweed (38) (1820), Cotula (7, 57) (1828–1917), Cotula bastarda (Portuguese) (186) (1814), Cotula fetida (Spanish, Italian) (186) (1814), Dillweed [Dilweed] (5, 7, 156, 157, 158) (1828–1929), Dilly (7) (1828), Dillydilweed [Dillidillweed] (92, 157, 158) (1876–1929), Dog camomile [Dog-chamomile, Dog's camomile] (5, 49, 93, 156, 157, 158) (1898–1936), Dog camovyne [Dog's camovyne] (157, 158) (1900–1929), Dog daisy [Dog-daisy] (5, 156, 157, 158) (1900–1929), Dog-banner (157, 158) (1900–1929), Dog-binder (157, 158) (1900–1929), Dog-fennel [Dog fennel, Dog's fennel, Dog's fennel] (3, 4, 5, 7, 49, 58, 62, 63, 72, 73, 80, 85, 92, 122, 145, 156, 157, 158, 186, 187) (1814–1986), Dog-finkle [Dog finkle] (5, 157, 158) (1900–1929), Eb kapor (Hungarian) (186) (1814), Fetid camomile (5, 93, 95, 97, 157, 158) (1900–1937), Fetid mayweed [Fetid may-weed] (157, 158) (1900–1929), Fieldweed [Field weed] (7, 92) (1828–1876), Fieldwort [Field wort] (92, 157, 158) (1876–1929), Flowan (157, 158) (1900–1929), Gaasedild (186) (1814), Gassedill (Norwegian) (186) (1814), Gasseguld (Norwegian) (186) (1814), Heilege dille (German) (186) (1814), Hog-fennel [Hog fennel, Hogfennel, Hog's fennel] (5, 156, 157, 158) (1900–1929), Horse daisy [Horse-daisy] (157, 158) (1900–1929), Hundekameelblomst (Danish) (186) (1814), Hundeurt (Danish) (186) (1814), Hundkamiller (Swedish) (186) (1814), Hundsbloom (German) (186) (1814), Hundsdill (German) (186) (1814), Hundskamille (German) (186) (1814), Hundsromey (German) (186) (1814), Hviteteja (186) (1814), Ironwort [Iron-wort, Ironwort] (46) (1671) accidentally introduced by 1671, Jayweed [Jay-weed] (157, 158) (1900–1929), Kanna perse hein (Estonian) (186) (1814), Kannapersed (Estonian) (186) (1814), Koedild (186) (1814), Krötendill (German) (186) (1814), Kuhdill (186) (1814), Llygad yr ych

(186) (1814), Macella fetida (Portuguese) (186) (1814), Madder (157, 158) (1900–1929), Madenweed [Maydenwede, Maden-weed] (157, 158, 179) (1526–1929), Maise (5, 156, 157, 158) (1900–1929), Maithen [Maythen] (165, 179, 186) (1633–1814), Maithes (165) (1807), Manzanilla fetida (Spanish) (187) (1818), Marg (157, 158) (1900–1929), Maroutte (French) (186) (1814), Mather (5, 156, 165) (1807–1923) no longer in use by 1923, Mathes (157, 158) (1900–1929), Mayflower [May flower, May-flower] (186) (1814), Mayweed [May-weed, May weed] (5, 7, 10, 19, 42, 46, 47, 49, 57, 58, 62, 63, 72, 80, 82, 92, 93, 106, 122, 131, 156, 157, 158, 186, 187) (1671–1937) accidentally introduced by 1671, Mayweed camomile (155) (1942), Maywort [May wort] (92) (1876), Middle consoulde [Myddle consoulde] (179) (1526), Morgan (5, 156, 157, 158) (1900–1929), Murg (158) (1900), Oil de vache (French) (186) (1814), Paddebloem (Dutch) (186) (1814), Pathweed [Path-weed] (156) (1923), Pigsty-daisy [Pig-sty-daisy, Pig-sty daisy] (5, 73, 156, 157, 158) (1892–1929) Ipswich MA, Pissweed (7) (1828), Poison daisy (157, 158) (1900–1929), Psi rumien (Polish) (186) (1814), Psy rmen (Bohemian) (186) (1814), Rumieniec smierdzacy (Polish) (186) (1814), Siurguld (Norwegian) (186) (1814), Solutucha trava (Russian) (186) (1814), Stinkende Kamille (Dutch, German) (7, 186) (1814–1828), Stinking camomile [Stinking chamomile] (50, 75, 92, 156, 157, 158, 165) (1807–present), Stinking mayweed (165) (1807), Stinkkamillen (German) (158, 186) (1814–1900), Streichblume (German) (186) (1814), Surkullor (Swedish) (186) (1814), Surtuppor (186) (1814), Wild camomile [Wild cammomile, Wild chamomile, Wild camomille] (7, 49, 57, 58, 92, 186) (1814–1917)

Anthemis **L.** – Camomile [Chamomile, Camomylle] (4, 10, 50, 156, 184) (1793–present), Corn camomile [Corn chamomile] (1) (1932), Dog camomile [Dog-chamomile, Dog's camomile] (1) (1932), Dog-fennel [Dog fennel, Dog's fennel, Dog's fennel] (1, 4, 93) (1932–1986), Ground-apple [Ground apple] (92) (1876), Mayweed [May-weed, May weed] (1, 10, 61, 93, 167) (1814–1936), Wild camomile [Wild cammomile, Wild chamomile, Wild camomille] (190) (~1759), Yellow camomile [Yellow chamomile] (1) (1932)

Anthemis nobilis **L.** – See *Chamaemelum nobile* (L.) All.

Anthemis repens **Walt.** – See *Acmella oppositifolia* (Lam.) R.K. Jansen var. *repens* (Walt.) R.K. Jansen

Anthemis tinctoria **L.** – Dill [Dyll] (46, 57, 103) (1671–1917), Golden camomile [Golden chamomile] (50) (present), Golden marguerite (109, 156) (1923–1949), Ox-eye camomile [Ox-eye chamomile] (5, 156) (1913–1923), Yellow camomile [Yellow chamomile] (3, 4, 5, 138, 156) (1913–1986)

Anthemum graveolens **L.** – possibly *Anethum graveolens* L.

Anthenantia rufa (**Ell..**) **Schultes** – See *Anthaenantia rufa* (Nutt.) J.A. Schultes

Anthericum **L.** – See Echeandia Ortega Greek "flower hedge" (109)

Anthericum torreyi – See *Echeandia flavescens* (J.A. & J.H. Schultes) Cruden

Anthoceros beltrani **Casares-Gil** – See *Phaeoceros laevis* (L.) Prosk.

Anthoceros curnowii **Steph.** – See *Phaeoceros laevis* (L.) Prosk.

Anthoceros dichotomus **Raddi var.** *gussonei* **Zodda** – See *Phaeoceros laevis* (L.) Prosk.

Anthoceros donnellii **Austin** – See *Phaeoceros laevis* (L.) Prosk.

Anthoceros laevis – See *Phaeoceros laevis* (L.) Prosk.

Anthoceros major **Smith** – See *Phaeoceros laevis* (L.) Prosk.

Anthoceros miyakeanus **Schiffn.** – See *Phaeoceros laevis* (L.) Prosk.

Anthoceros polymorphus **Raddi var.** *laevis* (**L.**) **Hampe** – See *Phaeoceros laevis* (L.) Prosk.

Anthoceros punctatus **L. var.** *laevis* (**L.**) **Hook. & Taylor ex Lindenb.** – See *Phaeoceros laevis* (L.) Prosk.

Anthoceros punctatus **L. var.** *major* (**Smith**) **Hook. & Wilson** – See *Phaeoceros laevis* (L.) Prosk.

Antholyza aethiopica – See *Chasmanthe aethiopica* (L.) N.E. Br.

Anthopogon **Necker.** – See *Gymnopogon* P. Beauv.

Anthopogon odoratum **L.** – possibly *Anthoxanthum odoratum* L.

Anthospermom (sic) – See *Acanthospermum* Schrank

Anthoxanthemum odoratum – possibly *Anthoxanthum odoratum* L.

Anthoxanthum arcticum **Veldkamp** – See *Hierochloe pauciflora* R. Br.

Anthoxanthum aristatum **Boiss.** – Annual sweet vernal grass (163) (1852), Annual vernal grass (50, 56) (1901–present), Long-awn vernal grass [Long-awned vernal grass] (5) (1913)

Anthoxanthum **L.** – Poverty grass [Poverty-grass, Povertygrass] (1) (1932), Spring grass [Spring-grass] (92, 184) (1793–1876), Sweet vernal grass [Sweet vernal-grass] (1) (1932), Sweet-scented vernal grass [Sweet-scented vernal-grass] (10, 45, 66) (1818–1912), Vernal grass [Vernalgrass, Vernal-grass] (155, 158) (1900–1942)

Anthoxanthum nitens **(Weber) Y. Schouten & Veldkamp** – See *Hierochloe odorata* (L.) Beauv.

Anthoxanthum odoratum **L.** – Prim grass (5) (1913), Spring grass [Spring-grass] (5) (1913), Sweet anthox (187) (1818), Sweet grass [Sweet-grass, Sweetgrass] (5, 7) (1828–1913), Sweet vernal (118) (1898), Sweet vernal grass [Sweet vernal-grass] (19, 45, 46, 50, 56, 67, 68, 87, 88, 90, 92, 94, 109, 111, 122, 129, 143, 163) (1840–present), Sweet-scented vernal grass [Sweet-scented vernal-grass] (90, 187) (1818–1885), Vernal grass [Vernalgrass, Vernal-grass] (92) (1876)

Anthoxanthum odoratum **L. var.** *puelii* **(Lecoq & Lamotte) Coss. & Durieu** – See *Anthoxanthum aristatum* Boiss.

Anthoxanthum puelii **Lecoq & Lamotte** – See *Anthoxanthum aristatum* Boiss.

Anthoxantum giganteum **Walt.** – See *Saccharum giganteum* (Walt.) Pers.

Anthriscus cerefolium **(L.) Hoffmann** – Beaked parsley (5) (1913), Chervil [Cheruell] (7, 110, 138, 156) (1828–1923), Garden chervil (5, 156) (1913–1923), Salad chervil [Saladchervil (109, 155) (1942–1949)

Anthriscus cerefolium **Hoffm.** – See *Anthriscus cerefolium* (L.) Hoffmann

Anthriscus **Hoffm.** – possibly *Anthriscus* Pers.

Anthriscus **Pers.** – Beakchervil (155) (1942), Chervil [Cheruell] (92, 179) (1526–1876)

Anthriscus sylvestris **(L.) Hoffmann** – Bur beakchervil (155) (1942), Wild chervil (92) (1876), Woodland beak-chervil [Woodland beakchervil] (155) (1942)

Anthriscus vulgaris – See *Torilis japonica* (Houtt.) DC.

Anthurium **Schott** – Anthurium (138, 155) (1923–1942)

Anthyllis **L.** – Anthyllis (155) (1942)

Anthyllis **L.** – Kidney-bean vetch [Kidney bean vetch] (92) (1876)

Anthyllis vulneraria **L.** – China-laurel [Chinalaurel] (155) (1942), Kidney vetch (3, 5, 68, 109) (1913–1977), Kidney-bean vetch [Kidney bean vetch] (92) (1876), Kidney-vetch anthyllis [Kidneyvetch anthyllis] (155) (1942), Lady's-fingers [Lady's fingers, Ladies'-fingers, Ladies' fingers] (5, 92) (1876–1913), Lamb's-toes [Lambs' toes] (92) (1876), Staunchwort (92) (1876), Woundwort [Wound-wort] (7, 92, 109, 155) (1828–1949)

Anticlea chlorantha **(Richardson) Rydb.** – See *Zigadenus elegans* Pursh subsp. *glaucus* (Nutt.) Hultén

Anticlea elegans **(Pursh) Rydb.** – See *Zigadenus elegans* Pursh subsp. *elegans*

Anticlea **Kunth.** – White camas [White camass] (1) (1932)

Antidesma **L.** – China-laurel [Chinalaurel] (155) (1942)

Antigonon **Endl.** – Coral vine [Coral-vine, Coralvine] (106, 155) (1930–1942)

Antigonon leptopus alba – See *Antigonon leptopus* Hook. & Arn.

Antigonon leptopus **Hook. & Arn.** – Confederate vine [Confederate-vine] (109) (1949), Coral vine [Coral-vine, Coralvine] (106, 109) (1930–1949), Corallita (106, 109) (1930–1949), Mountain-rose coralvine [Mountainrose coralvine] (155) (1942), Pink-vine (106, 109) (1930–1949), Rosa-de-montana (109, 138) (1923–1949), San Miguelito (106) (1930), White mountain-rose coralvine [White mountainrose coralvine] (155) (1942)

Antiphylla **Haw.** – See *Saxifraga* L.

Antiphylla oppositifolia **(L.) Fourr.** – See *Saxifraga oppositifolia* L. subsp. *oppositifolia*

Antirhinnum linaria **L.** – See *Linaria vulgaris* Mill.

Antirrhinum canadense – See *Nuttallanthus canadensis* (L.) D.A. Sutton

Antirrhinum coulterianum – See *Sairocarpus coulterianus* (Benth. ex A. DC.) D. A. Sutton

Antirrhinum coulterianum **subsp.** *orcuttianum* **(A. Gray) Pennell** – See *Sairocarpus coulterianus* (Benth. ex A. DC.) D.A. Sutton

Sairocarpus coulterianus **(Benth. ex A. DC.) D. A. Sutton** – Corn snapdragon (5, 155) (1913–1942), Orcutt's snapdragon [Orcutt snapdragon] (155) (1942)

Antirrhinum elatine **W.** – See *Knautia arvensis* (L.) Duby

Antirrhinum glandulosum **[Lej.]** – See *Linaria vulgaris* Mill.

Antirrhinum **L.** – Snapdragon [Snap dragon, Snap-dragon] (10, 50, 109, 138, 155, 156, 158) (1818–present), Toadflax [Toad flax, Toadflax] (10) (1818)

Antirrhinum majus **L.** – Bonny-rabbits [Bonny rabbits] (5) (1913), Bulldogs [Bull-dogs, Bull-dog] (5, 92, 156, 158) (1898–1923), Bunny-mouth (158) (1900), Bunny-rabbit [Bunny rabbits] (156, 158) (1900–1923), Calf's-mouth [Calf's mouth] (156) (1923), Calf-snout [Calf snout] (5, 158) (1900–1913), Catchfly [Catch fly] (158) (1900), Common snapdragon (109, 138, 155) (1923–1949), Dog's-mouth [Dogs' mouth, Dog's mouth] (5, 92, 156, 158) (1876–1923), Dragon's-mouth [Dragon's mouth] (5, 156, 158) (1900–1923), Garden snapdragon (50) (present), Great snapdragon (5, 158) (1900), Grosses Löwenmaul (German) (158) (1900), Guele de lion (French) (158) (1900), Guele de loup (French) (158) (1900), Large snapdragon (109) (1949), Lion's-mouth [Lion's mouth, Lion mouth] (5, 73, 156, 158) (1892–1923) Mansfield OH, Lion's-snap [Lion's snap] (5, 92, 156, 158) (1876–1923), Löwenmaul [Lowenmaul] (German) (158) (1900), Muflier (French) (158) (1900), Nuttall's snapdragon [Nuttall snapdragon] (155) (1942), Purple snapdragon (178) (1526), Rabbits (158) (1900), Rabbit's-mouth [Rabbit's mouth, Rabbits' mouth] (5, 92, 156, 158) (1876–1923), Snapdragon [Snap dragon, Snap-dragon] (4, 85, 92, 156, 158) (1876–1986), Tiger's-mouth [Tiger's mouth] (5, 156, 158) (1900–1923), Toad-mount (92) (1876), White snapdragon (178) (1526)

Antirrhinum multiflorum **Pennell** – See *Sairocarpus multiflorus* (Pennell) D. A. Sutton

Antirrhinum nuttallianum – possibly *Sairocarpus coulterianus* (Benth. ex A. DC.) D. A. Sutton

Antirrhinum orontium **L.** – See *Misopates orontium* (L.) Raf.

Antirrhinum speciosum **(Nutt.) Gray** – Gambel's snapdragon [Gambel's snap-dragon] (86) (1878) NM

Antirrhinum speciosum **Gray** – See *Antirrhinum speciosum* (Nutt.) Gray

Antirrhinum vulgare **Bubani** – See *Antirrhinum majus* L.

Anychia canadensis **(L.) B.S.P.** – See *Paronychia canadensis* (L.) Wood

Anychia capillacea **DC** – See *Paronychia canadensis* (L.) Wood

Anychia dichotoma **Michx.** – See *Paronychia canadensis* (L.) Wood

Anychia **Michx.** – See *Paronychia* Mill.

Anychia polygonoides **Raf.** – See *Paronychia fastigiata* (Raf.) Fern.

Anychiastrum montanum **Small.** – See *Paronychia montana* (Small) Pax & K. Hoffmann

Apargia autumnale **(L.) Hoffm.** – See *Leontodon autumnalis* L.

Apargia autumnalis **W.** – See *Leontodon autumnalis* L.

Apargia hispida **(L.) Willd.** – See *Leontodon hispidus* L. subsp. *hispidus*

Apargia nudicaulis **(L.) Britton** – See *Leontodon hirtus* L.

Apera spica venti **(L.) Beauv.** – See *Apera spica-venti* (L.) Beauv.

Apera spica-venti **(L.) Beauv.** – Aker-when (Swedish) (46) (1879), Bent grass [Bentgrass, Bent-grass] (19) (1840), Corn grass [Corn-grass, Corngrass] (5) (1913), Dropseed grass [Drop seed grass, Drop-seed grass, Drop-seed-grass] (92) (1876), Hwen (Swedish) (46) (1879), Kiosa (Swedish) (46) (1879), Loose silkybent (50) (present), Silky agrostis (45) (1896), Silky bent grass [Silky bent-grass] (5, 165) (1768–1913), Wind bent (5) (1913), Wind grass (5, 92) (1876–1913), Windlestraw (5) (1913), Wire bent grass (92) (1876)

Aphanes arvensis L. – Apahnostephus (158) (1900), Argentill (5) (1913), Bowel hivegrass (5) (1913), Breakstone (5) (1913), Colicwort (5) (1913), Field lady's-mantle [Field lady's mantle, Field ladysmantle] (5, 155) (1913–1942), Firegrass (5) (1913), Parsley breakstone (5) (1913), Parsley piert (5, 10, 19, 92, 156, 178) (1526–1923), Parsley vlix (5) (1913)

Aphanostephus DC. – Aphanostephus (158) (1900), Dozedaisy (50) (present), Lazy-daisy [Lazy daisy] (4) (1986), Poorland daisy [Poorland daisy] (122) (1937) TX, White-daisy [White daisy] (122) (1937) TX

Aphanostephus humilis (Benth.) Gray – See *Aphanostephus ramosissimus* DC.

Aphanostephus pilosus Buckl. – Lazy-daisy [Lazy daisy] (3) (1977)

Aphanostephus ramosissimus DC. – Hairy dozedaisy (50) (present), Lazy-daisy [Lazy daisy] (3) (1977), Plains dozedaisy (50) (present), Purplish-flower sand-daisy [Purplish-flowered sand-daisy] (97) (1937), Ridell's dozedaisy (50) (present), Sand-daisy (97) (1937) OK

Aphanostephus riddellii Torr. & Gray – Ridell's dozedaisy (50) (present)

Aphanostephus skirrobasis (DC.) Trelease – Aphanostephus (5, 97) (1913–1937), Arkansas doze-daisy [Arkansas dozedaisy] (50) (present), Lazy-daisy [Lazy daisy] (3) (1977), White-daisy [White daisy] (122) (1937) TX

Aphyllon fasciculatum Gray – See *Orobanche fasciculata* Nutt.

Aphyllon Mitch. – See *Orobanche* L. all US species

Aphyllon uniflorum (L.) Torr. & Gray – See *Orobanche uniflora* L.

Apinus flexilis (James) Rydb. – See *Pinus flexilis* James

Apinus Necker – See *Pinus* L.

Apios americana Medik. – Blo (Dakota Teton) (37) (1919), Blo (Lakota) (121) (1918?–1970?), Common wild potato (35) (1806), Do (Osage) (121) (1918?–1970?), Ground pea [Ground-pea, Ground peas] (38, 74, 156) (1820–1923) Northeastern US, Ground-apple [Ground apple] (35) (1806), Groundnut [Ground-nut, Ground nut, Ground nutts] (2, 3, 4, 5, 46, 50, 72, 85, 93, 97, 103, 107, 109, 114, 121, 131, 156) (1870–present), Hanke (Oregon tribes) (7) (1828), Himbaringa (38) (1820), Hopniss (Delaware) (7, 46) (1828–1879), Indian potato (7, 92, 121, 156) (1828–1970), Its (Pawnee) (37) (1919), Mdo (Dakota) (37) (1919), Modo (Sioux) (103) (1870), Nido (Sioux) (47) (1852), Noa (Missouri tribes) (7) (1828), Nu (Omaha-Ponca) (37) (1919), Openawk (46) (1879), Pea vine [Peavine, Peavine] (34, 38) (1820–1834), Pig-potato [Pig potato] (76, 156) (1896–1923) Western US, Pin (Chippewa, tuber) (105) (1932), Pomme de terre [Pommes de terre] (French) (27, 35, 47, 103) (1806–1870), Potato-bean [Potatobean, Potato bean] (109, 138, 156) (1923–1949), Potato-pea [Potato pea] (7, 92, 156) (1828–1923), Rabbit vine [Rabbit-vine] (156) (1923), Racine des chapelets (French) (105) (1932), Rosary (37) (1919), Tdo (Winnebago) (37) (1919), Trailing-pea [Trailing pea] (156) (1923), Traveler's-delight [Traveller's delight] (73, 156) (1892–1923) New Albany Miss, Tuberous wistaria (156) (1923), Tucaha (Southern tribes) (7) (1828), White-apple [White apple, White apples] (Oregon tribes)] (7, 92, 156) (1828–1923), Wild bean [Wild-bean, Wildbean, Wild beans] (5, 73, 93, 107, 109, 156) (1892–1949), Wild potato [Wild potatoe, Wild potatoes, Wild-potato] (35, 103) (1806–1870), Wild potato vine [Wild potato-vine, Wild potatoe vine, Wild potatoe-vine] (187) (1818), Wild wisteria [Wild-wisteria] (156) (1923), Dakota potato (76) (1896) MN, Håpniss [Hopniss, Hopnis] (Native American, Delaware) (7, 41, 46) (1770–1879)

Apios Fabr. – Groundnut [Ground-nut, Ground nut, Ground nutts] (2, 4, 50, 155) (1895–present), Potato-bean [Potatobean, Potato bean] (155) (1942), Wild bean [Wild-bean, Wildbean, Wild beans] (2) (1895)

Apios Medik. – See *Apios* Fabr.

Apios priceana B. L. Robins. – Price's groundnut [Price's ground nut] (5) (1913)

Apios tuberosa Moench – See *Apios americana* Medik.

Apium divaricatum Benth. & Hook.f. ex S.Wats. – Fool's-parsley [Fool's parsley, Fools' parsley] (19, 92) (1840–1876)

Apium echinatum (Nutt. ex DC.) Benth. & Hook. f. ex S. Wats. – See *Spermolepis echinata* (Nutt. ex DC.) Heller

Apium graveolens L. – Ache (107, 174) (1623–1753), Aipo (Potugual) (107) (1919), Apio (Spain) (107) (1919), Apium (57) (1917), Celeri (French) (107) (1919), Celery [Cellery] (7, 14, 57, 92, 106, 107, 109, 122, 138, 184) (1793–1949), Garden celery (110) (1886), Sedano (Italy) (107) (1919), Seldij (Flanders) (107) (1919), Selinon (110) (1886) in Odyssey, Selleree (German) (107) (1919), Selleri (Denmark) (107) (1919), Sellery (107) (1629), Smallage [Smalache] (46, 92, 107, 179) (1526–1919), Stammarche (179) (1526), Wild celery [Wildcelery] (50, 92, 155) (1876–present)

Apium graveolens L. var. *dulce* Pers. – See *Apium graveolens* L. var. *dulce* (Mill.) DC.

Apium graveolens L. var. *dulce* (Mill.) DC. – Ache parsley (5, 156, 158) (1900–1923), Celery (5, 85, 50, 109, 155) (1913–1949), Cultivated celery (93) (1936), Garden celery (92, 155) (1876–1942), March parsley (5) (1913), Marsh parsley (5) (1913), Mile (5) (1913), Smallage (5) (1913)

Apium L. – Celery (50, 155) (1942–present)

Apium nodiflorum (L.) Lag. – Water-parsnip [Water parsnip, Waterparsnip, Water parsnep, Water-parsnep] (92) (1876)

Apium petroselinum L. – See *Petroselinum crispum* (Mill.) Nyman ex A.W. Hill

Aplectrum hyemale (Muhl. ex Willd.) Torr. – Adam-and-Eve [Adam and Eve] (50, 92, 97, 109, 156, 158) (1876–present), Putty root [Putty-root, Puttyroot] (5, 72, 92, 109, 138, 156, 158) (1876–1949)

Aplectrum Nutt. – Adam-and-Eve [Adam and Eve] (1, 19, 158) (1840–1932), Putty root [Putty-root, Puttyroot] (1, 138, 155) (1923–1942)

Aplectrum spicatum (Walt.) B.S.P. – See *Aplectrum hyemale* (Muhl. ex Willd.) Torr.

Aplocera maritima Raf. – See *Ctenium aromaticum* (Walt.) Wood

Aplopappus acaulis – See *Stenotus acaulis* (Nutt.) Nutt. var. *acaulis*

Aplopappus acradenius – See *Isocoma acradenia* (Greene) Greene var. *acradenia*

Aplopappus arborescens – See *Ericameria arborescens* (Gray) Greene

Aplopappus bloomeri – See *Ericameria bloomeri* (Gray) J.F. Macbr.

Aplopappus brickellioides – See *Hazardia brickellioides* (Blake) W.D. Clark

Aplopappus canus – See *Hazardia cana* (Gray) Greene

Aplopappus Cass. – See *Haplopappus* Cass.

Aplopappus cooperi – See *Ericameria cooperi* (Gray) Hall

Aplopappus cuneatus – See *Ericameria cuneata* (Gray) McClatchie var. *cuneata*

Aplopappus eastwoodae (sic) – See *Ericameria fasciculata* (Eastw.) J.F. Macbr.

Aplopappus ericoides – See *Ericameria ericoides* (Less.) Jepson

Aplopappus falcatus – See *Stenotus acaulis* (Nutt.) Nutt.

Aplopappus fremonti – See *Oonopsis foliosa* (Gray) Greene var. *foliosa*

Aplopappus fruticosus – See *Isocoma tenuisecta* Greene

Aplopappus greenei – See *Ericameria greenei* (Gray) Nesom

Aplopappus integrifolius – See *Pyrrocoma integrifolia* (Porter ex Gray) Greene

Aplopappus junceus – See *Machaeranthera juncea* (Greene) Shinners

Aplopappus lanceolatus – See *Pyrrocoma lanceolata* (Hook.) Greene var. *lanceolata*

Aplopappus laricifolius – See *Ericameria laricifolia* (Gray) Shinners

Aplopappus linearifolius – See *Ericameria linearifolia* (DC.) Urbatsch & Wussow

Aplopappus linearifolius interior – See *Ericameria linearifolia* (DC.) Urbatsch & Wussow

Aplopappus macronema – See *Ericameria discoidea* (Nutt.) Nesom var. *discoidea*

Aplopappus megacephalus (Nash) Hitchc. – See *Rayjacksonia phyllocephala* (DC.) R.L. Hartman & M.L. Lane

Aplopappus nanus – See *Ericameria nana* Nutt.

Aplopappus nuttalli – See *Machaeranthera grindelioides* (Nutt.) Shinners var. *grindelioides*

Aplopappus palmeri – See *Ericameria palmeri* (Gray) Hall var. *palmeri*

Aplopappus parishi – See *Ericameria parishii* (Greene) Hall

Aplopappus pinifolius – See *Ericameria pinifolia* (Gray) Hall

Aplopappus propinquus – See *Ericameria brachylepis* (Gray) Hall

Aplopappus spinulosus (Pursh) DC. – See *Machaeranthera pinnatifida* (Hook.) Shinners subsp. *pinnatifida*

Aplopappus squarrosus – See *Hazardia squarrosa* (Hook. & Arn.) Greene var. *squarrosa*

Aplopappus suffruticossus – See *Ericameria suffruticosa* (Nutt.) G.L. Nesom

Aplopappus uniflorus – See *Pyrrocoma uniflora* (Hook.) Greene var. *uniflora*

Aplopappus venetus – See *Isocoma veneta* (Kunth) Greene

Aplopappus venetus vernonioides – See *Isocoma menziesii* (Hook. & Arn.) Nesom var. *vernonioides* (Nutt.) Nesom

Apocynum (Tourn.) L. – See *Apocynum* L.

Apocynum ×*floribundum Greene* – Intermediate dogbane (5) (1913), Miller's dogbane (5) (1913)

Apocynum album Greene – See *Apocynum cannabinum* L.

Apocynum ambigens Greene – See *Apocynum androsaemifolium* L.

Apocynum androsaemifolium L. – American dogbane (46) (1879), American ipecac (6) (1892), Apocyn Amer. (7) (1828), Apocynum radix (Official name of Materia Medica) (7) (1828), Bitter dogbane [Bitter dog-bane] (7, 92, 156, 157, 158) (1828–1929), Bitter-root [Bitter root, Bitterroot] (6, 7, 92, 101, 109, 148, 156) (1828–1949), Black Indian hemp (6, 58) (1869–1892), Buckbrush [Buck brush, Buck-brush] (156) (1923), Catchfly [Catch fly] (6, 7, 92, 156, 157, 158) (1828–1929), Chickasaw (77) (1898) ME, Clasping-leaf dogbane [Claspingleaf dogbane, Clasping-leaved dogbane] (122) (1937), Cliff dogbane (155) (1942), Colic root [Colic-root, Colicroot] (156, 157, 158) (1900–1929), Common dog's-bane (187) (1818), Dogbane [Dog-bane, Dog bane, Dog's bane, Dogs' bane, Dogsbane] (6, 19, 40, 49, 58, 63, 85, 92, 157, 158) (1840–1932), Fliegen Fangemdes (German) (7) (1828), Flytrap [Fly-trap, Fly trap] (6, 7, 92, 156, 157, 158) (1898–1929), Herbe à la puce (Fr. Can.) (41) (1770), Honey-bloom [Honey bloom] (6, 7, 92, 156, 157, 158) (1828–1929), Houatte (Canada, Louisiana) (7) (1828), Indian hemp [Indianhemp] (49, 101, 157, 158) (1898–1929), Ipecac (7) (1828), Kolicwurzel (German) (158) (1900), Low dogbane (155) (1942), Ma'kwona'gĭc odji'bĭk (Chippewa, bear entrails root) (40) (1928), Milk ipecac (156, 157, 158) (1900–1929), Milkweed [Milk weed [Milk-weed] (6, 7, 106, 156, 157) (1828–1930), Rheumatism-weed [Rheumatism weed] (75, 156, 157, 158) (1894–1929), Sasa'bikwan (Chippewa) (40) (1928), Silk-grass [Silk grass, Silke grass] (181) (~1678), Snake's-milk [Snake's milk, Snake milk, Snakemilk] (7) (1828), Spreading dogbane [Spreading dog-bane, Spreading dog's bane, Spreading dogsbane] (3, 4, 5, 6, 50, 62, 72, 80, 82, 93, 106, 122, 127, 131, 138, 148, 155, 156, 157, 158) (1892–present), Tutsan-leaf dogbane [Tutsan-leaved dogbane] (156) (1923), Wandering milkweed [Wandering milk weed] (6, 58, 92, 156, 157) (1869–1929), Western wallflower [Western wall flower, Western wall-flower] (156, 157, 158) (1900–1929), Wild ipecac (157, 158) (1900–1929), Wildweed (77) (1898) Paris & Harford ME

Apocynum androsaemifolium L. var. *woodsonii* Boivin – See *Apocynum androsaemifolium* L.

Apocynum androsemifolium L. – See *Apocynum androsaemifolium* L.

Apocynum cannabinum L. – American dogbane (46) (1879), American hemp (6, 64, 157, 158) (1892–1929), American Indian-hemp [American Indian hemp] (6, 59) (1892–1900), Amy root [Amy-root] (5, 62, 64, 156, 157, 158) (1900–1929), Apocynum (52, 54, 57, 59) (1905–1917), Bitter dogbane [Bitter dog-bane] (158) (1900), Bitter-root [Bitter root, Bitterroot] (49, 53, 54, 64, 156, 157, 158) (1900–1929),

Black Indian hemp (64, 92, 157, 158) (1876–1929), Bowman's root [Bowman's-root, Bowman root, Bowmanroot] (64, 158) (1900–1907), Canadian hemp [Canada hemp] (6, 14, 49, 52, 53, 54, 55, 57, 64, 106, 156, 157, 158) (1882–1930), Canadische Hanf (German) (6) (1892), Canadischer Hanf (German) (158) (1900), Chanure (46) (1879), Chanvre du Canada (French) (6, 158) (1892–1900), Choctaw root [Choctaw-root] (64, 106, 156) (1900–1923), Clasping-leaf dogbane [Claspingleaf dogbane, Clasping-leaved dogbane] (5, 72, 93, 97, 157, 158) (1900–1937), Common Indian hemp (2) (1895), Dogbane [Dog-bane, Dog bane, Dog's bane, Dogs' bane, Dogsbane] (6, 41, 105, 124, 125, 127, 148, 157) (1770–1933), Enequen (46) (1879), General Marion's weed (6) (1892), Hemp dogbane (3, 122, 138, 155, 156) (1923–1977), Houatte (Canada) (6) (1892), Hundskohl (German) (158) (1900), Hypericum-leaf dog's-bane [Hypericum leaved dog's bane] (42) (1814), Indian hemp [Indianhemp] (5, 19, 41, 46, 49, 50, 53, 54, 58, 61, 62, 63, 72, 80, 82, 85, 93, 97, 105, 106, 114, 125, 127, 131, 145, 148, 156, 157, 158, 177, 187, 189) (1762–present), Indian hemp dogbane (4) (1986), Indian physic [Indian-physic, Indianphysic, Indian physick] (64, 92, 156) (1898–1923), Indianischer Hanf (German) (158) (1900), Low dogbane (155) (1942), Milkweed [Milk weed [Milk-weed] (64, 156, 158) (1900–1923), Old Amy root (6) (1892), Prairie dogbane (3, 4, 155) (1942–1986), Rheumatism root [Rheumatism-root] (5, 64, 156, 157) (1900–1929), Rheumatism-weed [Rheumatism weed] (158) (1900), Sasáp-kwanins (Chippewa) (105) (1932), Silkgrass (35) (1806), Silk-grass [Silk grass, Silke grass] (35) (1806), Small-leaf milkweed [Small-leaved milkweed] (62) (1912), Snake's-milk [Snake's milk, Snake milk, Snakemilk] (6) (1892), St. John's dogs-bane [Saint John's-dogsbane] (5, 19, 92, 157, 158) (1840–1929), St.-John's-wort-leaf dogbane [St.-John's-wort-leaved dog's-bane] (187) (1818), Velvet dogbane (5, 64, 72, 97) (1907–1937), White Indian hemp (58) (1869), Wild cotton [Wild-cotton] (5, 64, 156, 157, 158) (1900–1929), Wilskt hampa (Swedish, wild hemp) (41) (1770), Riverbank dogbane (64) (1907)

Apocynum cordigerum Greene – See *Apocynum cannabinum* L.

Apocynum hypericifolium Aiton – See *Apocynum cannabinum* L.

Apocynum L. – Dogbane [Dog-bane, Dog bane, Dog's bane, Dogs' bane, Dogsbane] (2, 4, 50, 40, 93, 138, 155, 156, 158, 184, 190) (~1759–present), Indian hemp [Indianhemp] (2, 10, 93, 190) (~1759–1936)

Apocynum medium Greene – See *Apocynum* ×*floribundum* Greene

Apocynum medium Greene var. *vestitum* (Greene) Woods. – See *Apocynum* ×*floribundum* Greene

Apocynum milleri Britton – See *Apocynum* ×*floribundum* Greene

Apocynum pubescens Mitchell ex R. Br. – See *Apocynum cannabinum* L.

Apocynum pubescens R. Br. – See *Apocynum cannabinum* L.

Apocynum pumilum (Gray) Greene – See *Apocynum androsaemifolium* L.

Apocynum pumilum (Gray) Greene var. *rhomboideum* (Greene) Bég. & Bel. – See *Apocynum androsaemifolium* L.

Apocynum scopulorum Greene ex Rydb. – See *Apocynum androsaemifolium* L.

Apocynum sibiricum Jacq. – See *Apocynum cannabinum* L.

Apodanthera undulata Gray – Melon loco (149) (1904) NM

Apodanthera undulta (sic) – See *Apodanthera undulata* Gray

Aponogeton distachyos L. f. – Cape pond-weed [Cape-pondweed] (109, 138) (1923–1949), Cape water-hawthorn [Cape water hawthorn] (155) (1942), Water-hawthorn [Waterhawthorn] (109) (1949), possibly Gaint cape water-hawthorn [Gaint cape waterhawthorn] (155) (1942)

Aponogeton distachyus giganteus – possibly *Aponogeton distachyos* L. f. introduced

Aponogeton distachyus L.f. – See *Aponogeton distachyos* L. f.

Aponogeton L. f. – Water-hawthorn [Waterhawthorn] (155) (1942)

Aptenia cordifolia (L. f.) Schwant. – Dew plant [Dew-plant] (109) (1949), Heart-leaf fig-marigold [Heartleaf figmarigold] (138) (1923), Heart-leaf mesembryanthemum [Heartleaf mesembryanthemum] (155) (1942)

Aptenia cordifolia **Schwant** – See *Aptenia cordifolia* (L. f.) Schwant.

Aquilegia **(Tourn.) L.** – See *Aquilegia* L.

Aquilegia brevistyla **Hook.** – Small-flower columbine [Small-flowered columbine] (5, 85, 131) (1899–1932), Western columbine (3) (1977), Yukon columbine (155) (1942)

Aquilegia caerulea **James.** – Colorado columbine (138, 155) (1923–1942), Long-spur columbine [Long-spurred columbine] (2) (1895), Mountain columbine (38) (1820), Rocky Mountain columbine [Rockymountain columbine] (82) (1930)

Aquilegia canadensis **L.** – American columbine (138, 155, 187) (1818–1942), Bells (5, 76, 157, 158) (1896–1929) Sulphur Grove OH, Canadian columbine (46) (1879), Chuckles (157) (1929), Cluckies (5, 156) (1913–1923) no longer in use by 1923, Columbine [Collombines, Colombines] (82, 124, 127, 157) (1900–1930), Common columbine (122) (1937), Cory's columbine (122, 124) (1937), Culverwort (156) (1923), Honeysuckle [Honey suckle, Honey-suckle, Honisuckles] (5, 76, 156, 158) (1896–1923), Inubthon-kithe-sabe-hi (Omaha-Ponca, black perfume plant) (37) (1919), Jacket-and-breeches [Jacket and breeches] (76) (1896), Jack-in-trousers (5, 76, 156, 157, 158) (1896–1929) Lynn MA, children's name, Meetinghouses [Meeting houses] (5, 156, 157, 158) (1900–1929), Moɲbixoɲ (Osage) (121) (1918?–1970?), Red bells (156) (1923), Red columbine (7, 50, 92, 156, 157, 158) (1828–present), Red columbine of Virginia (181) (~1678), Rock bells (5) (1913), Rockbell [Rock-bells] (156) (1923), Rock-lily [Rock lily, Rock lilies] (5, 157, 158) (1900–1929), Scarlet columbine (42) (1814), Skalikatit (Pawnee, blackseed) (37) (1919), Skalikatit or Skarikatit (Pawnee, black-seed) (37) (1919), Skarikatit (Pawnee, black-seed) (37) (1919), Turk's-cap [Turk's cap, Turkscap] (156) (1923), Wild columbine (3, 4, 5, 19, 37, 42, 63, 82, 85, 97, 107, 114, 131, 157, 158, 190) (~1759–1986)

Aquilegia chrysantha **Gray** – Golden columbine (50, 86, 138, 155) (1878–present)

Aquilegia coerulea – See *Aquilegia caerulea* James.

Aquilegia coerulea **var.** *pinetorum* **(Tidestr.) Payson ex Kearney & Peebles** – Pine columbine (155) (1942)

Aquilegia elegantula **Greene** – Western red columbine (155) (1942)

Aquilegia flavescens **S. Wats.** – Yellow columbine (155) (1942)

Aquilegia formosa **Fisch. ex DC.** – California columbine (138, 155) (1931–1942), Columbine [Collombines, Colombines] (35) (1806), Fairies (76) (1896) Norridgewock ME, white varieties, Sitka columbine (138, 155) (1931–1942), Wild columbine (76) (1896)

Aquilegia formosa truncata – See *Aquilegia formosa* Fisch. ex DC.

Aquilegia formosa **var.** *truncata* **(Fisch. & C.A. Mey.) Baker** – See *Aquilegia formosa* Fisch. ex DC.

Aquilegia jonesi – See *Aquilegia jonesii* Parry

Aquilegia jonesii **Parry** – Jones' columbine [Jones columbine] (155) (1942)

Aquilegia **L.** – Columbine [Collombines, Colombines] (1, 2, 4, 10, 13, 15, 50, 82, 93, 138, 155, 156, 158, 167, 184) (1793–present), Honeysuckle [Honey suckle, Honey-suckle, Honisuckles] (2, 79) (1891–1895) Northeastern US

Aquilegia latiuscula **Greene** – See *Aquilegia canadensis* L.

Aquilegia longissima **Gray** – Long-spur columbine [Long spurred columbine, Longspur columbine] (122, 124, 155) (1937–1942) TX

Aquilegia phoenicantha **Cory** – See *Aquilegia canadensis* L.

Aquilegia pinetorum – See *Aquilegia coerulea* var. *pinetorum* (Tidestr.) Payson ex Kearney & Peebles

Aquilegia saximontana **Rydb.** – Rocky Mountain columbine [Rockymountain columbine] (155) (1942)

Aquilegia **Tourn.** – See *Aquilegia* L.

Aquilegia truncata **Fisch. & Mey.** – See *Aquilegia formosa* Fisch. ex DC.

Aquilegia vulgaris **L.** – Akeley (156) (1923), Bluebell [Blue-bell, Blue bell, Blue bells, Blue-bells] (5, 76, 156) (1896–1923) Northern OH, Capon's-tail [Capon's tail] (5, 156) (1913–1923), Cluverwort (5, 156) (1913–1923), Cock's-foot [Cocksfoot, Cocks-foot, Cock's foot, Cock-foot] (5, 156) (1913–1923) no longer in use by 1923,

Columbine [Collombines, Colombines] (46, 92, 114, 178) (1526–1894), Common garden columbine (2) (1895), European columbine (5, 15, 155, 156) (1895–1942), Garden columbine (19, 92, 156) (1840–1923), Lady's-shoes [Ladies-shoes, Lady's shoes] (5, 156) (1913–1923), Snapdragon [Snap dragon, Snap-dragon] (5, 156) (1913–1923)

Arabidopsis **Heynh.** – Mouse-ear cress [Mouseear cress [Mouse ear cress] (4) (1986), Rockcress [Rock-cress, Rock cress] (50) (present)

Arabidopsis novae-angliae **(Rydb.) Britton** – See *Braya humilis* (C.A. Mey.) B.L. Robins.

Arabidopsis thaliana **(L.) Britton** – Common wall cress (42) (1814), Mouse-ear [Mouse ear, Mouse ears, Mouse's ear, Mows eare] (5) (1913), Mouse-ear cress [Mouseear cress [Mouse ear cress] (1, 3, 4, 15, 50, 85, 92, 155, 156) (1876–present), Mouse-ear turkey-pod (187) (1818), Mouse-ear wallcress [Mouse-ear wall-cress] (42, 187) (1814–1818), Rockcress [Rock-cress, Rock cress] (92) (1876), Thalecress [Thale cress, Thale-cress] (5, 46, 156) (1879–1913), Turkeypod [Turkey pod, Turkey-pod] (5, 156) (1913–1923) no longer in use by 1923, Wallcress [Wall cress, Wall-cress] (5, 156) (1913–1923)

Arabidopsis thaliana **(L.) Heynh.** – See *Arabidopsis thaliana* (L.) Britton

Arabis **×***divaricarpa* **A. Nels.** – Spreading-pod rockcress [Spreadingpod rockcress] (50) (present)

Arabis albida – See *Arabis caucasica* Willd.

Arabis alpina **L.** – Alpine rockcress [Alpine rock cress] (5, 138, 155) (1913–1942), Bishop's-wig [Bishop's wig] (5) (1913), Dusty husband (5) (1913), Mountain rockcress [Mountain rock-cress] (109) (1949), Silver rockcress (155) (1942), Snowdrift [Snow drift] (5) (1913), White allison (5) (1913)

Arabis arenicola **(Richards.) Gelert.** – See *Arabis media* N. Busch

Arabis brachycarpa **(Torr. & Gray) Britton** – See *Arabis drummondii* Gray

Arabis breweri **S. Wats.** – Brewer's rockcress [Brewer rockcress] (155) (1942)

Arabis bulbosa **Schreber. ex Muhl.** – See *Cardamine bulbosa* (Schreb. ex Muhl.) Britton, Sterns & Poggenb.

Arabis canadensis **L.** – Canadian wall cress (42) (1814), Sickle-leaf wall cress [Sickle-leaved wall-cress] (187) (1818), Sicklepod [Sickle pod, Sickle-pod] (3, 4, 5, 15, 19, 50, 72, 92, 97, 131, 156, 158) (1840–present), Sickle-pod wall cress [Sickle-podded wall cress] (42) (1814), Tower mustard [Tower-mustard] (156) (1923)

Arabis canescens **Brocchi** – See *Arabis alpina* L.

Arabis caucasica **Willd.** – Wall rockcress [Wall rock-cress] (109, 155) (1942–1949), Wallcress [Wall cress, Wall-cress] (138) (1923)

Arabis collinsii **Fernald.** – See *Arabis holboellii* Hornem. var. *collinsii* (Fern.) Rollins

Arabis dentata **Torr. & Gray** – See *Arabis shortii* (Fern.) Gleason

Arabis drummondii **Gray** – Drummond's rockcress, Drummond's rock cress (5, 50, 155) (1913–present), Purple rockcress [Purple rock cress] (5, 72, 131) (1899–1913), Short-fruit rockcress [Shortfruit rockcress] (155) (1942)

Arabis exilis – See *Arabis holboellii* Hornem. var. *retrofracta* (Graham) Rydb.

Arabis falcata **Mich.** – See *Arabis canadensis* L.

Arabis fendleri **(S. Wats.) Greene** – Fendler's rockcress (50) (present)

Arabis glabra **(L.) Bernh.** – Rockcress [Rock-cress, Rock cress] (157) (1929), Tower cress (5, 156, 158) (1900–1923), Tower mustard [Tower-mustard] (2, 3, 4, 5, 15, 46, 72, 85, 92, 131, 156, 158) (1649–1986), Tower rockcress (50) (present), Tower-mustard rockcress [Towermustard rockcress] (155) (1942), Wallcress [Wall cress, Wall-cress] (157) (1929)

Arabis hirsuta **(L.) Scop.** – Hairy rockcress [Hairy rock cress, Hairy rock-cress] (2, 5, 50, 72, 131, 155) (1895–present)

Arabis hirsuta **(L.) Scop. var.** *pycnocarpa* **(M. Hopkins) Rollins** – Common hairy rockcress (155) (1942), Cream-flower rockcress [Creamflower rockcress] (50) (present), Rockcress [Rock-cress, Rock cress] (3, 4) (1977–1986)

Arabis hirsuta Scop. – See *Arabis hirsuta* (L.) Scop.

Arabis holboellii **Hornem.** – Holboell's rockcress [Holboell's rock cress, Holboell rockcress] (5, 50, 131, 155) (1899–present)

Arabis holboellii **Hornem. var. *collinsii* (Fern.) Rollins** – Collins' rock cress [Collin's rockcress] (5, 50) (1913–present), Rockcress [Rockcress, Rock cress] (3, 4) (1977–1986)

Arabis holboellii **Hornem. var. *pinetorum* (Tidestrom) Rollins** – Holboell's rockcress [Holboell's rock cress, Holboell rockcress] (50) (present)

Arabis holboellii **Hornem. var. *retrofracta* (Graham) Rydb.** – Slim rockcress (155) (1942)

Arabis horboellii **Hormen.** – See *Boechera holboellii* (Hornem.) Á.Löve & D.Löve

Arabis **L.** – Rockcress [Rock-cress, Rock cress] (1, 2, 4, 3, 15, 50, 93, 109, 155, 156, 158) (1895–present), Tower mustard [Tower-mustard] (1, 10, 13) (1818–1932), Turkeypod [Turkey pod, Turkey-pod] (42, 184) (1793–1814), Wall cress (10, 42, 158) (1814–1900), Wallcress [Wall cress, Wall-cress] (10, 158) (1818–1900), Wild candytuft (1) (1932)

Arabis laevigata **(Muhl. ex Willd.) Poir.** – Red rockcress (155) (1942), Smooth rockcress [Smooth rock cress, Smooth rock-cress] (2, 3, 4, 5, 50, 72, 97) (1895–present)

Arabis laevigata **Poir.** – See *Arabis laevigata* (Muhl. ex Willd.) Poir.

Arabis lemmoni – See *Arabis lemmonii* S. Wats.

Arabis lemmonii **S. Wats.** – Lemmon's rockcress [Lemmons rockcress] (155) (1942)

Arabis lyalli – See *Boechera lyallii* (S.Watson) Dorn

Arabis lyrata **L.** – Low rockcress [Low rock cress] (2, 156) (1895–1923), Lyre-leaf wallcress [Lyre leaved wall cress, Lyre-leaved rock cress] (5, 42, 72) (1814–1913)

Arabis media **N. Busch** – Arctic rockcress [Arctic rock cress] (5) (1913)

Arabis microphylla **Nutt.** – Little-leaf rockcress [Littleleaf rockcress] (155) (1942)

Arabis nuttalli – See *Arabis nuttallii* B.L. Robins.

Arabis nuttallii **B. L. Robins.** – Nuttall's rockcress [Nuttall rockcress] (155) (1942)

Arabis oregana **Rollins** – Oregon rockcress (155) (1942), Purple rockcress [Purple rock cress] (155) (1942)

Arabis patens **Sullivant** – Sreading rockcress [Sreading rock cress] (5) (1913)

Arabis perfoliata **Lam.** – See *Arabis glabra* (L.) Bernh.

Arabis petiolaris **(Gray) Gray** – Rockcress [Rock-cress, Rock cress] (122) (1937)

Arabis petiolaris **Gray** – See *Arabis petiolaris* (Gray) Gray

Arabis platysperma **Gray** – Pioneer rockcress (155) (1942)

Arabis purpurascens – See *Arabis oregana* Rollins

Arabis rhomboidea **Pers.** – See *Cardamine bulbosa* (Schreb. ex Muhl.) Britton, Sterns & Poggenb.

Arabis rhomboides **Michx.** – possibly *Cardamine bulbosa* (Schreb. ex Muhl.) Britton, Sterns & Poggenb.

Arabis shortii **(Fern.) Gleason** – Rockcress [Rock-cress, Rock cress] (3, 4, 85) (1932–1986), Short's rockcress (50) (Present), Toothed rock cress (5, 72) (1907–1913)

Arabis suffrutescens **S. Wats.** – Woody rockcress (155) (1942)

Arabis thaliana **L.** – See *Arabidopsis thaliana* (L.) Britton

Arabis virginica **(L.) Poir.** – See *Sibara virginica* (L.) Rollins

Arabis virginica **(L.) Trelease** – See *Sibara virginica* (L.) Rollins

Arachis hypogaea **L.** – Anchic (107) (1625) Peru, Earth-almond [Earth almond] (107) (1919), Earthnut [Earth-nut, Earth nut] (55, 92, 107) (1876–1919), Earthpea [Earth pea] (14) (1882), False groundnut [False ground nut] (19) (1840), Goobers [Goober] (73, 109) (1892–1949) Southern US, Ground pea [Ground-pea, Ground peas] (73) (1892) KY, Groundnut [Ground-nut, Ground nut, Ground nutts] (7, 14, 55, 73, 92, 109, 155) (1828–1949), Mandobi (107, 110) (1886–1919) Brazil, Mandois (107) (1682) Congo, Mandubi (107, 110) (1648–1919) Brazil, Mani (7, 107, 110) (1828–1919) South America, Monkey nut [Monkey-nut, Monkey-nuts] (110) (1886),

Mundubi (110) (1886), Peanut [Pea nut, Pea-nut] (7, 19, 55, 92, 107, 109, 110, 155) (1828–1942) Peru, Pindar [Pindars] (7, 107) (1828–1919) West Indies, Pinders (73) (1892) MS, Ynchic (Indian) (107) (1609)

Arachis hypogea – See *Arachis hypogaea* L.

Arachis **L.** – Peanut [Pea nut, Pea-nut] (155) (1942)

Aragalus lambertii **(Pursh) Kuntze** – possibly *Oxytropis lambertii* Pursh

Aragalus sericeus **(Nutt.) Greene** – See *Astragalus sericoleucus* Gray

Aralia **(Tourn.) L.** – See *Aralia* L.

Aralia californica **S. Wats.** – California aralia (155) (1942), California spikenard (64) (1907)

Aralia chinensis **L.** – Chinese angelica tree [Chinese angelica-tree] (109) (1949), Chinese aralia (138, 155) (1931–1942)

Aralia chinensis **L. var. *mandshurica*** – See *Aralia elata* (Miq.) Seem.

Aralia elata **(Miq.) Seem.** – Chinese angelica tree [Chinese angelica-tree] (135) (1910)

Aralia elata **Seem.** – See *Aralia elata* (Miq.) Seem.

Aralia hispida **Vent.** – Aralia (52) (1919), Bristle-stem elder [Bristle-stem elder] (19, 49, 53, 58, 92) (1840–1922), Bristle-stem sarsaparilla [Bristle stem sarsaparilla] (19, 49, 53, 58, 92) (1840–1922), Bristly aralia (42, 138, 155) (1814–1942), Bristly sarsaparilla (2, 5, 46, 109, 156) (1879–1949), Dwarf elder (5, 49, 52, 53, 57, 58, 61, 79, 92, 156) (1869–1923), Hyebele (156) (1923), Hyeble (5, 92) (1876–1913), Pigeon-berry [Pigeon berry] (5, 75, 156) (1894–1923) ME, Prickly elder (58) (1869), Rough sarsaparilla (5, 156) (1913–1923), Rough spikenard (7) (1828), Swamp-elder [Swamp elder] (29) (1869), Wild elder [Wild-elder] (5, 49, 53, 58, 92, 156) (1869–1923)

Aralia **L.** – Angelica or Angelica tree [Angelica-tree] (8) (1785), Aralia (138, 155, 158) (1900–1942), Aralie (French) (8) (1785), Sarsaparilla (1, 4, 93) (1932–1986), Spikenard (1, 4, 50) (1932–present), Wild ginseng (1, 93) (1932–1936)

Aralia nudicaulis **L.** – American sarsaparilla (49, 58, 64, 92, 157, 158) (1869–192908), Aralia radix (Official name of Materia Medica) (7) (1828), Aralie á tige nue (French) (158) (1900), Common sarsaparilla (38) (1820), Common wild sarsaparilla (2) (1895), False sarsaparilla (5, 49, 57, 58, 92, 156, 157, 158) (1869–1929), Ginseng (101) (1905) MT, true ginseng is Panax quinquefolia, Kada-kuns (Chippewa, little kada) (105) (1932), Life-of-man [Life of man, Life-o'-man] (7) (1828), Nackte Aralie (German) (158) (1900), Naked-stem sarsaparilla [Naked-stemmed sarsaparilla] (187) (1818), Nardus Americanus (Official name of Materia Medica) (7) (1828), Nardwurzel Aralie (German) (7) (1828), Petit nard (French) (7, 158) (1828–1900), Petty morel [Pettymorel, Petty-morel, Petty-morrel, Pettymorrel, Petty morrell, Petymorell] (7) (1828), Pigeon-weed [Pigeonweed, Pigeon weed] (7) (1828), Rabbit root (5) (1913), Rabbit's-foot [Rabbit foot, Rabbits' foot, Rabbitfoot] (156) (1923), Rabbit's-root [Rabbit's root, Rabbits' root] (64, 92, 157, 158) (1876–1929), Sarsaparilla (7, 43, 46, 101, 177) (1607–1905), Sasafafarilla (76) (1896) Bath ME, Sasafril (76) (1896) ME, Sasapril (76) (1896) ME, Sassafariller (75) (1894) Banner Elk NC, Sassaparil (7, 184) (1793–1828), S'assaparilla (190) (~1759), Saxapril (76) (1896) Bath ME, Shotbush [Shot bush, Shot-bush] (5, 7, 49, 64, 156, 157, 158) (1828–1929), Small spikenard (5, 7, 49, 58, 64, 92, 156, 157, 158) (1828–1929), Spiknard (7) (1828), Sweetroot [Sweet root] (7) (1828), Virginia sarsaparilla [Virginian sarsaparilla] (5, 64, 156, 157, 158) (1900–1929), Wabos'odji'bĭk (Chippewa, rabbit root) (40) (1928), Wild licorice [Wild liquorice] (5, 7, 49, 57, 64, 92, 156, 157, 158) (1828–1929), Wild sarsaparilla [Wild-sarsaparilla, Wild sarsaparilla] (3, 4, 5, 19, 22, 40, 42, 46, 47, 49, 50, 63, 64, 72, 85, 92, 93, 95, 105, 109, 131, 138, 155, 156, 157, 158, 187) (1814–present)

Aralia quinquefolia **Dec. & Planch** – See *Panax quinquefolius* L.

Aralia quinquefolia **Gray** – possibly *Panax quinquefolius* L.

Aralia racemosa **L.** – American spikehead (5, 6, 64, 72) (1892–1913), Amerikanische Nard (German) (158) (1900), Amerikanischer Aralie

(German) (6) (1892), Aralia (52) (1919), Aya'bĭdji'bikûgi'sĭn (Chippewa) (40) (1928), Berry-bearing aralia (42, 187) (1814–1818), Čikadak (Chippewa) (105) (1932), Hungry-root (156) (1923), Indian root [Indian-root] (64, 73, 92, 156, 157, 158) (1892–1929), Large spikenard (7) (1828), Life-of-man [Life of man, Life-o'-man] (5, 6, 64, 73, 75, 92, 156, 157, 158) (1892–1929), Nard Americain (French) (158) (1900), Nard d'Amerique (French) (6) (1892), O'kadak' (Chippewa) (40) (1928), Old-maid's-root [Old maid's root] (5, 156) (1913–1923), Old-man's-root [Old man's root] (64, 75, 76, 156, 157, 158) (1896–1929), Petty morel [Pettymorel, Pettymorel, Petty-morrel, Pettymorrel, Petty morell, Petymorell] (5, 6, 49, 53, 64, 73, 92, 157, 158, 184) (1793–1929), Pigeon-weed [Pigeonweed, Pigeon weed] (6) (1892), Spice bush [Spice-bush, Spicebush] (5, 75) (1894–1913) Hartford Conn, Spiceberry [Spice-berry, Spice berry] (64, 156, 157, 158) (1900–1929), Spignet (5, 49, 53, 58, 64, 75, 92, 156, 157, 158) (1869–1929), Spignut (73) (1892) VT, Spikenard (3, 4, 6, 19, 38, 40, 46, 47, 53, 58, 63, 79, 85, 92, 105, 157, 158, 187) (1818–1986) pronounced 'spicknard' in NH, Whiteroot [White-root, Whiteroot] (156) (1923), Wild licorice [Wild liquorice] (187) (1818)

Aralia racemosa L. subsp. *racemosa* – American spikenard (50) (present)

Aralia spinosa L. – Aaron's-rod [Aaron's rod] (156) (1923), Angelica or Angelica tree [Angelica-tree] (2, 5, 7, 14, 19, 38, 46, 49, 58, 106, 109, 156) (1617–1949), Angélique en arbre (French) (8) (1785), Aralie épineuse (French) (8) (1785), Devil's-club [Devil's club, Devilsclub] (106) (1930), Devil's-walkingstick [Devil's walking-stick, Devil's walking stick, Devil's-walking-stick] (138, 155, 156) (1923–1942), Hercules'-club [Hercules' club, Hercules club, Herculesclub] (2, 5, 49, 58, 63, 92, 97, 109, 124, 155, 156) (1869–1942), Pick tree [Pick-tree] (5, 156) (1913–1923), Pigeon tree [Pigeon-tree] (5, 92, 156) (1876–1923), Pigeon-weed [Pigeonweed, Pigeon weed] (187) (1818), Prickly elder (5, 7, 49, 92, 156) (1828–1923), Prickly-alder [Prickly alder] (58) (1869), Prickly-ash [Prickly ash, Pricklyash] (5, 177) (1762–1913), Shotbush [Shot bush, Shot-bush] (7, 19, 38, 92, 156) (1820–1923), Southern prickly-ash [Southern prickly ash] (49, 58, 92) (1869–1898), Southern prickly-elder [Southern prickly elder] (92) (1876), Spikenard tree [Spikenard-tree] (5, 7, 65, 92, 156) (1828–1931), Tear-blanket (156) (1923), Thorny aralia (187) (1818), Toothache bush [Toothache-bush, Toothe-ache bush] (49) (1898), Toothache tree [Toothache-tree] (5, 7, 49, 58, 156, 177) (1762–1923), Tree aralia (155) (1942), Virginia angelica tree [Virginian angelica tree] (8) (1785), Wild orange [Wild-orange] or Wild orange tree (5, 156) (1913–1923)

Aralia trifolia Decne. & Planch. – See Panax trifolius L.

Araujia Brot. – Bladder-flower [Bladderflower] (155) (1942)

Araujia sericifera Brot. – White bladder flower [White bladderflower] (155) (1942)

Arbutus arizonica (Gray) Sargent – Arizona madrone (155) (1942)

Arbutus L. – Arbousier (French) (8) (1785), Bearberry [Bear berry, Bear-berry] (8, 167) (1785–1814), Madrone (50, 155) (1942–present), Strawberry tree [Strawberry-tree] (8, 42) (1785–1814)

Arbutus menziesi – See *Arbutus menziesii* Pursh

Arbutus menziesii Pursh – Arbousier menzies (French) (20) (1857), Arbute tree (106) (1930), Madrona (106, 107) (1919–1930), Madroña (161) (1857), Madrone (109, 138) (1923–1949), Madroñe (75) (1894) CA, Madroño (109) (1949), Menzies' arbutus (103) (1870), Menzie's strawberry tree (20) (1857), Pacific madrone (155) (1942)

Arbutus texana Buckl. – See *Arbutus xalapensis* Kunth

Arbutus thymifolia Aiton – See *Gaultheria hispidula* (L.) Muhl. ex Bigelow

Arbutus uva-ursi L. – See *Arctostaphylos uva-ursi* (L.) Spreng.

Arbutus xalapensis Kunth – Mexican madrone (155) (1942), Texas madrone (155) (1942), Texas madrono (122, 124) (1937)

Arceuthobium Bieb. – Dwarf mistletoe [Dwarfmistletoe] (50, 155) (1942–present), Mistletoe [Misseltoe, Misletoe, Misleto] (121) (1970), Noŋnibatse (Osage, tobacco bunch) (121) (1918?–1970?)

Arceuthobium oxycedris M. Bieb. – See Arceuthobium oxycedri *(DC.) M. Bieb.*

Arceuthobium pusillum Peck – Small dwarf-mistletoe [Small dwarfmistletoe] (155) (1942), Small mistletoe (5, 156) (1913–1923)

Archangelica atropupureum – See Angelica atropurpurea L.

Archangelica atropurpurea Hoffn. – See Angelica atropurpurea L.

Archangelica hirsuta Torr. & Gray – See Angelica venenosa (Greenway) Fern.

Archangelica officinalis – See Angelica archangelica L.

Archemora ambigua Pursh – See *Oxypolis ternata* (Nutt.) Heller taxonomic status is unresolved (PL)

Archontophoenix alexandrae (F. Muell.) H. Wendl. & Drude – Alexandra palm (109) (1949) for Princess Alexandra of Denmark, Northern bangalow palm (109) (1949), Step palm (109) (1949)

Archontophoenix alexandrae Wendl. & Drude – See *Archontophoenix alexandrae* (F. Muell.) H. Wendl. & Drude for Princess Alexandra of Denmark

Archontophoenix alexandrae Wendl. & Drude var. *beatrice* C.T. White – See *Archontophoenix alexandrae* (F. Muell.) H. Wendl. & Drude

Arctagrostis arundinacea (Trin.) Beal – See *Arctagrostis latifolia* (R. Br.) Griseb. subsp. *arundinacea* (Trin.) Tzvelev

Arctagrostis latifolia (R. Br.) Griseb. – Arctogrostis (5, 19) (1840–1913), Broad-leaf arctic bent [Broad-leaved arctic bent] (94) (1901)

Arctagrostis latifolia (R. Br.) Griseb. subsp. *arundinacea* (Trin.) Tzvelev – Reed bent (4) (1986)

Arctium L. – Burdock (1, 4, 50, 69, 82, 93, 109, 155, 156, 158) (1900–present), Clote (179) (1526), Clyver [Clyuer] (179) (1526), Great bur [Grete burr, Grete burr, Grete burre] (179) (1526), Lesser burre (179) (1526), Little bur [Lytell burre] (179) (1526)

Arctium lappa L. – Arctium (174, 177) (1753–1762), Bachelor's-button [Bachelor's button, Bachelor's buttons, Batchelor's buttons] (158) (1900), Bardana (174, 177) (1753–1762), Bardana (Spanish) (92, 158) (1876–1900), Bardane (French) (5, 6, 64, 158) (1876–1913), Batweed [Bat weed] (6) (1892), Bazzies (158) (1900), Beggar's-button [Beggar's buttons] (5, 64, 69, 156, 158) (1900–1923), Billy-buttons (158) (1900), Bourgène (French) (158) (1900), Bourholm (French) (158) (1900), Burburr [Burr-bur] (69) (1904), Burdock (7, 10, 14, 19. 49, 52, 53, 55, 57, 58, 59, 64, 80, 85, 92, 106, 114, 145, 158, 184, 187) (1793–1930), Burdockbur (148) (1939), Burdock-grass [Burdock grass] (92) (1876), Burseed [Burr seed] (92) (1876), Buzzies (76) (1896) Southold Long Island, Clit-bur (158) (1900), Clive (158) (1900), Clotbur [Clot-bur, Clotburr, Clote-bur, Clot Burre] (6, 92, 93, 156, 158) (1892–1906), Clotebur [Clote-bur] (158) (1900), Cocklebur [Cockle-bur, Cockle-bur, Cockle-burr, Cockle burr, Cockleburr] (5, 156, 158) (1900–1923), Cockle-button [Cockle button] (5, 64, 69, 156) (1903–1923), Cockly-bur (158) (1900), Common burdock (6, 42) (1814–1892), Crocklety-bur (158) (1900), Cucklemoors (158) (1900), Cuckold-dock [Cuckold dock] (5, 64, 69, 156, 158) (1900–1923), Cuckoldy-bur (158) (1900), Cuckoo-button [Cuckoo button, Cuckoo-buttons] (158) (1900), Glouteron (French) (6, 158) (1892–1900), Gobo (of Japanese) (109) (1949), Great bur [Grete burr, Grete burr, Grete burre] (5, 156) (1913–1923), Great burdock (3, 5, 72, 82, 93, 109, 155, 158) (1900–1977), Great clotbur (5, 46) (1671–1913) accidentally introduced by 1671, Josselyn, Greater burdock [Greater burrdock] (50) (present), Hardane (156) (1923) no longer in use by 1923, Hardock (5, 64, 69, 92, 156, 158) (1876–1923) no longer in use by 1923, Harebur [Hareburr, Hare-bur] (92, 158) (1876–1900), Hoardock (158) (1900), Hurrbur [Hurr bur, Hurr-bur] (5, 64, 92, 156, 158) (1876–1923), Klette (German) (6) (1892), Klettenwurzel (German) (158) (1900), Lappa (6, 52, 55, 57, 64) (1892–1919), Perfonata (174) (1753), Stick-button [Stick button, Stick-buttons] (5, 64, 69, 156, 158) (1900–1923), Thistle [Thystle] (158) (1900), Turkey bur [Turkeybur, Turkey-bur] (158) (1900), Turkey-bur seed [Turkey bur seed, Turkeybur-seed] (2) (1895)

Arctium minus Bernh. – Burdock (37, 40, 63, 82, 122, 124, 125) (1899–1936), Common burdock (3, 4, 5, 62, 72, 82, 93, 95, 97, 109, 131,

157, 158) (1899–1986), Cuckoo-button [Cuckoo button, Cuckoo-buttons] (5) (1913), Lesser burdock [Lesser burrdock] (50, 157, 158) (1900–present), Smaller burdock (155) (1942), Wi'sûgibûg' (Chippewa, bitter leaf) (40) (1928)

Arctium minus Schkuhr – See *Arctium minus* Bernh.

Arctium tomentosum (Lam.) Schkuhr – See *Arctium tomentosum Mill.*

Arctium tomentosum Mill. – Cotton burdock (155) (1942), Cottony burdock (5) (1913), Woolly burdock [Woolly burrdock] (5, 50) (1913–present)

Arctomecon merriami – See *Arctomecon merriamii* Coville

Arctomecon merriamii Coville – Desert bear-poppy [Desert bear-poppy] (155) (1942)

Arctomecon Torr. & Frém. – Bear poppy [Bearpoppy] (155) (1942)

Arctophila fulva (Trin.) Rupr. ex Anderss. – Nodding colpodium (94) (1901), Yellow colpodium (94) (1901)

Arctostaphylos ×cinerea T. J. Howell [*canescens × viscida*] – Delnorte manzanita (155) (1942)

Arctostaphylos Adans. – Alpine bearberry (1) (1932), Bearberry [Bear berry, Bear-berry] (1, 2, 4, 106, 156) (1895–1986), Kinnikinnick [Kinnikinik, Kinnikinnick, Kinnikinic, Kinnikinnik] (1) (1932), Manzanita (1, 50, 106, 155) (1930–present), Ptarmigan-berry [Ptarmiganberry] (155) (1942)

Arctostaphylos alpina (L.) Spreng. – Alpine bearberry (5) (1913), Alpine ptarmigan-berry [Alpine ptarmiganberry] (155) (1942), Black bearberry [Black bear-berry] (5, 92, 156) (1876–1923)

Arctostaphylos andersonii Gray – Little-apple [Little apple] (77) (1898) CA, Manzanita (77) (1898) CA

Arctostaphylos bicolor – See *Xylococcus bicolor* Nutt.

Arctostaphylos bracteosa – See *Arctostaphylos tomentosa* (Pursh) Lindl.

Arctostaphylos canescens Eastw. – Hoary manzanita (50, 155) (1942–present)

Arctostaphylos cinerea – See *Arctostaphylos ×cinerea* T.J. Howell [*canescens × viscida*]

Arctostaphylos columbiana Piper – Hairy manzanita (155) (1942)

Arctostaphylos crustacea – See *Arctostaphylos tomentosa* (Pursh) Lindl.

Arctostaphylos densiflora M.S. Baker – Sonoma manzanita (155) (1942)

Arctostaphylos diversifolia – See *Comarostaphylis diversifolia* (Parry) Greene subsp. *diversifolia*

Arctostaphylos elegans – See *Arctostaphylos manzanita* Parry subsp. *elegans* (Eastw.) P.V. Wells

Arctostaphylos glandulosa Eastw. – Eastwood manzanita's [Eastwood manzanita] (155) (1942)

Arctostaphylos glauca Lindl. – Big-berry manzanita [Big-berried manzanita] (106) (1930), Great manzanita (138) (1923), Great-berry manzanita [Great-berried manzanita] (109) (1949), Manzanita (75, 92, 107, 161) (1857–1919) CA, Manzanito (57) (1917)

Arctostaphylos hispidula T.J. Howell – Howell's manzanita [Howell manzanita] (155) (1942)

Arctostaphylos hookeri G. Don – Hooker's manzanita [Hooker manzanita] (155) (1942)

Arctostaphylos insularis Greene ex Parry – Island manzanita (155) (1942)

Arctostaphylos manzanita Parry – Common manzanita (104, 106, 155) (1896–1942)

Arctostaphylos manzanita Parry subsp. *elegans* (Eastw.) P. V. Wells – Konouti manzanita (155) (1942)

Arctostaphylos mariposa – See *Arctostaphylos viscida* Parry subsp. *mariposa* (Dudley) P.V. Wells

Arctostaphylos mewukka Merriam – Indian manzanita (155) (1942)

Arctostaphylos morroensis Wies. & Schreib. – Morro manzanita (155) (1942)

Arctostaphylos myrtifolia Parry – Ione manzanita (155) (1942)

Arctostaphylos nevadensis Gray – Pinemat manzanita (155) (1942)

Arctostaphylos nissenana Merriam – Eldorado manzanita (155) (1942)

Arctostaphylos nummularia Gray – Dwarf manzanita (106) (1930), Fire manzanita (155) (1942), Little-berry manzanita [Littleberry manzanita] (155) (1942)

Arctostaphylos numularia – See *Arctostaphylos nummularia* Gray

Arctostaphylos obispoensis Eastw. – Serpentine manzanita (155) (1942)

Arctostaphylos otayensis Wies. & Schreib. – Otay's manzanita [Otay manzanita] (155) (1942)

Arctostaphylos pajaroensis (J.E. Adams ex McMinn) J.E. Adams – Pajaro manzanita (155) (1942)

Arctostaphylos parryana Lemmon – Parry's manzanita [Parry manzanita] (155) (1942)

Arctostaphylos parryana pinetorum – See *Arctostaphylos patula* Greene

Arctostaphylos patula Greene – Green-leaf manzanita [Greenleaf manzanita] (155) (1942), Pine manzanita (155) (1942)

Arctostaphylos pechoensis (Dudley ex Abrams) Dudley ex Munz – Pecho Mountain manzanita [PechoMountain manzanita] (155) (1942)

Arctostaphylos pilosula Jepson & Wies. ex Jepson – Stripe-berry manzanita [Stripeberry manzanita] (155) (1942)

Arctostaphylos pringlei Parry – Pringle's manzanita [Pringle manzanita] (155) (1942)

Arctostaphylos pumila Nutt. – Dune manzanita (155) (1942)

Arctostaphylos pungens H.B.K. – See *Arctostaphylos pungens* Kunth

Arctostaphylos pungens Kunth – Manzanita (122, 153) (1913–1937), Point-leaf manzanita [Pointleaf manzanita] (155) (1942)

Arctostaphylos rudis Jepson & Wies. ex Jepson – Shag-bark manzanita [Shagbark manzanita] (155) (1942)

Arctostaphylos sensitiva – See *Arctostaphylos nummularia* Gray

Arctostaphylos silvicola Jepson & Wies. ex Jepson – Silver-leaf manzanita [Silverleaf manzanita] (155) (1942)

Arctostaphylos stanfordiana Parry – Stanford's manzanita [Stanford manzanita] (155) (1942)

Arctostaphylos tomentosa (Pursh) Lindl. – Brittle-leaf manzanita [Brittleleaf manzanita] (155) (1942), Hairy manzanita (106) (1930), Manzanita (103, 107) (1870–1919), Manzañita (Spanish, little apple) (103) (1870), Monterey manzanita (155) (1942), Woolly manzanita (138, 155) (1931–1942)

Arctostaphylos uva-ursi (L.) Spreng. – At-tung-a-wi-at (Eskimo) (107) (1919), Barentraube (6) (1892), Barren bilberry (156) (1923), Barren myrtle (156, 157) (1923–1929), Bear whortleberry [Bear's whortleberry] (5, 157) (1913–1929), Bearberry [Bear berry, Bear-berry] (3, 4, 5, 6, 7, 8, 10, 14, 19, 34, 38, 40, 41, 42, 49, 52, 53, 55, 57, 58, 59, 85, 86, 92, 103, 106, 107, 108, 109, 112, 113, 130, 138, 153, 155, 156, 157) (1770–1986), Bear-bilberry [Bear's bilberry] (157) (1929), Beargrape [Bears' grape, Bear's grape] (6, 92, 106, 107, 156) (1892–1930), Bear's-grape bilberry [Bear's grape bilberry] (5) (1913), Boufferole (7, 8) (1785–1828), Box-leaf wintergreen [Box-leaved wintergreen] (156) (1923), Bralins (156) (1923) no longer in use by 1923, Brawlines (157) (1929), Brawlins (107) (1919), Busserolle (6) (1892), Checker-berry [Checker berry, Checkerberry, Chequer-berry, Chequer berry] (7) (1828), Creashak [Creashaks] (107, 156, 157) (1919–1929), Crowberry [Crow-berry, Crow berry] (73, 156, 157, 158) (1892–1929) Barnstable MA, Erdbeartege Sandbeere (German) (7) (1828), Foxberry [Fox berry, Fox-berry] (7) (1828), Fox-plum [Fox plum] (5, 156) (1913–1923), Ground-holly [Ground holly] (156) (1923), Heth (6) (1892), Hog crawberry (5) (1913), Hog-cranberry [Hog cranberry] (75, 156) (1894–1923) Provincetown MA, Iss-salth (Chinook) (107) (1919), Killikinic [Killikinick] (103) (1870), Kinikenich (34) (1834), Kinnikinnick [Kinnikinik, Kinnikinnick, Kinnikinic, Kinnikinnik] (5, 19, 50, 73, 85, 86, 92, 101, 106, 148, 155, 156, 157) (1840–present), Kleh (Chippewa) (107) (1919), Larb (6, 101, 103) (1870–1905) MT, Mealberry [Meal-berry, Meal berry] (5, 92, 156, 157) (1876–1923), Meal-plum (156) (1929), Meal-plum [Meal plum] (5) (1913), Mountain box (5, 6, 7, 92, 107, 156, 157) (1828–1929), Mountain cranberry (75, 92,

156, 157) (1894–1929) Southern ME, Mountain crawberry (5, 93) (1913–1936), Nakasis (Pawnee, little tree or short tree) (5) (1913), Raisin d'ours (French) (6, 7, 8) (1785–1892), Rapper dandies (5, 92, 156, 157) (1876–1929), Red bearberry [Red bear-berry] (131, 156, 157) (1899–1929), Redberry [Red-berry, Red berry] (6, 7) (1828–1892), Red-berry trailing arbutus [Red-berried trailing arbutus] (6) (1892), Rockberry [Rock-berry, Rock berry] (73, 156, 157) (1892–1929) Fortune Bay, Newfoundland, Sacacomis (101) (1905) MT, Sacacommé (35) (1806), Sakakomi (34) (1834), Tchakoshe-pukk (Crow) (107) (1919), Timiyah (Snake) (101) (1905) MT, Universe (6) (1892), Universe vine [Universe-vine] (5, 92, 156) (1898–1923), Upland crawberry (5, 6, 7, 49, 53, 58, 92, 156, 157) (1828–1929), Uva-ursa (156) (1923), Uva-ursi [Uva ursi, Uvae ursi] (Official name of Materia Medica) (7, 52, 53, 55, 58, 59, 92, 157, 174) (1753–1929), Uversy (156) (1923), Whortleberry [Whortle-berry] (6, 7) (1828–1892), Wild cranberry (92, 156) (1898–1923), Wild crawberry (5) (1913)

Arctostaphylos uva-ursi **Spreng.** – See *Arctostaphylos uva-ursi* (L.) Spreng.

Arctostaphylos viridissima **(Eastw.) McMinn** – Lompoc manzanita (155) (1942)

Arctostaphylos viscida **Parry** – White-leaf manzanita [Whiteleaf manzanita] (155) (1942)

Arctostaphylos viscida **Parry subsp.** *mariposa* **(Dudley) P. V. Wells** – Mariposa manzanita (155) (1942)

Arctotis grandis – See *Arctotis stoechadifolia* Berg.

Arctotis **L.** – Arctotis (138, 155) (1931–1942)

Arctotis stoechadifolia **Berg.** – African arctotis (155) (1942), African daisy (109) (1949), Bushy arctotis (138) (1923)

Arctotis stoechadifolius **Berg.** – See *Arctotis stoechadifolia* Berg.

Arctous **(Gray) Niedzu.** – See *Arctostaphylos* Adans.

Arctous alpina **(L.) Niedenzu** – See *Arctostaphylos alpina* (L.) Spreng.

Arctous ruber **(Rehder & E.H.Wilson) Nakai** – Red-fruit ptarmiganberry [Redfruit ptarmiganberry] (155) (1942)

Arctous ruber **[Nakai]** – See *Arctous ruber* (Rehder & E. H.Wilson) Nakai

Arctous rubra **(Rehd. & Wilson) Nakai** – possibly *Arctous ruber* (Rehder & E.H.Wilson) Nakai

Ardisia crenulata – See *Parathesis crenulata* (Vent.) Hook. f.

Ardisia solanacea **Roxb.** – Shoe-button ardisia [Shoebutton ardisia] (155) (1942)

Ardisia **Sw.** – Ardisia (138) (1923)

Arecastrum romanzoffianum **(Cham.) Becc.** – See *Syagrus romanzoffiana* (Cham.) Glassman

Arenaria **(Fenzl.) Hook.** – See *Arenaria* L.

Arenaria arctica **Stevar.** – See *Minuartia arctica* (Stev. ex Ser.) Graebn.

Arenaria burkei – See *Arenaria congesta* Nutt. var. *subcongesta* (S. Wats.) S. Wats.

Arenaria capillaris **Poir. subsp.** *americana* **Maguire** – Fescue sandwort (155) (1942)

Arenaria caroliniana **Walt.** – See *Minuartia caroliniana* (Walt.) Mattf.

Arenaria compacta – See *Arenaria kingii* (S. Wats.) M.E. Jones

Arenaria congesta **Nutt.** – Ballhead sandwort (155) (1942)

Arenaria congesta **Nutt. var.** *subcongesta* **(S. Wats.) S. Wats.** – Burke's sandwort [Burke sandwort] (155) (1942)

Arenaria cretica **Spreng.** – Cretan sandwort [Crete sandwort] (155) (1942)

Arenaria diffusa **Ell.** – See *Honckenya peploides* (L.) Ehrh. subsp. *diffusa* (Hornem.) Hultén

Arenaria drummondii **Shinners** – See *Minuartia drummondii* (Shinners) McNeill

Arenaria fendleri **Gray** – Fendler's sandwort [Fendler sandwort] (5, 50, 155) (1913–present)

Arenaria formosa – See *Arenaria capillaris* Poir. subsp. *americana* Maguire

Arenaria groenlandica **(Retz) Spreng.** – See *Minuartia groenlandica* (Retz.) Ostenf.

Arenaria hookeri **Nutt.** – Hooker's sandwort [Hooker sandwort] (5, 50,

131, 155) (1899–present), Sandwort [Sand wort] (157) (1929)

Arenaria hookeri **Nutt. subsp.** *hookeri* – Hooker's sandwort [Hooker sandwort] (50) (present)

Arenaria hookeri **Nutt. subsp.** *pinetorum* **(A. Nels.) W.A. Weber** – Hooker's sandwort [Hooker sandwort] (50) (present)

Arenaria kingi – See *Arenaria kingii* (S. Wats.) M.E. Jones

Arenaria kingii **(S. Wats.) M.E. Jones** – Compact sandwort (155) (1942), King's sandwort [Kings sandwort] (155) (1942), Uinta sandwort (155) (1942)

Arenaria **L.** – Rock sandwort (72) (1907), Sandwort [Sand wort] (1, 2, 4, 10, 15, 50, 93, 109, 138, 156, 167, 184) (1793–present)

Arenaria lanuginosa **(Michx.) Rohrb.** – Grass-leaf starwort [Grass-leaved star-wort] (187) (1818)

Arenaria laricifolia – See *Minuartia yukonensis* Hultén

Arenaria lateriflora **L.** – See *Moehringia lateriflora* (L.) Fenzl

Arenaria leptoclados **(Reichenb.) Guss.** – See *Arenaria serpyllifolia* L.

Arenaria litorea **Fernald** – See *Minuartia dawsonensis* (Britt.) House

Arenaria michauxii **Hook.f.** – See *Minuartia michauxii* (Fenzl) Farw. var. *michauxii*

Arenaria patula **Michx.** – See *Minuartia patula* (Michx.) Mattf.

Arenaria peploides **L.** – See *Honckenya peploides* (L.) Ehrh. subsp. *diffusa* (Hornem.) Hultén

Arenaria rubella – See *Minuartia rubella* (Wahlenb.) Hiern.

Arenaria rubra **L.** – See *Spergularia rubra* (L.) J.& K. Presl

Arenaria sajanesis **Willd.** – See *Minuartia biflora* (L.) Schinz & Thellung

Arenaria serpyllifolia **L.** – Sandwort [Sand wort] (85) (1932) SD, Slender sandwort (5) (1913), Thyme-leaf sandwort [Thymeleaf sandwort, Thyme-leaved sandwort] (4, 5, 15, 19, 50, 97, 155, 156, 187) (1818–present)

Arenaria stricta **Michx.** – See *Minuartia michauxii* (Fenzl) Farw. var. *michauxii*

Arenaria texana **(Robinson) Britton** – See *Minuartia michauxii* (Fenzl) Farw. var. *texana* (B.L. Robins.) Mattf.

Arenaria uintahensis – See *Arenaria kingii* (S. Wats.) M.E. Jones

Arenaria verna **L.** – See *Minuartia rubella* (Wahlenb.) Hiern.

Arequipa **Britton & Rose** – possibly *Echinocactus* Link & Otto

Arethusa bulbosa **L.** – Arethusa (5, 48, 138, 156, 174) (1753–1923), Bog rose (156) (1923), Bulbous arethusa (42) (1814), Bulbous-rooted arethusa (187) (1818), Dragon's-mouth [Dragon's mouth] (50, 73, 156) (1892–present), Laughing-jackass [Laughing jackass] (75) (1894), Meadow pink [Meadow-pink] (78) (1898) MA, Swamp pink [Swamppink, Swamp-pink] (78) (1898) MA, Wild pink (5, 73, 156) (1894–1923) Atlantic City NJ

Arethusa **L.** – Arethusa (138, 155) (1923–1942), Rose-lip [Rose lip] (1) (1932)

Arethusa ophioglossoides **L.** – See *Pogonia ophioglossoides* (L.) Ker Gawl.

Arethusa pendula – See *Triphora trianthophora* (Sw.) Rydb. subsp. *trianthophora*

Arethusa trianthophoros **Sw.** – See *Triphora trianthophora* (Sw.) Rydb.

Argemone alba **Lestib.** – See *Argemone albiflora* Hornem. subsp. *albiflora*

Argemone albiflora **Hornem. subsp.** *albiflora* – Prickly poppy [Pricklypoppy, Prickly-poppy] (38) (1820), White poppy (122, 124) (1937), White prickly-poppy [White prickly poppy, White prickly-poppy] (5, 97, 131, 155) (1899–1942)

Argemone gracilenta **Greene** – Leafy white prickly poppy (5) (1913), Prickly poppy [Pricklypoppy, Prickly-poppy] (85, 125, 157) (1900–1932), Thistle-poppy [Thistle poppy] (98, 157) (1926–1929), White-flower prickly-poppy [White-flowered prickly poppy] (65) (1931)

Argemone hispida **Gray** – Chialota (Spanish) (76) (1896), Hairy prickly-poppy [Hairy prickly poppy] (4) (1986), Hedgehog prickly poppy [Hedgehog pricklypoppy, Hedgehog prickly-poppy] (138, 155) (1923–1942), Rough prickly-poppy [Rough pricklypoppy] (50) (present), Thistle-poppy [Thistle poppy] (76) (1896)

Argemone intermedia **Sweet.** – See *Argemone gracilenta* Greene

43

Argemone L.

Argemone **L.** – Poppy-thistle [Poppy thistle] (106) (1930), Prickly poppy [Pricklypoppy, Prickly-poppy] (1, 2, 4, 13, 15, 50, 63, 82, 93, 106, 122, 109, 138, 155, 156, 158) (1895–present), Thistle-poppy [Thistle poppy] (1) (1932), Thorn-poppy [Thorn poppy] (7) (1828)

Argemone mexicana albiflora – See *Argemone polyanthemos* (Fedde) Ownbey

Argemone mexicana **L.** – Argemone (6, 174, 180) (1633–1892), Argemone (French) (6) (1892), Bird-in-the-bush [Birds-in-the-bush] (5, 73, 156) (1892–1923) Arlington MA, no longer in use by 1923, Chicalota (6) (1892), Devil's-fig [Devil's fig] (5, 6, 92, 156) (1876–1923), Flowering thistle (5, 73, 156) (1892–1923) Mansfield OH, Jamaica thistle (5, 156) (1913–1923), Mexican poppy (6, 72, 82, 92, 97) (1892–1937), Mexican prickly-poppy [Mexican prickly-poppy] (5, 155, 156) (1913–1942), Prickly poppy [Pricklypoppy, Prickly-poppy] (6, 10, 19, 49, 92) (1818–1898), Stachelmohn (German) (6) (1892), Thorn-apple [Thorn apple, Thornapple, Thorn apples, Thorne Apple] (6) (1892), Thorn-poppy [Thorn-poppy] (5, 6, 92, 156) (1876–1923), Yellow poppy (122) (1937) TX, Yellow thistle (5, 156) (1913–1923)

Argemone mexicana **L. var.** *albiflora* **Gray** – See *Argemone polyanthemos* (Fedde) Ownbey

Argemone platyceras [Otto & Dietr.] – possibly *Argemone pleiacantha* Greene

Argemone platyceras hispida – See *Argemone hispida* Gray

Argemone platyceras rosea – See *Argemone sanguinea* Greene

Argemone pleiacantha **Greene (possibly)** – Crested prickly-poppy [Crested pricklypoppy] (138, 155) (1923–1942)

Argemone polyanthemos **(Fedde) G. Ownbey** – Crested prickly-poppy [Crested pricklypoppy] (50) (present), Prickly poppy [Pricklypoppy, Prickly-poppy] (3, 4) (1977–1986), Mexican poppy (145) (1897)

Argemone sanguinea **Greene** – Red poppy (122) (1937) TX, Rosy prickly-poppy [Rosy pricklypoppy] (155) (1942)

Argemone squarrosa **Greene** – Hedgehog prickly poppy [Hedgehog pricklypoppy, Hedgehog prickly-poppy] (3, 4, 50) (1977–present)

Argentea **Lam.** – possibly *Argentina* Hill

Argentina anserina **(L.) Rydb.** – Anserine (French) (158) (1900), Argentina (158) (1900), Argentine (158) (1900), Buttercup [Butter cup, Buttercups] (158) (1900), Camoroche (157, 158) (1900–1929), Cinquefoil [Cink-foil, Cinque-foil] (35) (1806), Dog tansy [Dog's tansy] (156, 157, 158) (1900–1929) Scotland, Gänserich (German) (158) (1900), Goose-grass [Goosegrass] (92, 107, 156, 157, 158) (1898–1929), Goose-tansy [Goose tansy] (5, 107, 156, 157, 158) (1913–1929), Potentilla (174) (1753), Silberkraut (German) (158) (1900), Silver-feather [Silver feather] (156, 157, 158) (1900–1929), Silverweed [Silver weed, Silver-weed] (3, 4, 5, 41, 80, 85, 92, 107, 127, 131, 138, 156, 157, 158) (1770–1986), Silverweed cinquefoil (50, 155) (1942–present), Silvery cinquefoil (85) (1932), Tansey cinquefoil (19) (1840), Wild agrimony (157, 158) (1900–1929), Wild tansy [Wild tansey] (5, 156, 157, 158) (1900–1929)

Argentina argentea **Rydb.** – See *Argentina anserina* (L.) Rydb.

Argentina **Hill** – Silverweed [Silver weed, Silver-weed] (1, 50, 93) (1932–present), possibly Goose-tansy [Goose tansy] (1) (1932)

Argyreia **Lour.** – Asia-glory [Asiaglory] (155) (1942)

Argyreia nervosa **(Burm. f.) Bojer** – Woolly Asia glory [Woolly Asiaglory] (155) (1942), Woolly morning-glory (109) (1949)

Argyreia speciosa **Sweet** – See *Argyreia nervosa* (Burm. f.) Bojer

Argyrochosma **(Sm.) Windham** – False cloak fern (50) (present)

Argyrochosma dealbata **(Pursh) Windham** – Cloak fern [Cloakfern] (3, 97) (1937–1977), False cloak fern (4) (1986), Powdery false cloak fern (50) (present), Powdery notholaena (5, 122) (1913–1937)

Argyrochosma fendleri **(Kunze) Windham** – Cloak fern [Cloakfern] (4) (1986), Fendler's cloak fern [Fendler cloak fern] (4) (1986), Fendler's false cloak fern (50) (present), Zigzag cloak fern [Zigzag cloakfern] (155) (1942)

Argythamnia californica **Brandeg.** – California silverbush (155) (1942)

Argythamnia humilis **(Engelm. & Gray) Meull. Arg. var.** *laevis* **(Torr.) Shinners** – Low silverbush (50) (present)

Argythamnia humilis **(Engelm. & Gray) Muell. Arg. var.** *humilis* – Low ditaxis (5, 97) (1913–1937), Low silverbush (50) (present), Wild mercury (3) (1977)

Argythamnia humilis **(Engelm. & Gray) Muell.-Arg.** – Low silverbush (50) (present)

Argythamnia lanceolata **(Benth.) Muell.-Arg.** – Lance-leaf silverbush [Lanceleaf silverbush] (155) (1942) IA

Argythamnia mercurialina **(Nutt.) Muell. Arg.** – Tall ditaxis (5, 97) (1913–1937), Tall silverbush (50) (present), Wild mercury (3) (1977)

Argythamnia **P. Br.** – Ditaxis (155, 158) (1900–1942), Silver bush [Silver-bush, Silverbush] (50, 155) (1942–present), Silverbush [Silverbush] (50, 155) (1942–present), Wild mercury (4) (1986)

Arikuryroba – See *Syagrus* C. Martius

Ariocarpus fissuratus **(Engelm.) K. Schum.** – Dry whiskey (107) (1919), Living-rock [Livingrock, Living rock] (109, 122, 138) (1923–1949), Peyote (104) (1896)

Ariocarpus fissuratus **Schum.** – See *Ariocarpus fissuratus* (Engelm.) K. Schum.

Ariocarpus **Scheidw.** – Living-rock [Livingrock, Living rock] (138, 155) (1931–1942), Living-rock cactus [Livingrockcactus] (155) (1942)

Arisaema acuminatum **Small** – See *Arisaema triphyllum* (L.) Schott subsp. *pusillum* (Peck) Huttleston

Arisaema atrorubens **(Ait.) Blume** – See *Arisaema triphyllum* (L.) Schott subsp. *triphyllum*

Arisaema atrorubens **(Ait.) Blume var.** *stewardsonii* **(Britt.) G.T. Stevens** – See *Arisaema triphyllum* (L.) Schott subsp. *stewardsonii* (Britt.) Huttleston

Arisaema dracontium **(L.) Schott** – Drachen Aron (German) (6) (1892), Dragon arum (2) (1895), Dragonhead [Dragon-head, Dragon head, Dragon's head] (122, 124) (1937) TX, Dragonroot [Dragon root, Dragon-root, Dragon's root] (3, 5, 6, 72, 93, 97, 109, 138, 156, 157, 187) (1818–1977), Dragonroot jack-in-the-pulpit [Dragonroot jack-inthepulpit] (155) (1942), Dragon's-tail [Dragon-tail] (156) (1923), Gouet à Dragon (French) (6, 19) (1840–1892), Green dragon (6, 50, 57, 92, 93, 109, 125, 156, 157, 158, 187) (1818–present), Indian turnip (156) (1923), Pedate-leaf wakerobin [Pedate-leaved wake-robin] (187) (1818)

Arisaema **Martens** – Dragon arum (156) (1923), Dragonroot [Dragon root, Dragon-root, Dragon's root] (1) (1932), Green dragon (1) (1932), Indian turnip (1, 93, 158) (1932–1936), Jack-in-the-pulpit [Jack in the pulpit, Jackinthepulpit] (1, 93, 155) (1932–1942)

Arisaema pusillum **(Peck) Nash** – See *Arisaema triphyllum* (L.) Schott subsp. *pusillum* (Peck) Huttleston

Arisaema stewardsonii **Britton** – See *Arisaema triphyllum* (L.) Schott subsp. *stewardsonii* (Britt.) Huttleston

Arisaema triphyllum **(L.) Schott** – Arisarum trifolium (Official name of Materia Medica) (7) (1828), Aro (Spanish) (158) (1900), Arum (57, 64) (1908–1917), Arum radix (Official name of Materia Medica) (7) (1828), Bog-onion [Bog onion] (64, 73, 78, 92, 157) (1876–1929), Brown dragon [Brown-dragon] (5, 156, 158) (1896–1923), Common Indian turnip (2, 5) (1895–1913), Devil's-bit [Devil's bit, Devilbit] (7) (1828), Devil's-ear [Devil's ear] (156, 157, 158) (1900–1929), Dragon [Dragons] (46) (1879), Dragonroot [Dragon root, Dragon-root, Dragon's root] (7, 49, 53, 58, 79, 92, 107) (1828–1922), Dragon-turnip [Dragon turnip] (6, 7, 64, 92, 157, 158) (1828–1929), Dreiblättriger Aron [Dreyblättrige Aron] (German) (7, 158) (1828–1900), Gouet à Trois Feuilles (French) (6, 10, 19, 158) (1818–1982), Indian Jack-in-the-pulpit [Indian Jackinthepulpit] (155) (1942), Indian turnip (7, 37, 46, 49, 53, 57, 58, 64, 72, 86, 92, 93, 97, 156, 157, 158, 187) (1818–1937), Indianische Aronswurz (German) (158) (1900), Jack-in-the-pulpit [Jack in the pulpit, Jackinthepulpit] (3, 5, 6, 35, 40, 49, 50, 53, 57, 58, 64, 73, 85, 86, 92, 93, 97, 122, 124, 125, 127, 138, 156, 157, 158) (1806–present), Lady-in-a-chaise [Lady in a chaise] (79) (1891) NH, Lords-and-ladies [Lordsandladies] (64, 92, 156, 158) (1876–1923), Marsh-turnip [Marsh turnip] (37, 92, 158) (1830–1900),

Meadow turnip (64) (1908), Meadow-turnip (158) (1900), Memory root (6, 78) (1892–1898) MA, Mikasi-makan (Omaha-Ponca, coyote medicine) (37) (1830), Nikso kororik kahtsu nitawau (Pawnee, herb which bears what resembles an ear of corn) (5) (1913), Pepper-turnip [Pepper turnip] (5, 7, 64, 156, 158) (1828–1923), Pied-de-veautriphylle (French) (7) (1828), Preacher-in-the-pulpit [Preacher in the pulpit] (86) (1878), Priest's-pintl [Priest's pintle] (64, 92, 158) (1876–1908), Starchwort [Starch-wort] (5, 64, 92, 156, 158) (1876–1923), Swamp turnip (158) (1900), Three-leaf arum [Three-leaved arum] (7, 19, 64, 157, 158) (1828–1929), Three-leaf Indian turnip [Three-leaved Indian turnip] (5, 86, 156) (1878–1923), Three-leaf wild turnip [Three leaved wild turnip] (42) (1814), Wakerobin [Wake robin, Wake-robin] (5, 7, 49, 57, 58, 64, 75, 78, 92, 156, 157, 158) (1828–1929), Wild pepper (64, 156, 158) (1900–1929), Wild turnip [Wild-turnip] (5, 19, 64, 73, 156, 157, 158) (1840–1929), Wild turnip root (92) (1876), Zehrwurz (German) (158) (1900)

Arisaema triphyllum (L.) Schott subsp. *pusillum* (Peck) Huttleston – Jack-in-the-pulpit [Jack in the pulpit, Jackinthepulpit] (50) (present), Peck's Jack-in-the-pulpit (5) (1913)

Arisaema triphyllum (L.) Schott subsp. *stewardsonii* (Britt.) Huttleston – Stewardson Brown's Indian turnip (5) (1913)

Arisaema triphyllum (L.) Schott subsp. *triphyllum* – Brown dragon [Brown-dragon] (19) (1840), Common jack-in-the-pulpit [Common jackinthepulpit] (155) (1942), Indian turnip (107, 109) (1919–1949), Jack-in-the-pulpit [Jack in the pulpit, Jackinthepulpit] (50, 107, 109) (1919–present)

Arisaema triphyllum (L.) Torr. – See *Arisaema triphyllum* (L.) Schott

Aristea Aiton – Aristea (155) (1942)

Aristida adscensionis L. – Dog-town grass [Dog town grass, Dog-town-grass] (94) (1901), Needle grass [Needle-grass, Needlegrass] (5) (1913), Purple beard grass [Purple beard-grass] (5) (1913), Six-weeks threeawn (3, 50) (1977–present), Triple-awn beard grass [Triple-awned beard grass, Triple-awned beard-grass] (5, 99) (1913–1923)

Aristida affinis (J.A. Schultes) Kunth – See *Aristida purpurascens* Poir. var. *purpurascens*

Aristida arizonica Vasey – Arizona threeawn [Arizona three awn] (3, 122, 155) (1937–1977)

Aristida barbata Fourn. – See *Aristida havardii* Vasey

Aristida basiramea Engelm. ex Vasey – Beard grass [Beard-grass, Beardgrass] (119) (1938), Forked threeawn (3) (1977), Forked triple-awn grass [Forked triple-awned grass] (119) (1938), Fork-tip threeawn [Forktip threeawn] (155) (1942), Fork-tip three-awn grass [Forktip threeawn grass] (5) (1913), Tufted tripleawn [Tufted triple-awn, Tufted triple awn] (94) (1901–1915), Tufted triple-awn grass [Tufted triple awn grass] (56) (1901)

Aristida californica Thurb. ex S. Wats. – Hare's grass (94) (1901)

Aristida curtissii (A. Gray) Nash – See *Aristida dichotoma* Michx. var. *curtissii* Gray ex S. Wats. & Coult.

Aristida desmantha Trin. & Rupr. – Curly three-awn [Curly threeawn] (19, 155) (1840–1942), Western bunch grass [Western bunch-grass] (94) (1901), Western triple-awn grass [Western triple-awned grass] (50, 163) (1852–present)

Aristida dichotoma Michx. – Beard grass [Beard-grass, Beardgrass] (19) (1840), Branching aristida (187) (1818), Church-mouse threeawn [Churchmouse threeawn] (50, 155) (1942–present), Forked aristida (187) (1818), Poverty grass [Poverty-grass, Povertygrass] (5, 19, 56, 66, 80, 92, 94, 119, 163) (1840–1938)

Aristida dichotoma Michx. var. *curtissii* Gray ex S. Wats. & Coult. – Church-mouse threeawn [Churchmouse threeawn] (3) (1977), Curtiss' three-awn [Curtiss threeawn, Curtis threeawn] (3, 155) (1942–1977), Curtiss' triple-awn grass [Curtiss' triple-awned grass, Curtiss's triple-awned grass] (5, 99, 119) (1913–1938), Fork-tip three-awn grass [Forktip threeawn grass] (50) (present)

Aristida dichotoma Michx. var. *dichotoma* – Church-mouse threeawn [Churchmouse threeawn] (5) (1913)

Aristida divaricata H. & B. – Poverty threeawn [Poverty three awn (3, 122, 155) (1937–1977), Spreading triple-awn grass [Spreading triple-awned grass] (5) (1913)

Aristida divergens Vasey – See *Aristida ternipes* Cav.

Aristida divericata H. & B. – See *Aristida divaricata* H. & B.

Aristida fasciculata Torr. – See *Aristida adscensionis* L.

Aristida fendleriana Steud. – See *Aristida purpurea* Nutt. var. *fendleriana* (Steud.) Vasey

Aristida floridana (Chapman) Vasey – Florida curly-head [Florida curly head] (94) (1901)

Aristida glauca (Nees) Walp. – See *Aristida purpurea* Nutt. var. *nealleyi* (Vasey) Allred

Aristida gossypina Bosc – See *Aristida lanosa* Muhl. ex Elliott

Aristida gracilis Ell. – See *Aristida longispica* Poir. var. *longispica*

Aristida havardii Vasey – Havard's poverty grass (94) (1901), Havard's three-awn [Havard's threeawn, Havard three awn, Havard threeawn] (50, 122, 155) (1937–present)

Aristida intermedia Scribn. & Ball – See *Aristida longispica* Poir. var. *geniculata* (Raf.) Fern

Aristida L. – False needle grass [False needle-grass] (152) (1912) NM, Needle grass [Needle-grass, Needlegrass] (152) (1912) NM, Poverty grass [Poverty-grass, Povertygrass] (1, 93, 148) (1932–1939), Threeawn (50) (present), Three-awn grass [Three-awned grass] (66, 148) (1903–1939), Triple-awn grass (93) (1936), Wire grass [Wiregrass, Wiregrass] (1) (1932)

Aristida lanosa Muhl. ex Elliott – Woolly poverty grass [Woolly poverty-grass] (94) (1901), Woolly triple-awn grass [Woolly triple-awned grass] (5, 119, 163) (1852–1938), Woolly-sheaf threeawn [Woollysheaf threeawn] (50) (present)

Aristida longiseta Steud. – See *Aristida purpurea* Nutt. var. *longiseta* (Steud.) Vasey

Aristida longiseta Steud. var. *robusta* Merr. – See *Aristida purpurea* Nutt. var. *longiseta* (Steud.) Vasey

Aristida longispica Poir. – Slender triple-awn grass [Slender triple-awned grass] (119) (1938), Slim-spike threeawn [Slimspike threeawn] (3, 50) (1977–present)

Aristida longispica Poir. var. *geniculata* (Raf.) Fern – Intermediate aristida (56) (1901), Kearney's threeawn [Kearney threeawn] (155) (1942), Plains aristida (5, 163) (1852–1913), Slim-spike threeawn [Slimspike threeawn] (50) (present)

Aristida longispica Poir. var. *longispica* – Slender aristida (56) (1901), Slender beard grass (111) (1915), Slender triple-awn grass [Slender triple-awned grass] (5, 66, 99) (1903–1923), Slim-spike threeawn [Slimspike threeawn] (50) (present)

Aristida oligantha Michx – Branched aristida (5, 119) (1913–1938), Few-flower aristida [Few flowered aristida, Few-flowered aristida] (99, 119, 163) (1852–1938), Few-flower threeawn [Few-flowered threeawn] (3, 5) (1913–1977), Prairie threeawn (50, 155) (1942–present), Prairie three-awn grass [Prairie three awn grass] (122) (1937), Prairie tripleawn [Prairie triple-awn, Prairie triple awn] (56, 66, 94, 111) (1901–1915), S-curve threeawn (50, 155) (1942–present), Three-awn grass [Three-awned grass] (66) (1903), Wire grass [Wire-grass, Wiregrass] (145) (1897) KS

Aristida palustris (Chapman) Vasey – Swamp poverty grass [Swamp poverty-grass] (94) (1901)

Aristida parishii A.S. Hitchc. – See *Aristida purpurea* Nutt. var. *parishii* (A.S. Hitchc.) Allred

Aristida purpurascens Poir. – Arrow grass [Arrow-grass] (5, 119, 163) (1852–1938), Arrow-feather threeawn [Arrowfeather threeawn] (3, 50, 155) (1942–present), Beard grass [Beard-grass, Beardgrass] (87) (1884), Broom-sedge [Broom sedge, Broomsedge] (5, 119, 163) (1852–1938), Purple triple-awn [Purple triple awn] (66) (1903), Purplish aristida (119) (1938), Three-awn grass [Three-awned grass] (87) (1884)

Aristida purpurascens Poir. var. *minor* Vasey – See *Aristida purpurascens* Poir. var. *purpurascens*

Aristida purpurascens Poir. var. *purpurascens* – Arrow-feather

[Arrowfeather] (122) (1937), Long-leaf threeawn [Longleaf three-awn] (155) (1942)

Aristida purpurea Nutt. – Bunch grass [Bunchgrass, Bunch-grass] (129) (1894), Muskit grass (75) (1894) TX, Poverty grass [Poverty-grass, Povertygrass] (145) (1897), Purple aristida (119) (1938), Purple beard grass [Purple beard-grass] (111, 129) (1894–1915), Purple needle grass [Purple needle-grass] (152, 163) (1852–1912), Purple threeawn [Purple three awn] (50, 122, 155) (1937–present), Purple three-awn grass [Purple three-awned grass] (87) (1884), Spear grass [Spear-grass] (144) (1899), Western beard grass (87) (1884), Wire grass [Wire-grass, Wiregrass] (129) (1894), Beard grass [Beard-grass, Beardgrass] (3, 11, 50) (1888–present)

Aristida purpurea Nutt. var. *fendleriana* (Steud.) Vasey – Fendler's threeawn [Fendler three awn, Fendler threeawn] (5, 50, 119, 122, 155) (1913–present), Fendler's triple-awn grass [Fendler's triple-awned grass] (5, 50, 119) (1913–present)

Aristida purpurea Nutt. var. *longiseta* (Steud.) Vasey – Dog-town grass [Dog town grass, Dogtown-grass] (111, 163) (1852–1915), Fendler's threeawn [Fendler three awn, Fendler threeawn] (50) (present), Large purple aristida (56) (1901), Long-awn aristida [Long-awned aristida] (5, 163) (1852–1913), Long-awn needle grass [Long-awned needlegrass] (152) (1912), Poverty grass [Poverty-grass, Povertygrass] (85) (1932), Purple aristida (56) (1901), Red threeawn [Red three awn, Red three-awn] (3, 122, 140, 146, 155) (1937–1977)

Aristida purpurea Nutt. var. *nealleyi* (Vasey) Allred – Blue threeawn (50, 155) (1942–present)

Aristida purpurea Nutt. var. *parishii* (A.S. Hitchc.) Allred – Parish's threeawn (50) (present)

Aristida purpurea Nutt. var. *purpurea* – Purple threeawn [Purple three awn] (50) (present), Roemer's threeawn [Roemer threeawn] (155) (1942)

Aristida purpurea Nutt. var. *wrightii* (Nash) Allred – Wright's three-awn [Wright threeawn] (3, 50, 155) (1942–1977), Wright's three-awn grass [Wright's three-awned grass] (5) (1913), Wright's triple-awn grass [Wright's triple-awned grass] (99, 119, 163) (1852–1938)

Aristida purpurea Steud. – possibly *Aristida purpurea* Nutt.

Aristida ramosissima Engelm. – See *Aristida oligantha* Michx

Aristida roemeriana Scheele – See *Aristida purpurea* Nutt. var. *purpurea*

Aristida spiciformis Ell. – Spike-like poverty grass (94) (1901)

Aristida stricta Michx. – Downy triple-awn [Downy triple awn] (66) (1903), Pineland threeawn (155) (1942), Wire grass [Wire-grass, Wiregrass] (94) (1901)

Aristida ternipes Cav. – Texas poverty grass (94) (1901)

Aristida ternipes Cav. var. *gentilis* (Henr.) Allred – Spider grass (122) (1937) TX

Aristida ternipes Cav. var. *minor* (Vasey) Hitchc. – See *Aristida ternipes* Cav. var. *gentilis* (Henr.) Allred

Aristida tuberculosa Nutt. – Beach-woods threeawn [Beachwoods threeawn] (155) (1942), Long-awn poverty grass [Long-awned poverty grass, Long-awned poverty-grass] (5, 56, 66, 80, 94, 111) (1901–1915), Poverty grass [Poverty-grass, Povertygrass] (80) (1913) IA, Sea-beach aristida (163) (1852), Sea-beach triple-awn grass [Sea-beach triple-awned grass] (5) (1913), Seaside threeawn (50) (present)

Aristida wrightii Nash – See *Aristida purpurea* Nutt. var. *wrightii* (Nash) Allred

Aristida wrightii Nash var. *parishii* (A.S. Hitchc.) Gould – See *Aristida purpurea* Nutt. var. *parishii* (A.S. Hitchc.) Allred

Aristolochia brasiliensis – See *Aristolochia labiata* Willd. introduced

Aristolochia brasiliensis macrophylla – See *Aristolochia labiata* Willd. introduced

Aristolochia californica Torr. – California Dutchman's-pipe [California Dutchmanspipe] (155) (1942)

Aristolochia clematitis L. – Aristolochia clematitis (178) (1526), Birthwort [Birth wort, Birth-wort] (5, 10) (1818–1913), Birthwort

Dutchman's-pipe [Birthwort Dutchmanspipe] (155) (1942), Climbing birthwort [Climbing Birthwoort] (178) (1526), Upright birthwort (5, 92, 156) (1876–1923)

Aristolochia durior Hill. – See *Aristolochia macrophylla* Lam.

Aristolochia elegans Mast. – Calico Dutchman's-pipe [Calico Dutchmanspipe] (138) (1923), Calico flower [Calico-flower, Calicoflower] (109, 138) (1923–1949)

Aristolochia erecta L. – Swan flower [Swanflower] (122, 124) (1937) TX

Aristolochia frutescens [Marsh.] – See *Aristolochia macrophylla* Lam.

Aristolochia galeata – See *Aristolochia labiata* Willd. introduced

Aristolochia grandiflora hookeri – See *Aristolochia grandiflora* Sw.

Aristolochia grandiflora Sw. – Hooker's pelican Dutchman's-pipe [Hookers pelican Dutchmanspipe] (155) (1942), Pelican Dutchman's-pipe [Pelican Dutchmanspipe] (155) (1942), Pelican flower [Pelicanflower, Pelican-flower, Pellican flower] (109, 138) (1923–1949)

Aristolochia hastata Nutt. – See *Aristolochia serpentaria* L.

Aristolochia L. – Aristoloche (8, 50) (1785–prsent), Birthwort [Birth wort, Birth-wort] (2, 8, 10, 109, 158, 167) (1785–1949), Dutchman's-pipe [Dutchman's pipe, Dutchmanspipe, Dutchmans-pipe] (1, 50, 155) (1932–present), Heartwort [Heart-wort] (158) (1900), Snakeroot [Snake root, Snake-root] (1) (1932)

Aristolochia labiata Willd. – Brazilian Dutchman's-pipe [Brazil Dutchmanspipe] (155) (1942), Broad-blade Dutchman's-pipe [Broadblade Dutchmanspipe] (155) (1942), Large-leaf Dutchman's-pipe [Large-leaf Dutchmanspipe] (155) (1942)

Aristolochia longiflora Engelm. & Gray – See *Aristolochia erecta* L.

Aristolochia macrophylla Lam. – Aristoloche en arbre (French) (8) (1785), Big sarsaparilla (5, 156) (1913–1923), Birthwort [Birth wort, Birth-wort] (19) (1840), Broad-leaf birthwort [Broad leaved birth wort] (42) (1814), Broad-leaf snakeroot [Broad leaved snake root] (42) (1814), Common Dutchman's-pipe [Common Dutchmanspipe] (155) (1942), Dutchman's-pipe [Dutchman's pipe, Dutchmanspipe, Dutchmans-pipe] (2, 5, 7, 10, 92, 97, 109, 138, 156) (1818–1949), Pennsylvania shrubby birthwort [Pennsylvanian shrubby birthwort] (8) (1785), Pipevine [Pipe-vine, Pipe vine] (2, 5, 7, 92, 109, 156) (1828–1949), Wild ginger [Wildginger] (5, 156) (1913–1923)

Aristolochia odoratissima L. – Fragrant Dutchman's-pipe [Fragrant Dutchmanspipe] (155) (1942)

Aristolochia reticulata Nutt. – Red River snakeroot [Red River snakeroot] (6, 49, 53, 64) (1892–1922), Serpentaria (64) (1907), Texas serpentaria (64) (1907), Texas snakeroot (6, 49, 53, 57, 64, 92) (1876–1922), Texas snakeroot Dutchman's-pipe [Texas snakeroot Dutchmanspipe] (155) (1942)

Aristolochia ringens Vahl – Gaping Dutchman's-pipe [Gaping Dutchmanspipe] (155) (1942)

Aristolochia serpentaria L. – Aristoloche serpentaire (French) (186) (1814), Aristolochia root (92) (1876), Birthwort [Birth wort, Birthwort] (6, 58, 64, 92, 156, 184) (1793–1923), Black snakeroot [Black snake-root, Black-snake root] (5, 102, 156) (1886–1923), Herb Dutchman's-pipe [Herb Dutchmanspipe] (155) (1942), Nash's snakeroot [Nash snake root] (122, 124) (1937) TX, Ormrot (186) (1814), Pelican flower [Pelicanflower, Pelican-flower, Pellican flower] (5, 64, 92, 156, 158) (1876–1923), Pistolochia (186) (1814), Pistolochia Virginiana (181, 186) (~1678–1825) John Gerarde, Sangreeroot [Sangree root, Sangree-root] (5, 64, 92, 156, 158) (1876–1908, 1923), Sangrel (64, 92, 156, 158) (1898–1923), Sangrel snakeweed [Sangrel snake weed] (5) (1913), Sangrel snakeweed [Sangrel snake weed] (5) (1913), Schlangen Osterluzey [Schlangenosterluzey] (German) (7, 186) (1814–1828), Schlangenwurzel (German) (6) (1892), Septentaria Virginiana (Official name of Materia Medica) (7) (1828), Serpentairu ou couleuvrée de Virginie (French) (6) (1892), Serpentaria (6, 52, 53, 54, 58, 59, 60, 64, 92, 158) (1869–1922), Serpentary (5, 55, 64, 156, 158) (1900–1923), Serpentary-root [Serpentary root] (6, 55) (1892–1911), Slangenwortel (German) (186) (1814), Slangröd (German) (186) (1814), Snagrel (6, 7,

64, 92, 158) (1828–1908), Snakeroot [Snake root, Snake-root] (6, 34, 181) (~1678–1892), Snakeroot birthwort (7) (1828), Snakeweed [Snake-weed, Snake weed, Snake Weede] (6, 7, 64, 92, 156, 158, 181) (~1678–1923), Snakeweed-root (186) (1814), Snecrut (181) (~1678), Sperpentaria de Virginia (Spanish) (158) (1900), True snakeroot [True snake-root] (46) (1649), Unaste'tstiyû (Cherokee, very small root) (102) (1886), Vipérine de Virginie (French) (158) (1900), Virginia serpentaria (64) (1907), Virginia serpentary (55) (1911), Virginia snakeroot [Virginia snake root] (2, 3, 4, 5, 6, 7, 14, 43, 49, 50, 52, 53, 54, 57, 58, 59, 60, 64, 92, 97, 102, 122, 124, 138, 156, 158) (1820–present), Virginia snakeroot dutchman's-pipe [Virginia snakeroot dutchmanspipe] (155) (1942), Virginische Schlangenwurzel (German) (158) (1900)

Aristolochia sipho L'Her. – See *Aristolochia macrophylla* Lam.

Aristolochia tomentosa Sims. – Pipevine [Pipe-vine, Pipe vine] (3) (1977), Woolly dutchman's-pipe [Wooly dutchman's pipe] (50) (present), Woolly pipevine [Woolly pipe vine, Woolly pipe-vine] (4, 5, 97, 122, 124) (1913–1986)

Aristolochia watsoni – See *Aristolochia watsonii* Woot. & Standl.

Aristolochia watsonii Woot. & Standl. – Watson's Dutchman's-pipe [Watson Dutchmanspipe] (155) (1942)

Aristotelia chilensis (Molina) Stuntz – Chilean winterberry (155) (1942)

Aristotelia L'Hér. – Winter-berry [Winter berry, Winterberry] (155) (1942)

Aristotelia macqui [L'Her.] – See *Aristotelia chilensis* (Molina) Stuntz introduced

Armeniaca vulgaris – See *Prunus armeniaca* L.

Armeria (DC.) Willd. – Thrift (50, 109, 155) (1942–present)

Armeria maritima (Mill.) Willd. subsp. *sibirica* (Turcz. ex Boiss.) Nyman – Purple-head thrift [Purplehead thrift] (155) (1942), Rush-leaf thrift [Rushleaf thrift] (155) (1942)

Armeria maritima (Mill.) Willd – Cliff-rose [Cliff rose] (156) (1923), Common thrift (138, 155) (1923–1942), European thrift (5, 156) (1913–1923), Inkroot [Ink-root, Ink root] (58, 92) (1869–1876), Lady's-cushion [Ladies' cushion, ladies cuchion] (5, 156) (1913–1923), Maiden pink (156) (1923), Marsh daisy (156) (1923), Red-root [Red-root, Red root] (5, 156) (1913–1923), Rockrose [Rock-rose, Rock rose] (156) (1923), Sea gilliflower [sea gilly-flower] (5, 156) (1913–1923), Sea pink [Sea-pink] (5, 92, 156) (1876–1923), Sea thrift [Sea-thrift] (5, 156) (1913–1923), Sea-cushion [Sea cushion] (156) (1923), Sea-grass [Sea grass] (5, 156) (1913–1923), Summer-thrift (156) (1923), Thrift (5, 19) (1840–1913)

Armeria maritima var. *purpurea* (Koch) G.H.M. Lawr. – See *Armeria maritima* (Mill.) Willd. subsp. *sibirica* (Turcz. ex Boiss.) Nyman

Armeria purpurea Koch – See *Armeria maritima* (Mill.) Willd. subsp. *sibirica* (Turcz. ex Boiss.) Nyman

Armeria setacea [Delile ex Nyman] – possibly *Armeria maritima* (Mill.) Willd. subsp. sibirica (*Turcz. ex Boiss.*) Nyman

Armeria Willd. – See *Armeria* (DC.) Willd.

Armillaria (Fr.) Staude – Armillaria (155) (1942)

Armillaria matsutake S. Ito & S. Imai – Matsutake armillaria (155) (1942)

Armillaria mellea (Vahl ex Fr.) Kar. – See *Armillaria mellea* (Vahl) P. Kumm.

Armillaria mellea (Vahl) P. Kumm. – Honey mushroom (170) (1995), Honey-cap [Honey cap] (128) (1933) ND, Honey-color armillaria [Honeycolor armillaria] (155) (1942)

Armillaria ventricosa (Peck) Peck – Coarse armillaria (155) (1942)

Armoracia armoracia (L.) Britton – See *Armoracia rusticana* P.G. Gaertn., B. Mey. & Scherb.

Armoracia Gaertn. – See *Armoracia* P. Gaertn. & B. Mey. & Scherb.

Armoracia lacustris (A. Gray) Al-Shehbaz & V. Bates. (possibly) – Water horseradish (92) (1876)

Armoracia lacustris (Gray) Al-Shehbaz & Bates – See *Neobeckia aquatica* (Eat.) Greene

Armoracia P. Gaertn. & B. Mey. & Scherb. – Horseradish [Horse-radish, Horse radish] (93) (1936), Armoracia (50) (present)

Armoracia rusticana P. G. Gaertn., B. Mey. & Scherb. – Armoracia (50, 57, 107) (1917–present), Chren (Russia) (110) (1886), Cran (French) (110) (1886), Cran de Bretagne (French) (158) (1900), Cranson de Bretagne (French) (110) (1886), Draba (107) (100 AD), Horseradish [Horse-radish, Horse radish] (1, 3, 4, 5, 7, 15, 50, 55, 57, 58, 63, 85, 92, 107, 155, 156, 178, 184) (1633–present), Kreen (110) (1886), Krenai (Lithuania) (110) (1886), Meer-radys (Holland) (110) (1886), Meerretig [Meerrettig] (German) (110, 158) (1886–1900), Mérédi or méridi (Italian Swiss sea-radish) (110) (1886), Moutarde des moines (French) (158) (1900), Peppar-rot (Swedish) (110) (1886), Rabano rusticano (Spanish) (158) (1900), Raifort (French, strong root) (110, 128, 158) (1886–1933), Red cole (107) (1919), Rhuddygyl maurth (Welsh) (110) (1886), possibly Armoratia (180) (1633)

Arnica acaulis (Walt.) B.S.P. – Leopard's-bane [Leopardsbane, Leopard's bane, Leopardbane] (5) (1913)

Arnica alpina (L.) Olin. & Laden – possibly *Arnica angustifolia* Vahl

Arnica angustifolia Vahl. – possibly Arctic arnica (5, 131, 155, 156) (1899–1942), possibly Arctic leopard's-bane [Arctic leopard's bane] (5, 156) (1913–1923), possibly Mountain tobacco (5, 131, 156) (1899–1923)

Arnica betonicifolia Greene – See *Arnica latifolia* Bong.

Arnica chamissonis Less. – Chamisso's arnica [Chamisso arnica] (155) (1942)

Arnica chamissonis Less. subsp. *foliosa* (Nutt.) Maguire var. *andina* (Nutt.) Ediger & Barkl. – Hoary-leaf arnica [Hoaryleaf arnica] (155) (1942), Leafy arnica (155) (1942)

Arnica chionopappa Fernald – See *Arnica lonchophylla* Greene subsp. *lonchophylla*

Arnica cordifolia Hook. – Heart-leaf arnica [Heartleaf arnica] (5, 50, 133, 155) (1899–present)

Arnica cordifolius Hook. (sic.) – See *Arnica cordifolia* Hook.

Arnica foliosa – See *Arnica chamissonis* Less. subsp. *foliosa* (Nutt.) Maguire var. *andina* (Nutt.) Ediger & Barkl.

Arnica foliosa incana – See *Arnica chamissonis* Less. subsp. *foliosa* (Nutt.) Maguire var. *andina* (Nutt.) Ediger & Barkl.

Arnica fulgens Pursh – Arnica (3) (1977), Foothills arnica (50) (present), Orange arnica (155) (1942), Rayless arnica (155) (1942)

Arnica L. – Arnica (1, 50, 93, 138, 148, 155, 158) (1900–present), Leopard's-bane [Leopardsbane, Leopard's bane, Leopardbane] (7, 156) (1828–1900)

Arnica latifolia Bong. – Broad-leaf arnica [Broadleaf arnica] (155) (1942)

Arnica latifolia var. *viscidula* Gray – See *Arnica ovata* Greene

Arnica latifolia viscidula – See *Arnica ovata* Greene

Arnica lonchophylla Greene subsp. *arnoglossa* (Greene) Maguire – Seep arnica (50) (present)

Arnica lonchophylla Greene subsp. *lonchophylla* – Betony arnica (155) (1942), White-plume arnica [White-plumed arnica] (5) (1913)

Arnica longifolia D.C. Eat. – Long-leaf arnica [Longleaf arnica] (155) (1942)

Arnica mollis Hook – Hairy arnica (5, 155) (1913–1942)

Arnica montana var. *alpina* L. – See *Arnica angustifolia* Vahl

Arnica nevadensis Gray – Nevada arnica (155) (1942)

Arnica nudicaulis (Michx.) Nutt. – possibly *Arnica acaulis* (Walter) Britton, Sterns & Poggenb.

Arnica nudicaulis Nutt. – possibly *Arnica acaulis* (Walter) Britton, Sterns & Poggenb.

Arnica ovata Greene – Sticky broad-leaf arnica [Sticky broadleaf arnica] (155) (1942)

Arnica parryi Gray – Nevada arnica (155) (1942)

Arnica pedunculata Rydb. – See Arnica fulgens Pursh

Arnica rydbergii Greene – Rydberg's arnica (50) (present)

Arnica sororia Greene – Twin arnica (50) (present)

Arnoglossum atriplicifolium (L.) H.E. Robins. – Da'yewû (Cherokee, it sews itself up) (102) (1886) leaves are said to grow together again when torn, Horse-mint [Horsemint, Horse mint] (38) (1820), Indian plantain (47) (1852), Orache caraway (19) (1840), Orach-leaf caca-lia [Orach-leaved cacalia] (187) (1818), Pale Indian plantain (3, 4, 5, 50, 72, 82, 93, 97, 156, 157, 158) (1900–present), Tassel flower [Tas-sel-flower, Tasselflower, Tassell flower] (102) (1886), Wild caraway [Wild carraway] (5, 156, 157, 158) (1900–1929)

Arnoglossum muehlenbergii (Schultz-Bip.) H.E. Robins. – Great In-dian plantain (5, 72, 82, 156) (1907–1930), Wild cabbage (7) (1828), Wild caraway [Wild carraway] (92) (1876), Wild collard (5, 156) (1913–1923)

Arnoglossum plantagineum Raf. – Coltsfoot [Colt's foot, Colt's-foot, Colt foot] (124) (1937) TX, Groove-stem Indian plaintain [Groove-stem Indian plaintain] (50) (present), Indian plantain (4, 95, 124, 157) (1900–1986), Tuberous Indian plantain (5, 72, 82, 93, 97, 122) (1907–1937)

Arnoglossum Raf. – Caraway [Carawaies] (7) (1828), Indian plantain (1, 2, 4, 50, 63, 75, 82, 93, 156, 158) (1894–present)

Arnoseris Gaertn. – Lamb's-succory [Lambsuccory, Lamb succory] (155) (1942)

Arnoseris minima (L.) Dumort. – possibly *Arnoseris minima* (L.) Sch-weig. & Koerte

Arnoseris minima (L.) Schweig. & Koerte – Dwarf hog's succory (5) (1913), possibly Dwarf nipplewort (5, 156) (1913–1923), pos-sibly Dwarf succory (156) (1923), possibly Dwarf swine's-succory [Dwarf swine's succory] (5) (1913), possibly Hog-succory [Hog's succory] (156) (1923), possibly Lamb's-succory [Lambsuccory, Lamb succory] (5, 156) (1913–1923), possibly Small lamb-suc-cory [Small lambsuccory] (155) (1942), possibly Swine's-succory [Swine-succory, Swine's succory] (156) (1923)

Aronia arborea – See *Pyrus canadensis* (L.) Farw.

Aronia arbutifolia (L.) Ell. – See *Photinia pyrifolia* (Lam.) Robertson & Phipps

Aronia atropurpurea Britton – See *Photinia floribunda* (Lindl.) Rob-ertson & Phipps

Aronia botryapium P. – See *Amelanchier canadensis* (L.) Medik.

Aronia Medik. – See *Photinia* Lindl.

Aronia melanocarpa (Michx.) Britton – See *Photinia melanocarpa* (Michx.) Robertson & Phipps

Aronia nigra (Willd.) Britton – See *Photinia melanocarpa* (Michx.) Robertson & Phipps

Aronia ovalis P. – See *Amelanchier canadensis* (L.) Medik.

Aronia prunifolia (Marsh.) Rehd. – See *Photinia floribunda* (Lindl.) Robertson & Phipps

Aronia sanguinea – See *Amelanchier canadensis* (L.) Medik.

Arrabidaea DC. – Funnelvine (155) (1942)

Arracacha esculenta DC. – See *Arracacia xanthorrhiza* E.N. Bancroft

Arracacia Bancr. – See *Arracacia* E.N. Bancroft

Arracacia E.N. Bancroft – Arracacia (155) (1942)

Arracacia xanthorrhiza E.N. Bancroft – Arracacha (110) (1886)

Arrhenatherum avenaceum Beauv. – See *Arrhenatherum elatius* (L.) Beauv. ex J. Presl & C. Presl

Arrhenatherum Beauv. – Oat grass [Oatgrass, Oat-grass] (50, 93, 138, 155) (1923–present)

Arrhenatherum bulbosum – See *Arrhenatherum elatius* (L.) Beauv. ex J. Presl & C. Presl

Arrhenatherum elatius (L.) Beauv. ex J. Presl & C. Presl – Butter twitch (5) (1913), Button grass (5) (1913), Button twitch (5) (1913), Evergreen grass (5, 45, 67, 87, 88) (1884–1913), False oat grass [False oat-grass] (5, 45, 56, 68) (1896–1913), French rye grass [French rye-grass] (45) (1896), Grass-of-the-Andes [Grass of the Andes] (5) (1913), Hever grass (5) (1913), Knyl-hafre (Swedish) (46) (1879), Meadow oat grass (68, 87, 88) (1884–1890), Oat grass [Oatgrass, Oat-grass] (5, 56, 68, 85, 92) (1876–1932), Onion grass [Oniongrass, Onion-grass] (5) (1913), Onion twitch (5) (1913), Pearl grass (3, 5) (1913–1977), Randall's grass [Randall grass] (67)

(1890), Ray grass [Ray-grass] (66, 67) (1890–1903), Tall meadow oat grass (56, 66, 68, 87) (1884–1903), Tall oat grass [Tall oatgrass, Tall oatgrass] (11, 45, 50, 66, 68, 87, 88, 94, 109, 111, 129, 138, 140, 143, 155) (1884–present), Tuber oat grass [Tuber oatgrass] (138) (1923)

Arrhenatherum elatius (L.) Beauv. ex J.& K. Presl var. *elatius* – Ray grass of France (92) (1876), Tall oat grass [Tall oatgrass, Tall oat-grass] (42, 45, 50) (1814–present), possibly Oat grass [Oatgrass, Oat-grass] (72) (1907)

Arsenococcus ligustrinus (L.) Small – Airelle à feuilles de troène (French) (8) (1785), Privet-leaf whortle-berry [Privet-leaved whor-tle-berry] (8) (1785)

Artabotrys hexapetalus (L.f.) Bhandari – Climbing ylang-ylang (109) (1949), Fragrant tailgrape (138, 155) (1923–1942)

Artabotrys odoratissimus Wight & Arn. – See *Artabotrys hexapeta-lus* (L. f.) Bhandari

Artabotrys R. Br. – Tail-grape [Tailgrape] (109, 138, 155) (1931–1949)

Artabotrys uncinatus – possibly *Artabotrys hexapetalus* (L. f.) Bhan-dari

Artanthe elongata – See *Piper aduncum* L.

Artemisia (Tourn.) L. – See *Artemisia* L.

Artemisia abrotanum L. – Abrotano (158) (1900), Abrotanum (158) (1900), Apple-riennie (158) (1900), Aurone Mâle (French) (158) (1900), Averoyne (158) (1900), Boy's-love [Boy's-love] (5, 73, 92, 156, 157, 158) (1892–1929) Wellfleet MA, Citronelle (French) (158) (1900), Eberraute (German) (158) (1900), Eherreiskraut (German) (158) (1900), Gertwurz (German) (158) (1900), Kiss-me-quick-and-go (156, 157, 158) (1900–1929), Lad-savour (157, 158) (1900–1929), Lad's-love [Lad's love] (5, 73, 92, 156) (1876–1923) New England, for aphrodisiac qualitites or use in love divinations, Leam-ington (73) (1892) Ipswich MA, Maiden's-ruin (157, 158) (1900–1929), Maid's-love (157, 158) (1900–1929), Male southernwood (178) (1526), Old-man [Old man] (5, 57, 73, 92, 107, 156, 157, 158) (1876–1929) for aphrodisiac qualitites or use in love divinations, Old-man wormwood [Oldman wormwood] (155) (1942), Sloven-wood [Sloven-wood] (5, 92, 156, 157, 158) (1876–1929), Smelling-wood (156, 157, 158) (1900–1929), Southern wormwood (46, 72) (1671–1907), Southernwood [Southern-wood, Southern wood] (3, 4, 5, 19, 41, 46, 50, 57, 92, 107, 109, 135, 138, 156, 158) (1671–present), Stabwurzel (German) (158) (1900), Sweet Benjamin (5, 75, 156, 157, 158) (1894–1929) Concord MA

Artemisia absinthium L. – Absinthe [Absinth] (5, 6, 85, 107, 138, 156) (1892–1932), Absinthe Grande (158) (1900), Absinthium (50, 53, 55, 57, 92, 109, 157, 158) (1876–present), Ajenjos (Spanish) (158) (1900), Alsei (German) (158) (1900), Aluyne (French) (158) (1900), Boy's-love [Boy's-love] (5, 75, 156) (1894–1923) New England, for aphrodisiac qualitites or use in love divinations, Madderwort [Maderwort] (5, 156, 157, 158) (1900–1929), Mingwort (5, 156, 157, 158) (1900–1929), Mugwort [Mug-wort, Mugwoort] (5, 156) (1913–1923), Muse'odji'bĭk (Chippewa, worm root) (40) (1928), Old-woman [Old woman] (156, 157, 158) (1900–1929), War-mot (5, 156, 157, 158) (1900–1929), Weremod (157, 158) (1900–1929), Wermuth (German) (6, 158) (1892–1900), Wormit (157, 158) (1900–1929), Wormwood [Wormewood, Worm-wood] (3, 4, 6, 19, 40, 46, 49, 53, 55, 57, 58, 61, 92, 107, 157, 158, 179, 184) (1671–1986) accidentally introduced into US by 1671, Wurmtod (German) (158) (1900), possibly Common wormwood (5, 7, 63, 72, 85, 93, 95, 109, 138, 155, 156) (1828–1949)

Artemisia albula Woot. – See *Artemisia ludoviciana* Nutt. subsp. *al-bula* (Woot.) Keck

Artemisia annua L. – Annual wormwood (5, 72, 93) (1907–1936), Sweet mugwort (155) (1942), Sweet sagewort (3, 4, 50) (1977–pres-ent), Sweet wormwood (109, 138, 155) (1923–1949)

Artemisia arbuscula Nutt. – Low sagebrush (138, 155) (1931–1942)

Artemisia biennis Willd. – Biennial wormwood (3, 4, 5, 50, 72, 93, 131, 155) (1899–present), Woemwood (62) (1912), Wormwood [Worme-wood, Worm-wood] (80) (1913)

Artemisia bigelovii Gray – Bigelow's sage [Bigelow sage] (50) (present), Bigelow's sagebrush [Bigelow sagebrush] (122, 155) (1937–1942), Bigelow's sage-bush (5) (1913)

Artemisia bolanderi – See *Artemisia cana* Pursh subsp. *bolanderi* (Gray) G. H. Ward

Artemisia borealis Pallas – See *Artemisia campestris* L. subsp. *borealis* (Pallas) Hall & Clements

Artemisia californica Less. – California sagebrush (155) (1942)

Artemisia campestris L. – Čaŋxloǧaŋ waštemna (Lakota, odorous weed) (121) (1918?–1970?), Field sagewort (50) (present), Field wormwood (19) (1840), Sagewort wormwood (155) (1942), Sagewort wormwood (177) (1762)

Artemisia campestris L. subsp. *borealis* (Pallas) Hall & Clements – Canadian sagebrush [Canada sagebrush] (155) (1942), Canadian wormwood [Canada wormwood] (5, 72, 93, 95, 131, 156) (1899–1936), Field sagewort (50) (present), Northern wormwood (5, 112, 155) (1913–1942), Sagebrush [Sage-brush, Sage brush] (85) (1932), Sea wormwood (5, 156) (1913–1923), Wild wormwood (5, 19, 156) (1840–1923)

Artemisia campestris L. subsp. *caudata* (Michx.) Hall & Clem. – Field sagewort (50) (present)

Artemisia campestris L. subsp. *pacifica* (Nutt.) Hall & Clements – See *Artemisia campestris* L. subsp. *borealis* (Pallas) Hall & Clements

Artemisia campestris L. var. *douglasiana* (Bess.) Boivin – See *Artemisia campestris* L. subsp. *borealis* (Pallas) Hall & Clements

Artemisia campestris L. var. *pacifica* (Nutt.) M. E. Peck – See *Artemisia campestris* L. subsp. *borealis* (Pallas) Hall & Clements

Artemisia campestris L. var. *strutziae* Welsh – See *Artemisia campestris* L. subsp. *borealis* (Pallas) Hall & Clements

Artemisia camporum Rydb. – See *Artemisia campestris* L. subsp. *borealis* (Pallas) Hall & Clements

Artemisia cana Pursh – Blue sage (101) (1905), Dwarf sagebrush (3) (1977), Hoary sagebrush [Hoary sage-bush] (5, 93, 95, 131) (1899–1936), Little sage brush (113, 130) (1890), Sagebush [Sage bush, Sage-bush] (5, 36, 97) (1830–1937), Silver sagebrush (50) (Present), Smaller sagebrush (95) (1911), White sagebrush [White sage-brush] (108) (1878), Wild sage (10, 19, 36) (1818–1840), Wild wormwood (36) (1830)

Artemisia cana Pursh subsp. *bolanderi* (Gray) G. H. Ward – Bolander's sagebrush [Bolander sagebrush] (155) (1942)

Artemisia cana Pursh subsp. *cana* – Silver sagebrush (50) (present)

Artemisia canadensis Michx. – See *Artemisia campestris* L. subsp. *borealis* (Pallas) Hall & Clements

Artemisia carruthii Wood ex Carruth. – Carruth's sagebrush [Carruth sagebrush] (155) (1942), Carruth's sagewort (50) (present), Kansas mugwort (5, 97) (1913–1937), Wright's sagebrush [Wrights sagebrush] (155) (1942)

Artemisia columbiensis [Nutt.] – See *Artemisia cana* Pursh

Artemisia cuneata Rydb. – See *Artemisia ludoviciana* Nutt. var. *cuneata* (Rydb.) Fernald

Artemisia discolor Douglas ex Besser – See *Artemisia michauxiana* Besser

Artemisia diversifolia Rydb. – See *Artemisia ludoviciana* Nutt. subsp. *ludoviciana*

Artemisia dracunculoides Pursh – See *Artemisia dracunculus* L.

Artemisia dracunculus L. – Ba'sibûgûk' (Chippewa, small leaf) (40) (1928), Ba'sûnûkûk' (Chippewa) (40) (1928), Biting dragon [Biting-dragon] (157, 158) (1900–1929), Bû'giso'wîn (Chippewa, swimming or bath) (40) (1928), Common wormwood (131) (1899), Draco (180) (1633), Dragon (French) (180) (1633), Dragon [Dragons] (158) (1900), Dragoncellum (180) (1633), Dragunbeifuss (German) (158) (1900), Estragon (French) (Spanish) (158) (1900), False-tarragon sagebrush [Falsetarragon sagebrush] (155) (1942), Fuzzyweed [Fuzzy weed] (37) (1919), Ǐ'ckode'bûg (Chippewa, fire leaf) (40) (1928), Jǐn'gwakwan'dûg (Chippewa, pine) (40) (1928), Kaisersalat (German) (158) (1900), Kihapiliwus (Pawnee,

broom) (37) (1919), Linear-leaf wormwood [Linear-leaved wormwood] (5, 72, 93, 97, 122) (1907–1937), Mugwort [Mug-wort, Mugwoort] (40) (1928), O'gima'wûck (Chippewa, chief medicine) (40) (1928), Rake-hinshek (Winnebago, bushy weed or fuzzy weed) (37) (1919), Sagebrush [Sage brush, Sage-brush] (85, 124) (1932–1937), Sagebrush [Sage brush] (133) (1903), Silky wormwood (3, 4, 5, 85, 93, 98) (1913–1986), Tarragon (46, 50, 57, 92, 107, 109, 138, 155, 157, 158, 178, 180) (1596–present), Thasatahi (Omaha-Ponca) (37) (1919), Wormwood [Wormewood, Wormwood] (124) (1937), possiblyTarchon (180) (1633)

Artemisia filifolia Torr. – Sagebrush [Sage brush, Sage-brush] (96) (1891), Sand sage (65) (1931), Sand sagebrush (3, 4, 50, 156) (1923–present), Silvery wormwood (5, 85, 93, 97, 122, 131, 158) (1899–1937), Southernwood [Southern-wood, Southern wood] (158) (1900), Wormwood [Wormewood, Worm-wood] (103, 113) (1870–1890)

Artemisia franserioides Greene – Ragweed sagebrush (155) (1942)

Artemisia frigida Willd. – Bi'jikiwîn'gûck (Chippewa, cattle herb) (40) (1928), Colorado mountain sage (157) (1929), Fringed sage (146) (1939), Fringed sagebrush (155) (1942), Fringed wormwood (138) (1923), Kiwoh'ki (Pawnee) (37) (1919), Little sage (121, 127) (1937–1970), Little wild sage (37) (1919), Mountain sage [Mountain-sage] (57, 156, 157, 158) (1900–1929), Nasula jazaŋpi ipije (Lakota, no appetite cure) (121) (1918?–1970?), Pasture sage (146, 156) (1923–1939), Pasture sage-brush [Pasture sagebrush] (5, 85, 122, 156, 157, 158) (1900–1929), Pasture sage-bush (93) (1936), Pezhe-h'ota zhinga (Omaha-Ponca, little gray herb) (37) (1919), Pežixota waštemna (Lakota, odorous gray herb) (121) (1918?–1970?), Prairie sage (40) (1928), Prairie sagewort (3, 50) (1977–present), Sagebrush [Sage brush, Sage-brush] (101) (1905), Sagebrush [Sage brush] (6, 158) (1892–1900), Sierra salvia (157, 158) (1900–1929), Sweet sage (101, 146) (1905–1939) MT, Wia-ta-pezhihuta (Dakota, woman's medicine) (37) (1919), Wild sage (156, 157, 158) (1900–1929), Wormwood sage (5, 131, 156, 157, 158) (1899–1931)

Artemisia glauca Pallas – See *Artemisia dracunculus* L.

Artemisia gmelinii Webb ex Stechmann – Russian wormwood (109, 137, 155) (1931–1949), Summer-fir Russian wormwood [Summerfir Russian wormwood] (155) (1942)

Artemisia gnaphalodes Nutt. – See *Artemisia ludoviciana* Nutt. subsp. *ludoviciana*

Artemisia kansana Britton – See *Artemisia carruthii* Wood ex Carruth.

Artemisia L. – Cudweed [Cud-weed, Cud weed] (1) (1932), Hyssop [Hysop, Hysope] (27) (1811), Mugwort [Mug-wort, Mugwoort] (1, 4, 167) (1814–1986), Old-woman [Old woman] (73) (1892), Sagebrush [Sage brush, Sage-brush] (1, 50, 108, 155, 158) (1878–present), Southernwood [Southern-wood, Southern wood] (10, 184) (1793–1818), Wormweed [Worm weed, Worm-weed] (93) (1936), Wormwood [Wormewood, Worm-wood] (1, 2, 4, 10, 34, 38, 63, 138, 155, 158) (1820–1986) from Old World name

Artemisia longifolia Nutt. – Alkali sagebrush (155) (1942), Long-leaf mugwort [Long-leaved mugwort] (5, 72, 93, 131) (1899–1936), Long-leaf sage [Long-leaved sage] (3, 4) (1977–1986), Long-leaf sagebrush [Longleaf sagebrush, Long-leaf sage brush, Long-leaved sage brush] (85, 155) (1932–1942), Long-leaf wormwood [Longleaf wormwood] (50) (present)

Artemisia ludoviciana Nutt. – Absinthe (28) (1850), Cudweed [Cudweed, Cud weed] (156) (1923), Dark-leaf mugwort [Darkleaf mugwort, Dark-leaved mugwort] (5, 93, 97, 122) (1913–1937), Lobed cudweed [Lobed cud-weed] (72) (1907), Louisiana sagebrush (155) (1942), Mugwort [Mug-wort, Mugwoort] (156) (1923), Prairie sage (28, 156) (1850–1923), Sagebrush [Sage brush, Sage-brush] (85) (1932), Sagebrush [Sage brush] (158) (1900), Western mugwort (80, 108, 156) (1878–1923), Western sage (156) (1923), White sage (4, 156) (1923–1986), White sagebrush [White sage-brush] (50) (present), White wormwood (80) (1913), Wild sage (35) (1806), Woolly sage (156) (1923), Wormwood [Wormewood, Worm-wood] (48) (1882)

Artemisia ludoviciana **Nutt. subsp. *albula* (Woot.) Keck** – Silver-king artemisia [Silver king artemisia] (109) (1949), Silver-king sagebrush [Silverking sagebrush] (155) (1942)

Artemisia ludoviciana **Nutt. subsp. *candicans* (Rydb.) Keck** – Woolly herb (108) (1878)

Artemisia ludoviciana **Nutt. subsp. *ludoviciana*** – Cudweed [Cudweed, Cud weed] (5) (1913), Cudweed mugwort (157, 158) (1900–1929), Cudweed sagebrush (155) (1942), Cudweed wormwood (138) (1923), Hanwinska (Winnebago, white herb) (37) (1919), Kiwaut (Pawnee) (37) (1919), Mix-leaf sagebrush [Mixleaf sagebrush] (155) (1942), Mugwort [Mug-wort, Mugwoort] (5) (1913), Nokwe'jigûn (Chippewa, something soft) (40) (1928), Pezhe hot'a (Omaha-Ponca, gray herb) (37) (1919), Pezhih'ota blaska (Dakota, flat gray herb) (37) (1919), Prairie mugwort (131, 157, 158) (1899–1929), Prairie sage (5, 93, 97) (1913–1937), Prairie wormwood (72) (1907), Pursh's sagebrush [Pursh sagebrush] (4, 50) (1986–present), Saw-leaf mugwort [Saw-leaved mugwort] (5, 72, 131) (1899–1913), Sawtooth sagebrush (155) (1942), Sawtooth wormwood (138) (1923), Western mugwort (158) (1900), Western sage (5, 93, 157) (1900–1936), Western sagebrush [Western sage brush] (85) (1932), White mugwort (40) (1928), White sage (3, 98, 127, 158) (1900–1977), White sagebrush [White sage-brush] (50) (present), Wild sage (37, 157) (1919–1929), Wormwood [Wormewood, Worm-wood] (21) (1893)

Artemisia ludoviciana **Nutt. subsp. *mexicana* (Willd. ex Spreng.) Keck** – Mexican mugwort (5, 97, 122) (1913–1937), Mexican sagebrush (155) (1942), New Mexico sagebrush [New Mexican sagebrush] (155) (1942), White sagebrush [White sage-brush] (50) (present), Wormwood [Wormewood, Worm-wood] (124) (1937)

Artemisia ludoviciana **Nutt. subsp. *redolens* (Gray) Keck** – Chihuahua sagebrush (155) (1942)

Artemisia ludoviciana **Nutt. var. *latifolia* (Bess.) Torr. & Gray** – See *Artemisia ludoviciana* Nutt. subsp. *ludoviciana*

Artemisia ludoviciana **var. *cuneata* (Rydb.) Fernald** – Wild wormwood (122) (1937)

Artemisia ludoviciana **var. *latiloba*** – See *Artemisia ludoviciana* Nutt. subsp. *candicans* (Rydb*.*) Keck

Artemisia mexicana **Willd. ex Spreng.** – See *Artemisia ludoviciana* Nutt. subsp. *mexicana* (Willd. ex Spreng.) Keck

Artemisia michauxiana **Bess.** – Michaux's sagebrush [Michaux sagebrush] (155) (1942), Sweet sagebrush (155) (1942)

Artemisia mutellina **Vill.** – See *Artemisia umbelliformis* Lam. introduced

Artemisia natronensis **A. Nelson** – See *Artemisia longifolia* Nutt.

Artemisia neomexicana **Greene ex Rydb.** – See *Artemisia ludoviciana* Nutt. subsp. *mexicana* (Willd. ex Spreng.) Keck

Artemisia nova **A. Nels.** – Black sagebrush (155) (1942)

Artemisia pacifica **Nutt.** – See *Artemisia campestris* L. subsp. *borealis* (Pallas) Hall & Clements

Artemisia palmeri **Gray** – Palmer's sagebrush [Palmer sagebrush] (155) (1942)

Artemisia parishi – See *Artemisia tridentata* Nutt. subsp. *parishii* (Gray) Hall & Clements

Artemisia parishii **A. Gray** – See *Artemisia tridentata* Nutt. subsp. *parishii* (Gray) Hall & Clements

Artemisia pedatifida **Nutt.** – Bird's-foot sagebrush [Birdfoot sagebrush] (50, 155) (1942–present)

Artemisia pontica **L.** – Hungarian wormwood (5, 156) (1913–1923), Roman artemisia (19) (1840), Roman wormwood (5, 92, 109, 138, 155, 156) (1876–1942)

Artemisia purshiana **Bess.** – See *Artemisia ludoviciana* Nutt. subsp. *ludoviciana*

Artemisia pycnocephala **(Less.) DC.** – Sandhill wormwood (155) (1942)

Artemisia redolens – See *Artemisia ludoviciana* Nutt. subsp. *redolens* (Gray) Keck

Artemisia rigida **(Nutt.) Gray** – Stiff sagebrush (155) (1942)

Artemisia ripicola **Rydb.** – See *Artemisia campestris* L. subsp. *borealis* (Pallas) Hall & Clements

Artemisia rothrocki – See *Artemisia rothrockii* Gray

Artemisia rothrockii **Gray** – Rothrock's sagebrush [Rothrock sagebrush] (155) (1942)

Artemisia rupestris **L.** – Broad-leaf wormwood [Broad leafed wormwood] (179) (1526), Rock wormwood (155) (1942)

Artemisia sacrorum **Lebed.** – See *Artemisia gmelinii* Webb ex Stechmann

Artemisia sacrorum viridis – See *Artemisia gmelinii* Webb ex Stechmann

Artemisia scoparia **Waldst. & Kit.** – Oriental wormwood (138, 155) (1931–1942)

Artemisia scopulorum **Gray** – Alpine sagebrush (155) (1942)

Artemisia serrata **Nutt.** – See *Artemisia ludoviciana* Nutt. subsp. *ludoviciana*

Artemisia spinescens **D.C. Eat.** – See *Picrothamnus desertorum* Nutt.

Artemisia stelleriana **Bess.** – Beach wormwood (5, 109, 138, 155 156) (1913–1949), Dusty-miller [Dustymiller, Dusty miller] (109, 155, 156) (1923–1949), Old-woman [Old woman] (109, 156) (1923–1949)

Artemisia tridentata angustifolia – See *Artemisia tridentata* Nutt. subsp. *tridentata*

Artemisia tridentata **Nutt.** – Absinthe (28) (1850), Big sage (146) (1939), Big sagebrush (3, 4, 50, 146, 155) (1939–present), Black sage (156) (1923), Blue sage (156) (1923), Common sagebrush [Common sage-brush] (95, 108, 158) (1878–1911), Common sagebush [Common sage-bush] (5) (1913), Mountain sage [Mountain-sage] (5, 93, 156, 157, 158) (1900–1929), Prairie sage (44) (1845), Qémqem (Nez Perce) (35) (1806), Sage plant (14) (1882), Sagebrush [Sage brush, Sage-brush] (5, 57, 75, 101, 109, 113, 130, 138, 156, 157, 158) (1890–1949), Sagebush [Sage bush, Sage-bush] (3, 4, 5, 10, 40, 45, 48, 63, 80, 82, 97, 106 109, 124, 131, 156, 157, 158, 187, 190) (1818–1986), Sageplant [Sage plant] (14, 179) (1526–1882), Sagewood [Sage wood, sage-wood] (5, 156, 157) (1900–1929), Southernwood [Southern-wood, Southern wood] (35) (1806), Three-tooth sagebrush [Three-toothed sage-brush] (108) (1878), Wild hyssop (35) (1806), Wild sage (160) (1860)

Artemisia tridentata **Nutt. subsp. *parishii* (Gray) Hall & Clements** – Parish's sagebrush [Parish sagebrush] (155) (1942)

Artemisia tridentata **Nutt. subsp. *tridentata*** – Narrow-leaf big sagebrush [Narrowleaf big sagebrush] (155) (1942)

Artemisia tridentata **Nutt. subsp. *vaseyana* (Rydb.) Beetle** – Mountain big sagebrush (50) (present), Saw-wort [Saw woort, Saw wort, Sawwort] (190) (~1759)

Artemisia tridentata **Nutt. subsp. *wyomingensis* Beetle & Young** – Wyoming big sagebrush (50) (present)

Artemisia tridentata **Nutt. var. *pauciflora* Winward & Goodrich** – See *Artemisia tridentata* Nutt. subsp. *vaseyana* (Rydb.) Beetle

Artemisia tridentata **Nutt. var. *vaseyana* (Rydb.) Boivin** – See *Artemisia tridentata* Nutt. subsp. *vaseyana* (Rydb.) Beetle

Artemisia tripartita **Rydb.** – Three-tip sagebrush [Threetip sagebrush] (155) (1942)

Artemisia umbelliformis **Lam.** – Silver Alp wormwood [Silveralp wormwood] (155) (1942)

Artemisia vaseyana **Rydb.** – See *Artemisia tridentata* Nutt. subsp. *vaseyana* (Rydb.) Beetle

Artemisia vulgaris – See *Artemisia ludoviciana* Nutt.

Artemisia vulgaris **L.** – Apple-pie [Apple pie] (156, 157) (1923–1929), Bifuss (German) (6) (1892), Bulwand (156, 157) (1923–1929), Common mugwort (5, 95, 156, 157) (1911–1929), Common tansy [Common tansey] (19) (1840), Couronne de St. Jean (French) (6) (1892), Felon herb [Fellon-herb, Felon-herb] (107, 156, 157) (1919–1929), Green ginger (156, 157) (1923–1929), Mother-wort (179) (1526), Mother-of-herbs [Moder of herbes] (179) (1526), Motherwort [Mother wort, Mother-wort, Mother Woort] (156, 157)

(1923–1929), Mugweed (157) (1929), Mugwort [Mug-wort, Mug-woort] (6, 7, 19, 57, 107, 109, 138, 157, 178) (1526–1949), Mugwort sagebrush (155) (1942), Sailor's-tobacco [Sailor's tobacco] (156, 157) (1923–1929), Small jagged mugwoort [Small iagged mug-woort] (178) (1526), Smotherwood (156, 157) (1923–1929), Worm-wood [Wormewood, Worm-wood] (156) (1923)

Artemisia wrighti – See *Artemisia carruthii* Wood ex Carruth.

Artemisia wrightii **Gray** – See *Artemisia carruthii* Wood ex Carruth.

Arthrothamnus **Klotzsch & Garcke** – See *Euphorbia* L.

Artobotrys odoratissimus **R. Br.** – See *Artabotrys hexapetalus* (L. f.) Bhandari

Artobotrys **R. Br.** – See *Artabotrys* R. Br.

Artocarpus altilis **(Parkinson) Fosberg** – Breadfruit [Bread fruit, Bread-fruit] (92, 109, 110, 138, 155) (1876–1949)

Artocarpus altilis **Fosberg** – See *Artocarpus altilis* (Parkinson) Fosberg

Artocarpus heterophyllus **Lam.** – Jack fruit [Jack-fruit, Jackfruit] (109, 155) (1942–1949)

Artocarpus heterophyllus **Lam.** – Jakfruit (109, 155) (1942–1949)

Artocarpus incisa **L.** – See *Artocarpus altilis* (Parkinson) Fosberg

Artocarpus incisus **(Thunb.) L. f.** – See *Artocarpus altilis* (Parkinson) Fosberg

Artocarpus **J.R. & G. Forst.** – Breadfruit [Bread fruit, Bread-fruit] (138) (1923)

Arum atrorubens **W.** – See *Arisaema triphyllum* (L.) Schott subsp. *triphyllum*

Arum dracontium **L.** – See *Arisaema dracontium* (L.) Schott

Arum esculentum **L.** – See *Colocasia esculenta* (L.) Schott colocasia of Diosorides is actually nelumbo according to A. DC.

Arum italicum **Mill.** – Italian arum (138, 155) (1923–1942)

Arum **L.** – Arum (138, 155) (1923–1942) the ancient Latin name, Cuckoo-point [Cuckow-point] (184) (1793), Indian turnip (167) (1814), Wakerobin [Wake robin, Wake-robin] (10) (1818)

Arum triphyllum **L.** – See *Arisaema triphyllum* (L.) Schott

Arum virginicum **L.** – See *Hexastylis virginica* (L.) Small

Aruncus **(L.) Adans.** – See *Aruncus* L.

Aruncus **Adans.** – See *Aruncus* L.

Aruncus allegheniensis – See *Aruncus dioicus* (Walt.) Fern. var. *dioicus*

Aruncus allegheniensis pubescens – See *Aruncus dioicus* (Walt.) Fern. var. *pubescens* (Rydb.) Fern.

Aruncus aruncus **(L.) Karst.** – See *Aruncus dioicus* (Walt.) Fern. var. *vulgaris* (Maxim.) Hara

Aruncus dioicus **(Walt.) Fern. var. dioicus** – Allegheny goatsbread [Alleghany goatsbread] (155) (1942)

Aruncus dioicus **(Walt.) Fern. var. pubescens (Rydb.) Fern.** – Goat's-beard [Goat's beard, Goats-beard, Goatsbeard] (97) (1937), Hairy Allegheny goat's-bread [Hairy Alleghany goatsbread] (155) (1942)

Aruncus dioicus **(Walt.) Fern. var. vulgaris (Maxim.) Hara** – Aruncus (174, 177) (1753–1762), Birch-leaf meadowsweet [Birshleaf meadowsweet] (155) (1942), Common goatbeard (138) (1923), Goat's-beard [Goat's beard, Goats-beard, Goatsbeard] (2, 5, 63, 156) (1895–1923), Steeple-weed (19) (1840), Sylvan goatsbeard (155) (1942)

Aruncus **L.** – Goat's-beard [Goat's beard, Goats-beard, Goatsbeard] (1, 72, 109, 138, 155, 156) (1907–1949)

Aruncus pubescens **Rydb.** – See *Aruncus dioicus* (Walt.) Fern. var. *pubescens* (Rydb.) Fern.

Aruncus sylvester – See *Aruncus dioicus* (Walt.) Fern. var. *vulgaris* (Maxim.) Hara

Arundinacia macrosperma **var. suffruticosa Munro.** – See *Arundinaria gigantea* (Walter) Muhl.

Arundinaria gigantea **(Walt.) Chapm.** – possibly *Arundinaria gigantea* (Walter) Muhl.

Arundinaria gigantea **(Walt.) Muhl. subsp. gigantea** – Cane [Canes] (7, 12, 19, 38, 45, 66, 94, 182) (1791–1912)

Arundinaria gigantea **(Walt.) Muhl. subsp. tecta (Walt.) McClure** – Reed canebrake [Reed cane brake] (5) (1913), Scutch cane (5)

(1913), Small cane (5, 88, 138) (1885–1923), Switch cane [Switch-cane] (5, 45, 88, 122) (1885–1937), Small cane (45) (1896)

Arundinaria gigantea **(Walter) Muhl.** – Giant cane (5, 50, 119, 163) (1913–present), Large cane (2, 107, 163) (1852–1919), Smaller reed (2) (1895), Southern cane (122, 138) (1923–1937), Switch cane [Switch-cane] (2) (1895), possibly Cain (35) (1806), possibly Reed grass [Reedgrass, Reed-grass] (124) (1937)

Arundinaria gigantea **subsp. macrosperma (Michx.) McClure** – See *Arundinaria gigantea* (Walt.) Muhl. subsp. *gigantea*

Arundinaria japonica – See *Pseudosasa japonica* (Sieb. & Zucc. ex Steud.) Makino ex Nakai

Arundinaria macrosperma **Michx.** – See *Arundinaria gigantea* (Walter) Muhl.

Arundinaria macrosperma **Michx. var. tecta Walt.** – See *Arundinaria gigantea (Walter) Muhl.* subsp. *tecta* (Walter) McClure

Arundinaria **Michx.** – Cane [Canes] (10, 66, 155) (1818–1942), Cane brake (92) (1876)

Arundinaria tecta **(Walt.) Muhl.** – See *Arundinaria gigantea* (Walt.) Muhl. subsp. *tecta* (Walt.) McClure

Arundo arenaria – See *Ammophila arenaria* (L.) Link

Arundo donax **L.** – Giant reed [Giantreed] (109, 119, 122, 138, 163) (1852–1949), Giant reed grass [Giant reed-grass] (88) (1885), Reed fescue (129) (1894), Spanish cane (92) (1876)

Arundo **L.** – Giant reed [Giantreed] (41, 155) (1770–1942), Reed [Rede, Reeds] (10, 92) (1818–1876)

Arundo phragmites **L.** – See *Phragmites australis* (Cav.) Trin. ex Steud.

Asarum **(Tourn.) L.** – See *Asarum* L.

Asarum acuminatum **(Ashe) Bicknell** – See *Asarum canadense* L.

Asarum arifolium **Michx** – See *Hexastylis arifolia* (Michx.) Small var. *arifolia*

Asarum canadense **L.** – Agabwen (105) (1932), American asarabacca (186, 187) (1814–1818), Asarabacca (5, 64, 92, 156) (1876–1923), Asarabica (156) (1923), Asaret (French) (158) (1900), Asaret du Canada (French) (7) (1828), Asari Canadensis herba (Official name of Materia Medica) (7) (1828), Asarum (52, 181) (~1678–1919), Az-aro (158) (1900), Black snakeroot [Black snake-root, Black-snake root] (156, 158) (1900–1923), Black snakeweed [Black snake-weed] (64) (1907), Broad-leaf asarabacca [Broadleaved asarabacca, Broad-leaved asabaraca] (7, 64, 158) (1828–1907), Canadian ginger [Canada ginger] (49, 156) (1898–1923), Canadian snakeroot [Canada snakeroot, Canada snake root, Canada snake-root] (7, 53, 57, 58, 64, 92, 109, 156, 158, 186) (1814–1949), Canadian wild ginger [Canada wild ginger, Canada wildginger] (2, 50, 138, 155) (1895–present), Canadische Haselwurz (German) (7) (1828), Canadische Schlagen-wurz (German) (158) (1900), Cat's-foot [Cats foot, Cat's foot, Cat foot] (64, 92, 156, 158) (1898–1923), Colic root [Colic-root, Colic-root] (5, 75, 158) (1900–1913) WV, Coltsfoot [Colt's foot, Colt's-foot, Colt foot] (7, 49, 58, 64, 75, 77, 177, 186, 190) (~1759–1908), Coltsfoot snakeroot [Coltsfoot snakeroot, Colt's-foot snakeroot, Colt's-foot-snakeroot] (79, 92, 156, 158) (1876–1900) NH, Curly wild ginger [Curly wildginger] (138, 155) (1923–1942), False colts-foot [False colt's foot] (5, 19, 64, 92, 156, 158) (1840–1923), False crowfoot (156) (1923), Gingembre (French) (41) (1770), Hazelwort [Hazel wort] (156) (1923), Heart snakeroot [Heart snake root, Heart snake-root] (5, 7, 64, 92, 156, 158) (1828–1923), Indian ginger (5, 7, 49, 53, 58, 64, 92, 156, 158, 186) (1814–1923), Indischer Ingwer (German) (158) (1900), Kidney-leaf asarabacca [Kidney-leaved asarabacca] (186) (1814), Long-tip wild ginger [Long-tipped wild ginger] (5, 72) (1907–1913), Name'pĭn (Chippewa, sturgeon plant) (40) (1928), Short-lobe wild ginger [Short-lobed wild ginger] (5, 72) (1907–1913), Snakeroot [Snake root, Snake-root] (64, 79, 92, 107) (1891–1919), Southern snakeroot [Southern snake-root] (5, 64, 156) (1907–1923), Vermont snakeroot [Vermont snake root, Vermont snake-root] (5, 64, 156, 158) (1900–1923), White snakeroot [White snake root, White snake-root] (19, 42) (1814–1840), Wild ginger [Wildginger] (3, 5, 7, 19, 35, 40, 41, 42, 46, 47, 49, 52, 53, 57, 58, 64, 65, 72, 97, 105, 107, 109, 156, 157, 158, 186, 187) (1770–1949)

51

Asarum caudatum **Lindl.** – British Columbia wild ginger [British Columbia wildginger, BritishColumbia wildginger] (50, 155) (1942–present), Wild ginger [Wildginger] (35) (1806)

Asarum hartwegi – See *Asarum hartwegii* S. Wats.

Asarum hartwegii **S. Wats.** – Sierra wild ginger [Sierra wildginger] (155) (1942)

Asarum **L.** – Asarabacca (2, 10, 158, 167) (1814–1900), Indian ginger (10) (1818), Wild ginger [Wildginger] (2, 4, 50, 109, 138, 155) (1923–present)

Asarum lemmoni – See *Asarum lemmonii* S. Wats.

Asarum lemmonii **S. Wats.** – Lemmon's wild ginger [Lemmons wildginger] (155) (1942)

Asarum reflexum **Bicknell** – See *Asarum canadense* L.

Asarum shuttleworthi – See *Hexastylis shuttleworthii* (Britten & Baker) Small var. *shuttleworthii*

Asarum virginicum **L.** – See *Hexastylis virginica* (L.) Small

Asclepias (Tourn.) **L.** – See *Asclepias* L.

Asclepias amoena **L.** – See *Asclepias purpurascens* L.

Asclepias amplexicaulis **Sm.** – Blunt-leaf milkweed [Blunt leaf milkweed] (3, 4, 5, 72, 82, 93, 97, 122, 124) (1907–1986), Clasping milkweed (50) (present)

Asclepias arenaria **Torr.** – Sand milkweed (3, 4, 5, 50, 93, 97, 122) (1913–present)

Asclepias asperula (Dcne.) **Woods.** – Antelope-horns [Antelope horns, Antelopehorns, Antelopehorn] (4) (1986), Spider milkweed (50) (present)

Asclepias asperula (Dcne.) **Woods. subsp.** *asperula* – Spider milkweed (50) (present)

Asclepias asperula (Dcne.) **Woods. subsp.** *capricornu* (Woods.) **Woods.** – Antelope-horns [Antelope horns, Antelopehorns, Antelopehorn] (50, 122, 124) (1937–present), Creeping milkweed (5) (1913), Decumbent butterfly-weed [Decumbent butterfly weed] (5, 72, 122) (1907–1937), Decumbent milkweed (5, 97) (1913–1937), Spider antelope-horn [Spider antelopehorn] (155) (1942)

Asclepias asperula (Dcne.) **Woods. var.** *decumbens* (Nutt.) **Shinners** – See *Asclepias asperula* (Dcne.) Woods. subsp. *capricornu* (Woods.) Woods.

Asclepias brachystephana **Engelm. ex Torr.** – Bract milkweed (50) (present), Short-crown milkweed [Shortcrown milkweed, Short crowned milkweed, Short-crowned milkweed] (4, 5, 122) (1913–1986)

Asclepias brachystephana **Torr.** – See *Asclepias brachystephana* Engelm. ex Torr.

Asclepias cinerea **Walt.** – Artichoke-leaf milkweed [Artichoke leaved milk weed] (42) (1814), Artichoke-leaf swallow-wort [Artichoke leaved swallow wort] (42) (1814)

Asclepias cornuti **Dcne.** – See *Asclepias syriaca* L.

Asclepias curassavica **L.** – Bastard ipecac (92) (1876), Blood-flower [Bloodflower, Blood flower] (57, 109, 138) (1917–1949), Blood-flower milkweed [Bloodflower milkweed] (155) (1942), Bloodweed [Blood weed, Blood-weed] (92) (1876), Garden silkweed (58) (1869), Redhead [Red head] (92) (1876)

Asclepias decumbens **L.** – See *Asclepias asperula* (Dcne.) Woods. subsp. *capricornu* (Woods.) Woods.

Asclepias engelmanniana **Woods.** – Auricled milkweed (5, 93, 97) (1913–1937), Engelmann's milkweed (4, 50) (1986–present), Green milkweed (124) (1937)

Asclepias eriocarpa **Benth.** – Kotolo milkweed (155) (1942), Woolly-pod milkweed [Woollypod milkweed] (155) (1942)

Asclepias erosa **Torr.** – Desert milkweed (155) (1942)

Asclepias exaltata (**L.**) **Muhl.** – See *Asclepias exaltata* L.

Asclepias exaltata **L.** – Poke milkweed (2, 5, 63, 82, 156) (1895–1930), Poke-leaf milkweed [Poke leaved milk weed, Poke-leaved milkweed] (42, 187) (1814–1818), Poke-leaf swallow-wort [Poke leaved swallow wort] (42) (1814), Tall milkweed (5, 37, 72, 156) (1907–1923), Wah'tha-ska (Omaha-Ponca) (37) (1919), Westcoast milkweed (155) (1942)

Asclepias fascicularis **Dcne.** – Mexican milkweed (155) (1942)

Asclepias fremonti – See *Asclepias eriocarpa* Benth.

Asclepias galioides **Kunth** – See *Asclepias verticillata* L.

Asclepias grandiflora [**L.f.**] – possibly *Gomphocarpus grandiflorus* (L. f.) K. Schum.

Asclepias hallii **Gray** – Hall's milkweed [Halls milkweed] (4, 50, 155) (1942–present), Large-flower milkweed [Large flowered milk weed] (42) (1814)

Asclepias hirtella (Pennell) **Woods.** – Green milkweed (50) (present), Prairie milkweed (3, 4) (1977–1986)

Asclepias incarnata alba – See *Asclepias incarnata* L.

Asclepias incarnata **f.** *rosea* **B.Boivin** – See *Asclepias incarnata* L.

Asclepias incarnata **fo.** *albiflora* **A. Heller** – See *Asclepias incarnata* L.

Asclepias incarnata **L.** – Asclépiade incarnate (French) (158) (1900), Bû'giso'wĭn (Chippewa, swimming or bath) (40) (1928), Fleisch-farbige Schwalbenwurzel (German) (158) (1900), Flesh-colored asclepias (49, 52, 53, 92, 158) (1876–1922), Flesh-colored milkweed [Flesh-coloured milk-weed, Flesh-coloured milk weed] (42, 187) (1814–1818), Flesh-colored swallowwort, Flesh-coloured swallow wort (42, 158) (1814–1900), Indian hemp [Indianhemp] (46) (1879), Pink swamp milkweed (138, 155) (1931–1942), Rose milkweed (156) (1923), Rose silkweed (5, 158) (1900–1913), Rose-colored silkweed [Rose colored silkweed] (53, 92, 158) (1876–1922), Swallow-wort [Swallowwort, Swallow wort] (34) (1834), Swamp milkweed (3, 4, 5, 40, 49, 50, 52, 53, 57, 58, 62, 63, 64, 72, 82, 85, 92, 95, 97, 98, 109, 114, 122, 124, 127, 131, 138, 155, 156, 157, 158) (1869–present), Swamp silkweed (5, 49, 53, 58, 92, 156, 158) (1869–1923), Water Indian hemp (5, 49, 158) (1898–1913), Water nerveroot [Water nerve root, Water nerve-root] (5, 92, 156, 158) (1876–1923), White Indian hemp (53, 58, 92, 156, 157) (1869–1929), White swamp milkweed (155) (1942)

Asclepias incarnata **L. subsp.** *incarnata* – Swamp milkweed (50) (present)

Asclepias incarnata **L. subsp.** *pulchra* (Ehrh. ex Willd.) **Woods.** – Hairy milkweed [Hairy milk weed] (5, 42, 138, 156) (1814–1923) Neb

Asclepias incarnata **L. subsp.** *pulchra* (Ehrh. ex Willd.) **Woods.** – Hairy swallow-wort [Hairy swallow wort] (42) (1814)

Asclepias incarnata **L. subsp.** *pulchra* (Ehrh. ex Willd.) **Woods.** – Hairy swamp milkweed (155) (1942)

Asclepias incarnata **L. subsp.** *pulchra* (Ehrh. ex Willd.) **Woods.** – River milkweed [River milk weed] (42) (1814)

Asclepias incarnata **L. subsp.** *pulchra* (Ehrh. ex Willd.) **Woods.** – River swallow-wort [River swallow wort] (42) (1814)

Asclepias incarnata **L. subsp.** *pulchra* (Ehrh. ex Willd.) **Woods.** – White Indian hemp (5, 156) (1913–1923)

Asclepias incarnata pulchra – See *Asclepias incarnata* L. subsp. *pulchra* (Ehrh. ex Willd.) Woods.

Asclepias incarnata rosea – See *Asclepias incarnata* L.

Asclepias incarnata **Walt.** – possibly *Asclepias longifolia* Michx.

Asclepias intermedia **Vail.** – See *Asclepias syriaca* L.

Asclepias involucrata **Engelm. ex Torr.** – Dwarf milkweed (4, 50, 155) (1942–present)

Asclepias **L.** – Antelope-horns [Antelope horns, Antelopehorns, Antelopehorn] (155) (1942), Butterfly weed [Butter-fly weed, Butterfly-weed, Butterfly-weed] (1, 106) (1930–1932), Green milkweed (1, 2, 63, 93) (1895–1936), Milkweed [Milk weed [Milk-weed] (1, 2, 4, 45, 50, 63, 82, 106, 109, 125, 138, 155, 156, 158) (1895–present), Nepesha (Oregon and Western tribes) (7) (1828), Silkweed (1, 2, 61, 79, 106, 109, 158) (1870–1932), Spider milkweed (1) (1932), Swallow-wort [Swallowwort, Swallow wort] (10) (1818), Wild cotton [Wild-cotton] (10) (1818)

Asclepias lanceolata **Walt.** – Few-flower milkweed [Few flowered milkweed] (5, 122) (1913–1937), Pacific milkweed (155) (1942)

Asclepias lanceolata **Walt. var.** *paupercula* (Michx.) **Fern.** – See *Asclepias lanceolata* Walt.

Asclepias lanuginosa **Nutt.** – Side-cluster milkweed [Sidecluster milkweed] (50) (present), Woolly milkweed [Wooly milkweed] (3, 4, 85, 93, 131) (1899–1986)

Asclepias latifolia **(Torr.) Raf.** – Broad-leaf milkweed [Broadleaf milkweed] (3, 4, 5, 50, 97, 122, 155) (1913–present)

Asclepias lindheimeri **Engelm. & A. Gray** – See *Asclepias oenotheroides* Cham. & Schlecht.

Asclepias linearis **Scheele** – Linear-leaf milkweed [Linear-leaved milkweed] (97) (1937)

Asclepias longifolia **Michx.** – Florida milkweed (5, 72, 93, 97) (1907–1937), Long-leaf milkweed [Long leaved milk weed] (42) (1814), Long-leaf swallow-wort [Long leaved swallow wort] (42) (1814)

Asclepias macrotis **Torr.** – Long-hood milkweed [Longhood milkweed] (4, 50) (1986–present)

Asclepias meadii **Torr. ex Gray** – Mead's milkweed (4, 5, 50, 72, 82) (1907–present)

Asclepias mexicana – See *Asclepias fascicularis* Dcne.

Asclepias nummularia **Torr.** – Money milkweed (124) (1937) TX

Asclepias oenotheroides **Cham. & Schlecht.** – Lindheimer's milkweed (97) (1937), Side-cluster milkweed [Sidecluster milkweed] (4) (1986), Zizotes milkweed (50) (present)

Asclepias ovalifolia **Dcne.** – Dwarf milkweed (5, 85) (1913–1932), Early milkweed (127) (1933), Oval-leaf milkweed [Oval-leaf milk weed, Oval leaved milk weed, Ovalleaf milkweed, Oval-leaved milkweed] (4, 5, 50, 72, 82, 131) (1899–present)

Asclepias paupercula **Michx.** – See *Asclepias lanceolata* Walt.

Asclepias perennis **Walt.** – Thin-leaf milkweed [Thinleaf milkweed] (5, 122) (1913–1937)

Asclepias phytolaccoides **Pursh** – See *Asclepias exaltata* L.

Asclepias pulchra **Ehrh.** – See *Asclepias incarnata* L. subsp. *pulchra* (Ehrh. ex Willd.) Woods.

Asclepias pumila **(Gray) Vail** – Češlošlo pežuta (Lakota, diarrhea medicine) (121) (1918?–1970?), Dwarf milkweed (3) (1977), Dwarf poison milkweed (148) (1939), Low milkweed (5, 93, 97, 121, 122, 131) (1899–1937), Peži swula čikala (Lakota, small herb) (121) (1918?–1970?), Plains milkweed (4, 50, 155) (1942–present)

Asclepias purpurascens **L.** – Oval-leaf milkweed [Oval-leaf milk weed, Oval leaved milk weed, Ovalleaf milkweed, Oval-leaved milkweed] (42) (1814), Oval-leaf swallow-wort [Oval leaved swallow wort] (42) (1814), Purple milkweed [Purple milk weed (3, 4, 5, 42, 50, 63, 72, 82, 85, 97, 155, 156) (1814–present), Purple swallow-wort [Purple swallow wort] (42) (1814)

Asclepias quadrifolia **Jacq.** – Four-leaf milkweed [Four-leaved milkweed, Four leaved milk weed] (4, 5, 42, 50, 72, 97, 156) (1814–present), Four-leaf swallow-wort [Four leaved swallow wort] (42) (1814)

Asclepias rubra **L.** – Red milkweed (5, 122, 138, 155) (1913–1942)

Asclepias speciosa **Torr.** – Butterfly weed [Butter-fly weed, Butterflyweed, Butterfly-weed] (101) (1905), Common milkweed [Common milk weed] (148) (1939), Milkweed [Milk weed [Milk-weed] (101, 114) (1894–1905), Showy milkweed (3, 4, 5, 50, 72, 80, 82, 85, 93, 95, 97, 121, 126, 127, 131, 155, 156, 157) (1899–present), Silkweed (101) (1905), Waxča xča (Lakota, flower blossom) (121) (1918?–1970?)

Asclepias stenophylla **Gray** – Low milkweed (114) (1894), Narrowleaf milkweed [Narrowleaf milkweed, Narrow-leafed milkweed, Narrow-leaved milkweed] (3, 4, 5, 85, 93, 97, 122, 131) (1899–1986), Slim-leaf milkweed [Slimleaf milkweed] (50) (present), Tinpsila pežuta (Lakota, turnip medicine) (121) (1918?–1970?)

Asclepias subulata **Dcne.** – Skeleton milkweed (155) (1942)

Asclepias subverticillata **(Gray) Vail** – Horsetail milkweed (50) (present), Poison milkweed (3, 4) (1977–1986)

Asclepias sullivantii **Engelm. ex Gray** – Prairie milkweed (50) (present), Smooth milkweed (3, 4, 114, 138) (1894–1986), Sullivant's milkweed [Sullivants milkweed] (5, 72, 82, 93, 155) (1907–1942)

Asclepias syriaca **L.** – Asclepiade a la Soie (French) (6, 158) (1892–1900), Common milkweed [Common milk weed] (2, 4, 3, 5, 6, 19, 40, 50, 59, 53, 57, 62, 63, 64, 72, 80, 82, 85, 93, 95, 109, 114, 127, 131, 138, 155, 156, 157, 158) (1892–present), Common silk plant (42) (1814), Common silkweed [Common silk weed] (57, 58, 157, 158) (1869–1929), Cotonier (French Canadian) (41) (1770), Cotton tree [Cotton-tree] (107) (1760), Herbe a la ouate (French) (6, 158) (1892–1900), Inĭ'nĭwûnj (Chipewwa, man-like) (40) (1928), Intermediate milkweed (5) (1913), Karípiku (Pawnee) (37) (1919), Mahińtsh (Winnebago) (37) (1919), Milk plant (28) (1850), Milkweed [Milk weed [Milk-weed] (37, 53, 56, 58, 80, 107, 145, 187) (1818–1922), Schwalbenwurzel (German) (6) (1892), Seidenpflanzen (German) (6, 158) (1892–1900), Silk-grass [Silk grass, Silke grass] (156) (1923), Silkweed (5, 6, 49, 53, 62, 92, 107, 122, 157, 158) (1876–1937), Silky swallow-wort [Silky swallowwort, Silky swallowort] (5, 7, 92, 156, 157, 158) (1828–1929), Swallow-wort [Swallowwort, Swallow wort] (19, 92) (1840–1876), Sweet milkweed (156) (1923), Syrian swallow-wort (187) (1818), Virginia silk [Virginian silk] (5, 28, 156, 157, 158) (1850–1929), Virginia swallow-wort [Virginian swallow-wort] (6) (1892), Wah'tha (Omaha-Ponca) (37) (1919), Wild cotton [Wild-cotton] (5, 6, 49, 53, 62, 75, 156, 157, 158, 187) (1818–1929)

Asclepias tuberosa **L.** – Archangel (75) (1894) near Providence RI, Asclepiade tubereuse (French) (6, 158) (1892–1900), Asclepias (52, 54) (1905–1919), Asclepias tuberosa radix (Official name of Materia Medica) (7) (1828), Butterfly flower [Butterfly-flower, Butterflyflower] (5, 156) (1913–1923), Butterfly milkweed (4, 50, 122, 155) (1942–present), Butterfly weed [Butter-fly weed, Butterflyweed, Butterfly-weed] (5, 6, 7, 19, 37, 42, 47, 49, 53, 54, 58, 62, 63, 64, 82, 85, 92, 95, 97, 106, 107, 109, 131, 138, 156, 157, 158, 186, 187) (1814–1949), Canadian root [Canada root, Canada-root] (5, 7, 64, 92, 156, 158) (1828–1923), Chigger-flower [Chigger flower] (77) (1898) Southwest MO, said to harbor chigger mites, Colic root [Colic-root, Colicroot] (6, 19) (1840–1892), Fluxroot [Flux-root, Flux root] (5, 7, 92, 156, 186) (1814–1923) no longer in use by 1923, Houatte tubereuse (French) (7) (1828), Indian posy [Indian-posy, Indian posey] (5, 64, 156, 157, 158) (1900–1929), Kiu makan (Omaha-Ponca, wound medicine) (37) (1919), Knollige Schwalbenwurz (German) (7, 6, 158, 186) (1814–1900), Makan saka (Omaha-Ponca [raw medicine) (37) (1919), Milkweed [Milk weed [Milk-weed] (61, 103) (1870–1871), Orange apocynum (6, 186) (1814–1892), Orange milkweed [Orange milk-weed] (6, 64, 156, 157, 158) (1892–1929), Orange swallow-wort [Orange swallowwort (5, 6, 7, 49, 53, 64, 92, 156, 158) (1828–1923), Orange-root [Orangeroot, Orange root] (5, 64, 156, 158) (1900–1923), Pleurisy root [Pleurisy-root, Pleurisyroot] (5, 6, 7, 19, 37, 42, 49, 52, 53, 54, 58, 62, 64, 72, 77, 92, 95, 106, 107, 109, 131, 156, 157, 158, 186, 187) (1814–1949), Silg grass (190) (~1759), Silkweed (7, 92) (1828–1876), Swallow-wort [Swallowwort, Swallow wort] (58, 77) (1869–1898), Tuberous-root swallow-wort [Tuberous-rooted swallow-wort] (186) (1814), Tuber-root [Tuber-root, Tuberroot] (5, 49, 64, 92, 107, 156, 157, 158) (1898–1929), Whiteroot [White-root, Whiteroot] (5, 6, 7, 19, 58, 64, 73, 75, 92, 156, 158) (1828–1923), Windroot [Wind-root, Windroot] (5, 6, 7, 49, 58, 62, 64, 92, 156, 158) (1828–1923) no longer in use by 1923, Windweed [Wind weed] (6) (1892), Yellow milkweed [Yellow milk-weed] (5, 64, 73, 156, 157, 158) (1892–1929)

Asclepias tuberosa **L. subsp. *interior* Woods.** – Butterfly milkweed (3, 50) (1977–present)

Asclepias tuberosa **L. subsp. *terminalis* Woods.** – See *Asclepias tuberosa* L. subsp. *interior* Woods.

Asclepias uncialis **Greene** – Dwarf milkweed (4) (1986), Wheel milkweed (50) (present)

Asclepias variegata **L.** – Red-ring milkweed [Redring milkweed] (50) (present), White milkweed (5, 97, 122) (1913–1937), Bedstraw milkweed (5, 97, 122) (1913–1937), Dwarf milkweed (19) (1840), Horsetail milkweed (138) (1923), Milkweed [Milk weed [Milkweed] (148) (1939), Poison milkweed (148, 155) (1939–1942), Waxpe tiņpsila (Lakota, turnip leaf) (121) (1918?–1970?), Whorled milkweed (3, 4, 5, 50, 72, 82, 85, 93, 97, 114, 121, 122, 125, 126,

127, 131, 148, 155, 156) (1894–present), Whorl-leaf milkweed [Whorl leaved milk weed] (42) (1814), Whorl-leaf swallow-wort [Whorl leaved swallow wort] (42) (1814)

Asclepias vincetoxicum – See *Cynanchum vincetoxicum* (L.) Pers.

Asclepias viridiflora **Raf.** – Green acerates (155) (1942), Green comet milkweed (50) (present), Green milkweed (3, 4, 5, 19, 72, 85, 92, 93, 97, 131, 156) (1840–1986), Hucinška (Lakota, spoon plant) (121) (1918?–1970?)

Asclepias viridis **Walt.** – Green antelope-horn [Green antelopehorn] (50) (present), Oblong-leaf milkweed [Oblong-leaved milkweed] (5, 97) (1913–1937), Spider milkweed (4, 93) (1936–1986)

Asclepiodora decumbens (**Nutt.**) **Gray** – See *Asclepias asperula* (Dcne.) Woods. subsp. *capricornu* (Woods.) Woods.

Asclepiodora **Gray** – See *Asclepias* L.

Asclepiodora viridis (**Walt.**) **Gray** – See *Asclepias viridis* Walt.

Ascophyllum nodosum (**Linnaeus**) **Le Jolis** – Drug rockweep (155) (1942)

Ascophyllum **Stackhouse** – Rockweep (155) (1942)

Ascyrum crux-andreae **L.** – See *Hypericum crux-andreae* (L.) Crantz

Ascyrum hypericoides **L.** – See *Hypericum hypericoides* (L.) Crantz subsp. *hypericoides*

Ascyrum hypericoides **L. var.** *multicaule* (**Michx.**) **Fern.** – See *Hypericum hypericoides* (L.) Crantz subsp. *multicaule* (Michx. ex Willd.) Robson

Ascyrum **L.** – See *Hypericum* L.

Ascyrum multicaule **Mich.** – See *Hypericum hypericoides* (L.) Crantz subsp. *multicaule* (Michx. ex Willd.) Robson

Ascyrum multicaule **Willd.** – See *Hypericum hypericoides* (L.) Crantz subsp. *multicaule* (Michx. ex Willd.) Robson

Ascyrum mutilum – See *Hypericum crux-andreae* (L.) Crantz

Ascyrum setosum – possibly *Hypericum setosum* L.

Ascyrum stans **Michx.** – See *Hypericum crux-andreae* (L.) Crantz

Ascyrum villosum **L.** – possibly *Hypericum setosum* L.

Asimina **Adans.** – Assiminier [Asiminier] (French) (8, 13) (1785–1849), Papaw [Pawpaw, Paw-paw] or Papaw tree [Papaw-tree, Pappaw tree] (1, 2, 4, 6, 7, 8, 13, 15, 44, 47, 50, 93, 138, 155, 156, 158) (1845–present)

Asimina angustifolia **Raf.** – Slim-leaf pawpaw [Slimleaf pawpaw] (155) (1942)

Asimina incana (**W. Bartram**) **Exell** – Mountain soursop (155) (1942), Woolly pawpaw (155) (1942)

Asimina longifolia **Kral** – Sprawling pawpaw (155) (1942)

Asimina obovata (**Willd.**) **Nash** – Big-flower pawpaw [Bigflower pawpaw] (155) (1942), Custard-apple [Custardapple, Custard apple] (183) (~1756), Papaw-apple [Pawpaw apple] (183) (~1756)

Asimina parviflora (**Michx.**) **Dunal** – Bush pawpaw (124) (1937) TX, Small-flower pawpaw (2, 155) (1895–1942)

Asimina parviflora **Dunal.** – See *Asimina parviflora* (Michx.) Dunal

Asimina pulchella – See *Deeringothamnus pulchellus* Small

Asimina pygmaea – See *Asimina longifolia* Kral

Asimina rugeli – See *Deeringothamnus rugelii* (B.L. Robins.) Small

Asimina tetramera **Small** – St. Lucie's pawpaw [St. Lucie pawpaw] (155) (1942)

Asimina triloba (**L.**) **Dunal** – American custard-apple (6, 49) (1892–1898), American pawpaw (95, 157) (1911–1929), Assiminier [Asiminier] (French) (6, 7, 20, 49, 158) (1828–1900), Common papaw [Common pawpaw] (2, 63, 82, 155, 156) (1895–1942), Custard-apple [Custardapple, Custard apple] (5, 7, 8, 19, 35, 92, 156, 157, 158, 187) (1785–1929), Dreilappige (German) (6) (1892), False banana (5, 156, 157, 158) (1900–1929), Festid shrub [Festid-shrub] (157) (1929), Fetid shrub [Fetid-shrub] (5, 156, 157, 158) (1900–1929), Hindse hiu (Osage) (121) (1918?–1970?), Hindse waxtha (Osage) (121) (1918?–1970?), North American papaw (5, 97, 156, 158) (1900–1937), Papaw [Pawpaw, Paw-paw] or Papaw tree [Papaw-tree, Pappaw tree] (3, 6, 10, 18, 19, 25, 34, 35, 48, 49, 50, 65, 72, 109, 122, 158, 181, 184, 187) (~1678–present), Pappas Arbor (181) (~1678), Pennsylvania triple-fruit papaw [Pennsylvanian

triple-fruited papaw] (8) (1785), Popaw (12) (1821), Tožon hi (Osage, possibly meaning potato wood tree) (121) (1918?–1970?), Trifid-fruit custard-apple [Trifid-fruited custard apple] (165) (1807), Wild banana (156) (1923)

Asimina triloba **Dunal.** – See *Asimina triloba* (L.) Dunal

Asparagus asparagoides (**L.**) **Druce** – Boston smilax (92) (1876), Cape-smilax [Cape smilax] (92) (1876), Myrtle-leaf [Myrtle leaf] (92) (1876), Smilax (of florists) (109) (1949), Smilax asparagus (138, 155) (1923–1942)

Asparagus asparagoides **Wight** – See *Asparagus asparagoides* (L.) Druce

Asparagus densiflorus (**Kunth**) **Jessop** – Sprenger's asparagus [Sprenger asparagus] (138, 155) (1923–1942)

Asparagus **L.** – Asparagus (50, 138, 155, 158) (1900–present) ancient Greek name of Persian origin

Asparagus officinalis **L.** – Asparagus (3, 5, 19, 49, 57, 72, 85, 92, 97, 107, 114, 117, 124, 157, 158, 178) (1596–1977), Asperge (French) (158) (1900), Common asparagus (42, 109) (1814–1949), Esparraguera (Spanish) (158) (1900), Garden asparagus (50, 109, 138, 155) (1923–present), Grass (158) (1900), Paddock-cheese (157, 158) (1900–1929), Sparagus (46, 158) (1671–1900) cultivated by English colonists by 1671, Spargel (German) (158) (1900), Sparrow-grass [Sparrow grass] (5, 7, 92, 138, 158) (1828–1923), Sperage [Spearage] (5, 157, 158, 178, 179) (1526–1929)

Asparagus officinalis **L. var.** *altilis* **L.** – See *Asparagus officinalis* L.

Asparagus setaceus (**Kunth**) **Jessop** – Asparagus-fern (109) (1949), Fern asparagus (138, 155) (1923–1942)

Asparagus sprengeri [**Regel**] – See *Asparagus densiflorus* (Kunth) Jessop

Asparella hystrix (**L.**) **Moench** – See *Elymus hystrix* L.

Asperella californica (**Bol.**) **Beal** – See *Elymus californicus* (Bol. ex Thurb.) Gould

Asperugo (**Tourn.**) **L.** – See *Asperugo* L.

Asperugo **L.** – Catchweed [Catch-weed, Catch weed] (1) (1932), German madwort [German-madwort] (1, 50, 158) (1900–present), Madwort (4, 156) (1923–1986)

Asperugo procumbens **L.** – Catchweed [Catch-weed, Catch weed] (5, 156, 158) (1900–1923), German madwort [German-madwort] (5, 50, 156, 158) (1900–present), Great goose-grass [Great goose grass] (5, 92, 156, 158) (1876–1923), Madwort (156) (1923), Small wild bugloss (5, 156, 158) (1900–1923), Wild bugloss [Wilde bugloss] (92) (1876)

Asperula arvensis **L.** – Blue woodruff [Blew woodroofe] (50, 178) (1526–present)

Asperula galioides **Bieb.** – See *Galium glaucum* L.

Asperula **L.** – Woodruff (50, 109, 138, 155, 156, 158) (1900–present)

Asperula odorata **L.** – See *Galium odoratum* (L.) Scop.

Asperula orientalis **Boiss. & Hohen.** – Oriental asperula (50) (present), Oriental woodruff (138, 155) (1923–1942)

Asperula tinctoria **L.** – See *Galium tinctorium* L.

Asphodelus fistulosus **L.** – Hollow aphodill (178) (1596), Onion-weed [Onionweed] (50) (present)

Asphodelus **L.** – Asphodel (138, 155) (1923–1942)

Aspidium boottii **Tuckm.** – See *Dryopteris* ×*boottii* (Tuckerman) Underwood *[cristata × intermedia]*

Aspidium cristatum **Swartz.** – See *Dryopteris cristata* (L.) A. Gray

Aspidium filix mas – See *Dryopteris filix-mas* (L.) Schott

Aspidium fragrans **Swartz.** – See *Dryopteris fragrans* (L.) Schott

Aspidium goldieanum **Hook** – See *Dryopteris goldiana* (Hook. ex Goldie) Gray

Aspidium marginale **Swartz.** – See *Dryopteris marginalis* (L.) A. Gray

Aspidium munitum **Kaulfuss** – See *Polystichum munitum* (Kaulfuss) K. Presl

Aspidium nevadense **D.C. Eaton** – See *Thelypteris nevadensis* (Baker) Clute ex Morton for Sierra Nevadas not state

Aspidium noveboracense **Swartz.** – See *Thelypteris noveboracensis* (L.) Nieuwl.

Aspidium **Sm.** – possibly *Tectaria* Cav.

Aspidium spinulosum **Swartz.** – See *Dryopteris carthusiana* (Vill.) H.P. Fuchs

Aspidium **Sw.** – See *Dryopteris* Adans. Gn aspidion "little shield"

Aspidium thelypteris **Swartz.** – See *Thelypteris palustris* Schott

Aspidotis californica **(Hook.) Nutt. ex Copeland** – California lip fern [Californian lip-fern] (86) (1878), Shield-like lip fern [Shield-like lip-fern] (86) (1878)

Aspidotis densa **(Brack.) Lellinger** – Clayton's cliff-brake (5) (1913), Indian's-dream [Indian's dream] (50) (present), Oregon cliff-brake (5) (1913), Pod fern [Podfern] (138) (1923)

Asplenium ×*ebenoides* **R.R. Scott** [*platyneuron × rhizophyllum*] – Scott's spleenwort (5, 86) (1878–1913)

Asplenium ×*stotleri* **Wherry** – See *Asplenium bradleyi* D.C. Eaton

Asplenium acrostichoides **Sw.** – See *Deparia acrostichoides* (Sw.) M. Kato

Asplenium adiantum nigrum – See *Asplenium adiantum-nigrum* L.

Asplenium adiantum-nigrum **L.** – Black maidenhair [Black maiden's hair, Blacke maiden haire] (178) (1596), Black spleenwort (92) (1876)

Asplenium angustifolium **Michx.** – See *Diplazium pycnocarpon* (Spreng.) Broun

Asplenium bradleyi **D.C. Eaton** – Bradley's spleenwort (5, 50, 97) (1913–present)

Asplenium cryptolepis **Fern. var. ohionis Fern.** – See *Asplenium ruta-muraria* L. var. *lanceolum* Christ

Asplenium ebeneum **Ait.** – See *Asplenium platyneuron* (L.) Britton, Sterns & Poggenb.

Asplenium ebenoides **R. R. Scott** – See *Asplenium* ×*ebenoides* R.R. Scott [*platyneuron × rhizophyllum*]

Asplenium ebenum **W.** – See *Asplenium platyneuron* (L.) Britton, Sterns & Poggenb.

Asplenium exiguum **Bedd.** – Little spleenwort (50) (present), Rock spleenwort (5) (1913), Smooth rock spleenwort (5) (1913)

Asplenium filix-foemina **Bernh.** – See *Athyrium filix-femina* (L.) Roth

Asplenium fontanum **(L.) Bernh.** – See *Asplenium exiguum* Bedd.

Asplenium glenniei **Baker** – See *Asplenium exiguum* Bedd.

Asplenium **L.** – Erth-thought [Erththought] (178, 179) (1526–1596), Politryke (178, 179) (1526–1596), Resurrection fern [Resurrectionfern] (124) (1937) TX, Saxifrage (178, 179) (1526–1596), Spleen fern [Spleenfern] (7) (1828), Spleenwort [Spleen-wort, Spleenewort] (1, 4, 10, 50, 109, 138, 155, 158, 167) (1814–present), Walking fern [Walking-fern, Walkingfern] (1, 155, 158) (1900–1942), Walking-leaf [Walking leaf] (1) (1932), possibly Hart's-tongue [Hart's tongue, Hartstongue, Harts toong, Hertes tongue] (7) (1828)

Asplenium melanocaulon – See *Asplenium trichomanes* L. subsp. *Trichomanes*

Asplenium montanum **Willd.** – Mountain spleenwort (5, 50) (1913–present)

Asplenium nidus **L.** – Bird's-nest fern [Birdsnest fern, Birds-nest-fern] (109, 138) (1923–1949)

Asplenium pinnatifidum **Nutt.** – Lobed spleenwort (50) (present), Pinnatifid spleenwort (5, 97) (1913–1937), Pinnatified spleenwort [Pinnatified spleen-wort] (86) (1878)

Asplenium platyneuron **(L.) B.S.P.** – Ebony spleenwort [Ebony spleenwort, Ebony spleen wort] (3, 4, 5, 19, 42, 50, 86, 122, 138, 155, 187) (1814–present), Purple spleenwort (97) (1937)

Asplenium platyneuron **(L.) B.S.P. var. platyneuron** – Ebony spleenwort [Ebony spleen-wort, Ebony spleen wort] (50, 72) (1907–present)

Asplenium platyneuron **(L.) Oakes ex D.C.Eat.** – See *Asplenium platyneuron* (L.) Britton, Sterns & Poggenb.

Asplenium resiliens **Kunze.** – Black-stem spleenwort [Blackstem spleenwort] (3, 4, 5, 50) (1913–present), Little ebony (5) (1913), Small spleenwort (5, 122) (1913–1937)

Asplenium rhizophylla **L.** – See *Asplenium rhizophyllum* L.

Asplenium rhizophyllum **L.** – I'natû ga'n'ka (Cherokee, snake tongue) (102) (1885), Leaf-rooting spleenwort [Leaf-rooting spleen-wort] (187) (1818), Walking fern [Walking-fern, Walkingfern] (3, 4, 5, 50, 72, 102, 109) (1886–present), Walking leaf-fern [Walking leaf fern] (97) (1937), Walking-leaf [Walking leaf] (5, 19, 86, 92, 109) (1840–1949)

Asplenium rhizophyllum **W.** – See *Asplenium rhizophyllum* L.

Asplenium ruta muriaria – See *Asplenium ruta-muraria* L.

Asplenium ruta-muraria **L.** – Dwarf spleenwort (19, 92) (1840–1876), Paronychia (174) (1753), Rue maidenhair [Rue Maiden haire] (178) (1596), Stone fern (92) (1876), Tentwort (92) (1876), Wall-rue [Wall rue] (2, 50, 92) (1876–present), Wall-rue spleenwort [Wall rue spleenwort] (5) (1913)

Asplenium ruta-muraria **L. var. lanceolum Christ** – Lance spleenwort (50) (present)

Asplenium ruta-muraria **L. var. ohionis (Fern.) Wherry** – See *Asplenium ruta-muraria* L. var. *lanceolum* Christ

Asplenium ruta-muraria **L. var. subtenuifolium auct. non Christ** – See *Asplenium ruta-muraria* L. var. *lanceolum* Christ

Asplenium scolopendrium **L.** – Caterpillar fern (92) (1876), Spleen-wort [Spleen-wort, Spleenewort] (92) (1876), Spleenwort fern (92) (1876)

Asplenium scolopendrium **L. var. americanum (Fern.) Kartesz & Gandhi** – Hart's-tongue [Hart's tongue, Hartstongue, Harts toong, Hertes tongue] (2, 5, 138, 178, 179) (1526–1923), Hart's-tongue fern [Hart's tonguefern] (50) (present), Sea-weed fern [Sea weed fern] (5) (1913), Snake fern (5) (1913), Barren spleenwort [Barren spleenewort] (178) (1596), Branched Harts toong (178) (1596), Finger fern [Finger Ferne] (178) (1596)

Asplenium septentrionale **(L.) Huds.** – Forked spleenwort (4, 50) (1986–present), Northern spleenwort [Northern spleanwort (*sic*)] (131) (1899)

Asplenium thelypteroides **Michx.** – See *Deparia acrostichoides* (Sw.) M. Kato

Asplenium trichomanes **L.** – Common spleenwort (92) (1876), Dwarf spleenwort (5, 86) (1878–1913), English maidenhair [English maiden hair] (5, 86, 158) (1878–1923), Maidenhair spleenwort [Maiden hair spleenwort, Maiden hair spleen wort, Maidenhair spleanwort] (3, 4, 5, 42, 50, 97, 109, 122, 131, 138, 155, 156) (1814–present), Wall spleenwort (5) (1913), Waterwort [Water wort] (5, 158) (1900–1913)

Asplenium trichomanes **L. subsp. trichomanes** . – Rough-stem spleenwort [Ruff stemmed spleen wort] (42) (1814)

Asplenium trichomanes-ramosum **L.** – Bright-green spleenwort [Brightgreen spleenwort] (50) (present), Green spleenwort (3, 4, 5, 155) (1913–1986)

Asplenium viride **Huds.** – See *Asplenium trichomanes-ramosum* L.

Asprella hystrix **(L.) Moench** – possibly *Elymus hystrix* L.

Aspris **Adans.** – See *Aira* L. Old Greek name for a weed

Aspris caryophyllea **(L.) Nash** – See *Aira caryophyllea* L.

Aspris praecox **(L.) Nash** – See *Aira praecox* L.

Aster abatus – See *Xylorhiza tortifolia* (Torr. & Gray) Greene var. *tortifolia*

Aster acuminatus **Michx.** – See *Oclemena acuminata* (Michx.) Greene

Aster adscendens **Lindl.** – See *Symphyotrichum ascendens* (Lindl.) Nesom

Aster alpinus **L.** – Alpine aster (155) (1942), Rock aster (138) (1923)

Aster amethystinus **Nutt.** – See *Symphyotrichum* ×*amethystinum* (Nutt.) Nesom [*ericoides × novae-angliae*]

Aster amplexicaulis **[Michx.]** – possibly *Symphyotrichum patens* (Aiton) G. I. Nesom var. *patens* current species depends on author

Aster anomalus **Engelm.** – See *Symphyotrichum anomalum* (Engelm.) Nesom

Aster azureus **Lindl.** – See *Symphyotrichum oolentangiense* (Riddell) Nesom var. *oolentangiense*

Aster bigelovi – See *Machaeranthera bigelovii* (Gray) Greene var. *bigelovii*

Aster brachyactis **Blake** – See *Symphyotrichum ciliatum* (Ledeb.) Nesom

Aster canbyi **Kuntze** – See *Pyrrocoma integrifolia* (Porter ex Gray) Greene

Aster canescens **Pursh** – See *Machaeranthera canescens* (Pursh) Gray subsp. *canescens* var. *canescens*

Aster carmesinus **Burgess** – See *Eurybia divaricata* (L.) Nesom

Aster carolinianus – See *Ampelaster carolinianus* (Walt.) Nesom

Aster chapmani – See *Eurybia chapmanii* (Torr. & Gray) Nesom

Aster chilensis – See *Symphyotrichum chilense* (Nees) Nesom var. chilense

Aster chinensis – See *Callistephus chinensis* (L.) Nees

Aster ciliolatus **Lindl.** – See *Symphyotrichum ciliolatum* (Lindl.) A.& D. Löve

Aster claytoni **Burgess** – See *Eurybia divaricata* (L.) Nesom

Aster cognatus – See *Xylorhiza cognata* (Hall) T.J. Wats.

Aster commutatus **(Torr. & Gray) Gray** – See *Symphyotrichum falcatum* (Lindl.) Nesom var. *commutatum* (Torr. & Gray) Nesom

Aster concinnus **Willd.** – See *Symphyotrichum laeve* (L.) A.& D. Löve var. *concinnum* (Willd.) Nesom

Aster concolor **L.** – See *Symphyotrichum concolor* (L.) Nesom

Aster conspicuus **Lindl.** – See *Eurybia conspicua* (Lindl.) Nesom

Aster conyzoides **Willd. And Pursh** – See *Sericocarpus asteroides* (L.) Britton, Sterns & Poggenb.

Aster cordifolius **L.** – See *Symphyotrichum cordifolium* (L.) Nesom

Aster cordifolius **L. var.** *laevigatus* – See *Symphyotrichum lowrieanum* (Porter) Nesom

Aster cordifolius **L. var.** *laevigatus* – See *Symphyotrichum lowrieanum* (Porter) Nesom

Aster cornifolius **Muhl.** – See *Doellingeria infirma* (Michx.) Greene

Aster corymbosus **Ait.** – See *Eurybia divaricata* (L.) G.L. Nesom

Aster curtisi – See *Symphyotrichum retroflexum* (Lindl. ex DC.) Nesom

Aster curvescens **Burgess** – See *Eurybia schreberi* (Nees) Nees

Aster depauperatus **(Porter) Fernald** – See *Symphyotrichum depauperatum* (Fern.) Nesom

Aster diffusus – See *Symphyotrichum ontarione* (Wiegand) Nesom

Aster diffusus **Aiton var.** *hirsuticaulis* **Gray** – See *Symphyotrichum lateriflorum* (L.) Á.Löve & D.Löve

Aster divaricatus **L.** – See *Eurybia divaricata* (L.) Nesom

Aster drummondii **Lindl.** – See *Symphyotrichum drummondii* (Lindl.) Nesom

Aster dumosus **L.** – See *Symphyotrichum dumosum* (L.) Nesom var. *dumosum*

Aster dumosus **L. var.** *coridifolius* **(Michx.) Torr. & Gray** – See *Symphyotrichum dumosum* (L.) Nesom var. *dumosum*

Aster eatonii **(Gray) Howell** – See *Symphyotrichum eatonii* (Gray) Nesom

Aster engelmanni – See *Eucephalus engelmannii* (D.C. Eat.) Greene

Aster ericoides **L.** – See *Symphyotrichum ericoides* (L.) Nesom var. *ericoides*

Aster ericoides pilosus **(Willd.) Porter** – See *Symphyotrichum pilosum* (Willd.) Nesom var. *pilosum*

Aster exiguus **Rydb.** – See *Symphyotrichum ericoides* (L.) Nesom var. *prostratum* (Kuntze) Nesom

Aster exilis **Ell.** – See *Symphyotrichum divaricatum* (Nutt.) Nesom

Aster falcatus **Lindl.** – See *Symphyotrichum falcatum* (Lindl.) Nesom var. *falcatum*

Aster faxoni **Porter** – See *Symphyotrichum pilosum* (Willd.) Nesom var. *pringlei* (Gray) Nesom

Aster fendleri **Gray** – See *Symphyotrichum fendleri* (Gray) Nesom

Aster foliaceus apricus – See *Symphyotrichum foliaceum* (DC.) Nesom var. *apricum* (Gray) Nesom

Aster foliaceus frondeus – See *Symphyotrichum foliaceum* (DC.) Nesom var. *parryi* (D.C. Eat.) Nesom

Aster foliaceus **Lindl.** – See *Symphyotrichum foliaceum* (DC.) Nesom var. *foliaceum*

Aster foliaceus **Lindl. ex DC. var.** *burkei* **Gray** – See *Symphyotrichum foliaceum* (DC.) Nesom var. *canbyi* (Gray) Nesom

Aster forwoodii **S. Wats.** – See *Symphyotrichum puniceum* (L.) A.& D. Löve var. *puniceum*

Aster fremonti – See *Symphyotrichum spathulatum* (Lindl.) Nesom var. *spathulatum*

Aster frondosus – See *Symphyotrichum frondosum* (Nutt.) Nesom

Aster furcatus **Burgess** – See *Eurybia furcata* (Burgess) Nesom

Aster glabriusculus **(Nutt.) Torr. & Gray** – See *Xylorhiza glabriuscula* Nutt.

Aster glomeratus **(Nees) Bernh.** – See *Eurybia schreberi* (Nees) Nees

Aster gracilis **Nutt.** – See *Eurybia compacta* Nesom

Aster grandiflorus **L.** – See *Symphyotrichum grandiflorum* (L.) Nesom

Aster grandiflorus **Nutt.** – See *Symphyotrichum grandiflorum* (L.) Nesom

Aster greatae – See *Symphyotrichum greatae* (Parish) G.L. Nesom

Aster herveyi **Gray** – See *Eurybia* ×*herveyi* (Gray) Nesom [*macrophylla* × *spectabilis*]

Aster hesperius **Gray** – See *Symphyotrichum lanceolatum* (Willd.) Nesom subsp. *hesperium* (Gray) Nesom

Aster hirsuticaulis **Lindl.** – See *Symphyotrichum lateriflorum* (L.) A.& D. Löve var. *lateriflorum*

Aster hirsuticaulis **Lindl. in DC.** – See *Symphyotrichum lateriflorum* (L.) Á.Löve & D.Löve var. *lateriflorum*

Aster ianthinus **Burgess** – See *Eurybia macrophylla* (L.) Cass.

Aster incanopilosus **(Lindl.) Sheldon** – See *Symphyotrichum falcatum* (Lindl.) Nesom var. *commutatum* (Torr. & Gray) Nesom

Aster infirmus **Michx.** – See *Doellingeria infirma* (Michx.) Greene

Aster integrifolius – See *Eurybia integrifolia* (Nutt.) Nesom

Aster johannensis – See *Symphyotrichum novi-belgii* (L.) Nesom var. *villicaule* (Gray) J. Labrecque & L. Brouillet

Aster junceus **Aiton** – See *Symphyotrichum novi-belgii* (L.) Nesom var. novi-belgii

Aster junciformis **Rydb.** – See *Symphyotrichum boreale* (Torr. & Gray) A.& D. Löve

Aster kumleinii **Fries** – See *Symphyotrichum oblongifolium* (Nutt.) Nesom

Aster **L.** – Aster (1, 2, 50, 63, 109, 138, 155, 158) (1899–present), Daisy [Daisies, Daysy] (76, 158) (1896–1900), Fall-roses [Fall roses] (76) (1896), Frost flower [Frost flower, Frost-flower] (73, 76, 156, 158) (1892–1923), Goodby-summer [Good-by summer] (75, 158) (1894–1900) Lincolnton NC, It-brings-the-frost (Onondaga Indians) (75, 155) (1894–1942) NY, Michaelmas daisy [Michaelmas daisies] (75, 76, 109) (1894–1949), Star flower [Starflower, Star-flower] (167) (1814), Starwort [Star-wort, Star wort] (2, 7, 10, 42, 92, 109, 156) (1793–1949), Wild aster (4, 93, 114) (1894–1986)

Aster laetevirens **Greene** – See *Symphyotrichum lanceolatum* (Willd.) Nesom subsp. *hesperium* (Gray) Nesom

Aster laevis **L.** – See *Symphyotrichum laeve* (L.) A. & D. Löve var. *laeve*

Aster lateriflorus **(L.) Britton** – See *Symphyotrichum lateriflorum* (L.) A. & D. Löve var. *lateriflorum*

Aster latifolius **[Desf.]** – See *Eurybia macrophylla* (L.) Cass.

Aster ledifolius **[Pursh]** – See *Oclemena nemoralis* (Aiton) Greene

Aster leucathemifolius – See *Machaeranthera canescens* (Pursh) A. Gray subsp. *canescens* var. *canescens*

Aster leucelene **Blake** – See *Chaetopappa ericoides* (Torr.) Nesom

Aster linariifolius **L.** – See *Ionactis linariifolius* (L.) Greene

Aster linariifolius **L. var.** *victorinii* **Fern.** – See *Ionactis linariifolius* (L.) Greene

Aster lindleyana **Torr. & Gray** – See *Symphyotrichum ciliolatum* (Lindl.) A. & D. Löve

Aster lindleyanus **Torr. & Gray** – See *Symphyotrichum ciliolatum* (Lindl.) A. & D. Löve

Aster linearifolius **(sic)** – See *Ionactis linariifolius* (L.) Greene

Aster linifolius – possibly *Symphyotrichum subulatum* (Michx.) Nesom

Aster longifolius **Lam.** – See *Symphyotrichum novi-belgii* (L.) Nesom var. *novi-belgii*

Aster longulus **Sheld.** – See *Symphyotrichum* ×*longulum* (Sheldon) Nesom [*boreale* × *puniceum*]

Aster lowrieanus **Porter** – See *Symphyotrichum lowrieanum* (Porter) Nesom

Aster lucidulus **(Gray) Wiegand** – See *Symphyotrichum puniceum* (L.) A.& D. Löve var. *puniceum*

Aster lucidus – See *Cotoneaster lucidus* Schldl.

Aster macrophyllus **L.** – See *Eurybia macrophylla* (L.) Cass.

Aster marilandicus **Pluk.** – possibly *Sericocarpus asteroides* (L.) Britton, Sterns & Poggenb.

Aster miser **[Nutt.]** – possibly *Symphyotrichum lateriflorum* (L.) Á.Löve & D.Löve

Aster missouriensis **Britton** – See *Symphyotrichum ontarione* (Wiegand) Nesom

Aster modestus **Lindl.** – See *Canadanthus modestus* (Lindl.) Nesom

Aster multiflorus **Aiton** – See *Symphyotrichum ericoides* (L.) Nesom var. *ericoides*

Aster multiflorus **Aiton var. ciliatus** – See *Symphyotrichum ericoides* (L.) Nesom var. *ericoides*

Aster multiformis **Burgess** – See *Eurybia macrophylla* (L.) Cass.

Aster nebraskensis **Britton** – See *Symphyotrichum praealtum* (Poir.) Nesom var. *nebraskense* (Britton) Nesom

Aster nemoralis **Aiton** – See *Oclemena nemoralis* (Aiton) Greene

Aster nobilis **Burgess** – See *Eurybia macrophylla* (L.) Cass.

Aster nova belgii **L.** – See *Symphyotrichum novi-belgii* (L.) Nesom var. *novi-belgii*

Aster novae-angliae **L.** – See *Symphyotrichum novae-angliae* (L.) Nesom

Aster novae-angliae roseus – See *Symphyotrichum novae-angliae* (L.) Nesom

Aster novae-angliae **var. roseus (Desf.) DC.** – See *Symphyotrichum novae-angliae* (L.) Nesom

Aster novibelgi – See *Symphyotrichum novi-belgii* (L.) Nesom var. *novi-belgii*

Aster novi-belgi **L.** – See *Symphyotrichum novi-belgii* (L.) Nesom var. *novi-belgii*

Aster novi-belgii **L.** – See *Symphyotrichum novi-belgii* (L.) Nesom var. *novi-belgii*

Aster oblongifolius **Nutt.** – See *Symphyotrichum oblongifolium* (Nutt.) Nesom

Aster occidentalis – See *Symphyotrichum spathulatum* (Lindl.) Nesom var. *spathulatum*

Aster ontarionis **Wiegand** – See *Symphyotrichum ontarione* (Wiegand) Nesom

Aster oolentangiensis **Riddell** – See *Symphyotrichum oolentangiense* (Riddell) Nesom var. *oolentangiense*

Aster orcutti – See *Xylorhiza orcuttii* (Vasey & Rose) Greene

Aster oregonus **(Nutt.) Torr. & Gray** – See *Symphyotrichum eatonii* (Gray) Nesom

Aster paludosus **Aiton** – See *Eurybia paludosa* (Aiton) Nesom

Aster paludosus **Aiton subsp. hemisphericus (Alex.) Cronq.** – See *Eurybia hemispherica* (Alexander) Nesom

Aster paniculatus **Lam.** – See *Symphyotrichum lanceolatum* (Willd.) Nesom subsp. *lanceolatum*

Aster parryi **Gray** – See *Xylorhiza glabriuscula* Nutt. var. *glabriuscula*

Aster parviceps **(Burgess) Mackenzie & Bush** – See *Symphyotrichum parviceps* (Burgess) Nesom

Aster patens **Aiton** – See *Symphyotrichum patens* (Aiton) G. I. Nesom var. *patens*

Aster patens **Willd. And Pers.** – possibly *Symphyotrichum patens* (Aiton) G.L. Nesom var. *patens*

Aster pattersoni – See *Machaeranthera bigelovii* (Gray) Greene var. *bigelovii*

Aster pauciflorus **Nutt.** – See *Almutaster pauciflorus* (Nutt.) A.& D. Löve

Aster pendulus **Willd.** – possibly *Symphyotrichum lateriflorum* (L.) A. & D. Löve

Aster perelegans – See *Eucephalus elegans* Nutt.

Aster phlogifolius **Muhl.** – See *Symphyotrichum phlogifolium* (Muhl. ex Willd.) Nesom

Aster phyllodes **Rydb.** – See *Symphyotrichum foliaceum* (DC.) Nesom var. *canbyi* (Gray) Nesom

Aster polyphyllus **Willd.** – See *Symphyotrichum pilosum* (Willd.) Nesom var. *pringlei* (Gray) Nesom

Aster porteri – See *Symphyotrichum porteri* (Gray) Nesom

Aster praealtus **Poir.** – See *Symphyotrichum praealtum* (Poir.) Nesom var. *praealtum*

Aster praealtus **Poir. var. praealtum** – possibly *Symphyotrichum praealtum* (Poir.) Nesom var. *praealtum*

Aster prenanthoides **Muhl.** – See *Symphyotrichum prenanthoides* (Muhl. ex Willd.) Nesom

Aster prenantoides **Muhl.** – See *Symphyotrichum prenanthoides* (Muhl. ex Willd.) Nesom

Aster priceae **Britton** – See *Symphyotrichum priceae* (Britt.) Nesom

Aster pringlei **(Gray) Britton** – See *Symphyotrichum pilosum* (Willd.) Nesom var. *pringlei* (Gray) Nesom

Aster ptarmicoides **(Nees) Torr. & Gray** – See *Oligoneuron album* (Nutt.) Nesom

Aster puniceus **L.** – See *Symphyotrichum puniceum* (L.) A.& D. Löve var. *puniceum*

Aster purpuratus **Nees** – See *Symphyotrichum laeve* (L.) A.& D. Löve var. *purpuratum* (Nees) Nesom

Aster radula **Aiton** – See *Eurybia radula* (Aiton) Nesom

Aster rigidus **L.** – See *Ionactis linariifolius* (L.) Greene

Aster roscidus **Burgess** – See *Eurybia macrophylla* (L.) Cass.

Aster roseus **Desf.** – See *Symphyotrichum novae-angliae* (L.) Nesom

Aster rubrotinctus **Blake** – See *Machaeranthera bigelovii* (Gray) Greene var. *bigelovii*

Aster sagittifolius **auct. non Wedemeyer ex Willd.** – See *Symphyotrichum urophyllum* (Lindl.) Nesom

Aster sagittifolius **Wedemeyer ex Willd.** – See *Symphyotrichum cordifolium* (L.) Nesom

Aster sagittifolius **Willd.** – See *Symphyotrichum cordifolium* (L.) Nesom

Aster salicifolius **Aiton** – See *Symphyotrichum potosinum* (A.Gray) G.L.Nesom

Aster salicifolius **Lam** – possibly *Symphyotrichum praealtum* (Poir.) Nesom var. *praealtum*

Aster schreberi **Nees** – See *Eurybia schreberi* (Nees) Nees

Aster scopulorum – See *Ionactis alpina* (Nutt.) Greene

Aster sericeus **Vent.** – See *Symphyotrichum sericeum* (Vent.) Nesom

Aster shorti **Hook.** – See *Symphyotrichum shortii* (Lindl.) Nesom

Aster shortii **Hook.** – See *Symphyotrichum shortii* (Lindl.) Nesom

Aster sibiricus **L.** – See *Eurybia sibirica* (L.) Nesom

Aster sibiricus **L. var. meritus (A. Nels.) Raup** – See *Eurybia merita* (A. Nels.) Nesom

Aster simplex **Willd.** – See *Symphyotrichum lanceolatum* (Willd.) Nesom subsp. *lanceolatum*

Aster simplex **Willd. var. interior (Wiegand) Cronq.** – See *Symphyotrichum lanceolatum* (Willd.) Nesom subsp. *lanceolatum*

Aster simplex **Willd. var. ramosissimus (Torr. & Gray) Cronq.** – See *Symphyotrichum lanceolatum* (Willd.) Nesom subsp. *lanceolatum*

Aster simplex **Willd. var. simplex** – See *Symphyotrichum lanceolatum* (Willd.) Nesom subsp. *lanceolatum*

Aster solidagineus **Michx.** – See *Sericocarpus linifolius* (L.) Britton, Sterns & Poggenb.

Aster solidaginoides **Willd.** – See *Sericocarpus linifolius* (L.) Britton, Sterns & Poggenb.

Aster spectabilis **Aiton** – See *Eurybia spectabilis* (Aiton) Nesom

Aster spinosus **Benth.** – See *Chloracantha spinosa* (Benth.) Nesom

Aster spurius **Willd.** – See *Symphyotrichum novae-angliae* (L.) G.L.Nesom

Aster stenomeres – See *Ionactis stenomeres* (Gray) Greene

Aster subulatus **Michx.** – See *Symphyotrichum subulatum* (Michx.) Nesom

Aster subulatus Michx. var. *ligulatus* Shinners – See *Symphyotrichum divaricatum* (Nutt.) Nesom

Aster surculosus Michx. – See *Eurybia surculosa* (Michx.) Nesom

Aster tanacetifolius Kunth – See *Machaeranthera tanacetifolia* (Kunth) Nees

Aster tardiflorus L. – See *Symphyotrichum novi-belgii* (L.) Nesom var. *villicaule* (Gray) J. Labrecque & L. Brouillet

Aster tataricus L. f. – Tatarian aster (138, 155) (1931–1942)

Aster tenebrosus Burgess – See *Eurybia divaricata* (L.) Nesom

Aster tenuicaulis (Mohr) Burgess – See *Symphyotrichum patens* (Aiton) G. I. Nesom var. *patens*

Aster tenuifolius L. – See *Symphyotrichum tenuifolium* (L.) Nesom

Aster tortifolius Michx. – See *Sericocarpus tortifolius* (Michx.) Nees

Aster tradescantia – See *Symphyotrichum tradescantii* (L.) Nesom

Aster tradescantii – See *Symphyotrichum tradescantii* (L.) Nesom

Aster tradescenti L. – See *Symphyotrichum tradescantii* (L.) Nesom

Aster tripolium – See *Tripolium pannonicum* (Jacq.) Dobrocz.

Aster turbinellus Lindl. – See *Symphyotrichum turbinellum* (Lindl.) Nesom

Aster umbellatus Lamarck [Mill?] – See *Doellingeria umbellata* (Mill.) Nees var. *umbellata*

Aster umbellatus Mill. – See *Doellingeria umbellata* (Mill.) Nees var. *umbellata*

Aster undulata L. – See *Symphyotrichum undulatum* (L.) Nesom

Aster undulatus Ait. – possibly *Symphyotrichum patens* (Aiton) G.L. Nesom var. *patens*

Aster undulatus L. – See *Symphyotrichum undulatum* (L.) Nesom

Aster vimineus Lam. – See *Symphyotrichum lateriflorum* (L.) A.& D. Löve var. *lateriflorum*

Aster violaris Burgess – See *Eurybia macrophylla* (L.) Cass.

Aster virgatus Ell. – See *Symphyotrichum laeve* (L.) A.& D. Löve var. *purpuratum* (Nees) Nesom

Aster walteri – See *Symphyotrichum walteri* (Alexander) Nesom

Aster X amethystinus Nutt. – See *Symphyotrichum ×amethystinum* (Nutt.) Nesom [*ericoides × novae-angliae*]

Aster xylorrhiza Torr. & Gray – See *Xylorhiza glabriuscula* Nutt.

Astilbe biternata (Vent.) Britt. – Astilbe (5) (1913), False goat's-beard [False goat's-beard] (5, 156) (1913–1923), False goats-beard astilbe [False goatsbeard astilbe] (155) (1942)

Astilbe Buch.-Ham. ex D. Don – Astilbe (138, 155) (1931–1942)

Astilbe decandra Don. – See *Astilbe biternata* (Vent.) Britt.

Astilbe japonica (Morr. & Dcne.) Gray – Japanese astilbe (138, 155) (1931–1942)

Astragalus (Tourn.) L. – See *Astragalus* L.

Astragalus aboriginorum glabriusculus (Hook.) Rydb. – See *Astragalus australis* (L.) Lam.

Astragalus aboriginorum Richards – See *Astragalus australis* (L.) Lam.

Astragalus adsurgens Pallas – See *Astragalus laxmannii* Jacq.

Astragalus adsurgens Pallas var. *robustior* Hook. – See *Astragalus laxmannii* Jacq. var. *robustior* (Hook.) Barneby & Welsh

Astragalus agrestis Dougl. ex G. Don – Cock's-head [Cock's head] (5, 131, 156) (1899–1923), Field milkvetch [Field milk vetch] (4) (1986), Nickle-leaf milkvetch [Nickleleaf milkvetch] (155) (1942), Purple milkvetch [Purple milk vetch] (5, 50, 82, 85, 93, 155) (1913–present)

Astragalus allochrous Gray – Half-moon loco [Halfmoon loco] (155) (1942)

Astragalus allochrous Gray var. *playanus* Isely – Half-moon milkvetch [Halfmoon milkvetch] (50) (present), Wooton's loco [Wooton loco] (155) (1942)

Astragalus alpinus L. – Alpine milkvetch [Alpine milk vetch] (4, 5, 85, 131, 155) (1899–1986)

Astragalus alpinus var. *brunetianus* Fernald – One-sided milkvetch [One-sided milk vetch] (19) (1840)

Astragalus americana (Hook.) Rydb. – See *Astragalus americanus* (Hook.) M.E.Jones

Astragalus americanus (Hook.) M.E.Jones – American milkvetch [American milk vetch] (4, 50) (1986–present), Arctic milkvetch [Arctic milk vetch] (5, 131) (1899–1913), Rattlepod [Rattle pod, Rattle-pod] (85) (1932)

Astragalus araneosus – See *Astragalus lentiginosus* Dougl. ex Hook. var. *diphysus* (Gray) M.E. Jones

Astragalus arizonicus Gray – Arizona loco (155) (1942)

Astragalus asymmetricus E. Sheld. – Woolly-leaf loco [Woollyleaf loco] (155) (1942)

Astragalus australis (L.) Lam. – Astragalus (107) (1919), Indian milkvetch [Indian milk vetch] (4, 5, 131, 155) (1899–1986)

Astragalus barrii Barneby – Barr's milkvetch (50) (present), Barr's orphaca [Barr orphaca] (4) (1986)

Astragalus beckwithi – See *Astragalus beckwithii* Torr. & Gray

Astragalus beckwithii Torr. & Gray – Beckwith's milkvetch [Beckwith milkvetch] (155) (1942)

Astragalus bigelovi – See *Astragalus mollissimus* Torr. var. *bigelovii* (Gray) Barneby

Astragalus bisulcatus (Hook.) Gray – Grooved milkvetch [Grooved milk vetch] (131) (1899), Milkvetch [Milk vetch, Milk-vetch] (148) (1939), Two-groove loco [Twogrooved loco] (155) (1942), Two-groove milkvetch [Twogrooved milkvetch, Two-grooved milk vetch, Two-grooved milkvetch] (3, 4, 50, 93, 97, 126, 148) (1933–present), Two-tooth milkvetch [Two-toothed milk vetch] (5) (1913)

Astragalus bisulcatus (Hook.) Gray var. *bisulcatus* – Two-groove milkvetch [Twogrooved milkvetch] (50) (present)

Astragalus bisulcatus (Hook.) Gray var. *haydenianus* (Gray) Barneby – Hayden's poison vetch [Hayden poisonvetch] (155) (1942)

Astragalus blakei Eggleston – See *Astragalus robbinsii* (Oakes) Gray var. *minor* (Hook.) Barneby

Astragalus bodinii Sheldon – Bodin's milkvetch [Bodin milk vetch] (4, 50) (1986–present)

Astragalus calycosus Torr. ex S. Watson – Bare-stem loco [Barestem loco] (155) (1942)

Astragalus canadensis L. – Canadian milkvetch [Canada milkvetch, Canada milk vetch, Canadian milk vetch] (3, 4, 42, 50, 85, 155) (1814–present), Cow vetch [Cow-vetch] (82) (1930) IA, Little rattlepod [Little rattle-pod, Little rattle pod] (121) (1918?–1970?), Ločipišni pežixota (Lakota, gray appetite herb) (121) (1918?–1970?), Locoweed [Loco weed, Loco-weed] (121) (1970), Milkvetch [Milk vetch, Milk-vetch] (80, 82, 121) (1913–1930), Rattlebox [Rattle box, Rattle-box] (80) (1913), Woolly milkvetch [Woolly milk vetch] (19, 42) (1814–1840)

Astragalus canadensis L. var. *canadensis* – Canadian milkvetch [Canada milkvetch, Canada milk vetch, Canadian milk vetch] (5, 50, 93) (1913–present), Canadian rattleweed [Canadian rattle weed] (5) (1913), Carolina milkvetch [Carolina milk vetch] (5, 42, 93, 97, 131) (1814–1937), Gasantho (Omaha-Ponca, rattle) (37) (1919), Little rattlepod [Little rattle-pod, Little rattle pod] (37, 127) (1919–1933), Milkvetch [Milk vetch, Milk-vetch] (72, 114) (1894–1907)

Astragalus canadensis L. var. *mortonii* (Nutt.) S. Wats. – Morton's loco [Morton loco] (155) (1942)

Astragalus carolinianus L. – See *Astragalus canadensis* L. var. *canadensis*

Astragalus caryocarpus Ker-Gawl. – See *Astragalus crassicarpus* Nutt. var. *crassicarpus*

Astragalus ceramicus Sheldon – Bird's-egg astragalus [Bird egg astragalus] (98) (1926), Painted milkvetch [Painted milk-vetch, Painted milk vetch] (50) (present)

Astragalus ceramicus Sheldon var. *filifolius* (Gray) F.J. Herm. – Bird's-egg pea [Bird-egg pea] (158) (1900), Long-leaf milkvetch [Long-leaved milk vetch] (5, 97) (1913–1937), Long-leaf painted-pod [Long-leaved painted pod] (93) (1936), Painted milkvetch [Painted milk-vetch, Painted milk vetch] (4, 50, 98) (1926–present)

Astragalus cicer L. – Cicer milkvetch (50) (present)

Astragalus coltoni – See *Astragalus coltonii* M.E. Jones

Astragalus coltonii **M.E. Jones** – Colton's loco [Colton loco] (155) (1942)

Astragalus convallarius **Greene** – Timber poisonvetch (155) (1942)

Astragalus crassicarpus **Nutt.** – Bi'jikiwi'bûgesan (Chippewa, cattle plum) (40) (1928), Buffalo bean [Buffalo bean, Buffalo-bean, Buffalo beans] (158) (1900), Buffalo-apple [Buffalo apple] (158) (1900), Buffalo-pea [Buffalo pea, Buffalo peas] (131, 158) (1899–1900), Groundplum [Ground-plum, Ground plum, Ground plums] (4, 40, 72, 121, 127, 131, 158) (1899–1986), Ground-plum milkvetch [Groundplum milkvetch] (50, 155) (1942–present), Pte tawote (Lakota, buffalo food) (121) (1918?–1970?)

Astragalus crassicarpus **Nutt. var. berlandieri Barneby** – Buffalo-weed [Buffalo weed] (156) (1923), Earthplum [Earth-plum] (156) (1923), Groundplum [Ground-plum, Ground plum, Ground plums] (156, 158) (1900–1923), Ground-plum milkvetch [Groundplum milkvetch] (50) (present), Larger ground plum (5, 93, 97, 131) (1899–1937), Mexican ground-plum [Mexican ground plum] (124) (1937), Prairie-apple [Prairie apple, Prairie apples] (76, 156, 158) (1896–1923) Southwestern MO, fruit eaten by children

Astragalus crassicarpus **Nutt. var. crassicarpus** – Buffalo bean [Buffalo bean, Buffalo-bean, Buffalo beans] (5, 76, 85, 156) (1896–1932) ND SD, Buffalo-apple [Buffalo apple] (5, 76, 156) (1896–1923) ND, Buffalo-pea [Buffalo pea, Buffalo peas] (5, 37, 114) (1894–1919), Earthplum [Earth-plum] (156) (1923), Groundplum [Ground-plum, Ground plum, Ground plums] (2, 47, 63, 85, 92, 98, 101, 107, 108, 114, 156) (1852–1932), Ground-plum milkvetch [Groundplum milkvetch] (50) (present), Indian apple [Indian-apple, Indian-apples] (98) (1926) Neb, Indian pea (101) (1905), Indian wild plum (98) (1926) Neb, Milkvetch [Milk vetch, Milk-vetch] (156) (1923), Pte ta wote (Dakota, food of buffalo) (37) (1919), Tdika shande (Omaha-Ponca) (37) (1919), Wamide wenigthe (Omaha-Ponca) (37) (1919)

Astragalus curvicarpus **(E. Sheld.) J.F. Macbr.** – Curve-pod locoweed [Curvepod locoweed] (155) (1942)

Astragalus decumbens – See *Astragalus miser* Dougl. var. *decumbens* (Nutt. ex Torr. & Gray) Cronq.

Astragalus diphysus – See *Astragalus lentiginosus* Dougl. ex Hook. var. *diphysus* (Gray) M.E. Jones

Astragalus distortus **Torr. & Gray** – Bent milkvetch [Bent milk vetch] (5, 72, 82, 97) (1907–1937), Ozark milkvetch [Ozark milk vetch] (4) (1986)

Astragalus drummondii **Dougl. ex Hook.** – Drummond's milkvetch [Drummond milk vetch, Drummond milkvetch] (4, 5, 93, 131, 155) (1899–1986)

Astragalus earlei **Greene** – See *Astragalus mollissimus* Torr. var. *earlei* (Greene ex Rydb.) Tidestrom

Astragalus eucosmus **B.L. Rob.** – Pretty milkvetch [Pretty milk vetch] (5) (1913)

Astragalus flexuosus **(Hook.) Dougl. ex G. Don** – Flexile milkvetch [Flexile milk vetch] (5, 50, 131, 155) (1899–present), Pliant milkvetch [Pliant milk vetch] (4)(1986), Slender milkvetch [Slender milk vetch] (3) (1977)

Astragalus flexuosus **(Hook.) Dougl. ex G. Don var. elongatus (Hook.) M.E. Jones** – Flexile milkvetch [Flexile milk vetch] (50) (present)

Astragalus flexuosus **(Hook.) Dougl. ex G. Don var. flexuosus** – See *Astragalus flexuosus* (Hook.) Dougl. ex G. Don var. *elongatus* (Hook.) M.E. Jones

Astragalus giganteus **S. Watson** – Yaqui loco (155) (1942)

Astragalus gilviflorus **Sheldon** – Plains milkvetch (50) (present), Plains orophaca (4) (1986)

Astragalus gilviflorus **Sheldon var. gilviflorus** – Plains milkvetch (50) (present)

Astragalus glaux **L.** – Milkvetch [Milk vetch, Milk-vetch] (19, 92) (1840–1876)

Astragalus glycyphyllos **L.** – Common milk tare [Common milke tare] (178) (1526), Wild licorice [Wild liquorice] (92) (1876)

Astragalus goniatus **Nutt.** – See *Astragalus agrestis* Dougl. ex G. Don

Astragalus gracilis **Nutt.** – Notched milkvetch [Notched milk vetch]

(131) (1899), Slender milkvetch [Slender milk vetch] (3, 4, 5, 50, 85, 93, 97, 131) (1899–present)

Astragalus haydenianus – See *Astragalus bisulcatus* (Hook.) Gray var. *haydenianus* (Gray) Barneby

Astragalus horni – See *Astragalus hornii* Gray

Astragalus hornii **Gray** – Horn loco (155) (1942)

Astragalus hyalinus **M.E. Jones** – Silvery milkvetch [Silvery milk vetch] (5, 93) (1913–1936), Summer milkvetch (50) (present), Summer orophaca (4) (1986)

Astragalus hylophilus – See *Astragalus miser* Dougl. var. *hylophilus*

Astragalus hypoglottis **L.** – See *Astragalus agrestis* Dougl. ex G. Don

Astragalus kentrophyta **Gray** – Nuttall's kentrophyta (4) (1986), Spiny milkvetch (50) (present), Thistle milkvetch (155) (1942)

Astragalus kentrophyta **Gray var. kentrophyta** – Prickly milkvetch [Prickly milk vetch] (5, 85, 93, 131) (1899–1936), Spiny milkvetch (50) (present)

Astragalus **L.** – Buffalo bean [Buffalo bean, Buffalo-bean, Buffalo beans] (1, 93, 106) (1930–1936), Buffalo-pea [Buffalo pea, Buffalo peas] (1) (1932), Čaŋte jazaŋpi ičuwa (Lakota, heart pain treatment) (121) (1918?–1970?), Dipelta (138) (1923), Groundplum [Ground-plum, Ground plum, Ground plums] (103) (1870), Indian pea (103) (1870), Loco (148, 155) (1939–1942), Locoweed [Loco weed, Loco-weed] (1, 106) (1930–1932) loco from Spanish for crazy from symptoms of poisoning in horses, Milkvetch [Milk vetch, Milk-vetch] (1, 2, 4, 10, 38, 50, 82, 103, 106, 127, 155, 156, 158) (1818–present), Poison vetch [Poisonvetch] (155) (1942), Pop-pea (103) (1870), Prairie-apple [Prairie apple, Prairie apples] (1, 93) (1932–1936), Rattle-box weed (103) (1870), Sheep-pod (1) (1932)

Astragalus lambertii **(Pursh) Greene** – See *Oxytropis lambertii* Pursh

Astragalus laxmannii **Jacq.** – Ascending milkvetch [Ascending milk vetch] (5, 82, 131) (1899–1930), Laxmann's milkvetch (50) (present)

Astragalus laxmannii **Jacq. var. robustior (Hook.) Barneby & Welsh** – Prairie milkvetch (50) (present), Standing milkvetch [Standing milk vetch] (4) (1986)

Astragalus lentiginosus **Dougl. ex Hook.** – Speckle-pod loco [Specklepod loco] (155) (1942)

Astragalus lentiginosus **Dougl. ex Hook. var. diphysus (Gray) M.E. Jones** – Blue loco (155) (1942), Dry plains milkvetch [Dryplains milkvetch] (155) (1942)

Astragalus leptaleus **Gray** – Pežuta skuja (Lakota, sweet medicine) (121) (1918?–1970?), Slender milkweed (121) (1970)

Astragalus leucophyllus – See *Astragalus asymmetricus* E. Sheld.

Astragalus lindheimeri **Engelm. ex Gray** – Lindheimer's milkvetch [Lindheimer milk vetch] (4) (1986)

Astragalus lotiflorus **Hook** – Lotus milkvetch (3, 4, 50) (1977–present), Low milkvetch [Low milk vetch] (5, 72, 82, 93, 97, 131) (1899–1937), Reverchon's astragalus (97) (1937)

Astragalus menziesi – See *Astragalus nuttallii* (Torr. & Gray) J.T. Howell var. *nuttallii*

Astragalus menziesii **Gray** – See *Astragalus nuttallii* (Torr. & Gray) J.T. Howell var. *nuttallii*

Astragalus mexicanus **A. DC.** – See *Astragalus crassicarpus* Nutt. var. *berlandieri* Barneby

Astragalus microlobus **Gray** – See *Astragalus gracilis* Nutt.

Astragalus miser **Dougl. var. decumbens (Nutt. ex Torr. & Gray) Cronq.** – Decumbent milkvetch (155) (1942)

Astragalus miser **Dougl. var. hylophilus** – Timber milkvetch (148) (1939) CO, Woodland weedy milkvetch [Woodland weedy milk vetch] (4) (1986), Woody milkvetch (50) (present)

Astragalus miser **Dougl. var. hylophilus (Rydb.) Barneby** – See *Astragalus miser* Dougl. var. *hylophilus*

Astragalus miser **var. serotinus (Gray ex Cooper) Barneby** – Palliser's poison milkvetch [Palliser poisonmilkvetch] (155) (1942)

Astragalus missouriensis **Nutt.** – Missouri milkvetch [Missouri milk vetch] (3, 4, 5, 50, 93, 97, 131) (1899–present)

Astragalus missouriensis **Nutt. var. missouriensis** – Missouri milkvetch [Missouri milk vetch] (50) (present)

Astragalus mollissimus **Torr.** – Crazyweed [Crazy-weed, Crazy weed] (5, 71, 97, 156, 157, 158) (1898–1937), Loco (96) (1891), Loco plant (157, 158) (1900–1929), Locoweed [Loco weed, Loco-weed] (71, 76, 124, 150) (1894–1898), Milkvetch [Milk vetch, Milk-vetch] (156) (1923), Rattle-bag weed [Rattle bag weed] (5, 156) (1913–1923), Rattle-box weed (76) (1896), Rattleweed [Rattle-weed, Rattle weed] (156, 157, 158) (1900–1929), Stemmed loco (125) (1930), Texas locoweed [Texas loco-weed] (156, 157, 158) (1900–1929), Woolly loco (3, 125, 155) (1930–1977), Woolly locoweed [Woolly loco-weed, Woolly loco weed] (5, 50, 71, 92, 93, 157, 158) (1898–present)

Astragalus mollissimus **Torr. var.** *bigelovii* **(Gray) Barneby** – Bigelow's milkvetch [Bigelow milkvetch] (155) (1942), Earl loco (155) (1942), Narrow-leaf loco [Narrowleaf loco, Narrow-leafed loco] (122, 124) (1937)

Astragalus mollissimus **Torr. var.** *mollissimus* – Woolly locoweed [Woolly loco-weed, Woolly loco weed] (50) (present)

Astragalus mollissimus **Torr. var.** *thompsoniae* **(S. Wats.) Barneby** – Thompson's loco [Thompson loco] (155) (1942)

Astragalus mortoni – See *Astragalus canadensis* L. var. *mortonii* (Nutt.) S. Wats.

Astragalus neglectus **(Torr. & Gray) Sheldon** – Cooper's milkvetch [Cooper's milk vetch, Cooper milk vetch] (3, 4, 5, 50, 72) (1907–present)

Astragalus nothoxys **Gray** – Sheep loco (155) (1942)

Astragalus nuttallianus **DC.** – Annual astragalus (97) (1937)

Astragalus nuttallianus **DC.** – Small-flower milkvetch [Smallflower milkvetch, Small-flowered milk vetch] (4, 50) (1986–present)

Astragalus nuttallii **(Torr. & Gray) J.T. Howell var.** *nuttallii* – Menzies' loco [Menzies loco] (155) (1942)

Astragalus oocarpus **Gray** – Egg-pod loco [Eggpod loco] (155) (1942)

Astragalus palliseri – See *Astragalus miser* var. *serotinus* (Gray ex Cooper) Barneby

Astragalus pattersoni – See *Astragalus pattersonii* Gray

Astragalus pattersonii **Gray** – Patterson's loco [Patterson loco] (155) (1942)

Astragalus pauciflorus **Hook.** – See *Astragalus leptaleus* Gray

Astragalus pectinatus **(Hook.) Dougl. ex G. Don** – Narrow-leaf milkvetch [Narrowleaf milkvetch, Narrow-leaved milk vetch] (5, 50, 93) (1913–present), Narrow-leaf poison milkvetch [Narrowleaf poisonmilkvetch] (155) (1942), Narrow-leaf poison-vetch [Narrow-leaved poisonvetch] (3) (1977), Tine-leaf milkvetch [Tine-leaved milkvetch, Tine-leaved milk vetch] (4) (1986)

Astragalus plattensis **Nutt.** – Groundplum [Ground-plum, Ground plum, Ground plums] (3) (1977), Platte milkvetch [Platte milk vetch] (5, 72, 93, 97, 131) (1899–1937), Platte River milkvetch [Platte River milk vetch] (4, 50) (1986–present)

Astragalus praelongus **Sheldon var.** *ellisiae* **(Rydb.) Barneby** – Ellis' stinking milkvetch (50) (present), Stinking milkvetch [Stinking milk vetch] (4) (1986)

Astragalus preussi – See *Astragalus preussii* Gray

Astragalus preussii **Gray** – Preuss' milkvetch [Preuss milkvetch] (155) (1942)

Astragalus puniceus **Osterhout** – Trinidad milkvetch [Trinidad milk vetch] (4, 50) (1986–present)

Astragalus purshi – See *Astragalus purshii* Dougl. ex Hook.

Astragalus purshii **Dougl. ex Hook.** – Pursh's loco [Pursh loco] (155) (1942), Pursh's milkvetch [Pursh milk vetch] (4) (1986), Woolly-pod milkvetch [Woollypod milkvetch] (50) (present)

Astragalus racemosus **Pursh** – Alkali milkvetch [Alkali milk-vetch] (4) (1986)

Astragalus racemosus **Pursh** – Cream milkvetch (50) (present), Creamy poisonvetch (3, 4) (1977–1986), Locoweed [Loco weed, Loco-weed] (121) (1970), Pežuta ska hu (Lakota, white medicine plant) (121) (1918?–1970?), Racemed milkvetch [Racemed milk vetch] (93) (1936), Racemose milkvetch [Racemose milk vetch] (5, 97, 131) (1899–1937)

Astragalus racemosus **Pursh var.** *longisetus* **M. E. Jones** – Cream milkvetch (50) (present)

Astragalus racemosus **Pursh var.** *racemosus* – Cream milkvetch (50) (present)

Astragalus remulcus – See *Astragalus tephrodes* A. Gray var. *brachylobus* (Gray) Barneby

Astragalus reverchonii **Gray** – See *Astragalus lotiflorus* Hook

Astragalus robbinsii **(Oakes) Gray** – Robbins' milkvetch [Robbin's milk vetch, Robbins' milk vetch (5) (1913)

Astragalus robbinsii **(Oakes) Gray var.** *minor* **(Hook.) Barneby** – Blake's milkvetch [Blake's milk vetch] (5) (1913)

Astragalus sabulosus **M. E. Jones** – Straight-stem poison milkvetch [Straightstem poisonmilkvetch] (155) (1942)

Astragalus scaposus – See *Astragalus calycosus* Torr. ex S. Watson

Astragalus secundus **Michx.** – See *Astragalus alpinus* var. *brunetianus* Fernald

Astragalus sericea – See *Astragalus sericoleucus* Gray

Astragalus sericoleucus **Gray** – Hoary milkvetch [Hoary milk vetch] (5, 93) (1913–1936), Locoweed [Loco weed, Loco-weed] (95) (1911), Silk orophaca (4) (1986), Silky milkvetch [Silky milk vetch] (50) (present)

Astragalus shortianus **Nutt. ex Torr. & Gray** – Short's milkvetch [Short's milk vetch] (4, 5, 50, 93) (1913–present)

Astragalus sonneanus – See *Astragalus whitneyi* var. *sonneanus* (Greene) Jeps.

Astragalus spatulatus **Sheldon** – Draba milkvetch [Draba milk vetch] (4) (1986), Low milkvetch [Low milk vetch] (157) (1929), Prairie milkvetch (155) (1942), Sessile-flower milkvetch [Sessile flowered milk vetch, Sessile-flowered milk vetch] (5) (1913), Silky milkvetch [Silky milk vetch] (85) (1932), Tufted milkvetch [Tufted milk vetch] (3, 5, 50, 93, 127, 131) (1899–present), Tufted milky vetch (85) (1932)

Astragalus splendens – See *Oxytropis splendens* Dougl. ex Hook

Astragalus succulentus **Richards.** – See *Astragalus crassicarpus* Nutt. var. *crassicarpus*

Astragalus tenellus **Pursh** – Loose-flower milkvetch [Loose-flowered milk vetch] (3, 5, 50, 93, 131, 155) (1899–present), Pulse milkvetch [Pulse milk vetch] (4) (1986)

Astragalus tennesseensis **Gray ex Chapman** – Tennessee milkvetch [Tennessee milk vetch] (5, 97) (1913–1937)

Astragalus tephrodes **var.** *brachylobus* **(Gray) Barneby** – Towline loco (155) (1942)

Astragalus tetrapterus **Gray** – Four-wing poison milkvetch [Fourwing poisonmilkvetch] (155) (1942)

Astragalus thompsoniae – See *Astragalus mollissimus* Torr. var. *thompsoniae* (S. Wats.) Barneby

Astragalus thurberi **Gray** – Thurber's loco [Thurber loco] (155) (1942)

Astragalus utahensis **(Torr.) Torr. & Gray** – Utah loco (155) (1942)

Astragalus vexilliflexus **Sheldon** – Bent-flower milkvetch [Bent-flowered milk vetch] (4, 50) (1986–present)

Astragalus viridis **(Nutt.) Sheldon** – See *Astragalus kentrophyta* Gray var. *kentrophyta*

Astragalus wardi – See *Astragalus wardii* Gray

Astragalus wardii **Gray** – Ward's loco [Ward loco] (155) (1942)

Astragalus whitneyi **var.** *sonneanus* **(Greene) Jeps.** – Balloonpod milkvetch (155) (1942)

Astragalus wootoni – See *Astragalus allochrous* Gray var. *playanus* Isely

Astragalus wootonii **Sheld.** – See *Astragalus allochrous* Gray var. *playanus* Isely

Astragalus yaquianus – See *Astragalus giganteus* S. Watson

Astragalus zionis **M. E. Jones** – Zion milkvetch (155) (1942)

Astranthium integrifolium **(Michx.) Nutt.** – Daisy of America (12) (1821), Entire-leaf western daisy [Entireleaf western daisy] (50) (present), Western daisy (4, 5, 97, 156) (1913–1986)

Astranthium integrifolium **(Michx.) Nutt. subsp.** *ciliatum* **(Raf.) Dejong** – Western daisy (3) (1977)

Astrantia L. – Masterwort [Master-wort, Master wort, Masterwoorts] (109, 137, 155) (1923–1949)

Astrantia major L. – Black masterwort (92) (1876), Great masterwort (138) (1923), Imperial masterwort (92) (1876)

Astrantia minor L. – Dwarf masterwort (155) (1942)

Astrolepis sinuata (**Lag. ex Sw.**) **Benham & Windham subsp.** *sinuata* – Bulb cloak fern [Bulb cloakfern] (155) (1942), Long cloak fern [Long cloak-fern] (50) (present), Scaly notholaena (97) (1937)

Astrophytum asterias (**Zucc.**) **Lem.** – Sea-urchin cactus (109) (1949)

Astrophytum asterias **Lem.** – See *Astrophytum asterias* (Zucc.) Lem.

Astrophytum **Lem.** – Star cactus [Starcactus] (109, 138, 155) (1923–1949)

Atamasco atamosco (**L.**) **Greene** – See *Zephyranthes atamasca* (L.) Herbert) (())

Atelophragma **Rydb.** – See *Astragalus* L. all US species

Atenia gairdneri **Hook. & Arn.** – See *Perideridia gairdneri* (Hook. & Arn.) Mathias

Atenia **Hook. & Arn.** – Squawroot [Squaw-root, Squaw root] (1) (1932), Yamp (1) (1932)

Athanasia trinervia **Walt.** – See *Marshallia trinervia* (Walt.) Trel.

Atheropogon apludioides [**Muhl. ex Willd.**] – See *Bouteloua curtipendula* (Michx.) Torr. var. *curtipendula*

Atheropogon curtipendulus (**Michx.**) **Fourn.** – See *Bouteloua curtipendula* (Michx.) Torr. var. *curtipendula*

Atheropogon **Muhl.** – See *Bouteloua* Lag.

Atheropogon oligostachyum – See *Bouteloua gracilis* (Willd. ex Kunth) Lag. ex Griffiths

Athyrium acrostichoides (**Sw.**) **Diels** – See *Deparia acrostichoides* (Sw.) M. Kato

Athyrium asplenoides (**Michx.**) **Desv.** – See *Athyrium filix-femina* (L.) Roth var. *asplenoides* (Michx.) Farw.

Athyrium filixfemina – See *Athyrium filix-femina* (L.) Roth

Athyrium filix-femina (**L.**) **Roth** – A'sawan (Chippewa) (40) (1928), Backache brake (5, 92, 157) (1876–1929), Brake aspidium (42) (1814), Common lady fern [Common ladyfern] (50) (present), Female fern [Female Ferne] (5, 92, 157) (1876–1929), Lady fern [Ladyfern, Lady-fern] (2, 3, 4, 40, 46, 72, 97, 109, 131, 138, 155, 157) (1895–1986), Spleenwort [Spleen-wort, Spleenewort] (157) (1929)

Athyrium filix-femina (**L.**) **Roth subsp.** *angustum* (**Willd.**) **Clausen** – Subarctic lady fern [Subarctic ladyfern] (50) (present)

Athyrium filix-femina (**L.**) **Roth subsp.** *cyclosorum* (**Rupr.**) **C. Christens.** – Subarctic lady fern [Subarctic ladyfern] (50) (present)

Athyrium filix-femina (**L.**) *Roth* **var.** *asplenoides* (**Michx.**) **Farw.** – Asplenium lady's-fern [Asplenium ladyfern] (50) (present), Dark shield fern (187) (1818), Male fern [Malefern, Male-fern, Male ferne] (122) (1937) TX, Southern lady fern [Southern lady-fern] (4) (1986), Spleenwort shield fern [Spleen-wort shield-fern] (187) (1818)

Athyrium filix-foemina (**L.**) **Roth** – See *Athyrium filix-femina* (L.) Roth

Athyrium pycnocarpon (**Spreng**) **Tidest.** – See *Diplazium pycnocarpon* (Spreng.) Broun

Athyrium **Roth** – Lady fern [Ladyfern, Lady-fern] (1, 4, 50) (1932–present)

Athyrium thelypterioides (**Michx.**) **Desv.** – See *Deparia acrostichoides* (Sw.) M. Kato

Athyrium thelypteroides **Desv.** – See *Deparia acrostichoides* (Sw.) M. Kato

Atragene americana **Sims.** – See *Clematis occidentalis* (Hornem.) DC. var. *occidentalis*

Atragene **L.** – See *Clematis* L.

Atragene pseudalpina – See *Clematis columbiana* (Nutt.) Torr. & Gray var. *columbiana*

Atragene pseudoalpina – See *Clematis columbiana* (Nutt.) Torr. & Gray var. *columbiana*

Atriplex (**Tourn.**) **L.** – See *Atriplex* L.

Atriplex arenaria **Nutt.** – See *Atriplex cristata* Humb. & Bonpl. ex Willd.

Atriplex argentea **Nutt.** – Saltbush [Salt bush, Salt-bush] (1) (1932), Saltweed [Saltweed, Salt-weed] (5, 97, 145, 156) (1897–1937), Silver orache (131) (1899), Silver-scale saltbush [Silverscale saltbush] (3, 4, 50) (1977–present), Silvery orache (5, 93, 156) (1913–1936), Tumbling salt-sage (141) (1899) WY

Atriplex argentea **Nutt. subsp.** *argentea* – Silver-scale saltbush [Silverscale saltbush] (3, 50) (1977–present)

Atriplex argentea **Nutt. subsp.** *argentea* **var.** *argentea* – Silver-scale saltbush [Silverscale saltbush] (50) (present)

Atriplex argentea **Nutt. subsp.** *expansa* (**S. Wats.**) **Hall & Clements** – Spreading salt-sage (141) (1899) WY

Atriplex argenteum **Nutt.** – See *Atriplex argentea* Nutt.

Atriplex canescens (**Pursh**) **James** – See *Atriplex canescens* (Pursh) Nutt.

Atriplex canescens (**Pursh**) **Nutt.** – Bushy atriplex (5, 93, 131, 158) (1899–1936), Bushy salt-sage (141) (1899) WY, Cenizo (5, 158) (1900–1913), Chamiso (Mexican) (147) (1856), Chamiza (124) (1937) TX, Four-wing saltbush [Fourwing saltbush] (4, 50, 155) (1942–present), Greasewood [Grease-wood] (147) (1856), Sagebush [Sage bush, Sage-bush] (2, 5, 21, 50, 138, 155, 158) (1900–present), Shadscale [Shad scale] (3, 97, 118, 153) (1898–1977)

Atriplex canescens (**Pursh**) **Nutt. var.** *canescens* – Four-wing saltbush [Fourwing saltbush] (50) (present)

Atriplex confertifolia (**Torr. & Frem.**) **S. Wats.** – Shadscale saltbush (50, 155) (1942–present), Shadscales (1) (1932), Spiny saltbush (3, 4) (1977–1986)

Atriplex confertifolia (**Torr.**) **S. Wats.** – See *Atriplex confertifolia* (Torr. & Frem.) S. Wats.

Atriplex cristata **Humb. & Bonpl. ex Willd.** – Sand orache (19) (1840), Sea-beach atriplex (5) (1913)

Atriplex dioica (**Nutt.**) **Macbr.** – See *Endolepis dioica* (Nutt.) Standl.

Atriplex eremicola – See *Atriplex fruticulosa* Jepson

Atriplex expansa **Wats.** – See *Atriplex argentea* Nutt. subsp. *expansa* (S. Wats.) Hall & Clements) (())

Atriplex fruticulosa **Jepson** – Osterhout's salt-sage (141) (1899)

Atriplex halamoides **Raf.** – See *Atriplex prostrata* Boucher ex DC. Atriplex halimoides

Atriplex hastata **L.** – See *Atriplex prostrata* Bouchér ex DC. subsp. *calotheca* (Rafn) M.A.Gust.

Atriplex hastata **sensu Aellen, non L.** – See *Atriplex prostrata* Bouchér ex DC.

Atriplex hortensis **L.** – Areche (107, 158) (1538–1900) England, Arrach [Arache] (92, 158, 179) (1526–1900), Arroche (French)\ (158) (1900), Bonny-dame [Bonny-dame] (92, 158) (1876–1900), Butter leaves [Butter-leaves] (107, 158) (1900–1919), Flat blites (178) (1526), Garden orach [Garden orache] (3, 7, 19, 46, 50, 92, 138, 155, 158) (1649–present), Mountain spinach (107, 158) (1900–1919), Orach [Orache] (4, 107, 109, 184) (1793–1986), Orage (158) (1900), Red arach of the garden (178) (1526), Red blites (178) (1526), Red oreche (107) (1538), White blite [White blites] (178) (1526), White garden arach (178) (1526), Wild arrach (46) (1671)

Atriplex **L.** – Gooseweed [Goose-weeds] (156) (1923), Orach [Orache] (1, 2, 4, 7, 93, 156) (1828–1986) Old World annuals are known as orach, Saltbush [Salt bush, Salt-bush] (4, 50, 93, 109, 141, 146, 148, 138, 153, 155, 158) (1899–present), Saltsage [Salt-sage] (141) (1899) WY

Atriplex micrantha **Ledeb.** – Two-scale saltbush [Twoscale saltbush] (50) (present)

Atriplex nudicaulis **Boguslaw** – Dwarf oats (19) (1840)

Atriplex nuttallii **S. Wats.** – Moundscale (4) (1986), Nuttall's atriplex (5, 93) (1913–1936), Nuttall's saltbush (50) (present), Nuttall's salt-sage [Nuttall's salt-sage] (141) (1899), Salt sage (3) (1977)

Atriplex oblongifolia **Waldst. & Kit.** – Oblong-leaf orache [Oblongleaf orache] (50) (present)

Atriplex patula **L.** – Fat-hen saltbush (156) (1923), Orach [Orache] (156) (1923), Spear-scale [Spearscale] (3, 4) (1977–1986), Spreading aranche (72) (1907)

Atriplex patula L. subsp. *hastata* sensu Hall & Clements p.p. – See *Atriplex subspicata* (Nutt.) Rydb.

Atriplex patula L. var. *hastata* (L.) Gray – See *Atriplex prostrata* Bouchér ex DC. subsp. *calotheca* (Rafn) M.A.Gust.

Atriplex patula L. var. *hastata* auct. non (L.) Gray – See *Atriplex prostrata* Bouchér ex DC.

Atriplex patulum L. – See *Atriplex patula* L.

Atriplex patulum Nutt. – possibly *Atriplex patula* L.

Atriplex powellii S. Wats. – Powell's saltbush (4) (1986), Powell's saltweed (50) (present)

Atriplex praecox – See *Atriplex nudicaulis* Boguslaw

Atriplex prostrata Bouchér ex DC. – Sea orach (7) (1828), Spear-leaf fat-hen saltbush [Spearleaf fat-hen saltbush] (155) (1942), Triangle orach [Triangle orache] (50) (present)

Atriplex prostrata subsp. *calotheca* (Rafn) M.A.Gust. – Fat-hen [Fat hen] (156, 158) (1900–1923), Halberd-leaf arache [Halberd-leaved arache] (72) (1907), Hard-iron (158) (1900), Orach [Orache] (80) (1913), Sea-beach orach (46) (1649)

Atriplex rosea L. – Red orache (4, 5, 21, 93) (1893–1986), Redscale (3, 4) (1977–1986), Tumbling orach (155) (1942), Tumbling saltweed (50) (present)

Atriplex semibaccata R. Br. – Australian saltbush (118) (1898)

Atriplex semibaccatum – See *Atriplex semibaccata* R. Br.

Atriplex subspicata (Nutt.) Rydb. – Halberd-leaf orache [Halberd-leaved orache, Halberd-leaved orach, Halbert-leaved orache] (5, 62, 93, 131, 158, 187) (1818–1913), Lamb's-quarters [Lambs' quarter, Lamb's quarters, Lamb's-quarters, Lambsquarter, Lambsquarters] (5, 156, 158) (1900–1923), Saline saltbush (50) (present), Spreading orache (19, 21, 62) (1840–1912)

Atriplex truncata (Torr. ex S. Wats.) Gray – Utah saltbush (118) (1898), Utah salt-sage (141) (1899)

Atriplex volutans A. Nels. – See *Atriplex argentea* Nutt.

Atropa belladonna L. – See *Atropa bella-donna* L.

Atropa bella-donna L. – Banewort [Bane-wort] (156) (1923), Belladonna (52, 53, 54, 55, 57, 59, 60, 61, 92, 109, 138, 180) (1633–1949), Black nightshade [Black night-shade] (156) (1923), Black-cherry [Black cherry] (49) (1898), Daftberry [Daft-berry] (156) (1923), Deadly nightshade (19, 52, 53, 54, 55, 57, 60, 92, 156, 178, 180) (1596–1923), Death's herb (156) (1923), Dwale (49, 53, 92, 156) (1898–1923), Dwayberry (156) (1923), Great morel (156) (1923), More morell (179) (1526), Poison black cherry (156) (1923), Sleeping nightshade (156) (1923), possibly Solatrum furiale (59) (1450)

Atropa L. – Belladonna (138) (1923)

Atropis californica Munro ex A.Gray – See Poa fendleriana (Steud.) Vasey

Aubrieta Adans. – Aubrieta (138) (1923)

Aucuba japonica Thunb. – Japanese aucuba (138) (1923)

Aucuba Thunb. – Aucuba (138) (1923)

Audibertia polystachya Benth. – See *Salvia apiana* Jepson

Aureolaria flava (L.) Farw. var. *flava* – Downy false foxglove [Downy false fox glove] (5, 72, 156) (1907–1923), False foxglove (19) (1840), Gall-of-the-earth [Gall of the earth] (18) (1805), Wild fox-glove [Wild fox glove] (156) (1923), Yellow foxglove (5, 156) (1913–1923)

Aureolaria grandiflora (Benth.) Pennell – Western false foxglove (5, 72, 97) (1907–1937)

Aureolaria grandiflora (Benth.) Pennell var. *serrata* (Torr. ex Benth.) Pennell – Big-flower gerardia [Bigflower gerardia] (3) (1977), Large-flower yellow false foxglove [Largeflower yellow false foxglove] (50) (present)

Aureolaria laevigata (Raf.) Raf. – Entire-leaf foxglove [Entire-leaved foxglove] (5) (1913)

Aureolaria pedicularia (L.) Raf. ex Farw. – American foxglove (49, 92) (1876–1898), Fern-leaf false foxglove [Fern-leaved false foxglove, Fern-leaved false foxglove] (5, 86, 97, 156) (1878–1937), Lousewort foxglove [Louse wort foxglove, Lousewort fox-glove] (19) (1840), Yellow foxglove (156) (1923)

Aureolaria pedicularia (L.) Raf. var. *pedicularia* – Bushy gerardia (5, 49, 92, 156) (1898–1923), False foxglove (156) (1923), Fern-leaf foxglove [Fern-leaved foxglove] (97) (1937), Feverweed [Fever weed, Fever-weed] (5, 49, 92, 156) (1898–1923), Lousewort [Louse wort, Louse-wort] (5, 49, 92) (1876–1913), Lousewort false foxglove [Lousewort false fox-glove] (5, 156) (1913–1923), Yellow gerardia (156) (1923)

Aureolaria Raf. – False foxglove (1, 4, 50) (1932–present), Oakleech (155) (1942)

Aureolaria virginica (L.) Pennell – False foxglove (92) (1876), Goldenoak [Golden oak] (5, 7, 92, 156) (1828–1923), Oak-leaf foxglove [Oak-leaved foxglove] (19, 156) (1840–1923), Smooth false foxglove (5, 97, 156) (1913–1937)

Auricularia auricula-judae (Bulliard) J. Schröter – Jew's-ear [Jew's ear, Jews' ear] (92) (1876)

Aurinia saxatilis (L.) Desv. – Basket-of-gold (109) (1949), Cliff stonecress (155) (1942), Gold-dust [Gold dust] (156) (1923) no longer in use by 1923, Goldentuft [Golden-tuft] (109, 138, 156) (1923–1949), Golden-tuft alyssum [Goldentuft alyssum] (155) (1942), Madwort (156) (1923), Rock alyssum (156) (1923), Yellow madwort (165) (1768)

Avena (Tourn.) L. – See *Avena* L.

Avena americana Scribn. – See *Helictotrichon hookeri* (Scribn.) Henr.

Avena barbata Brot. – See *Avena barbata* Pott ex Link

Avena barbata Pott ex Link – Slender wild oat (109) (1949)

Avena elatior L. – See *Arrhenatherum elatius* (L.) Beauv. ex J.& K. Presl var. *elatius*

Avena elatius (L.) Beauv. – possibly *Arrhenatherum elatius* (L.) Beauv. ex J.& K. Presl var. *elatius*

Avena fatua L. – Drake (5, 107) (1913–1919), Flaver (107) (1919), Havercorn (5) (1913), Hever (5) (1913), Pin grass (103) (1871), Poor oat (5) (1913), Potato oat (107) (1919), Tartarian oat [Tartarian oats, Tartarean oat] (107) (1919), Wild oat [Wild oats] (3, 5, 45, 50, 56, 67, 70, 72, 80, 85, 87, 88, 94, 103, 107, 109, 111, 123, 140, 148, 152, 155) (1856–present)

Avena flavescens L. – See *Trisetum flavescens* (L.) Beauv.

Avena hookeri Scribn. – See *Helictotrichon hookeri* (Scribn.) Henr.

Avena L. – Oat [Oats, Otes] (42, 50, 87, 93, 138, 155, 158, 184) (1793–present), Oat grass [Oatgrass, Oat-grass] (10, 42, 87) (1814–1884)

Avena mortoniana Scribn. – See *Helictotrichon mortonianum* (Scribn.) Henrard

Avena orientalis Schreb – See *Avena sativa* L.

Avena pensylvanica L. – See *Sphenopholis pensylvanica* (L.) A.S. Hitchc.

Avena praecox – See *Aira praecox* L.

Avena pratensis [L.] – See *Helictotrichon pratense* (L.) Pilg.

Avena pubescens Huds. – See *Helictotrichon pubescens* (Huds.) Schult. & Schult.f.

Avena sativa L. – Aits (Scotland) (158) (1900), Ausas (Lettonian) (110) (1886), Avoine (French) (158) (1900), Awiza (Lithuanian) (110) (1886), Awts (158) (1900), Banner oats (67) (1890), Coirce, cuirce, or corca (Irish) (110) (1886), Common oats [Common oat, Common Otes] (7, 45, 49, 50, 53, 56, 66, 110, 140, 155, 158, 180) (1633–present), Cultivated oats [Cultivated oat] (93, 163) (1852–1936), Eastern oats (110) (1886), Grass-of-the-Andes [Grass of the Andes] (92) (1876), Hafer (German) (158) (1900), Hafer corn [Hafer-corn] (158) (1900), Haver (107, 158) (1900–1919), Haw [Haws] (158) (1900), Kaer (Esthonian) (110) (1886), Kari (Georgian) (110) (1886), Kerch (Armorican) (110) (1886), Oat [Oats, Otes] (5, 19, 46, 52, 53, 54, 67, 85, 92, 107, 109, 119, 138, 152, 178, 179, 180) (1526–1949), Oat grass [Oatgrass, Oat-grass] (92) (1876), Olba (Basque) (110) (1886), Oloa (Basque) (110) (1886), Ovesu (Russian) (110) (1886), Siberian oat (107) (1919), Side oats [Side-oats, Side oat] (155) (1942), Tartarian oat [Tartarian oats, Tartarean oat] (45, 107) (1896–1919), Tyetts (158) (1900), Woats (158) (1900), Wocks (158) (1900), Wots (158) (1900), Yaits (158) (1900), Zab (Hungarian) (110) (1886), Zob (Croat) (110) (1886)

Avena sativa L. var. *orientalis* (Schreb.) Alef. – See *Avena sativa* L.

Avena spicata L. – See *Danthonia spicata* (L.) Roem. & Schult..

Avena sterilis L. – Animated oats [Animated oat] (19, 45, 50, 109, 119, 138) (1840–present), Red oat (119) (1938)

Avena striata Michx. – See *Schizachne purpurascens* (Torr.) Swall.

Avena strigosa Schreb. – Bristle-point oat [Bristle-pointed oat] (107) (1919), Hairy oats (67) (1890), Meagre oat (107) (1919)

Avena torreyi Nash. – See *Schizachne purpurascens* (Torr.) Swall.

Avenella flexuosa (L.) Drej. – See *Deschampsia flexuosa* (L.) Trin. var *flexuosa*

Avenula pubescens (Huds.) Dumort. – Downy oat grass [Downy oat-grass] (66) (1903)

Averrhoa carambola L. – Carambola (109, 138) (1923–1949) from Oriental vernacular name

Avicennia germinans (L.) L. – Avicenne cotonneux (French) (20) (1857), Black mangrove or Black mangrove tree (106) (1930), Black tree (106) (1930), Blackwood [Black wood] (77, 106) (1898–1930) Florida Keys, Mangle (19, 92) (1840–1876), Soft-leaf avicenna [Soft-leaved avicenna] (20) (1857)

Avicennia nitida – See *Avicennia germinans* (L.) L.

Avicennia oblongifolia Nutt. – See *Avicennia germinans* (L.) L.

Avicennia tomentosa – See *Avicennia germinans* (L.) L.

Axonopus affinis Chase – See *Axonopus fissifolius* (Raddi) Kuhlm.

Axonopus compressus (Sw.) Beauv. – Carpet grass [Carpet-grass] (5, 94, 119, 122, 138, 163) (1852–1938), Flat crab grass [Flat crab-grass] (5) (1913), Flat joint grass [Flat joint-grass] (5, 163) (1852–1913), Louisiana grass (5, 56, 94) (1897–1913)

Axonopus compressus (Swartz.) Beauv. – See *Axonopus compressus* (Sw.) Beauv.

Axonopus fissifolius (Raddi) Kuhlm. – Carpet grass [Carpet-grass] (109) (1949)

Axonopus furcatus (Flueggé) A.S. Hitchc. – Flat crab grass [Flat crab-grass] (163) (1852)

Axyris amaranthoides L. – Russian pigweed (3, 4, 50, 155) (1942–present), Upright axyris (5) (1913)

Axyris amarantoides L. (*sic*) – See *Axyris amaranthoides* L.

Ayapana triplinervis (Vahl) R.M. King & H. Rob. – See *Eupatorium triplinerve* Vahl

Azadirachta indica A.Juss. – Margosa tree (92) (1876), possibly Bead tree [Beade tree] (7) (1828), possibly Hoop tree (7) (1828), possibly Pride tree (7) (1828), possibly Pride-of-China [Pride of China] (7) (1828)

Azalea arborescens Pursh – See *Rhododendron arborescens* (Pursh) Torr.

Azalea atlantica – See *Rhododendron atlanticum* (Ashe) Rehd.

Azalea calendulacea – See *Rhododendron calendulaceum* (Michx.) Torr.

Azalea canescens Michx. – See *Rhododendron canescens* (Michx.) Sweet

Azalea flammea – possibly *Rhododendron flammeum* (Michx.) Sarg. not in PL W3 US IPNI

Azalea japonica – See *Rhododendron japonicum* (Gray) Sur.

Azalea L. – See *Rhododendron* L. most US species

Azalea lutea L. – See *Rhododendron calendulaceum* (Michx.) Torr.

Azalea nitida – possibly *Rhododendron viscosum* (L.) Torr. taxonomic status is unresolved (PL)

Azalea nudiflora L. – See *Rhododendron periclymenoides* (Michx.) Shinners

Azalea occidentalis – See *Rhododendron occidentale* (Torr. & Gray ex Torr.) Gray var. *occidentale*

Azalea procumbens – See *Loiseleuria procumbens* (L.) Desv.

Azalea vaseyi – See *Rhododendron vaseyi* Gray

Azalea viscosa glauca – See *Rhododendron viscosum* (L.) Torr.

Azalea viscosa L. – See *Rhododendron viscosum* (L.) Torr.

Azalea viscosa L. subsp. *palustris* – possibly *Rhododendron viscosum* (L.) Torr.

Azedaraca amena – possibly *Azadirachta indica* A. Juss.

Azolla caroliniana Willd. – Atlantic azolla (155) (1942), Carolina azolla (5, 72) (1907–1913), Carolina mosquito-fern [Carolina mosquitofern] (50) (present), Floating chainfern (122) (1937) TX, Mosquito-fern [Mosquitofern, Mosquito fern] (155) (1942)

Azolla Lam. – Azolla (155) (1942), Mosquito-fern [Mosquitofern, Mosquito fern] (4, 50, 109) (1949–present), Water fern [Waterfern, Water-fern] (4) (1986)

Azolla mexicana Schlecht. & Cham. ex K. Presl – Mexican mosquito-fern [Mexican mosquitofern] (50) (present)

B

Baccharis glutinosa **Pers.** – Guatemote (Spanish) (106) (1930), Mule's-fat [Mule's fat, Mule fat] (50) (present)

Baccharis halimifolia **L.** – Bacchante de Virginie (8) (1785), Cotton seedtree [Cotton seedtree, Cotton – Seed-tree] (5, 156) (1913–1923), Groundsel bush [Groundselbush, Groundsel-bush] (5, 109, 138, 156) (1913–1949), Groundsel tree [Groundsel-tree] (5, 7, 19, 92, 122, 124, 156) (1828–1937), Kiks-bushes (156) (1923) no longer in use by 1923, Mangle (156) (1923), Pencil tree [Pencil-tree] (5, 7, 156) (1828–1923), Plowman's-spikenard [Ploughman's spikenard, Plowman's spikenard] (5, 75, 156) (1894–1923), See-myrtle [See myrtle] (106) (1930), Virginia groundsel tree [Virginian groundsel tree] (8) (1785), Water-brush (156) (1923), Water-gall (156) (1923), White mangle (156) (1923)

Baccharis **L.** – Bacchante (8) (1785), Baccharis (50, 155, 158) (1900–present), Groundsel [Groundsell] (158) (1900), Groundsel tree [Groundsel-tree] (1, 10, 93) (1818–1936), Plowman's-spikenard [Ploughman's spikenard, Plowman's spikenard] (8, 167) (1785–1814)

Baccharis pilularis **DC.** – Chaparral broom (106) (1930), Kidneywort [Kidney-wort] (138) (1923)

Baccharis salicifolia **(Ruiz & Pavón) Pers.** – Black willow (75) (1894) Santa Barbara Co. CA, Mule-fat baccharis [Mulefat baccharis] (155) (1942), Mule's-fat [Mule's fat, Mule fat] (106) (1930), – Seepwillow baccharis (155) (1942), Water-motor (106) (1930)

Baccharis salicina **Torr. & Gray** – Great Plains false willow (50) (present), Groundsel [Groundsell] (157) (1929), Linear-leaf baccharis [Linearleaf baccharis, Linear-leaved baccharis] (5, 93, 97, 122) (1913–1937), Willow baccharis (3, 4, 5, 97, 122, 124, 155) (1913–1986)

Baccharis sarothroides **Gray** – Desert broom (106) (1930)

Baccharis texana **(Torr. & Gray) Gray** – Prairie false willow (50) (present)

Baccharis viminea **DC.** – See *Baccharis salicifolia* (Ruiz & Pavón) Pers.

Baccharis wrightii **Gray** – Wright's baccharis (5, 50, 97, 122) (1913–present)

Bacopa acuminata **(Walt.) Robins.** – See *Mecardonia acuminata* (Walt.) Small var. *acuminata*

Bacopa **Aubl.** – Water-hyssop [Waterhyssop, Water hyssop] (1, 4, 50, 155, 156) (1923 present)

Bacopa caroliniana **(Walt.) B. L. Robins.** – Blue hedge-hyssop (5) (1913), Blue hyssop (122) (1937) TX

Bacopa monniera – See *Bacopa monnieri* (L.) Pennell

Bacopa monnieri **(L.) Pennell** – Hedge hyssop [Hedgehyssop] (156) (1923), Herb grace [Herb-grace] (5) (1913), Herb-of-grace [Herb of grace, Herb-o'-grace] (156) (1923), Monnier's hedge hyssop (5) (1913), Water hyssop (5, 107, 156) (1913–1923)

Bacopa rotundifolia **(Michx.) Wettst.** – Common wild hydrangea (187) (1818), Disk water-hyssop [Disk waterhyssop] (50, 155) (1942–present), Round-leaf hedge-hyssop [Round-leaved hedge hyssop, Round-leaved hedge-hyssop] (5, 72, 93, 97, 131) (1899–1937), Round-leaf water-hyssop [Round-leaved water hyssop] (120) (1938), Water-hyssop [Waterhyssop, Water hyssop] (3, 85, 95) (1911–1977)

Baeothryon alpinum **(L.) Egor.** – See *Trichophorum alpinum* (L.) Pers.

Baeothryon verecundum **(Fern.) A. & D. Löve** – See *Trichophorum planifolium* (Spreng.) Palla

Baeria **Fisch. & C. A. Mey.** – See *Lasthenia* Cass. (all US species now in this genus)

Bahia **Lag.** – Bahia (50, 155) (1942–present)

Bahia pedata **Gray** – Blunt-scale bahia [Bluntscale bahia] (50) (present)

Baileya **Harvey & Gray ex Gray** – Desert-marigold (109) (1949)

Balduina uniflora **Nutt.** – One-head actinospermum [One-headed actinospermum] (5) (1913)

Ballota **L.** – Ballota (155) (1942), Black horehound [Black hoarhound] (158) (1900), Fetid horehound [Fetid hoarhound] (156) (1923), Horehound [Hoarhound, Hore-hound, Horehounde] (50) (present)

Ballota nigra **L.** – Bastard horehound [Bastard hoarhound] (5, 92, 158) (1876–1913), Black angelica (156) (1923), Black archangel (5, 158) (1900), Black ballota (155) (1942), Black borehound (92) (1876), Black horehound [Black hoarhound] (5, 50, 92, 156, 158) (1876–present), Dunny-nettle [Dunny nettle] (158) (1900), False horehound [False hoarhound] (19, 156) (1840–1923), False motherwort (19) (1840), Fetid horehound [Fetid hoarhound] (5, 156, 158) (1900–1923), Gemeine Ballote (German) (158) (1900), Hairhound [Hair-hound] (5, 156, 158) (1900–1923), Henbit [hen-bit, Hen bit] (5, 156, 158) (1900–1923), Marube fétide (French) (158) (1900), Marube noir (French) (158) (1900), Schwarzer Andorn (German) (158) (1900), Stinking horehound (92, 158) (1876–1900), Stinking-Roger (158) (1900)

Balsamita major **Desf.** – Alecoast (5, 158) (1900–1913), Alecost [Alecost] (5, 107, 156, 158) (1900–1923) no longer in use by 1923, Balsamite odorante (French) (158) (1900), Balsamkraut (German) (158) (1900), Baume-coq (French) (158) (1900), Bible-leaf (156) (1923) no longer in use by 1923, Cockmint [Cock mint] (92, 158) (1876–1900), Cologne-plant (156) (1923), Coq des jardin (French) (158) (1900), Cost (5, 156, 158, 179) (1526–1923) no longer in use by 1923 (156) from Latin costus, Costmary (4, 5, 50, 107, 109, 138, 156, 158, 179) (1526–1986), Frauenminze (German) (158) (1900), Lavender (158) (1900), Marienblatt (German) (158) (1900), Maudlin (158) (1900), Menthe-coq (French) (158) (1900), Mint-geranium [Mint geranium] (3, 4, 5, 156, 158) (1900–1986), Sweet Mary (156) (1923)

Balsamita **Mill.** – Costmary (1) (1932), Mint-geranium [Mint geranium] (1) (1932)

Balsamorhiza **Hook.** – See *Balsamorhiza* Nutt.

Balsamorhiza hookeri **Nutt.** – Balsamroot [Balsam root, Balsam-root] (107) (1919)

Balsamorhiza **Nutt.** – Balsamroot [Balsam root, Balsam-root] (1, 4, 155, 158) (1900–1986)

Balsamorhiza sagittata **(Pursh) Nutt.** – Arrowleaf [Arrow-leaf, Arrow leaf] (101) (1905), Arrow-leaf balsamroot [Arrowleaf balsamroot] (50, 155) (1942–present), Balsamroot [Balsam root, Balsam-root] (3, 85, 131, 146) (1899–1977), Bigroot [Big-root, Big root] (101) (1905), Oregon sunflower (107) (1919)

Balsamorrhizia – See *Balsamorhiza* Nutt.

Bambusa disticha – See *Pseudosasa disticha (Mitford) Nakai*

Bambusa multiplex **(Lour.) Raeusch. ex Schult. & Schult. f.** – Hedge bamboo (138) (1923)

Bambusa nana **(Roxb.)** – See *Bambusa multiplex* (Lour.) Raeusch. ex Schult. & Schult. f.

Bambusa pygmaea **(Miq.)** – See *Arundinaria pygmaea (Miq.) Asch. & Graebn.*

Bambusa **Schreb.** – Bamboo (from Malayan name)

Bambusa tessellata **Munro** – See Indocalamus tessellatus (Munro) Keng f.

Bambusa vulgaris **Schrad. ex J.C. Wendl.** – Feather bamboo (138) (1923), Feathery bamboo (109) (1949)

Banisteria ciliata **Lam.** – See Stigmaphyllon ciliatum Juss.

Bannisteria lupuloides – See *Myrospermum frutescens* Jacq.

Baptisia ×sulphurea **Engelm.** [*alba* × *sphaerocarpa*] – Yellow wild indigo [Yellow wild-indigo] (97) (1937) OK

Baptisia alba **(L.) R. Br.** – See *Baptisia alba* (L.) Vent.

Baptisia alba (**L.**) **Vent.** – Prairie indigo (5, 92, 156) (1876–1923), White wild indigo [White wild-indigo, White wildindigo] (5, 50, 72, 155) (1907–present), Wild indigo [Wild-indigo, Wildindigo] (48) (1882)

Baptisia alba (**L.**) **Vent. var. macrophylla** (**Larisey**) **Isely** – Atlantic wild indigo [Atlantic wildindigo] (155) (1942), Large white indigo (97) (1937), Large white wild indigo (93) (1936), Large-leaf wild indigo [Largeleaf wild indigo] (50) (present), White false indigo (5) (1913), White wild indigo [White wild-indigo, White wildindigo] (4, 5, 138) (1913–1986), Wild indigo [Wild-indigo, Wildindigo] (3, 72, 124) (1907–1977)

Baptisia australis (**L.**) **R. Br. ex Aiton f.** – Blue false indigo (3, 4, 5, 97, 156) (1913–1937), Blue indigo (48, 156, 158) (1882–1923), Blue rattlebush [Blue rattle-bush] (158) (1900), Blue wild indigo [Blue wild-indigo, Blue wildindigo] (5, 50, 138, 155) (1913–present), False indigo [False-indigo] (92, 156, 158) (1876–1923), Spiked indigo-weed [Spiked indigo weed] (19) (1840), Wild indigo [Wild-indigo, Wildindigo] (156, 158) (1900–1923)

Baptisia australis (**L.**) **R. Br. ex Aiton f. var. minor** (**Lehm.**) **Fern.** – Blue false indigo (3, 4) (1977–1986)

Baptisia bracteata **Muhl. ex Ell.** – Black rattlepod [Black rattle pod] (37) (1919), Bracted false indigo (82) (1930), Cream wild indigo [Cream wild-indigo, Cream wildindigo] (138, 155) (1923–1942), Gasatho (Omaha-Ponca, rattle) (37) (1919), Large-bract wild indigo [Large-bracted wild indigo] (5, 72, 93, 97) (1907–1937), Long-bract wild indigo [Longbract wild indigo] (50) (present), Pira-kari (Pawnee, many children) (37) (1919), Tdika shande nuga (Omaha-Ponca) (37) (1919), Wild indigo [Wild-indigo, Wildindigo] (82) (1930), Yellow false indigo (5) (1913)

Baptisia bracteata **Muhl. ex Ell. var. glabrescens** (**Larisey**) **Isely** – See *Baptisia bracteata* Muhl. ex Ell. var. *leucophaea* (Nutt.) Kartesz & Gandhi

Baptisia bracteata **Muhl. ex Ell. var. leucophaea** (**Nutt.**) **Kartesz & Gandhi** – Long-bract wild indigo [Longbract wild indigo] (4, 50) (1986–present)

Baptisia bracteata **var. glabrescens** (**Larisey**) **Isely** – Cream-colored indigo (48) (1882), Plains wild indigo [Plains wildindigo] (3, 155) (1942–1977)

Baptisia caerulea **Eaton & Wright** – See *Baptisia australis* (L.) R. Br. ex Aiton f.

Baptisia cerulea – See *Baptisia australis* (L.) R. Br. ex Aiton f.

Baptisia lactea (**Raf.**) **Thieret** – See *Baptisia alba* (L.) Vent. var. *macrophylla* (Larisey) Isely

Baptisia lanceolata (**Walt.**) **Ell.** – Gopherweed [Gopher weed] (74) (1893)

Baptisia lanceolata **Ell.** – See *Baptisia lanceolata* (Walt.) Ell.

Baptisia leucantha **Torr. & Gray** – See *Baptisia alba* (L.) Vent. var. *macrophylla* (Larisey) Isely

Baptisia leucophaea **Nutt.** – See *Baptisia bracteata* Muhl. ex Ell. var. *glabrescens* (Larisey) Isely

Baptisia nuttalliana **Small** – Nuttall's false indigo (97) (1937)

Baptisia sphaerocarpa **Nutt.** – Round-fruit false indigo [Round-fruited false indigo] (97) (1937)

Baptisia sulphurea **Engelm.** – See *Baptisia ×sulphurea* Engelm. *[alba × sphaerocarpa]*

Baptisia tinctoria (**L.**) **R. Br. ex Aiton f.** – American indigo (64, 92, 157) (1876–1929), Baptisia (52, 54, 57, 60, 61, 64, 157) (1870–1929), Baptisia (German) (6) (1892), Baptisia tinctoria herba (Official name of Materia Medica) (7) (1828), Baptisia tinctoria radix (Official name of Materia Medica) (7) (1828), Broom (186) (1814), Broom clover (64, 157) (1908–1929), Bugleweed [Bugle weed, Bugle-weed] (106) (1930), Butterfly flower [Butterfly-flower, Butterflyflower] (190) (~1759), Clover broom (5, 6, 7, 64, 106, 156, 157) (1828–1930), Dyer's baptisia (6) (1892), False indigo [False-indigo] (6, 156) (1892–1923), Farbende Baptisia (German) (7) (1828), Färbende Podolyria (German) (186) (1814), Horse fleaweed (5, 92) (1876–1913), Horsefly-weed [Horse-fly weed, Horsefly weed, Horse fly weed] (5, 6, 7, 58, 64, 92, 106, 107, 156, 157, 186) (1814–1930), Indigo broom (5, 7, 58, 64, 92, 157) (1828–1929), Indigo Sauvage

(French) (6, 157) (1892–1929), Indigo trefle (French) (6, 7) (1828–1932), Indigofera (58) (1869), Indigoweed [Indigo weed, Indigo-weed] (5, 6, 7, 49, 53, 64, 92, 106, 157, 186) (1814–1930), Rattle bush [Rattlebush, Rattle-bush] (5, 6, 7, 58, 64, 92, 106, 156, 157) (1828–1930), Shoofly [Shoo fly] (5, 64, 74, 106, 156) (1893–1930), Show-fly (157) (1929), Smooth Virginia rattle-broom [Smooth Virginia rattle broom] (181) (~1678), Wild indigo [Wild-indigo, Wildindigo] (2, 5, 6, 7, 19, 46, 49, 52, 53, 54, 57, 58, 60, 64, 72, 92, 106, 107, 156, 157, 177, 184, 186, 187, 190) (1649–1930), Yellow broom (5, 6, 7, 64, 92) (1828–1913), Yellow indigo (7, 64, 92, 106, 156, 157) (1828–1930), Yellow indigo broom (7) (1828), Yellow wild indigo [Yellow wild-indigo] (6, 97, 138) (1892–1937)

Baptisia **Vent.** – False indigo [False-indigo] (2, 4, 63, 82, 125) (1899–1986), Keugthe hi (Osage) (121) (1918?–1970?), Wild indigo [Wild-indigo, Wildindigo] (1, 10, 50, 93, 109, 121, 122, 138, 155, 156, 158) (1818–present)

Baptisia villosa (**Walt.**) **Nutt.** – See *Thermopsis villosa* (Walt.) Fern. & Schub.

Baptisia villosa **Ell.** – See *Thermopsis villosa* (Walt.) Fern. & Schub.

Barbarea **Aiton f.** – Herb of Santa Barbara (13) (1849), Scurvy-grass [Scurvy grass] (1, 13) (1849–1932), Wintercress [Winter cress, Winter-cress] (1, 4, 13, 15, 63, 109, 138, 155, 156, 158) (1849–1986), Yellow cress (93) (1936), Yellow rocket [Yellowrocket, Yellow-rocket] (13, 50) (1849–present)

Barbarea americana [**Rydb.**] – See *Barbarea orthoceras* Ledeb.

Barbarea arcuata **Reichenb.** – See *Barbarea vulgaris* W.T. Aiton

Barbarea barbarea (**L.**) **MacM.** – See *Barbarea vulgaris* W.T. Aiton

Barbarea **Beckmann** – possibly *Barbarea* Aiton f.

Barbarea orthoceras **Ledeb.** – American yellow-rocket [American yellowrocket] (50) (present), Erect-pod wintercress [Erectpod wintercress] (155) (1942), Northern rockcress [Northern rock cress] (4) (1986), Tongue-grass [Tongue grass] (35) (1806), Wild cress (35) (1806), Winter salad [Winter sallad] (12) (1821), Wintercress [Winter cress, Winter-cress] (3) (1977)

Barbarea praecox **R. Br.** – See *Barbarea verna* (Mill.) Aschers.

Barbarea stricta **Andrz** – See *Barbarea stricta* Andrz. ex Besser

Barbarea stricta **Andrz. ex Besser** – Erect-fruit wintercress [Erect-fruited winter cress] (5) (1913)

Barbarea verna (**P. Mill.**) **Aschers.** – American cress (5, 156, 107) (1913–1923), Bank cress (5, 156) (1913–1923), Belle Isle cress [Belleisle cress] (46, 107, 109, 156) (1879–1949), Bermuda cress (5, 156) (1913–1923), Early cress (109, 156) (1923–1949), Early winter Belle Isle cress (5) (1913), Early wintercress [Early winter-cress. Early winter cress] (15, 46, 107, 138) (1879–1923), Land cress [Land-cress] (5, 107, 156) (1913–1923), Scurvy-grass [Scurvy grass, Scurvey grass] (5, 15, 107, 156) (1895–1923), Winter cress [Winter cresses] (19, 156) (1840–1923) IN

Barbarea vulgaris **L.** – possibly *Barbarea vulgaris* W.T. Aiton

Barbarea vulgaris **W. T. Aiton** – Bitter wintercress (138, 155) (1923–1942), Bittercress [Bitter cress, Bitter-cress] (5, 107, 156, 157) (1919–1929), Cassabully (157) (1929), Common winter cress (15, 156) (1895), French cress (157) (1929), Garden yellow-rocket [Garden yellowrocket] (50) (present), Hedge mustard [Hedgemustard, Hedge-mustard] (157) (1929), Herb Barbara [Herb-Barbara] (5, 92) (1876–1913), Land cress [Land-cress] (157) (1929), Normandy cress (157) (1929), Poor-man's-cabbage [Poor man's cabbage] (156) (1923), Rocket (107) (1919), Rocket cress [Rocket-cress] (5, 156, 157) (1900–1923), St. Barbara's cress (157) (1929), St. Barbara's herb (157) (1929), St. Barbara's-wort [S. Barbaraes woort, S. Barbaraes woorts] (178) (1526), Toi (107) (1919), Water rocket (19) (1840), Watercress [Water-cress, Water cress] (181) (~1678), Water-radish [Water radish] (19) (1840), Winter cress [Winter cresses] (178, 180) (1526–1633), Winter rocket (5, 156, 157) (1913–1929), Wintercress [Winter cress, Winter-cress] (3, 4, 5, 63, 80, 107, 157) (1899–1986), Wound rocket (5, 156, 157) (1913–1929), Yellow cress (5, 156) (1913–1923), Yellow rocket [Yellowrocket, Yellow-rocket] (5, 15, 72, 85, 107, 157) (1895–1929), Yellow scurvy-grass (157)

(1929), (possibly) Bastard bunium (180) (1633), (possibly) False bunium (180) (1633), (possibly) Herb Saint Barbara [Herbe Saint Barbara] (180) (1633), (possibly) S. Barbaeren kraut (Germanes) (180) (1633), (possibly) Winter kersse (Lowe Dutch) (180) (1633)

Bartonia **Muhl. ex Willd.** – Bartonia (155) (1942), Screw-stem [Screwstem, Screw stem] (50) (present)

Bartonia ornata **Nutt.** – possibly *Mentzelia decapetala* (Pursh ex Sims) Urban & Gilg ex Gilg

Bartonia paniculata **(Michx.) Muhl.** – Branched bartonia (5, 97) (1913–1937)

Bartonia paniculata **(Michx.) Muhl. subsp. *paniculata*** – Screw-stem [Screwstem, Screw stem] (19) (1840)

Bartonia paniculata **(Michx.) Robinson** – See *Bartonia paniculata* (Michx.) Muhl.

Bartonia tenella **Muhl. ex Willd.** – See *Bartonia virginica* (L.) Britton, Sterns & Poggenb.

Bartonia verna **(Michx.) Muhl.** – See *Bartonia verna* (Michx.) Raf. ex Bart.

Bartonia verna **(Michx.) Raf. ex Bart.** – White bartonia (5) (1913)

Bartonia verna **Muhl.** – See *Bartonia verna* (Michx.) Raf. ex Bart.

Bartonia virginica **(L.) Britton, Sterns & Poggenb.** – Panicle-flower andrewsia [Panicle-flowered andrewsia] (187) (1818), Screw-stem [Screwstem, Screw stem] (5, 156) (1913–1923), Yellow bartonia (5, 156) (1913–1923)

Bartramia pomiformis **Hedw.** – Bartramia moss (50) (present)

Bartramia vulgaris **Michx.** – See *Bartramia pomiformis* Hedw.

Bartsia coccinea **L.** – See *Castilleja coccinea* (L.) Spreng.

Bartsia **L.** Painted-cup [Painted cup, Paintedcup] (167) (1814)

Bartsia odontites **(L.) Huds.** – See *Odontites vulgaris* Moench

Basella **L.** Malabar nightshade [Malabar-nightshade] (109) (1949)

Bassia **All.** – Bassia (155) (1942), Smotherweed (50) (present)

Bassia hyssopifolia **(Pallas) Kuntze** – Five-hook bassia [Fivehook bassia] (4, 155) (1942–1986), Five-horn smotherweed [Fivehorn smotherweed] (50) (present)

Batatas edulis **Chois.** – See *Ipomoea batatas* (L.) Lam.

Batidaea strigosa **(Michx.) Greene** – See *Rubus idaeus* L. subsp. *strigosus* (Michx.) Focke

Batidea strigosa **(Michx.) Greene** – See *Rubus idaeus* L. subsp. *strigosus* (Michx.) Focke

Batidophaca **Rydb.** – See *Astragalus* L. (all US species)

Batis maritima **L.** – American saltwort (14) (1882), Turtleweed (50) (present)

Batodendron andrachniforme **Small** – See *Vaccinium arboreum* Marsh.

Batodendron arboreum **(Marsh.) Nutt.** – See *Vaccinium arboreum* Marsh.

Batodendron glaucescens **Greene** – See *Vaccinium arboreum* Marsh.

Batodendron **Nutt.** – See *Vaccinium* L.

Batrachium circinatum **(Sibth.) Rchb.** – See *Ranunculus longirostris* Godr.

Batrachium divaricatum **(Schrank) Wimm.** – See *Ranunculus trichophyllus* Chaix var. *trichophyllus*

Batrachium hederaceum **(L.) S. F. Gray** – See *Ranunculus hederaceus* L.

Batrachium **S. F. Gary** – See *Ranunculus* L.

Batrachium trichophyllum **(Chaix ex Vill.) Bosch** – See *Ranunculus trichophyllus* Chaix var. *trichophyllus*

Batrachium trichophyllum **(Chaix.) Bossch.** – See *Ranunculus trichophyllus* Chaix var. *trichophyllus*

Batschia canescens **Michx.** – See *Lithospermum canescens* (Michx.) Lehm.

Batschia longiflora **Nutt.** – possibly *Lithospermum canescens* (Michx.) Lehm.

Batschia **Michx.** – possibly *Lithospermum* L. all US species

Bauhinia **L.** – Bauhinia (138) (1923)

Bauhinia monandra **Kurz** – Butterfly bauhinia (138) (1923), Butterfly flower [Butterfly-flower, Butterflyflower] (109) (1949), Jerusalem date (109) (1949)

Bauhinia tomentosa **L.** – St. Thomas' tree [Saint Thomas' tree, Saint-Thomas-tree] (92, 109, 138) (1876–1949)

Bauhinia variegata **L.** – Buddhist bauhinia (138) (1923), Mountain ebony (109) (1949), Orchid tree [Orchid-tree] (109) (1949)

Beckmannia eruciformis **(L.) Host var. *uniflora* Scribn. ex Gray** – See *Beckmannia syzigachne* (Steud.) Fern.

Beckmannia **Host** – Slough grass [Slough-grass, Sloughgrass] (1, 50, 152, 155) (1912–present), Western slough grass [Western sloughgrass] (93) (1936)

Beckmannia syzigachne **(Steud.) Fern.** – American slough grass [American sloughgrass] (3, 50, 140, 155) (1942–present), possibly Beckmannia (72) (1907), possibly Beckmann's grass (5) (1913), possibly Slough grass [Slough-grass, Sloughgrass] (5, 56, 85, 94, 101, 111, 129, 152) (1894–1932), possibly Wild timothy (56) (1901) IA

Begonia coccinea **Hook.** – Scarlet begonia (138) (1923)

Begonia cucullata **Willd.** – Perpetual begonia (138) (1923)

Begonia **L.** – Begonia (138) (1923), Elephant's-ear [Elephants' ear, Elephant's ears, Elephants-ear] (92) (1876)

Begonia semperflorens – See *Begonia cucullata* Willd.

Belamcanda **Adans** – Blackberry lily [Black berry lily, Blackberry-lily] (138, 158) (1900–1923), Belamcanda (50) (present) from native Asian name

Belamcanda chinensis **(L.) DC.** – Blackberry lily [Black berry lily, Blackberry-lily] (3, 5, 19, 50, 72, 92, 93, 109, 138, 155, 158) (1840–present), Dwarf tiger-lily [Dwarf tiger lily] (5, 73, 156, 158) (1892–1923) Mansfield OH, Leopard flower [Leopard-flower] (156) (1923), Leopard flower [Leopard-flower] (5, 158) (1900–1913), Leopard lily (5, 158) (1900–1913)

Bellis integrifolia **Michx.** – See *Astranthium integrifolium* (Michx.) Nutt.

Bellis **L.** – Bellis (50) (present), Daisy [Daisies, Daysy] (1, 2, 10, 109, 155, 156, 158, 167) (1814–1949) cultivated varieties, English daisy (4) (1986)

Bellis perennis **L.** – Bairnwort [Bairn wort] (5, 92, 158) (1876–1913), Banwort [Ban wort] (5, 158) (1900–1913), Bennert (5, 158) (1900–1913), Boneflower [Bone flower, Bone-flower] (5, 158) (1900–1913), Bonewort [Bone wort] (5, 158, 179) (1526–1913), Bruisewort [Bruise wort, Bruise-wort, Bruse-wort] (5, 158, 179) (1526–1913), Catposy [Cat-posy] (158) (1900) archaic, Childing daisy (5, 158) (1900–1913), Cockiloorie (158) (1900) archiac, Consound (158) (1900), Daisy [Daisies, Daysy] (19, 92, 179) (1526–1876), Dazeg (158) (1900), Dicky daisy (158) (1900), Dog daisy [Dog-daisy] (158) (1900) North England, English daisy (4, 107, 109, 138, 155, 158) (1900–1986), European daisy (5, 158) (1900), Ewe-gown [Ewe gown] (5, 158) (1900), Garden daisy (5, 158) (1900–1913), Gowan [Gowans] (92) (1876) Scotland, Gowlan (158) (1900), Hen-and-chickens [Hen and chickens] (5, 92, 158) (1876–1913), Herb Margaret (5) (1913), Lawn daisy [Lawndaisy] (50) (present), Lesse consoulde (179) (1526), Little daisy [Little daysi *sic*] (190) (~1759), Maple bush (92) (1876), Maple-flower (158) (1900), March daisy (5) (1913), Margaret (158) (1900), Marguerite (5) (1913), Marguerite (French) (158) (1900), Masliebenblume (German) (158) (1900), May gowan (5, 158) (1900–1913), True daisy (109) (1949)

Beloperone guttat **Brandegee** – See *Justicia brandegeeana* Wasshausen & L. B. Sm.

Benincasa hispida **(Thunb.) Cogn.** – Benincasa (110) (1886), Chinese preserving melon (109) (1949), Cumbalam (110) (1886), Wax gourd [Waxgourd] (138) (1923), White gourd (109) (1949), White gourd-melon (110) (1886)

Benincasa **Savi** Wax gourd [Waxgourd] (138) (1923)

Benzoin aestivale **(L.) Nees** – See *Lindera benzoin* Blume.

Benzoin melissaefolium **(Walt.) Nees.** – See *Lindera melissifolia* (Walt.) Blume

Benzoin melissifolia **(Walt.) Nees.** – See *Lindera melissifolia* (Walt.) Blume

Benzoin odoriferum – See *Lindera benzoin* Blume.

Berberis (Tourn.) L. – See *Berberis* L.

Berberis aquifolium Pursh – See *Mahonia aquifolium* (Pursh) Nutt.

Berberis canadensis P. Mill. – Allegheny barberry (138) (1923), American barberry (5, 107, 156) (1913–1923), American barberry bush (7) (1828), Barberry (2, 7) (1828–1932), Barberry bush (7) (1828), Berberis baccae (Official name of Materia Medica) (7) (1828), Berberitze (German) (7) (1828), Berberry [Berberies] (156) (1923), Canadian barberry (8) (1785), Canadian berberry (42) (1814), Common American berberry (42) (1814), Épine vinette (French) (7) (1828), Epine vinette du Canada (French) (8) (1785), Pipperidge bush (7) (1828), Sourberry [Sour-berry, Sour berry] (7) (1828)

Berberis canadensis Pursh – See *Berberis canadensis* P. Mill.

Berberis darwini – See *Berberis darwinii* Hook.

Berberis darwinii Hook. – Darwin's barbarry [Darwin barbarry] (138) (1923)

Berberis fendleri Gray – Colorado barberry (138) (1923), Fendler's barberry (153) (1913)

Berberis fremontii – See *Mahonia fremontii* (Torr.) Fedde

Berberis glumacea Spreng. – See *Mahonia nervosa* (Pursh) Nutt.

Berberis iberica Stev. & Fisch. ex DC. – See *Berberis vulgaris* L.

Berberis julianae C.K. Schneid. – Wintergreen barberry (109, 138) (1923–1949)

Berberis L. – Barberry (1, 4, 50, 10, 13, 14, 15, 82, 93, 106, 109, 138, 155, 156, 158, 167) (1814–present), Barberry bush (8, 190) (~1759–1785), Berberry [Berberies] (15) (1895), Épine vinette (French) (8) (1785)

Berberis nervosa Pursh – See *Mahonia nervosa* (Pursh) Nutt.

Berberis pinnata Lag. – See *Mahonia pinnata* (Lag.) Fedde subsp. *pinnata*

Berberis piperiana (Abrams) McMinn – See *Mahonia aquifolium* (Pursh) Nutt.

Berberis repens Lindl. – See *Mahonia repens* (Lindl.) G. Don

Berberis sargentiana C.K. Schneid. – Sargent's barberry [Sargent barberry] (138) (1923)

Berberis swaseyi Buckl. – See *Mahonia swaseyi* (Buckl. ex Young) Fedde

Berberis thunbergii DC. – Dwarf barberry (135) (1910), Japanese barberry (50, 82, 85, 109, 112, 138, 155) (1923–present), Red-leaf barberry [Red leaf barberry] (112) (1937), Red-leaf Japanese barberry [Redleaf Japanese barberry] (155) (1942)

Berberis thunbergii DC. var. *atropurpurea* Chenault – See *Berberis thunbergii* DC.

Berberis Tourn. – See *Berberis* L.

Berberis trifoliolata Moric. – See *Mahonia trifoliolata* (Moric.) Fedde

Berberis vulgaris L. – American barberry (92) (1876), Babaraune (157, 158) (1900–1929), Barberry (6, 19, 49, 53, 55, 57, 58, 61, 85, 92, 107, 57, 158, 184) (1793–1932), Barberry tree [Barberry-trees] (46) (1671), Beberitze (German) (158) (1900), Berberis (French) (158) (1900), Berberos (Spanish) (158) (1900), Berberry [Berberies without stones] (178) (1526), Berberry [Berberies] (6, 58, 179) (1526–1892), Common barberry (6, 50, 53, 72, 82, 109, 112, 157) (1900–present), Common European barberry (158) (1900), Common green barberry (135) (1910), Épine vinette (French) (6, 158) (1892), European barberry (5, 15, 93, 138, 155, 156, 157) (1895–1936), Garden barberry (157, 158) (1900–1929), Great berberry [Great berberries] (178) (1526), Guild tree [Guild-tree] (157, 158) (1900–1929), Jaundice-berry [Jaundice berry] (5, 92, 107, 156, 157, 158) (1876–1929), Jaundice-tree [Jaundice tree] (5, 156) (1913–1923), Pepperridge bush [Pepperridge-bush (5, 92, 156, 157, 158) (1876–1929) England, Peprage (157, 158) (1900–1929), Pipperidge [Piperidge] (157, 158) (1900–1929), Pipperidge bush (76, 92) (1876–1896) Southern NH, almost out of use by 1896, Piprage (107) (1919), Saurach (German) (158) (1900), Saurdorn (German) (6) (1892), Vinettier (French) (158) (1900), Wood-sore (157, 158) (1900–1929), Wood-sour [Wood-sour] (5, 156, 157, 158) (1900–1929), Woodssow (157, 158) (1900–1929)

Berberis vulgaris purpurea – See *Berberis vulgaris* L.

Berberis vulgaris var. *canadensis* Willd. – See *Berberis canadensis* Mill.

Berchemia Neck. – Supple-Jack [Supplejack, Supple jack, Supple jacks] (13, 138) (1849–1923)

Berchemia scandens (Hill.) Trelease – Alabama supplejack (138) (1923) TX, Rattan (5, 122, 124, 156) (1913–1937), Rattan vine (5, 65, 106, 156) (1913–1931), Supple-Jack [Supplejack, Supple jack, Supple jacks] (2, 5, 12, 15, 58, 92, 97, 106, 122, 124, 156) (1819–1937)

Berchemia volubilis DC. – See *Berchemia scandens* (Hill.) Trelease

Bergerocactus emoryi (Engelm.) Engelm. – Velvet cactus [Velvetcactus] (138, 155) (1931–1942)

Bergia L. – Bergia (50, 155, 158) (1900–present)

Bergia texana (Hook.) Seub. ex Walp. – Texas bergia (4, 5, 50, 155) (1913–present)

Berlandiera DC. – Greeneyes [Green eyes] (4, 50) (1986–present)

Berlandiera lyrata Benth. – Lyrate-leaf berlandieria [Lyrateleaf berlandieria] (122) (1937), Lyre-leaf berlandiera [Lyre-leafed berlandiera] (5, 97, 124) (1913–1937), Lyre-leaf greeneyes [Lyreleaf greeneyes] (50) (present), Wire-leaf berlandiera [Wireleaf berlandiera] (3) (1977)

Berlandiera texana DC. – Berlandier's daisy [Berlandier daisy] (122, 124) (1937), Texas berlandiera [Texan berlandiera] (3, 5, 97) (1913–1977), Texas greeneyes (50) (present)

Bernardia myricaefolia (Scheele) S. Wats. – See *Bernardia myricifolia* (Scheele) S. Wats.

Bernardia myricifolia (Scheele) S. Wats. – Myrtle croton (122) (1937) TX, Myrtle-leaf croton [Myrtle-leafed croton] (124) (1937) TX

Berteroa (L.) DC. – See *Berteroa* DC.

Berteroa DC. – False madwort (50) (present), Hoary alyssum (1, 93) (1932–1936), Hoary false alyssum (3, 4) (1977–1986)

Berteroa incana (L.) DC. – Hoary alyssum (5, 72, 80, 85) (1907–1932), Hoary false madwort (50) (present), Hoary madwort (165) (1768)

Berthellotia borrealis (sic) – possibly *Pluchea borealis* Gray

Berthelotia borealis Wooton – possibly *Pluchea borealis* Gray

Berthelotia DC – See *Pluchea* Cass.

Berthelotia sericea (Nutt.) Rydb. – See *Pluchea sericea* (Nutt.) Coville

Berula Bess. ex W.D.J. Koch – Berula (155) (1942), Water-parsnip [Water parsnip, Waterparsnip, Water parsnep, Water-parsnep] (1, 4, 50, 158) (1900–present)

Berula erecta (Huds.) Coville – Creeping water-parsley (156) (1923), Creeping water-parsnip [Creeping water parsnip] (5, 158) (1900–1913), Cut-leaf water-parsley [Cut-leaved water-parsley] (156) (1923), Cut-leaf water-parsnip [Cutleaf waterparsnip, Cut-leaf water parsnip, Cut-leaved water parsnip] (5, 50, 93, 95, 131, 158) (1899–present), Lesser water-parsnip [Lesser water-parsnip] (5, 158) (1900–1913), Narrow-leaf water-parsnip [Narrow-leaved water-parsnip, Narrow-leaved water parsnip] (5, 158) (1900–1913), Stalky berula (155) (1942), Water-parsnip [Water parsnip, Waterparsnip, Water parsnep, Water-parsnep] (3, 4, 85) (1932–1986)

Berula erecta (Huds.) Coville var. *incisa* (Torr.) Cronq. – See *Berula erecta* (Huds.) Coville

Berula Hoffm. – See *Berula* Bess. ex W.D.J. Koch

Besseya bullii (Eat.) Rydb. – Bull's coraldrops (50) (present), Bull's synthyris (5, 72) (1907–1913)

Besseya rubra (Dougl. ex Hook.) Rydb. – Red besseya (50) (present), Western synthyris (5, 93) (1913–1936)

Besseya Rydb. – Kittentail [Kitten-tails] (1, 4, 50) (1932–present)

Besseya wyomingensis (A. Nels.) Rydb. – Kittentail [Kitten-tails] (3, 85) (1932–1977), Wyoming besseya (50) (present)

Betonica officinalis L. – See *Stachys officinalis* (L.) Trev.

Betula (Tourn.) L. – See *Betula* L.

Betula ×sandbergii Britt. [*papyrifera × pumila*] – Sandberg's birch (5) (1913)

Betula alba Fern. – possibly *Betula pubescens* Ehrh.

Betula alba L. – See *Betula pubescens* Ehrh.

Betula alba pendula – See *Betula pendula* Roth

Bidens aurea (Aiton) Sherff – Golden thick-seed sunflower [Golden thick seedSun-flower] (187) (1818)

Bidens backii Torr. *beckii* – See *Bidens beckii* Torr. ex Spreng.

Bidens beckii Torr. – See *Bidens beckii* Torr. ex Spreng.

Bidens beckii Torr. ex Spreng. – Water bur-marigold (156) (1923), Water marigold [Water marygold] (5, 19, 63, 76, 92, 156) (1840–1923)

Bidens bidentoides (Nutt.) Britton – Swamp beggarsticks [Swamp beggar's tick, Swamp beggars' tick, Swamp beggar-ticks] (5, 156) (1913–1923)

Bidens bigelovii Gray – Bigelow's beggarticks (50) (present)

Bidens bipinnata L. – Beggarticks [Beggar ticks, Beggar's ticks, Beggars' ticks, Beggars-ticks, Beggar-ticks] (58) (1869), Cuckold [Cuckolds] (5, 156, 157) (1900–1929), Hemlock beggarticks (19) (1840), Spanish needle [Spanish-needles, Spanishneedles, Spanish needles] (3, 4, 5, 41, 49, 50, 57, 58, 61, 62, 92, 93, 97, 122, 124, 145, 155, 156, 157, 158, 187) (1770–present)

Bidens cernua L. – Baclin (158) (1900), Beggar's-lice [Beggar lice, Beggar-lice, Beggarlice, Beggarslice] (156) (1923), Beggarticks [Beggar ticks, Beggar's ticks, Beggars' ticks, Beggars-ticks, Beggar-ticks] (76) (1896) Paris ME, Bur-marigold [Bur marigold, Bur-marigolds, Burr marigold, Burr marygold] (46, 62, 98) (1879–1926), Double-tooth (5, 156, 158) (1900–1923), Nodding beggarticks [Nodding beggar-ticks] (3, 4, 50, 98, 155) (1926–present), Nodding bur-marigold [Nodding burr marigold, Nodding burr marygold] (5, 72, 93, 97, 131, 156, 158) (1899), Nodding sticktight (82) (1930), Pitchforks [Pitch-forks] (5, 62, 156, 158) (1900–1923), Small bur-marigold (93, 156) (1923–1936), Smaller bar-marigold (158) (1900), Smaller bur-marigold [Smaller bar-marigold (sic, 158] (5, 158) (1900–1913), Sticktight [Stick-tight, Sticktights, Stick-tights, Stick tights] (156) (1923), Water beggarticks (19) (1840), Water-agrimony [Water agrimony] (5, 156, 158) (1900–1923)

Bidens chrysanthemoides Michx. – See *Bidens laevis* (L.) Britton, Sterns & Poggenb.

Bidens comosa (Gray) Wiegand – See *Bidens tripartita* L.

Bidens connata Michx. – possibly *Bidens connata* Muhl. ex Willd.

Bidens connata Muhl. ex Willd. – Beggarticks [Beggar ticks, Beggar's ticks, Beggars' ticks, Beggars-ticks, Beggar-ticks] (62, 76) (1896–1912), Bur-marigold [Bur marigold, Bur-marigolds, Burr marigold, Burr marygold] (62, 92, 114) (1876–1912), Cuckold [Cuckolds] (156) (1923), Devil's-bootjacks [Devil's bootjacks] (62) (1912) IN, Harvestlice [Harvest lice, Harvest-lice] (92, 156) (1876–1923), Pitchforks [Pitch-forks] (62, 156) (1912–1923), Purple-stem beggarticks [Purplestem beggarticks] (50, 131, 155) (1899–present), Purple-stem swamp beggarticks [Purple-stemmed swamp beggar-ticks] (5, 93, 97) (1913–1937), Spanish needle [Spanish-needles, Spanishneedles, Spanish needles] (48, 61) (1870–1882), Sticktight [Stick-tight, Sticktights, Stick-tights, Stick tights] (3) (1977), Swamp beggarsticks [Swamp beggar's tick, Swamp beggars' tick, Swamp beggar-ticks] (62, 63, 72, 82, 156) (1899–1930), Swamp marigold (82) (1930), Tick-seed sunflower [Tick seed sunflower, Tick- seed sunflower] (62) (1912), possibly Marsh-marigold [Marsh marigold, Marshmarigold, Marsh mary-gold, Marsh marygold] (42) (1814)

Bidens coronata (L.) Britton – Coreopsis (106) (1930) Delaware River valley, Crown beggarticks (155) (1942), Crowned beggarticks (50) (present), Cuckold [Cuckolds] (92) (1876), Ditch sunflower [Ditch sunflower] (138, 155, 156) (1923–1942), Southern tick seed-sunflower [Southern tick – Seed-sunflower] (5) (1913), Sticktight [Stick-tight, Sticktights, Stick-tights, Stick tights] (82) (1930), Tall tick seed sunflower [Tall tick-seed-sunflower] (5, 72, 93) (1907–1936), Tickseed sunflower [Tick seed sunflower, Tick- seed sunflower] (3, 4, 106, 156) (1923–1986)

Bidens coronata (L.) Fisch. – See *Bidens coronata* (L.) Britton

Bidens discoidea (Torr. & Gray) Britton Bootjack [Boot-jack, Boot-jacks, Boot jacks] (80) (1913), Small beggarticks [Small beggarticks] (5, 50, 72, 97) (1907–present), Spanish needle [Spanish-needles, Spanishneedles, Spanish needles] (80) (1913), Tall bootjack [Tall boot-jack] (80) (1913) IA

Bidens frondosa L. – Beggar's-lice [Beggar lice, Beggar-lice, Beggar-lice, Beggarslice] (5, 156, 158) (1900–1923), Beggarticks [Beggar ticks, Beggar's ticks, Beggars' ticks, Beggars-ticks, Beggar-ticks] (3, 4, 5, 63, 76, 80, 85, 92, 93, 145) (1896–1986), Black beggarticks [Black beggar-ticks] (97) (1937), Bootjack [Boot-jack, Boot-jacks, Boot jacks] (80) (1913), Bur-marigold [Bur marigold, Bur-marigolds, Burr marigold, Burr marygold] (19, 187) (1818–1840), Cockle [Cockles, Cokyll] (156) (1923), Common beggarticks [Common beggar's ticks, Common beggar-ticks] (2, 49, 62, 158) (1895–1912), Common bur-marigold (5, 156, 158) (1900–1923), Cow-lice [Cow-lice] (156, 158) (1900–1923), Cuckles [Cuckle] (5, 75, 79, 156, 158) (1891–1923) Concord MA, Cuckold [Cuckolds] (19, 158) (1840–1900), Devil's beggartick [Devils beggarticks] (50, 155) (1942–present), Devil's-pitchfork [Devil's pitchfork] (5, 75, 156, 158) (1900–1923) Ferrisburgh VT, Concord MA, Harvestlice [Harvest lice, Harvest-lice] (158) (1900), Old-lady's-clothespins [Old ladies' clothes-pin, Old-ladies clothes pins] (5, 76, 156) (1896–1923) MA, Pitchforks [Pitch-forks] (76) (1896), Rayless marigold (5, 156, 158) (1900–1923), Spanish needle [Spanish-needles, Spanishneedles, Spanish needles] (48, 61, 72, 114) (1870–1907), Stick seed [Stick-seed, Stickseed] (5, 92, 156) (1876–1923), Sticktight [Stick-tight, Sticktights, Stick tights] (5, 80, 82, 122, 131, 156, 158) (1899–1936)

Bidens involucrata (Nutt.) Britton – See *Bidens aristosa* (Michx.) Britton

Bidens L. Beggarticks [Beggar ticks, Beggar's ticks, Beggars' ticks, Beggars-ticks, Beggar-ticks] (1, 2, 4, 50, 93, 106, 155, 158) (1895–present), Bootjack [Boot-jack, Bootjacks, Boot jacks] (106) (1930), Bur-marigold [Bur marigold, Bur-marigolds, Burr marigold, Burr marygold] (1, 2, 10, 82, 93, 109, 156) (1818–1949), Double-tooth (184) (1793), Marigold [Marigolds, Mary gold, Marygold] (106) (1930), Pitchforks [Pitch-forks] (2) (1895), Spanish needle [Spanish-needles, Spanishneedles, Spanish needles] (7, 10, 12, 73, 106, 190) (~1759–1930), Sticktight [Stick-tight, Sticktights, Stick-tights, Stick tights] (75, 106, 109) (1894–1949), Tickseed [Tick- seed, Tick seed] (109) (1949), Water marigold [Water marygold] (1) (1932)

Bidens laevis (L.) Britton, Sterns & Poggenb. – Brook sunflower (5, 62, 156) (1912–1923), Bur-marigold [Bur marigold, Bur-marigolds, Burr marigold, Burr marygold] (114) (1894), Daisy beggarticks (19) (1840), False sunflower [False sun-flower] (86) (1878), Large-flower marigold [Large flowered marygold] (42) (1814), Larger bur-marigold (5, 62, 72, 93, 156) (1907–1936), Meadow sunflower (46) (1783), Ox-eye [Ox eye, Oxeye, Oxe eie] (19) (1840), Quill coreopsis (138) (1923), Showy bur-marigold (106) (1930), Smooth bur-marigold [Smooth burr marigold] (5, 97, 131, 156) (1899–1937), Smooth ox-eye [Smooth oxeye, Smooth ox-eye] (187) (1818), Smooth sticktight (82) (1930)

Bidens polylepis Blake – See *Bidens aristosa* (Michx.) Britton

Bidens trichosperma (Michx.) Britton – See *Bidens coronata* (L.) Britton

Bidens tripartita L. Agrimony (158) (1900), Beggarticks [Beggar ticks, Beggar's ticks, Beggars' ticks, Beggars-ticks, Beggar-ticks] (3) (1977), Bur beggarticks (155) (1942), Chanvre aquatique (French) (158) (1900), Leafy-bract beggarticks [Leafybract beggarticks] (155) (1942), Leafy-bract tick seed [Leafy-bracted tick seed] (5, 72, 93, 97) (1907–1937), Spanish needle [Spanish-needles, Spanishneedles, Spanish needles] (177) (1762), Sticktight [Stick-tight, Sticktights, Stick-tights, Stick tights] (82) (1930), Swamp beggarsticks [Swamp beggar's tick, Swamp beggars' tick, Swamp beggar-ticks] (92, 158) (1876–1900), Three-finger beggarticks [Three-fingered beggarticks] (19) (1840), Three-lobe beggarticks [Threelobe beggar-ticks] (50) (present), Wasserdürrwurz (German) (158) (1900), Wasserhanf (German) (158) (1900), Water-agrimony [Water agrimony] (158) (1900), Water-hemp [Water hemp, Waterhemp] (158) (1900), Water-hemp agrimony [Water hemp agrimony] (92) (1876)

Bidens vulgata Greene – Beggarticks [Beggar ticks, Beggar's ticks, Beggars' ticks, Beggars-ticks, Beggar-ticks] (3, 4, 82) (1930–1986),

Big devil's-beggarticks [Big devils beggartick] (50) (present), Sticktight [Stick-tight, Sticktights, Stick-tights, Stick tights] (82) (1930), Tall beggarticks [Tall beggarticks] (5, 93, 97, 155, 156) (1913–1942)

Bigelovia douglasii Gray – See *Chrysothamnus viscidiflorus* (Hook.) Nutt.

Bigelovia venata Gray – See *Isocoma veneta* (Kunth) Greene

Bigelowia nudata (Michx.) DC. – Broomweed [Broom-weed, Broom weed] (156) (1923), Brownweed [Brown-weed] (156) (1923), Horseweed [Horse-weed, Horse weed] (156) (1923), Matchweed [Match-weed] (156) (1923), Rayless goldenrod [Rayless goldenrod] (156) (1923), Torch-weed (156) (1923)

Bigelowia nudata (Michx.) DC. subsp. *nudata* – Goldilocks [Goldylocks, Goldy-locks] (19) (1840), Rayless goldenrod [Rayless golden-rod] (5, 122) (1913–1937)

Bigelowia venata (Kunth) A. Gray – See *Isocoma veneta* (Kunth) Greene

Bigelowia viscidiflora DC. – See *Chrysothamnus viscidiflorus* (Hook.) Nutt.

Bigleovia arborescens – See *Ericameria laricifolia* (Gray) Shinners

Bignonia alliacea Lam. – See *Mansoa alliacea* (Lam.) A. H. Gentry

Bignonia capreolata L. – Crossvine [Cross vine, Cross-vine] (5, 109, 122, 124, 138, 156) (1913–1949), Quarter vine [Quarter-vine] (5, 109, 156) (1913–1949), Tendrilled trumpet flower [Tendrilled trumpet-flower] (5, 97, 156) (1913–1937), Trumpet flower [Trumpet-flower, Trumpet-flowers] (109) (1949)

Bignonia catalpa [L.] – See *Catalpa ovata* G. Don

Bignonia crucigera – See *Pithecoctenium crucigerum* (L.) A.H. Gentry

Bignonia L. – Bignone (French) (8) (1785), Bignonia (155, 158) (1900–1942), Trumpet flower [Trumpet-flower, Trumpet-flowers] (8, 10, 14, 184) (1785–1882), Trumpet-creeper [Trumpetcreeper, Trumpet creeper] (138) (1923)

Bignonia radicans L. – See *Campsis radicans* (L.) – Seem. ex Bureau

Bignonia sempervirens L. – See *Gelsemium sempervirens* (L.) J. St.-Hil.

Bignonia unguis-cati L. – See *Macfadyena unguis-cati* (L.) A.H. Gentry

Bignonia venusta [Ker-Gawl.] – See *Pyrostegia venusta* (Ker-Gawl.) Miers

Bilderdykia convolvulus (L.) Dumort. – See *Polygonum convolvulus* L. var. *convolvulus*

Bilderdykia dumetorum (L.) Dumort. – See *Polygonum scandens* L. var. *dumetorum* (L.) Gleason

Bilderdykia Dumort. – See *Polygonum* L.

Bilderdykia scandens (L.) Greene – See *Polygonum scandens* L. var. *scandens*

Bisca orellana L. – possibly *Bixa orellana* L.

Bistorta (C. Bauhin) Mill. – See *Polygonum* L.

Bistorta vivipara (L.) S. F. Gray – See *Polygonum viviparum* L.

Bituminaria bituminosa (L.) Stirt. – Treacle clauuer (178) (1526)

Bixa L. Anatto or Anatto tree [Anatto-tree] (138) (1923)

Bixa orellana L. – Achiote (92, 177) (1762–1876), Annatto or Annatto tree (92, 109, 138) (1876–1949), Annotto tree (92) (1876), Arnotta (92) 1876), Arnotto (109, 110) (1886–1949), Bixa (174) (1753), Roucou (92) (1876), Urucu (174) (1753), possibly Rocou (French) (110) (1886) from Brazilian name

Blechnum boreale – See *Blechnum spicant* (L.) Sm.

Blechnum L. – Blechnum (138) (1923)

Blechnum radicans – See *Woodwardia radicans* (L.) J. Sm.

Blechnum serrulatum L.C. Rich. – Saw fern [Sawfern] (138) (1923)

Blechnum spicant (L.) Sm. – Deer fern [Deerfern] (86, 138) (1878–1923), Jointed pod fern [Jointed pod-fern] (86) (1878), Northern hard fern [Northern hard-fern] (86) (1878), Roman fern (19, 92) (1840–1876)

Blechnum virginicum – See *Woodwardia virginica* (L.) Sm.

Blepharidachne kingii (S. Wats.) Hack. – King's desert-grass (94) (1901)

Blephariglotis [Raf] – See *Platanthera* L.C. Rich all US species, Greek "having a strap or rein" referring to the lip or spur of some species

Blephariglotis ciliaris (L.) Rydb. – See *Platanthera ciliaris* (L.) Lindl.

Blephariglotis leucophaea (Nutt.) Farw. – See *Platanthera leucophaea* (Nutt.) Lindl.

Blephariglottis blephariglottis (Willd.) Rydb. – See *Platanthera blephariglottis* (Willd.) Lindl. var. *blephariglottis*

Blephariglottis ciliaris (L.) Rydb. – See *Platanthera ciliaris* (L.) Lindl.

Blephariglottis grandiflora (Bigel.) Rydb. – See *Platanthera grandiflora* (Bigelow) Lindl.

Blephariglottis lacera (Michx.) Farwell – See *Platanthera lacera* (Michx.) G. Don

Blephariglottis leucophaea (Nutt.) Farwell – See *Platanthera leucophaea* (Nutt.) Lindl.

Blephariglottis leucophaea Gray – See *Platanthera leucophaea* (Nutt.) Lindl.

Blephariglottis permoena (A. Gray) Rydb. – See *Platanthera peramoena* (Gray) Gray

Blephariglottis psycodes (L.) Rydb. – See *Platanthera psycodes* (L.) Lindl.

Blephariglottis Raf. – See *Platanthera* L.C. Rich all US species

Blepharoneuron tricholepis (Torr.) Nash – Hairy drop seed(122) (1937)

Blephilia ciliata (L.) Benth. – Downy blephilia (5, 72, 82) (1907–1930), Downy pagoda-plant (50) (present), Ohio horsemint [Ohio horse-mint] (4, 5, 156) (1913–1986)

Blephilia ciliata (L.) Raf. – See *Blephilia ciliata* (L.) Benth.

Blephilia ciliata Raf. – See *Blephilia ciliata* (L.) Benth.

Blephilia hirsuta (Pursh) Benth. – Hairy blephilia (5, 72, 97) (1907–1937), Hairy pagoda-plant (50) (present), Ohio horsemint [Ohio horse-mint] (157) (1929), Wood-mint [Wood mint] (3, 4, 82, 156) (1923–1986)

Blephilia hirsuta (Pursh) Benth. var. *hirsuta* – Hairy pagoda-plant (50) (present)

Blephilia hirsuta (Pursh) Torr. – See *Blephilia hirsuta* (Pursh) Benth.

Blephilia hirsuta Raf. – See *Blephilia hirsuta* (Pursh) Benth.

Blephilia Raf. – Pagoda plant [Pagoda-plant] (50) (present), Wood-mint [Wood mint] (82) (1930)

Bletilla Reichenb. f. Bletilla (138) (1923)

Blighia Koenig – Blighia (50) (present)

Blighia sapida Koenig Akee (109, 138) (1923–1949)

Blitum capitatum L. – See *Chenopodium capitatum* (L.) Asch.

Blitum L. – See *Chenopodium* L.

Blitum maritimum [Nutt.] – See *Chenopodium rubrum* L.

Blitum virgatum L. – See *Chenopodium foliosum* (Moench) Aschers.

Bloomeria crocea (Torr.) Coville var. *aurea* (Kellogg) Ingram – Goldenstar [Golden-star, Golden stars] (138) (1923)

Blumelia lanuginosa Pers. – possibly *Sideroxylon lanuginosum* Michx.

Blumelia Sw. – possibly *Sideroxylon* L.

Blysmopsis rufa (Huds.) Oteng-Yeboah – See *Blysmus rufus* (Huds.) Link

Blysmus rufus (Huds.) Link – Red bulrush (50) (present), Red clubrush (5) (1913)

Bocconia cordata Willd. – See *Macleaya cordata* (Willd.) R. Br.

Bocconia L. – Plume-poppy [Plumepoppy] (138) (1923)

Boebera papposa (Vent.) Rydb. – See *Dyssodia papposa* (Vent.) A.S. Hitchc.

Boebera Willd. – See *Dyssodia* Cav.

Boechera lyallii (S.Watson) Dorn – Lyall's rockcress [Lyall rockcress] (155) (1942)

Boehmeria cylindrica (L.) Sw. – Bog hemp (3) (1977), Cylindrical boehmeria (42) (1814), False nettle [Falsenettle] (4, 5, 72, 93, 95, 122, 156) (1907–1986), Small-spike false nettle [Smallspike false nettle, Smallspike falsenettle] (50, 155) (1942–present)

Boehmeria Jacq. – False nettle [Falsenettle] (1, 2, 50, 93, 155, 156) (1895–present), Ramie (158) (1900)

Boehmeria nivea (L.) Gaud. – China-grass [China grass] (92, 110) (1876–1886), Chinese silk plant [Chinese silk-plant] (109) (1949), Grass-cloth plant [Grass cloth plant] (92) (1876), Ramie (109) (1949)

Boehmeria nivea **Gaud.** – See *Boehmeria nivea* (L.) Gaud.

Boehmeria nivea **Hooker and Arnott** – possibly *Boehmeria nivea* (L.) Gaud. taxonomic status is unresolved (PL)

Boerhavia erecta **L.** – Erect spiderling (50, 155) (1942–present), Jiggerweed [Jigger weed] (77) (1898) Florida Keys

Boerhavia **L.** – Spiderling [Spiderlings] (4, 50, 155) (1942–present)

Boisduvalia glabella **(Nutt.) Walp.** – See *Epilobium pygmaeum* (Speg.) Hoch & Raven

Boisduvalia **Spach.** – See *Epilobium* L. all US species

Bolboschoenus novae-angliae **(Britt.) S.G. Sm.** – See *Schoenoplectus novae-angliae* (Britt.) M.T. Strong

Bolboschoenus robustus **(Pursh) Soják** – See *Schoenoplectus novae-angliae* (Britt.) M.T. Strong

Boletus agaricum **Pollini** – possibly Female agaric (92) (1876), possibly Oak agaric (92) (1876)

Boletus agaricus – possibly *Boletus agaricum Pollini*

Boletus fomentarius **L.** – Amadou (92) (1876), German tinder (92) (1876), Spunk (92) (1876)

Boletus **Fr.** – See *Boletus* L.

Boletus hepaticus **Schaeff.** – possibly Liver mushroom (92) (1876)

Boletus ignarius **[L.]** – See *Phellinus igniarius* (L.) Quél.

Boletus **L.** Cow mushroom (78) (1898) NH, Paddock-stools [Paddock stools] (92) (1876), Toadstool (92) (1876), Touchwood (7) (1828)

Boletus laricis **Jacquin** – See *Fomitopsis officinalis (Batsch) Bondartsev & Singer*

Boletus suaveolens – See *Boletus suaveolens L.* current species depends on author

Boletus suaveolens **L.** – Willow sponge (92) (1876)

Boletus tuberosus **Bull.** – Tuberous boletus (42) (1814)

Boltonia asteroides **(L.) L'Hér.** – Aster boltonia (122) (1937), Aster-like boltonia (5, 72, 131) (1899–1913), False aster (19, 127) (1840–1933), False camomile [False chamomile, False-chamomile] (19, 156) (1840–1923), False starwort (156) (1923), White boltonia (138, 155) (1923–1942), White doll's-daisy [White doll's daisy] (50) (present)

Boltonia asteroides **(L.) L'Her. var.** *latisquama* **(Gray) Cronq.** – Broad-scale boltonia [Broad-scaled boltonia] (5, 97) (1913–1937), Violet boltonia (3, 138, 155) (1923–1977), White doll's-daisy [White doll's daisy] (50) (present)

Boltonia asteroides **(L.) L'Hér. var.** *recognita* **(Fern. & Grisc.) Cronq.** – White boltonia (3) (1977), White doll's-daisy [White doll's daisy] (50) (present)

Boltonia asteroides **var.** *asteroides* **Cronquist** – Moonwort [Moonwort, Moon wort] (92) (1876)

Boltonia decurrens **(Torr. & Gray) Wood.** – Clasping-leaf boltonia [Clasping-leaved boltonia] (5) (1913)

Boltonia diffusa **Ell.** – Bolton's aster (124) (1937), Panicled boltonia (5, 97) (1913–1937)

Boltonia diffusa **L'Her.** – possibly *Boltonia diffusa* Ell.

Boltonia glastifolia **(L'Hér.)** – See *Boltonia asteroides* (L.) L'Hér.

Boltonia latisquama **Gray** – See *Boltonia asteroides* (L.) L'Her. var. *latisquama* (Gray) Cronq.

Boltonia **L'Hér.** – Boltonia (82, 138, 155, 158) (1900–1942), Doll's-daisy [Doll's daisy] (50) (present)

Bonamia **Thouars** – Breweria (155, 158) (1900–1942)

Borago **L.** – Borage (1, 50, 82, 109, 138) (1923–present)

Borago officinalis **L.** – Beebread [Bee-bread] (156) (1923), Borage (5, 19, 57, 92, 106, 107, 156, 184) (1793–1930), Burrage (92) (1876), Common borage (50, 82, 138) (1923–present), Common bugloss (92) (1876), Cool-tankard [Cool tankard] (107, 156) (1919–1923), Lang-de-beef [Langue-de-beef, Langdebefe] (156) (1923), Star flower [Starflower, Star-flower] (156) (1923), Tablewort (107) (1919), Talewort (156) (1923)

Borrichia arborescens **(L.) DC.** – Ox-eye [Ox eye, Oxeye, Oxe eie] (19) (1840)

Borrichia frutescens **(L.) DC.** – Jamaica samphire (156) (1923), Sea

ox-eye (5, 72, 124, 156) (1907–1937)

Borya porulosa **Michx.** – See *Forestiera segregata* (Jacq.) Krug & Urban var. *segregata*

Boschniakia **C.A. Mey. ex Bong.** – Squirrel's-grandfather [Squirrel's grandfather] (77) (1898) CA

Bossekia parviflora **[(Nutt.) Greene]** – See *Rubus parviflorus* Nutt.

Bothriochloa barbinodis **(Lag.) Herter** – Barbed beard grass [Barbed beard-grass] (119) (1938), Cane bluestem (3, 50, 155) (1942–present), Pinhole beard grass [Pinhole beardgrass] (155) (1942)

Bothriochloa bladhii **(Retz.) S.T. Blake** – Caucasian bluestem (3, 50) (1977–present)

Bothriochloa ischaemum **(L.) Keng var.** *songarica* **(Rupr. ex Fisch. & C.A. Mey.) Celarier & Harlan** – Turkestan bluestem (3) (1977), Yellow bluestem (50) (present)

Bothriochloa **Kuntze** – Beard grass [Beard-grass, Beardgrass] (1, 50) (1932–present)

Bothriochloa laguroides **(DC.) Herter** – Silver beard grass [Silver beard-grass, Silver beardgrass] (50) (present)

Bothriochloa laguroides **(DC.) Herter subsp.** *torreyana* **(Steud.) Allred & Gould** – Silver beard grass [Silver beard-grass, Silver beardgrass] (50) (present), Torrey's silver beard grass [Torrey's silver beard-grass] (94) (1901)

Bothriochloa saccharoides **(Sw.) Rydb.** – Broom grass [Broomgrass] (11) (1888), Feather sedge grass [Feather sedge-grass] (5) (1913), Silver beard grass [Silver beard-grass, Silver beardgrass] (138, 140, 163) (1852–1944), Silver bluestem (3, 140) (1944–1977), Silvery beard grass [Silvery beard-grass] (119) (1938), Torrey's beard grass (5) (1913)

Bothriochloa wrightii **(Hack.) Henr.** – Wright's broom-sedge [Wright's broom sedge] (94) (1901)

Botrophia serpentaria – See *Cimicifuga racemosa* (L.) Nutt.

Botrophis serpentaria **Raf.** – See *Actaea racemosa* L.

Botrychium biternatum **(Sav.) Underwood** – Cut-leaf grape fern [Cutleaf grape fern, Cutleaf grapefern, Cut-leaved grape-fern] (122) (1937), possibly Consumption brake (92) (1876), possibly Grape fern [Grape-fern, Grapefern] (19) (1840), possibly Moonwort [Moon-wort, Moon wort] (19) (1840), possibly Rattlesnake fern [Rattlesnake-fern, Rattlesnakefern] (92) (1876)

Botrychium campestre **W.H. Wagner & Farrar** – Iowa moonwort (50) (present)

Botrychium dissectum **Spreng.** – Common grape fern [Common grapefern] (155) (1942), Cut-leaf grape fern [Cutleaf grape fern, Cutleaf grapefern, Cut-leaved grape-fern] (4, 5, 50, 138, 155) (1913–present), Grape fern [Grape-fern, Grapefern] (97) (1937), Moonwort [Moon-wort, Moon wort] (5) (1913), Ternate grape fern [Ternate grape-fern] (5) (1913)

Botrychium dissectum **Spreng. var.** *tenuifolium* **(Underw.) Clute.** – See *Botrychium biternatum* (Sav.) Underwood

Botrychium fumarioides **[Willd.]** – possibly *Botrychium biternatum* (Sav.) Underwood taxonomic status is unresolved (PL)

Botrychium fumaroides – possibly *Botrychium biternatum* (Sav.) Underwood

Botrychium lanceolatum **(S.G. Gmel.) Angs.** – Lance-leaf grape fern [Lance-leaved grape-fern] (5, 50) (1913–present)

Botrychium lunaria **(L.) Sw.** – Common moonwort (50) (present), Lunary (158) (1900), Moon fern [Moon-fern] (5, 158) (1900–1913), Moonwort [Moon-wort, Moon wort] (4, 5, 155, 158) (1900–1986), Plentage (158) (1900), Small moonwort [Small moone woort] (178) (1596), Underwood's moonwort (5) (1913), Unshoe-the-horse (158) (1900)

Botrychium lunarioides **(Michx.) Sw.** – Kidney-leaf hemlock fern [Kidney leaved hemlock fern] (42) (1814)

Botrychium lunaroides – See *Botrychium lunarioides* (Michx.) Sw.

Botrychium matricariae **(Schrank) Spreng.** – See *Botrychium multifidum* (Gmel.) Trev.

Botrychium matricariaefolium **A. Br.** – See *Botrychium matricariifolium* (A. Braun ex Dowell) A. Braun ex Koch

71

Botrychium matricariifolium (A. Braun ex Dowell) A. Braun ex Koch – Matricary grape fern [Matricary grape-fern] (4, 50, 131, 155) (1899–present), Wood's grape fern (5) (1913)

Botrychium matricariifolium **A. Br.** – See *Botrychium matricariifolium* (A. Braun ex Dowell) A. Braun ex Koch

Botrychium minganense Vict. – Mingan moonwort (50) (present)

Botrychium multifidum (Gmel.) Trev. – Broad-leaf grape fern [Broad-leaf grapefern, Broadleaf grapefern] (138, 155) (1923–1942), Eaton's grape fern [Eaton's grape-fern] (5) (1913), Grape fern [Grape-fern, Grapefern] (45, 50) (1896–present), Leathery grape fern (5) (1913)

Botrychium neglectum Wood – See *Botrychium matricariifolium* (A. Braun ex Dowell) A. Braun ex Koch

Botrychium obliquum Muhl. – See *Botrychium dissectum* Spreng.

Botrychium onandagense Underw. – See *Botrychium lunaria* (L.) Sw.

Botrychium rugulosum W. H. Wagner – Ternate grape fern [Ternate grape-fern] (86) (1878)

Botrychium silaifolium Presl. – See *Botrychium multifidum* (Gmel.) Trev.

Botrychium simplex E. Hitchcock. – Hitchcock's grape-fern (5) (1913), Little grape fern [Little grape-fern] (4, 5, 50) (1913–present)

Botrychium Sw. – Grape fern [Grape-fern, Grapefern] (1, 4, 50, 138, 155, 156) (1923–present), Moonwort [Moon-wort, Moon wort] (1, 86) (1878–1932), Rattlesnake fern [Rattlesnake-fern, Rattlesnake-fern] (7) (1828)

Botrychium tenebrosum A. A. Eaton. – See *Botrychium multifidum* (Gmel.) Trev.

Botrychium ternatum Swartz. – See *Botrychium rugulosum* W.H. Wagner

Botrychium virginianum (L.) Sw. – Fern rattlesnake-root [Fern rattlesnake-root, Fern rattlesnake root] (177, 181) (~1678–1762), Hemlock-leaf moonwort [Hemlock-leaved moonwort] (5, 157, 158) (1900–1929), Indicator (78, 158) (1898–1900) Jackson WV, thought to indicate presence of ginseng, Moosewort (72) (1907) IA, Rattlesnake grape fern [Rattle-snake grape-fern] (86) (1878) for resemblane of spore cases to tail of rattlesnake, Small moonwort [Small moone woort] (181) (~1678), Virginia grape-fern [Virginia grape fern] (122, 131, 157, 158) (1899–1937), Virginia indicator (157, 158) (1900–1929), Moonwort [Moon-wort, Moon wort] (58) (1869), Rattlesnake fern [Rattlesnake-fern, Rattlesnakefern] (3, 4, 5, 19, 40, 50, 58, 97, 107, 109, 138, 155, 157, 158, 187) (1818–present)

Botrychium virginicum (L.) Sw. – See *Botrychium virginianum* (L.) Sw.

Botrypus lunarioides Michx. – See *Boltonia asteroides* (L.) L'Hér. var. *asteroides*

Bougainvillea Comm. ex Juss. – Bougainvillea (138) (1923)

Bougainvillea glabra Choisy – possibly Lesser bougainvillea (138) (1923)

Bougainvillea spectabilis Willd. – Great bougainvillea (138) (1923)

Bourainvillea glauca – possibly *Bougainvillea glabra* Choisy

Boussingaultia gracilis Miers var. pseudo-baselloides Bailey – See *Anredera cordifolia* (Ten.) Steenis

Bouteloua aristidoides (Kunth) Griseb. – Needle grama (163) (1852), Needle grass [Needle-grass, Needlegrass] (122) (1937) TX, Six-weeks grama [Six weeks grama] (151, 152, 163) (1852–1912), Six-weeks mesquit (94) (1901)

Bouteloua aristidoides Thurb. – See *Bouteloua aristidoides* (Kunth) Griseb.

Bouteloua barbata Lag. – Low gramma grass (87) (1884), Six-weeks grama [Six weeks grama, Sixweeks grama] (31, 50, 94, 151, 152, 155) (1847–present)

Bouteloua breviseta Vasey – Chino or Chino grass (122, 163) (1852–1937) TX, Gyp grass (163) (1852), Short-awn grama [Short-awned grama] (94) (1901)

Bouteloua bromoides Lag. – See *Bouteloua repens* (Kunth) Scribn. & Merr.

Bouteloua burkii Scribn. – See *Bouteloua trifida* Thurb.

Bouteloua chondrosioides (Kunth) Benth. ex S. Wats. – Havard's grama (94) (1901), Woolly-spike grama [Woolly-spiked grama] (163) (1852)

Bouteloua curtipendula (Michx) Torr. – Grama [Gramma] (119) (1938), Grama grass [Grama-grass, Gramma grass] (116) (1958), Hairy mesquite grass [Hairy mesquite-grass] (151) (1896), Hairy muskit (66) (1903), Mesquit grass (22) (1893), Mesquite grass [Mesquite-grass] (116, 118, 129) (1894–1958), Muskit (11) (1888), Prairie oats (144) (1899) KS, Side oats [Side-oats, Side oat] (56, 94, 119) (1901–1938), Side-oats grama [Side oats grama, Sideoats grama, Side-oat grama] (3, 50, 114, 116, 122, 134, 140, 155, 163) (1852–present), Tall grama (1, 94, 129, 151) (1894–1932), Tall grama grass [Tall grama-grass, Tall gramma grass] (56, 75, 85, 87, 111, 116, 118, 119, 134, 163) (1852–1932), Tall grama oats (56) (1901), Tall mesquite (87) (1884), Wiry grama (94) (1901)

Bouteloua curtipendula (Michx.) Torr. var. curtipendula – Fall gramma grass (99) (1923), Hairbread [Hair bread] (19) (1840), Mesquite grass [Mesquite-grass] (5) (1913), Prairie grama (93) (1936), Racemed bouteloua (72) (1907), Side-oats grama [Side oats grama, Sideoats grama] (5, 50) (1913–present), Tall grama (152) (1912), Tall grama grass [Tall grama-grass, Tall gramma grass] (5) (1913)

Bouteloua eriopoda (Torr.) Torr. – Black grama [Black gramma] (3, 50, 119, 122, 151, 152, 155, 163) (1852–present), Woolly-foot [Woolly foot] (152, 163) (1852–1912) NM, Woolly-joint grama [Woolly-jointed grama, Woolly jointed grama] (94, 151) (1896–1901)

Bouteloua filiformis (Fourn.) Griffith – See *Bouteloua repens* (Kunth) Scribn. & Merr.

Bouteloua gracilis (Willd. ex Kunth) Lag. ex Griffiths – Blue grama (3, 5, 50, 56, 75, 93, 94, 98, 111, 115, 116, 119, 122, 129, 134, 140, 151, 152, 155, 163) (1852–present), Blue grama grass (75) (1894), Buffalo grass [Buffalo-grass, Buffalograss] (5, 30, 75, 87, 88, 101, 108, 146) (1844–1939), Common grama (5) (1913), Crowfoot grama (152) (1912) NM, Grama [Gramma] (11, 30, 45, 88) (1844–1896), Grama grass [Grama-grass, Gramma grass] (5, 22, 72, 85, 87, 101, 118, 119, 152, 164) (1853–1938), Low mesquite (87) (1884), Mesquit grass (66) (1903), Mesquite (45) (1896), Mesquite grass [Mesquite-grass] (5, 30, 45, 56, 87, 88, 99, 118, 119, 151) (1844–1938), Mezquite grass (66) (1903), Muskit grass (66) (1903), Tall grama (144) (1899), White grama (152) (1912), Five-spike blue grama [Fivespike blue grama] (155) (1942)

Bouteloua gracilis stricta – See *Bouteloua gracilis* (Willd. ex Kunth) Lag. ex Griffiths

Bouteloua gracilis Vasey in Rothr. var. stricta Hitchc. – See *Bouteloua gracilis* (Willd. ex Kunth) Lag. ex Griffiths

Bouteloua havardi Vasey – See *Bouteloua chondrosioides* (Kunth) Benth. ex S. Wats.

Bouteloua hirsuta Lag. – Black grama [Black gramma] (5, 56, 65, 93, 111, 116, 129, 144, 152, 163) (1852–1936), Black grama grass (75) (1894), Bristly mesquite [Bristly mesquit] (5, 87, 94) (1884–1913), Bristly muskit (66) (1903), Buffalo grass [Buffalo-grass, Buffalograss] (5, 75, 129) (1894–1913), Grama grass [Grama-grass, Gramma grass] (87, 164) (1852–1884), Hairy grama (1, 3, 50, 65, 85, 116, 119, 121, 122, 134, 140, 152, 155, 163) (1912–present), Hairy mesquite (116) (1958), Hairy mesquite grass [Hairy mesquite-grass] (5, 56, 72, 119) (1893–1938), Mezquit grass (92) (1876), Peyiokiyata (Lakota, forked grass (121) (1918–1970?), Short grama (144) (1899), Tall grama (56) (1901)

Bouteloua hirsuta Lag. var. hirsuta – Hairy grama (50) (present)

Bouteloua hirsuta Lag. var. pectinata (Featherly) Cory – Hairy grama (122) (1937), Hairy mesquite grass [Hairy mesquite-grass] (119) (1938)

Bouteloua Lag. – Buffalo grass [Buffalo-grass, Buffalograss] (1) (1932), Grama [Gramma] (1, 50, 155) (1932–present), Grama grass [Grama-grass, Gramma grass] (1, 45, 66, 67, 87, 93, 152, 164) (1852–1936), Mesquite grass [Mesquite-grass] (1, 67, 87, 93) (1884–1936), Musquit grass (45) (1896), Side-oats grama [Side oats grama, Sideoats grama, Side-oat grama] (93) (1936), Side-oats grama [Side oats grama] (93) (1936), Tall grama (93) (1936)

Bouteloua oligostachya **(Nutt.) Torr.** – See *Bouteloua gracilis* (Willd. ex Kunth) Lag. ex Griffiths

Bouteloua parryi **(Fourn.) Griffiths** – Hairy grama (94) (1901)

Bouteloua pectinata **Featherly** – See *Bouteloua hirsuta* Lag. var. *pectinata* (Featherly) Cory

Bouteloua polystachya **[(Benth.) Torr.]** – See *Bouteloua barbata* Lag.

Bouteloua prostrata **Lag.** – See *Bouteloua simplex* Lag.

Bouteloua racemosa **L.** – See *Bouteloua curtipendula* (Michx) Torr.

Bouteloua repens **(Kunth) Scribn. & Merr.** – Griffith's slender grama (122) (1937), Large mesquite (163) (1852), Spruce-top [Spruce tops] (94) (1901)

Bouteloua rigidiseta **(Steud.) Hitchc.** – Mesquite grass [Mesquite-grass] (163) (1852), Seedmesquite (94) (1901), Texas grama (50, 119, 122, 155) (1937–present)

Bouteloua rothrockii **Vasey** – Rothrock's grama (94) (1901)

Bouteloua simplex **Lag.** – Mat grama (122, 155) (1937–1942), Matted grama (50) (present), Tufted grama (94) (1901)

Bouteloua texana **S. Wats.** – See *Bouteloua rigidiseta* (Steud.) Hitchc.

Bouteloua trifida **Thurb.** – Burk's grama (94) (1901), Red grama (122) (1937), Small grama (94) (1901)

Bouteloua uniflora **Vasey** – One-flower grama [One-flowered grama] (94) (1901)

Bouvardia **Salisb.** – Bouvardia (138) (1923)

Bouvardia ternifolia **(Cav.) Schltdl.** – Scarlet bouvardia (138) (1923)

Bouvardia triphylla **[Salisb.]** – See *Bouvardia ternifolia* (Cav.) Schltdl.

Boykinia aconitifolia **Nutt.** – Aconite saxifrage (5) (1913)

Boykinia jamesii **(Torr.) Engl.** – See *Telesonix jamesii* (Torr.) Raf.

Brachiaria **(Trin.) Griseb.** – Signal-grass [Signalgrass] (155) (1942)

Brachiaria ciliatissima **(Buckl.) Chase** – See *Urochloa ciliatissima* (Buckl.) R. Webster

Brachyactis angusta **(Lindl.) Britton** – See *Symphyotrichum ciliatum* (Ledeb.) Nesom

Brachyactis angustus **(Lindl.) Britton** – See *Symphyotrichum ciliatum* (Ledeb.) Nesom

Brachyactis **Ledeb** – See *Symphyotrichum* Nees all US species

Brachychaeta sphacelata **(Raf.) Britton** – See *Solidago sphacelata* Raf.

Brachychiton populneum **(Schott) R. Br.** – Kurrajong (109) (1949)

Brachychiton **Schott & Endl.** – Bottletree [Bottle-tree] (109) (1949)

Brachyelytrum aristatum **Beauv.** – See *Brachyelytrum erectum* (Schreb. ex Spreng.) Beauv.

Brachyelytrum **Beauv.** – Brachyelytrum (66) (1903), Shorthusk (50, 155) (1942–present)

Brachyelytrum erectum **(Schreb. ex Spreng.) Beauv.** – Awned brachyelytrum (66, 90) (1885–1903), Bearded shorthusk [Bearded short husk, Bearded short-husk] (5, 50, 94, 111, 119, 155) (1901–present), Erect muhlenbergia (66, 187) (1818–1903)

Brachyelytrum erectum **(Schreb.) Beauv.** – See *Brachyelytrum septentrionale* (Babel) G. Tucker

Brachyelytrum septentrionale **(Babel) G. Tucker** – Brachyelytrum (56) (1901), False drop seed(19) (1840), Northern shorthusk (50) (present)

Brachystemum linifolium **Willd.** – See *Pycnanthemum flexuosum* (Walt.) Britton, Sterns & Poggenb.

Brachystemum virginicum **Michx.** – See *Pycnanthemum virginianum* (L.) T. Dur. & B.D. Jackson ex B.L. Robins. & Fern.

Bradburya **Raf.** – See *Centrosema* (DC.) Benth.

Bradburya virginiana **(L.) Kuntze** – See *Centrosema virginianum* (L.) Benth.

Brahea **Mart. ex Endl.** – Hesper palm (109) (1949)

Brahea serrulata **(Michx.) H. Wendl.** – See *Serenoa repens* (Bartr.) Small

Bramia moniera **(L.) Drake** – See *Bacopa monnieri* (L.) Pennell

Bramia rotundifolia **(Michx.) Britton** – See *Bacopa rotundifolia* (Michx.) Wettst.

Brasenia hydropeltis **Schreber.** – See *Brasenia schreberi* Gmel.

Brasenia peltata **[Pursh]** – See *Brasenia schreberi* Gmel.

Brasenia purpurea **(Michx.) Casp.** – See *Brasenia schreberi* Gmel.

Brasenia **Schreber** – Brasenia (50) (present), Watershield [Water shield, Water-shield] (1, 2, 4, 10, 13, 15, 138, 155, 158) (1818–1986)

Brasenia schreberi **Gmel.** – Brasenia (Official name of Materia Medica) (7) (1828), Deerfood [Deer-food, Deer food] (5, 7, 92, 156) (1828–1923), Deer's-foot [Deer-foot] (156) (1923), Egg-bonnet (156) (1923), Frogleaf [Frog-leaf] (5, 7, 92, 156) (1828–1923), Gelatina aquatica (Official name of Materia Medica) (7) (1828), Hydropelte (French) (7) (1828), Little waterlily [Little water-lily, Little water lily] (5, 7, 92, 156) (1828–1923), Purple bonnet (156) (1923), Purple wen-dock (3) (1977), Round-leaf nympha [Round leafed nympha] (183) (~1756), Schreber's water-shield [Schreber watershield] (155) (1942), Wasserschild (German) (7) (1828), Water-jelly [Water jelly, Waterjelly] (7, 92, 156) (1828–1923), Waterleaf [Water leaf, Water-leaf] (92, 156) (1876–1923), Watershield [Water shield, Water-shield] (4, 5, 7, 19, 47, 50, 72, 92, 107, 109, 138, 156, 187) (1818–present), Water-target [Water target, Watertarget] (5, 19, 156) (1840–1923)

Brasenia **Willd.** – See *Brasenia* Schreber

Brassenia schreberi **Gmel.** – See *Brasenia schreberi* Gmel.

Brassia **R. Br. ex Ait. f.** – Spider orchid [Spider-orchid] (138) (1923)

Brassica **(Tourn.) L.** – See *Brassica* L.

Brassica alba **Hook.** – See *Sinapis alba* L.

Brassica arvensis **(L.) Ktze.** – See *Moricandia arvensis* (L.) DC.

Brassica arvensis **L.** – See *Moricandia arvensis* (L.) DC.

Brassica campestris **L.** – See *Brassica rapa* L. var. *rapa*

Brassica carinata **A. Br.** – See *Brassica juncea* (L.) Czern.

Brassica fimbriata **DC.** – See *Brassica oleracea* L.

Brassica hirta **Moench** – See *Sinapis alba* L.

Brassica integrifolia **(H. West) Rupr.** – See *Brassica juncea* (L.) Czern.

Brassica japonica **Thunb.** – See *Brassica juncea* (L.) Czern.

Brassica juncea **(L.) Czern.** – Broad-leaf mustard [Broad-leaved mustard] (109) (1949), Chinese mustard (107) (1919), Curled mustard (156) (1923), Indian mustard [India mustard] (3, 4, 5, 50, 97, 107, 155, 156, 157, 158) (1900–present), Japanese mustard (155) (1942), Leaf mustard (109) (1949), Ostrich-plume mustard [Ostrich plume mustard] (109) (1949), Potherb mustard (138, 155, 156) (1923–1942), Russian mustard (157, 158) (1900–1929), Sarepta mustard (157, 158) (1900–1929), Southern curled mustard (109) (1949)

Brassica juncea **(L.) Czern. var. crispifolia Bailey** – See *Brassica juncea* (L.) Czern.

Brassica juncea **Coss.** – See *Brassica juncea* (L.) Czern.

Brassica juncea **Coss. var. foliosa Bailey** – See *Brassica juncea* (L.) Czern.

Brassica kaber **(DC.) Wheeler** – See *Sinapis arvensis* L.

Brassica kaber **Wheeler** – See *Sinapis arvensis* L.

Brassica **L.** – Black mustard (1, 93) (1932–1936), Borecole (107) (1919), Broccoli (107) (1919), Brussel sprouts (107) (1919), Cabbage (1, 107, 184) (1793–1932), Cauliflower (107) (1919), Charlock (107) (1919), Chinese cabbage (107) (1919), Cole [Coles] (109) (1949), Collard [Collards] (107) (1919), Couve (Portuguese) (107) (1919), Kale (107) (1919), Kohlrabi [Kohl-rabi] (107) (1919), Mustard [Mustards] (4, 50, 63, 82, 107, 109) (1899–present), Portugal cabbage (107) (1919), Rape (1, 93, 107) (1919–1936), Red cabbage (107) (1919), Rutabaga [Ruta-baga] (107) (1919), Savoy cabbage (107) (1919), Turnip [Turnep, Turnips] (1, 106, 107, 156) (1919–1932)

Brassica orientalis **L.** – See *Conringia orientalis* (L.) Dumort.

Brassica sinapistrum **Boiss.** – See *Sinapis arvensis* L.

Brassica sinapstrum **Bois.** – See *Sinapis arvensis* L.

Brauneria angustifolia **(DC.) Heller** – See *Echinacea angustifolia* DC. var. *angustifolia*

Brauneria **Neck.** – See *Echinacea* Moench

Brauneria pallida **(Nutt.) Britton** – See *Echinacea pallida* (Nutt.) Nutt.

Brauneria purpurea **(L.) Britton** – See *Echinacea purpurea* (L.) Moench

Braxilia **Raf.** – See *Pyrola* L.

Braya humilis **(C. A. Mey.) B. L. Robins.** – Low rockcress [Low rock cress] (5) (1913), Northern rockcress [Northern rock cress] (5) (1913)

Breweria aquatica **Gray.** – See *Stylisma aquatica* (Walt.) Chapman

Breweria humistrata **Gray.** – See *Stylisma humistrata* (Walt.) Chapman

Breweria pickeringii **Gray.** – See *Stylisma pickeringii* (Torr. ex M.A. Curtis) Gray var. *pattersonii* (Fern. & Schub.) Myint

Breweria **R. Br.** – See *Bonamia* Thouars

Breynia disticha **J. R. & G. Forst.** – Snow bush [Snow-bush] (109) (1949), Star snowbush (138) (1923)

Breynia nivosa **Small** – See *Breynia disticha* J.R. & G. Forst.

Brickellia brachyphylla **(Gray) Gray** – Plumed brickellbush (50) (present)

Brickellia californica **(Torr. & Gray) Gray** – California brickellbush (50) (present), California brickellia (155) (1942)

Brickellia **Ell.** Brickellbush (50) (present), Brickellia (155) (1942), Coleosanthus (158) (1900), False boneset (1, 4, 93, 158) (1900–1986), Kuhnia (82) (1930), Thoroughwort [Thorough wort, Thoroughwort] (1) (1932)

Brickellia eupatorioides **(L.) Shinners** – False boneset (50) (present)

Brickellia eupatorioides **(L.) Shinners var.** *chlorolepis* **(Woot. & Standl.) B.L. Turner** – False boneset (50) (present)

Brickellia eupatorioides **(L.) Shinners var.** *corymbulosa* **(Torr. & Gray) Shinners** – False boneset (3, 50, 98) (1926–present)

Brickellia eupatorioides **(L.) Shinners var.** *eupatorioides* – False boneset (5, 19, 50, 72, 82, 85, 92, 93, 95, 97, 122, 124, 156) (1840–present), Prairie boneset (122) (1937), Prairie false boneset (5, 72, 93, 97, 124, 131, 156) (1899–1937)

Brickellia eupatorioides **(L.) Shinners var.** *texana* **(Shinners) Shinners** – False boneset (50) (present)

Brickellia grandiflora **(Hook.) Nutt.** Brickellia (3) (1977), Largeflower thoroughwort [Largeflower thoroughwort] (5, 122) (1913–1937), Tassel flower [Tassel-flower, Tasselflower, Tassell flower] (5, 156) (1913–1923), Tassel-flower brickell bush [Tasselflower brickellbush] (50) (present), Tassel-flower brickellia [Tasselflower brickellia] (155) (1942)

Briza canadensis **[Michx.]** – See *Glyceria canadensis* (Michx.) Trin.

Briza **L.** – Quake grass [Quake-grass] (1) (1932), Quaking grass [Quaking-grass] (1, 10, 45, 66, 109) (1818–1949)

Briza maxima **L.** – Big quaking grass (50, 138) (1923–present), Large quaking grass (42, 66) (1814–1903), Quake grass [Quake-grass] (92) (1876), Quaking grass [Quaking-grass] (92) (1876), Rattlesnake grass [Rattle snake grass] (19, 92) (1840–1876)

Briza media **L.** – Cowquake [Cow-quake, Cow quake] (5) (1913), Dithering grass (5) (1913), Dodder grass (5) (1913), Fairy grass (5) (1913), Jockey grass (5) (1913), Lady's-hair [Lady's hair] (5) (1913), Maidenhair [Maiden-hair, Maiden hair] (5) (1913), Maidenhair grass [Maiden hair grass] (92) (1876), Pearl grass (5) (1913), Perennial quaking grass (50) (present), Quake grass [Quake-grass] (5, 72) (1907–1913), Quaking grass [Quaking-grass] (5, 19, 56, 66, 67, 88, 92, 184) (1793–1912), Qualking grass [Qualking-grass] (94) (1901), Rattlesnake grass [Rattle snake grass] (19) (1840), Shakers (5) (1913), Wag wanton (5) (1913)

Briza minor **L.** – Lesser quaking grass (5) (1913), Little quaking grass (50, 138) (1923–present), Quaking grass [Quaking-grass] (88) (1885), Smaller quaking grass (5) (1913)

Brizopyrum boreale – See *Distichlis spicata* (L.) Greene

Brizopyrum spicata – possibly *Distichlis spicata* (L.) Greene

Brizopyrum spicatum **(L.) Hook. & Arn.** – See *Distichlis spicata* (L.) Greene

Brodiaea capitata **Benth.** – See *Dichelostemma capitatum* (Benth.) Wood subsp. *capitatum*

Brodiaea coccinea **A. Gray** – See *Dichelostemma ida-maia* (Wood) Greene

Brodiaea coronaria **(Salisb.) Engl.** – Harvest brodiaea (109) (1949)

Brodiaea grandiflora **Smith.** – See *Triteleia grandiflora* Lindl. var. *grandiflora*

Brodlaea coronaria **Engler** – See *Brodiaea coronaria* (Salisb.) Engl.

Bromelia ananas **L.** – See *Ananas comosus* (L.) Merr.

Bromelica **(Thurber) Farwell.** – See *Melica* L.

Bromopsis erectus **(Huds.) Fourr.** – See *Bromus erectus* Huds.

Bromopsis kalmii **(Gray) Holub** – See *Bromus kalmii* Gray

Bromus anomalus – See *Bromus porteri* (Coult.) Nash

Bromus arvensis **L.** – Chess (19) (1840), Field brome (3, 5, 50, 56, 155) (1901–present), Field brome grass (68) (1890), Field chess (5, 72) (1907–1913) IA

Bromus asper **Murr.** – See *Bromus racemosus* L.

Bromus breviaristatus **(Hook.) Buckl.** – See *Bromus marginatus* Nees ex Steud.

Bromus brizaeformis **Fisch. & Mey.** – See *Bromus briziformis* Fisch. & C. A. Mey.

Bromus briziformis **Fisch. & C. A. Mey.** – Awnless brome grass [Awnless brome-grass] (5) (1913), Briza-like brome grass [Briza-like brome-grass] (94) (1901), Quake grass [Quake-grass] (5, 109) (1913–1949), Quaking brome (138) (1923), Rattle brome (140, 155) (1942–1944), Rattlesnake brome (50) (present), Rattlesnake chess (3, 140) (1944–1977)

Bromus canadensis **Michx.** – See *Bromus ciliatus* L. var. *ciliatus*

Bromus carinatus **H. & A.** – California brome (3, 50) (1977–present), Great western brome (94) (1901), Keeled brome (56) (1901)

Bromus carinatus **var.** *hookerianus* **(Thurb.) Shear** – See *Bromus carinatus* H. & A.

Bromus catharticus **Vahl** – Australian oats (88) (1885), Brome grass [Bromegrass, Brome-grass] (152) (1912), Horn grass (92) (1876), Johnson grass [Johnson-grass, Johnsongrass] (5) (1913), Rescue brome (155) (1942), Rescue grass [Rescuegrass, Rescue-grass] (5, 45, 50, 56, 88, 94, 109, 118, 119, 122, 138, 155, 163) (1852–present), Schrader's brome [Schraders brome] (109) (1949), Schrader's brome grass (5, 56, 129) (1894–1913), Schrader's bromus (45) (1896), Schrader's grass (87, 88, 118, 163) (1852–1898), Southern chess (5, 85, 119) (1913–1938), Wild brome grass [Wild brome-grass] (5, 45) (1896–1913)

Bromus ciliatus **L.** – Brome grass [Bromegrass, Brome-grass] (58) (1869), Fringed brome (3, 50, 122, 140, 155) (1937–present), Fringed brome grass [Fringed brome-grass] (5, 56, 66, 68, 72, 90, 143, 163) (1852–1936), Hairy brome grass (5) (1913), Old-fog [Old fog] (75) (1894), Swamp chess [Swamp-chess] (5, 56, 75, 94, 111, 129, 163) (1852–1915), Wild brome grass [Wild brome-grass] (163) (1852), Wood chess (5) (1913), Woodland chess (56) (1901)

Bromus ciliatus **L. var.** *ciliatus* – Canadian brome grass [Canada brome grass] (42) (1814), Fringed brome (50) (present)

Bromus ciliatus **L. var.** *laeviglumis* **Scribn. ex Shear** – See *Bromus pubescens* Muhl. ex Willd.

Bromus ciliatus purgans **A. Gray** – See *Bromus kalmii* Gray

Bromus ciliatus **var.** *purgans* **Gray** – See *Bromus kalmii* Gray

Bromus commutatus **Schrad.** – Hairy brome (155) (1942), Hairy chess (122) (1937), Meadow brome (50) (present), Sunshine brome (155) (1942), Upright chess (119) (1938)

Bromus commutatus **Schrad. var.** *apricorum* **Simonkai** – See *Bromus commutatus* Schrad.

Bromus erectus **Huds.** – Erect brome (50) (present), Erect brome grass (87) (1884), Meadow brome (56, 66) (1901–1903), Meadow brome grass [Meadow bromegrass] (56, 66, 138) (1901–1923), Upright brome grass (5) (1913)

Bromus giganteus **L.** – See *Lolium giganteum* (L.) S.J. Darbyshire

Bromus hookerianus **Thur.** – See *Bromus carinatus* H. & A.

Bromus hordeaceus **L.** – Annual brome grass (80) (1913), Blubber grass (5) (1913), Bull grass [Bull-grass, Bull grass] (5) (1913), Hairy cheat (85) (1932), Haver grass (5) (1913), Hooded grass (5) (1913), Lob grass (5) (1913), Lop grass (5) (1913), Soft brome (5, 50) (1913–present), Soft chess (5, 56, 72, 80, 94, 111) (1901–1915)

Bromus hordeaceus **L. subsp.** *hordeaceus* – Hairy cheat (163) (1852), Lob grass (92) (1876), Lop grass (92) (1876), Smooth-spike soft chess [Smooth spiked soft chess] (56) (1901), Soft brome (50, 155)

(1942–present), Soft brome grass (42, 66) (1814–1903), Soft chess (3, 56, 66, 122, 129, 163) (1852–1977)

***Bromus hordeaceus* var. *glabrescens* (Coss.) Shear.** – See *Bromus hordeaceus* L. subsp. *hordeaceus*

***Bromus inermis* Leyss.** – Austrian brome grass (68) (1890), Austrian brome hay (68) (1890), Awnless brome grass [Awnless brome-grass] (5, 56, 68, 109, 111, 118, 119, 143, 146, 163) (1852–1949), Brome grass [Bromegrass, Brome-grass] (85) (1932), Common brome grass [Common bromegrass] (138) (1923), Hungarian brome (109, 118) (1898–1949), Hungarian brome grass [Hungarian brome-grass] (5, 56, 68, 72, 94, 119, 143, 163) (1852–1938), Hungarian fodder grass (68) (1890), Smooth brome (50, 56, 94, 140, 146, 155) (1901–present), Smooth brome grass [Smooth brome-grass] (68, 129, 143) (1890–1936), Unarmed brome grass (152) (1912)

Bromus inermis* Leyss. subsp. *inermis – Smooth brome (50) (present)

***Bromus inermis* Leyss. subsp. *pumpellianus* (Scribn.) Wagnon** – Pumpelly's brome (50) (present)

***Bromus inermis* Leyss. subsp. *pumpellianus* (Scribn.) Wagnon** – Smooth brome (3) (1977)

***Bromus japonicus* Thunb. ex Murr.** – Japanese brome (3, 50, 140, 155) (1942–present), Japanese chess (122, 140, 146) (1937–1944), Spreading brome grass [Spreading brome-grass] (5, 56, 163) (1852–1913)

***Bromus kalmii* Gray** – Arctic brome (50) (present), Brome grass [Bromegrass, Brome-grass] (56, 72) (1901–1907), Broom grass [Broom-grass] (7, 92) (1828–1876), Canadian brome [Canada brome] (155) (1942), Canadian brome grass [Canada brome grass] (122) (1937), Cathartic broom grass [Cathartic broom-grass] (187) (1818), Hairy wood chess [Hairy wood-chess] (5, 85, 119, 163) (1852–1938), Kalm's brome [Kalm brome] (155) (1942), Kalm's brome grass [Kalm's brome-grass] (56, 94) (1897–1901), Kalm's chess (5, 72) (1907–1913), Swamp chess [Swamp-chess] (75) (1894), Wild chess (5, 66, 75, 111, 119) (1894–1938)

Bromus kalmii* var. *porteri – See *Bromus porteri* (Coult.) Nash

***Bromus* L.** – Brome (50, 155) (1942–present), Brome grass [Bromegrass, Brome-grass] (1, 10, 41, 92, 93, 109, 138, 152, 158, 184) (1770–1949), Cheat (93) (1936), Chess (1, 93, 158) (1932–1936), Wild oat [Wild oats] (152) (1912) NM

***Bromus lanatipes* (Shear) Rydb.** – Woolly brome (50) (present)

***Bromus latiglumis* (Shear) A.S. Hitchc.** Broad-glume brome grass [Broad glumed brome grass] (56) (1901), Ear-leaf brome [Earleaf brome] (155) (1942), Early-leaf brome [Earlyleaf brome] (50) (present), Swamp chess [Swamp-chess] (56) (1901), Wood brome grass (56) (1901), Wood chess (56) (1901)

***Bromus madritensis* L.** – Compact brome (50) (present), Compact chess (5) (1913), Madrid brome grass [Madrid bromegrass] (138) (1923)

***Bromus marginatus* Nees ex Steud.** – Larger short-awn chess [Larger short-awned chess] (56) (1901), Mountain brome (50, 146) (1939–present), Short-awn brome grass [Short-awned brome grass, Short awned brome grass] (5, 56) (1901–1913), Short-awn chess [Short-awned chess] (5, 56, 72) (1901–1907), Slim-leaf brome [Slimleaf brome] (155) (1942)

***Bromus marginatus* Nees ex Steud. var. *latior* Shear** – See *Bromus marginatus* Nees ex Steud.

***Bromus mollis* L.** – See *Bromus hordeaceus* L. subsp. *hordeaceus*

***Bromus multiflorus* [Roth.]** – possibly *Bromus racemosus* L.

***Bromus patulus* Mert. & Koch** – See *Bromus japonicus* Thunb. ex Murr.

***Bromus porteri* (Coult.) Nash** – Nodding brome (3, 155) (1942–1977), Porter's brome [Porter brome] (50, 155) (1942–present), Porter's chess (5) (1913), Wild chess (75, 111) (1894–1915)

***Bromus pratensis* Lam.** – See *Bromus erectus* Huds.

***Bromus pubescens* Muhl. ex Willd.** – Bloom grass (92) (1876), Brome grass [Bromegrass, Brome-grass] (92) (1876), Broom grass [Broom-grass] (19) (1840), Canadian brome [Canada brome] (3) (1977), Hairy woodland brome (50) (present), Smooth fringed brome grass (56) (1901)

***Bromus purgans* L.** – See *Bromus kalmii* Gray

***Bromus purgans* var. *incanus* Shear** – See *Bromus latiglumis* (Shear) A.S. Hitchc.

***Bromus purgans* var. *latiglumis* (Scribn.) Shear.** – See *Bromus latiglumis* (Shear) A. S. Hitchc.

***Bromus purgens* L.** – See *Bromus kalmii* Gray

***Bromus racemosus* L.** – Bald brome (3, 50, 155) (1942–present), Hairy brome grass (5) (1913), Rough brome grass (129) (1894), Smooth brome grass [Smooth brome-grass (5, 66, 111) (1903–1915), Upright chess (5, 56, 66, 72) (1893–1912), possibly Many-flower cheat [Many-flowered cheat] (187) (1818)

***Bromus ramosus* Huds.** – Hairy brome (50) (present) TX

***Bromus rigidus* Roth** – Ripgut (163) (1852), Ripgut grass (122) (1937) TX

***Bromus schraderi* [Kunth]** – See *Bromus catharticus* Vahl

***Bromus secalinus* L.** – Cheat (1, 3, 5, 46, 56, 62, 66, 72, 75, 80, 85, 87, 88, 90, 93, 94, 119, 145, 158, 163, 187) (1818–1977), Cheat grass [Cheatgrass] (92, 158) (1876–1900), Chess (5, 45, 56, 62, 66, 67, 75, 80, 87, 88, 90, 94, 111, 119, 122, 158, 163) (1852–1938), Chess brome (155) (1942), Chess grass (92) (1876), Cock grass (5) (1913), Common chess (56) (1901), Cook grass [Cook-grass] (119) (1938) OK, Rye brome (50) (present), Smooth rye brome [Smooth rye-brome] (5, 158) (1900–1913), Wild chess (87) (1884), Willard's brome grass (88, 90) (1885), Willard's bromus (66) (1903), Willard's bromus grass (92) (1876?)

***Bromus squarrosus* L.** – Corn brome (5, 50, 56, 72) (1893–present)

***Bromus sterilis* L.** – Barren brome grass (5) (1913), Barren oats [Barren otes] (180) (1633), Black grass (5) (1913), Haver grass (5) (1913), Hedge-oats [Hedge-Otes] (180) (1633), Poverty brome (50) (present), Sterile brome grass (66) (1903)

***Bromus tectorum* L.** – Awned brome grass (80) (1913), Cheat grass [Cheatgrass] (50, 146) (1939–present), Cheatgrass brome (140, 155) (1942–1944), Downy brome (3, 146, 155) (1939–1977), Downy brome grass [Downy brome-grass, Downy bromegrass] (5, 56, 62, 72, 80, 85, 94, 119, 140, 143, 148, 185) (1901–1944), Downy chess (122, 140, 143, 146) (1936–1944), Military grass (146) (1939) MT, Slender chess (62) (1912), Taklosta (Swedish) (46) (1879)

***Bromus texensis* (Shear) A. S. Hitchc.** – Texas brome grass (122) (1937)

***Bromus unioloides* H.B.K.** – See *Bromus catharticus* Vahl

***Broussonetia* L'Hér. ex Vent.** – Broussonetia (50) (present), Paper mulberry [Papermulberry] (109, 155, 158) (1900–1949)

***Broussonetia papyrifera* (L.) L'Hér. ex Vent.** – Common paper-mulberry [Common papermulberry] (155) (1942), Cut-paper [Cut paper] (5, 75, 156, 158) (1894–1923) WV, Otaheite mulberry (5, 156) (1913–1923), Paper mulberry [Papermulberry] (3, 5, 19, 50, 92, 97, 107, 122, 124, 156, 158) (1840–present), Tahiti mulberry (158) (1900), Tapa-cloth tree (107) (1919)

***Broussonetia papyrifera* (L.) Vent.** – See *Broussonetia papyrifera* (L.) L'Hér. ex Vent.

***Broussonetia papyrifera* Vent.** – See *Broussonetia papyrifera* (L.) L'Hér. ex Vent.

Broussonetia secundiflora – See *Sophora secundiflora* (Ortega) Lag. ex DC.

***Bruckenthalia* Rchb.** – See *Erica* L. all current species

***Brugmansia candida* Pers.** Floripondio (138) (1923)

***Brugmansia suaveolens* (Humb. & Bonpl. ex Willd.) Bercht. & K. Presl** – Angel's-trumpets [Angel trumpets, Angel-trumpets] (138) (1923)

Brunella – See *Prunella* L.

***Brunella vulgaris* L.** – See *Prunella vulgaris* L.

***Brunfelsia americana* L.** – Lady-of-the night (109) (1949)

***Brunnichia cirrhosa* Banks.** – See *Brunnichia ovata* (Walt.) Shinners

***Brunnichia ovata* (Walt.) Shinners** – Brunnichia (5, 97) (1913–1937), Buckwheat vine (156) (1923), Eardrop vine [Ear-drop vine] (122, 124) (1937) TX, Lady's-eardrop [Ladies' ear drops, Ladies ear-drop]

(106, 156) (1923–1930), Rajana (182) (1791), Tendril-bearing smartweed (106, 156) (1923–1930)

***Bryonia alba* L.** – Bastard turnip (53) (1922), Bryonia (52, 54, 57, 60) (1902–1919), Bryony [Briony] (52, 53, 57, 60, 92) (1876–1922), Devil's-turnip [Devil's turnip] (53) (1922), Tetter-berry [Tetter berry] (92) (1876), White bryony [White brionie, Whyte bryony] (50, 92, 107, 179) (1526–present), White vine [Whyte vyne] (179) (1526), Wild bryony (92) (1876), Wild hop [Wild hops] (92) (1876), Wood vine [Wood-vine] (92) (1876)

***Bryonia cretica* L. subsp. *dioica* (Jacq.) Tutin** – Bryonia (57, 60) (1902–1917), Bryony [Briony] (55, 57, 60, 92, 179) (1526–1917), Cretan bryony (55) (1911), Devil's-turnip [Devil's turnip] (92) (1876), Red bryony (92, 107) (1876–1919), Wild gourd [Wylde gourde] (179) (1526), Wild hop [Wild hops] (107) (1919), Wild nep [Wylde neppe] (179) (1526), Wild vine (92) (1876), possibly White bryony [White brionie, Whyte bryony] (178) (1526)

***Bryonia dioica* Jacq.** – See *Bryonia cretica* L. subsp. *dioica* (Jacq.) Tutin

***Bryonia* L.** – Bryony [Briony] (109) (1949) from Greek for "to sprout" referring to the shoots that come annually from the tuber

Bryophyllum calycinum – See *Kalanchoe pinnata* (Lam.) Pers.

***Bryophyllum pinnatum* (Lam.) Oken** – See *Kalanchoe pinnata* (Lam.) Pers.

***Bryoria fremontii* (Tuck.) Brodo & D. Hawksw.** – Black moss (101) (1905) MT, Tree moss [Tree-moss] (101) (1905) MT

Brysonima crassifolia – See *Byrsonima crassifolia* (L.) Kunth

***Bryum* Hedw.** – Robin-wheat [Robin wheat] (73) (1892) Mansfield OH

***Buchloe dactyloides* (Nutt.) Engelm.** – Buffalo grass [Buffalo-grass, Buffalograss] (3, 5, 11, 22, 28, 30, 45, 50, 56, 67, 72, 75, 85, 87, 88, 94, 111, 119, 122, 129, 134, 140, 144, 146, 152, 155, 163, 164) (1844–present), Early mesquite (119) (1938), False mesquite grass (87) (1884), Mesquite (87) (1884), Mesquite grass [Mesquite-grass] (5) (1913), Moor grass [Moor-grass] (10, 36) (1818–1830)

***Buchloe* Engelm.** – Buffalo grass [Buffalo-grass, Buffalograss] (1, 45, 50, 93) (1896–present)

***Buchnera americana* L.** – American bluehearts (3, 50) (1977–present), American buchnera (42) (1814), Bluehearts [Blue hearts, Blue-hearts] (5, 19, 97, 122, 156) (1840–1937)

***Buchnera* L.** – Bluehearts [Blue hearts, Blue-hearts] (1, 2, 4, 158) (1895–1986)

***Buda rubra* Dum.** – See *Spergularia rubra* (L.) J.& K. Presl

***Buddleja davidii* Franch.** Butterfly bush (112) (1937)

***Buglossoides arvensis* (L.) I. M. Johnston** – Bastard alkanet (5, 92, 157, 158) (1876–1929), Corn gromwell (3, 5, 50, 62, 72, 80, 93, 97, 155, 156, 157, 158) (1900–present), False alkanet (156) (1923), Field gromwell (187) (1818), Gromwell (92) (1876), Hoorletta (Swedish) (46) (1879), Lichwale (157, 158) (1900–1929), Painting plant [Painting-plant] (156, 157, 158) (1900–1929), Pearl plant [Pearl-plant] (5, 156, 157, 158) (1900–1929), Pigeon-weed [Pigeonweed, Pigeon weed] (62, 156) (1912–1923), Puccoon (80, 85) (1913–1932), Redroot [Red-root, Red root] (62, 156) (1912–1923), Salfern (157, 158) (1900–1929), Salfern stone seed [Salfern-stone seed] (5, 156) (1913–1923), Sminckrot (Swedish) (46) (1879), Steen-crout (19) (1840), Stone seed [Stone Seed, Stone-Seed] (19, 92, 157, 158) (1840–1929), Wheat-thief [Wheat thief] (19, 62, 156) (1840–1923)

***Buglossoides* Moench** – Buglossoides (50) (present)

***Bugula* Juss.** – See *Ajuga* L.

***Bulbilis dactyloides* (Nutt.) Raf.** – See *Buchloe dactyloides* (Nutt.) Engelm.

***Bulbilis* Raf.** – See *Buchloe* Engelm.

***Bulbostylis capillaris* (L.) Kunth ex C.B. Clarke** – Dense-tuft hairsedge [Densetuft hairsedge] (50) (present)

Bulbostylis capillaris* (L.) Kunth ex C.B. Clarke subsp. *capillaris – Dense-tuft hairsedge [Densetuft hairsedge] (50) (present), Hair-like fimbristylis (66) (1903), Hair-like stenophyllus (5, 72) (1907–1913)

***Bulbostylis* Kunth** – Hair-sedge [Hairsedge] (50) (present)

Bumelia angustifolia – See *Sideroxylon celastrinum* (Kunth) T.D. Pennington

***Bumelia decandra* L.** – possibly *Sideroxylon lycioides* L.

***Bumelia foetidissima* (Jacq.) Willd.** – See *Sideroxylon foetidissimum* Jacq. subsp. *foetidissimum*

***Bumelia lanuginosa* (Michx.) Pers.** – See *Sideroxylon lanuginosum* Michx.

***Bumelia lanuginosa* (Michx.) Pers. var. *oblongifolia* (Nutt.) Clark** – See *Sideroxylon lanuginosum* Michx. subsp. *oblongifolium* (Nutt.) T.D. Pennington

***Bumelia lycioides* (L.) Pers.** – See *Sideroxylon lycioides* L.

***Bumelia lycopoides* Pers.** – See *Sideroxylon lycioides* L.

***Bumelia oblongifolia* Nutt.** – See *Sideroxylon lanuginosum* Michx. subsp. *oblongifolium* (Nutt.) T.D. Pennington

***Bumelia reclinata* Vent.** – See *Sideroxylon reclinatum* Michx. subsp. *reclinatum*

***Bumelia schottii* Britton** – See *Sideroxylon celastrinum* (Kunth) T.D. Pennington

***Bumelia* Swz.** – See *Sideroxylon* L.

***Bumelia tenax* Willd.** – See *Sideroxylon tenax* L.

***Bumellia lanuginosa* (Michx.) Pers.** – See *Sideroxylon lanuginosum* Michx.

***Bunias americana* Raf.** – See *Cakile maritima* Scop.

***Bunias cakile* L.** – See *Cakile maritima* Scop.

***Bunium bulbocastanum* L.** – Kipper nut (92) (1876)

***Buphthalmum frutescens* L.** – See *Borrichia arborescens* (L.) DC.

***Buphthalmum helianthoides* [L.]** – See *Heliopsis helianthoides* (L.) Sweet

***Bupleurum* L.** – Bupleurum (50) (present), Thorough-wax [Thorough wax, Thoroughwax, Thorough Waxe, Thorow-wax] (4) (1986)

***Bupleurum rotundifolium* L.** – Hare's-ear [Hare's ear, Hares ear, Haresear] (5, 50, 85, 92, 97, 156) (1876–present), Modesty (5, 131, 156) (1899–1923), Perfoliata (174, 178) (1523–1753), Thorough-wax [Thorough wax, Thoroughwax, Thorough Waxe, Thorow-wax] (5, 19, 107, 156, 178, 184) (1526–1923), Thoroughwort [Thorough wort, Thorough-wort] (5, 156) (1913–1923)

***Burmannia biflora* L.** – Northern bluethread (50) (present), Northern burmannia (5) (1913)

***Bursa bursa-pastoris* (L.) Britton** – See *Capsella bursa-pastoris* (L.) Medik.

***Bursera acuminata* Willd.** – See *Dacryodes excelsa* Vahl

***Bursera gummifera* L.** – See *Bursera simaruba* (L.) Sargent

***Bursera simaruba* (L.) Sargent** – Almicigo (Spanish) (20) (1857), American gum tree (107, 174) (1753–1919), Caranna gum (92) (1876), Gomart d'Amerique (French) (20) (1857), Gumbo limbo (15) (1895), Gummier (French) (20) (1857), Indian birch (107) (1919), Mastic tree (15, 20) (1857–1895), West Indian birch tree (20) (1857)

***Butomus* L.** – Flowering-rush [Flowering rush] (109) (1949)

***Butomus umbellatus* L.** – Flowering-rush [Flowering rush] (3, 50) (1977–present), Grassy rush (107) (1919), Water gladiolus (107) (1919)

***Buxus* L.** Box or Box tree [Box-tree, Box tre] (179) (1526)

***Buxus sempervirens* L.** – Box or Box tree [Box-tree, Box tre] (19, 49, 92, 107) (1840–1919), Boxwood [Box wood] (7) (1828), Common box (109) (1949)

***Byrsonima coriacea* (Sw.) DC.** – See *Byrsonima spicata* (Cav.) Kunth

***Byrsonima crassifolia* (L.) Kunth** – Alcornoque of Spain (92) (1876), Cork or Cork tree [Cork-tree, Corktree] (92) (1876)

***Byrsonima spicata* (Cav.) Kunth** – Locust-berry [Locust berry] (92) (1876)

C

Cabomba **Aubl.** – Fanwort (50, 109) (1949–present), Watershield [Water shield, Water-shield] (109) (1949)

Cabomba caroliniana **Gray** – Cabomba (5, 106) (1913–1930), Carolina fanwort (50) (present), Carolina watershield [Carolina water shield, Carolina water-shield] (5, 156) (1913–1923), Fanwort (3, 4, 156) (1923–1986), Fish-grass (109) (1949), Washington plant (109) (1949), Watershield [Water shield, Water-shield] (106) (1930)

Cacalia atriplicifolia **L.** – See *Arnoglossum atriplicifolium* (L.) H.E. Robins.

Cacalia **L. (GP species)** – See *Arnoglossum* Raf.

Cacalia plantaginea **(Raf.) Shinners** – See *Arnoglossum plantagineum* Raf.

Cacalia reniformis **Muhl.** – See *Arnoglossum muehlenbergii* (Schultz-Bip.) H. E. Robins.

Cacalia suaveolens **L.** – See *Hasteola suaveolens* (L.) Pojark.

Cacalia tuberosa **Nutt.** – See *Arnoglossum plantagineum* Raf.

Cactus ficus-indica **L.** – See *Opuntia ficus-indica* (L.) Mill.

Cactus grandiflorus **Haw.** – See *Selenicereus grandiflorus* (L.) Britt. & Rose

Cactus grandiflorus **L.** – See *Selenicereus grandiflorus* (L.) Britt. & Rose

Cactus **L.** – See Opuntia Mill.

Cactus missouriensis **(Sweet) Kuntze** – See *Escobaria missouriensis* (Sweet) D. R. Hunt var. *missouriensis*

Cactus opuntia **L.** – See *Opuntia ficus-indica* (L.) Mill.

Cactus phyllanthoides **DC.** – See *Disocactus phyllanthoides* (DC.) Barthlott.

Cactus pusillus **Kuntze** – possibly *Opuntia pusilla* (Haw.) Nutt.

Cactus serpentinus **Lag. & Rodr.** – See *Disocactus flagelliformis* (L.) Barthlott

Cactus viviparus **Nutt.** – See *Escobaria vivipara* (Nutt.) Buxbaum var. *vivipara*

Caesalpina california – See *Caesalpinia pannosa* Brandegee

Caesalpina pulcherrima **Sw.** – See *Caesalpinia pulcherrima* (L.) Sw.

Caesalpinia bijuga **(L.) Sw.)** – See *Caesalpinia vesicaria* L.

Caesalpinia bonduc **(L.) Roxb.** – Bonduc (52) (1919), Bonduc nuts (92) (1876), Indian hazel nut (92) (1876), Yellow nicker (50) (present)

Caesalpinia bonducella **[L.]** – See *Caesalpinia bonduc* (L.) Roxb.

Caesalpinia brasiliensis **L.** – See *Lonchocarpus punctatus* Kunth

Caesalpinia californica **Standl.** – See *Caesalpinia pannosa* Brandegee

Caesalpinia crista **auct. non L.** – See *Caesalpinia bonduc* (L.) Roxb.

Caesalpinia drepanocarpa **(Gray) Fisher** – Sickle-pod holdback [Sicklepod holdback] (50) (present), Sicklepod rushpea [Sicklepod rush-pea] (4) (1986)

Caesalpinia gilliesii **(Hook.) Wallich ex D. Dietr.** – Bird-of-paradise flower [Bird of paradise flower] (106, 124, 153) (1913–1937)

Caesalpinia jamesii **(Torr. & Gray) Fisher** – James' hoffmannseggia [James' hoffmanseggia] (5, 97) (1913–1937), James' holdback (50) (present), James' rushpea [James rush-pea] (4) (1986)

Caesalpinia **L.** – Bonduc (8) (1785), Brasiletto (167) (1814) tropical species, Caesalpinia (155) (1942), Cniquier (French) (8) (1785), Nickar tree [Nickar-tree] (8) (1785), Nicker (50) (present), Sappan (158) (1900)

Caesalpinia mexicana **Gray** – California wood (92) (1876)

Caesalpinia mexicana **var. californica A. Gray** – See *Caesalpinia pannosa* Brandegee

Caesalpinia pulcherrima **(L.) Sw.** – Barbados flowerfence [Barbados flower fence] (92, 109) (1876–1949), Barbados pride [Barbados pride] (92, 109) (1876–1949), Dwarf poinciana (109) (1949)

Cajanus cajan **(L.) Millsp.** – Angola pea (92) (1876), Cajan (109)

(1949), Doll (4, 110, 156) (1886–1986), Pigeon-pea [Pigeonpea, Pigeon pea] (92, 109, 110) (1876–1949), Pois d'Angola (French Antilles) (110) (1886), Pois de Congo (French Antilles) (110) (1886), Pois pigeon (French Antilles) (110) (1886)

Cajanus cajan **Millsp.** – See *Cajanus cajan* (L.) Millsp.

Cajanus **DC.** – See *Cajanus* Adans.

Cajanus indicus **Sprengel** – See *Cajanus cajan* (L.) Millsp.

Cakile **(Tour.) Ludwig.** – possibly *Cakile* Mill.

Cakile americana **Nutt.** – See *Cakile edentula* (Bigelow) Hook. subsp. *edentula* var. *edentula*

Cakile edentula **(Bigelow) Hook.** – American sea rocket (5, 156) (1913–1923)

Cakile edentula **(Bigelow) Hook. subsp. *edentula* var. *edentula*** – American sea rocket (2) (1895), Sea rocket (19) (1840)

Cakile geniculata **(B. L. Robins.) Millsp.** – Salt-water mustard [Salt water mustard] (122) (1937) TX

Cakile maritima **Scop.** – See *Cakile maritima* Scop., Sea cole [Seacole] (7, 92) (1828–1876), Sea rocket (41, 92, 107) (1170–1919), Sea-tears (46) (1671)

Cakile **P. Mill. (possibly)** – Sea rocket (1, 10, 13, 15, 156) (1818–1932)

Caladium esculentum – See *Colocasia esculenta* (L.) Schott

Caladium sagittifolium **(L.) Vent.** – See *Xanthosoma sagittifolium* (L.) Schott

Caladium seguinum – See *Dieffenbachia seguine* (Jacq.) Schott

Calamagrostis **Adans.** – Reed bent grass (10, 45, 66) (1818–1903) , Reed grass [Reedgrass, Reed-grass] (1, 50, 93, 155) (1932–present)

Calamagrostis arenaria – See *Ammophila arenaria* (L.) Link

Calamagrostis brevipilis – See *Calamovilfa brevipilis* (Torr.) Hack. ex Scribn. & Southw.

Calamagrostis breviseta **(Gray) Scribn.** – See *Calamagrostis pickeringii* Gray

Calamagrostis breweri **Thurb.** – Brewer's reed-grass (94) (1901)

Calamagrostis californica **Kearney** – See *Calamagrostis stricta* (Timm) Koel. subsp. *inexpansa* (Gray) C.W. Greene

Calamagrostis canadensis **(Michx.) Beauv.** – Bluejoint [Blue-joint, Blue joint] (3, 11, 45, 50, 56, 75, 87, 88, 115, 116, 129) (1884–present), Blue-joint grass [Blue-joint grass] (56, 66, 68, 90, 92, 93) (1885–1936), Blue-joint reed grass [Bluejoint reedgrass] (140, 155) (1942–1944), Canadian small-reed (90) (1885), Redtop [Redtop, Red top] (56) (1901), Reed grass [Reedgrass, Reed-grass] (19, 85) (1840–1932), Small reed grass (87, 90) (1884–1885), Yellowtop [Yellow-top, Yellow top, Yellowtops, Yellow-tops] (111) (1915) Neb

Calamagrostis canadensis **(Michx.) Beauv. var. acuminata Vasey ex Shear & Rydb.** – See *Calamagrostis stricta* (Timm) Koel. subsp. *inexpansa* (Gray) C. W. Greene

Calamagrostis canadensis **(Michx.) Beauv. var. canadensis** – Scribner's reed grass [Scribner reedgrass] (155) (1942)

Calamagrostis canadensis **(Michx.) Beauv. var. langsdorfii (Link) Inman** – Langsdorf's reed-bent (94) (1901)

Calamagrostis canadensis **(Michx.) Beauv. var. macouniana (Vasey) Stebbins** – Canadian bent grass [Canada bent grass] (68) (1890), Macoun's blue-joint reed grass [Macoun bluejoint reedgrass] (155) (1942), Macoun's reed bent [Macoun's reed-bent] (56, 94) (1897–1901), Macoun's reed grass [Macoun's reedgrass] (5, 50) (1913–present), Reed grass [Reedgrass, Reed-grass] (116) (1958), Sand grass [Sandgrass, Sand-grass] (68, 155) (1890–1942), Small reed grass (68) (1890)

Calamagrostis cinnoides **(Muhl.) Scribn.** – See *Calamagrostis coarctata* (Torr.) Eat.

Calamagrostis cinnoides **W. Bart. nom. super.** – See *Calamagrostis coarctata* (Torr.) Eat.

Calamagrostis coarctata (Torr.) Eat. – Arctic reedgrass (50) (present), Crowded calamagrostis (66) (1903), Glaucous small reed (66) (1903), Nuttall's reed grass [Nuttall's reed-grass] (5, 94) (1901–1913), Reed bent grass (5) (1913), Reed-like calamagrostis (187) (1818), Wild oat [Wild oats] (5) (1913)

Calamagrostis colorata Sibthorp – See *Phalaris arundinacea* L.

Calamagrostis confinis Nutt. – See *Calamagrostis lapponica* (Wahlenb.) Hartman

Calamagrostis curtissii (Vasey) Scribn. – See *Calamovilfa curtissii* (Vasey) Scribn.

Calamagrostis epigeios (L.) Roth – Small reed grass (42) (1814), possibly Reed [Rede, Reeds] (184) (1793)

Calamagrostis fascicularis Kearney – possibly *Calamagrostis rubescens* Buckley

Calamagrostis howellii Vasey – Howell's grass (87) (1884)

Calamagrostis hyperborea Lange – See *Calamagrostis stricta* (Timm) Koel. subsp. *inexpansa* (Gray) C.W. Greene

Calamagrostis hyperborea Lange var. *americana* (Vasey) Kearney – See *Calamagrostis stricta* (Timm) Koel. subsp. *inexpansa* (Gray) C.W. Greene

Calamagrostis inexpansa Gray – See *Calamagrostis stricta* (Timm) Koel. subsp. *inexpansa* (Gray) C.W. Greene

Calamagrostis labradorica Kearney – See *Calamagrostis stricta* (Timm) Koel. subsp. *inexpansa* (Gray) C.W. Greene

Calamagrostis langsdorfii (Link.) Trin. – See *Calamagrostis canadensis* (Michx.) Beauv. var. *langsdorfii* (Link) Inman

Calamagrostis lapponica (Wahlenb.) Hartman – Sand grass [Sandgrass, Sandgrass] (129) (1894)

Calamagrostis macouniana Vasey – See *Calamagrostis canadensis* (Michx.) Beauv. var. *macouniana* (Vasey) Stebbins

Calamagrostis montanensis Scribn. – Plains reed-grass [Plains reedgrass] (3, 50, 155, 185) (1936–present)

Calamagrostis neglecta (Ehrh.) Gaertn. – See *Calamagrostis stricta* (Timm) Koel. subsp. *stricta*

Calamagrostis pickeringi – See *Calamagrostis pickeringii* Gray

Calamagrostis pickeringii Gray – Alpine reed bent (66) (1903), Pickering's reed grass [Pickering reedgrass] (155) (1942), Short-awn reed grass [Short-awned reed-grass] (94) (1901)

Calamagrostis porteri Gray – Porter's reed bent (94) (1901)

Calamagrostis purpurascens R. Br. – Purple pine grass [Purple pine-grass] (140, 155) (1942–1944), Purple reed grass [Purple reedgrass] (3, 50, 140) (1944–present), Purple reed-bent (94) (1901)

Calamagrostis rubescens Buckley (possibly) – Couch bent grass [Couch bent-grass] (94) (1901)

Calamagrostis scopulorum M. E. Jones – Broom reed grass [Broom reed-grass] (94) (1901)

Calamagrostis scribneri Beal – See *Calamagrostis canadensis* (Michx.) Beauv. var. *canadensis*

Calamagrostis sesquiflora (Trin.) Tzvelev – Vasey's reed grass [Vasey's reed-grass] (94) (1901)

Calamagrostis stricta (Timm) Koel. – Bunch grass [Bunchgrass, Bunch-grass] (87) (1884), Slim-stem reed grass [Slimstem reedgrass] (50) (present)

Calamagrostis stricta (Timm) Koel. subsp. *inexpansa* (Gray) C. W. Greene – Bog reed grass [Bog reed-grass] (5, 56, 85, 93, 94, 116) (1901–1958), Close-flower small reed [Close-flowered small reed] (66) (1903), Labrador reed grass (5) (1913), Northern reed grass [Northern reed-grass, Northern reedgrass] (3, 5, 50, 93, 116, 155) (1913–present), Sharp-point red-top [Sharp pointed red top] (56) (1901), Sierra reed grass [Sierra reedgrass] (155) (1942)

Calamagrostis stricta (Timm) Koel. subsp. *stricta* – Narrow reed grass (5) (1913), Pony grass (5, 111, 115, 116) (1913–1958), Slim-stem reed grass [Slimstem reedgrass] (50, 155) (1942–present), Yellowtop [Yellow-top, Yellow top, Yellowtops, Yellow-tops] (5) (1913)

Calamagrostis vaseyi Beal – See *Calamagrostis sesquiflora* (Trin.) Tzvelev

Calamaria saccharata (Engelm.) Kuntze – See *Isoetes saccharata* Engelm.

Calamintha alpina (L.) Lam. – See *Clinopodium alpinum* (L.) Kuntze

Calamintha clinopodium Benth. – possibly *Clinopodium vulgare* L. (Spenn on PL)

Calamintha glabella Benth. – See *Clinopodium glabellum* (Michx.) Kuntze

Calamintha Mill. – Calamint [Calamynt] (1, 2, 179) (1895–1932), Nespyte (179) (1526) Neb OK Quebec SD

Calamintha Moench – See *Calamintha* Mill.

Calamintha nepeta (L.) Savi – Sweete calamint (178) (1526) Neb OK SD

Calamintha nepeta (L.) Savi subsp. *nepeta* – Basil-thyme [Basil thyme] (156) (1923) misapplied, Calamint [Calamynt] (156) (1923), Calaminth (156) (1923), Field balm [Field-balm] (5, 156) (1913–1923), Field calamint (5) (1913), Field thyme (156) (1923), Lesser calamint (5, 156) (1913–1923), Mountain-mint [Mountain mint, Mountainmint] (190) (~1759) San Diego Co. CA

Calamintha officinalis – See *Calamintha sylvatica* Bromf. subsp. *ascendens* (Jord.) P.W. Ball

Calamintha sylvatica Bromf. subsp. *ascendens* (Jord.) P. W. Ball – Calamint [Calamynt] (92) (1876), Calamint of the mountain [Calamynt of the mountayne] (179) (1526)

Calamovilfa (Gray) Hack. ex Scribn. & Southworth – Reed grass [Reedgrass, Reed-grass] (1) (1932), Sand grass [Sand-grass, Sand-grass] (1, 93) (1932–1936), Sand-reed [Sandreed] (50, 155) (1942–present), Pine Barren sandreed (50) (present), Purple bent (66) (1903), Purple bent grass (5, 92) (1876–1913), Short-hair reed grass [Short-haired reed grass] (5, 94) (1901–1913)

Calamovilfa curtissii (Vasey) Scribn. – Southern reed grass [Southern reed-grass] (94) (1901)

Calamovilfa gigantea (Nutt.) Scribn, & Merr. – Big sandreed [Big sand-reed] (3, 119, 155) (1938–1977), Carrizo [Carizo, Carizzo] (119) (1938) OK, Giant reed grass [Giant reed-grass] (5, 163) (1852–1913), Giant sandreed (50) (present)

Calamovilfa longifolia (Hook.) Scribn. – Big sand grass (5, 56, 129) (1901–1894), Carrizo [Carizo, Carizzo] (5) (1913), Long-leaf reed grass [Long-leaved reedgrass, Long-leaved reed-grass, Long-leaved reed grass] (5, 56, 94, 111, 116, 163) (1851–1958), Prairie sandreed (3, 50, 140, 155) (1942–present), Reed grass [Reedgrass, Reed-grass] (85, 116) (1932–1958), Sand grass [Sandgrass, Sand-grass] (56, 75, 116, 140) (1894–1944), Sand reed grass [Sand reed-grass] (115, 116) (1932–1958), Woolly bent (66) (1903)

Calamus draco Willd. – See *Daemonorops draco* (Willd.) Blume

Calandrinia ciliata (Ruiz & Pav.) DC. – Mother's-beauties [Mother's beauties] (74) (1893)

Calandrinia menziesii [(Hook.) Torr. & A.Gray] – See *Calandrinia ciliata* (Ruiz & Pav.) DC.

Calathea zebrina (Sims) Lindl. – Zebra plant (109) (1949)

Calceolaria Loefl. – See *Hybanthus* Jacq.

Calceolaria verticillata (Ort.) Kuntze – See *Hybanthus verticillatus* (Ort.) Baill.

Calea aspera Jacq. – See *Melanthera aspera* (Jacq.) Steud. ex Small var. *aspera*

Calendula L. – Marigold [Marigolds, Mary gold, Marygold] (92) (1876)

Calendula officinalis L. – Calendula (49, 52, 54, 55, 92) (1876–1919), Diuerse sorts of Marigoldes (178) (1526), Garden marigold (49, 53, 58) (1898–1922), Goldins gold (107) (1919), Marigold [Marigolds, Mary gold, Marygold] (46, 49, 52, 53, 54, 55, 57, 59, 61, 92) (1571–1922) cultivated by English colonists by 1671, Mary-buds [Mary bud] (92) (1876), Mary-gowles [Mary gowles] (179) (1526), Pot marigold [Pot marygold] (19, 42, 107) (1814–1919), Pot-marigold (109) (1949), Ruddes (179) (1526)

Calibrachoa parviflora (Juss.) D'Arcy – Wild petunia (122, 124) (1937) TX

Calla aethiopica – See *Zantedeschia aethiopica* (L.) Spreng.

Calla **L.** – Calla (1, 155, 158) (1900–1942) ancient name, calla or calla lily of florists is *Zantedeschia,* Water-arum [Water arum] (1, 109, 158, 167) (1814–1949)

Calla palustris **L.** – Arona (46) (1879), Bog arum (86) (1878), Faverole (158) (1900), Female dragon [Female-dragon] (5, 158) (1900–1913), Female water-dragon (156) (1923), Marsh calla (42) (1814), Missebroed (Lapland) (46, 86) (1878–1879), Starchwort [Starchwort] (86) (1878) old English name, Swamp-robin [Swamp robin] (5, 7, 92, 156, 157, 158) (1828–1929), Water-arum [Water arum] (5, 19, 50, 78, 86, 107, 156, 158) (1840–present), Water-dragon [Water dragon] (5, 107, 156, 158) (1900–1923), Waterlily [Water lily, Water-lily, Water-lilies] (5, 156) (1913–1923), Wild calla (3, 5, 155, 156, 158) (1900–1977)

Calla virginica **Michx.** – See *Hexastylis virginica* (L.) Small

Callicarpa americana **L.** – American beauty-berry [American beautyberry] (4, 50, 155) (1942–present), American callicarpa (42) (1814), Beauty-berry [Beautyberry] (156) (1923), Beauty-fruit (156) (1923), Bermuda mulberry (5, 65, 156, 158) (1900–1931), Callicarpa (174, 177) (1753–1762), Callicarpa d'Amerique (French) (8) (1785), Carolina shrubby callicarpa [Carolinian shrubby callicarpa] (8) (1785)**,** French-mulberry [French mulberry] (2, 5, 58, 77, 97, 106, 109, 122, 124, 156, 158) (1895–1949), Possum-berry [Possum berry] (156) (1923), Sour bush [Sourbush, Sour-bush] (58, 156, 158) (1869–1923), Sowerbush (7) (1828), Spanish mulberry [Spanish-mulberry] (156) (1923), White American beauty-berry [White American beautyberry] (155) (1942)

Callicarpa americana **L. var.** *lactea* **F.J. Muell.** – See *Callicarpa americana* L.

Callicarpa dichotoma **(Lour.) K. Koch** – Laver (107) (1919), Slokam (107) (1919), Sloke (107) (1919)

Callicarpa **L.** – Beauty-berry [Beautyberry] (109, 155) (1942–1949), Beauty-fruit (156) (1923), Bermuda mulberry (10) (1818), Callicarpa (8, 158) (1785–1900)

Callirhoe alcaeoides **(Michx.) Gray** – Callirhoe (114) (1894), Light poppy-mallow [Light poppymallow, Light poppy mallow] (5, 50, 97, 122) (1913–present), Pink poppy-mallow [Pink poppy mallow] (3, 4, 93) (1936–1986), Poppy-mallow [Poppy mallow, Poppymallow] (95, 156) (1911–1923)

Callirhoe alcaeoides **Gray.** – See *Callirhoe alcaeoides* (Michx.) Gray

Callirhoe bushii **Fern.** – Bush's poppy-mallow [Bush's poppymallow] (50) (present)

Callirhoe digitata **Nutt.** – Annual winecup [Annual wine cup] (124) (1937), Finger poppy-mallow [Finger poppymallow, Finger poppy mallow] (3, 4, 155) (1942–1986), Fringed poppy-mallow [Fringed poppy mallow] (5, 97, 122, 156) (1913–1937), Mallow-wort [Mallow wort] (92) (1876), Wild hollyhock [Wild hollyhocks] (156) (1923), Winecup [Wine cup, Wine-cup] (50, 156) (1923–present)

Callirhoe involucrata **(Nutt.) Gray** – See *Callirhoe involucrata* (Torr. & Gray) Gray

Callirhoe involucrata **(Torr. & Gray) Gray** – Clustered poppy mallow (156) (1923), Low poppy-mallow [Low poppymallow] (155) (1942), Perennial wine cup (124) (1937), Pezhuta nantiazilia (Dakota, smoke treatment medicine) (37) (1919), Purple mallow (37, 85, 107) (1919–1932), Purple poppy-mallow [Purple poppy mallow, Purple poppymallow] (2, 4, 50, 5, 72, 86, 93, 97) (187–present), Wild geranium (156) (1923), Winecup [Wine cup, Wine-cup] (122) (1937)

Callirhoe involucrata **(Torr. & Gray) Gray var.** *involucrata* – Purple poppy-mallow [Purple poppy mallow, Purple poppymallow] (50) (present)

Callirhoe leiocarpa **Martin** – Tall poppy-mallow [Tall poppy mallow, Tall poppymallow] (50, 155) (1942–present)

Callirhoe **Nutt.** – Poppy-mallow [Poppy mallow, Poppymallow] (1, 4, 50, 82, 93, 109, 155, 156, 158) (1900–present)

Callirhoe papaver **(Cav.) Gray** – Large purple poppy (97) (1937), Woodland poppy-mallow [Woodland poppy mallow, Woodland poppymallow] (50) (present)

Callirhoe pedata **(Nutt. ex Hook.) Gray** – Pimple mallow (103, 107) (1870–1919), Tall poppy-mallow [Tall poppy mallow, Tall poppymallow] (97) (1937)

Callirhoe pedata **Gray** – See *Callirhoe pedata* (Nutt. ex Hook.) Gray

Callirhoe triangulata **(Leavenworth) Gray** – Clustered poppy mallow (5, 72, 97, 122) (1907–1937), Moŋkoŋ toŋga žiŋga (Osage, Little big medicine) (121) (1918?–1970?), Poppy-mallow [Poppy mallow, Poppymallow] (121) (1970)

Callirhoe triangulata **Gray** – See *Callirhoe triangulata* (Leavenworth) Gray

Callirrhoe – See *Callirhoe* Nutt.

Callirrhoe alceoides – See *Callirhoe alcaeoides* (Michx.) Gray

Callisia graminea **(Small) G. Tucker** – Grass-leaf roseling [Grassleaf roseling] (50) (present), Grass-like spiderwort (5, 97) (1913–1937)

Callisia graminifolia **(Raf.) D. R. Hunt** – See *Callisia graminea* (Small) G. Tucker

Callisia rosea **(Vent.) D.R. Hunt** – Piedmont roseling (50) (present), Rose-colored spiderwort (156) (1923)

Callistemon **R. Br.** – Bottlebrush [Bottle brush, Bottle-brush] (109) (1949)

Callistephus chinensis **(L.) Nees** – China aster (19, 92, 109) (1840–1949), Christmas daisy (92) (1876), Fall-roses [Fall roses] (73) (1892) Mansfield OH

Callistephus chinensis **Nees** – See *Callistephus chinensis* (L.) Nees

Callitriche austinii **Engelm.** – See *Callitriche terrestris* Raf.

Callitriche autumnale **L.** – See *Callitriche hermaphroditica* L.

Callitriche bifida **(L.) Morong.** – See *Callitriche hermaphroditica* L.

Callitriche hermaphroditica **L.** – Autumn water-starwort [Autumn waterstarwort] (155) (1942), Autumnal starwort (131) (1899), Northern water-starwort (50) (present), Water-starwort [Water starwort, Waterstarwort] (3, 120) (1938–1977)

Callitriche heterophylla **Pursh** – Large water-starwort (120) (1938), Larger water-starwort [Larger waterstarwort] (5, 155) (1913–1942), Two-head water-starwort [Twoheaded water-starwort] (50) (present)

Callitriche heterophylla **Pursh subsp.** *heterophylla* – Two-head water-starwort [Twoheaded water-starwort] (50) (present)

Callitriche **L.** – Star-grass [Star grass, Stargrass] (92) (1876), Water-chickweed [Water chickweed] (23) (1826), Water-star [Water star] (10) (1818), Water-starwort [Water starwort, Waterstarwort] (1, 4, 50, 155) (1932–present)

Callitriche palustris **L.** – Callitriche (174, 177) (1753–1762), Common water starwort [Common waterstarwort, Common water-starwort] (155) (1942), Star-grass [Star grass, Stargrass] (184) (1793), Vernal water-starwort [Vernal water starwort] (5, 50, 72, 122, 156) (1907–present), Water-chickweed [Water chickweed] (5, 49, 92, 156) (1876–1923), Water-fennel [Water fennel] (5, 93, 131, 156, 157) (1899–1936), Water-starwort [Water starwort, Waterstarwort] (49, 85, 92, 93, 157) (1876–1929)

Callitriche terrestris **Raf.** – Terrestrial water-starwort [Terrestrial water starwort] (5, 50, 156) (1913–present)

Callitriche verna **L.** – See *Callitriche palustris* L.

Calluna **Salisb.** – Heather (109, 156) (1923–1949)

Calluna vulgaris **(L.) Hull** – Besom (5) (1913), Heath (107) (1919), Heather (5, 92, 106, 156) (1876–1930), Ling (5, 92, 156) (1876–1923), Moor-besom [Moor besom] (156) (1923) no longer in use by 1923, Moorwort [Moor-wort] (5) (1913)

Calluna vulgaris **(L.) Salisb.** – See *Calluna vulgaris* (L.) Hull

Calmia latifolia – See *Kalmia latifolia* L.

Calocarpum **Pierre** – See *Pouteria* Aubl.

Calocarpum sapota **Merr.** – See *Pouteria sapota* (Jacq.) H.E. Moore & Stearn

Calocedrus decurrens **(Torr.) Florin** – California incense-cedar (138) (1923), California white cedar (161) (1857), White cedar (75, 147) (1856–1894) CA

Calochortus albus **Dougl. ex Benth.** – Fairy lantern (109) (1949)

Calochortus amabilis **Purdy** – Golden fairy-lantern [Golden fairy lantern] (109) (1949)

Calochortus elegans **Pursh** – Star tulip (107) (1919)
Calochortus gunnisoni **Wats.** – See *Calochortus gunnisonii* S. Wats.
Calochortus gunnisonii **S. Wats.** – Butterfly lily [Butterfly-lily] (5) (1913), Gunnison's mariposa [Gunnison mariposa] (155) (1942), Gunnison's mariposa lily (5, 50, 93) (1913–present), Mariposa lily [Mariposa lilies, Mariposa-lily, Mariposalily] (85) (1932), Sego lily [Segolily] (3) (1977)
Calochortus gunnisonii **S. Wats. var.** *gunnisonii* – Gunnison's mariposa lily (50) (present)
Calochortus luteus **Dougl. ex Lindl.** – Butterfly tulip [Butter-fly tulip] (107) (1919), Butterfly weed [Butter-fly weed, Butterflyweed, Butterfly-weed] (86) (1878) CA, Mariposa lily [Mariposa lilies, Mariposa-lily, Mariposalily] (86) (1878), Sago (Utah Indians) (103) (1871), Sego lily [Segolily] (107) (1919), Wild sago (103) (1871), Wild tulip (86) (1878) CA, Yellow pretty-grass (86) (1878)
Calochortus nuttallii **Torr. & Gray** – Mariposa lily [Mariposa lilies, Mariposa-lily, Mariposalily] (3, 75, 85, 127, 157) (1894–1977), Nuttall's Mariposa lily (5, 93) (1913–1936), Sego lily [Segolily] (50, 155) (1942–present)
Calochortus **Pursh.** – Butterfly lily [Butterfly-lily] (1, 93, 109) (1932–1949), Globe-tulip (109) (1949), Mariposa lily [Mariposa lilies, Mariposa-lily, Mariposalily] (1, 75, 93, 101, 109, 155, 158) (1886–1949) Spanish for butterfly, Mariposa tulip [Mariposatulip] (155) (1942), Sago lily (1, 93, 190) (~1759–1936) Native Americans called roots "sego", Sego lily [Segolily] (101) (1905)
Calochortus venustus **Bentham.** – See *Calochortus venustus* Dougl. ex Benth.
Calochortus venustus **Dougl. ex Benth.** – Butterfly tulip [Butter-fly tulip] (86) (1878), Mariposa lily [Mariposa lilies, Mariposa-lily, Mariposalily] (86) (1878)
Calodendrum capense **Thunb.** – See *Calodendrum capense* (L.f.) Thunb.
Calonyction **Choisy** – See *Ipomoea* L.
Calonyction speciosum **[Choisy]** – See *Ipomoea alba* L.
Calopogon pulchellus **R. Br. ex Ait. f.** – See *Calopogon tuberosus* (L.) Britton, Sterns & Poggenb. var. *tuberosus*
Calopogon **R. Br. ex Ait. f.** – Grass-pink orchid (109) (1949), Calopogon, Grass-pink [Grass pink] (1, 75, 156) (1894–1932)
Calopogon tuberosus **(L.) B.S.P. var.** *latifolius* **(St. John) Boivin** – See *Calopogon tuberosus* (L.) Britton, Sterns & Poggenb. var. *tuberosus*
Calopogon tuberosus **(L.) B.S.P. var.** *tuberosus* – Bearded pink (5, 156) (1913–1923), Calopogon (5, 48, 156) (1913–1923), Grass-pink [Grass pink] (5, 72, 86, 122, 156) (1878–1937), Grass-pink orchid (138) (1923), Meadow-gift (156) (1923), Swamp pink [Swamppink, Swamp-pink] (5, 156) (1913–1923), Tuberous grasspink (50) (present), possibly Beautiful tuberous cymbidium (42) (1814)
Calopogon tuberosus **(L.) Britton, Sterns & Poggenb. var.** *tuberosus* – Grass-pink [Grass pink] (19) (1840)
Caltha **(Rupp.) L.** – See *Caltha* L.
Caltha dentata **[Muehl.]** – See *Caltha palustris* L.
Caltha flabellifolia **Pursh** – See *Caltha palustris* L.
Caltha **L.** – Cowslip [Cowslips, Cowslyp] (7) (1828), Marsh-marigold [Marsh marigold, Marshmarigold, Marsh mary-gold, Marsh mary-gold] (1, 4, 7, 10, 13, 15, 50, 93, 109, 155, 156, 158, 167) (1814–present), Meadow gowan (1) (1932), Meadow-bout [Meadow bouts, Meadow-bouts, Meadowbouts] (7) (1828)
Caltha leptosepala **DC.** – Marsh-marigold [Marsh marigold, Marsh-marigold, Marsh mary-gold, Marsh marygold] (190) (~1759)
Caltha natans **Pallas ex Georgi** – Floating marsh-marigold [Floating marsh marigold] (5) (1913)
Caltha palustris **L.** – American cowslip [American cowslips] (5, 6, 19) (1840–1913), Boots (5) (1913), Bullflower [Bull-flower] (5, 156, 157, 158) (1900–1929), Bull's-eyes [Bull's eyes, Bullseye, Bulls-eyes] (156) (1923), Buttercup [Butter cup, Buttercups] (14) (1882), Capers (5, 76, 157, 158) (1896–1929) Berwick ME, Coltsfoot [Colt's foot, Colt's-foot, Colt foot] (5, 76) (1896) ME, Coltsroot (76) (1896–1913) Sulphur Grove OH, Common marsh-marigold

[Common marshmarigold, Common marsh marygold] (42, 155) (1814–1942), Cowlily [Cow-lily, Cow lily] (5, 74, 156, 157, 158) (1893–1929), Cowlips [Cow lips] (6) (1892), Cowslip [Cowslips, Cowslyp] (2, 5, 6, 12, 5, 40, 92, 107, 156, 157, 158) (1892–1929), Cowslop [Cowslops] (74, 157, 158) (1893–1929) Ferrisburgh VT, Crazy bet [Crazy-bet] (5, 157) (1913–1929), Crowfoot [Crow-foot, Crow foot, Crowfote, Crow's foot] (5, 76, 156, 157, 158) (1896–1929) South Berwick ME, Drunkards (5, 157) (1913–1929), Gaged marsh marigold [Gaged marsh marygold] (42) (1814), Goldflower [Gold flower] (86) (1878), Gools (5, 156, 157) (1913–1929), Great bitter-flower [Great bitter flower] (5) (1913), Great butter-flower [Great butter flower] (157, 158) (1900–1929) IA, Horseblob [Horse blobs, Horse blob, Horse-blob] (5, 92, 156, 157) (1876–1929), Kingcup [King cup, King cups, Kingcups, King's cup, Kings' cup] (5, 156) (1913–1923), Mare blebs (6) (1892), Mare blobs (6) (1892), Marigold [Marigolds, Mary gold, Marygold] (72) (1907) IA, Marsh goldflower [Marsh gold-flower] (86) (1878), Marsh-marigold [Marsh marigold, Marshmarigold, Marsh mary-gold, Marsh marygold] (1, 3, 5, 6, 14, 15, 19, 63, 85, 86, 92, 105, 107, 127, 131, 3, 156, 157, 158, 187) (1818–1977) from Saxon merse mear-geallia "marsh-horse gold", May blobs [May-blob] (5, 156, 157) (1900–1929) England, Meadow buttercup [Meadow buttercups] (5, 74, 156, 158) (1893–1923), Meadow cowslip (187) (1818), Meadow-bout [Meadow bouts, Meadow-bouts, Meadowbouts] (5, 92, 157, 184) (1793–1929), Meadow-bright [Meadow bright] (107) (1919), Meadow-gowan [Meadow gowan (156, 157) (1900–1929), Mingde-beguk (Chippewa, wide leaf) (105) (1932), Mireblobs [Mireblob, Mire blobs] (5, 157) (1913–1929), Mountain marsh-marigold [Mountain marsh marigold] (5) (1913), O'gite'bŭg (Chippewa) (40) (1928), Open gowan (5, 157) (1900–1929), Palsy-wort [Palsy wort] (5, 6, 92, 157, 158) (1892–1929), Soldier's-buttons [Soldier's buttons, Soldiers buttons] (5, 156, 157, 158) (1900–1929), Spring cowslip [Spring cowslips] (5, 157, 158) (1900–1929), Sumpf Ringelblume (German) (6) (1892), Waterblob [Water blob, Water-blob, Water blobs] (5, 92, 157) (1876–1929), Waterbouts [Water bouts] (6) (1892), Water-dragon [Water dragon] (5, 6, 92, 157, 158) (1892–1929), Water-goggles [Water goggles] (5, 156, 157, 158) (1900–1929), Water-gowan [Water gowan] (5, 157) (1913–1929), Yellow marsh-marigold [Yellow marsh marigold] (50) (present)
Caltha palustris **L. var.** *palustris* – Yellow marsh-marigold [Yellow marsh marigold] (50) (present)
Calvatia bovista **(L.) Macbride** – See *Calvatia gigantea* (Batsch) Lloyd
Calvatia caelata **(Bull.) Morgan** – Carved puffball (128) (1933) ND
Calvatia craniformis **Schw.** – See *Calvatia craniiformis* (Schwein.) Fr. ex De Toni
Calvatia craniiformis **(Schwein.) Fr. ex De Toni** – Puffball [Puff-ball, Puff ball, Puffballs, Puff balls] (40) (1928), Skull-shaped puffball (170) (1995)
Calvatia gigantea **(Batsch) Lloyd** – Giant puff-ball (72) (1907)
Calycanthus ferax **Michx.** – See *Calycanthus floridus* L. var. *glaucus* (Willd.) Torr. & Gray
Calycanthus fertilis **Walt.** – See *Calycanthus floridus* L. var. *glaucus* (Willd.) Torr. & Gray
Calycanthus floridus **L.** – Allspice of Carolina (183) (~1756), American allspice (156) (1923), Bubby-blossoms (156) (1923), Calycant de Caroline (8) (1785), Carolina allspice [Carolinian allspice] (8, 19, 92, 107, 109, 156) (1785–1949), Florida allspice (57) (1917), Hairy strawberry shrub (5) (1913), Spice bush [Spice-bush, Spicebush] (5, 76, 156) (1896–1923) Middlesborough MA, Strawberry bush [Strawberry-bush, (5, 74) (1893–1913) Eastern MA, Strawberry shrub [Strawberry-shrub] (156) (1923), Sweet Betsies (76) (1896) Alabama, plantation negroes, Sweet Betty [Sweet Betties, Sweet Bettie] (5, 156) (1913–1923), Sweet bubbie [Sweet bubbies] (5, 156) (1913–1923), Sweet shrub (5, 7, 92, 112, 156) (1828–1937), Sweet-scented shrub [Sweet-sented (*sic*) Shrub] (74, 76, 156, 184) (1793–1923)

Calycanthus floridus L. var. *glaucus* (Willd.) Torr. & Gray – Bubby-bush [Bubbybush, Bubby bush] (5, 74, 156) (1913–1923) Banner Elk NC, Smooth strawberry shrub (5) (1913), Strawberry shrub [Strawberry-shrub] (156) (1923), Sweet shrub (156) (1923)

Calycanthus glaucus Willd. – See *Calycanthus floridus* L. var. *glaucus* (Willd.) Torr. & Gray

Calycanthus L. – Calycant (8) (1785), Carolina allspice [Carolinian all-spice] (2, 8, 10, 82, 167) (1785–1930), Sweet shrub [Sweet-shrub] (109) (1949), Sweet-scented shrub [Sweet-sented (*sic*) Shrub] (2, 109, 156) (1895–1949)

Calycanthus laevigatus Willd. – See *Calycanthus floridus* L. var. *glaucus* (Willd.) Torr. & Gray

Calycocarpum lyoni (Pursh) Nutt. – Cupseed [Cup-seed, Cup seed] (2, 4, 5, 50, 97, 156) (1895–present), Wild sarsaparilla [Wild-sarsaparilla, Wild sarsaparilla] (122) (1937)

Calycocarpum lyoni Nutt. – See *Calycocarpum lyoni* (Pursh) Nutt.

Calycocarpum Nutt. – Calycocarpum (50) (present), Cupseed [Cup-seed, Cup seed] (1, 158) (1900–1932)

Calydorea coelestina (Bartr.) Goldblatt & Henrich – Bartram's ixia (50) (present), Celestial (124) (1937) TX, Dragonhead [Dragon-head, Dragon head, Dragon's head] (124) (1937) TX, Southern grass-lily (97) (1937)

Calylophus berlandieri Spach. – Berlandier's evening primrose [Berlandier evening primrose] (4) (1986), Berlandier's sundrops (50) (present)

Calylophus drummondianus Spach subsp. *drummondianus* – possibly *Calylophus berlandieri* Spach subsp. *pinifolius* (Engelm. ex A. Gray) Towner

Calylophus hartwegii (Benth.) Raven – Hartweg's evening-primrose [Hartweg evening primrose] (4) (1986), Hartweg's sundrops (50) (present)

Calylophus hartwegii (Benth.) Raven subsp. *hartwegii* – Galpinsia (97) (1937) OK

Calylophus hartwegii (Benth.) Raven subsp. *pubescens* (Gray) Towner & Raven – Oblong-leaf primrose [Oblong-leaved primrose] (5, 97) (1913–1937)

Calylophus lavandulifolius (Torr. & Gray) Raven – Lavender-leaf evening-primrose [Lavenderleaf eveningprimrose] (155) (1942), Lavender-leaf primrose [Lavender-leaved primrose] (4, 5, 97) (1913–1986), Lavender-leaf sundrops [Lavenderleaf sundrops] (50) (present)

Calylophus serrulatus (Nutt.) Raven – Evening-primrose [Evening primrose, Eveningprimrose] (96, 98) (1891–1926), Large tooth-leaf primrose [Large tooth-leaved primrose] (97) (1937), Plains yellow primrose (4) (1986), Tooth-leaf primrose [Tooth-leaved primrose] (5, 72, 97, 127, 131) (1899–1937), Yellow evening-primrose [Yellow eveningprimrose, Yellow evening primrose] (3) (1977), Yellow primrose (85) (1932) SD, Yellow sundrops (50) (present)

Calylophus Spach – Galpinsia (158) (1900), Primrose (158) (1900), Sundrop [Sundrops, Sun-drops] (50) (present)

Calypso borealis (Sw.) Salisb. – See *Calypso bulbosa* (L.) Oakes

Calypso borealis Salisb. – See *Calypso bulbosa* (L.) Oakes

Calypso bulbosa (L.) Oakes – Calypso (86, 138, 156, 158) (1878–1923), Fairy slipper (50) (present), Venus'-slipper [Venus' slipper, Venus'slipper] (3, 156) (1923–1977)

Calypso bulbosa (L.) Oakes var. *americana* (R. Br. ex Ait. f.) Luer – Calypso (5) (1913), Fairy slipper (50) (present), Venus'-slipper [Venus' slipper, Venus'slipper] (85) (1932)

Calypso Salisb. – Calypso (1, 138, 158) (1900–1932) for Calypso of Greek mythology, Fairy slipper (50) (present), Venus'-slipper [Venus' slipper, Venus'slipper] (1) (1932)

Calyptocarpus vialis Less. – Prostrate sunflower (122, 124) (1937)

Calystegia macounii (Greene) Brummitt – Macoun's false bindweed (178) (1526)

Calystegia pellita (Ledeb.) G. Don – California rose [California-rose] (109) (1949), Rose convovulus (138) (1923)

Calystegia R. Br. – False bindweed (50) (present), Hedge bindweed [Hedge bind weed] (4) (1986)

Calystegia sepium (L.) R. Br. – Bindweed [Bind weed, Bind-weed] (47, 107) (1852–1919), Hedge false bindweed (50) (present)

Calystegia sepium (L.) R. Br. subsp. *angulata* Brummitt – Creeping bindweed [Creeping bind weed] (42) (1814), Field bindweed (19) (1840), Hedge bindweed [Hedge bind weed] (3, 4, 5, 14, 42, 62, 72, 80, 82, 93, 131, 138, 156, 158) (1814–1986), Hedge false bindweed (50) (present), Trailing bindweed (5, 72, 131) (1899–1913)

Calystegia sepium (L.) R. Br. subsp. *sepium* – Bear-bine (156) (1923), Bellbind [Bell bind, Bell-bind] (5, 156, 158) (1900–1923), Bindweed [Bind weed, Bind-weed] (178) (1526), Bracted bindweed (5, 62, 156, 158) (1900–1923), Common bindweed [Common bind weed] (56) (1901), Creeper [Creepers] (5, 73, 156, 158) (1892–1923), Devil's vine (5, 62, 156) (1912–1923) no longer in use by 1923, German scammony (5, 156, 158) (1900–1923), Great bearbind (42) (1814), Great bindweed [Great bind weed] (5, 85, 93, 97, 122, 156, 158) (1900–1932), Greater bearbind [Greater bear-bind] (158) (1900), Harvest-lily [Harvest lily] (5, 156) (1913–1923) no longer in use by 1923, Hedge glorybind (155) (1942), Hedgebell [Hedge-bells] (158) (1900), Hedge-lily [Hedge lily] (5, 156, 158) (1900–1923) no longer in use by 1923, Hellweed [Hell-weed, Hell weed] (156) (1923), Kentucky hunter (77) (1898) Sulphur Grove OH; Paris ME, Lady's-nightcap [Lady's nightcap, Ladies' nightcap, Ladies'-nightcap] (5, 156, 158) (1900–1923) no longer in use by 1923, Large bindweed [Large bind-weed] (95, 127) (1911–1933), Large-flower bindweed [Large-flowered bind-weed] (187) (1818), Lily vine [Lily-vine] (156) (1923) no longer in use by 1923, Lily-bind [Lily bind] (5, 158) (1900–1913), Morning-glory [Morningglory, Morning glory] (80) (1913), Pea vine [Peavine, Pea-vine] (77) (1898) Sulphur Grove OH, Pear vine (5) (1913), Rutland beauty [Rutland-beauty] (5, 73, 77, 109, 156, 158) (1892–1949), Virginia creeper [Virginian creeper] (156) (1923), White morning-glory [White morning glory] (145) (1897), Wild morning-glory [Wild morning glory] (62) (1912), Wood vine [Wood-vine] (156) (1923), Woodbind [Woodbinde, Wood bind, Woodbynde] (5, 156, 158) (1900–1923), Woodbine (75, 158) (1894–1913) NY

Calystegia silvatica (Kit.) Griseb. subsp. *fraterniflora* (Mackenzie & Bush) Brummitt – Short-stalk bindweed [Shortstalk bindweed, Short-stalked bindweed] (5, 50) (1913–present)

Calystegia soldanella (L.) R. Br. ex Roemer & J. A. Schultes – Scotch scurvy grass (92) (1876), Sea bindweed (92) (1876)

Calystegia spithamaea (L.) Pursh – Bracted bindweed (5, 156) (1913–1923), Dwarf bindweed [Dwarf bind weed] (42) (1814), Dwarf morning-glory [Dwarf morning glory] (5, 19, 156) (1840–1923), Low bindweed (5, 156) (1913–1923), Low false bindweed (4) (1986), Upright bindweed [Upright bind-weed] (5, 72, 97, 156) (1907–1937)

Camassia angusta (Engelm. & Gray) Blank. – Prairie camas (50) (present)

Camassia esculenta (Ker.) Robins – See *Camassia scilloides* (Raf.) Cory

Camassia esculenta Lindl. – See *Camassia scilloides* (Raf.) Cory

Camassia fraseri Torr. – See *Camassia scilloides* (Raf.) Cory

Camassia Lindl. – Blue camas (1) (1932), Camas [Camass, Kamas, Kmass] (2, 109, 155) (1895–1949) from camass or quamash the Indian name, Camash (1) (1932), Swamp sego (1) (1932), Wild hyacinth (1, 156) (1923–1932)

Camassia quamash (Pursh) Greene – Commass (35) (1806), Pashaquaw (35) (1806), Quamash (35) (1806), Small camas (50) (present)

Camassia quamash (Pursh) Greene subsp. *quamash* – Bear-grass [Bear grass, Bear's grass, Bears' grass] (7) (1828), Eastern camass (158) (1900), Eastern quamash (158) (1900)

Camassia scilloides (Raf.) Cory – Atlantic camas (50, 155) (1942–present), Biscuitroot [Biscuit root, Biscuit-root] (101) (1905) MT, Camas [Camass, Kamas, Kmass] (14, 35, 101, 106, 156) (1803–1930) William Clark, from Nootka 'chamash' (sweet), Common camass (107) (1919), Eastern camass (3, 5) (1913–1977), Etwoi (Flathead) (101)

(1905) MT, False hyacinth (156) (1923), Kamas (28) (1850), Kamass root (103) (1871), Kamosh (107) (1919), Kmass (78) (1898) CA, Light-blue wild hyacinth (65) (1931), Paseego (Snake, Shoshone) (101) (1905) MT, Pasiggo (Snake, Shoshone) (35) (1806) Meriwether Lewis – spelled Pas-she-co or Pas-shi-co, Quamash (7, 14, 92, 106, 107) (1828–1930), Quamash (2) (1895), Wild hyacinth (5, 7, 72, 78, 97, 103, 106, 158) (1828–1937), Wild hyacinth (2, 92) (1876–1895)

Camelina **Crantz** – False flax [Falseflax] (1, 4, 50, 93, 155, 156, 158) (1900–present)

Camelina microcarpa **Andrz.** – See *Camelina microcarpa* DC.

Camelina microcarpa **Andrz. ex DC.** – See *Camelina microcarpa* DC.

Camelina microcarpa **DC.** – Little-pod false flax [Littlepod falseflax, Littlepod false flax] (50, 155) (1942–present), Small-fruit false flax [Small-fruited false flax, Small-fruited false-flax] (5, 97) (1913–1937), Small-seed false flax [Small-seeded false flax] (3, 4) (1977–1986)

Camelina sativa **(L.) Crantz** – Big-seed false flax [Bigseed falseflax] (155) (1942), Camline (156, 157, 158) (1900–1929), Cheat (5, 156, 157, 158) (1900–1929), Dodder-cake [Dodder cake] (92) (1876) oil cakes made from refuse, Dutch flax (5, 156, 157, 158) (1900–1929), False flax [Falseflax] (5, 15, 70, 72, 80, 85, 97, 107, 131, 145, 156, 157, 158) (1895–1937), Gold-of-Pleasure [Gold of Pleasure] (3, 4, 5, 50, 107, 156, 157, 158) (1876–present), Leindotter (German) (158) (1900), Madwort (5, 19, 92, 156, 157, 158) (1840–1929), Myagrum (157, 158) (1900–1929), Oilseed [Oil-seed, Oil seed] (5, 156) (1913–1923), Oil-seed plant (107) (1919), Siberian oilseed [Siberian oil-seed] (5, 107, 156) (1913–1923), Wild flax [Wilde flaxe, Wilde-flax] (19, 157, 158) (1840–1929), possibly Camelina (180) (1633)

Camelina sativa **(L.) Crantz subsp.** *sativa* – Camline (184) (1793), Gold-of-Pleasure [Gold of Pleasure] (50) (present)

Camellia japonica **L.** – Camelia (92) (1876)

Camellia **L.** – Tea (7) (1828)

Camissonia bistorta **(Nutt. ex Torr. & Gray) Raven** – Twisted sundrop (138) (1923)

Camissonia contorta **(Dougl. ex Lehm.) Kearney** – Small-flower evening-primrose [Small-flowered evening primrose] (5) (1913)

Campanula **(Tourn.) L.** – See *Campanula* L.

Campanula acuminata **Michx.** – See *Campanulastrum americanum* (L.) Small

Campanula americana **L.** – See *Campanulastrum americanum* (L.) Small

Campanula amplexicaulis **Michx.** – See *Triodanis perfoliata* (L.) Nieuwl.

Campanula aparinoides **Pursh** – Bedstraw bellflower (5, 93, 155, 156) (1913–1942), Blue marsh bellflower (5, 93) (1913–1936), Marsh bellflower [Marsh belleflower] (3, 4, 5, 50, 72, 93, 95, 155, 156) (1907–present), Marsh bellwort (131) (1899), Slender bellflower (5, 156) (1913–1923)

Campanula carpatica **Jacq.** – Tussock bellflower (109) (1949)

Campanula divaricata **Michx.** – Harebell [Hare-bell, Hare bell] (44) (1845), Panicled bellflower (5) (1913)

Campanula elatines **Bout. ex Willk. & Lange** – See Campanula lusitanica subsp. specularioides (Coss.) Aldasoro & L.Sáez

Campanula flexuosa **Michx.** – See *Campanula divaricata* Michx.

Campanula glomerata **L.** – Canterbury bells (5, 156) (1913–1923), Clustered bellflower (5, 156) (1913–1923), Dane's blood (5, 92, 156) (1876–1923)

Campanula **L.** – Bellflower [Bell-flower] (1, 2, 4, 10, 50, 82, 93, 109, 122, 155, 156, 158, 184) (1793–present), Bluebell [Blue-bell, Blue bell, Blue bells, Blue-bells] (1, 93) (1932–1936), Harebell [Harebell, Hare bell] (1, 2, 93) (1895–1937)

Campanula lanuginosa **hort. ex Steud.** – See Campanula sibirica subsp. divergens (Waldst. & Kit. ex Willd.) Nyman

Campanula latifolia **L.** – Giant's-throatwort [Giants Throatwoort, Giants Throate woort] (178) (1526), Haskwort (92) (1876)

Campanula linifolia **[Schrank]** – See *Campanula rotundifolia* L.

Campanula linifolia **Scop.** – See Campanula carnica Schiede ex Mert. & W. D. J. Koch

Campanula media – possibly *Campanula medium* L.

Campanula medium **L.** – Canterbury bells (19, 82, 109) (1840–1949), Coventry bells [Couentrie bels] (92, 178) (1526–1876), Marian violets (Diuers sorts) (178) (1526)

Campanula persicifolia **L.** – Peach-leaf bellflower [Peach leafe belflower] (50, 178) (1526–present), White peach-leaf bellflower [White peach leafe belflower] (178) (1526)

Campanula petiolata **A. DC.** – See *Campanula rotundifolia* L.

Campanula rapunculoides **L.** – Creeping bellflower (3, 4, 5, 107, 155, 156) (1913–1986), European bellflower (5, 156) (1913–1923), Rampion (82, 109) (1930–1949), Rampion bellflower (50) (present), Rover bellflower (4, 109) (1949–1986), possibly Nettle-leaf bellflower [Nettle-leaved bellflower] (19) (1840)

Campanula rapunculus **L.** – See *Campanula rapunculoides* L.

Campanula rotundifolia **L.** – Air-bell (158) (1900), American harebell (155) (1942), Bellflower [Bell-flower] (92) (1876), Blaewort (158) (1900), Blaver (158) (1900), Bluebanners [Blue-banners] (158) (1900), Bluebell [Blue-bell, Blue bell, Blue bells, Bluebells] (95, 105, 109, 127, 155, 156, 158) (1900–1949), Bluebell bellflower (50) (present), Bluebell of Scotland [Blue bells of Scotland, Bluebells-of-Scotland] (5, 46, 86, 93, 156) (1878–1936), Bluebottle [Blue-bottle, Blue bottle, Blue bottles] (158) (1900), Campanule (French) (158) (1900), Common harebell (2) (1895), Flax bellflower [Flax bell-flower] (19) (1840), Glockenblume (German) (158) (1900), Gowk's-thumbs (158) (1900), Hairbell [Hair bell, Hair-bell] (19, 92, 158) (1840–1900), Harebell [Harebell, Hare bell] (3, 4, 5, 40, 44, 63, 72, 86, 92, 93, 105, 109, 131, 156, 158) (1845–1986) also in England, Heathbells [Heath bells, Heath-bells, Heath-bell] (5, 156, 158) (1900–1923), Heatherbells (156) (1923), Lady's-thimble [Lady thimble, Lady's thimble, Lady's thimbles] (158) (1900), Mekminswan (Chippewa) (105) (1932), Round-leaf bellflower [Round-leaved bellflower, Round leaved bell flower] (5, 42, 156) (1814–1923), Round-leaf bellwort [Round-leaved bellwort] (158) (1900), Scotch bluebell (40) (1928), Thimbles (5, 156) (1913–1923), Velvet bluebells-of-Scotland [Velvet bluebells of Scotland] (155) (1942), Windbells [Windbells] (156) (1923), Witche's-bell [Witches' bells, Witches bells, Witches'-bells, Witches' bells, Witches bells] (5, 156, 158) (1900–1923), Zi'gini'ce (Chippewa) (40) (1928)

Campanula rotundifolia **L. var.** *velutina* **A. DC.** – See *Campanula rotundifolia* L.

Campanula speculum – possibly *Legousia speculum-veneris* (L.) Fisch. ex A. DC. (taxonomic status is unresolved (PL)

Campanula trachelium **L.** – Canterbury bells (5, 156) (1913–1923), Great throatwort [Great throate woort] (178) (1526), Nettle-leaf bellflower [Nettle-leaved bellflower] (5, 156) (1913–1923)

Campanula uliginosa **Rydb.** – See *Campanula aparinoides* Pursh

Campanula uniflora **L.** – Arctic harebell (5) (1913), Bellflower [Bellflower] (5) (1913)

Campanula urticaefolia **W.** – possibly *Campanula rapunculoides* L.

Campanulastrum americanum **(L.) Small** – American bellflower (4, 50, 155) (1942–present), Hibelia (77) (1898) Sulphur Grove OH, spikes of flowers resembel Lobelia syphylitica (High lobelia) from a distance, Pointed bellflower [Pointed bell flower] (42) (1814), Pointed-leaf bellwort [Pointed-leaved bellwort] (187) (1818), Tall belleflower (72) (1907) IA, Tall bellflower [Tall bell-flower] (3, 4, 5, 63, 65, 82, 93, 95, 97, 114, 131, 156) (1894–1986)

Campanulastrum **Small** – Bellflower [Bell-flower] (50) (present)

Campe barbarea **(L.) W. Wight ex Piper** – See *Barbarea vulgaris* W.T. Aiton

Campe barbarea **Wight** – See *Barbarea vulgaris* W.T. Aiton

Camphora officinarum – See *Cinnamomum camphora* (L.) J. Presl

Campsis grandiflora **Loisel.** – possibly *Campsis grandiflora* (Thunb.) K. Schum.

Campsis **Lour.** – Campsis (50) (present), Trumpet-creeper [Trumpet-creeper, Trumpet creeper] (109, 155) (1942–1949)

Campsis radicans **(L.) Seem.** – See *Campsis radicans* (L.) Seem. ex Bureau

Campsis radicans **(L.) Seem. ex Bureau** – Bignone de Virginie (French) (8, 20) (1785–1857), Bignonia (158) (1900), Climbing trumpet-flower [Climbing trumpet flower] (8) (1785), Common trumpet-creeper [Common trumpetcreeper] (20, 155) (1857–1942), Common trumpet-flower [Common flower, Common trumpet flower] (20, 155) (1857–1942), Cowitch [Cow-itch, Cow itch] (5, 156) (1913–1923), Crossvine [Cross vine, Cross-vine] (5, 92, 106, 156, 158) (1876–1930), Evergreen bignonia [Ever-green bignonia] (8) (1785), Foxglove [Fox glove, Fox-glove, Foxgloves] (5, 73, 158) (1892–1913) Chesterton MD, Great orange-colored Virginia jasmine [Great orange coloured Virginia jasmine] (181) (~1678), Hellvine [Hell-vine] (156) (1923), Indian creeper (156) (1923), Shoestrings [Shoe strings, Shoe string, Shoestring, Shoe-string, Shoe-strings] (156) (1923), Trumpet flower [Trumpet-flower, Trumpet-flowers] (5, 10, 46, 62, 86, 97, 106, 156, 158, 189) (1767–1937), Trumpet vine [Trumpet-vine] (2, 3, 5, 86, 109, 156, 158) (1878–1949), Trumpet-ash [Trumpet ash] (5, 156, 158) (1900–1923), Trumpet-creeper [Trumpetcreeper, Trumpet creeper] (2, 4, 5, 50, 62, 63, 72, 82, 85, 86, 106, 112, 114, 122, 124, 138, 156, 158, 187) (1818–present), Virginia trumpet-flower (158) (1900), Yellow jasmine (8) (1785)

Camptosorus **Link.** – See *Asplenium* L.

Camptosorus rhizophyllus **(L) Link.** – See *Asplenium rhizophyllum* L.

Campulosus aromaticus **(Walt.) Scribn.** – See *Ctenium aromaticum* (Walt.) Wood

Campyloneurum angustifolium **(Sw.) Fée** – Callahuala root (92) (1876)

Campyloneurum phyllitidis **(L.) K. Presl** – Strap fern [Strapfern] (138) (1923)

Cana indica **L.** – See *Canna indica* L.

Canadanthus modestus **(Lindl.) Nesom** – Few-flower aster [Fewflower aster, Few-flowered aster] (155) (1942), Great northern aster (5, 82) (1913–1930)

Cananga **Hook. f. & Thomas** – See *Cananga* (DC.) Hook. f. & T. Thomson

Cananga odorata **(Lam.) Hook. f. & T. Thomson** – Ylang-ylang (109) (1949)

Cananga odorata **Hook. f. & Thomas** – See *Cananga odorata* (Lam.) Hook. f. & T. Thomson

Canavalia **DC.** – See *Canavalia* Adans.

Canavalia ensiformis **(L.) DC.** – Jack bean [Jack-bean] (109) (1949)

Canavalia ensiformis **DC.** – See *Canavalia ensiformis* (L.) DC.

Canavalia gladiata **(Jacq.) DC.** – Sword bean (109) (1949)

Canavalia gladiata **DC.** – See *Canavalia gladiata* (Jacq.) DC.

Canavalia obtusifolia **DC** – See *Canavalia rosea* (Sw.) DC.

Canavalia rosea **(Sw.) DC.** – Op (76) (1896) Florida Keys, Wild hop [Wild hops] (76) (1896) Florida Keys

Canella alba **Murray** – See *Canella winteriana* (L.) Gaertn.

Canella winterana **Gaertner** – See *Canella winteriana* (L.) Gaertn.

Canella winteriana **(L.) Gaertn.** – Canella (57, 58, 92) (1869–1917), False Winter's bark (92) (1876), White canella (15) (1895), White cinnamon (92) (1876), Whitewood [White wood, White-wood] or White-wood tree [White wood tree] (15, 49) (1895–1898), Wild cinnamon or Wild cinnamon tree (15, 49, 55, 92, 107) (1895–1919), Winter's-bark [Winter's bark] (15) (1895), Winteranus (174) (1753)

Canna edulis – See *Canna indica* L.

Canna indica **L.** – Adder's-spear [Adder's spear] (73) (1892) MA, African turmeric (92) (1876), Canna (92) (1876), Indian shot (92, 109) (1876–1949), Shot plant (92) (1876), St. Kitt's arrow-root [Saint Kitt's arrow root] (92) (1876), Tous-les-mois (French) (92) (1876), Wild plantain (92) (1876)

Canna indicus – See *Canna indica* L.

Canna **L.** – Flowering reed (10) (1818), Indian shot (2, 10) (1818–1895)

Canna speciosa – See *Canna indica* L.

Cannabis **(Tourn.) L.** – See *Cannabis* L.

Cannabis indica – See *Cannabis sativa* L. subsp. *indica* (Lam.) E. Small & Cronq.

Cannabis **L.** – Hemp (1, 4, 50, 82, 93, 138, 155, 158) (1900–present), Marijuana [Marihuana] (4) (1986)

Cannabis sativa **L.** – Bang (7, 110) (1828–1886), Barren hemp (157) (1929), Bhang (14, 59) (1882–1911) mentioned in Arabian nights, Chanvre (French) (6, 110) (1886), Common American hemp (92) (1876), Common hemp (7, 138, 157, 158) 1828–1923), Exciter-of-Desire [Exciter of Desire] (India) (6) (1892), Fimble (107, 156) (1919–1923), Gallow-grass [Gallow grass, Gallows-grass] (5, 92, 107, 156, 157, 158) (1876–1923), Ganga (Bengali) (53, 110) (1886), Ganja (6, 92) (1876–1892), Ganjah (53) (1922), Grass-of-fakirs [Grass of Fakirs] (India) (6) (1892), Guaza (6, 53) (1892), Gunjah (6, 14, 53) (1882), Hanf (German) (6, 110) (1886), Hashash (6) (1892), Hashisch (6) (1892), Hashish (6, 59) (1892–1911), Hemp (4, 5, 6, 14, 21, 19, 53, 57, 59, 61, 72, 80, 82, 85, 92, 93, 95, 107, 109, 110, 114, 131, 145, 148, 155, 156, 157, 158, 184) (1793–1986), Hempseed [Hemp seed] (92) (1876), Hempweed [Hempweed, Hemp weed] (92, 157, 158, 179) (1526–1900), Increaser-of-Pleasure [Increaser of Pleasure] (India) (6) (1892), Indian cannabis (57) (1917), Indian hemp [Indianhemp] (6, 57, 60, 125) (1876–1922), Kanas (Keltic and Breton) (110) (1886), Leaf-of-Delusion [Leaf of Delusion] (India) (6) (1892), Marijuana [Marihuana] (3, 4, 50, 109, 125) (1930–present), Neckweed [Neck-weed] (5, 92, 156, 157, 158) (1898–1929), Nickweed [Nick-weed] (157, 158) (1900–1929), Redroot [Red-root, Red root] (5, 93, 156, 158) (1900–1937), St. Andrew's-lace [St. Andrews-lace] (5, 93, 158) (1900–1936), Tristram's-knot (157, 158) (1900–1929), Welsh parsley (157, 158) (1900–1929)

Cannabis sativa **L. subsp.** *indica* **(Lam.) E. Small & Cronq.** – Bang (92) (1876), Bhang (92) (1876), Charas (92) (1876), Churrus (92) (1876) resinous substance, Gunjah (92) (1876) dried flower branches, Halish (92) (1876), Hashish (92) (1876), Indian hemp [Indianhemp] (52, 53, 54, 55, 92) (1905–1919), Marijuana [Marihuana] (50) (present)

Cannabis sativa **L. subsp.** *sativa* – Marijuana [Marihuana] (50) (present)

Cannabis sativa **L. subsp.** *sativa* **var.** *sativa* – Marijuana [Marihuana] (50) (present)

Cannabis sativa **L. var.** *indica* – See *Cannabis sativa* L. subsp. *indica* (Lam.) E. Small & Cronq.

Capnoides **Adans.** – See *Corydalis* DC.

Capnoides aureum **(Willd.) Kuntze** – See *Corydalis aurea* Willd.

Capnoides campestre **Britton** – See *Corydalis micrantha* (Engelm. ex Gray) Gray subsp. *australis* (Chapman) G. B. Ownbey

Capnoides curvisiliqua **(Engelm.) Kuntze** – See *Corydalis crystallina* Engelm.

Capnoides curvisiliquum **(Engelm.) Kuntze** **(sic)** – See *Corydalis crystallina* Engelm.

Capnoides flavulum **(Raf.) Kuntze** – See *Corydalis flavula* (Raf.) DC.

Capnoides micranthum **(Engelm.) Britton** – See *Corydalis micrantha* (Engelm. ex Gray) Gray subsp. *micrantha*

Capnoides montanum **(Engelm.) Britton** – See *Corydalis curvisiliqua* Engelm. subsp. *occidentalis* (Engelm. ex Gray) W. A. Weber

Capnoides sempervirens **(L.) Borck.** – Pink corydalis (5) (1913), Roman wormwood (5) (1913)

Capraria biflora **L.** – Carib tea (7, 92) (1828–1876), Goatweed [Goat's weed] (92) (1876), Shrubby goatweed [Shrubby goat weed] (92) (1876)

Caprifolium **Michx.** – possibly *Lonicera* L.

Caprifolium sempervirens **[(L.) Moench]** – See *Lonicera sempervirens* Aiton

Caprifolium **Tourn. Juss.** – possibly *Lonicera* L.

Capriola **Adans.** – See *Cynodon* L. C. Rich.

Capriola dactylon **(L.) Kuntze** – See *Cynodon dactylon* (L.) Pers.

Capsella bursa-pastoris **(L.) Medik.** – Blindweed [Blind-weed, Blind weed] (157, 158) (1900–1929), Bourse à pasteur (French) (158)

(1900), Bourse de Pasteur (French) (6) (1892), Bourse de pasteur on Cure (French) (180) (1633), Bozsekens eruyt (180) (1633), Capsella (52) (1919), Case-weed (Northen England) (180) (1633) John Gerarde, Caseweed [Case weed, Case-weed] (5, 156, 157, 158) (1900–1929), Casseweed [Casse-weed] (157, 158, 179) (1526–1929), Clappedepouch (157, 158) (1900–1929) archaic, Cocowort (92, 157, 158) (1876–1929), Fat-hen [Fat hen] (158) (1900), Gäsekresse (German) (158) (1900), Hen-pepper (156) (1923) Ferrisburgh VT, Hirtentäschel (German) (158) (1900), Hirtentäschlein (German) (6, 158) (1892–1900), Ĭ'ckode'wadji'bĭk (Chippewa, fire root) (40) (1928), Lady's-purse [Lady's purse] (5, 156, 157, 158) (1900–1929), Molette (French) (158) (1900), Mother's-heart [Mother's heart] (5, 62, 107, 156, 157, 158) (1900–1929), Pepper plant [Pepper-plant] (5, 73, 156, 157, 158) (1892–1923), Pepper-and-shot (157, 158) (1900–1929), Pepper-grass [Peppergrass, Pepper grass] (74) (1893), Pepper-weed [Pepperweed] (156) (1923), Pickpocket [Pick-pocket, Pick pocket] (5, 74, 92, 156, 157, 158) (1893–1929), Pickpurse [Pick-purse, Pick purse] (Northern England) (5, 92, 156, 157, 158, 180) (1633–1929), Poor-man's-parmacetie [Poor mans parmacetie] (180) (1633), Poor-man's-pharmacetty [Poor man's pharmacetty] (92, 157, 158) (1876–1929), Säckelkraut (German) (158) (1900), Shepherd's-bag [Shepherd's bag] (5, 156) (1913–1923), Shepherd's-pouch [Shepherd's pouch] (5, 156) (1913–1923), Shepherd's-purse [Shepherd's purse, Shepherds' purse, Shepherdspurse] (1, 3, 4, 5, 6, 15, 19, 40, 45, 46, 49, 50, 52, 53, 57, 62, 63, 72, 80, 82, 85, 92, 97, 107, 122, 131, 145, 155, 156, 157, 158) (1649–present) accidentally introduced by 1671, Shepherd's-sprout [Shepherd's sprout] (49, 53) (1898–1922), Shovelweed [Shovel weed, Shovel-weed] (5, 74, 156, 157) (1893–1929) Penobscot ME, from shape of pods, St. James'-weed [Saint James' weed, St. James weed] (5, 92) (1876–1913), Toothwort (5, 156, 158) (1900–1923), Towwort (Northen England) (180) (1633), Toy-weed (156) (1923) no longer in use by 1923, Toywort (5, 92, 157, 158) (1876–1929), Treacle mustard [Treakle mustard] (178) (1526), Wardseed [Ward-seed] (157, 158) (1900–1929), Windflower [Wind flower, Wind-flower, Wind-floures, Winde-floures] (5, 76, 158) (1896–1913) Fairhaven MA, Witch's-pouches [Witches' pouches, Wiches' pouches] (5, 156, 157, 158) (1900–1929)

Capsella **Medik.** – Capsella (50, 180) (present), Shepherd's-purse [Shepherdspurse, Sheperd's purse] (155, 158) (1900–1942)

Capsicum annuum **L.** – American pepper (92) (1876), Annual capsicum (110) (1886), Bell pepper (92, 109) (1876–1949), Bonnet pepper (92, 107) (1876–1919), Cayenne (59, 92) (1876–1911), Cayenne pepper (19, 58, 82, 92, 107) (1840–1930), Chillies (92, 107) (1876–1919), Chilly pepper (92) (1876), Common red pepper [Common redpepper] (138) (1923), Cone pepper (109) (1949), Ginnie Pepper (178) (1526), Guinea pepper (19, 92, 107) (1840–1919), Long pepper (109) (1949), Lunan pepper (107) (1919), Paprika (107) (1919), Pimento (107) (1919), Poivre de Guinée (French "Guinea pepper") (110) (1886), Poivre d'Indie (French, Indian pepper) (110) (1886), Poivre du Brézil (French, Brazilian pepper) (110) (1886), Quija (Brazil) (110) (1886), Quiya (Brazil) (110) (1886), Red cluster pepper (109) (1949), Red pepper [Redpepper] (19, 58, 92, 107) (1840–1919), Scotch bonnets (92) (1876), Spanish pepper (92) (1876), Sweet pepper (109) (1949), Turkish pepper (107) (1919), possibly Chile (Mexico) (7) (1828)

Capsicum annuum **L. var.** *annuum* – African chillies (53) (1922), Age (107) (1919), Aji (Peru) (107) (1532), Bird pepper [Bird's pepper, Birds' pepper] (53) (1922), Bush red pepper [Bush redpepper] (138) (1923), Cayenne pepper (50, 52, 53, 57, 110) (1917–present), Goat pepper (107) (1919), Guinea pepper (53) (1922), Indian Pepper (178) (1526), Red pepper [Redpepper] (53, 57, 107) (1917–1922), Shrubby capsicum (110) (1886), Spur pepper (107) (1919), Uchu (Peru) (107) (1532)

Capsicum annuum **L. var.** *aviculare* (Dierbach) **D'Arcy & Eshbaugh** – See *Capsicum annuum* L. var. *glabriusculum* (Dunal) Heiser & Pickersgill

Capsicum annuum **L. var.** *frutescens* (L.) **Kuntze** – See *Capsicum annuum* L. var. *annuum*

Capsicum annuum **L. var.** *glabriusculum* (Dunal) **Heiser & Pickersgill** – Cayenne pepper (107) (1919)

Capsicum annuus – possibly *Capsicum annuum* L.

Capsicum cerasiforme [Hort. ex Dun.] – See *Capsicum baccatum* L.

Capsicum fastigiatum **Blume** – See *Capsicum annuum* L.

Capsicum frutescens **L.** – See *Capsicum annuum* L. var. *annuum*

Capsicum frutescens **L. var.** *conoides* **Bailey** – See *Capsicum annuum* L.

Capsicum frutescens **L. var.** *fasciculatum* **Bailey** – See *Capsicum annuum* L.

Capsicum frutescens **L. var.** *grossum* **Bailey** – See *Capsicum annuum* L.

Capsicum frutescens **L. var.** *longum* **Bailey** – See *Capsicum annuum* L.

Capsicum **L.** – Cayenne pepper (7) (1828), Red pepper [Redpepper] (82, 109, 110, 138) (1923–1949)

Capsicum minimum **Roxb.** – See *Capsicum annuum* L. var. *glabriusculum* (Dunal) Heiser & Pickersgill

Capsicum tetragonum **Mill** – See *Capsicum annuum* L.

Caragana arborescens **Lam.** – Caragana (106, 112) (1930–1937), Pea tree [Pea-tree] (82, 106) (1930), Siberian pea tree [Siberian pea-tree] (106, 107, 112, 135, 138) (1910–1937), Siberian peashrub [Siberian pea shrub, Siberian pea-shrub] (4, 50, 155) (1942–present)

Caragana **Fabr.** – Pea shrub [Pea-shrub, Pea shrub] (4, 50, 138, 155) (1923–present), Pea tree [Pea-tree] (1, 82) (1930–1932)

Caragana frutex (L.) **K. Koch** – Pea tree [Pea-tree] (82) (1930), Russian pea-shrub (138) (1923), Siberian pea tree [Siberian pea-tree] (82) (1930)

Caragana frutex **Koch** – See *Caragana frutex* (L.) K. Koch

Caragana **Lam.** – See *Caragana* Fabr.

Carara coronopus (L.) **Medik.** – Buckhorn [Buck horn, Buck-horn, Buck's horn, Buckshorn, Buck's-horn, Bucks-horne, Bucks horne] (5) (1913), Herb ivy [Herb-ivy] (5) (1913), Sow-grass [Sow grass] (5) (1913), Swine cress [Swine-cress, Swine cresses] (5) (1913), Wart-cress [Wartcress, Wart cress] (5) (1913), Wartwort [Wart-wort] (5) (1913)

Carara didyma (L.) **Britton** – See *Coronopus didymus* (L.) Sm.

Cardamine (Tourn.) **L.** – See *Cardamine* L.

Cardamine angustata **O. E. Schulz** – Slender toothwort (5) (1913)

Cardamine aquatica **Nieuwl.** – See *Nasturtium officinale* W.T. Aiton

Cardamine arenicola **Britton** – See *Cardamine parviflora* L. var. *arenicola* (Britton) Schultz

Cardamine bellidifolia **L.** – Alpine cress (5, 156) (1913–1923), Daisy-leaf water cress [Daisy leaved water cress] (19) (1840)

Cardamine bulbosa (Schreber. ex Muhl.) **B.S.P.** – Bulb bittercress (138, 155) (1923–1942), Bulbous bittercress (50) (present), Bulbous cress (5, 93, 131) (1899–1936), Bulbous-rooted turkey-pod (187) (1818), Bulbous-rooted wall-cress (187) (1818), Meadow cress (7, 92) (1828–1876), Spring cress (3, 4, 72, 92, 156) (1876–1986), Tuberous wall cress (42) (1818)

Cardamine californica (Nutt.) **Greene var.** *californica* – California toothwort (138) (1923)

Cardamine clematitis **Shuttlew. ex Gray** – Mountain bittercress [Mountain bitter cress] (5) (1913)

Cardamine concatenata (Michx.) **Sw.** – Crowfoot [Crow-foot, Crow foot, Crowfote, Crow's foot] (5, 74, 156) (1913–1923) IN, no longer in use by 1923, Crow's-toes [Crow toes, Crow's toes, Crow-toes] (5, 76, 156) (1896–1923) Sulphur Grove OH, no longer in use by 1923, Cut toothwort (138) (1923), Cut-leaf pepper root [Cut-leaved pepper root] (5) (1913), Cut-leaf toothwort [Cutleaf toothwort, Cut-leaved toothwort, Cut-leaved tooth-wort] (5, 50, 86, 155) (1878–present), Jagged-leaf toothwort [Jagged-leaved tooth-wort, Jagged leaved tooth wort] (42, 181) (1678–1814), Pepper root [Pepper-root] (72, 97, 156) (1907–1937), Purple-flower toothwort [Purple flowered toothwort] (5) (1913), Tooth-cup [Tooth cup, Tooth-cup] (4) (1986), Toothwort (3, 156) (1923–1977), Coralwort [Coral wort] (184) (1793)

Cardamine diphylla (**Michx.**) **Wood** – Coralwort [Coral wort] (42) (1814)

Cardamine diphylla (**Michx.**) **Wood** – Crinkleroot [Crinkle-root, Crinkle root] (2, 5, 74, 92, 138, 156) (1876–1923), Pepper root [Pepper-root] (2, 13, 15, 19, 92, 107, 156) (1840–1923), Pepperwort [Pepper wort, Pepper wort, Pepper woort] (86) (1878), Tooth root (19, 92) (1840–1876), Toothwort (92, 156) (1876–1923), Trickle (5, 19, 92) (1840–1913), Trinle root [Trinle-root] (156) (1923) no longer in use by 1923, Two-leaf toothwort [Two-leaved toothwort, Two leaved tooth wort] (2, 5, 42, 72) (1814–1913), Two-tooth pepper root [Two-toothed pepper root] (5) (1913)

Cardamine diphylla **Wood.** – See *Cardamine diphylla* (Michx.) Wood

Cardamine douglassii (**Torr.**) **Britton** – See *Cardamine douglassii* Britt.

Cardamine douglassii **Britt.** – Mountain watercress [Mountain water cress, Mountain water-cress] (5, 156) (1913–1923), Northern bittercress (138) (1923), Purple cress (5, 156) (1913–1923), Spring cress (156) (1923)

Cardamine flexuosa **With.** – Wood bittercress [Wood bitter cress] (72) (1907), Woodland bittercress (50) (present)

Cardamine hirsuta **L.** – Hairy bittercress [Hairy bitter-cress, Hairy bitter cress] (5, 72, 93, 157) (1900–1936), Hairy cress (107) (1919), Hairy lady's-smock [Hairy lady's smock], Lamb's cress (5, 107, 156, 157) (1913–1929), Land cress [Land-cress] (5, 156, 157) (1913–1929), Scurvy-grass [Scurvy grass, Scurvey grass] (107) (1919), Small bitter cress [Small bitter-cress] (2, 156, 157) (1895–1929), Touch-me-not (5) (1913)

Cardamine **L.** – Bittercress [Bitter cress, Bitter-cress] (1, 2, 4, 13, 50, 93, 109, 138, 155, 156, 158) (1895–present), Lady's-smock [Ladies' smock, Lady's smock, Ladiesmock, Ladies-smock] (7, 10, 42) (1814–1828), Milkmaid [Milkmaids, Milk maid] (1) (1932), Pepper root [Pepper-root] (15, 109, 156) (1895–1949), Spring cress (156) (1923), Toothwort (1, 2, 10, 13, 15, 93, 109, 138, 156) (1818–1949)

Cardamine maxima (**Nutt.**) **Wood** – Large toothwort (5) (1913)

Cardamine nuttallii **Greene** – Cascade toothwort (138) (1923)

Cardamine nuttallii **Greene var.** *nuttallii* – Oregon toothwort (138) (1923)

Cardamine parviflora **L.** – Sand bittercress [Sand bitter cress] (50) (present), Small-flower bittercress [Small-flowered bitter cress, Small-flower bitter cress] (3, 4, 5, 72) (1907–1986)

Cardamine pensylvanica **Muhl. ex Willd.** – American water cress [American water-cress] (42, 46) (1814–1879), Bittercress [Bitter cress, Bitter-cress] (3, 4, 85) (1932–1986), Pennsylvania bittercress [Pennsylvania bitter cress] (5, 50, 72) (1907–present), Pennsylvania watercress [Pennsylvania water-cress] (187) (1818)

Cardamine pratensis **L.** – Bittercress [Bitter cress, Bitter-cress] (156) (1923), Cockoo flower (5, 107, 156) (1913–1923), Cockoo spit (5) (1913), Cuckoo-flower [Cuckooflower, Cuckoo flower, Cuckow flower] (2, 92, 109, 131) (1876–1949), Field watercress [Field water cress] (19) (1840), Lady's-smock [Ladies' smock, Lady's smock, Ladiesmock, Ladies-smock] (2, 5, 92, 107, 109, 156) (1876–1949), Mayflower [May flower, May-flower] (107, 156) (1919–1923), Meadow bittercress [Meadow bitter cress] (5) (1913), Meadow cress (107, 156) (1919–1923), Milkmaid [Milkmaids, Milk maid] (5, 156) (1913–1923) no longer in use by 1923, Smick-smock [Smick smock] (5) (1913), Spink (5) (1913)

Cardamine purpurea (**Torr.**) **Britton** – See *Cardamine purpurea* Cham. & Schlecht.

Cardamine purpurea **Cham. & Schlecht.** – Purple cress (72) (1907)

Cardamine rhomboidea (**Pers.**) **DC.** – See *Cardamine bulbosa* (Schreb. ex Muhl.) Britton, Sterns & Poggenb.

Cardamine rhomboides **DC.** – See *Cardamine bulbosa* (Schreb. ex Muhl.) Britton, Sterns & Poggenb.

Cardamine rotundifolia **Michx.** – American water cress [American water-cress] (5, 131, 156) (1899–1923), Mountain watercress [Mountain water cress, Mountain water-cress] (2, 5, 156) (1895–1923), Round-leaf cuckoo flower [Round-leaved cuckoo flower] (107)

(1919), Round-leaf watercress [Round-leaved water cress] (5, 156) (1913–1923), Watercress [Water-cress, Water cress] (107) (1919)

Cardamine virginica **L.** – See *Sibara virginica* (L.) Rollins

Cardaminopsis halleri (**L.**) **Hayek** – See *Arabidopsis halleri* (L.) O'Kane & Al-Shehbaz

Cardaria chalapensis (**L.**) **Hand.-Maz.** – Lens pepperweed (155) (1942), Lens-pod hoary cress [Lens-podded hoary cress] (4) (1986), Lens-pod whitetop [Lenspod whitetop] (50) (present)

Cardaria **Desv.** – Hoary cress (4) (1986), Whitetop [White top, White-top] (50, 155) (1942–present)

Cardaria draba (**L.**) **Desv.** – Hoary cress (3, 4, 5, 97, 107) (1913–1986), Whitetop [White top, White-top] (50) (present)

Cardaria pubescens (**C. A. Mey.**) **Jarmolenko** – Hairy whitetop (50, 155) (1942–present), Long-stalk hairy whitetop [Longstalk hairy whitetop] (155) (1942), Whitetop [White top, White-top] (3, 4) (1977–1986)

Cardaria pubescens (**C. A. Mey.**) **Jarmolenko var.** *elongata* **Rollins** – See *Cardaria pubescens* (C. A. Mey.) Jarmolenko

Cardiospermum halicacabum **L.** – Balloon vine [Balloonvine, Balloon-vine] (1, 2, 5, 13, 15, 76, 92, 97, 106, 107, 122, 124, 138, 156, 158) (1895–1937), Balloonvine heartseed (155) (1942), Common balloonvine [Common balloon vine] (4) (1986), Hart peas [Hart Pease] (178) (1526), Heart-pea [Heart pea] (5, 107, 156, 158) (1900–1923), Heartseed [Heart seed, Heart-seed] (1, 2, 5, 10, 13, 15, 92, 156, 158) (1818–1932), Indian heart [Indian-heart] (158) (1900), Love-in-a-puff [Love in a puff] (50, 92) (1876–present), Puffball [Puff-ball, Puff ball, Puffballs, Puff balls] (5, 76, 156, 158) (1896–1923) Sulphur Grove OH, Winter cherry [Winter-cherry, Winter cherries] (5, 107, 156, 158) (1900–1923)

Cardiospermum **L.** – Balloon vine [Balloonvine, Balloon-vine] (4, 50) (1986–present), Heartseed [Heart seed, Heart-seed] (109, 138, 155, 158, 167) (1814–1949)

Cardiospermum microcarpum **H.B.K.** – See *Cardiospermum microcarpum* Kunth

Cardiospermum microcarpum **Kunth** – Perennial balloon vine (124) (1937)

Carduncellus caeruleus **Less.** – See *Carthamus caeruleus* L.

Carduus acanthoides **L.** – Acanthus bristle-thistle [Acanthus bristlethistle] (155) (1942), Plumeless thistle (3, 4) (1977–1986), Spiny plumeless thistle (50) (present)

Carduus altissimus **L.** – See *Cirsium altissimum* (L.) Hill

Carduus arvensis (**L.**) **Robson** – See *Cirsium arvense* (L.) Scop.

Carduus austrinus **Small** – See *Cirsium texanum* Buckl.

Carduus benedictus **Gaert.** – possibly *Cnicus benedictus* L.

Carduus crispus **L.** – Crisped thistle (41) (1770) Curled thistle (5, 93, 156) (1913–1936), Welted thistle (5, 93, 156) (1913–1936)

Carduus discolor **Muhl.** – See *Cirsium discolor* (Muhl. ex Willd.) Spreng.

Carduus hillii (**Canby**) **Porter** – See *Cirsium pumilum* (Nutt.) Spreng.

Carduus horridus – See *Cirsium kosmelii* (Adams) Fisch. ex Hohen..

Carduus **L.** – Bristle-thistle [Bristlethistle] (155) (1942), Plumeless thistle (4, 50, 156) (1923–present), Tassel-bur (158) (1900), Thistle [Thystle] (1, 10, 93, 158, 179, 184, 190) (1526–1936)

Carduus lanceolatus **L.** – See *Cirsium vulgare* (Savi) Ten.

Carduus lecontei **Pollard** – See *Cirsium lecontei* Torr. & A. Gray

Carduus marianus **L.** – See *Silybum marianum* (L.) Gaertn.

Carduus muticus (**Michx.**) **Pers.** – See *Cirsium muticum* Michx.

Carduus nutans **L.** – Bank thistle [Bank-thistle] (5, 156, 158) (1900–1923), Buck thistle [Buck-thistle] (5, 156, 158) (1900–1923), Musk bristle-thistle [Musk bristlethistle] (155) (1942), Musk thistle [Musk-thistle] (3, 4, 5, 46, 156, 158) (1879–1986), Nodding plumeless thistle (50) (present), Nodding thistle (4) (1986), Plumeless thistle (5, 156, 158) (1900–1923), Queen Ann's thistle (5, 156, 158) (1900–1923), Scotch thistle (46, 158) (1879–1900)

Carduus ochrocentrus (**Gray**) **Green** – See *Cirsium ochrocentrum* Gray

Carduus pectinatus W. – See *Carduus defloratus L.*

Carduus plattensis Rydberg – See *Cirsium canescens* Nutt.

Carduus undulatus Nutt. – See *Cirsium undulatum* (Nutt.) Spreng. var. *undulatum*

Carduus virginianus Jacq. – possibly *Cirsium virginianum* (L.) Michx.

Carduus virginianus L. – See *Cirsium virginianum* (L.) Michx.

Carex (Rupp.) L. – See *Carex* L.

Carex ×*xanthocarpa* Degl. (possibly) – Yellow-fruit sedge [Yellowfruit sedge, Yellow-fruited sedge] (72) (1907)

Carex ×*aestivaliformis* Mackenzie [*aestivalis* × *gracillima*] – False summer sedge (5) (1913)

Carex ×*anticostensis* (Fern.) Lepage – See *Carex* × *stenolepis* Lessing [*saxatilis* × *vesicaria*]

Carex ×*stenolepis* Lessing [*saxatilis* × *vesicaria*] – Maine sedge (5) (1913)

Carex abacta Bailey – See *Carex michauxiana* Boeckl.

Carex abbreviata Prescott – See *Carex torreyi* Tuckerman

Carex abscondita Mackenzie – Thicket sedge (5, 50) (1913–present)

Carex acuta auct. non L. – See *Carex nigra* (L.) Reichard

Carex acutiformis Ehrh. – Lesser common sedge (5, 156) (1913–1923), Lesser pond sedge (50) (present), Marsh sedge (5, 156) (1913–1923), Sniddle [Sniddles] (5, 156) (1913–1923), Swamp sedge (5, 156) (1913–1923)

Carex adusta Boott. – Browned sedge (5) (1913), Lesser brown sedge (50) (present)

Carex aenea Fernald – See *Carex siccata* Dewey

Carex aestivaliformis Mackenzie – See *Carex* ×*aestivaliformis* Mackenzie [*aestivalis* × *gracillima*]

Carex aestivalis M.A. Curtis ex Gray – Summer sedge (5, 50) (1913–present), Winter-grass [Winter grass] (5) (1913)

Carex aggregata Mackenzie – Glomerate sedge (3, 5, 50) (1913–present)

Carex alata Torr. – Broad-wing sedge [Broadwing sedge, Broad-winged sedge] (5, 50, 72) (1907–present)

Carex albicans Willd. ex Spreng. – White-fringe sedge [White-fringed sedge] (5) (1913), White-tinge sedge [Whitetinge sedge] (50) (present)

Carex albicans Willd. ex Spreng. var. *albicans* – Black-edge sedge [Black-edged sedge] (5) (1913), Emmon's sedge (5, 72) (1907–1913), White-tinge sedge [Whitetinge sedge] (50) (present)

Carex albolutescens Schwein – Greenish-white sedge (5) (1913), Green-white sedge [Greenwhite sedge] (50) (present)

Carex albursina Sheldon – White bear sedge [Whitebear sedge] (5, 50, 72, 155) (1907–present)

Carex alopecoidea Tuckerman – Foxtail sedge (5, 50, 66, 72) (1893–present)

Carex amphibola Steud. – Eastern narrow-leaf sedge [Eastern narrowleaf sedge] (50) (present), Gray sedge (5, 72) (1907–1913), Narrow-leaf sedge [Narrowleaf sedge, Narrow-leaved sedge] (3, 5, 72) (1907–1977)

Carex amphibola Steud. var. *turgida* Fern. – See *Carex amphibola* Steud.

Carex amphigena (Fernald) MacKenzie – See *Carex glareosa* Schkuhr ex Wahlenb. subsp. *glareosa* var. *amphigena* Fern.

Carex anceps Muhl. – See *Carex laxiflora* Lam. var. *laxiflora*

Carex angustata Boott – Large bog sedge (66) (1903)

Carex angustior Mackenzie – See *Carex echinata* Murr. subsp. *echinata*

Carex annectens (Bickn.) Bickn. – Pale sedge (5) (1913), Yellow-fruit sedge [Yellowfruit sedge, Yellow-fruited sedge] (3, 5, 50) (1913–present)

Carex annectens Bickn. var. *annectens* – Yellow-fruit sedge [Yellowfruit sedge, Yellow-fruited sedge] (3) (1977)

Carex annectens Bickn. var. *xanthocarpa* (Bickn.) Wieg. – See *Carex annectens* (Bickn.) Bickn.

Carex aquatilis Wahlenb. – Water sedge (5, 50, 66, 72, 139, 155) (1907–present)

Carex aquatilis Wahlenb. var. *aquatilis* – Water sedge (50) (present)

Carex aquatilis Wahlenb. var. *dives* (Holm) Kükenth. – Sitka sedge (50) (present)

Carex aquatilis Wahlenb. var. *sitchensis* (Prescott ex Bong.) L. Kelso – See *Carex aquatilis* Wahlenb. var. *dives* (Holm) Kükenth.

Carex arapahoensis Clokey – Arapahoe sedge (139) (1944)

Carex arcta Boott – Northern cluster sedge (50) (present), Northern clustered sedge (5) (1913)

Carex arctata Boott. ex Hook. – Drooping wood sedge (5, 50) (1913–present), Short-beak woody sedge [Short-beaked woody sedge] (66) (1903)

Carex arenaria L. – German sarsaparilla (92) (1876), Red sedge (57) (1917), Sand sedge (5, 50, 156) (1913–present), Sandstar [Sand star] (5, 156) (1913–1923), Sarsaparilla germanica (57) (1917), Sea bent [Sea-bent] (5, 156) (1913–1923), Sea carex (66) (1903), Sea sedge [Sea-sedge] (5, 92, 156) (1913–1923), Stare (5, 156) (1913–1923)

Carex aristata R. Br. – See *Carex atherodes* Spreng.

Carex arkansana Bailey – Arkansas sedge (50) (present)

Carex artitecta Mack. – See *Carex albicans* Willd. ex Spreng. var. *albicans*

Carex asa-grayi Bailey – See *Carex grayi* Carey

Carex assiniboinensis W. Boott. – Assiniboia sedge (5, 50) (1913–present)

Carex atherodes Spreng. – Awned sedge (5, 66, 72) (1903–1913), Giant sedge (129) (1894) SD, Slough sedge (3) (1977), Wheat sedge (50) (present)

Carex athrostachya Olney – Slender-beak sedge [Slenderbeak sedge] (50) (present)

Carex atlantica Bailey – Eastern sedge (5) (1913), Prickly bog sedge (50) (present)

Carex atlantica Bailey subsp. *atlantica* – Prickly bog sedge (5) (1913), Prickly bog sedge (50) (present)

Carex atlantica Bailey subsp. *capillacea* (Bailey) Reznicek – Howe's sedge (5) (1913), Prickly bog sedge (50) (present)

Carex atlantica Bailey var. *incomperta* (Bickn.) F.J. Herm. – See *Carex atlantica* Bailey subsp. *atlantica*

Carex atra formis Britton – See *Carex atratiformis* Britt.

Carex atrata L. – See *Carex atratiformis* Britt.

Carex atratiformis Britt. – Black sedge (5, 139) (1913–1944)

Carex atrofusca Schk. – Dark-brown sedge (5, 50) (1913–present)

Carex aurea Nutt. – Golden sedge (5, 50, 139, 155) (1913–present), Golden-fruit sedge [Golden fruited sedge] (5, 66) (1903–1913)

Carex backii Boott – Back's sedge (5, 50, 66) (1903–present)

Carex baileyi Britton – Bailey's sedge (5, 50) (1913–present)

Carex barrattii Schw. & Torr. – Barratt's sedge (5, 50) (1913–present)

Carex bebbii Olney ex Fern. – Bebb's sedge [Bebb sedge] (5, 50, 139) (1913–present)

Carex bella Bailey – Southwestern showy sedge (50) (present)

Carex bicknellii Britt. – Bicknell's sedge (3, 5, 50, 72) (1893–present)

Carex bigelowii Torr. ex Schwein. – Rigid sedge (66) (1903), Washington's sedge (66) (1903)

Carex bipartita All. – See *Carex lachenalii* Schk.

Carex bipartita All. var. *amphigena* (Fern.) Polunin – See *Carex glareosa* Schkuhr ex Wahlenb. subsp. *glareosa* var. *amphigena* Fern.

Carex blanda Dewey – Eastern woodland sedge (50) (present), Pale smooth sedge (66) (1903), Woodland sedge (3, 5) (1913–1977)

Carex brevior (Dewey) Mackenzie – Fescue sedge (3) (1977), Short-beak sedge [Shortbeak sedge] (50) (Present)

Carex brittoniana Bailey – See *Carex tetrastachya* Scheele

Carex bromoides Schk. ex Willd. – Brome-like sedge (5, 50, 66) (1912–present)

Carex brunnescens (Pers.) Poir. – Brownish sedge (5, 50) (1913–present)

Carex bulbostylis Mackenzie – See *Carex bulbostylis* Mack.

Carex bullata Schk. – Button sedge (5, 50, 156) (1913–present), Inflated sedge (66) (1903), possibly Cylindrical-spike sedge [Cylindrical-spiked sedge] (66) (1903)

Carex bullata var. *cylindracea* Dewey – possibly *Carex tuckermani* Dewey

Carex bushii Mackenzie – Bush's sedge [Bush sedge] (3, 5, 50) (1913–present), Southern sedge (5, 50) (1913–present)

Carex buxbaumii Wahlenb. – Brown sedge (5) (1913), Buxbaum's sedge [Buxbaum sedge] (50, 66, 139, 187) (1818–present)

Carex camporum Mackenzie – See *Carex praegracilis* W. Boott

Carex canescens L. – Hoary sedge (5) (1913), Silvery sedge (5, 50) (1913–present), White sedge (66) (1903), Whitish sedge (5) (1913)

Carex capillaris L. – Hair-like sedge (5, 50) (1913–present)

Carex capillaris L. var. *elongata* Olney – See *Carex capillaris* L.

Carex capitata L. – Capitate sedge (5, 50) (1913–present), Small-head sedge (66) (1903)

Carex careyana Torr. ex Dewey – Carey's sedge (5, 50, 66) (1912–present)

Carex caroliniana Schwein. – Carolina sedge (5, 50) (1913–present)

Carex caroliniana Schwein. var. *cuspidata* (Dewey) Shinners – See *Carex bushii* Mackenzie

Carex caryophyllea Latourrette – Iron-grass [Iron grass] (5, 156) (1913–1923), Pink-grass [Pink grass] (5, 156) (1913–1923), Vernal sedge (50, 156) (1923–present)

Carex castanea Wahlenb. – Chestnut sedge (5) (1913), Fringed sedge (66) (1903)

Carex cephalantha (Bailey) Bickn. – See *Carex echinata* Murr. subsp. *echinata*

Carex cephaloidea (Dewey) Dewey – Thin-leaf sedge [Thinleaf sedge, Thin-leaved sedge] (5, 50, 72) (1907–present)

Carex cephalophora Muhl. ex Willd. – Head sedge (19, 187) (1818–1840), Oval-head sedge [Oval-headed sedge, Ovalhead sedge] (5, 66) (1903–1913), Oval-leaf sedge (50) (present), Oval-shaped sedge (72) (1907), Woodbank sedge (3, 155) (1942–1977)

Carex cherokeensis Schwein. – Cherokee sedge (5, 50) (1913–present)

Carex chordorrhiza Ehrh. Ex L. f. – Creeping sedge (5, 50, 72) (1893–present), Long-root sedge [Long-rooted sedge] (66) (1903), possibly Lesser-panicle sedge [Lesser-panicled sedge] (66, 72) (1903–1907)

Carex collinsii Nutt. – Collins' sedge [Collins sedge] (5, 50) (1913–present), possibly Awl-fruit sedge [Awl-fruited sedge] (66) (1903)

Carex colorata Mackenzie – See *Carex woodii* Dewey

Carex communis Bailey – See *Carex communis* Bailey, Fibrous-root sedge [Fibrousroot sedge, Fibrous-rooted sedge] (5, 50) (1913–present)

Carex comosa Boott. – Bristly sedge (5, 72) (1907–1913), Long-hair sedge [Longhair sedge] (50) (present)

Carex complanata Torr. – Hirsute sedge (5, 50) (1913–present)

Carex concinna Muhl. – See *Carex concinna* R. Br., Low northern sedge (5, 50) (1913–present)

Carex concolor R. Br. – See Carex aquatilis var. minor Boott

Carex conglomerata Thuill. – possibly *Carex viridula* Michx. subsp. *viridula* (taxonomic status is unresolved (PL))

Carex conjuncta Boott – Great fox sedge (42) (1814), Great fox seg (42) (1814), Raf-starr (46) (1879), Soft fox sedge (5, 50, 72) (1893–present)

Carex conoidea Schk. ex Willd. – Conical-fruit sedge [Conical-fruited sedge] (66) (1903), Field sedge (5, 72) (1907–1913), Mt. Katahdin sedge (5) (1913), Open-field sedge [Openfield sedge] (50) (present)

Carex convoluta Mack. – See *Carex rosea* Schkuhr ex Willd.

Carex costata Schwein. – See *Carex virescens* Muhl. ex Willd.

Carex crawei Dewey – Crawe's sedge (5, 50, 66, 72) (1893–present)

Carex crawfordii Fernald – Crawford's sedge (5, 50) (1913–present)

Carex crinita Lam. – Chaffy sedge (42, 187) (1814–1818), Chaffy seg (42) (1814), Drooping sedge (156) (1923), Fringed sedge (5, 50, 66, 155, 156) (1912–present), Sickle-grass [Sickle grass] (156) (1923)

Carex crinita Lam. var. *brevicrinis* Fern. – Fringed sedge (50) (present)

Carex crinita Lam. var. *gynandra* (Schwein.) Schwein. & Torr. – See *Carex gynandra* Schwein.

Carex cristatella Britt. – Crested sedge (5, 50, 72) (1893–present)

Carex cruscorvi – See *Carex crus-corvi* Shuttlew. ex Kunz.

Carex crus-corvi Shuttlew. ex Kunz. – Crowfoot sedge (155) (1942),

Raven-foot sedge [Ravenfoot sedge, Raven's foot sedge] (5, 50, 72) (1907–present)

Carex cryptocarpa C. A. Meyer – See *Carex lyngbyei* Hornem.

Carex cylindrica [Schwein] – possibly *Carex bullata* Schk. (current species depends on author)

Carex davisii Schwein. & Torr. – Davis' sedge (3, 5, 50, 66, 72) (1893–present)

Carex debilis Michx. – Weak sedge (66) (1903), White edge sedge (50) (present), White-edge sedge [White-edged sedge] (5) (1913)

Carex debilis Michx. var. *rudgei* Bailey – Slender-stalk sedge [Slender-stalked sedge] (5) (1913)

Carex debilis Michx. var. *rudgei* Bailey – White edge sedge (50) (present)

Carex decidua Boott – Fibrous-root sedge [Fibrousroot sedge, Fibrous-rooted sedge] (72) (1907)

Carex decomposita Muhl. – Cypress-knee sedge [Cypressknee sedge] (50) (present), Large-panicle sedge [Large-panicled sedge] (5, 66) (1903–1913)

Carex deflexa Hornem. – Northern sedge (5, 50) (1913–present)

Carex delicatula Bickn. – See *Carex atlantica* Bailey subsp. *capillacea* (Bailey) Reznicek

Carex deweyana Schwein. – Dewey's sedge [Dewey sedge] (5, 50, 66, 72, 139) (1903–present)

Carex diandra Schrank – Lesser-panicle sedge [Lesser-panicled sedge] (5, 50) (1913–present)

Carex digitalis Willd. – Slender wood sedge (5, 50, 66) (1912–present)

Carex dioica L. subsp. *gynocrates* (Wormsk. ex Drej.) Hultén – See *Carex gynocrates* Wormsk.

Carex dioica L. var. *gynocrates* (Wormsk. ex Drej.) Ostenf. – See *Carex gynocrates* Wormsk.

Carex disperma Dewey – Softleaf sedge (5, 50) (1913–present), Two-seed sedge [Two-seeded sedge] (66) (1903)

Carex douglasii Boott. – Douglas' sedge [Douglas sedge] (5, 50, 139, 155) (1913–present)

Carex drummondiana Dewey – See *Carex rupestris* All. var. *drummondiana* (Dewey) Bailey

Carex durifolia Bailey – See *Carex backii* Boott

Carex duriuscula C. A. Mey. – Involute-leaf sedge [Involute-leaved sedge] (5, 72) (1907–1913), Needle-leaf sedge [Needleleaf sedge] (3, 50, 139, 155) (1942–present), Squarrose sedge (50) (present)

Carex ebenea Rydb. – Ebony sedge (139) (1944)

Carex eburnea Boott. – Bristle-leaf sedge [Bristleleaf sedge, Bristleaved sedge] (50, 72) (1907–present), Bristle-leaf white sedge [Bristle-leaved white sedge] (66) (1903)

Carex echinata Murr. subsp. *echinata* – Little prickly sedge (5) (1913), Star sedge (50) (present), Yellow-fruit sedge [Yellowfruit sedge, Yellow-fruited sedge] (50) (present)

Carex echinata Murr. var. *angustata* (Carey) Bailey – See *Carex echinata* Murr. subsp. *echinata*

Carex echinata Murr. var. *conferta* (Chapman) Bailey – See *Carex atlantica* Bailey subsp. *atlantica*

Carex egglestonii Mackenzie – Eggleston's sedge [Eggleston sedge] (139) (1944)

Carex elachycarpa Fernald. – See *Carex sterilis* Willd.

Carex eleocharis Bailey – See *Carex duriuscula* C.A. Mey.

Carex emoryi Dewey – Emory's sedge [Emory sedge] (3, 50, 139, 155) (1942–present)

Carex engelmannii Bailey – Engelmann's sedge [Engelman sedge] (139) (1944)

Carex exilis Dewey – Coast sedge (5) (1913), Coastal sedge (50) (present), Slender sedge (66) (1903)

Carex extensa Goodenough – Long-bract sedge [Long-bracted sedge] (5, 50) (1913–present)

Carex festiva Dewey – See *Carex macloviana* d'Urv.

Carex festivella Mack. – See *Carex microptera* Mackenzie

Carex festucacea Schkuhr – Fescue sedge (5, 50, 72) (1893–present), Fescue-like sedge [Fescue-like-sedge] (187) (1818)

87

Carex filifolia **Nutt.** – Thread sedge (5) (1913), Thread-leaf sedge [Threadleaf sedge] (50, 139, 155) (1942–present), Three-leaf sedge [Three leaved sedge] (3) (1977)

Carex filiformis **L.** – See *Carex lasiocarpa* Ehrh.

Carex fissa **Mack.** – Hammock sedge (50) (present)

Carex flacca **Schreb.** – Carnation-grass [Carnation grass] (5, 92, 156) (1913–1923), Gilliflower-grass [Gilliflower grass] (5, 156) (1913–1923), Heath sedge (5, 50, 156) (1913–present), Pink-grass [Pink grass] (5, 156) (1913–1923)

Carex flaccosperma **Dewey** – Thin-fruit sedge [Thinfruit sedge, Thin-fruited sedge] (5, 50) (1913–present)

Carex flaccosperma **Dewey var.** *glaucodea* **(Tuckerman ex Olney) Kükenth.** – See *Carex glaucodea* Tuckerm. ex Olney

Carex flava **L.** – Hedgehog-grass [Hedge hog grass, Hedge-hog grass, Hedge-hog-grass] (46) (1671), Large yellow carex (66) (1903), Marsh hedgehog grass [Marsh hedgehog-grass] (5, 92, 156) (1913–1923), Meadow sedge (156) (1923), Yellow sedge (5, 50, 156) (1913–present)

Carex flava **L. var.** *lepidocarpa* **(Tausch) Gord.** – See *Carex viridula* Michx. subsp. *brachyrrhyncha* (Celak.) B. Schmid var. *elatior* (Schlecht.) Crins

Carex flava **L. var.** *nelmesiana* **(Raymond) Boivin** – See *Carex viridula* Michx. subsp. *brachyrrhyncha* (Celak.) B. Schmid var. *elatior* (Schlecht.) Crins

Carex flexilis **[Rudge]** – possibly *Carex castanea* Wahlenb. (current species depends on author)

Carex flexuosa **Muhl.** – See *Carex debilis* Michx. var. *rudgei* Bailey

Carex foenea **Willd.** – Dry-spike sedge [Dryspike sedge, [Dry-spiked sedge] (50) (present), Hay sedge (5, 72) (1907–1913)

Carex foenea **Willd. var.** *foenea* – See *Carex siccata* Dewey

Carex folliculata **L.** – All-yellow sedge [All yellow sedge] (66) (1903), Long sedge (5) (1913), Northern long sedge (50) (present), Round-spike sedge [Round-spiked sedge] (187) (1818)

Carex formosa **Dewey** – Handsome sedge (5, 50) (1913–present), Showy sedge (66) (1903)

Carex frankii **Kunth** – Frank's sedge [Franks sedge, Frank sedge] (3, 5, 50, 120, 155) (1913–present)

Carex fraseri **Andr.** – See *Cymophyllus fraserianus* (Ker-Gawl.) Kartesz & Gandhi

Carex fraseriana **Ker-Gawl.** – See *Cymophyllus fraserianus* (Ker-Gawl.) Kartesz & Gandhi

Carex fuliginosa **Schkuhr subsp.** *misandra* **(R. Br.) Nyman** – See *Carex misandra* R. Br.

Carex fulvescens **Mackenzie** – See *Carex hostiana* DC.

Carex fusca **All.** – See *Carex nigra* (L.) Reichard

Carex garberi **Fern.** – Elk sedge (50) (present)

Carex geyeri **Boott** – Elk sedge (139) (1944) CO

Carex gigantea **Rudge** – Giant sedge (50) (present), Large sedge (5) (1913)

Carex glareosa **Schkuhr ex Wahlenb. subsp.** *glareosa* **var.** *amphigena* **Fern.** – Lesser saltmarsh sedge (50) (present), Northern clustered sedge (5) (1913), Weak clustered sedge (5) (1913)

Carex glareosa **Wahl.** – See *Carex glareosa* Schkuhr ex Wahlenb. subsp. *glareosa* var. *amphigena* Fern.

Carex glauca **Murr.** – See *Carex flacca* Schreb.

Carex glaucescens **Ell.** – Southern glaucous sedge (5) (1913), Southern waxy sedge (50) (present)

Carex glaucodea **Tuckerm. ex Olney** – Blue sedge (50) (present), Glaucescent sedge (5) (1913)

Carex goodenowii **J. Gay.** – See *Carex nigra* (L.) Reichard

Carex gracilescens **Steud.** – Slender loose-flower sedge [Slender loose-flower sedge] (50) (Present), Slender nodding sedge (66) (1903)

Carex gracillima **Schwein.** – Graceful sedge (5, 50) (1913–present)

Carex grahamii **Boott.** – See *Carex ×stenolepis* Lessing [*saxatilis × vesicaria*]

Carex granularis **Muhl. ex Willd.** – Granular-spike sedge [Granular-spiked sedge] (66) (1903), Limestone meadow sedge (50) (present), Meadow sedge (5, 72) (1907–1913)

Carex granularis **Muhl. ex Willd. var.** *haleana* **(Olney) Porter** – Limestone meadow sedge (50) (present), Meadow sedge (3) (1977), Shriver's sedge (5) (1913)

Carex granularis **Muhl. var.** *granularis* – Meadow sedge (3) (1977)

Carex gravida **Bailey** – Heavy sedge (5, 50, 72) (1893–present)

Carex gravida **Bailey var.** *gravida* – Heavy sedge (3) (1977)

Carex gravida **Bailey var.** *lunelliana* **(Mack.) Herm.** – Heavy sedge (3) (1977)

Carex grayi **Carey** – Gray's sedge (5, 50, 66, 72) (1903–present)

Carex grisea **Wahl.** – See *Carex amphibola* Steud.

Carex gynandra **Schwein.** – Nodding sedge (5, 50) (1913–present)

Carex gynocrates **Wormsk.** – Northern bog sedge (5, 50) (1913–present), Short-beak sedge [Short beaked sedge] (66) (1903)

Carex halleri **Gunn.** – See *Carex hallii* Olney

Carex hallii **Olney** – Alpine sedge (5) (1913), Deer sedge (5) (1913), Hall's sedge [Hall sedge] (139) (1944)

Carex halophila **F. Nyl.** – See *Carex recta* Boott.

Carex hassei **Bailey** – Hasse's sedge (5) (1913), Salt sedge (50) (present)

Carex hawaiiensis **St. John** – See *Carex echinata* Murr. subsp. *echinata*

Carex haydeniana **Olney** – Cloud sedge (139) (1944) CO

Carex haydenii **Dewey** – Hayden's sedge (5, 50, 72) (1893–present)

Carex heleonastes **Ehrh.** – Hudson Bay sedge (5, 50) (1913–present)

Carex heliophila **Mack.** – See *Carex inops* Bailey subsp. *heliophila* (Mackenzie) Crins

Carex hepburnii **Boott.** – See *Carex nardina* Fries var. *hepburnii* (Boott) Kükenth.

Carex hirsutella **Mack** – Fuzzy-wuzzy sedge [Fuzzy wuzzy sedge] (50) (present), Three-head sedge [Three-headed sedge] (66) (1903)

Carex hirta **L.** – Carnation-grass [Carnation grass] (5, 156) (1913–1923), Goose-grass [Goose grass] (5, 156) (1913–1923), Hairy sedge (5, 156) (1913–1923), Hammer sedge (5, 50, 156) (1913–present), possibly Bastard sarsaparilla (92) (1876)

Carex hirtifolia **MacKenzie** – Pubescent sedge (5, 50, 66, 72) (1903–present)

Carex hitchcockiana **Dewey** – Hitchcock's sedge (5, 50, 66, 72) (1893–present)

Carex hoodi – See *Carex hoodii* Boott

Carex hoodii **Boott** – Hood's sedge [Hood sedge] (50, 139, 155) (1942–present)

Carex hookeriana **Dew** – Hooker's sedge [Hooker sedge] (139) (1944)

Carex hormathodes **Fernald** – Marsh straw sedge (5, 50) (1913–present)

Carex hostiana **DC.** – Tawny sedge (5) (1913)

Carex houghtoniana **Torr. ex Dewey** – Houghton's sedge (5, 50) (1913–present)

Carex houghtonii **Torr.** – See *Carex houghtoniana* Torr. ex Dewey

Carex howei **Mackenzie** – See *Carex atlantica* Bailey subsp. *capillacea* (Bailey) Reznicek

Carex hyalinolepis **Steud.** – Hart Wright's sedge (5) (1913), Shoreline sedge (50) (Present), Streambank sedge (155) (1942), Thin-scale sedge (3) (1977), possibly Strand carex (187)

Carex hystericina **Muhl. ex Willd.** – Bottle-brush sedge [Bottlebrush sedge] (3, 50, 139, 155) (1942–present), Porcupine sedge (5, 42, 66, 72, 156) (1814–1907), Porcupine seg (42) (1814)

Carex ignota **Dewey** – See *Carex striatula* Michx.

Carex illota **Bailey** – Sheep sedge (139) (1944) CO

Carex impressa **(S. H. Wright) Mackenzie** – See *Carex hyalinolepis* Steud.

Carex incomperta **Bicknell** – See *Carex atlantica* Bailey subsp. *atlantica*

Carex incondita **F.J. Herm.** – See *Carex macloviana* d'Urv.

Carex incurva **Lightf.** – See *Carex maritima* Gunn

Carex inops **Bailey** – Long-stolon sedge (50) (present)

Carex inops **Bailey subsp.** *heliophila* **(Mackenzie) Crins** – Sun sedge (50, 139, 155) (1942–present)

Carex interior **Bailey** – Inland sedge (5, 50, 72, 139, 155) (1907–present)

Carex interior **Bailey var. capillacea Bailey** – See *Carex atlantica* Bailey subsp. *capillacea* (Bailey) Reznicek

Carex intumescens **Rudge** – Bladder sedge (5, 72) (1907–1913), Great bladder sedge (50) (present), Swollen-fruit sedge [Swollen-fruited sedge] (66) (1903)

Carex jamesii **Schwein.** – James' sedge (5, 50, 72) (1893–present)

Carex joori **Bailey** – See *Carex joorii* Bailey

Carex joorii **Bailey** – Cypress swamp sedge (5, 50) (1913–present)

Carex josselynii **(Fern.) Mackenzie ex Pease** – See *Carex echinata* Murr. subsp. *echinata*

Carex katahdinensis **Fernald** – See *Carex conoidea* Schk. ex Willd.

Carex kelloggii **W. Boott.** – See *Carex lenticularis* Michx. var. *lipocarpa* (Holm) L. A. Standley

Carex **L.** – Sedge (1, 7, 10, 50, 85, 92, 93, 101, 109, 139, 152, 155, 156, 158, 167) (1814–present), Seg (184) (1793), Shere-grass [Shere grass] (92) (1876), Sword-grass [Sword grass] (41) (1770)

Carex lachenalii **Schk.** – Arctic hare's foot sedge (5) (1913)

Carex lachenalii **Schk.** – Two-tip sedge [Two-tipped sedge] (50) (present)

Carex lacustris **Willd.** – Great common sedge (5) (1913), Hairy sedge (50) (present), Lake bank sedge (5) (1913), Lake sedge (66) (1903)

Carex lacustris **Willd. var. laxiflora Dewey** – See *Carex hyalinolepis* Steud.

Carex laeviconica **Dewey** – Smooth-cone sedge [Smoothcone sedge] (3, 50) (1977–present)

Carex laevivaginata **(Kukenth.) Mack.** – Smooth-sheath sedge [Smoothsheath sedge] (50) (present)

Carex lagopodioides **Willd.** – See *Carex tribuloides* Wahlenb. var. *tribuloides*

Carex lanuginosa **(auct. non Michx.)** – See *Carex pellita* Muhl ex Willd.

Carex lanuginosa **Michx.** – See *Carex lasiocarpa* Ehrh. var. *americana* Fern.

Carex laricina **Mackenzie ex Bright** – See *Carex echinata* Murr. subsp. *echinata*

Carex lasiocarpa **Ehrh.** – Slender sedge (5, 72) (1907–1913), Slender-leaf sedge [Slender-leaved sedge] (66) (1903), Wool-fruit sedge [Woolfruit sedge] (155) (1942), Woolly-fruit sedge [Woollyfruit sedge, Woolly-fruited sedge] (50) (present)

Carex lasiocarpa **Ehrh. var. americana Fern.** – American woolly-fruit sedge [American woollyfruit sedge] (50) (present), Woolly sedge [Wooly sedge] (3, 5, 72, 139) (1907–1977)

Carex laxiculmis **Schwein.** – See *Carex laxiculmis* Schwein., Spreading sedge (5, 50, 72) (1893–present)

Carex laxiflora **Lam.** – Broad loose-flower sedge [Broad looseflower sedge] (50) (present), Loose-flower sedge [Loose-flowered sedge] (5, 66, 72) (1903–1893)

Carex laxiflora **Lam. var. angustifolia Dewey** – See *Carex striatula* Michx.

Carex laxiflora **Lam. var. laxiflora** – Two-edge sedge [Two-edged sedge] (5, 66, 187) (1818–1913)

Carex laxiflora **Lam. var. patulifolia (Dewey) Carey** – See *Carex laxiflora* Lam. var. *laxiflora*

Carex leavenworthii **Dewey** – Leavenworth's sedge (3, 5, 50, 72) (1893–present)

Carex leersii **Willd.** – See *Carex echinata* Murr. subsp. *echinata*

Carex lenticularis **Michx.** – Lake shore sedge [Lakeshore sedge] (50) (present), Lenticular sedge (5) (1913)

Carex lenticularis **Michx. var. lipocarpa (Holm) L. A. Standley** – Kellogg's sedge [Kellogg sedge] (139) (1944)

Carex lepidocarpa **Tausch.** – See *Carex viridula* Michx. subsp. *brachyrrhyncha* (Celak.) B. Schmid var. *elatior* (Schlecht.) Crins

Carex leporina **L.** – See *Carex ovalis* Goodenough

Carex leptalea **Wahl.** – Bristle-stalk sedge [Bristle-stalked sedge] (5) (1913), Bristly-stalk sedge [Bristlystalk sedge] (50) (present)

Carex leptalea **Wahl. subsp. leptalea** – Bristle-stalk sedge [Bristle-stalked sedge] (66) (1903)

Carex limosa **L.** – Mud sedge (5, 50, 66, 72, 155) (1907–present)

Carex livida **(Wahl.) Willd.** – Livid sedge (5, 50, 66) (1912–present)

Carex longirostris **Torr.** – See Carex sprengelii Dewey ex Spreng.

Carex louisianica **Bailey** – Louisiana sedge (5, 50) (1913–present)

Carex lucustris – See *Carex lacustris* Willd.

Carex lupuliformis **Sartwell ex Dewey** – False-hop sedge [False hop sedge] (50) (present), Hop-like sedge (5, 72) (1907–1913)

Carex lupulina **Muhl. ex Willd.** – Hop sedge (3, 5, 50, 66, 72, 155) (1907–present), Hop-like sedge (187) (1818)

Carex lurida **Wahl.** – Moŋhiŋ ts'azi (Osage, grass that never dies) (121) (1918–1970), Sallow sedge (5, 50) (1913–present), Sedge (121) (1918–1970)

Carex lurida **Wahlenb.** – Long-point sedge [Long-pointed sedge] (66, 187) (1818–1903)

Carex lyngbyei **Hornem.** – Hidden-fruit sedge [Hidden-fruited sedge] (5) (1913), Lyngbye's sedge (50) (present)

Carex macloviana **d'Urv.** – Falkland Island sedge (5) (1913), Thick-head sedge [Thickhead sedge] (50) (present)

Carex magellanica **Lam. subsp. irrigua (Wahlenb.) Hultén** – Bog sedge (5) (1913), Boreal bog sedge (50) (present)

Carex magnifolia **Mackenzie** – See *Carex abscondita* Mackenzie

Carex mainensis **Porter** – See *Carex ×stenolepis* Lessing [*saxatilis × vesicaria*]

Carex maritima **Gunn** – Curved sedge (5, 50) (1913–present), Seaside sedge (5) (1913)

Carex maritima **Mueller** – See *Carex maritima* Gunn

Carex meadii **Dewey** – Mead's sedge (3, 5, 50, 72) (1893–present)

Carex melanostachya **Bieb. ex Willd.** – Great Plains sedge (50) (present)

Carex melozitnensis **Porsild** – See *Carex rotundata* Wahl.

Carex membranacea **Hook.** – Fragile sedge (5, 50) (1913–present) IA

Carex membranopacta **Bailey** – See *Carex membranacea* Hook.

Carex mesochorea **MacKenzie** – Midland sedge (5, 50) (1913–present)

Carex michauxiana **Boeckl.** – Michaux's sedge (50) (present), Yellowish sedge (5) (1913)

Carex microdonta **T. & H.** – Little-tooth sedge [Littletooth sedge] (3, 50) (1977–present)

Carex microglochin **Wahl.** – False uncinia (5) (1913), Few-seed bog sedge [Fewseeded bog sedge] (50) (present)

Carex microptera **Mackenzie** – Mountain sedge (139) (1944), Oval-head sedge [Oval-headed sedge, Ovalhead sedge] (139, 155) (1942–1944), Small-wing sedge [Smallwing sedge] (50, 155) (1942–present)

Carex microrhyncha **Mack** – Little-snout sedge [Littlesnout sedge] (50) (present)

Carex miliacea **Muhl. ex Willd.** – See *Carex prasina* Wahlenb.

Carex miliaris **Michx.** – See *Carex saxatilis* L.

Carex misandra **R. Br.** – Short-leaf sedge [Short-leaved sedge] (5, 50) (1913–present)

Carex mohriana **Mackenzie** – See *Carex atlantica* Bailey subsp. *capillacea* (Bailey) Reznicek

Carex molesta **Mackenzie ex Bright** – Troublesome sedge (50) (present)

Carex monile **Tuckerm.** – See *Carex vesicaria* L. var. *monile* (Tuckerman) Fern.

Carex morrowi – See *Carex morrowii* Boott

Carex muehlenbergii **Schkuhr ex Willd. var. enervis Boott** – See *Carex muehlenbergii* Schkuhr ex Willd.

Carex muhlenbergii **Schkuhr var. australis Olney** – possibly *Carex vulpinoidea* Michx.

Carex multiflora **Willd.** – See *Carex vulpinoidea* Michx.

Carex muricata **L.** – Greater prickly sedge (5) (1913), Lesser prickly sedge (5, 156) (1913–1923), Little prickly sedge (66) (1903), Piggstarr (46) (1879), Prickly sedge (42) (1814), Prickly seg (42) (1814),

Rough sedge (50) (present)

Carex muricata L. var. *angustata* (Carey) Carey ex Gleason – See *Carex echinata* Murr. subsp. *echinata*

Carex muricata L. var. *cephalantha* (Bailey) Wieg. & Eames – See *Carex echinata* Murr. subsp. *echinata*

Carex muricata L. var. *laricina* (Mackenzie ex Bright) Gleason – See *Carex echinata* Murr. subsp. *echinata*

Carex muskingumensis Schwein. – Muskingum sedge (5, 72) (1907–1913)

Carex nardina Fried. – Nard sedge (5) (1913), Spike sedge (50) (present)

Carex nardina Fries var. *hepburnii* (Boott) Kükenth. – Hepburn's sedge (139) (1944)

Carex nebrascensis Dewey – Nebraska sedge (5, 50, 139, 155) (1913–present)

Carex nevadensis Boiss. & Reut. subsp. *flavella* (Krecz.) Janchen – See *Carex flava* L.

Carex nigra (L.) Reichard – Bog sedge (66) (1903), Brown sedge (72) (1907), Common sedge (5) (1913), Goodenough's sedge (5) (1913), Star (5) (1913), Stare (5) (1913), Torrets (5) (1913), Tufted sedge (5) (1913), Turrets (5) (1913)

Carex nigricans C. A. Mey. – Black alpine sedge (139) (1944)

Carex nigro-marginata Schwein. – See *Carex albicans* Willd. ex Spreng. var. *albicans*

Carex normalis Mackenzie – Greater straw sedge (50) (present), Larger straw sedge (5) (1913)

Carex norvegica Retz. subsp. *inferalpina* (Wahlenb.) Hultén – Vahl's sedge [Vahl sedge] (139) (1944)

Carex norvegica Willd. – Norway sedge (5, 50) (1913–present)

Carex novae-angliae Schwein. – New England sedge (5, 50, 66) (1912–present)

Carex nubicola Mackenzie – See *Carex haydeniana* Olney

Carex oblita Steud. – See *Carex venusta* Dewey var. *minor* Boeckl.

Carex obtusata Lilj. – Obtuse sedge (50) (present)

Carex oederi Michx. – possibly *Carex viridula* Michx. subsp. *viridula*

Carex oederi Retz. – See *Carex viridula* Michx. subsp. *viridula*

Carex oklahomensis Mack – Oklahoma sedge (50, 155) (1942–present)

Carex oligocarpa Schkuhr ex Willd. – Few-fruit sedge [Few-fruited sedge] (5, 72) (1907–1913), Few-seed sedge [Fewseed sedge] (155) (1942), Richwoods sedge (50) (present), Small few-fruit sedge [Small few-fruited sedge] (66) (1903)

Carex oligosperma Michx. – Few-fruit sedge [Few-fruited sedge] (66) (1903), Few-seed sedge [Fewseed sedge] (5, 50) (1913–present)

Carex ormantha (Fern.) Mackenzie – See *Carex echinata* Murr. subsp. *echinata*

Carex oronensis Fernald. – Orono sedge (5, 50) (1913–present)

Carex ovalis Goodenough – Egg-bract sedge [Eggbract sedge] (50) (present), Hare sedge (42) (1814), Hare seg (42) (1814), Hare-foot sedge [Hare's-foot sedge, Hare's foot sedge] (5) (1913)

Carex oxylepis Torr. & Hook – Sharp-scale sedge [Sharpscale sedge, Sharp-scaled sedge (5, 50) (1913–present)

Carex pairaei F. W. Schultz – See *Carex muricata* L.

Carex pallescens L. – Blek-starr (Swedish) (46) (1879), Pale pubescent sedge (66) (1903)

Carex panicea L. – Blue-grass [Blue grass, Bluegrass] (5, 156) (1913–1923), Carnation-grass [Carnation grass] (5, 156) (1913–1923), Gilliflower-grass [Gilliflower grass] (5, 156) (1913–1923), Grass-like sedge [Grasslike sedge] (5, 50, 156) (1913–present), Hirss-starr (Swedish) (46) (1879), Pink-leaf sedge [Pink-leaved sedge] (5, 156) (1913–1923)

Carex paniculata Willd. – See *Carex paniculata* L.

Carex parallela auct. non (Laestad.) Sommerf. – See *Carex gynocrates* Wormsk.

Carex parryana Dewey – Parry's sedge (5, 50) (1913–present)

Carex pauciflora Lightf. – Few-flower sedge [Fewflower sedge, Few-flowered sedge] (5, 50, 66) (1903–present)

Carex paupercula Michx. – See *Carex magellanica* Lam. subsp. *irrigua* (Wahlenb.) Hultén

Carex peckii Howe – Peck's sedge (50) (present)

Carex pedicellata (Dewey) Britton – See *Carex austrina* Mack.

Carex pedunculata Muhl – Long-stalk sedge [Longstalk sedge, Long-stalked sedge] (5, 42, 50, 66, 72) (1814–present), Long-stalk seg [Long stalked seg] (42) (1814)

Carex pellita Muhl ex Willd. – Woolly sedge [Wooly sedge] (3, 5, 50, 155) (1913–present), Woolly-fruit sedge [Woollyfruit sedge, Woolly-fruited sedge] (66) (1903)

Carex pennsylvanica Lam. – Marginated sedge (187) (1818), Pennsylvania sedge [Pennsylvanian sedge] (5, 50, 66, 72) (1893–present)

Carex perglobosa Mackenzie – Globose sedge (139) (1944)

Carex petasata Dewey – Liddon's sedge [Liddon sedge] (139) (1944)

Carex phaeocephala Piper – Dunhead sedge (139) (1944)

Carex phyllomanica W. Boott var. *angustata* (Carey) Boivin – See *Carex echinata* Murr. subsp. *echinata*

Carex phyllomanica W. Boott var. *ormantha* (Fern.) Boivin – See *Carex echinata* Murr. subsp. *echinata*

Carex physocarpa J. & K. Presl – See *Carex saxatilis* L.

Carex picta Steud. – Boott's sedge (5, 50) (1913–present)

Carex plantaginea Lam. – Plantain-leaf sedge [Plantainleaf sedge, Plantain-leaved sedge] (5, 50, 66, 138, 156) (1903–present), Plantain sedge [Plantane sedge] (187) (1818)

Carex platyphylla Carey – Broad-leaf sedge [Broad leaved sedge] (5, 50) (1913–present)

Carex polymorpha Muhl. – Variable sedge (5, 50) (1913–present)

Carex polytrichoides Muhl. ex Willd. – See *Carex leptalea* Wahlenb. subsp. *leptalea*

Carex practicola Rydb. – See *Carex praticola* Rydb.

Carex praegracilis W. Boott – Clustered field sedge [Clustered-field sedge] (3, 5, 50) (1913–present), Slender sedge (139) (1944)

Carex prairea Dewey – possibly *Carex prairea* Dewey ex Alph. Wood (taxonomic status is unresolved (PL))

Carex prairea Dewey ex Alph. Wood (possibly) – Prairie sedge (5, 50, 155) (1913–present)

Carex prarisa Dew. – possibly *Carex prairea* Dewey ex Alph. Wood

Carex prasina Wahl. – Drooping sedge (5, 50) (1913–present), Millet sedge (187) (1818), Millet-like sedge (66) (1903)

Carex praticola Rydb. – Meadow sedge (50) (present), Northern meadow sedge (5) (1913)

Carex projecta Mackenzie – Necklace sedge (5, 50) (1913–present)

Carex pseudo-cyperus L. – See *Carex pseudocyperus* L.

Carex pseudocyperus L. – Cyperus-like sedge (5, 50, 66, 72) (1893–present)

Carex pubescens [Muhl. ex Willd.] – See *Carex hirtifolia* MacKenzie

Carex radiata (Wahlenb.) Small – Eastern star sedge (50) (present)

Carex raeana Boott. – See *Carex vesicaria* L. var. *raeana* (Boott) Fern.

Carex rariflora (Wahlenb.) Sm. – Loose-flower alpine sedge [Loose-flowered alpine sedge] (5) (1913)

Carex raynoldsii Dewey – Raynold's sedge [Raynolds sedge] (139) (1944)

Carex recta Boott. – Cuspidate sedge (5) (1913), Esturary sedge (50) (present)

Carex retroflexa Muhl. – Reflexed sedge (5, 50, 66) (1912–present)

Carex retrorsa Schwein – Knot-sheath sedge [Knotsheath sedge] (50) (present), Late-fruit sedge [Late-fruited sedge] (66, 129) (1894–1903), Retrorse sedge (5, 72) (1907–1913)

Carex rhomalea (Fernald) Mackenzie – See *Carex saxatilis* L.

Carex richardsonii R. Br. – Richardson's sedge (5, 50, 72) (1893–present)

Carex rigida – See *Carex bigelowii* Torr. ex Schwein.

Carex riparia [non M. A. Curtis] – See *Carex hyalinolepis* Steud.

Carex riparia Curtis – See *Carex riparia* Curtis

Carex rosaeoides E. C. Howe – possibly *Carex seorsa* Howe (taxonomic status is unresolved (PL))

Carex rosea Schkuhr ex Willd. – Rose sedge (66, 187) (1818–1903), Rosy sedge (50) (present), Stellate sedge (5, 72) (1907)

Carex rossi – See *Carex rossii* Boott

Carex rossii **Boott** – Ross's sedge [Ross' sedge, Ross sedge] (5, 50, 139, 155) (1913–present)

Carex rostrata **Stokes** – Beaked sedge (5, 50, 139, 155, 187) (1814–present), Beaked seg (42) (1818)

Carex rostrata **Stokes var. anticostensis Fern.** – See *Carex ×stenolepis* Lessing [*saxatilis × vesicaria*]

Carex rotundata **Wahl.** – Round sedge (50) (present), Round-fruit sedge [Round-fruited sedge] (5) (1913)

Carex rotundata **Wahlenb. var. compacta (R.Br. ex Dewey) Boivin** – See *Carex saxatilis* L.

Carex rupestris **All.** – Curly sedge (50) (present), Rock sedge (5) (1913)

Carex rupestris **All. var. drummondiana (Dewey) Bailey** – Drummond's sedge [Drummond sedge] (139) (1944)

Carex salina **Wahlenb. var. kattegatensis (Fries) Almquist** – See *Carex recta* Boott.

Carex salina **Wahlenb. var. subspathacea (Wormsk. ex Hornem.) Tuckerman** – See *Carex subspathacea* Wormsk. ex Horner

Carex saliniformis **Mackenzie** – See *Carex hassei* Bailey

Carex saltuensis **Bailey** – See *Carex vaginata* Tausch.

Carex sartwelli – See *Carex sartwellii* Dewey

Carex sartwellii **Dewey** – Sartwell's sedge [Sartwell sedge] (5, 50, 66, 72, 139, 155) (1893–present)

Carex saxatilis **L.** – Moosehead Lake sedge (5) (1913), Northeastern sedge (5) (1913), Rock sedge (50) (present), Russet sedge (5) (1913)

Carex saximontana **MacKenzie** – Rocky Mountain sedge (50) (present)

Carex scabrata **Schwein** – Eastern rough sedge (50) (present), Rough-fruit sedge [Rough-fruited sedge] (66) (1903), possibly Rough sedge (5) (1913)

Carex scarbra **Schwein** – possibly *Carex scabrata* Schwein

Carex schweinitzii **Dewey ex Schwein.** – Schweinitz's sedge (5, 50, 66, 72) (1893–present)

Carex scirpiformis **Mack** – See *Carex scirpoidea* Michx. subsp. *scirpoidea*

Carex scirpoidea **Michx.** – Alpine sedge (66) (1903), Northern single-spike sedge [Northern singlespike sedge] (50) (present), Northern spike sedge [Northern spikesedge] (50) (present), Scirpus-like sedge (5) (1913)

Carex scirpoidea **Michx. subsp. scirpoidea** – Mountain sedge (5, 19) (1840–1913)

Carex scoparia **Schkuhr ex Willd.** – Broom sedge (50, 139, 155) (1942–present), Broom-like sedge (66) (1903), Pointed broom sedge (5, 72) (1907–1913)

Carex scopulorum **Holm** – Rock sedge (139) (1944)

Carex seorsa **Howe (possibly)** – Weak stellate sedge (5) (1913)

Carex setacea **Dewey** – See *Carex vulpinoidea* Michx. var. *vulpinoidea*

Carex setifolia **(Dewey) Britton** – See *Carex eburnea* Boott

Carex shortiana **Dewey** – Short's sedge (5, 50, 72) (1893–present)

Carex shriveri **Britton** – See *Carex granularis* Muhl. ex Willd. var. *haleana* (Olney) Porter

Carex siccata **Dewey** – Dry-spike sedge [Dryspike sedge, Dry-spiked sedge] (50) (present), Fernald's hay sedge (50) (present), Hillside sedge (5) (1913), Silver-top sedge [Silvertop sedge] (139, 155) (1942–1944), Silvery-top sedge [Silvery topped sedge] (129) (1894)

Carex silicea **Olney** – Beach sedge (50) (present), Sea-beach sedge [Sea beach sedge] (5) (1913)

Carex soperi **Raup** – See *Carex macloviana* d'Urv.

Carex sparganioides **Muhl. ex Willd.** – Bur-reed sedge (5, 50, 66, 72) (1893–present)

Carex sprengelii **Dewey ex Spreng.** – Long-beak sedge [Long-beaked sedge] (3, 5, 66, 72) (1903–1977), Sprengel's sedge [Sprengel sedge] (50, 139) (1944–present)

Carex squarrosa **L.** – Cat-tail sedge (72) (1907), Square-head sedge [Square-headed sedge] (66) (1903), Squarrose sedge (5, 50, 72) (1893–present)

Carex squarrosa **L. var. typhina (Michx.) Nutt.** – See *Carex typhina*

Michx.

Carex stellulata **auct. non Goodenough** – See *Carex muricata* L.

Carex stenophylla **Whal.** – See *Carex duriuscula* C.A. Mey.

Carex sterilis **Willd.** – Aroostook sedge (5) (1913), Barren sedge (19, 187) (1818–1840), Dioecious sedge (50) (present), Involute-leaf sedge [Involute-leaved sedge] (5) (1913), Little prickly sedge (72) (1907)

Carex stipata **Muhl. ex Willd.** – Awl-fruit sedge [Awl-fruited sedge] (5, 66, 72) (1903–1893), Close-spike sedge [Close-spiked sedge] (187) (1818), Owl-fruit sedge [Owlfruit sedge] (50) (present)

Carex stipata **Muhl. ex Willd. var. stipata** – Owl-fruit sedge [Owlfruit sedge] (50) (present)

Carex straminea **Willd. ex Schkuhr** – See *Carex straminea* Willd. ex Schkuhr, Dog-grass [Dog grass] (5, 156) (1913–1923), Eastern straw sedge (50) (present), Saw-beak sedge (3) (1977), Straw-color sedge [Straw-colored sedge] (66, 129) (1894–1903)

Carex straminea **Willd. ex Schkuhr var. invisa W. Boott** – See *Carex hormathodes* Fernald

Carex striata **Michx.** – Striate sedge [Striated sedge] (66) (1903)

Carex striata **Michx. var. striata** – Walter's sedge (5) (1913)

Carex striatula **Michx.** – Lined sedge (50) (present), Straw sedge (5, 19, 72, 156) (1840–1923), Striate sedge [Striated sedge] (5) (1913)

Carex stricta **Lam.** – Tussock sedge (5, 72, 86, 156) (1878–1923), Upright sedge (50, 129) (1894–present), Upright-leaf sedge [Upright-leaved sedge] (86) (1878)

Carex strictior **Dewey** – See *Carex stricta* Lam.

Carex styloflexa **Buckley** – Bent sedge (5, 50) (1913–present)

Carex stylosa **C. A. Meyer** – Variegated sedge (5, 50) (1913–present)

Carex suberecta **(Olney) Britton** – Prairie straw sedge (5, 50) (1913–present)

Carex subspathacea **Wormsk. ex Horner** – Hoppner's sedge (5, 50) (1913–present)

Carex subulata **[Michx.]** – possibly *Carex collinsii* Nutt. (current species depends on author)

Carex supina **Willd. ex Wahlenb.** – Weak arctic sedge (5, 50) (1913–present)

Carex swanii **(Fernald) Mackenzie** – Swan's sedge (5, 50) (1913–present)

Carex sychnocephala **Carey** – Dense long-beak sedge [Dense long-beaked sedge] (5, 72) (1907–1913), Many-head sedge [Manyhead sedge] (50) (present), Narrow-fruit sedge [Narrow-fruited sedge] (129) (1894)

Carex sylvaticae **Huds., affinis** – possibly *Carex debilis* Michx.

Carex tenera **Dewey** – Marsh straw sedge (72) (1907), Quill sedge (50) (present)

Carex tentaculata **Muhl. ex Willd.** – See *Carex lurida* Wahlenb.

Carex tenuiflora **Wahl.** – Cluster-spike sedge [Cluster-spiked sedge] (66) (1903), Sparse-flower sedge [Sparseflower sedge, Sparse-flowered sedge] (5, 50) (1913–present)

Carex teretiuscula – possibly *Carex chordorrhiza* Ehrh. Ex L. f. (current species depends on author)

Carex tetanica **Schkuhr** – Crooked-neck sedge [Crooked-necked sedge] (66) (1903), Rigid sedge (50) (present), Wood's sedge (5, 72) (1907–1913)

Carex tetanica **Schkuhr var. woodii (Dewey) Wood** – See *Carex woodii* Dewey

Carex tetrastachya **Scheele** – Britton's sedge (50) (present)

Carex texensis **(Torr.) Bailey** – Texas sedge (5, 50) (1913–present)

Carex tonsa **(Fernald) Bicknell** – Deep-green sedge (5) (1913), Shaved sedge (50) (present)

Carex torreyi **Tuckerman** – Torrey's sedge [Torrey sedge] (5, 50, 66, 139) (1903–present)

Carex torta **Boott. ex Tuckerman** – Twisted sedge (5, 50) (1913–present)

Carex tracyi **auct. non Mackenzie** – See *Carex ovalis* Goodenough

Carex triangularis **Boeckl.** – Eastern fox sedge (50) (present)

Carex tribuloides **Wahl.** – Blunt broom sedge (5, 50) (1913–present),

Bristle-bract sedge [Bristlebract sedge] (155) (1942)

Carex tribuloides* Wahl. var. *tribuloides – Blunt broom sedge (50, 72) (1907–present), Hare-foot sedge [Hare's-foot sedge, Hare's foot sedge] (187) (1818)

***Carex triceps* Mackenzie** – See *Carex hirsutella* Mack

***Carex trichocarpa* Muhl.** – Hairy-fruit sedge [Hairyfruit sedge, Hairy-fruited sedge] (5, 50, 66, 72) (1903–present)

***Carex trichocarpa* Muhl.** – Hairy-seed sedge [Hairyseed sedge] (155) (1942)

***Carex trisperma* Dewey** – Three-fruit sedge [Three-fruited sedge] (5) (1913), Three-seed sedge [Threeseeded sedge, Three-seeded sedge] (50, 66) (1903–present)

***Carex tuckermani* Dewey** – Tuckerman's sedge (5, 50, 66, 72) (1893–present)

***Carex typhina* Michx.** – Cat-tail sedge (5, 50) (1913–present)

***Carex typhinoides* Schwein.** – See *Carex squarrosa* L.

***Carex umbellata* Schkuhr ex Willd.** – Parasol sedge (50) (present), Umbel-like sedge (5) (1913), Umbel-spike sedge [Umbel-spiked sedge] (66) (1903)

***Carex ursina* Dewey** – Bear sedge (5) (1913)

***Carex utriculata* Boott** – Bladder-fruit sedge [Bladder-fruited sedge] (66) (1903), Northwest Territory sedge (50) (present)

***Carex vaginata* Tausch.** – Sheathed sedge (5, 50) (1913–present)

***Carex vahlii* Schkuhr.** – See *Carex norvegica* Retz. subsp. *inferalpina* (Wahlenb.) Hultén

***Carex vallicola* Dew.** – Valley sedge (50) (present)

***Carex varia* Muhl.** – See *Carex albicans* Willd. ex Spreng. var. *albicans*

***Carex venusta* Dewey var. *minor* Boeckl.** – Dark-green sedge (5, 50) (1913–present)

***Carex vesicaria* L.** – Blister sedge (50, 139, 155) (1942–present), Inflata sedge (5) (1913)

***Carex vesicaria* L. var. *monile* (Tuckerman) Fern.** – Necklace sedge (5, 50, 72) (1907–present)

***Carex vesicaria* L. var. *raeana* (Boott) Fern.** – Rae's sedge (5, 50) (1913–present)

***Carex vestita* Willd.** – Hairy-beak sedge [Hairy-beaked sedge] (187) (1818), Short woolly-spike sedge [Short woolly-spiked sedge] (66) (1903), Velvet sedge (5, 50) (1913–present)

***Carex villosa* [Stokes]** – possibly *Carex hirta* L. (current species depends on author)

***Carex virescens* Muhl. ex Willd.** – Green sedge (19, 187) (1818–1840), Green-spike sedge [Green-spiked sedge] (66) (1903), Ribbed sedge (5, 50) (1913–present)

***Carex virescens* Muhl. ex Willd. var. *swanii* Fern.** – See *Carex swanii* (Fernald) Mackenzie

***Carex viridula* Michx.** – Green sedge (139, 155) (1942–1944), Little green sedge (50) (present)

***Carex viridula* Michx. subsp. *brachyrrhyncha* (Celak.) B. Schmid var. *elatior* (Schlecht.) Crins** – Little green sedge (50) (present) Small yellow sedge (5) (1913)

Carex viridula* Michx. subsp. *viridula – Green sedge (5) (1913), Little green sedge (50) (present), Oeder's sedge (66) (1903)

***Carex vulpinoidea* Michx.** – Fox sedge (3, 5, 50, 66, 72, 129, 139, 155) (1894–present), Many-flower sedge [Many-flowered sedge] (187) (1818), Muhlenberg's sedge (5, 50, 66) (1903–present)

Carex vulpinoidea* Michx. var. *vulpinoidea – Bristly-spike sedge [Bristly-spiked sedge] (5, 66) (1903–1913), Fox sedge (50) (present), Northern fox sedge (50) (present)

***Carex walteriana* Bailey** – See *Carex striata* Michx. var. *striata*

***Carex washingtoniana* Dewey** – See *Carex bigelowii* Torr. ex Schwein.

***Carex willdenovii* Schk.** – See *Carex willdenowii* Schkuhr ex Willd.

***Carex willdenowii* Schkuhr ex Willd.** – Willdenow's sedge (5, 66) (1903–1913)

***Carex woodii* Dewey** – Pretty sedge (50) (present), Purplish-tinged sedge [Purplish-tinged sedge] (5) (1913)

***Carex wormskioldiana* Hornem.** – See *Carex scirpoidea* Michx. subsp. *scirpoidea*

Carex xanthocarpa – possibly *Carex ×xanthocarpa* Degl. (current species depends on author)

***Carex xerantica* Bailey** – White-scale sedge [Whitescale sedge] (50) (present)

***Carica* L.** – Papaya (138) (1923)

***Carica papaya* L.** – Ababai (110) (1886) Caribbean, Common melon tree (20) (1857), Melon tree [Melon-tree] (52, 54, 57, 107) (1905–1919), Olocoton (Nicaragua) (110) (1886), Papaw [Pawpaw, Pawpaw] or Papaw tree [Papaw-tree, Pappaw tree] (10, 14, 20, 52, 54, 92, 107, 109, 110) (1818–1949) possibly, from Caribbean name, Papaya (50, 52, 107, 109, 138) (1919–present), Papy (7) (1828), True papaw (57) (1917)

***Carissa grandiflora* A. DC.** – See *Carissa macrocarpa* (Ecklon) A. DC.

***Carissa* L.** – Carissa (138) (1923)

***Carissa macrocarpa* (Ecklon) A. DC.** – Carissa (138) (1923), Natal plum [Natal-plum] (109) (1949)

***Carnegia gigantea* (Engelm.) Britt. & Rose** – Giant cactus [Giantcactus] (76, 103, 104, 106, 109, 138, 155) (1870–1949), Har'-say (Pima) (132) (1855), Harsee (Indians, sic) (107, 147) (1856–1919), Monumental cactus (103) (1870), Pitahaya (Mexicans) (104) (1896), Saguaro (106, 109, 155) (1930–1949), Sahuaro [Sahauro] (9, 106) (1873–1930), Suhuara (104) (1896), Suwarrow (Mexicans) (107, 147) (1856–1919)

***Carnegiea* Britt. & Rose** – Giant cactus [Giantcactus] (138) (1923)

***Carnegiea gigantea* Britt. & Rose** – See *Carnegia gigantea* (Engelm.) Britt. & Rose

***Carpenteria californica* Torr.** – Carpenteria (138) (1923)

***Carpenteria* Torr.** – Carpenteria (138) (1923)

***Carphephorus odoratissimus* (J. F. Gmel.) Herbert** – Carolina vanilla [Carolina-vanilla] (5, 92, 107, 138, 156) (1876–1923), Deer's-tongue [Deer's tongue, Deer tongue, Deer-tongue] (5, 49, 53, 57, 92, 106, 107, 156) (1876–1930), Dog's-tongue [Dog's tongue] (5, 156) (1913–1923), Hound's-tongue [Hounds-tongue, Hound's tongue, Hounds' tongue, Hondes tonge] (5, 92, 156) (1876–1923), Setwall (107) (1919), Vanilla leaf [Vanilla leaf, Vanillaleaf] (5, 7, 57, 92, 156) (1828–1923), Vanilla plant [Vanilla-plant] (5, 106, 156) (1913–1930), Wild vanilla (92) (1876)

***Carphephorus paniculatus* (J. F. Gmel.) Herbert** – Hairy trilisa (5) (1913)

***Carpinus* (Tourn.) L.** – See *Carpinus* L.

***Carpinus americana* W.** – See *Carpinus caroliniana* Walt. subsp. *caroliniana*

***Carpinus betulus* L.** – Common hornbeam (14) (1882), European hornbeam (109, 138) (1923–1949), Hop hornbeam [Hop-hornbeam, Hophornbeam, Hophorn-bean] or Hop hornbeam tree [Hop horn beam tree] (14) (1882), Yoke elm (92) (1876)

Carpinus betulus virginiana – See *Carpinus caroliniana* Walt. subsp. *virginiana* (Marsh.) Furlow

***Carpinus caroliniana* Walt** – American hornbeam [American hornbeam] (2, 5, 41, 72, 93, 97, 109, 138, 156) (1770–1949)

***Carpinus caroliniana* Walt var. *virginiana* Fern.** – See *Carpinus caroliniana* Walt. subsp. *virginiana* (Marsh.) Furlow

***Carpinus caroliniana* Walt.** – Blue beech (2, 5, 82, 93, 95, 156) (1895–1936), Hornbeam [Horn beam] or Hornbeam tree (35, 78, 85, 105, 122) (1806–1937), Horse beech (156) (1923), Horst's beech [Horst beech] (156) (1923), Ironwood [Iron wood, Iron-wood] (5, 75, 156) (1894–1923), Ska'agon-minš (Chippewa) (105) (1932), Water beech (2, 5, 156) (1895–1923)

Carpinus caroliniana* Walt. subsp. *caroliniana – American hornbeam [American horn-beam] (20, 42, 187) (1814–1857), American ironwood [American iron-wood] (6) (1892), Blue beech (19, 92) (1840–1876), Charme (Upper Louisiana) (20) (1857), Hornbeam [Horn beam] or Hornbeam tree (19, 92) (1840–1876), Ironwood [Iron wood, Iron-wood] (92) (1876), Water beech (46, 92) (1649–1876)

***Carpinus caroliniana* Walt. subsp. *virginiana* (Marsh.) Furlow** – American hornbeam [American horn-beam] (8) (1785), Blue beech

Carya laciniosa (Michx. f.) G. Don

(109) (1949), Charme de Virginie (French) (8) (1785)

Carpinus carolinianum **Walt.** – See *Carpinus caroliniana* Walt

Carpinus **L.** – Blue beech (1) (1932), Bois dur (French) (41) (1770), Charme (8) (1785), Hornbeam [Horn beam] or Hornbeam tree (1, 2, 8, 10, 42, 109, 138, 167, 184) (1785–1949), Ironwood [Iron wood, Iron-wood] (1, 82, 156) (1923–1932), Water beech (41) (1770)

Carpinus laxiflora **Blume** – See *Carpinus laxiflora* (Siebold & Zucc.) Blume

Carpinus vulgaris **[Mill.]** – See *Carpinus betulus* L.

Carpobrotus edulis **(L.) N.E. Br.** – Hottentot-fig (109) (1949)

Carpobrotus edulis **L.** – See *Carpobrotus edulis* (L.) N.E. Br.

Carpoceros laevis **(L.) Dumort.** – See *Phaeoceros laevis* (L.) Prosk.

Carthamnus tinctorius **L.** – See *Carthamus tinctorius* L.

Carthamus **L.** – Distaff thistle (50) (present), False saffron (1) (1932), Safflower (1, 4, 158) (1900–1986)

Carthamus lanatus **L.** – Wild bastard saffron [Wilde bastard saffron] (178) (1526)

Carthamus tinctoria – See *Carthamus tinctorius* L.

Carthamus tinctorius **L.** – African saffron (49, 158) (1898–1900), Alazor (Spanish) (158) (1900), American saffron (49, 53, 57, 92, 158) (1876–1922), Azafrancillo (158) (1900), Bastard saffron (7, 49, 53, 92, 158, 178) (1526–1922), Cartamo (Spanish) (158) (1900), Carthame (French) (158) (1900), Carthamine (110) (1886), Deutscher safran (German) (158) (1900), Dyer's saffron [Dyers' saffron] (49, 53, 58, 92, 158) (1869–1922), False saffron (19, 49, 92, 107, 109, 158) (1840–1949), Farbersaflor (German) (158) (1900), Ihridh (Arabic) (110) (1886), Lady's-rouge [Ladies' rouge] (7) (1828), Parrot-corn [Parrot's corn, Parrots' corn] (92, 158) (1876–1900), Thistle-saffron [Thistle saffron] (158) (1900)

Carum carui **L.** – See *Carum carvi* L.

Carum carvi **L.** – Caraway [Carawaies] (1, 3, 4, 5, 19, 50, 53, 55, 57, 58, 59, 63, 72, 80, 85, 107, 109, 131, 138, 155, 156, 158, 178, 186) (1526–present), Caraway seed (92) (1876), Carui (179) (1526), Carum (57, 174, 178) (1523–1917), Carvies (5, 156, 158) (1900–1923), Cumich (German) (59, 107) (1911–1919), Kummel (107) (1919), Saxifrage (158) (1900)

Carum gairdneri **(Hook. & Arn.) Gray** – See *Perideridia gairdneri* (Hook. & Arn.) Mathias subsp. *gairdneri*

Carum gairdneri **Benth. & Hook.** – See *Perideridia gairdneri* (Hook. & Arn.) Mathias subsp. *gairdneri*

Carum **L.** – Carum (50) (present)

Carum petroselinum **Benth. & Hook. f.** – See *Petroselinum crispum* (P. Mill.) Nyman ex A. W. Hill

Carya **×lecontei** Little [*aquatica × illinoinensis*] – Texas hickory (97) (1937)

Carya alba **(L.) Nutt. ex Ell.** – Black hickory (5, 78, 156, 158) (1898–1923) , Bull nut [Bull-nut, Bullnut] (5, 73, 156, 158) (1892–1923) Peoria IL, Common hickory (20, 43, 177, 187) (1762–1857), Fragrant hickory (5, 158) (1900–1913), Hard-bark hickory (5, 156, 158) (1900–1923), Hickory nut (14) (1882), Hickory or Hickory tree [Hiccory-tree] (6, 34, 40, 41, 46, 92, 189) (1767–1928), Kingnut [King-nut, King nut] (5, 75, 156, 158) (1894–1923), Kiskytom (6, 75) (1892–1894) Ostego Co. NY, Koeskatoma nuts (33) (1827), Mï'tïgwabak' (Chippewa, bow-wood) (40) (1928), Mockernut [Mocker nut, Mocker-nut] (1, 5, 18, 72, 82, 93, 97, 107, 113, 138, 156, 158) (1805–1932), Mockernut hickory [Mocker-nut hickory] (3, 4, 20, 50, 155, 187) (1857–present), Pick hickory (181) (~1678), Red hickory (5, 158) (1900–1913), Shag walnut (19) (1840), Shagbark hickory [Shag-bark hickory] (6, 19, 57, 58, 107) (1840–1919), Shag-bark tree [Shag bark tree] (92) (1876), Shag-bark walnut [Shag bark walnut] (92) (1876), Shellbark hickory [Shell-bark hickory, Shell bark hickory] (2, 6, 20, 27, 46, 107) (1811–1879), Squarenut [Square nut] (107) (1919), Walnut [Wall nut, Wall nutte, Walnutt, Walnuts] or Walnut tree (46, 75) (1879–1894), White hickory [White hickery] (6, 158) (1892–1900), White walnut [White walnuts] or White walnut tree [White walnut-trees] (177, 189) (1762–1767), White-bark [White bark, Whitebark] (156) (1923), White-bark

hickory [White bark hickory] (5) (1913), Whiteheart [White heart] (82) (1930) IA, White-heart hickory [White-heart hiccory, White-heart hickory] (2, 5, 19, 97, 107, 156, 158) (1840–1923), White-heart pohickery (158) (1900)

Carya alba **Nutt.** – See *Carya alba* (L.) Nutt. ex Ell.

Carya amara **Nutt.** – See *Carya cordiformis* (Wangenh.) K. Koch

Carya aquatica **(Michx. f.) Nutt.** – Bitter pecan (5, 156) (1913–1923), Pignut [Pig-nut, Pig nut] (7) (1828), Swamp hickory (5, 97, 156) (1913–1937), Water bitternut (5, 156) (1900–1923), Water bitternut hickory (20) (1857), Water hickory (2, 5, 97, 156) (1895–1937)

Carya aquatica **Nutt.** – See *Carya aquatica* (Michx. f.) Nutt.

Carya buckleyi **Durand** – See *Carya texana* Buckl.

Carya carolinae-septentrionalis **(Ashe) Engl. & Graebn.** – Southern shagbark (5) (1913)

Carya cordiformis **(Wangenh.) K. Koch** – Bitter hickory (5, 9, 113, 156) (1890–1923), Bitter pignut (5) (1913), Bitternut [Bitter-nut, Bitter nut] (2, 5, 10, 19, 72, 92, 95, 109, 155, 156, 187) (1818–1949), Bitternut hickory [Bitter-nut hickory, Bitter nut hickory] (1, 3, 4, 20, 46, 50, 82, 93, 97, 138, 155) (1857–present), Broad-leaf bitternut hickory [Broadleaf bitternut hickory] (155) (1942), Heart nut [Heart-nut] (109) (1949), Pig hickory (5, 156) (1913–1923), Shell-barked hickory (8) (1785), Swamp hickory (1, 5, 82, 93, 97, 109, 156, 187) (1818–1949), possibly Noyer à fruit blanc ovale (French) (8) (1785), possibly Pignut [Pig-nut, Pig nut] (7) (1828), possibly White hickory [White hickery] (187) (1818)

Carya cordiformis **(Wangenh.) K. Koch var.** *latifolia* **Sargent** – See *Carya cordiformis* (Wangenh.) K. Koch

Carya cordiformis **K. Koch** – See *Carya cordiformis* (Wangenh.) K. Koch

Carya glabra **(Mill) Spach.** – See *Carya glabra* (Mill.) Sweet

Carya glabra **(Mill.) Sweet** – Balsam hickery (8) (1785), Black hickory (156) (1923), Broom hickory (82, 156) (1923–1930), **B**rown hickory (156) (1923), Little pignut (5) (1913), Little shagbark (5) (1913), Noyer blanc odorant (French) (8) (1785), Pignut hickory [Pig nut hickory, Pig-nut hickory, Pig-nut hickery] (20) (1857), Pignut hickory [Pig nut hickory, Pig-nut hickory, Pig-nut hickery] (1, 46, 82, 156) (1879–1932), Red hickory (156) (1923), Small pignut (5) (1913), Small-fruit hickory [Small fruited hickory] (5) (1913), Smalnuts (46) (1879), White hickory [White hickery] (156) (1923), possibly Pignut [Pig-nut, Pig nut] (7, 92) (1828–1876)

Carya glabra **(Mill.) Sweet var.** *glabra* – Black hickory (5, 78) (1898–1913) Sulphur Grove MO, Broom hickory (2, 5, 19, 107, 187) (1818–1919), Brown hickory (5) (1913), Hog nut (82, 187) (1818–1930), Little shagbark (156) (1923), Noyer à petit fruit (French) (20) (1857), Pignut [Pig-nut, Pig nut] (2, 14, 19, 95, 107, 113, 138) (1818–1923), Pignut hickory [Pig nut hickory, Pig-nut hickory, Pig-nut hickery] (5, 72, 85, 97) (1907–1937), Red hickory (5) (1913), Small pignut (156) (1923), Small-fruit hickory [Small fruited hickory] (20, 107, 156) (1857–1923), Spignut (78) (1898) IN, White hickory [White hickery] (5) (1913)

Carya glabra **var.** *odorata* **(Marshall) Little** – See *Carya glabra* (Mill.) Sweet

Carya illinoinensis **(Wangenh.) K. Koch** – Illinois hickory [Illinois hickery] (8) (1785), Illinois nut [Illinois-nut] (5, 156, 158) (1900–1923), Illinois pecan (158) (1900), Noyer pacanier (French) (8) (1785), Pacans (35) (1806), Pecan [Peccan] (1, 2, 3, 4, 5, 7, 8, 10, 12, 19, 27, 35, 50, 65, 72, 82, 92, 97, 107, 121, 138, 155, 156, 158) (1785–present), Pecan nut [Peccan nut] (19) (1840), Pecan-nut hickory [Pecannut hickory] (20) (1857), Pecaunes (Indians, sic) (107) (1919), Peccane (39) (1814), Soft-shell hickory (5, 156, 158) (1900–1923), WataΘtoΘta (Osage) (121) (1918?–1970?)

Carya **L. Willd.** – See *Carya* Nutt.

Carya laciniosa **(Michx. f.) G. Don** – Big hickory (158) (1900), Big shagbark [Big shag bark, Big shag-bark] (5, 72, 93, 97, 156, 158) (1900–1937), Big shellbark (107, 156) (1919–1923), Big shell-bark hickory [Big shellbark hickory] (2, 4, 109) (1895–1986), Big-bud hickory (109) (1949), Black walnut [Black wallnut, Black walnutt]

(190) (~1759), Bottom shellbark hickory (109) (1949), Gloucester-nut (187), Hard-nut hickory (46) (1879), Hickory or Hickory tree [Hiccory-tree] (92) (1876), Kingnut [King-nut, King nut] (2, 5, 82, 93, 109, 156, 158) (1895–1949), Kingnut hickory (3) (1977), Mockernut [Mocker nut, Mocker-nut] (78, 109) (1898–1949), Pull-nut [Pull-nut] (78) (1898), Shellbark [Shell bark] (7) (1828), Shell-bark hickory [Shell-bark hickory, Shell bark hickory] (50, 65, 78, 95, 138, 155, 158) (1876–present) MO, Thick hickory (158) (1900), Thick shellbark (5, 156) (1913–1923), Thick shell-bark hickory [Thick shellbark hickory] (20, 187) (1818–1857), Walnut [Wall nut, Wall nutte, Walnutt, Walnuts] or Walnut tree (46) (1879), Western hickory (158) (1900), Western shellbark [Western shell bark] (5) (1913), Western shellbark hickory (2) (1895), White-heart hickory [White-heart hiccory, Whiteheart hickory] (109) (1949), possibly Big hickory-nut (113) (1890)

Carya laciniosa **Loud.** – See *Carya laciniosa* (Michx. f.) G. Don

Carya microcarpa **Nutt.** – See *Carya glabra* (Mill.) Sweet var. *glabra*

Carya myristicarformis – See *Carya myristiciformis* (F. Michx.) Nutt.

Carya myristiciformis **(F. Michx.) Nutt.** – Nutmeg hickory (20, 65, 97) (1857–1937)

Carya **Nutt.** – Hickory or Hickory tree [Hiccory-tree] (7, 10, 35, 50, 82, 93, 106, 112, 138, 155, 156, 158, 167, 182, 190) (1791–present) from aboriginal hicori, Kisaktomas-nut (158) (1900), Kiskatom (158) (1900), Kiskatom (158) (1900) no longer in use by 1900, Kisky-Thomas-nut (158) (1900), Peeck hickory nut [Peeck hickerie nut] (181) (~1678)

Carya olivaeformis **Nutt.** – See *Carya illinoinensis* (Wangenh.) K. Koch

Carya ovata **(Mill.) K. Koch** – Ash-leaf shagbark hickory [Ashleaf shagbark hickory] (155) (1942), Chansu (Dakota) (37) (1919) Chansu-hu (Hickory tree), Green mountain spinnery (109) (1949), Hickory nut (37) (1919), Kingnut [King-nut, King nut] (5, 156) (1913–1923), Little-nut shagbark hickory [Littlenut shagbark hickory] (155) (1942), Nonsi (Omaha-Ponca) (37) (1919) Nonsi-hi (Hickory tree), Northern hickory (5) (1913), Panja (Winnebago, nut) (37) (1919) Panja-hu (Nut tree), Red-heart hickory [Red heart hickory] (5, 156) (1913–1923), Sahpakskiisu (Pawnee, skull nut) (37) (1919), Scaly-bark (156) (1923), Shagbark [Shag-bark] (5, 93, 158) (1900–1936), Shagbark hickory [Shag-bark hickory] (1, 3, 4, 50, 82, 93, 109, 138, 155, 156, 158) (1900–present), Shell-bark [Shell bark] (5) (1913), Shellbark hickory [Shell-bark hickory, Shell bark hickory] (5, 82, 95, 97, 113, 156, 158) (1890–1937), Southern shagbark hickory (155) (1942), Sweet walnut (5, 156, 158) (1900–1923), Upland hickory (5, 156) (1913–1923), Walnut [Wall nut, Wall nutte, Walnutt, Walnuts] or Walnut tree (5) (1913), White hickory [White hickery] (5, 156, 158) (1900–1923), White walnut [White walnuts] or White walnut tree [White walnut-trees] (5, 156, 158) (1900–1923)

Carya ovata **(Mill.) K. Koch var.** *fraxinifolia* **Sargent** – See *Carya ovata* (Mill.) K. Koch

Carya ovata **(Mill.) K. Koch var.** *nuttallii* **Sargent** – See *Carya ovata* (Mill.) K. Koch

Carya ovata **(Mill.) K. Koch var.** *pubescens* **Sargent** – See *Carya ovata* (Mill.) K. Koch

Carya ovata **K. Koch** – See *Carya ovata* (Mill.) K. Koch

Carya pallida **(Ashe) Engl. & Graebn.** – Pale hickory (5) (1913)

Carya pecan **(Marsh.) Schneid.** – See *Carya illinoinensis* (Wangenh.) K. Koch

Carya porcina **Nutt. ex Elliott** – See *Carya glabra* (Mill.) Sweet

Carya squamosa – See *Carya alba* (L.) Nutt. ex Ell.

Carya sulcata **Nutt.** – See *Carya laciniosa* (Michx. f.) G. Don

Carya texana **Buckl.** – Black hickory (3, 4, 50, 155) (1942–present), Buckley's hickory (97) (1937), Scurfy hickory (5) (1913), Woolly pignut (5, 97) (1913–1937)

Carya tomentosa **(Poir.) Nutt.** – See *Carya alba* (L.) Nutt. ex Ell.

Carya tomentosa **Nutt.** – See *Carya alba* (L.) Nutt. ex Ell.

Caryopteris **Bunge** – Bluebead [Blue bead] (109, 138) (1923–1949)

Caryota **L.** – Caryota (138) (1923), Fish-tail palm (109) (1949)

Caryota urens **L.** – Toddy palm (138) (1923), Wine palm (109) (1949)

Casasia clusiifolia **(Jacq.) Urban** – Seven-year apple [Seven year apple] (76) (1896) Florida

Casine yapon – possibly *Ilex vomitoria* Aiton

Cassandra calyculata **Don.** – See *Chamaedaphne calyculata* (L.) Moench

Cassandra **D. Don** – See *Eubotrys* Nutt.

Cassena vera **Catesb.** – possibly *Ilex cassine* L.

Cassia **(Tourn.) L.** – See *Cassia* L.

Cassia acutifolia **Delile** – See *Senna alexandrina* Mill.

Cassia alata **L.** – See *Senna alata* (L.) Roxb.

Cassia angustifolia **Vahl** – See *Senna alexandrina* Mill.

Cassia artemisioides **Gaudich. ex DC.** – See *Senna artemisioides* (Gaud. ex DC.) Randell

Cassia chamaecrista **L.** – See *Chamaecrista fasciculata* (Michx.) Greene var. *fasciculata*

Cassia corymbosa – See *Senna corymbosa* (Lam.) Irwin & Barneby

Cassia fasciculata **Michx.** – See *Chamaecrista fasciculata* (Michx.) Greene var. *fasciculata*

Cassia fistula **L.** – Cassia stick tree (92) (1876), Golden-shower (109, 138) (1923–1949), Pudding pipe tree [Pudding-pipe-tree] (92, 109) (1876–1949), Purging cassia (57, 92) (1876–1917)

Cassia grandis **L. f.** – Pink-shower (138) (1923)

Cassia **L.** – American senna (93) (1936), Cassia (50, 158) (1900–present), Purging bean [Purging beanes] (181) (~1678), Senna (1, 82, 106, 109, 155, 156) (1923–1949), Wild senna [Wild-senna] (93, 167) (1814–1936)

Cassia laevigata – See *Senna septentrionalis* (Viviani) Irwin & Barneby

Cassia ligustrina **L.** – possibly *Senna ligustrina* (L.) Irwin & Barneby

Cassia lindheimeriana **Scheele** – See *Senna lindheimeriana* (Scheele) Irwin & Barneby

Cassia marilandica **L.** – See *Senna marilandica* (L.) Link

Cassia medsgeri **Shafer** – See *Senna marilandica* (L.) Link

Cassia nictitans **L.** – See *Chamaecrista nictitans* (L.) Moench subsp. *nictitans* var. *nictitans*

Cassia occidentalis **L.** – See *Senna occidentalis* (L.) Link

Cassia roemeriana **Scheele** – See *Senna roemeriana* (Scheele) Irwin & Barneby

Cassia senna **L.** – See *Senna alexandrina* Mill.

Cassia siamea **Lam.** – See *Senna siamea* (Lam.) Irwin & Barneby

Cassia tomentosa – See *Senna hirsuta* (L.) Irwin & Barneby var. *hirsuta*

Cassia tora **L.** – See *Senna tora* (L.) Roxb.

Cassia toroides – See *Senna tora* (L.) Roxb.

Cassine **L.** – Cassine (8) (1785), Cassine (French) (8) (1785), South-sea tea tree [South-sea tea-tree] (8) (1785)

Cassine peragua **L. Schoepf.** – See *Ilex cassine* L.

Cassiope **D. Don.** – False white heather (106) (1930), Heather (106) (1930), Moss heather (106) (1930), Moss plant [Moss-plant] (1) (1932), White heather (1) (1932)

Cassiope mertensiana **(Bong.) D. Don** – False white heather (106) (1930)

Cassiope tetragona **(L.) D. Don** – Four-angled cassiope (5) (1913)

Castalia odorata **(Aiton) Wood** – See *Nymphaea odorata* Aiton subsp. *odorata*

Castalia odorata **(Dryand.) Woodvar. & Wood.** – See *Nymphaea odorata* Aiton subsp. *odorata*

Castalia **Salisb.** – See *Nymphaea* L.

Castalia tetragona **(Georgi) Lawson** – See *Nymphaea tetragona* Georgi

Castalia tuberosa **(Paine) Greene** – See *Nymphaea odorata* Aiton subsp. *tuberosa* (Paine) Wiersma & Hellquist

Castalis tragus **(Aiton) Norl.** – Cape-marigold [Cape marigold] (82) (1930) IA, Winter cape-marigold (138) (1923)

Castana pumila **Nutt.** – See *Castanea pumila* (L.) Mill.

Castana vulgaris – possibly *Castanea sativa* Mill.

Castanea **(Tourn.) Hill.** – See *Castanea* Mill.

Castanea alnifolia – See *Castanea pumila* (L.) Mill.var. *pumila*

Castanea americana **Raf.** – See *Castanea dentata* (Marsh.) Borkh.

Castanea chrysophylla **Dougl. Ex Hook.** – See *Chrysolepis chrysophylla* (Douglas ex Hook.) Hjelmq.

Castanea crenata **Sieb. & Zucc.** – Japanese chestnut (109, 138) (1923–1949)

Castanea dentata **(Marsh.) Borkh.** – American chestnut or American chestnut tree (2, 5, 8, 46, 82, 107, 109, 137, 138, 187) (1785–1949), Chesnut (19) (1840), Chestnut [Chestnuts, Chestnutte] or Chestnut tree (20, 46, 53, 57, 82, 106, 156, 182) (1791–1930), Prickly bur [Prickly-bur] (5, 156) (1913–1923), Sardian nut (5, 156) (1913–1923), Wompinish (Narraganset) (46) (1879), possibly Chataignier d'Amérique (French) (8) (1785)

Castanea dentata **Borkh.** – See *Castanea dentata* (Marsh.) Borkh.

Castanea floridana **(Sarg.) Ashe** – See *Castanea pumila* (L.) Mill.var. *pumila*

Castanea **Gaertn. Willd.** – possibly *Castanea* Mill.

Castanea japonica – See *Castanea crenata* Sieb. & Zucc.

Castanea **Mill.** – Chestnut [Chestnuts, Chestnutte] or Chestnut tree (10, 109, 112, 138, 156, 167) (1814–1949)

Castanea mollissima **Blume** – Chestnut [Chestnuts, Chestnutte] or Chestnut tree (112) (1937), Chinese chestnut (109) (1949), Hairy chestnut (138) (1923)

Castanea ozarkensis **Ashe** – See *Castanea pumila* (L.) Mill. var. *ozarkensis* (Ashe) Tucker

Castanea pumila **(L.) Mill.** – Chechniquamins (46) (1879), Chestnut [Chestnuts, Chestnutte] or Chestnut tree (156) (1923), Chinkapin [Chincapin] (20, 181, 189) (~1678–1857), Chinquapin [Chinquepin] (5, 8, 19, 38, 41, 46, 65, 92, 97, 106, 107, 109, 122, 137, 138, 156, 181, 1884) (~1678–1949), Chinquapin bush [Chinquapin-bush] (177, 181) (~1678–1762), possibly Chataignier nain (French) (8) (1785), possibly Chinquapin (French) (8) (1785), possibly Dwarf chestnut (8) (1785)

Castanea pumila **(L.) Mill. var. *ozarkensis* (Ashe) Tucker** – Chestnut [Chestnuts, Chestnutte] or Chestnut tree (65) (1931), Chinquapin [Chinquepin] (97) (1937)

Castanea pumila **(L.) Mill. var. *pumila*** – Chataignier à feuilles d'aune (French) (20) (1857), Chinquapin [Chinquepin] (124) (1937), Dwarf chestnut (20) (1857)

Castanea sativa **Mill.** – American chestnut or American chestnut tree (20) (1857), Castanea (178) (1526), Chatagnier (French) (6, 8) (1785–1892), Chesnut (182, 184) (1791–1793), Chestayne (179) (1526), Chestnut [Chestnuts, Chestnutte] or Chestnut tree (6, 7, 8, 18, 41, 52, 58, 110, 178, 179) (1526–1919), Common American chestnut (42) (1814), Common chestnut (10) (1818), Eurasian chestnut (109) (1949), European chestnut (107) (1919), Kastanie (German) (6) (1892), Marone (Italy) (110) (1170), Marrone (Italy) (110) (1170), possibly Spanish chestnut (92, 109, 138) (1876–1949)

Castanea sativa **var. *americana* Watson.** – See *Castanea dentata* (Marsh.) Borkh.

Castanea sempervirens **[Kellogg]** – See *Chrysolepis sempervirens* (Kellogg) Hjelmqvist

Castanea **Tourn.** – See *Castanea* Mill.

Castanea vesca **L.** – See *Castanea sativa* Mill.

Castanea vesca **L. var. *americana*** – See *Castanea dentata* (Marsh.) Borkh.

Castanea vulgaris **Lam.** – See *Castanea sativa* Mill.

Castanopsis chrysophylla – See *Chrysolepis chrysophylla* (Douglas ex Hook.) Hjelmq.

Castanopsis sempervirens – See *Chrysolepis sempervirens* (Kellogg) Hjelmqvist

Castela erecta **Turpin.** – possibly Armagosa (57) (1917), possibly Chaparro armagoso (57) (1917), possibly Goat bush [Goatbush, Goat's bush] (92) (1876)

Castela nicholsonii **Hook.** – possibly *Castela erecta* Turpin

Castela nicolsoni – possibly *Castela erecta* Turpin

Castela **Turpin** – Goat bush [Goatbush, Goat's bush] (13) (1849)

Castelaria nicholsoni **Small** – See *Castela erecta* Turpin

Castelaria nicholsonii **(Hook.) Small** – See *Castela erecta* Turpin

Castilla elastica **Sessé** – Mexican rubbertree (138) (1923)

Castilleia coccinea – See *Castilleja coccinea* (L.) Spreng.

Castilleia sessiliflora **Pursh** – See *Castilleja sessiliflora* Pursh

Castilleja acuminata **(Pursh) Spreng.** – See *Castilleja septentrionalis* Lindl.

Castilleja applegatei **Fern. subsp. *martinii* (Abrams) Chuang & Heckard** – Wavy-leaf Indian paintbrush [Wavyleaf Indian paintbrush] (50) (present)

Castilleja coccinea **(L.) Spreng.** – Bloody-warrior [Bloody warrior] (5, 75, 156, 158) (1894–1923) no longer in use by 1923, Election posies [Election-posies] (5, 73, 158) (1892–1913) Dudley MA, Indian paintbrush [Indian paint-brush, Indian paint brush] (3, 5, 73, 97, 138, 155, 156, 158) (1892–1977), Indian pink (5, 75, 156) (1894–1923) Peoria IL, Nosebleed [Nose-bleed, Nose bleed, Nose bleede (5, 75, 156) (1894–1923) CT, no longer in use by 1923, Paintbrush [Paintbrush, Paint brush] (73) (1892), Painted-cup [Painted cup, Painted-cup] (5, 12, 19, 47, 92, 187) (1852–1913), Prairie-fire [Prairie fire] (5, 73, 156, 158) (1892–1923) WI, no longer in use by 1923, Red Indians [Red-Indians] (5, 73, 156, 158) (1892–1923) MA, Scarlet bartsia (42) (1814), Scarlet Indian paintbrush (50) (present), Scarlet painted-cup [Scarlet painted-cup] (2, 5, 72, 97, 156, 158) (1895–1937), Wickawee (5, 73, 156, 158) (1892–1923) MA, from Indian name, no longer in use by 1923, Wĭnabojo' noko'mĭs wi'nĭzĭsûn (Chippewa, Winabojo's grandmother's hair) (40) (1928)

Castilleja flava **S. Wats.** – Yellow Indian paintbrush (50) (present), Yellow painted-cup [Yellow paintedcup] (155) (1942)

Castilleja foliolosa **Hook. & Arn.** – Woolly painted-cup (138) (1923)

Castilleja foliosa – See *Castilleja foliolosa* Hook. & Arn.

Castilleja indivisa **Engelm.** – Entire-leaf painted-cup [Entire-leaved painted-cup] (5, 97, 122) (1913–1937), Texas painted-cup [Texas painted cup] (124, 138) (1923–1937)

Castilleja integra **Gray** – Whole-leaf Indian paintbrush [Wholeleaf Indian paintbrush] (50) (present), Whole-leaf painted-cup [Wholeleaf paintedcup] (155) (1942)

Castilleja linariifolia **Benth.** – Wyoming Indian paintbrush (50) (present), Wyoming paintbrush (4) (1986), Wyoming painted-cup [Wyoming paintedcup] (155) (1942)

Castilleja lindheimeri **Gray** – See *Castilleja purpurea* (Nutt.) G. Don var. *lindheimeri* (Gray) Shinners

Castilleja luteovirens **Rydb.** – See *Castilleja sulphurea* Rydb.

Castilleja miniata **Dougl. ex Hook.** – Giant red Indian paintbrush (50) (present), Scarlet painted-cup [Scarlet paintedcup] (155) (1942)

Castilleja minor **(Gray) Gray** – Indian pink (5) (1913), Small-flower painted-cup [Small-flowered paintedcup] (5) (1913) SD

Castilleja minor **Gray** – See *Castilleja minor* (Gray) Gray

Castilleja **Mutis ex L. f.** – Indian paintbrush [Indian paint-brush, Indian paint brush] (1, 4, 50, 93) (1932–present), Painted-cup [Painted cup, Paintedcup] (1, 2, 10, 93, 138, 155, 156, 158) (1818–1942), Painter's-brush [Painter's brush] (1) (1932), Squaw-feather [Squaw feather] (1, 93) (1932–1936)

Castilleja purpurea **(Nutt.) G. Don var. *citrina* (Pennell) Shinners** – Citron paintbrush (3) (1977), Prairie Indian paintbrush (50) (present)

Castilleja purpurea **(Nutt.) G. Don var. *lindheimeri* (Gray) Shinners** – Indian paintbrush [Indian paint-brush, Indian paint brush] (97, 124) (1937)

Castilleja purpurea **(Nutt.) G. Don var. *purpurea*** – Downy Indian paintbrush (50) (present)

Castilleja purpurea **(Nutt.) G. Don.** – Downy Indian paintbrush (50) (present), Purple painted-cup (97) (1937)

Castilleja rhexifolia **Rydb.** – See *Castilleja sulphurea* Rydb.

Castilleja septentrionalis **Lindl.** – Lance-leaf painted-cup [Lance-leaved painted-cup] (5) (1913), Painted-cup [Painted cup, Painted-cup] (131) (1899), Pale painted-cup (5) (1913)

Castilleja sessiliflora **Pursh** – Downy paintbrush [Downy paintbrush] (3, 4) (1977–1986), Downy paintedcup [Downy painted-cup,

Downy painted cup] (5, 50, 72, 93, 97, 122) (1907–present), Honeysuckle [Honey suckle, Honey-suckle, Honisuckles] (77) (1898) Burnside SD, Prairie painted-cup [Prairie painted cup] (131) (1899) SD, Waxpe jazokapi (Lakota, suck leaf) (121) (1918?–1970?)

Castilleja sulphurea **Rydb.** – Downy paintbrush [Downy paint-brush] (85) (1932) SD, Indian paintbrush [Indian paint-brush, Indian paint brush] (85) (1932), Split-leaf painted-cup [Splitleaf paintedcup] (155) (1942), Sulfur Indian paintbrush [Sulphur Indian paintbrush] (50) (present), Sulfur painted-cup [Sulfur paintedcup] (155) (1942), Yellow-green painted-cup [Yellowgreen paintedcup] (155) (1942)

Casuarina cunninghamiana **Miq.** – Cunningham beefwood's [Cunningham beefwood] (138) (1923)

Casuarina equisetifolia **L.** – Horsetail tree [Horsetail-tree] (109, 138) (1923–1949)

Casuarina **L.** – See *Casuarina* Rumph. ex L.

Casuarina **Rumph. ex L.** – Australian-pine (109) (1949), Beefwood (109, 138) (1923–1949), She-oak (109) (1949)

Catabrosa aquatica **(L.) Beauv.** – Brook grass [Brook-grass, Brook-grass] (3, 85, 140, 155) (1932–1977), Float grass [Flote grass] (46) (1879), Floating manna grass [Floating manna-grass] (56, 67) (1890–1901), Kiarr-tatel (Swedish) (46) (1879), Reed meadow grass [Reed meadow-grass] (66, 87, 90) (1885–1903), Sweet grass [Sweet-grass, Sweetgrass] (101) (1905) MT, Water aira grass [Water aira-grass] (165) (1768), Water grass [Water-grass] (5, 111, 157) (1913–1929), Water hair grass (5, 19, 66) (1840–1912), Water meadow grass (68) (1890), Water spear grass (66) (1903), Water whorl grass [Water whorl-grass, Water whorlgrass] (5, 50, 94) (1901–present), White spear grass (87, 90) (1884–1885)

Catabrosa **Beauv.** – Brook grass [Brook-grass, Brookgrass] (1, 93) (1932–1936), Whorl grass [Whorlgrass] (50) (present)

Catalpa bignonioides **Walt.** – Bean tree [Beantree, Bean-tree (5, 6, 49, 53, 156) (1892–1923), Candle tree [Candle-tree, Candletree] (5, 156) (1913–1923) IA, Catalpa or Catalpa tree [Catalpa-tree] (5, 6, 12, 14, 20, 38, 49, 58, 63, 97, 122, 124, 156) (1820–1937), Catawba or Catawba tree (5, 75, 156) (1894–1923) WV, Cigar tree [Cigar-tree] (5, 49, 53, 156) (1898–1923), Common catalpa (2, 109, 138) (1895–1949), Indian bean [Indian-bean] or Indian bean tree [Indian bean-tree] (5, 6, 49, 63, 72, 109, 156) (1892–1949), Indian cigar tree (5, 156) (1913–1923), Patalpa (156) (1923), Smoking bean (156) (1923), Southern catalpa (50) (present)

Catalpa bungei **C. A. Mey.** – Manchurian catalpa (138) (1923)

Catalpa catalpa **(L.) Karst.** – See *Catalpa bignonioides* Walt.

Catalpa cordifolia **Nutt.** – possibly *Catalpa bignonioides* Walt.

Catalpa **Jussieu** – See *Catalpa* Scop.

Catalpa kaempferi **(Siebold & Zucc.)** – See *Catalpa ovata* G. Don

Catalpa **L.** – See *Catalpa* Scop.

Catalpa ovata **G. Don** – Bois shavanon (French Creole) (17, 20) (1796–1857), Catalpa (French) (8, 20) (1785–1857), Catalpa or Catalpa tree [Catalpa-tree] (8, 92, 189) (1767–1876), Catawba or Catawba tree (20, 92) (1857–1876) for Indian tribe, Chinese catalpa (50, 155) (1942–present), Japanese catalpa (138) (1923)

Catalpa **Scop.** – Catalpa or Catalpa tree [Catalpa-tree] (1, 10, 26, 50, 82, 138, 155, 158) (1818–present), Cigar tree [Cigar-tree] (1) (1932), Indian bean [Indian-bean] or Indian bean tree [Indian bean-tree] (1, 2) (1895–1932), Indian cigar tree (4) (1986), Petalfra (38) (1820)

Catalpa speciosa **(Warder) Warder ex Engelm.** – Candle tree [Candle-tree, Candletree] (156) (1923), Catalpa or Catalpa tree [Catalpa-tree] (3, 82, 106, 114, 156) (1894–1977), Catawba or Catawba tree (4, 5, 63, 82, 158) (1899–1986), Cigar tree [Cigar-tree] (4, 5, 156, 158) (1900–1986), Hardy catalpa (5, 112, 156, 158) (1900–1937), Indian bean [Indian-bean] or Indian bean tree [Indian bean-tree] (106, 156) (1923–1930), Larger Indian bean (5, 63, 72, 158) (1899–1913), Northern catalpa (4, 50, 155) (1942–present), Shawnee-wood [Shawnee-wood] (5, 156, 158) (1900–1923), Western catalpa (5, 85, 97, 109, 122, 124, 135, 138, 156, 158) (1900–1949), White mahogany (156) (1923)

Catalpa syringaefolia – possibly *Catalpa bignonioides* Walter (current species depends on author)

Catanache caerulea – See *Catananche caerulea L.*

Catananche caerulea **L.** – Blue Cupid's-daisy [Blue Cupids-daisy] (138) (1923)

Catananche **L.** – Cupid's-daisy [Cupids-daisy] (109, 138) (1923–1949)

Catapodium rigidum **(L.) C. E. Hubbard ex Dony** – See *Desmazeria rigida* (L.) Tutin

Catathelasma ventricosum (Peck) Singer – Swollen-stalk cat [Swollen-stalked cat] (170) (1995)

Catesbaea **L.** – Lily-thorn [Lilythorn] (138) (1923)

Catharanthus roseus **(L.) G. Don** – Madagascar periwinkle (109, 138) (1923–1949)

Cathartolinum berlandieri **(Hook.) Small** – See *Linum berlandieri* Hook. var. *berlandieri*

Cathartolinum catharticum **(L.) Small** – See *Linum catharticum* L.

Cathartolinum curtissii **(Small) Small** – See *Linum medium* (Planch.) Britton var. *texanum* (Planch.) Fern.

Cathartolinum floridanum **(Planch.) Small.** – See *Linum floridanum* (Planch.) Trel. var. *floridanum*

Cathartolinum medium **(Planch.) Small.** – See *Linum medium* (Planch.) Britt. var. *medium*

Cathartolinum **Reichenb.** – See *Linum* L.

Cathartolinum rigidum **(Pursh) Small** – See *Linum rigidum* Pursh var. *rigidum*

Cathartolinum striatum **(Walt.) Small** – See *Linum striatum* Walt.

Cathartolinum sulcatum **(Riddell) Small** – See *Linum sulcatum* Riddell var. *sulcatum*

Cathartolinum virginianum **(L.) Reichenb.** – See *Linum virginianum* L.

Caucalis daucoides **L.** – See *Caucalis platycarpos* L. (taxonomic status is unresolved (PL))

Caucalis platycarpos **L.** – Bastard parsley (92) (1876), Hen's-foot [Hen's foot] (92) (1876)

Caucauis daucoides – See *Caucalis platycarpos* L.

Caulanthus crassicaulis **(Torr.) S. Wats.** – Wild cabbage (74, 106, 107) (1893–1930)

Caulanthus crassicaulis **S. Wats.** – See *Caulanthus crassicaulis* (Torr.) S. Wats.

Caulanthus procerus – See *Guillenia flavescens* (Hook.) Greene

Caulanthus **S. Wats.** – Wild cabbage (15) (1895)

Caulinia flexilis **[Willd.]** – See *Najas flexilis* (Willd.) Rostk. & Schmidt

Caulophyllum **Michx.** – Blue cohosh (13, 93, 155, 158) (1849–1942), Cohosh [Co-hosh] (50) (present), Lion's-leaf (158) (1900), Pappoose root [Pappoose-root] (13) (1849)

Caulophyllum thalictroides **(L.) Michx.** – Be'cigodji'bigŭk (Chippewa) (40) (1928), Blau cohosch (German) (6, 7) (1828–1932), Blue cohosh (3, 4, 5, 6, 15, 37, 40, 49, 50, 52, 53, 54, 55, 57, 58, 63, 72, 85, 92, 109, 131, 138, 155, 156, 157, 158) (1869–present), Blue ginseng (5, 6, 7, 64, 92, 156, 157, 158) (1828–1929), Blueberry [Blueberries, Blue berries, Blue berry] (5, 6, 7, 58, 92, 156) (1828–1923), Blue-berry cohosh [Blueberry cohosh] (7) (1828), Blue-berry root [Blueberry-root] (5, 64, 156, 157, 158) (1900–1929), Caulophyllum radix (Official name of Materia Medica) (7) (1828), Cohoche bleu (French) (6, 7) (1828–1932), Cohosh [Co-hosh] (7, 29, 187) (1818–1869), Cohush (7) (1828), False cohosh (19) (1840), Papoose root (2, 5, 6, 7) (1828–1913), Pappoose root [Pappoose-root] (19, 49, 53, 55, 58, 64, 156, 157, 158) (1840–1929), Squawroot [Squaw-root, Squaw root] (5, 6, 7, 49, 53, 55, 57, 58, 64, 92, 156, 157, 158) (1828–1929), Yellow ginseng (6, 7, 64, 156, 157, 158) (1828–1929), Zhu-nakada-tanga-makan (Omaha-Ponca. great fever medicine) (37) (1919)

Ceanothus americanus **L.** – American ceanothus (8) (1785), Céanote d'Amérique (French) (8) (1785), Céanothe (French) (158) (1900), Ceanothus (52, 54, 57, 174) (1753–1917), Common New Jersey tea tree (42) (1814), Indian tea (37, 156) (1919–1923), Jersey tea [Jersey-tea] (7, 92, 138, 157, 158) (1828–1929), Jersey-tea ceanothus [Jerseytea ceanothus] (155) (1942), Kadegimnedu (Chippewa) (105)

(1932), Konjibik (Chippewa) (105) (1932), Mountain-sweet [Mountain sweet] (5, 92, 107, 156, 157, 158) (1876–1929), New Jersey tea [New-Jersey-tea, New-Jersey tea] (3, 4, 5, 15, 19, 49, 50, 52, 53, 54, 57, 58, 65, 72, 82. 92, 95, 97, 104, 105, 106, 107, 109, 113, 122, 124, 156, 157, 158, 184, 187) (1793–present), New Jersey tea shrub (14) (1882), New Jersey tea tree [New-Jersey tea-tree] (8) (1785), Redrod for dying (177) (1762), Redroot [Red-root, Red root] (5, 7, 14, 35, 47, 49, 52, 53, 54, 57, 58, 61, 82, 92, 106, 156, 157, 158, 184, 187) (1793–1929), Seckelblume (German) (158) (1900), Spangles (5) (1913), Sprangle [Sprangles] (156, 157, 158) (1900–1929), Tabehi (Omaha-Ponca) (37) (1919), Walpole tea (5, 92, 156, 157, 158) (1876–1929), Wild pepper (5, 76, 156) (1896–1923) Greene Co. MO, Wild snowball (5, 49, 58, 92, 107, 156, 157, 158) (1869–1929)

Ceanothus americanus **L.** *var.* *pitcheri* **Torr. & Gray** – See *Ceanothus americanus* L.

Ceanothus arboreus **Greene** – Catalina ceanothus (109) (1949), Feltleaf ceanothus [Feltleaf ceanothus] (109) (1949)

Ceanothus azureus – possibly *Ceanothus caeruleus* Lag. (current species depends on author)

Ceanothus caeruleus **Lag.** – possibly Azure ceanothus (138) (1923)

Ceanothus cuneatus **(Hook.) Nutt.** – Buckbrush [Buck brush, Buckbrush] (106) (1930) CA

Ceanothus cyaneus **Eastw.** – San Diego ceanothus (109) (1949)

Ceanothus divaricatus **Nutt.** – See *Ceanothus oliganthus* Nutt.

Ceanothus fendleri **Gray** – Fendler's ceanothus [Fendler ceanothus] (50, 130, 138, 155) (1895–present), Fendler's redroot (131) (1899)

Ceanothus greggii **Gray** – Gregg's ceanothus (124) (1937)

Ceanothus herbaceus **Raf.** – Downy redroot [Downy red-root] (72) (1907) IA, Inland ceanothus (155) (1942), Inland Jersey-tea (138) (1923), Jersey tea [Jersey-tea] (50) (present), Mountain laurel [Mountain Lawrell] (85) (1932), New Jersey tea [New-Jersey-tea, New-Jersey tea] (3, 4, 40, 85) (1928–1986), Odiga'dimanido (Chippewa) (40) (1928), Redroot [Red-root, Red root] (95, 113, 122, 124, 130, 145) (1890–1937), Small redroot [Small red root] (72, 151) (1896–1907), Smaller redroot [Smaller red root] (5, 97) (1913–1937), Uŋpaŋ tawota (Lakota, elk food) (121) (1918?–1970?)

Ceanothus herbaceus **Raf.** *var.* *pubescens* **(Torr. & Gray ex S. Wats.) Shinners** – See *Ceanothus herbaceus* Raf.

Ceanothus hirsutus **Nutt.** – See *Ceanothus oliganthus* Nutt.

Ceanothus **L.** – California lilac (15) (1895), Céanote (French) (8) (1785), Ceanothus (50, 138, 155) (1923–present), Deer brush (1) (1932), Mountain laurel [Mountain Lawrell] (1) (1932), Mountain lily [Mountaine Lillie, Mountaine Lilly] (106) (1930), New Jersey tea [New-Jersey-tea, New-Jersey tea] (1, 10, 13, 15, 93) (1818–1936), New Jersey tea tree [New Jersey tea-tree] (8) (1785), Redroot [Red-root, Red root] (10, 13, 82, 93, 156, 158, 190) (~1759–1936), Snow brush (1) (1932)

Ceanothus officinalis **Raf.** – See *Ceanothus americanus* L.

Ceanothus oliganthus **Nutt.** – Lilac (76) (1896) Santa Barbara CA, Tall mountain-lilac (138) (1923)

Ceanothus ovatus **Desf.** – See *Ceanothus herbaceus* Raf.

Ceanothus ovatus **Desf.** *var.* *pubescens* **Torr. & Gray ex S. Wats.** – See *Ceanothus herbaceus* Raf.

Ceanothus prostratus **Benth.** – Mahala mat [Mahala mats, Mahalamats] (76, 106, 109, 138) (1896–1949), Squaw-carpet [Squaw carpet, Squaw carpets] (106, 109) (1930–1949)

Ceanothus sanguineus **Pursh** – Buckbrush [Buck brush, Buck-brush] (106) (1930) CA, Redroot [Red-root, Red root] (35) (1806)

Ceanothus spinosus **Nutt.** – Greenbark ceanothus (109) (1949), Redheart ceanothus [Redheart ceanothus] (109) (1949)

Ceanothus thyrsiflorus **Esch.** – Blueblossom [Blue-blossom] (109, 138) (1923–1949), California lilac (52, 76) (1896–1919) CA, Ceanothe thyrsiflore (French) (20) (1857), Ceanothus (52) (1919), Deer bush (52) (1919), Tree ceanothus (20) (1857), Wild lilac (76, 161) (1857–1896) CA

Ceanothus velutinus **Dougl. ex Hook.** – Fragrant laurel (106) (1930) Western Washington, Mountain balm (4) (1986), Snow brush (106)

(1930), Snowbrush ceanothus (50, 155) (1942–present), Velvety ceanothus (130) (1895), Velvety redroot (131) (1899)

Cecropia peltata **L.** – Trumpet tree (92) (1876), Trumpet-wood [Trumpet wood] (92) (1876)

Cedrela **L.** – See *Cedrela* P. Br.

Cedrela odorata **L.** – Barbados cedar [Barbadoes cedar] (92) (1876), Cigarbox cedar [Cigarbox-cedar] (138) (1923), Spanish cedar [Spanish-cedar] (109) (1949), Sweet-scented cedar [Sweet scented cedar] (92) (1876), West Indian cedar [West-Indian-cedar] (109) (1949)

Cedrela **P. Br.** – Cedrela (138) (1923)

Cedronella cana – See *Cedronella canariensis* (L.) Willd. ex Webb & Berth.

Cedronella canariensis **(L.) Willd. ex Webb & Berth.** – Balm-of-Gilead herb [Balm of Gilead herb] (19, 92) (1840–1876), Canary-balm [Canarybalm] (138) (1923), Hoary cedronella (138) (1923), Sweet balm (92) (1876)

Cedronella mexicana **[(Kunth) Benth.]** – See *Agastache mexicana* (Kunth) Lint & Epling

Cedronella **Moench** – Cedronella (138) (1923)

Cedronella triphylla **Moench** – See *Cedronella canariensis* (L.) Willd. ex Webb & Berth.

Cedrus deodara **(Roxb. ex D. Don) G. Don f.** – Deodar (138) (1923) deodar is native name in Himalayas, Deodar cedar (109) (1949), Fountain tree (92) (1876)

Cedrus deodora **Loud.** – See *Cedrus deodara* (Roxb. ex D. Don) G. Don f.

Cedrus libani **A.Rich.** – Cedar of Lebanon (20) (1857)

Cedrus libani **Loud.** – See *Cedrus libani* A. Rich. (Libani for Lebanon)

Cedrus **Loud.** – See *Cedrus* Trew (from Kedrus the ancient Greek name)

Cedrus **Trew** – Cedar or Cedar tree (109, 138) (1923–1949) from Kedrus the ancient Greek name

Ceiba **Adans.** – See *Ceiba* Mill.

Ceiba **Mill.** – Ceiba (138) (1923) from aboriginal name

Ceiba pentandra **(L.) Gaertn.** – Cabbage-wood (107) (1919), Ceiba (107, 138) (1919–1923), God tree (92) (1876), Silk-cotton tree [Silk-cotton-tree] (109) (1949)

Ceiba pentandra **Gaertn.** – See *Ceiba pentandra* (L.) Gaertn.

Celastrus articulata **Thunb.** – See *Celastrus orbiculatus* Thunb. ex Murray

Celastrus articulatus **Thunb.** – See *Celastrus orbiculatus* Thunb. ex Murray

Celastrus **L.** – Bittersweet [Bitter sweet, Bitter-sweet] (50, 93, 138, 155, 156) (1923–present), Célastre (French) (8) (1785), Shrubby bittersweet (1, 13) (1849–1932), Staff tree [Staff-tree] (1, 8, 10, 13, 15, 82, 158) (1785–1932), Waxwork [Wax work, Wax-work] (1, 13) (1849–1932)

Celastrus orbiculatus **Thunb. ex Murray** – Chinese bittersweet (82) (1930) IA, Oriental bittersweet (138) (1923)

Celastrus scandens **L.** – American bittersweet [American bitter-sweet] (50, 109 122, 124, 138, 155) (1923–present), American climbing staff-tree (8) (1785), Bima'kwûd (Chippewa, twisting around) (40) (1928), Bi-na-quat (Chippewa) (47) (1852), Bittersweet [Bitter sweet, Bitter-sweet] (9, 22, 37, 40, 65, 85, 103, 105, 106, 107, 112, 130, 131, 156, 158) (1870–1937), Bois retors (French) (103) (1870), Celaster (German) (158) (1900), Celastre (French) (158) (1900), Climbing bittersweet [Climbing bitter-sweet] (3, 5, 15, 42, 47, 49, 72, 82, 92, 95, 97, 106, 108, 125, 126, 156, 157, 158) (1814–1977), Climbing celastrus (187) (1818), Climbing orangeroot [Climbing orange root, Climbing orange-root] (5, 92, 156, 157, 158) (1876–1929), Climbing staff-tree (49, 57, 92) (1876–1917), False bittersweet [False bitter-sweet or false bitter sweet] (5, 19, 49, 57, 58, 61, 92, 109, 135, 156, 157) (1840–1949), Fever-twig [Fever-twig] (5, 7, 49, 92, 156, 157, 158) (1828–1929), Fever-twitch [Fever twitch] (92) (1876), Jacob's-ladder [Jacob's ladder, Jacobs-ladder] (5, 73, 158) (1892–1913) Stratham NH, Redroot [Red-root, Red root] (19, 156) (1840–1923), Roxbury waxwork [Roxbury wax work, Roxbury wax-work] (5, 73, 92, 156, 157, 158) (1892–1929) Eastern MA, Shrubby bittersweet (5, 15, 156, 157, 158) (1895–1929), Staff tree [Staff-tree] (5, 7, 14, 19, 47, 49, 92, 103, 107, 156, 157, 158, 184) (1793–1929), Waxwork [Wax work, Wax-work] (2, 5, 14, 49, 58, 92, 106, 107, 109, 138, 156, 158, 187) (1818–1949), Yellowroot [Yellow root, Yellow-root] (92, 157, 158) (1876–1929), Zuzecha-ta-wote (Dakota, snake food) (37) (1919)

***Celeri graveolens* (L.) Britton** – See *Apium graveolens* L. var. *dulce* (P. Mill.) DC.

***Celosia argentea* L.** – Cockscomb [Cock's comb, Cocks-comb, Cock's-comb] (184) (1793), Feather cockscomb (138) (1923), Hutton's cockscomb [Hutton cockscomb] (138) (1923)

***Celosia argentea* L. var. *cristata* Kuntze** – See *Celosia cristata* L.

Celosia castrensis – See *Celosia argentea* L.

***Celosia cristata* L.** – Cockscomb [Cock's comb, Cocks-comb, Cock's-comb] (19, 92, 109) (1840–1949), Common cockscomb (138) (1923), Purple flower-gentle [Purple flower gentle] (178) (1526)

Celosia huttoni – See *Celosia argentea* L.

***Celosia huttonii* Mast.** – See *Celosia argentea* L.

***Celosia* L.** – Cockscomb [Cock's comb, Cocks-comb, Cock's-comb] (138) (1923)

***Celsia* L.** – See *Verbascum* L.

***Celtis* (Tourn.) L.** – See *Celtis* L.

***Celtis australis* L.** – Date-plum [Dateplum, Date plum] (178) (1526), European hackberry (138) (1923), Nettle tree [Nettle-tree] (178) (1526)

***Celtis canina* Raf.** – See *Celtis occidentalis* L.

***Celtis crassifolia* Lam.** – See *Celtis occidentalis* L.

***Celtis douglasii* Planch.** – See *Celtis laevigata* Willd. var. *reticulata* (Torr.) L. Benson

***Celtis georgiana* Small.** – See *Celtis tenuifolia* Nutt.

***Celtis integrifolia* [Lam.]** – See *Celtis tenuifolia* Nutt.

***Celtis* L.** – Hackberry [Hack-berry] or Hackberry tree (1, 4, 50, 7, 10, 82, 93, 106, 109, 138, 155) (1923–present), Lote (189) (1767), Micocoulier (French) (8) (1785), Nettle tree [Nettle-tree] (2, 7, 8, 10, 42, 158) (1814–1900)

***Celtis laevigata* Willd.** – Nettle tree of America [Nettle-tree of America] (189) (1767), Smooth-leaf hackberry [Smooth-leafed hackberry] (124) (1937), Sugar hackberry (155) (1942), Sugarberry [Sugar-berry, Sugar berry] or Sugar-berry tree [Sugar berry tree] (3, 4, 50, 109) (1949–present)

***Celtis laevigata* Willd. var. *reticulata* (Torr.) L. Benson** – Cumaro (153) (1913) NM, Douglas' hackberry [Douglas hackberry] (155) (1942), Hackberry [Hack-berry] or Hackberry tree (35, 65, 149, 153) (1806–1931), Micocoulier riticule (French) (20) (1857), Netleaf hackberry [Netleaf hackberry] (3, 4, 50, 155) (1942–present), Oklahoma hackberry (155) (1942), Palo blanco [Paloblanco] (138) (1923), Rough-leaf hackberry [Rough leafed hackberry] (124) (1937), Small-leaf nettle tree [Small-leaved nettle tree] (20) (1857), Thick-leaf hackberry [Thick-leaved hackberry] (5, 97) (1913–1937)

***Celtis laevigata* Willd. var. *smallii* (Beadle) Sargent** – See *Celtis tenuifolia* Nutt.

***Celtis longifolia* Nutt.** – See *Celtis occidentalis* L.

***Celtis longifolia* Raf.** – See *Celtis tenuifolia* Nutt.

***Celtis mississippiensis* Bosc** – See *Celtis tenuifolia* Nutt.

Celtis occidentalis crassifolia – See *Celtis occidentalis* L. var. *occidentalis*

***Celtis occidentalis* L.** – American hackberry (2) (1895), American nettle tree [American nettle-tree] (6, 20, 158, 187) (1818–1900), American yellow-fruit nettle-tree [American yellow-fruited nettletree] (8) (1785), Bastard elm (5, 158) (1900–1913), Beaver wood [Beaver-wood] (5, 6, 75, 156, 158) (1892–1923), Bois connu (Illinois French) (17) (1796), Bois inconnu (Illinois French, New Orleans, Illinois) (17, 20) (1796–1857) Illinois French, Common American nettle tree (42) (1814), Common hackberry (50, 155) (1942–present), False elm (5, 156, 158) (1900–1923), Goŋe (Osage) (121) (1918?–1970?), Gube (Omaha-Ponca) (37) (1919), Hackberry [Hack-berry] or Hackberry tree (3, 4, 5, 6, 9, 14, 17, 20, 27, 28, 34, 35, 37, 44,

46, 82, 85, 92, 93, 95, 97, 107, 112, 113, 121, 130, 131, 135, 138, 156, 158) (1796–1986), Hagberry [Hag-berry] (19) (1840), Hedgeberry [Hedge-berry] (156) (1923), Hoop ash (5, 19, 20, 27, 75, 156, 158) (1811–1923), Juniper or Juniper tree [Juniper-tree] (5, 156, 158) (1900–1923), Kaapsit (Pawnee) (37) (1919), Lote tree (181) (~1678), Micocoulier d'Occident (French) (8) (1785), Minny-berry (156) (1923), Nettle tree [Nettle-tree] (5, 27, 34, 41, 92, 107, 156, 181, 184) (~1678–1923), Northern hackberry (106) (1930), One-berry [One-berry, One berry] (5, 156, 158) (1900–1923), Rim ash (5, 156, 158) (1900–1923), Rough-leaf hackberry [Rough-leaved hackberry] (5, 85, 93, 97) (1913–1937), Sucré Baie (French) (6) (1892), Sugarberry [Sugar-berry, Sugar berry] or Sugar-berry tree [Sugar berry tree] (5, 6, 14, 46, 92, 106, 107, 156, 158, 187) (1818–1930), Thick-leaf nettle tree [Thick-leaved nettle tree] (20) (1857), Wake-warutsh (Winnebago, raccoon food) (37) (1919), Yamnumnugapi (Dakota, to crunch) (37) (1919), Zuckerbeere (German) (6) (1892), possibly Hedge beech (46) (1649)

***Celtis occidentalis* L. var. *crassifolia* (Lam.) Gray** – See *Celtis occidentalis* L. var. *occidentalis*

Celtis occidentalis* L. var. *occidentalis – Big-leaf hackberry [Bigleaf hackberry] (138, 155) (1923–1942), Hackberry [Hack-berry] or Hackberry tree (112) (1937)

***Celtis pallida* Torr.** – Cranjero (Mexico) (107) (1919), Cranxero (Mexico) (107) (1919), Granejo (106) (1930), Granjeno (122, 124) (1937) TX

***Celtis pumila* Pursh var. *georgiana* (Small) Sargent** – See *Celtis tenuifolia* Nutt.

***Celtis reticulata* Torr.** – See *Celtis laevigata* Willd. var. *reticulata* (Torr.) L. Benson

***Celtis reticulata* Torr. var. *vestita* Sargent** – See *Celtis laevigata* Willd. var. *reticulata* (Torr.) L. Benson

***Celtis tala* Gill.** – See *Celtis pallida* Torr.

***Celtis tenuifolia* Nutt.** – Dwarf hackberry (3, 4, 50) (1977–present), Entire-leaf nettle tree [Entire-leaved nettle tree] (12) (1821), Georgia hackberry (5, 97, 155) (1913–1942), Hackberry [Hack-berry] or Hackberry tree (12) (1821), Long-leaf nettle-tree [Long-leaved nettle-tree] (20) (1857), Micocoulier à longues feuilles (French) (20) (1857), Small's sugar hackberry [Smalls sugar hackberry] (155) (1942), Southern hackberry (5, 97, 106) (1913–1937), Sugarberry [Sugar-berry, Sugar berry] or Sugar-berry tree [Sugar berry tree] (106, 138) (1923–1930), Thin-leaf nettle-tree [Thin-leaved nettle-tree] (20) (1857)

***Cenchrus carolinianus* Walt.** – See *Cenchrus longispinus* (Hack.) Fern.

***Cenchrus echinatus* L.** – Bur grass [Bur-grass, Burr grass] (19) (1840), Cockspur grass [Cockspur-grass] (187) (1818), Hedgehog grass [Hedge hog grass, Hedge-hog grass, Hedge-hog-grass] (19, 92, 163, 184, 187) (1818–1876), Rough-seed hedgehog grass [Rough seeded hedge hog grass] (42) (1814) CO Neb, Southern sandbur [Southern sand-bur] (50) (present)

***Cenchrus incertus* M. A. Curtis** – See *Cenchrus spinifex* Cav.

***Cenchrus* L.** – Bur grass [Bur-grass, Burr grass] (1, 10, 92, 93) (1818–1936), Hedgehog grass [Hedge hog grass, Hedge-hog grass, Hedge-hog-grass] (42) (1814), Sandbur [Sand bur, Sand-bur] (1, 50, 93, 122, 155, 163) (1852–present), Sandspur (1) (1932)

***Cenchrus longispinus* (Hack.) Fern.** – Field sandbur (3, 140) (1944–1977), Mat sandbur (50, 140) (1944–present), Small bur grass (5) (1913)

***Cenchrus macrocephalus* Scribn.** – See *Cenchrus tribuloides* L.

***Cenchrus myosuroides* Kunth** – Long-spike sandbur [Long-spiked sand-bur] (94) (1901)

***Cenchrus pauciflorus* Benth.** – See *Cenchrus spinifex* Cav.

***Cenchrus racemosus* L.** – See *Tragus racemosus* (L.) All.

***Cenchrus spinifex* Cav.** – Bur grass [Bur-grass, Burr grass] (119) (1938), Coast sandbur (122) (1937), Coastal sandbur (50) (present), Field sandbur (122) (1937), Mat sandbur (155) (1942), Sandbur [Sand bur, Sand-bur] (85, 119, 163) (1852–1938), Southern sandbur [Southern sand-bur] (94) (1901)

Cenchrus tribuloides L. – Bear grass (5, 75) (1894–1913), Bur grass [Bur-grass, Burr grass] (2, 5, 46, 62, 66, 150) (1894–1912), Hedge-hog grass [Hedge hog grass, Hedge-hog grass, Hedge-hog-grass] (2, 5, 62, 66, 75) (1894–1913), Large sand-bur (94) (1901), Roseta (150) (1894) NM, Sand bar (78) (1898) TX, Sand bur [Sand burr, Sandbur, Sand-bur] (5, 11, 56, 62, 73, 80, 94, 111, 131, 148, 150, 152) (1888–1939), Sandbur [Sand bur, Sand-bur] (145) (1897), Sand-dune sand-bur [Sanddune sandbur] (50) (present), Sandspur [Sand spur] (5, 78) (1898–1913) FLA

Centaurea americana Nutt. – American centaury (86) (1878), American knapweed (106) (1930), American star thistle [American star-thistle] (5, 50, 97, 158) (1913–present), Basket-flower [Basketflower] (3, 4, 109, 138) (1923–1986), Basket-flower centaurea [Basketflower centaurea] (155) (1942), Sultana star thistle (122, 124) (1937) TX

Centaurea benedicta L. – See *Cnicus benedictus* L.

Centaurea calcitrapa L. – Caltrappe (179) (1526), Caltrop [Caltrops] (5, 107, 156) (1913–1923), Knapweed [Knap weed] (7, 92) (1828–1876), Knopweed [Knop weed, Knop-weed] (5, 156) (1913–1923), Maize thorn [Maize-thorn] (5, 156) (1913–1923), Mouse-thorn [Mouse thorn] (5, 156) (1913–1923), Star thistle [Star-thistle] (5, 42, 92, 107, 156) (1814–1923), Starry thistle [Starrie thistle] (178) (1526)

Centaurea cineraria L. – Dusty-miller [Dustymiller, Dusty miller] (109, 138) (1923–1949)

Centaurea cyanus L. – Bachelor's-button [Bachelor's button, Bachelor's buttons, Batchelor's buttons] (3, 4, 5, 106, 109, 114, 156, 157, 158) (1894–1986), Barbeau (French) (5, 76, 156, 158) (1896–1923) LA, for M. Barbeau who brought it from France, Blaver (5, 156, 157, 158) (1900–1929), Blawort (157, 158) (1900–1929), Blue centaury (92) (1876), Blue poppy (5, 156, 158) (1900–1923), Blueblow [Blue-blow] (157, 158) (1900–1929), Bluebonnet [Blue bonnets, Blue-bonnets, Bluebonnets] (5, 92, 157, 158) (1876–1929), Bluebottle [Blue-bottle, Blue bottle, Blue bottles] (5, 7, 10, 14, 19, 42, 92, 93, 106, 109, 114, 131, 156, 157, 158) (1814–1949), Bluecaps [Blue caps, Blue-caps] (5, 156, 157, 158) (1900–1929), Bluet (French) (158) (1900), Bluets [Bluet] (106) (1930), Break-your-spectacles (157, 158) (1900–1929), Brushes (5, 64, 73, 78, 92, 156, 157, 158) (1900–1929), Casse-lunette (French) (158) (1900), Common cornflower (106) (1930), Corn bluebottle [Corn blue-bottle] (5, 156, 157, 158) (1900–1929), Corn centaury (5, 156, 157, 158) (1900–1929), Cornbinks [Corn binks, Corn-binks] (5, 156, 157, 158) (1900–1929), Cornbottles [Corn bottles, Corn-bottle] (5, 156, 157, 158) (1900–1929), Cornflower [Corn-flower, Corn flower] (4, 5, 82, 85, 93, 97, 109, 131, 138, 155, 156, 157, 158, 178) (1526–1986), French pink [French pinks] (5, 76, 156, 157, 158) (1896–1929), Garden cornflower (50) (present), Hurt-sickle [Hurtsickle, Hurt sickle] (5, 156, 157, 158) (1900–1929), Knapweed [Knap weed] (157, 158) (1900–1929), Kornblume (German) (158) (1900), Ragged-robin [Ragged robin] (76) (1896) Rutalnd MA, Ragged-sailor [Ragged sailor, Ragged sailors] (106) (1930), Witche's-bell [Witches' bells, Witches bells, Witches'-bells, Witches' bells, Witches bells] (5, 156, 157, 158) (1900–1929), Witch's-thimble [Witches thimbles, Witches' thimbles, Witches'-thimbles, Witches'thimbles] (5, 156, 157, 158) (1900–1929)

Centaurea dealbata Willd. – Persian centaruea (138) (1923)

Centaurea diffusa Lam. – Diffuse knapweed (4) (1986), White knapweed (50) (present)

Centaurea iberica Trev. ex Spreng. – Iberian centuarea (155) (1942), Iberian knapweed (50) (present), Iberian star-thistle [Iberian star thistle] (4) (1986)

Centaurea jacea L. – Brown knapweed (5) (1913), Knapweed [Knap weed] (19, 42) (1814–1840), Rayed knapweed (5) (1913)

Centaurea L. – Bachelor's-button [Bachelor's button, Bachelor's buttons, Batchelor's buttons] (1) (1932), Barnaby's thistle (106) (1930), Bluebottle [Blue-bottle, Blue bottle, Blue bottles] (1, 158, 167) (1814–1900), Centaurea (138, 155) (1923–1942), Centaury (4, 184) (1793–1986), Cornflower [Corn-flower, Corn flower] (1, 93)

(1932–1936), Dusty-miller [Dustymiller, Dusty miller] (75) (1894) Boston Florists' catalogue, Knapweed [Knap weed] (4, 10, 50) (1818–present), Star thistle [Star-thistle] (1, 4, 82, 106, 156) (1923–1986)

Centaurea macrocephala Puschk. ex Willd. – Globe centaurea (138) (1923)

Centaurea maculosa Lam. – Spotted centaurea (155) (1942), Spotted knapweed (3, 4, 5, 50) (1913–present)

Centaurea melitensis L. – Lombardy star thistle (106) (1930) Southeast, Napa thistle (106) (1930) CA, Pasture weed (76) (1896) CA, Rayless winged centaury (5, 122, 124) (1913–1937), Tacalote (106) (1930), Tocalote (106) (1930), Tocolote (76) (1896)

Centaurea montana L. – Cantaurea (82) (1930), Great cornflower [Great corne flower] (178) (1526), Mountain bluet (109) (1949), Mountain-bluet (138) (1923)

Centaurea moschata – See *Amberboa moschata* (L.) DC.

Centaurea muricata L. – See *Cyanopsis muricata* (L.) Dostál

Centaurea nigra L. – Bachelor's-button [Bachelor's button, Bachelor's buttons, Batchelor's buttons] (5, 156) (1913–1923) no longer in use by 1923, Black knapweed (5, 14, 19, 156) (1840–1923), Blue-tops [Blue tops, Blue-tops] (5, 156) (1913–1923) no longer in use by 1923, Boleweed [Bole weed] (5) (1913), Bowlweed [Bowl-weed] (156) (1923), Bullweed [Bull-weed] (5, 156) (1913–1923), Button-weed [Button-weed, Button weed] (5, 156) (1913–1923), Centaury (5, 156) (1913–1923), Clubweed [Club-weed] (156) (1923), Clunweed [Clun weed] (5) (1913), Cropweed [Crop weed, Crop-weed] (5, 156) (1913–1923), Hardheads [Hard-head] (5, 156) (1913–1923), Hardweed [Hard weed, Hard-weed] (5, 156) (1913–1923), Horse-knobs [Horse knobs, Horse knob] (5, 92) (1876–1913), Horse-knops [Horse knops] (5, 156) (1913–1923), Hurt-sickle [Hurtsickle, Hurt sickle] (5, 156) (1913–1923), Ironhead [Iron head] (5) (1913), Ironweed [Iron weed, Iron weed] (5, 156) (1913–1923), Knapweed [Knap weed] (7, 82, 138, 156) (1828–1930), Knobweed [Knobweed, Knob weed] (5, 156) (1913–1923), Lady's-cushion [Lady's cushion, Ladies' cushion] (5, 156) (1913–1923) no longer in use by 1923, Loggerheads [Logger-heads] (5, 92, 156) (1876–1923) no longer in use by 1923, Mat felon [Matfelon] (5, 156) (1913–1923) no longer in use by 1923, Spanish buttons (156) (1923), Sweeps (5, 156) (1913–1923) no longer in use by 1923, Tassel [Tasyll] (5, 156) (1913–1923) no longer in use by 1923

Centaurea nigrescens Willd. – Tyrol knapweed (5) (1913)

Centaurea repens L. – See *Rhaponticum repens* (L.) Hidalgo

Centaurea scabiosa L. – Great purple knapweed [Great purple knapweede] (178) (1526), Greater centaury (4, 5, 156) (1923–1986), Greater knapweed (14, 50) (1882–present), Mat felon [Matfelon] (178) (1526), Scabiosa centaurea (155) (1942), Scabious knapweed (5, 156) (1913–1923), Scabrous centaury (19) (1840)

Centaurea solstitialis L. – Another sort of great Knapweede (178) (1526), Barnaby's thistle (3, 5, 19, 93, 156) (1840–1977), Knapweed [Knap weed] (7, 80) (1828–1913), Phalaritha (46) (1879), St. Barnaby's thistle (5, 19, 93, 157) (1840–1936), Star thistle [Star-thistle] (80, 157) (1913–1929), Yellow centaurium (155) (1942), Yellow star-thistle [Yellow star thistle] (4, 50, 106, 157) (1900–present)

Centaurea vochinensis Bernh. – See *Centaurea nigrescens* Willd.

Centaurella paniculata M. – See *Bartonia paniculata* (Michx.) Muhl. subsp. *paniculata*

Centaurium beyrichii (T. & G.) Fernald – See *Centaurium beyrichii* (Torr. & Gray ex Torr.) B.L. Robins.

Centaurium beyrichii (Torr. & Gray ex Torr.) B. L. Robins. – Centaury (97) (1937), Mountain pink [Mountain-pink] (100, 122) (1850–1937), Tausengüldenkraut (German, thousand guelders herb) (100) (1850)

Centaurium calycosum (Buckley) Fernald – Buckley's centaury (5, 122) (1913–1937)

Centaurium centaurium (L.) W. F. Wright – See *Centaurium erythraea* Raf.

Centaurium erythraea Raf. – Bitter herb (5) (1913), Bitter-herb (156)

(1923), Bloodwort [Blood wort, Blood-wort] (5, 156) (1913–1923), Centory (179) (1526), Christ's ladder (156) (1923), Earthgall [Earthgall, Earth gall, Erthe galle] (5, 156, 179) (1526–1923), Erithraea (174) (1753), European centaury (5, 156) (1913–1923), Feverfew [Fever few, fever-few] (156) (1923), Lesser centaury (5, 156) (1913–1923), Mountain flax [Mountain-flax] (156) (1923), Sanctuary (5, 156) (1913–1923) no longer in use by 1923, White centory [White centorie] (178) (1526), possibly Common centaury (14) (1882), possibly Common centorie (180) (1633)

Centaurium exaltatum (Griseb.) W. Wight ex Piper – Desert centaury (50) (present), Tall centaury (5) (1913), Western centaury (5, 93) (1913–1936)

Centaurium Hill – Centaurium (155) (1942), Centaury (1, 50, 82, 93, 109, 156) (1923–present)

Centaurium pulchellum (Sw.) Druce – Branched centaury (50) (present), Branching centaury (5) (1913), Dwarf chironia (42) (1814)

Centaurium spicatum (L.) Fernald. – Centaury (82) (1930), Spiked centaury (5) (1913)

Centaurium texense (Griseb.) Fernald – Lady Bird's centaury (50) (present), Texas centaury [Texan centaury] (5, 122) (1913–1937)

Centaurium umbellatum auct. non Gilib. – See *Centaurium erythraea* Raf.

Centaurium venustum (Gray) B. L. Robins. – Pink centaurium (138) (1923)

Centella asiatica (L.) Urban – Codagam (174) (1753), Ovate-leaf marsh penny-wort [Ovate-leaved marsh penny-wort] (5) (1913), Thick-leaf pennywort [Thick leaved pennywort] (92) (1876)

Centenculus minimus L. – See *Anagallis minima* (L.) Krause

Centranthus DC. – See *Centranthus* Neck. ex Lam. & DC.

Centranthus Neck. ex Lam. & DC. – Centranth (109) (1949) from Greek for spurred flower

Centranthus ruber (L.) DC. – Jupiter's-beard [Jupiter's beard, Jupitersbeard, Jupiters-beard] (109, 138) (1923–1949), Red valerian (109, 178) (1526–1949)

Centromadia pungens (Hook. & Arn.) Greene – Spikeweed (106) (1930)

Centrosema (DC.) Benth. – Butterfly pea [Butterfly-pea] (138, 158) (1900–1923), Spurred butterfly-pea [Spurred butterfly pea] (2) (1895)

Centrosema virginianum (L.) Benth. – Gulf Coast pea (124) (1937) TX, Piedmont butterfly-pea (138) (1923), Spurred butterfly (5) (1913), Spurred butterfly-pea [Spurred butterfly pea] (97, 156) (1923–1937)

Centrosema virginianum Benth. – See *Centrosema virginianum* (L.) Benth.

Centunculus L. – See *Anagallis* L.

Centunculus lanceolatus Michx. – See *Anagallis minima* (L.) Krause

Centunculus minimus L. – See *Anagallis minima* (L.) Krause

Cepa – See *Allium* L.

Cephalanthus L. – Bois bouton (French) (8) (1785), Button tree [Button-tree] (8) (1785), Buttonbush [Button bush, Button-bush] (1, 2, 4, 41, 50, 82, 109, 138, 155, 156, 158) (1770–present), Buttonwood [Button wood, Button-wood] (42) (1814), Céphalante (French) (8) (1785)

Cephalanthus occidentalis L. – American button-wood, American button wood (42, 187) (1814–1818), Americansiche Weissball (German) (6, 7) (1828–1932), Bois bouton (French) (8) (1785), Bois de Marais (French, Louisiana Purchase) (7) (1828), Bois de plomb (French) (6) (1892), Box (5, 156, 158) (1900–1923), Buckbrush [Buck brush, Buck-brush] (156) (1923), Button tree [Button-tree] (5, 6, 7, 8, 156, 157, 158) (1828–1929), Buttonbush [Button bush, Button-bush] (19, 72, 92, 114, 127, 131, 156) (1828–1937), Button-willow [Button willow] (5, 106, 156) (1913–1930), Buttonwood [Button wood, Button-wood] (6, 10, 14, 41, 49, 177) (1762–1898), Buttonwood shrub [Button-wood shrub] (5, 7, 92, 156, 158) (1828–1923), Carolina globe tree (177) (1762), Céphalante d'Occident (French) (8) (1785), Cephalanthe d'Amerique (French) (6, 7)

(1828–1932), Cephalanthus Cortex (Official name of Materia Medica) (7) (1828), Common buttonbush (4, 50, 138, 155) (1923–present), Crane-willow [Crane willow] (5, 6, 49, 156, 157, 158) (1892–1929), Crooked-wood (156) (1923), Crouper bush [Crouper-bush] (5, 75, 156, 158) (1900–1923) Ferrisbrugh VT, Elbowbush [Elbowbush, Elbow bush] (156) (1923), Globeflower [Globe-flower, Globe flower] (5, 6, 7, 49, 58, 92, 156) (1828–1923), Globe-flower shrub [Globe-flower-shrub, Globe-flowered-shrub] (184, 187) (1793–1818), Honeyballs [Honey-balls, Honey-ball] (5, 156, 157, 158) (1913–1929), Knopfbusch (German) (6) (1892), Little snowball [Little snow-ball] (5, 7, 92, 156, 158) (1828–1923), Mountain globeflower [Mountain globe-flower, Mountain globe flower] (92, 157, 158) (1876–1929), Pinball [Pin-ball, Pin ball] (5, 73, 156, 157, 158) (1892–1929) NH, Pond buttonwood (75) (1894), Pond-dogwood [Pond dog-wood, Pond dog wood, Pond dogwood] (5, 6, 7, 19, 49, 57, 58, 92, 156, 157, 158, 187) (1818–1929), River bush [Riverbush] (5, 156, 157, 158) (1900–1929), Snowball [Snow ball, Snowballs, Snow-balls] (6) (1892), Southern buttonbush (155) (1942), Swamp dogwood [Swamp-dogwood (58, 157, 158) (1869–1929), Swampwood [Swamp wood, Swamp-wood] (5, 7, 92, 156, 157, 158) (1828–1929), Whiteball [White ball] (7, 92) (1828–1876)

Cephalanthus occidentalis L. var. *pubescens* Raf. – See *Cephalanthus occidentalis* L.

Cephalaria gigantea (Ledeb.) Bobr. – Tatarian cephalaria (138) (1923)

Cephalaria Schrad. ex Roemer & J. A. Schultes – Cephalaria (138) (1923)

Cephalaria tatarica [auct. non Roemer & J. A. Schultes] – See *Cephalaria gigantea* (Ledeb.) Bobr.

Cephalophora scaposa DC. – See *Tetraneuris scaposa* (DC.) Greene var. *scaposa*

Cerassus pennsylvanica Loisel. – See *Prunus pensylvanica* L. f. var. *pensylvanica*

Cerassus pumila Michx. (sic) – See *Prunus pumila* L. var. *pumila*

Cerassus virginianum D.C. (sic) – See *Prunus virginiana* L.

Cerastium alpinum L. – See *Cerastium beeringianum* Cham. & Schlecht. subsp. *earlei* (Rydb.) Hultén

Cerastium arvense L. – Barren chickweed (5) (1913), Corn pink (42) (1814), Field chickweed (5, 50, 72, 131, 156) (1899–present), Field mouse ear [Field mouse-ear] (156) (1923), Field mouse-ear chickweed (86) (1878), Large-flower mouse-ear chickweed [Large-flowered mouse-ear chickweed] (187) (1818), Meadow chickweed (5, 156) (1913–1923), Mouse-ear chickweed [Mouse ear chickweed [Mouse-eared chickweed] (42) (1814), Prairie chickweed (4, 127) (1933–1986), Starry cerastium (138, 155) (1923–1942), Starry grassweed (156) (1923), Starry grasswort (109) (1949)

Cerastium arvense L. subsp. *strictum* (L.) Ugborogho – Common cerastium (155) (1942), Field chickweed (50) (present), Long-peduncle mouse-ear chickweed [Long peduncled mouse-ear chickweed] (187) (1818)

Cerastium beeringianum Cham. & Schlecht. subsp. *earlei* (Rydb.) Hultén – Alpine chickweed (5) (1913)

Cerastium brachypetalum Desportes ex Pers. – Gray chickweed (50) (present), Short-stalk chickweed [Shortstalk chickweed, Short-stalked chickweed] (5, 93, 97, 131) (1899–1937)

Cerastium cerastoides (L.) Britton – Starwort chickweed (5) (1913)

Cerastium diffusum Pers. – Four-stamen chickweed [Fourstamen chickweed] (50) (present)

Cerastium fontanum Baumg. – Common mouse-ear chickweed [Common mouse ear chickweed] (50) (present)

Cerastium fontanum Baumg. subsp. *vulgare* (Hartman) Greuter & Burdet – Big cerastium (155) (1942), Big chickweed (50) (present), Broader mouse-ear chickweed (187) (1818), Chickweed [Chickweed, Chick weed] (19, 80, 102) (1840–1913), Common mouse-ear chickweed [Common mouse ear chickweed] (4, 15, 156) (1895–1986), Large mouse-ear chickweed (72, 93, 156, 187) (1818–1936), Larger mouse-ear (80) (1913), Larger mouse-ear chickweed (5, 97) (1913–1937), Mouse-ear [Mouse ear, Mouse ears, Mouse's ear,

Mows eare] (5, 19, 80, 156) (1840–1923), Mouse-ear chickweed [Mouse ear chickweed [Mouse-eared chickweed] (145) (1897), Mouse-ear chickweed [Mouse-eared chickweed] (85) (1932), Narrow-leaf mouse-ear chickweed [Narrow-leaved mouse-ear chickweed] (187) (1818)

Cerastium glomeratum **Thuill.** – Clammy chickweed [Clammy chickweed, Clammy chick weed] (42) (1814), Clammy mouse-ear chickweed (156, 187) (1818–1923), Mouse-ear chickweed [Mouse ear chickweed [Mouse-eared chickweed] (5, 15, 45, 72, 92, 97, 122, 156) (1876–1937), Sticky cerastium (155) (1942), Sticky chickweed (19, 50) (1840–present)

Cerastium **L.** – Cerastium (138, 155) (1923–1942), Chickweed [Chickweed, Chick weed] (42, 158) (1814–1900), Mouse-ear [Mouse ear, Mouse ears, Mouse's ear, Mows eare] (184) (1793), Mouse-ear chickweed [Mouse ear chickweed [Mouse-eared chickweed] (1, 4, 50, 10, 13, 15, 93, 109, 156, 167, 190) (~1759–present)

Cerastium longipedunculatum **Muhl.** – See *Cerastium nutans* Raf.

Cerastium nitidum **Greene** – See *Cerastium arvense* L. subsp. *strictum* (L.) Ugborogho

Cerastium nutans **Raf.** – Chickweed [Chick-weed, Chick weed] (145) (1897), Clammy chickweed [Clammy chick-weed, Clammy chick weed] (5, 156) (1913–1923), Clammy mouse-ear chickweed (187) (1818), Nodding chickweed (4, 5, 50, 72, 80, 93, 97, 156) (1907–present), Powder horn [Powder-horn, Powderhorn] (5, 93, 122, 131, 156) (1899–1937)

Cerastium nutans **Raf. var. *nutans*** – Nodding chickweed (50) (present)

Cerastium semidecandrum **L.** – Five-stamen chickweed [Fivestamen chickweed] (50) (present), Five-stamen mouse-ear chickweed [Fivestamened mouse-ear chickweed] (5) (1913), Least chickweed [Least chick weed] (42) (1814), Least mouse-ear chickweed (187) (1818), Small chickweed (156) (1923), Small mouse-ear chickweed (5) (1913), Spring mouse-ear (5, 156) (1913–1923)

Cerastium strictum **L.** – See *Cerastium arvense* L. subsp. *strictum* (L.) Ugborogho

Cerastium tomentosum **L.** – Snow-in-summer [Snow-in-summer] (50, 109, 138) (1923–present)

Cerastium trigynum **Vill.** – See *Cerastium cerastoides* (L.) Britton

Cerastium velutinum **Raf.** – See *Cerastium arvense* L.

Cerastium viscosum **L.** – See *Cerastium glomeratum* Thuill.

Cerastium vulgatum **L.** – See *Cerastium fontanum* Baumg. subsp. *vulgare* (Hartman) Greuter & Burdet

Cerasus avium – See *Prunus avium* (L.) L.

Cerasus borealis **Michx.** – possibly *Prunus nigra* Aiton (taxonomic status is unresolved (PL))

Cerasus carolinaensis – possibly *Prunus caroliniana* (Mill.) Aiton

Cerasus caroliniana **Michx.** – possibly *Prunus caroliniana* (Mill.) Aiton

Cerasus carolinianum – possibly *Prunus caroliniana* (Mill.) Aiton

Cerasus cerasus **(L.) Eaton & Wright** – See *Prunus cerasus* L.

Cerasus depressa **Pursh** – See *Prunus pumila* L.

Cerasus emarginata **[Dougl. ex Hook.]** – See *Prunus emarginata* (Dougl. ex Hook.) D. Dietr.

Cerasus ilicifolia **Nutt. ex Hook. & Arn.** – See *Prunus ilicifolia* (Nutt. ex Hook. & Arn.) D. Dietr.

Cerasus lauro cerasus – See *Prunus laurocerasus* L.

Cerasus laurocerasus **Lois** – See *Prunus laurocerasus* L.

Cerasus mahaleb **[(L.) Miller]** – See *Prunus mahaleb* L.

Cerasus mollis **Douglas ex Hook.** – See *Prunus emarginata* (Douglas ex Hook.) D. Dietr. var. *mollis* (Douglas ex Hook.) W.H. Brewer

Cerasus padus **(L.) DC.** – See *Prunus padus* L.

Cerasus pennsylvanica **Torr. & Gray** – See *Prunus pensylvanica* L. f. var. *pensylvanica*

Cerasus pensylvanica – See *Prunus pensylvanica* L. f. var. *pensylvanica*

Cerasus pumila **Michx.** – See *Prunus pumila* L. var. *pumila*

Cerasus serotina **[(Ehrh.) Loisel.]** – See *Padus serotina* (Ehrh.) Borkh.

Cerasus virginiana **(L.) Michx.** – See *Prunus virginiana* L.

Cerasus virginianum – See *Prunus virginiana* L.

Ceratocephala **Moench** – Curve-seed butterwort [Curveseed butterwort] (50) (present)

Ceratocephala testiculata **(Crantz) Bess.** – Curve-seed butterwort [Curveseed butterwort] (50) (present)

Ceratochloa pendula **[Schrad.]** – See *Bromus catharticus* Vahl

Ceratoides lanata **(Pursh) J. T. Howell** – See *Krascheninnikovia lanata* (Pursh) A. D. J. Meeuse & Smit

Ceratonia **L.** – Carob or Carob tree (138) (1923)

Ceratonia siliqua **L.** – Agarrobo (Spanish) (110) (1886), Algaroba [Algarroba] (92) (1876), Algaroba bean (92) (1876), Bean tree [Beantree, Bean-tree (92) (1876), Bread of St. John (110) (1886), Carob or Carob tree (92, 110, 138) (1876–1923), Caroubier (French) (92, 110) (1876–1886), Carrubo, currabio, or carubio (Italian) (110) (1886), Honey-bread [Honey bread] (92) (1876), Husks-of-the-ancient [Husks of the ancient] (92) (1876), Johannis brodbaum (German) (110) (1886), Karoub (92) (1876) tree is takharrout, Locust bean (92) (1876), Locust or Locust tree (178) (1526), St. John's-bread [Saint John's bread] (92) (1876) Christians claim that St. John the Baptist fed upon this tree in the desert, Sweetpod [Sweet pod] (92) (1876)

Ceratophyllum demersum **L.** – Cedar-moss [Cedar moss] (156) (1923), Coon's-tail [Coon's tail, Coontail, Coon-tail] (50, 97, 156) (1923–present), Fish-blankets (156) (1923), Hornwort [Horn wort] (3, 5, 19, 72, 85, 92, 93, 97, 120, 131, 155, 156, 157, 158) (1840–1977), Morassweed [Morass-weed] (5, 156, 157, 158) (1900–1929)

Ceratophyllum echinatum **Gray** – Spineless hornwort (50) (present)

Ceratophyllum **L.** – Coon's-tail [Coon's tail, Coontail, Coon-tail] (4, 109) (1949–1986), Hornwort [Horn wort] (1, 4, 50, 10, 109, 155, 158, 167) (1814–present)

Ceratopteris **Brongn.** – Floating fern [Floating-fern] (109) (1949), Water fern [Waterfern, Water-fern] (109, 138) (1923–1949)

Ceratopteris thalictroides **(L.) Brongn.** – Horned fern (86) (1878)

Ceratoschoenus corniculata **[(Lam.) Nees]** – See *Rhynchospora corniculata* (Lam.) A.Gray

Ceratoschoenus macrostachya – See *Rhynchospora macrostachya* Torr. ex A.Gray

Ceratoschoenus macrostachys **(Torr. ex A. Gray) A. Gray** – See *Rhynchospora macrostachya* Torr. ex A.Gray

Ceratostigma plumbaginoides **Bunge** – Larpente's plumbago [Larpente plumbago] (138) (1923)

Cercidiphyllum japonicum **Sieb. & Zucc. ex J. Hoffmann & H. Schult.** – Chinese katsura tree [Chinese katsura-tree] (138) (1923), Katsura tree [Katsura-tree] (109, 138) (1923–1949)

Cercidiphyllum japonicum sinense – See *Cercidiphyllum japonicum* Sieb. & Zucc. ex J. Hoffmann & H. Schult.

Cercidiphyllum japonicum **var. *sinense* Rehder & E. H. Wilson** – See *Cercidiphyllum japonicum* Sieb. & Zucc. ex J. Hoffmann & H. Schult.

Cercidium floridum **Benth. ex Gray** – See *Parkinsonia florida* (Benth. ex Gray) S. Wats.

Cercidium floridum **subsp. *floridum*** – possibly *Parkinsonia florida* (Benth. ex Gray) S. Wats. (taxonomic status is unresolved (PL))

Cercidium macrum **Johnston** – See *Parkinsonia texana* (Gray) S. Wats. var. *macra* (I. M. Johnston) Isely

Cercidium torreyana – See *Parkinsonia florida* (Benth. ex A. Gray) S. Watson

Cercidium torreyanum **(S. Watson) Sarg.** – See *Parkinsonia florida* (Benth. ex A. Gray) S. Watson

Cercis canadensis **L.** – American Judas-tree [American Judas tree] (5, 42, 93, 157, 158) (1814--1936), American redbud [American red bud] (2, 42, 137, 138) (1814–1895), Bois noir (French, black wood) (17) (1796), Bouton rouge (French) (158) (1900), Eastern redbud (5, 50, 95, 50, 97, 106, 112, 122, 124, 131, 155, 156, 158) (1899–present), Gainier (French) (158) (1900), Garnier du Canada (French) (8) (1785), Judas tree [Judas' tree, Judas-tree] (8, 10, 19, 58, 92, 95, 106,

107, 156, 187) (1785–1930), Judée du Canada (French) (8) (1785), June-bud [June bud] (156) (1923) no longer in use by 1923, Red Judas tree [Red Judas-tree] (5, 157, 158) (1900–1929), Redbud [Redbud, Red bud, Red-budds] or Redbud tree [Red bud tree, Redbud-tree, Redbud tree] (3, 4, 7, 10, 57, 93, 107, 121, 157, 181, 184, 187) (~1678–1986), Salad tree [Salad-tree, Sallad tree] (5, 41, 156, 157, 158) (1770–1929), Žoŋšabethe hi (Osage, dark-wood tree) (121) (1918?–1970?)

Cercis canadensis **L. var.** *canadensis* – Eastern redbud (50) (present)

Cercis canadensis **L. var.** *texensis* **(S. Wats.) M. Hopkins** – California redbud (138) (1923), Mountain redbud (122, 124) (1937) TX, Texas redbud [Texan redbud, Texan red-bud] (106, 138) (1923–1930), Western redbud (106) (1930)

Cercis **L.** – Abre de Judée (8) (1785), Gainier (French) (8) (1785), Judas tree [Judas' tree, Judas-tree] (1, 8, 93, 158, 167) (1785–1936), June-bud [June bud] (106) (1930), Redbud [Red-bud, Red bud, Red-budds] or Redbud tree [Red bud tree, Redbud-tree, Redbud tree] (1, 50, 82, 93, 109, 138, 155, 156) (1923–present), Salad tree [Salad-tree, Sallad tree] (106) (1930)

Cercis occidentalis **Torr.** – See *Cercis canadensis* L. var. *texensis* (S. Wats.) M. Hopkins

Cercis reniformis **Engelm. ex A. Gray** – See *Cercis canadensis* L. var. *texensis* (S. Wats.) M. Hopkins

Cercocarpus **Kunth** – Mountain-mahogany [Mountain mahogany, Mountainmahogany] (50, 93, 106, 122, 153, 155) (1913–present)

Cercocarpus ledifolius **Nutt.** – Buissonn à plumes (French) (20) (1857), Feather bush (20) (1857), Mountain-mahogany [Mountain mahogany, Mountainmahogany] (76, 101, 125, 138) (1896–1930)

Cercocarpus montanus **Raf.** – Alder-leaf mountain-mahogany [Alderleaf mountain mahogany] (50) (present), Mountain-mahogany [Mountain mahogany, Mountainmahogany] (1, 3, 85, 95, 113, 130, 137, 157, 158) (1890–1977), Small-leaf cercocarpus [Small-leaved cercocarpus] (5, 131) (1899–1913), True mountain-mahogany [True mountainmahogany] (155) (1942), Valley-mahogany [Valley mahogany] (112, 137, 138) (1923–1937)

Cercocarpus parviflorus **H. & A.** – See *Cercocarpus montanus* Raf.

Cerefolium cerefolium **(L.) Britton** – See *Anthriscus cerefolium* (L.) Hoffmann

Cereus giganteus **Engelm.** – See *Carnegia gigantea* (Engelm.) Britt. & Rose

Cereus grandiflorus **(L.) Mill.** – See *Selenicereus grandiflorus* (L.) Britt. & Rose

Cereus greggi **Engelm.** – See *Peniocereus greggii* (Engelm.) Britt. & Rose var. *greggii*

Cereus hildmannianus **K. Schum.** (possibly) – Pine torch (178) (1526)

Cereus **Mill.** – Cereus (14, 155) (1882–1942), Torch thistle [Torch thistles] (14) (1882)

Cereus pectinatus **Engelm.** – See *Echinocereus pectinatus* (Scheidw.) Engelm.

Cereus peruvianus **auct. non (L.) Mill.** – See *Cereus hildmannianus* K. Schum.

Cereus peruvianus **Mill.** – See *Cereus repandus* (L.) Mill.

Cereus repandus **(L.) Mill.** – Hedge cactus (109) (1949), Peruvian cereus [Peru cereus] (155) (1942)

Cereus thurberi **[Engelm.]** – See *Stenocereus thurberi* (Engelm.) Buxbaum

Cerinthe **L.** – Honeywort (138) (1923)

Cerinthe major **L.** – Great honeywort [Great honie woort] (178) (1526)

Cerinthe retorta **Sm.** – Greek honeywort (138) (1923)

Cesalpina brasiliensis **L.** – See *Lonchocarpus punctatus* Kunth

Cestrum aurantiacum **Lindl.** – Orange cestrum (138) (1923)

Cestrum diurnum **L.** – Day cestrum (138) (1923), Day jessamine (109) (1949)

Cestrum fasciculatum **(Schlecht.) Miers** – Early cestrum (138) (1923)

Cestrum **L.** – Cestrum (138) (1923)

Cestrum nocturnum **L.** – Night-blooming cestrum [Nightblooming cestrum] (138) (1923), Night-jessamine [Night jessamine] (109) (1949)

Cestrum parqui **L'Hér.** – Chilean parqui (138) (1923), Willow-leaf jessamine [Willow-leaved jessamine] (109) (1949)

Cetraria islandica **(L.) Acharius** – Iceland moss (49, 55, 57, 58, 92, 107) (1869–1911)

Cetraria islandica **L.** – See *Cetraria islandica* (L.) Acharius

Cevallia **Lag.** – Cevallia (158) (1900)

Cevallia sinuata **Lag.** – Stinging-serpent [Stinging serpent] (50) (present)

Chaenactis angustifolia **Greene** – See *Chaenactis douglasii* (Hook.) Hook. & Arn. var. *douglasii*

Chaenactis brachiata **Greene** – See *Chaenactis douglasii* (Hook.) Hook. & Arn. var. *douglasii*

Chaenactis brachiata **Greene var.** *stansburiana* **Stockwell** – See *Chaenactis douglasii* (Hook.) Hook. & Arn. var. *douglasii*

Chaenactis cineria **Stockwell** – See *Chaenactis douglasii* (Hook.) Hook. & Arn. var. *douglasii*

Chaenactis **DC.** – Chaenactis (155, 158) (1900–1942), False yarrow [Falseyarrow] (155) (1942), Morning-brides [Morning brides] (1) (1932)

Chaenactis douglasii **(Hook.) Hook. & Arn.** – Douglas' chanaectis [Douglas chanaectis] (155) (1942), Douglas' dusty-maiden [Douglas' dustymaiden] (50) (present), Morning-brides [Morning brides] (85) (1932) SD

Chaenactis douglasii **(Hook.) Hook. & Arn. var.** *achilleifolia* **(Hook. & Arn.) Gray** – See *Chaenactis douglasii* (Hook.) Hook. & Arn. var. *douglasii*

Chaenactis douglasii **(Hook.) Hook. & Arn. var.** *douglasii* – Douglas' dusty-maiden [Douglas' dustymaiden] (50) (present)

Chaenactis douglasii **(Hook.) Hook. & Arn. var.** *glandulosa* **Cronq.** – See *Chaenactis douglasii* (Hook.) Hook. & Arn. var. *douglasii*

Chaenactis douglasii **(Hook.) Hook. & Arn. var.** *montana* **M.E. Jones** – See *Chaenactis douglasii* (Hook.) Hook. & Arn. var. *douglasii*

Chaenactis douglasii **(Hook.) Hook. & Arn. var.** *nana* **Stockwell** – See *Chaenactis douglasii* (Hook.) Hook. & Arn. var. *douglasii*

Chaenactis douglasii **(Hook.) Hook. & Arn. var.** *rubricaulis* **Rydb.** – See *Chaenactis douglasii* (Hook.) Hook. & Arn. var. *douglasii*

Chaenactis douglasii **(Hook.) Hook. & Arn. var.** *typicus* **Cronq.** – See *Chaenactis douglasii* (Hook.) Hook. & Arn. var. *douglasii*

Chaenactis humilis **Rydb.** – See *Chaenactis douglasii* (Hook.) Hook. & Arn. var. *douglasii*

Chaenactis panamintensis **Stockwell** – See *Chaenactis douglasii* (Hook.) Hook. & Arn. var. *douglasii*

Chaenactis ramosa **Stockwell** – See *Chaenactis douglasii* (Hook.) Hook. & Arn. var. *douglasii*

Chaenactis rubricaulis **Rydb.** – See *Chaenactis douglasii* (Hook.) Hook. & Arn. var. *douglasii*

Chaenactis suksdorfii **Stockwell** – See *Chaenactis douglasii* (Hook.) Hook. & Arn. var. *douglasii*

Chaenomeles japonica **(Thunb.) Lindl. ex Spach** – Dwarf Japanese quince (109) (1949), Flowering quince (73, 138) (1892–1923), Japanese quince (107, 112) (1919–1937)

Chaenomeles japonica **Lindl.** – See *Chaenomeles japonica* (Thunb.) Lindl. ex Spach

Chaenomeles lagenaria **Koidz.** – See *Chaenomeles speciosa* (Sweet) Nakai

Chaenomeles **Lindl.** – Flowering quince (109) (1949)

Chaenomeles sinensis **Koehne** – See *Pseudocydonia sinensis* (Dum.-Cours.) Schneid.

Chaenomeles speciosa **(Sweet) Nakai** – Japanese quince (109) (1949)

Chaenorhinum **(DC.) Reichenb.** – Dwarf snapdragon (50) (present)

Chaenorhinum minus **(DC.) Lange** – See *Chaenorhinum minus* (L.) Lange

Chaenorhinum minus **(L.) Lange** Dwarf snapdragon (4, 50) (1986–present), Small snapdragon [Small snap dragon] (1, 5) (1913–1932)

Chaerophyllum bulbosum **L.** – Turnip-chervil (138) (1923), Turnip-root chervil [Turnip-rooted chervil] (109) (1949)

Chaerophyllum L. – Chervil [Cheruell] (1, 4, 50, 155, 158) (1900–present)

Chaerophyllum procumbens (L.) Crantz – Chervil [Cheruell] (3) (1977), Procumbent chervil (187) (1818), Spreading chervil (5, 50, 155, 156) (1913–present), Wild chervil (4, 156) (1923–1986)

Chaerophyllum procumbens (L.) Crantz var. *procumbens* – Spreading chervil (50, 72, 97) (1907–present)

Chaerophyllum sativum Lam. – See *Anthriscus cerefolium* (L.) Hoffmann

Chaerophyllum tainturieri Hook. – Chervil [Cheruell] (4) (1986), Hairy-fruit chervil [Hairyfruit chervil] (50) (present), Tainturier's chervil (5, 97) (1913–1937)

Chaerophyllum tainturieri Hook. var. *tainturieri* – Hairy-fruit chervil [Hairyfruit chervil] (50) (present), Texas chervil (97) (1937)

Chaerophyllum texanum Coult. & Rose – See *Chaerophyllum tainturieri* Hook. var. *tainturieri*

Chaetochloa composita Scribn. – See *Setaria vulpiseta* (Lam.) Roemer & J.A. Schultes

Chaetochloa corrugata (Ell.) Scribn. – See *Setaria corrugata* (Ell.) J.A. Schultes

Chaetochloa glauca (L.) Scribn. – See *Pennisetum glaucum* (L.) R. Br.

Chaetochloa imberbis (Poir.) Scribn. – See *Setaria parviflora* (Poir.) Kerguélen

Chaetochloa italica (L.) Scribn. – See *Setaria italica* (L.) Beauv.

Chaetochloa lutescens (Weigel) Stuntz – See *Pennisetum glaucum* (L.) R. Br.

Chaetochloa magna (Griseb.) Scribn. – See *Setaria magna* Griseb.

Chaetochloa palmifolia – See *Setaria palmifolia* (Koenig) Stapf

Chaetochloa Scribn. – See *Setaria* Beauv

Chaetochloa verticillata (L.) Scribn. – See *Setaria verticillata* (L.) Beauv.

Chaetochloa viridis (L.) Scribn. – See *Setaria viridis* (L.) Beauv. var. *viridis*

Chaetochloa vulpiseta (Lam.) A. S. Hitchc. & Chase – See *Setaria vulpiseta* (Lam.) Roemer & J.A. Schultes

Chaetopappa asteroides (Nutt.) DC. – Arkansas least-daisy [Arkansas leastdaisy] (50) (present), Chaetopappa (5, 97) (1913–1937), Least daisy (122) (1937)

Chaetopappa DC. – Chaetopappa (158) (1900), Heath aster (158) (1900), Least-daisy [Leastdaisy] (50) (present), Rose heath-aster [Rose heath aster] (93) (1936), White aster (4) (1986)

Chaetopappa ericoides (Torr.) Nesom – Baby-white aster [Baby-white aster] (155) (1942), Rose heath-aster [Rose heath aster] (5, 97) (1913–1937), Rose-heath [Rose heath] (50) (present), White aster (3) (1977)

Chaiturus marrubiastrum (L.) Reichenb. – Horehound lion's-tail [Hoarhound lion's-tail] (158) (1900), Horehound motherwort [Hoarhound motherwort, Hoarhound motherwort] (5, 156, 158) (1900–1923), Lion's-tail [Lion's tail, Lions' tail, Lionstail, Lions-tail] (5, 50) (1913–present)

Chaiturus Willd. – Lion's-tail [Lion's tail, Lions' tail, Lionstail, Lions-tail] (50) (present), *possibly* Bristle-tail grass [Bristle tailed grass] (92) (1876)

Chalcas exotica (L.) Millsp. – See *Murraya exotica* L.

Chamaebatia foliolosa Benth. – Bear clover (106) (1930), Bearmat [Bear-mat] (106) (1930), Mountain-misery [Mountain misery] (106) (1930), Tar bush (76) (1896) CA, Tarweed [Tar weed, Tar-weed] (76, 106) (1896–1930)

Chamaecistus procumbens (L.) Kuntze – See *Loiseleuria procumbens* (L.) Desv.

Chamaecrista (L.) Moench – Partridge pea [Partridge-pea, Partridgepea] (1, 93, 155) (1932–1942), Sensitive pea (1, 50, 93) (1932–present) Neb, Wild sensitive plant [Wild sensitive-plant] (1) (1932)

Chamaecrista fasciculata (Michx.) Greene – Dwarf cassia (5) (1913), Large-flower sensitive-pea [Large-flowered sensitive pea] (5) (1913), Maggoty boy bean [Magoty boy bean] (5) (1913), Partridge pea [Partridge-pea, Partridgepea] (5, 97, 125) (1913–1937), Prairie

senna (5) (1913), Sensitive pea (85, 125) (1930–1932) KS, Showy partridge pea [Showy partridgepea] (155) (1942)

Chamaecrista fasciculata (Michx.) Greene – Sleeping plant [Sleeping-plant, Sleepingplant] (50) (present)

Chamaecrista fasciculata (Michx.) Greene var. *fasciculata* – Acoumack-pea (187) (1818), Bundled cassia (42) (1814), Cassia (19) (1840), Dwarf partridge pea (42) (1814), Dwarf senna (156, 158) (1900–1923), Large-flower sensitive-pea [Large-flowered sensitive pea] (5, 86) (1878–1913), Larger sensitive-pea (158) (1900), Maggoty boy bean [Magoty boy bean] (74, 156) (1893–1923) NY, no longer in use by 1923, Partridge (187) (1818), Partridge pea [Partridge-pea, Partridgepea] (3, 75, 109) (1894–1977), Prairie senna (92, 156, 158) (1876–1923), Sensitive pea (47, 92, 106, 131) (1852–1930) SD, Sensitive plant (156) (1923), Sensitive senna (92) (1876), Showy partridge pea [Showy partridgepea] (4) (1986), Sleeping plant [Sleeping-plant, Sleepingplant] (50, 156) (1923–present), Wild senna [Wild-senna] (114) (1894), Dwarf cassia (92, 187) (1818–1876)

Chamaecrista Moench – See *Chamaecrista* (L.) Moench

Chamaecrista nictitans (L.) Moench – Partridge pea [Partridge-pea, Partridgepea] (50) (present), Sensitive pea [Sensitive-pea] (5, 97) (1913–1937) OK

Chamaecrista nictitans (L.) Moench subsp. *nictitans* var. *nictitans* – Nodding cassia (42) (1814), Sensitive cassia (38) (1820), Sensitive partridgepea [Sensitive partridge pea] (4) (1986), Sensitive pea [Sensitive-pea] (3, 156, 158) (1900–1977), Sensitive plant (92, 156) (1898–1923), Small-flower wild sensitive pea [Small-flowered wild sensitive pea] (86) (1878), Twinkling cassia (86) (1878), Twinkling senna (86) (1878), Wild sensitive plant [Wild sensitive-plant] (2, 5, 19, 158, 187) (1818–1900)

Chamaecyparis henryae Li – See *Chamaecyparis thyoides* (L.) Britton, Sterns & Poggenb.

Chamaecyparis lawsoniana (A. Murr.) Parl. – Ginger-pine [Ginger pine] (75) (1894), Lawson's cypress [Lawson cypress] (109, 138) (1923–1949) for Charles Lawson, 1794–1873, Britain, Oregon cedar (75) (1894), Port Orford cedar (14, 50) (1882–present), Scarab cypress (109) (1949), White cedar (75) (1894) NW

Chamaecyparis lawsoniana Parl. – See *Chamaecyparis lawsoniana* (A. Murr.) Parl.

Chamaecyparis lawsoniana Parl. var. *allumii* Beissn. – See *Chamaecyparis lawsoniana* (A. Murr.) Parl.

Chamaecyparis lawsoniana Parl. var. *alluminii* Beissn. – See *Chamaecyparis lawsoniana* (A. Murr.) Parl.

Chamaecyparis nootkatensis (D. Don) Spach – Alaska cedar (75) (1894) WA, Nootka cypress (138) (1923), Yellow cedar (75) (1894) AK

Chamaecyparis nutkaensis Hartw. – See *Chamaecyparis nootkatensis* (D. Don) Spach

Chamaecyparis Spach. – Cedar or Cedar tree (50) (present), False cypress [False-cypress] (2, 109) (1895–1949)

Chamaecyparis sphaeroidea Spach. – possibly *Chamaecyparis thyoides* (L.) Britton, Sterns & Poggenb.

Chamaecyparis thyoides (L.) Britton, Sterns & Poggenb. – Atlantic white cedar (50) (present), Cèdre blanc (French) (8) (1785), Cipres (46) (1879), Cipressi (46) (1879), Cyprès à feuilles d'Thuya (French) (8) (1785), Juniper or Juniper tree [Juniper-tree] (5, 20) (1857–1913), Maryland blue-berry cypress [Maryland blue-berried cypress] (8) (1785), Post cedar (5) (1913), Southern white cedar (5) (1913), Swamp-cedar [Swamp cedar] (5) (1913), White cedar (7, 10, 14, 19, 20, 41, 46, 92) (1770–1882), White juniper or White juniper tree (41) (1770), White-cedar [Whitecedar] (109, 138) (1923–1949)

Chamaecystis prolifera (L. f.) Link – Tagasaste (106) (1930), Tree alfalfa [Tree alfalfa] (106) (1930), Tree clover [Tree-clover] (106) (1930), White broom (106) (1930)

Chamaedaphne calyculata (L.) Moench – Andromede Caliculée (French) (8) (1785), Box-leaf andromeda [Box-leaved andromeda] (42, 187) (1814–1818), Calycled andromeda (165) (1807),

Cassandra (86, 156) (1878–1923), Dwarf cassandra (5) (1913), Evergreen andromeda (187) (1818), Evergreen dwarf andromeda [Ever-green dwarf andromeda] (8) (1785), Leather-leaf [Leatherleaf, Leather leaf] (5, 19, 86, 92, 109, 138, 156) (1840–1949)

Chamaedaphne calyculata **Moench** – See *Chamaedaphne calyculata* (L.) Moench

Chamaelirion carolinianum **Willd.** – See *Chamaelirium luteum* (L.) A. Gray

Chamaelirion lutea – See *Chamaelirium luteum* (L.) A. Gray

Chamaelirion **Willd.** – See *Chamaelirium* Willd.

Chamaelirium carolinianum **Willd.** – See *Chamaelirium luteum* (L.) A. Gray

Chamaelirium luteum **(L.) A. Gray** – Blazing star [Blazing-star, Blazingstar] (2, 5, 6, 7, 19, 52, 53, 58, 64, 156, 187) (1818–1922), Colic root [Colic-root, Colicroot] (6) (1892), Devil's-bit [Devil's bit, Devilbit] (5, 6, 7, 53, 58, 64, 92, 156, 187) (1818–1923), Devil's-root [Devil's root] (7) (1828), Drooping starwort [Drooping star-wort] (5, 6, 53, 58, 64, 92, 156, 187) (1818–1923), Eenhorn (7, 92) (1828–1876), Fairy wand [Fairywand] (50, 138, 156) (1923–present), False unicorn (58, 92) (1869–1876), False unicorn plant (5, 6) (1892–1913), False unicornroot [False unicorn root] (19, 57, 64) (1840–1917), Grub-root (156) (1923), Helonias (52, 54) (1905–1919), Rattlesnake-root [Rattlesnake root, Rattle-Snake-Root, Rattlesnakes' root, Rattlesnakeroot] (7, 177) (1762–1828), Redseed [Red-seed, Red seed] (53, 57, 64, 156) (1908–1923), Star-grass [Star grass, Stargrass] (64, 156) (1908–1923), Starwort [Star-wort, Star wort] (6, 53, 54, 64) (1892–1922), Unicorn (58) (1869), Unicorn plant [Unicorn-plant, Unicornplant] (6, 156) (1892–1923), Unicorn root [Unicorn-root] (5, 52, 53, 61, 64) (1870–1922), Unicorn-horn [Unicorn's horn, Unicorns' horn, Unicorn horn] (5, 64, 92) (1876–1913)

Chamaelirium obovale **Small** – See *Chamaelirium luteum* (L.) A. Gray

Chamaelirium **Willd.** – Blazing star [Blazing-star, Blazingstar] (1, 2, 109) (1895–1949), Devil's-bit [Devil's bit, Devilbit] (1, 2, 156) (1895–1932), Fairy wand [Fairywand] (109) (1949)

Chamaemelum nobile **(L.) All.** – Anthemis (52, 57, 59) (1911–1919), Camomile [Chamomile, Camomylle] (19, 49, 52, 53, 54, 58, 92, 107, 109, 179) (1526–1949), Common camomile [Common chamomile] (10, 138, 165) (1807–1923), Double camomile [Double Cammomill] (178) (1526), English camomile [English chamomile] (46, 49, 57, 155) (1649–1942), Garden camomile [Garden chamomile] (5, 49, 57, 155) (1649–1942), Garden camomile [Garden chamomile] (5, 58, 92, 156) (1869–1923), Ground-apple [Ground apple] (92) (1876) flowers, Low camomile [Low chamomile] (5, 92, 156) (1876–1923), Roman camomile [Roman chamomile] (49, 50, 53, 55, 57, 58, 59, 92, 155) (1869–present), Scotch camomile [Scotch chamomile] (5, 156) (1913–1923), Sweet camomile [Sweet chamomile] (165) (1807), Whig plant (92) (1876), White camomile [White chamomile] (5, 156) (1913–1923)

Chamaenerion **(Gesn.) Ludw.** – See *Chamerion* Raf. ex Holub (all US species)

Chamaenerion **(Tourn.) Adans** – See *Chamerion* Raf. ex Holub (all US species)

Chamaenerion angustifolium **(L.) Scop.** – See *Chamerion angustifolium* (L.) Holub subsp. *angustifolium*

Chamaenerion latifolium **(L.) Sweet** – See *Chamerion latifolium* (L.) Holub

Chamaepericlimenum **Aschers. & Graebn.** – See *Cornus* L.

Chamaepericlymenum canadense **(L.) Asch. & Graebn.** – See *Cornus canadensis* L.

Chamaepericlymenum suecicum **(L.) Asch. & Graebn.** – See *Cornus suecica* L.

Chamaeraphis italica – See *Setaria italica* (L.) Beauv.

Chamaeraphis italica **(L.) Kuntze** – See *Setaria italica* (L.) Beauv.

Chamaeraphis viridis **(L.) Porter** – See *Setaria viridis* (L.) Beauv.

Chamaerhodos **Bunge** – Chamaerhodos (158) (1900), Little rose (50) (present)

Chamaerhodos erecta **(L.) Bunge** – Little ground-rose [Little ground rose] (4) (1986), Little rose (50) (present)

Chamaerhodos erecta **(L.) Bunge subsp.** *nuttallii* **(Pickering ex Rydb.) Hultén** – American chamaerhodos (5) (1913), Little rose (3) (1977), Nuttall's little rose (50) (present)

Chamaerhodos erecta **(L.) Bunge var.** *parviflora* **(Nutt.) A.S. Hitchc** – See *Chamaerhodos erecta* (L.) Bunge subsp. *nuttallii* (Pickering ex Rydb.) Hultén

Chamaerhodos nuttallii **(Torr. & Gray) Pickering** – See *Chamaerhodos erecta* (L.) Bunge subsp. *nuttallii* (Pickering ex Rydb.) Hultén

Chamaerops acaulis **Michx.** – See *Sabal minor* (Jacq.) Pers.

Chamaerops **Michx.** – possibly *Sabal* Adans.

Chamaerops palmetto **[(Walter) Michx.]** – See *Sabal palmetto* (Walt.) Lodd. ex J.A. & J.H. Schultes

Chamaerops serrulata **Pursh** – See *Serenoa repens* (Bartr.) Small

Chamaesaracha coniodes **(Moric. ex Dunal) Britton** – Chamaesaracha (3, 4) (1977–1986), Gray five-eyes [Gray fiveeyes] (50) (present), Hairy chamaesaracha (5, 97) (1913–1937)

Chamaesaracha coronopus **(Dunal) Gray** – Green false nightshade (3, 4) (1977–1986), Green-leaf five-eyes [Greenleaf fiveeyes] (50) (present), Smoothish chamaesaracha (5, 97) (1913–1937)

Chamaesaracha sordida **(Dunal) Gray** – Hairy five-eyes [Hairy five eyes] (3) (1977)

Chamaesyce albicaulis **Rydb.** – See *Chamaesyce serpyllifolia* (Pers.) Small subsp. *serpyllifolia*

Chamaesyce albomarginata **(Torr. & Gray) Small** – White-margin euphorbia [Whitemargin euphorbia] (155) (1942), White-margin sandmat [Whitemargin sandmat] (50) (present)

Chamaesyce carunculata **(Waterfall) Shinners** – Sand dune sandmat [Sanddune sandmat] (50) (present)

Chamaesyce fendleri **(Torr. & Gray) Small** – Fendler's euphorbia [Fendler euphorbia] (3, 4, 155) (1942–1986), Fendler's sandmat (50) (present), Fendler's spurge (5, 93, 97) (1913–1937)

Chamaesyce geyeri **(Engelm.) Small** – Carpetweed [Carpet weed, Carpet-weed] (85) (1932) SD, Geyer's sandmat (50) (present), Geyer's spurge (5, 93, 97) (1913–1937)

Chamaesyce geyeri **(Engelm.) Small var.** *geyeri* – Čaŋxlogaŋ wapoštaŋ (Lakota, hat weed) (121) (1918?–1970?), Geyer's euphorbia [Geyer euphorbia] (155) (1942), Geyer's sandmat (50) (present), Geyer's spurge (3, 4, 72, 121, 131) (1899–1986)

Chamaesyce glyptosperma **(Engelm.) Small** – Rib-seed sandmat [Ribseed sandmat] (50) (present), Ridge-seed euphorbia [Ridgeseed euphorbia] (155) (1942), Ridge-seed spurge [Ridge-seeded spurge] (3, 4, 5, 72, 93, 97, 98, 131) (1899–1986), Spurge (85, 157) (1929–1932)

Chamaesyce hirta **(L.) Millsp.** – Cat's-hair [Cat's hair] (53) (1922), Pill-bearing spurge (53) (1922), Pill-pod euphorbia [Pillpod euphorbia] (155) (1942), Queensland asthma weed (53) (1922)

Chamaesyce humistrata **(Engelm.) Small** – Hairy spreading spurge (5, 93, 97, 122) (1913–1937), Spreading sandmat (50) (present), Spreading spurge (3, 4) (1977–1986)

Chamaesyce hypericifolia **(L.) Millsp.** – Black pursely (7) (1828), Black puslane (6, 49) (1892–1898), Black spurge (7) (1828), Black-parsley [Black parsley] (6) (1892), Common spurge (6) (1892), Corn pusley (78) (1898) Southold LI, Eyebright [Eye-bright, Eye bright] (6, 19, 49, 82) (1840–1930), Fluxweed [Flux weed, Flux-weed] (49) (1898), Garden spurge (49, 53) (1898–1922), Johanneskraut-Blattrige Wolfsmilch (German) (6) (1892), Large spotted spurge [Large spotted-spurge] (6, 49, 53, 92) (1876–1922), Milk parsley (6) (1892), Milk purslane [Milk-purslain] (6, 49) (1892–1898), Milkweed [Milk weed [Milk-weed] (102) (1886), Spotted pursely (7) (1828), Spurge (19) (1840), St.-John's-wort-leaf spurge [St.-John's-wort-leaved spurge] (187) (1818), U'ga-atasgi'skĭ (Cherokee, the pus oozes out) (102) (1886)

Chamaesyce hyssopifolia **(L.) Small** – See *Chamaesyce nutans* (Lag.) Small

Chamaesyce lata **(Engelm.) Small** – Hoary euphorbia (3, 4, 155)

(1942–1986), Hoary sandmat (50) (present), Hoary spurge (5, 97, 122) (1913–1937)

Chamaesyce maculata (L.) Small – Black purslane (158) (1900), Black pursley (92) (1876), Black pusley (5, 156) (1913–1923), Black spurge (5, 92, 156) (1876–1923), Blotched spurge (5, 156, 158) (1900–1923), Corn pusley (78) (1898) Southold Long Island, Creeping spurge (80) (1913), Fench pursley (78) (1898), French pursley (78) (1898) Sulphur Grove OH, Milk purslane [Milk-purslain] (5, 62, 72, 93, 131, 156, 158) (1899–1936), Milkweed [Milk weed [Milk-weed] (5, 73, 80, 156, 158) (1892–1930), Prostrate spurge (80) (1913), Rupter-wort, with the white flower (46) (1671), Spotted euphorbia (155) (1942), Spotted eyebright [Spotted eyebright, Spotted eye-bright] (5, 156, 158) (1900–1923), Spotted purslane (158) (1900), Spotted pursley (158) (1900), Spotted pusley (5, 92, 156) (1898–1923), Spotted sandmat (50) (present), Spotted spurge (3, 4, 5, 62, 92, 97, 122, 156, 158) (1876–1986), Spurge (125) (1930)

Chamaesyce missurica (Raf.) Shinners – Missouri spurge (3, 4) (1977–1986), Prairie sandmat (50) (present), Prairie spurge (4, 5, 97, 122) (1913–1986), White-flower spurge [White flowered spurge. White-flowered spurge] (5, 85, 93, 97, 122, 131) (1899–1937)

Chamaesyce nutans (Lag.) Small – Eyebane (4, 50) (1986–present), Large spotted spurge [Large spotted-spurge] (5, 62, 93, 156, 158) (1900–1936), Nodding spurge (156) (1923), Spurge (80, 125) (1913–1930), Stubble spurge (62) (1912) IN, Upright blotched spurge (158) (1900), Upright spotted spurge (5, 62, 93, 97, 131, 156, 158) (1899–1937), possibly Spotted spurge (80, 85, 187) (1817–1932)

Chamaesyce petaloidea (Engelm.) Small. – See *Chamaesyce missurica* (Raf.) Shinners

Chamaesyce polygonifolia (L.) Small – Knotgrass spurge (156) (1923), Knotweed spurge (5, 156) (1913–1923), Seaside spurge (5, 122, 156) (1913–1937) TX, Shore spurge (5, 156) (1913–1923), Spurge-time (46) (1671)

Chamaesyce preslii (Guss.) Arthur – See *Chamaesyce nutans* (Lag.) Small

Chamaesyce prostrata (Aiton) Small – Gollindrinera (92) (1876), Prostrate sandmat (50) (present), Prostrate spurge (158) (1900), Swallow-wort [Swallowwort, Swallow wort] (158) (1900)

Chamaesyce rafinesquei (Greene) Arthur – See *Chamaesyce vermiculata* (Raf.) House

Chamaesyce revoluta (Engelm.) Small – Thread-stem sandmat [Threadstem sandmat] (50) (present)

Chamaesyce S. F. Gray – Carpetweed [Carpet weed, Carpet-weed] (1) (1932), Sandmat (50) (present), Spurge (1, 93) (1932–1936)

Chamaesyce serpens (Kunth) Small – Matted sandmat (50) (present), Round-leaf spreading spurge [Round-leaved spreading spurge] (5, 72, 93, 97) (1913–1937), Round-leaf spurge [Round-leaved spurge] (3, 4, 131) (1899–1986), Serpent euphorbia (155) (1942), Spurge (85) (1932)

Chamaesyce serpyllifolia (Pers.) Small – Naze-ni pezhi (Omaha-Ponca [milkweed] (37) (1919), Thyme-leaf sandmat [Thymeleaf sandmat] (50) (present), Thyme-leaf spurge [Thymeleaf spurge, Thyme-leaved spurge] (5, 93, 97) (1913–1937)

Chamaesyce serpyllifolia (Pers.) Small subsp. *serpyllifolia* – Thyme-leaf euphorbia [Thymeleaf euphorbia] (155) (1942), Thyme-leaf sandmat [Thymeleaf sandmat] (50) (present), Thyme-leaf spurge [Thymeleaf spurge, Thyme-leaved spurge] (3, 4, 72, 122, 131) (1899–1986) Neb, White-stem spurge [White-stemmed spurge] (5, 93) (1913–1936)

Chamaesyce stictospora (Engelm.) Small – Mat spurge (3, 4) (1977–1986), Narrow-seed spurge [Narrowseeded spurge, Narrow-seeded spurge] (5, 93, 97, 122, 131) (1899–1937), Slim-seed sandmat [Slimseed sandmat] (50) (present), Spurge (85) (1932)

Chamaesyce vermiculata (Raf.) House – Hairy spurge (5) (1913)

Chamaesyce zygophylloides (Boiss.) Small. – See *Chamaesyce missurica* (Raf.) Shinners

Chamerion angustifolium (L.) Holub subsp. *circumvagum* (Mosquin)

Kartesz – Fireweed [Fire weed, Fire-weed] (50) (present), Willow herb [Willow-herb, Willowherb] (4) (1986)

Chamerion angustifolium (L.) Holub subsp. *angustifolium* – Bay willowherb [Bay willow-herb] (5, 156) (1913–1923), Bay-willow [Bay willow] (5, 156, 157, 158) (1900–1929), Blooming Sally (5, 138, 156, 157, 158) (1900–1929), Blooming-willow [Blooming willow] (5, 156, 157, 158) (1900–1929), Burntweed [Burnt weed, Burnt-weed] (5, 74, 156, 157, 158) (1893–1929) Penobscot River ME, lumberman, Epilobium (52, 57) (1917–1919), Firetop [Fire top, Fire-top] (5, 74, 156, 157, 158) (1893–1929) Penobscot River ME, lumberman, Fireweed [Fire weed, Fire-weed] (3, 40, 50, 63, 82, 85, 92, 106, 107, 109, 137, 131, 156, 157, 158) (1876–present), Flowering-willow [Flowering willow] (5, 92, 156, 157, 158) (1876–1929), French willow (5, 156, 157, 158) (1900–1929), French willowherb [French willow herb, French willow-herb] (5, 156, 157, 158) (1900–1929), Great willowherb [Great willow herb, Great willow-herb] (2, 5, 49, 53, 63, 72, 93, 109, 131, 156, 157, 158) (1895–1949), Herb wickopy [Herb-wicopy, Herb-wickopy] (5, 156, 157, 158) (1900–1929), Indian wickopy (157, 158) (1900–1929), Indian wickup (5) (1913), Moose's-tongue [Moose-tongue] (156) (1923), Narrow-leaf willowherb [Narrow leaved willow herb] (42) (1814), Oja'cidji'bĭk (Chippewa, slippery root) (40) (1928), Persian willow (5, 156, 157, 158) (1900–1929), Pigweed [Pig-weed, Pig weed] (5, 76, 156, 158) (1896–1923), Purple fireweed [Purple fire-weed] (157, 158) (1900–1929), Purple rocket (5, 76, 156, 157, 158) (1896–1929), Rose-bay [Rose bay, Rosebay] (5, 49, 53, 58, 92, 156, 157, 158) (1869–1929), Sally-bloom [Sally bloom] (76, 156) (1896–1923), Siberian flax (76) (1896) Westmoreland Co. NB, Spiked willow herb [Spiked willow-herb, Spiked willow herbe] (156) (1923), Wickup [Wickop] (49, 52, 53, 76, 79, 92, 156, 157, 158) (1876–1929), Wicopy herb (92) (1876), Wicopy root (92) (1876), Willow herb [Willow-herb, Willowherb] (19, 49, 52, 53, 57, 58, 92, 106, 107) (1840–1930), Willow herbe with flowers like the Rose Bay (178) (1526)

Chamerion angustifolium (L.) Holub. – Spiked willow herb [Spiked willow-herb, Spiked willow herbe] (5, 157, 158) (1900–1929)

Chamerion latifolium (L.) Holub – Broad-leaf willowherb [Broad-leaved willow-herb] (5) (1913)

Chamerion Raf. ex Holub – Fireweed [Fire weed, Fire-weed] (1, 4, 50, 93) (1932–present)

Chamerops palmetto – See *Serenoa repens* (Bartr.) Small (Chamaerops?)

Chamomila (Hall.) Gilib. – possibly *Matricaria* L.

Chamomilla maritima (L.) Rydb. – See *Tripleurospermum maritima* (L.) W.D.J. Koch subsp. *maritima*

Chamomilla suaveolens (Pursh) Rydb. – See *Matricaria discoidea* DC.

Chaptalia tomentosa Vent. – Gowins (183) (~1756), Leather-leaf [Leatherleaf, Leather leaf] (183) (~1756)

Chara fragilis Lois. – Stonewort (120) (1938) OK

Chara L. – Stonewort (92) (1876), Water-feather [Water-feather, Water feathers] (7) (1828)

Chara vulgaris L. – Feather beds (19, 187) (1818–1840), Water-feather [Water-feather, Water feathers] (92) (1876)

Chara vulgaris W. – See *Chara vulgaris* L.

Charturus – See *Chaiturus* Willd.

Chasmanthe aethiopica (L.) N.E. Br. – Ethiopian madflower (155) (1942)

Chasmanthium latifolium (Michx.) Yates – Broad-flower fescue grass [Broad-flowered fescue grass] (87) (1884), Broad-leaf spike grass [Broad-leaved spike grass, Broad-leaved spike-grass] (5, 56, 66, 72, 94, 99, 119, 163) (1852–1938), Broad-leaf uniola [Broadleaf uniola] (122, 138, 155) (1923–1942), Indian woodoats (50) (present), Wild fescue grass [Wild fescue-grass] (144) (1899), Wild oat [Wild oats] (5) (1913)

Chasmanthium laxum (L.) Yates – Slender spike grass [Slender spike-grass] (5, 66, 119, 163) (1852–1938), Slender wood-oats [Slender woodoats] (50) (present), Union grass (5) (1913)

Chasmanthium sessiliflorum (Poir.) Yates – Long-leaf spike grass

[Long-leaved spike-grass] (94) (1901), Short-stalk uniola [Short-stalked uniola] (94) (1901)

Chayota edulis [Jacq.] – See *Sechium edule* (Jacq.) Sw.

Chayota Jacq. – See *Sechium* P. Browne (introduced)

Cheilanthes alabamensis (Buckl.) Kunze – Alabama lip-fern [Alabama lipfern] (4, 5, 50, 97, 122, 155) (1913–present)

Cheilanthes californica Mettenius – See *Aspidotis californica* (Hook.) Nutt. ex Copeland

Cheilanthes covillei Maxon – Coville's lipfern [Coville lipfern] (138) (1923)

Cheilanthes eatonii Baker – Eaton's lip fern [Eaton lipfern, Eaton's lipfern] (155) (1942)

Cheilanthes feei T. Moore – Fee's lip fern [Fee lipfern] (155) (1942), Lip fern [Lipfern, Lip-fern] (3, 72) (1907–1977), Slender lip fern [Slender lipfern, Slender lip-fern] (4, 5, 50, 97, 122) (1913–present)

Cheilanthes fendleri Hook. – Fendler's lip fern [Fendler lipfern, Fendler's lip-fern] (4, 50, 97, 138, 155) (1923–present)

Cheilanthes gracilis (Fee.) Mett. – See *Cryptogramma stelleri* (S. G. Gmel.) Prantl.

Cheilanthes gracillima D.C. Eat. – Lace fern [Lace-fern] (109) (1949)

Cheilanthes horridula Maxon – Spinose lip fern [Spinose lip-fern] (97) (1937)

Cheilanthes lanosa (Michx.) D.C. Eat. – Clothed lip fern (5, 19) (1840–1913), Hairy lip fern [Hairy lipfern, Hairy lip-fern] (3, 5, 50, 86, 97, 122, 155) (1878–present), Lip fern [Lipfern, Lip-fern] (19) (1840), Woolly lip fern [Woolly lip-fern, Woolly lipfern] (4) (1986)

Cheilanthes lindheimeri (Sm.) Hook. – Fairy sword [Fairyswords] (50) (present), Lindheimer's lip fern [Lindheimer lipfern] (4, 155) (1942–1986)

Cheilanthes siliquosa Maxon – See *Aspidotis densa* (Brack.) Lellinger

Cheilanthes Sw. – Lip fern [Lipfern, Lip-fern] (1, 4, 50, 138, 155, 158) (1900–present)

Cheilanthes tomentosa Link. – Webby lip fern (5) (1913), Woolly lip fern [Woolly lip-fern, Woolly lipfern] (4, 5, 50, 97, 122, 138, 155) (1913–present)

Cheilanthes vestita Swartz. – See *Cheilanthes lanosa* (Michx.) D.C.Eat.

Cheilanthes wootonii Maxon – Beaded lipfern (4, 50) (1986–present), Wooton's lip-fern (97) (1937)

Cheiranthus annuus L. – See *Matthiola incana* (L.) Aiton f.

Cheiranthus asper Nutt. – See *Erysimum capitatum* (Dougl. ex Hook.) Greene var. *capitatum*

Cheiranthus cheiri L. – See *Erysimum cheiri* (L.) Crantz

Cheiranthus fenestralis L. – See *Matthiola incana* (L.) Aiton f.

Cheiranthus incanus L. – See *Matthiola incana* (L.) Aiton f.

Cheiranthus L. – See *Erysimum* L.

Cheiranthus syrticola Greene – See *Erysimum inconspicuum* (S. Wats.) MacM.

Cheirinia aspera (DC.) Britton – See *Erysimum capitatum* (Dougl. ex Hook.) Greene var. *capitatum*

Cheirinia asperrima (Greene) Rydb. – See *Erysimum capitatum* (Dougl. ex Hook.) Greene var. *capitatum*

Cheirinia cheiranthoides (L.) Link. – See *Erysimum cheiranthoides* L.

Cheirinia inconspicua (S. Wats.) Britton – See *Erysimum inconspicuum* (S. Wats.) MacM.

Cheirinia Link. – See *Erysimum* L.

Cheirinia repanda (L.) Link. – See *Erysimum repandum* L.

Chelidonium (Tourn.) L. – See *Chelidonium* L.

Chelidonium glaucum – See *Glaucium flavum* Crantz

Chelidonium L. – Celandine (1, 15, 50, 57, 109, 155, 156, 158, 167) (1814–present), Swallow-wort [Swallowwort, Swallow wort] (15) (1895)

Chelidonium majus L. – Celandine (5, 7, 10, 19, 46, 49, 50, 53, 54, 82, 92, 156, 158, 184, 187) (1671–present), Celidonia mayor (Spanish) (158) (1900), Cellydony (179) (1526), Chelandine (49) (1898), Chélidoine (French) (158) (1900), Chelidonium (54, 57) (1905–1917), Cock's-foot [Cocksfoot, Cocks-foot, Cock's foot,

Cock-foot] (158) (1900), Common celandine (6, 42) (1814–1892), Devil's-milk [Devil's milk] (156, 158) (1900–1923), Felonwort [Fellenwort] (156, 158) (1900–1923), Garden celandine (52, 92, 158) (1876–1919), Great celandine (49, 52, 53) (1919–1922), Greater celandine (42, 155, 156, 158) (1814–1942), Herbe a l'hirondelle (French) (6) (1892), Jacob's-ladder [Jacob's ladder, Jacobs-ladder] (156, 158) (1900–1923), Kenningwort (46, 156) (1671–1923), Killwart [Kill-wart] (158) (1900), Killwort (5, 156) (1913–1923), Saladine (158) (1900), Schellkraut (German) (158) (1900), Schollkraut or Schöllkraut (German) (6, 158) (1892–1900), Sightwort (156) (1923), Swallow-wort [Swallowwort, Swallow wort] (5, 156, 158) (1900–1923), Tetterwort (5, 6, 49, 52, 53, 54, 92, 156, 158) (1892–1923), Wart flower [Wartflower, Wart-flower] (156, 158) (1900–1923), Wartweed [Wartweed] (158) (1900), Wartwort [Wart-wort] (5, 156, 158) (1900–1923), Wretweed [Wret-weed] (158) (1900)

Chelone glabra L. – Balmony (5, 6, 49, 53, 57, 58, 61, 86, 92, 156) (1869–1923), Bammony (73) (1892) Belleisle NB, Bitter herb (5, 92) (1876–1913), Bitterweed [Bitter weed, Bitter-weed] (156) (1923), Chelone (French) (6) (1892), Chelone (German) (6) (1892), Chelonide glabre (French) (7) (1828), Cod-head [Cod head] (5, 156) (1913–1923) no longer in use by 1923, Common snakehead (7) (1828), Fish-mouth [Fish mouth] (5, 92, 156) (1876–1923) no longer in use by 1923, Glatte (German) (6) (1892), Rheumatism root [Rheumatism-root] (156) (1923), Salt rheumweed [Salt rheum weed] (5, 6, 49, 92, 156) (1876–1923), Shell flower [Shell-flower, Shellflower] (5, 6, 7, 49, 58, 86, 92, 156) (1828–1923), Snakehead [Snake head, Snake-head, Snakeheads] (5, 19, 46, 53, 57, 58, 72, 86, 92, 156) (1840–1923), Turtle bloom [Turtlebloom, Turtle-bloom] (5, 7, 53, 58, 92, 156) (1828–1923), Turtle-head [Turtlehead, Turtle head] (5, 6, 7, 53, 86, 92, 156) (1828–1923), White hummingbird tree (42) (1814), White turtlehead (138) (1923)

Chelone L. – Balmony (2) (1895), Hummingbird tree [Humming bird tree] (42) (1814), Snakemouth [Snake mouth, Snake-mouth] (75) (1894) Banner Elk NC, Snake's-head [Snake head, Snake-head, Snakehead, Snakeheads] (2, 6) (1892–1895), Turtle-head [Turtle-head, Turtle head] (1, 2, 63, 109, 138, 156) (1895–1949) from shape of flower

Chelone lyoni Pursh – See *Chelone lyonii* Pursh

Chelone lyonii Pursh – Lion's-turtlehead [Lyon's turtle head] (5) (1913), Pink turtlehead (138) (1923)

Chelone obliqua L. – Red turtlehead [Red turtle head] (5, 72) (1907–1913), Rose turtlehead (138) (1923)

Chenopodium (Tourn.) L. – See *Chenopodium* L.

Chenopodium album L. – Ansérine sauvage (French) (158) (1900), Baconweed [Bacon-weed] (5, 156, 157, 158) (1900–1929), Blackweed [Black weed] (77) (1898) Eastern Long Island, stains fingers black, Calite (150) (1894) NM, Čanxlǒǧan iŋkpa gmigmela (Lakota, small end rounded weed) (121) (1918?–1970?), Common lamb's-quarter [Common lamb's quarter] (42) (1814), Dirty Dick [Dirty-Dick] (156, 157, 158) (1900–1929), Fat-hen [Fat hen] (5, 156, 157, 158) (1900–1929), Frostblite [Frost-blite, Frost blite] (5, 156, 157, 158) (1900–1929), Goosefoot [Goose-foot, Goose foot] (41, 150) (1770–1894), Green pigweed [Green pig-weed] (19) (1840), Kitsarius (Pawnee, green juice) (37) (1919), Lamb's-quarters [Lambs' quarter, Lamb's quarters, Lamb's-quarters, Lambsquarter, Lambsquarters] (3, 4, 5, 35, 37, 45, 50, 62, 72, 80, 85, 92, 93, 95, 97, 103, 107, 121, 122, 125, 131, 145, 150, 156, 157, 158, 187) (1818–present), Lambs-quarters goosefoot [Lambsquarters goosefoot] (155) (1942), Mails (157, 158) (1900–1929), Meals (156, 157, 158) (1900–1929), Melge (157, 158) (1900–1929), Miles (157, 158) (1900–1929), Motton-tops (157) (1929), Muckweed [Muck-weed] (5, 156, 157, 158) (1900–1929), Mutton-tops (156, 158) (1900–1923), Pigweed [Pig-weed, Pig weed] (5, 45, 62, 80, 93, 107, 131, 150, 156, 157, 158) (1894–1936), Ragjag [Rag-jag] (156, 157, 158) (1900–1929), Wah'pe toto (Dakota, greens) (37) (1919), Weisser Gänsefuss (German) (158) (1900), White goosefoot [White goose-foot] (5, 62, 93,

107, 157, 158) (1900–1936), Wild spinach (5, 156, 157, 158) (1900–1929)

Chenopodium album L. var. *album* – Lamb's-quarters [Lambs' quarter, Lamb's quarters, Lamb's-quarters, Lambsquarter, Lambsquarters] (50) (present), Pigweed [Pig-weed, Pig weed] (156, 158) (1900–1923)

Chenopodium album L. var. *missouriense* (Aellen) I. J. Bassett & C. W. Crompton – Missouri lamb's-quarters [Missouri lambsquarters] (50) (present) , Pigweed goosefoot (155) (1942)

Chenopodium ambrosoides L. – Late-flowering goosefoot [Lateflowering goosefoot] (50) (present) (French) (158) (1900), Ambrosia (69, 156, 158) (1900–1904), American wormseed (49, 52, 55, 57, 60, 62, 69, 109) (1902–1949), Chenipodium (52) (1919), Culen (Chile) (14) (1882), Epazotl (Mexico) (107) (1919), Fragrant Jerusalem-oak [Fragrant Jerusalem oak] (7) (1828), Jerusalem tea (69, 92, 156, 157, 158) (1898–1929), Jesuit tea (69, 156, 157, 158) (1900–1929), Mexican tea (3, 4, 5, 50, 7, 14, 62, 69, 72, 80, 92, 93, 95, 97, 107, 125, 156, 157, 158) (1828–present), Mexikanisches Traubenkraut (German) (158) (1900), Spanish tea (69, 156, 157, 158) (1900–1929), Stinkweed [Stink-weed, Stink weed] (156) (1923), Sweet pigweed (19) (1840), Wohlreichender Gänsefuss (German) (158) (1900), Wormseed [Worm-seed, Worm seed] (21, 49, 122) (1893–1937), Wormseed goosefoot (155) (1942)

Chenopodium ambrosioides L. var. *ambrosioides* – American wormseed (6, 53, 54, 92, 158) (1892–1922), Americanische Wormsaamen (German) (6) (1892), Anserine anthelmintique (French) (186) (1814), Anserine vermifuge (6, 7, 186) (1814–1892), Ceniglo antelmintico (186) (1814), Chénopode Anthelmintique (French) (6) (1892), Chenopodio vermifugo (186) (1814), Drug wormseed goosefoot (155) (1942), Fishweed [Fish-weed] (156) (1923), Goosefoot [Goose-foot, Goose foot] (92) (1876), Jerusalem oak [Jerusalem-oak] (6, 7, 41, 58, 92, 156, 158, 186, 187) (1770–1923), Jerusalem oak leaves (92) (1876), Jerusalem oak seed (92) (1876), Mexican tea (50) (present), Oak-of-Jerusalem [Oak of Jerusalem] (92) (1876), Sowbank (7) (1828), Stinking-weed [Stinkingweed, Stinking weed] (7, 92) (1828–1876), Stinkweed [Stink-weed, Stink weed] (6) (1892), Wild wormseed (92) (1876), Worm goosefoot [Worm goose-foot] (186) (1814), Wormseed [Worm-seed, Worm seed] (6, 7, 19, 41, 48, 53, 58, 62, 92, 156, 158, 186) (1770–1923), Wormseed goosefoot (7) (1828), Wormseed plant (92) (1876), Wormwood [Wormewood, Worm-wood] (7) (1828), Wurmdryvend ganzevoet (186) (1814), Wurmmelde [Wurm-melde, Wurmmelte] (186) (1814), Wurmsaamen Gansefuss (German) (6, 7) (1828–1892), Wurmsamen (German) (186) (1814), Wurmtreibender Gänsfuss (German) (186) (1814)

Chenopodium ambrosioides L. var. *anthelminticum* (L.) Aellen – See *Chenopodium ambrosioides* L. var. *ambrosioides*

Chenopodium anthelminticum L. – See *Chenopodium ambrosioides* L. var. *ambrosioides*

Chenopodium atrovirens Rydb. – Piñon goosefoot [Pinyon goosefoot] (50) (present)

Chenopodium berlandieri Moq. – Pit-seed goosefoot [Pitseed goosefoot] (3, 4, 50, 155) (1942–present)

Chenopodium berlandieri Moq. var. *bushianum* (Aellen) Cronq. – Bush's goosefoot (50) (present), Pigweed goosefoot (155) (1942)

Chenopodium berlandieri Moq. var. *zschackii* (J. Murr) J. Murr ex Aschers. – Zschack's goosefoot (50) (present)

Chenopodium bonus-henricus L. – All-good [All good] (5, 107, 156) (1913–1923), Blite (5, 156) (1913–1923), English mercury (5, 19, 92, 156) (1840–1923), False mercury [False mercurie] (178) (1526), Fat-hen [Fat hen] (5, 107, 156) (1913–1923), Good King Henry [Good-King-Henry] (5, 72, 92, 107, 109, 138, 156) (1876–1949), Goosefoot [Goose-foot, Goose foot] (107) (1919), Markery (5, 156) (1913–1923) no longer in use by 1923, Mercury (107, 156) (1919–1923), Mercury goosefoot (5) (1913), Perennial goosefoot (5, 156) (1913–1923), Roman plant (5, 156) (1913–1923) no longer in use by 1923, Shoemaker's-heels [Shoemaker's heels] (156) (1923), Smear-dock (156) (1923), Smiddy-leaves [Smiddy leaves] (5, 156)

(1913–1923) no longer in use by 1923, Tota bona (107, 177) (1762–1919), Wild spinach (5, 107, 156) (1913–1923)

Chenopodium boscianum Moq. – See *Chenopodium standleyanum* Aellen

Chenopodium botrys L. – Ambrose (5, 156, 157, 158) (1900–1929), Ambrosia (75) (1894) Concord MA, Chénopode à grappes (French) (158) (1900), Feather-geranium [Feather geranium] (5, 92, 93, 95, 109, 156, 157, 158) (1876–1949), Hindheal [Hind-heal, Hindheel] (5, 156, 157, 158) (1900–1929), Jerusalem oak [Jerusalem-oak] (1, 3, 4, 72, 85, 122, 138, 156, 157, 158) (1900–1929), Jerusalem-oak goosefoot [Jerusalemoak goosefoot] (50, 155) (1942–present), Oak-of-Hierusalem [Oak of Hierusalem] (46) (1671), Oak-of-Jerusalem [Oak of Jerusalem] (19, 178) (1526–1840) deliberately introduced by colonists by 1671, Sweet Jerusalem-oak [Sweet Jerusalem oak] (7) (1828), Traubenkraut (German) (158) (1900), Turnpike-geranium [Turnpike geranium] (5, 156, 157, 158) (1900–1929)

Chenopodium bushianum Aellen – See *Chenopodium berlandieri* Moq. var. *bushianum* (Aellen) Cronq.

Chenopodium capitatum (L.) Ambrosi – See *Chenopodium capitatum* (L.) Asch.

Chenopodium capitatum (L.) Asch. – Blette (French) (46) (1879), Blite (46, 92, 184) (1793–1879), Blite goosefoot (50, 155) (1942–present), Common strawberry blite (42) (1814), Indian paint [Indian-paint] (5, 75, 156, 158) (1894–1923) from bright color of fruit, Indian strawberry [India-strawberry] (5, 19, 92, 156, 158) (1840–1923), Strawberry blite [Strawberry blight] (2, 4, 5, 19, 85, 92, 107, 122, 156, 158) (1840–1986), Strawberry spinach [Strawberry-spinage] (2, 5, 46, 92, 107, 156, 158) (1859–1913), Strawberry spinage [Strawberry-spinage] (46) (1879), possibly Garden strawberry (77) (1898) Paris ME

Chenopodium capitatum Watson – possibly *Chenopodium capitatum* (L.) Asch.

Chenopodium cycloides A. Nels. – Sandhill goosefoot (3, 4, 50) (1977–present)

Chenopodium dacotacum – See *Chenopodium watsonii* A. Nels.

Chenopodium dacoticum Standl. – See *Chenopodium watsonii* A. Nels.

Chenopodium desiccatum A. Nels. – Arid-land goosefoot [Aridland goosefoot] (50) (present), Oblong-leaf chenopod [Oblong-leaved chenopod] (131) (1899)

Chenopodium foetidum Lam. – See *Chenopodium vulvaria* L.

Chenopodium foetidus – possibly *Chenopodium vulvaria* L. (current species depends on author)

Chenopodium foliosum (Moench) Aschers. – Leafy goosefoot (50) (present), Slender blite (19) (1840), Slender-stalk strawberry blite [Slender stalked strawberry blite] (42) (1814)

Chenopodium fremontii S. Wats. – Fremont's goosefoot [Fremont goosefoot] (3, 4, 50, 93, 131, 155) (1899–present)

Chenopodium fremontii S. Wats. var. *fremontii* – Fremont's goosefoot [Fremont goosefoot] (50) (present)

Chenopodium gigantospermum Aellen – See *Chenopodium simplex* (Torr.) Raf.

Chenopodium glaucum L. – Glaucous goosefoot [Glaucous goose foot] (42) (1814), Goosefoot [Goose-foot, Goose foot] (85) (1932), Oak-leaf goosefoot [Oak-leaved goosefoot] (3, 4, 5, 50, 72, 93, 131, 155, 156) (1899–present)

Chenopodium humile Hook. – See *Chenopodium rubrum* L.

Chenopodium hybridum auct. non L. – See *Chenopodium simplex* (Torr.) Raf.

Chenopodium incanum (S. Wats.) Heller – Mealy goosefoot (5, 50, 93, 97, 122) (1913–present), Hoary goosefoot [Hoary goose foot] (42) (1814)

Chenopodium incanum (S. Wats.) Heller var. *incanum* – Mealy goosefoot (50) (present)

Chenopodium L. – Blite (7) (1828), Goosefoot [Goose-foot, Goose foot] (1, 2, 4, 42, 50, 10, 93, 109, 138, 155, 158) (1814–present), Lamb's-quarters [Lambs' quarter, Lamb's quarters, Lamb's-quarters,

Lambsquarter, Lambsquarters] (1, 4, 7, 93, 146, 190) (~1759–1986), Pigweed [Pig-weed, Pig weed] (1, 7, 92) (1828–1932), Sowbank (7, 92) (1828–1876), Strawberry blite [Strawberry blight] (1, 42, 158) (1814–1932), Strawberry pigweed (1) (1932), Strawberry spinage [Strawberry-spinage] (10) (1818)

Chenopodium lanceolatum **Muhl. ex Willd.** – See *Chenopodium album* L. var. *album*

Chenopodium leptophyllum **(Moq.) Nutt. ex S. Wats.** – Narrow goosefoot (50) (present), Narrow-leaf goosefoot [Narrowleaf goosefoot, Narrow-leaved goosefoot] (5, 93, 97, 122, 131) (1899–1937), Slim-leaf goosefoot [Slimleaf goosefoot] (155) (1942)

Chenopodium leptophyllum oblongifolium **S. Wats.** – See *Chenopodium desiccatum* A. Nels.

Chenopodium maritimum **L.** – See *Suaeda maritima* (L.) Dumort.

Chenopodium murale **L.** – Nettle-leaf goosefoot [Nettle-leaved goosefoot] (50, 62, 72, 97, 133) (1907–present)

Chenopodium olidum **Curtis** – See *Chenopodium vulvaria* L.

Chenopodium paganum **auct. non Reichenb.** – See *Chenopodium album* L. var. *missouriense* (Aellen) I.J. Bassett & C.W. Crompton

Chenopodium paganum **Reich.** – See *Chenopodium berlandieri* Moq. var. *bushianum* (Aellen) Cronq.

Chenopodium pallescens **Standl.** – Slim-leaf goosefoot [Slimleaf goosefoot] (50) (present)

Chenopodium polyspermum **L.** – All-seed [All seed] (156) (1923), Many-seed goosefoot [Many-seeded goosefoot] (5) (1913)

Chenopodium pratericola **Rydb.** – Desert goosefoot (50) (present)

Chenopodium rubrum **L.** – Alkali blite (1, 3, 4) (1932–1986), Coast blite (1, 156) (1923–1932), Fat-hen [Fat hen] (158) (1900), French spinach (156, 158) (1900–1923), Maple-leaf goosefoot [Maple-leaf goosefoot, Maple-leaved goose-foot, Maple-leaved goose-foot] (85) (1932), Pigweed [Pig-weed, Pig weed] (156) (1923), Red goosefoot [Red goose-foot] (19, 50, 93, 122, 131, 155, 156, 158) (1840–present), Red pigweed [Red pig-weed] (19, 156, 158) (1840–1923), Swine's-bane [Swine's bane, Swinesbane] (92, 156, 158) (1876–1923)

Chenopodium salinum **Standl.** – Rocky Mountain goosefoot (50) (present)

Chenopodium scoparium **[L.]** – See *Kochia scoparia* (L.) Schrad.

Chenopodium simplex **(Torr.) Raf.** – Hog-bane [Hog's-bane] (158) (1900), Maple-leaf goosefoot [Mapleleaf goosefoot, Maple-leaved goose-foot, Maple-leaved goosefoot] (3, 4, 21, 50, 62, 72, 80, 93, 95, 131, 145, 155, 156, 158) (1893–present), Maple-leaf pigweed [Maple-leaved pigweed] (2, 158) (1895–1900), Nightshade [Nightshade, Night shade, Nyght shade] (158) (1900), Sowbane [Sowbane] (156, 158) (1900–1923), Stramonium-leaf goosefoot [Stramonium-leaved goosefoot] (46) (1879), Swine's-bane [Swine's bane, Swinesbane] (156, 158) (1900–1923), Tufted goosefoot [Tufted goose foot] (42) (1814)

Chenopodium standleyanum **Aellen** – Bosc's goosefoot (72, 93, 97, 131) (1899–1937), Standley's goosefoot (50) (present)

Chenopodium subglabrum **(S. Wats.) A. Nels.** – Smooth goosefoot (50) (present)

Chenopodium urbicum **L.** – City goosefoot (50, 62, 155) (1912–present), Upright goosefoot (62, 72) (1907–1913), Dirty John (156) (1923), Goosefoot [Goose-foot, Goose foot] (92) (1876), Notchweed (92) (1876), Notchwort (156) (1923), Stinking arach (178) (1526), Stinking goosefoot (5, 92, 122, 156) (1876–1937), Stinking motherwort [Stinking Mother woort] (156, 178) (1526–1923), Stinking orache (92) (1876)

Chenopodium watsonii **A. Nels.** – Lamb's-quarters [Lambs' quarter, Lamb's quarters, Lamb's-quarters, Lambsquarter, Lambsquarters] (21) (1893), Watson's goosefoot (50) (present)

Chilopsis **D. Don** – Desert-willow [Desertwillow, Desert willow] (138) (1923)

Chilopsis linearis **(Cav.) Sweet** – Catalpa willow (77) (1898) TX, Desert-willow [Desertwillow, Desert willow] (4, 50, 77, 109, 122, 124, 138, 149, 153, 155) (1898–present), Jano (153) (1913) NM, Mimbres (149) (1904) NM

Chilopsis linearis **(Cavar.) DC.** – See *Chilopsis linearis* (Cav.) Sweet

Chilopsis saligna **Don.** – See *Chilopsis linearis* (Cav.) Sweet

Chimanthus amygdalinus **Raf.** – possibly *Prunus caroliniana* (P. Mill.) Aiton

Chimaphila corymbosa **Pursh** – See *Chimaphila umbellata* (L.) Bart.

Chimaphila maculata **(L.) Pursh** – Dragon's-tongue [Dragon's tongue] (5, 156) (1913–1923) no longer in use by 1923, Ground-holly [Ground holly] (7) (1828), Here a pisser (Canada) (7) (1828), King-cure (7) (1828), King's-cure [King's cure, King's-cure, Kings' cure] (92) (1876), Lion's-tongue [Lion's tongue] (156) (1923), Paigne (Canada) (7) (1828), Pipperidge [Piperidge] (156) (1923), Poison pippsissewa (187) (1818), Psiseva (7) (1828), Pyrole à feuilles maculées (French) (8) (1785), Pyrole blanche (French) (7) (1828), Rat's-bane [Rat's bane, Ratsbane, Rat's-bane] (5, 73, 156) (1892–1923) Blue Ridge VA, no longer in use by 1923, Rheumatism root [Rheumatism-root] (5, 156) (1913–1923), Rheumatism-weed [Rheumatism weed] (7) (1828), Spotted pipsiseway (7) (1828), Spotted pipsissiwa [Spotted-pipsissiwa] (5) (1913), Spotted pyrola (8) (1785), Spotted wintergreen (5, 19, 92, 156) (1840–1923), Striped pipsissewa (138, 156) (1923), Wax flower (77) (1898) Southold Long Island, White pipsiseway (7) (1828), Whiteleaf [White leaf, White-leaf] (7) (1828), Wild arsenic (5, 73, 156) (1892–1923), Wintergreen [Winter greene, Winter-green] (7, 92) (1828–1876)

Chimaphila maculata **Pursh** – See *Chimaphila maculata* (L.) Pursh

Chimaphila occidentalis **Rydb.** – See *Chimaphila umbellata* (L.) Bart.

Chimaphila **Pursh** – Pipsissewa [Pippsissewa] (1, 2, 109, 138, 155, 156) (1923–1942), Prince's-pine [Prince's pine, Princespine, Princes-pine] (2, 4) (1895–1986), Rheumatism-weed [Rheumatism weed] (92) (1876), Umbellated pyrola (10) (1818), Wintergreen [Winter greene, Winter-green] (158) (1900)

Chimaphila umbellata **(L.) Bart.** – Bitter wintergreen (5, 6, 19, 92, 158) (1840–1913), Bittersweet [Bitter sweet, Bitter-sweet] (5, 73, 156, 158) (1892–1923) NH, Chimaphila (52, 54) (1905–1919), Common pipsissewa (138, 155) (1931–1942), Doldenblüthiges Harnkraut (German) (6, 158) (1892–1900), Doldentragendes Wintergrün (186) (1814), Ga'gige'bûg (Chippewa, everlasting leaf) (40) (1928), Ground-holly [Ground holly] (5, 6, 49, 53, 58, 92, 156, 158) (1869–1923), Herbe de Paigne (French) (186) (1814), King's-cure [King's cure, King's-cure, Kings' cure] (5, 92, 156, 158, 186) (1825–1923) no longer in use by 1923, L'Herbe a Pisser (French) (186) (1814), Love-in-winter (5, 73, 156, 158) (1892–1923) no longer in use by 1923, Noble-pine [Noble pine] (5, 73, 92, 156, 158) (1876–1923) no longer in use by 1923, Oder Wintergrün (German) (6) (1892), Phipsesawa (8) (1785), Pine tulip (5, 92, 156) (1876–1923) no longer in use by 1923, Pine-tulip [Pine tulip] (5, 156, 158) (1900–1923), Pipsissewa [Pippsissewa] (5, 6, 40, 47, 49, 52, 53, 54, 55, 57, 58, 59, 61, 72, 92, 105, 156, 158, 186, 187) (1814–1932), Pirola (186) (1825), Prince's-pine [Prince's pine, Princespine, Princes-pine] (1, 3, 4, 5, 6, 19, 53, 49, 57, 58, 92, 101, 105, 155, 156, 158) (1840–1986), Prince's-pone [Prince's pone] (*sic*) (85) (1932) SD, Princess pine (29, 156) (1869–1923), Pyrola (92, 158) (1876–1900), Pyrole (186) (1825), Pyrole à fleurs en ombelle (French) (8) (1785), Pyrole ombellée (French) (6, 158) (1892–1900), Rheumatism-weed [Rheumatism weed] (156, 158) (1900–1923), Umbellated pyrola (8) (1785), Wintergreen [Winter greene, Winter-green] (6, 49, 55, 59, 75, 77, 92, 156, 186, 187) (1818–1923) SD, Wintergroen (186) (1825), Wintergrün (German) (158, 186) (1825–1900), Yaskopteg (Chippewa) (105) (1932)

Chimaphila umbellata **Nutt.** – See *Chimaphila umbellata* (L.) Bart.

Chimaphila umbellata **var.** *cisatlantica* **S. F. Blake** – Prince's-pine [Prince's pine, Princespine, Princes-pine] (109) (1949)

Chimonanthus **Lindl.** – Winter-sweet [Wintersweet] (138) (1923)

Chimophila **(*sic*)** *umbellata* **Nutt.** – See *Chimaphila umbellata* (L.) Bart.

Chiococca alba **(L.) A.S. Hitchc.** – Cahinca (49) (1898), Cahinca root

(92) (1876), Cainca (49) (1898), Cluster-flower snowberry [Cluster-flowered snowberry] (49) (1898), David root (7, 49, 92) (1828–1898), Snowberry [Snow berry, Snow-berry] (7, 49, 92) (1828–1898)

Chiococca racemosa **L.** – See *Chiococca alba* (L.) A.S. Hitchc.

Chiogenes hispudula **(L.) Torr. & Gray** – See *Gaultheria hispidula* (L.) Muhl. ex Bigelow

Chiogenes hispudula **Torr. & Gray** – See *Gaultheria hispidula* (L.) Muhl. ex Bigelow

Chiogenes **Salisb.** – See *Gaultheria* L.

Chiogenes serpyllifolia **Aiton** – See *Gaultheria hispidula* (L.) Muhl. ex Bigelow

Chionanthus **L.** – Chionanthe (French) (8) (1785), Fringe tree [Fringetree, Fringe-tree] (2, 7, 8, 10, 26, 82, 109, 138, 156, 189) (1767–1949), Snowdrop [Snowdrops, Snow-drops, Snow drop] (8) (1785)

Chionanthus virginica **L.** – See *Chionanthus virginicus* L.

Chionanthus virginicus **L.** – American fringe (5, 156) (1913–1923), Arbre de niege (French) (8) (1785), Chionanthe (French) (6) (1892), Chionanthe de Virginie (French) (8, 20) (1785–1857), Chionanthus (52, 54) (1905–1919), Common fringe tree (20) (1857), Flowering-ash [Flowering ash] (5, 156) (1913–1923), Fringe flower (14, 52) (1882–1919), Fringe tree [Fringetree, Fringe-tree] (5, 6, 19, 20, 49, 53, 54, 57, 58, 61, 65, 92, 97, 135, 156, 174, 184) (1753–1937), Grandfather graybeard (156) (1923), Gray-beard tree [Gray beard tree, Graybeard-tree] (5, 92, 156) (1876–1923), Oder Schneeblume (German) (6) (1892), Old-man's-beard [Old man's beard, Old-mans-beard] (5, 6, 49, 53, 58, 82, 92, 156) (1869–1930), Poison ash (5, 6, 156) (1892–1923), Schneebaum (German) (6) (1892), Shavings (5, 156) (1913–1923), Slaw bush [Slaw-bush] (156) (1923), Snow flower [Snowflower] or Snow flower tree [Snowflower-tree] (5, 6, 92, 156) (1876–1923), Snowdrop tree [Snowdrop-tree, Snow drop tree] (6, 19, 49, 53) (1840–1922), Virginia snowdrop tree [Virginian snow-drop tree] (8) (1785), White ash (5, 156) (1913–1923), White fringe tree [White fringetree] (122, 124, 138) (1923–1937), White-fringe [White fringe] (5, 92, 112, 135, 156) (1876–1937)

Chionodoxa **Boiss.** – Glory-of-the-snow (109, 138) (1923–1949)

Chionodoxa luciliae **Boiss.** – Glory-of-the-snow (138) (1923)

Chironia angularis **L.** – possibly *Sabatia angularis* (L.) Pursh (taxonomic status is unresolved (PL))

Chironia campanulata **L.** – See *Sabatia campanulata* (L.) Torr.

Chironia chloroides **Michx.** – See *Sabatia chloroides* Pursh

Chironia dodecandra **L.** – See *Sabatia chloroides* Pursh

Chironia gracilis **Michx.** – possibly *Sabatia campanulata* (L.) Torr.

Chironia pulchella **[Willd.]** – See *Centaurium pulchellum* (Sw.) Druce

Chlamydomonas augustae **Skuja** – Red snow (46) (1879)

Chloracantha spinosa **(Benth.) Nesom** – Devilweed aster (155) (1942), Mexican devilweed [Mexican devil-weed] (4) (1986), Scoba (150) (1894) NM, Skeleton-weed [Skeleton weed, Skeletonweed] (150) (1894), Spiny aster (150) (1894), Spiny chlorocantha (50) (present)

Chloris cucullata **Bisch.** – Hooded windmill grass [Hooded windmillgrass] (50, 155) (1942–present)

Chloris elata **Desv.** – Many-spike chloris [Many-spiked chloris] (94) (1901)

Chloris gayana **Kunth** – Rhodes grass [Rhodes-grass] (109, 122, 138) (1923–1949)

Chloris glauca **(Chapm.) Vasey** – See *Eustachys glauca* Chapman

Chloris petraea **Sw.** – See *Eustachys petraea* (Sw.) Desv.

Chloris pluriflora **(Fourn.) W. D. Clayton** – Many-flower trichloris [Many-flowered trichloris] (94) (1901)

Chloris polydactyla **(L.) Sw.** – See *Chloris elata* Desv.

Chloris **Sw.** – Chloris (155) (1942), Finger grass [Fingergrass, Finger-grass] (138) (1923), Windmill grass [Windmill-grass, Windmillgrass] (50, 155) (1942–present)

Chloris verticillata **Nutt.** – Branching foxtail (5, 163) (1852–1913), Chloris (144) (1899), Prairie chloris (5, 119) (1913–1938), Tumble windmill grass [Tumble windmillgrass] (50, 155) (1942–present),

Windmill grass [Windmill-grass, Windmillgrass] (3, 5, 94, 99, 119, 122, 134, 163) (1852–1977)

Chloris virgata **Sw.** – Feather finger grass [Feather finger-grass] (50, 138, 163) (1852–present), Feather-finger [Featherfinger] (122) (1937) TX, Showy chloris (3, 155) (1942–1977)

Chlorogalum pomeridianum **(DC.) Kunth** – Amole (78) (1898) CA, Soap bulb (14) (1882) CA, used in washing, Soap plant [Soap-plant] (78, 161) (1857–1898) CA, used in washing, Soaproot [Soap-root, Soap root] (78) (1898), Wavy-leaf soap plant [Wavyleaf soap plant] (50) (present)

Chlorogalum pomeridianum **Kunth** – See *Chlorogalum pomeridianum* (DC.) Kunth

Choisya **H.B.K.** – See *Choisya* Kunth

Choisya **Kunth** – Mexican orange [Mexican-orange] (138) (1923)

Chondrilla juncea **L.** – Chondrilla (70) (1895), Devil's-grass [Devil's grass] (5, 75, 156) (1894–1923) WV, Gum succory (5, 156) (1913–1923), Hog-bite [Hog bite] (5, 75, 156) (1894–1923) WV, Naked-weed [Naked-weed, Naked weed] (5, 75, 156) (1894–1923) WV, Skeleton-grass [Skeleton grass] (5) (1913), Skeleton-weed [Skeleton weed, Skeletonweed] (75, 156) (1894–1923) WV, Succory gum (92) (1876)

Chondrophora nudata **(Michx.) Britton** – See *Bigelowia nudata* (Michx.) DC. subsp. *nudata*

Chondrophora virgata **(Nutt.) Greene** – See *Bigelowia nudata* (Michx.) DC. subsp. *nudata*

Chondrosea aizoon **(Jacq) Haw.** – See *Saxifraga paniculata* Mill. subsp. *neogaea* (Butters) D. Löve

Chondrosea **Haw.** – See *Saxifraga* L. (US species)

Chondrosium foeneum **[Torr.]** – See *Bouteloua hirsuta* Lag.

Chondrosium papillosum **[(Engelm.) Torr.]** – See *Bouteloua hirsuta* Lag.

Chondrosum **[Desv.]** – See *Bouteloua* Lag.

Chondrus crispus **(L.) J. Stackhouse** – Carageenan (57, 58) (1917–1869), Carrageen moss [Carragheen moss] (92) (1876), Chondrus (57) (1917), Irish moss (55, 57, 58, 59, 92) (1869–1917), Pearl moss (92) (1876), Salt rock moss (92) (1876)

Chorisia speciosa **St. Hil.** – Floss-silk tree [Floss-silk-tree] (138) (1923), Vegetable silk (92) (1876)

Chorispora **R. Br. ex DC.** – Chorispora (50) (present)

Chorispora tenella **(Pallas) DC.** – Blue mustard (3, 4, 97) (1937–1986), Crossflower (50) (present)

Chrosperma muscaetoxicum **(Walt.) Kuntze** – See *Amianthium muscitoxicum* (Walt.) Gray

Chrosperma muscitoxicum **(Walt.) Kuntze** – See *Amianthium muscitoxicum* (Walt.) Gray

Chrosperma **Raf.** – See *Amianthium* A. Gray (all US species)

Chrysactinia mexicana **Gray** – False damiana (122) (1937) TX

Chrysalidocarpus lutescens **Wendl.** – See *Dypsis lutescens* (H. Wendl.) Beentje & Dransf.

Chrysanthemum **(Tourn.) L.** – See *Chrysanthemum* L.

Chrysanthemum ×*morifolium* **Ramat. (possibly)** – Common chrysanthemum (138) (1923)

Chrysanthemum arcticum **L.** – See *Dendranthema arcticum* (L.) Tzvelev subsp. *arcticum*

Chrysanthemum balsamita **L.** – See *Balsamita major* Desf.

Chrysanthemum carinatum **L.** – See *Chrysanthemum carinatum* Schousboe

Chrysanthemum carinatum **Schousboe** – Annual chrysanthemum (138) (1923), Three-color daisy [Three-colored daisy] (19) (1840), Tricolor chrysanthemum (109) (1949)

Chrysanthemum coccineum **Willd.** – Caucasian insect powder (92) (1876), Common pyrethrum (109) (1949), German insect powder (92) (1876), Guirila (92) (1876), Painted-lady [Painted lady] (138) (1923), Persian feverfew (92) (1876)

Chrysanthemum coronarium **L.** – Crown daisy [Crowndaisy] (109, 138) (1923–1949), Garden chrysanthemum (19) (1840), Garland chrysanthemum (109) (1949)

Chrysanthemum frutescens **L.** – Marguerite (82, 109, 138) (1923–1949), Paris daisy (109) (1949)

Chrysanthemum hortorum **Bailey** – possibly *Chrysanthemum* ×*morifolium* Ramat.

Chrysanthemum **L.** – Chrysanthemum (4, 138, 155, 158) (1900–1986), Corn marigold [Corn-marigold] (92) (1876), Daisy [Daisies, Daysy] (50) (present), Large daisy (190) (~1759), Ox-eye [Ox eye, Oxeye, Oxe eie] (10) (1818), Ox-eye daisy [Oxeye daisy, Oxeyedaisy, Ox-eyed daisy] (82, 93, 156, 167) (1814–1936)

Chrysanthemum lacustre **Brot.** – See *Leucanthemum lacustre* (Brot.) Samp.

Chrysanthemum leucanthemum **L.** – See *Leucanthemum vulgare* Lam.

Chrysanthemum leucanthemum **L. var. pinnatifidum Lecoq & Lamotte** – See *Leucanthemum vulgare* Lam.

Chrysanthemum maximum **Ramond** – See *Leucanthemum maximum* (Ramond) DC.

Chrysanthemum morifolium **Ramat.** – See *Dendranthema* ×*grandiflorum* Kitam. [*indicum* × *japonicum*]

Chrysanthemum nipponicum **Matsum.** – See *Leucanthemum nipponicum* Franch. ex Maxim.

Chrysanthemum parthenium **(L.) Pers.** – See *Tanacetum parthenium* (L.) Schultz-Bip.

Chrysanthemum parthenium **Pers. var. aureum Hort.** – See *Tanacetum parthenium* (L.) Schultz-Bip.

Chrysanthemum segetum **L.** – Corn chrysanthemum (107, 109, 156) (1919–1949), Corn daisy [Corne daisie] (178) (1526), Corn marigold [Corn-marigold] (5, 107, 109, 138, 156) (1913–1949), Pasture marigold (178) (1526), Yellow ox-eye (5, 156) (1913–1923)

Chrysanthemum uliginosum **Pers.** – See *Tanacetum vulgare* L.

Chrysobalanus icaco **L.** – Cocoa plum [Coco-plum, Coco plum] (92, 106, 107, 138) (1876–1930), Gopher-plum [Gopher plum] (106) (1930)

Chrysobalanus **L.** – Cocoa plum [Coco-plum, Coco plum] (10) (1818)

Chrysobalanus oblongifolius **Michx.** – See *Licania michauxii* Prance

Chrysocoma graveolens **Nutt.** – See *Ericameria nauseosa* (Pallas ex Pursh) Nesom & Baird subsp. *nauseosa* var. glabrata (Gray) Nesom & Baird

Chrysogonum **L.** – Gold-joint (167) (1814)

Chrysogonum virginianum **L.** – Chrysogonum (5, 174, 181) (~1678–1913), Goldenstar [Golden-star, Golden stars] (109, 138) (1923–1949)

Chrysolepis chrysophylla **(Douglas ex Hook.) Hjelmq.** – Chinquapin [Chinquepin] (161) (1857), Giant chinquapin (106) (1930), Golden chinquapin (106) (1930), Golden-leaf chestnut [Golden-leaved chestnut] (20) (1857), Western chinquapin (161) (1857)

Chrysolepis chrysophylla **(Douglas ex Hook.) Hjelmqvist var. chrysophylla** – Giant chinquapin (138) (1923)

Chrysolepis sempervirens **(Kellogg) Hjelmqvist** – Bush chinquapin (106) (1930), California chinquapin (138) (1923)

Chrysophyllum cainito **L.** – Cainito (174) (1753), Star-apple [Star apple] (109, 110, 138) (1886–1949)

Chrysophyllum **L.** – Star-apple [Star apple] (138) (1923)

Chrysopogon avenaceus **Benth.** – See *Sorghastrum nutans* (L.) Nash

Chrysopogon nutans **Benth.** – See *Sorghastrum nutans* (L.) Nash

Chrysopogon pauciflorus **(Chapm.) Benth. ex Vasey** – Few-flower sorghum [Few-flowered sorghum] (94) (1901)

Chrysopogon zizanioides **(L.) Roberty** – See *Vetiveria zizaniodes* (L.) Nash

Chrysopsis argentea **[(Pers.) Elliott]** – See *Pityopsis graminifolia* var. *latifolia* (Fernald) Semple & F.D. Bowers

Chrysopsis berlandieri **Greene** – See *Heterotheca canescens* (DC.) Shinners & Gray

Chrysopsis falcata **(Pursh) Ell.** – See *Pityopsis falcata* (Pursh) Nutt.

Chrysopsis falcata **Ell.** – See *Pityopsis falcata* (Pursh) Nutt.

Chrysopsis foliosa **(Nutt.) Shinners** – See *Heterotheca villosa* (Pursh) Shinners var. *foliosa* (Nutt.) Harms

Chrysopsis foliosa **Nutt.** – See *Heterotheca villosa* (Pursh) Shinners var. *foliosa* (Nutt.) Harms

Chrysopsis fulcrata **Greene** – See *Heterotheca fulcrata* (Greene) Shinners var. *fulcrata*

Chrysopsis gossypina **(Michx.) Ell.** – Cottony golden aster (5) (1913)

Chrysopsis gossypina **Nutt.** – See *Chrysopsis gossypina* (Michx.) Ell.

Chrysopsis graminifolia **(Michx.) Ell.** – See *Pityopsis graminifolia* (Michx.) Nutt. var. *graminifolia*

Chrysopsis graminifolia **Nutt.** – See *Pityopsis graminifolia* (Michx.) Nutt. var. *graminifolia*

Chrysopsis hispida **(Hook.) DC.** – See *Heterotheca villosa* (Pursh) Shinners var. *minor* (Hook.) Semple

Chrysopsis hispida **(Hook.) Nutt.** – See *Heterotheca villosa* (Pursh) Shinners var. *minor* (Hook.) Semple

Chrysopsis mariana **(L.) Ell.** – Caucasian inula (138) (1923), Goldenstar [Golden-star, Golden stars] (5, 156) (1913–1923), Maryland golden aster [Maryland golden-aster] (5, 138, 156) (1913–1923), Wild elecampane (187) (1818), Yellow-aster (187) (1818), possibly Maryland golden star (86) (1878) name created by Thomas Meehan

Chrysopsis mariana **Nutt.** – possibly *Chrysopsis mariana* (L.) Ell.

Chrysopsis **Nutt.** – Goldaster (155) (1942), Golden aster [Golden-aster] (1, 2, 4, 82, 106, 109, 138, 156, 158) (1895–1986)

Chrysopsis pilosa **Nutt.** – Golden aster [Golden-aster] (124) (1937), Nuttall's golden-aster [Nuttall's golden aster] (5, 97) (1913–1937), Soft golden-aster [Soft golden aster, Soft goldenaster] (3, 4, 50) (1977–present)

Chrysopsis scabrifolia **A. Nels.** – See *Heterotheca stenophylla* (Gray) Shinners var. *stenophylla*

Chrysopsis stenophylla **(Gray) Greene** – See *Heterotheca stenophylla* (Gray) Shinners var. *stenophylla*

Chrysopsis villosa **(Pursh) Nutt.** – See *Heterotheca villosa* (Pursh) Shinners var. *villosa*

Chrysopsis villosa **(Pursh) Nutt. var. angustifolia (Rydb.) Cronq.** – See *Heterotheca stenophylla* (Gray) Shinners var. *angustifolia* (Rydb.) Semple

Chrysopsis villosa **(Pursh) Nutt. var. canescens (DC.) Gray** – See *Heterotheca canescens* (DC.) Shinners & Gray

Chrysopsis villosa **(Pursh) Nutt. var. foliosa (Nutt.) DC.Eat.** – See *Heterotheca villosa* (Pursh) Shinners var. *foliosa* (Nutt.) Harms

Chrysopsis villosa **(Pursh) Nutt. var. hispida (Hook.) Gray** – See *Heterotheca villosa* (Pursh) Shinners var. *minor* (Hook.) Semple

Chrysopsis villosa **(Pursh) Nutt. var. villosa** – possibly *Heterotheca villosa* (Pursh) Shinners var. *villosa*

Chrysopsis villosa **Nutt.** – See *Heterotheca villosa* (Pursh) Shinners var. *villosa*

Chrysosplenium **(Tourn.) L.** – See *Chrysosplenium* L.

Chrysosplenium alternifolium **L.** – See *Chrysosplenium iowense* Rydb.

Chrysosplenium iowense **Rydb.** – Golden saxifrage (107) (1919), Iowa golden saxifrage (5, 72) (1907–1913)

Chrysosplenium **L.** – Golden saxifrage (1, 10, 167) (1814–1932), Water-carpet [Water carpet] (1, 7, 156) (1828–1932)

Chrysosplenium oppositifolium **L.** – Golden saxifrage (5, 19, 63, 156) (1840–1923), Opposite-leaf golden-saxifrage [Opposite-leaved golden saxifrage] (187) (1818), Water-carpet [Water carpet] (5, 19, 156) (1840–1923)

Chrysosplenium tetrandrum **(Lund ex Malmgr.) Th. Fries in NW** – See *Chrysosplenium iowense* Rydb.

Chrysothamnus baileyi **Woot. & Standl.** – Bailey's rabbitbrush (50) (present)

Chrysothamnus douglasii **(Gray) Clem. & E. G. Clem.** – See *Chrysothamnus viscidiflorus* (Hook.) Nutt.

Chrysothamnus douglasii **Gray** – See *Chrysothamnus viscidiflorus* (Hook.) Nutt.

Chrysothamnus frigidus **Greene** – See *Ericameria nauseosa* (Pallas ex Pursh) Nesom & Baird subsp. *nauseosa* var. *nauseosa*

Chrysothamnus graveolens **(Nutt.) Greene** – See *Ericameria nauseosa*

(Pallas ex Pursh) Nesom & Baird subsp. *nauseosa* var. glabrata (Gray) Nesom & Baird

Chrysothamnus howardi (Parry) Greene – See *Ericameria parryi* (Gray) Nesom & Baird var. *howardii* (Parry ex Gray) Nesom & Baird

Chrysothamnus howardii (Parry ex Gray) Greene – See *Ericameria parryi* (Gray) Nesom & Baird var. *howardii* (Parry ex Gray) Nesom & Baird

Chrysothamnus lanceolatus – See *Chrysothamnus viscidiflorus* (Hook.) Nutt. subsp. *lanceolatus* (Nutt.) Hall & Clements

Chrysothamnus naseosus (Pallas) Britton subsp. *graveolens* (Nutt.) Piper – See *Ericameria nauseosa* (Pallas ex Pursh) Nesom & Baird subsp. *nauseosa* var. glabrata (Gray) Nesom & Baird

Chrysothamnus nauseosus (Pallas ex Pursh) Britton – See *Ericameria nauseosa* (Pallas ex Pursh) Nesom & Baird subsp. *nauseosa* var. *nauseosa*

Chrysothamnus Nutt. – Chrysothamnus (158) (1900), Rabbitbrush [Rabbit-brush, Rabbit brush] (1, 4, 50, 93, 106, 122, 146, 155) (1930–present), Rayless goldenrod [Rayless golden-rod] (122) (1937)

Chrysothamnus plattensis Greene – See *Ericameria nauseosa* (Pallas ex Pursh) Nesom & Baird subsp. *nauseosa* var. *nauseosa*

Chrysothamnus pulchellus (Gray) Greene – Rayless goldenrod [Rayless golden-rod] (124) (1937), Southwestern rabbitbrush [Southwest rabbitbrush] (50, 155) (1942–present)

Chrysothamnus viscidiflorus (Hook.) Nutt. – Douglas' rabbitbrush [Douglas rabbitbrush] (155) (1942), Douglas' rayless goldenrod [Douglas's rayless goldenrod] (131) (1899), Yellow rabbitbrush (50) (present)

Chrysothamnus viscidiflorus (Hook.) Nutt. subsp. *lanceolatus* (Nutt.) Hall & Clements – Rabbitbrush [Rabbit-brush, Rabbit brush] (106) (1930)

Chrysothamnus viscidiflorus (Hook.) Nutt. subsp. *viscidiflorus* var. *viscidiflorus* – Low Douglas' rabbitbrush [Low Douglas rabbitbrush] (155) (1942), Yellow rabbitbrush (50) (present)

Chrysothamnus viscidiflorus (Hook.) Nutt. subsp. *pumilus* (Nutt.) Hall & Clements – See *Chrysothamnus viscidiflorus* (Hook.) Nutt. subsp. *viscidiflorus* var. *viscidiflorus*

Chrysurus aureus – See *Lamarckia aurea* (L.) Moench

Chrysurus cynosuroides [Pers.] – See *Lamarckia aurea* (L.) Moench

Cibotium Kaulfuss – Cibotium (138) (1923)

Cicendia pulchella Griseb. – See *Centaurium pulchellum* (Sw.) Druce

Cicer arietinum L. – Chick pea (19, 50, 92, 107, 109) (1840–present), Chickpea [Chick-pea] (107, 110, 138) (1886–1923), Chyches (179) (1526), Coffee pea (92) (1876), Egyptian pea (107) (1919), Garbantzua (Basque) (110) (1886), Garbanzo (109) (1949), Garbanzo (Castilean) (110) (1886), Garvance (French) (110) (1886), Nachius (Turkish and Armenian) (110) (1886), Nachuda (Georgian) (110) (1886), Nachunt (Turkish and Armenian) (110) (1886)

Cicer L. – Chickpea [Chick-pea] (138) (1923)

Cichorium (Tourn.) L. – See *Cichorium* L.

Cichorium endivia L. – Endive [Endyue] (92, 107, 109, 110, 179) (1526–1949), Garden chicory (92) (1876), Garden endive (19, 92) (1840–1876)

Cichorium intybus L. – Bachelor's-button [Bachelor's button, Bachelor's buttons, Batchelor's buttons] (5, 75, 106, 156, 158) (1894–1930), Barbe de capuchin (French) (107) (1919), Blue chicory [Blue chiccory] (6) (1892), Blue succory (6) (1892), Blue-daisy [Blue daisy, Blue daisies] (5, 76, 106, 157, 158) (1896–1929) Southold Long Island, Blue-dandelion [Blue dandelion] (5, 73, 79, 106, 156, 157) (1891–1930) IA, Blue-sailors [Blue sailors, Bluesailors] (5, 73, 82, 93, 106, 122, 124, 156, 157, 158) (1892–1937), Bunk (5, 156, 157, 158) (1900–1929), Chicoreé sauvage (French) (6, 158) (1892–1900), Chicorium (57) (1917), Chicory [Chycory] (5, 45, 49, 50, 57, 62, 63, 72, 80, 82, 85, 92, 93, 95, 97, 98, 106, 107, 109, 122, 124, 148, 156, 157, 158, 179) (1526–present), Chicorie (German) (6, 158) (1892–1900), Coffee weed

[Coffee-weed] (5, 106, 158) (1900–1930), Common chicory (3, 156) (1923–1977), Endive (10, 19) (1818–1840), Endivie (German) (158) (1900), Ragged-sailor [Ragged sailor, Ragged sailors] (76) (1896) Southold LI, Scleropis (5) (1913), Succory (7, 10, 19, 45, 49, 80, 92, 107, 109, 156) (1818–1949), Wegewart (German) (6) (1892), Wild bachelor's-buttons [Wild bachelor's buttons] (76) (1896) Worcester MA, Wild chicory (6, 110) (1886–1892), Wild cicory [Wilde cicorie] (178) (1526), Wild endive (6) (1892), Wild succory (5, 6, 49, 62, 92, 106, 156, 157, 158, 187) (1818–1930), Witloof (107) (1919)

Cichorium L. – Chicory [Chycory] (1, 4, 50, 82, 155, 156, 158) (1900–present), Endive (184) (1793), Succory (42) (1814)

Cicuta bolanderi S. Wats. – See *Cicuta maculata* L. var. *bolanderi* (S. Wats.) Mulligan

Cicuta bulbifera L. – Bulb water hemlock [Bulb waterhemlock] (155) (1942), Bulb-bearing cowbane [Bulb bearing cow bane] (42) (1814), Bulb-bearing water hemlock [Bulb-bearing water-hemlock] (5, 72, 93, 131, 156, 158) (1899–1936), Bulblet-bearing water hemlock (50) (present), Bulbous water hemlock (3, 4) (1977–1986), Water hemlock [Waterhemlock, Water-hemlock] (41, 157) (1770–1929)

Cicuta curtissii Coult. & Rose – See *Cicuta maculata* L. var. *maculata*

Cicuta douglasii (DC.) J. M. Coult. & Rose – Cicuta (71) (1898), Douglas' water hemlock [Douglas waterhemlock] (155) (1942), Oregon water hemlock (71) (1898), Water hemlock [Waterhemlock, Water-hemlock] (71) (1898)

Cicuta L. – Cowbane (1, 93) (1932–1936), Poison hemlock [Poison-hemlock, Poisonhemlock] (1) (1932), Water cowbane (10) (1818), Water hemlock [Waterhemlock, Water-hemlock] (1, 2, 4, 10, 50, 93, 109, 138, 155, 156, 158) (1818–present)

Cicuta maculata L. – American hemlock (7, 92) (1828–1876), American spotted cowbane [American spotted cow bane] (42) (1814), American water hemlock [American water-hemlock] (6, 57, 71, 92, 158) (1876–1917), Americanische Schierling (German) (7) (1828), Amerikanischer Wasserschierling (German) (6) (1892), Beaver-poison [Beaver poison] (2, 6, 71, 92, 156, 158) (1876–1923), Children's-bane [Children's bane] (6, 7, 71, 92, 133, 156, 158) (1828–1923) no longer in use by 1923, Cicuta (92, 125) (1876–1930), Cicuta Americana (Official name of Materia Medica) (7) (1828), Cique d'Amerique (French) (6, 7) (1828–1932), Common water hemlock (4) (1986), Cowbane (56, 71, 80, 125, 133, 184) (1793–1898), Death-of-man [Death of man] (6, 7, 71, 92, 156, 158) (1828–1923), Muskratweed [Muskrat weed] (71) (1898), Musquash root [Musquash-root] (2, 5, 6, 62, 71, 109, 133, 156, 158) (1892–1949), Musquash-poison (156, 158) (1900–1923), Poison hemlock [Poison-hemlock, Poisonhemlock] (40, 47, 85, 158) (1852–1932), Poison snakeweed (158) (1900), Poison-root [Poisonroot, Poison root] (7) (1828), Snakeweed [Snake-weed, Snake weed, Snake Weede] (6, 7, 71, 76, 156) (1828–1923) no longer in use by 1923, Spotted beaver-poison [Spotted beaver poison] (133) (1903) ND, Spotted cowbane [Spotted cow-bane] (2, 6, 62, 71, 92, 114, 133, 156) (1892–1923), Spotted hemlock (5, 71, 92) (1876–1913), Spotted parsley (71, 133, 158) (1898–1903) ND, Spotted water-hemlock [Spotted water-hemlock, Spotted water hemlock] (50, 138, 155) (1923–present), Wanûkons' (Chippewa) (40) (1928), Water hemlock [Waterhemlock, Water-hemlock] (3, 5, 62, 63, 71, 97, 121, 126, 131, 133, 156) (1898–1977), Water-parsley [Water parsley] (7) (1828), Wild hemlock (7, 71, 72, 92, 93, 98, 158) (1828–1936), Wild parsnip [Wild-parsnip, Wilde parsnep] (122, 124, 158) (1900–1937), Žoŋxaštoŋga (Osage, large wood) (121) (1918?–1970?)

Cicuta maculata L. var. *angustifolia* Hook. – Hemlock [Hemloc, Hemlocke] (148) (1939), Indian suicide plant (157) (1929), Poison hemlock [Poison-hemlock, Poisonhemlock] (148) (1939), Spotted water-hemlock [Spotted waterhemlock, Spotted water hemlock] (50) (present), Water hemlock [Waterhemlock, Water-hemlock] (101, 146, 148) (1905–1939), Water-parsnip [Water parsnip, Water-parsnip, Water parsnep, Water-parsnep] (101) (1905), Western water hemlock [Western water-hemlock, Western waterhemlock] (95, 155,

157) (1929–1942), Wyoming water hemlock [Wyoming water-hemlock] (157) (1929)

Cicuta maculata **L. var.** *bolanderi* **(S. Wats.) Mulligan** – Bolander's water hemlock [Bolander waterhemlock] (155) (1942), Spotted water-hemlock [Spotted waterhemlock, Spotted water hemlock] (50) (present)

Cicuta maculata **L. var.** *maculata* – Curtiss' water hemlock [Curtiss waterhemlock] (155) (1942), Spotted water-hemlock [Spotted waterhemlock, Spotted water hemlock] (50) (present)

Cicuta occidentalis **Greene** – See *Cicuta maculata* L. var. *angustifolia* Hook.

Cicuta vagans **Greene** – See *Cicuta douglasii* (DC.) J.M.Coult. & Rose

Cicuta virosa **L.** – Cowbane (92) (1876), Water hemlock [Waterhemlock, Water-hemlock] (19) (1840)

Cimicifuga americana **Michx.** – American bugbane (2, 5, 156) (1895–1923), Mountain rattletop [Mountain rattle top] (5) (1913), Stinking bugwort [Stinking bug wort] (42) (1814)

Cimicifuga cordifolia **Pursh** – See *Cimicifuga racemosa* (L.) Nutt.

Cimicifuga **L.** – See *Cimicifuga* Wernischeck

Cimicifuga racemosa **(L.) Nutt.** – Actee a grappe (French) (6) (1892), Black snakeroot [Black snake-root, Black-snake root] (2, 5, 6, 7, 14, 15, 19, 42, 49, 55, 57, 60, 64, 92, 109, 156, 177) (1814–1949), Bugbane [Bug-bane, Bug bane] (6, 19, 58, 64, 92, 156) (1840–1923), Bugwort (64, 92, 156) (1898–1923), Cimicifuga (54, 55, 57, 59, 60, 64) (1902–1917), Cohosh bugbane (138) (1923), Fairy candles (156) (1923), Heart-leaf rattletop [Heart-leaved rattle top] (5) (1913), Heart-leaf snakeroot [Heart-leaved snake root] (5) (1913), Macrotys (53, 54, 59) (1905–1922), Rattle-root [Rattleroot, Rattle root] (5, 6, 49, 58, 64, 92, 156) (1869–1923), Rattle-top [Rattle top, Rattletop] (5, 64, 156) (1907–1923), Richweed [Rich-weed, Rich weed] (5, 7, 49, 64, 92, 177, 187) (1762–1913) Banner Elk NC, Squaw-weed [Squawweed, Squaw-weed] (156) (1923), Swarze Cohosche (German) (6) (1892), Tall bugbane (2) (1895), Traubenformiges Christophskraut (German) (6) (1892), possibly Cohosh [Cohosh] (19) (1840)

Cimicifuga racemosa **Nutt.** – See *Cimicifuga racemosa* (L.) Nutt.

Cimicifuga **Wernischeck** – Black cohosh (13) (1849), Black snakeroot [Black snake-root, Black-snake root] (10, 13) (1818–1849), Bugbane [Bug-bane, Bug bane] (13, 15, 109, 156, 167) (1814–1949)

Cineraria heterophylla **Ph.** – See *Packera tomentosa* (Michx.) C. Jeffrey

Cineraria integrifolia **var.** *minor* **Pursh** – See *Packera tomentosa* (Michx.) C.Jeffrey

Cineraria integrifolia **var.** *minor* **W.** – possibly *Packera tomentosa* (Michx.) C.Jeffrey

Cineraria **L.** – See *Senecio* L.

Cinna arundinacea **L.** – Common reed grass [Common reed-grass] (56) (1901), Indian reed (19, 66, 92, 94) (1840–1903), Indian reed grass [Indian reed-grass] (5, 56, 92, 119, 129) (1894–1938), Reed-like grass (187) (1818), Reedy cinna (42, 66) (1814–1903), Stout woodreed (155) (1942), Stout woodreed grass (122) (1937), Sweet reed grass [Sweet reed-grass] (5, 119) (1913–1938), Sweet wood grass [Sweet wood-grass] (163) (1852), Sweet woodreed (50) (present), Wood reed [Woodreed] (3) (1977), Wood reed grass [Wood reed-grass] (5, 66, 87, 88, 90, 92, 111, 119, 163) (1852–1938)

Cinna bolanderi **Scribn.** – California reed grass [Californian reed-grass] (94) (1901)

Cinna glomerata **Walt.** – See *Andropogon glomeratus* (Walt.) Britton, Sterns & Poggenb.

Cinna **L.** – Reed grass [Reedgrass, Reed-grass] (1, 93) (1932–1936), Wood reed [Woodreed] (50, 155) (1942–present), Wood reed grass [Wood reed-grass] (66) (1903)

Cinna latifolia **(Trev. ex Goepp.) Griseb.** – Drooping reed grass (66) (1903), Drooping woodreed (3, 50, 155) (1942–present), Slender Indian reed (94) (1901), Slender reed grass (56) (1901), Slender wood reed grass [Slender wood reed-grass] (5, 99) (1913–1923), Sweet

reed grass [Sweet reed-grass] (5) (1913), Wood reed grass [Wood reed-grass] (85) (1932)

Cinna pendula **[Trin]** – See *Cinna latifolia* (Trev. ex Goepp.) Griseb.

Cinnamomum camphora **(L.) J. Presl** – Camphor tree [Camphor-tree] (19, 20, 92, 109) (1840–1949), Dutch amphor (92) (1876)

Cinnamomum camphora **Nees & Eberm.** – See *Cinnamomum camphora* (L.) J. Presl

Cinnamomum loureirii – See *Cinnamomum verum* J. Presl

Cinnamomum **Schaeffer** – possibly, Canell (179) (1526), possibly Cynamome (179) (1526)

Cinnamomum verum **J. Presl** – Cassia buds (92) (1876), Cassia-flower tree [Cassiaflower-tree] (138) (1923), Ceylon cinnamom (92) (1876), Cinnamon (110, 138) (1886–1923), Cinnamon tree [Cinnamon-tree] (109) (1949)

Cinnamomum zelyanicum **Blume** – See *Cinnamomum verum* J. Presl

Cinnamonium **Blume** – possibly *Cinnamomum* Schaeffer

Cinnamonum zeylandicum **Breyn.** – See *Cinnamomum verum* J. Presl

Cinnamonum zeylanicum **Breyn.** – See *Cinnamomum verum* J. Presl

Circaea ×*intermedia* **Ehrh.** [*alpina* × *lutetiana*] – Enchanter's nightshade [Inchanters night-shade] (92) (1876)

Circaea alpina **L.** – Alpine circaea (155) (1942), Alpine enchanter's nightshade (131) (1899) SD, Low enchanter's nightshade (156) (1923), Mountain enchanter's-nightshade [Mountain enchanter's nightshade] (41, 42) (1770–1814), Small enchanter's-nightshade [Small enchanter's nightshade] (50) (present), Smaller enchanter's-nightshade [Smaller enchanter's nightshade] (5, 72) (1907–1913), Tissavoyanne jaune (French) (41) (1770)

Circaea **L.** – Circaea (155) (1942), Enchanter's nightshade [Inchanters night-shade] (1, 2, 4, 10, 50, 158, 190) (~1759–present), Nightshade [Night-shade, Night shade, Nyght shade] (42) (1814)

Circaea latifolia **Hill** – See *Circaea lutetiana* L. subsp. *canadensis* (L.) Asch. & Magnus

Circaea lutetiana **L.** – Bindweed-nightshade [Bindweed nightshade, Binde-weed nightshade] (156, 158, 180) (1633–1923) no longer in use by 1923, Broad-leaf enchanter's-nightshade [Broadleaf enchanter's nightshade] (50) (present), Common enchanter's-nightshade [Common enchanter's nightshade] (158) (1900), Common nightshade [Common night shade, Common night-shade] (42) (1814), Enchanter's nightshade [Inchanters night-shade] (5, 19, 72, 93, 97, 131, 156, 178) (1526–1937), Enchanter's-wort [Entchanters-wort] (184) (1793), Mandrake (156) (1923), Paris circaea (155) (1942), Water-nettle [Water nettle] (79) (1891), Wild mandrake (158) (1900)

Circaea lutetiana **L. subsp.** *canadensis* **(L.) Asch. & Magnus** – Broad-leaf circaea [Broadleaf circaea] (155) (1942), Enchanter's night-shade [Inchanters night-shade] (3) (1977)

Cirsium **(Tourn.) Mill.** – See *Cirsium* Mill

Cirsium ×*iowense* **(Pammel) Fern.** [*altissimum* × *discolor*] – Iowa thistle (80, 82, 97) (1930–1937), Thistle [Thystle] (56) (1901)

Cirsium altissimum **(L.) Hill** – Fall prairie thistle (47) (1852), Roadside-thistle [Roadside thistle] (4, 62, 131, 156) (1899–1986), Tall thistle (3, 4, 5, 50, 62, 72, 82, 93, 95, 97, 122, 155) (1907–present), Tall thistle (19, 114, 145) (1840–1897)

Cirsium altissimum **(L.) Spreng** – See *Cirsium altissimum* (L.) Hill

Cirsium arvense **(L.) Scop.** – Boar thistle [Boar-thistle] (157, 158) (1900–1929), California thistle (156) (1923), Canadian thistle [Canada thistle] (3, 4, 5, 19, 45, 49, 50, 56, 57, 58, 62, 63, 72, 75, 80, 82, 85, 93, 95, 106, 131, 145, 155, 156, 157, 158, 187, 195) (1814–present), Corn thistle [Corn-thistle] (5, 156, 157, 158) (1900–1929), Creeping thistle [Creeping-thistle] (5, 62, 156, 157, 158) (1900–1929), Cursed thistle [Cursed-thistle] (5, 49, 62, 92, 156, 157, 158) (1898–1929), Dashel (157, 158) (1900–1929), Dodger (157, 158) (1900–1929), Dog thistle [Dog-thistle] (157, 158) (1900–1929), Field thistle (4) (1986), Hard thistle [Hard-thistle] (5, 156, 157, 158) (1913–1929), Prickly thistle [Prickly-thistle] (5, 156, 157, 158) (1900–1929), Pricky thistle [Pricky-thistle] (158) (1900), Sharp thistle [Sharp-thistle] (157) (1929), Way thistle [Way-thistle] (5, 156, 157, 158) (1900–1929)

Cirsium austrinum (**Small**) **E. D. Schulz** – See *Cirsium texanum* Buckl.

Cirsium canescens **Nutt.** – Nebraska thistle (5, 93) (1913–1936), Platte thistle (3, 4) (1977–1986), Prairie thistle (5, 50, 93, 131) (1899–present), Woolly thistle (80, 82) (1913–1930)

Cirsium discolor (**Muhl. ex Willd.**) **Spreng.** – Field thistle (3, 5, 62, 72, 93, 95, 97, 122, 131, 156) (1899–1977), Prairie thistle (80) (1913), Wood thistle (80, 82) (1913–1930)

Cirsium drummondii **Torr. & Gray** – Drummond's thistle [Drummond thistle] (4, 155) (1942–1986), Thistle [Thystle] (85) (1932)

Cirsium eatonii var. *eriocephalum* (**A. Gray**) **D. J. Keil** – Mountain thistle (101) (1905) MT, Thistle-root (101) (1905) MT, Tsinah (Snake) (101) (1905) MT

Cirsium edule **Nutt.** – Edible thistle (50) (present), I/lšanáta(n)qi (35) (1806)

Cirsium flodmanii (**Rydb.**) **Arthur** – Flodman's thistle (4, 5, 50) (1913–present), Prairie thistle (3) (1977)

Cirsium flodmanii (**Rydb.**) **Britton** – See *Cirsium flodmanii* (Rydb.) Arthur

Cirsium foliosum (**Hook.**) **DC.** – Elk thistle (155) (1942)

Cirsium hillii (**Canby**) **Fernald** – Hill's thistle (5) (1913)

Cirsium horridulum **Michx.** – Yellow thistle (2, 5, 46, 124, 187) (1783–1937)

Cirsium iowense – See *Cirsium ×iowense* (Pammel) Fern. [*altissimum × discolor*]

Cirsium iowense (**Pammel**) **Fern.** – See *Cirsium ×iowense* (Pammel) Fern. [*altissimum × discolor*]

Cirsium kosmelii (**Adams**) **Fisch. ex Hohen.** – Thorny thistle (42) (1814)

Cirsium lanceolatum (**L.**) **Hill.** – See *Cirsium vulgare* (Savi) Ten.

Cirsium **Mill** – Ma'zana'tĭg (Chippewa) (40) (1928), Thistle [Thystle] (1, 50, 82, 92, 93, 155, 156, 179) (1526–present), True thistle (4) (1986)

Cirsium muticum **Michx.** – Swamp thistle (3, 4, 5, 50, 72, 155, 156) (1907–present)

Cirsium nebraskense **Britton** – See *Cirsium canescens* Nutt.

Cirsium ochrocentrum **Gray** – Western thistle (145) (1897), Yellow-spine thistle [Yellow spine thistle, Yellowspine thistle, Yellow spined thistle, Yellow-spined thistle] (3, 4, 5, 50, 93, 97) (1899–present)

Cirsium odoratum (**Muhl.**) **Britton** – See *Cirsium pumilum* (Nutt.) Spreng.

Cirsium palustre (**L.**) **Scop.** – Marsh thistle (5) (1913)

Cirsium pitcheri (**Torr. ex Eat.**) **Torr. & Gray** – Pitcher's thistle (5) (1913)

Cirsium plattense (**Rydb.**) **Britton** – See *Cirsium canescens* Nutt.

Cirsium plattense **Cockerell** – See *Cirsium canescens* Nutt.

Cirsium pulcherrimum (**Rydb.**) **K. Schum.** – Wyoming thistle (50) (present)

Cirsium pumilum (**Nutt.**) **Spreng.** – Bull thistle [Bull-thistle] (73, 156) (1892–1923), Fragrant thistle (5, 156) (1913–1923), Hill's thistle (72) (1907), Pasture thistle (5, 156) (1913–1923), Star thistle [Star-thistle] (46) (1783)

Cirsium texanum **Buckl.** – Red thistle (124) (1937) TX, Texas thistle (4, 50) (1986–present)

Cirsium undulatum (**Nutt.**) **Spreng** – Canadian thistle [Canada thistle] (3, 160) (1860–1977), Prairie thistle (127) (1933), Wavy-leaf thistle [Wavyleaf thistle, Wavy-leaved thistle] (3, 4, 5, 50, 93, 97, 122, 155) (1913–present)

Cirsium undulatum (**Nutt.**) **Spreng. var.** *undulatum* – Pasture thistle (145) (1897) KS, Wavy-leaf thistle [Wavyleaf thistle, Wavy-leaved thistle] (50, 72, 131) (1899–present), White thistle [White thistle] (95) (1911)

Cirsium virginianum (**L.**) **Michx.** – Virginia thistle [Virginian thistle] (5, 97, 122, 131) (1899–1937)

Cirsium vulgare (**Savi**) **Ten.** – Bank thistle [Bank-thistle] (5, 156, 158) (1900–1923), Bell thistle [Bell-thistle] (5, 158, 156) (1913–1923), Bird thistle [Bird-thistle] (5, 156, 158) (1913–1923), Blue thistle [Blue-thistle] (5, 156) (1913–1923), Blue-thistle (158) (1900), Boar thistle [Boar-thistle] (5, 75, 156, 158) (1894–1923) WV, Bull thistle [Bull-thistle] (3, 4, 5, 50, 56, 62, 80, 82, 155, 156, 158) (1900–present), Bur thistle [Bur-thistle, Burr thistle, Burthistle] (156, 158) (1900–1923), Button thistle [Button-thistle] (5, 156, 158) (1900–1923), Common bur (5) (1913), Common bur thistle (93, 95) (1911–1936), Common field thistle (72) (1907), Common thistle (19, 62, 63, 92, 158, 187) (1818–1900), English thistle (145) (1897) KS, Horse thistle [Horse-thistle] (5, 156, 158) (1900–1923), Lance-leaf thistle [Lance leaved thistle] (56) (1901), Milk thistle [Milk-thistle] (92) (1876), Plume thistle [Plume-thistle] (5, 156, 158) (1900–1923), Roadside-thistle [Roadside thistle] (5, 156, 158) (1900–1923), Scotch thistle (158) (1900) emblem of Scotland, Spear thistle [Spear-thistle] (5, 85, 156, 158) (1900–1932), Buck thistle [Buck-thistle] (158) (1900)

Cissampelos pareira **L.** – Ice vine (92) (1876), Velvetleaf [Velvet leaf, Velvet-leaf] (92) (1876)

Cissus ampelopsis **Pers.** – See *Ampelopsis cordata* Michx.

Cissus arborea (**L.**) **Des Moul.** – possibly *Ampelopsis arborea* (L.) Koehne (taxonomic status is unresolved (PL))

Cissus erosa **Rich.** – Sandhill grape (7) (1828)

Cissus hederacea [**Pers.**] – See *Parthenocissus quinquefolia* (L.) Planch.

Cissus incisa (**Nutt.**) **Des Moul.** – See *Cissus trifoliata* (L.) L.

Cissus **L.** – Possum-grape [Possum grape] (4) (1986), Treebine (50, 155) (1942)

Cissus quinquefolia – See *Parthenocissus quinquefolia* (L.) Planch.

Cissus stans **Pers.** – See *Ampelopsis arborea* (L.) Koehne

Cissus trifoliata (**L.**) **L.** – Cowitch [Cow-itch, Cow itch] (106, 124) (1930–1937), Cut-leaf cissus [Cut-leaved cissus] (5, 97) (1913–1937), Ivy treebine (155) (1942), Possum-grape [Possum grape] (3, 4) (1977–1986), Sorrel vine [Sorrelvine] (50) (present), Yerba del buey (106, 122, 124) (1930–1937) Southern US

Cissus verticillata (**L.**) **Nicolson & C. E. Jarvis** – Mistletoe [Misseltoe, Misletoe, Misleto] (12) (1819)

Cistus canadensis **L.** – See *Helianthemum canadense* (L.) Michx.

Cistus carolinianus **Walt.** – possibly *Helianthemum carolinianum* (Walt.) Michx.

Cistus creticus – See *Cistus incanus* L. subsp. *creticus* (L.) Heywood

Cistus incanus **L. subsp.** *creticus* (**L.**) **Heywood** – Ladanum (92) (1876)

Cistus **L.** – Rockrose [Rock-rose, Rock rose] (42, 109, 138) (1814–1949)

Cistus ladaniferus **L.** – Gum rockrose (138) (1923), Labdanum (92) (1876)

Cistus monspeliensis **L.** – Montpelier roskrose (138) (1923)

Cistus salvifolius **L.** – Holly-rose [Holly rose] (92) (1876), Salvia rock-rose (138) (1923)

Citrullus amarus **Schrad.** – See *Citrullus lanatus* (Thunb.) Matsumura & Nakai

Citrullus citrullus (**L.**) **Karst.** – See *Citrullus lanatus* (Thunb.) Matsumura & Nakai

Citrullus colocynthis (**L.**) **Schrad.** – Bitter apple (19, 38, 55, 57, 92) (1820–1917), Bitter cucumber (92) (1876), Bitter gourd (92, 107) (1876–1919), Colloquintide [Colloquintida] (179) (1526), Colocynth (50, 52, 57, 92, 107) (1876–present), Colocynth-apple [Colocynth apple] (92) (1876), Colocynthis (54) (1905), Gourd of Alexandry [Gowrde of Alexandry] (179) (1526), Koloquinten (German) (57) (1917), Wild gourd [Wylde gourde] (179) (1526)

Citrullus colocynthis **Schrad.** – See *Citrullus colocynthis* (L.) Schrad.

Citrullus lanatus (**Thunb.**) **Matsumura & Nakai** – Abbatitchim (Hebrew) (110) (1886), Arbus (Russian) (110) (1886), Carpousia or carpousea (Modern Greek) (110) (1886), Ché-m t-toh (Cuchan Yuma) (132) (1855), Ché-mĕt-on-ya (Cuchan Yuma) (132) (1855), Chimico (Albanian) (110) (1886), Cindria (Spanish) (110) (1886), Citron melon (92) (1876), Citruels (182) (1791), Citrulle [Cytrulle] (179) (1526), Citruls (182) (1791), Karpus (Turkey) (110) (1886),

113

Melon [Melons] (182) (1791), Musk (181) (~1678), Pastèque (French) (110) (1886), Saka thide (Omaha-Ponca, eaten raw) (37) (1919) introducd from Africa by Spanish very early or Gilmore felt they may be indigenous as Lewis & Clark and others report that they were grown by natives, Saka yutapi (Dakota Santee) (37) (1919), Shpanshni yutapi (Dakota Yankton and Teton, eaten raw) (37) (1919), Sindria (Sardinian) (110) (1886), Watermelon [Water melon, Water-melon, Water mellons, Water Melons] (7, 19, 35, 37, 41, 50, 52, 54, 57, 58, 82, 92, 106, 107, 109, 110, 114, 155, 158, 181, 182) (~1678–present), Water-millon (181) (~1678), Wathaka ratdshe (Oto) (37) (1919), Wild melon (92) (1876), Zandria (Spanish) (110) (1886)

Citrullus vulgaris **Schrad** – See *Citrullus lanatus* (Thunb.) Matsumura & Nakai

Citrus ×*aurantium* **L.** [*maxima* × *reticulata*] – Apfelsine (German) (110) (1886), Arancio dolce (Italian) (110) (1886), Arange (178) (1526), Bergamont (107) (1919), Bigarade (92) (1876), Bitter orange (107) (1919), Golden-apple [Golden apple] (92) (1876), Neroli (92) (1876), Orange [Oranges, Orenge] or Orange tree (7, 19, 106, 110, 178, 182) (1526–1930), Seville orange (107, 109) (1919–1949), Sour orange (109) (1949), Sweet orange (107) (1919)

Citrus ×*limonia* **Osbeck** [*limon* × *reticulata*] – Grapefruit [Grape fruit] (109) (1949), Lemon or Lemon tree (92, 107) (1876–1919), Pomelo (109) (1949), Tahiti orange (138) (1923)

Citrus acida **Pers.** – See *Citrus aurantifolia* (Christm.) Swingle

Citrus aurantifolia **(Christm.) Swingle** – Lime or Lime tree [Lime-tree, Limetree] (106, 109) (1930–1949)

Citrus aurantifolia **Swingle** – See *Citrus aurantifolia* (Christm.) Swingle

Citrus decumana **(L.) L.** – See *Citrus maxima* (Burm. f.) Merr.

Citrus decumana **Murr.** – possibly *Citrus maxima* (Burm. f.) Merr.

Citrus grandis **Osbeck** – See *Citrus maxima* (Burm. f.) Merr.

Citrus japonica **Thunb.** – See *Fortunella japonica* (Thunb.) Swingle

Citrus limetta **Risso** – Adam's-apple [Adams' apple] (92) (1876), Lime tree fruit (92) (1876), Sweet lime (110) (1886)

Citrus limon **(L.) Burm. f.** – Lemon or Lemon tree (50, 52, 58, 92, 106, 109) (1869–present), Lemonis succus (52) (1919), Lymon (179) (1526)

Citrus limonia **Osbeck** – See *Citrus* ×*limonia* Osbeck [*limon* × *reticulata*]

Citrus limonum – See *Citrus* ×*limonia* Osbeck [*limon* × *reticulata*]

Citrus maxima **(Burm. f.) Merr.** – Grapefruit [Grape fruit] (106, 107, 138) (1919–1930), Pompelmous (109) (1949), Pummelo (107, 109) (1919–1949), Shaddock (109) (1949) from name of captain who first introducd species to West Indies

Citrus medica **L.** – Cedrat (92) (1876) oil from fruit rind, Citron [Cytron] (107, 109, 110, 138, 179) (1526–1949), Lemon or Lemon tree (7, 19, 110) (1828–1886), Lumias (Italian) (110) (1260), possibly Citronnier (French) (110) (1886)

Citrus medica limetta – See *Citrus limetta* Risso

Citrus medica limonum – possibly *Citrus medica* L.

Citrus medica var. *limetta* **Engl.** – See *Citrus limetta* Risso

Citrus nobilis deliciosa – See *Citrus reticulata* Blanco

Citrus nobilis **Loureiro** – See *Citrus reticulata* Blanco

Citrus nobilis var. *deliciosa* **(Ten.) Swingle** – See *Citrus reticulata* Blanco

Citrus paradisi **Macf.** – See *Citrus* ×*limonia* Osbeck [*limon* × *reticulata*]

Citrus reticulata **Blanco** – Kan (China) (110) (1886), King orange (138) (1923), Mandarin (109, 110) (1886–1949), Mandarin orange (138) (1923), Satsuma orange (109) (1949), Tangerine (109) (1949)

Citrus sinensis **(L.) Osbeck** – Orange [Oranges, Orenge] or Orange tree (138, 179) (1526–1923), Sweet orange (109) (1949)

Citrus taitensis – See *Citrus* ×*limonia* Osbeck [*limon* × *reticulata*]

Citrus trifoliata **L.** – See *Poncirus trifoliata* (L.) Raf.

Cladina rangiferina **(L.) Nyl.** – Gray-green reindeer lichen [Greygreen reindeer lichen] (50) (present)

Cladium effusum **Torr.** – See *Cladium mariscus* (L.) Pohl subsp. *jamaicense* (Crantz) Kükenth.

Cladium jamaicense **Crantz** – See *Cladium mariscus* (L.) Pohl subsp. *jamaicense* (Crantz) Kükenth.

Cladium leptostachyum **Nees & Meyen** – See *Cladium mariscus* (L.) Pohl subsp. *jamaicense* (Crantz) Kükenth.

Cladium mariscoides **(Muhl.) Torr.** – Water bog-rush [Water bog rush] (5, 19) (1840–1913), Bog-rush (156) (1923), Smooth twig rush (66) (1903), Twig rush [Twig-rush] (5, 156) (1913–1923)

Cladium mariscus **(L.) Pohl subsp.** *jamaicense* **(Crantz) Kükenth.** – Jamaica swamp sawgrass (50) (present), Saw-grass [Sawgrass, Saw grass] (5, 19, 75, 92, 156) (1840–1923)

Cladium **P. Br.** – Saw-grass [Sawgrass, Saw grass] (1, 155) (1932–1942), Twig rush [Twig-rush] (1) (1932)

Cladonia bellidiflora **(Ach.) Schaer.** – Red-cup moss (73) (1892)

Cladonia rangiferina **(L.) F. H. Wigg.** – See *Cladina rangiferina* (L.) Nyl.

Cladothrix lanuginosa **Nutt.** – See *Tidestromia lanuginosa* (Nutt.) Standl.

Cladothrix **Nutt.** – See *Tidestromia* Standl.

Cladrastis kentukea **(Dum.-Cours.) Rudd.** – American yellow-wood (5, 14, 97, 156) (1882–1937), Fustic tree [Fustic-tree] (5, 7, 92, 156) (1828–1923), Gopher wood [Gopher-wood] (5, 156) (1913–1923), Kentucky yellow-wood [Kentucky yellow wood] (5, 92, 156) (1876–1923), Virgilia (156) (1923), Yellow locust (5, 7, 156) (1828–1923), Yellow-wood [Yellowwood, Yellow wood] (20, 82, 92, 106, 156) (1857–1930), Yellow-ash [Yellow ash] (5, 7, 92) (1828–1913)

Cladrastis lutea **(Michx. f.) Koch.** – See *Cladrastis kentukea* (Dum.-Cours.) Rudd .

Cladrastis **Raf.** – Yellow-wood [Yellowwood, Yellow wood] (2, 82, 138, 156) (1895–1930)

Cladrastis tinctoria **Raf.** – See *Cladrastis kentukea* (Dum.-Cours.) Rudd .

Clarkia amoena **(Lehm.) A. Nels. & J. F. Macbr. subsp.** *amoena* – Farewell-to-spring (109, 138) (1923–1949)

Clarkia amoena **subsp.** *lindleyi* **(Douglas) H. F. Lewis & M. R. Lewis** – Whitney's godetia [Whitney godetia] (138) (1923)

Clarkia **Pursh** – Clarkia (138) (1923), Godetia (138) (1923)

Clavaria coralloides **L.** – Coral-like clavaria [Coral like clavaria] (42) (1814)

Clavaria cristata – See *Clavulina cristata* (Fr.) Schroer.

Clavaria **L.** – Club mushroom [Club mushrooms] (7, 184) (1793–1828), Coral mushrooms (7) (1828)

Clavaria **Tul.** – possibly *Clavaria* L.

Claviceps purpurea **(Fr.) Tul.** – Ergot (7, 49, 52, 55, 57, 59, 60, 61, 92, 148) (1828–1939), Ergot of rye (54, 55, 57, 60) (1902–1917), Ergota (55, 57, 59, 60) (1902–1917), Pulvis parturiens (59) (1807), Smut (49) (1898), Spur (49) (1898), possibly Spurred rye (52, 54, 92) (1876–1919)

Clavicorona pyxidata **(Fr.) Doty** – Crown-tipped coral (170) (1995), Cup-tip coral fungus (128) (1933) ND

Clavulina cristata **(Fr.) Schroer.** – Crested coral (170) (1995), Crested coral fungus (128) (1933) ND

Claytonia **(Gron.) L.** – See *Claytonia* L.

Claytonia asarifolia **Bong.** – See *Claytonia sibirica* L.

Claytonia assarifolia **Bong.** – See *Claytonia sibirica* L.

Claytonia caroliniana **Michx.** – Broader-leaf spring-beauty [Broader-leaved spring beauty] (2) (1895), Carolina spring-beauty [Carolina spring beauty, Carolina springbeauty] (5, 138, 156) (1913–1923), White-leaf spring beauty [White-leaved spring beauty] (5, 156) (1913–1923)

Claytonia cubensis – See *Claytonia perfoliata* Donn ex Willd.

Claytonia **L.** – Groundnut [Ground-nut, Ground nut, Ground nutts] (1, 93) (1932–1936), Miners' lettuce (1) (1932), Pigroot [Pig-root] (7) (1828), Seaside portulaca (106) (1930), Spanish lettuce (1) (1932), Spring-beauty [Spring beauty, Springbeauty] (1, 2, 4, 13, 15, 50, 82,

93, 109, 155, 156) (1895–present), Squaw-cabbage [Squaw cab-
bage] (1) (1932), Squaw-lettuce [Squaw lettuce] (1) (1932)
Claytonia lanceolata **Pall. ex Pursh** – Groundnut [Ground-nut, Ground
nut, Ground nutts] (101) (1905) MT, Pigeon-root [Pigeon root] (92)
(1876), Spring-beauty [Spring beauty, Springbeauty] (101) (1905) MT
Claytonia parviflora **Dougl. ex Hook. var.** *depressa* **Gray** – See *Clay-
tonia rubra* (T.J. Howell) Tidestrom subsp. *depressa* (Gray) J.M.
Miller & K. Chambers
Claytonia perfoliata amplectens **Greene** – See *Claytonia perfoliata*
Donn ex Willd.
Claytonia perfoliata **Donn ex Willd.** – Cuban spinach (107) (1919),
Spanish lettuce (5, 131) (1899–1913), Wild lettuce [Wild-lettuce,
Wylde letuse] (74) (1893) Santa Barbara CA, sometimes eaten by
children
Claytonia perfoliata **Donn ex Willd. subsp.** *perfoliata* – Indian lettuce
(156) (1923), Miner's lettuce (156) (1923), Squaw-lettuce [Squaw
lettuce] (101) (1905), Winter purslane (156) (1923)
Claytonia perfoliata **Donn.** – See *Claytonia perfoliata* Donn ex Willd.
Claytonia perfoliata **var.** *amplectens* **Greene** – See *Claytonia perfoli-
ata* Donn ex Willd.
Claytonia rubra **(T.J. Howell) Tidestrom subsp.** *depressa* **(Gray)
J.M. Miller & K. Chambers** – Squaw-lettuce [Squaw lettuce] (85)
(1932) SD
Claytonia sibirica **L.** – Siberian purslane (107) (1919)
Claytonia simsii **Sweet** – See *Claytonia virginica* L. var. *acutiflora* DC.
Claytonia virginica **L.** – Good-morning-spring [Good morning spring]
(5, 73, 158) (1892–1913) Hemmingford Quebec, Grassflower
[Grass-flower, Grass flower] (5, 158) (1900–1913), Mayflower
[May flower, May-flower] (5, 73, 158) (1892–1913), Notch-petal
claytonia [Notch-petalled claytonia] (86) (1878), Spring-beauty
[Spring beauty, Springbeauty] (5, 19, 65, 72, 86, 92, 97, 106, 107,
158) (1840–1937), Virginia spring-beauty [Virginia springbeauty,
Virginia spring beauty] (3, 4, 50, 155) (1942–present), Wild potato
[Wild potatoe, Wild potatoes, Wild-potato] (5, 72, 158) (1900–1913)
Claytonia virginica **L. var.** *acutiflora* **DC.** – White Texas star (124)
(1937) TX
Claytonia virginica **L. var.** *virginica* – Virginia spring-beauty [Virginia
springbeauty, Virginia spring beauty] (50) (present)
Cleistes divaricata **(L.) Ames** – Rosebud orchid (50) (present), Spread-
ing pogonia (5) (1913)
Clematis ×jackmanii **T. Moore** [*lanuginosa* × *viticella*] – Clematis
(112) (1937), Jackman's clematis [Jackman clematis] (138) (1923)
Clematis addisonii **Britt.** – Addison Brown's leather flower (5) (1913)
Clematis alpina **subvar.** *teniloba* **A. Gray in H. Newton & W. P. Jen-
ney** – See *Clematis columbiana* (Nutt.) Torr. & Gray var. *tenuiloba*
(Gray) J. Pringle
Clematis alpina tenuiloba **(Gray) Rydberg** – See *Clematis columbiana*
(Nutt.) Torr. & Gray var. *tenuiloba* (Gray) J. Pringle
Clematis bigelovii **Torr.** – Leather flower [Leatherflower, Leather-
flower] (153) (1913) NM
Clematis columbiana **(Nutt.) Torr. & Gray var.** *columbiana* – Purple
virgin's-bower [Purple virgin's bower] (3, 153) (1913–1977)
Clematis columbiana **(Nutt.) Torr. & Gray var.** *tenuiloba* **(Gray)
J. Pringle** – Alpine clematis (131) (1899) SD, Rock clematis (50)
(present)
Clematis crispa **L.** – Also another kind of Clematis having long tough
roots not unline those of licorice (181) (~1678) IA, Blue jessamine
(5, 156) (1913–1923), Bluebell [Blue-bell, Blue bell, Blue bells,
Blue-bells] (5, 156) (1913–1923), Clematis (156) (1923), Curl-
flower (156) (1923), Curl-flower clematis [Curl-flowered clematis]
(5) (1913), Curly clematis (138) (1923), Marsh leather flower (5)
(1913), Sims' clematis (72) (1907) IA
Clematis dioscoreifolia **Levl. & Vaniot** – See *Clematis terniflora* DC.
Clematis douglasii **Hook.** – See *Clematis hirsutissima* Pursh
Clematis drummondii **Torr. & Gray** – Drummond's clematis [Drum-
mond clematis] (155) (1942), Old-man's-beard [Old man's beard,
Old-mans-beard] (124) (1937) TX, Texas virgin's-bower [Texas

virgin bower] (122) (1937) TX
Clematis erecta **L.** – See *Clematis recta* L.
Clematis florida **Thunb.** – Cream clematis (138) (1923)
Clematis fremontii **S. Wats.** – Fremont's clematis [Fremont clematis]
(4, 125, 138, 155) (1923–1986), Fremont's leather flower (5, 50)
(1913–present)
Clematis glaucophylla **Small** – Glaucous leather flower (5) (1913)
Clematis grata **[Wall.]** – See *Clematis orientalis* L.
Clematis hirsutissima **Pursh** – Douglas' clematis [Douglas clematis]
(138) (1923), Hairy clematis (50) (present), Headache-weed (101)
(1905), Lion's-beard [Lion's beard, Lions'beard] (101) (1905)
Clematis hirsutissima **Pursh var.** *scottii* **(Porter) Erickson** – Scott's
clematis [Scott clematis] (50, 131, 155) (1899–present), Scott's
leather flower (5) (1913)
Clematis integrifolia **L.** – Bush lady's-bower [Bush Ladies Bowre]
(178) (1526)
Clematis jackmani – See *Clematis ×jackmanii* T. Moore [*lanuginosa*
× *viticella*]
Clematis **L.** – Bell-rue [Bell rue] (1) (1932), Clematis (109, 112, 155,
156) (1923–1949), Lady's-bower [Lady's bower] (190) (~1759),
Leather flower [Leatherflower, Leather-flower] (1, 50, 93) (1932–
present), Lion's-beard [Lion's beard, Lions'beard] (1) (1932), Old-
man's-whiskers [Old man's whiskers] (1) (1932), Pipestem [Pipe-
stem, Pipe stem] (1) (1932), Purple virgin's bower [Purple virgin's
bower] (1) (1932), Traveler's-joy [Traveler's joy, Traveller's joy,
Traveller's-joy, Travellers Ioy] (1, 184) (1793–1932), Vase vine [Va-
sevine, Vase-vine] (1) (1932), Virgin's-bower [Virgins-bower, Virgin's bower, Virgin bower] (1, 2, 4, 7, 10, 13, 15, 63, 82, 93, 109,
158, 167) (1814–1986), White clematis (1) (1932)
Clematis lasiantha **Nutt.** – Pipestem clematis (109) (1949)
Clematis ligusticifolia **Nutt.** – Čaŋjuwi skaska naxča (Lakota, possibly meaning loose white vine) (121) (1918?–1970?), Common wild
clematis (135) (1910), Hill clematis (106, 156) (1923–1930), Pipestem [Pipe-stem, Pipe stem] (156) (1923), Virgin's-bower [Vir-
gins-bower, Virgin's bower] (101) (1905), Western clematis (4, 85,
142, 156) (1902–1986), Western virgin's-bower [Western virgin's
bower, Western virgins-bower, Western virginsbower, Western vir-
gin-bower, Western virgin bower] (5, 93, 108, 121, 138, 142, 155,
156, 157) (1878–1942), Western white clematis (50) (present), Wild
clematis (101, 114) (1894–1905), Windflower [Wind flower, Wind-
flower, Wind-floures, Winde-floures] (156, 157) (1923–1929)
Clematis ligusticifolia **Nutt. var.** *californica* **S. Wats.** – Virgin's-bower
[Virgins-bower, Virgin's bower, Virgin bower] (76) (1896), Wind-
flower [Wind flower, Wind-flower, Wind-floures, Winde-floures]
(76) (1896)
Clematis ligusticifolia **Nutt. var.** *ligusticifolia* – Suksdorf's clematis
[Suksdorf clematis] (155) (1942), Western white clematis (50) (present)
Clematis missouriensis **Rydb.** – See *Clematis virginiana* L.
Clematis occidentalis **(Hornem.) DC.** – Rock clematis (138) (1923),
possibly Blue clematis (156) (1923), possibly Purple virgin's-bower
[Purple virgin's bower] (156) (1923)
Clematis occidentalis **(Hornem.) DC. var.** *occidentalis* – American
atragene (42) (1814), False virgin's-bower [False virgin bower] (19)
(1840), Mountain clematis (5, 156) (1913–1923), Purple virgin's-
bower [Purple virgin's bower] (5, 63, 72, 82) (1899–1930), Whorl-
leaf clematis [Whorl-leaved clematis] (5) (1913)
Clematis ochroleuca **Aiton** – Curly heads (5) (1913), Curly-heads (156)
(1923), Dwarf clematis (5) (1913), Erect mountain leather-flower
[Erect mountain leather flower] (5) (1913), Erect silky leather-flower
[Erect silky leather flower] (5) (1913), Pale clematis (2) (1895)
Clematis orientalis **L.** – Heavy-scent clematis [Heavy-scented clema-
tis] (2) (1895), Himalayan clematis (138) (1923), Oriental clema-
tis (138) (1923)
Clematis paniculata **Thunb.** – See *Clematis terniflora* DC.
Clematis pitcheri **Torr. & Gray** – Bluebill (50) (present), Leather flower
[Leatherflower, Leather-flower] (82) (1930), Pitcher's clematis

[Pitcher clematis] (4, 155) (1942–1986), Red-flower clematis pipe-vine [Red-flowered clematis pipe vine] (124) (1937)

Clematis pitcheri* Torr. & Gray var. *pitcheri – Pitcher's leather flower (5, 97) (1913–1937)

***Clematis pseudoalpina* [A. Nelson]** – See *Clematis columbiana* (Nutt.) Torr. & Gray var. *columbiana*

***Clematis recta* L.** – Ground clematis (138) (1923)

***Clematis recta* L.** – Upright virgin's-bower [Upright virgin's bower] (2, 82, 92) (1876–1930)

***Clematis scottii* Porter** – See *Clematis hirsutissima* Pursh var. *scottii* (Porter) Erickson

***Clematis sericea* Michx.** – See *Clematis ochroleuca* Aiton

***Clematis simsii* Sweet** – See *Clematis crispa* L.

***Clematis suksdorfii* B.L. Robins.** – See *Clematis ligusticifolia* Nutt. var. *ligusticifolia*

***Clematis tangutica* (Maxim.) Korsh.** – Golden clematis (109) (1949)

***Clematis tenuiloba* (Gray) C. L. A.S. Hitchc.** – See *Clematis columbiana* (Nutt.) Torr. & Gray var. *tenuiloba* (Gray) J. Pringle

***Clematis terniflora* DC.** – Sweet autumn clematis [Sweetautumn clematis] (138, 155) (1923–1942), Sweet autumn virgin's-bower [Sweet autumn virginsbower] (50) (present), White clematis (82) (1930), Yam-leaf clematis [Yamleaf clematis] (138) (1923)

***Clematis texensis* Buckl.** – Clematis pipe vine (124) (1937) TX, Scarlet clematis (109) (1949)

***Clematis versicolor* Small ex Rydb.** – Pale leather flower (5, 97) (1913–1937)

***Clematis verticillaris* DC.** – See *Clematis occidentalis* (Hornem.) DC.

Clematis verticillata – possibly *Clematis occidentalis* (Hornem.) DC.

***Clematis viorna* L.** – Headache-weed (156) (1923), Leather flower [Leatherflower, Leather-flower] (2, 5, 15, 19, 63, 72, 92, 138, 156) (1840–1923), Vase vine [Vasevine, Vase-vine] (156) (1923), Viorna (109, 156) (1923–1949)

***Clematis virginiana* L.** – Clematis (112) (1937), Common virgin's-bower [Common virgin's bower] (13, 38, 63, 158) (1820–1900), Common wild virgin's-bower [Common wild virgin's bower] (2) (1895), Devil's-darning-needle [Devil's darning needle] (5, 50, 156, 158) (1900–present), Devil's-hair [Devil's hair] (5, 74, 156, 158) (1893–1923) VA, Devil's-thread [Devil's thread] (156) (1923), Lady's-bower [Ladies' bower] (49) (1898), Love vine [Love-vine] (5, 49, 156, 158) (1898–1923), Missouri virgin's-bower [Missouri virginsbower] (155) (1942), Pipestem [Pipe-stem, Pipe stem] (156) (1923), Traveler's-ivy [Traveler's ivy] (49) (1898), Traveler's-joy [Traveler's joy, Traveller's joy, Traveller's-joy, Travellers Ioy] (5, 19, 158, 187) (1818–1900), Upright virgin's-bower [Upright virgin's bower] (181) (~1678), Virginia virgin's-bower [Virginia virgin's bower, Virginian virgin's bower] (5, 131) (1899–1913), Virgin's-bower [Virgins-bower, Virgin's bower, Virginsbower] (4, 15, 19, 48, 49, 61, 72, 82, 85, 127, 138, 155, 156) (1840–1986), Wild clematis (114) (1894), Wild hop [Wild hops] (5, 76, 156) (1896–1923) Hartford & Oxford Co ME, Woodbine (5, 76, 156, 158) (1896–1923) Hartford & Oxford Co ME

***Clematis virginiana* L. var. *missouriensis* (Rydb.) Palmer & Steyermark** – See *Clematis virginiana* L.

***Clematis vitalba* L.** – Lady's-bower [Ladies' bower] (92) (1876), Old-man's-beard [Old man's beard, Old-mans-beard] (92, 109) (1876–1949), Smokewood [Smoke wood] (92) (1876), Traveler's-joy [Traveler's joy, Traveller's joy, Traveller's-joy, Travellers Ioy] (92, 109, 138, 178) (1526–1949), Virgin's-bower [Virgins-bower, Virgin's bower, Virgin bower] (92) (1876), White vine [Whyte vyne] (92) (1876), Wild vine (92) (1876)

***Clematis viticella* L.** – Blue lady's-bower [Blew Ladies Bowre] (178) (1526), Italian clematis (138) (1923), Italian leather flower (50) (present), Purple virgin's-bower [Purple virgin's bower] (19) (1840), Red lady's-bower [Red ladies bowre] (178) (1526), Vine bower (2) (1895)

Cleome dodecandra – See *Polanisia dodecandra* (L.) DC.

***Cleome hassleriana* Chod.** – Cleome (92) (1876), Electric-light plant [Electric light plant] (156) (1923), Giant spider-flower (109) (1949), Spider flower [Spiderflower [Spider-flower (5, 72, 74, 82, 97, 138, 156) (1893–1937), Spider plant (106) (1930)

***Cleome integrifolia* Torr & Gray** – See *Cleome serrulata* Pursh

***Cleome* L.** – Base-mustard [Base mustard] (42) (1814), Bee plant [Beeplant] (4) (1986), Bee-flower [Beeflower, Bee flower] (1, 93) (1932–1936), Cleome (93, 158) (1900–1936), Indian pink (1, 93) (1932–1936), Spiderflower [Spider flower, Spider-flower] (4, 50, 82, 155, 158) (1900–present), Stink flower [Stinkflower] (1, 93) (1932)

***Cleome lutea* Hook.** – Yellow cleome (4, 5, 93) (1913–1986), Yellow spiderflower (50, 155) (1942–present)

Cleome lutea* Hook. var. *lutea – Yellow spiderflower (50, 155) (1942–present)

***Cleome pungens* auct. non Willd.** – See *Cleome hassleriana* Chod.

***Cleome pungens* Willd.** – See *Cleome spinosa* Jacq.

***Cleome serrulata* Pursh** – Bee plant [Beeplant] (85) (1932), Bee spiderflower (155) (1942), Bee-flower [Beeflower, Bee flower] (98) (1926), Cleome (106) (1930), Pink cleome (5, 72, 85, 93, 97, 131, 156) (1899–1937), Rocky Mountain beeplant [Rocky Mountain bee plant, Rocky Mountain bee-plant, Rocky Mt. bee plant] (2, 3, 4, 5, 50, 80, 82, 98, 106, 127, 145, 156) (1895–present), Rocky Mountain honey plant (114, 124) (1894–1937), Spiderflower [Spider flower, Spider-flower] (156) (1923), Stinking clover (80, 106, 156) (1913–1930), Stinkweed [Stink-weed, Stink weed] (98) (1926)

***Cleome spinosa* Jacq.** – Prickly cleome (5, 86, 156) (1878–1923), Spiderflower [Spider flower, Spider-flower] (86) (1878)

***Cleome spinosa* L.** – See *Cleome hassleriana* Chod.

***Cleome viscosa* L.** – Bastard mustard (92) (1876), Clammy mustard (92) (1876), Clammyweed [Clammy-weed, Clammy weed] (92) (1876), Wormweed [Worm weed, Worm-weed] (92) (1876)

***Cleomella angustifolia* Torr.** – Cleomella (3, 106) (1930–1977), Eastern cleomella (4) (1986), Narrow-leaf rhombopod [Narrowleaf rhombopod] (50) (present), Northern cleomella (5, 97) (1913–1937)

***Cleomella* DC.** – Cleomella (158) (1900), Stinkweed [Stink-weed, Stink weed] (50) (present)

Clerodendron – See *Clerodendrum* L.

***Clerodendron foetidum* [Bunge]** – See *Clerodendrum bungei* Steud.

Clerodendron thomsonae – See *Clerodendrum thompsoniae* Balf. f.

***Clerodendrum bungei* Steud.** – Rose glory-bower [Rose glorybower] (138) (1923)

***Clerodendrum indicum* (L.) Kuntze** – Tube flower [Tube-flower] (109) (1949), Turk's-turban [Turks-turban] (109) (1949)

***Clerodendrum indicum* Kuntze** – See *Clerodendrum indicum* (L.) Kuntze

***Clerodendrum inerme* (L.) Gaertn.** – Volkameria (92) (1876)

***Clerodendrum* L.** – Glorybower (109, 138) (1923–1949)

***Clerodendrum thompsoniae* Balf. f.** – Thomson's glory-bower [Thomson glorybower] (138) (1923)

***Clerodendrum trichotomum* Thunb.** – Harlequin glory-bower [Harlequin glorybower] (138) (1923)

***Clethra acuminata* Michx.** – Cinnamon clethra (138, 156) (1923), Mountain-sweet pepperbush [Mountain sweet pepperbush] (5) (1913)

***Clethra alnifolia* L.** – Alder-leaf clethra [Alder-leaved clethra] (8, 187) (1785–1818), Clethra à feuilles d'aune (French) (8) (1785), Fragrant clethra (187) (1818), Pepper bush [Pepper-bush, Pepperbush] (106) (1930), Speckled alder (5) (1913), Spiked alder (19, 92, 156) (1840–1923), Summer-sweet [Summersweet, Summer sweet] (109, 138, 156) (1923–1949), Sweet pepperbush [Sweet pepper-bush] (5, 19, 92, 106, 109, 156) (1840–1949), Ti-Ti [Titi] (156) (1923), White alder (5, 92, 106, 156) (1876–1930), White bush [White-bush] (5, 19, 92, 156) (1840–1923), Woolly clethra (138) (1923)

***Clethra* L.** – Clethra (8) (1785), Clethra (French) (8) (1785), Sweet pepperbush [Sweet pepper-bush] (167) (1814), White alder (2, 156) (1895–1942), White-alder (109) (1949)

***Clethra tomentosa* [Lam.]** – See *Clethra alnifolia* L.

***Cleyera japonica* Thunb.** – Sakaki (109) (1949)

Cliftonia **Banks ex Gaertn. f.** – Buckwheat tree [Buckwheat-tree] (15) (1895), Ti-Ti [Titi] (15) (1895)

Cliftonia ligustrina **[Sims ex Spreng.]** – See *Cliftonia monophylla* (Lam.) Britton

Cliftonia monophylla **(Lam.) Britton** – Buckwheat tree [Buckwheat-tree] (20, 106) (1857–1930), Cliftonie á feuilles de troene (French) (20) (1857), possibly Black ti-ti [Black titi] (106) (1930), possibly Ironwood [Iron wood, Iron-wood] (106) (1930), possibly Ti-Ti [Titi] (106) (1930)

Clinopodium acinos **(L.) Kuntze** – See *Acinos arvensis* (Lam.) Dandy

Clinopodium arkansanum **(Nutt.) House** – Arkansas calamint (4) (1986), Bed's-foot [Bed's foot] (5) (1913), Limestone calamint (50) (present), Low calamint (5, 97) (1913–1937), Slender calamint (5) (1913)

Clinopodium douglasii **(Benth.) Kuntze** – Yerba buena (57, 77, 106) (1898–1930)

Clinopodium glabrum **(Nutt.) Kuntze** – See *Clinopodium arkansanum* (Nutt.) House

Clinopodium incanum **L.** – See *Pycnanthemum incanum* (L.) Michx.

Clinopodium **L.** – Basilweed [Basil-weed, Basil weed] (184) (1793), Clinopodium (50) (present), Dogmint [Dog mint, Dog-mint] (7) (1828), Field balm [Field-balm] (5) (1913)

Clinopodium nepeta **(L.) Kuntze** – See *Calamintha nepeta* (L.) Savi subsp. *nepeta*

Clinopodium vulgare **L.** – Basil (1, 2) (1895–1932), Basil-thyme [Basil thyme] (156) (1923), Basilweed [Basil-weed, Basil weed] (5, 156) (1913–1923), Bed's-foot [Bed's foot] (5, 156) (1913–1923), Common wild basil (187) (1818), Dogmint [Dog mint, Dog-mint] (5, 92, 156) (1876–1923), Field basil (5, 156) (1913–1923), Field thyme (5, 19, 92, 156) (1840–1923), Horse-thyme [Horse thyme] (5, 156) (1913–1923), Stone basil (5, 156) (1913–1923), Wild basil (5, 10, 156) (1818–1923), possibly Horse-thyme [Horse thyme] (92) (1876)

Clintonia alleghaniensis **Harned** – See *Clintonia umbellulata* (Michx.) Morong

Clintonia borealis **(Ait.) Raf.** – Bear plum (75) (1894) Franconia NH, Bear's-tongue [Bear tongue, Bear-tongue] (5, 156) (1913–1923), Bluebead [Blue bead] (50, 156) (1923–present), Calf corn (78) (1898) Hartford ME, Clintonia (5, 40, 156) (1913–1928), Clinton's lily (5) (1913), Corn lily [Corn-lily] (156) (1923), Cowtongue [Cow tongue, Cow-tongue] (5, 73, 156) (1892–1923) Aroostock Co ME; NB, Dogberry [Dog-berry, Dog berry] (5, 75, 156) (1894–1923) Bath ME, Dragoness plant (19, 92) (1840–1876), He loll (79) (1891) NH, Heal-all [Healall] (2, 73, 79, 156) (1891–1923), Hound's-tongue [Hounds-tongue, Hound's tongue, Hounds' tongue, Hondes tonge] (78) (1898) ME, Northern clintonia (156) (1923), Northern lily (5, 75) (1894–1913), Oval-leaf dracaena [Oval leaved dracaena] (42) (1814), Quaffidilla (46) (1783), Wild corn (5, 75) (1894–1913) ME, Wild lily-of-the-valley [Wild lily of the valley] (5, 19, 73, 156) (1840–1923), Wood lily (156) (1923), Yellow clintonia (5) (1913)

Clintonia borealis **Raf.** – See *Clintonia borealis* (Ait.) Raf.

Clintonia umbellata **Torr.** – See *Clintonia umbellulata* (Michx.) Morong

Clintonia umbellulata **(Michx.) Morong** – Dog-plum [Dog plum] (5, 50, 156) (1913–present), White clintonia (5, 156) (1913–1923), Wild corn (156) (1923)

Clintonia uniflora **(Menzies ex J. A. & J. H. Schultes) Kunth** – Queen-cup (109) (1949)

Clintonia uniflora **Kunth** – See *Clintonia uniflora* (Menzies ex J.A. & J.H. Schultes) Kunth

Clitoria **L.** – Butterfly pea [Butterfly-pea] (1, 2, 4, 109, 138, 156, 158) (1895–1986), Pigeon-wings [Pigeon wings] (155) (1942)

Clitoria mariana **L.** – Atlantic pigeonwings (50, 155) (1942–present), Butterfly pea [Butterfly-pea] (4, 5, 97, 122, 124, 156) (1913–1986), Clabber-spoon [Clabber spoon] (5) (1913), Pigeon-wings [Pigeon wings] (4) (1986), Porcelain butterfly-pea (138) (1923)

Clitoria virginiana **L.** – See *Centrosema virginianum* (L.) Benth.

Clusia galactodendron **Desvaux** – See *Clusia minor* L.

Clusia **L.** – Balsam tree [Balsam-tree] (167) (1814)

Clusia minor **L.** – Cow tree (92) (1876), Milk tree (92) (1876)

Cnemidophacos **Rydb.** – See *Astragalus* L. (all US species)

Cnicus altissimus **Willd.** – See *Cirsium altissimum* (L.) Hill

Cnicus arvensis **Hoffm.** – See *Cirsium arvense* (L.) Scop.

Cnicus benedictus **L.** – Bitter thistle (5, 69, 156) (1903–1923), Blessed thistle (5, 7, 19, 49, 57, 58, 69, 92, 156) (1828–1923), Holy thistle [Holy thystle] (5, 49, 58, 69, 92, 156, 179) (1526–1923), Lovely thistle (7) (1828), Our Lady's thistle (5, 69, 156) (1903–1923), Spotted cardus (92) (1876), Spotted thistle (69) (1904), St Benedict's thistle (5, 69, 156) (1903–1923), Sweet sultan (5, 75, 156) (1894–1923) Mattapoisett MA, possibly Hairy bastard saffron [Hairie bastard saffron] (178) (1526)

Cnicus eriocephalus **Gray** – See *Cirsium eatonii* (A. Gray) B. L. Rob. var. *eriocephalum* (A.Gray) D. J. Keil

Cnicus horridulus **Pursh** – See *Cirsium horridulum* Michx.

Cnicus **L.** – Blessed thistle (2, 7, 63) (1828–1899), Stickers (73) (1892) St. John NB, Thistle [Thystle] (2, 7, 63) (1828–1899)

Cnicus lanceolatus **L.** – See *Cirsium vulgare* (Savi) Ten.

Cnicus muticus **Pursh** – See *Cirsium muticum* Michx.

Cnicus ochrocentrus **Gray** – See *Cirsium ochrocentrum* Gray

Cnicus pumilus **Torr.** – See *Cirsium pumilum* (Nutt.) Spreng.

Cnicus spinossimus, affine – possibly *Cirsium horridulum* Michx.

Cnicus undulatus **Gray** – See *Cirsium undulatum* (Nutt.) Spreng. var. *undulatum*

Cnidium canadense **S. T.** – possibly *Conioselinum chinense* (L.) Britton, Sterns & Poggenb. (taxonomic status is unresolved (PL))

Cnidoscolus **J. Pohl** – Bull nettle [Bull-nettle] (4) (1986), Cnidoscolus (50) (present), Tread-softly [Treadsoftly, Tread softly] (155) (1942)

Cnidoscolus stimulans – See *Cnidoscolus stimulosus* (Michx.) Engelm. & Gray

Cnidoscolus stimulosus **(Michx.) Engelm. & Gray** – Bull nettle [Bull-nettle] (78) (1898) Southern US, Milky ricinus of Virginia [Milkey ricinus of Virginia] (181) (~1678), Sand-nettle [Sandnettle, Sand nettle] (5, 92, 156) (1876–1923), Spurge nettle (5, 97, 156) (1913–1937), Stinging bush [Stinging-bush] (5, 156) (1913–1923), Tread-softly [Treadsoftly, Tread softly] (5, 19, 92, 156) (1840–1923)

Cnidoscolus texanus **(Muell.-Arg.) Small** – Bull nettle [Bull-nettle] (4, 122) (1937–1986), Malo mujer (Spanish) (122) (1937) TX, Texas bull-nettle [Texas bull nettle, Texas bullnettle] (50) (present), Texas tread-softly [Texas treadsoftly] (155) (1942), Tread-softly [Tread-softly, Tread softly] (97) (1937)

Cnidoscolus urens **(L.) Arthur** – Spurge nettle (107) (1919), Tread-softly [Treadsoftly, Tread softly] (107) (1919)

Coccinia cordifolia **Cogn.** – See *Coccinia grandis* (L.) Voigt

Coccinia grandis **(L.) Voigt** – Ivy gourd [Ivy-gourd] (109, 138) (1923–1949)

Coccolaba uvifera **L.** – See *Coccoloba uvifera* (L.) L.

Coccoloba diversifolia **Jacq.** – possibly, Sea-grape [Seagrape, Sea grape] (106) (1930)

Coccoloba laurifolia **Jacq.** – See *Coccoloba diversifolia* Jacq.

Coccoloba pubescens **L.** – Messamine (181) (~1678)

Coccoloba uvifera **(L.) L.** – Caraccas kino (92) (1876), Columbia kino (92) (1876), Kino (107) (1919), Lobeberry [Lobe berry] (92) (1876), Raisinier à grappe (French) (20) (1857), Raisinier de mer (French) (20) (1857), Sea-grape [Seagrape, Sea grape] (106, 109, 138) (1923–1949), Seaside-grape [Sea-side grapes, Sea side grapes] (7, 20, 92, 107) (1828–1919), Seaside-plum [Seaside plum] (106) (1930), Side-grape [Side grape] (20) (1857)

Coccolobis uvifera – See *Coccoloba uvifera* (L.) L.

Coccolobis laurifolia – possibly *Coccoloba diversifolia* Jacq.

Coccothrinax **Sarg.** – Seamberry palm (109) (1949)

Cocculus **(Pluk.) DC.** – See *Cocculus* DC.

Cocculus carolinus **(L.) DC.** – Carolina cocculus (2, 4) (1895–1986), Carolina coralseed (50) (present), Carolina moonseed [Carolinian moonseed] (5, 8, 97, 109) (1785–1949), Carolina snailseed (138, 155) (1923–1942), Coralberry [Coral-berry, Coral berry] (122, 124) (1937) TX, Ménisperme de Caroline (French) (8) (1785), Red-berry moonseed (5) (1913), Sarsaparilla (156) (1923), Snailseed [Snail-seed] (3, 4, 156) (1923–1986)

Cocculus DC. – Coralbead [Coral bead] (1, 50) (1932), Snailseed [Snail seed] (138, 155) (1923–1942)

Cocculus diversifolius DC. – Snailseed [Snail seed] (122, 124) (1937)

Cocculus orbiculatus (L.) DC. – Japanese snailseed (138) (1923)

Cocculus trilobus [(Thunb.) DC.] – See *Cocculus orbiculatus* (L.) DC.

Cochlearia aquatica – possibly *Armoracia lacustris* (A.Gray) Al-Shehbaz & V.Bates.

Cochlearia armoracia L. – See *Armoracia rusticana* P.G. Gaertn., B. Mey. & Scherb.

Cochlearia L. – Scurvy-grass [Scurvy grass, Scurvey grass] (7, 109) (1828–1949), Survy-grass (158) (1900)

Cocos australis – See *Syagrus romanzoffiana* (Cham.) Glassman (introduced)

Cocos datil [Drude & Griseb.] – See *Syagrus romanzoffiana* (Cham.) Glassman

Cocos L. – Coconut [Cocoanuts] (109) (1949)

Cocos nucifera L. – Cocoanut palm [Cocoa-nut palm] (106, 110) (1886–1930), Coyolli (Mexico) (110) (16th century) Mexico

Codiaeum variegatum – See *Codiaeum variegatum* (L.) Juss.

Codiaeum Juss. – Croton (109) (1949)

Codiaeum variegatum (L.) Juss. – Croton (138) (1923)

Coeloglossum bracteatum (Willd.) Parl. – See *Coeloglossum viride* (L.) Hartman var. *virescens* (Muhl. ex Willd.) Luer

Coeloglossum Hartm. – Frog orchid (50) (present)

Coeloglossum viride (L.) Hartman – Long-bract frog orchid [Long-bract frog orchid] (50) (present)

Coeloglossum viride (L.) Hartman var. *virescens* (Muhl. ex Willd.) Luer – Bracted green orchis (5, 156) (1913–1923), Long-bract frog orchid [Longbract frog orchid] (50) (present), Long-bract orchis [Long-bracted orchis] (3, 5, 72, 93, 156, 158) (1907–1977), Satyr orchid (138) (1923), Vegetable satyr (5, 19, 156, 158) (1840–1923)

Coelopleurum actaeifolium (Michx.) Coult. & Rose – See *Angelica gmelinii* (DC.) Pimenov

Coelorachis cylindrica (Michx.) Nash – Carolina joint-tail [Carolina jointtail] (155) (1942), Cheat (3) (1977), Cylinder joint grass (50) (present), Pitted joint grass [Pitted joint-grass] (5, 119, 163) (1852–1938), Rat-tail grass [Rat-tail-grass] (119) (1938), Slender rat-tail grass [Slender rat-tail-grass] (94) (1901)

Coelorachis rugosa (Nutt.) Nash – Rough-flower rat-tail-grass [Rough-flowered rat-tail-grass] (94) (1901), Tall rat-tail grass [Tall rat-tail-grass] (94) (1901), Wrinkled joint grass [Wrinkled joint-grass] (5) (1913), Wrinkled joint-tail grass [Wrinkled jointtail grass] (50) (present)

Coelorachis tessellata (Steud.) Nash – Tall rat-tail grass [Tall rat-tail-grass] (94) (1901)

Coffea arabica L. – Arabian coffee (109, 138) (1923–1949), Coffee (110) (1886), Common coffee (109) (1949)

Coffea L. – Coffee (138) (1923)

Coffea liberica Bull ex Hiern. – Liberian coffee (138) (1923)

Cogswellia daucifolia (Nutt.) M. E. Jones – See *Lomatium foeniculaceum* (Nutt.) Coult. & Rose subsp. *daucifolium* (Torr. & Gray) Theobald

Cogswellia foeniculacea (Nutt.) Coult. & Rose – See *Lomatium foeniculaceum* (Nutt.) Coult. & Rose subsp. *foeniculaceum*

Cogswellia montana (J. M. Coult. & Rose) M. E. Jones – See *Lomatium cous* (S. Wats.) Coult. & Rose

Cogswellia nudicaulis M. E. Jones – See *Lomatium nudicaule* (Pursh) J.M. Coult. & Rose

Cogswellia orientalis (Coult. & Rose) M. E. Jones – See *Lomatium orientale* Coult & Rose

Cogswellia Spreng. – See *Lomatium* Raf.

Cogswellia villosa M. E. Jones – See *Lomatium foeniculaceum* (Nutt.)

Coult. & Rose subsp. *foeniculaceum*

Coix L. – Job's-tear [Job's tear, Job's tears, Jobs-tears, Job's tear's, Iobs Teares] (138, 167) (1814–1923)

Coix lachryma L. – See *Coix lacryma-jobi* L.

Coix lacryma-jobi L. – Christ's tears (163) (1852), Diospiros (180) (1633), Gromell reed (180) (1633), Job's-drops [Iobs drops] (180) (1633), Job's-tear [Job's tear, Job's tears, Jobs-tears, Job's tear's, Iobs Teares] (19, 45, 50, 56, 67, 88, 92, 94, 122, 138, 178, 180, 184) (1596–present), Tear grass (67) (1890)

Cola acuminata (P. Beauv.) Schott & Endl. – Abata cola (50) (present), Cola (57, 107) (1917–1919), Colanut [Cola nut] (107, 109) (1919–1949), Colla (107) (1919), Gooba nut (109) (1949), Gooranut (107) (1919), Kola (52, 53, 57) (1917–1922), Kolanut [Kola nut] (52, 107) (1919), Kolla (107) (1919)

Cola acuminata Schott. & Endl. – See *Cola acuminata* (P. Beauv.) Schott & Endl.

Colchicum autumnale L. – Autumn crocus (50) (present), Autumn-crocus (109) (1949), Colchicum (52, 54, 57, 59, 60, 92) (1876–1919), Common autumn-crocus (138) (1923), Deadly meade saffron (178) (1596), Hungary mead saffron [Hungarie meade saffron] (178) (1596), Meadow saffron (52, 54, 55, 57, 60, 92) (1876–1919), Naked-ladies [Naked ladies] (92) (1876), Son-before-the-father [Sonne before the Father] (180) (1633), Tilteloosen (Low Dutch) (180) (1633), Upstart (92) (1876)

Colchicum L. – Autumn-crocus (138) (1923), Meadow saffron (180) (1633)

Coleanthus subtilis (Tratt.) Seidel – Moss grass [Moss-grass] (94) (1901)

Coleanthus subtilis Seid. – See *Coleanthus subtilis* (Tratt.) Seidel

Coleogeton filiformis (Pers.) D. H. Les & Haynes subsp. *occidentalis* (J.W. Robbins) D. H. Les & Haynes – See *Stuckenia filiformis* (Pers) Boerner subsp. *occidentalis* (J.W. Robbins) Haynes, D. H. Les, & M. Kral

Coleogeton filiformis subsp. *occidentalis* (J.W. Robbins) Les & R. R. Haynes – See *Stuckenia filiformis* (Pers) Boerner subsp. *occidentalis* (J. W. Robbins) Haynes, D. H. Les, & M. Kral

Coleosanthus Cass. – See *Brickellia* Ell.

Coleosanthus grandiflorus (Hook.) Kuntze – See *Brickellia grandiflora* (Hook.) Nutt.

Coleus bluemi Benth. – See *Coleus scutellarioides* (L.) Benth.

Coleus bluemi verschaffelti – See *Plectranthus scutellarioides* (L.) R.Br. (introduced)

Coleus blumei var. *verschaffeltii* (Lem.) Lem. – See *Plectranthus scutellarioides* (L.) R.Br. (introduced)

Coleus Lour. – Coleus (138) (1923)

Coleus scutellarioides (L.) Benth. – Common coleus (138) (1923), Joseph's-coat [Joseph's coat] (75) (1894)

Collinsia bartsiaefolia – See *Collinsia bartsiifolia* Benth.

Collinsia bartsiifolia Benth. – Seaside collinsia (138) (1923)

Collinsia bicolor Benth. – See *Collinsia heterophylla* Graham

Collinsia grandiflora Lindl. – Bluelips [Blue lips] (138) (1923)

Collinsia heterophylla Graham – Chinese houses (138) (1923)

Collinsia L. – possibly *Collinsia* Nutt.

Collinsia Nutt. – Blue-eyed Mary [Blue eyed Mary, Blue eyed Marys] (1, 4, 50) (1932–present), Bluelips [Blue lips] (1) (1932), Collinsia (138, 155, 158) (1923–1942), possibly Horseweed [Horse-weed, Horse weed] (10) (1818), possibly Knotroot [Knot-root, Knot root] (10) (1818)

Collinsia parviflora Dougl. – See *Collinsia parviflora* Lindl.

Collinsia parviflora Lindl. – Blue-eyed Mary [Blue eyed Mary, Blue eyed Marys] (85) (1932) SD, Bluelips [Blue lips] (3, 4) (1977–1986), Little-flower collinsia [Littleflower collinsia] (155) (1942), Maiden blue-eyed-Mary [Maiden blue eyed Mary] (50) (present), Slender collinsia (155) (1942), Small-flower collinsia [Small-flowered collinsia] (5, 131) (1899–1913)

Collinsia tenella (Pursh) Piper – See *Collinsia parviflora* Lindl.

Collinsia vera Nutt. – possibly *Collinsia verna* Nutt.

Collinsia verna **Nutt.** – Blue-bonnet-white-apron (156) (1923), Blue-eye [Blue eye, Blue eyes] (156) (1923), Blue-eyed Mary [Blue eyed Mary, Blue eyed Marys] (3, 4, 5, 72, 75, 97, 138, 156, 158) (1894–1986), Blue-eyed-Mary collinsia (155) (1942) Concord MA, Broad-leaf collinsia [Broad-leaved collinsia] (5, 158) (1900–1913), Collinsia (19, 92) (1840–1876), Innocence (5, 156, 158) (1900–1923), Lady-by-the-lake (156) (1923), Spring blue-eyed Mary [Spring blue eyed Mary] (50) (present), Tall pink (19) (1840)

Collinsia violacea **Nutt.** – Collinsia (3, 4) (1977–1986), Narrow-leaf collinsia [Narrow-leaved collinsia] (5, 65, 97) (1913–1937), Violet blue-eyed Mary [Violet blue eyed Mary] (50) (present), Violet collinsia (5, 122) (1913–1937)

Collinsonia canadensis **L.** – Aniseroot [Anise root, Anise-root] (7) (1828), Archangel (19) (1840), Baume de Cheval (French) (6) (1892), Broad-leaf collinsia [Broadleaf collinsia] (7) (1828), Canadische Collinsonie (German) (6, 7) (1828–1932), Citronella (5, 64, 156) (1907–1923), Citronella horsebalm (138) (1923), Collinsia (Official name of Materia Medica) (7, 52, 54, 57, 64) (1828–1919), Collinsone du Canada (French) (7) (1828), Collinson's flower (5, 86) (1878–1913), Common horsebalm [Common horse balm] (42) (1814), Gravelroot [Gravel root, Gravel-root] (6) (1892), Hardhack [Hard-hack] (6, 58, 92) (1869–1892), Heal-all [Healall] (6, 7, 55, 58, 86, 92) (1828–1911), Horsebalm [Horse-balm, Horse balm] (5, 6, 19, 41, 46, 53, 64, 86, 92, 156) (1770–1923), Horseweed [Horse-weed, Horse weed] (5, 6, 7, 58, 64, 86, 92, 184, 190) (~1759–1913), Knob-grass [Knob grass] (5, 64, 92) (1876–1913), Knobroot [Knob root] (5, 6, 55, 64, 92) (1876–1913), Knobweed [Knob-weed, Knob weed] (5, 7, 64, 86, 156) (1828–1923), Knotgrass [Knot grass, Knotgrass, Knotgrasse] (156) (1923) no longer in use by 1923, Knotroot [Knot-root, Knot root] (6, 7, 64, 86, 92, 156) (1828–1923), Oxbalm [Ox balm, Ox-balm] (5, 6, 58, 64, 92, 156) (1869–1923), Richleaf [Rich-leaf, Rich leaf] (5, 6, 7, 64, 92, 156) (1828–1923), Richweed [Rich-weed, Rich weed] (2, 5, 6, 7, 19, 46, 50, 53, 64, 86, 92, 156) (1878–present), Stone root [Stoneroot, stone-root] (2, 5, 6, 7, 52, 53, 54, 55, 57, 58, 61, 64, 86, 92, 156) (1869–1923), possibly Horseweed [Horse-weed, Horse weed] (41) (1770)

Collinsonia **L.** – Horsebalm [Horse-balm, Horse balm] (2, 50, 155, 156, 158) (1895–present)

Collomia grandiflora **Douglas** – Big-flower gilia [Bigflower gilia] (138) (1923)

Collomia linearis **Nutt.** – Collomia (157) (1929), Narrow-leaf collomia [Narrow-leaved collomia] (5, 93, 131) (1899–1936), Tiny-trumpet [Tiny trumpet] (50) (present)

Collomia **Nutt.** – Collomia (4, 158) (1900–1986), Horseweed [Horse-weed, Horse weed] (138) (1923), Trumpet (50) (present)

Collybia dryophila **(Bull. Ex Fr.) Kum.** – See *Collybia dryophila* (Bull.) P. Kumm.

Collybia dryophila **(Bull.) P. Kumm.** – Oak-loving collybia (170) (1995), Oak-loving mushroom (128) (1933)

Collybia velutipes **(Curtis) P. Kumm.** – Velvet-stem mushroom [Velvet-stemmed mushroom] (128) (1933)

Colocasia antiquorum **Schott** – See *Colocasia esculenta* (L.) Schott

Colocasia esculenta **(L.) Schott** – Ado (182) (1791), Alcoleaz (Portugal) (110) (1886), Aro di Egitto (Italian) (110) (1886), Black caco (92) (1876), Colocasia (110) (1886) colocasia of Diosorides is actually nelumbo according to Alfonse DeCandolle, Culcas (Egypt) (110) (16th century), Dasheen (109, 138) (1923–1949), Eddo (109) (1949), Eldoes (7) (1828), Elephant's-ear [Elephants' ear, Elephant's ears, Elephants-ear] (138) (1923), Imo (Japan) (110) (1886), Indian kale (92) (1876), Kandalla (Ceylon, cultivated plant) (110) (1886), Tanniers (7) (1828), Taro (109, 138) (1923–1949), Ynayah (86) (1878) Southern states

Colocasia esculenta **Schott** – See *Colocasia esculenta* (L.) Schott

Colocynthis vulgaris **Schrad.** – See *Citrullus colocynthis* (L.) Schrad.

Colpodium fulvum **(Trin.) Griseb.** – See *Arctophila fulva* (Trin.) Rupr. ex Anderss.

Colpodium pendulinum **(Laest.) Griseb.** – See *Arctophila fulva* (Trin.)

Rupr. ex Anderss.

Colubrina americana – See *Colubrina arborescens* (Mill.) Sarg.

Colubrina arborescens **(P. Mill.) Sargent** – Bois de couleuvre (French) (20) (1857) , Snakewood [Snake wood] (20) (1857)

Colubrina colubrina **(Jacq.) Millsp.** – See *Colubrina arborescens* (Mill.) Sarg.

Colubrina elliptica **(Sw.) Brizicky & W. L. Stern** – Cottony jujube (109) (1949), Indian jujube [India jujube] (109, 138) (1923–1949)

Colubrina texensis **(Torr. & Gray) Gray** – Hog-plum [Hog plum, Hog's plum] (122, 124) (1937) TX, Rockbrush (106) (1930)

Colutea arborescens **L.** – Bastard sena (178) (1526), Bladder senna [Bladder-senna] (19, 92) (1840–1876), Common bladder-senna (138) (1923)

Colutea **L.** – Bladder senna [Bladder-senna] (7, 138) (1828–1923)

Comandra livida **Richards.** – See *Geocaulon lividum* (Richardson) Fernald

Comandra **Nutt.** – Bastard toadflax [Bastard toad flax, Bastard toad-flax] (1, 50, 93, 158) (1900–present), Comandra (155) (1942), False toadflax [False toad-flax, False toad flax] (156) (1923), Toadflax [Toad flax, Toad-flax] (7) (1828)

Comandra pallida **A. DC.** – See *Comandra umbellata* (L.) Nutt. subsp. *pallida* (A. DC.) Piehl

Comandra richardsiana **Fern.** – See *Comandra umbellata* (L.) Nutt. subsp. *umbellata*

Comandra umbellata **(L.) Nutt.** – Bastard toadflax [Bastard toad flax, Bastard toad-flax] (5, 50, 72, 93, 131, 158, 187) (1818–present), Common comandra (155) (1942), Flaxweed [Flax-weed] (184) (1793), Toadflax [Toad flax, Toad-flax] (95) (1911), possibly False toadflax [False toad-flax, False toad flax] (19, 156) (1840–1923)

Comandra umbellata **(L.) Nutt. subsp. *pallida* (A. DC.) Piehl** – Bastard toadflax [Bastard toad flax, Bastard toad-flax] (3) (1977), Pale bastard toadflax (50) (present), Pale comandra (5, 93, 97, 131) (1899–1937)

Comandra umbellata **(L.) Nutt. subsp. *umbellata*** – Bastard toadflax [Bastard toad flax, Bastard toad-flax] (3, 50) (1977–present), Richard's comandra [Richards comandra] (155) (1942)

Comarostaphylis diversifolia **(Parry) Greene subsp. *diversifolia*** – Toothed manzanita (155) (1942)

Comarum palustra – See *Comarum palustre* L.

Comarum palustre **L.** – Bĭne'bûg (Chippewa, prairie chiken or grouse leaf) (40) (1928), Bog-strawberry [Bog strawberry] (5, 156) (1913–1923), Cowberry [Cow-berry, Cow berry] (5, 156) (1913–1923), Marsh cinquefoil [Marsh cinque-foil] (5, 72, 156) (1907–1923), Marsh five-finger (2, 5, 19, 92, 156) (1840–1942), Marshlocks (40) (1928), Meadow-nuts [Meadow nuts] (5) (1913), Purple cinquefoil (5, 156) (1913–1923), Purple marshlocks [Purple marsh-locks] (5, 50, 156) (1913–present), Purplewort [Purple-wort, Purple woort] (5, 156) (1913–1923) no longer in use by 1923

Commelina angustifolia **Michx.** – See *Commelina erecta* L. var. *angustifolia* (Michx.) Fern.

Commelina coelestis **Willd.** – Mexican dayflower (138) (1923)

Commelina communis **L.** – Asiatic dayflower [Asiatic day flower] (5, 50, 57) (1913–present), Common dayflower [Common day-flower] (155) (1942), Creeping dayflower [Creeping day-flower] (98) (1926), Dayflower [Day flower, Day-flower] (3, 98) (1926–1977)

Commelina communis **L. var. *communis*** – Asiatic dayflower [Asiatic day flower] (50) (present)

Commelina crispa **Wooton** – See *Commelina erecta* L. var. *angustifolia* (Michx.) Fern.

Commelina diffusa **Burm. f.** – Climbing dayflower (50) (present), Creeping dayflower [Creeping day-flower] (3) (1977)

Commelina elegans **Kunth** – White-mouth dayflower [Whitemouth dayflower] (50) (present)

Commelina erecta **L.** – Erect dayflower (155) (1942), Great upright-branch Virginia bastard spiderwort [Great upright branct Virginia bastard spiderwort] (181) (~1678), Slender dayflower [Slender day-flower] (5, 97) (1913–1937), White-mouth dayflower [Whitemouth dayflower] (50) (present)

Commelina erecta L. var. *angustifolia* (Michx.) Fern. – Curly-leaf dayflower [Curly-leaved dayflower, Curly-leaved day-flower] (5, 97, 155) (1913–1942), Dayflower [Day flower, Day-flower] (19, 85, 92) (1840–1932), Erect dayflower (3) (1977), Narrow-leaf dayflower [Narrowleaf dayflower] (155) (1942), White-mouth dayflower [Whitemouth dayflower] (50) (present)

Commelina erecta L. var. *erecta* – Erect dayflower (3) (1977), White-mouth dayflower [Whitemouth dayflower] (50) (present)

Commelina hirtella Vahl – See *Commelina virginica* L.

Commelina L. – Dayflower [Day flower, Day-flower] (1, 7, 50, 93, 109, 122, 124, 138, 155, 156, 158) (1828–present), Dew flower [Dew-flowers] (1) (1932)

Commelina nudiflora L. – See *Murdannia nudiflora* (L.) Brenan

Commelina saxicola Small – White-mouth dayflower [Whitemouth dayflower] (50) (present) OK

Commelina virginica L. – Bearded day-flower (97) (1937), Common dayflower [Common day-flower] (86) (1878), Dayflower [Day flower, Day-flower] (65) (1931), Virginia dayflower [Virginia dayflower] (5, 50, 93, 97, 155) (1913–present), Virginia spider-flower [Virginia spiderflower] (117) (1908)

Comptonia Aiton – See *Comptonia* L'Hér. ex Aiton

Comptonia asplenifolia [(L.) L'Hér. ex Aiton] – See *Comptonia peregrina* (L.) Coult.

Comptonia Banks. – possibly *Comptonia* L'Hér. ex Aiton

Comptonia L'Hér. ex Aiton – Sweet-fern [Sweetfern, Sweet fern] (1, 10, 50, 138, 167) (1814–present)

Comptonia peregrina (L.) Coult. – Astringent root (7) (1828), Canadian sweet gale [Canada sweet gale] (5, 156) (1913–1923), Comptonia (Official name of Materia Medica) (7) (1828), Comptonier odorant (French) (7) (1828), Dulcifilix folia (Official name of Materia Medica) (7) (1828), Fern bush [Fern-bush] (7) (1828), Ferngale [Fern gale, Fern-gale] (5, 7, 92, 156) (1828–1923), Fern-leaf gale [Fern-leaved gale] (187) (1818), Fernwort bush [Fern wort bush] (5) (1913), Meadow fern (5, 7, 156) (1828–1923), Ricket plant (58) (1869), Shrubby fern (5, 92, 156) (1876–1923), Shrubby sweetfern [Shrubby sweet fern] (7, 8) (1785–1828), Spleenwort [Spleen-wort, Spleenewort] (58) (1869), Spleenwort bush [Spleen wort-bush] (5, 7, 92, 156) (1828–1923), Spleenwort fern (92) (1876), Spleenwort-leaf gale [Spleenwort-leaved gale] (8) (1785), Streifenfarren (German) (7) (1828), Streifenfarrenblättrige comptonia (German) (186) (1814), Sweet bush [Sweet-bush] (5, 7, 58, 92, 156) (1828–1923), Sweet-fern [Sweetfern, Sweet fern] (7, 10, 19, 42, 46, 57, 58, 92, 109, 138, 186, 187) (1671–1949), Sweet-ferry [Sweet ferry] (5, 7, 92, 156, 186) (1814–1923), possibly Baybush [Bay-bush] (156) (1923), possibly Fern meadow-burs (156) (1923), possibly Kba'agne-minš (Chippewa) (105) (1932)

Comptonia peregrina Coulter – See *Comptonia peregrina* (L.) Coult.

Condalia Cav. – Snakewood [Snake wood] (50) (present)

Condalia ericoides (Gray) M. C. Johnston – Javelina brush (122) (1937) TX, Little buckthorn (122) (1937) TX

Condalia ferrea Griseb – See *Krugiodendron ferreum* (Vahl) Urb.

Condalia hookeri M. C. Johnston var. *hookeri* – Bluewood [Bluewood] (107) (1919), Brasil (122, 124) (1937) TX, Brazil (106) (1930, Texas logwood [Texan logwood] (107) (1919)

Condalia obovata Hook. – See *Condalia hookeri* M.C. Johnston var. *hookeri*

Condalia obtusifolia (Hook.) Weberb. – See *Ziziphus obtusifolia* (Hook. ex Torr. & Gray) Gray var. *obtusifolia*

Conferva L. – Crow silk (92) (1876), Water moss [Watermoss] (7) (1828)

Conioselinum canadense (Michx.) – See *Conioselinum chinense* (L.) Britton, Sterns & Poggenb.

Conioselinum chinense (L.) Britton, Sterns & Poggenb. – Appalachian hemlock-parsley [Appalachian hemlockparsley] (155) (1942), Chinese hemlock-parsley [Chinese hemlockparsley] (50) (present), Hemlock-parsley [Hemlockparsley, Hemlock parsley] (1, 5, 92,

93, 95, 156) (1876–1936), Marsh parsley (10) (1818), Persil (46) (1879), Wild chervil (7) (1828)

Conioselinum Hoffmann – Hemlock-parsley [Hemlockparsley, Hemlock parsley] (50, 155, 158) (1900–present)

Conium L. – Poison hemlock [Poison-hemlock, Poisonhemlock] (50, 158) (1900)

Conium maculatum L. – Bad-man's-oatmeal [Bad-man's oatmeal] (69, 158) (1900–1904), Bunk (5, 69, 156, 158) (1900–1923), Cashes (5, 69, 71, 156, 158) (1898–1923), Cicuta mayor (158) (1900), Cicuta officinalis (Official name of Materia Medica) (7) (1828), Ciguë officinale (French) (158) (1900), Cique commune (French) (7) (1828), Cique ordinaire (French) (6) (1892), Common hemlock (7, 42) (1814–1828) IA, Conium (Official name of Materia Medica) (7, 57, 60, 92) (1828–1917), European hemlock (148) (1939) CO, Gefleckter Schierling (German) (158) (1900), Gemeine Schierling (German) (7) (1828), Grand ciguë (French) (6, 158) (1892–1900), Heck-how (69, 158) (1900–1904), Hemlock [Hemloc, Hemlocke] (10, 14, 49, 53, 55, 60, 71, 92, 148, 179, 184, 187) (1526–1939), Herb Bennet [Herb Bennett] (6, 71, 107) (1892–1919), Poison hemlock [Poison-hemlock, Poisonhemlock] (1, 3, 4, 5, 6, 19, 49, 50, 52, 53, 57, 59, 62, 63, 71, 72, 92, 107, 109, 125, 126, 155, 156, 158) (1892–present) hemlock = leek of the shore or border (Saxon), Poison humlock (158) (1900), Poison humly (158) (1900), Poison snakeroot (156, 158) (1900–1923), Poison snakeweed (71, 158) (1898–1900), Poison-parsley [Poison parsley] (5, 7, 49, 52, 69, 92, 156, 158) (1828–1923), Poison-root [Poisonroot, Poison root] (71, 92) (1876–1898), Schierling (German) (6) (1892), Snakeweed [Snake-weed, Snake weed, Snake Weede] (5, 156) (1913–1923), Spotted cowbane [Spotted cow-bane] (69, 156, 158) (1900–1923), Spotted hemlock (49, 53, 60) (1897–1922), Spotted parsley (5, 7, 69, 71, 92, 156, 158) (1828–1923), Spotted poison-parsley [Spotted poison parsley] (6) (1892), St. Bennet's herb [St. Bennet's-herb] (5, 69, 156, 158) (1900–1923), Stinkweed [Stink-weed, Stink weed] (6, 71) (1892–1898), Water-parsley [Water parsley] (92) (1876), Wild hemlock (6, 71) (1892–1898), Winter-fern (71, 109) (1898–1949), Wode-whistle [Wode-whistle] (5, 69, 71, 156, 158) (1898–1923)

Conobea multifida (Michx.) Benth. – See *Leucospora multifida* (Michx.) Nutt.

Conocarpus erecta L. – See *Conocarpus erectus* L.

Conocarpus erectus L. – Button tree [Button-tree] (20) (1857) Jamaica, Buttonbush [Button bush, Button-bush] (7) (1828), Conocarpe droit (20) (1857), Silky button tree (20) (1857), White mangrove (20) (1857)

Conoclinium coelestinum (L.) DC. – Blue boneset (5, 75, 122, 124, 156, 158) (1900–1937), Blue mistflower (50) (present), Mistflower [Mist-flower, Mist flower] (3, 4, 5, 63, 75, 92, 97, 109, 138, 156, 158) (1876–1986), Mistflower eupatorium (155) (1942), Violet boneset (7) (1828)

Conoclinium DC. – Thoroughwort [Thorough wort, Thorough-wort] (50) (present)

Conopholis americana (L. f.) Wallr. – American broomrape (92, 156) (1876–1923), Beechdrops [Beech drops, Beech-drops] (156) (1923), Broomrape [Broom-rape, Broom rape] (7) (1828), Cancer-root [Cancer root] (5, 156) (1913–1923), Clapwort [Clap-wort] (5, 7, 92) (1828–1913), Earthclub [Earth club, Earth-club] (5, 7, 92, 156) (1876–1923), One-flower orobanche [One-flowered orobanche] (187) (1818), Squaw-drops [Squaw drops] (156) (1923), Squawroot [Squaw-root, Squaw root] (5, 156) (1913–1923)

Conopholis americana Wallr. – See *Conopholis americana* (L. f.) Wallr.

Conopholis Wallr. – Cancer-root [Cancer root] (2) (1895), Squawroot [Squaw-root, Squaw root] (2, 158) (1895–1900)

Conostylis americana Ph. – See *Lophiola aurea* Ker-Gawl.

Conradina canescens Gray – Wild rosemary (75) (1894) FL

Conringia (Heist.) Adans. – See *Conringia* Heister ex Fabr.

Conringia (Heist.) Link. – See *Conringia* Heister ex Fabr.

Conringia Heister ex Fabr. – Hare's-ear [Hare's ear, Hares ear,

Haresear] (1, 93, 155, 158) (1900–1942), Hare's-ear mustard [Hare's ear mustard] (50, 97) (1937–present)

***Conringia orientalis* (L.) Dumort.** – Hare's-ear [Hare's ear, Hares ear, Haresear] (5, 158) (1900–1913), Hare's-ear mustard [Hare's ear mustard] (3, 4, 50, 80, 131, 156) (1899–present), Perfoliate cabbage (19) (1840), Treacle hare's-ear [Treacle haresear] (155) (1942), Treacle mustard [Treakle mustard] (5, 85, 158) (1900–1932)

***Consolida ajacis* (L.) Schur** – Common larkspur (158) (1900), Doubtful knight's spur (50) (present), Doubtful larkspur (155) (1942), Garden larkspur (97, 114) (1894–1937), Rocket larkspur (2, 4, 5, 92, 109, 138, 155) (1876–1986)

***Consolida regalis* S. F. Gray** – Field larkspur (2, 63, 72, 82, 138, 156) (1895–1930), Forking larkspur (109) (1949), Knight's-spur [Knights' spur] (92, 156) (1898–1923), Larkheel [Lark heel] (92) (1876), Lark's-claw [Larks' claw] (92) (1876), Lark's-heel [Lark's heel] (156) (1923), Larkspur [Lark-spur] (19, 57, 71, 92) (1840–1917), Staggerweed [Stagger-weed, Stagger weed] (92) (1876)

***Consolida* S. F. Gray** – Knight's-spur [Knights' spur] (50) (present)

***Convallaria bifolia* L.** – See *Maianthemum dilatatum* (Wood) A. Nels. & J. F. Macbr.

***Convallaria borealis* W.** – See *Clintonia borealis* (Ait.) Raf.

***Convallaria* L.** – Lily-of-the-valley [Lily of the valley] (2, 10, 50, 109, 138, 156, 158) (1818–present), Solomon's-seal [Solomon's seal, Solomon seal, Solomon's seal, Solomons-seal, S'alomon's seal, Salamons seale] (167, 184, 190) (~1759–1814)

***Convallaria latifolia* Mill.** – See *Convallaria majalis* L.

***Convallaria majalis* L.** – Common lily-of-the-valley [Common lily of the valley] (42) (1814), Conval lily [Conval-lily] (5, 156, 158, 178) (1596–1923) no longer in use by 1923, Convallaria (52, 54, 59, 60) (1905–1919), European lily-of-the-valley [European lily of the valley] (50) (present), Lily-of-the-valley [Lily of the valley] (5, 7, 49, 52, 53, 54, 55, 57, 59, 60, 85, 92, 138, 148, 155, 156, 158) (1828–1942), Liricon-fancy (158) (1900), Liris de los valles (Spanish) (158) (1900), Maiblume (German) (158) (1900), Maiglocken (German) (158) (1900), May blossoms [May-blossom] (5, 158) (1900–1913), May lily [May Lillie] (5, 49, 92, 158, 178) (1596–1913), Mayflower [May flower, May-flower] (156) (1923), Muguet (French) (158) (1900), Park lily (158) (1900), Valleys (158) (1900), Wood lily (5, 156, 158) (1900–1923)

***Convallaria multiflora* L.** – See *Polygonatum biflorum* (Walt.) Ell.

***Convallaria racemosa* L.** – See *Maianthemum racemosum* (L.) Link subsp. *racemosum*

***Convallaria stellata* L.** – See *Maianthemum stellatum* (L.) Link

***Convallaria trifolia* L.** – See *Maianthemum trifolium* (L.) Sloboda

***Convolvulus* (Tourn.) L.** – See *Convolvulus* L.

***Convolvulus althaeoides* L.** – Mediterranean convolvulus (138) (1923)

***Convolvulus ambigens* House** – See *Convolvulus arvensis* L.

***Convolvulus americanus* (Sims) Greene** – See *Calystegia sepium* (L.) R. Br. subsp. *sepium*

***Convolvulus arvensis* L.** – Bearbind [Bear-bind] (92, 156, 157, 158) (1898–1929), Bellbind [Bell bind, Bell-bind] (156, 157, 158) (1900–1923), Bindweed [Bind weed, Bind-weed] (6, 19, 106, 122, 145, 178) (1596–1937), Black bindweed [Black bind-weed] (80) (1913), Cornbind [Corn-bind, Corn bind] (62, 156, 157, 158) (1900–1929), Corn-lily [Corn-lilly] (157, 158) (1900–1929), Creeping Jenny [Creeping Jennie, Creeping-Jennie, Creeping-jenny] (85) (1932) SD, Die Winde (German) (6) (1892), European bindweed [European bind-weed] (56, 80) (1901–1913), European glorybind (155) (1942), European morning glory (80, 82) (1913–1930) IA, Field bindweed (3, 4, 50, 62, 82, 107) (1912–present), Field-corn [Field corn] (42) (1814), Hairy bindweed (93) (1936), Hedgebell [Hedge-bells] (92, 156, 157, 158) (1876–1929), Hoary bindweed (5, 97, 122) (1913–1937), Lap-love (156, 157, 158) (1900–1929), Le Liseron (French) (6) (1892), Morning-glory [Morninggglory, Morning glory] (106) (1930), Nebraska glorybind (155) (1942), Perennial morning-glory [Perennial morning glory] (80) (1913), Sheepbine (156) (1923) no longer in use by 1923, Sheep-blue (157, 158)

(1900–1929), Small bindweed [Small bind-weed] (5, 72, 93, 95, 97, 156, 157, 158) (1900–1937), Western bindweed (85) (1932), Wind (157, 158) (1900–1929), With-wind [Withwind] (156, 157, 158) (1900–1929)

***Convolvulus batatus* L.** – See *Ipomoea batatas* (L.) Lam.

***Convolvulus equitans* Benth.** – Red-centered vine morning-glory (124) (1937), Texas bindweed (50) (present)

***Convolvulus fraterniflorus* (Mackenzie & Bush) Mackenzie & Bush** – See *Calystegia silvatica* (Kit.) Griseb. subsp. *fraterniflora* (Mackenzie & Bush) Brummitt

***Convolvulus hermannoides* Gray** – See *Convolvulus equitans* Benth.

***Convolvulus incanus* Vahl.** – See *Convolvulus arvensis* L.

***Convolvulus japonicus* Thunb.** – See *Calystegia pellita* (Ledeb.) G. Don

***Convolvulus* L.** – Bindweed [Bind weed, Bind-weed] (1, 2, 10, 14, 50, 63, 82, 93, 109, 125, 156, 158, 184) (1793–present), Convovulus (138) (1923), Field bindweed (4) (1986), Gaybine (92) (1876), Glorybind (155) (1942), Morning-glory [Morningglory, Morning glory] (1, 93) (1932–1936), Woodbind [Woodbinde, Wood bind, Woodbynde] (179) (1526)

Convolvulus nil – See *Ipomoea nil* (L.) Roth

***Convolvulus panduratus* Michx.** – See *Ipomoea pandurata* (L.) G.F.W. Mey.

***Convolvulus pellitus* Ledeb.** – See *Calystegia pellita* (Ledeb.) G. Don

***Convolvulus purpureus* [L.]** – See *Ipomoea purpurea* (L.) Roth

***Convolvulus purpureus* Pursh** – possibly *Ipomoea purpurea* (L.) Roth

***Convolvulus repens* L.** – See *Calystegia sepium* (L.) R. Br. subsp. *angulata* Brummitt

***Convolvulus sagittifolius* Michx.** – See *Ipomoea sagittata* Lam.

***Convolvulus sepium* L.** – See *Calystegia sepium* (L.) R. Br. subsp. *sepium*

***Convolvulus soldanella* L.** – See *Calystegia soldanella* (L.) R. Br. ex Roemer & J. A. Schultes

***Convolvulus speciosus* Walt.** – See *Argyreia nervosa* (Burm. f.) Bojer

***Convolvulus spithamaeus* L.** – See *Calystegia spithamaea* (L.) Pursh

***Convolvulus tricolor* L.** – Dwarf convolvulus (138) (1923), Dwarf morning-glory [Dwarf morning glory] (109) (1949), Three-color bindweed [Three colored bindweed, 3-colored bindweed] (19) (1840)

Convolvulus turpethum – See *Operculina turpethum* (L.) J. Silva Manso

***Conyza canadensis* (L.) Cronq.** – Canadian horseweed (50) (present), Horseweed [Horse-weed, Horse weed] (3, 4, 98, 121) (1918–1986)

Conyza canadensis* (L.) Cronq. var. *canadensis – Beschreikraut (German) (158) (1900), Bitterweed [Bitter weed, Bitter-weed] (5, 69, 156, 157, 158) (1900–1929), Bloodstaunch [Blood staunch, Bloodstaunch] (5, 69, 92, 157, 158) (1876–1929), Butterweed [Butter weed, Butter-weed] (2, 5, 6, 49, 58, 62, 69, 92, 156, 157, 158) (1869–1929), Canadian erigeron [Canada erigeron] (157, 158) (1900–1929), Canadian fleabane [Canada fleabane] (5, 6, 7, 49, 53, 55, 57, 58, 61, 85, 92, 93, 122, 156, 157, 158) (1828–1937), Canadisches Berufkraut (German) (6, 158) (1892–1900), Colt's-tail [Colt's tail, Coltstail] (5, 6, 19, 49, 53, 58, 69, 92, 156, 157, 158) (1840–1929), Conyzella (177) (1762), Cow's-tail [Cows' tail] (5, 69, 73, 92, 156, 157, 158) (1876–1929) Normal, IL, Erigeron (52, 54) (1905–1919), Erigeron de Canada (French) (6) (1892), Fireweed [Fire weed, Fireweed] (5, 69, 92, 156, 157, 158) (1876–1929), Fleabane [Flea-bane, Flea bane] (19, 45, 52, 54) (1840–1919), Hogweed [Hog-weed, Hog weed] (5, 156, 157, 158) (1900–1929), Horsetail [Horse tail, Horsetail] (92, 145) (1876–1897), Horseweed [Horse-weed, Horse weed] (2, 5, 6, 7, 40, 45, 49, 58, 62, 63, 69, 72, 80, 92, 93, 95, 97, 114, 125, 131, 148, 156, 157, 158) (1828–1939), Horseweed fleabane (155) (1942), Mare's-tail [Marestail, Mare's tail, Mare's-tails] (2, 5, 45, 62, 125, 156, 157, 158) (1895–1929), Prideweed [Pride weed, Pride-weed] (5, 6, 19, 49, 53, 69, 92, 156, 157, 158) (1840–1929),

121

Scabious [Scabius, Scabyous] (6, 49, 53, 92, 156, 157, 158) (1892–1929), Wild daisy (114) (1894)

Conyza L. – See *Conyza* Less.

Conyza Less. – Canadian fleabane [Canada fleabane] (1, 93) (1932–1936), Fleabane [Flea-bane, Flea bane] (10, 42, 167) (1814–1818), Horseweed [Horse-weed, Horse weed] (1, 50, 93, 158) (1900–present), Plowman's-wort [Ploughman's wort, Plowmans'-wort, Plowmans'-wort, Plowmanwort] (7) (1828)

Conyza linifolia L. – See *Sericocarpus linifolius* (L.) Britton, Sterns & Poggenb.

Conyza marilandica Michx. – See *Pluchea foetida* (L.) DC.

Conyza ramosissima Cronq. – Dwarf fleabane [Dwarfe Fleabane] (5, 85, 122, 156) (1913–1937), Dwarf horseweed (50) (present), Low horseweed [Low horse-weed, Low horse weed] (5, 72, 93, 97, 156) (1907–1937), Purple horseweed [Purple horse-weed, Purple horse weed] (5, 93, 131, 156) (1899–1936), Spreading fleabane (3, 4) (1977–1986)

Cooperia drummondii Herb. – Drummond's cooperia (5, 97) (1913–1937), Evening rain lily (50) (present), Evening star [Evening-star] (138) (1923), Evening-star rainlily [Eveningstar rainlily] (155) (1942), Kansas rainlily [Kansas rain lily] (155) (1942), Prairie lily [Prairie-lily] (5, 156) (1913–1923), Rain lily [Rainlily, Rain-lily, Rain lilies] (78) (1898), Star flower [Starflower, Star-flower] (78) (1898) TX, White rain lily (124) (1937)

Cooperia Herb. – Prairie lily [Prairie-lily] (1, 109, 158) (1900–1949), Rain lily [Rainlily, Rain-lily, Rain lilies] (50, 109, 138, 155) (1923–present), White rain lily (122) (1937)

Cooperia kansensis W. C. Stevens – See *Cooperia drummondii* Herb.

Cooperia pedunculata Herbert – Great rainlily (138) (1923), White rain lily (124) (1937)

Coprinus atramentarius (Bull.) Fr., – Inky cap (128) (1933)

Coprinus comatus (O. F. Müll.) Gray – Shaggy mane (128) (1933)

Coprinus fimetarius Fr. – Mealy ink cap (128) (1933)

Coprosma J. R. & G. Forst. – Coprosma (138) (1923)

Coptis Salisb. – Goldthread [Gold-thread, Gold thread] (1, 13, 53, 109, 138, 156) (1849–1949)

Coptis trifolia (L.) Salisb. – Canker-root [Cankerroot, Canker root] (5, 49, 53, 64, 76, 92, 156) (1896–1923) Oxford Co. ME, Common goldthread (7) (1828), Coptide (156) (1923) no longer in use by 1923, Coptis (Official name of Materia Medica) (7, 57, 64) (1828–1917), Coptis triphylle (French) (7) (1828), Fibraurea (Official name of Materia Medica) (7) (1828), Goldenthread [Golden thread] (10) (1818), Goldthread [Gold-thread, Gold thread] (5, 7, 14, 19, 40, 49. 53, 57, 58, 64, 92, 105, 138, 156, 186) (1814–1932), Helleborus trifolius (Official name of Materia Medica) (7) (1828), Kleinste Christwurz (German) (7, 186) (1814–1828), Mouthroot [Mouth-root, Mouth root] (5, 7, 49, 53, 64, 92, 156, 186) (1814–1923), Nigella (186) (1814), Oza'widji'bĭk (Chippewa [yellow root) (40) (1928), Sau-tiskan (Chippewa) (105) (1932), Three-leaf goldthread [Three-leaved goldthread] (2) (1895), Three-leaf hellebore [Three-leaved hellebore] (41) (1770), Tissavoyame jaune (Canada) (7) (1828), Yellowroot [Yellow root, Yellow-root] (5, 64, 92, 156) (1876–1923)

Coptis trifolia Salisb. – See *Coptis trifolia* (L.) Salisb.

Corallorhiza multiflora Nutt. – See *Corallorrhiza maculata* (Raf.) Raf. var. *maculata*

Corallorhiza R. Br. (*sic*) – See *Corallorrhiza* Gagnebin

Corallorhiza wisteriana Conrad. – See *Corallorrhiza wisteriana* Conrad

Corallorrhiza (Haller) Chatelain – See *Corallorrhiza* Gagnebin

Corallorrhiza corallorrhiza (L.) Karst. – See *Corallorrhiza trifida* Chat.

Corallorrhiza Gagnebin – Coralroot [Coral-root, Coral root] (1, 50, 93, 156, 158) (1900–present), Crawley (75) (1894) NC

Corallorrhiza maculata (Raf.) Raf. – Crawley root [Crawley-root] (157) (1929), Dragon's-claws [Dragon's claws] (5, 156, 158) (1900–1923), Large coralroot [Large coral-root, Large coral root] (5, 93,

122, 156, 157) (1900–1937), Larger coral-root (157) (1929), Spotted coralroot (3) (1977), Summer coralroot (50) (present)

Corallorrhiza maculata (Raf.) Raf. var. *maculata* – Dragon's-claws [Dragon's claws] (75) (1894), Large coralroot [Large coral-root, Large coral root] (72) (1907)

Corallorrhiza maculata (Raf.) Raf. var. *occidentalis* (Lindl.) Ames – Summer coralroot (50) (present)

Corallorrhiza maculata Raf. f. *flavida* – See *Corallorrhiza maculata* (Raf.) Raf. var. *maculata*

Corallorrhiza maculata Raf. f. *maculata* – See *Corallorrhiza maculata* (Raf.) Raf. var. *maculata*

Corallorrhiza multiflora Nutt. – See *Corallorrhiza maculata* (Raf.) Raf. var. *maculata*

Corallorrhiza ochroleuca Rydb. – See *Corallorrhiza striata* Lindl. var. *striata*

Corallorrhiza odontorhiza (Willd.) Nutt. – See *Corallorrhiza odontorhiza* (Willd.) Poir.

Corallorrhiza odontorhiza (Willd.) Poir. – Autumn coralroot (50) (present), Autumn Virginia ladies'-Traces [Autum Virginia ladies Traces] (181) (~1678), Chicken's-toes [Chicken toe, Chickens'-toes, Chickens' toes, Chicken's toes] (49, 53, 64, 158) (1900–1922), Corallorhiza (52, 64) (1908–1919), Coralroot [Coral-root, Coral root] (49, 53, 57, 64, 92) (1876–1922), Coral-teeth [Coral teeth] (19) (1840), Crawley (158) (1900), Crawley root [Crawley-root] (5, 49, 52, 53, 57, 64, 92, 156, 158) (1900–1923), Dragon's-claws [Dragon's claws] (5, 19, 49, 53, 64, 92, 156, 158) (1840–1923), Fever-root [Fever root, Feverroot] (64, 92, 158) (1876–1923), Large tooth-root cymbidium [Large tooth rooted cymbidium] (42) (1814), Late coralroot [Late coral-root, Late coral root] (3, 64, 122, 156, 158) (1900–1977), Scaly dragon's-claw [Scaly dragons' claw] (92) (1876), Small coralroot [Small coral-root] (5, 64, 156, 158) (1900–1923), Small-flower coralroot [Small-flowered coralroot, Small-flowered coral root, Small-flowered coral-root] (64, 72, 158) (1900–1908), Turkey-claw [Turkey claw] (5, 64, 92, 156, 158) (1900–1923)

Corallorrhiza R. Br. – See *Corallorrhiza* Gagnebin

Corallorrhiza striata Lindl. – Hooded coralroot (50) (present), Striped coralroot (3, 5) (1913–1977)

Corallorrhiza striata Lindl. var. *striata* – Hooded coralroot (50) (present), Yellow coralroot [Yellow coral root, Yellow coral-root] (5, 93, 157) (1900–1936)

Corallorrhiza striata Lindl. var. *vreelandii* (Rydb.) L.O. Williams – Vreeland's coralroot (50) (present)

Corallorrhiza trifida Chat. – Coralroot [Coral-root, Coral root] (19, 85) (1840–1932), Early coral root [Early coral-root] (5, 93, 156, 157) (1900–1936), Fever-root [Fever root, Feverroot] (157) (1929), Pale coralroot (3) (1977), Yellow coralroot [Yellow coral root, Yellow coral-root] (50) (present)

Corallorrhiza trifida Chatelain var. *verna* (Nutt.) Fern. – See *Corallorrhiza trifida* Chat.

Corallorrhiza verna T. – See *Corallorrhiza trifida* Chat.

Corallorrhiza wisteriana Conrad – Spring coralroot (50) (present), Spring Virginia lady's-traces [Spring Virginia ladies traces] (181) (~1678), Western coralroot [Western coral root] (122) (1937), Wister's coralroot [Wister's coral-root] (3, 5, 97) (1913–1977)

Corchorus olitorius L. – Jew's-mallow [Jew's mallow, Jews-mallow] (92, 109) (1876–1949), Nalta jute (109) (1949)

Cordia boisseri – See *Cordia boissieri* A. DC.

Cordia boissieri A. DC. – Anachuite wood (92) (1876), Texas wild olive (124) (1937) TX, Wild olive [Wilde oliue] or Wild olive tree [Wild olive-tree] (122) (1937) TX

Cordia collococca L. – Turkey-berry tree [Turkey berry tree] (92) (1876)

Cordia L. – Cordia (138) (1923)

Cordia laevigata Lam. – Glossy cordia (138) (1923)

Cordia myxa L. – Sebesten (92) (1876)

Cordia nitida – See *Cordia laevigata* Lam.

Cordia sebestena L. – Geiger tree [Geiger-tree] (109, 138) (1923–1949),

Rough-leaf cordia [Rough-leaved cordia] (20) (1857), Sebestier domestique (French) (20) (1857)

Cordyline australis (G. Forst.) Endl. – Green dracena (138) (1923)

Cordyline Comm. ex R. Br. – Dracena (138) (1923)

Cordyline fruticosa (L.) Chev. – Common dracena (138) (1923)

Cordyline guineensis (L.) Britton – See *Sansevieria hyacinthoides* (L.) Druce

Cordyline terminalis – See *Cordyline fruticosa* (L.) Chev.

Corema conradii (Torr.) Torr. ex Loud. – Broom crowberry [Broomcrowberry] (138, 156) (1923), Brown crowberry (5, 156) (1913–1923), Conrad's broom crowberry (5) (1913), Crapeberry [Crapeberry] (156) (1923), Plymouth crowberry (5, 156) (1913–1923), Poverty-grass [Poverty grass] (5, 75, 156) (1894–1923) Provincetown MA

Corema conradii Torr. – See *Corema conradii* (Torr.) Torr. ex Loud.

Coreopsis angustifolia L. – Pinewoods coneflower (106, 114) (1894–1930)

Coreopsis angustifolia L. – Purple coneflower [Purple cone-flower, Purple cone flower] (106, 114) (1894–1930)

Coreopsis aurea Aiton – See *Bidens aurea* (Aiton) Sherff

Coreopsis auriculata L. – Eared coreopsis (138) (1923), Lobed tickseed (5) (1913), Running tickseed (5) (1913)

Coreopsis basalis (A. Dietr.) Blake – Goldenwave [Golden-wave] (109, 138) (1923–1949), Lady's-breastpin [Lady's breast-pin] (76) (1896) Sulphur Grove OH

Coreopsis cardaminaefolia (DC.) Torr. & Gray – See *Coreopsis tinctoria* Nutt. var. *tinctoria*

Coreopsis crassifolia Aiton – See *Coreopsis lanceolata* L.

Coreopsis delphiniifolia Lam. – Larkspur coreopsis (109, 138) (1923–1949), Larkspur tickseed (5) (1913)

Coreopsis douglasii (DC.) Hall – Douglas' coreopsis [Douglas coreopsis] (138) (1923)

Coreopsis drummondi – See *Coreopsis basalis* (A. Dietr.) Blake

Coreopsis drummondii Torr. & Gray – See *Coreopsis basalis* (A. Dietr.) Blake

Coreopsis grandiflora Hogg ex Sweet – Big coreopsis (138) (1923), Big-flower coreopsis [Bigflower coreopsis] (3, 4, 155) (1942–1986), Large-flower tickseed [Largeflower tickseed] (5, 50, 97) (1913–present)

Coreopsis grandiflora Hogg ex Sweet var. *harveyana* (Gray) Sherff – Harvey's coreopsis (97) (1937)

Coreopsis harveyana Gray – See *Coreopsis grandiflora* Hogg ex Sweet var. *harveyana* (Gray) Sherff

Coreopsis L. – Coreopsis (138, 155) (1923–1942), Dye flowers (75) (1894) Banner Elk NC, Old-maid's-breastpin [Old maid's breastpin] (75) (1894) Plymouth OH, Tickseed [Tick-seed, Tick seed] (1, 2, 7, 50, 63, 93, 106, 109, 156, 167) (1814–present), Tickseed sunflower [Tick seed sunflower, Tick-seed sunflower] (158) (1900), Tickweed [Tick weed, Tick-weed] (92) (1876)

Coreopsis lanceolata L. – Coreopsis (174) (1753), Hairy tickseed (5) (1913), Lance coreopsis (138, 155) (1923–1942), Lance-leaf coreopsis [Lanceleaf coreopsis] (122) (1937), Lance-leaf tickseed [Lanceleaf tickseed, Lance-leaved tickseed] (5, 50) (1913–present), Thick-leaf tickseed [Thickleaf tickseed, Thick-leaved tickseed] (5, 97, 122) (1913–1937), Tickseed [Tick-seed, Tick seed] (156) (1923)

Coreopsis major Walt. – Greater tickseed (5) (1913), Trefoil coreopsis (138) (1923), Wood tickseed (5) (1913)

Coreopsis maritima (Nutt.) Hook.f. – Saxifrage tunic-flower [Saxifrage tunicflower] (5, 156) (1913–1923), Sea coreopsis (138) (1923)

Coreopsis palmata Nutt. – Finger coreopsis (3, 4, 138, 155) (1923–1986), Stiff coreopsis (122) (1937), Stiff tickseed (5, 50, 72, 93, 97, 131) (1899–present), Tickseed [Tick-seed, Tick seed] (85) (1932)

Coreopsis perfoliata Walt. – See *Bidens laevis* (L.) Britton, Sterns & Poggenb.

Coreopsis pubescens Ell. – Hairy coreopsis (138) (1923) SD, Star tickseed (5, 50, 97, 156) (1913–present)

Coreopsis radiata [Mill.] – See *Bidens laevis* (L.) Britton, Sterns & Poggenb.

Coreopsis rosea Nutt. – Pink tickseed (5) (1913), Rose coreopsis (138) (1923), Rose tickseed (156) (1923) OK, Small pink tickseed (156) (1923), Small rose tickseed (5) (1913), Swamp tickseed (156) (1923), Tickseed [Tick-seed, Tick seed] (19) (1840)

Coreopsis senifolia Michx. – See *Coreopsis major* Walt.

Coreopsis stillmanii (Gray) Blake – Stillman's coreopsis [Stillman coreopsis] (138) (1923)

Coreopsis tinctoria Nutt. – Calliopsis (138) (1923), Čaŋxloǧaŋ wakaljapi (Lakota, boiling weed) (121) (1918?–1970?), Coreopsis (114, 127) (1894), Garden coreopsis (93) (1936), Garden tickseed (5, 72, 131, 156) (1899–1923), Golden coreopsis (5, 85, 92, 93, 97, 122, 156, 158) (1876–1937), Golden tickseed (50, 121) (1920–present), Nuttall's weed [Nuttall-weed] (5, 92, 156, 158) (1876–1923), Plains coreopsis (3, 155) (1942–1977), Rocky Mountain flower [Rocky Mt. flower] (73) (1892) Mansfield OH, Tickseed [Tick-seed, Tick seed] (95, 114, 127) (1894–1933)

Coreopsis tinctoria Nutt. var. *tinctoria* – Cardamine coreopsis (155) (1942), Cress-leaf coreopsis [Cressleaf coreopsis, Cress leaf coreopsis] (122, 124) (1937), Cress-leaf tickseed [Cress-leaved tickseed] (5, 97) (1913–1937), Golden tickseed (50) (present)

Coreopsis tripteris L. – Atlantic coreopsis (155) (1942), Tall coreopsis (3, 4) (1977–1986), Tall tickseed (5, 50, 72, 97, 156) (1907–present), Tickseed sunflower [Tick seed sunflower, Tick-seed sunflower] (19, 92) (1840–1876)

Coreopsis verticillata L. – Thread-leaf coreopsis (109, 138) (1923–1949), Whorled tickseed (5, 93, 97) (1913–1937), Whorl-leaf sunflower [Whorl leaved sun flower] (42) (1814)

Coriandrum L. – Coriander (138) (1923) from Latin and Greek connected with word for bug

Coriandrum sativum (L.) Britt. – See *Coriandrum sativum* L.

Coriandrum sativum (Tourn.) L. – See *Coriandrum sativum* L.

Coriandrum sativum L. – Coliander (92) (1876), Coriander [Coryandre] (1, 5, 19, 46, 49, 50, 53, 55, 57, 58, 59, 85, 92, 97, 107, 109, 122, 138, 156, 179) (1526–present) cultivated by English colonists by 1671, Coriandrum (57, 59) (1911–1917)

Corispermum (A. Juss.) L. – See *Corispermum* L.

Corispermum americanum (Nutt.) Nutt. – American bugseed (50) (present)

Corispermum americanum (Nutt.) Nutt. var. *rydbergii* Mosyakin – Bugseed [Bug seed, Bug-seed] (3, 93, 97, 131, 145, 156) (1897–1977), Bugweed [Bug-weed] (5, 156, 158) (1900–1923), Hyssop-leaf tickseed [Hyssopleaf tickseed] (4, 155) (1942–1986), Tumbleweed [Tumble weed, Tumble-weed] (5, 93, 156, 158) (1900–1936)

Corispermum hyssopifolium L. – See *Corispermum americanum* (Nutt.) Nutt. var. *rydbergii* Mosyakin

Corispermum L. – Bugseed [Bug seed, Bug-seed] (1, 2, 50, 93, 158) (1900–present), Tickseed [Tick-seed, Tick seed] (10, 14, 155, 158) (1818–1942)

Corispermum nitidum Kit. ex J.A. Schultes – Bugseed [Bug seed, Bug-seed] (3, 4) (1977–1986), Shiny bugseed (50) (Present)

Cornus alba L. – See *Cornus sericea* L. subsp. *sericea*

Cornus alterna – See *Cornus alternifolia* L.f.

Cornus alternifolia L. f. – Alternate branched dogwood (8) (1785), Alternate-leaf cornel [Alternate-leaved cornel] (5, 156) (1913–1923), Alternate-leaf dogwood [Alternate-leaved dogwood, Alternate leaved dog wood] (5, 42, 72) (1814–1913), Blue dogwood (5, 156) (1913–1923), Cornouiller à feuilles alternes (French) (8) (1785), Dogwood [Dog-wood, Dog wood] or Dogwood tree [Dogwood-tree, Dogwood trees] (47) (1852), Female Virginia dogwood [Female virginian dogwood] (8) (1785), Green osier [Green-osier] (5, 29, 76, 156) (1869–1923), Muj'omȋj' (Chippewa, moose plant) (40) (1928), Pagoda dogwood (109, 138, 156) (1923–1949), Pigeon-berry [Pigeon berry] (5, 156) (1913–1923), Purple dogwood (5, 156) (1913–1923), Umbrella tree [Umbrella-tree] (5, 156) (1913–1923)

Cornus amomum Mill. – Blue-berry cornel [Blueberry cornel, Blue berry cornel, Blue-berried cornel, Blueberry cornell] (5, 156, 157, 158) (1900–1929), Chan-shasha (Dakota, red wood) (37) (1919), Cornouiller soyeaux (French) (158) (1900), Dogwood [Dog-wood, Dog wood] or Dogwood tree [Dogwood-tree, Dogwood trees] (85) (1932), Female dogwood (157, 158) (1900–1929), Killikinic [Killi-kinick] (158) (1900), Kinnikinnick [Kinnikinik, Kinnikinnick, Kin-nikinic, Kinnikinnik] (5, 37, 72, 85, 93, 95, 107, 156, 157, 158) (1900–1932), Ninigahi (Omaha-Ponca, pipe-mix) (37) (1919), Pale dogwood (4) (1986), Rapahat (Pawnee, red stick) (37) (1919), Red brush [Red-brush] (5, 156, 158) (1900–1923), Red dogwood [Red dog wood] (37) (1919), Red osier [Red-osier] (5, 156, 158) (1900–1923), Red-bush (157) (1929), Red-rod (156, 157, 158) (1900–1923), Red-willow [Red willow] (5, 156, 158) (1900–1923), Rose-willow [Rose willow] (5, 156, 158) (1900–1923), Ruh'i-shutsh (Winnebago) (37) (1919), Silky cornel (5, 82, 93, 97, 131, 156, 157, 158) (1899–1930), Silky dogwood (50, 109, 138, 155, 157) (1923–present), Squaw bush [Squawbush, Squaw-bush] (5, 155, 156, 157, 158) (1900–1942), Sumpfcornel [Sumpf cornel] (German) (6, 158) (1892–1900), Swamp dogwood [Swamp-dogwood (5, 156, 157, 158) (1900–1929)

Cornus amomum **Mill. subsp.** *obliqua* **(Raf.) J. S. Wils.** – See *Cornus foemina* Mill.

Cornus asperifolia **Michx.** – Dogwood [Dog-wood, Dog wood] or Dogwood tree [Dogwood-tree, Dogwood trees] (22) (1893), Mansa-h'te-hi (Omaha-Ponca [real arrow tree) (37) (1919), Mansi-hotsh (Winnebago) (37) (1919), Nakipistatu (Pawnee, real arrow tree) (37) (1919), Rough cornel (5) (1913), Rough dogwood (5, 37) (1913–1919), Rough-leaf cornel [Rough-leaved cornel] (72, 156) (1907–1923), Rough-leaf dogwood [Rough leaf dogwood, Roughleaf dog-wood] (93, 95, 97, 113, 122, 124, 130, 131, 138) (1890–1937)

Cornus baileyi **Coult & Evans.** – See *Cornus sericea* L. subsp. *sericea*

Cornus canadensis **L.** – Bearberry [Bear berry, Bear-berry] (156) (1923), Bunchberry [Bunch berry] (3, 4, 5, 40, 92, 107, 109, 138, 156, 158) (1876–1986), Bunchberry dogwood (50, 155) (1942–present), Bunch-plum [Bunch plums, Bunch plum] (5, 73, 156, 158) (1892–1923) NH, Caca'gomĭn (Chippewa) (40) (1928), Canadian dogwood [Canadian dog wood] (42) (1814), Cracker-berry (156, 158) (1900–1923), Dwarf cornel (2, 5, 19, 46, 92, 107, 131, 156, 158) (1840–1923), Low cornel (5, 156, 158) (1900–1923), Pigeon-berry [Pigeon berry] (46, 73) (1879–1892), Pudding-berry [Pudding berries, Pudding berry (14, 73, 79) (1882–1891) probably from in-sipid nature, Puppy-wood (156) (1923), Small flowering-cornel (158) (1900), Šul(a)mix (Chinookan) (35) (1806), Trailing dogwood (156) (1923)

Cornus candidissima **Marsh.** – See *Cornus foemina* Mill.

Cornus candidissima **Mill.** – See *Cornus florida* L.

Cornus circinata **L'Her.** – See *Cornus rugosa* Lam.

Cornus circinnata **[Cham. & Schltdl.]** – See *Cornus sericea* L. subsp. *occidentalis* (Torr. & Gray) Fosberg

Cornus drummondii **C. A. Mey.** – Miss Price's cornel (5) (1913), MoηΘa hi (Osage, arrow tree) (121) (1918?–1970?), Rough-leaf dogwood [Rough leaf dogwood, Roughleaf dogwood] (3, 4, 50, 121) (1918–present)

Cornus femina **Mill.** – See *Cornus foemina* Mill.

Cornus florida **L.** – American boxwood [American box-wood] (158) (1900), American cornelian tree (158) (1900), American dogwood (158) (1900), Arrow-wood [Arrow wood] (5, 156) (1913–1923), Bitter redberry (6, 7) (1828–1932), Bloodtwig [Blood twig] (92) (1876), Bois bouton (French) (7) (1828), Bois de fleche (French, Louisiana Purchase) (7) (1828), Box tree [Box-tree, Box tre] (6, 7, 14, 186) (1825–1892), Boxwood [Box wood] (5, 49, 58, 92, 156, 158) (1869–1923), Budwood (92) (1876), Coenuillier a Grandes Fleurs (French) (6) (1892), Common dogwood [Common dog-wood, Common dog wood] (7, 42) (1814–1828), Cornel [Cor-nels] or Cornel tree [Cornell tree] (6, 92) (1876–1892), Cornelian cherry [Cornelian-cherry] (41) (1770), Cornelian tree [Cornelian-tree] (5, 156) (1913–1923), Cornouiller à grandes fleurs (French)

(158) (1900), Cornouiller fleuri (French) (7) (1828), Cornouilles de la Floride (French) (8) (1785), Cornus (52, 54, 60) (1902–1919), Cornus florida (Official name of Materia Medica) (7) (1828), Cross-bluthige Cornel (German) (6) (1892), Dog tree [Dog-tree] (6, 7, 92, 186) (1825–1892), Dogwood [Dog-wood, Dog wood] or Dog-wood tree [Dogwood-tree, Dogwood trees] (7, 12, 19, 20, 38, 41, 49, 52, 53, 54, 57, 58, 60, 92, 158, 177, 182, 184, 186, 187, 189, 190) (~1759–1922), False box (5, 19, 92) (1840–1913), False boxwood [False box-wood, False box wood] (5, 156) (1913–1923), Florid cornel (7, 186) (1825–1828), Florida cornel (92, 156, 158) (1898–1923), Florida dogwood (5, 92, 156, 158) (1898–1923), Flower-ing cornel (49, 53, 58, 92, 156, 158) (1869–1923), Flowering dog-wood (2, 3, 4, 5, 6, 49, 53, 82, 97, 105, 122, 124, 138, 155, 156, 158) (1892–1986), Great-flower dogwood [Great-flowered dog-wood] (186) (1814), Gross blüthige Kornel (German) (158) (1900), Hat-ta-wa-no-min-schi (6, 186) (1825–1892), Hornbaum (German) (158) (1900), Indian arrow-wood [Indian arrow wood, Indian arrow-wood] (5, 156, 158) (1900–1923), Large-flower cornel [Large-flow-ered cornel] (186, 187) (1814–1818), Male Virginia dogwood [Male Virginian dogwood] (8, 186) (1785–1825), Mon-ha-can-ni-min-schi (6, 7, 186) (1825–1932), Nature's-mistake [Nature's mistake] (5, 75, 156, 158) (1844–1923) Abington Mass, no longer in use by 1923, Nemwatik (Chippewa) (105) (1932), New England boxwood [New England box-wood] (6, 158, 186) (1825–1892), Schonbluhender Hartriegel (German) (7) (1828), Virginia dogwood (92, 158) (1876–1900), White cornel (5, 156, 158) (1900–1923)

Cornus foemina **Mill.** – Cornouiller a feuilles glauques (French) (8) (1785), Dogwood [Dog-wood, Dog wood] or Dogwood tree [Dog-wood-tree, Dogwood trees] (9, 19, 113) (1840–1910), Gray dog-wood (4) (1986), Gray-bark dogwood [Gray-barked dogwood] (85) (1932), Panicled cornel (5, 156) (1913–1923), Panicled dogwood (5, 72, 93, 97) (1907–1937), Stiff cornel (5, 156) (1913–1923), Stiff cornel dogwood (155) (1942), Stiff dogwood (5, 50) (1913–present), Swamp American dogwood (8) (1785), Upright dogwood [Upright dog wood] (42) (1814), White cornel (5) (1913), White-fruit dog-wood [White-fruited dogwood] (5) (1913)

Cornus foemina **Mill. subsp.** *racemosa* **(Lam.) J. S. Wilson** – See *Cornus racemosa* Lam.

Cornus kousa **Hance** – Kousa dogwood (138) (1923)

Cornus **L.** – Bunchberry [Bunch berry] (1, 85) (1932) SD, Cornel [Cor-nels] or Cornel tree [Cornell tree] (1, 2, 8, 10, 82, 158, 184) (1785–1932), Cornouiller (French) (8) (1785), Dogberry [Dog-berry, Dog berry] or Dogberry tree [Dogberrie tree] (8) (1785), Dogwood [Dog-wood, Dog wood] or Dogwood tree [Dogwood-tree, Dogwood trees] (1, 2, 10, 50, 82, 93, 106, 109, 138, 155, 158) (1818–present), Flow-ering dogwood (1) (1932), Kinnikinnick [Kinnikinik, Kinnikinnick, Kinnikinic, Kinnikinnik] (1) (1932)

Cornus mas **L.** – Cornel [Cornels] or Cornel tree [Cornell tree] (92, 178) (1526–1876), Cornel cherry (20) (1857), Cornelian cherry [Cornelian-cherry] (19, 92, 109, 138) (1840–1949), Male cornell tree (178) (1526)

Cornus mascula – See *Cornus mas* L.

Cornus nuttalli – See *Cornus nuttallii* Audubon ex Torr. & Gray

Cornus nuttallii **Audubon ex Torr. & Gray** – Cornouiller de Nuttall (French) (20) (1857), Large-flower dogwood [Large-flowered dog-wood] (20) (1857), Nuttall's cornel (161) (1857), Oregon dogwood (160) (1860), Pacific dogwood (138) (1923)

Cornus obliqua **Raf.** – Pale dogwood (3, 138, 155) (1923–1977), Silky dogwood (50) (Present)

Cornus occidentalis **Coville** – See *Cornus sericea* L. subsp. *occidenta-lis* (Torr. & Gray) Fosberg

Cornus paniculata **L'Her.** – See *Cornus racemosa* Lam.

Cornus priceae **Small** – See *Cornus drummondii* C.A. Mey.

Cornus pubescens – See *Cornus sericea* L. subsp. *occidentalis* (Torr. & Gray) Fosberg

Cornus racemosa **Lam.** – Buckbrush [Buck brush, Buck-brush] (106) (1930) Arkansas, Bush dogwood [Bush dog-wood] (19) (1840),

Dogwood [Dog-wood, Dog wood] (63, 82) (1899–1930), Gray dogwood (3, 50, 121, 138, 155, 156) (1918–present), MoŋΘa xota hu (Osage, blackbird arrow tree) (121) (1918?–1970?), Panicled cornel (63, 156) (1899–1923), Panicled dogwood (109) (1949), Paniculated dogwood [Paniculated dog wood] (42) (1814), Smooth dogwood (106) (1930), Spicewood [Spice-wood, Spice wood] (106) (1930) Arkansas

Cornus rugosa **Lam.** – Alder dogwood (6, 7) (1828–1932), Alder-leaf dogwood [Alder-leaved dogwood] (5, 92, 156) (1898–1923), Cornuile a Feuilles Rondie (French) (6) (1892), Green osier [Green-osier] (5, 6, 156) (1892–1923), Green ozier (92) (1876), Hairy dogwood [Hairy dog wood] (42) (1814), Pennsylvania dogwood (6) (1892), Round-leaf cornel [Round-leaved cornel, Round leaved cornel] (5, 6, 7, 58, 92, 156) (1828–1923), Round-leaf dogwood [Roundleaf dogwood, Round-leaved dogwood, Round leaved dogwood] (5, 6, 58, 72, 92, 138, 156) (1869–1923), Rundblätterige Cornel (German) (6) (1892), Swamp sassafras [Swamp-sassfras] (6) (1892), possibly Broad-leaf dogwood [Broad-leaved dogwood] (92) (1876), possibly Dogachamus (92) (1876)

Cornus sanguinea **Forsk.** – See *Cornus sanguinea* L.

Cornus sanguinea **L.** – American red-rod cornus (8) (1785), Blood-red dogwood [Blood red dogwood] (82) (1930), Blood-twig dogwood [Bloodtwig dogwood] (109, 138) (1923–1949), Bloody dogwood [Bloody dog wood] (42) (1814), Common dogwood [Common dogwood, Common dog wood] (19) (1840), Cornel dogwood (107) (1919), Cornelian cherry [Cornelian-cherry] (41) (1770), Cornouiller sanguin (French) (8) (1785), Dogberry [Dog-berry, Dog berry] or Dogberry tree [Dogberrie tree] (92, 107, 178) (1526–1919), Dogwood [Dog-wood, Dog wood] (14, 107) (1882–1919) bark once used for washing mangy dogs, Gutter tree [Gutter-tree] (92) (1876), Hound's tree (14) (1882), Hound's-berry tree [Hounds' berry tree] (92) (1876), Pegwood [Peg-wood] (107) (1919), Red dogwood [Red dog wood] (27) (1811)

Cornus sericea **L.** – American red-rod cornel (186) (1814), Arrow-wood [Arrow wood] (35) (1806) William Clark, Blue-berry cornel [Blueberry cornel, Blue berry cornel, Blue-berried cornel, Blueberry cornell] (6, 7, 92, 187) (1818–1932), Blue-berry cornus [Blue-berried cornus] (186) (1814), Blue-berry dogwood [Blue berry dog wood, Blueberry dogwood, Blue-berried dogwood] (42, 186) (1814), Bois rouge (French) (35) (1806) Meriwether Lewis, Cornuille Soyeux (French) (6) (1892), Female dogwood (6, 186) (1825–1892), Ki-ni-ha-nick (186) (1814), Kinnikinnick [Kinnikinik, Kinnikinnick, Kinnikinic, Kinnikinnik] (2, 6, 46, 47, 58, 63, 113, 130) (1852–1899), Kinnikinnick bark (92) (1876), Milawapamule (6) (1892), New England dogwood (186) (1814), Red brush [Red-brush] (76) (1896), Red osier [Red-osier] (19, 58, 92) (1840–1892), Red rod (19, 92) (1840–1876), Red rood (92) (1876), Red-osier dogwood [Red-osier dogwood, Redosier dogwood] (50) (present), Red-willow [Red willow] (34, 35, 38, 76, 92, 186, 187) (1806–1906), Rose-willow [Rose willow] (7, 58, 92, 186, 187) (1818–1892), Silky cornel (6, 58, 63, 92, 130) (1869–1899), Silky dogwood (6) (1892), Squaw bush [Squawbush, Squaw-bush] (46, 76) (1879–1896), Swamp dogwood [Swamp-dogwood (6, 7, 58, 92) (1828–1892)

Cornus sericea **L. subsp.** *occidentalis* **(Torr. & Gray) Fosberg** – Woolly-leaf cornus [Woolly-leaved cornus] (20) (1857)

Cornus sericea **L. subsp.** *sericea* – Bailey's cornel (5, 130) (1895–1913), Bailey's dogwood [Bailey dogwood] (5, 131, 138, 155) (1899–1942), Bois rouge (French) (35, 101) (1806–1905), Chanshasha-hinchake (Dakota) (37) (1919), Creeping dogwood [Creeping dog wood] (42) (1814), Dogberry [Dog-berry, Dog berry] or Dogberry tree [Dogberrie tree] (5, 156, 158) (1900–1923), Dogwood [Dog-wood, Dog wood] (105, 112) (1932–1937), Golden-twig dogwood [Goldentwig dogwood] (109) (1949), Gutter tree [Gutter-tree] (5, 156, 158) (1900–1923), Indian tobacco [Indian-tobacco] (107) (1919), Killikinic [Killikinick] (158) (1900), Kinnikinnick [Kinnikinik, Kinnikinnick, Kinnikinic, Kinnikinnik] (5, 37, 101, 156, 158) (1900–1923), Magnoxigill (Indians of Maine) (107) (1919),

Mĭs'kwabi'mĭc (Chippewa, reddish) (40) (1928), Muns-minš (105) (1932), Native red-osier dogwood (112) (1937), Ningahi h'te (Omaha-Ponca) (37) (1919), Pigeon-berry bush [Pigeonberry bush] (46) (1783), Red brush [Red-brush] (5, 37, 73, 156, 158) (1892–1923), Red cornel (156) (1923), Red dogwood [Red dog wood] (156) (1923), Red osier [Red-osier] (3, 47, 85, 131, 156) (1852–1977), Red osier cornel (5, 158) (1900–1913), Red osier dogwood (5, 9, 40, 63, 72, 97, 108, 155, 158) (1873–1942), Red-osier dogwood [Red-osier dogwood, Redosier dogwood] (5, 9, 40, 50, 63, 72, 93, 95, 97, 108, 113, 138) (1873–present), Red-willow [Red willow] (47, 101) (1852–1905), Redwood [Red wood] (35) (1806), Squaw bush [Squawbush, Squaw-bush] (5, 75, 156) (1894–1923), Tartarian dogwood (109, 138, 155) (1923–1949), Waxberry cornel [Waxberry cornell, Wax-berry cornel] (5, 7, 92, 156, 158) (1828–1923), White cornel (20) (1857), White-berry dogwood [White berry dog wood] (42) (1814), Wild red-osier [Wild red osier] (2) (1895)

Cornus stolonifera **fo.** *flaviramea* **(Späth ex Koehne) Rickett** – See *Cornus sericea* L. subsp. *sericea*

Cornus stolonifera **Michx.** – See *Cornus sericea* L. subsp. *sericea*

Cornus stolonifera **Michx. var.** *flaviramea* **Rehd.** – See *Cornus sericea* L. subsp. *sericea*

Cornus stricta **Lam.** – See *Cornus foemina* Mill.

Cornus suecica **L.** – Dwarf honeysuckle (156) (1923), Kinnikinnick [Kinnikinik, Kinnikinnick, Kinnikinic, Kinnikinnik] (107) (1919), Lapland cornel (5, 156) (1913–1923), Northern dwarf cornel (5, 156) (1913–1923), Plant-of-gluttony (156) (1923)

Cornus tomentulosa **Michx.** – See *Cornus rugosa* Lam.

Coronilla **L.** – Axseed (158) (1900), Coronilla (138, 155) (1923–1942), Crownvetch [Crown vetch] (4, 50, 156) (1923–present)

Coronilla securidaca **L.** – See *Securigera securidaca* (L.) O. Deg. & Dorf.

Coronilla valentina **L.** – Dwarf bastard senna [Dwarfe Bastard Sena] (178) (1526), Mediterranean crownvetch (50) (present)

Coronilla varia **L.** – Axseed (5, 156, 158) (1900–1923) no longer in use by 1923, Axwort (5, 156, 158) (1900–1923) no longer in use by 1923, Coronilla (5, 85, 156) (1913–1932), Crownvetch [Crown vetch] (3, 4, 109, 138, 156) (1923–1986), Crownvetch coronilla (155) (1942), Hatchet vetch (178) (1526), Hedysarum (178) (1526), Hive vine [Hive-vine, Hivevine] (5, 156, 158) (1900–1923), Purple crownvetch (50) (present)

Coronopus didyma **S.** – See *Coronopus didymus* (L.) Sm.

Coronopus didymus **(L.) Sm.** – Lesser watercress [Lesser water cress] (5) (1913), Swine cress [Swine-cress, Swine cresses] (19) (1840)

Coronopus **Gaertn.** – possibly *Coronopus* Zinn

Coronopus procumbens **[Gilib]** – See *Coronopus squamatus* (Forsk.) Aschers.

Coronopus ruellii **All.** – See *Lepidium coronopus* (L.) Al-Shehbaz

Coronopus squamatus **(Forsk.) Aschers.** – Buckesshorne (179) (1526), Buckhorn [Buck horn, Buck-horn, Buck's horn, Buckshorn, Buck's-horn, Bucks-horne, Bucks horne] (156, 178) (1526–1923) no longer in use by 1923, Carpet cress [Carpet-cress] (156) (1923), Herb ivy [Herb-ivy] (156) (1923), Sow's-grass [Sow's grass] (156) (1923), Swine cress [Swine-cress, Swine cresses] (156) (1923), Wart-cress [Wartcress, Wart cress] (107, 156) (1919–1923), Wartwort [Wartwort] (156, 179) (1526–1923)

Coronopus **Zinn** – Wart-cress [Wartcress, Wart cress] (10, 13, 156) (1818–1923), possibly Pepper-grass [Peppergrass, Pepper grass] (7) (1828), possibly Swine cress [Swine-cress, Swine cresses] (15) (1895)

Corrigiola litoralis **L.** – Bastard knot grass (92) (1876)

Cortaderia argentea – See *Cortaderia selloana* (J. A. & J. H. Schultes) Aschers. & Graebn.

Cortaderia selloana **(J. A. & J. H. Schultes) Aschers. & Graebn.** – Common pampas grass [Common pampasgrass] (138) (1923), Pampas grass [Pampas-grass, Pampasgrass] (56, 67, 92, 109, 163) (1852–1949)

Cortaderia selloana **Aschers. & Graebn.** – See *Cortaderia selloana* (J. A. & J. H. Schultes) Aschers. & Graebn.

Corydalis aurea Willd.

Cortaderia Stapf – Pampas grass [Pampas-grass, Pampasgrass] (138) (1923)

Corydalis aurea Willd. – Golden corydalis (2, 3, 4, 5, 72, 85, 97, 122, 127, 131, 145, 155, 156) (1897–1986), Golden-flower corydalis [Golden-flowered corydalis] (187) (1818), Scrambled-eggs [Scrambled eggs] (50, 124) (1937–present)

Corydalis aurea Willd. var. *aurea* – See *Corydalis aurea* Willd. (accepted in PL not in US)

Corydalis aurea Willd. var. *occidentalis* Engelm. – See *Corydalis curvisiliqua* Engelm. subsp. *occidentalis* (Engelm. ex Gray) W.A. Weber

Corydalis bulbosa DC. – See *Corydalis solida* (L.) Clairv.

Corydalis canadensis Goldie – See *Dicentra canadensis* (Goldie) Walp.

Corydalis crystallina Engelm. – Curve-fruit corydalis [Curved-fruited corydalis] (97, 131) (1899–1937), Curve-pod fumewort [Curve-pod fumewort] (50) (present), Mealy corydalis (3, 4) (1977–1986), Mealy fumewort (50) (present), Scrambled-eggs [Scrambled eggs] (122) (1937) TX, Vesicular corydalis (5, 72, 97) (1907–1937)

Corydalis cucullaria [**Pers.**] – See *Dicentra cucullaria* (L.) Bernh.

Corydalis curvisiliqua Engelm. – See *Corydalis crystallina* Engelm.

Corydalis curvisiliqua Engelm. subsp. *grandibracteata* (Fedde) G. B. Ownbey – Curve-pod fumewort [Curvepod fumewort] (50) (present), Large-bract corydalis [Large-bracted corydalis] (4) (1986)

Corydalis curvisiliqua Engelm. subsp. *occidentalis* (Engelm. ex Gray) W. A. Weber – Curve-pod fumewort [Curvepod fumewort] (50) (present), Golden corydalis (3) (1977), Mountain corydalis (5, 85, 93, 97, 155) (1913–1942), Squirrel-corn [Squirrel corn, Squirrel-corn] (157) (1929)

Corydalis DC. – Corydalis (1, 138, 155, 158) (1900–1942), Fumeroots [Fume-roots] (156) (1923), Fumewort (4, 50) (1896–present)

Corydalis flavula (Raf.) DC. – Colic weed [Colic-weed, Colicweed] (5, 156, 158) (1900–1923), Pale corydalis (4, 5, 72, 97, 156, 158) (1900–1986), Yellow corydalis (5, 156) (1913–1923), Yellow fumewort (50) (present), Yellow harlequin (3, 4) (1977–1986), Yellowish corydalis (2) (1895)

Corydalis formosa Pursh – See *Dicentra canadensis* (Goldie) Walp.

Corydalis glauca Pursh – See *Corydalis sempervirens* (L.) Pers.

Corydalis lutea – See *Pseudofumaria lutea* (L.) Borkh.

Corydalis micrantha (Engelm. ex Gray) Gray – Slender fumewort (3) (1977), Small-flower fumewort [Smallflower fumewort] (50) (present)

Corydalis micrantha (Engelm. ex Gray) Gray subsp. *australis* (Chapman) G. B. Ownbey – Golden corydalis (5) (1913), Plains corydalis (5, 93, 97) (1913–1937), Small-flower fumewort [Smallflower fumewort] (50) (present)

Corydalis micrantha (Engelm. ex Gray) Gray subsp. *micrantha* – American hazel (46) (1879), Slender fumewort (4) (1986), Small-flower corydalis [Small flowered corydalis] (5, 72, 97, 122) (1907–1937), Small-flower fumewort [Smallflower fumewort] (50) (present)

Corydalis micrantha (Engelm.) Gray – See *Corydalis micrantha* (Engelm. ex Gray) Gray

Corydalis montana Engelm. – See *Corydalis curvisiliqua* Engelm. subsp. *occidentalis* (Engelm. ex Gray) W.A. Weber

Corydalis rosea [**Eaton**] – possibly *Capnoides sempervirens* (L.) Borck.

Corydalis sempervirens (L.) Pers. – Loridales plant (76) (1896) ME, Pale corydalis (2, 156) (1895–1923), Pink corydalis (156) (1923), Rock fumewort (156) (1923), Roman wormwood (76, 109, 156) (1923–1949) Paris ME, possibly Rosy corydalis (42) (1814)

Corydalis solida (L.) Clairv. – Fumewort (107) (1919), Holewort (92) (1876), Hollow-wort [Hollow wort] (92) (1876), Purple hollow roote (178) (1526), White hollow-root [White hollow roote] (178) (1526)

Corydalis Vent. – See *Corydalis* DC.

Corydalis Vent. Bernh. – possibly *Corydalis* DC.

Corylus (Tourn.) L. – See *Corylus* L.

Corylus americana Marsh. – possibly *Corylus americana* Walt.

Corylus americana Walt. – American common hazel nut (42) (1814),

American filbert (155) (1942), American hazelnut [American hazel-nut] (1, 2, 8, 50, 82, 109, 138, 157, 187) (1818–present), Avellane (46) (1879), Bagan' (Chippewa) (40) (1928), Bonneted hazel (95, 97, 113, 130, 156) (1890–1937), Corylus (46) (1879), Cuckold-nut (8) (1785), Dwarf filbert (8) (1785), Dwarf hazel nut [Dwarf hazle nut] (42) (1814), Filbert [Philburt, Filberts, Filberds, or Philberds] (5, 42, 46, 97, 156, 177) (1762–1937), Hasill (46) (1617), Hazel [Hazle] or Hazel tree (12, 40, 92) (1821–1928), Hazel brush (22) (1893), Hazelnut [Hazel nut, Hazel-nut, Hasel nuts, Hazle-nut] or Hazelnut tree [Hasel nut tree] (4, 5, 19, 37, 38, 46, 47, 72, 82, 85, 92, 93, 97, 105, 106, 107, 113, 130, 131, 156) (1820–1986), Huksik (Winnebago) (37) (1919), Noisetier d'Amérique (French) (8) (1785), Pikanin-minš (Chippewa) (105) (1932), Quà-ing-yǎ (Oto) (38) (1820), Uma (Dakota) (37) (1919), Unzhinga (Omaha-Ponca) (37) (1919) Unzhinga-hi (Hazel-bush), Weech (46) (1879), possibly Wild filbert (187) (1818)

Corylus americana Willd. – See *Corylus americana* Walt.

Corylus avellana L. – Barcelona nuts (107) (1919), Cobnut [Cob nut] (107) (1919), Common filbert (109) (1949), European common hazel nut [European common hazle nut] (42) (1814), European filbert (109) (1949), Filbert [Philbert, Filberts, Filberds, or Philberds] (19, 107, 138) (1840–1932) for Philibert King of France, Hazel [Hazle] or Hazel tree (41, 92) (1770–1876), Hazelnut [Hazel nut, Hazel-nut, Hasel nuts, Hazle-nut] or Hazelnut tree [Hasel nut tree] (107, 112) (1919–1937), Heraclotic nuts (107) (1919)

Corylus cornuta H.R.P. – See *Corylus cornuta* Marsh

Corylus cornuta Marsh – Bagan' (Chippewa) (40) (1928), Beaked filbert (155) (1942), Beaked hazel (19, 92, 158) (1840–1900), Beaked hazelnut [Beaked hazel-nut] (1, 2, 4, 5, 50, 82, 85, 107, 109, 130, 131, 138) (1895–present), Cuckold hazel nut [Cuckold hazle nut] (42) (1814), Cuckold-nut (8) (1785), Dwarf filbert (8) (1785), Filbert [Philburt, Filberts, Filberds, or Philberds] (35, 46) (1617–1806), Hazelnut [Hazel nut, Hazel-nut, Hasel nuts, Hazle-nut] or Hazelnut tree [Hasel nut tree] (35) (1806), Noisetier à fruit cornu (French) (8) (1785)

Corylus humilis – See *Corylus americana* Walt.

Corylus L. – Filbert [Philburt, Filberts, Filberds, or Philberds] (2, 7, 14, 92, 109, 138, 155) (1828–1949), Hazel [Hazle] or Hazel tree (8, 155, 156, 184) (1785–1942), Hazelnut [Hazel nut, Hazel-nut, Hasel nuts, Hazle-nut] or Hazelnut tree [Hasel nut tree] (2, 4, 8, 10, 14, 50, 7, 42, 82, 93, 112, 138, 167) (1785–present), Noisetier (8) (1785)

Corylus rostrata Aiton – See *Corylus cornuta* Marsh

Corymbia citriodora (Hook.) K. D. Hill & L. A. S. Johnson – Bloodwood [Blood wood] (92) (1876)

Corypha Jacq. – possibly *Sabal* Adans.

Corypha minor Jacq. – See *Sabal minor* (Jacq.) Pers.

Corypha palma – possibly *Sabal palmetto* (Walt.) Lodd. ex J.A. & J.H. Schultes

Corypha palmetto Walt. – See *Sabal palmetto* (Walt.) Lodd. ex J.A. & J.H. Schultes

Corypha pumila Walt. – See *Sabal minor* (Jacq.) Pers.

Corypha repens Bartr. – See *Serenoa repens* (Bartr.) Small

Coryphantha (Engelm.) Lem. – Ball cactus (93) (1936), Coryphantha (155) (1942)

Coryphantha Engelm. – See *Coryphantha* (Engelm.) Lem.

Coryphantha Lem. – See *Coryphantha* (Engelm.) Lem.

Coryphantha missouriensis (Sweet) Britton & Rose – See *Escobaria missouriensis* (Sweet) D.R. Hunt var. *missouriensis*

Coryphantha neomexicana Engelm. – See *Escobaria vivipara* (Nutt.) Buxbaum var. *neomexicana* (Engelm.) Buxbaum

Coryphantha vivipara (Nutt.) Britton & Rose – See *Escobaria vivipara* (Nutt.) Buxbaum var. *vivipara*

Cosmos bipinnatus Cav. – Common cosmos (138) (1923), Cosmos (82) (1930) IA

Cosmos Cav. – Cosmos (138) (1923)

Cosmos parviflorus (Jacq.) H.B.K. – See *Cosmos parviflorus* (Jacq.) Pers.

Cosmos parviflorus (Jacq.) Pers. – Small pink-flower cosmos [Small pink flowered cosmos] (124) (1937) TX

Cosmos sulphureus **Cav.** – Yellow cosmos (109, 138) (1923–1949)

Cota **J. Gay.** – See *Anthemis* L.

Cotinus americanus **Nutt.** – See *Cotinus obovatus* Raf.

Cotinus coggygria **Scop.** – Aaron's-beard [Aaron's beard, Aaronsbeard] (19, 92) (1840–1876), American smoke tree [American smoketree, American smoke-tree] (112) (1937), Burningbush [Burning bush, Burning-bush] (156) (1923), Common smoketree (138) (1923), False fringe tree (19, 92) (1840–1876), Feather tree [Feather-tree] (7, 92) (1828–1876), Poison ash (92) (1876), Purple fringe (92, 156) (1898–1923), Smoke bush (135) (1910), Smoke plant (92, 107) (1876–1919), Smoke tree [Smoke-tree] (82, 92, 109) (1876–1949), Venice sumac [Venice sumach] (92) (1876), Wig tree (92) (1876), Young fustic (92) (1876), Zant wood (92) (1876)

Cotinus obovatus **Raf.** – American smoke tree [American smoketree, American smoke-tree] (5, 15, 65, 138, 156) (1895–1931), Chittam wood [Chittam-wood, Chittem wood, Chittim wood, Chittim-wood] (15, 97, 135, 156) (1895–1937), Chottam wood (5) (1913), Large-leaf cotinus [Large leaved cotinus] (20) (1857), Smoke tree [Smoke-tree] (93, 124) (1936–1937), Sumac fustet d'Amerique (French) (20) (1857), Wild smoke tree (5) (1913), Yellow-wood [Yellowwood, Yellow wood] (5, 156) (1913–1923), possibly Feather tree [Feather-tree] (156) (1923)

Cotoneaster acutifolia – See *Cotoneaster acutifolius* Turcz.

Cotoneaster acutifolius **Turcz.** – Peking cotoneaster (112, 138) (1923–1937)

Cotoneaster adpressa – See *Cotoneaster adpressus* Boiss.

Cotoneaster adpressus **Boiss.** – Creeping cotoneaster (138) (1923)

Cotoneaster bullata macrophylla – See *Cotoneaster bullatus* var. *macrophyllus* Rehder & E. H. Wilson

Cotoneaster bullatus var. *macrophyllus* **Rehder & E. H. Wilson** – Big-leaf cotoneaster [Bigleaf cotoneaster] (138) (1923)

Cotoneaster dielsiana – See *Cotoneaster dielsianus* E. Pritz.

Cotoneaster dielsianus **E. Pritz.** – Diel's cotoneaster [Diels cotoneaster] (138) (1923)

Cotoneaster divaricata – See *Cotoneaster divaricatus* Rehd. & Wilson

Cotoneaster divaricatus **Rehd. & Wilson** – Spreading cotoneaster (138) (1923)

Cotoneaster francheti – See *Cotoneaster franchetii* Boiss.

Cotoneaster franchetii **Boiss.** – Franchet's cotoneaster [Franchet cotoneaster] (138) (1923)

Cotoneaster horizontalis **Dcne.** – Rock cotoneaster (138) (1923)

Cotoneaster lucidus **Schldl.** – Shining aster (155) (1942)

Cotoneaster **Medik.** – Cotoneaster (138) (1923), Firethorn [Fire thorn] (156) (1923)

Cotoneaster pannosa – See *Cotoneaster pannosus* Franch.

Cotoneaster pannosus **Franch.** – Silver-leaf cotoneaster [Silverleaf cotoneaster] (138) (1923)

Cotoneaster pyracantha **(L.) Spach** – See *Pyracantha coccinea* M. Roemer

Cotoneaster simonsi – See *Cotoneaster simonsii* Baker

Cotoneaster simonsii **Baker** – Simon's cotoneaster [Simons cotoneaster] (138) (1923)

Cottea pappophoroides **Kunth** – Cotta grass [Cotta-grass] (94) (1901)

Cotyledon californica **[Baker]** – See *Dudleya cymosa* (Lem.) Britt. & Rose

Cotyledon **L.** – Cotyledon (138) (1923), Hipwort [Hip-wort, Hip wort] (86) (1878) old European name, Kidneywort [Kidney-wort] (86) (1878) old European name, Navelwort [Navel-wort] (86) (1878) old European name, Renney-wort (86) (1878) old European name, Shield-of-heaven [Shield of heaven] (86) (1878) old European name

Cotyledon laxa **(Lindley) S. Watson** – possibly *Dudleya cymosa* (Lem.) Britt. & Rose

Cotyledon laxa **Benth. & Hook. f. ex Jeps.** – possibly *Dudleya cymosa* (Lem.) Britt. & Rose

Cotyledon nevadensis **Wats.** – See *Dudleya cymosa* (Lem.) Britt. & Rose

Couroupita guianensis **Aubl.** – Cannon-ball tree [Cannon ball tree] (92, 109) (1876–1949)

Coursetia axillaris **Coult. & Rose** – Baby bonnets (122, 124) (1937) TX

Coursetia **DC.** – Catgut [Cat gut, Cat-gut] (1) (1932), Goat's-rue [Goatsrue, Goat's rue, Goats-rue] (1, 158) (1900–1932)

Covillea glutinosa **[(Engelm.) Rydb.]** – See *Larrea tridentata* (Sessé & Moc. ex DC.) Coville var. *tridentata*

Covillea tridentata **[(Sessé & Moc. ex DC.) Vail]** – See *Larrea tridentata* (Sessé & Moc. ex DC.) Coville var. *tridentata*

Cowania **D. Don** – Quinine bush [Quinine-bush] (122) (1937)

Cowania mexicana **[D.Don]** – See *Purshia mexicana* (D. Don) Henrickson

Cowania stansburiana – See *Purshia stansburiana* (Torr.) Henrickson

Cracca hispidula **(Michx.) Kuntze** – See *Tephrosia hispidula* (Michx.) Pers.

Cracca **L.** – See *Coursetia* DC.

Cracca spicata **(Walt.) Luntze** – See *Tephrosia spicata* (Walt.) Torr. & Gray

Cracca virginiana **L.** – See *Tephrosia virginiana* (L.) Pers

Crambe **L.** – Sea-kale [Seakale, Sea kale] (138) (1923)

Crambe maritima **L.** – Common seakale (138) (1923), Sea-kale [Seakale, Sea kale] (92, 109) (1876–1949)

Craniolaria annua **L.** – Sugar root [Sugar-root] (138) (1923)

Crantzia lineata **Nutt.** – See *Lilaeopsis chinensis* (L.) Kuntze

Crassina grandiflora **(Nutt.) Kuntze** – See *Zinnia grandiflora* Nutt.

Crassina pumila **[(A. Gray) Kuntze]** – See *Zinnia acerosa* (DC.) Gray

Crassina **Scepin** – See *Zinnia* L.

Crassula aquatica **(L.) Schoenl.** – Pygmy-weed [Pigmy weed, Pygmy-weed] (5, 19, 92, 156) (1840–1923)

Crassula **L.** – Crassula (155) (1942)

Crassula saginoides **(Maxim.) Bywater & Wickens** – Vaillant's pigmy-weed [Vaillant's pigmy weed] (5) (1913)

Crataegus ×*anomala* **Sargent (pro sp.) [*intricata* × *mollis*]** – Arnold's hawthorn [Arnold hawthorn] (138) (1923), Arnold's thorn (5) (1913), Oblong-leaf thorn [Oblong-leaved thorn] (5) (1913)

Crataegus aestivalis **Torr. & Gray.** – Apple haw (20, 74) (1857–1893), Crataegus (107) (1919), Naked-flower hawthorn [Naked-flowered hawthorn] (20) (1857), Summer haw (2) (1895)

Crataegus albicans **Ashe** – See *Crataegus mollis* Scheele

Crataegus alnorum **Sargent** – See *Crataegus schuettei* Ashe

Crataegus anomala **Sargent** – See *Crataegus* ×*anomala* Sarg. [*intricata* × *mollis*]

Crataegus apiifolia **[Michx.]** – possibly *Crataegus oxyacantha* L. var. *apiifolia* Michx.

Crataegus arborescens – See *Crataegus viridis* L.

Crataegus arkansana **Sargent** – See *Crataegus mollis* Scheele

Crataegus arnoldiana **Sargent** – See *Crataegus* ×*anomala* Sarg. [*intricata* × *mollis*]

Crataegus aspera **Sargent** – See *Crataegus pruinosa* (Wendl.) K. Koch

Crataegus beata **Sarg.** – Dunbar's thorn (5) (1913)

Crataegus berberifolia **Torr. & Gray** – See *Crataegus crus-galli* L.

Crataegus bicknellii **Eggleston** – See *Crataegus succulenta* Schrad. ex Link

Crataegus boyntoni **Beadle** – See *Crataegus intricata* Lange

Crataegus brachyacantha **Sarg. & Engelm.** – Hog's haw (74) (1893), Pomette bleue (French) (74) (1893)

Crataegus brainerdi **Sargent** – See *Crataegus brainerdii* Sarg.

Crataegus brainerdii **Sarg.** – Brainerd's thorn (5) (1913)

Crataegus calpodendron **(Ehrh.) Medik.** – Black thorn [Black-thorn] (5, 157) (1900–1929), Common thorn (5, 157) (1900–1929), Globose-fruit thorn [Globose-fruited thorn] (5) (1913), Pear haw (5, 157) (1900–1929), Pear hawthorn (155) (1942), Pear thorn (5, 50, 157) (1900–present), Red haw (5, 93) (1913–1936), Thorn-apple [Thorn apple, Thornapple, Thorn apples, Thorne Apple] or Thorn-apple tree [Thorn apple tree] (5) (1913), Thorn-plum [Thorn plum] (5) (1913), Urn-tree hawthorn (4) (1986), White thorn [Whitethorn,

White thorne] (5, 157) (1913–1929)

Crataegus canbyi **Sargent** – See *Crataegus crus-galli* L.

Crataegus chrysocarpa **Ashe** – Black haw [Black-haw, Blackhaw] (101) (1905) MT, Chosanwa (Winnebago) (37) (1919), Eastern fire-berry hawthorn (155) (1942), Fire-berry hawthorn [Fireberry hawthorn] (50, 155) (1942–present), Glandular thorn (72) (1907), Jack's thorn (5) (1913), Northern hawthorn (4) (1986), Red haw (35, 37, 101) (1806–1919), Round-leaf hawthorn [Roundleaf hawthorn] (137, 138) (1923–1931), Round-leaf thorn [Round-leaved thorn] (5) (1913), Stlak (Flathead) (101) (1905) MT, fruit, Taspan (Omaha-Ponca) (37) (1919)

Crataegus chrysocarpa **Ashe var.** *phoenicea* **Palmer** – See *Crataegus chrysocarpa* Ashe

Crataegus coccinioides **Ashe** – Eggert's thorn (5, 97) (1913–1937), Hawthorn (4) (1986), Kansas hawthorn (50, 155) (1942–present)

Crataegus coleae **Sarg.** – Miss Macauley's thorn (5) (1913)

Crataegus collina **Chapman** – See *Crataegus punctata* Jacq.

Crataegus columbiana **How.** – See *Crataegus chrysocarpa* Ashe

Crataegus cordata **Aiton** – See *Crataegus phaenopyrum* (L. f.) Medik.

Crataegus crusgalli **L.** – See *Crataegus crus-galli* L.

Crataegus crus-galli **L.** – Barberry-leaf haw [Barberry-leaved haw] (5, 97) (1913–1937), Barberry-leaf hawthorn [Barberryleaf hawthorn] (155) (1942), Canby's thorn (5) (1913), Cockspur hawthorn [Cockspur hawthorn, Cockspur-hawthorn] (3, 4, 50, 63, 155, 187) (1818–present), Cockspur thorn [Cock-spur thorn] (2, 5, 19, 41, 72, 97, 109, 132, 137, 138, 156, 158) (1770–1949), Eureka Springs hawthorn (155) (1942), Fruitful thorn (5) (1913), Hawthorn (5) (1913), Martha's Vineyard thorn (5) (1913), Mississippi hawthorn (155) (1942), Missouri hawthorn (138, 155) (1923–1942), Mohr's hawthorn [Mohrs hawthorn] (155) (1942), Newcastle thorn (5, 74, 158) (1893–1913), Palmer's hawthorn [Palmer hawthorn (4, 155) (1942–1986), Palmer's thorn (5, 97) (1913–1937), Piedmont hawthorn (155) (1942), Pin thorn [Pin-thorn] (5, 156, 158) (1900–1923), Pineland hawthorn (155) (1942), Red haw (5, 156) (1913–1923), Thorn bush [Thorn-bush] (5, 156) (1913–1923), Thorn or Thorn tree (19) (1840), Thorn-apple [Thorn apple, Thornapple, Thorn apples, Thorne Apple] or Thorn-apple tree [Thorn apple tree] (5, 156) (1913–1923), Thorn-plum [Thorn plum] (5) (1913), Virginia azarole [Virginian azarole] (41) (1770), White thorn [Whitethorn, White thorne] (7, 92) (1828–1876), possibly Epine à feuilles luisantes (French) (8) (1785), possibly Pear-leaf thorn [Pear leaved thorn] (8) (1785)

Crataegus cuneiformis (**Marsh.**) **Eggleston** – See *Crataegus disperma* Ashe

Crataegus cuneiformis **Eggl.** – See *Crataegus disperma* Ashe

Crataegus curvisepala **auct. non Lindm.** – See *Crataegus monogyna* Jacq.

Crataegus delosi – See *Crataegus dodgei* Ashe

Crataegus delosii **Sarg.** – See *Crataegus dodgei* Ashe

Crataegus denaria **Beadle** – See *Crataegus crus-galli* L.

Crataegus disjuncta **Sargent** – See *Crataegus pruinosa* (Wendl.) K. Koch

Crataegus disperma **Ashe** – Marshall's thorn (5) (1913)

Crataegus dispessa **Ashe** – Bush's thorn (5) (1913), Épine à feuilles en coin (French) (8) (1785), Wedge-leaf mespilus [Wedge leaved mespilus] (8) (1785)

Crataegus dodgei **Ashe** – Bunch hawthorn (138) (1923)

Crataegus douglasii **Lindl.** – Black haw [Black-haw, Blackhaw] (35, 106, 135) (1806–1930), Black hawthorn (50, 138) (1923–present), Brook thorn (108) (1878), Douglas' thorn (5) (1913), Purple haw (35) (1806)

Crataegus durobrivensis **Sarg.** – See *Crataegus suborbiculata* Sarg.

Crataegus ellwangeriana **Sarg.** – See *Crataegus pedicellata* Sarg.

Crataegus engelmanni **Sargent** – See *Crataegus engelmannii* Sarg.

Crataegus engelmannii **Sarg.** – Engelmann's hawthorn [Engelmann hawthorn] (155) (1942)

Crataegus fecunda **Sargent** – See *Crataegus crus-galli* L.

Crataegus filipes **Ashe** – See *Crataegus jesupii* Sarg.

Crataegus flabellata (**Bosc.**) **K. Koch** – See *Crataegus flabellata* (Spach) Kirchn.

Crataegus flabellata (**Spach**) **Kirchn.** – Asa Gray's thorn (5) (1913), Bosc's thorn (5) (1913), Fan-leaf thorn [Fan-leaved thorn] (72) (1907)

Crataegus flava **Aiton** – Red haw (5) (1913), Summer haw (2, 5, 107) (1895–1919), Yellow haw (2, 5) (1895–1913), Yellow-berry thorn [Yellow-berried thorn] (19) (1840), Yellow-fruit hawthorn [Yellow fruited hawthorn] (42) (1814), Yellow-fruit thorn [Yellow-fruited thorn] (107) (1919)

Crataegus foetida [**Ashe**] – See *Crataegus intricata* Lange

Crataegus fructuosa **Sargent** – West Chester hawthorn (138) (1923)

Crataegus gattingeri **Ashe** – See *Crataegus pruinosa* (Wendl.) K. Koch

Crataegus globosa **Sargent** – See *Crataegus calpodendron* (Ehrh.) Medik.

Crataegus grayana **Eggl.** – See *Crataegus flabellata* (Spach) Kirchn.

Crataegus induta **Sargent** – See *Crataegus mollis* Scheele

Crataegus intricata **Lange** – Allegheny thorn [Alleghany thorn] (5, 97) (1913–1937), Beadle's yellow-fruit thorn [Beadle's yellow-fruited thorn] (5) (1913), Biltmore thorn (5) (1913), Boynton's hawthorn [Boynton hawthorn] (138) (1923), Boynton's thorn (5) (1913), Lange's thorn (5) (1913), Padus-leaf thorn [Padus-leaved thorn] (5) (1913), Peck's thorn (5) (1913), Russet hawthorn (138) (1923), Stone's thorn (5) (1913)

Crataegus iracunda **Beadle** – Gruber's thorn (5) (1913)

Crataegus irrasa **Sarg.** – Blanchard's thorn (5) (1913), Oakes' thorn (5) (1913)

Crataegus jackii **Sargent** – See *Crataegus chrysocarpa* Ashe

Crataegus jesupii **Sarg.** – Jesup's thorn (5) (1913), Miss Beckwith's thorn (5) (1913)

Crataegus jonesiae **Sarg.** – Fernald's thorn (5) (1913), Miss Jones' thorn (5) (1913)

Crataegus kelloggii **Sarg.** – Kellogg's thorn (5) (1913)

Crataegus **L.** – Haw [Haws] or Haw tree (1, 35, 93, 106) (1806–1936), Hawthorn (1, 2, 4, 7, 10, 50, 82, 105, 106, 109, 112, 138, 156, 158, 184) (1793–present), Mespilus (8) (1785), Mĭne'saga'wûnj (Chippewa, having fruit and thorns) (40) (1928), Minesgan-winš (Chippewa) (105) (1932), Red haw (122, 124) (1937), Thorn or Thorn tree (7, 93) (1828–1936), Thorn-apple [Thorn apple, Thornapple, Thorn apples, Thorne Apple] or Thorn-apple tree [Thorn apple tree] (40, 73) (1892–1928), White hawthorn (82) (1930), White thorn [Whitethorn, White thorne] (2) (1895), Wild service tree [Wild service-tree] (8) (1785)

Crataegus lacera **Sargent** – See *Crataegus mollis* Scheele

Crataegus lanuginosa **Sarg.** – Woolly hawthorn (4, 50) (1986–present), Woolly thorn (5) (1913)

Crataegus laurentiana **Sargent** – See *Crataegus jonesiae* Sarg.

Crataegus leiophylla **Sargent** – See *Crataegus pruinosa* (Wendl.) K. Koch

Crataegus lucorum **Sarg.** – Grove thorn (5) (1913)

Crataegus macauleyae **Sargent** – See *Crataegus coleae* Sarg.

Crataegus macracantha **Lodd.** – See *Crataegus succulenta* Schrad. ex Link

Crataegus macrosperma **Ashe** – Roan Mountain thorn (5) (1913), Variable thorn (5) (1913)

Crataegus margaretta **Ashe.** – See *Crataegus margarettiae* Ashe

Crataegus margarettiae **Ashe** – Brown's thorn (5, 82) (1913–1930), Mrs. Ashes's thorn (5) (1913)

Crataegus marshallii **Eggl.** – Épine à feuilles de perfil (French) (8) (1785), Parsley haw (5, 122) (1913–1937), Parsley-leaf haw [Parsley-leaved haw] (5) (1913), Parsley-leaf thorn [Parsley-leaved thorn] (97) (1937), Virginia parsley-leaf mespilus [Virginian parsley leaved mespilus] (8) (1785)

Crataegus mohrii **Beadle** – See *Crataegus crus-galli* L.

Crataegus mollis **Scheele** – Arkansas hawthorn (138, 155) (1923–1942), Arnold's hawthorn [Arnold hawthorn] (50) (present), Common red haw (82) (1930), Downy haw (93) (1936), Downy hawthorn (3, 4,

137, 138, 155) (1923–1986), Downy thorn (5) (1913), Hairy haw-thorn (130) (1895), Hawthorn (82) (1930), Red haw (82, 85, 156) (1923–1932), Red-fruit thorn [Red fruited thorn, Red-fruited thorn] (5, 72, 93, 97, 131) (1907–1937), Summer haw (4) (1986), Tatnall's thorn (5) (1913), Thorn-apple [Thorn apple, Thornapple, Thorn ap-ples, Thorne Apple] or Thorn-apple tree [Thorn apple tree] (85, 156) (1923–1932), Turkey-apple hawthorn [Turkeyapple hawthorn] (155) (1942), White thorn [Whitethorn, White thorne] (190) (~1759), Wild thorn (82) (1930)

Crataegus monogyna **Jacq.** – Common quickset (187) (1818), Cra-taegus (54) (1905), Hathorn (5) (1913), Haw [Haws] or Haw tree (5) (1913), Hawthorn (5, 19, 54, 107) (1840–1919), Hedge thorn (5) (1913), May bush (5) (1913), May thorn (5) (1913), Noble epine (92) (1876), Quickset (5, 19, 92) (1840–1913), Quickthorn (5) (1913), Thorn-apple [Thorn apple, Thornapple, Thorn apples, Thorne Apple] or Thorn-apple tree [Thorn apple tree] (92) (1876), Wick [Wicke, Wicks] (5) (1913), Wicken [Wickens] (5) (1913)

Crataegus multiflora **Bunge** – Ink-berry hawthorn [Inkberry hawthorn] (138) (1923)

Crataegus neofluvialis **Ashe** – See *Crataegus succulenta* Schrad. ex Link

Crataegus nigra **Waldst. & Kit.** – European black hawthorn (137, 138) (1923–1931)

Crataegus nitida **(Englem.) Sargent** – Glossy hawthorn (138) (1923), Shining thorn (5) (1913)

Crataegus oakesiana **Eggleston** – See *Crataegus irrasa* Sarg.

Crataegus ovata **Sargent** – Ovate-leaf thorn [Ovate-leaved thorn] (5) (1913)

Crataegus oxyacantha **auct. non L.** – See *Crataegus monogyna* Jacq.

Crataegus oxyacantha **L.** – See *Crataegus curvisepala* Lindm.

Crataegus oxyacantha **L. var. apiifolia Michx.** – Parsley hawthorn (138) (1923)

Crataegus padifolia **Sargent** – See *Crataegus intricata* Lange

Crataegus pallens **Beadle** – See *Crataegus intricata* Lange

Crataegus palmeri **Sargent** – See *Crataegus crus-galli* L.

Crataegus pedicellata **Sarg.** – Cockspur hawthorn [Cock-spur haw-thorn, Cockspur-hawthorn] (181) (~1678), Ellwanger's hawthorn [Ellwanger hawthorn] (138) (1923)

Crataegus persimilis **Sarg.** – Plum-leaf hawthorn [Plumleaf hawthorn] (138) (1923)

Crataegus pertomentosa **Ashe** – See *Crataegus succulenta* Schrad. ex Link

Crataegus phaenopyrum **(L. f.) Medik.** – Maple-leaf hawthorn [Ma-ple leaved hawthorn] (42) (1814), Poplar-leaf haw [Poplar-leaved haw] (5) (1913), Red haw (5) (1913), Virginia heart-leaf thorn [Vir-ginia heart-leaved thorn] (5) (1913), Virginia hedge thorn (5) (1913), Virginia thorn (92) (1876), Washington hawthorn (137, 138) (1923–1931), Washington thorn (2, 5, 109) (1895–1949)

Crataegus populifolia **Walter** – See *Crataegus phaenopyrum* (L. f.) Medik.

Crataegus populnea **Ashe** – See *Crataegus iracunda* Beadle

Crataegus pringlei **Sarg.** – Pringle's thorn (5) (1913)

Crataegus pruinosa **(Wendl.) K. Koch** – Fretz's thorn (5) (1913), Frosted hawthorn (138, 155) (1923–1942), Frosty hawthorn (4) (1986), Gattinger's thorn (5) (1913), Maine's thorn (5) (1913), Mis-souri thorn (5) (1913), Rough-leaf thorn [Rough-leaved thorn] (5) (1913), Waxy-fruit hawthorn [Waxyfruit hawthorn, Waxy-fruited thorn] (5, 50) (1913–present)

Crataegus prunifolia **[Pers.]** – See *Crataegus persimilis* Sarg.

Crataegus punctata **Jacq.** – Chapman's hill thorn (5) (1913), Common thorn tree (19) (1840), Dotted haw (5) (1913), Dotted hawthorn (50, 137, 138, 155) (1923–present), Dotted-fruit thorn [Dotted-fruited thorn] (156) (1923), Hillside hawthorn (4) (1986), Large-fruit haw-thorn [Large fruited hawthorn] (42) (1814), Large-fruit thorn [Large-fruited thorn] (5, 72) (1907–1913), White thorn [Whitethorn, White thorne] (5) (1913), Yellow dotted hawthorn (155) (1942)

Crataegus punctata **Jacq. var. aurea Aiton** – See *Crataegus punctata* Jacq.

Crataegus punctata **Jacq. var. canescens Britton** – See *Crataegus punctata* Jacq.

Crataegus pyrifolia **A.** – See *Photinia pyrifolia* (Lam.) Robertson & Phipps

Crataegus regalis **Beadle** – See *Crataegus crus-galli* L.

Crataegus reverchoni **Sargent** – See *Crataegus reverchonii* Sarg.

Crataegus reverchoni **Sargent var. discolor (Sargent) Palmer** – See *Crataegus reverchonii* Sarg.

Crataegus reverchoni **Sargent var. stevensiana (Sargent) Palmer** – See *Crataegus reverchonii* Sarg.

Crataegus reverchonii **Sarg.** – Reverchon's thorn (5) (1913)

Crataegus rivularis **Nutt.** – River hawthorn (20, 137, 138) (1857–1931)

Crataegus roanensis **Ashe** – See *Crataegus macrosperma* Ashe

Crataegus rotundifolia **Moench** – See *Crataegus chrysocarpa* Ashe

Crataegus rugosa **Ashe** – See *Crataegus pruinosa* (Wendl.) K. Koch

Crataegus schizophylla **Eggleston** – See *Crataegus crus-galli* L.

Crataegus schuettei **Ashe** – Edson's thorn (5) (1913)

Crataegus signata **Beadle** – See *Crataegus crus-galli* L.

Crataegus spathulata **Michx.** – Narrow-leaf thorn [Narrow-leaved thorn] (5) (1913), Small-fruit haw [Small-fruited haw] (5) (1913), Small-fruit thorn [Small-fruited thorn] (5, 97) (1913–1937), White thorn [Whitethorn, White thorne] (106) (1930)

Crataegus stonei **Sargent** – See *Crataegus intricata* Lange

Crataegus straminea **Beadle** – See *Crataegus intricata* Lange

Crataegus submollis **Sarg.** – Emerson's thorn (5) (1913), Quebec haw-thorn (138) (1923)

Crataegus suborbiculata **Sarg.** – Caughuawaga thorn (5) (1913), Christmas hawthorn (138) (1923)

Crataegus subpilosa **Sargent** – See *Crataegus crus-galli* L.

Crataegus succulenta **Link var. pertomentosa (Ashe) E. J. Palm.** – See *Crataegus succulenta* Schrad. ex Link

Crataegus succulenta **Link var. succulenta** – See *Crataegus succu-lenta* Schrad. ex Link

Crataegus succulenta **Schrad. ex Link** – American hawthorne (85) (1932), Bicknell's thorn (5) (1913), Fleshy hawthorn (50, 138, 155) (1923–present), Hawthorn (3, 112) (1937–1977), Long-spine thorn [Long-spined thorn] (5, 72, 93) (1907–1936), Long-spine thorn-ap-ple [Long spined thorn apple] (131) (1899), New River thorn (5) (1913), Prairie thorn (5) (1913), Red haw (112) (1937), Spike haw-thorn (137, 138, 155) (1923–1942), Succulent hawthorn (4) (1986)

Crataegus succulenta **Schrader** – See *Crataegus succulenta* Schrad. ex Link

Crataegus triflora **Chapman** – Three-flower hawthorn [Threeflower hawthorn] (138) (1923)

Crataegus uniflora **Muench.** – Dwarf thorn (5) (1913), One-flower hawthorn (138) (1923)

Crataegus vailiae **Britton** – Miss Vail's thorn (5) (1913)

Crataegus viridis **L.** – Alixier arborescent (French) (20) (1857), Green haw (4, 122) (1937–1986), Green hawthorn (50, 155) (1942–pres-ent), Green-leaf hawthorn [Green leaved hawthorn] (42) (1814), Hawthorn (3) (1977), Long-leaf hawthorn [Long-leaved hawthorn] (20) (1857), Red haw (5) (1913), Southern thorn (5, 97) (1913–1937), Tree haw (5) (1913), Tree thorn (5) (1913)

Crepis acuminata **Nutt.** – Taper-tip hawk's-beard [Taper-tip hawks-beard, Tapertip hawksbeard] (50, 155) (1942–present)

Crepis atribarba **Heller** – Slender hawk's-beard [Slender hawksbeard] (50) (Present)

Crepis biennis **L.** – Rough hawk's-beard [Rough hawksbeard] (5) (1913)

Crepis capillaris **(L.) Wallr.** – Hawk's-beard [Hawk's beard, Hawk beard, Hawksbeard] (92) (1876), Smooth hawk's-beard [Smooth hawksbeard] (5, 50, 155) (1913–present)

Crepis glauca **(Nutt.) Torr. & Gray** – See *Crepis runcinata* (James) Torr. & Gray

Crepis intermedia **Gray** – Small-flower gray hawk's-beard [Small-flowered gray hawksbeard] (5) (1913)

Crepis **L.** – Hawk's-beard [Hawk's beard, Hawk beard, Hawksbeard] (4, 50, 93, 155, 156, 158) (1900–present)

Crepis occidentalis **Nutt.** – Large-flower gray hawk's-beard [Large-flowered gray hawksbeard] (5, 50) (1913–present), Western hawk's-beard [Western hawksbeard] (155) (1942)

Crepis pulchra **L.** – Small-flower hawk's-beard [Small-flowered hawk's-beard] (156) (1923), Small-flower hawkweed [Small-flowered hawkweed] (5) (1913)

Crepis runcinata **(James) Torr. & Gray** – Dandelion hawk's-beard [Dandelion hawksbeard] (155) (1942), Fiddle-leaf hawksbeard [Fiddleleaf hawksbeard] (50) (present), Glaucous hawksbeard (5) (1913), Hawk's-beard [Hawk's beard, Hawk beard, Hawksbeard] (3, 85, 127) (1932–1977), Naked-stem hawksbeard [Naked stemmed hawksbeard] (5, 131) (1899–1913)

Crepis runcinata **(James) Torr. & Gray** subsp. *runcinata* – Dandelion hawk's-beard [Dandelion hawksbeard] (155) (1942), Fiddle-leaf hawksbeard [Fiddleleaf hawksbeard] (50) (present)

Crepis tectorum **L.** – Narrow-leaf hawk's-beard [Narrowleaf hawksbeard] (5, 50, 155) (1913–present)

Crepis virens – See *Crepis capillaris* (L.) Wallr.

Crescentia cujete **L.** – Calabash tree [Calabash-tree] (109, 138) (1923–1949), Calabassier cujete (20) (1857), Long-leaf calabash tree [Long leaved calabash tree] (20) (1857)

Crescentia **L.** – Calabash tree [Calabash-tree] (138) (1923)

Cressa **L.** – Alkali-weed [Alkaliweed, Alkali weed] (4, 50) (1986–present), Cressa (158) (1900)

Cressa truxillensis **Kunth** – Spreading alkaliweed (50) (present)

Crinum americanum **L.** – Crinum (174) (1753), Florida crinum (138) (1923), Louisiana squill (7, 92) (1828–1876), Seven-sisters [Seven sisters] (50) (present), Southern swamp crinum (109) (1949), Southern swamp lily (109) (1949)

Crinum asiaticum **L.** – Asiatic poison bulb (92) (1876), Poison bulb [Poisonbulb] (92, 138) (1876–1923), Tanghekolli (174) (1753)

Crinum bulbispermum **(Burm. f.) Milne-Redhead & Schweickerdt** – Hardy crinum (138) (1923)

Crinum floridanum **Fraser ex Steud.** – See *Crinum americanum* L.

Crinum **L.** – Crinum (138) (1923) Greek for lily, Crinum lily (109) (1949)

Crinum longifolium – See *Crinum bulbispermum* (Burm. f.) Milne-Redhead & Schweickerdt

Crinum strictum **Herbert** – See *Crinum americanum* L.

Criosanthes arietina **(Ait. f.) House** – See *Cypripedium arietinum* R.Br.

Criosanthes **Raf.** – See *Cypripedium* L. (US species)

Cristatella jamesii **Torr. & Gray** – See *Polanisia jamesii* (Torr. & Gray) Iltis

Cristatella **Nutt.** – See *Polanisia* Raf.

Critesion brachyantherum **(Nevski) Barkworth & D. R. Dewey** – See *Hordeum brachyantherum* Nevski subsp. *brachyantherum*

Critesion jubatum **(L.) Nevski** subsp. *breviaristatum* **(Bowden) A. & D. Löve** – See *Hordeum brachyantherum* Nevski subsp. *brachyantherum*

Crocanthemum canadense **(L.) Britton** – See *Helianthemum canadense* (L.) Michx.

Crocanthemum corymbosum **(Michx.) Britton** – See *Helianthemum corymbosum* Michx.

Crocanthemum majus **sensu Britt.** – See *Helianthemum bicknellii* Fern.

Crocanthemum **Spach** – See *Helianthemum* Mill.

Crocosmia ×*crocosmiiflora* **(V. Lemoine) N.E. Br.** [*aurea* × *pottsii*] – Common montbretia (109) (1949)

Crocosmia crocosmaeflora **N.E. Br.** – See *Crocosmia* ×*crocosmiiflora* (V. Lemoine) N.E. Br. [*aurea* × *pottsii*]

Crocosmia **Planch.** – Coppertip (138) (1923)

Crocus angustifolia **Weston** – Cloth-of-gold crocus (109, 138) (1923–1949), Common crocus (138) (1923), Golden crocus (92) (1876), Saffron of the spring (178) (1596), Spring crocus (92) (1876)

Crocus imperati **Ten.** – Early crocus (138) (1923)

Crocus **L.** – Crocus [Crocuses] (138) (1923)

Crocus susianus **Ker.** – See *Crocus angustifolia* Weston

Crocus vernus – See *Crocus angustifolia* Weston

Croomia pauciflora **(Nutt.) Torr.** – Few-flower croomia [Few-flowered croomia] (86) (1878)

Croomia pauciflora **Torr.** – See *Croomia pauciflora* (Nutt.) Torr.

Croptilon divaricatum **(Nutt.) Raf.** – Isopappus (5, 97) (1913–1937)

Croptilon hookerianum **(Torr. & Gray) House** var. *validum* **(Rydb.) E. B. Sm.** – Hooker's scratchdaisy (50) (present), Slender goldenweed (4) (1986)

Crotalaria angulata **Mill.** – See *Crotalaria rotundifolia* Walt. ex J.F. Gmel.

Crotalaria juncea **L.** – Sunn hemp (109) (1949)

Crotalaria **L.** – Crotalaria (155) (1942), Rattlebox [Rattle box, Rattle-box] (1, 2, 10, 50, 93, 122, 156, 158) (1818–present), Rattlepod [Rattle pod, Rattle-pod] (4) (1986)

Crotalaria ovalis **Pursh** – See *Crotalaria rotundifolia* Walt. ex J.F. Gmel.

Crotalaria rotundifolia **Walt. ex J. F. Gmel.** – Prostrate rattlebox [Prostrate rattle-box, Prostrate rattle box] (5, 97) (1913–1937), Rabbit-bells [Rabbit bells] (156) (1923)

Crotalaria sagittalis **L.** – Arrow crotolaria (155) (1942), Arrow rattle-box [Arrow rattle box] (187) (1818), Arrow-head rattlebox [Arrowhead rattlebox] (50) (present), Arrow-leaf crotolaria [Arrow leaved crotolaria] (42) (1814), Crazyweed [Crazy-weed, Crazy weed] (156) (1923), Hoary Virginia rattlebroom [Hoary Virginia rattle broom] (181) (~1678), Locoweed [Loco weed, Loco-weed] (5, 76, 156, 157, 158) (1896–1929) Rattlebox [Rattle box, Rattle-box] (3, 4, 5, 71, 19, 63, 72, 80, 85, 92, 93, 97, 125, 131, 156, 157, 158) (1840–1986), Rattleweed [Rattle-weed, Rattle weed] (71, 156) (1898), Wild pea (71, 74, 156, 157, 158) (1893–1929)

Croton balsamifer **Jacq.** – See *Croton flavens* L.

Croton capitatus **Michx.** – Bear's-fright [Bearfright] (7, 92) (1828–1876), Capitate croton (5, 97) (1913–1937), Goatweed [Goat's weed] (106) (1930), Hogwort [Hog wort] (5, 7, 50, 72, 92, 106, 156) (1828–present), Woolly croton [Wooly croton] (4, 106, 155) (1930–1986)

Croton capitatus **Michx.** *lindheimeri* **(Engelm. & Gray) Muell.** – Woolly croton [Wooly croton] (3, 155) (1942–1977)

Croton capitatus **Michx.** var. *capitatus* – Hogwort [Hog wort] (50) (present), Woolly croton [Wooly croton] (3) (1977)

Croton capitatus **Michx.** var. *lindheimeri* **(Engelm. & Gray) Muell.** – Lindheimer's hogwort (50) (present)

Croton corymbosus **Engelm.** – See *Croton pottsii* (Klotzsch) Muell.-Arg. var. *pottsii*

Croton corymbulosum **Rothr.** – See *Croton pottsii* (Klotzsch) Muell.-Arg. var. *pottsii*

Croton corymbulosus **Engelm. ex C. F. Wheeler** – See *Croton pottsii* (Klotzsch) Muell.-Arg. var. *pottsii*

Croton dioicus **Cav.** – Grassland croton (50) (present)

Croton flavens **L.** – Seaside balsam [Sea side balsam] (92) (1876), Small seaside balsam (92) (1876)

Croton fruticulosus **Engelm. ex Torr.** – Shrubby croton (122) (1937)

Croton glandulosus **L.** – Glandular croton (5, 72, 97) (1907–1937), Tropic croton (4) (1986), Vente conmigo (50) (present)

Croton glandulosus **L.** var. *septentrionalis* **Muell. Arg.** – Tropic croton (3) (1977), Vente conmigo (50) (present)

Croton humilis **L.** – Pepper-rod [Pepper rod] (92) (1876)

Croton **L.** – Croton (1, 4, 50, 93, 106, 158) (1900–present), Rush foil (4) (1986)

Croton lindheimerianus **Scheele** – Lindheimer's croton (5, 97) (1913–1937), Three-seed croton [Threeseed croton, Three-seeded croton] (3, 50) (1977–present)

Croton lineare – See *Croton linearis* Jacq.

Croton linearis **Jacq.** – Cascarilla bark (92) (1876), Wild rosemary (92) (1876)

Croton michauxii **G. L. Webster** – Crotonopsis (5, 97) (1913–1937)

Croton monanthogynus **Michx.** – One-seed croton [One-seeded croton] (3, 4) (1977–1986), Prairie tea (5, 50, 75, 158) (1900–present), Single-fruit croton [Single-fruited croton] (5, 97) (1913–1937)

Croton pavana **Buch.-Ham.** – See Croton tiglium L.

Croton pottsii **(Klotzsch) Muell. Arg.** – Leatherweed [Leather-weed, Leather weed] (4, 50) (1986–present)

Croton pottsii **(Klotzsch) Muell.-Arg. var.** *pottsii* – Chaparral tea (104, 107) (1896–1919), Encemilla (104, 107) (1896–1919)

Croton sebifera **L.** – See *Triadica sebifera* (L.) Small

Croton setigerus **Hook.** – Coyote weed (106) (1930), Turkey mullein (75, 106) (1894–1930) Santa Barbara Co. CA, White drought-weed [White drought weed] (106) (1930), Yerba del pescado (Spanish California) (106) (1930) used to stupefy fish

Croton texensis **(Klotzsch) Muell.-Arg.** – Croton (85, 148) (1932–1939), Skunkweed (skunk weed, skunk-weed) (5, 121, 156) (1913–1923), Texas croton (3, 4, 5, 50, 72, 93, 97, 121, 125, 131, 148, 155) (1899–present), Waxpe xča xča (Lakota, flower leaf) (121) (1918?–1970?)

Croton texensis **(Klotzsch) Muell.-Arg. var.** *texensis* – Texas croton (50) (present)

Croton willdenowii **G. L. Webster** – Crotonopsis (3) (1977), Wildenow's croton (50) (present)

Crotonopsis elliptica **Willd.** – See *Croton willldenowii* G. L. Webster

Crotonopsis linearis **Michx.** – See *Croton michauxii* G. L. Webster

Crotonopsis **Michx.** – See *Croton* L.

Crucianella **L.** – Crosswort [Cross wort, Cross-wort, Crosse woort] (109, 138) (1923–1949)

Cruciata laevipes **Opiz** – Crosswort [Cross wort, Cross-wort, Crosse woort] (178) (1526), Smooth bedstraw (50) (present)

Crunocallis chamissoi **(Ledeb. ex Spreng.) Rydb.** – See *Montia chamissoi* (Ledeb. ex Spreng.) Greene

Crunocallis chamissonis **(Ledeb.) Rydb.** – See *Montia chamissoi* (Ledeb. ex Spreng.) Greene

Crunocallis **Rydb.** – possibly *Mimosa* L. (all US species)

Crupina vulgaris **Cass.** – Common crupina (50) (present)

Cryophytum crystallinum **(L.) N.E. Br.** – See *Mesembryanthemum crystallinum* L.

Cryophytum **N.E. Br.** – possibly *Mesembryanthemum* L.

Crypsis **Ait** – Prickle grass [Prickle-grass, Pricklegrass] (50) (present), Thorn grass (24) (1817)

Crypsis **Lamarck** – See *Crypsis* Ait

Crypsis schoenoides **(L.) Lam.** – Rush cat-tail grass [Rush cat's-tail grass] (5) (1913), Rush-like timothy (5, 94) (1901–1913), Swamp prickle grass [Swamp pricklegrass] (50) (present)

Crypta minima **Nutt.** – See *Elatine americana* (Pursh) Arn.

Cryptantha cana **(A. Nels.) Payson** – Mountain cryptantha (50) (present)

Cryptantha celosioides **(Eastw.) Payson** – Butte candle [Buttecandle] (50) (present), Clustered oreocarya (5, 93, 131) (1899–1936), Sheldon cryptantha (155) (1942)

Cryptantha cinerea **(Greene) Cronq.** – James' cryptantha [James cryptantha] (50) (present)

Cryptantha cinerea **(Greene) Cronq. var.** *jamesii* **Cronq.** – James' cryptantha [James cryptantha] (3, 50, 98, 155) (1926–present), Shrubby oreocarya (5, 93, 97) (1913–1937)

Cryptantha crassisepala **(Torr. & Gray) Greene** – Rosita (5) (1913), Thick-sepal cryptantha [Thicksepal cryptantha] (3, 50) (1977–present), Thick-sepal cryptanthe [Thick-sepaled cryptanthe] (5, 122) (1913–1937), Thick-sepal cype [Thick-sepaled cype] (131) (1899)

Cryptantha fendleri **(Gray) Greene** – Fendler's cryptanthe (5) (1913), Patterson's cryptanthe (131) (1899), Sand-dune cryptantha [Sand-dune cryptantha] (50) (present), Sand-dune cryptantha [Sanddune cryptantha] (50) (present)

Cryptantha fulvocanescens **(S. Wats.) Payson var.** *fulvocanescens* – Tawny cryptantha (50) (present), Tawny oreocarya (5) (1913)

Cryptantha jamesii **(Torr.) Payson** – See *Cryptantha cinerea* (Greene) Cronq. var. *jamesii* Cronq.

Cryptantha **Lehm. ex G. Don** – Cryptantha (50, 155) (1942–present),

Cryptanthe (158) (1900), White forget-me-not [White-forget-me-nots] (75, 158) (1894–1900) Santa Barbara Co. CA

Cryptantha minima **Rydb.** – Least cryptantha (97) (1937), Little cryptantha (50) (present)

Cryptantha pattersonii **(Gray) Greene** – See *Cryptantha fendleri* (Gray) Greene

Cryptantha sericea **(Gray) Payson** – Low oreocarya (5, 93) (1913–1936)

Cryptantha sheldonii **(Brand) Payson** – See *Cryptantha celosioides* (Eastw.) Payson

Cryptantha thyrsiflora **(Greene) Payson** – Calcareous cryptantha (50) (present)

Cryptantha torreyana **(Gray) Greene** – Torrey's cryptantha (50) (present)

Cryptanthe **Lehm.** – See *Cryptantha* Lehm. ex G. Don

Cryptanthe crassisepala **(Torr. & Gray) Greene** – See *Cryptantha crassisepala* (Torr. & Gray) Greene

Cryptogramma acrostichoides **R. Br.** – American parsley-fern (109) (1949), American rockbrake [American rock-brake, American rock brake] (5, 50, 138) (1913–present)

Cryptogramma crispa **(L.) R. Br. ex Hook.** – See *Cryptogramma acrostichoides* R. Br.

Cryptogramma densa **(Brack.) Diels** – See *Aspidotis densa* (Brack.) Lellinger

Cryptogramma **R. Br.** – American rockbrake [American rock-brake, American rock brake] (50) (present), Rock brake [Rockbrake, Rock-brake] (1, 109, 138, 155, 158) (1900–1949)

Cryptogramma stelleri **(S. G. Gmel.) Prantl.** – Fragile rock brake (50) (present), Slender cliff-brake (5, 72) (1907–1913), Slender lip fern [Slender lipfern, Slender lip-fern] (131) (1899), Slender rockbrake (138) (1923)

Cryptomeria **D. Don** – Cryptomeria (138) (1923)

Cryptomeria japonica **(L. f.) D. Don** – Common cryptomeria (138) (1923)

Cryptostegia grandiflora **(Roxb. ex R. Br.) R. Br.** – Palay rubbervine (138) (1923)

Cryptostegia madagascariensis **Bojer ex Dcne.** – Madagascar rubbervine (138) (1923)

Cryptostegia **R. Br.** – Rubber vine [Rubber-vine, Rubbervine] (109, 138) (1923–1949)

Cryptotaenia canadensis **(L.) DC.** – Canadian honewort (50) (present), Canadian honeywort [Canadian honey-wort] (187) (1818), Cerfeuil sauvage (French Canadians) (41) (1770), Chervil [Cheruell] (187) (1818), Honewort [Hone wort] (1, 3, 5, 72, 85, 95, 97, 107, 131, 184) (1793–1977), Pipevine [Pipe-vine, Pipe vine] (92) (1876)

Cryptotaenia **DC.** – Honewort [Hone wort] (50, 93, 158) (1900–present)

Ctenium americanum – See *Ctenium aromaticum* (Walt.) Wood

Ctenium aromaticum **(Walt.) Wood** – Lemon grass [Lemon-grass] (5) (1913), Toothache grass [Toothache-grass] (5, 7, 45, 50, 66, 92, 94, 166) (1828–present), Wild ginger [Wildginger] (5) (1913)

Cubelium concolor **(Forst.) Raf.** – See *Hybanthus concolor* (T.F.Forst) Spreng.

Cubelium **Raf.** – See *Hybanthus* Jacq.

Cucubalus behen **L.** – See *Silene vulgaris* (Moench) Garcke

Cucubalus **L.** – See *Silene* L.

Cucubalus stellatus **L.** – possibly *Silene stellata* (L.) W.T. Aiton (taxonomic status is unresolved (PL))

Cucumis anguina **W.** – See *Trichosanthes anguina* L.

Cucumis anguira **L.** – See *Trichosanthes anguina* L.

Cucumis dipsaceus **C. G. Ehrenb. ex Spach** – Hedgehog gourd (109) (1949), Teasel gourd [Teaselgourd] (109, 138) (1923–1949)

Cucumis **L.** – Cucumber (138) (1923), Wild cowcumber (190) (~1759)

Cucumis melo dudaim – See *Cucumis melo* L.

Cucumis melo flexuosus – See *Cucumis melo* L.

Cucumis melo **L.** – Cantaloupe (50, 82, 107, 138) (1919–present), Cassaba melon (109) (1949), Ché-mĕt-a-qúis (Cuchan Yuam) (132)

(1855), Dudaim melon (109, 138) (1923–1949), Mango melon (109) (1949), Mellone (Italy) (107) (1919), Melon [Melons] (92, 106, 107, 109, 110, 138, 179) (1526–1949) possibly introduced into America by Columbus, Melone (107) (1617), Melone (Italy) (107) (1919), Meloni (Sardinia) (107) (1919), Million (107) (1919), Muskmelon [Muske-melon, Musk-melon, Muskmelon] (7, 19, 107, 109, 114, 132, 138) (1828–1949), Oriental pickling melon (109) (1949), Pepo (107) (15th Century), Pepone (107) (1617), Pepone (Italy) (107) (1919), Pompion [Pompions] (107) (1919), Pompon [Pompons] (177) (1762), Serpent cucumber (92) (1876), Serpent melon (92) (1876), Sikuos pepon (107) (1919), Snake melon (109, 138) (1923–1949), Sugar and muske melons, diuers sorts (178) (1526), Winter melon (109) (1949)

Cucumis melo L. var. *chito* Naud. – See *Cucumis melo* L.

Cucumis melo L. var. *conomon* Makino – See *Cucumis melo* L.

Cucumis melo L. var. *dudaim* Naud. – See *Cucumis melo* L.

Cucumis melo var. *chito* (Morren) Naudin – See *Cucumis melo* L.

Cucumis melo var. *conomon* (Thunb.) Makino – See *Cucumis melo* L.

Cucumis melo var. *flexuosus* Naudin – See *Cucumis melo* L.

Cucumis perennis [Gray] – See *Cucurbita foetidissima* Kunth

Cucumis sativus L. – Aggouria (Modern Greek) (110) (1886), Agurka (Bohemian) (110) (1886), Coucommer (179) (1526), Cowgourde (179) (1526), Cucumber (7, 19, 57, 82, 92, 106, 107, 109, 110, 114, 138, 184) (1793–1949), Gurke (German) (110) (1886), Krastavak (Slavic) (110) (1886), Sikua (Modern Greek) (110) (1886), Uggurits (Estonian) (110) (1886), Ukkurits (Estonian) (110) (1886)

Cucurbita (Tourn.) L. – See *Cucurbita* L.

Cucurbita aurantia – See *Cucurbita pepo* L.

Cucurbita ficifolia Bouche – Fig-leaf gourd [Figleaf gourd] (109) (1949), Fig-leaf pumpkin [Fig-leafed pumpkin] (110) (1886), Malabar gourd (109) (1949), Siamese melon (110) (1886)

Cucurbita foetidissima Kunth – American colycinth (38) (1820), Arizona gourd (156) (1923), Buffalo gourd [Buffalogourd] (3, 4, 121, 138, 155) (1923–1986), Calabazilla (5, 74, 156, 157, 158) (1893–1929) Southern CA, Chili cojote (74, 157, 158) (1893–1929) Southern CA, Fetid gourd (121) (1918?–1970?), Fetid wild pumpkin (156) (1923), Gourd [Gourde, Gowrde] (157) (1929), Missouri gourd (5, 50, 72, 93, 97, 156, 157, 158) (1900–present), Moŋkoŋ nikašiga (Osage, human being medicine) (121) (1918?–1970?), Moŋkoŋ toŋga (Osage, big medicine) (121) (1918?–1970?), Niashiga makan (Omaha-Ponca, human-being medicine) (37) (1919), Wagamun pezhuta (Dakota, pumpkin medicine) (37) (1919), Wild gourd [Wylde gourde] (37, 124) (1919–1937), Wild pumpkin (121, 156, 157, 158) (1900–1970)

Cucurbita L. – Diuers sorts of Gourds (178) (1526), Gourd [Gourde, Gowrde] (1, 50, 93, 138, 167) (1814–present), Macock [Macocks] (181) (~1678), Pumpkin [Pumpkins] (1, 82, 93, 109, 138, 156, 158, 181) (~1678–1949), Squash [Squashes] (1, 82, 93, 109, 138, 156) (1923–1949)

Cucurbita lagenaria L. – See *Lagenaria siceraria* (Molina) Standl.

Cucurbita lagenaria W. – See *Lagenaria siceraria* (Molina) Standl.

Cucurbita maxima Dcne. – Autumn squash (109) (1949), Canadian crookneck [Canada crookneck, Canada crook-neck] (158) (1900), Cashaw (110) (1886), China crook-neck (158) (1900), Crook-neck squash (158) (1900), Cushaw (110) (1886), Cushaw crook-neck (158) (1900), Gourd [Gourde, Gowrde] (110) (1886), Hubbard squash (107) (1919), Macock [Macocks] (110) (1886) early Anglo-American travelers, Marrow (107) (1919), Melon pumpkin (55) (1911), Na'bûogwis'simaün (Chippewa [flat pumpkin) (40) (1928), Pumpkin [Pumpkins] (14) (1882), Simnens (35) (1806), Squash [Squashes] (40, 82, 106, 110, 138) (1923–1930), Turban nouveau du Brésil (French) (107) (1856), Turban rouge (French) (107) (1856), Turban squash [Turban squashes] (107, 109) (1919–1949), Wàttàng (Omaha) (38) (1820), Wat-twòing (Oto) (38) (1820), Winter crook-neck squash [Winter crookneck squashes] (158) (1900), Winter squash [Winter squashes] (50, 109, 155) (1942–present), Zapilliot (107) (1919)

Cucurbita maxima subsp. *turbaniformis* (M. Roem.) Vass. – See *Cucurbita maxima* Dcne.

Cucurbita melopepo L. – See *Cucurbita pepo* L.

Cucurbita melopepo W. – possibly *Cucurbita pepo* L. var. *melopepo* (L.) Alef.

Cucurbita moschata (Duchesne ex Lam.) Duchesne ex Poir. – Canadian crookneck [Canada crookneck, Canada crook-neck] (107) (1919), Courge de la Florida (French) (107) (1919), Crane-neck (107) (1776), Crooked-neck [Crooked neck] (107) (1772), Cushaw (107, 109, 138) (1919–1949) Indian name, Ecushaw (107) (1586), Melon pumpkin (110) (1886), Musk pumpkin (110) (1886), Pompion [Pompions] (182) (1791), Pumpkin [Pumpkins] (182) (1791), Squash [Squashes] (106) (1930), Sweet pumpkin (82) (1930), Winter crookneck (107) (1919), Winter crook-neck squash [Winter crookneck squashes] (109) (1949)

Cucurbita moschata Duchesne – See *Cucurbita moschata* (Duchesne ex Lam.) Duchesne ex Poir.

Cucurbita ovifera W. – See *Cucurbita pepo* L. var. *ovifera* (L.) Alef.

Cucurbita pepo condensa – See *Cucurbita pepo* L. var. *melopepo* (L.) Alef.

Cucurbita pepo L. – Askutasquash (Northeastern Indians) (107) (1919) source of English name "squash," Calabassa (Spanish) (107) (1561), Cauwoord (Belgium, gourd) (107) (1586), Cimnel [Cimnell] (summer squash) (107, 181) (~1678–1675), Citrouilles (107) (1703), Citrulle [Cytrulle] (179) (1526), Club squash (19) (1840), Cohurden (French, gourd) (107) (1536), Common squash (92) (1876), Coucourde (gourd) (107) (1587), Courgen (France, gourd) (107) (1536), Cymling (summer squash) (107) (1803) Thomas Jefferson, Field pumpkin (50, 82, 109) (1930–present), Gourd [Gourde, Gowrde] (107, 179) (1526–1919), Idianisch apfel (German) (107) (1552), Kurbs (German, gourd) (107) (1919), Macock gourd (46) (1610), Ogwis'simaün (Chippewa) (40) (1928), Orange vine (7, 92) (1828–1876), Pepo (53, 57, 59, 60) (1902), Pompeon (107) (1683), Pompion [Pompions] (92, 158) (1876–1900), Pompon [Pompons] (107) (1822), Pumions (107) (1822), Pumpkin [Pumpkins] (7, 40, 53, 57, 58, 59, 60, 82, 92, 106, 107, 110, 121, 138, 155, 158) (1828–1942), Quaasiens (107) (1650) New Netherlands, Sitroules (107) (1605), Squash [Squashes] (7, 107, 121, 114) (1828–1919), Squoutersquashes (Northeastern Indians) (107) (1919), Symnels (summer squash) (107) (1648), Vineapple [Vine apple] (107) (1919), Wagmu (Lakota, possibly from wagmuŋ "twisted thing") (121) (1918?–1970?), Warted squash (10) (1818), Watoŋ (Osage, possibly from watoŋga "big thing") (121) (1918?–1970?) Osage have many named varieites, Wild pumpkin (124) (1937), Zucca (Italy, gourd) (107) (1919), Zucco de Peru (107) (1552), Zucco de Syria (107) (1552)

Cucurbita pepo L. var. *melopepo* (L.) Alef. – Bush squash [Bush squashes] (109) (1949), Pumpkin [Pumpkins] (109) (1949), Summer crookneck squash (138) (1923), Summer-squashes [Summersquashes] (109) (1949), possibly Flat squash (19) (1840)

Cucurbita pepo L. var. *ovifera* (L.) Alef. – Egg squash (19, 92) (1840–1876), Gourd [Gourde, Gowrde] (138) (1923), Wild gourd [Wylde gourde] (122) (1937), Yellow-flower gourds [Yellow-flowered gourds] (109) (1949)

Cucurbita pepo L. var. *pepo* – Pumpkin [Pumpkins] (37) (1919), Wagamun (Dakota Teton) (37) (1919) Omaha did not distinguish squash or pumpkin, but recognized many varieties of this species, Wamnu (Dakota) (37) (1919), Watan (Omaha-Ponca) (37) (1919)

Cucurbita perennis Gray – See *Cucurbita foetidissima* Kunth

Cucurbita polymorpha [Duchesne] – See *Cucurbita pepo* L.

Cucurbita verrucosa W. – See *Cucurbita pepo* L.

Cuminum cyminum L. – Comyn (179) (1526), Cumin (92, 107, 109, 122, 138) (1876–1949), Cumin seede (178) (1526), Cummin (92) (1876), Cummin seed (92) (1876)

Cunila L. – Cunila (50) (present), Dittany (2, 4) (1895–1986), Mountain dittany (10) (1818), Pennyroyal [Penny-royal, Penny royal, Penniroyal] (167, 184) (1814), Stonemint [Stone mint, Stone-mint] (4,

155, 158) (1900–1986)

Cunila mariana L. – See *Cunila origanoides* (L.) Britton

Cunila origanoides (L.) Britton – American dittany (5, 7, 49, 92, 122, 158) (1828–1937), Americanische Cunile (German) (7) (1828), Basil (156) (1923), Common dittany (50) (present), Cunila herba (Official name of Materia Medica) (7) (1828), Cunile d'Amerique (French) (7) (1828), Dittany (4, 19, 57, 58, 57, 58, 156, 177, 181, 184, 186) (~1678–1986), Frostweed [Frost weed, Frost-weed] (156) (1923), High pennyroyal (156, 158) (1900–1923), Maryland cunila (186) (1814), Maryland dittany (2, 109, 155) (1895–1949), Maryland stonemint (155) (1942), Mint-leaf cunila [Mint leaved cunila, Mint-leaved cunila] (42, 186) (1814), Mountain dittany (7, 49, 58, 92, 156, 158, 186) (1814–1923), Stonemint [Stone mint, Stonemint] (5, 7, 49, 58, 92, 97, 109, 138, 156, 158) (1828–1949), Sweet horse-mint [Sweet horsemint, Sweet horse-mint] (5, 7, 92, 156, 158) (1828–1923), Wild basil (5, 7, 92, 158, 186) (1814–1913), possibly Wisoccan (refers to any kind of medicine) (181) (~1678)

Cunila pulegioides L. – See *Hedeoma pulegioides* (L.) Pers.

Cunninghamia lanceolata (Lamb.) Hook. – Chinese fir [Chinese-fir] (138) (1923)

Cunninghamia R. Br. – China-fir (109, 138) (1923–1949)

Cuphea hyssopifolia Kunth – Clammy cuphea (187) (1818)

Cuphea ignea A. DC. – Fiery cuphea (138) (1923), possibly Cigar flower [Cigar-flower] (86, 109) (1878–1949)

Cuphea P. Br. – Blue waxweed [Blue wax weed] (1) (1932), Cuphea (138, 155) (1923–1942), Waxbush [Wax bush, Wax-bush] (1) (1932), Waxweed [Wax-weed] (50) (present)

Cuphea petiolata (L.) Koehne – See *Cuphea viscosissima* Jacq

Cuphea platycentra [Lem.] – possibly *Cuphea ignea* A. DC. (current species depends on author)

Cuphea viscosissima Jacq – Blue waxweed [Blue wax weed]s (3, 4, 5, 50, 86, 97, 156) (1878–present), Clammy cuphea (5, 155, 156, 158) (1900–1942), Grass-poly [Grass poly, Grass-poley, Grass poley, Grase-poley, Grass-polley, Grasspoly] (184) (1793), Tarweed [Tar weed, Tar-weed] (5, 74, 156, 158) (1893–1923) WV, Waxbush [Wax bush, Wax-bush] (5, 19, 92, 156, 158) (1840–1923), Waxweed [Wax-weed] (158) (1900)

Cupressus arizonica Greene – Arizona cypress (122, 124, 138, 153) (1913–1937), Rough-bark Arizona cypress [Rough-barked Arizona cypress] (109) (1949)

Cupressus arizonica Greene subsp. *arizonica* – Smooth Arizona cypress (109) (1949), Smooth cypress (138) (1923)

Cupressus arizonica Greene var. *bonita* Lemmon – See *Cupressus arizonica* Greene

Cupressus disticha L. – See *Taxodium distichum* (L.) L. C. Rich.

Cupressus forbesii Jepson – Blue cypress (75) (1894) CA, Guadalupe cypress (109, 138) (1923–1949) found on Guadalupe Isl. Mex., Tecate cypress (109) (1949)

Cupressus glabra Sudw. – See *Cupressus arizonica* Greene subsp. *arizonica*

Cupressus goveniana Gord. – Gowen's cypress [Gowen cypress] (109, 138) (1923–1949) for James Robert Gowen, Secr. Royal Hort Soc. 1845–1850

Cupressus guadalupensis Wats. – See *Cupressus forbesii* Jepson (found on Guadalupe Isl. Mex.)

Cupressus L. – Cyprès (French) (8) (1785), Cypress or Cypress tree [Cypress-tree, Cypresse tree] (8, 10, 20, 50, 109, 138, 167) (1785–present) from ancient Latin name

Cupressus lawsoniana – See *Chamaecyparis lawsoniana* (A. Murr.) Parl.

Cupressus macnabiana A. Murr. – Macnab's cypress [Macnab cypress] (138) (1923)

Cupressus macrocarpa Hartw. ex Gord. – Monterey cypress (75, 109, 138) (1894–1949)

Cupressus nutkatensis Hook. – See *Xanthocyparis nootkatensis* (D. Don) Farjon & D. K. Harder

Cupressus thuioides – See *Chamaecyparis thyoides* (L.) Britton, Sterns & Poggenb.

Cupressus thuyoïdes L. – See *Chamaecyparis thyoides* (L.) Britton, Sterns & Poggenb.

Curcas purgans [Medic.] – See *Jatropha curcas* L.

Curcuma longa L. – Curcuma (92) (1876)

Cuscuta (Tourn.) L. – See *Cuscuta* L.

Cuscuta americana L. – American dodder (42) (1814), Devil's-gut [Devil's gut, Devil's-guts, Devil's guts, Devil's-guts] (7, 92) (1828–1876), Dodder (7, 19, 92, 187) (1818–1876), Love vine [Love-vine] (19, 92, 187) (1818–1876), Scaldweed (92) (1876)

Cuscuta approximata Bab. – Alfalfa dodder (50, 82) (1930–present), Little-seed alfalfa dodder [Littleseed alfalfa dodder] (155) (1942)

Cuscuta arvensis Beyrich. – See *Cuscuta pentagona* Engelm. var. *pentagona*

Cuscuta cephalanthi Engelm. – Buttonbush dodder [Button-bush dodder] (3, 4, 5, 50, 72, 122) (1907–present), Buttonwood dodder (124) (1937)

Cuscuta compacta Juss. ex Choisy – Compact dodder (5, 50, 97) (1913–present), Love vine [Love-vine] (5, 73) (1892)

Cuscuta compacta Juss. ex Choisy var. *compacta* – Compact dodder (50) (present)

Cuscuta coryli Engelm. – Hazel dodder (3, 5, 50, 72, 82, 85, 93, 95, 97, 122, 124) (1907–present)

Cuscuta cuspidata Engelm. – Cusp dodder (3, 4, 50) (1977–present), Cuspidate dodder (5, 72, 93, 97) (1907–1937)

Cuscuta decora Engelm. – See *Cuscuta indecora* Choisy

Cuscuta epilinum Weihe. – Beggarweed [Beggar weed, Beggarweed] (156) (1923), Devil's-gut [Devil's gut, Devil's-guts, Devil's guts, Devil's-guts] (156) (1923), Flax dodder (5, 14, 80, 82, 156) (1882–1937), Flax vine [Flax-vine] (156) (1923), Hell-bind (156) (1923), Lover's-knot [Lover's knot] (156) (1923), Strangle tare [Strangle-tare] (156) (1923), Strangleweed [Strangle-weed] (156) (1923)

Cuscuta epithymum (L.) L. – Alfalfa dodder (68) (1913) Ottawa, Clover dodder (3, 5, 50, 62, 80, 85, 131, 155, 156, 158) (1900–present), Devil's-gut [Devil's gut, Devil's-guts, Devil's guts, Devil's-guts] (62) (1912) IN, Hailweed [Hail weed] (5) (1913), Hairweed [Hair weed, Hair-weed] (5, 156) (1913–1923) no longer in use by 1923, Hellweed [Hell-weed, Hell weed] (156) (1923), Lesser clover dodder (82) (1930), Lesser dodder (158) (1900), Lesser lucerne dodder (5, 156) (1913–1923), Lucerne dodder (45, 158) (1896–1900), Thyme dodder (5, 82, 156, 158) (1900–1930)

Cuscuta epithymum Murray – See *Cuscuta epithymum* (L.) L.

Cuscuta europaea L. – Flax drop (92) (1876), Flax vine [Flax-vine] (19, 92) (1840–1876), Flaxweed [Flax weed] (92) (1876), Hellweed [Hell-weed, Hell weed] (92) (1876), Strangle tare [Strangle-tare] (92) (1876)

Cuscuta europea – See *Cuscuta europaea* L.

Cuscuta glabrior (Engelm.) Yunck. – See *Cuscuta pentagona* Engelm. var. *glabrior* (Engelm.) Gandhi, R. D. Thomas & S. L. Hatch

Cuscuta glomerata Choisy – American dodder (5, 82, 85, 93) (1913–1936), Cluster dodder (3) (1977), Dodder (37, 46) (1610–1879), Glomerate dodder (5, 72, 95, 97, 122, 131) (1899–1937), Hakastahkata (Pawnee, yellow vine) (37) (1919), Love vine [Love-vine] (37) (1919), Rope dodder (50) (present)

Cuscuta gronovii Willd. ex J. A. Schultes – Angel's-hair [Angel's hair] (77) (1898) LA, Common American dodder (86) (1878), Common dodder (47, 62, 156) (1852–1923), Devil's-gut [Devil's gut, Devil's-guts, Devil's guts, Devil's-guts] (5, 156) (1913–1923), Goldthread [Gold-thread, Gold thread] (156) (1923), Gronovi's dodder (131) (1899), Gronovius' dodder [Gronovius dodder] (3, 4, 5, 72, 82, 155) (1907–1986), Love vine [Love-vine] (5, 86, 97, 156) (1878–1937), Onion dodder (62) (1912), Scaldweed [Scald weed, Scald-weed] (5, 50, 156) (1913–present), Wild dodder (62) (1912)

Cuscuta indecora Choisy – Big-seed alfalfa dodder [Bigseed alfalfa dodder] (50, 155) (1942–present), Dodder (85) (1932), Large alfalfa dodder (3, 4) (1977–1986), Prairie dodder (124) (1937), Pretty dodder (5, 93, 95, 97) (1911–1937)

133

Cuscuta indecora Choisy var. *neuropetala* (Engelm.) A. S. Hitchc. – Big-seed dodder [Bigseed dodder] (50) (present)

Cuscuta inflexa Engelm. – See *Cuscuta coryli* Engelm.

Cuscuta L. – Coral vine [Coral-vine, Coralvine] (1, 93) (1932–1936), Cornsilk [Corn silk] (77) (1898) Southold Long Island, Dodder [Dodyr] (1, 2, 4, 14, 50, 82, 93, 106, 158, 179, 184) (1526–present), Love vine [Love-vine] (1, 4, 73, 77, 93, 106) (1892–1986)

Cuscuta megalocarpa Rydb. – Big-fruit dodder [Bigfruit dodder] (50) (present)

Cuscuta obtusiflora Kunth – Smartweed dodder [Smartweed dodder, Smart-weed dodder] (82) (1930)

Cuscuta paradoxa Raf. – See *Cuscuta glomerata* Choisy

Cuscuta pentagona Engelm. – Field dodder (3, 4) (1977–1986), Five-angle dodder [Fiveangled dodder] (50) (present)

Cuscuta pentagona Engelm. var. *glabrior* (Engelm.) Gandhi, Thomas & Hatch – Bush-clover dodder [Bushclover dodder] (50) (present)

Cuscuta pentagona Engelm. var. *pentagona* – Dodder (145) (1897), Field dodder (5, 62, 72, 80, 82, 93, 95, 97, 131, 156) (1899–1937) Five-angle dodder [Fiveangled dodder] (50) (present), Goldthread [Gold-thread, Gold thread] (156) (1923), Love vine [Love-vine] (5, 85, 156) (1913–1932), Orabauke (46) (1610), Strangleweed [Strangle-weed] (156) (1923)

Cuscuta planiflora Ten. – See *Cuscuta approximata* Bab.

Cuscuta polygonorum Engelm. – Smartweed dodder [Smartweed dodder, Smart-weed dodder] (3, 4, 5, 50, 72, 93, 122) (1907–present)

Cuscuta rostrata Shuttlw. ex Engelm. & Gray – Beaked dodder (5) (1913)

Cuscuta squamata Engelm. – Scale-flower dodder [Scaleflower dodder] (50) (present)

Cuscuta suaveolens Ser. – Chile dodder (155) (1942), Fringed dodder (50) (present)

Cuscuta umbellata Kunth – Flat-globe dodder [Flatglobe dodder] (50) (present)

Cuthbertia graminea Small. – See *Callisia graminea* (Small) G. Tucker

Cuthbertia rosea (Vent.) Small – See *Callisia graminea* (Small) G. Tucker

Cyanococcus (Gray) Rydb. – See *Vaccinium* L.

Cyanococcus vacillans (Kalm) Rydb. – See *Vaccinium fuscatum* Aiton

Cyanopsis muricata (L.) Dostál – Spiny amberboa (138) (1923)

Cyathea Sm. – Tree fern [Treefern] (138) (1923)

Cyathus vernicosus (Bull.) DC. – Bird's-nest fungus [Birds' nest fungus] (128) (1933) ND

Cycas revoluta Thunb. – Sago cycas (138) (1923), Sago-palm (109) (1949)

Cyclachaena Fresen. – See *Iva* L.

Cyclachaena xanthifolia (Nutt.) Fresen. – See *Iva xanthifolia* Nutt.

Cyclanthera dissecta (Torr. & Gray) Arn. – Bur cucumber [Bur-cucumber, Burcucumber, Burr cucumber] (122) (1937) TX, Cut-leaf cyclanthera [Cutleaf cyclanthera] (5, 50) (1913–present), Cyclanthera (3, 4) (1977–1986)

Cyclanthera Schrad. – Cyclanthera (4, 50, 155) (1942–present)

Cycloloma atriplicifolium (Spreng.) Coult. – Cycloloma (21, 72, 131) (1893–1899), Plains tumbleweed (122) (1937), Sandhill tumbleweed [Sand-hill tumble-weed] (145) (1897), Tumble ringwing (4, 155) (1942–1986), Tumbleweed [Tumble weed, Tumble-weed] (5, 93, 96, 156) (1891–1936), Western tumbleweed (80) (1913), Winged pigweed (3, 4, 5, 50, 80, 85, 93, 97, 156) (1913–present)

Cycloloma Moq. – Cycloloma (50) (present), Ringwing (155) (1942), Tumbleweed [Tumble weed, Tumble-weed] (1, 158) (1900–1932), Winged pigweed (1, 2) (1895–1932)

Cycloloma platyphylla Moq. – See *Cycloloma atriplicifolium* (Spreng.) Coult.

Cycloma atriciplicifolium (Spreng.) Coult. – See *Cycloloma atriplicifolium* (Spreng.) Coult.

Cydonia europaea Savi – See *Cydonia oblonga* Mill.

Cydonia japonica – See *Chaenomeles japonica* (Thunb.) Lindl. ex Spach

Cydonia Mill. – Quince (138) (1923)

Cydonia oblonga Mill. – Aiva (Russian) (110) (1886), Apple (179) (1526), Armuda (Armenian) (110) (1886), Codogno (Italian) (110) (1886), Common quince (137, 138) (1923–1931), Coudougner or coing (French) (110) (1886), Cydonia (Greek) (110) (1886), Cydonium (57) (1917), Golden-apple [Golden apple] (92) (1876), Kudonea (107) (1919), Pigwa (Polish) (110) (1886), Quince (19, 54, 55, 57, 58, 92, 107, 110) (1840–1919), Quince [Quynce] (179) (1526), Quitte (German) (110) (1886), Tunja (Slavic) (110) (1886)

Cydonia sinensis – See *Pseudocydonia sinensis* (Dum.-Cours.) Schneid.

Cydonia vulgaris Pers. – See *Cydonia oblonga* Mill.

Cylindropuntia leptocaulis (DC.) F. M. Knuth – Block-head cactus [Blockhead cactus] (100) (1850) TX, Rat-tail cactus [Rattail cactus] (76) (1896) AZ

Cymbalaria cymbalaria (L.) Wettst. – See *Cymbalaria muralis* P.G. Gaertn., B. Mey. & Scherb.

Cymbalaria Hill – Basket-ivy [Basketivy] (155) (1942), Cymbalaria (50) (present), Kenilworth ivy [Kenilworthivy] (158) (1900)

Cymbalaria Medik. – See *Cymbalaria* Hill

Cymbalaria muralis P. G. Gaertn., B. Mey., & Scherb. – Aaron's-beard [Aaron's beard, Aaronsbeard] (5, 155) (1913–1942), Climbing sailor (5, 156) (1913–1923) no longer in use by 1923, Coliseum (156) (1923), Coliseum ivy (5) (1913), Ivy-leaf toadflax [Ivy-leaved toad flax, Ivy-leaved toadflax] (5, 92, 156) (1876–1923), Ivyweed [Ivy weed] (5, 156) (1913–1923), Kenilworth (5) (1913), Kenilworth ivy [Kenilworthivy] (4, 50, 107, 138, 155, 156) (1919–present), Mother-of-thousands (5, 92, 156) (1876–1923), Oxford weed (5, 156) (1913–1923), Pennywort [Penny-wort, Penny wort] (5, 107, 156) (1913–1923), Roving-sailor [Roving sailor] (5, 156) (1913–1923) no longer in use by 1923, Wandering-Jew [Wandering Jew] (5, 156) (1913–1923)

Cymbia occidentalis (Nutt.) Standley – See *Krigia occidentalis* Nutt.

Cymbidium odontorhizon [Willd.] – See *Corallorrhiza odontorhiza* (Willd.) Poir.

Cymbidium pulchellum Sw. – See *Calopogon tuberosus* (L.) Britton, Sterns & Poggenb. var. *tuberosus*

Cymbopogon citratus (DC. ex Nees) Stapf – Lemon grass [Lemongrass] (92, 109) (1876–1949)

Cymbopogon citratus Stapf. – See *Cymbopogon citratus* (DC. ex Nees) Stapf

Cymbopogon nardus (L.) Rendle – Citronella grass [Citronella-grass] (109) (1949), Citronelle oil (92) (1876)

Cymbopogon nardus Rendle – See *Cymbopogon nardus* (L.) Rendle

Cymophyllus fraseri (Andr.) Mackenzie – See *Cymophyllus fraserianus* (Ker-Gawl.) Kartesz & Gandhi

Cymophyllus fraserianus (Ker-Gawl.) Kartesz & Gandhi – Fraser's cymophyllus (50) (present), Fraser's sedge [Fraser sedge] (5, 66, 138) (1903–1923)

Cymopterus acaulis (Pursh) Raf. – Plains cymopterus (5, 97, 131) (1899–1937), Plains spring-parsley [Plains springparsley] (50) (present), Wild parsley [Wildparsley] (98) (1926) Neb

Cymopterus acaulis (Pursh) Raf. var. *acaulis* – Plains spring-parsley [Plains springparsley] (50) (present)

Cymopterus acaulis (Pursh) Rydb. – See *Cymopterus acaulis* (Pursh) Raf.

Cymopterus macrorhizus Buckl. – Big-root spring-parsley [Bigroot springparsley] (50) (present)

Cymopterus montanus Nutt. ex Torr. & Gray – Gamote (Mexican) (14, 107) (1882–1919), Mountain corkwing (3) (1977) IA, Mountain cymopterus (5, 97, 131) (1899–1937), Mountain spring-parsley [Mountain springparsley] (50) (present)

Cymopterus Raf. – Corkwing (155) (1942), Phellopterus (158) (1900), Spring-parsley [Springparsley] (50) (present)

Cynanchum L. – Anglepod [Angle pod, Angle-pod] (1) (1932), Dogbane [Dog-bane, Dog bane, Dog's bane, Dogs' bane, Dogsbane] (10) (1818), Sandvine [Sand vine, Sand-vine] (4, 158) (1900–1986),

134

Swallow-wort [Swallowwort, Swallow wort] (50, 155, 158) (1900–present)

Cynanchum laeve (Michx.) Pers. – Anglepod [Angle pod, Angle-pod] (82, 106, 156) (1923–1930), Bluevine [Blue-vine] (106, 156) (1923–1930), Climbing milkweed (4, 80, 82, 106, 156) (1923–1986), Devil's-shoestring [Devil's shoe-string, Devil's shoe string, Devil's-shoestrings, Devil's shoe-strings, Devil's shoestrings, Devil's shoe strings] (106, 156) (1923–1930), Enslen's vine (5, 156) (1913–1923), Honey vine [Honeyvine] (50) (present), Sandvine [Sand vine, Sand-vine] (3, 5, 93, 95, 97, 106, 156, 157) (1900–1977), Vine milkweed (122) (1937), Wild sweet-potato vine [Wild sweet potato vine] (106, 156) (1923–1930)

Cynanchum louiseae Kartesz & Gandhi – Black swallow-wort [Blacke swallowwoort] (4, 5, 156, 178) (1526–1986), Louis' swallow-wort (50) (present)

Cynanchum nigrum (L.) Pers. – See *Cynanchum louiseae* Kartesz & Gandhi

Cynanchum suberosum – possibly *Matelea gonocarpos* (Walt.) Shinners (current species depends on author)

Cynanchum vincetoxicum (L.) Pers. – German contrayerva (92) (1876), White swallow-wort [White swallow wort, White Swallowwoort] (92) (1876)

Cynara cardunculus L. – Artichoke (107) (1919), Cardoon (19, 92, 107, 109, 110, 138) (1840–1949), Girello (Italian) (110) (1886), Hirschuffor kerschouff (Arabic) (110) (1886), Scolimos (Greek) (110) (1886), possibly Kactos (Greek) (110) (1886), possibly Kinara (Greek) (110) (1886)

Cynara L. – Artichoke (10) (1818), Common artichoke (10) (1818)

Cynara scolymus L. – Artichoke (92, 109, 110, 138) (1876–1949), Garden artichoke (19, 92) (1840–1876)

Cynoctonum mitreola (L.) Britton – See *Mitreola petiolata* (J.F. Gmel.) Torr. & Gray

Cynoctonum succulentum R. W. Long – See *Mitreola petiolata* (J.F. Gmel.) Torr. & Gray

Cynodon dactylon (L.) Pers. – Bahama grass [Bahama-grass] (5, 109, 158) (1900–1949), Bermud grass (45) (1896), Bermuda grass [Bermudagrass, Bermuda-grass] (3, 5, 7, 10, 45, 50, 56, 66, 67, 87, 88, 90, 92, 94, 99, 109, 111, 119, 122, 138, 144, 152, 155, 158, 163) (1818–present), Cane grass (5) (1913), Dog grass [Dog's grass, Dogs-grasse] (7) (1828), Dogtooth [Dogs tooth, Dog's tooth, Dogs-tooth] (67) (1890), Dogtooth grass [Dog's tooth grass, Dog's-tooth grass, Dogtoothgrass] (5, 158) (1900–1913), Indian couch grass [Indian couch-grass] (158) (1900), Indian doob (5) (1913), Scotch grass (158) (1900), Scutch grass [Scutch-grass] (5, 45, 66, 90, 92, 158) (1876–1913), Wire grass [Wire-grass, Wiregrass] (5, 45, 163) (1852–1896)

Cynodon L. C. Rich. – Bermuda grass [Bermudagrass, Bermuda-grass] (50, 66, 158) (1900–present), Dogtooth grass [Dog's tooth grass, Dog's-tooth grass, Dogtoothgrass] (155) (1942)

Cynodon transvaalensis Burtt-Davy – African dogtooth grass (50) (present), Trasvaal dog-tooth grass [Trasvaal dogtoothgrass] (155) (1942)

Cynoglossum (Tourn.) L. – See *Cynoglossum* L.

Cynoglossum amabile Stapf & Drummond – Chinese forget-me-not (109) (1949)

Cynoglossum amplexicaule Michx. – See *Cynoglossum virginianum* L.

Cynoglossum boreale Fern. – See *Cynoglossum virginianum* L. var. *boreale* (Fern.) Cooperrider

Cynoglossum L. – Beggar's-lice [Beggar lice, Beggar-lice, Beggarlice, Beggarslice] (77) (1898) Sulphur Grove OH, Dog bur [Dog-bur] (75) (1894) WV, Hound's-tongue [Hounds-tongue, Hound's tongue, Hounds' tongue, Hondes tonge] (1, 2, 4, 7, 10, 50, 93, 107, 109, 138, 155, 156, 158, 184) (1793–present), Stickseed [Stick seed, Stickseed] (75) (1894) WV, Woolmat [Wool-mat] (75) (1894)

Cynoglossum officinale L. – Beggar's-lice [Beggar lice, Beggarlice, Beggarslice] (156) (1923), Beggarticks [Beggar ticks, Beggar's ticks, Beggars' ticks, Beggars-ticks, Beggar-ticks]

(156) (1923), Canadian bur (92, 156, 157, 158) (1876–1929), Common hound's-tongue [Common houndstongue, Common hound's tongue] (42, 138, 155, 156) (1814–1942), Dog bur [Dog-bur] (62, 75, 156, 157, 158) (1900–1929), Dog's-tongue [Dog's tongue] (156, 157, 158) (1900–1929), Gipsy flower [Gypsy flower, Gipsy-flower, Gypsyflower, Gypsy-flower] (5, 50, 62, 85, 156, 157, 158) (1900–present), Hound's-tongue [Hounds-tongue, Hound's tongue, Hounds' tongue, Hondes tonge] (3, 4, 5, 19, 45, 47, 49, 62, 63, 72, 80, 92, 106, 145, 157, 158, 178, 179) (1526–1986), Hundszunge (German) (158) (1900), Langue de chien (French) (158) (1900), Officinal houndstongue (187) (1818), Rose-noble [Rose noble] (156, 157, 158) (1900–1923) no longer in use by 1923, Sheep-lice (73, 156, 157, 158) (1892–1929) N. OH, Sticktight [Stick-tight, Sticktights, Stick-tights, Stick tights] (75) (1894) Anderson IN, Tory-bur (75) (1894) NY, possibly obsolete by 1894, Toryweed [Tory weed, Tory-weed] (19, 29, 92, 157, 158) (1840–1929), Venusfinger (German) (92) (1876), Wood-mat (156) (1923), Woolmat [Wool-mat] (62) (1912)

Cynoglossum officinalis – See *Cynoglossum officinale* L.

Cynoglossum virginianum L. – Common hound's-tongue [Common houndstongue, Common hound's tongue] (187) (1818), Dog bur [Dog-bur] (5, 156) (1913–1923), Wild comfrey (2, 3, 5, 19, 50, 80, 92, 97, 156) (1840–present)

Cynoglossum virginianum L. var. *boreale* (Fern.) Cooperrider – Northern wild comfrey (3, 4, 5) (1913–1986), Wild comfrey (50) (present)

Cynomaranthrum (Nutt.) Coult. & Rose – See *Lomatium* Raf.

Cynomarathrum nuttallii (Gray) Coult. & Rose – See *Lomatium nuttallii* (Gray) J.F. Macbr.

Cynosciadium pinnatum DC. – See *Limnosciadium pinnatum* (DC.) Math. & Const.

Cynosurus aegyptius L. – See *Dactyloctenium aegyptium* (L.) Willd.

Cynosurus cristatus L. – Crested dog's-tail [Crested dogtail] (45, 56, 66, 68, 109, 138) (1896–1949) IA NM, Crested dog's-tail grass [Crested dog's tail grass] (5, 50, 92) (1876–present), Dog-tail grass [Dog's tail grass, Dogs' tail grass, Dog's-tail grass, Dog's-tail-grass] (5, 68, 92, 94) (1876–1913), Hendon's bent grass [Hendon bent grass] (5) (1913), Leghorn straw grass (5) (1913)

Cynosurus echinatus L. – Cockscomb [Cock's comb, Cocks-comb, Cock's-comb] (92) (1876)

Cynosurus indicus L. – See *Eleusine indica* (L.) Gaertn.

Cynoxylon floridum (L.) Raf. – See *Cornus florida* L.

Cynoxylon Raf. – See *Cornus* L.

Cynthia D. Don – See *Krigia* Schreb. (all US species)

Cynthia dandelion (L.) DC. – See *Krigia dandelion* (L.) Nutt.

Cynthia virginica (L.) D. Don. – See *Krigia biflora* (Walt.) Blake var. *biflora*

Cyperus acuminatus Torr. & Hook. ex Torr. – Pointed-sedge [Pointed sedge] (66) (1903), Short-point cyperus [Short-pointed cyperus] (5, 72) (1907), Tape-leaf flatsedge [Tapeleaf flatsedge] (3) (1977), Taper-leaf flatsedge (139) (1944), Taper-leaf sedge [Taperleaf sedge] (155) (1942), Taper-tip flatsedge [Tapertip flat sedge] (50) (present)

Cyperus adenophorus Schrader – See *Cyperus haspan* L.

Cyperus aggregatus (Willd.) Endl. – Cayenne cyperus (5) (1913), Inflated-scale flatsedge [Inflatedscale flatsedge] (50) (present)

Cyperus albomarginatus (Mart. & Schrad. ex Nees) Steud. – See *Cyperus flavicomus* Michx.

Cyperus alternifolius L. – See *Cyperus involucratus* Rottb.

Cyperus bipartitus Torr. – Brook flatsedge (3, 155) (1942–1977), Nutgrass [Nutgrass, Nut grass] (85) (1932), Shining cyperus (5, 72) (1907), Slender flatsedge (50) (present)

Cyperus cayennensis (Lam.) Britton – See *Cyperus aggregatus* (Willd.) Endl.

Cyperus compressus L. – Flat cyperus (5) (1913), Flat-stem sedge [Flat stemmed sedge] (42) (1814), Poorland flatsedge (50) (present)

Cyperus croceus Vahl – Baldwin's cyperus (5) (1913), Baldwin's flatsedge (50) (present)

***Cyperus cylindricus* (Ell.) Britt.** – See *Cyperus retrorsus* Chapman var. *retrorsus*

***Cyperus dentatus* Torr.** – Small-flower cyperus galingale [Small flowered alum-root] (42) (1814), Toothed cyperus (5) (1913), Cypress-grass [Cypress grass, Cyprus grass] (5, 156) (1913–1923), Diandrus sedge (66) (1903), Galingal (5, 156) (1913–1923), Galingale (5, 156) (1913–1923), Low cyperus (5, 72, 156) (1907–1923), Low flatsedge (3) (1977), Umbrella flatsedge (50) (present)

***Cyperus difformis* L.** – Variable flatsedge (50) (present)

***Cyperus dipsaciformis* Fern.** – See *Cyperus retrofractus* (L.) Torr.

***Cyperus echinatus* (L.) Wood** – Globe flatsedge (3, 4, 50) (1977–present), Globose cyperus (5, 156) (1913–1923), Hedgehog club-rush [Hedge-hog club rush] (5, 19, 156) (1840–1923), Rough-spike mariscus [Rough spiked mariscus] (187) (1818)

***Cyperus engelmanni* Steud.** – See *Cyperus odoratus* L.

***Cyperus entrerianus* Boeckl.** – Baldwin's cyperus (5) (1913)

***Cyperus erythrorhizos* Muhl.** – Chesnut-colored sedge (129) (1894), Chestnut sedge (66) (1903), Hale's cyperus (5) (1913), Red-root cyperus [Redrooted cyperus, Red-rooted cyperus] (3, 5, 72) (1893–1977), Red-root flatsedge [Redroot flatsedge] (50) (present)

***Cyperus esculentus* L.** – Amandes de terre (French) (158) (1900), Chufa (2, 109, 138, 155, 158) (1895–1949), Chufa flatsedge (50, 155) (1942–present), Earth-almond [Earth almond] (5, 156, 158) (1900–1923), Earthnut [Earth-nut, Earth nut] (158) (1900), Edible galingale (5, 156) (1913–1923), Galingale (62) (1912) IN, Ground almond (158) (1900), Northern nut-grass [Northern nut grass] (80, 122) (1913–1937), Nut-grass [Nutgrass, Nut grass] (145, 152, 157, 158) (1897–1929), Rush nut [Rush-nut] (5, 156, 158) (1900–1923), Souchet comestible (French) (158) (1900), Straw-sedge [Straw sedge] (66) (1903), Tiger-nut (156) (1923), Tuberous cyperus galingale (42) (1814), Yellow nut-grass [Yellow nut grass] (5, 62, 72, 156) (1907–1912), Yellow nut-sedge [Yellow nutsedge] (3) (1977)

***Cyperus fendlerianus* Boeckl.** – Fendler's flatsedge (139) (1944)

***Cyperus ferax* L. C. Richard** – See *Cyperus odoratus* L.

***Cyperus ferruginescens* Boeck.** – See *Cyperus odoratus* L.

***Cyperus filicinus* Vahl.** – Fern flatsedge (50) (present), Nuttall's cyperus (5) (1913), Nuttall's sedge (66) (1903)

***Cyperus filiculmis* Vahl** – See *Cyperus lupulinus* (Spreng.) Marcks subsp. *lupulinus*

***Cyperus filiculmis* Vahl var. *oblitus* Fern. & Grisc.** – See *Cyperus grayi* Torr.

***Cyperus flavescens* L.** – Galingale (5, 156) (1913–1923), Yellow cyperus (5, 72, 156) (1907–1923), Yellow dwarf-sedge [Yellow dwarf sedge] (66) (1903), Yellow flatsedge (50) (present), Yellow-grass [Yellow grass] (19) (1840)

***Cyperus flavicomus* Michx.** – Brown sedge (66) (1903), Elegant cyperus (5) (1913), White-edge flatsedge [Whiteedge flatsedge] (50) (present)

***Cyperus flavus* (Vahl) Nees, non J. & K. Presl** – See *Cyperus aggregatus* (Willd.) Endl.

***Cyperus fuscus* L.** – Brown cyperus (5) (1913), Brown flatsedge (50) (present)

***Cyperus globulosus* Aubl.** – See *Cyperus entrerianus* Boeckl.

***Cyperus globulosus* auct. non Aubl.** – See *Cyperus croceus* Vahl

***Cyperus grayi* Torr.** – Gray's cyperus (5) (1913), Gray's flatsedge (50) (present), Gray's galingale (66) (1903)

***Cyperus halei* Torr.** – See *Cyperus erythrorhizos* Muhl.

***Cyperus hallii* Britton** – See *Cyperus setigerus* Torr. & Hook.

***Cyperus haspan* L.** – Brazilian flat-sedge (138) (1923)

***Cyperus holosericeus* Link** – See *Cyperus polystachyos* Rottb. var. *texensis* (Torr.) Fern.

***Cyperus houghtonii* Torr.** – Houghton's cyperus (5) (1913), Houghton's flatsedge [Houghton flatsedge] (50) (present)

***Cyperus huarmensis* (Kunth) M. C. Johnston** – See *Cyperus aggregatus* (Willd.) Endl.

***Cyperus hydra* [Michx.]** – See *Cyperus rotundus* L.

***Cyperus hystricinus* Fernald.** – Bristly cyperus (5) (1913), Bristly flatsedge (50) (present)

***Cyperus inflexus* Muhl.** – See *Cyperus squarrosus* L.

***Cyperus involucratus* Rottb.** – Umbrella plant [Umbrella-plant] (109) (1949), Umbrella-sedge [Umbrella sedge] (138) (1923)

***Cyperus iria* L.** – Yellow cyperus (5) (1913)

***Cyperus* L.** – Bulrush [Bull rush, Bullrush, Bul-Rush, Bulrushes] (7) (1828), Cypress-grass [Cypress grass, Cyprus grass] (10, 158) (1818–1900), Flatsedge [Flat-sedge] (50, 138, 139) (1923–present), Galingale (1, 109, 158, 184) (1793–1949), Nut-grass [Nutgrass, Nut grass] (1) (1932), Rysshe (178, 179) (1526–1596)

***Cyperus lancastriensis* Porter** – See *Cyperus lancastriensis* Porter ex Gray

***Cyperus lancastriensis* Porter ex Gray** – Lancaster cyperus (5) (1913), Many-flower flatsedge [Manyflower flatsedge] (50) (present)

***Cyperus longispicatus* J. B. S. Norton** – See *Cyperus odoratus* L.

***Cyperus lupulinus* (Spreng) Marcks** – Great Plains flatsedge (50) (present), Houghton's flatsedge [Houghton flatsedge] (3) (1977)

Cyperus lupulinus* (Spreng.) Marcks subsp. *lupulinus – Fern flatsedge (3) (1977), Great Plains flatsedge (50) (present), Slender cyperus (5, 72) (1907–1913), Wiry sedge (66) (1903)

***Cyperus lupulinus* (Spreng.) Marcks subsp. *macilentus* (Fern.) Marcks** – Bush's cyperus (5) (1913), Bush's flatsedge (139) (1944), Great Plains flatsedge (50) (present)

***Cyperus michauxianus* Schult.** – See *Cyperus odoratus* L.

***Cyperus microdontus* Torr.** – See *Cyperus polystachyos* Rottb. var. *texensis* (Torr.) Fern.

***Cyperus multiflorus* (Britt.) Small** – See *Cyperus croceus* Vahl

***Cyperus niger* Ruiz & Pavón** – Black flatsedge (50) (present)

***Cyperus nuttallii* Eddy** – See *Cyperus filicinus* Vahl.

***Cyperus obesus* Liebm.** – See *Cyperus aggregatus* (Willd.) Endl.

***Cyperus odoratus* L.** – Coarse cyperus (5) (1913), Engelmann's cyperus (5) (1913), Engelmann's flatsedge [Engelmann flatsedge] (155) (1942), Engelmann's sedge [Engelman sedge] (66) (1903), Fragrant flatsedge (50) (present), Long-spike flatsedge [Longspike flatsedge] (155) (1942), Michaux's cyperus (5, 72) (1907–1913), Michaux's sedge (66) (1903), Slender flatsedge (3) (1977)

***Cyperus officinalis* [T. Nees]** – possibly *Cyperus esculentus* L. (current species depends on author)

***Cyperus ovularis* (Michx.) Torr.** – See *Cyperus echinatus* (L.) Wood

***Cyperus paniculatus* Rottb.** – See *Cyperus polystachyos* Rottb. var. *polystachyos*

***Cyperus papyrus* L.** – Paper plant (180) (1633), Paper reed (180) (1633), Papyrus (109, 138) (1923–1949)

***Cyperus parviflorus* [Muhl.]** – See *Cyperus dentatus* Torr.

***Cyperus phymatodes* (Muhl.)** – See *Cyperus esculentus* L.

***Cyperus polystachyos* Rottb. var. *filicinus* (Vahl) C. B. Clarke** – See *Cyperus filicinus* Vahl.

***Cyperus polystachyos* Rottb. var. *macrostachyus* Boeckl.** – See *Cyperus filicinus* Vahl.

Cyperus polystachyos* Rottb. var. *polystachyos – Many-spike flatsedge [Manyspike flatsedge] (50) (present), Panicled cyperus (5) (1913)

***Cyperus polystachyos* Rottb. var. *texensis* (Torr.) Fern.** – Coast cyperus (5) (1913), Texas flatsedge [Texan flatsedge] (50) (present)

***Cyperus pseudovegetus* Steud.** – Marsh cyperus (5) (1913), Marsh flatsedge (50) (present)

***Cyperus refractus* Engelm. ex Boeckl.** – Reflexed cyperus (5) (1913), Reflexed flatsedge (50) (present)

***Cyperus retroflexus* Buckl.** – One-flower flatsedge [Oneflower flatsedge] (50, 155) (1942–present)

***Cyperus retrofractus* (L.) Torr.** – Rough cyperus (5) (1913), Rough flatsedge (50) (present)

Cyperus retrorsus* Chapman var. *retrorsus – Cylinder flatsedge (155) (1942), Pine Barren cyperus [Pine-barren cyperus] (5) (1913), Pine Barren flatsedge [Pine-barren flatsedge] (50) (present)

***Cyperus rivularis* Kunth** – See *Cyperus bipartitus* Torr.

***Cyperus rotundus* L.** – Coco-grass [Coco grass] (2, 5, 156) (1895–1923),

Nut-grass [Nutgrass, Nut grass] (2, 3, 5, 50, 66, 92, 156) (1895–present), Nutgrass flatsedge (155) (1942), Round-root [Round root] (5, 156) (1913–1923), Southern nut-grass [Southern nut grass] (122) (1937) TX

Cyperus sabulosus **Mart. & Scrad.** – See *Cyperus flavicomus* Michx.

Cyperus schweinitzii **Torr.** – Schweinitz's flatsedge [Schweinitz flatsedge] (3, 50, 155) (1942–present), Schweintiz's cyperus [Schweinitz cyperus] (5, 72) (1907–1913), Schweintiz's galingale (66) (1903)

Cyperus schweintzi – See *Cyperus schweinitzii* Torr.

Cyperus setigerus **Torr. & Hook.** – Hall's cyperus (5) (1913), Lean flatsedge (50) (present)

Cyperus speciosus **Vahl** – See *Cyperus odoratus* L.

Cyperus squarrosus **L.** – Awned cyperus (5, 72) (1907–1913), Bearded flatsedge (50, 155) (1942–present), Curve-tip flatsedge (139) (1944), Dwarf odorous galingale (66) (1903), Fragrant cyperus galingale (42) (1814), Rice-field flatsedge [Ricefield flatsedge] (50) (present)

Cyperus strigosus **L.** – Bristle-spike galingale [Bristle-spiked galingale] (66) (1903), False nutgrass (3) (1977), Ground-moss [Ground moss] (156) (1923), Lank galingale (156) (1923), Nut-grass [Nutgrass, Nut grass] (75, 156) (1894–1923) tubers eaten by children, Rough bristle-spike cyperus galingale [Rough bristle spiked cyperus galingale] (42) (1814), Straw-color cyperus [Straw-colored cyperus] (5, 72, 120, 156) (1907–1938), Straw-color flatsedge [Straw-colored flatsedge] (50) (present)

Cyperus surinamensis **Rottb.** – Tropical flatsedge (4, 50) (1986–present)

Cyperus tenuifolius **(Steud.) Dandy** – See *Kyllinga pumila* Michx.

Cyperus torreyi **Britton** – See *Cyperus retrorsus* Chapman var. *retrorsus*

Cyperus virens **Michx.** – Green flatsedge (4, 155) (1942–1986)

Cyperus virens **Michx.** – Green sedge (66) (1903)

Cypripedium acaule **Ait.** – Camel's-foot [Camel's foot] (5, 156) (1913–1923) no longer in use by 1923, Dwarf umbil (7, 86) (1828–1878), Indian mocassin (5, 156) (1913–1923), Indian slipper (78) (1898) ME, Low ladyslipper [Low ladies' slipper] (19) (1840), Moccasin flower [Mocasin flower, Mocassin flower, Moccasin-flower, Moccason flower, Mockasin flower] (5, 46, 48, 50, 156, 187) (1818–present), Nerve root [Nerve-root] (5, 73, 78, 156) (1892–1923), Noah's ark (5, 86, 156, 187) (1878–1923) no longer in use by 1923, Old-goose [Old goose] (5, 156) (1913–1923) no longer in use by 1923, Pink ladyslipper [Pink lady's slipper, Pink lady-slipper, Pink ladies' slipper] (5, 109, 138, 156) (1913–1949), Pitcherplant [Pitcher plant, Pitcher-plant] (156) (1923), Priest's-shoe [Priest's shoe] (46) (1649), Purple cypripedium (156) (1923), Purple lady's-slipper [Purple ladies' slipper, Purple ladies'-slipper, Purple lady's slipper] (5, 86) (1878–1913), Purple moccasin flower (86) (1878), Red lady's-slipper [Red ladies' slipper] (7) (1828), Squirrel's-shoes [Squirrel's shoes, Squirrels' shoes] (5, 75, 156) (1894–1923) CT, no longer in use by 1923, Stemless dwarf ladyslipper [Stemless dwarf lady's slipper] (42) (1814), Stemless ladyslipper [Stemless ladies' slipper, Stemless lady's slipper] (2, 5, 92, 156) (1876–1923), Stemless moccasin flower (86) (1878), Two-lips [Two lips] (5, 156) (1913–1923), Valerian (75, 78) (1894–1898) ME, for reported efficacy for nervous disorders, Whippoorwill [Whip-poor-will] (73) (1892), Whippoorwill-shoes [Whipoorwill shoes, Whip-poor-will's shoe, Whip-poor-will shoe, Whip-poor-will shoes, Whippoorwill's shoes, Whip-poor-will's shoes] (75, 92) (1876–1894)

Cypripedium arietinum **R. Br.** – American valerian (5, 156) (1913–1923), Ram's-head [Ramshead, Ram's-head] (5, 92) (1876–1913), Ram's-head lady's-slipper [Ram's head ladies' slipper, Ram's head lady slipper, Ram's head lady's slipper, Ramshead ladyslipper, Rams-head lady-slipper (2, 5, 50, 109, 138, 156) (1895–present), Ram's-head moccasin flower [Ram's head moccasin flower] (86) (1878)

Cypripedium calceolus **L. var. *parviflorum* (Salisb.) Fern.** – See

Cypripedium parviflorum Salisb.

Cypripedium calceolus **L. var. *planipetalum* (Fern.)** – See *Cypripedium parviflorum* Salisb. var. *pubescens* (Willd.) Knight

Cypripedium californicum **Gray** – California lady-slipper [California ladyslipper] (138) (1923)

Cypripedium candidum **Muhl. ex Willd.** – Ducks (5, 156) (1913–1923), Small white lady's-slipper [Small white lady's slipper, Small white ladies' slipper, Small white ladies'-slipper] (2, 5, 19, 72, 127, 156, 158) (1840–1933), White lady's-slipper [White lady's slipper, White ladies' slipper, White lady-slipper, White ladyslipper] (3, 7, 85, 109, 138) (1828–present), White moccasin flower (86) (1878), White umbel [White umbil] (7, 92) (1828–1876), White-foot lady's-slipper [White footed ladies' slipper] (92) (1876)

Cypripedium fasciculatum **Kellogg ex S. Wats.** – Brownie lady-slipper [Brownie ladyslipper] (138) (1923)

Cypripedium hirsutum **Mill** – See *Cypripedium reginae* Walt.

Cypripedium humile **Willd.** – possibly *Cypripedium acaule* Ait.

Cypripedium **L.** – Cypripedium (57) (1917), Ducks (75) (1894) PA, Dwarf umbil (92) (1876), Lady's-slipper [Lady's slipper, Ladies' slipper, Lady-slipper, Ladyslipper, Ladie-slipper, Lady's slippers] (1, 50, 57, 92, 93, 109, 127, 138, 155, 156, 158, 167, 184) (1793–present), Moccasin flower [Mocasin flower, Mocassin flower, Moccasin-flower, Moccason flower, Mockasin flower] (1, 2, 35, 92, 109, 181) (~1678–1949), Moccasin plant (92) (1876), Moccasin root (92) (1876), Monkey flower [Monkey-flower, Monkeyflower] (92) (1876), Ram's-head [Ramshead, Ram's-head] (1) (1932), Ram's-head lady's-slipper [Ram's head ladies' slipper, Ram's head lady slipper, Ram's head lady's slipper, Ramshead ladyslipper, Rams-head lady-slipper (1) (1932), Umbil (92) (1876), Venus'-cup [Venus' cup] (92) (1876), Venus'-shoe [Venus' shoe] (86, 92) (1876–1878), Venus'-slipper [Venus' slipper, Venus'slipper] (86) (1878), Venus'-sock [Venus' sock] (86) (1878), Whippoorwill-shoes [Whippoorwill shoes, Whip-poor-will's shoe, Whip-poor-will shoe, Whip-poor-will shoes, Whippoorwill's shoes, Whip-poor-will's shoes] (75) (1894) NY, from Indian name

Cypripedium luteum **[Ait. Ex Raf.]** – See *Cypripedium parviflorum* Salisb. var. *parviflorum*

Cypripedium luteum **[Raf.]** – See *Cypripedium parviflorum* Salisb. var. *parviflorum*

Cypripedium montanum **Dougl. ex Lindl.** – Lady's-slipper [Lady's slipper, Ladies' slipper, Lady-slipper, Ladyslipper, Ladie-slipper, Lady's slippers] (35) (1806), Moccasin flower [Mocasin flower, Mocassin flower, Moccasin-flower, Moccason flower, Mockasin flower] (35) (1806), Mountain lady's-slipper [Mountain lady's slipper, Mountain ladyslipper] (50, 138) (1923–present)

Cypripedium parviflorum **Salisb.** – Common lady's-slipper [Common ladies' slipper] (19) (1840), Downy lady's-slipper [Downy ladies' slipper, Downy ladies'-slipper, Downy lady's slipper] (5, 97, 156) (1913–1937), Ducks (5, 156) (1913–1923), Indian shoe (5, 156) (1913–1923), K'kwĕ ulasu'la (Cherokee, partridge mocassin) (102) (1885), Lady's-slipper [Lady's slipper, Ladies' slipper, Lady-slipper, Ladyslipper, Ladie-slipper, Lady's slippers] (55, 64, 102) (1886–1911), Lesser yellow lady's-slipper [Philotria minor (Engelm.) Small.] (50) (present), Male nervine (156) (1923), Monkey flower [Monkey-flower, Monkeyflower] (156) (1923), Slipper root [Slipper-root] (5, 156) (1913–1923), Small yellow lady's-slipper [Small yellow lady's slipper, Small yellow ladies' slipper, Small yellow ladies'-slipper] (64, 72, 127, 157, 158) (1900–1937), Smaller yellow lady's-slipper [Smaller yellow lady's slipper] (2) (1895), Small-flower lady's-slipper [Small-flowered ladies' slipper] (42, 53) (1814–1922), Venus'-cup [Venus' cup] (156) (1923), Venus'-shoe [Venus' shoe] (156) (1923), Whippoorwill-shoes [Whipoorwill shoes, Whip-poor-will's shoe, Whip-poor-will shoe, Whip-poor-will shoes, Whippoorwill's shoes, Whip-poor-will's shoes] (5, 156) (1913–1923), Yellow downy lady's-slipper [Yellow

brittle bladderfern] (50) (present)

Cytherea bulbosa **(L.) House.** – See *Calypso bulbosa* (L.) Oakes var. *americana* (R. Br. ex Ait. f.) Luer

Cytherea **Salisb.** – See *Calypso* Salisb. (all US species)

Cytisus ×racemosus **Nichols.** – See *Genista canariensis* L.

Cytisus cajan – See *Cajanus cajan* (L.) Millsp.

Cytisus canariensis **[(L.) Kuntze]** – See *Genista canariensis* L.

Cytisus **Desf.** – Broom (106, 138, 156) (1923–1930)

Cytisus laburnum **L.** – See *Laburnum anagyroides* Medik.

Cytisus maderensis – See *Genista stenopetala* Webb & Berth.

Cytisus multiflorus **(L'Hér.) Sweet** – White Spanish broom (109, 138) (1923–1949)

Cytisus proliferus **L.f.** – See *Chamaecystis prolifera* (L. f.) Link

Cytisus racemosus – See *Genista canariensis* L.

Cytisus scoparius **(L.) Link** – Bannal (5) (1913), Besom (5, 156) (1913–1923), Brome (179) (1526), Broom (5, 49, 52, 53, 57, 59, 60, 107) (1898–1919), Broom herb (92) (1876), Broomflower [Broom flowers] (92) (1876), Broomtops [Broom tops] (49, 53, 55, 58) (1911–1922), Common broom (59) (1911), Genesta (Italian & German) (59) (1911), Ginster (156) (1923), Green broom (5, 156) (1913–1923), Hagweed (5) (1913), Irish broom (49, 53, 92) (1876–1922), Scoparius (52) (1919), Scotch broom (5, 19, 106, 107, 138, 156) (1840–1930)

Cytisus triflorus **(L'Her.)** – See *Cytisus villosus* Pourret

Cytisus villosus **Pourret** – Greek broom (138) (1923)

Cytisus scoparius (L.) Link [as *Sarothamnus scoparius* (L.) Koch]
(O.W. Thomé, 1885)

D

Dacryodes excelsa **Vahl** – Caranna (92) (1876)

Dactylis glomerata **L.** – American cock's foot (56, 66) (1901–1903), Cock's-foot [Cocksfoot, Cocks-foot, Cock's foot, Cock-foot] (5, 45, 46, 68, 109, 143) (1896–1949), Cock's-foot grass [Cocksfoot grass, Cocks' foot grass, Cock's-foot-grass, Cock's foot-grass] (19, 87, 90, 92, 119, 184) (1793–1938), Dew grass (5, 92) (1876–1913), Hard grass [Hardgrass] (5, 92) (1876–1913), Orchard grass [Orchardgrass, Orchard-grass] (3, 5, 10, 11, 21, 45, 46, 50, 56, 66, 67, 68, 72, 85, 87, 88, 90, 92, 94, 109, 111, 119, 125, 129, 138, 140, 143, 155, 163, 187) (1818–present), Rough cock's-foot [Rough cock's foot] (66, 90, 92) (1885–1903) ME, England, Rough grass (92) (1876)

Dactylis glomerata **L. subsp.** *glomerata* – Orchard grass [Orchardgrass, Orchard-grass] (50) (present)

Dactylis **L.** – Cock's-foot [Cocksfoot, Cocks-foot, Cock's foot, Cock-foot] (66, 155) (1903–1942), Orchard grass [Orchardgrass, Orchard-grass] (50, 93, 138, 155) (1923–present)

Dactyloctenium aegyptium **(L.) Willd.** – Crabgrass [Crab-grass, Crab grass] (5) (1913), Crowfoot [Crow-foot, Crow foot, Crowfote, Crow's foot] (5) (1913), Crowfoot grass [Crow-foot-grass, Crowfoot-grass] (94, 163) (1852–1901), Egyptian grass [Egyptian-grass] (5, 50, 66, 92, 163) (1852–present), Finger-comb grass (5) (1913), Yard grass [Yard-grass, Yardgrass] (5) (1913)

Dactyloctenium radulans **(R. Br.) Beauv.** – possibly Comb fringe grass (92) (1876)

Dactylorhiza **Neck. ex Nevski** – possibly Fool's-stones [Fools' stones, Fooles stone, Fool-stone] (184) (1793), possibly Orchis (1) (1930), possibly Salep (7) (1828), possibly Twinroot (7) (1828)

Dahlia **Cav.** – Dahlia (82, 138) (1923-930)

Dahlia gracilis **Ortgies** – See *Dahlia coccinea* Cav.

Dahlia pinnata **Cav.** – Aztec dahlia (138) (1923), Common dahlia (82, 109) (1930–1949), Dahlia (92, 107) (1876–1919), Garden dahlia (109) (1949), Old garden dahlia (138) (1923)

Dahlia rosea – See *Dahlia pinnata* Cav.

Dahlia variabilis **Desf.** – See *Dahlia pinnata* Cav.

Dalbergia **L. f.** – Rosewood [Rose wood] (138) (1923)

Dalbergia sissoo **Roxb. ex DC.** – Sissoo (138) (1923)

Daldinia concentrica **(Bolton) Ces. & De Not.,** Spherical black fungus (128) (1933)

Dalea alopecuroides **Willd.** – See *Dalea leporina* (Aiton) Bullock

Dalea aurea **Nutt. ex Pursh** – Golden parosela (5, 85, 93, 97, 131) (1899–1937), Golden prairie-clover [Golden prairie clover] (4, 50) (1986–present), Pezhuta pa (Dakota, bitter medicine) (37) (1919), Silk-top dalea [Silktop dalea] (3, 155) (1942–1977)

Dalea candida **Michx. ex Willd.** – Prairie clover [Prairieclover] (156) (1923), White tassel-flower [White tassel flower] (5, 76, 156) (1896–1923) Southwestern MO, Small-leaf petalostemum [Small-leafed petalostemum] (124) (1937)

Dalea candida **Michx. ex Willd. var.** *candida* – Prairie clover [Prairieclover] (85) (1932), White prairie clover [White prairieclover] (3, 4, 5, 50, 65, 72, 82, 93, 97, 98, 114, 131, 138, 155) (1894–present)

Dalea candida **Michx. ex Willd. var.** *oligophylla* **(Torr.) Shinners** – Pussyfoot [Pussy foot, Pussy's foot] (122, 124) (1937), Slender white prairie clover [Slender white prairieclover] (5, 93, 97, 155) (1913–1942), Western prairie clover (3) (1977), White prairie clover [White prairieclover] (50, 85) (1932–present)

Dalea compacta **Spreng.** – Compact prairie clover (50) (present), Dense-flower prairie clover [Dense-flowered prairie clover] (131) (1899)

Dalea compacta **Spreng. var.** *compacta* – Tennessee prairie clover [Tennessee prairieclover] (138) (1923)

Dalea cylindriceps **Barneby** – Andean prairie clover (50) (present), Compact prairie clover (3) (1977), Dense-flower prairie clover [Dense-flowered prairie clover] (5, 93) (1913–1936), Massive-spike prairie clover [Massive spike prairie clover] (4) (1986)

Dalea enneandra **Nutt.** – Nine-anther dalea (3) (1977), Nine-anther prairie clover [Nineanther prairie clover] (4, 50) (1986–present), Slender parosela (5, 72, 93, 97, 131) (1899–1936)

Dalea foliosa **(Gray) Barneby** – Leafy prairie clover (5, 72) (1907–1913), possibly Prairie clover [Prairieclover] (2) (1895)

Dalea formosa **Torr.** – Feather dalea (155) (1942), Feather-plume [Featherplume, Feather plume] (4, 50) (1986–present)

Dalea frutescens **Gray** – Black dalea (4, 155) (1942–1986), Black prairie clover (50) (present)

Dalea jamesii **(Torr.) Torr. & Gray** – James' dalea [James dalea] (3, 4, 155) (1942–1986), James' parosela (97) (1937), James' prairie clover (50) (present)

Dalea **L.** – Dalea (106, 155) (1930–1942), Parosela (158) (1900), Prairie clover [Prairieclover] (50) (present)

Dalea lanata **Spreng.** – Woolly dalea (3) (1977), Woolly parosela (5, 97) (1913–1937), Woolly prairie clover (50) (present)

Dalea leporina **(Aiton) Bullock** – Foxtail dalea (4, 155) (1942–1986), Foxtail prairie clover (50) (present), Parosela (80) (1913), Pink parosela (5, 72, 80, 85, 93, 131) (1899–1936)

Dalea multiflora **(Nutt.) Shinners** – Prairie clover [Prairieclover] (93, 156) (1923–1936), Round-head prairie clover [Roundhead prairie clover, Roundheaded prairie clover, Round-headed prairie clover, Roundheaded prairieclover] (3, 4, 50) (1977-prsent)

Dalea nana **Torr. ex Gray** – Dwarf dalea (3, 4, 155) (1942–1986), Low parosela (5, 97) (1913–1937)

Dalea obovata **(Torr. & A. Gray) Shinners** – Pussyfoot [Pussy foot, Pussy's foot] (122, 124) (1937) TX, Round-head prairie clover [Roundhead prairie clover, Roundheaded prairie clover, Round-headed prairie clover, Roundheaded prairieclover] (5, 93, 97, 155) (1913–1942)

Dalea phleoides **(Torr. & Gray) Shinners var.** *microphylla* **(Torr. & Gray) Barneby** – Red tassel-flower [Red tassel flower] (101) (1905), Small-leaf petalostemum [Small-leafed petalostemum] (124) (1937)

Dalea pinnata **(J. F. Gmel.) Barneby var.** *pinnata* – Pine Barren prairie clover [Pine-barren prairie clover] (106) (1930), Summer-farewell [Summer farewell] (106) (1930) because of late blooming

Dalea purpurea **Vent.** – Prairie clover [Prairieclover] (22) (1893), Purple prairie clover [Purple prairieclover] (4, 72, 95, 98, 114) (1894–1986), Red tassel-flower [Red tassel flower] (76) (1896), Violet prairie clover (50, 131) (1899–present)

Dalea purpurea **Vent. var.** *arenicola* **(Wemple) Barneby** – Violet prairie clover (50) (present)

Dalea purpurea **Vent. var.** *purpurea* – Ba'sibûgûk' (Chippewa, small leaves) (40) (1928), Kahts-pidipatski (Pawnee, small medicine) (37) (1919), Kiha piliwus hawastat (Pawnee, broom weed) (37) (1919), Makan skithe [Makan-skithe] (Omaha-Ponca, sweet medicine) (37) (1919), Prairie clover [Prairieclover] (1, 63, 82, 106, 127, 138, 155, 156) (1899–1942), Purple clover (93) (1936), Purple prairie clover [Purple prairieclover] (3, 5, 37, 82, 85, 97, 121, 155) (1913–1977), Red tassel-flower [Red tassel flower] (5, 156) (1913–1923), Thimbleweed [Thimble weed, Thimble-weed] (5, 156) (1913–1923), Tokala tapežuta hu wiŋjela (Lakota, female fox-medicine plant) (121) (1918?–1970?), Violet clover (93) (1936), Violet prairie clover (5, 50) (1913–present), Wanah'cha (Dakota) (37) (1919)

Dalea spinosa **[Gray]** – See *Psorothamnus spinosus* (Gray) Barneby

Dalea tenuifolia **(Gray) Shinners** – Prairie clover [Prairieclover] (40) (1928), Silky prairie clover [Silky prairieclover] (5, 72, 97)

(1907–1937), Slim-leaf prairie clover [Slimleaf prairie clover] (3, 4, 50) (1977–present)

Dalea villosa (**Nutt.) Spreng** – Blaje zitkatačaŋ hu stola (Lakota, little wild tea of the plains) (121) (1918?–1970?), Hairy prairie clover (5, 93, 95, 97, 121, 131) (1899–1970), Silky prairie clover [Silky prairieclover] (3, 4, 5, 50, 85, 93, 138, 155) (1932–present)

Dalibarda **L.** – Dalibarda (138) (1923), False violet (156) (1923)

Dalibarda repens **L.** – Creeping strawberry (156) (1923), Dalibarda (5, 138) (1913–1923), Dewdrop [Dew drop] (5, 74, 156) (1893–1923) NY, False violet (19, 156) (1840–1923), Franklin's plant [Franklin plant] (76) (1896) Oxford Co ME, Heart-leaf dalibarda [Heart leaved dalibarda] (42) (1814), Robin-run-away [Robin runaway, Robin run away] (5, 76, 156) (1896–1923) Oxford Co ME, Spiceroot [Spice root] (19) (1840), Star violet (156) (1923)

Dammara robusta – See *Agathis robusta* (C. Moore ex F. Muell.) Bailey

Danthonia allenii **Austin** – See *Danthonia compressa* Austin ex Peck

Danthonia californica **Boland.** – California oat grass (87) (1884)

Danthonia compressa **Austin ex Peck** – Flattened oat grass [Flattened oatgrass] (50) (present), Flattened wild oat grass (5) (1913), Mountain oat grass (87, 88) (1884–1885), Tennesoat grass (5) (1913), Tennessee oat grass [Tennessee oat-grass] (94) (1901)

Danthonia **DC.** – Danthonia (155) (1942), Oat grass [Oatgrass, Oatgrass] (50) (present), Wild oat grass [Wild oat-grass, Wild oats grass] (1, 92, 93, 152) (1912–1936)

Danthonia decumbens **(L.) DC.** – Common heath grass [Common heathgrass] (50) (present), Heath grass (5) (1913), Heather grass [Heather-grass] (5, 94) (1901–1913)

Danthonia epilis **Scribn.** – Carolina oat grass [Carolina oatgrass] (50) (present), Smooth wild oat grass (5) (1913)

Danthonia intermedia **Vasey** – Timber danthonia (140, 155) (1942–1944), Timber oat grass [Timber oatgrass] (3, 50, 140) (1944–present), Vasey's wild oat grass (5) (1913)

Danthonia parryi **Scribn.** – Parry's danthonia [Parry danthonia] (140) (1944), Parry's oatgrass [Parry oatgrass] (140) (1944)

Danthonia sericea **Nutt.** – Downy danthonia (50) (present), Silky oat grass [Silky oat-grass], Silky wild oat grass (5) (1913), Silky-flower oat grass [Silky-flowered oat grass] (87) (1884)

Danthonia sericea **Nutt. var. epilis (Scribn.) Blomquist** – See *Danthonia epilis* Scribn.

Danthonia spicata **(L.) Beauv. ex Roemer & J. A. Schultes** – June grass [June-grass, Junegrass] (75, 90) (1885–1894), Old-fog [Old fog] (66, 75, 90) (1885–1903), Poverty danthonia (155) (1942), Poverty grass [Poverty-grass, Povertygrass] (143) (1936), Poverty oat grass [Poverty oat-grass, Poverty oatgrass (3, 50, 122, 143) (1936–present), Spiked oat grass (42) (1814), Spiked wild oat grass (87, 90) (1884–1885), Whitetop [White top, White-top] (66, 90) (1885–1903), Wild oat [Wild oats] (19) (1840), Wild oat grass [Wild oatgrass, Wild oats grass] (56, 66, 85, 90, 94, 119, 143) (1885–1938), Wire grass [Wire-grass, Wiregrass] (90) (1885) ME, Witch grass [Witch-grass, Witchgrass] (78) (1898) ME

Danthonia unispicata **(Thurb.) Munro ex Macoun** – One-spike danthonia [Onespike danthonia] (50) (present)

Daphne **L.** – Daphne (138) (1923) Greek name for Laurus nobilis

Daphne laureola **L.** – Spurge laurel (92) (1876), Spurge-laurel [Spurgelawrel] (109) (1949), Layreole (179) (1526)

Daphne mezereum **L.** – Dwarf bay [Dwarfe Bay] or Dwarf bay tree [Dwarfe Bay tree] (5, 156, 178) (1526–1923), February daphne (138) (1923), Flax-olive (156) (1923), Lady laurel (5, 156) (1913–1923), Mezerei cortex (49) (1898), Mezereon (19, 41, 49, 55, 57, 60, 92, 156) (1770–1923), Mezereum (57, 59, 60, 156) (1902–1917), Mysterious plant (5, 156) (1913–1923) no longer in use by 1923, Paradise plant [Paradise-plant] (5, 156) (1913–1923) no longer in use by 1923, Spurge flax (5, 92) (1876–1913), Spurge laurel (5, 156) (1913–1923), Spurge-olive [Spurge olive] (5, 92, 156) (1876–1923), Wild pepper (5, 92, 156)

Daphnopsis americana **(Mill.) J. R. Johnst. (possibly)** – Noseburn tree (92) (1876)

Daphnopsis tenuifolia – possibly *Daphnopsis americana* (Mill.) J. R. Johnst.

Daphnopsis tinifolia **Griseb.** – possibly *Daphnopsis americana* (Mill.) J. R. Johnst.

Darlingtonia californica **Torr.** – California pitcher plant [Californian pitcher plant, Californian pitcherplant] (14, 138) (1882–1923), Saddle flower (92) (1876)

Darmera peltata **(Torr. ex Benth.) Voss** – Umbrella plant [Umbrellaplant] (109) (1949), Umbrella saxifrage (138) (1923)

Dasiphora floribunda **(Pursh) Kartesz** – American shrubby cinquefoil (8) (1785), Bush cinquefoil (155) (1942), Cinquefoil [Cink-foil, Cinque-foil] (112) (1937), Hardhack [Hard-hack] (5, 76, 156, 158) (1896–1923) MA, Kouril-skoi-tchai (Siberia "Kurile tea") (107) (1919), Prairie weed [Prairie-weed] (5, 156, 158) (1900–1923), Quinte-feuille en arbrisseau (French) (8) (1785), Shrubby cinquefoil [Shrubby cinque-foil] (2, 3, 5, 19, 38, 50, 72, 82, 85, 86, 107, 108, 130, 131, 138, 153, 156, 158) (1840–present), Yellow rockrose [Yellow rock-rose] (156) (1923)

Dasiphora fruticosa **(L.) Rydb.** – See *Dasiphora floribunda* (Pursh) Kartesz

Dasiphora **Raf.** – Shrubby cinquefoil [Shrubby cinque-foil] (1) (1932), Yellow rose (1) (1932)

Dasistoma flava **(L.) Wood.** – See *Aureolaria flava* (L.) Farw. var. *flava*

Dasistoma macrophylla **(Nutt.) Raf.** – Mullein false foxglove (156) (1923), Mullein foxglove [Mullen foxglove] (2, 3, 5, 50, 63, 93, 157, 158) (1895–present)

Dasistoma pedicularia **(L.) Benth.** – See *Aureolaria pedicularia* (L.) Raf. var. *pedicularia*

Dasistoma **Raf.** – Dasistoma (50) (present), False foxglove (158) (1900), Mullein foxglove [Mullen foxglove] (1, 4) (1932–1986)

Dasistoma virginica **(L.) Britton** – See *Aureolaria virginica* (L.) Pennell

Dasylirion graminifolium **[(Zuc.) Zucc.]** – See *Yucca whipplei* Torr. var. *whipplei*

Dasylirion texanum **Scheele** – Sotol (122, 124) (1937)

Dasylirion wheeleri **S. Wats.** – Bear-grass [Bear grass, Bear's grass, Bears' grass] (78, 151) (1896–1898) AZ NM, Wheeler's sotol [Wheeler sotol] (138) (1923), possibly Sotol (149, 151, 153) (1896–1913)

Dasylirion whelleri – See *Dasylirion wheeleri* S.Watson ex Rothr.

Dasylirion **Zucc.** – Sotol (106, 138) (1923–1930)

Dasyochloa pulchella **(Kunth) Willd. ex Rydb.** – Fluff grass (122) (1937) TX

Dasypyrum villosum **(L.) P. Candargy** – Tufted rye (66) (1903)

Dasystephana **Adans.** – See *Gentiana* L.

Dasystephana affinis **(Griseb.) Rydb.** – See *Gentiana affinis* Griesb.

Dasystephana andrewsii **(Griseb.) Small.** – See *Gentiana andrewsii* Griseb.

Dasystephana flavida **(Gray) Britton** – See *Gentiana alba* Muhl. ex Nutt.

Dasystephana grayi **(Kusnezow) Britton** – See *Gentiana rubricaulis* Schwein.

Dasystephana linearis **(Froel.) Britton** – See *Gentiana linearis* Froel.

Dasystephana parvifolia **(Chapman) Small.** – See *Gentiana catesbaei* Walt.

Dasystephana porphyrio **(J. F. Gmel.) Small.** – See *Gentiana autumnalis* L.

Dasystephana puberula **(Michx.) Small.** – See *Gentiana puberulenta* J. Pringle

Dasystephana saponaria **(L.) Small.** – See *Gentiana saponaria* L. var. *saponaria*

Dasystephana villosa **(L.) Small.** – See *Gentiana villosa* L.

Dasystoma grandiflora **(Benth.) Wood.** – See *Aureolaria grandiflora* (Benth.) Pennell ((Dasistoma))

Dasystoma laevigata **Raf. (Dasistoma)** – See *Aureolaria laevigata* (Raf.) Raf.

Dasystoma pedicularia (**L.**) **Benth.** – See *Aureolaria pedicularia* (L.) Raf. var. *pedicularia*

Dasystoma **Raf.** – See *Dasistoma* Raf.

Dasystoma serrata (**Benth.**) **Small.** – See *Aureolaria grandiflora* (Benth.) Pennell var. *serrata* (Torr. ex Benth.) Pennell ((Dasistoma))

Dasystoma virginica (**L.**) **Britton** – See *Aureolaria virginica* (L.) Pennell

Datisca hirta **L.** – See *Rhus hirta* (L.) Sudworth

Datisca **L.** – Bastard hemp [Bastard-hemp] (167) (1814)

Datura alba – See *Datura metel* L.

Datura arborea **L.** – See *Brugmansia candida* Pers.

Datura fastuosa [**auct. non L.**] – See *Datura inoxia* P. Mill.

Datura inoxia **P. Mill.** – Apple-of-Peru [Apple of Peru, Appleofperu] (180) (1633), Cornucopia floripondio (138) (1923), Entire-leaf thorn-apple [Entire leaf thorn apple, Entire-leaved thorn apple, Entire-leaved thorn-apple] (5) (1913), Henbane of Peru (180) (1633), Indian apple [Indian-apple, Indian-apples] (4) (1986), Jamestown-weed [Jamestown weed] (77) (1898), Main-oph-weep (6) (1892), Paracoculi (Italian) (180) (1633), Prickly bur [Pricklyburr] (50) (present), Sacred datura (138, 155) (1923–1942), Thorn-apple [Thorn apple, Thornapple, Thorn apples, Thorne Apple] (77) (1898), Toloachi (Spanish) (104) (1896)

Datura **L.** – Datura (138, 155) (1923–1942), Jamestown-weed [Jamestown weed] (1, 10) (1818–1932), Jimsonweed [Jimson-weed, Jimson weed] (1, 50, 156) (1923–present), Stramonium (1, 18) (1805–1932), Thorn-apple [Thorn apple, Thornapple, Thorn apples, Thorne Apple] (1, 4, 10, 156, 158) (1818–1986), Thorny-apple [Thornie-apples] (180) (1633)

Datura metel **auct. non L.** – See *Datura inoxia* P. Mill.

Datura metel **L.** – Downy thornapple (107) (1919), Entire-leaf thorn-apple [Entire leaf thorn apple, Entire-leaved thorn apple, Entire-leaved thorn-apple] (97, 124) (1937), Hindu datura (138, 155) (1931–1942), Indian datura (92) (1876), Smooth thorn-apple [Smooth thorne apples] (178) (1526), Toloachi (Spanish) (123) (1856)

Datura meteloides **DC.** – See *Datura inoxia* P. Mill.

Datura quercifolia **Kunth** – Chinese thorn-apple [Chinese thornapple] (50) (present), Oak-leaf datura [Oakleaf datura] (155) (1942), Oak-leaf thorn-apple [Oak leaf thorn apple] (4, 124) (1937–1986), Toloachi (104) (1896)

Datura stramonium **L.** – Angel's trumpet-flower [Angel's trumpet flower] (106) (1930), Apple-of-Peru [Apple of Peru, Appleofperu] (6, 49, 69, 71, 157, 158) (1892–1929), Blue thornapple [Blue thorn apple] (42) (1814), Common stramonium (71) (1898), Common thorn-apple [Common thorn apple] (7, 42, 80) (1814–1913), Datura (57) (1917), Devil's-apple [Devil's apple] (5, 6, 62, 69, 71, 92, 156, 157, 158) (1892–1929), Devil's-trumpet [Devil's trumpet] (5, 69, 156, 158) (1900–1929), Dewtry (5, 69, 156, 158) (1900–1923) no longer in use by 1923, Doranapfel (German) (158) (1900), Estramonio (Spanish) (158) (1900), Fireweed [Fire weed, Fire-weed] (5, 69, 156, 158) (1900–1923), Gemeine Stechappel (German) (7) (1828), Green thorn-apple [Green thorn apple] (19) (1840), Jamestown lily (5, 69, 71, 75, 156, 158) (1894–1923), Jamestown-weed [Jamestown weed] (5, 6, 42, 49, 52, 53, 54, 59, 61, 69, 71, 92, 106, 109, 156, 157, 158, 187) (1814–1949), James-weed [James weed] (18) (1805), Jimpson seed (92) (1876), Jimsonweed [Jimson-weed, Jimson weed] (3, 4, 5, 6, 49, 50, 52, 53, 57, 59, 62, 63, 69, 71, 72, 73, 80, 85, 92, 97, 106, 109, 124, 125, 148, 156, 157) (1892–present), Jimsonweed datura (155) (1942), L'endormie (French) (6) (1892), Mad-apple [Mad apples, Mad-apples] (5, 6, 69, 71, 92, 156, 158) (1892–1923), Night-blooming cactus (71) (1898) trade name, Pear-apple (6) (1892), Peru-apple [Peru apple] (5, 156) (1913–1923), Pomme épineuse (French) (6, 158) (1892–1900), Purple jimson (62) (1912), Purple jimsonweed [Purple jimson weed] (80, 145) (1897–1913), Purple stramonium (80, 92, 158) (1876–1913), Purple thorn-apple [Purple thornapple, Purple thorn apple] (19, 62, 69, 72, 80, 156, 158) (1840–1913, 1923), Purple-stem jimson weed [Purple-stemmed jimson weed] (71) (1898), Sinkweed (6, 7, 49) (1828–1898), Steckapfel (German) (6, 156) (1892–1923), Stink (158) (1900), Stink-apple (157) (1929), Stinkweed [Stink-weed, Stink weed] (69, 71, 75, 156, 157, 158) (1898–1929), Stinkwort (69, 71, 92) (1876–1904), Stramoine (French) (158) (1900), Stramoine vulgaire (French) (7) (1828), Stramonium (5, 18, 52, 53, 55, 59, 60, 92, 156, 158, 187) (1805–1923), Stramonium (Official name of Materia Medica) (7) (1828), Stramony (6) (1892), Tatula (174) (1753), Thorn-apple [Thorn apple, Thornapple, Thorn apples, Thorne Apple] (5, 6, 14, 41, 49, 53, 57, 60, 62, 63, 69, 71, 92, 93, 156, 157, 158, 178, 184, 187) (1526–1936), Thorny apples-of-Peru [Thorny apples of Peru] (180) (1633), Toloache (Spanish) (158) (1900), White jimsonweed [White jimson weed] (145) (1897), White-man's-plant [White man's plant] (7, 71) (1828–1898), Wild datura (106) (1930)

Datura suaveolens [**Humb. & Bonpl. ex Willd.**] – See *Brugmansia suaveolens* (Humb. & Bonpl. ex Willd.) Bercht. & K. Presl

Datura tatula **L.** – See *Datura stramonium* L.

Datura wrightii **Regel** – Sacred thorn-apple (50) (present), Sweet-scented datura [Sweet scented datura] (92) (1876)

Daucus (**Tourn.**) **L.** – See *Daucus* L.

Daucus carota **L.** – Bee's-nest [Bee's nest] (157) (1929), Bee's-nest plant [Beesnest plant] (92, 158) (1876–1900), Bird's-nest [Bird's nest, Birds-nest, Birds nest, Birds' nest, Birdsnest] (62, 75, 76, 156) (1896–1923), Bird's-nest plant [Bird's nest plant, Birds' nest plant] (106, 156, 157, 158) (1900–1930), Bird's-nest root [Birds' nest root] (92) (1876), Carota (57) (1917), Carotte (French) (158) (1900), Carrot [Carot] (62, 106, 107, 184) (1793–1930), Common carrot (138) (1923), Crow's-nest (57, 156) (1917–1923) obsolete by 1923, Dawke (157, 158, 179) (1526–1929), Devil's-plague [Devil's plague] (62, 75, 106, 156, 157, 158) (1900–1930), Fiddle (157, 158) (1900–1929), Gallicam (107) (27 AD), Garden carrot (92) (1876), Gelbe Rübe (German) (158) (1900), Hill-trot (157, 158) (1900–1929), Laceflower [Lace flower, Lace-flower] (75, 106, 156, 157, 158) (1894–1929) Philadelphia PA, Mirrot (157, 158) (1900–1929), Möhre (German) (158) (1900), Parsnip [Parsnep] (73) (1892) Harmony ME, Queen Anne's lace (50, 62, 75, 93, 106, 156) (1912–present), Rantipole (156, 157, 158) (1900–1923) no longer in use by 1923, Wild carrot (3, 4, 5, 49, 62, 70, 72, 80, 85, 92, 93, 95, 97, 106, 122, 131, 155, 156, 157, 158, 187) (1818–1986), Zanahoria (Spanish) (158) (1900), Cultivated carrot (109) (1949)

Daucus carota **L.** **subsp.** *sativus* (**Hoffm.**) **Arcang.** – See *Daucus carota* L.

Daucus carota **L.** **var.** *sativa* **DC.** – See *Daucus carota* L.

Daucus **L.** – Carrot [Carot] (1, 4, 10, 138, 155, 156, 158) (1818–1986), Wild carrot (50) (present)

Daucus pusillus **Michx.** – American carrot (72, 97, 122) (1907–1937), American wild carrot (50) (present), Rattlesnake-bite cure [Rattlesnake bite cure] (76) (1896), Rattlesnake-weed [Rattlesnake weed, Rattlesnake weede, Rattlesnakes' weed] (4) (1986), Southwestern carrot (3, 155) (1942–1977), Yerba del vibora (Spanish) (76) (1896) CA

Davallia **Smith.** – See *Dennstaedtia* Bernh. (for Edmund Davall, 1763–1798, Swiss botanist)

Decemium **Raf.** – See *Hydrophyllum* L. (US species)

Decodon **J. F. Gmel.** – Swamp loosestrife (1) (1932), Water-willow [Water willow, Waterwillow, Water willoe] (138, 156) (1923), Wild oleander (1) (1932)

Decodon verticillatus (**L.**) **Ell.** – Grass-poly [Grass poly, Grass-poley, Grass poley, Grase-poley, Grass-polley, Grasspoly] (5, 7, 19, 106, 156) (1828–1930), Milk willow herb [Milk willow-herb, Milk willow herb] (5, 156) (1913–1923), Peatweed [Peat weed, Peat-weed] (5, 106, 156) (1913–1930), Slinkweed [Slink weed, Slink-weed] (5, 156) (1913–1923), Stinkweed [Stink-weed, Stink weed] (106) (1930), Swamp loosestrife (5, 106, 156) (1913–1930), Swamp willow herb [Swamp willow-herb] (19, 92) (1840–1876), Water-willow [Water willow, Waterwillow, Water willoe] (106, 138, 156) (1923–1930), Whorled loosestrife (187) (1818), Wild oleander (5, 106, 156) (1913–1930), Willow herb [Willow-herb, Willowherb] (5, 106, 156) (1913–1930)

Dentaria tenella [Pursh]

Decumaria barbara L. – Decumaria (5) (1913), Decumary (19) (1840)

Decumaria forsythia Michx. – See *Decumaria barbara* L.

Decumaria sarmentosa [Bosc] – See *Decumaria barbara* L.

Deeringothamnus pulchellus Small – Slim-petal pawpaw [Slimpetal pawpaw] (155) (1942)

Deeringothamnus rugelii (B. L. Robins.) Small – Rugel's papaw [Rugel pawpaw] (155) (1942)

Delairea odorata Lem. – Climbing groundsel (138) (1923), German ivy [German-ivy] (92, 109) (1876–1949), Ivy groundsel (138) (1923)

Delonix regia (Bojer ex Hook.) Raf. – Peacock flower [Peacock-flower] (109) (1949), Royal poiciana (138) (1923), Royal poinciana (109) (1949)

Delonix regia Raf. – See *Delonix regia* (Bojer ex Hook.) Raf.

Delopyrum articulatum (L.) Small – See *Polygonella articulata* (L.) Meisn.

Delopyrum Small. – See *Polygonella* Michx. (all US species)

Delphidium Raf. – See *Delphinium* L.

Delphinium (Tourn.) L. – See *Delphinium* L.

Delphinium ×*occidentale* (S. Wats.) S. Wats. [*barbeyi* × *glaucum*] – Tall larkspur (146) (1939)

Delphinium ajacis L. – See *Consolida ajacis* (L.) Schur

Delphinium albescens Rydb. – See *Delphinium carolinianum* Walt. subsp. *virescens* (Nutt.) Brooks

Delphinium ambiguum L. – See *Consolida ajacis* (L.) Schur

Delphinium azureum Michx. – See *Delphinium carolinianum* Walt. subsp. *carolinianum*

Delphinium bicolor Nutt. – Blue larkspur (127) (1933), Larkspur [Larkspur] (126) (1933), Little larkspur (4, 50, 155) (1942–present), Low larkspur (126, 146) (1933–1939), Mewzie's larkspur (131) (1899)

Delphinium cardinale Hook. – Cardinal larkspur (138) (1923), Scarlet larkspur (76, 109) (1896–1949)

Delphinium carolinianum Walt. – Azure larkspur (5, 158) (1900–1913), Blue larkspur (5, 122, 124, 158) (1900–1937), Carolina larkspur (5, 50, 97, 131, 133, 155, 158) (1899–present), Prairie larkspur (5, 72, 158) (1900–1913)

Delphinium carolinianum Walt. subsp. *carolinianum* – Azure larkspur (2) (1895)

Delphinium carolinianum Walt. subsp. *virescens* (Nutt.) Brooks – Early larkspur (98) (1926), Plains larkspur (155) (1942), Prairie larkspur (3, 4, 5, 72, 80, 82, 85, 93, 97, 98, 125) (1907–1986), Tall white larkspur (127) (1933), White larkspur (122, 124) (1937), Wild larkspur (95) (1911)

Delphinium consolida L. – See *Consolida regalis* S.F. Gray

Delphinium consolidum – See *Consolida regalis* S.F. Gray

Delphinium cucullatum – See *Delphinium* ×*occidentale* (S. Wats.) S. Wats. [*barbeyi* × *glaucum*]

Delphinium decorum Fisch. & C. A. Mey. – Blue larkspur (76) (1896)

Delphinium elatum Ait. – possibly *Delphinium elatum* L.

Delphinium elatum L. – Bee larkspur (2, 138) (1895–1923), Candle larkspur (109) (1949), possibly Lark-heel wolf's-bane [Larks heele Wolfesbane] (178) (1526)

Delphinium exaltatum Aiton – Tall larkspur (5, 72, 93, 131, 138, 156) (1899–1936) ND, Tall wild larkspur (2) (1895)

Delphinium geyeri Greene – Geyer's larkspur [Geyer larkspur] (50, 155) (1942–present), Poisonweed [Poison weed] (71) (1898), Wyoming larkspur (71) (1898)

Delphinium grandiflorum L. – Bouquet larkspur (82, 109) (1930–1949), Cultivated larkspur (82) (1930), Great-leaf larkspur [Great leaved larkspur] (2) (1895), Siberian larkspur (138)

Delphinium L. – Larkspur [Lark-spur] (1, 2, 4, 7, 10, 13, 15, 50, 63, 82, 93, 148, 138, 155, 158, 167, 184) (1793–present), Poisonweed [Poison weed] (148) (1939) CO, Purple larkspur (71) (1898)

Delphinium menziesii DC. – Larkspur [L'arks S'pur] (190) (~1759), Purple larkspur (71) (1898)

Delphinium nelsoni Greene – See *Delphinium nuttallianum* Pritz ex. Walp.

Delphinium nelsonii Greene – See *Delphinium nuttallianum* Pritz ex. Walp.

Delphinium nudicaule Torr. & Gray – Orange larkspur (138) (1923), Red larkspur (109) (1949)

Delphinium nuttallianum Pritz ex. Walp. – Blue larkspur (4) (1986), Larkspur [Lark-spur] (85) (1932), Nelson's larkspur (5) (1913), Nuttall's larkspur [Nuttall larkspur] (155) (1942), Two-lobe larkspur [Twolobe larkspur] (50) (present)

Delphinium parryi Gray – Parry's larkspur [Parry larkspur] (138) (1923)

Delphinium penardii Huth – See *Delphinium carolinianum* Walt. subsp. *virescens* (Nutt.) Brooks

Delphinium Tourn. – See *Delphinium* L.

Delphinium treleasei Bush ex K. C. Davis – Trelease's larkspur (5) (1913)

Delphinium tricorne Michx. – Dwarf larkspur (4, 5, 50, 63, 71, 72, 93, 97, 125) (1898–present), Dwarf wild larkspur (2, 156) (1895), Rock larkspur (138, 155) (1923–1942), Staggerweed [Stagger weed, Stagger-weed] (71, 156) (1898–1923) OH

Delphinium tridactylum Michx. – See *Delphinium exaltatum* Aiton

Delphinium trolliifolium Gray – Cow poison (71) (1898), Tall mountain larkspur (71) (1898)

Delphinium urceolatum Jacq. – See *Delphinium exaltatum* Aiton

Delphinium virescens Nutt. – See *Delphinium carolinianum* Walt. subsp. *virescens* (Nutt.) Brooks

Demidofia repens Gmel. – See *Dichondra carolinensis* Michx.

Dendranthema ×*grandiflorum* Kitam. [*indicum* × *japonicum*] – Florist's chrysanthemum [Florists chrysanthemum] (109) (1949), Mulberry chrysanthemum (138) (1923)

Dendranthema arcticum (L.) Tzvelev subsp. *arcticum* – Arctic chrysanthemum (138) (1923), Arctic daisy (5) (1913)

Dendrocalamus latiflorus – See *Sinocalamus latiflorus* (Munro) McClure

Dendromecon Benth. – Tree poppy [Treepoppy] (138) (1923)

Dendromecon rigida Benth. – Bush poppy [Bush-poppy] (109) (1949), Tree poppy [Treepoppy] (74, 138) (1894–1923)

Dendromecon rigidum – See *Dendromecon rigida* Benth.

Dennstaedtia Bernh. – Cup fern [Cup-fern, Cupfern] (109, 138) (1923–1949), Davallia (138) (1923)

Dennstaedtia bipinnata (Cav.) Maxon – Glossy cupfern (138) (1923)

Dennstaedtia cicutaria (Sw.) T. Moore – Common cupfern (138) (1923)

Dennstaedtia punctiloba Moore – See *Dennstaedtia punctilobula* (Michx.) T. Moore

Dennstaedtia punctilobula (Michx.) T. Moore – Boulder fern (5) (1913), Eastern hay-scented fern (50) (present), Fine-haired fern [Fine haired fern] (5) (1913), Hairy dicksonia (5) (1913), Hay-scented cup fern [Hay-scented cupfern] (138) (1923), Hay-scented fern [Hay-scented-fern] (5, 109) (1913–1949)

Dennstedtia – See *Dennstaedtia* Bernh.

Dennstedtia adiantoides – See *Dennstaedtia bipinnata* (Cav.) Maxon

Dennstedtia cicutaria – See *Dennstaedtia cicutaria* (Sw.) T. Moore

Denslovia clavellata (Michx.) Rydb. – See *Platanthera clavellata* (Michx.) Luer

Denslovia Rydb. – See *Habenaria* Willd.

Dentaria (Tourn.) L. – See *Cardamine* L.

Dentaria californica – See *Cardamine californica* (Nutt.) Greene var. *californica*

Dentaria diphylla L. – See *Cardamine diphylla* (Michx.) Wood

Dentaria diphylla Michx. – See *Cardamine diphylla* (Michx.) Wood

Dentaria heterophylla Nutt. – See *Cardamine angustata* O.E. Schulz

Dentaria L. – See *Cardamine* L.

Dentaria lacinata Muhl. – See *Cardamine concatenata* (Michx.) Sw.

Dentaria macrocarpa Nutt. – See *Cardamine nuttallii* Greene

Dentaria maxima Nutt. – See *Cardamine maxima* (Nutt.) Wood

Dentaria tenella [Pursh] – See *Cardamine nuttallii* Greene var. *nuttallii*

Deparia acrostichoides (**Sw.**) **M. Kato** – Silvery spleenwort (5, 19, 72, 138) (1840–1923)

Deringa **Adans.** – See *Cryptotaenia* DC.

Deringa canadensis (**L.**) **Kuntze** – See *Cryptotaenia canadensis* (L.) DC.

Deschampsia atropurpurea (**Wahl.**) **Scheele** – See *Vahlodea atropurpurea* (Wahlenb.) Fries ex Hartman

Deschampsia **Beauv.** – Hair grass [Hairgrass, Hair-grass] (1, 50, 152, 155) (1912–present)

Deschampsia caespitosa (**L.**) **Beauv.** – Bullpates (5) (1913), Bullpates (5) (1913), Bull-poll [Bull poll] (5) (1913), Bunch grass [Bunchgrass, Bunch-grass] (88) (1885), Hair grass [Hairgrass, Hair-grass] (45, 85, 87, 90) (1884–1932), Hassock grass (5, 92) (1876–1913), Tufted hair grass [Tufted hair-grass] (3, 5, 50, 56, 66, 90, 140, 155) (1885–present), Turfy aira grass [Turfy aira-grass] (165) (1768), Windlestraw (5) (1913)

Deschampsia calycina **Presl.** – See *Deschampsia danthonioides* (Trin.) Munro

Deschampsia danthonioides (**Trin.**) **Munro** – Oat-like hair grass [Oat-like hair-grass] (94) (1901)

Deschampsia flexuosa (**L.**) **Trin.** – Common hair grass (90) (1885), Crinkled hair-grass (119) (1938), Tufted hair grass [Tufted hair-grass] (94) (1901), Wavy hair grass (5, 50) (1913–present), Wood hair grass (5, 87, 90, 111) (1885–1916)

Deschampsia flexuosa (**L.**) **Trin. var** *flexuosa* – Common hair grass (66) (1903), Flexuose hair-grass (187) (1818), Hair grass [Hairgrass, Hair-grass] (19, 50) (1840–present), Heath aira grass [Heath aira-grass] (165) (1768), Wavy hair grass (50) (present), Wood hair grass (66) (1901–1903)

Deschampsia holciformis **J. Presl** – California hair grass [Californian hair-grass] (94) (1901)

Deschampsia pacifica **Tatew. & Ohwi** – See *Vahlodea atropurpurea* (Wahlenb.) Fries ex Hartman

Descurainia incana (**Bernh. ex Fisch. & C. A. Mey.**) **Dorn subsp.** *incana* – Hoary hedge mustard (156) (1923), Mountain tansy-mustard [Mountain tansymustard] (50) (present), Richardson's tansy-mustard [Richardson tansymustard] (155) (1942), Tansy-mustard [Tansy mustard, Tansymustard] (156) (1923), Tansy mustard (101) (1905), Western tansy-mustard [Western tansymustard, Western tansy mustard] (5, 93, 97, 131) (1899–1937)

Descurainia incana (**Bernh. ex Fisch. & C. A. Mey.**) **Dorn subsp.** *procera* (**Greene**) **Kartesz & Gandhi** – Hartweg's tansy mustard (5) (1913), Hastings' tansy mustard (131) (1899)

Descurainia incana **var.** *major* (**Hook.**) **Dorn** – See *Descurainia incana* (Bernh. ex Fisch. & C. A. Mey.) Dorn subsp. *incana*

Descurainia pinnata (**Walt.**) **Britton** – Pinnate tansy-mustard [Pinnate tansymustard] (50) (present), Tansy-mustard [Tansy mustard, Tansymustard] (3, 4) (1977–1986), Western tansy-mustard [Western tansymustard, Western tansy mustard] (155) (1942)

Descurainia pinnata (**Walt.**) **Britton subsp.** *brachycarpa* (**Richards.**) **Detling** – Tansy-mustard [Tansy mustard, Tansymustard] (3, 5, 72, 93, 97) (1907–1977), Western tansy-mustard [Western tansymustard, Western tansy mustard] (50) (present)

Descurainia pinnata (**Walt.**) **Britton subsp.** *intermedia* (**Rydb.**) **Detling** – Western tansy-mustard [Western tansymustard, Western tansy mustard] (50, 72) (1907–present)

Descurainia pinnata (**Walter**) **Britton subsp.** *pinnata* – Tansy-mustard [Tansy mustard, Tansymustard] (15, 107, 145) (1895–1929), Water-radish [Water radish] (181) (1818)

Descurainia richardsonii (**Sweet**) **O. E. Schulz** – See *Descurainia incana* (Bernh. ex Fisch. & C.A. Mey.) Dorn subsp. *incana*

Descurainia sophia (**L.**) **Webb ex Prantl** – Descurea (174) (1753), Fine-leaf hedge-mustard [Fine-leaved hedge mustard, Fine-leaved hedge-mustard] (5, 157, 158) (1900–1929), Flaxweed [Flax-weed] (5, 93, 156) (1913–1936), Flixweed [Flix-weed, Flix weed, Flixe weede] (3, 4, 5, 72, 92, 156, 157, 158, 178) (1526–1986) from German for thread or hair, Herb Sophia (5, 50, 92, 97, 156, 157, 158) (1876–present), Scrambling rocket (157, 158) (1900–1929)

Descurainia **Webb & Berth.** – Tansy-mustard [Tansy mustard, Tansy-mustard] (1, 4, 50, 155, 158) (1900–present)

Desmanthus brachylobus **Benth.** – See *Desmanthus illinoensis* (Michx.) MacM. ex B.L. Robins. & Fern.

Desmanthus cooleyi (**Eat.**) **Trel.** – Bundle-flower [Bundleflower] (3) (1977), Cooley's bundle-flower [Cooley's bundleflower] (50) (present), James' bundle-flower [James bundleflower] (155) (1942), James' mimosa (97) (1937)

Desmanthus illinoensis (**Michx.**) **MacM. ex B. L. Robins. & Fern.** – Atikatsatsiks (Pawnee, spider bean) (37) (1919), Bundle-flower [Bundleflower] (3) (1977), Illinois acacia (5, 86) (1878–1913), Illinois bundleflower (4, 155) (1942–1986), Illinois mimosa (5, 72, 97, 157) (1900–1937), Kitsitsaris (Pawnee, bad plant) (37) (1919), Mimosa (93) (1936) Neb, Pezhe gagtho (Omaha-Ponca, rattle plant) (37) (1919), Prairie bundleflower (50) (present), Prairie mimosa (85) (1932), Spider bean (37, 157) (1919–1929), Wild sensitive plant [Wild sensitive-plant] (114) (1894)

Desmanthus leptolobus **Torr. & Gray** – Bundle-flower [Bundleflower] (3) (1977), Prairie mimosa (5, 97, 122) (1913–1937), Slender-lobe bundleflower [Slenderlobe bundleflower, Slender-lobed bundleflower] (4, 50) (1986–present)

Desmanthus **Willd.** – Bundle-flower [Bundleflower] (50, 155) (1942–present), Mimosa (158) (1900), Prairie mimosa (1) (1932)

Desmazeria **Dumort.** – Spike grass [Spike-grass, Spikegrass] (138) (1923)

Desmazeria rigida (**L.**) **Tutin** – Fern grass [Ferngrass] (50) (present), Hard meadow grass (19) (1840)

Desmodium acuminatum **DC.** – See *Desmodium glutinosum* (Muhl. ex Willd.) Wood

Desmodium canadense (**L.**) **DC.** – Beggar's-lice [Beggar lice, Beggarlice, Beggarlice, Beggarslice] (74, 156, 158) (1893–1923) MA, Beggarticks [Beggar ticks, Beggar's ticks, Beggars' ticks, Beggars-ticks, Beggar-ticks] (156, 158) (1900–1923), Bush trefoil (19, 156) (1840–1923), Canadian tickclover [Canada tickclover, Canadian tick-trefoil] (3, 4, 5, 72, 93, 155, 158) (1907–1986), Canadian tick-trefoil [Canada tick-trefoil] (5, 72, 93, 158) (1900–1936), Clover (158) (1900), Hairy tick-trefoil (93) (1936), Hoary tickclover (3, 4, 138, 155) (1923–1986), Hoary tick-trefoil [Hoary ticktrefoil, Hoary tick trefoil] (5, 50, 62, 72, 97) (1907–present), Lucerne [Lucern] (158) (1900), Sainfoin (5) (1913), Seed ticks (62) (1912), Seed ticks (5, 155) (1913–1942), Showy tick-trefoil [Showy tick trefoil, Showy ticktrefoil] (5, 50, 93, 97, 158) (1900–present), Tick trefoil [Tick-trefoil] (114, 156) (1894–1923)

Desmodium canescens (**L.**) **DC.** – See *Desmodium canadense* (L.) DC.

Desmodium ciliare (**Muhl. ex Willd.**) **DC.** – Hairy small-leaf tick-trefoil [Hairy small-leaved tick trefoil, Hairy small-leaved tick-trefoil] (50) (present), Little-leaf tickclover [Littleleaf tickclover] (155) (1942), Slender tick clover [Slender tickclover] (4) (1986)

Desmodium cuspidatum (**Muhl. ex Willd.**) **DC. ex Loud.** – Large-bract tick trefoil [Largebract ticktrefoil, Large-bracted tick trefoil] (5, 50, 97) (1913–present), Long-leaf tickclover [Longleaf tickclover] (3, 4) (1977–1986)

Desmodium cuspidatum (**Muhl. ex Willd.**) **DC. ex Loud. var.** *cuspidatum* – Beggarticks [Beggar ticks, Beggar's ticks, Beggars' ticks, Beggars-ticks, Beggar-ticks] (5, 85, 93) (1913–1936), Broad-leaf tick-trefoil [Broad-leaved tick-trefoil] (131) (1899), Pointed-leaf tick trefoil [Pointed leaved tick trefoil, Pointedleaf ticktrefoil, Pointed-leaved tick-trefoil] (5, 72, 93, 97) (1907–1937), Tick trefoil [Tick-trefoil] (65) (1931)

Desmodium cuspidatum (**Muhl. ex Willd.**) **DC. ex Loud. var.** *longifolium* (**Torr. & Gray**) **Schub.** – Large-bract tick trefoil [Largebract ticktrefoil] (50) (present), Long-leaf ticktrefoil [Long-leaved tick trefoil] (72) (1907)

Desmodium **Desv.** – Beggarticks [Beggar ticks, Beggar's ticks, Beggars' ticks, Beggars-ticks, Beggar-ticks] (1, 93) (1932–1936), Tick clover [Tickclover] (4, 138, 155, 156) (1923–1986), Tick trefoil [Tick-trefoil] (1, 2, 4, 50, 87, 156, 158) (1884–present), Tickseed

[Tick-seed, Tick seed] (87) (1884), Trick trefoil [Trick-trefoil (*sic*)] (93) (1936)

Desmodium dillenii **Darl.** – See *Desmodium perplexum* Schub.

Desmodium glabellum (**Michx.**) **DC.** – Dillenius' ticktrefoil (50) (present), Trailing tick-trefoil [Trailing tick trefoil] (5) (1913)

Desmodium glutinosum (**Muhl. ex Willd.**) **Wood** – Large-flower tick-clover [Largeflower tickclover] (3, 4, 155) (1942–1986), Pointed-leaf tick trefoil [Pointed leaved tick trefoil, Pointedleaf ticktrefoil, Pointed-leaved tick-trefoil] (50) (present), Tickseed [Tick-seed, Tick seed] (14) (1882)

Desmodium illinoense **Gray** – Illinois tickclover (3, 4) (1977–1986), Illinois ticktrefoil [Illinois tick-trefoil, Illinois tick trefoil] (5, 50, 72, 93, 97, 131) (1899–present)

Desmodium laevigatum (**Nutt.**) **DC.** – Smooth tick trefoil [Smooth tick-trefoil] (5, 97) (1913)

Desmodium lineatum **DC.** – Sand tick trefoil (5) (1913)

Desmodium marilandicum (**L.**) **DC.** – Maryland tickclover (4, 155) (1942–1986), Smooth small-leaf tick trefoil [Smooth small-leaf tick-trefoil] (50) (present)

Desmodium michauxii (**Vail**) **Daniels** – See *Desmodium rotundifolium* DC.

Desmodium nudiflorum (**L.**) **DC.** – Bare-stem tickclover [Barestem tick-clover (155) (1942), Naked-flower tick trefoil [Naked-flowered tick trefoil, Naked-flowered tick-trefoil] (5, 50, 72, 97) (1907–present), Scapose tickclover (4) (1986), Tickseed [Tick-seed, Tick seed] (14) (1882)

Desmodium obtusum (**Muhl. ex Willd.**) **DC.** – Hairy small-leaf tick-trefoil [Hairy small-leaved tick trefoil, Hairy small-leaved tick-trefoil] (5, 97) (1913–1937), Rigid tick trefoil (5, 72) (1907–1913), Stiff tick trefoil [Stiff ticktrefoil] (50) (present)

Desmodium ochroleucum **M. A. Curtis ex Canby** – Cream-flower ticktrefoil [Cream-flowered tick trefoil] (5) (1913)

Desmodium paniculatum (**L.**) **DC.** – Panicled tick clover [Panicled tickclover] (3, 4) (1977–1986), Panicle-leaf tick clover [Panicledleaf tickclover] (155) (1942), Panicle-leaf tick trefoil [Panicledleaf tick-trefoil] (50) (present)

Desmodium paniculatum (**L.**) **DC. var. paniculatum** – Panicled tick trefoil [Panicled tick-trefoil] (5, 72, 93, 97) (1907–1937), Panicle-leaf tick trefoil [Panicledleaf ticktrefoil] (50) (present)

Desmodium pauciflorum (**Nutt.**) **DC.** – Few-flower tickclover [Few-flowered tickclover] (4) (1986), Few-flower ticktrefoil [Few-flowered tick-trefoil, Few-flowered tick trefoil] (5, 50, 72, 97) (1907–present)

Desmodium perplexum **Schub.** – Dillen's tickclover [Dillen tickclover] (155) (1942), Dillen's ticktrefoil [Dillen's tick trefoil, Dillen's tick-trefoil] (5, 72, 93, 97) (1907–1937), Perplexed tick trefoil [Perplexed ticktrefoil] (50) (present)

Desmodium rigidum **DC.** – See *Desmodium obtusum* (Muhl. ex Willd.) DC.

Desmodium rotundifolium **DC.** – Dollarleaf [Dollar-leaf, Dollar leaf] (156) (1923), Hive vine [Hive-vine, Hivevine] (5, 74, 156) (1893–1923) WV, Prostrate tick trefoil [Prostrate ticktrefoil] (5, 50) (1913–present), Round-leaf tick clover [Roundleaf tickclover] (155) (1942), Round-leaf tick trefoil [Round-leaved tick trefoil] (5) (1913), Tick trefoil [Tick-trefoil] (156) (1923), Trailing tick-trefoil [Trailing tick trefoil] (5) (1913)

Desmodium sessilifolium (**Torr.**) **Torr. & Gray** – Sessile tickclover (2, 155) (1895–1942), Sessile-leaf tickclover [Sessile-leaved tick-clover] (4) (1986), Sessile-leaf tick-trefoil [Sessileleaf ticktrefoil, Sessile-leaved tick trefoil, Sessile-leaved tick-trefoil] (4, 5, 50, 72) (1907–present)

Desmodium strictum (**Pursh**) **DC.** – Stiff tick trefoil [Stiff ticktrefoil] (5) (1913)

Desmodium tortuosum (**Sw.**) **DC.** – Beggarweed [Beggar weed, Beggar-weed] (109, 118) (1898–1949)

Desmodium tortuosum **DC.** – See *Desmodium tortuosum* (Sw.) DC.

Desmodium viridiflorum (**L.**) **DC.** – Velvet-leaf tick trefoil [Velvet-leaved tick trefoil] (5, 97) (1913–1937)

Desmodium viridiflorum **Beck.** – See *Desmodium viridiflorum* (L.) DC.

Deutzia gracilis **Sieb. & Zucc.** – Deutzia (92) (1876), Slender deutzia (112, 138) (1923–1937)

Deutzia parviflora **Bunge** – Mongolian deutzia (138) (1923)

Deutzia purpurascens (**Franch. ex L. Henry**) **Rehder** – Red-bud deutzia [Redbud deutzia] (138) (1923)

Deutzia scabra **Thunb.** – Deutzia (82) (1930), Fuzzy deutzia (138) (1923)

Deutzia **Thunb.** – Deutzia (82, 138) (1923-930)

Deyeuxia canadensis **Beauv.** – See *Calamagrostis canadensis* (Michx.) Beauv.

Deyeuxia **Clarion** – See *Calamagrostis* Adans.

Deyeuxia howellii – See *Calamagrostis howellii* Vasey

Deyeuxia sylvatica [**Kunth**] – See *Calamagrostis stricta* (Timm) Koel.

Diamorpha cymosa (**Nutt.**) **Britton ex Small** – See *Sedum smallii* (Britton) H.E.Ahles

Diamorpha pusilla **Nutt.** – See *Sedum smallii* (Britton) H.E.Ahles

Dianthera americana **L.** – See *Justicia americana* (L.) Vahl

Dianthera humilis **Engelm. & Gray.** – See *Justicia ovata* (Walt.) Lindau var. *ovata*

Dianthera **L.** – See *Justicia* L.

Dianthera lanceolata (**Chapman**) **Small.** – See *Justicia ovata* (Walt.) Lindau var. *lanceolata* (Chapman) R.W. Long

Dianthera ovata **Walt.** – See *Justicia ovata* (Walt.) Lindau var. *ovata*

Dianthus armeria **L.** – Deptford pink (4, 5, 50, 15, 46, 72, 155, 156) (1879–present), Dianthus (92) (1876), Grass-pink [Grass pink] (76, 156) (1896) Paris ME, Maiden (46) (1879), Pink (19) (1840), Wild pink (85, 156, 187) (1818–1932)

Dianthus barbatus **L.** – Blooming-down (158) (1900), Bloomy down (5, 156) (1913–1923) no longer in use by 1923, Bouncing Bet [Bouncing-Bet, Bouncingbet] (74) (1893) Ferrisburgh VT, Bunch pink (5, 73, 92, 156, 158) (1892–1923), Double Sweet Williams [Double Sweete Williams] (178) (1526), French pink [French pinks] (5, 74, 156, 158) (1893–1923) Brunswick, NY, London pride [London-pride] (5, 156) (1913–1923), London tuft (5, 156) (1913–1923), Scarlet lightning (74) (1893) Quebec, scarlet variety, Snowflake [Snow flake] (5, 74, 156) (1893–1923) Quebec, white variety, no longer in use by 1923, Sweet John [Sweet johns] (5, 92, 156) (1898–1923) no longer in use by 1923, Sweet William [Sweetwilliam, Sweet-william] (1, 5, 15, 19, 50, 79, 92, 109, 138, 155, 156, 158) (1840–present), Sweet William of a bright red [Sweete William of a bright red] (178) (1526), Sweet William, many in a hose [Swette Williams, many in a hose] (178) (1526)

Dianthus caesius [**Smith**] – See *Dianthus gratianopolitanus* Vill.

Dianthus carthusianorum **L.** – Carthusian pink (138) (1923), Double red Johns [Double red Iohns] (178) (1526), White sweet Johns [White Sweete Iohns] (178) (1526), Wild Sweet Johns [Wilde Sweete Iohns] (178) (1526)

Dianthus caryophyllus **L.** – Carnation (19, 109, 138) (1840–1949), Clove pink (92, 109, 138) (1876–1949), Gilliflower (92) (1876), Gilloflowers of diuers sort and colours (178) (1526), Grenadine (109) (1949), Gylofre (179) (1526), Orange tawny gilloflowers [Orange tawnie gilloflowers] (178) (1526), Picotee (109) (1949)

Dianthus chinensis **L.** – China pink (19, 92, 114) (1840–1894), Chinese pink (138) (1923), Rainbow pink (109)

Dianthus deltoides **L.** – Maiden pink (5, 15, 109, 138, 156) (1895–1949), Meadow pink [Meadow-pink] (5, 156) (1913–1923), Spink (5, 156) (1913–1923)

Dianthus gratianopolitanus **Vill.** – Cheddar pink (109, 138) (1923–1949)

Dianthus **L.** – Carnation (1, 7, 15, 138, 155, 156, 158) (1828–1942), Clove pink (7) (1828), Pink (1, 10, 15, 50, 92, 109, 138, 155, 156, 158, 167) (1814–present)

Dianthus plumaris – See *Dianthus plumarius* L.

Dianthus plumarius **L.** – Cottage pink (109) (1949), Garden pink (138) (1923), Grass-pink [Grass pink] (138) (1923), Pheasant's-eye [Pheasantseye, Pheasant's-eye] (92) (1876), Single pink (19) (1840)

(Lam.) Gould & C. A. Clark var. *patulum* (Scribn. & Merr.) Gould & C. A. Clark

***Dichanthelium commutatum* (J. A. Schultes) Gould** – Ashe's panicum (5) (1913), Linear-leaf panicum [Linear-leaved panicum] (72) (1907), Tall fringed panic grass [Tall fringed panic-grass] (119) (1938), Tall fringed panicum (5) (1913), Variable panic grass [Variable panicgrass] (50) (present), Variable panicum (5) (1913)

***Dichanthelium consanguineum* (Kunth) Gould & C. A. Clark** – Blood panic grass [Blood panicgrass] (50) (present), Kunth's panicum (5) (1913)

***Dichanthelium depauperatum* (Muhl.) Gould** – Few-flower panic grass [Few-flowered panic grass] (90) (1885), Starved panic grass [Starved panic-grass, Starved panicgrass] (5, 50, 85, 93, 163) (1852–present), Starved panicum (56, 72, 131) (1899–1907), Stunted panicum (3) (1977), Worthless panic (66, 90) (1885–1903)

***Dichanthelium dichotomum* (L.) Gould** – Cypress panic grass [Cypress panicgrass] (50) (present)

Dichanthelium dichotomum* (L.) Gould var. *dichotomum – Barbed panic grass [Barbed panic-grass] (119, 163) (1852–1938), Barbed panicum (5) (1913), Bearded joint [Bearded-joint] (94) (1901), Bearded joint grass (5) (1913), Bog panic grass [Bog panic-grass] (163) (1852), Bog panicum (5) (1913), Clute's panicum (5) (1913), Forked panic grass [Forked panic-grass] (119, 163) (1852–1938), Forked panicum (5, 72, 131) (1899–1907), Large-fruit panicum [Large-fruited panicum] (72) (1907), Panic grass [Panic-grass, Panicgrass, Panick grass] (19) (1840), Polymorphous panic (66) (1903), Polymorphus panic grass (90) (1885), Ringed panicum (5) (1913), Small panic grass [Small panicgrass] (11) (1888), Spotted-sheath panicum [Spotted-sheathed panicum] (5) (1913), Spreading witch grass [Spreading witch-grass] (99) (1923)

***Dichanthelium dichotomum* (L.) Gould var. *ensifolium* (Baldw. ex Ell.) Gould & C. A. Clark** – Britton's panic grass [Britton's panicgrass] (94) (1901), Small-leaf panicum [Small-leaved panicum] (5) (1913)

***Dichanthelium dichotomum* (L.) Gould var. *tenue* (Muhl.) Gould & C. A. Clark** – White-edge panicum [White-edged panicum] (5) (1913)

***Dichanthelium ensifolium* (Baldw. ex Ell.) Gould** – See *Dichanthelium dichotomum* (L.) Gould var. *ensifolium* (Baldw. ex Ell.) Gould & C. A. Clark

***Dichanthelium ensifolium* (Baldw. ex Ell.) Gould var. *unciphyllum* (Trin.) B. F. Hansen & Wunderlin** – See *Dichanthelium dichotomum* (L.) Gould var. *tenue* (Muhl.) Gould & C. A. Clark

***Dichanthelium joorii* (Vasey) Mohlenbrock** – See *Dichanthelium commutatum* (J. A. Schultes) Gould

***Dichanthelium latifolium* (L.) Gould & C. A. Clark** – Broad-leaf panic grass [Broad-leaved panic grass] (66, 90) (1885–1903), Broad-leaf panicum [Broad-leaved panicum] (3, 5) (1913–1977), Broad-leaf rosette grass [Broadleaf rosette grass] (50) (present), Porter's panicum (56) (1901)

***Dichanthelium laxiflorum* (Lam.) Gould** – Lax-flower panicum [Lax-flowered panicum] (5) (1913), Open-flower rosette grass [Open-flower rosette grass] (50) (present)

***Dichanthelium leibergii* (Vasey) Freckmann** – Leiberg's panicum [Leiberg panicum] (3, 50, 155) (1942–present), Lieberg's panicum (5, 56, 72) (1893–1901)

***Dichanthelium leucothrix* (Nash) Freckmann** – Rough panic grass [Rough panic-grass, Rough panicgrass] (50) (present), Roughish panicum (5) (1913)

***Dichanthelium linearifolium* (Scribn. ex Nash) Gould** – Elongate panicum [Elongated panicum] (3, 72) (1907–1977), Linear-leaf panicum [Linear-leaved panicum] (56) (1901), Long-stalk panic grass [Long-stalked panic-grass, Long-stalked panic grass] (5, 163) (1852–1913), Low white-hair panic grass [Low white-haired panic-grass, Low white-haired panic grass] (5, 163) (1852–1913), Slender panic grass (56) (1901), Slim-leaf panic grass [Slimleaf panic-grass] (50) (present), Slim-leaf panicum [Slimleaf panicum] (3, 155)

(1942–1977), Werner's panic grass [Werner's panic-grass] (5, 163) (1852–1913), Werner's panicum [Werner panicum] (155) (1942)

***Dichanthelium malacophyllum* (Nash) Gould** – Soft-leaf panic grass [Soft-leaved panic-grass] (119, 163) (1852–1938), Soft-leaf panicum [Softleaf panicum, Soft-leaved panicum] (3, 5, 155) (1913–1977), Soft-leaf rosette grass [Softleaf rosette grass] (50) (present)

***Dichanthelium mattamuskeetense* (Ashe) Mohlenbrock** – See *Dichanthelium dichotomum* (L.) Gould var. *dichotomum*

***Dichanthelium meridionale* (Ashe) Freckmann** – Matting panicum (5) (1913), Matting rosette grass (50) (present)

***Dichanthelium microcarpon* (Muhl. ex Ell.) Mohlenbrock** – See *Dichanthelium dichotomum* (L.) Gould var. *dichotomum*

***Dichanthelium nitidum* (Lam.) Mohlenbrock** – See *Dichanthelium dichotomum* (L.) Gould var. *dichotomum*

Dichanthelium oligosanthes* (J. A. Schultes) Gould var. *oligosanthes – Few-flower panic grass [Few-flowered panic grass] (119) (1938), Few-flower panicum [Few-flowered panicum] (5) (1913), Heller's rosette grass (50) (present), Peyijuhiṇta (Lakota, grass + to rake) (121) (1918–1970?), Small panic grass [Small panicgrass] (3) (1977)

***Dichanthelium oligosanthes* (J.A. Schultes) Gould var. *scribnerianum* (Nash) Gould** – Heller's panicum [Heller panicum] (155) (1942), Large-fruit panicum [Large-fruited panicum] (56) (1901), Panic grass [Panic-grass, Panicgrass, Panick grass] (119, 121) (1918–1970), Scribner's panic grass (56) (1901), Scribner's panicum [Scribner panicum] (5, 56, 72, 131, 140, 155) (1899–1944), Scribner's rosette grass (50) (present)

***Dichanthelium ovale* (Ell.) Gould & C. A. Clark var. *addisonii* (Nash) Gould & C. A. Clark** – Addison's rosette grass (50) (present), Commons' panicum (5) (1913), Low stiff panicum (5) (1913), Mrs. Owen's panicum (5) (1913)

***Dichanthelium polyanthes* (J. A. Schultes) Mohlenbrock** – See *Dichanthelium sphaerocarpon* (Ell.) Gould var. *isophyllum* (Scribn.) Gould & C.A. Clark

***Dichanthelium portoricense* (Desv. ex Hamilton) B. F. Hansen & Wunderlin** – See *Dichanthelium sabulorum* (Lam.) Gould & C.A. Clark var. *thinium* (A.S. Hitche. & Chase) Gould & C.A. Clark

***Dichanthelium ravenelii* (Scribn. & Merr.) Gould** – Ravenel's panicum (5) (1913), Ravenel's rosette grass (50) (present)

***Dichanthelium sabulorum* (Lam.) Gould & C. A. Clark var. *patulum* (Scribn. & Merr.) Gould & C. A. Clark** – Hemlock panicum (5) (1913), Hemlock rosette grass (50) (present), Nash's panic grass [Nash's panic-grass] (94) (1901), Nash's panicum (5) (1913), Webber's panic grass [Webber's panic-grass] (94) (1901)

***Dichanthelium sabulorum* (Lam.) Gould & C. A. Clark var. *thinium* (A. S. Hitche. & Chase) Gould & C. A. Clark** – American panic grass [American panic-grass] (94) (1901), American panicum (5) (1913), Hairy panicum (72) (1907), Hemlock rose grass (50) (present), Hemlock rosette grass (50) (present)

***Dichanthelium scabriusculum* (Ell.) Gould & C. A. Clark** – Hairy panicum (56) (1901), Tall rough panicum (5) (1913), Tall swamp panic grass [Tall swamp panic-grass] (163) (1852), Tall swamp panicum (5) (1913), Woolly panic grass [Woolly panic-grass] (163) (1852), Woolly panicum (5, 155) (1913–1942), Woolly rosette grass (50) (present)

***Dichanthelium scoparium* (Lam.) Gould** – Sticky panic grass (66) (1903), Velvet pancium (50) (present), Velvet panic grass [Velvet panic-grass] (119) (1938), Velvety panic grass [Velvety panic-grass] (163) (1852), Velvety panicum (3, 5, 72, 131, 155) (1899–1977)

***Dichanthelium sphaerocarpon* (Ell.) Gould** – Round-seed panic grass [Roundseed panicgrass] (50) (present)

***Dichanthelium sphaerocarpon* (Ell.) Gould var. *isophyllum* (Scribn.) Gould & C. A. Clark** – Barbed panicum (5) (1913), Bearded joint grass (5) (1913), Round-seed panic grass [Roundseed panicgrass] (50) (present), Small-fruit panic grass [Small-fruited panic-grass] (119) (1938), Small-fruit panicum [Small-fruited panicum] (5) (1913)

Dichanthelium sphaerocarpon (Ell.) Gould var. *polyanthes* (J. A. Schultes) Gould – See *Dichanthelium sphaerocarpon* (Ell.) Gould var. *isophyllum* (Scribn.) Gould & C. A. Clark

Dichanthelium sphaerocarpon (Ell.) Gould var. *sphaerocarpon* – Round-flower panic [Round-flowered panic] (94) (1901), Round-fruit panic grass [Round-fruited panic grass, Round-fruited panic-grass] (5, 163) (1852–1913), Round-seed panic grass [Roundseed panicgrass] (50) (present), Round-seed panicum [Roundseed panicum] (3, 155) (1942–1977)

Dichanthelium spretum (J. A. Schultes) Freckmann – Eaton's panic grass [Eaton's panic-grass] (163) (1852), Eaton's panicum (5) (1913), Eaton's rosette grass (50) (present), Eight-joint panicum [Eight-jointed panicum] (5, 50) (1913–present), Purple panicum (5, 50) (1913–present)

Dichanthelium strigosum (Muhl. ex Ell.) Freckmann var. *leucoblepharis* (Trin.) Freckmann – Dwarf panicum (5, 50) (1913–present), Rough-hair rosette grass [Roughhair rosette grass] (50)

Dichanthelium strigosum (Muhl. ex Ell.) Freckmann var. *strigosum* – Rough-hair rosette grass [Roughhair rosette grass] (50) (present), Rough-hairy panicum (5) (1913), Long-stalk panic [Long-stalked panic] (94) (1901)

Dichanthelium villosissimum (Nash) Freckmann – White-hair rosette grass [Whitehair rosette grass] (50) (present)

Dichanthelium villosissimum (Nash) Freckmann var. *praecocius* (A. S. Hitchc. & Chase) Freckmann – Early branching panic grass [Early-branching panic-grass] (163) (1852), Early branching panicum (5) (1913), Early panicum (3) (1977), Panic grass [Panic-grass, Panicgrass, Panick grass] (119) (1938), White-hair rosette grass [Whitehair rosette grass] (50) (present)

Dichanthelium villosissimum (Nash) Freckmann var. *villosissimum* – White-hair panic grass [White-haired panic-grass] (163) (1852), White-hair panicum [White-haired panicum] (5) (1913), White-hair rosette grass [Whitehair rosette grass] (50) (present)

Dichanthelium wilcoxianum (Vasey) Freckmann – Fall rosette grass (50) (present), Wilcox's panic grass (111) (1915), Wilcox's panicum [Wilcox panicum] (3, 5, 56, 72, 131, 155) (1899–1977)

Dichanthelium xanthophysum (Gray) Freckmann – Slender panicum (5, 56) (1901–1913), Slender rosette grass (50) (present), Yellow panic grass (66, 90) (1885–1903)

Dichanthelium yadkinense (Ashe) Mohlenbrock – See *Dichanthelium dichotomum* (L.) Gould var. *dichotomum*

Dichelostemma capitatum (Benth.) Wood subsp. *capitatum* – Hog-onion [Hog onion] (75) (1894) CA, corm tastes like elm bark and is eaten by children, Spanish lily (75) (1894) CA

Dichelostemma ida-maia (Alph. Wood) Greene – Fire-cracker flower [Fire cracker flower] (86, 109) (1878–1949), Scarlet California hyacinth (86) (1878)

Dichodon cerastoides (L.) Rchb. – See *Cerastium cerastoides* (L.) Britton

Dichondra carolinensis Michx. – Dichondra (5) (1913), Moneywort [Money wort] (124) (1937) TX

Dichondra repens Forst. var. *carolinensis* (Michx.) Choisy – See *Dichondra carolinensis* Michx.

Dichromena colorata (L.) Hitchc. – See *Rhynchospora colorata* (L.) H. Pfeiffer

Dichromena latifolia Baldw. – See *Rhynchospora latifolia* (Baldw. ex Ell.) Thomas

Dichromena leucocephala Michx. – See *Rhynchospora colorata* (L.) H. Pfeiffer

Dichromena nivea (Boeckl.) Britt. – See *Rhynchospora nivea* Boeckl.

Dichrophyllum Kl. & Garcke – See *Euphorbia* L.

Dichrophyllum marginatum (Pursh) KL. & Garcke. – See *Euphorbia marginata* Pursh

Dicliptera brachiata (Pursh) Spreng. – Branched foldwing (50) (present), Diapedium (5, 97) (1913–1937), Dicliptera (3) (1977)

Dicliptera Juss. – Foldwing (50) (present), Diapedium (158) (1900)

Diclythra Raf. – possibly *Dicentra* Bernh.

Dicranum bonjeanii De Not in Lisa – Bonjean's dicranum moss (50) (present), Woodmoss (40) (1928)

Dictamnus alba – See *Dictamnus albus* L.

Dictamnus albus L. – Bastard dittany [Bastard dittanie] (92, 178) (1526–1876), Burningbush [Burning bush, Burning-bush] (109) (1949), Fraxinella (178) (1526), Gasplant [Gas-plant] (109, 138) (1923–1949) will often give a flash of light when a burning match is held under the flower cluster, White fraxinella (92)

Dictamnus L. – Dittany (109) (1949), Fraxinella (109) (1949), Gasplant [Gas-plant] (138) (1923)

Didiplis diandra (Nutt. ex DC.) Wood – Water purslane [Water purslain, Water-purslane, Waterpurslane] (1, 3, 4, 5, 50, 72, 93, 155, 156) (1907–present)

Didiplis Raf. – Dididplis (50) (present), possibly Water purslane [Water purslain, Water-purslane, Waterpurslane]] (10) (1818)

Dieffenbachia Schott – Tuftroot (138)

Dieffenbachia seguine (Jacq.) Schott – Dumb cane (92, 109) (1876–1949) West Indies, those who chew it said to lose power of speech

Dielytra canadensis [(Goldie) G. Don] – See *Dicentra canadensis* (Goldie) Walp.

Dielytra cucullaria DC. – See *Dicentra cucullaria* (L.) Bernh.

Diervilla (Tourn.) Mill. – See *Diervilla* Mill.

Diervilla Adans. – possibly *Diervilla* Mill.

Diervilla canadensis Muhl. – See *Diervilla lonicera* Mill.

Diervilla diervilla (L.) MacM. – See *Diervilla lonicera* Mill.

Diervilla diervilla MacMill. – See *Diervilla lonicera* Mill.

Diervilla florida (Bunge) Siebold & Zucc., possibly Diervilla (112) (1937), possibly Pink weigela (138) (1923), possibly Rose weigela (138) (1923)

Diervilla lonicera Mill. – Bush honeysuckle [Bush honey suckle, Bush-honeysuckle] (5, 19, 40, 49, 58, 61, 72, 92, 105, 106, 156) (1840–1930), Diervilla (174) (1753), Dierville (French) (8) (1785), Dwarf bush-honeysuckle (138) (1923), Dwarf diervilla (42) (1814), Gravelweed [Gravel-weed, Gravel weed] (5, 49, 58, 92, 156) (1869–1923), Life-of-man [Life of man, Life-o'-man] (5, 76, 156) (1896–1923) Oak Bay NB, Marsh diervilla (42) (1814), Wežauškwagmik (Chippewa) (105) (1932), Yellow-flower diervilla [Yellow flowered diervilla] (8, 42) (1785–1814)

Diervilla lutea – See *Diervilla lonicera* Mill.

Diervilla Mill. – Bush honeysuckle [Bush honey suckle, Bush-honey-suckle] (1, 2, 82, 109, 138, 156) (1895–1949), Weigela (2) (1895)

Diervilla rivularis Gattinger – Georgia bush-honeysuckle (138) (1923)

Diervilla sessilifolia Buckley – Bush honeysuckle [Bush honey suckle, Bush-honeysuckle] (82) (1930), Southern bush-honeysuckle (138) (1923)

Diervilla tourneforti Michx. – See *Diervilla lonicera* Mill.

Diervilla tournefortii Michx. – See *Diervilla lonicera* Mill.

Diervilla trifida Moench – See *Diervilla lonicera* Mill.

Dieteria canescens var. *leucanthemifolia* (Greene) D. R. Morgan & R. L. Hartm. – See *Machaeranthera canescens* (Pursh) A. Gray subsp. *canescens* var. *canescens*

Digitalis (Tourn.) L. – See *Digitalis* L.

Digitalis ambigua [Murr.] – See *Digitalis grandiflora* P. Mill.

Digitalis grandiflora P. Mill. – Yellow foxglove (109, 138, 190) (~1759–1949)

Digitalis L. – Foxglove [Fox glove, Fox-glove, Foxgloves] (50, 82, 109, 138, 155, 156, 158, 184) (1793–present)

Digitalis lanata Ehrh. – Grecian foxglove (50, 109 138, 155) (1923–present)

Digitalis lutea L. – Straw foxglove (109, 138) (1923–1949), Yellow foxglove (92) (1876)

Digitalis pupurea L. – Common foxglove (109, 138) (1923–1949), Cottagers (5, 69) (1903–1913), Dead-men's-bells [Dead men's bells] (92) (1876), Digitalis (54, 55, 59, 60) (1902–1905), Dog's-finger [Dog's finger] (5, 69, 92) (1876–1913), Fairy bells [Fairy-bells, Fairy bells] (5, 69, 156) (1903–1923), Fairy cap (5, 69, 156) (1903–1923), Fairy fingers (5, 69, 92) (1876–1913), Fairy gloves

[Fairy glove, Fairy's glove] (5, 92, 156) (1876–1923), Fairy thimbles (5, 69) (1903–1913), Fairy weed (5) (1913), Finger flower (69, 92) (1876–1904), Flapdock (69) (1904), Folk's-glove [Folk's glove] (5, 92, 156) (1876–1923), Foxglove [Fox glove, Fox-glove, Foxgloves] (4, 19, 49, 52, 53, 54, 55, 57, 60, 61, 69, 82, 92, 106, 148, 156) (1840–1939), Lady's-fingers [Lady fingers, Ladyfingers] (5, 69) (1903–1913), Lady's-glove [Ladies' glove, Lady glove, Lady's glove, Lady's-gloves] (5, 69, 92) (1876–1913), Lady's-thimble [Lady thimble, Lady's thimble, Lady's thimbles] (5, 69, 156) (1904–1923), Lion's-mouth [Lion's mouth, Lion mouth] (5, 69, 156) (1903–1923) no longer in use by 1923, Popdock [Pop-dock, Pop dock] (5, 69, 156) (1903–1923) no longer in use by 1923, Popglove [Pop glove] (5) (1913), Purple foxglove [Purple foxe gloues (5, 49, 50, 53, 60, 69, 92, 178) (1526–present), Rabbit-flower [Rabbit's flower, Rabbit flower] (5, 69, 156) (1903–1923), Scotch mercury (5, 69) (1903–1913), Thimbles (5, 69, 156) (1903–1923), Throatwort [Throat wort, Throat-wort] (5, 69, 156) (1903–1923) no longer in use by 1923, White foxglove [White foxe gloues] (178) (1526), Witch's-thimble [Witches thimbles, Witches' thimbles, Witches'-thimbles, Witches'thimbles] (5, 156) (1913–1923), American foxglove (92) (1876)

***Digitaria californica* (Benth.) Henr.** – Arizona cotton grass [Arizona cotton-grass] (94) (1901), Arizona cottontop (3, 50, 155) (1942–present), Cottontop [Cotton top] (122) (1937) TX

***Digitaria ciliaris* (Retz.) Koel.** – Fringed crabgrass [Fringed crab-grass] (5, 99) (1913–1923), Southern crabgrass (50) (present)

***Digitaria cognata* (J. A. Schultes) Pilger** – Diffuse panicum (72) (1907), Diffuse purple panicum (56) (1901), Fall witch grass [Fall witchgrass, Fall witch-grass] (94) (1901)

Digitaria cognata* (J. A. Schultes) Pilger var. *cognata – Carolina crabgrass (50) (present), Diffuse crabgrass [Diffuse crab-grass] (5, 119, 163) (1852–1938), Fall witch grass [Fall witchgrass, Fall witch-grass] (3, 122, 155, 163) (1852–1977)

***Digitaria cognata* (J. A. Schultes) Pilger var. *pubiflora* Vasey ex L.H. Dewey** – Autumn panic (66) (1903)

***Digitaria filiformis* (L.) Koel.** – Erect digitaria (187) (1818), Slender crabgrass [Slender crab grass] (3, 50, 56, 66) (1901–present), Slender finger grass [Slender finger-grass, Slender fingergrass] (5, 72, 119, 155, 163) (1852–1942), Wire grass [Wire-grass, Wiregrass] (5, 119) (1913–1938)

***Digitaria gracillima* (Scribn.) Fernald** – Slender panicum (94) (1901)

***Digitaria* Haller** – Crabgrass [Crab-grass, Crab grass] (1, 7, 10, 50, 93, 110) (1818–present), Crop grass [Crop-grass] (7) (1828), Fall witch grass [Fall witchgrass, Fall witch-grass] (1) (1932), Finger grass [Fingergrass, Finger-grass] (155) (1942)

***Digitaria humifusa* Pers.** – See *Digitaria ischaemum* (Schreb.) Schreb. ex Muhl.

***Digitaria insularis* (L.) Mez ex Ekman** – Cotton grass[Cotton-grass] (94) (1901), Sour grass [Sourgrass] (92, 122, 163) (1852–1937)

***Digitaria ischaemum* (Schreb.) Schreb. ex Muhl.** – Big smooth crabgrass (155) (1942), Crabgrass [Crab-grass, Crab grass] (119, 145) (1897–1938), Finger grass [Fingergrass, Finger-grass] (119) (1938), Small crabgrass [Small crab grass, Small crab-grass] (5, 85, 62, 72, 131, 143) (1852–1936), Smooth crabgrass [Smooth crab grass, Smooth crab-grass] (94) (1901), Smooth crabgrass [Smooth crab grass, Smooth crab-grass] (3, 50, 56, 66, 80, 90, 140, 143, 155) (1885–present)

***Digitaria* Mich.** – See *Digitaria* Haller

***Digitaria sanguinalis* (L.) Scop.** – Blutfennich (Bohemian) (67) (1890), Common crab grass (66) (1903), Crabgrass [Crab-grass, Crab grass] (3, 11, 19, 45, 56, 62, 67, 87, 88, 92, 94, 107, 111, 119, 122, 134, 145, 152) (1840–1977), Crowfoot [Crow-foot, Crow foot, Crowfote, Crow's foot] (5) (1913), Finger grass [Fingergrass, Finger-grass] (5, 19, 45, 56, 62, 66, 80, 92, 107, 119, 143, 155) (1840–1938), Hairy crabgrass (50, 140, 155) (1942–present), Hairy finger grass (5) (1913), Large crab grass [Large crab-grass] (5, 72, 99, 131, 143, 163) (1852–1937), Pigeon grass [Pigeon-grass, Pigeongrass,

Pigeon's- grass, Pigeon's grass] (5, 75) (1894–1913) Hopkinton IA, Purple crabgrass [Purple crab-grass] (187) (1818)

***Digitaria serotina* (Walt.) Michx.** – Dwarf crabgrass (50) (present), Late-flowering finger grass [Late-flowering finger-grass] (5) (1913)

***Digitaria tenuis* (Nees) Henrard** – Slender woolly panic (94) (1901)

***Digitaria villosa* (Walt.) Pers.** – Shaggy crabgrass (50) (Present), Shaggy finger grass [Shaggy fingergrass] (155) (1942), Silvery panic grass [Silvery panic-grass] (94) (1901), Southern slender finger grass [Southern slender finger-grass] (5, 99, 119, 163) (1852–1938)

***Digraphis arundinacea* [Trin.]** – See *Phalaris arundinacea* L.

***Diholcos* Rydb.** – See *Astragalus* L. (US species)

Dilatris heritiera – See *Lachnanthes caroliana* (Lam.) Dandy

***Dilatris* Persoon** – See *Lachnanthes* Ell.

***Dillenia indica* L.** – Indian dillenia (138) (1923)

***Dillenia* L.** – Dillenia (138) (1923)

***Dimorphocarpa candicans* (Raf.) Rollins** – Palmer's spectacle-pod [Palmer's spectaclepod] (50) (present), Spectacle-pod [Spectacle pod] (3, 4, 97) (1937–1986), Wislizenus' spectacle-pod [Wislizenus spectaclepod] (155) (1942)

***Dimorphocarpa palmeri* (Pays.) Rollins** – See *Dimorphocarpa candicans* (Raf.) Rollins

***Dimorphotheca aurantiaca* DC.** – See *Castalis tragus* (Aiton) Norl.

***Dimorphotheca* Moench** – Cape-marigold [Cape marigold] (82, 109, 138) (1923–1949)

***Dimorphotheca sinuata* DC.** – Blue-eyed cape-marigold (138)

***Diodia* L.** – Buttonweed [Button-weed, Button weed] (1, 4, 155, 156) (1923–1986)

***Diodia teres* Walt.** – Buttonweed [Button-weed, Button weed] (3, 106, 145, 156) (1897–1977), Poor Joe [Poorjoe] (5, 50, 156) (1913–present), Poorland-weed [Poor land weed] (5, 156) (1913–1923), Poorweed [Poor-weed] (156) (1923), Poverty-weed [Povertyweed, Poverty weed] (5, 156) (1913–1923), Rough buttonweed [Rough button weed, Rough button-weed] (4, 5, 97, 122, 155, 156) (1923–1986)

***Diodia virginiana* L.** – Buttonweed [Button-weed, Button weed] (92, 156) (1876–1923), Jacob's-ladder [Jacob's ladder, Jacobs-ladder] (156) (1923), Large buttonweed [Large button-weed] (97) (1937), Larger buttonweed [Larger button weed] (5, 122, 124) (1913–1937)

Diodia virginica – possibly *Diodia virginiana* L.

***Dionaea* Ell.** – Venus flytrap [Venus' fly-trap, Venus's flytrap] (2, 10, 13, 138, 167) (1814–1923)

***Dionaea muscipula* Ellis.** – Tipitiwitchet (183) (~1756), Venus flytrap [Venus' fly-trap, Venus's flytrap] (14, 19, 92, 109, 138) (1840–1949)

***Dioscorea* (Plum) L.** – See *Dioscorea* L.

***Dioscorea alata* L.** – Ubi (Pacific Isles) (110) (1886), Water yam (50) (present), Winged yam (138) (1923), Yams (41) (1770)

***Dioscorea batatas* Dcne.** – See *Dioscorea oppositifolia* L.

***Dioscorea bulbifera* L.** – Air-potato [Airpotato] (109, 138) (1923–1949)

***Dioscorea cayenensis* Lam.** – Attoto yam (109) (1949), Negro-country yam (Guiana) (110) (1886), Yellow yam (109) (1949)

***Dioscorea glauca* Barton** – See *Dioscorea quaternata* J.F. Gmel.

***Dioscorea* L.** – Igname or inhame (Africa) (110) (1886) may refer to several species, Wild yam root [Wild yam-root] (1) (1932), Yam (1, 50, 92, 93, 109, 138, 155, 158, 167) (1814–present) means "to eat" in several dialects of Guinea (110), Yam root (10) (1818–1828)

***Dioscorea oppositifolia* L.** – Chinese yam (50, 109) (1949–present), Cinnamon vine [Cinnamon-vine, Cinnamonvine] (109, 138, 155) (1923–1949)

***Dioscorea paniculata* Michx.** – See *Dioscorea villosa* L.

***Dioscorea quaternata* J. F. Gmel.** – Smooth-leaf yamroot [Smooth-leaved yam-root] (187) (1818)

***Dioscorea sativa* [L.]** – possibly *Dioscorea villosa* L. (current species depends on author)

***Dioscorea trifida* L. f.** – Cush-cush (109) (1949), Yampee (109) (1949)

***Dioscorea villosa* L.** – American yam (42) (1814), Atlantic yam (155) (1942), China root [China-root] (58, 92) (1869–1876), Colic root [Colic-root, Colicroot] (5, 6, 49, 53, 57, 58, 64, 75, 92, 93, 156, 158) (1892–1936), Devil's-bones [Devil's bones] (6, 64, 92, 156, 158)

(1892–1923), Dioscorea (52, 54, 57, 64) (1905–1919), Iguame Indigené (French) (6) (1892), Rheumatism root [Rheumatism-root] (6, 49, 64, 156, 158) (1892–1923), Wild yam (3, 7, 48, 49, 52, 53, 54, 57, 58, 61, 64, 92, 122, 124, 156, 158) (1828–1937), Wild yam root [Wild yam-root] (2, 5, 6, 72, 92, 93, 97, 156) (1874–1937), Wilde Yam (German) (6) (1892), Yam root (19) (1840), possibly Common yam (138) (1923), possibly Yam (110) (1886)

***Diospyros* L.** – Date-plum [Dateplum, Date plum] (1, 2, 8, 10, 158) (1818–1932), Diospyros (50) (present), Ebony (109, 156) (1900–1949), Guaiacana (8) (1785), Ougoust (Western tribes) (7) (1828), Persimmon [Persimon, Persimons] or Persimmon tree [Persimon tree, Persimon-tree] (1, 2, 8, 10, 27, 18, 20, 106, 109, 138, 155, 156, 181) (1785–1949), Piakmin (Western tribes) (7) (1828), Plaqueminier (French) (8, 20) (1785–1857)

***Diospyros texana* Scheele** – Black persimmon (107, 122, 124) (1919–1937), Date-plum [Dateplum, Date plum] (106) (1930), Mexican persimmon (106, 122, 124) (1930–1937), Sapote-pieto (Mexican) (107) (1919)

***Diospyros virginiana* L.** – American date-plum [American date plum] (14) (1882), Amerikanische Dattellpflaume (German) (158) (1900), Common persimmon (2, 50, 109, 138, 155, 158) (1900–present), Date-plum [Dateplum, Date plum] (5, 49, 92, 156) (1898–1923), Diospyros (Official name of Materia Medica) (7, 57) (1828–1917), Eastern persimmon (122, 124) (1937) TX, Fuzzy common persimmon (155) (1942), Guaiacan (7) (1828), Guajacana (174, 177, 189) (1753–1767), Jove's-fruit [Jove's fruit] (92, 156, 158) (1876–1923) no longer in use by 1923, Lotus tree [Lotus-tree] (5, 92, 156, 158) (1876–1923), Medlar [Medlars] (46, 107, 181) (~1678–1919), Mespila (107) (1919), Mespilorum (107) (1919), North American ebony (156, 158) (1900–1923), Oklahoma persimmon (155) (1942), Orange [Oranges, Orenge] (46) (1879), Ougoufle (Louisiana) (46, 107) (1879), Parsimon (158) (1900), Pascimmon (181) (~1678), Persimmon [Persimon, Persimons] or Persimmon tree [Persimon tree, Persimon-tree] (3, 4, 5, 7, 19, 41, 44, 46, 49, 57, 58, 63, 65, 72, 92, 97, 103, 107, 121, 135, 156, 184) (1770–1986), Persimmon bark (7, 92, 187, 189) (1767–1876), Persimon Baum (German) (7) (1828), Pesimmon [Pessimon] (107, 182) (1791–1919), Pessemmins (46) (1879), Piakmine (46, 107) (1879–1919), Pishamin (177) (1762), Pishamon (181) (~1678), Pishmin (7) (1828), Plaqueminier (French) (7) (1828), Plaqueminier de Virginie (French) (8, 158) (1785–1900), Possum-wood [Possum wood] (5, 106, 156, 158) (1900–1930), Rutilo colore (46) (1879), Seeded-plum [Seeded plums] (7, 19, 92, 156, 158) (1828–1923), Virginia persimmon tree [Virginian persimmon tree] (8) (1785), Winter-plum [Winter plum, Winter plums] (7, 92, 156, 158) (1828–1923), Yellow-plums [Yellow plums] (7, 82) (1828–1930), Θta-iŋge (Osage) (121) (1918?–1970?)

***Diospyros virginiana* L. var. *platycarpa* Sargent** – See *Diospyros virginiana* L.

***Diospyros virginiana* L. var. *pubescens* (Pursh) Dippel** – See *Diospyros virginiana* L.

***Dipelta* [Maxim.]** – See *Astragalus* L.

***Diphasiastrum sabinifolium* (Willd.) Holub** – See *Lycopodium clavatum* L.

***Diphasiastrum sitchense* (Rupr.) Holub** – See *Lycopodium sitchense* Rupr.

***Diphasiastrum tristachyum* (Pursh) Holub** – See *Lycopodium tristachyum* Pursh

***Diphasium chamicyparissus* (A. Braun) A. & D. Löve** – See *Lycopodium tristachyum* Pursh

***Diphasium complanatum* (L.) Rothm. subsp. *chamicyparissus* (A. Braun) Kukkonen** – See *Lycopodium tristachyum* Pursh

***Diphasium sitchense* (Rupr.) A. & D. Löve** – See *Lycopodium sitchense* Rupr.

***Diphasium tristachyum* (Pursh) Rothm.** – See *Lycopodium tristachyum* Pursh

***Diphylleia cymosa* Michx.** – Umbrella-leaf [Umbrellaleaf, Umbrella leaf] (5, 138, 156) (1913–1923)

***Diphylleia* Michx.** – Umbrella-leaf [Umbrellaleaf, Umbrella leaf] (138) (1923)

***Diplachne acuminata* Nash** – See *Leptochloa fusca* (L.) Kunth subsp. *fascicularis* (Lam.) N. Snow

***Diplachne* Beauv.** – See *Leptochloa* Beauv. (US species)

***Diplachne fascicularis* (Lam.) Beauv.** – See *Leptochloa fusca* (L.) Kunth subsp. *fascicularis* (Lam.) N. Snow

***Diplachne maritima* Bicknell** – See *Leptochloa fusca* (L.) Kunth subsp. *fascicularis* (Lam.) N. Snow

Diplacus aurantiacus* (W. Curtis) Jepson subsp. *aurantiacus – Bush monkeyflower [Bush monkey-flower] (138) (1923)

***Diplacus glutinosus* (J. C. Wendl.) Nutt.** – See *Diplacus aurantiacus* (W. Curtis) Jepson subsp. *aurantiacus*

***Diplazium pycnocarpon* (Spreng.) Broun** – Glade fern (3, 4) (1977–1986), Narrow-leaf spleenwort [Narrowleaf spleenwort, Narrow-leaved spleenwort] (5, 138, 155) (1913–1942), Swamp spleenwort (5, 19, 50, 92) (1840–present)

***Diplopappus cornifolius* (Muhl. ex Willd.) Less. ex Darl.** – See *Doellingeria infirma* (Michx.) Greene

***Diplopappus cornifolius* (Muhl. ex Willd.) Lindl. ex Torr. & Gray** – See *Doellingeria umbellata* (Mill.) Nees

***Diplopappus linariifolius* Hook.** – possibly *Ionactis linariifolius* (L.) Greene (taxonomic status is unresolved (PL))

***Diplotaxis* DC.** – Crossweed [Cross weed, Cross-weed] (158) (1900), Rocket (158) (1900), Wall-rocket [Wallrocket, Wall rocket] (50, 155) (1942–present)

***Diplotaxis muralis* (L.) DC.** – Annual wallrocket (50) (present), Crossweed [Cross weed, Cross-weed] (5, 158) (1900–1913), Flixweed [Flix-weed, Flix weed, Flixe weede] (5, 156, 158) (1900–1923), Sand rocket (3, 4, 5, 85, 156, 158) (1900–1986), Stinking wallrocket (155) (1942)

***Diplotaxis tenuifolia* (L.) DC.** – Crossweed [Cross weed, Cross-weed] (5, 156) (1913–1923), Wall-rocket [Wallrocket, Wall rocket] (5, 156) (1913–1923)

***Dipogon lignosus* (L.) Verdc.** – Australian pea [Australian-pea] (109, 138) (1923–1949)

***Dipsacus fullonum* L.** – Bottonweed [Botton weed] (5) (1913), Buttonweed [Button-weed, Button weed] (5, 156) (1913–1923), Card teasel [Card-teasel] (5, 122, 124, 156, 158) (1900–1937), Card thistle (5, 156) (1913–1923), Churchbrooms [Church brooms, Church broom] (5, 156, 158) (1900–1923), Clothier's-brush [Clothier's brush] (5, 156, 158) (1900–1923), Common teasel (4, 5, 62, 156, 158) (1900–1986), Draper's teasel (5, 156, 158) (1900–1923), English thistle (62, 75) (1894–1912), Fuller's teasel [Fullers teasel] (5, 50, 62, 106, 138, 155, 156, 158) (1898–present), Fuller's thistle [Fullers thistle] (5, 109, 156) (1913–1949), Fuller's weed [Fuller's-weed] (158) (1900), Gipsy-combs [Gypsy combs] (5, 156, 158) (1900–1923), Huttonweed [Hutton-weed] (75, 158) (1894–1900) WV, found on Hutton farm, Indian thistle (5, 75, 156, 158) (1900–1923) WV, Prickly-back [Prickly back] (5, 156) (1913–1923), Prickly-bark (158) (1900), Pricky-bark (158) (1900), Shepherd's-staff [Shepherd's staff] (5, 156, 158) (1900–1923), Shepherd's-thistle [Shepherd's thistle] (156) (1923), Tassel [Tasyll] (156, 158) (1900–1923), Teasel [Teazel] (3, 14, 19, 92, 106, 132, 158, 184) (1793–1977), Tezils (62) (1912) IN, Old English name, Venus'-bath [Venus' bath] (5, 92, 156, 158) (1876–1923), Venus'-cup [Venus' cup] (5, 156, 158) (1900–1923), Venus'-cup teasel [Venus-cup teasel, Venuscup teasel] (155) (1942), Water-thistle [Water thistle] (5, 75, 156) (1894–1923) WV, water collects in leaf axils, Wild teasel (5, 19, 42, 62, 156, 158, 187) (1814–1923), Wood-broom [Wood brooms, Wood broom] (5, 92, 156, 158) (1876–1923), Wy'-wy (Pima) (132) (1855)

Dipsacus fullonum* L. subsp. *fullonum – Fuller's teasel [Fullers teasel] (50) (present), Wild tassel [Wylde tasyll] (179) (1526)

***Dipsacus* L.** – Teasel [Teazel] (1, 4, 7, 10, 50, 109, 138, 155, 156, 158) (1828–present)

***Dipsacus laciniatus* L.** – Cut-leaf teasel [Cutleaf teasel, Cut-leaved teasel] (3, 4, 50, 155) (1942–present)

Dipsacus sylvestris **Huds.** – See *Dipsacus fullonum* L.

Dirca **L.** – Dirca (French) (8) (1785), Leatherwood [Leather-wood, Leather wood] (1, 2, 8, 10, 109, 138, 167) (1814-949), Moosewood [Moose-wood, Moose wood] (1, 2) (1895–1932), Wicopy [Wick-opy] (1) (1932)

Dirca palustris **L.** – American mezereon (5, 6, 19, 49, 92, 156) (1840–1923), Bois de cuir (French) (8) (1785), Bois de plomb (French Can, lead wood) (6, 7, 41) (1770–1892), Čibagup (Chippewa) (105) (1932), Dirca des marais (French) (8) (1785), Dircier triflore (French) (7) (1828), Djibe'gûb (Chippewa) (40) (1928), Indian wickape (78) (1898) Western US, Jibagup (Chippewa) (105) (1932), Leather bush [Leather-bush] (5, 92, 156) (1876–1923), Leatherwood [Leather-wood, Leather wood] (5, 6, 7, 14, 19, 23, 41, 49, 65, 72, 92, 105, 138, 156) (1770–1932), Leaverwood [Leaver wood, Leaver-wood] (5, 92, 156) (1876–1923), Leder-Holz (German) (6, 7) (1828–1892), Marsh leatherwood [Marsh leather wood] (42) (1814), Moosewood [Moose-wood, Moose wood] (5, 6, 7, 19, 40, 41, 42, 47, 49, 92, 156) (1770–1928), Poison-berry [Poison berry] (7) (1828), Rope-bark [Rope bark] (5, 6, 7, 92, 156) (1828–1923), Swamp leatherwood (7) (1828), Swampwood [Swamp-wood, Swamp wood] (5, 6, 7, 92, 156) (1828–1923), Thong wood (6) (1892), Virginia marsh leather-wood [Virginian marsh leather-wood] (8) (1785), Wickeryby bush [Wickeryby-bush] (156) (1923), Wickup [Wickop] (5, 156) (1913–1923), Wicopy [Wickopy] (5, 6, 49, 78, 75, 156) (1892–1923) from Indian name, Wicopy bark (92)

Disporum lanuginosum **(Michx.) Nichols** – Fairy bells [Fairybells, Fairy bells] (156) (1923), Hairy disporum (3) (1977), Liverberry [Liver-berry, Liver berry] (156) (1923), Twisted-stalk [Twistedstalk, Twisted stalk] (156) (1923), Yellow fairybells (50) (present)

Disporum lanuginosum **Benth. & Hook.** – See *Disporum lanuginosum* (Michx.) Nichols

Disporum **Salisb. ex D. Don** – Fairy bells [Fairybells, Fairy bells] (50, 138, 155, 156) (1923–present)

Disporum trachycarpon **(Wats.) Benth. & Hook.** – See *Disporum trachycarpum* (S. Wats.) Benth. & Hook. f.

Disporum trachycarpum **(S. Wats.) Benth. & Hook. f.** – Fairy bells [Fairybells, Fairy bells] (3) (1977), Rough-fruit disporum [Rough-fruited disporum] (5, 93) (1913–1936), Rough-fruit fairybells [Rough-fruit fairybells] (50) (present), Wartberry fairybells (155) (1942)

Distegia **Raf.** – possibly *Lonicera* L.

Distichlis maritima **Raf.** – See *Distichlis spicata* (L.) Greene

Distichlis **Raf.** – Alkali grass [Alkali-grass, Alkaligrass] (1, 93) (1932–1936), Salt grass [Saltgrass, Salt-grass] (1, 50, 93) (1932–present), Spike grass [Spike-grass, Spikegrass] (1) (1932)

Distichlis spicata **(L.) Greene** – Alkali grass [Alkali-grass, Alkaligrass] (5, 94, 116, 119, 144, 146) (1899–1958), Alkaline grass (88, 151) (1885–1896), Desert salt grass [Desert saltgrass] (140) (1944), Inland salt grass [Inland saltgrass] (50, 140, 155) (1942–present), Marsh grass [Marshgrass, Marsh-grass] (87, 90) (1884–1885), Marsh spike grass [Marsh-spike-grass] (5, 119) (1913–1938), Pey-isuksuta (Lakota, tough or hard grass) (121) (1918–1970?), Salt grass [Saltgrass, Salt-grass] (5, 11, 75, 85, 87, 90, 111, 116, 119, 121, 129, 134, 144, 146, 151, 163) (1852–1939), Seashore saltgrass (3, 155) (1942–1977), Spiked quaking grass (92) (1876), Wire grass [Wire-grass, Wiregrass] (116) (1958), possibly Spike grass [Spike-grass, Spikegrass] (66, 90, 92) (1876–1903)

Distichlis spicata **(L.) Greene subsp. *stricta* (Torr.) Thorne** – See *Distichlis spicata* (L.) Greene

Distichlis spicata **(L.) Greene var. *stricta* (Torr.) Beetle** – See *Distichlis spicata* (L.) Greene

Distichlis stricta **(Torr.) Rydb.** – See *Distichlis spicata* (L.) Greene

Ditaxis humilis **(Engelm. & Gray) Pax.** – See *Argythamnia humilis* (Engelm. & Gray) Muell. Arg. var. *humilis*

Ditaxis mercurialina **(Nutt.) Coult.** – See *Argythamnia mercurialina* (Nutt.) Muell. Arg.

Ditaxis **Vahl.** – See *Argythamnia* P. Br.

Dithyrea wislizenii **Engelm.** – See *Dimorphocarpa candicans* (Raf.) Rollins

Dithyrea wislizenii **Engelm. var. *palmeri* Pays.** – See *Dimorphocarpa candicans* (Raf.) Rollins

Ditrichum pallidum **(Hedw.) Hampe** – Hair-mouth moss (19) (1840)

Ditrysinia fruticosa **(W. Bartram) Govaerts & Frodin** – Privet-leaf stillingia [Privet-leaved stillingia] (20) (1857)

Dodecatheon clevelandi – See *Dodecatheon clevelandii* Greene

Dodecatheon clevelandii **Greene** – Cleveland shootingstar (138) (1923)

Dodecatheon hendersoni – See *Dodecatheon hendersonii* Gray

Dodecatheon hendersonii **Gray** – Henderson's shootingstar [Henderson shootingstar] (138) (1923)

Dodecatheon hugeri **Small.** – See *Dodecatheon meadia* L. subsp. *meadia*

Dodecatheon jeffreyi **Van Houtte** – Jeffrey's shootingstar [Jeffrey shootingstar] (138) (1923)

Dodecatheon **L.** – American cowslip [American cowslips] (1, 10, 82, 156) (1818–1932), Bird's-bill [Birds' bill, Birds'-bill] (1) (1932), Cowslip [Cowslips, Cowslyp] (93) (1936), Shooting-star [Shooting star, Shootingstar] (1, 4, 50, 72, 109, 138, 155, 158) (1900–present)

Dodecatheon meadia **L.** – American cowslip [American cowslips] (2, 5, 14, 82, 97, 131, 156) (1882–1937), Common shooting-star [Common shootingstar] (138) (1923), Cyclamen (77) (1898) Alabama, False cowslip (19) (1840), Gentlemen-and-ladies [Gentlemen and ladies] (156) (1923), Greatest blush bear's-ears [Greatest blush Bears' ears] (181) (~1678), Indian chief (5, 75, 156) (1894–1923) Rockford IL, Johnny-jump [Johnny jump] (5, 75, 156) (1894–1923) Southern CA, Lamb's-noses [Lamb's noses] (156) (1923), Meadia (174) (1753), Mosquito-bells (156) (1923), Prairie-pointer [Prairie pointer] (156) (1923), Pride-of-Ohio [Pride of Ohio] (5, 50, 156) (1913–present), Rooster-head [Rooster heads] (5, 75, 156) (1894–1923) Santa Barbara CA, Sanicula (181) (~1678), Shooting-star [Shooting star, Shooting stars] (3, 4, 5, 14, 63, 75, 92, 97, 122, 124, 131, 156) (1882–1986), Snake's-head [Snake head, Snake-head, Snakehead, Snakeheads] (156) (1923)

Dodecatheon meadia **L. subsp. *meadia*** – White American cowslip (97) (1937)

Dodecatheon pauciflorum **(Durand) Greene** – See *Dodecatheon pulchellum* (Raf.) Merr. subsp. *pulchellum*

Dodecatheon pauciflorum **Greene** – See *Dodecatheon pulchellum* (Raf.) Merr. subsp. *pulchellum*

Dodecatheon pulchellum **(Raf.) Merr.** – Dark-throat shootingstar [Darkthroat shootingstar] (50) (present), Shooting-star [Shooting star] (4) (1986)

Dodecatheon pulchellum **(Raf.) Merr. subsp. *pulchellum*** – Cowslip [Cowslips, Cowslyp] (127) (1933), Dark-throat shootingstar [Dark-throat shootingstar] (50, 155) (1942–present), Shooting-star [Shooting star] (3, 85, 127) (1932–1977), Southern shooting-star [Southern shootingstar] (138, 155) (1923–1942), Yellow-throat shooting-star [Yellowthroat shootingstar] (155) (1942)

Dodecatheon radicatum **Greene** – See *Dodecatheon pulchellum* (Raf.) Merr. subsp. *pulchellum*

Dodecatheon salinum **A. Nels.** – See *Dodecatheon pulchellum* (Raf.) Merr. subsp. *pulchellum*

Dodonaea **Mill.** – Hopbush (138) (1923)

Dodonea **L.** – See *Dodonaea* Mill.

Doellingeria humilis **(Willd.) Britton** – See *Doellingeria infirma* (Michx.) Greene

Doellingeria infirma **(Michx.) Greene** – Broad-leaf flat-top white aster [Broad-leaved flat-top white aster] (5, 72) (1907–1913), Cornel-leaf aster [Cornel-leaved aster] (5, 156) (1913–1923), Dogwood-leaf aster [Dogwood-leaved aster] (187), Weak starwort [Weak star wort] (42) (1814)

Doellingeria **Nees** – White aster (158) (1900), Whitetop [White top, White-top] (50) (present)

Doellingeria umbellata **(P. Mill.) Nees** – Flat-top white aster [Flat-topped white aster] (131) (1899), Parasol whitetop (50) (present)

Doellingeria umbellata (P. Mill.) Nees var. *pubens* (Gray) Britton – Parasol whitetop (50) (present)

Doellingeria umbellata (P. Mill.) Nees var. *umbellata* – Corymbed aster (82) (1930), Flat-top aster [Flattop aster] (138, 155) (1931–1942), Tall flat-top white aster (5, 72, 156) (1907–1923), Umbell-flower starwort [Umbelled-flowered star-wort] (187) (1818)

Dolicholus erectus (Walt.) Vail – See *Rhynchosia tomentosa* (L.) Hook. & Arn. var. *tomentosa*

Dolicholus simplicifolius (Walt.) Vail – See *Rhynchosia reniformis* DC.

Dolichos lablab L. – See *Lablab purpureus* (L.) Sweet

Dolichos lignosus L. – See *Dipogon lignosus* (L.) Verdc.

Dolichos pruriens – See *Mucuna pruriens* (L.) DC. var. *pruriens*

Dolichos purpureus L. – See *Lablab purpureus* (L.) Sweet

Dolichos sinensis L. – See *Vigna unguiculata* (L.) Walp.

Dolichos soja L. – See *Glycine max* (L.) Merr.

Dolichos sphaerospermus – See *Vigna unguiculata* (L.) Walp.

Dondia Adans. – See *Suaeda* Forsk. ex J. F. Gmel. (all US species)

Dondia depressa (Pursh) Britton – See *Suaeda calceoliformis* (Hook.) Moq.

Dondia linearis (Ell.) Heller – See *Suaeda linearis* (Ell.) Moq.

Dondia maritima (L.) Druce – See *Suaeda maritima* (L.) Dumort. subsp. *maritima*

Doronicum L. – Leopard's-bane [Leopardsbane, Leopard's bane, Leopardbane] (109, 138, 167) (1814–1949)

Doronicum pardalianches L. – Great leopard's-bane [Great leopardsbane] (92) (1876), Leopard's-bane [Leopardsbane, Leopard's bane, Leopardbane] (178) (1526)

Dovyalis hebecarpa (G. Gardn.) Warb. – Ceylon-gooseberry (109) (1949), Kitembilla (109) (1949)

Dovyalis hebecarpa Warb. – See *Dovyalis hebecarpa* (G. Gardn.) Warb.

Doxantha unguis-cati Rehd. – See *Macfadyena unguis-cati* (L.) A.H. Gentry

Draba (Dill.) L. – See *Draba* L.

Draba alpina L. – Alpine whitlow grass (5) (1913)

Draba arabisans Michx. – Rockcress whitlow-grass [Rock cress whitlow grass] (5) (1913)

Draba aurea Vahl ex Hornem. – Golden draba (50, 155) (1942–present), Golden whitlow-grass [Golden whitlow grass] (5, 133) (1899–1913)

Draba brachycarpa Nutt. – Short-fruit whitlow [Short-fruited whitlow] (5) (1913), Short-fruit whitlow-grass [Short-fruited whitlow-grass] (97) (1937), Short-pod draba [Shortpod draba] (3, 4, 50) (1977–present)

Draba breweri S. Wats. var. *cana* (Rydb.) Rollins – Canescent whitlow-grass [Canescent whitlow grass] (5) (1913), Cushion draba (50) (present), Hunger flower [Hunger-flower] (156) (1923), Lanceolate draba (155) (1942), Nailwort (156) (1923)

Draba caroliniana Walt. – See *Draba reptans* (Lam.) Fern.

Draba cuneifolia Nutt. ex Torr. & Gray – Wedge-leaf draba [Wedgeleaf draba] (3, 4, 50) (1977–present), Wedge-leaf whitlow-grass [Wedge-leaved whitlow grass, Wedge-leaved whitlow-grass] (5, 97) (1913–1937), Whitlow-grass [Whitlow grass, Whitlowgrass] (122) (1937)

Draba cuneifolia Nutt. ex Torr. & Gray var. *cuneifolia* – Wedge-leaf draba [Wedgeleaf draba] (50) (present)

Draba fladnizensis Wulf. – Arctic whitlowgrass (138) (1923), White arctic whitlow-grass [White arctic whitlow grass] (5) (1913)

Draba glabella Pursh – Rough whitlow-grass [Rough whitlow grass] (19) (1840)

Draba hirta L. – See *Draba glabella* Pursh

Draba incana L. – Hoary whitlow-grass [Hoary whitlow grass] (5) (1913), Hunger flower [Hunger-flower] (92) (1876), Nailwort (92) (1876), Twisted whitlow-grass [Twisted whitlow grass] (5) (1913), Whitlow-grass [Whitlow grass, Whitlowgrass] (92) (1876)

Draba L. – Draba (1, 50, 155) (1932–present), Nailwort (158) (1900),

Whitlow-grass [Whitlow grass, Whitlowgrass] (1, 2, 4, 10, 13, 93, 138, 158, 184) (1793–1986), Whitlow-wort [Whitlow wort, Whitlowwort] (155) (1942)

Draba lanceolata Royle – See *Draba breweri* S. Wats. var. *cana* (Rydb.) Rollins

Draba nemorosa L. – Wood whitlow-grass [Wood whitlow grass] (5, 131) (1899–1913), Woodland draba (50) (present), Woods draba [Woods draba] (155) (1942), Yellow whitlow-wort [Yellow whitlowwort] (3, 4) (1977–1986)

Draba nivalis Lilj. – Yellow arctic whitlow-grass [Yellow arctic whitlow grass] (5) (1913)

Draba ramosissima Desv. – Branching whitlow-grass [Branching whitlow grass] (5) (1913)

Draba reptans (Lam.) Fern. – Carolina draba (50) (present), Carolina whitlow-grass [Carolina whitlow grass] (5, 72, 97, 131) (1907–1937), White whitlow-wort [White whitlowwort] (3, 4) (1977–1986)

Draba stenoloba Ledeb. – Alaska draba (50) (present)

Draba stylaris J. Gay – See *Draba breweri* S. Wats. var. *cana* (Rydb.) Rollins

Draba verna L. – Chickweed nailwort [Chickweede naile woort] (178) (1526), Nailwort (5, 156) (1913–1923), Shad-blossom (187) (1818), Shad-blow [Shadblow] (156) (1923), Shad-flower [Shadflower, Shad flower] (5, 74) (1893–1913) WV, Spring whitlow-grass [Spring whitlow grass] (42) (1814), Vernal whitlow-grass [Vernal whitlow grass] (5) (1913), White-blow [White blow] (5, 156) (1913–1923) no longer in use by 1923, Whitlow-grass [Whitlow grass, Whitlowgrass] (15, 92, 156, 187) (1818–1923)

Dracaena borealis Ait. – See *Clintonia borealis* (Ait.) Raf.

Dracaena L. – Dracaena (109, 138) (1923–1949) Greek 'female dragon', juice when thickened said to resemble dragon's blood

Dracocephalum (Tourn.) L. – See *Dracocephalum* L.

Dracocephalum canariense L. – See *Cedronella canariensis* (L.) Willd. ex Webb & Berth.

Dracocephalum denticulatum Aiton – See *Physostegia virginiana* (L.) Benth. subsp. *virginiana*

Dracocephalum intermedium Nutt. – See *Physostegia intermedia* (Nutt.) Engelm. & Gray

Dracocephalum L. – Dragonhead [Dragon-head, Dragon head, Dragon's head] (1, 4, 10, 50, 93, 109, 138, 155, 156, 158, 184) (1793–present), False dragonhead [False dragon-head, False-dragonhead, False dragon's headFalse dragonshead] (1) (1932)

Dracocephalum moldavica L. – Dragonhead [Dragon-head, Dragon head, Dragon's head] (114) (1894), Moldavian balm (5, 92) (1876–1913), Moldavian dragonhead [Moldavian dragon head, Moldavica dragonshead] (5, 50, 155) (1913–present), Turkey balm [Turkie balme] (178) (1526)

Dracocephalum nuttallii Britton – See *Physostegia parviflora* Nutt. ex Gray

Dracocephalum parviflorum Nutt. – American dragonhead [American dragon head, American dragon-head] (5, 50, 72, 93, 131, 155) (1899–present), Dragonhead [Dragon-head, Dragon head, Dragon's head] (3, 85, 156) (1923–1977), Lion's-heart [Lion's heart, Lionsheart, Lyonsheart] (156) (1923)

Dracocephalum speciosum Sweet – See *Physostegia virginiana* (L.) Benth. subsp. *virginiana*

Dracocephalum thymiflorum L. – Thyme-leaf dragonhead [Thymeleaf dragonhead] (50, 155) (1942–present)

Dracocephalum virginianum L. – See *Physostegia virginiana* (L.) Benth.

Dracontium foetidum L. – See *Symplocarpus foetidus* (L.) Salisb. ex Nutt.

Dracontium foetidum L. Steud. – See *Symplocarpus foetidus* (L.) Salisb. ex Nutt. (taxonomic status is unresolved (PL))

Dracontium polyphyllum L. – Labaria plant (92) (1876)

Dracopis amplexicaulis (Vahl.) Cass. – Clasping coneflower (50, 124) (1937–present), Clasping-leaf brown-eyed Susan [Clasping-leaf brown-eyed-Susan, Clasping leaf brown-eyed-Susan] (5, 97, 122)

(1913–1937), Clasping-leaf coneflower [Claspingleaf coneflower] (5, 97, 138, 155) (1913–1942), Coneflower [Cone-flower, Cone flower] (4) (1986)

Dracunculus **Mill.** – Dragon [Dragons] (138) (1923)

Dracunculus **Schott.** – possibly *Dracunculus* Mill.

Dracunculus vulgaris **Schott** – Common dragon (138) (1923), Dragon [Dragons] (178) (1596), Serpentona maior (178) (1596)

Drimophyllum pauciflorum **[Nutt.]** – possibly *Umbellularia californica* (Hook. & Arn.) Nutt.

Drosera americana **Willd.** – See *Drosera intermedia* Hayne

Drosera anglica **Huds.** – Dew-grass [Dew grass] (46) (1671), Long-leaf sundew [Long-leaved sun-dew] (187) (1818), Narrow-leaf sundew [Narrowleaf sundew] (138) (1923), Oblong-leaf sundew [Oblong-leaved sundew] (5) (1913)

Drosera brevifolia **Pursh** – Dwarf sundew (50) (present), Short-leaf sundew [Short-leaved sundew] (2) (1895)

Drosera filiformis **Raf.** – Thread-leaf sundew [Threadleaf sundew, Thread-leaved sundew] (2, 5, 138, 156) (1895–1923), possibly Hairy sundew [Hairy sun dew] (42) (1814)

Drosera intermedia **Hayne** – American long-leaf sundew [American long leaved sun dew] (42) (1814), Spatulate-leaf sundew [Spatulate-leaved sundew] (5) (1913)

Drosera intermedia **var.** *americana* **Dcne.** – See *Drosera intermedia* Hayne

Drosera **L.** – Sundew [Sun-dew] (1, 2, 4, 7, 10, 13, 50, 109, 138, 155, 158) (1818–present)

Drosera linearis **Goldie** – Slender-leaf sundew [Slender-leaved sundew] (5, 6) (1892–1913)

Drosera longifolia **L.** – See *Drosera anglica* Huds.

Drosera rotundifolia **L.** – Common sundew (158) (1900), Dew plant [Dew-plant] (92, 156, 158) (1898–1923), Dew-grass [Dew grass] (46) (1671), Drosera (52, 54, 57) (1905–1917), Drosere a Feuilles Rondes (French) (6) (1892), Edler Wiederthon (German) (158) (1900), Eyebright [Eye-bright, Eye bright] (5, 73, 156, 158) (1892–1923) NH, Lustwort [Lust wort, Lust-wort] (5, 52, 92, 107, 156, 158) (1876–1923), Moor-grass [Moor grass] (5, 6, 156, 158) (1892–1923), Moorwort [Moor-wort] (158) (1900), Red-rot [Red rot] (5, 6, 156, 158) (1892–1923), Rosa solis [Rosa-solis] (5, 156, 158) (1900–1923), Rosée du soleil (French) (6, 158) (1892–1900), Ros-solis (158) (1900), Round-leaf dew plant [Round leaved dew plant] (5) (1913), Round-leaf sundrew [Round leaved sundew, Round-leaved sundew] (2, 3, 4, 5, 42, 49, 50, 53, 107, 138, 155, 158, 187) (1814–present), Rundblattriger Sonnenthau (German) (6) (1892), Sin-dew (156) (1923), Sinnthau (German) (158) (1900), Sonnenthau (German) (158) (1900), Sundew [Sun-dew] (19, 47, 49, 52, 53, 54, 57, 61, 92, 156) (1840–1923), Wathaessa (177) (1762), Youthwort [Youth wort] (5, 6, 52, 92, 156, 158) (1892–1923), Yungfernblüthe (German) (158) (1900)

Dryas drummondii **Richards. ex Hook.** – Drummond's mountain avens (5) (1913)

Dryas integrifolia **Vahl.** – Entire-leaf mountain avens [Entire-leaved mountain avens] (5) (1913)

Dryas **L.** – Dryad (1) (1932), Mountain avens (1, 10) (1818–1932)

Dryas octopetala **L.** – Dryas (174) (1753), Mountain avens (19, 107) (1840–1919), White mountain avens (5) (1913), Wild betony (5) (1913)

Drymocallis agrimonioides **(Purch) Rydb.** – See *Potentilla arguta* Pursh subsp. *arguta*

Drymocallis arguta **(Pursh) Rydb.** – See *Potentilla arguta* Pursh subsp. *arguta*

Drymocallis **Fourr.** – See *Potentilla* L. (all US species)

Dryopteris ×*boottii* **(Tuckerman) Underwood** [*cristata* × *intermedia*] – Boott's shield-fern (5, 50) (1913–present), Boott's woodfern [Boott woodfern] (138) (1923)

Dryopteris ×*poyseri* **Wherry** – See *Dryopteris clintoniana* (D. C. Eaton) Dowell.

Dryopteris **Adans.** – Male fern [Malefern, Male-fern, Male ferne] (1)

(1932), Oak fern [Oak-fern, Oakfern, Oke ferne] (1) (1932), Shield fern (1, 158) (1900–1932), Wood fern [Woodfern] (4, 50, 131, 155) (1923–present)

Dryopteris assimilis **S. Walker** – See *Dryopteris expansa* (K. Presl) Fraser-Jenkins & Jermy

Dryopteris austriaca **(Jacq.) Woyn. ex Schinz & Thell.** – See *Dryopteris campyloptera* (Kunze) Clarkson

Dryopteris austriaca **(Jacq.) Woynar ex Schinz & Thellung var.** *intermedia* **(Muhl. ex Willd.) Morton** – See *Dryopteris intermedia* (Muhl. ex Willd.) Gray

Dryopteris boottii **(Tuckerman.) Underw.** – See *Dryopteris* ×*boottii* (Tuckerman) Underwood [*cristata* × *intermedia*]

Dryopteris campyloptera **(Kunze) Clarkson** – Broad prickly-tooth wood fern [Broad prickly-toothed wood fern] (5) (1913), Mountain wood fern [Mountain woodfern] (138) (1923), Spreading shield fern (5) (1913)

Dryopteris campyloptera **Clarkson** – See *Dryopteris campyloptera* (Kunze) Clarkson

Dryopteris carthusiana **(Vill.) H. P. Fuchs** – Prickly-tooth fern [Prickly-toothed fern] (4, 5) (1913–1986), Spinulose shield fern [Spinulose shield-fern] (5, 72) (1907–1913), Spinulose wood fern [Spinulose wood-fern] (4, 50, 109) (1949–present), Toothed wood fern [Toothed woodfern] (138, 155) (1923–1942), Wood fern [Woodfern] (3) (1977), possibly Common wood fern [Common wood-fern, Common woodfern] (158) (1900)

Dryopteris clintoniana **(D. C. Eaton) Dowell.** – Clinton's fern (5) (1913), Clinton's woodfern [Clinton woodfern] (50, 138) (1923–present)

Dryopteris cristata **(L.) A. Gray** – Crested fern (5, 86) (1878–1913), Crested shield fern [Crested shield-fern] (4, 5, 72, 86) (1878–1986), Crested wood fern [Crested woodfern] (3, 5, 50, 138, 155) (1911–present)

Dryopteris cristata **(L.) Gray var.** *clintoniana* **(D.C. Eat.) Underwood** – See *Dryopteris clintoniana* (D.C. Eaton) Dowell.

Dryopteris cristola **(L.) A. Gray** – possibly *Dryopteris cristata* (L.) A. Gray (not in US PL W3 IPNI)

Dryopteris dentata – See *Thelypteris dentata* (Forsk.) E. St. John

Dryopteris dilatata **(Hoffm.) Gray** – See *Dryopteris campyloptera* (Kunze) Clarkson

Dryopteris dilatata **(Hoffmann) Gray subsp.** *americana* **(Fisch.) Hultén** – See *Dryopteris expansa* (K. Presl) Fraser-Jenkins & Jermy

Dryopteris dilatata **auct. non (Hoffmann) Gray** – See *Dryopteris expansa* (K. Presl) Fraser-Jenkins & Jermy

Dryopteris disjuncta **(Lebed.) Morton** – See *Gymnocarpium disjunctum* (Rupr.) Ching

Dryopteris dryopteris **(L.) Britton** – Oak fern [Oak-fern, Oakfern, Oke ferne] (3, 5, 46, 72, 131, 138, 158) (1899–1977), Western oak fern [Western oakfern] (50) (present)

Dryopteris expansa **(K. Presl) Fraser-Jenkins & Jermy** – Broad prickly-tooth wood fern [Broad prickly-toothed wood fern] (5) (1913), Spreading shield fern (5) (1913), Spreading wood fern [Spreading woodfern] (50) (present)

Dryopteris filix-mas **(L.) Schott** – Aspidium (53, 57, 59) (1911–1922), Basket fern (5, 158) (1900–1913), Bearpaw root [Bears' paw root, Bear's-paw root] (5, 92, 158) (1876–1913), Felix mas (54) (1905), Filix mas (55, 178) (1596–1911), Fougère male (French) (158) (1900), Helecho macho (Spanish) (158) (1900), Johanniswurzel (German) (158) (1900), Knotty brake (5, 92, 158) (1876–1913), Male fern [Malefern, Male-fern, Male ferne] (4, 5, 49, 50, 52, 53, 54, 55, 57, 58, 60, 61, 92, 97, 109, 122, 131, 133, 138, 158, 178) (1696–present), Male shield fern [Male shield-fern (5, 92, 158) (1876–1913), Shield fern (3, 58) (1869–1977), Shield root [Shield roots] (5, 92) (1876–1913), Sweet brake (5, 92, 158) (1876–1913), Waldfarn (German) (158) (1900), Wurmfarn (German) (158) (1900), Fragrant shield fern [Fragrant shield-fern] (5) (1913), Fragrant wood fern (5, 50) (1913–present), Sweet shield fern (86) (1878)

Dryopteris goldiana **(Hook. ex Goldie) Gray** – Goldie's fern [Goldie fern, Goldie's-fern] (5, 72, 109, 138) (1907–1949), Goldie's wood fern [Goldie woodfern] (4, 5, 50, 155) (1913–present)

***Dryopteris goldieana* (Hook.) A. Gray** – See *Dryopteris goldiana* (Hook. ex Goldie) Gray

***Dryopteris hexagonoptera* (Michx.) C. Chr.** – See *Phegopteris hexagonoptera* (Michx.) Fee

***Dryopteris intermedia* (Muhl. ex Willd.) Gray** – American shieldfern [American shield-fern] (5, 122) (1913–1937), Common wood fern [Common wood-fern, Common woodfern] (5, 138) (1913–1923), Intermediate wood fern [Intermediate woodfern] (50) (present)

***Dryopteris intermedia* (Muhl.) Gray.** – See *Dryopteris intermedia* (Muhl. ex Willd.) Gray

***Dryopteris linnaeana* C. Christens.** – See *Gymnocarpium dryopteris* (L.) Newman

***Dryopteris marginalis* (L.) A. Gray** – Aspidium (64) (1908), Evergreen wood fern, Evergreen wood-fern (3, 5, 64, 158) (1900–1977), Leather wood fern [Leather woodfern] (138, 155) (1923–1942), Marginal aspidium (42) (1814), Marginal shield fern [Marginal shield-fern (4, 5, 49, 53, 109, 187) (1818–1986), Marginal wood fern [Marginal woodfern] (50) (present), Marginal-fruit shield fern [Marginal-fruited shield-fern, Marginal fruited shield fern] (64, 158) (1900–1908), Shield fern (97) (1937)

***Dryopteris noveboracensis* (L.) A. Gray** – See *Thelypteris noveboracensis* (L.) Nieuwl.

***Dryopteris phegopteris* (L.) C. Chr.** – See *Phegopteris connectilis* (Michx.) Watt

***Dryopteris robertiana* (Hoffm.) C. Chr.** – See *Gymnocarpium robertianum* (Hoffmann) Newman

***Dryopteris simulata* Davenp.** – See *Thelypteris simulata* (Davenport) Nieuwl.

***Dryopteris spinulosa* (O. F. Muell.) Watt** – See *Dryopteris carthusiana* (Vill.) H. P. Fuchs

***Dryopteris spinulosa* (O. F. Muell.) Watt var. *concordiana* (Davenport) Eastman** – See *Dryopteris intermedia* (Muhl. ex Willd.) Gray

***Dryopteris spinulosa* (O. F. Muell.) Watt var. *dilatata* auct. non (Hoffmann) Underwood** – See *Dryopteris expansa* (K. Presl) Fraser-Jenkins & Jermy

***Dryopteris spinulosa* (O. F. Muell.) Watt var. *intermedia* (Muhl. ex Willd.) Underwood** – See *Dryopteris intermedia* (Muhl. ex Willd.) Gray

***Dryopteris spinulosa* (Retz) Kuntze** – possibly *Dryopteris carthusiana* (Vill.) H. P. Fuchs

***Dryopteris thelypteris* (L.) A. Gray** – See *Thelypteris palustris* Schott var. *pubescens* (Lawson) Fern.

***Drypetes crocea* Poit.** – See *Drypetes lateriflora* (Sw.) Krug & Urb.

***Drypetes glauca* Vahl** – Glaucous drypetes (20) (1857)

***Drypetes lateriflora* (Sw.) Krug & Urb.** – Small-flower drypetes [Small-flowered drypetes] (20) (1857)

***Duchesnea indica* (Andr.) Focke** – Barren-strawberry [Barren strawberry] (156) (1923), Indian strawberry [India-strawberry] (5, 50, 92, 156, 158) (1876–present), Mock strawberry [Mock-strawberry] (5, 97, 138, 156) (1913–1937), Yellow strawberry (158) (1900)

***Duchesnea* Sm.** – Duchesnea (50) (present), Indian strawberry [India-strawberry] (109, 156) (1923–1949), Mock strawberry [Mock-strawberry, Mockstrawberry] (109, 138, 155, 158) (1900–1929)

***Dudleya* Britt. & Rose** – Dudleya (138) (1923)

***Dudleya cymosa* (Lem.) Britt. & Rose** – Nevada cotyledon (86) (1878), possibly Rock-moss [Rock moss] (74) (1893)

***Dudleya nevadensis* (S. Wats.) Britt. & Rose** – See *Dudleya cymosa* (Lem.) Britton & Rose

***Dulichium arundinaceum* (L.) Britt.** – Three-way sedge (3, 50) (1977–present)

Dulichium arundinaceum* (L.) Britt. var. *arundinaceum – Dulichium (5, 66, 72) (1903–1913), Galingale (19) (1840), Sheathed dulichium (187) (1818)

***Dulichium* Rich.** – Dulichium (50) (present)

***Dulichium spathaceum* Pers.** – See *Dulichium arundinaceum* (L.) Britton var. *arundinaceum*

***Dumontinia tuberosa* (Bull.) L.M. Kohn** – Tuberous cup fungus (128) (1933)

***Dupontia cooleyi* [Gray]** – See *Trisetum melicoides* (Michx.) Vasey ex Scribn.

***Dupontia fisheri* R. Br.** – Fisher's dupontia (5, 94) (1901–1913), Fisher's tundra grass [Fisher's tundragrass] (50) (present), Slender dupontia (94) (1901)

***Dupontia psilosantha* (Rupr.) Griseb.** – See *Dupontia fisheri* R. Br.

***Duranta erecta* L.** – Golden dewdrop (106, 109) (1930–1949), Pigeonberry [Pigeon berry] (109) (1949), Sky flower [Skyflower, Sky-flower] (109) (1949), Tropical lilac (106) (1930)

***Duranta* L.** – Sky flower [Skyflower, Sky-flower] (138) (1923)

***Duranta plumiere* (Jacq.)** – See *Duranta erecta* L.

***Duranta repens* L.** – See *Duranta erecta* L.

***Dypsis lutescens* (H. Wendl.) Beentje & Dransf.** – Madagascar palm (109) (1949), Yellow palm (138) (1923)

***Dyschoriste linearis* (Torr. & Gray) Kuntze** – Polka dots [Polkadots] (50)

***Dyschoriste* Nees** – Calophanes (158) (1900), Snakeherb (50) (present)

***Dyschoriste oblongifolia* (Michx.) Kuntze** – Dyschoriste (5) (1913)

***Dysodia aurea* (Gray) A. Nels. (sic)** – See *Thymophylla aurea* (Gray) Greene ex Britton var. *aurea*

***Dyssodia acerosa* DC.** – See *Thymophylla acerosa* (DC.) Strother

***Dyssodia* Cav.** – Dogweed [Dog weed] (155) (1942), Dyssodia (50) (present), Fetid marigold [Foetid marigold] (1, 2, 158) (1895–1932)

***Dyssodia chrysanthemoides* Lag.** – See *Dyssodia papposa* (Vent.) A.S. Hitchc.

***Dyssodia papposa* (Vent.) A.S. Hitchc.** – Askutstat (Pawnee) (37) (1919), Boebera (125) (1930) KS, False dogfennel [False dog-fennel, False dog fennel] (5, 97, 122, 156, 158) (1900–1937), Fetid marigold [Foetid marigold] (3, 4, 5, 37, 50, 63, 62, 72, 80, 85, 93, 95, 121, 131, 148, 156, 158) (1899–present), Pezhe piazhi (Omaha-Ponca, vile weed) (37) (1919), Pispiza tawote (Lakota, prairie dog food) (121) (1918?–1970?), Pizpiza-ta-wote (Dakota, prairie dog food) (37) (1919), Prairie-dog food [Prairie dog food] (37) (1919), Prairie-dog weed [Prairie dogweed (5, 76, 155, 156, 158) (1896–1942), Stinkweed [Stink-weed, Stink weed] (145) (1897), Tiny-Tim [Tiny Tim] (122, 124) (1937) TX, Yellow dog-fennel (62) (1912)

***Dyssodia tagetoides* Torr. & Gray** – False dogfennel [False dog-fennel, False dog fennel] (50) (present)

***Dyssodia tenuiloba* (DC. Robinson** – See *Dyssodia papposa* (Vent.) A. S. Hitchc.)

E

Eatonia obtusata **Gr.** – See *Sphenopholis obtusata* (Michx.) Scribn.

Eatonia pennsylvanica **Gray** – See *Sphenopholis nitida* (Biehler) Scribn.

Eatonia pensylvanica – See *Sphenopholis nitida* (Biehler) Scribn.

Ecballium **A. Rich.** – Squirting cucumber [Squirting-cucumber] (109, 138) (1923–1949)

Ecballium elaterium **(L.) A. Rich.** – Elaterium (92) (1876), Elaterium cucumber (92) (1876), Squirting cucumber [Squirting-cucumber] (92, 138) (1876–1923), Wild balsam-apple [Wild balsam apple] (92) (1876), Wild cowcomer [Wylde cowcomer] (179) (1526), Wild cucumber [Wild-cucumber, Wilde cucumbers] (92, 178) (1526–1876)

Echeandia flavescens **(J. A. & J. H. Schultes) Cruden** – Torrey's anthericum [Torry anthericum] (155) (1942)

Echeandia **Ortega** – Anthericum (155) (1942)

Echeveria **DC.** – Echeveria (138, 155) (1931–1942)

Echinacea angustifolia **DC.** – Black Sampson (47, 49, 52, 54) (1852–1919), Black Samson echinacea [Black-samson echinacea, Blacksamson echinacea] (50, 155) (1942–present), Comb (76) (1896) Burnside SD, Comb plant (37) (1919), Coneflower [Coneflower, Cone flower] (49, 52, 53, 54) (1905–1922), Echinacea (52, 54, 57) (1905–1917), Ichah'pe-hu (Dakota, whip plant) (37) (1919), Ksapitahako (Pawnee, to whirl in the hand) (37) (1919), Mika-hi (Omaha-Ponca, comb plant) (37) (1919), Narrow-leaf coneflower [Narrow leaf cone flower] (124) (1937), Narrow-leaf purple coneflower [Narrowleaf purplecone flower, Narrow-leaved purple cone-flower] (5, 37, 49, 53, 97, 122) (1898–1937), Pale purple coneflower [Pale purple cone-flower, Pale purple cone flower] (63) (1899), Pale-purple coneflower (63) (1899), Purple coneflower [Purple cone-flower, Purple cone flower] (49, 52, 53, 93, 127) (1919–1936), Rattlesnake-weed [Rattlesnake weed, Rattlesnake weede, Rattlesnakes' weed] (101) (1905) MT, Saparidu kahts (Pawnee, mushroom medicine) (37) (1919), Snakeroot [Snake root, Snake-root] (101) (1905) MT

Echinacea angustifolia **DC. var. *angustifolia*** – Comb (156) (1923), Echinacea (64) (1907), Narrow-leaf coneflower [Narrow-leaved cone-flower] (72) (1907), Pale-purple coneflower (64) (1907), Purple coneflower [Purple cone-flower, Purple cone flower] (3, 85, 156) (1923–1977), Purple daisy (156) (1923), Sampson-root (64, 156) (1908–1923)

Echinacea angustifolia **DC. var. *strigosa* McGreg.** – Purple coneflower [Purple cone-flower, Purple cone flower] (3) (1977), Strigose black-Sampson [Strigose blacksampson] (50) (present)

Echinacea atrorubens **Nutt.** – Topeka purple coneflower (50) (present)

Echinacea **Moench** – Echinacea (155) (1942), Hedgehog coneflower [Hedgehog-coneflower] (138) (1923), Purple coneflower [Purple cone-flower, Purple cone flower] (1, 2, 50, 109, 158) (1895–present), possibly Red sunflower (7) (1828)

Echinacea pallida **(Nutt.) Britton** – See *Echinacea pallida* (Nutt.) Nutt.

Echinacea pallida **(Nutt.) Nutt.** – Comb (Dakota) (158) (1900), Echinacea (158) (1900, Pale echinacea (3, 4, 155) (1942–1986), Pale purple coneflower [Pale purple cone-flower, Pale purple cone flower] (5, 50, 72, 97, 124, 131, 158) (1899–present)

Echinacea paradoxa **(J.B.S. Norton) Britt.** – Bush's cone flower (5) (1913)

Echinacea purpurea **(L.) Moench** – Black Sampson (5, 92, 156) (1876–1923), Bobartia (174) (1753), Comb flower [Comb-flower] (156) (1923), Eastern purple coneflower (50) (present), Hedgehog coneflower [Hedgehog cone-flower] (156) (1923), Purple coneflower [Purple cone-flower, Purple cone flower] (5, 63, 72, 92, 97,

156) (1876–1923), Purple daisy (156) (1923), Purple echinacea (155) (1942), Red sunflower (5, 92, 156) (1876–1923)

Echinocactus hamatocanthus **Muehlenpf.** – See *Ferocactus hamatacanthus* (Muehlenpfordt) Britt. & Rose var. *hamatacanthus*

Echinocactus **Link & Otto** – Barrel cactus [Barrelcactus] (104) (1896), Echinocactus (155, 158) (1900–1942), Hedgehog thistle [Hedge hog thistle] (14) (1882), possibly Arequipa (155) (1942)

Echinocactus polycephalus **Engelm. & Bigelow** – Cottontop echinocactus (155) (1942), Many-head hedgehog cactus [Many-headed hedgehog cactus] (86) (1878)

Echinocactus texensis **Hopffer.** – Barrel cactus [Barrelcactus] (4) (1986), Devil's-head [Devil's head] (4) (1986), Devils-head echinocactus (155) (1942), Hedgehog cactus [Hedge hog cactus] (92) (1876), Horse-crippler [Horse crippler] (50) (present), Horse-crippler cactus [Horse crippler cactus] (109) (1949), Viznaga (122) (1937) TX

Echinocactus wislizeni **Engelm.** – See *Ferocactus wislizeni* (Engelm.) Britt. & Rose

Echinocereus albispinus **Lahman** – See *Echinocereus reichenbachii* (Terscheck ex Walp.) Haage f. var. *baileyi* (Rose) N.P. Taylor

Echinocereus baileyi **[Rose]** – See *Echinocereus reichenbachii* (Terscheck ex Walp.) Haage f. var. *baileyi* (Rose) N.P. Taylor

Echinocereus caespitosus **Engelm. & Gray** – See *Echinocereus reichenbachii* (Terscheck ex Walp.) Haage f.

Echinocereus **Engelm.** – Echinocereus (155, 158) (1900–1942), Hedgehog cereus (1, 50) (1932–present)

Echinocereus enneacanthus **Engelm.** – Petaya (122) (1937) TX

Echinocereus pectinatus **(Scheidw.) Engelm.** – Rainbow cactus (76) (1896) AZ

Echinocereus perbellus **Britton & Rose** – See *Echinocereus reichenbachii* (Terscheck ex Walp.) Haage f. var. *perbellus* (Britt. & Rose) L. Benson

Echinocereus reichenbachii **(Terscheck ex Walp.) Haage f.** – Cob cactus (109) (1949), Lace cactus (4, 97, 109) (1937–1986), Lace echinocereus (155) (1942), Lace hedgehog cactus (50) (present), Tufted hedgehog cactus (5) (1913)

Echinocereus reichenbachii **(Terscheck ex Walp.) Haage f. var. *baileyi* (Rose) N. P. Taylor** – Bailey's echinocereus [Bailey echinocereus] (155) (1942), Bailey's hedgehog cactus (50) (present), Whitespine echinocereus [Whitespine echinocereus] (155) (1942)

Echinocereus reichenbachii **(Terscheck ex Walp.) Haage f. var. *perbellus* (Britt. & Rose) L. Benson** – Small lace cactus (97) (1937) OK

Echinocereus reichenbachii **Haage Jr.** – See *Echinocereus reichenbachii* (Terscheck ex Walp.) Haage f.

Echinocereus rigidissimus **(Engelm.) Haage f.** – Rainbow cactus (138) (1923), Rainbow echinocereus (155) (1942)

Echinocereus triglochidiatus **Engelm.** – Claret-cup cactus (109) (1949), Claret-cup echinocereus [Claretcup echinocereus] (155) (1942)

Echinocereus viridiflorus **Engelm.** – Green-flower hedgehog cactus [Green-flowered hedgehog cactus] (5) (1913), Green-pitaya echinocereus [Greenpitaya echinocereus] (155) (1942), Hedgehog cactus [Hedge hog cactus] (4, 85) (1932–1986), Nylon hedgehog cactus (50) (present), Pitaya (97) (1937) OK

Echinocereus viridiflorus **Engelm. var. *viridiflorus*** – Nylon hedgehog cactus (50) (present)

Echinochloa **Beauv.** – Barnyard grass [Barnyard-grass] (1, 93) (1932–1936), Cockspur (155) (1942), Cockspur grass [Cockspur-grass] (50) (present), Jungle grass (1) (1932), Prickly grass (92) (1876)

Echinochloa colona **(L.) Link** – Jungle-rice [Jungle rice, Junglerice]

(5, 50, 56, 94, 119, 122, 155, 163) (1852–present), Millet [Myllet] (107) (1919), Shama millet (45, 56) (1896–1901), Shanwa millet [Shanwamillet] (155) (1942)

Echinochloa colonum (L.) Link – See *Echinochloa colona* (L.) Link

Echinochloa crus-galli (L.) Beauv. – Ankee millet (56) (1901), Barn grass [Barngrass, Barn-grass] (5, 66, 90, 92, 119) (1885–1938), Barnyard grass [Barnyard-grass] (3, 11, 21, 19, 45, 50, 56, 62, 66, 68, 72, 80, 85, 87, 88, 90, 92, 94, 109, 111, 118, 119, 122, 129, 131, 138, 140, 143, 144, 145, 151, 152, 155) (1840–present), Barnyard millet (68) (1890), Cock's-foot [Cocksfoot, Cocks-foot, Cock's foot, Cock-foot] (151) (1896), Cock's-foot grass [Cocksfoot grass, Cocks' foot grass, Cock's-foot-grass, Cock's foot-grass] (92) (1876), Cocks'-foot panicum (187) (1818), Cockspur grass [Cockspur-grass] (5, 62, 99, 119) (1912–1938), Hedgehog grass [Hedge hog grass, Hedge-hog grass, Hedge-hog-grass] (92) (1876), Large crowfoot grass (151) (1896), Loose panic grass [Loose panic-grass] (5) (1913), Water grass [Water-grass] (5, 119, 151) (1896–1938)

Echinochloa crus-galli (L.) Beauv. var. *frumentacea* Wight – See *Echinochloa frumentacea* Link

Echinochloa crus-galli (L.) Beauv. var. *mitis* (Pursh) Peterm. – See *Echinochloa muricata* (Beauv.) Fern. var. *microstachya* Wieg.

Echinochloa crusgalli edulis – See *Echinochloa frumentacea* Link

Echinochloa crus-galli var. *edulis* A. S. Hitchc. – See *Echinochloa frumentacea* Link

Echinochloa crus-galli var. *mitis* (Pursh) Peterm. – See *Echinochloa muricata* (Beauv.) Fern. var. *microstachya* Wieg.

Echinochloa crus-pavonis (H.B.K.) Schult. var. *macera* (Wieg.) Gould – Gulf cockspur (155) (1942), Gulf cockspur grass (50) (present)

Echinochloa frumentacea Link – Billion-dollar grass [Billion dollar grass, Billion-dollar-grass] (1, 50, 109) (1932–present), Japanese barnyard millet (109, 163) (1852–1949), Japanese millet (1, 138, 155) (1923–1942), Sanwa millet (56) (1901), Shamalo (158) (1900), Shamaloo (158) (1900), Sonwa millet (45) (1896)

Echinochloa microstachya (Wieg.) Rydb. – See *Echinochloa muricata* (Beauv.) Fern. var. *microstachya* Wieg.

Echinochloa muricata (Beauv.) Fern. – Rough barnyard grass [Rough barnyardgrass] (50) (present)

Echinochloa muricata (Beauv.) Fern. var. *microstachya* Wieg. – Awnless barnyard grass (56) (1901), Beardless barnyard grass [Beardless barnyardgrass] (155) (1942), Rough barnyard grass [Rough barnyardgrass] (50) (present)

Echinochloa muricata (Beauv.) Fern. var. *muricata* – Rough barnyard grass [Rough barnyardgrass] (50) (present)

Echinochloa schinata – See *Echinochloa crus-galli* (L.) Beauv.

Echinochloa walteri (Pursh) Nash – Coast cockspur grass (50) (present), Long-awn barnyard grass [Long-awned barnyard-grass] (119) (1938), Saltmarsh cockspur grass [Salt-marsh cockspur grass [Salt-marsh cockspur-grass (5, 56, 72, 163) (1852–1913)

Echinocystis fabacea [Naudin] – See *Marah fabaceus* (Naud.) Naud. ex Greene

Echinocystis lobata (Michx.) Torr. & Gray – Balsam-apple [Balsam apple, Balsamapple] (157) (1929), Bladder cucumber (114) (1894), Creeper [Creepers] (5, 76, 158) (1896–1913) ME, Creeping Jenny [Creeping Jennie, Creeping-Jennie, Creeping-jenny] (5, 76, 156, 158) (1896–1923), Mock apple (5, 156) (1913–1923), Mock cucumber [Mock-cucumber, Mockcucumber] (138, 155) (1923–1942), Mock orange [Mock-orange, Mockorange] (5, 156, 158) (1900–1923), Prickly cucumber (79) (1891) NH, Wah'nah'hecha (Dakota) (37) (1919), Watangtha (Omaha-Ponca, ghost melon) (37) (1919), Wild balsam-apple [Wild balsam apple] (5, 72, 82, 97, 106, 131, 142, 156, 158) (1899–1930), Wild climbing cucumber (142) (1902) WY, Wild cucumber [Wild-cucumber, Wilde cucumbers] (3, 4, 5, 35, 37, 50, 63, 73, 82, 93, 106, 109, 114, 122, 127, 156) (1806–present), Wild mock cucumber [Wild mockcucumber] (155) (1942)

Echinocystis Torr. & Gray – Balsam-apple [Balsam apple, Balsamapple] (1, 82) (1930–1932), Echinocystis (50) (present), Mock apple (1) (1932), Mock cucumber [Mock-cucumber, Mockcucumber] (138, 156) (1923), Wild balsam-apple [Wild balsam apple] (2, 158) (1895–1900), Wild cucumber [Wild-cucumber, Wilde cucumbers] (2, 4) (1895–1986)

Echinocystis wrightii Cogn. – See *Echinopepon wrightii* (Gray) S. Watson

Echinodorus berteroi (Spreng.) Fassett – Burhead [Bur-head, Burrhead] (3, 158) (1900–1977), Upright burhead [Upright bur-head, Upright burrhead] (50) (present)

Echinodorus cordifolius (L.) Griseb. – Burhead [Bur-head, Burrhead] (85, 156) (1923–1932), Creeping burhead [Creeping bur-head, Creeping burrhead] (5, 50, 97, 120) (1913–present), Upright burhead [Upright bur-head, Upright burrhead] (5, 72, 93, 97, 120, 131) (1899–1938)

Echinodorus L.C. Rich. ex Engelm. – Burhead [Bur-head, Burrhead] (1, 50, 122, 155) (1932–present)

Echinodorus parvulus Engelm. – See *Echinodorus tenellus* (Mart.) Buch.

Echinodorus radicans (Nutt.) Engelm. – See *Echinodorus cordifolius* (L.) Griseb.

Echinodorus rostratus Engelm. – See *Echinodorus berteroi* (Spreng.) Fassett

Echinodorus tenellus (Mart.) Buch. – Dwarf water-plantain [Dwarf water plantain] (72) (1907) IA, Mud-babies [Mudbabies] (50) (present)

Echinopanax horridus (J. E. Smith) Dcne. & Planch. – See *Oplopanax horridus* Miq.

Echinopepon Naud. – Spring-gourd (167) (1814)

Echinopepon wrightii (Gray) S. Watson – Balsam-apple [Balsam apple, Balsamapple] (122) (1937) TX

Echinops exaltatus Schrad. – Tall globethistle (138) (1923)

Echinops L. – Globethistle [Globe thistle] (1, 82, 109, 138) (1923–1949)

Echinops ritro L. – Globethistle [Globe thistle] (82) (1930), Steel globe-thistle [Steel globethistle] (138) (1923)

Echinops sphaerocephalus L. – Chapman's honey plant [Chapman honey plant] (106) (1930), Common globethistle (138) (1923), Globethistle [Globe thistle] (19, 106, 156) (1840–1930)

Echinospermum floribundum Lehm. – See *Hackelia floribunda* (Lehm.) I.M. Johnston

Echinospermum lappula Lehm. – See *Lappula squarrosa* (Retz.) Dumort.

Echinospermum Lehm. – See *Lappula* Moench

Echinospermum redkowskii occidentale Wats. – See *Lappula occidentalis* (S. Wats.) Greene var. *occidentalis*

Echinospermum virginicum Lehm. – See *Hackelia virginiana* (L.) I.M. Johnston

Echites suaveolens [(Lindl.) A. DC.] – See *Mandevilla laxa (Ruiz & Pav.) Woodson*

Echium candicans L. f. – Pride-of-Madeira (138) (1923)

Echium fastuosum – See *Echium candicans* L. f.

Echium L. – Blueweed [Blue-weed, Blue weed] (1, 4) (1932–1986), Viper's bugloss [Vipersbugloss, Viper's-bugloss, Vipers bugloss] (1, 4, 10, 19, 50, 109, 155, 156, 158) (1818–present)

Echium vulgare L. – Adder's-wort, [Adder's wort, Adderswort] (5, 92, 156, 157, 158) (1876–1929), Blue cat-tail [Blue cat's-tail] (156, 157, 158) (1900–1929), Blue thistle [Blue-thistle] (5, 7, 19, 75, 92, 106, 156, 157, 158) (1828–1930), Blue-devil [Blue devil, Blue devils, Blue-devils] (5, 75, 109, 156, 157, 158) (1894–1949), Bluestem [Blue-stem, Blue stem] (5, 75, 156, 157, 158) (1900–1929) WV, Blueweed [Blue-weed, Blue weed] (3, 5, 62, 63, 75, 77, 92, 106, 109, 156, 157, 158) (1876–1977), Cat-tail [Cat's tail, Cats Taile, Cat's-tail, Cats tails] (5, 156) (1913–1923) no longer in use by 1923, Common bugloss (42) (1814), Common viper's-bugloss [Common vipersbugloss] (50, 155) (1942–present), Natterkopf (German) (158) (1900), Snake flower [Snakeflower, Snake-flower] (5, 156, 157, 158) (1900–1929), Vipérine (French) (158) (1900),

Viper's bugloss [Vipersbugloss, Viper's-bugloss, Vipers bugloss] (5, 62, 63, 72, 85, 92, 97, 106, 131, 156, 157, 158) (1899–1937), Viper's-grass [Viper's grass] (5, 156, 157, 158) (1900–1929), Viper's-herb [Viper's herb] (5, 156, 157, 158) (1900–1929)

Eclipta alba (L.) Hassk. – See *Eclipta prostrata* (L.) L.

Eclipta L. – Eclipta (50, 158) (1900), Yerba de tajo (Spanish) (1) (1932)

Eclipta prostrata (L.) L. – Eclipta (72) (1907), False daisy (50) (present), Tuber verbena (181) (~1678), White vervain (181) (~1678), Yerba de tajo [Yerba-de-tajo, Yerbadetajo] (3, 4, 5, 93, 97, 122, 155) (1913–1986)

Edgeworthia chrysantha – See *Edgeworthia papyrifera* Sieb. & Zucc.

Edgeworthia Meisn. – Paper tree [Papertree] (138) (1923)

Edgeworthia papyrifera Sieb. & Zucc. – Golden papertree (138) (1923)

Edosmia gairdneri Hook. & Arn. – See *Perideridia gairdneri* (Hook. & Arn.) Mathias subsp. *gairdneri*

Edraianthus A. Dc. – See *Wahlenbergia* Schrad. ex Roth

Egeria densa Planch. – Brazilian waterweed (50) (present), Dense-leaf elodea [Denseleaved elodea] (155) (1942)

Egeria Planch. – Egeria (50) (present)

Ehrendorferia chrysantha (Hook. & Arn.) Rylander – Golden eardrops (138) (1923)

Ehretia anacua (Berl.) Johnston – See *Ehretia anacua* (Teran & Berl.) I.M. Johnston

Ehretia anacua (Teran & Berl.) I. M. Johnston – Anaqua (106, 122) (1930–1937), Knockaway (106) (1930)

Ehretia elliptica DC. – See *Ehretia anacua* (Teran & Berl.) I.M. Johnston

Eichhornia azurea (Sw.) Kunth – Saw-petal water-hyacinth [Sawpetal water-hyacinth] (138) (1923)

Eichhornia crassipes (Mart.) Solms – Common water-hyacinth (138) (1923), Water hyacinth [Water-hyacinth] (109, 122, 124) (1937–1949)

Eichhornia crassipes Solms. – See *Eichhornia crassipes* (Mart.) Solms

Eichhornia Kunth – Water hyacinth [Water-hyacinth] (138) (1923) (for J. A. F. Eichhorn, 1779–1856, Prussian statesman)

Eichornia crassipes (Mart.) Solms – See *Eichhornia crassipes* (Mart.) Solms

Elaeagnus (Tourn.) L. – See *Elaeagnus* L.

Elaeagnus angustifolia L. – Oleaster (82, 106, 107, 109, 135) (1910–1949), Russian oleaster (82) (1930), Russian olive [Russian-olive, Russianolive] (3, 4, 50, 82, 85, 93, 106, 112, 135, 137, 138, 155) (1910–present), Russian wild olive (153) (1913), Tree-of-paradise [Tree of paradise] (137) (1931), Var songorica (106) (1930), Wild olive [Wilde oliue] or Wild olive tree [Wild olive-tree] (82, 106, 107, 137) (1919–1931), Zinzeyd (107) (1919)

Elaeagnus argentea Pursh – See *Elaeagnus commutata* Bernh. ex Rydb.

Elaeagnus commutata Bernh. ex Rydb. – Buckbrush [Buck brush, Buck-brush] (156) (1923), Silver bush [Silver-bush, Buck-brush] (101) (1905), Silverberry [Silver berry, Silver-berry] (2, 3, 4, 5, 50, 85, 93, 106, 108, 109, 130, 131, 138, 155, 156, 158) (1878–present), Silverbush [Silver-bush] (101) (1905) MT, Wolfberry [Wolf berry, Wolf-berry] (156) (1923), Wolf-willow [Wolf willow] (106, 156) (1923–1930)

Elaeagnus hortensis L. – See *Elaeagnus angustifolia* L.

Elaeagnus L. – Elaeagnus (50, 138, 155) (1923–present), Oleaster (2, 4, 10) (1818–1986), Silver bush [Silver-bush, Silverbush] (1) (1932), Silverberry [Silver berry, Silver-berry] (1, 158) (1900–1932), Silverbush [Silver-bush] (1) (1932)

Elaeagnus longipes (A.Gray) – See *Elaeagnus multiflora* Thunb.

Elaeagnus multiflora Thunb. – Cherry elaeagnus (138) (1923)

Elaeagnus parvifolia [Royle] – See *Elaeagnus umbellata* Thunb. var. *parvifolia* (Royle) Schneid.

Elaeagnus pungens Thunb. – Thorny elaeagnus (138) (1923)

Elaeagnus umbellata Thunb. – Autumn elaeagnus (155) (1942), Autumn olive (50, 138) (1923–present)

Elaeagnus umbellata Thunb. var. *parvifolia* (Royle) Schneid. – Chinese elaeagnus (138) (1923)

Elaeis guineensis Jacq. – African oil palm (138) (1923), Elaeis (110) (1886)

Elaeis Jacq. – Oil palm (109) (1949)

Elaphomyces granulatus Fr. – Deer-balls [Deer balls] (92) (1876)

Elaterium L. – See *Echinopepon* Naud. (US species)

Elatine americana (Pursh) Arn. – Mud-purslane [Mud purslane] (19) (1840), Waterwort [Water wort] (3, 5, 156) (1913–1977)

Elatine brachysperma Gray – Short-seed waterwort [Shortseed waterwort, Short-seeded water wort] (5, 50, 155) (1913–present)

Elatine hydropiper L. – Waterwort [Water wort] (92) (1876), Hydropiper (174, 177) (1753–1762)

Elatine L. – Mud-purslane [Mud purslane] (1, 158) (1900–1932), Waterwort [Water wort] (1, 4, 13, 15, 50, 155) (1849–present)

Elatine rubella Rydb. – American waterwort (155) (1942), Long-stem waterwort [Long-stemmed water wort, Long-stemmed waterwort] (5, 131) (1899–1913), Mud-purslane [Mud purslane] (5, 156) (1913–1923), Southwestern waterwort (50) (present)

Elatine triandra Schkuhr – See *Elatine rubella* Rydb.

Eleagnus angustifolia L. – See *Elaeagnus angustifolia* L.

Eleagnus argentea Pursh – See *Elaeagnus commutata* Bernh. ex Rydb.

Eleocharis acicularis (L.) Roemer & J. A. Schultes – Hair club-rush (66) (1903), Least spike-rush [Least spike rush] (5, 156) (1913–1923), Needle spike-rush [Needle spike rush, Needle spikerush] (5, 50, 72, 156) (1907–present), Needle spike-sedge [Needle spikesedge] (3, 139) (1944–1977)

Eleocharis acuminata (Muhl.) Nees. – See *Eleocharis compressa* Sullivant

Eleocharis albida Torr. – White spike-rush [White spike rush, White spikerush] (5, 50) (1913–present)

Eleocharis arenicola Torr. – See *Eleocharis montevidensis* Kunth

Eleocharis atropurpurea (Retz) Kunth – See *Eleocharis atropurpurea* (Retz.) J.& K. Presl

Eleocharis atropurpurea (Retz.) J. & K. Presl – Purple spikerush [Purple spike rush] (5, 50, 72) (1907–present)

Eleocharis capitata (L.) R. Br. – See *Eleocharis geniculata* (L.) Roemer & J.A. Schultes

Eleocharis caribaea (Rottb.) S. F. Blake – See *Eleocharis geniculata* (L.) Roemer & J. A. Schultes

Eleocharis compressa Sull. var. *compressa* – Flat-stem spikerush [Flat-stem spikerush, Flat-stemmed spike rush] (5, 50) (1913–present)

Eleocharis compressa Sullivant – Flat-stem spikesedge [Flatstem spikesedge] (3) (1977), Flat-stem tufted spikerush [Flat stemmed tufted spike-rush] (129) (1894), Narrow-tip spikesedge (139) (1944), Tufted rush (66) (1903)

Eleocharis diandra C. Wright – possibly Tufted spike-rush (129) (1894)

Eleocharis engelmanni Steud. – Blunt spike-rush [Blunt spike rush] (5, 50) (1913–present), Engelmann's spikerush [Engelmann's spikerush, Engelmann's spike rush] (5, 50) (1913–present)

Eleocharis equisetoides (Ell.) Torr. – Horsetail rush (66) (1903)

Eleocharis erythropoda Steud. – Bald spikerush (50) (present)

Eleocharis filiculmis Kunth – Thread-like rush [Threadlike rush] (66) (1903)

Eleocharis flaccida (Rchb.) Urban – See *Eleocharis flavescens* (Poir.) Urban

Eleocharis flavescens (Poir.) Urban – Pale spikerush [Pale spike rush] (5) (1913)

Eleocharis geniculata (L.) Roemer & J. A. Schultes – Canadian spikesedge [Canada spikesedge] (50) (present), Capitate spike-rush [Capitate spike rush] (5) (1913)

Eleocharis intermedia (Muhl.) Schult – Matted spike-rush [Matted spike rush] (5, 50) (1913–present), Mediate spike rush (66, 72) (1903–1907)

Eleocharis interstincta (Vahl) R. & S. – Knotted spike-rush [Knotted spike rush] (5, 50, 156) (1913–present)

Eleocharis lanceolata Fern. – Dagger-leaf spikerush [Daggerleaf spikerush] (50) (present)

Eleocharis macrostachya Britt. – See *Eleocharis palustris* (L.) Roemer & J. A. Schultes

Eleocharis melanocarpa Torr. – Black club-rush (66) (1903), Blackfruit spike rush [Blackfruit spikerush, Black-fruit spikerush] (5, 50) (1913–present)

Eleocharis microcarpa Torr. – Small-fruit spikerush [Smallfruit spikerush] (50) (present), Torrey's spike-rush [Torrey's spike rush] (5) (1913)

Eleocharis montevidensis Kunth – Sand spike-rush [Sand spikerush] (50) (present), Sand spike-sedge [Sand spikesedge] (139) (1944)

Eleocharis obtusa (Willd.) J. A. Schultes – Blunt spike-rush [Blunt spike rush] (120) (1938), Obtuse spike-rush (66) (1903), Wire grass [Wire-grass, Wiregrass] (85) (1932)

Eleocharis obtusa (Willd.) Schult. var. *ovata* (Roth) Drapalik & Mohlenbrook – See *Eleocharis engelmanni* Steud.

Eleocharis obtusa R. Br. – possibly *Eleocharis diandra* C. Wright

Eleocharis olivacea Torr. – Bright-green spike-rush [Bright green spike rush] (5, 50) (1913–present), Olive spikerush [Olive spike rush] (66) (1903)

Eleocharis ovata (Roth) Roemer & J. A. Schultes – Blunt spike-sedge [Blunt spikesedge] (3) (1977), Ovate spikerush (50) (present), Ovoid spikerush [Ovoid spike rush] (5, 72) (1907–1913)

Eleocharis palustris (L.) Roemer & J. A. Schultes – Aglet-head rush [Aglet-headed rush] (5) (1913), Aglet-head spike-rush [Aglet-headed spike-rush] (156) (1923), Common spikerush [Common spike-rush] (50, 66, 129) (1894–present), Common spikesedge (139) (1944), Creeping spike rush [Creeping spike-rush] (5, 72, 120, 156) (1907–1938), Pale spikerush [Pale spike rush] (5) (1913), Small's spikerush [Small's spike rush] (5) (1913), Spike-rush [Spike rush, Spikerush] (3) (1977), Bayonet-grass (156) (1923), Tule (156) (1923)

Eleocharis parvula (R. & S.) var. *anachaeta* (Torr.) Svens – See *Eleocharis parvula* (Roem. & Schult.) Link ex Bluff, Nees & Schauer

Eleocharis parvula (Roem. & Schult.) Link ex Bluff, Nees & Schauer – Colorado bulrush (139) (1944), Dwarf spike rush [Dwarf spikerush, Dwarf spikerush] (50, 66) (1903–present)

Eleocharis pauciflora (Lightf.) Link – See *Eleocharis quinqueflora* (F.X. Hartmann) Schwarz

Eleocharis pygmaea Torr. – See *Eleocharis parvula* (Roem. & Schult.) Link ex Bluff, Nees & Schauer

Eleocharis quadrangulata (Michx.) Roemer & J. A. Schultes – Angled spike-rush (120) (1938), Quadrangular rush (66) (1903), Square-stem spike-rush [Squarestem spikerush] (50) (present)

Eleocharis quinqueflora (F. X. Hartmann) Schwarz – Dwarf club rush (5) (1913), Few-flower clubrush [Few-flowered club rush] (5) (1913), Few-flower spikerush [Fewflower spikerush] (50) (present)

Eleocharis R. Br. – Spike-rush [Spike rush, Spikerush] (1, 50, 93, 121, 152, 156) (1912–present), Spike-sedge [Spikesedge] (139) (1944), Wire-grass [Wire grass] (1, 93) (1932–1936), Θažiŋga (Osage, little rush) (121) (1918–1970)

Eleocharis robbinsii Oakes – Robbins' club-rush (66) (1903), Robbins' spikerush [Robbins spike rush] (5, 50) (1913–present)

Eleocharis rostellata (Torr.) Torr. – Beaked spike rush [Beaked spikerush] (5, 50) (1913–present), Brake spike rush (66) (1903)

Eleocharis smallii Britt. – See *Eleocharis palustris* (L.) Roemer & J.A. Schultes

Eleocharis tenuis (Willd.) J. A. Schultes – Club rush [Club-rush] (19) (1840), Kill-cow [Kill cow] (5, 75, 156) (1894–1923) WV, Poverty-grass [Poverty grass] (5, 75, 156) (1894–1923) WV, Slender club-rush (66) (1903), Slender spike-rush [Slender spike rush, Slender spikerush] (5, 50, 156) (1913–present)

Eleocharis tenuis (Willd.) J. A. Schultes var. *verrucosa* (Svens.) Svens. – Slender spike-rush [Slender spike rush, Slender spikerush] (50) (present)

Eleocharis tricostata Torr. – Flat stemrush [Flat stem-rush] (66) (1903), Three-angle spikerush [Three-angled spikerush] (50) (present), Three-rib spike-rush [Three-ribbed spike rush] (5) (1913)

Eleocharis tuberculosa (Michx.) Roemer & J. A. Schultes – Conecup spikerush (50) (present), Large-tubercle spike rush [Large-tubercled spike rush] (5) (1913), Tubercled spike-rush (66) (1903), Twisted spike-rush [Twisted spike rush] (5) (1913)

Eleocharis uniglumis (Link) J.A. Schultes – One-scale spikerush [Onescale spikerush] (50) (present)

Eleocharis wolfii (Gray) Gray ex Britt. – Wolf's spike-rush [Wolf's spike rush, Wolf's spikerush] (5, 50, 72) (present), Wolf's spike-sedge [Wolf spikesedge] (3) (1977)

Eleocharis xyridiformis Fern. & Brackett – See *Eleocharis palustris* (L.) Roemer & J. A. Schultes

Elephantella groenlandica (Retz.) Rydb. – See *Pedicularis groenlandica* Retz.

Elephantella Rydb. – See *Pedicularis* L. (all US species)

Elephantopus carolinianus Willd. – Carolina elephant's-foot (Carolina elephant's foot or Carolina elephantsfoot, Carolina elephant-foot Carolina elephant foot) (5, 50, 97, 122, 124, 156) (1913–present), Elephant's-foot [Elephant's foot, Elephantsfoot] (3, 19) (1840–1977)

Elephantopus L. – Elephant's-foot [Elephant's foot, Elephantsfoot] (1, 4, 10) (1818–1986)

Elephantopus nudatus Gray – Smoothish elephant's foot (5) (1913)

Elephantopus tomentosus L. – Devil's-grandmother [Devil's grandmother] (5, 75, 156) (1894–1923), Elephant's-foot [Elephant's foot, Elephantsfoot] (57) (1917), Tobacco-weed [Tobacco weed] (5, 75, 156) (1894–1923), Woolly elephant's-foot [Woolly elephant's foot, Woolley elephant's-foot, Woolly elephantfoot] (5, 97, 122, 124, 156) (1913–1937), possibly *Elephantopus tomentosus* L.

Eleusine coracana (L.) Gaertn. – African millet (109, 138) (1923–1949), Big crow's-foot [Big crow's foot] (129) (1894), Coracan (110) (1886)

Eleusine Gaertn. – Crabgrass [Crab-grass, Crab grass] (93) (1936), Goose grass [Goosegrass, Goose-grass] (50) (present), Wire grass [Wire-grass, Wiregrass] (93) (1936), Yard grass [Yard-grass, Yardgrass] (93) (1936)

Eleusine indica (L.) Gaertn. – Crabgrass [Crab-grass, Crab grass] (5, 66, 72, 87, 88, 92, 119, 145, 187) (1818–1938), Crop grass [Cropgrass] (5, 66, 187) (1818–1913), Crowfoot [Crow-foot, Crow foot, Crowfote, Crow's foot] (66, 87, 88) (1884–1903), Crowfoot grass [Crow-foot-grass, Crowfoot-grass] (80, 187) (1818–1913), Dog's-tail [Dog's tail, Dog's-tails, Dog-tails] (5) (1913), Dog-tail grass [Dog's tail grass, Dogs' tail grass, Dog's-tail grass, Dog's-tail-grass] (19, 75, 92, 145, 184) (1793–1897), Goose grass [Goosegrass, Goose-grass] (3, 5, 85, 94, 111, 119, 122, 134, 140, 163) (1852–1977), Indian goose grass [Indian goosegrass] (50) (present), Wire grass [Wire-grass, Wiregrass] (5, 19, 56, 66, 75, 80, 87, 88, 92, 119) (1840–1938), Yard grass [Yard-grass, Yardgrass] (5, 87, 88, 92, 94, 99, 119, 134, 140, 163) (1852–1944)

Eleutherococcus Maxim. – Acanthopanax (155) (1942)

Eliocharis acuminata (Muhl.) Nees. – See *Eleocharis compressa* Sull. var. *compressa*

Eliocharis palustris (L.) R. & S. – See *Eleocharis palustris* (L.) Roemer & J. A. Schultes

Eliocharis simplex (Ell.) A. Dietr. – See *Eleocharis tuberculosa* (Michx.) Roemer & J. A. Schultes

Eliocharis torreyana Boeckl. – See *Eleocharis microcarpa* Torr.

Eliocharis tuberculosa (Michx.) R. & S. – See *Eleocharis tuberculosa* (Michx.) Roemer & J. A. Schultes

Ellisia L. – Ellisia (50, 155) (1942–present)

Ellisia nyctelea (L.) L. – Aunt Lucy (50) (present), Common ellisia (80) (1913), Ellisia (80) (1913), Nyctelea (5, 93, 97) (1913–1937), Water-pod (3, 4) (1977–1986)

Elodea Adans. – possibly *Hypericum* L.

Elodea bifoliata St. John – Two-leaf waterweed [Twoleaf waterweed] (50) (present)

Elodea canadensis Michx. – American waterweed [American waterweed] (156, 158) (1900–1923) England, Babington's curse [Babington's-curse] (156, 158) (1900–1923) introduced into England by botanist of that name, Canadian waterweed [Canada waterweed] (50, 155) (1942–present), Canadian weed (156) (1923), Cat-tail [Cat's tail, Cats Taile, Cat's-tail, Cats tails] (158) (1900), Choke pondweed [Choke pond-weed] (5, 14, 93, 156) (1882–1936), Ditch-moss [Ditch moss, Ditchmoss] (19, 72, 109, 131, 156, 158) (1840–1949), Elodea (109) (1949), Little snakeweed [Little snake weed] (19) (1840), Narrow-leaf waterweed [Narrowleaf waterweed, Narrow-leafed water-weed] (155) (1942), Raave (158) (1900), Thyme-weed [Thyme-weed] (158) (1900), Water-thyme [Water thyme] (92, 156, 158) (1876–1923), Waterweed [Water weed, Water-weed] (3, 5, 85, 92, 93, 138, 156) (1876–1977)

Elodea densa **(Planch.) Casp.** – See *Egeria densa* Planch.

Elodea linearis **(Rydb.) St. John** – See *Elodea canadensis* Michx.

Elodea **Michx.** – Des-shean (Monomonie) (23) (1810), Elodea (155) (1942), Waterweed [Water weed, Water-weed] (50, 120, 138) (1923–present)

Elodea minor **(Engelm. ex Caspary) Farw.** – See *Elodea nuttallii* (Planch.) St. John

Elodea nuttallii **(Planch.) St. John** – Lesser water-weed (5, 120) (1913–1938), Narrow-leaf waterweed [Narrowleaf waterweed, Narrow-leafed water-weed] (5) (1913), Nuttall's water-weed (5) (1913), Waterweed [Water weed, Water-weed] (3) (1977), Western water-weed (50, 155) (1942–present)

Elodea virginica **Nutt.** – See *Triadenum virginicum* (L.) Raf.

Elodes – possibly *Hypericum* L.

Elsholtzia ciliata **(Thunb.) Hyl.** – Elsholtzia (5) (1913)

Elsholtzia cristata **Willd.** – See *Elsholtzia ciliata* (Thunb.) Hyl.

Elsholtzia patrina **(Lepech.) Garcke** – See *Elsholtzia ciliata* (Thunb.) Hyl.

Elsholtzia patrinii **(Lepech.) Garcke** – See *Elsholtzia ciliata* (Thunb.) Hyl.

Elyhordeum iowense **Pohl** – Iowa barley (50) (present)

Elyhordeum macounii **(Vasey) Barkworth & D. R. Dewey** [*Elymus trachycaulus* × *Hordeum jubatum*] – Macoun's barley (50) (present), Macoun's lyme grass [Macoun's lyme-grass] (56, 94, 111) (1901–1915), Macoun's wild rye [Macoun wildrye (5, 72, 155) (1907–1942)

Elyhordeum **Mansf. ex Zizin & Petrowa** – Barley (50) (present)

Elyhordeum montanense **(Scribn.) Bowden** [*Elymus virginicus* × *Hordeum jubatum*] – Montana barley (94, 155) (1901–1942), Mountain barley (50) (present), Pammel's barley (5) (1913), Pammel's wild barley (56, 72) (1901–1907)

Elymus ×*hansenii* **Scribn.** [*glaucus* × *elymoides* or *multisetus*] – Hansen's sitanion (94) (1901)

Elymus ×*pseudorepens* **(Scribn. & J. G. Sm.) Barkworth & D.R. Dewey** [*lanceolatus* × *trachycaulus*] – False couch grass (5, 56, 94) (1901–1913), False quackgrass (140, 155) (1942–1944)

Elymus alaskanus **(Scribn. & Merr.) A. Löve subsp. latiglumis (Scribn. & J.G. Sm.) A. Löve** – Northern wheat grass [Northern wheat-grass] (94) (1901), Violet wheatgrass (155) (1942)

Elymus albicans **(Scribn. & J.G. Sm.) A. Löve** – Griffith's wheatgrass [Griffiths wheatgrass] (140, 155) (1942–1944), Montana wheatgrass (50, 155) (1942–present)

Elymus ambigua **Vasey and Scribn.** – See *Leymus ambiguus* (Vasey & Scribn.) D.R. Dewey

Elymus ambiguus – See *Leymus ambiguus* (Vasey & Scribn.) D.R. Dewey

Elymus arenarius **L.** – See *Leymus arenarius* (L.) Hochst.

Elymus arizonicus **(Scribn. & J.G. Sm.) Gould** – Arizona wheat grass [Arizona wheat-grass] (94) (1901)

Elymus arkansanus **Scribn. & Ball** – See *Elymus villosus* Muhl. ex Willd.

Elymus australis **Scribn. & Ball** – See *Elymus virginicus* L. var. *virginicus*

Elymus brachystachys **Scribn. & Ball** – See *Elymus canadensis* L.

Elymus californicus **(Bol. ex Thurb.) Gould** – California bottle-brush (94) (1901)

Elymus canadensis **L.** – Canadian lyme grass [Canada lyme grass, Canada lyme-grass, Canadian lime grass] (5, 42, 56, 66, 90, 119) (1814–1938), Canadian wild rye [Canada wildrye, Canada wild rye, Canada wild-rye] (3, 11, 50, 116, 140, 143, 146, 155) (1888–present), Great lyme grass [Great lyme-grass] (94) (1901), Lyme grass (87, 88, 143) (1884–1936), Nodding wild rye [Nodding wildrye, Nodding wild-rye] (5, 72, 85, 87, 93, 116, 119, 140, 143, 163) (1852–1958), Robust Canadian wild rye [Robust Canada wildrye] (155) (1942), Robust lyme grass (56) (1901), Rye grass [Rye-grass, Rye-grass] (88) (1885), Short-spike rye grass [Short spiked rye grass] (56) (1901), Short-spike wild rye [Short-spiked wild rye] (5) (1913), Smooth-scale Canada wild rye [Smoothscale Canada wildrye] (155) (1942), Stout wild rye (72) (1907), Terrell's grass [Terrell-grass, Terrell grass, Terril grass] (87, 90) (1884–1885), Wild rye [Wild-rye, Wildrye] (21, 35, 88, 90, 115, 116, 118, 122, 129, 144, 152) (1806–1958), Wild rye grass (111) (1915)

Elymus canadensis **L. var. brachystachys (Scribn. & Ball) Farw.** – See *Elymus canadensis* L.

Elymus canadensis **L. var. robustus (Scribn. & J.G. Sm.) Mackenzie & Bush** – See *Elymus canadensis* L.

Elymus caninus **(L.) L.** – Awned wheat grass [Awned wheat-grass] (5, 56, 72, 90, 93, 111) (1885–1936), Bearded wheat grass (5, 56, 66, 129) (1894–1913), Chien-dent (French) (46) (1879), Dog grass [Dog's grass, Dogs-grasse] (46, 92) (1876–1879), Dogtooth grass [Dog's tooth grass, Dog's-tooth grass, Dogtoothgrass] (5, 46) (1892–1913), Fibrous-root wheat grass [Fibrous-rooted wheat grass] (5, 90) (1885–1913), Hound grass (46) (1879), Slender wheat grass [Slender wheatgrass] (5) (1913)

Elymus cinereus **Scribn.** – See *Leymus cinereus* (Scribn. & Merr.) A.Löve

Elymus condensatus **J. Presl** – See *Leymus condensatus* (J. Presl) A. Löve

Elymus condensatus **J. Presl var. pubens Piper** – See *Leymus cinereus* (Scribn. & Merr.) A.Löve

Elymus curvatus **Piper** – See *Elymus submuticus* (Hook.) Smyth & Smyth

Elymus diversiglumis **Scribn. & Ball** – Diverse-glume wild rye [Diverseglume wildrye] (50) (present), Various-glume wild rye [Various-glumed wild rye] (5) (1913)

Elymus elymoides **(Raf.) Swezey** – Orchard barley (94) (1901), Squirrel-tail [Squirrel tail, Squirreltail] (3, 50) (1977–present)

Elymus elymoides **(Raf.) Swezey subsp. brevifolius (J.G. Sm.) Barkworth** – Squirrel-tail [Squirrel tail, Squirreltail] (3, 50) (1977–present)

Elymus elymoides **(Raf.) Swezey subsp. elymoides** – Bottle-brush squirreltail [Bottlebrush squirreltail] (140, 155) (1942–1944), Long-bristle wild rye [Long-bristled wild rye, Long-bristled wild-rye] (5, 163) (1852–1913), Squirrel-tail [Squirrel tail, Squirreltail] (50, 122, 140) (1937–present), Wild rye [Wild-rye, Wildrye] (145) (1897), Wild rye grass (111) (1915)

Elymus flavescens **Scribn. & J.G. Sm.** – See *Leymus flavescens* (Scribn. & J.G. Sm.) Pilger

Elymus geniculatus – possibly *Leymus arenarius* (L.) Hochst. (current species depends on author)

Elymus giganteus – See *Leymus racemosus* (Lam.) Tzvelev

Elymus glaber **(J.G. Sm.) Burtt Davy** – See *Elymus elymoides* (Raf.) Swezey subsp. *elymoides*

Elymus glabriflorus **(Vasey) Scribn. & Ball** – See *Elymus virginicus* L. var. *virginicus*

Elymus glaucifolius **Muhl. ex Willd.** – See *Elymus canadensis* L.

Elymus glaucus **Buckl.** – Blue wild rye [Blue wildrye] (3, 50, 109, 155) (1942–present) , Smooth wild rye (5) (1913)

Elymus glausifilius – See *Elymus canadensis* L.

Elymus halophilus **Bicknell** – See *Elymus virginicus* L. var. *halophilus* (Bickn.) Wieg.

Elymus hirsutiglumis **Scribn.** – See *Elymus virginicus* L. var. *virginicus*

Elymus hystrix **L.** – Bottlebrush [Bottle brush, Bottle-brush] (94) (1901), Eastern bottle-brush grass [Eastern bottlebrush grass] (50) (present), possibly Bottle-brush grass [Bottlebrush grass, Bottle-brushgrass] (45, 56, 66, 90) (1885–1903), possibly Hedgehog grass [Hedge hog grass, Hedge-hog grass, Hedge-hog-grass] (19, 88) (1840–1885)

Elymus hystrix **L. var.** *bigeloviana* **(Fern.) Bowden** – Eastern bottle-brush grass [Eastern bottlebrush grass] (50) (present)

Elymus hystrix **L. var.** *hystrix* – Bottlebrush [Bottle brush, Bottle-brush] (111) (1915), Bottle-brush grass [Bottlebrush grass, Bottle-brushgrass] (3, 5, 72, 92, 119, 155) (1876–1977), Bottle-rush [Bottle rush] (5) (1913), Eastern bottle-brush grass [Eastern bottlebrush grass] (50) (present)

Elymus innovatus **Beal** – See *Leymus innovatus* (Beal) Pilger

Elymus interruptus **Buckl.** – Texas wild rye [Texas wildrye] (50, 155) (1942–present)

Elymus jejunus **(Ramaley) Rydb.** – See *Elymus virginicus* L. var. *virginicus*

Elymus junceus **Fisch.** – See *Psathyrostachys juncea* (Fisch.) Nevski

Elymus **L.** – Bottle-brush grass [Bottlebrush grass, Bottlebrushgrass] (93, 155) (1936–1942), Lime grass [Lime-grass] (184) (1793), Long-awn wild rye [Long-awned wild rye] (93) (1936), Lyme grass (35, 66) (1806–1903), Rye grass [Rye-grass, Ryegrass] (1, 10) (1818–1932), Squirrel-tail [Squirrel tail, Squirreltail] (155) (1942), Wild rye [Wild-rye, Wildrye] (1, 10, 35, 50, 87, 138, 155) (1806–present), Wild rye grass (87) (1884)

Elymus lanceolatus **(Scribn. & J.G. Sm.) Gould** – Elmer's wheatgrass [Elmer wheatgrass] (155) (1942), Northern wheat grass [Northern wheat-grass] (5, 85) (1913–1932) SD, Riverside wheat grass [Riverside wheat-grass] (94) (1901), Streambank wheat grass [Streambank wheatgrass] (50, 155) (1942–present), Thick-spike wheatgrass [Thickspike wheatgrass] (3, 146, 155) (1939–1977)

Elymus lanceolatus **(Scribn. & J.G. Sm.) Gould subsp.** *lanceolatus* – Northern wheat grass [Northern wheat-grass] (50) (present)

Elymus macounii **Vasey** – See *Elyhordeum macounii* (Vasey) Barkworth & D.R. Dewey

Elymus mollis **Trin** – See *Leymus mollis* (Trin.) Pilger subsp. *mollis*

Elymus pungens **auct. non (Pers.) Melderis** – See *Thinopyrum pycnanthum* (Godr.) Barkworth

Elymus pycnanthus **(Godr.) Melderis** – See *Thinopyrum pycnanthum* (Godr.) Barkworth

Elymus repens **(L.) Gould** – Bluejoint [Blue-joint, Blue joint] (5) (1913), Chandler's grass [Chandler grass] (45, 64, 66, 69, 90) (1885–1908), Chiendent (92) (1876), Chiendent officinal (French) (158) (1900), Colorado blue grass (5) (1913), Common couch grass (45) (1896), Common quack grass (56) (1901), Common witch grass [Common witchgrass] (45) (1896), Cooch grass [Cooch-grass] (158) (1900), Couch grass [Couch-grass] (5, 19, 45, 49, 52, 53, 54, 55, 59, 56. 62, 64, 66, 67, 69, 87, 88, 90, 92, 94, 111, 118, 119, 129, 143, 157, 158, 163) (1840–1938), Creeping wheat (45) (1896), Creeping wheat grass [Creeping wheat-grass] (64, 69) (1904–1908), Cutch grass [Cutch-grass] (158) (1900), Devil's grass (62, 64, 69) (1904–1912) IN, Dog grass [Dog's grass, Dogs-grasse] (5, 45, 49, 53, 62, 64, 66, 69, 78, 87, 90, 92) (1876–1922) dog's eat it for medicinal qualities in exciting vomit, Dogweed [Dog weed] (92) (1876), Durfa grass [Durfa-grass] (64, 69) (1904–1908), Durfee grass (45, 64, 69) (1896–1904), Dutch grass (64, 69) (1904–1908), False wheat (5) (1913), Fin's grass (45, 64, 69) (1896–1904), Graswurzel (German) (158) (1900), Knot grass [Knotgrass] (5, 92) (1876–1913), Petit chiendent (French) (158) (1900), Pond grass (5) (1913), Quack grass [Quack-grass, Quackgrass] (5, 11, 19, 45, 50, 56, 62, 64, 69, 72, 80, 85, 87, 88, 90, 92, 93, 118, 119, 122, 129, 140, 143, 155, 163) (1840–present), Quake grass [Quake-grass] (45, 64, 66, 69, 90) (1896–1904), Queckenwurzel (German) (158) (1900), Quekes (178, 179) (1526–1596), Quichens (5) (1913), Quick grass [Quick-grass]

(45, 49, 53, 64, 69, 80, 90, 92, 108, 158, 163) (1852–1922), Quickens (92, 158) (1876–1900), Quitch (49, 53, 92) (1876–1922), Quitch grass [Quitch-grass] (5, 45, 49, 64, 66, 69, 87, 90, 92, 119, 158, 163) (1852–1938), Rye grass [Rye-grass, Ryegrass] (45) (1896), Scutch grass [Scutch-grass] (45, 64, 69, 80, 158) (1896–1913), Shear grass (5) (1913), Sheep's-cheese (158) (1900), Shelly grass (5, 92) (1876–1913), Slough grass [Slough-grass, Sloughgrass] (5) (1913), Squitch (5, 45) (1896–1913), Squitch grass [Squitch-grass] (90, 158) (1885–1900), Stroil (5) (1913), Summer wheat (19) (1840), Triticum (57, 59, 64, 157) (1908–1929), Twitch grass [Twitch-grass] (5, 45, 64, 66, 69, 78, 87, 90, 92, 157, 158) (1884–1929), Wheat grass [Wheatgrass, Wheatgrass] (64, 69, 87, 90) (1884–1908), Wick [Wicke, Wicks] (158) (1900), Wicken [Wickens] (5, 158) (1900–1913), Witch grass [Witch-grass, Witchgrass] (5, 45, 64, 67, 69, 5, 78, 90, 92, 157, 158) (1876–1929)

Elymus robustus **Scribn. & J.G. Sm.** – See *Elymus canadensis* L.

Elymus salinus **Jones** – See *Leymus salinus* (M.E. Jones) A. Löve subsp. *salinus*

Elymus scribneri **(Vasey) M. E. Jones** – Scribner's wheat grass [Scribner wheatgrass] (140) (1944), Spreading wheatgrass (140) (1944)

Elymus sierrae **Gould** – Short-leaf wheat grass [Short-leafed wheatgrass] (94) (1901)

Elymus simplex **Scribn. & Williams** – See *Leymus simplex* (Scribn. & Williams) D. R. Dewey

Elymus sitanion **J. A. Schultes** – See *Elymus elymoides* (Raf.) Swezey subsp. *elymoides*

Elymus stebbinsii **Gould** – Parish's wheat grass [Parish's wheat-grass] (94) (1901)

Elymus striatus **var.** *villosus* **Gray** – See *Elymus villosus* Muhl. ex Willd.

Elymus striatus **Willd.** – See *Elymus virginicus* L. var. *virginicus*

Elymus striatus **Willd. var.** *ballii* **Pammel** – See *Elymus villosus* Muhl. ex Willd.

Elymus submuticus **(Hook.) Smyth & Smyth** – Awnless terrell grass (56) (1901), Beardless Virginia wild rye [Beardless Virginia wild-rye] (155) (1942), Short-awn wild rye [Short-awned wild rye (5) (1913), Virginia wild rye [Virginia wild-rye, Virginia wildrye] (50) (present)

Elymus trachycaulus **(Link) Gould ex Shinners** – Slender wheat grass [Slender wheatgrass] (50) (present)

Elymus trachycaulus **(Link) Gould ex Shinners subsp.** *subsecundus* **(Link) A. & D. Löve** – Awned wheat grass [Awned wheat-grass] (68) (1890), Bearded wheat grass (56, 85) (1901–1932), Richardson's wheat grass (56, 72, 94) (1901–1907), Slender wheat grass [Slender wheatgrass] (50) (present)

Elymus trachycaulus **(Link) Gould ex Shinners subsp.** *trachycaulus* – Awned wheat grass [Awned wheat-grass] (5) (1913), Bald wheat grass (68) (1890), Bearded wheat grass (5) (1913), Dog couch grass (143) (1936) Quebec, Dogtooth grass [Dog's tooth grass, Dog's-tooth grass, Dogtoothgrass] (5) (1913), Fibrous-root wheat grass [Fibrous-rooted wheat grass] (5) (1913), Purple wheat grass (111) (1915), Purplish wheat grass (5) (1913), Rye grass [Rye-grass, Rye-grass] (93) (1936), Slender wheat grass [Slender wheatgrass] (1, 3, 4, 5, 50, 56, 68, 72, 80, 85, 94, 111, 115, 118, 119, 129, 40, 141, 143, 146, 152, 155, 163) (1852–present), Western rye grass [Western rye-grass] (68, 143) (1852–1936), Wheat grass [Wheat-grass, Wheatgrass] (68) (1890)

Elymus triticoides **Buckl.** – See *Leymus triticoides* (Buckl.) Pilger

Elymus villosissimus **Scrib.** – See *Leymus mollis* subsp. *villosissimus* (Scribn.) Á. Löve & D. Löve

Elymus villosus **Muhl. ex Willd.** – Arkansas wild rye (56, 72) (1901–1907), Ball's slender lyme grass (56) (1901), Hairy wild rye [Hairy wildrye] (50, 155) (1942–present), Lime grass (19, 92) (1840–1876), Little rye grass (119) (1938) OK, Lyme grass (45) (1896), Slender wild rye (3, 163) (1852–1977), Smooth slender wild rye (5) (1913)

Elymus virginicus **L.** – Bald rye grass (68) (1890), Lyme grass (66, 92, 111, 129, 143) (1894–1936), Smooth rye grass (87, 90) (1884–1885),

Terrell's grass [Terrell-grass, Terrell grass, Terril grass] (5, 56, 68, 87, 88, 90, 94, 118, 119, 143, 163) (1852–1938), Virginia lyme grass (5, 68, 90) (1885–1913), Virginia wild rye [Virginia wild-rye, Virginia wildrye] (3, 5, 50, 72, 119, 122, 143, 155, 163) (1907–present), Wheat grass [Wheat-grass, Wheatgrass] (68) (1890), Wild rye [Wild-rye, Wildrye] (19, 66, 85, 87, 129, 144) (1840–1932), Wild rye grass (88, 90) (1885)

Elymus virginicus L. f. *australis* (Scribn. & Ball) A. S. Hitchc. – See *Elymus virginicus* L. var. *virginicus*

Elymus virginicus L. var. *glabriflorus* (Vasey) Bush – See *Elymus virginicus* L. var. *virginicus*

Elymus virginicus L. var. *halophilus* (Bickn.) Wieg. – Saltmarsh wild rye [Salt marsh wild rye] (5) (1913), Virginia wild rye [Virginia wild-rye, Virginia wildrye] (50) (present)

Elymus virginicus L. var. *intermedius* (Vasey) Bush – See *Elymus virginicus* L. var. *virginicus*

Elymus virginicus L. var. *submuticus* Hook. – See *Elymus submuticus* (Hook.) Smyth & Smyth

Elymus virginicus L. var. *virginicus* – Dennett grass (5, 87, 111, 129) (1885–1915), Hairy-flower lyme grass [Hairy flowered lyme grass] (56, 94) (1901), Hairy-scale Virginia wild rye [Hairyscale Virginia wildrye] (155) (1942), Long-awn Virginia wild rye [Longawn Virginia wildrye] (155) (1942), Prairie wild rye [Prairie wildrye] (155) (1942), Slender hairy lyme grass (66) (1903), Slender lyme grass [Slender lyme-grass] (56, 94) (1901), Slender wild rye (5, 72, 93) (1907–1936), Smaller rye grass (87) (1884), Smaller wild rye (88) (1885), Smooth southern wild rye [Smooth southern wild-rye] (5, 163) (1852–1913), Southern wild rye (5) (1913), Strict wild rye [Strict wild-rye] (5, 72, 158, 163) (1852–1913) IA, Virginia wild rye [Virginia wild-rye, Virginia wildrye] (50) (present), Western wild rye (5) (1913)

Elymus vulpinus Rydb. – Rydberg's wild rye [Rydberg's wildrye] (5, 50) (1913–present), Swale wheat grass [Swale wheatgrass] (155) (1942)

Elyna bellardii (All.) Degl. – See *Kobresia myosuroides* (Vill.) Fiori

Elytrigia pungens auct. non (Pers.) Tutin – See *Thinopyrum pycnanthum* (Godr.) Barkworth

Elytrigia pycnanthes (Godr.) A. Löve – See *Thinopyrum pycnanthum* (Godr.) Barkworth

Emblica officinalis [Gaertn.] – See *Phyllanthus emblica* L.

Emilia coccinea (Sims) G. Don – Flora's-paintbrush [Flora's paint brush, Flora's paint-brush, Floras-paintbrush] (109) (1949), Tassel flower [Tassel-flower, Tasselflower, Tassell flower] (109, 138) (1923–1949)

Emilia flammea [Cass.] – See *Emilia coccinea* (Sims) G. Don

Emilia sagittata DC. – See *Emilia coccinea* (Sims) G. Don

Emilia sonchifolia (L.) DC. – Tassel flower [Tassel-flower, Tasselflower, Tassell flower] (92) (1876)

Emmenanthe Benth. – Yellowbell [Yellow-bell, Yellow bell, Yellow bells, Yellow-bells, Yellowbells] (138) (1923)

Emmenanthe penduliflora Benth. – Yellowbell [Yellow-bell, Yellow bell, Yellow bells, Yellow-bells, Yellowbells] (77, 138) (1898–1923)

Empetrum L. – Crowberry [Crow-berry, Crow berry] (1, 138, 167) (1814–1932)

Empetrum nigrum L. – Black crowberry (5, 19, 156) (1840–1923), Blackberry-heath [Black-berry heath, Black berried heath] (5, 156) (1913–1923), Crakeberry [Crake berry, Crake-berry] (5, 10, 107, 156) (1818–1923) no longer in use by 1923, Crowberry [Crow-berry, Crow berry] (5, 10, 92, 103, 107, 109, 138) (1870–1949), Crow-peas [Crow pea] (5, 156) (1913–1923), Curlew-berry [Curlew berry] (5, 156) (1913–1923), Heath (5) (1913), Heathberry [Heath-berry] (5, 156) (1913–1923), Hog-cranberry [Hog cranberry] (5, 75, 156) (1894–1923) Islands of Penobscot Co. ME, no longer in use by 1923, Monox (107, 156) (1919–1923), Monox heather (5, 156) (1913–1923), Pigeon-berry [Pigeon berry] (156) (1923), Squirt-plum [Squirt plum] (78) (1898) Rumford ME, Wire-ling [Wire ling] (5, 156) (1913–1923) Neb

Empetrum nigrum Michx. – possibly *Empetrum nigrum* L.

Endolepis dioica (Nutt.) Standl. – Rillscale (3) (1977), Sillscale (4) (1986), Suckley's endolepis (50) (present)

Endolepis Torr. – Endolepis (50) (present)

Endorima uniflora (Nutt.) Barnhart – See *Balduina uniflora* Nutt.

Enemion biternatum Raf. – Atlantic isopyrum (155) (1942), Climbing milkweed (145) (1897) KS, Eastern false rue-anemone [Eastern false rue anemone] (50) (present), False anemone (156) (1923), False meadowrue [False meadow rue] (82) (1930) IA, False rue-anemone [False rue anemone] (1, 4, 5, 72, 97) (1907–1986), Honey vine [Honeyvine] (77) (1898) TX, Rue-anemone [Rue anemone] (156) (1923)

Enemion Raf. – False anemone (156) (1923), False rue-anemone [False rue anemone] (50, 158) (1900–present), Isopyrum (155) (1942)

Engelmannia peristenia (Raf.) Goodman & Lawson – Cut-leaf Engelmann's flower [Cut-leaved Engelmann flower] (84, 86) (1878–1880), Engelmannia (5) (1913), Engelmann's daisy [Engelmanns daisy] (3, 4, 50, 122, 124) (1937–present)

Engelmannia pinnatifida Torr. & Gray – See *Engelmannia peristenia* (Raf.) Goodman & Lawson

Enicostema verticillatum (L.) Engl. ex Gilg – Axillary gentian (7) (1828)

Enneapogon desvauxii Desv. ex Beauv. – Feather pappus grass [Feather pappusgrass] (155) (1942), Nine-awn pappus grass [Nineawn pappusgrass] (50) (present), Purple grass [Purple-grass] (94) (1901), Spike pappus grass (122) (1937)

Enslenia albida Nutt. – See *Enemion biternatum* Raf.

Entada phaseoloides (L.) Merr. – Sea beans (92) (1876)

Entada scandens [(L.) Benth.] – See *Entada phaseoloides* (L.) Merr.

Ephedra altissima Desf. – Climbing jointfir (138) (1923)

Ephedra antisyphilitica Berl. ex C. A. Mey. – Clapweed (4, 50) (1986–present), Ephedra (3, 57) (1917–1977), Joint-fir [Jointfir, Joint fir] (124, 158) (1900–1937), Mountain rush (158) (1900), Shrubby horsetail (158) (1900), Vine ephedra (155) (1942)

Ephedra coryi E. L. Reed – Cory's jointreed (50) (present)

Ephedra distachya L. – Common jointfir (138) (1923)

Ephedra L. – Canatillo (153) (1913) NM, Ephedra (155) (1942), Joint-fir [Jointfir, Joint fir] (50, 138, 155, 158) (1900–present), Mexican tea (4) (1986), Mormon tea (4, 153) (1913–1986), Popotillo (153) (1913) NM, Seaside grape [Sea-side grape] (167) (1814), Seaside-grape [Sea-side grapes, Sea side grapes] (167) (1814)

Ephedra pedunculata Engelm. ex S. Wats. – Vine ephedra (124) (1937)

Ephedra torreyana Wats. – Torrey's ephedra [Torrey ephedra] (3, 4, 155) (1942–1986), Torrey's jointfir (50) (present)

Ephemerum congestum Moench – See *Tradescantia virginiana* L.

Epibaterium carolinum (L.) Britton – See *Cocculus carolinus* (L.) DC.

Epicampes rigens (Boland.) Benth. – See *Muhlenbergia rigens* (Benth.) A. S. Hitchc.

Epidendrum conopseum Ait. f. – Bartram's tree-orchis (86) (1878), Green fly orchid (50) (present)

Epidendrum conopseum R. Br. – See *Epidendrum magnoliae* Muhl.

Epidendrum L. – Epidendron (86) (1878) meaning 'upon a tree'

Epidendrum magnoliae Muhl. – Epidendrum tree-grass (183) (1756), Ipedendrum (183) (1756)

Epifagus Nutt. – Beechdrops [Beech drops, Beech-drops, Beech-drops] (1, 2, 10, 50) (1818–present) parasitic on beeches, Cancer-root [Cancer root] (2, 10) (1818–1895)

Epifagus virginiana (L.) W. Bart. – Beechdrops [Beech drops, Beech-drops] (5, 7, 19, 49, 57, 61, 86, 92, 122, 157, 186, 187) (1814–1937), Cancer-drops [Cancer drops] (5, 92, 156) (1876–1923), Cancer-root [Cancer root] (5, 7, 19, 49, 57, 92, 156, 186, 187) (1814–1923) thought to be cure for cancer, Fir rape [Fir-rape] (92) (1876), Virginia brown-rape (5, 156) (1913–1923)

Epigaea L. – Épigée (French) (8) (1785), Trailing arbutus [Trailing-arbutus] (8, 138, 156, 167) (1785–1923)

Epigaea repens L. – Arbutus (106) (1930), Creeping epigaea (187) (1818), Creeping ground laurel (41, 187) (1770–1818), Creeping

Epilobium **(Gesn.) L.**

pigeon-berry [Creeping pigeon berry] (42) (1814), Crocus [Crocuses] (5, 156) (1913–1923), Epigaea (52, 54) (1905–1919), Épigée rampante (French) (8) (1785), Gravel plant [Gravel-plant] (5, 6, 53, 57, 92, 156) (1876–1923), Gravelweed [Gravel-weed, Gravel weed] (6, 49, 53, 58, 92) (1869–1922), Ground laurel (1, 2, 5, 6, 49, 53, 58, 92, 106, 156) (1869–1932), May cherry [May-cherry] (92) (1876), Mayflower [May flower, May-flower] (2, 5, 6, 49, 58, 53, 109, 156) (1869–1949), Moss-beauty [Moss beauty] (6) (1892), Mountain pink [Mountain-pink] (5, 6, 49, 58, 92, 156) (1869–1923), Real mayflower (77) (1898) Norridgewock ME, Hepatica is also called mayflower in this area, Rough-leaf [Rough leaf] (156) (1923), Shad-flower [Shadflower, Shad flower] (5, 73, 77, 156) (1892–1923) New England & NJ, Trailing arbutus [Trailing-arbutus] (1, 2, 5, 6, 8, 10, 19, 47, 49, 52, 53, 54, 57, 58, 61, 92, 106, 109) (1840–1949), Winter pink (5, 6, 49, 58, 92, 156) (1869–1923) no longer in use by 1923

Epilobium **(Gesn.) L.** – See *Epilobium* L.

Epilobium adenocaulon **Haussk.** – See *Epilobium ciliatum* Raf. subsp. *ciliatum*

Epilobium alpinum **L.** – See *Epilobium anagallidifolium* Lam.

Epilobium anagallidifolium **Lam.** – Alpine willow herb (5) (1913), Pimpernel willowherb [Pimpernel willow herb] (5) (1913)

Epilobium angustifolium **L.** – See *Chamerion angustifolium* (L.) Holub subsp. *angustifolium*

Epilobium brachycarpum **K. Presl** – Autumn willowherb (155) (1942), Panicled willowherb [Panicled willow herb] (5, 131) (1899–1913), Tall annual willow herb [Tall annual willowherb] (50) (present), Willow herb [Willow-herb, Willowherb] (3) (1977)

Epilobium brevistylum **Barbey** – See *Epilobium ciliatum* Raf. subsp. *ciliatum*

Epilobium canum **(Greene) Raven subsp.** *angustifolium* **(Keck) Raven** – California fuchsia [California-fuchsia] (109) (1949), Hummingbird-trumpet (138) (1923) Santa Barbara Co. CA, Wild fuschia (76) (1896) Santa Barbara Co. CA

Epilobium ciliatum **Raf.** – Fringed willowherb (50) (present), Willow herb [Willow-herb, Willowherb] (4) (1986)

Epilobium ciliatum **Raf. subsp.** *ciliatum* – Fringed willowherb (50) (present), Northern willow-herb [Northern willowherb, Northern willow herb] (5, 72, 93, 131) (1899–1936), Sierra willow-weed [Sierra willow weed, Sierra willowweed] (155) (1942), Sticky willow-weed [Sticky willow weed, Sticky willowweed] (155) (1942), Willow herb [Willow-herb, Willowherb] (3) (1977)

Epilobium coloratum **Biehler** – Coloured willow herb (42) (1814), Purple-leaf willowherb [Purpleleaf willow herb, Purple-leaved willow herb, Purple-leaved willow-herb] (3, 4, 5, 50, 72, 93, 131, 156) (1899–present), Purple-vein willowherb [Purple-veined willow herb, Purple-veined willow-herb] (5, 156) (1913–1923), Small willowherb [Small willow-herb, Small willow herb] (156) (1923)

Epilobium drummondii **Hausskn.** – See *Epilobium saximontanum* Hausskn.

Epilobium halleanum **Hausskn** – Glandular willowherb (50) (present)

Epilobium hirsutum **L.** – Apple-pie [Apple pie] (5, 156) (1913–1923), Cherry-pie [Cherry pie] (5, 156) (1913–1923), Codded willow herbe [Codded Willow-herbe] (178, 180) (1526–1633), Codlins-and-cream (5, 92, 156) (1876–1923), Fiddle-grass [Fiddle-grass] (5, 156) (1913–1923), Gooseberry-pie [Gooseberry pie] (5, 156) (1913–1923), Great hairy willowherb [Great hairy willow-herb, Great hairy willow herb] (5, 156) (1913–1923), Hairy willowherb [Hairy willow-herb] (156) (1923), Hairy willowweed [Hairy willow-weed] (138) (1923)

Epilobium hornemannii **Reichenb.** – Hornemann's willow herb [Hornemann's willowherb, Hornemann willowherb] (5, 50, 131, 155) (1899–present)

Epilobium **L.** – Boisduvalia (158) (1900), Cottonweed [Cotton-weed, Cotton weed] (1) (1932), Spike primrose [Spikeprimrose] (155) (1942), Willow herb [Willow-herb, Willowherb] (1, 2, 10, 50, 82, 93, 109, 138, 156, 158, 167, 184) (1793–present), Willow-weed

[Willow weed, Willowweed] (155) (1942)

Epilobium leptophyllum **Raf.** – Bog willowherb (50) (present), Narrow-leaf willowherb [Narrow-leaved willow herb] (3, 4) (1977–1986)

Epilobium lineare **Muhl.** – See *Epilobium palustre* L.

Epilobium palustre **L.** – Antonskraut (German) (6) (1892), Herbe de St. Antoine (French) (6) (1892), Linear-leaf willow herb [Linear-leaved willow herb, Linear-leaved willow-herb] (5, 42, 72, 93, 187) (1814–1936), Marsh epilobium (6, 49, 53) (1892–1922), Marsh willowherb [Marsh willow herb [Marsh willow-herb (5, 19, 50, 156, 158) (1840–present), Narrow-leaf willowherb [Narrow-leaved willow herb] (6) (1892), Swamp willow herb [Swamp willow-herb] (5, 6, 49, 53, 158) (1892–1922), Swamp-willow [Swamp willow] (6) (1892), Wickup [Wickop] (5, 6, 49, 53, 156, 158) (1892–1923)

Epilobium paniculatum **Nutt. ex Torr. & Gray** – See *Epilobium brachycarpum* K. Presl

Epilobium parviflorum **Schreb.** – Small-flower hairy willow herb [smallflower hairy willowherb] (50) (present)

Epilobium pubescens **[Roth]** – See *Epilobium parviflorum* Schreb.

Epilobium pygmaeum **(Speg.) Hoch & Raven** – Smooth spike-primrose (50) (present)

Epilobium saximontanum **Hausskn.** – Drummond's willowherb [Drummond's willow herb] (131) (1899), Rocky Mountain willowherb [Rockymountain willowherb] (50) (present)

Epilobium spicatum **Lk.** – See *Chamerion angustifolium* (L.) Holub subsp. *angustifolium*

Epilobium strictum **Muhl. ex Spreng.** – Downy willow herb (5) (1913), Soft willow herb (5, 42) (1814–1913), Upright willow herb (42) (1814)

Epimedium hexandrum – possibly *Vancouveria hexandra* (Hook.) C. Morren & Decne.

Epimedium **L.** – Epimedium (138) (1923) Dioscorides name for this species

Epipactis gigantea **Dougl. Ex Hook.** – Great helleborine (109) (1949), Helleborine (3, 85) (1932–1977), Stream orchid (50) (present)

Epipactis helleborine **(L.) Crantz** – Bastard hellebore (5, 92) (1876–1913), Broad-leaf helleborine [Broadleaf helleborine] (50) (present), Creeping wild white hellebore [Creeping wilde white Hellebore] (178) (1596), Elleborine (178) (1596), False helleborine (156) (1923), Helleborine (5, 156) (1913–1923)

Epipactis latifolia **(L.) All.** – See *Epipactis helleborine* (L.) Crantz

Epipactis pubescens – See *Goodyera pubescens* (Willd.) R. Br. ex Ait. f.

Epipactis **R. Br.** – possibly *Epipactis* Zinn.

Epipactis repens **[(L.) Crantz]** – See *Goodyera repens* (L.) R. Br. ex Ait. f.

Epipactis **Zinn. (possibly)** – Helleborine (1, 50, 158) (1900–present), possibly Rattlesnake-plantain [Rattlesnake plantain, Rattle snake plantain, Rattle-snake plantane, Rattlesnakes' plantain] (156) (1923)

Epiphegus americanus **Nuttall** – See *Epifagus virginiana* (L.) W. Bart.

Epiphegus **Nutt.** – possibly *Epifagus* Nutt.

Epiphegus virginiana **Bart.** – possibly *Epifagus virginiana* (L.) W. Bart.

Epiphyllum oxypetalum **(DC.) Haw.** – Broad-leaf cactus [Broadleaf cactus] (138) (1923), Broad-leaf epiphyllum [Broadlaef epiphyllum] (155) (1942)

Epithelantha micromeris **(Engelm.) A. Weber ex Britt. & Rose var.** *micromeris* – Button cactus (138) (1923)

Epixiphium wislizeni **(Engelm. ex Gray) Munz** – Maurandia vine (149) (1904) NM

Equisetum **(Tourn.) L.** – See *Equisetum* L.

Equisetum **×***ferrissii* **Clute (pro sp.)** [*hyemale* × *laevigatum*] – Intermediate scouring-rush [Intermediate scouring rush] (4) (1986)

Equisetum **×***litorale* **Kühlewein ex Rupr. (pro sp.)** [*arvense* × *fluviatile*] – Shore horsetail (5) (1913)

Equisetum arvense **L.** – Bottlebrush [Bottle brush, Bottle-brush] (5, 157, 158) (1900–1929), Cat-tail [Cat's tail, Cats Taile, Cat's-tail,

Cats tails] (5, 157, 158) (1900–1929), Common horsetail (80) (1913), Corn-field horsetail [Cornfield horsetail] (5) (1913), Devil's-gut [Devil's gut, Devil's-guts, Devil's guts, Devil's-guts] (79) (1891) NH, Dubock (German) (158) (1900), Field horsetail [Field horse-tail] (3, 4, 5, 50, 72, 131, 155, 157, 158, 187) (1818–present), Horse-pipe [Horse pipe, Horsepipe] (5, 157, 158) (1900–1929), Horsetail [Horse tail, Horse-tail] (19) (1840), Kleiner Schachtelbalm (German) (158) (1900), Pferdschwanz (German) (158) (1900), Scheuerkraut (German) (158) (1900), Scouring-rush [Scouring rush, Scouringrush] (157) (1929), Snake-pipes [Snake pipes] (5) (1913), Zinnkraut (German) (158) (1900)

Equisetum fluviatile **L.** – Great scouring-rush [Great scouring rush] (6) (1892), Horsetail [Horse tail, Horse-tail] (107) (1919), Joint-grass [Joint grass] (107) (1919), Paddock-pipe [Paddock pipe, Paddock pipes, Paddock-pipes] (5, 158) (1900–1913), Scrub-grass [Scrub grass] (107) (1919), Swamp horsetail (5, 72, 131, 155) (1899–1942), Water horsetail (3, 4, 5, 50, 155) (1913–present)

Equisetum hyemale **L.** – Common rush (4, 5) (1913–1986), Common scouring rush [Common scouring-rush] (38, 97) (1820–1937), Dutch rush (5, 6, 14, 92, 107, 158) (1871–1919), Equisteum (52, 57) (1917–1919), Gijib'inŭskon' (Chippewa, it is round) (40) (1928), Gunbright [Gun bright, Gun-bright] (5, 78, 92, 158) (1876–1913) ME, said to have been used by Indians to polish guns, Horse-pipe [Horse pipe, Horsepipe] (5, 92, 158) (1876–1913), Horsetail [Horse tail, Horse-tail] (49, 53, 92, 107) (1919–1922), Mare's-tail [Marestail, Mare's tail, Mare's-tails] (5, 92) (1876–1913), Pewterwort [Pewterwort, Pewter wort] (5, 92, 158) (1876–1913), Polirschachtelhalm (German) (158) (1900), Polishing-rush [Polishing rush] (158) (1900), Prêle (French) (6, 17, 46) (1796–1892), Rough horsetail [Rough horse-tail] (5, 158, 187) (1818–1913), Rush [Rushes] (27, 28) (1811–1850), Sand-rush [Sand rush] (35) (1806), Schaaf-stroo (Dutch) (46) (1879), Schachtelhalm (German) (6) (1892), Schaffthew (German) (46) (1879), Scour-grass (187), Scouring-rush [Scouring rush, Scouringrush] (3, 6, 19, 40, 46, 49, 52, 53, 57, 72, 107, 124, 155, 158, 187) (1818–1977), Scouring-rush horsetail [Scouringrush horsetail, Scouring rush horsetail] (50) (present), Scouring-rush horsetail [Scouringrush horsetail] (50) (present), Scrubbing-rush [Scrubbing rush] (6, 35) (1806–1892), Scrub-grass [Scrub grass] (12) (1821), Shave-grass [Shave grass] (5, 6, 10, 46, 49, 53, 92, 107, 158) (1818–1919), Shaveweed [Shave weed] (5) (1913), Snakeweed [Snake-weed, Snake weed, Snake Weede] (78) (1898) IA, Tischlerschachtelhalm (German) (158) (1900), Winter horsetail (6) (1892)

Equisetum hyemale **L. var. *affine* (Engelm.) A.A. Eat.** – Great scouring-rush [Great scouring rush] (72) (1907), Scouring-rush horsetail [Scouring rush horsetail] (50) (present), Stout scouring-rush [Stout scouringrush] (5, 97, 131, 138, 155) (1899–1942), Western scouring-rush [Western scouringrush] (155) (1942)

Equisetum hyemale **L. var. *californicum* Milde** – See *Equisetum hyemale* L. var. *affine* (Engelm.) A.A. Eat.

Equisetum **L.** – Horsetail [Horse tail, Horse-tail] (1, 4, 10, 14, 37, 50, 126, 138, 148, 155, 158) (1793–present), Joint-rush [Joint rush] (37) (1830), Mande idhe shnaha (Omaha-Ponca, to make a bow smooth) (37) (1830), Mares tayle (178, 179) (1526–1596), Pakarut (Pawnee) (37) (1830), Prele (28) (1850), Pull-pipes [Pull pipes] (92) (1876), Rush [Rushes] (35) (1806), Scouring-rush [Scouring rush, Scouringrush] (4, 37, 126, 148) (1919–1986), Shangga wathata (Omaha-Ponca) (37) (1830), Snake-grass [Snake grass, Snakegrass] (37) (1830)

Equisetum laevigatum **A. Br.** – Prairie scouring-rush [Prairie scouring rush] (72) (1907), Smooth horsetail (3, 50, 155) (1942–present), Smooth scouring-rush [Smooth scouring rush] (4, 5, 97, 131) (1899–1986)

Equisetum limosum **L.** – See *Equisetum fluviatile* L.

Equisetum littorale **Kuehl.** – See *Equisetum* ×*litorale* Kühlewein ex Rupr. [*arvense* × *fluviatile*]

Equisetum palustre **L.** – Cat-whistle [Cat whistle, Cat-whistles] (5,

158) (1900–1913), Marsh horsetail (4, 5, 50, 155, 158) (1900–present), Marsh-reed [Marsh reed] (158) (1900), Marshweed [Marsh weed] (5) (1913), Meadow horsetail (3) (1977), Paddock-pipe [Paddock pipe, Paddock pipes, Paddock-pipes] (92) (1876), Snake-pipes [Snake pipes] (5, 158) (1900–1913), Tad-pipes (158) (1900), Toadpipes (158) (1900)

Equisetum praealtum **Raf.** – See *Equisetum hyemale* L. var. *affine* (Engelm.) A.A. Eat.

Equisetum pratense **Ehrh.** – Meadow horsetail (3, 4, 5, 50, 155) (1913–present), Thicket horsetail (5, 72) (1907–1913)

Equisetum robustum **A. Br.** – See *Equisetum hyemale* L. var. *affine* (Engelm.) A.A. Eat.

Equisetum scirpoides **Michx.** – Dwarf scouring rush (3, 4, 50) (1977–present), Sedge-like equisetum (5) (1913), Sedge-like horsetail [Sedgelike horsetail] (155) (1942)

Equisetum sylvaticum **L.** – Bottlebrush [Bottle brush, Bottle-brush] (5) (1913), Grangas (Swedish) (46) (1879), Hastgroning (Swedish) (46) (1879), Sylvan horsetail (155) (1942), Wood horsetail (3, 4, 131) (1899–1986), Woodland horsetail (50, 72) (1907–present)

Equisetum variegatum **Schleich. ex F. Weber & D.M.H. Mohr** – Northern scouring-rush [Northern scouring rush] (157) (1929), Variegated equisetum (5, 97) (1913–1937), Variegated horsetail (3, 155) (1942–1977), Variegated scouring-rush [Variegated scouring rush] (4, 50) (1986–present)

Eragrostis abyssinica **L.** – See *Eragrostis tef* (Zuccagni) Trotter

Eragrostis arida **Hitchc.** – See *Eragrostis pectinacea* (Michx.) Nees ex Steud.

Eragrostis barrelieri **Daveau** – Mediterranean love grass [Mediterranean lovegrass] (3, 155) (1942–1977)

Eragrostis **Beauv.** – See *Eragrostis* von Wolf

Eragrostis beyrichii **J. G. Smith.** – See *Eragrostis secundiflora* J. Presl subsp. *oxylepis* (Torr.) S.D. Koch

Eragrostis capillaris **(L.) Nees** – Blowout grass [Blow-out grass, Blowoutgrass] (75) (1894) Neb, Branching spear grass (66) (1903), Capillary eragrostis (56, 72) (1901–1907), Hair-panicle meadow grass [Hair-paniled meadow grass] (66, 187) (1818–1903), Lace grass [Lace-grass, Lacegrass] (3, 5, 50, 93, 94, 119, 122, 155, 163) (1852–present), Slender meadow grass [Slender meadow-grass] (187) (1818), Tiny love grass [Tiny love-grass] (5, 93, 99, 119, 163) (1852–1938)

Eragrostis cilianensis **(All.) Link.** – See *Eragrostis cilianensis* (All.) Vign. ex Janchen

Eragrostis cilianensis **(All.) Vign. ex Janchen** – Candy grass [Candygrass] (94, 119, 129) (1894–1938), Love grass [Love-grass, Lovegrass] (140) (1944), Pungent meadow grass (56) (1901), Skunk grass [Skunk-grass] (119) (1938) OK, Stink grass [Stink-grass, Stinkgrass] (3, 50, 56, 75, 80, 111, 122, 125, 129, 140, 155) (1894–present), Stinking grass (56, 145) (1897–1901), Strong-scented eragrostis (72) (1907), Strong-scented love grass [Strong-scented love-grass] (5, 99, 119, 163) (1852–1938)

Eragrostis curtipedicellata **Buckl.** – Gummy love grass [Gummy lovegrass] (3, 50, 155) (1942–present), Short-stalk eragrostis [Short-stalked eragrostis] (94) (1901), Short-stalk love grass [Short-stalked love grass, Short-stalked love-grass] (5, 99, 119, 163) (1852–1938)

Eragrostis curvula **(Schrad.) Nees** – Weeping love grass [Weeping lovegrass] (3, 50, 155) (1942–present)

Eragrostis diffusa **Buckl.** – See *Eragrostis pectinacea* (Michx.) Nees ex Steud. var. *pectinacea*

Eragrostis eragrostis **(L.) Beauv.** – See *Eragrostis minor* Host

Eragrostis frankii **C. A. Mey. ex Steud.** – Frank's eragrostis (72) (1907), Frank's love grass [Frank's love-grass] (5, 99, 163) (1852–1923), Sand-bar love grass [Sandbar lovegrass] (3, 50, 155) (1942–present), Short-stalk meadow grass [Short-stalked meadow grass, Short-stalked meadow-grass] (5, 6, 66, 94) (1901–1912)

Eragrostis hirsuta **(Michx.) Nees** – Big-top love grass [Bigtop lovegrass] (50) (present), Stout love grass [Stout love-grass] (5, 163)

(1852–1913)

Eragrostis hypnoides (**Lam.**) **Britton, Sterns & Poggenb.** – Creeping eragrostis (56, 72) (1901–1907), Creeping meadow grass [Creeping meadow-grass] (111) (1915), Smooth creeping grass [Smooth creeping-grass] (163) (1852), Smooth creeping love grass [Smooth creeping love-grass] (5, 93, 119) (1913–1938), Stink grass [Stink-grass, Stinkgrass] (85) (1932), Teal love grass [Teal lovegrass] (3, 50, 155) (1942–present)

Eragrostis intermedia **Hitchc.** – Plains love grass [Plains lovegrass, Plains love-grass] (3, 50, 122, 155) (1937–present)

Eragrostis major **Host** – See *Eragrostis cilianensis* (All.) Vign. ex Janchen

Eragrostis megastachya (**Koel.**) **Link** – See *Eragrostis cilianensis* (All.) Vign. ex Janchen

Eragrostis mexicana (**Hornem.**) **Link subsp. *mexicana*** – Crabgrass [Crab-grass, Crab grass] (94, 152) (1901–1912), Mexican eragrostis (56) (1901), Mexican love grass [Mexcian lovegrass] (50, 122, 155) (1937–present), Mexican spear grass (56) (1901), New Mexico love grass [NewMexico lovegrass] (155) (1942)

Eragrostis mexicana **Link** – See *Eragrostis mexicana* (Hornem.) Link subsp. *mexicana*

Eragrostis minor **Host** – Little love grass [Little lovegrass] (3, 50) (1977–present), Low eragrostis (72) (1907), Low love grass [Low love-grass] (5, 155) (1913–1942), Low meadow grass (56) (1901), Pungent meadow grass (66, 87) (1884–1903), Strong-scented meadow grass (66) (1903)

Eragrostis neomexicana **Vasey** – See *Eragrostis mexicana* (Hornem.) Link subsp. *mexicana*

Eragrostis neo-mexicana **Vasey** – See *Eragrostis mexicana* (Hornem.) Link subsp. *mexicana*

Eragrostis obtusiflora (**Fourn.**) **Scribn.** – Mexican salt grass [Mexican salt-grass] (94, 152) (1901–1912)

Eragrostis obtusiflora **Scribn.** – See *Eragrostis obtusiflora* (Fourn.) Scribn.

Eragrostis oxylepis (**Torr.**) **Torr.** – See *Eragrostis secundiflora* J. Presl subsp. *oxylepis* (Torr.) S. D. Koch

Eragrostis pectinacea (**Michx.**) **Nees ex Steud.** – Carolina love grass [Carolina lovegrass] (3, 155) (1942–1977), Comb grass (111) (1915), Desert love grass [Desert lovegrass] (155) (1942), False redtop [False red-top, False red top] (5) (1913), Meadow comb grass (56, 66) (1901–1903), Pink grass [Pink-grass] (5) (1913), Purple eragrostis (72) (1907), Purple love grass [Purple love-grass, Purple lovegrass] (5, 93, 99) (1913–1936), Pursh's love grass [Pursh's love-grass] (163) (1852), Tufted love grass [Tufted lovegrass] (50) (present)

Eragrostis pectinacea (**Michx.**) **Nees ex Steud. var. *miserrima* (Fourn.) J. Reeder** – Gulf love grass [Gulf lovegrass] (155) (1942)

Eragrostis pectinacea (**Michx.**) **Nees ex Steud. var. *pectinacea*** – Love grass [Love-grass, Lovegrass] (93) (1936), Pursh's eragrostis (72) (1907), Pursh's love grass [Pursh's love-grass] (5, 99) (1913–1923), Southern eragrostis (66) (1903), Southern spear grass [Southern spear-grass] (5, 56, 94, 119, 129) (1894–1938), Spreading love grass [Spreading lovegrass] (155) (1942), Tufted love grass [Tufted lovegrass] (50) (present)

Eragrostis pilifera **Scheele** – See *Eragrostis trichodes* (Nutt.) Wood

Eragrostis pilosa (**L.**) **Beauv.** – Hairy love grass [Hairy love-grass] (99) (1923), Hairy meadow grass [Hairy meadow-grass] (187) (1818), Indian love grass [Indian lovegrass, India love grass, India lovegrass] (3, 4, 50, 122, 140, 155) (1937–present), Slender meadow grass [Slender meadow-grass] (66, 94, 111, 129) (1894–1915), Small tufted love grass [Small tufted love-grass, Small tufted lovegrass] (5, 119, 140) (1913–1944), Southern spear grass [Southern spear-grass] (80) (1913)

Eragrostis pilosa (**L.**) **Beauv. var. *perplexa* (Harvey)** – See *Eragrostis pilosa* (L.) Beauv.

Eragrostis pilosa (**L.**) **Beauv. var. *pilosa*** – possibly *Eragrostis pilosa* (L.) Beauv.

Eragrostis poaeoides **Beauv. ex Roemer & J. A. Schultes** – See

Eragrostis minor Host

Eragrostis poaeoides **Beauv. ex Roemer & J. A. Schultes var. *megastachya*** – See *Eragrostis minor* Host

Eragrostis purshii **Schrad.** – See *Eragrostis pectinacea* (Michx.) Nees ex Steud. var. *pectinacea*

Eragrostis refracta (**Muhl.**) **Scribn.** – Meadow love grass [Meadow love-grass] (163) (1852)

Eragrostis reptans (**Michx.**) **Nees** – See *Neeragrostis reptans* (Michx.) Nicora

Eragrostis secundiflora **J. Presl** – Clustered love grass [Clustered lovegrass] (5, 99, 119) (1913–1938), Purple love grass [Purple lovegrass, Purple lovegrass] (94, 152) (1901–1912), Red love grass [Red lovegrass] (50, 155) (1942–present)

Eragrostis secundiflora **J. Presl subsp. *oxylepis* (Torr.) S. D. Koch** – Beyrich's love grass [Beyrich's love-grass] (119) (1938), Red love grass [Red lovegrass] (3, 50) (1977–present), Wichita love grass [Wichita lovegrass] (155) (1942)

Eragrostis sessilispica **Buckl.** – Stiff prairie grass (5) (1913), Tumble love grass [Tumble lovegrass] (3, 50, 155) (1942–present)

Eragrostis spectabilis (**Pursh**) **Steud.** – False redtop [False red-top, False red top] (119) (1938), Love grass [Love-grass, Lovegrass] (163) (1852), Pink grass [Pink-grass] (119) (1938) OK, Purple love grass [Purple love-grass, Purple lovegrass] (3, 50, 119, 122, 155, 163) (1852–present)

Eragrostis tef (**Zuccagni**) **Trotter** – Crabgrass [Crab-grass, Crab grass] (56) (1901), Teff (56, 107, 109, 138) (1901–1949)

Eragrostis tenuifolia (**A. Rich.**) **Hochst. ex Steud.** – Bunch grass [Bunchgrass, Bunch-grass] (45, 87, 88) (1885–1896), Oregon blue grass (87) (1884), Redtop [Red-top, Red top] (45, 87, 88) (1884–1896), Red-top buffalo grass [Red-topped buffalo-grass] (45, 87, 88) (1884–1896)

Eragrostis tenuis **Gray** – See *Eragrostis capillaris* (L.) Nees

Eragrostis tephrosanthes **Schult.** – See *Eragrostis pectinacea* (Michx.) Nees ex Steud. var. *miserrima* (Fourn.) J. Reeder

Eragrostis trichodes (**Nutt.**) **Nash** – See *Eragrostis trichodes* (Nutt.) Wood

Eragrostis trichodes (**Nutt.**) **Wood** – Blowout grass [Blow-out grass, Blowoutgrass] (5, 93, 111, 116, 119) (1913–1958), Branching spear-grass (94) (1901), Hair-like eragrostis (56, 72) (1901–1907), Hair-like love grass [Hair-like love-grass] (5, 119) (1913–1938), Love grass [Love-grass, Lovegrass] (116) (1958), Sand love grass [Sand lovegrass] (3, 50, 155) (1942–present), Sand-hill love grass [Sand-hill lovegrass] (155) (1942)

Eragrostis von Wolf – Love grass [Love-grass, Lovegrass] (50, 92, 93, 122, 155) (1936–present), Skunk grass [Skunk-grass] (1) (1932), Stink grass [Stink-grass, Stinkgrass] (1, 93) (1932–1936)

Eragrostis weigeltiana (**Reichenb.**) **Bush** – See *Neeragrostis reptans* (Michx.) Nicora

Eranthis hyemalis (**L.**) **Salisb.** – Christmas flower (5, 156) (1913–1923), Hellebore (156) (1923), Winter aconite [Winter-aconite] (5, 15, 109, 138, 156) (1895–1949), Winter hellebore (5, 92) (1876–1913), Winter wolf's-bane [Winter wolfesbane] (178) (1526), Winter-aconite (138) (1923), Wolf's-bane [Wolfbane, Wolf bane, Wolf's bane, Wolfsbane, Wolfs-bane] (5, 156) (1913–1923)

Eranthis **Salisb.** – Winter aconite [Winter-aconite] (156) (1923)

Erechtites hieracifolius – See *Erechtites hieraciifolia* (L.) Raf. ex DC.

Erechtites hieraciifolia (**L.**) **Raf. ex DC.** – American burnweed (50, 155) (1942–present), Burnweed (50) (present), Butterweed [Butter weed, Butter-weed] (156) (1923), Feuerkraut (German) (6) (1892), Fireweed [Fire weed, Fire-weed] (5, 6, 19, 48, 49, 53, 57, 58, 61, 62, 63, 72, 80, 92, 93, 122, 156, 157, 158, 187) (1818–1936), Herbe de Feu (French) (6) (1892), Pileweed [Pile-weed] (156) (1923), Pilewort [Pile-wort, Pile wort] (5, 62, 92, 156, 157, 158) (1876–1929)

Erechtites hieraciifolia (**L.**) **Raf. ex DC. var. *hieraciifolia*** – Fireweed [Fire weed, Fire-weed] (19, 187) (1818–1840), Groundsel [Groundsell] (187) (1818), Hawkweed [Hawk-weed, Hawk weed,

Hawke-weed] (187) (1818)

Erechtites **Raf.** – Burnweed (50, 155) (1942–present), Fireweed [Fire weed, Fire-weed] (1, 3, 4, 158) (1900–1986), Pilewort [Pile-wort, Pile wort] (1) (1932)

Eremocarpus setigerus **Benth.** – See *Croton setigerus* Hook.

Eremochloa ophiuroides **(Munro) Hack.** – Centipede grass [Centipede-grass] (109) (1949), Lazy-man's grass [Lazy-mans-grass] (109) (1949) needs little mowing

Eremopyrum orientale **(L.) Jaubert & Spach** – Dwarf oriental rye (66) (1903)

Erianthus **Michx.** – See *Saccharum* L. (Greek for wool-flower for silky hairs)

Erianthus alopecuroides **(L.) Ell.** – See *Saccharum alopecuroidum* (L.) Nutt.

Erianthus brevibarbus **Michx.** – See *Saccharum brevibarbe* (Michx.) Pers. var. *brevibarbe*

Erianthus compactus **Nash.** – See *Saccharum giganteum* (Walt.) Pers.

Erianthus contorta **Ell.** – See *Saccharum brevibarbe* (Michx.) Pers. var. *contortum* (Ell.) R. Webster

Erianthus contortus **Bald.** – See *Saccharum brevibarbe* (Michx.) Pers. var. *contortum* (Ell.) R. Webster

Erianthus contortus **Ell.** – See *Saccharum brevibarbe* (Michx.) Pers. var. *contortum* (Ell.) R. Webster

Erianthus divaricatus **(L.) Hitchc.** – See *Saccharum alopecuroidum* (L.) Nutt.

Erianthus giganteus **(Walt.) Muhl.** – See *Saccharum giganteum* (Walt.) Pers.

Erianthus laxus **Nash** – See *Saccharum giganteum* (Walt.) Pers.

Erianthus ravennae **(L.) Beauv.** – See *Saccharum ravennae* (L.) L.

Erianthus ravennae **(L.) Beauv. var. purpurascens (Anderss.) Hack.** – See *Saccharum ravennae* (L.) L.

Erianthus saccharoides **Michx.** – See *Saccharum giganteum* (Walt.) Pers.

Erianthus tracyi **Nash** – See *Saccharum alopecuroidum* (L.) Nutt.

Erica cinerea **L.** – Twisted heath (109, 138) (1923–1949)

Erica **L.** – Heath (92, 109, 138) (1876–1949)

Erica lusitanica **K. Rudolphi** – Spanish heather (109) (1949)

Erica tetralix **L.** – Cross-leaf heath [Crossleaf heath] (138) (1923)

Erica vagans **L.** – Cornish heath (109, 138) (1923–1949)

Erica vulgaris **L.** – See *Calluna vulgaris* (L.) Hull

Ericameria arborescens **(Gray) Greene** – Fleece goldenweed (155) (1942), Rabbit-brush goldenweed [Rabbitbrush goldenweed] (155) (1942)

Ericameria bloomeri **(Gray) J. F. Macbr.** – Rabbit-brush goldenweed [Rabbitbrush goldenweed] (155) (1942)

Ericameria brachylepis **(Gray) Hall** – Chaparral goldenweed (155) (1942)

Ericameria cooperi **(Gray) Hall** – Cooper's goldenweed [Cooper goldenweed] (155) (1942)

Ericameria cuneata **(Gray) McClatchie var. cuneata** – Heather goldenweed (155) (1942), Wedge-leaf goldenweed [Wedgeleaf goldenweed] (155) (1942)

Ericameria discoidea **(Nutt.) Nesom var. discoidea** – White-stem goldenweed [Whitestem goldenweed] (155) (1942)

Ericameria ericoides **(Less.) Jepson** – Heather goldenweed (155) (1942)

Ericameria fasciculata **(Eastw.) J. F. Macbr.** – Monterey goldenweed (155) (1942)

Ericameria **Gray** – See *Ericameria* Nutt.

Ericameria greenei **(Gray) Nesom** – Greene's goldenweed [Greenes goldenweed] (155) (1942)

Ericameria laricifolia **(Gray) Shinners** – Herba del pasmo (52, 54) (1905–1919), Larch-leaf goldenweed [Larchleaf goldenweed] (155) (1942), Turpentine bush (52) (1919)

Ericameria linearifolia **(DC.) Urbatsch & Wussow** – Desert goldenweed (155) (1942), Narrow-leaf goldenweed [Narrowleaf goldenweed] (155) (1942)

Ericameria nana **Nutt.** – Dwarf goldenweed (155) (1942)

Ericameria nauseosa **(Pallas ex Pursh) Nesom & Baird** – Rubber rabbitbrush (50) (present)

Ericameria nauseosa **(Pallas ex Pursh) Nesom & Baird subsp. nauseosa var. glabrata (Gray) Nesom & Baird** – Fetid rayless goldenrod [Fetid rayless golden-rod] (5, 93, 112, 158) (1900–1937), Green-plume rabbitbrush [Greenplume rabbitbrush] (155) (1942), Rabbitbrush [Rabbit-brush, Rabbit brush] (3, 5, 85, 93, 127) (1913–1977), Rayless goldenrod [Rayless golden-rod] (130) (1895), Rubber rabbitbrush (50) (present)

Ericameria nauseosa **(Pallas ex Pursh) Nesom & Baird subsp. nauseosa var. nauseosa** – Rabbitbrush [Rabbit-brush, Rabbit brush] (112, 158) (1900–1937), Rubber rabbitbrush (50, 155) (1942–present), Woolly rabbitbrush [Woolly rabbit brush] (85) (1932)

Ericameria **Nutt.** – Ericameria (158) (1900), Goldenbush (50) (present)

Ericameria palmeri **(Gray) Hall var. palmeri** – Palmer's goldenweed [Palmer goldenweed] (155) (1942)

Ericameria parishii **(Greene) Hall** – Parish's goldenweed [Parish goldenweed] (155) (1942), Pine goldenweed (155) (1942)

Ericameria parryi **(Gray) Nesom & Baird** – Parry's rabbit-brush [Parry's rabbitbrush] (50) (present)

Ericameria parryi **(Gray) Nesom & Baird var. howardii (Parry ex Gray) Nesom & Baird** – Howard's rabbitbrush [Howard rabbitbrush] (155) (1942), Howard's rayless goldenrod [Howard's rayless golden-rod] (5) (1913), Parry's rabbit-brush [Parry's rabbitbrush] (50) (present)

Ericameria pinifolia **(Gray) Hall** – Chaparral goldenweed (155) (1942), Pine goldenweed (155) (1942)

Ericameria suffruticosa **(Nutt.) G.L. Nesom** – Plantain goldenweed (155) (1942), Single-head goldenweed [Singlehead goldenweed] (155) (1942)

Erigenia bulbosa **(Michx.) Nutt.** – Groundnut [Ground-nut, Ground nut, Ground nutts] (156) (1923), Harbinger-of-spring [Harbinger of spring] (4, 5, 50, 138, 155, 156, 158) (1900–present), Pepper-and-salt (5, 76, 156, 158) (1896–1923), Turkey-foot [Turkey foot, Turkeyfoot] (156) (1923), Turkey-pea [Turkey pea] (5, 73, 75, 76, 156, 158) (1892–1923) OH

Erigenia **Nutt.** – Harbinger-of-spring [Harbinger of spring] (1, 2, 138, 155, 158) (1900–1942), Pepper-and-salt (1, 156) (1923–1932), Turkey-pea [Turkey pea] (1) (1932)

Erigeron acris **L.** – Bitter fleabane (5, 50, 155, 50, 156) (1913–present), Blue fleabane (5, 156) (1913–1923)

Erigeron alpinum – See *Erigeron elatus* (Hook.) Greene

Erigeron alpinus **L.** – See *Erigeron elatus* (Hook.) Greene

Erigeron annuus **(L.) Pers.** – Annual fleabane [Annual flea bane] (3, 4, 155) (1942–1986), Common fleabane (156) (1923), Daisy fleabane [Daisy-fleabane] (5, 62, 63, 80, 82, 97, 121, 122, 145, 156, 158) (1897–1937), Eastern daisy fleabane (50) (present), Fleabane [Fleabane, Flea bane] (80, 82) (1913–1930), Inijaŋ pežuta or inijaŋpi (Lakota, sore mouth medicine) (121) (1918?–1970?), Lace-buttons [Lace-button, Lace buttons] (5, 156, 158) (1900–1923), Larger daisy fleabane (72, 156) (1907–1923), Oŋwahiŋjuŋtoŋpi (Lakota, tanning substance) (121) (1918?–1970?), Scabious [Scabius, Scabyous] (46) (1617), Scabius (46) (1617), Sweet scabious [Sweet-scabious] (5, 46, 62, 97, 131, 156, 158, 186, 187) (1814–1937), Tall daisy (156) (1923), Whitetop [White top, White-top] (5, 62, 93, 122, 156) (1912–1937), White-top weed [White top weed] (76) (1896), Whiteweed [White weed, White-weed] (80, 156) (1913–1923), Yerba del pasmore (Spanish) (76) (1896) CA

Erigeron asper **Nutt.** – See *Erigeron glabellus* Nutt. var. *pubescens* Hook.

Erigeron bellidiastrum **Nutt.** – Western daisy fleabane (5, 50, 93, 97) (1913–present), Western fleabane (3, 4, 85) (1932–1986)

Erigeron bellidiastrum **Nutt. var. bellidiastrum** – Western daisy fleabane (50) (present)

Erigeron bellidiastrum **Nutt. var. robustus Cronq.** – Western daisy fleabane (50) (present)

Erigeron bellidifolium **Muhl.** – See *Erigeron pulchellus* Michx.

Erigeron bellidifolius **Muhl.** – See *Erigeron pulchellus* Michx.

Erigeron caespitosus **Nutt.** – Tufted erigeron (5, 50, 93) (1913–present), Tufted fleabane (155) (1942)

Erigeron camphoratum **L.** – possibly *Pluchea foetida* (L.) DC.

Erigeron camphoratus **L.** – See *Pluchea foetida* (L.) DC.

Erigeron canadensis **L.** – See *Conyza canadensis* (L.) Cronq. var. *canadensis*

Erigeron canus **Gray** – Hoary erigeron (5, 50, 85, 93, 97, 131) (1899–present), Hoary fleabane (155) (1942)

Erigeron compositus **Pursh** – Cut-leaf daisy [Cutleaf daisy] (50) (present), Dwarf fleabane [Dwarfe Fleabane] (131) (1899), Fern-leaf fleabane [Fernleaf fleabane] (155) (1942), Mountain fleabane (85) (1932), Trifid fleabane (155) (1942)

Erigeron corymbosus **Nutt.** – Long-leaf fleabane [Longleaf fleabane] (50) (present), Purple-daisy fleabane [Purpledaisy fleabane] (155) (1942)

Erigeron divaricatus **Michx.** – See *Conyza ramosissima* Cronq.

Erigeron divergens **Torr. & Gray** – Spreading fleabane (5, 50, 93, 97, 122, 155) (1913–present)

Erigeron elatus **(Hook.) Greene** – Alpine fleabane (138) (1923)

Erigeron flagellaris **Gray** – Running fleabane (5, 122, 131) (1899–1937), Sprawling fleabane (155) (1942), Trailing fleabane (3, 50, 155) (1942–present)

Erigeron formosissimus **Greene** – Beautiful fleabane (50) (present)

Erigeron glabellus **Nutt.** – Fleabane [Flea-bane, Flea bane] (85) (1932), Smooth fleabane (138, 155) (1923–1942), Streamside fleabane (50) (present)

Erigeron glabellus **Nutt. var.** *pubescens* **Hook.** – Rough erigeron (5, 93, 131) (1899–1936), Streamside fleabane (50) (present)

Erigeron glaucus **Ker-Gawl.** – Beach aster (109) (1949), Beach fleabane (138) (1923), Seaside daisy (109) (1949)

Erigeron hyssopifolius **Michx.** – Hyssop-leaf erigeron [Hyssop-leaved erigeron] (5) (1913)

Erigeron integrifolia – possibly *Erigeron strigosus* Muhl. ex Willd.

Erigeron integrifolius **Bigelow** – possibly *Erigeron strigosus* Muhl. ex Willd.

Erigeron karvinskianus **DC.** – Pointed erigeron (86) (1878)

Erigeron **L.** – Daisy fleabane [Daisy-fleabane] (57) (1917), Erigeron (158) (1900), Fleabane [Flea-bane, Flea bane] (1, 2, 4, 10, 50, 57, 63, 93, 109, 138, 155, 156, 184) (1793–1986)

Erigeron **L.** – Less fleabane [Less flea bane] (167) (1814)

Erigeron lonchophyllus **Hook.** – Bog fleabane (85) (1932), Short-ray fleabane [Shortray fleabane] (50) (Present), Spearleaf (155) (1942)

Erigeron macranthus **Nutt.** – See *Erigeron speciosus* (Lindl.) DC. var. *macranthus* (Nutt.) Cronq.

Erigeron modestus **Gray** – Plains fleabane (50) (present)

Erigeron mucronatum **DC.** – See *Erigeron karvinskianus* DC.

Erigeron nudicaulis **Michx.** – See *Erigeron vernus* (L.) Torr. & A.Gray

Erigeron nudiflorus **Buckl.** – See *Erigeron flagellaris* Gray

Erigeron ochroleucus **Nutt.** – Buff fleabane (50) (present)

Erigeron philadelphicus **L.** – Cocash (7) (1828), Common fleabane (63) (1899), Daisy [Daisies, Daysy] (7, 76, 156, 158) (1828–1923), Daisy fleabane [Daisy-fleabane] (5, 156, 158) (1900–1923), Erigeron de Philadelphie (French) (7) (1828), Fieldweed [Field weed] (7) (1828), Fleabane [Flea-bane, Flea bane] (127) (1933), Frostweed [Frost weed, Frost-weed] (7) (1828), Philadelphia fleabane [Philadelphia flea-bane] (3, 5, 50, 62, 72, 93, 97, 122, 124, 155, 158, 186, 187) (1818–present), Scabious [Scabius, Scabyous] (186, 187) (1814–1818), Scabish (7) (1828), Skevish (5, 7, 92, 131, 156, 158) (1828–1923) no longer in use by 1923, Skevish fleabane (7) (1828), Skewisch Berungskraut (German) (7) (1828), Squaw-weed [Squaw-weed, Squaw-weed] (7) (1828), Sweet scabious [Sweet-scabious] (5, 7, 92, 156, 158) (1828–1923), Wood daisy (124) (1937)

Erigeron philadelphicus **L. var.** *philadelphicus* – Philadelphia fleabane [Philadelphia flea-bane] (50) (present), Purple fleabane (7) (1828)

Erigeron pulchellus **Michx.** – Blue spring daisy [Blue spring-daisy]

(5, 156, 158) (1900–1923), Daisy fleabane [Daisy-fleabane] (7, 86) (1828–1878), Daisy-leaf fleabane [Daisy-leaved flea-bane] (86) (1878), Early-flowering fleabane [Early-flowering flea-bane] (86) (1878), Fleabane [Flea-bane, Flea bane] (86) (1878), New England daisy (46) (1671), Poor Robert's-plantain [Poor Robert's Plantane, Poor Robert's plantain] (86, 187) (1818–1878), Poor Robin's-plantain [Poor robins plantain, Poor-robins-plantain, Poorrobins-plantain, Poor robin's plantain, Poor robin plantain] (5, 86, 109, 138, 155, 156, 158) (1878–1949), Robert's plantain (5, 7, 19, 92, 156, 158) (1828–1923), Robin's-plantain [Robin's plantain, Robin plantain] (2, 3, 4, 5, 50, 63, 72, 97, 122, 131, 156, 158) (1895–present), Rose-Betty [Rose Betty, Rosebety] (7, 92, 158) (1828–1900), Rose-petty [Rose petty] (5, 156) (1913–1923)

Erigeron pulcherrimus **Heller** – Basin fleabane (50) (present)

Erigeron pulcherrimus **Heller var.** *wyomingia* **(Rydb.) Cronq.** – See *Erigeron pulcherrimus* Heller

Erigeron pumilus **Nutt.** – Čaŋxloğaŋ hu ptepteċela (Lakota, short buffalo-weed) (121) (1918?–1970?), Daisy [Daisies, Daysy] (5, 76, 158) (1896–1913), Daisy fleabane [Daisy-fleabane] (121) (1970), Low erigeron (5, 93, 131, 158) (1899–1937), Low fleabane (3, 155) (1942–1977), Shaggy fleabane (50) (Present)

Erigeron pumilus **Nutt. subsp.** *pumilus* – Shaggy fleabane (50) (Present)

Erigeron purpureum **[Aiton]** – See *Erigeron philadelphicus* L. var. *philadelphicus*

Erigeron ramosus **(Walt.) B.S.P.** – See *Erigeron strigosus* Muhl. ex Willd. var. *strigosus*

Erigeron speciosus **(Lindl.) DC.** – Aspen fleabane (50) (present), Oregon fleabane (138, 155) (1923–1942)

Erigeron speciosus **(Lindl.) DC. var.** *macranthus* **(Nutt.) Cronq.** – Aspen fleabane (50, 155) (1942–present)

Erigeron strigosum – See *Erigeron strigosus* Muhl. ex Willd.

Erigeron strigosus **Muhl. ex Willd.** – Daisy fleabane [Daisy-fleabane] (3, 4, 145) (1897–1986), Prairie fleabane (50) (present), Rough fleabane (7) (1828), possibly Slender fleabane (7) (1828)

Erigeron strigosus **Muhl. ex Willd. var.** *strigosus* – Common daisy-fleabane (158) (1900), Daisy fleabane [Daisy-fleabane] (5, 72, 80, 93, 97, 131, 156) (1899–1937), Prairie fleabane (50) (present), Rough-stem fleabane [Rough-stemmed fleabane] (156) (1923), Slender daisy fleabane (62) (1912), Whitetop [White top, White-top] (5, 156) (1913–1923)

Erigeron subtrinervis **Rydb. ex Porter & Britton** – Three-nerve fleabane [Threenerve fleabane, Three-nerved fleabane] (5, 50, 93, 95, 131, 155) (1899–present)

Erigeron subtrinervis **Rydb. ex Porter & Britton var.** *subtrinervis* – Three-nerve fleabane [Threenerve fleabane, Three-nerved fleabane] (50, 155) (1942–present)

Erigeron tenuis **Torr. & Gray** – Slender rough fleabane (5, 97) (1913–1937), Slender-leaf fleabane [Slenderleaf fleabane] (50) (present)

Erigeron trifidus **Hook.** – See *Erigeron compositus* Pursh

Erigeron uniflorus **L.** – Arctic erigeron (5) (1913)

Erigeron vernus **(L.) Torr. & Gray** – Early fleabane (5) (1913)

Erigeron vetensis **Rydb.** – Early bluetop fleabane (50) (present)

Eriobotrya japonica **(Thunb.) Lindl.** – Japanese plum (107, 109) (1919–1949), Loquat (106, 107, 109, 138) (1919–1949)

Eriobotrya japonica **Lindl.** – See *Eriobotrya japonica* (Thunb.) Lindl.

Eriobotrya **Lindl.** – Loquat (138) (1923)

Eriocarpum grindelioides **Nutt.** – See *Machaeranthera grindelioides* (Nutt.) Shinners var. *grindelioides*

Eriocarpum megacephalum **Nash** – See *Rayjacksonia phyllocephala* (DC.) R. L. Hartman & M. L. Lane

Eriocarpum **Nutt.** – See *Xanthisma* DC.

Eriocarpum spinulosum **(Pursh) Greene** – See *Machaeranthera pinnatifida* (Hook.) Shinners subsp. *pinnatifida*

Eriocaulon anceps **Walt.** – See *Lachnocaulon anceps* (Walter) Morong

Eriocaulon aquaticum **(Hill) Druce** – Pipewort [Pipe-wort, Pipe wort] (19, 46) (1840–1879), Sevenangle pipewort [Sevenangle pipewort,

Seven-angled pipewort] (5, 50) (1913–present)

Eriocaulon compressum **Lam.** – Flattened pipewort (5, 50) (1913–present)

Eriocaulon decangulare **L.** – Hatpins (156) (1923), Pipewort [Pipe-wort, Pipe wort] (156) (1923), Tall pipewort (19) (1840), Ten-angle pipewort [Tenangle pipewort, Ten-angled pipewort] (5, 50, 156) (1913–present), White shoe-buttons [White shoe buttons] (156) (1923)

Eriocaulon **L.** – Pipewort [Pipe-wort, Pipe wort] (1, 10, 50, 167) (1814–present)

Eriocaulon parkeri **B. L. Robinson** – Estuary pipewort (50) (present), Parker's pipewort (5) (1913)

Eriocaulon pellucidum **Michx.** – See *Eriocaulon aquaticum* (Hill) Druce

Eriocaulon rollandii **Rouss.** – See *Eriocaulon parkeri* B. L. Robinson

Eriocaulon septangulare **With.** – See *Eriocaulon aquaticum* (Hill) Druce

Eriocaulon septangulare **Withering var. *parkeri* (B. L. Robins.) Boivin & Cayouette** – See *Eriocaulon parkeri* B. L. Robinson

Eriocaulon villosum **Michx.** – See *Lachnocaulon anceps* (Walt.) Morong

Eriochloa acuminata **(J. Presl) Kunth var. *acuminata*** – Southwestern cupgrasss (155) (1942), Taper-tip cup grass [Tapertip cupgrass] (50) (present)

Eriochloa contracta **Hitchc.** – Dotted millet (119) (1938), Prairie cup grass [Prairie cupgrass] (3, 50, 122, 155) (1937–present)

Eriochloa gracilis **(Fourn.) Hitchc.** – See *Eriochloa acuminata* (J. Presl) Kunth var. *acuminata*

Eriochloa **Kunth** – Cup grass [Cupgrass] (50, 155) (1942–present), Dotted millet (93) (1936)

Eriochloa lemmonii **Vasey & Scribn.** – Canyon cup grass [Canyon cupgrass] (50, 155) (1942–present), Lemmon's wool grass [Lemmon's wool-grass] (94) (1901)

Eriochloa lemmonii **Vasey & Scribn. var. *gracilis* (Fourn.) Gould** – Taper-tip cup grass [Tapertip cupgrass] (50) (present)

Eriochloa michauxii **(Poir.) A. S. Hitchc. var. *michauxii*** – Soft wool grass [Soft wool-grass] (94) (1901)

Eriochloa mollis **(Michx.) Kunth.** – See *Eriochloa michauxii* (Poir.) A.S. Hitchc. var. *michauxii*

Eriochloa punctata **(L.) Desv. ex Hamilton** – Dotted millet (5, 99) (1913–1923), Everlasting grass [Everlasting-grass] (5, 94, 155, 163) (1852–1942), Louisiana cup grass [Louisiana cupgrass] (50, 155) (1942–present)

Eriochloa sericea **(Scheele) Munro ex Vasey** – Silky everlasting grass [Silky everlasting-grass] (94) (1901), Texas cup grass [Texas cupgrass] (50, 155) (1942–present)

Eriochloa villosa **(Thunb.) Kunth** – Hairy cup grass [Hairy cupgrass] (50, 155) (1942–present)

Eriocoma cuspidata **Nutt.** – See *Achnatherum hymenoides* (Roemer & J. A. Schultes) Barkworth

Eriocoma hymenoides **(R. & S.) Rydb.** – See *Oryzopsis hymenoides* (R. & S.) Ricker

Eriocoma **Nutt.** – See *Achnatherum* P. Beauv.

Eriodendron anfractuosum **DC.** – See *Ceiba pentandra* (L.) Gaertn.

Eriodendron anfrectuosum – See *Ceiba pentandra* (L.) Gaertn.

Eriodictyon californicum **(Hook. & Arn.) Torr.** – California yerba santa (50) (present), Consumptive's-weed [Consumptive's weed] (57) (1917), Eriodictyon (52, 54) (1905–1919), Mountain balm (53, 54, 57, 106) (1905–1930), Mountain balsam (77) (1898) CA, Palo santo (54) (1905) CA, Yerba santa (52, 53, 54, 55, 57, 75, 106) (1894–1930) CA

Eriodictyon glutinosum **Benth** – See *Eriodictyon californicum* (Hook. & Arn.) Torr.

Eriogonum alatum **Torr.** – Wing eriogonum (155) (1942), Winged buckwheat (50) (present), Winged eriogonum (4, 5, 93, 97) (1913–1986)

Eriogonum alatum **Torr. var. *alatum*** – Winged buckwheat (50) (present)

Eriogonum alatum **Torr. var. *glabriusulum* Torr.** – Winged buckwheat (50) (1977)

Eriogonum alleni **S. Wats.** – Allen's eriogonum (5) (1913)

Eriogonum annuum **Nutt.** – Annual buckwheat (50) (present), Annual eriogonum (3, 4, 5, 93, 97, 98, 131, 155) (1899–1986), Umbrella plant [Umbrella-plant] (85, 98) (1926)

Eriogonum brevicaule **Nutt.** – Short-stem buckwheat [Shortstem buckwheat] (50) (Present), Short-stem eriogonum [Shortstem eriogonum] (4) (1986)

Eriogonum brevicaule **Nutt. var. *brevicaule*** – Narrow-leaf eriogonum [Narrow-leaved eriogonum] (5) (1913), Short-stem buckwheat [Shortstem buckwheat] (50) (Present)

Eriogonum campanulatum **Nutt.** – See *Eriogonum brevicaule* Nutt. var. *brevicaule*

Eriogonum cernuum **Nutt.** – Nodding buckwheat (50) (present), Nodding eriogonum (5, 93, 155) (1913–1942), Nodding wild buckwheat (4) (1986)

Eriogonum cernuum **Nutt. var. *cernuum*** – Nodding buckwheat (50) (present)

Eriogonum correllii **Reveal** – Correll's buckwheat (50) (present), Correll's eriogonum (4) (1986), James' eriogonum (5, 97, 155) (1913–1942), James' wild buckwheat (4) (1986)

Eriogonum corymbosum **Benth.** – Crisp-leaf eriogonum [Crisp-leaved eriogonum] (5) (1913)

Eriogonum effusum **Nutt.** – Effuse eriogonum (5, 93) (1913–1936), Heather (106) (1930) CO, Slender eriogonum (5, 93) (1913–1936), Slender-bush eriogonum [Slenderbush eriogonum] (155) (1942), Spreading buckwheat (50) (present), Spreading wild buckwheat (4) (1986)

Eriogonum effusum **Nutt. var. *effusum*** – Spreading buckwheat (50) (present)

Eriogonum fasciculatum **Benth.** – Wild buckwheat (106) (1930)

Eriogonum flavum **Nutt.** – Alpine golden buckwheat (50) (present), Eriogonum (127) (1933)

Eriogonum flavum **Nutt.** – Yellow eriogonum (5, 93, 131, 155) (1899–1942), Yellow wild buckwheat (4) (1986)

Eriogonum gordonii **Benth.** – Gordon's buckwheat (50) (present), Gordon's eriogonum (4) (1986)

Eriogonum jamesii **Benth.** – See *Eriogonum correllii* Reveal

Eriogonum lachnogynum **Torr.** – Long-root eriogonum [Long-rooted eriogonum] (5, 97) (1913–1937), Woolly-cup buckwheat [Woolycup buckwheat] (50) (present)

Eriogonum longifolium **Nutt.** – Long-leaf buckwheat [Longleaf buckwheat] (50) (present), Long-leaf eriogonum [Long-leaved eriogonum, Long leaved eriogonum] (5, 97) (1913–1937), Wild buckwheat (156) (1923)

Eriogonum longifolium **Nutt. var. *lindheimeri* Grand.** – See *Eriogonum longifolium* Nutt. var. *longifolium*

Eriogonum longifolium **Nutt. var. *longifolium*** – Lindheimer's long-leaf eriogonum [Lindheimer's longleaf eriogonum] (4) (1986), Long-leaf buckwheat [Longleaf buckwheat] (50) (present), Long-leaf eriogonum [Longleaf eriogonum] (3) (1977)

Eriogonum **Michx.** – Buckwheat [Buck-wheat] (50) (present), Eriogonum (155, 158) (1900–1942), Flat-top [Flat top] (106) (1930), Umbrella plant [Umbrella-plant] (1, 93) (1932–1936) Neb, Wild buckwheat (4, 106, 122) (1930–1986), Woolly knotweed [Woolly knot weed] (167) (1814)

Eriogonum microthecum **Nutt.** – See *Eriogonum effusum* Nutt.

Eriogonum multiceps **Nees** – See *Eriogonum pauciflorum* Pursh var. *pauciflorum*

Eriogonum pauciflorum **Pursh** – Few-flower buckwheat [Fewflower buckwheat] (50) (present), Few-flower eriogonum [Few-flowered eriogonum] (5, 131) (1899–1913)

Eriogonum pauciflorum **Pursh var. *gnaphalodes* (Benth.) Reveal** – Few-flower buckwheat [Fewflower buckwheat] (50) (present)

Eriogonum pauciflorum **Pursh var. *pauciflorum*** – Branched eriogonum (5, 93, 131) (1899–1936), Few-flower buckwheat [Fewflower buckwheat] (50) (present)

Aiton

***Erodium moschatum* Willd.** – See *Erodium moschatum* (L.) L'Hér. ex Aiton

***Erodium texanum* Gray** – Large-flower stork's-bill [Large flowered stork's bill] (122, 124) (1937), Texas heronbill (155) (1942), Texas stork's-bill [Texas stork's bill] (50) (present)

***Eruca* (Tourn.) Mill.** – See *Eruca* Mill.

***Eruca eruca* (L.) Britton** – See *Eruca vesicaria* (L.) Cav. subsp. *sativa* (Mill.) Thellung

***Eruca* Mill.** – Garden rocket (1) (1932), Rocket-salad [Rocketsalad] (4, 50) (1986–present)

***Eruca sativa* Mill.** – See *Eruca vesicaria* (L.) Cav. subsp. *sativa* (Mill.) Thellung

***Eruca vesicaria* (L.) Cav.** – Rocket-salad [Rocketsalad] (50) (present)

***Eruca vesicaria* (L.) Cav. subsp. *sativa* (Mill.) Thellung** – Garden rocket (5, 85, 156) (1913–1932), Rocket (80, 107) (1913–1919), Rocket-salad [Rocketsalad] (3, 4, 50, 109, 155) (1942–present), Roqueta (French) (107) (1919), Roquette (109) (1949), Skyrwyt (179) (1526)

***Erucastrum gallicum* (Willd.) O. E. Schulz** – Common dog-mustard [Common dogmustard] (50) (present), Dog-mustard [Dog mustard] (3, 4) (1977–1986), Rocketweed (155) (1942)

***Ervatamia coronaria* Stapf.** – See *Tabernaemontana divaricata* (L.) R. Br. ex Roemer & J. A. Schultes

***Ervum hirsutum* W.** – See *Vicia hirsuta* (L.) Gray

***Ervum lens* L.** – See *Lens culinaris* Medik.

***Eryngium* (Tourn.) L.** – See *Eryngium* L.

***Eryngium amethystinum* L.** – Amethyst eryngo (138) (1923)

***Eryngium aquaticum* L.** – See *Eryngium yuccifolium* Michx.

Eryngium aquaticum* L. var. *aquaticum – Virginia eryngo [Virginian eryngo] (5) (1913)

***Eryngium articulatum* Hook.** – Blue thistle [Blue-thistle] (106) (1930)

***Eryngium campestre* L.** – Mediterranean sea holly [Mediterranean sea hollie] (178) (1526), Wild eryngo (92) (1876)

***Eryngium diffusum* Torr.** – Diffuse eryngo (4, 97) (1937–1986), Spreading eryngo (50) (present)

***Eryngium* L.** – Briery-thistle [Briery thistle] (158) (1900), Button snakeroot [Button-snakeroot, Button snake root] (7) (1828), Eryngo (1, 4, 10, 50, 109, 138, 155, 156, 158) (1818–present), Rattlesnake-master [Rattlesnake master, Rattlesnake's master, Rattlesnakes' master, Rattlesnake's-master] (1) (1932), Sea holly (10) (1818)

***Eryngium leavenworthii* Torr. & Gray** – Briery-thistle [Briery thistle] (5, 76, 156) (1896–1923) Waco TX, Button snakeweed (156) (1923), Leavenworth's eryngo [Leavenworth eryngo] (3, 4, 5, 50, 97, 155) (1913–present), Purple eryngium (124) (1937), Purple thistle (106) (1930)

***Eryngium maritimum* L.** – Reed brier [Reed brere] (179) (1526), Sea-holly [Seaholly, Sea holly, Sea hollie] (138, 178) (1526–1923), Tassel [Tasyll] (179) (1526), Thistle-of-the-sea [Thystle of the see] (179) (1526), Yringe (179) (1526)

***Eryngium planum* L.** – Mountain sea-holly [Mountain sea hollie] (178) (1526), Plains eryngo (50) (present)

***Eryngium prostratum* Nutt. ex DC.** – Creeping eryngo (50) (present), Prostrate eryngo (5, 97) (1913–1937)

***Eryngium virginianum* Lam.** – See *Eryngium aquaticum* L. var. *aquaticum*

***Eryngium yuccaefolium* Michx.** – See *Eryngium yuccifolium* Michx.

Eryngium yuccafolium – See *Eryngium yuccifolium* Michx.

Eryngium yuccefolium – See *Eryngium yuccifolium* Michx.

***Eryngium yuccifolium* Michx.** – Button eryngo (50) (present), Button snakeroot [Button-snakeroot, Button snake root] (2, 3, 4, 5, 6, 19, 49, 52, 53, 54, 58, 63, 64, 72, 85, 92, 97, 104, 109, 122, 124, 131, 138, 156, 157, 158) (1840–1937), Button-snakeroot eryngo [Button-snakeroot eryngo] (155) (1942), Corn snakeroot [Corn snake root] (5, 6, 7, 49, 53, 58, 64, 92, 156, 157, 158) (1828–1929), Eryngium (52, 64) (1907–1919), Eryngo (6, 53, 64) (1892–1922), Panicant

D'eau (French) (6) (1892), Rattlesnake-flag [Rattlesnake flag] (5, 7, 64, 92, 156, 157, 158) (1828–1929), Rattlesnake-master [Rattlesnake master, Rattlesnake's master, Rattlesnakes' master, Rattlesnake's-master] (5, 6, 49, 53, 58, 57, 64, 92, 109, 156, 157, 158) (1869–1949), Rattlesnake-root [Rattlesnake root, Rattle-Snake-Root, Rattlesnakes' root, Rattlesnakeroot] (47) (1852), Rattlesnake-weed [Rattlesnake weed, Rattlesnake weede, Rattlesnakes' weed] (5, 64, 92, 156, 157, 158) (1876–1929), Wassermannstreu (German) (6) (1892), Water eryngo [Water-eryngo] (5, 49, 53, 54, 57, 61, 64, 92, 156, 157, 158) (1870–1929)

***Erysibe vera* Wallroth** – possibly Corn ergot [Corn-ergot] (49, 52, 53) (1919–1922), possibly Corn smut (49, 53) (1922), possibly Corn-brand [Corn brand] (49, 53) (1922), possibly Smut (19) (1840)

***Erysimum* (Tourn.) L.** – See *Erysimum* L.

***Erysimum alliaria* L.** – See *Alliaria petiolata* (Bieb.) Cavara & Grande

***Erysimum arkansanum* Nutt.** – See *Erysimum capitatum* (Dougl. ex Hook.) Greene var. *capitatum*

***Erysimum asperum* (Nutt.) DC.** – See *Erysimum capitatum* (Dougl. ex Hook.) Greene var. *capitatum*

Erysimum asperum arkansanum – See *Erysimum capitatum* (Dougl. ex Hook.) Greene var. *capitatum*

***Erysimum capitatum* (Dougl. ex Hook.) Greene** – Coast blistercress (138) (1923), Coast erysimum (155) (1942), Sand-dune wallflower [Sanddune wallflower] (50) (present), Western wallflower [Western wall flower, Western wall-flower] (4) (1986)

Erysimum capitatum* (Dougl. ex Hook.) Greene var. *capitatum – Arkansas bittercress (138) (1923), Arkansas erysimum (155) (1942), Bitter-root [Bitter root, Bitterroot] (7) (1828), False wallflower [False wall flower] (156) (1923), Orange mustard (5, 76, 156, 158) (1896–1923), Plains ersysimum (155) (1942), Prairie rocket [Prairie-rocket] (5, 156, 158) (1900–1923), Rough blistercress (138) (1923), Sand-dune wallflower [Sanddune wallflower] (5, 64, 156, 157, 158) (1900–present), Tall erysimum (155) (1942), Wallflower [Wall-flower, Wallflowers] (85, 122) (1932–1937), Western wallflower [Western wall flower, Western wall-flower] (3, 4, 5, 15, 63, 93, 98, 121, 127, 131, 145, 156, 158) (1895–1986), Yellow phlox (85, 93, 97, 157, 158) (1900–1937)

***Erysimum cheiranthoides* L.** – O'zawa'bigwûn (Chippewa [yellow flower] (40) (1928), Tarrify (5, 157) (1913–1929), Treachle mustard (131) (1899), Treacle erysimum (155) (1942), Treacle mustard [Treakle mustard] (5, 156, 157, 158) (1900–1929), Treacle wormseed (157, 158) (1900–1929), Wallflower [Wall-flower, Wallflowers] (156) (1923), Wormseed [Worm-seed, Worm seed] (5) (1913), Wormseed mustard [Worm-seed mustard] (15, 40, 63, 72, 85, 93, 95, 156, 157, 158) (1895–1936), Wormseed wallflower (3, 4, 50) (1977–present)

***Erysimum cheiri* (L.) Crantz** – Common wallflower (138) (1923), Double yellow wallflower [Double yellow wall flowers] (178) (1526), Gilly flower [Gilly flowers, Gillyflowers] (46) (1671) cultivated by English colonists by 1671, Wallflower [Wall-flower, Wallflowers] (19, 92, 109) (1840–1949)

***Erysimum elatum* Nutt.** – See *Erysimum capitatum* (Dougl. ex Hook.) Greene var. *capitatum*

***Erysimum inconspicuum* (S. Wats.) MacM.** – Sand erysimum (131) (1899), Shy wallflower (50) (Present), Small erysimum (131) (1899), Small-flower erysimum [Smallflower erysimum] (155) (1942), Small-flower prairie rocket [Small-flowered prairie rocket, Small-flowered prairie-rocket] (5, 93) (1913–1936), Small-flower wallflower [Smallflower wallflower] (3, 4) (1977–1986)

***Erysimum* L.** – Blistercress [Blistercress] (109, 138) (1923–1949), Erysimum (155) (1942), False wallflower [False wall flower] (13) (1849), Hedge mustard [Hedgemustard, Hedge-mustard] (1, 10, 93) (1818–1936), Prairie rocket [Prairie-rocket] (1, 93) (1932–1936), Stock [Stocks] (10) (1818), Treacle mustard [Treakle mustard] (13, 15, 156) (1849–1923), Wallflower [Wall-flower, Wallflowers] (4, 7, 10, 50, 138) (1818–present), Wild wallflower [Wild wall flower, Wild wall-flower] (1, 93) (1932–1936), Winter cress [Winter cresses] (10) (1818), Wormseed [Worm-seed, Worm seed] (184) (1793), Yellow phlox (1, 93) (1932–1936)

Erysimum officinale (L.) Scop. – See *Sisymbrium officinale* (L.) Scop

Erysimum officinale L. – See *Sisymbrium officinale* (L.) Scop

Erysimum parviflorum Nutt. – See *Erysimum inconspicuum* (S. Wats.) MacM.

Erysimum perofskianum Fisch. & C. A. Mey. – Afghan blistercress (138) (1923)

Erysimum repandum L. – Bushy wallflower (3, 4) (1977–1986), Repand cheirinia (5, 97) (1913–1937), Spreading erysimum (155) (1942), Spreading wallflower (50) (present)

Erysimum syrticolum Sheldon – See *Erysimum inconspicuum* (S. Wats.) MacM.

Erythea Wats. – See *Brahea* Mart. ex Endl.

Erythraea centaurium L. – See *Centaurium erythraea* Raf.

Erythraea douglasii A. Gray – See *Zeltnera exaltata* (Griseb.) G. Mans.

Erythraea douglassi A. Gray – See *Zeltnera exaltata* (Griseb.) G. Mans.

Erythraea muehlenbergia Griseb. – See *Zeltnera muehlenbergii* (Griseb.) G. Mans.

Erythraea muehlenbergii Griseb. – See *Zeltnera muehlenbergii* (Griseb.) G. Mans.

Erythrina arborea [(Chapman) Small] – See *Erythrina herbacea* L.

Erythrina corallodendron L. – Coral tree [Coral-tree, Coraltree] (138) (1923), Moricou (174) (1753)

Erythrina crista galli – See *Erythrina crista-galli* L.

Erythrina crista-galli L. – Cockscomb [Cock's comb, Cocks-comb, Cock's-comb] (92) (1876), Cockspur coral-tree (109) (1949), Coral tree [Coral-tree, Coraltree] (92) (1876), Coxscomb evergreen (19) (1840)

Erythrina flabelliformis Kearney – Western coralbean (138) (1923)

Erythrina herbacea L. – Coral bean [Coralbean] (122, 124, 138) (1923–1937), Coral tree [Coral-tree, Coraltree] (10) (1818), Coralbloom [Coral bloom] (7, 92) (1828–1876), Dwarf coral plant (86) (1878)

Erythrina L. – Coral tree [Coral-tree, Coraltree] (109, 138) (1923–1949), Immortelle [Immortelles] (109) (1949)

Erythroea centaurium – possibly *Centaurium erythraea* Raf.

Erythronium albidum Nutt. – Deer's-tongue [Deer's tongue, Deer tongue, Deer-tongue] (5, 75) (1894–1913) Anderson IN, Dogtooth-violet [Dog's tooth violet, Dog's-tooth violet, Dog-tooth violet, Dog-toothed violet] (85, 122, 124, 156) (1923–1937), Easter lily (156) (1923), Fawn lily [Fawn-lily, Fawnlily] (156) (1923), Spring lily [Spring-lily] (5, 156, 157, 158) (1900–1929), Trout lily [Trout-lily, Troutlily] (156) (1923), Tulip (78) (1898) MO, White adder's-tongue [White adder's tongue] (5, 72, 93, 156, 157, 158) (1900–1936), White dog-tooth violet [White dog's-tooth violet] (3, 5) (1913–1977), White fawn-lily [White fawnlily] (50, 155) (1942–present), White snakeleaf (7) (1828), White trout-lily [White troutlily] (138) (1923), Wild tulip (156) (1923)

Erythronium americanum Ker. – Adder's-leaf [Adder leaf, Adder's leaf] (7, 92, 157) (1828–1929), Adder's-tongue [Adder tongue, Adders tongue, Adder's tongue, Adders toong, Adderstongue] (2, 19, 49, 57, 58, 92) (1840–1917), Adder's-violet [Adder's violet, Adders' violet] (157) (1929), American dog's-tooth-violet [American dog's-tooth violet] (187) (1818), Common adder's-tongue [Common adderstongue] (157) (1929), Common trout lily [Common troutlily] (138) (1923), Cornflower [Corn-flower, Corn flower] (78) (1898) ME, Deer's-tongue [Deer's tongue, Deer tongue, Deer-tongue] (5, 75, 92, 157) (1876–1929) Anderson IN, Dent de chiene jaune (French) (7) (1828), Dogtooth-violet [Dog's tooth violet, Dog's-tooth violet, Dog-tooth violet, Dog-toothed violet] (5, 19, 49, 50, 57, 58, 92, 156, 157) (1840–present), Dog-violet [Dog violet] (7) (1828), Erythronium (92) (1876), Erythronium (Official name of Materia Medica) (7) (1828), Fawn lily [Fawn-lily, Fawnlily] (156) (1923), Fellow snowdrop (49) (1898), Fishhook [Fishhooks] (156) (1923), Gelb Hundzahn (German) (7) (1828), Jonquil

(78) (1898) ME, Lamb's-tongue [Lambs tongue, Lambs tongue, Lambs' tongues] (5, 7, 75, 86, 92, 156, 157) (1828–1929) Banner Elk NC, Rattlesnake-violet [Rattle snake violet, Rattle-snake violet, Rattlesnakes' violet, Rattlesnake's violet] (5, 7, 49, 58, 92, 156, 157) (1828–1929), Scrofula root [Scrofula-root] (5, 7, 92, 157) (1828–1929), Snakeleaf [Snake leaf] (92, 156) (1876–1923), Snakeroot [Snake root, Snake-root] (5, 156) (1913–1923), Trout flower [Trout-flower] (5, 156, 157) (1913–1929), Trout lily [Trout-lily, Troutlily] (5, 75, 156, 157) (1894–1929), Wild yellow lily (78) (1898) ME, Yellow adder's-tongue [Yellow adder's tongue] (5, 7, 72, 92, 93, 97, 156, 157) (1828–1937), Yellow bastard daffodil (46) (1671), Yellow dogtooth-violet [Yellow dogtooth violet, Yellow dog-tooth violet] (2, 86) (1878–1895), Yellow erythronium (9, 92) (1873–1876), Yellow hookers (156) (1923), Yellow lily (5, 75, 156, 157) (1894–1929) Ferrisburgh VT, Yellow snakeleaf [Yellow snake-leaf, Yellow snake leaf] (7, 86, 92, 157) (1828–1929), Yellow snowdrop [Yellow snow drop] (5, 7, 58, 86, 92, 156, 157) (1828–1929), Yellowbell [Yellowbell, Yellow bell, Yellow bells, Yellow-bells, Yellowbells] (5, 73, 75, 156, 157) (1892–1929)

Erythronium californicum Purdy – California trout lily [California troutlily] (138) (1923)

Erythronium citrinum S. Wats. – Lemon trout lily [Lemon troutlily] (138) (1923)

Erythronium flavum Smith. – See *Erythronium americanum* Ker.

Erythronium grandiflorum Pursh – Dogtooth-violet [Dog's tooth violet, Dog's-tooth violet, Dog-tooth violet, Dog-toothed violet] (35, 101, 107) (1806–1919), Glacier lily [Glacierlily] (138) (1923), Yellow avalanche lily (50) (present)

Erythronium hendersoni – See *Erythronium hendersonii* S. Wats.

Erythronium hendersonii S. Wats. – Henderson troutlily [Henderson troutlily]'s (138) (1923)

Erythronium L. – Adder's-tongue [Adder tongue, Adders tongue, Adder's tongue, Adders toong, Adderstongue] (1, 93, 156, 158) (1900–1936), Deer's-tongue [Deer's tongue] (Missouri tribes) (7) (1828), Dogtooth [Dogs tooth, Dog's tooth, Dogs-tooth] (184, 190) (~1759–1793), Dogtooth-violet [Dog's tooth violet, Dog's-tooth violet, Dog-tooth violet, Dog-toothed violet] (1, 10, 93, 167) (1814–1936), Fawn lily [Fawn-lily, Fawnlily] (50, 109, 155) (1942–present), Star-strikers [Star strikers] (1, 93) (1932–1936), Tarmia (Missouri tribes) (7) (1828), Trout lily [Trout-lily, Troutlily] (138) (1923)

Erythronium mesachoreum Knerr – See *Erythronium mesochoreum* Knerr

Erythronium mesochoreum Knerr – Hedte-shutsh (Winnebago) (37) (1830), Midland adder's-tongue [Midland adder's tongue, Midlands adder's-tongue] (5, 72, 93, 97) (1907–1937), Midland fawnlily (50) (present), Spring lily [Spring-lily] (37) (1830), White dog-tooth violet [White dog's-tooth violet] (3) (1977)

Erythronium oregonum Applegate – Dogtooth-violet [Dog's tooth violet, Dog's-tooth violet, Dog-tooth violet, Dog-toothed violet] (35) (1806), Giant white fawnlily (50) (present)

Erythronium propullans A. Gray – Minnesota adder's-tongue [Minnesota adder's tongue] (5) (1913)

Erythronium purpurascens S. Wats. – Sierra trout-lily [Sierra trout-lily] (138) (1923)

Erythronium revolutum Sm. – Mahogany fawn lily [Mahogany fawnlily] (50) (present), Mahogany trout lily [Mahogany troutlily] (138) (1923)

Erythronium rostratum C. B. Wolf – Yellow fawn-lily [Yellow fawnlily] (50) (present)

Escallonia Mutis ex L. f. – Escallonia (138) (1923)

Escholtzia californica – See *Eschscholzia californica* Cham.

Eschscholzia californica Cham. – California poppy [California-poppy, Californiapoppy] (2, 50, 82, 106, 109, 155) (1895–present), Common California poppy [Common California-poppy] (138) (1923), Cups-of-flame [Cups of flame] (76) (1896), Cups-of-gold [Cups of gold] (76) (1896) CA, Eschscholtzia (92) (1876), Torosa (Spanish) (76) (1896)

Eschscholzia californica **Cham. subsp.** *californica* – California poppy [California-poppy, Californiapoppy] (28, 50) (1850–present), Douglas' California poppy [Douglas California-poppy] (138) (1923), Orange California poppy [Orange California-poppy] (138) (1923)

Eschscholzia californica crocea – See *Eschscholzia californica* Cham. subsp. *californica*

Eschscholzia californica douglasi – See *Eschscholzia californica* Cham. subsp. *californica*

Eschscholzia californica **var.** *crocea* **(Benth.) Jeps.** – See *Eschscholzia californica* Cham. subsp. *californica*

Eschscholzia **Cham.** – California poppy [California-poppy, Californiapoppy] (50, 73, 122, 123, 138, 158) (1856–present), Cups-of-flame [Cups of flame] (73) (1892) CA

Eschscholzia crocea **Benth.** – See *Eschscholzia californica* Cham. subsp. *californica*

Eschscholzia tenuifolia **Benth.** – See *Eschscholzia caespitosa* Benth.

Escobaria **Britt. & Rose** – Foxtail cactus (50) (present)

Escobaria missouriensis **(Sweet) D. R. Hunt** – Missouri foxtail cactus (50) (present)

Escobaria missouriensis **(Sweet) D. R. Hunt var.** *missouriensis* – Ball cactus (156) (1923), Bird's-nest cactus [Bird's nest cactus] (145) (1897), Cushion cactus (101) (1905) MT, Michkideamachwa (Crow) (101) (1905) MT, Missouri cactus (5, 93, 131, 156) (1899–1936), Missouri coryphantha (155) (1942), Missouri foxtail cactus (50) (present), Nipple cactus (5, 93, 97, 156) (1913–1937), Pincushion cactus [Pin-cushion cactus] (85) (1932)

Escobaria missouriensis **(Sweet) D. R. Hunt var.** *similis* **(Engelm.) N.P. Taylor** – Missouri foxtail cactus (50) (present), Purple cactus (156) (1923)

Escobaria vivipara **(Nutt.) Buxbaum** – Spiny-star [Spiny star, Spiny-star] (50) (present)

Escobaria vivipara **(Nutt.) Buxbaum var.** *neomexicana* **(Engelm.) Buxbaum** – Spiny-stars coryphantha [Spinystars coryphantha] (155) (1942), Western coryphantha (97) (1937)

Escobaria vivipara **(Nutt.) Buxbaum var.** *radiosa* **(Engelm.) D.R. Hunt** – Spiny-star [Spiny star, Spinystar] (50) (present)

Escobaria vivipara **(Nutt.) Buxbaum var.** *vivipara* – Ball cactus (127) (1933) Globe cactus (145) (1897) KS, Pincushion cactus [Pin-cushion cactus] (4) (1986), Purple cactus (5, 93, 97, 131, 157) (1899–1937), Spiny-star [Spiny star, Spinystar] (50) (present), Tuberculated cactus (108) (1878), Turk's-head [Turk's-head, Turks-head] (108) (1878)

Eubotrys **Nutt.** – Leather-leaf [Leatherleaf, Leather leaf] (1, 2, 138, 156) (1895–1932)

Eubotrys racemosa **(L.) Nutt.** – See *Leucothoe racemosa* (L.) Gray

Eubotrys recurva **(Buckl.) Britton** – See *Leucothoe recurva* (Buckl.) Gray

Eucalyptis citriodora – See *Corymbia citriodora* (Hook.) K. D. Hill & L. A. S. Johnson

Eucalyptus amygdalina **Labill.** – Almond eucalyptus (138) (1923)

Eucalyptus botryoides **Sm.** – Bangalay (138) (1923)

Eucalyptus calophylla **R. Br.** – Port Gregory gum (138) (1923)

Eucalyptus camaldulensis **Dehnhardt** – Creek gum (57, 138) (1917–1923), Kino (57) (1917), Murray's red gum [Murray red gum] (57, 109) (1917–1949), Red gum (57) (1917), White gum [White-gum] or White gum tree (92) (1876) native of Australia

Eucalyptus citriodora **Hook.** – Lemon gum (138) (1923), Lemon-scent spotted gum [Lemon-scented spotted gum] (109) (1949)

Eucalyptus cladocalyx **F. Muell. (possibly)** – Sugar gum (109) (1949)

Eucalyptus cladothrix **F. Muell.** – possibly *Eucalyptus cladocalyx* F. Muell.

Eucalyptus cornuta **Labill.** – Yate tree [Yate-tree] (138) (1923)

Eucalyptus crebra **F. Muell.** – Narrow-leaf ironbark [Narrowleaf ironbark] (138) (1923)

Eucalyptus ficifolia **F. Muell.** – Scarlet bloom (106) (1930), Scarlet gum (138) (1923), Scarlet-flower gum [Scarlet-flowering gum] (109) (1949)

Eucalyptus globulus **Labill.** – Blue gum or Blue gum tree (60, 92, 106, 138) (1876–1930), Eucalyptus (57) (1917), Fever tree (92) (1876), Tasmanian blue gum (109) (1949)

Eucalyptus gomphocephala **DC.** – Tooart (138) (1923)

Eucalyptus goniocalyx **F. Muell. ex Miq.** – Bastard box [Bastardbox] (138) (1923)

Eucalyptus **L'Hér.** – Eucalyptus (106, 138) (1923–1930), Gum or Gum tree [Gum-tree] (106, 109) (1930–1949), Gumwood [Gum-wood] (92) (1876), Woolly-but [Woolybut] (92) (1876)

Eucalyptus maculata citriodora – See *Eucalyptus citriodora* Hook.

Eucalyptus maculata **Hook. var.** *citriodora* **Bailey** – See *Eucalyptus citriodora* Hook.

Eucalyptus pilularis **Sm.** – Blackbutt (138) (1923)

Eucalyptus polyanthemos **Schauer** – Australian-beech (109) (1949), Redbox [Red-box] (109, 138) (1923–1949)

Eucalyptus resinifera **Sm.** – Botany baybkino (92) (1876), Mahogany gum (138) (1923)

Eucalyptus robusta **Sm.** – Brown gum (138) (1923), Swamp-mahogony (109) (1949)

Eucalyptus rostrata **Schlecht** – See *Eucalyptus camaldulensis* Dehnhardt

Eucalyptus rudis **Sm.** – Desert gum (109, 138) (1923–1949), Moitch (109) (1949)

Eucalyptus sideroxylon **A. Cunningham** – Mugga (109) (1949), Red ironbark (109, 138) (1923–1949)

Eucalyptus tereticornis **Sm.** – Forest red gum (109) (1949)

Eucalyptus viminalis **Labill.** – Manna gum (109, 138) (1923–1949), Ribbon gum (109) (1949)

Eucephalus elegans **Nutt.** – Nuttall's aster [Nuttall aster] (155) (1942)

Eucephalus engelmannii **(D.C. Eat.) Greene** – Engelmann's aster [Engelmann aster] (155) (1942)

Eucharis grandiflora **Planch. & Linden** – Amazon-lily [Amazonlily] (109) (1949), Great Amazon lily [Great Amazonlily] (138) (1923)

Eucharis **Planch. & Linden** – Amazon-lily [Amazonlily] (138) (1923)

Euchlaena mexicana **Schrad.** – See *Zea mexicana* (Schrad.) Kuntze

Euchlaena **Schrad.** – See *Zea* L.

Euchroma coccinea **W.** – See *Castilleja coccinea* (L.) Spreng.

Euchroma **Nutt.** – See *Castilleja* Mutis ex L. f.

Euclidium **Aiton f.** – Mustard [Mustards] (50) (present)

Euclidium syriacum **(L.) Aiton f.** – Syrian mustard (50) (present)

Eudistemon **Raf.** – possibly *Coronopus* Zinn

Eugenia apiculata **DC.** – Short-leaf eugenia [Shortleaf eugenia] (138) (1923)

Eugenia aromatica **O. Berg** – See *Myrcianthes fragrans* (Sw.) McVaugh

Eugenia buxifolia **(Sw.) Willd.** – See *Eugenia foetida* Pers.

Eugenia dichotoma – See *Myrcianthes fragrans* (Sw.) McVaugh

Eugenia foetida **Pers.** – Box-leaf eugenia [Box-leaved eugenia] (20) (1857), Tambosier à feuilles de buis (French) (20) (1857)

Eugenia jambos **L.** – See *Syzygium jambos* (L.) Alston

Eugenia **L.** – Eugenia (138) (1923)

Eugenia malaccensis **L.** – See *Syzygium malaccense* (L.) Merr. & Perry

Eugenia pimenta **[(L.) DC.]** – See *Pimenta dioica* (L.) Merr.

Eugenia procera **(Sw.) Poir.** – Ironwood [Iron wood, Iron-wood] (107) (1919), Tall eugenia (20) (1857), Tambosier élevé (French) (20) (1857)

Eugenia procera **Poir.** – See *Eugenia procera* (Sw.) Poir.

Eugenia uniflora **L.** – Pitanga (109) (1949), Surinam-cherry (109, 138) (1923–1949)

Eulophus americanus **Nutt.** – See *Perideridia americana* (Nutt. ex DC.) Reichenb.

Eulophus **Nutt.** – See *Perideridia* Reichnb.

Eunanus **Gray** – possibly *Mimulus* L. (all US species)

Euonymus **(Tourn.) L.** – See *Euonymus* L.

Euonymus alata **(Thunb.) Sieb.** – Winged euonymus (112, 138) (1923–1937)

Euonymus alatus – See *Euonymus alata* (Thunb.) Sieb.

Euonymus americanus L. – See *Euonymus americanus* L., American strawberry bush (2, 82) (1895–1930), Bishop's-cap [Bishop's cap, Bishops-cap, Bishopscap] (156) (1923), Brook euonymus (122, 138, 156) (1923–1937), Burningbush [Burning bush, Burning-bush] (5, 19, 92, 156) (1840–1923), Burning-heart [Burning heart] (5, 156) (1913–1923), Creeping-root burning-bush [Creeping-rooted burning-bush] (187) (1818), Creeping-root spindle-tree [Creeping-rooted spindle-tree] (187) (1818), Fishwood [Fish wood, Fishwood] (5, 156) (1913–1923), Prickwood [Prick-wood, Prick wood] (92) (1876), Running euonymus (138) (1923), Running strawberry-bush [Running strawberry bush] (5, 109, 156) (1913–1949), Spindle tree [Spindletree, Spindle-tree] (92) (1876), Strawberry bush [Strawberry-bush (5, 15, 65, 92, 97, 109, 113, 122, 124, 156) (1890–1949), Strawberry shrub [Strawberry-shrub] (7, 92) (1828–1876), Wahoo [Waahoo, Wa-a-hoo, Wauhoo, Whahoo] (59, 156) (1911–1923), possibly Evergreen spindletree [Ever-greenspindle tree] (8) (1785), possibly Fusain toujours vert (French) (8) (1785)

Euonymus americanus L. var. *sarmentosus* – See *Euonymus americanus* L.

Euonymus atropurpurea Jacq. – American spindle tree [American spindle-tree] (157, 158) (1900–1929), Arrow-wood [Arrow wood] (5, 7, 92, 156) (1828–1923), Bitter-ash [Bitter ash] (92, 156, 158) (1876–1923), Burningbush [Burning bush, Burning-bush] (2, 5, 6, 15, 37, 49, 53, 72, 85, 93, 95 109, 121, 130, 131, 135, 157, 158) (1892–1949), Bursting-heart [Bursting heart] (156, 157, 158) (1900–1929), Dogwood [Dog-wood, Dog wood] (156) (1923), Eastern burningbush (155) (1942), Eastern wahoo (50, 155) (1942–present), Euonymous (52, 55, 57) (1911–1917), Fusain (French) (6) (1892), Indian arrow (73, 92, 156) (1876–1923), Indian arrow-wood [Indian arrow wood, Indian arrowwood] (5, 6, 49, 53, 58, 92, 157, 158) (1876–1929), Ninebark [Nine bark, Nine-bark] (59) (1911), Niniba žoŋ (Osage, pipestem wood) (121) (1918?–1970?), Ou Bonnet de Pretre (French) (6) (1892), Pegwood [Peg-wood] (92) (1876), Seven-bark [Seven barks, Seven bark] (59) (1911), Skewerwood [Skewer wood, Skewer-wood] (156) (1923), Spindelbaum (German) (6) (1892), Spindle tree [Spindletree, Spindle-tree] (2, 5, 6, 19, 49, 53, 58, 135, 155, 156) (1840–1942), Strawberry bush [Strawberry-bush (5, 157, 158) (1900–1929), Strawberry tree [Strawberry-tree] (5, 156, 157, 158) (1900–1929), Wahoo [Waahoo, Wa-a-hoo, Wauhoo, Whahoo] (3, 5, 6, 9, 15, 22, 48, 49, 52, 53, 57, 58, 59, 61, 65, 72, 85, 92, 97, 109, 112, 125, 131, 138, 157, 158) (1869–1986), Wahoon (6, 7) (1828–1932), Wananh'a-i-monthin (Omaha-Ponca, ghost walking stick) (37) (1919), possibly Carolina spindle tree [Carolinian spindle tree] (8) (1785), possibly Fusain de Caroline à fleurs noires (French) (8) (1785)

Euonymus atropurpurea Jacq. var. *atropurpurea* – Eastern wahoo (50) (present)

Euonymus carolinienensis [Marsh.] – See *Euonymus atropurpureus* Jacq.

Euonymus europaea L. – Arrowbeam [Arrow beam, Arrow-beam] (5, 156) (1913–1923), Butcher's prick tree [Bitcher's prick-tree] (5, 156) (1913–1923), Cat tree [Cat-tree] (5, 156) (1913–1923), European burningbush (138) (1923), European dogwood [European dog-wood] (5, 156) (1913–1923), European spindle-tree [European spindle tree] (82) (1930) IA, Gaiter tree [Gaiter-tree] (5, 156) (1913–1923), Gatten or Gatten tree [Gatten-tree] (5, 156) (1913–1923), Gatteridge (5, 156) (1913–1923), Louseberry or Louseberry tree [Louseberry-tree, Louse berry tree] (5, 92, 156) (1876–1923), Pegwood [Peg-wood] (5, 156) (1913–1923), Pincushion shrub [Pincushion-shrub (5, 156) (1913–1923), Prick timber [Prick-timber] (5, 156) (1913–1923), Prickwood [Prick-wood, Prick wood] (5, 156) (1913–1923), Skewerwood [Skewer wood, Skewer-wood] (5, 156) (1913–1923), Skiverwood [Skiver-wood, Skiver wood] (5, 156) (1913–1923), Spindle tree [Spindletree, Spindle-tree] (5, 156, 178) (1526–1923), Witchwood [Witch-wood, Witch wood] (5, 156) (1913–1923)

Euonymus fortunei (Turcz.) Hand.-Maz. var. *fortunei* – Big-leaf winter-creeper [Bigleaf wintercreeper] (138) (1923)

Euonymus fortunei (Turcz.) Hand.-Maz. var. *radicans* (Sieb. ex Miq.) Rehd. – Winter-creeper [Wintercreeper, Winter creeper] (112, 138) (1923–1937)

Euonymus hamiltonianus Wall subsp. *sieboldianus* (Blume) Hara – Yeddo euonymus (138) (1923)

Euonymus hamiltonianus Wall. – Lance-leaf euonymus [Lanceleaf euonymus] (138) (1923)

Euonymus japonicus Thunb. – Chinese box (92) (1876), Evergreen burningbush (138) (1923), Japanese spindle-tree [Japanese spindle tree] (107) (1919)

Euonymus L. – Burningbush [Burning bush, Burning-bush] (1, 13, 93, 156) (1932–1936), Euonymus (138, 155) (1923–1942), Fusain (French) (8) (1785), Skewerwood [Skewer wood, Skewer-wood] (92) (1876), Spindle bush [Spindlebush] (7) (1828), Spindle tree [Spindletree, Spindle-tree] (8, 10, 13, 15, 50, 82, 109) (1785–present), Strawberry tree [Strawberry-tree] (13) (1849), Wahoo [Waahoo, Wa-a-hoo, Wauhoo, Whahoo] (1, 7, 158) (1828–1932), Wahoon (7) (1828)

Euonymus lanceifolius (Loes.) – See *Euonymus hamiltonianus* Wall.

Euonymus nanus M. Bieb. – Dwarf burningbush (138) (1923)

Euonymus obovatus Nutt. – See *Euonymus americanus* L.

Euonymus radicans – See *Euonymus fortunei* (Turcz.) Hand.-Maz. var. *radicans* (Sieb. ex Miq.) Rehd.

Euonymus radicans var. *vegeta* Rehder – See *Euonymus fortunei* (Turcz.) Hand.-Maz. var. *fortunei*

Euonymus radicans vegetus – See *Euonymus fortunei* (Turcz.) Hand.-Maz. var. *fortunei*

Euonymus sempervirens [Marsh] – possibly *Euonymus americanus* L. (current species depends on author)

Euonymus yedoensis – See *Euonymus hamiltonianus* Wall subsp. *sieboldianus* (Blume) Hara

Eupatoriadelphus maculatus (L.) King & H. Rob. var. *bruneri* (A. Gray) King & H. Rob. – Rydberg's Joe-pye weed (72) (1907)

Eupatorium (Tourn.) L. – See *Eupatorium* L.

Eupatorium ageratoides L. – See *Ageratina altissima* (L.) King & H.E. Robins.

Eupatorium album L. – White thoroughwort (5, 122, 156) (1913–1937)

Eupatorium altissimum L. – Tall boneset (72, 82) (1907–1930), Tall eupatorium (155) (1942), Tall Joe-Pye weed (3) (1977), Tall thoroughwort (5, 50, 93, 95, 97, 122, 131) (1899–present)

Eupatorium aromaticum L. – See *Ageratina aromatica* (L.) Spach var. *aromatica*

Eupatorium aromaticum melissoides – See *Ageratina aromatica* (L.) Spach

Eupatorium aromaticum var. *melissoides* (Willd.) A. Gray – See *Ageratina aromatica* (L.) Spach

Eupatorium ayapana Vent. – See *Eupatorium triplinerve* Vahl

Eupatorium bruneri Gray – See *Eupatorium maculatum* L. var. *bruneri* (Gray) Breitung

Eupatorium cannabinum L. – Hemp agrimony (92) (1876), King Kunigundus herbe (178) (1526), Sweet-smelling trefoil [Sweet smelling trefoil] (92) (1876), Water maudlin (92) (1876), Wild hemp [Wylde hempe] (179) (1526)

Eupatorium capillifolium (Lam.) Small – Dog-fennel [Dog fennel, Dog's fennel, Dog's fennel] (5, 156) (1913–1923), Hogweed [Hogweed, Hog weed] (5) (1913), Sneezeweed hog-weed (156) (1923)

Eupatorium coelestinum L. – See *Conoclinium coelestinum* (L.) DC.

Eupatorium compositifolium Walt. – Yankee-weed [Yankee weed] (124) (1937) TX

Eupatorium glechonophyllum – See *Ageratina glechonophylla* (Less.) R.M. King & H. Rob.

Eupatorium holzingeri Rydb. – See *Eupatorium purpureum* L. var. *holzingeri* (Rydb.) E. Lamont

Eupatorium hyssipifolium L. – Hempweed [Hemp-weed, Hemp weed] (19) (1840), Hyssop-leaf eupatorium [Hyssop-leaved eupatorium]

(187) (1818), Hyssop-leaf thoroughwort [Hyssopleaf thoroughwort, Hyssop-leaved thoroughwort] (5, 19, 122) (1840–1937), Justice-weed [Justice weed, Justice-weed, Justices' weed] (92) (1876)

Eupatorium hyssopifolium **L. var.** *hyssopifolium* – Torrey's thoroughwort (5) (1913)

Eupatorium incarnatum **Walt.** – See *Fleischmannia incarnata* (Walt.) King & H.E.

Eupatorium **L.** – Boneset (1, 2, 93, 106, 109, 122, 156) (1895–1949), Eupatorium (138, 155) (1923–1942), Hempweed [Hemp-weed, Hemp weed] (184) (1793), Joe Pye weed [Joe-Pye-weed, Joe-pye weed] (93) (1936), Mistflower [Mist-flower, Mist flower] (1) (1932), Thoroughwort [Thorough wort, Thorough-wort] (1, 2, 50, 82, 93, 109, 122, 158) (1895–present), White snakeroot [White snake root, White snake-root] (1, 93) (1932–1936)

Eupatorium lanceolatum **Muhl ex Willd** – See *Eupatorium pilosum* Walter

Eupatorium leucolepis **(DC.) Torr. & Gray** – Justiceweed [Justice weed, Justice-weed, Justices' weed] (5, 92, 156) (1876–1923), White-bract thoroughwort [Whitebracted thoroughwort, White-bracted thoroughwort, White-bracted thorough-wort] (5, 156) (1913–1923)

Eupatorium leucolepis **Torr. & Gray** – See *Eupatorium leucolepis* (DC.) Torr. & Gray

Eupatorium maculatum **L.** – Joe Pye weed [Joe-Pye-weed, Joe-pye weed] (4, 40, 109) (1929–1986), Maculated hempweed [Maculated hemp-weed] (187) (1818), Purple boneset (156) (1923), Spotted boneset (5, 7, 64, 92, 157, 158) (1828–1929), Spotted eyebright [Spotted eyebright, Spotted eye-bright] (157, 158) (1900–1929), Spotted joepye weed [Spotted joepyeweed, Spotted Joe-pye-weed] (5, 50, 64, 72, 85, 93, 95, 97, 122, 131, 155, 156, 157, 158) (1899–present)

Eupatorium maculatum **L. var.** *bruneri* **(Gray) Breitung** – Bruner's joe-pye weed [Bruner joepyeweed] (155) (1942), Bruner's trumpetweed [Bruner's trumpet weed] (5) (1913), Spotted joe-pye weed [Spotted joepyeweed, Spotted Joe-pye-weed] (3, 38, 50) (1977–present)

Eupatorium maculatum **L. var.** *maculatum* – Rough Joe-Pye-weed (138) (1923), Spotted joe-pye weed [Spotted joepyeweed, Spotted Joe-pye-weed] (82) (1930)

Eupatorium melissoides **Willd.** – See *Ageratina aromatica* (L.) Spach

Eupatorium micranthum **[Lag.]** – possibly *Ageratum corymbosum* Zuccagni (current species depends on author)

Eupatorium perfoliatum **L.** – Agueweed [Ague weed, Ague-weed] (5, 6, 7, 52, 53, 69, 92, 156, 157, 158) (1814–1929), Boneset (3, 4, 5, 6, 7, 12, 19, 40, 49, 52, 53, 55, 57, 58, 59, 61, 62, 63, 69, 72, 92, 93, 105, 114, 122, 124, 131, 138, 155, 156, 157, 158, 186, 187) (1814–1986), Bonset (7) (1828), Common boneset (50) (present), Common thoroughwort (5, 62, 95, 97, 157, 158) (1900–1937), Cross-wort [Cross wort, Cross-wort, Crosse woort] (5, 6, 7, 53, 69, 92, 156, 158, 186, 187) (1814–1923), Durchwachsener Wasserdost (German) (158, 186) (1814–1900), Durchwachsener Wasserhanf (German) (6, 158) (1892–1900), Durchwasser Wasserdost (German) (7) (1828), Durchwasserdost (German) (7) (1828), Eupatoire percefeuille (French) (7) (1828), Eupatorie perfoliée (French) (6, 158) (1892–1900), Eupatorio (Spanish) (158) (1900), Eupatorium (52, 57) (1917–1919), Feverwort [Fever wort, Fever-wort] (6, 7, 69, 92, 156, 157, 158) (1828–1929), Herbe à fiévre (French) (6, 158) (1892–1900), Herbe Parfaite (French) (6, 158) (1892–1900), Indian sage [Indian-sage] (5, 6, 7, 49, 53, 69, 93, 156, 157, 158, 186, 187) (1814–1936), Joe-Pye [Joe pye, Joe Pie, Joepye] (7) (1828), Marsh-sage (156) (1923), Niya'wibûkûk (Chippewa) (40) (1928), Šašabwaksing (Chippewa) (105) (1932), Šiabuksing (Chippewa) (105) (1932), Sweating plant [Sweating-plant] (69, 92, 156, 157, 158) (1898–1929), Sweating-weed [Sweating weed, Sweatingweed] (6) (1892), Tearal [Tearel] (69, 92) (1876–1904), Teasel [Teazel] (7, 69) (1828–1904), Thorough-growth [Thorough growth] (156) (1923), Thorough-stem [Thorough stem] (5, 7, 53, 69, 92, 156, 158, 186) (1814–1923), Thorough-wax [Thorough wax, Thoroughwax,

Thorough Waxe, Thorow-wax] (5, 6, 7, 53, 69, 92, 156, 158, 186) (1814–1923), Thoroughwort [Thorough wort, Thorough-wort] (6, 7, 19, 49, 53, 55, 57, 58, 59, 69, 92, 106, 156, 184, 187) (1814–1930), Throughgrow (5, 76, 156) (1896–1923) Eastern PA, Vegetable antimony (6, 7, 53, 69, 92, 156, 157, 158) (1828–1929), Wild Isaac (69) (1904), Wild sage (5, 156, 158) (1900–1923), Wood boneset (69, 92) (1876–1904)

Eupatorium pilosum **Walter** – Spear-leaf hempweed [Spear-leafed hemp-weed] (187) (1818)

Eupatorium pubescens – See *Eupatorium rotundifolium* L. var. *ovatum* (Bigelow) Torr.

Eupatorium purpureum **L.** – Ămādita'tĭ (Cherokee, water dipper) (102) (1886) stem was used as straw for sucking water, Biaškagemesek (Chippewa) (105) (1932), Blue-stem joepye weed [Bluestem joepyeweed] (155) (1942), Eupatorium (52) (1919), Gravelroot [Gravel root, Gravel-root] (5, 6, 7, 49, 53, 54, 58, 64, 75, 92, 102, 157, 158) (1828–1929) said to be a remedy for calculi, Gravelweed [Gravelweed, Gravel weed] (49, 52, 53) (1919–1922), Hollow-stem hempweed [Hollow-stemmed hemp-weed] (187) (1818), Indian gravelroot [Indian gravel-root, Indian gravel root] (5, 64, 156, 158) (1900–1923), Indian marsh milkweed [Indian marsh milk-weed] (157) (1929), Joe Pye weed [Joe-Pye-weed, Joe-pye weed] (2, 49, 53, 58, 62, 63, 64, 72, 82, 92, 93, 97, 105, 106, 109, 122, 127, 138, 156) (1869–1937), Joe pye's weed (19) (1840), Joe-Pye [Joe pye, Joe Pie, Joepye] (5, 6, 7, 19, 49, 92, 95) (1828–1911), Joe-the-weed (157) (1929), Jopiweed (6) (1892), Kidney-bean root [Kidney bean root] (92) (1876), Kidneyroot [Kidney root] (5, 64) (1907–1908), Kidneywort [Kidneywort] (156) (1923), King-of-the-meadow [King of the meadow] (5, 64, 76, 156, 158) (1896–1923), Marsh milkweed [Marsh milk-weed, Marsh milk weed] (5, 64, 73, 75, 156, 158) (1892–1923), Motherwort [Mother wort, Mother-wort, Mother Woort] (5, 64, 73, 156, 157, 158) (1892–1929), Pride-of-the-meadow [Pride of the meadow] (156) (1923), Purple boneset (5, 6, 7, 49, 62, 64, 85, 92, 93, 156, 157, 158) (1828–1936), Purple hempweed [Purple hemp-weed] (6) (1892), Purple thoroughwort (2, 6, 19) (1840–1895), Purpurfarbener Wasserhanf (German) (6) (1892), Queen-of-the-meadow [Queen of the meadow] (5, 6, 49, 52, 53, 54, 58, 61, 64, 73, 75, 76, 92, 102, 156, 157, 158) (1869–1929), Quillwort [Quill-wort, Quill wort] (5, 64, 75, 156, 158) (1900–1923) no longer in use by 1923, Skunkweed, [Skunk weed, Skunk-weed] (5, 156) (1913–1923), Slunkweed [Slunk-weed] (64, 156, 158) (1900–1923), Sweet Joe-pye weed (3, 4) (1977–1986), Sweet-scented joe-pye weed [Sweetscented joepyeweed] (50) (present), Tall boneset (5, 7, 64, 92, 156, 157, 158) (1828–1929), Trumpet-weed [Trumpet weed, Trumpetweed] (5, 6, 19, 49, 54, 62, 64, 92, 95, 156, 157, 158) (1840–1929), Turnip-weed [Turnip weed, Turnipweed] (106, 156) (1923–1930), possibly Whorl-leaf hempweed [Whorled-leaved hemp-weed] (187) (1818)

Eupatorium purpureum **L. var.** *holzingeri* **(Rydb.) E. Lamont** – Holzinger's eupatorium (50) (present), Holzinger's trumpet-weed (97) (1937)

Eupatorium purpureum **L. var.** *purpureum* – Three-leaf hempweed [Three-leaved hemp-weed] (187) (1818), Wood boneset (7) (1828)

Eupatorium purpureum maculatum – See *Eupatorium maculatum* L. var. *maculatum*

Eupatorium purpureum **var.** *maculatum* **(L.) Darl.** – See *Eupatorium maculatum* L. var. *maculatum*

Eupatorium resinosum **Torr. ex DC.** – Resin boneset (5) (1913)

Eupatorium rotundifolium **L.** – Boneset (80) (1913), Horehound [Hoarhound, Hore-hound, Horehounde] (156) (1923), Rough boneset (7, 92) (1828–1876), Rough-leaf thoroughwort [Roughleaf thoroughwort] (122, 156) (1923–1937), Roundish-leaf Hempweed [Roundish-leaved Hemp-weed] (187) (1818), Round-leaf thoroughwort [Roundleaf thoroughwort] (5, 97, 122) (1913–1937), Wild horehound [Wild hoarhound] (5, 7, 58, 61, 92, 156) (1828–1923)

Eupatorium rotundifolium **L. var.** *ovatum* **(Bigelow) Torr.** – Hairy thoroughwort (5) (1913)

Eupatorium rotundifolium **L. var.** *rotundifolium* – Rough boneset

(156) (1923), Rough thoroughwort (5, 156) (1913–1923), Vervain thoroughwort (5, 156) (1913–1923), Wild horehound [Wild hoarhound] (5, 156) (1913–1923)

Eupatorium rugosum Houtt. – See *Ageratina altissima* (L.) King & H.E. Robins.

Eupatorium semiserratum DC. – Small-flower thoroughwort [Small-flowered thoroughwort] (5) (1913)

Eupatorium serotinum Michx. – Late eupatorium (3, 155) (1942–1977), Late thoroughwort (138) (1923), Late-flowering thoroughwort [Lateflowering thoroughwort, Late flowering thoroughwort] (5, 50, 72, 82, 97, 122) (1907–present), Silver-rod (156) (1923)

Eupatorium sessilifolium L. – Bastard boneset (5, 7) (1828–1932), Sessile-leaf eupatorium [Sessile-leaved eupatorium] (187) (1818), Upland boneset (5, 156) (1913–1923)

Eupatorium teucrifolium Willd. – See *Eupatorium rotundifolium* L.

Eupatorium torreyanum Short. – See *Eupatorium hyssopifolium* L. var. *hyssopifolium*

Eupatorium trifoliatum L. – See *Eupatorium purpureum* L. var. *purpureum*

Eupatorium triplinerve Vahl – Ayapana (92) (1876)

Eupatorium urticaefolium Reicherd. – See *Ageratina altissima* (L.) King & H.E. Robins.

Eupatorium urticefolium – See *Ageratina altissima* (L.) King & H. E. Robins.

Eupatorium urticifolium Reicherd. – See *Ageratina altissima* (L.) King & H.E. Robins.

Eupatorium verbenaefolium Michx. – See *Eupatorium rotundifolium* L. var. *rotundifolium*

Eupatorium verbenifolium Reichard – See *Eupatorium rotundifolium* L. var. *rotundifolium*

Eupatorium verticillatum [Lam.] – See *Eupatorium purpureum* L.

Eupatorium violaceum Raf. – See *Conoclinium coelestinum* (L.) DC.

Euphorbia agraria Bieb. – Leafy spurge (3) (1977), Urban spurge (50) (present)

Euphorbia albomarginata T.& G. – See *Chamaesyce albomarginata* (Torr. & Gray) Small

Euphorbia antisyphilitica Zucc. – Candelilla (122) (1937) TX, Wax euphorbia (155) (1942)

Euphorbia bicolor Engelm. & Gray – Snow-on-the-mountain [Snow on the mountain] (124) (1937) TX

Euphorbia brachycera Engelm. – Horned spurge (50) (present), Robust euphorbia (155) (1942), Rocky Mountain spurge (5, 85, 93, 131) (1899–1936)

Euphorbia commutata Engelm. – Tinted spurge (5, 72, 122) (1907–1937)

Euphorbia corollata L. – Apple root [Apple-root] (5, 7, 49, 92, 156, 157, 158) (1828–1929), Blooming spurge (5, 6, 7, 49, 53, 92, 93, 156, 157, 158) (1828–1936), Blum Wolfsmilch (German) (7) (1828), Bowman's root [Bowman's-root, Bowman root, Bowmanroot] (5, 6, 7, 49, 61, 92, 156, 157, 158) (1828–1929), Correlated spurge (187) (1818), Emetic root [Emetic-root] (7, 49, 92, 157, 158) (1828–1929), Euphorbe à grandes fleurs (French) (6) (1892), Euphorbia (52) (1919), Euphorbia radix (Official name of Materia Medica) (7) (1828), Flowering spurge (3, 4, 5, 6, 47, 50, 62, 72, 80, 82, 85, 86, 93, 97, 109, 122, 125, 138, 156, 157, 158) (1852–present), Flowering-spurge euphorbia [Floweringspurge euphorbia] (155) (1942), Hippo (7, 49, 92) (1828–1898), Indian physic [Indian-physic, Indianphysic, Indian physick] (6, 7, 49) (1828–1898), Ipecac (7, 49) (1828–1898), Ipecacuana (7) (1828), Ipecacuana (Official name of Materia Medica) (7) (1828), Large flowering-spurge [Large flowering spurge, Large-flowering spurge] (49, 52, 53, 57, 92, 157, 158) (1876–1929), Large-flower spurge [Large flowered spurge, Large-flowered spurge] (6, 156) (1892–1923), Maryland spurge (5) (1913), Milk ipecac (5, 92, 156, 157, 158) (1898–1929), Milk purslane [Milk-purslain] (5, 7, 49, 53, 156, 157, 158) (1828–1929), Milk pusley [Milk pussley] (5, 92, 156, 158) (1876–1923), Milkweed [Milk weed (Milk-weed] (5, 7, 78, 92, 156, 158) (1828–1923), Pehaca

(Louisiana) (7) (1828) means emetic root, Persely (7) (1828), Picac (5, 7, 49, 92, 156) (1828–1923) no longer in use by 1923, Purge root (5, 49) (1898–1923), Purging root [Purging-root] (92, 156, 157, 158) (1876–1929), Pursley (157) (1929), Showy spurge (157) (1929), Snake-milk [Snake milk, Snake's milk] (5, 6, 7, 49, 53, 92, 156, 157, 158) (1828–1929), Snake's-milk [Snake's milk, Snake milk, Snake-milk] (5, 6, 7, 49, 53, 92, 156, 157, 158) (1828–1929), Tithymale Fleuri (French) (7) (1828), Wandering milkweed [Wandering milk weed] (6) (1892), White pursely (7, 92) (1828–1876), White purslane (5, 156, 157, 158) (1900–1929), White-flower spurge [White flowering spurge] (82) (1930), White-top spurge [White-topped spurge] (62) (1912), Wild hippo [Wild hipp] (5, 6, 156, 157, 158) (1892–1929), Wild ipecac (6) (1892)

Euphorbia corollata Willd. – See *Euphorbia corollata* L.

Euphorbia cuphosperma (Engelm.) Boiss. – Warty spurge (122) (1937)

Euphorbia cyathophora Murray – Cruel plant (82) (1930), Fire-on-the-mountain [Fire on the mountain] (3, 4, 50, 156) (1923–present), Hypocrite plant (156) (1923), Painted spurge (138) (1923), Painted-leaf [Painted leaf] (82, 156) (1923–1930), Various-leaf spurge [Various-leaved spurge] (5, 72, 93, 97, 131) (1899–1937), Wild poinsettia (124) (1937)

Euphorbia cyparissias L. – Balsam (5, 75, 156) (1894–1923), Balsam spurge (156, 158) (1900–1923), Bonaparte's crown [Bonaparte's-crown] (5, 156, 158) (1900–1923) no longer in use by 1923, Butternut [Butter nuts, Butter nut] (73) (1892) Harmony ME, Cypress (5, 73, 156, 158) (1892–1923), Cypress euphorbia (155) (1942), Cypress spurge (3, 4, 50, 62, 72, 80, 92, 109, 122, 138, 156, 158) (1876–present), Cypresse spurge (178, 180) (1526–1633), Euphorbia (45) (1896), Garden spurge (5, 156) (1913–1923), Graveyard moss (78) (1898) IN, Graveyard spurge (62, 156) (1912–1923) IN, Graveyard weed (5, 75, 156, 158) (1894–1923) WV, Irish moss (5, 73, 158) (1892–1913) New Brunswick, Kiss-me-Dick (5, 156) (1913–1923), Kiss-me-quick [Kiss me quick] (156, 158) (1900–1923), Milkweed [Milk weed (Milk-weed] (78) (1898), Quacksalver's-spurge [Quacksalver's spurge, Quack salver's spurge] (5, 156, 158) (1900–1923) no longer in use by 1923, Spurge (148) (1939), Tree moss [Tree-moss] (5, 73, 93, 156, 158) (1892–1936), Welcome-to-our-house (5, 156, 158) (1900–1923)

Euphorbia davidii Subils – David's spurge (50) (present)

Euphorbia dendroides L. – Tree spurge (178) (1526)

Euphorbia dentata Michx. – Toothed euphorbia (155) (1942), Toothed spurge (3, 4, 5, 50, 72, 93, 97, 122, 131) (1899–1937), Warty spurge (5, 85, 93) (1913–1936)

Euphorbia dictyosperma Fisch. & Meyer. – See *Euphorbia spathulata* Lam

Euphorbia epithymoides L. – Cushion euphorbia (155) (1942), Cushion spurge (138) (1923)

Euphorbia esula L. – Faitour's grass [Faitour's-grass] (156, 158) (1900–1923), Leafy euphorbia (155) (1942), Leafy spurge (4, 50, 156, 158) (1900–present), Tithymal (156, 158) (1900–1923)

Euphorbia esula L. var. esula – Faitour's grass [Faitour's-grass] (5) (1913), Leafy spurge (5, 50, 93) (1913–present), Tithymal (5) (1913)

Euphorbia esula L. var. uralensis (Fisch. ex Link) Dorn – Narrow-leaf leafy spurge (4) (1986), Russian leafy spurge (50) (present)

Euphorbia exigua L. – Dwarf spurge [Dwarfe Spurge] (50, 178) (1526–present)

Euphorbia fendleri Torr. & Gray – See *Chamaesyce fendleri* (Torr. & Gray) Small

Euphorbia geyeri Engelm. – See *Chamaesyce geyeri* (Engelm.) Small var. *geyeri*

Euphorbia glyptosperma Engelm. – See *Chamaesyce glyptosperma* (Engelm.) Small

Euphorbia helioscopia L. – Cat's-milk, [Cats milk, Cat's milk, Catmilk] (5, 92, 156) (1876–1923), Churnstaff [Churn-staff] (5, 92, 156) (1876–1923) no longer in use by 1923, Devil's-milk [Devil's milk] (5, 92, 156) (1876–1923), Little-good [Little good, Littlegood] (5, 82) (1913–1930), Madwomen's-milk [Mad woman's milk, Madwomen's milk, Madwoman's milk, Mad-woman's-milk] (5, 50, 156) (1913–present), Mouse-milk [Mouse milk] (5, 156) (1913–1923) no longer in use by 1923, Saturday's-pepper [Saturday's pepper] (156) (1923), Seven sisters (5, 156) (1913–1923) obsolete by 1923, Sun euphorbia (155) (1942), Sun spurge (5, 156) (1913–1923), Sunweed [Sun-weed] (5, 156) (1913–1923), Turnsole (5, 156) (1913–1923), Wart spurge [Wart-spurge] (5, 85, 122, 156) (1913–1937), Wartgrass [Wartgrass] (5, 156) (1913–1923), Wartweed [Wart-weed] (5, 156) (1913–1923), Wartwort [Wart-wort] (5, 92) (1876–1913), Wolf's-milk [Wolf's milk] (5, 156) (1913–1923) no longer in use by 1923

Euphorbia heterophylla **L.** – See *Euphorbia cyathophora* Murray

Euphorbia hexagona **Nutt. ex Spreng.** – Angled spurge (5, 93, 97, 131) (1899–1937), Six-angle euphorbia [Sixangle euphorbia] (155) (1942), Six-angle spurge [Sixangle spurge, Six-angled spurge] (3, 4, 50) (1977–present), Spurge (85) (1932)

Euphorbia humistrata **Engelm.** – See *Chamaesyce humistrata* (Engelm.) Small

Euphorbia hypercifolio **L.** – See *Chamaesyce hypericifolia* (L.) Millsp.

Euphorbia hypericifolia **L.** – See *Chamaesyce hypericifolia* (L.) Millsp.

Euphorbia hypericifolia **Willd.** – See *Chamaesyce hypericifolia* (L.) Millsp.

Euphorbia ipecacuanha – See *Euphorbia ipecacuanhae* L.

Euphorbia ipecacuanhae **L.** – American ipecac (6, 49, 53, 92) (1892–1922), American ipecacuanha (53, 186, 187) (1814–1922), American white ipecac (5, 156) (1913–1923), Anne Arundel's spurge [Anne Arundel spurge] (5) (1913), Black spurge (156) (1923), Brechenmachende Wolfsmilch (German) (156) (1923), Brechwolfsmilch (German) (6) (1892), Carolina hippo (6) (1892), Carolina ipecac (6, 49, 156) (1892–1923), Euphorbe vomitive (French) (6) (1892), Euphorbia (92) (1876), Ipecac euphorbia (155) (1942), Ipecac spurge (2, 5, 53, 92, 156) (1876–1923), Ipecacuanha spurge (6, 7, 49, 57) (1828–1917), Spurge (92) (1876), Spurge ipecac (5, 92, 156) (1898–1923), White ipecac (92, 156) (1898–1923), White secac (49) (1898), Wild hippo [Wild hipp] (156) (1923), Wild ipecac (5, 6, 49, 53, 61, 92, 156, 186) (1870–1923) TX

Euphorbia **L.** – Euphorbia (155) (1942), Kombu (155) (1942), Poinsettia (93, 138) (1923–1939), Snow-on-the-mountain [Snow on the mountain] (1, 93) (1932–1936), Spourge (179) (1526), Spurge (1, 2, 4, 10, 50, 82, 93, 109, 138, 156, 158, 167, 184) (1793–present), Tintymall of Babylon (179) (1526)

Euphorbia lata **Engelm.** – See *Chamaesyce lata* (Engelm.) Small

Euphorbia lathyris **L.** – Antigopher plant (71) (1898), Caper bush [Caper-bush] (5, 71, 156) (1898–1923) OK, Caper euphorbia (155) (1942), Caper spurge (5, 6, 71, 92, 107, 109, 156) (1876–1949), Capper plant (7) (1828), Catepuce (156) (1923), Garden spurge (6, 71, 92) (1876–1898), Gopher plant [Gopher-plant] (71, 156) (1898–1923), Mole plant [Mole-plant, Moleplant] (5, 6, 7, 71, 109, 155, 156, 187) (1818–1949), Mole tree [Mole-tree] (5, 6, 71, 73, 156) (1892–1923) Northern OH, said to keep moles out of gardens, Moleweed [Mole weed] (71, 75, 155) (1898–1942) WV, Myrtle spurge [Mirtle spurge] (5, 122, 156) (1913–1937), Purgienkörner (German) (6) (1892), Springwort [Spring wort] (5, 71, 1923) (1898–1923), Spurge caper (7, 19, 92) (1828–1876), Wild caper (5, 71, 156) (1898–1923), Wolf's-milk [Wolf's milk] (71, 156) (1898–1923)

Euphorbia lathyris **Willd.** – See *Euphorbia lathyris* L.

Euphorbia longicruris **Scheele** – Wedge-leaf spurge [Wedgeleaf spurge] (50) (present)

Euphorbia lucida **Waldst. & Kit.** – Shining spurge (5) (1913)

Euphorbia maculata **L.** – See *Chamaesyce maculata* (L.) Small

Euphorbia marginata **Pursh** – Ghostweed [Ghost-weed] (78) (1898) Waco TX, Ice plant [Ice-plant, Iceplant] (106) (1930) TX, Itopta sapa tapežuta (Lakota, black-footed ferret medicine) (121) (1918?–1970?), Kalipika tsitsiks (Pawnee) (37) (1919), Karipika (Pawnee) (37) (1919), Milkweed [Milk weed [Milk-weed] (78, 106)

(1898–1930), Mountain spurge (5) (1913), Mountain-snow [Mountain snow] (156, 157, 158) (1900–1929), Snow-on-the-mountain [Snow on the mountain] (3, 4, 5, 37, 50, 71, 73, 78, 80, 82, 85, 86, 93, 97, 106, 109, 121, 122, 124, 138, 145, 148, 155, 156, 157, 158) (1878–present), Spurge (106, 125) (1930), Variegated spurge (5, 38, 156, 157, 158) (1820–1929), White-margin spurge [White margined spurge, White-margined spurge] (5, 72, 93, 131, 156, 157, 158) (1899–1936)

Euphorbia marilandica **Greene** – See *Euphorbia corollata* L.

Euphorbia milii **Des Moulins** – Crown-of-thorn euphorbia [Crownofthorneuphorbia] (155) (1942), Crown-of-thorns (109) (1949)

Euphorbia missouriensis **(Norton) Small.** – See *Euphorbia spathulata* Lam

Euphorbia missurica **Raf.** – See *Chamaesyce missurica* (Raf.) Shinners

Euphorbia montana robusta **Engelm.** – See *Euphorbia brachycera* Engelm.

Euphorbia myrsinites **L.** – Myrtle spurge [Mirtle spurge] (50, 178) (1526–present)

Euphorbia nutans **Lag.** – See *Chamaesyce nutans* (Lag.) Small

Euphorbia obtusata **Pursh** – See *Euphorbia spathulata* Lam

Euphorbia paralias **L.** – Sea spurge (50, 178)

Euphorbia peplus **L.** – Devil's-milk [Devil's milk] (5, 156) (1913–1923), Hyssop spurge [Hyssope spurge] (178) (1526), Peplios (178) (1526), Peplis (178) (1526), Petty euphorbia (155) (1942), Petty spurge (5, 72, 122, 156) (1907–1937), Pretty spurge (156) (1923), Round spurge (178) (1526), Round-leaf spurge [Round leafed spurge] (178) (1526), Seven-sisters [Seven sisters] (5, 156) (1913–1923), Wartweed [Wart-weed] (5, 156) (1913–1923), Wild caper (19) (1840)

Euphorbia peplus **W.** – See *Euphorbia peplus* L.

Euphorbia petaloidea **Engelm.** – See *Chamaesyce missurica* (Raf.) Shinners

Euphorbia pilulifera – See *Chamaesyce hirta* (L.) Millsp.

Euphorbia platyphyllos **L.** – Broad-leaf spurge [Broad-leaved spurge] (5) (1913)

Euphorbia podperae **Croizat** – See *Euphorbia agraria* Bieb.

Euphorbia polygonifolia **L.** – See *Chamaesyce polygonifolia* (L.) Small

Euphorbia preslii **Guss.** – See *Chamaesyce nutans* (Lag.) Small

Euphorbia prostrata **Aiton** – See *Chamaesyce prostrata* (Aiton) Small

Euphorbia pulcherrima **Willd. ex Klotzsch** – Common poinsettia (155) (1942), Poinsettia (92, 106, 138) (1876–1930)

Euphorbia purpurea **(Raf.) Fern.** – Darlington's spurge (5) (1913)

Euphorbia revoluta **Engelm.** – See *Chamaesyce revoluta* (Engelm.) Small

Euphorbia robusta **(Engelm.) Small** – See *Euphorbia brachycera* Engelm.

Euphorbia serpens **Kunth** – See *Chamaesyce serpens* (Kunth) Small

Euphorbia serpillifolia **Pers.** – See *Chamaesyce serpyllifolia* (Pers.) Small subsp. *serpyllifolia*

Euphorbia serpyllifolia **Lam.** – See *Chamaesyce serpyllifolia* (Pers.) Small subsp. *serpyllifolia*

Euphorbia spathulata **Lam** – Arkansas spurge (5, 93, 97) (1913–1937), Blunted spurge (122) (1937), Blunt-leaf spurge [Blunt-leaved spurge] (5, 72, 93, 97) (1907–1937), Purple spurge (85) (1932), Reticulate-seed spurge [Reticulate seeded spurge, Reticulate-seeded spurge] (5, 72, 93, 97, 131) (1899–1937), Warted spurge (5, 156) (1913–1923), Warty spurge (50) (present)

Euphorbia stictospora **Engelm.** – See *Chamaesyce stictospora* (Engelm.) Small

Euphorbia strictior **Holz.** – Panhandle spurge (50) (present)

Euphorbia tirucalli **L.** – Indian tree spurge (109) (1949), Malabar-tree euphorbia [Malabartree euphorbia] (155) (1942), Milk bush [Milk-bush] (109) (1949)

Euphorbia uralensis **Fisch. ex Link** – See *Euphorbia esula* L. var.

uralensis (Fisch. ex Link) Dorn

Euphorbia variegata **Sims** – See *Euphorbia marginata* Pursh

Euphorbia **x** *pseudovirgata* **(Schur) Soo** – See *Euphorbia esula* L. var. *esula*

Euphorbia zygophylloides **Boiss.** – See *Chamaesyce missurica* (Raf.) Shinners

Euphrasia **(Tourn.) L.** – See *Euphrasia* L.

Euphrasia americana **Wettst.** – See *Euphrasia nemorosa* (Pers.) Wallr.

Euphrasia **L.** – Eufrace (179) (1526), Eyebright [Eye-bright, Eye bright] (1, 10, 156, 167) (1814–1932)

Euphrasia nemorosa **(Pers.) Wallr.** – Eyebright [Eye-bright, Eye bright] (5, 156) (1913–1923), Hairy eyebright (5) (1913)

Euphrasia oakesii **Wettst.** – Oakes' eyebright (5) (1913)

Euphrasia officinalis **L.** – See *Euphrasia stricta* D. Wolff ex J. F. Lehm.

Euphrasia randii **Robinson** – Rand's eyebright (5) (1913)

Euphrasia stricta **D. Wolff ex J. F. Lehm.** – Augentrost (German) (6) (1892), Euphraise (French) (6) (1892), Euphrasia (52, 54) (1905–1919), Euphrasy (6) (1892), Eyebright [Eye-bright, Eye bright] (6, 7, 10, 19, 49, 52, 53, 54, 57, 58, 92) (1818–1922)

Euploca convolvulacaea **Nutt.** – possibly *Heliotropium convolvulaceum* (Nutt.) Gray

Euploca **Nutt.** – See *Heliotropium* L. (most US species)

Eurotia **Adans.** – See *Krascheninnikovia* Guldenstaedt

Eurotia lanata **(Pursh) Moq.** – See *Krascheninnikovia lanata* (Pursh) A. D. J. Meeuse & Smit

Eurotium glabrum **Blaser (possibly)** – Green mould (56) (1901)

Eurotium glaucus – possibly *Eurotium glabrum* Blaser

Eurybia **×*herveyi* (Gray) Nesom** [*macrophylla* × *spectabilis*] – Hervey's aster (5) (1913)

Eurybia chapmanii **(Torr. & Gray) Nesom** – Savannah aster (138, 155) (1931–1942)

Eurybia compacta **Nesom** – Slender aster (5, 156) (1913–1923), Tuber aster (5, 156) (1913–1923)

Eurybia conspicua **(Lindl.) Nesom** – Eastern showy aster (50) (present), Rough aster (3, 50, 85) (1932–present), Showy aster (155) (1942), Western showy aster (50) (present)

Eurybia divaricata **(L.) Nesom** – Clayton's aster (5) (1913), Clustered aster (42) (1814), Corymbed aster (156) (1923), Crimson-disk aster (5) (1913), Early aster (156) (1923), Long-leaf wood aster [Long-leaved wood aster] (5) (1913), White wood aster (5, 72, 155) (1907–1942), Wood aster (156) (1923)

Eurybia furcata **(Burgess) Nesom** – Forking aster (5) (1913)

Eurybia hemispherica **(Alexander) Nesom** – Single-stem bog aster [Single-stemmed bog aster] (4) (1986), Southern showy aster (50) (present)

Eurybia integrifolia **(Nutt.) Nesom** – Thick-stem aster [Thickstem aster] (155) (1942)

Eurybia macrophylla **(L.) Cass.** – Big-leaf aster [Bigleaf aster] (138, 155) (1931–1942), Broad-leaf starwort [Broad leaved star wort] (42) (1814), Dewy-leaf aster (5) (1913), Large-leaf aster [Large-leaved aster] (5, 72, 95, 106, 156) (1907–1930), Rough-tongues (156) (1923), Stately aster (5) (1913), Various-leaf aster [Various-leaved aster] (5) (1913), Violet wood aster (5) (1913), Violet-leaf aster (5) (1913)

Eurybia merita **(A. Nels.) Nesom** – Arctic aster (4) (1986), Subalpine aster (50) (present)

Eurybia paludosa **(Aiton) Nesom** – Single-stem bog aster [Single-stemmed bog aster] (155) (1942), Southern swamp aster (5, 97, 122) (1913–1937)

Eurybia radula **(Aiton) Nesom** – File-blade aster (5) (1913), Low rough aster (5) (1913), Rough aster (155) (1942)

Eurybia schreberi **(Nees) Nees** – Bernhardi's aster (5) (1913), Dome-top aster [Dome-topped aster] (5) (1913), Schreber's aster [Schreber aster] (5, 155) (1913–1942)

Eurybia sibirica **(L.) Nesom** – Siberian aster (131, 155) (1899–1942)

Eurybia spectabilis **(Aiton) Nesom** – Low showy aster (5, 156) (1913–1923), Seaside aster (138, 155) (1931–1942), Seaside purple aster (5, 156) (1913–1923)

Eurybia surculosa **(Michx.) Nesom** – Creeping aster (5) (1913)

Eurystemon mexicanum **(Wats.) Alex.** – See *Heteranthera mexicana* S. Wats.

Eurytaenia texana **Torr. & Gray** – Texas spread-wing [Texas spread-wing] (4, 50) (1986–present)

Eustachys glauca **Chapman** – Smooth chloris (94) (1901)

Eustachys petraea **(Sw.) Desv.** – Pinewoods finger grass [Pinewoods fingergrass] (50) (present), Seaside chloris [Sea side chloris] (19) (1840), Seaside finger grass [Seaside finger-grass] (94) (1901)

Eustoma exaltatum **(L.) Salisb.** – Catchfly gentian [Catchfly-gentian] (138) (1923), Catchfly prairie gentian (50) (present)

Eustoma exaltatum **(L.) Salisb. ex G. Don subsp.** *russellianum* **(Hook) Kartesz** – Canada-pest [Canada pest] (75, 158) (1894–1900) Deer Lodge MT, Prairie gentian [Prairiegentian] (3, 122, 124, 155) (1937–1977), Russell's eustoma (5, 93, 97) (1913–1937), Russell's prairie-gentian [Russel prairiegentian] (155) (1942), Showy prairie gentian (50) (Present)

Eustoma grandiflorum **(Raf.) Shinners** – See *Eustoma exaltatum* (L.) Salisb. ex G. Don subsp. *russellianum* (Hook) Kartesz

Eustoma russellianum **(Hook.) G. Don** – See *Eustoma exaltatum* (L.) Salisb. ex G. Don subsp. *russellianum* (Hook) Kartesz

Eustoma russellianum **Griseb.** – See *Eustoma exaltatum* (L.) Salisb. ex G. Don subsp. *russellianum* (Hook) Kartesz

Eustoma **Salisb. ex G. Don** – Canada-pest [Canada pest] (158) (1900), Catchfly gentian [Catchfly-gentian] (4) (1986), Prairie gentian [Prairiegentian] (4, 50) (1986–present)

Eustoma silenifolium **[Salisb.]** – See *Eustoma exaltatum* (L.) Salisb. ex G. Don

Euthamia caroliniana **(L.) Greene** – See *Euthamia tenuifolia* (Pursh) Nutt. var. *tenuifolia*

Euthamia floribunda **Greene** – See *Euthamia graminifolia* (L.) Nutt. var. *nuttallii* (Greene) W. Stone

Euthamia graminifolia **(L.) Nutt.** – Flat-top goldentop (50) (present), Goldenrod [Golden-rod, Golden rod] (40) (1928), Narrow-leaf goldenrod [Narrowleaf goldenrod, Narrow-leaf golden-rod, Narrow-leaved goldenrod, Narrow-leaved golden-rod] (127) (1933), Spear-leaf goldenrod [Spear-leaved Golden-rod] (187) (1818), Swamp goldenrod [Swamp golden-rod] (62) (1912)

Euthamia graminifolia **(L.) Nutt. var.** *graminifolia* – Bushy goldenrod [Bushy golden-rod] (5, 62, 72, 82, 85, 93, 106, 156, 158) (1923–1930), Flat-top goldenrod [Flat-top golden-rod, Flat-topped golden-rod, Flat-topped goldenrod] (5, 50, 93, 156, 158) (1900–present), Flat-top goldentop (50) (present), Fragrant goldenrod [Fragrant golden-rod] (5, 62, 82, 93, 95, 131, 156) (1899–1936), Goldenrod [Golden-rod, Golden rod] (4) (1986), Grass-leaf goldenrod [Grass-leaf golden-rod, Grassleaf goldenrod] (19, 155) (1840–1942), Narrow-leaf goldenrod [Narrowleaf goldenrod, Narrow-leaf golden-rod, Narrow-leaved goldenrod, Narrow-leaved golden-rod] (3) (1977)

Euthamia graminifolia **(L.) Nutt. var.** *major* **(Michx.) Fern.** – See *Euthamia graminifolia* (L.) Nutt. var. *graminifolia*

Euthamia graminifolia **(L.) Nutt. var.** *nuttallii* **(Greene) W. Stone** – Small-head bushy goldenrod [Small-headed bushy golden-rod] (5) (1913)

Euthamia gymnospermoides **Greene** – Narrow-leaf goldenrod [Narrowleaf goldenrod, Narrow-leaf golden-rod, Narrow-leaved goldenrod, Narrow-leaved golden-rod] (3) (1977), Texas goldentop (50) (present), Viscid bush goldenrod (122) (1937), Viscid bushy goldenrod [Viscid bushy golden-rod] (5, 97) (1913–1937), Viscid euthamia (4) (1986)

Euthamia leptocephala **(Torr. & Gray) Greene** – Western bushy goldenrod [Western bushy golden-rod] (5) (1913)

Euthamia minor **(Michx.) Greene** – See *Euthamia tenuifolia* (Pursh) Nutt. var. *tenuifolia*

Euthamia **Nutt. ex Cass.** – Bushy goldenrod [Bushy golden-rod] (1, 93) (1932–1936), Fragrant goldenrod [Fragrant golden-rod] (158)

(5, 156) (1913–1923)

(1900), Goldentop [Golden-top, Golden top] (50) (present)

Euthamia occidentalis **Nutt.** – Western goldenrod (106, 155) (1930–1942), Western goldentop (50) (present)

Euthamia tenuifolia **(Pursh) Nutt. var.** *tenuifolia* – Narrow-leaf bushy goldenrod [Narrow-leaved bushy golden-rod] (5) (1913), Narrow-leaf goldenrod [Narrowleaf goldenrod, Narrow-leaf golden-rod, Narrow-leaved goldenrod, Narrow-leaved golden-rod] (122) (1937), Pygmy goldenrod [Pigmy golden-rod, Pygmy golden-rod] (19) (1840), Slender fragrant goldenrod (72, 131) (1899–1907), Slender-leaved goldenrod [Slender-leaved Golden-rod] (187) (1818)

Evax **Gaertn.** – Pygmy cudweed (50) (present), Rabbit-tobacco [Rabbit tobacco, Rabbittobacco] (4) (1986)

Evax prolifera **Nutt. ex DC.** – Big-head pygmy cudweed [Bighead pygmycudweed] (50) (present), Cudweed [Cud-weed, Cud weed] (124) (1937) TX, Filago (5, 97, 131) (1899–1937), Rabbit-tobacco [Rabbit tobacco, Rabbittobacco] (4) (1986)

Evax verna **Raf. var.** *verna* – Rabbit-tobacco [Rabbit tobacco, Rabbit-tobacco] (97) (1937)

Evernia prunastri **(L.) Ach.** – Ring lichen (50) (present)

Evernia prunastri **L.** – See *Evernia prunastri* (L.) Ach.

Evernia vulpina **(L.) Ach.** – See *Letharia vulpina* (L.) Hue

Evodia **J. R. Forst. & G. Forst.** – See *Tetradium* Lour. (Euodia J. R. Forst. & G. Forst.)

Evolvulus **L.** – Dwarf morning-glory [Dwarf morning glory] (50) (present), Evolvulus (155, 158) (1900–1942)

Evolvulus nuttallianus **J.A. Schultes** – Evolvulus (5, 93, 97, 131) (1899–1937), Nuttall's evolvulus [Nuttall evovulus] (3, 4, 155) (1942–1986), Shaggy dwarf morning-glory (50) (Present)

Evolvulus nuttallianus **R. & S.** – See *Evolvulus nuttallianus* J.A. Schultes

Evolvulus pilosus **Nutt.** – See *Evolvulus nuttallianus* J.A. Schultes

Exaecaria lucida – See *Gymnanthes lucida* Sw.

Excoecaria lucida **(Sw.) Sw.** – See *Gymnanthes lucida* Sw.

Exobasidium **Woronin** – May apple [Mayapple, May-apple] (78) (1898)

Exochorda grandiflora – See *Exochorda racemosa* (Lindl.) Rehd.

Exochorda **Lindl.** – Pearl bush [Pearl-bush, Pearlbush] (109, 138) (1923–1949)

Exochorda racemosa **(Lindl.) Rehd.** – Common pearlbush (138) (1923), Pearl bush [Pearl-bush, Pearlbush] (112) (1937) Neb

Exothea paniculata **(Juss.) Radlk.** – Genip tree (20) (1857), Honey-berry [Honey berries] (92) (1876), Kniepier panicale (20) (1857), Round-fruit honeyberry [Round fruited honeyberry] (20) (1857)

Eysenhardtia polystachya **(Ortega) Sargent** – Rockbrush (106) (1930)

Eysenhardtia texana **Scheele** – Rock brush (122, 124) (1937) TX

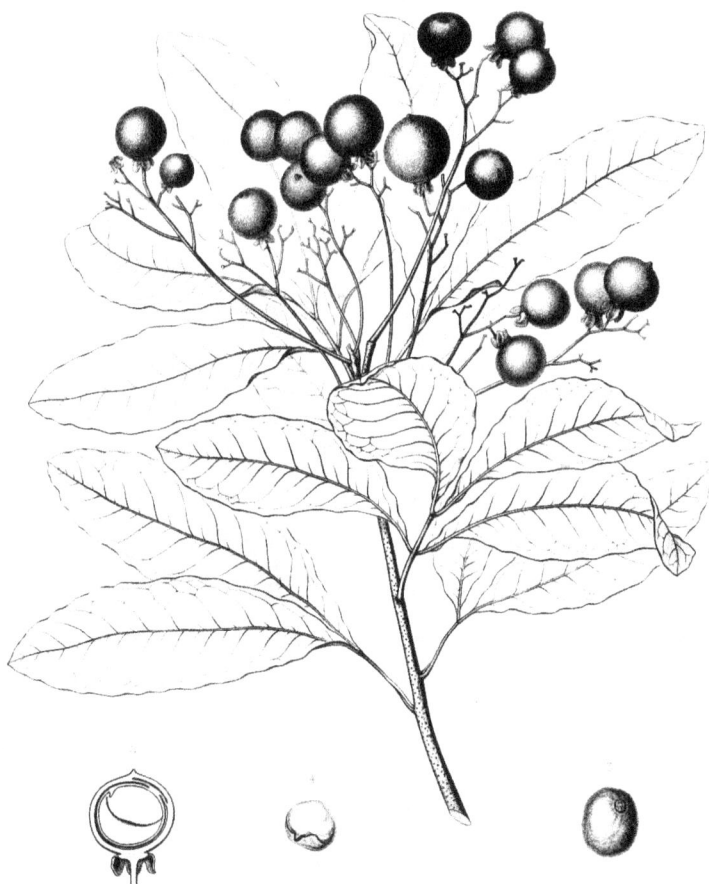

C. E. Faxon. del.

Picart fr sc

Exothea paniculata (Juss.) Radlk.
(C.E. Faxon, 1898)

F

Fagara Clava-Herculis **L.** – See *Zanthoxylum clava-herculis* L.

Fagopyrum **(Tourn.) Mill.** – See *Fagopyrum* Mill.

Fagopyrum esculentum **Moench** – Alforfon (Spanish) (46) (1879), Beckenweidt (180) (1633), Beech-wheat [Beech wheat] (5, 6, 156, 180) (1633–1923), Blé Noir (French) (158) (1900), Blé sarrasin (French "Saracen wheat") (110) (1886), Brank (5, 14, 107, 156, 158) (1882–1923), Buchweizen [Buchweitzen] (German) (6, 110, 158) (1886–1900) corrupted into buckwheat in English, Bucke (180) (1633), Buckwheat [Buck-wheat] (3, 4, 5, 6, 19, 50, 72, 85, 92, 93, 95, 106, 107, 110, 114, 156, 158, 180) (1633–present), Bullimong (180) (1633), Common buckwheat (109, 138, 155) (1923–1949), Corn heath (5) (1913), Corn-heath (156) (1923), Crap (5, 156, 158) (1900–1923), Dragee aux cheueaux (French) (180) (1633), Ed-du (Breton "black wheat") (110) (1886), Faggina (Italian) (46, 110) (1879–1886), Fajol (Spanish) (46) (1879), French wheat (180) (1633), Goat's-wheat [Goats wheat] (180) (1633), Gwinis-du (Breton "black corn") (110) (1886), Heath corn (92, 158) (1876–1900), Heidekorn (German) (6) (1892), Heydencorn (180) (1633), Heydenkorn (107) (1552), India-wheat (158) (1900), Kjo (Japanese) (46) (1879), Le Blé Noir (French) (6) (1892), Le Blé Sarrasin (French) (6) (1892), Notch-seed buckwheat [Notch-seeded buckwheat] (107, 110) (1886–1919), Saracen's-corn [Saracen's corn] (5, 92, 156, 158) (1876–1923), Saracen's-wheat [Saracen's wheat] (5) (1913), Sarrasin (French) (158) (1900), Soba (Japanese) (46) (1879), Tatarka (Bohemian) (46) (1879), Tatrika (Slavic languages) (110) (1886), Tatrikat (Estonian) (46) (1879), Tatrka (Slavic languages) (110) (1886), Tattar (Polish) (46) (1879), Tattar (Slavic languages) (110) (1886)

Fagopyrum fagopyrum **(L.) Karst** – See *Fagopyrum esculentum* Moench

Fagopyrum **Gaertn.** – See *Fagopyrum* Mill.

Fagopyrum **Mill.** – Buckwheat [Buck-wheat] (1, 14, 50, 82, 109, 138, 155, 158) (1882–present)

Fagopyrum sagittatum **Gilib.** – See *Fagopyrum esculentum* Moench

Fagopyrum tataricum **(L.) Gaertn.** – Indian buckwheat (92) (1876), Indian tartaricum (92) (1876), Indian wheat [India-wheat] (109, 156) (1923–1949), Kangra buckwheat (138) (1923), Rough buckwheat (5) (1913), Tartarian buckwheat (107) (1919), Tartary buckwheat (5, 110) (1886–1913)

Fagopyrum tatricum **(L.) Gaertn.** – See *Fagopyrum tataricum* (L.) Gaertn.

Fagopyrum tatricum **Gaertn.** – See *Fagopyrum tataricum* (L.) Gaertn.

Fagus **(Tourn) L.** – See *Fagus* L.

Fagus americana – See *Fagus grandifolia* Ehrh.

Fagus castanea – See *Castanea sativa* Mill.

Fagus ferruginea **Aiton** – See *Fagus grandifolia* Ehrh.

Fagus grandifolia **Ehrh.** – American beech (2, 5, 57, 65, 97, 107, 109, 112, 138, 158) (1895–1949), Beech [Beach] or Beech tree [Beech-tree] (35, 43, 65, 105, 106, 122, 124, 182, 184) (1791–1932), Black beech (78) (1898) Western US, Chestnut [Chestnuts, Chestnutte] (190) (~1759), Common beech (46) (1649), Red beech (5, 19, 20, 78, 156, 187) (1814–1923), Rusty-leaf beech [Rusty-leaved beech] (14) (1882), Ŝewe-minŝ (Chippewa) (105) (1932), Stone beech (156) (1923)

Fagus grandifolia **Ehrh. subsp.** *grandifolia* – Beech [Beach] or Beech tree [Beech-tree] (41, 187) (1770–1818), White beech (5, 19, 20, 78, 156) (1840–1923), possibly White beech (187) (1818)

Fagus grandifolia **Ehrh. var.** *caroliniana* **(Loud.) Fern. & Rehder** – See *Fagus grandifolia* Ehrh.

Fagus **L.** – American beech (112, 138) (1923–1937), Beech [Beach] or Beech tree [Beech-tree] (1, 7, 8, 10, 109, 137, 138, 156, 167, 190) (~1759–1949), Hètre (8) (1785)

Fagus pumila – See *Castanea pumila* (L.) Mill.

Fagus sylvatica atropunicea – See *Fagus sylvatica* L.

Fagus sylvatica **f.** *pendula* **(Perr.) Domin** – See *Fagus sylvatica* L.

Fagus sylvatica **L.** – American beech tree (8) (1785), Beech [Beach] or Beech tree [Beech-tree] (18) (1805), Copper beech (109) (1949), Cut-leaf beech [Cutleaf beech] (109) (1949), European beech (107, 109, 135, 138) (1910–1949), Fern-leaf beech [Fernleaf beech] (109) (1949), Hêtre des bois à feuilles pourpres (French) (8) (1785), Purple beech (109) (1949), Weeping birch (109) (1949)

Fagus sylvatica **L. var.** *atropunicea* **West.** – See *Fagus sylvatica* L.

Fagus sylvatica **L. var.** *heterophylla* **Loud.** – See *Fagus sylvatica* L.

Fagus sylvatica **L. var.** *pendula* **Loud.** – See *Fagus sylvatica* L.

Fagus sylvatica **var.** *americana* **[Pers.]** – See *Fagus grandifolia* Ehrh. subsp. *grandifolia*

Fagus sylvestris **Michx.** – See *Fagus grandifolia* Ehrh. subsp. *grandifolia*

Fagus-castanea dentata – possibly *Castanea dentata* (Marsh.) Borkh.

Fagus-castanea pumila – possibly *Castanea pumila* (L.) Mill.

Fagus-castenea – possibly *Castanea sativa* Mill.

Falcaria **Fabr.** – Falcaria (50) (present)

Falcaria vulgaris **Bernh.** – Sickleweed [Sickle weed, Sickle-weed] (50) (present)

Falcata comosa **(L.) Kuntze** – See *Amphicarpaea bracteata* (L.) Fern. var. *comosa* (L.) Fern.

Falcata **Gmel.** – See *Amphicarpaea* Ell. ex Nutt.

Falcata pitcheri **(Torr. & Gray) Kuntze** – See *Amphicarpaea bracteata* (L.) Fern. var. *comosa* (L.) Fern.

Fallugia paradoxa **(D. Don) Endl.** – Apache-plume [Apache plume, Apacheplume] (4, 50, 122, 124, 153, 155) (1913–present), Poñel (Mexicans) (149) (1904), Ponil (122) (1937) TX

Fatsia horrida **Benth. & Hook.** – See *Oplopanax horridus* Miq.

Fedia chenopodifolia **Pursh** – See *Valerianella chenopodiifolia* (Pursh) DC.

Fedia radiata **Michx.** – See *Valerianella radiata* (L.) Dufr.

Ferocactus **Britt. & Rose** – Barrel cactus [Barrelcactus] (109, 155) (1942–1949)

Ferocactus covillei – See *Ferocactus emoryi* (Engelm.) Orcutt

Ferocactus emoryi **(Engelm.) Orcutt** – Sonora water cactus (138) (1923)

Ferocactus hamatacanthus **(Muehlenpfordt) Britt. & Rose var.** *hamatacanthus* – Fishhook [Fish-hooks] (122) (1937) TX

Ferocactus uncinatus – See *Sclerocactus uncinatus* (Galeotti) N. P. Taylor var. *wrightii* (Engelm.) N. P. Taylor

Ferocactus wislizeni **(Engelm.) Britt. & Rose** – Arizona water cactus (138) (1923), Barrel cactus [Barrelcactus] (76, 149) (1896–1904), Bisnaga (9, 149) (1873–1910) NM, Biznacha (Spanish, Mexican) (103, 107) (1870–1919), Fish-hawk cactus (76) (1896) AZ, Southwest barrel cactus [Southwest barrelcactus] (155) (1942), Visnada (Mexicans) (107, 147) (1856–1919)

Festuca altaica **Trin.** – Altai fescue (50) (present), Buffalo bunch grass [Buffalo bunch-grass] (45, 87) (1884–1896), Bunch grass [Bunchgrass, Bunch-grass] (75, 87, 88, 161) (1857–1894), Great bunch grass [Great bunch-grass] (45, 56, 87) (1884–1901), Rough fescue (3, 155) (1942–1977), Rough fescue grass (5, 111) (1913–1915)

Festuca arizonica **Vasey** – Arizona fescue (152) (1912) NM, Pine grass (152) (1912) NM

Festuca arundinacea **Schreb.** – See *Lolium arundinaceum* (Schreb.) S.J. Darbyshire

Festuca arvernensis **Auquier, Kerguélen & Markgr.-Dannenb.** – Blue fescue (109, 138) (1923–1949)

Festuca brachyphylla **J. A. Schultes ex J. A. & J. H. Schultes** – Alpine fescue (50) (present), Short-leaf fescue grass [Short-leaved fescue grass] (5) (1913)

Festuca brachyphylla **Schultes** – See *Festuca brachyphylla* J. A. Schultes ex J. A. & J. H. Schultes

Festuca brevipila **Tracey** – Hard fescue (45, 50, 56, 68, 109, 129, 138, 155) (1890–present), Hard fescue grass (19, 50, 66) (1840–present)

Festuca campestris **Rydb.** – Rough fescue (50) (present)

Festuca capillata **Lam.** – See *Festuca filiformis* Pourret

Festuca confinis **Vasey** – See *Leucopoa kingii* (S. Wats.) W. A. Weber

Festuca dasyclada **Hack. ex Beal** – Hackel's fescue (94) (1901)

Festuca decumbens **L.** – See *Danthonia decumbens* (L.) DC.

Festuca duriuscula **L.** – See *Festuca brevipila* Tracey

Festuca elatior arundinacea **(Schreb.) Hack.** – See *Lolium arundinaceum* (Schreb.) S.J. Darbyshire

Festuca elatior **L.** – See *Lolium pratense* (Huds.) S.J. Darbyshire

Festuca elatior **L. subsp. *arundinacea* (Schreb.) Hack.** – See *Lolium arundinaceum* (Schreb.) S.J. Darbyshire

Festuca elatior pratensis **(Huds.) Hack.** – See *Lolium pratense* (Huds.) S.J. Darbyshire

Festuca filiformis **Pourret** – Fair fescue (138) (1923), Filiform fescue grass (5) (1913), Fine-leaf sheep fescue [Fineleaf sheep fescue, Fine-leaf sheep's fescue, Fine-leaved sheep's fescue] (50, 68) (1890–present)

Festuca fluitans – See *Glyceria fluitans* (L.) R. Br.

Festuca gigantea **(L.) Vill.** – See *Lolium giganteum* (L.) S.J. Darbyshire

Festuca glauca – See *Festuca arvernensis* Auquier, Kerguélen & Markgr.-Dannenb.

Festuca heterophylla **Lam.** – Shade fescue (138) (1923), Various-leaf fescue [Various-leaved fescue] (56, 68) (1901–1913)

Festuca idahoensis **Elmer** – Blue bunch grass [Blue bunchgrass] (3) (1977), Idaho fescue (50, 146, 155) (1939–present)

Festuca jonesii **Vasey** – See *Festuca subulata* Trin.

Festuca kingii **(S. Wats.) Cassidy** – See *Leucopoa kingii* (S. Wats.) W.A. Weber

Festuca kingii **(S. Wats.) Scribn.** – See *Leucopoa kingii* (S. Wats.) W.A. Weber

Festuca **L.** – Fescue (50, 109, 138, 155, 184) (1793–present), Fescue grass [Fescue-grass] (1, 10, 66, 93, 152, 163) (1818–1936), Rescue grass [Rescuegrass, Rescue-grass] (152) (1912) NM, Spike fescue [Spikefescue] (155) (1942)

Festuca loliacea **[Huds.]** – possibly *Schedonorus ×festucaceus* (Link) Kartesz *[arundinaceus × pratensis]*

Festuca megalura **Nutt.** – See *Vulpia myuros* (L.) K.C. Gmel.

Festuca microstachys **Nutt.** – See *Vulpia microstachys* (Nutt.) Munro var. *microstachys*

Festuca myuros **L.** – See *Vulpia myuros* (L.) K.C. Gmel.

Festuca nutans **Willd.** – See *Festuca paradoxa* Desv.

Festuca obtusa **Biehler** – See *Festuca subverticillata* (Pers.) Alexeev

Festuca occidentalis **Hook** – Western fescue grass (5, 50) (1913–present)

Festuca octoflora **Walt.** – See *Vulpia octoflora* (Walt.) Rydb. var. *octoflora*

Festuca octoflora **Walt. var. *hirtella* (Piper) Piper ex A.S. Hitchc.** – See *Vulpia octoflora* (Walt.) Rydb. var. *hirtella* (Piper) Henr.

Festuca ovina **L.** – Bunch grass [Bunchgrass, Bunch-grass] (45) (1896), Sheep fescue [Sheep's fescue, Sheeps fescue] (2, 5, 11, 45, 50, 56, 66, 67, 68, 90, 92, 94, 109, 111, 129, 140, 143, 138, 155) (1885–present), Sheep's fescue grass [Sheep's fescue-grass] (72, 87, 157) (1885–1929)

Festuca ovina **L. subsp. *tenuifolia* (Sibth.) Peterm.** – See *Festuca filiformis* Pourret

Festuca ovina **L. var. *capillata* (Lam.) Alef.** – See *Festuca filiformis* Pourret

Festuca ovina **L. var. *duriuscula* auct. non (L.) W. D. J. Koch** – See *Festuca brevipila* Tracey

Festuca ovina **L. var. *glauca* Koch** – See *Festuca arvernensis* Auquier, Kerguélen & Markgr.-Dannenb.

Festuca ovina **L. var. *polyphylla* Vasey ex Beal** – See *Festuca occidentalis* Hook

Festuca ovina **L. var. *rydbergii* St. Yves** – See *Festuca saximontana* Rydb. var. *saximontana*

Festuca ovina **L. var. *saximontana* (Rydb.) Gleason** – See *Festuca filiformis* Pourret

Festuca ovina **L. var. *tenuifolia* (Sibthorp) Sm.** – See *Festuca filiformis* Pourret

Festuca paradoxa **Desv.** – Clustered fescue [Cluster fescue] (3, 50, 155) (1942–present), Nodding fescue (56, 66) (1901–1903), Nodding fescue grass [Nodding fescue-grass] (5, 72, 163, 187) (1818–1913), Short's fescue (56) (1901), Short's fescue grass [Short's fescue-grass] (5, 72, 119) (1907–1938)

Festuca pratensis **Huds.** – See *Lolium pratense* (Huds.) S.J. Darbyshire

Festuca rubra glaucescens **Hack.** – See *Festuca rubra* L. subsp. *rubra*

Festuca rubra **L.** – Chewing's fescue [Chewings fescue] (109, 155) (1942–1949), Creeping fescue (68) (1890), Red fescue (3, 50, 56, 66, 68, 109, 129, 138, 140, 143, 155) (1894–present), Red fescue grass (5, 56, 72) (1893–1901)

Festuca rubra **L. subsp. *rubra*** – Tennessee fescue (94) (1901)

Festuca rubra **L. var. *commutata* Gaud.** – See *Festuca rubra* L.

Festuca saximontana **Rydb.** – Rocky Mountain fescue (50) (present)

Festuca saximontana **Rydb. var. *saximontana*** – Rocky Mountain fescue (50) (present), Sheep's fescue (3) (1977)

Festuca scabrella **Torr.** – See *Festuca altaica* Trin.

Festuca sciurea **Nutt.** – See *Vulpia sciurea* (Nutt.) Henr.

Festuca shortii **Kunth ex Wood** – See *Festuca paradoxa* Desv.

Festuca subulata **Trin.** – Bearded fescue (50, 155) (1942–present), Jones's fescue (94) (1901)

Festuca subverticillata **(Pers.) Alexeev** – Nodding fescue (3, 50, 122, 155) (1937–present), Nodding fescue grass [Nodding fescue-grass] (163) (1852)

Festuca tenella **Willd.** – See *Vulpia octoflora* (Walt.) Rydb. var. *glauca* (Nutt.) Fern.

Festuca tenuifolia **Sibthorp** – See *Festuca filiformis* Pourret

Festuca thalasica – See *Puccinellia maritima* (Huds.) Parl.

Festuca thurberi **Vasey** – Thurber's fescue [Thurber fescue] (140) (1944)

Festuca versuta **Beal** – Texas fescue (50, 155) (1942–present), Texas fescue grass [Texas fescue-grass] (119) (1938)

Festulolium loliaceum **(Huds.) P.Fourn.** – See *Schedonorus ×festucaceus* (Link) Kartesz *[arundinaceus × pratensis]*

Ficaria ficaria **(L.) Karst.** – See *Ranunculus ficaria* L.

Ficus altissima **Blume** – Lofty fig (138) (1923)

Ficus aurea **Nutt.** – Figuier doré (French) (20) (1857), Florida strangler fig (138) (1923), Small-fruit fig tree [Small fruited fig tree] (20) (1857)

Ficus bengalensis **L.** – See *Ficus benghalensis* L.

Ficus benghalensis **L.** – Banyan (107, 109) (1919–1949)

Ficus benjamina **L.** – Benjamin fig (138) (1923)

Ficus brevifolia **Nutt.** – See *Ficus citrifolia* Mill.

Ficus carica **L.** – Common fig (109, 138) (1923–1949), Dwarf fig tree [Dwarfe Fig tree] (178) (1526), Erineos (Greek) (110) (1886), Ficus de Algarua (178) (1526), Fig or Fig tree (7, 19, 53, 55, 57, 92, 107, 110, 178) (1526–1922), Sukai (Greek) (110) (1886)

Ficus citrifolia **Mill.** – Cherry fig tree (20) (1857), Figuier à feuilles courtes (French) (20) (1857), Figuier peduncule (French) (20) (1857), Short-leaf fig tree [Short-leaved fig-tree] (20) (1857)

Ficus elastica **Roxb. ex Hornem.** – Indian rubber tree [India rubber tree, India rubbertree] (138) (1923), Rubber-plant (109) (1949)

Ficus **L.** – Fig or Fig tree (109, 138) (1923–1949), Fygge (179) (1526)

Ficus lutea **Vahl** – Zulu fig (138) (1923)

Ficus pedunculata – See *Ficus citrifolia* Mill.

Ficus pumila **L.** – Climbing fig (138) (1923), Creeping fig (109) (1949)

Ficus religiosa **L.** – Bo tree [Bo-tree] (109) (1949), Peepul (107, 109) (1919–1949), Sacred bo tree (138) (1923), Sacred fig (107) (1919)

Ficus rubiginosa **Desf.** – Rusty fig (138) (1923)

Ficus utilis [Sim.] – See *Ficus lutea* Vahl

Filago germanica – See *Filago pyramidata* L.

Filago L. – Cotton-rose [Cotton rose, Cottonrose] (156) (1923), Everlasting (158) (1900), Filago (158) (1900), Fluffweed (155) (1942)

Filago nivea Small. – See *Evax verna* Raf. var. *verna*

Filago prolifera (Nutt.) Britton – See *Evax prolifera* Nutt. ex DC.

Filago pyramidata L. – Cat's-foot [Cats foot, Cat's foot, Cat foot] (184) (1793), Cotton-rose [Cotton rose, Cottonrose] (92) (1876)

Filago vulgaris Lam. – Chafeweed [Chafe-weed, Chafe weed] (5, 156) (1913–1923), Childing cudweed (5, 156) (1913–1923), Cotton-rose [Cotton rose, Cottonrose] (5, 156) (1913–1923), Cudweed [Cud-weed, Cud weed] (5, 156) (1913–1923), Downweed [Downweed] (5, 156) (1913–1923), Herb Impius (5) (1913), Herba impia (156) (1923), Hoarwort (5, 156) (1913–1923), Owl's-crown [Owl's crown] (5, 156) (1913–1923)

Filinguis Raf. – possibly *Asplenium* L.

Filipendula (Tourn.) Mill. – See *Filipendula* Mill.

Filipendula Adans. – possibly *Filipendula* Mill.

Filipendula hexapetala Gilib. – See *Filipendula vulgaris* Moench

Filipendula Mill. – Meadow-queen [Meadow queen] (1) (1932), Queen-of-the-prairie [Queen of the prairie] (1) (1932), possibly Meadowsweet [Meadow-sweet, Meadow sweet] (109, 138) (1923–1949)

Filipendula rubra (Hill.) Robinson – Prairie meadowsweet (138) (1923), Queen-of-the-prairie [Queen of the prairie] (5, 72, 156) (1907–1923)

Filipendula ulmaria (L.) Maxim. – Bridewort [Bride wort, Bridewort] (5, 156) (1913–1923), European meadowsweet (138) (1923), Herb Christopher [Herb-Christopher] (5) (1913), Honeysweet [Honey-sweet, Honey sweet] (5, 156) (1913–1923), Meadow-queen [Meadow queen] (5, 156) (1913–1923), Meadowsweet [Meadowsweet, Meadow sweet] (5, 156) (1913–1923), Meadow-wort [Meadowwort, Meadow wort] (5, 156) (1913–1923), My-lady's-belt [My lady's belt] (5) (1913), Sweet bay [Sweet-bay, Sweetbay] (156) (1923), Sweet hay (5) (1913)

Filipendula ulmaria (L.) Maxim. subsp. *ulmaria* – Meadow-queen [Meadow queen] (92) (1876), Meadowsweet [Meadow-sweet, Meadow sweet] (92) (1876), Meadow-wort [Meadowwort, Meadow wort] (92) (1876), Meadsweete (178) (1526), Pride-of-the-meadow [Pride of the meadow] (92) (1876), Queen-of-the-meadow [Queen of the meadow] (19, 92, 156) (1840–1923), Spiraea [Spirea] (92) (1876)

Filipendula vulgaris Moench – Dropwort (109, 138, 179) (1526–1949)

Filix Adans. – See *Cystopteris* Bernh.

Filix bulbifera (L.) Underw. – See *Cystopteris bulbifera* (L.) Bernh.

Filix bulbifera L. Andrew. – possibly *Cystopteris bulbifera* (L.) Bernh.

Filix fragilis (L.) Underw. – See *Cystopteris fragilis* (L.) Bernh.

Filix montana (Lam.) Underw. – See *Cystopteris montana* (Lam.) Bernh. ex Desv.

Fimbristylis annua (All.) R. & S. – Annual fimbry (50) (present), Olney's bulrush [Olney bulrush] (5, 155) (1913–1942), Olney's rush (66) (1903), Spreading fimbristylis (66) (1903), Weak fimbristylis (5) (1913)

Fimbristylis autumnalis (L.) Roemer & J. A. Schultes – Autumnal scirpus (187) (1818), Low fimbristylis (5) (1913), Slender fimbristylis (5, 72) (1907–1913), Slender fimbry (50) (present), Tufted fimbristylis (66) (1903)

Fimbristylis baldwiniana Torr. – See *Fimbristylis annua* (All.) R. & S.

Fimbristylis capillaris (L.) Gray – See *Bulbostylis capillaris* (L.) Kunth ex C.B. Clarke subsp. *capillaris*

Fimbristylis caroliniana (Lam.) Fern. – Carolina fimbry (50) (present)

Fimbristylis castanea (Michx.) Vahl – Marsh fimbristylis (5) (1913), Marsh fimbry (50) (present)

Fimbristylis dichotoma (L.) Vahl – Forked fimbry (50) (present)

Fimbristylis geminata (Nees) Kunth – See *Fimbristylis autumnalis* (L.) Roemer & J.A. Schultes

Fimbristylis interior Britton – See *Fimbristylis puberula* (Michx.) Vahl var. *interior* (Britt.) Kral

Fimbristylis laxa Vahl – See *Fimbristylis annua* (All.) R. & S.

Fimbristylis puberula (Michx.) Vahl – Hairy fimbristylis (5) (1913), Hairy fimbry (50) (present)

Fimbristylis puberula (Michx.) Vahl var. *interior* (Britt.) Kral – Hairy fimbry (50) (present), Plains fimbristylis (5, 50) (1913–present)

Fimbristylis puberula (Michx.) Vahl var. *puberula* – Hairy fimbry (50) (present)

Fimbristylis spadicea auct. non (L.) Vahl – See *Fimbristylis thermalis* S. Wats.

Fimbristylis spathacea Roth – Pee-mottenga (174) (1753)

Fimbristylis thermalis S. Wats. – Hotsprings fimbry (50) (present), Tall fimbristylis (66) (1903)

Fimbristylis Vahl. – Club rush [Club-rush] (10) (1818), Fimbry (50) (present)

Fimbristylis vahlii (Lam.) Link. – Vahl's fimbristylis (5) (1913), Vahl's fimbry (50) (present)

Firmiana simplex (L.) W. Wight – Chinese parasol tree [Chinese parasoltree, Chinese parasol-tree] (109, 138) (1923–1949), Phoenix tree [Phoenix-tree] (109) (1949), Sourwood [Sour-wood, Sour wood] or Sourwood tree (106) (1930), Varnish tree (106) (1930)

Fissipes acaulis (Ait.) Small – See *Cypripedium acaule* Ait.

Flacourtia indica (Burm. f.) Merr. – Batoko-plum (109) (1949), Governor's-plum [Governors-plum] (109) (1949), Ramontchi (109) (1949)

Flacourtia indica Merr. – See *Flacourtia indica* (Burm. f.) Merr.

Flammulina velutipes (Curtis) Singer (possibly) – Velvet foot (170) (1995)

Flammulina velutipes (Fr.) Kar. – possibly *Flammulina velutipes* (Curtis) Singer

Flaveria campestris Johnst. – Alkali yellowtops (50) (present), Flaveria (3) (1977), Plains flaveria (5, 97) (1913–1937)

Flaveria Juss. – Flaveria (158) (1900), Yellowtop [Yellow-top, Yellow top, Yellowtops, Yellow-tops] (50) (present)

Flavoparmelia caperata (L.) Hale – Shield lichen [Shield-lichen] (92) (1876)

Fleischmannia incarnata (Walt.) King & H.E. – Mata (92) (1876), Pink thoroughwort (5, 122, 124) (1913–1937)

Floerkea proserpinacoides Willd. – False mermaid (5, 13, 15, 19, 156) (1840–1923), Mermaid-weed [Mermaid weed] (156) (1923)

Floerkea uliginosa Muhl. – See *Floerkea proserpinacoides* Willd.

Floerkea Willd. – False mermaid (1, 2) (1895–1932), Sweet-salad [Sweet sallad] (7) (1828)

Floerkia proserpinacoides Willd. – See *Floerkea proserpinacoides* Willd.

Flourensia DC. – Blackbrush [Black brush] (153) (1913) NM

Fluminia [Fries] – See *Scolochloa* Link

Fluminia festucacea (Willd.) A. S. Hitchc. – See *Scolochloa festucacea* (Willd.) Link

Fodder legumes in general – Artificial grass (92) (1876)

Foeniculum capillaceum Gilib – See *Foeniculum vulgare* Mill.

Foeniculum dulce Loefl. – See *Foeniculum vulgare* Mill.

Foeniculum foeniculum (L.) Karst. – See *Foeniculum vulgare* Mill.

Foeniculum officinale All. – See *Foeniculum vulgare* Mill.

Foeniculum officinalis – See *Foeniculum vulgare* Mill.

Foeniculum P. Mill. – Fennel [Fenell] (50, 155, 156, 158) (1900–present)

Foeniculum vulgare Gaertn. – See *Foeniculum vulgare* Mill.

Foeniculum vulgare Mill. – Azorian fennel (165) (1807), Bitter fennel (107) (1919), Common fennel (92, 138, 155, 165) (1807–1942), Cultivated fennel (106) (1930), Dill [Dyll] (5, 93, 156, 158) (1900–1923), Fenchel (German) (158) (1900), Fennel [Fenell] (1, 5, 7, 19, 46, 49, 53, 55, 57, 59, 72, 95, 107, 109, 122, 156, 157, 158, 165) (1671–1937), Fenouil (French) (158) (1900), Finckle (107, 165) (1686–1807), Fingel (158) (1900), Finkel (5, 156, 158) (1900–1923), Finochio (107, 165) (1807–1919), Foeniculum (57, 107) (1586–1917), Foennel (107) (1538), Fyncle (107) (1538), Giant fennel [Giantfennel] (157, 158) (1900–1929), Large fennel

Fragaria vesca L.

(157, 158) (1900–1929), Meetin seed [Meetin-seed] (156) (1923), Roman fennel (49) (1898), Spingel (5, 156, 158) (1900–1923), Sweet fennel (42, 49, 50, 92, 106, 165) (1807–present), Wild fennel (92) (1876)

Fomes applanatus **(Pers.) Gillet** – Shelf bracket fungus (128) (1933), Shelf fungus (40) (1928)

Fomes fomentarius **(L.) Fr.** – Hoof-shaped bracket fungus (128) (1933), Surgeon's-agaric [Surgeon's agaric] (57) (1917)

Fomes fomentarius **(L.) J.J. Kickx** – possibly *Fomes fomentarius* (L.) Fr.

Fomes fraxinophilus **(Peck) Sacc.** – Ash-loving bracket fungus (128) (1933)

Fomes igniarius **(L.) Fr.** – Punkwood bracket fungus (128) (1933)

Fomes igniarius **Speg.** – possibly *Fomes igniarius* (L.) Fr.

Fomitopsis officinalis **(Batsch) Bondartsev & Singer** – Agaricus albus (53, 92) (1876–1922), Boletus (52) (1919), Fungus agaric (52) (1919), Larch agaric (49, 52, 53, 57, 92) (1876–1922), Male agaric (92) (1876), Purging agaric (49, 53, 57, 92) (1876–1922), Spunk (52) (1919), White agaric (49, 53, 57, 92) (1876–1922)

Fomitopsis pinicola **(Sw.) P. Karst.** – Pine bracket fungus (128) (1933) ND

Fontanesia – See *Fontanesia* Labill.

Fontanesia fortunei – See *Fontanesia phillyreoides* Labill. subsp. *fortunei* (Carr.) Yaltirik

Fontanesia **Labill.** – Fontanesia (138) (1923)

Fontanesia phillyreoides **Labill.** – Syrian-privet (138) (1923)

Fontanesia phillyreoides **Labill. subsp. *fortunei* (Carr.) Yaltirik** – Fortune's fontanesia [Fortune fontanesia] (138) (1923)

Forestiera acuminata **(Michx.) Poir.** – Adelia (5, 97) (1913–1937), Eastern swamp-privet [Eastern swampprivet] (50) (present), Privet adelia (138) (1923), Swamp privet (3, 4, 156) (1923–1986), Swamp-privet [Swampprivet, Swamp privet] (3, 4, 156) (1923–1986), Texas adelia (122, 138) (1923–1937), Texas forestiera (155) (1942)

Forestiera ligustrina **[Gray]** – See *Forestiera acuminata* (Michx.) Poir.

Forestiera **Poir.** – Adelia (138) (1923), Swamp-privet [Swampprivet, Swamp privet] (50) (present)

Forestiera porulosa – See *Forestiera segregata* (Jacq.) Krug & Urban var. *segregata*

Forestiera pubescens **Nutt.** – Downy forestiera (155) (1942), Elbow-bush [Elbow-bush, Elbow bush] (4, 124) (1937–1986), Stretchberry [Stretch berry, Stretch-berry] (50) (present)

Forestiera segregata **(Jacq.) Krug & Urban var. *segregata*** – Dotted borya (19) (1840)

Forsellesia planitierum **Ensign** – See *Glossopetalon planitierum* (Ensign) St. John

Forsythia ×*intermedia* **Zabel [*suspensa* × *viridissima*]** – Goldenbell [Golden-bell, Golden bell, Golden bells, Golden-bells, Goldenbells] (112) (1937)

Forsythia intermedia – See *Forsythia* ×*intermedia* Zabel [*suspensa* × *viridissima*]

Forsythia scandens **Walt.** – See *Decumaria barbara* L.

Forsythia suspensa **(Thunb.) Vahl** – Fortune's forsythia [Fortune forsythia] (138) (1923), Goldenbell [Golden-bell, Golden bell, Golden bells, Golden-bells, Goldenbells] (112) (1937), Siebold's forsythia [Siebold forsythia] (138) (1923), Weeping forsythia (138) (1923)

Forsythia suspensa fortunei – See *Forsythia suspensa* (Thunb.) Vahl

Forsythia suspensa sieboldi – See *Forsythia suspensa* (Thunb.) Vahl

Forsythia suspensa **var. *fortunei* (Lindl.) Rehder** – See *Forsythia suspensa* (Thunb.) Vahl

Forsythia suspensa **var. *sieboldii* Zabel** – See *Forsythia suspensa* (Thunb.) Vahl

Forsythia **Vahl** – Forsythia (138) (1923), Goldenbell [Golden-bell, Golden bell, Golden bells, Golden-bells, Goldenbells] (82, 109) (1930–1949)

Forsythia viridissima **Lindl.** – Green-stem forsythia [Greenstem forsythia] (138) (1923)

Forsythia **Walt.** – See *Forsythia* Vahl

Fortunella japonica **(Thunb.) Swingle** – Kumquat (107, 138) (1919–1923), Round kumquat (109) (1949)

Fortunella japonica **Swingle** – See *Fortunella japonica* (Thunb.) Swingle

Fortunella margarita **(Lour.) Swingle** – Nagami kumquat (109) (1949)

Fortunella margarita **(Lour.) Swingle** – Oval kumquat (109) (1949)

Fortunella margarita **Swingle** – See *Fortunella margarita* (Lour.) Swingle

Fortunella **Swingle** – Kumquat (109) (1949)

Fothergilla alnifolia **W.** – See *Fothergilla gardenii* L.

Fothergilla gardeni **L.** – See *Fothergilla gardenii* L.

Fothergilla gardeni **Murray** – possibly *Fothergilla gardenii* L.

Fothergilla gardenii **L.** – Carolina fothergilla [Carolinian fothergilla] (8) (1785), Dwarf fothergilla (138) (1923), Fothergilla de Caroline (French) (8) (1785), Witch-alder [Witch alder] (5, 19, 92, 156) (1840–1923), possibly Dwarf alder (5, 156) (1913–1923), possibly Fothergilla (5, 156) (1913–1923)

Fothergilla **L.** – Fothergilla (8, 138) (1785–1923), Fothergilla (French) (8) (1785)

Fothergilla major **(Sims) Lodd.** – Alabama fothergilla (138) (1923), Large fothergilla (138) (1923)

Fothergilla monticola **(Ashe)** – See *Fothergilla major* (Sims) Lodd.

Fothergilla **Murr.** – See *Fothergilla* L.

Fouquiera splendens **Engelm.** – See *Fouquieria splendens* Engelm.

Fouquieria **Kunth** – Candlewood [Candelwood, Candle wood] (15) (1895)

Fouquieria splendens **Engelm.** – Candlewood [Candelwood, Candle wood] (149, 153) (1904–1913), Coach-whip [Coach whip] (15) (1895), Coach-whip cactus [Coach whip cactus] (153) (1913), Ocotillo (124, 149, 153, 155) (1904–1949) NM TX

Fragaria **(Tourn.) L.** – See *Fragaria* L.

Fragaria ×*ananassa* **Duchesne var. *cuneifolia* (Nutt. ex T. J. Howell)** – Pineapple strawberry [Pine apple strawberry] (19) (1840)

Fragaria americana **(Porter) Britton** – See *Fragaria vesca* L. subsp. *americana* (Porter) Staudt

Fragaria californica – See *Fragaria vesca* L. subsp. *californica* (Cham. & Schlecht.) Staudt

Fragaria canadensis **Michx.** – See *Fragaria virginiana* Duchesne subsp. *virginiana*

Fragaria chiloensis **(L.) Mill.** – Chili strawberry (110) (1886), Chiloe strawberry (138) (1923), Cultivated strawberry (82) (1930), Garden strawberry (82, 107) (1919–1930), Green strawberry (107) (1919), Pine strawberry (107) (1919), Quelghen (Chili) (107) (1919)

Fragaria chiloensis **Duchesne** – See *Fragaria chiloensis* (L.) Mill.

Fragaria collina **Ehrh.** – See *Fragaria chiloensis* (L.) Mill.

Fragaria glauca **(S. Wats.) Rydb.** – See *Fragaria virginiana* Duchesne subsp. *glauca* (S. Wats.) Staudt

Fragaria grandiflora – See *Fragaria* ×*ananassa* Duchesne var. *cuneifolia* (Nutt. ex T. J. Howell)

Fragaria grayana **Vilmorin** – See *Fragaria virginiana* Duchesne subsp. *grayana* (Vilm. ex J. Gay) Staudt

Fragaria indica **[Andr.]** – See *Duchesnea indica* (Andr.) Focke

Fragaria **L.** – De-min (Chippewa, heart berry) (105) (1932), Fragalo (Italian) (107) (1571), Fraghe (Italian) (107) (1571), Fraises (107) (1542), Fraysas (107) (1554), Fresa (Spanish) (107) (1919), Fresas (French) (107) (1536), Fresera (Spanish) (107) (1919), Strawberry [Straw-berry, Strawberries, Strawberye, Strawberyes] (1, 4, 10, 35, 50, 63, 82, 105, 106, 107, 108, 109, 138, 155, 156, 158, 167, 182, 190) (~1759–present), Strawberry vine [Strawberry vines] (182) (1791), Terresteria mora (Earth mulberry) (107) (1540), Wild strawberry [Wild strawberries] (93) (1936)

Fragaria vesca americana – See *Fragaria vesca* L. subsp. *americana* (Porter) Staudt

Fragaria vesca **L.** – Alpine strawberry (49, 107, 138) (1919–1932), American strawberry (7) (1828), Common strawberry (7, 92) (1828–1876), English strawberry (19, 49) (1840–1898), Erdbeere (German) (6, 158) (1892), European hedge strawberry (5) (1913), European strawberry (155) (1942), European wood strawberry (5, 72, 158) (1900–1913), Fragraria baccae (Official name of Materia Medica) (7) (1828), Fraisier Sauvage (French) (7) (1828), Le Fraisier (French) (6, 158) (1892–1900), Perpetual strawberry (107) (1919), Sheep-nose [Sheep nose, Sheep noses] (5, 76, 158) (1896–1913) Central VT, Sowtit [Sow tit, Sow-tit] (5, 76, 158) (1896–1913) Central VT, Strawberry [Straw-berry, Strawberries, Strawberye, Strawberyes] (57, 110, 179, 184) (1526–1886), Wild strawberry [Wild strawberries] (6, 7) (1828–1932), Wood strawberry (6, 47, 49, 82, 92, 107) (1852–1930), Woodland strawberry (4, 50) (1986–present)

Fragaria vesca L. subsp. *americana* (Porter) Staudt – American strawberry (138, 155) (1923–1942), American wood strawberry (5, 93, 97, 157, 158) (1900–1937), Aparu-huradu (Pawnee, ground berry) (37) (1919), Bashte (Omaha-Ponca) (37) (1919) Bashte-hi (Strawberry vine), Haz-scheck (Winnebago) (37) (1919), Indian strawberry [India-strawberry] (131) (1899), Wazhushtecha (Dakota) (37) (1919) Wazhushtecha-hu (Strawberry vine), Wild strawberry [Wild strawberries] (37) (1919), Wood strawberry (3, 72, 131) (1899–1977), Woodland strawberry (50) (present), Woods strawberry (85) (1932)

Fragaria vesca L. subsp. *californica* (Cham. & Schlecht.) Staudt – California strawberry (138) (1923)

Fragaria virginiana Duchesne – Aparu-huradu (Pawnee, ground berry) (37) (1919), Bashte (Omaha-Ponca) (37) (1919) Bashte-hi (Strawberry vine), Common field strawberry (157, 158) (1900–1929), Greenish strawberry [Greenish strawberrie] (178) (1526), Haz-scheck (Winnebgao) (37) (1919), Ode'imīnĭdji'bĭk (Chippewa [heart berry root] (40) (1928), Red strawberry [Red Strawberrie] (178) (1526), Scarlet strawberry (5, 97, 107, 110, 157, 158) (1886–1937), Strawberry [Straw-berry, Strawberries, Strawberye, Strawberyes] (114, 131, 156) (1894–1923), Strayberry (156) (1923), Wazhushtecha (Dakota) (37) (1919) Wazhushtecha-hu (Strawberry vine), White strawberry [White strawberrie] (178) (1526), Wild strawberry [Wild strawberries] (2, 4, 19, 37, 40, 72, 85, 92, 95, 103, 127, 187) (1818–1986), Wuttahimneash (New England natives) (46, 107) (1879–1919) New England natives, possibly Common strawberry (47) (1852), Virginia strawberry [Virginian strawberry] (5, 50, 93, 97, 107, 110, 138, 155, 157) (1886–present)

Fragaria virginiana Duchesne subsp. *glauca* (S. Wats.) Staudt – Blue-leaf strawberry [Blueleaf strawberry] (155) (1942), Virginia strawberry [Virginian strawberry] (50) (present), Wild strawberry [Wild strawberries] (3) (1977)

Fragaria virginiana Duchesne subsp. *grayana* (Vilm. ex J. Gay) Staudt – Gray's strawberry (5, 97) (1913–1937), Illinois strawberry (155) (1942), Scarlet strawberry (72) (1907) IA, Virginia strawberry [Virginian strawberry] (50) (present), Wild strawberry [Wild strawberries] (3, 82) (1930–1977)

Fragaria virginiana Duchesne subsp. *virginiana* – Mountain strawberry (5, 19) (1840–1913), Northern wild strawberry (5) (1913)

Fragaria virginiana Duchesne var. *illinoensis* Gray – See *Fragaria virginiana* Duchesne subsp. *grayana* (Vilm. ex J. Gay) Staudt

Fragaria virginiana Ehrh. – possibly *Fragaria virginiana* Duchesne

Frangula alnus Mill. – Alder buckthorn [Alder-buckthorn] (5, 49, 53, 55, 82, 109, 156, 158) (1898–1949), Alder dogwood (158) (1900), Arrow-wood [Arrow wood] (5, 156, 158) (1900–1923), Berry alder [Berry-alder] (5, 156, 158) (1900–1923), Black alder [Blacke aller] or Black alder tree (5, 92, 156, 158, 178) (1526–1923), Black-dogwood [Black dogwood] (5, 92, 156, 158) (1876–1923), Bourdaine (French) (158) (1900), Buckthorn [Bucke thorne] (53, 57, 59) (1911–1922), Butcher's prick tree [Bitcher's prick-tree] (156, 158) (1900–1923), European black alder (158) (1900), European buckthorn (156) (1923), Faulbaum (German) (158) (1900), Frangula (55, 57, 59, 174) (1753–1917), Glatter Wegedorn (German) (158) (1900), Glossy buckthorn (138, 155) (1923–1942), Narrow-leaf glossy buckthorn [Narrowleaf glossy buckthorn] (155) (1942), Persian berry [Persian-berry] (5, 156) (1913–1923), Pulverholz (German) (158) (1900)

Frangula californica (Eschsch.) Gray – Bearberry [Bear berry, Bearberry] (74) (1893) Santa Barbara CA, California buckthorn (53, 138) (1922–1923), California coffee tree (53) (1922), Coffee-berry [Coffee berry] (106, 109) (1930–1949), Pigeon-berry [Pigeon berry] (106) (1930), Wild coffee [Wild-coffee] (74) (1893) Santa Barbara CA

Frangula californica (Eschsch.) Gray subsp. *tomentella* (Benth.) Kartesz & Gandhi – White-leaf buckthorn [Whiteleaf buckthorn] (138) (1923)

Frangula caroliniana (Walt.) Gray – Alder-leaf buckthorn [Alder-leaf buckthorn, Alder-leaved buckthorn] (5, 156) (1913–1923), Bog birch (5, 156) (1913–1923), Buckthorn [Bucke thorne] (107) (1919), Carolina buckthorn (5, 20, 93, 97, 138, 156) (1857–1937), Indian cherry [Indian-cherry] (2, 5, 62, 5, 106, 107, 109, 113, 122, 156) (1890–1949), Nerprun de la Caroline (French) (20) (1857), Pole-cat tree [Polecat tree, Polecat-tree] (106, 156) (1923–1930), Tree buckthorn (122) (1937), Yellow buckthorn (106, 156) (1923–1930), Yellow-wood [Yellowwood, Yellow wood] (156) (1923)

Frangula Mill. – Alder buckthorn [Alder-buckthorn] (13) (1849), Buckthorn [Bucke thorne] (50) (present)

Frangula purshiana (DC.) Cooper – Bearberry [Bear berry, Bearberry] (52, 107) (1919), Bearwood [Bear-wood] (52, 160) (1860–1919), Cascara buckthorn (138) (1923), Cascara sagrada (52, 53, 54, 55, 57, 59, 101, 106, 109) (1905–1949), Cascara tree (101) (1905), Chittam (106) (1930), Chittam wood [Chittam-wood, Chittem wood, Chittim wood, Chittim-wood] (59) (1911), Chittem bark (49, 52, 53, 57, 59) (1911–1922), Oregon buckthorn (160) (1860), Pursh's buckthorn (20) (1857), Sacred bark (49, 52, 53, 54, 55, 59) (1905–1922)

Frangula Tourn. – See *Frangula* Mill.

Frankenia grandiflora Chamisso et Schlechtendal – See *Frankenia salina* (Molina) I.M. Johnston

Frankenia grandifolia Cham. & Schlecht. – See *Frankenia salina* (Molina) I.M. Johnston

Frankenia salina (Molina) I. M. Johnston – Yerba reuma (53, 57) (1917–1922)

Frankenia salina Chamisso and Schlectendal – See *Frankenia salina* (Molina) I.M. Johnston

Franklinia alatamaha Bartr. ex Marsh. – Franklinia (2, 8, 13, 20) (1785–1895)

Franklinia americana Marsh. – possibly *Franklinia alatamaha* Bartr. ex Marsh.

Franklinia Bartr. ex Marsh. – Franklinia (8, 138) (1785–1923), Franklinia (French) (8) (1785)

Franklinia Marsh – See *Franklinia* Bartr. ex Marsh.

Franseria Cavar. – See *Ambrosia* L.

Franseria discolor Nutt. – See *Ambrosia tomentosa* Nutt.

Franseria hokeriana Nutt. – See *Ambrosia acanthicarpa* Hook.

Franseria tenuifolia Harvar. & Gray – See *Ambrosia confertiflora* DC.

Franseria tomentosa Gray – See *Ambrosia grayi* (A. Nels.) Shinners

Frasera caroliniensis Walt. – American calumba (14) (1882), Columbo (156, 186) (1814–1923), Columbo-root (186) (1814), Deer's-ears [Deer's ears] (156) (1923), Frasera (57, 64) (1907–1917), Frasera officinalis (186) (1814), Ground centaury (156) (1923), Ground century (64) (1907), Marietta Columbo (186) (1814), Monument plant [Monument-plant] (156) (1923), Pyramid flower [Pyramid-flower] (5, 64, 92, 156) (1876–1923), Pyramid plant [Pyramid-plant] (5, 64, 92, 156) (1876–1923), Wild columbo (186) (1814), possibly American columbo (5, 7, 49, 57, 61, 64, 92, 186) (1814–1923), possibly Colombo (Official name of Materia Medica) (7) (1828), possibly Colombo root (7) (1828), possibly Colombo Wurzel (German) (7) (1828), possibly Columbia (7, 186) (1814–1828), possibly Cucurma (7) (1828), possibly Frasera radix (Official name of Materia Medica) (7) (1828), possibly Frasere colombo (French) (7) (1828), possibly Goldenseal [Golden-seal, Golden seal] (7) (1828), possibly Indian lettuce (7, 64, 92, 156, 182, 186) (1791–1923), possibly Meadowpride [Meadow-pride, Meadow pride] (7, 64, 92, 156)

(1828–1928), possibly Pyramid (7) (1828), possibly Yellow gentian (5, 7, 64, 92, 156) (1828–1923)

Frasera speciosa **Dougl. ex Griseb.** – Columbo (106) (1930), Deer's-ears [Deer's ears] (106) (1930) translation of Navaho name, Elkweed (50) (present), Frasera (106) (1930), Monument plant [Monument-plant] (106) (1930), Pyramid flower [Pyramid-flower] (122, 124) (1937), Showy frasera (131, 155) (1899–1942)

Frasera verticillata **Raf.** – possibly *Frasera caroliniensis* Walt.

Frasera **Walt.** – American calumba (2, 158) (1895–1900), American columbo (156) (1923), Elkweed (155) (1942), Frasera (155) (1942), Green gentian (50) (present), Whiteroot [White-root, Whiteroot] (23) (1810)

Frasera walteri **Michx.** – See *Frasera caroliniensis* Walt.

Fraxinus **(Tourn.) L.** – See *Fraxinus* L.

Fraxinus acuminata **Lam.** – See *Fraxinus americana* L.

Fraxinus acuminatus **Lk.** – See *Fraxinus americana* L.

Fraxinus alba **[Marsh.]** – See *Fraxinus americana* L.

Fraxinus americana **L.** – American white ash (6, 8, 157, 158) (1785–1929), Ash or Ash tree [Asshe tre] (157, 158) (1900–1929), Biltmore ash (5, 138, 155) (1913–1942), Black ash (52) (1919), Bo-yak (Chippewa, straight-grained ash) (105) (1932), Cane ash (5, 156, 157, 158) (1900–1929), Carolina ash [Carolinian ash] (8) (1785), Elder-leaf ash [Elder-leaved ash] (52, 53) (1919–1922), Fraxinus (52) (1919), Frêne blanc (French) (8) (1785), Frêne d'Amérique (French) (8) (1785), Le Fréne Blanc (French) (6) (1892), Nitiminš (Chippewa, spear timber) (105) (1932), Red ash (8) (1785), Small-seed white ash [Smallseed white ash] (155) (1942), Swamp ash (19) (1840), Walnut-leaf ash (19) (1840), Walnut-leaf white ash [Walnut-leaf white ash] (155) (1942), Weisse Esche (German) (6) (1892), White ash (2, 4, 5, 9, 18, 19, 20, 35, 46, 48, 50, 52, 53, 57, 63, 72, 82, 85, 92, 93, 95, 97, 105, 108, 109, 113, 122, 124, 130, 131, 135, 138, 155, 156, 157, 158) (1840–present)

Fraxinus americana **L. var.** *juglandifolia* **(Lam.) Rehd.** – See *Fraxinus americana* L.

Fraxinus americana **L. var.** *microcarpa* **Gray** – See *Fraxinus americana* L.

Fraxinus americana **var.** *juglandifolia* **(Lam.) Rehder** – See *Fraxinus americana* L.

Fraxinus americana **var.** *sambucifolia* **(Lam.) D. J. Browne** – See *Fraxinus nigra* Marshall

Fraxinus anomala **Torr. ex S. Wats.** – Single-leaf ash [Singleleaf ash] (138) (1923)

Fraxinus biltmoreana **Beadle** – See *Fraxinus americana* L.

Fraxinus campestris **Britton** – See *Fraxinus pennsylvanica* Marsh.

Fraxinus caroliniana **Mill.** – Carolina ash [Carolinian ash] (5, 20, 156) (1857–1923), Fréne à petites fleurs (French) (20) (1857), Pop ash [Pop-ash] (5, 156) (1913–1923), Poppy ash [Poppy-ash] (5, 156) (1913–1923), Small-leaf ash [Small-leaved ash] (20) (1857), Three-wing ash [Three-winged ash] (20) (1857), Water ash (5, 97, 122, 124, 156) (1913–1937) NM

Fraxinus cuspidata **Torr.** – Fragrant ash (122, 138) (1923–1937)

Fraxinus darlingtonii **Britton** – See *Fraxinus pennsylvanica* Marsh.

Fraxinus dipetala **Hook. & Arn.** – California flowering ash [Californian flowering ash] (20) (1857), California shrub ash (138) (1923), Le frêne à fleurs de Californie (French) (20) (1857)

Fraxinus excelsior **L.** – Ash or Ash tree [Asshe tre] (41, 107, 179) (1526–1919), Bird's-tongue [Birds tongue] (92) (1876), Common European ash (20) (1857), European ash (109, 112, 138) (1923–1949)

Fraxinus greggii **Gray** – Gregg's ash [Gregg ash] (122, 138) (1923–1937)

Fraxinus juglandifolia **W.** – See *Fraxinus americana* L.

Fraxinus **L.** – A'gimak' (Chippewa, snowshoe wood) (40) (1928), Ash or Ash tree [[Asshe tre] (1, 3, 4, 7, 8, 10, 35, 40, 50, 82, 93, 106, 109, 138, 155, 156, 158) (1785–present), Frêne (French) (8) (1785), possibly Flowering ash (10) (1818)

Fraxinus lanceolata **Borkh.** – See *Fraxinus pennsylvanica* Marsh.

Fraxinus latifolia **Benth.** – Fréne de l'Oregon (French) (20) (1857), Oregon ash (106, 138, 160, 161) (1857–1930), Oregon black ash (20) (1857)

Fraxinus michauxii **Britton** – See *Fraxinus profunda* (Bush) Bush

Fraxinus nigra **Marsh** – Basket ash (5, 156, 158) (1900–1923), Brown ash (5, 156) (1913–1923), Fréne noir (French) (8) (1785), Hoop ash (5, 156, 158) (1900–1923), Swamp ash (5, 156, 158) (1900–1923), Water ash (5, 20, 156, 158) (1857–1923), Black ash (2, 3, 20, 19, 53, 57, 63, 72, 80, 92, 138, 155, 156, 158) (1840–1977), Elder-leaf ash [Elder-leaved ash] (53) (1922)

Fraxinus oregona – See *Fraxinus latifolia* Benth.

Fraxinus pauciflora **Nutt.** – See *Fraxinus caroliniana* Mill.

Fraxinus pennsylvanica **Marsh.** – Ash or Ash tree [Asshe tre] (37) (1919), Black ash (5, 93, 156) (1913–1936), Blue ash (5, 156, 157) (1913–1929), Darlington's ash (5) (1913), Field ash (95) (1911) Neb, Fréne de Pensylvanie (French) (8) (1785), Green ash (2, 4, 5, 9, 20, 46, 50, 63, 72, 82, 85, 93, 97, 101, 112, 113. 124, 130, 131, 135, 138, 156) (1857–present), Kiditako (Pawnee) (37) (1919), Pennsylvania sharp-key ash [Pennsylvanian sharp-keyed ash] (8) (1785), Pseh'tin (Dakota) (37) (1919), Red ash (2, 3, 4, 5, 19, 63, 72, 82, 93, 97, 109, 113, 130, 131, 138, 155, 156) (1840–1986), River ash (5, 156) (1913–1923), Swamp ash (5, 156, 157) (1913–1929), Tashnánga-hi (Omaha-Ponca) (37) (1919), Water ash (5) (1913), Western green ash (85) (1932), Yellow ash (77) (1898)

Fraxinus pennsylvanica **Marsh. var.** *lanceolata* **(Borkh.) Sargent** – See *Fraxinus pennsylvanica* Marsh.

Fraxinus pennsylvanica **Marsh. var.** *pennsylvanica* – See *Fraxinus pennsylvanica* Marsh.

Fraxinus pennsylvanica **Marshall var.** *pubescens* **(Lam.) Lingelsh.** – See *Fraxinus pennsylvanica* Marsh.

Fraxinus platicarpa – See *Fraxinus caroliniana* Mill.

Fraxinus platycarpa **Michx.** – See *Fraxinus caroliniana* Mill.

Fraxinus platycarpa **var.** *triptera* **(Nutt.) Alph.Wood** – See *Fraxinus caroliniana* Mill.

Fraxinus profunda **(Bush) Bush** – Ash or Ash tree [Asshe tre] (187) (1818), Michaux's ash (5) (1913), Pumpkin ash (5) (1913), Red ash (20, 187) (1818–1857)

Fraxinus profunda **Bush** – See *Fraxinus profunda* (Bush) Bush

Fraxinus pubescens **Lam.** – See *Fraxinus pennsylvanica* Marsh.

Fraxinus quadrangulata **Michx.** – Blue ash (3, 4, 5, 10, 19, 20, 35, 63, 72, 82, 92, 97, 109, 138, 155, 158) (1818–1986)

Fraxinus rotundifolia **[Mill.]** – See *Fraxinus angustifolia* Vahl

Fraxinus sambucifolia **Lam.** – See *Fraxinus nigra* Marshall

Fraxinus texensis **(Gray) Sargent** – Texas ash (138) (1923)

Fraxinus tomentosa **[Michx. f.]** – See *Fraxinus profunda* (Bush) Bush

Fraxinus triptera **[Nutt.]** – See *Fraxinus caroliniana* Mill.

Fraxinus velutina coriacea – See *Fraxinus velutina* Torr.

Fraxinus velutina **Torr.** – Arizona ash (112) (1937), Fresno (153) (1913) NM, Mountain ash [Mountain-ash, Mountainash] (149, 153) (1904–1919)

Fraxinus velutina **Torr. var.** *coriacea* **(S. Wats.) Rehd.** – See *Fraxinus velutina* Torr.

Fraxinus viridis **Michx.** – See *Fraxinus pennsylvanica* Marsh.

Frazera walteri – See *Frasera caroliniensis* Walt.

Freesia corymbosa **(Burm. f.) N.E. Br.** – Common freesia (138) (1923)

Freesia **Ecklon ex Klatt** – Freesia (138) (1923)

Freesia refracta alba – See *Freesia corymbosa* (Burm. f.) N.E. Br.

Fremontia californica **Torr.** – See *Fremontodendron californicum* (Torr.) Coville

Fremontia **Torr.** – See *Fremontodendron* Coville

Fremontodendron californicum **(Torr.) Coville** – Flannel bush [Flannel-bush] (109) (1949), Fremontia (138) (1923)

Fremontodendron **Coville** – Fremontia (138) (1923)

Fritillaria affinis **(Schult.) Sealy var.** *affinis* – Narrow-leaf fritillary [Narrow-leaved fritillary] (107) (1919)

Fritillaria atropurpurea **Nutt.** – Čaŋxlogaŋ makatola (Lakota, green earth weed) (121) (1918?–1970?), Chocolate lily (127) (1933) ND, Leopard lily (3, 85, 121, 127) (1918–1977), Purple fritillaria (5, 93) (1913–1936), Purple-spot fritillary [Purplespot fritillary] (155) (1942), Spotted fritillary (50) (present)

Fritillaria **L.** – Checkered-lily [Chequered lily] (10) (1818), Frittillary (50, 109, 138, 155) (1923–present), Guinea-hen flower [Guinea hen flower] (158) (1900) no longer in use by 1900, Leopard lily (1, 93) (1932–1936), Tiger lily [Tiger-lily] (1, 93) (1932–1936)

Fritillaria lanceolata **Pursh** – See *Fritillaria affinis* (Schult.) Sealy var. *affinis*

Fritillaria liliacea **Lindl.** – White fritillary (138) (1923)

Fritillaria pudica **(Pursh) Spreng** – Yellow fritillary (50, 155) (1942–present), Yellowbell [Yellow-bell, Yellow bell, Yellow bells, Yellow-bells, Yellowbells] (101) (1905) MT

Froelichia campestris **Small** – See *Froelichia floridana* (Nutt.) Moq. var. *campestris* (Small) Fern.

Froelichia drummondii **Moq.** – Snake-cotton [Snake cotton, Snakecotton] (122, 124) (1937) TX

Froelichia floridana **(Nutt.) Moq.** – Field snakecotton [Field snake cotton] (4) (1986), Florida froelichia (72) (1907), Plains snakecotton [Plains snakecotton] (50) (present), Prairie froelichia (97) (1937)

Froelichia floridana **(Nutt.) Moq. var.** *campestris* **(Small) Fern.** – Plains snake-cotton [Plains snakecotton] (50) (present), Prairie froelichia (5, 93) (1913–1936), Snake-cotton [Snake cotton, Snakecotton] (3) (1977)

Froelichia gracilis **(Hook.) Moq.** – Cottonweed [Cotton-weed, Cotton weed] (3) (1977), Slender froelichia (5, 93, 97, 98) (1913–1937), Slender snake-cotton [Slender snake cotton, Slender snakecotton] (4, 50, 122) (1937–present)

Froelichia **Moench** – Froelichia (93, 158) (1900–1936), Snake-cotton [Snake cotton, Snakecotton] (4, 50) (1986–present)

Fuchsia **L.** – Fuchsia (138) (1923)

Fuchsia magellanica conica – See *Fuchsia magellanica* Lam.

Fuchsia magellanica gracilis – See *Fuchsia magellanica* Lam.

Fuchsia magellanica **Lam.** – Cone fuchsia (138) (1923), Eardrop [Ear-drop, Ear-drops] (19, 92) (1840–1876), Fuchsia (92) (1876), Magellan's fuchsia [Magellan fuchsia] (138) (1923), Naiad fuchsia (138) (1923)

Fuchsia magellanica **Lk.** – See *Fuchsia magellanica* Lam.

Fuchsia magellanica **var.** *conica* **(Lindl.) Bailey** – See *Fuchsia magellanica* Lam.

Fucus helminthocorton – See *Alsidium helminthochorton* (Schwendimann) Kützing

Fucus **L.** – Seaweeds (7) (1828), Wrack [Wracks] (7) (1828)

Fucus natans **[L.]** – See *Sargassum natans* (L.) Gaillon

Fucus vesiculosus **L.** – Anit-fat (60) (1902) commercial name, Black tang (53) (1922), Bladder fucus (92) (1876), Bladder wrack (52, 53, 55, 57, 60, 92) (1876–1922), Kelp ware (52, 53) (1919–1922), Rockweed [Rockweed, Rockweed] (57) (1917), Sea wrack [Seawrack, Sea-wrack] (52, 53, 60, 92) (1876–1922)

Fuirena hispida **Ell.** – See *Fuirena squarrosa* Michx.

Fuirena **Rottb.** – Umbrella-grass [Umbrella grass] (1, 93) (1932–1936), Umbrella-sedge [Umbrella sedge] (50) (present)

Fuirena simplex **Vahl** – Fuirena (3) (1977), Western umbrella-grass [Western umbrella grass] (5) (1913), Western umbrella-sedge [Western umbrella sedge] (50) (present)

Fuirena simplex **Vahl var.** *aristulata* **(Torr.) Kral** – Western umbrella-sedge [Western umbrella sedge] (50) (present)

Fuirena squarrosa **Michx.** – Hairy fuirena (5) (1913), Hairy umbrella-sedge [Hairy umbrella sedge] (50) (present), Rough-head fuirena [Rough-headed fuirena] (187) (1818), Umbrella-grass [Umbrella grass] (5, 19, 66, 156) (1840–1913)

Fumaria **L.** – Fumitory (50, 155, 158, 184) (1793–present)

Fumaria officinalis **L.** – Beggary (156, 158) (1900–1923), Drug fumitory (50, 155) (1942–present), Earthsmoke [Earth-smoke, Earth smoke] (92, 156) (1876–1923), Erdrauch (German) (158) (1900), Feldraute (German) (158) (1900), Fume-of-the-earth [Fume of the erthe] (179) (1526), Fumeterre (French) (158) (1900), Fumitory (1, 5, 7, 10, 19, 49, 92, 156, 158) (1818–1932), Fumyterry (179) (1526), Hedge fumitory (5, 156, 158) (1900–1923), Hiel de tierra (Spanish) (158) (1900), Pajarilla (French) (158) (1900), Smoke plant (124) (1937) TX, Smoke-of-the-earth [Smoke of the erthe] (179) (1526), Wax-dolls [Wax dolls] (156, 158) (1900–1923)

Fumaria officinalis **L. subsp.** *wirtgenii* **(W. D. J. Koch) Arcang.** – Drug fumitory (50) (present)

Fumaria vaillantii **Loisel.** – Earthsmoke [Earth-smoke, Earth smoke] (50, 158) (1900–present)

Funaria hygrometrica **Hedw.** – Funaria moss (50) (present), Hygrometer moss (19) (1840)

Funastrum clausum **(Jacq.) Schltr.** – Sweet philibertia (138) (1923)

Funastrum crispum **(Benth.) Schlechter** – Wavy-leaf twinevine [Wavyleaf twinevine] (50) (present), Waxy-leaf twinevine [Waxy-leaf twine vine] (4) (1986)

Funastrum cynanchoides **(Dcne.) Schlechter subsp.** *cynanchoides* – Arroyo twinevine [Arroyo twine vine] (4) (1986), Fringed twinevine (50) (present)

Funastrum **Fourn.** – Philibertia (138) (1923)

Funastrum **Fourn.** – Twine vine [Twinevine] (4, 50) (1986–present)

Funkia **[Spreng.]** – See *Hosta* Tratt.

Funkia grandiflora **[Siebold & Zucc.]** – See *Hosta plantaginea* (Lam.) Aschers.

Funkia subcordata **Spreng.** – See *Hosta plantaginea* (Lam.) Aschers.

G

Gaertneria acanthicarpa (**Hook.**) **Britton** – See *Ambrosia acanthicarpa* Hook.

Gaertneria discolor (**Nutt.**) **Kuntze** – See *Ambrosia tomentosa* Nutt.

Gaertneria **Med.** – See *Ambrosia* L.

Gaertneria tomentosa (**Nutt.**) **Heller** – See *Ambrosia tomentosa* Nutt.

Gaillardia aestivalis (**Walt.**) **H. Rock var.** *flavovirens* (**C. Mohr**) **Cronq.** – Yellow gaillardia (5, 97) (1913–1937)

Gaillardia aestivalis (**Walt.**) **Rock** – Lance-leaf blanket-flower [Lance-leaf blanketflower] (50) (present), Lance-leaf gaillardia [Lance-leaved gaillardia] (97) (1937), Prairie gaillardia (3, 4) (1977–1986)

Gaillardia amblyodon **J. Gay** – Blunt-tooth blanket-flower [Blunt-toothed blanketflower] (86) (1878), Maroon gaillardia (138) (1923), Red gaillardia (124) (1937)

Gaillardia aristata **Pursh** – Blanket-flower [Basketflower, Blanket flower] (3, 4, 85, 156) (1923–1986), Common gaillardia (50) (present), Common perennial gaillardia (138, 155) (1923–1942), Great-flower gaillardia [Great-flowered gaillardia, Great flowered gaillardia] (5, 131) (1899–1913)

Gaillardia bicolor **Lam.** – See *Gaillardia pulchella* Foug.

Gaillardia fastigata **Greene** – See *Gaillardia aestivalis* (Walt.) Rock

Gaillardia **Foug.** – Blanket-flower [Basketflower, Blanket flower] (1, 4, 50, 93, 158) (1900–present), Gaillardia (138, 155) (1923–1942), Othake (155) (1942)

Gaillardia lanceolata **Michx.** – See *Gaillardia aestivalis* (Walt.) Rock

Gaillardia lutea **Greene** – See *Gaillardia aestivalis* (Walt.) Rock var. *flavovirens* (C. Mohr) Cronq.

Gaillardia picta – See *Gaillardia pulchella* Foug. var. *picta* (Sweet) Gray

Gaillardia pinnatifida **Torr.** – Pinnate-leaf gaillardia [Pinnate-leaved gaillardia] (97) (1937), Red-dome blanket-flower [Red dome blanketflower] (50) (present)

Gaillardia pulchella **Foug.** – Firewheel (50) (present), Flowerwheel [Flower wheel] (124) (1937) TX, Indian blanket (124) (1937) TX, Indian blanket flower (4) (1986), Marigold [Marigolds, Mary gold, Marygold] (106) (1930), Niggar-toe (145) (1897) KS, Rose-ring gaillardia [Rosering gaillardia] (3, 4, 138, 155) (1923–1986), Showy gaillardia (5, 93, 97, 122) (1913–1937), possibly Snakeroot [Snake root, Snake-root] (34) (1834)

Gaillardia pulchella **Foug. var.** *picta* (**Sweet**) **Gray** – Painted gaillardia (92, 138) (1876–1923)

Gaillardia pulchella **Foug. var.** *pulchella* – Firewheel (50) (present)

Gaillardia pulchella picta – See *Gaillardia pulchella* Foug. var. *picta* (Sweet) Gray

Gaillardia suavis (**Gray & Engelm.**) **Britton & Rusby** – Perfume-balls [Perfumeballs] (50) (present), Rayless gaillardia (5, 97) (1913–1937)

Gaillardia trinervata **Small** – See *Gaillardia suavis* (Gray & Engelm.) Britton & Rusby

Galactea pilosa **Ell.** – See *Galactia regularis* (L.) Britton, Sterns & Poggenb.

Galactia glabella **Michx.** – See *Galactia regularis* (L.) Britton, Sterns & Poggenb.

Galactia **P. Br.** – Milk-pea [Milk pea] (2, 50, 155, 158) (1895–present)

Galactia regularis (**L.**) **Britton, Sterns & Poggenb.** – Downy milk-pea [Downy milk pea] (4) (1986), Eastern milkpea (50) (present), Milk-pea [Milk pea] (5, 97, 156) (1913–1937), Milky Way plant (19) (1840), Shapely milk-pea [Shapely milkpea] (155) (1942)

Galactia volubilis (**L.**) **Britt.** – Downy milk-pea [Downy milk pea] (5, 72, 97) (1907–1937)

Galactia volubilis (**L.**) **Britton var.** *mississippiensis* **Vail** – See *Galactia regularis* (L.) Britton, Sterns & Poggenb.

Galactia volubilis (**L.**) **Britton var.** *volubilis* – possibly *Galactia volubilis* (L.) Britton

Galanthus elwesii **Hook. f.** – Giant snowdrop (109) (1949)

Galanthus **L.** – Snowdrop [Snowdrops, Snow-drops, Snow drop] (109, 138) (1923–1949)

Galanthus nivalis **L.** – Common snowdrop (109, 138) (1923–1949), Erangelia (174) (1753), Galanthus (174) (1753), Snowdrop [Snowdrops, Snow-drops, Snow drop] (19, 92) (1840–1876), White snowdrop (92) (1876)

Galardia bicolor – possibly *Gaillardia pulchella* Foug.

Galarrhoeus **Haw.** – See *Euphorbia* L.

Galax aphylla **auct. non L.** – See *Galax urceolata* (Poir.) Brummitt

Galax aphylla **L.** – See *Nemophila aphylla* (L.) Brummitt (taxonomic status is unresolved (PL))

Galax **L.** – See *Galax* Sims

Galax rotundifolia **L.** – See *Galax urceolata* (Poir.) Brummitt

Galax **Sims** – Galax (138) (1923)

Galax urceolata (**Poir.**) **Brummitt** – Carpenter's-leaf [Carpenters' leaf] (7, 92) (1828–1876) Banner Elk NC

Galearis **Raf.** – Galearis (50) (present), Showy orchid (1) (1932)

Galearis spectabilis (**L.**) **Raf.** – Gay orchis (5, 19, 156, 158) (1840–1913), Preacher-in-the-pulpit [Preacher in the pulpit] (86, 156, 158) (1878–1923) PA, Purple orchis (5, 75, 158) (1894–1913), Showy orchid (50) (Present), Showy orchis (3, 5, 72, 86, 93, 109, 138, 156, 158) (1878–1977) IA Neb, Spring orchis (156, 158) (1900–1923)

Galega **L.** – Goat's-rue [Goatsrue, Goat's rue, Goats-rue] (138, 155, 158) (1923–1942)

Galega officinalis **L.** – Common goat's-rue [Common goatsrue] (138, 155) (1923–1942), Geisraute (German) (158) (1900), Goat's-rue [Goatsrue, Goat's rue, Goats-rue] (49, 57, 82, 92, 107, 109, 129, 158, 178) (1526–1949), Pestilenzkraut (German) (158) (1900), Professorweed (50) (present), Rue de chère (French) (158) (1900)

Galeobdolon luteum – See *Lamiastrum galeobdolon* (L.) Ehrend. & Polatschek

Galeopsis bifida **Boenn.** – Bastard hemp [Bastard-hemp] (5, 92, 158) (1876–1913), Bee nettle [Bee-nettle] (5, 156, 158) (1900–1923), Bisbee weed (77) (1898) Paris ME, Blind nettle [Blind-nettle] (5, 156, 158) (1900–1923), Brittle-stem hemp nettle [Brittlestem hempnettle] (155) (1942), Burweed [Bur weed, Bur-weed, Burr weed, Burrweed, Burr-weed] (77) (1898) Paris ME, Chanvre bâtard (French) (158) (1900), Common hemp nettle (4) (1986), Dog-nettle [Dog-nettle] (5, 156, 158) (1900–1923), False hemp (156) (1923), Flowering nettle [Flowering-nettle] (5, 19, 92, 156, 158) (1840–1923), Hanfnessel (German) (158) (1900), Hemp deadnettle [Hemp dead nettle, Hemp dead-nettle] (5, 19, 156, 158) (1840–1923), Hemp nettle [Hemp-nettle, Hempnettle] (1, 3, 5, 10, 63, 72, 85, 92, 156, 158) (1899–1977), Hohlzahn (German) (158) (1900), Holy rope [Holy-rope] (156, 158) (1900–1923) obsolete by 1923, Ironwort [Iron-wort, Ironwort] (5, 156, 158) (1900–1923), Keays' weed [Keays weed] (77) (1898) Paris ME, Nettle-hemp [Nettle hemp] (5, 156, 158) (1900–1923), Simon's weed (5) (1913), Split-lip hemp-nettle [Splitlip hempnettle] (50) (present), Stinging nettle (5) (1913), Wild hemp [Wylde hempe] (5, 158) (1900–1913)

Galeopsis **L.** – Hemp nettle [Hemp-nettle, Hempnettle] (4, 50, 155, 156, 158) (1900–present)

Galeopsis ladanum **L.** – Dog-nettle [Dog-nettle] (5, 156) (1913–1923), Ironwort [Iron-wort, Ironwort] (5, 92, 156) (1876–1923), Red hemp-nettle (5, 19, 156) (1840–1923)

Galeopsis tetrahit **L.** – See *Galeopsis bifida* Boenn.

Galeorchis **Rybd.** – See *Galearis* Raf.

Galeorchis spectablis (**L.**) **Rydb.** – See *Galearis spectabilis* (L.) Raf.

Galinsoga ciliata (Raf.) Blake – See *Galinsoga quadriradiata* Cav.

Galinsoga parviflora Cav. – Frenchweed [French weed, French weed] (106) (1930), Galinsoga (5, 72, 97, 106) (1907–1937), Gallant-soldier (50) (present), Little-flower quickweed [Littleflower quickweed] (155) (1942)

Galinsoga quadriradiata Cav. – Fringed quickweed (3, 4, 155) (1942–1986), Shaggy-soldier (50) (Present)

Galinsoga Ruiz & Pavón – Galinsoga (158) (1900), Gallant-soldier (50) (present), Quickweed (4, 155) (1942–1986)

Galium aparine L. – Airif (5, 156, 158) (1900–1923) no longer in use by 1923, Bedstraw [Bed straw] (49, 53, 85, 92, 93, 107) (1876–1936), Beggar's-lice [Beggar lice, Beggar-lice, Beggarlice, Beggarslice] (5, 93, 156, 157, 158) (1900–1929), Bird-lime [Bird lime] (156) (1923), Burhead [Bur-head, Burrhead] (5, 156, 157, 158) (1900–1929), Burweed [Bur weed, Bur-weed, Burr weed, Burrweed, Burrweed] (107) (1919), Catchweed [Catch-weed, Catch weed] (5, 19, 49, 53, 92, 107, 156, 158, 187) (1818–1923), Catchweed bedstraw (3, 4, 155) (1942–1986), Cheese rennet-herb [Cheese rennet herb] (92) (1876), Clabber-grass [Clabbergrass] (92) (1876), Claver-grass [Claver grass, Clayver-grass] (5, 156, 158) (1900–1923), Cleavers [Cleaver] (1, 2, 5, 49, 52, 53, 57, 61, 72, 92, 93, 107, 131, 156, 157, 158) (1870–1936), Cleavers' goose-grass (187) (1818), Cleaverwort [Cleaver-wort, Cleaver wort] (5, 92, 156, 157, 158) (1876–1923), Cling-rascal [Cling rascal] (5, 156, 158) (1900–1923) no longer in use by 1923, Clivers (46, 92, 158) (1671–1900), Clyvers [Clyuers] (179) (1526), Common cleavers (187) (1818), Galium (57) (1917), Goose-grass [Goose grass] (2, 5, 19, 46, 49, 53, 92, 105, 122, 131, 156, 157, 158) (1671–1923), Goose's-hare [Gooses hare] (92) (1876), Gosling-weed [Gosling weed] (5, 156, 157, 158) (1900–1929), Grip or Grip-grass [Grip grass] (5, 92, 156, 158) (1876–1923) no longer in use by 1923, Hairif (5, 156, 158) (1900–1923) no longer in use by 1923, Harvestlice [Harvest lice, Harvest-lice] (156) (1923), Klebkraut (German) (158) (1900), Lady's bedstraw [Ladies' bedstraw, Lady's bedstraws, Lady's-bedstraw] (57) (1917) from legend that Mother of Jesus rested on hay containing one of the species, Loveman [Love-man] (5, 156, 158) (1900–1923) no longer in use by 1923, Maid's-hair [Maid's hair, Maids' hair] (158) (1900), Milksweet [Milk sweet] (92) (1876), Pertimugget (158) (1900), Pezukškuns (Chippewa, partridge berry) (105) (1932), Pigtail [Pigtail] (5, 156, 158) (1900–1923) no longer in use by 1923, Poor Robin [Poor-robin] (5, 92, 156, 158) (1876–1923) no longer in use by 1923, Rièbel (French) (158) (1900), Savoyan (92) (1876), Scratch-grass [Scratch grass] (5, 156) (1913–1923), Scratch-weed [Scratch weed] (5, 92, 156) (1876–1923), Snatch-weed (157, 158) (1900–1929), Stick-a-back [Stickaback] (5, 156, 158) (1900–1923) no longer in use by 1923, Stickle-back [Stickleback] (5, 156, 158) (1900–1923), Sticky-willy [Stickywilly] (50) (present), Sweetheart [Sweethearts, Sweet-hearts] (5, 156, 158) (1900–1923) no longer in use by 1923, Turkey-grass [Turkey grass] (5, 156, 157, 158) (1900–1929), Vaillantii goose-grass [Vaillantii goosegrass] (5, 97, 122) (1913–1937), Wild hedge bur [Wild hedge-burs] (5, 158) (1900–1913), Wild rosemary (158) (1900)

Galium aristatum L. – False baby's-breath [False babys-breath] (109) (1949)

Galium arkansanum Gray – Arkansas bedstraw (5, 97) (1913–1937)

Galium asprellum Michx. – Catchweed [Catch-weed, Catch weed] (156) (1923), Clivers (156) (1923), Pointed cleavers (5, 49, 92, 156) (1876–1923), Rough bedstraw (5, 19, 49, 63, 72, 93, 156) (1840–1936), Rough cleavers (156) (1923)

Galium bermudense L. – See *Galium circaezans* Michx. var. *circaezans*

Galium boreale L. – Mattara (Finland) (46) (1879), Northern bedstraw (3, 4, 5, 50, 63, 72, 82, 85, 93, 109, 122, 127, 131, 138, 155, 156) (1899–present)

Galium brachiatum Pursh – See *Galium triflorum* Michx.

Galium circaezans Michx. – Cross cleavers [Crosscleavers, Cross-cleavers] (5, 19, 72, 92, 93, 97, 122, 156, 158) (1840–1937), Cross-branch goose-grass [Cross-branched goose-grass] (187) (1818),

Licorice bedstraw (50) (present), Upright cockspur (46) (1783), Wild licorice [Wild liquorice] (2, 5, 19, 63, 93, 97, 156, 158) (1840–1937), Woods bedstraw (3, 4) (1977–1986)

Galium circaezans Michx. var. *circaezans* – Coast bedstraw (5) (1913)

Galium circaezans Michx. var. *hypomalacum* Fern. – Licorice bedstraw (50) (present)

Galium claytonii Michx. – See *Galium tinctorium* L.

Galium concinnum Torr. & Gray – Shining bedstraw (3, 4, 5, 50, 72, 93) (1907–present)

Galium cruciata (L.) Scop. – See *Cruciata laevipes* Opiz

Galium glaucum L. – Bedstraw asperula (5, 156) (1913–1923), Bedstraw woodruff (155) (1942)

Galium hispidulum Michx. – Madder (190) (~1759)

Galium kamtschaticum Steller – See *Galium kamtschaticum* Steller ex J.A. & J.H. Schultes

Galium kamtschaticum Steller ex J.A. & J.H. Schultes – Northern wild licorice [Northern wild liquorice] (5) (1913)

Galium L. – Bedstraw [Bed straw] (1, 2, 4, 10, 50, 82, 93, 109, 138, 155, 156, 158) (1818–present), Beggar's-lice [Beggar lice, Beggarlice, Beggarlice, Beggarslice] (76) (1896) Southwest MO, Cleavers [Cleaver] (2, 4, 10, 76, 93, 156, 158) (1818–1986), Clivers (2) (1895), Goose-grass [Goose grass] (184) (1793), Lady's bedstraw [Ladies' bedstraw, Lady's bedstraws, Lady's-bedstraw] (109) (1949), Robin-run-ahead (76) (1896) Sulphur Grove OH

Galium labradoricum Wiegand – Bog bedstraw (155) (1942), Labrador bedstraw (4) (1986), Labrador marsh bedstraw (5) (1913), Northern bog bedstraw (50) (present)

Galium lanceolatum Torr. – Torrey's wild licorice [Torrey's wild liquorice] (5) (1913), Wild licorice [Wild liquorice] (156) (1923)

Galium latifolium Michx. – Purple bedstraw (5, 156) (1913–1923)

Galium luteum [Lam.] – See *Galium verum* L.

Galium mollugo L. – Baby's-breath [Babies' breath, Baby's breath, Babies'-breath, Babysbreath] (75, 156) (1894–1923) Eastern MA, Bedstraw [Bed straw] (82) (1930), False baby's-breath [False babysbreath] (109) (1949), Great hedge bedstraw [Great hedge-bedstraw] (5, 156) (1913–1923), Infant's-breath [Infant's breath] (156) (1923), Mist (75) (1894) Eastern MA, Mollugo (178) (1526), Whip-tongue (92, 156) (1898–1923) no longer in use by 1923, White bedstraw (5, 109, 138, 156) (1913–1949), White lady's-bedstraw [White ladies bedstraw] (178) (1526), Wild madder [Wild-madder] (5, 72, 156) (1907–1923) IA

Galium obtusum Bigelow – Blunt-leaf bedstraw [Bluntleaf bedstraw] (3, 4, 50) (1977–present)

Galium odoratum (L.) Scop. – Hay plant (5) (1913), Mugget (5) (1913), Mugwet (5) (1913), Rockweed [Rockweed, Rockweed] (5) (1913), Star-grass [Star grass, Stargrass] (5) (1913), Sweet hairhoof (5) (1913), Sweet woodruff (5, 109, 138, 155) (1913–1949), Sweetgrass [Sweet grass, Sweetgrass] (5) (1913), Wood root (92) (1876), Wood rue [Woodrue] (179) (1526), Woodrip (5) (1913), Woodroof (107) (1919), Wood-rowel [Woodrowel] (5) (1913), Woodruff-weed (156) (1923)

Galium palustre L. – Marsh bedstraw (5, 72, 156) (1907–1923), Marsh cleavers (92) (1876), White lady's-bedstraw [White ladies bedstraw] (178) (1526)

Galium parisiense L. – Wall bedstraw (5) (1913)

Galium pilosum Aiton – Hairy bedstraw (3, 4, 5, 50, 97, 122, 155) (1913–present)

Galium pilosum Aiton var. *puncticulosum* (Michx.) Torr. & Gray – Hairy bedstraw (50) (present), Hairy goose-grass (187) (1818)

Galium puncticulosum Michx. – See *Galium pilosum* Aiton var. *puncticulosum* (Michx.) Torr. & Gray

Galium sylvaticum L. – Baby's-breath [Babies' breath, Baby's breath, Babies'-breath, Babysbreath] (156) (1923), Scotch mist (156) (1923), Wood bedstraw (5, 156) (1913–1923)

Galium texense Gray – Texas bedstraw (4, 50) (1986–present)

Galium tinctorium L. – Clayton's bedstraw [Claytons bedstraw] (5, 155) (1913–1942), Dye bedstraw (155) (1942), Dyer's cleavers

[Dyers' cleavers] (19, 92, 156, 157, 158) (1840–1923), Dyer's goose-grass [Dyers' goose-grass] (187) (1818), Dyers woodruff (109, 155) (1942–1949), Smaller wild madder (157, 158) (1900–1929), Stiff marsh bedstraw (stiff marsh-bedstraw) (5, 50, 72, 93, 97, 122, 156) (1907–present), Wild madder [Wild-madder] (5, 19, 85, 131, 156, 187) (1818–1932)

Galium tricorne Stokes – See *Galium tricornutum* Dandy

Galium tricornutum **Dandy** – Rough-fruit corn bedstraw [Rough-fruited corn bedstraw] (5, 156) (1913–1923)

Galium trifidum L. – Bedstraw [Bed straw] (19) (1840), Lady's bed-straw [Ladies' bedstraw, Lady's bedstraws, Lady's-bedstraw] (187) (1818), Small bedstraw (3, 4, 5, 47, 63, 72, 85, 93, 155) (1852–1986), Small cleavers (5, 49, 92, 95, 131) (1898–1936), Three-petal bedstraw [Threepetal bedstraw] (50) (present), Three-petal goose-grass [Three-petaled goose-grass] (187) (1818), Tisavojaune rouge (French Canadian) (41) (1770)

Galium trifidum **L. subsp.** *trifidum* – Three-petal bedstraw [Threepetal bedstraw] (50) (present)

Galium triflorum **Michx.** – Bedstraw [Bed straw] (19) (1840), Fragrant bedstraw [Fragrant bed-straw] (5, 37, 50, 72, 97, 122, 131, 156, 157, 158) (1899–present), Lady's-bouquet [Lady's bouquet] (37) (1919), Sweet-scented bedstraw [Sweetscented bedstraw] (3, 4, 5, 49, 63, 85, 93, 155, 156, 157, 158) (1898–1986), Three-flower bedstraw [Three-flowered bedstraw] (5, 156) (1913–1923), Trailing cockspur (46) (1783), Wau-inu-makan (Omaha-Ponca, woman's perfume) (37) (1919), Wau-pezhe (Omaha-Ponca, woman's herb) (37) (1919), Woodruff (156) (1923)

Galium uliginoso – See *Galium tinctorium* L.

Galium vaillant **DC.** – See *Galium aparine* L.

Galium vaillantii **DC.** – See *Galium aparine* L.

Galium verum **L.** – Bedflower [Bed-flower] (156, 158) (1900–1923) no longer in use by 1923, Bedstraw [Bed straw] (5, 7) (1828–1913), Brum (158) (1900), Caillelait commune (French) (7) (1828), Caille-lait jaune (French) (158) (1900), Cheese-rennet [Cheese-rennet] (107, 156, 158) (1919–1923), Clabber-grass [Clabbergrass] (7) (1828), Cleaverwort [Cleaver-wort, Cleaver wort] (7) (1828), Common cleavers (7) (1828), Cuajaloche (Spanish) (158) (1900), Curd-wort [Cud-wort] (156, 158) (1900–1923), Fleawort [Fleawort, Flea wort] (156, 158) (1900–1923) no longer in use by 1923, Goose-grass [Goose grass] (7) (1828), Hundred-fold (108) (1878), Keeslip (158) (1900), Labkraut (158) (1900), Lady's bedstraw [Ladies' bedstraw, Lady's bedstraws, Lady's-bedstraw] (5, 92, 156) (1876–1923), La-dy's-cleavers [Ladies' cleavers] (158) (1900), Liebfrauenstroh (German) (158) (1900), Maid's-hair [Maid's hair, Maids' hair] (92, 156, 158) (1898–1923) no longer in use by 1923, Megerkraut (German) (158) (1900), Milksweet [Milk sweet] (7) (1828), Our Lady's bed-straw [Our-Lady's bedstraw] (158) (1900), Poor Robin [Poor-robin] (7) (1828), Runnet (158) (1900), Savoyan (7) (1828) Canada, Yel-low bedstraw (3, 4, 19, 41, 49, 85, 92, 107, 109, 138, 155, 156, 158) (1770–1986), Yellow cleavers (92, 156, 158) (1876–1923), Yel-low lady's-bedstraw [Yellow ladies bedstraw] (178) (1526), Yellow spring bedstraw (50) (present)

Galium virgatum **Nutt.** – Southwest bedstraw (4) (1986), Southwestern bedstraw (5, 50, 97, 122) (1913–present)

Galpinsia **Britton** – See *Calylophus* Spach (all US species)

Galpinsia hartwegii **(Benth.) Britton** – See *Calylophus hartwegii* (Benth.) Raven subsp. *hartwegii*

Galpinsia interior **Small.** – See *Calylophus hartwegii* (Benth.) Raven subsp. *pubescens* (Gray) Towner & Raven

Galpinsia lavendulaefolia **(Torr. & Gray) Small** – See *Calylophus lavandulifolius* (Torr. & Gray) Raven

Gamochaeta purpurea **(L.) Cabrera** – Purple cudweed (3, 4, 122, 155) (1937–1986), Purplish cudweed (5, 97, 156) (1913–1937), Spoon-leaf purple everlasting [Spoonleaf purple everlasting] (50) (present)

Garcinia mangostana **L.** – Mangosteen (109, 110, 138) (1886–1949)

Gardenia cluiaefolia **Jaque** – See *Casasia clusiifolia* (Jacq.) Urban

Gardenia clusiifolia **Jacq.** – See *Casasia clusiifolia* (Jacq.) Urban

Gardenia jasminoides **J. Ellis** – Cape-jasmine [Cape jasmine] (92, 109, 138) (1876–1949), Dwarf cape-jasmine (138) (1923)

Gardenia radicans **Thunb.** – See *Gardenia jasminoides* J.Ellis

Garrya **Dougl. ex Lindl.** – Silk-tassel bush [Silktassel-bush] (138) (1923)

Garrya fremontii **Torr.** – California feverbush [California fever bush] (57) (1917)

Garrya goldmanii **Woot. & Standl.** – See *Garrya ovata* Benth. subsp. *goldmannii* (Woot. & Standl.) Dahling

Garrya lindheimeri **Torr.** – See *Garrya ovata* Benth. subsp. *lindheimeri* (Torr.) Dahling

Garrya ovata **Benth.** – Egg-leaf silktassel [Eggleaf silktassel] (50) (present)

Garrya ovata **Benth. subsp.** *goldmannii* **(Woot. & Standl.) Dahling** – Mexican silk-tassel [Mexican silk tassel] (4) (1986)

Garrya ovata **Benth. subsp.** *lindheimeri* **(Torr.) Dahling** – Silk tassel bush (124) (1937)

Gastridium australe – See *Gastridium phleoides* (Nees & Meyen) C.E. Hubbard

Gastridium lendigerum **(L.) Gaudin** – See *Gastridium phleoides* (Nees & Meyen) C.E. Hubbard

Gastridium phleoides **(Nees & Meyen) C. E. Hubbard** – Nit grass [Nit-grass] (92, 94, 163) (1852–1901)

Gastridium ventricosum **(Gouan) Schinz & Thell.** – See *Gastridium phleoides* (Nees & Meyen) C.E. Hubbard

Gastrolychnis apetala **(L.) Tolm. & Kozhanch.** – See *Silene uralensis* (Rupr.) Bocquet subsp. *uralensis*

Gastrolychnis **Rchb.** – See *Silene* L. (all US species)

Gaultheria hispidula **(L.) Muhl. ex Bigelow** – Cancer wintergreen (92) (1876), Capillaire (73, 156) (1892–1923), Maidenhair [Maiden-hair, Maiden hair] (73) (1892), Moxie (77) (1898), Running tea (77) (1898), Spiceberry [Spice-berry, Spice berry] (77) (1898), Sugarberry [Sugar-berry, Sugar berry] (77) (1898), Teaberry [Tea-berry, Tea berry, Tea-berries] (73, 77) (1892–1898), Creeping snow-berry [Creeping snow-berry] (2, 5, 40, 41, 107, 109, 156) (1770–1949), Creeping wintergreen (19, 92) (1840–1876), Grains de perdix (French, partridge grains) (41) (1770), Ivory plum [Ivory plums] (5, 73, 156) (1892–1923) no longer in use by 1923, Maid-enhair-berry [Maidenhair berry] (5, 156) (1913–1923) no longer in use by 1923, Mountain partridge-berry [Mountain partridge berry] (5, 156) (1913–1923), Moxieberry [Moxie-berry, Moxie berry] (5, 75, 156) (1894–1923), Moxie-plum [Moxie plum] (41, 156) (1770–1923), Running birch (5, 75, 156) (1894–1923), Sugar-plum [Sugar plum, Sugar-plums, Sugar plums] (156) (1923) no longer in use by 1923, Tea bush (41) (1770), Wabos'obûgons' (Chippewa, small rab-bit-leaf) (40) (1928), White cranberry (92, 156) (1876–1923), White pollum (156) (1923), White teaberry (156) (1923), White winter-green [White winter-green] (156) (1923), possibly Airelle de marais (French) (8) (1785), possibly American cranberry (41) (1770), possi-bly Atopa or atocas (French Canadians) (41) (1770), possibly Marsh cranberry (8) (1785), possibly Marsh vaccinium (8) (1785), possibly Sweetberry [Sweet berry, Sweet-berry] (92) (1876), possibly Tran-bär (Swedish) (41) (1770), possibly White pollom (92) (1876)

Gaultheria hispidula **M.** – See *Gaultheria hispidula* (L.) Muhl. ex Bi-gelow

Gaultheria humilis **Salisb.** – See *Gaultheria procumbens* L.

Gaultheria **L.** – Aromatic wintergreen (156) (1923), Capillaire (1) (1932), Creeping snowberry [Creeping snow-berry] (1, 156) (1923–1932), Gaulther (French) (8) (1785), Gaultheria (8) (1785), Gin-gerberry [Ginger berry, Ginger-berry] (167) (1814), Mountain tea [Mountain-tea] (8, 10, 167) (1785–1818), Moxie-plum [Moxie plum] (1) (1932), Partridge-berry [Partridgeberry, Partridge berry] (10) (1818), Wintergreen [Winter greene, Winter-green] (2) (1895)

Gaultheria procumbens **L.** – Bergthee (German) (6) (1892), Berried-tea (186) (1814), Boxberry [Box berry, Box-berry] (2, 5, 6, 7, 14, 49, 53, 79, 92) (1828–1922), Canadian gaultheria (8) (1785), Ca-nadian mountain tea (8) (1785), Canadian tea [Canada tea] (5,

92, 156) (1876–1923), Checker-berry [Checker berry, Checker-berry, Chequer-berry, Chequer berry] (1, 2, 5, 6, 7, 49, 57, 79, 92, 107, 109, 156) (1828–1949), Chickaberry (75) (1894) Stonington CT, Chicken-berry [Chicken berry] (5, 73, 156) (1892–1923) NH, no longer in use by 1923, Chink [Chinks] (5, 73, 92, 156) (1876–1923), Common wintergreen (47) (1852), Creeping wintergreen (1, 2, 5, 6, 156) (1892–1932), Deerberry [Deer-berry, Deer berry] (5, 7, 49, 73, 92, 156, 186) (1814–1892), Dewberry [Dew-berry, Dew berry] (6) (1892), Drunkards (5, 73, 156) (1892–1923) Barnstable MA, young children believed plant caused intoxication, no longer in use by 1923, Eyeberry [Eye-berry] (156) (1923), Gaulther rampant (French) (8) (1785), Gaultheria (52) (1919), Gingerberry [Ginger berry, Ginger-berry] (5, 156) (1913–1923), Greenberry [Green berry] (5) (1913), Groundberry [Ground-berry, Ground berry] (5, 7, 92, 156) (1828–1923), Grouseberry [Grouse-berry, Grouse berry] (5, 6, 7, 92, 156) (1828–1923), Hillberry [Hill-berry, Hill berry] (5, 6, 7, 92, 156) (1828–1923), Ivory plum [Ivory plums] (5, 73, 79, 92, 156) (1876–1923), Ivory-leaves [Ivory leaves] (73) (1892) Ipswich MA, Ivyberry [Ivy berry, Ivy-berry] (5, 73, 156) (1892–1923) NB, Jinks (73, 156) (1892–1923), Kinnikinnick [Kinnikinik, Kinni-kinnick, Kinnikinic, Kinnikinnik] (156) (1923), Little Johnnies (75) (1894) Calais ME, Mountain tea [Mountain-tea] (5, 6, 7, 14, 49, 53, 73, 92, 156, 184, 186, 187) (1793–1882), Niederliegende Gaultheria (German) (186) (1814), Oneberry [One-berry, One berry] (5, 73, 156) (1892–1923), Partridge plant (75) (1894) NH, Partridge-berry [Partridgeberry, Partridge berry] (5, 7, 14, 49, 57, 59, 75, 92, 156, 186, 187) (1814–1923), Pipius (79) (1891) NH, young shoots, Pippins (73, 156) (1892–1923) young shoots, Pollom (186) (1814), Procalm (156) (1923) no longer in use by 1923, Red berry tea [Redberry tea] (92, 156) (1876–1923), Red pollom (5, 92, 156) (1876–1923) no longer in use by 1923, Redberry [Red-berry, Red berry] (6, 7) (1828–1892), Red-berry tea [Red berry tea, Redberry tea] (7, 92, 156) (1828–1923), Spice wintergreen (156) (1923), Spiceberry [Spiceberry, Spice berry] (5, 6, 7, 92, 156) (1828–1923), Spicy wintergreen (5, 19, 92) (1840–1913), Spring wintergreen (5, 156) (1913–1923), Teaberry [Tea-berry, Tea berry, Tea-berries] (5, 6, 7, 49, 53, 92, 107, 156, 186, 187) (1814–1923), Tea-leaves (156) (1923), Thé de montagne (French) (8) (1785), The du Canada (French) (6) (1892), Thebuske (186) (1814), Trailing gaultheria (186) (1814), Wax-cluster [Wax cluster] (92) (1876), Wini'sîbûgons' (Chippewa, dirty leaf) (40) (1928), Winsibog (Chippewa) (105) (1932), Wintergreen [Winter greene, Winter-green] (6, 7, 14, 40, 49, 52, 53, 55, 57, 61, 71, 92, 103, 104, 105, 107, 109, 138, 156, 186, 187) (1814–1949), Young chinks (73) (1892), Young come-ups (75) (1894) Ferrisburgh VT, young shoots, Young ivories (73) (1892) NH, Youngsters (73) (1892) ME, young shoots, Bergbeere (German) (7) (1828), Gaultheria (Official name of Materia Medica) (7) (1828), Gautiere rampante (French) (7) (1828) TX, Ground ivy [Ground-ivy] (7) (1828), Ground-holly [Ground holly] (7) (1828), Moschar (Missouri tribes) (7) (1828) indicates poor soil

Gaultheria shallon **Pursh** – Salad (75) (1894) CA, Salal [Sallal] (33, 106, 107, 138, 160, 161) (1827–1930), Shallon (14, 35) (1806–1882)

Gaultiera repens **Raf.** – See *Gaultheria procumbens* L.

Gaura biennis **L.** – Biennial gaura (5, 72, 82, 93, 97, 156) (1907–1937), Common gaura (156) (1923), Gaura (82, 145) (1897–1930), Virginia loosestrife [Virginian loosestrife] (19) (1840)

Gaura coccinea **Nutt. ex Pursh** – Bee-blossom [Bee blossom] (124) (1937), Butterfly weed [Butter-fly weed, Butterflyweed, Butterfly-weed] (156) (1923), Gaura (127) (1933), Oŋsunkoju spapi (Lakota, possibly meaning dog-catcher) (121) (1918?–1970?), Ragged-lady [Ragged lady] (106) (1930), Red gaura (82, 106) (1930), Scarlet beeblossom (50) (present), Scarlet gaura (3, 4, 5, 72, 85, 93, 97, 121, 131, 155, 156, 157) (1899–1986), Tatawabluška tačaŋxlogaŋ (Lakota, horsefly weed) (121) (1918?–1970?), Waving butterfly (127) (1933) ND, Wild buckwheat (124) (1937) TX, Wild honeysuckle [Wild honey-suckle] (5, 156) (1913–1923)

Gaura coccinea **Pursh** – See *Gaura coccinea* Nutt. ex Pursh

Gaura **L.** – Bee-blossom [Bee blossom] (50) (present), Butterfly weed [Butter-fly weed, Butterflyweed, Butterfly-weed] (1, 4, 93) (1932–1986), Gaura (82, 138, 155) (1930–1942), Virginia loosestrife [Virginian loosestrife] (167) (1814), Wild honeysuckle [Wild honeysuckle] (76, 158) (1896–1900)

Gaura lindheimeri **Engelm. & Gray** – White gaura (138) (1923)

Gaura longiflora **Spach** – Long-flower beeblossom [Longflower beeblossom] (50) (present), Long-flower gaura [Long-flowered gaura] (4) (1986)

Gaura mollis **James** – Small-flower gaura [Small-flowered gaura] (5, 72, 93, 97, 131) (1899–1937), Velvet-leaf gaura [Velvet leaf gaura] (124) (1937), Velvetweed [Velvet weed, Velvet-weed] (50) (present), Velvety gaura (3, 4, 145) (1897–1986)

Gaura neomexicana **Woot.** – New Mexico beeblossom (50) (present)

Gaura neomexicana **Woot. subsp.** *coloradensis* **(Rydb.) Raven & Gregory** – Colorado beeblossom (50) (present)

Gaura parviflora **Dougl.** – See *Gaura mollis* James

Gaura sinuata **Nutt. ex Ser.** – Sinuate-leaf gaura [Sinuate-leaved gaura] (4) (1986), Wavy-leaf beeblossom [Wavyleaf beeblossom] (50) (present), Wavy-leaf gaura [Wavy-leaved gaura] (5, 97) (1913–1937), Wild honeysuckle [Wild honey-suckle] (5) (1913)

Gaura suffulta **Engelm. ex Gray** – Gaura (4) (1986), Kisses (50) (present), Woody gayra (124) (1937) TX

Gaura triangulata **Buckl.** – Prairie beeblossom (50) (present)

Gaura villosa **Torr.** – Hairy gaura (3, 4) (1977–1986), Wild honey-suckle [Wild honey-suckle] (5) (1913), Woolly beeblossom (50) (present), Woolly gaura [Wooly guara] (5, 97) (1913–1937)

Gaurella **Small.** – See *Oenothera* L. (all US species)

Gautiera repens **Kalm.** – See *Gaultheria procumbens* L.

Gaylussacia baccata **(Wang.) K. Koch** – Attitaash (Narrangansett) (46) (1879), Black huckleberry (2, 5, 47, 49, 63, 72, 82, 106, 107, 109, 138, 156) (1852–1949), Black whortleberry [Black whortleberry] (19, 49) (1840–1898), Blacksnap [Black snap, Black snaps] (5, 75, 156) (1894–1923), Clammy whortle-berry (42) (1814), Common huckleberry (2) (1895), Crackers (5, 156) (1913–1923), Highbush huckleberry (5, 156) (1913–1923), Highland huckleberry (72) (1907), Huckleberry (2, 46, 58, 92) (1869–1895), Hurtleberry [Hurtleberye] (46) (1879), Sautaash (46) (1879), Whinberry [Whin berry] (92) (1876), Whortleberry [Whortle-berry] (46) (1879)

Gaylussacia baccata **K. Koch** – See *Gaylussacia baccata* (Wang.) K. Koch

Gaylussacia brachycera **(Michx.) Gray** – Box huckleberry (5, 138, 156) (1913–1923), Juniper-berry [Juniper berries] (156) (1923)

Gaylussacia dumosa **(Andr.) Torr. & Gray** – Bush huckleberry (5, 156) (1913–1923), Bush whorleberry (19, 92, 187) (1818–1876), Dwarf huckleberry (2, 5, 156) (1895–1923), Gopherberry [Gopherberry, Gopher berry] (5, 156) (1913–1923), Hairy huckleberry (46) (1879), Small bush whortleberry (43) (1820), Swamp whortle-berry (5, 156) (1913–1923), possibly Bush whoitle-berry [Bush-whoitleberry] (177) (1762)

Gaylussacia dumosa **Torr. & Gray.** – See *Gaylussacia dumosa* (Andr.) Torr. & Gray

Gaylussacia frondosa **(L.) Torr. & Gray** – Airelle à fleurs accompagnées de feuilles (French) (8) (1785), Blue dangleberry (49) (1898), Blue huckleberry (46, 49, 156) (1879–1923), Blue whortleberry (5, 19, 49, 92) (1840–1913), Blueberry [Blueberries, Blue berries, Blue berry] (92, 187) (1818–1876), Bluetangle [Blue-tangle, Blue tangle, Blue tangles, Blue-tangles] (2, 5, 92, 107, 156, 187) (1818–1923), Bluets [Bluet] (92) (1876), Dangleberry [Dangle-berry] (2, 5, 46, 107, 138, 156) (1879–1932), Dwarf huckleberry (107) (1919), High blueberry [High blue-berry] (49, 156) (1898–1923), Huckleberry (5) (1913), Indian gooseberry (8) (1785), Leafy vaccinium (8) (1785), Low whortle-berry (43) (1820), Tangleberry [Tangle-berry] (5, 156) (1913–1923)

Gaylussacia frondosa **Torr. & Gray.** – See *Gaylussacia frondosa* (L.) Torr. & Gray

Gaylussacia **H.B.K.** – See *Gaylussacia* Kunth

Gaylussacia **Kunth** – Black hurts (73) (1892) Newfoundland, short for whortleberries, Huckleberry (1, 2, 106, 109, 138, 156) (1895–1949)

Gaylussacia resinosa **(Aiton) Torr. & Gray** – See *Gaylussacia baccata* (Wang.) K. Koch

Gaylussacia resinosa **Torr. & Gray.** – See *Gaylussacia baccata* (Wang.) K. Koch

Gaylussacia ursina **(M. A. Curtis) Torr. & Gray ex Gray** – Bear huckleberry [Bear-huckleberry] (77, 156) (1898–1923) Mountains of New England, Buckberry [Buck-berry] (138) (1923)

Gaylussacia ursina **Torr. & Gray** – See *Gaylussacia ursina* (M.A. Curtis) Torr. & Gray ex Gray

Gayophytum diffusum **Torr. & Gray subsp.** *parviflorum* **Lewis & Szweykowski** – Baby's-breath [Babies' breath, Baby's breath, Babies'-breath, Babysbreath] (3) (1977), Spreading groundsmoke (50) (present)

Gayophytum **Juss.** – Baby's-breath [Babies' breath, Baby's breath, Babies'-breath, Babysbreath] (1) (1932), Gayophytum (158) (1900), Groundsmoke (50, 155) (1942–present)

Gayophytum ramosissimum **Torr. & Gray** – Baby's-breath [Babies' breath, Baby's breath, Babies'-breath, Babysbreath] (85) (1932), Bushy gayophyton (131) (1899)

Gazania **Gaertn.** – Gazania (138) (1923) for Theodore of Gaza, 1398–1478, translator of Aristotle and Theophrastus

Geastrum archeri **Berk.** – Archer's earthstar (128) (1933) ND

Geastrum **Pers.** – Groundstar [Ground star] (7) (1828)

Geastrum triplex **Jungh.** – Collar earthstar (128) (1933) ND

Gelidium corneum **(Hudson) J. V. Lamouroux** – Kanteen (107) (1919)

Gelidium corneum **Lam.** – See *Gelidium corneum* (Hudson) J. V. Lamouroux

Gelsemium **Juss.** – Yellow jessamine (2, 156) (1895–1923)

Gelsemium lucidum **Poir.** – See *Gelsemium sempervirens* (L.) J. St.-Hil.

Gelsemium nitidum **L.** – See *Gelsemium sempervirens* (L.) J. St.-Hil.

Gelsemium nitidum **Michx.** – See *Gelsemium sempervirens* (L.) J. St.-Hil.

Gelsemium sempervirens **(L.) Aiton f.** – See *Gelsemium sempervirens* (L.) J. St.-Hil.

Gelsemium sempervirens **(L.) J. St.-Hil.** – Bignone toujours verte (French) (8) (1785), Cancer-root [Cancer root] (1) (1932), Carolina jasmine [Carolina jasmin] (49, 53, 64, 86, 156) (1878–1923), Carolina jessamine [Carolina-jessamine] (5, 10, 49, 59, 64, 92, 138) (1876–1923), Carolina wild woodbine (5, 64, 156) (1907–1923), Carolina yellow jessamine (109) (1949), Evening trumpet-flower [Evening trumpet flower] (5, 64, 156) (1907–1923), Evergreen bignonia [Ever-green bignonia] (8) (1785), False jasmine (6) (1892), Gelber Jasmin (German) (6) (1892), Gelsemium (54, 57, 60, 64) (1902–1917), Jasmin Jaune (French) (6) (1892), Jessamine (7, 59) (1828–1911), White jessamine (59) (1911), White poison vine (59) (1911), Wild jessamine (6, 92, 156) (1876–1923), Wild woodbine (49, 59) (1898–1911), Woodbine (6, 7, 92) (1828–1892), Yellow false jessamine (156) (1923), Yellow jasmine (6, 8, 49, 52, 53, 54, 57, 60, 106, 122, 124, 182) (1785–1937), Yellow jessamine (5, 6, 49, 53, 59, 61, 86, 92, 106, 182, 189) (1767–1930), Yellow yessamy (177) (1762)

Gelsemium sempervirens **Aiton** – See *Gelsemium sempervirens* (L.) J. St.-Hil.

Gelsemium sempervirens **Aiton f.** – See *Gelsemium sempervirens* (L.) J. St.-Hil.

Gelsemium sempervirens **J.** – See *Gelsemium sempervirens* (L.) J. St.-Hil.

Gemmingia chinensis **(L.) Kuntze** – See *Belamcanda chinensis* (L.) DC.

Gemmingia **Fabr.** – See *Belamcanda* Adans

Genista aetnensis **(Biv.) DC.** – Aetna broom (138) (1923)

Genista canariensis **L.** – Canary broom (138) (1923), Easter broom (138) (1923)

Genista **L.** – Broom (138) (1923), Woad-waxen [Woadwaxen, Woad waxen] (156) (1923)

Genista monosperma **(L.) Lam.** – See *Retama monosperma* (L.) Boiss.

Genista scoparia **Lam.** – possibly *Cytisus scoparius* (L.) Link (taxonomic status is unresolved (PL))

Genista stenopetala **Webb & Berth.** – Madeira broom (138) (1923)

Genista tinctoria **L.** – Alleluia (5) (1913), Base broom (5, 156) (1913–1923), Dyer's broom [Dyers' broom, Dyers-broom] (5, 6, 7, 19, 49, 92, 107, 156) (1828–1923), Dyer's greenweed [Dyer's green weed] (5, 6, 49, 92, 109) (1876–1949), Dyer's weed [Dyers' weed, Dyer's-weed] (49, 92, 156) (1876–1923), Dyer's whin (5) (1913), Dye-weed [Dye-weed] (5, 156) (1913–1923), Farbeginster (German) (6) (1892), Furze (92) (1876), Genet des Teintuiers (French) (6) (1892), Green broom (92) (1876), Greenweed [Green weed, Green-weed] (6, 49, 92, 156) (1876–1923), Greenwood [Green wood, Green-wood] (5, 6, 7, 92, 156) (1828–1923) IA, Whin (6, 92, 156) (1876–1923), Woad-wax (156) (1923), Woad-waxen [Woadwaxen, Woad waxen] (5, 6, 138, 156) (1892–1923), Wood-wash (156) (1923), Woodwax [Wood wax] (5, 73) (1892–1913), Woodwaxen [Wood waxen] (6, 7, 19, 49, 92, 107) (1828–1919)

Gentiana acuta **Michx.** – See *Gentianella amarella* (L.) Boerner subsp. *acuta* (Michx.) J. Gillett

Gentiana affinis **Griesb.** – Bigelow's gentian [Bigelow gentian] (155) (1942), Gentian (85) (1932), Northern gentian (3, 4) (1977–1986), Oblong-leaf gentian [Oblong-leaved gentian] (5) (1913), Oregon gentian (155) (1942), Pleated gentian (50) (present), Rocky Mountain pleated gentian [RockyMountain pleated gentian] (155) (1942)

Gentiana alba **Muhl. ex Nutt.** – Plain gentian (50) (present), Sampson root (92) (1876), Sampson snakeroot [Sampson snake root] (49, 92) (1898), White gentian (48) (1882), Yellow gentian (156) (1923), Yellowish gentian (5, 72, 156) (1907–1923)

Gentiana amarella **(p.p. non L.)** – See *Gentianella amarella* (L.) Boerner subsp. *acuta* (Michx.) J. Gillett

Gentiana amarella **auct. p.p. non L.** – See *Gentianella amarella* (L.) Boerner subsp. *acuta* (Michx.) J. Gillett

Gentiana amarella **L. var.** *acuta* – See *Gentianella amarella* (L.) Boerner subsp. *acuta* (Michx.) J. Gillett

Gentiana andrewsii **Griseb.** – Andrew's gentian [Andrews gentian] (155) (1942), Barrel gentian (5, 75, 156, 157) (1894–1929) MA, Belmony (79) (1891) NH, Blind gentian (5, 73, 75, 156, 157) (1892–1929) Northeast US, Blue gentian [Blue-gentian] (85, 156) (1923–1932), Bottle gentian (4, 5, 75, 93, 156, 157) (1894–1986), Cloistered-heart [Cloistered heart] (5, 156, 157) (1913–1929), Closed blue gentian (5) (1913), Closed bottle gentian (50) (present), Closed gentian (3, 63, 72, 86, 93, 109, 127, 131, 138, 156, 157) (1878–1977), Dumb foxglove (156) (1923), Sampson's snakeroot (156) (1923)

Gentiana andrewsii **Griseb. var.** *dakotica* **A. Nels.** – Dakota gentian (50) (present)

Gentiana autumnalis **L.** – Autumnal peranual gentian (183) (~1756), One-flower gentian [One-flowered gentian] (5) (1913)

Gentiana axillaris **Raf.** – See *Enicostema verticillatum* (L.) Engl. ex Gilg

Gentiana bigelovii **Gray** – See *Gentiana affinis* Griesb.

Gentiana catesbaei **Walt.** – American gentian (92) (1876), Bitter-root [Bitter root, Bitterroot] (7) (1828), Blue gentian (7, 92) (1828–1876), Bluebell [Blue-bell, Blue bell, Blue bells, Blue-bells] (7, 92) (1828–1876), Catesby's gentian [Catesbian gentian] (7) (1828), Elliot's gentian (5) (1913), Fluxroot [Flux-root, Flux root] (92) (1876), Gentiane de Catesby (French) (7) (1828), Katesbys Enzian (German) (7) (1828), Rough gentian (92) (1876), Simpson's root [Simpson root] (7) (1828), Snakeroot [Snake root, Snake-root] (7) (1828), Southern gentian (7, 92) (1828–1876)

Gentiana catesbei **Walt. & Ell.** – See *Gentiana catesbaei* Walt.

Gentiana centaurium **L.** – See *Centaurium erythraea* Raf.

Gentiana clausa **Raf.** – Closed gentian (7) (1828)

Gentiana collinsiana **Raf.** – See *Gentiana saponaria* L.

Gentiana crinita Froel. – See *Gentianopsis crinita* (Froel) Ma.

Gentiana cruciata L. – Cross gentian (138) (1923), Crosswort gentian [Crossewoort gentian, Crosse woort gentian] (178, 180) (1526–1633)

Gentiana detonsa Rottb. – See *Gentianopsis detonsa* (Rottb.) Ma subsp. *detonsa*

Gentiana elliottea Raf. – See *Gentiana saponaria* L.

Gentiana flavida Gray – See *Gentiana alba* Muhl. ex Nutt.

Gentiana heterophylla Raf. – See *Gentiana villosa* L.

Gentiana L. – Gentian (1, 93) (1932–1936)

Gentiana linearis Froel. – Autumn bell-flower (46) (1671), Linear gentian (7) (1828), Narrow-leaf gentian [Narrow-leaved gentian] (5) (1913)

Gentiana linerais Willd. – See *Gentiana linearis* Froel.

Gentiana ochroleuca Froel. – See *Gentiana villosa* L.

Gentiana ochroleuca var. *heterophylla* (Raf.) Griseb. In A. DC. – See *Gentiana villosa* L.

Gentiana ochroleuca Willd. – possibly *Gentiana villosa* L.

Gentiana oregana Engelm. ex Gray – See *Gentiana affinis* Griesb.

Gentiana plebeja Ledeb. ex Spreng. – See *Gentianella amarella* (L.) Boerner subsp. *acuta* (Michx.) J. Gillett

Gentiana procera Holm. – See *Gentianopsis virgata* (Raf.) Holub

Gentiana propinqua Richards. – See *Gentianella propinqua* (Richards.) J. Gillett subsp. *propinqua*

Gentiana puberula Michx. – See *Gentiana puberulenta* J. Pringle

Gentiana puberulenta J. Pringle – Downy gentian (4, 5, 50, 85, 93, 131, 138, 155, 157) (1899–present), Gentian (37) (1919), Makan chahiwi-cho (Winnebago, blue medicine) (37) (1919), Pezhuta-zi (Dakota, yellow medicine) (37) (1919), Prairie gentian [Prairie gentian] (4, 72) (1907–1986)

Gentiana quinquefolia L. – See *Gentianella quinquefolia* (L.) Small subsp. *quinquefolia*

Gentiana quinquefolia Lam. – possibly *Gentianella quinquefolia* (L.) Small subsp. *quinquefolia*

Gentiana rigida Raf. – See *Gentiana saponaria* L.

Gentiana rubricaulis Schwein. – Gray's gentian (5) (1913), Red-stem gentian [Red-stemmed gentian] (72) (1907)

Gentiana saponaria L. – Blue gentian (156) (1923), Calathian violet (156) (1923), Collinsian gentian (7) (1828), Elliottian gentian (7) (1828), Harvestbells [Harvest bells] (156) (1923), Marsh gentian (156) (1923), Rough gentian (156) (1923), Samson's snakeroot [Sampson snakeroot, Samson snake-root] (156) (1923), Shortian's gentian [Shortian gentian] (7) (1828), Soap gentian (7, 19) (1828–1840), Soapwort gentian [Soapwort-gentian] (2, 48, 92, 156, 187) (1818–1923), Stiff gentian (7) (1828), Swamp gentian (122, 124) (1937) TX, Torreyan gentian (7) (1828)

Gentiana saponaria L. var. *saponaria* – Blue gentian [Blue-gentian] (5) (1913), Calathian violet (5) (1913), Harvestbells [Harvest bells] (5) (1913), Marsh gentian (5) (1913), Rough gentian (5) (1913), Samson's snakeroot [Sampson snakeroot, Samson snake-root] (5) (1913), Soapwort [Soap-wort, Sope woort, Sope-wort] (5) (1913)

Gentiana serpentaria Raf. – See *Gentiana villosa* L.

Gentiana shortiana Raf. – See *Gentiana saponaria* L.

Gentiana torreyana Raf. – See *Gentiana saponaria* L.

Gentiana ventricosa Griseb. – See *Gentianopsis crinita* (Froel) Ma.

Gentiana villosa L. – Fluxroot [Flux-root, Flux root] (7) (1828), Gray gentian [Grey gentian] (7) (1828), Marsh gentian (5, 156) (1913–1923), Samson's snakeroot [Sampson snakeroot, Samson snake-root] (5, 156) (1913–1923), Snakeroot gentian [Snake root gentian] (7) (1828), Straw-color gentian [Straw colored gentian, Straw-colored gentian] (5, 49, 92, 156) (1876–1923), Striped gentian (5, 156) (1913–1923), Yellowish-white gentian [Yellowish white gentian] (49, 92) (1876–1898), possibly Marsh gentian (19, 49, 92) (1840–1898), possibly Pale gentian (7) (1828), possibly Snakeroot [Snake root, Snake-root] (14) (1882)

Gentianella amarella (L.) Boerner subsp. *acuta* (Michx.) J. Gillett – Annual gentian (155) (1942), Autumn dwarf gentian (50) (present), Autumnal gentian (92) (1876), Baldmoney [Bald-money] (5, 156)

(1913–1923), Bastard gentian (5, 92) (1876–1913), False gentian (156) (1923), Felwort [Fellwort] (5, 156) (1913–1923), New World annual gentian [NewWorld annual gentian] (50) (present), Northern gentian (5, 131, 155, 156) (1899–1942)

Gentianella Moench – Baldmony (179) (1526), Felwort [Fellwort] (179) (1526)

Gentianella propinqua (Richards.) J. Gillett subsp. *propinqua* – Four-part gentian [Four-parted gentian] (5) (1913)

Gentianella quinquefolia (L.) Small subsp. *quinquefolia* – Agueweed [Ague weed, Ague-weed] (5, 156) (1913–1923), Five-flower gentian [Five-flowered gentian] (5, 7, 49, 156) (1828–1923), Gall flower [Gall-flower] (156) (1923), Gall-of-the-earth [Gall of the earth] (5, 156) (1913–1923), Gallweed [Gall-weed] (5, 49, 92, 156) (1876–1923), Narrow-leaf gentian [Narrow leaved gentian] (7) (1828), Stiff gentian (5, 72, 156) (1907–1923), Yellow bunch gentian (7) (1828)

Gentianopsis crinita (Froel) Ma. – Blue fringed gentian (92, 156) (1876–1923), Fringed gentian (1, 2, 5, 7, 19, 47, 63, 72, 85, 109, 138, 155, 156) (1828–1949), Greater fringed gentian (50) (present), Swollen gentian (5) (1913)

Gentianopsis detonsa (Rottb.) Ma subsp. *detonsa* – Fringed gentian (1, 2, 5, 7, 19, 47, 63, 72, 85, 109, 133, 138, 155, 156) (1899–1949), Smalled fringed gentian (72) (1907)

Gentianopsis Ma. – Fringed gentian (4) (1986)

Gentianopsis virgata (Raf.) Holub – Amber tree (92) (1876), Lesser fringed gentian (50) (present), Smaller fringed gentian (5) (1913)

Geocaulon lividum (Richardson) Fernald – Northern comandra (5) (1913)

Geoffrea inermis W. Wright – See *Andira inermis* (W. Wright) Kunth ex DC.

Geoprumnon crassicarpum (Nutt.) Rydb. – See *Astragalus crassicarpus* Nutt. var. *crassicarpus*

Geoprumnon mexicanum (A. DC.) Rydb. – See *Astragalus crassicarpus* Nutt. var. *berlandieri* Barneby

Geoprumnon plattense (Nutt.) Rydb. – See *Astragalus plattensis* Nutt.

Geoprumnon Rydb. – See *Astragalus* L. (all US species)

Geoprumnon tennesseense (Gray) Rydb. – See *Astragalus tennesseensis* Gray ex Chapman

Geranium (Tourn.) L. – See *Geranium* L.

Geranium bicknellii Britton – Bicknell's cranesbill (50) (present), Bicknell's gentian [Bicknell gentian] (155) (1942), Slender crane's-bill [Slender cranesbill, Slender cranebill] (85) (1932)

Geranium caespitosum James var. *fremontii* (Torr. ex Gray) Dorn – Rocky Mountain cranebill [Rocky Mountain cranesbill] (138) (1923)

Geranium carolinianum L. – Carolina cranebill [Carolina cranesbill, Carolina crane-bill, Carolina crane's bill, Carolina crane's-bill] (3, 4, 5, 72, 85, 97, 131, 157) (1899–1986), Carolina geranium (50, 155, 157) (1900–present), Dove's-foot [Dove's foot, Doues foote, Doues fote, Dovefoot, Dove-foot] (35, 46) (1671–1806), White-flower cranesbill [White-flowered crane's-bill] (187) (1818), Wild geranium (145) (1897)

Geranium columbinum L. – Long-stalk crane's-bill [Long-stalked crane's-bill, Long-stalked crane's bill] (5, 131, 156) (1899–1923), Long-stalk geranium [Long stalked geranium] (19) (1840)

Geranium dissectum L. – Australian geranium (107) (1919), Cut-leaf cranebill [Cut-leaved crane's bill] (5, 131) (1899–1913), Native carrot (107) (1919), Wood geranium (5, 19, 92) (1840–1913)

Geranium fremonti – See *Geranium caespitosum* James var. *fremontii* (Torr. ex Gray) Dorn

Geranium ibericum Cav. – Iberian cranesbill (138) (1923)

Geranium incisum Nutt. – See *Geranium oreganum* Howell

Geranium L. – Cranebill [Cranesbill, Cranesbill, Crane's-bill, Crane's bill] (1, 2, 4, 13, 15, 82, 93, 106, 109, 138, 156, 158, 184) (~1759–1986), Dove's-foot [Dove's foot, Doues foote, Doues fote, Dove-foot, Dove-foot] (179) (1526), Wild cranebill [Wild cranesbill, Wild cranesbill, Wild crane's bill, Wild crane's-bill] (92) (1876), Wild geranium (1, 93, 106) (1930–1936)

Geranium lucidum L. – Shining geranium (50) (present)

Geranium maculatum L. – Aguja (Portuguese) (186) (1814), Agulha (186) (1814), Alumbloom [Alum-bloom, Alum bloom] (5, 64, 76, 156, 157, 158) (1896–1929), Alumroot [Alum-root, Alum root] (5, 6, 7, 49, 52, 55, 64, 76, 92, 156, 157, 158, 186) (1814–1929), American kino root (5, 92, 156) (1876–1923), American tomentil (92) (1876), Anda'nkalagi'skĭ (Cherokee, it removes things from the gums) (102) (1886), Astringent root (92, 156) (1876–1923), Bec de Grue (French) (6, 186) (1814–1892), Becco di gru (Italian) (186) (1814), Bec-de-grue tacheté (French) (158) (1900), Be'cigodji'bigûk (Chippewa, one root) (40) (1928), Bico de cegonha (Portuguese) (186) (1814), Bico de grou (Portuguese) (186) (1814), Capjnusek (Bohemian) (186) (1814), Chocolate flower [Chocolate-flower] (5, 64, 73, 156, 157, 158) (1892–1929) Stratham NH, Common crane's-bill (186, 187) (1814–1818), Cranebill [Cranesbill, Cranesbill, Crane's-bill, Crane's bill] (19, 46, 49, 52, 53, 54, 55, 57, 59, 61, 64, 92, 102, 156, 157, 158, 186) (1649–1929), Crowfoot [Crow-foot, Crow foot, Crowfote, Crow's foot] (5, 6, 7, 52, 53, 64, 76, 92, 156, 158, 186) (1814–1923) from shape of root, Crowfoot geranium (19) (1840), Darru oru fu (Hungarian) (186) (1814), Dove's-foot [Dove's foot, Doues foote, Doues fote, Dovefoot, Dove-foot] (64, 157, 158) (1900–1907), Fleckstorchschnabel (German) (158) (1900), Geflleckter Storchsnabel (German) (6, 7, 186) (1814–1932), Geraine (French) (186) (1814), Geranio (Spanish, Portuguese) (158, 186) (1814–1900), Geranion (186) (1814), Geranium (52, 54, 57, 59, 114) (1894–1917), Geranium maculé (French) (7, 158) (1828–1900), Geranium radix (7) (1828), Hierba de pico (186) (1814), Jerenio (Spanish) (186) (1814), Kapu nos (Bohemian) (186) (1814), Karvamozenzel (Ukranian) (186) (1814), Kino Americanus (Official name of Materia Medica) (7) (1828), Kraanhals (Dutch) (186) (1814), Oijevaarsbek (Dutch) (186) (1814), Old-maid's-nightcap [Old maid's night-caps, Old-maid's night-cap, Old-maid's-night-cap, Old maid's nightcap] (64, 76, 156, 157, 158) (1896–1929) Madison WI, Ou de cicogne (French) (186) (1814), Pamplilla (186) (1814), Pesigunk (Chippewa, bitter) (105) (1932), Pico de ciguenä (Spanish) (186) (1814), Pico de grulla (Spanish) (186) (1814), Pied-de-corneille (French) (158) (1900), Pychaweic (Polish) (186) (1814), Racine a becquet (Canada, Louisiana) (7, 186) (1814–1828), Raven's-claw [Raven's claw] (46) (1671), Rockweed [Rockweed, Rockweed] (5, 156) (1913–1923), Sailor's-knot [Sailor's knot] (5, 156, 186) (1814–1923) no longer in use by 1923, Schnabel kraut (German) (186) (1814), Schuratelinei nos (Russian) (186) (1814), Shame-face [Shameface] (5, 64, 156, 157, 158) (1900–1929), Spotted cranebill [Spotted crane's bill, Spotted cranesbill, Spotted crane's-bill] (5, 6, 7, 64, 86, 92, 156, 157, 158) (1828–1929), Spotted geranium (6, 49, 50, 53, 64, 74, 92, 155, 156, 158) (1892–present), Spotted-leaf cranebill [Spotted-leaved crane's bill] (86) (1878), Storchschnabel (German) (186) (1814), Storkenaab (Danish) (186) (1814), Storknäf (Swedish) (186) (1814), Stork's-bill [Storks' bill, Storksbill, Stork's bill, Storks bill] (6, 7, 64, 157, 158) (1828–1932), Tormentil (6, 92) (1876–1892), Wild alum (102) (1886), Wild cranebill [Wild cranesbill, Wild cranesbill, Wild crane's bill, Wild crane's-bill] (3, 4, 5, 6, 49, 53, 64, 72, 97, 157, 158) (1892–1986), Wild geranium (6, 40, 44, 64, 82, 105, 138, 156, 157, 158, 187) (1818–1932), Zorawei nozki (186) (1814)

Geranium molle L. – Cranebill [Cranesbill, Cranesbill, Crane's-bill, Crane's bill] (5) (1913), Culverfoot [Culver-foot] (5, 156) (1913–1923), Dove-foot crane's-bill [Dove's foot crane's bill, Dove's-foot crane's-bill] (72, 156) (1907–1923) obsolete by 1923, Dove's-foot [Dove's foot, Doues foote, Doues fote, Dovefoot, Dove-foot] (5, 178) (1526–1913), Pigeon-foot [Pigeon foot, Pigeon's foot] (5, 156) (1913–1923), Starlights [Starlight] (5, 156) (1913–1923)

Geranium oreganum Howell – Cranebill [Cranesbill, Cranesbill, Crane's-bill, Crane's bill] (76) (1896), Wild red geranium (101) (1905)

Geranium ornatum A. Nelson – See *Geranium oreganum* Howell

Geranium pratense L. – Meadow cranesbill (138) (1923), Meadow geranium (5) (1913), Small crane's-bill [Small cranesbill] (3, 4, 19, 92) (1840–1986), Small geranium (50, 155) (1942–present), Smallest-flower crane's-bill [Smallest-flowered crane's-bill] (187) (1818), Small-flower crane's-bill [Small-flowered crane's bill, Small-flower cranebill] (5, 85) (1913–1932), Small-leaf crane's-bill [Small-leaved cranebill, Small-leaved crane's bill] (72) (1907)

Geranium pusillum – See *Geranium pratense* L.

Geranium richardsonii Fisch. & Trautv. – Richardson's cranebill [Richardson's cranesbill, Richardson's cranes bill] (4, 131) (1899–1986), Richardson's geranium [Richardson geranium] (50, 155) (1942–present)

Geranium robertianum L. – Bockstorchschnabel (German) (158) (1900), Cranebill [Cranesbill, Cranesbill, Crane's-bill, Crane's bill] (41) (1770), Death-come-quickly (156, 157, 158) (1900–1929), Dragon's-blood [Dragon's blood] (5, 156, 158) (1900–1923), Fox geranium (5, 156, 157, 158) (1900–1929), Herb Robert [Herb-Robert, Herbe Robert] (2, 4, 7, 15, 19, 46, 92, 109, 138, 156, 157, 158, 178) (1526–1986) deliberately introduced by colonists by 1671, Herbe à Robert (French) (158) (1900), Herb-robert geranium [Herbrobert geranium] (155) (1942), Jenny-wren [Jenny wren] (5, 156, 157, 158) (1900–1929), Mountain geranium (5, 76, 156, 157, 158) (1896–1929), Red bird's-eye [Red-bird's-eye] (156, 157, 158) (1900–1929), Red Robin [Red-Robin] (5, 109, 156, 157) (1900–1949), Red-bird (157, 158) (1900–1929), Red-Robin (158) (1900), Redshank [Red shank, Red-shank, Red shanks, Redshanks, Red-shanks] (5, 92, 156, 157, 158) (1898–1929), Robert's geranium [Robert geranium] (50) (present), Rockweed [Rockweed, Rockweed] (7, 92, 157, 158) (1828–1929), Ruprechtskraut (German) (158) (1900), Sailor's-knot [Sailor's knot] (157, 158) (1900–1929), Stinking cranebill [Stinking cranesbill] (157, 158) (1900–1929), Wild geranium (5, 74, 156) (1893–1923), Wren's-flower [Wren's flower] (5, 156, 157, 158) (1900–1929)

Geranium rotundifolium L. – Round-leaf cranebill [Round-leaved crane's bill] (5, 72) (1907–1913), Round-leaf geranium [Roundleaf geranium] (50) (present)

Geranium sanguineum L. – Blood geranium (92) (1876), Blood-red cranesbill [Bloodred cranesbill] (138) (1923), Bloody geranium (19) (1840), Stork's-bill [Storks' bill, Storksbill, Stork's bill, Storks bill] (178) (1526)

Geranium sibiricum L. – Siberian crane's-bill [Siberian crane's bill] (5) (1913)

Geranium sylvaticum L. – Dove's-foot [Dove's foot, Doues foote, Doues fote, Dovefoot, Dove-foot] (92) (1876), Crowfoot cranebill [Crowefoote Cranes bill] (178) (1526), Stork's-bill with white flowers [Storks bill with white flowers] (178) (1526)

Geranium texanum (Trel.) Heller – Geranium (122) (1937)

Geranium viscosissimum Fisch. & C. A. Mey. ex C. A. Mey. – Sticky geranium (155) (1942), Sticky purple geranium (50) (present), Viscid cranebill [Viscid cranesbill, Viscid crane's bill] (4, 131) (1899–1986)

Gerardia – See *Agalinis* Raf.

Gerardia aspera Dougl. – See *Agalinis aspera* (Dougl. ex Benth.) Britton

Gerardia aspera Dougl. ex Benth. – See *Agalinis aspera* (Dougl. ex Benth.) Britton

Gerardia auriculata Michx. – See *Agalinis auriculata* (Michx.) Blake

Gerardia flava L. – See *Aureolaria flava* (L.) Farw. var. *flava*

Gerardia gattingeri Small – See *Agalinis gattingeri* (Small) Small

Gerardia glauca Eddy – See *Aureolaria virginica* (L.) Pennell

Gerardia grandiflora Benth. – See *Aureolaria grandiflora* (Benth.) Pennell var. *grandiflora*

Gerardia heterophylla Nutt. – See *Agalinis heterophylla* (Nutt.) Small ex Britton

Gerardia laevigata Raf. – See *Aureolaria laevigata* (Raf.) Raf.

Gerardia linifolia Nutt. – See *Agalinis linifolia* (Nutt.) Britt.

Gerardia maritima Raf. – See *Agalinis maritima* (Raf.) Raf. var. *maritima*

191

Gerardia maritima **Raf. var. *grandiflora* Benth.** – See *Agalinis maritima* (Raf.) Raf. var. *grandiflora* (Benth.) Shinners

Gerardia paupercula **(Gray) Britton** – See *Agalinis paupercula* (Gray) Britton var. *paupercula*

Gerardia pedicularia **L.** – See *Aureolaria pedicularia* (L.) Raf. ex Farw.

Gerardia purpurea **L.** – See *Agalinis purpurea* (L.) Pennell

Gerardia quercifolia **Pursh** – See *Aureolaria virginica* (L.) Pennell

Gerardia skinneriana **Wood** – See *Agalinis skinneriana* (Wood) Britton

Gerardia strictiflora **Benth.** – See *Agalinis strictifolia* (Benth.) Pennell

Gerardia tenuifolia **Vahl.** – See *Agalinis tenuifolia* (Vahl) Raf.

Gerardia virginica **[(L.) B.S.P.]** – See *Aureolaria virginica* (L.) Pennell

Gerbera **Cass.** – See *Gerbera* Gmel.

Gerbera **Gmel.** – Gerbera (138) (1923)

Gerbera jamesonii **Bolus** – See *Gerbera jamesonii* Bolus ex Hooker f.

Gerbera jamesonii **Bolus ex Hooker f.** – Barberton daisy (109) (1949), Flame-ray gerbera (138) (1923), Transvaal daisy (109) (1949)

Gesneria **L.** – Gesneria (138) (1923)

Geum aleppicum **Jacq.** – Avens (40) (1928), Blackbur [Black bur, Black-bur] (5, 156, 158) (1900–1923), Camp root (5) (1913), Cramp-root (156) (1923), Field avens (2) (1895), Herb Bennet [Herb Bennett] (5, 19, 156) (1840–1923), Redroot [Red-root, Red root] (5, 156) (1913–1923), Upright avens (19) (1840), White bennet (187) (1818), Yellow avens (3, 4, 5, 50, 72, 85, 93, 131, 155, 156, 158) (1899–present), Yellow bennet (156, 158) (1900–1923)

Geum aleppicum **Jacq. var. *strictum* (Aiton) Fern.** – See *Geum aleppicum* Jacq.

Geum canadense **Jacq.** – American white avens (156, 158) (1900–1923), Chocolate root [Chocolate-root] (156) (1923), Herb Bennet [Herb Bennett] (5, 156) (1913–1923), Stickweed [Stick-weed, Stick weed] (80) (1913) WV, Throatroot [Throat root, Throat-root] (156) (1923)

Geum ciliatum **Pursh** – See *Geum triflorum* Pursh var. *ciliatum* (Pursh) Fassett

Geum flavum **(Porter) Bicknell** – See *Geum virginianum* L.

Geum **L.** – Avens (1, 2, 4, 10, 50, 92, 93, 109, 138, 155, 156, 158, 167) (1814–present), Bennet (184) (1793), Old-man's-whiskers [Old man's whiskers] (1) (1932), Sieversia (155) (1942)

Geum laciniatum **Murray** – Rough avens (4, 50) (1986–present)

Geum laciniatum **Murray var. *trichocarpum* Fern.** – Rough avens (50) (present)

Geum macrophyllum **Willd.** – Avens (157) (1929), Large-leaf avens [Largeleaf avens, Large-leaved avens] (5, 50, 72, 131, 155) (1899–present), Long-leaf avens [Long-leaved avens] (3) (1977)

Geum odoratum **Bart.** – See *Sieversia radiata* (Michx.) G. Don

Geum peckii **Pursh** – Yellow mountain avens (5) (1913)

Geum radiatum **Mich.** – See *Sieversia radiata* (Michx.) G. Don

Geum rivale **L.** – Benoite aquatique (French) (6, 158) (1892–1900), Chocolate (74, 76) (1893–1896) NH ME, root used in beverage, Chocolate root [Chocolate-root] (5, 6, 92, 156, 158) (1876–1923), Cure-all [Cure all, Cureall] (5, 156, 158) (1900–1923), Drooping avens (5, 158) (1900–1913), Evan's root [Evans-root, Evan root] (5, 92, 156, 158) (1876–1923), Indian chocolate (5, 6, 92, 107, 156, 158) (1892–1923), Maidenhair [Maiden-hair, Maiden hair] (5, 74, 76, 158) (1893–1913), Purple avens (2, 3, 4, 5, 6, 19, 49, 50, 92, 107, 156, 158) (1892–present), River avens (156) (1923), Sumpfnelkenwurzel (German) (6, 158) (1892–1900), Throatroot [Throat root, Throat-root] (5, 158) (1900–1913), Throatwort [Throat wort, Throat-wort] (156) (1923), Wasserbenediktenwurzel (German) (158) (1900), Water avens (2, 4, 5, 6, 49, 57, 92, 107, 155, 156, 158) (1892–1986)

Geum strictum **Aiton** – See *Geum aleppicum* Jacq.

Geum triflorum **Pursh** – Johnny-smokers [Johnny smokers] (74) (1893) Rockford IL, fruits have conspicuous plumose styles, Maidenhair [Maiden-hair, Maiden hair] (4) (1986), Old-man's-whiskers [Old man's whiskers] (50) (present), Prairie-smoke [Prairie smoke] (76) (1896), Purple avens (3) (1977), Three-flower avens [Three-flowered avens] (86) (1878), Torch flower [Torch-flower] (4) (1986)

Geum triflorum **Pursh var. *ciliatum* (Pursh) Fassett** – Apacheplume [Apache plume, Apacheplume] (156) (1923), Johnny smokers (5, 156) (1913–1923), Long-plume purple avens [Long-plumed purple avens, Long plumed purple avens] (5, 72, 131) (1899–1913), Maidenhair [Maiden-hair, Maiden hair] (127) (1933) ND, Ne'baneya'nekweäg' (Chippewa, it is one-sided) (40) (1928), Old-man's-whiskers [Old man's whiskers] (127, 156) (1923–1939) ND, Prairie-smoke [Prairie smoke] (5, 40, 127, 156) (1913–1933), Prairie-smoke sieversia [Prairiesmoke sieversia] (155) (1942), Purple avens (85) (1932) SD, Torch flower [Torch-flower] (127, 156) (1923–1933) ND

Geum urbanum **L.** – Avens (57, 107) (1917–1919), Blessed herb (92) (1876), Clove-root (107) (1919), European avens (57, 92) (1876–1917), Herb Bennet [Herb Bennett] (107) (1919), Star-of-the-earth [Star of the earth] (92) (1876)

Geum vernum **(Raf.) Torr. & Gray** – Early water avens (5) (1913), Heart-leaf avens [Heartleaf avens] (3, 4) (1977–1986), Spring avens (2, 5, 50, 97) (1895–present)

Geum virginianum **L.** – American bennet (157, 158) (1900–1929), Avens (7, 19) (1828–1840), Benner (5) (1913), Bennet (7, 92) (1828–1876), Bennet (German) (7) (1828), Benoite de Virginie (French) (7) (1828), Chocolate plant (156) (1923), Chocolate root [Chocolate-root] (5, 7, 49, 157, 158) (1828–1929), Cream-colored avens (5) (1913), Cure-all [Cure all, Cureall] (7, 92) (1828–1876), Evan's root [Evans-root, Evan root] (7) (1828), Geum radix (Official name of Materia Medica) (7) (1828), Herb Bennet [Herb Bennett] (5, 92) (1876–1913), Redroot [Red-root, Red root] (156, 157, 158) (1900–1929), Rough avens (5, 72, 85, 97, 131, 156, 157, 158) (1899–1937), Throatroot [Throat root, Throat-root] (5, 7, 49, 92, 157, 158) (1828–1929), Throatwort [Throat wort, Throat-wort] (156) (1923), Virginia geum (49) (1898), White avens (2, 3, 4, 5, 7, 48, 50, 72, 80, 85, 92, 93, 97, 122, 131, 155, 156, 157, 158) (1828–present)

Gifola – See *Filago* L.

Gifola germanica **(L.) Dumort** – See *Filago vulgaris* Lam.

Gilenia trifoliata **Moench** – See *Porteranthus trifoliatus* (L.) Britton

Gilia abrotanifolia **(Nutt. ex Greene)** – See *Gilia capitata* Sims subsp. *abrotanifolia* (Nutt. ex Greene) V. Grant

Gilia acerosa **(Gray) Britton** – See *Gilia rigidula* Benth.

Gilia achilleaefolia – See *Gilia achilleifolia* Benth.

Gilia achilleifolia **Benth.** – Yarrow gilia (138) (1923)

Gilia aggregata **(Pursh) Spreng.** – See *Ipomopsis aggregata* (Pursh) V. Grant subsp. *aggregata*

Gilia aggregata **Spreng.** – See *Ipomopsis aggregata* (Pursh) V. Grant subsp. *aggregata*

Gilia californica **Benth.** – See *Linanthus californicus* (Hook. & Arn.) J. M. Porter & L. A. Johnson

Gilia capitata **Dougl.** – See *Gilia capitata* Sims

Gilia capitata **Sims** – Gilia (82) (1930), Globe gilia (138) (1923)

Gilia capitata **Sims subsp. *abrotanifolia* (Nutt. ex Greene) V. Grant** – Santa Barbara gilia (138) (1923)

Gilia congesta **Hook.** – See *Ipomopsis congesta* (Hook.) V. Grant subsp. *congesta*

Gilia coronopifolia **Pers.** – See *Ipomopsis rubra* (L.) Wherry

Gilia grandiflora **Gray** – See *Collomia grandiflora* Douglas

Gilia iberidifolia **Benth.** – See *Ipomopsis congesta* (Hook.) V. Grant

Gilia incisa **Benth.** – False flax [Falseflax] (122, 124) (1937), Pheasant's-eye [Pheasantseye, Pheasant's-eye] (124) (1937)

Gilia longiflora **(Torr.) G. Don** – See *Ipomopsis longiflora* (Torr.) V. Grant subsp. *longiflora*

Gilia micrantha **[Steud.]** – See *Linanthus parviflorus* (Benth.) Greene

Gilia pinnatifida **Nutt. ex Gray** – Small-flower gilia [Small-flowered gilia] (5) (1913), Sticky gilia (50) (present)

Gilia pumila **Nutt.** – See *Ipomopsis pumila* (Nutt.) V. Grant

Gilia rigidula **Benth.** – Bluebowls (50) (present), Needle-leaf gilia [Needle-leaved gilia] (5, 97) (1913–1937)

Gilia rubra (L.) **Heller** – See *Ipomopsis rubra* (L.) Wherry

Gilia spicata capitata **Gray** – See *Ipomopsis spicata* (Nutt.) V. Grant subsp. *capitata* (Gray) V. Grant

Gilia spicata **Nutt.** – See *Ipomopsis spicata* (Nutt.) V. Grant subsp. *spicata*

Gilia tricolor **Benth.** – Bird's-eye [Bird's eye, Bird's-eyes, Birds-eyes] (109) (1949), Bird's-eye gilia [Birdseye gilia] (138) (1923), Tri-colored gilia (86) (1878)

Gillenia **Moench** – American ipecac (2) (1895)

Gillenia stipulacea **Nutt.** – See *Porteranthus stipulatus* (Muhl. ex Willd.) Britt.

Gillenia stipulata **(Muhl.) Baill.** – See *Porteranthus stipulatus* (Muhl. ex Willd.) Britt.

Gillenia trifoliata **(L.) Moench** – American ipecac (156, 186) (1825–1923), Beaumont's root [Beaumont root] (186) (1814), Bowman's root [Bowman's-root, Bowman root, Bowmanroot] (2, 5, 19, 49, 64, 138, 156, 186) (1840–1923), Common Indian physic (2) (1895), Dreyblättrige Spierstaude (German) (186) (1814), Dropwort (156, 186) (1825–1923), False ipecac (64, 156) (1907–1923), Gillenia (156) (1923), Indian hippo (5, 64, 92, 156, 186) (1814–1923), Indian physic [Indian-physic, Indianphysic, Indian physick] (5, 19, 49, 61, 64, 92, 109, 156, 181, 184, 186, 187) (~1678–1949), Ipecacuan (186) (1814), Ipecacuanhua (181, 186) (~1678–1825), Meadowsweet [Meadow-sweet, Meadow sweet] (5, 92, 186) (1825–1913), Three-leaf spiraea [Three-leaved spiraea] (186) (1814), Trifoliate Virginia meadow-sweet (181) (~1678)

Gillenia trifoliata **Moench** – See *Gillenia trifoliata* (L.) Moench

Ginkgo biloba **L.** – Gingo tree (92) (1876), Ginkgo or Gingko tree (92, 107, 109, 137) (1876–1949) from Chinese name Gink-go, Maidenhair tree [Maiden hair tree, Maidenhair-tree, Maiden-hair tree] (92, 107, 109, 136, 138) (1876–1949)

Ginkgo **L.** – Maidenhair tree [Maiden hair tree, Maidenhair-tree, Maiden-hair tree] (138) (1923)

Githago **Desf.** – See *Agrostemma* L.

Glabaria geniculata **(Walt.) Britton** – possibly *Litsea aestivalis* (L.) Fern.

Glabraria geniculata **(Marsh.) Britton** – See *Litsea aestivalis* (L.) Fern.

Gladiolus communis **L.** – Corn flag [Corn-flag, Corne-flag] (92) (1876), French corne glaaden (178) (1596), French sword-flag (180) (1633), Gladiolus (92) (1876), Round mandrake (92) (1876), Round ransom (92) (1876), Sword lily (92) (1876), Sword-grass [Sword grass] (92) (1876)

Gladiolus **L.** – Corn flag [Corn-flag, Corne-flag] (180) (1633), Corn gladin [Corne gladin] (180) (1633), Corn-sedge [Corne-Sedge] (180) (1633), Gladiolus (138, 180) (1633–1923), Glais (French) (180) (1633), Jacob's-ladder [Jacob's ladder, Jacobs-ladder] (75) (1894) Lincolnton NC, Moacuccio (Italian) (180) (1633), Siegwurtz (German) (180) (1633), Sword flag [Sword-flag] (180) (1633), Sword lily (75) (1894) NY

Gladiolus papilio **Hook. f.** – Orchid gladiolus (138) (1923)

Glandularia **×*hybrida* (Grönland & Rümpler) Nesom & Pruski** [*peruviana × phlogiflora* or *platensis*] – Common garden verbena (109) (1949), Wild verbena (174) (1753)

Glandularia bipinnatifida **(Nutt.) Nutt.** – Dakota mock vervain (50) (present)

Glandularia bipinnatifida **(Nutt.) Nutt. var.** *bipinnatifida* – Dakota mock vervain (50) (present), Dakota vervain (4, 138, 155) (1923–1986), Hairy vervain (97) (1937), Small-flower verbena [Small-flowered verbena, Smallflowered verbena] (5, 19, 97, 122) (1840–1937), Vervain (3) (1977), Western pink verbena (122) (1937), Western vervain (145) (1897), White vervain (3, 4, 5, 80, 93, 95, 156, 157, 158, 187) (1818–1986), Wright's verbena [Wrights verbena] (155) (1942)

Glandularia canadensis **(L.) Nutt.** – Clump verbena (109) (1949), Large-flower verbena [Large-flowered verbena] (5, 72, 97, 158) (1900–1937), Rose mock vervain (50) (present), Rose verbena

(155) (1942), Rose vervain (3, 4, 138) (1923–1986), Sweet William [Sweetwilliam, Sweet-william] (77) (1898) Southwestern MO, from sweetish taste of flowers, Verbena (122) (1937), possibly Aublet's verbena (86) (1878)

Glandularia carolinensis **Gmel.** – See *Glandularia canadensis* (L.) Nutt.

Glandularia **J. F. Gmel.** – Mock vervain (50) (present)

Glandularia peruviana **(L.) Druce (possibly)** – Cultivated verbena (114) (1894) Neb

Glandularia pumila **(Rydb.) Umber** – Pink mock vervain (50) (present), Pink vervain (3) (1977), Vervain (97) (1937)

Glandularia pumila **Rydb.** – See *Glandularia pumila* (Rydb.) Umber

Glandularia wrightii **(Gray) Umber** – Davis Mountain mock vervain (50) (present)

Glaucium corniculatum **(L.) J. H. Rudolph** – Black-spot horn-poppy [Blackspot hornpoppy] (50, 155) (1942–present), Red horned-poppy [Red horned poppy, Red horned poppie] (4, 178) (1526–1986)

Glaucium flavum **Crantz** – Bruiseroot [Bruise root] (92, 156) (1876–1923), Horned poppy [Horned-poppy] (10, 15, 23, 19, 92, 156) (1810–1923), Sea celandine (92, 156) (1876–1923), Sea poppy [Sea-poppy] (5, 156) (1913–1923), Squatmore (156) (1923), Yellow horned-poppy [Yellow horned poppie, Yellow hornpoppy] (5, 138, 156, 178) (1526–1923), possibly Bruiseroot [Bruise root] (7) (1828), possibly Horn poppy [Hornpoppy] (7) (1828)

Glaucium glaucium **(L.) Karst.** – See *Glaucium flavum* Crantz

Glaucium luteum **Pursh** – See *Glaucium flavum* Crantz

Glaucium **Mill.** – Horn poppy [Hornpoppy] (138, 155) (1923–1942), Horned poppy [Horned-poppy] (4, 109, 156, 158) (1900–1986), Sea-poppy (109) (1949)

Glaucothea **[O. F. Cook]** – See *Brahea* Mart. ex Endl.

Glaux **(Tourn.) L.** – See *Glaux* L.

Glaux **L.** – Black saltwort (1, 10) (1818–1932), Milkwort (50, 190) (~1759–present), Sea milkwort [Seamilkwort] (1, 4, 41, 155, 156, 158) (1770–1986)

Glaux maritima **L.** – Black saltwort (5, 92, 156, 158) (1876–1923), Glauce (French) (158) (1900), Milchkraut (German) (158) (1900), Sea milkwort [Seamilkwort] (3, 4, 5, 19, 50, 92, 155, 156, 158) (1840–present), Sea trifoly (5, 156, 158) (1900–1923)

Glechoma hederacea **L.** – Ale gill (156) (1923) no longer in use by 1923, formerly used in brewing, Alehoof [Ale hoof, Ale-hoof] (5, 7, 10, 46, 92, 107, 156, 157, 158, 187) (1671–1929), Alehoue (178) (1526), Bluebell [Blue-bell, Blue bell, Blue bells, Blue-bells] (77) (1898) Cambridge MA, Carrion-flower [Carrionflower, Carrion flower] (92) (1876), Cat's-foot [Cats foot, Cat's foot, Cat foot] (5, 49, 92, 157, 158) (1876–1929), Cat's-paw [Cat's paws, Cat's-paws] (157, 158) (1900–1929), Common ground ivy (93) (1936), Creeping charlie [Creeping-charlie, Creeping charley] (5, 73, 80, 82, 156, 157, 158) (1892–1930), Creeping Jenny [Creeping Jennie, Creeping-Jennie, Creeping-jenny] (156) (1923), Crow victuals [Crow-victuals] (5, 73, 158) (1892–1900) Chestertown MD, name used by Negroes, Field balm [Field-balm] (5, 109, 157, 158) (1900–1949) Gill (106) (1930) Gill-go-by-the-ground (92, 156) (1876–1923), Gill-go-over-the-ground (49) (1898), Gill-over-the-ground (1, 63, 73, 75, 106, 109, 156) (1892–1949), Gillrun (92) (1876), Gill-run-over (156) (1923), Gill-run-over-grass (77) (1898) Cambridge MA, Glechoma (57) (1917), Ground ivy [Ground-ivy] (49, 63, 80, 82, 92, 106, 107, 109, 138, 156) (1671–1949), Gundelreben (German) (158) (1900), Hayhofe [Hay hofe] (5, 156, 157, 158) (1900–1929), Hayhove [Hay hove] (156) (1923), Haymaids [Hay maids, Hay-maids] (5, 92, 156, 157, 158) (1876–1929), Hedgemaids [Hedge maids, Hedge-maids] (5, 92, 156, 157, 158) (1876–1929), Hove (5, 92, 157, 158) (1876–1929), Jack-over-the-ground (73) (1892) Eastern MA, Lierre terrestre (French) (158) (1900), Nepeta (107) (1919), Robin-run-away [Robin runaway, Robin run away] (5, 7, 73, 92, 156, 157, 158) (1828–1929), Robin-run-in-the-hedge (92, 158) (1876–1900), Robin-running-in-the-hedge (157) (1929), Roving Charley (156)

(1923), Run-away Jack (77) (1898) Cambridge MA, Run-away Nell (77) (1898) Medford MA, Tanhoof (157, 158) (1900–1929), Tunhoof [Tun hoof] (5, 92, 156) (1876–1923), Wild snakeroot [Wild snake root, Wild snake-root] (5, 73, 156) (1892–1923)

Glechoma L. – Gill-over-the-ground (1) (1932), Glechoma (50) (present), Ground ivy [Ground-ivy] (1, 158) (1900–1932)

Gleditschia aquatica – See *Gleditsia aquatica* Marsh.

Gleditschia L. – See *Gleditsia L.*

Gleditsia ×texana **Sargent (pro sp.)** [*aquatica × triacanthos*] – Texas locust (122, 124) (1937) TX

Gleditsia aquatica **Marsh.** – Févier aquatique (French) (8) (1785), One-seed honey locust [One-seeded honey locust] (12) (1821), Swamp locust (5, 19, 97, 158) (1840–1937), Water locust [Waterlocust] (2, 5, 8, 20, 50, 97, 122, 124, 138, 155, 156, 158) (1857–present)

Gleditsia brachycarpa **(Michaux) Pursh** – See *Gleditsia triacanthos* L.

Gleditsia L. – Févier (French) (8) (1785), Honey locust [Honeylocust, Honey-locust] (1, 2, 4, 7, 8, 10, 82, 93, 109, 138, 155, 156, 167) (1814–1986), Locust or Locust tree (50) (present), Triple-thorn acaia [Triple-thorned acaia, 3-thorned acacia] (8, 167) (1785–1814)

Gleditsia monosperma **Walter** – See *Gleditsia aquatica* Marsh.

Gleditsia spinosa – See *Gleditsia triacanthos* L.

Gleditsia texana **Sarg.** – See *Gleditsia ×texana* Sarg. [*aquatica × triacanthos*]

Gleditsia triacanthos inermis – See *Gleditsia triacanthos* L.

Gleditsia triacanthos L. – Black locust (5, 157, 158) (1900–1929), Common honey-locust [Common honeylocust] (138, 155) (1923–1942), Févier à épines à trois pointes (French) (8) (1785), Fevier épineux (French) (17) (1796), Honey (5, 158) (1900–1913), Honey locust [Honeylocust, Honey-locust] (3, 4, 5, 8, 9, 10, 18, 19, 27, 35, 38, 41, 50, 63, 72, 82, 85, 92, 95, 97, 106, 107, 109, 112, 113, 114, 122, 124, 130, 135, 156, 157, 158, 177, 184, 187) (1762–present), Honey-shucks [Honey shucks] (5, 156, 157, 158) (1900–1929), Large-thorn acacia [Large-thorned acacia] (189) (1767), Locust thorn (158) (1900), Short-pod honey locust [Short-podded honey locust] (12) (1821), Squeak-bean (156) (1923), Sweet bean [Sweet-bean] (5, 156, 157, 158) (1900–1929), Sweet locust (5, 17, 20, 109, 131, 135, 156, 157, 158) (1796–1949), Thorn locust [Thorn-locust] (5, 74, 156, 157) (1893–1929), Thornless honey locust [Thornless honeylocust] (112, 138) (1923–1937), Thorny locust (106) (1930), Three-thorn acacia [Three-thorned acacia, Three thorned acacia] (5, 92, 156, 157, 158) (1876–1929), Three-thorn locust [Three-thorned locust] (187) (1818), Triple-thorn acaia [Triple-thorned acaia] (8) (1785)

Glinus lotoides L. – Lotus sweetjuice (50) (present)

Gliricidia sepium **(Jacq.) Kunth ex Walp. (possibly)** – Madre (109) (1949)

Gliricidia sepium **Steud.** – possibly *Gliricidia sepium* (Jacq.) Kunth ex Walp.

Gloriosa L. – Climbing lily [Climbing-lily] (109) (1949), Glorylily [Glory lily] (109, 138) (1923–1949)

Gloriosa rothschildiana **O'Brien** – See *Gloriosa superba* L.

Gloriosa superba L. – Malabar glorylily (138) (1923), Rothschild's glory-lily [Rothschild glorylily] (138) (1923)

Glossopetalon planitierum **(Ensign) St. John** – Greasebush [Greasebush, Grease bush] (3, 4) (1977–1986), Plains greasebush (50) (present)

Glyceria acutiflora **Torr.** – Creeping manna grass [Creeping manna-grass] (50) (present), Pointed spear grass (66, 90) (1885–1903), Sharp-flower manna grass [Sharp-flowered manna-grass] (90, 94) (1885–1901), Sharp-scale manna grass [Sharp-scaled manna grass] (5) (1913)

Glyceria americana **Pammel** – See *Glyceria grandis* S. Wats.

Glyceria aquatica **Smith** – See *Catabrosa aquatica* (L.) Beauv.

Glyceria arundinacea **Kunth** – Reed meadow grass [Reed meadow-grass] (88) (1885), Tall meadow grass (88) (1885)

Glyceria borealis **(Nash) Batchelder** – Northern manna grass [Northern manna-grass, Northern mannagrass] (3, 5, 94, 155) (1901–1977),

Slender manna grass (56, 72) (1901–1907), Small floating manna grass [Small floating mannagrass] (50) (present)

Glyceria borreri **(Bab.) Bab.** – See *Puccinellia fasciculata* (Torr.) Bicknell

Glyceria canadensis **(Michx.) Trin.** – Meadow rattlesnake grass (19) (1840), Pearl grass (75) (1894) MA, children's name, Quake grass [Quake-grass] (43) (1820), Rattlesnake grass [Rattle snake grass] (5, 66, 87, 88, 90, 92, 94) (1876–1913), Rattlesnake manna grass [Rattlesnake mannagrass] (50, 155) (1942–present), Tall quaking grass (5, 87, 88, 90) (1884–1913)

Glyceria distans **[(Jacq.) Wahlenb.]** – See *Puccinellia distans* (Jacq.) Parl.

Glyceria elata **(Nash ex Rydb.) M. E. Jones** – See *Glyceria striata* (Lam.) A. S. Hitchc.

Glyceria elongata – See *Glyceria melicaria* (Michx.) F.T. Hubb.

Glyceria fluitans **(L.) R. Br.** – Common manna grass (66, 90) (1885–1903), Float grass [Flote grass] (5, 92, 107) (1876–1919), Floating manna grass [Floating manna-grass] (5, 56, 72, 87, 88, 90, 94) (1885–1913), Floating meadow grass [Floating meadow-grass] (45, 66, 129) (1894–1903), Manna (92) (1876), Manna croup grass (5) (1913), Manna grass [Manna-grass, Mannagrass] (3, 56, 92, 107) (1876–1977), Manna seed (92) (1876), Poland manna (5, 107) (1913–1919), River festuca [River-festuca] (187) (1818), Russian grass [Russia grass] (5) (1913), Russian seeds [Russia seeds] (92) (1876), Sweet grass [Sweet-grass, Sweetgrass] (5, 92, 101) (1876–1913), Water manna grass [Water mannagrass] (50, 155) (1942–present), Water-fescue [Water fescue] (19) (1840)

Glyceria grandis **S. Wats.** – American manna grass [American manna-grass] (50, 140, 143, 155) (1936–present), Reed manna grass [Reed mannagrass, Reed manna-grass] (140) (1944), Reed meadow grass [Reed meadow-grass] (56, 72, 94, 111, 129, 143) (1894–1936), Tall glyceria (143) (1852–1936), Tall manna grass [Tall mannagrass] (3) (1977)

Glyceria grandis **S. Wats. var. grandis** – Reed meadow grass [Reed meadow-grass] (5) (1913), Tall manna grass [Tall mannagrass] (5) (1913), Water meadow grass (5) (1913), White spear grass (5) (1913)

Glyceria laxa **(Scribn.) Scribn.** – Limp manna grass [Limp manna-grass] (50) (present), Northern manna grass [Northern manna-grass, Northern mannagrass] (5) (1913)

Glyceria maritima **(Huds.) Wahlenb.** – See *Puccinellia maritima* (Huds.) Parl.

Glyceria maritima **Whal.** – See *Puccinellia maritima* (Huds.) Parl.

Glyceria maxima **(Hartm.) Holmb.** – Reed meadow grass [Reed meadow-grass] (94) (1901), Water manna grass [Water mannagrass] (138) (1923), Water meadow grass (56) (1901)

Glyceria melicaria **(Michx.) F. T. Hubb.** – Long-panicle manna grass [Long paniceled manna grass] (66, 90) (1885–1903)

Glyceria nervata **Trin.** – See *Glyceria striata* (Lam.) A.S. Hitchc.

Glyceria obtusa **(Muhl.) Trin.** – Atlantic manna grass [Atlantic manna-grass] (50) (present), Blunt manna grass (5) (1913), Blunt-flower meadow grass [Blunt-flowered meadow-grass] (187) (1818), Densely-flowered manna grass [Densely flowered manna-grass] (94) (1901), Obtuse spear grass (66, 90) (1885–1903)

Glyceria pallida **(Torr.) Trin.** – See *Torreyochloa pallida* (Torr.) Church var. *pallida*

Glyceria pauciflora **Presl.** – See *Torreyochloa pallida* (Torr.) Church var. *pauciflora* (J. Presl) J. I. Davis

Glyceria R. Br. – Manna grass [Manna-grass, Mannagrass] (1, 45, 50, 66, 93, 152, 155) (1896–present)

Glyceria septentrionalis **A. S. Hitchc.** – American flote grass (5) (1913), Eastern manna grass [Eastern mannagrass] (122) (1937), Floating manna grass [Floating manna-grass] (5, 163) (1852–1913)

Glyceria spectabilis **[Mert. & W. D. J. Koch]** – See *Glyceria maxima* (Hartm.) Holmb.

Glyceria striata **(Lam.) A. S. Hitchc.** – Fowl grass [Fowl-grass] (5, 119) (1913–1938), Fowl manna grass [Fowl mannagrass] (3, 50, 122,

140, 143, 155) (1936–present), Fowl meadow grass [Fowl meadow-grass] (94, 111, 119, 129, 143, 163) (1894–1938), Manna grass [Manna-grass, Mannagrass] (85, 152) (1912–1932), Meadow grass [Meadow-grass, Medow Grasse] (5, 119) (1913–1938), Meadow spear grass [Meadow spear-grass] (5, 66, 119) (1903–1938), Nerved manna grass [Nerved-manna-grass, Nerved manna-grass] (5, 56, 66, 72, 87, 90, 119, 129, 143, 163) (1852–1938), Nerved meadow grass (88, 90) (1884–1885), Tall manna grass [Tall mannagrass] (155) (1942)

Glycine apios L. – See *Apios americana* Medik.

Glycine frutescens L. – See *Wisteria frutescens* (L.) Poir.

Glycine frutescens Michx. – See *Wisteria frutescens* (L.) Poir.

Glycine gracilis Skvortzov – See *Glycine max* (L.) Merr.

Glycine hispida (Moench) Maxim. – See *Glycine max* (L.) Merr.

Glycine hispida Maxim. – See *Glycine max* (L.) Merr.

Glycine L. – See *Glycine* Willd.

Glycine max (L.) Merr. – Green gram (158) (1900), Miso (158) (1900), Sahuca bean (158) (1900), Shu (Ancient Chinese) (110) (1886), Slender groundnut (155) (1942), Soja bean (68, 118) (1898–1913), Soy (110) (1886), Soybean [Soy bean] (50, 68, 109, 118, 138, 158) (1898–present), Ta-tou (Chinese) (110) (1886), White gram (158) (1900)

Glycine priceana (Robinson) Britton – See *Apios priceana* B.L. Robins.

Glycine soja Sieb. & Zucc. – Coffee bean (107) (1919), Soja bean (106, 107) (1919–1930), Soy (106) (1930), Soybean [Soy bean] (106, 107) (1919–1930)

Glycine tomentosa L. – See *Rhynchosia tomentosa* (L.) Hook. & Arn. var. *tomentosa*

Glycine Willd. – Glycine (French) (8) (1785), Groundnut [Ground-nut, Ground nut, Ground nutts] (93, 155) (1936–1942), Perennial kidney bean [Perennial kidney-bean] (8) (1785), Soybean [Soy bean] (50, 158) (1900–present)

Glycyrrhiza (Tourn.) L. – See *Glycyrrhiza* L.

Glycyrrhiza glabra L. – Black liquorice (92) (1876), Common licorice (138, 178) (1526–1923), Cultivated licorice (50) (present), Glycyrrhiza (52, 57) (1917–1919), Italian juice (92) (1876), Licorice root [Licorice-root, Licorice roots, Liquorice roots] (92) (1876), Licorice tree [Lycoryce tre] (179) (1526), Nakhalsa (Mongolia) (107) (1919), Spanish juice (92) (1876), Sweetwood [Sweet wood, Sweet-wood] (92) (1876), possibly Licorice [Liquorice] (19, 52, 55, 57, 92, 107, 109) (1793–1949)

Glycyrrhiza L. – Cahohamo (7) (1828), Licorice [Liquorice] (1, 4, 7, 50, 93, 138, 155, 156, 158) (1828–present)

Glycyrrhiza lepidota Pursh – American licorice (5, 50, 92, 93, 97, 155, 156, 157, 158) (1876–present), Buffalo bur [Buffalo-bur, Buffalo burr] (131) (1899) SD, Deseret-weed (156) (1923), Licorice [Liquorice] (106, 122) (1930–1937), Licorice root [Licorice-root, Licorice roots, Liquorice roots] (5, 76, 124, 156) (1896–1936), Pithahatusakitstsuhast (Pawnee) (37) (1919), Sweetroot [Sweet root] (156) (1923), Sweetwood [Sweet wood, Sweet-wood] (156) (1923), Wild licorice [Wild liquorice] (3, 4, 5, 35, 37, 38, 47, 72, 80, 85, 93, 95, 107, 108, 114, 121, 126, 131, 146, 156, 157, 158) (1878–1986), Wild licorice root [Wild liquorice root] (101) (1905), Wi-nawizi (Dakota, jealous woman) (37) (1919), Winawizi čikala (Lakota, little burr) (121) (1918?–1970?)

Glycyrrhiza officinalis [Lepech.] – possibly *Glycyrrhiza glabra* L.

Gnaphalium chilense Spreng. – See *Pseudognaphalium stramineum* (Kunth) W. A. Weber

Gnaphalium decurrens Ives – See *Pseudognaphalium macounii* (Greene) Kartesz

Gnaphalium dioicum (Michx.) – See *Antennaria dioica* (L.) Gaertn.

Gnaphalium helleri Britton – See *Pseudognaphalium helleri* (Britt.) A. Anderb. subsp. *helleri*

Gnaphalium L. – Cudweed [Cud-weed, Cud weed] (1, 2, 4, 7, 10, 50, 93, 155, 156, 158, 167, 184) (1793–present), Everlasting (1, 2, 4, 10, 92, 93, 158) (1818–1986), Lady's-tobacco [Ladies' tobacco] (76)

(1896) Madison WI, Life-everlasting [Life everlasting] (92) (1876), Mouse-ear [Mouse ear, Mouse ears, Mouse's ear, Mows eare] (79) (1891) NH, Petty-cotton [Petty cotton] (156) (1923)

Gnaphalium lanceolata Nutt. – See *Grindelia lanceolata* Nutt.

Gnaphalium luteo-album – See *Pseudognaphalium luteoalbum* (L.) Hilliard & Burtt

Gnaphalium luteoalbum L. – See *Pseudognaphalium luteoalbum* (L.) Hilliard & Burtt

Gnaphalium macounii Greene – See *Pseudognaphalium macounii* (Greene) Kartesz

Gnaphalium margaritaceum [L.] – See *Anaphalis margaritacea* (L.) Benth. & Hook

Gnaphalium obtusifolium L. – See *Pseudognaphalium obtusifolium* (L.) Hilliard & Burtt subsp. *obtusifolium*

Gnaphalium palustre Nutt. – Everlasting (3) (1977), Western marsh cudweed (5, 50) (1913–present)

Gnaphalium plantagineum [L.] – possibly *Antennaria plantaginifolia* (L.) Richards (current species depends on author)

Gnaphalium plantaginifolia – See *Antennaria plantaginifolia* (L.) Richards

Gnaphalium plantaginifolium L. – See *Antennaria plantaginifolia* (L.) Richards

Gnaphalium purpureum L. – See *Gamochaeta purpurea* (L.) Cabrera

Gnaphalium supinum L. – See *Omalotheca supina* (L.) DC.

Gnaphalium sylvaticum L. – See *Omalotheca sylvatica* (L.) Schultz-Bip. & F.W. Schultz

Gnaphalium uliginosum L. – Cudweed [Cud-weed, Cud weed] (19, 92) (1840–1876), Dysentery weed [Dysentery-weed] (158) (1900), Low cudweed (3, 4, 5, 155, 156, 158) (1900–1986), Marsh cudweed (5, 50, 156, 158) (1900–present), Mouse-ear [Mouse ear, Mouse ears, Mouse's ear, Mows eare] (5, 76, 156, 158) (1896–1923) Paris ME, Mud life-everlasting (19) (1840), Small life-everlasting [Small life everlasting] (156, 158) (1900–1923), Wartwort [Wart-wort] (5, 156, 158) (1900–1923)

Gnaphalium viscosum Kunth – See *Pseudognaphalium viscosum* (Kunth) W. A. Weber

Gnaphalium wrightii Gray – See *Pseudognaphalium canescens* (DC.) W. A. Weber subsp. *canescens*

Godetia amoena Don – See *Clarkia amoena* (Lehm.) A. Nels. & J.F. Macbr. subsp. *amoena*

Godetia grandiflora Lindl. – See *Clarkia amoena* subsp. *lindleyi* (Douglas) H. F. Lewis & M. R. Lewis

Godetia Spach – See *Clarkia* Pursh (all US species)

Gomphocarpus grandiflorus (L. f.) K. Schum. – Large-flower swallow-wort [Large flowered swallow wort] (42) (1814)

Gomphrena decumbens Jacq. – See *Gomphrena serrata* L.

Gomphrena globosa L. – Bachelor's-button [Bachelor's button, Bachelor's buttons, Batchelor's buttons] (19, 77, 92) (1840–1898), Common globe-amaranth (138) (1923), French clover (73) (1892) Northern OH, Globe [Globes] (73) (1892) Southern VT, Globe-amaranth [Globe amaranth] (19, 77, 92, 156) (1840–1923), Immortelle [Immortelles] (156) (1923)

Gomphrena L. – Globe-amaranth [Globe amaranth] (138) (1923)

Gomphrena nealleyi Coult. & Fisher – Gulf Coast amaranth (124) (1937)

Gomphrena serrata L. – Wild globe amaranth (124) (1937)

Gonolobus baldwynianus Sweet in Loudon – See *Matelea baldwyniana* (Sweet) Woods.

Gonolobus biflorus Raf. – See *Matelea biflora* (Raf.) Woods

Gonolobus hirsutus Mich. – See *Matelea obliqua* (Jacq.) Woods.

Gonolobus laevis Michx. – See *Cynanchum laeve* (Michx.) Pers.

Gonolobus Michx. – Anglepod [Angle pod, Angle-pod] (82, 92, 156) (1876–1930), Choke-dog [Choke dog] (92) (1876)

Gonolobus obliquus R. Br. – See *Matelea obliqua* (Jacq.) Woods.

Gonolobus suberosus auct. non (L.) R. Br. – See *Matelea gonocarpos* (Walt.) Shinners

Gonotheca helianthoides – See *Tetragonotheca helianthoides* L.

Goodyera decipiens (Hook.) **F.T. Hubbard** – See *Goodyera oblongifolia* Raf.

Goodyera oblongifolia Raf. – Menzies' rattlesnake plantain (5) (1913), Rattlesnake-plantain [Rattlesnake plantain, Rattle snake plantain, Rattle-snake plantane, Rattlesnakes' plantain] (3) (1977), Western rattlesnake-plantain [Western rattlsenake plantain] (50, 138) (1923–present)

Goodyera pubescens (**Willd.**) **R. Br. ex Ait. f.** – Adder's-violet [Adder's violet, Adders' violet] (5, 19, 49, 82, 156) (1840–1930), Downy rattlesnake-plantain [Downy rattlesnake plantain] (5, 50, 72, 109, 138, 156) (1907–present), Netleaf [Net-leaf] (7, 156) (1828–1923), Net-leaf plantain [Net leaf plantain, Netleaf plantain] (5, 49, 92) (1876–1913), Networt (7, 92) (1828–1876), Rat's-bane [Rat's bane, Ratsbane, Rat's-bane] (5, 75, 156) (1894–1923) Banner Elk NC, no longer in use in 1923, Rattlesnake leaf [Rattle snake leaf] (5, 7, 19, 49, 92, 156) (1828–1923), Rattlesnake-plantain [Rattlesnake plantain, Rattle snake plantain, Rattle-snake plantane, Rattlesnakes' plantain] (46, 187) (1818–1849), Rattlesnake-weed [Rattlesnake weed, Rattlesnake weede, Rattlesnakes' weed] (5, 92, 156) (1876–1923), Scrofula-weed [Scrofula weed] (5, 7, 18, 49, 92, 156) (1805–1923), Spotted plantain (5, 92, 156) (1876–1923)

Goodyera pubescens **R. Br.** – See *Goodyera pubescens* (Willd.) R. Br. ex Ait. f.

Goodyera R. Br. – Goodyera (158) (1900), Rattlesnake-plantain [Rattlesnake plantain, Rattle snake plantain, Rattle-snake plantane, Rattlesnakes' plantain] (1, 50, 109, 138) (1923–present)

Goodyera repens (**L.**) **R. Br. ex Ait. f.** – Adder's-tongue [Adder tongue, Adders tongue, Adder's tongue, Adders toong, Adderstongue] (78) (1898) ME, Creeping rattlesnake-plantain (138) (1923), Creeping root plant (5) (1913), Creeping-root plant (156) (1923), Dwarf rattlesnake-plantain [Dwarf rattlesnake plantain] (3) (1977), Lesser rattlesnake-plantain [Lesser rattlesnake plantain] (5, 50, 109, 156) (1913–present), Rattlesnake-plantain [Rattlesnake plantain, Rattle snake plantain, Rattle-snake plantane, Rattlesnakes' plantain] (85, 92) (1876–1932), Satyrion without stones (178) (1596), Squirrel's-ear [Squirrel ear] (5, 92, 156) (1876–1923), White-plantain [White plantain] (5, 92, 156) (1876–1923)

Goodyera tesselata **Lodd.** – Checkered rattlesnake-plantain [Checkered rattlesnake plantain] (50, 138) (1923–present), Loddiges' rattlesnake-plantain [Loddiges' rattlesnake plantain] (5) (1913)

Gordonia Ell. – Gordonia (138) (1923), Loblolly bay [Lobblloly bay, Loblolly-bay] (13, 15, 156) (1849–1923)

Gordonia lasianthus (**L.**) **Ellis** – Loblolly bay [Lobblloly bay, Loblolly-bay] (2, 5, 13, 12, 5, 20, 46, 109, 138, 156, 189) (1767–1949), Bay tree [Bay-tree] (46) (1610), Black laurel (5, 156) (1913–1923), Holly bay (5, 19, 92, 156) (1840–1923), Red bay [Redbay] (156) (1923), Swamp bay (5) (1913), Swamp laurel (7, 92, 156) (1828–1923), Tan bay (5, 156) (1913–1923), Tree-of-peace [Tree of peace] (46) (1879), White bay [White-bay] (46) (1879)

Gordonia pubescens **Cav.** – See *Franklinia alatamaha* Bartr. ex Marsh.

Gordonia pubescens **Lam.** – See *Franklinia alatamaha* Bartr. ex Marsh.

Gordonia pubescens **L'Her.** – See *Franklinia alatamaha* Bartr. ex Marsh.

Gossypianthus lanuginosus (**Poir.**) **Moq.** – Woolly cotton flower [Woolly cottonflower] (4, 50) (1986–present)

Gossypianthus lanuginosus (**Poir.**) **Moq. var.** *lanuginosus* – Cottonflower [Cottonflower] (4) (1986), Sheldon's gossypianthus (97) (1937), Woolly cotton flower [Woolly cottonflower] (50) (present)

Gossypianthus sheldonii (**Uline & Bray**) **Small** – See *Gossypianthus lanuginosus* (Poir.) Moq. var. *lanuginosus*

Gossypium barbadense **L.** – Cotton (55) (1911), Long-staple cotton [Long staple cotton] (110) (1886), Sea-island cotton [Sea island cotton] (109, 110, 138) (1886–1949), West Indian cotton (182) (1791)

Gossypium herbaceum **L.** – Algodon (Southern Europe) (110) (1886), Barbados cotton (110) (1886), Bombast (178) (1526), Cotton (19, 52, 54, 55, 61, 92, 106, 107, 110, 114, 125) (1840–1930), Cotton tree [Cotton-tree] (178) (1526), Gossypium (52, 54) (1905–1919), Levant cotton (109) (1949), Tree cotton [Tree-cotton] (110) (1886), Upland cotton (15) (1895), Xylon (178) (1526)

Gossypium hirsutum **L.** – Upland cotton (109, 138) (1923–1949)

Gossypium hirsutum **L. var.** *hirsutum* – Jamaica cotton (109) (1949)

Gossypium hirsutum **L. var.** *punctatum* **J. B. Hutchins** – See *Gossypium hirsutum* L. var. *hirsutum*

Gossypium L. – Cotton (7, 15, 109, 138) (1828–1949)

Gouania lupuloides (**L.**) **Urban** – Chaw-stick [Chaw stick] (92, 107) (1876–1919)

Gouannia domingensis [**(Jacq.) L.**] – See *Gouania lupuloides* (L.) Urban

Gouannia domingensis **L.** – See *Gouania lupuloides* (L.) Urban

Gracilaria lichenoides [**Greville**] – See *Hydropuntia edulis* (S.G.Gmelin) Gurgel & Fredericq

Gracilaria lichenoides **L. Harv.** – possibly *Hydropuntia edulis* (S.G.Gmelin) Gurgel & Fredericq

Graphephorum melicoides (**Michx.**) **Desv.** – See *Trisetum melicoides* (Michx.) Vasey ex Scribn.

Graphephorum melicoideum (**Michx.**) **Beauv.** – See *Trisetum melicoides* (Michx.) Vasey ex Scribn.

Graphephorum wolfii (**Vasey**) **Vasey ex Coult.** – See *Trisetum wolfii* Vasey

Gratiola aurea **Muhl.** – Golden hedge-hyssop [Golden hedgehyssop] (5, 50, 155, 158) (1900–present), Goldenpert [Golden pert] (4, 5, 46, 158) (1783–1986), Hedge hyssop [Hedgehyssop] (19, 92) (1840–1876)

Gratiola L. – Hedge hyssop [Hedgehyssop] (1, 2, 4, 10, 26, 50, 155, 156) (1826–present)

Gratiola lutea **Raf.** – See *Gratiola aurea* Muhl.

Gratiola neglecta **Torr.** – Clammy hedge-hyssop [Clammy hedge hyssop, Clammy hedgehyssop] (50) (present), Hedge hyssop [Hedgehyssop] (3, 4) (1977–1986)

Gratiola pilosa **Michx.** – Hairy hedge-hyssop [Hairy hedge hyssop] (5, 122) (1913–1937)

Gratiola sphaerocarpa **Ell.** – See *Gratiola virginiana* L. var. *virginiana*

Gratiola virginiana **L.** – Clammy hedge (5) (1913), Clammy hedgehyssop [Clammy hedge hyssop, Clammy hedgehyssop] (72, 97, 120, 122, 156) (1907–1938), Creeping hedgehyssop [Creeping hedge hyssop] (19) (1840), Goldenpert [Golden pert] (156) (1923), Hedge hyssop [Hedgehyssop] (4, 85, 93) (1932–1986), Round-fruit hedge-hyssop [Roundfruit hedgehyssop] (50) (present), Virginia hedge-hyssop [Virginia hedge hyssop, Virginia hedgehyssop] (3, 155) (1942–1977), Water jessamine (7, 92, 157, 158) (1828–1929)

Gratiola virginiana **L. var.** *virginiana* – Round-fruit hedge-hyssop [Round-fruited hedge-hyssop] (5, 72, 97) (1907–1937)

Gratiola virginica **Pursh** – See *Gratiola virginiana* L.

Gratiola viscidula **Pennell** – Viscid hedge-hyssop (5) (1913)

Gratiola viscosa **Schwein.** – See *Gratiola viscidula* Pennell

Grevillea R. Br. ex Knight – Grevillea (138) (1923), Silk-bark oak (107) (1919)

Grevillea robusta **A. Cunningham ex R. Br.** – Silk-oak (109, 138) (1923–1949)

Grindelia camporum **Greene** – Grindelia (57) (1917)

Grindelia camporum **Greene var.** *camporum* – Great Valley gumweed (50) (present), Grindelia (52, 60) (1902–1919), Gum plant [Gumplant, Gum-plant] (52, 54, 69, 75) (1903–1919), Hardy grindelia (49) (1898), Wild sunflower [Wild sun-flower] (52, 54) (1905–1919), Yellow tarweed [Yellow tar weed] (54) (1905)

Grindelia camporum **Greene var.** *parviflora* **Steyermark** – See *Grindelia camporum* Greene var. *camporum*

Grindelia cuneifolia **Nutt.** – See *Grindelia stricta* DC. var. *angustifolia* (Gray) M. A. Lane

Grindelia grandiflora **Hook.** – Giant tarweed [Giant tar weed] (124) (1937)

Grindelia inornata **Greene** – Colorado gumweed (50) (present)

Grindelia lanceolata **Nutt.** – Narrow-leaf gum plant [Narrow-leaved gum-plant] (5, 97) (1913–1937), Narrow-leaf gumweed [Narrowleaf gumweed] (50, 122) (1937–present), Spiny-tooth gumweed [Spinytooth gumweed] (3, 4) (1977–1986)

Grindelia nuda **Wood var. *nuda*** – Curly-top gumweed [Curlytop gumweed] (3, 50) (1977–present)

Grindelia paludosa **Greene** – See *Grindelia camporum* Greene var. *camporum*

Grindelia papposa **Nesom & Suh** – Goldenweed (4) (1986), Prionopsis (5, 97) (1913–1937), Spanish gold (50) (present), Wax goldenweed (3) (1977)

Grindelia procera **Greene** – See *Grindelia camporum* Greene var. *camporum*

Grindelia revoluta **Steyerm.** – Rolled gumweed (50) (present)

Grindelia robusta **Nutt.** – See *Grindelia camporum* Greene var. *camporum*

Grindelia squarrosa **(Pursh) Dunal** – Agueweed [Ague weed, Agueweed] (54) (1905), Aslimtka (Sioux) (101) (1905), Bakskitits (Pawnee, stick head) (37) (1919), Broad-leaf gumplant [Broad-leaved gum-plant, Broad-leaved gum plant] (5, 72, 97, 122, 131, 157, 158) (1899–1937), Curlycup gumweed (50, 155) (1942–present), Curlytop gumweed [Curlytop gumweed] (4, 98) (1926–1986), Epinettes des prairies (28) (1850), Gum plant [Gumplant, Gum-plant] (85, 156) (1923–1932), Gumweed [Gum weed] (95, 98, 106, 114, 145, 148) (1894–1939), Pezhe-wasek (Omaha-Ponca, strong herb) (37) (1919), Pte-ichi-yuh'a (Dakota, curly buffalo) (37) (1919), Rosinweed [Rosin-weed, Rosin weed] (101, 106, 156) (1905–1930), Scaly grindelia (49, 69) (1903), Slimpi (Sioux) (101) (1905) MT, Stickyhead [Sticky head] (37, 156) (1919–1923), Tarweed [Tar weed, Tarweed] (156) (1923), Wild arnica (101) (1905) MT, possibly Grindelia (53, 57, 60, 157) (1900–1929)

Grindelia squarrosa **(Pursh) Dunal var. *nuda* (Wood.) Gray** – See *Grindelia nuda* Wood var. *nuda*

Grindelia squarrosa **(Pursh) Dunal var. *quasiperennis* Lunell** – Curlycup gumweed (3, 50) (1977–present)

Grindelia squarrosa **(Pursh) Dunal var. *serrulata* (Rydb.) Steyermark** – Curlycup gumweed (50) (present)

Grindelia squarrosa **(Pursh) Dunal var. *squarrosa*** – Curlycup gumweed (3, 50) (1977–present)

Grindelia squarrosa **(Pursh.) Nuttall** – possibly *Grindelia squarrosa* (Pursh) Dunal

Grindelia stricta **DC. var. *angustifolia* (Gray) M. A. Lane** – Grindelia (57) (1917)

Grindelia **Willd.** – Gum plant [Gumplant, Gum-plant] (1, 156, 158) (1900–1932), Gumweed [Gum weed] (4, 50, 93, 146, 155) (1936–present), Prionopsis (158) (1900), Tarweed [Tar weed, Tar-weed] (82, 158) (1900–1930)

Grossularia **(Tourn.) Mill.** – See *Ribes* L.

Grossularia cynosbati **(L.) Mill.** – See *Ribes cynosbati* L.

Grossularia hirtella **(Michx.) Spach** – See *Ribes hirtellum* Michx.

Grossularia missouriensis **(Nutt.) Coville & Britton** – See *Ribes missouriense* Nutt.

Grossularia oxyacanthioides **(L.) Mill.** – See *Ribes oxyacanthoides* L. subsp. *oxyacanthoides*

Grossularia reclinata **(L.) Mill.** – See *Ribes uva-crispa* L. var. *sativum* DC.

Grossularia rotundifolia **(Michx.) Covar. & Britton** – See *Ribes rotundifolium* Michx.

Grossularia setosa **(Lindl.) Covar. & Britton** – See *Ribes oxyacanthoides* L. subsp. *setosum* (Lindl.) Sinnott

Guaiacum angustifolium **Engelm.** – Guayacan (124) (1937), Lignum-vitae [Lignum vitae] or Lignum-vitae tree (106) (1930), Soap bush [Soapbush] (106) (1930)

Guaiacum **L.** – Lignum-vitae [Lignum vitae] or Lignum-vitae tree (13, 15) (1849–1895)

Guaiacum officinale **L.** – Guaiac (92) (1876), Guaiacum (92) (1876), Guayac (7) (1828), Lignum-vitae [Lignum vitae] or Lignum-vitae tree (7, 60, 92) (1828–1902), Gayac bois saint (20) (1857), Holy wood (20) (1857), Lignum benedictum (49) (1898), Lignum

sanctum (49) (1898), Lignum-vitae [Lignum vitae] or Lignum-vitae tree (49, 57) (1898–1917), Palus sanctus (49) (1898), Small-leaf lignum-vitae [Small-leaved lignum vitae] (20) (1857), Wood-of-life [Wood of life] (20) (1857)

Guajacum angustifolium **Engelm.** – See *Guaiacum angustifolium* Engelm.

Guajacum **L.** – See *Guaiacum* L.

Guajacum officinale **L.** – See *Guaiacum officinale* L.

Guajacum sanctum **L.** – See *Guaiacum sanctum* L.

Guanabanus – See *Annona* L.

Guarella canescens **(Torr.) Small.** – See *Oenothera canescens* Torr. & Frem.

Guayacum officinale **L.** – possibly *Guaiacum officinale* L.

Guazuma tomentosa **H.B.K.** – See *Guazuma ulmifolia* Lam.

Guazuma ulmifolia **Lam.** – Bastard cedar (92, 107) (1876–1919)

Guilandina bonduc **L.** – See *Caesalpinia bonduc* (L.) Roxb.

Guilandina bonducella **L.** – See *Caesalpinia bonduc* (L.) Roxb.

Guilandina crista **auct. non (L.) Small** – See *Caesalpinia bonduc* (L.) Roxb.

Guilandina dioica **L.** – See *Gymnocladus dioicus* (L.) K. Koch

Guilandina **L.** – See *Caesalpinia* L.

Guilandina moringa **L.** – See *Moringa oleifera* Lam.

Guilleminea densa **(Willd.) Moq.** – Dense cotton-flower [Dense cottonflower] (4) (1986), Small matweed (50) (present)

Guilleminea lanuginosa **(Poir.) Hook. f.** – See *Gossypianthus lanuginosus* (Poir.) Moq. var. *lanuginosus*

Guillenia flavescens **(Hook.) Greene** – Wild cabbage (74) (1893)

Guizotia abyssinica **(L. f.) Cass.** – Ramtil (92) (1876), Ramtilla (50) (present)

Guizotia oleifera **[DC.]** – See *Guizotia abyssinica* (L. f.) Cass.

Gunnera chilensis **(Lam.) O** – See *Gunnera tinctoria* (Molina) Mirbel

Gunnera **L.** – Gunnera (138) (1923)

Gunnera tinctoria **(Molina) Mirbel** – Chilean gunnera (138) (1923)

Gutierrezia dracunculoides **(DC.) Blake** – See *Amphiachyris dracunculoides* (DC.) Nutt.

Gutierrezia euthamia **Torr. & Gray** – See *Gutierrezia sarothrae* (Pursh) Britton & Rusby

Gutierrezia **Lag.** – Broomweed [Broom-weed, Broom weed] (93, 122) (1936–1937), Brownweed [Brown-weed] (158) (1900), Snakeweed [Snake-weed, Snake weed, Snake Weede] (50, 155) (1942–present)

Gutierrezia sarothrae **(Pursh) Britton & Rusby** – Broom snakeweed (3, 50, 155) (1942–present), Broomweed [Broom-weed, Broom weed] (5, 37, 76, 93, 97, 121, 122, 127, 148, 156) (1896–1939), Brownweed [Brown-weed] (156) (1923), Green greasewood (113, 130) (1890–1895), Matchweed [Match-weed] (146) (1939) MT, Peži zizi (Lakota, yellow herb) (121) (1918?–1970?), Rabbitbrush [Rabbit-brush, Rabbit brush] (5, 156) (1913–1923), Rabbitweed [Rabbit-weed] (156) (1923), Snakeweed [Snake-weed, Snake weed, Snake Weede] (4) (1986)

Gutierrezia texana **(DC.) Torr. & Gray** – Broomweed [Broom-weed, Broom weed] (106) (1930), Texas snakeweed (50) (present)

Gymnadenia conopsea **(L.) R. Br.** – Fragrant orchid (50) (present), Sweet-smelling satyrion [Sweete smelling satyrion] (178) (1596)

Gymnadenia conopsea **R. Br.** – See *Gymnadenia conopsea* (L.) R. Br.

Gymnadeniopsis clavellata **(Michx.) Rydb.** – See *Platanthera clavellata* (Michx.) Luer

Gymnadeniopsis integra **(Nutt.) Rydb.** – See *Platanthera integra* (Nutt.) Gray ex Beck

Gymnadeniopsis nivea **(Nutt.) Rydb.** – See *Platanthera nivea* (Nutt.) Luer

Gymnanthes lucida **Sw.** – Agalboche luisant (French) (20) (1857), Shingin-leaf poison wood [Shingin-leaved poison wood] (20) (1857)

Gymnocarpium disjunctum **(Rupr.) Ching** – Oak fern [Oak-fern, Oke ferne] (109, 155) (1942–1949)

Gymnocarpium dryopteris **(L.) Newman** – Pale mountain polypody (158) (1900), Small-leaf fern [Small leafed ferne] (178) (1596), Western oak fern [Western oakfern] (50) (present)

Gymnocarpium dryopteris (L.) Newman var. *pumilum* (DC.) Boivin – See *Gymnocarpium robertianum* (Hoffmann) Newman

Gymnocarpium robertianum (Hoffmann) Newman – Scented oak fern [Scented oak-fern] (5, 50) (1913–present)

Gymnocladus canadensis Lam. – See *Gymnocladus dioicus* (L.) K. Koch

Gymnocladus dioica (L.) Koch – See *Gymnocladus dioicus* (L.) K. Koch

Gymnocladus dioicus (L.) K. Koch – American coffee bean [American coffee-bean] or American coffee-bean tree (5, 6, 49, 92, 156, 157) (1892–1929), American coffee tree (61, 157, 158) (1870–1929), Bonduc (38) (1820), Bondue (6, 7) (1828–1932), Canadian dioiceous bonduc (8) (1785), Chicot (5, 38, 156, 157, 158) (1820–1929), Chicot (French) (6, 20, 107) (1857–1919), Cniquier dioïque (French) (8) (1785), Coffee bean tree (10, 12) (1818–1820), Coffee nut [Coffee-nuts, Coffee-nut] or Coffee nut tree (5, 35, 44, 156, 157, 158) (1806–1929), Coffee tree [Coffee-tree, Coffeetree] (7, 8, 18, 20, 27, 38, 49, 82, 112, 125, 156) (1785–1937), Gourganes (French) (20) (1857), Hardy bonduc (38) (1820), Kentucky coffee bean (76) (1896), Kentucky coffee tree [Kentucky coffee-tree, Kentucky coffeetree] (1, 2, 3, 4, 5, 6, 9, 14, 37, 48, 50, 63, 72, 76, 82, 85, 92, 97, 107, 109, 112, 113, 130, 131, 138, 155, 156, 157, 158) (1873–present), Kentucky mahogany (5, 6, 49, 92, 156, 157, 158) (1892–1929), Mahogany or Mahogany tree (7, 8) (1785–1828), Nanpashakanak (Winnebago) (37) (1919), Nantita (Omaha-Ponca) (37) (1919), Nickar tree [Nickar-tree] (5, 6, 7, 8, 92, 157, 158) (1785–1929), Nicker tree [Nicker-tree] (107, 156) (1919–1923), Nicker-nut (156) (1923), Stump tree [Stump-tree, Stumptree] (38, 107, 156) (1820–1923), Tohuts (Pawnee) (37) (1919), Wah'nah'na (Dakota) (37) (1919)

Gymnocladus Lam. – Coffee tree [Coffee-tree, Coffeetree] (50, 155) (1942–present), Kentucky coffee tree [Kentucky coffee-tree, Kentucky coffeetree] (93) (1936)

Gymnogramma triangularis Kaulfuss – See *Pentagramma triangularis* (Kaulfuss) Yatskievych, Windham & Wollenweber

Gymnolomia porteri (Gray) Gray – See *Helianthus porteri* (A.Gray) Pruski

Gymnolomia porteri Gray – See *Helianthus porteri* (A.Gray) Pruski

Gymnopogon ambiguus (Michx.) Britton, Sterns & Poggenb. – Bearded skeleton grass [Bearded skeletongrass] (3, 50, 155) (1942–present), Broad-leaf beard grass [Broad-leaved beard grass, Broad-leaved beard-grass] (5, 119, 163) (1852–1938), Naked beard grass [Naked beard-grass] (5, 66, 92, 94, 119) (1876–1938)

Gymnopogon brevifolius Trin. – Short-leaf beard grass [Short-leaved-beard grass, Short-leaved beard grass] (5, 66, 94, 163) (1852–1903), Short-leaf skeleton grass [Shortleaf skeleton grass] (50) (present)

Gymnopogon P. Beauv. – Beard grass [Beard-grass, Beardgrass] (66) (1903), Skeleton grass [Skeletongrass] (50, 155) (1942–present)

Gymnopogon racemosus [Beauv.] – See *Gymnopogon ambiguus* (Michx.) Britton, Sterns & Poggenb.

Gynandropsis DC. – See *Cleome* L.

Gynema balsamica Raf. – See *Pluchea foetida* (L.) DC.

Gynerium argenteum Nees. – See *Cortaderia selloana* (J. A. & J. H. Schultes) Aschers. & Graebn.

Gynerium saccharoides – See *Gynerium sagittatum* (Aubl.) Beauv.

Gynerium sagittatum (Aubl.) Beauv. – Uva grass [Uva-grass] (109, 138, 163) (1852–1949)

Gynerium sagittatum Beauv. – See *Gynerium sagittatum* (Aubl.) Beauv.

Gynura aurantiaca (Blume) DC. – Velvet plant [Velvet-plant, Velvet-plant] (109, 138) (1923–1949)

Gynura aurantiaca DC. – See *Gynura aurantiaca* (Blume) DC.

Gypsophila acutifolia Stev. ex Spreng. – Green gypsophila (138) (1923)

Gypsophila elegans Bieb. – Common gypsophila (138, 155) (1923–1942)

Gypsophila L. – Baby's-breath [Babies' breath, Baby's breath, Babies'-breath, Babysbreath] (50, 93, 156, 158) (1900–present), Gypsophill [Gypsophila, Gypsophyll] (138, 155, 158) (1900–1942)

Gypsophila muralis L. – Baby's-breath [Babies' breath, Baby's breath, Babies'-breath, Babysbreath] (3, 85) (1932–1977), Cushion gypsophila (138, 155) (1923–1942), Low babysbreath (50) (present), Low gypsophyll (5) (1913)

Gypsophila paniculata L. – Baby's-breath gypsophila [Babysbreath gypsophila] (50) (present), Baby's-breath [Babies' breath, Baby's breath, Babies'-breath, Babysbreath] (4, 5, 76, 85, 109, 138, 155, 156, 158) (1896–1986), Chalk plant [Chalk-plant] (156) (1923), Gypsophill [Gypsophila, Gypsophyll] (158) (1900), Levant soapwort (57) (1917), Mist (5, 76, 156, 158) (1907–1923) Eastern MA, Panicled gypsophila (156) (1923), Saponaria levantica (57) (1917), Tall gypsophyll (5, 72, 156, 158) (1900–1923)

Gypsophila repens L. – Creeping gypsophila (138) (1923)

Gypsophila scorzonerifolia Ser. – Garden baby's-breath [Garden babysbreath] (50) (present)

Gyrnerium sagittatum Beauv. – See *Gynerium sagittatum* (Aubl.) Beauv.

Gyromia L. – See *Medeola* L.

Gyromia virginica – See *Medeola virginiana* L.

Gyrophora Ach. – Rock moss (92) (1876)

Gyrophora muhlenbergia Ach. – See *Umbilicaria muehlenbergii* (Ach.) Tuck.

Gyrophora vellea L. – See *Umbilicaria vellea* (L.) Ach.

Gyrostachys cernua (L.) Kuntze – See *Spiranthes cernua* (L.) L. C. Rich.

Gyrostachys gracilis (Bigel.) Kuntze – See *Spiranthes lacera* (Raf.) Raf. var. *gracilis* (Bigelow) Luer

Gyrostachys stricta [Rydb.] – See *Spiranthes romanzoffiana* Cham.

Gyrotheca tinctoria (J. F. Gmel.) Salisb. – See *Lachnanthes caroliana* (Lam.) Dandy

Gyrotheca tinctoria (Walt.) Salisb. – See *Lachnanthes caroliana* (Lam.) Dandy

H

Habenaria blephariglottis **Torr.** – See *Platanthera blephariglottis* (Willd.) Lindl. var. *blephariglottis*

Habenaria bracteata **W.** – See *Coeloglossum viride* (L.) Hartman var. *virescens* (Muhl. ex Willd.) Luer

Habenaria ciliaris **R. Br.** – See *Platanthera ciliaris* (L.) Lindl.

Habenaria clavellata **(Michx.) Spreng.** – See *Platanthera clavellata* (Michx.) Luer

Habenaria dilatata **(Pursh) Hook** – See *Platanthera dilatata* (Pursh) Lindl. ex Beck var. *dilatata*

Habenaria fimbriata **R. Br.** – See *Platanthera grandiflora* (Bigelow) Lindl.

Habenaria flava **(L.) R. Br.** – See *Platanthera flava* (L.) Lindl. var. *flava*

Habenaria hookeri – See *Platanthera hookeri* (Torr. ex Gray) Lindl.

Habenaria hyperborea **(L.) R. Br.** – See *Platanthera hyperborea* (L.) Lindl. var. *hyperborea*

Habenaria integra **(Nutt.) Spreng.** – See *Platanthera integra* (Nutt.) Gray ex Beck

Habenaria lacera **(Michx.) Lodd.** – See *Platanthera lacera* (Michx.) G. Don

Habenaria lacera **Lodd.** – See *Platanthera lacera* (Michx.) G. Don

Habenaria leucophaea **(Nutt.) Gray** – See *Platanthera leucophaea* (Nutt.) Lindl.

Habenaria obtusata **(Banks ex Pursh) Richards.** – See *Platanthera obtusata* (Banks ex Pursh) Lindl.

Habenaria orbiculata **Torr.** – See *Platanthera orbiculata* (Pursh) Lindl.

Habenaria peramoena – See *Platanthera peramoena* (Gray) Gray

Habenaria psycodes **Gray.** – See *Platanthera psycodes* (L.) Lindl.

Habenaria psycodes **Spreng.** – See *Platanthera psycodes* (L.) Lindl.

Habenaria saccata **Greene** – See *Platanthera stricta* Lindl.

Habenaria scutellata **(Nutt.) F. Morris** – See *Platanthera flava* (L.) Lindl. var. *flava*

Habenaria unalascensis **(Spreng.) Wats.** – See *Piperia unalascensis* (Spreng.) Rydb.

Habenaria viridis **(L.) R. Br. var. bracteata (Muhl.) Gray** – See *Coeloglossum viride* (L.) Hartman var. *virescens* (Muhl. ex Willd.) Luer

Habenaria **Willd.** – Bog orchid (50) (present), Fringed orchis (156) (1923), Orchis (158) (1900), Rein orchis (2) (1895), Wood orchid (1) (1932)

Habranthus tubispathus **(L'Hér.) Traub** – Yellow rainlily [Yellow rain lily] (122, 124) (1937) TX

Hackelia deflexa **(Wahlenb.) Opiz** – Nodding stickseed (50) (present)

Hackelia deflexa **(Wahlenb.) Opiz var. americana (Gray) Fern. & I.M. Johnston** – American stickseed (50) (present), Nodding stickseed (5, 72, 93, 131) (1899–1936)

Hackelia floribunda **(Lehm.) I. M. Johnston** – Large-flower stickseed [Large-flowered stickseed] (4, 5, 93, 131) (1899–1986), Large-flower sticktight [Large-flowered sticktight] (85) (1932), Many-flower stickseed [Manyflower stickseed] (50) (present), Stickweed [Stick-weed, Stick weed] (77) (1898) CA

Hackelia **Opiz** – Stickseed [Stick seed, Stick-seed] (4, 50) (1986–present)

Hackelia virginiana **(L.) I. M. Johnston** – Beggar's-lice [Beggar lice, Beggar-lice, Beggarlice, Beggarslice] (2, 5, 50, 62, 63, 80, 145, 156, 157, 158) (1895–present), Beggarticks [Beggar ticks, Beggar's ticks, Beggars' ticks, Beggars-ticks, Beggar-ticks] (5, 77, 156, 157, 158) (1898–1929), Dysentery root [Dysentery-root] (5, 156, 157, 158) (1900–1929), Dysentery weed [Dysentery-weed] (5, 156, 157, 158) (1900–1929), Hairy stickseed [Hairy stick seed] (5) (1913), Hound's-tongue with a very small flower [Hounds tongue with a very small flower] (181) (~1678), Small

sheep-bur (156, 157, 158) (1900–1929), Soldiers (5, 73, 156, 157, 158) (1892–1929) Eastern MA, Sticktight [Stick-tight, Sticktights, Stick-tights, Stick tights] (5, 75, 156, 157, 158) (1894–1929), Virginia mouse-ear (5, 156, 157, 158) (1900–1929), Virginia stickseed (5, 62, 72, 93, 97, 131, 156, 157, 158) (1899–1929), Virginia stickweed (3) (1977)

Hackelochloa granularis **(L.) Kuntze** – Lizard-tail grass [Lizard-tail-grass] (93, 94, 163) (1852–1936)

Haematoxylum campechianum **L.** – Blockwood (92) (1876), Campeachy wood (92) (1876), Logwood (106, 138) (1923–1930)

Haematoxylum **L.** – Logwood (7, 138) (1828–1923)

Halenia deflexa **(Sm.) Griseb.** – American spur-gentian [American spurgentian] (155) (1942), American spurred gentian (50) (present), Spurred gentian (1, 3, 4, 131, 156) (1899–1986)

Halerpestes cymbalaria **(Pursh) Greene** – See *Ranunculus cymbalaria* Pursh

Halerpestes **Greene** – See *Ranunculus* L. (all US species)

Halesia carolina **L.** – Bell-olive tree [Bell olive tree, bell olive-tree] (5, 156) (1913–1923), Bellwood [Bell-wood] (156) (1923), Calico wood [Calico-wood] (5, 156) (1913–1923), Halesia à fruit à deux (French) (8) (1785), Possum-wood [Possum wood] (156) (1923), Rattlebox [Rattle box, Rattle-box] (156) (1923), Shittim-wood [Shittimwood, Shittim wood] (5) (1913), Silverbell [Silverbell] or Silver-bell tree [Silverbell-tree, Silver bell tree, Silver-bell tree] (5, 97, 124, 156) (1913–1937), Snowdrop tree [Snowdrop-tree, Snow drop tree] (5, 122, 124, 156) (1937–1949), Tisswood [Tiss wood, Tiss-wood] (5, 156) (1913–1923), Two-wing fruited halesia [Two-winged fruited halesia] (8) (1785), Two-wing halesia [Two-winged halesia] (2) (1895), Two-wing silverbell (138) (1923), Wild olive [Wilde oliue] or Wild olive tree [Wild olive-tree] (5, 156) (1913–1923)

Halesia diptera **Ell.** – See *Halesia carolina* L.

Halesia diptera **L.** – See *Halesia carolina* L.

Halesia **Ellis ex L.** – Halesia (8) (1785), Halesia (French) (8) (1785), Silverbell [Silver-bell] or Silver-bell tree [Silverbell-tree, Silver bell tree, Silver-bell tree] (2, 8, 109, 138, 156) (1785–1949), Snowdrop [Snowdrops, Snow-drops, Snow drop] (2) (1895), Snowdrop tree [Snowdrop-tree, Snow drop tree] (10, 109) (1818–1949)

Halesia **L.** – See *Halesia* Ellis ex L.

Halesia monticola **[(Rehd.) Sarg.]** – See *Halesia tetraptera* Ellis var. *monticola* (Rehd.) Reveal & Seldin

Halesia tetraptera **Ellis var. monticola (Rehd.) Reveal & Seldin** – Mountain silverbell (138) (1923), Silverbell [Silver-bell] or Silver-bell tree [Silverbell-tree, Silver bell tree, Silver-bell tree] (65) (1931) OK

Halesia tetraptera **L.** – Four-wing fruited halesia [Four-winged fruited halesia] (8) (1785), Four-wing halesia [Four-winged halesia] (2) (1895), Great silverbell (138) (1923), Halesia à fruit à quatre (French) (8) (1785), Shittim-wood [Shittimwood, Shittim wood] (75) (1894) WV, Silverbell [Silver-bell] or Silver-bell tree [Silver-bell-tree, Silver bell tree, Silver-bell tree] (92, 107) (1876–1919), Snowdrop tree [Snowdrop-tree, Snow drop tree] (14, 19, 92) (1840–1882), Wild olive [Wilde oliue] or Wild olive tree [Wild olive-tree] (107) (1919)

Halimodendron **Fischer ex DC.** – Salt tree [Salt-tree] (138) (1923), Saltbush [Salt-bush, Salt bush] (112) (1937) Neb

Halimodendron halodendron **(L. f.) Voss** – Salt tree [Salt-tree] (138) (1923), Saltbush [Salt-bush, Salt bush] (112) (1937) Neb

Halogeton **C. A. Mey.** – Salt-lover [Saltlover] (50) (present)

Halogeton glomeratus **(Bieb.) C. A. Mey.** – Salt-lover [Saltlover] (50) (present)

Hamamelis **L.** – Hamamelis (French) (8) (1785), Witch hazel [Witch-hazel, Witchhazel, Witch hazle] (1, 2, 8, 10, 109, 138, 156, 190) (~1759–1949)

Hamamelis macrophylla – See *Hamamelis virginiana* L.

Hamamelis vernalis **Sargent** – Vernal witch-hazel (138) (1923)

Hamamelis virginiana **L.** – Big-leaf witch hazel [Bigleaf witch hazel] (7) (1828), Common witch-hazel (138) (1923), Hamamelier d'Hyver (French) (7) (1828), Hamamelis (52, 53, 54, 55, 57, 174, 177, 189) (1753–1922), Hamamelis Cortex (Official name of Materia Medica) (7) (1828), Hamamelis de Virginie (French) (8) (1785), Hexehasel (German) (7) (1828), Nsakemižinš (Chippewa) (105) (1932), Pistachio (5, 92, 156) (1876–1923), Pistachoe nut (7) (1828), Shemba (Osage) (7) (1828), Snapping hazel (5, 53, 92, 156) (1876–1923), Snapping hazel nut [Snapping hazelnut] (6, 7, 49) (1828–1898), Spotted alder (5, 6, 49, 92, 156) (1876–1923), Striped alder (92) (1876), Tobacco-wood [Tobacco wood] (5, 92, 156) (1876–1923), Virginia witch hazel [Virginian witch hazel] (8) (1785), Water seeker (6) (1892), Winter witchhazel [Winter witch hazel] (7) (1828), Winterbloom [Winter bloom, Winter-bloom] (5, 6, 7, 49, 53, 92, 156) (1828–1923), Witch hazel [Witch-hazel, Witchhazel, Witch hazle] (5, 6, 7, 19, 40, 41, 46, 49, 52, 53, 54, 55, 57, 59, 61, 63, 72, 92, 105, 107, 112, 113, 122, 124, 156, 177, 183, 184, 187) (~1756–1937)

Hamamelis virginica **[L.]** – See *Hamamelis virginiana* L.

Hamatocactus setispinus **(Engelm.) Britton & Rose** – See *Thelocactus setispinus* (Engelm.) E. F. Anderson

Hamiltonia oleifera **W.** – See *Pyrularia oleifera* (Muhl. ex Willd.) A. Gray

Hamosa **Medik.** – See *Astragalus* L. (US species)

Haploesthes **Gray** – False broomweed (4, 50) (1986–present), Haploesthes (158) (1900)

Haploesthes greggii **Gray** – False broomweed (50) (present), Gregg's haploesthes (5, 97) (1913–1937)

Haplopappus acaulis **(Nutt.) Gray** – See *Stenotus acaulis* (Nutt.) Nutt. var. *acaulis*

Haplopappus acradenius **(Greene) Blake** – See *Isocoma acradenia* (Greene) Greene var. *acradenia*

Haplopappus annuus **(Rydb.) Cory** – See *Rayjacksonia annua* (Rydb.) R. L. Hartman & M. A. Lane

Haplopappus **Cass.** – Goldenweed (4) (1986), Haplopappus (50) (present)

Haplopappus ciliatus **(Nutt.) DC.** – See *Grindelia papposa* Nesom & Suh

Haplopappus divaricatus **(Nutt.) Gray** – See *Croptilon divaricatum* (Nutt.) Raf.

Haplopappus eastwoodae **H.M.Hall** – See *Ericameria fasciculata* (Eastw.) J. F. Macbr.

Haplopappus engelmannii **(Gray) Hall** – See *Oonopsis engelmannii* (Gray) Greene

Haplopappus falcatus **(Rydb.) S.F. Blake** – See *Stenotus acaulis* (Nutt.) Nutt.

Haplopappus fremontii **(Gray) Greene** – See *Oonopsis foliosa* (Gray) Greene var. *foliosa*

Haplopappus greenei **A. Gray** – See *Ericameria greenei* (Gray) Nesom

Haplopappus heterophyllus **(Gray) Blake)** – See *Isocoma pluriflora* (Torr. & Gray) Greene

Haplopappus integrifolius **Porter ex Gray** – See *Pyrrocoma integrifolia* (Porter ex Gray) Greene

Haplopappus junceus **Greene** – See *Machaeranthera juncea* (Greene) Shinners

Haplopappus lanceolatus **(Hook.) Torr. & Gray** – See *Pyrrocoma lanceolata* (Hook.) Greene var. *lanceolata*

Haplopappus laricifolius **Gray** – See *Ericameria laricifolia* (Gray) Shinners

Haplopappus megacephalus **(Nash) Hitchc.** – See *Rayjacksonia phyllocephala* (DC.) R. L. Hartman & M. L. Lane

Haplopappus phyllocephalus **DC.** – See *Rayjacksonia phyllocephala* (DC.) R. L. Hartman & M. L. Lane

Haplopappus spinulosus **(Pursh) DC.** – See *Machaeranthera pinnatifida* (Hook.) Shinners subsp. *pinnatifida*

Haplopappus validus **(Rydb.) Cory** – See *Croptilon hookerianum* (Torr. & Gray) House var. *validum* (Rydb.) E. B. Sm.

Haplopappus venetus **(Kunth) Blake subsp. *vernonioides* (Nutt.) Hall** – See *Isocoma menziesii* (Hook. & Arn.) Nesom var. *vernonioides* (Nutt.) Nesom

Happlopappus venetus – See *Isocoma veneta* (Kunth) Greene

Harrimanella hypnoides **(L.) Coville** – Moss plant [Moss-plant] (5, 156) (1913–1923)

Hartmania **Spach.** – See *Oenothera* L.

Hartmannia speciosa **(Nutt.) Small.** – See *Oenothera speciosa* Nutt.

Hasteola **Raf.** – Sweet-scented Indian plantain (5, 72) (1907–1913)

Hasteola suaveolens **(L.) Pojark.** – Indian plantain (82) (1930) IA, Sweet-scented Indian plantain (5, 72, 156) (1907–1923), Wild caraway [Wild carraway] (5, 19, 156) (1840–1923)

Havardia pallens **(Benth.) Britt. & Rose** – Gulf Coast guajillo (124) (1937) TX, Gulf guajillo tenaza (122) (1937) TX

Hazardia brickellioides **(Blake) W. D. Clark** – Brickell's goldenweed [Brickell goldenweed] (155) (1942), Hoary goldenweed (155) (1942)

Hazardia cana **(Gray) Greene** – Hoary goldenweed (155) (1942)

Hazardia squarrosa **(Hook. & Arn.) Greene var. *squarrosa*** – Sawtooth goldenweed [Sawtooth goldenweed] (155) (1942), Singlehead goldenweed [Singlehead goldenweed] (155) (1942)

Hebe speciosa **(R. Cunningham ex A. Cunningham) J. C. Andersen** – Showy speedwell (138) (1923)

Hechtia **Klotzsch** – Ballmoss [Ball moss] (122) (1937) TX

Hechtia texensis **S. Wats.** – False agave (122, 124) (1937) TX

Hedeoma drummondii **Benth.** – Drummond's false pennyroyal [Drummond false pennyroyal, Drummond falsepennyroyal] (3, 4, 50, 155) (1942–present), Drummond's pennyroyal (131) (1899), False pennyroyal [Falsepennyroyal] (124) (1937), Lemon mint (124) (1937) TX, Long-flower pennyroyal [Long-flowered pennyroyal] (5, 97) (1913–1937)

Hedeoma hispida **Pursh** – Hairy pennyroyal (82) (1930), Maka chiaka (Dakota) (37) (1919), Pennyroyal [Penny-royal, Penny royal, Penniroyal] (85) (1932), Rough false pennyroyal [Rough falsepennyroyal] (4, 50, 155) (1942–present), Rough pennyroyal (3, 5, 37, 72, 93, 95, 97, 122, 131) (1907–1977)

Hedeoma longiflora **Rydb.** – See *Hedeoma drummondii* Benth.

Hedeoma **Pers.** – American pennyroyal (156) (1923), False pennyroyal [Falsepennyroyal] (50, 155) (1942–present), Mock pennyroyal (1, 4, 82, 93) (1930–1986), Pennyroyal [Penny-royal, Penny royal, Penniroyal] (158) (1900), Wild pennyroyal (10) (1818)

Hedeoma pulegioides **(L.) Pers.** – American false penny-royal [American false pennyroyal, American falsepennyroyal] (50, 155) (1942–present), American pennyroyal (1, 2, 5, 6, 7, 46, 49, 53, 55, 57, 59, 63, 72, 82, 85, 93, 95, 156, 157, 158) (1879–1936), Americanischer Polei [Amerikanischer Poley] (German) (6, 158) (1892–1900), Hedeoma (55, 59) (1911–1917), Hedeoma herba (Official name of Materia Medica) (7) (1828), Hedeome pouliot (French) (7) (1828), Mock pennyroyal (6, 156, 157, 158) (1892–1929), Mosquito plant [Mosquitoplant] (157) (1929), Peneriall (46) (1879), Pennyroyal [Pennyroyal, Penny royal, Penniroyal] (3, 7, 19, 41, 49, 53, 61, 62, 121, 157, 158, 184, 186) (1770–1977), Pennyroyal-leaf cunila [Penny royal leaved cunila] (42) (1814), Peže tuhu (Osage, green herb) (121) (1918–1970?), Poleyblattrige (German) (7) (1828), Poleyblattrige Cunila (German) (186) (1814), Pouliot Americain (French) (158) (1900), Pouliot d'Amerique (French) (6) (1892), Pudding-grass [Pudding grass] (77) (1898) Western US, Squaw-mint [Squawmint, Squaw mint] (5, 6, 7, 49, 53, 92, 156, 157, 158) (1828–1929), Squawweed [Squawweed, Squaw-weed] (156) (1923), Stinking balm (6, 7, 92, 158) (1828–1900), Stinking tich-weed (157) (1929), Thickweed [Thick weed] (92) (1876), Tickseed [Tick-seed, Tick seed] (156) (1923), Tickweed [Tick weed, Tick-weed] (5, 6, 7, 49, 53, 92, 158) (1828–1922), Upright pennyroyal [Upright peniroyal] (46) (1879)

Hedeoma reverchonii **Gray** – Reverchon's false pennyroyal [Reverchon false pennyroyal] (4, 50) (1986–present)

Hedera canariensis **Willd.** – See *Hedera helix* L. subsp. *canariensis* (Willd.) Cout.

Hedera colchica **(K. Koch) K. Koch** – Colchis ivy (109, 138) (1923–1949)

Hedera colchica **Koch** – See *Hedera colchica* (K. Koch) K. Koch

Hedera helix **L.** – Black yew [Blacke yuy] (179) (1526), Common ivy (49) (1898), English ivy (19, 106, 109, 138) (1840–1949), Ivy (7, 49, 92, 106) (1828–1930), Yuy (179) (1526)

Hedera helix **L. subsp.** *canariensis* **(Willd.) Cout.** – Algerian ivy (109, 138) (1923–1949)

Hedera **L.** – American ivy (1) (1932), Ivy (8, 138, 155, 158, 184) (1785–1923), Lierre (French) (8) (1785), Virginia creeper [Virginian creeper] (1) (1932), Woodbine (1, 82) (1930–1932)

Hedera quinquefolia – See *Parthenocissus quinquefolia* (L.) Planch.

Hedychium coronarium **Koenig** – Common ginger-lily [Common gingerlily] (138) (1923), Garland flower [Garland-flower] (109) (1949)

Hedychium gardnerianum **Shepard ex Ker-Gawl.** – Indian ginger-lily [India ginger-lily, India gingerlily] (138) (1923)

Hedychium **Koenig** – Garland flower [Garland-flower] (92) (1876), Ginger-lily [Gingerlily] (109, 138) (1923–1949)

Hedychloe pumila **Raf.** – possibly *Kyllinga pumila* Michx.

Hedyotia glomerata **Michx.** – See *Oldenlandia uniflora* L.

Hedyotis crassifolia **Raf.** – See *Houstonia pusilla* Schoepf

Hedyotis glomerata **(Michx.) Elliott** – See *Oldenlandia uniflora* L.

Hedyotis humifusa **Gray** – See *Houstonia humifusa* (Gray) Gray

Hedyotis **L.** – Bluets [Bluet] (4) (1986), Star-violet [Starviolet] (50) (present)

Hedyotis longifolia **(Gaertn.) Hook** – See *Houstonia longifolia* Gaertn.

Hedyotis nigricans **(Lam.) Fosberg** – Diamond flower [Diamondflower, Diamond-flower, Diamondflowers] (50) (present), Narrowleaf bluet [Narrowleaf bluet] (3, 4) (1977–1986)

Hedyotis nigricans **(Lam.) Fosberg var.** *nigricans* – Baby's-breath [Babies' breath, Baby's breath, Babies'-breath, Babysbreath] (156) (1923), Bluets [Bluet] (156) (1923), Common bluets (155) (1942), Diamond flower [Diamondflower, Diamond-flower, Diamondflowers] (50) (present), Innocence (156) (1923), Narrow-leaf houstonia [Narrow-leaved houstonia] (5, 72, 93, 97) (1907–1937), Star-violet [Star violet] (5, 156, 158) (1900–1923), Venus'-pride [Venus' pride, Venus' pride] (5, 156) (1913–1923)

Hedypnois **Mill.** – Swine's-lettuce [Swine's lettuce] (167) (1814)

Hedysarum **(Tourn.) L.** – See *Hedysarum* L.

Hedysarum alpinum **L.** – Alpine sweet-vetch [Alpine sweetvetch] (50) (present), Hedysarum (131) (1899), Sweet broom (4) (1986)

Hedysarum americanum **(Michx.) Britton** – See *Hedysarum alpinum* L.

Hedysarum boreale **Nutt.** – Boreal sweetvetch (50) (present), Hedysarum (5) (1913), Northern sweetvetch (155) (1942), Sweet broom (4) (1986), Sweetvetch [Sweet vetch] (3) (1977)

Hedysarum boreale **subsp.** *mackenzii* **(Richardson) S. L.Welsh** – Licorice root [Licorice-root, Licorice roots, Liquorice roots] (107) (1919)

Hedysarum canadense **L.** – See *Desmodium canadense* (L.) DC.

Hedysarum **L.** – Hedysarum (1, 4, 158) (1900–1986), Saintfoin (184) (1793), Sweet broom (4) (1986), Sweetvetch [Sweet vetch] (50, 155) (1942–present)

Hedysarum mackenzii **Richards** – See *Hedysarum boreale* Nutt. subsp. *mackenzii* (Richardson) S. L.Welsh

Hedysarum onobrychis **L.** – See *Onobrychis viciifolia* Scop.

Helenium amarum **(Raf.) H. Rock** – Bitter sneezeweed (4) (1986), Yellowdicks (50) (present)

Helenium amarum **(Raf.) H. Rock var.** *amarum* – Bitter sneezeweed (4, 155) (1942–1986), Bitterweed [Bitter weed, Bitter-weed] (106, 138, 156) (1923–1930), Fine-leaf sneezeweed [Fine-leaved sneezeweed] (5, 72, 97, 158) (1900–1937), Narrow-leaf sneezeweed [Narrow-leaved sneezeweed] (106) (1930), Slender-leaf sneezeweed

[Slender-leaved sneezeweed] (86) (1878), Sneezeweed [Sneeze weed, Sneeze-weed] (156) (1923), Southern sneezeweed (106) (1930), Yellowdicks (50) (present)

Helenium amarum **(Raf.) H. Rock var.** *badium* **(Gray ex S. Wats.) Waterfall** – Sneezeweed [Sneeze weed, Sneeze-weed] (97) (1937), Yellowdicks (50) (present)

Helenium autumnale **L.** – Autumn sneezeweed (71) (1898), Autumn sneezewort (71, 86) (1878–1898) used as snuff to cause sneezing, Common sneezeweed (7, 50, 138, 155) (1828–present), Dog-fennel [Dog fennel, Dog's fennel, Dog's fennel] (156) (1923), False sunflower [False sun-flower] (5, 7, 19, 71, 86, 92, 93, 156, 157, 158) (1828–1936), Helenie d'Automne (French) (7) (1828), Helenium (Official name of Materia Medica) (7) (1828), Niessenkraut (German) (7) (1828), Northern sneezeweed (106) (1930), Ox-eye [Ox eye, Oxeye, Oxe eie] (5, 7, 92, 156, 157, 158) (1828–1929), Rosilla de puebla (Spanish) (158) (1900) Mexico, Sneezeweed [Sneeze weed, Sneeze-weed] (3, 4, 5, 7, 49, 56, 62, 63, 71, 80, 82, 92, 95, 97, 126, 156, 157, 158) (1898–1986), Sneezewort [Sneeze-wort, Sneeze woort] (48, 49, 57, 71, 72, 92, 131, 156, 157, 158) (1882–1929), Staggerweed [Stagger-weed, Stagger weed] (71) (1898) SC, Swamp sneezewort (92) (1876), Swamp sunflower (5, 7, 49, 62, 71, 86, 92, 93, 156, 157, 158) (1828–1936), Wild sunflower [Wild sunflower] (49) (1898), Yellow star [Yellow-star] (5, 7, 92, 156, 157, 158) (1828–1929)

Helenium autumnale **L. var.** *montanum* **(Nutt.) Fern.** – Mountain sneezeweed (50, 155) (1942–present), Sneezeweed [Sneeze weed, Sneeze-weed] (85) (1932)

Helenium autumnalis – See *Helenium autumnale* L.

Helenium badium **(Gray) Greene** – See *Helenium amarum* (Raf.) H. Rock var. *badium* (Gray ex S. Wats.) Waterfall

Helenium bigelovi – See *Helenium bigelovii* Gray

Helenium bigelovii **Gray** – Bigelow's sneezeweed [Bigelow sneezeweed] (138) (1923)

Helenium flexuosum **Raf.** – Purple sneezeweed (50) (present), Purple-head sneezeweed [Purplehead sneezeweed (5, 97, 122, 155) (1913–1942)

Helenium hoopesii – See *Hymenoxys hoopesii* (Gray) Bierner

Helenium **L.** – American sneezewort (10) (1818), False sunflower [False sun-flower] (167) (1814), Sneezeweed [Sneeze weed, Sneeze-weed] (1, 2, 4, 50, 82, 109, 125, 138, 155, 156, 158) (1895–present)

Helenium microcephalum **DC.** – Small-head sneezeweed [Smallhead sneezeweed, Small headed sneeze weed] (50, 124) (1937–present)

Helenium montanum **Nutt.** – See *Helenium autumnale* L. var. *montanum* (Nutt.) Fern.

Helenium nudiflorum **Nutt.** – See *Helenium flexuosum* Raf.

Helenium puberulum **DC.** – Rosilla (76) (1896) CA

Helenium tenuifolium **Nutt.** – See *Helenium amarum* (Raf.) H. Rock var. *amarum*

Heleochloa schoenoides **(L.) Host** – See *Crypsis schoenoides* (L.) Lam.

Helianthella quinquenervis **(Hook.) Gray** – False sunflower [False sun-flower] (3, 4) (1977–1986), Five-nerve false sunflower [Five-nerved false sunflower] (131) (1899), Five-nerve helianthella [Five-nerve helianthella] (50) (present)

Helianthemum **Adans.** – See *Helianthemum* Mill.

Helianthemum bicknellii **Fern.** – Frostweed [Frost weed, Frost-weed] (3, 4, 157) (1929–1986), Hoary frostweed [Hoary frost-weed] (5, 50, 72, 85, 97, 131, 156) (1899–present), Rockrose [Rock-rose, Rock rose] (93, 156) (1923–1936)

Helianthemum canadense **(L.) Michx.** – Canadian cistus [Canada cistus] (42) (1814), Canadian rockrose [Canada rock rose] (5, 42, 156) (1814–1923), Canadisches Sonnenroschen (German) (6) (1892), Frost plant [Frostplant] (6, 19, 49, 92) (1840–1898), Frost-flower (156) (1923), Frostweed [Frost weed, Frost-weed] (2, 5, 6, 15, 49, 92, 156) (1876–1923), Frostwort [Frost wort] (5, 6, 7, 49, 57, 72, 92) (1828–1917), Heliantheme du Canada (French) (6) (1892), Hollyrose [Holly rose] (6) (1892), Long-branch frostweed [Long-branched frostweed, Long-branched frost-weed] (5, 156) (1913–1923), Male fluellin (46) (1671), Rockrose [Rock-rose, Rock rose] (5, 7, 6, 19, 49, 61, 92, 156, 187) (1818–1923), Scrofula plant [Scrofula-plant] (5, 92, 156) (1876–1923), Speedwell (46) (1671), Sunrose [Sun-rose] (92, 156) (1898–1923)

Helianthemum canadense **Michx.** – See *Helianthemum canadense* (L.) Michx.

Helianthemum carolinianum **(Walt.) Michx.** – Carolina rockrose [Carolina rock rose] (86) (1878), Carolina sun rockrose [Carolina sun rock-rose] (86) (1878)

Helianthemum carolinianum **Michx.** – See *Helianthemum carolinianum* (Walt.) Michx.

Helianthemum corymbosum **Michx.** – Pine Barren frostweed [Pine-barren frostweed] (5) (1913)

Helianthemum majus **(L.) B.S.P.** – See *Helianthemum bicknellii* Fern.

Helianthemum **Mill.** – Frostweed [Frost weed, Frost-weed] (1, 4, 13, 50, 93) (1849–present), Frostwort [Frost wort] (155) (1942), Rockrose [Rock-rose, Rock rose] (13, 15, 156, 158) (1849–1923), Sunrose [Sun-rose] (109, 138, 155) (1923–1949)

Helianthemum salicifolium **(L.) Mill.** – Dwarf hollyrose [Dwarfe hollyrose] (178) (1526), Willow-leaf frostweed [Willowleaf frostweed] (178) (1526)

Helianthemum **Tourn.** – See *Helianthemum* Mill.

Helianthium **Engelm.** – See *Echinodorus* L.C. Rich. ex Engelm.

Helianthus **(Vaill.) L.** – See *Helianthus* L.

Helianthus ×*ambiguus* **(Gray) Britt. (pro sp.)** [*divaricatus* × *giganteus*] – Ambiguous sunflower (72) (1907), Oblong-leaf sunflower [Oblong-leaved sunflower] (5, 97) (1913–1937)

Helianthus ×*kellermanii* **Britt.** [*grosseserratus* × *salicifolius*] – Kellerman's sunflower (5) (1913)

Helianthus ×*laetiflorus* **Pers.** [*pauciflorus* × *tuberosus*] – Cheerful sunflower (50) (present), Prairie artichoke (156) (1923), Prairie sunflower [Prairie sun-flower] (138) (1923), Showy sunflower (5, 72, 109, 138, 156) (1907–1949), Stiff sunflower (5, 72, 82, 97, 131) (1899–1937)

Helianthus ×*multiflorus* **L.** [*annuus* × *decapetalus*] – Dahlia sunflower (76) (1896) Sulphur Grove OH, Flower-of-the-sun [Flower of the sunne, many on one stalk] (178) (1526)

Helianthus ambiguus **(T. & G.) Britton** – See *Helianthus* ×*ambiguus* (Gray) Britt. [*divaricatus* × *giganteus*]

Helianthus angustifolius **L.** – Narrow-leaf sunflower [Narrow-leaved sunflower] (5) (1913), Swamp sunflower (5, 109, 122, 124, 138) (1913–1949)

Helianthus annuus **L.** – Chimalati (107) (1919), Chrysis (174) (1753), Comb flower [Comb-flower] (5, 92, 156, 157, 148) (1876–1939), Common sunflower (2, 3, 4, 5, 19, 41, 50, 57, 62, 63, 72, 80, 82, 92, 93, 95, 97, 105, 109, 122, 127, 131, 138, 145, 155, 157, 158) (1770–present), Flower-of-the-sun [Flower of the sunne] (178) (1526), Garden sunflower (92, 156, 157, 158) (1898–1929), Gold (5, 156, 158) (1900–1923), Golden (5, 156, 157, 158) (1900–1929), Great flower-of-the-sun [Great flower of the sunne] (178) (1526), Kirik-tara-kata (Pawnee, yellow eyes) (37) (1919), Larea ball (5) (1913), Larea-bell (156) (1923), Larrabell (157, 158) (1900–1929), Le Tournesol (French) (6) (1892), Mira sol (150) (1894) NM, Soleil (37) (1919), Sonnenblume (German) (6) (1892), Sunflower [Sun-flower] (6, 37, 49, 57, 107, 108, 114, 150, 157, 158) (1878–1929), Wah'cha-zizi (Dakota, yellow flower) (37) (1919), Wallflower [Wall-flower, Wallflowers] (158) (1900), Western sunflower (108) (1878), Wild sunflower [Wild sun-flower] (80, 85, 101) (1905–1932), Zha-zi (Omaha-Ponca, yellow weed) (37) (1919)

Helianthus argophyllus **Torr. & Gray** – Silver-leaf sunflower [Silverleaf sunflower] (109, 122, 124, 138) (1923–1949)

Helianthus atrorubens **L.** – Dark-eye sunflower [Darkeye sunflower] (109, 138) (1923–1949), Hairy wood sunflower (5, 97, 156) (1913–1937), Purple disk sunflower (purple-disk sunflower) (5, 156) (1913–1923)

Helianthus besseyi **Bates** – possibly *Helianthus tuberosus* L.

Helianthus californicus **DC.** – California sunflower (138) (1923)

Helianthus ciliaris **DC.** – Blueweed [Blue-weed, Blue weed] (150) (1894) NM, Plains sunflower (122) (1937) TX, Smooth sunflower (97) (1937), Texas blueweed (3, 4, 50) (1977–present), Yerba parda (Spanish) (150) (1894) NM

Helianthus cucumerifolius **Torr. & Gray** – See *Helianthus debilis* Nutt. subsp. *cucumerifolius* (Torr. & Gray) Heiser

Helianthus dalyi **Britton** – See *Helianthus maximiliani* Schrad.

Helianthus debilis **Nutt.** – Cucumber sunflower (138) (1923)

Helianthus debilis **Nutt. subsp. *cucumerifolius* (Torr. & Gray) Heiser** – Cucumber-leaf sunflower (109) (1949), Sand sunflower (124) (1937) TX

Helianthus debilis **Nutt. var. *cucumerifolius* (Torr. & Gray) Gray** – See *Helianthus debilis* Nutt. subsp. *cucumerifolius* (Torr. & Gray) Heiser

Helianthus decapetalus **L.** – River sunflower (156) (1923), Ten-petal sunflower [Ten-petalled sun-flower] (187) (1818), Ten-ray sunflower [Ten-rayed sunflower] (156) (1923), Thin-leaf sunflower [Thinleaf sunflower] (5, 62, 97, 109, 138) (1912–1949), Throatwort sunflower (5, 72, 97, 122) (1907–1937), Throatwort-leaf sunflower [Throatwort-leaved sun-flower] (187) (1818), Wild sunflower [Wild sunflower] (5, 62, 72, 156) (1907–1923)

Helianthus divaricatus **L.** – Marygold-of-Peru [Marygold of Peru] (46) (1671), Rough sunflower (5, 92, 93, 97) (1876–1937), Rough-leaf sunflower [Rough-leaved sun-flower] (187) (1818), Small-flower sunflower [Small-flowered sun-flower] (187) (1818), Woodland sunflower (5, 72, 156) (1907–1923), Woods sunflower (93) (1936)

Helianthus doronicoides **Lam.** – See *Helianthus* ×*ambiguus* (Gray) Britt. [*divaricatus* × *giganteus*]

Helianthus giganteus **L.** – Giant sunflower (5, 72, 107, 109, 138) (1907–1949), Great sunflower (38) (1820), Indian potato (5, 156) (1913–1923), Tall sunflower (5, 93, 97, 156) (1913–1937), Wild sunflower [Wild sun-flower] (5, 56, 92, 156) (1876–1923)

Helianthus grosseserratus **Martens** – Meadow sunflower (80) (1913), Prairie sunflower [Prairie sun-flower] (82) (1930), Saw-tooth sunflower [Sawtooth sunflower, Saw toothed sunflower] (3, 4, 5, 50, 72, 80, 93, 97, 122, 131, 138, 155) (1899–present), Sunflower [Sunflower] (145) (1897)

Helianthus hirsutus **Raf.** – Big-leaf woodland sunflower [Bigleaf woodland sunflower] (138) (1923), Hairy sunflower (3, 4, 50) (1977–present), Stiff-hair sunflower [Stiff-haired sunflower, Stiff-haired sunflower] (5, 72, 93, 97, 122) (1907–1937), Wood sunflower (72) (1907)

Helianthus kellermani **Britton** – See *Helianthus* ×*kellermanii* Britt. [*grosseserratus* × *salicifolius*]

Helianthus **L.** – Ground-artichoke [Ground artichoke] (1) (1932), Sunflower [Sun-flower] (1, 4, 7, 21, 35, 50, 63, 82, 93, 106, 109, 122, 127, 138, 146, 155, 156, 158, 167, 184) (1793–present)

Helianthus laetiflorus **Pers.** – See *Helianthus* ×*laetiflorus* Pers. [*pauciflorus* × *tuberosus*]

Helianthus laevigatus **Torr. & Gray** – Smooth sunflower (5) (1913)

Helianthus laevis **Pers.** – See *Bidens laevis* (L.) Britton, Sterns & Poggenb.

Helianthus lenticularis **Dougl.** – See *Helianthus annuus* L.

Helianthus maximiliani **Schrad.** – Judge Daly's sunflower (5) (1913), Maximilian's sunflower [Maximilian sunflower, Maximillian's sunflower, Maximilians sunflower] (3, 4, 5, 50, 72, 80, 82, 85, 86, 97, 122, 124, 131, 138, 155) (1878–present), Narrow-leaf sunflower [Narrow-leaved sunflower] (127) (1933), Sunflower [Sun-flower] (145) (1897), Wild artichoke (101) (1905)

Helianthus maximilianii **Schrad.** – See *Helianthus maximiliani* Schrad.

Helianthus microcephalus **Torr. & Gray** – Small wood sunflower (5, 97) (1913–1937)

Helianthus mollis **Lam.** – Ashy sunflower (3, 4, 50, 109, 138, 155) (1923–present), Hairy sunflower (5, 65, 72, 97, 122) (1907–1937), Soft-leaf sunflower [Soft-leaved Sun-flower] (187) (1818)

Helianthus mollis **Willd.** – See *Helianthus mollis* Lam.

Helianthus multiflorus – See *Helianthus ×multiflorus* L. [*annuus × decapetalus*]

Helianthus nuttallii **Torr. & Gray** – Nuttall's sunflower (4, 50) (1986–present)

Helianthus nuttallii **Torr. & Gray subsp.** *nuttallii* – Nuttall's sunflower (3, 50) (1977–present)

Helianthus nuttallii **Torr. & Gray subsp.** *rydbergii* **(Britton) Long** – Nuttall's sunflower (3) (1977), Rydberg's sunflower (50) (present)

Helianthus occidentalis **Riddell** – Few-leaf sunflower [Few leaved sunflower, Few-leaved sunflower] (5, 72, 122) (1907–1937), Western sunflower (82) (1930)

Helianthus orgyalis **DC.** – See *Helianthus salicifolius* A. Dietr.

Helianthus pauciflorus **Nutt.** – Stiff sunflower (50) (present)

Helianthus pauciflorus **Nutt. subsp.** *pauciflorus* – Rough sunflower (127) (1933), Stiff sunflower (3, 4, 50, 93, 155) (1936–present)

Helianthus pauciflorus **Nutt. subsp.** *subrhomboideus* **(Rydb.) O. Spring & E. Schilling** – Rhombic-leaf sunflower [Rhombicleaf sunflower, Rhombic-leaved sunflower] (5, 155) (1913–1942), Stiff sunflower (3, 50) (1977–present)

Helianthus petiolaris **Nutt** – Plains sunflower (3) (1977), Prairie sunflower [Prairie sun-flower] (5, 50, 72, 80, 85, 93, 95, 97, 122, 124, 131, 155, 156) (1899–present), Sand sunflower (127) (1933), Sand-hill sunflower (145) (1897), Western sunflower (80) (1913)

Helianthus petiolaris **Nutt. subsp.** *petiolaris* – Prairie sunflower [Prairie sun-flower] (50) (present)

Helianthus porteri **(A. Gray) Pruski** – Stone-mountian star (86) (1878)

Helianthus pumilus **Nutt.** – Little sunflower (50) (present)

Helianthus rigidus **(Cass.) Desf.** – See *Helianthus pauciflorus* Nutt. subsp. *pauciflorus*

Helianthus rigidus **(Cass.) Desf. subsp.** *rigidus* – See *Helianthus pauciflorus* Nutt. subsp. *pauciflorus*

Helianthus salicifolius **A. Dietr.** – Linear-leaf sunflower [Linear-leaved sunflower] (5, 93, 97) (1913–1937), Sunflower [Sun-flower] (145) (1897), Willow-leaf sunflower [Willowleaf sunflower, Willow-leaved sunflower] (3, 4, 50, 155) (1986–present)

Helianthus scaberrimus **Ell.** – See *Helianthus ×laetiflorus* Pers. [*pauciflorus × tuberosus*]

Helianthus strumosus **L.** – Pale-leaf wood sunflower [Pale-leaved wood sunflower] (5, 72, 82, 97) (1907–1937), Pale-leaf woodland sunflower [Paleleaf woodland sunflower] (50) (present), Woodland sunflower (138, 155) (1923–1942), Yellow creeping starwort of Virginia (181) (~1678)

Helianthus strumosus macrophyllus **(Willd.) Britton** – See *Helianthus hirsutus* Raf.

Helianthus subrhomboideus **Rydb.** – See *Helianthus pauciflorus* Nutt. subsp. *subrhomboideus* (Rydb.) O. Spring & E. Schilling

Helianthus subtuberosus **Bourgeau** – See *Helianthus giganteus* L.

Helianthus tomentosus **Michx.** – See *Helianthus tuberosus* L.

Helianthus tracheliifolius **Mill.** – See *Helianthus decapetalus* L.

Helianthus tuberosus **L.** – Artichoke (35, 80, 85) (1806–1923) Lewis & Clark, Arzeneykräftige Osterluzey (German) (186) (1814), A'skibwan' (Chippewa, raw thing) (40) (1928), Battatas de Canada (107) (1629), Canadian potato [Canada potato] (5, 156, 158) (1900–1923), Chiquebi (Native Americans) (110) (1618), Common artichoke (47) (1852), Earth-apple [Earth apple] (5, 62, 92, 156, 158) (1876–1923), Erdapfel (German) (158) (1900), Erdartischocke (German) (158) (1900), Girasole (5, 92, 109, 156) (1876–1949), Hierusalem artichoke (107, 177) (1762–1919), Jerusalem artichoke (3, 5, 50, 7, 14, 19, 37, 40, 62, 63, 72, 82, 92, 93, 95, 97, 105, 107, 110, 122, 124, 127, 131, 138, 145, 155, 156, 158) (1882–present), Jerusalem potato (156) (1923), Jerusalem sunflower [Jerusalemsunflower] (3, 5, 50, 7, 14, 19, 37, 40, 62, 63, 72, 82, 92, 93, 95, 97, 105, 107, 110, 122, 124, 127, 131, 138, 145, 155, 156, 158) (1882–present), Jerusalem-artichoke sunflower [Jerusalemartichoke sunflower] (155) (1942), Kisu-sit (Pawnee, long tapering) (37) (1919), Pangi (Dakota) (37) (1919), Panhe (Omaha-Ponca) (37) (1919), Panh'e (Winnebago) (37) (1919), Potatoes of Canada (107) (1657), Topinambaus

(French) (110) (1618), Topinambour (French) (5, 156, 158) (1900–1923), Ush-keobuag (Chippewa) (47) (1852), Wild artichoke (103) (1870), Woolly sunflower (5, 155) (1913–1942), possibly Bessey's sunflower (97) (1937) OK

Helichroa **Raf.** – possibly *Echinacea* Moench

Helichrysum bracteatum **(Vent.) Andr.** – Everlasting (109) (1949), Immortal flower (92) (1876), Strawflower [Straw-flower] (109, 138) (1923–1949)

Helichrysum bracteatum **Andr.** – See *Helichrysum bracteatum* (Vent.) Andr.

Helichrysum **Gaertn.** – possibly *Helichrysum* Mill.

Helichrysum **Mill.** – Everlasting (138) (1923), Paper flower [Paperflower, Paper flowers] (73) (1892) Northern OH

Helichrysum petiolare **Hilliard & Burtt** – Cudweed everlasting (138) (1923)

Helichrysum petiolatum **[(L.) DC.]** – See *Helichrysum petiolare* Hilliard & Burtt

Heliconia bihai **(L.) L.** – Carib heliconia (138) (1923)

Heliconia caribaea **Lam.** – Balisier (109) (1949), Wild plantain (109) (1949)

Heliconia **L.** – Heliconia (138) (1923) for Mt. Helicon, seat of the muses

Helictotrichon hookeri **(Scribn.) Henr.** – American oat (94) (1901), Hooker's oat (5) (1913), Spike-oat [Spike oat, Spikeoat] (3, 50, 155) (1942–present)

Helictotrichon mortonianum **(Scribn.) Henrard** – Alpine oat (140) (1944) CO, Morton's oat grass [Morton's oat-grass] (94) (1901)

Helictotrichon pratense **(L.) Pilg.** – Meadow oat grass (66) (1903), Narrow-leaf oat grass [Narrow-leaved oat-grass] (45) (1896)

Helictotrichon pubescens **(Huds.) Bess. ex Pilger** – See *Avenula pubescens* (Huds.) Dumort.

Helictotrichon pubescens **(Huds.) Schult. & Schult.f.** – possibly *Avenula pubescens* (Huds.) Dumort.

Helietta parvifolia **(Gray ex Hemsl.) Benth.** – Baretta (122) (1937)

Heliopsis helianthoides **(L.) Sweet** – False sunflower [False sunflower] (4, 5, 156) (1923–1986), Ox-eye [Ox eye, Oxeye, Oxe eie] (4, 5, 156) (1923–1986), Smooth ox-eye [Smooth oxeye, Smooth ox-eye] (42, 50, 62) (1814–present) Manasseh Cutler, Sunflower heliopsis (138, 155) (1923–1942)

Heliopsis helianthoides **(L.) Sweet var.** *occidentalis* **(T.R. Fisher) Steyermark** – Smooth ox-eye [Smooth oxeye, Smooth ox-eye] (50) (present)

Heliopsis helianthoides **(L.) Sweet var.** *scabra* **(Dunal) Fern.** – False sunflower [False sun-flower] (4, 5, 62, 93, 95, 156) (1911–1986), Gi'zĭso'bûgons' (Chippewa, sun small leaf) (40) (1928), Orange sunflower (156) (1923), Ox-eye [Ox eye, Oxeye, Oxe eie] (40, 82) (1928–1930), Rough heliopsis (138, 155) (1923–1942), Rough ox-eye [Rough ox-eye or rough ox eye] (5, 62, 63, 72, 82, 97, 121, 131, 156) (1899–1937), Rough ox-eye daisy (85) (1932), Smooth ox-eye [Smooth oxeye, Smooth ox-eye] (50) (present), Sunflower heliopsis (155) (1942)

Heliopsis laevis **Pers.** – See *Bidens laevis* (L.) Britton, Sterns & Poggenb.

Heliopsis **Pers.** – False sunflower [False sun-flower] (158) (1900), Heliopsis (50, 155) (1942–present), Ox-eye [Ox eye, Oxeye, Oxe eie] (1, 2, 80, 82, 156) (1923–1932)

Heliopsis scabra **Dunal.** – See *Heliopsis helianthoides* (L.) Sweet var. *scabra* (Dunal) Fern.

Heliotropium **(Tourn.) L.** – See *Heliotropium* L.

Heliotropium arborescens **L.** – Big heliotrope (138) (1923), Common heliotrope (82, 109, 138) (1923–1949), Girasol (92) (1876)

Heliotropium convolvulaceum **(Nutt.) Gray** – Bindweed heliotrope (5, 97) (1913–1937), Phlox heliotrops (50) (present), Saltflat heliotrope [Salt flat heliotrope] (124) (1937) TX, Wild heliotrope (3) (1977), possibly Bindweed euploca (155) (1942)

Heliotropium corymbosum **[Ruiz & Pavar.]** – See *Heliotropium arborescens* L.

Heliotropium curassavicum **L.** – Wild heliotrope (106) (1930)

203

Heliotropium curassavicum L. var. *curassavicum* – Salt heliotrope (50, 155) (1942–present)

Heliotropium curassavicum L. var. *obovatum* DC. – Heliotrope (93, 157) (1900–1936), Seaside heliotrope [Sea-side heliotrope (50, 157) (1929–present), Spatulate-leaf heliotrope [Spatulate-leaved heliotrope] (5) (1913), Wild heliotrope (85, 155) (1932–1942)

Heliotropium europaeum L. – European heliotrope (5, 122) (1913–1937), Heliotrope (156) (1923), Turnsole (156) (1923)

Heliotropium indicum L. – Indian heliotrope (5, 50, 97, 122) (1913–present), Introduced heliotrope (124) (1937), Turnsole (3, 5, 19, 92) (1840–1977)

Heliotropium L. – Heliotrope (1, 2, 4, 50, 82, 106, 138, 155, 156, 158) (1895–present), Turnsole (10, 158) (1818–1900) means "turning to the sun"

Heliotropium peruvianum L. – See *Heliotropium arborescens* L.

Heliotropium spathulatum Rydb. – See *Heliotropium curassavicum* L. var. *obovatum* DC.

Heliotropium tenellum (Nutt.) Torr. – Pasture heliotrope (3, 50) (1977–present), Slender heliotrope (5, 97) (1913–1937)

Helleborus fetidus – See *Helleborus foetidus* L.

Helleborus foetidus L. – Bastard bearsfoot (92) (1876), Bear's-foot [Bear's foot, Bearsfoot] (7, 92) (1828–1876), Fetid hellebore (15, 92) (1876–1895), Hellebore (19) (1840), Oxheal (92) (1876), Setterwort [Setterwoort] (178) (1526), Settiswort (7, 92) (1828–1876), Stinking black hellebore (92) (1876)

Helleborus hyemalis – See *Eranthis hyemalis* (L.) Salisb.

Helleborus L. – Hellebore (109, 138, 156, 167) (1814–1949)

Helleborus niger L. – Black hellebore [Blacke elebore] (2, 15, 49, 52, 53, 55, 57, 61, 92, 179) (1526–1922), Christmas rose [Christmas-rose] (2, 15, 49, 53, 55, 92, 109, 138) (1876–1949) for time of flowering under mild climates, Elebore (179) (1526), Helleborus (52) (1919), Lion's-foot [Lion's foot, Lions' foot, Lyons fote] (179) (1526), Pedelyon (179) (1526), True black hellebore [True blacke hellebore] (178) (1526)

Helleborus trifolium – See *Coptis trifolia* (L.) Salisb.

Helleborus trifolius L. – See *Coptis trifolia* (L.) Salisb.

Helleborus viridis L. – Chris root (5, 76) (1896–1913) Sulphur Grove OH, probably short for Christmas root, Christmas flower (106) (1930), Christmas rose [Christmas-rose] (5, 76, 156) (1896–1923) Sulphur Grove OH, Elebore Vert (French) (6) (1892), Green hellebore (2, 5, 6, 15, 57, 106, 156) (1892–1930), Grune Niesswurz (German) (6) (1892), Hellebore (184) (1793), Peg-root (156) (1923), Wild black hellebore [Wilde blacke hellebore] (178) (1526)

Helonias asphodeloides L. – See *Xerophyllum asphodeloides* (L.) Nutt.

Helonias bullata L. – Helonias (19, 174) (1753–1840), Stud flower [Stud-flower] (5, 86, 156) (1878–1923), Swamp pink [Swamppink, Swamp-pink] (5, 138, 156) (1913–1923)

Helonias dioica Wr. – See *Chamaelirium luteum* (L.) A. Gray

Helonias erythrosperma Michx. – See *Amianthium muscitoxicum* (Walt.) Gray

Helonias L. – Swamp pink [Swamppink, Swamp-pink] (109, 138) (1923–1949)

Helonias latifolia Michx. – See *Helonias bullata* L.

Helonias tenax Pursh – See *Xerophyllum tenax* (Pursh) Nutt.

Helxine dumetorum – See *Polygonum scandens* L. var. *dumetorum* (L.) Gleason

Helxine soleirolii Req. – See *Soleirolia soleirolii* (Req.) Dandy

Hemerocallis aurantiaca Baker – See *Hemerocallis fulva* L. var. *aurantiaca* (Baker) M. Hotta

Hemerocallis aurantiaca major – See *Hemerocallis fulva* L. var. *aurantiaca* (Baker) M. Hotta

Hemerocallis flava L. – See *Hemerocallis lilioasphodelus* L.

Hemerocallis fulva (L.) L. – Beautiful-for-a-day [Beautiful for a day] (180) (1633), Brown lily (187) (1818), Common orange daylily (109) (1949), Copper-flower daylily [Copper-flowered day lily] (187) (1818), Daylily [Day lily, Day-lily, Day-Lillie] (3, 10, 72, 93) (1818–1977), Eve's-thread [Eve's thread] (75, 156) (1894–1923)

WV, Fiare-for-a-day [Fiare for a day] (180) (1633), Fire-lily (156) (1923), Homestead lily (156) (1923), Liliago (180) (1633), Lily-for-a-day [Lillie for a day] (180) (1633), Lirionconfancie (180) (1633), Orange daylily [Orange day-lily] (50, 156) (1923–present), Orange tawny lily [Orange tawnie lillie] (178) (1596), Tawny daylily [Tawny day lily, Tawny day-lily] (19, 138, 155, 156) (1840–1942), Tiger lily [Tiger-lily] (156) (1923)

Hemerocallis fulva var. *aurantiaca* (Baker) M. Hotta – Golden summer daylily [Golden summer day-lily] (109) (1949), Great orange daylily (138) (1923), Orange daylily [Orange day-lily] (138) (1923)

Hemerocallis L. – Daylily [Day lily, Day-lily, Day-Lillie] (50, 107, 109, 138, 156, 158) (1900–present)

Hemerocallis lilioasphodelus L. – Common yellow day-lily (109) (1949), Dayflower [Day flower, Day-flower] (92) (1876), Daylily [Day lily, Day-lily, Day-Lillie] (92, 180) (1633–1876), Lemon day-lily (138) (1923), Lemon lily (78, 156) (1898–1923), Yellow daylily [Yellow day-lily] (19, 50, 156) (1840–present)

Hemerocallis minor Mill. – Dwarf daylily (138) (1923), Dwarf yellow daylily [Dwarf yellow day-lily] (109) (1949)

Hemicarpha aristulata (Coville) Smyth – See *Lipocarpha aristulata* (Coville) G. Tucker

Hemicarpha drummondii Nees – See *Lipocarpha drummondii* (Nees) G. Tucker

Hemicarpha micrantha (Vahl) Pax – See *Lipocarpha micrantha* (Vahl) G. Tucker

Hemicarpha subsquarosa ((Muhl.) Nees) – See *Lipocarpha micrantha* (Vahl) G. Tucker

Hemionitis palmata L. – Strawberry fern (138) (1923)

Hemizonia DC. – Tarweed [Tar weed, Tar-weed] (106) (1930), Vinegar weed [Vinegar-weed] (106) (1930) San Joaquin Valley CA, Yellowtop [Yellow-top, Yellow top, Yellowtops, Yellow-tops] (106) (1930) Fresno Co, CA

Hemizonia fasciculata (DC.) Torr. & Gray – Balsamio (76) (1896) CA, Tarweed [Tar weed, Tar-weed] (76) (1896)

Hemizonia pungens (Hook. & Arn.) Torr. & Gray – Tarweed [Tar weed, Tar-weed] (75) (1894)

Hemizonia pungens Torr. & Gray – See *Hemizonia pungens* (Hook. & Arn.) Torr. & Gray

Hemizonia ramosissima [Benth.] – See *Hemizonia fasciculata* (DC.) Torr. & Gray

Hemizonia virgata – See *Holocarpha virgata* (Gray) Keck

Hepatica (Rupp.) Hill. – See *Hepatica* Mill.

Hepatica acuta (Pursh) Britt. – See *Hepatica nobilis* Schreb. var. *acuta* (Pursh) Steyermark

Hepatica acutiloba DC. – See *Hepatica nobilis* Schreb. var. *acuta* (Pursh) Steyermark

Hepatica americana (DC.) Ker. – See *Hepatica nobilis* Schreb. var. *obtusa* (Pursh) Steyermark

Hepatica americana DC. – See *Hepatica nobilis* Schreb. var. *obtusa* (Pursh) Steyermark

Hepatica americana Ker. – See *Hepatica nobilis* Schreb. var. *obtusa* (Pursh) Steyermark

Hepatica Dill. – See *Hepatica* Mill.

Hepatica hepatica (L.) Karst – See *Hepatica nobilis* Schreb. var. *obtusa* (Pursh) Steyermark

Hepatica Mill. – Crystalwort [Crystal wort, Crystal-wort] (92) (1876), Hepatica (1, 2, 138) (1895–1932), Liverleaf [Liver-leaf, Liver leaf] (1, 2, 7, 13, 15, 82, 109) (1828–1949), Liverwort [Liver-wort, Liver wort] (156) (1923)

Hepatica nobilis Schreb. – American liverwort (53) (1922), Animu'sĭd (Chippewa) (40) (1928), Blue anemone (156) (1923), Common liverwort (7) (1828), Crystalwort [Crystal wort, Crystal-wort] (92, 156) (1876–1923), Edel leberkraut (German) (46) (1879), Golden-trefoil (156) (1923) no longer in use by 1923, Gulden klee (German) (46) (1879), Heart liverwort (74) (1893), Heart-leaf liverwort [Heart-leaved liverwort] (156) (1923), Hepatica (40, 82, 105, 156) (1923–1932), Hepatica (Official name of Materia Medica) (7) (1828), Hepatique

(French) (46) (1879), Hepatique trilobe (French) (7) (1828), Herb Trinity [Herb-Trinity] (92, 156) (1876–1923), Ivy flower [Ivy-flower] (156) (1923), Kidneywort [Kidney-wort] (156) (1923), Leberkraut (German) (7) (1828), Liverleaf [Liver-leaf, Liver leaf] (53, 82, 156) (1922–1930), Liver-moss [Livermoss, Liver moss] (156) (1923), Liverweed [Liver-weed, Liver weed] (7) (1828), Liverwort [Liver-wort, Liver wort] (53, 79, 92, 156, 190) (~1759–1923) Northeastern US, Mayflower [May flower, May-flower] (156) (1923), Noble blue liverwort [Noble blew liuerwoort] (178) (1526), Noble liverwoort with white flowers [Noble liuerwoort with white flowers] (178) (1526), Noble liverwort (7, 10, 46, 74, 76, 79, 156, 178) (1671–1923), Noble red liverwort [Nobel red liuerwort] (178) (1526), Paas blumes (156) (1923), Pne-obogons (Chippewa) (105) (1932), Pne-uzidin (Chippewa, partridge foot) (105) (1932), Round-lobe hepatica [Roundlobe hepatica, Round-lobed hepatica] (2, 138) (1895–1923), Spring-beauty [Spring beauty, Springbeauty] (74, 156) (1893–1923) NY, Three-leaf liverwort [Three-leaved liverwort] (156) (1923), Three-lobe liverwort [Three-lobed liver-wort] (187) (1818), Trefoil (7) (1828), Windflower [Wind flower, Wind-flower, Wind-floures, Winde-floures] (79) (1891)

Hepatica nobilis **Schreb. var.** ***acuta*** **(Pursh) Steyermark** – Heart liverleaf [Heart liver-leaf, Heart liver leaf] (5, 19, 49, 53, 72, 92) (1840–1922), Heart liverwort (5) (1913), Heartleaf [Heart leaves, Heartleaf] (102) (1886), Hepatica (82) (1930), Liverwort [Liver-wort, Liver wort] (102) (1886), Mayflower [May flower, May-flower] (5) (1913), Pass blummies (76) (1896) Brodhead WI, Sharp-lobe hepatica [Sharplobe hepatica, Sharp-lobed hepatica] (2, 138) (1895–1923), Sharp-lobe liver-leaf [Sharp-lobed liver-leaf] (5) (1913), Sharp-lobe liverwort [Sharp-lobed liverwort] (5) (1913), Skwa'lĭ (Cherokee) (102) (1886), Spring-beauty [Spring beauty, Springbeauty] (5, 76) (1896–1913) Brodhead WI, American liverleaf (49) (1898), Blåblomster (Swedish, blue flower) (41) (1770), Crystalwort [Crystal wort, Crystal-wort] (5) (1913), Edellebere (German) (6) (1892), Gabisan'ikeäg' (Chippewa, it is silent) (40) (1928), Golden trefoil (5) (1913), Heart liverwort (5) (1913), Hepatica (6, 40, 42, 49, 165, 174, 177) (1753–1892), Hepatique (French) (6) (1892), Herb Trinity [Herb-Trinity] (5, 6) (1892–1913), Ivy flower [Ivy-flower] (5) (1913), Kidney liverleaf [Kidney liver-leaf] (5, 19, 49, 53) (1840–1922), Kidneywort [Kidney-wort] (6) (1892), Liverleaf [Liver-leaf, Liver leaf] (6, 49, 61, 92) (1870–1898), Liver-moss [Livermoss, Liver moss] (5, 92) (1876–1913), Liverweed [Liverweed, Liver weed] (6, 92) (1876–1892), Liverwort [Liver-wort, Liver wort] (6, 42, 49, 57, 92) (1814–1917), Mouse-ear [Mouse ear, Mouse ears, Mouse's ear, Mows eare] (5) (1913), Noble liverwort (5, 41, 49, 92) (1770–1913), Round-lobe hepatica [Roundlobe hepatica, Round-lobed hepatica] (6) (1892), Round-lobe liver-leaf [Round-lobed liver-leaf] (5) (1913), Spring-beauty [Spring beauty, Springbeauty] (5) (1913), Squirrel cup [Sqirrel cup, Squirrel cups, Squirrel-cups] (5) (1913), Three-leaf liverwort [Three-leaved liverwort] (5) (1913), Trefoil (6, 92) (1876–1892)

Hepatica triloba **Chaix.** – See *Hepatica nobilis* Schreb.

Heptallon graveolens **Raf.** – See *Croton capitatus* Michx.

Heracleum **L.** – Cow-cabbage [Cow cabbage] (1) (1932), Cowparsnip [Cow parsnip, Cow-parsnip] (1, 2, 4, 10, 40, 50, 82, 93, 101, 138, 155, 156, 158) (1818–present)

Heracleum lanatum **Michx.** – See *Heracleum maximum* Bartr.

Heracleum mantegazzianum **Sommier & Levier** – Big-leaf cow-parsnip [Bigleaf cow-parsnip] (138) (1923)

Heracleum maximum **Bartr.** – American cow-parsnip [American cow parsnip] (107) (1919), Beaver-root [Beaver root] (37) (1919), Bi'bigwe'wûnûck (Chippewa, flute-reed) (40) (1928), Common cowparsnip [Common cow-parsnip] (50, 138, 155) (1923–present), Cowparsnep [Cow parsnep] (7, 19) (1828–1840), Cowparsnip [Cow parsnip, Cow-parsnip] (4, 5, 37, 49, 52, 62, 63, 72, 80, 82, 85, 92, 95, 106, 127, 131, 146, 156, 157, 158, 187) (1818–1986), Eltrot (3) (1977), Madnep [Mad-nep] (92, 157, 158) (1876–1929), Madness (157, 158) (1900–1929), Masterwort [Master-wort, Master wort, Masterwoorts] (5, 7, 49, 52, 61, 62, 92, 156, 158) (1828–1923),

Royal cow-parsnip [Royal cow parsnip] (92) (1876), Youthwort [Youth wort] (92, 157, 158) (1876–1929), Zhaba-makan (Omaha-Ponca, beaver-medicine) (37) (1919)

Heracleum sphondylium **L.** – Cow parsley (92) (1876), Cowparsnep [Cow parsnep] (48) (1527–1793), Cowparsnip [Cow parsnip, Cowparsnip] (14, 107) (1882–1919), Meadow parsnip [Medow parsnep] (178) (1526)

Heracleum sphondylium **L. subsp.** ***montanum*** **(Schleicher) Briq.** – See *Heracleum maximum* Bartr.

Herissantia crispa **(L.) Briz.** – Curly abutilon (155) (1942)

Hernandia sonora **L.** – Jack-in-a-box [Jack in a box] (92) (1876)

Herniaria glabra **L.** – Burstwort (138) (1923), Rupturewort [Rupture woort, Rupture-wort] (178) (1526)

Herniaria **L.** – Burstwort [Burstwoort] (138, 180) (1633–1923), Rupturewort [Rupture woort, Rupture-wort] (109) (1949) reported as a cure of rupture or hernia

Herniera glabra – See *Herniaria glabra* L.

Herpestis monnieri **HBK.** – See *Bacopa monnieri* (L.) Pennell

Hesperaloe parviflora **(Torr.) Coult.** – Red-flower yucca [Red flowered yucca] (122, 124) (1937) TX

Hesperaloe parviflora **(Torr.) Coulter var.** ***engelmani*** **(Krauskopf) Trel.** – See *Hesperaloe parviflora* (Torr.) Coult.

Hesperis **L.** – Dame's-rocket [Dame's rocket, Dames rocket] (4) (1986), Dame's-violet [Dame's violet, Dames-violet, Dames Violets] (156) (1923), Rocket (10, 15, 50, 92, 109, 138, 155, 158) (1818–present)

Hesperis matronalis **L.** – Damask-violet [Damask violet] (5, 156, 158) (1900–1923), Dame's-gilliflower [Dame's gilliflower] (5, 158) (1900–1913), Dame's-rocket [Dame's rocket, Dames rocket] (1, 3, 4, 5, 50, 72, 85, 138, 155, 156, 158) (1900–present), Dame's-violet [Dame's violet, Dames-violet, Dames violets] (1, 5, 15, 74, 92, 109, 156, 158, 178, 180) (1526–1949), Damewort [Dame-wort] (156) (1923), Eveweed [Eve-weed] (156) (1923), Garden rocket (92, 158) (1876–1900), Night-rocket [Night rocket] (156) (1923), Night-scented gilliflower (5, 156, 158) (1900–1923), Night-violet [Night violet] (156) (1923), Queen's gilliflower (5, 156, 158) (1900–1923), Queen's gilloflowers (178) (1526), Rogue's gilliflower (5, 156, 158) (1900–1923), Summer-lilac [Summer lilac] (5, 156, 158) (1900–1923), Sweet rocket (5, 76, 92, 156, 158) (1896–1923) Paris ME, Winter gilliflower (5, 156, 158) (1900–1923)

Hesperocallis undulata **Gray** – California daylily (78) (1898)

Hesperochloa **(Piper) Rydb.** – See *Festuca* L.

Hesperochloa kingii **(Wats.) Rydb.** – See *Leucopoa kingii* (S. Wats.) W.A. Weber

Hesperostipa **(M. K. Elias) Barkworth** – Needle-and-thread [Needle-andthread, Needle and thread] (50) (present)

Hesperostipa comata **(Trin. & Rupr.) Barkworth** – Short-awn porcupine grass [Shortawn porcupinegrass] (155) (1942), Short-bristle needle-and-thread [Shortbristle needle and thread] (50) (Present), Silk grass [Silkgrass, Silk-grass] (5) (1913)

Hesperostipa comata **(Trin. & Rupr.) Barkworth subsp.** ***comata*** – Blowout grass [Blow-out grass, Blowoutgrass] (5) (1913), Bunch grass [Bunchgrass, Bunch-grass] (5, 45) (1896–1913), Needle grass [Needle-grass, Needlegrass] (5, 56, 93, 94, 111, 115, 126, 129, 140) (1894–1944), Needle-and-thread [Needleandthread, Needle and thread] (3, 50, 98, 140, 146, 155, 185) (1926–present), Needle-and-thread grass [Needle and thread grass, Needle-and-thread-grass] (122, 163) (1852–1937), Porcupine grass [Porcupine-grass, Porcupinegrass] (5, 108) (1878–1913), Silk grass [Silkgrass, Silk-grass] (5) (1913), Spear grass [Spear-grass] (108, 146) (1878–1939), Western needle grass [Western needlegrass, Western needle-grass] (116, 146) (1939–1958), Western stipa (56) (1901)

Hesperostipa curtiseta **(A. S. Hitchc.) Barkworth** – See *Hesperostipa comata* (Trin. & Rupr.) Barkworth

Hesperostipa neomexicana **(Thurb. ex Coult.) Barkworth** – New Mexico feather grass [New Mexico feather-grass, New Mexico feathergrass] (3, 50, 94, 122, 140, 155) (1901–present), New Mexico stipa (152) (1912)

Hesperostipa spartea (**Trin.) Barkworth** – Buffalo grass [Buffalo-grass, Buffalograss] (56) (1901) IA, Darning-needle [Darning needle] (56) (1901) IA, Mičapeča (Lakota) (121) (1918–1970), Mika-hi (Omaha-Ponca, comb plant) (37) (1830), Mikapšse (Osage, from word for raccoon) (121) (1918–1970), Needle grass [Needle-grass, Needlegrass] (37, 56, 93, 116, 121) (1830–1970), Paari pitsuts (Pawnee, Pawnee hairbrush) (37) (1830), Pitsuts (Pawnee, hairbrush) (37) (1830), Porcupine grass [Porcupine-grass, Porcupinegrass] (3, 45, 50, 56, 66, 67, 85, 93, 94, 111, 115, 119, 121, 129, 134, 155) (1890–present), Spanish needle [Spanish-needles, Spanishneedles, Spanish needles] (5, 11, 35, 37) (1806–1913), Spear grass [Spear-grass] (85) (1932), Wild oat [Wild oats] (56) (1901) IA

Hesperoyucca whipplei – See *Yucca whipplei* Torr. var. *whipplei*

Heteranthera dubia (**Jacq.) MacM.** – Buffalo grass [Buffalo-grass, Buffalograss] (156) (1923), Grass-leaf mudplantain [Grassleaf mudplantain] (50) (present), Grass-leaf schollera [Grass-leaved schollera] (187) (1818), Low-water star (187) (1818), Water star-grass [Water star grass, Water stargrass] (2, 3, 5, 72, 93, 120, 122, 156, 158) (1895–1977), Yellow-eyed water-grass [Yellow-eyed water grass] (19) (1840)

Heteranthera graminea **Vahl** – See *Heteranthera dubia* (Jacq.) MacM.

Heteranthera limosa (**Sw.) Vahl.** – Blue mud-plantain [Blue mud plantain] (50) (present), Mud-plantain [Mudplantain, Mud plantain] (3, 85, 158) (1900–1977), Smaller mud-plantain [Smaller mud plantain] (5, 92, 97) (1913–1937)

Heteranthera mexicana **S. Wats.** – Mexican mudplantain (50) (present)

Heteranthera multiflora (**Griseb.) Horn** – Bouquet mud-plantain [Bouquet mudplantain] (50) (present)

Heteranthera peduncularis **Benth.** – Blue mud-plantain [Blue mud plantain] (5) (1913), Egret mudplantian (50) (present)

Heteranthera reniformis **R. & P.** – Kidney-leaf heteranthera [Kidney-leaved heteranthera] (187) (1818), Kidney-leaf mudplantain [Kidneyleaf mudplantain] (50) (present), Mud-plantain [Mudplantain, Mud plantain] (5, 92, 97, 156) (1876–1937)

Heteranthera rotundifolia (**Kunth) Griseb.** – Round-leaf mud-plantain [Roundleaf mudplantain] (50) (present)

Heteranthera **Ruiz & Pavón** – Mud-plantain [Mudplantain, Mud plantain] (32, 50, 155, 156) (1895–present), Water star-grass [Water star grass] (1) (1932)

Heterochloa maritima – possibly *Puccinellia maritima* (Huds.) Parl.

Heteromeles arbutifolia (**Lindl.) M. Roemer** – California holly (74, 106) (1893–1930) Santa Barbara CA, Chistmas berry (106) (1930), Tollon (74, 109) (1893–1949) CA, Tollonweed (106) (1930), Toyon [Toy-on] (74, 106, 109) (1893–1949) CA

Heteromeles arbutifolia (**Lindl.) M. Roemer var.** *arbutifolia* – Christmas berry [Christmasberry, Christmas-berry] (109, 138) (1923–1949)

Heteropogon contortus (**L.) Beauv.** – See *Heteropogon contortus* (L.) Beauv. ex Roemer & J.A. Schultes

Heteropogon contortus (**L.) Beauv. ex Roemer & J. A. Schultes** – Tangle-head [Tangle head] (122) (1937) TX, Twisted beard grass [Twisted beard-grass] (94) (1901)

Heteropogon melanocarpus (**Ell.) Ell. ex Benth.** – Large-fruit beard grass [Large-fruited beard-grass] (94) (1901), Sweet tanglehead [Sweet tangle head] (122) (1937) TX

Heterotheca canescens (**DC.) Shinners & Gray** – Berlandier's golden aster (97) (1937), Golden aster [Golden-aster] (4, 50) (1986–present), Hoary false goldenaster (50) (present)

Heterotheca **Cass.** – Camphorweed [Camphor-weed, Camphor weed] (4) (1986), False golden-aster [False goldenaster] (50) (present), Heterotheca (158) (1900)

Heterotheca fulcrata (**Greene) Shinners** – See *Heterotheca fulcrata* (Greene) Shinners var. *fulcrata*

Heterotheca fulcrata (**Greene) Shinners var.** *fulcrata* – Rocky-scree false golden-aster [Rockyscree false goldenaster'] (50) (present)

Heterotheca stenophylla (**Gray) Shinners** – Stiff-leaf false golden-aster [Stiffleaf false goldenaster, Stiff-leaf false goldenaster] (50) (present)

Heterotheca stenophylla (**Gray) Shinners var.** *angustifolia* (**Rydb.) Semple** – Golden aster [Golden-aster] (3) (1977), Stiff-leaf false golden-aster [Stiffleaf false goldenaster, Stiff-leaf false goldenaster] (50) (present)

Heterotheca stenophylla (**Gray) Shinners var.** *stenophylla* – Narrow-leaf gold-aster [Narrowleaf goldaster] (155) (1942), Stiff-leaf false golden-aster [Stiffleaf false goldenaster, Stiff-leaf false goldenaster] (50) (present), Stiff-leaf golden-aster [Stiffleaf golden aster, Stiff-leaved golden aster] (5, 97, 122) (1913–1937)

Heterotheca subaxillaris (**Lam.) Britton & Rusby** – Camphorweed [Camphor-weed, Camphor weed] (50, 122, 124) (1937–present), Heterotheca (5, 97) (1913–1937)

Heterotheca villosa (**Pursh) Shinners** – Hairy false golden-aster [Hairy false goldenaster] (50) (present)

Heterotheca villosa (**Pursh) Shinners var.** *ballardii* (**Rydb.) Semple** – Hairy false golden-aster [Hairy false goldenaster] (50) (present)

Heterotheca villosa (**Pursh) Shinners var.** *foliosa* (**Nutt.) Harms** – Golden aster [Golden-aster] (3, 85) (1932–1977), Hairy false golden-aster [Hairy false goldenaster] (50) (present), Leafy gold-aster [Leafy goldaster] (155) (1942)

Heterotheca villosa (**Pursh) Shinners var.** *minor* (**Hook.) Semple** – Golden aster [Golden-aster] (3) (1977), Hairy false golden-aster [Hairy false goldenaster] (50) (present), Hispid golden-aster [Hispid golden aster] (5, 97) (1913–1937), Rough gold-aster [Rough goldaster] (155) (1942)

Heterotheca villosa (**Pursh) Shinners var.** *nana* (**Gray) Semple** – Hairy false golden-aster [Hairy false goldenaster] (50) (present)

Heterotheca villosa (**Pursh) Shinners var.** *villosa* – Golden aster [Golden-aster] (3, 82, 127, 156) (1923–1977), Goldeneye [Golden eye, Golden-eye] (156) (1923), Hairy false golden-aster [Hairy false goldenaster] (50) (present), Hairy gold-aster [Hairy goldaster] (155) (1942), Hairy golden-aster [Hairy golden aster] (5, 72, 93, 97, 122, 131, 138, 158) (1899–1937), Rosinweed [Rosin-weed, Rosin weed] (156) (1923), Rosinwood [Rosin wood, Rosin-wood] (5, 76, 158) (1896–1913)

Heuchera acerifolia [**Raf.**] – possibly *Heuchera villosa* Michx.

Heuchera americana **L.** – Alumroot [Alum-root, Alum root] (5, 14, 49, 57, 92, 158, 186, 187) (1814–1913), American alumroot (50, 138, 155) (1923–present), American sanicle (5, 49, 92, 156, 158, 186) (1814–1923), Cliffweed [Cliff-weed] (156, 158) (1900–1923), Common alumroot [Common alum root, Common alum-root] (2, 5, 156, 158) (1895–1923), Heuchera (57, 174, 177) (1917), Rock geranium (156) (1923), Split-rock [Split rock] (156, 158) (1900–1923)

Heuchera americana **L. var.** *americana* – Curtis' heuchera (5) (1913)

Heuchera americana **L. var.** *hirsuticaulis* (**Wheelock) Rosendahl, Butters & Lakela** – Ciwade'imïnaga'wûnj (Chippewa, sour fruit) (40) (1928), Rough alumroot (155) (1942), Rough heuchera (5, 72, 93, 131) (1899–1936), Rough-stem heuchera [Rough-stemmed heuchera] (5, 97) (1913–1937)

Heuchera curtisii **Torr. & Gray** – See *Heuchera americana* L. var. *americana*

Heuchera hirsuticaulis (**Wheelock) Rydb.** – See *Heuchera americana* L. var. *hirsuticaulis* (Wheelock) Rosendahl, Butters & Lakela

Heuchera hispida **Pursh** – See *Heuchera americana* L. var. *hirsuticaulis* (Wheelock) Rosendahl, Butters & Lakela

Heuchera **L.** – Allum root (10) (1818), Alumroot [Alum-root, Alum root] (2, 4, 50, 40, 82, 93, 109, 138, 155, 156, 158) (1895–present), Ciwade'imïn'ïbûg (Chippewa, sour leaf) (40) (1928), Kalispell (1) (1932)

Heuchera longiflora **Rydb.** – Long-flower heuchera [Long-flowered heuchera] (5) (1913)

Heuchera macrorhiza **Small.** – See *Heuchera villosa* Michx. var. *villosa*

Heuchera parviflora **Bartl.** – Rugel's heuchera (5) (1913), Small-flower alum-root [Small flowered alum-root] (131) (1899)

Heuchera parviflora **Bartl. var.** *puberula* (**Mackenzie & Bush) E. Wells** – Puberulent heuchera (5) (1913)

Heuchera parviflora **Nutt.** – See *Heuchera parviflora* Bartl.

Heuchera puberula **Mackenzie & Bush.** – See *Heuchera parviflora* Bartl. var. *puberula* (Mackenzie & Bush) E. Wells

Heuchera pubescens **Pursh** – Downy heuchera (5, 97) (1913–1937), Marbled alumroot (138) (1923)

Heuchera richardsonii **R. Br.** – Alumroot [Alum-root, Alum root] (3, 121) (1918–1977), Richardson's alumroot (50) (present), Waxpetaga (Lakota, possibly meaning frothy leaves) (121) (1918?–1970?)

Heuchera sanguinea **Engelm.** – Coralbells [Coral bells] (82, 109, 138) (1923–1949)

Heuchera villosa **Michx.** – Hairy alumroot (138) (1923), Hairy heuchera (5) (1913), possibly Alaunwurzel (German) (7) (1828), possibly Alumroot [Alum-root, Alum root] (7) (1828), possibly American sanicle (5, 92, 156) (1876–1923), possibly Cliffweed [Cliff-weed] (7, 92) (1828–1876), possibly Ground-maple [Ground maple] (7, 92, 156) (1828–1923), possibly Heuchera radix (Official name of Materia Medica) (7) (1828), possibly Heuchere Erable (French) (7) (1828), possibly Maple-leaf alumroot [Maple leaf alum root, Maple-leaf alumroot] (7, 92) (1828–1876), possibly Sanicle (7) (1828), possibly Split-rock [Split rock] (7, 92) (1828–1876)

Heuchera villosa **Michx. var.** *villosa* – Big-root heuchera (5) (1913)

Hexalectris aphylla **[Raf.]** – See *Hexalectris spicata* (Walt.) Barnh

Hexalectris spicata **(Walt.) Barnh** – Crested coralroot [Crested coral root] (3, 5, 122, 156) (1913–1977), Spiked crested coralroot (50) (present)

Hexastylis arifolia **(Michx.) Small var.** *arifolia* – Arum wild ginger [Arum wildginger] (138, 155) (1931–1942), Heartleaf [Heart leaves, Heart-leaf] (75, 156) (1894–1923) GA, Jug plant [Jug-plant] (156) (1923)

Hexastylis arifolia **(Michx.) Small.** – Halberd hexastylis (5) (1913), Heart-leaf hexastylis [Heart-leaved hexastylis] (5) (1913)

Hexastylis memmingeri **(Ashe) Small** – See *Hexastylis virginica* (L.) Small

Hexastylis shuttleworthii **(Britten & Baker) Small var.** *shuttleworthii* – Mottled wild ginger [Mottled wildginger] (138, 155) (1931–1942)

Hexastylis shuttleworthii **(Britten & Baker) Small.** – Large-flower hexastylis [Large-flowered hexastylis] (5) (1913)

Hexastylis virginica **(L.) Small** – Black snakeweed [Black snakeweed] (5, 92, 156) (1876–1923), Great snakeroot (181) (~1678), Heart snakeroot [Heart snake root, Heart snake-root] (186) (1814), Heartleaf [Heart leaves, Heart-leaf] (5, 75, 156) (1894–1923), Heart-leaf wild ginger [Heartleaf wildginger] (138) (1923), Large turtle liver (46) (1879), Luchau loobe thlucco (Creek) (46) (1879), Memminger's hexastylis (5) (1913), Pigs (156) (1923), Round-leaf Virginia foal's-foot [Round leaved Virginia foals-foot] (181) (~1678), Southern wild ginger (5, 156) (1913–1923), Taw-him (41) (1770), Taw-ho (41) (1770), Tuckáh (Native American) (41) (1770), Tuckahoo (41) (1770), Virginia heartleaf (50) (present), Virginia hexastylis (5) (1913), Virginia wakerobin [Virginian wake robin] (41) (1770), Virginia wild ginger [Virginia wildginger] (2, 155) (1895–1942)

Hibiscus abelmoschus **L.** – See *Abelmoschus moschatus* Medik.

Hibiscus aculeatus **Walt.** – Prickly rose mallow (2) (1895)

Hibiscus californicus **Kellogg** – See *Hibiscus moscheutos* L. subsp. *lasiocarpos* (Cav.) O. J. Blanchard

Hibiscus cardiophyllus **Gray** – See *Hibiscus martianus* Zucc.

Hibiscus coccineus **Walt** – American scarlet rose-mallow (86) (1878), Crimson hibiscus (183) (~1756), Great red hibiscus (2) (1895), Great red rosemallow [Great red rose mallow] (2) (1895), Scarlet hibiscus (86) (1878), Scarlet rose-mallow [Scarlet rose mallow, Scarlet rosemallow] (138) (1923)

Hibiscus elatus **Sw.** – Mountain rosemallow (138) (1923)

Hibiscus esculentus **L.** – See *Abelmoschus esculentus* (L.) Moench

Hibiscus grandiflorus **Michx.** – Great rosemallow (138) (1923)

Hibiscus incanus **Wendl.** – See *Hibiscus moscheutos* L. subsp. *moscheutos*

Hibiscus **L.** – Hibiscus (138, 155, 158) (1923–1942), Marshmallow [Marsh mallow, Marsh mallows, Marsh-mallow] (1) (1932), Rose Hibiscus (183) (~1756), Rose-mallow [Rose mallow, Rosemallow] (1, 2, 4, 13, 15, 50, 82, 93, 109, 138, 155, 156, 158) (1895–present), Sweatweed [Sweat weed, Sweat-weed] (7) (1828), Water-mallow [Water mallow] (7) (1828)

Hibiscus laevis **All.** – Halberd-leaf mallow [Halberd-leaved mallow] (156) (1923), Halberd-leaf rose-mallow [Halbard leaf rose mallow, Halberdleaf rosemallow, Halberd-leaved rose mallow, Halberd-leaved rose-mallow] (2, 4, 5, 50, 72, 93, 92, 97, 124, 156, 158) (1895–present), Scarlet rose-mallow [Scarlet rose mallow] (3) (1977), Soldier rose-mallow [Soldier rosemallow] (138) (1923), Sweating-weed [Sweating weed, Sweatingweed] (5, 156, 158) (1900–1923)

Hibiscus lasiocarpos **Cavar.** – See *Hibiscus moscheutos* L. subsp. *lasiocarpos* (Cav.) O. J. Blanchard

Hibiscus martianus **Zucc.** – Heart-leaf rose-mallow [Heartleaf rosemallow] (50) (present), Silver-leaf hibiscus [Silver leaf hibiscus] (124) (1937) TX

Hibiscus militaris **Cavar.** – See *Hibiscus laevis* All.

Hibiscus moscheutos **L.** – Common rose-mallow [Common rosemallow] (138) (1923), Crimson-eye rosemallow [Crimson-eyed rose mallow, Crimsoneyed rosemallow] (50) (present), Mallow-rose [Mallow rose] (5, 74, 156, 158) (1893–1923) NY, Marshmallow [Marsh mallow, Marsh mallows, Marsh-mallow] (156, 181) (~1678–1923), Rose-mallow [Rose mallow, Rosemallow] (4) (1986), Sea hollyhock (5, 156, 158) (1900–1923), Swamp rose-mallow [Swamp rose mallow] (2, 5, 82, 156, 158) (1895–1930), Swamp-mallow [Swamp mallow] (5, 156, 158) (1900–1923), Water-mallow [Water mallow] (5, 92, 156, 158) (1876–1923)

Hibiscus moscheutos **L. subsp.** *lasiocarpos* **(Cav.) O. J. Blanchard** – California rose-mallow [California rosemallow] (155) (1942), Hairy-fruit rosemallow [Hairy fruited rose mallow, Hairy-fruited rose mallow, Hairy-fruited rose-mallow] (2, 5, 97, 124) (1895–1937), Rose-mallow [Rose mallow, Rosemallow] (4) (1986), Woolly rose-mallow [Woolly rosemallow] (155) (1942)

Hibiscus moscheutos **L. subsp.** *moscheutos* – Bamia (178) (1526), Common rose-mallow [Common rosemallow] (155) (1942), Crimson-eye rosemallow [Crimson-eyed rose mallow, Crimsoneyed rosemallow] (5, 50, 138, 156) (1913–present), Marsh hibiscus (92, 187) (1818–1876), Strange marsh mallow (178) (1526), Velvety rose-mallow [Velvety rose mallow] (5) (1913), White hibiscus (156) (1923), White rose-mallow [White rose mallow] (156) (1923)

Hibiscus moscheutus **L.** – See *Hibiscus moscheutos* L.

Hibiscus mutabilis **L.** – Confederate-rose (109) (1949), Cotton rose-mallow (138) (1923), Cotton-rose [Cotton rose, Cottonrose] (109) (1949)

Hibiscus oculiroseus **[Britton]** – See *Hibiscus moscheutos* L. subsp. *moscheutos*

Hibiscus palustris **L.** – See *Hibiscus moscheutos* L. subsp. *moscheutos*

Hibiscus rosa sinensis – See *Hibiscus rosa-sinensis* L.

Hibiscus rosa-sinensis **L.** – Chinese hibiscus (107, 109, 138) (1919–1949), Rose-of-China [Rose of China] (92, 109) (1876–1949), Shoeblack plant (92) (1876)

Hibiscus sabdariffa **L.** – Guinea sorrel (92) (1876), Jamaica sorrel (109) (1949), Roselle (109, 138) (1923–1949), Sabdarissa (178) (1526), Thorny mallow [Thornie mallow] (178) (1526)

Hibiscus scaber **Michx.** – possibly *Hibiscus aculeatus* Walt.

Hibiscus schizopetalus **(Dyer) Hook. f.** – Fringed hibiscus (138) (1923)

Hibiscus speciosus **Aiton** – possibly *Hibiscus aculeatus* Walt.

Hibiscus syriacus **L.** – Rose-of-Sharon [Rose of Sharon] (5, 92, 107, 109, 112, 156) (1876–1949), Shrub althea [Shrub-althea] (109, 138) (1923–1949), Shrubby althaea (5, 15, 92, 109, 156) (1895–1949), Tree hibiscus (156) (1923), Tree mallow [Tree mallows, Tree mallowes] (178) (1526)

Hibiscus tiliaceus **L.** – Hau tree (106) (1930), Linden hibiscus (138) (1923)

207

Hibiscus trionum L. – Black-eyed Susan [Blackeyed Susan] (5, 73, 156, 158) (1892–1923) NH, New Brunswick, Bladder ketmia (5, 72, 80, 92, 145, 156, 158) (1876–1923), Devil's-head-in-a-bush [Devil's head-in-a-bush] (5, 73, 156, 158) (1892–1923) NH, New Brunswick; no longer in use by 1923, Flower-of-an-hour [Flower of an hour, Flowerofanhour] (3, 4, 5, 15, 50, 92, 93, 97, 109, 114, 127, 131, 138, 155, 156, 158) (1894–present), Modesty (5, 76, 93, 156, 158) (1896–1936), Shoofly [Shoofly] (80, 156) (1913–1923) no longer in use by 1923, Venice mallow (4, 5, 85, 131, 156, 158) (1899–1986)

Hickoria glabra **Britton.** – See *Carya glabra* (Mill.) Sweet

Hicoria alba (**L.**) **Britton** – See *Carya alba* (L.) Nutt. ex Ell.

Hicoria aquatica (**Michx. F.**) **Britton** – See *Carya aquatica* (Michx. f.) Nutt.

Hicoria borealis **Ashe** – See *Carya ovata* (Mill.) K. Koch

Hicoria buckleyi (**Dur.**) **Sud.** – See *Carya texana* Buckl.

Hicoria carolinae-septentrionalis **Ashe** – See *Carya carolinae-septentrionalis* (Ashe) Engl. & Graebn.

Hicoria cordiformis (**Wangenh.**) **Britton** – See *Carya cordiformis* (Wangenh.) K. Koch

Hicoria glabra (**Mill.**) **Britton** – See *Carya glabra* (Mill.) Sweet var. *glabra*

Hicoria laciniosa (**Michx. f.**) **Sargent** – See *Carya laciniosa* (Michx. f.) G. Don

Hicoria microcarpa (**Nutt.**) **Britton** – See *Carya glabra* (Mill.) Sweet

Hicoria minima (**Marsh**) **Britton** – See *Carya cordiformis* (Wangenh.) K. Koch

Hicoria myristicaeformis (**Michx. F.**) **Britton** – See *Carya myristiciformis* (F. Michx.) Nutt.

Hicoria myristiciformis (**F. Michx.**) **Britton** – See *Carya myristiciformis* (F. Michx.) Nutt.

Hicoria ovata (**Mill.**) **Britton** – See *Carya ovata* (Mill.) K. Koch

Hicoria pallida **Ashe** – See *Carya pallida* (Ashe) Engl. & Graebn.

Hicoria pecan (**Marsh.**) **Britton** – See *Carya illinoinensis* (Wangenh.) K. Koch

Hicoria **Raf.** – See *Carya* Nutt.

Hicoria sulcata [**Raf.**] – possibly *Carya laciniosa* (Michx. f.) G. Don

Hicoria texana (**LeConte**) **Britton** – See *Carya* ×*lecontei* Little [*aquatica* × *illinoinensis*]

Hicoria villosa (**Sargent**) **Ashe** – See *Carya texana* Buckl.

Hicorius glabra (**Mill.**) **Britt.** – possibly *Carya glabra* (Mill.) Sweet var. *glabra* (taxonomic status is unresolved (PL))

Hicorya alba – See *Carya alba* (L.) Nutt. ex Ell.

Hicorya amara – See *Carya cordiformis* (Wangenh.) K. Koch

Hicorya oliva – See *Carya illinoinensis* (Wangenh.) K. Koch

Hicorya porcina [**Raf.**] – possibly *Carya glabra* (Mill.) Sweet

Hicorya sulcata [**Raf.**] – possibly *Carya laciniosa* (Michx. f.) G. Don

Hieracium (**Tourn.**) **L.** – See *Hieracium* L.

Hieracium ×*floribundum* **Wimmer & Grab.** (pro sp.) [*caespitosum* × *lactucella*] – Smoothish hawkweed (5) (1913)

Hieracium ×*marianum* **Willd.** (pro sp.) [*gronovii* × *venosum*] – Maryland hawkweed (5) (1913)

Hieracium albiflorum **Hook** – White hawkweed (50, 155) (1942–present)

Hieracium aurantiacum **L.** – Devil's-paintbrush [Devil's paint-brush] (5, 62, 106, 109, 156) (1912–1949), Fairy paintbrush [Fairy's paintbrush] (156) (1923), Flora's-paintbrush [Flora's paint brush, Flora's paint-brush, Floras-paintbrush] (5, 75, 156) (1894–1923) Oxford Co. & Penobscot Co. ME, Golden hawkweed (62) (1912) IN, Golden mouse-ear hawkweed [Golden mouse-ear hawk-weed] (5, 156) (1913–1923), Grim-the-collier (5, 156) (1913–1923), Hawkweed [Hawk-weed, Hawk weed, Hawke-weed] (106) (1930), Missionary weed [Missionary-weed] (5, 76, 156) (1896–1923) East Sangerville ME, Orange hawkweed [Orange hawk-weed] (5, 19, 106, 109, 138, 156) (1840–1949), Red daisy (5, 156) (1913–1923), Tawny hawkweed [Tawny hawk-weed] (5, 156) (1913–1923)

Hieracium caespitosum **Dumort.** – Field hawkweed (5) (1913), King devil [King-devil] (156) (1923)

Hieracium canadense **Michx.** – Canadian hawkweed [Canada hawkweed] (5, 50, 72, 85, 131, 155, 156, 158) (1899–present), Hawkweed [Hawk-weed, Hawk weed, Hawke-weed] (3) (1977), High dandelion (5, 158) (1900–1913), Yellow succory (46) (1783)

Hieracium fendleri **Schultz-Bip.** – Fendler's hawkweed (131) (1899)

Hieracium fendleri **Schut** – See *Hieracium fendleri* Schultz-Bip.

Hieracium florentinum **All.** – See *Hieracium piloselloides* Vill.

Hieracium floribundum **Wimm. & Grab.** – See *Hieracium* ×*floribundum* Wimmer & Grab. [*caespitosum* × *lactucella*]

Hieracium greenii **Porter & Britton** – Green's hawkweed (5) (1913)

Hieracium gronovii **L.** – Cat's-ear [Cat's ear, Cats-ear] (5, 156) (1913–1923), Gronovius' hawkweed (5) (1913), Hairy hawkweed [Hairy hawk-weed] (5, 97, 156, 158) (1900–1937), Hawkweed [Hawk-weed, Hawk weed, Hawke-weed] (19) (1840), Queen-devil [Queendevil] (50) (present), Vein-leaf [Vein leaf] (19) (1840)

Hieracium **L.** – Accippitrina (180) (1633), Cichorea iaulne (French) (180) (1633), Eperviére (French) (158) (1900), Habichtskraut (German) (158) (1900), Hawkweed [Hawk-weed, Hawk weed, Hawke-weed] (1, 2, 4, 10, 50, 63, 93, 109, 138, 155, 156, 158, 180, 184, 190) (~1759–present) sap said to sharpen eyesight, Lampuca (180) (1633), Porcellia (180) (1633), Speer-hawk (158) (1900)

Hieracium lachenalii **K. C. Gmel.** – Hawkweed [Hawk-weed, Hawk weed, Hawke-weed] (5) (1913)

Hieracium longipilum **Torr.** – Hairy hawkweed [Hairy hawk-weed] (50) (present), Long-beard hawkweed [Long-bearded hawkweed] (3, 5, 63, 72, 93, 97, 122) (1899–1977)

Hieracium marianum **Willd.** – See *Hieracium* ×*marianum* Willd. [*gronovii* × *venosum*]

Hieracium murorum **L.** – French lungwort (5, 156) (1913–1923), Golden lungwort (5, 156) (1913–1923), Ling-gowan [Ling gowans] (156) (1923) no longer in use by 1923, Mouse bloodwort [Mouse-bloodwort] (156) (1923) no longer in use by 1923, Wall hawkweed [Wall hawk-weed] (5, 156) (1913–1923)

Hieracium paniculatum **L.** – Panicled hawkweed (5) (1913)

Hieracium pilosella **L.** – Felon herb [Fellon-herb, Felon-herb] (5, 156) (1913–1923), Ling-gowan [Ling gowans] (5) (1913), Mouse bloodwort [Mouse blood wort (5, 92, 156) (1876–1923), Mouse-ear [Mouse ear, Mouse ears, Mouse's ear, Mows eare] (92, 156, 178, 179) (1526–1923), Mouse-ear hawkweed (5) (1913)

Hieracium piloselloides **Vill.** – King devil [King-devil] (5, 156) (1913–1923)

Hieracium pratense **Tausch.** – See *Hieracium caespitosum* Dumort.

Hieracium scabriusculum **Schwein.** – See *Hieracium umbellatum* L.

Hieracium scabrum **Michx.** – Rough hawkweed (5, 62, 63, 72, 97, 157) (1899–1937)

Hieracium umbellatum **L.** – Lungenhabichtskraut (German) (158) (1900) plant used in asthma, Narrow-leaf hawkweed [Narrow-leaved hawkweed] (5, 50, 93, 131, 155) (1899–present)

Hieracium venosum **L.** – Adder's-tongue [Adder tongue, Adders tongue, Adder's tongue, Adders toong, Adderstongue] (5, 156) (1913–1923), Bloodwort [Blood wort, Blood-wort] (7, 92, 157) (1828–1929), Early hawkweed [Early hawk-weed] (5, 156, 157) (1913–1929), Hawkbit [Hawk bit] (5, 92, 156) (1876–1923), Hawkweed [Hawk-weed, Hawk weed, Hawke-weed] (7, 49, 92) (1828–1898), Poor Robert's-plantain [Poor Robert's Plantane, Poor Robert's plantain] (187) (1818), Poor Robin's-plantain [Poor robins plantain, Poor-robins-plantain, Poorrobins-plantain, Poor robin's plantian, Poor robin plantain] (5, 44, 46, 156, 157) (1845–1929), Rattlesnake-weed [Rattlesnake weed, Rattlesnake weede, Rattlesnakes' weed] (2, 5, 44, 46, 49, 92, 156, 157) (1845–1929), Snake-plantian [Snake plantian] (5, 7, 92, 156, 157) (1828–1929), Striped bloodwort (5, 92, 156, 157) (1876–1929), Striped woodwort (49) (1898), Vein-leaf hawkbit [Vein leaf hawk's-bit] (156, 158) (1900–1923), Vein-leaf hawkweed (5, 157) (1913–1929), Veiny-leaf hawkweed [Veiny-leaved hawkweed, Veiny leaved hawkweed] (49, 92, 156, 157) (1898–1929)

Hieracium vulgatum **Fries** – See *Hieracium lachenalii* K. C. Gmel.

Hierochloa alpina – See *Hierochloe alpina* (Sw. ex Willd.) Roemer & J. A. Schultes

Hierochloa arborealis – possibly *Hierochloe odorata* (L.) Beauv.

Hierochloa borealis Sch. – See *Hierochloe odorata* (L.) Beauv.

Hierochloe alpina (Sw. ex Willd.) Roemer & J. A. Schultes – Alpine holy grass [Alpine holygrass] (66, 90) (1885–1903)

Hierochloe alpina (Sw. ex Willd.) Roemer & J. A. Schultes subsp. *alpina* – Alpine holy grass [Alpine holygrass] (5, 45, 94) (1896–1913), Alpine sweet grass [Alpine sweetgrass] (50) (present), Alpine vanilla grass (45) (1896)

Hierochloe hirta (Schrank) Borbás – Northern sweet grass [Northern sweetgrass] (50) (present)

Hierochloe hirta (Schrank) Borbás subsp. *arctica* (J. Presl) G. Weim. – Northern sweet grass [Northern sweetgrass] (50) (present)

Hierochloe odorata (L.) Beauv. – Holy grass [Holygrass] (5, 80, 85, 87, 90, 92, 140) (1876–1944) strewn before church doors in N. Europe, Kataaru (Pawnee) (37) (1830), Manuska (Winnebago) (37) (1830), Nodding vanilla grass (5) (1913), Northern holy grass (45) (1896), Pezhe zonsta (Omaha-Ponca) (37) (1830), Seneca grass (5, 19, 45, 66, 87, 90, 92) (1840–1903), Sweet grass [Sweet-grass, Sweetgrass] (3, 35, 37, 40, 85, 140, 155) (1806–1977), Sweet summer grass (19) (1840), Vanilla grass [Vanilla-grass, Vanillagrass] (5, 45, 50, 56, 66, 67, 80, 87, 90, 92, 94, 140) (1885–present), Wachanga (Dakota) (37) (1830), Wicko'bĭmûcko'si (Chippewa, sweet grass) (40) (1928), possibly Summer grass [Summer-grass] (92) (1876)

Hierochloe odorata auct. non (L.) Beauv. p.p. – See *Hierochloe alpina* (Sw. ex Willd.) Roemer & J. A. Schultes subsp. *alpina*

Hierochloe pauciflora R. Br. – Arctic holy grass (5) (1913), Arctic sweet grass [Arctic sweetgrass] (50) (present)

Hierochloe R. Br. – Sweet grass [Sweet-grass, Sweetgrass] (1, 50, 155) (1932–present)

Hilaria belangeri (Steud.) Nash – Creeping mesquite (163) (1852), Curly mesquite (65, 163) (1852–1931), Curly mesquite grass (122) (1937) NM

Hilaria cenchroides Kunth – Curly mesquite (94) (1901), Texas curly mesquite (152) (1912)

Hilaria jamesii (Torr.) Benth. – See *Pleuraphis jamesii* Torr.

Hilaria Kunth – Hilaria (155) (1942)

Hilaria mutica (Buckl.) Benth. – See *Pleuraphis mutica* Buckl.

Hilaria rigida – See *Pleuraphis rigida* Thurb.

Hippeastrum equestre [(Aiton) Herb.] – See *Hippeastrum puniceum* (Lam.) Kuntze

Hippeastrum puniceum (Lam.) Kuntze – House-amaryllis (138) (1923)

Hippocrepis L. – Horseshoe-vetch (109) (1949)

Hippomane L. – Manchineel or Manchineel tree [Manchineel-tree] (167) (1814)

Hippomane mancinella L. – Manchenil tree (7) (1828), Manchineel or Manchineel tree [Manchineel-tree] (20, 92, 106) (1857–1930), Mancillier (20) (1857)

Hippophae canadensis W. – See *Shepherdia canadensis* Nutt.

Hippophae L. – Rhamnoide (French) (8) (1785), Sallow thorn [Sallow-thorn] (8) (1785), Sea-buckthorn [Sea buckthorn] (8, 109, 138, 167) (1785–1949)

Hippophae rhamnoides L. – Common sea-buckthorn (138) (1923), Sea-buckthorn [Sea buckthorn] (135) (1910)

Hipposelinum levisticum (L.) Britton & Rose – See *Levisticum officinale* W. D. J. Koch

Hippuris L. – Mare's-tail [Marestail, Mare's tail, Mare's-tails] (1, 26, 50, 155, 158) (1826–present)

Hippuris tetraphylla L. f. – Four-leaf mare's-tail [Four-leaved mare's tail] (5) (1913)

Hippuris vulgaris L. – Bottlebrush [Bottle brush, Bottle-brush] (5, 93, 131, 156, 158) (1899–1936), Cat-tail [Cat's tail, Cats Taile, Cat's-tail, Cats tails] (5, 156, 158) (1900–1923), Common mare's-tail (50) (present), Female knot-grass (158) (1900), Jointweed [Joint-weed, Joint weed] (5, 93, 156, 158) (1900–1923), Knotgrass [Knot grass, Knot-grass, Knotgrasse] (5, 156) (1913–1923), Mare's-tail [Marestail, Mare's tail, Mare's-tails] (3, 4, 5, 10, 19, 85, 92, 93, 155, 156, 158) (1818–1986), Paddock-pipe [Paddock pipe, Paddock pipes, Paddock-pipes] (5, 156, 158) (1900–1923), Pesse d'eau (French) (158) (1900), Schafthalm (German) (158) (1900), Witch's-milk [Witches' milk, Witches milk, Witches'-milk, Witche's-milk] (5, 156, 158) (1900–1923)

Hippurus tetraphylla L. f. – See *Hippuris tetraphylla* L. f.

Hocoria texana (LeConte) Britton – See *Carya* ×*lecontei* Little [*aquatica* × *illinoinensis*]

Hoffmannseggia Cav. – Rush pea (4, 50) (1986–present)

Hoffmannseggia densiflora Benth. – See *Hoffmannseggia glauca* (Ortega) Eifert

Hoffmannseggia drepanocarpa Gray – See *Caesalpinia drepanocarpa* (Gray) Fisher

Hoffmannseggia falcaria Cavar. – See *Hoffmannseggia glauca* (Ortega) Eifert

Hoffmannseggia glauca (Ortega) Eifert – Indian rushpea [Indian rush-pea] (4, 50, 155) (1942–present), Pignut [Pig-nut, Pig nut] (3, 4) (1977–1986), Sickle-fruit hoffmanseggia [Sickle-fruited hoffmanseggia] (5, 97) (1913–1937)

Hoffmannseggia jamesii Torr. & Gray – See *Caesalpinia jamesii* (Torr. & Gray) Fisher

Hoffmanseggia jamesii Torr. & Gray – See *Caesalpinia jamesii* (Torr. & Gray) Fisher

Holcophacos Rydb. – See *Astragalus* L. (all current species)

Holcus halapensis L. – See *Sorghum halepense* (L.) Pers.

Holcus L. – Johnson grass [Johnson-grass, Johnsongrass] (93) (1936) Neb, Meadow soft grass (66) (1903), Soft grass [Soft-grass] (10, 92, 184) (1793–1876), Velvet grass [Velvet-grass, Velvetgrass] (1, 50, 155) (1932–present)

Holcus lanatus L. – Calf-kill [Calf kill] (5) (1913), Common velvet grass [Common velvetgrass] (50, 155) (1942–present), Couch grass [Couch-grass] (46) (1671) accidentally introduced by 1671, Dart grass (5) (1913), Feather grass [Feathergrass, Feather-grass] (5, 75) (1894–1913) WV, Meadow soft grass (5, 45, 66, 87, 90) (1884–1913), Old whitetop [Old white top] (5, 75) (1894–1913) WV, Rot grass (5) (1913), Salem grass [Salem-grass] (5, 45, 187) (1818–1913), Soft grass [Soft-grass] (19, 88) (1840–1885), Soft meadow grass (92) (1876), Soft woolly grass (45) (1896), Velvet grass [Velvet-grass, Velvetgrass] (3, 5, 45, 56, 66, 72, 75, 88, 90, 92, 94, 109, 111, 119, 122, 138, 163) (1852–1977), Velvet mesquite (5, 88) (1885–1913), Velvet mesquite grass [Velvet mesquit grass] (45, 87, 90) (1884–1896), White timothy (5, 45) (1896–1913), Whites (5) (1913), Woolly soft grass [Wooly soft grass] (5) (1913), Yorkshire fog (5, 45) (1896–1913)

Holcus mollis L. – Creeping soft grass (45, 66) (1896–1903), Creeping velvet grass [Creeping velvetgrass] (50) (present)

Holcus saccharatus L. – See *Sorghum bicolor* (L.) Moench

Holcus sorghum L. – See *Sorghum bicolor* (L.) Moench subsp. *bicolor*

Holcus sorghum sudanensis – See *Sorghum bicolor* (L.) Moench subsp. *drummondii* (Nees ex Steud.) de Wet & Harlan

Holcus striatus L. – See *Sacciolepis striata* (L.) Nash

Holmskioldia sanguinea Retz. – Chinese hat plant [Chinese-hat-plant] (109) (1949)

Holocarpha virgata (Gray) Keck – Yellow tarweed [Yellow tar weed] (106) (1930)

Holodiscus australis [A. Heller] – See *Holodiscus dumosus* (Nutt. ex Hook.) Heller

Holodiscus discolor (Pursh) Maxim. – Rock-spiraea [Rock spiraea] (138) (1923)

Holodiscus dumosus (Nutt. ex Hook.) Heller – Wild crape myrtle (149) (1904) NM

Holosteum L. – Holosteum (50) (present), Jagged chickweed (158) (1900)

Holosteum umbellatum L. – Chickweed [Chick-weed, Chick weed] (184) (1793), Jagged chickweed (4, 5, 50, 156) (1913–present)

Homalobus caespitosus Nutt. – See *Astragalus spatulatus* Sheldon

Homalobus montanus (Nutt.) Britton – See *Astragalus kentrophyta* Gray var. *kentrophyta*

Homalobus Nutt. – See *Astragalus* L. (all US species)

Homalobus tenellus (Pursh) Britton – See *Astragalus tenellus* Pursh

Homalocenchrus lenticularis (Michx.) Scribn. – See *Leersia lenticularis* Michx.

Homalocenchrus Meig. – See *Leersia* Sw.

Homalocenchrus monandrus (Sw.) Britton – See *Leersia monandra* Sw.

Homalocenchrus oryzoides (L.) Poll. – See *Leersia oryzoides* (L.) Sw.

Homalocenchrus virginicus (Willd.) Britton – See *Leersia virginica* Willd.

Homalocephala Britt. & Rose – See *Echinocactus* Link & Otto (all US species)

Homalocephala texensis Britton & Rose – See *Echinocactus texensis* Hopffer.

Homalocladium platycladum (F. J. Muell.) Bailey – Centipede-plant (109) (1949), Ribbon bush [Ribbonbush, Ribbon-bush] (109, 138) (1923–1949)

Homalocladium platycladum Bailey – See *Homalocladium platycladum* (F. J. Muell.) Bailey

Honckenya Ehrh. – Sea sandwort (13) (1849)

Honckenya peploides (L.) Ehrh. – Sea chickweed (5) (1913), Sea pimpernel (5) (1913), Sea-beach sandwort [Seabeach sandwort, Sea beach sandwort] (5) (1913), Sea-purslane [Sea purslane] (5) (1913)

Honckenya peploides (L.) Ehrh. subsp. *diffusa* (Hornem.) Hultén – Sea chickweed (19, 107, 156) (1840–1923), Sea pimpernel (156) (1923), Sea sandwort (2, 156) (1895–1923), Sea-beach sandwort [Seabeach sandwort, Sea beach sandwort] (155, 156) (1923–1942), Sea-purslane [Sea purslane] (156) (1923), Spreading sandwort (2) (1895)

Hopea L. – See *Symplocos* Jacq.

Hopea tinctorea L. – See *Symplocos tinctoria* (L.) L'Her.

Hordeum boreale Scribn. & J. G. Sm. – See *Hordeum brachyantherum* Nevski subsp. *brachyantherum*

Hordeum brachyantherum Nevski – Meadow barley (5, 50) (1913–present), Northern meadow barley (3) (1977)

Hordeum brachyantherum Nevski subsp. *brachyantherum* – Northern wild barley [Northern wild-barley] (94) (1901)

Hordeum bulbosum L. – Barley grass [Barley-grass] (87) (1884), Meadow barley (5, 50, 56, 72, 94, 122, 152) (1901–present), Wild barley (56, 94, 152) (1901–1912)

Hordeum deficiens Steud. ex A. Braun – See *Hordeum vulgare* L.

Hordeum distichon L. – See *Hordeum vulgare* L.

Hordeum distichon nudum L. – See *Hordeum vulgare* L.

Hordeum distichon var. *nudum* L. – See *Hordeum vulgare* L.

Hordeum distichum – See *Hordeum vulgare* L.

Hordeum hexastichon L. – See *Hordeum vulgare* L.

Hordeum jubatum L. – A'djidamo'wano (Chippewa, squirrel tail) (40) (1928), Barley (108) (1878), Foxtail barley (3, 50, 122, 140, 143, 155, 163) (1852–present), Foxtail grass [Fox tail grass, Foxtail grass, Foxtail-grass] (45, 87) (1884–1896), Maned barley (107) (1919), Skunk grass [Skunk-grass] (62) (1912) IN, Squirrel-tail [Squirrel tail, Squirreltail] (85, 93, 140) (1932–1944), Squirrel-tail barley (107) (1919), Squirrel-tail grass [Squirreltail grass, Squirrel-tail-grass, Squirreltail-grass] (5, 11, 19, 40, 45, 56, 62, 66, 72, 75, 80, 87, 88, 90, 92, 94, 109, 111, 119, 129, 138, 143, 145, 148, 152, 163) (1840–1949), Wall barley [Wall-barley] (19, 56, 62, 80, 87, 88, 115, 126, 143, 148) (1840–1939)

Hordeum jubatum L. subsp. *breviaristatum* Bowden – See *Hordeum brachyantherum* Nevski subsp. *brachyantherum*

Hordeum jubatum L. subsp. *intermedium* Bowden – Intermediate barley (50) (present)

Hordeum jubatum L. subsp. *jubatum* – Foxtail barley (50) (present)

Hordeum jubatum L. var. *boreale* (Scribn. & J. G. Sm.) Boivin – See *Hordeum brachyantherum* Nevski subsp. *brachyantherum*

Hordeum L. – Barley (10, 45, 50, 155, 184) (1793–present), Barley grass [Barley-grass] (66, 92) (1876–1903), Bear (158) (1900), Bigg [Big] (158) (1900), Foxtail [Fox tail, Fox-tail, Fox tails, Foxetaile, Fox-taile] (1, 93) (1932–1936), Haules (158) (1900), Hoils (158) (1900), Pillards (158) (1900), Squirrel-tail [Squirrel tail, Squirrel-tail] (1, 93) (1932–1936), Wild barley (93) (1936)

Hordeum marinum Huds. – Sea barley [Sea-barley] (45) (1896), Seaside barley (94) (1901)

Hordeum maritimum With. – See *Hordeum marinum* Huds.

Hordeum montanense Scribn. – See *Elyhordeum montanense* (Scribn.) Bowden

Hordeum murinum L. – Barley grass [Barley-grass] (163) (1852), Foxtail [Fox tail, Fox-tail, Fox tails, Foxetaile, Fox-taile] (88) (1885), Foxtail barley (155) (1942), Mouse barley [Mouse-barley (5, 50, 119, 163) (1852–present), Sea barley [Sea-barley] (155) (1942), Squirrel grass (88) (1885), Squirrel-tail [Squirrel tail, Squirreltail] (5, 88) (1885–1913), Wall barley [Wall-barley] (5, 45, 94, 163) (1852–1913), Way barley (5) (1913), Way bent (5, 45) (1896–1913), White oats (88) (1885), Wild barley (5) (1913)

Hordeum nodosum L. – See *Hordeum bulbosum* L.

Hordeum pammelii Scribn. & Ball. – See *Elyhordeum montanense* (Scribn.) Bowden

Hordeum pratense [Huds.] – See *Hordeum secalinum* Schreb.

Hordeum pusillum Nutt. – Barley grass [Barley-grass] (66) (1903), Little barley (3, 5, 50, 56, 72, 80, 93, 94, 119, 122, 134, 140, 155, 163) (1852–present), Wild barley (85) (1932)

Hordeum secalinum Schreb. – Barley (108, 161) (1857–1878), Wild meadow barley (87) (1884)

Hordeum vulgare L. – Barley (7, 19, 49, 53, 85, 92, 107, 109, 119, 138, 140, 155, 178, 179, 180) (1526–1944), Barley Big (180) (1633), Battledore barley (107) (1919), Bear barley [Beare barley] (158, 180) (1633–1900), Beardless barley (155, 163) (1942–1952), Bere (107) (1919), Big barley (107, 180) (1633–1919), Bigg [Big] (180) (1633), Black barley (158) (1900) variety, Cenada (Spanish) (180) (1633), Common barley (50, 110, 119, 180) (1633–present), Common English barley (158) (1900), Crimmon (180) (1633), Cultivated barley (56, 163) (1852–1901), Dinkel barley (158) (1900) variety, Fan-shaped barley (110) (1886), Four-row barley [Four rowed barley] (56, 66) (1901–1903), French barley (158) (1900) variety, Galaticum (180) (1633), Gerste (German) (158) (1900), Gersten (High Dutch) (180) (1633), Gersten (Low Dutch) (180) (1633), Golden barley (158) (1900) variety, Hulless barley (119) (1938), Italian barley (158) (1900) variety, Naked barley (158) (1900) variety, Nepal barley (107) (1919), Orge (French) (180) (1633), Orge à café (French, "coffee barley) (110) (1886), Orge du Pérou (French, Peruvian coffee) (110) (1886), Orgre (French) (158) (1900), Orzo (Italian) (180) (1633), Pearl barley (49, 55, 92) (1876–1911), Red barley (158) (1900) variety, Red Sea barley (107) (1919), Russian barley (158) (1900) variety, Scotch barley (158) (1900) variety, Siberian barley (158) (1900) variety, Six-lines barley (107) (1919), Six-row barley [Sixrow barley, Six rowed barley, Six-rowed barley] (66, 67, 110, 155) (1886–1942), Sprat barley (66, 107) (1903–1919), Spring barley (158) (1900) variety, Square barley (166, 58) (1900–1903), Two-row barley [Tworow barley, Two rowed barley, Two-rowed barley, Two-rowed barley] (56, 66, 67, 110, 155, 158) (1890–1942), Wheat barley (158) (1900), Winter barley (107, 158) (1900–1919) variety

Hordeum vulgare L. var. *trifurcatum* (Schlecht.) Alef. – See *Hordeum vulgare* L.

Hordeum zeocriton L. – See *Hordeum vulgare* L.

Hosackia americana (Nutt.) Piper. – See *Lotus unifoliolatus* (Hook.) Benth. var. *unifoliolatus*

Hosackia purshiana Benth. – See *Lotus unifoliolatus* (Hook.) Benth.

Hosta caerulea [(Andr.) Tratt.] – See *Hosta ventricosa* (Salisb.) Stearn

Hosta lancifolia Engl. – Lance-leaf plantain-lily [Lanceleaf plantain-lily] (138) (1923), Narrow-leaf plantain-lily [Narrow-leaved plantain-lily] (109) (1949)

Hosta plantaginea (**Lam.**) **Aschers.** – August lily (156) (1923), Big plantain-lily [Big plantainlily] (138) (1923), Daylily [Day lily, Day-lily, Day-Lillie] (156) (1923), Fragrant plantain-lily (109) (1949), Plantain-lily [Plantainlily] (156) (1923), White day-lily (156) (1923), White plantain-lily [White plantainlily] (138) (1923)

Hosta plantaginea **Aschers** – See *Hosta plantaginea* (Lam.) Aschers.

Hosta plantaginea **f.** *grandiflora* (**Siebold & Zucc.**) **Asch. & Graebn.** – See *Hosta plantaginea* (Lam.) Aschers.

Hosta plantaginea grandiflora – See *Hosta plantaginea* (Lam.) Aschers.

Hosta **Tratt.** – Daylily [Day lily, Day-lily, Day-Lillie] (156) (1923), Plantain-lily [Plantainlily] (109, 138) (1923–1949)

Hosta ventricosa (**Salisb.**) **Stearn** – Blue plantain-lily [Blue plantain-lily] (109, 138) (1923–1949)

Hosta ventricosa **Stearn** – See *Hosta ventricosa* (Salisb.) Stearn

Hottonia inflata **Ell.** – American featherfoil [American feather foil] (5, 97, 122, 124) (1913–1937), Featherfoil [Feather foil] (156) (1923), Water gilliflower (156) (1923), Water-feather [Water-feather, Water feathers] (5, 10, 156) (1818–1923), Water-milfoil [Water milfoil, Water mill-foil, Watermillfoil] (156) (1923), Water-violet [Water violet] (5, 19, 46, 156) (1783–1923), Water-yarrow [Water yarrow] (5, 156) (1913–1923)

Hottonia **L.** – Featherfoil [Feather foil] (2) (1895), Water-violet [Water violet] (2, 156) (1895–1942)

Houstonia angustifolia **Michx.** – See *Hedyotis nigricans* (Lam.) Fosberg var. *nigricans*

Houstonia caerulea **L.** – American daisy (86) (1878), Angel's-eye [Angeleyes, Angel eyes, angel-eyes] (5, 73, 156) (1892–1923) no longer in use by 1923, Blue-eyed babies (5, 73, 156) (1892–1923) Springfield MA, no longer in use by 1923, Blue-eyed-grass [Blue-eyed grass] (5, 76, 156) (1896–1923) Brodhead WI, Bluets [Bluet] (2, 5, 86, 109, 138, 156, 187) (1818–1949), Bright-eyes [Bright eyes] (5, 73, 156) (1892–1923) Baltimore MD, no longer in use by 1923, Common houstonia (2) (1895), Dwarf pink (19, 86, 156) (1840–1923), Eyebright [Eye-bright, Eye bright] (5, 73, 75, 156) (1892–1923) Isles of Shoals ME, Forget-me-not [Forget me not, For-get-me-not, For-get-me-nots, Forgetmenot] (73, 76, 156) (1892–1923), Innocence (5, 19, 73, 86, 156) (1840–1923) Boston MA, Little washerwoman (5, 76, 156) (1896–1923) Bethlehem PA, no longer in use by 1923, Nuns (5, 73, 156) (1892–1923) no longer in use by 1923, Quaker beauty (73) (1892), Quaker bonnet [Quaker bonnets, Quaker-bonnets] (5, 86, 156) (1878–1923) Philadelphia PA, Quaker lady [Quaker ladies, Quaker-ladies] (5, 73, 156) (1892–1923) MA, Sky-blue houstonia (187) (1818), Starlights [Starlight] (75) (1894) Cambridge MA, Star-of-Bethlehem [Star of Bethlehem, Starre of Bethlem, Stars of Bethlehem] (5, 73, 156) (1892–1923) MS, Venus'-pride [Venus' pride, Venus' pride] (5, 19, 75, 156) (1840–1923), Wild forget-me-not (5) (1913)

Houstonia canadensis **Willd. ex Roemer & J. A. Schultes** – Fringed houstonia (5, 97) (1913–1937)

Houstonia ciliolata **Torr.** – See *Houstonia canadensis* Willd. ex Roemer & J. A. Schultes

Houstonia coerulea **L.** – See *Houstonia caerulea* L.

Houstonia coliolata **Torr.** – possibly *Houstonia canadensis* Willd. ex Roemer & J. A. Schultes

Houstonia humifusa (**Gray**) **Gray** – Innocence (97) (1937) OK, Matted bluet (50) (present), Pink houstonia (124) (1937), Rough small bluet (4) (1986)

Houstonia **L.** – Bluets [Bluet] (1, 50, 155, 156, 158) (1900–present), Houstonia (138) (1923), Star-violet [Star violet] (76) (1896) Waco TX, Venus'-pride [Venus' pride, Venus' pride] (76, 158) (1896–1900), Wild forget-me-not (76) (1896) Waco TX

Houstonia lanceolata (**Poir.**) **Britton** – See *Houstonia purpurea* L. var. *calycosa* Gray

Houstonia longifolia **Gaertn.** – Bluets [Bluet] (3) (1977), Long-leaf bluets [Longleaf bluets] (138, 155) (1923–1942), Long-leaf houstonia [Long-leaved houstonia] (5, 97) (1913–1937), Long-leaf

summer bluet [Longleaf summer bluet] (50) (present), Slender-leaf bluets [Slender-leaved bluets] (4) (1986), Slender-leaf houstonia [Slenderleaf houstonia] (5, 122) (1913–1937)

Houstonia minima **Beck.** – See *Houstonia pusilla* Schoepf

Houstonia patens **Ell.** – See *Houstonia pusilla* Schoepf

Houstonia purpurea **L.** – Large houstonia (5, 97) (1913–1937), Mountain houstonia (138) (1923), Purple bluets (155) (1942), Venus'-pride [Venus' pride, Venus' pride] (5, 50) (1913–present)

Houstonia purpurea **L. var.** *calycosa* **Gray** – Calycose houstonia (5, 97) (1913–1937), Venus'-pride [Venus' pride, Venus' pride] (50) (present)

Houstonia purpurea **var.** *ciliolata* **Gray.** – See *Houstonia canadensis* Willd. ex Roemer & J. A. Schultes

Houstonia purpurea **var.** *longifolia* **Gray.** – See *Houstonia longifolia* Gaertn.

Houstonia pusilla **Schoepf** – Least bluet [Least bluets] (5, 63, 65, 72, 97) (1899–1937), Small bluet [Small bluets] (3, 4, 5, 97, 156) (1913–1986), Star-violet [Star violet] (5, 156) (1913–1923), Tiny bluet [Tiny bluets] (50, 155) (1942–present)

Houstonia serpyllifolia **Michx.** – Creeping bluets (109, 138) (1923–1949), Houstonia with a small purple Flower (183) (~1756), Thyme-leaf bluets [Thyme-leaved bluets] (5) (1913)

Houstonia tenuifolia **Nutt.** – See *Houstonia longifolia* Gaertn.

Houttoynia californica **Benth. & Hook.** – See *Anemopsis californica* (Nutt.) Hook. & Arn.

Hovenia dulcis **Thunb.** – Japanese raisin-tree (109) (1949), Raisin tree [Raisin-tree, Raisintree] (138) (1923)

Hovenia **Thunb.** – Raisin tree [Raisin-tree, Raisintree] (138) (1923)

Hoya carnosa (**L. f.**) **R. Br.** – Common waxplant (138) (1923), Wax plant [Wax-plant, Waxplant] (92, 109) (1876–1949)

Hoya carnosa **R. Br.** – See *Hoya carnosa* (L. f.) R. Br.

Hoya **R. Br.** – Wax plant [Wax-plant, Waxplant] (138) (1923)

Hudsonia ericoides **L.** – American heath (5, 156) (1913–1923), False heath (19) (1840), Field pine (5, 156) (1913–1923), Goldheather [Gold heather] (156) (1923), Heath-like hudsonia (5) (1913), Hudsonia (156) (1923), Lingwort (46) (1649), Poverty-grass [Poverty grass] (5, 156) (1913–1923)

Hudsonia **L.** – Beach-heather [Beachheather, Beach heather] (1, 155) (1932–1942), False heather (158) (1900), Golden-heather [Goldenheather, Golden heather] (50) (present), Poverty-grass [Poverty grass] (4) (1986)

Hudsonia tomentosa **Nutt.** – Anonymos yellow sandbind (46) (1783), Beach-heather [Beachheather, Beach heather] (4, 5, 156, 158) (1900–1986), Bear-grass [Bear grass, Bear's grass, Bears' grass] (5, 156, 158) (1900–1923), Dog's-dinner [Dog's dinner] (5, 76, 156, 158) (1896–1923) Wellfleet MA, False heather (5, 156, 158) (1900–1923), Ground-cedar [Groundcedar, Ground cedar] (5, 156, 158) (1900–1923), Ground-moss [Ground moss] (5, 156, 158) (1900–1923), Heath (76, 156, 158) (1896–1923) Wellfleet MA, Heath-like hudsonia (5) (1913), Hudsonia (156) (1923), Poverty plant [Poverty-plant (5, 156) (1913–1923), Poverty-grass [Poverty grass] (3, 5, 15, 76, 158) (1895–1977), Woolly beach-heather [Woolly beachheather] (50, 155) (1942–present), Woolly hudsonia (5, 158) (1900–1913)

Humulus americana **Nutt.** – See *Humulus lupulus* L. var. *lupuloides* E. Small

Humulus americanus **Nutt.** – See *Humulus lupulus* L. var. *lupuloides* E. Small

Humulus japonicus **Sieb. & Zucc.** – Hop [Hops, Hoppes] (21) (1893), Japanese hop (3, 4, 50, 93, 138, 155) (1923–present)

Humulus **L.** – Hop [Hops, Hoppes] (1, 4, 50, 93, 106, 109, 138, 155, 156, 158, 167) (1814–present), Hop vine [Hop vine] (153) (1913)

Humulus lupulus **L.** – Apini (110) (1886), Apwynis (Lithuanian) (110) (1886), Bine (107, 157, 158) (1919–1929), Blust (110) (1886), Bur (157, 158) (1900–1929), Chmeli (Slavic) (110) (1886), Common hop [Common hops] (3, 4, 6, 7, 38, 47, 50, 93, 106, 108, 138, 155, 156, 187) (1818–present), European hop (109) (1949), Hop [Hops, Hoppes] (5, 7, 10, 27, 49, 52, 53, 55, 57, 59, 60, 72, 85, 92, 92, 95,

107, 110, 131, 157, 179, 184, 187) (1526–1936), Hop vine [Hop vine] (7, 44, 60, 92, 157, 158) (1828–1929), Hopfen (German) (6, 7) (1828–1932), Houblon (French) (6) (1892), Houblon commune (French) (7) (1828), Humle (Scandinavian) (110) (1886), Humuli strobili (Official name of Materia Medica) (7) (1828), Humulus (59, 60, 174, 177) (1753–1911), Lupuli coni (Official name of Materia Medica) (7) (1828), Lupulo (Italian) (110) (1886), Lupulus (6, 55) (1892–1911), Northern vine (6) (1892), Seeder (157, 158) (1900–1929), Tap (Estonian) (110) (1886), Wild hop [Wild hops] (7, 142) (1828–1902)

Humulus lupulus L. var. *lupuloides* E. Small – American hop (109) (1949), Chan iyuwe (Dakota, twining on a tree) (37) (1919), Hop [Hops, Hoppes] (37) (1919), Makan skithe [Makan-skithe] (Omaha-Ponca, sweet medicine) (37) (1919), Wah'pe onapoh'ye (Dakota, leaves and to puff up) (37) (1919), Wiunabih'u (37) (1919)

Humulus lupulus L. var. *neomexicanus* A. Nels. & Cockerell – Hop vine [Hop vine] (149) (1904), New Mexico hop [New Mexican hop, NewMexican hop] (138, 155) (1923–1942), Wild hop [Wild hops] (153) (1913)

Humulus lupulus neomexicanus – See *Humulus lupulus* L. var. *neomexicanus* A. Nels. & Cockerell

Hunnemannia fumariaefolia Sweet – See *Hunnemannia fumariifolia* Sweet

Hunnemannia fumariifolia Sweet – Goldencup [Golden-cup, Golden cup] (109, 138) (1923–1949)

Hunnemannia Sweet – Goldencup [Golden-cup, Golden cup] (138) (1923), Mexican tulip-poppy (109) (1949)

Huperzia lucidula (Michx.) Trevisan – Moon-fruit pine [Moon fruit pine, Moonfruit pine] (5, 19, 92) (1840–1913), Shining clubmoss [Shining club-moss] (5, 50, 138) (1913–present), Trailing evergreen (5) (1913)

Huperzia porophila (Lloyd & Underwood) Holub – Lloyd's clubmoss [Lloyd's club-moss] (5) (1913), Rock clubmoss (50) (present)

Huperzia selago (L.) Bernh. ex Mart. & Schrank var. *selago* – Fir club-moss (5, 50, 92) (1876–present), Fir moss (5) (1913), Foxfeet [Fox feet] (5) (1913), Tree moss [Tree-moss] (5) (1913), Upright clubmoss [Upright club moss] (5) (1913)

Huperzia selago (L.) Bernh. subsp. *lucidula* (Michx.) A. & D. Löve – See *Huperzia lucidula* (Michx.) Trevisan

Huperzia selago (L.) Bernh. var. *patens* (Beauv.) Trevisan – See *Huperzia porophila* (Lloyd & Underwood) Holub

Huperzia selago (L.) Bernh. var. *porophila* (Lloyd & Underwood) A. & D. Löve – See *Huperzia porophila* (Lloyd & Underwood) Holub

Hura crepitans L. – Sandbox tree (7, 92, 138) (1828–1923)

Hutchinsia procumbens (L.) Desv. – Prostrate hutchinsia (5) (1913)

Hutchinsia R. Br. – See *Hutchinsia* Aiton f.

Hyacinthoides hispanica (Mill.) Rothm. – Spanish bluebell (109) (1949)

Hyacinthoides hispanica (Mill.) Rothm. – Spanish squill (138) (1923)

Hyacinthoides nonscripta (L.) Chouard ex Rothm. – Blue harebells [Blew hare-bels] (180) (1633), Common blue squill (138) (1923), English blue hyacinth [English blew iacint] (178) (1596), English bluebell (109) (1949), English harebell [English hare-bels] (180) (1633), English hyacinth [English iacint] (180) (1633), English reddish hyacinth [English reddish iacint] (178) (1596), English white hyacinth [English white iacint] (178) (1596)

Hyacinthoides non-scripta (L.) Chouard ex Rothm. – See *Hyacinthoides nonscripta* (L.) Chouard ex Rothm.

Hyacinthus comosus L. – See *Muscari comosum* (L.) Mill.

Hyacinthus L. – Hyacinth (109, 138, 184) (1793–1949)

Hyacinthus muscari L. – See *Muscari neglectum* Guss. ex Ten.

Hyacinthus orientalis L. – Blue Oriental Iacint [Blew Orientall Iacint, Blue Oriental Iacinth, Blew Orientall Iacinth] (178, 180) (1596–1633), Common hyacinth (109, 138) (1923–1949), Garden hyacinth (19) (1840), Jacinth (92) (1876), Jacob's-ladder [Jacob's ladder, Jacobs-ladder] (75) (1894) OH, Sky-color oriental hyacinth [Skie

coloured Orientall Iacint] (178) (1596)

Hyacinthus racemosus [(L.) Mill.] – See *Muscari neglectum* Guss. ex Ten.

Hybanthus concolor (T. F. Forst) Spreng. – Eastern green violet (50) (present), Green violet [Greenviolet] (2, 3, 4, 5, 19, 156) (1840–1986)

Hybanthus Jacq. – Calceolaria (155, 158) (1900–1942), Green violet [Greenviolet] (1, 4, 50, 122, 158) (1937–present), White ipecacuanha (13) (1849)

Hybanthus verticillatus (Ort.) Baill. – Baby's-slippers [Baby's slippers, Babysslippers] (50) (present), Nodding green violet (4) (1986), Nodding violet (5, 65, 97, 158) (1900–1937), North American calceolaria [NorthAmerican calceolaria] (3, 155) (1942–1977), Whorl-leaf [Whorl leaf] (5) (1913), Whorl-leaf violet [Whorl-leaved violet] (158) (1900)

Hybiscus syriacus – See *Hibiscus syriacus* L.

Hydatica foliolosa (R. Br.) Small. – See *Saxifraga foliolosa* R. Br.

Hydatica petiolaris (Raf.) Small. – See *Saxifraga michauxii* Britt.

Hydatica stellaris (L.) S. F. Gray – See *Saxifraga stellaris* L.

Hydrangea (Gron.) L. – See *Hydrangea* L.

Hydrangea arborescens L. – Bissum (156, 158) (1900–1923), High geranium (156) (1923), Hills-of-snow (5, 156) (1913–1923), Hydrangea [Hydrangia] (19, 54, 57, 60, 64, 92, 158, 174, 177) (1753–1917), Hydrangea de Virginie (French) (8) (1785), Seven-bark [Seven barks, Seven bark] (5, 49, 52, 53, 54, 61, 64, 92, 156, 158) (1870–1923), Smooth hydrangea (138, 155) (1923–1942), Wild hydrangea (3, 4, 5, 49, 50, 52, 53, 63, 64, 72, 92, 97, 156, 158) (1898–present)

Hydrangea cinerea Small – Ashy hydrangea (5, 138) (1913–1923), Ninebark [Nine bark, Nine-bark] (156) (1923), Silverleaf [Silver leaf, Silver-leaf] (156) (1923), Wild hydrangea (156) (1923)

Hydrangea L. – Bissum (7) (1828), Hydrangea (French) (8) (1785), Hydrangea [Hydrangia] (1, 8, 50, 138, 155, 158) (1785–present)

Hydrangea paniculata Sieb. – Panicled hydrangea [Panicle hydrangea] (138) (1923)

Hydrangea quercifolia Bartram. – Oak-leaf hydrangea [Oakleaf hydrangea] (2, 138) (1895–1923)

Hydrangea radiata Walt. – Purple-stem hydrangea [Purplestem hydrangea] (138) (1923)

Hydrangea vulgaris Pursh – See *Hydrangea arborescens* L.

Hydranthelium rotundifolium (Michx.) Pennell – See *Bacopa rotundifolia* (Michx.) Wettst.

Hydrastis canadensis L. – Canadische Gelbwurzel (German) (6) (1892), Canadische Hydrastis (German) (186) (1814), Curcuma (49, 64) (1907–1908), Curcume (29) (1869), Eyebalm [Eye-balm, Eye balm] (5, 7, 49, 64, 92, 156) (1828–1923), Eyeroot [Eye-root, Eye root] (5, 49, 64, 92, 156) (1876–1923), Gelb Puckuhn (German) (7) (1828), Goldenroot [Golden root] (49, 64) (1907–1908), Goldenseal [Golden-seal, Golden seal] (1, 2, 5, 6, 7, 15, 49, 52, 53, 54, 55, 57, 59, 60, 61, 63, 64, 72, 92, 97, 138, 156) (1870–1937), Ground-raspberry [Ground raspberry] (5, 6, 7, 49, 59, 64, 92, 156) (1828–1923), Hydraste du Canada [Hydraste de Canada] (French) (7, 186) (1814–1828), Hydrastis (53, 54, 55, 57, 59) (1905–1922), Hydrastis (French) (6) (1892), Hydrastis radix (Official name of Materia Medica) (7) (1828), Ice-root (156) (1923), Indian dye [Indian-dye] (5, 6, 49, 64, 156) (1892–1923), Indian iceroot (5) (1913), Indian paint [Indian-paint] (7, 49) (1828–1898), Indian plant (92) (1876), Indian turmeric [Indian-turmeric] (5, 6, 49, 64, 156) (1892–1923), Jaundice-root (49, 64, 92) (1876–1908), Mild turmeric (49) (1898), Ohio curcuma (5, 49, 64) (1898–1913), Orange-root [Orangeroot, Orange root] (1, 2, 5, 6, 7, 19, 49, 53, 63, 64, 72, 92, 97, 156) (1840–1937), Seal (64) (1907), Turmeric root [Turmeric-root] (5, 6, 19) (1840–1913), Wild curcuma (6, 49, 64) (1892–1908), Wild turmeric (64) (1907), Yellow Indian paint (5, 64, 156) (1907–1923), Yellow paint root (92) (1876), Yellow puccoon (2, 5, 6, 7, 15, 49, 52, 53, 54, 57, 59, 64, 92, 156) (1892–1923), Yellow-eye [Yellow eye] (5, 49, 64, 92, 156) (1876–1923), Yellowpaint [Yellow paint] (7, 64) (1828–1908), Yellowroot [Yellow root, Yellow-root] (5, 6, 7, 14, 35, 49, 53, 59, 64, 92, 156) (1806–1923), Yellow-seal (156) (1923)

Hydrastis **Ellis** – possibly *Hydrastis* L.

Hydrastis **L.** – Goldenseal [Golden-seal, Golden seal] (109, 156) (1923–1949), Orange-root [Orangeroot, Orange root] (13, 109) (1849–1949), Yellow puccoon (13) (1849), possibly Yellowroot [Yellow root, Yellow-root] (15, 167) (1814–1895)

Hydrocharis cordifolia **[Nutt.]** – See *Limnobium spongia* (Bosc) L.C. Rich. ex Steud.

Hydrocharis **L.** – Frogbit [Frog bit, Frogs-bit, Frog's bit, Frogs-bit] (138, 155, 167) (1814–1923)

Hydrocharis morsus-ranae **L.** – Frogbit [Frog bit, Frogs-bit, Frog's bit, Frogs-bit] (109, 138) (1923–1949)

Hydrocleis – See *Hydrocleys* Rich. ((Spelling variant))

Hydrocleys nymphoides **(Humb. & Bonpl. ex Willd.) Buch.** – Water-poppy [Waterpoppy] (109, 138) (1923–1949)

Hydrocleys nymphoides **Buchenau** – See *Hydrocleys nymphoides* (Humb. & Bonpl. ex Willd.) Buch.

Hydrocleys **Rich.** – Water-poppy [Waterpoppy] (138) (1923)

Hydrocotyle americana **L.** – American marsh pennywort [American marsh penny wort] (5, 156) (1913–1923), American pennywort [American penny-wort] (187) (1818), Jagged rose pennywort [Jagged rose-penny wort] (46) (1671), Penny-post [Penny post] (5, 76, 156) (1896–1923) Western US, no longer in use by 1923, Pennywort [Penny-wort, Penny wort] (184) (1793)

Hydrocotyle asiatica – See *Centella asiatica* (L.) Urban

Hydrocotyle canbyi **C. & R.** – See *Hydrocotyle prolifera* Kellogg

Hydrocotyle ficarioides **Michx.** – See *Centella asiatica* (L.) Urban

Hydrocotyle ficaroides **Michx.** – See *Centella asiatica* (L.) Urban

Hydrocotyle **L.** – Fairy table [Fairy-table] (158) (1900), Hydrocotyle (50) (present), Marsh pennywort (1, 10, 158) (1818–1932), Pennywort [Penny-wort, Penny wort] (155) (1942), Shilling-grass (158) (1900), Shilling-grass (158) (1900), Wassernabel (German) (158) (1900), Water pennywort (4, 156) (1923–1986)

Hydrocotyle lineata **Michx.** – See *Lilaeopsis chinensis* (L.) Kuntze

Hydrocotyle prolifera **Kellogg** – Canby's marsh pennywort [Canby's marsh penny wort] (5) (1913)

Hydrocotyle ranunculoides **L. f.** – Floating marsh pennywort [Floating marsh penny wort, Floating marsh-penny-wort] (5, 50, 97, 158) (1913–present), Floating pennywort (155) (1942)

Hydrocotyle umbellata **L.** – Erva de capitaon (174, 177) (1753–1762), Many-flower marsh pennywort [Many-flowered marsh penny-wort] (5) (1913), Marsh pennywort (156, 181) (~1678–1923), Sheep's-bane [Sheepsbane] (156) (1923), Umbellate marsh penny-wort (5) (1913), Umbelled penny-wort (187) (1818), Water navelwort [Water-navelwort] (5, 19, 92, 156) (1840–1923), Water-grass [Water grass] (5, 156) (1913–1923)

Hydrocotyle umbellulata **Michx.** – See *Hydrocotyle umbellata* L.

Hydrocotyle verticillata **Thunb.** – Whorled marsh pennywort [Whorled marsh penny wort, Whorled marsh-penny-wort] (5, 97) (1913–1937)

Hydrolea affinis **Gray.** – See *Hydrolea uniflora* Raf.

Hydrolea caroliniana **Michx.** – See *Hydrolea quadrivalvis* Walt.

Hydrolea **L.** – Nama (106) (1930)

Hydrolea ovata **Nutt. ex Choisy** – Ovate-leaf nama [Ovate-leaved nama] (5, 97, 106) (1913–1937)

Hydrolea quadrivalvis **Walt.** – Hairy nama (5) (1913)

Hydrolea uniflora **Raf.** – Smooth nama (5, 97) (1913–1937)

Hydropeltis purpurea **[Michx.]** – See *Brasenia schreberi* Gmel.

Hydrophyllum **(Tourn.) L.** – See *Hydrophyllum* L.

Hydrophyllum appendiculatum **Michx.** – Appendaged water-leaf (5, 72) (1907–1913), Great waterleaf (50) (present), Hairy waterleaf (107) (1919), Notch-bract waterleaf [Notchbract waterleaf] (3, 4) (1977–1986), Shawnee salad [Shawnee sallad] (7) (1828), Woolen-breeches [Woollen breeches] (107, 156) (1919–1923)

Hydrophyllum canadense **L.** – Broad-leaf water-leaf [Broad-leaved water-leaf] (5) (1913), Canadian waterleaf (156) (1923), Rough bur flower [Rough burr flower] (19) (1840), Stag cabbage (29) (1869)

Hydrophyllum **L.** – Waterleaf [Water leaf, Water-leaf] (1, 2, 4, 10, 50, 63, 82, 93, 155, 156, 158) (1818–present)

Hydrophyllum macrophyllum **Nutt.** – Large-leaf waterleaf [Large-leaved water-leaf] (5, 72) (1907–1913)

Hydrophyllum virginianum **L.** – Brookflower [Brook-flower, Brook flower] (5, 156, 158) (1900–1923), Burflower [Burr flower, Burr-flower, Bur flower] (6, 19, 92, 156, 158) (1840–1923), Indian salad (107, 156) (1919–1923), John's cabbage (6) (1892), Shawanese lettuce (6) (1892), Shawnee salad [Shawnee sallad] (50, 107, 156) (1919–present), Virginia waterleaf [Virginia water leaf, Virginia water-leaf, Virginia water leaf, Virginian waterleaf] (5, 6, 72, 93, 106, 131, 155, 156) (1892–1942), Waterleaf [Water leaf, Water-leaf] (3, 4, 6, 82, 85, 127, 184) (1793–1986)

Hydrophyllum virginicum **L.** – See *Hydrophyllum virginianum* L.

Hydropuntia edulis **(S. G. Gmelin) Gurgel & Fredericq** – Agar agar (92, 107) (1876–1919), Ceylon moss (92) (1876), Jaffna moss (92) (1876)

Hydrotrida caroliniana **(Walt.) Small.** – See *Bacopa caroliniana* (Walt.) B. L. Robins.

Hylocereus **(Berger) Britt. & Rose** – Night-blooming cereus [Night-blooming cereus, Night blooming cereus] (109, 137, 155) (1923–1949)

Hylocereus **Britt. & Rose** – See *Hylocereus* (Berger) Britt. & Rose

Hylotelephium erythrostictum **(Miq.) H. Ohba.** – Blush stonecrop (138) (1923)

Hylotelephium spectabile **(Boreau) H. Ohba.** – Showy stonecrop (138, 155) (1931–1942)

Hylotelephium telephioides **(Michx.) H. Ohba.** – Sweetheart [Sweethearts, Sweet-hearts] (156) (1923), Wild live-forever [Wild liveforever, Wild live forever] (138, 156) (1923)

Hylotelephium telephium **(L.) H. Ohba. subsp.** *telephium* – Aaron's-rod [Aaron's rod] (5, 73, 76, 79, 156) (1891–1923), Bag-leaves (156) (1923), Blowleaf [Blow leaf] (79) (1891) NH, Bogleaves [Bog leaves] (5) (1913), Evergreeen (5, 73, 156) (1892–1923) Chesterton MD, Everlasting (5, 73, 156) (1892–1923) Hemmingford Quebec, Frog plant [Frog-plant, Frog plants] (5, 73, 156) (1892–1923) NH, Frog's-bladder [Frog's bladder] (5, 73, 156) (1892–1923) NY, Frog's-mouth [Frog-mouth, Frog's mouth] (5, 73, 156) (1892–1923) NY, Frog's-throats [Frogs' throats] (73) (1892) Bedford MA, Garden orpine (5, 156) (1913–1923), Great orpin (178) (1526), Great Spanish orpin (178) (1526), Harping Johnny (156) (1923) no longer in use by 1923, Houseleek [House leek] (79) (1891) NH, Leek [Leeks, Leke, Leekes] (5, 73) (1892–1913) Stowe VT, Life-of-man [Life of man, Life-o'-man] (5, 74, 76, 156) (1993–1923) Concord MA, Live-forever [Liveforever, Live forever] (5, 19, 63, 82, 92, 156) (1840–1930), Live-forever stonecrop [Liveforever stonecrop] (155) (1942), Live-long [Live long] (5, 92, 156) (1876–1923), Midsummer-men [Midsummer men] (5, 156) (1913–1923) no longer in use by 1923, Orpine (5, 19, 63, 72, 92, 107, 156) (1840–1923), Pudding-bag plant [Pudding bag plant] (73) (1892) MA, Toad-bellies (156) (1923), Witch's-money bags [Witches' money bags, Witches' money-bags] (5, 73, 156) (1892–1923) Western MA

Hymenaea courbaril **L.** – Anime (92) (1876), Courbaril (138) (1923), Gum anime (92) (1876)

Hymenocallis bidentata **Small** – See *Hymenocallis rotata* (Ker-Gawl.) Herbert

Hymenocallis caribaea **(L.) Herbert** – Caribbean spider lily [Caribbean spiderlily] (138) (1923)

Hymenocallis caroliniana **(L.) Herbert** – Carolina spider-lily [Carolina spiderlily] (50) (present), Hymenocallis (5) (1913), Western spider-lily [Western spiderlily, Western spider lily] (97, 138) (1923–1937)

Hymenocallis coronaria **(Le Conte) Kunth** – See *Hymenocallis caroliniana* (L.) Herbert

Hymenocallis galvestonensis **(Herbert) Baker** – White spider lily (124) (1937)

Hymenocallis galvestonensis **Baker** – See *Hymenocallis galvestonensis* (Herbert) Baker

213

Hymenocallis georgiana **Traub** – See *Hymenocallis caroliniana* (L.) Herbert

Hymenocallis lacera **Salisb.** – See *Pancratium maritimum* L.

Hymenocallis occidentalis **(LeConte) Kunth.** – See *Hymenocallis caroliniana* (L.) Herbert

Hymenocallis occidentalis **Kunth.** – See *Hymenocallis caroliniana* (L.) Herbert

Hymenocallis palusvirensis **Traub ex J. E. Laferriere** – See *Hymenocallis caroliniana* (L.) Herbert

Hymenocallis rotata **(Ker-Gawl.) Herbert** – Streambank spiderlily (50) (present)

Hymenocallis **Salisb.** – Spider lily [Spider-lily] (109, 122, 138) (1923–1949)

Hymenocallis traubii **Moldenke** – See *Hymenocallis rotata* (Ker-Gawl.) Herbert

Hymenoclea monogyra **Torr. & Gray ex Gray** – Burro brush (122) (1937) TX, Burrow brush (124) (1937) TX

Hymenomycetes **Fr.** – Devil's-umbrellas [Devil's umbrellas] (73) (1892) Baltimore MD

Hymenopappus artemisiifolius **DC.** – Wild cauliflower (124) (1937) TX

Hymenopappus artimisaefolius **DC.** – See *Hymenopappus artemisiifolius* DC.

Hymenopappus carolinensis **(Lam.) Porter** – See *Hymenopappus scabiosaeus* L'Hér. var. *scabiosaeus*

Hymenopappus corymbosus **Torr. & Gray** – See *Hymenopappus scabiosaeus* L'Her. var. *corymbosus* (Torr. & Gray) B. L. Turner

Hymenopappus filifolius **Hook.** – Fine-leaf hymenopappus [Fineleaf hymenopappus] (50, 155) (1942–present), Low tufted hymneopappus (5, 93) (1913–1936), Tufted hymenopappus (131) (1899)

Hymenopappus filifolius **Hook. var. cinereus (Rydb.) I. M. Johnst.** – Fine-leaf hymenopappus [Fineleaf hymenopappus] (50) (present)

Hymenopappus filifolius **Hook. var. polycephalus (Osterhout) B. L. Turner** – Many-head hymenopappus [Manyhead hymenopappus] (50) (present)

Hymenopappus flavescens **Gray** – College-flower [Collegeflower] (50) (present), Woolly yellow hymenopappus (5, 97) (1913–1937)

Hymenopappus **L'Hér.** – Hymenopappus (50, 155, 158) (1900–present)

Hymenopappus scabiosaeus **L'Hér.** – Carolina woolly-white [Carolina woollywhite] (50) (present)

Hymenopappus scabiosaeus **L'Her. var. corymbosus (Torr. & Gray) B. L. Turner** – Corymbed hymenopappus (5) (1913), Old plainsmen (3, 4) (1977–1986), Smooth white hymenopappus (5, 97) (1913–1937)

Hymenopappus scabiosaeus **L'Hér. var. scabiosaeus** – White-bract hymenopappus [White-bracted hymenopappus] (5, 97) (1913–1937)

Hymenopappus tenuifolius **Pursh** – Chalk Hill hymenopappus (50) (present), Slim-leaf hymenopappus [Slimleaf hymenopappus] (3) (1977), Šuŋkuštipije (Lakota, horse hoof cure) (121) (1918?–1970?), Woolly hymenopappus (131) (1899), Woolly white hymenopappus [Wooly white hymenopappus] (5, 93, 97, 121, 122) (1913–1970)

Hymenothecium **Lag.** – See *Aegopogon* Humb. & Bonpl. ex Willd.

Hymenoxys acaulis **(Pursh) Parker** – See *Tetraneuris acaulis* (Pursh) Greene var. *acaulis*

Hymenoxys **Cass.** – Bitterweed [Bitter weed, Bitter-weed] (4) (1986), Colorado rubber plant (1) (1932), Picradenia (158) (1900), Rubberweed (50) (present)

Hymenoxys floribunda **[(A. Gray) Cockerell]** – See *Hymenoxys richardsonii* (Hook.) Cockerell var. *floribunda* (Gray) Parker

Hymenoxys hoopesii **(Gray) Bierner** – Orange sneezeweed (138) (1923), Sneezeweed [Sneeze weed, Sneeze-weed] (148) (1939) CO, Western sneezeweed (148) (1939) CO, Yellow-weed [Yellow weed] (148) (1939) CO

Hymenoxys linearifolia **Hook.** – See *Tetraneuris linearifolia* (Hook.) Greene var. *linearifolia*

Hymenoxys odorata **DC.** – Bitter rubberweed (50) (present), Bitterweed [Bitter weed, Bitter-weed] (3, 4) (1977–1986), Fragrant picradenia

(158) (1900), Limonillo (5, 97) (1913–1937)

Hymenoxys richardsonii **(Hook.) Cockerell var. floribunda (Gray) Parker** – Colorado rubber plant (3, 4, 148) (1939–1986), Pingue (148) (1939) CO

Hymenoxys richardsonii **(Hook.) Cockerell var. richardsonii** – Pingue actinea (155) (1942)

Hymenoxys richardsonii **(Hook.) Cockll.** – Colorado rubber plant (3, 4) (1977–1986), Pingue rubberweed (50) (present)

Hymenoxys scaposa **(DC.) K. F. Parker** – See *Tetraneuris scaposa* (DC.) Greene var. *scaposa*

Hymenoxys texana **(Coult. & Rose) Cockerell** – Texas bitterweed (122) (1937)

Hyociamus alba – See *Hyoscyamus albus* L.

Hyoscyamus albus **L.** – White henbane (92, 178) (1526–1876)

Hyoscyamus **L.** – Henbane (50, 109 138, 155, 158) (1900–present)

Hyoscyamus niger **L.** – Belene (5, 156) (1913–1923) no longer in use by 1923, Belene chenile (158) (1900), Beleño negro (Spanish) (158) (1900), Bilsenkraut (German) (6, 158, 180) (1633–1900), Black henbane [Blacke henbane] (5, 6, 7, 46, 50, 92, 148, 155, 156, 158, 178, 180) (1526–present) accidently introduced by 1671, Chenile (156) (1923) no longer in use by 1923, Fetid nightshade (5, 156, 158) (1900–1923), Henbane (1, 3, 4, 6, 7, 10, 14, 20, 49, 52, 53, 54, 55, 57, 59, 60, 61, 85, 92, 126, 138, 156, 158, 179, 184) (1793–1986), Henbell (158) (1900), Henkam (158) (1900), Hogbean [Hog bean, Hog's bean, Hog's-bean] (5, 6, 92, 156, 158) (1876–1923), Hyosciamus (Official name of Materia Medica) (7) (1828), Hyoscyamus (54, 57, 59, 60) (1902–1905), Insaneroot [Insane root, Insaneroot] (5, 156, 158) (1900–1923), Jusquiame noir (French) (6, 7, 158) (1828–1900), Loaves-of-bread (158) (1900), Poison-tobacco [Poison tobacco] (5, 6, 7, 92, 156, 158) (1828–1923), Schwarz Bilsenkraut [Schwarzes Bilsenkraut] (German) (7, 158) (1828–1900), Stinking nightshade (6, 7, 92, 156, 158) (1828–1923), Teufelsaugenkraut (German) (158) (1900)

Hyoseris amplexicaulis **Michx.** – See *Krigia biflora* (Walt.) Blake

Hyoseris biflora **Walt.** – See *Krigia biflora* (Walt.) Blake

Hyoseris **L.** – See *Hedypnois* Mill.

Hyoseris virginica **L.** – See *Krigia virginica* (L.) Willd.

Hypelate trifoliata **Swartz.** – White ironwood (15) (1895)

Hypericum **(Tourn.) L.** – See *Hypericum* L.

Hypericum ×moserianum **Luquet ex André [*calycinum* × *patulum*]** – Goldflower [Gold flower] (109, 138) (1923–1949)

Hypericum adpressum **Bartram.** – See *Hypericum adpressum* Raf. ex W. Bart.

Hypericum adpressum **Raf. ex W. Bart.** – Creeping St. John's-wort [Creeping St. John's wort, Creeping St. Johnswort] (5, 156) (1913–1923)

Hypericum androsaemum **L.** – Park leaves [Parke leaues] (178) (1526), Tutsan (109, 178) (1526–1949)

Hypericum angulosum **Michx.** – See *Hypericum denticulatum* Walt.

Hypericum ascyron **L.** – Giant St. John's-wort [Giant St. John's wort, Giant St. Johnswort] (5, 93, 124, 155, 156, 158) (1900–1942), Great St. John's-wort [Great St. Johnswort, Great St. John's wort] (2, 4, 5, 50, 72, 156, 158) (1900–present), Greater St. John's wort [Greater St. John's-wort] (3) (1977), Great-flower St. John's-wort [Great flowered St. John's-wort] (156) (1923)

Hypericum aureum **Bartram.** – See *Hypericum frondosum* Michx.

Hypericum axillare **Michx.** – possibly *Triadenum virginicum* (L.) Raf.

Hypericum boreale **(Britton) Bicknell** – Northern St. John's-wort [Northern St. John's wort] (5) (1913)

Hypericum canadense **L.** – Canadian St. John's-wort [Canadian St. John's wort] (5, 72, 93, 131) (1899–1936), Slender St. John's-wort [Slender St. John's wort] (187) (1818)

Hypericum cistifolium **Lam.** – See *Hypericum sphaerocarpum* Michx.

Hypericum corymbosum **[Muhl. ex Willd.]** – See *Hypericum punctatum* Lam.

Hypericum crux-andreae **(L.) Crantz** – Atlantic St. Peter's-wort [Atlantic St. Peterswort] (155) (1942), Common Andrew's cross (42)

Hypericum punctatum Lam.

(1814), Common St. Peter's-wort [Common St. Peter's wort] (2) (1895), St. Andrew's-cross [Saint Andrew's cross, St. Andrews-cross] (2, 92, 97, 157) (1876–1937), St. Peter's-wort [St. Peter's wort, Saint Peters wort] (19, 5, 97, 156) (1840–1937), Upright Andrew's-cross [Upright Andrew's cross] (42) (1814)

Hypericum densiflorum **Pursh** – Bushy St. John's-wort [Bushy St. John's wort] (5) (1913), Cluster St. Johns-wort [Cluster St. Johnswort] (138) (1923), Dense-flower St. John's-wort [Dense-flowered St. John's wort] (5) (1913)

Hypericum denticulatum **Walt.** – Branchy St. John's-wort [Branchy St. John's wort] (2) (1895), Copper-colored St. John's-wort [Copper-colored St. John's wort] (5) (1913), Virgate St. John's-wort [Virgate St. John's wort] (5) (1913)

Hypericum dolabriforme **Vent.** – Straggling St. John's-wort [Straggling St. John's wort] (5) (1913)

Hypericum drummondii **(Grev. & Hook.) Torr. & Gray** – Drummond's pineweed [Drummond pineweed] (155) (1942), Drummond's St. John's-wort [Drummond's St. John's wort] (5, 72, 97) (1907–1937), Nits-and-lice (3, 4, 50) (1977–present)

Hypericum ellipticum **Hook.** – Elliptical-leaf St. John's-wort [Elliptical-leaved St. John's wort] (2) (1895), Elliptic-leaf St. John's-wort [Elliptic-leaved St. John's wort] (5) (1913), Pale St. John's-wort [Pale St. John's wort] (5) (1913)

Hypericum fasciculatum **Lam.** – Myrtle-leaf St. John's-wort [Myrtle-leaved St. John's wort] (2) (1895)

Hypericum frondosum **Michx.** – Golden St. John's-wort [Golden St. John's wort, Golden St. Johnswort] (2, 5, 97, 138) (1895–1937)

Hypericum galioides **Lam.** – Bedstraw St. John's-wort [Bedstraw St. John's wort] (5, 138) (1913–1923)

Hypericum gentianoides **(L.) Britton, Sterns & Poggenb.** – False John's-wort [False John's wort, False johnswort] (5, 19, 92, 157) (1840–1929), False St. John's-wort (156) (1923), Groundbroom (7) (1828), Groundpine [Ground-pine, Ground pine] (5, 7, 156, 177, 184, 187) (1762–1923), Knitweed [Knit-weed] (156) (1923), Nitweed [Nit-weed, Nit weed] (5, 19, 92, 157) (1840–1929), Orangegrass [Orangegrass, Orange grass] (2, 5, 19, 72, 92, 156, 157) (1840–1929), Pine tassel (156) (1923), Pineweed [Pine-weed, Pine weed] (2, 5, 19, 92, 156, 157) (1840–1929), Poverty-grass [Poverty grass] (156) (1923), Sarothra (174, 177) (1753–1762)

Hypericum glomeratum [**Small**] – See *Hypericum densiflorum* Pursh

Hypericum graveolens **Buckley** – Mountain St. John's-wort [Mountain St. John's wort, Mountain St. Johnswort] (5, 156) (1913–1923)

Hypericum gymnanthum **Engelm. & Gray** – Clasping-leaf St. John's-wort [Clasping leaved St. John's wort] (5, 72, 97) (1907–1937)

Hypericum hypericoides **(L.) Crantz subsp.** *hypericoides* – Ascyre à feuilles de mille pertuis (French) (8) (1785), Ascyre perforée (French) (8) (1785), Crux Sancti Andraeae (181) (~1678), Hypericum-like andrew's-cross [Hypericum like andrew's cross] (42) (1814), Peter's wort (92) (1876), St. Andrew's-cross [Saint Andrew's cross, St. Andrewscross] (5, 155, 156) (1913–1942), St. Andrew's-wort [Saint Andrews wort, St. Andrews wort] (177, 181) (~1678–1762), St. Peter's-wort [St. Peter's wort, Saint Peters wort] (8) (1785)

Hypericum hypericoides **(L.) Crantz subsp.** *multicaule* **(Michx. ex Willd.) Robson** – Many-stem Andrew's-cross [Many stemmed Andrew's cross] (42) (1814), Many-stem St. Peter's-wort [Many-stemmed St. Peter's-wort] (187) (1818), St. Andrew's-cross [Saint Andrew's cross, St. Andrewscross] (3, 4, 50) (1977–present)

Hypericum kalmianum **L.** – Kalm's St. John's-wort [Kalm's St. John's wort, Kalm St. Johnswort] (2, 5, 138, 156) (1895–1923), Mille-pertuis de Kalm (French) (8) (1785), Shrubby St. John's wort [Shrubby St. John's-wort] (5, 156) (1913–1923), Virginia St. John's-wort [Virginian St. John's wort] (8) (1785)

Hypericum **L.** – Andrew's cross (42) (1814), Ascyre (French) (8) (1785), John's-wort [Johns-wort, Johnswort, John's wort] (184) (1793), Orange-grass [Orangegrass, Orange grass] (1, 93, 158) (1900–1936), Pineweed [Pine-weed, Pine weed] (1, 93, 155) (1932–1942), St.

Andrew's-cross [Saint Andrew's cross, St. Andrewscross] (1, 4) (1932–1986), St. John's-wort [St. John's wort, St. Johnswort, Saynt Johns wort] (1, 2, 4, 8, 10, 13, 15, 50, 93, 109, 138, 155, 156, 158, 167, 190) (~1759–present), St. Peter's-wort [St. Peter's wort, Saint Peters wort] (1, 2, 8, 10, 13, 15, 158, 167) (1814–1932), possibly Marsh St. John's-wort [Marsh St. John's wort, Marsh St. Johnswort] (2, 13) (1849–1895)

Hypericum lobocarpum **Gattinger** – Gattinger's hypericum [Gattinger hypericum] (138) (1923)

Hypericum maculatum **Walter** – Spotted St. John's-wort [Spotted St. John's wort, Spotted St. Johnswort] (2, 72) (1895–1907)

Hypericum majus **(Gray) Britton** – Greater St. John's wort [Greater St. John's-wort] (3, 4) (1977–1986), Large St. John's-wort [Large St. Johnswort] (50) (present), Larger Canadian St. John's-wort [Larger Canadian St. John's wort] (5, 93) (1913–1936), St. John's-wort [St. John's wort, St. Johnswort, Saynt Johns wort] (85) (1932)

Hypericum moserianum **Andre** – See *Hypericum* ×*moserianum* Luquet ex André [*calycinum* × *patulum*]

Hypericum mutilum **L.** – Dwarf St. John's-wort [Dwarf St. John's wort] (3, 4, 5, 50, 72, 156) (1907–present), Low centaury (19, 92) (1840–1876), Slender St. John's-wort [Slender St. John's wort] (5) (1913), Small St. John's-wort [Small St. John's wort] (2) (1895), Small-flower St. John's-wort [Small-flowered St. John's wort, Small-flowered St. John's-wort] (5, 97, 156) (1913–1937)

Hypericum nudicaule **Walt.** – See *Hypericum gentianoides* (L.) Britton, Sterns & Poggenb.

Hypericum nudiflorum **Michx. ex Willd.** – Naked-cluster St. John's-wort [Naked-clustered St. John's wort] (2) (1895)

Hypericum parviflorum **W.** – See *Hypericum mutilum* L.

Hypericum perforatum **L.** – Amber (5, 156, 158) (1900–1923), Balm-of-warrior's-wound [Balm of warrior's wound] (156, 157, 158) (1900–1929), Cammock (5, 156, 157, 158) (1900–1929), Casse Diable (French) (158) (1900), Chasse diable (French) (6) (1892), Common St John's-wort [Common St. John's wort, Common St. Johnswort] (3, 4, 5, 50, 62, 72, 93, 155, 156, 157, 158, 187) (1818–present), Devil's-scourge [Devil's scourge] (6) (1892), European St. John's-wort (156) (1923), God's wonder plant (6) (1892), Hartheu (German) (6, 158) (1892–1900), Hasenkraut (German) (158) (1900), Herb John [Herb-John, Herbe John] (5, 62, 156, 157, 158, 179) (1526–1929), Herbe St. Jean (French) (6) (1892), Hexenkraut (German) (6, 158) (1892–1900), Hypericon (Spanish) (158) (1900), Hypericum (57) (1917), Hyssop [Hysop, Hysope] (158) (1900), Johannisblut (German) (158) (1900), Johanniskraut (German) (6, 158) (1892–1900), John's-wort [Johns-wort, Johnswort, John's wort] (5, 92, 157, 158) (1876–1929), Millepertuis (50) (present), Mille-Pertuis [Millepertuis] (French) (6, 158) (1892–1900), Penny-John [Penny John] (5, 156, 157, 158) (1900–1929), Rosin-rose [Rosin rose] (5, 156, 157, 158) (1900–1929), Saint Johannis wort [Saynt Johannis wort] (179) (1526), St. John (74, 156, 158) (1893–1929) WV, St. John's bush [St. John's-bush] (74, 157) (1893–1929) WV, St. John's-wort [St. John's wort, St. Johnswort, Saynt Johns wort] (6, 7, 46, 48, 49, 52, 53, 57, 80, 92, 179) (1526–1922), Teufelsflucht (German) (158) (1900), Touch-and-heal (5, 156, 157, 158) (1900–1929), Toute saine (French) (156) (1923), Tutsan (156) (1923), Witche's-herb [Witches' herb, Witches'-herb] (6) (1892)

Hypericum petiolatum **Walt., non L.** – See *Triadenum walteri* (J.G. Gmel.) Gleason

Hypericum pilosum **Walt.** – See *Hypericum setosum* L.

Hypericum prolificum **L.** – Broom brush (5, 74) (1893–1913) WV, Brown-brush (156) (1923), Bush broom (156) (1923), Paintbrush [Paint-brush, Paint brush] (5, 76, 156) (1896–1923) Oakdam IN, Rockrose [Rock-rose, Rock rose] (5, 156) (1913–1923), Shrubby St. John's wort [Shrubby St. Johnswort, Shrubby St. John's-wort] (2, 5, 45, 72, 97, 138, 156) (1895–1937)

Hypericum pseudomaculatum **Bush** – See *Hypericum punctatum* Lam.

Hypericum punctatum **Lam.** – Black St. John's-wort (187) (1818), Corymbed St. John's-wort [Corymbed St. John's wort] (5) (1913),

Large-spot St. John's-wort [Large-spotted St. John's wort] (5, 97) (1913–1937), Spotted St. John's-wort [Spotted St. John's wort, Spotted St. Johnswort] (3, 4, 5, 50, 97, 155, 156) (1913–present), St John's-wort [St John's wort] (46) (1879)

Hypericum pyramidatum **Aiton** – See *Hypericum ascyron* L.

Hypericum quinquenervium **Walt.** – See *Hypericum mutilum* L.

Hypericum sarothra **Michx.** – See *Hypericum gentianoides* (L.) Britton, Sterns & Poggenb.

Hypericum setosum **L.** – Crux Saint Andraeae (181) (~1678), Hairy St. John's-wort [Hairy St. John's wort] (2) (1895), possibly Ascyre velue (French) (8) (1785), possibly Villose St. Peter's-wort [Villose St. Peter's wort] (8) (1785)

Hypericum simplex **Michx.** – See *Hypericum setosum* L.

Hypericum sphaerocarpum **Michx.** – Cistus-leaf St. John's-wort [Cistus-leaved St. John's wort] (2) (1895), Round-fruit St. John's-wort [Roundfruit St. John's wort, Round-fruited St. John's wort] (3, 4, 72) (1907–1986), Round-pod St. John's-wort [Round-podded St. John's wort] (5, 97) (1913–1937), Round-seed St. John's-wort [Roundseed St. Johnswort] (50) (present)

Hypericum villosum **[(L.) Crantz]** – See *Hypericum setosum* L.

Hypericum virgatum **Lam.** – See *Hypericum denticulatum* Walt.

Hypericum virginicum **L.** – See *Triadenum virginicum* (L.) Raf.

Hypochaeris **L.** – Cat's-ear [Cat's ear, Cats-ear] (1, 138) (1923–1932), Gosmore (1) (1932)

Hypochaeris radicata **L.** – California dandelion (106, 156) (1923–1930), Cat's-ear [Cat's ear, Cats-ear] (106, 156) (1923–1930), Gosmore (5, 156) (1913–1923), Long-root cat's-ear [Long-rooted cat's ear, Longrooted catsear] (5, 122) (1913–1937), Spotted cat's-ear [Spotted cat's ear] (107) (1919)

Hypopitys **(Dill.) Adans.** – See *Monotropa* L.

Hypopitys **Adans.** – possibly *Monotropa* L.

Hypopitys americana **(DC.) Small** – See *Monotropa hypopithys* L.

Hypopitys hypopitys **(L.) Small.** – See *Monotropa hypopithys* L.

Hypopitys lanuginosa **(Michx.) Nutt.** – See *Monotropa hypopithys* L.

Hypopitys latisquama **Rydb.** – See *Monotropa hypopithys* L.

Hypopythis **Dill.** – See *Monotropa* L.

Hypoxis erecta **L.** – See *Hypoxis hirsuta* (L.) Cov.

Hypoxis hirsuta **(L.) Cov.** – Common goldstar (50) (present), Common goldstar-grass [Common goldstargrass] (155) (1942), Gold-eye (156) (1923), Goldeye-grass [Gold-eye-grass] (138) (1923), Star root (92) (1876), Star-grass [Star grass, Stargrass] (7, 19, 72, 85, 86, 92, 127, 157, 158) (1828–1933), Star-of-Bethlehem [Star of Bethlehem, Starre of Bethlem, Stars of Bethlehem] (156, 157) (1923–1929), Yellow star-grass [Yellow stargrass] (3, 5, 93, 97, 156, 157, 158) (1900–1977), Yellow-eyed-grass [Yellow-eyed grass, Yellow eyed grass] (156) (1923)

Hypoxis **L.** – Goldeye-grass [Gold-eye-grass] (138) (1923), Gold-star-grass [Goldstargrass] (155) (1942), Star-grass [Star grass, Stargrass] (1, 50, 93, 109, 156, 158, 167) (1814–present)

Hypsizygus ulmarius **(Bull.) Redhead** – Elm cap (3, 37) (1830–1977), Elm mushroom (128) (1933)

Hyptis mutabilis **(A. Rich.) Briq.** – Purple-flower mint [Purple-flowered mint] (106) (1930)

Hyptis mutabilis **(A. Rich.) Briq. var. spicata (Poit.) Briq.** – See *Hyptis mutabilis* (Rich.) Briq.

Hyptis radiata **Willd.** – See *Hyptis alata* (Raf.) Shinners

Hyptis spicata **Poit.** – See *Hyptis mutabilis* (Rich.) Briq.

Hyssopus **L.** – Hyssop [Hysop, Hysope] (10, 109, 138, 167, 184) (1793–1949) possibly ancient hyssop of bible

Hyssopus nepetoides **W.** – See *Agastache nepetoides* (L.) Kuntze

Hyssopus officinalis **L.** – Broad-leaf hyssopus [Broad leafed hyssopus] (178) (1526), Curled hyssop [Curlde hyssope] (178) (1526), English white hyssop [English white hyssope] (178) (1526), Hyssop [Hysop, Hysope] (5, 7, 19, 46, 49, 57, 85, 92, 107, 131, 138, 156) (1617–1932), Hyssop of Candie [Hyssope of Candie] (178) (1526), Hyssopus (57) (1917), Iagged leafed hyssope (Jagged-leaf hyssop) (178) (1526), Thin-leaf hyssop (Thinne leafed Hyssope) (178) (1526), White-flower hyssop [White flowred hyssope] (178) (1526), Yellow-leaf hyssop [Yellow leafed hyssope] (178) (1526), Ysope (179) (1526)

Hyssopus scrophulariifolius **Willd. and Pursh** – See *Agastache scrophulariifolia* (Willd.) Kuntze

Hystix **Moench** – See *Elymus* L.

Hystrix hystrix **(L.) Millsp.** – See *Elymus hystrix* L. var. *hystrix*

Hystrix patula **Moench** – See *Elymus hystrix* L. var. *hystrix*

I

Iberis amara **L.** – Annual candytuft (50) (present), Bitter candy-tuft [Bitter candy tuft] (52, 92) (1876–1919), Candytuft [Candy-tuft, Candy tuft] (92) (1876), Common white candytuft (138) (1923), Peasant's-mustard [Pesants Mustard] (178) (1526), Rocket candytuft (109) (1949)

Iberis carnosa **Willd.** – Tenore's candytuft [Tenore candytuft] (138) (1923)

Iberis coronaria **[D. Don]** – possibly *Iberis umbellata* L

Iberis gibraltarica **L.** – Gibraltar candytuft (109, 138) (1923–1949)

Iberis **L.** – Candytuft [Candy-tuft, Candy tuft] (109, 138, 155, 158, 190) (~1759–1949)

Iberis sempervirens **L.** – Edging candytuft (109) (1949), Evergreen candytuft (138) (1923)

Iberis tenoreana **DC.** – See *Iberis carnosa* Willd.

Iberis umbellata **L.** – Arabis (178) (1526), Candy mustard [Candie mustard] (178) (1526), Candytuft [Candy-tuft, Candy tuft] (19) (1840), Common candy tuft (92) (1876), Globe candytuft (109) (1949), Purple candytuft (138) (1923), possibly Rocket candytuft (92) (1876)

Ibervillea **Greene** – Globeberry [Globe berry, Globe berries] (4, 50) (1986–present), Ibervillea (158) (1900)

Ibervillea lindheimeri **(Gray) Greene** – Globeberry [Globe berry, Globe berries] (4) (1986), Lindheimer's globeberry (50) (present), Wild balsam (122) (1937) TX, Wild balsam-apple [Wild balsam apple] (124) (1937) TX, Yerba de vibrona (Spanish) (122) (1937) TX

Ibicella lutea **(Lindl.) Van Eselt.** – Yellow unicorn plant [Yellow unicornplant] (138) (1923)

Ibidium beckii **(Lindl.) House.** – See *Spiranthes lacera* (Raf.) Raf. var. *gracilis* (Bigelow) Luer

Ibidium cernuum **(L.) House.** – See *Spiranthes cernua* (L.) L. C. Rich.

Ibidium gracile **(Bigel.) House.** – See *Spiranthes lacera* (Raf.) Raf. var. *gracilis* (Bigelow) Luer

Ibidium ovale **(Lindl.) House.** – See *Spiranthes ovalis* Lindl. var. *ovalis*

Ibidium plantagineum **(Raf.) House** – See *Spiranthes lucida* (H. H. Eat.) Ames

Ibidium praecox **(Walt.) House.** – See *Spiranthes praecox* (Walt.) S. Wats.

Ibidium **Salisb.** – See *Spiranthes* Rich.

Ibidium strictum **(Rydb.) House** – See *Spiranthes romanzoffiana* Cham.

Ibidium vernale **(Engelm. & Gray) House.** – See *Spiranthes vernalis* Engelm. & Gray

Ilex ambigua **(Michx.) Torr.** – Carolina holly [Carolinian holly] (97) (1937) OK, Yaupon (106) (1930)

Ilex aquifolium **L.** – American common holly (8) (1785), Dahoon holly (189) (1767), English holly (109, 138) (1923–1949), European holly (92) (1876), Holly or Holly tree (41) (1770), Houx ordinaire d'Amérique (French) (8) (1785), Mountain holly (92) (1876)

Ilex bronxensis **Britton** – See *Ilex verticillata* (L.) Gray

Ilex caroliniana **(Walt.) Trelease** – See *Ilex ambigua* (Michx.) Torr.

Ilex caroliniana **[Trel. ex Small]** – See *Ilex ambigua* (Michx.) Torr.

Ilex cassena **Michx.** – possibly *Ilex cassine* L.

Ilex cassine **L.** – Appalachian tea (156) (1923), Black drink (7) (1828), Carolina holly [Carolinian holly] (8) (1785), Cassena (2, 7) (1828–1932), Cassena bush [Cassena-bush] (156) (1923), Cassina (107) (1919), Cassine (174, 177) (1753–1762), Cassine de Caroline (8) (1785), Dahoon (8, 109, 138) (1785–1949), Dahoon holly (2, 5, 15, 107, 156) (1895–1923), Evergreen cassine [Ever-green cassine] (8) (1785), Holly or Holly tree (107) (1919), Houx de la Caroline (French) (8) (1785), South-sea tea tree [South-sea tea-tree] (8) (1785), Vulgairement Apalachine (French) (8) (1785), Yapon (8, 189) (1767–1785), Yapoon (5) (1913), Yaupon (2, 5, 38, 46, 107, 156) (1820–1923)

Ilex coriacea **(Pursh) Chapman** – Holly of America (189) (1767), Shining inkberry [Shining ink berry] (5) (1913)

Ilex cornuta **Lindl. & Paxton** – Chinese holly (138) (1923)

Ilex crenata fo. *microphylla* **Rehder** – See *Ilex crenata* Thunb.

Ilex crenata microphylla – See *Ilex crenata* Thunb.

Ilex crenata **Thunb.** – Bearberry [Bear berry, Bear-berry] (5, 156, 158) (1900–1923), Buzzard's-berry [Buzzard's berry] (106) (1930) Arkansas, Curtiss' possum-haw [Curtiss possumhaw] (155) (1942), Deciduous holly (3, 4, 5, 97, 106, 122, 124, 156) (1913–1986), Japanese holly (109, 138) (1923–1949), Little-leaf Japanese holly [Littleleaf Japanese holly] (138) (1923), Meadow holly [Meadow-holly] (5, 97, 156, 158) (1900–1937), Posum-haw [Possum haw, Possum-haw] (4, 5, 50, 106, 109, 122, 124, 138, 155, 156, 158) (1900–present), Privet (106) (1930), Redberry [Red-berry, Red berry] (156) (1923), Swamp holly (5, 156, 158) (1900–1923)

Ilex curtissii **(Fern.) Small** – See *Ilex crenata* Thunb.

Ilex dahoon **Walt.** – See *Ilex cassine* L.

Ilex decidua **Walt.** – See *Ilex crenata* Thunb.

Ilex glabra **(L.) Gray** – Apalachine tea (92) (1876), Apalanche glabre (French) (8) (1785), Appalachian tea (5, 107, 156) (1913–1923), Bear bush [Bear-bush] (156) (1923), Evergreen winterberry [Evergreen winter-berry] (5, 8, 156) (1785–1923), Gallberry [Gall berry] (5, 106, 156) (1913–1930), Inkberry [Ink-berry, Ink berry] (2, 5, 12, 19, 48, 92, 106, 107, 109, 122, 156) (1840–1949), Prinos (French) (8) (1785), Winter-berry [Winter berry, Winterberry] (109) (1949), Winterberry tea (14) (1882)

Ilex krugiana **Loes.** – Krug holly (106) (1930)

Ilex **L.** – Apalanche (French) (8) (1785), Black-alder [Black alder] (7) (1828), Bois de marque (French) (41) (1770), Fever bush [Fever-bush, Fever-bush] (7) (1828), Holly or Holly tree (1, 4, 8, 10, 15, 106, 109, 138, 155, 158) (1785–1986), Houx (French) (8) (1785), Inkberry [Ink-berry, Ink berry] (41) (1770), Winter-berry [Winter berry, Winterberry] (7, 8, 10, 14, 158, 167) (1785–1900)

Ilex laevigata **(Pursh) Gray** – Can-hoop [Can hoop] (5, 156) (1913–1923), Hoop-wood (156) (1923), Smooth winterberry [Smooth winter berry] (2, 5, 138, 156) (1895–1923)

Ilex laevigata **Gray.** – See *Ilex laevigata* (Pursh) Gray

Ilex longipes **Chapman ex Trel.** – Large-leaf holly [Largeleaf holly, Large-leaved holly] (122) (1937)

Ilex lucida **Torr. & Gray ex S. Watson** – Tall gallberry (106) (1930)

Ilex montana **(Torr. & Gray) Gray** – Large-leaf holly [Largeleaf holly, Large-leaved holly] (5, 156) (1913–1923), Mountain holly (5, 156) (1913–1923), Mountain winterberry (138) (1923)

Ilex monticola **Gray.** – See *Ilex montana* (Torr. & Gray) Gray

Ilex mucronata **(L.) M. Powell, Savol. & S. Andrews** – Absconda (46) (1879), Brick timber (5, 73) (1892–1913) Fortune Bay, Newfoudland, Canadian holly (8) (1785), Catberry [Cat berry, Cat-berry] (5, 73, 156) (1892–1923) Fortune Bay, Newfoundland, Hedgehog holly [Hedgehog holly] (8) (1785), Houx de Canada (French) (8) (1785), Mountain-holly [Mountain holly] (5, 19, 107, 109, 138, 156) (1840–1949), Prick-timber (156) (1923), Wild holly (5, 19, 156) (1840–1923)

Ilex myrtifolia **Walt.** – Myrtle-leaf dahoon holly (106) (1930)

Ilex opaca **Aiton** – American holly (2, 5, 7, 15, 20, 38, 49, 92, 97, 107, 108, 109, 122, 124, 138, 147, 156) (1828–1949), Bird-lime [Bird lime] (92) (1876), Christmas holly (65) (1931) OK, Common holly (106) (1930), Evergreen holly (19) (1840), Holly or Holly tree (12, 57) (1821–1917), Houx (French) (7) (1828), White holly (5, 156) (1913–1923)

Ilex paraguensis **St.Hilaire** – Brazilian tea [Brazil tea] (92) (1876), Maté (107, 110) (1886–1919), Yerba de maté (107) (1919), Yerba maté (109) (1949)

Ilex quercifolia **Meerb.** – possibly *Ilex opaca* Aiton

Ilex verticillata **(L.) Gray** – Apalachine à Feuilles de Prunier (French) (6) (1892), Apalanche a feuilles de prunier (French) (186) (1814), Apalanche verticillée (French) (8) (1785), Black-alder [Black alder] (2, 5, 6, 15, 49, 53, 57, 61, 72, 92, 106, 107, 109, 156, 186, 187) (1814–1949), Brook alder (92) (1876), Common winterberry [Common winter berry] (2, 138) (1895–1923), Deciduous service-bush (186) (1814), Deciduous winter-berry (186) (1814), Dogberry [Dog-berry, Dog berry] (156) (1923), False alder (5, 92, 156) (1876–1923), False berry (19) (1840), Fever bush [Feverbush, Fever-bush] (5, 6, 106, 156) (1892–1930), Northern holly (156) (1923), Northern winterberry (5) (1913), Pigeon-berry [Pigeon berry] (156) (1923), Prinos (6, 53, 53, 57, 174, 177) (1753–1922), Prinos (French) (8) (1785), Striped alder (5, 92, 156) (1876–1923), Virginia winterberry [Virginian winterberry, Virginian winter-berry] (5, 6, 8, 41, 156) (1770–1923), Virginische Winterbeere (German) (6) (1892), White alder (5, 76, 156) (1896–1923) Oxford Co. ME, Whorled winterberry (186) (1814), Winter-berry [Winter berry, Winterberry] (6, 15, 19, 49, 53, 57, 92, 106, 107, 109, 156, 184, 186, 187) (1793–1949), Wortelförmige Winterbeer (German) (186) (1814)

Ilex verticilliata **Gray.** – See *Ilex verticillata* (L.) Gray

Ilex vomitoria **Aiton** – Appalachian tea (5, 156) (1913–1923), Carolina tea (5, 156) (1913–1923), Cassena (5, 15, 109, 156) (1895–1949), Cassena bush [Cassena-bush] (156) (1923), Cassine (104, 182) (1791–1896), Dahoon holly (92) (1876), Deerberry [Deer-berry, Deer berry] (156) (1923), Emetic holly (5, 156) (1913–1923), Evergreen cassena (5, 156) (1913–1923), Evergreen holly (122, 124) (1937) TX, Indian black-drink [Indian black drink] (5, 92, 156) (1876–1923), Indian tea (156) (1923), South Sea tea (5, 14, 92, 156) (1876–1923) no longer in use by 1923, Yaupon (5, 15, 92, 97, 109, 122, 124, 138, 156) (1895–1949), Yupon (104) (1896) Southern Indians, possibly Beloved tree (182) (1791)

Iliamna remota **Greene** – See *Iliamna rivularis* (Dougl. ex Hook.) Greene var. *rivularis*

Iliamna rivularis **(Dougl. ex Hook.) Greene** – Maple-leaf mallow [Maple-leaved mallow] (85) (1932) SD

Iliamna rivularis **(Dougl. ex Hook.) Greene var. *rivularis*** – Globemallow [Globe-mallow, Globe mallow] (156) (1923), Maple-leaf globemallow [Maple-leaved globe mallow] (5, 156) (1913–1923)

Illecebrum achyrantha **Walt.** – possibly *Alternanthera pungens* Kunth

Illicium anisatum **[Gaertn.]** – possibly *Illicium parviflorum* Michx. (taxonomic status is unresolved (PL))

Illicium floridanum **Ellis** – Badiane de al Floride (French) (7) (1828), Florida anise (92) (1876), Florida anise tree (7) (1828), Poison bay (14) (1882), Star anise [Star-anis] (7) (1828), Sweet laurel (7, 92) (1828–1876), Wild anise (92) (1876)

Illicium **L.** – Anise tree [Anisetree] (138) (1923), Anise-seed tree [Anise seed tree] (10) (1818), Star anise [Star-anis] (2, 13, 15, 167) (1814–1895)

Illicium parviflorum **Michx.** – Badiane (92) (1876), Japanese anise-tree [Japanese anisetree] (138) (1923), Star anise [Star-anis] (92) (1876)

Ilyanthes **Raf.** – possibly *Lindernia* All.

Ilysanthes attenuata **(Spreng.) Small** – See *Lindernia dubia* (L.) Pennell var. *dubia*

Ilysanthes dubia **(L.) Barnhart** – See *Lindernia dubia* (L.) Pennell var. *dubia*

Ilysanthes gratioloides **(L.) Benth.** – See *Lindernia dubia* (L.) Pennell

Ilysanthes inequalis **(Walt.) Pennell** – See *Lindernia dubia* (L.) Pennell var. *anagallidea* (Michx.) Cooperrider

Ilysanthes **Raf.** – See *Lindernia* All.

Impatiens **(Rivinius) L.** – See *Impatiens* L.

Impatiens aurea **Muhl.** – See *Impatiens pallida* Nutt.

Impatiens balsamina **L.** – Balsamweed [Balsam weed, Balsam-weed] (19) (1840), Garden balsam (14, 82, 92, 109, 138) (1882–1949), Lady's-slipper [Lady's slipper, Ladies' slipper, Lady-slipper, Ladyslipper, Ladie-slipper, Lady's slippers] (73, 92) (1876–1892), Male balsam-apple [Male balsam apple] (178) (1526)

Impatiens biflora **Walt.** – See *Impatiens capensis* Meerb.

Impatiens capensis **Meerb.** – Balsam (5, 156) (1913–1923), Balsamweed [Balsam weed, Balsam-weed] (73, 158) (1892–1900), Brook celandine (5, 156, 157, 158) (1900–1929), Brook solentine (158) (1900), Celandine (74, 76) (1893–1896), Ceroline (157, 158) (1900–1929), Cowslip [Cowslips, Cowslyp] (5, 76, 156, 158) (1896–1923) OH, Eardrop [Ear drop, Ear-drops] (5) (1913), Earjewel [Ear jewel, Ear-jewel] (5, 74, 156, 157, 158) (1893–1929) VT, Fulvous-flower touch-me-not [Fulvous-flowered touch-me-not] (187) (1818), Jewelweed [Jewel-weed, Jewel weed] (5, 50, 53, 86, 156) (1878–present), Kicking-colt [Kicking colt] (5, 73, 156, 157, 158) (1892–1929) E. MA, Kicking-horses [Kicking horses] (5, 76, 156, 157, 158) (1896–1929) Paris ME, because ripe seed vessels burst open when touched, Lady's-eardrop [Ladies'-eardrop] (73, 156, 157, 158) (1892–1929), Lady's-pocket [Ladies'-pocket] (73, 157, 158) (1892–1929), Lady's-slipper [Lady's slipper, Ladies' slipper, Lady-slipper, Ladyslipper, Ladie-slipper, Lady's slippers] (5, 73, 156) (1892–1923) NY, Noli-me-tangere [Noli me tangere] (181) (~1678), Orange jewelweed (157, 158) (1900–1929), Pale touch-me-not [Pale touch me not] (92) (1876), Pocket-drop [Pocket drop] (5) (1913), Shining-grass [Shining grass] (5, 73, 156, 157, 158) (1892–1929) Weathersfield, VT, Silver plant (157, 158) (1900–1929), Silverleaf [Silver leaf, Silver-leaf] (5, 86, 157, 158) (1878–1929), Silverweed [Silver weed, Silver-weed] (5, 74, 156) (1893–1923) NY, Slipperweed [Slipper weed, Slipper-weed] (5, 73, 156, 157, 158) (1892–1929) Mansfield OH, Snapdragon [Snap dragon, Snap-dragon] (5, 73, 156, 158) (1892–1923) NH, Snapweed [Snap weed, Snap-weed] (46, 73, 86, 156, 157, 158) (1878–1929), Solentine (5, 74, 156, 157) (1893–1929), Speckled jewels (19, 49, 92, 156, 158) (1840–1923), Speckled jewelweed [Speckled jewel-weed] (158) (1900), Speckled touch-me-not (53) (1922), Spotted jewelweed (105, 157, 158) (1900–1932), Spotted snapweed [Spotted snap-weed] (86, 138, 155) (1878–1942), Spotted touch-me-not (2, 3, 4, 5, 15, 49, 72, 82, 86, 93, 95, 97, 131, 156, 157, 158) (1878–1986), Sullendine (79) (1891) NH, Tawny impatiens (86) (1878), Touch-me-not (46, 127) (1879–1933), Weathercock [Weather cock, Weather-cock, Weathercocks] (5, 156, 157, 158) (1900–1929), Wild balsam (5, 74, 156, 158) (1893–1923), Wild celandine (5, 74, 156, 157) (1893–1929), Wild lady's-slipper [Wild ladies'-slipper] (157, 158) (1900–1929), Wild touch-me-not (5, 76, 93, 114) (1894–1936)

Impatiens fulva **Nutt.** – See *Impatiens capensis* Meerb.

Impatiens **L.** – Balsam (2, 10, 13, 15, 85) (1818–1930), Celandine (7) (1828), Jewelweed [Jewel-weed, Jewel weed] (1, 2, 7, 13, 15, 106) (1828–1932), Quick-in-the-hand [Quick in the hand, Quickinthehand] (7) (1828), Slippers [Slipper] (7) (1828), Snapweed [Snap weed, Snap-weed] (109, 155) (1942–1949), Touch-me-not (1, 2, 4, 7, 10, 13, 50, 106, 156, 158) (1818–present), Weathercock [Weather cock, Weather-cock, Weathercocks] (7) (1828), Wild balsamina (190) (~1759)

Impatiens nolitangere **L.** – See *Impatiens noli-tangere* L.

Impatiens noli-tangere **L.** – Noli-me-tangere [Noli me tangere] (174) (1753), Nolitangere (92) (1876), Touch-me-not (15, 184) (1793–1895), Yellow balsam (92) (1876)

Impatiens pallida **Nutt.** – Balsam (5, 156) (1913–1923), Balsam jewelweed [Balsam jewel weed] (49, 53) (1898–1922), Balsamweed [Balsam weed, Balsam-weed] (49, 53, 92) (1876–1922), Ceroline (157) (1929), Cream-colored jewelweed [Cream-colored jewel-weed] (156) (1923), Golden jewelweed (157) (1929), Jewelweed [Jewel-weed, Jewel weed] (4, 5, 19, 53, 57, 92) (1840–1986), Pale balsam-weed (157) (1929), Pale jewelweed (105, 157) (1929–1932), Pale snapweed (138, 155) (1923–1942), Pale touch-me-not [Pale touch me not] (2, 4, 5, 50, 49, 53, 72, 82, 93, 95, 97, 131, 156, 157) (1895–present), Pale-flower touch-me-not [Pale-flowered touch-me-not] (187) (1818), Quick-in-the-hand [Quick in the hand, Quickinthehand] (5, 92, 156, 157) (1876–1929), Silverweed [Silver weed, Silver-weed] (5, 74, 156, 157) (1893–1929) Mansfield O, Slippers [Slipper] (5, 92, 156, 157) (1876–1929), Slipperweed [Slipper weed,

Slipper-weed] (156, 157) (1923–1929), Snapweed [Snap weed, Snap-weed] (5, 92, 156, 157) (1876–1929), Touch-me-not (19, 48, 85, 92) (1840–1932), Weathercock [Weather cock, Weather-cock, Weathercocks] (92, 156, 157) (1876–1929), Wild balsam (5, 157) (1913–1929), Wild celandine (5, 92, 156, 157) (1876–1929), Wild lady's-slipper [Wild ladies'-slipper] (157) (1929), Wild touch-me-not (37, 114) (1894–1919), Yellow jewelweed [Yellow jewel-weed] (156, 157) (1923–1929)

Impatiens sultani – See *Impatiens walleriana* Hook. f.

Impatiens sultanii **Hook. f.** – See *Impatiens walleriana* Hook. f.

Impatiens walleriana **Hook. f.** – Sultan's snapweed [Sultan snapweed] (138) (1923)

Imperata brasiliensis **Trin.** – Brazilian blady-grass (94) (1901)

Imperata brevifolia **Vasey** – Satin-tail [Satintail] (122) (1937) TX, Western blady grass [Western blady-grass] (94) (1901)

Imperata hookeri **Rupr.** – See *Imperata brevifolia* Vasey

Imperatoria lucida **(L.) Spreng.** – See *Angelica lucida* L.

Imperatoria ostruthium **L.** – See *Peucedanum ostruthium* (L.) W.D.J. Koch

Indigofera anil **L.** – See *Indigofera suffruticosa* Mill.

Indigofera caroliniana **Mill.** – Amil (10) (1818), Nil (10) (1818)

Indigofera decora **Lindl.** – Chinese indigo (138) (1923)

Indigofera kirilowii **Maxim. ex Palibin** – Kirilow's indigo [Kirilow indigo] (138) (1923)

Indigofera **L.** – Devil's-dye [Devil's dye] (92) (1876), Indigo (4, 10, 92, 138, 155, 158) (1818–1986), Indigo plant (1, 92) (1876–1932)

Indigofera leptosepala **Nutt.** – See *Indigofera miniata* Ort. var. *leptosepala* (Nutt.) B.L.Turner

Indigofera miniata **Ort. var.** *leptosepala* **(Nutt.) B. L.Turner** – Scarlet pea (4) (1986), Scarlet-pea [Scarlet pea] (4) (1986), Western indigo (50, 155) (1942–present), Western indigo plant [Western indigo-plant] (5, 97) (1913–1937), Wild indigo plant [Wild indigo-plant] (5) (1913)

Indigofera suffruticosa **Mill.** – Anil (92) (1876), Masterwort [Masterwort, Master wort, Masterwoorts] (190) (~1759)

Indigofera tinctoria **L.** – Dyer's indigo (110) (1886), Indigo (19, 55, 182) (1791–1922), True indigo (138) (1923)

Inga guadalupensis **(Pers.) Desvar.** – See *Pithecellobium unguis-cati* (L.) Benth.

Inga laurina **(Sw.) Willd.** – Guama (138) (1923)

Inga unguis-cati **(L.) Willd.** – See *Pithecellobium unguis-cati* (L.) Benth.

Inodes schwarzii **O. F. Cook** – See *Sabal palmetto* (Walt.) Lodd. ex J. A. & J. H. Schultes

Inula britannica **L.** – British inula (138) (1923)

Inula dysenterica – See *Pulicaria dysenterica* (L.) Bernh.

Inula glandulosa **Lam.** – See *Chrysopsis mariana* (L.) Ell.

Inula graminifolia **Michx.** – See *Pityopsis graminifolia* (Michx.) Nutt.

Inula helenium **L.** – Alant (German) (6) (1892), Aunee (French) (6) (1892), Elecampane (57, 61, 62, 63, 64, 72, 92, 109, 138, 156) (1870–1949), Elecampine (5, 6, 7, 19, 49, 52, 53, 54, 55) (1828–1922), Elfdock [Elf-dock, Elfe docke] (5, 64, 156, 179) (1526–1923), Elfwort (5, 64, 156) (1907–1923), Horse-elder [Horse elder] (5, 64, 156) (1907–1923), Horseheal [Horse-heal, Horse heal, Horshele] (5, 62, 64, 92, 156, 179) (1526–1923), Inul (64) (1907), Inula (54, 55, 57, 64) (1905–1917), Scabwort (5, 6, 49, 53, 64, 92, 156, 179) (1526–1923), Starwort [Star-wort, Star wort] (76) (1896) Western US, Velvet dock (64, 156) (1908–1923), Wild sunflower [Wild sun-flower] (5, 64, 156) (1907–1923), Yellow starwort (5, 64, 156) (1907–1923)

Inula **L.** – Elecampane (167) (1814), Elecampine (1, 158) (1900–1932), Fleabane [Flea-bane, Flea bane] (10) (1818), Inula (138, 155) (1923–1942)

Inula mariana – See *Chrysopsis mariana* (L.) Ell.

Inula salicina – See *Inula salicina* L.

Inula salicina **L.** – Willow-leaf inula [Willowleaf inula] (138) (1923)

Iodanthus pinnatifidus **(Michx.) Steud.** – False rocket (5, 156)

(1913–1923), Purple mustard (85) (1932), Purple rocket (3, 4, 5, 50, 72, 97, 156) (1907–present)

Iodanthus **Torr. & Gray** – False rocket (13, 158) (1849–1900), Iodanthus (50) (present), Purple rocket (158) (1900)

Ionactis alpina **(Nutt.) Greene** – Crag aster (155) (1942)

Ionactis **Greene** – Aster (50) (present), Pine starwort (158) (1900)

Ionactis linariifolius **(L.) Greene** – Double-bristle aster [Double-bristled aster] (156) (1923), Flax-leaf whitetop aster [Flaxleaf whitetop aster] (50) (present), Pine starwort (5, 158) (1900–1913), Pine-starwort (156) (1923), Sand-paper starwort [Sandpaper starwort, Sandpaper star-wort] (5, 84, 86, 156, 158) (1878–1923), Savorleaf aster [Savorleaf aster] (122) (1937), Savory-leaf aster [Savoryleaf aster, Savory-leaved aster] (5, 155, 156, 158) (1900–1942), Savory-leaf starwort [Savory-leaved star-wort] (187) (1818), Stiff aster (5, 156, 158) (1900–1923), Stiff-leaf starwort [Stiff leaved star wort] (42) (1814)

Ionactis stenomeres **(Gray) Greene** – Northwest aster (155) (1942)

Ionaoxalis violacea **(L.) Small.** – See *Oxalis violacea* L.

Ionidium concolor **Forst.** – possibly *Hybanthus concolor* (T.F.Forst) Spreng. (taxonomic status is unresolved (PL))

Ionidium **Vent.** – See *Hybanthus* Jacq.

Ionopsidium acaule **(Desf.) Reichenb.** – Diamond flower [Diamond-flower, Diamond-flower, Diamondflowers] (138) (1923)

Ionopsidium **Reichenb.** – Diamond flower [Diamondflower, Diamond-flower, Diamondflowers] (109, 138) (1923–1949)

Ionoxalis **Small.** – See *Oxalis* L.

Ipheion uniflorum **Raf.** – See *Tristagma uniflorum* (Lindl.) Traub

Ipomea batatus **Poir.** – See *Ipomoea batatas* (L.) Lam.

Ipomea pandurata – See *Ipomoea pandurata* (L.) G. F. W. Mey.

Ipomoea alba **L.** – Moon flower [Moon-flower, Moonflower] (2) (1895), Moon vine [Moon-vine] (142) (1902)

Ipomoea batatas **(L.) Lam.** – Ajes (110) (1886), Amote (110) (1886), Batatas (110, 182) (1791–1886), Bermuda potatos [Bermudas-Potatos] (177) (1762), Camote (110) (1886), Carolina potato [Carolina potatoe] (19, 92) (1840–1876), Cumar (Quichuen) (110) (1886), Gumara (New Zealand) (110) (1886), Hetich (181) (~1678), Potato [Potatoes] (181, 182) (~1678–1791), Spanish potato [Spanish potatoes] (178) (1526), Sweet potato [Sweet potatoe, Sweet-potato, Sweetpotato] (7, 19, 92, 107, 109, 110, 138) (1828–1949)

Ipomoea batatas **Lam.** – See *Ipomoea batatas* (L.) Lam.

Ipomoea biloba **Forsk** – See *Ipomoea pes-caprae* (L.) R. Br.

Ipomoea bona-nox **L.** – See *Ipomoea alba* L.

Ipomoea carnea **Jacq. subsp.** *fistulosa* **(Mart. ex Choisy) D. Austin** – Tall bush morning-glory (124) (1937)

Ipomoea coccinea **L.** – American jasmine (5, 156, 158) (1900–1923), Red morning-glory [Red morning glory] (3, 4) (1977–1986), Redsater (50) (present), Scarlet star-glory [Scarlet starglory] (138, 155) (1923–1942), Small red morning-glory [Small red morning glory] (5, 97, 158) (1900–1937), Star ipomoea (109) (1949), Wild red morning-glory (156) (1923)

Ipomoea cordatotriloba **Dennst. var.** *cordatotriloba* – Small-flower pink morning-glory [Small-flowered pink morning glory] (5, 97) (1913–1937)

Ipomoea cordatotriloba **Dennst. var.** *torreyana* **(Gray) D. Austin** – Tievine (106) (1930)

Ipomoea crassicaulis **(Benth.) Robinson** – See *Ipomoea carnea* Jacq. subsp. *fistulosa* (Mart. ex Choisy) D. Austin

Ipomoea cristulata **Hallier f.** – Trans-Pecos morning-glory [Transpecos morningglory] (50) (present)

Ipomoea hederacea **Jacq.** – Blue field morning-glory (80) (1913), Blue morning-glory [Blue morning glory] (77, 157, 158) (1898–1929) Southwest MO, Ivy-leaf morning-glory [Ivyleaf morning-glory, Ivyleaf morningglory, Ivy-leaved morning glory, Ivy-leaved morning-glory] (3, 4, 5, 50, 62, 72, 85, 93, 97, 131, 138, 155, 157) (1899–present), Kaladana (55, 157) (1900–1929), Kengashi (157) (1929), Morning-glory [Morningglory, Morning glory] (80, 145) (1897–1913), Wild blue morning-glory [Wild blue morning glory] (82) (1930)

(1898–present), Texas plume [Texasplume] (77, 138, 155) (1898–1942), Trailing fire (156) (1923)

Ipomopsis spicata **(Nutt.) V. Grant** – Spiked ipomopsis (50) (present)

Ipomopsis spicata **(Nutt.) V. Grant subsp.** *capitata* **(Gray) V. Grant** – Capitate gilia (131) (1899)

Ipomopsis spicata **(Nutt.) V. Grant subsp.** *spicata* – Spicate gilia (5) (1913), Spike gilia (3, 155) (1942–1977), Spiked ipomopsis (50) (present)

Iresine celosia **L.** – **Rydberg** – See *Iresine rhizomatosa* Standl.

Iresine celosiodes **L.** – See *Iresine diffusa* Humb. & Bonpl. ex Willd.

Iresine diffusa **Humb. & Bonpl. ex Willd.** – Bloodleaf [Blood leaf, Blood-leaf] (5, 97, 156) (1913–1937), Juba's-bush [Juba's bush, Juba-bush] (5, 156) (1913–1923)

Iresine lindeni – See *Iresine lindenii* Van Houtte

Iresine lindenii **Van Houtte** – Linden bloodleaf (138) (1923)

Iresine **P. Br.** – Bloodleaf [Blood leaf, Blood-leaf] (109, 138, 155) (1923–1949)

Iresine paniculata **(L.) Kuntze** – See *Iresine diffusa* Humb. & Bonpl. ex Willd.

Iresine rhizomatosa **Standl.** – Bloodleaf [Blood leaf, Blood-leaf] (4) (1986), Juba's-bush [Juba's bush, Juba-bush] (50) (present), Juba's-bush bloodleaf [Jubasbush bloodleaf] (155) (1942)

Iris **(Tourn.) L.** – See *Iris* L.

Iris aphylla **L.** – Stool iris (138) (1923)

Iris biliotti **Foster** – See *Iris germanica* L.

Iris bracteata **S. Wats.** – Bracted iris (138) (1923)

Iris brevicaulis **Raf.** – Lamance iris (3, 138, 155) (1923–1977), Leafy blue flag (5) (1913), Mississippi iris (155) (1942), Zigzag iris (50) (present)

Iris carolina **Radius** – See *Iris prismatica* Pursh ex Ker-Gawl.

Iris cengialti **[Ambrosi]** – See *Iris pallida* Lam. subsp. *cengialti* (Ambrosi ex A. Kern.) Foster

Iris cristata **Ait.** – Crested dwarf iris (5, 97) (1913–1937), Crested iris (107, 138) (1919–1923), Dwarf crested iris (50) (present)

Iris cristata **Ait. subsp.** *lacustris* **(Nutt.) Iltis** – See *Iris lacustris* Nutt.

Iris cristata lacustris – See *Iris lacustris* Nutt.

Iris cypriana **Foster & Baker** – See *Iris germanica* L.

Iris douglasiana **Herb.** – Douglas' iris [Douglas iris] (138) (1923), Watson's iris [Watson iris] (138) (1923)

Iris douglasiana watsoniana – See *Iris douglasiana* Herb.

Iris ecristata **Alexander** – See *Iris fulva* Ker.-Gawl.

Iris ensata **Thunb.** – Japanese iris (109, 138) (1923–1949)

Iris foetidissima **L.** – Gladwine (92) (1876), Gladwin's iris [Gladwin iris] (138) (1923), Scarlet-seed iris [Scarlet-seeded iris] (109) (1949), Spurgewort (180) (1633), Stinking gladen (178) (1596)

Iris foliosa **Mackenzie & Bush** – See *Iris brevicaulis* Raf.

Iris fulva **Ker.-Gawl.** – Bronze iris (124) (1937) TX, Copper iris (50, 138, 156) (1923–present), Red-brown flag [Red brown flag] (5) (1913)

Iris georgiana **Britton** – See *Iris hexagona* Walt. var. *hexagona*

Iris germanica **L.** – Blue flower-de-lyce [Blewe flourdelyce] (178, 179) (1526–1596), Cyprian iris (138) (1923), Elder-scented iris (19) (1840), Fleur-de-lis [Fleur de lis] (5) (1913), Garden iris (19) (1840), German iris (50, 109, 138) (1923–present), Mardin iris (138) (1923), Orris root (57) (1917), Phrygian iris (138) (1923), Purple flower-de-luce [Purple flowerdeluce] (178) (1596), Trojan iris (138) (1923)

Iris hartwegi – See *Iris hartwegii* Baker

Iris hartwegii **Baker** – Foothill iris (138) (1923)

Iris hexagona **Walt.** – See *Iris virginica* L.

Iris hexagona **Walt. var.** *hexagona* – Carolina blue flag (5) (1913), Dixie iris (50) (present)

Iris hookeri **Penny** – See *Iris setosa* Pallas ex Link var. *canadensis* M. Foster ex B.L. Robins. & Fern.

Iris kaempferi **Sieb.** – See *Iris ensata* Thunb.

Iris **L.** – Blue flag (1, 93, 158) (1900–1936), Flag (10, 184) (1793–1818), Flag-lily [Flag-lilly, Flag lily] (7, 156) (1828, 1923), Flambe (French) (180) (1633), Fleur-de-lis [Fleur de lis] (1, 7, 93, 109, 156,

158) (1828–1949), Flower-de-luce [Flower de luce, Floure-de-luce] (2, 10, 180, 190) (1633–1895), Giglio azurro (Italian) (180) (1633), Gilgen Schwertel (German) (180) (1633), Iris (50, 138, 155) (1923–present), Lischdoden (Dutch) (180) (1633)

Iris lacustris **Nutt.** – Dwarf lake iris (5, 50) (1913–present), Lake iris (138) (1923)

Iris laevigata **Fisch.** – Japanese iris (109) (1949), Rabbit-ear iris (138) (1923)

Iris longipetala **Herbert** – See *Iris missouriensis* Nutt.

Iris macrosiphon **Torr.** – Tube iris (138) (1923)

Iris mesopotamica **Dykes** – See *Iris germanica* L.

Iris mississippiensis **Alexander** – See *Iris brevicaulis* Raf.

Iris missouriensis **Nutt.** – Blue flag (3, 85, 101) (1905–1977), Coast iris (138, 155) (1923–1942), Common small blue flag (35) (1806), Flag (148) (1939), Fleur-de-lis [Fleur de lis] (85) (1932) SD, Rocky Mountain iris [RockyMountain iris] (50, 86, 138, 155) (1878–present), Western blue flag (5) (1913), Wild blue flag (148) (1939), Wild blue iris (148) (1939), Wild flag (101) (1905)

Iris pallida **Lam.** – Flower-de-luce of Dalmatia [Flowerdeluce of Dalmatia] (178) (1596), Great flower-de-luce of Dalmatia [Great floure-de-luce of Dalmatia] (180) (1633), Little Dalmatian Flower-de-luce [Little Dalmatian Flowerdeluce] (178) (1596), Orris root (57) (1917), Small Dalmatian iris (180) (1633), Sweet iris (138) (1923)

Iris pallida **subsp.** *cengialti* **(Ambrosi ex A. Kern.) Foster** – Tyrolean iris (138) (1923)

Iris prismatica **Pursh ex Ker-Gawl.** – Cube-seed iris [Cubeseed iris] (138) (1923), Narrow blue flag (5, 156) (1913–1923), Poison flag root [Poison flag-root] (75, 156) (1894–1923) Concord MA, Slender blue flag (2) (1895), Slender blue iris (50) (present)

Iris prismatica **Pursh.** – See *Iris prismatica* Pursh ex Ker-Gawl.

Iris pseudacorus **L.** – Bastard floure-de-luce (180) (1633), Common water flags [Common Waterflags] (178) (1596), Corn flag [Corn-flag, Corne-flag] (5, 156, 158) (1900–1923), Daggers (5, 156, 158) (1900–1923) no longer in use by 1923, False sweet flag [False sweet-flag] (5, 156, 158) (1900–1923), Flagons (5, 156, 158) (1900–1923) no longer in use by 1923, Flower-de-luce [Flower de luce, Floure-de-luce] (180) (1633), Gladon (178, 179) (1526–1596), Jacob's-sword [Jacob's sword] (5, 156, 158) (1900–1923) no longer in use by 1923, Pale-yellow iris [Paleyellow iris] (50) (present), Seggs (180) (1633), Sword flag [Sword-flag] (5, 156, 158) (1900–1923), Water-seg (158) (1900), Water-skegs (156) (1923) no longer in use by 1923, Yellow flag (5, 156, 158) (1900–1923), Yellow flag iris [Yellowflag] (138, 155) (1923–1942), Yellow iris (3, 107) (1919–1977), Yellow water flag [Yellow water-flag] (5, 156, 158) (1900–1923), Yellow water skegs [Yellow water-skegs] (5, 158) (1900–1913)

Iris pumila **L.** – Broad-leaf dwarf flower-de-luce [Broad leafed Dwarfe Flowerdeluce] (178) (1596), Changeable flowerdeluce [Changeable floure de-luce] (178) (1596), Crocus [Crocuses] (73) (1892) NH, Dwarf flower-de-luce (19) (1840), Dwarf flower-de-luce with reddish flowers [Dwarfe Flowerdeluce with reddish flowers] (178) (1596), Dwarf iris (50) (present), Little violet flower-de-luce [Little violet flowerdeluce] (178) (1596), Narrow-leaf dwarf flower-de-luce [Narrow leafed Dwarfe Flowerdeluce] (178) (1596), Narrow-leaf flower-de-luce [Narrow leafed Floure-de-luce] (180) (1633), Purple flower-de-luce [Purple flowerdeluce] (178) (1596), Red-flower dwarf iris [Red floured Dwarfe Iris] (180) (1633), Snow-white Dwarfe Flowerdeluce [Snowe white Dwarfe Flowerdeluce] (178) (1596)

Iris purdyi **Eastw.** – Purdy's iris [Purdy iris] (138) (1923)

Iris sambucina **L.** – See *Iris germanica* L.

Iris setosa **Pallas ex Link** – Arctic iris (138) (1923)

Iris setosa **Pallas ex Link var.** *canadensis* **M. Foster ex B. L. Robins. & Fern.** – Canadian beach-head iris [Canada beachhead iris] (50) (present), Hooker's blue flag (5) (1913)

Iris shrevei **Small** – See *Iris virginica* L. var. *shrevei* (Small) E. Anders.

Iris sibirica **L.** – Siberian iris (107, 138) (1919–1923)

Iris spuria L. – Little French flower-de-luce [Little French flowerde-luce] (178) (1596), Seashore iris (138) (1923)

Iris spuria L. subsp. *ochroleuca* (L.) Dykes – Seashore iris (50) (present), Yellow iris (19) (1840), Yellow-band iris [Yellowband iris] (138) (1923)

Iris tectorum Maxim. – Roof iris (138) (1923)

Iris tridentata Pursh – Savannah iris (50) (present)

Iris tripetala Walt – See *Iris tridentata* Pursh

Iris trojana A. Kern. ex Stapf – See *Iris germanica* L.

Iris variegata L. – Hungarian iris (138) (1923)

Iris verna L. – Dwarf iris (5, 156) (1913–1923), Dwarf violet iris (50) (present), Low spring sweet iris (183) (1756), Slender blue flag (5, 156) (1913–1923), Slender dwarf iris (2) (1895), Spring iris (5, 86, 156) (1878–1923), Vernal iris (138) (1923), Violet (156) (1923)

Iris versicolor L. – American fleur-de-lis (64, 158) (1900–1908), American flower-de-luce (64, 158) (1900–1908), Amerikanischer Schwertel (German) (158) (1900), Blue flag iris [Blueflag iris] (3, 6, 7, 19, 37, 40, 46, 49, 52, 53, 54, 55, 57, 58, 61, 64, 86, 92, 138, 155, 157, 158) (1649–1977), Blue flower-de-luce [Blew flower-deluce] (46) (1671), Blue lily (78) (1898) Madison WI, Common blue flag (156) (1923), Flag-lily [Flag-lilly, Flag lily] (5, 6, 49, 64, 92, 156, 157, 158) (1892–1929), Flambe varié (French) (158) (1900), Flambe variée (French) (158) (1900), Fleur-de-luce [Fleur de luce] (53) (1922), Flower-de-luce [Flower de luce, Floure-de-luce] (6, 49, 92, 157) (1876–1929), Flowering flag (156) (1923), Glaieul bleu (French) (6, 158) (1892–1900), Harlequin blue flag (50) (present), Iris (57, 64) (1908–1917), Iris root (157) (1929), Iris varié (French) (158) (1900), Large blue flag [Large blue-flag] (93, 156) (1923–1936), Large blue iris (72) (1907), Larger blue flag (2, 5, 6, 53, 157) (1874–1922), Liria Americana (Spanish) (158) (1900), Liver-lily [Liver lilly, Liver lily] (5, 6, 49, 64, 92, 156, 157, 158) (1892–1929), Makan skithe [Makan-skithe] (Omaha-Ponca, sweet medicine) (37) (1830), Mercury (61) (1870) termed the mercury of Eclectic practice, Poison flag (5, 49, 64, 92, 156, 157, 158) (1900–1929), Poison flag root [Poison flag-root] (75) (1894) Concord MA, Snake-lily [Snake lily, Snake lilly] (5, 19, 49, 64, 92, 156, 157, 158) (1840–1929), Verschiedenfarbige Schwertlilie (German) (6, 158) (1892–1900), Water flag (5, 49, 64, 92, 93, 156, 157, 158) (1900–1936)

Iris virginica L. – Common blue flag (187) (1818), Dixie iris (50, 138) (1923–present), Fleur-de-luce [Fleur de luce] (187) (1818), Southern blue flag (5) (1913), Virginia iris (50, 155) (1942–present)

Iris virginica L. var. shrevei (Small) E. Anders. – Interior iris (155) (1942), Shreve's iris (50) (Present)

Iris watsoniana Purdy – See *Iris douglasiana* Herb.

Iris xiphium L. – Bulbous flower-de-luce [Bulbous flowerdeluce] (178) (1596), Changeable flowerdeluce [Changeable floure de-luce] (180) (1633), Over-worn flower-de-luce [Ouerworne flowerdeluce] (178) (1596), Spanish iris (109, 138) (1923–1949)

Isanthus brachiatus (L.) Britton, Sterns & Poggenb. – Blue-gentian [Blue gentian] (5, 156, 158) (1900–1923), False pennyroyal [Falsepennyroyal] (3, 5, 72, 85, 93, 97, 122, 156, 158) (1900–1977), Fluxweed [Flux weed, Flux-weed] (5, 50, 155, 50, 156, 158) (1900–present)

Isanthus caeruleus Michx. – See *Trichostema brachiatum* L.

Isanthus coeruleus Michx. – See *Trichostema brachiatum* L.

Isanthus Michx. – False pennyroyal [Falsepennyroyal] (2, 155, 156, 158) (1895–1942), Fluxweed [Flux weed, Flux-weed] (50, 155) (1942–present)

Isatis indigofera Fortune – possibly *Isatis tinctoria* L.

Isatis indigotica Fortune – See *Isatis tinctoria* L.

Isatis L. – Woad [Woade] (109) (1949)

Isatis tinctoria L. – Dyer's weed [Dyers' weed, Dyer's-weed] (92) (1876), Dyer's woad [Dyers woad] (109) (1949), Glastum (178) (1526), Pastel leaves (92) (1876), possibly Woad [Woade] (19, 92, 107, 178) (1526–1919)

Isnardia L. – See *Ludwigia* L.

Isnardia palustris L. – See *Ludwigia palustris* (L.) Ell.

Isocoma acradenia (Greene) Greene var. *acradenia* – Fleece goldenweed (155) (1942), Pale-leaf goldenweed [Paleleaf goldenweed] (155) (1942)

Isocoma menziesii (Hook. & Arn.) Nesom var. *vernonioides* (Nutt.) Nesom – Coast goldenweed (155) (1942), Dogbane [Dog-bane, Dog bane, Dog's bane, Dogs' bane, Dogsbane] (82) (1930)

Isocoma Nutt. – Rayless goldenrod [Rayless golden-rod] (106) (1930)

Isocoma pluriflora (Torr. & Gray) Greene – Southern goldenbush (50) (present)

Isocoma tenuisecta Greene – Burro weed [Burroweed] (155) (1942)

Isocoma veneta (Kunth) Greene – Damiana (Spanish) (76) (1896), Damiana goldenweed (155) (1942), Rheumatic plant (76) (1896)

Isoetes ×dodgei A. A. Eat. [*riparia* × *tenella*] – Dodge's quillwort (5, 50) (1913–present)

Isoetes ×eatonii Dodge [*engelmannii* × *tenella*] – Eaton's quillwort (5) (1913), Grave's quillwort (5) (1913)

Isoetes ×foveolata A. A. Eat. ex Dodge [*engelmannii* × *tuckermannii*] – Pitted quillwort (5) (1913)

Isoetes braunii Durieu – See *Isoetes tenella* Léman

Isoetes butleri Engelman – Butler's quillwort (4, 5) (1913–1986), Limestone quillwort (50) (present), Quillwort [Quill-wort, Quill wort] (3) (1977)

Isoetes dodgei A.A. Eaton – See *Isoetes ×dodgei* A. A. Eat. [*riparia* × *tenella*]

Isoetes eatoni Dodge – See *Isoetes ×eatonii* Dodge [*engelmannii* × *tenella*]

Isoetes echinospora Durieu – See *Isoetes tenella* Léman

Isoetes engelmanni A. Br. – Appalachian quillwort (50) (present), Engelmann's quillwort [Engelman's quillwort] (5) (1913)

Isoetes foveolata A. A. Eaton – See *Isoetes ×foveolata* A. A. Eat. ex Dodge [*engelmannii* × *tuckermannii*]

Isoetes gravesii A. A. Eaton – See *Isoetes ×eatonii* Dodge [*engelmannii* × *tenella*]

Isoetes heiroglyphica A. A. Eaton – See *Isoetes lacustris* L.

Isoetes L. – Quillwort [Quill-wort, Quill wort] (1, 4, 10, 50, 155) (1818–present)

Isoetes lacustris L. – Braknagras (Swedish) (46) (1879), Lake quillwort (5) (1913), Quillwort [Quill-wort, Quill wort] (19, 46, 92) (1840–1879), Warty quillwort (5) (1913)

Isoetes macrospora Durieu – See *Isoetes lacustris* L.

Isoetes melanopoda Gay & Durieu ex Durieu – Black-base quillwort [Black-based quillwort] (5) (1913), Black-foot quillwort [Blackfoot quillwort] (50) (present), Midland quillwort (4) (1986), Quillwort [Quill-wort, Quill wort] (3) (1977)

Isoetes muricata Durieu – See *Isoetes tenella* Léman

Isoetes riparia Engelm. ex A. Braun – Riverbank quillwort (5) (1913), Shore quillwort (50) (present)

Isoetes saccharata Engelm. – Sugar quillowrt (50) (present), Sugary quillwort (5) (1913)

Isoetes setacea Lam. p.p. – See *Isoetes tenella* Léman

Isoetes tenella Léman – Braun's quillwort [Braun quillwort] (5) (1913), Spiny-spore quillwort (50) (present)

Isoetes tuckermani A. Br. – Tuckerman's quillwort (5, 50) (1913–present)

Isolepis carinata Hook. & Arn. ex Torr. – Keeled bulrush (50) (present)

Isolepis cernua (Vahl) Roemer & J.A. Schultes – Weeping bulrush (138) (1923)

Isoloba elatior (Michx.) Raf. – Butterwort [Butter wort, Butter woorts] (19, 92, 183) (~1756–1840), Tat-grass [Tat grass] (92) (1876)

Isopappus diivaricatus (Nutt.) Torr. & Gray – See *Croptilon divaricatum* (Nutt.) Raf.

Isopyrum biternatum (Raf.) Torr. & Gray – See *Enemion biternatum* Raf.

Isopyrum L. – See *Enemion* Raf.

Isotria affinis **(Austin) Rydb.** – See *Isotria medeoloides* (Pursh) Raf.

Isotria medeoloides **(Pursh) Raf.** – Small whorled pogonia (156) (1923), Smaller whorled pogonia (5) (1913)

Isotria verticillata **(Muehl. ex Willd.) Raf.** – Purple five-leaf orchid [Purple fiveleaf orchid] (50) (present), Whorled pogonia (5, 156) (1913–1923), Whorled snakemouth [Whorled snake mouth, Whorled snake-mouth] (5, 156) (1913–1923)

Itea **L.** – Itea (8) (1785), Itea (French) (8) (1785), Sweetspire [Sweet spire] (138) (1923)

Itea virginica **L.** – Chaste shrub (156) (1923), Doconangia (174, 177) (1753–1762), Itea (5, 19, 174, 177) (1753–1913), Itéa de Virginie (French) (8) (1785), Sweetspire [Sweet spire] (109, 138, 156) (1923–1949), Virginia itea [Virginian itea] (8) (1785), Virginia tea (156) (1923), Virginia willow [Virginia-willow] (97, 109, 156) (1937–1949)

Iuglans – See *Juglans* L.

Iva angustifolia **Nutt.** – Narrow-leaf marsh elder [Narrowleaf marsh elder, Narrowleaf marshelder, Narrow-leaved marsh elder] (50, 97, 122) (1937–present)

Iva angustifolia **Nutt.** – Narrow-leaf sumpweed [Narrowleaf sumpweed] (155) (1942)

Iva annua **L.** – Annual marsh-elder [Annual marshelder] (50) (present)

Iva annua **L. var.** *annua* – Marshelder [Marsh elder, Marsh-elder] (4, 21, 125) (1893–1986), Rough marsh-elder [Rough marsh elder] (5, 93, 97, 122) (1913–1937), Seacoast sumpweed (155) (1942)

Iva axillaris **Pursh** – Marshelder [Marsh elder, Marsh-elder] (85) (1932), Poverty sumpweed (155) (1942), Poverty-weed [Poverty-weed, Poverty weed] (3, 4, 50) (1977–present), Small-flower marshelder [Small flower marsh elder, Small flower marsh elder, Small-flowered marsh elder] (5, 93, 97, 122, 131) (1899–1937)

Iva ciliata **Willd.** – See *Iva annua* L. var. *annua*

Iva frutescens **L.** – Bastard Jesuit bark (7) (1828), False Jesuit's bark [False Jesuit's-bark] (5) (1913), High-water shrub [Highwater-shrub] (5, 19) (1840–1913), Jesuit's-bark [Jesuit's bark] (5, 75) (1894–1913) NY, Marshelder [Marsh elder, Marsh-elder] (5, 10, 122) (1818–1937) TX

Iva frutescens **L. subsp.** *oraria* **(Bartlett) R.C. Jackson** – False Jesuit's bark [False Jesuit's-bark] (156) (1923), Green mangle (156) (1923), High-water shrub [Highwater-shrub] (156) (1923), Jacko-bush (156) (1923), Jesuit's-bark [Jesuit's bark] (156) (1923), Mangle (156) (1923), Marshelder [Marsh elder, Marsh-elder] (156) (1923), Poverty-weed [Povertyweed, Poverty weed] (156) (1923)

Iva imbricata **Walt.** – Sea-coast marsh-elder [Sea-coast marsh elder] (5, 156) (1913–1923)

Iva **L.** – Bozzleweed (1) (1932), Carelessweed [Careless-weed, Careless weed] (1) (1932), False bark-tree (167) (1814), Horseweed [Horse-weed, Horse weed] (1) (1932), Marshelder [Marsh elder, Marsh-elder] (1, 2, 4, 50, 93, 156, 158) (1895–present), Poverty-weed [Povertyweed, Poverty weed] (1, 93) (1932–1936), Salt sage (1, 93) (1932–1936), Sumpweed (155) (1942)

Iva oraria – See *Iva frutescens* L. subsp. *oraria* (Bartlett) R. C. Jackson

Iva xanthifolia **Nutt.** – Burweed [Bur weed, Bur-weed, Burr weed, Burrweed, Burr-weed] (131) (1899) SD, Burweed marsh-elder [Burweed marsh elder] (5, 21, 72, 93, 97, 122) (1893–1937), Carelessweed [Careless-weed, Careless weed] (156) (1923), Giant sumpweed (50) (present), Half-breed weed [Halfbreed weed] (80) (1913), Horseweed [Horse-weed, Horse weed] (85) (1932), Marshelder [Marsh elder, Marsh-elder] (3, 4, 63, 80, 121, 126, 131, 145) (1897–1986), Prairie ragweed [Prairie rag-weed] (156) (1923), Rag sumpweed (155) (1942), Waxpe šiča (Lakota, bad leaves) (121) (1918?–1970?)

Ixia campanulata **Houtt.** – Scarlet ixia (138) (1923)

Ixia chinensis **L.** – See *Belamcanda chinensis* (L.) DC.

Ixia coccinea **[Thunb.]** – See *Ixia campanulata* Houtt.

Ixia coelestina **Bartr.** – See *Calydorea coelestina* (Bartr.) Goldblatt & Henrich

Ixia **L.** – Ixia (138, 155) (1923–1942) Greek "bird lime" perhaps referring to juice

Ixia maculata **L.** – Spotted ixia (138) (1923)

Ixia speciosa **Andrews** – See *Ixia campanulata* Houtt.

Ixophorus glaucus **(L.) Nash** – See *Pennisetum glaucum* (L.) R. Br.

Ixophorus glaucus **L.** – See *Pennisetum glaucum* (L.) R. Br.

Ixophorus italicus **(L.) Nash** – See *Setaria italica* (L.) Beauv.

Ixophorus viridis **L.** – See *Setaria viridis* (L.) Beauv.

Ixora coccinea **L.** – Scarlet ixora (138) (1923), Schetti (174) (1753)

Ixora **L.** – Ixora (138) (1923)

Ixora parviflora **[Vahl]** – See *Ixora pavetta* Andrews

Ixora pavetta **Andrews** – White ixora (138) (1923)

Iva xanthifolia Nutt.
J. Kops, 1915

223

J

Jacaranda **Juss.** – Jacaranda (138) (1923)

Jacaranda mimosifolia **D. Don** – Green-ebony (138) (1923)

Jacaranda ovalifolia **[R. Br.]** – See *Jacaranda mimosifolia* D. Don

Jacobea aurea – possibly *Packera aurea* (L.) A.& D. Löve

Jacobea lobata – possibly *Packera glabella* (Poir) C. Jeffrey

Jacobea obovata – possibly *Packera obovata* (Muhl. ex Willd.) W. A. Weber & A. Löve

Jacobinia **(Nees)** – See *Justicia* L.

Jacquemontia tamnifolia **(L.) Griseb.** – Clustered blue morning-glory (122, 124) (1937)

Janipha **Kunth.** – See *Manihot* Mill.

Janipha stimulosa **Raf.** – See *Cnidoscolus stimulosus* (Michx.) Engelm. & Gray

Jasione **L.** – Sheep's-bit [Sheep's bit] (156) (1923)

Jasione montana **L.** – Sheep's-bit [Sheep's bit] (5, 156) (1913–1923)

Jasminum azoricum – See *Jasminum fluminense* Vell.

Jasminum dichotomum **Vahl** – Gold coast jasmine (109) (1949)

Jasminum fluminense **Vell.** – Azores jasmine (138) (1923)

Jasminum fruiticans – See *Jasminum fruticans* L.

Jasminum gracillimum **Hook. f.** – See *Jasminum multiflorum* (Burm. f.) Andr. (introduced)

Jasminum grandiflorum – See *Jasminum officinale* L.

Jasminum **L.** – Jasmine (109, 138) (1923–1949) from ancient Arabic name, Jessamine (109) (1949)

Jasminum multiflorum **(Burm. f.) Andr.** – Furry jasmine (138) (1923), Slender jasmine (138) (1923)

Jasminum nudiflorum **Lindl.** – Winter jasmine (138) (1923)

Jasminum officinale **L.** – Common white jasmine (138) (1923), Gelsiminum (178) (1526), Jasmine (19, 92) (1840–1876), Poet's jessamine [Poets jessamine] (109) (1949), Spanish jasmine (138) (1923), White gessemin (178) (1526), White jassamine (92) (1876), Yasmyn (92) (1876)

Jasminum pubescens **[(Retz.) Willd.]** – See *Jasminum multiflorum* (Burm. f.) Andr.

Jasminum sambac **(L.) Aiton** – Arabian jasmine (109, 138) (1923–1949)

Jasminum sambac **Aiton** – See *Jasminum sambac* (L.) Aiton

Jatropha curcas **L.** – Barbados nuts [Barbadoes nuts] (92) (1876), Physic nut [Physic nuts, Physick Nut, Physic-nut] (92) (1876), Purging nuts (92) (1876)

Jatropha dioica **Sessé** – Leatherweed [Leather-weed, Leather weed] (124) (1937)

Jatropha gossypiifolia **L.** – Bastard French physic nut (92) (1876)

Jatropha **L.** – Spurge nettle (158) (1900), Tread-softly [Treadsoftly, Tread softly] (156) (1923)

Jatropha manihot – See *Manihot esculenta* Crantz

Jatropha spathulata **(Ortega) Müll. Arg.** – See *Jatropha dioica* Sessé

Jatropha stimulosa **Michx.** – See *Cnidoscolus stimulosus* (Michx.) Engelm. & Gray

Jatropha urens **L.** – See *Cnidoscolus urens* (L.) Arthur

Jeffersonia **Bart.** – Twinleaf [Twin leaf, twin-leaf] (15, 138) (1895–1923)

Jeffersonia bartoni **Michx.** – See *Jeffersonia diphylla* (L.) Pers.

Jeffersonia diphylla **(L.) Pers.** – Common twinleaf (7) (1828), Ground-squirrel pea [Ground squirrel pea] (5, 7, 49, 64, 92, 156) (1828–1923), Helmetpod [Helmet-pod, Helmet pod] (5, 7, 64, 92, 156) (1828–1923), Jefferson (French) (7) (1828), Jeffersonia (64) (1907), Rheumatism root [Rheumatism-root] (2, 5, 13, 49, 53, 64, 92, 156) (1849–1923), Squirrel's-ear [Squirrel ear] (92) (1876), Twinleaf [Twin leaf, twin-leaf] (2, 5, 13, 19, 49, 53, 57, 61, 64, 92, 109, 138, 156) (1840–1949), Yellowroot [Yellow root, Yellow-root]

(7, 64, 92, 156) (1828–1929)

Jeffersonia diphylla **Barton** – See *Jeffersonia diphylla* (L.) Pers.

Jeffersonia diphylla **Pers.** – See *Jeffersonia diphylla* (L.) Pers.

Juglans ailanthifolia **Carr.** – Japanese walnut (138) (1923), possibly Flat walnut (138) (1923)

Juglans alba **L. p.p.** – See *Carya alba* (L.) Nutt. ex Ell.

Juglans alba odorata – See *Carya glabra* (Mill.) Sweet

Juglans alba ovata – possibly *Carya cordiformis* (Wangenh.) K. Koch

Juglans amara **[Michx.]** – See *Carya cordiformis* (Wangenh.) K. Koch

Juglans aquatica – See *Carya aquatica* (Michx. f.) Nutt.

Juglans californica **S. Wats.** – California black walnut (138) (1923)

Juglans cathartica **Michx** – See *Juglans cinerea* L.

Juglans cinerea **L.** – Butternut [Butter nuts, Butter nut] (1, 2, 3, 4, 5, 6, 7, 9, 10, 19, 20, 40, 46, 49, 50, 52, 53, 54, 57, 61, 72, 82, 85, 92, 93, 95, 105, 107, 109, 113, 138, 155, 156, 157, 158) (1857–present), Butternutsträ (Swedish) (41) (1770), Daheya (46) (1879), Lemon walnut (5, 92, 156, 157, 158) (1898–1929), Noix (46) (1879), Noyer gris (French) (6) (1892), Noyers (46) (1879), Oil nut [Oilnut, Oil-nut] or Oil-nut tree [Oil nut tree] (5, 6, 49, 78, 92, 156, 157, 158) (1892–1929), Pkanak (Chippewa) (105) (1932), Quaheya (46) (1879), Small oilnut [Small oil nut] (46) (1649), Wallnuss (German) (6) (1892), White walnut [White walnuts] or White walnut tree [White walnut-trees] (1, 2, 5, 6, 7, 35, 49, 53, 78, 82, 85, 92, 104, 109, 156, 158) (1806–1949), Wussoquat (Narragansett) (46, 107) (1879–1919)

Juglans cordiformis **Maxim.** – See *Carya cordiformis* (Wangenh.) K. Koch

Juglans exaltata – possibly *Carya ovata* (Mill.) K. Koch

Juglans hindsi – See *Juglans hindsii* (Jepson) Jepson ex R.E. Sm.

Juglans hindsii **(Jepson) Jepson ex R. E. Sm.** – Hinds' walnut [Hinds walnut] (138) (1923)

Juglans **L.** – Ack-root [Ackroot] (92) (1876) from Indian name for walnut, Butternut [Butter nuts, Butter nut] (156, 190) (~1759–1923), Hickory or Hickory tree [Hiccory-tree] (167, 190) (~1759–1814), Noyer (French) (8) (1785), Walnut [Wall nut, Wall nutte, Walnutt, Walnuts] or Walnut tree (4, 8, 10, 50, 82, 92, 93, 106, 109, 138, 155, 156, 158, 184) (1793–present)

Juglans laciniosa **[F. Michx.]** – See *Carya laciniosa* (Michx. f.) G. Don

Juglans major **(Torr.) Heller** – Walnut [Wall nut, Wall nutte, Walnutt, Walnuts] or Walnut tree (112) (1937)

Juglans microcarpa **Berl.** – Little walnut (4, 50, 97) (1937–present), Nogal (149) (1904) NM, River walnut (122) (1937) TX, Texas walnut (4) (1986)

Juglans microcarpa **Berl. var. microcarpa** – Texas black walnut (155) (1942), Texas walnut (138) (1923), Walnut [Wall nut, Wall nutte, Walnutt, Walnuts] or Walnut tree (149) (1904), Western black walnut (65) (1931)

Juglans myristicaeformis – See *Carya myristiciformis* (F. Michx.) Nutt.

Juglans myristiciformis **F. Michx.** – See *Carya myristiciformis* (F. Michx.) Nutt.

Juglans nigra **L.** – Black walnut [Black wallnut, Black walnutt] (1, 4, 5, 7, 9, 12, 14, 20, 19, 27, 35, 37, 41, 44, 46, 50, 57, 65, 72, 82, 85, 91, 92, 93, 95, 97, 105, 107, 109, 112, 113, 121, 122, 124, 125, 130, 131, 135, 138, 153, 156, 157, 158, 181, 182, 187, 189) (~1678–present), Chak (Winnebago) (37) (1919), Chan-sapa (Dakota Teton, black wood) (37) (1919), Eastern black walnut (155) (1942), Hma (Dakota) (37) (1919), Large oilnut [Large oil nut] (46) (1649), Milk hickory [Milke Hickerie] (181) (~1678), Noyer à fruit noir (French) (8) (1785), Round black Virginia walnut [Round black Virginian walnut] (8) (1785), Sahtaku (Pawnee) (37) (1919), Schwartznussbaum (German) (41) (1770), Swartnöttbom (Swedish) (41) (1770),

Tage (Osage) (121) (1918?–1970?), Tdage (Omaha-Ponca) (37) (1919), Walnut [Wall nut, Wall nutte, Walnutt, Walnuts] or Walnut tree (157, 181) (~1678–1929), Zwartnootboom (Dutch) (41) (1770)

Juglans olivaeformis – See *Carya illinoinensis* (Wangenh.) K. Koch

Juglans oliviformis **Michx.** – See *Carya illinoinensis* (Wangenh.) K. Koch

Juglans pecan **[Marshall]** – See *Carya illinoinensis* (Wangenh.) K. Koch

Juglans porcina **[Michx. f.]** – See *Carya glabra* (Mill.) Sweet

Juglans regia **L.** – Common European walnut (20) (1857), Common walnut (92) (1876), English walnut or English walnut tree (41, 92, 107) (1770–1919), Jupiter's-nuts [Jupiter's nuts] (92) (1876), Madeira nut (19, 92, 107) (1840–1919), Persian walnut (107, 109, 138) (1919–1949), Walnut [Wall nut, Wall nutte, Walnutt, Walnuts] or Walnut tree (110, 178, 179) (1526–1886), Walsh nut tree (178) (1526)

Juglans rupestris **Engelm.** – See *Juglans microcarpa* Berl. var. *microcarpa*

Juglans sieboldiana – See *Juglans ailanthifolia* Carr.

Juglans sieboldiana cordiformis – possibly *Juglans ailanthifolia* Carr.

Juglans sieboldiana **var.** *cordiformis* **Makino** – possibly *Juglans ailanthifolia* Carr.

Juglans squamosa **[Poir.]** – See *Carya alba* (L.) Nutt. ex Ell.

Juglans tomentosa **Poir.** – See *Carya alba* (L.) Nutt. ex Ell.

Juncoides **Adans. (Seg.)** – See *Luzula* DC.

Juncoides arcticum **(Blytt) Coville** – See *Luzula arctica* Blytt subsp. *arctica*

Juncoides campestre **(L.) Kuntze** – See *Luzula campestris* (L.) DC.

Juncoides carolinae **(S. Wats.) Kuntze.** – See *Luzula acuminata* Raf. var. *carolinae* (S. Wats.) Fern.

Juncoides nemorosum **(Poll.) Kuntze.** – See *Luzula luzuloides* (Lam.) Dandy & Wilmott

Juncoides parviflorum **(Ehrh.) Coville** – See *Luzula parviflora* (Ehrh.) Desv.

Juncoides spicatum **(L.) Kuntze** – See *Luzula spicata* (L.) DC.

Juncus **(Tourn.) L.** – See *Juncus* L.

Juncus ×*oronensis* **Fern.** [*tenuis* × *vaseyi*] – Maine rush (5) (1913)

Juncus acuminatus **Michx.** – Green rush (66) (1903), Knotty-leaf rush [Knotty-leaved rush] (156) (1923), Sharp-fruit rush [Sharp-fruited rush, Sharp fruited rush] (5, 66, 72, 120) (1903–1938), Sharp-point rush [Sharp-pointed rush] (156) (1923), Taper-tip rush [Tapertip rush] (50) (present)

Juncus alpinoarticulatus **Chaix** – Northern green rush (50) (present)

Juncus alpinoarticulatus **Chaix subsp.** *nodulosus* **(Wahlenb.) Hämet-Ahti** – Alpine rush (155) (1942), Northern green rush (50) (present), Richardson's rush (5, 93) (1913–1936)

Juncus alpinus **[Vill.]** – See *Juncus alpinoarticulatus* Chaix subsp. *nodulosus* (Wahlenb.) Hämet-Ahti

Juncus ambiguus **Guss.** – Seaside rush (50) (present)

Juncus arizonicus **Wiegand** – See *Juncus interior* Wieg. var. *arizonicus* (Wieg.) F.J. Herm.

Juncus articulatus **L.** – Brownish-fruit rush [Brownish-fruited rush] (66) (1903), Jointed rush (5, 156) (1913–1923), Joint-leaf rush [Jointleaf rush] (50) (present), Ryll-togh (46) (1879), Spart (5, 156) (1913–1923)

Juncus ater **Rydb.** – See *Juncus balticus* Willd. var. *montanus* Engelm.

Juncus balticus **Willd.** – Baltic rush (3, 5, 50, 66, 72, 93, 155) (1907–present), Wire-grass [Wire grass] (87, 101) (1884–1905)

Juncus balticus **Willd. var.** *montanus* **Engelm.** – Black rush [Black-rush] (139) (1944), Mountain rush (50) (present)

Juncus biglumis **L.** – Two-flower rush [Two-flowered rush] (5, 50) (1913–present)

Juncus brachycarpus **Engelm.** – Short-fruit rush [Short-fruited rush] (5) (1913), White-root rush [Whiteroot rush] (50) (present)

Juncus brachycephalus **(Engelm.) Buch.** – Small headed rush (5)

(1913), Small-head rush [Smallhead rush, Small headed rush] (3, 5, 50) (1913–present)

Juncus brachyphyllus **Wieg.** – Small-headed rush (3) (1977), Tufted-stem rush [Tuftedstem rush] (50) (present)

Juncus brevicaudatus **(Engelm.) Fernald** – Narrow-panicle rush [Narrowpanicle rush, Narrow-panicled rush] (5, 50) (1913–present)

Juncus brunnescens **Rydb.** – See *Juncus saximontanus* A. Nels.

Juncus bufonius **L.** – Bog rush [Bogrush] (85) (1932) SD, Coegrass [Coe grass] (5, 156) (1913–1923), Frog-grass [Frog grass, Frog grasse, Frogge-grasse] (156) (1923), Frogweed [Frog weed] (5) (1913), Holosteum (174) (1753), Rush-grass [Rushgrass, Rush grass, Rush-grasse] (178, 180) (1526–1633), Saltweed [Salt weed, Salt-weed] (5, 156) (1913–1923), Toad rush (3, 5, 19, 50, 66, 92, 93, 139, 155, 156) (1840–present), Toad-grass [Toad-grasse] (156, 178, 180) (1596–1923), Toadweed [Toad weed] (5) (1913)

Juncus bufonius **L. var.** *bufonius* – Toad rush (50) (present)

Juncus bufonius **L. var.** *occidentalis* **F. J. Herm.** – Round-fruit rush [Roundfruited rush] (139) (1944)

Juncus bulbosus **L.** – Black rush [Black-rush] (19) (1840), Black-grass [Black grass, Blackgrass] (66) (1903), Bulbous rush (5) (1913)

Juncus caesariensis **Coville** – New Jersey rush (5, 50) (1913–present)

Juncus campestris – See *Luzula multiflora* (Ehrh.) Lej. subsp. *multiflora* var. *multiflora*

Juncus canadensis **J. Gay ex Laharpe** – Canadian rush [Canada rush] (5, 50, 72, 155) (1907–present)

Juncus castaneus **Smith.** – Chestnut rush (5, 50) (1913–present), Clustered alpine rush (5) (1913)

Juncus compressus **Jacq.** – Round-fruit rush [Roundfruit rush] (50) (present)

Juncus conglomeratus **L.** – See *Juncus effusus* L. var. *conglomeratus* (L.) Engelm.

Juncus conradi **[Tuckerm. ex Torr.]** – See *Juncus pelocarpus* E. Meyer.

Juncus conradii **Tuck.** – See *Juncus pelocarpus* E. Meyer.

Juncus coriaceus **Mackenzie** – Awl-leaf rush [Awl-leaved rush] (5) (1913), Bristly rush (66) (1903), Leathery rush (50) (present)

Juncus crassifolius **Buch.** – See *Juncus validus* Coville var. *validus*

Juncus debilis **A. Gray** – Weak rush (5, 50, 66) (1912–present)

Juncus dichotomus **Ell.** – Forked rush (5, 50) (1913–present)

Juncus diffusissimus **Buckl.** – Diffuse rush (5) (1913), Slim-pod rush [Slimpod rush] (3, 50) (1977–present)

Juncus drummondii **E. Mey.** – Drummond's rush [Drummond rush] (139) (1944)

Juncus dudleyi **Wieg.** – Dudley's rush [Dudley rush] (3, 5, 50, 93, 139) (1913–present)

Juncus echinatus **Muhl.** – See *Juncus polycephalus* Michx.

Juncus effusus **L.** – Bog rush [Bogrush] (5, 28, 120, 156) (1850–1938), Bulrush [Bull rush, Bullrush, Bul-Rush, Bulrushes] (19, 92) (1840–1876), Candle rush (5, 156) (1913–1923), Common rush (5, 50, 72, 138, 155, 156) (1907–present), Hard rush (5, 156) (1913–1923), Pin rush (5, 156) (1913–1923), Round rush (5, 156) (1913–1923), Small bulrush [Small bull-rush] (187) (1818), Soft rush [Soft-rush] (5, 19, 66, 120, 156) (1840–1938), Sugar rush [Sugar-rush] (156) (1923), Water rush (5, 92, 156) (1913–1923)

Juncus effusus **L. var.** *caeruleomontanus* **St. John** – See *Juncus effusus* L. var. *conglomeratus* (L.) Engelm.

Juncus effusus **L. var.** *compactus* **auct. non Lej. & Court.** – See *Juncus effusus* L. var. *conglomeratus* (L.) Engelm.

Juncus effusus **L. var.** *conglomeratus* **(L.) Engelm.** – Common rush (50) (present), Glomerate rush (5) (1913), Pith rush (5, 156) (1913–1923), Staff rush (5, 156) (1913–1923)

Juncus effusus **L. var.** *solutus* **Fern. & Wieg.** – Bog rush [Bogrush] (3) (1977), Lamp rush (50) (present)

Juncus ensifolius **Wikst. var.** *montanus* **(Engelm.) C. L. Hitchc.** – See *Juncus saximontanus* A. Nels.

Juncus ensifolius **Wikstr. var.** *brunnescens* **(Rydb.) Cronq.** – See *Juncus saximontanus* A. Nels.

Juncus filiformis **L.** – Slender rush (66) (1903), Thread rush (5, 50, 156) (1913–present)

Juncus gerardi **Lois.** – Black-grass [Black grass, Blackgrass] (3, 5, 46, 156) (1879–1977), Salt-meadow rush [Saltmeadow rush] (138, 155) (1923–1942), Salt-meadow rush [Saltmeadow rush] (50, 155) (1942–present)

Juncus greenei **Oakes & Tuckerm.** – Greene's rush (5, 50, 66) (1912–present)

Juncus gymnocarpus **Coville** – Pennsylvania rush (5, 50) (1913–present)

Juncus hallii **Engelm.** – Hall's rush [Hall rush] (139) (1944)

Juncus interior **Wieg.** – Inland rush (3, 5, 50, 93, 139, 155) (1911–present)

Juncus interior **Wieg. var. *arizonicus* (Wieg.) F. J. Herm.** – Arizona rush (139) (1944)

Juncus interior **Wieg. var. *interior*** – Inland rush (50) (present)

Juncus **L.** – Binken (High Dutch) (180) (1633), Bog rush [Bogrush] (41, 158) (1770–1900), Giunco (Italian) (180) (1633), Ioue (French) (180) (1633), Iunco (Spanish) (180) (1633), Rush [Rushes] (1, 7, 10, 50, 93, 138, 139, 155, 158, 180, 181, 184) (1633–present), Rysshe (178, 179) (1526–1596), Siefen (Low Dutch) (180) (1633), Sourgrass [Sourgrass, Sour grass] (75) (1894) Neb, Wire-grass [Wire grass] (1, 93) (1932–1936)

Juncus longistylis **Torr.** – Long-style rush [Longstyle rush, Longstyled rush, Long-styled rush] (5, 50, 93, 139) (1913–present)

Juncus longistylis **Torr. var. *longistylis*** – Long-style rush [Longstyle rush, Longstyled rush, Long-styled rush] (50) (present)

Juncus macer **S. F. Gray** – See *Juncus tenuis* Willd.

Juncus marginatus **Rostk.** – Awn-petal rush [Awn-petaled rush] (5) (1913), Grass-leaf rush [Grassleaf rush, Grass-leaved rush] (3, 5, 50, 66, 72, 93) (1903–present)

Juncus maritimus **Lam.** – Sea rush (5, 50, 66) (1912–present)

Juncus megacephalus **M. A. Curtis** – Carolina rush (72) (1907) IA

Juncus militaris **Bigel.** – Bayonet rush (5, 50, 156) (1913–present), Marshall's rush [Marshall rush] (66) (1903)

Juncus nodatus **Cov.** – Stout rush (3, 5, 50, 120) (1913–present)

Juncus nodosus **L. var. *nodosus*** – Knotted rush (50) (present)

Juncus nodosus **L.** – Big-head bog rush [Big-headed bog-rush] (129) (1894), Jointed rush (139, 155) (1942–1944), Knotted rush (3, 5, 50, 72, 93, 156) (1907–present), Round-headed rush (66) (1903)

Juncus oronensis **Fernald** – See *Juncus ×oronensis* Fern. *[tenuis × vaseyi]*

Juncus paradoxus **[E. Mey.]** – See *Juncus acuminatus* Michx.

Juncus parryi **Engelm.** – Parry's rush [Parry rush] (139) (1944)

Juncus pelocarpus **E. Meyer.** – Brown-fruit rush [Brownfruit rush, Brown-fruited rush] (5, 50) (1913–present), Conrad's rush (66) (1903)

Juncus platyphyllus **(Wieg.) Fern.** – See *Juncus dichotomus* Ell.

Juncus polycephalus **Michx.** – Many-head rush [Manyhead rush, Many-headed rush] (3, 5, 50) (1913–present), Rough-head rush [Rough-headed rush] (187) (1818)

Juncus repens **Michx.** – Creeping rush (5) (1913), Lesser creeping rush (50) (present)

Juncus robustus **(Engelm.) Coville** – See *Juncus nodatus* Cov.

Juncus roemerianus **Scheele.** – Needle-grass rush [Needlegrass rush] (50) (present), Roemer's rush (5) (1913)

Juncus saximontanus **A. Nels.** – Button rush (139) (1944), Rocky Mountain rush [RockyMountain rush] (50, 139, 155) (1942–present)

Juncus scirpoides **Lam.** – Needle-pod rush [Needlepod rush] (50) (present), Pale rush (66) (1903), Scirpus-like rush (5) (1913)

Juncus secundus **Beauv. ex Poir.** – Lop-sided rush [Lopsided rush] (50) (present), Secund rush (5) (1913)

Juncus setaceus **Rostk.** – See *Juncus coriaceus* Mackenzie

Juncus setosus **(Coville) Small** – See *Juncus marginatus* Rostk.

Juncus sphaerocarpus **Nees.** – See *Juncus bufonius* L. var. *occidentalis* F. J. Herm.

Juncus stygius **L.** – Long-fruit rush [Long-fruited rush] (66) (1903), Moor rush (5, 50) (1913–present)

Juncus subtilis **E. Meyer** – Creeping rush (5) (1913), Greater creeping rush (50) (present)

Juncus tenuis **Willd.** – Path rush (3) (1977), Poverty rush (50, 155) (1942–present), Poverty-grass [Poverty grass] (5, 75, 156) (1894–1923) WV, Slender bog rush (129) (1894), Slender rush (5, 61, 66, 72, 80, 93, 156) (1870–1936), Soft rush [Soft-rush] (155) (1942), Wire-grass [Wire grass] (5, 62, 75, 80, 156) (1894–1923), Yard rush (5, 62, 156) (1912–1923)

Juncus tenuis **Willd. var. *platyphyllus* (Wieg.) F. J. Herm.** – See *Juncus dichotomus* Ell.

Juncus torreyi **Coville** – Torrey's rush [Torrey rush] (3, 5, 50, 72, 93, 139, 155) (1907–present)

Juncus trifidus **L.** – Highland rush (5, 50) (1913–present), Three-leaf rush [Three-leaved rush] (66) (1903)

Juncus triglumis **L.** – Three-flower rush [Three-flowered rush] (5) (1913), Three-hull rush [Three hulled rush] (50) (present)

Juncus validus **Coville** – Round-head rush [Roundhead rush] (50) (present)

Juncus validus **Coville var. *validus*** – Round-head rush [Roundhead rush] (50) (present)

Juncus vaseyi **Engelm.** – Vasey's rush [Vasey rush] (5, 50, 72, 139) (1893–present)

Juniperus alpina **(Sm.) S. F. Gray** – See *Juniperus communis* L. var. *montana* Ait.

Juniperus andina **[Nutt.]** – See *Juniperus occidentalis* Hook.

Juniperus barbadensis – See *Juniperus virginiana* L. var. *silicicola* (Small) J. Silba

Juniperus barbadensis **var. *australis* (Endl.) ined.** – Coast juniper (122) (1937), Gulf Coast cedar (124) (1937), Southern red cedar [Southern redcedar] (138) (1923)

Juniperus californica **Carr.** – California juniper (138) (1923)

Juniperus caroliniana **Du Roi** – See *Juniperus virginiana* L.

Juniperus coahuilensis **(Martinez) Gaussen ex R.P. Adams** – Red-fruit juniper [Red fruited juniper] (122) (1937)

Juniperus communis **L.** – Aiten (5, 157, 158) (1900–1929), Aitnach (157, 158) (1900–1929), Common juniper (2, 4, 7, 10, 20, 41, 50, 85, 109, 130, 136, 138, 155) (1770–present), Dwarf juniper (3, 4, 136) (1930–1986), Enebro (Spanish) (158) (1900), Etnach (157, 158) (1900–1929), Fairy circle [Fairy circles, Fairy-circle] (73, 157, 158) (1892–1929) Eastern MA, Ga'gawan'dagisïd (Chippewa, deceptive) (40) (1928), Genévrier commun (French) (158) (1900), Geniev commun (French) (7) (1828), Gorst (157, 158) (1900–1929), Hackmatack [Hack-matack, Hacmatack] (5, 73, 157, 158) (1892–1929) Ipswich Mass, Horse savin (5, 157, 158) (1900–1929), Irish juniper (109) (1949), Jachendel (German) (158) (1900), Jenepre (178, 179) (1526–1596), Johandel (German) (158) (1900), Juniper bark (92) (1876), Juniper bush [Juniper-bush] (92) (1876), Juniper or Juniper tree [Juniper-tree] (5, 19, 35, 40, 52, 53, 57, 58, 60, 72, 78, 92, 107, 113, 157, 158, 187) (1806–1929), Juniper-berry [Juniper berries] (92) (1876), Kaddig (German) (158) (1900), Kranewett (German) (158) (1900), Röd en (German) (41) (1770), Swedish juniper (109, 138) (1923–1949), Trailing juniper (136) (1930), Wachholder (German) (158) (1900)

Juniperus communis **L. subsp. *alpina* (Sm.) Celak.** – See *Juniperus communis* L. var. *montana* Ait.

Juniperus communis **L. subsp. *nana* (Willd.) Syme** – See *Juniperus communis* L. var. *montana* Ait.

Juniperus communis **L. subsp. *saxitilis* (Pallas) E. Murr.** – See *Juniperus communis* L. var. *montana* Ait.

Juniperus communis **L. var. *alpina* Sm.** – See *Juniperus communis* L. var. *montana* Ait.

Juniperus communis **L. var. *depressa* Pursh** – Andorra juniper (112) (1937), Old-field common juniper [Oldfield common juniper] (155) (1942)

Juniperus communis L. var. *jackii* Rehd. – See *Juniperus communis* L. var. *montana* Ait.

Juniperus communis L. var. *montana* Ait. – Fairy circle [Fairy circles, Fairy-circle] (5) (1913), Juniper or Juniper tree [Juniper-tree] (131) (1899), Low juniper (5, 85) (1913–1932), Mountain juniper (136, 138) (1923–1930), Siberian juniper (153) (1913) NM

Juniperus communis L. var. *saxatilis* Pallas – See *Juniperus communis* L. var. *montana* Ait.

Juniperus communis montana – See *Juniperus communis* L. var. *montana* Ait.

Juniperus communis suecica – See *Juniperus communis* L.

Juniperus communis var. *hispanica* Endl. – See *Juniperus communis* L.

Juniperus communis var. *suecica* Aiton – See *Juniperus communis* L.

Juniperus deppeana Steud. – Alligator bark juniper (153) (1913), Alligator juniper (109, 122, 124, 138) (1923–1949), Juniper or Juniper tree [Juniper-tree] (149) (1904), Mountain cedar (122) (1937), Rough-bark juniper [Rough barked juniper] (124) (1937), Sweet-fruit juniper [Sweet-fruited juniper] (107) (1919)

Juniperus deppeana Steud. var. *pachyphloea* Martinez – See *Juniperus deppeana* Steud.

Juniperus erythrocarpa Cory – See *Juniperus coahuilensis* (Martinez) Gaussen ex R. P. Adams

Juniperus flaccida Schlecht. – Drooping juniper (122) (1937)

Juniperus horizontalis Moench – Andorra juniper (109) (1949), Bar Harbor juniper (112) (1937), Creeping juniper (3, 4, 50, 109, 130, 136, 138, 155) (1895–present), Creeping red cedar (131, 136) (1899–1930), Dwarf cedar (7, 35) (1806–1828), Dwarf red cedar (92) (1876), Ground cedar (108) (1878), Ground juniper (46) (1879), Prostrate savin juniper (136) (1930), Running cedar (108) (1878), Savin (73) (1892) Newfoundland, berries are called face-and-eye berries, Shrubby red cedar (5) (1913), Spreading red cedar (85) (1932), Trailing juniper (101) (1905), Waukegan juniper (109, 112, 136) (1930–1949)

Juniperus horizontalis Moench var. *douglasii* Hort. – See *Juniperus horizontalis* Moench

Juniperus horizontalis Moench var. *plumosa* Rehd. – See *Juniperus horizontalis* Moench

Juniperus L. – Cedar or Cedar tree (121, 148, 167) (1814–1970), Genevrier (French) (8) (1785), Juniper or Juniper tree [Juniper-tree] (1, 4, 8, 10, 38, 50, 109, 121, 122, 148, 155, 158, 167, 184) (1785–present) from Latin meaning "renewing its youth," Red cedar [Red-cedar, Redcedar] or Red cedar tree (148) (1939), Wath'-pith (Comanche Shoshonee) (132) (1855), Xaŋte (Lakota) (121) (1918–1970), Xoŋdse (Osage) (121) (1918–1970)

Juniperus lucayana auct. non Britt. – See *Juniperus virginiana* L. var. *silicicola* (Small) J. Silba

Juniperus lucayana Britt. – See *Juniperus barbadensis* var. *australis (Endl.) ined.*

Juniperus mexicana Spreng. – See *Juniperus deppeana* Steud.

Juniperus monosperma (Engelm.) Sarg. – Brown cedar (113) (1890), Cedar or Cedar tree (153) (1913), Cherry-stone juniper [Cherrystone juniper] (112, 138) (1923–1937), One-seed juniper [One-seeded juniper] (3, 4, 50, 112, 155) (1937–present), Sabina (153) (1913) NM, White juniper or White juniper tree (97) (1937) OK

Juniperus nana Willd. – See *Juniperus communis* L. var. *montana* Ait.

Juniperus occidentalis Hook. – California juniper (107) (1919), Cedar or Cedar tree (149) (1904), Sierra juniper (155) (1942), Western juniper (103, 161) (1857–1871)

Juniperus occidentalis Hook. var. *monosperma* Engelm. – See *Juniperus monosperma* (Engelm.) Sarg.

Juniperus pachyphloea Torr. – See *Juniperus deppeana* Steud.

Juniperus pinchotii Sudw. – Mountain cedar (124) (1937) TX, Pinchot's juniper [Pinchot juniper] (4, 50, 122) (1937–present), Redberry juniper [Redberry juniper] (3, 155) (1942–1977)

Juniperus prostrata N. – See *Juniperus horizontalis* Moench

Juniperus rigida Sieb. & Zucc. – See *Juniperus sabina* L.

Juniperus sabina L. – Common savin [Common sauin] (178) (1596), Juniper leaves (92) (1876), Juniper or Juniper tree [Juniper-tree] (78) (1898) Western US, Needle juniper (109, 138) (1923–1949), Sabina (55, 57, 59) (1911–1917), Sauyn (178, 179) (1526–1596), Savin (7, 10, 19, 41, 55, 58, 61, 92, 109, 138) (1770–1949), Savin bearing berries [Sauin bearing berries] (178) (1596), Savin juniper (112) (1937), Savine (57) (1917), Savin-tops (49) (1898), Tamarix savin (136) (1930)

Juniperus sabina L. var. *tamariscifolia* Ait. – See *Juniperus sabina* L. (introduced)

Juniperus sabina procumbens Pursh – See *Juniperus horizontalis* Moench

Juniperus sabina prostrata (Pers.) Loud. – See *Juniperus horizontalis* Moench

Juniperus sabina var. *procumbens* – See *Juniperus horizontalis* Moench

Juniperus sabina var. *tamariscifolia* Aiton – See *Juniperus sabina* L.

Juniperus scopulorum Sarg. – Cedro (153) (1913) NM, Colorado juniper (112, 136, 138) (1923–1937), Colorado red cedar (112) (1937) Neb, Platte cedar (157) (1929), Red cedar [Red-cedar, Redcedar] or Red cedar tree (101) (1905) MT, Rocky Mountain cedar (112) (1937), Rocky Mountain juniper [RockyMountain juniper] (4, 50, 109, 136, 155) (1930–present), Rocky Mountain red cedar (3) (1977), Silver cedar (136) (1930), Western red cedar (85, 97, 136, 157) (1930–1937)

Juniperus sibirica Burgsd. – See *Juniperus communis* L. var. *montana* Ait.

Juniperus silicicola (Small) Bailey – See *Juniperus virginiana* L. var. *silicicola* (Small) J. Silba

Juniperus virginiana L. – American savin (46) (1879), American savine (57) (1917), Carolina cedar (5, 92, 157, 158) (1876–1929), Cedar of North America (189) (1767), Cedar or Cedar tree (37, 39, 46, 65) (1830–1931), Cedar-apple [Cedar apple, Cedar-apples, Cedar apples] (92) (1876) insect galls, Cédre de Virginie (French) (6) (1892), Cédre rouge (French) (41) (1770), Cèdre rouge de Caroline (French) (8) (1785), Common red cedar (7, 112) (1828–1937), Cypress-leaf savin [Cypress-leav'd savin] (181) (~1678), Eastern cedar (149) (1904) NM, Eastern red cedar [Eastern redcedar] (50, 155) (1942–present), Genevrier de Virginie (French) (8) (1785), Genevrier des Andes (French) (20) (1857), Hante or h'ante sha (Dakota) (37) (1830) seeds were hante itika (cedar eggs), Juniper bush [Juniperbush] (5) (1913), Juniper or Juniper tree [Juniper-tree] (78, 106, 108) (1878–1930), Maazi (Omaha-Ponca) (37) (1830), Mishquawtuck (Narraganset) (46) (1879), Miskwa'wak (Chippewa, red wood) (40) (1928), Pencil cedar (6, 157, 158) (1892–1929), Pencilwood [Pencil wood, Pencil-wood] (5, 92, 157, 158) (1876–1929), Red Carolinian cedar (8) (1785), Red cedar [Red-cedar, Redcedar] or Red cedar tree (3, 4, 5, 6, 8, 9, 12, 14, 20, 19, 27, 35, 38, 40, 41, 46, 55, 57, 58, 72, 85, 92, 97, 106, 108, 109, 112, 113, 114, 130, 131, 135, 136, 138, 147, 157, 158, 164, 184, 187) (1770–1986), Red juniper (5, 6, 41, 157, 158) (1770–1929), Red savin (5, 6, 157, 158) (1892–1929), Rocky Mountain juniper [RockyMountain juniper] (20) (1857), Roth Ceder (German) (6) (1892), Savin (2, 5, 46, 106, 158) (1895–1930), Stinking cedar (20) (1857), Tawatsaako (Pawnee) (37) (1830), Virginia cedar [Virginian cedar] (14, 157, 158) (1882–1929), Virginia red cedar (122, 124) (1937), Virginische Ceder (German) (6) (1892), possibly Silver red cedar (136) (1930)

Juniperus virginiana L. subsp. *silicicola* (Small) E. Murr. – See *Juniperus virginiana* L. var. *silicicola* (Small) J. Silba

Juniperus virginiana L. var. *crebra* Fern. & Grisc. – See *Juniperus virginiana* L. var. *virginiana*

Juniperus virginiana L. var. *glauca* Carr – possibly *Juniperus virginiana* L.

Juniperus virginiana L. var. *silicicola* (Small) J. Silba – Barbados cedar [Barbadoes cedar] (20) (1857), Southern red cedar [Southern redcedar] (50) (present)

Juniperus virginiana L. var. *virginiana* – Eastern red cedar [Eastern redcedar] (50) (present), Northeastern red cedar [North Eastern redcedar] (155) (1942), Red cedar [Red-cedar, Redcedar] or Red cedar tree (1) (1932)

Juniperus vulgaris **Tragus ex Bubani** – See *Juniperus communis* L.

Jussiaea californica – See *Ludwigia peploides* (Kunth) Raven subsp. *peploides*

Jussiaea decurrens **(Walt.) DC.** – See *Ludwigia decurrens* Walt.

Jussiaea decurrens **DC.** – See *Ludwigia decurrens* Walt.

Jussiaea diffusa **Forskal** – See *Ludwigia peploides* (Kunth) Raven

Jussiaea **L.** – See *Ludwigia* L.

Jussiaea longifolia – See *Ludwigia longifolia* (DC.) H. Hara

Jussiaea repens **L.** – See *Ludwigia peploides* (Kunth) Raven subsp. *glabrescens* (Kuntze) Raven

Jussiaea suffruticosa **L.** – See *Ludwigia octovalvis* (Jacq.) Raven subsp. *octovalvis*

Justicia americana **(L.) Vahl** – American dianthera (3, 4) (1977–1986), American water-willow [American water willow] (50) (present), Dense-flower water-willow [Dense-flowered water willow, Dense-flowered waterwillow, Denseflowered water willow] (5, 72, 97, 122) (1907–1937), Dianthera (174, 177) (1753–1762), Water-willow [Water willow, Waterwillow, Water willoe] (4, 19, 106, 120, 124, 156) (1840–1986), Bastard hedgehysop (184) (1793)

Justicia brandegeeana **Wasshausen & L. B. Sm.** – Shrimp plant [Shrimp-plant] (109) (1949)

Justicia **L.** – Dianthera (155) (1942), Jacobinia (138) (1923), Water-willow [Water willow, Waterwillow, Water willoe] (1, 50, 158) (1900–present)

Justicia ovata **(Walt.) Lindau var.** *lanceolata* **(Chapman) R. W. Long** – Narrow-leaf water-willow [Narrowleaf water willow, Narrow-leaved water willow] (5, 97, 122) (1913–1937)

Justicia ovata **(Walt.) Lindau var.** *ovata* – Loose-flower water-willow [Looseflowered water willow] (5) (1913)

Juniperus virginiana
(J.J. Audubon, 1827)

K

Kalanchoe **Adans** – Kalanchoe (138) (1923)

Kalanchoe pinnata (**Lam.**) **Pers.** – Airplant [Air-plant] (109) (1949), Floppers (109) (1949), Leaf plant (19) (1840), Life plant [Life-plant] (73, 109) (1892–1949), Sproutleaf [Sprout leaf] (19) (1840)

Kalanchoë pinnata **Pers.** – See *Kalanchoe pinnata* (Lam.) Pers.

Kallstroemia grandiflora **Torr. ex Gray** (**possibly**) – Arizona poppy (106) (1930)

Kallstroemia grandifolia – possibly *Kallstroemia grandiflora* Torr. ex Gray

Kallstroemia hirsutissima **Vail ex Small** – Hirsute caltrop (5, 97) (1913–1937)

Kallstroemia intermedia **Rydb.** – See *Kallstroemia parviflora* J.B.S. Norton

Kallstroemia maxima (**L.**) **Hook. & Arn.** – Caltrop [Caltrops] (10) (1818), Greater caltrop (156) (1923)

Kallstroemia parviflora **J. B. S. Norton** – Greater caltrop (5, 97) (1913–1937), Warty caltrop (50) (present)

Kallstroemia **Scop.** – Caltrop [Caltrops] (50, 155, 158) (1900–present)

Kalmia angustifolia **L.** – Calf-kill [Calf kill] (5, 156) (1913–1923), Dwarf laurel (5, 19, 41, 71, 86, 156) (1770–1923), Dwarf sheep laurel (71) (1898), Ivy (75, 177) (1762–1894) VA, Ivy tree [Ivytree] (189) (1767), Kill-kid [Kill-kid] (5, 156) (1913–1923), Kill-lamb [Kill lamb] (92) (1876), Lambkill [Lamb-kill, Lamb kill] (2, 5, 71, 92, 106, 109, 138, 156) (1895–1949), Lamb's laurel [Lamb laurel] (71) (1898), Laurel [Laurell the small kind] (190) (~1759), Low laurel (71) (1898), Narrow-leaf kalmia [Narrow leaved kalmia] (8) (1785), Narrow-leaf laurel [Narrow-leaved laurel, Narrow leaved laurel] (71, 92, 156) (1876–1923), Poison-berry [Poyson berry] (46) (1671), Sheep laurel [Sheep-laurel] (2, 5, 7, 19, 71, 92, 106, 109) (1828–1949), Sheep-poison [Sheep poison] (5, 71, 73, 92, 156) (1876–1923) Northeastern US, Small laurel (71) (1898), Spoonwood ivy [Spoonwood-ivy] (5, 73, 156) (1892–1923) CT, Spurge-laurel [Spurge-lawrel] (46) (1671), Wicky (5, 71, 156) (1898–1923)

Kalmia carolina **Small.** – Karolina kalmia (138) (1923), Southern sheep laurel (5) (1913)

Kalmia ciliata **Bart.** – possibly *Kalmia hirsuta* Walt. (taxonomic status is unresolved (PL))

Kalmia glauca **Ait** – See *Kalmia polifolia* Wangenh.

Kalmia hirsuta **Walt.** – Hairy laurel (5) (1913), possibly Swine's-lettuce [Swine's lettuce] (167) (1814)

Kalmia **L.** – American laurel (1, 2, 8, 10) (1818–1932), Calico bush [Calico-bush] (10) (1818), Dwarf laurel (167) (1814), Ivy (167) (1814), Kalmia (8, 138) (1785–1923), Kalmia (French) (8) (1785), Laurel (106, 112, 184) (1793–1937), Mountain laurel [Mountain Lawrell] (2, 92, 156) (1876–1923), Small laurel (187) (1818), Swamp laurel (1) (1932)

Kalmia latifolia **L.** – American laurel (5, 6, 14, 71, 156, 187) (1818–1923), Big ivy (6, 7, 71) (1828–1898), Big-leaf ivy [Big leaved ivy] (5, 49, 92, 156) (1876–1923), Broad-leaf kalmia [Broad-leaved kalmia] (5, 7, 8, 20, 92) (1785–1913), Broad-leaf laurel [Broad-leaved laurel] (19, 71, 92) (1840–1898), Calico bush [Calico-bush] (2, 5, 6, 7, 49, 71, 92, 106, 109, 138, 156) (1892–1949), Calico tree (18, 187) (1805–1818), Clamoun (5, 156) (1913–1923) no longer in use by 1923, Common Laurel (177) (1762), Grande kalmie (French) (6, 7) (1828–1932), Gross Kalmie (German) (6) (1892), High laurel (71) (1898), Ivy (49, 71, 75, 77, 156, 177) (1762–1923), Ivy bush [Ivybush] (5, 71, 156, 187) (1818–1923), Ivy tree of Virginia [Ivy-tree of Virginia] (189) (1767), Ivywood [Ivy wood] (71) (1898), Joy (181) (~1678), Kalmia (52, 57, 71, 138) (1898–1923), Lambkill [Lamb-kill, Lamb kill] (6, 7, 49, 53) (1828–1932), Large laurel [Large laurell] (190) (~1759), Large mountain laurel (2) (1895), Laurel (7, 18,
46, 49, 53, 71, 187) (1649–1922), Mountain laurel [Mountain Lawrell] (5, 6, 7, 20, 41, 49, 52, 53, 57, 71, 106, 156) (1770–1930), Mountain-laurel (109, 138) (1923–1949), Poison ivy (71, 106, 156) (1898–1930) Southern states, Poison laurel (71) (1898), Rose laurel (6, 7, 71, 92) (1828–1898), Rose tree (46) (1609), Round-leaf laurel [Round-leaved laurel] (6) (1892), Sheep laurel [Sheep-laurel] (6, 49, 53, 61, 71) (1870–1922), Sheep-poison [Sheep poison] (7) (1828), Sheep's-bane [Sheepsbane] (77) (1898) Long Island NY, Small laurel (5, 71, 156) (1898–1923), Spoon tree (41) (1770), Spoonhunt [Spoon hunt] (5, 73, 92) (1876–1913) Mason NH, Spoonwood [Spoon wood [Spoon-wood] (5, 6, 7, 20, 49, 57, 71, 92, 106, 156) (1828–1930), Stud-flower Virginia cistus [Studded flowered Virginia cistus] (181) (~1678), Wick [Wicke, Wicks] (6, 7, 92) (1828–1892), Wicky (71) (1898), Wood laurel (5, 71, 156) (1898–1923)

Kalmia microphylla (**Hook.**) **Heller** – Alpine bog kalmia (138) (1923)

Kalmia polifolia microphylla – See *Kalmia microphylla* (Hook.) Heller

Kalmia polifolia **Wangenh.** – American laurel (1, 2, 8, 10) (1818–1932), Bog kalmia (109, 138) (1923–1949), Glaucous-leaf laurel [Glaucous-leaved laurel] (187) (1818), Pale laurel (5, 92, 156) (1876–1923), Swamp laurel (5, 7, 19, 92. 156) (1828–1923)

Kalmia polifolia **Wangenh. var.** *microphylla* (**Hook.**) **Hall** – See *Kalmia microphylla* (Hook.) Heller

Kalmiella hirsuta (**Walt.**) **Small.** – See *Kalmia hirsuta* Walt.

Kalopanax septemlobus (**Thunb.**) **Koidz.** – Painted maple (138, 165) (1768–1923)

Karwinskia humboldtiana (**J. A. Schultes**) **Zucc.** – Coyotillo (122, 124) (1937) TX

Keckiella antirrhinoides (**Benth.**) **Straw subsp.** *antirrhinoides* – Snapdragon penstemon (138) (1923)

Keckiella cordifolia (**Benth.**) **Straw** – Heart-leaf penstemon [Heartleaf penstemon] (138) (1923)

Kentrophyllum lanatum **DC** – See *Carthamus lanatus* L.

Kentrophyta montana **Nutt. ex Torr. & A. Gray** – See *Astragalus kentrophyta* Gray var. *kentrophyta*

Kentrophyta **Nutt.** – See *Astragalus* L. (all US species)

Kerria **DC.** – Kerria (138) (1923)

Kerria japonica (**L.**) **DC.** – Japanese globeflower [Japan globe-flower] (156) (1923), Jew's-mallow [Jew's mallow, Jews-mallow] (156) (1923), Kerria (138) (1923)

Kickxia elatine (**L.**) **Dumort.** – Cancerwort (5) (1913), Canker-root [Cankerroot, Canker root] (3, 4, 5) (1913–1986), Female fluellin (5) (1913), Round-leaf toad-flax [Round-leaved toad-flax] (5) (1913), Sharp-leaf cancerwort [Sharpleaf cancerwort] (50) (Present), Sharp-point fluellin [Sharppoint fluellin, Sharp-pointed fluellin] (5, 155) (1913–1942), Sharp-point toadflax [Sharp-pointed toad flax] (5) (1913)

Kigelia africana (**Lam.**) **Benth.** – Sausage tree [Sausage-tree] (109) (1949)

Kigelia pinnata **DC.** – See *Kigelia africana* (Lam.) Benth.

Killingia monocephala – possibly *Kyllinga brevifolia* Rottb. (current species depends on author)

Knautia arvensis (**L.**) **Duby** – Bluebuttons [Blue-buttons, Blue buttons] (3, 4, 5, 156, 158) (1900–1986), Bluecaps [Blue caps, Blue-caps] (4, 5, 156, 158) (1900–1986), Cancer-root [Cancer root] (156) (1923), Creeping snapdragon (19) (1840), Eastening-wort [Easteningwort] (158) (1900), Egyptian rose (5, 156, 158) (1900–1923), Elatine (177, 178) (1526–1762), Female fluellin (156) (1923), Field scabiosa (50) (present), Field scabious (4, 5, 92, 155, 156, 158) (1876–1986), Gipsy-rose [Gypsy rose] (5, 156, 158) (1900–1923), Pincushion [Pincushions, Pin-cushion, Pin cushions] (5, 156, 158) (1923), Scabish (156) (1923), Snapdragon [Snap dragon, Snap-dragon] (10, 50, 109, 138, 155, 156, 158, 184) (1793–present)

Kneiffia alleni (Britton) Small. – See *Oenothera fruticosa* L. subsp. *fruticosa*

Kneiffia fruticosa (L.) Raimann. – See *Oenothera fruticosa* L. subsp. *fruticosa*

Kneiffia glauca (Michx.) Spach. – See *Oenothera fruticosa* L. subsp. *glauca* (Michx.) Straley

Kneiffia linearis (Michx.) Spach. – See *Oenothera fruticosa* L. subsp. *fruticosa*

Kneiffia linifolia (Nutt.) Spach – See *Oenothera linifolia* Nutt.

Kneiffia longipedicellata Small – See *Oenothera fruticosa* L. subsp. *fruticosa*

Kneiffia pratensis Small. – See *Oenothera pilosella* Raf. subsp. *pilosella*

Kneiffia pumila (L.) Spach – See *Oenothera perennis* L.

Kneiffia Spach. – See *Oenothera* L. (all US species)

Knieffia spachiana (T. & G.) Small. – See *Oenothera spachiana* Torr. & Gray

Kniphofia alooides Moench – See *Kniphofia uvaria* (L.) Oken

Kniphofia Moench – Torch lily [Torchlily] (138) (1923)

Kniphofia uvaria (L.) Oken – Giant torchlily (138) (1923), Poker-plant (109) (1949), Red-hot-poker plant [Red hot poker plant] (92) (1876), Torch flower [Torch-flower] (109) (1949)

Kniphofia uvaria var. *nobilis* (Guillon) Baker – See *Kniphofia uvaria* (L.) Oken

Kniphofia uvarua nobilis – See *Kniphofia uvaria* (L.) Oken

Kobresia bellardi (all.) Degland – See *Kobresia myosuroides* (Vill.) Fiori

Kobresia bipartita (All.) Della Torre – See *Kobresia simpliciuscula* (Wahlenb.) Mackenzie

Kobresia myosuroides (Vill.) Fiori – Bellardi's bog-sedge [Bellardi bog sedge] (50) (present), Bellard's kobresia (5) (1913)

Kobresia simpliciuscula (Wahlenb.) Mackenzie – Arctic kobresia (5) (1913), Simple bog-sedge [Simple bog sedge] (50) (present)

Kochia Roth – Kochia (93) (1936), Molly (50) (present), Summer-cypress [Summercypress, Summer cypress] (138, 155) (1923–1942), White-sage [White sage] (158) (1900)

Kochia scoparia (L.) Roth – See *Kochia scoparia* (L.) Schrad.

Kochia scoparia (L.) Schrad. – Belvedere [Belvidere] (4, 5, 109, 138, 158, 180) (1633–1986), Belvedere cypress [Belvidere cypress] (156, 157) (1923–1929), Belvedere summer-cypress [Belvedere summercypress] (155) (1942), Broom cypress (5, 156, 157, 158) (1913–1929), Broom-like ragwort [Broomlike ragwort] (50) (present), Brown cypress (156, 157, 158) (1900–1929), Burningbush [Burning bush, Burning-bush] (93) (1936), Common summer-cypress (138) (1923), Firebush [Fire bush] (21) (1893), Kochia (3, 4, 5, 93, 97) (1913–1986), Mexican firebush [Mexican fire bush] (4) (1986), Mexican fireweed [Mexican-fireweed] (50, 80) (1913–present), Mock cypress (4) (1986), Osyris (174) (1753), Standing-cypress [Standing cypress] (156) (1923), Summer cypress (19) (1840), Summer-cypress [Summercypress, Summer cypress] (4, 5, 19, 85, 97, 109, 125, 156, 157, 158) (1840–1986), World's Fair plant (156) (1923)

Kochia trichophylla [Stapf] – See *Kochia scoparia* (L.) Schrad.

Koeberlinia spinosa Zucc. – Allthorn (122, 124) (1937)

Koeberlinia Zucc. – Junco (122, 153) (1913–1937) NM TX

Koeleria cristata (L.) Pers. – See *Koeleria macrantha* (Ledeb.) J.A. Schultes

Koeleria macrantha (Ledeb.) J.A. Schultes – Crested hair grass (5, 92) (1876–1913), Crested koeleria (66, 87) (1884–1903), June grass [June-grass, Junegrass] (3, 45, 75, 85, 87, 98, 115, 116, 122, 134, 140, 146, 152, 185) (1884–1977), Koeleria (56, 72) (1901–1907), Koeler's grass (5, 116, 119, 163) (1852–1958), Prairie grass [Prairie-grass] (11, 144) (1888–1899), Prairie June grass (134) (1932), Prairie June grass [Prairie June-grass, Prairie Junegrass] (5, 50, 111, 119, 129, 140, 155) (1894–present)

Koeleria pennsylvanica DC. – See *Sphenopholis nitida* (Biehler) Scribn.

Koeleria Pers. – June grass [June-grass, Junegrass] (1, 50, 93, 152) (1912–present), Koeleria (155) (1942)

Koeleria truncata – See *Sphenopholis obtusata* (Michx.) Scribn.

Koellia albescens (Torr. & Gray) Kuntze – See *Pycnanthemum albescens* Torr. & Gray ex Gray

Koellia aristata (Michx.) Kuntze – See *Pycnanthemum setosum* Nutt.

Koellia clinopodioides (Torr. & Gray) Kuntze – See *Pycnanthemum clinopodioides* Torr. & Gray

Koellia flexuosa (Walt.) MacM. – See *Pycnanthemum flexuosum* (Walt.) Britton, Sterns & Poggenb.

Koellia hyssopifolia (Benth.) Britton – See *Pycnanthemum flexuosum* (Walt.) Britton, Sterns & Poggenb.

Koellia incana (L.) Kuntze – See *Pycnanthemum incanum* (L.) Michx. var. *incanum*

Koellia lanceolata (Pursh) Kuntze – See *Pycnanthemum virginianum* (L.) T. Dur. & B. D. Jackson ex B. L. Robins. & Fern.

Koellia Moench – See *Pycnanthemum* Michx.

Koellia montana (Michx.) Kuntze – See *Pycnanthemum montanum* Michx.

Koellia mutica (Michx.) Britton – See *Pycnanthemum muticum* (Michx.) Pers.

Koellia pilosa (Nutt.) Britton – See *Pycnanthemum verticillatum* (Michx.) Pers. var. *pilosum* (Nutt.) Cooperrider

Koellia pycnanthemoides (Leavenw.) Kuntze – See *Pycnanthemum pycnanthemoides* (Leavenworth) Fern. var. *pycnanthemoides*

Koellia verticillata (Michx.) Kuntze – See *Pycnanthemum verticillatum* (Michx.) Pers. var. *verticillatum*

Koellia virginiana (L.) MacM. – See *Pycnanthemum virginianum* (L.) T. Dur. & B. D. Jackson ex B. L. Robins. & Fern.

Koelreuteria Laxm. – Goldenrain tree [Goldenrain-tree, Golden-rain tree] (109, 138) (1923–1949)

Koelreuteria paniculata Laxm. – Goldenrain tree [Goldenrain-tree, Golden-rain tree] (112, 138) (1923–1937)

Koenigia islandica L. – Macounastrum (5) (1913)

Kolkwitzia amabilis Graebn. – Beauty-bush [Beauty bush] (109, 112) (1937–1949)

Koniga Adans. – See *Lobularia* Desv.

Koniga maritima (L.) R. Br. – See *Lobularia maritima* (L.) Desv.

Korycarpus arundinaceus Zea. – See *Diarrhena americana* Beauv.

Korycarpus diandrus (Michx.) Kuntze. – See *Diarrhena americana* Beauv.

Kosteletskya virginica Gray. – See *Kosteletzkya virginica* (L.) K. Presl ex Gray

Kosteletzkya virginica (L.) Gray – See *Kosteletzkya virginica* (L.) K. Presl ex Gray

Kosteletzkya virginica (L.) K. Presl ex Gray – Virginia kosteletzkya [Virginian kosteletzkya] (2, 5) (1895–1913)

Krameria (Loefl.) L. – See *Krameria* L.

Krameria L. – Krameria (155, 158) (1900–1942), Ratany (4, 155) (1942–1986), Rhatany (13) (1849)

Krameria lanceolata Torr. – Linear-leaf krameria [Linear-leaved krameria] (5, 97, 158) (1900–1937), Ratany (3, 4) (1977–1986), Trailing krameria (50, 155) (1942–present)

Krameria Loefl. – See *Krameria* L.

Krameria secundiflora DC. – See *Krameria lanceolata* Torr.

Krascheninnikovia Guldenstaedt – Eurotia (158) (1900), White-sage [White sage] (1) (1932), Winterfat [Winter fat, Winter-fat] (1, 50, 93, 155) (1932–present)

Krascheninnikovia lanata (Pursh) A.D.J. Meeuse & Smit – American eurotia (5, 93) (1913–1936), Common winterfat (155) (1942), Romeria (5) (1913), Sweet-sage [Sweet sage] (118) (1898) TX, White-sage [White sage] (4, 5, 85, 93, 108, 131, 153, 157, 158) (1899–1986), Winterfat [Winter fat, Winter-fat] (3, 5, 50, 93, 118, 122, 124, 141, 146, 153, 157, 158) (1898–present)

Kraunhia frutescens (L.) Greene – See *Wisteria frutescens* (L.) Poir.

Kraunhia macrostachys (Torr. & Gray) Small. – See *Wisteria frutescens* (L.) Poir.

Krigia amplexicaulis (Michx.) Nutt. – See *Krigia biflora* (Walt.) Blake

Krigia biflora (Walt.) Blake – Cynthia (156) (1923), False dandelion (75, 156) (1894–1923), Stem-clasping swine's-succory [Stem-clasping swines'-succory] (187) (1818), Two-flower dwarf-dandelion [Twoflower dwarfdandelion] (50) (present), Virginia goatbeard [Virginia's goat's-beard] (156) (1923), Yellow goat's-beard [Yellow goats'-beard, Yellow goats-beard, Yellow goat's beard] (177) (1762)

Krigia biflora (Walt.) Blake var. *biflora* – Cynthia (5) (1913), False dandelion (5) (1913), Two-flower dwarf-dandelion [twoflower dwarfdandelion] (50) (present), Virginia goatbeard [Virginia's goat's-beard] (5, 97) (1913–1937)

Krigia caespitosa (Raf.) Chambers – Common dwarf-dandelion [Common dwarf dandelion] (3) (1977), Common serinia (155) (1942), Serinia (5, 97) (1913–1937), Weedy dwarf-dandelion [Weedy dwarf-dandelion] (50) (present)

Krigia dandelion (L.) Nutt. – Dandelion cynthia (86) (1878), Dwarf goat's-beard [Dwarf goatsbeard] (5, 156) (1913–1923), Dwarf-dandelion [Dwarfdandelion, Dwarf dandelion] (5, 65, 72, 97, 156) (1907–1937), Potato dandelion (3) (1977), Potato dwarf-dandelion [Potato dwarfdandelion] (50) (present)

Krigia montana (Michx.) Nutt. – Mountain-dandelion (138) (1923)

Krigia occidentalis Nutt. – Western dwarf-dandelion [Western dwarf dandelion, Western dwarfdandelion] (3, 5, 50, 97, 155) (1913–present)

Krigia oppositifolia Raf. – See *Krigia caespitosa* (Raf.) Chambers

Krigia Schreb. – Dwarf-dandelion [Dwarfdandelion, Dwarf dandelion] (2, 50, 156) (1895–present), Serinia (155, 158) (1900–1942)

Krigia virginia Willd. – possibly *Krigia virginica* (L.) Willd.

Krigia virginica (L.) Willd. – Carolina dwarf dandelion (5, 97, 122) (1913–1937), Cynthia (72) (1907), Dwarf-dandelion [Dwarfdandelion, Dwarf dandelion] (19, 138, 156) (1840–1923), Mouse-ear minor (46) (1671), Swine's-succory [Swine-succory, Swine's succory] (184) (1793), possibly Krigia (156) (1923)

Krigia virginica Michx. – See *Krigia virginica* (L.) Willd.

Krugiodendron ferreum (Vahl) Urb. – Black ironwood (15) (1895)

Krynitzkia Fisch & Mey. – See *Cryptantha* Lehm. ex G. Don

Kuhnia chlorolepis Woot. & Standl. – See *Brickellia eupatorioides* (L.) Shinners var. *chlorolepis* (Woot. & Standl.) B. L. Turner

Kuhnia eupatorioides L. – See *Brickellia eupatorioides* (L.) Shinners var. *eupatorioides*

Kuhnia eupatorioides L. var. *corymbulosa* Torr. & Gray – See *Brickellia eupatorioides* (L.) Shinners var. *corymbulosa* (Torr. & Gray) Shinners

Kuhnia eupatorioides L. var. *texana* Gray & Englem. – See *Brickellia eupatorioides* (L.) Shinners var. *texana* (Shinners) Shinners

Kuhnia glutinosa Ell. – See *Brickellia eupatorioides* (L.) Shinners var. *eupatorioides*

Kuhnia L. – See *Brickellia* Ell.

Kuhniastera candida (Willd.) OK. – possibly *Dalea candida* Michx. ex Willd. var. *candida* (taxonomic status is unresolved (PL))

Kuhnistera compacta (Spreng.) Kuntze. – See *Dalea compacta* Spreng.

Kuhnistera foliosa (A. Gray) Kuntze – See *Dalea foliosa* (Gray) Barneby

Kuhnistera pinnati – See *Dalea pinnata* (J. F. Gmel.) Barneby var. *pinnata*

Kuhnistera purpurea (Vent.) MacM. – See *Dalea purpurea* Vent.

Kuhnistera tenuifolia (A. Gray) Kuntze – See *Dalea tenuifolia* (Gray) Shinners

Kuhnistera villosa (Nutt.) Kuntze. – See *Dalea villosa* (Nutt.) Spreng

Kummerowia Schindl. – Kummerowia (50) (present)

Kummerowia stipulacea (Maxim.) Makino – Korean clover (3, 50) (1977–present)

Kummerowia stipulacea (Maxim.) Makino – Korean lespedeza (4, 155) (1942–1986)

Kummerowia striata (Thunb.) Schindl. – Common lespedeza (4, 155) (1942–1986), Hoopkoop plant (5, 158) (1900–1913), Japanese clover [Japan clover] (3, 5, 45, 50, 66, 87, 97, 109, 158) (1884–present), Japanese lespedeza (4) (1986), Wild clover (5, 158) (1900–1913)

Kyllinga brevifolia Rottb. – False bog rush (19) (1840), possibly Bog rush [Bogrush] (92) (1876)

Kyllinga monocephala – See *Kyllinga brevifolia* Rottb.

Kyllinga pumila Michx. – Low kyllinga (5) (1913), Low spikesedge (50) (present), Round-head sedge [Roundhead sedge] (66) (1903), possibly Sweet grass [Sweet-grass, Sweetgrass] (7) (1828)

231

L

Lablab purpureus **(L.) Sweet** – Bonavist (109, 183) (~1756–1949), Bonavista bean (107) (1919), Hyacinth-bean [Hyacinth bean] (109, 138, 156) (1923–1949), Jack bean [Jack-bean] (156) (1923), Lablab (110) (1886), Oh-no-more lablab [Oh no more lab lab] (183) (~1756), Wall (110) (1886), Wild cowhage (19) (1840)

Lablab vulgaris **[Savi]** – See *Lablab purpureus* (L.) Sweet

Laburnum anagyroides **Medik.** – Bean tree [Beantree, Bean-tree (109) (1949), Goldenchain [Golden-chain, Golden chain] (92, 109, 138) (1876–1949), Laburnum or Laburnum tree (92) (1876)

Laburnum **Medik.** – Laburnum or Laburnum tree (138) (1923) from ancient latin name

Laburnum vulgare **J. Presl** – See *Laburnum anagyroides* Medik.

Lachnanthes caroliana **(Lam.) Dandy** – Bloodroot [Blood-root, Blood root] (86) (1878), Bloodwort [Blood wort, Blood-wort] (86) (1878), Carolina redroot [Carolina red-root, Carolina red root] (5, 50, 156) (1913–present), Dyer's dilatris [Dyers' dilatris] (6) (1892), Indian redroot [Indian red-root, Indian red root] (5, 92, 156) (1876–1923), Paint root [Paint-root] (5, 156) (1913–1923), Redroot [Red-root, Red root] (5, 6, 49, 86, 106, 156, 187) (1818–1930), Spirit-weed [Spirit weed] (5, 6, 49, 92, 156) (1876–1923), Wool flower (86) (1878)

Lachnanthes **Ell.** – Redroot [Red-root, Red root] (2, 10) (1818–1895) root used for dye

Lachnanthes tinctoria **(J. F. Gmel.) Ell.** – See *Lachnanthes caroliana* (Lam.) Dandy

Lachnanthes tinctoria **Ell.** – See *Lachnanthes caroliana* (Lam.) Dandy

Lachnocaulon anceps **(Walt.) Morong** – White-head bogbutton [Whitehead bogbutton] (50) (present), possibly Hairy pipewort (5, 156) (1913–1923)

Lacinaria acidota **(Engelm. & Gray) Kuntze** – See *Liatris acidota* Engelm. & Gray

Lacinaria cylindracea **(Michx.) Kuntze** – See *Liatris cylindracea* Michx

Lacinaria elegans **(Walt.) Kuntze** – See *Liatris elegans* (Walt.) Michx. var. *elegans*

Lacinaria graminifolia **(Walt.) Kuntze** – See *Liatris pilosa* (Aiton) Willd. var. *pilosa*

Lacinaria **Hill.** – See *Liatris* Gaertn. ex Schreber.

Lacinaria pilosa **(Aiton) Heller** – See *Liatris pilosa* (Aiton) Willd. var. *pilosa*

Lacinaria punctata **(Hook.) Kuntze** – See *Liatris punctata* Hook. var. *punctata*

Lacinaria pycnostachya **(Michx.) Kuntze** – See *Liatris pycnostachya* Michx. var. *pycnostachya*

Lacinaria scariosa **(L.) Hill** – See *Liatris scariosa* (L.) Willd. var. *scariosa*

Lacinaria smallii **Britton** – See *Liatris virgata* Nutt.

Lacinaria spicata **(L.) Kuntze.** – See *Liatris spicata* (L.) Willd. var. *spicata*

Lacinaria squarrosa **(L.) Hill** – See *Liatris squarrosa* (L.) Michx. var. *squarrosa*

Laciniaria spicata **Willd.** – See *Liatris spicata* (L.) Willd.

Lactuca **(Tourn.) L.** – See *Lactuca* L.

Lactuca biennis **(Moench) Fern.** – Blue lettuce (155) (1942), Blue wood-lettuce [Blue wood lettuce] (3, 4) (1977–1986), Milkweed [Milk weed [Milk-weed]] (5, 76) (1896–1913), Tall blue lettuce (5, 50, 62, 72, 131) (1899–present)

Lactuca campestris **Greene** – See *Lactuca ludoviciana* (Nutt.) Riddell

Lactuca canadensis **L.** – American lettuce (157) (1929), American wild lettuce (158) (1900), Arrow-leaf lettuce [Arrow-leaved lettuce] (5, 62, 72, 97, 158) (1899–1937), Butterweed [Butter weed, Butter-weed] (5, 76, 156, 157, 158) (1896–1929) Sulphur Grove OH, Canadian lettuce [Canada lettuce] (50, 80, 155, 157) (1900–present), Canadian wild lettuce [Canada wild lettuce] (158) (1900), Canadische Lattich (German) (6) (1892), Devil's weed [Devil's-weed] (5, 75, 156, 158) (1900–1923) WV, Devil's-ironweed [Devil's iron weed, Devil's ironweed] (5, 75, 156, 157, 158) (1894–1929) WV, Fall lettuce (156) (1923), Fireweed [Fire weed, Fire-weed] (5, 6, 156, 158, 187) (1818–1923), Horseweed [Horse-weed, Horse weed] (5, 75, 156) (1894–1923) WV, Laitue du Canada (French) (6) (1892), Odjici'gomīn (Chippewa) (40) (1928), Snakebite [Snake bite, Snake-bite] (157, 158) (1900–1929), Snakeweed [Snake-weed, Snake weed, Snake Weede] (158) (1900), Steele's wild lettuce (5) (1913), Tall lettuce (5, 62, 131, 156, 157, 158) (1899–1929), Tall wild lettuce (93) (1936), Trumpet [Trumpets] (5, 156, 158) (1900–1923), Trumpet milkweed [Trumpet milk-weed] (5, 156, 157, 158) (1900–1929), Trumpet-weed [Trumpet weed, Trumpetweed] (5, 6, 156, 158) (1923), Wild lettuce [Wild-lettuce, Wylde letuse] (3, 4, 5, 6, 19, 40, 47, 62, 63, 72, 76, 80, 82, 85, 92, 95, 97, 122, 145, 156, 157, 158, 187) (1818–1986), Wild opium (5, 156, 157, 158) (1900–1929), possibly Buttonweed [Button-weed, Button weed] (29) (1869), possibly Long-leaf wild lettuce [Long-leaved wild-lettuce] (187) (1818), possibly Milkweed [Milk weed [Milk-weed] (29) (1869), possibly Richweed [Rich-weed, Rich weed] (29) (1869)

Lactuca elongata **Michx.** – possibly *Lactuca canadensis* L. (taxonomic status is unresolved (PL))

Lactuca floridana **(L.) Gaertn.** – Blue lettuce (82) (1930), Blue-flower sowthistle [Blue-flowered sow-thistle] (187) (1818), False lettuce (5, 85) (1913–1932), Florida lettuce (3, 4, 5, 72, 97) (1907–1986), Gall-of-the-earth [Gall of the earth] (187) (1818), Lettuce [Lettice, Lettise, Letuse] (106) (1930), Tall wood lettuce (122, 124) (1937), Wild blue lettuce (106) (1930), Woodland lettuce (50) (present)

Lactuca floridana **(L.) Gaertn. var.** *floridana* – Woodland lettuce (50) (present)

Lactuca floridana **(L.) Gaertn. var.** *villosa* **(Jacq.) Cronq.** – Blue lettuce (82, 85) (1930–1932), False lettuce (5) (1913), Hairy-vein blue lettuce [Hairy-veined blue lettuce] (5, 72, 93) (1907–1936), Woodland lettuce (50) (present)

Lactuca hirsuta **Muhl. ex Nutt.** – Hairy wood lettuce [Hairy wood-lettuce] (5, 72, 97, 122) (1907–1937), Red wood-lettuce (5) (1913)

Lactuca integrifolia **Bigel** – See *Lactuca canadensis* L.

Lactuca **L.** – Lettuce [Lettice, Lettise, Letuse] (1, 4, 7, 10, 50, 63, 82, 93, 138, 155, 156, 158, 184) (1793–present), Milkweed [Milk weed [Milk-weed] (73, 79) (1891–1892) NB

Lactuca leucophaea **Gray** – See *Lactuca biennis* (Moench) Fern.

Lactuca ludoviciana **(Nutt.) Riddell** – Biannual lettuce (50) (present), Prairie lettuce (97) (1937), Western lettuce (5, 72, 93, 97, 122, 131) (1899–1937), Western wild lettuce (3, 4, 95) (1911–1986)

Lactuca oblongifolia **Nutt.** – See *Lactuca tatarica* (L.) C. A. Mey. var. *pulchella* (Pursh) Breitung

Lactuca pulcella **(Pursh) DC.** – See *Lactuca tatarica* (L.) C. A. Mey. var. *pulchella* (Pursh) Breitung

Lactuca pulchella **(Pursh) DC.** – See *Lactuca tatarica* (L.) C. A. Mey. var. *pulchella* (Pursh) Breitung

Lactuca sagittifolia **Ell.** – See *Lactuca canadensis* L.

Lactuca saligna **L.** – Willow lettuce (5) (1913), Willow-leaf lettuce [Willowleaf lettuce, Willow-leaved lettuce] (3, 4, 50) (1977–present)

Lactuca sativa **convar.** *asparagina* **L. H. Bailey ex Holub** – See *Lactuca sativa* L.

Lactuca sativa **L.** – Alface (Spanish) (180) (1633), Asparagus lettuce

(109) (1949), Cabbage lettuce (180) (1633), Common lettuce (92) (1876), Crompled lettuce (180) (1633), Curled lettuce (180) (1633), Entire-leaf prickly lettuce [Entire-leaved prickly lettuce] (82) (1930), Garden lettuce (50, 92, 138, 180) (1633–present), Head lettuce (109) (1949), Lactucarium (92) (1876), Laictue (French) (180) (1633), Latouwe (Low Dutch) (180) (1633), Lattich (Germanes) (180) (1633), Lechuga (Spanish) (180) (1633), Lettuce [Lettice, Lettise, Letuse] (19, 109, 110, 178, 179, 180) (1526–1949), Loved lettuce [Loued lettuce] (180) (1633), Lumbard lettuce (180) (1633), Prickly lettuce (80) (1913), Red lettuce (180) (1633), Salad (92) (1876), Savoy lettuce [Savuoy lettuce] (180) (1633), Sleepwort (92) (1876), Tridax (Greek) (110) (1886)

Lactuca sativa L. var. *asparagina* Bailey – See *Lactuca sativa* L.
Lactuca sativa var. *capitata* L. – See *Lactuca sativa* L.
Lactuca scariola L. – See *Lactuca serriola* L.
Lactuca scariola L. var. *integrata* Gren. & Godr. – See *Lactuca sativa* L.
Lactuca scariola L. var. *sativa* (Moris) – See *Lactuca sativa* L.
Lactuca serriola L. – Compass plant [Compass-plant, Compassplant] (70, 156, 158) (1895–1923), English thistle (70) (1895), Horse thistle [Horse-thistle] (156, 158) (1900–1923), Lettuce [Lettice, Lettise, Letuse] (46) (1671), Milk thistle [Milk-thistle] (62, 70, 156) (1895–1923), Prickly lettuce (3, 4, 50, 56, 62, 63, 70, 72, 80, 82, 98, 107, 131, 145, 155, 156, 158) (1895–present), Scaryole (179) (1526), Wild lettuce [Wild-lettuce, Wylde letuse] (156, 158, 179) (1526–1923)
Lactuca spicata (Lam.) A.S. Hitchc. – See *Lactuca biennis* (Moench) Fern.
Lactuca steelei Britton – See *Lactuca canadensis* L.
Lactuca tatarica (L.) C.A. Mey. – Blue lettuce (50) (present)
Lactuca tatarica (L.) C.A. Mey. var. *pulchella* (Pursh) Breitung – Azuŋtka jazaŋpi onpijapi (Lakota, kidney pain treatment) (121) (1918?–1970?), Blue lettuce (3, 4, 50, 80, 95, 148, 156) (1911–present), Blue-flower lettuce [Blue flowered lettuce] (80) (1913), Chicory lettuce (155) (1942), Large blue lettuce (122) (1937), Large-flower blue lettuce [Large-flowered blue lettuce] (5, 72, 93, 97, 131) (1899–1937), Wild blue lettuce (127) (1933), Wild lettuce [Wild-lettuce, Wylde letuse] (114, 121, 145, 148) (1894–1970)
Lactuca villosa Jacq. – See *Lactuca floridana* (L.) Gaertn. var. *villosa* (Jacq.) Cronq.
Lactuca virosa L. – Acid lettuce (60) (1902), Acrid lettuce (92, 157, 158) (1876–1929), Bitter lettuce (155) (1942), German lactucarium (92) (1876), Gift-Lattich (German) (158) (1900), Green endive (157, 158) (1900–1929), Horse thistle [Horse-thistle] (5) (1913), Laitue vireuse (French) (158) (1900), Lettuce [Lettice, Lettise, Letuse] (55) (1911), Lettuce opium (53, 57) (1917–1922) dried milk, Milk thistle [Milk-thistle] (5) (1913), Prickly letuce (5, 92, 93, 97) (1876–1937), Sleeping wild lettuce [Sleeping wilde Lettise] (178) (1526), Stink-Lattich (158) (1900), Strong-scented lettuce (49, 62, 92, 157, 158) (1876–1929), Wild lettuce [Wild-lettuce, Wylde letuse] (5, 85, 93, 157) (1899–1936)
Laelia Adans. – Laelia (138) (1923)
Lagenaria leucantha Rusby – See *Lagenaria siceraria* (Molina) Standl.
Lagenaria Ser. – Bottle gourd (109) (1949), Gourd [Gourde, Gowrde] (138) (1923), Mock orange [Mock-orange, Mockorange] (73) (1892) Northern OH
Lagenaria siceraria (Molina) Standl. – Bottle gourd (10, 50, 107, 121) (1818–present), Calabash (7, 10, 19, 110) (1818–1886), Calabash gourd (92, 138, 155) (1876–1942), Common bottle gourd (92) (1876), Dipper gourd (37) (1919), Dolma (Turkey) (107) (1919), Gourd [Gourde, Gowrde] (7, 19, 92, 110, 182) (1791–1886), Ini-iže (Osage) (121) (1918?–1970?), Peh'e (Omaha-Ponca) (37) (1919), Taquera (110) (1658), Trumpet gourd (107) (1919), Wagmuha (Lakota) (121) (1918?–1970?), Wakmu (Dakota) (37) (1919), Wamnuha (Dakota) (37) (1919), White-flower gourd [White-flowered gourd] (109) (1949)

Lagenaria siceraria Standl. – See *Lagenaria siceraria* (Molina) Standl.
Lagenaria vulgaris Ser. – See *Lagenaria siceraria* (Molina) Standl.
Lagerstroemia indica L. – Common crapemyrtle (138) (1923), Crapemyrtle [Crapemyrtle, Crape myrtle] (109, 122, 124) (1937–1949)
Lagerstroemia L. – Crape-myrtle [Crapemyrtle, Crape myrtle] (138) (1923), Hare's-foot [Hares foot, Hares foote, Hairs foot] (190) (~1759)
Lagerstroemia speciosa (L.) Pers. – Queen crape-myrtle [Queen crape-myrtle] (109, 138) (1923–1949)
Laguncularia racemosa – See *Laguncularia racemosa* (L.) Gaertn. f.
Laguncularia racemosa (L.) Gaertn. f. – Buttonwood [Button wood, Button-wood] (106) (1930), Manglier à grappes (French) (20) (1857), White mangrove (20, 106) (1857–1930)
Lagurus ovatus L. – Foxtail [Fox tail, Fox-tail, Fox tails, Foxtaile, Fox-taile] (178, 180) (1596–1633), Hare-tail grass [Hare's-tail grass, Hares' tail grass, Hare's-tail-grass] (45, 92, 109) (1896–1949)
Lamarckia aurea (L.) Moench – Goldentop [Golden-top, Golden top] (94, 109, 122, 163) (1852–1949), Goldentop grass (138) (1923)
Lamiastrum galeobdolon (L.) Ehrend. & Polatschek – Weasel-snout (92) (1876), Yellow archangel [Yellow archangell] (92, 178) (1526–1876)
Laminaria digitata (Hudson) J. V. Lamouroux – Red-ware (107) (1919), Sea tangles (57) (1917), Sea-girdles [Sea girdles] (57, 107) (1917–1919), Sea-wand (107) (1919), Sea-ware (107) (1919), Tangle (107) (1919)
Laminaria longicruris [Bachelot de la Pylaie] – See *Saccharina longicruris* (Bachelot de la Pylaie) Kuntze
Laminaria saccharina (Linnaeus) J. V. Lamouroux – Devil's-apron [Devil's apron] (92) (1876), Venus'-apron-strings [Venus's apron strings] (73) (1892)
Lamium (Tourn.) L. – See *Lamium* L.
Lamium album L. – Archangel (107) (1919), Bee nettle [Bee-nettle] (5, 156) (1913–1923), Blind nettle [Blind-nettle] (5, 92, 156) (1876–1923), Day nettle (5) (1913), Deadnettle [Dead-nettle, Dead nettle] (6, 57, 107) (1892–1919), Dog-nettle [Dog-nettle] (156) (1923), Dumb-nettle [Dumb nettle] (5, 107, 156) (1913–1923), L'Ortie Blanche (French) (6) (1892), Snake flower [Snakeflower, Snake-flower] (5, 156) (1913–1923) no longer in use by 1923, Suck-bottle [Suck bottle] (5, 156) (1913–1923) no longer in use by 1923, Weissbienensang (German) (6) (1892), Weisse Taubnessel (German) (6) (1892), White archangel [White archangell] (5, 6, 92, 156, 178) (1526–1923) no longer in use by 1923, White dead nettle (white dead-nettle) (5, 156) (1913–1923), White lamium (106) (1930), White nettle (92) (1876)
Lamium amplexicaule L. – Deadnettle [Dead-nettle, Dead nettle] (19, 62, 63, 85, 92, 122, 124, 187) (1818–1937), Dumb-nettle [Dumb nettle] (92) (1876), Great henbit (187) (1818), Greater henbit (5, 158) (1900–1913), Henbit [Hen-bit, Hen bit] (3, 4, 5, 19, 62, 72, 75, 92, 93, 97, 122, 124, 156, 158, 178) (1596–1986), Henbit archangel (187) (1818), Henbit deadnettle [Henbit dead-nettle, Henbit dead nettle] (5, 50, 155, 50, 156, 158) (1900–present), Stem-clasping sr-changel (187) (1818)
Lamium L. – Archangel (10, 184) (1793–1818), Archaungell (179) (1526), Blind nettle [Blynde nettell] (179) (1526), Deadnettle [Dead-nettle, Dead nettle, Deed nettel] (1, 4, 50, 7, 10, 93, 106, 109, 138, 155, 156, 158, 167, 179) (1526–present), Henbit [hen-bit, Hen bit] (1, 7, 93) (1828–1936)
Lamium maculatum L. – Spotted dead-nettle [Spotted deadnettle, Spotted dead nettle] (5, 138) (1913–1923), Spotted lamium (106) (1930), Variegated dead-nettle [Variegated dead nettle] (5) (1913)
Lamium purpureum L. – Day nettle (5, 158) (1900–1913), Deaf-nettle [Deaf nettle] (5, 158) (1900–1913), Dog-nettle [Dog-nettle] (156, 158) (1900–1923), French nettle (5, 158) (1900–1913), Purple deadnettle [Purple deadnettle] (3, 4, 50, 138, 155) (1932–present), Rabbit-meat [Rabbit meat] (5, 158) (1900–1913), Red archangel (5, 158) (1900–1913), Red dead-nettle [Red dead nettle] (5, 97, 106, 107, 156, 158) (1900–1937), Sweet archangel (5, 158) (1900–1913)

Lamium purpureum L. var. *purpureum* – Purple dead-nettle [Purple deadnettle] (50) (present)

Lamprocapnos spectabilis (L.) Fukuhara – Bleeding-heart [Bleeding heart, Bleeding hearts, Bleedingheart] (76, 92, 109, 138) (1876–1949), Dielytra (92) (1876), Diethra (73) (1892) MA, Eardrop [Ear drop, Ear-drops] (76) (1896) Sulphur Grove OH, Lady-in-a-boat [Lady in a boat] (74) (1893) Fanconia NH, Lady's-eardrops [Lady's ear drop [Lady's ear drops, Ladies'-eardrop] (74) (1893) Concord MA, Love-lies-bleeding [Love lies bleeding] (76) (1896) Northern OH

Lantana camara L. – Bahama tea (7) (1828), Cailleau (92) (1876), Common lantana (138) (1923), Sage tree [Sagetree] (92) (1876), Yellow lantana (138) (1923)

Lantana camara L. var. *flava* (Medik.) Moldenke – See *Lantana camara* L.

Lantana flava – See *Lantana camara* L.

Lantana involucrata L. – Sage tree [Sagetree] (77) (1898) Florida Keys, White-flower lantana [White flowered lantana] (124) (1937)

Lantana involucrata var. *floridana* Chapm. – See *Lantana involucrata* L.

Lantana L. – Blueberry [Blueberries, Blue berries, Blue berry] (7) (1828), Cailleau (Louisiana) (7) (1828), Lantana (138) (1923), Sage tree [Sagetree] (7) (1828), Tea plant [Tea-plant] (75) (1894) LA

Lantana montevidensis (Spreng.) Briq. – Trailing lantana (109) (1949), Weeping lantana (109, 138) (1923–1949)

Lantana sellowiana [Spreng.] – See *Lantana montevidensis* (Spreng.) Briq.

Laportea canadensis (L.) Gaudisch – See *Laportea canadensis* (L.) Weddell

Laportea canadensis (L.) Weddell – Albany hemp (5, 19, 92, 156, 157, 158) (1840–1929), Canadian nettle [Canada nettle] (5, 19, 92, 93, 156, 157, 158) (1840–1936), Canadian woodnettle (50, 155) (1942–present), False nettle [Falsenettle] (40) (1928), Kentucky hemp (14) (1882), Star nettle (62) (1912) IN, Woodland nettle (46) (1879), Wood-nettle [Wood nettle, Woodnettle] (3, 4, 5, 63, 72, 78, 85, 92, 93, 95, 97, 131, 156, 157, 158) (1876–1986), Ze'sûb (Chippewa) (40) (1928)

Laportea Gaud. – Laportea (50) (present), Wood-nettle [Wood nettle, Woodnettle] (1, 155, 156, 158) (1900–1942)

Lappula (Rivar.) Moench – See *Lappula* Moench

Lappula americana (Gray) Rydb. – See *Hackelia deflexa* (Wahlenb.) Opiz var. *americana* (Gray) Fern. & I. M. Johnston

Lappula cenchrusoides A. Nels. – Great Plains stickseed (50) (present)

Lappula deflexa (Wahlenb.) Garcke p.p. – See *Hackelia deflexa* (Wahlenb.) Opiz var. *americana* (Gray) Fern. & I.M. Johnston

Lappula echinata Gilib. – See *Lappula squarrosa* (Retz.) Dumort.

Lappula floribunda (Lehm.) Greene – See *Hackelia floribunda* (Lehm.) I.M. Johnston

Lappula Gilib. – See *Lappula* Moench

Lappula lappula (L.) Karst. – See *Lappula squarrosa* (Retz.) Dumort.

Lappula Moench – Beggarticks [Beggar ticks, Beggar's ticks, Beggars' ticks, Beggars-ticks, Beggar-ticks] (1, 93) (1932–1936), Burseed [Bur-seed] (1, 93) (1932–1936), Stickseed [Stick seed, Stick-seed] (1, 4, 50, 93, 155, 156, 158) (1895–present), Sticktight [Stick-tight, Sticktights, Stick-tights, Stick tights] (1, 93) (1932–1936)

Lappula myosotis var. Wolf – See *Lappula squarrosa* (Retz.) Dumort.

Lappula occidentalis (S. Wats.) Greene – Flat-spine stickseed [Flatspine stickseed] (50) (present), Hairy sticktight (85) (1932), Western stickseed (97) (1937)

Lappula occidentalis (S. Wats.) Greene var. *cupulata* (Gray) Higgins – Cup-seed stickseed [Cupseed stickseed] (3, 4) (1977–1986), Flatspine stickseed [Flatspine stickseed] (50) (present), Hairy stickseed [Hairy stick seed] (72, 93, 97, 122) (1907–1937)

Lappula occidentalis (S. Wats.) Greene var. *occidentalis* – Flat-spine stickseed [Flatspine stickseed] (50) (present), Small beggar's-lice (145) (1897), Sticktight [Stick-tight, Sticktights, Stick-tights, Stick tights] (75) (1894), Western stickseed (131) (1899), possibly Low stickseed (3) (1977)

Lappula redowskii (Hornem.) Greene – See *Lappula occidentalis* (S. Wats.) Greene var. *occidentalis* (authors not (Hornem.) Greene (IT))

Lappula redowskii occidentalis (S. Wats.) Rydb. – See *Lappula occidentalis* (S. Wats.) Greene var. *occidentalis*

Lappula redowskii subsp. *occidentalis* (S. Watson) Á. Löve & D. Löve – See *Lappula occidentalis* (S. Wats.) Greene var. *occidentalis*

Lappula squarrosa (Retz.) Dumort. – Blue bur (62) (1912) IN, Blue stickseed (3, 4) (1977–1986), Burseed [Bur-seed] (5, 62, 72, 80, 93, 131, 156, 158) (1899–1923), European stickseed (5, 50, 93, 155, 156, 158) (1900–present), Small sheep-bur (5, 156, 158) (1900–1923), Stickseed [Stick seed, Stick-seed] (47, 80) (1852–1913), Sticktight [Stick-tight, Sticktights, Stick-tights, Stick tights] (5, 75, 85, 156, 158) (1894–1932)

Lappula texana (Scheele) Britton – See *Lappula occidentalis* (S. Wats.) Greene var. *cupulata* (Gray) Higgins

Lappula virginiana (L.) Greene – See *Hackelia virginiana* (L.) I.M. Johnston

Lapsana communis L. – Ballogan (5) (1913), Bolgan leaves (5) (1913), Common nipplewort (50, 155) (1942–present), Dock cress [Docke Cresses, Dock Cresses] (5, 178, 180) (1526–1913), Lampsana (178) (1526), Nipplewort (4, 5, 92, 107, 156) (1876–1986), Succory (5) (1913), Succory dock cress [Succory dock-cress] (92, 156) (1898–1923), possibly Napium (180) (1633), possibly Papillaris (Prussia) (180) (1633)

Lapsana L. – Nipplewort (156) (1923)

Larix (Tourn.) Adans. – See *Larix* Mill

Larix americana L. – See *Larix laricina* (Du Roi) Koch.

Larix cedrus Mill. – See *Cedrus libani* A.Rich.

Larix decidua Mill. – Common larch (19) (1840), European larch (28, 107, 109, 112, 138) (1850–1949), False manna (92) (1876), possibly Larch or Larch tree (8) (1785), possibly Méleze (French) (8) (1785)

Larix europaea DC. – See *Larix decidua* Mill.

Larix kaempferi (Lam.) Carr. – Japanese larch (109, 138) (1923–1949)

Larix laricina (Du Roi) Koch. – American black larch (58) (1869), American larch (1, 5, 10, 20, 41, 46, 49, 57, 61, 92, 109, 138) (1770–1949), Black larch (5, 7, 19, 49, 92) (1828–1913), Cypress or Cypress tree [Cypress-tree, Cypresse tree] (75, 78) (1894–1898), Epinette rouge (French Canada) (20, 41, 168) (1770–1857), Hackmack (5) (1913), Hackmatack [Hack-matack, Hacmatack] (5, 19, 46, 58, 92, 109) (1840–1949), Hackmetack (49, 92) (1876–1879), Juniper cypress (5) (1913), Juniper or Juniper tree [Juniper-tree] (73, 75, 78, 79) (1891–1898), Lereckhout (46) (1617), Mû'ckigwa'tĭg (Chippewa, swamp tree) (40) (1928), Red larch (5, 7, 19) (1828–1913), Tamarack [Tamarac] (1, 5, 19, 29, 40, 49, 50, 57, 58, 92, 109, 135) (1840–present), Tamarisk [Tamarix] (19, 43) (1820–1840), possibly Black American larch-tree (8) (1785), possibly Méleze blanc (French) (8) (1785), possibly Méleze noir (French) (8) (1785), possibly Red American larch-tree (8) (1785), possibly White American larch tree [White American larch-tree] (8) (1785)

Larix larix (L.) Karst. – See *Larix decidua* Mill.

Larix leptolepis Gord. – See *Larix kaempferi* (Lam.) Carr.

Larix microcarpa – See *Larix laricina* (Du Roi) Koch.

Larix Mill – Hackmatack [Hack-matack, Hacmatack] (7) (1828), Larch or Larch tree (1, 7, 50, 109, 138) (1828–present) from ancient Latin name, Tamarisk [Tamarix] (1, 7) (1828–1932)

Larix occidentalis Nutt. – Larch or Larch tree (35) (1806), Sapin d'Occident (French) (20) (1857), Tamerack (35) (1806), Western larch (20, 50, 138, 161) (1857–present)

Larix pendula – See *Larix laricina* (Du Roi) Koch.

Larrea glutinosa Engelm. – See *Larrea tridentata* (Sessé & Moc. ex DC.) Coville var. *tridentata*

Larrea mexicana Moricand. – See *Larrea tridentata* (Sessé & Moc. ex DC.) Coville

Larrea Ort. – Creosote plant (13) (1849), Gobernadora (Spanish) (13) (1849) Mexico, Guamis (Spanish) (13) (1849) Mexico

Larrea tridentata (DC.) Coville – See *Larrea tridentata* (Sessé & Moc. ex DC.) Coville

Larrea tridentata (Sessé & Moc. ex DC.) Coville – Creosote bush [Creasote bush] (14, 124) (1882–1937), Creosote plant (15, 107, 147) (1856–1919), Gobernadora (15) (1895)

Larrea tridentata (Sessé & Moc. ex DC.) Coville var. *tridentata* – Creosote bush (106, 149, 153) (1904–1930), Greasewood [Grease-wood] (106, 153) (1913–1930), Hediodilla (149) (1904) NM, Hediodillo (106) (1930), Hediondillo (Spanish, stinking) (153) (1913) NM

Lasiacis divaricata (L.) A. S. Hitchc. – Cane-like paṅicum (87) (1884), Small cane (94) (1901)

Lasiagrostis – See *Achnatherum* Beauv.

Lasthenia Cass. – Goldfields (138) (1923)

Lasthenia gracilis (DC.) Greene – Slender goldfields (138) (1923)

Lastraea Filix-mas Presl. (Lastrea) – See *Dryopteris filix-mas* (L.) Schott

Lastrea phegopteris (L.) Bory – See *Phegopteris connectilis* (Michx.) Watt

Lathyrus (Tourn.) L. – See *Lathyrus* L.

Lathyrus brachycalyx Rydb. subsp. *Brachycalyx* – Hinbthi-si-tanga (Omaha-Ponca, large-seeded bean) (37) (1919), Showy vetchling (5, 93, 97, 131) (1899–1937), Wild pea (85) (1932) SD, Wild sweet pea (37) (1919)

Lathyrus cicera L. – Cicera (110) (1886), Ervilia (110) (1886), Flat-pod pea [Flat-podded pea] (110) (1886), Lesser chickpea [Lesser chick-pea] (107) (1919), Mochi (Italian) (110) (1886), Vetch (107) (1919)

Lathyrus incanus (Sm. & Rydb.) Rydb. – See *Lathyrus polymorphus* Nutt. subsp. *incanus* (Sm. & Rydb.) A.S. Hitchc.

Lathyrus japonicus Willd. var. *maritimus* (L.) Kartesz & Gandhi – Beach pea (2, 5, 19, 41, 46, 47, 92, 109, 156) (1770–1949), Feetches (46) (1617), Heath pea [Heath-pea] (107, 156) (1919–1923), Sea pea (5) (1913), Seaside everlasting pea (5) (1913), Wild pea (46) (1617)

Lathyrus L. – Bitter vetch (10) (1818), Everlasting pea [Euerlasting Pease] (10, 82, 156) (1818–1930), Marsh pea (158) (1900), Pea [Peas, Pease] (50, 138) (1923–present), Pea vine [Peavine, Peavine] (155) (1942), Vetchling (4, 10, 93, 109, 158) (1818–1986), Wild sweet pea (93) (1936)

Lathyrus latifolius L. – Everlasting pea [Euerlasting Pease] (3, 4, 5, 19, 46, 109, 156, 158) (1879–1986), Perennial pea (50, 138, 156) (1923–present), Perennial peavine (155) (1942), Perennial sweet pea [Perennial sweetpea] (4) (1986), Pois eternel (French) (46) (1879)

Lathyrus maritimus (L.) Bigelow – See *Lathyrus japonicus* Willd. var. *maritimus* (L.) Kartesz & Gandhi

Lathyrus maritimus Bigelow – See *Lathyrus japonicus* Willd. var. *maritimus* (L.) Kartesz & Gandhi

Lathyrus myrtifolius Muhl. ex Willd. – See *Lathyrus palustris* L.

Lathyrus nissolia L. – Catanance (178) (1526), Enchanting vetch [Inchaunting vetch] (178) (1526), Grass pea (50) (present)

Lathyrus ochroleucus Hook. – Yellow vetchling (3, 4) (1977–1986), Cream pea (50) (present), Cream peavine (155) (1942), Cream-colored pea (85) (1932), Cream-colored vetchling (5, 72, 93, 131) (1899–1936), Pale vetchling (5) (1913)

Lathyrus odorata – See *Lathyrus odoratus* L.

Lathyrus odoratus L. – Chick vetch (92) (1876), Posy peas (74) (1893) Franconia NH, Sweet pea [Sweetpea, Sweet peas] (19, 46, 82, 92, 109, 114, 138) (1840–1949)

Lathyrus ornatus Nutt. – See *Lathyrus brachycalyx* Rydb. subsp. *brachycalyx*.

Lathyrus palustris L. – Marsh pea (19, 50, 158) (1840–present), Marsh peavine (155) (1942), Marsh vetchling (3, 4, 5, 72, 131, 156, 158) (1899–1986), Myrtle-leaf marsh pea [Myrtle-leaved marsh pea] (5, 158) (1900–1913), Myrtle-leaf pea vine [Myrtle-leaved pea-vine] (187) (1818), Pogotč-minjimin (Chippewa [wild pea) (105) (1932), Wild pea (5, 76, 82, 105, 156, 158) (1896–1930)

Lathyrus polymorphus Nutt. – Hoary peavine (3, 98) (1926–1977), Hoary vetchling (4) (1986), Many-stem pea [Manystem pea] (50) (present), Sweet pea [Sweetpea, Sweet peas] (38) (1820)

Lathyrus polymorphus Nutt. subsp. *incanus* (Sm. & Rydb.) A. S. Hitchc – Hoary pea [Hoarypea, hoary-pea] (50) (present), Hoary peavine (155) (1942)

Lathyrus polymorphus Nutt. subsp. *polymorphus* – Everlasting pea [Euerlasting Pease] (5, 158) (1900–1913), Prairie vetchling (5, 72, 156, 158) (1900–1923)

Lathyrus pratensis L. – Angle-berries [Angleberries] (5, 156) (1913–1923), Craw peas [Craw-peas] (5) (1913), Crow peas [Crow-peas] (156) (1923), Lady's-fingers [Lady's fingers, Ladies'-fingers, Ladies' fingers] (5, 156) (1913–1923), Meadow pea (5, 82) (1913–1930), Mouse pea (5, 156) (1913–1923), Tare-vetch [Tare vetch] (5) (1913), Tom-thumb [Tom thumb] (5, 156) (1913–1923), Yellow tarfitch (5) (1913), Yellow vetchling (5, 156) (1913–1923)

Lathyrus pusillus Ell. – Low peavine (3, 155) (1942–1977), Low vetchling (5, 97) (1913–1937), Singletary vetchling (4) (1986), Tiny pea (50) (present)

Lathyrus sativus L. – Chickling vetch (107, 110) (1886–1919), Grass pea (68, 109) (1913–1949)

Lathyrus splendens Kellogg – Pride-of-California [Pride of California] (76, 109) (1896–1949)

Lathyrus sylvestris L. – Everlasting pea [Euerlasting Pease] (178) (1526), Flat pea (68, 109, 118) (1898–1949)

Lathyrus tingitanus L. – Tangier pea (109) (1949)

Lathyrus tuberosus L. – Dutch mice (107) (1919), Eearthnut pea (107) (1919), Groundnut peavine (155) (1942), Tuberous sweet pea [Tuberous sweetpea] (50) (present)

Lathyrus venosus Muhl. – Bushy vetch (3, 127, 156) (1923–1977), Bushy vetchling (4) (1986), Mĭs'nĭsĭno'wûck (Chippewa, island medicine) (40) (1928), Veiny pea (5, 50, 72, 82, 131) (1899–present), Veiny peavine (155) (1942), Wild pea (40, 85, 131) (1899–1932)

Lathyrus venosus Muhl. ex Willd. var. *intonsus* Butters & St. John – See *Lathyrus venosus* Muhl.

Laurencia obtusa (Hudson) Lamouroux – Corsican moss (107) (1919)

Laurencia obtusa Berk. – See *Laurencia obtusa* (Hudson) Lamouroux

Laurencia pinnatifida (Hudson) J. V. Lamouroux – See *Osmundea pinnatifida* (Hudson) Stackhouse

Laurocerasus – See *Prunus* L. (all US species)

Laurocerasus caroliniana [(Mill.) M. Roem.] – See *Prunus caroliniana* (P. Mill.) Aiton

Laurocerasus officinalis – See *Prunus laurocerasus* L.

Laurus aestivalis L. – See *Litsea aestivalis* (L.) Fern.

Laurus albida N. – See *Sassafras albidum* (Nutt.) Nees

Laurus benzoin L. – See *Lindera benzoin* Blume.

Laurus borbonia L. – See *Persea borbonia* (L.) Spreng.

Laurus camphora L. – See *Cinnamomum camphora* (L.) J. Presl

Laurus caroliniensis Michx. – possibly *Persea borbonia* (L.) Spreng.

Laurus catesbiana Michx. – See *Nectandra coriacea* (Sw.) Griseb.

Laurus cinnamomum Loureiro – See *Cinnamomum verum* J. Presl

Laurus geniculata Walt. – See *Litsea aestivalis* (L.) Fern.

Laurus L. – Bay [Baye] or Bay tree [Bay-tree] (7, 8, 184) (1785–1828), Bayes (179) (1526), Laurel (7, 109, 138) (1828–1949), Laurier (French) (8) (1785), Sassafras [Sassaphras] or Sassafras tree [Sassafras-tree] (10, 167, 190) (~1759–1818), Spicewood [Spicewood, Spice wood] (10) (1818), Sweet bay [Sweet-bay, Sweetbay] or Sweet bay tree [Sweet bay trees] (109) (1949)

Laurus nobilis L. – Bay [Baye] or Bay tree [Bay-tree] (46, 107, 92) (1671–19191), Bay laurel (55) (1911), Grecian laurel (138) (1923), Indian bay (92) (1876), Laurel (57, 107, 179) (1526–1919), Laurel leaves (92) (1876), Laurel-berry [Laurel berries] (92) (1876), Sweet bay [Sweet-bay, Sweetbay] or Sweet bay tree [Sweet bay trees] (57, 92, 107) (1876–1919), Wild allspice [Wild all Spice] (190) (~1759)

Laurus persea L. – See *Persea americana* Mill.

Laurus regalis – See *Umbellularia californica* (Hook. & Arn.) Nutt. var. *californica*

Laurus sassafras **L.** – See *Sassafras albidum* (Nutt.) Nees

Laurus winterana **L.** – See *Canella winteriana* (L.) Gaertn.

Lavandula angustifolia **Mill.** – Aspic (92) (1876), Garden lavender (57) (1917), Lavender (19, 53, 61, 107) (1840–1922), Lavender-cotton [Lavendercotton, Lavender cotton] (46) (1671), Male lavender (92) (1876), Naked Sticadoue (178) (1526), Spike lavender (92, 138) (1876–1923), True lavender (138) (1923)

Lavandula **L.** – Lavender [Lauendre] (82, 106, 109, 138, 179) (1526–1949) from Latin lavo "to wash" referring to the use of lavender in the bath

Lavandula officinalis **[Chaix]** – See *Lavandula angustifolia* Mill.

Lavandula spica **Cavar.** – See *Lavandula angustifolia* Mill.

Lavandula spica **E.** – See *Lavandula angustifolia* Mill.

Lavandula stoechas **L.** – Arabian lavender (92) (1876), Arabian sticadoue (178) (1526), Stickadore (92) (1876)

Lavandula vera **DC.** – See *Lavandula angustifolia* Mill.

Lavatera arborea **L.** – Tree mallow [Tree mallows, Tree mallowes] (19, 92) (1840–1876)

Lavatera arborea **L.** – Velvet tree-mallow [Velvet treemallow] (138) (1923)

Lavatera assurgentiflora **Kellogg** – California tree-mallow [California treemallow] (138) (1923), Tree mallow [Tree mallows, Tree mallowes] (76) (1896) Santa Barbara CA

Lavatera **L.** – Tree mallow [Treemallow, Tree mallow, Tree mallows, Tree mallowes] (82, 109, 138) (1923–1949)

Lavatera olbia **L.** – French mallow (178) (1526)

Lavatera thuringiaca **L.** – Gay mallows (19) (1840)

Lavatera trimestris **L.** – Herb treemallow (138) (1923)

Lavauxia brachycarpa **(Gray) Britton** – See *Oenothera brachycarpa* Gray

Lavauxia **Spach.** – See *Oenothera* L.

Lavauxia triloba **(Nutt.) Spach** – See *Oenothera triloba* Nutt.

Lavauxia watsonii **(Britton) Small** – See *Oenothera triloba* Nutt.

Lavendula spica **(Lavandula)** – See *Lavandula angustifolia* Mill.

Lawsonia alba **Lam.** – See *Lawsonia inermis* L.

Lawsonia inermis **L.** – Alcamet (179) (1526), Alcanna (92) (1876), Gopher wood [Gopher-wood] (92) (1876), Hanna (Persian) (110) (1886), Henna (109, 110, 138) (1886–1949), Henne (92) (1876), Kinna (Modern Greek) (110) (1886), Mignonetter tree [Mignonetter-tree] (109) (1949), Sakachera (110) (1886)

Lawsonia **L.** – Henna (138) (1923)

Layia platyglossa **(Fisch. & C. A. Mey.) Gray** – Tidy-tips [Tidytip] (76) (1896)

Leavenworthia aurea **Torr.** – Golden gladecress (50) (present)

Leavenworthia michauxii **Torr.** – See *Leavenworthia uniflora* (Michx.) Britt.

Leavenworthia **Torr.** – Gladecress (50) (present)

Leavenworthia torulosa **Gray** – Necklace leavenworthia (5) (1913)

Leavenworthia uniflora **(Michx.) Britt.** – Michaux's leavenworthia (5, 97) (1913–1937)

Lecanora affinis **Eversm.** – Crab's-eye [Crab's eye] (107) (1919)

Lecanora affinis **L.** – See *Lecanora affinis* Eversm.

Lecanora esculenta **(Pall.) Eversm.** – Cup moss (107) (1919)

Lecanora esculenta **L.** – See *Lecanora esculenta* (Pall.) Eversm.

Lecanora tartarea **(L.) Ach.** – Cudbear (92) (1876), Tartarian moss (92) (1876)

Lechea **(Kalm.) L.** – See *Lechea* L.

Lechea intermedia **Leggett** – Large-pod pinweed [Largepod pinweed, Largepodded pin-weed] (5, 50) (1913–present), Pinweed [Pin-weed, Pin weed] (3, 4) (1977–1986)

Lechea intermedia **Leggett ex Britt. var. *juniperina* (Bickn.) B.L. Robins.** – Maine pinweed [Maine pin-weed] (5) (1913)

Lechea juniperina **Bicknell** – See *Lechea intermedia* Leggett ex Britt. var. *juniperina* (Bickn.) B.L. Robins.

Lechea **Kalm** – See *Lechea* L.

Lechea **L.** – Pinweed [Pin-weed, Pin weed] (1, 4, 13, 15, 50, 93, 155, 156, 158) (1849–present)

Lechea leggettii **Brit. & Holl.** – See *Lechea pulchella* Raf. var. *pulchella*

Lechea major **L.** – See *Helianthemum canadense* (L.) Michx.

Lechea major **Michx.** – See *Helianthemum canadense* (L.) Michx.

Lechea maritima **Leggett ex B.S.P.** – Beach pinweed [Beach pin-weed] (5) (1913)

Lechea minor **L.** – Lesser lechea (187) (1818), Pinweed [Pin-weed, Pin weed] (47) (1852), Smaller pinweed (2) (1895), Thyme-leaf pinweed [Thyme-leaved pin-weed, Thyme-leaved pinweed] (5, 72, 156) (1907–1923)

Lechea mucronata **Raf.** – Greater pinweed [Greater pin-weed] (157, 158) (1900–1929), Hairy pinweed [Hairy pin-weed] (4, 5, 50, 72, 93, 97, 155, 157, 158) (1900–present), Large pinweed [Large pin-weed] (5) (1913)

Lechea pulchella **Raf. var. *pulchella*** – Leggett's pinweed [Leggett pinweed] (5) (1913)

Lechea stricta **Leggett ex Britton** – Bushy pinweed [Bushy pin-weed] (5, 93) (1913–1936), Pinweed [Pin-weed, Pin weed] (3, 4) (1977–1986), Prairie pinweed [Prairie pin-weed] (5, 50, 72, 93) (1907–present)

Lechea tenuifolia **Michx.** – Narrow-leaf pinweed [Narrowleaf pinweed, Narrow-leaved pin-weed] (5, 50, 72, 93, 97) (1907–present), Pinweed [Pin-weed, Pin weed] (3, 4, 85) (1932–1986)

Lechea villosa **Ell.** – See *Lechea mucronata* Raf.

Lechia tenuifolia **Michx.** – See *Lechea tenuifolia* Michx.

Lecticula resupinata **(B. D. Greene) Barnhart** – See *Utricularia resupinata* B. D. Greene ex Bigelow

Ledum decumbens **(Aiton) Lodd.** – See *Ledum palustre* L. subsp. *decumbens* (Aiton) Hultén

Ledum glandulosum **Nutt.** – Labrador tea [Labrador-tea] (148) (1939)

Ledum groenlandica **Oeder** – See *Ledum groenlandicum* Oeder

Ledum groenlandicum **Oeder** – Bog Labrador tea (50) (present), Labrador tea [Labrador-tea] (5, 19, 40, 49, 57, 92, 104, 106, 107, 109, 156) (1840–1949) leaves used as tea substitute during the Revolutionary War, Muckig'obûg (Chippewa, swamp leaf) (40) (1928), True Labrador tea [True Labrador-tea] (138) (1923), possibly Gowiddie (77) (1898) Newfoundland, possibly James' tea (49) (1898), possibly Labrador (75, 77) (1894–1898) ME, possibly Labrador tea plant (43) (1820), possibly Ledum (57) (1917), possibly Marsh tea (47) (1852)

Ledum **L.** – Labrador tea [Labrador-tea] (1, 2, 7, 10, 138, 156) (1818–1932), Ledum (French) (8) (1785), Marsh cistus (8) (1785), Marsh tea (7) (1828), Marsh-rosemary [Marsh rose-mary, Marsh rosemary] (167) (1814), Wild rosemary (8) (1785)

Ledum latifolium **[Jacq.]** – possibly *Ledum groenlandicum* Oeder

Ledum latifolium **Aiton** – possibly *Ledum groenlandicum* Oeder

Ledum palustre **L.** – Crystal tea [Crystal-tea] (138) (1923), Labrador tea [Labrador-tea] (14) (1882), Marsh tea (19, 92, 104) (1840–1896), Marsh-rosemary [Marsh rose-mary, Marsh rosemary] (107) (1919), Wild rosemary (92) (1876)

Ledum palustre **L. subsp. *decumbens* (Aiton) Hultén** – Narrow-leaf Labrador tea [Narrow-leaved Labrador tea] (5) (1913)

Ledum palustre **L. var. *latifolium* (Jacq.) Michx.** – See *Ledum groenlandicum* Oeder

Leersia hexandra **Sw.** – Zacate (Philippines) (88) (1885)

Leersia lenticularis **Michx.** – Catchfly grass [Catch-fly-grass, Catchfly-grass, Catchflygrass, Catch-fly grass] (3, 5, 19, 45, 56, 66, 94, 122, 155, 163) (1840–1977), White grass [White-grass, Whitegrass] (88) (1885)

Leersia monandra **Sw.** – Bunch cut grass [Bunch cutgrass] (50) (present), Slender cut grass [Slender cut-grass] (94) (1901), Slender cut grass [Slender cut-grass] (94) (1901)

Leersia oryzoides **(L.) Sw.** – Cut grass [Cut-grass, Cutgrass] (19, 66, 81, 80, 187) (1818–1951), False grass (5) (1913), False rice (66, 87, 88, 90) (1885–1903), Prickle grass [Prickle-grass, Pricklegrass] (90)

(1885) ME, Rice cut grass [Rice cutgrass, Rice-cut-grass, Rice cut-grass] (3, 5, 45, 50, 56, 90, 92, 94, 99, 111, 119, 122, 129, 131, 155, 163) (1852–present), Rice grass [Ricegrass] (85) (1932), Rice's-cousin [Rice's cousin] (5, 45) (1896–1913), Sickle-grass [Sickle grass] (187) (1818), White grass [White-grass, Whitegrass] (66, 87, 90, 92) (1876–1903)

Leersia Sw. – Cut grass [Cut-grass, Cutgrass] (50, 155) (1942–present), Rice cut grass [Rice cutgrass, Rice-cut-grass, Rice cut-grass] (1, 93) (1932–1936), Rice grass [Ricegrass] (10) (1818), White grass [White-grass, Whitegrass] (66) (1903)

Leersia virginica Willd. – Cut grass [Cut-grass, Cutgrass] (88) (1885), Rice grass [Ricegrass] (19) (1840), Small-flower white grass [Small-flowered white grass] (66, 87) (1884–1903), Virginia cut grass [Virginia cut-grass, Virginian cut grass] (66, 111, 129, 163) (1852–1915), White grass [White-grass, Whitegrass] (3, 5, 19, 50, 94, 99, 119, 122, 131, 163) (1840–present), White rice (45) (1896)

Legousia perfoliata (L.) Britton – See *Triodanis perfoliata* (L.) Nieuwl. var. *perfoliata*

Legousia speculum-veneris (L.) Fisch. ex A. DC. – Corn spurry [Corn spurrey, Corn-spurrey] (1) (1932), possibly Venus'-looking-glass [Venus' looking glass, Venus looking glass, Venus's looking glass, Venus lookingglass, Venuslookingglass] (19, 92, 107, 109, 138) (1840–1949)

Leguminosae – See Fabaceae

Leiophyllum buxifolium (Berg.) Ell. – Allegheny sandmyrtle (138) (1923), Box sandmyrtle (138) (1923), Sand myrtle (19, 156) (1840–1923), Sand-myrtle [Sandmyrtle] (92) (1876), Sleek-leaf [Sleekleaf, Sleek leaf] (19, 92, 156) (1840–1923)

Leiophyllum buxifolium (Berg.) Ell. var. *prostratum* (Loud.) Gray – See *Leiophyllum buxifolium* (Berg.) Ell.

Leiophyllum buxifolium Ell. – See *Leiophyllum buxifolium* (Berg.) Ell.

Leiophyllum buxifolium prostratum – See *Leiophyllum buxifolium* (Berg.) Ell.

Leiophyllum Hedw. f. – Sand myrtle (2, 156) (1895–1942), Sand-myrtle [Sandmyrtle] (109, 138) (1923–1949)

Leitneria floridana Chapman – Cork wood [Cork-wood, Corkwood] (5, 122, 156) (1913–1937), Leitneria (5) (1913)

Lemanea Bory de Saint-Vincent – Small River Stone Horsetail (181) (~1678)

Lemna aequinoctialis Welw. – Lesser duckweed (50) (present)

Lemna cyclostasa (Ell.) Chev. – See *Lemna minor* L.

Lemna gibba L. – Gibbous duckweed (93) (1936), Swollen duckweed (50, 155) (1942–present)

Lemna – Duckmeat [Duck-meat, Duck-meat, Ducke meate, Duck's meat, Ducks' meat, Duck'smeat, Duck's-meat] (122, 158, 167, 184) (1793–1937), Duckweed (1, 10, 50, 93, 155, 158) (1818–present), Mardling (158) (1900), Toad-spit [Toadspit, Toad spit] (158) (1900), Water-lentil [Water-lentils, Water lentils] (158) (1900)

Lemna minima Philipi. – See *Lemna minor* L.

Lemna minor L. – Common duckweed (50, 155) (1942–present), Duckmeat [Duck-meat, Duck-meat, Ducke meate, Duck's meat, Ducks' meat, Duck'smeat, Duck's-meat] (5, 92, 178, 179) (1526–1913), Duckweed (3, 92) (1876–1977), Frog's-foot [Frogges Fote] (178, 179) (1526–1596), Green duckmeat [Green duck meat] (19) (1840), Grenes (178, 179) (1526–1596), Least duckweed (5, 155) (1913–1942), Lentils of the water [Lentylles of the water] (178, 179) (1526–1596), Lesser duckweed (5, 72, 93, 97) (1907–1937), Mardling (5) (1913), Toad-spit [Toadspit, Toad spit] (5) (1913), Valdivia duckweed (5, 97) (1913–1937), Water-lentil [Water-lentils, Water lentils] (5) (1913)

Lemna minuta Kunth – Least duckweed (50) (present)

Lemna obscura (Austin) Daubs – Little duckweed (50) (present)

Lemna perpusilla Torr. – Minute duckweed (3, 5, 50, 93, 97, 155) (1911–present)

Lemna polyrrhiza [L.] – See *Spirodela polyrhiza* (L.) Schleid.

Lemna trisulca L. – Duckmeat [Duck-meat, Duck-meat, Ducke meate, Duck's meat, Ducks' meat, Duck'smeat, Duck's-meat] (19,

156) (1840–1923), Duckweed (85) (1932), Ivy-leaf duckweed [Ivy-leaved duckweed] (5, 72, 93, 156) (1907–1936), Star duckweed (3, 5, 50, 155, 156) (1911–present)

Lemna turionifera Landolt – Turion duckweed (50) (present)

Lemna valdiviana Phil. – Valdivia duckweed (50) (present)

Lenophyllum texanum (J. G. Sm.) Rose – Texas sedum (122) (1937) TX

Lens culinaris Medik. – Adaschum or adaschim (Hebrew) (110) (1886), Fakos or fakai (Greek) (110) (1886), Lenszic (Lithuanian) (110) (1886), Lentil [Lentils, Lentyle] (92, 107, 109, 110, 178, 179) (1526–1949) from ancient Latin 'lens' for the shape of seed, Tillseed [Tilseed] (92) (1876)

Lens esculenta Moench – See *Lens culinaris* Medik.

Lentibularia vulgaris var. *americana* Nieuwl. & Lunell, *Utricularia vulgaris* L. – See *Utricularia macrorhiza* Le Conte

Leonotis (Pers.) Aiton f. – Lion's-ear [Lions' ear, Lion ears, Lion's ear, Lions-ear] (109, 138) (1923–1949)

Leonotis leonurus (L.) Aiton f. – Lion's-ear [Lions' ear, Lion ears, Lion's ear, Lions-ear] (138) (1923)

Leonotis nepetaefolia A. Br. – See *Leonotis nepetifolia* (L.) Aiton f.

Leonotis nepetifolia (L.) Aiton f. – Lion's-head [Lion's head, Lion head] (122, 124) (1937) TX

Leonotis T. Br. – See *Leonotis* (Pers.) Aiton f.

Leontice thalictroides L. – See *Caulophyllum thalictroides* (L.) Michx.

Leontodon autumnale – See *Leontodon autumnalis* L.

Leontodon autumnalis L. – Arnica (73, 156) (1892–1923), Arnica bud [Arnica-bud] (5, 75, 156) (1894–1923) Allston MA, Autumnal hawkbit (5, 156) (1913–1923), Common hawkbit (5) (1913), Dog dandelion [Dog-dandelion] (5, 75, 156) (1894–1923) Allston MA, Fall dandelion (5, 46, 156) (1879–1923), Hawkweed [Hawk-weed, Hawk weed, Hawke-weed] (19) (1840), Lion's-tooth [Lion's tooth, Lions' tooth] (5, 156) (1913–1923), Summer dorn (46) (1879)

Leontodon erythrospermum (Andrz. ex Bess.) Britton – See *Taraxacum laevigatum* (Willd.) DC.

Leontodon hastilis L. – See *Leontodon hispidus* L.

Leontodon hirtus L. – Hairy hawkbit (5) (1913), Rough hawkbit (5) (1913)

Leontodon hispidus L. – Bristly hawkbit (50) (present)

Leontodon hispidus L. subsp. *hispidus* – Common hawkbit (5) (1913), Hairy hawkbit (5) (1913)

Leontodon L. – Hawkbit [Hawk bit] (4, 155, 156, 158) (1900–1986)

Leontodon latilobum (DC.) Britton – See *Taraxacum officinale* G.H. Weber ex Wiggers subsp. *vulgare* (Lam.) Schinz & R. Keller

Leontodon palustre S. – See *Taraxacum palustre* (Lyons) Symons

Leontodon palustris Lyons – See *Taraxacum palustre* (Lyons) Symons

Leontodon taraxacum L. – See *Taraxacum officinale* G. H. Weber ex Wiggers

Leontodon vulgaris [Lam.] – See *Taraxacum officinale* G. H. Weber ex Wiggers

Leonurus cardiaca L. – Agripaume (158) (1900), Cardiaire (French) (158) (1900), Common motherwort (3, 50, 82, 138, 155) (1923–present), Cowthwort (5, 156, 157, 158) (1900–1929), Herzgespann (German) (158) (1900), Leonurus (57) (1917), Lion's-ear [Lions' ear, Lion ears, Lion's ear, Lions-ear] (5, 92, 156, 157, 158) (1876–1929), Lion's-tail [Lion's tail, Lions' tail, Lionstail, Lions-tail] (7, 92, 156, 157, 158, 184) (1793–1929), Motherwort [Mother wort, Mother-wort, Mother Woort] (4, 5, 10, 19, 47, 49, 52, 53, 57, 61, 62, 63, 72, 80, 82, 85, 92, 93, 97, 106, 114, 122, 131, 145, 156, 157, 158, 178, 187) (1526–1986), Mugwort [Mug-wort, Mugwoort] (187) (1818), Throwort [Throw wort, Throwwort] (7, 92, 157, 158) (1828–1929), Wolfstrapp (German) (158) (1900)

Leonurus L. – Lion's-tail [Lion's tail, Lions' tail, Lionstail, Lions-tail] (158) (1900), Motherwort [Mother wort, Mother-wort, Mother Woort] (1, 4, 50, 82, 93, 138, 155, 156, 158, 167) (1814–present)

Leonurus marrubiastrum L. – See *Chaiturus marrubiastrum* (L.) Reichenb.

Leonurus sibiricus L. – Honeyweed (50) (present), Lion's-tail [Lion's tail, Lions' tail, Lionstail, Lions-tail] (5) (1913), Siberian motherwort (5, 155) (1913–1942)

Leopoldia comosa **(L.) Parl.** – See *Muscari comosum* (L.) Mill.

Lepachys columnaris **(Sims) Torr. & Gray.** – See *Ratibida columnifera* (Nutt.) Wood & Standl.

Lepachys columnifera **(Nutt.) J. F. Macbr.** – See *Ratibida columnifera* (Nutt.) Wood & Standl.

Lepachys pinnata **Torr. & Gray.** – See *Ratibida columnifera* (Nutt.) Wood & Standl.

Lepachys **Raf.** – See *Ratibida* Raf (all US species)

Lepachys tagetes **(James) Gray** – See *Ratibida tagetes* (James) Barnhart

Lepadena marginata **(Pursh) Niewl.** – See *Euphorbia marginata* Pursh

Lepadena **Raf.** – See *Euphorbia* L.

Lepargyraea argentea **(Nutt.) Greene** – See *Shepherdia argentea* (Pursh) Nutt.

Lepargyraea canadensis **(L.) Greene** – See *Shepherdia canadensis* Nutt.

Lepargyraea **Raf.** – See *Shepherdia* Nutt. (all US species)

Lepargyrea **Raf.** – See *Shepherdia* Nutt. (all US species)

Lepidium **(Tourn.) L.** – See *Lepidium* L.

Lepidium austrinum **Small.** – Pepper-grass [Peppergrass, Pepper grass] (4) (1986), Southern pepperwort (50) (present)

Lepidium bidentatum **Montin** – Fish poison (92, 107) (1876–1919)

Lepidium bipinnatifidum **auct. non Desvar.** – See *Lepidium oblongum* Small var. *oblongum*

Lepidium campestre **(L.) Aiton f.** – Bastard cress (5, 92, 158) (1876–1913), Cow cress [Cow-cress] (5, 15, 156, 158) (1895–1923), Crowdweed [Crowd-weed, Crowd weed] (5, 74, 156, 158) (1893–1923) WV, English pepper-grass [English pepper grass] (5, 156, 158) (1900–1923), False flax [Falseflax] (5, 92, 156, 158) (1876–1932), Field cress (5, 156, 158) (1900–1923), Field peppergrass [Field pepper-grass, Field pepper grass] (3, 4, 62) (1912–1986), Field pepperweed (50, 155) (1942–present), Garlic mustard [Garlicmustard, Garlicke mustard] (178) (1526), Glen pepper [Glen-pepper, Glenn pepper] (5, 74, 156, 158) (1893–1923) WV, Glen weed [Glenn-weed] (5, 74, 158) (1893–1913) WV, first noticed on Glenn farm, Konung Salomons ljusstake (Swedish) (46) (1879), Mithridate mustard (5, 156, 158) (1900–1923), Mithridate pepperwort (158) (1900), Pepper-grass [Peppergrass, Pepper grass] (156) (1923), Poor-man's-pepper [Poor-man's pepper, Poor man's pepper] (5, 156, 158) (1900–1923) no longer in use by 1923, Yellowseed [Yellow seed, Yellow-seed] (5, 156, 148) (1913–1939)

Lepidium campestre **(L.) R. Br.** – See *Lepidium campestre* (L.) Aiton f.

Lepidium densiflorum **Schrad.** – Common pepperweed (50) (present), Pepper-grass [Peppergrass, Pepper grass] (3, 4, 5, 85, 121) (1913–1986), Prairie pepperweed (155) (1942), Wild peppergrass [Wild pepper-grass] (97) (1937), Wild tongue-grass [Wild tonguegrass, Wild tongue grass] (5) (1913), Zitkala tawote (Lakota, small bird's food) (121) (1918?–1970?)

Lepidium draba **L.** – See *Cardaria draba* (L.) Desv.

Lepidium **L.** – Birdseed [Bird-seed, Bird seed] (1) (1932), Canary-grass [Canary grass] (1) (1932), Cress (2, 10) (1818–1895), Dittander (184) (1793), Pepper-grass [Peppergrass, Pepper grass] (1, 2, 4, 13, 15, 35, 63, 93, 109, 122, 138, 156, 158) (1895–1986), Pepper-weed [Pepperweed] (50, 155) (1942–present), Pepperwort [Pepper wort, Pepper wort, Pepper woort] (13, 63) (1849–1899)

Lepidium latifolium **L.** – Broad-leaf pepperweed [Broadleaved pepperweed] (50) (present), Dittander (46, 92, 107, 180) (1633–1919), Pepperwort [Pepper wort, Pepper wort, Pepper woort] (46, 178, 180) (1526–1671) cultivated by English colonists by 1671, Poor-man's-pepper [Poor-man's pepper, Poor man's pepper] (107) (1919)

Lepidium oblongum **Small** – Pepper-grass [Peppergrass, Pepper grass] (97) (1937), Veiny pepperweed (50) (present)

Lepidium oblongum **Small var.** *oblongum* – Veiny pepperweed (50) (present), Wayside pepperweed (155) (1942)

Lepidium perfoliatum **L.** – Clasping peppergrass (3, 4) (1977–1986), Clasping pepperweed (50, 155) (1942–present)

Lepidium piscidium **Forst.** – See *Lepidium bidentatum* Montin

Lepidium ramosissimum **A. Nels.** – Bushy peppergrass (3, 4)

(1977–1986), Many-branch pepperweed [Manybranched pepperweed, Many-branched pepperweed] (50) (present)

Lepidium repens **(Schrenk) Boiss.** – See *Cardaria chalapensis* (L.) Hand.-Maz.

Lepidium ruderale **L.** – Bowyer's mustard [Bowyers mustard] (178, 180) (1526–1633), Little mustard (178) (1526), Narrow-leaf pepper-grass [Narrow-leaved pepper grass] (5) (1913), Roadside pepper-grass [Roadside pepper grass] (5) (1913)

Lepidium sativa – See *Lepidium sativum* L.

Lepidium sativum **L.** – Cress (5, 92, 107, 179) (1526–1919), Curled Cresses (178) (1526), Diéges (Albanian) (110) (1886), Garden cress [Garden-cress, Gardyne cress] (3, 4, 15, 109, 110, 138, 155, 156, 158, 179) (1526–1986), Garden garth (158) (1900), Garden karse (158) (1900), Garden pepper-cress (158) (1900), Garden pepper-grass [Garden pepper grass, Garden peppergrass] (5, 72, 158) (1900–1913), Garden-cress pepperweed [Gardencress pepperweed] (50, 155) (1942–present), Golden cress (156, 158) (1900–1923), Golden peppergrass [Golden pepper-grass, Golden pepper grass] (5, 156, 158) (1900–1923), Nasturtium (107) (1919), Pepper-grass [Pepper-grass, Pepper grass] (19, 92, 156) (1840–1923), Pepperwort [Pepper wort, Pepper wort, Pepper woort] (92) (1876), Poor-man's-pepper [Poor-man's pepper, Poor man's pepper] (92, 158) (1876–1900), Sauce-alone [Sauce alone] (92, 158) (1876–1900), Tame cress (179) (1526), Tongue-grass [Tongue grass] (5, 92, 156, 158) (1876–1923), Town pepper-grass [Town pepper grass, Town peppergrass] (5, 158) (1900–1913), Upland cress (156) (1923)

Lepidium virginicum **L.** – Bird pepper [Bird's pepper, Birds' pepper] (5, 73, 156, 157, 158) (1892–1929), Birdseed [Bird-seed, Bird seed] (156) (1923), Canary-grass [Canary grass] (62) (1912), Chickweed [Chick-weed, Chick weed] (156) (1923), Crow cress [Crowcress] (157) (1929), Field cress (157) (1929), Large peppergrass (80) (1913), Peppercress [Pepper cress] (7, 92) (1828–1876), Pepper-grass [Peppergrass, Pepper grass] (4, 15, 145) (1895–1986), Tall speedwell [Tall speed-well] (187) (1818), Tongue-grass [Tongue grass] (5, 35, 62, 74, 156, 157, 158) (1806–1929), Virginia peppergrass [Virginia peppergrass, Virginia pepper grass] (3, 72, 80) (1907–1977), Virginia pepperweed (50, 155) (1942–present), Wild peppergrass [Wild pepper-grass] (2, 5, 19, 46, 62, 63, 85, 97, 131, 156, 157, 158, 187) (1818–1937), Wild pepperwort [Wild pepperwort] (181) (~1678)

Lepidium virginicum **L. var.** *medium* **(Greene) C. L. Hitchc.** – Pepper-grass [Peppergrass, Pepper grass] (145) (1897), Wild tongue-grass [Wild tonguegrass, Wild tongue grass] (76) (1896)

Lepidium virginicum **L. var.** *virginicum* – Virginia pepperweed (50) (present)

Lepidotis alopecuroides **(L.) Rothm.** – See *Lycopodiella alopecuroides* (L.) Cranfill

Lepidotis inundata **(L.) C. Borner** – See *Lycopodiella inundata* (L.) Holub

Lepigonum rubrum **Fries** – possibly *Spergularia rubra* (L.) J.& K. Presl

Leptamnium virginianum **(L.) Raf.** – See *Epifagus virginiana* (L.) W. Bart.

Leptandra **Nutt.** – See *Veronicastrum* Heister ex Fabr.

Leptandra purpurea **[Raf.]** – possibly *Veronicastrum virginicum* (L.) Farw. (taxonomic status is unresolved (PL))

Leptandra virginica **(L.) Nutt.** – See *Veronicastrum virginicum* (L.) Farw.

Leptasea aizoides **(L.) Haw.** – See *Saxifraga aizoides* L.

Leptasea **Haw.** – See *Saxifraga* L.

Leptasea hirculus **(L.) Small.** – See *Saxifraga hirculus* L. subsp. *hirculus*

Leptasea tricuspidata **(Retz.) Haw.** – See *Saxifraga hirculus* L. subsp. *hirculus*

Leptilon canadense **(L.) Britton** – See *Conyza canadensis* (L.) Cronq. var. *canadensis*

Leptilon divaricatum **(Michx.) Raf.** – See *Conyza ramosissima* Cronq.

Lespedeza leptostachya **Engelm.**

Leptilon **Raf.** – See *Conyza* Less. (most US species)

Leptochloa attenuata **Nutt.** – See *Leptochloa panicea* (Retz.) Ohwi subsp. *mucronata* (Michx.) Nowack

Leptochloa **Beauv.** – Slender grass [Slender-grass] (66, 92) (1876–1903), Sprangle-top [Sprangletop, Sprangle top] (50, 155) (1942–present)

Leptochloa dubia **(H.B.K.) Nees** – Green sprangletop (3, 50, 122, 155) (1937–present), Prangle (119) (1938) OK, Sprangle [Sprangles] (152) (1912) NM, Sprangle-top [Sprangletop, Sprangle top] (163) (1852), Texas crowfoot (163) (1852)

Leptochloa fascicularis **(Lam.) Gray** – See *Leptochloa fusca* (L.) Kunth subsp. *fascicularis* (Lam.) N. Snow

Leptochloa filiformis **(Lam.) Beauv.** – See *Leptochloa panicea* (Retz.) Ohwi subsp. *brachiata* (Steudl.) N. Snow

Leptochloa fusca **(L.) Kunth** – Malabar sprangletop (50) (present)

Leptochloa fusca **(L.) Kunth subsp. *fascicularis* (Lam.) N. Snow** – Bearded sprangletop (3, 50, 155) (1942–present), Clustered love grass [Clustered love-grass] (99) (1923), Clustered salt grass [Clustered salt-grass] (5, 94) (1901–1913), Clustering slender grass (66) (1903), Leptochloa (119) (1938), Long-awn diplachne [Long-awned diplachne] (5) (1913), Salt meadow diplachne (155) (1942), Salt meadow diplachne (5, 72) (1907–1913), Salt meadow grass [Salt meadow-grass] (163) (1852), Salt-meadow grass [Salt meadow grass, Salt meadow-grass] (163) (1852), Sharp-scale diplachne [Sharp-scaled diplachne] (5) (1913), Spike grass [Spike-grass, Spikegrass] (5, 87, 129) (1885–1894)

Leptochloa mucronata **(Michx.) Kunth** – See *Leptochloa panicea* (Retz.) Ohwi subsp. *mucronata* (Michx.) Nowack

Leptochloa nealleyi **Vasey** – Nealley's leptochloa (94) (1901)

Leptochloa panicea **(Retz.) Ohwi subsp. *brachiata* (Steudl.) N. Snow** – Feather grass [Feathergrass, Feather-grass] (5, 87, 119) (1884–1938), Mucronate sprangletop (50) (present), Red sprangletop [Red sprangle-top] (3, 155, 163) (1852–1977), Salt grass [Saltgrass, Salt-grass] (5, 119) (1913–1938), Slender grass [Slender-grass] (5, 119, 163) (1852–1938)

Leptochloa panicea **(Retz.) Ohwi subsp. *mucronata* (Michx.) Nowack** – Feather grass [Feather-grass, Feathergrass] (94) (1901), Mucronate sprangletop (50) (present), Pointed slender grass (66) (1903), Sharp-scale leptochloa [Sharp-scaled leptochloa] (5, 99) (1913–1923), Slender grass [Slender-grass] (87) (1884)

Leptochloa scabra **Nees** – Rough leptochloa (94) (1901)

Leptochloa viscida **(Scribn.) Beal** – Viscid leptochloa (94) (1901)

Leptocoryphium lanatum **(Kunth) Nees** – Rough panic grass [Rough panic-grass, Rough panicgrass] (94) (1901), Rough-stalk witch grass [Roughstalk witchgrass] (155) (1942)

Leptodactylon caespitosum **Nutt.** – See *Linanthus caespitosus* (Nutt.) J. M. Porter & L. A. Johnson

Leptodactylon **Hook. & Arn.** – Prickly-phlox [Pricklyphlox] (50) (present)

Leptodactylon pungens **(Torr.) Torr. ex Nutt.** – Granite gilia (155) (1942), Granite prickly-phlox [Granite prickly phlox] (50) (present)

Leptoglottis angustisiliqua **Britton & Rose** – See *Mimosa microphylla* Dry.

Leptoglottis chapmanii **Small ex Britton & Rose** – See *Mimosa microphylla* Dry.

Leptoglottis **DC.** – See *Mimosa* L. (all US species)

Leptoglottis microphylla **(Dry.) Britton & Rose** – See *Mimosa microphylla* Dry.

Leptoloma **Chase** – See *Digitaria* Haller

Leptoloma cognatum **(Schult.) Chase** – See *Digitaria cognata* (J.A. Schultes) Pilger var. *cognata*

Leptopus phyllanthoides **(Nutt.) G. L. Webster** – Northern andrachne (5, 97) (1913–1937)

Leptorchis liliifolia **(L.) Kuntze** – See *Liparis liliifolia* (L.) L.C. Rich. ex Ker-Gawl.

Leptorchis liliifolia **(Rich. ex Lindl.) Kuntze** – Large twayblade [Large tway-blade] (72) (1907)

Leptorchis loeselii **(L.) MacMill.** – See *Liparis loeselii* (L.) Rich.

Leptorchis **Thouars.** – See *Liparis* L. C. Rich.

Leptospermum laevigatum **(Gaertner) F. Muell.** – Australian tea-tree (109, 138) (1923–1949), Manuka tea-tree (109) (1949)

Leptospermum laevigatum **F. Muell.** – See *Leptospermum laevigatum* (Gaertner) F. Muell.

Leptospermum scoparium **Forst.** – See *Leptospermum laevigatum* (Gaertner) F. Muell.

Leptosyne **[DC.]** – See *Coreopsis* L.

Leptosyne douglasi – See *Coreopsis douglasii* (DC.) Hall

Leptosyne maritima – See *Coreopsis maritima* (Nutt.) Hook.f.

Leptosyne stillmanii **[Gray]** – See *Coreopsis stillmanii* (Gray) Blake

Leptotaenia multifida **Nutt.** – See *Lomatium dissectum* (Nutt.) Mathias & Constance var. *multifidum* (Nutt.) Mathias & Constance

Lepturus incurvatus **(L.) Trin.** – See *Parapholis incurva* (L.) C.E. Hubb.

Lepturus paniculatus **[Nutt.]** – See *Schedonnardus paniculatus* (Nutt.) Trel.

Lerchenfeldia flexuosa **(L.) Schur** – See *Deschampsia flexuosa* (L.) Trin. var *flexuosa*

Lespedeza ×brittonii **Bickn.** [*procumbens × virginica*] – Britton's bush clover (5) (1913)

Lespedeza ×longifolia **DC.** [*capitata × hirta*] – Long-leaf bush-clover [Long-leaved bush-clover] (97) (1937)

Lespedeza ×manniana **Mackenzie & Bush (pro sp.)** [*capitata × violacea*] – Mann's bush clover (5) (1913)

Lespedeza ×neglecta **Mackenzie & Bush** [*stuevei × virginica*] – Bush clover [Bush-clover, Bushclover] (97) (1937)

Lespedeza ×nuttallii **Darl.** [*hirta × intermedia*] – Nuttall's bush clover (5) (1913)

Lespedeza ×simulata **Mackenzie & Bush (pro sp.)** [*capitata × virginica*] – Intermediate bush-clover [Intermediate bush clover] (5, 97) (1937)

Lespedeza angustifolia **(Pursh) Ell.** – Narrow-leaf bush clover [Narrow-leaved bush clover] (5) (1913)

Lespedeza angustifolia **Ell.** – See *Lespedeza angustifolia* (Pursh) Ell.

Lespedeza bicolor **Turcz.** – Shrub bush clover [Shrub bushclover] (138) (1923)

Lespedeza brittonii **Bicknell** – See *Lespedeza ×brittonii* Bickn. [*procumbens × virginica*]

Lespedeza capitata **Michx.** – Bush clover [Bush-clover, Bushclover] (3, 85, 114, 156) (1894–1977), Dusty clover (5, 156, 158) (1900–1923), Parus-as (Pawnee, rabbitfoot) (37) (1919), Rabbit's-foot [Rabbit foot, Rabbits' foot, Rabbitfoot] (37) (1919), Round-head bush clover [Roundhead bushclover, Round-headed bush clover, Round-headed bush-clover] (5, 93, 97, 131, 138, 158) (1899–1937), Round-head lespedeza [Roundhead lespedeza] (4, 50, 155) (1942–present), Tall bush clover (72) (1907), Te-hunton-hi nuga (Omaha-Ponca, male buffalo bellow plant) (37) (1919)

Lespedeza cuneata **(Dumort.-Cours.) G. Don** – Chinese bush clover (4) (1986), Chinese lespedeza (50, 155) (1942–present), Sericea lespedeza (3, 4) (1977–1986)

Lespedeza divergens **Pursh** – See *Lespedeza violacea* (L.) Pers.

Lespedeza formosa **(Vogel) Koehne** – Purple bush clover [Purple bush-clover] (138) (1923)

Lespedeza frutescens **(L.) Hornem.** – Shrubby lespedeza (50) (Present), Wand-like bush clover [Wand-like bush-clover] (5, 72, 97) (1907–1937)

Lespedeza frutescens **(Willd.) Ell.** – See *Lespedeza capitata* Michx.

Lespedeza hirta **(L.) Hornem.** – Hairy bush-clover [Hairy bush clover] (5, 72, 97) (1907–1937), Hairy lespedeza (3, 4, 50, 155) (1942–present)

Lespedeza intermedia **(S. Wats.) Britton** – See *Lespedeza violacea* (L.) Pers.

Lespedeza leptostachya **Engelm.** – Prairie bush clover (5) (1913), Prairie clover [Prairieclover] (72) (1907), Prairie lespedeza (50) (present), Slender-spike lespedeza [Slender spike lespedeza] (4) (1986)

239

Lespedeza longifolia **DC.** – See *Lespedeza* ×*longifolia* DC. [*capitata* × *hirta*]

Lespedeza manniana **Mackenzie & Bush** – See *Lespedeza* ×*manniana* Mackenzie & Bush [*capitata* × *violacea*]

Lespedeza **Michx.** – Bush clover [Bush-clover, Bushclover] (1, 2, 4, 63, 93, 109, 138, 156, 158) (1895–1986), Lespedeza (4, 50, 155) (1942–present)

Lespedeza neglecta **(Britton) Mack. & Bush** – See *Lespedeza* ×*manniana* Mackenzie & Bush [*capitata* × *violacea*]

Lespedeza nuttallii **Darl.** – See *Lespedeza* ×*nuttallii* Darl. [*hirta* × *intermedia*]

Lespedeza prairea **(Mackenzie & Bush) Britton** – See *Lespedeza virginica* (L.) Britton

Lespedeza procumbens **Michx** – Trailing bush clover [Trailing bush-clover] (5, 97) (1913–1937), Trailing lespedeza (3, 4, 50, 155, 187) (1818–present)

Lespedeza repens **(L.) Bart.** – Creeping bush-clover [Creeping bush clover] (5, 97) (1913–1937), Creeping lespedeza (3, 4, 155) (1942–1986)

Lespedeza reticulata **Pers.** – See *Lespedeza virginica* (L.) Britton

Lespedeza sessiliflora **Michx.** – See *Lespedeza virginica* (L.) Britton

Lespedeza simulata **Mackenzie & Bush** – See *Lespedeza* ×*simulata* Mackenzie & Bush [*capitata* × *virginica*]

Lespedeza stipulacea **Maxim.** – See *Kummerowia stipulacea* (Maxim.) Makino

Lespedeza striata **(Thunb.) Hook. & Arn.** – See *Kummerowia striata* (Thunb.) Schindl.

Lespedeza stuevei **Nutt.** – Stuve's bush clover [Stuve's bush-clover] (5) (1913), Stuve's lespedeza [Stuves lespedeza] (3, 155) (1942–1977), Tall bush lespedeza (4, 124) (1937–1986), Tall lespedeza (50) (present)

Lespedeza violacea **(L.) Pers.** – Bush clover [Bush-clover, Bushclover] (5, 72, 97) (1907–1937), Diverging lespedeza (187) (1818), Prairie lespedeza (4) (1986), Violet lespedeza (3, 50, 155) (1942–present), Wand lespedeza (155) (1942)

Lespedeza virginica **(L.) Britton** – Bush clover [Bush-clover, Bush-clover] (19, 92) (1840–1876), Prairie clover [Prairieclover] (124) (1937), Slender bush clover (5, 72) (1907–1913), Slender bush lespedeza (4) (1986), Slender lespedeza (3, 50, 155) (1942–present)

Lesquerella alpina **(Nutt.) S. Wats.** – Alpine bladderpod (50) (present)

Lesquerella alpina **(Nutt.) S. Wats. var. spathulata (Rydb.) Payson** – Low bladderpod [Low bladder-pod, Low bladder pod] (5, 93, 131) (1899–1936)

Lesquerella arctica **(DC.) S. Wats.** – Arctic bladderpod [Arctic bladder pod] (5, 50) (1913–present)

Lesquerella arenosa **(Richards.) Rydb.** – Great Plains bladderpod (50) (present)

Lesquerella arenosa **(Richards.) Rydb. var. arenosa** – Great Plains bladderpod (50) (present), Silvery bladderpod [Silvery bladder-pod] (131) (1899)

Lesquerella arenosa **(Richards.) Rydb. var. argillosa Rollins & Shaw** – Great Plains bladderpod (50) (present)

Lesquerella argentea **(Pursh) MacM.** – See *Lesquerella ludoviciana* (Nutt.) S. Wats.

Lesquerella auriculata **(Engelm. & Gray) S. Wats.** – Auricled bladderpod [Auricled bladder-pod] (97) (1937), Ear-leaf bladderpod [Earleaf bladderpod] (50) (present)

Lesquerella condensata **A. Nels.** – Dense bladderpod (50) (present)

Lesquerella fendleri **(Gray) Wats** – Fendler's bladderpod (50) (present)

Lesquerella globosa **(Desv.) S. Wats.** – Bladderpod [Bladder pod, Bladder-pod] (156) (1923), Globe bladderpod (50, 155) (1942–present), Short's bladderpod [Short's bladder pod] (5) (1913)

Lesquerella gordonii **(Gray) S. Wats.** – Bladderpod [Bladder pod, Bladder-pod] (106) (1930), Gordon's bladderpod [Gordon's bladder-pod] (50, 97) (1937–present)

Lesquerella gracilis **(Hook.) S. Wats.** – Slender bladderpod [Slender bladder pod, Slender bladder-pod] (5, 93, 97) (1913–1937),

Spreading bladderpod (50) (present)

Lesquerella gracilis **(Hook.) S. Wats. subsp. nuttallii (T. & G.) Rollins & Shaw** – Nuttall's bladderpod (50) (present), Spreading bladderpod (3, 4) (1977–1986)

Lesquerella grandiflora **(Hook.) S. Wats.** – Bladderpod [Bladder pod, Bladder-pod] (124) (1937), Field-of-the-cloth-of-gold [Field of the cloth of gold] (124) (1937) TX

Lesquerella grandiflora **S.Wats.** – See *Lesquerella grandiflora* (Hook.) S. Wats.

Lesquerella ludoviciana **(Nutt.) S. Wats.** – Bladderpod [Bladder pod, Bladder-pod] (3, 4, 98) (1926–1986), Foothill bladderpod (50) (present), Silver bladderpod (155) (1942), Silvery bladderpod [Silvery bladder-pod, Silvery bladder pod] (5, 93, 97) (1913–1937)

Lesquerella montana **(Gray) S. Wats.** – Mountain bladderpod (50) (present)

Lesquerella ovalifolia **Rydb. ex Britton** – Oval-leaf bladderpod [Oval leaved bladder pod, Oval-leaf bladder pod, Oval-leaved bladderpod] (3, 4, 5, 93, 97) (1913–1986), Round-leaf bladderpod [Round-leaf bladderpod] (50) (present)

Lesquerella ovalifolia **Rydb. ex Britton subsp. ovalifolia** – Oval-leaf balddderpod (3) (1977), Round-leaf bladderpod [Roundleaf bladderpod] (50) (present)

Lesquerella **S. Wats.** – Bladderpod [Bladder pod, Bladder-pod] (1, 4, 50, 93, 122, 127, 155, 156, 158) (1900–present)

Lesquerella spathula **Rydb.** – See *Lesquerella alpina* (Nutt.) S. Wats. var. *spathulata* (Rydb.) Payson

Letharia vulpina **(L.) Hue** – Tree moss [Tree-moss] (101) (1905) MT

Leucadendron argenteum R. Br. – See *Leucadendron argenteum* (L.) R. Br.

Leucaena glauca **Benth.** – See *Leucaena leucocephala* (Lam.) de Wit

Leucaena leucocephala **(Lam.) de Wit** – White popinac (109) (1949)

Leucaena pulverulenta **(Schlecht.) Benth.** – Tepehuaje (124) (1937) TX

Leucanthemum **(Tourn.) Mill.** – See *Leucanthemum* Mill.

Leucanthemum lacustre **(Brot.) Samp.** – Portuguese chrysanthemum (138) (1923), Portuguese daisy (109) (1949)

Leucanthemum leucanthemum **(L.) Rydb.** – See *Leucanthemum vulgare* Lam.

Leucanthemum maximum **(Ramond) DC.** – Max daisy (109) (1949), Pyrenees chrysanthemum (138) (1923)

Leucanthemum **Mill.** – Daisy [Daisies, Daysy] (50) (present), Ox-eye daisy [Oxeye daisy, Oxeyedaisy, Ox-eyed daisy] (1) (1932)

Leucanthemum nipponicum **Franch. ex Maxim.** – Nippon daisy (109) (1949), Nippon oxeye daisy (138) (1923)

Leucanthemum vulgare **Lam.** – Big daisy (5, 156) (1913–1923), Bull daisy [Bull-daisy] (5, 156, 158) (1900–1923), Bull's-eye daisy [Bull's eye daisy, Bullseye daisy] (5, 156, 158) (1900–1923), Bull's-eyes [Bull's eyes, Bullseye] (73, 75) (1892–1894), Butter daisy [Butter-daisy] (5, 156, 158) (1900–1923), Common field daisy (158) (1900), Daisy [Daisies, Daysy] (7) (1828), Devil's daisy [Devil's-daisy] (158) (1900), Dog blow [Dog-blow] (5, 158) (1900–1913), Dog daisy [Dog-daisy] (5, 156, 158) (1900–1923), Dutch curse (156) (1923), Dutch morgan (5, 156, 158) (1900–1923), Eastern ox-eye daisy (56) (1901) IA, Field daisy [Field-daisy] (5, 49, 53, 82, 93, 106, 156) (1898–1936), Field ox-eye daisy [Field oxeyedaisy] (155) (1942), Golden daisy [Golden-daisy] (92, 158) (1876–1900), Goldens (7, 49) (1828–1898), Goldins (184) (1793), Grande marguarite (French) (49) (1898), Great daisy [Great-daisy] (158) (1900), Great field daisy [Great field daisie] (178) (1526), Great oxeye [Great ox-eye] (49) (1898), Great white oxeye [Great white ox-eye] (5, 158) (1900–1913), Herb Margaret (5, 92, 156, 158) (1876–1923), Horse daisy [Horse-daisy] (5, 156, 158) (1900–1923), Horse gowan [Horse-gowan] (49, 158) (1898–1900), Kellup's weed [Kellup weed, Kellip-weed] (75, 158) (1894–1900) Montpelier VT, Magdalene daisy [Magdalene-daisy] (158) (1900), Marguerite (4, 107, 156, 158) (1900–1986), Maudlin daisy [Maudlin-daisy] (5, 49, 156, 158) (1898–1923), Maudlinwort [Maudlin wort] (92, 158) (1876–1900),

Midsummer daisy [Midsummer-daisy] (5, 156, 158) (1900–1923), Moon daisy [Moon-daisy] (5, 49, 156, 158) (1898–1923), Moon flower [Moon-flower, Moonflower] (5, 156, 158) (1900–1923), Moon-penny [Moon penny] (5, 156, 158) (1900–1923), Ox-eye [Ox eye, Oxeye, Oxe eie] (45) (1896), Ox-eye daisy [Oxeye daisy, Ox-eyedaisy, Ox-eyed daisy] (3, 4, 5, 19, 42, 49, 50, 53, 58, 62, 63, 72, 80, 82, 85, 92, 97, 106, 107, 109, 114, 122, 124, 138, 145, 155, 156, 158, 187) (1814–present), Pismire (73, 158) (1892–1900) East Weymouth MA, Poorland daisy [Poor-land daisy] (5, 156, 158) (1900–1923), Poverty-weed [Povertyweed, Poverty weed] (5, 156, 158) (1900–1923), Rhode Island clover (75) (1894) Montpelier VT, Richardson's clover (187) (1818), Sheriff-pink [Sheriff pink] (5, 75, 156) (1894–1923) WV, no longer in use by 1923, Sheriffweed [Sheriffweed] (158) (1900), White daisy (5, 45, 49, 62, 63, 92, 107, 131, 156, 158) (1876–1923), White oxeye daisy [White ox-eye daisy] (45) (1896), White-man's-weed [White man's weed, White-man's weed] (5, 156) (1913–1923), Whiteweed [White weed, White-weed] (5, 7, 19, 49, 58, 62, 92, 106, 107, 109, 122, 156, 158, 187) (1818–1949)

Leucelene ericoides (Torr.) Greene – See *Chaetopappa ericoides* (Torr.) Nesom

Leucelene Greene – See *Chaetopappa* DC.

Leucocoma (Ehrh.) Rydb. – See *Trichophorum* Pers. (US species)

Leucocoma alpina (L.) Rydb. – See *Trichophorum alpinum* (L.) Pers.

Leucocrinum montanum Nutt. ex Gray – Common star lily [Common starlily] (50, 155) (1942–present), Ecopa (Crow) (101) (1905) MT, Mountain lily [Mountaine Lillie, Mountaine Lilly] (3, 157) (1900–1977), Sand lily [Sand-lily] (93, 157) (1929–1936), Shoestring lily [Shoe-string lilies] (156) (1923), Spring lily [Spring-lily] (101) (1905) MT, Star lily [Star-lily, Starlily] (138) (1923), Star-of-Bethlehem [Star of Bethlehem, Starre of Bethlem, Stars of Bethlehem] (85) (1932), Wild hyacinth (157) (1929), Wild tuberose [Wild tube-rose, Wild tube rose] (101) (1905) MT

Leucocrinum Nutt. ex Gray – Mountain lily [Mountaine Lillie, Mountaine Lilly] (1, 93) (1932–1936), Sand lily [Sand-lily] (109) (1949), Soaproot [Soap-root, Soap root] (158) (1900), Star lily [Star-lily, Starlily] (50, 109, 138, 155) (1923–present), Star-of-Bethlehem [Star of Bethlehem, Starre of Bethlem, Stars of Bethlehem] (1, 93) (1932–1936)

Leucoium vernum – See *Leucojum vernum* L.

Leucojum aestivum L. – Early summer fools [Early Sommer fooles] (178) (1596), Summer snowflake [Summer-snowflake] (138) (1923), Summer sottekins [Sommer sottekins] (178) (1596), Summer-fools [Sommer fooles] (178) (1596)

Leucojum L. – Bulbous-violet [Bulbous violets] (180) (1633), Snowflake [Snow flake] (109, 138) (1923–1949)

Leucojum vernum L. – Bulbed-violet [Bulbed violet] (180) (1633), Dryskens (Dutch) (180) (1633), Early bulbous stock gilloflower [Early bulbous stocke gilloflower] (178) (1596), Snowdrop [Snowdrops, Snow-drops, Snow drop] (180) (1633), Snowflake [Snow flake] (92) (1876), Sommer l(?)ottekins (Dutch) (180) (1633), Spring snowflake (138) (1923), Summer-fools [Sommer fooles] (180) (1633), Timely-flowerung bulbous Violet [Timely flouring bulbous Violet] (180) (1633), White-violet [White violet] (92) (1876)

Leucophyllum frutescens (Berl.) I. M. Johnston – Ceniza (124) (1937) TX, Cenizo (109) (1949)

Leucophyllum frutescens L. – See *Leucophyllum frutescens* (Berl.) I.M. Johnston

Leucophysalis grandiflora (Hook.) Rydb. – Large white ground-cherry [Large white ground cherry] (5) (1913), Wild tomato (75) (1894) MN

Leucopoa Griseb. – Spike fescue [Spikefescue] (50) (present)

Leucopoa kingii (S. Wats.) W. A. Weber – King's fescue (94) (1901), Spike fescue [Spikefescue] (50, 140, 155) (1942–present), Watson's fescue grass (5) (1913)

Leucospora multifida (Michx.) Nutt. – Conobea (5, 72, 97) (1907–1937), Leucospora (3, 4) (1977–1986), Narrow-leaf paleseed [Narrowleaf paleseed] (50) (present)

Leucospora Nutt. – Leucospora (50) (present)

Leucothoe acuminata (Aiton) G. Don – See *Agarista populifolia* (Lam.) W.S. Judd

Leucothoe axillaris (Lam.) D. Don. – Andromeda (183) (~1756), Branch ivy (71) (1898), Calf-kill [Calf kill] (71) (1898), Catesby's leucothoe (5) (1913), Dog-hobble [Dog hobble] (5, 156) (1913–1923), Dog-laurel [Dog laurel] (5, 71, 156) (1898–1923), Downy leucothoe (5) (1913), Drooping leucothoe (138) (1923), Fetter bush [Fetterbush, Fetter-bush] (5, 71) (1898–1913), Hemlock [Hemloc, Hemlocke] (71) (1898), Leucothoe (71, 156) (1898–1923), Pipestem wood [Pipe-stem-wood, Pipe-stem wood] (183) (~1756), Poison hemlock [Poison-hemlock, Poisonhemlock] (156) (1923)

Leucothoe axillaris Don. – See *Leucothoe axillaris* (Lam.) D. Don.

Leucothoe catesbaei (Walt.) Gray – See *Leucothoe axillaris* (Lam.) D. Don.

Leucothoe catesbaei Gray. – See *Leucothoe axillaris* (Lam.) D. Don.

Leucothoe D. Don – Fetter bush [Fetterbush, Fetter-bush] (156) (1923), Hemlock [Hemloc, Hemlocke] (75) (1894) NC, Leucothoe (138) (1923) named for the daughter of Orchamus, king of Babylonia

Leucothoe racemosa (L.) Gray – Swamp eubotrys (5) (1913), Swamp leucothoe (156) (1923), Sweetbells (109, 138) (1923–1949), White osier (7, 92, 156) (1828–1923), White ozier (5) (1913), White pepper (156) (1923), White pepper bush [White pepperbush, White pepper-bush] (5, 7, 92) (1828–1913), possibly Andromede à grappe (French) (8) (1785), possibly Andromede paniculée (French) (8) (1785), possibly Branching andromeda (165) (1807), possibly Panicled andromeda (8, 165) (1785–1807), possibly Pennsylvania redbud andromeda [Pennsylvanian red-bud andromeda] (8) (1785), possibly Pepper bush [Pepper-bush, Pepperbush] (19, 92, 156) (1840–1923), possibly Redbud [Red-bud, Red bud, Red-budds] or Redbud tree [Red bud tree, Redbud-tree, Redbud tree] (187) (1818), possibly Sweet-scented andromeda (187) (1818), possibly White bush [White-bush] (19, 92) (1840–1876)

Leucothoe racemosa Gray. – See *Leucothoe racemosa* (L.) Gray

Leucothoe recurva (Buckl.) Gray – Mountain eubotrys (5) (1913), Red-twig leucothoe [Redtwig leucothoe] (138) (1923)

Levisticum Koch – Lovage [Louage] (1) (1932)

Levisticum officinale W. D. J. Koch – Common lovage [Common Louage] (178) (1526), Lavose (92) (1876), Levisticum (57) (1917), Levose (92) (1876), Lovage [Louage] (5, 10, 57, 107, 109, 179, 184) (1526–1949), Sea-parsley [Sea parsley] (92) (1876), Smellage (10, 92) (1818–1876)

Lewisia Pursh – Bitter-root [Bitter root, Bitterroot] (15) (1895)

Lewisia rediviva Pursh – Bitter-root [Bitter root, Bitterroot] (15, 101, 109, 138) (1895–1949), Butter-root (107) (1919), Canadian bitterroot [Canadian bitter root] (14) (1882), Konah (Snake) (101) (1905) MT, Racine amare (French) (101) (1905) MT, Racine d'amare (French Canada) (25) (1834), Racine d'amère (French) (15) (1895), Spatlum (Flathead) (101, 107) (1905–1919), Spatulum (103) (1870) MT, from Indian name, Spoet'lum (Sailish or Flat-head) (25) (1834), White lewisia (103) (1870)

Leycesteria formosa Wallich – Himalayan honeysuckle [Himalaya-honeysuckle] (109, 138) (1923–1949)

Leymus ambiguus (Vasey & Scribn.) D. R. Dewey – Colorado wild rye [Colorado wildrye] (140) (1944), Wild rye [Wild-rye, Wildrye] (140) (1944)

Leymus arenarius (L.) Hochst. – Downy Lyme grass (5) (1913), European dune grass [European dunegrass] (138) (1923), Marram grass [Marram-grass] (92) (1876), Marram sea grass (5) (1913), Narrow bent (5) (1913), Rancenria grass (75) (1894), Rancheria grass (5, 45, 56, 161) (1857–1901), Raucheria grass (45) (1896), Sand rye grass [Sand ryegrass] (50) (present), Sea lyme grass [Sea lyme-grass] (5, 41, 92, 94, 109) (1770–1949), Sielge de mer (French, sea rye) (41) (1770), Upright sea lyme grass, Upright sea lime grass (56, 66

(1901–1903), possibly Lyme grass (92) (1876)

Leymus cinereus **(Scribn. & Merr.) A. Löve** – Basin wild rye [Basin wildrye] (50) (present), Corn grass [Corn-grass, Corngrass] (35) (1806), Pacific giant wildrye (155) (1942)

Leymus condensatus **(J. Presl) A. Löve** – Buffalo rye (101) (1905) MT, Giant rye grass [Giant rye-grass] (45, 56, 87, 88, 94, 111, 157) (1885–1929), Giant wild rye [Giant wild-rye, Giant wildrye] (140, 50, 146, 155) (1939–present), Lyme-grass (45) (1896), Rye grass [Rye-grass, Ryegrass] (101, 157) (1900–1929), Western rye grass [Western rye-grass (87) (1884), Wild rye [Wild-rye, Wildrye] (45) (1896), Wild-rye grass (87) (1884)

Leymus flavescens **(Scribn. & J.G. Sm.) Pilger** – Yellow wild rye [Yellow wildrye] (50) (present), Yellow-hair lyme grass [Yellow-haired lyme-grass] (94) (1901)

Leymus **Hochst.** – Wild rye [Wild-rye, Wildrye] (50) (present)

Leymus innovatus **(Beal) Pilger** – Brown's wild rye (94) (1901), Downy rye grass [Downy ryegrass] (50) (present), Fuzzy-spike wildrye [Fuzzyspike wildrye] (155) (1942)

Leymus mollis **(Trin.) Pilger subsp.** *mollis* – American dune grass [American dunegrass] (138) (1923), Soft lyme grass (66, 90) (1885–1903)

Leymus mollis **subsp.** *villosissimus* **(Scribn.) Á. Löve & D. Löve** – Northern lyme grass [Northern lyme-grass] (94) (1901)

Leymus racemosus **(Lam.) Tzvelev** – Siberian wild rye [Siberian wild-rye] (138) (1923)

Leymus salinus **(M.E. Jones) A. Löve subsp.** *salinus* – Alkali lyme grass [Alkali lyme-grass] (94) (1901)

Leymus simplex **(Scribn. & Williams) D.R. Dewey** – Alkali wildrye (50) (present), Salt lyme grass [Salt lyme-grass] (94) (1901)

Leymus triticoides **(Buckl.) Pilger** – Beardless wild rye [Beardless wild-rye, Beardless wildrye] (50, 163) (1852–present), Creeping wild rye [Creeping wildrye] (155) (1942)

Liatris acidota **Engelm. & Gray** – Slender button snakeroot [Slender button-snakeroot] (5, 72, 97, 122, 124) (1907–1937), Slender snakeroot (93) (1936)

Liatris aspera **Michx.** – Backache root [Backache-root] (48) (1828) KS, Blue blazing-star [Blue blazing star] (86, 156) (1878–1923), Broadleaf Virginia knapweed [Broad-leaved Virginia Knapweed, with a knobbed root] (181) (~1678), Button snakeroot [Button-snakeroot, Button snake root] (14, 156) (1882–1923), Devil's-bite [Devil's bite, Devilsbite] (75, 156) (1894–1923), Gayfeather [Gay-feather, Gay feather] (5, 49, 106, 156) (1898–1930), Large button snakeroot [Large button-snakeroot [Large button sanke-root, Large button snakeroot] (82, 122) (1930–1937), Rattlesnake-master [Rattlesnake master, Rattlesnake's master, Rattlesnakes' master, Rattlesnake's-master] (156) (1923), Tall blazing star (50) (present), Tall gayfeather (155) (1942), Devil's-bit [Devil's bit, Devilbit] (49, 156) (1898–1923)

Liatris aspera **Michx. var.** *aspera* – Tall blazing star (50) (present)

Liatris **Auct.** – See *Liatris* Gaertn. ex Schreber.

Liatris cylindracea **Michx** – Blazing star [Blazing-star, Blazingstar] (82) (1930), Cylindrical blazing star [Cylindric blazing star] (5, 72) (1907–1913)

Liatris densispicata **(Bush) Gaiser** – Dense-spike blazing star [Densespike blazing star] (50) (present)

Liatris densispicata **(Bush) Gaiser var.** *interrupta* **Gaiser** – Densespike blazing star [Densespike blazing star] (50) (present)

Liatris dubia **Barton** – possibly *Liatris pilosa* (Aiton) Willd.

Liatris elegans **(Walt.) Michx.** – Handsome blazing star (122, 124) (1937), Pink-scale gayfeather [Pinkscale gayfeather] (138) (1923)

Liatris elegans **(Walt.) Michx. var.** *elegans* – Handsome blazing star (5, 97) (1913–1937)

Liatris **Gaertn. ex Schreber.** – Backache root [Backache-root] (7) (1828), Blazing star [Blazing-star, Blazingstar] (1, 2, 4, 7, 50, 63, 82, 86, 93, 106, 109, 114, 127, 158) (1878–present), Button-root [Button-snakeroot, Button snake root] (1, 2, 7, 63, 93, 106, 109, 156) (1828–1949), Devil's-ironweed [Devil's iron weed, Devil's ironweed] (7) (1828) Concord MA, because the corm or tuber

is thought to look as if bitten off, Gayfeather [Gay-feather, Gay feather] (4, 7, 86, 98, 109, 138, 155) (1828–1986), Pinette de prairie (French Canadian boatmen) (10) (1818), Prairie-pine [Prairie pine, Prairie pines] (7) (1828), Rattlesnake-master [Rattlesnake master, Rattlesnake's master, Rattlesnakes' master, Rattlesnake's-master] (7) (1828), Rough-root [Rough root] (7) (1828), Sawort (7) (1828), Throatwort [Throat wort, Throat-wort] (7) (1828)

Liatris glabrata **Rydb.** – See *Liatris squarrosa* (L.) Michx. var. *glabrata* (Rydb.) Gaiser

Liatris graminifolia **Willd.** – See *Liatris pilosa* (Aiton) Willd. var. *pilosa*

Liatris hirsuta **Rydb.** – See *Liatris squarrosa* (L.) Michx. var. *hirsuta* (Rydb.) Gaiser

Liatris intermedia **Lindl.** – See *Liatris cylindracea* Michx

Liatris lancifolia **(Greene) Kittell** – Gayfeather [Gay-feather, Gay feather] (3) (1977), Lance-leaf blazing star [Lanceleaf blazing star] (50) (present)

Liatris ligulistylis **(A. Nels.) K. Schum.** – Gayfeather [Gay-feather, Gay feather] (3) (1977), Rocky Mountain blazing star (50) (present), Rocky Mountain gayfeather (138, 155) (1923–1942)

Liatris macrostachya **Michx.** – See *Liatris spicata* (L.) Willd.

Liatris mucronata **DC.** – Cusp blazing star (50) (present), Gayfeather [Gay-feather, Gay feather] (3) (1977)

Liatris odoratissima – See *Carphephorus odoratissimus* (J.F. Gmel.) Herbert

Liatris pilosa **(Aiton) Willd.** – Blue blazing-star [Blue blazing star] (186) (1814), possibly Button snakeroot [Button-snakeroot, Button snake root] (186) (1814), possibly Rattlesnake-master [Rattlesnake master, Rattlesnake's master, Rattlesnakes' master, Rattlesnake's-master] (186) (1814)

Liatris pilosa **(Aiton) Willd. var.** *pilosa* – Fine-leaf blazingstar [Fine-leaved blazing-star] (156) (1923), Grass-leaf gayfeather [Grassleaf gayfeather] (138) (1923), Loose-flower button-snakeroot [Loose-flowered button-snakeroot] (5) (1913), Mountain button-snakeroot (5) (1913), Purple-rod (156) (1923)

Liatris punctata **Hook** – Blazing star [Blazing-star, Blazingstar] (3, 98, 148) (1926–1977), Dotted blazing star (50, 121) (1918–present), Dotted button-snakeroot [Dotted button snake root, Dotted button snakeroot] (82, 122) (1930–1937), Dotted gayfeather (138, 155) (1923–1942) Neb, Gayfeather [Gay-feather, Gay feather] (98) (1926), Tatečaŋnuǵa (Lakota, lumpy carcass or lumps in carcass) (121) (1918?–1970?), Western snakeweed [Western snake-weed] (148) (1939)

Liatris punctata **Hook. var.** *nebraskana* **Gaiser** – Nebraska blazing star (50) (present)

Liatris punctata **Hook. var.** *punctata* – Dotted blazing star (50) (present), Dotted button-snakeroot [Dotted button snake root, Dotted button snakeroot] (5, 72, 97, 131) (1899–1937), Snakeroot [Snake root, Snake-root] (93) (1936) Neb, Spotted blazing star (85) (1932)

Liatris pycnostachya **Michx.** – Cat-tail gayfeather [Cattail gayfeather] (138) (1923), Hairy button snakeroot [Hairy button snake root, Hairy button snake-root] (122, 124, 156) (1923–1937), Kansas gayfeather [Kansas gay feather] (155, 156) (1923–1942), Prairie blazing star (50, 82) (1930–present), Prairie button-snakeroot (156) (1923), Pride-of-the-prairies [Pride of the prairies] (38) (1820), Tall blazing star (3) (1977)

Liatris pycnostachya **Michx. var.** *pycnostachya* – Hairy button snakeroot [Hairy button snake root, Hairy button snake-root] (5, 93) (1913–1936), Prairie blazing star (50, 72) (1907–present), Prairie button-snakeroot (5, 97) (1913–1937)

Liatris scariosa **(L.) Willd. var.** *scariosa* – Aontashe (Omaha-Ponca) (37) (1919), Blazing star [Blazing-star, Blazingstar] (37, 40, 131, 157) (1899–1929), Blue blazing-star [Blue blazing star] (157, 158) (1900–1929), Devil's-bit [Devil's bit, Devilbit] (157, 158) (1900–1929), Gayfeather [Gay-feather, Gay feather] (158) (1900), Gray-feather (157) (1929), Kahtsu-dawidu or Kahtsu-rawidu (Pawnee, round medicine) (37) (1919), Large blazing star (72) (1907), Large blue blazing star (93) (1936), Large button snakeroot [Large button-snakeroot, Large button snake-root, Large button snakeroot] (5, 97, 131, 157, 158) (1899–1937), Makan-sagi (Omaha-Ponca, hard medicine) (37) (1919), O'mucko'zowa'no (Chippewa, elk tail) (40) (1928), Rattlesnake-master [Rattlesnake master, Rattlesnake's master, Rattlesnakes' master, Rattlesnake's-master] (158) (1900)

Liatris scariosa **Willd.** – See *Liatris aspera* Michx.

Liatris **Schreber.** – See *Liatris* Gaertn. ex Schreber.

Liatris spheroidea **Michx.** – Spherical blazing star (50) (present)

Liatris spicata **(L.) Willd. var. *macrostachya*** – See *Liatris spicata* (L.) Willd.

Liatris spicata **(L.) Willd.** – Backache root [Backache-root] (92, 156) (1876–1923), Blue blazing-star [Blue blazing star] (187) (1818), Button snakeroot [Button-snakeroot, Button snake root] (19, 49, 53, 57, 61, 156) (1840–1923), Colic root [Colic-root, Colicroot] (52, 156) (1919–1923), Corn snakeroot [Corn snake root] (156) (1923), Dense button-snakeroot [Dense button snakeroot] (156) (1923), Devil's-bite [Devil's bite, Devilsbite] (156) (1923), Gayfeather [Gay-feather, Gay feather] (19, 49, 52, 92, 156) (1840–1923), Liatris (52) (1919), Prairie-pine [Prairie pine, Prairie pines] (92, 156) (1876–1923), Rattlesnake-master [Rattlesnake master, Rattlesnake's master, Rattlesnakes' master, Rattlesnake's-master] (92) (1876), Rough-root [Rough root] (92, 156) (1876–1923), Saw-wort [Saw woort, Saw wort, Sawwort] (72, 92, 156) (1876–1923), Spike gayfeather (138) (1923), Throatwort [Throat wort, Throat-wort] (92, 156) (1898–1923), Throat-wort, Radix est discutiens (177) (1762)

Liatris spicata **(L.) Willd. var. *spicata*** – Backache root [Backache-root] (5, 157) (1913–1929), Button snakeroot [Button-snakeroot, Button snake root] (157) (1929), Colic root [Colic-root, Colicroot] (5) (1913), Corn snakeroot [Corn snake root] (157) (1929), Dense button-snakeroot [Dense button snakeroot] (5, 131, 157) (1899–1923), Devil's-bit [Devil's bit, Devilbit] (5, 92, 131, 157) (1876–1929), Gayfeather [Gay-feather, Gay feather] (5, 93, 157) (1913–1936), Prairie-pine [Prairie pine, Prairie pines] (5, 157) (1913–1929), Rough-root [Rough root] (5) (1913), Saw-wort [Saw woort, Saw wort, Sawwort] (157) (1929), Spike (157) (1929), Throatwort [Throat wort, Throatwort] (5) (1913)

Liatris spicata **Willd.** – See *Liatris spicata* (L.) Willd.

Liatris squarrosa **(L.) Michx.** – Blazing star [Blazing-star, Blazingstar] (49, 53, 82, 92, 156) (1876–1930), Button snakeroot [Button-snakeroot, Button snake root] (14) (1882), Colic root [Colic-root, Colicroot] (156) (1923), Common blazing star (2) (1895), Rattlesnakemaster [Rattlesnake master, Rattlesnake's master, Rattlesnakes' master, Rattlesnake's-master] (92, 156) (1876–1923), Rattlesnakeroot [Rattlesnake root, Rattle-Snake-Root, Rattlesnakes' root, Rattlesnakeroot] (156) (1923), Scaly blazing star [Scaly blazing-star] (50, 92, 122, 156) (1876–present)

Liatris squarrosa **(L.) Michx. var. *glabrata* (Rydb.) Gaiser** – Gayfeather [Gay-feather, Gay feather] (3, 98) (1926–1977), Scaly blazing star [Scaly blazing-star] (50) (present)

Liatris squarrosa **(L.) Michx. var. *hirsuta* (Rydb.) Gaiser** – Gayfeather [Gay-feather, Gay feather] (3, 4) (1977–1986), Scaly blazing star [Scaly blazing-star] (50) (present)

Liatris squarrosa **(L.) Michx. var. *squarrosa*** – Blazing star [Blazing-star, Blazingstar] (85, 95) (1911–1932), Colic root [Colic-root, Colicroot] (131, 157) (1899–1929), Rattlesnake-master [Rattlesnake master, Rattlesnake's master, Rattlesnakes' master, Rattlesnake's-master] (157) (1929), Scaly blazing star [Scaly blazing-star] (5, 72, 93, 97, 157) (1900–1937)

Liatris squarrosa **Willd.** – See *Liatris squarrosa* (L.) Michx.

Liatris squarrosa **Willd. var. *intermedia* (Lindl.) DC.** – See *Liatris cylindracea* Michx

Liatris virgata **Nutt.** – Small's button-snakeroot (5) (1913)

Liatris **Willd.** – possibly *Serratula* L.

Libanotis vulgaris **[DC.]** – See *Seseli libanotis* (L.) W. D. J. Koch

Libocedrus decurrens **Torr.** – See *Calocedrus decurrens* (Torr.) Florin

Licania michauxii **Prance** – Deer plum (106) (1930) Alabama, Gopher-apple [Gopher apple] (106) (1930), Ground-oak [Ground oak] (106) (1930)

Lichen caninus **L.** – Dogmoss (7) (1828)

Lichen caperata – See *Lichen caperatus* L.

Lichen caperatus **L.** – Stone crottles (92) (1876)

Lichen islandicus **L.** – See *Cetraria islandica* (L.) Acharius

Lichen parietinus **L.** – Wall moss (92) (1876)

Lichen rangiferinus **L.** – Reindeer moss (14, 41, 92) (1770–1882)

Lichen roccella **L.** – All-bone [Allbone, All bones, All-bones] (92) (1876)

Ligusticum actaeifolium **Michx.** – See *Angelica gmelinii* (DC.) Pimenov

Ligusticum canadense **(L.) Britton** – Angelico (5, 156) (1913–1923), Nonda (5) (1913), Nondo (156) (1923)

Ligusticum levisticum **L.** – See *Levisticum officinale* W. D. J. Koch

Ligusticum scoticum **L.** – Lovage [Louage] (10) (1818), Scotch lovage (5, 107, 156) (1913–1923), Sea lovage (5, 156) (1913–1923), Seaparsley [Sea parsley] (5, 156) (1913–1923), Shunis (5, 156) (1913–1923)

Ligustrum **(Tourn.) L.** – See *Ligustrum* L.

Ligustrum amurense **Carr.** – Amur privet (112, 138) (1923–1937), Chinese privet (82) (1930)

Ligustrum japonicum **Thunb.** – Japanese privet [Japan privet] (138) (1923)

Ligustrum **L.** – Japanese privet [Japan privet] (106) (1930), Lovage [Louage] (156) (1923), Privet (1, 50, 82, 106, 109, 112, 126, 138, 155, 156) (1826–present)

Ligustrum lucidum **Aiton f.** – Glossy privet (138) (1923)

Ligustrum ovalifolium **Hassk.** – California privet (109, 122, 124, 135, 138) (1910–1949)

Ligustrum quihoui **Carrière** – Quihou privet (138) (1923)

Ligustrum sinense **Lour.** – Chinese privet (138) (1923)

Ligustrum vulgare **L.** – Common privet (41, 109) (1770–1949), European privet (50, 122, 138, 155) (1923–present), Prie (156, 158) (1900–1923), Prim (5, 19, 26, 49, 53, 92, 156, 158, 187) (1818–1923), Prim-print (156) (1923), Primwort (5, 92, 156, 158) (1876–1923), Print (5, 158, 187) (1818–1913), Privet (5, 7, 49, 53, 57, 82, 92, 156, 158, 182, 184, 187) (1791–1930), Privy (7, 49, 53, 92, 158) (1828–1922), Rainweide (German) (158) (1900), Reimveide (7) (1828), Saugh (158) (1900), Skedge (5, 156, 158) (1900–1923), Skedgwith (5, 156, 158) (1900–1923), Skerrish (158) (1900)

Lilaca vulgaris **Tt.** – possibly *Syringa vulgaris* L.

Lilaeopsis chinensis **(L.) Kuntze** – Lilaeopsis (5, 72) (1907–1913)

Lilaeopsis lineata **(Michx.) Greene** – See *Lilaeopsis chinensis* (L.) Kuntze

Lilium **(Tourn.) L.** – See *Lilium* L.

Lilium ×testaceum **(Lindl.) Turrill** – Nankeen lily (109, 138) (1923–1949)

Lilium auratum **L.** – Gold-band lily [Goldband lily] (109, 138) (1923–1949), Golden-band lily [Golden-banded lily] (107) (1919)

Lilium auratum **Lindl.** – See *Lilium auratum* L.

Lilium bolanderi **S. Wats.** – Thimble lily (109, 138) (1923–1949)

Lilium bulbifera – See *Lilium bulbiferum* L.

Lilium bulbiferum **L.** – Blood-red lily [Blood Red Lillie] (178) (1596), Bulb-bearing lily (107) (1919), Bulbed red lillie (178) (1596), Comosandalos (Hermonians) (180) (1633), Fiery red lily [Fierie red lilly] (180) (1633), Orange lily (19, 50, 138) (1840–present), Red bulb-bearing lily [Red bulbe-bearing Lilly] (180) (1633), Red lily [Red lilly] (180) (1633), Shan-tan (107) (1919) China, Tiger lily [Tiger-lily] (92) (1876)

Lilium canadense **L.** – American yellow lily (86) (1878), Canadian lily [Canada lily] (2, 5, 50, 138, 155, 156, 157, 158) (1895–present), Field lily (156, 157, 158) (1900–1929), File lily (5) (1913), Meadow lily (5, 75, 109, 157, 158) (1894–1949), Nodding lily [Nodding lilies] (5, 19, 75, 92, 156, 157, 158) (1840–1929), Wild field lily (93)

(1936), Wild red lily (156) (1923), Wild yellow lily (5, 72, 85, 93, 156, 157, 158) (1907–1936), Wĭnabojo'bikwûk' (Chippewa, Winabojo's arrow) (40) (1928), Yellow lily (109) (1949)

Lilium canadense **L. subsp.** *michiganense* **(Farw.) Boivin & Cody** – See *Lilium michiganense* Farw.

Lilium canadense **L. var.** *parviflorum* **Hook.** – See *Lilium columbianum* Leichtlin

Lilium candidum **L.** – Giglio (180) (1633), Juno's-rose [Iuno's rose] (180) (1633), Lily [Lylly] (178, 179) (1526–1596), Lirio blanco (Spanish) (180) (1633), Lys blance (French) (180) (1633), Madonna lily (50, 109, 138) (1923–present) NY, Meadow lily (49, 92) (1876–1898) NY, Sultan zambach (Turks) (180) (1633), White lily [White lilies] (19, 49, 92) (1840–1876)

Lilium carolinianum **Michx., non Bosc ex Lam.** – See *Lilium michauxii* Poir.

Lilium catesbaei **Walt.** – Pine lily (50) (present), Southern lily (19) (1840), Southern red lily (2, 5) (1895–1913)

Lilium columbianum **hort. ex Baker** – See *Lilium columbianum* Leichtlin

Lilium columbianum **Leichtlin** – Columbia lily (138) (1923), Panther lily (138) (1923)

Lilium croceum **Chaix** – See *Lilium bulbiferum* L.

Lilium fortunofulgidum **Roane & Henry** – See *Lilium michauxii* Poir.

Lilium grayi **S. Wats.** – Asa Gray's lily (5) (1913), Gray's lily [Grays lily] (50, 138) (1923–present)

Lilium harrisianum **Beane & Vollmer** – See *Lilium pardalinum* Kellogg subsp. *pardalinum*

Lilium humboldti – See *Lilium humboldtii* Roezl & Leichtl. ex Duchartre

Lilium humboldtii **Roezl & Leichtl. ex Duchartre** – Humboldt's lily [Humboldt lily] (138) (1923)

Lilium **L.** – Lily [Lylly] (1, 7, 10, 50, 93, 109, 138, 155, 156, 158, 167, 184) (1793–present)

Lilium lancifolium **Thunb.** – Tiger lily [Tiger-lily] (5, 50, 52, 53, 54, 72, 107, 109, 138, 156) (1907–present), Easter lily (138) (1923), White trumpet lily (109) (1949)

Lilium maritimum **Kellogg** – Coast lily (138) (1923)

Lilium martagon **L.** – Goldwerz (High Dutch) (180) (1633), Great mountain lily [Great mountaine lilly] (180) (1633), Imperial crown (190) (~1759), Lirio Amarillo (Spanish) (180) (1633), Lys sauvage (French) (180) (1633), Martagon Imperiale (Flanders) (180) (1633), Martagon lily (92, 109, 138) (1923–1949), Mountain lily [Mountaine Lillie, Mountaine Lilly] (178, 180) (1596–1633), Small mountain lily [Small mountaine lilly] (180) (1633), Turban lily (107) (1919), Turk's-cap [Turk's cap, Turkscap] (92, 107) (1876–1919), Turk's-cap lily [Turk's cap lily, Turkscap lily] (92, 109) (1876–1949)

Lilium michauxii **Poir.** – Carolina lily (5, 50, 122, 138) (1913–present)

Lilium michiganense **Farw.** – Michigan lily (50, 155) (1942–present), Turk's-cap lily [Turk's cap lily, Turkscap lily] (3) (1977)

Lilium occidentale **Purdy** – Eureka lily (138) (1923)

Lilium pardalinum **Kellogg** – Leopard lily (138) (1923)

Lilium pardalinum **Kellogg subsp.** *pardalinum* – Santa Cruz lily (138) (1923), Sunset lily (109) (1949)

Lilium pardalinum **Kellogg var.** *giganteum* **Hort.** – See *Lilium pardalinum* Kellogg subsp. *pardalinum*

Lilium parryi **S. Wats.** – Lemon lily (138) (1923)

Lilium parviflorum **[(Hook.) W. G. Sm.]** – See *Lilium columbianum* Leichtlin

Lilium parvum **Kellogg** – Sierra lily (138) (1923)

Lilium philadelphicum **L.** – American tiger lily (158) (1900), Fire lily (156) (1923), Flame lily (5, 156, 158) (1900–1923), Freckled lily (78) (1898) ME, Glade lily [Glade-lily] (5, 75, 156, 158) (1894–1923) WV, Huckleberry lily [Huckleberry-lily] (5, 156, 158) (1900–1923), Mouse-root (156) (1923), Orange-cup lily [Orangecup lily] (109, 138) (1923–1949), Philadelphia lily (5, 156, 187) (1818–1923), Red lily [Red lilly] (5, 19, 156, 158) (1840–1923), Tiger lily [Tiger-lily] (5, 75, 156) (1894–1923), Wild orange lily (5, 156, 158) (1900–1923), Wild orange-red lily (2) (1895), Wood lily (5, 50, 72, 155, 156, 158) (1900–present)

Lilium philadelphicum **L. var.** *andinum* **(Nutt.) Ker.-Gawl.** – Mountain wood lily (155) (1942), Tiger lily [Tiger-lily] (127) (1933), Western orange-cup lily [Western orangecup lily] (138, 155) (1923–1942), Western red lily (5, 72, 85, 93) (1907–1936), Western wild lily (157) (1929), Western wood lily (155) (1942), Wild lily (3, 127) (1933–1977), Wood lily (50) (present)

Lilium philadelphicum **L. var.** *montanum* **(A. Nels.) Wherry** – See *Lilium philadelphicum* L. var. *andinum* (Nutt.) Ker.-Gawl.

Lilium regale **E. E. Wilson** – Regal lily (109) (1949), Royal lily (138) (1923)

Lilium roezlii **Regel** – See *Lilium pardalinum* Kellogg subsp. *pardalinum*

Lilium rubescens **S. Wats.** – Chaparral lily (109, 138) (1923–1949)

Lilium superbum **L.** – American Turk's-cap lily [American Turk's cap lily, American Turkscap lily, American Turks-cap lily] (2, 109, 138) (1895–1949), Martagon de Canada (French) (46) (1619), Meadow lily (158) (1900), Nodding lily [Nodding lilies] (5, 73, 75, 158) (1892–1894), Nodding tiger lily [Nodding tiger-lily] (156) (1923), Superb lily (19, 156) (1840–1923), Swamp lily [Swamp-lily] (156) (1923), Tiger lily [Tiger-lily] (156) (1923), Turk's-cap [Turk's cap, Turkscap] (107) (1919), Turk's-cap lily [Turk's cap lily, Turkscap lily] (5, 6, 50, 72, 155, 158) (1874–present), Turk's-head [Turk's-head, Turks-head] (73, 156) (1892–1923) MA, Turk's-head lily [Turk's head lily] (5, 158) (1900–1913), Wild lily (158) (1900), Wild tiger lily (5, 6, 75) (1892–1913)

Lilium superbum **var.** *carolinianum* **Chapm.** – See *Lilium michauxii* Poir.

Lilium testaceum **Lindl.** – See *Lilium × testaceum* (Lindl.) Turrill

Lilium tigrinum **Andr.** – See *Lilium lancifolium* Thunb.

Lilium tigrinum **Ker-Gawl.** – See *Lilium lancifolium* Thunb.

Lilium umbellatum **Pursh** – See *Lilium philadelphicum* L. var. *andinum* (Nutt.) Ker.-Gawl.

Lilium washingtonianum **Kellogg** – Washington lily (109, 138) (1923–1949)

Limnanthemum **[S. G. Gmel.]** – See *Nymphoides* Hill

Limnanthemum lacunosum **Griseb.** – See *Nymphoides cordata* (Ell.) Fern.

Limnanthemum trachyspermum **Gray.** – possibly *Nymphoides aquatica* (J. F. Gmel.) Kuntze

Limnanthes douglasii **R. Br.** – Meadow foam (106) (1930), Meadowfoam [Meadow-foam] (109, 138) (1923–1949)

Limnanthes douglassi – See *Limnanthes douglasii* R. Br.

Limnetis cynosuroides **W.** – See *Spartina cynosuroides* (L.) Roth

Limnetis juncea **Michx.** – See *Spartina patens* (Ait.) Muhl.

Limnetis **Richard** – See *Spartina* Schreber

Limnia depressa **(A. Gray) Rydb.** – See *Claytonia rubra* (T. J. Howell) Tidestrom subsp. *depressa* (Gray) J. M. Miller & K. Chambers

Limnia **L.** – See *Claytonia* L.

Limnia perfoliata **(Donn) Haw.** – See *Claytonia perfoliata* Donn ex Willd.

Limnia perfoliata **Haw.** – See *Claytonia perfoliata* Donn ex Willd.

Limnobium **Rich.** – Frogbit [Frog bit, Frogs-bit, Frog's bit, Frogs-bit] (1, 2, 158) (1895–1932), Occident frogbit [Occident-frogbit] (155) (1942), Sponge plant [Spongeplant] (50) (present)

Limnobium spongia **(Bosc) L. C. Rich. ex Steud.** – American frog's-bit [American frog's bit] (156) (1923), American spongeplant (50) (present), Common occident frogbit [Common occident-frogbit] (155) (1942), Frogbit [Frog bit, Frogs-bit, Frog's bit, Frogs-bit] (5, 10, 122) (1818–1937)

Limnodea arkansana **(Nutt.) L. H. Dewey** – Ozark grass [Ozarkgrass] (50, 155) (1942–present)

Limnomium arborescens – possibly *Limonium arborescens* (Brouss.) Kuntze

Limnorchis dilatata **(Pursh) Rydb.** – See *Platanthera dilatata* (Pursh) Lindl. ex Beck var. *dilatata*

Limnorchis hyperborea **(L.) Rydb.** – See *Platanthera hyperborea* (L.) Lindl. var. *hyperborea*

Limnorchis **Rydb.** – See *Platanthera* L.C. Rich

Limnorchis viridiflora **(Cham.) Rydb.** – See *Platanthera hyperborea* (L.) Lindl. var. *viridiflora* (Cham.) Luer

Limnosciadium pinnatum **(DC.) Math. & Const.** – Pinnate cynosciadium (5, 97) (1913–1937), Tansy dogshade (50) (present)

Limodorum **L.** – See *Calopogon* R. Br. ex Ait. f. (all U.S. species)

Limodorum tuberosum **L.** – See *Calopogon tuberosus* (L.) Britton, Sterns & Poggenb. var. *tuberosus*

Limonium arborescens **(Brouss.) Kuntze** – Tree sea-lavender (138) (1923)

Limonium carolinianum **(Walt.) Britt.** – American thrift (5, 92, 156) (1876–1923), Canker-root [Cankerroot, Canker root] (92) (1876), Inkroot [Ink-root, Ink root] (5, 49, 58, 92, 156) (1876–1923), Lavender thrift [Lavender-thrift] (5, 92, 156) (1876–1923), Marshroot [Marsh root] (5, 92) (1876–1913), Marsh-rosemary [Marsh rosemary, Marsh rosemary] (5, 49, 58, 92, 156) (1869–1923), Meadow root (92) (1876), Sea gilliflower [sea gilly-flower] (92) (1876), Sea-lavender [Sea lavender, Sea lauender] (5, 49, 58, 122, 156, 178) (1526–1936), Seaside lavender [Sea-side lavender] (5) (1913), Sea-thrift [Sea thrift] (58, 92) (1869–1876)

Limonium limbatum **Small.** – Trans-Pecos sea-lavender [Transpecos sealavender] (50) (present)

Limonium **P. Mill.** – Sea-lavender [Sea lavender, Sea lauender] (109, 122, 138) (1923–1949), Statice (122) (1937), Thrift (138, 156) (1923)

Limonium sinuatum **(L.) P. Mill.** – Notch-leaf sea-lavender [Notchleaf sea-lavender] (138) (1923)

Limonium vulgare **Mill.** – Inkroot [Ink-root, Ink root] (49) (1898), Marsh-rosemary [Marsh rose-mary, Marsh rosemary] (2, 19, 57) (1840–1917), Sea-lavender [Sea lavender, Sea lauender] (2, 19) (1840–1895), Statice (57) (1917)

Limosella aquatica **L.** – Mudweed [Mud-weed] (5, 156, 157) (1900–1929), Mudwort [Mud wort] (3, 5, 85, 156) (1913–1977), Water mudwort (50, 155) (1942–present)

Limosella aquatica **var. *tenuifolia* Hoffm.** – See *Limosella australis* R. Br.

Limosella australis **R. Br.** – Mudwort [Mud wort] (19, 92) (1840–1876)

Limosella **L.** – Mudweed [Mud-weed] (158) (1900), Mudwort [Mud wort] (1, 2, 10, 50, 155, 158) (1818–present)

Limosella subulata **Ives** – See *Limosella australis* R. Br.

Linanthus androsaceus **subsp. *micranthus* (Steud.) H. Mason** – See *Linanthus parviflorus* (Benth.) Greene

Linanthus caespitosus **(Nutt.) J. M. Porter & L. A. Johnson** – Mat prickly-phlox [Mat prickly phlox] (50) (present), Tufted sharp-leaf gilia [Tufted sharp-leaved gilia] (5, 93) (1913–1936)

Linanthus californicus **(Hook. & Arn.) J. M. Porter & L. A. Johnson** – Shrubby gilia (138) (1923), See *Linanthus californicus* (Hook. & Arn.) J. M. Porter & L. A. Johnson

Linanthus parviflorus **(Benth.) Greene** – Thread-flower gilia [Thread-flower gilia] (138) (1923)

Linanthus septentrionalis **Mason** – Northern limnanthus (50) (present)

Linaria **(Tourn.) L.** – See *Linaria* Mill.

Linaria **(Tourn.) Mill.** – See *Linaria* Mill.

Linaria bipartita **(Vent.) Willd.** – Cloven-lip toadflax (138) (1923)

Linaria canadensis **(L.) Dumort** – See *Nuttallanthus canadensis* (L.) D.A. Sutton

Linaria canadensis **(L.) Dumort var. *canadensis*** – possibly *Nuttallanthus canadensis* (L.) D. A. Sutton

Linaria canadensis **(L.) Dumort var. *texana* (Scheele) Pennell** – See *Nuttallanthus texanus* (Scheele) D. A. Sutton

Linaria cymbalaria **(L.) Mill.** – See *Cymbalaria muralis* P. G. Gaertn., B. Mey. & Scherb.

Linaria dalmatica **(L.) Mill. subsp. *dalmatica*** – Dalmatian toadflax (50, 155) (1942–present)

Linaria dalmatica **(L.) P. Mill.** – Dalmatian toadflax (50, 138, 155) (1923–present), Toadflax [Toad flax, Toad-flax] (3) (1977)

Linaria elatine **(L.) Mill.** – See *Knautia arvensis* (L.) Duby

Linaria **Juss.** – See *Linaria* Mill.

Linaria linaria **(L.) Karst.** – See *Linaria vulgaris* Mill.

Linaria maroccana **Hook. f.** – Moroccan toadflax [Morocco toadflax] (138) (1923)

Linaria **Mill.** – Butter-and-eggs [Butter & eggs, Butter and eggs] (1, 93) (1932–1936), Toadflax [Toad flax, Toad-flax] (2, 4, 7, 50, 82, 93, 109, 138, 155, 156) (1828–present)

Linaria purpurea **(L.) Mill.** – Purple toadflax [Purple toad flax, Purple toad flaxe] (50, 178) (1526–present)

Linaria repens **(L.) P. Mill.** – Pale-blue toad-flax (5) (1913)

Linaria reticulata **(Sm.) Desf.** – Purple-net toadflax [Purplenet toadflax] (138) (1923)

Linaria supina **(L.) Chaz.** – Supine linaria (5) (1913), Toadflax of Valentia [Toade flaxe of Valentia] (178) (1526)

Linaria supina **Desf.** – See *Linaria supina* (L.) Chaz.

Linaria texana **Scheele** – See *Nuttallanthus texanus* (Scheele) D.A. Sutton

Linaria vulgaris **Hill** – See *Linaria vulgaris* Mill.

Linaria vulgaris **Mill.** – Bread-and-biscuit [Bread and biscuit] (73) (1892), Bread-and-butter (5, 157, 158) (1900–1929) Ipswich MA, Bread-and-butter toadflax (155) (1942), Brideweed [Bride-weed] (5, 156, 157, 158) (1900–1929), Bridewort [Bride wort, Bride-wort] (156) (1923) no longer in use by 1923, Butter-and-eggs [Butter & eggs, Butter and eggs] (3, 5, 6, 45, 48, 49, 50, 62, 63, 72, 77, 80, 82, 85, 93, 95, 97, 109, 122, 124, 127, 131, 148, 155, 156, 157, 158) (1882–present), Chopped-eggs (157, 158) (1900–1929), Common toadflax [Common toad-flax, Common toad flax] (42, 138, 157, 158) (1814–1929), Continental weed (5, 6) (1892–1913), Deadmen's-bones [Dead men's bones] (5, 73, 157, 158) (1892–1929) Troy NY, Devil's flower (5) (1913), Devil's-flax [Devil's flax] (5, 75, 156, 157, 158) (18994–1929) WV, Eggs-and-bacon (5, 156) (1913–1923), False flax [Falseflax] (6) (1892), Flachskraut (German) (158) (1900), Flax snapdragon [Flax snap dragon] (19) (1840), Flaxweed [Flax-weed] (5, 156, 157, 158) (1900–1929), Frauenflachs (German) (6) (1892), Gallweed [Gall-weed] (156) (1923) no longer in use by 1923, Gallwort [Gall-wort, Gall wort] (5, 92, 157, 158) (1876–1929), Haycocks (157, 158) (1900–1929), Impudent-lawyer [Impudent lawyer] (5, 75, 156, 157, 158) (1894–1929) WV, Indian hemp [Indianhemp] (75, 156) (1894–1923) WV, Jacob's-ladder [Jacob's ladder, Jacobs-ladder] (5, 6, 73, 158) (1892–1923) parts of NE US, Lady's-slipper [Lady's slipper, Ladies' slipper, Lady-slipper, Ladyslipper, Ladie-slipper, Lady's slippers] (77) (1898) MA, Larkspur [Lark-spur] (158) (1900), Leinkraut (German) (6, 158) (1892–1900), Linaire commune (French) (6, 158) (1892–1900), Löwenmaul [Lowenmaul] (German) (6, 158) (1892–1900), Mother-of-millions [Mother of millions] (156) (1923), Rabbit-ears [Rabbit ears] (156) (1923), Rabbit-flower [Rabbit's flower, Rabbit flower] (5, 156) (1913–1923), Ramstead [Ramsted] (49, 157, 158) (1898–1929), Rancid (5, 156, 158) (1900–1923) no longer in use by 1923, Ranstead [Ransted] (5, 6, 62, 156, 157, 184) (1793–1929), Ransteadweed (187) (1818), Sierra snapdragon (155) (1942), Snapdragon [Snap dragon, Snap-dragon] (5, 19, 75, 92, 93, 156, 158) (1840–1936), Toadflax [Toad flax, Toad-flax] (6, 18, 45, 46, 48, 49, 62, 80, 82, 127, 148, 156, 187) (1671–1933), Wild flax [Wilde flaxe, Wilde-flax] (5, 75, 93, 157, 158) (1894–1936), Wild snapdragon [Wild snap-dragon] (187) (1818), Wild tobacco [Wild-tobacco, Wildtobacco] (5, 75, 157, 158) (1894–1929) WV, Yellow flax (6) (1892), Yellow toadflax [Yellow toad flax, Yellow toad-flax] (5, 95, 131, 56, 157, 158) (1899–1936), Yellow-rod (157, 158) (1900–1929)

Lindera benzoin **Blume.** – Allspice (7) (1828), Allspice bush (6, 186) (1814–1892), Benjamin bush [Benjamin-bush] (2, 5, 6, 49, 58, 92, 107, 156) (1869–1923), Benjamin tree [Benjamin-tree] (8) (1785),

Benjamins [Benjamin] (46) (1879), Bensoin officinarum (177) (1762), Benzoelorbeer (German) (6) (1892), Benzoin (6) (1892), Benzoin Lorbeer (German) (186) (1814), Canonotha (46) (1879), Common spicebush (2, 6, 155) (1895–1942), Fever bush [Feverbush, Fever-bush] (5, 6, 7, 19, 46, 58, 92, 156, 157, 186, 187) (1814–1929), Feverwood [Fever wood, Fever-wood] (49, 92, 186) (1814–1898), Goroffle (46) (1879), Kapak-minš (Chippewa, brittle tree) (105) (1932), Laurier benzoin (French) (6) (1892), Laurier beujoin (French) (8) (1785), Northern spicebush (50) (present), Poivrier (French) (17) (1796), Snapweed [Snap weed, Snap-weed] (5, 92, 156) (1876–1923) no longer in use by 1923, Snapwood [Snap wood, Snap-wood] (5, 92, 156) (1876–1923), Spice bush [Spice-bush, Spicebush] (3, 12, 19, 49, 57, 58, 65, 92, 104, 107, 109) (1820–1977), Spiceberry [Spice-berry, Spice berry] (6, 186, 187) (1814–1892), Spicewood [Spice-wood, Spice wood] (5, 7, 8, 14, 17, 34, 35, 49, 58, 92, 97, 138, 156) (1785–1937), Wild allspice [Wild all Spice] (5, 49, 58, 92, 156, 177, 186, 187) (1753–1923), Wild pimento (177) (1762)

Lindera melissaefolia **Blume.** – See *Lindera melissifolia* (Walt.) Blume

Lindera melissifolia **(Walt.) Blume** – Hairy spicebush [Hairy spice bush, Hairy spice-bush] (5, 156) (1913–1923), Jove's-fruit [Jove's fruit] (5, 156) (1913–1923)

Lindera **Thunb.** – Fever bush [Feverbush, Fever-bush] (2) (1895), Spice bush [Spice-bush, Spicebush] (1, 2, 4, 50, 138, 155, 156) (1895–present), Wild allspice [Wild all Spice] (2) (1895)

Lindernia **All.** – False pimpernel [Falsepimpernel] (1, 2, 50, 155, 158) (1895–present)

Lindernia anagallidea **(Michx.) Pennell** – See *Lindernia dubia* (L.) Pennell var. *anagallidea* (Michx.) Cooperrider

Lindernia attenuata **Muhl.** – See *Lindernia dubia* (L.) Pennell

Lindernia diffusa **(L.) Wettst.** – Bitter-blain [Bitter blain] (92) (1876)

Lindernia dilatata **Muhl.** – See *Lindernia dubia* (L.) Pennell

Lindernia dubia **(L.) Pennell** – False pempernel (131) (1899), False pimpernel [Falsepimpernel] (3, 4) (1977–1986), Pimpernel (19) (1840), Yellow-seed false pimpernel [Yellowseed false pimpernel] (50) (present)

Lindernia dubia **(L.) Pennell var.** *anagallidea* **(Michx.) Cooperr.** – Water hedge-hyssop [Water hedge hyssop] (19) (1840), False pimpernel [Falsepimpernel] (3) (1977), Long-stalk false pimpernel [Long-stalked false pimpernel] (97) (1937), Yellow-seed false pimpernel [Yellowseed false pimpernel] (50) (present)

Lindernia dubia **(L.) Pennell var.** *dubia* – False hedgehyssop [False hedge hyssop] (19) (1840), False pimpernel [Falsepimpernel] (93, 95, 156) (1911–1936), Long-stalk false pimpernel [Long-stalked false pimpernel] (5, 72, 97) (1907–1937), Short-stalk false pimpernel [Short-stalked false pimpernel] (5, 72) (1907–1913), Sweetweed (184) (1793), Yellow-seed false pimpernel [Yellowseed false pimpernel] (50) (present)

Lindernia pyxidaria – See *Lindernia dubia* (L.) Pennell var. *dubia*

Lindheimera texana **Gray & Engelm.** – Lindheimer's daisy (124) (1937), Texas star daisy (97) (1937), Texas yellow-star [Texas yellowstar] (50) (present), Yellow Texas star (122) (1937)

Linnaea americana **Forbes** – See *Linnaea borealis* L.

Linnaea borealis americana – See *Linnaea borealis* L. subsp. *americana* (Forbes) Hultén ex Clausen

Linnaea borealis **L.** – Benwarksgras (Swedish) (46) (1879), Cinnamon vine [Cinnamon-vine, Cinnamonvine] (156) (1923), Deer vine [Deer-vine] (5, 75, 156, 158) (1894–1923) ME, Eglantine [Eglentyne] (156) (1923), Grand vine (72) (1907) IA, Ground vine [Ground-vine] (5, 7, 92, 156, 158) (1828–1923), Hwita klacker (Swedish) (46) (1879), Klasgras (Swedish) (46) (1879), Norrislegrass (Norway) (46) (1879), Torrwarksgras (Swedish) (46) (1879), Twin flower [Twinflower, Twin-flower] (3, 4, 5, 7, 19, 50, 72, 92, 109, 131, 156, 158) (1828–present), Two-eyed berry [Two-eyed berries, Two-eyes berry, Two-eye berry] (5, 73, 156, 158) (1892–1923) St. Stephen NB, Windgras (Swedish) (46) (1879)

Linnaea borealis **L. subsp.** *americana* **(Forbes) Hultén ex Clausen** – American twin-flower [American twinflower] (138, 155) (1923–1942)

Linnaea **L.** – Twin flower [Twinflower, Twin-flower] (1, 2, 4, 50, 138, 155, 156, 158) (1895–present)

Linneusia borealis **L.** – See *Linnaea borealis* L.

Linum **(Tourn.) L.** – See *Linum* L.

Linum angustifolium **Huds.** – See *Linum bienne* Mill.

Linum aristatum **Engelm.** – Bristle flax (50) (present), Broom flax (4) (1986)

Linum austriacum **L.** – Austrian flax (138) (1923)

Linum berlandieri **Hook.** – Berlandier's yellow flax (50, 122, 155) (1937–present), Large yellow flax (124) (1937)

Linum berlandieri **Hook. var.** *berlandieri* – Berlandier's flax (4) (1986), Berlandier's yellow flax (5, 50, 97, 155) (1913–present), Stiff-stem flax [Stiffstem flax] (3) (1977)

Linum bienne **Mill.** – Pale flax (50) (present), Wild flax [Wilde flaxe, Wilde-flax] (178) (1526)

Linum catharticum **L.** – Cathartic flax (5, 156) (1913–1923), Dwarf flax [Dwarfe flaxe] (5, 156, 178) (1526–1923), Dwarf wild flax (92) (1876), Fairy flax (5, 156) (1913–1923), Fairy lint (5, 156) (1913–1923), Mill mountain (92) (1876), Mill mountain flax (5) (1913), Mountain flax [Mountain-flax] (5, 156) (1913–1923), Purging flax (5, 92, 156) (1876–1923)

Linum compactum **A. Nels.** – Compact stiff-stem flax [Compact stiffstem flax] (4) (1986), Stiff-stem flax [Stiffstem flax] (3) (1977), Wyoming flax (50) (present)

Linum floridanum **(Planch.) Trel. var.** *floridanum* – Florida yellow flax (5) (1913)

Linum grandiflorum **Desf.** – Flowering flax (50, 109 138, 155) (1923–present)

Linum hudsonioides **Planch.** – Texas flax (50) (present)

Linum humile **Mill.** – See *Linum usitatissimum* L.

Linum **L.** – Blue flax (1) (1932), Flax (1, 4, 10, 13, 15, 50, 82, 93, 109, 138, 155, 158, 184) (1793–present), Yellow flax (1, 93) (1932–1936)

Linum lewisi – See *Linum lewisii* Pursh

Linum lewisii **Pursh** – Blue flax (101, 122) (1905–1937), Lewis' flax [Lewis flax] (155) (1942), Lewis' wild flax (5, 97, 131) (1899–1937), Perennial blue flax [Perrennial blue flax] (124) (1937), Prairie flax (5, 50, 109, 138, 156, 157) (1900–present), Wild blue flax (127) (1933), Wild flax [Wilde flaxe, Wilde-flax] (37, 93, 101, 156) (1905–1936)

Linum lewisii **Pursh var.** *lewisii* – Blue flax (3, 4) (1977–1986), Prairie flax (50) (present)

Linum medium **(Planch.) Britt. var.** *medium* – Stiff yellow flax (5, 97) (1913–1937)

Linum medium **(Planch.) Britton var.** *texanum* **(Planch.) Fern.** – Stiff yellow flax (50, 122) (1937–present), Sucker flax (4) (1986)

Linum perenne **L.** – Blue flax (50) (present), Flax (35) (1806), Flowering flax (44) (1845), Perennial flax (2, 86, 92, 138, 155) (1878–1942), Perennial wild flax (108) (1878)

Linum perenne **L. var.** *lewisii* **(Pursh) Eat. & Wright** – See *Linum lewisii* Pursh var. *lewisii*

Linum pratense **(Nort.) Small** – Meadow flax (50) (present), Norton's flax (4) (1986)

Linum puberulum **(Engelm.) Heller** – Plains flax (4, 50) (1986–present)

Linum rigidum **Pursh** – Flax (148) (1939), Large-flower yellow flax [Large-flowered yellow flax] (72, 122, 131) (1899–1937), Stiff-stem flax [Stiffstem flax] (50, 155) (1942–present), Wild flax [Wilde flaxe, Wilde-flax] (126, 148) (1933–1939), Wild yellow flax (127) (1933), Yellow flax (47, 125) (1852–1930)

Linum rigidum **Pursh var.** *berlandieri* **(Hook.) T.& G.** – See *Linum berlandieri* Hook. var. *berlandieri*

Linum rigidum **Pursh var.** *compactum* **(A. Nels.) Rogers** – See *Linum compactum* A. Nels.

Linum rigidum **Pursh var.** *rigidum* – Large-flower yellow flax [Large-flowered yellow flax] (5, 97) (1913–1937), Stiff-stem flax [Stiffstem flax] (3, 4, 50, 98) (1926–present), Yellow flax (85) (1932)

Linum rigidum **Pursh** var. *simulans* **Rogers** – Stiff-stem flax [Stiff-stem flax] (50) (present)

Linum striatum **Walt.** – Ridged yellow flax (5, 97) (1913–1937)

Linum sulcatum **Riddell** – Grooved flax (3, 4, 50, 155) (1942–present), Grooved yellow flax (72, 122, 131) (1899–1907), Yellow flax (98) (1926)

Linum sulcatum **Riddell** var. *sulcatum* – Grooved flax (50) (present), Grooved yellow flax (5, 97) (1913–1937), Yellow flax (85) (1932)

Linum usitatissimum **L.** – Aiwina (Finnish) (110) (1886), Atasi (110) (1886), Common flax (3, 4, 50, 82, 155, 156) (1923–present), Cultivated flax (5, 93) (1913–1936), Flax (5, 19, 72, 85, 95, 97, 107, 109, 110, 114, 138, 158, 179, 180) (1526–1949), Flaxseed [Flax seed] (53, 57, 59, 92, 157) (1876–1922), Flix (5, 156, 158) (1900–1923), Haar (German near Salzburg) (110) (1886) from German for thread or hair, Hor (Danish) (110) (1886), Hor härr (Danish) (110) (1886), Klanglein (German) (110) (1886), Li (Basque) (110) (1886), Liho (Basque) (110) (1886), Lin (Keltic) (110) (1886), Linn [Lynn] (156) (1923), Lino (Basque) (110) (1886), Linseed (5, 53, 57, 59, 92, 95, 156, 157) (1876–1936), Lint (156, 158) (1900–1923), Lintbells [Lint-bells, Lint bells] (5, 97, 156, 158) (1900–1937), Linum (59) (1911), Low flax (155) (1942), Lyne (179) (1526), Pellawa (Finnish) (110) (1886), Springlein (German) (110) (1886), Vlix (158) (1900), Winterlien (German) (92) (1876)

Linum usitatissimum **L.** var. *humile* (**Mill.**) **Pers.** – See *Linum usitatissimum* L.

Linum virginianum **L.** – Slender yellow flax (5) (1913), Wechkenah (Missouri tribes) (7) (1828), Wild flax [Wilde flaxe, Wilde-flax] (2, 7, 19, 92) (1828–1895), Wild Virginia flax [Wild Virginian flax] (41) (1770), Wild yellow flax (5) (1913)

Liparis **L.C. Rich.** – Twayblade [Tway blade, Tway-blade] (1, 109, 138) (1923–1949), Wide-lip orchid [Widelip orchid] (50) (present)

Liparis liliifolia (**L.**) **L. C. Rich** – See *Liparis loeselii* (L.) Rich

Liparis liliifolia (**L.**) **L. C. Rich. ex Ker-Gawl.** – Brown wide-lip orchid [Brown widelip orchid] (50) (present), Large twayblade [Large tway-blade] (5, 156) (1913–1923), Lily-leaf malaxis [Lily-leaved malaxis] (187) (1818), Twayblade [Tway blade, Tway-blade] (19) (1840)

Liparis loeselii (**L.**) **L. C. Rich** – Fen orchis (72, 93) (1907–1936), Lily twaybalde (138) (1923), Loesel's twayblade [Loesel twayblade] (3, 5, 138) (1913–1977), Long-leaf malaxis [Long-leaved malaxis] (187), Twayblade [Tway blade, Tway-blade] (93, 122) (1936–1937), Yellow wide-lip orchid [Yellow widelip orchid] (50) (present)

Liparis **Rich.** – See *Liparis* L. C. Rich.

Lipocarpha aristulata (**Coville**) **G. Tucker** – Awned half-chaff sedge [Awned halfchaff sedge] (50) (present), Awned hemicarpha (5) (1913)

Lipocarpha drummondii (**Nees**) **G. Tucker** – Drummond's halfchaff sedge (50) (present), Drummond's hemicarpha [Drummond hemicarpha] (3) (1977)

Lipocarpha maculata (**Michx.**) **Torr.** – American halfchaff sedge (50) (present), American lipocarpha (5) (1913)

Lipocarpha micrantha (**Vahl**) **G. Tucker** – Common hemicarpha (3, 5) (1913–1977), Dwarf hemicarpha (66) (1903), Hemicarpha (72) (1907) IA, Small-flower half-chaff sedge [Smallflower halfchaff sedge] (50) (present)

Lipocarpha **R. Br.** – Half-chaff sedge [Halfchaff sedge] (50) (present)

Lippia (**Houstaon**) **L.** – See *Lippia* L.

Lippia berlandieri **Schauer** – See *Lippia graveolens* Kunth

Lippia canescens – See *Phyla nodiflora* (L.) Greene

Lippia citriodora – See *Aloysia triphylla* (L'Hér.) Britt.

Lippia cuneifolia (**Torr.**) **Steud.** – See *Lippia cuneifolia* (Torr.) Greene

Lippia cuneifolia **Steud** – See *Phyla cuneifolia* (Torr.) Greene

Lippia dulcis **Trevar.** – See *Phyla scaberrima* (Juss.) Moldenke

Lippia graveolens **Kunth** – Red brush [Red-brush] (122) (1937) TX

Lippia **L.** – Carpet-grass [Carpet grass] (106) (1930), Fogfruit [Fogfruit, Fog fruit] (82, 158) (1900–1930), Lippia (138, 155) (1923–1942)

Lippia lanceolata **Michx.** – See *Phyla lanceolata* (Michx.) Greene

Lippia lanceolata **Michx.** var. *recognita* **Fern. & Grisc.** – See *Phyla lanceolata* (Michx.) Greene

Lippia ligustrina (**Lag.**) **Britton** – See *Aloysia gratissima* (Gillies & Hook.) Troncoso

Lippia macrostachya **S. Watson** – See *Aloysia macrostachya* (Torr.) Moldenke

Lippia nodiflora (**L.**) **Michx.** – See *Phyla nodiflora* (L.) Greene

Lippia repens (**Spreng.**) – See *Phyla nodiflora* (L.) Greene

Liquidambar asplenifolia (**L.**) **C.F. Ludw.** – See *Comptonia peregrina* (L.) Coult.

Liquidambar **L.** – Bilsted (2) (1895), Liquidambar (French) (8) (1785), Liquidambar [Liquidamber] (8) (1785), Sweetgum [Sweet gum, Sweet-gum] or Sweetgum tree [Sweet gum-tree] (2, 8, 138, 167) (1785–1923)

Liquidambar peregrina – See *Comptonia peregrina* (L.) Coult.

Liquidambar styraciflua **L.** – Ahite Franckincense, Olibanum or Thus (181) (~1678), Alligator tree [Alligator-tree] (5, 156) (1913–1923), Alligator wood (74) (1893) WV, Bilsted (5, 49, 156) (1898–1923), Byl steel (Belgis Noveboracensibus) (177) (1762), Copalm (156) (1923), Copalm (French) (17, 20, 49, 92) (1796–1898), Gum or Gum tree [Gum-tree] (27) (1811), Gum wax (49) (1898), Gumwood [Gum-wood] (177) (1762), Incense tree [Incense-tree] (156) (1923), Liquidambar [Liquidamber] (5, 57, 156) (1913–1923), Liquidambar à feuilles d'erable (French) (8) (1785), Maple-leaf liquidambar tree [Maple-leaved liquidambar-tree] (8) (1785), Mountain-mahogany [Mountain mahogany, Mountainmahogany] (156) (1923), Opossum tree [Opossum-tree] (5, 92, 156) (1876–1923), Red gum (5, 65, 156) (1913–1931) OK, Satin walnut (5, 156) (1913–1923), Star-leaf gum [Star-leaved gum] (5, 156) (1913–1923), Storax or Storax tree [Storax trees] (34, 178) (1526–1834), Styrax (178) (1526), Sweetgum [Sweet gum, Sweet-gum] or Sweetgum tree [Sweet gum-tree] (5, 7, 8, 10, 12, 18, 20, 19, 41, 49, 53, 57, 61, 65, 92, 97, 109, 122, 124, 138, 156, 177, 181, 182, 189) (~1678–1949), White gum [White-gum] or White gum tree (5, 7, 92, 156, 177) (1762–1923)

Liriodendron **L.** – Poplar or Poplar tree [Poplar-tree] (181) (~1678), Tulip tree [Tulip-tree, Tuliptree] (8, 15, 138, 167) (1785–1923)

Liriodendron tulipifera **L.** – American poplar (186, 187) (1814–1818), American tulip-tree [American tuliptree, American tulip tree] (186) (1814), Basswood [Bass wood, Bass-wood] (5, 156) (1913–1923), Blue poplar (5) (1913), Bois blanc (French) (43) (1820), Bois jaune (French, yellow wood) (17, 186) (1796–1814), Canoe tree (41) (1770), Canoe wood [Canoe-wood] (20, 49, 92, 156) (1649–1923), Cucumber tree [Cucumber-tree, Cucumbertree] (5, 74, 156) (1893–1923), Cypress tree [Cypress-tree, Cypresse tree] (186) (1814), Espetonga (Osage) (7) (1828), Hickory poplar (5, 74) (1893–1913) WV, Kanœträd (186) (1814), Knuträd (186) (1814), Knutræ (186) (1814), Lime or Lime tree [Lime-tree, Limetree] (5, 156) (1913–1923), Linn [Lynn] or Linn tree [Linn-tree] (156) (1923), Lynn tree (5) (1913), Lyre tree [Lyre-tree] (92, 156) (1898–1923), Magnolia (74) (1893) White Haven PA, Old-wife's-shirt [Old wife's shirt] (186) (1814), Old-woman's-smock [Old woman's smock] (41) (1770), Poplar or Poplar tree [Poplar-tree] (2, 18, 20, 41, 46, 49, 107, 177, 184, 186) (1770–1919), Rakiock (46, 181) (~1678–1879), Saddle tree [Saddle-tree] (5, 156) (1913–1923), Saddle-leaf [Saddle leaf] (5, 156) (1913–1923), Tree-of-peace [Tree of peace] (181) (~1678), Tsue-u (186) (1814), Tulip poplar (5, 7) (1828–1932), Tulip tree [Tulip-tree, Tuliptree] (2, 5, 7, 10, 12, 13, 14, 15, 20, 19, 41, 46, 49, 57, 82, 92, 106, 107, 109, 138, 156, 181, 182, 186, 187, 189, 190) (~1678–1949), Tulip-poplar (106, 156) (1923–1930), Tulpboom (186) (1814), Tulpinbaum (186) (1814), Tzue-u (186) (1814), Virginia tulip tree [Virginian tulip-tree] (8) (1785), White poplar or White poplar tree (2, 5, 13, 18, 46, 49, 74, 92, 186, 187) (1818–1913), Whitewood [White wood, White-wood] (2, 5, 7, 13, 15, 20, 19, 49, 92, 107, 109, 156, 177, 186) (1762–1949), Wild poplar (92) (1876), Yellow poplar (5, 13, 18, 49, 61, 74, 82, 92, 106, 156) (1805–1930), Yellow-wood [Yellowwood, Yellow wood] (7,

46, 49, 186) (1825–1898)

Liriope **Lour.** – Lily-turf (109) (1949)

Lisianthius glaucifolius **Jacq.** – See *Eustoma exaltatum* (L.) Salisb. ex G. Don

Lisimachia ciliata **L.** – See *Lysimachia ciliata* L.

Lisimachia racemosa – possibly *Lysimachia terrestris* (L.) Britton, Sterns & Poggenb.

Listera auriculata **Wieg.** – Auricled twayblade (5, 50) (1913–present)

Listera australis **Lindl.** – Southern twayblade (5, 50) (1913–present)

Listera convallarioides **(Sw.) Nutt. ex Ell.** – Broad-leaf twayblade [Broad-leaved tway-blade] (5) (1913), Broad-lip twayblade [Broad-lipped twayblade] (50) (present), Lily orchis (19) (1840), Twayblade [Tway blade, Tway-blade] (3, 5) (1913–1977)

Listera cordata **(L.) R. Br. ex Ait. f.** – Double-leaf (5, 156) (1913–1923), Twinfoil (156) (1923), possibly Heart-leaf listeria [Heart-leaved listeria] (187) (1818)

Listera cordata **(L.) R. Br. ex Ait. f. var.** *cordata* – Heart-leaf twayblade [Heartleaf twayblade] (5, 50) (1913–present), Twi-foil (5) (1913)

Listera smallii **Wieg.** – Kidney-leaf twayblade [Kidneyleaf twayblade] (5, 50) (1913–present)

Listeriacordata **Willd.** – possibly *Listera cordata* (L.) R. Br. ex Ait. f.

Lithocarpus densiflorus **(Hook. & Arn.) Rehd.** – California chestnut oak (161) (1857), Chêne à fleurs denses (French) (20) (1857), Dense-flower oak [Dense flowered oak] (20) (1857), Tan bark (106) (1930)

Lithophragma **(Nutt.) Torr. & Gray** – Prairie-star [Prairie star] (1) (1932), Star flower [Starflower, Star-flower] (1) (1932), Woodland-star [Woodland star, Woodlandstar] (1, 50, 155) (1932–present)

Lithophragma bulbiferum **Rydb.** – See *Lithophragma glabrum* Nutt.

Lithophragma glabrum **Nutt.** – Woodland star (3) (1977)

Lithophragma parviflora **(Hook.) Nutt.** – See *Lithophragma parviflorum* (Hook.) Nutt. ex Torr. & Gray

Lithophragma parviflorum **(Hook.) Nutt. ex Torr. & Gray** – Prairie-star [Prairie star] (3, 4, 5) (1913–1986), Small-flower tellima [Small flowered tellima] (131) (1899), Small-flower woodland-star [Small-flower woodland-star] (50) (present), Woodland-star [Woodland star, Woodlandstar] (85) (1932)

Lithops **N.E. BRr.** – possibly *Mesembryanthemum* L.

Lithospermum **(Tourn.) L.** – See *Lithospermum* L.

Lithospermum angustifolium **Michx.** – See *Lithospermum incisum* Lehm.

Lithospermum arvense **L.** – See *Buglossoides arvensis* (L.) I. M. Johnston

Lithospermum canescens **(Michx.) Lehm.** – Alconet (92) (1876), American alkanet (156, 157, 158) (1900–1929), American anchusa (92, 157, 158) (1876–1929), Bazu-hi (Omaha-Ponca) (37) (1919), Bloodroot [Blood-root, Blood root] (77) (1898) Southwest MO, False bugloss (19) (1840), Hoary gromwell (155) (1942), Hoary puccoon (2, 4, 47, 50, 5, 63, 72, 85, 93, 97, 127, 131, 156, 157, 158) (1852–present), Indian paint [Indian-paint] (3, 75, 77, 156, 157, 158) (1898–1977), Indian puccoon (156, 157, 158) (1900–1929), Orange puccoon (156) (1923), Pocones (46) (1879), Puccoon (19, 46, 109, 138) (1840–1949)

Lithospermum canescens **Lehm.** – See *Lithospermum canescens* (Michx.) Lehm.

Lithospermum carolinense **(Walt.) MacM.** – See *Lithospermum caroliniense* (Walt. ex J.F. Gmel.) MacM.

Lithospermum caroliniense **(Walt. ex J. F. Gmel.) MacM.** – Carolina gromwell (138, 155) (1923–1942), Carolina puccoon (50) (present), Gmelin's puccoon (5, 93) (1913–1936), Gromwell (48) (1882), Hairy puccoon (2, 5, 63, 93, 97, 98, 121, 156) (1895–1937), Hoary puccoon (98) (1926), Odji'bĭknamûn' (Chippewa) (40) (1928), Pežuta ha sapa (Lakota, black skin medicine) (121) (1918?–1970?), Pežuta waxe ša (Lakota, black-skin medicine) (121) (1918?–1970?), Puccoon (3, 4, 40) (1929–1986), Sand-barren puccoon (156) (1923),

Woolly puccoon (124) (1937)

Lithospermum caroliniense **(Walt. ex J. F. Gmel.) MacM. var.** *croceum* **(Fern.) Cronq.** – Shrubby gromwell (138) (1923)

Lithospermum caroliniense **(Walter ex J. F. Gmel.) MacMill. var.** *caroliniense* – Smooth bugloss (42) (1814), possibly Alkanet (184) (1793)

Lithospermum croceum **Fern.** – See *Lithospermum caroliniense* (Walt. ex J. F. Gmel.) MacM. var. *croceum* (Fern.) Cronq.

Lithospermum gmelinii **(Michx.) Hitch.** – possibly *Lithospermum caroliniense* (Walt. ex J. F. Gmel.) MacM.

Lithospermum hirsuta **Lehm.** – See *Lithospermum caroliniense* (Walt. ex J. F. Gmel.) MacM.

Lithospermum incisum **Lehm.** – Fringed puccoon (85) (1932), Indian paint [Indian-paint] (101) (1905), Narrow-leaf gromwell [Narrowleaf gromwell] (155) (1942), Narrow-leaf puccoon [Narrow leaf puccoon, Narrow-leaved puccoon] (3, 5, 72, 93, 97, 98, 121, 124, 127, 131, 156) (1899–1977), Narrow-leaf stoneseed [Narrowleaf stoneseed] (50) (present), Pežuta sapsapa (Lakota, black medicine) (121) (1918?–1970?), Puccoon (109, 114) (1894–1949), Yellow puccoon (5, 156) (1913–1923), possibly Long-flower puccoon [Long-flowered puccoon] (38) (1820)

Lithospermum **L.** – Gromwell (1, 2, 7, 10, 93, 109, 138, 155, 156, 158, 184) (1793–1949), Indian paint [Indian-paint] (1, 93) (1932–1936), Puccoon (1, 2, 7, 93, 127, 156) (1828–1933), Stoneseed [Stone seed, Stone-seed] (50) (present), possibly Red paint (7) (1828)

Lithospermum latifolium **Michx.** – American gromwell (3, 5, 72, 155, 156) (1907–1977), American stoneseed (50) (present), Gromwell (4) (1986)

Lithospermum linearifolium **Goldie** – See *Lithospermum incisum* Lehm.

Lithospermum officinale **L.** – Common gromwell (49, 156) (1898–1923), Graymile (5, 156) (1913–1923), Gromwell (5, 19, 63, 72) (1840–1907), Gromyll (179) (1526), Lichwale (156) (1923), Little gromell (178) (1526), Little mile (156) (1923) no longer in use by 1923, Little-wale [Littlewale] (5) (1913), Lychwale (179) (1526), Lychworte (179) (1526), Pearl plant [Pearl-plant] (5, 92, 156) (1876–1923), Stony-card (156) (1923)

Lithospermum pilosum **Nutt.** – See *Lithospermum ruderale* Dougl. ex Lehm.

Lithospermum ruderale **Dougl. ex Lehm.** – Woolly gromwell (5, 93) (1913–1936)

Lithospermum virginianum **L.** – See *Onosmodium virginianum* (L.) A. DC.

Litsea aestivalis **(L.) Fern.** – Carolina spicewood tree [Carolinian spice wood tree] (8) (1785), Laurier articulé (French) (8) (1785), Pond bush [Pond-bush] (5, 20, 156) (1857–1923), Pond-spice [Pond spice] (2, 5, 92, 156) (1876–1923), Spicewood [Spice-wood, Spice wood] (41, 184) (1770–1793)

Litsea geniculata **Benth. & Hook.** – See *Litsea aestivalis* (L.) Fern.

Littorella **Berg.** – Shoreweed [Shore-weed, Shore weed] (1) (1932)

Littorella uniflora **(L.) Ascherson** – Plaintain shoreweed [Plantain shore-weed, Plaintain shore weed] (5, 156) (1913–1923), Shore-grass [Shore grass] (5, 156) (1913–1923)

Livistona chinensis **(Jacq.) R. Br. ex Mart.** – Chinese fan palm [Chinese fan-palm] (109, 138) (1923–1949), Fountain palm (109) (1949)

Livistona chinensis **R. Br.** – See *Livistona chinensis* (Jacq.) R. Br. ex Mart.

Livistona **R. Br.** – Fountain palm (109) (1949)

Livistona rotundifolia **(Lam.) Mart.** – Java fan palm (138) (1923)

Lobaria pulmonaria **(L.) Hoffm.** – Lung lichen (50, 107) (1919–present), Lung moss (53, 92) (1876–1922), Lungs-of-the-oak [Lungs of the oak] (92) (1876), Lungwort [Lung-wort] (52, 54, 107) (1905–1919), Lungwort lichen (53) (1922), Maple lungwort (92) (1876), Oak lungwort (53) (1922), Sticta (52, 54) (1905–1919), Tree lungwort (53, 92) (1876–1922)

Lobelia **(Plum.) L.** – See *Lobelia* L.

Lobelia amoena **Michx.** – Southern lobelia (5) (1913)

Lolium multiflorum **Lam.**

Lobelia canbyi **Gray** – Canby's lobelia (5) (1913)

Lobelia cardinalis **L.** – Cardealina (186) (1814), Cardinal plant (186, 187) (1814–1818), Cardinale (French) (186) (1814), Cardinal-flower [Cardinal flower, Cardinalflower, Cardinal's flower, Cardinals' flower] (1, 3, 4, 6, 5, 7, 19, 34, 37, 44, 46, 50, 63, 72, 82, 86, 92, 95, 97, 109, 122, 124, 125, 138, 148, 155, 157, 158, 184, 186) (1793–present), Cardinalizia (186) (1814), Escurripa (186) (1814), Fior cardinale (Italian) (186) (1814), High-belia [Highbelia, High belia] (6) (1892), Hog-physic [Hog physic, Hog's physic] (5, 75, 156, 157, 158) (1894–1929) Plymouth Co. Mass, Indian tobacco [Indian-tobacco] (148) (1939) CO, Kardinaals bloem (186) (1814), Lobélie cardinale (French) (6, 186) (1814–1892), Mexican lobelia (138, 155) (1923–1942), Queen-of-the-meadow [Queen of the meadow] (77) (1898) Southold Long island, Red bay [Red-bay] (156) (1923), Red Betty [Red-Betty] (5, 37, 75, 156, 157, 158) (1900–1929) Ferrisburgh VT, Red cardinal (156, 157, 158) (1900–1929), Red cardinal flower (92) (1876), Red lobelia (5, 6, 37, 92, 156, 157, 158) (1892–1929), Rothe Kardinals Blume (German) (6, 186) (1814–1892), Scarlet lobelia (6, 156, 186) (1814–1892), Slinkweed [Slink weed, Slink-weed] (5, 73, 156, 158) (1892–1923) Princeton MA, Stinkweed [Stink-weed, Stink weed] (157) (1929), Western cardinal flower [Western cardinalflower] (155) (1942)

Lobelia claytoniana **Michx.** – See *Lobelia spicata* Lam.

Lobelia dortmanna **L.** – Water gladiole (5, 75, 156) (1894–1923) NY, Water lobelia (5, 19, 156) (1840–1923)

Lobelia elongata **Small.** – Long-leaf lobelia [Long-leaved lobelia] (5, 97) (1913–1937)

Lobelia erinus **L.** – Edging lobelia (138) (1923)

Lobelia feayana **Gray** – Dr. Feay's lobelia (86) (1878)

Lobelia flaccidifolia **Small** – Great blue lobelia (124) (1937) TX

Lobelia fulgens **Humb. & Bonpl. ex Willd.** – See *Lobelia cardinalis* L.

Lobelia glandulosa **Walt.** – Glandular lobelia (5) (1913)

Lobelia halei **Small.** – See *Lobelia flaccidifolia* Small

Lobelia inflata **L.** – Asthmaweed [Asthma weed, Asthma-weed] (5, 6, 7, 62, 69, 92, 156, 157, 158) (1828–1929), Aufgeblasene Lobelie (German) (186) (1814), Bladderpod [Bladder pod, Bladder-pod] (6, 69, 157, 158) (1892–1929), Bladder-pod lobelia [Bladder-podded lobelia, Bladder podded lobelia] (5, 92, 156, 186) (1814–1923), Common lobelia (7) (1828), Emetic herb (53, 92) (1876–1922), Emetic root [Emetic-root] (6) (1892), Emeticweed [Emetic weed, Emetic-weed] (5, 6, 7, 46, 53, 59, 92, 156, 186, 187) (1814–1923), Eyebright [Eye-bright, Eye bright] (5, 6, 69, 92, 156, 157, 158, 186) (1814–1929), Gagroot [Gag-root, Gag root] (5, 69, 92, 156, 157, 158) (1876–1929), Indian tobacco [Indian-tobacco] (3, 4, 5, 6, 7, 46, 47, 49, 50, 52, 53, 55, 57, 59, 60, 61, 62, 63, 69, 72, 92, 97, 101, 109, 125, 138, 156, 157, 158, 186, 187) (1814–present), Indian tobacco lobelia [Indiantobacco lobelia] (155) (1942), Kinnikinnick [Kinnikinik, Kinnikinnick, Kinnikinic, Kinnikinnik] (156) (1923), Lobelia (49, 52, 53, 54, 55, 57, 59, 60, 69, 92, 157, 158) (1876–1922), Lobelie (German) (6) (1892), Lobélie enflée (French) (6, 7, 158) (1828–1900), Lobelienkraut (German) (158) (1900), Low-belia [Low belia] (5, 69, 75, 156, 158) (1900–1923) somewhat general among herb gatherers, Pukeweed [Puke-weed, Puke weed] (5, 6, 7, 53, 69, 92, 156, 157, 158) (1828–1929), Vomitweed [Vomit weed] (53, 54) (1905–1922), Vomitwort [Vomit wort] (69, 92, 157, 158) (1876–1929), Wild tobacco [Wild-tobacco, Wildtobacco] (5, 6, 7, 19, 53, 69, 92, 156, 157, 158, 186, 187) (1814–1929)

Lobelia kalmi – See *Lobelia kalmii* L.

Lobelia kalmii **L.** – Brook lobelia (5, 131) (1899–1913), Kalm's lobelia (3, 4, 5, 156) (1913–1986), Ontario lobelia (50, 138, 155) (1923–present)

Lobelia **L.** – Lobelia (1, 50, 82, 93, 107, 138, 158) (1900–present) for Matthias de Lobel or L'obel, 1538–1616, Flemish botanist and author

Lobelia **L.** – Red cardinal flower (190) (~1759)

Lobelia leptostachys **A. DC.** – See *Lobelia spicata* Lam. var. *leptostachys* (A. DC.) Mackenzie & Bush

Lobelia nuttallii **J. A. Schultes** – Nuttall's lobelia (5) (1913)

Lobelia paludosa **Nutt.** – Swamp lobelia (5) (1913)

Lobelia puberula **Michx.** – Downy lobelia (5, 65, 72, 97) (1907–1937)

Lobelia pubula **Michx.** – possibly *Lobelia puberula* Michx.

Lobelia siphilitica **L.** – Big blue lobelia [Bigblue lobelia] (155) (1942), Blaue Kardinals blume (German) (186) (1814), Blue cardinal (92) (1876), Blue cardinal plant (186) (1814), Blue cardinal-flower [Blue cardinal flower, Blue cardinal's flower] (3, 4, 5, 6, 7, 93, 97, 98, 131, 156, 157, 158, 186, 187) (1814–1986), Blue lobelia (6, 92, 125, 127, 157, 158, 186) (1814–1933), Cardinale bleue (French) (186) (1814), Gemeine Lobelie (German) (6, 186) (1814–1892), Great blue lobelia (6, 50, 82, 156) (1892–present), Great lobelia (4, 5, 6, 62, 63, 72, 82, 93, 98, 106, 114, 156, 157, 158) (1882–1986), High-belia [Highbelia, High belia] (5, 6, 75, 92, 156, 158) (1876–1923), Kopper-Lobebliae (186) (1814), Large blue lobelia (138) (1923), Lebelie syphilitique (French) (6) (1892), Lobelie siphylitique (French) (186) (1814), Pokkige Lobelia (186) (1814), Tan tuttipang (186) (1814)

Lobelia siphilitica **L. var. *ludoviciana* A. DC.** – Great blue lobelia (50) (present)

Lobelia spicata hirtella **Gray** – See *Lobelia spicata* Lam. var. *hirtella* Gray

Lobelia spicata **Lam.** – Clayton's lobelia (187) (1818), Lobelia (126, 127) (1933), Pale lobelia (93, 95) (1911–1936), Pale-spike lobelia [Pale spiked lobelia, Palespike lobelia] (3, 4, 5, 50, 72, 97, 155) (1907–present), Spiked lobelia (156) (1923)

Lobelia spicata **Lam. var. *hirtella* Gray** – Pale-spike lobelia [Pale spiked lobelia, Palespike lobelia] (50) (present), Prairie lobelia (131) (1899), Rough lobelia (72) (1907)

Lobelia spicata **Lam. var. *leptostachys* (A. DC.) Mackenzie & Bush** – Spiked lobelia (5, 72, 97) (1907–1937)

Lobelia splendens **Willd.** – See *Lobelia cardinalis* L.

Lobelia syphilitica **L.** – See *Lobelia siphilitica* L.

Lobularia **Desv.** – Lobularia (50) (present), Sweet alyssum [Sweetalyssum] (155, 156) (1923–1942), Sweet alyssum [Sweet-alyssum] (155, 156) (1923–1942)

Lobularia maritima **(L.) Desv.** – Leafy madwort (165) (1768), Madwort (5, 92, 156) (1876–1923), Seaside koniga (5) (1913), Snowdrift [Snow drift] (5, 156) (1913–1923), Sweet Allison (5, 156) (1913–1923) no longer in use by 1923, Sweet alyssum [Sweet-alyssum] (5, 15, 50, 92, 109, 114, 138, 156) (1876–present), possibly Alyssum (92) (1876)

Loeflingia **L.** – Loeflingia (50, 158) (1900–present)

Loeflingia squarrosa **Nutt.** – Spreading pygmy-leaf [Spreading pygmyleaf] (50) (present)

Loeflingia squarrosa **Nutt. subsp. *squarrosa*** – Spreading pygmy-leaf [Spreading pygmyleaf] (50) (present), Texas loeflingia (5) (1913)

Loeflingia texana **Hook.** – See *Loeflingia squarrosa* Nutt. subsp. *squarrosa*

Logfia arvensis **(L.) Holub** – Field cottonrose (50) (present)

Logfia **Cass.** – Cotton-rose [Cotton rose, Cottonrose] (50) (present)

Loiseleuria **Desv.** – Alpine azalea (156) (1923–1932), Alpine-azalea (138) (1923)

Loiseleuria procumbens **(L.) Desv.** – Alpine azalea (5) (1913), Alpine-azalea [Alpine azalea] (109, 138, 156) (1923–1949), Trailing azalea (5, 19, 156) (1840–1923)

Loiseleuria procumbens **Desvar.** – See *Loiseleuria procumbens* (L.) Desv.

Lolium arundinaceum **(Schreb.) S. J. Darbyshire** – Reed fescue (68, 94, 155) (1890–1942), Tall fescue (3, 50) (1977–present), Tall meadow fescue (45, 129) (1894–1896)

Lolium arvense **With.** – See *Lolium temulentum* L.

Lolium giganteum **(L.) S. J. Darbyshire** – Giant fescue (50) (present), Great fescue grass (5) (1913)

Lolium italicum **A. Br.** – See *Lolium multiflorum* Lam.

Lolium **L.** – Darnel (1, 7, 10, 66) (1818–1932), Ray grass [Ray-grass] (14) (1882), Rye grass [Rye-grass, Ryegrass] (1, 50, 93, 109, 155, 158) (1900–present)

Lolium multiflorum **Lam.** – See *Lolium perenne* L. subsp. *multiflorum*

(Lam.) Husnot

Lolium perenne L. – Common darnel (68, 90, 143) (1890–1936), Crap (5) (1913), Darnel (19, 45, 85, 92, 184, 187) (1793–1932), Darnel grass (92) (1876), English bluegrass [English blue-grass, English blue grass] (5, 75) (1894–1913) WV, English ray grass (67, 68) (1890–1913) Ottawa, English rye (56) (1901) IA, English rye grass [English rye-grass] (68, 109, 119, 163) (1890–1949), Ever grass [Ever-grass] (5, 119) (1913–1938), Italian rye grass [Italian ryegrass, Italian rye-grass] (87, 90, 118) (1884–1898), Perennial ray grass [Perennial ray-grass] (45) (1896), Perennial rye (5, 56) (1901–1913), Perennial rye grass [Perennial rye-grass, Perennial ryegrass] (45, 50, 56, 66, 68, 90, 92, 109, 111, 119, 122, 129, 138, 140, 143, 152, 155, 163) (1852–present), Ray grass [Ray-grass] (5, 56, 90, 92, 119, 157, 163) (1852–1938), Red dare (5) (1913), Red darnel (5) (1913), Red ray (5, 119) (1913–1938), Rye grass [Rye-grass, Ryegrass] (5, 72, 87, 88, 90, 92, 94, 119) (1884–1938), White nonesuch (5) (1913)

Lolium perenne L. subsp. *multiflorum* (**Lam.**) **Husnot** – Australian rye grass [Australian rye-grass] (119) (1938), Awned darnel (85) (1932), Awned ray grass [Awned ray-grass] (72) (1907), Awned rye grass [Awned rye-grass] (5, 119) (1913–1938), Italian ray grass [Italian ray-grass] (45, 56, 66, 67, 157) (1890–1929), Italian rye (45) (1896), Italian rye grass [Italian ryegrass, Italian rye-grass] (5, 50, 68, 87, 88, 92, 94, 109, 110, 119, 122, 129, 138, 143, 155, 163) (1852–present), Many-flower darnel [Many-flowered darnel] (66) (1903), Perennial rye grass [Perennial rye-grass, Perennial ryegrass] (3) (1977)

Lolium perenne L. var. *aristatum* **Willd.** – See *Lolium perenne* L. subsp. *multiflorum* (Lam.) Husnot

Lolium perenne L. var. *cristatum* **Pers. ex B. D. Jackson** – See *Lolium perenne* L. var. *perenne*

Lolium perenne L. var. *italicum* – See *Lolium perenne* L. subsp. *multiflorum* (Lam.) Husnot

Lolium perenne L. var. *perenne* – Crested rye grass [Crested ryegrass] (155) (1942), Perennial rye grass [Perennial rye-grass, Perennial ryegrass] (3, 50) (1977–present)

Lolium persicum **Boiss. & Hohen. ex Boiss.** – Persian rye grass [Persian ryegrass] (50) (present)

Lolium pratense (**Huds.**) **S. J. Darbyshire** – Dover grass (5) (1913), English bluegrass [English blue-grass, English blue grass] (68) (1890), Evergreen grass (5, 45, 66, 68, 87) (1884–1913), Fescue grass [Fescue-grass] (19, 92) (1840–1876), Frisky grass (5) (1913), Frisky meadow grass (5) (1913), Meadow fescue (3, 11, 45, 56, 66, 67, 68, 90, 94, 109, 111, 129, 138, 140, 143, 152, 155) (1885–1977), Meadow fescue grass [Meadow fescue-grass] (5, 56, 87, 119) (1885–1938), Meadow rye grass [Meadow ryegrass] (50) (present), Randall's grass [Randall grass] (5, 45, 56, 66, 68, 88) (1885–1913), Tall fescue (56, 68, 87, 88, 92, 109, 118, 129, 152) (1884–1949), Tall fescue grass [Tall fescue-grass] (5, 45, 56, 72, 119, 187) (1818–1938), Tall meadow fescue (45) (1896), Taller fescue (45, 90) (1885–1896)

Lolium temulentum L. – Bearded darnel (5, 66, 111, 157, 158) (1903–1929), Beardless darnel rye grass [Beardless darnel ryegrass] (155) (1942), Bragge (157, 158) (1900–1929), Cheat (75, 119, 157, 158) (1894–1938), Cokyll (178, 179) (1526–1596), Darnel (5, 14, 56, 67, 72, 88, 92, 94, 119, 155, 157, 158, 163, 178, 179) (1526–1942), Darnel grass (92) (1876), Darnel rye grass [Darnel ryegrass] (50, 155) (1942–present), Dragge (5, 157, 158) (1900–1929), Drake (157, 158) (1900–1929), Drank (158) (1900), Dravick (157, 158) (1900–1929), Drawke (5) (1913), Droke (157, 158) (1900–1929), Drunk (5, 157, 158) (1900–1929), Eaver (158) (1900), Ivory (119) (1938) OK, Ivraie (French) (158) (1900), Ivray (157, 158) (1900–1929), Lolch (German) (158) (1900), Lover's-steps (157, 158) (1900–1929), Neele (158) (1900), Nelle (157) (1929), Poison darnel [Posison-darnel] (3, 4, 45, 56, 80, 88, 119, 163) (1852–1986), Ray (157, 158, 178, 179) (1526–1929), Ray grass [Ray-grass] (157, 158) (1900–1929), Riely (157, 158) (1900–1929), Sturdy (157, 158) (1900–1929), Sturdy ryle (5) (1913), Tare [Tares] (5, 56, 92, 119) (1901–1938) thought to be the biblical tares, Taummelkorn (German) (158) (1900)

Lolium temulentum L. var. *leptochaeton* **A. Br.** – See *Lolium*

temulentum L.

Lomaria spicant **Desv.** – See *Blechnum spicant* (L.) Sm. (gn from GR. loma "fringe")

Lomatium ambiguum (**Nutt.**) **Coult. & Rose** – Biscuitroot [Biscuit root, Biscuit-root] (101, 103, 107) (1870–1919), Bread-and-biscuit [Bread and biscuit] (76) (1896) CA, from Indian use of plant, Breadroot [Bread root, Bread-root] (101, 103, 107) (1870–1919) MT, Cous (101) (1905) MT, Cous root (101) (1905) MT, Konse (Indians of Orgeon and Idaho) (107) (1919), Kouse root (76, 103) (1870–1896), Racine blanc (French Canadians) (103) (1870), Racine blanche (French) (101) (1905) MT

Lomatium ambiguum **Coult. & Rose** – See *Lomatium ambiguum* (Nutt.) Coult. & Rose

Lomatium cous (**S. Wats.**) **Coult. & Rose** – A-sáblal (35) (1806), Biscuitroot [Biscuit root, Biscuit-root] (101, 146) (1905–1939) CA, Breadroot [Bread root, Bread-root] (101) (1905) MT, Cous (101) (1905) MT, Cous root (101) (1905) MT, Racine blanche (French) (101) (1905) MT, Wild carrot (146) (1939), Wild parsley [Wildparsley] (146) (1939)

Lomatium cous **Coult. & Rose** – See *Lomatium cous* (S. Wats.) Coult. & Rose

Lomatium dissectum (**Nutt.**) **Mathias & Constance var.** *multifidum* (**Nutt.**) **Mathias & Constance** – Wild parsnip [Wild-parsnip, Wilde parsnep] (101) (1905) MT

Lomatium foeniculaceum (**Nutt.**) **Coult. & Rose** – Desert biscuitroot (50) (present), Hairy parsley (131) (1899), Racine blanc (French Canadians) (107) (1919), Wild parsley [Wildparsley] (4) (1986)

Lomatium foeniculaceum (**Nutt.**) **Coult. & Rose subsp.** *daucifolium* (**Torr. & Gray**) **Theobald** – Desert biscuitroot (50) (present), Wild parsley [Wildparsley] (3) (1977)

Lomatium foeniculaceum (**Nutt.**) **Coult. & Rose subsp.** *foeniculaceum* – Carrot-leaf parsley [Carrot-leaved parsley] (5, 93, 97, 122) (1913–1937), Desert biscuitroot (50) (present), Hairy parsley (5, 85, 93, 97) (1913–1937), Loveseed [Love seed] (37) (1919), Pezhe bthaska (Omaha-Ponca, flat herb) (37) (1919)

Lomatium graveolens (**S. Watson**) **Dorn & R. L. Hartm.** – Fennel-leaf parsley [Fennel-leaved parsley] (131) (1899), Yampeh (Snake and Shoshoni Indians) (107) (1919)

Lomatium macrocarpum (**Nutt. ex Torr. & Gray**) **Coult. & Rose** – Big-seed biscuitroot [Bigseed biscuitroot] (50) (present), Big-seed lomatium [Bigseed lomatium] (155) (1942)

Lomatium montanum **J. M. Coult. & Rose** – See *Lomatium cous* (S. Wats.) Coult. & Rose

Lomatium nudicaule (**Pursh**) **J. M. Coult. & Rose** – Symrnium (107) (1919), White-flower parsley [White-flowered parsley] (131) (1899) SD

Lomatium nuttallii (**Gray**) **J. F. Macbr.** – Dog-parsley [Dog parsley, Dogparsley] (4, 93) (1936–1986), Nuttall's biscuitroot (50) (present), Nuttall's dog-parsley [Nuttall dogparsley, Nuttall's dog parsley] (5, 155) (1913–1942)

Lomatium orientale **Coult & Rose** – Northern Idaho biscuitroot (50) (present), Šahijela tatiŋpsiŋla (Lakota, Cheyenne turnip) (121) (1918?–1970?), White-flower parsley [White-flowered parsley] (5, 93) (1913–1936), Wild parsley [Wildparsley] (3, 121, 85, 127) (1918–1977)

Lomatium platycarpum **Coult. & Rose** – See *Lomatium simplex* (Nutt.) J.F. Macbr. var. *simplex*

Lomatium **Raf.** – Biscuitroot [Biscuit root, Biscuit-root] (1) (1932), Cous (1) (1932), Desert parsley [Desert-parsley, Desertparsley] (50) (present), Dog-parsley [Dog parsley, Dogparsley] (155) (1942), Lomatium (155) (1942), Whisk-broom parsley (1, 93) (1932–1936) Neb, Wild parsley [Wildparsley] (4) (1986)

Lomatium simplex (**Nutt.**) **J. F. Macbr. var.** *simplex* – Biscuitroot [Biscuit root, Biscuit-root] (101) (1905), Breadroot [Bread root, Bread-root] (101) (1905) MT, Cous (101) (1905) MT, Cous root (101) (1905) MT, Racine blanche (French) (101) (1905) MT

Lomatium triternatum (**Pursh**) **Coult. & Rose** – Biscuitroot [Biscuit root, Biscuit-root] (101) (1905) MT, Breadroot [Bread root, Bread-root] (101) (1905) MT, Cous (101) (1905) MT, Cous root (101) (1905) MT, Racine blanche (French) (101) (1905) MT, Sour-grape [Sour grape] (181) (~1678)

Lomatium triternatum **Coult. & Rose** – See *Lomatium triternatum* (Pursh) Coult. & Rose

Lomatogonium **A. Braun** – Marsh felwort (1) (1932)

Lomatogonium rotatum **(L.) Fries ex Fern.** – Marsh felwort (5, 156) (1913–1923)

Lonchocarpus **Kunth** – Lancepod (138) (1923)

Lonchocarpus punctatus **Kunth** – Braziletto (92) (1876), Brazilwood [Brazil wood] (7) (1828)

Lonchocarpus sepium **DC.** – See *Gliricidia sepium* (Jacq.) Kunth ex Walp.

Lonercera peryclymenum – See *Lonicera periclymenum* L.

Lonicera ×bella **Zabel** [*morrowii × tatarica*] – White-bell honeysuckle [White bell honeysuckle] (112) (1937)

Lonicera albiflora **Torr. & Gray** – Western white honeysuckle (50) (present), White honeysuckle [White honey-suckle] (3, 4, 149) (1904–1986), White-flower honeysuckle [White-flowered honey-suckle] (97) (1937)

Lonicera bela albida – See *Lonicera ×bella* Zabel [*morrowii × tatarica*]

Lonicera caerulea **L.** – Blue fly honeysuckle [Blue fly-honeysuckle] (5, 156) (1913–1923), Mountain fly honeysuckle [Mountain fly-honeysuckle] (5, 156) (1913–1923) IA, Sweetberry honeysuckle (138, 156) (1923)

Lonicera canadensis **Bartr. ex Marsh.** – American fly honeysuckle (American fly-honeysuckle) (5, 138, 156) (1913–1923), Canadian dwarf-cherry honeysuckle (8) (1785), Chamœ-cerasus de Canada (8) (1785), Medaddy bush [Medaddy-bush, Medaddybush] (5, 156) (1913–1923), Vernal honeysuckle (156) (1923)

Lonicera canadensis **Marsh** – See *Lonicera canadensis* Bartr. ex Marsh.

Lonicera caprifolium **L.** – American honeysuckle (156) (1923), American woodbine (5, 156) (1913–1923), Common honeysuckle (156) (1923), Double honeysuckles [Double honisuckles] (178) (1526), Fragrant woodbine (5, 156) (1913–1923), Honeysuckle [Honey suckle, Honey-suckle, Honisuckles] (19, 92) (1840–1876), Italian honeysuckle (5, 156) (1913–1923), Italian woodbine (156) (1923), Perfoliate honeysuckle (5, 156) (1913–1923), Sweet honeysuckle (138) (1923)

Lonicera chrysantha **Turcz. ex Ledeb.** – Coralline honeysuckle (138) (1923), Creamy-bell honeysuckle (112) (1937)

Lonicera ciliosa **(Pursh) DC.** – See *Lonicera ciliosa* (Pursh) Poir. ex DC.

Lonicera ciliosa **(Pursh) Poir. ex DC.** – Honeysuckle [Honey suckle, Honey-suckle, Honisuckles] (35) (1806)

Lonicera coerulea **L.** – See *Lonicera caerulea* L.

Lonicera diervilla **L.** – See *Diervilla lonicera* Mill.

Lonicera dioica **L.** – Bittersweet [Bitter sweet, Bitter-sweet] (156) (1923), Donald's honeysuckle [Donald honeysuckle] (155) (1942), Douglas' honeysuckle (5, 72, 97, 131, 158) (1899–1937), Glaucous honeysuckle (5, 72, 156, 158) (1900–1923), Limber honeysuckle (4, 50, 138, 155, 156) (1923–present), Northern yellow honeysuckle (158) (1900), Small honeysuckle (156) (1923), Small woodbine (156, 158) (1900–1923), Small yellow honeysuckle (158) (1900), Smooth-leaf honeysuckle [Smooth-leaved honeysuckle, Smooth leaved honeysuckle] (5, 93, 95) (1911–1936), Wild honeysuckle [Wild honey-suckle] (4, 82) (1930–1986), Yellow honeysuckle (156, 158) (1900–1923), possibly Honeysuckle [Honey suckle, Honey-suckle, Honisuckles] (105) (1932)

Lonicera divica **L** – possibly *Lonicera dioica* L.

Lonicera etrusca **Santi** – Etruscan honeysuckle (138) (1923)

Lonicera flava **Sims.** – Southern yellow honeysuckle (158) (1900), Yellow honeysuckle (4, 5, 50, 97, 113, 138, 155, 156) (1890–present)

Lonicera fragrantissima **Lindl. & Paxton** – Winter honeysuckle (112, 138) (1923–1937)

Lonicera glaucescens **(Rydb.) Rydb.** – See *Lonicera dioica* L.

Lonicera glaucescens **Rydb.** – See *Lonicera dioica* L.

Lonicera hirsuta **Eaton** – Hairy honeysuckle (2, 5, 130, 138, 156) (1895–1913), Rough woodbine (19, 92, 156) (1840–1923)

Lonicera involucrata **(Richards.) Banks.** – See *Lonicera involucrata* Banks ex Spreng.

Lonicera involucrata **Banks ex Spreng.** – Bearberry [Bear berry, Bear-berry] (101, 112, 160) (1860–1937), Bearberry honeysuckle (103, 138) (1870–1923), Fly blossom (160) (1860), Involucred fly-honeysuckle (5) (1913), Twinberry [Twin-berry, Twin berry] (101) (1905) MT

Lonicera japonica **Thunb.** – Chinese honeysuckle (5, 156) (1913–1923), Japanese honeysuckle [Japan honeysuckle] (3, 4, 5, 50, 138, 155, 156) (1913–present), Purple Japanese honeysuckle (155) (1942)

Lonicera japonica **Thunb. var. *chinensis* (P.W. S. Wats.) Baker** – See *Lonicera japonica* Thunb.

Lonicera korolkowi – See *Lonicera korolkowii* Stapf

Lonicera korolkowii **Stapf** – Blue-leaf honeysuckle [Blueleaf honey-suckle] (138) (1923)

Lonicera **L.** – Bush honeysuckle [Bush honey suckle, Bush-honey-suckle] (1) (1932), Chevre-feuille (French) (8) (1785), Fly honeysuckle [Fly honey-suckle, Fly-honeysuckle] (1) (1932), Honey-suckle [Honey suckle, Honey-suckle, Honisuckles] (1, 2, 4, 8, 7, 40, 50, 82, 93, 106, 109, 138, 155, 156, 158, 190) (~1759–present) for nectar at bottom of flower, Twinberry [Twin-berry, Twin berry] (1) (1932), Woodbine (2, 8) (1785–1932), possibly Bearberry [Bear berry, Bear-berry] (1) (1932), possibly Coral honeysuckle (10) (1818), possibly Swamp honeysuckle (1) (1932), possibly With-wind [Withwind] (92) (1876)

Lonicera maackii **(Rupr.) Herder** – Amur honeysuckle (50, 138, 155) (1923–present)

Lonicera marilandica [**L.**] – See *Spigelia marilandica* (L.) L. (taxonomic status is unresolved (PL))

Lonicera morrowi **Gray** – Bush honeysuckle [Bush honey suckle, Bush-honeysuckle] (82) (1930), Morrow's honeysuckle [Morrow honeysuckle] (112, 138) (1923–1937), Winter honeysuckle (106) (1930)

Lonicera oblongifolia **(Goldie) Hook.** – Swamp fly honeysuckle [swamp fly-honeysuckle] (5, 138, 156) (1913–1923)

Lonicera oblongifolia **Muhl.** – possibly *Lonicera oblongifolia* (Goldie) Hook.

Lonicera periclymenum **L.** – Chervil [Cheruell] (179) (1526), Goat's leaf [Goat's leaves, Gotes leues] (92, 179) (1526–1876), Honey-suckle [Honey suckle, Honey-suckle, Honisuckles] (178) (1526), Woodbind [Woodbinde, Wood bind, Woodbynde] (178, 179) (1526), Woodbine (19, 109, 138) (1840–1949)

Lonicera pileata **Oliv.** – Privet honeysuckle (138) (1923)

Lonicera prolifera **(Kirchn.) Rehd.** – See *Lonicera reticulata* Raf.

Lonicera reticulata **Raf.** – Grape honeysuckle (3, 4, 50, 138, 155) (1923–present), Honeysuckle [Honey suckle, Honey-suckle, Honisuckles] (63) (1899), Sullivant's honeysuckle (5, 72, 82, 97) (1907–1937)

Lonicera ruprechtiana **Regel** – Manchurian honeysuckle (138) (1923)

Lonicera sempervirens **Ait.** – possibly *Lonicera sempervirens* L.

Lonicera sempervirens **L.** – Caçapililol xochitl (177) (1762), Coral honeysuckle (5, 46, 97, 112, 156, 158) (1879–1937), Evergreen coral honeysuckle (122, 124) (1937), Evergreen honeysuckle [Evergreen honeysuckle] (8) (1785), Perfoliate ever-flowering woodbind [Perfoliate ever flowring Woodbind] (181) (~1678), Scarlet coral honeysuckle (86) (1878), Scarlet honeysuckle (156) (1923), Scarlet honeysuckle (156) (1923), Scarlet trumpet honeysuckle (5, 86, 158) (1878–1913), Trumpet honeysuckle [Trumpet honey-suckle] (2, 3, 5, 46, 50, 86, 93, 95, 109, 113, 138, 155, 156, 158) (1878–present), Trumpet-leaf honeysuckle [Trumpet leaf honeysuckle] (92) (1876), Woodbine (156, 158) (1900–1923), possibly Chevre-feuille toujours vert (French) (8) (1785), possibly Honeysuckle [Honey suckle,

Honey-suckle, Honisuckles] (114) (1894)

Lonicera sempervirens **L. var.** *virginiana* **(Marshall) Castigl.** – Chevre-feuille de Virginie (French) (8) (1785), Virginia scarlet honeysuckle [Virginian scarlet honeysuckle] (8) (1785)

Lonicera standishi – See *Lonicera standishii* Jacques

Lonicera standishii **Jacques** – Standish' honeysuckle [Standish honeysuckle] (138) (1923)

Lonicera sullivanti **Gray** – See *Lonicera reticulata* Raf.

Lonicera symphoricarpos **L.** – See *Symphoricarpos orbiculatus* Moench

Lonicera tatarica **L.** – Bush honeysuckle [Bush honey suckle, Bush-honeysuckle] (63, 93, 112, 156) (1899–1936), Garden fly-honeysuckle (5, 156) (1913–1923), Tartarian bush honeysuckle [Tartarian bush-honeysuckle] (5, 72, 156) (1907–1923), Tatarian honeysuckle [Tartarian honeysuckle] (3, 50, 82, 106, 109, 135, 138, 155, 156) (1910–present), Twin-sisters [Twin sisters] (75) (1894) La Crosse WI

Lonicera thibetica (Bureau & Franch.) – See *Lonicera rupicola* var. *rupicola*

Lonicera utahensis **S. Wats.** – Utah honeysuckle (138) (1923)

Lonicera villosa **(Michx.) J. A. Schultes var.** *solonis* **(Eat.) Fern.** – Twinberry [Twin-berry, Twin berry] (19) (1840)

Lonicera xylosteum **L.** – European fly honeysuckle (European fly-honeysuckle) (109, 138, 156) (1923–1949), Fly honeysuckle [Fly honey-suckle, Fly-honeysuckle] (5) (1913), Tree honeysuckle [Tree honisuckles] (178) (1526), Xylosteum (174) (1753)

Lophanthus **[J. R. Forst. & G. Forst.]** – See *Waltheria* L.

Lophanthus anisatus **Benth.** – See *Agastache foeniculum* (Pursh) Kuntze

Lophanthus nepetoides **Benth.** – See *Agastache nepetoides* (L.) Kuntze

Lophanthus scrophulariaefolius **Benth.** – See *Agastache scrophulariifolia* (Willd.) Kuntze

Lophiola americana **(Pursh) Coville** – See *Lophiola aurea* Ker-Gawl.

Lophiola americana **(Pursh) Wood** – See *Lophiola aurea* Ker-Gawl.

Lophiola aurea **Ker-Gawl.** – Goldencrest [Golden crest] (50, 156) (1923–present), Lophiola (5) (1913), Weed-grass [Weed grass] (19) (1840)

Lophiola septentrionalis **Fern.** – See *Lophiola aurea* Ker-Gawl.

Lophophora **Coult.** – Peyote (138, 155) (1931–1942)

Lophophora lewinii **(Hennings ex Lewin) C. H. Thomps.** – Ah'-o-ly (Pima) (132) (1855), Crossvine [Cross vine, Cross-vine] (5) (1913), Mescal (57) (1917), Mescal buttons (104) (1896), Mezcal (132) (1855), Nat-tar (Pinal Leño Apache) (132) (1855), Peyote (104) (1896), Peyotl (104) (1896)

Lophophora williamsii **(Lem. ex Salm-Dyck) Coult.** – Makan (Omaha-Ponca, the medicine) (37) (1919), Mescal-button peyote [Mescalbutton peyote] (155) (1942), Peyote (37, 50, 52, 138) (1919–present)

Lophophora williamsii **(Lem. ex Salm-Dyck) Coult. var.** *echinata* **(Croizat) H. Bravo** – See *Lophophora williamsii* (Lem. ex Salm-Dyck) Coult.

Lophostemon confertus **(R. Br.) P. G. Wilson & Waterhouse** – Brisbane box [Brisbane-box, Brisbanebox] (109, 138) (1923–1949)

Lophotocarpus calcycinus **(Engelm.) J. G. Smith** – See *Sagittaria calycina* Engelm. var. *spongiosa* Engelm.

Lophotocarpus depauperatus **J. G. Smith** – See *Sagittaria calycina* Engelm. var. *calycina*

Lophotocarpus spathulatus **J. G. Smith** – See *Sagittaria calycina* Engelm. var. *spongiosa* Engelm.

Lophotocarpus spongiosus **(Engelm.) J. G. Smith** – See *Sagittaria calycina* Engelm. var. *spongiosa* Engelm.

Lophotocarpus **T. Durand** – See *Sagittaria* L. (all US species)

Lorrinseria areolata **(L.) Presl.** – See *Woodwardia areolata* (L.) T. Moore

Lotus americanus **(Nutt.) Bisch.** – See *Lotus unifoliolatus* (Hook.) Benth. var. *unifoliolatus*

Lotus corniculatus **L.** – Bird's-eye [Bird's eye, Bird's-eyes, Birds-eyes] (5, 156, 158) (1900–1923), Bird's-foot deervetch [Birdfoot deervetch] (50, 155) (1942–present), Bird's-foot trefoil [Birds-foot trefoil, Birdsfoot trefoil] (3, 4, 5, 45, 85, 109, 138) (1896–1986), Bloomfell [Bloom fell, Bloom-fell] (5, 156, 158) (1900–1923), Butterjags [Butter-jags, Butter jags] (92, 158) (1876–1900), Cat clover [Cat's clover, Catclover, Cat-clover] (5, 156) (1913–1923), Cat-in-clover (158) (1900), Claver (5, 158) (1900–1913), Cross-toes [Cross-toes, Crosstoes] (5, 92, 156, 158) (1876–1923), Crow's-toes [Crow toes, Crow's toes, Crow-toes] (5, 156, 158) (1900–1923), Devil's-fingers [Devil's fingers] (5, 158) (1900–1913), Eggs-and-bacon (158) (1900), Ground honeysuckle (5, 156, 158) (1900–1923), Jack-jump-about (158) (1900), Lady's-fingers [Ladies' finger, Ladies'-fingers] (5, 156) (1913–1923), Lady's-glove [Ladies' glove, Lady glove, Lady's glove, Lady's-gloves] (158) (1900), Lady's-shoes-and-stockings (158) (1900), Lady's-slipper [Lady's slipper, Ladies' slipper, Lady-slipper, Ladyslipper, Ladie-slipper, Lady's slippers] (158) (1900), Sheep-foot [Sheep-foot] (5, 156, 158) (1900–1923), Shoes-and-stockings [Shoes-and-stockings] (5, 92, 156) (1876–1923)

Lotus glaber **Mill.** – Deer-clover [Deer clover] (106) (1930), Deerweed (106) (1930), Tanglefoot [Tangle foot] (106) (1930), White alfalfa (106) (1930), Wild broom (106) (1930)

Lotus **L.** – Bird's-foot trefoil [Birds-foot trefoil, Birdsfoot trefoil] (156, 158) (1900–1923), Deervetch [Deer vetch] (155) (1942), Trefoil (4, 50) (1986–present)

Lotus major **[Sm.]** – possibly *Lotus pedunculatus* Cav. (current species depends on author)

Lotus pedunculatus **Cav. (possibly)** – Large-foot trefoil [Large foot trefoil] (45) (1896)

Lotus purshianus **(Benh.) Clem. & Clem.** – See *Lotus unifoliolatus* (Hook.) Benth. var. *unifoliolatus*

Lotus tenuis **Waldst. & Kit. ex Willd.** – Narrow-leaf bird's-foot trefoil [Narrowleaf bird's-foot trefoil] (50) (present), Narrow-leaf trefoil [Narrow-leaved trefoil] (4) (1986)

Lotus tetragonolobus **L.** – See *Tetragonolobus purpureus* Moench

Lotus uliginosus **Schkuhr** – See *Lotus pedunculatus* Cav.

Lotus unifoliolatus **(Hook.) Benth.** – American bird's-foot trefoil (50) (present), Big lotus (114) (1894) Neb, Bird's-foot trefoil [Birds-foot trefoil, Birdsfoot trefoil] (156) (1923), Prairie bird's-foot trefoil [Prairie bird's foot trefoil] (5, 93, 97, 121, 131, 156) (1899–1937), Trefoil (156) (1923), Wild vetch (5, 93, 156) (1913–1936)

Lotus unifoliolatus **(Hook.) Benth. var.** *unifoliolatus* – Dakota vetch (131) (1899) SD, Deervetch [Deer vetch] (4, 98) (1926–1986), Prairie bird's-foot [Prairie bird's foot] (72) (1907), Prairie trefoil (4, 98) (1926–1986), Spanish-clover deervetch [Spanishclover deervetch] (155) (1942), Zitkala tawote (Lakota, small bird's food) (121) (1918?–1970?)

Lucuma mammosa **Gaertn.** – See *Manilkara zapota* (L.) van Royen

Ludwigea alternifolia **L.** – See *Ludwigia alternifolia* L.

Ludwigea hirtella **Raf.** – See *Ludwigia hirtella* Raf.

Ludwigia alata **Ell.** – Wing-stem ludwigia [Wing-stemmed ludwigia] (5) (1913)

Ludwigia alternifolia **L.** – Bowman's root [Bowman's-root, Bowman root, Bowmanroot] (158) (1900), Bushy seedbox (3, 4) (1977–1986), Ludvigia (174) (1753), Rattlebox [Rattle box, Rattle-box] (5, 93, 97, 158) (1900–1937), Rattlepod [Rattle pod, Rattle-pod] (156) (1923), Seedbox [Seed box, Seed-box] (2, 5, 19, 50, 63, 72, 74, 92, 156, 158) (1840–present), Yellow Virginia bottlekin (181) (~1678)

Ludwigia alternifolia **L. var.** *pubescens* **Palm. & Steyerm.** – See *Ludwigia alternifolia* L.

Ludwigia angustifolia **Michx.** – See *Ludwigia linearis* Walt.

Ludwigia arcuata **Walt.** – Long-stalk ludwigiantha [Long-stalked ludwigiantha] (5) (1913)

Ludwigia brevipes **(B. H. Long ex Britt., A. Braun & Small) Eames** – Short-stalk ludwigiantha [Short-stalked ludwigiantha] (5) (1913)

Ludwigia cylindrica **Ell.** – See *Ludwigia glandulosa* Walt. subsp. *glandulosa*

Ludwigia decurrens **Walt.** – Upright primrose-willow [Upright primrose willow] (5, 97) (1913–1937)

Ludwigia glandulosa **Walt.** – Cylindric-fruit ludwigia [Cylindric-fruited ludwigia] (4, 5, 97) (1913–1986), Cylindric-fruit primrose-willow [Cylindricfruit primrose-willow] (50) (present)

Ludwigia hirtella **Raf.** – Hairy ludwigia (5, 97) (1913–1937)

Ludwigia jussiaeoides **Michx.** – See *Ludwigia decurrens* Walt.

Ludwigia **L.** – False loosestrife [False loose-strife] (1, 2, 4, 93, 106, 156, 158) (1895–1986), Marsh purslane [Marshpurslane] (1, 158) (1900–1932), Primrose-willow [Primrose willow] (1, 50, 122, 138, 156, 158) (1900–present), Seedbox (4, 122, 138, 155) (1923–1986), Water purslane [Water purslain, Water-purslane, Waterpurslane]] (106) (1930), Water-primrose [Water primrose, Waterprimrose] (155) (1942)

Ludwigia linearis **Walt.** – Linear-leaf ludwigea [Linear-leaved ludwigea] (5) (1913)

Ludwigia longifolia **(DC.) H. Hara** – Brazilian primrose-willow (138) (1923)

Ludwigia natans **Ell.** – See *Ludwigia repens* Forst.

Ludwigia octovalvis **(Jacq.) Raven subsp. *octovalvis*** – Primrose-willow [Primrose willow] (124) (1937)

Ludwigia palustris **(L.) Ell.** – Bastard loosestrife (5) (1913), False loosestrife [False loose-strife] (5, 156, 157, 158) (1900–1929), Marsh purslane [Marshpurslane] (5, 63, 72, 93, 97, 155, 156, 157, 158) (1899–1942), Marsh seedbox (4, 50) (1986–present), Phthisic-weed [Phthsic weed] (5, 156, 157, 158) (1900–1929), Water purslane [Water purslain, Water-purslane, Waterpurslane] (3, 5, 19, 63, 76, 106, 120, 156, 157, 158) (1840–1977)

Ludwigia peploides **(Kunth) Raven** – Clove-strip [Clove strip] (5, 156, 158) (1900–1923), Creeping primrose-willow [Creeping primrose willow] (5, 156, 158) (1900–1923), Floating evening-primrose [Floating evening primrose] (4, 50) (1986–present), Floating primrose-willow [Floating primrose willow] (5, 97, 156, 158) (1900–1937), Floating water-primrose [Floating waterprimrose] (155) (1942), Primrose-willow [Primrose willow] (120, 124) (1937–1938), Water pusley [Water-pusley] (156) (1923)

Ludwigia peploides **(Kunth) Raven subsp. *glabrescens* (Kuntze) Raven** – Clove-strip [Clove strip] (158) (1900), Creeping primrose-willow [Creeping primrose willow] (158) (1900), Creeping water-primrose [Creeping waterprimrose] (155) (1942), Floating evening-primrose [Floating evening primrose] (4) (1986), Floating primrose-willow [Floating primrose willow] (50, 158) (1900–present), Nir-Carambu (174) (1753)

Ludwigia peploides **(Kunth) Raven subsp. *peploides*** – California waterweed (106) (1930), Waterweed [Water weed, Water-weed] (106) (1930)

Ludwigia polycarpa **Short & Peter** – False loosestrife [False loose-strife] (5, 156) (1913–1923), Many-fruit ludwigia [Many-fruited ludwigia] (5, 72) (1907–1913), Many-fruit primrose-willow [Many-fruit primrose-willow] (50) (present), Many-seed seedbox [Many-seeded seedbox] (3, 4) (1977–1986)

Ludwigia repens **Forst.** – Creeping primrose-willow [Creeping primrose willow] (50) (present), Water seedbox (155) (1942), Water-primrose [Water primrose, Waterprimrose] (4) (1986)

Ludwigia sphaerocarpa **Ell.** – Globe-fruit ludwigia [Globe-fruited ludwigia] (5) (1913)

Ludwigiantha arcuata **(Walt.) Small.** – See *Ludwigia arcuata* Walt.

Ludwigiantha brevipes **Long** – See *Ludwigia brevipes* (B.H. Long ex Britt., A. Braun & Small) Eames

Luetkea caespitosa **(Nutt.) Kuntze** – See *Petrophytum caespitosum* (Nutt.) Rydb.

Luffa acutangula **(L.) Roxb.** – Angular luffa (110) (1886), Papengaye (Senegambia) (110) (1886), Singkwa towel gourd [Singkwa towel-gourd] (138) (1923)

Luffa acutangulla **Roxb.** – See *Luffa acutangula* (L.) Roxb.

Luffa aegyptiaca **Mill.** – Suakwa towel gourd [Suakwa towelgourd] (138) (1923), Towel gourd [Towelgourd] (110) (1886)

Luffa cylindrica **[(L.) M. Roemer]** – See *Luffa aegyptiaca* Mill.

Luffa **Mill.** – Towel gourd [Towelgourd] (138) (1923)

Lugustrum – See *Ligustrum* L.

Lunaria annua **L.** – Bolbonac (107, 180) (1633–1919), Matrimony plant [Matrimony-plant] (5, 156) (1913–1923), Matrimony vine [Matrimony-vine, Matrimonyvine] (5, 76) (1896–1913) Paris ME, Money plant [Money-plant] (5, 156) (1913–1923), Money-in-both-pockets (156) (1923), Moonwort [Moon-wort, Moon wort] (10, 156) (1818–1923), Penny flower [Penny-flower] (5, 107, 156) (1913–1923), Satin (5) (1913), Satin flower [Satin-flower] (5, 156) (1913–1923), Satin-pod [Satin pod] (19, 156) (1840–1923), possibly Gold-and-silver plant [Gold and silver plant, Gold-and-silver plants, Gold and silver plants, Gold-and-silver-plants] (74, 156) (1893–1923) NJ, possibly Honesty [Honestie] (5, 19, 92, 107, 109, 138, 156, 178) (1526–1949), possibly Money flower (92) (1876), possibly Silver-leaf [Silver leaf, Silver-leaf] (156) (1923), possibly White satin [White sattin, White satten] (178) (1526)

Lunaria biennis **L.** – possibly *Lunaria annua* L. subsp. *annua* L.

Lunaria biennis **Moench.** – See *Lunaria annua* L. subsp. *annua* L.

Lunaria **L.** – Honesty [Honestie] (138, 156) (1923), Moonwort [Moon-wort, Moon wort] (109) (1949), Satin flower [Satin-flower]

Lunaria rediviva **L.** – Honesty [Honestie] (19) (1840), Never-dying white satin [Neuer dying white Sattin] (178) (1526), Perennial honesty (138) (1923), Perennial satin flower [Perennial satin-flower] (156) (1923), Perennial satin-pod [Perennial satin pod] (5) (1913), Satin flower [Satin-flower] (5, 92, 156) (1876–1923), Satin-pod [Satin pod] (156) (1923), Sweet-smelling white satin [Sweete smelling white sattin] (178) (1526), White satin [White sattin, White satten] (46) (1671) cultivated by English colonists by 1671

Lunaris biennis – possibly *Lunaria annua* L. subsp. *annua* L.

Lunellia rubra **(Douglas ex Hook.) Nieuwl.** – Western wulfena (131) (1899)

Lupinus **(Tourn.) L.** – See *Lupinus* L.

Lupinus ×*alpestris* **A. Nels.** – Great Basin lupine (50) (present)

Lupinus acclivatatis **C. P. Sm.** – See *Lupinus* ×*alpestris* A. Nels.

Lupinus adscendens **Rydb.** – See *Lupinus* ×*alpestris* A. Nels.

Lupinus affinis **J. G. Agardh** – Early lupine (138) (1923)

Lupinus albus **L.** – Common lupines (178) (1526), Egyptian lupin (110) (1886), Field lupine (107) (1919), Lupin (49, 110) (1886–1898), Termos (Greek) (110) (1886), White lupin (49) (1898), White lupine (19, 109, 138) (1840–1949), Wolf bean [Wolf-bean] (107) (1919)

Lupinus alexanderae **C.P. Sm.** – See *Lupinus* ×*alpestris* A. Nels.

Lupinus aliesicola **C.P. Sm.** – See *Lupinus* ×*alpestris* A. Nels.

Lupinus angustifolius **L.** – Blue lupine [Blew Lupines] (178) (1526)

Lupinus annieae **C.P. Sm.** – See *Lupinus* ×*alpestris* A. Nels.

Lupinus arborea **Sims.** – Sundial [Sun-dial, Sun dial] (76) (1896) CA, Tree lupine (76, 109, 138) (1896–1949)

Lupinus argenteus **Pursh** – Blue bean (148) (1939), Blue lupine (127) (1933), Bluebead [Blue bead] (148) (1939), Lupine (148) (1939), Silvery lupine (4, 50, 126, 133, 155) (1903–present), Wild bean [Wild-bean, Wildbean, Wild beans] (148) (1939) CO

Lupinus argenteus **Pursh subsp. *argenteus*** – Silvery lupine (3, 5, 50, 93, 98) (1913–present)

Lupinus argenteus **Pursh var. *aristovatus* C.P. Sm.** – See *Lupinus* ×*alpestris* A. Nels.

Lupinus argenteus **Pursh var. *krauchianus* C.P. Sm.** – See *Lupinus* ×*alpestris* A. Nels.

Lupinus argenteus **Pursh var. *macounii* (Rydb.) R. J. Davis** – See *Lupinus* ×*alpestris* A. Nels.

Lupinus argenteus **Pursh var. *parviflorus* (Nutt.) C.L.A.S. Hitchc.** – See *Lupinus parviflorus* Nutt. ex Hook. & Arn. subsp. *parviflorus*

Lupinus argenteus **Pursh var. *prati-harti* C.P. Sm.** – See *Lupinus* ×*alpestris* A. Nels.

Lupinus argenteus **Pursh var. *submanens* C.P. Sm.** – See *Lupinus* ×*alpestris* A. Nels.

Lupinus argenteus **Pursh var. *wallianus* C.P. Sm.** – See *Lupinus*

×*alpestris* A. Nels.

Lupinus calcicola C.P. Sm. – See *Lupinus* ×*alpestris* A. Nels.

Lupinus capitisamniculi C.P. Sm. – See *Lupinus* ×*alpestris* A. Nels.

Lupinus caudatus Kellogg – Tail-cup lupine [Tailcup lupine] (4, 50, 155) (1942–present)

Lupinus caudatus Kellogg subsp. *argophyllus* (Gray) L. Phillips – Kellogg's spurred lupine (50) (present)

Lupinus caudatus Kellogg subsp. *caudatus* – Tail-cup lupine [Tailcup lupine] (50) (present)

Lupinus chamissonis Eschsch. – Chamisso's lupine [Chamisso lupine] (138) (1923)

Lupinus clokeyanus C.P. Sm. – See *Lupinus* ×*alpestris* A. Nels.

Lupinus cytisoides – See *Lupinus latifolius* Lindl. ex J.G. Agardh subsp. *latifolius*

Lupinus decumbens Torr. – See *Lupinus argenteus* Pursh subsp. *argenteus*

Lupinus flavopinum C.P. Sm. – See *Lupinus* ×*alpestris* A. Nels.

Lupinus havardi S. Wats. – See *Lupinus havardii* S. Wats.

Lupinus havardii S. Wats. – Chisos bluebonnet (122) (1937) TX, Chisos Mountain bluebonnet (124) (1937) TX

Lupinus junipericola C.P. Sm. – See *Lupinus* ×*alpestris* A. Nels.

Lupinus L. – Bluebonnet [Blue bonnets, Blue-bonnets, Bluebonnets] (1, 93) (1932–1936), Fingerleaf [Finger leaf] (7) (1828), Lupin (7, 10, 158) (1818–1900), Lupine (1, 4, 45, 50, 93, 106, 138, 155, 156, 158, 190) (~1759–present), Monkey face [Monkey's-face, Monkey faces] (76) (1896) Sulphur Grove OH, Old-maid's-bonnet [Old maids' bonnet, Old maid's bonnets] (158) (1900), Quaker bonnet [Quaker bonnets, Quaker-bonnets] (1, 158) (1900–1932), Sundial [Sun-dial] (76, 158) (1896–1900) Sulphur Grove OH, Wild lupine (158) (1900), Wolf's-bean [Wolf's bean] (1) (1932)

Lupinus lariversianus C.P. Sm. – See *Lupinus* ×*alpestris* A. Nels.

Lupinus latifolius Lindl. ex J. G. Agardh subsp. *latifolius* – Broom lupine (138) (1923)

Lupinus laxus Rydb. – See *Lupinus* ×*alpestris* A. Nels.

Lupinus littoralis Dougl. – Chinook licorice [Chinook liquorice] (74) (1893) Washington, DC, Cul-wha-mo (Chinook) (35) (1806), Somûchtan (Chenook) (33) (1827)

Lupinus luteus L. – European yellow lupine (138) (1923), Spanish violets (178) (1526), Yellow lupine [Yellow lupines] (19, 107, 109, 178) (1526–1949)

Lupinus macounii Rydb. – See *Lupinus* ×*alpestris* A. Nels.

Lupinus nanus Douglas ex Benth. – Common dwarf lupine (138) (1923)

Lupinus parviflorus Nutt. ex Hook. & Arn. – Lodgepole lupine (50, 155) (1942–present), Small-flower lupine [Small-flowered lupine] (131) (1899)

Lupinus parviflorus Nutt. ex Hook. & Arn. subsp. *parviflorus* – Silvery lupine (3) (1977)

Lupinus patulipes C.P. Sm. – See *Lupinus* ×*alpestris* A. Nels.

Lupinus perennis L. – Butterfly flower [Butterfly-flower, Butterflyflower] (190) (~1759), Indian beet (156) (1923), Lupine (41, 92) (1770–1876), Middle sort of great blew lupine (181) (~1678), Oldmaid's-bonnet [Old maids' bonnet, Old maid's bonnets] (5, 76, 156) (1896–1923) no longer in use by 1923, Perennial lupin (187) (1818), Quaker bonnet [Quaker bonnets, Quaker-bonnets] (5, 156) (1913–1923) no longer in use by 1923, Sundial [Sun-dial, Sun dial] (5, 76, 156) (1896–1923), Sundial lupine [Sun-dial lupine] (138) (1923), Wild lupine (2, 5, 19, 63, 72, 107, 156) (1840–1923), Wild pea (5, 73, 76, 156) (1892–1923)

Lupinus perennis L. fo. *roseus* Britton – See *Lupinus perennis* L. subsp. *perennis*

Lupinus perennis L. subsp. *perennis* – Pink bluebonnet (122) (1937) TX

Lupinus plattensis S. Wats. – Nebraska lupine (4, 5, 50, 93, 97, 155) (1913–present), Platte lupine (4) (1986)

Lupinus polyphyllus Lindl. – Washington lupine (138) (1923)

Lupinus populorum C.P. Sm. – See *Lupinus* ×*alpestris* A. Nels.

Lupinus pulcherrimus Rydb. – See *Lupinus* ×*alpestris* A. Nels.

Lupinus pusillus Pursh – Low lupine (5, 93, 97, 125, 131, 133) (1899–1937), Rusty lupine (4, 50, 155) (1942–present), Small lupine (3, 4) (1977–1986)

Lupinus pusillus Pursh subsp. *pusillus* – See *Lupinus sericeus* Pursh subsp. *sericeus* var. *sericeus*

Lupinus sericeus Pursh – Silky lupine (4, 50, 155) (1942–present), Woolly lupine (131) (1899)

Lupinus sericeus Pursh subsp. *sericeus* var. *sericeus* – Rusty lupine (50) (present)

Lupinus siccosilvae C.P. Sm. – See *Lupinus* ×*alpestris* A. Nels.

Lupinus subcarnosus Hook. – Blue lupine (106) (1930), Bluebonnet [Blue bonnets, Blue-bonnets, Bluebonnets] (106, 122) (1930–1937), Sandy-land bluebonnet [Sandy land bluebonnet] (124) (1937), Texas lupine (138) (1923)

Lupinus termis Forsk. – See *Lupinus albus* L.

Lupinus texensis Hook. – Purple bluebonnet (124) (1937), Rock bluebonnet (124) (1937)

Lupinus Tourn. – See *Lupinus* L.

Lupinus trainianus C.P. Sm. – See *Lupinus* ×*alpestris* A. Nels.

Lupinus varius L. – See *Lupinus angustifolius* L.

Lupinus villosus Willd. – Hairy lupine (19) (1840), Monkey face [Monkey's-face, Monkey faces] (73) (1892), Sundial [Sun-dial] (73) (1892) Northern OH

Luziola fluitans (Michx.) Terrell & H. Rob. – Wild rice [Wildrice] (29, 45) (1869–1896)

Luzula acuminata Raf. var. *acuminata* – Hairy wood rush (66, 72) (1903–1907), Il-togh (Swedish) (46) (1879)

Luzula acuminata Raf. var. *carolinae* (S. Wats.) Fern. – Carolina woodrush (50) (present), Hairy wood rush (5) (1913)

Luzula arctica Blytt subsp. *arctica* – Arctic woodrush [Arctic wood rush] (5, 50) (1913–present)

Luzula arcuata (Wahlenb.) Sw. – Pointed-rush [Pointed rush] (66) (1903)

Luzula bulbosa (Wood) Smyth & Smyth – Bulbous woodrush (50) (present), Woodrush [Wood rush] (3) (1977)

Luzula campestris (L.) DC. – Common wood rush [Common woodrush] (5, 66) (1903–1913), Cuckoo-grass [Cuckoo grass] (92) (1876), Field woodrush (50, 155) (1942–present)

Luzula campestris (L.) DC. var. *bulbosa* Wood – See *Luzula bulbosa* (Wood) Smyth & Smyth

Luzula campestris (L.) DC. var. *multiflora* (Ehrh.) Celak – See *Luzula multiflora* (Ehrh.) Lej. subsp. *multiflora* var. *multiflora*

Luzula carolinae S. Wats. – See *Luzula acuminata* Raf. var. *carolinae* (S. Wats.) Fern.

Luzula confusa Lindeberg – Northern woodrush [Northern wood rush] (5, 50) (1913–present)

Luzula DC. – Woodrush [Wood rush] (1, 50, 139, 152, 158) (1912–present)

Luzula echinata (Small.) Hermann – Hedgehog woodrush (50) (present), Herdgehog woodrush (50) (present)

Luzula hyperborea R. Br. p.p. – See *Luzula arctica* Blytt subsp. *arctica*

Luzula intermedia (Thuill) A. Nelson – See *Luzula multiflora* (Ehrh.) Lej. subsp. *frigida* (Buch.) Krecz.

Luzula luzuloides (Lam.) Dandy & Wilmott – Forest wood rush (5) (1913), Oak-forest woodrush [Oakforest woodrush] (50) (present)

Luzula multiflora (Ehrh.) Lej. – Common woodrush (50) (present), Grove woodrush (155) (1942), Woodrush [Wood rush] (85) (1932)

Luzula multiflora (Ehrh.) Lej. subsp. *frigida* (Buch.) Krecz. – Field woodrush (139) (1944)

Luzula multiflora (Ehrh.) Lej. subsp. *multiflora* var. *multiflora* – Field rush [Field-rush] (187) (1818), Woodrush [Wood rush] (3) (1977)

Luzula multiflora (Retz.) Lej. – See *Luzula multiflora* (Ehrh.) Lej.

Luzula nivalis (Laestad.) Beurling – See *Luzula arctica* Blytt subsp. *arctica*

Luzula parviflora (Ehrh.) Desv. – Millet woodrush (139, 155) (1942–1944), Small woodrush [Small wood rush] (66) (1903), Small-flower

254

woodrush [Small-flowered wood rush] (5, 50) (1913–present)

Luzula pilosa (L.) Willd. – See *Luzula acuminata* Raf. subsp. *acuminata*

Luzula spicata (L.) DC. – Brown rush (66) (1903), Spike woodrush (139) (1944), Spiked woodrush [Spiked wood rush] (5, 50) (1913–present)

Lychnis affinis Vahl. – See *Silene involucrata* (Cham. & Schltdl.) Bocquet

Lychnis alba Mill. – See *Silene latifolia* Poir. subsp. *alba* (Mill.) Greuter & Burdet

Lychnis alpina L. – See *Silene suecica* (Lodd.) Greuter & Burdet

Lychnis apetala L. – See *Silene uralensis* (Rupr.) Bocquet subsp. *uralensis*

Lychnis chalcedonica L. – Campion of Constantinople (178) (1526), Cross-of-Jerusalem [Cross of Jerusalem] (5, 156, 158) (1900–1923), Fireballs [Fire balls, Fire-balls] (5, 73, 156, 158) (1892–1923) Mansfield OH, no longer in use by 1923, Jerusalem cross [Jerusalem-cross] (92, 158) (1876–1900), Knight's-cross [Knight's cross, Knight-cross] (5, 156, 158) (1900–1923), London pride [London-pride] (79) (1891) Northeastern US, Maltese cross [Maltese-cross, Maltese-cross] (5, 50, 92, 109, 138, 156, 158) (1876–present), Maltese-cross campion [Maltesecross campion] (155) (1942), Mock sweet william [Mock sweet-william] (158) (1900), Nonesuch [None-such, Nonesuch] (5, 156, 158, 178) (1526–1923) no longer in use by 1923, Scarlet lightning (5, 73, 156, 158) (1892–1923) Hemmingford N.J., Scarlet lychnis (4, 5, 19, 156, 158) (1840–1986), Scarlet-cross (158) (1900), Sweet William [Sweetwilliam, Sweet-william] (5, 73, 156, 158) (1892–1923)

Lychnis coelirosa – See *Silene coeli-rosa* (L.) Godr.

Lychnis coeli-rosa Desr. – See *Silene coeli-rosa* (L.) Godr.

Lychnis coronaria (L.) Desr. – Crown-of-the-field [Crown of the field] (92) (1876), Double red campions (178) (1526), Dusty-miller [Dustymiller, Dusty miller] (109, 156) (1923–1949), Gardener's-delight [Gardener's delight] (5, 156) (1913–1923) no longer in use by 1923, Gardener's-eye [Gardener's eye] (5, 156) (1913–1923) no longer in use by 1923, Mullein lychnis (156) (1923), Mullein pink [Mullen pink] (5, 15, 109, 156) (1895–1949), Rose-campion [Rose campion] (5, 92, 109, 138, 156, 165) (1768–1949), White campion [White campions] (178) (1526)

Lychnis coronaria Desr. – See *Lychnis coronaria* (L.) Desr.

Lychnis dioica L. – See *Silene dioica* (L.) Clairville

Lychnis drummondii (Hook.) S. Wats. – See *Silene drummondii* Hook. var. *drummondii*

Lychnis flos cuculi – See *Lychnis flos-cuculi* L.

Lychnis floscuculi – See *Lychnis flos-cuculi* L.

Lychnis flos-cuculi L. – Bachelor's-button [Bachelor's button, Bachelor's buttons, Batchelor's buttons] (92) (1876), Crow-flower [Crow flower] (5, 156) (1913–1923) no longer in use by 1923, Cuckoo-flower [Cuckooflower, Cuckoo flower] (5, 92, 156, 178) (1526–1923), Cuckoos [Cuckoo] (5, 156) (1913–1923) no longer in use by 1923, Indian pink (5, 156) (1913–1923) no longer in use by 1923, Marsh gilliflower (5, 156) (1913–1923) no longer in use by 1923, Meadow campion (5, 156) (1913–1923), Meadow pink [Meadow-pink] (5, 156) (1913–1923), Ragged-Jack [Ragged Jack] (5, 156) (1913–1923) no longer in use by 1923, Ragged-robin [Ragged robin] (5, 15, 19, 92, 109, 138, 156) (1840–1949), Wild field pinks [Wilde field pinks] (178) (1526)

Lychnis fulgens Fisch. ex Sims – Brilliant campion (138) (1923)

Lychnis L. – Campion (50, 138, 155, 156) (1923–present), Cockle [Cockel, Cokyll] (15) (1895), Lychnis (138, 156, 158) (1900–1923)

Lychnis Tourn. – See *Lychnis* L.

Lychnis vespertina Sibthorp – See *Silene latifolia* Poir. subsp. *alba* (Mill.) Greuter & Burdet

Lychnis viscaria L. – Bird-lime wort [Birdlime woort] (178) (1526), Clammy campion (138) (1923), Clammy lichnia (19) (1840), German catchfly (109) (1949)

Lycium barbarum L. – Barbary matrimony-vine (138) (1923), Barbary wolfberry (155) (1942), Bastard jasmine (75, 158) (1894–1900) IA, Bastard jesssamine (5) (1913), Boxthorn [Box-thorn, Box thorn] (5, 75, 92, 156, 158) (1876–1923), Common matrimony-vine (138) (1923), Duke of Argyll's tea-tree (158) (1900), False jessamine (156) (1923), Fever-twig [Fever-twig] (156) (1923), Jackson vine [Jackson-vine] (5, 73, 156, 158) (1892–1923) Mansfield OH, Jasmine (5, 73) (1892–1913) Mansfield OH, Jessamine (73, 158) (1892–1900) Stratham NH, Matrimony vine [Matrimony-vine, Matrimonyvine] (1, 3, 5, 19, 50, 63, 72, 82, 85, 92, 93, 95, 106, 114, 148, 155, 156, 158) (1840–present), Morel (156) (1923), Privy (73) (1892) Mansfield OH, Tether-devil [Tether devil] (156) (1923), Violet-bloom [Violet bloom] (156) (1923), Washington's bower (77) (1898) Southwest MO, Wolf-grape [Wolf grape] (156) (1923)

Lycium berlandieri Dunal – Berlandier's wolfberry (50) (present), Silver wolfberry (4) (1986)

Lycium carolinianum Walt. var. *quadrifidum* (Dunal) C. L. Hitchc. – Large-fruit matrimony vine [Large-fruited matrimony vine] (124) (1937)

Lycium carolinianum Walt. var. *quadrifidum* Moc. and Sess ex Dunal – See *Lycium carolinianum* Walt. var. *quadrifidum* (Dunal) C.L. Hitchc.

Lycium chinense Mill. – Chinese matrimony-vine (138) (1923), Matrimony vine [Matrimony-vine, Matrimonyvine] (112) (1937)

Lycium fremonti – See *Lycium fremontii* Gray

Lycium fremontii Gray – Desert matrimony (106) (1930), Squaw bush [Squawbush, Squaw-bush] (106) (1930) Phoenix AZ, Squawberry [Squaw berry, Squaw-berry] (106) (1930) Phoenix AZ

Lycium halimifolium Mill. – See *Lycium barbarum* L.

Lycium L. – Boxthorn [Box-thorn, Box thorn] (10, 109) (1818–1949), Desert thorn [Desert-thorn, Desertthorn] (50, 155) (1942–present), Matrimony vine [Matrimony-vine, Matrimonyvine] (82, 93, 109, 156, 158) (1900–1949), Squaw bush [Squawbush, Squaw-bush] (106, 155) (1930–1942), Wolfberry [Wolf berry, Wolf-berry] (4, 155) (1942–1986)

Lycium pallidum Miers. – Pale desert-thorn (50) (present), Pale wolfberry (4, 155) (1942–1986)

Lycium torreyi Gray – Garrambullo (149, 153) (1904–1919) NM

Lycium vulgare Dunal – See *Lycium barbarum* L.

Lycoperdon gemmatum Batsch. – possibly *Lycoperdon perlatum* Pers.

Lycoperdon L. – possibly *Lycoperdon* Pers.

Lycoperdon perlatum Pers. (possibly) – Hokshi chekpa (Dakota, baby's navel) (37) (1830), possibly Kaho rahik (Pawnee, old name) (37) (1830), possibly Puffball [Puff-ball, Puff ball, Puffballs, Puff balls] (37) (1830)

Lycoperdon Pers. – Devil's-snuffbox [Devil's snuff box] (14) (1882), Fuss-balls (46) (1671), Puffball [Puff-ball, Puff ball, Puffballs, Puff balls] (7, 14) (1828–1882), possibly Truffle [Truffles] (184) (1793)

Lycoperdon proteus Bull. – Frog cheese (92) (1876), Puffball [Puffball, Puff ball, Puffballs, Puff balls] (92) (1876)

Lycoperdon solidum L. – Indian head (103) (1871), Tuckaho [Tuckaho, Tuckahoe] (103) (1871)

Lycoperdon tuber L. – Truffle [Truffles] (41) (1770), Tuber (174) (1753), Tuckahoo (177) (1762)

Lycopersicon esculentum Mill. – See *Solanum lycopersicum* L. var. *lycopersicum*

Lycopersicon esculentum P. Mill var. *cerasiforme* Alef. – See *Solanum lycopersicum* L. var. *cerasiforme* (Dunal) Spooner, J. Anderson & R. K. Jansen

Lycopersicon Hill. – See *Solanum* L. (all species in US)

Lycopersicon lycopersicon (L.) Karst – See *Solanum lycopersicum* L. var. *lycopersicum*

Lycopersicon Mill. – See *Solanum* L. (all species in US)

Lycopersicon pimpinellifolium (Jusl.) Mill. – See *Solanum pimpinellifolium* Jusl.

Lycopersicum – See *Solanum* L. (all species in US)

Lycopersicum pimpinellifolium – See *Solanum pimpinellifolium* Jusl.

Lycopodiella alopecuroides (L.) Cranfill – Foxtail clubmoss [Fox-tail

Lycopodiella appressa (Chapman)   SCIENTIFIC NAMES INDEX

club-moss] (5, 50) (1913–present)

Lycopodiella appressa (Chapman) **Cranfill** – Chapman's club-moss (5) (1913), Southern bog clubmoss (50) (present)

Lycopodiella caroliniana (L.) **Pichi Sermolli var.** *caroliniana* – Carolina clubmoss [Carolina club-moss] (5, 122) (1913–1937), Slender clubmoss (50) (present)

Lycopodiella cernua var. *cernua* (L.) **Pichi Sermolli** – Bellon-patsia (174) (1753)

Lycopodiella inundata (L.) **Holub** – Bog club-moss (5) (1913), Clubmoss [Club-moss, Club moss] (46) (1879), Inundated clubmoss (50) (present), Marsh clubmoss [Marsh club-moss] (5) (1913)

Lycopodium adpressum (Chapm.) **Lloyd & Underw.** – See *Lycopodiella appressa* (Chapman) Cranfill

Lycopodium alopecuroides **L.** – See *Lycopodiella alopecuroides* (L.) Cranfill

Lycopodium alopecuroides **L. subsp.** *appressum* (Chapman) **Clute** – See *Lycopodiella appressa* (Chapman) Cranfill

Lycopodium alopecuroides **L. var.** *appressum* **Chapman** – See *Lycopodiella appressa* (Chapman) Cranfill

Lycopodium alpinum **L.** – Alpine club-moss (5, 50) (1913–present), Cypress moss (5) (1913), Heath cypress (5) (1913), Savin-leaf club moss [Savin-leaved club moss] (5) (1913)

Lycopodium annotinum **L.** – Bristly clubmoss (3) (1977), Interrupted clubmoss [Interrupted club moss] (5) (1913), Running ground-pine [Running ground pine] (19) (1840), Stiff clubmoss [Stiff club moss] (5, 50) (1913–present)

Lycopodium apodum **L.** – See *Selaginella apoda* (L.) Spring

Lycopodium armatum **Desv.** – See *Lycopodium sabinifolium* Willd.

Lycopodium carolinianum **L.** – See *Lycopodiella caroliniana* (L.) Pichi Sermolli var. *caroliniana*

Lycopodium cernuum **L.** – See *Lycopodiella cernua* var. *cernua* (L.) Pichi Sermolli

Lycopodium chamicyparissus **A. Braun** – See *Lycopodium tristachyum* Pursh

Lycopodium chapmanii **Underwood ex Maxon p.p.** – See *Lycopodiella appressa* (Chapman) Cranfill

Lycopodium clavatum **L.** – Buckhorn [Buck horn, Buck-horn, Buck's horn, Buckshorn, Buck's-horn, Bucks-horne, Bucks horne] (5) (1913), Buck's-grass [Buck's grass] (5) (1913), Clubmoss [Clubmoss, Club moss] (6, 14, 19, 46, 49, 52, 53, 55, 59, 92) (1840–1922), Common club moss (6) (1892), Coral evergreen (5, 73) (1892–1913), Creeping bur (5) (1913), Creeping Jenny [Creeping Jennie, Creeping-Jennie, Creeping-jenny] (5, 73) (1892–1913), Foxtail [Fox tail, Fox-tail, Fox tails, Foxetaile, Fox-taile] (5, 92) (1876–1913), Gemeines Bürlapp (German) (6) (1892), Ground-pine [Ground-pine, Ground pine] (5, 6) (1892–1913), Hogbed [Hog bed, Hog-bed, Hog's bed] (6) (1892), Kalben-Moos (German) (6) (1892), Kalfwerefwor (Swedish) (46) (1879), Lamb's-tail [Lamb's tail, Lamb's tails] (5) (1913), Lycopodium (52, 55, 57, 59, 92) (1876–1919), Mattegras (Swedish) (46) (1879), Pied de loup (French) (6) (1892), Ralf-mossa (Swedish) (46) (1879), Running clubmoss [Running club-moss] (50) (present), Running moss (5) (1913), Running-pine [Runningpine, Running pine] (72, 138) (1907–1923), Running-pine club-moss (5) (1913), Snake moss (5, 6) (1892–1913), Staghorn [Stag-horn, Stag's horn] (6, 92) (1876–1892), Stag-horn evergreen [Stag horn evergreen] (78) (1898) Concord MA, Staghorn moss (5) (1913), Toad's-tail [Toad's tail] (5) (1913), Vegetable brimstone (92) (1876), Vegetable powder (92) (1876), Vegetable sulphur (14, 57, 92) (1882–1917), Wisp-mossa (Swedish) (46) (1879), Witches (14) (1882), Wolf's claw [Wolf claw, Wolf's claw] (5, 6, 92) (1876–1913) IA

Lycopodium complanatum **L.** – Creeping Jenny [Creeping Jennie, Creeping-Jennie, Creeping-jenny] (5, 73, 158) (1892–1913) Bedford MA, Creeping vine (78) (1898) Ferrisburgh VT, Crowfoot [Crow-foot, Crow foot, Crowfote, Crow's foot] (5, 158) (1900–1913), Evergreen (78) (1898), Festoon-pine [Festoon pine] (5) (1913), Ground-cedar [Groundcedar, Ground cedar] (5, 50, 73, 138,

158) (1892–present), Ground-festoon (158) (1900), Groundpine [Ground-pine, Ground pine] (5, 19, 92, 158) (1840–1913), Hogbed [Hog bed, Hog-bed, Hog's bed] (5, 92, 158) (1876–1913), Joemna (Sweden) (46) (1879), Liberty (73) (1892) Chestertown MD, Running vine (78) (1898) Ferrisburgh VT, Trailing Christmas-green (5, 72, 78, 158) (1898–1913), Trailing vine (78) (1898) Ferrisburgh VT, possibly Flat club-moss (187) (1818)

Lycopodium complanatum **L. subsp.** *chamicyparissus* (A. Braun) **Nyman** – See *Lycopodium tristachyum* Pursh

Lycopodium complanatum **L. var.** *chamicyparissus* (A. Braun) **Doell** – See *Lycopodium tristachyum* Pursh

Lycopodium complanatum **L. var.** *patentifolium* **Spring** – See *Lycopodium tristachyum* Pursh

Lycopodium dendroideum **Michx.** – Bunch evergreen (73) (1892) NH, Crowfoot [Crow-foot, Crow foot, Crowfote, Crow's foot] (73) (1892) Chestertown MD, Groundpine [Ground-pine, Ground pine] (4, 10, 187) (1818–1986), Tree ground-pine [Tree groundpine] (50) (present), Treeweed [Tree weed] (19) (1840)

Lycopodium inundatum **L.** – See *Lycopodiella inundata* (L.) Holub

Lycopodium inundatum **L. var.** *alopecuroides* (L.) **Tuckerman** – See *Lycopodiella alopecuroides* (L.) Cranfill

Lycopodium inundatum **L. var.** *appressum* **Chapman** – See *Lycopodiella appressa* (Chapman) Cranfill

Lycopodium inundatum **L. var.** *bigelovii* **Tuckerman** – See *Lycopodiella appressa* (Chapman) Cranfill

Lycopodium **L.** – Clubmoss [Club-moss, Club moss] (1, 4, 10, 50, 138, 155, 158, 184) (1793–present), Foxtail [Fox tail, Fox-tail, Fox tails, Foxetaile, Fox-taile] (78) (1898) St. Andrews NB, Groundpine [Ground-pine, Ground pine] (1, 7) (1828–1932), Hogbed [Hog bed, Hog-bed, Hog's bed] (7) (1828)

Lycopodium lucidulum **Michx.** – See *Huperzia lucidula* (Michx.) Trevisan

Lycopodium lucidulum **Michx. var.** *porophilum* (Lloyd & Underwood) **Clute** – See *Huperzia porophila* (Lloyd & Underwood) Holub

Lycopodium obscurum **L.** – Bunch evergreen (5, 158) (1900–1913), Crowfoot [Crow-foot, Crow foot, Crowfote, Crow's foot] (5, 155, 158) (1900–1942), Groundpine [Ground-pine, Ground pine] (3, 5, 40, 131, 138, 155, 158) (1899–1977), Rare club moss (50) (present), Spiral-pine [Spiral pine] (5, 158) (1900–1913), Tree-like clubmoss [Tree-like club-moss, Tree-like club moss] (5, 158) (1900–1913)

Lycopodium porophilum **Lloyd & Underw.** – See *Huperzia porophila* (Lloyd & Underwood) Holub

Lycopodium reflexum **Sw., non Lam.** – See *Huperzia lucidula* (Michx.) Trevisan

Lycopodium rupestre – See *Selaginella rupestris* (L.) Spring

Lycopodium sabinaefolium **Willd.** – See *Lycopodium sabinifolium* Willd.

Lycopodium sabinifolium **Willd.** – Cedar-like club-moss (5) (1913), Savin-leaf ground-pine [Savinleaf groundpine] (50) (present)

Lycopodium sabinifolium **Willd. subsp.** *sitchense* (Rupr.) **Calder & Taylor** – See *Lycopodium sitchense* Rupr.

Lycopodium sabinifolium **Willd. var.** *sitchense* (Rupr.) **Fern.** – See *Lycopodium sitchense* Rupr.

Lycopodium selago **L.** – See *Huperzia selago* (L.) Bernh. ex Mart. & Schrank var. *selago*

Lycopodium selago **L. subsp.** *patens* (Beauv.) **Calder & Taylor** – See *Huperzia porophila* (Lloyd & Underwood) Holub

Lycopodium selago **L. var.** *patens* (Beauv.) **Desv.** – See *Huperzia porophila* (Lloyd & Underwood) Holub

Lycopodium selago **L. var.** *porophilum* (Lloyd & Underwood) **Clute** – See *Huperzia porophila* (Lloyd & Underwood) Holub

Lycopodium sitchense **Rupr.** – Alaska club-moss [Alaskan club-moss] (5) (1913), Sitka clubmoss (50) (present)

Lycopodium tristachyum **Pursh** – Deep-root clubmoss [Deeproot clubmoss] (50) (present), Groundpine [Ground-pine, Ground pine] (5) (1913)

256

Lycopsis arvensis **L.** – See *Anchusa arvensis* (L.) Bieb.

Lycopsis **L.** – See *Anchusa* L. (US species)

Lycopus (**Tourn.**) **L.** – See *Lycopus* L.

Lycopus americanus **Muhl. ex W. Bart.** – American bugleweed (4, 138, 155) (1923–1986), American water-horehound [American water-hoarhound, American water horehound] (50) (present), Bitter bugle (5, 156, 158) (1900–1923), Bugle (57) (1917), Cut-leaf horehound [Cutleaf hoarhound (122) (1937), Cut-leaf water-horehound [Cut-leaved water horehound, Cut-leaved water hoarhound] (5, 72, 93, 97, 131, 158) (1907–1937), Gipsyweed [Gypsy weed, Gipsy weed, Gypsy-weed, Gypsyweed (5, 156, 158) (1900–1923), Gipsywort [Gypsywort, Gypsy-wort, Gypsiewort] (5, 156, 158) (1900–1923), Lycopus (57) (1917), Paul's betony [Pauls' betony] (5, 158) (1900–1913), Rattlesnake-weed [Rattlesnake weed, Rattlesnake weede, Rattlesnakes' weed] (77) (1898) Southwest MO, said to be an antidote for rattlesnake bite, Water horehound [Water hoarhound, Waterhorehound] (47, 95, 114, 156) (1852–1923)

Lycopus amplectens **Raf.** – Sessile-leaf water-hoarhound [Sessile-leaved water hoarhound] (5) (1913) W. US

Lycopus asper **Greene** – Ande'gopĭn (Chippewa, crow plant) (40) (1928), Bugleweed [Bugle weed, Bugle-weed] (40) (1928), Rough bugleweed (3, 4, 50) (1977–present), Water horehound [Water hoarhound, Waterhorehound] (85) (1932), Western water horehound [Western water hoarhound] (5, 72, 93, 131) (1899–1936)

Lycopus europaeus **L.** – Bitter bugle (156) (1923), Bitter bugleweed (5) (1913), European bugleweed (138) (1923), European water horehound [European water hoarhound] (156) (1923), Gipsy herb [Gypsy herb] (5) (1913), Gipsy plant [Gipsy-plant, Gypsy-plant] (156) (1923) no longer in use by 1923, Gipsyweed [Gypsy weed, Gipsy weed, Gypsy-weed, Gypsyweed (5, 156) (1913–1923) no longer in use by 1923, Glidewort [Glide woort] (178) (1526), Green archangel (5, 92, 156) (1876–1923) no longer in use by 1923, Marsh horehound [Marsh hoarhound] (156) (1923), Water horehound [Water hoarhound, Waterhorehound] (5, 19) (1840–1913)

Lycopus **L.** – Bugleweed [Bugle weed, Bugle-weed] (1, 4, 93, 106, 138, 155, 158) (1900–1986), Gipsyweed [Gypsy weed, Gipsy weed, Gypsy-weed, Gypsyweed (158) (1900), Gipsywort [Gypsywort, Gypsy-wort, Gypsiewort] (158, 180, 184) (1793–1900), Water horehound [Water hoarhound, Waterhorehound] (1, 2, 10, 26, 50, 93, 106, 156, 190) (~1759–present)

Lycopus lucidus **Turcz** – See *Lycopus asper* Greene

Lycopus rubellus **Moench** – Gipsyweed [Gypsy weed, Gipsy weed, Gypsy-weed, Gypsyweed (5, 156) (1913–1923), Gipsywort [Gypsywort, Gypsy-wort, Gypsiewort] (5, 156) (1913–1923), Stalked water-horehound [Stalked water hoarhound, Stalked water horehound] (5, 72, 122, 131) (1899–1936), Taper-leaf water horehound [Taper-leaf water hoarhound] (50) (present), Water horehound [Water hoarhound, Waterhorehound] (4, 156) (1923–1986)

Lycopus sessilifolius **Gray** – See *Lycopus amplectens* Raf.

Lycopus sinuatus **Ell.** – See *Lycopus americanus* Muhl. ex W. Bart.

Lycopus uniflorus **Michx.** – Bugleweed [Bugle weed, Bugle-weed] (3, 156) (1923–1977), Northern bugleweed [Northern bugle weed] (5, 50, 93) (1913–present), One-flower horehound [One flower horehound] (4) (1986)

Lycopus virginicus **L.** – American water-horehound [American water-hoarhound, American water horehound] (157, 158) (1900–1929), Archangel (77) (1898) Dixfield ME, Betony (92) (1876), Bugle (57) (1917), Bugleweed [Bugle weed, Bugle-weed] (2, 5, 6, 7, 19, 47, 49, 52, 53, 54, 61, 63, 92, 93, 95, 122, 156, 157, 158) (1840–1937), Buglewort [Bugle wort, Bugle-wort] (5, 7, 92, 156, 158) (1828–1923), Carpenter's-herb [Carpenter's herb] (92, 157, 158) (1876–1929), Gipsyweed [Gypsy weed, Gipsy weed, Gypsy-weed, Gypsy-weed (6, 7, 49, 92, 157, 158) (1828–1929), Gipsywort [Gypsywort, Gypsy-wort, Gypsiewort] (6, 92) (1876–1892), Green archangel (158) (1900), Lycope de Virginie (French) (6, 7, 158) (1828–1900), Lycopus (52, 54, 57) (1905–1917), Paul's betony [Pauls' betony] (6, 7, 49, 53, 92, 158) (1828–1922), Purple archangel (92) (1876),

Purple bugleweed [Purple bugle-weed] (72) (1907), Spring-of-Jerusalem [Spring of Jerusalem] (77) (1898) S. Berwick ME, Sweet bugle (49, 53, 92) (1876–1922), Sweet bugleweed (158) (1900), Virginia bugleweed (3, 4, 155) (1942–1986), Virginia water horehound (50) (present), Virginischer Wolfsfuss (German) (6, 158) (1892–1900), Water bugle (6, 7, 49, 92) (1828–1898), Water horehound [Water hoarhound, Waterhorehound] (6, 7, 49, 92, 157) (1828–1929), Wolf's-foot [Wolf foot, Wolf-foot] (92, 157, 158) (1876–1929), Wood betony [Wood-betony, Woodbetony] (5, 156, 157, 158) (1900–1929)

Lycoris **Herbert** – Cluster-amaryllis (138) (1923)

Lycoris squamigera **Maxim.** – Hardy cluster-amaryllis (138) (1923)

Lycurus **Kunth** – Wolf's-tail [Wolfstail, Wolftail] (50, 155) (1942–present)

Lycurus phleoides **H.B.K.** – Common wolf's-tail [Common wolfstail] (50) (present), Texas timothy [Texan timothy] (94, 152, 163) (1852–1912), Wolf's-tail [Wolfstail, Wolftail] (3, 119, 122, 140, 155, 163) (1852–1977)

Lygodesmia **D. Don** – Lygodesmia (158) (1900), Prairie pink (1) (1932), Skeleton plant [Skeletonplant] (50) (present), Skeleton-plant [Skeletonplant] (50) (Present), Skeleton-weed [Skeleton weed, Skeletonweed] (1, 4, 155) (1932–1986), Wild asparagus (1) (1932)

Lygodesmia grandiflora (**Nutt.**) **Torr. & Gray** – Large-flower skeletonplant [Largeflower skeletonplant] (50) (present)

Lygodesmia juncea (**Pursh**) **D. Don ex Hook.** – Lygodesmia (80, 125, 157) (1900–1913), Makačaŋšiŋhu (Lakota, skunk resin plant) (121) (1918?–1970?), Prairie pink (85, 121, 148) (1932–1939), Rush skeleton plant [Rush skeletonplant] (50) (present), Rush skeleton-weed [Rush skeletonweed] (155) (1942), Rush-like lygodesmia [Rushlike lygodesmia] (5, 72, 80, 97, 122, 131) (1899–1937), Skeleton-weed [Skeleton weed, Skeletonweed] (3, 37, 80, 121, 148) (1919–1977)

Lygodesmia rostrata **Gray** – See *Shinnersoseris rostrata* (Gray) S. Tomb

Lygodesmia texana (**Torr. & Gray**) **Greene** – Flowering straw (97) (1937) OK, Skeleton-weed [Skeleton weed, Skeletonweed] (124) (1937), Texas skeleton-plant [Texas skeletonplant] (50) (present), Texas skeleton-weed (3) (1977)

Lygodium japonicum (**Thunb. ex Murr.**) **Sw.** – Japanese climbing fern (138) (1923)

Lygodium microphyllum (**Cav.**) **R. Br.** – Feathery climbing fern (138) (1923)

Lygodium palmatum (**Bernh.**) **Sw.** – American climbing fern (50) (present), Climbing fern [Climbing-fern] (5, 19) (1840–1913), Creeping fern (5) (1913), Hartford climbing fern (2, 5, 109, 138) (1895–1949), Hartford fern [Hartford-fern] (2, 5) (1895–1913), Windsor fern (5) (1913)

Lygodium scandens – See *Lygodium microphyllum* (Cav.) R. Br.

Lygodium **Swartz** – Climbing fern [Climbing-fern] (2, 50, 108, 138, 161) (1857–present), Snake's-tongue [Snake's tongue, Snakes' tongue] (10) (1818)

Lyonia ferruginea (**Walt.**) **Nutt.** – Wicky (106) (1930), Ximenia (182) (1791), possibly Ferruginous andromeda (42) (1814), possibly Rusty andromeda (165) (1807)

Lyonia ligustrina (**L.**) **DC.** – He-huckleberry (109, 138, 156) (1923–1949), Maleberry [Male berry, Male-berry] (77, 109, 156) (1898–1949), Pepper bush [Pepper-bush, Pepperbush] (156) (1923), Privet-andromeda [Privet andromeda] (5, 97, 156) (1913–1937), Seedy buckberry [Seedy buck-berry] (75, 156) (1894–1923), Swamp andromeda (156) (1923), White alder (124, 156) (1923–1937), White bush [White-bush] (156) (1923), White pepper (156) (1923), Whitewood [White wood, White-wood] (156) (1923), possibly White pepper bush [White pepperbush, White pepper-bush] (46) (1783)

Lyonia ligustrina (**L.**) **DC. var.** *foliosiflora* (**Michx.**) **Fern.** – White alder (122) (1937)

Lyonia ligustrina (**L.**) **DC. var.** *ligustrina* – Lyon's andromeda (5)

***Lyonia ligustrina* DC.**

(1913), Maleberry [Male berry, Male-berry] (97) (1937) OK, Seedy buckberry [Seedy buck-berry] (5) (1913), White alder (5) (1913), White pepper bush [White pepperbush, White pepper-bush] (5) (1913), Whitewood [White wood, White-wood] (5) (1913), Wicky (182) (1791), Wild lime or Wild lime tree [Wild lime-tree] (174) (1753)

Lyonia ligustrina **DC.** – See *Lyonia ligustrina* (L.) DC.

Lyonia lucida **(Lam.) K. Koch** – Andromede luisante (French) (8) (1785), Carolina redbud [Carolinian red-buds] (8) (1785), Evergreen andromeda (183) (~1756), Evergreen shining-leaf andromeda [Evergreen shining-leaved andromeda] (8) (1785), Fetter bush [Fetterbush, Fetter-bush] (5, 109, 156) (1913–1949), Pipestem [Pipe-stem, Pipe stem] (5, 7, 92, 156) (1828–1923), Sourwood [Sour-wood, Sour wood] or Sourwood tree (7) (1828)

Lyonia lucida **Koch** – See *Lyonia lucida* (Lam.) K. Koch

Lyonia mariana **(L.) D. Don** – Andromede de Maryland (French) (8) (1785), Broad-leaf andromeda [Broad-leaved andromeda] (8) (1785), Kill-lamb [Kill lamb] (71) (1898), Maryland andromeda (8, 165) (1785–1807), Moorwort [Moor-wort] (86) (1878), Oval-leaf andromeda [Oval leaved andromeda, Oval-leaved andromeda] (42, 187) (1814–1818), Sorrel tee [Sorel tee, Sorrel-tree] (5, 92, 156) (1876–1923), Stagger brush [Stagger-brush, Staggerbrush] (2) (1895), Stagger bush [Stagger-bush, Staggerbush] (2, 5, 71, 86, 92, 109, 122, 138, 156) (1878–1949) thought to cause "staggers" in sheep, Wick [Wicke, Wicks] (5, 7, 86, 156) (1828–1923), Wicopy [Wickopy] (156) (1923)

Lyonia mariana **D. Don.** – See *Lyonia mariana* (L.) D. Don

Lyonothamnus floribunda – See *Lyonothamnus floribundus* Gray

Lyonothamnus floribundus asplenifolius – See *Lyonothamnus floribundus* Gray subsp. *aspleniifolius* (Greene) Raven

Lyonothamnus floribundus **Gray** – Catalina lyon shrub [Catalina lyonshrub] (138) (1923), Ironwood [Iron wood, Iron-wood] (74) (1893) CA

Lyonothamnus floribundus **Gray subsp.** *aspleniifolius* **(Greene) Raven** – Fern-leaf lyonshrub [Fernleaf lyonshrub] (138) (1923)

Lyonothamnus **Gray** – Lyon-shrub [Lyonshrub] (138) (1923)

Lysias hookeriana **(A. Gray) Rydb.** – See *Platanthera hookeri* (Torr. ex Gray) Lindl.

Lysias orbiculata **(Pursh) Rydb.** – See *Platanthera orbiculata* (Pursh) Lindl.

Lysiella obtusata **(Pursh) Richards.** – See *Platanthera obtusata* (Banks ex Pursh) Lindl.

Lysiella **Rydb.** – See *Platanthera* L.C. Rich (US species)

Lysiloma latisiliquum **(L.) Benth.** – Acacia à large silique (French) (20) (1857), Broad-pod acacia [Broad-podded acacia] (20) (1857)

Lysimachia **(Tourn.) L.** – See *Lysimachia* L.

Lysimachia ciliata **L.** – Fringed loosestrife (3, 4, 5, 50, 72, 82, 85, 93, 97, 122, 127, 131, 138, 156) (1899–present), Fringed steironema (155) (1942), Heart-leaf loosestrife [Heart-leaved loose-strife] (187) (1818), Loosestrife [Loose strife, Loose-strife] (109) (1949), Low steironema (155) (1942), Moneywort [Money wort] (19) (1840)

Lysimachia clethroides **Duby** – Clethra loosestrife (138) (1923)

Lysimachia hybrida **Michx.** – Lance-leaf loosestrife [Lanceleaf loose-strife] (122) (1937), Loosestrife [Loose strife, Loose-strife] (3, 4) (1977–1986), Lowland yellow loosestrife (50) (present)

Lysimachia japonica **Thunb.** – Japanese loosestrife (138) (1923)

Lysimachia **L.** – Loosestrife [Loose strife, Loose-strife] (1, 2, 4, 10, 82, 109, 138, 155, 156, 158, 184) (1793–1986), Lysimaque (French) (158) (1900), Steironema (155) (1942), Tufted loosestrife (1, 158) (1900–1932), Weiderich (German) (158) (1900), Yellow loosestrife [Yellow loose strife] (50) (present)

Lysimachia lanceolata **Walt.** – Loosestrife [Loose strife, Loose-strife] (3) (1977), Lance-leaf loosestrife [Lance-leaved loosestrife] (5, 50, 72, 82, 85, 97) (1907–present)

Lysimachia nummularia **L.** – Creeping charlie [Creeping-charlie, Creeping charley] (109) (1949), Creeping Jenny [Creeping Jennie, Creeping-Jennie, Creeping-jenny] (5, 50, 109, 158) (1900–present),

Creeping loosestrife (156, 158) (1900–1923), Creeping Sally (5, 156) (1913–1923), Down-hill-of-life (5, 75, 156, 158) (1900–1923) Lincolnton NC, Herb tuppence (158) (1900), Herb twopence [Herb-twopence, Herbe Two pence] (5, 156, 158, 178) (1526–1923), Infant's-breath [Infant's breath] (77) (1898) Oxford Co. ME, Meadow run-a-gates [Meadow-runagates] (156, 158) (1900–1923), Money plant [Money-plant] (77, 156) (1898–1923) Oxford Co. ME, Money-bags [Money bags] (77) (1898) Medford MA, Money-myrtle (156) (1923), Moneywort [Money wort] (3, 4, 5, 72, 92, 109, 138, 155, 156, 158) (1876–1986), Monnayère (French) (158) (1900), Myrtle (156) (1923), Pfennigkraut (German) (158) (1900), String-of-sovereigns [Strings of sovereigns] (156, 158) (1900–1923), Two-penny-grass [Two-penny grass] (5, 92, 156, 158) (1876–1923), Wandering-Jenny [Wandering Jenny] (5, 156, 158) (1900–1923), Wandering-sailor [Wandering sailor] (156, 158) (1900–1923), Wandering-Sally [Wandering Sally] (5, 156) (1913–1923)

Lysimachia punctata **L.** – Garden loosestrife (3) (1977), Large yellow loosestrife (50) (present), Spotted loosestrife (5, 138, 155, 156) (1913–1942)

Lysimachia quadrifolia **L.** – Crosswort [Cross wort, Cross-wort, Crosse woort] (5, 7, 92, 156, 158) (1828–1923), Five-sisters [Five-sisters] (5, 156, 158) (1900–1923), Four-leaf loosestrife [Fourleaf loosestrife] (86, 155) (1878–1942), Liberty tea [liberty-tea] (5, 156) (1913–1923), Linear-leaf loosestrife [Linear-leaved loosestrife] (5, 158) (1900–1913), Prairie loosestrife (72) (1907), Prairie money-wort (5, 82, 158) (1900–1930), Prairie steironema (155) (1942), Whorled loosestrife (3, 4, 5, 72, 156, 158) (1900–1986), Whorled yellow loosestrife (50) (present), Yellow balm (5, 7, 156, 158) (1828–1923)

Lysimachia racemosa – possibly *Lysimachia terrestris* (L.) Britton, Sterns & Poggenb.

Lysimachia radicans **Hook.** – Fringed loosestrife (1) (1932), Trailing loosestrife (5, 122) (1913–1937)

Lysimachia terrestris **(L.) Britton, Sterns & Poggenb.** – Bulb-bearing loosestrife [Bulb-bearing loose-strife] (5, 72, 156, 187) (1818–1923), Swamp-candle [Swampcandle, Swamp candles] (5, 138, 156) (1913–1923), possibly Cluster-flower loose-strife [Cluster-flowered loose-strife] (187) (1818)

Lysimachia thyrsiflora **L.** – Tufted loosestrife (3, 4, 5, 50, 72, 85, 93, 95, 131, 156) (1899–present), Water loosestrife (138, 155) (1923–1942)

Lysimachia tonsa **(Wood) Wood ex Pax & R. Knuth** – Southern loosestrife (5) (1913)

Lysimachia vulgaris **L.** – Golden loosestrife (5, 138, 156) (1913–1923), Golden willowherb [Golden willow-herb] (5, 156) (1913–1923), Willow-wort [Willow wort, Willowort] (5, 156) (1913–1923), Yellow loosestrife [Yellow loose strife] (5, 92, 156) (1876–1923), Yellow rocket [Yellowrocket, Yellow-rocket] (5, 156) (1913–1923), Yellow willow herb [Yellow willowherb, Yellow willow herbe] (5, 92, 178) (1526–1913)

Lythrum alatum **Pursh** – Loosestrife [Loose strife, Loose-strife] (82, 85, 157) (1900–1930), Milk willow herb [Milk willow-herb, Milk willow herb] (5, 156, 158) (1900–1923), Wing-angle loosestrife [Wing-angled loosestrife] (5, 63, 72, 97, 120, 131, 158) (1857–1938), Winged loosestrife (4, 93, 122, 124, 155, 156) (1923–1986), Winged lythrum (50, 138) (1923–present)

Lythrum alatum **Pursh var.** *alatum* – Loosestrife [Loose strife, Loose-strife] (3) (1977), Winged lythrum (50) (present)

Lythrum alatum **Pursh var.** *lanceolatum* **(Ell.) Rothr.** – Loosestrife [Loose strife, Loose-strife] (97) (1937), Winged lythrum (50) (present)

Lythrum californicum **Torr. & Gray** – California loosestrife (50) (present), Loosestrife [Loose strife, Loose-strife] (3) (1977)

Lythrum dacotanum **Nieuwl.** – See *Lythrum alatum* Pursh var. *alatum*

Lythrum hyssopifolia **L.** – Dwarf grass poley (19) (1840), Grass-poly [Grass poly, Grass-poley, Grass poley, Grase-poley, Grass-polley, Grasspoly] (5, 46, 156) (1879–1923), Hyssop loosestrife (5, 156)

(1913–1923)

Lythrum hyssopifolium L. – See *Lythrum hyssopifolia* L.

Lythrum L. – Loosestrife [Loose strife, Loose-strife] (1, 2, 4, 10, 50, 82, 122, 156, 158) (1818–present), Lythrum (138, 155) (1923–1942), Purple loosestrife (106) (1930), Willow herb [Willow-herb, Willow-herb] (167) (1814)

Lythrum lanceolatum Ell. – See *Lythrum alatum* Pursh var. *lanceolatum* (Ell.) Rothr.

Lythrum lineare L. – Linear-leaf loosestrife [Linear-leaved loosestrife] (5) (1913)

Lythrum petiolatum L. – See *Cuphea viscosissima* Jacq

Lythrum salicaria L. – Herba salicariae (49) (1898), Killweed [Kill-weed] (156) (1923), Long purples [Long-purples] (156, 158) (1900–1923), Loosestrife [Loose strife, Loose-strife] (7, 49, 92, 158) (1828–1900), Milk willow herb [Milk willow-herb, Milk willow herb] (92, 156, 158) (1898–1923), Purple loosestrife (3, 4, 5, 50, 109, 138, 155, 156, 158) (1900–present), Purple willowherb [Purple willow-herb] (49, 92, 156, 158) (1898–1923), Purple-grass [Purple grass] (156, 158) (1900–1923), Rainbow-weed [Rainbow-weed] (92, 156, 158) (1898–1923), Rebelweed [Rebel-weed] (106) (1930), Red Sally [Red-Sally] (156, 158) (1900–1923), Red-weed [Red-weed, Red weed] (156) (1923), Rosy strife (156) (1923), Rother Weiderich (German) (158) (1900), Sage-willow [Sage willow] (92, 156, 158) (1898–1923), Salicaire (French) (158) (1900), Soldiers (156, 158) (1900–1923), Spiked loosestrife (5, 82, 106, 109, 156, 158) (1913–1949), Spiked willow herb [Spiked willow-herb, Spiked willow herbe] (156, 158) (1900–1923), Wand lythrum (138) (1923), Willowort (7) (1828), Willow-weed [Willow weed, Willowweed] (92, 156, 158) (1898–1923), Willow-wort [Willow wort, Willowort] (7, 92, 158) (1828–1900)

Lythrum verticillatum L. – See *Decodon verticillatus* (L.) Ell.

Lythrum salicaria L.
(J. Zorn & D. L. Oskamp, 1796)

M

Macadamia **F. Muell.** – Macadamia (138) (1923) for John Amadam M.D., 1827–1865, Secr. Philosophical Insitute Victoria Asutralia

Macadamia ternifolia **F. Muell.** – Queensland nut [Queensland-nut] (109, 138) (1923–1949)

Macfadyena unguis-cati **(L.) A. H. Gentry** – Cat-claw trumpet [Catclaw trumpet] (138) (1923), Cat's-claw [Catclaw, Cat-claw, Catsclaw, Cats-claw, Cat's-claws, Cat's claws] (109) (1949)

Machaeranthera bigelovii **(Gray) Greene var.** *bigelovii* – Bigelow's aster [Bigelow aster] (138, 155) (1931–1942), Patterson's aster [Patterson aster] (155) (1942)

Machaeranthera canescens **(Pursh) A. Gray subsp.** *canescens* **var.** *canescens* – Daisy-leaf aster [Daisyleaf aster] (155) (1942)

Machaeranthera canescens **(Pursh) Gray** – Hoary aster (4) (1986)

Machaeranthera canescens **(Pursh) Gray subsp.** *canescens* – Hoary tansyaster (50) (present)

Machaeranthera canescens **(Pursh) Gray subsp.** *canescens* **var.** *canescens* – Hoary aster (155) (1942), Hoary tansyaster (50) (present), Nebraska tansy-aster [Nebraska tansyaster] (50) (present)

Machaeranthera canescens **(Pursh) Gray subsp.** *glabra* **(Gray) B. L. Turner** – Hoary tansyaster (50) (present), Viscid aster (5, 93, 131) (1899–1936)

Machaeranthera canescens **(Pursh) Gray var.** *latifolia* **(A. Nels.) Welsh, non Gray** – See *Machaeranthera canescens* (Pursh) Gray subsp. *canescens* var. *canescens*

Machaeranthera grindelioides **(Nutt.) Shinners** – Goldenweed (3, 4) (1977–1986)

Machaeranthera grindelioides **(Nutt.) Shinners var.** *grindelioides* – Nutall's goldenweed [Nuttall goldenweed] (155) (1942), Nuttall's goldenweed [Nuttall goldenweed] (155) (1942), Rayless eriocarpum (131) (1899), Rayless sideranthus (5, 93) (1913–1936), Rayless tansy-aster [Rayless tansyaster] (50) (present)

Machaeranthera juncea **(Greene) Shinners** – Lance-leaf goldenweed [Lanceleaf goldenweed] (155) (1942), Rush goldenweed (155) (1942)

Machaeranthera linearis **Greene** – See *Machaeranthera canescens* (Pursh) Gray subsp. *glabra* (Gray) B. L. Turner var. *glabra* Gray

Machaeranthera **Nees** – Aster (158) (1900), Iron plant (93) (1936) Neb, Tansy [Tansey, Tansie] (1, 93) (1932–1936) Neb, Tansy-aster [Tansy aster, Tansyaster] (50) (present), Viscid aster (1, 93) (1932–1936)

Machaeranthera pinnatifida **(Hook.) Shinners** – Lacy tansy-aster [Lacy tansyaster] (50) (present)

Machaeranthera pinnatifida **(Hook.) Shinners subsp.** *pinnatifida* – Cut-leaf aplopappus [Cutleaf aplopappus] (122) (1937), Cut-leaf eriocarpum [Cut-leaved eriocarpum] (131) (1899), Cut-leaf ironplant [Cutleaf ironplant] (3, 4, 98) (1926–1986), Cut-leaf sideranthus [Cut-leaved sideranthus] (5, 93, 97) (1913–1937), Glabrous sideranthus (97) (1937), Glandular sideranthus (97) (1937), Iron-plant goldenweed [Ironplant goldenweed] (155) (1942), Saw-tooth goldenweed [Sawtooth goldenweed] (155) (1942), Sideranthus (93, 97, 127) (1936–1937)

Machaeranthera sessiliflora **(Nutt.) Greene** – See *Machaeranthera canescens* (Pursh) Gray subsp. *glabra* (Gray) B. L. Turner

Machaeranthera tanacetifolia **(Kunth) Nees** – Dagger-flower (5) (1913), Tahoka daisy (4) (1986), Tansey-leaf tansy-aster [Tansey-leaf tansyaster] (50) (present), Tansy-aster [Tansy aster, Tansyaster] (3, 4, 5, 85, 93, 97, 124, 145) (1897–1986), Tansy-leaf aster [Tansyleaf aster] (155) (1942)

Macleaya cordata **(Willd.) R. Br.** – Bocconia (92, 114) (1876–1894), Celandine tree (92) (1876), Pink plume-poppy [Pink plumepoppy] (138) (1923), Plume-poppy [Plumepoppy] (109) (1949), Tree celandine [Tree celandine] (109) (1949)

Macleaya cordata **R. Br.** – See *Macleaya cordata* (Willd.) R. Br.

Maclura aurantiaca **Nutt.** – See *Maclura pomifera* (Raf.) Schneid.

Maclura **Nutt.** – Bow-wood [Bow wood] (12) (1821), Maclura (50) (present), Osage orange [Osageorange, Osage-orange] (4, 93, 109, 138, 155, 156, 158) (1900–1986), Yellow-wood [Yellowwood, Yellow wood] (12) (1821)

Maclura pomifera **(Raf.) Schneid.** – Ayac (7) (1828), Bodark (158) (1900), Bois d'arc (French) (2, 20, 30, 37, 44, 78, 121, 124, 156, 158, 164) (1844–1937), Bois jaune (French, yellow wood) (39) (1814), Bowdark (30, 156, 158) (1844–1923), Bow-wood [Bow wood] (2, 5, 7, 10, 12, 30, 34, 38, 92, 156) (1818–1923), Hedge plant (5, 156, 158) (1900–1923), Hedge tree (78) (1898) Southwest MO, Hedge-apple [Hedge apple] (156) (1923), Miŋdsešta hi (Osage, smooth bow tree) (121) (1918?–1970?), Mock orange [Mock-orange, Mockorange] (39, 156) (1814–1923), Nakitsu (Pawnee) (37) (1919), North American bow-wood (158) (1900), Osage (158) (1900), Osage apple [Osage-apple] (5, 33, 35, 92, 156, 158) (1806–1923) William Clark, Osage orange [Osageorange, Osage-orange] (1, 3, 4, 5, 14, 20, 34, 37, 38, 44, 50, 72, 78, 85, 92, 93, 97, 112, 121, 145, 138, 155, 158, 164) (1834–present), Stinkingwood [Stinking wood] (7) (1828), Wild orange [Wild-orange] or Wild orange tree (5, 75, 93, 156) (1894–1936), Yellow-wood [Yellowwood, Yellow wood] (5, 7, 10, 20, 34, 156, 158) (1818–1923), Zhon-zi-zhu (Omaha-Ponca, yellow flesh wood) (37) (1919)

Maclura tinctoria **(L.) D. Don ex Steud.** – Fustic (92) (1876), Fustic wood (92) (1876)

Macounastrum islandicum **(L.) Small.** – See *Koenigia islandica* L.

Macrocalyx nyctelea **(L.) Kuntze** – See *Ellisia nyctelea* (L.) L.

Macrosiphonia brachysiphon **Gray** – See *Mandevilla brachysiphon* (Torr.) Pichon

Macrotrys actraeoides **Sweet** – possibly *Actaea racemosa* L. (taxonomic status is unresolved (PL))

Macrotrys racemosa of Eaton – possibly *Cimicifuga racemosa* (L.) Nutt.

Macrotrys racemosa **Raf.** – possibly *Cimicifuga racemosa* (L.) Nutt.

Macrotrys racemosa **Sweet** – possibly *Actaea racemosa* L.

Macrotrys serpentaria – possibly *Cimicifuga racemosa* (L.) Nutt.

Macuillamia **Raf.** – See *Bacopa* Aubl.

Macuillamia rotundifolia **(Michx.) Raf.** – See *Bacopa rotundifolia* (Michx.) Wettst.

Madia glomerata **Hook.** – Cluster tarweed (155) (1942), Mountain tarweed (50) (present), Tarweed [Tar weed, Tar-weed] (4, 101) (1905–1986)

Madia sativa **Molina** – Madia (110) (1886), Madia-oil plant (107) (1919), Tarweed [Tar weed, Tar-weed] (75) (1894)

Magnolia acuminata **(L.) L.** – Black linn (5, 156) (1913–1923), Blue magnolia (49, 156) (1898–1923), Canoe wood [Canoe-wood] (2, 5) (1895–1913), Cucumber tree [Cucumber-tree, Cucumbertree] (8, 10, 13, 14, 15, 18, 20, 19, 49, 82, 92, 106, 109, 137, 138, 156, 182, 184) (1785–1949), Heart-leaf cucumber tree [Heart-leaved cucumber tree] (20) (1857), Long-leaf mountain magnolia [Long leaved mountain magnolia] (8) (1785), Magnolia rustique (French) (8) (1785), Mountain magnolia (5, 49, 156) (1898–1923), Yellow cucumber magnolia (2) (1895), Yellow cucumber tree [Yellow cucumbertree] (138) (1923), Yellow linn (5, 74, 156) (1893–1923) WV

Magnolia ashei **Weatherby** – Cucumber tree [Cucumber-tree, Cucumbertree] (122, 124) (1937)

Magnolia auriculata **Hook.** – See *Magnolia macrophylla* Michx.

Magnolia cordata **Michx.** – See *Magnolia acuminata* (L.) L.

Magnolia fraseri **Walt.** – Cucumber tree [Cucumber-tree, Cucumbertree] (5, 156) (1913–1923), Ear-leaf umbrella tree [Ear-leaved umbrella tree, Ear-leaved umbrella-tree] (2, 5, 109, 156) (1895–1949), Fraser's magnolia [Fraser magnolia] (5, 138) (1913–1923), Indian physic [Indian-physic, Indianphysic, Indian physick] (5, 156) (1913–1923), Long-leaf umbrella tree [Long-leaved umbrella tree] (5) (1913), North Carolina bay (5, 156) (1913–1923), Water-lily tree [Water lily tree] (5, 156) (1913–1923)

Magnolia glauca L. – See *Magnolia virginiana* L.

Magnolia grandiflora L. – Big laurel (19, 20) (1840–1857), Bull bay or Bull bay tree (106, 109) (1930–1949), Evergreen laurel-leaf tulip-tree [Ever-green laurel-leaved tulip-tree] (8) (1785), Grand magnolia (8) (1785), Great laurel tree (182) (1791), Great-flower magnolia [Great-flowered magnolia] (2) (1895), Large magnolia (20) (1857), Large-flower magnolia [Large-flowered magnolia] (20) (1857), Laurier tulipier (French) (8, 20) (1785–1857), Magnolia (19, 106, 107, 122) (1840–1937), Pyramidal laurel (182) (1791), Southern magnolia (138) (1923), Tolochlucco (Big bay) (182) (1791)

Magnolia halleana Hort. – See *Magnolia stellata* (Sieb. & Zucc.) Maxim.

Magnolia kobus DC. – Kobus magnolia (138) (1923)

Magnolia L. – Laurel (92) (1876), Laurel-leaf tuliptree [Laurel-leaved tulip-tree] (8) (1785), Laurier tulipier (French) (8) (1785), Magnolia (8, 82, 138) (1785–1930), Magnolia (French) (8) (1785), Red laurel [Redlaurel] (92) (1876)

Magnolia macrophylla Michx. – Beaver tree [Beavertree] (7) (1828), Bigbloom [Big-bloom, Bigbloom] (5, 7, 92, 156) (1828–1923), Bi-gleaf (7) (1828), Big-leaf magnolia [Bigleaf magnolia] (7, 138) (1828–1923), Cucumber tree [Cucumber-tree, Cucumbertree] (5, 156) (1913–1923), Ear-leaf magnolia [Ear-leaved magnolia] (20) (1857), Elkbark [Elk-bark, Elk bark] (5, 7, 92, 156) (1828–1923), Elkwood [Elk-wood, Elk wood] (7) (1828), Great-leaf magnolia [Great-leaved magnolia] (2, 156) (1895–1942), Indian physic [Indian-physic, Indianphysic, Indian physick] (20) (1857), Itomico (7) (1828), Large-leaf cucumber tree [Large-leaved cucumber-tree] (109, 156) (1923–1949), Large-leaf umbrella tree [Large-leaved umbrella tree, Large-leaved umbrella-tree] (5, 20, 156) (1857–1923), Laurel (7) (1828), Long-leaf cucumber tree [Long leaved cucumber tree] (20) (1857), Long-leaf magnolia [Long-leaved magnolia] (20) (1857), Magnolia grande feuille (French) (7) (1828), Silverleaf [Silver leaf, Silver-leaf] (5, 7, 92, 156) (1828–1923), Whitebay (7) (1828)

Magnolia pyramidata Bartr. – Pyramid magnolia (138) (1923)

Magnolia stellata (Sieb. & Zucc.) Maxim. – Star magnolia (137, 138) (1923–1931), Starry magnolia (109) (1949)

Magnolia stellata Maxim. – See *Magnolia stellata* (Sieb. & Zucc.) Maxim.

Magnolia tripetala L. – Cucumber tree [Cucumber-tree, Cucumbertree] (5, 156) (1913–1923), Elkwood [Elk-wood, Elk wood] (5, 156) (1913–1923), Magnolia ombrelle (French) (8) (1785), Umbrella magnolia (138) (1923), Umbrella tree [Umbrella-tree] (2, 5, 8, 10, 13, 14, 15, 20, 19, 49, 92, 97, 109, 156, 184) (1785–1949)

Magnolia umbrella Lam. – See *Magnolia tripetala* L.

Magnolia virginiana L. – Bay (106) (1930), Beaver tree [Beavertree] (5, 6, 19, 41, 49, 52, 92, 106, 156, 186) (1770–1930), Beaver wood [Beaver-wood] (6, 20, 186, 187) (1818–1892), Biberbaum (German) (186) (1814), Brewster (6) (1892), Castor wood [Castor-wood] (6, 186) (1825–1892), Eisengraue Magnolie (German) (186) (1814), Elkbark [Elk-bark, Elk bark] (6, 186) (1825–1892), Fo no ki (186) (1814), Gach-hach-gik (186) (1814), Graue Magnolia (German) (186) (1814), Indian bark [Indian-bark] (5, 6, 92, 156, 186) (1825–1923), Kobuks (186) (1814), Kobus (186) (1814), Kobusi (186) (1814), Konsusi (186) (1814), Laurel magnolia [Laurel-magnolia] (2, 5, 6, 106, 156) (1892–1930), Laurel tree of Carolina [Laurel-tree of Carolina] (189) (1767), Laurel-leaf tuliptree [Laurel-leaved tulip-tree] (41) (1770), Magnolia (57, 82) (1917–1930), Magnolia glauque (French) (8, 186) (1785–1825), Magnolia of Pennsylvania (189) (1767), Magnolie (German) (6) (1892), Magnolier bleue (French) (186) (1814), Magnolier des marais (French)

(186) (1814), Magnolier glauque (French) (6) (1892), Meergrüne magnolie (186) (1814), Mitsmata (186) (1814), Mockkwuren (186) (1814), Red bay [Redbay] (92, 156) (1876–1923), Red laurel [Red-laurel] (49, 52) (1898–1919), Rose-bay [Rose bay, Rosebay] (189) (1767), Small magnolia (2, 6, 8, 13, 20, 186, 187) (1785–1895), Swamp bay (156) (1923), Swamp laurel (5, 6, 19, 106, 156, 187) (1818–1930), Swamp magnolia (5, 156) (1913–1923), Swamp sassafras [Swamp-sassfras] (5, 6, 8, 41, 49, 52, 92, 156, 184, 186, 187) (1785–1923), Sweet bay [Sweet-bay, Sweetbay] or Sweet bay tree [Sweet bay trees] (2, 5, 6, 15, 41, 76, 92, 106, 109, 122, 124, 138, 156, 1770, 183) (1818–1949), Sweet magnolia [Sweet-magnolia] (6, 49, 52, 92, 186) (1825–1892), Sweet-flower bay [Sweet-flowering bay] (186, 189) (1767–1814), Umbrella tree [Umbrella-tree] (177, 189) (1762–1767), White bay [White-bay] (5, 6, 15, 20, 49, 52, 92, 156, 186) (1825–1923), White laurel [White-laurel] (5, 15, 41, 49, 52, 156, 186) (1770–1923), possibly Elkbark [Elk-bark, Elk bark] (156) (1923), possibly Holly-bay (156) (1923)

Magnolia virginica L. – possibly *Magnolia virginiana* L.

Mahonia aquifolium (**Pursh) Nutt.** – Barberry (59, 60, 103, 148) (1870–1939), Berberis (54, 59, 60, 64) (1902–1911), California barberry (64, 157) (1908–1929), False Oregon grape (103) (1870), Graperoot [Grape root] (5, 76, 157) (1896–1929) Northern UT, Holly barberry (2, 109, 135) (1895–1949), Holly mahonia (109) (1949), Holly-leaf barberry [Hollyleaved barberry, Holly-leaved barberry] (5, 50, 64, 157, 160) (1860-prsent), Mahonia (2, 52, 92, 107) (1876–1919), Mountain-grape [Mountain grape] (49, 52, 53, 107) (1919–1922), Mountain-holly [Mountain holly] (64) (1907), Oregon grape [Oregon-grape] (5, 49, 52, 53, 54, 60, 64, 74, 76, 85, 93, 95, 107, 148, 157, 160) (1860–1949), Oregon holly-grape [Oregon hollygrape] (138) (1923), Rocky Mountain grape (5, 64, 157) (1908–1929), Trailing mahonia (5, 64, 131, 157) (1899–1929)

Mahonia aquifolium **Nutt.** – See *Mahonia aquifolium* (Pursh) Nutt.

Mahonia bealei (**Fortune) Carr.** – Leather-leaf holly-grape [Leather-leaf hollygrape] (138) (1923)

Mahonia fremontii (**Torr.) Fedde** – Yellow barberry (106) (1930)

Mahonia haematocarpa (**Woot.) Fedde** – Barberry (149) (1904)

Mahonia nervosa (**Pursh) Nutt.** – Long-leaf hollygrape [Longleaf hollygrape] (138) (1923), Oregon grape [Oregon-grape] (106, 107, 109, 161) (1857–1949)

Mahonia nevini – See *Mahonia nevinii* (Gray) Fedde

Mahonia nevinii (**Gray) Fedde** – Fernando's holly-grape [Fernando hollygrape] (138) (1923)

Mahonia **Nutt.** – Barberry (50) (present), Holly-grape [Hollygrape] (138) (1923), Mahonia (155) (1942), Mountain-holly [Mountain holly] (7) (1828), Oregon grape [Oregon-grape] (1) (1932)

Mahonia pinnata (**Lag.) Fedde** – Cluster hollygrape (138) (1923)

Mahonia pinnata (**Lag.) Fedde subsp.** *pinnata* – Barberry (76) (1896), Blue barberry (107) (1919), California barberry (106) (1930), Leña amarilla (Spanish) (74, 76, 107) (1893–1919) CA Mexico, Linna amorilla (Spanish) (14, 147) (1856–1882) Mexico, Oregon grape [Oregon-grape] (76, 161) (1857–1896)

Mahonia piperiana **Abrams** – See *Mahonia aquifolium* (Pursh) Nutt.

Mahonia pumila (**Greene) Fedde** – See *Mahonia repens* (Lindl.) G. Don

Mahonia repens (**Lindl.) G. Don** – Creeping barberry (2, 50, 113, 130) (1890–present), Creeping hollygrape (138) (1923), Creeping mahonia (155) (1942), Mountain-holly [Mountain holly] (35) (1806), Oregon grape [Oregon-grape] (3, 4, 101, 135, 153) (1905–1986), Pygmy mahonia (155) (1942)

Mahonia swaseyi (**Buckl. ex Young) Fedde** – Blue agarita (124) (1937) TX, Texas barberry (4, 50) (1986–present), Texas mahonia (155) (1942)

Mahonia trifoliolata (**Moric.) Fedde** – Agarita (Spanish) (106, 124) (1930–1937) TX, Mexico, Agreeto (Italian) (180) (1633), Agrito (122) (1937) TX, Algerita [Algeritas] (15, 50, 155) (1895–present), Currant [Currants] (15) (1895) TX, Laredo mahonia (155) (1942), Triple-leaf barberry [Triple-leaved barberry (106) (1930), Wild currant [Wild currants] (106) (1930) TX

Maianthemum bifolium **DC** – See *Maianthemum dilatatum* (Wood) A. Nels. & J. F. Macbr.

Maianthemum canadense **Desf.** – Beadruby [Bead ruby, Bead-ruby (5, 75, 155, 158) (1894–1942) NY, Canadian beedruby [Canada beedruby] (155) (1942), Canadian mayflower [Canada mayflower] (50) (present), Cowslip [Cowslips, Cowslyp] (5, 73, 156, 158) (1892–1923), False lily-of-the-valley (5, 127, 158) (1900–1933), Heartleaf [Heart leaves, Heart-leaf] (156) (1923), Lily-of-the-valley [Lily of the valley] (73) (1892) NH, Mayflower [May flower, May-flower] (156) (1923), One leaf [One-leaf] (5, 158) (1900–1913), One-blade [One blade] (5, 158) (1900–1913), One-leaf [One leaf] (5, 158) (1900–1913), Ruby-bead (156) (1923), Two-leaf convallary [Two-leaved convallary] (187) (1818), Two-leaf Solomon's-seal [Two-leaved Solomon's seal, Two-leaf Solomon's seal] (5, 72, 73, 156, 158) (1892–1923), Wild lily-of-the-valley [Wild lily of the valley] (3, 5, 75, 85, 156, 158) (1894–1977)

Maianthemum dilatatum **(Wood) A. Nels. & J. F. Macbr.** – Dwarf Solomon's-seal [Dwarf Solomon's-seal, Dwarf Solomon seal] (19, 92) (1840), One-blade [One blade] (46, 92, 178) (1596–1876), Two-leaf small Solomon's-seal [Two leaved small Solomon's seal] (42) (1814), Wild lily-of-the-valley [Wild lily of the valley] (78) (1898)

Maianthemum **G. H. Weber ex Wiggers** – Adder's-tongue [Adder tongue, Adders tongue, Adder's tongue, Adders toong, Adder-stongue] (7) (1828), Beadruby [Bead ruby, Bead-ruby (155) (1942), False lily-of-the-valley (109) (1949), False Solomon's-seal [False Solomon's seal, False Solomonseal, False Solomons-seal] (2, 109, 138, 155, 156) (1895–1949), Harewost (7) (1828), Matasbuck (Algic tribes) (7) (1828), Mayflower [May flower, May-flower] (50) (present), Smilacina (158) (1900), Smilacine (158) (1900), Solomon's-plume [Solomonplume, Solomon's plume, Solomon-plume] (155) (1942), Solomon's-seal [Solomon's seal, Solomon seal, Solomon's seal, Solomons-seal, S'alomon's seal, Salamons seale] (158) (1900), Two-leaf Solomon's-seal [Two-leaved Solomon's seal, Two-leaf Solomon's seal] (1) (1932), Wild lily-of-the-valley [Wild lily of the valley] (1, 93) (1932–1936), Wild spikenard (1, 93) (1932–1936)

Maianthemum racemosum **(L.) Link** – Feathery false lily-of-the-valley [Feathery false lily of the valley] (50) (present)

Maianthemum racemosum **(L.) Link subsp.** *racemosum* – Agoŋg'osimīnûn' (Chippewa) (40) (1928), Clustered Solomon's-seal [Clustered Solomon's seal, Clustered Solomon seal] (92, 156) (1876–1923), Cluster-flower convallary [Cluster-flowered convallary] (187) (1818), Cluster-flower Solomon's-seal [Cluster flowered Solomon's seal] (42) (1814), False Solomon's-seal [False Solomon's seal, False Solomonseal, False Solomons-seal] (40, 121, 138, 156, 157, 158) (1918–1970), False spikenard (3, 5, 46, 65, 85, 93, 97, 107, 158) (1900–1977), Feather Solomon's-plume [Feather Solomonplume] (155) (1942), Feathery false lily-of-the-valley [Feathery false lily of the valley] (50) (present), Goldenseal [Goldenseal, Golden seal] (5, 75, 156, 157, 158) (1894–1929) Banner Elk NC, Japizapi hu (Lakota, mouth organ plant) (121) (1918–1970), Job's-tear [Job's tear, Job's tears, Jobs-tears, Job's tear's, Iobs Teares] (5, 75, 156, 157, 158) (1894–1929) NY, Salomon's seal (46) (1671), Small Solomon's seal [Small Solomon's-seal] (5, 92, 157, 158) (1876–1929), Solomon's-plume [Solomonplume, Solomon's plume, Solomon-plume] (156) (1923), Solomon's-seal of Virginia [Salomons Seale of Virginia] (181) (~1678), Spiked Solomon's seal [Spiked Solomon seal] (19, 50) (1840–present), Treacle-berry [Treackleberries] (46, 107, 156) (1879–1923), Wild spikenard (5, 93, 97, 156, 157, 158) (1900–1937), Zigzag Solomon's-seal [Zigzag Solomon's seal] (5, 156, 158) (1900–1923)

Maianthemum stellatum **(L.) Link** – False Solomon's-seal [False Solomon's seal, False Solomonseal, False Solomons-seal] (5, 85, 156) (1913–1932), Slim Solomon-plume [Slim Solomonplume] (155) (1942), Sol me (35) (1806), Spikenard (3) (1977), Star-flower Solomon's seal [Star-flowered Solomon's seal (5, 42, 93, 127, 156) (1814–1936), Starry false lily-of-the-valley (50) (present), Starry false Solomon's-seal [Starry false Solomonseal] (138) (1923),

Starry Solomon's-plume [Starry Solomonplume, Starry Solomonplume] (155) (1942), Starry Solomon's-seal [Starry Solomon's seal] (156) (1923), Virginia Solomon's-seal [Virginian's Salomon's seale] (46) (1879)

Maianthemum trifolium **(L.) Sloboda** – Labrador Solomon's-plume [Labrador Solomonplume] (155) (1942), Three-leaf false lily-of-the-valley [Threeleaf false lily of the valley] (50) (present), Three-leaf Solomon's-seal [Three leaved Solomon's seal] (5, 42) (1814–1913)

Mairania alpina **(L.) Desvar.** – See *Arctostaphylos alpina* (L.) Spreng.

Majorana hortensis **Moench** – See *Origanum majorana* L.

Malacothrix **DC.** – Desert dandelion (1) (1932)

Malacothrix sonchoides **(Nutt.) Torr. & Gray** – Malacothrix (5) (1913)

Malaxis brachypoda **(Gray) Fern.** – White adder's-mouth orchid [White adder's mouth orchid] (50) (present)

Malaxis liliifolia **Sw.** – See *Liparis liliifolia* (L.) L. C. Rich. ex Ker-Gawl.

Malaxis liliifolia **Willd. And Pursh** – See *Liparis liliifolia* (L.) L. C. Rich. ex Ker-Gawl.

Malaxis longifolia **Bart.** – See *Liparis loeselii* (L.) Rich.

Malaxis monophyllos **(L.) Sw.** – White adder's-mouth [White adder's mouth] (5) (1913)

Malaxis monophyllos **(L.) Sw. subsp.** *brachypoda* **(Gray) A. & D. Löve** – See *Malaxis brachypoda* (Gray) Fern.

Malaxis ophioglossoides **Willd.** – See *Malaxis unifolia* Michx.

Malaxis **Soland. ex Sw.** – Adder's-mouth [Adder mouth, Adder's mouth (1) (1932), Adder's-mouth orchid [Adder's mouth orchid] (50) (present), Adder's-meat [Adder's meat] (92) (1876), Adder's-mouth [Adder mouth, Adder's mouth (19) (1840), Adder's-tongue malaxis [Adder-tongue malaxis] (187) (1818), Anomalos (46) (1783), Green adder's-mouth [Green adder's mouth] (5, 72) (1907–1913), Green adder's-mouth orchid [Green adder's mouth orchid] (50) (present), One-leaf malaxis [One-leaved malaxis] (187) (1818)

Malcolmia maritima **(L.) Aiton f.** – Virginia stock [Virginian stock] (109) (1949)

Malcolmia maritima **R. Br.** – See *Malcolmia maritima* (L.) Aiton f.

Malcolmia **R. Br.** – Malcolm's stocks [Malcolm stocks] (109) (1949)

Mallotus philippensis **(Lam.) Muell.-Arg.** – Wurrus (92) (1876)

Malosma laurina **(Nutt.) Nutt. ex Abrams** – Laurel sumac (106, 109) (1930–1949)

Malpighia coccigera **L.** – Holly malpighia (138) (1923)

Malpighia cocigera – See *Malpighia coccigera* L.

Malpighia coriacea **[Sw.]** – See *Byrsonima crassifolia* (L.) Kunth

Malpighia glabra **L.** – Barbados-cherry [Barbadoes-cherry, Barbadoes cherry] (92, 107, 109) (1876–1949), Wild crape myrtle (122, 124) (1937) TX

Malpighia **L.** – Malphigia (138) (1923)

Malpigia **L.** – See *Malpighia* L.

Malus ×*dawsoniana* **Rehd.** [*fusca* × *pumila*] – Dawson's crab [Dawson crab] (138) (1923)

Malus ×*soulardii* **(Bailey) Britt.** [*ioensis* × *pumila*] – Soulard's crab [Soulard crab] (137, 138) (1923–1931), Soulard's crab apple [Soulard crab apple] (106) (1930)

Malus angustifolia **(Aiton) Michx.** – Southern crab apple (106) (1930)

Malus angustifolia **(Aiton) Michx. var.** *angustifolia* – American crab (107) (1919), Narrow-leaf crab apple [Narrow-leaved crab apple] (2, 20) (1857–1895), possibly Wild crab of North Carolina (183) (~1756)

Malus baccata **(L.) Borck.** – Siberian crab (82, 107, 135, 137, 138) (1910–1931), Siberian crab apple (5, 109) (1913–1949)

Malus baccata **Borkhausen** – See *Malus baccata* (L.) Borck.

Malus baccata L. var. manshurica Maxim – See *Malus mandshurica* (Maxim.) Kom.

Malus coronaria **(L.) Mill.** – American crab apple (72, 106) (1907–1930), Crab apple [Crab-apple, Crabapple] (5, 20) (1857–1913), Crab tree [Crab-tree] (5) (1913), Eastern wild crab apple (112) (1937), Narrow-leaf crab apple [Narrow-leaved crab apple] (5) (1913), Southern wild crab (5) (1913), Wild apple [Wylde apple] or Wild apple tree (20) (1857), Wild sweet crab (138) (1923)

Malus coronaria (L.) Mill. var. *coronaria* – American crab apple (2, 107) (1895–1919), Anchor tree (41) (1770), Crab apple [Crab-apple, Crabapple] (19, 41, 47, 92, 103) (1770–1876), Crab tree [Crab-tree] (41) (1770), Dwarf pear (19) (1840), Fragrant crab or Fragrant crab tree [Fragrant crab-tree] (156) (1923), Garland crab (107, 156) (1919–1923), Garland crab apple (2) (1895), Garland tree (156) (1923), Russet pear (19) (1840), Souring (92) (1876), Sweet-scented crab or Sweet-scented crab tree [Sweet-scented crab-tree] (107, 187) (1818–1919), Wild crab apple (22, 113) (1890–1893), Wild crab or Wild crab tree (5, 92, 182) (1791–1913)

Malus dawsoniana – See *Malus ×dawsoniana* Rehd. [*fusca × pumila*]

Malus diversifolia – See *Malus fusca* (Raf.) Schneid.

Malus floribunda Sieb. ex Van Houtte – Japanese flowering crab (138) (1923)

Malus fusca (Raf.) Schneid. – Crab apple [Crab-apple, Crabapple] (106) (1930), Indian pear (103) (1870), Oregon crab (138) (1923), Oregon crab apple [Oregon crab-apple, Oregon crabapple] (7, 106, 107, 160) (1828–1930), Poirier rivulaire (French) (20) (1857), Pow-itch (Chinook) (107) (1919), River crab (20) (1857)

Malus glaucescens Rehdr. – American crab apple (5) (1913), Dunbar's crab [Dunbar crab] (138) (1923), Fragrant crab or Fragrant crab tree [Fragrant crab-tree] (5) (1913), Sweet-scented crab or Sweet-scented crab tree [Sweet-scented crab-tree] (5) (1913), Wild crab or Wild crab tree (5) (1913)

Malus halliana Koehne – Hall's crab [Hall crab] (138) (1923)

Malus ioensis (Wood) Britton – Crab apple [Crab-apple, Crabapple] (37) (1919), Elk River wild crab (137) (1931) SD, Native wild crab apple (112) (1937), Nevis' wild crab [Nevis wild crab] (137) (1931) SD, Prairie crab (137, 138) (1923–1931), Prairie crab apple [Prairie crabapple] (50, 155) (1942–present), She (Omaha-Ponca) (37) (1919) She-hi (Apple tree), She-si (Apple seed), Western crab apple (5, 72, 85, 93, 95, 97, 137, 157) (1900–1937), Wild American crab apple [Wild American crabapple] (137) (1931)

Malus ioensis (Wood) Britton var. *bushii* Rehd. – See *Malus ioensis* (Wood) Britton var. *ioensis*

Malus ioensis (Wood) Britton var. *ioensis* – Bechtel's crab [Bechtel crab] (4, 112, 137) (1931–1986), Double-flower crab [Double flowering crab] (112) (1937), Iowa crab (4) (1986), Iowa wild crab apple (82) (1930) IA, Missouri crabapple (155) (1942), Palmer's crab apple [Palmer crabapple] (155) (1942), Prairie crab apple [Prairie crabapple] (50) (present), Western crab apple (2, 63) (1895–1899), Wild crab or Wild crab tree (82) (1930)

Malus ioensis (Wood) Britton var. *palmeri* Rehd. – See *Malus ioensis* (Wood) Britton var. *ioensis*

Malus ioensis (Wood) Britton var. *plena* – See *Malus ioensis* (Wood) Britton var. *ioensis*

Malus ioensis (Wood) Britton var. *texana* Rehd. – Texas crabapple (124) (1937) TX

Malus Juss. – See *Malus* Mill.

Malus malus (L.) Britton – See *Malus sylvestris* (L.) Mill.

Malus Mill. – Apple or Apple tree (1, 8, 50, 109, 138, 155, 158, 179) (1526–present), Crab (138) (1923), Crab apple [Crab-apple, Crabapple] (106, 155) (1930–1942), Crab tree [Crab-tree] (158) (1900), Wild crab apple (93) (1936)

Malus niedzwetskyana Hemsl. – See *Malus pumila* Mill.

Malus prunifolia (Willd.) Borkh. – Pear-leaf crab [Pearleaf crab] (137, 138) (1923–1931), Plum-leaf apple [Plum-leaved apple] (107) (1919), Siberian crab (19) (1840)

Malus prunifolia Borkh. – See *Malus prunifolia* (Willd.) Borkh.

Malus pumila Mill. – Red-vein crab [Redvein crab] (137, 138) (1923–1931)

Malus sargenti – See *Malus sargentii* Rehd.

Malus sieboldi Rehd. – See *Malus sieboldii* (Regel) Rehd.

Malus sieboldii (Regel) Rehd. – Dwarf crab (137) (1931), Toringo crab (137, 138) (1923–1931)

Malus sieboldii (Regel) Rehd. var. *zumi* (Matsumura) Asami – Zumi crab (137, 138) (1923–1931)

Malus soulardi Britt. – See *Malus ×soulardii* (Bailey) Britt. [*ioensis × pumila*]

Malus spectabilis (Aiton) Borkh. – Chinese flowering crab (138) (1923)

Malus sylvestris (L.) Mill. – See *Malus sylvestris* (L.) Mill.

Malus sylvestris Mill. – Apli (Scandinavian) (110) (1886), Apple or Apple tree (57, 61, 92) (1870–1917), Commo apple (63) (1899), Common apple or Common apple tree (1, 49, 63, 137) (1898–1932), Crab stock (5) (1913), Crab tree [Crab-tree] (5) (1913), Cultivated apple (137) (1931), Iabloko (Russian) (110) (1886), Malus (57) (1917), Molé (Albanian) (110) (1886), Nurse garden (5) (1913), Obolys (Lithuanian) (110) (1886), Paradise apple (178) (1526), Sagara (Basque) (110) (1886), Scarb tree (5) (1913), Sêf (Persian) (110) (1886), Wild apple [Wylde apple] or Wild apple tree (19, 179) (1526–1840), Wilding tree (5) (1913), Wood crab [Wood crabbe] (179) (1526), Wyldynge (179) (1526)

Malus zumi Rehd. – See *Malus sieboldii* (Regel) Rehd. var. *zumi* (Matsumura) Asami

Malva (Tourn.) L. – See *Malva* L.

Malva alcea L. – European mallow (5, 156) (1913–1923), Hollyhock mallow (138) (1923), Vervain mallow (5, 92, 156) (1876–1923)

Malva crispa (L.) L. – Curled mallow [Curled mallows, Curled Mallowes] (19, 72, 109, 178) (1526–1949), Curly mallow (50, 138, 155) (1923–present), French mallowes (178) (1526), Whorled mallow (131) (1899)

Malva L. – Cheeses (Fruit) (1) (1932), Mallow [Mallows, Mallowes, Malowe] (1, 4, 7, 10, 13, 15, 50, 82, 93, 106, 109, 138, 155, 156, 158, 179, 184) (1526–present)

Malva moschata L. – Mush (76) (1896) ME, Musk (5, 73, 76, 156) (1892–1923), Musk mallow (5, 15, 19, 82, 109, 138, 156) (1840–1949), Musk plant [Musk-plant, Muskplant] (5, 73, 156) (1892–1923), Musk-rose [Musk rose] (156) (1923), Stork-bill mallow [Storks bill mallow] (178) (1526)

Malva neglecta Wallr. – Common mallow (3, 4, 50) (1977–present)

Malva parviflora L. – Cheeseweed mallow (50) (present), Little mallow (155) (1942), Small-fruit mallow [Small-fruited mallow] (3, 4) (1977–1986)

Malva rotundifolia L. – Blue mallow (5, 92, 106, 156, 157, 158) (1876–1930), Buttonweed [Button-weed, Button weed] (156) (1923), Cheese plant (73) (1892), Cheeseflower [Cheese flower, Cheeseflower] (156) (1923), Cheeses (5, 62, 73, 80, 92, 97, 156) (1892–1937), Cheese's running mallow (131) (1899), Cheesetts (76) (1896) Oxford Co., ME, Common mallow (3, 4, 5, 15, 80, 145, 156, 157, 158) (1895–1986), Common maul (158) (1900), Common maws (158) (1900), Country mallow (5, 106, 156, 157, 158) (1900–1930), Creeping charlie [Creeping-charlie, Creeping charley] (62) (1912) IN, Doll-cheese [Doll cheeses] (5, 106, 156, 157, 158) (1900–1930), Dutch-cheese [Dutch cheese] (5, 106, 156, 157, 158) (1900–1930) from shape of seed pods, Dwarf mallow (5, 15, 85, 92, 156, 157, 158) (1895–1932), Fairy cheeses [Fairy-cheese, Fairy-cheeses] (5, 106, 156, 157, 158) (1900–1930), Kässekraut (German) (158) (1900), Low mallow (5, 19, 50, 62, 92, 93, 156, 157, 158) (1840–present), Low maul (158) (1900), Low maws (158) (1900), Malice (5, 74, 156, 158) (1893–1923) Ferrisburgh VT, Mallow [Mallows, Mallowes, Malowe] (46, 57, 107, 114, 158) (1649–1919) accidentally introduced by 1671, Pancake plant [Pancake-plant] (156) (1923), Pellas (5, 156, 157, 158) (1900–1929), Petite mauve (French) (158) (1900), Round-leaf mallow [Round-leaved mallow] (62, 72) (1907–1913), Running mallow (5, 93, 95, 155, 156, 157, 158) (1900–1936)

Malva silvestris L. – See *Malva sylvestris* L.

Malva sylvestris L. – Cheesecake [Cheese-cake, Cheese cake] (5, 156) (1913–1923), Cheese-cake plant (157, 158) (1900–1929), Cheeseflower [Cheese flower, Cheese-flower] (5, 156, 157, 158) (1900–1929), Cheeses (107) (1919), Chock-cheese (157, 158) (1900–1929), Common mallow (92, 158) (1876–1900), Country mallow (5, 156, 158) (1900–1923), Grande mauve (French) (158) (1900), High mallow (3, 4, 5, 15, 50, 72, 92, 93, 107, 114, 122, 131, 155,

156, 157, 158) (1894–present), Käsepappel (German) (158) (1900), Mallow [Mallows, Mallowes, Malowe] (19, 57, 85, 190) (~1759–1932), Malva (57, 92) (1876–1917), Marshmallow [Marsh mallow, Marsh mallows, Marsh-mallow] (107, 156) (1919–1923), Maul (5, 156) (1913–1923) no longer in use by 1923, Mauve (French) (158) (1900), Mauve sauvage (French) (158) (1900), Pancake plant [Pancake-plant] (157, 158) (1900–1929), Pick-cheese [Pick cheese] (5, 157, 158) (1900–1929), Pisk-cheese (156) (1923), Round dock (5, 156, 157, 158) (1900–1929), Wladmalve (German) (158) (1900)

Malva verticillata crispa **L.** – See *Malva crispa* (L.) L.

Malva verticillata **L.** – Cluster mallow [Clustered mallow] (3, 4, 50, 155) (1942–present), Curled mallow [Curled mallows, Curled Mallowes] (5, 107, 156) (1913–1923), Whorled mallow (5, 93, 156) (1913–1936)

Malvastrum angustum **Gray** – See *Malvastrum hispidum* (Pursh) Hochr.

Malvastrum coccineum **(Pursh) Gray** – See *Sphaeralcea coccinea* (Nutt.) Rydb. subsp. *coccinea*

Malvastrum **Gray** – False mallow [False-mallow, Falsemallow, False mallows] (2, 15, 50, 93, 109, 155, 158) (1895–present), Scarlet mallow (1) (1932)

Malvastrum hispidum **(Pursh) Hochr.** – Hispid false mallow (50) (present), Narrow-leaf globe mallow [Narrowleaf globemallow (3, 4, 155) (1942–1986), Yellow false mallow (5, 72, 97, 156) (1907–1937)

Malvaviscus arboreus **Dill. ex Cav.** – Wax-mallow [Waxmallow] (138) (1923)

Malvaviscus arboreus **Dill. ex Cav. var. drummondii (Torr. & Gray) Schery** – Texas mallow (122) (1937) TX

Malvaviscus drummondii **Torr. & Gray** – See *Malvaviscus arboreus* Dill. ex Cav. var. *drummondii* (Torr. & Gray) Schery

Malvella leprosa **(Ortega) Krapov** – Alkali mallow (50) (present), Alkali sida (155) (1942), Melonsilla (Mexican, little melon) (150) (1894), Round-leaf sida [Round-leaved sida] (5, 97) (1913–1937)

Malvella sagittifolia **(Gray) Fraxell.** – Arrow-leaf mallow [Arrowleaf mallow] (50) (present)

Malviscus drummondii **Torr. & Gray** – See *Malvaviscus arboreus* Dill. ex Cav. var. *drummondii* (Torr. & Gray) Schery

Mamea americana **Jacq.** – possibly *Mammea americana* L.

Mammea americana **L.** – Mamay (174) (1753), Mamey (109, 110, 138) (1886–1949) from West Indies aboriginal name, Mammee-apple [Mammee apple] (109, 110) (1886–1949)

Mammea **L.** – Mamey (138) (1923)

Mammillaria fissurata **Engelm.** – See *Ariocarpus fissuratus* (Engelm.) K. Schum.

Mammillaria grahamii **Engelm.** – Pincushion cactus [Pin-cushion cactus] (76) (1896) AZ

Mammillaria **Haw.** – Globe cactus (50) (present), Mammal thistle (14) (1882), Mammillaria (155) (1942), Nipple thistle (14) (1882)

Mammillaria heyderi **Muehlenpfordt** – Heyder's mammillaria [Heyder mammillaria] (155) (1942), Little nipple cactus (50) (present), Pincushion [Pincushions, Pin-cushion, Pin cushions] (122) (1937) TX

Mammillaria micromeris **[Engelm.]** – See *Epithelantha micromeris* (Engelm.) A. Weber ex Britt. & Rose var. *micromeris*

Mammillaria missouriensis **Sweet** – See *Escobaria missouriensis* (Sweet) D.R. Hunt var. *missouriensis*

Mammillaria vivipara **[(Nutt.) Haw.]** – See *Escobaria vivipara* (Nutt.) Buxbaum var. *vivipara*

Mammillaria vivipara **Haw.** – See *Escobaria vivipara* (Nutt.) Buxbaum var. *vivipara*

Mandevilla brachysiphon **(Torr.) Pichon** – Jessamine (75) (1894)

Mandevilla laxa **(Ruiz & Pav.) Woodson** – Savannah flower (92) (1876)

Mandevilla laxa **Woodson** – See *Mandevilla laxa* (Ruiz & Pav.) Woodson

Mandevilla **Lindl.** – See *Fernaldia* Woodson

Mandevilla suaveolens – See *Mandevilla laxa* (Ruiz & Pav.) Woodson

Manfreda tigrina **(Engelm.) Small** – See *Manfreda virginica* (L.) Salisb. ex Rose

Manfreda variegata **(Jacobi) Rose** – Texas tuberose (122, 124) (1937) TX

Manfreda virginica **(L.) Salisb. ex Rose** – Agave (19) (1840), American aloe (58) (1869), False aloe [False-aloe] (5, 49, 50, 58, 92, 97, 156) (1869–present), Rattlesnake-master [Rattlesnake master, Rattlesnake's master, Rattlesnakes' master, Rattlesnake's-master] (5, 7, 46, 49, 58, 75, 92, 156) (1828–1923), Virginia agave [Virginian agave] (165) (1768), Virginia aloes (7, 92) (1828–1876)

Mangifera indica **L.** – Mango (106, 107, 110) (1886–1930)

Manihot **Adans.** – See *Manihot* Mill.

Manihot dulcis **Pax** – See *Manihot esculenta* Crantz

Manihot esculenta **Crantz** – Aipi (109) (1949), Bitter cassava (92, 109) (1876–1949), Cassava (138) (1923), Cassava plant (92) (1876), Mandioca (92) (1876), Manioc (109, 110) (1886–1949), Sweet cassava (109) (1949), Tapioca-plant (109) (1949), Yuca (109) (1949), Yuca (Brazil) (110) (1886)

Manihot **Mill.** – Manpelaan (Modern India) (110) (1886), Sand-nettle [Sandnettle, Sand nettle] (7) (1828)

Manihot utilissima **Pohl** – See *Manihot esculenta* Crantz

Manilkara achras **(Mill.) Fosberg** – See *Manilkara zapota* (L.) van Royen

Manilkara zapota **(L.) van Royen** – American sapota (165) (1768), Common sapota (165) (1768), Mammee sapota (110) (1886), Marmalade-plum [Marmalade plum] (110) (1886), Naseberry (92, 107) (1876–1919), Naseberry bully tree (20) (1857), Nisberry tree (165) (1768), Sapodilla (20, 107, 109, 110, 138, 155, 165) (1768–1949), Sapota (107) (1919), Sapote (138) (1923), Sapotillier commun (French) (20) (1857), Small sapodilla (20) (1857), possibly Sapodil (7, 92) (1828–1876), possibly Sapodilla plum (92) (1876)

Manisuris **[L.]** – See *Rottboellia* L. f. (US species all reassigned)

Manisuris corrugata **(Baldw.) Kuntze** – See *Coelorachis rugosa* (Nutt.) Nash

Manisuris cylindrica **(Michx.) O. Ktze.** – See *Coelorachis cylindrica* (Michx.) Nash

Manisuris rugosa **(Nutt.) Kuntze** – See *Coelorachis rugosa* (Nutt.) Nash

Manisuris tessellata **Steud.** – See *Coelorachis tessellata* (Steud.) Nash

Mansoa alliacea **(Lam.) A. H. Gentry** – Garlic shrub (92) (1876)

Marah fabaceus **(Naud.) Naud. ex Greene** – California bitter-root [Californian bitter root] (14) (1882)

Marah macrocarpus **(Greene) Greene var. macrocarpus** – Bigroot [Big-root, Big root] (14, 123) (1856–1882), Giant root (123) (1856), Man-in-the-ground [Man in the ground] (74) (1893)

Maranta arundinacea **L.** – Arrowplant [Arrow-plant] (92) (1876), Arrowroot (49, 50, 107, 109, 110) (1886–present), Bermuda arrowroot [Bermuda arrow-root] (49, 138) (1898–1923), Indian arrowroot [Indian arrow root] (92) (1876)

Maranta **L.** – Arrowroot (7, 138) (1828–1923), Maranta (138) (1923) for B. Maranta, Venetian physician and botanist, died 1754

Marbosia tinctoria **Wm.** – See *Xanthorhiza simplicissima* Marsh.

Marchantia polymorpha **L.** – Brook liverwort (92) (1876), Lichen (174) (1753), Liverwort [Liver-wort, Liver wort] (92) (1876), Woodrow [Wood row] (92) (1876)

Marginaria polypodioides **(L.) Tidestrom** – See *Pleopeltis polypodioides* (L.) Andrews & Windham subsp. *polypodioides*

Mariana **Hill** – See *Silybum* Adans.

Mariana mariana **(L.) Hill** – See *Silybum marianum* (L.) Gaertn.

Marilaunidium hispidum **(Gray) Kuntze** – See *Nama hispidum* Gray

Mariscus **(Hall.) Zinn.** – See *Cladium* P. Br.

Mariscus cayennensis **(Lam.) Urban** – See *Cyperus aggregatus* (Willd.) Endl.

Mariscus echinatus **[Ell.]** – See *Cyperus echinatus* (L.) Wood

Mariscus flavus **Vahl** – See *Cyperus aggregatus* (Willd.) Endl.

Mariscus globulosus **auct. non (Aubl.) Urban** – See *Cyperus croceus* Vahl

Mariscus jamaicensis (Crantz) Britton – See *Cladium mariscus* (L.) Pohl subsp. *jamaicense* (Crantz) Kükenth.

Mariscus mariscoides (Muhl.) Kuntze – Water bog-rush [Water bog rush] (50) (present)

Marrubium (Tourn.) L. – See *Marrubium* L.

Marrubium L. – Horehound [Hoarhound, Hore-hound, Horehounde] (50, 82, 93, 109, 138, 155, 156, 158, 167) (1814–present)

Marrubium vulgare L. – Andornkraut (German) (158) (1900), Common horehound [Common hoarhound] (3, 4, 5, 82, 93, 97, 109, 138, 155, 157, 158) (1913–1986), Herehoune (158) (1900), Horehound [Hoarhound, Hore-hound, Horehounde] (1, 7, 19, 49, 50, 53, 55, 57, 59, 85, 92, 106, 107, 158, 179, 184, 187) (1526–present), Horhowne (158) (1900), Horone (158) (1900), Houndbene (5, 158) (1900), Hound's-bane [Hound's bane] (156) (1923), Houndsbene (69) (1904), Marrube (5, 69, 156) (1903–1923) no longer in use by 1923, Marrube blanc (French) (158) (1900), Marrubia (Spanish) (158) (1900), Marrubium (59) (1911), Marvel (5, 69, 156, 158) (1900–1923) no longer in use by 1923, Mawroll (158) (1900), Weisser Andorn (German) (158) (1900), White horehound [White hoarhound] (5, 10, 55, 63, 72, 92, 93, 95, 156, 157, 178) (1596–1936)

Marselea quadrifolia L. – See *Marsilea quadrifolia* L.

Marshalia obovata – See *Marshallia obovata* (Walt.) Beadle & F. E. Boynt.

Marshallia caespitosa Nutt. – Narrow-leaf marshallia [Narrow-leaved marshallia] (5, 97) (1913–1937), Puffball [Puff-ball, Puff ball, Puff-balls, Puff balls] (50) (present) *Marshallia grandiflora* Beadle & F. E. Boynt. – Large-flower marshallia [Large-flowered marshallia] (5) (1913)

Marshallia obovata (Walt.) Beadle & F. E. Boynt. – False scabish (156) (1923)

Marshallia Schreb. – Barbara's buttons (50) (present), Marshallia [Marshalia] (138, 155) (1923–1942)

Marshallia trinervia (Walt.) Porter – See *Marshallia trinervia* (Walt.) Trel.

Marshallia trinervia (Walt.) Trel. – Broad-leaf marshallia [Broad-leaved marshallia] (5) (1913)

Marshallia trinervia (Walter) lesquereux ex Trel. – See *Marshallia trinervia* (Walt.) Trel.

Marsilea L. – Pepperwort [Pepper wort, Pepper wort, Pepper woort] (4, 50, 138, 155) (1923–present), Water-clover [Waterclover, Water clover] (3, 4, 50) (1977–present)

Marsilea quadrifolia L. – European marsilea (5) (1913), European water-clover [European waterclover] (50) (present), Four-leaf marsilia [Four-leaved marsilia] (3) (1977), Pepperwort [Pepper wort, Pepper wort, Pepper woort] (5) (1913)

Marsilea uncinata A. Braun – See *Marsilea vestita* Hook. & Grev. subsp. *vestita*

Marsilea vestita Hook. & Grev. – Hairy marsilea (131) (1899), Hairy pepperwort (5, 97, 122) (1913–1937), Hairy water-clover [Hairy waterclover] (50) (present), Pepperwort [Pepper wort, Pepper wort, Pepper woort] (3) (1977), Western water-clover [Western water clover] (4) (1986)

Marsilea vestita Hook. & Grev. subsp. *vestita* – Four-leaf clover fern [Four-leafed clover fern] (122) (1937) TX, Hairy water-clover [Hairy waterclover] (50) (present), Hooked pepperwort (155) (1942)

Marsilia quadrifolia L. – See *Marsilea quadrifolia* L.

Martynia fragrans Lindl. – See *Proboscidea louisianica* (Mill.) Thell. subsp. *fragrans* (Lindl.) Bretting

Martynia L. – Martynia (155) (1942), Unicorn plant [Unicorn-plant, Unicornplant] (2, 138) (1895–1923)

Martynia louisiana Miller – See *Proboscidea louisianica* (Mill.) Thell.

Martynia lutea [Lindl.] – See *Ibicella lutea* (Lindl.) Van Eselt.

Martynia proboscidea Pursh – See *Proboscidea louisianica* (Mill.) Thell.

Martynia proboscides Gloxin – See *Proboscidea louisianica* (Mill.) Thell.

Martynia violacea [Engelm.] – See *Proboscidea louisianica* (Mill.) Thell. subsp. *fragrans* (Lindl.) Bretting

Maruta Cass. – See *Anthemis* L.

Maruta cotula (L.) DC. – See *Anthemis cotula* L.

Matelea Aubl. – Anglepod [Angle pod, Angle-pod] (4) (1986), Climbing milkweed (4) (1986), Milkvine (50) (present)

Matelea baldwyniana (Sweet) Woods. – Baldwin's milkvine (50) (present), Baldwin's vincetoxicum (5, 97) (1913–1937), Climbing milkweed (4) (1986)

Matelea biflora (Raf.) Woods – Pearl milkweed (124) (1937) TX, Prairie angle-pod (97) (1937), Star milkvine (50) (present), Star milkweed (124) (1937) TX, Two-flower milkvine [Two-flowered milkvine] (4) (1986), White perwinkle [White peruinkle] (174) (1753), Wintergreen [Winter greene, Winter-green] (178) (1526)

Matelea carolinensis (Jacq.) Woods. – Carolina vincetoxicum (5, 97) (1913–1937), Hairy vincetoxicum (5) (1913), Negro vine [Negro-vine] (5, 156) (1913–1923), Running milkweed (5, 156) (1913–1923)

Matelea cynanchoides (Engelm.) Woods – Milk vine [Milk-vine, Milkvine] (4) (1986), Prairie milkvine (50) (present)

Matelea decipiens (Alex.) Woods. – Climbing milkweed (4) (1986), Old-field milkvine [Oldfield milkvine] (50) (present)

Matelea gonocarpa (Walt.) Shinners – See *Matelea gonocarpos* (Walt.) Shinners

Matelea gonocarpos (Walt.) Shinners – White swallow-wort [White swallow wort, White Swallowwoort] (178) (1526), Angle-fruit milkvine [Anglefruit milkvine] (50) (present), Anglepod [Angle pod, Angle-pod] (4) (1986), Angle-pod milkvetch [Anglepod milkvetch] (155) (1942), Coast vincetoxicum (5) (1913), Cork-pod milkvine [Corkpod milkvine] (155) (1942), Large-leaf anglepod [Largeleaf angle pod, Large-leaved angle-pod] (5, 97, 122, 156) (1913–1937), possibly Bastard dog's-bane [Bastard Dogs-bane] (184) (1793)

Matelea obliqua (Jacq.) Woods. – False choak-dog (19) (1840), Large-flower vincetoxicum [Large-flowered vincetoxicum] (5) (1913), Negro vine [Negro-vine] (7, 92) (1828–1876), Short's vincetoxicum (5) (1913)

Mateuccia strutiopteris (L.) Lodaro – See *Matteuccia struthiopteris* (L.) Todaro

Mathiola incana R. Br. – See *Matthiola incana* (L.) Aiton f.

Matricaria chamomila L. – See *Matricaria recutita* L.

Matricaria discoidea DC. – Camomile [Chamomile, Camomylle] (85) (1932), Disc mayweed (50) (present), Green dogfennel [Green dog-fennel, Green dog fennel] (101) (1905), Lavender-cotton [Lavendercotton, Lavender cotton] (10, 19) (1818–1840), Pineapple-weed [Pineappleweed (3, 4, 155, 156) (1923–1986), Rayless camomile [Rayless chamomile] (5, 97, 156) (1913–1937), Rayless dogfennel (101) (1905), Wild marigold (5, 75, 156) (1894–1923)

Matricaria inodora L. – See *Tripleurospermum perforata* (Merat) M. Lainz

Matricaria L. – Camomile [Chamomile, Camomylle] (1, 93, 158) (1900–1936), False camomile [False chamomile, False-chamomile] (138) (1923), Featherfen (7) (1828), Feverfew [Fever few, fever-few] (184) (1793), Green dogfennel [Green dog-fennel, Green dog fennel] (1, 93) (1932–1936), Matricary (109) (1949), Mayweed [May-weed, May weed] (50, 155) (1942–present), Wild camomile [Wild cammomile, Wild chamomile, Wild camomille] (156) (1923), possibly Pineapple-weed [Pineappleweed] (1) (1932)

Matricaria maritima L. – See *Tripleurospermum maritima* (L.) W. D. J. Koch subsp. *maritima*

Matricaria matricarioides (Less.) Porter – See *Matricaria discoidea* DC.

Matricaria parthenium L. – See *Tanacetum parthenium* (L.) Schultz-Bip.

Matricaria parthenoides – See *Tanacetum parthenium* (L.) Schultz-Bip.

Matricaria perforata Mérat – See *Tripleurospermum perforata* (Mérat)

M. Lainz

Matricaria recutita **L.** – Apple-riennie (158) (1900), Camomille commune on d'Allemagne (French) (158) (1900), Corn feverfew (158) (1900), Dog camovyne [Dog's camovyne] (158) (1900), False camomile [False chamomile, False-chamomile] (4) (1986), Feldkamille (German) (158) (1900), German camomile [German-camomile, German chamomile] (5, 49, 50, 52, 53, 55, 57, 58, 59, 92, 122, 155, 156, 158) (1869–present), Horse gowan [Horse-gowan] (5, 156, 158) (1900–1923), Manzanilla comun (Spanish) (158) (1900), Matricaria (55) (1911), Mayweed [May-weed, May weed] (158) (1900), Sweet false camomile [Sweet false chamomile] (109) (1949), Wild camomile [Wild cammomile, Wild chamomile, Wild camomille] (5, 19, 53, 158) (1840–1922)

Matricaria suaveolens – See *Matricaria discoidea* DC.

Matteuccia struthiopteris **(L.) Todaro** – Ostrich fern [Ostrich-fern, Ostrichfern] (1, 2, 3, 4, 19, 50, 72, 131, 138, 155, 158) (1840–present)

Matteuccia **Todaro** – Ostrich fern [Ostrich-fern, Ostrichfern] (1, 109) (1932–1949)

Matthiola **Aiton f.** – Stock [Stocks] (109, 138) (1923–1949)

Matthiola annua **(L.) Sweet** – July flower [July-flower] (19, 92) (1840–1876), Stock [Stocks] (19) (1840)

Matthiola bicornis **DC.** – See *Matthiola longipetala* (Vent.) DC.

Matthiola fenestralis **R. Br.** – See *Matthiola incana* (L.) Aiton f.

Matthiola incana **(L.) Aiton f.** – Brampton stock (109) (1949), Broadwort [Broad wort] (92) (1876), Brompton queens (19, 92) (1840–1876), Brompton stocks [Brompton stock] (19, 92) (1840–1876), Common stock (82, 138) (1923–1930), Diuers sorts of double Stocke gilloflowers (178) (1526), Gilly flower [Gilly flowers, Gillyflowers] (46, 92) (1671–1876), Stock [Stocks] (92, 107, 109, 131) (1876–1949), Waved wall flower (19) (1840), Yellow-violet [Yellow violet] (92) (1876)

Matthiola incana **(L.) R. Br.** – See *Matthiola incana* (L.) Aiton f.

Matthiola incana **Br.** – See *Matthiola incana* (L.) Aiton f.

Matthiola longipetala **(Vent.) DC.** – Evening stock (109) (1949), Greek stock (138) (1923)

Matthiola **R. Br.** – See *Matthiola* Aiton f.

Mattuschia **Gmel.** – See *Saururus* L.

Maurandella antirrhiniflora **(Humb. & Bonpl. ex Willd.) Rothm.** – Blue vine-snapdragon [Blue vine snapdragon] (124) (1937) TX, Vine blue snapdragon (122) (1937) TX

Maurandia – See *Maurandya* Ortega

Maurandia barclaiana – See *Maurandya barclaiana* Lindl.

Maurandia wislizeni – See *Epixiphium wislizeni* (Engelm. ex Gray) Munz

Maurandya antirrhiniflora **Humb. & Bonpl.** – See *Maurandella antirrhiniflora* (Humb. & Bonpl. ex Willd.) Rothm.

Maurandya barclaiana **Lindl.** – Barclay's maurandia [Barclay maurandia] (138) (1923)

Maurandya **Ortega** – Maurandia (138) (1923)

Maurandya wislizeni **Engelm. ex Gray** – See *Epixiphium wislizeni* (Engelm. ex Gray) Munz

Mayaca aubleti **Michx.** – See *Mayaca fluviatilis* Aubl.

Mayaca fluviatilis **Aubl.** – Mayaca (5) (1913), Stream bogmoss (50) (present)

Maytenus boaria **Molina** – Mayten (109, 138) (1923–1949)

Maytenus phyllanthoides **Benth.** – Leather-leaf [Leatherleaf, Leather leaf] (122) (1937) TX

Mayzea cerealis **Tt. Raf.** – See *Zea mays* L.

Mecardonia acuminata **(Walt.) Small** – Axil-flower [Axilflower] (50) (present), Purple hedge-hyssop [Purple hedge hyssop] (5, 97) (1913–1937)

Mecardonia acuminata **(Walt.) Small var.** *acuminata* – Purple hedge-hyssop [Purple hedge hyssop] (122) (1937)

Meconopsis heterophylla **[Benth.]** – See *Stylomecon heterophylla* (Benth.) G. Taylor

Medeola **L.** – Cucumber root [Cucumber-root] (138) (1923), Indian cucumber (10, 50, 167) (1814–present), Indian cucumber-root [Indian cucumber root] (1, 109, 156) (1923–1949)

Medeola virginiana **L.** – Cucumber root [Cucumber-root] (7, 138, 186) (1814–1923), Gyromia (46) (1879), Indian cucumber (19, 46, 50, 86, 186, 187) (1814–present) Native Americans ate roots which taste like cucumbers, Indian cucumber-root [Indian cucumber root] (5) (1913)

Medicago **(Tourn.) L.** – See *Medicago* L.

Medicago arabica **(L.) Huds.** – Bur clover [Burr clover] (45) (1896), Bur-heart clover [Bur heart clover] (5) (1913), California clover (5, 45) (1896–1913), California spotted clover (5) (1913), German medic fodder [Germaine Medicke Fodder] (178) (1526), Heart trefoil (5) (1913), Heartleaf [Heart leaf] (5) (1913), Medicke fodder of Arabia (178) (1526), Purple-grass [Purple grass] (5) (1913), Spotted bur clover (109, 122, 124) (1937–1949), Spotted medic [Spotted medick] (5, 45, 85, 97, 156) (1896–1937)

Medicago denticulata **Willd.** – See *Medicago polymorpha* L.

Medicago hispida **Gaertn.** – See *Medicago polymorpha* L.

Medicago **L.** – Alfalfa (1, 4, 50, 93) (1932–present), Lucerne [Lucern] (1) (1932), Medic (1, 10, 109, 138, 155, 156, 184) (1793–1949), Medick (1, 4, 10, 82, 109, 138, 156) (1818–1986), Nonesuch [None-such, Nonesuch] (1) (1932), Snail clover (158) (1900)

Medicago lupulina **L.** – Black clover (85) (1932), Black medic [Black medick] (3, 4, 5, 45, 50, 62, 68, 80, 82, 92, 97, 106, 107, 109, 155, 156, 158) (1896–present), Black nonesuch (5, 156, 158) (1900–1923), Black trefoil (5, 158) (1900–1913), Black-grass [Black grass, Blackgrass] (5, 156, 158) (1900–1923), Blackseed [Black seed] (5, 156, 158) (1900–1923), Black-seed hop clover [Black-seed hop clover] (72) (1907), Bur clover [Burr clover] (103) (1870), Dutch clover (19, 92) (1840–1876), Hop clover [Hop-clover] (5, 85, 93, 109, 122, 156, 158) (1900–1949), Hop medick [Hop-medick] (5, 14, 19, 62, 92, 156, 158) (1840–1923), Hop trefoil [Hop-trefoil] (92, 158) (1876–1900), Horned clover (5, 156, 158) (1900–1923), Medick (92) (1876), Melilot trefoil (5, 92, 158) (1876–1913), Natural-grass [Natural grass] (5, 158) (1900–1913), Nonesuch [Nonesuch, Nonesuch] (5, 19, 45, 62, 92, 107, 156, 158) (1840–1923), Nonsuch (46) (1879), Prostrate yellow clover (62) (1912), Sainfoin (5, 156) (1913–1923), Shamrock (5, 156, 158) (1900–1923), Yellow hop clover [Yellow hop-clover] (156) (1923), Yellow trefoil (68, 95, 109, 146) (1911–1949)

Medicago maculata **Willd.** – See *Medicago arabica* (L.) Huds.

Medicago minima **L.** – Bur clover [Burr clover] (3) (1977), Bur-medick [Burr medick] (50) (present), Little medic (155) (1942), Prickly medic [Prickly medick] (4) (1986), Small bur clover (4) (1986)

Medicago polymorpha **L.** – Bur clover [Burr clover] (5, 45, 50, 76, 87, 93, 97, 106, 107, 122, 124, 156) (1884–present), California clover (87) (1884) Southern states, Common bur clover (124) (1937), Shanghai trefoil (107) (1919), Toothed bur clover (109) (1949), Toothed medic (5, 93, 97) (1913–1937)

Medicago sativa **L.** – Alfafa (Spanish from Arabic) (45, 110) (1886–1896), Alfalfa (3, 4, 5, 32, 45, 50, 52, 63, 66, 68, 72, 82, 85, 87, 93, 95, 97, 106, 107, 109, 114, 118, 122, 124, 125, 129, 138, 151, 155, 156, 157, 158) (1884–present) from alfacfacah = best sort of fodder in Arabian or from Al-chelfa that which grows after something else, Alfasafat (Spanish from Arabic) (110) (1886), Brazilian clover (5, 118, 157, 158) (1898–1929), Burgundy clover (5, 157, 158) (1900–1929), Burgundy hay [Burgundy-hay, Burgundie hay] (157, 158, 178) (1526–1929), Burgundy trefoil (156) (1923), California clover (52) (1919), Chilean clover [Chilian clover] (5, 45, 118, 157, 158) (1896–1929), Dutch clover (157, 158) (1900–1929), Erurye (Spanish, old name) (110) (1886), Fisfisat (Arabic) (110) (1886), French clover (45, 118) (1896–1898), Great trefoil (5, 157, 158) (1900–1929), Herba spagna (Itallian) (110) (1886), Holy hay [Holyhay, Holy-hay] (5, 157, 158) (1900–1929), Laouzerdo (Southern France) (110) (1886) morphed into luzerne, hence source of name, Lucerne [Lucern] (5, 14, 19, 45, 63, 66, 68, 82, 87, 92, 93, 95, 107, 109, 118, 129, 151, 156, 157, 158) (1840–1949), Lucifer

266

(158) (1900), Medick (14, 19, 45, 118) (1840–1898), Melga (Spanish) (110) (1886), Mielga (Spanish) (110) (1886), Purple medic [Purple medick] (5, 45, 156, 157, 158) (1896–1929) England, Sainfoin (5, 110, 156) (1913–1923), Snail clover (5, 157, 158) (1900–1929), Snail flower [Snail-flower] (156) (1923), Spanish clover (52, 157, 158) (1900–1929), Spanish medick (156) (1923), Spanish trefoil (5, 45, 118, 157, 158) (1896–1929), Userdas (Catalan) (110) (1886)

Medicago sativa L. subsp. *falcata* (L.) Arcang. – Russian alfalfa (82) (1930) IA, Siberian alfalfa (82) (1930) IA, Sickle alfalfa (155) (1942), Sickle medic [Sickle medick] (68) (1913), Yellow alfalfa (3, 50, 85) (1932–present), Yellow lucerne (68) (1913) Ottawa

Medicago sativa L. subsp. *sativa* – Medick (82) (1930)

Medicago sativa subsp. *varia* (Martyn) Arcang. – See *Medicago sativa* L. subsp. *sativa*

Medicago scutellata (L.) Mill. – Beehive [Bee-hive] (19, 92) (1840–1876), Snail medick (138) (1923), Snail plant (92) (1876), Snails (107) (1919), Snail-shell (19) (1840), possibly Medicke fodder (178) (1526)

Medicago scutellata Mill. – See *Medicago scutellata* (L.) Mill.

Medinilla Gaud. – Medinilla (138) (1923)

Meehania cordata (Nutt.) Britton – Meehania (5) (1913)

Megalodonta beckii (Torr. ex Spreng.) Greene – See *Bidens beckii* Torr. ex Spreng.

Megalodonta beckii (Torr. ex Spreng.) Greene var. *beckii* – See *Bidens beckii* Torr. ex Spreng.

Megalodonta beckii (Torr.) Greene – See *Bidens beckii* Torr. ex Spreng.

Megalodonta Greene. – See *Bidens* L. (US species)

Megapterium (S. Wats.) Britton – See *Oenothera* L.

Megapterium argophyllum R. R. Gates – See *Oenothera macrocarpa* Nutt. subsp. *incana* (Gray) Reveal

Megapterium missouriense (Sims) Spach – See *Oenothera macrocarpa* Nutt. subsp. *macrocarpa*

Megapterium oklahomense Norton – See *Oenothera macrocarpa* Nutt. subsp. *oklahomensis* (J. B. S. Norton) Wagner

Megarrhiza californica Torr. – See *Marah macrocarpus* (Greene) Greene var. *macrocarpus*

Meibomia Adans – See *Desmodium* Desv.

Meibomia arenicola Vail. – See *Desmodium lineatum* DC.

Meibomia bracteosa (Michx.) Kuntze – See *Desmodium cuspidatum* (Muhl. ex Willd.) DC. ex Loud.

Meibomia canadense (L.) Kuntze – See *Desmodium canadense* (L.) DC.

Meibomia canescens L. – See *Desmodium canadense* (L.) DC.

Meibomia dillenii (Darl.) Kuntze – See *Desmodium perplexum* Schub.

Meibomia glabella (Michx.) Kuntze – See *Desmodium glabellum* (Michx.) DC.

Meibomia grandiflora (Walt.) Kuntze – See *Desmodium cuspidatum* (Muhl. ex Willd.) DC. ex Loud. var. *cuspidatum*

Meibomia Heister – See *Desmodium* Desv.

Meibomia illinoensis (Gray) Kuntze – See *Desmodium illinoense* Gray

Meibomia laevigata (Nutt.) Kuntze – See *Desmodium laevigatum* (Nutt.) DC.

Meibomia longifolia (Torr. & Gray) Vail – See *Desmodium cuspidatum* (Muhl. ex Willd.) DC. ex Loud. var. *longifolium* (Torr. & Gray) Schub.

Meibomia michauxii Vail – See *Desmodium rotundifolium* DC.

Meibomia nudiflora (L.) Kuntze – See *Desmodium nudiflorum* (L.) DC.

Meibomia obtusa (Muhl.) Vail. – See *Desmodium obtusum* (Muhl. ex Willd.) DC.

Meibomia ochroleuca (M. A. Curtis) – See *Desmodium ochroleucum* M.A. Curtis ex Canby

Meibomia paniculata (L.) Kuntze – See *Desmodium paniculatum* (L.) DC. var. *paniculatum*

Meibomia pauciflora (Nutt.) Kuntze – See *Desmodium pauciflorum* (Nutt.) DC.

Meibomia rigida (Ell.) Kuntze – See *Desmodium obtusum* (Muhl. ex

Willd.) DC.

Meibomia sessilifolia (Torr.) Kuntze – See *Desmodium sessilifolium* (Torr.) Torr. & Gray

Meibomia stricta (Pursh) Kuntze – See *Desmodium strictum* (Pursh) DC.

Meibomia viridiflora (L.) Kuntze – See *Desmodium viridiflorum* (L.) DC.

Melaleuca L. – Bottlebrush [Bottle brush, Bottle-brush] (109) (1949), Melaleuca (138) (1923) Greek "black white" for black trunk and white branches of some species

Melampodium australe Loefl. – See *Acanthospermum australe* (Loefl.) Kuntze

Melampodium cinereum DC. – Rock daisy (124) (1937)

Melampodium leucanthum Torr. & Gray – Black-foot daisy (4) (1986), Plains blackfoot (50, 155) (1942–present), Plains melampodium (5, 97) (1913–1937)

Melampyrum (Tourn.) L. – Cow-wheat [Cow wheat] (1, 2, 10, 180) (1633–1932), Horse flower [Horse-floure] (180) (1633)

Melampyrum americanum Michx. – See *Melampyrum lineare* Desr. var. *lineare*

Melampyrum latifolium Muhl. – See *Melampyrum lineare* Desr. var. *latifolium* Bart.

Melampyrum lineare Desr. (possibly) – Cow-wheat [Cow wheat] (156, 187) (1818–1923), possibly Narrow-leaf cow-wheat [Narrow-leaved cow-wheat] (5) (1913)

Melampyrum lineare Desr. var. *latifolium* Bart. – Broad-leaf cow-wheat [Broad-leaved cow-wheat] (5) (1913)

Melampyrum lineare Desr. var. *lineare* – Cow-wheat [Cow wheat] (19, 46, 63) (1783–1899)

Melampyrum lineare Lam. – possibly *Melampyrum lineare Desr.*

Melandrium Roehl. – See *Silene* L.

Melanthium hybridum Wr. – See *Melanthium latifolium* Desr.

Melanthium L. – Blackflower [Black flower, Black-flower] (167) (1814), Bunchflower [Bunch-flower, Bunch flower] (1, 50, 138, 155) (1923–present), Melanthium (158) (1900) from Greek meaning 'black flower'

Melanthium latifolium Desr. – Bunchflower [Bunch-flower, Bunch flower] (19, 92) (1840–1876), Crisped bunchflower [Crisped bunch flower] (5) (1913), Slender bunchflower (50) (present)

Melanthium parviflorum (Michx.) S. Wats. – Appalachian bunchflower (50) (present), Small-flower veratrum [Small-flowered veratrum] (5) (1913)

Melanthium virginicum L – Blackflower [Black flower, Black-flower] (5, 19, 92, 156, 158) (1840–1913), Bunchflower [Bunch-flower, Bunch flower] (3, 5, 72, 122, 124, 155, 156, 158) (1900–1977), Common bunch flower (80) (1913), Quafidil (7) (1828), Quafodil (5, 92, 156, 158) (1876–1923), Virginia bunchflower (50) (present)

Melanthium woodii (J. W. Robbins ex Wood) Bodkin – Indian pokeweed [Indian poke weed] (5) (1913), Wood's bunchflower (50) (present), Wood's false hellbore (5, 72, 97) (1907–1937)

Melia azadirachta – See *Melia azedarach* L.

Melia azedarac L. – See *Melia azedarach* L.

Melia azedarach L. – African lilac (49) (1898), Azedarach (57) (1917), Azedarach bark (92) (1876), Bead tree [Beade tree] (19, 49, 92, 178) (1526–1898), Bean tree [Beantree, Bean-tree (107) (1919), China tree [China-tree] (15, 106, 107, 109) (1895–1949), Chinaberry [China-berry, China berry] or Chinaberry tree (37, 106, 109, 122, 138, 153) (1913–1949), False sycamore (107) (1919), Hoop tree (92) (1876), Indian lilac (49) (1898), Makanzhide sabe (Omaha-Ponca, black 'red medicine') (37) (1919), Margosa bark (57) (1917), Neem bark (92) (1876), Persian lilac (49) (1898), Piocha (153) (1913) NM, Pride-of-India [Pride of India] (15, 20, 44, 49, 92, 106, 107, 109) (1845–1949), Syrian bean tree (107) (1919), Texas umbrella-tree (138) (1923), Umbrella china (122, 124) (1937) TX, Umbrella tree [Umbrella-tree] (153) (1913) NM, Zizyphus (178) (1526), Pride tree (92) (1876)

Melia azedarach L. var. *umbraculiformis* Berck. & Bailey – See

Melia azedarach L.

Melia azedarach umbraculiformis – See *Melia azedarach* L.

Melia azedarachta L. – See *Melia azedarach* L.

Melia azedarch – See *Melia azedarach* L.

Melia indica (A. Juss.) Brandis – See *Azadirachta indica* A.Juss.

Melia L. – Bead tree [Beade tree] (109) (1949)

Melianthus L. – Honeybush (138) (1923)

Melianthus major L. – Big-leaf honeybush [Bigleaf honeybush] (138) (1923)

Melica aristata Thurb. ex Boland. – Bearded melic grass [Bearded melic-grass] (94) (1901)

Melica bulbosa Geyer ex Porter & Coult. – Bulbous melic grass (87) (1884), Infalted melic-grass (94) (1901), Inflated melic grass [Inflated melic-grass] (94) (1901), Onion gràss [Oniongrass, Oniongrass] (50, 122, 155, 163) (1852–present), Thick-root bunch grass [Thick-rooted bunch-grass] (94) (1901)

Melica californica Scribn. – California melic grass [California melic-grass] (94) (1901), Woody melic grass [Woody melic-grass] (94) (1901)

Melica diffusa Pursh – See *Melica mutica* Walt.

Melica frutescens Scribn. – See *Melica californica* Scribn.

Melica fugax Boland. – Small melic grass [Small melic-grass] (94) (1901)

Melica harfordii Boland. – Harford's melic grass [Harford's melic-grass] (94) (1901)

Melica imperfecta Trin. – Small-flower melic grass [Small-flowered melic-grass] (94) (1901)

Melica inflata (Boland.) Vasey – See *Melica bulbosa* Geyer ex Porter & Coult.

Melica L. – Melic (155) (1942), Melic grass [Melic grass, Melic-grass] (1, 10, 41, 50, 93, 152) (1770–present), Onion grass [Oniongrass, Onion-grass] (155) (1942)

Melica mutica Walt. – Melic grass [Melic grass, Melic-grass] (19, 66, 87, 179) (1793–1903), Narrow melic grass [Narrow melic-grass (5, 56, 72, 163) (1852–1913), Tall melic grass [Tall melic-grass] (56, 72) (1901–1907), Two-flower melic [Two flower melic, Two-flower melic, Two-flowered melic] (3, 122, 155) (1937–1977), Two-flower melic grass [Twoflower melicgrass] (3, 50) (1977–present)

Melica nitens (Scribn.) Nutt. ex Piper – Melic grass [Melic grass, Melic-grass] (111) (1915), Tall melic grass [Tall melic-grass] (5, 119, 163) (1852–1938), Three-flower melic [Threeflower melic] (3, 155) (1942–1977), Three-flower melic grass [Threeflower melic-grass] (50) (present)

Melica parviflora Scribn. – See *Melica porteri* Scribn.

Melica porteri Scribn. – Porter's melic [Porter melic] (3, 122, 155) (1937–1977), Porter's melic grass [Porter's melicgrass] (50) (present), Small melic grass [Small melic-grass] (5, 72) (1907–1913), Small-flower melic [Small flowered melic] (56) (1901)

Melica smithii (Porter ex Gray) Vasey – Melic grass [Melic grass, Melic-grass] (3, 85) (1932–1977), Smith's melic [Smith melic] (155) (1942), Smith's melic grass [Smith's melicgrass, Smith's melic-grass] (50, 94) (1901–present), Smith's oat (5) (1913)

Melica speciosa M. – See *Melica mutica* Walt.

Melica stricta Boland. – Large-flower melica [Large-flowered melica] (94) (1901)

Melica subulata (Griseb.) Scribn. – Slender-flower melic grass [Slender-flowered melic-grass] (94) (1901)

Melica torreyana Scribn. – Torrey's melic grass [Torrey's melic-grass] (94) (1901)

Melicocca bijuga L. – See *Melicoccus bijugatus* Jacq.

Melicocca paniculata Juss. – See *Exothea paniculata* (Juss.) Radlk.

Melicoccus bijugatus Jacq. – Genip (109) (1949), Mamoncillo (109, 138) (1923–1949), Spanish lime [Spanish-lime] (109) (1949)

Melilotus (Tourn.) Hill. – See *Melilotus* Mill.

Melilotus alba Lam. – possibly *Melilotus officinalis* (L.) Lam.

Melilotus albus Desr. – possibly *Melilotus officinalis* (L.) Lam.

Melilotus albus Medik. – See *Melilotus officinalis* (L.) Lam.

Melilotus albus Medik. var. *annuus* Coe – See *Melilotus officinalis* (L.) Lam.

Melilotus indica (L.) All. – Indian clover (122) (1937) TX, Indian yellow clover (124) (1937) TX, Yellow sweet clover [Yellow sweet-clover, Yellow sweetclover] (148) (1939) CO

Melilotus Mill. – Honey clover [Honey-clover] (1) (1932), Honysocle (179) (1526), King's-crown [King's crown, King's-crown, Kynges crowne] (179) (1526), Melilot (82, 109, 156) (1923–1949), Mellilot (179) (1526), Mellilot clover (7) (1828), Sweet clover (1, 50, 93, 106, 109, 156) (1923–present)

Melilotus officinalis (L.) Lam. – Balsam-flowers [Balsam flowers] (5, 156) (1913–1923), Buffalo clover [Buffalo-clover] (187) (1818), Hart's clover (5, 156, 157, 158) (1900–1929), Hart's trefoil (157, 158) (1900–1929), Heartwort [Heart-wort] (5, 156, 157, 158) (1900–1929), Hubam sweet clover [Hubam sweetclover] (155) (1942), King's clover [Kings' clover] (5, 92, 156, 157, 158) (1876–1929), King's-crown [King's crown, King's-crown, Kynges crowne] (5, 156, 157, 158) (1900–1929), Least hop trefoil [Least hop-trefoil] (5) (1913), Melilot (6, 14, 92, 107, 156) (1876–1923), Melilot (French) (6) (1892), Mélilot officinal (French) (158) (1900), Melilotenklee (German) (6, 156) (1892–1900), Meliloto (Spanish) (158) (1900), Melilotus (57) (1917), Melist (107) (1919), Mellilot clover (92) (1876), Plaster clover [Plaster-clover] (5, 156, 158) (1900–1923), Plater clover (157) (1929), Steinklee (German) (6, 158) (1892–1900), Sweet clover (6, 37, 45, 48, 49, 57, 63, 80, 92, 107, 114, 129, 156) (1876–1923), Sweet yellow clover (131) (1899), Trebol oloroso (Spanish) (158) (1900), Whuttle-grass (157, 158) (1900–1929), Wild laburnum (157, 158) (1900–1929) England, Yellow melilot (5, 6, 45, 49, 53, 129, 156, 157, 158) (1892–1929), Yellow melilot clover (19, 49, 53, 92) (1840–1922), Yellow millet (5, 157, 158) (1900–1929), Yellow sweet clover [Yellow sweet-clover, Yellow sweetclover] (3, 4, 5, 6, 50, 53, 62, 80, 82, 85, 93, 95, 97, 106, 109, 122, 124, 129, 145, 155, 156, 157, 158) (1892–present), German clover [Germaine Clauer] (178) (1526) John Gerarde, possibly Bokara clover (129) (1894), possibly Bokhara clover (5, 45, 68, 82, 156, 157, 158) (1896–1929), possibly Cabul clover (5, 156, 157, 158) (1900–1929), possibly Honey (5) (1913), possibly Honey clover [Honey-clover] (5, 76, 156) (1896–1923), possibly Honey lotus [Honey-lotus] (5, 92, 156, 157, 158) (1876–1929), possibly Sweet lucerne (157, 158) (1900–1929), possibly Sweet melilot (157, 158) (1900–1929), possibly Tree clover [Tree-clover] (5, 62, 156, 157, 158) (1900–1929), possibly Wachanga iyechecha (Dakota, similar to sweet grass) (37) (1919), possibly White melilot (5, 6, 45, 62, 63, 92, 129, 156, 157, 158) (1892–1929), possibly White melilot clover (19) (1840), possibly White millet (5, 157, 158) (1900–1929), White sweet clover [White sweet-clover, White sweetclover] (3, 4, 5, 50, 62, 68, 72, 80, 82, 85, 93, 95, 97, 106, 109, 122, 124, 125, 131, 138, 145, 155, 156, 157, 158) (1897–present)

Melilotus officinalis (L.) Pallas – See *Melilotus officinalis* (L.) Lam.

Melilotus officinalis Willd. – See *Melilotus officinalis* (L.) Lam.

Melilotus vulgaris Eat. & Wright – See *Melilotus officinalis* (L.) Lam.

Melinis repens (Willd.) Zizka – Natal grass [Natal-grass] (109, 122, 138, 163) (1852–1949), Ruby grass [Ruby-grass] (109) (1949), Wine grass [Wine-grass] (109) (1949)

Melissa L. – Balm (7, 10, 138, 156, 167) (1814–1923), Beebalm [Bee balm, Bee-balm] (1) (1932), Lemon balm [Lemon-balm] (1) (1932)

Melissa officinalis L. – Balm (10, 19, 49, 57, 107, 156) (1818–1923), Balm mint [Balm-mint] (5, 156) (1913–1923), Balmleaf [Balm leaf, Balm-leaf] (5, 156) (1913–1923), Bawme (179) (1526), Bawme tre (179) (1526), Beebalm [Bee balm, Bee-balm] (1, 5, 106, 109, 156) (1913–1949), Citronelle (92) (1876), Common balm [Common balme] (3, 75, 138, 178) (1526–1977), Cure-all [Cure all, Cureall] (92) (1876), Dropsy plant (5, 92) (1876–1913), Dropsy-wort (156) (1923), Garden balm (5) (1913), Garden bee balm (93) (1936), Goose-tongue [Goose tongue] (5, 75) (1894–1913) Concord MA, Honey plant [Honey-plant] (5, 156) (1913–1923), Lemon balm

[Lemon-balm] (5, 49, 75, 92, 109, 156) (1876–1949), Lemon lobe-lia (5, 75) (1894–1913) Northeastern US, Melissa (57, 114) (1894–1917), Melisse (179) (1526), Pimentary (5, 156) (1913–1923) no longer in use by 1923, Sweet Mary (5, 75, 156) (1894–1923) Northeastern US, no longer in use by 1923, Yellow sweet clover [Yellow sweet-clover, Yellow sweetclover] (63, 72) (1899–1912)

Melissa pulegioides [L.] – See *Hedeoma pulegioides* (L.) Pers.

Melocactus communis [(Aiton) Link & Otto] – See *Melocactus intortus* (Mill.) Urb.

Melocactus communis Link & Otto – See *Melocactus intortus* (Mill.) Urb.

Melocactus intortus (Mill.) Urb. – Melon cactus [Meloncactus] (92, 107) (1876–1919), Melon thistle [Melon thistles] (14) (1882), Turk's-cap cactus (107) (1919)

Melocactus Link & Otto – Melon cactus [Meloncactus] (155) (1942), Turk's-cap [Turk's cap, Turkscap] (92) (1876)

Melosmon Raf. – See *Teucrium* L.

Melothria L. – Creeping cucumber (4, 158) (1900–1986), Melothria (50) (present)

Melothria pendula L. – Creeping cucumber (3, 4, 5, 19, 92, 97, 122, 124, 156) (1840–1986), Guadalupe cucumber [Guadaloupe cucumber] (50) (present), Shagahinga (Missouri tribes) (7) (1828), Small creeping Virginia cucumber (181) (~1678)

Menispermum canadense L. – Bittersweet [Bitter sweet, Bitter-sweet] (23) (1810) NY, Canadian moonseed [Canada moonseed] (5, 6, 8, 49, 53, 64, 97, 131, 156, 158) (1892–1937), Canadisches Mond-korn (German) (158) (1900), Common moonseed (50, 109 138, 155) (1923–present), Hakakut (Pawnee, sore mouth) (37) (1919), Ingath-ahe-hazi-i-ta (Omaha-Ponca, thunder grapes) (37) (1919), Maple vine (6) (1892), Ménisperme de Canada (French) (8) (1785), Mé-nisperme du Canada (French) (158) (1900), Menispermum (57, 64) (1908–1917), Moodseed (*sic*) (72) (1907), Moonseed [Moon seed, Moon-seed] (1, 3, 4, 7, 19, 37, 85, 92, 93, 113, 125, 126, 130, 157, 187) (1818–1986), Moon-seed root [Moon seed root] (92) (1876), Moonseed sarsaparilla (49) (1898), Pisswort (7) (1828), Sarsaparilla (38, 76) (1820–1896) Parke Co. ID; Sulphur Grove OH, Texas sar-saparilla (5, 6, 49, 64, 92, 156, 157, 158) (1892–1929), Vine-maple [Vine maple] (49, 156, 157, 158) (1900–1929), Wanaghi-haz (Win-nebago, ghost fruit) (37) (1919), Wananha hazi etai (Ponca, grapes of the ghosts) (37) (1919), Yellow parilla (5, 6, 48, 49, 53, 57, 61, 64, 92, 130, 156, 157, 158) (1870–1929), Yellow sarsaparilla (5, 6, 7, 64, 92, 156, 157, 158) (1828–1929)

Menispermum carolinum [L.] – See *Cocculus carolinus* (L.) DC.

Menispermum L. – Menisperme (French) (8) (1785), Moonseed [Moon seed, Moon-seed] (8, 10, 13, 15, 50, 63, 109, 138, 155, 156, 158, 167, 184) (1785–present)

Menodora heterophylla Moric. ex DC. – Redbud [Red-bud, Red bud, Red-budds] or Redbud tree [Red bud tree, Redbud-tree, Redbud tree] (124) (1937)

Mentha (Tourn.) L. – See *Mentha* L.

Mentha ×*gracilis* Sole [*arvensis* × *spicata*] – Ginger mint [Gingermint] (50) (present), Little-leaf mint [Littleleaf mint] (155) (1942), Red mint (155) (1942), Small-leaf mint [Small-leaved mint] (5) (1913)

Mentha ×*piperita* L. [*aquatica* × *spicata*] – Balm mint [Balm-mint] (5, 158) (1900–1913), Brandy mint [Brandy-mint] (5, 156, 157) (1900–1929), Crisp-leaf mint [Crisped-leaved mint, Crispleaf mint] (5, 155, 158) (1900–1942), Cross mint (5, 158) (1900–1913), Curled mint (5, 92, 158) (1876–1913), Curled mint (5, 156, 157) (1900–1929), Lamb's mint [Lamb mint] (5, 156, 157) (1900–1929), Lammint (157) (1929), Manzania (77) (1898) CA, Mentha (52) (1919), Men-the poivree (French) (6) (1892), Peppermint [Peper-mint] (3, 5, 6, 19, 49, 50, 52, 53, 54, 55, 57, 59, 60, 62, 63, 80, 82, 92, 93, 95, 97, 106, 107, 109, 120, 138, 156, 157) (1704–present), Pfeffermünze (German) (6) (1892)

Mentha ×*rotundifolia* (L.) Huds. [*longifolia* × *suaveolens*] – Ap-ple-mint [Apple mint] (5, 109, 138, 156) (1913–1949), Horse mint [Horse-mint, Horsemint, Horsmynte] (5, 156) (1913–1923),

Patagonian mint [Patagonia-mint] (5, 92, 156) (1876–1923), Round-leaf mint [Round-leaved mint] (5, 109) (1913–1949), Wild mint [Wylde mynte] (5, 156) (1913–1923)

Mentha ×*villosa* Huds. [*spicata* × *suaveolens*] – Woolly mint (5) (1913)

Mentha alopecuroides Hull. – See *Mentha* ×*villosa* Huds. [*spicata* × *suaveolens*]

Mentha aquatica L. – Bergamot herb (92) (1876), Bergamot mint (1, 5, 109, 138, 155, 156, 158) (1900–1949), Bishop's-weed [Bishop's weed, Bishop weed] (158) (1900), Fish mint [Fish-mint] (5, 156, 158) (1900–1923), Orange peppermint (155) (1942), Water mint [Water-mint] (5, 50, 92, 155, 156) (1876–present), American mint (156) (1923), American wild mint (5, 72, 82, 93, 131, 138, 157, 158) (1899–1936), Canadian mint [Canada mint] (155) (1942), Čaŋ pežuta čikala (Lakota, little wood medicine) (121) (1918?–1970?), Čejaka or šejaka (Lakota, mint) (121) (1918?–1970?), Chiaka (Da-kota) (37) (1919), Corn mint (5, 156, 158) (1900–1923), Cow basil [Cow basill] (178) (1526), Cow-basil [Cow basil, Cow-Basill, Cow basill] (178) (1526), Creeping whorled mint (5, 93) (1913–1936), Downy whorled mint (5, 93) (1913–1936), Feldminze (German) (158) (1900), Field mint (3, 4, 5, 19, 93, 98, 138, 155, 156, 158) (1840–1986), Horse mint [Horse-mint, Horsemint, Horsmynte] (19) (1840), Kahts-kiwahaaru (Pawnee, swamp medicine) (37) (1919), Lamb's-tongue [Lambs tongue, Lambs tongue, Lambs' tongues] (5, 156, 158) (1900–1923) no longer in use by 1923, Mint (80, 82, 107) (1913–1930), Northern mint (19) (1840), Peppermint [Peper-mint] (85) (1932), Pezhe nubthon (Omaha-Ponca, fragrant herb) (37) (1919), Red mint (155) (1942), Sarazyne mynt (Saracen's-mint) (179) (1526), Spearmint [Spear mint, Spear-mint, Spere Mynt] (5, 85) (1913–1932), Water calamint (92, 158) (1876–1900), Wild ber-gamont [Wildbergamont] (77) (1898) Oxford ME, Wild bergamot (77) (1898), Wild mint [Wylde mynte] (1, 2, 4, 35, 37, 46, 47, 48, 50, 63, 95, 105, 114, 121, 127) (1671–present), Wild pennyroyal (5, 156, 158) (1900–1923), Wild peppermint (101) (1905), Wytmynt (179) (1526)

Mentha arvensis L. var. *canadensis* (L.) Kuntze – See *Mentha arven-sis* L.

Mentha arvensis subsp. *borealis* (Michx.) Roy L. Taylor & Mac-Bryde – See *Mentha arvensis* L.

Mentha borealis Michx. – See *Mentha arvensis* L.

Mentha canadensis L. – See *Mentha arvensis* L.

Mentha cardiaca Gerarde – See *Mentha* ×*gracilis* Sole [*arvensis* × *spicata*]

Mentha citrata Ehrh. – See *Mentha aquatica* L.

Mentha crispa L. – See *Mentha* ×*piperita* L. [*aquatica* × *spicata*]

Mentha gentilis auct. non L. – See *Mentha* ×*gracilis* Sole [*arvensis* × *spicata*]

Mentha gentilis L. – See *Mentha arvensis* L.

Mentha L. – Menthe (French) (158) (1900), Mint (1, 2, 4, 7, 10, 50, 82, 93, 106, 109, 138, 156, 158, 178, 181, 184) (1526–present), Minze (German) (158) (1900), Peppermint [Peper-mint] (1) (1932), Spear-mint [Spear mint, Spear-mint, Spere Mynt] (1) (1932)

Mentha longifolia (L.) Huds. – See *Mentha spicata* L.

Mentha palustris – See *Mentha* ×*piperita* L. [*aquatica* × *spicata*]

Mentha piperita L. – See *Mentha* ×*piperita* L. [*aquatica* × *spicata*]

Mentha piperita L. subsp. *citrata* (Ehrh.) Briq. – See *Mentha aquat-ica* L.

Mentha pulegium L. – Great pennyroyal [Great penniroyall] (178) (1526), Hillwort (92) (1876), Lesser pennyroyal [Lesser penniroy-all] (178) (1526), Pennyroyal [Penny-royal, Penny royal, Pen-niroyal] (46, 106, 107, 109, 138, 190) (1671–1949), Pudding-grass [Pudding grass] (92) (1876)

Mentha rotundifolia (L.) Huds. – See *Mentha* ×*rotundifolia* (L.) Huds. [*longifolia* × *suaveolens*]

Mentha rotundifolia Huds. – See *Mentha* ×*rotundifolia* (L.) Huds. [*longifolia* × *suaveolens*]

Mentha spicata L. – American spearmint [America spear mint] (19)

Mentha tenuis Michx.

(1840), Baume vert (French) (158) (1900), Brook mint [Brook-mint] (5, 156, 158) (1900–1923), Brown mint (5, 158) (1900–1913), Common mint (5, 62, 156) (1912–1923), European horse mint [European horsemint] (5, 158) (1900–1913), Fish mint [Fish-mint] (5, 156, 158) (1900–1923), Garden mint [Gardyn mynte] (5, 156, 158, 179) (1526–1923), Green mint (156) (1923), Grüne Minze (German) (158) (1900), Horse mint [Horse-mint, Horsemint, Horsmynte] (5, 155, 156, 179) (1526–1942), Lamb's mint [Lamb mint] (5, 156, 158) (1900–1923), Lammint (158) (1900), Mackerel mint [Mackerel-mint (5, 156, 158) (1900–1923), Menthe romaine (French) (158) (1900), Menthe vert (French) (158) (1900), Mint (55, 92, 158) (1876–1911), Our Lady's mint (5, 62, 156, 158) (1900–1923), Römische minze (German) (158) (1900), Sage-of-Bethlehem (5, 156, 158) (1900–1923), Spearmint [Spear mint, Spear-mint, Spere Mynt] (1, 4, 5, 19, 49, 50, 53, 55, 57, 59, 60, 61, 62, 63, 72, 92, 97, 106, 107, 109, 120, 124, 138, 155, 156, 158) (1568–present), Tame mint [Tame mynte] (179) (1526), Water horse mint (5) (1913), Water mint [Water-mint] (156, 158) (1900–1923), Wild mint [Wylde mynte] (85, 179) (1526–1932), Yerba buena (Spanish) (158) (1900)

Mentha tenuis Michx. – See *Mentha spicata* L.

Mentha viridis L. – See *Mentha spicata* L.

Mentzelia (Plum.) L. – See *Mentzelia* L.

Mentzelia albescens (Gill. & Arn.) Griseb. – Wavy-leaf blazing star [Wavyleaf blazingstar] (50) (present)

Mentzelia albicaulis (Dougl. ex Hook.) Dougl. ex Torr. & Gray – Prairie-lily [Prairie lily] (107) (1919), Sand-lily [Sand lily] (101) (1905) MT, Stickleaf [Stick leaf] (106) (1930), White-stem blazing star [Whitestem blazingstar] (50) (present), White-stem mentzelia [Whitestem mentzelia, White-stemmed mentzelia] (5, 93, 155) (1913–1942)

Mentzelia aspera L. – Mentzelia (174) (1753)

Mentzelia decapetala (Pursh ex Sims) Urban & Gilg ex Gilg – Evening star [Evening-star] (127) (1933) ND, Gumbo-lily [Gumbo lily] (156) (1923), Gunebo lily (5, 158) (1900–1913), Mentzelia (127) (1933), Prairie-lily [Prairie lily] (5, 85, 93, 97, 156, 158) (1900–1937), Sand-lily [Sand lily] (3) (1977), Scoria-lily [Scoria lily] (127) (1933) ND, Showy mentzelia (5, 131, 156) (1899–1923), Ten-petal blazing star [Tenpetal blazingstar] (50, 155) (1942–present), Tenpetal menzelia [Tenpetal mentzelia] (4, 155) (1942–1986)

Mentzelia dispersa S. Wats. – Bushy blazing star [Bushy blazingstar] (50) (present)

Mentzelia L. – Blazing star [Blazing-star, Blazingstar] (1, 4, 50, 138) (1923–present), Mentzelia (93, 148, 155) (1936–1942) for Christian Mentzel, 1622–1701, German botanist, Prairie-lily [Prairie lily] (158) (1900), Sand-lily [Sand lily] (1, 4) (1932–1986), Stickleaf [Stick leaf] (1, 4, 148) (1932–1986)

Mentzelia laevicaulis (Dougl. ex Hook.) Torr. & Gray – Blazing star [Blazing-star, Blazingstar] (157) (1929), Gunebo lily (76) (1896) ND, Loasa (157) (1929), Yellow sandlily [Yellow sand lily] (101) (1905) MT

Mentzelia laevicaulis Torr. & Gray – See *Mentzelia laevicaulis* (Dougl. ex Hook.) Torr. & Gray

Mentzelia multiflora (Nutt.) Gray – Adonis blazing star [Adonis blazingstar] (50) (present), Desert blazing star [Desert blazingstar] (155) (1942), Desert mentzelia (155) (1942)

Mentzelia nuda (Pursh) Torr. & Gray – Bractless blazing star [Bractless blazingstar] (50, 155) (1942–present), Bractless mentzelia (3, 131, 155) (1899–1977)

Mentzelia nuda (Pursh) Torr. & Gray var. nuda – Branched nuttallia (5, 93, 97) (1913–1937), Prairie-lily [Prairie lily] (85) (1932), Toka hupepe (Dakota) (37) (1919)

Mentzelia nuda (Pursh) Torr. & Gray var. stricta (Osterhout) Harrington – Stiff nuttallia (5, 93, 97) (1913–1937)

Mentzelia oligosperma Nutt. ex Sims – Chicken-thief [Chickenthief] (50) (present), Few-seed mentzelia [Few-seeded mentzelia] (5, 97, 131) (1913–1937) , Stickleaf [Stick leaf] (4, 156) (1923–1986) , Stick-leaf mentzelia [Stickleaf mentzelia] (3) (1977)

Mentzelia ornata Torr. – See *Mentzelia laevicaulis* (Dougl. ex Hook.)

Torr. & Gray

Mentzelia ornata Torr. & Gray. – See *Mentzelia laevicaulis* (Dougl. ex Hook.) Torr. & Gray

Mentzelia reverchonii (Urban & Gilg) Thomps. & Zavortink – Reverchon's blazing star [Reverchon's blazingstar] (50) (present)

Menyanthes (Tourn.) L. – See *Menyanthes* L.

Menyanthes L. – Bogbean [Bog-bean, Bog bean] (1, 138, 155) (1923–1942), Buckbean [Buck bean, Buck-bean] (2, 4, 50, 85, 92, 156, 158) (1895–present), Marsh-trefoil [Marsh trefoil] (1) (1932)

Menyanthes nymphoides L. – See *Nymphoides peltata* (Gmel.) Kuntze

Menyanthes trachysperma Michx. – See *Nymphoides aquatica* (J. F. Gmel.) Kuntze

Menyanthes trifoliata L. – American buckbean (7) (1828), Bachsbohne (6) (1892), Bean trefoil (5, 92, 156, 158) (1876–1923), Bieberklee (158) (1900), Bitter trefoil (5, 92, 158) (1876–1913), Bitterklee (German) (6, 158) (1892–1900), Bitter-root [Bitter root, Bitterroot] (6, 7) (1828–1892), Bitterworm [Bitter worm, Bitter-worm] (5, 92, 158) (1876–1913), Bitterwort [Bitter wort] (156) (1923), Bog hop (156, 158) (1900–1923), Bogbean [Bog-bean, Bog bean] (5, 6, 49, 92, 109, 131, 156, 158) (1892–1949), Bog-myrtle [Bog myrtle] (5, 92, 156, 158) (1876–1923) ME, Bognut [Bog-nut, Bog nut] (5, 156, 158) (1900–1923), Brookbean [Brook-bean] (5, 92, 156, 158) (1876–1923), Buckbean [Buck bean, Buck-bean] (1, 3, 5, 6, 10, 19, 49, 50, 57, 63, 72, 93, 109, 131, 148, 156, 158, 184) (1793–present), Common bogbean (138, 155) (1923–1942), Dreiblatt (German) (158) (1900), Fieberklee (German) (6, 158) (1892), Marsh-clover [Marsh clover] (5, 6, 92, 156, 158) (1892–1923), Marsh-trefoil [Marsh trefoil] (5, 6, 7, 10, 49, 77, 92, 107, 156, 158, 187) (1818–1923), Menyanthe (French) (158) (1900), Menyanthe trefle (French) (6) (1892), Menyanthe trefle d'eau (French) (7) (1828), Menyanthes (57) (1917), Moon flower [Moon-flower, Moonflower] (5, 92, 158) (1876–1913), Moor flower [Moor-flower] (156) (1923), Three-leaf bogbean [Three-leaved bog-bean] (187) (1818), Three-leaf buckbean [Three-leaved buck-bean] (187) (1818), Trébal acuatico (Spanish) (158) (1900), Trefle d'eau (French) (6, 158) (1892–1900), Wasserklee (German) (158) (1900), Water shamrock (5, 6, 7, 57, 92, 156, 158) (1828–1923), Water trefoil (5, 49, 156, 158) (1898–1923)

Menyanthes verna (Raf.) – See *Menyanthes trifoliata* L.

Menziesia ferruginea Sm. – Mountain heath (156) (1923), Smooth menziesia (5) (1913)

Menziesia glabella Gray – See *Menziesia ferruginea* Sm.

Menziesia pilosa (Michx. ex Lam.) Juss. ex Pers. – Allegheny menziesia [Alleghany menziesia] (5, 138) (1913–1923), Minnie bush [Minnie-bush] (5, 156) (1913–1923)

Menziesia pilosa (Michx.) Pers. – See *Menziesia pilosa* (Michx. ex Lam.) Juss. ex Pers.

Menziesia Smith. – Menziesia (138) (1923)

Meratia (Loisel) – See *Chimonanthus* Lindl.

Mercurialis annua L. – Annual mercury (107) (1919), Female mercury [Female mercurie] (178, 180) (1526–1633), Herb mercury (5, 156) (1913–1923), Male mercury [Male mercurie] (178) (1526), Mercury herb (92) (1876), Mercury-weed [Mercury weed] (57) (1917)

Mercurialis L. – Mercury (156) (1923)

Meriolix intermedia Rydb. – See *Calylophus serrulatus* (Nutt.) Raven

Meriolix Raf. – See *Calylophus* Spach (all US species)

Meriolix serrulata (Nutt.) Walp. – See *Calylophus serrulatus* (Nutt.) Raven

Merremia dissecta (Jacq.) Hallier f. – Alamo-vine [Alamo vine] (122, 124) (1937) TX

Mertensia ciliata (James) D. Don – Mountain bluebells (138, 155) (1923–1942), Tall fringed bluebells (50) (present)

Mertensia foliosa A. Nels. – See *Mertensia oblongifolia* (Nutt.) G. Don

Mertensia fusiformis Greene – See *Mertensia oblongifolia* (Nutt.) G. Don

Mertensia lanceolata (Pursh) DC. – Lance-leaf bluebells [Lanceleaf bluebells] (155) (1942), Lance-leaf lungwort [Lance-leaved lungwort] (5, 131) (1899–1913), Prairie bluebells (50) (present), Wild forget-me-not (3, 127) (1933–1977)

Mertensia lanceolata (**Pursh**) **DC. var.** *lanceolata* – Prairie bluebells (50) (present)

Mertensia maritima (**L.**) **Gray** – Oyster plant [Oyster-plant, Oyster-plant] (156) (1923), Sea bugloss (156) (1923), Sea lungwort (2, 156) (1895–1942)

Mertensia maritima (**L.**) **Gray var.** *maritima* – Oyster plant [Oyster-plant, Oysterplant] (5) (1913), Sea bugloss (5) (1913), Sea lungwort (5) (1913)

Mertensia oblongifolia (**Nutt.**) **G. Don** – Green-leaf bluebells [Green-leaf bluebells] (155) (1942), Leafy bluebells (155) (1942), Oblong bluebells (50) (present), Oblong-leaf bluebells [Oblongleaf bluebells] (155) (1942), Spindle-root bluebells [Spindleroot bluebells] (155) (1942)

Mertensia paniculata (**Aiton**) **G. Don.** – Bluebell [Blue-bell, Blue bell, Blue bells, Blue-bells] (35, 85) (1806–1923), Tall lungwort (5, 72, 131) (1899–1913)

Mertensia platyphylla **Heller** – Cowslip [Cowslips, Cowslyp] (35) (1806)

Mertensia **Roth** – Bluebell [Blue-bell, Blue bell, Blue bells, Blue-bells] (1, 50, 93, 109 138, 155) (1923–present), Languid lady (1) (1932), Lungwort [Lung-wort] (1, 93, 156, 158) (1900–1936)

Mertensia virginica (**L.**) **DC.** – possibly *Mertensia virginica* (L.) Pers. ex Link

Mertensia virginica (**L.**) **Pers. ex Link** – American lungwort (46) (1879), Cowslip [Cowslips, Cowslyp] (35, 92) (1806–1876) William Clark, Lungwort [Lung-wort] (47, 63, 184) (1793–1899), Mountain cowslip (177) (1762), Virginia bluebells (50, 109, 138, 156) (1923–present), possibly Bluebell [Blue-bell, Blue bell, Blue bells, Blue-bells] (5, 63, 156) (1899–1923), possibly Blue-iris [Blue iris] (156) (1923), possibly Bunchflower [Bunch-flower, Bunch flower] (156) (1923), possibly Old-lady's-bonnet [Old lady's bonnet] (156) (1923), possibly Roanoke bells (5, 156) (1913–1923) no longer in use by 1923, possibly Smooth lungwort (2, 156) (1895–1923), possibly Tree lungwort (5, 156) (1913–1923) no longer in use by 1923, possibly Virginia cowslip (5, 63, 72, 92, 93, 101, 156) (1876–1949), possibly Virginia lungwort (48, 92, 156) (1882–1923)

Mertensia virginica **DC.** – possibly *Mertensia virginica* (L.) Pers. ex Link

Mertensia virginica **Pers.** – See *Mertensia virginica* (L.) Pers. ex Link

Mertensia viridis (**A. Nels.**) **A. Nels.** – See *Mertensia oblongifolia* (Nutt.) G. Don

Mesadenia atriplicifolia (**L.**) **Raf.** – See *Arnoglossum atriplicifolium* (L.) H. E. Robins.

Mesadenia **Raf.** – See *Arnoglossum* Raf. (all US species)

Mesadenia tuberosa (**Nutt.**) **Britton** – See *Arnoglossum plantagineum* Raf.

Mesadenis reniformis (**Muhl.**) **Raf.** – See *Arnoglossum muehlenbergii* (Schultz-Bip.) H. E. Robins.

Mesembryanthemum cordifolium – See *Aptenia cordifolia* (L. f.) Schwant.

Mesembryanthemum crystallinum **L.** – Diamond plant (92) (1876), Ice plant [Ice-plant, Iceplant] (15, 19, 107, 109, 138) (1840–1949), Iceplant mesembryanthemum (155) (1942)

Mesembryanthemum **L.** – Dew plant [Dew-plant] (73) (1892) Northern OH, Fig-marigold [Figmarigold, Figmarigold] (138, 155) (1931–1942), Mesembryanthemum (155) (1942), Rat-tail pink (73) (1892) Dorchester MA, possibly Stoneface (109) (1949)

Mesosphaerum spicatum [**Rusby**] – See *Hyptis mutabilis* (A. Rich.) Briq.

Mespilus apiifolia [**Marsh.**] – See *Crataegus marshallii* Eggl. (taxonomic status is unresolved (PL))

Mespilus arborea **Michx. f.** – See *Amelanchier arborea* (Michx. f.) Fern.

Mespilus arbutifolia **L.** – See *Adenorachis arbutifolia* (L.) Nieuwl.

Mespilus canadensis **L.** – See *Pyrus canadensis* (L.) Farw.

Mespilus canadensis oligocarpa **Michx.** – See *Amelanchier bartramiana* (Tausch) M. Roem.

Mespilus crus galli – possibly *Crataegus crus-galli* L.

Mespilus cuneiformis [**Marsh.**] – See *Crataegus cuneiformis* (Marshall) Eggl.

Mespilus **L.** – Epine (8) (1785), Medlar [Medlars] or Medlar tree (8, 109, 138, 184) (1785–1949), White thorn [Whitethorn, White thorne] (167) (1814)

Mespilus prunifolia – See *Photinia floribunda* (Lindl.) Robertson & Phipps

Metopium toxiferum (**L.**) **Krug & Urban** – Poison ash (92, 165) (1807–1876), Poisonwood [Poison wood, Poison-wood] (165) (1807), Torchwood [Torch wood] (46) (1879)

Metrosideros **Banks ex Gaertn.** – Iron tree [Irontree] (138) (1923)

Micrampelis lobata (**Michx.**) **Greene** – See *Echinocystis lobata* (Michx.) Torr. & Gray

Micrampelis **Raf.** – See *Echinocystis* Torr. & Gray

Micranthemum micranthemoides (**Nutt.**) **Wettst.** – Nuttall's micranthemum (5) (1913)

Micranthes caroliniana (**Gray**) **Small.** – See *Saxifraga caroliniana* Gray

Micranthes **Haw.** – See *Saxifraga* L.

Micranthes micranthidifolia (**Haw.**) **Small.** – See *Saxifraga micranthidifolia* (Haw.) Steud.

Micranthes nivalis (**L.**) **Small.** – See *Saxifraga nivalis* L.

Micranthes pennsylvanica (**L.**) **Haw.** – See *Saxifraga pensylvanica* L.

Micranthes pensylvanica (**L.**) **Haw.** – See *Saxifraga pensylvanica* L.

Micranthes texana (**Buckl.**) **Small.** – See *Saxifraga texana* Buckl.

Micranthes virginiensis (**Michx.**) **Small.** – See *Saxifraga virginiensis* Michx. var. *virginiensis*

Microchloa **R. Br.** – Small grass (92) (1876)

Micromeris chamissonis [(**Benth.**) **Greene**] – See *Clinopodium douglasii* (Benth.) Kuntze

Micropetalon lanceolatum **Michx.** – See *Stellaria lanceolata* (Michx.) Torr.

Microphacos **Rydb.** – See *Astragalus* L.

Microrhamnus ericoides **Gray** – See *Condalia ericoides* (Gray) M.C. Johnston

Microseris cuspidata (**Pursh**) **Sch. Bip.** – See *Nothocalais cuspidata* (Pursh) Greene

Microseris **D. Don** – Microseris (155, 158) (1900–1942) Greek for "little endive"

Microseris nutans (**Hook.**) **Schultz-Bip.** – Wild dandelion (101) (1905) MT

Microseris nutans **Gray** – See *Microseris nutans* (Hook.) Schultz-Bip.

Microsorum scolopendria (**Burm. f.**) **Copeland** – See *Phymatosorus scolopendria* (Burm. f.) Pic. Serm.

Microsteris micrantha (**Kellogg**) **Greene** – See *Phlox gracilis* (Hook.) Greene subsp. *humilis* (Greene) Mason

Microstylis monophyllos – See *Malaxis monophyllos* (L.) Sw.

Microstylis **Nutt.** – See *Malaxis* Soland. ex Sw.

Microstylis ophioglossoides [(**Muhl. ex Willd.**) **Nutt. ex Eaton**] – See *Malaxis unifolia* Michx.

Microstylis ophioglossoides **W.** – See *Malaxis unifolia* Michx.

Microstylis unifolia (**Michx.**) **B.S.P.** – See *Malaxis unifolia* Michx.

Microthlaspi perfoliatum (**L.**) **F. K. Mey.** – Clasp-leaf pennycress [Claspleaf pennycress] (50) (present), Perfoliate pennycress [Perfoliate penny cress] (4, 5) (1913–1986), Small-flower microsteris [Small-flowered microsteris] (5) (1913)

Miegia macrosperma **Pers.** – See *Arundinaria gigantea* (Walt.) Muhl. subsp. *gigantea*

Miegia **Persoon** – See *Arundinaria* Michx.

Mikania scandens (**L.**) **Willd.** – Climbing boneset (5, 97, 106, 122, 124, 156) (1913–1937), Climbing hempweed (5, 92, 106, 109, 156) (1876–1949), Climbing mikania (187) (1818), Climbing thoroughwort (19) (1840), Duckblind (106) (1930) Kankakee IL

Mikania scandens **Willd.** – See *Mikania scandens* (L.) Willd.

Mikania **Willd.** – Climbing hempweed (2) (1895)

Milium compressum **Sw.** – See *Axonopus compressus* (Sw.) Beauv.

Milium effusum **L.** – American millet grass [American milletgrass] (50) (present), Millet grass [Milletgrass] (19, 92) (1840–1876), Tall millet grass (5, 85) (1913–1932), Wild millet (56, 87, 94) (1885–1915)

Milium **L.** – Millet grass [Milletgrass] (1, 10, 50, 66, 155) (1818–present)

Milium nigricans – See *Sorghum bicolor* (L.) Moench

Milium pungens **T. & G.** – See *Piptatherum pungens (Torr.) Barkworth*

Milla biflora **Cav.** – Mexican star [Mexican-star] (138) (1923)

Milla **Cav.** – Mexican star [Mexican-star] (109) (1949)

Millegrana radiola **(L.) Druce** – See *Radiola linoides* Roth

Millettia **Wight & Arn.** – Millettia (138) (1923)

Millium **(Tourn.) L.** – See *Milium* L.

Mimetanthe pilosa **(Benth.) Greene** – Hairy monkey-flower (49) (1898)

Mimosa aculeaticarpa **Ortega var.** *biuncifera* **(Benth.) Barneby** – Cat-claw mimosa [Catsclaw mimosa, Catclaw mimosa] (4, 50, 155) (1942–present), Cat's-claw [Catclaw, Cat-claw, Catsclaw, Catsclaw, Cat's-claw, Cat's claws] (124) (1937)

Mimosa biuncifera **Benth.** – See *Mimosa aculeaticarpa* Ortega var. *biuncifera* (Benth.) Barneby

Mimosa borealis **Gray** – Cat's-claw [Catclaw, Cat-claw, Catsclaw, Cats-claw, Cat's-claws, Cat's claws] (97) (1937), Fragrant mimosa (50, 155) (1942–present) , Mimosa (3) (1977), Pink mimosa (4, 97, 122) (1937–1986)

Mimosa cineraria **L.** – See *Prosopis cineraria* (L.) Druce

Mimosa filicioides **Cav.** – See *Acacia angustissima* (Mill.) Kuntze

Mimosa fragrans **Gray** – See *Mimosa borealis* Gray

Mimosa glandulosa **Michx.** – See *Desmanthus illinoensis* (Michx.) MacM. ex B. L. Robins. & Fern.

Mimosa horridula **Michx.** – See *Mimosa microphylla* Dry.

Mimosa **L.** – Acacia (7) (1828), Cat's-claw [Catclaw, Cat-claw, Catsclaw, Cats-claw, Cat's-claws, Cat's claws] (4, 152) (1913–1986), Gatunas (153) (1913) NM, Mimosa (4, 138, 155, 158) (1900–1986), Sensitive brier [Sensitivebrier, Sensitive briar] (1, 2, 4, 155, 158) (1895–1986), Sensitive plant (50) (Present), Shame vine (73) (1892) Northern MS, Shame vine [Shame-vine] (73) (1892)

Mimosa latisiliqua **L.** – See *Lysiloma latisiliquum* (L.) Benth.

Mimosa microphylla **Dry.** – Balsam-apple [Balsam apple, Balsamapple] (167) (1814), Be-shamed-Mary [Be shamed Mary] (156) (1923), Cat-claw sensitive brier [Catclaw sensitive brier, Catclaw sensitive brier] (155) (1942), Gander's-teeth [Gander teeth] (156) (1923), Little-leaf sensitive-brier [Littleleaf sensitive-briar, Little-leaf sensitivebrier] (50, 155) (1942–present), Narrow-leaf sensitive brier [Narrow-leaved sensitive brier] (, 97, 158) (1900–1937), Prairie sensitive plant (44) (1845), Saw brier [Saw-brier] (12, 38) (1820–1821), Sensitive brier [Sensitivebrier, Sensitive-brier, Sensitive briar, Sensitive-briar] (5, 19, 76, 85, 92, 93, 95, 97, 131, 156, 158) (1840–1937), Sensitive plant [Sensitive-plant, Sensitiveplant] (5, 158) (1900–1913), Sensitive-rose [Sensitive rose] (5, 73, 76, 156, 158) (1892–1923) Burnside SD, Shame vine [Shame-vine] (5, 122, 156, 158) (1900–1937), Shame-faced brier (76) (1896) Southwestern MO, Wild sensitive plant [Wild sensitive-plant] (28, 164) (1850–1854)

Mimosa nuttallii **(DC.) B. L. Turner** – Cat-claw sensitive brier [Catclaw sensitive brier, Catclaw sensitive brier] (4) (1986), Nuttall's sensitive-brier [Nuttall's sensitive-briar] (50) (present), Sensitive brier [Sensitivebrier, Sensitive briar] (4) (1986)

Mimosa pudica **L.** – Humble plant [Humble-plant] (92, 109, 182) (1791–1949), Sensitive plant [Sensitive-plant, Sensitiveplant] (92, 109, 138) (1876–1949), Touch-weed (92) (1876)

Mimosa quadrivalvis **L. var.** *angustata* **(Torr. & Gray) Barneby** – See *Mimosa microphylla* Dry.

Mimosa rupertiana **B. L. Turner** – Eastern sensitive brier [Eastern sensitive briar] (50) (present), Sensitive brier [Sensitivebrier, Sensitive

briar] (3) (1977), Western sensitive brier (4) (1986)

Mimosa scorpioides **L.** – See *Acacia nilotica* (L.) Willd. ex Delile

Mimulus alatus **Aiton** – Sharp-wing monkeyflower [Sharpwing monkeyflower, Sharpwing monkey-flower, Sharp-winged monkey flower, Sharp winged monkey flower, Sharp-winged monkeyflower] (3, 4, 5, 50, 72, 97, 122, 155) (1907–present), possibly Wingstem monkey flower [Wing-stemmed monkey-flower] (187) (1818)

Mimulus alatus **Soland.** – See *Mimulus alatus* Aiton

Mimulus brevipes **Benth.** – Canary monkey-flower [Canary monkey-flower] (138) (1923)

Mimulus cardinalis **Dougl. ex Benth.** – Crimson monkey-flower [Crimson monkeyflower] (138) (1923)

Mimulus floribundus **Dougl. ex Lindl.** – Many-flower monkey-flower [Manyflowered monkeyflower] (50) (present)

Mimulus fremonti – See *Mimulus fremontii* (Benth.) Gray

Mimulus fremontii **(Benth.) Gray** – Fremont's monkey-flower [Fremont monkeyflower] (50) (present)

Mimulus geyeri **Torr.** – See *Mimulus glabratus* Kunth var. *jamesii* (Torr. & Gray ex Benth.) Gray

Mimulus glabratus **Kunth** – Round-leaf monkey flower [Roundleaf monkeyflower, Roundleaf monkey-flower] (50) (present)

Mimulus glabratus **Kunth var.** *fremontii* **(Benth.) A. L. Grant** – See *Mimulus glabratus* Kunth var. *jamesii* (Torr. & Gray ex Benth.) Gray

Mimulus glabratus **Kunth var.** *jamesii* **(Torr. & Gray ex Benth.) Gray** – Geyer's monkey-flower (97) (1937), Geyer's yellow monkey-flower [Geyer's yellow monkey flower] (5) (1913), James' mimulus (72) (1907), James' monkey-flower [James' monkeyflower, James' monkey flower] (50, 86, 131) (1878–present), Round-leaf monkey flower [Roundleaf monkeyflower, Roundleaf monkey-flower] (3, 4) (1977–1986), Yellow monkey flower [Yellow monkey-flower] (85, 93, 95, 157) (1929–1936)

Mimulus glutinosus **J. C. Wendl.** – See *Diplacus aurantiacus* (W. Curtis) Jepson subsp. *aurantiacus*

Mimulus guttatus **DC.** – Common monkey-flower [Common monkey-flower] (155) (1942), Common yellow monkey-flower [Common yellow monkey flower] (4) (1986), Langsdorff's yellow monkey flower (5) (1913), Monkey flower [Monkey-flower, Monkeyflower] (3, 85) (1932–1977), Seep monkey-flower [Seep monkeyflower] (50) (present)

Mimulus jamesii **Torr. & Gray.** – See *Mimulus glabratus* Kunth var. *jamesii* (Torr. & Gray ex Benth.) Gray

Mimulus **L.** – Dog's-snout [Dogs-snout] (184) (1793), Monkey flower [Monkey-flower, Monkeyflower] (1, 4, 50, 10, 41, 63, 93, 109, 138, 156, 158) (1818–present), possibly Eunanus (158) (1900)

Mimulus langsdorfii **Donn ex Greene** – See *Mimulus guttatus* DC.

Mimulus lewisi – See *Mimulus lewisii* Pursh

Mimulus lewisii **Pursh** – Lewis' monkey-flower [Lewis monkeyflower] (138) (1923)

Mimulus luteus alpinus – possibly *Mimulus tilingii* Regel var. *caespitosus* (Greene) A. L. Grant

Mimulus luteus **L. var.** *alpinus* **Gray, non Lindl.** – possibly *Mimulus tilingii* Regel var. *caespitosus* (Greene) A. L. Grant

Mimulus moschata – See *Mimulus moschatus* Dougl. ex Lindl.

Mimulus moschatus **Dougl. ex Lindl.** – Eyebright [Eye-bright, Eye bright] (156) (1923), Musk flower [Musk-flower] (5, 156) (1913–1923), Musk plant [Musk-plant, Muskplant] (5, 14, 109, 138, 156) (1882–1949), Vegetable musk (92) (1876)

Mimulus pilosus **Wats.** – See *Mimetanthe pilosa* (Benth.) Greene

Mimulus ringens **L.** – Allegheny monkey-flower [Allegheny monkey-flower, Alleghany monkey-flower, Allegany monkeyflower] (3, 4, 50, 109, 138, 155) (1923–present), Blue monkey-flower (85) (1932), Eyebright [Eye-bright, Eye bright] (156) (1923), Gaping monkey flower [Gaping monkey-flower] (187) (1818), Monkey flower [Monkey-flower, Monkeyflower] (19, 72, 92, 114, 127, 131, 156) (1840–1933), Square-stem monkey-flower [Square-stemmed monkey-flower] (5, 93, 97) (1913–1937)

Mimulus tilingii **Regel var.** *caespitosus* **(Greene) A. L. Grant** – Alpine monkey-flower [Alpine monkeyflower] (138) (1923)

Minuartia arctica (**Stev. ex Ser.**) **Graebn.** – Arctic sandwort (5) (1913)

Minuartia biflora (**L.**) **Schinz & Thellung** – Siberian sandwort (5, 156) (1913–1923)

Minuartia caroliniana (**Walt.**) **Mattf.** – Carolina sandwort (155) (1942), Long-root (156) (1923), Mountain sandwort (156) (1923), Pine Barren sandwort [Pine-barren sandwort] (2, 5, 156) (1895–1923)

Minuartia dawsonensis (**Britt.**) **House** – Beach sandwort (5) (1913)

Minuartia drummondii (**Shinners**) **McNeill** – Drummond's stitchwort (50) (present)

Minuartia groenlandica (**Retz.**) **Ostenf.** – Greenland sandwort (138, 155) (1931–1942), Mountain sandwort (5, 156) (1913–1923), Mountain starwort (5, 156) (1913–1923)

Minuartia **L.** – Sandwort [Sand wort] (1) (1932)

Minuartia **L.** – Stitchwort [Stitch wort] (50) (present)

Minuartia michauxii (**Fenzl**) **Farw.** – Michaux's stitchwort (50) (present)

Minuartia michauxii (**Fenzl**) **Farw. var.** *michauxii* – Rock sandwort (5, 97, 131, 155) (1899–1942), Sandwort [Sand wort] (85) (1932), Upright sandwort (42) (1814)

Minuartia michauxii (**Fenzl**) **Farw. var.** *texana* (**B. L. Robins.**) **Mattf.** – Rock sandwort (4, 156) (1923–1986), Texas sandwort (5, 97) (1913–1937), Texas stitchwort (50) (present)

Minuartia patula (**Michx.**) **Mattf.** – Pitcher's sandwort (5, 97) (1913–1937), Pitcher's stitchwort (50) (present)

Minuartia rubella (**Wahlenb.**) **Hiern.** – Beautiful sandwort (50) (present), Tall nasturtium (178) (1526) CA, Tufted sandwort (138, 155) (1923–1942), Vernal sandwort (5, 131) (1899–1913)

Minuartia yukonensis **Hultén** – Larch-leaf sandwort [Larchleaf sandwort] (155) (1942)

Mirabilis albida (**Walt.**) **Heimerl** – Pale umbrella-wort [Pale umbrella wort, Pale umbrellawort] (5, 97, 131) (1899–1937), White four-o'clock [White four-o-clock] (4, 50) (1986–present)

Mirabilis carletonii (**Standl.**) **Standl.** – See *Mirabilis glabra* (S. Wats.) Standl.

Mirabilis dichotoma – See *Mirabilis jalapa* L.

Mirabilis exaltata (**Standl.**) **Standl.** – See *Mirabilis glabra* (S. Wats.) Standl.

Mirabilis glabra (**S. Wats.**) **Standl.** – Carleton's four-o'clock [Carleton four-o'clock] (4) (1986), Carleton's umbrella wort [Carleton's umbrella-wort] (5, 97) (1913–1937), Smooth four-o'clock (4, 50) (1986–present), Smooth umbrella-wort (97) (1937), Tall four-o'clock (4) (1986)

Mirabilis hirsuta (**Pursh**) **MacM.** – Hairy four-o'clock [Hairy four o'clock] (4, 50, 98) (1926–present), Hairy umbrella-wort [Hairy umbrellawort, Hairy umbrella-wort] (5, 72, 93, 97, 131, 158) (1899–1937), Musk (158) (1900)

Mirabilis jalapa **L.** – Beauty-of-the-night [Beauty of the night] (92) (1876), Common four-o'-clock (138) (1923), False jalap (92) (1876), Four-o'-clock [Four-o'clock, Four-o-clock, Four-o'-clocks] (3, 92, 109) (1876–1977), Jalap plant (92) (1876), Marvel-of-Peru [Marvel of Peru] (92, 109, 178) (1526–1949), Mexican four-o'clock [Mexican four o'clock] (19) (1840), Nyctage (174) (1753), Prett-per-night (77) (1898) Sulphut Grove OH, Pretty-by-night (73) (1892) Fort Worth TX, World's-wonder [World's wonder] (92) (1876)

Mirabilis **L.** – False jalap (7) (1828), Four-o'-clock [Four-o'clock, Four-o-clock, Four-o'-clocks] (4, 7, 50, 122, 138, 155) (1828–present), Marvel-of-Peru [Marvel of Peru] (147) (1856)

Mirabilis linearis (**Pursh**) **Heimerl** – Narrow-leaf four-o'clock [Narrowleaf four-o'clock] (4, 50) (1986–present), Narrow-leaf umbrella-wort [Narrow-leaved umbrella wort, Narrow-leaved umbrellawort] (5, 93, 97, 131) (1899–1937), Umbrella-wort [Umbrella wort] (85) (1932)

Mirabilis longiflora **L.** – Afternoon ladies (92) (1876), Evening beauty (92) (1876), Marvel-of-Peru [Marvel of Peru] (92) (1876), Sweet four-o'-clock (138) (1923)

Mirabilis nyctaginea (**Michx.**) **MacM.** – Four-o'-clock [Four-o'clock, Four-o-clock, Four-o'-clocks] (80) (1913), Heart-leaf four-o'clock [Heartleaf four o'clock] (50) (present), Heart-leaf umbrella-wort [Heart-leaved umbrella-wort, Heart-leaved umbrella wort] (5, 93, 97, 131) (1899–1936), Kahtstakat (Pawnee, yellow medicine) (37) (1919), Makan-wasek (Omaha-Ponca, strong medicine) (37) (1919), Poípie (Dakota) (37) (1919), Umbrella plant [Umbrella-plant] (80) (1913) IA, Umbrella-wort [Umbrella wort] (156) (1923), Wild four-o'clock [Wild four o'clock] (4, 37, 72, 80, 82, 93, 121, 127, 145, 156) (1897–1986)

Mirabilis oxybaphoides (**Gray**) **Gray** – Smooth spreading four-o'clock (50) (present), Spreading four-o'clock (4) (1986)

Miscanthus **Anderss.** – Silver grass [Silvergrass] (50, 155) (1942–present)

Miscanthus japonicus **Anders.** – See *Miscanthus sinensis* Anderss.

Miscanthus sacchariflorus (**Maxim.**) **Franch.** – Amur silver grass [Amur silvergrass] (50) (present)

Miscanthus sinensis **Anderss.** – Chinese silver grass [Chinese silvergrass] (50) (present), Eulalia (56, 94, 109, 138, 163) (1852–1949), Japanese plume grass (5) (1913)

Misopates orontium (**L.**) **Raf.** – Corn snapdragon (5, 155) (1913–1942), Lesser snapdragon (5) (1913)

Mitchella **L.** – Mitchella (8) (1785), Mitchella (French) (8) (1785), Partridge-berry [Partridgeberry, Partridge berry] (1, 2, 10, 138, 156) (1818–1932), Squawberry [Squaw berry, Squaw-berry] (2) (1895), Twinberry [Twin-berry, Twin berry] (1) (1932)

Mitchella repens **L.** – Boxberry [Box berry, Box-berry] (73, 156) (1892–1923) Bedford MA, Checker-berry [Checker berry, Checkerberry, Chequer-berry, Chequer berry] (18, 49, 53, 92, 156) (1805–1923), Chicken-berry [Chicken berry] (76, 156) (1896–1923) Western US, no longer in use by 1923, Cowberry [Cow-berry, Cow berry] (73, 156) (1892–1923) Ulster Co NY, Creeping checker-berry [Creeping checker berry] (6) (1892), Creeping evergreen mitchella (8) (1785), Creeping mitchella (187) (1818), Deerberry [Deer-berry, Deer berry] (6, 49, 53, 92, 156) (1892–1923) no longer in use by 1923, Eyeberry [Eye-berry] (156) (1923), Foxberry [Fox berry, Fox-berry] (76, 156) (1896–1923) Lynn MA, no longer in use by 1923, Groundberry [Ground-berry, Ground berry] (34) (1834), Hive vine [Hive-vine, Hivevine] (92, 156) (1876–1923) no longer in use by 1923, Jesuit-berry (156) (1923), Mitchella (54, 57, 174, 177) (1753–1917), Mitchella rampant (French) (8) (1785), Mountain-tea (156) (1923), Oneberry [One-berry, One berry] (49, 53, 76, 156) (1896–1923) no longer in use by 1923, One-berry leaves [One berry leaves] (92) (1876), Partridge vine [Partridge-vine] (156) (1923), Partridge-berry [Partridgeberry, Partridge berry] (5, 6, 7, 19, 49, 52, 53, 54, 57, 61, 72, 92, 107, 109, 122, 124, 138, 156) (1828–1949), Partridge-berry vine [Partridge berry vine] (92) (1876), Pigeon-berry [Pigeon berry] (76, 156) (1896–1923) MA, no longer in use by 1923, Pigeon-plum [Pigeon plum] (156) (1923) no longer in use by 1923, Pudding-plum [Pudding plum] (156) (1923) no longer in use by 1923, Running box (156) (1923), Snakeberry [Snake berry, Snake-berry] (73, 156) (1892–1923) NY, no longer in use by 1923, Snake-plum [Snake plum] (76) (1896) Oxford Co. ME, Squaw vine [Squaw-vine] (6, 49, 52, 53, 54, 57, 73, 92, 107, 156) (1892–1923) parts of Northeastern US, Squawberry [Squaw berry, Squaw-berry] (6, 53, 109, 156) (1892–1949), Squawberry vine (49) (1898), Squaw-plum [Squaw plum] (156) (1923), Teaberry [Tea-berry, Tea berry, Tea-berries] (156) (1923), Twinberry [Twin-berry, Twin berry] (5, 97, 109, 156) (1913–1949), Two-eyed berry [Two-eyed berries, Two-eyes berry, Two-eye berry] (73, 156) (1892–1923) Wakefield MA, no longer in use by 1923, Two-eyed chequer-berry (6) (1892), Two-eyes plum (76) (1896) Oxford Co. ME, Winter-clover [Winter clover] (6, 49, 92, 156) (1876–1923) no longer in use by 1923

Mitella (**Tourn.**) **L.** – See *Mitella* L.

Mitella cordifolia (**Lam.**) – See *Mitella nuda* L.

Mitella diphylla **L.** – American bastard-sanicle (187) (1818), American mitella (190) (~1759), Bishop's-cap [Bishop's cap, Bishops-cap,

Bishopscap] (63, 92, 156) (1876–1923), Common bishop's-cap [Common bishopscap] (138) (1923), Common miterwort (2) (1895), Coolwort (79) (1891) NH, Currant-leaf [Currant leaf] (5, 19, 92, 156) (1840–1923), Fairy cup (5, 74, 156) (1893–1923) NY, False sanicle (5, 74, 156) (1893–1923) NY, Fringe cup [Fringe-cup] (5, 74, 156) (1893–1923) NY, Mitrewort [Mitre-wort, Mitre wort] (5, 63, 156) (1899–1923), Two-leaf bishop's-cap [Two-leaved bishop's cap, Two-leaved bishop's-cap] (5, 72, 156) (1907–1923), Two-leaf miterwort [Two-leaved miterwort] (2) (1895)

Mitella L. – Bishop's-cap [Bishop's cap, Bishops-cap, Bishopscap] (1, 2, 109, 138) (1895–1949), Miterwort [Mitrewort] (1, 2, 155, 158) (1895–1942), Mitrewort [Mitre-wort, Mitre wort] (109, 156) (1923–1949)

Mitella nuda L. – Bishop's-cap [Bishop's cap, Bishops-cap, Bishopscap] (3, 4, 156) (1923–1986), Coolwort (57) (1917), Crystal flower (156) (1923), Naked miterwort (155) (1942), Naked-stalk miterwort [Naked-stalked miterwort] (2, 156) (1895–1923), Stoloniferous bishop's-cap [Stoloniferous bishop's cap] (5) (1913), Stoloniferous mitrewort (5) (1913)

Mitreola petiolata (**J. F. Gmel.**) **Torr. & Gray** – Lax hornpod (50) (present), Mitreola (174, 177) (1753–1762), Mitrewort [Mitre-wort, Mitre wort] (5, 156) (1913–1923), Pink snakeroot [Pink snake root] (7, 92) (1828–1876)

Mnesithea rugosa (**Nutt.**) **Koning & Sosef** – See *Coelorachis rugosa* (Nutt.) Nash

Modiola caroliniana (**L.**) **G. Don** – Bristly-fruit mallow [Bristly fruited mallow] (5, 156) (1913–1923)

Modiola multifida **Moench** – See *Modiola caroliniana* (L.) G. Don

Modiolus carolinianus – See *Modiola caroliniana* (L.) G. Don

Moehringia L. – Sandwort (5) (1913), Sandwort [Sand wort] (50, 93, 158) (1900–present)

Moehringia lateriflora (**L.**) **Fenzl** – Blunt-leaf moehringia [Blunt-leaved moehringia] (5) (1913), Blunt-leaf sandwort [Bluntleaf sandwort] (50, 5, 72, 131, 155) (1899–present), Broad-leaf chickweed [Broad-leaved chickweed] (127) (1933), Grove sandwort (4) (1986), Lateral-flowered sandwort [Lateral flowered sandwort] (42) (1814), Sandwort [Sand wort] (19) (1840), Showy sandwort (156) (1923), Side-flower sandwort [Side-flowered sandwort, Side-flowering sandwort] (2, 156) (1895–1923)

Moehringia macrophylla (**Hook.**) **Fenzl** – Large-leaf moehringia [Large-leaved moehringia] (5) (1913), Large-leaf sandwort [Large-leaved sandwort] (5) (1913)

Moehringia macrophylla (**Hook.**) **Torr.** – See *Moehringia macrophylla* (Hook.) Fenzl

Moldavica (**Tourn.**) **Adans.** – possibly *Dracocephalum* L.

Moldavica moldavica (**L.**) **Britton** – See *Dracocephalum moldavica* L.

Moldavica parviflora (**Nutt.**) **Britton** – See *Dracocephalum parviflorum* Nutt.

Molina salicifolia **Ruiz & Pavón** – See *Baccharis salicifolia* (Ruiz & Pavón) Pers.

Molinia caerulea (**L.**) **Moench** – Blue pearl grass (56) (1901), Indian grass [Indian-grass, Indiangrass] (5) (1913), Lavender grass (5) (1913), Molinia (94) (1901), Moor grass [Moor-grass] (5) (1913), Purple melic grass (5) (1913)

Mollugo L. – Carpetweed [Carpet weed, Carpet-weed] (1, 13, 50, 93, 155, 158, 184) (1793–present), Indian chickweed (1, 13, 15, 158) (1849–1932)

Mollugo verticillata L. – Carpetweed [Carpet weed, Carpet-weed] (4, 5, 15, 19, 62, 63, 72, 85, 92, 93, 97, 122, 145, 155, 156, 158, 187) (1818–1986), Devil's-grip [Devil's grip] (5, 76, 156, 158) (1896–1923) North Berwick ME, name given by section hands along railroad because the plant is so hard to eradicate, Green carpetweed (50) (present), Indian chickweed (5, 62, 156, 187) (1818–1923)

Moluccella L. – Molucca balm [Molucca-balm] (138) (1923)

Moluccella laevis L. – Molucca balm [Molucca-balm] (19, 77, 92, 109, 138) (1840–1949), Old-maid's-bonnet [Old maids' bonnet, Old maid's bonnets] (77) (1898) Sulphut Grove OH, Shell flower

[Shell-flower, Shellflower) (19, 77, 109) (1840–1949), East Indian balm [East Indian balme] (178) (1526)

Momordica balsamina L. – Balsam opfel (180) (1633), Balsam-apple [Balsam apple, Balsamapple] (19, 61, 92, 107, 109, 138) (1840–1949), Balsamina (92) (1876), Female balsam-apple [Female balsam apple] (178, 180) (1526–1633), possibly Balsam vine (7, 92) (1828–1876)

Momordica charantia L. – Balsam-pear (109, 138) (1923–1949)

Momordica cylindrica L. – See *Luffa aegyptiaca* Mill.

Momordica elaterium – See *Ecballium elaterium* (L.) A. Rich.

Momordica L. – Balsam-apple [Balsam apple, Balsamapple] (138) (1923)

Monachne [**Beauv.**] – See *Panicum* L.

Monanthochloe littoralis **Engelm.** – Salt-cedar [Salt cedar, Saltcedar] (94, 163) (1852–1901), Salt-cedar grass [Salt cedar grass] (122) (1937)

Monarda bradburiana **Beck** – Bradbury's monarda [Bradbury monarda] (4, 5, 97) (1913–1986), Eastern beebalm (50) (present)

Monarda citriodora **Cerv. ex Lag.** – Lemon beebalm (3, 4, 50, 155) (1942–present), Lemon mint (4, 156) (1923–1986), Lemon monarda (156) (1923), Prairie bergamot (156) (1923), Purple lemon monarda (5, 97) (1913–1937)

Monarda citriodora **Cerv. ex Lag. subsp.** *citriodora* **var.** *citriodora* – Lemon beebalm (50) (present)

Monarda clinopodia L. – Balsam balm (5) (1913), Basil-balm [Basil balm] (156) (1923)

Monarda clinopodioides **Gray** – Basil beebalm (3, 4, 50) (1977–present), False balm (97) (1937) OK

Monarda coccinea **Raf.** – See *Monarda didyma* L.

Monarda didyma L. – American beebalm [American bee balm] (5) (1913), Beebalm [Bee balm, Bee-balm] (2, 86, 92, 107, 109, 156) (1878–1949), Blue balm (92) (1876), Fragrant balm (2, 5, 109, 156) (1895–1949), Horse-mint [Horsemint, Horse mint] (5, 7, 156) (1828–1923), Indian plume [Indian's plume] (5, 156) (1913–1923), Low balm (5, 92, 156) (1876–1923), Monarde ecarlatte (French) (7) (1828), Mountain balm (7, 92) (1828–1876), Mountain-mint [Mountain mint, Mountainmint] (5, 7, 19, 92, 156) (1828–1923), O-gee-chee (Fiery or flaming flowers) (86) (1878) possibly from native Oswego language, Oswego beebalm (138) (1923), Oswego tea [Oswego-tea] (2, 5, 7, 14, 86, 92, 107, 109, 138, 156, 184) (1828–1949), Red balm (5, 7, 92, 156) (1828–1923), Red bergamot (156) (1923), Red mint (190) (~1759), Rose-balm [Rose balm] (92, 156) (1876–1923), Scarlet rose-balm [Scarlet rosebalm, Scarlet rose balm] (7, 92) (1828–1876), Squarestalk [Square-stalk, Square stalk] (7) (1828), Square-stem monkey-flower [Square-stemmed monkey-flower] (156) (1923), Sweet Mary (156) (1923)

Monarda dispersa **Small.** – See *Monarda citriodora* Cerv. ex Lag.

Monarda fistulosa f. *oblongata* (**Aiton**) **Voss** – See *Monarda fistulosa* L. subsp. *fistulosa*

Monarda fistulosa L. – Bergamot (85) (1932), H'eh'aka ta pezhuta (Dakota, elk medicine) (37) (1919), Hexaka tawote (Lakota, elk food) (121) (1918?–1970?), Horse-mint [Horsemint, Horse mint] (37, 85, 114, 121, 124, 156) (1894–1937), Nidsida (Osage) (121) (1918?–1970?), Oswego tea [Oswego-tea] (5, 93, 156, 157) (1900–1936), Parakaha (Pawnee) (37) (1919) The Pawnee recognized four varietes of the species distinguished by odor and growth form, Pezhe pa (Omaha-Ponca, bitter herb) (37) (1919), Tsakus tawirat (Pawnee) (37) (1919), Tsusahtu (Pawnee, ill smelling) (37) (1919), Waxpe waštemna (Lakota, odorous leaves) (121) (1918?–1970?), Wild bergamont [Wildbergamont] (2, 5, 37, 47, 48, 50, 57, 63, 72, 93, 95, 97, 106, 109, 121, 127, 131, 138, 156, 157) (1852–present), Wild bergamot beebalm (155) (1942), possibly Izna-kithe-iga hi (Omaha-Ponca) (37) (1919), possibly Tsostu (Pawnee) (37) (1919), possibly Wah'pe washtemma (Dakota, fragrant leaves) (37) (1919)

Monarda fistulosa L. subsp. *fistulosa* – Wild bergamot [Wildbergamont] (3, 50) (1977–present), Wild bergamot (19, 92) (1840–1876)

Monarda fistulosa L. subsp. *fistulosa* var. *menthifolia* (**Graham**)

Morella caroliniensis (P. Mill.) Smalla

Fern. – Mint-leaf beebalm [Mintleaf beebalm] (50) (present), Wild bergamont [Wildbergamont] (3, 50) (1977–present)

Monarda fistulosa L. subsp. *fistulosa* var. *mollis* (L.) Benth. – Bibig-wûnûkûk' (Chippewa, resembling a flute) (40) (1928), Hairy wild bergamot [Hairy wildbergamot] (138) (1923), Horse-mint [Horse-mint, Horse mint] (40, 101) (1905–1928), Okarini pisten (Sioux) (101) (1905) MT, Pale bergamot (85) (1932), Pale wild bergamot (5, 72, 93, 131) (1899–1936), Taken skina zuhapi (Sioux) (101) (1905) MT, Wabino'wûck (Chippewa, Eastern medicine) (40) (1928), Wild bergamot (50, 97) (1937–present)

Monarda fistulosa media – See *Monarda media* Willd.

Monarda fistulosa var. *washtemma* – possibly *Monarda fistulosa* L.

Monarda L. – Balmony (2) (1895), Beebalm [Bee balm, Bee-balm] (4, 50, 106, 138, 155, 156) (1923–present), Horse-mint [Horsemint, Horse mint] (1, 2, 4, 93, 106, 109, 156, 158) (1895–1986), Lemon mint (1) (1932), Mountain balm (10) (1818), Oswego tea [Oswego-tea] (34) (1834), Sweet Mary (75) (1894) NH, Wild bergamot (1, 93, 106, 158) (1900–1932)

Monarda media Willd. – Purple bergamot (5) (1913), possibly Purple wild bergamot [Purple wildbergamot] (138) (1923)

Monarda menthaefolia – See *Monarda fistulosa* L. subsp. *fistulosa* var. *menthifolia* (Graham) Fern.

Monarda menthifolia Graham – See *Monarda fistulosa* L. subsp. *fistulosa* var. *menthifolia* (Graham) Fern.

Monarda mollis L. – See *Monarda fistulosa* L. subsp. *fistulosa* var. *mollis* (L.) Benth.

Monarda oblongata A. – See *Monarda fistulosa* L. subsp. *fistulosa*

Monarda pectinata Nutt. – Lemon mint (1) (1932), Lemon monarda (97, 98) (1926–1937), Plains beebalm (4) (1986), Plains lemon monarda (5, 93) (1913–1936), Pony beebalm (50, 155) (1942–present), Prairie bergamot (5) (1913), Spotted beebalm (3, 4) (1977–1986)

Monarda punctata L. – Horse-mint [Horsemint, Horse mint] (1, 2, 5, 49, 52, 53, 57, 63, 72, 82, 97, 124, 156) (1895–1937), Monarda (52, 57, 92, 174) (1753–1917), Mountain-mint [Mountain mint, Mountainmint] (48) (1882), Rignum (5, 156) (1913–1923), Spotted beebalm (50, 138) (1923–present), Wild balm [Wild baulm] (181) (~1678)

Monarda punctata L. subsp. *punctata* var. *occidentalis* (Epling) Palmer & Steyermark – Dotted beebalm (4) (1986), Horse-mint [Horsemint, Horse mint] (3) (1977), Spotted beebalm (50) (present)

Monarda russeliana Nutt. ex Sims – Russell's beebalm [Russell beebalm] (138) (1923)

Monarda scabra Beck – See *Monarda fistulosa* L. subsp. *fistulosa* var. *mollis* (L.) Benth.

Monarda stanfieldii Small – Standfield's monarda (97) (1937)

Monese grandiflora Salisb. – See *Moneses uniflora* (L.) Gray

Moneses Salisb. ex S. F. Gray – One-flower pyrola [One-flowered pyrola] (2, 158) (1895–1900), One-flower wintergreen [One-flowered wintergreen] (1) (1932), Single-beauty [Single beauty] (1) (1932)

Moneses uniflora (L.) Gray – Consumption-weed [Consumption weed] (7) (1828), Moneses (155) (1942), Mossberry [Moss-berry, Moss berry] (107) (1919), One-flower pipsissewa [One-flowered pipsissewa] (103) (1870), One-flower pyrola [One-flowered pyrola] (107, 156, 158) (1900–1923), One-flower wintergreen [One-flowered wintergreen] (3, 4, 5, 85, 156, 158) (1900–1986), Single delight (50) (Present), Single-delight [Single delight] (50) (present), Snowdrop [Snowdrops, Snow-drops, Snow drop] (156) (1923)

Monita L. (possibly) – Water spring-beauty [Water spring beauty] (1) (1932)

Monniera rotundifolia Michx. – See *Bacopa rotundifolia* (Michx.) Wettst.

Monolepis nuttalliana (J. A. Schultes) Greene – Monolepis (5, 93, 131) (1899–1936), Nuttall's monolepis [Nuttall monolepis] (155) (1942), Nuttall's poverty-weed [Nuttall's povertyweed] (50) (present), Poverty-weed [Povertyweed, Poverty weed] (3, 4, 85, 122) (1932–1986)

Monolepis Schrad. – Monolepis (155, 158) (1900–1942), Poverty-weed [Povertyweed, Poverty weed] (1, 50) (1932–present)

Monotropa hypopithys L. – False beechdrops [False beech-drops, False beech drops] (2, 5, 92, 156) (1840–1923), Fir rape [Fir-rape] (156) (1923), Fir rope (5, 156) (1913–1923) no longer in use by 1923, Hairy pinesap [Hairy pine sap] (5) (1913), Pine sap (5, 72) (1907–1913), Pinesap [Pine sap, Pine-sap] (2, 4, 50, 92, 155, 156) (1876–present), Woolly bird's-nest [Woolly birds-nest] (187) (1818), Yellow birds-nest [Yellow bird's nest] (187) (1818), Yellow pinesap [Yellow pine-sap] (156) (1923)

Monotropa L. – Bird's-nest [Bird's nest, Birds-nest, Birds nest, Birds' nest, Birdsnest] (7, 167, 184) (1793–1828), possibly Indian pipe [Indianpipe, Indian-pipe] (2, 4, 50, 138, 155, 156, 158) (1895–present), possibly Pine sap (10) (1818), possibly Pinesap [Pine sap, Pine-sap] (1, 158) (1900–1932)

Monotropa lanuginosa Michx. – See *Monotropa hypopithys* L.

Monotropa uniflora L. – American iceplant [American ice-plant] (5, 157, 158) (1900–1929), Bird's-nest [Bird's nest, Birds-nest, Birds nest, Birds' nest, Birdsnest] (6, 19, 49, 156) (1840–1923), Bird's-nest plant [Bird's nest plant, Birds' nest plant] (5, 92, 158) (1876–1913), Broomrape [Broom-rape, Broom rape] (177) (1762), Common Indian pipe (2) (1895), Convulsion root [Convulsion-root] (5, 6, 73, 79, 157, 158) (1891–1929), Convulsion weed [Convulsion-weed] (5, 92, 156, 158) (1876–1923), Corpse plant [Corpse-plant] (2, 5, 6, 63, 92, 156, 157, 158) (1895–1929), Dutchman's-pipe [Dutchman's pipe, Dutchmanspipe, Dutchmans-pipe] (5, 75, 156, 158) (1900–1923), Einblüthige Monotropa (German) (6) (1892), Eyebright [Eye-bright, Eye bright] (5, 156, 158) (1900–1923), Fairy smoke [Fairy-smoke] (5, 75, 156, 157, 158) (1900–1929) Deering ME, Fir rape [Fir-rape] (92) (1876), Fit plant (5, 49) (1898–1913), Fit root [Fit-root, Fitroot] (5, 6, 7, 158) (1828–1892), Fit-root plant [Fit root plant] (92, 156) (1876–1923), Ghost-flower (5, 73, 77, 156, 157, 158) (1892–1929) NB, S. Berick ME, Ice plant [Ice-plant, Iceplant] (6, 7, 49, 61, 156) (1828–1923), Indian pipe [Indianpipe, Indian-pipe] (1, 3, 4, 5, 6, 19, 49, 50, 63, 72, 92, 95, 131, 138, 155, 156, 157, 158) (1892–present), Nest plant (6) (1892), Nest root [Nest-root] (7, 92, 158) (1828–1900), Ova-ova (6, 49, 92, 157, 158) (1876–1929), Pipe plant [Pipe-plant] (5, 6, 7, 49, 92, 156, 157, 158) (1828–1929), Tobacco-pipe [Tobacco pipe] (6) (1892)

Monotropsis odorata Ell. – See *Monotropsis odorata* Schwein. ex Ell.

Monotropsis odorata Schwein. ex Ell. – Carolina beechdrops [Carolina beech-drops] (5, 156) (1913–1923), Sweet pine-sap [Sweet pine sap] (5, 156) (1913–1923)

Monroa squarrosa (Nutt.) Torr. – False buffalo grass [False buffalo-grass, False buffalo-grass] (3, 5, 11, 50, 75, 85, 94, 122, 129, 140, 145, 152, 155, 163) (1852–present), Munro's grass [Munroe's grass, Munro-grass] (5, 119, 163) (1852–1938)

Monroa Torr. – False buffalo grass [False buffalograss, False buffalo-grass] (1, 50, 93) (1932–present)

Monstera deliciosa Liebm. – Ceriman (109, 138) (1923–1949)

Montia chamissoi (Ledeb. ex Spreng.) Greene – Crunocallis (5) (1913)

Montia fontana L. – Blinking chickweed [Blinking-chickweed] (5, 156) (1913–1923), Blinks (5, 156) (1913–1923), False springbeauty [False spring beauty] (19) (1840), Water chickweed (5, 156) (1913–1923), Water-blinks [Water blinks] (5, 156) (1913–1923)

Montia perfoliata Howell – See *Claytonia perfoliata* Donn ex Willd. subsp. *perfoliata*

Montropa – possibly *Monotropa* L.

Montropa hypopitys L. – See *Monotropa hypopithys* L.

Montropa uniflora L. – See *Monotropa uniflora* L.

Moraea Mill. – Moraea (138) (1923)

Morchella angusticeps Peck – Morelle [Morel] (35) (1806)

Morchella Dill. ex Pers – Carved Virginia Puffball (181) (~1678), Gerarde (181) (~1678), Morelle [Morel] (101) (1905)

Morchella esculenta (L.) Pers. – Mikai hthi (Omaha-Ponca, star sore) (37) (1830), Morelle [Morel] (37, 128) (1830–1933) Banister

Morella californica (Cham. & Schlecht.) Wilbur – California wax myrtle (106) (1930)

Morella caroliniensis (P. Mill.) Small – Bayberry [Bay berry] (5, 156)

(1913–1923), Northern bayberry (138) (1923), Small waxberry (5, 156) (1913–1923), Waxberry [Wax-berry, Wax berry] (106) (1930)

Morella cerifera (L.) Small – Arbre à Suif (French) (6) (1892), Arbre de Cire (French) (8) (1785), Bayberry [Bay berry] (2, 6, 19, 46, 49, 52, 53, 57, 61, 92, 156) (1840–1923), Bayberry bush (41) (1770), Candleberry [Candle berry, Candle-berry] or Candleberry tree [Candel berry tree, Candle-berry-tree] (5, 6, 41, 49, 52, 53, 73, 92, 156) (1770–1923), Candleberry myrtle [Candelberry myrtle, Candle-berry myrtle] (5, 8, 14, 92, 156, 177, 189) (1762–1923), Cirier (French) (8) (1785), Gale (184) (1793), Medomhumar (46) (1879) Nantucket natives, Myrkle bush [Myrkle-bushes] (156) (1923), Myrtles (182) (1791), Southern waxmyrtle (138) (1923), Sweet oak (5, 156) (1913–1923), Tallow bayberry [Tallow bay-berry] (5, 156) (1913–1923), Tallow shrub (5, 6, 41, 92, 156) (1770–1923), Wachs-busch (German) (6) (1892), Wachsgagle (German) (6) (1892), Wax myrtle [Wax-myrtle, Waxmyrtle] (2, 5, 6, 46, 49, 52, 53, 57, 92, 106, 109, 124, 156) (1879–1949), Wax tree (34) (1834), Waxberry [Wax-berry, Wax berry] (5, 49, 52, 53, 92, 156) (1898–1923), possibly Arbre de cire nain (French) (8) (1785), possibly Cirier nain (French) (8) (1785), possibly Dwarf candleberry myrtle (8) (1785)

Morella faya (Aiton) Wilbur – Fayal myrtle (20) (1857)

Morella inodora (Bartr.) Small – Cirier inodore (French) (20) (1857), Inodoruous candle tree (20) (1857), Odorless myrtle (106) (1930), Wax tree (182) (1791)

Morella pensylvanica (Mirbel) Kartesz – Bayberry [Bay berry] (109) (1949)

Moricandia arvensis (L.) DC. – Carlick (158) (1900), Carlock (158) (1900), Chadlock (158) (1900), Charlock (62, 138, 156, 158) (1900–1923) IN, Common mustard (82) (1930), Corn kale [Corn-kale] (156, 158) (1900–1923), Corn mustard (156, 158) (1900–1923), Crowd-grass (156) (1923), Crowdweed [Crowd-weed, Crowd weed] (158) (1900), Crunchweed [Crunch-weed] (156) (1923), Curlock (158) (1900), English charlock (80) (1913) IA, Field kale [Field-kale] (156, 158) (1900–1923), Kedlock (158) (1900), Kellock (158) (1900), Kerlock (158) (1900), Kilk (158) (1900), Kraut-grass (156) (1923), Krautweed [Kraut-weed, Kraut weed] (158) (1900), Mustard [Mustards] (80) (1913), Runchweed [Runch-weed, Runch weed] (156, 158) (1900–1923), Warlock (158) (1900), Watercress [Watercress, Water cress] (74) (1893) WV, Wild mustard (62, 80, 82, 131, 156, 158) (1899–1930), Yellow-flower [Yellow flower] (156, 158) (1900–1923)

Morinda citrifolia L. – Awl tree (92, 107) (1876–1919), Indian mulberry [Indian-mulberry] (92, 107, 138) (1876–1923)

Morinda L. – Indian mulberry [Indian-mulberry] (138) (1923)

Morinda roioc L. – See *Morinda royoc* L.

Morinda royoc L. – Redroot [Red-root, Red root] (76) (1896) West Indies

Moringa Adans. – Horseradish tree [Horseradish-tree, Horse-radish-tree] (138) (1923)

Moringa oleifera Lam. – Ben nuts (92) (1876), Ben oil (92) (1876), Horseradish tree [Horseradish-tree, Horse-radish-tree] (109, 138) (1923–1949)

Morongia angustata (Torr. & Gray) Britton – See *Mimosa microphylla* Dry.

Morongia Brit. – See *Mimosa* L.

Morongia microphylla (Dryand.) Britton – See *Mimosa microphylla* Dry.

Morongia uncinata (Willd.) Britton – See *Mimosa microphylla* Dry.

Morongia uncinata Willd. – See *Mimosa microphylla* Dry.

Morus (Tourn.) L. – See *Morus* L.

Morus acidosa [Griff.] – See *Morus australis* Poir.

Morus alba L. – European mulberry trees (182) (1791), Many-stem mulberry [Many-stemmed mulberry] (19) (1840), Pe-sang (Chinese) (110) (1886), Russian mulberry (95, 109, 112, 122, 124, 135, 138, 155) (1910–1949), Silkworm mulberry (138) (1923), Sycamine (92) (1876), Whit mulberry [Whit mulberries] (181) (~1678), White mulberry [White mulberrie] (1, 3, 4, 5, 19, 50, 82, 85, 93, 95, 97, 107,

109, 110, 138, 153, 155, 156, 178) (1526–present)

Morus alba L. var. *tatarica* (L.) Ser. – See *Morus alba* L.

Morus alba L. var. *tatarica* Loud. – See *Morus alba* L.

Morus alba tatarica – See *Morus alba* L.

Morus alba var. *multicaulis* (Perr.) Loudon – See *Morus alba* L.

Morus australis Poir. – Acid mulberry (138) (1923)

Morus L. – Meurier (41) (1770), Mulberry [Molberye] or Mulberry tree (1, 8, 10, 50, 57, 82, 93, 109, 138, 155, 158, 167, 184) (1785–present), Murier (French) (8) (1785)

Morus microphylla Buckl. – Mountain mulberry (122, 124) (1937) TX, Mulberry [Molberye] or Mulberry tree (153) (1913), Texas mulberry (155) (1942), White mulberry [White mulberrie] (149) (1904) NM

Morus multicaulis – See *Morus alba* L.

Morus nigra L. – Black mulberry (1, 19, 92, 93, 97, 107, 109, 110, 122, 124, 138) (1840–1937), Mulberry [Molberye] or Mulberry tree (179) (1526), Purple mulberry [Purple mulberrie] (178) (1526), Red mulberry [Red mulberrie] (178) (1526)

Morus rubra L. – American mulberry (109, 156, 158) (1900–1949), Large-leaf Virginia mulberry tree [Large-leaved Virginian mulberry tree] (8) (1785), Mulberry [Molberye] or Mulberry tree (35, 41, 103) (1770–1870), Murier rouge (French) (8) (1785), Native mulberry (180) (1791), Red mulberry [Red mulberrie] (1, 3, 4, 5, 7, 9, 22, 20, 19, 46, 49, 50, 72, 82, 85, 92, 93, 95, 97, 107, 109, 113, 122, 124, 130, 131, 138, 155, 156, 157, 158, 187) (1818–present)

Morus rubra L. var. *rubra* – Red mulberry [Red mulberrie] (50) (present)

Mucuna Adans. – Velvet bean [Velvetbean] (138) (1923)

Mucuna pruriens (L.) DC. – Ass's-eyes [Asses' eyes] (92) (1876), Cowhage (92, 107) (1876–1919), Cowitch [Cow-itch, Cow itch] (92, 107) (1876–1919), Donkey's-eyes [Donkeys' eyes] (92) (1876), Kitedzi (107) (1919), Sea beans (92) (1876)

Mucuna pruriens (L.) DC. var. *pruriens* – Chinese velvetbean (138) (1923), Cowage (19, 138) (1840–1923), Cowhitch (19) (1840), Lyon bean (109) (1949)

Mucuna pruriens (L.) DC. var. *utilis* (Wallich ex Wight) Baker ex Burck – Deering's velvetbean [Deering velvetbean] (138) (1923), Velvet bean [Velvetbean] (106) (1930), Yokohama bean (109) (1949), Yokohama velvetbean (138) (1923)

Mucuna puriens DC. – See *Mucuna pruriens* (L.) DC.

Mucuna utilis (Wall.) – See *Mucuna pruriens* (L.) DC. var. *utilis* (Wallich ex Wight) Baker ex Burck

Muehlenbeckia complexa Meisn. – Maidenhair vine [Maidenhair-vine] (109) (1949), Wire plant [Wire-plant] (109) (1949), Wire vine [Wirevine] (138) (1923)

Muehlenbeckia platyclada – See *Homalocladium platycladum* (F. J. Muell.) Bailey

Muhlenbergia ambigua Torr. – See *Muhlenbergia mexicana* (L.) Trin.

Muhlenbergia andina (Nutt.) A. S. Hitchc. – Foxtail muhly (50) (present), Hairy dropseed (5) (1913), Woolly dropseed [Woolly drop-seed] (94) (1901), Woolly-seed muhlenbergia [Wooly-seeded muhlenbergia] (88) (1885)

Muhlenbergia arenicola Buckl. – Sand muhly (3, 50, 155) (1942–present)

Muhlenbergia asperifolia (Nees & Meyen ex Trin.) Parodi – Alkali muhly (140, 155) (1942–1944), Prairie grass [Prairie-grass] (111) (1915), Rough-leaf dropseed [Rough-leaved dropseed, Rough-leaved drop-seed] (3, 5, 93, 163) (1852–1977), Rough-leaf prairie grass [Rough-leaved prairie grass] (129) (1894), Rough-leaf salt grass [Rough-leafed salt-grass] (94) (1901), Scratch grass [Scratch-grass] (3, 50, 119, 140, 146) (1938–present)

Muhlenbergia brachyphylla Bush – See *Muhlenbergia bushii* Pohl

Muhlenbergia brevifolia (Nutt.) Nash – See *Muhlenbergia cuspidata* (Torr. ex Hook.) Rydb.

Muhlenbergia bushii Pohl – Nodding muhly (50, 155) (1942–present)

Muhlenbergia capillaris (Lam.) Trin. – Awned hair grass (92) (1876), Bearded hair grass [Bearded hair-grass] (94) (1901), Hair grass [Hairgrass, Hair-grass] (3, 66) (1903–1977), Hair-awn muhly

[Hairawn muhly] (50, 155) (1942–present), Long-awn hair grass [Long-awned hair-grass] (5, 119, 163) (1852–1938)

Muhlenbergia capillaris **(Lam.) Trin. var.** *trichopodes* **(Ell.) Vasey** – Bunch hair grass [Bunch hair-grass] (94) (1901)

Muhlenbergia comata **(Thurb.) Benth.** – See *Muhlenbergia andina* (Nutt.) A.S. Hitchc.

Muhlenbergia commutata **(Scribn.) Bush** – See *Muhlenbergia frondosa* (Poir.) Fern.

Muhlenbergia cuspidata **(Torr. ex Hook.) Rydb.** – Plains muhly (3, 50) (1977–present), Prairie grass [Prairie-grass] (129) (1894), Prairie rush-grass [Prairie rush grass] (5, 56, 119) (1901–1938), Short-leaf rush grass [Short-leaved rush grass] (5) (1913)

Muhlenbergia cuspidata **(Torr.) Nash** – possibly *Muhlenbergia cuspidata* (Torr. ex Hook.) Rydb.

Muhlenbergia diffusa **Sr.** – See *Muhlenbergia schreberi* J.F. Gmel.

Muhlenbergia dubia **Fourn. ex Hemsl.** – Pine-needle [Pineneedle] (122) (1937) TX

Muhlenbergia dumosa **Scribn. ex Vasey** – Shrubby dropseed [Shrubby drop-seed] (94) (1901)

Muhlenbergia emersleyi **Vasey** – Bull grass [Bull-grass, Bull grass] (122) (1937) TX

Muhlenbergia expansa **(Poir.) Trin.** – See *Muhlenbergia capillaris* (Lam.) Trin. var. *trichopodes* (Ell.) Vasey

Muhlenbergia filiculmis **Vasey** – Slim-stem muhly [Slimstem muhly] (50, 155) (1942–present), Thread-like muhlenbergia (94) (1901)

Muhlenbergia filiformis **(Thurb. ex S. Wats.) Rydb.** – Mountain dropseed [Mountain drop-seed] (94) (1901), Pullup muhly (3, 155) (1942–1977), Slender dropseed (5, 50) (1913–present), Slender rush grass [Slender rush-grass] (94) (1901)

Muhlenbergia foliosa **(Roemer & J. A. Schultes) Trin. subsp.** *setiglumis* **(S. Wats.) Scribn.** – See *Muhlenbergia mexicana* (L.) Trin.

Muhlenbergia frondosa **(Poir.) Fern.** – Wire-stem muhly [Wirestem muhly] (3, 50) (1977–present), Woolly-seed muhlenbergia [Wooly-seeded muhlenbergia] (87) (1884)

Muhlenbergia glauca **(Nees) B. D. Jackson** – Lemmon's dropseed [Lemmon's drop-seed] (94) (1901)

Muhlenbergia glomerata **(Willd.) Trin.** – Clustering muhlenbergia (66, 90) (1885–1903), Cluster-spike muhlenbergia [Cluster-spiked muhlenbergia] (90) (1885), Dropseed grass [Drop seed grass, Drop-seed grass, Drop-seed-grass] (45) (1896), Fine prairie grass (45) (1896), Fine slough grass (45) (1896), Limber Bill (45) (1896), Marsh muhlenbergia (56) (1901), Muhlenberg's grass [Muhlenberg grass] (11, 45) (1888–1896), Nimblewill [Nimble will, Nimble-will] (45) (1896), Small willow-top [Small willow top] (45) (1896), Spiked muhlenbergia (87, 88, 90) (1884–1885), Spiked muhly (50) (present), Wild timothy (45, 56, 144) (1896–1901)

Muhlenbergia gracillima **Torr.** – See *Muhlenbergia torreyi* (Kunth) A.S. Hitchc. ex Bush

Muhlenbergia jonesii **(Vasey) Hitchc.** – Jones' rush grass [Jones' rush-grass] (94) (1901)

Muhlenbergia lemmoni **Scribn.** – See *Muhlenbergia glauca* (Nees) B. D. Jackson

Muhlenbergia mexicana **(L.) Trin.** – Bearded leafy muhly (155) (1942), Knot-root grass [Knot root grass] (5, 56) (1901–1913), Leafy muhly (155) (1942), Mexican bent grass [Mexican bent-grass] (165, 187) (1818–1768), Mexican dropseed [Mexican drop-seed] (56, 94, 119) (1901–1938), Mexican drop-seed grass (80) (1913), Mexican muhlenbergia (66, 90) (1885–1903), Mexican muhly (50) (present), Mexican wood grass (129) (1894), Minnesota dropseed (5) (1913), Muhlenberg's grass [Muhlenberg grass] (11) (1888), Nimblewill [Nimble will, Nimble-will] (80, 87) (1884–1913), Orchard grass [Orchardgrass, Orchard-grass] (80) (1913) IA, Satin grass [Satin-grass] (5, 56, 119) (1901–1938), Turkey grass (80) (1913), Wild timothy (144) (1899) KS, Wire-stem muhly [Wirestem muhly] (3, 155) (1942–1977), Wood grass [Wood-grass] (5, 87, 90, 93, 99, 111, 119) (1885–1936), possibly Thread-form bent grass (42) (1814)

Muhlenbergia minutissima **(Steud.) Swall.** – Annual muhly (50) (present), Dropseed [Drop-seed, Drop seed] (93) (1936), Prairie grass [Prairie-grass] (111) (1915), Vasey's dropseed [Vasey's drop-seed] (5) (1913)

Muhlenbergia montana **(Nutt.) A. S. Hitchc.** – Mountain muhly (122, 140) (1937–1944)

Muhlenbergia monticola **Buckl.** – See *Muhlenbergia tenuifolia* (Kunth) Trin.

Muhlenbergia palustris **Scribn.** – See *Muhlenbergia schreberi* J. F. Gmel.

Muhlenbergia parviglumis **Vasey** – Small-glume dropseed [Small-glumed drop-seed] (94) (1901)

Muhlenbergia pauciflora **Buckl.** – New Mexico muhly [New Mexican muhly] (122) (1937)

Muhlenbergia porteri **Scribn. ex Beal** – Bush grass [Bush-grass] (163) (1852), Bush muhly (50, 122, 155) (1937–present), Hoe grass [Hoe-grass] (155) (1942), Mesquite grass [Mesquite-grass] (152, 163) (1852–1912), Porter's muhly (3) (1977)

Muhlenbergia pungens **Thurb.** – Blowout grass [Blow-out grass, Blowoutgrass] (93, 111) (1915–1936), Muhlenberg's grass [Muhlenberg grass] (11) (1888), Prairie dropseed (5) (1913), Purple hair grass [Purple hair-grass] (93, 163) (1852–1936), Sand Hills muhly [Sandhills muhly, Sandhill muhly] (50, 140, 155) (1942–present), Sand muhly (3) (1977)

Muhlenbergia racemosa **(Michx.) Britton, Sterns & Poggenb.** – Dropseed grass [Drop seed grass, Drop-seed grass, Drop-seed-grass] (80) (1913), Green muhly (140, 155) (1942–1944), Knot-root grass [Knot root grass] (68) (1890), Marsh muhlenbergia (80) (1913), Marsh muhly (3, 50, 140) (1944–present), Orchard grass [Orchardgrass, Orchard-grass] (80) (1913) IA, Satin grass [Satin-grass] (5, 56, 119, 163) (1852–1938), Spiked muhlenberg's grass (129) (1894), Wild timothy (5, 80, 93, 94, 111, 119) (1901–1938)

Muhlenbergia repens **(J. Presl) A. S. Hitchc.** – Creeping muhly (122) (1937)

Muhlenbergia richardsonis **(Trin.) Rydb.** – False buffalo grass [False buffalograss, False buffalo-grass] (111) (1915) Neb, Mat muhly (3, 50, 155, 185) (1936–present)

Muhlenbergia rigens **(Benth.) A. S. Hitchc.** – Deer-grass [Deergrass, Deer grass] (94, 122, 163) (1852–1937), Purple muhly (122) (1937)

Muhlenbergia rigida **(H.B.K.) Kunth** – See *Muhlenbergia rigens* (Benth.) A.S. Hitchc.

Muhlenbergia **Schreb.** – Dropseed grass [Drop seed grass, Drop-seed grass, Drop-seed-grass] (66, 87) (1884–1903), Muhlenberg's grass [Muhlenberg grass] (93) (1936) for Dr. Muhlenberg, distinguished American botanidst, Muhly (50, 155) (1942–present)

Muhlenbergia schreberi **J. F. Gmel.** – Dropseed [Drop-seed, Drop seed] (45, 87, 92) (1876–1896), Dropseed grass [Drop seed grass, Drop-seed grass, Drop-seed-grass] (19, 119) (1840–1938), Nimblewill [Nimble will, Nimble-will] (3, 16, 45, 50, 56, 66, 80, 87, 93, 94, 99, 111, 119, 122, 155, 163) (1837–present), Satin grass [Satin-grass] (119, 163) (1852–1938), Spreading muhlenbergia (187) (1818), Swamp dropseed (5, 50) (1913–present), Wire grass [Wire-grass, Wiregrass] (87, 93, 119) (1884–1938), Wood grass [Wood-grass] (90) (1885), Wood muhlenbergia (90) (1885)

Muhlenbergia simplex **(Scribn.) Rydb.** – See *Muhlenbergia filiformis* (Thurb. ex S. Wats.) Rydb.

Muhlenbergia sobolifera **(Muhl. ex Willd.) Trin.** – Awnless muhlenbergia (66) (1903), Bearded rock muhly (155) (1942), Rock dropseed [Rock drop-seed, Rock-dropseed] (5, 99, 119, 163) (1852–1938), Rock muhlenbergia (56, 163) (1852–1901), Rock muhly (3, 50, 155) (1942–present), Slender satin grass [Slender satin-grass] (163) (1852)

Muhlenbergia sobolifera **var.** *setigera* **Scribn.** – See *Muhlenbergia sobolifera* (Muhl. ex Willd.) Trin.

Muhlenbergia spica-venti **[(L.) Trin.]** – See *Apera spica-venti* (L.) Beauv.

Muhlenbergia squarrosa (**Trin.**) **Rydb.** – See *Muhlenbergia richardsonis* (Trin.) Rydb.

Muhlenbergia sylvatica **Torr. ex Gray** – Forest muhly (3, 155) (1942–1977), Sylvan muhlenbergia (66) (1903), Wood dropseed (5) (1913), Wood grass [Wood-grass] (87, 129) (1884–1894), Woodland dropseed [Woodland drop seed, Woodland drop-seed] (5, 56, 94, 163) (1852–1933), Woodland muhly (50) (present)

Muhlenbergia tenuiflora (**Willd.**) **Britton, Sterns & Poggenb.** – Colonial bent (109) (1949), Rhode Island bent (109) (1949), Slender muhlenbergia (56) (1901), Slender muhly (50) (present), Slender satin grass [Slender satin-grass] (5) (1913), Slender-flower dropseed [Slender flowered dropseed, Slender-flowered dropseed] (5, 94) (1901–1913), Slim-flower muhly [Slimflower muhly] (155) (1942), Willdenow's muhlenbergia (66) (1903)

Muhlenbergia tenuifolia (**Kunth**) **Trin.** – Mesa muhly (122) (1937)

Muhlenbergia texana **Buckl.** – Grama grass [Grama-grass, Gramma grass] (151) (1896) NM, Mesquite grass [Mesquite-grass] (151) (1896) NM, Texas dropseed grass [Texas drop seed grass] (151) (1896)

Muhlenbergia thurberi (**Scribn.**) **Rydb.** – Thurber's rush grass [Thurber's rush-grass] (94) (1901)

Muhlenbergia torreyana (**J. A. Schultes**) **A. S. Hitchc.** – Close-flower dropseed [Close-flowered drop seed] (66) (1903), Flat-stem dropseed [Flat-stemmed dropseed] (5) (1913), Flat-stem sporobolus [Flat-stemmed sporobolus] (94) (1901), New Jersey muhly (50) (present)

Muhlenbergia torreyi (**Kunth**) **A. S. Hitchc. ex Bush** – Filiform dropseed (5) (1913), Pancake grass [Pancakegrass] (119, 140) (1938–1944), Ring grass [Ringgrass Ring-grass] (119, 122, 140, 163) (1852–1944), Ring muhly (50, 140, 155) (1942–present), Ring-grass muhly [Ringgrass muhly] (3) (1977)

Muhlenbergia trichopodes (**Ell.**) **Chapm.** – See *Muhlenbergia capillaris* (Lam.) Trin. var. *trichopodes* (Ell.) Vasey

Muhlenbergia umbrosa **Scribn.** – See *Muhlenbergia sylvatica* Torr. ex Gray

Muhlenbergia uniflora (**Muhl.**) **Fern.** – Blue ruin (78) (1898) ME, Bog muhly (50) (present), Late dropseed [Late drop-seed, Late drop seed] (66, 94) (1901–1903), Late-flowering dropseed (5) (1913), Late-flowering sporobolus [Late flowering sporobolus] (90) (1885)

Muhlenbergia utilis (**Torr.**) **A. S. Hitchc.** – Aparejo grass (94, 152, 163) (1852–1912)

Muhlenbergia utilis (**Torr.**) **Rydb.** – See *Muhlenbergia utilis* (Torr.) A.S. Hitchc.

Muhlenbergia willdenovii **Trin.** – See *Muhlenbergia tenuiflora* (Willd.) Britton, Sterns & Poggenb.

Mulgedium macrophyllum (**Willd.**) **DC.** – See *Lactuca macrophylla* Gray

Munroa squarrosa (**Nutt.**) **Torr.** – See *Monroa squarrosa* (Nutt.) Torr.

Munroa **Torr.** – See *Monroa* Torr.

Murdannia nudiflora (**L.**) **Brenan** – Creeping dayflower [Creeping day-flower] (5, 97, 138) (1913–1937), Naked-stem dewflower [Nakedstem dewflower] (50) (present)

Muricauda **Small.** – See *Arisaema* Martens

Murraya exotica **L.** – Chinese box (107) (1919)

Murraya exotica **L.** – Orange-jasmine (138) (1923)

Musa ×*paradisiaca* **L.** [*acuminata* × *balbisiana*] – Abellana (107) (1570), Adam's-fig [Adam's fig] (107) (1919), Apple-of-paradice [Apple of paradice] (178, 179) (1526–1596), Banana (92, 109, 110) (1876–1949), Common banana (138) (1923), Paco (107) (1578), Plaintain (92, 109) (1876–1949), Plane (Spanish) (110) (1886) for resemblance to plane tree, Plantain [Plantayne] (107) (1919), Tachouner (107) (1616)

Musa acuminata **Colla** – Cavendish banana (138) (1923), Dwarf banana (109) (1949)

Musa cavendishi – See *Musa acuminata* Colla

Musa **L.** – Banana (7, 50, 138) (1828–present), Plaintain tree (7, 92) (1828–1876)

Musa nana **Lour.** – See *Musa acuminata* Colla

Musa paradisiaca **L.** – See *Musa* ×*paradisiaca* L. [*acuminata* × *balbisiana*]

Musa paradisiaca **L. var. sapientum Kuntze.** – See *Musa* ×*paradisiaca* L. [*acuminata* × *balbisiana*]

Musa sapientum **L.** – See *Musa* ×*paradisiaca* L. [*acuminata* × *balbisiana*] (for resemblance to plane tree)

Musa troglodytarum **L.** – Fe'i banana (109) (1949)

Muscadina (**Planch.**) **Small.** – possibly *Vitis* L.

Muscari atlanticum **Boiss. & Reut.** – See *Muscari neglectum* Guss. ex Ten.

Muscari botryoides (**L.**) **Mills** – Baby's-breath [Babies' breath, Baby's breath, Babies'-breath, Babysbreath] (5, 73) (1892–1913), Blue grape-flower [Blew grape-floure] (180) (1633), Bluebell [Blue-bell, Blue bell, Blue bells, Blue-bells] (5, 73, 156, 158) (1892–1923) Chestertown MD, Bluebottle [Blue-bottle, Blue bottle, Blue bottles] (5, 73, 156) (1892–1923) Mansfield O, Common globe-hyacinth [Common globe hyacinth] (158) (1900), Common grape-hyacinth [Common grape hyacinth, Common grapehyacinth] (50, 138, 155) (1923–present), Globe hyancinth (92) (1876), Grape flower (5, 178) (1596–1913), Grape-hyacinth [Grapehyacinth, Grape hyacinth] (5, 156) (1913–1923), Great grape-flower [Great grape-floure] (180) (1633), Pearls-of-Spain [Pearls of Spain] (156, 158) (1900–1923), Sky-color grape flower [Sky-coloured Grape-floure, Skie coloured Grape flower] (178, 180) (1596–1633), Starch-hyacinth [Starch hyacinth] (156) (1923)

Muscari comosum (**L.**) **Mill.** – Fair curled-hair branched hyacinth [Faire curld-haire branched Iacinth] (180) (1633), Fair-hair hyacinth [Faire-haired Iacinth] (180) (1633), Fair-hair hyacinth of Turkey [Faire haired Iacint of Turkie] (178) (1596), Greater fair-hair hyacinth [Greater faire haired Iacint] (178) (1596), Lesser fair-hair hyacinth [Lesser faire haired Iacint] (178) (1596), Purple grape hyacinth (19) (1840)

Muscari **L.** – See *Muscari* Mill.

Muscari **Mill.** – Grape-hyacinth [Grapehyacinth, Grape hyacinth] (109, 138, 155, 156) (1923–1949)

Muscari moschatum – See *Muscari neglectum* Guss. ex Ten.

Muscari muscarimi **Medik.** – See *Muscari neglectum* Guss. ex Ten.

Muscari neglectum **Guss. ex Ten.** – Ash-colored Grapeflower [Ash coloured Grape flower, Ash-coloured Grape-floure] (178, 180) (1596–1633), Grape flower (5) (1913), Grape-hyacinth [Grapehyacinth, Grape hyacinth] (92, 107) (1876–1919), Harebell hyacinth [Hare bell hyacinth] (19) (1840), Musk hyacinth (19) (1840), Pearls-of-Spain [Pearls of Spain] (5) (1913), Starch grape-hyacinth [Starch grape hyacinth] (5, 50) (1913–present), Starch-hyacinth [Starch hyacinth] (5) (1913), Tipcadi (180) (1633)

Muscari racemosa (**L.**) **Mill.** – See *Muscari neglectum* Guss. ex Ten.

Muscari racemosa **Mill.** – See *Muscari neglectum* Guss. ex Ten.

Muscari racemosum (**L.**) **Lam. & DC.** – See *Muscari neglectum* Guss. ex Ten.

Muscari racemosum (**L.**) **Mill.** – See *Muscari neglectum* Guss. ex Ten.

Muscaria caespitosa (**L.**) **Haw.** – See *Saxifraga caespitosa* L. subsp. *caespitosa*

Musineon divaricatum (**Pursh**) **Nutt.** – See *Musineon divaricatum* (Pursh) Raf.

Musineon divaricatum (**Pursh**) **Raf.** – Leafy musineon (5, 131) (1899–1913), Leafy wild parsley [Leafy wildparsley] (50) (present)

Musineon divaricatum (**Pursh**) **Raf. var. divaricatum** – Leafy wild parsley [Leafy wildparsley] (50) (present)

Musineon divaricatum (**Pursh**) **Raf. var. hookeri** (**Torr. & Gray**) **Mathias** – Marshaspita (Crow) (101) (1905) MT, Wild parsley [Wildparsley] (101) (1905) MT

Musineon hookeri **Nutt.** – See *Musineon divaricatum* (Pursh) Raf. var. *hookeri* (Torr. & Gray) Mathias

Musineon **Raf.** – Musiineon (158) (1900), Wild parsley [Wildparsley] (50) (present)

Musineon tenuifolium (**Nutt. ex Torr. & Gray**) **Coult. & Rose**

– Scapose musineon (5, 131) (1899–1913), Slender wild parsley [Slender wildparsley] (50) (present)

Mutinus caninus (**Huds.**) **Fr.** – Dog-prick mushroom [Dog's prick mushroom] (181) (~1678)

Mutinus caninus (**Pers.**) **Fr.** – See *Mutinus caninus* (Huds.) Fr.

Myagrum perfoliatum **L.** – Myagrum (5) (1913)

Myagrum sativum **L.** – See *Camelina sativa* (L.) Crantz subsp. *sativa*

Mynphoides indicum **Kuntze** – See *Nymphoides indica* (L.) Kuntze

Myosotis (**Rupp.**) **L.** – See *Myosotis* L.

Myosotis alpestris **F. Schmidt** – See *Myosotis sylvatica* Ehrh. ex Hoffmann

Myosotis arvense **Hoffm.** – See *Myosotis arvensis* (L.) Hill

Myosotis arvensis (**L.**) **Hill** – Field mouse ear [Field mouse-ear] (5, 156) (1913–1923), Field scorpion-grass [Field scorpion grass] (5, 156) (1913–1923), Forgat mig ei (Swedish) (46) (1879), Forget-me-not [Forget me not, For-get-me-not, For-get-me-nots, Forgetmenot] (19) (1840), Scorpion-grass [Scorpion grass] (92) (1876)

Myosotis azorica **H. C. Wats. ex Hook.** – Azores forget-me-not (138) (1923)

Myosotis **L.** – Forget-me-not [Forget me not, For-get-me-not, For-get-me-nots, Forgetmenot] (1, 2, 4, 50, 82, 109, 138, 155, 158) (1895–present), Scorpion-grass [Scorpion grass] (2, 10, 77, 82, 156, 184) (1793–1930)

Myosotis laxa **Lehm.** – Bay forget-me-not [Bay forgetmenot] (50, 138, 155) (1923–present), Forget-me-not [Forget me not, For-get-me-not, For-get-me-nots, Forgetmenot] (156) (1923), Smaller forget-me-not (5) (1913)

Myosotis macrosperma **Engelm.** – Large-seed forget-me-not [Large-seeded forget-me-not] (50, 131) (1899–present), Southern scorpion-grass (97) (1937) OK

Myosotis micrantha – See *Myosotis stricta* Link ex Roemer & J. A. Schultes

Myosotis palustris (**L.**) **Hill** – See *Myosotis scorpioides* L.

Myosotis scorpioides **L.** – Caterpillars (156, 158) (1900–1923), Forget-me-not [Forget me not, For-get-me-not, For-get-me-nots, Forgetmenot] (5, 92, 158) (1876–1913), Love-me (5, 156, 158) (1900–1923), Marsh scorpion-grass [Marsh scorpion grass] (5, 156, 158) (1900–1923), Mouse-ear [Mouse ear, Mouse ears, Mouse's ear, Mows eare] (158) (1900), Mouse-ear scorpion-grass [Mouse-ear scorpion grass] (5, 92, 156, 187) (1818–1923), Scorpion-grass [Scorpion grass] (158) (1900), Scorpion-weed [Scorpion weed] (19, 92) (1840–1876), Snake-grass [Snake grass, Snakegrass] (5, 156, 158) (1900–1923), True forget-me-not [True forgetmenot] (3, 50, 82, 109, 138, 155, 156) (1923–present), Water scorpion-grass [Water scorpion grass] (92) (1876)

Myosotis stricta **Link ex Roemer & J. A. Schultes** – Blue scorpion-grass (156) (1923), Strict forget-me-not (50) (present)

Myosotis sylvatica **Ehrh. ex Hoffmann** – Alpine forget-me-not [Alpine forgetmenot] (138, 155) (1923–1942), Forget-me-not [Forget me not, For-get-me-not, For-get-me-nots, Forgetmenot] (85) (1932), Garden forget-me-not (3, 4) (1977–1986), Sylvan forget-me-not (131) (1899), Woodland forget-me-not [Woodland forgetmenot] (50, 138, 155) (1923–present)

Myosotis verna **Nutt.** – Early scorpion-grass [Early scorpion grass] (5, 97, 122, 156) (1913–1937), Forget-me-not [Forget me not, For-get-me-not, For-get-me-nots, Forgetmenot] (5, 156) (1913–1923), Spring forget-me-not (50) (present), Spring scorpion-grass [Spring scorpion grass] (5, 72, 97, 156) (1907–1937), Virginia forget-me-not (3) (1977)

Myosotis versicolor (**Pers.**) **J. E. Smith** – Blue scorpion-grass (156) (1923), Yellow scorpion-grass (156) (1923), Yellow-and-blue scorpion-grass [Yellow and blue scorpion grass] (5) (1913)

Myosotis virginiana **L.** – See *Hackelia virginiana* (L.) I.M. Johnston

Myosotis virginica (**L.**) **B.S.P.** – See *Myosotis verna* Nutt.

Myosoton aquaticum (**L.**) **Moench** – Giant chickweed [Giantchickweed] (50) (present), Water chickweed (5, 156, 158) (1900–1923), Water mouse-ear chickweed (5, 156, 158) (1900–1923)

Myosoton **Moench** – Myosoton (50) (present)

Myosurus **Dill.** – See *Myosurus* L.

Myosurus **L.** – Mouse-tail [Mousetail, Mouse-tail, Mousetaile] (4, 13, 15, 50, 93, 155, 156, 158) (1849–present)

Myosurus minimus **L.** – Bloodstrange [Blood strange, Blood-strange] (5, 156, 158, 180) (1633–1923), Little mouse-tail [Little mouse tail] (5) (1913), Mouse-tail [Mousetail, Mouse-tail, Mousetaile] (1, 3, 5, 63, 72, 85, 95, 97, 122, 131, 156, 178) (1526–1977), Small mouse-tail (158) (1900), Tiny mouse-tail [Tiny mousetail] (50, 155) (1942–present)

Myrcianthes fragrans (**Sw.**) **McVaugh** – Clove tree [Clovetree] (138) (1923), Small-leaf eugenia [Small-leaved eugenia] (20) (1857), Tambosier dichotome (French) (20) (1857)

Myrica asplenifolia **Endl.** – See *Comptonia peregrina* (L.) Coult.

Myrica aspleniifolia **L.** – See *Comptonia peregrina* (L.) Coult.

Myrica californica – See *Morella californica* (Cham. & Schlecht.) Wilbur

Myrica carifers – See *Morella cerifera* (L.) Small

Myrica caroliniensis **Mill.** – See *Morella caroliniensis* (Mill.) Small

Myrica cerifera humilis – possibly *Morella cerifera* (L.) Small

Myrica cerifera **L.** – See *Morella cerifera* (L.) Small

Myrica faya – See *Morella faya* (Aiton) Wilbur

Myrica gale **L.** – American bog gale (8) (1785), Bay bush [Bay-bush] (5, 92, 156) (1876–1923), Bayberry [Bay berry] (47) (1852), Bog myrtle (5, 14, 19, 156) (1840–1923), Burton's myrtle [Burton myrtle, Burton-myrtle] (5, 156) (1913–1923), Dutch myrtle (5, 92, 156) (1876–1923), Gale (41) (1770), Galé d'Amérique (French) (8) (1785), Gall bush [Gall-bush] (156) (1923), Gaul (46) (1671), Gaule (178) (1526), Golden osier (5, 156) (1913–1923), Golden withy (156) (1923), Laurier (French) (41) (1770), Meadow fern (5, 75, 92, 156) (1876–1923) Dover ME, Meadow-burs (156) (1923), Meadow-fern bur [Meadow fern burrs] (92) (1876), Moor myrtle [Moor-myrtle] (5, 156) (1913–1923), Noble myrtle [Noble mirtle] (46) (1671), Poivrier (French) (41) (1770), Scotch gael (156) (1923), Sweetgale [Sweet gale] (2, 5, 14, 19, 92, 109, 138, 156) (1840–1949), Sweet-willow [Sweet willow, Sweete willow] (5, 41, 92, 156, 178) (1526–1923)

Myrica hartwegii **S. Wats.** – Sweet bayberry [Sweet bay-berry] (106) (1930)

Myrica inodora – See *Morella inodora* (Bartr.) Small

Myrica **L.** – Arbre de Cire (French) (8) (1785), Bayberry [Bay berry] (2, 7, 138, 167) (1814–1923), Candleberry myrtle [Candelberry myrtle, Candle-berry myrtle] (8, 10, 14) (1785–1882), Cirier (French) (8) (1785), Gale (10) (1818), Sweetgale [Sweet gale] (1, 7) (1828–1932), Wax myrtle [Wax-myrtle, Waxmyrtle] (7, 106, 138) (1828–1930), Waxberry [Wax-berry, Wax berry] (7) (1828)

Myrica pennsylvanica **Loisel** – See *Morella pensylvanica* (Mirbel) Kartesz

Myrica pensylvanica **Loisel** – See *Morella pensylvanica* (Mirbel) Kartesz

Myriophyllum (**Vaill.**) **L.** – See *Myriophyllum* L.

Myriophyllum alterniflorum **DC.** – Loose-flower water milfoil [Loose-flowered water milfoil] (5) (1913)

Myriophyllum aquaticum (**Vell.**) **Verdc.** – Brazilian parrotfeather (138) (1923), Chilean water milfoil (120) (1938) OK, Parrot-feather [Parrotfeather, Parrot's feather, Parrots-feather] (109) (1949)

Myriophyllum brasiliense **Cambess** – See *Myriophyllum aquaticum* (Vell.) Verdc.

Myriophyllum exalbescens **Fern.** – See *Myriophyllum sibiricum* Komarov

Myriophyllum farwellii **Morong** – Farwell's water milfoil (5) (1913)

Myriophyllum heterophyllum **Michx.** – Two-leaf water-milfoil [Twoleaf watermilfoil] (50) (present), Various-leaf water-milfoil [Various-leaved water milfoil, Various-leaved water millfoil] (5, 72, 131) (1899–1913), Water-milfoil [Water milfoil, Water mill-foil, Watermillfoil] (3) (1977)

Myriophyllum humile (**Raf.**) **Morong.** – Low water milfoil (5) (1913)

Myriophyllum L. – Parrot-feather [Parrotfeather, Parrot's feather, Parrots-feather] (138, 155) (1923–1942), Water-milfoil [Water milfoil, Water mill-foil, Watermillfoil] (1, 4, 10, 50, 63, 93, 158, 167) (1814–present), Water-rope [Water rope] (124) (1937) TX

Myriophyllum pinnatum **(Walt.) Britton, Sterns & Poggenb.** – Cut-leaf water milfoil [Cutleaf watermilfoil] (50) (present), Green parrot's-feather [Green parrot's feather, Green parrotfeather] (4, 155) (1942–1986), Pinnate water-milfoil [Pinnate water milfoil] (5, 72, 97) (1907–1937), Water-milfoil [Water milfoil, Water mill-foil, Watermillfoil] (3) (1977)

Myriophyllum proserpinacoides **[Gillies ex Hook. & Arn.]** – See *Myriophyllum aquaticum* (Vell.) Verdc.

Myriophyllum sibiricum **Komarov** – American milfoil (4) (1986), Short-spike water-milfoil [Shortspike watermilfoil] (50) (Present), Water-milfoil [Water milfoil, Water mill-foil, Watermillfoil] (3, 46) (1879–1977)

Myriophyllum spicatum L. – Meakin (5, 156, 158) (1900–1923) no longer in use by 1923, Navelwort [Navel-wort] (158) (1900), Spike water-milfoil [Spike watermilfoil, Spiked water milfoil, Spiked water-milfoil] (5, 50, 72, 95, 120, 131, 156, 158) (1899–present), Spiked water milfoil [Spiked water-milfoil] (5, 72, 95, 120, 131, 156, 158) (1899–1937), Water navelwort [Water-navelwort] (5, 156, 158) (1900–1923), Water-milfoil [Water milfoil, Water mill-foil, Watermillfoil] (85) (1932)

Myriophyllum spicatum L. var. *exalbescens* **(Fern.) Jeps.** – See *Myriophyllum sibiricum* Komarov

Myriophyllum tenellum **Bigelow** – Slender parrot's-feather [Slender parrotfeather] (155) (1942), Slender water-milfoil [Slender water milfoil] (5, 50) (1913–present)

Myriophyllum verticillatum L. – Canadian parrot-feather [Canada parrotfeather] (138, 155) (1923–1942), Myriad-leaf (156) (1923), Parrot-feather [Parrotfeather, Parrot's feather, Parrots-feather] (156) (1923), Water-milfoil [Water milfoil, Water mill-foil, Watermillfoil] (3, 19, 92) (1840–1977), Whorled milfoil (85) (1932), Whorled water-milfoil [Whorled water milfoil, Whorled water millfoil] (5, 72, 131, 156) (1899–1923), Whorl-leaf water milfoil [Whorl-leaf watermilfoil] (50) (present)

Myristica fragrans **Houtt.** – Common nutmeg (138) (1923), Mace (92) (1876), Nutmeg (92, 110) (1876–1886), Nutmygge (179) (1526)

Myristica **Gronov.** – Nutmeg (109) (1949)

Myristica L. – See *Myristica* Gronov.

Myrospermum frutescens **Jacq.** – Wild hopseed [Wilde hop seed, Wilde hop-seed] (181) (~1678), Wilde hop-seed Barbadensibus dicta (181) (~1678)

Myrrhis canadensis **Michx.** – See *Cryptotaenia canadensis* (L.) DC.

Myrrhis **Mill.** – Chervil [Cheruell] (10) (1818), possibly Myrrh (109, 138) (1923–1949) from Greek word for perfume

Myrrhis **Morison** – possibly *Myrrhis* Mill.

Myrrhis odorata **(L.) Scop.** – Myrrh (138) (1923), Sweet chervil [Sweete cheruill] (178) (1526), Sweet cicely (of Europe) (109) (1949)

Myrrhis odorata **Scop.** – See *Myrrhis odorata* (L.) Scop.

Myrrhis **Scop.** – possibly *Myrrhis* Mill.

Myrsiphyllum asparagoides – See *Asparagus asparagoides* (L.) Druce

Myzorrhiza ludoviciana **(Nutt.) Rydb.** – See *Orobanche ludoviciana* Nutt. subsp. *ludoviciana*

Myzorrhiza **Philippi** – See *Orobanche* L.

N

Nabalus albus (L.) Hook. – See *Prenanthes alba* L.

Nabalus altissimus (L.) Hook. – See *Prenanthes altissima* L.

Nabalus asper (Michx.) Torr. & Gray – See *Prenanthes aspera* Michx.

Nabalus boottii DC. – See *Prenanthes boottii* (DC.) Gray

Nabalus Cass. – See *Prenanthes* L.

Nabalus crepidineus (Michx.) DC. – See *Prenanthes crepidinea* Michx.

Nabalus nanus (Bigelow) DC. – See *Prenanthes nana* (Bigelow) Torr.

Nabalus racemosus (Michx.) DC. – See *Prenanthes racemosa* Michx. subsp. *multiflora* Cronq.

Nabalus serpentarius (Pursh) Hook. – See *Prenanthes serpentaria* Pursh

Nabalus trifoliolatus Cass. – See *Prenanthes trifoliolata* (Cass.) Fern.

Nabalus virgatus (Michx.) DC. – See *Prenanthes autumnalis* Walt.

Naias guadalupenis (Spreng.) Morong – See *Najas guadalupensis* (Spreng.) Magnus

Naias L. – See *Najas* L.

Naias marina L. – See *Najas marina* L.

Najas canadensis Michx. – See *Najas flexilis* (Willd.) Rostk. & Schmidt

Najas flexilis (Willd.) Rostk. & Schmidt – Naiad (3) (1977), Water knotgrass [Water knot-grass, Water knot grass] (19) (1840), Nodding waternymph (50) (present), Shiny najas (85) (1932), Waternymph [Water nymph, Waternymph] (19, 92) (1840–1876), Slender naias (5, 72, 93, 131) (1899–1936), Naiad (3) (1977), Southern water nymph (50) (present), Southern water-nymph [Southern water nymph, Southern waternymph] (50) (present), Slender najas (85) (1932), Southern naiad (155) (1942), Guadalupe naias [Guadaloupe naias] (5, 93, 97, 120) (1913–1938)

Najas guadalupensis (Spreng.) Magnus subsp. *guadalupensis* – Southern water-nymph [Southern water nymph, Southern waternymph] (50) (present)

Najas L. – Naias (93) (1936), Naiad (120, 155) (1938–1942), Waternymph [Water nymph, Waternymph] (50, 158) (1900–present)

Najas marina L. – Spiny naiad (50) (present), Spiny naias (155) (1942), Naiad (156) (1923), Pondweed [Pondweeds, Pond weed] (156) (1923), Large naias (5, 97) (1913–1937)

Nama affinis (Gray) Kuntze – See *Hydrolea uniflora* Raf.

Nama hispida Gray (sic) – See *Nama hispidum* Gray

Nama hispidum Gray – Bristly nama (50) (present), Sand bells (97, 122) (1937)

Nama hispidum Gray var. *spathulatum* (Torr.) C.L. Hitchc. – See *Nama hispidum* Gray

Nama jamaicense L. – Fiddleleaf (122) (1937)

Nama L. – Fiddleleaf (50) (present), Nama (138) (1923)

Nama ovata (Nutt.) Britton – See *Hydrolea ovata* Nutt. ex Choisy

Nama quadrivalvis (Walt.) Kuntze – See *Hydrolea quadrivalvis* Walt.

Nama stevensii A. S. Hitchc – Stevens' fiddleleaf (50) (present), Stevens' fiddlehead (3, 4) (1977–1986)

Nandina domestica Thunb. – Nandina (138) (1923)

Nandina Thunb. – Nandina (138) (1923)

Napaea (Clayton) L. – See *Napaea* L.

Napaea dioica L. – Glade mallow (5, 72, 156) (1907–1923), possibly False mallow [False-mallow, Falsemallow, False mallows] (19) (1840)

Napaea L. – Glade mallow (1, 2, 13, 15) (1849–1932)

Narcissus ×*incomparabilis* Mill. [*poeticus* × *pseudonarcissus*] – Butter-and-eggs [Butter & eggs, Butter and eggs] (92) (1876), Half-skirt daffodil [Halfskirt daffodil] (138) (1923), Single yellow daffodil (178) (1596)

Narcissus ×*medioluteus* Mill. [*poeticus* × *tazetta*] – Primrose peerless narcissus (109) (1949), Primrose narcissus (138) (1923), Daffodill with the yellow circle (178) (1596), Common white daffodil (180) (1633), French daffodill (180) (1633), King's-chalice [King's chalice] (180) (1633), Primrose pearls [Primrose pearles] (180) (1633), Serin cade (180) (1633)

Narcissus ×*odorus* L. [*jonquilla* × *pseudonarcissus*] – Yellow jonquil (92) (1876), Campernelle jonquil (109) (1949)

Narcissus aurantius [Schult.f.] – See *Narcissus* × *incomparabilis* Mill. [*poeticus* × *pseudonarcissus*]

Narcissus biflorus Curt. – See *Narcissus* ×*medioluteus* Mill. [*poeticus* × *tazetta*]

Narcissus bulbocodium L. – Hoop-petticoat [Hoop petticoat] (92) (1876), Medusa's-trumpet [Medusa's trumpet] (92) (1876), Hoop-petticoat daffodil (109) (1949), Petticoat daffodil (138) (1923)

Narcissus incomparabilis Mill. – See *Narcissus* × *incomparabilis* Mill. [*poeticus* × *pseudonarcissus*]

Narcissus jonquilla L. – Jonquil flower (92) (1876), Junquilia [Iunquilia] (180) (1633), Late-flowering rush daffodill [Late flouring Rush Daffodill] (180) (1633), Rush daffodill (178, 180) (1596–1633), Jonquil (19, 50, 92, 109, 138) (1840–present)

Narcissus L. – Easter flower [Easter-flower, Easter flowers] (78) (1898) OH, Daffodilly (180) (1633), Daffodowndilly (180) (1633), Iennetten (180) (1633), Narcissen (Dutch) (180) (1633), Primrose peerelesse (180) (1633), Narcissus (92, 107, 138) (1876–1923) probably for narcotic qualities

Narcissus odorus L. – See *Narcissus* ×*odorus* L. [*jonquilla* × *pseudonarcissus*]

Narcissus papyraceus Ker Gawl. – Paper-white narcissus (109) (1949)

Narcissus poeticus L. – Single daffy (73) (1892) NH, Pheasant's-eye [Pheasantseye, Pheasant's-eye] (109) (1949), Double white daffodill (178) (1596), Timely purple-ring daffodil [Timely purple ringed Daffodill] (180) (1633), Early purple-circle daffolill [Early purple circle daffolill] (178, 180) (1526–1633), Purple-circle daffodil [Purple circled Daffodill] (178, 180) (1526–1633), Timeliest purple-circle daffodil [Timeliest purple circled Daffodill] (178, 180) (1526–1633), Poet's narcissus [Poets narcissus] (19, 109, 138, 156) (1840–1949)

Narcissus pseudo-narcissus L. – See *Narcissus pseudonarcissus* L.

Narcissus pseudonarcissus L. – Easter flower [Easter-flower, Easter flowers] (73) (1892), Butter-and-eggs [Butter & eggs, Butter and eggs] (75) (1894), Trumpet narcissus (109) (1949), Common daffodil (138) (1923), Double yellow daffodill (180) (1633), Double yellow narcissus (180) (1633), Geel Spozckel bloemen (Dutch) (180) (1633), Common yellow daffodil (178, 180) (1596–1633), Daffodilly (5, 180) (1633–1913), Daffodowndilly (5, 180) (1633–1913), Daffodil (5, 19, 49, 50, 92, 109, 156) (1840–present), Daffy (5, 73) (1892–1913) NH

Narcissus tazeta – See *Narcissus tazetta* L.

Narcissus tazetta L. – Polyanthus (19) (1840), Cream naricissus (50) (present), Primrose peerless [Primrose peerelesse] (178) (1596), Polyanthus narcissus (109, 138) (1923–1949), Italian daffodill [Italian dafodil] (178, 180) (1596–1633)

Narcissus tazetta L. var. *papyraceus* Hort. – See *Narcissus papyraceus* Ker Gawl.

Nardus L. – Mat grass [Mat-grass, Matgrass] (10, 50, 19) (1818–present)

Nardus stricta L. – Common nard (92) (1876), Mat grass [Mat-grass, Matgrass] (92) (1876), Wire bent (94) (1901)

Narthecium americanum Ker-Gawl. – Yellow asphodel (50) (present), Asphodel (92) (1876), Bog asphodel (156) (1923), Bastard asphodel (158) (1900), Lancashire asphodel [Lancashire asphodill] (158, 178) (1596–1900), Yellow-grass [Yellow grass] (5, 156) (1913–1923), Moor-grass [Moor grass] (5, 156, 158) (1900–1923), Rosa solis [Rosa-solis] (5, 156, 158) (1900–1923), American bog asphodel (5, 158) (1900–1913)

Narthecium glutinosum **Michx.** – See *Tofieldia glutinosa* (Michx.) Pers. subsp. *glutinosa*

Narthecium ossifragum **(L.) Huds. var. *americanum* (Ker-Gawl.) Gray** – See *Narthecium americanum* Ker-Gawl.

Narthecium pubens **Michx.** – See *Tofieldia racemosa* (Walt.) Britton, Sterns & Poggenb.

Narthecium pusillum **Michx.** – See *Tofieldia pusilla* (Michx.) Pers.

Nassella **(Trin.) Desv.** – Tussock grass [Tussockgrass] (50) (present)

Nassella lepida **(Hitchc.) Barkworth** – Hasse's feather grass [Hasse's feather-grass] (94) (1901)

Nassella leucotricha **(Trin. & Rupr.) Pohl** – Spear grass [Spear-grass] (163) (1852), Texas needle grass [Texas needlegrass] (119, 122) (1937–1938)

Nassella neesiana **(Trin. & Rupr.) Barkworth** – Bear grass (87) (1884), Bunch grass [Bunchgrass, Bunch-grass] (87) (1884)

Nassella tenuissima **(Trin.) Barkworth** – Slender feather grass [Slender feather-grass] (94) (1901), Wiry spear grass [Wiry spear-grass] (163) (1852)

Nassella viridula **(Trin.) Barkworth** – Wild oat grass [Wild oat-grass, Wild oats grass] (5) (1913), Green stipa (56) (1901), Sleepy grass [Sleepygrass, Sleepy-grass] (56) (1901) IA, Western bunch grass [Western bunch-grass] (56) (1901), Bunch grass [Bunchgrass, Bunch-grass] (87) (1884), Feathery bunch grass [Feathery bunch-grass] (157) (1929), Green needle grass [Green needlegrass] (3, 50, 140, 155) (1942–present), Feather bunch grass [Feather bunch-grass] (5, 56, 93, 94, 111, 129) (1901–1936)

Nasturtium amphibium **R. Br.** – See *Rorippa amphibia* (L.) Bess.

Nasturtium aquatica – possibly *Nasturtium officinale* W. T. Aiton

Nasturtium aquaticum – possibly *Nasturtium officinale* W. T. Aiton

Nasturtium armoracia **Fries.** – See *Armoracia rusticana* P. G. Gaertn., B. Mey. & Scherb.

Nasturtium hispidum **DC** – See *Rorippa palustris* (L.) Bess. subsp. *hispida* (Desv.) Jonsell

Nasturtium lacustre **Fries** – See *Neobeckia aquatica* (Eat.) Greene

Nasturtium officinale **R. Br.** – possibly *Nasturtium officinale* W. T. Aiton

Nasturtium officinale **W. T. Aiton (possibly)** – Nasturtium (92) (1876), possibly Lake cress (156) (1923) OK, possibly Lake watercress [Lake water cress, Lake water-cress] (156) (1923), possibly River cress (156) (1923), possibly Well-cress (156) (1923), possibly Crashes (156, 158) (1900–1923) no longer in use by 1923, possibly Watercress [Water-cress, Water cress] (3, 4, 15, 50, 72, 85, 92, 107, 109, 122, 131, 138, 155, 156, 157, 158) (1895–present), possibly Brooklime [Brook-lime, Brook lime] (5, 156, 157, 158) (1900–1929), possibly Brown cress (5, 156, 157, 158) (1900–1929), possibly Water-grass [Water grass] (5, 156, 157, 158) (1900–1929) Ireland, possibly Well-grass [Well grass] (5, 158) (1900–1913), possibly True water-cress [True water cress] (5, 63, 97, 120, 157, 158) (1899–1938)

Nasturtium palustre – See *Rorippa palustris* (L.) Bess.

Nasturtium palustris **DC.** – See *Rorippa palustris* (L.) Bess

Nasturtium **R. Br.** – Nasturtion (92) (1876), Watercress [Water-cress, Water cress] (1, 4, 13, 63, 156, 179) (1526–1986)

Nasturtium sessiliflorum **Nutt.** – See *Rorippa sessiliflora* (Nutt.) A.S. Hitchc.

Nasturtium sinuatum **Nutt.** – See *Rorippa sinuata* (Nutt.) A. S. Hitchc.

Nasturtium sylvestre **R. Br.** – See *Rorippa palustris* (L.) Bess.

Naumbergia **Moench** – See *Lysimachia* L.

Naumburgia thyrsiflora **(L.) Duby** – See *Lysimachia thyrsiflora* L.

Navarretia intertexta **(Benth.) Hook.** – Needle-leaf navarretia [Needle-leaf navarretia] (50) (present)

Navarretia intertexta **(Benth.) Hook. subsp. *propinqua* (Suksdorf) Day** – Near navarretia (50) (present)

Navarretia leucocephala **Benth. subsp. *minima* (Nutt.) Day** – Small navarretia (5) (1913)

Navarretia minima **Nutt.** – See *Navarretia leucocephala* Benth. subsp. *minima* (Nutt.) Day

Navarretia **Ruiz & Pavón** – Pincushion plant [Pincushionplant] (50) (present)

Nazia aliena **Spreng.** – See *Tragus berteronianus* J.A. Schultes

Nazia racemosa **(L.) Kuntze** – See *Tragus racemosus* (L.) All.

Nectandra coriacea **(Sw.) Griseb.** – Red bay [Redbay] (7) (1828), Red laurel [Redlaurel] (7) (1828), Sweet bay [Sweet-bay, Sweetbay] or Sweet bay tree [Sweet bay trees] (7) (1828), Toluchluco (Indians) (7) (1828)

Nectris **Schreb.** – See *Cabomba* Aubl.

Neeragrostis **Bush** – Creeping love grass [Creeping lovegrass] (50) (present)

Neeragrostis reptans **(Michx.) Nicora** – Hairy creeping love grass [Hairy creeping love-grass] (5, 93, 99, 119) (1913–1938), Creeping love grass [Creeping lovegrass] (50, 155) (1942–present), Creeping meadow grass [Creeping meadow-grass] (66, 163, 187) (1818–1903)

Negundo **(Ray) Ludwig.** – See *Acer* L. (all US species)

Negundo aceroides **(L.) Moench** – See *Acer negundo* L. var. *negundo*

Negundo aceroides **Moench** – See *Acer negundo* L. var. *negundo*

Negundo californicum – See *Acer negundo* L. var. *californicum* (Torr. & Gray) Sarg.

Negundo californieum – See *Acer negundo* L. var. *californicum* (Torr. & Gray) Sarg.

Negundo fraxinifolium – possibly *Acer negundo* L.

Negundo fraxinifolius – possibly *Acer negundo* L.

Negundo nuttallii **(Nieuwl.) Rydb.** – See *Acer negundo* L. var. *violaceum* (Kirchn.) Jaeger

Neltuma **Raf.** – See *Prosopis* L. (all US species)

Nelumbium codophyllum **Raf.** – possibly *Nelumbo lutea* Willd.

Nelumbium **Juss.** – See *Nelumbo* Adans. (all US species)

Nelumbium luteum **Juss.** – possibly *Nelumbo lutea* Willd.

Nelumbium luteum **Willd.** – See *Nelumbo lutea* Willd.

Nelumbo **(Tourn.) Adans** – See *Nelumbo* Adans.

Nelumbo **Adans.** – Duck-acorn [Duck acorn] (1) (1932)

Nelumbo **Adans.** – Taluwa (Quapaws) (7) (1828), Terowa (Oto) (7) (1828), Nelumbo (13) (1849), Wankapin (15) (1895), Big yellow waterlily [Big yellow water-lily] (93) (1936), Lotus-lily [Lotus lily] (158) (1900), Water-bean (158) (1900), Lotus (1, 4, 50, 82, 93, 138, 155) (1923–present)

Nelumbo lutea **Willd.** – Big yellow waterlily [Big yellow water-lily] (5) (1913), Grains de volaille (French) (35) (1806) William Clark, Po kish' a co mah (Kickapoo) (35) (1806), Pois de Shicoriat (French) (35) (1806), Pokus haki (35) (1806), Swan root (35) (1806), Volies (35) (1806), Wab-bis-sa-pin (Chipewa) (35) (1806), Tethawe (Omaha-Ponca) (37) (1919), Tewape (Dakota) (37) (1919), Tsherop (Winnebago) (37) (1919), Tukawiu (Pawnee) (37) (1919), Waterlily [Water lily, Water-lily, Water-lilies] (74) (1893) Peoria IL, Nelumbo (82) (1930), Kewapa (Lakota) (121) (1918?–1970?), Tewapa (Lakota) (121) (1918?–1970?), Tsewathe (Osage) (121) (1918?–1970?), Alligator buttons (156) (1923), Water-bean (156) (1923), Yankapin bonnets (156) (1923), Colocasia (183) (~1756), Egyptian bean hibiscus [Egyptian bean hybiscus] (183) (~1756), Yankapin (106, 156, 157, 158) (1900–1930), Yoncopin (106, 156, 157, 158) (1900–1930), Duck-acorn [Duck acorn] (106, 156, 158) (1900–1930), Youquepin (122, 124) (1937) TX, American lotus-lily [American lotus lily] (157, 158) (1900–1929), Great waterlily [Great water-lily] (157, 158) (1900–1929), Great yellow lily (157, 158) (1900–1929), Water lotus (157, 158) (1900–1929), American lotus (3, 5, 50, 72, 82, 97, 106, 109, 120, 121, 138, 158, 183) (~1756–present), Yellow lotus (37, 156) (1919–1923), Lotus (4, 7, 92, 120, 124) (1828–1986), American nelumbo (5, 111, 157, 158) (1900–1929), Rattle nut [Rattle-nut] (7, 92, 156, 158) (1828–1923), Great yellow waterlily [Great yellow water lily, Great yellow water-lily] (74, 156) (1893–1923) NY, Wankapin (76, 156, 157, 158) (1896–1929), Wonkapin (76, 156, 157, 158) (1896–1929) Southern IN, supposedly an Indian name, possibly Nelumbo jaune (French) (7) (1828), possibly Pond-lily [Pond lily] (7) (1828), possibly Watershield [Water shield, Wa-ter-shield] (7) (1828), possibly Yellow waterlily [Yellow water lily, Yellow water-lily, Yellow water lilly] (7) (1828), possibly Great pondlily [Great pond lily] (12) (1821), possibly Te-row-a (Oto, bi-son-beaver) (38) (1820), possibly Water-nut [Water-nuts, Waternuts] (1, 92, 106, 156, 158) (1828–1932), possibly Yellow nelumbo (2, 7, 63, 107) (1828–1919), possibly American water-lotus [American water lotus] (46, 107) (1879–1919), possibly Napoleon plant (7, 92) (1828–1876)

Nelumbo nelumbo (L.) Karst – possibly *Nelumbo nucifera* Gaertn.

Nelumbo nucifera Gaertn. – East Indian lotus (109) (1949), possibly Indian lotus (5) (1913), possibly Sacred bean (5) (1913), possibly Hindu lotus (138, 155) (1923–1942)

Nelumbo speciosa Willd. – See *Nelumbo nucifera* Gaertn.

Nemastylis acuta (Bart.) Herb. – See *Nemastylis geminiflora* Nutt.

Nemastylis coelestina (Bart.) Nutt. – See *Calydorea coelestina* (Bartr.) Goldblatt & Henrich

Nemastylis coelestina Nutt. – See *Calydorea coelestina* (Bartr.) Goldblatt & Henrich

Nemastylis geminiflora Nutt. – Prairie-lily [Prairie lily] (3) (1977), Prairie pleatleaf (50) (present), Celestial (124) (1937) TX, Dragon-head [Dragon-head, Dragon head, Dragon's head] (124) (1937) TX, Northern nemastylis (5, 97) (1913–1937)

Nemastylis Nutt. – Pleatleaf (50) (present), Nemastylis (158) (1900)

Nemesia strumosa Benth. – Pouched nemesia (138) (1923)

Nemesia Vent. – Nemesia (138) (1923)

Nemexia leptanthera (Pennell) Small – See *Smilax pseudochina* L.

Nemexia Raf. – See *Smilax* L. (all US species)

Nemexia tamnifolia (Michx.) Small – See *Smilax pseudochina* L.

Nemopanthes canadensis Raf. – See *Ilex mucronata* (L.) M. Powell, Savol. & S. Andrews

Nemopanthes fascicularis Raf. – See *Ilex mucronata* (L.) M. Powell, Savol. & S. Andrews

Nemopanthes Raf. – See *Nemopanthus* Raf.

Nemopanthus canadensis (Michx.) DC. – possibly *Ilex mucronata* (L.) Powell, Savolainen & Andrews

Nemopanthus mucronata (L.) Trelease – See *Ilex mucronata* (L.) M. Powell, Savol. & S. Andrews

Nemopanthus mucronatus (L.) Loes. – See *Ilex mucronata* (L.) M. Powell, Savol. & S. Andrews

Nemopanthus mucrunatus Trel. – See *Ilex mucronata* (L.) M. Powell, Savol. & S. Andrews

Nemopanthus Raf. – Catberry [Cat berry, Cat-berry] (1) (1932), Mountain-holly [Mountain holly] (1, 15, 138, 156) (1895–1932)

Nemophila aphylla (L.) Brummitt – Small-flower nemophila [Small-flowered nemophila] (5) (1913), Wand flower [Wand-flower, Wand flower] (156) (1923), Beetleweed [Beetle weed, beetle-weed] (5, 10, 156) (1818–1923), Galax (5, 138, 156) (1913–1923), Galaxy (5, 156) (1913–1923), Coltsfoot [Colt's foot, Colt's-foot, Colt foot] (5, 75, 156) (1894–1923)

Nemophila insignis Dougl. – See *Nemophila menziesii* Hook. & Arn. var. *menziesii*

Nemophila maculata Benth. ex Lindl. – Five-spot (109) (1949), Spotted nemophila (138) (1923)

Nemophila menziesi insignis – See *Nemophila menziesii* Hook. & Arn. var. *menziesii*

Nemophila menziesii Hook. & Arn. – Menzies nemophila (138) (1923), Baby-blue eyes [Baby blue-eyes] (75, 77, 109, 138) (1894–1949)

Nemophila menziesii Hook. & Arn. var. *menziesii* – Bluebell [Blue-bell, Blue bell, Blue bells, Blue-bells] (75) (1894) Santa Barbara CA, Love-grove [Love grove] (92) (1876)

Nemophila microcalyx Fisch & Mey. – See *Nemophila aphylla* (L.) Brummitt

Nemophila Nutt. – Nemophila (138) (1923)

Nemophila phacelioides Nutt. – Large-flower baby-blue-eyes

[Largeflower baby blue eyes] (50) (present), Baby-blue eyes [Baby blue-eyes] (3, 97) (1937–1977)

Neobeckia aquatica (Eat.) Greene – Lake watercress [Lake water cress, Lake water-cress] (5) (1913), River cress (5) (1913), Lake cress (2, 63) (1895–1899)

Neobessya missouriensis (Nutt.) Britton & Rose – See *Escobaria missouriensis* (Sweet) D.R. Hunt var. *missouriensis*

Neolentinus lepideus (Fr.) Redhead & Ginns 1985 – Railroad-tie mushroom (128) (1933), Scaly mushroom (128) (1933)

Neopieris mariana (L.) Britton – See *Lyonia mariana* (L.) D. Don

Neopieris nitida (Bartr.) Britton – See *Lyonia lucida* (Lam.) K. Koch

Neottia cernua [(L.) Sw.] – See *Spiranthes cernua* (L.) L. C. Rich.

Neottia pubescens Willd. – See *Goodyera pubescens* (Willd.) R. Br. ex Ait. f.

Neottia tortilis W. – See *Spiranthes torta* (Thunb.) Garay & H. R. Sweet

Nepeta cataria L. – Gajugĕns'ĭbûg (Chippewa, little cat leaf) (40) (1928), Nepe (46) (1617), Herba catariae (49) (1898), Herba nepetae (49) (1898), Cataria (57) (1917), Cat's heal-all (156) (1923), Ground ivy [Ground-ivy] (157) (1929), Cataire (French) (158) (1900), Ca-trup (158) (1900), Chataire (French) (158) (1900), Herbe aux chats (French) (158) (1900), Katzenkraut (German) (158) (1900), Kat-zenminze (German) (158) (1900), Menthe des chats (French) (158) (1900), Catnip (1, 3, 4, 7, 19, 37, 40, 47, 49, 50, 53, 57, 61, 62, 69, 72, 80, 82, 85, 92, 93, 95, 97, 106, 107, 109, 114, 131, 138, 145, 155, 156, 157, 158) (1852–present), Catmint [Cat mint, Cat-mint] (1, 5, 7, 10, 19, 46 (1671), 49, 53, 62, 63, 69, 85, 92, 93, 95, 109, 156, 157, 187) (1671–1949), Nep (5, 184, 187) (1793–1913), Catnep (5, 49, 53, 63, 109, 157, 158, 187) (1818–1949), Field mint (69, 156, 158) (1900–1904), Catwort [Cat's wort, Cats wort, Cat's-wort] (69, 92, 157, 158) (1876–1929)

Nepeta glechoma Benth. – See *Glechoma hederacea* L.

Nepeta hederacea (L.) Trevisan – See *Glechoma hederacea* L.

Nepeta hederacea Trevisan – See *Glechoma hederacea* L.

Nepeta L. – Catnep (158) (1900), Nepeta (138, 155) (1923–1942), Cat-mint [Cat mint, Cat-mint] (167, 190) (~1759–1814), Catnip (50, 82, 156) (1923–present)

Nepeta virginica L. – See *Pycnanthemum flexuosum* (Walt.) Britton, Sterns & Poggenb.

Nephrodium arcrostichoides Michx. – See *Polystichum acrostichoides* (Michx.) Schott

Nephrodium asplenoides Michx. – possibly *Athyrium filix-femina* (L.) Roth var. *asplenoides* (Michx.) Farw.

Nephrodium marginale Michx. – See *Dryopteris marginalis* (L.) A. Gray

Nephrolepis cordifolia (L.) K. Presl – Ladder fern (107) (1919)

Nephrolepis exaltata (L.) Schott – Common sword fern [Common swordfern] (138) (1923)

Nephrolepis Schott – Sword fern [Sword-fern, Swordfern] (109, 138) (1923–1949)

Neptunia Lour. – Puff (50) (present), Sensitive brier [Sensitive-brier, Sensitivebriar] (155) (1942), Neptunia (4, 155, 158) (1900–1986)

Neptunia lutea (Leavenworth) Benth. – Lemon acacia (155) (1942), Yellow neptunia (155) (1942), Yellow sensitive brier [Yellow sensitive briar] (122, 124) (1937), Yellow-puff (4, 50) (1986–present)

Nerium L. – Oleander [Oleandre] (138) (1923)

Nerium odorum [Sol.] – See *Nerium oleander* L.

Nerium oleander L. – Laurier rose (49) (1898), Common oleander (138) (1923), Rhododendrum (174) (1753), Rose-bay [Rose bay, Rosebay] (178) (1526), Oleander [Oleandre] (49, 57, 92, 109, 124, 126, 178, 179) (1526–1949), Rose laurel (7, 92) (1828–1876), Sweet oleander (92, 138) (1876–1923)

Nertera depressa [Banks & Sol. ex Gaertn.] – See *Nertera granadensis* (L. f.) Druce

Nertera granadensis (L. f.) Druce – Bead plant [Bead-plant, Bead-plant] (109, 138) (1923–1949)

Nertera granadensis Druce – See *Nertera granadensis* (L. f.) Druce

Neslia paniculata (L.) Desv. – Ballmustard [Ball mustard] (3, 4, 5, 50,

80, 155, 156) (1913–present)

Nestronia umbellula **Raf.** – Nestronia (5) (1913), Conjurer's nut (183) (~1756), Fascinating nut (183) (~1756), Physic nut [Physic nuts, Physick Nut, Physic-nut] (183) (~1756)

Neviusia alabamensis **Gray** – Alabama snow-wreath (86) (1878), Neviusa (86) (1878), Snow-wreath (138) (1923)

Neviusia **Gray** – Snow-wreath (138) (1923)

Nevrosperma balsaminica **Raf.** – possibly *Momordica balsamina* L.

Nicandra **Adans.** – Nicandra (50) (present) for Nicandra poet of Colophon who wrote on plants about 100 BC, Apple-of-Peru [Apple of Peru, Appleofperu] (138, 155, 158) (1900–1942)

Nicandra physalodes **(L.) Gaertn.** – Globe [Globes] (77) (1898) Sulphur Grove OH, Peruvian bluebell (158) (1900), Apple-of-Peru [Apple of Peru, Appleofperu] (1, 4, 5, 50, 63, 109, 138, 155, 156, 158) (1899–present), Shoofly plant [Shoo-fly plant] (109, 156) (1923–1949)

Nicotiana **(Tourn.) L.** – See *Nicotiana* L.

Nicotiana alata **Link & Otto** – Winged tobacco (138) (1923)

Nicotiana angustifolia **[Mill.]** – See *Nicotiana rustica* L.

Nicotiana attenuata **Torr. ex S. Wats.** – Tobacco (148) (1939), Wild tobacco [Wild-tobacco, Wildtobacco] (148) (1939)

Nicotiana bigelovii **Wats.** – See *Nicotiana quadrivalvis* Pursh var. *bigelovii* (Torr.) DeWolf

Nicotiana clevelandi **Gray** – See *Nicotiana clevelandii* Gray

Nicotiana clevelandii **Gray** – Tobacco (107) (1919)

Nicotiana glauca **Graham** – Tobacco tree (77) (1898) CO, Tronadora (122) (1937) TX, Sacred mustard (122, 124) (1937) TX, Tree tobacco (75, 138) (1894–1923) Santa Barbara CA

Nicotiana **L.** – A-óobe (Cuchan Yuma) (132) (1855), A-ú-ba (Diegeño Yuma) (132) (1855), Co-ap'-e (Chemehuevi Shoshone) (132) (1855), Ha'mi (Kiwomi Keres) (132) (1855), Ha'-o-mi (Kiwomi Keres) (132) (1855), He'-to-co-ni (Zuñi) (132) (1855), Oh-oúbe (Mohave Yuma) (132) (1855), Pah'-mon (Comanche Shoshonee) (132) (1855), Pi'-bŭt (Cahuillo Shoshonee) (132) (1855), Qutschar'-tai (Delaware) (132) (1855), Ta'-po (Kioway) (132) (1855), T'thai-a-mer' (Shawnee) (132) (1855), Vib (Pima) (132) (1855), Weh'-ec (Hueco Pawnee) (132) (1855), Tobacco (1, 7, 10, 14, 50, 138, 156) (1818–present)

Nicotiana longiflora **Cav.** – Long-flower tobacco [Long-flowered tobacco] (5) (1913)

Nicotiana quadrivalvis **Pursh** – Chan-di (Dakota) (37) (1919), Chan-li (Dakota Teton) (37) (1919), Nini-hi (Omaha-Ponca) (37) (1919), Tobacco (34, 35, 37, 107) (1806–1919), Nonehaw (Missouri tribes) (6, 7) (1828–1932), Wild tobacco [Wild-tobacco, Wildtobacco] (85, 101) (1905–1932)

Nicotiana quadrivalvis **Pursh var.** *bigelovii* **(Torr.) DeWolf** – Wild tobacco [Wild-tobacco, Wildtobacco] (75) (1894)

Nicotiana repanda **Willd. ex Lehm.** – Tobacco (107) (1919), Yetl (Mexico) (107) (1919), Wild tobacco [Wild-tobacco, Wildtobacco] (124) (1937)

Nicotiana rustica **L.** – Common tobacco (19) (1840), Tabacco del daiblo (Chili) (110) (1886), Pachyphylla (174) (1753), Yellow henbane (178) (1526), Tobacco (27, 107) (1811–1919), Syrian tobacco (5, 156) (1913–1923), Wild tobacco [Wild-tobacco, Wildtobacco] (5, 156) (1913–1923), Indian tobacco [Indian-tobacco] (5, 75, 156) (1894–1923) NY, Real tobacco (5, 75, 156) (1894–1923) NY, Aztec tobacco (75, 138) (1894–1923) NY

Nicotiana tabacum **L.** – Tabac (French) (6) (1892), Yaqui tobacco (6) (1892), Drunkwort (92) (1876) young plants, believed by children to intoxicate (73) obsolete by 1923, Tobacco plant (106) (1930), Docchan (Arabic, "smoke") (110) (1886), Petum (110) (1886), Tabaco (110) (after 1600), Tabok (110) (1886), Tamboc (110) (1886), Tambuco (110) (after 1600), Henbane of Peru (178) (1526), Tabaco (178) (1526), Arianocoe (181) (~1678), Old Tom (181) (~1678), One-and-all [One & All] (181) (~1678), Prior (181) (~1678), Sweet-scented tobacco (181) (~1678), Virginia tobacco [Virginian tobacco] (19, 92) (1840–1876), Common tobacco (43, 138) (1820–1923), Tabacum (57, 60) (1902–1917), Tabak (German) (6, 110) (1886–1892),

Tobacco (6, 45, 48, 57, 60, 92, 106, 107, 109, 110, 182, 184) (1793–1949), Cohiba (Haiti) (6, 7) (1828–1932)

Nicotiana ybarrensis **Kunth** – See *Nicotiana tabacum* L.

Nierembergia frutescens **Durieu** – Tall cup flower [Tall cup-flower, Tall cupflower] (109, 138) (1923–1949)

Nierembergia **Ruiz & Pavón** – Cupflower [Cup flower] (109, 138) (1923–1949)

Nigella **(Tourn.) L.** – See *Nigella* L.

Nigella damascena **L.** – Common fennel flower (2) (1895), Nigella (57) (1917), Jack-in-the-bush (76) (1896) Worcester MA, Jack-in-the-pulpit [Jack in the pulpit, Jackinthepulpit] (76) (1896) Rutalnd MA, Maid-in-the-mist [Maid in the mist] (76) (1896) Acton MA, Ragged-sailor [Ragged sailor, Ragged sailors] (76) (1896) Rutalnd MA, Lady-in-the-green [Lady in the green] (79) (1891) Northeast US, Devil's-in-a-bush [Devil's in a bush] (92) (1876), Wild fennel (107) (1919), Damask nigella [Damaske nigella] (178) (1526), Love-in-a-mist [Love in a mist] (1, 2, 79, 92, 109, 138, 156) (1876–1949), Fennel-flower [Fennel flower] (19, 156) (1840–1923), Ragged-lady [Ragged lady] (2, 92) (1876–1895), Devil-in-the-bush (Devil in the bush) (79, 156) (1891–1923)

Nigella **L.** – Love-in-a-mist [Love in a mist] (138) (1923), Fennel-flower [Fennel flower] (1, 109, 156) (1923–1949)

Nigella sativa **L.** – Bishop's-wort [Bishop's wort, Bishopswort] (92) (1876), Black caraway (92) (1876), Black cummin (92) (1876), Nigella seed (92) (1876), Small fennel flower (92) (1876), Black cumin (107) (1919), Fennel-flower [Fennel flower] (107) (1919), Nigella (107) (1919), Roman camomile [Roman chamomile] (107) (1919), Double nigella (178) (1526), White nigella (178) (1526), Cokyll (179) (1526), Gith (179) (1526), Nutmeg flower (19, 92, 107) (1840–1919)

Nigella sativus – See *Nigella sativa* L.

Nolina lindheimeriana **(Scheele) S. Wats.** – Ribbon grass [Ribbon-grass] (122, 124) (1937) TX

Nolina **Michx.** – Nolina (138) (1923), Bear-grass [Bear grass, Bear's grass, Bears' grass] (149) (1904)

Nolina microcarpa **S. Wats.** – Bear-grass [Bear grass, Bear's grass, Bears' grass] (153) (1913) NM

Nolina parryi **S. Wats.** – Parry's nolina [Parry nolina] (138) (1923)

Nolina texana **S. Wats.** – Texas sacahuista (50) (present), Sacahuiste (122) (1937) TX, Bunch grass [Bunchgrass, Bunch-grass] (122, 124) (1937) TX

Nopalea cochinellifera **Salm-Dyck** – See *Opuntia cochenillifera* (L.) Mill.

Nopalea **Salm-Dyck** – See Opuntia Mill.

Norta **Adans.** – See *Sisymbrium* L.

Norta altissima **(L.) Britton** – See *Sisymbrium altissimum* L.

Nothocalais **(Gray) Greene** – Prairie-dandelion [Prairie dandelion] (50) (present), False calais (158) (1900), False dandelion (158) (1900)

Nothocalais cuspidata **(Pursh) Greene** – Sharp-point prairie-dandelion [Sharppoint prairie-dandelion] (50) (Present), Dandelion (76) (1896) Burnside SD, Wavy-leaf agoseris [Wavyleaf agoseris] (155) (1942), False dandelion (3, 5, 85, 93, 95, 98) (1911–1936), Prairie false dandelion (5, 97, 156) (1913–1937), False calais (72, 131) (1899–1907)

Nothoholcus lanatus **(L.) Nash** – See *Holcus lanatus* L.

Notholaena dealbata **(Pursh) Kunze** – See *Argyrochosma dealbata* (Pursh) Windham

Notholaena fendleri **Kunze** – See *Argyrochosma fendleri* (Kunze) Windham

Notholaena **R. Br.** – Notholaena (158) (1900), Cloak fern [Cloakfern] (50, 155) (1942–present)

Notholaena sinuata **(Sw.) Kaulf** – See *Astrolepis sinuata* (Lag. ex Sw.) Benham & Windham subsp. *sinuata*

Notholaena standleyi **Maxon** – Star cloak fern [Star cloakfern] (50, 97, 155) (1937–present)

Nothoscordum bivalve **(L.) Britt.** – Yellow false garlic [Yellow falsegarlic] (5, 93, 97, 155) (1913–1942), Crow-poison [Crow poison, Crowpoison] (50, 122) (1937–present), possibly

　　　Nymphaea mexicana Zucc.

Ornithogalum stagger-grass [Ornathogalum (*sic*) Staggergrass] (183) (1756)

Nothoscordum borbonicum **Kunth** – False snowdrop [False snow drop] (19) (1840), Fragrant false garlic (50) (present), possibly Carolina garlick (165) (1768)

Nothoscordum fragrans **auct. non (Vent.) Kunth** – See *Nothoscordum borbonicum* Kunth

Nothoscordum gracile **Stearn, non (Ait.) Stearn** – See *Nothoscordum borbonicum* Kunth

Nothoscordum **Kunth.** – False garlic [Falsegarlic] (1, 50, 155) (1932–present)

Nothoscordum striatum **Kunth.** – See *Nothoscordum bivalve* (L.) Britt.

Nuphar advena **Aiton f.** – See *Nuphar lutea* (L.) Sm. subsp. *advena* (Aiton) Kartesz & Gandhi

Nuphar kalmiana **(Michx.) W. T. Aiton** – See *Nuphar lutea* (L.) Sm. subsp. *pumila* (Timm) E. O. Beal

Nuphar lutea **(L.) Sibth. & Sm. subsp. *macrophylla* (Small) Beal** – See *Nuphar lutea* (L.) Sm. subsp. *advena* (Aiton) Kartesz & Gandhi

Nuphar lutea **(L.) Sm.** – Yellow pond-lily [Yellow pond lily] (50) (present), Water-can [Water can] (92) (1876), Yellow waterlily [Yellow water lily, Yellow water-lily, Yellow water lilly] (107) (1919), European cowlily (155) (1942)

Nuphar lutea **(L.) Sm. subsp. *advena* (Aiton) Kartesz & Gandhi** – Tukawisi (Pawnee Skidi) (37) (1919), Tut (Pawnee Chawi) (37) (1919), Goldwatch [Gold watch] (74) (1893) Mauch Chunk PA, Hog-lily [Hog lily] (74) (1893) Concord MA, Yellow lily-root [Yellow lily root] (92) (1876), Tah-wah-pah (Dakota Indians) (103) (1870), Common spatterdock (109) (1949), Θiŋmoŋnoŋta (Osage) (121) (1918?–1970?), Spatterdock cow-lily [Spatterdock cowlily] (155) (1942), Flatterdock [Flatter-dock, Flatter dock] (156) (1923), Globe-lily (156) (1923), Mule-foot bonnets (156) (1923), Mule-foot lily (156) (1923), Three-color lily [Three-colored lily] (156) (1923), Tuckaho [Tuckaho, Tuckahoe] (156) (1923), Tucky (156) (1923), Tucky-lily (156) (1923), Yellow lanterns (156) (1923), Houselily [House lilly] (157) (1929), Common yellow pondlily [Common yellow pond lily] (158) (1900), Dog-lily [Dog lily] (158) (1900), Pond-lily [Pond lily] (106, 127) (1930–1933), Beaver-lily (156, 158) (1900–1923), Splatter-dock (156, 187) (1818–1923), Yellow waterlily [Yellow water lily, Yellow water-ily, Yellow water lilly] (3, 19, 46, 76, 92, 101, 106, 124, 157) (1840–1977), Spatterdock [Spatter dock, Spatter-dock] (46, 92, 106, 107, 138, 156, 157, 158) (1879–1930), Yellow pond-lily [Yellow pond lily] (48, 50, 57, 72, 74, 85, 92, 93, 97, 103, 107, 120, 121, 122, 156, 157, 158) (1840–present), Large yellow pondlily [Large yellow pond lily] (5, 37, 131, 158) (1900–1919), Bonnets (74, 158) (1893–1900), Horselily [Horse-lily, Horse lily] (76, 156, 158) (1896–1923) Hartford ME, Kelp (76, 158) (1896–1900) South Berwick ME, Bull-head lily [Bullhead lily] (79, 158) (1891–1900) NH, Brandy-bottle [Brandy bottles] (92, 156) (1876–1923), Froglily [Frog-lilly, Frog lily] (92, 156, 157, 158) (1876–1929), Beaver-root [Beaver root] (92, 156, 158) (1876–1923), Cowlily [Cow-lily, Cow lily] (92, 97, 156, 157, 158) (1876–1937)

Nuphar lutea **(L.) Sm. subsp. *pumila* (Timm) E. O. Beal** – Small yellow pondlily [Small yellow pond lily] (5) (1913), Small waterlily [Small water lily] (187) (1818)

Nuphar lutea **(L.) Sm. subsp. *sagittifolia* (Walt.) E. O. Beal** – Arrowleaf pondlily [Arrow-leaved pond lily] (5) (1913), Alligator bonnets (5, 156) (1913–1923)

Nuphar lutea **(L.) Sm. subsp. *variegata* (Dur.) E. O. Beal** – Yellow waterlily [Yellow water lily, Yellow water-lily, Yellow water lilly] (3) (1977), Variegated yellow pond-lily (50) (present), Painted cowlily (155) (1942)

Nuphar luteum **Sibth. & Sm.** – See *Nuphar lutea* (L.) Sm.

Nuphar microcarpum **(Miller & Standl.) Standl. (*sic*)** – See *Nuphar lutea* (L.) Sm. subsp. *advena* (Aiton) Kartesz & Gandhi

Nuphar sagittifolia **(Walt.) Pursh** – See *Nuphar lutea* (L.) Sm. subsp. *sagittifolia* (Walt.) E. O. Beal

Nuphar sagittifolium **Pursh** – See *Nuphar lutea* (L.) Sm. subsp. *sagittifolia* (Walt.) E. O. Beal

Nuphar **Sm.** – Pond-lily [Pond lily] (50) (present), Nenufar (179) (1526), Yellow pond-lily [Yellow pond lily] (1, 10, 13, 15, 63) (1818–1932), Cowlily [Cow-lily, Cow lily] (1, 109, 155) (1932–1949), Spatterdock [Spatter dock, Spatter-dock] (1, 4, 13, 15, 109, 138) (1849–1986)

Nuphar variegatum **Engelm.** – See *Nuphar lutea* (L.) Sm. subsp. *variegata* (Dur.) E. O. Beal

Nuttallanthus canadensis **(L.) D. A. Sutton** – Canadian toadflax [Canada toadflax] (50) (present), Small upright blue fkaxweed [Small upright blew Fkaxeweed] (181) (~1678), Purple toadflax [Purple toad flax, Purple toad flaxe] (187) (1818), Canadian snapdragon [Canadian snap dragon] (42) (1814), Chaparral snapdragon (138, 155) (1923–1942), Wild toadflax [Wild toad flax, Wild toad-flax] (2, 5, 93, 97) (1895–1937), Old-field toadflax [Oldfield toadflax] (4, 155) (1942–1986), Blue toadflax [Blue toad flax, Blue toad-flax] (5, 72, 93, 95, 97, 122, 131) (1899–1937)

Nuttallanthus **D. A. Sutton** – Toadflax [Toad flax, Toad-flax] (50) (present)

Nuttallanthus texanus **(Scheele) D. A. Sutton** – Old-field toadflax [Oldfield toadflax] (3) (1977), Blue toadflax [Blue toad flax, Blue toad-flax] (124) (1937), Texas toadflax [Texas toad flax, Texas toad-flax] (4, 50, 122) (1937–present)

Nuttallia cerasiformis **Torr. & Gray** – See *Oemleria cerasiformis* (Torr. & Gray ex Hook. & Arn.) Landon

Nuttallia decapetala **(Pursh) Greene** – See *Mentzelia decapetala* (Pursh ex Sims) Urban & Gilg ex Gilg

Nuttallia nuda **(Pursh) Greene** – See *Mentzelia nuda* (Pursh) Torr. & Gray var. *nuda*

Nuttallia **Raf.** – See *Mentzelia* L.

Nuttallia reverchonii **(Urban & Gilg) W. A. Weber** – See *Mentzelia reverchonii* (Urban & Gilg) Thomps. & Zavortink

Nuttallia stricta **(Osterhout) Greene** – See *Mentzelia nuda* (Pursh) Torr. & Gray var. *stricta* (Osterhout) Harrington

Nyctaginia capitata **Choisy** – Devil's-bouquet [Devil's bouquet] (124) (1937)

Nyctelea nyctelea **(L.) Britton** – See *Ellisia nyctelea* (L.) L.

Nymphaea **(Tourn.) L.** – See *Nymphaea* L.

Nymphaea advena **Soland.** – See *Nuphar lutea* (L.) Sm. subsp. *advena* (Aiton) Kartesz & Gandhi

Nymphaea alba **L.** – European waterlily [European water lily] (92) (1876), Water-rocket [Water rocket] (92) (1876), Flatterdock [Flatter-dock, Flatter dock] (107) (1919), White waterlily [White water lily, White water-lily] (107) (1919), European white waterlily [European white water-lily] (109, 138, 155) (1923–1949)

Nymphaea caerulea **Savigny** – Blue lotus (of Egypt) (109) (1949), Blue Egyptian lotus (138) (1923)

Nymphaea capensis **Thunb.** – Cape blue water-lily (109) (1949), Cape waterlily (138, 155) (1931–1942)

Nymphaea coerulea **Savar.** – See *Nymphaea caerulea* Savigny

Nymphaea elegans **Hook.** – White waterlily [White water lily, White water-lily] (122) (1937) TX, Pond-lily [Pond lily] (124) (1937) TX, Señorita waterlily (138, 155) (1931–1942)

Nymphaea flava **Leitn.** – See *Nymphaea mexicana* Zucc.

Nymphaea **L.** – Splatter-dock (93) (1936), Nymphaea (109) (1949), Nenufar (179) (1526), Water-can [Water can] (184) (1793), Waterlily [Water lily, Water-lily, Water-lilies] (1, 10, 50, 82, 106, 109, 138, 167) (1814–present), Pond-lily [Pond lily] (1, 156, 158) (1900–1932), Yellow pond-lily [Yellow pond lily] (93, 158) (1900–1936)

Nymphaea longifolia Michx. – See *Nuphar longifolia* (Michx.) Sm.

Nymphaea lotus **L.** – Egyptian waterlily [Egyptian water lily] (107) (1919), Lotus (107) (1919), White lotus (of Egypt) (109) (1949), Ambel (174) (1753), White Egyptian waterlily (138, 155) (1931–1942)

Nymphaea mexicana **Zucc.** – Audubon's yellow water-lily (86) (1878), Golden waterlily [Golden water-lily] (86) (1878), Yellow Mexican waterlily (138, 155) (1931–1942), Yellow waterlily [Yellow water lily, Yellow water-lily, Yellow water lilly] (2, 109) (1895–1949)

Nymphaea microphylla **Pers.** – See *Nuphar lutea* (L.) Sm. subsp. *pumila* (Timm) E. O. Beal

Nymphaea odorata **(Dryand.) Woods. & Wood.** – possibly *Nymphaea odorata* Aiton

Nymphaea odorata **Aiton** – Fragrant white waterlily [Fragrant white water lily] (4) (1986), Large white waterlily [Large white water lily] (6) (1892), Nenuphar odorant (French) (7) (1828), Sweet-scented pondlily [Sweet-scented pond lily] (49) (1898), American white water-lily [American white waterlily] (50) (present), Sweet-scented waterlily [Sweet-scented water lily, Sweet scented water lily] (92) (1876), Fragrant waterlily [Fragrant water-lily] (109, 187) (1818–1949), White waterlily [White water lily, White water-lily] (2, 92) (1876–1895), American water-lily [American water lily, American waterlily] (3, 138, 155) (1932–1977), Pond-lily [Pond lily] (49, 131) (1898–1899) IA, Water-nymph [Water nymph, Waternymph] (6, 49) (1892–1898), Waterlily [Water lily, Water-lily, Water-lilies] (6, 49, 57, 92) (1876–1917), White pond-lily [White pond lily] (6, 7, 19, 48, 49, 61, 92) (1828–1898), Sweet waterlily [Sweet water lily] (6, 7, 63, 86) (1828–1932), Cow-cabbage [Cow cabbage] (7, 92) (1828–1876), Toad-lily [Toadlily, Toad lily] (7, 92) (1828–1876), Water-cabbage [Water cabbage] (7, 92) (1828–1876)

Nymphaea odorata **Aiton subsp.** *tuberosa* **(Paine) Wiersma & Hellquist** – See *Nymphaea odorata* Aiton subsp. *tuberosa* (Paine) Wiersma & Hellquist

Nymphaea odorata **Aiton subsp.** *odorata* – Richfield American waterlily (155) (1942), Small American waterlily (155) (1942), Alligator bonnets (156) (1923), Waterlily [Water lily, Water-lily, Water-lilies] (156) (1923), White pond-lily [White pond lily] (158) (1900), Cape Cod waterlily [Capecod waterlily] (138, 155) (1923–1942), White waterlily [White water lily, White water-lily] (40, 156) (1923–1928), Pond-lily [Pond lily] (5, 156) (1913–1923), Toad-lily [Toadlily, Toad lily] (5, 156, 158) (1900–1923), Water-cabbage [Water cabbage] (5, 156, 158) (1900–1923), Water-nymph [Water nymph, Waternymph] (5, 156, 158) (1900–1923), Sweet-scented white waterlily [Sweet-scented white water-lily] (5, 72, 97, 156, 158) (1900–1937)

Nymphaea odorata **Aiton subsp.** *tuberosa* **(Paine) Wiersma & Hellquist** – Moc-cup-pin (Chipewa) (35) (1806), Tuber-bearing waterlily [Tuber-bearing water lily] (63) (1899), Common white waterlily [Common white water lily] (82) (1930), Tuberous waterlily [Tuberous water-lily] (109, 156) (1923–1949), Magnolia waterlily (138, 155) (1923–1942), White waterlily [White water lily, White water-lily] (3, 4, 82, 85, 120, 157) (1900–1986), Tuberous white waterlily [Tuberous white water lily, Tuberous white water-lily] (5, 72, 93, 97, 120) (1907–1938)

Nymphaea odorata **Aiton var.** *gigantea* **Tricker** – See *Nymphaea odorata* Aiton subsp. *odorata*

Nymphaea odorata **Aiton var.** *minor* **Sims** – See *Nymphaea odorata* Aiton subsp. *odorata*

Nymphaea odorata **Aiton var.** *rosea* **Pursh** – See *Nymphaea odorata* Aiton subsp. *odorata*

Nymphaea odorata rosea – See *Nymphaea odorata* Aiton subsp. *odorata*

Nymphaea reniformis **DC.** – See *Nymphaea odorata* Aiton subsp. *tuberosa* (Paine) Wiersma & Hellquist

Nymphaea sagittaefolia **Walt.** – See *Nuphar lutea* (L.) Sm. subsp. *sagittifolia* (Walt.) E. O. Beal

Nymphaea sagittifolia **Walt.** – See *Nuphar lutea* (L.) Sm. subsp. *sagittifolia* (Walt.) E. O. Beal

Nymphaea tetragona **Georgi** – Small white waterlily [Small white water lily] (5) (1913), Pygmy water-lily [Pygmy waterlily] (109, 137, 155) (1923–1949)

Nymphaea **Tourn.** – See *Nymphaea* L.

Nymphaea tuberosa **Paine** – See *Nymphaea odorata* Aiton subsp.

tuberosa (Paine) Wiersma & Hellquist

Nymphoides **(Tourn.) Hill.** – See *Nymphoides* Hill

Nymphoides aquatica **(J. F. Gmel.) Kuntze** – Larger floating-heart [Larger floating heart] (5) (1913), Floatingheart [Floating-heart, Floating heart] (122, 124) (1937) TX

Nymphoides aquaticum **(Walt.) Kuntze.** – See *Nymphoides aquatica* (J. F. Gmel.) Kuntze

Nymphoides cordata **(Ell.) Fern.** – Floatingheart [Floating-heart, Floating heart] (19) (1840), Spur-stem (19) (1840), Wild violet (41) (1770), Floatingheart [Floating-heart, Floating heart] (5, 86, 156) (1878–1923)

Nymphoides **Hill** – Floatingheart [Floating-heart, Floating heart] (1, 2, 109, 138) (1895–1949)

Nymphoides indica **(L.) Kuntze** – Water-snowflake (109, 138) (1923–1949)

Nymphoides indicum – See *Nymphoides indica* (L.) Kuntze

Nymphoides lacunosa – See *Nymphoides cordata* (Ell.) Fern.

Nymphoides lacunosum **(Vent.) Kuntze.** – See *Nymphoides cordata* (Ell.) Fern.

Nymphoides nymphacaeoides **(L.) Britton** – possibly *Nymphoides peltata* (Gmel.) Kuntze

Nymphoides nymphaeoides **(L.) Britt.** – See *Nymphoides peltata* (Gmel.) Kuntze

Nymphoides peltata **(Gmel.) Kuntze** – Fringed waterlily [Fringed water-lily] (156) (1923), Floatingheart [Floating-heart, Floating heart] (5, 138, 156) (1913–1923), Waterlily [Water lily, Water-lily, Water-lilies] (5, 156) (1913–1923), Dwarf waterlily [Dwarf water-lily, Dwarf water lily] (92, 156) (1876–1923), Fringed bog-bean [Fringed bog bean] (92, 156) (1876–1923)

Nymphoides peltatum – See *Nymphoides peltata* (Gmel.) Kuntze

Nyssa angulisans **Michx.** – See *Nyssa aquatica* L.

Nyssa aquatica **L.** – Black gum or Black gum tree (5) (1913), Olive tree (along Mississiippi) (8) (1785), Tupélo aquatique (French) (8) (1785), Virginia water tupelo tree [Virginian water tupelo tree] (8) (1785), Gum or Gum tree [Gum-tree] (20) (1857), Ogeechee lime [Ogechee lime, Ogeeche limes] (107) (1919), Black-berry-bearing gum [Black-berry-bearing-gum] (177) (1762), Big tupelo (122, 124, 138) (1923–1937), Tupelo or Tupelo tree [Tupelo-tree] (14, 20, 41, 177, 189) (1762–1882), Water tupelo [Water-tupelo] (177, 189) (1762–1767), Wild olive (Lower Louisiana) (2, 10, 20, 107) (1818–1919), Large tupelo (2, 5, 20, 107, 156) (1857–1923), Peperidge (Dutch near New York) (20, 187) (1818–1857), Cotton gum [Cotton-gum] (5, 106, 109) (1913–1949), Tupelo gum (Tupelo-gum) (5, 106, 109, 156) (1913–1949), Swamp hornbeam (5, 156) (1913–1923), Swamp tupelo (5, 156) (1913–1923), Sour gum [Sour-gum] or Sour-gum tree [Sour gum tree] (5, 20, 19, 187) (1818–1913)

Nyssa biflora **Walt.** – Southern tupelo (5) (1913), Swamp hornbeam (5) (1913), Water gum (5) (1913), Tupelo or Tupelo tree [Tupelo-tree] (14) (1882), Horne-bound tree [Horne bound tree] (46) (1879), Swamp tupelo (46) (1879), Vine tree (46) (1879), Wenomesippaguash (Narraganset) (46) (1879), Southern black-gum (106) (1930), Water-gum (106) (1930), Black haw [Black-haw, Blackhaw] (181) (~1678), Water tupelo [Water-tupelo] (2, 5) (1895–1913)

Nyssa canadensis **Poir.** – See *Nyssa sylvatica* Marsh.

Nyssa candicans **Michx.** – See *Nyssa ogeche* Bartr. ex Marsh.

Nyssa capitata **Walt.** – See *Nyssa ogeche* Bartr. ex Marsh.

Nyssa coccinea **[Bart.]** – See *Nyssa ogeche* Bartr. ex Marsh.

Nyssa denticulata **[Aiton]** – See *Nyssa aquatica* L.

Nyssa grandidentata **[Michx. F.]** – See *Nyssa aquatica* L.

Nyssa **L.** – Black gum or Black gum tree (7) (1828), Tupélo (French) (8) (1785), Olivier (French, olive) (17) (1796), Pepperage tree (190) (~1759), Pepperidge [Peperidge] (2, 7) (1828–1895), Sour gum [Sour-gum] or Sour-gum tree [Sour gum tree] (2, 7, 10) (1818–1895), Tupelo or Tupelo tree [Tupelo-tree] (2, 7, 8, 10, 109, 138, 182, 184) (1785–1949)

Nyssa montana [**Gaertn.**] – See *Nyssa ogeche* Bartr. ex Marsh.

Nyssa multiflora **Walt.** – possibly *Nyssa sylvatica* Marsh.

Nyssa multiflora **Wangenh.** – See *Nyssa sylvatica* Marsh.

Nyssa ogeche **Bartr. ex Marsh.** – Tupélo ogeche (French) (8) (1785), Black gum or Black gum tree (17) (1796), Oliver sauvage (French Creole) (17) (1796), Sour tupelo (20) (1857), Ogeechee plum [Ogeche plum] (106) (1930), White tupelo (106) (1930), Ogeeche limes (182) (1791), Tupilo (183) (~1756), Wild lemon [Wild lemmon] (183) (~1756), Tupelo or Tupelo tree [Tupelo-tree] (14, 17) (1796–1882), Wild lime or Wild lime tree [Wild lime-tree] (2, 20, 106, 183) (~1756–1930), Ogeechee lime [Ogechee lime, Ogeeche limes] (2, 8, 10, 107) (1785–1919), Ogeechee [Ogeeche] or Ogeechee tree (92, 182, 183) (~1756–1876)

Nyssa ogeche **Marsh.** – See *Nyssa ogeche* Bartr. ex Marsh.

Nyssa sylvatica **Marsh.** – Common tupelo (2) (1895), Tupélo de montagne (French) (8) (1785), Battledoe (46) (1758), Old-man's-beard [Old man's beard, Old-mans-beard] (75) (1894) Lincolnton NC, M'gos atik (Chippewa, awl wood) (105) (1932), Highland blackgum (106) (1930), Stinkwood (106) (1930), Yellow-gum (106) (1930), Water-gum (156) (1923), Water-tupelo (156) (1923), Gum or Gum tree [Gum-tree] (18, 35) (1805–1806), Swamp hornbeam (19, 92, 156) (1840–1923), Peppe: 107, 109, 156) (1840–1949), Sour gum [Sour-gum] or Sour-gum tree [Sour gum tree] (2, 5, 8, 10, 20, 92, 97, 106, 107, 109, 156, 182) (1791–1949), Tupelo or Tupelo tree [Tupelo-tree] (5, 14, 19, 34, 92, 106, 138, 156) (1834–1930), Beetlebung [Beetle-bung, Beetle bung] (5, 156) (1913–1923) no longer in use by 1923, Hornpipe (5, 156) (1913–1923) no longer in use by 1923, Snag tree (snag-tree) (5, 156) (1913–1923) no longer in use by 1923, Yellow gum tree [Yellow gum-tree] (5, 20, 156) (1857–1923), Black gum or Black gum tree (5, 20, 46, 65, 106, 107, 109, 122, 156) (1857–1949), Hornbeam [Horn beam] or Hornbeam tree (5, 73, 156) (1892–1923) NH, no longer in use by 1923, Hornbine [Horn-bine, Horn bine] (5, 75, 156) (1894–1923) Southern states, no longer in use by 1923, Horn-pine [Hornpipe, Horn pine] (5, 75, 156) (1894–1923) Southern states, no longer in use by 1923

Nyssa sylvatica **Marsh.** – Upland tupelo or Upland tupelo tree (8, 46, 124, 107) (1785–1937)

Nyssa tomentosa [**Michx.**] – See *Nyssa aquatica* L.

Nyssa uniflora **Walt.** – possibly *Nyssa aquatica* L.

Nyssa uniflora **Wangenh.** – See *Nyssa aquatica* L.

Nyssa villosa **Michx.** – See *Nyssa sylvatica* Marsh.

Black Gum.
Nyssa sylvatica

Nyssa sylvatica Marsh.
(F. A. Michaux, 1819)

O

Oakesia puberula **Watson.** – See *Uvularia puberula* Michx.

Oakesiella puberula **(Michx.) Small** – See *Uvularia puberula* Michx.

Oaksiella sessilifolia **(L.) Sm.** – See *Uvularia sessilifolia* L.

Oaksiella **Small.** – possibly *Uvularia* L.

Obione canescens – See *Atriplex canescens* (Pursh) Nutt.

Obolaria virginica **L.** – Round Virginia Rape with a stringy root (181) (~1678), Pennywort [Penny-wort, Penny wort] (5, 19, 156) (1840–1923)

Oceanorus leimanthoides **(A. Gray) Small** – See *Zigadenus leimanthoides* Gray

Ocimum basilicum **L.** – Great basil [Great basill] (178) (1526), Basil (19, 109) (1840–1949), Sweet basil [Sweet-basil] (7, 57, 92, 107, 184) (1793–1919), Common basil (138) (1923), Basel [Basyll] (179) (1526)

Ocimum **L.** – Basil (138) (1923)

Ocimum salinum **Molina** – See *Frankenia salina* (Molina) I. M. Johnston

Oclemena acuminata **(Michx.) Greene** – Swamp aster (106) (1930), Acuminatus aster (155) (1942), Mountain aster (5, 156) (1913–1923), Whorled aster (5, 156) (1913–1923)

Oclemena nemoralis **(Aiton) Greene** – Wood aster (19) (1840), Winǐ'sǐkĕns (Chippewa, dirty, little) (40) (1928), Bog aster (5, 155) (1913–1942)

Ocymum basilicum **L.** – See *Ocimum basilicum* L.

Odontites rubra **[(Baumg.) Opiz]** – See *Odontites vulgaris* Moench

Odontites vulgaris **Moench** – Red eyebright (156) (1923)

Odostemon aquifolium **(Pursh) Rydb.** – See *Mahonia aquifolium* (Pursh) Nutt.

Odostemon **Raf.** – See *Mahonia* Nutt.

Odostemon repens **(Lindl.) Cockerell** – See *Mahonia repens* (Lindl.) G. Don

Oemleria cerasiformis **(Torr. & Gray ex Hook. & Arn.) Landon** – Fringe tree [Fringetree, Fringe-tree] (35) (1806), Osoberry [Oso berry] (76) (1896) Northwestern US

Oenanthe **L.** – Filipendula (10) (1818), Water dropwort [Water dropwort] (10) (1818)

Oenoplia volubilis – possibly *Berchemia scandens* (Hill.) Trelease

Oenothera albicaulis **Nutt.** – See *Oenothera albicaulis* Pursh

Oenothera albicaulis **Pursh** – White-stalk primrose [White-stalked primrose] (38) (1820), Whitest evening-primrose (50) (present), White evening-primrose [White evening primrose] (85) (1932), Evening-primrose [Evening primrose, Eveningprimrose] (158) (1900), Pale evening-primrose [Pale evening primrose] (3, 4) (1977–1986), Prairie evening-primrose [Prairie evening primrose] (4, 97) (1937–1986)

Oenothera argillicola **Mackenzie** – Narrow-leaf evening-primrose [Narrow-leaved evening primrose] (5) (1913)

Oenothera biennis **L.** – Cure-all [Cure all, Cureall] (6) (1892), Nachtkerz (German) (6) (1892), Primrose tree (7) (1828), Sundrop [Sundrops, Sun-drops] (7) (1828), Biennial oenothera (41) (1770), Yellow lysimachus of Virginia (46) (1671), Nachtkerze (German) (158) (1900), Codded loose-strife of Virginia (181) (~1678), Tree primrose of Virginia (181) (~1678), Evening tree-primrose (187) (1818), German rampion (107, 156) (1919–1923), Evening-primrose [Evening primrose, Eveningprimrose] (14, 46, 49, 53, 57, 80, 85, 92, 107, 114, 122, 124, 131, 145, 157) (1879–1937), Field evening-primrose [Field evening primrose] (157, 158) (1900–1929), Wild evening-primrose [Wild evening primrose] (157, 158) (1900–1929), Common evening-primrose [Common evening primrose, Common eveningprimrose] (2, 3, 4, 5, 6, 50, 62, 72, 93, 97, 109, 127, 138, 155, 156, 157, 158) (1892–present), Northern

evening-primrose [Northern evening primrose] (5, 138) (1913–1923), Large rampion (5, 156, 157, 158) (1900–1929), Four-o'-clock [Four-o'clock, Four-o-clock, Four-o'-clocks] (5, 156, 158) (1900–1923), Night willowherb [Night willow-herb, Night willow herb] (5, 6, 156, 157, 158) (1892–1929), Tree primrose [Tree-primrose] (5, 6, 19, 46, 49, 53, 156, 157, 158, 180) (1633–1929), Scabish (5, 6, 7, 19, 76, 92, 156, 158) (1828–1923), Coffee plant [Coffee-plant] (5, 74, 156) (1893–1923) Eastern states, used to make beverage in harvest fields, Fever plant [Fever-plant] (5, 74, 156, 157, 158) (1893–1929) Eastern states, used as diaphoretic, archiac, King's cure-all [King's-cure-all] (5, 74, 156, 157, 158) (1893–1929) Southern states, Scurvish (5, 74, 156, 158) (1893–1923) Franconia NH, no longer in use by 1923, Onagre (French) (6, 158) (1892–1900)

Oenothera biennis **L.** *grandiflora* **Lindl.** – See *Oenothera grandiflora* L'Hér. ex Aiton

Oenothera biennis **L. subsp.** *centralis* **Munz.** – See *Oenothera biennis* L.

Oenothera bistorta – See *Camissonia bistorta* (Nutt. ex Torr. & Gray) Raven

Oenothera brachycarpa **Gray** – Short-fruit evening-primrose [Short-fruit evening primrose] (50) (Present), Short-pod primrose [Short-podded primrose] (5, 97) (1913–1937)

Oenothera caespitosa **Nutt.** – Gumbo evening-primrose [Gumbo evening primrose] (4) (1986), Stemless western primrose (108) (1878), Scapose primrose (5, 131) (1899–1913), Tufted evening-primrose [Tufted eveningprimrose] (50, 138, 155) (1923–present), possibly Rockrose [Rock-rose, Rock rose] (85) (1932) SD, possibly Butte primrose (127) (1933) ND, possibly Gumbo-lily [Gumbo lily] (85, 127) (1932–1933) name widely used "much to writer's disapproval" (127)

Oenothera caespitosa **Nutt. subsp.** *caespitosa* – Gumbo evening-primrose [Gumbo evening primrose] (4) (1986), Tufted evening-primrose [Tufted eveningprimrose] (50) (present), Gumbo-lily [Gumbo lily] (3, 4) (1977–1986)

Oenothera caespitosa **Nutt. subsp.** *marginata* **(Nutt. ex Hook. & Arn.) Munz** – White evening-primrose [White evening primrose] (138) (1923)

Oenothera caespitosa **Nutt. subsp.** *montana* **(Nutt.) Munz** – See *Oenothera caespitosa* Nutt. subsp. *caespitosa*

Oenothera canescens **Torr. & Frem.** – Beak-pod evening primrose [Beakpod evening primrose] (3) (1977), Spotted primrose (5) (1913), Spotted evening-primrose [Spotted evening primrose] (4, 50) (1986–present)

Oenothera coronopifolia **Torr. & Gray** – Gray-leaf evening-primrose [Gray-leaved evening primrose] (5) (1913), Crown-leaf evening-primrose [Crownleaf evening-primrose] (50) (present), Comb-leaf evening primrose [Combleaf evening primrose] (3, 4) (1977–1986), Cut-leaf evening-primrose [Cut-leaved evening primrose] (5, 131) (1899–1913)

Oenothera cruciata **Nutt.** – See *Camissonia contorta* (Dougl. ex Lehm.) Kearney

Oenothera drummondii **Hook.** – Drummond's evening-primrose [Drummond evening-primrose] (138) (1923)

Oenothera elata **Kunth subsp.** *hirsutissima* **(Gray ex S. Wats.) W. Dietr.** – Hooker's evening-primrose [Hooker eveningprimrose, Hooker's evening primrose] (3, 50, 155) (1942–present)

Oenothera engelamanii **(Small) Munz** – Engelmann's evening-primrose [Engelmann's evening primrose] (4, 50) (1986–present)

Oenothera eximia **(Gray)** – See *Oenothera caespitosa* Nutt. subsp. *marginata* (Nutt. ex Hook. & Arn.) Munz

Oenothera flava (A. Nels.) Garrett – Yellow evening-primrose [Yellow eveningprimrose, Yellow evening primrose] (50, 155) (1942–present)

Oenothera flava (A. Nels.) Garrett subsp. *flava* – Yellow evening-primrose [Yellow eveningprimrose, Yellow evening primrose] (50) (present)

Oenothera fremontii S. Wats. – See *Oenothera macrocarpa* Nutt. subsp. *fremontii* (S. Wats.) W. L. Wagner

Oenothera fruticosa L. – Common sundrops (138) (1923), Shrubby oenothera (187) (1818), Shrubby tree-primrose (187) (1818), Sundrop [Sundrops, Sun-drops] (19, 63, 109, 156) (1840–1949), Scabbish [Scabish] (73, 156) (1892–1923) NH, Wild beet (74, 156) (1893–1923) WV, used as pot herb

Oenothera fruticosa L. subsp. *fruticosa* – Allen's sundrops (5) (1913), Long-stem sundrops [Long-stemmed sundrops] (5) (1913), Scabish (5) (1913), Wild beet (5) (1913), Common sundrops (5, 72) (1907–1913) IA, Narrow-leaf sundrops [Narrow leaved sundrops, Narrow-leaved sundrops] (5, 97) (1913–1937)

Oenothera fruticosa L. subsp. *glauca* (Michx.) Straley – Glaucous sundrops (5) (1913), Scabish (5) (1913), Blue-leaf sundrops [Blue-leaf sundrops] (138) (1923), Fraser's sundrops [Fraser sundrops] (138) (1923), Sundrop [Sundrops, Sun-drops] (92, 109) (1876–1949)

Oenothera glauca fraseri – See *Oenothera fruticosa* L. subsp. *glauca* (Michx.) Straley

Oenothera glauca Michx. – See *Oenothera fruticosa* L. subsp. *glauca* (Michx.) Straley

Oenothera glazioviana Micheli – Lamarck's evening-primrose [Lamarck evening-primrose] (138) (1923)

Oenothera grandiflora – See *Oenothera grandiflora* L'Hér. ex Aiton

Oenothera grandiflora L'Hér. ex Aiton – Golden oenothera (183) (~1756)

Oenothera grandis (Britton) Smyth – Showy evening-primrose [Showy evening primrose] (50) (Present)

Oenothera heterophylla Spach – Tall sand primrose (122) (1937) TX, Tall evening-primrose [Tall evening primrose] (124) (1937) TX

Oenothera hookeri Torr. & Gray – See *Oenothera elata* Kunth subsp. *hirsutissima* (Gray ex S. Wats.) W. Dietr.

Oenothera howardii (A. Nels.) W. L. Wagner – Howard's evening-primrose [Howard's evening primrose] (50) (present)

Oenothera humifusa Nutt. – Seaside evening-primrose [Seaside evening primrose] (5) (1913), Hoary-pod Virginia willowherb [Hoary podded Virginia willow herb] (181) (~1678)

Oenothera jamesii Torr. & Gray – Trumpet evening-primrose [Trumpet evening primrose] (50) (present)

Oenothera L. – Mountain-primrose [Mountain primrose] (1) (1932), Fremont's primrose (5) (1913), Scapose primrose (158) (1900), Night willowherb [Night willow-herb, Night willow herb, Night-willowherb] (184) (1793), Sundrop [Sundrops, Sun-drops] (1, 138, 155, 158) (1900–1942), Evening-primrose [Evening primrose, Eveningprimrose] (1, 2, 50, 63, 93, 109, 138, 155, 156, 158) (1895–present), Rockrose [Rock-rose, Rock rose] (1, 93) (1932–1936) Neb, White evening-primrose [White evening primrose] (1, 93) (1932–1936), Primrose (1, 93, 158) (1900–1936), Spotted primrose (1, 93, 158) (1900–1936), Tree primrose [Tree-primrose] (10, 167) (1814–1818)

Oenothera laciniata Hill – White evening-primrose [White evening primrose] (3) (1977), Mexican evening-primrose [Mexican evening primrose] (124) (1937), Scollop-leaf oenothera [Scollop-leaved oenothera] (187) (1818), Cut-leaf evening-primrose [Cut-leaved evening primrose] (4, 5, 50, 85, 93, 97, 155) (1899–present), Sinuate-leaf evening-primrose [Sinuate-leaved evening primrose] (72, 131) (1899–1907)

Oenothera latifolia (Rydb.) Munz – Pale evening-primrose [Pale evening primrose] (4) (1986), Mountain evening-primrose (50) (present), Gray-leaf evening-primrose [Gray-leaved evening primrose] (97) (1937)

Oenothera lavandulifolia Torr. & Gray – See *Calylophus lavandulifolius* (Torr. & Gray) Raven

Oenothera linifolia Nutt. – Thread-leaf evening-primrose [Threadleaf evening primrose] (50) (present), Narrow-leaf evening-primrose [Narrow-leaved evening primrose] (3, 4) (1977–1986), Thread-leaf sundrops [Thread-leaved sundrops] (5, 97) (1913–1937)

Oenothera macrocarpa Nutt. – Big-fruit evening-primrose [Bigfruit evening-primrose] (50) (present)

Oenothera macrocarpa Nutt. subsp. *fremontii* (S. Wats.) W. L. Wagner – Fremont's evening-primrose [Fremont's evening primrose] (3, 4, 50) (1977–present)

Oenothera macrocarpa Nutt. subsp. *incana* (Gray) Reveal – Hoary evening-primrose [Hoary evening primrose] (4) (1986), Canescent primrose (97) (1937)

Oenothera macrocarpa Nutt. subsp. *macrocarpa* – Missouri evening-primrose [Missouri evening primrose] (4) (1986), Large-fruit evening-primrose [Large-fruited evening primrose] (86) (1878), Ozark sundrops (138, 155) (1923–1942), Missouri primrose (5, 97, 156) (1913–1937)

Oenothera macrocarpa Nutt. subsp. *oklahomensis* (J.B.S. Norton) Wagner – Oklahoma evening-primrose [Oklahoma evening primrose] (4) (1986), Oklahoma primrose (5, 97) (1913–1937) OK

Oenothera missouriensis Sims – See *Oenothera macrocarpa* Nutt. subsp. *macrocarpa*

Oenothera mollissima L. – Mithon (177) (1762)

Oenothera muricata L. – See *Oenothera biennis* L.

Oenothera nuttallii Sweet – Prairie evening-primrose [Prairie evening primrose] (98) (1926), White-stem evening-primrose [White-stemmed evening primrose] (3, 4, 98) (1926–1986), Nuttall's evening-primrose [Nuttall's evening primrose] (5, 50) (1913–present)

Oenothera oakesiana (Gray) J. W. Robbins ex S. Wats. & Coult. – Oakes' evening primrose [Oakes evening primrose] (5) (1913)

Oenothera oakesiana Robbins – See *Oenothera oakesiana* (Gray) J.W. Robbins ex S. Wats. & Coult.

Oenothera pallida Lindl. – White-stem evening-primrose [White-stemmed evening primrose] (127) (1933), Prairie evening-primrose [Prairie evening primrose] (156) (1923), Tall white evening-primrose [Tall white evening primrose] (156) (1923)

Oenothera perennis L. – Sundrop [Sundrops, Sun-drops] (109) (1949), Small evening-primrose [Small evening primrose] (156) (1923), Small sundrops (5, 156) (1913–1923)

Oenothera pilosella Raf. subsp. *pilosella* – Meadow sundrops (5, 156) (1913–1923)

Oenothera pratensis [(Small) B.L. Rob.] – See *Oenothera pilosella* Raf. subsp. *pilosella*

Oenothera pumila L. – See *Oenothera perennis* L.

Oenothera rhombipetala Nutt. ex Torr. & Gray – Four-point evening-primrose [Fourpoint evening primrose] (3, 4, 50) (1977–present), Rhombic evening-primrose [Rhombic evening primrose] (5, 72, 97) (1907–1937)

Oenothera rosea L'Hér. ex Aiton – Rose sundrops (138) (1923)

Oenothera serrulata Nutt. – See *Calylophus serrulatus* (Nutt.) Raven

Oenothera sinuata L. – See *Oenothera laciniata* Hill

Oenothera spachiana Torr. & Gray – Small sundrops (97) (1937)

Oenothera speciosa Nutt. – Showy evening-primrose [Showy evening primrose] (4) (1986), Pink-ladies [Pinkladies] (50) (present), Mexican evening-primrose [Mexican evening primrose] (109) (1949), Hartmannia (124) (1937) TX, Red primrose (124) (1937), Prairie-poppy [Prairie poppy] (156) (1923), White evening-primrose [White evening primrose] (156) (1923), Showy primrose (5, 97) (1913–1937)

Oenothera speciosa Nutt. var. *childsii* Munz – See *Oenothera speciosa* Nutt.

Oenothera strigosa (Rydb.) Mack. & Bush subsp. *canovirens* (Stell) Munz – See *Oenothera villosa* Thunb. subsp. *villosa*

Oenothera strigosa (Rydb.) Mack. & Bush subsp. *strigosa* – See *Oenothera villosa* Thunb. subsp. *strigosa* (Rydb.) W. Dietr. & P. H. Raven

Oenothera tetragona **Roth** – See *Oenothera fruticosa* L. subsp. *glauca* (Michx.) Straley

Oenothera tetragona **Roth var.** *fraseri* **(Pursh) Munz** – possibly *Oenothera fruticosa* L. subsp. *glauca* (Michx.) Straley

Oenothera triloba **Nutt.** – Three-leaf primrose [Three-leaved primrose] (5) (1913), Three-lobe primrose [Three-lobed primrose] (97) (1937), Watson's lavauxia (97) (1937), Stemless evening-primrose [Stemless evening primrose] (3, 4, 50) (1977–present), Common evening-primrose [Common evening primrose, Common eveningprimrose] (4) (1986), Hairy evening-primrose (50) (present)

Oenothera villosa **Thunb. subsp.** *strigosa* **(Rydb.) W. Dietr. & P. H. Raven** – Common evening-primrose [Common evening primrose, Common eveningprimrose] (3, 95) (1911–1977), Hairy evening-primrose (50) (present)

Oenothera villosa **Thunb. subsp.** *villosa* – Hairy evening-primrose (50) (present)

Oldenlandia corymbosa **L.** – Flat-top mille graines (50) (present)

Oldenlandia glomerata **Michx.** – See *Oldenlandia uniflora* L.

Oldenlandia **L.** – Buttonweed [Button-weed, Button weed] (156) (1923), Bluets [Bluet] (158) (1900)

Oldenlandia uniflora **L.** – Creeping greenhead [Creeping green head] (19, 156) (1840–1923), Clustered bluets (5, 156) (1913–1923)

Olea americana – See *Osmanthus americanus* (L.) Benth. & Hook. f. ex Gray var. *americanus*

Olea europaea **L.** – Olive bark (92) (1876), Azebuche (Andalusian) (110) (1886), Elaia (Greek) (110) (1886), Olivio (Spain) (110) (1886), Common olive (138) (1923), Oleaster (178) (1526), Wild olive [Wilde oliue] or Wild olive tree [Wild olive-tree] (178) (1526), Olyue (179) (1526), Olive or Olive tree (8, 20, 92, 106, 107, 110) (1785–1930)

Olea **L.** – Olivier (French, olive) (8) (1785), Olive or Olive tree (8, 10, 109, 138) (1785–1949)

Oligoneuron album **(Nutt.) Nesom** – Prairie goldenrod (50) (present), Late white aster (82) (1930), Upland aster (127) (1933), White upland aster (109, 155, 156) (1923–1949), Sneezewort aster (3, 4) (1977–1986), Upland white aster (5, 72, 131, 156) (1899–1923)

Oligoneuron canescens **Rydb.** – See *Oligoneuron rigidum* (L.) Small var. *humile* (Porter) Nesom

Oligoneuron houghtonii **(Torr. & Gray ex Gray) Nesom** – Houghton's goldenrod [Houghton's golden-rod] (5) (1913)

Oligoneuron nitidum **(Torr. & Gray) Small** – Narrow-leaf goldenrod [Narrowleaf goldenrod, Narrow-leaf golden-rod, Narrow-leaved goldenrod, Narrow-leaved golden-rod] (97) (1937)

Oligoneuron ohioense **(Frank ex Riddell) G. N. Jones** – Ohio goldenrod [Ohio golden-rod] (5) (1913)

Oligoneuron riddellii **(Frank ex Riddell) Rydb.** – Riddell's goldenrod [Riddell's golden-rod, Riddell goldenrod] (5, 50, 72, 155) (1907–present)

Oligoneuron rigidum **(L.) Small** – Stiff goldenrod [Stiff golden-rod] (50) (present)

Oligoneuron rigidum **(L.) Small var.** *humile* **(Porter) Nesom** – Stiff goldenrod [Stiff golden-rod] (50) (present), Rough goldenrod [Rough golden-rod] (85) (1932)

Oligoneuron rigidum **(L.) Small var.** *rigidum* – A'djidamo'wano (Chippewa, squirrel tail) (40) (1928), Large yellow-flower goldenrod [Large yellow-flowered goldenrod] (80) (1913), Large-flower goldenrod [Large-flowered goldenrod] (80) (1913), Rigid goldenrod (3, 4, 92) (1876–1986), Hard-leaf goldenrod [Hardleaf golden-rod, Hard-leaved golden-rod, Hard-leaved goldenrod] (5, 19, 122, 131) (1840–1937), Stiff goldenrod [Stiff golden-rod] (5, 50, 72, 82, 95, 97, 127, 138, 155) (1907–present), Goldenrod [Golden-rod, Golden rod] (56, 145, 148) (1897–1901)

Oligoneuron **Small** – Sneezewort aster (1) (1932), Goldenrod [Golden-rod, Golden rod] (1, 50) (1932–present)

Oligosporus campestris **(L.) Cass. subsp.** *pacificus* **(Nutt.) W. A. Weber** – See *Artemisia campestris* L. subsp. *borealis* (Pallas) Hall & Clements

Oligosporus pacificus **(Nutt.) Poljakov** – See *Artemisia campestris* L. subsp. *borealis* (Pallas) Hall & Clements

Olneya tesota **Gray** – Mexican ironwood (106) (1930), Palo de Hierro (Mexican) (106) (1930), Sonora ironwood (106) (1930), Olneya (107) (1919), Tesota (Mexicans) (123) (1856), Ironwood [Iron wood, Iron-wood] (103, 106, 107) (1870–1930), Arbol de Hierro (Mexican) (106, 123) (1856–1930)

Omalotheca norvegica **(Gunnerus) Sch. Bip. & F. W. Schultz** – Norwegian cudweed (5) (1913)

Omalotheca supina **(L.) DC.** – Dwarf cudweed (5, 156) (1913–1923), Mountain cudweed [Mountain cud-weed] (5, 156) (1913–1923)

Omalotheca sylvatica **(L.) Schultz-Bip. & F. W. Schultz** – Chafeweed [Chafe-weed, Chafe weed, Chafweed] (5) (1913), Chafeweed [Chafe-weed, Chafe weed] (156) (1923), English cudweed [English cudweede] (178) (1526), Owl's-crown [Owl's crown] (5, 156) (1913–1923), Wood cudweed (5, 156) (1913–1923), Golden motherwort (5, 92, 156) (1876–1923)

Omphalodes linifolia **(L.) Moench** – Flax-leaf navelseed [Flaxleaf navelseed] (138) (1923)

Omphalodes **Mill.** – Navelwort [Navel-wort] (109) (1949), Navelseed [Navel-seed] (109, 138) (1923–1949)

Omphalodes **Moench** – See *Omphalodes* Mill.

Omphalodes verna **Moench** – Creeping forget-me-not (109) (1949), Venus'-button [Venusbutton] (138) (1923)

Onagra **Adans.** – See *Oenothera* L.

Onagra biennis **(L.) Scop.** – See *Oenothera biennis* L.

Onagra biennis **L.** – See *Oenothera biennis* L.

Onagra strigosa **[Rydb.]** – See *Oenothera villosa* Thunb. subsp. *strigosa* (Rydb.) W. Dietr. & P.H. Raven

Onanbrychis **Scop.** – See *Onobrychis* Mill.

Onobrychis **Gaertn.** – possibly *Onobrychis* Mill.

Onobrychis **Mill.** – Sand-foin (1) (1932), Sainfoin (45, 46, 50, 155) (1879–present)

Onobrychis onobrychis **(L.) Rydb.** – See *Onobrychis viciifolia* Scop.

Onobrychis sativa **[Lam.]** – See *Onobrychis viciifolia* Scop.

Onobrychis **Tourn.** – See *Onobrychis* Mill.

Onobrychis viciaefolia **Scop.** – See *Onobrychis viciifolia* Scop.

Onobrychis viciifolia **Scop.** – Wild clover (28) (1850), Foin francais (French) (46) (1879), Sand-foin (85) (1932) SD, Holy clover (109) (1949), Saintfoin (109) (1949), Lupinella (110) (1886), Esparsette (129) (1894), Common sainfoin (155) (1942), Cinquefoil [Cink-foil, Cinque-foil] (158) (1900), Cockscomb [Cock's comb, Cocks-comb, Cock's-comb] (158) (1900), Cock's-head plant (158) (1900), Everlasting-grass (158) (1900), Hen's-bill (158) (1900), Lucerne [Lucern] (158) (1900), Medick fitch (158) (1900), Dutch cock's-head [Dutch Cocks Head] (178) (1526), Esparcet (106, 109) (1930–1949), Esparcette (French) (28, 46, 68, 158) (1850–1913), Sainfoin (45, 50, 68, 92, 107, 109, 110, 129) (1886–present), French-grass [French grass] (46, 92) (1876–1879), Sanfoin (66, 158) (1900–1903)

Onoclea **L.** – Sensitive fern (1, 4, 10, 50, 72, 138, 158) (1818–present)

Onoclea sensibilis **L.** – Polypod brakes (78) (1898) ME, usually Polypodium, Sugar brakes (78) (1898) ME, Angiopteris (174, 177) (1753–1762), Dragon-bridges (177, 181) (~1678–1762), Sensitive fern [Sensitive-fern, Sensitivefern] (3, 4, 5, 19, 50, 86, 92, 97, 109, 122, 131, 155, 157, 158) (1840–present) fronds wilt quickly when cut and are very sensitive to frost

Onoclea struthiopteris **(L.) Hoffmann** – See *Matteuccia struthiopteris* (L.) Todaro

Ononis campestris **G. Koch & Ziz** – Cammock (92) (1876), Petty whin (92) (1876), Rest harrow (92) (1876), Stay-plough [Stay plough] (92) (1876), Field restharrow (178) (1526), Rest harrow with white flowers (178) (1526), Rest harrow without prickles (178) (1526)

Ononis spinosa – See *Ononis campestris* G. Koch & Ziz

Onopordon – See *Onopordum* L.

Onopordon acanthium **L.** – See *Onopordum acanthium* L.

Onopordon tauricum – See *Onopordum tauricum* Willd.

Onopordum **(Vaill.) L.** – See *Onopordum* L.

Onopordum acanthium L. – Eseldistel (German) (3) (1977), Scardiccione (Italian) (46) (1879), Oak thistle [Oak-thistle] (156) (1923), Argentine thistle (158) (1900), Crab thistle [Crab-thistle] (158) (1900), Scotch thistle (3, 4, 5, 46, 109, 156, 158) (1879–1986), Ass's-thistle [Ass's thistle, Asse's thistle] (5, 156) (1913–1923), Silver-thistle [Silver thistle] (5, 156) (1913–1923), Down thistle [Down-thistle] (5, 156, 158) (1900–1923), Musk thistle [Musk-thistle] (5, 156, 158) (1900–1923), Queen Mary's thistle (5, 156, 158) (1900–1923), Oat thistle [Oat-thistle] (5, 158) (1900–1913), Cotton thistle [Cottonthistle] (5, 19, 92, 107, 156, 158) (1840–1923), Scotch cotton-thistle [Scotch cottonthistle] (50, 155) (1942–present)

Onopordum L. – White thistle [White thistle] (7) (1828), Scotch thistle (1, 4) (1932–1986), Cotton thistle [Cottonthistle] (1, 50, 138, 155, 158) (1900–present)

Onopordum tauricum Willd. – Taurus cotton-thistle [Taurus cottonthistle] (138) (1923)

Onosmodium carolinianum (Lam.) DC. – See *Lithospermum caroliniense* (Walter ex J. F. Gmel.) MacMill. var. *caroliniense*

Onosmodium hispidissimum Mackenzie – See *Onosmodium molle* Michx. subsp. *hispidissimum* (Mackenzie) Boivin

Onosmodium hispidum Michx. – possibly *Onosmodium virginianum* (L.) A. DC.

Onosmodium Michx. – False gromwell (1, 2, 4, 82, 156, 158) (1895–1986), Marbleseed (50, 155) (1942–present)

Onosmodium molle Michx. – Soft-hair marbleseed [Softhair marbleseed] (50) (present), Shaggy false gromwell (72) (1907), False gromwell (82) (1930), Soft-hairy false gromwell (5, 72, 131) (1899–1913)

Onosmodium molle Michx. subsp. *hispidissimum* (Mackenzie) Boivin – False gromwell (3) (1977), Soft-hair marbleseed [Softhair marbleseed] (50) (present), Shaggy false gromwell (5, 97) (1913–1937)

Onosmodium molle Michx. subsp. *occidentale* (Mackenzie) Cochrane – Šuŋkčaŋkahuipije (Lakota, horse spine cure) (121) (1918?–1970?), Soft false gromwell (122) (1937), False gromwell (3, 85) (1932–1977), Western false gromwell [Western false-gromwell] (5, 93, 97, 121, 157) (1900–1937), Western marbleseed (50, 155) (1942–present)

Onosmodium molle Michx. subsp. *subsetosum* (Mackenzie & Bush) Cochrane – Ozark false gromwell (5) (1913)

Onosmodium occidentale Mackenzie – See *Onosmodium molle* Michx. subsp. *occidentale* (Mackenzie) Cochrane

Onosmodium subsetosum Mack. & Bush – See *Onosmodium molle* Michx. subsp. *subsetosum* (Mackenzie & Bush) Cochrane

Onosmodium virginianum (L.) A. DC. – Corn gromwell (92) (1876), Necklace-weed [Necklace weed] (156) (1923), Pearl plant [Pearlplant] (156) (1923), Hispid purshia (187) (1818), False gromwell (19, 40, 48, 49, 58, 92) (1840–1928), Virginia false gromwell (5, 156) (1913–1923), Wild's Job's-tears [Wild's Job's tears] (5, 58) (1869–1913), Gravelweed [Gravel-weed, Gravel weed] (58, 92, 156) (1869–1923), Wild Job's-tears [Wild Job's tears] (92, 156) (1876–1923), possibly Mi'gĭsnĕs'ĭbûg (Chippewa, little shell leaf) (40) (1928)

Onosmodium virginianum DC. – See *Onosmodium virginianum* (L.) A. DC.

Onospordon acanthium (sic) – See *Onopordum acanthium* L.

Onychium densum Brack. – See *Aspidotis densa* (Brack.) Lellinger

Oonopsis engelmannii (Gray) Greene – Engelmann's oonopsis [Engelman's oonopsis] (5) (1913), Engelmann's false goldenweed (50) (present), Engelmann's goldenweed (3, 4, 5) (1913–1986)

Oonopsis foliosa (Gray) Greene var. *foliosa* – Leafy false goldenweed (50) (present), Burro weed [Burroweed] (155) (1942), Fremont's goldenweed [Fremont goldenweed] (155) (1942), Jimmyweed (155) (1942)

Oonopsis Greene – See *Oonopsis* Nutt.

Oonopsis multicaulis (Nutt.) Greene – Branched false goldenweed (50) (present)

Oonopsis Nutt. – False goldenweed (50) (present), Oonopsis (158) (1900)

Operculina dissecta (Jacq.) House – See *Merremia dissecta* (Jacq.) Hallier f.

Operculina turpethum (L.) J. Silva Manso – Turpeth root (92) (1876)

Ophioglossum (Tourn) L. – See *Ophioglossum* L.

Ophioglossum arenarium E. G. Britton – See *Ophioglossum vulgatum* L.

Ophioglossum engelmannii Prantl. – Adder's-tongue fern [Addertongue fern, Adder's tongue fern] (124) (1937) TX, Engelmann's adder's-tongue [Engelmann's addertongue, Engelmann adderstongue] (122, 155) (1937–1942), Adder's-tongue [Adder tongue, Adders tongue, Adder's tongue, Adders toong, Adderstongue] (3, 5, 97) (1913–1977), Limestone adder's-tongue [Limestone adder's tongue, Limestone adderstongue] (4, 50) (1986–present)

Ophioglossum L. – Adder's-fern [Adder's fern] (158) (1900), Adder's-grass (158) (1900), Adder's-spear [Adder's spear] (158) (1900), Edder's-tongue (158) (1900), Serpent's-tongue [Serpent's tongue] (158) (1900), Snake's-tongue [Snake's tongue, Snakes' tongue] (158) (1900), Adder's-tongue [Adder tongue, Adders tongue, Adder's tongue, Adders toong, Adderstongue] (1, 4, 10, 50, 138, 155, 158) (1818–present)

Ophioglossum pusillum Raf. – Northern adder's-tongue [Northern adderstongue] (50) (present)

Ophioglossum vulgare L. – See *Ophioglossum vulgatum* L.

Ophioglossum vulgatum L. – Adder's-fern [Adder's fern] (5) (1913), Adder's-spear [Adder's spear] (5) (1913), Sand adder's-tongue [Sand adder's tongue] (5) (1913), Serpent's-tongue [Serpent's tongue] (5) (1913), Snakeleaf [Snake leaf] (7) (1828), Southern adder's-tongue [Southern adderstongue] (50) (present), Common adder's-tongue [Common adderstongue] (138, 155, 187) (1818–1942), Adder's-tongue fern [Adder-tongue fern, Adder's tongue fern] (19, 92) (1840–1876), Adder's-tongue [Adder tongue, Adders tongue, Adder's tongue, Adders toong, Adderstongue] (3, 5, 14, 46, 122, 178) (1596–1977) accidentally introduced by 1671, Snake's-tongue [Snake's tongue, Snakes' tongue] (5, 92) (1876–1913)

Ophiopogon jaburan (Sieb.) Lodd. – Jaburan (138) (1923)

Ophiopogon Ker-Gawl. – Lily-turf (109) (1949), Snakebeard (138) (1923)

Ophiorhiza mitreola L. – See *Mitreola petiolata* (J.F. Gmel.) Torr. & Gray

Ophiorrhiza mitreola L. – See *Mitreola petiolata* (J.F. Gmel.) Torr. & Gray

Ophrys auriculata (Wiegand) House. – See *Listera auriculata* Wieg.

Ophrys australis (Lindl.) House. – See *Listera australis* Lindl.

Ophrys convallarioides (Sw.) W. F. Wright – See *Listera convallarioides* (Sw.) Nutt. ex Ell.

Ophrys cordata L. – See *Listera cordata* (L.) R. Br. ex Ait. f. var. *cordata*

Ophrys smallii (Wiegand) House. – See *Listera smallii* Wieg.

Oplismenus compositus (L.) Beauv. – Basket grass (138) (1923)

Oplismenus hirtellus (L.) Beauv. – Creeping beard grass [Creeping beard-grass] (94) (1901)

Oplismenus hirtellus (L.) P. Beauv. subsp. *hirtellus* – Scotch grass (182) (1791)

Oplismenus hirtellus (L.) R. & S. – See *Oplismenus hirtellus* (L.) Beauv.

Oplopanax horridus Miq. – Devil's-walkingstick [Devil's walking-stick, Devil's walking stick, Devil's-walking-stick] (101, 160) (1860–1905), Devil's-club [Devil's club, Devilsclub] (5, 138, 156) (1913–1923), Noachist (stinking medicine Cheyenne & Crow) (101) (1905) MT, Ginseng (103) (1870)

Opulaster intermedius Rydb. – See *Physocarpus opulifolius* (L.) Maxim. var. *intermedius* (Rydb.) B.L. Robins.

Opulaster Medik. – See *Physocarpus* (Camb.) Raf.

Opulaster monogyna (Torr.) Kuntze – possibly *Physocarpus monogynus* (Torr.) J. M. Coult.

Opulaster monogynus Torr. – possibly *Physocarpus monogynus* (Torr.) J. M. Coult.

Opulaster opulifolius (L.) Kuntze – See *Physocarpus opulifolius* (L.) Maxim. var. *opulifolius*

Opuntia (Tourn.) Mill. – See Opuntia Mill.

Opuntia arborescens Engelm. – See *Opuntia imbricata* (Haw.) DC. var. *imbricata*

Opuntia arenaria Engelm. – Sand cactus (138) (1923)

Opuntia basilaris Engelm. & Bigelow – Beaver-tail prickly-pear [Beavertail pricklypear] (155) (1942), Beaver-tail cactus [Beavertail cactus] (109, 138) (1923–1949)

Opuntia camanchica Engelm. & Bigel. – See *Opuntia phaeacantha* Engelm. var. *camanchica* (Engelm. & Bigelow) L. Benson

Opuntia cochenillifera (L.) Mill. – Cochineal fig (92) (1876), Cochineal nopalaea (155) (1942), Cochineal cactus (109, 138) (1923–1949)

Opuntia cochinilifera – See *Opuntia cochenillifera* (L.) Mill.

Opuntia compressa [J. F. Macbr.] – possibly *Opuntia ficus-indica* (L.) Mill. (current species depends on author)

Opuntia davisii Engelm. & Bigelow – See *Opuntia tunicata* (Lehm.) Link & Otto var. *davisii* (Engelm. & Bigelow) L. Benson

Opuntia engelmannii Salm-Dyck – Cactus-apple [Cactus apple] (50) (present), Prickly-pear cactus [Pricklypear cactus, Prickly pear cactus] (76) (1896), Indian fig [Indian-fig, Indianfig] (107) (1919), Engelmann's prickly-pear [Engelmann pricklypear] (155) (1942)

Opuntia engelmannii Salm-Dyck var. *lindheimeri* (Engelm.) Parfitt & Pinkava – Texas prickly pear [Texas pricklypear] (36, 50) (1986–present)

Opuntia erinacea Engelm. & Bigelow ex Engelm. – Grizzly-bear cactus (109) (1949), Grizzly-bear pricklypear [Grizzlybear pricklypear] (155) (1942)

Opuntia ficus-indica (L.) Mill. – Broad-leaf cactus [Broad-leafed cactus] (44) (1845), Metaquesunnauk (46) (1879) natives on Roanoke, Barberry fig (107) (1919), Fig of the Christians (Moors) (110) (1886), Tuna [Tunas] (Spanish) (110) (1886), Barbary fig (156) (1923), Barberry (156) (1923), Hedgehog-thistle (156) (1923), Prickly-pear cactus [Pricklypear cactus, Prickly pear cactus] (156) (1923), Fig of India (178) (1526), Common Indian fig (42) (1814), Ficus indica (177, 178) (1526–1762), Common prickly-pear [Common prickly pear, Common pricklypear] (2, 138, 155) (1895–1942), Indian fig [Indian-fig, Indianfig] (6, 42, 109, 110, 155, 156, 182) (1791–1949) OK, Prickly pear [Pricklypear, Prickly-pear] (6, 19, 27, 46, 92, 107, 110, 156, 177) (1762–1923), Devil's-tongue [Devil's tongue, Devilstongue] (73, 156) (1892–1923) Northern OH

Opuntia ficus-indica Haw. – See *Opuntia ficus-indica* (L.) Mill.

Opuntia fragilis (Nutt.) Haw. – Little prickly pear (4) (1986), Tuna (5) (1913), Brittle opuntia (5, 93, 131) (1899–1936), Brittle prickly-pear [Brittle pricklypear] (50, 155) (1942–present)

Opuntia fragilis (Nutt.) Haw. var. *fragilis* – Brittle prickly-pear [Brittle pricklypear] (50) (present)

Opuntia frutescens [Engelm.] – See *Cylindropuntia leptocaulis* (DC.) F. M. Knuth

Opuntia fulgida Engelm. – Jumping cholla (50) (present), Straw cactus (76) (1896) AZ, Sonoran jumping cholla (155) (1942)

Opuntia grandiflora Engelm. – See *Opuntia macrorhiza* Engelm. var. *macrorhiza*

Opuntia humifusa (Raf.) Raf. – Eastern prickly-pear [Eastern prickly pear] (4) (1986), Pidahatus (Pawnee) (37) (1919), Prickly pear [Pricklypear, Prickly-pear] (37) (1919), Unchela (Dakota) (37) (1919) fruit was called Unchela taspun, Devil's-tongue [Devil's tongue, Devilstongue] (5, 50) (1913–present), Western prickly pear [Western prickly-pear] (5, 72, 85, 93, 95, 131) (1899–1936)

Opuntia humifusa (Raf.) Raf. var. *humifusa* – Barberry (5) (1913), Barbary fig (158) (1900), Hedgehog thistle [Hedge hog thistle] (158) (1900), Eastern prickly-pear [Eastern prickly pear] (5, 158) (1900–1913), Indian fig [Indian-fig, Indianfig] (5, 158) (1900–1913), Prickly-pear cactus [Pricklypear cactus, Prickly pear cactus] (5, 158) (1900–1913), Devil's-tongue [Devil's tongue, Devilstongue] (50,

73, 158) (1892–present) Northern OH, Prickly pear [Pricklypear, Prickly-pear] (63, 107, 145) (1897–1919)

Opuntia imbricata (Haw.) DC. – Tree cactus (97) (1937), Walking-stick cactus [Walkingstick cactus] (138, 155) (1923–1942), Tree cholla (4, 50) (1986–present)

Opuntia imbricata (Haw.) DC. var. *imbricata* – Candelabrum cactus (149) (1904) NM, Cholla (149) (1904), Tree cactus (5, 76, 153) (1896–1913)

Opuntia leptocaulis DC. – Pencil cholla (4) (1986), Christmas cactus (50) (present), Tassajilla (97) (1937) OK, Tassijilla (106) (1930), Tasajillo (122) (1937) TX, Tesajo (155) (1942)

Opuntia leucotricha DC. – Aaron's-beard cactus [Aaronsbeard cactus] (138) (1923), Aaron's-beard [Aaron's beard, Aaronsbeard] (155) (1942), Aaron's-beard prickly-pear [Aaronsbeard pricklypear] (155) (1942)

Opuntia lindheimeri Engelm. – See *Opuntia engelmannii* Salm-Dyck var. *lindheimeri* (Engelm.) Parfitt & Pinkava

Opuntia mackensenii Rose – See *Opuntia macrorhiza* Engelm. var. *macrorhiza*

Opuntia macrorhiza Engelm. – Plains prickly pear [Plains pricklypear] (4) (1986), Twist-spine prickly pear [Twistspine pricklypear, Twist-spine pricklypear] (50) (present), Prickly pear [Pricklypear, Prickly-pear] (97) (1937)

Opuntia macrorhiza Engelm. var. *macrorhiza* – Large-flower opuntia [Large-flowered opuntia] (97) (1937), Big-flower prickly-pear [Big-flower pricklypear] (155) (1942), Mackensen's prickly pear [Mackensen pricklypear] (155) (1942), Twisted-spine cactus (5, 97) (1913–1937), Twist-spine prickly pear [Twistspine pricklypear, Twist-spine pricklypear] (50, 155) (1942–present)

Opuntia microdasys (Lehm.) Lehm. Ex Pfeiff. – Bunny-ears (109) (1949), Gold-plush prickly-pear [Goldplush pricklypear] (155) (1942)

Opuntia microdasys Pfeiffer – See *Opuntia microdasys* (Lehm.) Lehm. Ex Pfeiff.

Opuntia Mill. – Tree cactus (1) (1932), Common Indian fig (10) (1818), Melon thistle [Melon thistles] (10) (1818), Pomme de racquette (French) (89) (1820), Tuna [Tunas] (Spanish) (103) (1870), Uŋkčela blaska (Lakota, flat cactus) (121) (1918?–1970?), Nopal cactus [Nopalcactus] (155) (1942), Opuntia (158) (1900), Metack sunancks (181) (~1678), Mettaquesunnauks (181) (~1678), Indian fig [Indian-fig, Indianfig] (1, 2, 10, 14, 106) (1818–1882), Prickly pear [Pricklypear, Prickly-pear] (1, 4, 7, 10, 14, 35, 103, 106, 109, 121, 138, 149, 151, 155, 158, 167) (1814–1986), Cholla (1, 4, 93, 155) (1932–1986) flat-stemmed species are pricklypear, cylindrical-stemmed species are cholla, Nopal [Nopales] (149, 151) (1896–1904) NM, Prickly-pear cactus [Pricklypear cactus, Prickly pear cactus] (2, 93, 146) (1895–1936)

Opuntia missouriensis DC. – See *Opuntia polyacantha* Haw. var. *trichophora* (Engelm. & Bigelow) Coult.

Opuntia opuntia (L.) Coult. – See *Opuntia humifusa* (Raf.) Raf. var. *humifusa*

Opuntia opuntia (L.) Karst. – See *Opuntia humifusa* (Raf.) Raf. var. *humifusa*

Opuntia phaeacantha Engelm. – Prickly pear [Pricklypear, Prickly-pear] (4) (1986), Tulip prickly pear [Tulip pricklypear] (50) (present)

Opuntia phaeacantha Engelm. var. *camanchica* (Engelm. & Bigelow) L. Benson – Comanche cactus (5) (1913), Bastard fig (107) (1919)

Opuntia polyacantha Haw. – Cactus (101) (1905), Michkidea (Crow) (101) (1905) MT, Pomme de racquette (French) (101) (1905), Prickly pear [Pricklypear, Prickly-pear] (101) (1905), Tuna [Tunas] (Spanish) (101) (1905), Prickly-pear cactus [Pricklypear cactus, Prickly pear cactus] (127) (1933), Plains prickly pear [Plains pricklypear] (4, 50, 155) (1942–present), Many-spine opuntia [Many-spined opuntia] (5, 93, 97) (1913–1937)

Opuntia polyacantha Haw. var. *polyacantha* – Hair-spine prickly-pear [Hairspine pricklypear] (50) (present)

Opuntia polyacantha Haw. var. *trichophora* (Engelm. & Bigelow) Coult. – Limber-spine cactus [Limber-spined cactus] (97) (1937) OK, Missouri cactus (108) (1878), Prickly pear [Pricklypear, Prickly-pear] (145) (1897)

Opuntia rafinesquei Engelm. – See *Opuntia humifusa* (Raf.) Raf. var. *humifusa*

Opuntia rufida Engelm. – Blind-pear (109) (1949), Blind prickly-pear [Blind pricklypear] (155) (1942)

Opuntia tortispina Engelm. & Bigelow – See *Opuntia macrorhiza* Engelm. var. *macrorhiza*

Opuntia trichophora (Engelm.) Britton & Rose – See *Opuntia polyacantha* Haw. var. *trichophora* (Engelm. & Bigelow) Coult.

Opuntia tunicata (Lehm.) Link & Otto – Thistle cholla (50) (present), Jeff Davis' cholla [JeffDavis cholla] (155) (1942)

Opuntia tunicata (Lehm.) Link & Otto var. *davisii* (Engelm. & Bigelow) L. Benson – Thistle cholla (50) (present), Cholla (97) (1937)

Opuntia vulgaris Mill. – See *Opuntia ficus-indica* (L.) Mill.

Orbexilum onobrychis (Nutt.) Rydb. – Psoralea (5) (1913), Sainfoin (5) (1913), Sainfoin psoralea (156) (1923), French-grass [French grass] (5, 156) (1913–1923)

Orbexilum pedunculatum (P. Mill.) Rydb. – Samson's snakeroot [Sampson snakeroot, Samson snake-root] (49) (1898), Bob's root (5, 49, 156) (1898–1923)

Orbexilum pedunculatum (P. Mill.) Rydb. var. *pedunculatum* – Bab's root [Bab's-root] (158) (1900), Samson's snakeroot [Sampson snakeroot, Samson snake-root] (3, 4, 50) (1977–present), Congo root [Congo-root] (5, 49, 156, 158) (1898–1923)

Orbexilum Raf. – Leather-root (50) (present)

Orbexilum stipulatum (Torr. & Gray) Rydb. – Large-stipule psoralea [Large-stipuled psoralea] (5) (1913)

Orchidocarpum Michx. – See *Annona* L.

Orchidocarpum parviflorum Michx. – See *Asimina parviflora* (Michx.) Dunal

Orchis (Tourn.) L. – possibly *Dactylorhiza* Neck. ex Nevski (US species)

Orchis clavellata subsp. *tridentata* – See *Platanthera clavellata* (Michx.) Luer

Orchis cristata Willd. And Michx. – See *Platanthera cristata* (Michx.) Lindl.

Orchis fimbriata Willd. – possibly *Platanthera grandiflora* (Bigelow) Lindl.

Orchis macrophylla – possibly *Platanthera macrophylla* (Goldie) Lindl.

Orchis orbiculata [Pursh] – See *Platanthera orbiculata* (Pursh) Lindl.

Orchis spectabilis L. – See *Galearis spectabilis* (L.) Raf.

Orcuttia greenei Vasey – See *Tuctoria greenei* (Vasey) J. Reeder

Oreocarya suffruticosa (Torr.) Greene – See *Cryptantha cinerea* (Greene) Cronq. var. *jamesii* Cronq.

Oreocarya fulvocanescens (Gray) Greene – See *Cryptantha fulvocanescens* (S. Wats.) Payson var. *fulvocanescens*

Oreocarya glomerata (Pursh) Greene – See *Cryptantha celosioides* (Eastw.) Payson

Oreocarya Greene – See *Cryptantha* Lehm. ex G. Don (all US species)

Oreocarya sericea (Gray) Greene – See *Cryptantha sericea* (Gray) Payson

Oreodaphne californica (Hook. & Arn.) Nees – See *Umbellularia californica* (Hook. & Arn.) Nutt.

Origanum incanum Walt. – See *Pycnanthemum setosum* Nutt.

Origanum L. – Wild margoran (190) (~1759), Marjoram (109, 138, 156, 184) (1793–1949)

Origanum majorana L. – Majorana (57) (1917), Marjorana (107) (13th Century), Annual marjoram (109) (1949), Marierome (178) (1526), Margetym gentyll (179) (1526), Mariorayne (179) (1526), Sweet marjoram [Sweete marjoram] (19, 57, 92, 107, 109, 138) (1840–1949), possibly Marjoram (92) (1876)

Origanum marjoram – possibly *Origanum majorana* L.

Origanum vulgare L. – Sweet marjoram [Sweete marjoram] (46) (1629), Winter marjoram (92) (1876), Agrioriganum (178) (1526), Field organie (178) (1526), Brotherwort (179) (1526), Orygan (179) (1526), Marjoram (10, 106) (1818–1930), Organy (5, 106, 107, 156) (1913–1930), Organs (5, 156) (1913–1923) no longer in use bu 1923, Pot marjoram [Pot marjorum] (5, 156) (1913–1923), Wild marjoram (5, 7, 19, 46, 49, 92, 107, 109, 138, 156) (1649–1949), Winter sweet [Winter-sweet] (5, 92, 106, 156) (1876–1930), Origanum (61, 92) (1870–1876), Common marjoram (92, 187) (1818–1876)

Ormosia G. Jackson – Ormosia (138) (1923)

Ornithogalum hirsutum L. – See *Hypoxis hirsuta* (L.) Cov.

Ornithogalum L. – Bethlehem-star [Bethlehemstar] (7) (1828), Ackers wibel (High Dutch) (180) (1633), Feldz Wibel (High Dutch) (180) (1633), Star-of-Bethlehem [Star of Bethlehem, Starre of Bethlem, Stars of Bethlehem] (1, 10, 50, 138, 155, 156, 158, 180) (1633–present)

Ornithogalum nutans L. – Drooping star-of-Bethlehem (5, 50) (1913–present)

Ornithogalum pyrenaeicum L. – See *Ornithogalum pyrenaicum* L.

Ornithogalum pyrenaicum L. – Pyrenees star-of-Bethlehem [Pyrenees star of Bethlehem] (50) (present), French sparrow-grass [French sparrow grass] (92) (1876), Bulbous asphodill (178) (1596), Bulbed asphodill (180) (1633), Onion asphodill (180) (1633), Dove's-dung [Dove's dung] (107) (1919), Star lily [Star-lily, Starlily] (156) (1923), John-go-to-bed-at-noon (158) (1900), Common star-of-Bethlehem (138, 155) (1923–1942), Star-of-Bethlehem [Star of Bethlehem, Starre of Bethlem, Stars of Bethlehem] (3, 5, 19, 92, 93, 97, 107, 109, 156, 158, 178, 180, 187) (1596–1977), Ten o'clock lady (5, 156) (1913–1923), Nap-at-noon (5, 156, 158) (1900–1923), Star flower [Starflower, Star-flower] (5, 156, 158) (1900–1923), Summer snowflake [Summer-snowflake] (5, 156, 158) (1900–1923), Eleven-o'-clock-lady [Eleven o'clock lady] (5, 158) (1900–1913), Sleepy-Dick [Sleepydick, Sleepy Dick] (5, 50, 156, 158) (1900–present), Ten o'clock [Ten-o'-clock] (92, 158) (1876–1900)

Ornithopus perpusillus L. – Little white bird's-foot [Little white bird's foot] (50) (present), Bird's-foot [Birdes foote] (178) (1526), Caterpillar scorpion-grass [Caterpillar Scorpion grasse] (178) (1526)

Ornithopus sativus Brot. – Bird's-foot [Bird's foot] (110) (1886)

Ornus dipetala [Nutt.] – See *Fraxinus dipetala* Hook. & Arn.

Ornus Pers. – possibly *Fraxinus* L.

Orobanche americana L. – See *Conopholis americana* (L. f.) Wallr.

Orobanche fasciculata Nutt. – Clustered broomrape (50) (present), Yellow broomrape [Yellow broom rape] (85) (1932), Cancer-root [Cancer root] (101) (1905), Naked broomrape [Naked broom-rape, Naked broom rape] (2, 63) (1895–1899), Yellow cancer-root [Yellow cancer root] (5, 131, 156, 157, 158) (1899–1929), Clustered cancer root [Clustered cancer-root] (5, 93, 158) (1900–1936)

Orobanche L. – One-flower cancer-root [One-flowered cancer root] (2) (1895), Cancerweed [Cancer weed, Cancer-weed] (35) (1806) Meriwether Lewis, Squirrel's-grandfather [Squirrel's grandfather] (77) (1898), One-flower broomrape [One-flowered broom-rape, One-flowered broomrape] (86) (1878), Ghost-pipe [Ghostpipe] (155) (1942), Cancer-root [Cancer root] (1, 158) (1900–1932), Broomrape [Broom-rape, Broom rape] (1, 4, 10, 14, 50, 155, 158, 184) (1793–present), Naked broomrape [Naked broom-rape, Naked broom rape] (2, 63) (1895–1899)

Orobanche ludoviciana Nutt. – Broomrape [Broom-rape, Broom rape] (3, 4, 93, 157) (1900–1986), Strangle tare [Strangle-tare] (5, 156) (1913–1923), Louisiana broomrape [Louisiana broom rape, Louisiana broom-rape] (5, 50, 72, 97, 122, 124, 131, 155) (1899–present)

Orobanche ludoviciana Nutt. subsp. *ludoviciana* – Louisiana broomrape [Louisiana broom rape, Louisiana broom-rape] (50) (present), Broomrape [Broom-rape, Broom rape] (85) (1932)

Orobanche ludoviciana Nutt. subsp. *multiflora* (Nutt.) Collins – Many-flower broomrape [Manyflower broomrape] (50) (present)

Orobanche minor **J. E. Smith** – Clover broom-rape (5, 156) (1913–1923), Devil's-root [Devil's root] (5, 156) (1913–1923), Hellroot [Hell root, hell-root] (5, 156) (1913–1923), Herb bane [Herb-bane] (5, 156) (1913–1923), Lesser broomrape [Lesser broom-rape] (5, 156) (1913–1923), Strangle tare [Strangle-tare] (5, 156) (1913–1923)

Orobanche multiflora **Nutt.** – See *Orobanche ludoviciana* Nutt. subsp. *multiflora* (Nutt.) Collins

Orobanche ramosa **L.** – Branched broom-rape (5) (1913), Strangle tare [Strangle-tare] (5) (1913), Hemp broom-rape (5, 156) (1913–1923)

Orobanche riparia **Collins** – River broomrape (50) (present)

Orobanche uniflora **L.** – Cancer-drops [Cancer drops] (7) (1828), Broomrape [Broom-rape, Broom rape] (19) (1840), Squawroot [Squaw-root, Squaw root] (19) (1840), One-flower (122) (1937), Ghost-pipe [Ghostpipe] (155) (1942), Beechdrops [Beech drops, Beech-drops] (157) (1929), Agutiguepo-obi (174) (1753), Einblumige Sommerwurz (German) (186) (1814), One-flower cancer-root [One-flowered cancer root] (3, 156, 186) (1814–1977), Cancer-root [Cancer root] (5, 19, 93, 157, 158) (1840–1936), Squaw-drops [Squaw drops] (5, 7, 92, 156) (1828–1923), Pale broomrape [Pale broom-rape] (5, 72, 93, 156, 157, 158) (1900–1936), Naked broom-rape [Naked broom-rape, Naked broom rape] (5, 93, 156, 157, 158) (1900–1936), One-flower broomrape [One-flowered broom-rape Oneflowered broomrape] (5, 50, 86, 93, 97, 156, 157, 158) (1878–present)

Orobanche uniflora **L.** var. *purpurea* (Heller) Munz – See *Orobanche uniflora* L.

Orobanche virginiana **L.** – See *Epifagus virginiana* (L.) W. Bart.

Orobus **L.** – See *Lathyrus* L. (US species)

Orontium aquaticum **L.** – Ocoughtanamins (46) (1879) James River, Sacquenummener (Roanoke) (46) (1879), Taw-kee (86) (1878) Indian name, Never-wets (156) (1923), Aronia (177) (1762), Floating arum [Floating-arum] (5, 156) (1913–1923), Water-dock [Water dock] (5, 156) (1913–1923), Goldenclub [Golden club, Golden-club] (5, 19, 41, 46, 50, 86, 92, 107, 138, 156, 187) (1770–present), Tawkin (5, 7, 41, 92, 156) (1770–1923)

Orontium **L.** – Floating arum [Floating-arum] (167) (1814), Golden-club [Golden club, Golden-club] (2, 10, 50, 109, 138, 156) (1818–present)

Orophaca argophylla (Nutt.) **Rydb.** – See *Astragalus hyalinus* M.E. Jones

Orophaca **Britton** – See *Astragalus* L. (all US species)

Orophaca caespitosa (Nutt.) **Britton** – See *Astragalus spatulatus* Sheldon

Orophaca sericea (Nutt.) **Britton** – See *Astragalus sericoleucus* Gray

Orthilia **Raf.** – Orthilia (50) (present)

Orthilia secunda (L.) **House** – Serrated wintergreen (5) (1913), Shinleaf [Shin leaf, Shinleaf] (5) (1913), Yethering bells (46) (1879), Yevering bells (46) (1879), Sidebells wintergreen (50) (Present), Side-bells wintergreen [Sidebells wintergreen] (50) (present), Low shin-leaf (156) (1923), Side-bells pyrola [Sidebells pyrola, Side-bell pyrola] (138, 155, 156) (1923–1942), One-sided wintergreen (3, 4, 5, 19, 72, 85, 95, 131, 156) (1840–1986)

Orthocarpus luteus **Nutt.** – Owl clover [Owl's-clover, Owl's clover, Owlclover] (1, 3, 4, 85) (1932–1986), Yellow orthocarpus (5, 131) (1899–1913), Yellow owl clover [Yellow owl's-clover, Yellow owl-clover] (50, 155) (1942–present)

Orthocarpus **Nutt.** – Orthocarpus (50) (present), Owl clover [Owl's-clover, Owl's clover, Owlclover] (50, 93, 155) (1936–present)

Oryza **L.** – Rice (138) (1923) adaptation of Arabic name eruz

Oryza mutica – See *Oryza sativa* L.

Oryza sativa **L.** – Mountain rice (7) (1828), Paddy (92) (1876), Arous (Arabic) (110) (1886), Arroz (Spanish) (110) (1886), Newaree (Telinga) (110) (1886), Ora Za (180) (1633), Rice (180) (1633), Risz (German) (180) (1633), Riz (French) (180) (1633), Rys (German) (180) (1633), Rys (178, 179) (1526–1596), Cultivated rice (56, 163) (1852–1901)

Oryzopsis asperifolia **Michx.** – White-grain mountain-rice [Whitegrained mountain rice] (5) (1913), Large white-grain mountain-rice [Large white-grained mountain-rice] (90) (1885), Mountain-rice [Mountain rice] (19, 107) (1840–1919), Rough-leaf rice grass [Roughleaf ricegrass] (3, 50, 140, 155) (1942–present), White mountain-rice [White mountain rice] (66, 90, 94) (1885–1903)

Oryzopsis bloomeri (Bol.) **Ricker** – See *Achnatherum* ×*bloomeri* (Boland.) Barkworth [*hymenoides* × *occidentale*]

Oryzopsis canadensis (Poir.) **Torr.** – See *Piptatherum canadense* (Poir) Barkworth

Oryzopsis cuspidata **Benth.** – See *Achnatherum hymenoides* (Roemer & J. A. Schultes) Barkworth

Oryzopsis exigua **Thurb.** – See *Piptatheropsis exigua* (Thurb.) Romasch., P. M. Peterson & R. J. Soreng

Oryzopsis hymenoides (R. & S.) **Ricker** – Silky grass [Silky-grass] (85) (1932) SD

Oryzopsis juncea (Michx.) **B.S.P.** – See *Piptatherum canadense* (Poir) Barkworth

Oryzopsis melanocarpa **Muhl.** – See *Patis racemosa* (Sm.) Romasch., P. M. Peterson & R. J. Soreng

Oryzopsis **Michx.** – Mountain-rice [Mountain rice] (1, 93) (1932–1936), Rice grass [Ricegrass] (50, 155) (1942–present)

Oryzopsis micrantha (Trin. & Rupr.) **Thurb.** – See *Piptatherum micranthum* (Trin. & Rupr.) Barkworth

Oryzopsis pungens (Torr.) **Hitchc.** – See *Piptatherum pungens (Torr.) Barkworth*

Oryzopsis racemosa (J. E. Smith) **Ricker** – See *Patis racemosa* (Sm.) Romasch., P. M. Peterson & R. J. Soreng

Osmanthus americana (sic) **Benth. & Hook. f.** – See *Osmanthus americanus* Benth. & Hook.

Osmanthus americanus (L.) **Benth. & Hook. f. ex Gray var. americanus** – Olivier d'Amérique (French) (8) (1785), Devil wood [Devilwood, Devil-wood, Devil's wood] (19, 20, 92) (1840–1876), American olive or American linden tree (8, 19, 92, 107) (1785–1876)

Osmanthus americanus **Benth. & Hook.** – Olive or Olive tree (182) (1791), Purple-berry bay [Purple berried bay] (182) (1791), Purple-berry Bay of Catesby [Purple berr'd Bay of Catesby] (183) (~1756), Devil wood [Devilwood, Devil-wood, Devil's wood] (2, 75, 107) (1894–1919)

Osmanthus **Gray** – possibly *Osmanthus* Lour.

Osmanthus **Lour.** – Osmanthus (138) (1923), possibly Devil wood [Devilwood, Devil-wood, Devil's wood] (109) (1949)

Osmaronia cerasiformis (Torr. & Gray) **Greene** – See *Oemleria cerasiformis* (Torr. & Gray ex Hook. & Arn.) Landon

Osmorhiza aristata var. *brevistylis* (DC.) **B. Boivin**) – See *Osmorhiza claytonii* (Michx.) C. B. Clarke

Osmorhiza berteroi **DC.** – Sweet cicely [Sweetcicely, Sweet cicily] (50) (present), Spreading sweetroot (155) (1942), Western sweet cicely (5, 85) (1913–1932)

Osmorhiza brevistylis – See *Osmorhiza claytonii* (Michx.) C. B. Clarke

Osmorhiza chilensis **Hook. & Arn.** – See *Osmorhiza berteroi* DC.

Osmorhiza claytoni – See *Osmorhiza claytonii* (Michx.) C. B. Clarke

Osmorhiza claytonii (Michx.) **C. B. Clarke** – Osaga'tigom' (Chippewa, tangled branches) (40) (1928), Sweet cecily (40) (1928), Sweet chervil [Sweete cheruill] (158) (1900), Sweet jarvil (3, 5, 76, 156, 158) (1896–1977), Hairy sweet cicely (5, 158) (1900–1913), Woolly sweet cicely [Wooly sweet cicely] (5, 85, 72, 131, 156, 158) (1899–1936), Clayton's sweetroot [Clayton sweetroot] (50, 155) (1942–present)

Osmorhiza depauperata **Phil.** – Squawroot [Squaw-root, Squaw root] (3) (1977), Blunt-fruit sweet cicely [Blunt-fruited sweet cicely] (5) (1913), Blunt-seed sweetroot [Bluntseed sweetroot] (50, 155) (1942–present)

Osmorhiza divaricata **Nutt.** – See *Osmorhiza berteroi* DC.

Osmorhiza longistylis (Torr.) **DC.** – Chan-pezhuta (Dakota, wood-medicine) (37) (1919), Kahtstaraha (Pawnee, buffalo medicine) (37) (1919), Shanga-makan (Omaha-Ponca, horse-medicine) (37)

(1919), American sweet cicely (46) (1879), Carvell (46) (1879), Sicily root (92) (1876), Sweet sicily (92) (1876), Segede bwens (Chippewa) (105) (1932), Smooth sweet cicely (156) (1923), Cicely root [Cicely-root] (156, 157, 158) (1900–1929), Sweet cicely [Sweetcicely, Sweet cicily] (19, 37, 49, 85, 92, 93, 105, 127, 158) (1840–1936), Aniseroot [Anise root, Anise-root] (3, 4, 5, 92, 93, 157, 158) (1876–1986), Sweet cecily (47, 57) (1852–1917), Smoother sweet cicely [Smoother sweet-cicely] (5, 49, 72, 97, 131, 157, 158) (1898–1937), Sweet anise (5, 76, 156, 157, 158) (1896–1929) Sulphur Grove OH, from anise-like odor and taste, Sweet jarvil (5, 76, 156, 157, 158) (1896–1929), Sweet chervil [Sweete cheruill] (5, 92, 156, 157) (1876–1929), Long-style sweetroot [Longstyle sweetroot] (50, 155) (1942–present)

Osmorhiza longistylis* (Torr.) DC. var. *longistylis – See *Osmorhiza longistylis* (Torr.) DC.

***Osmorhiza longistylis* (Torr.) DC. var. *villicaulis* Fern.** – See *Osmorhiza longistylis* (Torr.) DC.

***Osmorhiza obtusa* (Coult. & Rose) Fern.** – See *Osmorhiza depauperata* Phil.

***Osmorhiza occidentalis* (Nutt. ex Torr. & Gray) Torr.** – Sweet myrrh (35) (1806)

***Osmorhiza* Raf.** – Sweet cicely [Sweetcicely, Sweet cicily] (1, 2, 4, 93, 156, 158) (1895–1986), Sweetroot [Sweet root] (50, 155) (1942–present)

***Osmorrhiza longistylis* DC. (*sic*)** – See *Osmorhiza longistylis* (Torr.) DC.

***Osmorrhiza occidentalis* (Nutt.) Torr.** – See *Osmorhiza occidentalis* (Nutt. ex Torr. & Gray) Torr.

***Osmorrhiza* Raf.** – See *Osmorhiza* Raf.

***Osmunda* (Tourn) L.** – See *Osmunda* L.

***Osmunda cinnamomea* L.** – Breadroot [Bread root, Bread-root] (5) (1913), Swamp brake (5) (1913), Flowering fern [Flowering-fern] (19) (1840), Tall osmunda (187) (1818), Cinnamon fern [Cinnamon-fern] (1, 5, 50, 72, 92, 97, 109, 122, 124, 138, 187) (1818–present), Fiddleheads [Fiddle heads] (5, 73) (1892–1913)

***Osmunda claytoniana* L.** – Clayton's flowering fern (5) (1913), Clayton's fern (1, 5, 72) (1893–1932), Interrupted fern [Interrupted-fern] (5, 50, 109, 138) (1913–present)

***Osmunda* L.** – Rattlesnake fern [Rattlesnake-fern, Rattlesnakefern] (7) (1828), Osmunda (50) (present) for Osmunder, a Saxon god, Fiddleheads [Fiddle heads] (73) (1892), Royal fern [Royal-fern, Royal-fern] (1, 4) (1932–1986), Flowering fern [Flowering-fern] (10, 158, 184) (1793–1900)

***Osmunda regalis* L.** – Bracken (5) (1913), Water fern [Waterfern, Water-fern] (5) (1913), Buckhorn [Buck horn, Buck-horn, Buck's horn, Buckshorn, Buck's-horn, Bucks-horne, Bucks horne] (73) (1892), Fern brake (92) (1876), Male fern [Malefern, Male-fern, Male ferne] (92) (1876), Flowering-fern (109) (1949), Buckhorn male fern [Buckhorn male-fern] (157) (1929), Lady brake (157) (1929), Royal brake (157) (1929), Bog-onion [Bog onion] (158) (1900), Royal osmunda (187) (1818), Osmund-the-waterman [Osmund the waterman] (157, 178) (1596–1929), Royal fern [Royal-fern, Royalfern] (3, 5, 50, 72, 92, 97, 109, 138, 155, 157) (1907–present), Ditch fern (5, 157) (1900–1913), Royal osmund (5, 157) (1900–1929), Snake fern (5, 157) (1913–1929), Tree fern [Treefern] (5, 157) (1913–1929), Buckhorn brake (5, 49, 92, 157) (1876–1929), Hartshorn bush [Harts horn bush] (5, 92, 157) (1876–1929), Herb Christopher [Herb-Christopher] (5, 92, 157) (1876–1929), King's fern [Kings' fern, King fern] (5, 92, 157) (1876–1929), Flowering fern [Flowering-fern] (5, 92, 157, 187) (1818–1929), Royal flowering fern (52, 157) (1919–1929), Buckthorn brake [Buck thorn brake] (52, 57) (1917–1919), Flowering brake (92, 157) (1876–1929), St. Christopher's herb [Saint Christopher herb, St. Christopher's-herb, S. Christophers herbe] (92, 157) (1876–1929)

***Osmunda regalis* L. var. *spectabilis* (Willd.) A. Gray** – Regal fern (124) (1937), Royal fern [Royal-fern, Royalfern] (4, 50, 122) (1937–present)

***Osmunda spectabilis* Willdenow** – See *Osmunda regalis* L.

Osmunda spicant – See *Blechnum spicant* (L.) Sm.

***Osmunda virginiana* L.** – See *Botrychium virginianum* (L.) Sw.

***Osmundea pinnatifida* (Hudson) Stackhouse** – Pepper dulse (107) (1919)

***Osteospermum uvedalia* L.** – See *Smallanthus uvedalius* (L.) Mackenzie ex Small

Osterdamia japonica – See *Zoysia japonica* Steud.

***Osterdamia matrella* (L.) Kuntze** – See *Zoysia matrella* (L.) Merr.

Osterdamia tenuifolia – See *Zoysia tenuifolia* Willd. ex Thiele

***Ostrya* (Michx.) Scop.** – See *Ostrya* Scop.

***Ostrya baileyi* Rose** – See *Ostrya knowltonii* Coville

***Ostrya carpinifolia* Scop.** – Charme à fruit d'houblon (French) (8) (1785), Bois dur (French) (20) (1857), Leverwood [Lever-wood, Lever wood] (20) (1857), Yzerhout (Belgis Noveboracensibus) (177) (1762), Ironwood [Iron wood, Iron-wood] (20, 177) (1762–1857), Hop hornbeam [Hop-hornbeam, Hophornbeam, Hophorn-bean] or Hop hornbeam tree [Hop horn beam tree] (8, 10, 38, 42, 49) (1785–1898)

***Ostrya knowltonii* Coville** – Hop hornbeam [Hop-hornbeam, Hophornbeam, Hophorn-bean] or Hop hornbeam tree [Hop horn beam tree] (153) (1913)

***Ostrya* Scop.** – Hop hornbeam [Hop-hornbeam, Hophornbeam, Hophorn-bean] or Hop hornbeam tree [Hop horn beam tree] (1, 2, 4, 50, 82, 109, 138, 155, 156, 58) (1895–present), Ironwood [Iron wood, Iron-wood] (1, 2, 93) (1932–1986)

***Ostrya virginiana* (Mill.) K. Koch** – Ma'nanons (Chippewa) (40) (1928), American hop tree (82) (1930), Hornbeam [Horn beam] or Hornbeam tree (82) (1930), Ispaŋapŋheča (Lakota) (121) (1918?–1970?), Hop-horn beans (157) (1929), Black hazel (156, 157, 158) (1900–1929), Deer wood [Deer-wood] (156, 157, 158) (1900–1929), Indian cedar (156, 157, 158) (1900–1929), Leverwood [Lever-wood, Lever wood] (156, 157, 158) (1900–1929), Ironwood [Iron wood, Iron-wood] (4, 5, 9, 40, 57, 65, 72, 85, 93, 97, 109, 113, 130, 156, 157, 158) (1873–1986)

***Ostrya virginiana* (Mill.) K. Koch var. *lasia* Fern.** – See *Ostrya virginiana* (Mill.) K. Koch var. *virginiana*

Ostrya virginiana* (Mill.) K. Koch var. *virginiana – Hopfenhausche (German) (6) (1892), American box (38) (1820), Blue beech (38) (1820), American hop-hornbeam [American hop hornbeam, American hophornbeam] (2, 6, 109, 138, 155) (1892–1949), Ironwood [Iron wood, Iron-wood] (2, 6, 19, 47, 49, 92, 131) (1840–1899), Leverwood [Lever-wood, Lever wood] (2, 6, 19, 49, 75, 92) (1840–1895), Hop hornbeam [Hop-hornbeam, Hophornbeam, Hophorn-bean] or Hop hornbeam tree [Hop horn beam tree] (4, 5, 19, 40, 50, 57, 75, 92, 93, 97, 112, 121, 122, 124, 130, 156, 158) (1840–present), Hardhack [Hard-hack] (75, 156, 157, 158) (1894–1929) Franconia NH

***Ostrya virginiana* (Mill.) Willd.** – See *Ostrya virginiana* (Mill.) K. Koch

***Ostrya virginica* Willd.** – See *Ostrya virginiana* (Mill.) K. Koch var. *virginiana*

***Ostrya* Willd.** – possibly *Carpinus* L.

***Othake callosum* (Nutt.) Bush** – See *Palafoxia callosa* (Nutt.) Torr. & Gray

***Othake* Raf.** – See *Gaillardia* Fouq. (all US species)

***Othake sphacelatum* (Nutt.) Rydb.** – See *Palafoxia sphacelata* (Nutt. ex Torr.) Cory

***Othake texana* (DC.) Gray** – See *Palafoxia texana* DC.

***Othake texanum* (DC.) Bush** – See *Palafoxia texana* DC.

***Othonna* L.** – See *Senecio* L.

***Otophylla auriculata* (Michx.) Small.** – See *Agalinis auriculata* (Michx.) Blake

***Otophylla* Benth.** – See *Agalinis* Raf. (all US species)

***Oxalis acetosella* (auct. non L.)** – See *Oxalis montana* Raf.

***Oxalis acetosella* L.** – Welch sorrel (92) (1876), Greensauce [Greensauce, Green sauce] (92, 156) (1898–1923)

***Oxalis acetosella* var. *oregana* Trelease** – See *Oxalis oregana* Nutt.

Oxypolis rigidior (L.) Raf. – possibly Hemlock [Hemloc, Hemlocke] (156) (1923), possibly Hemlock dropwort [Hemlock-dropwort] (5, 156) (1913–1923), possibly Pig-potato [Pig potato] (5, 156) (1913–1923), possibly Water dropwort [Water drop-wort] (5, 156) (1913–1923), possibly Cowbane (5, 72, 97, 156) (1907–1937)

Oxypolis rigidus (L.) Raf. – possibly *Oxypolis rigidior* (L.) Raf.

Oxypolis ternata (Nutt.) Heller – Sulfurwort [Sulphurwort, Sulphur wort, Sulpher wort] (19) (1840), Milk parsley (92) (1876), possibly Water dropwort [Water drop-wort] (19) (1840)

Oxyria digyna (L.) Hill – Oxyrie reniforme (French) (7) (1828), Welsh sorrel (7) (1828), Sorrel [Sorell, Sorrell] (46) (1610), Round-leaf sorrel [Round-leafed sorrel] (103, 156) (1870–1923), Sour dock (5, 156) (1913–1923), Mountain sorrel (5, 7, 92, 101, 107, 122, 156) (1828–1937), Boreal sourdock [Boreal sour dock] (7, 92) (1828–1876)

Oxyria reniformis R. Brown – See *Oxyria digyna* (L.) Hill

Oxytria albiflora (Raf.) Pollard – See *Schoenolirion albiflorum* (Raf.) R.R. Gates

Oxytria crocea (Michx.) Raf. – See *Schoenolirion croceum* (Michx.) Wood

Oxytropis arctica R. Br. – Arctic oxytrope (5) (1913)

Oxytropis arctica var. *bellii* (Britton ex Macoun) B. Boivin – See *Oxytropis bellii* (Britton ex Macoun) Palib.

Oxytropis belli (Britton) Palibine – See *Oxytropis bellii* (Britton ex Macoun) Palib.

Oxytropis bellii (Britton ex Macoun) Palib. – Bell's oxytropis (5) (1913)

Oxytropis besseyi (Rydb.) Blank. – Red loco (4) (1986), Bessey's point vetch [Bessey pointvetch] (155) (1942), Bessey's locoweed (4, 50) (1986–present)

Oxytropis borealis DC. var. *viscida* (Nutt.) Welsh – Viscid loco-weed (131) (1899)

Oxytropis campestris (L.) DC. – Field oxytropis (5) (1913), Yellow oxytropis (5) (1913), Field locoweed (50) (present)

Oxytropis campestris (L.) DC. var. *gracilis* (A. Nels.) Barneby – See *Oxytropis monticola* Gray

Oxytropis DC. – Rattlepod [Rattle pod, Rattle-pod] (1) (1932), Bastard vetch (10) (1818), Painted pod (93) (1936) Neb, Crazyweed [Crazy-weed, Crazy weed] (155) (1942), Pointvetch (155) (1942), Rattleweed [Rattle-weed, Rattle weed] (1, 93, 106) (1932–1936), Locoweed [Loco weed, Loco-weed] (4, 45, 50, 82, 93, 156) (1896–present), possibly Pea tree [Pea-tree] (1) (1932)

Oxytropis deflexa (Pallas) DC. – Locoweed [Loco weed, Loco-weed] (85) (1932)

Oxytropis deflexa (Pallas) DC. var. *sericea* Torr. & Gray – Pendulous-pod locoweed (4) (1986), Blue nodding locoweed (50) (present)

Oxytropis lagopus Nutt. var. *atropupurea* (Rydb.) Barneby – Hare's locoweed (4) (1986), Hare-foot locoweed [Haresfoot locoweed] (50) (present)

Oxytropis Lam. – possibly *Oxytropis* DC.

Oxytropis lamberti Pursh – See *Oxytropis lambertii* Pursh

Oxytropis lambertii Pursh – Loco (76) (1896), Loco vetch (133) (1903), White loco (146) (1939), Lambert's crazyweed [Lambert crazyweed] (155) (1942), Purple locoweed [Purple loco weed] (3, 4, 50, 80, 98) (1926–present), Stemless locoweed [Stemless loco weed, Stemless loco weed] (5, 63, 71, 72, 80, 97, 156) (1898–1937), Colorado locoweed [Colorado loco weed] (5, 71) (1898–1913), Stemless crazyweed [Stemless crazy weed, Stemless crazy-weed] (5, 97) (1913–1937) OK, Crazyweed [Crazy-weed, Crazy weed] (71, 133, 146, 156) (1898–1939), Locoweed [Loco weed, Loco-weed] (71, 76, 82, 85, 95, 126, 127, 133, 156) (1896–1933), Colorado loco-vetch [Colorado loco vetch] (86, 156) (1878–1923), Stemless loco (93, 125) (1930–1936)

Oxytropis lambertii Pursh var. *lambertii* – Purple locoweed [Purple loco weed] (50) (present)

Oxytropis monticola Gray – Slender locoweed (4) (1986), Yellow-flower locoweed [Yellowflower locoweed] (50) (present), Hairy crazyweed (155) (1942)

Oxytropis multiceps Nutt. – Dwarf locoweed (4) (1986), Tufted oxytropis (5) (1913), Nuttall's oxytrope (50) (present)

Oxytropis nana Nutt. – Dwarf locoweed (4) (1986), Wyoming locoweed (50) (present)

Oxytropis podocarpa Gray – Inflated oxytrope (5) (1913)

Oxytropis richardsonii (Hook.) K. Schum – See *Oxytropis splendens* Dougl. ex Hook

Oxytropis sericea Nutt. – Silky crazyweed (155) (1942), White locoweed (3, 4, 50) (1977–present)

Oxytropis sericea Nutt. var. *sericea* – White locoweed (50) (present)

Oxytropis splendens Dougl. ex Hook – Showy oxytropis (5) (1913), Showy loco (126) (1933), Crazyweed [Crazy-weed, Crazy weed] (133) (1903), Loco vetch (133) (1903), Locoweed [Loco weed, Loco-weed] (133) (1903), Showy crazyweed (155) (1942), Whorled crazyweed (155) (1942), Showy locoweed [Showy loco weed] (3, 4, 50, 133) (1903–present)

Oxytropis villosa (Rydb.) K. Schum – See *Oxytropis monticola* Gray

Ozonium auricomum Grev. – See *Ozonium auricomum* Link

Ozonium auricomum Link – Stinking bearded mushroom (181) (~1678)

P

Pachira aquatica **Aubl.** – Guiana-chestnut (138) (1923)

Pachira **Aubl.** – Pachira (138) (1923)

Pachistima – See *Paxistima* Raf.

Pachylophus caespitosa **(Nutt.) Raimann** – possibly *Oenothera caespitosa* Nutt.

Pachylophus **Spach.** – See *Oenothera* L.

Pachyma cocos **(Schwein.) Fr.** – Tockohow (46) (1610)

Pachyma **Fr.** – Tuckaho [Tuckaho, Tuckahoe] (7) (1828), Tuckahoo (7) (1828)

Pachysandra **Michx.** – Pachysandra (138) (1923)

Pachysandra procumbens **Michx.** – Allegheny mountain spurge [Alleghany mountain spurge] (5, 156) (1913–1923), Allegheny pachysandra [Allegany pachysandra] (109) (1949), American thick-stamen (86) (1878) Meehan knew no common name and made this up, Mountain pachysandra (138) (1923)

Pachysandra terminalis **Sieb. & Zucc.** – Japanese pachysandra (109, 138) (1923–1949)

Pachystima canbyi **Gray** – See *Paxistima canbyi* Gray

Packera **A. & D. Löve** – Ragwort [Rag-wort] (50) (present)

Packera anonyma **(Alph.Wood) W. A. Weber & Á. Löve** – Small's squaw weed (5) (1913)

Packera antennariifolia **(Britt.) W. A. Weber & A. Löve** – Cat-paw ragwort [Cat's paw ragwort] (5) (1913)

Packera aurea **(L.) A. & D. Löve** – Cocash weed [Cocash-weed] (92, 156, 158) (1898–1923), Coughweed [Cough weed, Cough-weed] (92, 156, 158) (1898–1923), False valerian (5, 6, 19, 49, 92, 156, 158) (1840–1923), Female-regulator [Female regulator] (6, 49, 53, 58, 92, 158) (1869–1922)

Packera aurea **(L.) A.& D. Löve** – Fireweed [Fire weed, Fire-weed] (6, 92, 156, 158) (1876–1923), Golden groundsel (138, 155) (1931–1942), Golden ragwort (2, 5, 6, 58, 63, 97, 109, 131, 156, 158) (1869–1949), Golden senecio (6, 48, 49, 53, 92, 158) (1876–1922), Goldenes Kreuzkraut (German) (6) (1892), Golden-flower groundsel [Golden-flowered groundsel] (187), Groundsel [Groundsell] (6, 58) (1869–1892), Grundy-swallow [Grundy swallow] (5, 156, 158) (1900–1923), Liferoot [Life-root, Life root] (5, 6, 7, 48, 49, 52, 53, 54, 57, 58, 61, 156, 158) (1828–1923), Life-root plant [Life root plant] (92) (1876), Mequot (158) (1900), Nunqua (158) (1900), Nutqua (158) (1900), Piunkum (156) (1923), Senecio (54) (1905), Seneçon (French) (6) (1892), Snakeroot [Snake root, Snake-root] (75, 156, 158) (1894–1923) Concord MA, odor and taste of roots similar to Polygala senega, Squaw-weed [Squawweed, Squaw-weed] (2, 6, 49, 58, 156, 158) (1869–1923), Swamp squaw-weed [Swamp squaw weed (5, 72, 122, 156, 158) (1900–1936), Uncum (2, 158) (1895–1900), Uncum-piuncum (156) (1923), Unkum (6, 58, 92, 158) (1869–1900), Waw-weed [Waw weed] (92) (1876), possibly Anumguah (7) (1828), Ragwort [Rag-wort] (7, 19, 49, 53, 57, 92, 106, 114, 158) (1828–1930)

Packera cana **(Hook.) W. A. Weber & A. Löve** – Gray ragwort (3, 4) (1977–1986), Pursh's groundsel [Pursh groundsel] (155) (1942), Silvery groundsel (5, 93, 131) (1899–1936), Woolly groundsel (50, 155) (1942–present)

Packera glabella **(Poir) C. Jeffrey** – Butterweed [Butter weed, Butterweed] (2, 3, 4, 5, 7, 50, 92, 156) (1828–present), Cress-leaf groundsel [Cressleaf groundsel, Cress-leaved groundsel] (5, 97, 155, 156) (1913–1942)

Packera obovata **(Muhl. ex Willd.) W. A. Weber & A. Löve** – Long-stem groundsel (19) (1840), Obovate-leaf groundsel [Obovate-leaved groundsel] (187), Old Robert's root (92) (1876), Robert's-root [Roberts root] (7) (1828), Round-leaf groundsel [Roundleaf groundsel] (3, 4, 138) (1923–1986), Round-leaf ragwort [Roundleaf ragwort] (50) (present), Round-leaf squaw-weed [Round-leaf squaw weed] (5, 72, 97) (1907–1937), Squaw-weed [Squawweed, Squaw-weed] (92) (1876)

Packera pauciflora **(Pursh) A. & D. Löve** – Northern squaw-weed [Northern squaw weed] (5, 131) (1899–1913)

Packera paupercula **(Michx.) A. & D. Löve** – Balsam groundsel (3, 4, 5, 19, 50, 72, 93, 93, 122, 131, 155, 158) (1840–present), Crawford's squaw-weed [Crawford's squaw weed] (5) (1913), Gaspe's groundsel [Gaspe groundsel] (155) (1942), Groundsel balsam (158) (1900)

Packera plattensis **(Nutt.) W. A. Weber & A. Löve** – Groundsel [Groundsell] (148) (1939) CO, Prairie groundsel (50, 155) (1942–present), Prairie ragwort (3, 4, 5, 93, 97, 98, 122, 131) (1899–1986)

Packera pseudaurea **(Rydb.) W. A. Weber & A. Löve** – False-gold groundsel [Falsegold groundsel] (50) (present)

Packera pseudaurea **(Rydb.) W. A. Weber & A. Löve var. semicordata (Mackenzie & Bush) T. M. Barkl.** – False-gold groundsel [Falsegold groundsel] (50) (present)

Packera schweinitziana **(Nutt.) W. A. Weber & A. Löve** – Robbins' squaw-weed [Robbins' squaw weed] (5) (1913)

Packera tomentosa **(Michx.) C. Jeffrey** – Ashweed [Ash-weed, Ash weed, Ashe weed, Ashe-weed] (156) (1923), Ashwort [Ash wort] (5, 19, 92) (1840–1913), Rag woolwort (156) (1923), Woolly ragweed (5, 122, 156) (1913–1937), possibly Mountain fleawort [Mountain flea wort] (19) (1840)

Packera tridenticulata **(Rydb.) W. A. Weber & A. Löve** – Three-tooth ragwort [Threetooth ragwort] (50) (present), Western squaw-weed [Western squaw weed] (5, 93, 97) (1913–1937)

Padus melanocarpa **(A. Nels.) Shafer** – See *Prunus virginiana* L. var. *melanocarpa* (A. Nels.) Sarg.

Padus **Mill.** – See *Prunus* L.

Padus nana **(Du Roi) M. Roemer** – See *Prunus virginiana* L. var. *virginiana*

Padus serotina **(Ehrh.) Borkh.** – American black cherry (46) (1879), Chokecherry [Choke cherry, Choke-cherry, Choke cherries, Chokecherries, Choak cherry] (19) (1840), Rum cherry (46) (1879)

Padus virginiana **(L.) Mill.** – See *Prunus virginiana* L. var. *virginiana*

Padus virginiana **subsp. *melanocarpa* (A. Nelson) W. A. Weber** – Black western chokecherry (138) (1923), Chokecherry [Choke cherry, Choke-cherry, Choke cherries, Choke-cherries, Choak cherry] (112) (1937)

Paeonia brownii **Dougl. ex Hook.** – Western peony (109) (1949)

Paeonia **L.** – Peony [Paeony] (7, 15, 82, 109, 138) (1828–1949), Pyony (179) (1526)

Paeonia lactiflora **Pallas** – Chinese peony (138) (1923), Peony [Paeony] (107) (1919)

Paeonia officinalis **L.** – Common peony (92, 138) (1876–1923), Double peony [Double pionie] (178) (1526), Female peony [Female Pionie] (178) (1526), Misbegotten peony [Misbegotten pionie] (178) (1526), Paeonia (92) (1876), Peony [Paeony] (7, 19, 49, 52, 57, 82) (1828–1930), Piney (49, 52) (1898–1919), Whitish peony [Whitish pionie] (178) (1526)

Palafoxia callosa **(Nutt.) Torr. & Gray** – Rayless othake (5, 97, 106) (1913–1937), Rayless polypteris (122, 124) (1937)

Palafoxia hookeriana **Torr. & A. Gray var. hookeriana** – Palafoxia (138) (1923)

Palafoxia **Lag.** – Palafox (50) (present), Palafoxia (155, 158) (1900–1942), Polypteris (155, 158) (1900–1942)

Palafoxia rosea **(Bush) Cory** – Rosy palafox (50) (present)

Palafoxia sphacelata **(Nutt. ex Torr.) Cory** – Hooker's othake (5, 97) (1913–1937), Othake (3, 50) (1977–present)

Palafoxia texana **DC.** – Texas othake (97) (1937)

Paliurus aculeatus **Lam.** – See *Paliurus spina-christi* Mill.

Paliurus spina-christi **Mill.** – Christ's thorn [Christ-thorn] (92) (1876), Christ's thorn [Christ-thorn] (109, 138) (1923–1949)

Pallasia **Houtt.** – See *Crypsis* Ait.

Palmaria palmata **(L.) Weber & Mohr** – Dillisk (92, 107) (1876–1919), Dulse (92, 107) (1876–1919), Waterleaf [Water leaf, Waterleaf] (92) (1876)

Panaeolus retirugus **(Fr.) Gillet** – Net-cap mushroom (128) (1933)

Panax horridum – See *Oplopanax horridus* Miq.

Panax **L.** – Ginseng (1, 10, 50, 93, 138, 155, 158) (1818–present)

Panax quinquefolium **L.** – See *Panax quinquefolius* L.

Panax quinquefolius **L.** – American ginseng (7, 50, 64, 92, 109, 138, 155, 157, 158) (1828–present), Amerikanische Kraftwurzel (German) (158) (1900), Dsindsom (186) (1814), Five-finger [Fivefinger, Five finger] (6, 7, 64, 156, 157, 158) (1828–1929), Five-fingers root [Fivefingers root] (92) (1876), Fünfblättrige Kraftwurzel (German) (186) (1814), Garangtoging (Iroquois, a child) (41, 177) (1762–1770), Garantogen (7, 92) (1828–1876), Garantoquen [Garantoquen] (6, 158, 186) (1814–1900), Garantquen (157) (1929), Garent-Oguen (Iroquois, a child) (41, 177) (1750–1770), Gensang (7) (1828), Ginsano (186) (1814), Ginsem [Gin-sem] (177, 186) (1762–1814), Ginseng (2, 3, 4, 5, 6, 14, 19, 37, 41, 47, 49, 52, 53, 57, 61, 63, 64, 72, 92, 95, 97, 102, 105, 107, 156, 158, 182, 184, 186, 187) (1770–1986), Ginseng root (7) (1828), Ginshang (75, 156) (1894–1923) VT, Ginsing (92, 57) (1876–1900), Gin-zeng (177) (1762), Gin-zing (177) (1762), Grantogen (157, 158) (1900–1929), Jin chen [Jin-chen] (6, 186) (1814–1892), Jin-seng (186) (1814), Jinshang (158) (1900), Junshand (157) (1929), Kraftwurzel (German) (6, 186) (1814–1892), Mandchon orkoda (186) (1814), Nindsin (186) (1814), Ninsin (7, 158) (1828–1900), Ninsin root (92) (1876), Panax (52, 53, 57) (1917–1922), Redberry [Red-berry, Red berry] (5, 6, 64, 92, 156, 157, 158) (1876–1929), Sang (5, 64, 75, 102, 156, 157, 158) (1886–1929) WV, Schinseng (German) (158) (1900), Seng (64) (1907), Šuniau-jibik (Chippewa, money root) (105) (1932), possibly Â'talĭ kûlĭ (Cherokee, it climbs the mountain) (102) (1886) addressed in Cherokee rituals as "great man" or "little man", possibly Ginseng d'Amerique (French) (6) (1892), possibly Man's-health [Man's health] (6) (1892), possibly Tartar root (6) (1892)

Panax trifolius **L.** – Dwarf ginseng (2, 5, 138, 156) (1895–1923), Dwarf groundnut [Dwarf ground-nut] (19, 92) (1840–1876)

Panax trifolius **L.** – Groundnut [Ground-nut, Ground nut, Ground nutts] (2, 5, 76, 156) (1895–1923)

Pancratium **L.** – Pancratium (50) (present), Sea-dafodil (167) (1814), Squilily (7) (1828)

Pancratium maritimum **L.** – Agria skilla (46) (1879), Sea daffodil (2, 107) (1895–1919), Sea-onion of Valentia [Sea Onions of Valentia] (178) (1596), Sousan (46) (1879), Squilily (92) (1876)

Pandanus **L. f.** – Screw-pine [Screwpine, Screw pine] (107, 109, 138) (1919–1949)

Pandanus pacificus **Hort.Veitch** – See Pandanus dubius Spreng.

Pandanus tectorius **Parkinson ex Zucc.** – Breadfruit [Bread fruit, Bread-fruit] (107) (1919), Pandang (107) (1919), Screw-pine [Screwpine, Screw pine] (107) (1919)

Pandanus utilis **Bory** – Common screwpine (138) (1923)

Pandanus veitchi – See *Pandanus veitchii* hort. Veitch ex Masters & T. Moore

Pandanus veitchii **hort. Veitch ex Masters & T. Moore** – Veitch's screwpine [Veitch screwpine] (138) (1923)

Pandorea jasminoides **Schum.** – See *Pandorea jasminoides* (Lindl.) K. Schum.

Pandorea ricasoliana – See *Podranea ricasoliana* (Tanfani) Sprague

Panicularia acutiflora **(Torr.) Kuntze** – See *Glyceria acutiflora* Torr.

Panicularia americana **(Torr.) MacM.** – See *Glyceria grandis* S. Wats.

Panicularia borealis **Nash** – See *Glyceria borealis* (Nash) Batchelder

Panicularia **Fabr.** – See *Glyceria* R. Br.

Panicularia fluitans **(L.) Kuntze** – See *Glyceria fluitans* (L.) R. Br.

Panicularia laxa **Scribn.** – See *Glyceria laxa* (Scribn.) Scribn.

Panicularia nervata **(Willd.) Kuntze** – See *Glyceria striata* (Lam.) A.S. Hitchc.

Panicularia obtusa **(Muhl.) Kuntze** – See *Glyceria obtusa* (Muhl.) Trin.

Panicularia pallida **(Torr.) Kuntze** – See *Torreyochloa pallida* (Torr.) Church var. *pallida*

Panicularia septentrionalis **(Hitchc.) Bicknell** – See *Glyceria septentrionalis* A. S. Hitchc.

Panicum acuminatum **Sw. var. consanguineum (Kunth) J. W. Wipff & S. D. Jones** – See *Dichanthelium consanguineum* (Kunth) Gould & C. A. Clark

Panicum acuminatum **Sw. var. leucothrix (Nash) Lelong** – See *Dichanthelium leucothrix* (Nash) Freckmann

Panicum acuminatum **Sw. var. unciphyllum (Trin.) Lelong** – See *Dichanthelium meridionale* (Ashe) Freckmann

Panicum agrostoides **Spreng.** – See *Panicum rigidulum* Bosc ex Nees var. *elongatum* (Pursh) Lelong

Panicum agrostoides **Spreng. var. elongatum (Pursh) Scribn.** – See *Panicum rigidulum* Bosc ex Nees var. *elongatum* (Pursh) Lelong

Panicum alabamense **Ashe** – See *Dichanthelium ovale* (Ell.) Gould & C. A. Clark var. *addisonii* (Nash) Gould & C. A. Clark

Panicum amarum **Ell.** – Bitter grass [Bittergrass] (50) (present), Bitter panic grass [Bitter panic-grass, Bitter panicgrass] (50, 94) (1901–present), Smaller sea-beach grass (5, 7) (1828–1913)

Panicum amarum **Ell. var. amarulum (A. S. Hitchc. & Chase) P.G. Palmer** – Bitter panic (5, 66) (1903–1913), Southern sea-beach grass (5) (1913)

Panicum anceps **Michx.** – Beaked panic grass [Beaked panicgrass, Beaked panic-grass] (50, 99, 119, 163) (1852–present), Beaked panicum (3, 5, 155) (1913–1977), Double-head panic [Double-headed panic] (66) (1903), Flat-stem panic [Flat-stemmed panic] (5, 94, 119, 163) (1852–1938), Two-edge panic grass [Two-edged panic grass, Two-edged panic-grass] (87, 187) (1818–1884)

Panicum angustifolium **Ell.** – See *Dichanthelium aciculare* (Desv. ex Poir.) Gould & C. A. Clark

Panicum arenicoloides **Ashe** – See *Dichanthelium aciculare* (Desv. ex Poir.) Gould & C. A. Clark

Panicum autumnale – See *Digitaria cognata* (J.A. Schultes) Pilger var. *pubiflora* Vasey ex L. H. Dewey

Panicum barbipulvinatum **Nash** – See *Panicum capillare* L.

Panicum barbulatum **Michx.** – See *Dichanthelium dichotomum* (L.) Gould var. *dichotomum*

Panicum bicknellii **Nash** – See *Dichanthelium boreale* (Nash) Freckmann

Panicum boreale **Nash** – See *Dichanthelium boreale* (Nash) Freckmann

Panicum bulbosum **Kunth** – Alkali saccatone (94) (1901) TX, Bulb panicum (122) (1937), Bulbous panic grass [Bulbous panic-grass] (163) (1852)

Panicum bushii **Nash** – See *Dichanthelium boreale* (Nash) Freckmann

Panicum caerulescens **Hack. ex A. S. Hitchc.** – See *Dichanthelium dichotomum* (L.) Gould var. *dichotomum*

Panicum calliphyllum **Ashe** – See *Dichanthelium boreale* (Nash) Freckmann

Panicum capillare **L.** – Barbed witch grass [Barbed witch-grass] (5, 85, 163) (1852–1932), Capillary panic grass [Capillary panic-grass] (143) (1936), Common witch grass [Common witchgrass] (140, 155) (1942–1944), Cushion witch grass [Cushion witchgrass] (155) (1942), Fool hay [Fool-hay] (5, 94, 119) (1901–1938), Hair-stalk panic grass [Hair-stalked panic grass] (66, 87, 90) (1885–1903), Old witch grass [Old witch-grass, Old-witch-grass] (2, 5, 11, 45, 56, 62, 80, 87, 90, 92, 94, 111, 119, 129, 143, 163) (1852–1938), Tickle grass [Ticklegrass, Tickle-grass] (5, 56, 62, 75, 78, 80, 119, 129, 140, 145, 152) (1894–1944), Tumble grass [Tumble-grass, Tumblegrass] (2, 56) (1895–1901), Tumbleweed [Tumble weed, Tumble-weed] (5, 62, 119) (1912–1938), Western witch grass [Western witch-grass] (93) (1936), Witch grass [Witch-grass, Witchgrass] (3,

(1886), Worga (Telinga) (110) (1886)

Panicum miliaceum L. subsp. *miliaceum* –

Panicum minimum **Scrib. & Merr.** – See *Panicum philadelphicum* Bernh. ex Trin.

Panicum minus **Nash** – See *Panicum philadelphicum* Bernh. ex Trin.

Panicum molle **Sw.** – See *Urochloa mutica* (Forsk.) T. Q. Nguyen

Panicum nashianum **Scribn.** – See *Dichanthelium sabulorum* (Lam.) Gould & C. A. Clark var. *patulum* (Scribn. & Merr.) Gould & C. A. Clark

Panicum nitidum **Lam.** – See *Dichanthelium dichotomum* (L.) Gould var. *dichotomum*

Panicum nudicaule **Vasey** – See *Dichanthelium dichotomum* (L.) Gould var. *dichotomum*

Panicum obtusum **H.B.K.** – Blunt panic grass [Blunt panic-grass] (5, 99, 119) (1913–1938), Grape-vine grass [Grape vine grass, Grape-vine-grass] (5, 119) (1913–1938), Grape-vine mesquite (151, 163) (1852–1896), Obtuse-flower panicum [Obtuse-flowered panicum] (87) (1884), Range grass (5) (1913), Vine mesquite [Vine-mesquite] (3, 5, 50, 119, 140, 155) (1911–present), Vine mesquite grass [Vine mesquite-grass] (94, 122, 152) (1901–1937), Wire grass [Wiregrass, Wiregrass] (5) (1913)

Panicum oligosanthes **Schukt.** var. *scribnerianum* (Nash) **Fern.** – See *Dichanthelium oligosanthes* (J. A. Schultes) Gould var. *oligosanthes*

Panicum oligosanthes **Schult.** – See *Dichanthelium oligosanthes* (J. A. Schultes) Gould var. *oligosanthes*

Panicum onslowense **Ashe** – See *Dichanthelium sabulorum* (Lam.) Gould & C. A. Clark var. *patulum* (Scribn. & Merr.) Gould & C. A. Clark

Panicum pacificum **A. S. Hitchc. & Chase** – See *Dichanthelium acuminatum* (Sw.) Gould & C. A. Clark var. *fasciculatum* (Torr.) Freckmann

Panicum paspaloides **Pers.** – See *Paspalidium geminatum* (Forssk.) Stapf

Panicum paucipilum **Nash** – See *Dichanthelium spretum* (J. A. Schultes) Freckmann

Panicum perlongatum **Nash.** – See *Dichanthelium linearifolium* (Scribn. ex Nash) Gould

Panicum perlongum **Nash** – See *Dichanthelium linearifolium* (Scribn. ex Nash) Gould

Panicum philadelphicum **Bernh. ex Trin.** – Philadelphia panic grass [Philadelphia panicgrass] (50) (present), Philadelphia witch grass [Philadelphia witchgrass] (155) (1942), Small tumble grass (56) (1901), Small witch grass [Small witch-grass] (94) (1901), Tuckerman's witch grass [Tuckerman witchgrass] (155) (1942), Wood witch grass [Wood witch-grass] (5, 163) (1852–1913)

Panicum porterianum **Nash.** – See *Dichanthelium boscii* (Poir.) Gould & C. A. Clark

Panicum proliferum var. *decompositum* **(R. Br.) Thell.** – See Panicum decompositum R. Br.

Panicum proliferum var. *geniculatum* – See *Panicum dichotomiflorum* Michx.

Panicum prostratum **L.** – See *Urochloa reptans* (L.) Stapf

Panicum purpurascens **Raddi** – See *Urochloa mutica* (Forsk.) T. Q. Nguyen

Panicum recognitum **Fern.** – See *Dichanthelium scabriusculum* (Ell.) Gould & C. A. Clark

Panicum repens **L.** – Creeping panic (94) (1901)

Panicum reverchonii **Vasey** – See *Setaria reverchonii* (Vasey) Pilger

Panicum rigidulum **Bosc ex Nees** –

Panicum rigidulum **Bosc ex Nees** var. *condensum* **(Nash) Mohlenbrock** – See *Panicum rigidulum* Bosc ex Nees var. *elongatum* (Pursh) Lelong

Panicum rigidulum **Bosc ex Nees** var. *elongatum* **(Pursh) Lelong** – Agrostis-like panic grass (66) (1903), Dense panic grass [Dense panic-grass] (5, 99) (1913–1923), Long-leaf panic grass [Long-leaved panic-grass, Long-leaved panic grass] (5, 163) (1852–1913), Munro's grass [Munroe's grass, Munro-grass] (94, 163)

(1852–1901), Red-top panic (5, 119, 163) (1852–1938), Red-top panic grass [Redtop panicgrass] (50) (present), Red-top panicum [Redtop panicum] (87, 155) (1884–1942), Tall flat panic grass [Tall flat panic-grass] (5, 163) (1852–1913)

Panicum rigidulum **Bosc ex Nees** var. *rigidulum* – See *Panicum rigidulum* Bosc ex Nees var. *elongatum* (Pursh) Lelong

Panicum rostratum **Muhl.** – See *Panicum anceps* Michx.

Panicum saccharatum **Buckl.** – See *Digitaria californica* (Benth.) Henr.

Panicum scoparioides **Ashe** – See *Dichanthelium* ×*scoparioides* (Ashe) Mohlenbrock [*acuminatum* × *oligosanthes*]

Panicum scoparium **Lam.** – See *Dichanthelium scoparium* (Lam.) Gould

Panicum scribnerianum **Nash** – See *Dichanthelium oligosanthes* (J.A. Schultes) Gould var. *scribnerianum* (Nash) Gould

Panicum serotinum **(Walt.) Trin.** – See *Setaria italica* (L.) Beauv.

Panicum serotinum **(Walter) C. C. Gmel.** – See *Digitaria serotina* (Walt.) Michx.

Panicum shastense **Scribn. & Merr.** – See *Dichanthelium* ×*scoparioides* (Ashe) Mohlenbrock [*acuminatum* × *oligosanthes*]

Panicum spretum **Schult.** – See *Dichanthelium spretum* (J. A. Schultes) Freckmann

Panicum squarrosum **(L. f.) Lam.** – See *Pseudoraphis spinescens* (R. Br.) Vickery

Panicum stenodes **Griseb.** – Small-joint panic grass [Small-jointed panic-grass] (94) (1901)

Panicum striatum **Lam.** – See *Sacciolepis striata* (L.) Nash

Panicum strigosum **Muhl. ex Elliott** – See *Dichanthelium strigosum* (Muhl. ex Elliott) Freckmann var. *strigosum*

Panicum subspicatum **Vasey** – See *Setaria ramiseta* (Scribn.) Pilger

Panicum tennesseense **Ashe** – See *Dichanthelium acuminatum* (Sw.) Gould & C. A. Clark var. *fasciculatum* (Torr.) Freckmann

Panicum texanum **Buckl.** – See *Urochloa texana* (Buckl.) R. Webster

Panicum trifolium **Nash** – See *Dichanthelium dichotomum* (L.) Gould var. *tenue* (Muhl.) Gould & C. A. Clark

Panicum tuckermanii **Fern.** – See *Panicum philadelphicum* Bernh. ex Trin.

Panicum unciphyllum **Trin.** var. *thinium* **A. S. Hitchc. & Chase** – See *Dichanthelium sabulorum* (Lam.) Gould & C. A. Clark var. *thinium* (A. S. Hitchc. & Chase) Gould & C. A. Clark

Panicum urvilleanum **Kunth** – Woolly-flower panic [Wooly-flowered panic] (94) (1901)

Panicum verrucosum **Muhl.** – Warty panic grass [Warty panic-grass] (5, 50, 66, 94) (1901–present)

Panicum villosissimum **Nash** – See *Dichanthelium villosissimum* (Nash) Freckmann var. *villosissimum*

Panicum virgatum **L.** – Black bent (129) (1894) SD, Black bent grass [Black-bent grass] (5) (1913), False redtop [False red-top, False red top] (129) (1894) SD, H'ade wathazhinde (Ponca) (37) (1830), Switchgrass [Switch grass, Switch-grass] (3, 50, 56, 75, 78, 85, 87, 88, 90, 94, 98, 99, 109, 111, 115, 119, 122, 129, 140, 144, 155, 163) (1852–present), Tall panic grass (87, 88, 90, 129) (1884–1894), Tall smooth panic grass (66, 90) (1885–1903), Tall smooth panicum (72, 131) (1894–1907), Thatch grass (5, 11, 37) (1888–1913), Wild redtop [Wild red-top] (5, 75, 93, 119) (1894–1938), Wobsqua grass (5) (1913)

Panicum virgatum **L.** var. *virgatum* – Switchgrass [Switch grass, Switch-grass] (50) (present)

Panicum viscidum **Ell.** – See *Dichanthelium scoparium* (Lam.) Gould

Panicum walteri **Pursh** – See *Echinochloa walteri* (Pursh) Nash

Panicum webberianum **Nash** – See *Dichanthelium sabulorum* (Lam.) Gould & C.A. Clark var. *patulum* (Scribn. & Merr.) Gould & C. A. Clark

Panicum werneri **Scribn.** – See *Dichanthelium linearifolium* (Scribn. ex Nash) Gould

Panicum wilcoxianum **Vasey** – See *Dichanthelium wilcoxianum* (Vasey) Freckmann

Panicum wilmingtonense **Ashe** – See *Dichanthelium ovale* (Ell.) Gould

& C. A. Clark var. *addisonii* (Nash) Gould & C. A. Clark

Panicum xalapense **Kunth** – See *Dichanthelium laxiflorum* (Lam.) Gould

Panicum xanthophysum **A. Gray** – See *Dichanthelium xanthophysum* (Gray) Freckmann

Pantheon **Cutler** – possibly *Rhododendron* L.

Papaver (**Tourn.**) **L.** – See *Papaver* L.

Papaver alpinum **L.** – Alpine poppy (109, 138) (1923–1949)

Papaver argemone **L.** – Headache [Head-ache] (5, 156) (1913–1923), Long rough-fruit poppy [Long rough-fruited poppy] (5) (1913), Pale rough-fruit poppy [Pale rough-fruited poppy] (5) (1913), Prickly poppy [Pricklypoppy, Prickly-poppy] (156) (1923), Wind rose (5, 156) (1913–1923)

Papaver dubium **L.** – Blaver (5, 156, 158) (1900–1923), Blindeyes [Blind-eyes, Blind eyes] (4, 5, 50, 156) (1913–present), Headache [Head-ache] (5, 156, 158) (1900–1923), Long smooth-fruit poppy [Long smooth-fruited poppy] (5, 158) (1900–1913), Long-head poppy [Longhead poppy] (4) (1986), Long-pod poppy [Longpod poppy] (138, 155) (1923–1942)

Papaver glaucum **Boiss. & Hausskn.** – Tulip poppy (19, 138) (1840–1923)

Papaver hybridum **L.** – Bastard poppy [Bastard poppie] (178) (1526), Round prickly-head poppy [Round pricklyhead poppy] (50)

Papaver **L.** – Cheese-bowl [Cheese bowl, Cheesebowl, Cheesebowls] (180) (1633), Poppy (1, 4, 7, 10, 15, 50, 82, 106, 109, 138, 155, 156, 158, 179, 184) (1793–present)

Papaver nudicaule **L.** – Arctic poppy (5, 107) (1913–1919), Iceland poppy (5, 109, 138) (1913–1949), Yellow poppy (19) (1840)

Papaver orientale **L.** – Aphion (107) (1919) Turks & Armenians, Oriental poppy (82, 107, 109, 138) (1919–1949)

Papaver rheas – See *Papaver rhoeas* L.

Papaver rhoeas **L.** – African rose (5, 156, 158) (1913–1923), Ampola (158) (1900), Blindeyes [Blind-eyes, Blind eyes] (158) (1900), Blue-eye [Blue eye, Blue eyes] (5, 156) (1913–1923), Canker (158) (1900), Canker-rose [Canker rose] (5, 156, 158) (1900–1923), Chasbowl (158) (1900), Cheese-bowl [Cheese bowl, Cheesebowl, Cheesebowls] (5, 92, 156, 158) (1876–1923) no longer in use by 1923, Cockeno (158) (1900), Common poppy (82) (1930), Copper-rose [Copper rose] (158) (1900), Coquelicot (French) (158) (1900), Corn pope (158) (1900), Corn popple (158) (1900), Corn poppy (3, 5, 50, 15, 49, 92, 107, 109, 138, 155, 156, 158) (1895–present), Corn puppy (158) (1900), Corn-rose [Corn Rose] (5, 50, 92, 156, 158) (1876–present), Cuprose-rose [Cuprose rose] (158) (1900), Double red poppy [Double red poppie] (178) (1526), Feldrose (German) (158) (1900), Field poppy (4, 5, 107, 156, 158) (1900–1986), Headache [Head-ache] (5, 156, 158) (1900–1923), Headwark (158) (1900), Joan silverpin [Joan silver-pin, Joan silver pin] (92) (1876), Klapperrose (German) (158) (1900), Klatschrose (German) (158) (1900), Pavot rouge (French) (158) (1900), Purple single poppy [Purple single poppie] (178) (1526), Red poppy (5, 55, 57, 92, 156, 158) (1876–1923), Redweed [Red-weed, Red weed] (5, 156) (1913–1923), Reed poppy (179) (1526), Rhoeas (57) (1917), Thunder flower [Thunder-flower] (5, 156, 158) (1900–1923) no longer in use by 1923, Wild poppy [Wylde poppy] (19, 179) (1526–1840)

Papaver somniferum **L.** – Balewort (5, 156) (1913–1923) no longer in use by 1923, Black poppy [Blacke poppy] (92, 179) (1526–1876), Cheese-bowl [Cheese bowl, Cheesebowl, Cheesebowls] (5, 156) (1913–1923) no longer in use by 1923, Common garden poppy (148) (1939), Common poppy (156) (1923), Double white poppy [Double white poppie] (178) (1526), Garden poppy (5, 15, 106, 156) (1895–1930), Joan silverpin [Joan silver-pin, Joan silver pin] (5, 156) (1913–1923), Mack (South of Caucasus) (110) (1886), Makon (Dorian) (110) (1886), Maple-leaved viburnum (5, 156) (1913–1923), Mawseed [Maw-seed] (5, 92, 156) (1876–1923), Meconium (49) (1898), Opium (53, 54, 55, 57, 59, 60, 92) (1876–1922), Opium poppy (5, 15, 19, 82, 92, 107, 109, 138, 156) (1840–1949), Poppy (92, 110, 148) (1876–1939), Succus thebaicus (49) (1898), White poppy (54, 60) (1526–1902), White single poppy [White single poppie] (178) (1526)

Papaya carica **Gaertner** – See *Carica papaya* L.

Pappophorum **Schreber.** – Pappus grass [Pappusgrass] (155) (1942)

Pappophorum wrightii **S. Wats.** – See *Enneapogon desvauxii* Desv. ex Beauv.

Papyrius papyrifera (**L.**) **Kuntze** – See *Broussonetia papyrifera* (L.) L'Hér. ex Vent.

Parapholis incurva (**L.**) **C. E. Hubb.** – Curly hard grass [Curly hard-grass] (94) (1901)

Paraserianthes lophantha (**Willd.**) **I. Nielsen** – Plume albizia [Plume albizzia] (109, 138, 155) (1923–1949)

Parathesis crenulata (**Vent.**) **Hook. f.** – Coral ardisia (138) (1923)

Parietaria diffusa – See *Parietaria judaica* L.

Parietaria judaica **L.** – Pireter (179) (1526), Walworde (179) (1526)

Parietaria **L.** – Pellitory (1, 2, 7, 10, 50, 122, 155, 158, 167) (1814–present)

Parietaria officinalis **L.** – Helxine (178) (1526), Pellitorie of the wall (178) (1526), Pellitory (107) (1919), Wall pellitory (92) (1876)

Parietaria pensylvanica **Muhl. ex Willd.** – American pellitory (157) (1929), Hammerwort (5, 93, 156, 157) (1900–1936), Helxine (156, 157) (1900–1923), Pellitory (19, 80, 85, 93, 95, 156, 157) (1840–1936), Pennsylvania pellitory [Pennsylvanian pellitory] (3, 4, 5, 50, 72, 97, 131, 155) (1899–present)

Paris – See *Paris quadrifolia* L.

Paritium tiliaceum [(**L.**) **A. Juss.**] – See *Hibiscus tiliaceus* L.

Parkinsonia aculeata **L.** – Horsebean [Horse-bean, Horse bean] (106) (1930), Jerusalem thorn [Jerusalem-thorn] (109) (1949), Parkinsonia (174) (1753), Retama (106, 109, 122, 124) (1930–1949)

Parkinsonia florida (**Benth. ex Gray**) **S. Wats.** – Green acacia (154) (1857), Green bark acacia (106) (1930), Greenwood [Green wood, Green-wood] (76) (1896), Palo verde (106) (1930), Palo verde (Spanish) (154) (1857)

Parkinsonia **L.** – Horsebean [Horse-bean, Horse bean] (106) (1930), Jerusalem thorn [Jerusalem-thorn] (106) (1930), Parkinsonia (138) (1923)

Parkinsonia microphylla **Torr.** – Desert bush (106) (1930), Jerusalem thorn [Jerusalem-thorn] (106) (1930), Palo verde (Spanish) (106) (1930) Mexico

Parkinsonia texana (**Gray**) **S. Wats. var. *macra* (I. M. Johnston) Isely** – Palo verde (124) (1937) TX

Parmelia **Ach.** – Lichen (121) (1918–1970)

Parmelia borreri **Turn.** – See *Punctelia borreri* (Sm.) Krog

Parmelia caperata – See *Flavoparmelia caperata* (L.) Hale

Parmelia caperata (**L.**) **Ach.** – See *Flavoparmelia caperata* (L.) Hale

Parmelia esculenta (**Pall.**) **Spreng.** – Manna (of Bible) (107) (1886)

Parmelia jubata (**L.**) **Ach.** – Bearded moss (103) (1871), possibly Rockhair alectoria (155) (1942)

Parmelia pseudoborreri **Asah.** – See *Punctelia borreri* (Sm.) Krog

Parmentiera cereifera **Seem.** – Candle tree [Candle-tree, Candletree] (138) (1923)

Parnassia americana **Muhl.** – See *Parnassia glauca* Raf.

Parnassia asarifolia **Vent.** – Brook parnassia (138) (1923), Kidney-leaf grass-of-parnassus [Kidney-leaved grass-of-parnassus] (5) (1913)

Parnassia california – See *Parnassia caroliniana* Michx.

Parnassia caroliniana **Michx.** – California parnassia (138) (1923), Carolina grass-of-Parnassus (5, 156) (1913–1923), Carolina parnassia (138) (1923), Grass-of-Parnassus [Grass of Parnassus] (72, 92, 131, 156) (1876–1923)

Parnassia fimbriata **Koenig** – Rocky Mountain parnassia (138) (1923)

Parnassia glauca **Raf.** – Fen grass-of-Parnassus [Fen grass of Parnassus] (50) (present), Flowering-plantain [Flowering plantain] (19) (1840), Grass-of-Parnassus [Grass of Parnassus] (3, 4) (1977–1986), Parnassus-grass [Parnassus grasse] (19) (1840)

Parnassia grandifolia **DC.** – Large-leaf grass-of-parnassus [Large-leaved grass-of-parnassus] (5) (1913)

Parnassia kotzebuei **Cham. ex Spreng.** – Kotzebue's grass-of-parnassus

(5) (1913)

Parnassia L. – Grass-of-Parnassus [Grass of Parnassus] (1, 2, 10, 13, 109, 158) (1818–1949) plant called Grass-of-Parnassus by Dioscorides from Mt. Parnassus, Parnassia (138, 155) (1923–1942), White buttercup (156, 158) (1900–1923), White liverwort (156, 158) (1900–1923)

Parnassia palustris L. – Bog star (127) (1933) ND, Flenort (Swedish) (46) (1879), Grass-of-Parnassus [Grass of Parnassus] (46, 127) (1879), Harnacker (Swedish) (46) (1879), Hiarteblad (Swedish) (46) (1879), Hwit-wisil (Swedish) (46) (1879), Marsh grass-of-parnassus [Marsh grass of Parnassus] (5, 50, 156) (1913–present), Northern grass-of-Parnassus (3, 4, 5) (1913–1986), Parnassia (174) (1753), Parnassus-grass [Parnassus grasse] (178) (1526), Slotter-blomster (Swedish) (46) (1879), Wide-world parnassia [Wideworld parnassia] (155) (1942)

Parnassia palustris L. var. *parviflora* (DC.) Boivin – Grass-of-Parnassus [Grass of Parnassus] (3, 85) (1932–1977), Marsh grass-of-parnassus [Marsh grass of Parnassus] (50) (present), Small-flower grass-of-Parnassus [Small-flowered grass-of-Parnassus, Small-flowered grass of Parnassus] (4, 5, 131) (1899–1986), Small-flower parnassia [Smallflower parnassia] (155) (1942)

Parnassia parviflora DC. – See *Parnassia palustris* L. var. *parviflora* (DC.) Boivin

Paronychia argyrocoma (Michx.) Nutt. – Allegheny nailwort (138) (1923), Nailwort (86) (1878), Silver chickweed (5, 156) (1913–1923), Silver whitlow-wort [Silver whitlow wort] (5, 156) (1913–1923), Silverhead [Silver-head] (5, 86, 156) (1878–1923)

Paronychia argyrocoma Nutt. – See *Paronychia argyrocoma* (Michx.) Nutt.

Paronychia canadensis (L.) Wood – Fork chickweed (19) (1840), Forked chickweed (1, 2, 4, 13, 158) (1849–1986), Forked whitlow wort [Forked whitlow-wort] (5, 97, 156) (1913–1937), Forking nailwort (155) (1942), Forking whitlow-wort [Forking whitlowwort] (5, 97, 156) (1913–1937), Nailwort (5, 156) (1913–1923), Slender forked chickweed (5, 72, 93) (1907–1936), Smooth forked nailwort (50) (present), Whitlow-wort [Whitlow wort, Whitlowwort] (156) (1923)

Paronychia depressa (Torr. & Gray) Nutt. ex A. Nels. – Depressed whitlow wort (5, 93) (1913–1936), Spreading nailwort (50) (present)

Paronychia dichotoma (L.) Nutt. – See *Paronychia canadensis* (L.) Wood

Paronychia fastigiata (Raf.) Fern. – Forked chickweed (4) (1986), Hairy forked nailwort (50) (present), Mountain ancychiastrum (5) (1913)

Paronychia jamesii Torr. & Gray – James' nailwort [James nailwort] (4, 50, 155) (1942–present), James' whitlow-wort [James' whitlow wort] (5, 93, 97, 131) (1899–1937), Ward's whitlow-wort [Ward's whitlow wort] (5) (1913)

Paronychia Mill. – Dutchman's-pipe plant [Dutchmans' pipe plant] (92) (1876), Forked chickweed (1, 2, 5, 13, 97, 156, 158) (1849–1937), Knotgrass [Knot grass, Knot-grass, Knotgrasse] (158) (1900), Nailwort (4, 50, 138, 155, 158) (1900–present) said to be used for felons and whitlows diseases of nails and joints of fingers, Whitlow-wort [Whitlow wort, Whitlowwort] (1, 2, 4, 13, 86, 155, 158) (1878–1986)

Paronychia montana (Small) Pax & K. Hoffmann – Mountain ancychiastrum (5) (1913)

Paronychia scoparia Small. – See *Paronychia virginica* Spreng.

Paronychia sessiliflora Nutt. – Creeping nailwort (50) (present), Low whitlow-wort [Low whitlow wort] (5, 97) (1913–1937)

Paronychia virginica Spreng. – Strict whitlow-wort (97) (1937)

Paronychia wardii Rydb. – See *Paronychia jamesii* Torr. & Gray

Parosela alopecuroides (Willd.) Rydb. – See *Dalea leporina* (Aiton) Bullock

Parosela aurea (Nutt.) Britton – See *Dalea aurea* Nutt. ex Pursh

Parosela Cavar. – See *Dalea* L.

Parosela dalea (L.) Britton – See *Dalea cliffortiana* Willd.

Parosela enneandra (Nutt.) Britton – See *Dalea enneandra* Nutt.

Parosela jamesii (Torr. & Gray) Vail – See *Dalea jamesii* (Torr.) Torr. & Gray

Parosela nana (Torr.) Heller. – See *Dalea nana* Torr. ex Gray

Parsonsia petiolata (L.) Rusby – See *Cuphea viscosissima* Jacq

Parthenium argentatum Gray – Guayule (109, 122) (1937–1949)

Parthenium auriculatum Britton – See *Parthenium integrifolium* L. var. *auriculatum* (Britt.) Cornelius ex Cronq.

Parthenium hispidum Raf. – See *Parthenium integrifolium* L. var. *hispidum* (Raf.) Mears

Parthenium hysterophorus L. – Bastard feverfew (158) (1900), Brown-bush (158) (1900), Feverfew [Fever few, fever-few] (124) (1937), Indian mugwort (158) (1900), Santa Maria (3, 4, 5, 97, 124) (1913–1986), Santa Maria feverfew (50, 122) (1937–present), Whitehead [White-head] (158) (1900) West Indies, Wild wormwood (158) (1900)

Parthenium incanum Kunth – Mariola (4, 50, 153) (1913–present)

Parthenium integrifolium L. – American feverfew [American fever-few, American fever few] (5, 72, 97, 156, 158) (1900–1937), Cutting-almond [Cutting almond] (92, 156, 158) (1898–1923), Nephritic plant (92, 158) (1876–1900), Pellitory of Spain (46) (1610), Prairie dock (5, 63, 92, 156, 158) (1876–1923), Prairie feverfew (122) (1937), White-flower Virginia sengreen [White flowred Virginia Sengreen] (181) (~1678), Wild quinine (31, 50, 75, 156, 158) (1847–present)

Parthenium integrifolium L. var. *auriculatum* (Britt.) Cornelius ex Cronq. – Auricled parthenium (5) (1913)

Parthenium integrifolium L. var. *hispidum* (Raf.) Mears – Creeping parthenium (5) (1913), Hairy feverfew (122) (1937), Hairy parthenium (5) (1913), Wild quinine (50) (present)

Parthenium L. – False feverfew [False fever-few] (167) (1814), Feverfew [Fever few, fever-few] (1) (1932)

Parthenocissus heptaphylla (Buckl.) Britt. ex Small – Cowitch [Cowitch, Cow itch] (106) (1930), Seven-leaf ivy [Seven-leaved ivy, Seven-leafed ivy] (106, 124) (1930–1937)

Parthenocissus inserta (Kerner) Fritsch – See *Parthenocissus quinquefolia* (L.) Planch.

Parthenocissus Planch. – Creeper [Creepers] (7, 50, 155) (1828–present), Virginia creeper [Virginian creeper] (4) (1986)

Parthenocissus quinquefolia (L.) Planch. – American ivy (5, 6, 8, 13, 49, 57, 58, 92, 106, 142, 156, 157, 158) (1785–1929), American joy [American-joy] (74, 157, 158) (1893–1929), American woodbine (92, 158) (1876–1900), Amerikanischer Epheu (German) (158) (1900), Common creeper (187) (1818), Common woodbine (38) (1820), Creeper [Creepers] (19, 92) (1840–1876), False grape [False grapes] (3, 6, 19, 37, 49, 58, 92, 156, 157, 158) (1840–1929), False Virginia creeper (131) (1899), Five-finger [Fivefinger, Five finger] (76, 157, 158) (1896–1929), Five-finger creeper [Five-fingered creeper] (156) (1923), Five-finger ivy [Five-fingered ivy] (74, 156, 158) (1893–1923), Five-leaf creeper [Five-leaved creeper] (46) (1879), Five-leaf ivy [Five-leaved ivy] (130, 156, 158) (1895–1923), Five-leaf wild ivy [Five leaved wild ivy] (42) (1814), Five-leaves (6, 49, 92) (1876–1892), Hairy creeper (138) (1923), Ingtha hazi itai (Omaha-Ponca) (37) (1919), Ivy (41) (1770), Manido'bima'kwûd (Chippewa) (40) (1928), Thicket creeper (155) (1942), Vigne vierge (French) (8, 158) (1785–1900), Virginia creeper [Virginian creeper] (2, 3, 4, 5, 6, 8, 13, 15, 48, 49, 50, 58, 65, 72, 80, 82, 85, 92, 93, 95, 97, 101, 106, 109, 112, 113, 122, 130, 135, 142, 149, 155, 156, 157, 158) (1785–present), Wall creeper (138) (1923), Wild wood vine [Wild wood-vine] (6, 49, 157, 158) (1892–1929), Wild woodbine (92, 158) (1876–1900), Wilder Wein (German) (158) (1900), Wood vine [Wood-vine] (156) (1923), Woodbine (2, 6, 15, 40, 46, 49, 57, 58, 82, 85, 92, 106, 109, 131, 142, 156, 158) (1671–1949), Woody climber (92, 158) (1876–1900), possibly St. Paul's creeper [St. Paul creeper] (138) (1923)

Parthenocissus tricuspidata (Sieb. & Zucc.) Planch. – Boston ivy (106, 109) (1930–1949), Japanese creeper (138) (1923), Japanese

Paspalum urvillei **Steud.** – Vasey's paspalum (94) (1901)

Paspalum vaginatum **Sw.** – Sand knot-grass (163) (1852), Seashore paspalum (50, 155) (1942–present)

Paspalum vaseyanum **Scribn.** – See *Paspalum urvillei* Steud.

Paspalum virgatum pubiflorum – See *Paspalum urvillei* Steud.

Paspalum walterianum **Schultes** – See *Paspalum dissectum* (L.) L.

Passiflora caerulea **L.** – Blue passion-flower [Blue passion flower, Blue passionflower] (19, 107) (1840–1919), Blue-crown passion-flower [Bluecrown passionflower] (138) (1923), Passionflower [Passion-flower, Passion flower] (92) (1876)

Passiflora coccinea **Aubl.** – Scarlet passionflower (138) (1923)

Passiflora edulis **Sims** – Granadilla (92) (1876), Purple granadilla (109, 138) (1923–1949)

Passiflora foetida **L.** – White passionflower [White passion flower] (122) (1937)

Passiflora gracilis **Jacq. ex Link** – Crinkled passionflower (138) (1923)

Passiflora incarnata **L.** – Apricot-vine (156) (1923), Granadilla (181, 182) (~1678–1791), Ground ivy [Ground-ivy] (156) (1923), Maracock vine (46) (1879), Marucuia (181) (~1678), May apple [May-apple, May-apple] (182) (1791), Maypop [May-pop, May pop, Maypops, May pops] (3, 4, 5, 49, 53, 92, 106, 107, 109, 122, 124, 138, 156) (1876–1986), Maypop passion-flower [Maypop passion-flower] (155) (1942), Passiflora (54, 57) (1905–1917), Passion vine [Passion-vine] (5, 156) (1913–1923), Passionflower [Passion-flower, Passion flower] (5, 46, 49, 52, 53, 54, 57, 156, 164) (1854–1923), Purple passion-flower [Purple passionflower] (50) (present), Wild passion vine [Wild passion-vine] (158) (1900), Wild passionflower [Wild passionflower, Wild passion flower] (109, 158, 164) (1854–1949)

Passiflora **L.** – Maracock (181) (~1678), Mariock-apple (181) (~1678), Moracocks (181) (~1678), Passionflower [Passion-flower, Passion flower] (1, 2, 4, 7, 10, 106, 109, 138, 155, 158) (1818–1986) for passion of Christ because flowers resemble crown of thorns

Passiflora laurifolia **L.** – Jamaica-honeysuckle (109) (1949), Marquiaas (174) (1753), Water-lemon [Waterlemon, Water lemon] (109, 138) (1923–1949), Yellow granadilla (109) (1949)

Passiflora ligularis **Juss.** – Sweet granadilla (109, 138) (1923–1949)

Passiflora lutea **L.** – Passionflower [Passion-flower, Passion flower] (3, 4) (1977–1986), Yellow passionflower [Yellow passion-flower, Yellow passion flower] (5, 19, 48, 50, 122, 138, 155) (1840–present)

Passiflora lutea **L. var.** *glabrifolia* **Fern.** – See *Passiflora lutea* L.

Passiflora maliformis **L.** – Conch nut (107) (1919), Conch-apple [Conch apple] (107) (1919), Sweet calabash (107) (1919), Water-lemon [Waterlemon, Water lemon] (107) (1919)

Passiflora manicata **(Juss.) Pers.** – Red passionflower (138) (1923)

Passiflora mollissima **(Kunth) Bailey** – Soft-leaf passionflower [Soft-leaf passionflower] (138) (1923)

Passiflora quadrangularis **L.** – Giant granadilla (109, 138) (1923–1949), Granadilla (107) (1919)

Passiflora rubra **L.** – Dutchman's-laudunum [Dutchmans' laudunum] (92) (1876)

Passiflora suberosa **L.** – Cork passion-flower [Cork passionflower] (138) (1923), Devil's-pumpkin [Devil's pumpkin] (76) (1896) Florida Keys

Passiflora tenuiloba **Engelm.** – Small white passion-flower [Small white passion flower] (124) (1937)

Passiflora warei **Nutt.** – See *Passiflora suberosa* L.

Pastinaca **L.** – Parsnip [Parsnep] (1, 50, 82, 93, 138, 155, 156, 158) (1900–present), Skyrwyt (179) (1526), Wild parsnip [Wild-parsnip, Wilde parsnep] (4) (1986)

Pastinaca opopanax **L.** – See Opopanax opopanax (L.) H. Karst.

Pastinaca sativa **L.** – Bird's-nest [Bird's nest, Birds-nest, Birds nest, Birds' nest, Birdsnest] (5, 156) (1913–1923), Common parsnip (45) (1896), Cultivated parsnip (109) (1949), Elaphoboscon (107) (1919), Garden parsnip (6, 155) (1892–1942), Hart's-eye [Hart's eye (5, 157, 158) (1900–1929), Heart's-eye (156) (1923), Madnep [Mad-nep] (156, 157, 158) (1900–1929), Milk parsley (107) (1919),

Mypes (157, 158) (1900–1929), Panais Potager (French) (6) (1892), Parsenep (158) (1900), Parsnip [Parsnep] (6, 7, 10, 19, 46, 80, 85, 92, 106, 107, 122, 138, 148, 156, 157, 158, 184) (1671–1939) cultivated by English colonists by 1671, Pasnet (158) (1900), Pastinake (German) (6) (1892), Pastnip (158) (1900), Queenweed [Queen weed, Queen-weed] (5, 62, 75, 156, 157, 158) (1894–1929), Tank (156, 157, 158) (1900–1929), Wild parsley [Wildparsley] (5, 72) (1907–1913), Wild parsnip [Wild-parsnip, Wilde parsnep] (3, 4, 50, 62, 80, 82, 93, 95, 97, 131, 133, 148, 156, 178, 187) (1526–present), Pestnachen (German) (107) (1550)

Patis racemosa **(Sm.) Romasch., P. M. Peterson & R. J. Soreng** – Black mountain rice (66, 94, 129) (1894–1903), Black-fruit mountain-rice [Black-fruited mountain rice] (5, 50, 56) (1901–present), Black-seed millet grass [Black seed millet grass] (19) (1840), Black-seed ricegrass [Blackseed ricegrass] (50, 155) (1942–present), Clustered millet grass (19) (1840)

Paullinia **L.** – Paullinia (138) (1923)

Paulownia **Sieb. & Zucc.** – Paulownia (138) (1923) for Anna Paulownia, 1795–1865, princess of the Netherlands

Paulownia tomentosa **(Thunb.) Baill.** – See *Paulownia tomentosa* (Thunb.) Sieb. & Zucc. ex Steud.

Paulownia tomentosa **(Thunb.) Sieb. & Zucc. ex Steud.** – possibly Blue catalpa (156) (1923), possibly Cootnwood (156) (1923), possibly Empress tree (156) (1923), possibly Napoleon (156) (1923), possibly Neckweed [Neck-weed] (156) (1923), possibly Paulownia (5) (1913), possibly Princess tree (156) (1923), possibly Royal paulownia (138) (1923)

Pavia **Lam.** – possibly *Aesculus* L.

Pavia lutea **[Poir]** – possibly *Aesculus flava* Aiton

Pavia macrostachya **[DC.]** – possibly *Aesculus parviflora* Walt. (taxonomic status is unresolved (PL))

Pavia ohioensis **[Michx. f.]** – possibly *Aesculus glabra* Willd. (taxonomic status is unresolved (PL))

Pavia rubra **[Moench.]** – possibly *Aesculus pavia* L.

Pavonia **Cav.** – Pavonia (138) (1923) for Joseh Pavon, Spanish botanist

Paxistima canbyi **Gray** – Canby's mountain-lover [Canby's mountain-lover] (5, 86, 156) (1878–1923), Rat-stripper [Rat stripper] (5, 73, 156) (1892–1923), Canby's pachistima [Canby pachistima] (138) (1923)

Paxistima myrsinites **(Pursh) Raf.** – Myrtle pachistima (138) (1923)

Paxistima **Raf.** – Pachistima (138) (1923)

Pectis angustifolia **Torr.** – Lemon-scent [Lemonscent, Lemon scent] (50) (present), Lemon-scent pectis [Lemon scented pectis] (5, 93, 122, 124) (1913–1937), Pectis (3, 157) (1929–1977)

Pectis angustifolia **Torr. var.** *angustifolia* – Narrow-leaf pectis [Narrowleaf pectis] (50) (present)

Pectis **L.** – Cinchweed (50) (present), Lemon-scent [Lemonscent, Lemon scent] (1) (1932), Pectis (155, 158) (1900–1942)

Pectis papposa **Gray** – See *Pectis papposa* Harvey & Gray

Pectis papposa **Harvey & Gray** – Manzanilla coyote (76, 154) (1857–1896) CA, Mexico

Pedicularis **(Tourn.) L.** – See *Pedicularis* L.

Pedicularis canadensis **L.** – Beefsteak plant [Beefsteak-plant, Beefsteakplant] (5, 156) (1913–1923), Canadian lousewort (50) (present), Chicken's-heads [Chicken's heads] (77) (1898) Southold Long Island, Common lousewort, Common louse-wort (4, 63, 72, 187) (1818–1986), Common wood betony (86) (1878), Early pedicularis (155) (1942), Early wood-betony [Early woodbetony] (138) (1923), Head-betony [Head betony] (5, 92, 156) (1876–1923), High heal-all [High healall] (5, 156) (1913–1923), Lousewort [Louse wort, Louse-wort] (3, 5, 19, 122, 131, 156) (1840–1977), Lousewort foxglove [Louse wort foxglove, Lousewort fox-glove] (5, 92) (1876–1913), Pedicularia (156) (1923), Red rattle (92) (1876), Snaffles (5, 92, 156) (1876–1923), Wood betany (131) (1899), Wood betony [Wood-betony, Woodbetony] (2, 4, 5, 92, 97, 105, 156) (1876–1986), Wood lousewort (93) (1936)

Pedicularis canadensis **L. subsp.** *canadensis* – Heal-all [Healall] (7)

Pedicularis capitata Adams.

(1828), High heal-all [High healall] (92) (1876)

Pedicularis capitata **Adams.** – Capitate pedicularis (5) (1913)

Pedicularis crenulata **Benth.** – Meadow lousewort (50) (present), Meadow pedicularis (155) (1942)

Pedicularis euphrasioides **Stephan ex Willd.** – See *Pedicularis labradorica* Wirsing

Pedicularis flammea **L.** – Red-tip pedicularis [Red-tipped pedicularis] (5) (1913)

Pedicularis furbishiae **S. Wats.** – Miss Furbish's pedicularis (5) (1913)

Pedicularis gladiata **Michx.** – See *Pedicularis canadensis* L. subsp. *canadensis*

Pedicularis grayi **A. Nels.** – See *Pedicularis procera* Gray

Pedicularis groenlandica **Retz.** – Long-beak pedicularis [Long-beaked pedicularis] (5) (1913), Red elephants (156) (1923)

Pedicularis **L.** – Duck's-bill [Duck-bill] (1) (1932), Elephant flower (1) (1932), Elephant's-head [Elephant's head] (1) (1932), Indian warrior (1) (1932), Little red elephant (1) (1932), Lousewort [Louse wort, Louse-wort] (1, 2, 4, 7, 10, 50, 63, 109, 155, 156, 158, 184) (1793–present) cows and sheep were thought to get lice from this plant in N. Europe, Pedicularis (155) (1942), Wood betony [Wood-betony, Woodbetony] (109, 138, 155) (1923–1949), Yellow rattle (190) (~1759)

Pedicularis labradorica **Wirsing** – Eyebright [Eye-bright, Eye bright] (5) (1913)

Pedicularis lanceolata **Michx.** – Pale-flower lousewort [Pale-flowered louse-wort] (187) (1818), Swamp betony (85) (1932), Swamp louse-wort (4, 5, 50, 72, 93, 131) (1899–present), Swamp pedicularis (155) (1942), Swamp wood-betony [Swamp woodbetony] (138) (1923)

Pedicularis lapponica **L.** – Lapland pedicularis (5) (1913)

Pedicularis pallida **Nutt.** – See *Pedicularis lanceolata* Michx.

Pedicularis palustris **L.** – Cow-wort [Cow's wort, Cow's-wort] (5, 156) (1913–1923), European wood betony [European woodbetony] (138) (1923), Marsh lousewort (5, 156) (1913–1923), Purple pedicularis (5, 156) (1913–1923), Rattle (190) (~1759), Red rattle (5, 156) (1913–1923) misapplied

Pedicularis procera **Gray** – Giant lousewort (50) (present), Gray's lousewort (4) (1986), Gray's pedicularis [Grays pedicularis] (155) (1942), Tall pedicularis (85) (1932)

Pedilanthus **Neck. ex Poit.** – Slipper flower [Slipper-flower, Slipperflower] (155) (1942)

Pedilanthus tithymaloides **(L.) Poit.** – Jewbush [Jewbush] (92, 155) (1876–1942), Red-bird cactus [Redbird-cactus] (109) (1949), Redbird slipper-flower [Redbird slipperflower] (155) (1942), Slipper flower [Slipper-flower, Slipperflower] (109) (1949)

Pedilanthus tithymaloides **Poit.** – See *Pedilanthus tithymaloides* (L.) Poit.

Pediocactus **Britton & Rose** – Hedgehog cactus [Hedge hog cactus] (50) (present), Nipple cactus (4) (1986)

Pediocactus simpsoni – See *Pediocactus simpsonii* (Engelm.) Britton & Rose

Pediocactus simpsonii **(Engelm.) Britton & Rose** – Hedgehog thistle [Hedge hog thistle] (5) (1913), Simpson's cactus (5) (1913), Simpson's hedgehog cactus (50) (present), Snowball cactus [Snowball-cactus] (138, 155) (1923–1942)

Pediomelum argophyllum **(Pursh) J. Grimes** – Gi'zǐso'bûgons' (Chippewa, sun, little leaf) (40) (1928), Nebraska psoralea (5, 93) (1913–1936), Psoralea (40, 125) (1928–1930), Silver-leaf Indian breadroot [Silverleaf Indian breadroot] (50) (Present), Silver-leaf psoralea (5, 72, 93, 97, 131) (1899–1937), Silver-leaf scurf pea [Silverleaf scurf-pea] (3, 4, 155) (1942–1986), Silver-leaf surf-pea [Silverleaf surf-pea] (121) (1970), Tičaničahu xloxota (Lakota, possibly meaning gray hollow curlew plant) (121) (1918?–1970?)

Pediomelum cuspidatum **(Pursh) Rydb.** – Large-bract Indian breadroot [Largebract Indian breadroot] (50) (present), Large-bract psoralea [Large-bracted psoralea] (5, 93, 97, 131) (1899–1937), Tallbread scurfpea [Tallbread scurfpea] (4, 155) (1942–1986)

Pediomelum digitatum **(Nutt. ex Torr. & Gray) Isely** – Palm-leaf Indian breadroot [Palmleaf Indian breadroot] (50) (present), Palm-leaf

scurf pea [Palm-leaved scurf pea] (4) (1986)

Pediomelum esculentum **(Pursh) Rydb.** – Aha (Crow) (101) (1905) MT, Breadroot [Bread root, Bread-root] (14, 19, 28, 49, 92, 101, 103, 107, 127) (1811–1933), Breadroot scurf pea (3, 4) (1977–1986), Cree potato (5, 156, 158) (1900–1923), Cree turnip (158) (1900), Dakota tipsinna (76) (1896) Burnside SD, from Indian name, Dakota turnip (76, 158) (1896–1900) MN, Dogthe (Osage) (121) (1918?–1970?), Esharusha (Crow) (101) (1905) MT, Ground-potato [Ground potato] (35) (1806) William Clark, Hankee (35) (1806) William Clark, Indian breadroot [Indian bread-root, Indian bread root] (5, 93, 122, 138, 156, 158) (1900–1937), Indian plant-root [Indian plant root] (124) (1937) TX, Indian turnip (47, 49, 85, 101, 103, 107, 127, 131) (1870–1933), Large Indian breadroot (50) (present), Missouri breadnut [Missouri bread-nut] (156) (1923), Missouri breadroot [Missouri bread-root, Missouri bread root] (5, 158) (1900–1913), Mu-gar-re (Omaha) (38) (1820), Noo (Omaha) (38) (1820), Nugthe (Omaha-Ponca) (37) (1919), Patsuroka (Pawnee) (37) (1919), Pomme blanche [Pomme blanch] (French) (2, 5, 34, 36, 37, 38, 83, 85, 93, 95, 101, 107, 121, 156, 158) (1830–1936), Pomme blanche des praires (French) (108) (1878), Pomme de prairie (French) (47, 83, 89, 101, 103, 156, 158) (1820–1923), Pomme de terre [Pommes de terre] (French) (38) (1820), Prairie-apple [Prairie apple, Prairie apples] (5, 63, 93, 97, 156, 158) (1899–1937), Prairie-potato [Prairie potato] (5, 28, 103, 107, 156) (1850–1923), Prairie-turnip [Prairie turnip] (4, 5, 14, 34, 49, 72, 83, 92, 97, 121, 131, 156) (1834–1986), Tdokewihi (Winnebago, hungry) (37) (1919) MN, Teep-se-nah (Assiniboin) (83) (1850) IA, Tiŋpsila (Lakota) (121) (1918?–1970?), Tipsin (5, 37, 76, 127, 156, 158) (1896–1937), Tipsinah (Sioux) (47) (1852), Tipsinla (Dakota Teton) (37) (1919), Tipsinna (5, 156, 158) (1900–1923), Tipsinna (Dakota) (37) (1919), Tipsin-nah or Tip-sin-nah (Sioux) (101, 103) (1870–1905), Turnip-of-the-plains [Turnip of the plains] (33) (1827), White-apple [White apple, White apples] (35) (1806)

Pediomelum hypogaeum **(Nutt. ex Torr. & Gray) Rydb.** – Subterranean Indian breadroot (50) (present)

Pediomelum hypogaeum **(Nutt. ex Torr. & Gray) Rydb. var. *hypogaeum*** – Indian breadroot [Indian bread-root, Indian bread root] (156) (1923), Little breadroot scurfpea [Little breadroot scurf pea] (3, 4) (1977–1986), Prairie breadroot [Prairie bread-root] (157) (1929), Prairie-potato [Prairie potato] (157) (1929), Small Indian breadroot [Small Indian bread root, Small Indian bread-root] (5, 93, 97) (1913–1937), Smaller Indian breadroot [Smaller Indian bread-root] (157) (1929), Subterranean Indian breadroot (50) (present)

Pediomelum linearifolium **(Torr. & Gray) J. Grimes** – Narrow-leaf Indian breadroot [Narrowleaf Indian breadroot] (50) (present), Narrow-leaf psoralea [Narrow-leaved psoralea] (5, 93, 97) (1913–1937), Slim-leaf scurf pea [Slimleaf scurf pea] (3, 4) (1977–1986)

Pediomelum reverchonii **(S. Wats.) Rydb.** – Reverchon's psoralea (97) (1937)

Pediomelum **Rydb.** – Breadroot [Bread root, Bread-root] (1) (1932), Indian breadroot [Indian bread-root, Indian bread root] (50) (present), Indian turnip (1) (1932), Pomme blanche [Pomme blanch] (French) (1) (1932), Pomme de prairie (French) (1) (1932)

Peganum harmala **L.** – Harmal peganum (50) (present), Harmala (178) (1526), Wild rue (178) (1526)

Pelargonium **×*domesticum* Bailey [*angulosum* × *cucullatum*]** – Fancy geranium (109) (1949), Fancy pelargonium (109) (1949), Lady Washington's geranium [Lady Washington geranium] (138) (1923), Show geranium (109) (1949), Show pelargonium (109) (1949)

Pelargonium **×*hortorum* Bailey [*inquinans* × *zonale*]** – Fish geranium (109, 138) (1923–1949)

Pelargonium acerifolium **(Mill.) L'Hér.** – See *Pelargonium cucullatum subsp. strigifolium* Volschenk

Pelargonium capitatum **(L.) L'Hér. ex Aiton** – Rose geranium (74) (1893), Rose-scent geranium [Rose-scented geranium] (19, 74) (1840–1893), Sweet-scented geranium (74) (1893)

Pelargonium domesticum **Bailey** – See *Pelargonium* ×*domesticum*

Bailey [*angulosum* × *cucullatum*]

Pelargonium graveolens **L'Hér. ex Aiton** – Rose geranium (138) (1923), Sweet-rose geranium (19) (1840)

Pelargonium hortorum **Bailey** – See *Pelargonium* ×*hortorum* Bailey [*inquinans* × *zonale*]

Pelargonium inquinans **(L.) L'Hér. ex Aiton** – Scarlet geranium (19) (1840)

Pelargonium **L'Hér. ex Aiton** – Geranium (138) (1923), Pelargonium (138) (1923) from Greek for "stork's bill," Stork's-bill [Storks' bill, Storksbill, Stork's bill, Storks bill] (109) (1949)

Pelargonium odoratissimum **(L.) L'Hér. ex Aiton** – Apple geranium (109) (1949), Garden geranium (92) (1876), Geranium (92) (1876), Nutmeg geranium (109, 138) (1923–1949), Pelargonium (92) (1876), Rose geranium (92) (1876), Sweet-scented geranium (19) (1840)

Pelargonium peltatum **(L.) L'Hér. ex Aiton** – Ivy geranium (109) (1949), Ivy-leaf geranium [Ivyleaf geranium] (138) (1923)

Pelargonium peltatum **Aiton** – See *Pelargonium peltatum* (L.) L'Hér. ex Aiton

Pelargonium quercifolium **(L. f.) L'Hér. ex Aiton** – Oak-leaf geranium [Oak-leaved geranium] (19, 109) (1840–1949)

Pelargonium quercifolium **Aiton** – See *Pelargonium quercifolium* (L. f.) L'Hér. ex Aiton

Pelargonium zonale **(L.) L'Hér. ex Aiton** – Horseshoe geranium [Horse-shoe geranium] (19, 109, 138) (1840–1949), Zonal geranium (109) (1949)

Pelargonium zonale **Aiton** – See *Pelargonium zonale* (L.) L'Hér. ex Aiton

Pellaea atropurpurea **(L.) Link** – Clayton's cliff-brake (5, 158) (1900–1913), Cliffbrake [Cliff-brake] (97) (1937), Dark-purple rockbrake [Dark purple rock brake] (86) (1878), Indian dream (92) (1876), Indian's-dream [Indian's dream] (5, 158) (1900–1913), Mountain brake (92) (1876), Purple cliff brake [Purple cliff-brake, Purple cliffbrake] (3, 50, 122, 138, 155) (1923–present), Purple-stem cliff brake [Purple-stemmed cliff-brake] (4, 131, 158) (1899–1986), Rock brake [Rock-brake, Rockbrake] (5, 19, 49, 61, 72, 92) (1840–1913), Winter brake (5, 92) (1876–1913), Winter fern (92) (1876)

Pellaea breweri **D.C. Eat.** – Brewer's cliff-brake (131) (1899)

Pellaea glabella **Mett. Ex Kuhn** – Smooth cliff-brake [Smooth cliff-brake] (50) (present)

Pellaea glabella **Mett. ex Kuhn subsp.** *occidentalis* **(E. Nels.) Windham** – Dwarf cliff brake [Dwarf cliffbrake] (4, 155) (1942–1986), Smooth cliff-brake [Smooth cliff brake, Smooth cliffbrake] (3, 97) (1937–1977), Western dwarf cliff-brake [Western dwarf cliffbrake] (50) (present)

Pellaea glabella **Mett. ex Kuhn var.** *glabella* – Smooth cliff-brake [Smooth cliff brake, Smooth cliffbrake] (3, 50) (1977–present)

Pellaea gracilis **Hook.** – See *Cryptogramma stelleri* (S. G. Gmel.) Prantl.

Pellaea **Link** – Cliffbrake [Cliff-brake] (4, 50, 109, 138, 155, 158) (1900–present)

Pellaea mucronata **(D.C. Eat.) D.C. Eat.** – Bird rock-brake (86) (1878), Bird's-foot cliffbreak [Birdfoot cliffbreak] (50, 155) (1942–present)

Pellaea mucronata **D.C. Eat.** – See *Pellaea mucronata* (D.C. Eat.) D.C. Eat.

Pellaea ornithopus **Hook.** – See *Pellaea mucronata* (D.C. Eat.) D.C. Eat. (sp means bird foot)

Pellaea pumila **Rydb.** – See *Pellaea glabella* Mett. ex Kuhn subsp. *occidentalis* (E. Nels.) Windham (taxonomic status is unresolved (PL))

Pellaea viridis **(Forsk.) Prantl** – Green cliffbrake (138) (1923)

Pellaea wrightiana **Hook.** – Cliffbrake [Cliff-brake] (97) (1937)

Pellaea wrightiana **Hook.** – Wright's cliff-brake [Wright's cliffbrake, Wright's cliff brake] (4, 50) (1986–present)

Peltandra alba **Raf.** – See *Peltandra sagittifolia* (Michx.) Morong

Peltandra glauca **(Ell.) Feay** – See *Peltandra sagittifolia* (Michx.) Morong

Peltandra **Raf.** – Arrow-arum [Arrow arum] (2, 50, 109, 138, 156) (1895–present), Taroho (Indian tribes) (7) (1828), Tuckah (Indian tribes) (7) (1828), Wampee (Indian tribes) (7) (1828)

Peltandra sagittifolia **(Michx.) Morong** – White arrow arum (50) (present)

Peltandra virginica **(L.) Schott.** – Arrow-arum [Arrow arum] (107, 156) (1919–1923), Cuttanimmons (181) (~1678), Green arrow-arum [Green arrow arum, Green arrowarum] (5, 50, 97, 109, 156) (1913–present), Kattanemmons (181) (~1678), Kuttanemmons (181) (~1678), Ocoughtanausnis (181) (~1678), Ocoughtawmins (181) (~1678), Poison arum (5, 156) (1913–1923), Tockawaugh (181) (~1678), Tockawhoughe (181) (~1678), Tuckaho [Tuckaho, Tuck-ahoe] (156, 181) (~1678–1923), Virginia arrow-arum (138) (1923), Virginia wakerobin [Virginian wake robin] (107, 156) (1919–1923)

Peltiphyllum **(Engler) Engler in Engler & Prantl** – See *Darmera* Voss

Penicillaria spicata **[Willd.]** – See *Pennisetum glaucum* (L.) R. Br.

Penicillium glaucum **Link** – Common blue mould (56) (1901), Vinegar plant (92) (1876)

Peniocereus greggi – See *Peniocereus greggii* (Engelm.) Britt. & Rose

Peniocereus greggii **(Engelm.) Britt. & Rose** – Deer-horn cactus [Deerhorn cactus, Deerhorncactus] (138, 155) (1931–1942)

Peniocereus greggii **(Engelm.) Britt. & Rose var.** *greggii* – Three-corner cactus [Three-cornered cactus] (76) (1896)

Peniophyllum **Pennel.** – See *Oenothera* L. (US species)

Pennisetum alopecuroides **(L.) Spreng.** – Crimson fountain grass (138) (1923)

Pennisetum glaucum **(L.) R. Br.** – African cane (87) (1884), African millet (109) (1949), Barn grass [Barngrass, Barn-grass] (7, 78) (1828–1898) ME, Bottle grass [Bottle-grass] (87, 90, 92) (1876–1903), Bristly foxtail [Bristly fox tail, Bristly fox-tail] (92) (1876), Cat grass [Catgrass] (7) (1828), Cat-tail grass [Cat's tail grass, Cats-tail grass] (56) (1901), Cat-tail millet [Cattailmillet, Cattails millet] (45, 87, 151, 155) (1884–1942), East Indian millet [East India millet] (87) (1884), Egyptian millet (87) (1884), Foxtail [Fox tail, Fox-tail, Fox tails, Foxetaile, Fox-taile] (45, 66, 80, 90, 131, 152) (1896–1913), Foxtail grass [Fox tail grass, Fox-tail grass, Foxtail-grass] (85, 92) (1876–1932), Foxtail panic [Fox-tail panic] (19) (1840), Glaucous bristly foxtail (5) (1913), Herneh (46) (1879), Horse millet (45) (1896), Indian millet (45, 109) (1896–1949), Millet a chandlles (French) (46) (1879), Pearl millet [Pearlmillet] (45, 50, 56, 67, 68, 87, 109, 138, 151, 155, 163) (1884–present), Pigeon grass [Pigeon-grass, Pigeongrass, Pigeon's- grass, Pigeon's grass] (56, 80, 87, 88, 90, 119, 131, 134, 143, 163) (1852–1938), Pussy grass (56) (1901) IA, Red panic [Red panicke] (178) (1596), Spiked millet (107) (1919), Yellow bristle grass [Yellow bristle-grass] (143) (1936), Yellow bristly foxtail (5) (1913), Yellow foxtail [Yellow fox tail] (3, 5, 56, 93, 94, 99, 111, 119, 129, 134, 143, 145, 155, 163) (1852–1977)

Pennisetum **L. C. Rich. ex Pers.** – Bristly panick grass (10) (1818), Egyptian millet (158) (1900), Fountain grass (50) (present), Pennisetum (155) (1942)

Pennisetum purpureum **Schumacher** – Elephant grass [Elephants grass, Elephant's grass] (138, 163) (1852–1923), Napier grass (138, 163) (1852–1923)

Pennisetum typhoideum **Rich.** – See *Pennisetum glaucum* (L.) R. Br.

Pennisetum villosum **R. Br. ex Fresen.** – Feathertop (138) (1923)

Penstemon **(Mitchell) Soland.** – See *Penstemon* Schmidel

Penstemon acuminatus **Dougl. ex Lindl.** – Beardtongue [Beardtongue, Beard tongue] (156) (1923), Sharp-leaf beard-tongue [Sharp-leaved beard-tongue] (5, 93, 97) (1913–1937), Sharp-leaf penstemon [Sharpleaf penstemon] (122) (1937), St. Joseph's-wand [St. Joseph's wand] (5, 156) (1913–1923), Stiff penstemon (138) (1923)

Penstemon albidus **Nutt.** – White beardtongue [White beard-tongue] (3, 4, 85, 93, 131) (1899–1986), White penstemon (50, 155) (1942–present), White-flower beardtongue [White-flowered beard-tongue] (5, 97) (1913–1937), White-flower penstemon [White flower

subsp. *torreyi* (Benth.) Keck

Penstemon tubaeflorus Nutt. – See *Penstemon tubiflorus* Nutt.

Penstemon tubiflorus Nutt. – Funnel-form beardtongue [Funnel-form beard-tongue] (5, 97) (1913–1937), Tube penstemon (3, 4, 138, 155) (1923–1986), White wand beardtongue (50) (present)

Penstemon tubiflorus Nutt. var. *tubiflorus* – White wand beardtongue (50) (present)

Penstemon virens Pennell – Front Range beardtongue (50) (present), Green penstemon (155) (1942)

Pentaglottis sempervirens (L.) Tausch ex Bailey – Evergreen alkanet (165) (1807), Evergreen bugloss (138, 155) (1931–1942), Ever-living borage [Euerliuing Borage] (178) (1526)

Pentagramma triangularis (Kaulfuss) Yatskievych, Windham & Wollenweber – California gold fern [California goldfern] (86, 138) (1878–1923), Gold fern [Gold-fern, Goldfern] (109) (1949)

Penthorum L. – Ditch stonecrop [Ditch stone crop] (1, 2, 4, 156, 158) (1895–1986), Penthorum (50, 155) (1942–present), Virginia orpine [Virginian orpine] (167) (1814)

Penthorum sedoides L. – American penthorum (187) (1818), Ditch stonecrop [Ditch stone crop] (4, 5, 49, 50, 53, 63, 72, 97, 120, 155, 156, 157, 158) (1898–present), Dutch stonecrop (157) (1929), Nightshade [Night-shade, Night shade, Nyght shade] (177) (1762), Penthorum (57, 174, 177) (1753–1917), Virginia orpine [Virginian orpine] (19) (1840), Virginia penthorum (155) (1942), Virginia stonecrop [Virginia stone crop, Virginia stone-crop] (6, 48, 49, 52, 53, 57, 85, 93, 120, 131, 156, 157, 158) (1882–1936)

Pentstemon Aiton – See *Penstemon* Schmidel

Peonia L. – See *Paeonia* L.

Peonia officinalis – See *Paeonia officinalis* L.

Peperomia humilis A. Dietr. – Florida pepper (19) (1840)

Peperomia maculosa (L.) Hook. – Peperomia (138) (1923), Spotted peperomia (138) (1923)

Peperomia Ruiz & Pavón – Peperomia (138) (1923), Piney (52) (1919)

Peplis L. – possibly *Lythrum* L. (US species is Didiplis and Lythrum)

Pepo (Tourn.) Mill. – See *Cucurbita* L.

Pepo foetidissima (Kunth) Britton – See *Cucurbita foetidissima* Kunth

Pepo pepo L. – See *Cucurbita pepo* L. var. *pepo*

Peramium decipiens (Hook.) Piper – See *Goodyera oblongifolia* Raf.

Peramium ophioides (Fernald) Rydb. – See *Goodyera repens* (L.) R. Br. ex Ait. f.

Peramium pubescens (Willd.) MacM. – See *Goodyera pubescens* (Willd.) R. Br. ex Ait. f.

Peramium tesselatum (Lodd.) Heller – See *Goodyera tesselata* Lodd.

Perdicum semiflosculare Walt. – possibly *Chaptalia tomentosa* Vent.

Pereskia aculeata Mill. – Barbados-gooseberry [Barbadoes gooseberry, Barbadoes-gooseberry] (14, 107, 109, 155) (1882–1949), Blade-apple [Bladeapple] (138) (1923), Lemon vine [Lemon-vine] (109) (1949)

Pereskia grandifolia Haw. – Bush pereskia (138) (1923), Lemon vine [Lemon-vine] (109) (1949)

Pereskia Mill. – Barbados-gooseberry [Barbadoes gooseberry, Barbadoes-gooseberry] (14) (1882), Pereskia (138, 155) (1931–1942)

Pericallis cuneata (L'Hér.) Bolle – Cineraria (138) (1923), Florist's cineraria [Florsits cineraria] (109) (1949)

Pericome caudata Gray – Mountain tail-leaf (50) (present), Tall-leaf pericome [Tallleaf pericome] (155) (1942)

Perideridia americana (Nutt. ex DC.) Reichenb. – Eastern eulophus (5) (1913), Eastern yampah (50) (present), Eulophus (3) (1977)

Perideridia gairdneri (Hook. & Arn.) Mathias – Gairdner's yampah (50) (present), Mock bishop's-weed [Mock bishop's weed, Mock bishop-weed, Mock Bishopweed] (3) (1977), Squawroot [Squaw-root, Squaw root] (4, 85, 101) (1905–1986), Stuaertia (189) (1767), Yamp (158) (1900), Yámpa (Shoshone) (35) (1806), Yampah [Yampa] (155) (1942)

Perideridia gairdneri (Hook. & Arn.) Mathias subsp. *gairdneri* – Edible-rooted caraway (107) (1919), Gairdner's caraway (131) (1899), Indian paper tree [India paper tree, India papertree] (138) (1923),

Yamp (101) (1905)

Perideridia Reichnb. – Eulophus (158) (1900), Yampah [Yampa] (50) (present)

Perilla frutescens (L.) Britton – Beefsteak plant [Beefsteak-plant, Beefsteakplant] (4, 5, 50, 156, 158) (1900–present), Common perilla (3, 4, 155) (1942–1986), Green perilla (138) (1923), Perilla (5, 72, 158) (1900–1913)

Perilla frutescens (L.) Britton var. *frutescens* – Beefsteak plant [Beefsteak-plant, Beefsteakplant] (50) (present)

Perilla L. – Perilla (50, 138, 155, 158) (1923–present)

Periploca graeca L. – Climbing dogbane [Climbing dog's-bane, Climing dogs bane] (158, 178) (1526–1900), Climbing dogbane [Climing Dogs bane] (178) (1526), Grecian silkvine (138, 155) (1923–1942), Milk vine [Milk-vine, Milkvine] (19, 158) (1840–1900), Silk vine [Silkvine, Silk-vine] (4, 50, 158) (1900–present)

Periploca L. – Climbing dogbane [Climbing dog's-bane, Climing dogs bane] (158) (1900), Milk vine [Milk-vine, Milkvine] (158) (1900), Silk vine [Silkvine, Silk-vine] (1, 4, 109, 138, 155, 158) (1900–1986)

Peritoma DC. – See *Cleome* L.

Peronia stricta Laroch – See *Thalia dealbata* Fraser ex Roscoe

Persea americana Mill. – Avocado (109, 138) (1923–1949), Avocat (Louisiana) (7) (1828), Avogado pear (7) (1828), Red bay [Redbay] (2) (1895), Trapp's avocado [Trapp avocado] (109, 138) (1923–1949)

Persea borbonia (L.) Spreng. – Avocado (109, 138) (1923–1949), Bay galls [Bay-galls] (5, 156) (1913–1923), Dwarf sweet bay (182) (1791), Eto-mico (King's tree) (182) (1791), False mahoggany (5) (1913), Florida mahogany (106, 156) (1923–1930), Isabella wood [Isabella-wood] (5, 156) (1913–1923), Laurel tree [Laurel-tree] (106) (1930), Laurier de Bourbon (French) (8) (1785), Laurus borbonia (182) (1791), Red bay [Redbay] (5, 20, 46, 75, 106, 138, 156, 182, 189) (1767–1930), Red-stalk Carolina bay tree [Red-stalked Carolinian bay-tree] (8) (1785), Shore bay (106) (1930), Sweet bay [Sweet-bay, Sweetbay] or Sweet bay tree [Sweet bay trees] (5, 106, 122, 124, 156, 182) (1791–1937), Tisswood [Tiss wood, Tiss-wood] (5, 106, 156) (1913–1930)

Persea carolinensis (Raf.) Nees – Ascopo (Natives of Roanoke) (46) (1879), Carolina red bay (2) (1895), White bay [White-bay] (5, 75, 156) (1894–1923)

Persea caroliniensis Nees. – See *Persea carolinensis* (Raf.) Nees

Persea Gaertn. – See *Persea* Mill.

Persea gratissima Gaertn. – See *Persea americana* Miller var. *americana*

Persea humilis Nash – Scrub bay (106) (1930)

Persea leiogyna Blake – See *Persea americana* Mill.

Persea littoralis [Small] – See *Persea borbonia* (L.) Spreng.

Persea Mill. – Alligator-pear [Alligator pear] (106) (1930), Avocado (106) (1930), Persea (138) (1923), Red bay [Redbay] (2) (1895)

Persea palustris (Raf.) Sargent – Swamp bay (5, 156) (1913–1923), Swamp red bay (106) (1930)

Persicaria (C. Bauhin) Mill. – See *Polygonum* L.

Persicaria (Tourn.) Mill. – See *Polygonum* L.

Persicaria amphibia (L.) Delarbre – Ground-willow [Ground willow] (5) (1913), Redshank [Red shank, Red-shank, Red shanks, Redshanks, Red-shanks] (5) (1913), Water persicaria (5, 93) (1913–1936), Willow-grass [Willow grass] (5) (1913), Willow-weed [Willow weed, Willowweed] (5) (1913)

Persicaria arifolia (L.) Haraldson – Halberd-leaf tear-thumb [Halbardleaf tear thumb, Halberd-leaved tear thumb, Halberd-leaved tear-thumb] (5, 86, 122, 156) (1878–1937)

Persicaria careyi (Olney) Greene – See *Polygonum careyi* Olney

Persicaria hydropiper (L.) Opiz. – See *Polygonum hydropiper* L.

Persicaria hydropiperoides (Michx.) Small var. *breviciliata* (Fern.) C. F. Reed – See *Polygonum hydropiperoides* Michx.

Persicaria lapathifolia (L.) S. F. Gray – See *Polygonum lapathifolium*

309

L.

Persicaria longiseta **(de Bruyn) Moldenke** – See *Polygonum caespitosum* Blume var. *longisetum* (de Bruyn) A.N. Steward

Persicaria longistyla **Small.** – See *Polygonum pensylvanicum* L.

Persicaria maculosa **Gray** – Blackheart [Black-heart, Black heart] (5, 75, 77, 156, 158) (1894–1923) ME, VT, from the shape of dark spots on the leaves, Common persicary (5) (1913), Heart's-ease [Heart's ease, Heartsease, Hearts' ease] (5, 19, 75, 79, 92, 106, 156, 158) (1840–1930) from shape of dark spots on leaves, Heartweed [Heart weed, Heart-weed] (5, 62, 75, 77, 156, 158) (1898–1923), Lady's-thumb [Ladies' thumb, Lady's thumb] (3, 4, 5, 19, 45, 62, 72, 80, 82, 92, 93, 97, 106, 114, 122, 124, 125, 156) (1818–1986), Lover's-pride [Lover's pride] (5, 156, 158) (1900–1923), Peachwort [Peach-wort] (5, 92, 156, 158) (1898–1923), Pinkweed [Pink weed, Pink-weed] (5, 92, 156, 158) (1876–1923), Redshank [Red shank, Red-shank, Red shanks, Redshanks, Red-shanks] (5, 92, 156, 158) (1876–1923), Redweed [Red-weed, Red weed] (5, 156, 158) (1900–1923), Spotted knotweed [Spotted knot weed, Spotted knot-weed] (5, 92, 156, 158) (1876–1923), Willow-weed [Willow weed, Willowweed] (5, 156, 158) (1900–1923)

Persicaria muehlenbergii **(S. Wats.) Small** – See *Polygonum amphibium* L. var. *emersum* Michx.

Persicaria opelousana **(Riddell) Small** – See *Polygonum hydropiperoides* Michx.

Persicaria orientalis **(L.) Spach** – See *Polygonum orientale* L.

Persicaria paludicola **Small** – See *Polygonum hydropiperoides* Michx.

Persicaria pennsylvanica **(L.) Small.** – possibly *Persicaria pensylvanica* (L.) M. Gómez

Persicaria pensylvanica **(L.) G. Maza** – See *Polygonum pensylvanicum* L.

Persicaria pensylvanica **(L.) M. Gómez** – Heart's-ease [Heart's ease, Heartsease, Hearts' ease] (82, 85, 114) (1894–1932)

Persicaria portoricensis **(Betero) Small.** – See *Polygonum densiflorum* Meisn.

Persicaria pratincola **Greene** – See *Polygonum amphibium* L. var. *emersum* Michx.

Persicaria setacea **(Baldw.) Small** – See *Polygonum hydropiperoides* Michx.

Perularia scutellata **(Nutt.) Small** – See *Platanthera flava* (L.) Lindl. var. *flava*

Petalospermum foliosus **Gray.** – possibly *Dalea foliosa* (Gray) Barneby

Petalostemon arenicola **Wemple** – See *Dalea purpurea* Vent. var. *arenicola* (Wemple) Barneby

Petalostemon candidus **(Willd.) Michx.** – See *Dalea candida* Michx. ex Willd. var. *candida*

Petalostemon candidus **Michx.** – See *Dalea candida* Michx. ex Willd. var. *candida*

*Petalostemon compactus***(Spreng.) Swezey** – See *Dalea cylindriceps* Barneby

Petalostemon decumbens **(Nutt.)** – See *Dalea compacta* Spreng. var. *compacta*

Petalostemon foliosum **Gray** – See *Dalea foliosa* (Gray) Barneby

Petalostemon **Michx.** – See *Dalea* L.

Petalostemon mollis **Rydb.** – See *Dalea purpurea* Vent. var. *purpurea*

Petalostemon occidentale **(Gray) Fern.** – See *Dalea candida* Michx. ex Willd. var. *oligophylla* (Torr.) Shinners

Petalostemon oligophyllus **(Torr.) Rydb.** – See *Dalea candida* Michx. ex Willd. var. *oligophylla* (Torr.) Shinners

Petalostemon oligophyllus **(Torr.) Torr. ex Smyth** – See *Dalea candida* Michx. ex Willd. var. *oligophylla* (Torr.) Shinners

Petalostemon purpureum **(Vent.) Rydb.** – See *Dalea purpurea* Vent. var. *purpurea*

Petalostemon tenuifolium **Gray** – See *Dalea tenuifolia* (Gray) Shinners

Petalostemon villosum **Nutt.** – See *Dalea villosa* (Nutt.) Spreng

Petalostemon villosus **Nutt.** – See *Dalea villosa* (Nutt.) Spreng

Petalostemon violaceum **Michx.** – See *Dalea purpurea* Vent.

Petalostemum microphyllum **(Torr. & Gray) Heller** – See *Dalea phleoides* (Torr. & Gray) Shinners var. *microphylla* (Torr. & Gray) Barneby

Petalostemum candidum **(Willd.) Michx.** – See *Dalea candida* Michx. ex Willd.

Petalostemum compactum **(Spreng.) Swezey** – See *Dalea cylindriceps* Barneby

Petalostemum multiflorum **Nutt.** – See *Dalea multiflora* (Nutt.) Shinners

Petalostemum purpureum **(Vent.) Rydb.** – See *Dalea purpurea* Vent. var. *purpurea*

Petalostemum purpureus **(Vent.) Rydb.** – See *Dalea purpurea* Vent. var. *purpurea*

Petalostemum tenuifolium **Gray** – See *Dalea tenuifolia* (Gray) Shinners

Petalostemum villosum **Nutt.** – See *Dalea villosa* (Nutt.) Spreng

Petasites **×*vitifolius* Greene [*frigidus* × *sagittatus*]** – Arctic sweet-colt's-foot [Arctic sweet colts foot, Arctic sweet coltsfoot] (5) (1913)

Petasites arcticus **Porsild** – See *Petasites frigidus* (L.) Fries var. *palmatus* (Aiton) Cronq.

Petasites fragrans **C.Presl** – Arctic sweet-colt's-foot [Arctic sweet colts foot, Arctic sweet coltsfoot] (50) (present), Mountain colt's-foot [Mountain colt's foot] (19) (1840), Sweet butterbur (138) (1923)

Petasites frigidus **(L.) Fries** – See *Petasites fragrans* C.Presl

Petasites frigidus **(L.) Fries subsp. *arcticus* (Porsild) Cody** – See *Petasites frigidus* (L.) Fries var. *palmatus* (Aiton) Cronq.

Petasites frigidus **(L.) Fries var. *palmatus* (Aiton) Cronq.** – Arctic sweet-colt's-foot [Arctic sweet colts foot, Arctic sweet coltsfoot] (50) (present), Butterbur [Butter bur, Butter-bur] (5, 85, 156) (1913–1932), Palmate butterbur (155) (1942), Palmate-leaf sweet coltsfoot (5, 156) (1913–1923), Silky prairie clover [Silky prairieclover] (5, 85, 93) (1913–1936)

Petasites **Gaertn.** – See *Petasites* Mill.

Petasites hybridus **(L.) G. Gaertn., B. Mey. & Scherb.** – Arctic sweet-colt's-foot [Arctic sweet colts foot, Arctic sweet coltsfoot] (5) (1913), Batter-dock [Batter dock] (5, 156) (1913–1923), Bog rhubarb (5) (1913), Bog-rhubarb (156) (1923), Butterbur [Butter bur, Butter-bur] (5, 156) (1913–1923), Butterfly-dock [Butterfly dock] (5, 156) (1913–1923), Eldin (5, 156) (1913–1923) no longer in use by 1923, Fleadock [Flea-dock, Flea dock] (5, 156) (1913–1923) no longer in use by 1923, Gallon (5, 156) (1913–1923) no longer in use by 1923, Oxwort [Ox wort] (5, 156) (1913–1923) no longer in use by 1923, Pestilence-weed [Pestilence weed] (92) (1876), Pestilence-wort [Pestilence wort] (5, 156) (1913–1923) no longer in use by 1923, Poison rhubarb (5, 156) (1913–1923), Umbrella-leaf [Umbrellaleaf, Umbrella leaf] (156, 158) (1900–1923)

Petasites japonica – See *Petasites japonicus* (Sieb. & Zucc.) Maxim.

Petasites japonicus **(Sieb. & Zucc.) Maxim.** – Japanese butterbur (138) (1923)

Petasites **L.** – possibly *Petasites* Mill.

Petasites **Mill.** – Arctic sweet-colt's-foot [Arctic sweet colts foot, Arctic sweet coltsfoot] (50) (present), Sweet coltsfoot (1, 4, 158) (1900–1986), possibly Butterbur [Butter bur, Butter-bur] (1, 50, 138, 155) (1923–present), possibly Japanese butterbur (138) (1923)

Petasites officinalis **Moench** – See *Petasites hybridus* (L.) G. Gaertn., B. Mey. & Scherb.

Petasites palmata **(Aiton) Gray** – See *Petasites frigidus* (L.) Fries var. *palmatus* (Aiton) Cronq.

Petasites sagittata **(Pursh) Gray** – Arrow-leaf sweet-colt's-foot [Arrowleaf sweet coltsfoot] (5, 50) (1913–present), Batter-dock [Batter dock] (5) (1913), Sweet coltsfoot (3, 131, 156) (1899–1977), possibly Coltsfoot [Colt's foot, Colt's-foot, Colt foot] (35) (1806) Meriwether Lewis

Petasites speciosus **(Nutt.) Piper** – See *Petasites frigidus* (L.) Fries var.

palmatus (Aiton) Cronq.

Petasites vulgaris [Hill] – See *Petasites hybridus* (L.) G. Gaertn., B. Mey. & Scherb.

Petrea L. – Purple wreath (109) (1949)

Petrea volubilis L. – Queen's-wreath [Queens wreath] (109) (1949)

Petrophyton caespitosum (Nutt.) Rydb. – Mat rock-spirea [Mat rockspirea] (50) (present), Rock-plant spirea [Rockplant spirea] (3) (1977), Rock-spiraea [Rock spiraea] (4) (1986), Tufted meadowsweet (131) (1899) SD, Tufted rockmat (155) (1942)

Petrophyton Rydb. – See *Petrophytum* Rydb.

Petrophytum Rydb. – Rockmat (155) (1942), Rock-spiraea [Rock spiraea] (4, 50) (1986–present)

Petrorhagia (Ser.) Link – Tunic flower [Tunic-flower, Tunicflower] (138) (1923)

Petrorhagia prolifera (L.) P. W. Ball & Heywood – Childing pink (5, 156) (1913–1923), Childing sweet william (5, 156) (1913–1923), Proliferous pink (5) (1913)

Petrorhagia saxifraga (L.) Link – Coat-flower (109) (1949), Saxifrage pink (5, 156) (1913–1923), Saxifrage tunic-flower [Saxifrage tunicflower] (138) (1923), Tunic flower [Tunic-flower, Tunicflower] (109) (1949)

Petroselinum crispum (P. Mill.) Nyman ex A. W. Hill – Ache (156, 158) (1900–1923), Apium (107) (1919), Common parsley (5, 7, 49, 92, 93, 156, 158) (1828–1936), Garden parsley (5, 58, 93, 158) (1869–1936), Goldenweed (155) (1942), March (92, 158) (1876–1900), Parsley (8, 19, 45, 46, 49, 50, 52, 53, 54, 55, 57, 85, 92, 107, 109, 110, 122, 138, 158, 184) (1671–present), Percely (179) (1526), Peregil (Spanish) (158) (1900), Persil (French) (158) (1900), Petersilge (German) (158) (1900), Petersilie (German) (158) (1900), Petroselinum (110) (1886), Selinon (107) (322 BC), possibly Crisp parsley [Crispe parsley] (178) (1526), possibly Curled parsley (178) (1526)

Petroselinum Hoffm. – See *Carum* L.

Petroselinum hortense Hoffm. – See *Petroselinum crispum* (Mill.) Nyman ex A.W. Hill

Petroselinum J. Hill –

Petroselinum sativum Moench – possibly *Petroselinum crispum* (Mill.) Nyman ex A.W. Hill

Petroselinum vulgare Lagasca – See *Petroselinum crispum* (Mill.) Nyman ex A.W. Hill

Petunia ×*atkinsiana* D. Don ex Loud. [*axillaris* × *integrifolia*] – Common garden petunia (109) (1949), Common petunia (138) (1923), Garden petunia (82) (1930)

Petunia axillaris (Lam.) Britton, Sterns & Poggenb. – Large white petunia (109) (1949), White petunia (5, 85) (1913–1932)

Petunia hybrida Vilm. – See *Petunia* ×*atkinsiana* D. Don ex Loud. [*axillaris* × *integrifolia*]

Petunia integrifolia (Hook.) Schinz & Thellung – Violet petunia (5, 85) (1913–1932), Violet-flower petunia [Violet-flowered petunia] (109) (1949)

Petunia parviflora Juss. – See *Calibrachoa parviflora* (Juss.) D'Arcy

Petunia violacea Lindl. – See *Petunia integrifolia* (Hook.) Schinz & Thellung

Peucedanum ambiguum Nutt. – See *Lomatium ambiguum* (Nutt.) Coult. & Rose

Peucedanum foeniculaceum Nutt. ex. Torr. & Gray – See *Lomatium foeniculaceum* (Nutt.) Coult. & Rose

Peucedanum graveolens [Wats.] – See *Lomatium graveolens* (S. Watson) Dorn & R. L. Hartm.

Peucedanum graveolens Benth. & Hook. – See *Anethum graveolens* L.

Peucedanum L. – Hog-fennel [Hog fennel, Hogfennel, Hog's fennel] (155, 158) (1900–1942), Sulfurwort [Sulphur wort, Sulpher wort] (10) (1818)

Peucedanum nudicaule Nutt. – See *Lomatium nudicaule* (Pursh) J. M. Coult. & Rose

Peucedanum ostruthium (L.) W. D. J. Koch – Astrantia (178) (1526),

Broad-leaf hog's-fennel [Broad-leaved hog's fennel] (5) (1913), Divinum remedium (92) (1876), Felon-grass [Felon grass] (5, 156) (1913–1923), Felonwort [Fellonwort] (5, 156) (1913–1923), Hog-fennel [Hog fennel, Hogfennel, Hog's fennel] (156) (1923), Imperatoria (57) (1917), Imperial masterwort (5, 7, 92, 156) (1828–1923), Masterwort [Master-wort, Master wort, Masterwoorts] (5, 57, 92, 107, 156, 178) (1526–1923), Pellitory of Spain (5, 156) (1913–1923), Symrnium (107) (1919)

Peucedanum ostruthium Koch – See *Peucedanum ostruthium* (L.) W. D. J. Koch

Peucedanum palustre (L.) Moench – Marsh hog's-fennel [Marsh hog's fennel] (107) (1919), Masterwort [Master-wort, Master wort, Masterwoorts] (107) (1919), Swamp sowfennel (92) (1876)

Peucedanum palustre Moench – See *Peucedanum palustre* (L.) Moench

Peucedanum sativum Benth. & Hook. f. – See *Pastinaca sativa* L.

Peucedanum ternatum Nutt. – See *Oxypolis ternata* (Nutt.) Heller

Peziza auricula [(L.) Lightf.] – See *Auricularia auricula-judae* (Bulliard) J. Schröter

Peziza badia Pers. – Large brown cup fungus (128) (1933)

Peziza Fr. – Cup-mushroom (184) (1793)

Phaca americana (Hook.) Rydb. – See *Astragalus americanus* (Hook.) M. E. Jones

Phaca L. – See *Oxytropis* DC.

Phaca longifolia (Pursh) Nutt. – See *Astragalus ceramicus* Sheldon var. *filifolius* (Gray) F. J. Herm.

Phaca neglecta Torr. & Gray – See *Astragalus neglectus* (Torr. & Gray) Sheldon

Phacelia alpina Rydb. – See *Phacelia hastata* Dougl. ex Lehm. var. *hastata*

Phacelia bipinnatifida Michx. – Bipinnate phacelia (86) (1878), Loose-flower phacelia [Loose-flowered phacelia] (5) (1913)

Phacelia campanularia Gray – Harebell phacelia (138) (1923)

Phacelia congesta Hook. – Bluecurls [Blue curls, Blue-curl, Blue-curls] (122) (1937), Caterpillars (50) (present)

Phacelia covillei S. Wats. – Coville's phacelia (5) (1913)

Phacelia distans Benth. – Hill vervenia (106) (1930)

Phacelia dubia (L.) Small. – Small-flower phacelia [Small-flowered phacelia] (5, 97) (1913–1937)

Phacelia fimbriata Michx. – Fringed phacelia (5) (1913), Mountain phacelia (5) (1913)

Phacelia franklinii (R. Br.) Gray – See *Phacelia linearis* (Pursh) Holz.

Phacelia gilioides Brand. – Brand's phacelia (50) (present), Hairy phacelia (3, 4) (1977–1986)

Phacelia hastata Dougl. ex Lehm. – Silver-leaf phacelia [Silverleaf phacelia] (50) (Present)

Phacelia hastata Dougl. ex Lehm. var. *hastata* – Alpine phacelia (155) (1942), Phacelia (127) (1933), Scorpion-weed [Scorpion weed, Scorpionweed] (3, 4, 93) (1936–1986) Neb, Silky phacelia (5, 85) (1913–1932), Silver-leaf phacelia [Silverleaf phacelia] (50, 155) (1942–present)

Phacelia hirsuta Nutt. – Fuzzy phacelia (50) (present), Hairy phacelia (5, 97, 122) (1913–1937)

Phacelia hispida [Buckley] – See *Phacelia patuliflora* (Engelm. & Gray) Gray

Phacelia hursuta Nutt. – See *Phacelia hirsuta* Nutt.

Phacelia integrifolia Torr. – Crenate-leaf phacelia [Crenateleaf phacelia, Crenate-leaved phacelia] (5, 97, 122) (1913–1937), Gyp phacelia (3, 4) (1977–1986), Gypsum phacelia (50) (present)

Phacelia integrifolia Torr. var. *texana* (J. Voss) Atwood – Texas phacelia (50) (present)

Phacelia Juss. – Phacelia (50, 106, 138, 155, 158) (1900–present), Scorpion weed (1) (1932)

Phacelia leucophylla Torr. – See *Phacelia hastata* Dougl. ex Lehm. var. *hastata*

Phacelia linearis (Pursh) Holz. – Franklin's phacelia [Franklin phacelia] (5, 155) (1913–1942), Thread-leaf phacelia [Threadleaf phacelia] (50, 138, 155) (1923–present)

Phacelia minor (**Harvey**) **Thellung ex F. Zimmerman** – Bluebell phacelia (138) (1923), California bluebell (109) (1949)

Phacelia minor **Thell.** – See *Phacelia minor* (Harvey) Thellung ex F. Zimmerman

Phacelia parryi **Torr.** – Parry's phacelia [Parry phacelia] (138) (1923)

Phacelia parviflora **Pursh** – See *Phacelia dubia* (L.) Small.

Phacelia patuliflora (**Engelm. & Gray**) **Gray** – Caterpillar phacelia (106) (1930)

Phacelia popei **Torr. & Gray** – Pope's phacelia (50) (present)

Phacelia purshii **Buckl.** – Miami mist (156) (1923), Pursh's phacelia (5, 97) (1913–1937)

Phacelia robusta (**Macbr.**) **Johnst.** – Stout phacelia (50) (present)

Phacelia strictiflora (**Engelm. & Gray**) **Gray** – Prairie phacelia (50) (present)

Phacelia tanacetifolia **Benth.** – Fiddleneck [Fiddle neck] (106) (1930), Tansy phacelia (138) (1923), Tansy-leaf phacelia (77) (1898), Valley vervenia (106) (1930)

Phacelia texana **Voss** – See *Phacelia integrifolia* Torr. var. *texana* (J. Voss) Atwood

Phacelia viscida (**Benth. ex Lindl.**) **Torr.** – Phacelia (92) (1876)

Phacelia whitlavia – See *Phacelia minor* (Harvey) Thellung ex F. Zimmerman

Phaeoceros laevis (**L.**) **Prosk.** – Phaeoceros (50) (present), Wax liverwort (19) (1840)

Phaethusa helianthoides (**Michx.**) **Britton** – See *Verbesina helianthoides* Michx.

Phaethusa occidentalis (**L.**) **Britton** – See *Verbesina occidentalis* (L.) Walt.

Phaethusa virginica (**L.**) **Brittton** – See *Verbesina virginica* L. var. *virginica*

Phalangium quamash – See *Camassia quamash* (Pursh) Greene subsp. *quamash*

Phalaris angusta **Nees ex Trin.** – California timothy (94) (1901)

Phalaris arundinacea **L.** – Aiguillettes d'armes (French) (180) (1633), Bride's-laces [Brides' laces] (5, 158) (1900–1913) Neb, Canary grass [Canary-grass, Canary grass, Canarie grasse] (158) (1900), Coloured calamagrostis (187) (1818), Coloured reed-grass (187) (1818), Daggers (158) (1900), Doggers (5) (1913), Flack (Swedish) (46) (1879), Furrowed grass [Furrowed grasse] (180) (1633), Gardener's-garters [Gardener's garters] (163) (1852), Lady grass (5) (1913), Lady's-laces [Ladies laces, Ladies' laces, Ladies'-laces, Lady-laces] (5, 158, 178, 180) (1526–1913), London lace [London-lace] (5, 158) (1900–1913), Painted grass [Painted-grass, Painted grasse] (5, 158, 163, 180) (1633–1913), Reed canary (88) (1885), Reed canary grass [Reed canarygrass, Reed canary-grass] (3, 45, 50, 56, 66, 68, 85, 87, 90, 92, 93, 94, 109, 111, 115, 129, 138, 143, 144, 155, 163) (1852–present), Reed grass [Reedgrass, Reed-grass] (67) (1890), Ribbon grass [Ribbon-grass] (5, 22, 46, 90, 92, 144, 158, 163) (1852–1913), Ror-flen (Swedish) (46) (1879), Spires (5) (1913), Streaked grasse (180) (1633), Striped grass (92) (1876), Sword grass (5) (1913), Wild prairie timothy [Wild prairie timothey] (35) (1806)

Phalaris arundinacea **L. var.** *picta* **L.** – See *Phalaris arundinacea* L.

Phalaris arundinacea **L. var.** *variegata* – See *Phalaris arundinacea* L.

Phalaris canariensis **L.** – Alpist (158) (1900) Europe and Canary Islands, Alpisti (178, 180) (1596–1633), Annual canary grass [Annual canarygrass] (50) (present), Bird-seed grass [Bird-seed-grass] (5, 93, 119) (1913–1938), Canary bird seed (12) (1819), Canary corn [Canarie corne] (180) (1633), Canary grass [Canary-grass, Canary grass, Canarie grasse] (3, 56, 67, 85, 86, 90, 92, 107, 109, 111, 119, 122, 131, 155, 157, 158, 163, 180) (1633–1977), Canary seed [Canarie seed, Canarie seede] (92, 178, 180) (1596–1876), Common canary grass (66) (1903), Gardener's-garters [Gardener's garters] (92) (1876)

Phalaris caroliniana **Walt.** – Alpist (158) (1900), California timothy (5,

11, 19, 45) (1840–1888), California timothy grass (87, 88) (1884–1885), Canary grass [Canary-grass, Canary grass, Canarie grasse] (45, 88, 158) (1885–1900), Carolina canary grass [Carolina canarygrass, Carolina canary-grass] (5, 50, 119, 155) (1913–present), Foxtail grass [Fox tail grass, Fox-tail grass, Foxtail-grass] (5) (1913), Gilbert's relief grass (45, 87, 88) (1885–1896), May grass [Maygrass] (3) (1977), Ribbon grass [Ribbon-grass] (5, 19, 92) (1840–1913), Southern canary grass [Southern canary-grass] (5, 94, 163) (1852–1913), Southern reed (45, 88) (1885–1896), Southern reed canary grass (87) (1884), Southern reed grass [Southern reed-grass] (5) (1913), Stewart's canary grass [Stewart's canary-grass] (45, 87, 88) (1885–1896), Wild canary grass (5, 19) (1840–1913)

Phalaris colorata [**Beauv.**] – See *Phalaris arundinacea* L.

Phalaris intermedia **Bosc.** – See *Phalaris caroliniana* Walt.

Phalaris **L.** – Canary (184) (1793), Canary grass [Canary-grass, Canary grass, Canarie grasse] (1, 45, 50, 66, 93, 152, 155, 158) (1896–present), Canary seed [Canarie seed, Canarie seede] (7, 10) (1818–1828)

Phalaris lemmoni **Vasey** – See *Phalaris lemmonii* Vasey

Phalaris lemmonii **Vasey** – Lemmon's canary grass [Lemmon's canary-grass] (94) (1901)

Phallus impudicus **L.** – Stinkhorn (92) (1876)

Phallus Junius ex **L.** – Carrion-flower [Carrionflower, Carrion flower] (78) (1898) MA, Death baby (76) (1896) MA, appearance near house supposedly foretold a death in the family, Morille (184) (1793)

Phallus umpudicus – See *Phallus impudicus* L.

Phanopyrum gymnocarpon (**Ell.**) **Nash** – Marsh panic grass [Marsh panic-grass] (94) (1901)

Pharbitis nil **Chois.** – See *Ipomoea nil* (L.) Roth

Phaseolus (**Tourn.**) **L.** – See *Phaseolus* L.

Phaseolus acutifolius **Gray** – Teparies (105) (1932)

Phaseolus acutifolius **Gray var.** *latifolius* **Freeman** – Tepary bean (109) (1949)

Phaseolus acutifolius latifolius – See *Phaseolus acutifolius* Gray var. *latifolius* Freeman

Phaseolus aureus **Roxb.** – See *Vigna radiata* (L.) R. Wilczek var. *radiata*

Phaseolus coccineus **L.** – Multiflora bean (109) (1949), Scarlet runner (19, 82, 92, 107, 109, 138) (1840–1949), Spanish bean (92) (1876)

Phaseolus helvolus **L.** – See *Strophostyles helvula* (L.) Ell.

Phaseolus **L.** – Asasment (181) (~1678), Beane [Beane] (1, 7, 106, 109, 138) (1828–1949), Diuers sorts of beanes (178) (1526), Faselen (German) (107) (1919), French beanes (diuers sorts) (178) (1526), Kidney bean [Kidney-bean] (82, 103, 178, 184) (1526–1930), Okindgier (181) (~1678), Purutu (Peru) (107) (1919), Welsch bonen (107) (1552)

Phaseolus limensis **Macf.** – See *Phaseolus lunatus* L.

Phaseolus lunatus **L.** – Bushel bean (107) (1814), Carolina bean (109) (1949), Civet bean (107, 109, 138) (1919–1949), Dwarf sieva bean (109) (1949), French bean (Anglo-Indians) (110) (1886), Lima bean (19, 82, 107, 109, 138, 148) (1840–1949), Lima haricot (110) (1886), Scimitar-pod kidney bean [Scimetar-podded kidney bean] (110) (1886), Sewee bean (109) (1949), Sieva bean (107, 109) (1919–1949), Sugar bean (107, 110) (1886–1919)

Phaseolus lunatus **L. var.** *lunonanus* **Bailey** – See *Phaseolus lunatus* L.

Phaseolus macrocarpus [**Moench**] – See *Phaseolus lunatus* L.

Phaseolus max **L.** – See *Glycine max* (L.) Merr.

Phaseolus multiflorus **Willd.** – See *Phaseolus coccineus* L.

Phaseolus mungo **L.** – See *Vigna mungo* (L.) Hepper

Phaseolus polystachios (**L.**) **B.S.P.** – Kidney bean [Kidney-bean] (10) (1818), Perennial kidney bean [Perennial kidney-bean] (187) (1818), Thicket bean (50) (present), Wild bean [Wild-bean, Wildbean, Wild beans] (3, 5, 85, 93, 97) (1913–1977), Wild kidney beans (5) (1913)

Phaseolus polystachys (**L.**) **B.S.P.** – See *Phaseolus polystachios* (L.) Britton, Sterns & Poggenb.

Phaseolus retusa **Benth.** – See *Phaseolus ritensis* M.E.Jones

Phaseolus ritensis **M. E. Jones** – Metcalfe's bean [Metcalfe bean]

(138) (1923), Prairie bean [Prairie-bean] (107) (1919)

Phaseolus vulgaris L. – Alubia (Spanish) (107) (1919), American beans (107) (1670), A'teba'kwe (Abenaki) (107) (1919), Atit (Pawnee) (37) (1919), Ayacotle (Mexico) (107) (1919), Beane [Beane] (82) (1930), Bush bean (107, 109) (1919–1949), Common bean (107, 138) (1919–1923), Common pole bean (19) (1840), Etl (Aztec) (107) (1919), Fagiuolo (Italian) (107) (1919), Febues du Bresil (Brazilian beans) (107) (1605), Garden bean [Garden beans] (37, 121) (1918–1919), Haricot (107) (1919) corrpution of Greek arachos used for several legumes, Haricot (French) (6, 110) (1886–1892), Haricot bean (138) (1923), Hinbthinge (Omaha-Ponca) (37) (1919), Honink (Winnebago) (37) (1919), Hoŋbthiŋ (Osage) (121) (1918?–1970?) Osage have at least two named varieties, Kidney bean [Kidney-bean] (6, 107, 109, 110, 138) (1886–1949), Loubion (Modern Greek) (107) (1919), Malachxil (Delaware) (107) (1919), Mushaquissedes (Pequod) (107) (1919), Ogaressa (Huron) (107) (1919), Okindgier (Roanoke) (107) (1919), Omniča (Lakota) (121) (1918?–1970?), Onmnicha (Dakota) (37) (1919), Phaseole (French) (107) (1919), Pole bean (6, 107) (1892–1919), Sahe (46, 107) (1879–1919) St Lawrence River, Sahu (107) (1919), Schminkbohne (German) (6) (1892), String bean (6) (1892), Tuppuhguam-ash (Algonquin "twiners") (107) (1919), White bean (6) (1892), Wild kidney beans (41) (1770) possibly – Common haricot (110) (1886), possibly Dolichos (110) (1886) Theophrastus, possibly Fagiolo (Italian) (110) (1886), possibly Faséole or fazéole (French) (110) (until end of 17th century), possibly Fasiolos (110) (1886) Dioscorides, probably this species), possibly Fasiolum (110) (1886) Charlemagne, possibly Fasoler (Spanish) (110) (1886), possibly Fasoulia (Modern Greek) (110) (1886), possibly Fasulé (Albanian) (110) (1886), possibly Frajol (Spanish) (110) (1886), possibly Frisoles (Peru) (110) (1886), possibly Frisoles (Spanish) (110) (1886), possibly Palares (Peru) (110) (1886), possibly Paller (Native S. American) (110) (1886), possibly Turkish bean (110) (16th century)

Phaseolus vulgaris Savi – possibly *Phaseolus vulgaris* L.

Phaulothamnus spinescens Gray – Snake-eyes [Snake eyes] (122, 124) (1937) TX

Phedimus hybridus (L.) Hart – See *Sedum hybridum* L.

Phegopteris connectilis (Michx.) Watt – Common beech fern (5) (1913), Long beech-fern (5, 72, 109) (1907–1949), Narrow beechfern [Narrow beech-fern] (109, 138) (1923–1949), Sun fern (5, 50) (1913–present)

Phegopteris hexagonoptera (Michx.) Fee – Beech fern (97) (1937), Broad beech fern [Broad beech-fern, Broad beechfern] (5, 50, 109, 155) (1913–present), Hexagon beech fern (5) (1913), Winged wood fern [Winged woodfern] (138) (1923)

Phellinus igniarius (L.) Quél. – Boletus (of the oak) (92) (1876), Spunk (92) (1876)

Phellodendron amurense Rupr. – Amur corktree (137, 138) (1923–1931), Chinese cork tree [Chinese corktree] (137) (1931), Manchurian corktree (137) (1931)

Phellodendron Rupr. – Cork or Cork tree [Cork-tree, Corktree] (109, 138) (1923–1949)

Phellodendron sachalinense (F. Schmidt) Sargent – Sakhalin corktree (138) (1923)

Phellopterus montanus Nutt. – See *Cymopterus montanus* Nutt. ex Torr. & Gray

Phellopterus Nutt. – See *Cymopterus* Raf.

Phemeranthus rugospermus (Holz.) Kiger – Prairie talinum (5) (1913)

Phemeranthus teretifolius (Pursh) Raf. – Fameflower [Fame flower, Fame-flower] (5, 72, 86, 97, 131) (1878–1937), Flameflower [Flame flower, Flame-flower] (72, 156) (1907–1923), Rock purslane (156) (1923), Taliny (19) (1840), Terete talinum (86) (1878), Terete-leaf talinum [Terete-leaved talinum] (2) (1895), Wild portulaca (156) (1923)

Philadelphicus coronarius – possibly *Philadelphus coronarius* L.

Philadelphus coronarius L. – Common mock orange (135) (1910), False syringa (19, 92, 156) (1840–1923), Garden syringa (5, 156) (1913–1923), Mock orange [Mock-orange, Mockorange] (5, 19, 82, 85, 92, 97, 156, 184) (1793–1937), Orange-flower tree (5, 156) (1913–1923), Sweet mock orange [Sweet mockorange] (112, 138) (1923–1937), Whitepipe [White pipe] (178) (1526), possibly Syringia (92) (1876)

Philadelphus floridus Beadle – Beadle's mock orange [Beadle mockorange] (138) (1923)

Philadelphus gordonianus [Lindl.] – See *Philadelphus lewisii* Pursh

Philadelphus grandiflorus Willd. – See *Philadelphus inodorus* L.

Philadelphus hirsutus Nutt. – Hairy mock orange [Hairy mockorange] (2, 138) (1895–1923)

Philadelphus inodorus L. – Big scentless mockorange (138) (1923), Carolina scentless syringa [Carolinian scentless syringa] (8) (1785), Flowery syringa (19) (1840), Large-flower mock orange [Large flowering mock orange] (2, 135) (1895–1910), Large-flower syringa [Large-flowered syringa] (5) (1913), Scentless mock orange [Scentless mockorange] (2, 138) (1895–1923), Scentless syringa (5, 19) (1840–1913), Syringa sans odeur (French) (8) (1785)

Philadelphus L. – Mock orange [Mock-orange, Mockorange] (2, 8, 10, 109, 112, 138, 146, 149, 153) (1785–1949), Syringa (2, 8, 82, 149, 167) (1785–1930), Syringa (French) (8) (1785)

Philadelphus lewisii Pursh – Gordon's mockorange [Gordon mockorange] (138) (1923), Lewis' mock orange [Lewis mockorange] (138) (1923), Privey (35) (1806), Wild syringa (101) (1905)

Philadelphus microphyllus Gray – Little-leaf mock orange [Littleleaf mockorange] (138) (1923)

Philadelphus pubescens Loisel. – Hoary mock orange [Hoary mockorange] (138) (1923)

Philadelphus serpyllifolius Gray – Syringa (124) (1937)

Philibertia clausa (Jacq.) K. Schum. – See Funastrum clausum (Jacq.) Schltr.

Philibertia Kunth – See *Funastrum* Fourn.

Philodendron giganteum Schott – Climbing philodendron (138) (1923)

Philodendron Schott – Philodendron (138) (1923)

Philotria angustifolia (Muhl.) Britton – See *Elodea nuttallii* (Planch.) St. John

Philotria minor (Engelm.) Small. – See *Elodea nuttallii* (Planch.) St. John

Philotria planchonii (Casp.) Rydb. – See *Elodea canadensis* Michx.

Phippsia algida (C. J. Phipps) R. Br. – Icegrass (50) (present), Phippsia (5, 94) (1901–1913)

Phlebodium (R. Br.) J. Sm. – Golden polypody (50) (present)

Phlebodium aureum (L.) J. Sm. – Golden polypody (50, 138) (1923–present), Hare-foot fern [Hares-foot-fern] (109) (1949)

Phleum alpinum L. – Alpine cat-tail [Alpine cat's tail] (5) (1913), Alpine timothy (45, 50, 94, 146, 152, 155) (1896–present), Fiallkampe (46) (1879), Mountain cat's-tail [Mountain cat's tail] (66) (1903), Mountain foxtail (5) (1913), Mountain timothy (3, 45, 88) (1885–1977), Native timothy (45, 87) (1884–1896), Timothy grass [Timothy-grass] (35) (1806)

Phleum boehmeri Wibel – See *Phleum phleoides* (L.) H. Karst.

Phleum L. – Cat-tail [Cat's tail, Cats Taile, Cat's-tail, Cats tails] (66) (1903), Cat-tail grass [Cat's tail grass, Cats-tail grass] (10) (1818), Timothy (1, 50, 93, 138, 155) (1923–present), Timothy grass [Timothy-grass] (10) (1818)

Phleum pratense L. – Cat-tail grass [Cat's tail grass, Cats-tail grass] (19, 92, 108) (1840–1876), Common timothy (45, 87) (1884–1896), Herd's grass [Herds-grass, Herd's-grass, Herds-grass, Herd grass] (5, 45, 46, 56, 66, 68, 87, 90, 92, 109, 119, 143) (1884–1949), Herd's grass of New England [Herds grass of New England] (92) (1876), Meadow cat's-tail [Meadow cat's tail] (5, 19, 68) (1840–1913), Rattail [Rattail] (5) (1913), Round bent grass [Round bent-grasse] (180) (1633), Small cat-tail grass [Small cats-taile grasse] (180) (1633), Soldier's-feather [Soldier's feather] (5) (1913), Timothy (3, 45, 46, 50, 56, 66, 67, 68, 85, 87, 88, 90, 94, 109, 111, 115, 119, 122, 125,

129, 138, 140, 143, 146, 155, 163, 184) (1793–present), Timothy grass [Timothy-grass] (11, 19, 92, 187) (1818–1888)

Phlomis fruticosa L. – French sage (178) (1526), Jerusalem sage [Jerusalem-sage] (109) (1949) possibly a corruption of Girasole articocco, Italian for sunflower artichoke, name dates back to at least 1686, Sweet French sage [Sweete French sage] (178) (1526)

Phlomis L. – Jerusalem sage [Jerusalem-sage] (138, 156) (1923)

Phlomis tuberosa L. – Bodmon sok (Kalmuck) (107) (1919), Jerusalem sage [Jerusalem-sage] (5, 92) (1876–1913), Sage-leaf mullein [Sage leaf mullein] (92, 158, 156) (1898–1923), Sage-leaf mullen (5) (1913), Tuber jerusalem-sage [Tuber jerusalemsage] (155) (1942), Tuberous Jerusalem-sage [Tuberous Jerusalemsage] (50) (present)

Phlox affinis – possibly *Phlox carolina* L.

Phlox alyssifolia **Greene** – Alyssum-leaf phlox [Alyssumleaf phlox] (50) (present)

Phlox amoena **Sims.** – Amoena phlox (138) (1923), Hairy phlox (5) (1913)

Phlox amplifolia **Britton** – Large-leaf phlox [Large-leaved phlox] (5) (1913)

Phlox andicola **E. Nels.** – Creeping phlox (98) (1926), Moss phlox (3) (1977), Plains phlox (4, 155) (1942–1986), Prairie phlox (50) (present), Rock phlox (98) (1926) Neb, Spreading phlox (98) (1926)

Phlox andicola **E. Nels. subsp.** *andicola* – Prairie phlox (50) (present)

Phlox bifida **Beck** – Cleft phlox (5) (1913), Crawling phlox (72) (1907) IA, Sand phlox (109, 156) (1923–1949)

Phlox bifida **Beck subsp.** *stellaria* **(Gray) Wherry** – Chickweed phlox (5, 156) (1913–1923), Mauve phlox (138) (1923)

Phlox bifida **Beck.** – See *Phlox bifida* Beck

Phlox brittonii **Small.** – See *Phlox subulata* L. subsp. *brittonii* (Small) Wherry

Phlox bryoides **Nutt.** – See *Phlox hoodii* Richards. subsp. *muscoides* (Nutt.) Wherry

Phlox caespitosa **Nutt.** – Douglas' phlox (5, 93, 131) (1899–1936)

Phlox canescens **Torr. & Gray** – See *Phlox hoodii* Richards. subsp. *canescens* (Torr. & Gray) Wherry

Phlox carolina **L.** – Carolina phlox (64) (1907), Thick-leaf phlox (109) (1949)

Phlox diffusa **Benth.** – Spreading phlox (50, 155) (1942–present)

Phlox diffusa **Benth. subsp.** *scleranthifolia* **(Rydb.) Wherry** – Spreading phlox (50) (present)

Phlox divaricata **L.** – Blue phlox (138, 156) (1923), Sweet William [Sweetwilliam, Sweet-william] (122, 124) (1937), Sweet William phlox [Sweetwilliam phlox] (155) (1942), Wild blue phlox (5, 50, 72, 85, 93, 97, 122, 124) (1907–present), Wild Sweet William [Wild Sweet-William] (5, 109, 156) (1913–1949)

Phlox divaricata **L. subsp.** *laphamii* **(Wood) Wherry** – Blue phlox (3, 4) (1977–1986), Lapham's phlox (50) (present)

Phlox douglasii **Hook.** – See *Phlox caespitosa* Nutt.

Phlox drummondii **Hook.** – Annual phlox (109) (1949), Drummond's phlox [Drummond phlox] (82, 109, 122, 138) (1923–1949), Phlox (92) (1876)

Phlox glaberrima **L.** – Smooth phlox (5, 72, 138, 156) (1907–1923), Smooth pink phlox (122, 124) (1937)

Phlox gracilis **(Hook.) Greene** – Slender phlox (50) (present)

Phlox gracilis **(Hook.) Greene subsp.** *humilis* **(Greene) Mason** – Slender phlox (50) (present)

Phlox hoodii **Richards.** – Hood's phlox [Hoods phlox] (3, 85, 93, 155) (1932–1977), Moss phlox (1) (1932), Moss pink [Moss-pink] (1, 127) (1932–1933), Spiny phlox (50) (present)

Phlox hoodii **Richards. subsp.** *canescens* **(Torr. & Gray) Wherry** – Hoary phlox (85) (1932)

Phlox hoodii **Richards. subsp.** *glabrata* **(E. Nels.) Wherry** – Carpet phlox (50) (present), Smooth Hood's phlox [Smooth Hoods phlox] (155) (1942)

Phlox hoodii **Richards. subsp.** *hoodii* – Spiny phlox (50) (present)

Phlox hoodii **Richards. subsp.** *muscoides* **(Nutt.) Wherry** – Dwarf Hood's phlox [Dwarf Hoods phlox] (155) (1942), Moss phlox (5, 93, 158) (1900–1936), Musk phlox (50) (present), Square-stem phlox [Squarestem phlox] (155) (1942)

Phlox kelseyi **Britton** – Kelsey's phlox (5, 85, 93, 131) (1899–1936)

Phlox **L.** – Lychnidia (156) (1923), Phlox (1, 4, 50, 82, 93, 138, 155, 158) (1900–present), Sweet William [Sweetwilliam, Sweet-william] (77) (1898), Wild Sweet William [Wild Sweet-William] (158) (1900)

Phlox latifolia **Michx.** – Mountain phlox (5, 109, 138, 156) (1913–1949), Sweet William [Sweetwilliam, Sweet-william] (77) (1898) Sulphur Grove OH

Phlox longipilos **Waterfall** – Long-hair phlox [Longhair phlox] (50) (present)

Phlox maculata **L.** – Litchnidia (79) (1891) NH, Spotted lichnidia (19) (1840), Spotted-stalk lychnidea [Spotted-stalked lychnidea] (187) (1818), Spotted-stem phlox [Spotted-stemmed phlox] (187) (1818), Sweet William phlox [Sweetwilliam phlox] (138) (1923), Wild Sweet William [Wild Sweet-William] (5, 72, 156) (1907–1923)

Phlox oklahomensis **Wherry** – Oklahoma phlox (50) (present)

Phlox ovata **L.** – See *Phlox latifolia* Michx.

Phlox paniculata **L.** – Fall phlox (3, 4, 50) (1977–present), Garden phlox (5, 72, 85, 93, 95, 97, 138, 156) (1907–1937), Smooth-stem lichnidia (19) (1840), Summer perennial phlox (109) (1949), Summer phlox (155) (1942)

Phlox pilosa **L.** – Creeping lichnidia (19) (1840), Downy phlox (5, 50, 93, 97, 131, 138, 155, 156) (1899–present), Frenchman's-buttons [Frenchman's buttons] (156) (1923), Hairy lychnidea (187) (1818), Hairy phlox (5, 156) (1913–1923), Prairie phlox (4, 5, 72, 85, 93, 122, 124, 156) (1907–1986), Sweet William [Sweetwilliam, Sweetwilliam] (5, 73, 77, 156) (1892–1923), Wild phlox (114) (1894)

Phlox pilosa **L. subsp.** *fulgida* **(Wherry) Wherry** – Downy phlox (50) (present), Prairie downy phlox (155) (1942), Prairie phlox (3) (1977)

Phlox pilosa **L. subsp.** *ozarkana* **(Wherry) Wherry** – Ozark downy phlox (155) (1942), Ozark phlox (50) (present), Prairie phlox (3) (1977)

Phlox pilosa **L. subsp.** *pilosa* – Downy phlox (50) (present), Eastern downy phlox (155) (1942), Prairie phlox (3) (1977)

Phlox pilosa **L. var.** *virens* **(Michx.) Wherry** – See *Phlox pilosa* L. subsp. *pilosa*

Phlox stellaria **Gray** – See *Phlox bifida* Beck subsp. *stellaria* (Gray) Wherry

Phlox stolonifera **Sims.** – Crawling phlox (5) (1913), Creeping phlox (109, 138) (1923–1949)

Phlox suaveolens **Aiton** – possibly *Phlox maculata* L. (taxonomic status is unresolved (PL))

Phlox subulata **L.** – Creeping phlox (77) (1898) Sulphur Grove OH, Flowering-moss [Flowering moss] (5, 73, 156) (1892–1923) Northern OH, Ground-pink [Ground pink] (2, 5, 63, 86, 108, 109, 156) (1878–1949), Moss phlox (138) (1923), Moss pink [Moss-pink] (2, 5, 63, 72, 77, 86, 92, 108, 109, 156) (1878–1949), Mountain pink [Mountain-pink] (5, 19, 86, 156) (1840–1923), Small savory-leaf Virginia stitchwort [Small savory leaved Virginia stitchwort] (181) (~1678), Wild pink (5, 187) (1818–1913)

Phlox subulata **L. subsp.** *brittonii* **(Small) Wherry** – Britton's phlox (5) (1913)

Phoenix canariensis **hort. ex Chabaud** – Canary date palm (138) (1923), Date [Dates] or Date tree (178, 179) (1526–1596)

Phoenix dactylifera **L.** – Date [Dates] or Date tree (92) (1876), Date palm (107, 110, 138) (1886–1923), Date-plum [Dateplum, Date plum] (92) (1876)

Phoenix humilis **Royle** – See *Chamaerops humilis* L.

Phoenix **L.** – Date palm (138) (1923)

Pholiota praecox **(Pers.) P. Kumm.** – Early mushroom (128) (1933) ND

Pholisma sonorae **(Torr. ex Gray) Yatskievych** – Sand-food [Sand food] (103, 104) (1870–1896)

Phoradendron flavescens **Nutt.** – See *Phoradendron leucarpum* (Raf.)

Reveal & M. C. Johnston

Phoradendron juniperinum **Engelm. ex Gray** – Cedar mistletoe (122, 124) (1937)

Phoradendron leucarpum **(Raf.) Reveal & M. C. Johnston** – American mistletoe (2, 5, 49, 53, 97, 122, 124, 138, 156, 174) (1753–1937), Christmas American mistletoe [Christmas American-mistletoe] (155) (1942), Eastern mistletoe (4) (1986), False mistletoe (2, 156) (1895), Goldenbough [Golden bough] (92) (1876), Mistletoe [Misseltoe, Misletoe, Misleto] (35, 48, 49, 53, 92, 106, 161) (1806–1930), Oak mistletoe (50) (present)

Phoradendron rubrum **(L.) Griseb.** – Gui rouge (French) (8) (1785), Mahogany mistletoe (50) (present), Red-berry mistletoe [Red berried mistletoe] (8) (1785)

Phoradendron serotinum **(Raf.) M. C. Johnst.** – See *Phoradendron leucarpum* (Raf.) Reveal & M. C. Johnston

Phoradendron tomentosum **(DC.) Engelmann. ex Gray** – Christmas mistletoe (50) (present), Hairy mistletoe (4) (1986)

Phormium cookianum **Le Jolis** – See Phormium colensoi Hook.f.

Phormium **J. R. & G. Forst.** – Flax-lily [Flaxlily] (138) (1923)

Phormium tenax **J. R. & G. Forst.** – New Zealand flax (109, 138) (1923–1949)

Photinia arbutifolia – See *Heteromeles arbutifolia* (Lindl.) M. Roemer var. *arbutifolia*

Photinia floribunda **(Lindl.) Robertson & Phipps** – Épine à feuilles de prunier (French) (8) (1785), Plum-leaf medlar [Plumb leaved medlar] (8) (1785), Purple chokeberry [Purple choke-berry] (138) (1923), Purple-fruit chokeberry [Purple-fruited choke berry] (5) (1913), Red-fruit swamp-service [Red-fruited swamp-service] (187) (1818)

Photinia **Lindl.** – Chokeberry [Choke-berry, Choke berry] (1, 50, 138, 155) (1923–present), Photinia (138) (1923)

Photinia melanocarpa **(Michx.) Robertson & Phipps** – Black chokeberry [Black choak-berry] (5, 19, 72, 138) (1840–1923), Black-fruit medlar [Black-fruited medlar] (187) (1818), Black-fruit swamp-service [Black-fruited swamp-service] (187) (1818), Chokepear [Choke-pear, Choke pear] (5) (1913)

Photinia pyrifolia **(Lam.) Robertson & Phipps** – Arbutus-leaved aronia (187) (1818), Chokepear [Choke-pear, Choke pear] (5, 73, 156) (1892–1923), Common chokeberry (2) (1895), Dogberry [Dog-berry, Dog berry] (5, 73) (1892–1913) Northeastern US, Pear-leaf hawthorn [Pear leaved hawthorn] (42) (1814), Pear-leaf thorn [Pear leaved thorn] (19) (1840), Purple chokeberry [Purple choke-berry] (138, 156) (1923), Red chokeberry [Red choke berry, Red choke-berry, Red choak-berry] (5, 19, 124, 135, 138, 155) (1840–1942), Red-fruit medlar [Red-fruited medlar] (187) (1818)

Photinia serratifolia **(Desf.) Kalkm.** – Low photinia (138) (1923)

Phragmites **Adans.** – Cane grass (1) (1932), Carrizo [Carizo, Carizzo] (152) (1912) NM, Common reed grass [Common reed-grass] (93) (1936), Pšištoŋža (Osage, from word for crooked) (121) (1918–1970), Reed [Rede, Reeds] (1, 50, 121, 155) (1918–present), Reed grass [Reedgrass, Reed-grass] (66) (1903)

Phragmites australis **(Cav.) Trin. ex Steud.** – Abo'djigûn (Chippewa, something turned out or over) (40) (1928), Bennels (5, 107) (1913–1919), Bog reed [Bog-reed] (5, 119) (1913–1938), Cane grass (101) (1905) MT, Carrizo [Carizo, Carizzo] (149, 152) (1904–1912) NM, Common reed (3, 50, 94, 140, 155) (1977–present), Common reed grass [Common reed-grass] (2, 5, 66, 99, 107, 119, 152) (1895–1938), Dutch reed [Dutch-reed] (5, 119) (1913–1938), Plume grass [Plume-grass, Plumegrass] (85) (1932) SD, Pole-reed [Pole reed] (5, 119) (1913–1938), Reed [Rede, Reeds] (40, 56, 72, 90, 107, 178, 179) (1526–1928), Reed grass [Reedgrass, Reed-grass] (11, 19, 22, 45, 87, 101, 124, 129) (1840–1937), Spires (5) (1913), Tall reed grass [Tall reed-grass] (163) (1852), Wild broom-corn [Wild broom corn] (5) (1913)

Phragmites communis **Trin.** – See *Phragmites australis* (Cav.) Trin. ex Steud.

Phragmites communis **Trin. var. *berlandieri* (Fourn.) Fern.** – See

Phragmites australis (Cav.) Trin. ex Steud.

Phragmites **Trin.** – See *Phragmites* Adans.

Phragmites vulgaris **(Lam.) B.S.P.** – See *Phragmites australis* (Cav.) Trin. ex Steud.

Phryma **L.** – Lopseed [Lop-seed] (1, 2, 93, 155, 158) (1895–1942), Phryma (50) (present)

Phryma leptostachya **L.** – American lopseed (50, 155) (1942–present), Lopseed [Lop-seed] (3, 4, 5, 19, 40, 63, 65, 72, 85, 92, 93, 95, 97, 131, 156) (1840–1986), Phryma (174, 177) (1753–1762)

Phyla cuneifolia **(Torr.) Greene** – Chapparal (77) (1898), Mexican heliotrope (77) (1898), Wedgeleaf (50) (present), Wedge-leaf fogfruit [Wedgeleaf fog-fruit, Wedge-leaved fog-fruit] (4, 5, 97, 122) (1913–1986), Wedge-leaf frogfruit [Wedge-leaved frog-fruit] (93) (1936)

Phyla incisa **Small** – See *Phyla nodiflora* (L.) Greene

Phyla lanceolata **(Michx.) Greene** – Carpetweed [Carpet weed, Carpetweed] (124) (1937) TX, Fogfruit [Fog-fruit, Fog fruit] (2, 3, 5, 63, 72, 82, 97, 120, 122, 133, 156) (1857–1977), Frog-fruit [Frog fruit] (93, 124, 156) (1923–1937), Lance-leaf fogfruit [Lanceleaf fogfruit] (50) (present), Northern fogfruit [Northern fog-fruit] (4) (1986)

Phyla **Lour.** – Fogfruit [Fog-fruit, Fog fruit] (50) (present)

Phyla nodiflora **(L.) Greene** – Carpet-grass [Carpet grass] (106) (1930), Carpetweed [Carpet weed, Carpet-weed] (124) (1937) TX, Creeping lippia (138) (1923), Fogfruit [Fog-fruit, Fog fruit] (106) (1930), Frog-fruit [Frog fruit] (124) (1937), Lawn plant (106) (1930), Lippia (106) (1930), Mat grass [Mat-grass, Matgrass] (106) (1930), Spatulate-leaf fogfruit [Spatulate-leaved fog-fruit] (5, 97) (1913–1937), Turkey-tangle fogfruit [Turkey tangle fogfruit] (50) (present)

Phyla scaberrima **(Juss.) Moldenke** – Lippia mexicana (57) (1917), Rough fogfruit (50) (present)

Phyllanthus abnormis **Baill.** – Drummond's leaf-flower (50) (present)

Phyllanthus acidus **(L.) Skeels** – Gooseberry tree [Gooseberry-tree] (109) (1949), Otaheite gooseberry [Otaheite-gooseberry] (109) (1949), Star-gooseberry (138) (1923)

Phyllanthus acidus **Skeels** – See *Phyllanthus acidus* (L.) Skeels

Phyllanthus avicularia **Small.** – See *Phyllanthus pudens* L. C. Wheeler

Phyllanthus carolinensis **Walt.** – Carolina leaf-flower (50) (present), Carolina phyllanthus (5, 97) (1913–1937)

Phyllanthus emblica **L.** – Emblic (107, 109) (1919–1949) Arabic, Myrobalan (109) (1949), White galls (92) (1876)

Phyllanthus **L.** –

Phyllanthus niruri **L.** – Kirganeli (174) (1753)

Phyllanthus nivosus – See *Breynia disticha* J. R. & G. Forst.

Phyllanthus polygonoides **Nutt.** – Knotweed leaf-flower [Knotweed leafflower] (155) (1942), Smartweed leaf-flower [Smart-weed leaf-flower] (50) (present)

Phyllanthus pudens **L. C. Wheeler** – Texas star gooseberry (124) (1937) TX

Phyllitis japonica **Komarov subsp. *americana* (Fern.) A. & D. Löve** – See *Asplenium scolopendrium* L. var. *americanum* (Fern.) Kartesz & Gandhi

Phyllitis scolopendrium **(L.) Newman var. *americana* Fern.** – See *Asplenium scolopendrium* L. var. *americanum* (Fern.) Kartesz & Gandhi

Phyllodoce caerulea **(L.) Bab.** – Mountain heath (5, 156) (1913–1923)

Phyllodoce coerula **(L.) Bab.** – See *Phyllodoce caerulea* (L.) Bab.

Phyllodoce empetriformis **(Sm.) D. Don** – Red false heather (106) (1930), Red fill-o-do-see (106) (1930)

Phyllostachys aurea **Carr. ex A. & C. Rivière** – Yellow bamboo (109) (1949)

Phyllostachys aurea **Riv.** – See *Phyllostachys aurea* Carr. ex A.& C. Rivière

Phyllostachys bambusoides **Sieb. & Zucc.** – Japanese timber bamboo (138) (1923)

Phyllostachys nigra **(Lodd.) Munro** – Black bamboo (109) (1949), Black-joint bamboo [Blackjoint bamboo] (138) (1923)

Phyllostachys nigra **Munro** – See *Phyllostachys nigra* (Lodd.) Munro

Phyllostachys ruscifolia **Siebenl. ex Satow** – See *Shibataea kumasaca*

(Steud.) Makino

Phymatosorus scolopendria (Burm. f.) Pic. Serm. – East Indian polypody (138) (1923)

Phymosia cuspidata (**Gray**) **Britton** – See *Sphaeralcea angustifolia* (Cav.) G. Don

Phymosia rivularis (**Dougl.**) **Rydb.** – See *Iliamna rivularis* (Dougl. ex Hook.) Greene

Physalis alkekengi **L.** – Alkakengie (180) (1633), Alkegnegi berries (92) (1876), Alkegneki (109) (1949), Alkékenge coqueret (French) (158) (1900), Alkekengi (158) (1900), Alkekengi (of shops) (180) (1633), Bladder herb [Bladder-herb] (158) (1900), Blasenkirschen (German) (158) (1900), Cape gooseberry [Cape-gooseberry] (92) (1876), Chinese lantern plant [Chinese lantern-plant] (109, 156) (1923–1949), Common winter-cherry [Common winter cherry] (19) (1840), Halicacabum (178) (1526), Husk-tomato [Husk tomato] (156) (1923), Judenkirschen (German) (158) (1900), Keravoulia (Modern Boeotians) (107) (1919), Schlutten (German) (158) (1900), Strawberry groundcherry [Strawberry groundcherry] (50, 138, 155) (1923–present), Strawberry-tomato [Strawberry tomato] (107, 156, 158) (1900–1923), Winter cherry [Winter-cherry, Winter cherries] (178) (1526), Wintercherry [Winter cherry] (92, 107, 109, 156, 158) (1876–1949)

Physalis angulata **L.** – Cut-leaf ground-cherry [Cutleaf ground cherry, Cut-leaved ground cherry] (3, 4, 5, 50, 72, 97, 122, 124) (1907–present), Ground-cherry [Groundcherry, Ground cherry] (107) (1919), Lance-leaf ground-cherry [Lanceleaf ground cherry] (5, 122) (1913–1937), Pops (107) (1750)

Physalis barbadensis **Jacq.** – See *Physalis pubescens* L. var. *pubescens*

Physalis bunyardi – See *Physalis bunyardii* Makino (taxonomic status is unresolved (PL))

Physalis cinerascens (**Dunal**) **A. S. Hitchc.** var. *cinerascens* – Ground-cherry [Ground cherry, Groundcherry] (4) (1986), Ground-cherry [Groundcherry, Ground cherry] (4) (1986)

Physalis edulis – See *Physalis peruviana* L.

Physalis grandiflora **Hook.** – See *Leucophysalis grandiflora* (Hook.) Rydb.

Physalis hederifolia **Gray** – Ivy-leaf ground-cherry [Ivyleaf groundcherry] (50) (present), Prairie ground-cherry [Prairie groundcherry, Prairie ground cherry] (4) (1986)

Physalis hederifolia **Gray** var. *comata* (**Rydb.**) **Waterfall** – Hillside ground-cherry [Hillside ground cherry] (5, 72, 97, 122) (1907–1937), Ivy-leaf ground-cherry [Ivyleaf groundcherry] (50) (present), Round-leaf ground-cherry [Round-leaved ground cherry, Round-leaved ground-cherry (5, 93, 97, 122, 131) (1899–1937)

Physalis heterophylla **Nees** – Cape gooseberry [Cape-gooseberry] (5) (1913), Clammy groundcherry [Clammy ground cherry, Clammy ground cherry, Clammy ground-cherry] (3, 4, 5, 50, 62, 72, 85, 93, 97, 122, 131, 155) (1899–present), Ground-cherry [Groundcherry, Ground cherry] (37, 98, 121) (1919–1977), Nikakitspak (Pawnee, forehead-pop) (37) (1919), Pe igatush (Omaha-Ponca, forehead pop) (37) (1919), Peruvian ground-cherry [Peruvian groundcherry, Peruvian ground cherry] (5) (1913), Strawberry-tomato [Strawberry tomato] (5) (1913), Tamanioh'pe (Dakota) (37) (1919), Tamnioxpi hu (Lakota, placenta or womb plant) (121) (1918?–1970?)

Physalis heterophylla **Nees** var. *heterophylla* –

Physalis hispida (**Waterfall**) **Cronq.** – Ground-cherry [Groundcherry, Ground cherry] (3) (1977), Prairie ground-cherry [Prairie ground-cherry, Prairie ground cherry] (50) (present)

Physalis ixocarpa **Brot.** – See *Physalis philadelphica* Lam. var. *immaculata* Waterfall

Physalis **L.** – Cherry tomato [Cherry tomatoes] (77) (1898) Eastern end of Long Island, Ground-cherry [Groundcherry, Ground cherry] (1, 2, 4, 7, 10, 50, 63, 93, 109, 138, 145, 155, 156, 158) (1818–present), Husk-tomato [Husk tomato] (2, 109, 156) (1895–1949), Strawberry-tomato [Strawberry tomato] (1, 2, 93) (1895–1936), Tomatillo (1) (1932), Wild cherry (75) (1894) NJ, Winter cherry [Winter-cherry, Winter cherries] (10, 184, 190) (~1759–1818), Winter-cherry

[Winter cherry] (10) (1818)

Physalis lanceolata **Michx.** – Ground-cherry [Ground cherry, Ground-cherry] (80, 114) (1894–1932), Ground-cherry [Groundcherry, Ground cherry] (80, 114) (1894–1913), Hanpok-hischasu (Winnebago, owl eyes) (37) (1919), Makan bashahon-shon (Omaha-Ponca, crooked medicine) (37) (1919), Prairie ground-cherry [Prairie groundcherry, Prairie ground cherry] (5, 37, 62, 72, 85, 93, 97, 131) (1899–1937), Strawberry-tomato [Strawberry tomato] (107) (1919)

Physalis lobata **Torr.** – See *Quincula lobata* (Torr.) Raf.

Physalis longifolia **Nutt.** – Common groundcherry [Common groundcherry, Common ground cherry] (4) (1986), Long-leaf ground-cherry [Longleaf ground cherry, Longleaf groundcherry, Long-leaved ground-cherry, Long-leaved ground cherry] (5, 50, 72, 85, 93, 97, 122, 131) (1899–present)

Physalis longifolia **Nutt.** var. *longifolia* – Ground-cherry [Ground-cherry, Ground cherry] (3) (1977), Long-leaf ground-cherry [Longleaf ground cherry, Longleaf groundcherry, Long-leaved ground-cherry, Long-leaved ground cherry] (50) (present)

Physalis longifolia **Nutt.** var. *subglabrata* (**Mackenzie & Bush**) **Cronq.** – Ground-cherry [Groundcherry, Ground cherry] (3) (1977), Lantern plant (124) (1937) TX, Large-bladder ground-cherry [Large bladder ground cherry] (5, 122, 124) (1913–1937), Long-leaf ground-cherry [Longleaf ground cherry, Longleaf groundcherry, Long-leaved ground-cherry, Long-leaved ground cherry] (50) (present), Smooth ground-cherry [Smooth ground cherry] (5, 97) (1913–1937), Taper-leaf ground-cherry [Taperleaf groundcherry] (97) (1937)

Physalis macrophysa **Rydb.** – See *Physalis longifolia* Nutt. var. *subglabrata* (Mackenzie & Bush) Cronq.

Physalis missouriensis **Mackenzie & Bush** – Downy ground-cherry [Downy ground cherry] (3) (1977), Missouri ground-cherry [Missouri groundcherry, Missouri ground cherry] (5, 50, 97) (1913–present)

Physalis mollis **Nutt.** – Field ground-cherry [Field groundcherry] (50) (present), Velvety ground-cherry (97) (1937)

Physalis obscura **Michx.** – See *Physalis pubescens* L.

Physalis pendula **Rydb.** – See *Physalis angulata* L.

Physalis pennsylvanica **Willd.** – See *Physalis viscosa* L.

Physalis peruviana **L.** – Alkekengi (107) (1919), Barbados-gooseberry [Barbadoes gooseberry, Barbadoes-gooseberry] (107) (1919), Cape gooseberry [Cape-gooseberry] (109, 138) (1923–1949), Cherry tomato [Cherry tomatoes] (107) (1919), Ground-cherry [Groundcherry, Ground cherry] (85, 107) (1919–1932), Husk-tomato [Husk tomato] (85) (1932), Peruvian ground-cherry [Peruvian groundcherry, Peruvian ground cherry] (138) (1923), Sousourouscurou (Carib) (107) (1919), Winter cherry [Winter-cherry, Winter cherries] (107) (1919)

Physalis philadelphica **Lam.** – Miltomatl (107) (1651) Mexico, Petite tomato du Mexique (French) (107) (1883), Philadelphia ground-cherry (72) (1907), Purple ground-cherry [Purple ground cherry] (107) (1919), Purple strawberry-tomato [Purple strawberry tomato] (107) (1919), Purple winter-cherry [Purple winter cherry] (107) (1919), Strawberry-tomato [Strawberry tomato] (107) (1885)

Physalis philadelphica **Lam.** var. *immaculata* **Waterfall** – Mexican ground-cherry [Mexican ground cherry] (5, 97, 122, 124, 156) (1913–1937), Strawberry-tomato [Strawberry tomato] (5, 156) (1913–1923), Tomatillo (5, 109, 138, 156) (1913–1949)

Physalis pruinosa [**auct. non L.**] – possibly *Physalis pubescens* L. var. *integrifolia* (Dunal) Waterfall

Physalis pubescens **L.** – Camaru (107) (1648), Cape gooseberry [Cape-gooseberry] (156) (1923), Common groundcherry [Common ground-cherry, Common ground cherry] (138) (1923), Common husk-tomato [Common husk tomato] (2) (1895), Downy ground-cherry [Downy ground cherry] (4) (1986), Dwarf cape-gooseberry [Dwarf cape gooseberry] (2, 5, 158) (1895–1913), Dwarf strawberry-tomato [Dwarf strawberry tomato] (158) (1900), Ground-cherry

[Groundcherry, Ground cherry] (19, 107, 156) (1840–1923), Husk-tomato [Husk tomato] (50, 107, 156) (1919–present), Low hairy ground-cherry [Low hairy ground cherry] (5, 62, 72, 97, 122, 158) (1900–1937), Strawberry-tomato [Strawberry tomato] (2, 5, 62, 107, 156) (1895–1923), Winter cherry [Winter-cherry, Winter cherries] (181) (~1678)

Physalis pubescens **L. var.** *integrifolia* **(Dunal) Waterfall** – Downy ground-cherry [Downy ground cherry] (3) (1977), Husk-tomato [Husk tomato] (50) (present), possibly Tall hairy ground-cherry [Tall hairy ground cherry] (5, 72, 97) (1907–1937)

Physalis pubescens **L. var.** *missouriensis* **(Mack. & Bush) Waterfall** – See *Physalis missouriensis* Mackenzie & Bush

Physalis pubescens **L. var.** *pubescens* – Barbados ground cherry [Barbadoes ground cherry, Barbadoes ground-cherry] (5, 97, 122) (1913–1937)

Physalis pumila **Nutt.** – Dwarf groundcherry (50) (present), Low ground-cherry [Low ground cherry] (5, 97, 122) (1913–1937), Prairie ground-cherry [Prairie groundcherry, Prairie ground cherry] (3, 4, 155) (1942–1986)

Physalis pumila **Nutt. subsp.** *hispida* **(Waterfall) Hinton** – See *Physalis hispida* (Waterfall) Cronq.

Physalis rotundata **Rydb.** – See *Physalis hederifolia* Gray var. *comata* (Rydb.) Waterfall

Physalis subglabrata **Mackenzie & Bush** – See *Physalis longifolia* Nutt. var. *subglabrata* (Mackenzie & Bush) Cronq.

Physalis virginiana **Mill.** – Accomodation plant (156) (1923), Ground-cherry [Groundcherry, Ground cherry] (156) (1923), Hing-flower (156) (1923), Husk-tomato [Husk tomato] (156) (1923), Strawberry-tomato [Strawberry tomato] (107) (1919), Virginia ground-cherry [Virginia ground cherry, Virginia groundcherry, Virginian ground cherry] (4, 5, 50, 62, 72, 93, 97, 131, 155) (1899–present), Wild cherry (5, 75, 156) (1894–1923) Northern MN, Wild ground-cherry [Wild ground cherry] (85) (1932)

Physalis virginiana **Mill. var.** *sonorae* **(Torr.) Waterfall** – See *Physalis longifolia* Nutt. var. *longifolia*

Physalis virginiana **Mill. var.** *subglabrata* **(Mack. & Bush) Waterfall** – See *Physalis longifolia* Nutt. var. *subglabrata* (Mackenzie & Bush) Cronq.

Physalis virginiana **Mill. var.** *virginiana* – Ground-cherry [Groundcherry, Ground cherry] (3) (1977), Virginia ground-cherry [Virginia ground cherry, Virginia groundcherry] (50) (present)

Physalis viscosa **L.** – Ground-cherry [Groundcherry, Ground cherry] (19, 49, 92) (1840–1898), Pennsylvania winter-cherry [Pennsylvanian winter-cherry] (187) (1818), Stellate ground cherry (5) (1913), Yellow henbane (5, 19, 49, 92, 156) (1840–1923)

Physalodes physalodes **(L.) Britton** – See *Nicandra physalodes* (L.) Gaertn.

Physaria **(Nutt. ex Torr. & Gray) Gray** – Bladderpod [Bladder pod, Bladder-pod] (158) (1900), Double bladderpod [Double bladder pod, Double bladder-pod] (1, 4, 93) (1932–1986), Twinpod (50, 155) (1942–present)

Physaria brassicoides **Rydb.** – Common twinpod (155) (1942), Double bladderpod [Double bladder pod, Double bladder-pod] (3, 4, 5, 131) (1913–1986), Double twinpod (50) (present)

Physaria didymocarpa **(Hook.) Gray** – See *Physaria brassicoides* Rydb.

Physocarpus **(Camb.) Raf.** – Ninebark [Nine bark, Nine-bark] (1, 4, 50, 82, 93, 109, 138, 155, 156, 158) (1900–present)

Physocarpus capitatus **(Pursh) Kuntze** – Ninebark [Nine bark, Nine-bark] (35) (1806), Sevenbark [Seven-bark, Seven bark, Seven barks] (35) (1806)

Physocarpus intermedius **(Rydb.) Schneid.** – See *Physocarpus opulifolius* (L.) Maxim. var. *intermedius* (Rydb.) B. L. Robins.

Physocarpus malvaceus **(Greene) Kuntze** – Mallow ninebark (138) (1923)

Physocarpus **Maxim** – See *Physocarpus* (Camb.) Raf.

Physocarpus monogynus **(Torr.) Coult.** – Dwarf ninebark (112)

(1937), Mountain ninebark (4, 155) (1942–1986), possibly Small-flower ninebark [Small-flowered ninebark] (131) (1899), possibly Western ninebark (130) (1895)

Physocarpus opulifolius **(L.) Maxim.** – Common ninebark (50, 109, 138, 155) (1923–present), Miskwazi-wušk (Chippewa, water-strider herb) (105) (1932), Ninebark [Nine bark, Nine-bark] (3, 4, 63, 82, 105, 112) (1899–1986), Ninebark syringa (156) (1923)

Physocarpus opulifolius **(L.) Maxim. var.** *intermedius* **(Rydb.) B.L. Robins.** – Atlantic ninebark (50) (present), Illinois ninebark (138, 155) (1923–1942), Ninebark [Nine bark, Nine-bark] (82) (1930), Prairie ninebark [Prairie nine-bark, Prairie nine bark] (5, 72, 93) (1907–1936)

Physocarpus opulifolius **(L.) Maxim. var.** *opulifolius* – Double bridal-wreath [Double bridal wreath] (112) (1937), Eastern ninebark [Eastern nine bark] (72) (1907), Guelder-rose-leaf spiraea [Guelder rose-leaved spiraea] (8) (1785), Ninebark [Nine bark, Nine-bark] (5, 8, 19, 85, 95, 130, 131) (1785–1913), Sevenbark [Seven-bark, Seven bark, Seven barks] (177) (1762), Snowball hard-hack (19) (1840), Spiraea à feuilles d'obier (French) (8) (1785)

Physostegia angustifolia **Fern.** – False dragonhead [False dragonhead, False-dragonhead, False dragon's headFalse dragonshead] (4) (1986), Narrow-leaf false dragonhead [Narrowleaf false dragonhead] (50) (present)

Physostegia **Benth.** – False dragonhead [False dragon-head, False-dragonhead, False dragon's headFalse dragonshead] (2, 4, 138) (1895–1986), Lion's-heart [Lion's heart, Lionsheart, Lyonsheart] (4, 50, 155, 158) (1900–present), Obedient plant [Obedient-plant] (4, 156) (1923–1986)

Physostegia intermedia **(Nutt.) Engelm. & Gray** – Intermediate lion's-heart [Intermediate lionsheart] (3) (1977), Slender false dragonhead (50) (present), Slender lion's-heart [Slender lion's heart] (5) (1913)

Physostegia ledinghamii **(Boivin) Cantino** – Ledingham's false dragonhead (50) (present)

Physostegia parviflora **Nutt. ex Gray** – Obedient plant [Obedient-plant] (3, 4, 127) (1933–1986), Purple lion's-heart [Purple lion's heart] (5, 72, 93) (1907–1936), Western false dragonhead (50) (present), Western lion's-heart [Western lion's heart] (5, 93) (1913–1936)

Physostegia virginiana **(L.) Benth.** – American heath (5, 156) (1913–1923), American heather (156) (1923), Dragonhead [Dragon-head, Dragon head, Dragon's head] (5, 19, 85, 92, 93, 97, 124) (1840–1937), False dragonhead [False dragon-head, False-dragonhead, False dragon's headFalse dragonshead] (3, 63, 72, 82, 131, 156, 158) (1899–1977), Lion's-heart [Lion's heart, Lionsheart, Lyonsheart] (5, 156, 158) (1900–1923), Obedient plant [Obedient-plant] (5, 50, 156, 158) (1900–present), Virginia false dragonhead [Virginia false-dragonhead] (138) (1923), Virginia lion's-heart [Virginia lionsheart] (4, 155) (1942–1986)

Physostegia virginiana **(L.) Benth. subsp.** *praemorsa* **(Shinners) Cantino** – Obedient plant [Obedient-plant] (50) (present)

Physostegia virginiana **(L.) Benth. subsp.** *virginiana* – Few-flower lion's-heart [Few-flowered lion's heart] (5) (1913), Himalayan dragonshead (155) (1942), Obedient plant [Obedient-plant] (50) (present), Tall cluster false dragonhead [Tall cluster false-dragonhead] (138) (1923)

Physostegia virginiana speciosa – See *Physostegia virginiana* (L.) Benth. subsp. *virginiana*

Phytolacca americana **L.** – American nightshade (5, 69, 181) (~1678–1913), American pokeweed (50) (present), Branching phytolacca (186) (1814), Cancer jalap [Cancer-jalap] (5, 69) (1903–1913), Coakum [Coacum] (5) (1913), Cocum (77) (1898) Sulphur Grove OH, Common pokeberry (138, 155) (1923–1942), Garget (5, 69) (1903–1913), Gthebe moŋkoŋ (Osage, vomit medicine) (121) (1918?–1970?), Haystack weed (77) (1898), Ink bush (77) (1898) Southold Long Island, Inkberry [Ink-berry, Ink berry] (5, 37) (1913–1919), Ink-berry bush (77) (1898), Pachone (181) (~1678), Påk (Swedish) (41) (1770), Phytolacca (54) (1905), Pigeon-berry [Pigeon berry]

(5, 14, 69, 77, 93) (1882), Pocan bush [Pocan-bush] (5, 71) (1898–1913), Pocum (77) (1898) Sulphur Grove OH, friends of J. K. Polk used this plant as their symbol when he was running for president, Poke (5, 14, 52, 54, 69, 71, 97, 109, 124, 177, 187) (1762–1949), Pokeberry [Poke-berry, Poke berry] (4, 37, 77, 93, 95) (1898–1986), Pokeroot [Poke root, Poke-root] (77) (1898), Pokeweed [Pokeweed, Poke-weed] (4, 5, 41, 121, 125, 187) (1770–1986), Red ink plant [Red ink-plant, Red-ink plant] (5, 71) (1898–1913), Red nightshade (181) (~1678), Redweed [Red-weed, Red weed] (5, 37, 69) (1903–1913), Redweed of Virginia [Red weed of Virginia] (181) (~1678), Scoke (5, 69, 109) (1903–1949)

Phytolacca americana L. var. *americana* – Agouman (French) (158) (1900), American nightshade (6, 41, 49, 64, 71, 156, 157, 158, 186) (1770–1929), Americanisher Nachteschatten (German) (186) (1814), Amerikanische Kermesbeere (German) (6) (1892), Amerikanische Rermesbeere (German) (186) (1814), Amerikanische Scharlachbeere (German) (6, 186) (1814–1892), Cancer jalap [Cancer-jalap] (64, 156, 158) (1900–1923), Cancer-root [Cancer root] (6, 49, 71) (1892–1898), Chongras (Louisiana) (6, 7, 71) (1828–1898), Chou-gras (107) (1817), Coakum [Coacum] (7, 49, 64, 69, 92, 156, 158, 186) (1814–1923), Cocum (6, 71, 186) (1814–1892) Northern tribes, Cokan (Virginian tribes) (6) (1892), Common poke (157) (1929), Common pokeweed (2) (1895), Crowberry [Crowberry, Crow berry] (6, 71) (1892–1898), Cuechiliz (Mexico) (7) (1828), Foxglove [Fox glove, Fox-glove, Foxgloves] (158) (1900), Garget (2, 6, 7, 49, 53, 64, 71, 92, 107, 152, 157, 158, 186) (1814–1929), Garget plant (59) (1911), Gargetweed [Garget weed] (49) (1898), Gemeine Rermesbeere (German) (186) (1814), Grande morelle des Indes (French) (186) (1814), Herbe de la lache (186) (1814), Herbe de la Laque (French) (6) (1892), Hierba carmin (186) (1814), Inkberry [Ink-berry, Ink berry] (62, 64, 69, 156) (1903–1923), Ink-berry roots (157) (1929), Jabonera (Spanish) (158) (1900), Jalap (6, 71) (1892–1898), Jalap cancer-root [Jalap cancer root] (49, 186) (1814–1898), Jucato (Jamaica) (7) (1828), Keermesbeer (German) (158) (1900), Kokum (48) (1882), Mazorquilla (Spanish) (158) (1900), Mechoacan (49) (1898), Mechoacan du Canada (French) (186) (1814), Morelle a gràppes (French) (6, 158, 186) (1814–1900), Mountain calalae (186) (1814), Namoll (Spanish) (158) (1900), Phytolacca (59, 60, 64) (1902–1911), Pianta laca (186) (1814), Pigeon-berry [Pigeon berry] (2, 6, 7, 19, 49, 62, 64, 71, 92, 152, 157, 158, 186) (1814–1929), Pocan (Virginian tribes) (6, 7, 64, 69, 107, 158) (1828–1908), Pocan bush [Pocan-bush] (92, 156) (1876–1923), Poke (7, 10, 38, 49, 53, 55, 60, 61, 64, 158, 184, 186) (1793–1922), Pokeberry [Poke-berry, Poke berry] (62, 156) (1912–1923), Pokeroot [Poke root, Poke-root] (6, 49, 53, 57, 59, 71, 92, 157) (1892–1929), Pokeweed [Poke-weed, Poke-weed] (6, 19, 44, 49, 53, 62, 64, 71, 72, 92, 145, 156, 157, 158, 186, 190) (~1759–1929), Pök-weed (186) (1814), Rasin d'Amerique (French) (186) (1814), Red ink plant [Red ink-plant, Red-ink plant] (92, 156, 157, 158) (1876–1929), Red inkberry [Red ink berry] (64, 69) (1903–1907), Red nightshade (49) (1898), Red-ink plant (158) (1900), Redweed [Red-weed, Red weed] (49, 64, 71, 92, 156, 157, 158) (1876–1929), Scharlachbeere (German) (158) (1900), Scoke (2, 6, 49, 62, 64, 92, 107, 152, 157, 158, 186) (1814–1929), Scoke jalap (49) (1898), Skoke (48, 71, 92) (1876–1898), Skokeweed [Skoke weed] (49) (1898), Tienmannige lakplant (186) (1814), Virginia poke [Virginian poke] (49, 64, 69, 92, 107, 158) (1876–1919), Virginia pole [Virginian pole] (158) (1900)

Phytolacca decandra L. – See *Phytolacca americana* L. var. *americana*

Phytolacca L. – Poke (167) (1814), Pokeberry [Poke-berry, Poke berry] (1, 109, 138, 155, 158) (1900–1949), Pokeweed [Poke-weed, Poke-weed] (2, 50, 109) (1895–present), Scoke (2) (1895)

Picea A. Dietr. – Spruce (4, 50, 109, 138, 155, 158) (1900–present)

Picea abies (L.) H. Karst. – Abies (178) (1596), Burgundy pitch (92) (1876), Common fir (92) (1876), Épicéa (French) (158) (1900), Faux sapin (French) (158) (1900), Fichte (German) (158) (1900), Fir or Fir tree [Firre tree] (178, 180) (1596–1633), Galipot tree (158)

(1900), Gallpot (92) (1876), Himalayan pine (138) (1923), Norway spruce (58, 92, 107, 109, 112, 135, 136, 138, 158) (1857–1949), Norway Spurce fir (20) (1857), Pesse (French) (158) (1900), Spruce (92, 106) (1876–1930), Spruce fir (158) (1900), Spruce-top [Spruce tops] (92) (1876), possibly Sapin (French) (8) (1785)

Picea abies Karst. – See *Picea abies* (L.) H. Karst.

Picea amabilis Dougl. – See *Abies amabilis* (Dougl. ex Loud.) Dougl. ex Forbes

Picea australis Small – See *Picea rubens* Sarg.

Picea balsamea [(L.) Loudon] – See *Abies balsamea* (L.) Mill.

Picea bicolor (Maxim.) Mayr – See *Picea alcoquiana* (H.J.Veitch ex Lindl.) Carrière

Picea canadensis (Mill.) B.S.P. – See *Picea glauca* (Moench) Voss

Picea canadensis albertiana – See *Picea glauca* (Moench) Voss

Picea engelmannii Parry ex Engelm. – Engelmann's spruce [Engelman spruce] (135, 136, 138, 153) (1910–1930), White spruce (149) (1904) NM

Picea glauca (Moench) Voss – Alberta spruce (109, 112, 136, 138) (1923–1949), Black Hills spruce (4, 40, 109, 112, 136) (1928–1986), Black spruce (5, 158) (1900–1913), Cat pine (5, 75, 158) (1894–1913) Buckfield ME, Cat spruce (5, 158) (1900–1913), Épinette blanche du Canada (French) (8) (1785), Newfoundland spruce (8) (1785), Pine spruce (5, 158) (1900–1913), Pine tops (92) (1876), Silvery Black Hills spruce (136) (1930) SD, Single spruce (5, 158) (1900–1913), Skunk spruce [Skunk-spruce] (75, 158) (1894–1913) ME, from supposedly unpleasant smell of foliage, White pine (41) (1770), White spruce (1, 2, 3, 5, 50, 85, 109, 112, 130, 131, 135, 136, 138, 155, 158) (1895–present)

Picea grandis [Douglas ex Loudon] – See *Abies grandis* (Dougl. ex D. Don) Lindl.

Picea Link. – possibly *Picea* A. Dietr.

Picea mariana (Mill.) Britton, Sterns & Poggenb. – Abeti (46) (1879), Austrian pine (112) (1937), Black spruce (5, 6, 10, 20, 19, 46, 49, 50, 92, 109, 136, 138, 158) (1818–1949), Blue spruce (5) (1913), Cat spruce (5, 75) (1894–1913), Double spruce (2, 5, 6, 20, 49, 107) (1895–1919), Epinette à la bière (Canada) (20) (1857), Epinette noire (Canada) (20) (1857), He balsam (5) (1913), Juniper or Juniper tree [Juniper-tree] (5) (1913), Spruce gum tree [Spruce gum-tree] (5, 92) (1876–1913), Spruce pine (5, 75) (1894–1913) WV, White spruce (5) (1913), Yew pine (5, 75) (1894–1913)

Picea mariana B.S.P. – See *Picea mariana* (Mill.) Britton, Sterns & Poggenb.

Picea nigra Link. – See *Picea mariana* (Mill.) Britton, Sterns & Poggenb.

Picea polita (Siebold & Zucc.) Carr. – See *Picea torano* (Siebold ex K. Koch) Koehne

Picea pungens Engelm. – Blue spruce (50, 136, 149) (1899–present), Colorado blue spruce (135, 136, 153) (1910–1930), Colorado spruce (109, 112, 136, 138) (1923–1949), Silver spruce (136) (1930)

Picea rubens Sarg. – Cĭngob' (Chippewa) (40) (1928), Pitch pine (14) (1882), Red spruce (5, 10, 19, 38, 50, 109, 138) (1818–present), Spruce (40) (1928), Spruce fir (19) (1840)

Picea sitchensis (Bong.) Carr. – Sitka spruce (109, 138) (1923–1949)

Picradenia acaulis (Nutt.) Britton – See *Tetraneuris acaulis* (Pursh) Greene var. *acaulis*

Picradenia Hook – See *Hymenoxys* Cass.

Picradenia odorata (DC.) Britton – See *Hymenoxys odorata* DC.

Picradenia richardsonii Hook. – See *Hymenoxys richardsonii* (Hook.) Cockerell var. *richardsonii*

Picradeniopsis oppositifolia (Nutt.) Rydb. ex Britton – Bahia (131, 148) (1899–1948), Opposite-leaf bahia [Oppositeleaf bahia] (50) (present), Picradeniopsis (5, 97) (1913–1937), Plains bahia (155) (1942)

Picradeniopsis oppositifolius (Nutt.) Rydb. – See *Picradeniopsis oppositifolia* (Nutt.) Rydb. ex Britton

Picradeniopsis Rydb. ex Britton – Bahia (50) (present)

Picradeniopsis woodhousei (Gray) Rydb. – Woodhouse's bahia (50)

(present)

Picrasma excelsa (Sw.) Planch. – Bitter-ash [Bitter ash] (92) (1876), Bitter-bark [Bitter bark] (92) (1876), Bitterwood [Bitter-wood, Bitter wood] (15, 92) (1876–1895), Quassia (92) (1876)

Picris echioides L. – Bristly ox-tongue [Bristly oxtongue] (5, 50, 155, 50, 156, 158) (1900–present), Bugloss [Buglos, Buglosse] (5, 156, 158) (1900–1923), Bugloss picris [Bugloss-picris] (5, 156, 158) (1900–1923), Oxtongue [Ox-tongue] (3, 4, 107, 156) (1919–1986)

Picris hieracioides L. – Hawkweed [Hawk-weed, Hawk weed, Hawkeweed] (156) (1923), Hawkweed picris (5) (1913), Lang-de-beef [Langue-de-beef, Langbebefe] (5, 156) (1913–1923), Picris (92) (1876)

Picrothamnus desertorum Nutt. – Bud sagebrush (155) (1942)

Pieris floribunda (Pursh) Benth. & Hook. – See *Pieris floribunda* (Pursh) Benth. & Hook. f.

Pieris floribunda (Pursh) Benth. & Hook. f. – Mountain andromeda (138) (1923), possibly Mountain fetter-bush (5, 156) (1913–1923)

Pieris lucida (H. Levar.) – See *Vaccinium bracteatum* var. *bracteatum*

Pilea fontana (Lunell) Rydb. – Lesser clearweed (50) (present)

Pilea involucrata (Sims) Urban – Panamigo (109) (1949)

Pilea Lindl. – Clearweed [Clear weed] (1, 4, 50, 155, 158) (1900–present), Coolweed [Cool weed] (158) (1900), Richweed [Rich-weed, Rich weed] (1) (1932)

Pilea microphylla (L.) Liebm. – Artillery (109) (1949)

Pilea microphylla Liebm. – See *Pilea microphylla* (L.) Liebm.

Pilea nummularifolia Wedd. – See *Pilea nummulariifolia* (Sw.) Weddell

Pilea nummulariifolia (Sw.) Weddell – Creeping Cherley (109) (1949)

Pilea pumila (L.) Gray – Canadian clearweed [Canada clearweed] (50, 155) (1942–present), Clearweed [Clear weed] (3, 5, 97, 156) (1913–1977), Coolweed [Cool weed] (5, 155, 156) (1913–1942), Deadnettle [Dead-nettle, Dead nettle] (156) (1923), False nettle [Falsenettle] (156) (1923), Richweed [Rich-weed, Rich weed] (5, 35, 155, 156) (1806–1942), Silverweed [Silver weed, Silver-weed] (156) (1923), Stingless nettle (5, 93, 156) (1913–1936), Waterweed [Water weed, Water-weed] (78) (1898) Sulphur Grove OH

Pilea pumila (L.) Gray var. *pumila* – Clearweed [Clear weed] (19, 92, 95, 131, 158) (1840–1911), Coolweed [Cool weed] (7, 92, 158) (1828–1900), Pellucid nettle (187) (1818), Richweed [Rich-weed, Rich weed] (9, 72, 92, 158) (1840–1907), Stingless nettle (19, 92, 158) (1840–1900)

Pilea serpyllifolia (Poir.) Wedd. – See *Pilea trianthemoides* (Sw.) Lindl.

Pilea trianthemoides (Sw.) Lindl. – Artillery plant (92) (1876)

Piloblephis rigida (Bartr. ex Benth.) Raf. – Wild pennyroyal (106) (1930)

Pilobolus Tode – Horse Dung Mushroom with dewey heads (181) (~1678)

Pilostyles thurberi Gray – Thurber's stem-sucker [Thurber's stem-sucker] (50) (present)

Pilularia americana A. Braun – American pillwort (4, 50) (1986–present)

Pilularia globulifera L. – See *Calamistrum globuliferum* (L.) Kuntze

Pilularia L. – Pillwort [Pill-wort] (4, 50) (1986–present)

Pimenta dioica (L.) Merr. – Allspice (92, 107, 109, 138) (1876–1949), Clove pepper (92) (1876)

Pimenta officinalis Lindl. – See *Pimenta dioica* (L.) Merr.

Pimenta racemosa (P. Mill.) J. W. Moore – Bay tree [Bay-tree] (109) (1949), Bay-rum tree [Bay-rum-tree] (109) (1949)

Pimpinella anisum L. – Anise (53, 55, 57, 107, 138) (1917–1923), Anise-seed [Anise seed, Anniseede] (92, 178) (1526–1876), Anisum (57, 59, 178) (1596–1917), Anys (179) (1526), Commyn (179) (1526), Roman fennel (107) (13th century)

Pimpinella L. – Anise (138) (1923)

Pimpinella magna – See *Pimpinella major* (L.) Huds.

Pimpinella major (L.) Huds. – Pimpinella (92) (1876)

Pimpinella nigra [Mill.] – See *Pimpinella saxifraga* L. subsp. *nigra*

(Mill.) Gaudin

Pimpinella saxifraga L. – Bennet (5, 156) (1913–1923), Burnet saxifrage [Burnet-saxifrage] (5, 156) (1913–1923), Pimpernel (5, 92, 156) (1876–1923), Pimpernell [Pympernell] (179) (1526), Pimpinel [Pimpinell] (92, 179) (1526–1876), Pimpinella (174) (1753), Self-heal [Self heal, Selfheal, Selfe heale] (179) (1526), Small burnet saxifrage (92) (1876), Small pimpernel (92) (1876), Small saxifrage (92) (1876)

Pimpinella saxifraga L. subsp. *nigra* (Mill.) Gaudin – False pimpernel [Falsepimpernel] (92) (1876)

Pinaropappus roseus (Less.) Less. – White rock-lettuce [White rock-lettuce] (50) (present), White-dandelion [White dandelion] (124) (1937) TX

Pinckneya bracteata (Bartr.) Raf. – Bitter-bark [Bitter bark] (7, 92) (1828–1876), Carolina bark (92) (1876), Fever tree (7, 92) (1828–1876), Florida bark (7, 92) (1828–1876), Georgia bark (7, 20, 92) (1828–1876), Pinckney bark (7, 92) (1828–1876), Quinquina pinckney (French) (7) (1828)

Pinckneya Michx. – Fever tree (2) (1895), Georgia bark (2) (1895)

Pinguicula (Tourn.) L. – See *Pinguicula* L.

Pinguicula elatior Michx – See *Isoloba elatior* (Michx.) Raf.

Pinguicula L. – Butterwort [Butter wort, Butter woorts] (1, 2, 10, 156) (1818–1932), Rot-grass [Rot grass] (92) (1876)

Pinguicula lutea Walt. – Yellow butterwort (86) (1878)

Pinguicula pumila Michx. – Low butterwort (122) (1937) TX

Pinguicula villosa L. – Hairy butterwort (5) (1913)

Pinguicula vulgaris L. – Beanweed [Bean-weed] (5, 156) (1913–1923), Bog-violet [Bog violet] (5, 156) (1913–1923), Butterwort [Butter wort, Butter woorts] (156, 178) (1526–1923), Common butterwort (5) (1913), Earning grass [Earning-grass] (5, 156) (1913–1923), Rot-grass [Rot grass] (5, 156) (1913–1923), Sheep root [Sheep-root] (5, 156) (1913–1923), Sheep rot [Sheep-rot] (5, 156) (1913–1923), Sheepweed [Sheep weed, Sheep-weed] (5, 156) (1913–1923), Steepgrass [Steep grass] (5, 156) (1913–1923), Yorkshire sanicle (5, 86, 156) (1878–1923) old British name

Pinus abies-americana – See *Tsuga canadensis* (L.) Carr.

Pinus alba [Ait.] – See *Picea glauca* (Moench) Voss

Pinus albicaulis Engelm. – Alpine pine (101) (1905) MT, Nut pine [Nut-pine] (101) (1905) MT, Sliva (inner bark) (101) (1905) MT, Tibap (Snake, nuts) (101) (1905) MT, White-bark pine [Whitebark pine] (138) (1923)

Pinus alcoquiana (Vietch ex Lindley) Parl. ex Lindl. – See Picea alcoquiana (H. J.Veitch ex Lindl.) Carrière

Pinus aristata Engelm. – Bristle-cone pine [Bristle cone pine, Bristlecone pine] (109, 138, 153) (1923–1949), Bull pine (153) (1913) NM, Foxtail pine (153) (1913) NM, Hickory pine (109, 153) (1913–1949)

Pinus arizonica Engelm. – Arizona pine (138) (1923)

Pinus attenuata Lemmon – Knob-cone pine [Knobcone pine] (109, 138) (1923–1949)

Pinus australis – See *Picea rubens* Sarg.

Pinus balfouriana Grev. & Balf. – Foxtail pine (138) (1923)

Pinus balsamea L. – See *Abies balsamea* (L.) Mill.

Pinus banksiana Lamb. – Bank's pine (5) (1913), Banksia pine [Banksian pine] (1, 20) (1857–1932), Black pine (5) (1913), Black-jack [Black jack, Black-jacks] (32) (1895) Neb, Gray pine [Grey pine] (1, 5, 10, 20, 136) (1818–1932), Hudson Bay pine (5, 19) (1840–1913), Jack pine (5, 50, 75, 109, 112, 136, 138, 155) (1894–present), Labrador pine (5) (1913), Northern scrub pine (1, 20, 136) (1857–1932), Rock pine (5, 32, 75) (1894–1913), Scrub pine (10, 20) (1818–1857), Shore pine (5, 19, 75) (1840–1913), Shrub pine (78) (1898) Western US, Unlucky tree (5, 75) (1894–1913) Adirondacks, unlucky especially for women to stand under this tree

Pinus brachyptera Engelm. – See *Pinus ponderosa* P. & C. Lawson var. *ponderosa*

Pinus canadensis L. – See *Tsuga canadensis* (L.) Carr.

Pinus caribaea Morelet. – See *Pinus elliottii* Engelm. var. *elliottii*

Pinus cembra L. – Carpathian balsam (92) (1876), Cembra pine (92)

(1876), Pine nuts (92) (1876), Riga balsam (92) (1876), Russian cedar (107) (1919), Stone pine (92) (1876), Swiss stone pine (92, 106, 107, 138) (1876–1930)

Pinus cembroides **Zucc.** – Mexican stone pine (109, 138) (1923–1949), Nut pine of northeastern Mexico (147) (1856), Piñon [Pinyon] (109) (1949)

Pinus cembroides **Zucc. var.** *edulis* **(Engelm.) Voss** – See *Pinus flexilis* James

Pinus contorta **Dougl. ex Loud.** – Lodgepole pine [Lodge-pole pine] (3, 50) (1977–present), Pitch pine (35) (1806), Shore pine (3, 109, 138) (1923–1977), Twisted pine (161) (1857), Twisted-branch pine [Twisted-branched pine] (20) (1857)

Pinus contorta **Dougl. ex Loud. subsp.** *murrayana* **(Grev. & Balf.) Critchfield** – See *Pinus contorta* Dougl. ex Loud. var. *latifolia* Engelm. ex Wats

Pinus contorta **Dougl. ex Loud. var.** *latifolia* **Engelm. ex Wats** – Lodgepole pine [Lodge-pole pine] (1, 85, 101, 112, 136, 138, 155) (1886–1942), Murray's lodgepole pine [Murray lodgepole pine] (50) (present), Wazi (Dakota) (37) (1830)

Pinus contorta **Loud.** – See *Pinus contorta* Dougl. ex Loud.

Pinus coulteri **D. Don** – Big-cone pine (109) (1949)

Pinus coulteri **D. Don** – Coulter's pine [Coulter pine] (20, 50, 109, 138) (1857–present) for Thomas Coulter, 1793–1843, Irish botanit

Pinus douglasii **[Sabine ex D. Don]** – See *Pseudotsuga menziesii* (Mirb.) Franco

Pinus echinata **Mill.** – Bull pine (5) (1913), Carolina pine (5) (1913), Pin à cône épineux (French) (8) (1785), Pitch pine (5) (1913), Short-leaf pine [Shortleaf pine, Short-leafed pine, Short-leaved pine] (5, 20, 50, 65, 109, 122, 124, 138, 155) (1857–present), Short-leaf yellow pine [Short leaf yellow pine, Short-leaved yellow pine] (2, 97) (1895–1937), Short-shot pine [Short shot pine] (5, 35) (1806–1913), Slash pine (5) (1913), Spruce pine (5, 20) (1857–1913), Three-leaf prickly-cone bastard pine [Three leaved prickly-coned bastard pine] (8) (1785), Three-leaf yellow pine [Three-leaved yellow pine] (19) (1840), Yellow pine (1, 2, 10, 147) (1818–1932)

Pinus edulis **Engelm.** – Edible pine (103) (1871), New Mexico pinyon (158) (1900), Nut pine [Nut-pine] (75, 107, 138) (1894–1923), Nut pine of New Mexico (75, 147) (1856–1894), Piñon [Pinyon] (75, 97, 147, 149, 153, 158) (1856–1937) NM, Mexico, Piñon pine [Pinon pine] (3, 107, 147) (1856–1977), Two-needle pinyon [Twoneedle pinyon] (50) (present)

Pinus elliottii **Engelm. var.** *elliottii* – Slash pine (109) (1949)

Pinus excelsa **[Lam.]** – See *Picea abies* (L.) H. Karst.

Pinus flexilis **James** – American cembra pine (4, 20) (1857–1986), Colorado pinyon pine (155) (1942), Flexible pine (108) (1878), Limber pine (1, 3, 5, 17, 19, 50, 85, 109, 112, 122, 136, 138, 153, 155) (1796–present), Nut pine [Nut-pine] (109) (1949), Pin cembrot d'Amerique (French) (20) (1857), Piñon pine [Pinyon pine] (122, 124) (1937) TX, Rocky Mountain white pine (147) (1856), Western white pine (136, 153) (1913–1930)

Pinus griffithii **McClelland** – See *Pinus wallichiana* A.B. Jacks.

Pinus halepensis **Mill.** – Aleppo pine (109, 138) (1923–1949)

Pinus inops **Ait.** – See *Pinus virginiana* Mill.

Pinus inops **Lam.** – possibly *Pinus virginiana* Mill. (not in US PL W3 IPNI)

Pinus jeffreyi **Grev. & Balf.** – Black pine (109) (1949), Jeffrey's pine [Jeffrey pine] (109, 138) (1923–1949)

Pinus **L.** – A'-she-ki (Zuñi) (132) (1855), BaΘoŋ (Osage) (121) (1918–1970), Cembra pine (50) (present), Hah'-ñi (Kiwomi Keres) (132) (1855), Ha-shi (Navajo) (132) (1855), Hemlock [Hemloc, Hemlocke] or Hemlock tree (167) (1814), I'-pah (Kioway) (132) (1855), Ku'-we (Delaware) (132) (1855), Pin (French) (8) (1785), Pine or Pine tree (4, 7, 8, 50, 109, 121, 158, 155, 167, 184) (1785–present) Classic Latin name of Celtic origin, S'she-quoi (Shawnee) (132) (1855), Ti-ak(Choctaw) (132) (1855), Wazi (Lakota) (121) (1918–1970), Wŏr-co-bith (Comanche Shoshonee) (132) (1855)

Pinus lambertiana **Dougl.** – Giant pine (107) (1919), Gigantic pine (10,

20) (1818–1857), Pin gigantique de Lambert (French) (20) (1857), Sugar pine (50, 75, 107, 109, 138, 145, 161) (1894–present), False manna (92) (1876)

Pinus larix **L.** – See *Larix decidua* Mill.

Pinus larix **var.** *alba* **Castigl.** – See *Larix laricina* (Du Roi) Koch

Pinus leucodermis **Antoine** – See *Pinus heldreichii* H. Christ

Pinus monophylla **Torr. & Frém.** – Nut pine [Nut-pine] (107, 147) (1856–1919), Nut pine of California (147) (1856), Piñon [Pinyon] (147) (1856), Single-leaf pine [Singleleaf pine] (138) (1923), Stone pine (107) (1919)

Pinus monticola **Dougl. ex D. Don** – Mountain white pine (109, 138) (1923–1949), Western white pine (50, 109) (1949–present), White pine (20, 35) (1806–1857)

Pinus mughus – See *Pinus mugo* Turra

Pinus mugo **Turra** – Dwarf mountain pine (136) (1930), Dwarf pine (57) (1917), Mugho pine (112, 135, 136, 138) (1910–1937), Shrubby Swiss pine (138) (1923), Swiss mountain pine (109, 136, 138) (1923–1949)

Pinus muricata **D. Don** – Bishop's pine [Bishop pine] (50, 109, 138) (1923–present), Smaller prickly-cone pine [Smaller prickly-coned pine] (20) (1857)

Pinus nigra **Arnold** – Austrian pine (109, 112, 136, 138) (1923–1949), Corsican pine (138) (1923)

Pinus nigra poiretiana – See *Pinus nigra* Arnold

Pinus osteosperma **[Engelm.]** – See *Pinus cembroides* Zucc.

Pinus palustris **Mill.** – Broom pine (20, 92, 182) (1791–1876), Colophony (92) (1876) source, Fat pine (5, 19) (1840–1913), Florida pine (5) (1913), Georgia pine (5, 52) (1913–1919), Georgia pitch pine (20) (1857), Great long-lived pine (182) (1791), Hard pine (5) (1913), Heart pine (5) (1913), Longest three-leaf marsh pine [Longest three leaved marsh pine] (8) (1785), Long-leaf pine [Longleaf pine, Long-leafed pine, Long-leaved pine] (2, 50, 52, 109, 122, 138, 182) (1791–present), Long-leaf pitch pine [Long-leaved pitch pine] (182) (1791), Long-straw pine (5, 10, 20, 19) (1818–1913), Pin de marais (French) (8) (1785), Pine broom (5) (1913), Pitch pine (5, 52, 92, 182) (1791–1919), Red pine (20) (1857), Southern pine (5) (1913), Southern yellow pine (2, 20) (1857–1895), Terebintha (57) (1917) source. Terebinthinae laricis (57) (1917) source, Texas yellow pine (5) (1913), Thus americanum (55) (1911) source, Turpentine pine (5) (1913), Virginia pine (5) (1913), White rosin or White rosin tree (5, 92) (1876–1913), Yellow pine (5) (1913), Yellow pitch pine (10, 20, 92) (1818–1876)

Pinus parryana **[Engelm.]** – See *Pinus quadrifolia* Parl. ex Sudworth

Pinus pinaster **Aiton** – Cluster pine (92, 109, 138) (1923–1949)

Pinus pinea **L.** – Italian stone pine (50, 109, 139) (1944–present), Pine nuts (92) (1876), Stone pine (20, 107) (1857–1919) SD

Pinus ponderosa **P. & C. Lawson** – Sinclair's pine (5, 8, 10, 20, 19, 40) (1818–1928), Bluff pine (108) (1878), Bull pine (32, 135, 158) (1895–1910), Gambier Parry's pine (158) (1900), Heavy-wood pine [Heavy-wooded pine] (1, 20, 136) (1857–1932), Long-leaf pine [Longleaf pine, Long-leafed pine, Long-leaved pine] (35, 158) (1806–1900) of the West, Meriwether Lewis, Missoula pine (101) (1905) MT, Ponderosa pine (3, 50, 155) (1942–present), Rocky Mountain yellow pine (4, 32) (1895–1986), Trucker pine (158) (1900), Western pitch pine (158) (1900), Western yellow pine (97, 109, 112, 138, 155, 158, 161) (1857–1949), Yellow pine (75, 101, 108, 135, 161) (1857–1910)

Pinus ponderosa **P. & C. Lawson subsp.** *coulteri* **(D. Don) E. Murr.** – See *Pinus coulteri* D. Don

Pinus ponderosa **P. & C. Lawson var.** *ponderosa* – Bull pine (153) (1913), New Mexico yellow pine [New Mexican yellow pine] (147) (1856), Pitch pine (75, 147) (1856–1894), Western yellow pine (122) (1937) TX, Yellow pine (75, 147, 153) (1856–1913)

Pinus ponderosa **P.& C. Lawson var.** *scopulorum* **Engelm.** – Black Hills pine (136) (1930) SD, Bull pine (1, 75, 136, 149) (1894–1932), Gambier Parry's pine (5) (1913), Long-leaf pine [Longleaf pine, Long-leafed pine, Long-leaved pine] (5) (1913), Ponderosa pine (50) (present), Red pine (5) (1913), Rock pine (1, 136) (1930–1932), Rocky Mountain ponderosa pine [RockyMountain ponderosa pine] (155) (1942), Rocky Mountain yellow pine (136, 138) (1923–1930), Western pitch pine (5) (1913), Western yellow pine (85, 122, 131, 136) (1899–1937), Yellow pine (113, 130) (1890–1895)

Pinus ponderosa scopulorum **Engelm.** – See *Pinus ponderosa* P. & C. Lawson var. *scopulorum* Engelm.

Pinus pumila **Regel** – See *Pinus pumila* (Pall.) Regel

Pinus pumilio **Haenke in Jirazek et al** – See *Pinus mugo* Turra

Pinus pungens **Lamb.** – Hickory pine (5) (1913), Prickly pine (2) (1895), Southern mountain pine (5) (1913), Table Mountain pine (2, 50, 138) (1895–present)

Pinus quadrifolia **Parl. ex Sudworth** – Parry's pine [Parry pine] (138) (1923)

Pinus radiata **D. Don** – Monterey pine (50, 109, 138) (1923–present), Oregon pitch pine (20) (1857), Seal pine (147) (1856), Spreading-cone pine [Spreading-coned pine] (5, 10, 20, 19) (1818–1857)

Pinus radiata **D. Don var.** *binata* **auct. non (S. Wats.) Lemmon** – See *Pinus radiata* D. Don

Pinus resinosa **Ait.** – See *Pinus resinosa* Aiton

Pinus resinosa **Aiton** – Canadian pine (5) (1913), Hard pine (5, 78) (1898–1913) ME, Jĩŋgwak' (Chippewa) (40) (1928), Norway pine (1, 20, 75, 78, 92, 136) (1857–1932), Pin rouge (French Canada) (20) (1857), Pitch pine (5, 10, 19) (1818–1840), Red pine (1, 20, 43, 50, 109, 112, 136, 138) (1820–present), Yellow pine (5, 19, 40) (1840–1928)

Pinus resinosa **Soland.** – See *Pinus resinosa* Aiton

Pinus rigida **Lambert** – possibly *Pinus rigida* Mill.

Pinus rigida **Mill.** – Black pine (10, 38, 43, 187) (1818–1820), Common three-leaf Virginia pine [Common three leaved Virginian pine] (8, 20) (1785–1857), Northern pitch pine (2) (1895), Pin de Virginie à trois feuilles (French) (8) (1785), Pitch pine (5, 46, 50, 109, 138, 187) (1818–present), Pitch tree (46) (1879), Sap pine (10, 19, 20) (1805–1857), Three-leaf Virginia pine [Three-leaved Virginian pine] (20) (1857), Torch pine (5) (1913)

Pinus rigida **Mill. subsp.** *serotina* **(Michx.) Clausen** – See *Pinus serotina* Michx.

Pinus sabiniana **Dougl. ex Dougl.** – California foothill pine (50) (present), Digger pine (107, 109, 138) (1919–1949), Nut pine [Nut-pine] (161) (1857) CA, Pin de sabine à grands cones epineux (French) (20) (1857), Prickly coned pine (20) (1857), Sabine's pine (20, 147, 161) (1856–1857)

Pinus scopulorum **(Engelman.) Lemmon.** – See *Pinus ponderosa* P. & C. Lawson var. *scopulorum* Engelm.

Pinus serotina **Michx.** – Pond pine (2, 50, 138) (1895–present)

Pinus strobiformis **Engelm.** – Mexican white pine (138) (1923)

Pinus strobus **L.** – Ameda (46) (1879), Apple pine (5, 10, 19, 20) (1818–1913), Cowaw-esuck (Narragansett) (46) (1879), Deal pine (5, 92) (1876–1913), Eastern white pine (50) (present), Jĩŋgwak' (Chippewa) (40) (1928), New England pine (8) (1785), Northern pine (5) (1913), Pin du Lord Weymouth (French) (8) (1785), Pumpkin pine (20) (1857), Sapling pine (20) (1857), Soft pine (5) (1913), Spruce pine (5) (1913), Weymouth pine (5, 46, 57) (1913–1917), White pine (1, 2, 10, 46, 57, 72, 92, 109, 112, 136, 138) (1818–1949), Yellow pine (78) (1898) Western US, possibly Board pine (46) (1879)

Pinus sylvestris **L.** – Pinaster (178) (1596), Pine wool (92) (1876) leaf fiber, Red deal (England) (20) (1857), Riga pine (136, 138) (1923–1930), Scotch fir (20, 55) (1857–1911), Scotch pine (32, 50, 107, 112, 136) (1895–present), Scots pine (109, 136, 138) (1923–1949), Wild pine (20, 92) (1857–1876), Yellow deal (20) (1857)

Pinus sylvestris rigensis – See *Pinus sylvestris* L.

Pinus taeda **L.** – Bastard pine (5) (1913), Foxtail pine (5) (1913), Frankincense tree (181) (~1678), Frankinsence pine (5) (1913), Indian pine (5, 8, 14) (1785–1882), Loblolly (92) (1876), Loblolly pine (2, 50, 97, 109, 122, 138) (1895–present), Long-shucks (5, 20,

19) (1840–1913), Long-straw pine (5) (1913), New Jersey fir tree (41) (1770), Old-field pine (2) (1895), Pin à l'encens (French) (5, 8, 10, 19) (1785–1913), Rosemary pine (5) (1913), Sap pine (5) (1913), Short-leaf pine [Shortleaf pine, Short-leafed pine, Short-leaved pine] (5) (1913), Slash pine (5) (1913), Swamp pine (5) (1913), Torch pine (5) (1913), Virginia swamp pine [Virginian swamp pine] (8) (1785), White pine (20) (1857)

Pinus thunbergiana **Franco** – Japanese black pine (109, 138) (1923–1949)

Pinus torreyana **Parry ex Carr.** – Soledad pine (109) (1949), Torrey's pine [Torrey pine] (109, 138) (1923–1949) For John Torrey, 1796–1873, New York

Pinus variabilis **Lb.** – See *Pinus echinata* Mill.

Pinus virginiana **Mill.** – Cedar pine (5) (1913), Jersey pine (5, 10) (1818–1913), Jersey scrub pine (2, 19) (1840–1895), New Jersey pine (20, 187) (1818–1857), Pin de Jersey (French) (8) (1785) misapplied, Pin de Virginies à dois feuilles (French) (8) (1785), River pine (5) (1913), Scrub pine (5, 20, 109, 138, 187) (1818–1949), Short shot pine (5) (1913) OK TX, Short shucks (5) (1913), Short-leaf pine [Shortleaf pine, Short-leafed pine, Short-leaved pine] (5) (1913), Spruce pine (5) (1913), Two-leaf Virginia pine [Two-leaved Virginian pine] (8) (1785), Virginia pine (50) (present), possibly Pitch pine (187) (1818)

Pinus wallichiana **A. B. Jacks.** – Himalayan pine (109) (1949)

Pinus-abies – possibly *Picea abies* (L.) H. Karst.

Pinus-abies balsamea – possibly *Abies balsamea* (L.) Mill.

Pinus-larix – possibly *Larix decidua* Mill.

Pinus-larix nigra – possibly *Larix laricina* (Du Roi) Koch

Pinus-larix rubra – possibly *Larix laricina* (Du Roi) Koch

Piper aduncum **L.** – Soldier's-herb [Soldiers' herb] (92) (1876)

Piper **L.** – Pepper (109, 138) (1923–1949)

Piper leptostachyon **Nutt.** – See *Peperomia humilis* A. Dietr.

Piperia **Rydb.** – Rein orchid (50) (present), Wood orchid (1) (1932)

Piperia unalascensis **(Spreng.) Rydb.** – Alaska piperia (5) (1913), Alaskan orchis (3) (1977), Slender-spire orchid (50) (present)

Piptatheropsis exigua **(Thurb.) Romasch., P. M. Peterson & R. J. Soreng** – Little mountain-rice [Little mountain rice] (94) (1901), Little rice grass [Little ricegrass] (50, 155) (1942–present)

Piptatherum **Beauv.** – Rice grass [Ricegrass] (50) (present)

Piptatherum canadense **(Poir) Barkworth** – Canadian rice [Canada rice] (66, 90) (1885–1903), Canadian rice grass [Canadian ricegrass] (50) (present), Macoun's feather grass (5, 19) (1840–1913), Macoun's stipa (94) (1901), Richardson's feather grass [Richardson's feather-grass] (5) (1913), Small mountain rice (94) (1901), Smallest oryzopsis (66, 90) (1885–1903)

Piptatherum micranthum **(Trin. & Rupr.) Barkworth** – Indian millet (94, 129) (1894–1901), Little-seed ricegrass [Littleseed ricegrass] (3, 50, 155) (1942–present), Mountain-rice [Mountain rice] (111) (1915), Small Indian millet (3, 5) (1913–1977), Small-flower mountain rice [Small-flowered mountain rice] (5, 94) (1901–1913)

Piptatherum pungens **(Torr.) Barkworth** – Dwarf millet grass (19) (1840), Mountain rice grass [Mountain ricegrass] (3, 50) (1977–present), Mountain-rice [Mountain rice] (85) (1932), Short-horn rice grass [Shorthorn ricegrass] (155) (1942), Slender mountain rice (5) (1913)

Piptatherum pungens **(Torr.) Dorn** – See *Piptatherum pungens* (Torr.) Barkworth

Piptochaetium avenaceum **(L.) Parodi** – Black oat grass [Black oat-grass] (5, 45, 66, 92, 94, 163) (1852–1913), Black-seed needlegrass [Blackseed needlegrass] (92, 122) (1876–1937), Black-seed spear grass [Blackseed speargrass] (50) (present), Feather grass [Feather-grass, Feather-grass] (5, 92, 184) (1793–1913)

Piptochaetium avenacioides **(Nash) Valencia & Costas** – Feather grass [Feathergrass, Feather-grass] (94) (1901)

Piptochaetium bicolor **(Vahl) É. Desv.** – Two-color feather grass [Two-coloured feather-grass] (187) (1818)

Piptochaetium fimbriatum **(Kunth) A. S. Hitchc.** – Piñon grass [Pinon grass] (152) (1912) NM, Piñon rice grass [Pinyon ricegrass, Pinyon

Piptochaetium pringlei (Beal) Parodi

rice grass] (122) (1937) TX

***Piptochaetium pringlei* (Beal) Parodi** – Pringle's feather grass [Pringle's feather-grass] (94) (1901), Pringle's needle grass [Pringle needlegrass] (122) (1937)

***Pirus malus* L.** – See *Malus sylvestris* (L.) Mill.

***Piscidia erythrina* L.** – See *Piscidia piscipula* (L.) Sarg.

***Piscidia piscipula* (L.) Sargent** – Boisivrant de la Jamaique (French) (20) (1857), Jamaica dogwood (20, 52, 53, 55, 57, 60, 92, 106) (1857–1930), Piscidia (55) (1911)

***Pisonia aculeata* L.** – Fingrigo (20) (1857), Pisone épineusse (French) (20) (1857), Pisonia (174) (1753), Prickly pisonia (20) (1857)

***Pisophaca* Rydb.** – See *Astragalus* L.

Pistachia atlantica – See *Pistacia atlantica* Desf.

***Pistacia atlantica* Desf.** – Mount Atlas pistache (138) (1923), Terebinth (138) (1923)

***Pistacia chinensis* Bunge** – Chinese pistache (138) (1923)

***Pistacia* L.** – Pistache (138) (1923)

***Pistacia mutica* Fisch. & C. A. Mey.** – See *Pistacia atlantica* Desf.

***Pistacia simaruba* L.** – See *Bursera simaruba* (L.) Sarg.

***Pistia* L.** – Water-lettuce [Waterlettuce] (138) (1923)

***Pistia stratiotes* L.** – Water-lettuce [Waterlettuce] (109, 138) (1923–1949)

***Pisum* L.** – Pea [Peas, Pease] (1, 10, 45, 109, 138) (1818–1949)

***Pisum maritimum* L.** – See *Lathyrus japonicus* Willd. var. *maritimus* (L.) Kartesz & Gandhi

***Pisum ochrus* L.** – See *Lathyrus ochrus* (L.) DC.

***Pisum sativum* L.** – Common pea (92, 138) (1876–1923), Early dwarf pea (109) (1949), Edible-pod pea [Edible-podded pea] (109) (1949), Field pea [Field-pea] (107, 109, 110) (1886–1949), Garden pea [Garden-pea] (3, 109, 110) (1886–1977), Gray pea [Grey pea] (107) (1919), Herbilia (Italian) (110) (930 AD), Mahometan pea (China) (110) (16th century), Pea [Peas, Pease] (19, 92, 107, 184) (1793–1919), Pea without parchment in the cods [Pease without parchment in the cods] (178) (1526), Rubiglia (Italian) (110) (1886), Scottish pease (178) (1526), Sweet pea [Sweetpea, Sweet peas] (7) (1828), Tufted peas [Tufted pease] (178) (1526)

***Pisum sativum* L. var. *arvense* (L.) Poir.** – See *Pisum sativum* L.

***Pisum sativum* L. var. *humile* Poir.** – See *Pisum sativum* L.

***Pisum sativum* L. var. *macrocarpon* Ser.** – See *Pisum sativum* L.

***Pithecellobium dulce* (Roxb.) Benth.** – Guamachil (138) (1923), Guamuchil (107) (1919), Guaymochil (109) (1949), Huamuchil (109) (1949), Manila tamarind (109) (1949), Opiuma (109) (1949)

***Pithecellobium dulce* Benth.** – See *Pithecellobium dulce* (Roxb.) Benth.

***Pithecellobium saman* Benth.** – See *Samanea saman* (Jacq.) Merr.

***Pithecellobium unguis-cati* (L.) Benth.** – Blunt-leaf inga [Blunt leaved inga] (20) (1857), Guadalupe inga [Guadaloupe inga] (20) (1857), Inga de la Guadaloupe (20) (1857), Inga ongle de chat (20) (1857)

***Pithecoctenium crucigerum* (L.) A. H. Gentry** – Bignone porte-croix (French) (8) (1785), Crossvine [Cross vine, Cross-vine] (8) (1785), Mexican monkeycomb (138) (1923)

***Pithecoctenium* Mart. ex Meisn.** – Monkey comb [Monkeycomb] (138) (1923)

***Pithecoctenium muricatum* [Moc. ex DC.]** – See *Pithecoctenium crucigerum* (L.) A. H. Gentry

***Pithecolobium flexicaule* (Benth.) Coulter** – See *Ebenopsis ebano* (Berland.) Barneby & J. W. Grimes

***Pittosporum* Banks ex Soland.** – Pittosporum (138) (1923)

***Pittosporum crassifolium* Banks & Soland. ex A. Cunningham** – Karo (109, 138) (1923–1949)

***Pittosporum crassifolium* Cunn.** – See *Pittosporum crassifolium* Banks & Soland. ex A. Cunningham

***Pittosporum tenuifolium* Banks & Soland.** – See *Pittosporum tenuifolium* Gaertn.

***Pittosporum tenuifolium* Gaertn.** – Kohuhu (109) (1949), Tawhiwhi (109, 138) (1923–1949)

***Pittosporum tobira* (Thunb.) Aiton f.** – Japanese pittosporum (109) (1949), Pitch-seed plant [Pitch seed plant] (92) (1876), Tobira (138) (1923)

***Pittosporum tobira* Aiton** – See *Pittosporum tobira* (Thunb.) Aiton f.

***Pittosporum undulatum* Vent.** – Orange pittosporum (138) (1923), Victorian-box (109) (1949)

***Pittosporum viridiflorum* Sims** – Cape pittosporum (138) (1923)

***Pityopsis falcata* (Pursh) Nutt.** – Golden aster [Golden-aster] (156) (1923), Ground goldflower [Ground gold-flower] (156) (1923), Sickle-leaf aster [Sickle-leaved aster] (5) (1913)

Pityopsis graminifolia* (Michx.) Nutt. var. *graminifolia – Golden aster [Golden-aster] (156) (1923), Goldenstar [Golden-star, Golden stars] (156) (1923), Grass-leaf golden aster [Grassleaf golden aster] (5, 97, 122) (1913–1937), Scurvy-grass [Scurvy grass, Scurvey grass] (5, 156) (1913–1923), Silver aster (156) (1923), Silver-grass [Silver grass] (5, 156) (1913–1923)

***Pityopsis graminifolia* var. *latifolia* (Fernald) Semple & F. D. Bowers** – Silver aster (92) (1876)

***Pityrogramma austroamericana* Domin** – Gold fern [Gold-fern, Goldfern] (109) (1949)

***Pityrogramma calomelanos* (L.) Link** – Silver fern [Silver-fern] (109) (1949)

***Pityrogramma calomelanos* Link** – See *Pityrogramma calomelanos* (L.) Link

***Pityrogramma calomelanos* Link var. *aureo-flava* Weatherby** – See *Pityrogramma austroamericana* Domin

***Pityrogramma ebenea* (L.) Proctor** – Silver fern [Silver-fern] (138) (1923)

***Pityrogramma* Link** – Gold fern [Gold-fern, Goldfern] (109, 138) (1923–1949), Silver fern [Silver-fern] (109) (1949)

***Pityrogramma sulphurea* (Sw.) Maxon** – Jamaica goldfern (138) (1923)

Pityrogramma tartarea – See *Pityrogramma ebenea* (L.) Proctor

***Pityrogramma triangularis* Maxon** – See *Pentagramma triangularis* (Kaulfuss) Yatskievych, Windham & Wollenweber

***Plagiobothrys* Fisch. & C. A. Mey.** – Allocarya (158) (1900), Popcorn flower [Popcorn-flower, Popcornflower] (50, 155) (1942–present)

***Plagiobothrys hispidulus* (Greene) I. M. Johnston** – See *Plagiobothrys scouleri* (Hook. & Arn.) I. M. Johnston var. *hispidulus* (Greene) Dorn

***Plagiobothrys scouleri* (Hook. & Arn.) I. M. Johnston** – Popcorn flower [Popcorn-flower, Popcornflower] (3, 4) (1977–1986), Scouler's popcorn-flower [Scouler's popcornflower, Scouler popcornflower] (50, 155) (1942–present)

***Plagiobothrys scouleri* (Hook. & Arn.) I. M. Johnston var. *hispidulus* (Greene) Dorn** – Hairy popcorn-flower [Hairy popcornflower] (155) (1942), Mountain allocarya (5, 93, 131) (1899–1936), Sleeping popcorn flower [Sleeping popcorn-flower, Sleeping popcornflower] (50) (present)

***Planera aquatica* Gmel.** – See *Planera aquatica* J.F. Gmel.

***Planera aquatica* J. F. Gmel.** – American planer tree (2) (1895), Sycamore or Sycamore tree [Sycamore-tree] (5, 156) (1913–1923), Water elm [Water-elm] (5, 97, 156) (1913–1937)

***Plantago* (Tourn.) L.** – See *Plantago* L.

***Plantago arenaria* Waldst. & Kit.** – See *Plantago psyllium* L.

***Plantago aristata* Michx.** – Bottle-rush Indian wheat [Bottlerush Indian-wheat] (155) (1942), Bracted plantain (3, 4, 62, 70, 80, 145) (1895–1986), Bristly buckhorn (62) (1912) IN, Buckhorn [Buck horn, Buckhorn, Buck's horn, Buckshorn, Buck's-horn, Bucks-horne, Bucks horne] (4) (1986), Large-bract plantain [Large-bracted plantain, Largebracted plantain] (5, 50, 72, 93, 97, 131, 156) (1899–present)

***Plantago asiatica* L.** – See *Plantago major* L.

***Plantago cordata* Lam** – Heart-leaf plantain [Heart-leaved plantain] (5, 156) (1913–1923), Water plantain (5, 48, 61, 92, 156) (1870–1923)

***Plantago coronopus* L.** – Buckhorn plantain [Buckshorn plantain] (92,

107) (1876–1919), Hartshorn [Harts horne] (178) (1526), Hartshorn plantain [Harts horn plantain] (92) (1876), Star-of-the-earth [Star of the earth] (107) (1919)

Plantago decipiens **Barn.** – See *Plantago maritima* L. var. *juncoides* (Lam.) Gray

Plantago elongata **Pursh** – Prairie plantain (50) (present), Slender plantain (4, 85, 97, 131) (1899–1986)

Plantago elongata **Pursh subsp.** *elongata* – Prairie plantain (50) (present)

Plantago eriopoda **Torr.** – Alkali plantain (3, 4) (1977–1986), Red-wool plantain [Redwool plantain] (50) (present), Saline plantain (5, 93, 95, 131) (1899–1936)

Plantago heterophylla **Nutt.** – Many-seed plantain [Many seeded plantain, Many-seeded plantain] (5, 97, 122) (1913–1937)

Plantago indica **L.** – See *Plantago psyllium* L.

Plantago juncoides **var.** *decipiens* **(Barnéoud) Fernald** – See *Plantago maritima* L. var. *juncoides* (Lam.) Gray

Plantago kentuckensis **Michx.** – possibly *Plantago cordata* Lam

Plantago **L.** – Plantain [Plantayne] (1, 2, 4, 10, 50, 63, 82, 93, 156, 158, 184) (1793–present), Rib-grass [Ribgrass, Rib grass] (1, 2, 93) (1932–1936)

Plantago lagopus **Pursh** – See *Plantago patagonica* Jacq.

Plantago lanceolata **L.** – Black-jack [Black jack, Black-jacks] (5, 156, 158) (1900–1923) no longer in use by 1923, Buck plantain [Buck-plantain] (5, 75, 156) (1894–1923) WV, Buckhorn [Buck horn, Buck-horn, Buck's horn, Buckshorn, Buck's-horn, Bucks-horne, Bucks horne] (4, 21, 62, 80, 82, 156) (1893–1986), Buck-horn plantain [Buck-horn plantain, Buck-horne plantaines] (75, 155, 156, 180) (1633–1942), Buckthorn plantain (5, 93) (1913–1936), Cat's-cradles [Cat's cradles] (5, 156) (1913–1923) no longer in use by 1923, Chimney-sweeps [Chimney sweeps] (5, 156, 157, 158) (1900–1929), Clock (5, 158) (1900–1913), Cocks (5, 156, 158) (1900–1923), Dog's-rib [Dogs rib, Dog-ribs] (5, 156, 158, 180) (1633–1923) no longer in use by 1923, English buckhorn plantain (85) (1932) SD, English plantain (3, 4, 5, 62, 63, 75, 82, 97, 145, 156, 157, 158) (1894–1986), Headsman [Headsmen] (5, 156, 158) (1900–1923), Hen plant [Hen-plant] (5, 156, 157, 158) (1900–1929), Hock-cockle [Hock cockle] (77) (1898) Southold Long Island, Jack-straws [Jack straws] (5, 156, 158) (1900–1923) no longer in use by 1923, Kemps [Kemp] (5, 62, 156, 157, 158) (1900–1929) IN, old English, Kempseed [Kemp-seed] (5, 62, 156, 158) (1900–1923) IN, old English, Klops (156) (1923) no longer in use by 1923, Knock-heads (156) (1923), Lance-leaf plantain [Lance-leaved plantain] (5, 45) (1896–1913), Lauten (Spanish) (158) (1900), Leechwort [Leech-wort] (5, 156, 157, 158) (1900–1929), Little plantain [Lytell plantayn] (179) (1526), Long plantain [Longe plantayn] (5, 156, 158, 179) (1526–1923), Narrow plantain (62) (1912), Narrow-leaf plantain [Narrowleaf plantain, Narrow-leaved plantain] (45, 50, 156) (1896–present), Plantain (French) (158) (1900), Ram's-tongue [Ram's tongue] (5, 156, 157, 158) (1900–1929), Rat-tail [Rattail] (5, 156, 158) (1900–1923), Rib plantain (56) (1901), Rib-grass [Ribgrass, Rib grass] (5, 45, 62, 82, 72, 80, 92, 95, 156, 157, 158) (1896–1929), Ribwort [Rib wort, Rib-wort, Rybwort] (5, 19, 62, 75, 92, 131, 156, 157, 158, 179, 187) (1526–1929), Ripple (75) (1894), Ripple plantain (5, 19, 97, 156) (1840–1937), Ripple-grass [Ripple grass] (5, 19, 62, 92, 156, 157, 158) (1840–1929) IN, Old English name, Rose ribwort [Rose ribwoort] (178) (1526), Snake plantain [Snake-plantain] (5, 92, 156, 157, 158) (1876–1929), Soldiers (77) (1898) Cambridge MA, Spitzer Wegetritt (German) (158) (1900), Way-bread [Way bread, Waybread] (158) (1900), Windles (5, 156, 158) (1900–1923) no longer in use by 1923

Plantago major **L.** – Asiatic plantain (155) (1942), Bird-seed plantain (157, 158) (1900–1929), Broad plantain (41) (1770), Broadleaf plantain [Broad-leaved plantain] (6, 156, 157, 158) (1892–1929), Cart-track plant (107, 156) (1919–1923), Common dooryard plantain (62) (1912), Common great plantain [Common great-plantane] (187) (1818), Common plantain (3, 4, 5, 43, 45, 47, 50, 63, 72, 80, 85, 93, 92, 97, 131, 145, 156, 157, 158) (1820–present), Dooryard plantain [Door-yard plantain] (5, 93, 122, 156, 157, 158) (1900–1937), Englishman's foot (41, 92) (1770–1876), Gine'biwŭck (Chippewa, snake-like) (40) (1928), Great plantain [Grete plantayne] (5, 7, 62, 179) (1526–1913), Greater plantain (156, 157, 158) (1900–1929), Grosser Wegerich (German) (158) (1900), Grosser Wegetritt (German) (6) (1892), Healing-blade [Healing blade] (5, 62, 156, 157, 158) (1900–1929) IN, old English name, Hen plant [Hen-plant] (5, 156, 157, 158) (1900–1929), Kemps [Kemp] (158) (1900), Lamb's-foot [Lamb's foot] (5, 156, 157, 158) (1900–1929), O'mûkiki'bûg (Chippewa, frog leaf) (40) (1928), Plaintain ordinaire (French) (6) (1892), Plantago (57) (1917), Plantain [Plantayne] (6, 19, 37, 40, 46, 49, 52, 53, 57, 107, 157, 158, 179) (1526–1939), Rib-grass [Ribgrass, Rib grass] (6, 49, 52, 53) (1892–1922), Ribwort [Rib wort, Rib-wort, Rybwort] (6, 49, 52, 53) (1892–1922), Ripple-grass [Ripple grass] (49, 52) (1898–1919), Ripple-seed plantain [Rippleseed plantain] (155) (1942), Round-leaf plantain [Round-leaved plantain] (5, 92, 156, 157, 158) (1876–1929), Sauohr (German) (158) (1900), Sinie makan (Omaha-Ponca) (37) (1919), Way-bread [Way bread, Way-bread] (5, 6, 92, 156, 157, 158, 187) (1818–1929), Way-bred [Way bred] (6) (1892), Wayside plantain [Way-side plantain] (5, 156) (1913–1923), Weybrede (179) (1526), White-man's-foot [White-man's foot] (5, 6, 158) (1892–1913), Woundweed [Wound weed] (62) (1912) IN, Old English name

Plantago maritima **L.** – Buckhorn [Buck horn, Buck-horn, Buck's horn, Buckshorn, Buck's-horn, Bucks-horne, Bucks horne] (5) (1913), Gibbals (5) (1913), Sea plantain [Sea Plantaine] (5, 19, 41, 180) (1526–1913), Sea-kemps [Sea kemps] (5) (1913), Sea-plantain [Sea-plantane] (46) (1671), Seaside plantain (5, 107) (1913–1919)

Plantago maritima **L. var.** *juncoides* **(Lam.) Gray** – Buckhorn [Buck horn, Buck-horn, Buck's horn, Buckshorn, Buck's-horn, Bucks-horne, Bucks horne] (156) (1923), Gibbals (156) (1923), Goose-tongue [Goose tongue] (156) (1923), Sea-kemps [Sea kemps] (156) (1923), Seaside plantain (156) (1923)

Plantago media **L.** – Fireleaves [Fire leaves, fire-leaves] (5, 156) (1913–1923), Fireweed [Fire weed, Fire-weed] (5, 156) (1913–1923), Healing herb [Healing-herb] (5, 156) (1913–1923), Hoary plantain (5, 156) (1913–1923), Kemps [Kemp] (92) (1876), Lamb's-legs (156) (1923), Lamb's-lettuce [Lamb's lettuce, Lamb lettuce] (5, 92) (1876–1913), Lamb's-tongue [Lambs tongue, Lambs tongue, Lambs' tongues] (5, 156) (1913–1923), Rib-grass [Ribgrass, Rib grass] (92) (1876)

Plantago patagonica aristata **Gray** – See *Plantago aristata* Michx.

Plantago patagonica **Jacq.** – Buckhorn [Buck horn, Buck-horn, Buck's horn, Buckshorn, Buck's-horn, Bucks-horne, Bucks horne] (3) (1977), India-wheat (146) (1939) MT, Large-bract plantain [Large-bracted plantain, Largebracted plantain] (97) (1937), Patagonian Indian wheat [Patagonia Indianwheat] (155) (1942), Plantain [Plantayne] (146) (1939), Prairie plantain (80, 108) (1878–1913), Pursh's plantain (5, 72, 97, 131, 156) (1899–1937), Rabbit's-foot plantain [Rabbit's foot plantain] (38) (1820), Salt-and-pepper plant [salt-and-pepper-plant] (5, 156) (1913–1923), Salt-and-pepper plant [Salt-and-pepper-plant] (5, 156) (1913–1923), Western plantain (93) (1936), Woolly Indian wheat [Woolly Indianwheat] (155) (1942), Woolly plantain (50, 85) (1932–present)

Plantago patagonica **Jacq. var.** *gnaphalioides* **(Nutt.) Gray** – See *Plantago patagonica* Jacq.

Plantago patagonica **Jacq. var.** *spinulosa* **(Dcne.) Gray** – See *Plantago patagonica* Jacq.

Plantago psyllium **L.** – Dwarf fleabane [Dwarfe Fleabane] (178) (1526), Flax-seed plantain [Flaxseed plantain] (155) (1942), Fleabane [Flea-bane, Flea bane] (178) (1526), Fleaseed [Flea seed] (92) (1876), Fleawort [Fleawort, Flea wort] (92) (1876), Indian plantain

(4) (1986), Psyllium (178) (1526), Sand plantain (5, 50) (1913–present), Whorled plantain (155) (1942)

Plantago psyllum – See *Plantago psyllium* L.

Plantago purshii **Roemer & J. A. Schultes** – See *Plantago patagonica* Jacq.

Plantago pusilla **Nutt.** – Slender plantain (3, 5) (1913–1977)

Plantago rhodosperma **Dcne.** – Pale plantain (5) (1913), Red-seed plantain [Redseed plantain, Red-seeded plantain] (3, 4, 50, 97, 155) (1937–present), White-man's-foot [White-man's foot] (5) (1913)

Plantago rugelii **Dcne.** – Black-seed plantain [Blackseed plantain] (50, 155) (1942–present), Pale plantain (62, 93, 156) (1912–1936), Plantain [Plantayne] (145) (1897), Rugel's plantain (3, 4, 5, 72, 80, 97, 131) (1899–1986), Silk plant [Silk-plant] (75, 156) (1894–1923), Silk-plant (75, 156) (1894–1923) FL, White-man's-foot [White-man's foot] (156) (1923)

Plantago spinulosa **Dcne.** – See *Plantago patagonica* Jacq.

Plantago virginica **L.** – Dwarf plantain (5, 19, 72, 93, 97) (1840–1937), Pale-seed plantain [Paleseed plantain, Pale-seeded plantain] (3, 155) (1942–1977), Virginia plantain (50) (present), White dwarf plantain (5, 62) (1912–1913)

Plantago wrightiana **Dcne.** – Wright's plantain [Wright plantain] (4, 97, 155) (1937–present)

Plantanthera lacera – See *Platanthera lacera* (Michx.) G. Don

Planus occidentalis – possibly *Platanus occidentalis* L.

Platanthera blephariglottis **(Willd.) Lindl. var.** *blephariglottis* – Feather-leaf orchis [Feather-leaved orchis] (5) (1913), White fringed orchid [White fringe-orchid] (138) (1923), White fringed orchis (2, 5, 109, 156) (1895–1949)

Platanthera ciliaris **(L.) Lindl.** – Orchis (19) (1840), Rattlesnake-master [Rattlesnake master, Rattlesnake's master, Rattlesnakes' master, Rattlesnake's-master] (156) (1923), Yellow fringed orchis [Yellow-fringed orchis] (2, 5, 109, 122, 156) (1895–1949), Yellow fringe-orchid (138) (1923)

Platanthera clavellata **(Michx.) Luer** – Three-tooth orchis [Three-toothed orchis] (156, 187) (1818–1923), Green wood orchis (156) (1923), Green woodland orchis (3) (1977), Small green wood orchid (5, 50) (1913–present), Wood orchid (85) (1932)

Platanthera cristata **(Michx.) Lindl.** – Short-spur orchis [Short-spurred orchis] (187) (1818)

Platanthera dilatata **(Pursh) Lindl. ex Beck** – Giant orchis (19) (1840), Scent-bottle [Scentbottle] (50) (present)

Platanthera dilatata **(Pursh) Lindl. ex Beck var.** *albiflora* **(Cham.) Ledeb.** – Scent-bottle [Scentbottle] (50) (present)

Platanthera dilatata **(Pursh) Lindl. ex Beck var.** *dilatata* – Scent-bottle [Scentbottle] (50) (present), Tall white bog orchis (5, 93, 109) (1913–1949), White bog orchid [White bog-orchid] (138) (1923), White orchis (3) (1977)

Platanthera dilatata **Lind.** – See *Platanthera dilatata* (Pursh) Lindl. ex Beck

Platanthera fimbriata **Lindl.** – See *Platanthera grandiflora* (Bigelow) Lindl.

Platanthera fissa – See *Platanthera psycodes* (L.) Lindl.

Platanthera flava **(L.) Lindl. var.** *flava* – Dog's-stones [Dogstones] (46) (1671), Green orchis (85) (1932), Green rein orchis (5, 156) (1913–1923), Greenish orchis (5, 156) (1913–1923), Pale-green orchid [Palegreen orchid] (50) (present), Small pale-green orchis (156) (1923), Tubercled orchis (5, 97, 156) (1913–1937), Yellow orchis (5, 156) (1913–1923)

Platanthera grandiflora **(Bigelow) Lindl.** – Dead-man's-fingers [Dead man's fingers] (156) (1923) no longer in use by 1923, Early purple-fringe orchis [Early purple-fringed orchis, Early purple fringed orchis] (5) (1913), Greater purple fringed orchid (50) (present), Large fringed orchis (156) (1923), Large purple fringed orchis (5) (1913), Large purple fringe-orchid (138) (1923), Larger purple fringed orchis (2) (1895), Long purples [Long-purples] (156) (1923) no longer in use by 1923, Meadow pink [Meadow-pink] (5, 73, 156)

(1892–1923) MA, Purple fringed orchis [Purple-fringed orchis] (156, 187) (1818–1923), Tattered fringed orchis (5, 156) (1913–1923), Wild hyacinth (78) (1898) ME

Platanthera hookeri **(Torr. ex Gray) Lindl.** – Hooker's orchid [Hooker orchid] (50, 138) (1923–present), Hooker's orchis (5, 72) (1907–1913) IA, Small two-leaved orchis (5) (1913), Solomon's-seal [Solomon's seal, Solomon seal, Solomon's seal, S'alomon's seal, Salamons seale] (5) (1913)

Platanthera hyperborea **(L.) Lindl.** – Northern green orchid (50) (present)

Platanthera hyperborea **(L.) Lindl. var.** *hyperborea* – Northern green orchid (50, 138) (1923–present), Northern green orchis (3, 5) (1913–1977), Tall leafy green orchis (5, 72, 93) (1907–1936)

Platanthera hyperborea **(L.) Lindl. var.** *viridiflora* **(Cham.) Luer** – Bog orchid (85) (1932)

Platanthera integra **(Nutt.) Gray ex Beck** – Small southern yellow orchis (5) (1913), Yellow fringeless orchid (50) (present)

Platanthera **L. C. Rich** – Bog orchid (1, 93) (1932–1936), Fringed orchid (1, 50) (1932–present)

Platanthera lacera **(Michx.) G. Don** – Dog's-stones [Dogstones] (46) (1671), Green fringed orchid (5, 50, 109, 156) (1913–present), Ragged fringed orchis (2) (1895), Ragged orchis (3, 5, 109, 156, 187) (1818–1977)

Platanthera leucophaea **(Nutt.) Lindl.** – Greenish fringed orchis [Greenish fringed-orchis] (158) (1900), Prairie fringed orchid (3) (1977), Prairie white fringed orchis [Prairie white fringed-orchis] (5, 50, 72, 93, 158) (1900–present), Western greenish fringed orchis (5) (1913), White fringed orchis (127) (1933), White-flower prairie orchis [White-flowered prairie orchis] (156) (1923), possibly Heal-all [Healall] (7) (1828)

Platanthera nivea **(Nutt.) Luer** – Snowy orchid (50) (present), Southern small white orchis (5) (1913)

Platanthera obtusata **(Banks ex Pursh) Lindl.** – Blunt-leaf orchid [Bluntleaved orchid] (50) (present), Dwarf orchis (5) (1913), One-leaf orchis [One-leaved orchis] (5) (1913), Small northern bog orchis (5) (1913)

Platanthera orbiculata **(Pursh) Lindl.** – Bear's-ear [Bears' ear] (156) (1923), Elephant's-ear [Elephants' ear, Elephant's ears, Elephants-ear] (156) (1923), Gall-of-the-earth [Gall of the earth] (156) (1923), Great green orchis (2, 156) (1895–1923), Heal-all [Healall] (5, 7, 156, 158) (1828–1923), Large round-leaf orchis [Large round-leaved orchis] (5) (1913), Large two-leaf orchis [Large two-leaved orchis] (5, 156) (1913–1923), Lesser round-leaf orchid [Lesser roundleaved orchid] (50) (present), Round-leaf orchis [Round-leaved orchis] (3, 156) (1923–1977), Shin-leaf [Shin leaf, Shinleaf] (156) (1923), Shin-plasters [Shinplasters] (156) (1923) no longer in use by 1923, Solomon's-seal [Solomon's seal, Solomon seal, Solomon's seal, Solomons-seal, S'alomon's seal, Salamons seale] (73, 75) (1892–1894) VT

Platanthera peramoena **(Gray) Gray** – Fringeless purple orchis (5) (1913), Great purple orchis (5) (1913)

Platanthera praeclara **Sheviak & Bowles** – Great Plains white fringed orchid (50) (present)

Platanthera psycodes **(L.) Lindl.** – Flaming orchis (5, 156) (1913–1923), Lesser purple fringed orchid (50) (present), Pink-fringe orchis [Pink-fringed orchis] (5, 156) (1913–1923), Small purple fringed orchid [Small purple fringe-orchid] (109, 138, 156) (1923–1949), Smaller purple fringed orchis (2, 5) (1895–1913), Soldier's-plume [Soldier's plume] (3, 5, 75, 156) (1894–1977), Wild hyacinth (78) (1898) ME

Platanthera stricta **Lindl.** – Lesser bog orchid (50) (present)

Platanus **(Tourn.) L.** – See *Platanus* L.

Platanus acerifolia **Willd.** – See *Platanus hybrida* Brot.

Platanus hybrida **Brot.** – London plane (109) (1949) variegated variety

Platanus **L.** – Buttonwood [Button wood, Button-wood] (12) (1821), Plane tree [Planetree, Plane-tree] (1, 2, 4, 8, 109, 138, 155, 158, 167, 184) (1793–1986), Platane (French) (8) (1785), Sycamore or

Sycamore tree [Sycomore-tree] (4, 50, 93, 109) (1936–present)

Platanus mexicana **Moric.** – See *Platanus racemosa* Nutt.

Platanus occidentalis **L.** – American plane or American plane tree [American planetree] (2, 8, 19, 38, 92, 109, 138, 155, 158) (1785–1949), American sycamore (46, 50) (1879–present), Buttonball [Button balls, Button ball, Button-ball] or Buttonball tree (5, 75, 95, 106, 156, 157) (1900–1930), Buttonwood [Button wood, Button-wood] (5, 10, 14, 20, 19, 38, 41, 44, 97, 106, 109, 113, 158, 187) (1770–1949), Cotonier (French, cotton tree) (17, 41) (1770–1796), Cotton tree [Cotton-tree] (20, 187) (1818–1857) Canada & upper Louisiana (Louisiana Purchase), False sycamore (5, 19, 92, 156, 158) (1840–1923), Large buttonwood [Large button wood] (8) (1785), Monkey balls [Monkeyballs] (156) (1923), Occidental plane tree (38) (1820), Palm tree [Palm trees] (18) (1805), Plane tree [Planetree, Plane-tree] (4, 5, 9, 18, 72, 92, 93, 95, 113, 156, 187) (1805–1986), Platane d'Occident (French) (8) (1785), Porcupine-eggs [Porcupine eggs] (156) (1923), Smooth American plane tree [Smooth American planetree] (155) (1942), Sycamore or Sycamore tree [Sycomore-tree] (3, 4, 10, 17, 20, 27, 35, 38, 65, 72, 93, 97, 106, 112, 113, 122, 124, 156, 158) (1818–1986), Vassbok (Swedish) (41) (1770), Vattenbok (Swedish) (41) (1770), Virginia maple [Virginian maple] (41) (1770), Water beech (5, 20, 41, 156, 158, 187) (1770–1923), Western plane tree [Western plane-tree] (14, 189) (1767–1882)

Platanus occidentalis **L. var. glabrata (Fern.) Sargent** – See *Platanus occidentalis* L.

Platanus racemosa **Nutt.** – California buttonwood (20) (1857), California planetree (138) (1923), California sycamore (106, 147) (1856–1930), Mexican sycamore (161) (1857), Platane de Californie (French) (20) (1857), Sycamore or Sycamore tree [Sycomore-tree] (161) (1857)

Platanus wrighti – See *Platanus wrightii* S. Wats.

Platanus wrightii **S. Wats.** – Aliso (153) (1913) NM, Arizona planetree (138) (1923), Sycamore or Sycamore tree [Sycomore-tree] (149, 153) (1904–1919)

Platycerium bifurcatum **(Cav.) C. Chr.** – Common staghorn fern (138) (1923)

Platycerium **Desv.** – Staghorn fern (138) (1923)

Platycladus orientalis **(L.) Franco** – Chinese arborvitae (112) (1937), Oriental arborvitae [Oriental arbor-vitae] (109, 112, 138) (1923–1937)

Platycodon **A. DC.** – Balloon-flower [Balloonflower] (138) (1923)

Platycodon grandiflorum **(Jacq.) A. DC.** – Balloon-flower [Balloonflower] (109) (1949) from the inflated buds, Blue Bellflower of China [Blew Belflower of China] (178) (1526)

Platystemon **Benth.** – Creamcups [Cream-cups, Cream cups] (15) (1895), Platystemon (138) (1923)

Platystemon californicus **Benth.** – Creamcups [Cream-cups, Cream cups] (74, 106, 109, 138) (1893–1949) Santa Barbara Co, CA

Platystigma linearis **Benth.** – Creamcups [Cream-cups, Cream cups] (74) (1893) Santa Barbara Co, CA

Plectranthus scutellarioides **(L.) R. Br.** – Verschaffelt's coleus [Verschaffelt coleus] (138) (1923)

Pleiotaenia nuttallii **(DC.) Coult. & Rose** – See *Polytaenia nuttallii* DC.

Pleopeltis polypodioides **(L.) Andrews & Windham subsp. *michauxiana* (Weatherby) Andrews & Windham** – Resurrection fern [Resurrectionfern] (3, 4, 50, 138) (1923–present)

Pleopeltis polypodioides **(L.) Andrews & Windham subsp. *polypodioides*** – Caprock fern (97) (1937) OK, Gray polypody (5, 122) (1913–1937), Resurrection fern [Resurrectionfern] (50, 155) (1942–present)

Pleuraphis jamesii **Torr.** – Black bunch grass [Black bunch-grass] (94) (1901), Galleta (3, 119, 140, 151, 155) (1896–1977), Galleta grass [Galleta-grass] (122, 151, 152, 163) (1852–1937), James' galleta (50) (present)

Pleuraphis mutica **Buckl.** – Black grama [Black gramma] (45, 94, 151)

(1896–1901), Galleta [Guyeta, Gietta, Gieta] (151) (1896), Galleta grass [Galleta-grass] (151) (1896), Tobosa grass [Tobosa-grass, Tobosagrass] (3, 50, 65, 119, 122, 152, 155, 163) (1852–present)

Pleuraphis rigida **Thurb.** – Galleta (94) (1901)

Pleurogyna rotata **(L.) Griseb.** – See *Lomatogonium rotatum* (L.) Fries ex Fern.

Pleurogyne **Eschsch.** – See *Lomatogonium* A. Braun

Pleuropogon californica **(Nees) Vasey** – See *Pleuropogon californicus* (Nees) Benth. ex Vasey

Pleuropogon californicus **(Nees) Benth. ex Vasey** – California pleuropogon (94) (1901)

Pleuropogon refractum **(Gray) Benth.** – See *Pleuropogon refractus* (Gray) Benth. ex Vasey

Pleuropogon refractus **(Gray) Benth. ex Vasey** – Nodding pleuropogon (94) (1901)

Pleuropogon sabinei **R. Br.** – False semaphore grass [False semaphore-grass] (50) (present), Sabine's pleuropogon (5) (1913)

Pleuropogon sabinii **R. Br.** – See *Pleuropogon sabinei* R. Br.

Pleuropterus zuccarinii **Small** – See *Polygonum cuspidatum* Sieb. & Zucc.

Pleurotus ostreatus **(Jacq.) P. Kumm.** – Oyster mushroom (128) (1933)

Pleurotus ulmarius **Bull.** – See *Pleurotus ulmarius* (Bull.) P. Kumm.

Pluchea bifrons **DC.** – See *Pluchea foetida* (L.) DC.

Pluchea camphorata **(L.) DC.** – Camphor pluchea (50) (present), Inland marsh fleabane (5, 97, 122) (1913–1937), Plowman's-wort [Ploughman's wort, Plowmans'-wort, Plowmans'-wort, Plowmanwort] (5, 156) (1913–1923), Salt-marsh fleabane [Salt marsh fleabane] (5, 122, 134, 156) (1913–1937), Skunkweed [Skunk-weed, Skunk weed] (106) (1930), Spicy fleabane (5, 97, 156) (1913–1937), Stinkweed [Stink-weed, Stink weed] (3) (1977)

Pluchea **Cass.** – Camphorweed [Camphor-weed, Camphor weed] (50) (present), Marsh fleabane [Marsh flea bane] (1, 4, 106, 158) (1930–1986), Pluchea (155) (1942), Stinkweed [Stink-weed, Stink weed] (4) (1986)

Pluchea foetida **(L.) DC.** – Baume des sauvages (French) (7) (1828), Fetid marsh-fleabane [Fetid marsh fleabane] (5, 156) (1913–1923), Marsh fleabane [Marsh flea bane] (19, 42, 92) (1814–1876), Plowman's-wort [Ploughman's wort, Plowmans'-wort, Plowmans'-wort, Plowmanwort] (19, 92) (1840–1876), Viscid marsh fleabane [Viscid marsh-fleabane] (5, 156) (1913–1923)

Pluchea odorata **(L.) Cass** – Inland marsh fleabane (124) (1937), Riverside tobacco (158) (1900), Sweetscent (50) (present)

Pluchea petiolata **Cass.** – See *Pluchea camphorata* (L.) DC.

Pluchea sericea **(Nutt.) Coville** – Arrow-wood [Arrow wood] (106) (1930), Cachanilla (Spanish) (106) (1930) NM

Plumbago auriculata **Lam.** – Cape plumbago (138) (1923)

Plumbago capensis – See *Plumbago auriculata* Lam.

Plumbago indica **L.** – Rose plumbago (138) (1923), Scarlet plumbago (138) (1923)

Plumbago **L.** – Leadwort [Lead wort] (109) (1949), Plumbago (138) (1923)

Plumbago rosea – See *Plumbago indica* L.

Plumbago rosea coccinea – See *Plumbago indica* L.

Plumbago rosea **var. coccinea (Lour.) Hook.** – See *Plumbago indica* L.

Plumbago scandens **L.** – Texas plumbago (122, 124) (1937) TX

Plumeria acutifolia **[Poir.]** – See *Plumeria rubra* L.

Plumeria **L.** – Frangipani (109, 138) (1923–1949)

Plumeria rubra **L.** – Mexican frangipani (138) (1923), Nosegay frangipani (138) (1923)

Pluteus cervinus **(Schaeff.) P. Kumm.** – Fawn-colored mushroom (128) (1933)

Pluteus cervinus **[P. Kumm.]** – See *Pluteus cervinus* (Schaeff.) P. Kumm.

Pneumaria maritima **(L.) Hill.** – See *Mertensia maritima* (L.) Gray var. *maritima*

Poa abbreviata **R. Br.** – Low spear grass [Low spear-grass] (5) (1913),

325

***Poa abbreviata* R. Br.**

Short bluegrass (50) (present)

***Poa abbreviata* R. Br. subsp. *pattersonii* (Vasey) A. & D. Löve & Kapoor** – Patterson's bluegrass [Patterson's blue-grass] (94) (1901)

***Poa abyssinica* Jacq.** – See *Eragrostis tef* (Zuccagni) Trotter

***Poa alpina* L.** – Alpine bluegras (140) (1944), Fiall-groe (Swedish) (46) (1879), Mountain spear grass [Mountain spear-grass] (94) (1901)

***Poa alsodes* Gray** – Grove bluegrass (50, 155) (1942–present), Grove meadow grass (5) (1913), Tall spear grass (87) (1884), Wood spear grass (66, 87) (1884–1903), Woodland bluegrass [Woodland blue-grass, Woodland blue grass] (94) (1901), Woods grass (87) (1884)

***Poa ampla* Merr.** – See *Poa secunda* J. Presl

***Poa angustifolia* L.** – See *Poa pratensis* L. subsp. *pratensis*

***Poa annua* L.** – Annual blue grass [Annual bluegrass, Annual blue-grass] (3, 50, 119, 122, 140, 143, 155, 163) (1852–present), Annual meadow grass [Annual meadow-grass] (5, 56, 72, 143, 187) (1818–1936), Annual poa (45) (1896), Annual spear grass (66, 87, 90) (1885–1903), Causeway grass (5) (1913), Dwarf lawn grass (85) (1932) SD, Dwarf meadow grass [Dwarf meadow-grass] (5, 119, 163) (1852–1938), Goose grass [Goosegrass, Goose-grass] (87) (1884), Low spear grass [Low spear-grass] (5, 45, 56, 90, 92, 94, 111, 119, 143, 163) (1852–1938), May grass [Maygrass] (5) (1913), Six-weeks grass (5) (1913), Suffolk grass (90) (1885) ME, Summer grass [Summer-grass] (94) (1901), possibly Small meadow grass [Small Medow-grasse] (178) (1596)

Poa aquatica – See *Glyceria maxima* (Hartm.) Holmb.

***Poa arachnifera* Torr.** – Texas bluegrass [Texas blue-grass, Texas blue grass] (3, 5, 45, 50, 56, 72, 87, 88, 94, 119, 122, 155, 163) (1852–present)

***Poa arachnifera* var. *glabrata* Vasey** – See *Poa arachnifera* Torr.

***Poa arctica* R. Br.** – Arctic bluegrass (140) (1944)

Poa arctica* R. Br. subsp. *arctica – Arctic spear grass (5) (1913)

***Poa argentea* Howell** – See *Poa pringlei* Scribn.

***Poa arida* Vasey** – Bunch grass [Bunchgrass, Bunch-grass] (163) (1852), Bunch spear grass (5, 129) (1894–1913), Mountain blue grass (11) (1888), Mountain spear grass [Mountain spear-grass] (87) (1884), Plains bluegrass (3, 50, 122, 140, 155) (1937–present), Prairie bunch grass [Prairie bunch-grass] (119) (1938), Prairie grass [Prairie-grass] (163) (1852), Prairie meadow grass (5) (1913), Prairie spear grass [Prairie spear-grass] (5, 94, 119) (1901–1938)

***Poa autumnalis* Muhl. ex Ell.** – Autumn blue grass [Autumn blue-grass] (50) (present), Flexuous spear grass [Flexuous spear-grass] (5, 163) (1852–1913), Southern spear grass [Southern spear-grass] (66) (1903)

***Poa bigelovii* Vasey & Scribn.** – Bigelow's blue grass [Bigelow's blue-grass, Bigelow's bluegrass] (94, 122) (1901–1937)

***Poa bolanderi* Vasey** – Bolander's spear-grass (94) (1901)

***Poa brachyphylla* Schult.** – See *Poa cuspidata* Nutt.

***Poa brevifolia* Muhl.** – See *Poa cuspidata* Nutt.

***Poa buckleyana* Nash** – See *Poa secunda* J. Presl

***Poa bulbosa* L.** – Bulbous blue grass [Bulbous bluegrass] (3, 50, 155) (1942–present), possibly Red dwarf grass [Red dwarfe-grasse] (178, 180) (1526–1633)

***Poa canadensis* Michx.** – See *Glyceria canadensis* (Michx.) Trin.

***Poa canbyi* (Scribn.) Piper** – Sandberg's blue grass [Sandberg blue-grass] (50) (present), Yellow spear grass [Yellow spear-grass] (94) (1901)

***Poa capillaris* L.** – See *Eragrostis capillaris* (L.) Nees

***Poa cenisia* All. var. *arctica* (R. Br.) Richter** – See *Poa arctica* R. Br. subsp. *arctica*

***Poa chapmaniana* Scribn.** – Chapman's bluegrass [Chapman blue-grass] (3, 50, 155) (1942–present), Chapman's spear grass [Chapman's spear-grass] (5, 56, 72, 119, 163) (1852–1938)

***Poa cilianensis* All.** – See *Eragrostis cilianensis* (All.) Vign. ex Janchen

***Poa compressa* L.** – Blue grass [Bluegrass, Blue-grass] (3, 19, 45, 66, 87, 90, 92, 187) (1818–1977), Canadian blue grass [Canadian bluegrass, Canadian blue-grass, Canada bluegrass, Canada blue grass, Canada blue-grass] (3, 27, 50, 56, 68, 85, 94, 109, 111, 119, 122, 138, 140, 143, 155, 163) (1819–present), Creeping poa (68) (1890), Creeping spear grass [Creeping spear-grass] (129) (1894), English bluegrass [English blue-grass, English blue grass] (5, 56, 68, 88, 119, 129) (1885–1938), Flat-stalk grass [Flat stalked grass] (90) (1885), Flat-stalk meadow grass [Flat-stalked meadow grass] (45) (1896), Flat-stem meadow grass [Flat-stemmed meadow grass, Flat-stemmed meadow-grass] (5, 119, 143) (1913–1938), Flat-stem poa [Flat-stemmed poa] (45) (1896), June grass [June-grass, Junegrass] (56) (1901) IA, Smaller bluegrass [Smaller blue grass] (68) (1890), Squitch grass [Squitch-grass] (5) (1913), Virginia blue grass (68) (1890), Wire grass [Wire-grass, Wiregrass] (5, 45, 56, 66, 68, 72, 87, 88, 90, 92, 109, 119, 129, 143) (1884–1949)

***Poa confusa* Rydb.** – See *Poa secunda* J. Presl

***Poa crocata* Michx.** – See *Poa palustris* L.

***Poa cusickii* Vasey** – Cusick's bluegrass [Cusick bluegrass] (50, 155) (1942–present), Purple-top bluegrass [Purple-top blue-grass] (94) (1901)

***Poa cuspidata* Nutt.** – Early bluegrass (50) (present), Short-leaf spear grass [Short-leaved spear grass] (5, 66) (1903–1913), Southern spear grass [Southern spear-grass] (94) (1901), Three-flower hair grass [Three-flowered hair-grass] (187) (1818)

***Poa debilis* Torr.** – See *Poa saltuensis* Fern. & Wieg.

***Poa douglasii* Nees** – Douglas' sand grass [Douglas' sand-grass] (94) (1901)

***Poa eminens* Presl.** – Large-flower bluegrass [Large-flowered blue-grass, Large-flowered blue-grass] (94) (1901), Large-flower spear grass [Large-flowered spear grass, Largeflower speargrass] (5, 50) (1913–present)

***Poa fendleriana* (Steud.) Vasey** – Fendler's blue grass [Fendler's blue-grass, Fendler bluegrass] (94, 155) (1901–1942), Mutton bluegrass (140, 155) (1942–1944), Mutton grass [Muttongrass, Mutton-grass] (3, 50, 94, 122, 152, 155, 163) (1852–present)

Poa fendleriana* (Steud.) Vasey subsp. *fendleriana – Mutton grass [Muttongrass, Mutton-grass] (50) (present)

***Poa fendleriana* (Steud.) Vasey subsp. *longiligula* (Scribn. & Williams) Soreng** – Long-tongue mutton bluegrass [Longtongue mutton bluegrass] (155) (1942), Mutton grass [Mutton-grass, Mutton-grass] (50) (present)

***Poa flabellata* Hook.f.** – See *Poa flabellata* (Lam.) Raspail

***Poa flava* L.** – See *Poa palustris* L.

***Poa flexuosa* Muhl., non Sm.** – See *Poa autumnalis* Muhl. ex Ell.

***Poa glauca* Vahl subsp. *rupicola* (Nash ex Rydb.) W. A. Weber** – Timberline blue grass [Timberline bluegrass] (50, 140, 155) (1942–present)

***Poa glauca* Vahl.** – Glaucous blue grass [Glaucous bluegrass] (50) (present), Glaucous spear grass (5) (1913), Green grass [Greengrass] (187) (1818), Green meadow grass [Green meadow-grass] (187) (1818), Greenland bluegrass (155) (1942)

***Poa glaucifolia* Scribn. & Williams** – See *Poa arida* Vasey

***Poa glumaris* Trin.** – See *Poa eminens* Presl.

***Poa gracillima* Vasey** – See *Poa secunda* J. Presl

***Poa interior* Rydb.** – See *Poa nemoralis* L. subsp. *interior* (Rydb.) W. A. Weber

***Poa juncifolia* Scribn.** – See *Poa secunda* J. Presl

***Poa kelloggii* Vasey** – Kellogg's spear-grass (94) (1901)

***Poa* L.** – Blue grass [Bluegrass, Blue-grass] (1, 50, 93, 119, 138, 146, 152, 155) (1912–present), Bunch grass [Bunchgrass, Bunch-grass] (45) (1896), Meadow grass [Meadow-grass, Medow Grasse] (1, 45, 108, 152, 184) (1793–1932), Spear grass [Spear-grass] (45) (1896)

***Poa laevigata* Scribn.** – See *Poa secunda* J. Presl

326

Podophyllum peltatum L.

Poa languida A. S. Hitchc. – See *Poa saltuensis* Fern. & Wieg.

Poa laxa Haenke – Alpine spear grass (5) (1913), Few-flower alpine meadow grass [Few-flowered alpine meadow grass] (90) (1885), Mountain spear grass [Mountain spear-grass] (5) (1913), Mt. Washington bluegrass (50) (present), Wavy meadow grass (66) (1903)

Poa leckenbyi Scribn. – See *Poa secunda* J. Presl

Poa leibergii Scribn. – Vasey's bluegrass [Vasey's blue-grass] (94) (1901)

Poa leptocoma Trin. – Slender mountain bluegrass [Slender mountain blue-grass] (94) (1901)

Poa lettermani Vasey – See *Poa lettermanii* Vasey

Poa lettermanii Vasey – Letterman's bluegrass [Letterman's blue-grass] (94) (1901)

Poa maritima Huds. – See *Puccinellia maritima* (Huds.) Parl.

Poa nemoralis L. – Lund-groe (Swedish) (46) (1879), Northern spear grass [Northern spear-grass] (94) (1901), Spear grass [Spear-grass] (111) (1915), Wood blue grass [Wood bluegrass] (50, 138, 155) (1923–present), Wood grass [Wood-grass] (56) (1901), Wood meadow grass [Wood meadow-grass] (56, 66, 68, 72, 92, 94, 109, 129) (1894–1949)

Poa nemoralis L. subsp. *interior* (Rydb.) W. A. Weber – Inland blue grass [Inland bluegrass, Inland blue-grass] (3, 50, 122, 155, 163) (1852–present)

Poa nervosa (Hook.) Vasey – Wheeler's bluegrass [Wheeler bluegrass] (140) (1944)

Poa nudata Scribn. – See *Poa secunda* J. Presl

Poa obtusa Muhl. – See *Glyceria obtusa* (Muhl.) Trin.

Poa occidentalis Vasey – Western bluegrass [Western blue-grass] (94) (1901) OK

Poa palustris L. – Duck grass (5, 56, 90) (1885–1913), False red-top [False red-top, False red top] (2, 5, 45, 66, 68, 72, 90, 92, 129) (1876–1913), Fowl bluegrass [Fowl blue-grass] (3, 50, 143, 155) (1936–present), Fowl meadow grass [Fowl meadow-grass] (2, 5, 45, 56, 66, 68, 87, 88, 90, 92, 109, 129, 143) (1884–1949), Northern spear grass [Northern spear-grass] (5) (1913), Swamp meadow grass [Swamp meadow-grass] (143) (1852–1936), Swamp wire grass (56, 90) (1885–1901), Wood meadow grass [Wood meadow-grass] (5) (1913)

Poa pattersoni Vasey – See *Poa abbreviata* R. Br. subsp. *pattersonii* (Vasey) A. & D. Löve & Kapoor

Poa phoenicea Rydb. – See *Poa arctica* R. Br.

Poa pilosa L. – See *Eragrostis pilosa* (L.) Beauv.

Poa pratense L. – Bird grass (68) (1890), Blue grass [Bluegrass, Blue-grass] (45, 56, 68, 125, 152) (1896–1930), Browntop [Brown-top, Brown top] (90) (1885) ME, Common meadow grass [Common Medow Grasse] (5, 68, 90, 178, 180) (1596–1913), Common spear grass [Common spear-grass] (66, 92, 187) (1818–1903), English grass (19, 68) (1840–1913) Ottawa, Green grass [Green-grass] (5, 45, 68) (1896–1913), Green meadow grass [Green meadow-grass] (66, 90) (1885–1903), Herd's grass [Herds-grass, Herd's-grass, Herds-grass, Herd grass] (45) (1896), June grass [June-grass, June-grass] (2, 45, 56, 66, 67, 87, 88, 90, 92, 109, 125, 134, 143, 163) (1852–1949), Kentucky bluegrass [Kentucky blue grass, Kentucky blue-grass] (3, 5, 45, 50, 56, 66, 67, 68, 72, 85, 87, 90, 92, 94, 109, 111, 115, 118, 119, 122, 129, 134, 138, 140, 143, 144, 146, 155, 163, 185) (1852–present), Meadow cat's-tail [Meadow cat's tail] (45) (1896), Meadow grass [Meadow-grass, Medow Grasse] (2, 5, 10, 19, 92, 178, 180) (1596–1913), Natural grass (5) (1913), Smooth-stalk meadow grass [Smooth-stalked meadow grass] (45, 68, 90) (1885–1913), Spear grass [Spear-grass] (19, 45, 68, 87, 88) (1840–1913), Timothy (45) (1896)

Poa pratensis L. subsp. *pratensis* – Kentucky bluegrass [Kentucky blue grass, Kentucky blue-grass] (50) (present), Narrow-leaf meadow grass [Narrow-leaved meadow grass] (41) (1770)

Poa pringlei Scribn. – Pringle's bluegrass [Pringle's blue-grass] (94) (1901), Silvery bluegrass [Silvery blue-grass] (94) (1901)

Poa pseudopratensis Scribn. & Rydb. – See *Poa arida* Vasey

Poa purpurascens Vasey – See *Poa cusickii* Vasey

Poa reflexa Vasey & Scribn. ex Vasey – Nodding bluegass [Nodding blue-gass] (94) (1901)

Poa saltuensis Fern. & Wieg. – Old-pasture bluegrass [Oldpasture bluegrass] (50) (present), Slender spear grass [Slender spear-grass] (94) (1901), Torrey's bluegrass [Torrey bluegrass] (155) (1942), Weak meadow grass (66) (1903), Weak spear grass (5, 45, 56, 72) (1893–1901)

Poa sandbergii Vasey – See *Poa secunda* J. Presl

Poa secunda J. Presl – Alkali bluegrass (155) (1942), Big blue grass [Big bluegrass] (146, 155) (1939–1944), Big bluestem [Big bluestem Big blue stem] (146, 155) (1939–1942), Buckley's spear grass (5) (1913), Bunch redtop [Bunch red-top] (5, 94) (1901–1913), Canby's blue grass [Canby's bluegrass, Canby bluegrass] (3, 155) (1942–1977), Fine-leaf blue grass [Fine-leaf bluegrass, Fine-leafed blue-grass] (94) (1901), Nevada bluegrass [Nevada blue-grass] (94, 146, 155, 185) (1901–1942), Oregon blue grass (5) (1913), Pine bluegrass (155) (1942), Sand blue grass [Sand blue-grass] (94) (1901), Sandberg's blue grass [Sandberg bluegrass] (50) (present), Slender blue grass [Slender bluegrass] (155) (1942), Smooth spear grass (5, 10) (1818–1913), Tufted spear grass (5, 11) (1888–1913)

Poa serotina Ehrh. – See *Poa palustris* L.

Poa sylvestris Gray – Sylvan spear grass [Sylvan spear-grass] (5, 66, 72, 163) (1852–1907), Woodland bluegrass [Woodland blue-grass, Woodland blue grass] (3, 50, 155) (1942–present), Woodland spear grass [Woodland spear-grass] (94) (1901)

Poa tenerrima Scribn. – Slender-flower blue-grass [Slender-flowered blue-grass] (94) (1901)

Poa tenuis Elliot – See *Eragrostis capillaris* (L.) Nees

Poa tracyi Vasey – Tracy's bluegrass [Tracy's blue-grass] (94) (1901)

Poa trivialis L. – Bird grass (5) (1913), Fowl meadow grass [Fowl meadow-grass] (5) (1913), Natural grass (5) (1913), Pasture gass (19) (1840), Rough blue grass [Rough bluegrass, Rough blue-grass] (50, 138, 143) (1923–present), Rough meadow grass [Rough meadow-grass] (45) (1896), Roughish meadow grass (72) (1907), Rough-stalk bluegrass [Roughstalk bluegrass] (155) (1942), Rough-stalk meadow-grass [Rough-stalked meadowgrass, Rough-stalked meadow grass, Rough-stalked meadow-grass] (3, 45, 56, 66, 68, 92, 94, 109, 143) (1896–1977), Rough-stem meadow grass [Rough-stemmed meadow-grass] (187) (1818)

Poa unilateralis Scribn. – One-sided bluegrass [One-sided blue-grass] (94) (1901) Neb

Poa vaseyochloa Scribn. – See *Poa leibergii* Scribn.

Poa viridis Muhl. – See *Poa glauca* Vahl.

Poa wolfii Scribn. – Wolf's blue grass [Wolf's bluegrass, Wolfs bluegrass] (50, 155) (1942–present), Wolf's meadow grass (56) (1901), Wolf's spear grass (5, 72) (1907–1913)

Pocilla biloba (L.) W. A. Weber – See *Veronica biloba* L.

Podalyria tinctoria Michx. – See *Baptisia tinctoria* (L.) R. Br. ex Aiton f.

Podalyria uniflora Michx. – See *Baptisia lanceolata* (Walt.) Ell.

Podalyria villosa Michx. – See *Thermopsis villosa* (Walt.) Fern. & Schub.

Podocarpus L'Hér. ex Pers. – Podocarpus (138) (1923)

Podocarpus macrophylla – See *Podocarpus macrophyllus* (Thunb.) Sweet

Podocarpus macrophyllus (Thunb.) Sweet – Yew podocarpus (138) (1923)

Podophyllum diphyllum L. – See *Jeffersonia diphylla* (L.) Pers.

Podophyllum L. – Mandrake (93, 158) (1900–1936), May apple [May-apple, May-apple] (50, 93, 138, 155, 156, 167) (1814–present)

Podophyllum peltatum L. – American mandrake (64, 92, 158) (1876–1908), Behen (156) (1923), Citron (French) (43) (1820), Common mayapple (138, 155) (1923–1942), Devil's-apple [Devil's apple] (5, 64, 156, 158) (1900–1923), Duck's-foot [Duck foot, Duck's foot,

Ducks foot, Ducks' foot] (6, 7, 14, 64, 92, 156, 158, 186) (1814–1923) no longer in use by 1923, Eendenpoot (186) (1814), Entenfuss (186) (1814), Fluss Blatt (German) (186) (1814), Fussblatt (6) (1892), Ground-lemon [Ground lemon] (5, 7, 64, 92, 156, 157, 158) (1828–1923), Herbe a serpente a sonnetes (French) (43) (1820), Hog-apple [Hog-apple] (5, 6, 64, 76, 92, 156, 157, 158) (1892–1929) fruit eaten by pigs and boys (76), Indian apple [Indian-apple, Indian-apples] (5, 6, 49, 64, 92, 156, 157, 158) (1892–1929), Ipecacuana (186) (1814), Ipecacuanha (186) (1814), Lemon apple (53) (1922), Mandrake (1, 2, 6, 7, 13, 15, 46, 49, 52, 53, 54, 55, 57, 58, 59, 64, 107, 109, 121, 125, 156, 157, 158, 186, 187) (1671–1949), Mandrake-pear [Mandrake pear] (74) (1893), May apple [Mayapple, May-apple] (1, 3, 4, 5, 6, 10, 13, 14, 15, 19, 41, 46, 49, 50, 53, 54, 55, 57, 58, 59, 61, 63, 64, 65, 72, 92, 97, 105, 107, 109, 121, 122, 124, 125, 156, 157, 158, 177, 184, 186, 187) (1762–present), Mayflower [May flower, May-flower] (49, 156) (1898–1923), Mountain May-apple [Mountain May apple] (7) (1828), Peca (6, 7) (1828–1932), Podophylle (French) (6) (1892), Podophylle de montagne (French) (7) (1828), Podophyllum (54, 59, 64, 174, 177) (1753–1911), Puck's-foot [Puck's foot] (5) (1913), Raccoon-berry [Raccoon berry, Raccoonberry] (5, 6, 7, 49, 53, 64, 92, 107, 156, 157, 158) (1828–1923), Rattlesnake plant (43) (1820), Schildblattinger Entenfuss (German) (6) (1892), Schildblättringer Entenfuss (German) (6, 186) (1814–1892), Šoŋgthiŋdse (Osage) (121) (1918?–1970?), Umbrella plant [Umbrella-plant] (64, 156, 158) (1900–1923), Vegetable calomel (64, 156, 158) (1900–1923), Wild jalap (6, 156) (1892–1923), Wild lemon [Wild lemmon] (5, 6, 7, 49, 53, 64, 92, 107, 156, 157, 158, 186, 187) (1814–1929), Wild mandrake (5, 19, 49, 64, 92, 157, 158) (1840–1929), Yellow-berry [Yellow berry] (7, 92) (1828–1876)

Podostemum ceratophyllum **Michx.** – Banister's naked waterweed [Banister's naked water-weed] (181) (~1678), Riverweed [Riverweed, River weed] (5, 156) (1913–1923), Thread-foot (5, 19, 156) (1840–1923)

Podostemum **Michx.** – Riverweed [River-weed, River weed] (1) (1932), Thread-foot (1) (1932)

Podranea ricasoliana (**Tanfani**) **Sprague** – Ricasol's pandorea [Ricasol pandorea] (138) (1923)

Pogonia affinis **Austin** – See *Isotria medeoloides* (Pursh) Raf.

Pogonia divaricata (**L.**) **R. Br.** – See *Cleistes divaricata* (L.) Ames

Pogonia **Juss.** – Pogonia (50, 138) (1923–present), Snakemouth [Snake mouth, Snake-mouth] (1, 158) (1900–1932)

Pogonia ophioglossoides (**L.**) **Ker-Gawl.** – Adder's pogonia (158) (1900), Adder's-mouth orchis (158) (1900), Adder's-mouth pogonia [Adder's mouth pogonia] (5, 156, 158) (1900–1923)

Pogonia ophioglossoides (**L.**) **Ker-Gawl.** – Adder's-tongue-leaf arethusa [Adder's tongue leaved arethusa] (42) (1814), Rose pogonia (5, 122, 138, 156, 158) (1900–1937), Snakemouth [Snake mouth, Snake-mouth] (5, 86, 156, 158) (1878–1923), Snake-mouth orchid [Snakemouth orchid] (50) (present)

Pogonia trianthophora – See *Triphora trianthophora* (Sw.) Rydb.

Pogonia verticillata (**Muhl. ex Willd.**) **Nutt.** – See *Isotria verticillata* (Muehl. ex Willd.) Raf.

Poinciana gilliesii **Hook.** – See *Caesalpinia gilliesii* (Hook.) Wallich ex D. Dietr.

Poinciana gilliesii **Wallich ex Hook.** – See *Caesalpinia gilliesii* (Hook.) Wallich ex D. Dietr.

Poinciana **L.** – See *Caesalpinia* L.

Poinciana pulcherrima **L.** – See *Caesalpinia pulcherrima* (L.) Sw.

Poinciana regia – See *Delonix regia* (Bojer ex Hook.) Raf.

Poinsettia cuphosperma (**Engelm.**) **Small.** – See *Euphorbia dentata* Michx.

Poinsettia dentata (**Michx.**) **Small.** – See *Euphorbia dentata* Michx.

Poinsettia heterophylla (**L.**) **Kl. & Garcke.** – See *Euphorbia cyathophora* Murray

Polanisia dodecandra (**L.**) **DC.** – Clammy base mustard (42) (1814), Red-whisker clammyweed [Redwhisker clammyweed] (50)

(present)

Polanisia dodecandra (**L.**) **DC. subsp.** *dodecandra* – Clammy mustard (7) (1828), Clammyweed [Clammy-weed, Clammy weed] (5, 72, 80, 85, 95, 97, 156, 157, 158) (1900–1937), Common clammy weed (7) (1828), False mustard (5, 7, 19, 92, 156, 157, 158) (1828–1929), Polanise graveole (French) (7) (1828), Red-whisker clammy-weed [Redwhisker clammyweed] (50) (present), Stinking clammy-weed [Stinking clammyweed] (155) (1942), Stinkweed [Stink-weed, Stink weed] (7, 80) (1828–1913), Wormweed [Worm weed, Wormweed] (5, 7, 156, 157, 158) (1828–1929)

Polanisia dodecandra (**L.**) **DC. subsp.** *trachysperma* (**Torr. & Gray**) **Iltis** – Clammyweed [Clammy-weed, Clammy weed] (3, 4, 82, 131) (1899–1986), Large-flower clammy-weed [Large-flowered clammy weed, Large-flowered clammy-weed] (4, 5, 72, 97) (1907–1986), Polanisia (114) (1894), Rough-seed clammy-weed [Roughseed clammyweed] (155) (1942), Sandy-seed clammy-weed [Sandyseed clammyweed] (50) (present), Stinkweed [Stink-weed, Stink weed] (80) (1913)

Polanisia graveolens **Raf.** – See *Polanisia dodecandra* (L.) DC. subsp. *dodecandra*

Polanisia icosandra – See *Cleome viscosa* L.

Polanisia jamesii (**Torr. & Gray**) **Iltis** – Cristatella (3, 4) (1977–1986), James' clammy-weed [James' clammyweed] (50) (present), James' cristatella (5, 72, 97) (1907–1937)

Polanisia **Raf.** – Clammyweed [Clammy-weed, Clammy weed] (1, 4, 50, 93, 155, 158) (1900–present), Cristatella (158) (1900), Polanisia (82) (1930)

Polanisia trachysperma **Torr. & Gray** – See *Polanisia dodecandra* (L.) DC. subsp. *trachysperma* (Torr. & Gray) Iltis

Polanisia viscosa – See *Cleome viscosa* L.

Polemonium brandegeei (**Gray**) **Greene** – Brandegee's Jacob's-ladder [Brandegee's Jacob's ladder] (50) (present)

Polemonium caeruleum **L.** – Charity (109) (1949), Greek valerian [Greeke valerian, Greek-valerian] (92, 109, 138, 178) (1526–1949), Jabon's-ladder [Jabons-ladder] (109) (1949), Jacob's-ladder [Jacob's ladder, Jacobs-ladder] (2) (1895), Polemonium (174, 177) (1753–1762)

Polemonium coeruleum – See *Polemonium caeruleum* L.

Polemonium humile **Willd.** – See *Polemonium pulcherrimum* Hook. subsp. *lindleyi* (Wherry) V. Grant

Polemonium **L.** – Greek valerian [Greeke valerian, Greek-valerian] (2, 19, 82, 156, 158) (1840–1930), Jacob's-ladder [Jacob's ladder, Jacobs-ladder] (1, 10) (1818–1932), Polemonium (138, 155) (1923–1942), Skunkweed [Skunk-weed, Skunk weed] (1) (1932)

Polemonium pulcherrimum **Hook. subsp.** *lindleyi* (**Wherry**) **V. Grant** – Dwarf polemonium (138) (1923), Low phlox (82) (1930)

Polemonium reptans **L.** – Abcess root [Abscess-root] (57, 92, 158) (1876–1917), American abscess-root [American abscess root] (5, 156) (1913–1923), American great valerian (5, 156) (1913–1923), American Greek valerian (49, 92, 158) (1876–1900), Blue valerian (77) (1898) Parke Co. IN, Bluebell [Blue-bell, Blue bell, Blue bells, Blue-bells] (5, 49, 73, 92, 156, 158) (1879–1923) Mansfield O, Creeping great valerian (5, 156) (1913–1923), Creeping Greek valerian (86, 158) (1878–1900), Creeping polemonium (3, 4, 138, 155) (1923–1986), Creeping-root Jacob's-ladder [Creeping-rooted Jacob's-ladder] (187) (1818), Forget-me-not [Forget me not, Forget-me-not, For-get-me-nots, Forgetmenot] (86, 156, 158) (1878–1923), Geschwürwurzel (German) (158) (1900), Greek valerian [Greeke valerian, Greek-valerian] (5, 50, 72, 82, 156) (1907–present), Green valerian (92) (1876), Jacob's-ladder [Jacob's ladder, Jacobs-ladder] (49, 61, 86, 92, 156, 158, 184) (1793–1923) for ladder-like leaf, Saint Jacob's ladder (82) (1930) IA, Snakeroot [Snake root, Snake-root] (77) (1898) Parke Co. IN, St. Jacob's-ladder [Saint Jacob's ladder] (82) (1930), Sweat root [Sweatroot, Sweat-root] (5, 92, 156) (1876–1923), Sweetroot [Sweet-root] (158) (1900)

Polemonium van-bruntiae **Britton** – See *Polemonium vanbruntiae*

Britton

Polemonium vanbruntiae Britton – American Jacob's-ladder [American Jacob's ladder] (5) (1913), Bluebell [Blue-bell, Blue bell, Blue bells, Blue-bells] (156) (1923), Jacob's-ladder [Jacob's ladder, Jacobs-ladder] (156) (1923)

Polianthes virginica (L.) Shinners – See *Manfreda virginica* (L.) Salisb. ex Rose

Polycodium melanocarpum (C. Mohr) Small – See *Vaccinium stamineum* L.

Polycodium stamineum (L.) Greene – See *Vaccinium stamineum* L.

Polygala alba Nutt. – Angel's-wings [Angel wings, Angelwings] (122, 124) (1937) TX, Milkwort (127) (1933), Southern senega (55) (1911), White milkwort [White milke woort] (3, 4, 5, 50, 93, 97, 122, 131) (1899–present), White polygala (155) (1942)

Polygala ambigua Nutt. – Loose-spike milkwort [Loose spiked milkwort] (5, 72, 97) (1907–1937)

Polygala brevifolia Nutt. – Short-leaf milkwort [Short-leaved milkwort] (5) (1913)

Polygala corymbosa Michx. – possibly *Polygala cymosa* Walt.

Polygala cruciata L. – Cross-leaf milkwort [Cross-leaved milkwort] (5, 72) (1907–1913), Drumheads (5, 156) (1913–1923), Marsh milkwort (5, 156) (1913–1923)

Polygala curtissii Gray – Curtiss' milkwort (5) (1913)

Polygala cymosa Walt. – Tall pine-barren milkwort (5) (1913)

Polygala incarnata L. – Common milkweed [Common milk weed] (92) (1876), Milkwort (19) (1840), Pink milkwort (5, 72, 97, 122, 156, 158) (1907–1937), Procession flower [Procession-flower] (5, 50, 92, 156, 158) (1876–present), Rogation flower [Rogation-flower] (5, 92, 156, 158) (1876–1923), Slender milkwort (4) (1986)

Polygala L. – Milkwort (1, 4, 10, 13, 15, 93, 109, 156, 158, 184) (1793–present), Polygala (50, 138, 155) (1923–present), Snakeroot [Snake root, Snake-root] (13, 190) (~1759–1849)

Polygala lindheimeri Gray var. parvifolia Wheelock – Shrubby milkwort (50) (Present)

Polygala lutea L. – Candy-weed (156) (1923), Orange milkwort (5, 156) (1913–1923), Wild batchelor's-button [Wild batchelor's button] (5) (1913), Yellow bachelor's-buttons [Yellow bachelor's button, Yellow bachelor's buttons] (2, 86, 156) (1878–1923) Southern US, Yellow clover (156) (1923), Yellow milkwort (5, 19, 86, 156) (1840–1923), Yellow-flower milkwort [Yellow-flowered milk-wort] (187) (1818)

Polygala mariana Mill – Maryland milkwort (5) (1913)

Polygala nuttallii Torr & Gray. – Ground centaury (5, 92) (1876–1913), Nuttall's milkwort (5, 72) (1907–1913)

Polygala paucifolia Willd. – Baby's-feet [Baby's feet, Babies' feet] (5, 73, 79, 156) (1891–1923) NH, Baby's-slippers [Baby's slippers, Babysslippers] (5, 74, 156) (1893–1923) Western MA, Baby's-toes [Baby's toes, Babies' toes] (5, 73, 156) (1892–1923) Hubbardston MA, Bird-on-the-wing [Bird on the wing] (5, 76, 156) (1896–1923) ME, Dwarf milkwort (5, 7, 92, 156) (1828–1923), Evergreen snakeroot [Evergreen snake root, Evergreen snake-root] (5, 7, 92, 156) (1828–1923), Flowering wintergreen (5, 15, 19, 92, 109, 156) (1840–1949), Fringed milkwort (5, 156) (1913–1923), Fringed polygala (2, 15, 92, 109, 138, 156) (1895–1949), Gaywings [Gay wings] (5, 74, 156) (1893–1923) NY, Indian pink (5, 74, 156) (1893–1923) Montague MA, Lady's-slipper [Lady's slipper, Ladies' slipper, Lady-slipper, Ladyslipper, Ladie-slipper, Lady's slippers] (5, 76, 156) (1896–1923) Gardiner ME, Little pollom (5, 7, 92, 156) (1828–1923), May-wings [May wings] (5, 74, 156) (1893–1923), Polygale naine (French) (7) (1828), Purple May-wing [Purple May wing] (76) (1896), Satin flower [Satin-flower] (156) (1923)

Polygala polygama Walt. – Bitter milkwort (5, 156) (1913–1923), Centaury (156) (1923), Pink milkwort (5, 156) (1913–1923), Racemed milkwort (5, 97, 122, 156) (1913–1937)

Polygala ramosa Ell. – Low pine-barren milkwort (5) (1913), Pine Barren milkwort (122) (1937) TX

Polygala sanguinea L. – Blodworte (179) (1526), Blood polygala (3,

4, 155) (1942–1986), Field milkwort (5, 72, 93, 156, 157) (1900–1929), Prairie wintergreen (156) (1923), Purple milkwort (5, 50, 93, 97, 156, 157) (1900–present), Strawberry-tassel [Strawberry tassel] (5, 156, 157) (1913–1929), Wild wintergreen (156) (1923)

Polygala senega L. – Bi'jikiwûck' (Chippewa, cattle medicine) (40) (1928), Milkwort (6) (1892), Mountain flax [Mountain-flax] (5, 6, 19, 64, 92, 156, 158) (1840–1923), Northern senega (55) (1911), Polygale de Virginie (French) (6) (1892), Rattlesnake snakeroot [Rattlesnake snake-root] (5, 41, 156, 177) (1762–1923), Rattlesnake-root [Rattlesnake root, Rattle-Snake-Root, Rattlesnakes' root, Rattlesnakeroot] (59, 64, 158, 186) (1814–1900), Seneca root (92, 158) (1876–1900), Seneca snakeroot [Seneca snake root, Seneca-snakeroot] (3, 5, 6, 7, 19, 35, 40, 47, 49, 50, 52, 53, 63, 64, 72, 85, 92, 93, 138, 156, 158) (1892–present), Seneca-snakeroot polygala (155) (1942), Senega (46, 52, 53, 59, 61, 64) (1870–1922), Senega root [Senega-root] (5, 53, 55, 92, 156) (1876–1923), Senega snakeroot [Senega snake root] (4, 6, 15, 49, 53, 57, 64, 92, 158) (1895–1986), Senega Wurzel [Senegawurzel] (German) (6, 158) (1892–1900), Seneka root (92) (1876), Seneka snakeroot [Seneka snake root] (6, 48, 49, 57, 92) (1876–1917) KS, Small senega (156) (1923), Snakeroot [Snake root, Snake-root] (14) (1882), Southern senega (156) (1923), Western senega (55) (1911), possibly Official milkwort [Official milk-wort] (186) (1814)

Polygala senega L. var. latifolia Torr. & Gray – See *Polygala senega* L.

Polygala seneka – possibly *Polygala senega* L. (taxonomic status is unresolved (PL))

Polygala verticillata L. – Dwarf snakeroot (19) (1840), Whorled milkwort (3, 4, 5, 50, 72, 85, 93, 97, 122, 131, 156) (1899–present)

Polygala verticillata L. var. isocycla Fern. – Whorled milkwort (50) (present)

Polygala virgata Thunb. – See Polygala lancifolia A. St.-Hil. & Moq.

Polygala viridescens L. – See *Polygala sanguinea* L.

Polygala vulgaris L. – Blue milkwort [Blew Milke woort] (178, 180) (1526–1633), Gang flower (92) (1876), Milkwort (107) (1919), Red milkwort [Red Milke woort] (178) (1526), White milkwort [White milke woort] (178) (1526)

Polygonatum Adans. – See *Polygonatum* Mill.

Polygonatum biflorum (Walt.) Ell. – Conquer-John [Conquer John] (5, 10, 75, 157, 158) (1818–1929), Conqueror John (156) (1923), Dropberry [Drop-berry, Drop berry] (92) (1876), Dwarf seal-wort (158) (1900), Dwarf Solomon's-seal [Dwarf Solomon's-seal, Dwarf Solomon seal] (5, 157, 158) (1900–1929), Giant Solomon's-seal [Giant Solomon's seal, Giant Solomon seal] (19, 58, 92) (1840–1876), Hairy Solomon's-seal [Hairy Solomon's seal] (5, 72, 157, 158) (1900–1929), Larger Solomon's-seal [Larger Solomon's seal] (2) (1895), Many-flower Solomon's-seal [Manny flowered Solomon's seal, Many-flowered Solomon's-seal] (42) (1814), Polygonatum (57) (1917), Sealroot (92, 178, 181) (`1526–1876), Sealwort (5, 92, 156, 157) (1876–1929), Small Solomon's seal [Small solomonseal] (138, 155, 156) (1923–1942), Smaller Solomon's-seal [Smaller Solomon's seal] (2) (1895), Smooth Solomon's-seal [Smooth Solomon's seal (50) (present), Solomon's-seal [Solomon's seal, Solomon seal, Solomon's seal, Solomons-seal, S'alomon's seal, Salamons seale] (3, 48, 57, 102, 157) (1886–1977), Twin-flower Solomon's-seal [Twin-flower Solomon's seal, Twin-flowered Solomon's-seal] (158) (1900), possibly Utīstugī (Cherokee) (102) (1885)

Polygonatum biflorum (Walt.) Ell. var. commutatum (J. A. & J. H. Schultes) Morong – Dropberry [Drop-berry, Drop berry] (156, 157, 158) (1900–1929), Giant Solomon's-seal [Giant Solomon's seal, Giant Solomon seal] (5, 157, 158) (1900–1929), Great Solomon's-seal [Great solomonseal, Great Solomon's seal] (138, 155, 156, 157, 158) (1900–1942), Sealwort (5, 156, 157, 158) (1900–1929), Smooth Solomon's-seal [Smooth Solomon's seal] (5, 50, 72, 93, 97, 157, 158) (1900–present), Solomon's-seal [Solomon's seal, Solomon seal, Solomon's seal, Solomons-seal, S'alomon's seal, Salamons seale] (40,

57, 65, 85, 127) (1917–1933)

Polygonatum commutatum **(R. & S.) Dietr.** – See *Polygonatum biflorum* (Walt.) Ell. var. *commutatum* (J. A. & J. H. Schultes) Morong

Polygonatum giganteum **Dietr.** – See *Polygonatum biflorum* (Walt.) Ell.

Polygonatum **Mill.** – Solomon's-seal [Solomon's seal, Solomon seal, Solomon's seal, Solomons-seale, S'alomon's seale, Salamons seale] (1, 50, 93, 109, 138, 155, 156, 158) (1900–present)

Polygonatum multiflorum **(L.) All.** – European Solomon's-seal [European Solomonseal] (138) (1923), Many-flower Solomon's-seal [Manny flowered Solomon's seal, Many-flowered Solomon's-seal] (187) (1818), Our Lady's seal [Our Ladyes seale] (178, 179) (1526–1596), Polygonatum (178) (1596), Solomon's-seal [Solomon's seal, Solomon seal, Solomon's seal, Solomons-seal, S'alomon's seal, Salamons seale] (107, 178, 179) (1526–1919)

Polygonatum multiflorum **All.** – See *Polygonatum multiflorum* (L.) All.

Polygonatum multiflorum latifolium – See *Polygonatum multiflorum* (L.) All.

Polygonatum officinale All. – See *Polygonatum odoratum* (Mill.) Druce

Polygonatum perfoliatum – possibly *Uvularia perfoliata* L.

Polygonatum pubescens **(Willd.) Pursh** – Blue seal [Blew seal] (46) (1671), Hairy Solomon's-seal [Hairy Solomon's seal] (42) (1814), Solomon's-seal [Solomon's seal, Solomon seal, Solomon's seal, Solomons-seal, S'alomon's seal, Salamons seale] (46) (1649)

Polygonella americana **(F & M) Small** – Jointweed [Joint-weed, Joint weed] (4, 124) (1937–1986), Small jointweed (122) (1937) TX, Southern jointweed (5, 50, 155) (1913–present)

Polygonella articulata **(L.) Meisn.** – Coast jointweed [Coast joint weed, Coast joint-weed] (5, 50, 122, 124, 156) (1913–present), Jointed-leaf knotweed [Jointed-leaved knot-weed] (187) (1818), Jointweed [Joint-weed, Joint weed] (19, 47, 92) (1840–1876), Sandgrass [Sand grass] (5, 75, 156) (1894–1923) Wellfleet MA

Polygonella **Michx.** – Jointweed [Joint-weed, Joint weed] (1) (1932)

Polygonum **(Tourn.) L.** – See *Polygonum* L.

Polygonum achoreum **Blake** – Erect knotweed [Erect knot-weed] (3) (1977), Knotweed [Knot-weed] (4) (1986), Leathery knotweed (50, 155) (1942–present)

Polygonum acre **Kunth** – See *Polygonum punctatum* Ell. var. *punctatum*

Polygonum amphibium **L.** – Colubrina (46) (1879), Ground-willow [Ground willow] (156, 157, 158) (1900–1929), Heart's-ease [Heart's ease, Heartsease, Hearts' ease] (77, 156, 158) (1898–1923), Mud knotweed (19) (1840), Naterwurtz (German) (46) (1879), Redshank [Red shank, Red-shank, Red shanks, Redshanks, Red-shanks] (156, 157, 158) (1900–1929), Serpentaria (46) (1879), Water knot-weed (50) (present), Water lady's-thumb [Water ladysthumb] (155) (1942), Water peachwort (46) (1879), Water persicaria (72, 122, 131, 156, 157, 158) (1899–1937), Water polygonum (2) (1895), Water smartweed [Water smart weed, Water smart-weed] (2, 4, 82, 156, 157) (1900–1930), Water-willow [Water willow, Waterwillow, Water willoe] (156) (1923), Willow-grass [Willow grass] (157, 158) (1900–1929), Willow-weed [Willow weed, Willowweed] (157, 158) (1900–1929)

Polygonum amphibium **L. var. emersum Michx.** – Aquatic knotweed (187) (1818), Arsmart [Arsesmart, Aarse-smart, Arssmert] (181) (~1678), Big-root lady's-thumb [Bigroot ladysthumb] (155) (1942), Creeping knotweed (19) (1840), Dense-flower persicaria [Dense-flowered persicaria] (5) (1913), Devil's-shoestring [Devil's shoe-string, Devil's shoe string, Devil's-shoestrings, Devil's shoe-strings, Devil's shoestrings, Devil's shoe strings] (80) (1913) IA, Heart's-ease [Heart's ease, Heartsease, Hearts' ease] (5, 114) (1894–1913), Lake knotweed (19) (1840), Long-root smartweed [Longroot smartweed] (50) (present), Marsh smartweed (80, 82) (1913–1930) IA, Muhlenberg's smartweed [Muhlenberg's smart weed] (56, 80) (1901–1913), Potincoba (181) (~1678), Scarlet knotweed [Scarlet knot-weed] (187) (1818), Shoestring [Shoe string] (80) (1913) IA,

Swamp persicaria (5, 72, 93, 97, 120, 131) (1899–1938), Swamp smartweed (3, 4) (1977–1986), Tannin plant (114) (1894) Neb, Tanweed (80, 82) (1913–1930) IA, Water smartweed [Water smart weed] (145) (1897)

Polygonum amphibium **L. var. hartwrightii (Gray) Bissell** – See *Polygonum amphibium* L. var. *stipulaceum* Coleman

Polygonum amphibium **L. var. stipulaceum Coleman** – Floating lady's-thumb [Floating ladysthumb] (155) (1942), Hart Wright's persicaria (72) (1907), Hartwright's persicaria (131) (1899), Swimming knotweed (19) (1840), Water smartweed [Water smart weed, Water smart-weed] (50, 82) (1930–present)

Polygonum amplexicaule **D. Don** – See *Persicaria amplexicaulis (D. Don) Ronse Decr.*

Polygonum arenastrum **Jord. ex Boreau** – Common knotweed (3) (1977), Knotweed [Knot-weed] (4) (1986), Oval-leaf knotweed (50) (present)

Polygonum arifolium **L.** – Halberd knotweed [Halbert knotweed] (19) (1840), Hastate knot-grass [Hastate knot grass] (92) (1876), Sickle-grass [Sickle grass] (5, 92, 156) (1876–1923), Tear-thumb [Tear thumb, Tear-thumb] (86, 92) (1876–1878) from sharp prickles

Polygonum ariifolium **(sic) L.** – See *Polygonum arifolium* L.

Polygonum articulata **(L.) Meisn.** – See *Polygonella articulata* (L.) Meisn.

Polygonum articulatum – See *Polygonella articulata* (L.) Meisn.

Polygonum atlanticum **(B.L. Robins.) Bickn. p.p.** – See *Polygonum ramosissimum* Michx. var. *ramosissimum*

Polygonum aubertii **Henry** – China fleecevine [China fleece-vine] (109, 138) (1923–1949), Silver lace vine [Silver lace-vine] (109) (1949)

Polygonum aviculare **L.** – All-seed [All seed] (158) (1900), Armstrong (158) (1900), Beggarweed [Beggar weed, Beggar-weed] (5, 156, 158) (1900–1923), Bird knotgrass [Bird knot-grass] (156) (1923), Birdgrass [Bird's grass, Bird-grass, Bird grass] (5, 158) (1900–1913), Bird's-tongue [Birds tongue] (5, 156, 158) (1900–1923), Birdweed [Bird weed, Bird-weed] (5, 7, 92, 156, 158) (1828–1923), Centinode (158) (1900), Common knot-grass (187) (1818), Common knotweed (2, 7) (1828–1932), Cow-grass [Cow grass] (5, 156, 158) (1900–1923) no longer in use by 1923, Crab-grass [Crab-grass, Crab grass] (5) (1913), Crabweed [Crab-weed] (158) (1900), Dog's-tail [Dog's tail, Dog's-tails, Dog-tails] (77) (1898), Door-grass [Door grass] (5, 73, 156, 158) (1892–1923) Southern IN, Doorweed [Door-weed, Door weed] (2, 47, 62, 72, 145, 156, 158) (1852–1923), Dooryard grass [Door-yard grass] (129, 156) (1894–1923) SD, Dooryard knotweed (80) (1913) IA, Finzach (158) (1900), Goose-grass [Goose grass] (5, 62, 92, 129, 156, 158) (1894–1923), Hogweed [Hog-weed, Hog weed] (158) (1900), Iron-grass [Iron grass] (156, 158) (1900–1923), Knotgrass [Knot grass, Knot-grass, Knotgrasse] (5, 7, 19, 45, 46, 62, 92, 97, 122, 129, 131, 156, 158, 179) (1526–1937) accidentally introduced by 1671, Knotweed [Knot-weed] (4, 125, 129) (1894–1986), Knotwort [Knot-wort] (158, 179) (1526–1900), Male knotgrass [Male knot-grass] (158) (1900), Mantil (158) (1900), Ninety-knot [Ninety knot] (5, 92, 156, 158) (1876–1923), Pinkweed [Pink weed, Pinkweed] (5, 93, 156, 158) (1900–1936), Prostrate knotweed (50, 155) (1942–present), Renouee vulgaire (French) (7) (1828), Sparrow's-tongue [Sparrow tongue, Sparrow-tongue] (5, 156, 158, 179, 180) (1526–1923), Stoneweed [Stone weed, Stone-weed] (5, 156, 158) (1900–1923), Swine-grass [Swine grass, Swines' grass, Swine's-grass] (5, 92, 156, 158) (1876–1923) no longer in use by 1923, Swine-grass [Swynes grasse] (179) (1526), Tacker-grass [Tacker grass] (156, 158) (1900–1923), Way-grass [Way grass] (5, 156, 158) (1900–1923), Wire-grass [Wire grass] (5, 73, 156, 158) (1892–1923) Northern OH, Wireweed [Wire weed, Wire-weed] (5, 156, 158) (1900–1923), Yardgrass (85) (1932) SD

Polygonum baldschuanicum **Regel** – Silver fleece vine [Silver fleece-vine] (138) (1923)

Polygonum baldschunicum – See *Polygonum baldschuanicum*

Regel

Polygonum bellardii All. – Bearded knot-weed (187) (1818), Knotweed [Knot-weed] (4) (1986), Narrow-leaf knotweed [Narrowleaf knotweed, Narrow-leaved knotweed] (5, 50, 122) (1913-prresent)

Polygonum bicorne Raf. – See *Polygonum pensylvanicum* L.

Polygonum bistorta L. – Bistort (57, 92, 107) (1876–1919), Bistorta (57) (1917), Bistorte (179) (1526), Dragonwort [Dragon wort] (92) (1876), Easter giant (92) (1876), Great snakeweed [Great snake weede] (178) (1526), Ma-shu (Western Eskimo) (107) (1919), Patience dock (92) (1876), Red-legs [Red legs] (92) (1876), Snakeweed [Snake-weed, Snake weed, Snake Weede] (92, 107, 178) (1526–1919)

Polygonum buxiforme Small – Box knotweed (50, 155) (1942–present), Knotweed [Knot-weed] (4) (1986), Shore knotweed (5, 93) (1913–1936)

Polygonum caespitosum Blume – Oriental lady's-thumb [Oriental ladysthumb] (50) (present)

Polygonum caespitosum Blume var. *longisetum* (de Bruyn) A. N. Steward – Oriental lady's-thumb [Oriental ladysthumb] (50) (present), Smartweed [Smart-weed, Smart weed] (4, 85) (1932–1986)

Polygonum camporum Meisn. – See *Polygonum striatulum* B.L. Robins.

Polygonum careyi Olney – Carey's persicaria (5) (1913)

Polygonum cilinode Michx. – Black bindweed [Black bind-weed] (2) (1895), Fringed black bindweed (5) (1913)

Polygonum coccineum Muhl. – See *Polygonum amphibium* L. var. *emersum* Michx.

Polygonum convolvulus L. – Bearbind [Bear-bind] (5, 156, 158) (1900–1923), Bind knotweed (19) (1840), Bindweed [Bind weed, Bind-weed] (95, 106) (1911–1930), Bindweed polygonum [Bindweed polygonum] (187) (1818), Black bindweed [Black bind-weed, Blacke bindeweed] (5, 50, 62, 72, 80, 82, 93, 131, 156, 178187) (1526–present), Black birdweed (92, 106, 158) (1876–1930), Black-bird bindweed (5, 156, 158) (1900–1923), Chizahaw (Osage) (7) (1828), Climbing bindweed (5, 156, 158) (1900–1923), Climbing buckwheat (4, 92, 156, 158, 187) (1818–1986), Corn bindweed (5, 93, 97, 122, 156, 158) (1900–1937), Cornbind [Corn-bind, Corn bind] (5, 156, 158) (1900–1923), Dull-seed knotweed [Dullseed knotweed] (155) (1942), Ivy bindweed (5, 156, 158) (1900–1923), Knot bindweed (5, 156, 158) (1900–1923), Wild bean [Wild-bean, Wildbean, Wild beans] (77) (1898) Oxford ME, Wild buckwheat (3, 4, 62, 80, 82, 106, 145) (1897–1986), With-wind [Withwind] (158) (1900), Devil's-tether [Devil's tether] (5, 156, 158) (1900–1923)

Polygonum convolvulus L. var. *convolvulus* – Bindweed [Bind weed, Bind-weed] (85) (1932)

Polygonum cuspidatum Sieb. & Zucc. – Crested false buckwheat (72) (1907), Japanese bamboo (4) (1986), Japanese fleeceflower (138, 155) (1923–1942) IA, Japanese knotweed (3, 5, 50, 109) (1913–present) NM, Mexican bamboo [Mexican-bamboo] (4, 109) (1949–1986)

Polygonum densiflorum Meisn. – Southwestern persicaria (5) (1913)

Polygonum douglasii Greene – Douglas' knotweed [Douglas knotweed, Douglas knotweed] (5, 50, 72, 97, 131, 155) (1899–present), Knotweed [Knot-weed] (4) (1986)

Polygonum douglasii Greene subsp. *douglasii* – Douglas' knotweed [Douglas knot-weed, Douglas knotweed] (50) (present)

Polygonum douglasii Greene subsp. *johnstonii* (Munz) Hickman – Johnston's knotweed (50) (present), Knotweed [Knot-weed] (4) (1986), Sawatch knotweed (155) (1942), Western persicaria (131) (1899)

Polygonum dumetorum L. var. *scandens* (L.) Gray – See *Polygonum scandens* L. var. *scandens*

Polygonum dumetorum var. *scandens* Gray. – See *Polygonum scandens* L. var. *scandens*

Polygonum emarginatum Roth – See *Fagopyrum esculentum* Moench

Polygonum emersum (Michx.) Britt. – See *Polygonum amphibium* L.

var. *emersum* Michx.

Polygonum erectum L. – Dooryard grass [Door-yard grass] (129) (1894) SD, Erect knotweed [Erect knot-weed] (4, 5, 50, 62, 72, 80, 93, 97, 131, 155) (1899–present), Goose-grass [Goose grass] (77, 129) (1894–1898), Upright knotweed (129) (1894)

Polygonum exsertum Small – See *Polygonum ramosissimum* Michx. var. *ramosissimum*

Polygonum fagopyrum L. – See *Fagopyrum esculentum* Moench

Polygonum fluitans Eat – See *Polygonum amphibium* L. var. *stipulaceum* Coleman

Polygonum fowleri Robinson – Fowler's knotweed (5) (1913)

Polygonum hartwrightii Gray – See *Polygonum amphibium* L. var. *stipulaceum* Coleman

Polygonum hydropiper L. – Arsenick (158) (1900), Arsmart [Arsesmart, Aarse-smart, Arssmert] (46, 157, 158, 179) (1526–1929) deliberately introduced by colonists by 1671, Josselyn, Bite-tongue [Bite tongue] (5, 156, 157, 158) (1900–1929), Biting knotweed [Biting knot-weed, Biting knot weed] (5, 92, 156, 157, 158) (1876–1929), Biting persicaria (5, 156, 157, 158) (1900–1929), Ciderage (157, 158) (1900–1929), Common smartweed (2, 62, 80, 156) (1895–1923), Culrage (157, 158, 179) (1526–1929), Doorweed [Door-weed, Door weed] (92) (1876), Lakeweed [Lake weed, Lakeweed] (92, 157, 158) (1876–1929), Marsh-pepper knotweed [Marsh-pepper knotweed] (50) (present), Marsh-pepper smartweed [Marsh-pepper smartweed] (155) (1942), Pepper plant [Pepper-plant] (5, 156, 157, 158) (1900–1923), Red-knees [Red knees] (5, 92, 156, 157, 158) (1876–1929), Red-leaves (156) (1923), Redshank [Red shank, Red-shank, Red shanks, Redshanks, Red-shanks] (5, 156, 157, 158) (1900–1929), Sanguinary (179) (1526), Sickleweed [Sickle-weed, Sickle weed] (5, 92, 156, 158) (1876–1923), Smartweed [Smart-weed, Smart weed] (5, 49, 72, 79, 93, 97, 131, 157, 158) (1891–1937), Snakeweed [Snake-weed, Snake weed, Snake Weede] (5, 156) (1913–1923), Water-pepper [Water pepper] (3, 4, 5, 47, 48, 49, 62, 80, 82, 92, 93, 97, 122, 124, 125, 156, 157, 158) (1852–1986), possibly Culrage (French) (180) (1633)

Polygonum hydropiperoides Michx. – Arsmart [Arsesmart, Aarse-smart, Arssmert] (46, 92) (1671–1876), Bristly persicaria (5) (1913), Mild water-pepper [Mild water pepper] (4, 5, 62, 72, 93, 97, 120, 156) (1907–1986), Opelousus persicaria (72) (1907), Ragged-sailor [Ragged sailor, Ragged sailors] (5) (1913), Small waterpepper [Small water pepper] (124) (1937), Smartweed [Smart-weed, Smart weed] (80) (1913), Southwest smartweed (3) (1977), Southwestern persicaria (5, 122) (1913–1937), Swamp smartweed (50, 155) (1942–present), Tasteless knotweed (19) (1840), Water-pepper [Water pepper] (80) (1913)

Polygonum incarnatum Ell. – See *Polygonum lapathifolium* L.

Polygonum L. – Bindweed [Bind weed, Bind-weed] (1, 93) (1932–1936), Bistort (1) (1932), Blindweed [Blind-weed, Blind weed] (77) (1898) Sulphur Grove OH, twining species, Buckwheat [Buckwheat] (10, 167) (1814–1818), Doorweed [Door-weed, Door weed] (1, 93, 106) (1930–1936), False buckwheat (5) (1913), Heart's-ease [Heart's ease, Heartsease, Hearts' ease] (77, 106) (1898–1930), Jointweed [Joint-weed, Joint weed] (2) (1895), Knotgrass [Knot grass, Knot-grass, Knotgrasse] (1, 93, 167) (1814–1936), Knotweed [Knot-weed] (1, 4, 50, 82, 93, 106, 109, 158) (1900–present), Lady's-thumb [Ladies' thumb, Lady's thumb] (1, 106) (1930–1932), Persicaria (10, 106) (1818–1930), Pull-down (77) (1898), Smartweed [Smart-weed, Smart weed] (1, 4, 82, 93, 106, 122) (1930–1986), Tear-thumb [Tear thumb, Tear-thumb] (1, 155) (1932–1942), Tovara (155) (1942), Water smartweed [Water smart weed] (106) (1930), Water-pepper [Water pepper] (1, 93, 106) (1930–1936)

Polygonum lapathifolium L. – Curly-top knotweed [Curlytop knotweed] (50) (present), Curly-top ladysthumb [Curlytop ladysthumb] (155) (1942), Dock-leaf persicaria [Dock-leaved persicaria] (5, 93, 131, 156) (1899–1936), Heart's-ease [Heart's ease, Heartsease, Hearts' ease] (82) (1930), Nodding smartweed (80, 82) (1913–1930),

Pale persicaria (72, 93, 97, 156) (1907–1937), Pale smartweed (3, 4, 98) (1926–1986), Pink nodding smartweed (82) (1930), Pink persicaria (72) (1907), Pink smartweed (80, 82) (1913–1930), Smartweed [Smart-weed, Smart weed] (85, 145) (1897–1932), Upland heart's-ease [Upland hearstease] (114) (1894), Willow-weed [Willow weed, Willowweed] (156) (1923), Woolly smartweed (155) (1942)

Polygonum leptocarpum **Robinson** – See *Polygonum ramosissimum* Michx.

Polygonum littorale **Link** – See *Polygonum buxiforme* Small

Polygonum longistylum **Small** – See *Polygonum pensylvanicum* L.

Polygonum maritimum **L.** – Coast knotgrass (5) (1913), Seaside knotweed (5) (1913)

Polygonum mite **(Pers.)** – See *Polygonum hydropiperoides* Michx.

Polygonum muhlenbergii **Watson.** – See *Polygonum amphibium* L. var. *emersum* Michx.

Polygonum natans **Eat.** – See *Polygonum amphibium* L. var. *stipulaceum* Coleman

Polygonum neglectum **Besser** – See *Polygonum bellardii* All.

Polygonum opelousanum **Riddell ex Small** – See *Polygonum hydropiperoides* Michx.

Polygonum orientale **L.** – Garden persicary (156, 158) (1900–1923), Gentleman's-cane [Gentleman's cane] (5, 75, 77, 156, 158) (1894–1923) OH, stems cut by children into canes, Kiss-me-over-the-fence (77) (1898) Sulphur Grove OH, Kiss-me-over-the-garden-gate (3, 4, 50) (1977–present), Love-lies-bleeding [Love lies bleeding] (156) (1923), Opelousas persicaria (5) (1913), Prince's-feather [Prince's feather, Princes-feather, Princesfeather] (5, 19, 77, 82, 93, 109, 156, 158) (1913–1949), Prince's-plume [Prince's plume, Princesplume] (138) (1923), Prince's-plume lady's-thumb [Princesplume ladysthumb] (155) (1942), Princess feather (72, 122) (1907–1937), Ragged-sailor [Ragged sailor, Ragged sailors] (77, 82, 92, 156, 158) (1898–1930), Tall persicaria (187) (1818)

Polygonum pensylvanicum **L.** – Glandular persicary (62) (1912), Heartseed [Heart seed, Heart-seed] (105) (1932), Knee knotweed (19) (1840), Long-style persicaria [Longstyled persicaria, Long-styled persicaria] (5, 97, 122) (1913–1937), Pebigumškike (Chippewa) (105) (1932), Pennsylvania knotweed [Pennsylvanian knot-weed] (187) (1818), Pennsylvania persicaria (5, 93, 97, 131) (1899–1937), Pennsylvania smartweed (4, 19, 50, 62, 72, 80, 82, 155) (1840–present), Persicaria (122) (1937), Pink smartweed (4) (1986), Smartweed [Smart-weed, Smart weed] (80, 125, 145) (1897–1930)

Polygonum periscarioides **Kunth** – See *Polygonum hydropiperoides* Michx.

Polygonum persicaria **L.** – Arsmart [Arsesmart, Aarse-smart, Arssmert] (46) (1671) deliberately introduced by colonists by 1671, Josselyn, Asmart [Ass-smart] (7) (1828), Crab's-claw (158) (1900), Doorweed [Door-weed, Door weed] (92) (1876), Heart's-ear (158) (1900), Heart-spot knotweed (19) (1840), Persicaria (158) (1900), Persicary (158) (1900), Plumbago (158) (1900), Smartweed [Smart-weed, Smart weed] (7, 40) (1828–1928), Spotted knotweed (92) (1876), Spotted lady's-thumb [Spotted ladysthumb] (50, 155) (1942–present), Spotted smartweed (62) (1912), Water-pepper [Water pepper] (7) (1828), Curage (French, Louisiana) (7, 180) (1633–1828) Louisiana Purchase

Polygonum prolificum **(Small) Robinson** – See *Polygonum ramosissimum* Michx.

Polygonum punctatum **Ell.** – American smartweed (157, 158) (1900–1929), Arsmart [Arsesmart, Aarse-smart, Arssmert] (157, 158) (1900–1929), Biting knotweed [Biting knot-weed, Biting knot weed] (19) (1840), Dotted smartweed [Dotted smart-weed] (5, 50, 93, 97, 155, 157, 158) (1900–present), Hydropiper (157, 158) (1900–1929), Ojig'imïn (Chippewa, fisher berry) (40) (1928), Smartweed [Smart-weed, Smart weed] (1, 40, 48, 52, 92, 125) (1876–1932), Turkey-troop [Turkey troop] (5, 157, 158) (1900–1929), Water smartweed [Water smart weed, Water smart-weed] (3, 4, 5, 72, 93, 97, 122, 131, 157, 158) (1899–1986), Water-pepper [Water pepper] (5, 19, 61, 157, 158) (1840–1929), Water-pepper knotweed [Water-pepper

knot-weed] (187) (1818)

Polygonum punctatum **Ell. var.** *confertiflorum* **(Meisn.) Fassett** – Dotted smartweed [Dotted smart-weed] (50) (present)

Polygonum punctatum **Ell. var.** *punctatum* – American water-pepper (46) (1879), Arsmart [Arsesmart, Aarse-smart, Arssmert] (46) (1671), Biting knotweed [Biting knot-weed, Biting knot weed] (6) (1892), Bitter smartweed (155) (1942), Dotted smartweed [Dotted smart-weed] (50, 156) (1923–present), Knöterich (German) (6) (1892), Smartweed [Smart-weed, Smart weed] (6, 57) (1892–1917), Turkey-troop [Turkey troop] (73, 156) (1892–1923) Long Island NY, Water smartweed [Water smart weed, Water smart-weed] (2, 6, 80, 82, 156) (1892–1932), Water-pepper [Water pepper] (6, 57, 156) (1892–1923), Wild smartweed (48) (1882), Asmart [Ass-smart] (6) (1892)

Polygonum raii **Bab.** – Ray's knotweed (72) (1907)

Polygonum ramosissimum **Michx.** – Bush knotweed (122) (1937) TX, Bushy knotweed [Bushy knot-weed] (3, 5, 50, 72, 80, 93, 97, 98, 131, 155) (1899–present), Erect knotweed [Erect knot-weed] (80) (1913), Knotweed [Knot-weed] (4, 85) (1932–1986), Long-fruit knotweed [Long fruited knotweed] (72, 93) (1907–1936), Narrow-point knotweed [Narrow-pointed knotweed] (5) (1913), Proliferous knotweed [Proliferous knot-weed] (5, 97) (1913–1937), Wireweed [Wire weed, Wire-weed] (145) (1897)

Polygonum ramosissimum **Michx. var.** *ramosissimum* – Atlantic coast knotweed (5) (1913), Knotweed (4, 85) (1932–1986), Long-fruit knotweed [Long fruited knotweed] (5, 72, 93) (1907–1936), Missouri knotweed (5) (1913)

Polygonum rayi **Babingt.** – See *Polygonum raii* Bab.

Polygonum sachalinense **F. Schmidt ex Maxim.** – Sacaline (109, 138) (1923–1949)

Polygonum sagittatum **L.** – Arrow-leaf tearthumb [Arrowleaf tearthumb, Arrow-leaved tear-thumb, Arrow-leaved tear thumb] (5, 50, 62, 72, 82, 93, 155, 156, 158) (1899–present), Cowtongue [Cow tongue, Cow-tongue] (177) (1762), Prickly knotweed (19) (1840), Scratch-grass [Scratch grass] (19, 79) (1840–1891), Tear-thumb [Tear thumb, Tear-thumb] (2, 4, 85) (1895–1986)

Polygonum sawatchense **Small** – See *Polygonum douglasii* Greene subsp. *johnstonii* (Munz) Hickman

Polygonum scandens **L.** – American climbing buckwheat (187) (1818), Bindweed [Bind weed, Bind-weed] (62) (1912), Climbing buckwheat (19, 82) (1840–1930), Climbing false buckwheat (3, 50, 62, 72, 131, 156) (1899–present), False buckwheat (4, 158) (1900–1986), Hedge cornbind (155) (1942), Vine false buckwheat (122) (1937)

Polygonum scandens **L. var.** *cristatum* **(Engelm. & Gray) Gleason** – Crested false buckwheat (5) (1913)

Polygonum scandens **L. var.** *dumetorum* **(L.) Gleason** – Chokeweed [Choak weed] (46) (1610), Climbing buckwheat (46) (1879), Climbing false buckwheat (2) (1895), Copse buckwheat (5) (1913), False buckwheat (5) (1913), Hedge buckwheat (5, 72, 97) (1907–1937)

Polygonum scandens **L. var.** *scandens* – Climbing false buckwheat (5, 50, 93, 97) (1913–present), False buckwheat (1, 85) (1932), Wild buckwheat (77) (1898) Burnside SD

Polygonum setaceum **Baldw.** – Bristle persicaria (122) (1937)

Polygonum striatulum **B. L. Robins.** – Prairie knotweed [Prairie knot-weed] (72, 131) (1899–1907) Neb NM

Polygonum tataricum **L.** – See *Fagopyrum tataricum* (L.) Gaertn.

Polygonum tenue **Michx.** – Doorweed [Door-weed, Door weed] (93) (1936), Knotweed [Knot-weed] (4) (1986), Pleat-leaf knotweed [Pleatleaf knotweed] (50) (present), Slender knot-grass [Slender knot grass] (19) (1840), Slender knotweed [Slender knot-weed] (3, 5, 72, 93, 97, 122, 131) (1899–1977), Slim knotweed (155) (1942)

Polygonum terrestre **[Hegetschw.]** – See *Polygonum amphibium* L.

Polygonum tinctorium **Aiton** – See Persicaria tinctoria (Aiton) H. Gross

Polygonum tomentosum **Schrank** – See *Polygonum lapathifolium* L.

Polygonum triangulum **Bickn.** – See *Polygonum ramosissimum*

Michx. var. *ramosissimum*

Polygonum virginianum **L.** – Camomile [Chamomile, Camomylle] (82) (1930), Knotweed [Knot-weed] (122, 184) (1793–1937), Virginia bistort (157, 158) (1900–1929), Virginia knotweed (5, 72, 93, 97, 157, 158) (1900–1937), Virginia tovara (155) (1942), possibly Jumpseed [Jump-seed] (50, 156) (1923–present)

Polygonum viviparum **L.** – Alpine bistort (3, 5, 131) (1899–1977), Bistort (4) (1986), Mortog (Sweden "swine grass") (107) (1919), Serpent-grass [Serpent grass] (5, 107) (1913–1919), Small snakeweed [Small snake weede] (178) (1526), Viviparous bistort (155) (1942)

Polymnia canadensis L – Leafcup [Leaf-cup, Leaf cup] (82) (1930), Small-flower leaf-cup [Small-flowered leaf-cup] (5, 72, 97) (1907–1937), White leaf-cup (19) (1840), White-flower leaf-cup [White-flower leafcup] (50) (present)

Polymnia **L.** – Leafcup [Leaf-cup, Leaf cup] (1, 2, 4, 82, 155, 158) (1895–1986), Polymnia (50) (present)

Polymnia uvedalia **L.** – See *Smallanthus uvedalius* (L.) Mackenzie ex Small

Polypodium amorphum **Suksdorf** – Irregular polypody (50) (present)

Polypodium aureum **L.** – See *Phlebodium aureum* (L.) J. Sm.

Polypodium calaguala – See *Campyloneurum angustifolium* (Sw.) Fée

Polypodium californicum **Kaulfuss** – California polypody [Californian polypody] (86) (1878)

Polypodium dryopteris [**L.**] – See *Gymnocarpium dryopteris* (L.) Newman

Polypodium falcatum **Kellogg** – See *Cyrtomium falcatum* (L. f.) C. Presl

Polypodium fragile [**L.**] – See *Cystopteris fragilis* (L.) Bernh.

Polypodium glycyrrhiza **D.C. Eat.** – Licorice fern [Liquorice fern] (138) (1923)

Polypodium hesperium **Maxon** – Western polypody (3, 50) (1977–present)

Polypodium **L.** – Polypody (1, 50, 109, 138, 155, 158, 167) (1814–present) "many feet" for creeping rootstocks

Polypodium noveboracense **L.** – See *Thelypteris noveboracensis* (L.) Nieuwl.

Polypodium phyllitidis – See *Campyloneurum phyllitidis* (L.) K. Presl

Polypodium polypoides – See *Pleopeltis polypodioides* (L.) Andrews & Windham subsp. *polypodioides*

Polypodium polypoides (**L.**) **Watt var. michauxinaum Weath.** –

Polypodium virginianum **L.** – Brakeroot [Brake root] (7, 49, 58, 92) (1828–1869), Common polypody (3, 4, 49, 86, 109, 122, 131, 138, 155, 158, 187) (1818–1986), Evergreen fern (86) (1878), Female fern [Female Ferne] (2, 5, 7, 49, 58, 92) (1828–1895), Fernroot [Fern-root, Fern root] (7, 49, 92) (1828–1898), Licorice fern [Liquorice fern] (124) (1937) TX, Polypode common (French) (7) (1828), Polypodium (57) (1917), Polypody (14, 46, 57, 61, 72, 92) (1649–1917), Rock brake [Rock-brake, Rockbrake] (7, 19, 49, 92, 158) (1828–1840), Rock polypod (50, 58, 92) (1869–present)

Polypodium vulgare **L.** – See *Polypodium virginianum* L. (US species)

Polypodium vulgare **L. subsp. columbianum** (**Gilbert**) **Hultén** – See *Polypodium hesperium* Maxon

Polypogon **Desf.** – Beard grass [Beard-grass, Beardgrass] (1, 66, 93, 152) (1903–1932), Polypogon (155) (1942), Rabbit-foot grass [Rabbitfoot-grass, Rabbitfoot grass] (50) (present)

Polypogon interruptus **Kunth** – Ditch rabbits-foot grass [Ditch rabbits-foot grass] (50) (present)

Polypogon littoralis (**With.**) **Smith** – See *Agropogon littoralis* (Sm.) C. E. Hubbard

Polypogon lutosus (**Poir**) **Hitchc.** – See *Agropogon littoralis* (Sm.) C. E. Hubbard

Polypogon maritimus **Willd.** – Seaside beard grass [Sea-side beard-grass] (94) (1901)

Polypogon monspeliensis (**L.**) **Desf.** – Annual beard grass [Annual beard-grass, Annual beardgrass] (5, 45, 66, 119, 140, 163) (1852–1944), Annual rabbit's-foot grass [Annual rabbitsfoot grass] (50)

(present), Beard grass [Beard-grass, Beardgrass] (87) (1884), Bearded fox-tail grass (165) (1768), Rabbit-foot grass [Rabbitfoot-grass, Rabbitfoot grass] (3, 109, 122) (1937–1977), Rabbit-foot polypogon [Rabbitfoot polypogon] (140, 155) (1942–1944)

Polypogon viridis (**Gouan**) **Breistr.** – Beardless rabbit's-foot grass [Beardless rabbitsfoot grass] (50) (present), Water bent grass [Water bent-grass, Water bentgrass] (94, 122, 155) (1901–1942)

Polyporus arcularius (**Batsch**) **Fr.** – Fringed pore fungus (128) (1933)

Polyporus fomentarium **Fries** – possibly *Fomes fomentarius* (L.) Fr.

Polyporus igniarius (**L.**) **Fr.** – Touchwood (92) (1876)

Polyporus officinalis (**Batsch**) **Fr.** – Agaryk (178, 179) (1526–1596)

Polyporus officinalis **Fries** – See *Polyporus officinalis* (Batsch) Fr.

Polyporus **P. Micheli ex Adans.** – Spunck (46) (1879), Touchwood (46) (1879)

Polyporus pargamenus **Fr.** – Paper pore fungus (128) (1933)

Polyporus sulphureus (**Bull.**) **Fr.** – Sulfur pore fungus [Sulphur pore fungus] (128) (1933)

Polypremum procumbens **L.** – Polyprenum (5, 97) (1913–1937)

Polypteris callosa (**Nutt.**) **Gray** – See *Palafoxia callosa* (Nutt.) Torr. & Gray

Polypteris hookeriana – See *Palafoxia hookeriana* Torr. & A. Gray var. *hookeriana*

Polypteris **Nutt.** – See Palafoxia Lag. (all US species)

Polyscias – See *Polyscias* J. R. & G. Forst.

Polyscias balfouriana – See *Polyscias scutellaria* (Burm. f.) Fosberg

Polyscias cumingiana (**K. Presl**) – Fern-leaf polyscias [Fernleaf polyscias] (138) (1923)

Polyscias filicifolia – See *Polyscias cumingiana* (K. Presl)

Polyscias guilfoylei (**Bull ex Cogn. & E. March.**) **Bailey** – Guilfoyle's polyscias [Guilfoyle polyscias] (138) (1923)

Polyscias **J. R. & G. Forst.** – Polyscias (138) (1923)

Polyscias scutellaria (**Burm. f.**) **Fosberg** – Balfour polyscias (138) (1923)

Polystichum acrostichoides (**Michx.**) **Schott** – Christmas fern [Christmasfern, Christmas-fern] (3, 50, 72, 97, 109, 122, 138, 155) (1907–present), Dagger fern [Dagger-fern] (109) (1949), Terminal shield fern (187)

Polystichum adiantiforme – See *Rumohra adiantiformis* (G. Forst.) Ching

Polystichum brauni – See *Polystichum braunii* (Spenner) Fee

Polystichum braunii (**Spenner**) **Fee** – Braun's holly fern [Braun holly-fern, Braun's holly-fern] (4, 5, 19, 50, 138) (1840–present), Prickly shield fern [Prickly shield-fern] (5) (1913), Shield fern [Shield-fern] (109) (1949)

Polystichum braunii (**Spenner**) **Fée subsp. purshii** (**Fern.**) **Calder & Taylor** – See *Polystichum braunii* (Spenner) Fee

Polystichum lonchitis (**L.**) **Roth.** – Holly fern [Hollyfern, Holly-fern] (4) (1986), Mountain holly fern [Mountain hollyfern, Mountain holly-fern] (109, 138, 155) (1923–1949), Northern holly fern [Northern hollyfern] (50) (present), Rough alpine fern (5) (1913)

Polystichum mohrioides (**Bory**) **K. Presl var. scopulinum** (**D. C. Eat.**) **Fern.** – See *Polystichum scopulinum* (D. C. Eaton) Maxon.

Polystichum munitum (**Kaulfuss**) **K. Presl** – Chamisso's shield fern (86) (1878) for botanist on Vancouver's voyage, Christmas fern [Christmasfern, Christmas-fern] (3) (1977), Giant holly fern [Giant hollyfern] (138) (1923), Sword fern [Sword-fern, Swordfern] (4) (1986), Western sword fern [Western swordfern, Western sword-fern] (50, 109, 155) (1942–present)

Polystichum **Roth.** – Christmas fern [Christmasfern, Christmas-fern] (4) (1986), Holly fern [Hollyfern, Holly-fern] (1, 4, 50, 109, 138, 155) (1923–present)

Polystichum scopulinum (**D. C. Eaton**) **Maxon.** – Eaton's shield fern [Eaton's shield-fern] (1, 5) (1913–1932), Mountain holly fern [Mountain hollyfern, Mountain holly-fern] (50) (present)

Polystictus versicolor (**L.**) **Fr.** – Channankpa (Dakota, tree ears) (37) (1830)

Polytaenia **DC.** – Hairy moss (50) (present), Polytaenia (158) (1900),

Prairie parsley (1) (1932)

Polytaenia nuttallii **DC.** – Nuttall's prairie-parsley [Nuttall's prairie parsley] (5, 50, 97) (1913–present), Polytaenia (72) (1907), Prairie parsley (3, 4, 122) (1937–1986)

Polytrichum apiculatum **Kindb.** – See *Polytrichum juniperinum* Hedw.

Polytrichum commune **Hedw.** – Bear-grass [Bear grass, Bear's grass, Bears' grass] (78) (1898) ME, Bear's-bread [Bears' bread] (73) (1892) Dennysville ME, Bird wheat [Bird's wheat] (78) (1898) Kennebec Valley ME, Rum suckers (73) (1892) NH, unripe spores supposedly have a spirituous taste

Polytrichum juniperinum **Hedw.** – Bearbed [Bear's bed] (50, 58, 92) (1869–present), Ground moss (50, 92) (1876–present), Hair-cap moss (19, 49, 52, 54, 57, 58, 61, 92) (1840–1917), Juniper polytrichum moss (50) (present), May-queen moss [May queen moss] (92) (1876), Robin's-rye [Robin's rye] (50, 58, 92) (1869–present

Poncirus trifoliata **(L.) Raf.** – Bitter orange (122, 124) (1937) TX, Orange [Oranges, Orenge] (138) (1923), Trifoliate-orange (109) (1949)

Poncirus trifoliata **Raf.** – See *Poncirus trifoliata* (L.) Raf.

Pontederia cordata **L.** – Alligator wampee (158) (1900), Common pickerel weed (2) (1895), Heart-leaf pontederia [Heart-leaved pontederia] (187) (1818), Lance pickerelweed (155) (1942), Michelia (177) (1762), Mouse-ear [Mouse ear, Mouse ears, Mouse's ear, Mows eare] (78) (1898) Grand Lake NB, Pickerel weed [Pickerelweed, Pickerel-weed] (5, 50, 72, 92, 97, 106, 109, 120, 122, 124, 138, 155, 156, 187) (1818–present), Pond-shovel [Pond shovel] (7) (1828), Shovel pickerel-weed [Shovel pickerelweed] (7) (1828), Shovel-leaf [Shovel leaf] (7) (1828), Shovelweed [Shovel weed, Shovel-weed] (92) (1876), Uniseme deltine (French) (7) (1828), Wampee (106) (1930) Southern US, Water hyacinth [Water-hyacinth] (156) (1923), Water-plantain [Water plantain, Waterplantain] (7) (1828)

Pontederia cordata **L. var.** *lancifolia* **(Muhl. ex Ell.) Torr.** – See *Pontederia cordata* L.

Pontederia **L.** – Golden maidenhair [Golden-maidenhair, Golden-maiden-hair] (184) (1793), Pickerel weed [Pickerelweed, Pickerel-weed] (1, 19, 138, 155, 158) (1840–1942), Pontederia (50) (present), Wampee (1) (1932)

Populus ×*acuminata* **Rydb.** [*angustifolia* × *deltoides*] – Acuminate-leaf cottonwood [Acuminate leaved cottonwood] (149, 153) (1904–1913), Black cottonwood (5, 93, 112, 130, 131, 157) (1895–1937), Lance-leaf cottonwood [Lanceleaf cottonwood] (4, 50, 85) (1932–present), Rydberg's cottonwood (130) (1895), Smooth-bark cottonwood [Smoothbark cottonwood, Smooth-barked cottonwood] (1, 3, 93, 138) (1923–1977)

Populus ×*berolinensis* **K. Koch** – Poplar or Poplar tree [Poplar-tree] (112) (1937)

Populus ×*brayshawii* **Boivin** [*angustifolia* × *balsamifera*] – Hybrid balsam poplar (4, 50) (1986–present)

Populus ×*canadensis* **Moench** [*deltoides* × *nigra*] – Canadian poplar (20) (1857), Carolina poplar [Carolinian poplar] (4, 50, 82, 109, 135, 155) (1910–present), Cotton tree [Cotton-tree] (17) (1796), Cottonwood [Cotton wood, Cotton-wood] or Cottonwood tree [Cotton wood tree] (12, 20) (1820–1857), Eugene poplar (109) (1949), Late Carolina poplar (155) (1942), Liard (French Creole) (17, 23, 27) (1796–1811)

Populus ×*canescens* **(Aiton) Sm.** [*alba* × *tremula*] – Common white poplar (20) (1857), Gray poplar (4, 50, 20, 138) (1857–present), Peuplier grisaille (French) (20) (1857)

Populus ×*jackii* **Sargent** [*balsamifera* × *deltoides*] – Balm-of-Gilead [Balm of Gilead] or Balm-of-Gilead tree [Balm of Gilead tree] (4, 50) (1986–present)

Populus acuminata **Rydb.** – See *Populus* ×*acuminata* Rydb. [*angustifolia* × *deltoides*]

Populus alba **L.** – Abbey (158) (1900), Abel (5, 158) (1900–1913), Abele or Abele tree [Abele-tree] (5, 72, 92, 109, 156, 158) (1876–1949), Arbell (158) (1900), Aspen [Aspin] or Aspen tree [Aspen-tree] (5, 156) (1913–1923), Aspen poplar (158) (1900), Awbel (158)

(1900), Bolle's poplar [Bolles poplar] (135) (1910), Dutch beech (5, 156, 158) (1900–1923), Great aspen (5, 156, 158) (1900–1923), Poplar or Poplar tree [Poplar-tree] (92) (1876), Rattler tree [Rattler-tree] (5, 156, 158) (1900–1923), Silver poplar (1, 3, 4, 93, 112, 158) (1900–1986), Silver popple (158) (1900), Silver-leaf poplar [Silver-leaved poplar] (5, 85, 97, 156, 158) (1900–1937), White asp (158) (1900), White aspen (5, 156) (1913–1923), White poplar or White poplar tree (1, 5, 14, 20, 50, 72, 92, 93, 107, 109, 112, 138, 155, 156, 158) (1857–present), White-bark [White bark, Whitebark] (5, 156, 158) (1900–1923), Whiteleaf [White leaf, White-leaf] (156) (1923)

Populus alba **var.** *pyramidalis* **Bunge** – Bolleana poplar (112, 138) (1923–1937)

Populus angulata **Aiton** – See *Populus deltoides* Bartr. ex Marsh. subsp. *deltoides*

Populus angulosa **Michx.** – possibly *Populus deltoides* Bartr. ex Marsh. subsp. *deltoides* (taxonomic status is unresolved (PL))

Populus angustifolia **James** – Balsam poplar (160) (1860), Bitter balsam (160) (1860), Bitter cottonwood (30) (1844), Black cottonwood (1, 5, 113, 156) (1890–1932), Liard amere (French) (28) (1850), Long-leaf cottonwood [Long-leaved cotton wood] (38) (1820), Mountain cottonwood (149, 153) (1904–1913), Narrow-leaf balsam poplar [Narrow-leaved balsam poplar] (20) (1857), Narrow-leaf black cottonwood [Narrow-leaved black cottonwood] (130) (1895), Narrow-leaf cottonwood [Narrow-leaved cottonwood] (1, 3, 4, 5, 28, 50, 85, 93, 131, 135, 138, 157) (1850–present), Narrow-leaf poplar [Narrowleaf poplar, Narrow-leafed poplar, Narrow-leaved poplar] (28, 112, 155) (1850–1942), Peuplier baumier à feuilles atroites (French) (20) (1857), Tweedy poplar (155) (1942), Willow cottonwood (5, 156) (1913–1923), Willow-leaf cottonwood (30) (1844), Willow-leaf poplar [Willow-leaved poplar] (108) (1878)

Populus argentea **Michx. f.** – See *Populus heterophylla* L.

Populus balsamifera **L.** – Balm-of-Gilead [Balm of Gilead] or Balm-of-Gilead tree [Balm of Gilead tree] (57) (1917), Balsam poplar (1, 3, 4, 5, 10, 14, 20, 19, 40, 50, 57, 85, 91, 92, 93, 105, 108, 109, 112, 130, 131, 135, 138, 156, 157, 158) (1818–1986), Balsam tree [Balsam-tree] (8) (1785), Canadian poplar (135) (1910) MT, Carolina poplar [Carolinian poplar] (5, 85, 92, 156) (1876–1932), Gilead buds (157) (1929), Leaf-buds (157) (1929), Man'asa'dĭ (Chippewa) (40) (1928), Man-saté (Chippewa, strange aspen) (105) (1932), Ontario poplar (5, 156) (1913–1923), Peuplier laird (French) (8) (1785), Poplar of Carolina (189) (1767), Rough-bark poplar [Rough bark poplar] (5, 156) (1913–1923), Simon's poplar [Simon poplar] (138) (1923), Tacamahac or Tacamahac tree (5, 8, 14, 20, 92, 108, 109, 156, 157, 158) (1785–1949), Tacamahac poplar (92) (1876), Tacamahaca (2) (1857) Indian name, possibly Athenian poplar (19) (1840)

Populus balsamifera **L. subsp.** *balsamifera* – American balm Gilead (92) (1876), Balm-of-Gilead [Balm of Gilead] or Balm-of-Gilead tree [Balm of Gilead tree] (1, 5, 72, 85, 91, 92, 108, 109, 156, 158) (1876–1949), Balm-of-Gilead poplar (138, 155) (1923–1942), Balsam poplar (113) (1890), Heart-leaf balsam poplar [Heart-leaved balsam poplar] (20) (1857), Lance-leaf balsam tree [Lance-leaved balsam tree] (8) (1785), Peuplier baumier (French) (8) (1785), Tacamahac or Tacamahac tree (46) (1879), Tacamahac poplar (155) (1942)

Populus balsamifera **L. var.** *angustifolia* **(James) S. Wats.** – See *Populus angustifolia* James

Populus balsamifera **L. var.** *candicans* **Gr.** – See *Populus balsamifera* L. subsp. *balsamifera*

Populus balsamifera lanceolata – See *Populus balsamifera* L. subsp. *balsamifera*

Populus balsamifera **var.** *candicans* **Gray** – See *Populus balsamifera* L. subsp. *balsamifera*

Populus berolinensis – See *Populus* ×*berolinensis* C. Koch [*laurifolia* × *nigra var. italica*]

Populus betulifolia **Pursh** – See *Populus nigra* L. var. *betulifolia* (Pursh) Torr.

Populus bolleana **Mast.** – See *Populus alba* L.

Populus canadensis **Moench** – See *Populus* ×*canadensis* Moench [*deltoides* × *nigra*]

Populus canadensis **Moench var. *eugenei* (Simon-Louis) Schelle** – See *Populus* ×*canadensis* Moench [*deltoides* × *nigra*]

Populus canadensis **Moench var. *serotina* (T. Hartig) Rehd.** – See *Populus* ×*canadensis* Moench [*deltoides* × *nigra*]

Populus candicans **Aiton** – See *Populus balsamifera* L. subsp. *balsamifera*

Populus candicans **Michx.** – See *Populus balsamifera* L. subsp. *balsamifera*

Populus canescens **[(Aiton) Sm.]** – See *Populus* ×*canescens* (Aiton) Sm. [*alba* × *tremula*]

Populus caroliniana **[Hort. ex McMinn & Maino]** – See *Populus* ×*canadensis* Moench [*deltoides* × *nigra*]

Populus deltoide – See *Populus deltoides* Bartr. ex Marsh.

Populus deltoides **Bartr. ex Marsh.** – Alamo (5, 156) (1913–1923), Berry-bearing poplar (5, 158) (1900–1913), Big cottonwood (5, 156, 158) (1900–1923), Black Italian poplar (5) (1913), Carolina poplar [Carolinian poplar] (5, 156, 158) (1900–1923), Common cottonwood (112) (1937), Cotton tree [Cotton-tree] (5, 156, 158) (1900–1923), Cotton tree of Carolina (8) (1785), Cottonwood [Cotton wood, Cotton-wood] or Cottonwood tree [Cotton wood tree] (5, 35, 72, 82, 91, 97, 109, 131, 156, 158) (1806–1949), Eastern cottonwood (50) (present), Eastern poplar (155) (1942), Italian black poplar (158) (1900), Necklace poplar (5, 156, 158) (1900–1923), Northern cottonwood (109) (1949), Peuplier à feuilles triangulaires (French) (8) (1785), Poplar or Poplar tree [Poplar-tree] (112) (1937) Neb, River poplar (5, 156, 158) (1900–1923), Southern cottonwood (138) (1923), Water poplar (5, 156, 158) (1900–1923), Western cottonwood [Western cotton-wood] (65) (1931), White poplar or White poplar tree (8) (1785), Yellow cottonwood (5, 156, 158) (1900–1923)

Populus deltoides **Bartr. ex Marsh. subsp. *deltoides*** – Angled cottonwood (108) (1878), Angle-twig poplar [Angletwig poplar] (155) (1942), Balm-of-Gilead [Balm of Gilead] or Balm-of-Gilead tree [Balm of Gilead tree] (19) (1840), Carolina cottonwood (138) (1923), Carolina poplar [Carolinian poplar] (20, 112) (1857–1937), Cotton tree [Cotton-tree] (10) (1818), Cottonwood [Cotton wood, Cotton-wood] or Cottonwood tree [Cotton wood tree] (1, 3, 23, 27, 19, 92, 164) (1810–1977), Cottonwood poplar (12) (1821), Eastern cottonwood (50) (present), Necklace poplar (1) (1932), Northern poplar (155) (1942), Palmer's poplar [Palmer poplar] (155) (1942), Southern poplar (155) (1942), Sweet cottonwood (30) (1844), Water poplar (19, 92) (18401876)

Populus deltoides **Bartr. ex Marsh. subsp. *monilifera* (Aiton) Eckenwalder** – Alamo (Spanish) (147) (1856), Baka hi (Osage) (121) (1918?–1970?), Čaŋčjaxu (Lakota, chewing wood) (121) (1918?–1970?), Carolina poplar [Carolinian poplar] (2) (1895), Common cottonwood (130) (1895), Cottonwood [Cotton wood, Cotton-wood] or Cottonwood tree [Cotton wood tree] (2, 3, 4, 9, 20, 32, 37, 46, 92, 108, 113, 114, 147, 160, 161) (1852–1986), Great Plains cottonwood (109) (1949), Italian black poplar (14) (1882), Natakaaru (Pawnee) (37) (1919), Necklace poplar (92, 130) (1876–1895), Northern cottonwood (138) (1923), Plains cottonwood (50, 155) (1942–present), Plains poplar (155) (1942), Poplar or Poplar tree [Poplar-tree] (147) (1856), River cottonwood (1, 85) (1932), Sargent's cottonwood [Sargent cottonwood] (138) (1923), Swiss poplar (20) (1857), Texas cottonwood (155) (1942), Texas poplar (155) (1942), Virginia poplar [Virginian poplar] (20) (1857), Wága chan (Dakota) (37) (1919), Wagačaŋ (Lakota) (121) (1918?–1970?), Western cottonwood [Western cotton-wood] (1, 5, 93, 95, 97, 121) (1911–1937), Western poplar (155) (1942), White poplar or White poplar tree (12) (1821), Yellow cottonwood (130) (1895), Maa zhon (Omaha-Ponca, cotton tree) (37) (1919)

Populus deltoides **Bartr. ex Marsh. subsp. *wislizeni* (S. Wats.) Eckenwalder** – Valley cottonwood (149, 153) (1904–1913)

Populus deltoides **Bartr. ex Marsh. var. *missouriensis* (A. Henry) A.**

Henry – See *Populus deltoides* Bartr. ex Marsh. subsp. *deltoides*

Populus deltoides **Bartr. ex Marsh. var. *virginiana* (Foug.) Sudworth** – See *Populus deltoides* Bartr. ex Marsh. subsp. *deltoides*

Populus deltoides **Marsh. var. *occidentalis* Rydb.** – See *Populus deltoides* Bartr. ex Marsh. subsp. *monilifera* (Aiton) Eckenwalder

Populus deltoides **var. *carolinensis*** – See *Populus* ×*canadensis* Moench [*deltoides* × *nigra*]

Populus dilatata **W.** – See *Populus nigra* L.

Populus fremontii **S. Wats.** – Fremont's cottonwood [Fremont cottonwood] (138) (1923)

Populus fremontii wislizenii – See *Populus deltoides* Bartr. ex Marsh. subsp. *wislizeni* (S. Wats.) Eckenwalder

Populus graeca **Willd.** – possibly *Populus balsamifera* L.

Populus grandidentata **Michx.** – American large aspen (20) (1857), Big-tooth aspen [Bigtooth aspen] (4, 50, 155) (1942–present), Great aspen (158) (1900), Larger American abele (2) (1895), Large-tooth aspen [Largetooth aspen] (5, 72, 109, 138, 156, 158) (1900–1949), Southern big-tooth aspen [Southern bigtooth aspen] (155) (1942), Tree poplar (19) (1840), White poplar or White poplar tree (5, 156) (1913–1923), possibly Large aspen (187) (1818)

Populus heterophylla **L.** – Balm-of-Gilead [Balm of Gilead] or Balm-of-Gilead tree [Balm of Gilead tree] (5, 156) (1913–1923), Black cottonwood (156) (1923), Cotton tree [Cotton-tree] (20) (1857), Cottonwood [Cotton wood, Cotton-wood] or Cottonwood tree [Cotton wood tree] (20) (1857), Downy poplar (2, 5, 156) (1895–1923), Peuplier argentés (French) (8) (1785), River cottonwood (5, 156) (1913–1923), Swamp cottonwood (5, 156) (1913–1923), Swamp poplar (5, 156) (1913–1923), Various-leaf poplar [Various leaved poplar] (19) (1840), Virginia poplar tree [Virginian poplar-tree] (8) (1785)

Populus hudsonica **[Michx.]** – See *Populus nigra* L. var. *hudsonica* C.K.Schneid.

Populus italica **(Du Roi) Moench** – See *Populus nigra* L.

Populus **L.** – Alamo (Spanish) (147) (1856), Aspen [Aspin] or Aspen tree [Aspen-tree] (1, 2, 4, 109, 155, 158, 167) (1814–1986), Cotton tree [Cotton-tree] (17) (1796), Cottonwood [Cotton wood, Cotton-wood] or Cottonwood tree [Cotton wood tree] (1, 4, 50, 35, 93, 109, 122, 125, 155) (1806–present), Hi'-e-tran (Kiwomi Keres) (132) (1855), Liard (French in Illinois) (17, 35) (1796–1806), Peuplier (French) (8) (1785), Poplar or Poplar tree [Poplar-tree] (1, 2, 4, 7, 8, 10, 34, 35, 82, 108, 109, 138, 155, 156, 158, 167, 184) (1785–1986) from classic Latin name

Populus monilifera **Aiton** – See *Populus deltoides* Bartr. ex Marsh. subsp. *monilifera* (Aiton) Eckenwalder

Populus nigra **L.** – Black pepillary (158) (1900), Black pipple (158) (1900), Black popillary (158) (1900), Black poplar (4, 5, 8, 14, 92, 109, 138, 155, 156, 158) (1882–1986), Black-lady [Black lady] (156, 158) (1900–1923), Cat-foot poplar [Cat foot poplar] (5, 156, 158) (1900–1923), Cotton tree [Cotton-tree] (158) (1900), Devil's-fingers [Devil's fingers] (5, 156) (1913–1923), House poplar (43) (1820), Italian poplar (19) (1840), Lombardy poplar (4, 19, 50, 85, 109, 112, 158) (1840–present), Mormon tree (156) (1923), Old English poplar (5, 156, 158) (1900–1923), Peuplier de Virginie (French) (8) (1785), Water poplar (158) (1900), Willow poplar (5, 156, 158) (1900–1923)

Populus nigra **L. var. *betulifolia* (Pursh) Torr.** – Birch-leaf poplar (19) (1840)

Populus nigra **L. var. *hudsonica* C. K. Schneid.** – American black poplar (20) (1857)

Populus occidentalis **(Rydb.) Britton ex Rydb.** – See *Populus deltoides* Bartr. ex Marsh. subsp. *monilifera* (Aiton) Eckenwalder

Populus palmeri **Sarg.** – See *Populus deltoides* Bartr. ex Marsh. subsp. *deltoides*

Populus sargentii **Dode.** – See *Populus deltoides* Bartr. ex Marsh. subsp. *monilifera* (Aiton) Eckenwalder

Populus tacamahaca **[Mill.]** – See *Populus balsamifera* L. subsp. *balsamifera*

Populus tacamahacca **Mill** – See *Populus balsamifera* L.

Populus texana **Sargent** – See *Populus deltoides* Bartr. ex Marsh.

335

subsp. *monilifera* (Aiton) Eckenwalder

Populus tomentosa **Carr.** – Chinese white poplar (138) (1923)

Populus tremula – possibly *Populus tremuloides* Michx. (US species)

Populus tremuloides **Michx.** – American asp (158) (1900), American aspen or American aspen tree (5, 6, 8, 20, 19, 49, 53, 57, 72, 82, 92, 93, 108, 109, 131, 156, 157, 158, 160) (1785–1949), American espen (158) (1900), American haspen (158) (1900), American poplar (5, 6, 49, 52, 53, 156, 157, 158) (1892–1929), Asa'dĭ (Chippewa) (37) (1919), Aspe (46) (1617), Aspen [Aspin] or Aspen tree [Aspen-tree] (28, 35, 40, 47, 92, 108, 112) (1806–1937), Aspen poplar (38) (1820), Aspen popple (122, 124) (1937) TX, Auld-wive's-tongues (37, 158) (1900–1919), Ever-trembling asp (46) (1629), Golden qualing aspen (155) (1942), Mountain ash [Mountain-ash, Mountainash] (156) (1923), Mountain asp (157, 158) (1900–1929), Mountain aspen (5) (1913), Pappel (German) (6) (1892), Poplar or Poplar tree [Poplar-tree] (61) (1870), Pople (6) (1892), Quaking ash (156) (1923), Quaking asp (28, 75, 92, 113, 130, 156, 157, 158) (1850–1923), Quaking aspen (1, 3, 4, 5, 17, 49, 50, 52, 53, 82, 85, 92, 93, 109, 138, 149, 153, 155, 161) (1857–present), Quiverleaf [Quiver leaf, Quiver-leaf] (5, 92, 156, 157, 158) (1876–1929), Tow-heads (156) (1923), Trembling tree (92) (1876), Upland poplar (6) (1892), Vancouver qualing aspen (155) (1942), White poplar or White poplar tree (5, 6, 19, 49, 52, 57, 92, 156, 157, 158) (1840–1929), possibly Peuplier de Canada (French) (8) (1785), possibly Tremble (French Canadians) (17) (1796)

Populus tremuloides **Michx. var. *aurea* (Tidestrom) Daniels** – See *Populus tremuloides* Michx.

Populus tremuloides **Michx. var. *vancouveriana* (Trel.) Sargent** – See *Populus tremuloides* Michx.

Populus tremulus – See *Populus tremula* L.

Populus tweedyi **Britton** – See *Populus angustifolia* James

Populus virginiana **Foug.** – See *Populus deltoides* Bartr. ex Marsh. subsp. *deltoides*

Populus wislizeni – See *Populus deltoides* Bartr. ex Marsh. subsp. *wislizeni* (S. Wats.) Eckenwalder

Populus x brayshawii **Boivin** – See *Populus* ×*brayshawii* Boivin [*angustifolia* × *balsamifera*]

Populus x jackii **Sargent** – See *Populus* ×*jackii* Sarg. [*balsamifera* × *deltoides*]

Porcelia triloba [**(L.) Pers.)**] – See *Asimina triloba* (L.) Dunal

Porlieria angustifolia **(Engelm.) Gray** – See *Guajacum angustifolium* Engelm.

Porophyllum gracile **Benth.** – Poison flower [Poison-flower] (75) (1894) Colorado River, Sweet-scented herb (76) (1896) CA, Yerba del vernada (76) (1896) CA

Porphyra laciniata **Agardh.** – See *Callicarpa dichotoma* (Lour.) K. Koch

Porrum – possibly *Allium porrum* L.

Porteranthus **Britt. ex Small** – American ipecac (1) (1932), Porteranthus (50) (present)

Porteranthus stipulatus **(Muhl. ex Willd.) Britt.** – American ipecac (2, 3, 5, 64, 49, 57, 92, 97, 109, 122, 156, 158) (1895–1977), Beaumont's root [Beaumont root] (7) (1828), Bowman's root [Bowman's-root, Bowman root, Bowmanroot] (7, 49, 92) (1828–1898), Gillenia (57) (1917), Gillenia occidentale (French) (7) (1828), Gillenia radix (7) (1828), Gillenwurzel (German) (7) (1828), Indian hippo (7, 49) (1828–1898), Indian physic [Indian-physic, Indianphysic, Indian physick] (3, 4, 7, 49, 50, 61, 92, 102, 138, 155, 158)) (1828–present), Injin physic (74) (1893) Banner Elk NC, Ipecac (7) (1828), Large-stipule Indian physic [Large stipuled Indian physic] (2) (1895), Meadowsweet [Meadow-sweet, Meadow sweet] (7) (1828), Small-flower Indian physic [Small-flowered Indian-physic] (186) (1814), Ûnlĕ Ukĭ'ltĭ (Cherokee, the locust frequents it) (102) (1886), Western dropwort (7, 92) (1828–1876)

Porteranthus trifoliatus **(L.) Britton** – Gilenia (64) (1907), Papiconah (Illinois French) (17) (1796), Western dropwort (5, 64) (1907–1908)

Portulaca **(Tourn.) L.** – See *Portulaca* L.

Portulaca grandiflora **Hook.** – Common portulaca (138, 155) (1923–1942), French purslane (158) (1900), French pursley (156) (1923), French pussley [French pusley] (5, 73) (1892–1913) Southern VT, Garden portulaca (5, 97, 156, 158) (1900–1937), Garden purslane (5, 156, 158) (1900–1923), Kentucky moss (5, 76, 156, 158) (1896–1923) Sulphur Grove OH, Mexican rose (5, 73, 156, 158) (1892–1923) Chestertown MD, Moss (74) (1893) Southern IN, Portulaca (92, 114) (1876–1894), Rose-moss [Rose moss] (5, 50, 73, 76, 109, 156, 158) (1893–present) SD, Showy portulaca (5, 156, 158) (1900–1923), Sun plant [Sun-plant] (5, 156, 158) (1900–1923), Wax pink [Wax pinks] (5, 92, 156, 158) (1876–1923)

Portulaca halimoides **L.** – Silk-cotton purslane [Silkcotton purslane] (50) (Present), Slender-leaf purslane [Slenderleaf purslane] (3, 4) (1977–1986)

Portulaca **L.** – Moss flower (124) (1937) TX, Portulaca (138, 155, 158) (1923–1942), Purslane [Purslain] (1, 4, 7, 13, 15, 50, 82, 158, 167) (1828–present), Pussley [Pusley] (1) (1932)

Portulaca mundula **I. M. Johnst.** – See *Portulaca pilosa* L.

Portulaca oleracea **L.** – Andrache (Greek) (110) (1886), Andrachen (107) (1919), Cholza (Persian) (110) (1886), Common purslane (3, 4, 15, 38, 103, 4, 138, 155) (1870–1986), Garden purslane (57, 92) (1876–1917), Kitchen-garden purslane (109) (1949), Kreusel (German) (110) (1886), Kurj-noha (Bohemian) (110) (1886), Kurza noka (Polish) (110) (1886), Little hogweed (50) (present), Notched purslane (5, 72, 156) (1907–1923), Parsley (85) (1932), Pigweed [Pigweed, Pig weed] (5, 156) (1913–1923), Porcelayne (179) (1526), Portulaca (41) (1770), Purselin (46) (1879), Purselyn (46) (1617), Purslane [Purslain] (5, 10, 19, 41, 62, 72, 76, 80, 82, 85, 92, 93, 95, 97, 107, 110, 131, 145, 156, 157, 158, 184, 187) (1605–1937), Pursley (76, 92, 131, 157, 158) (1896–1936), Pussley [Pusley] (5, 62, 73, 76, 80, 93, 122, 156, 158) (1892–1923), Schrucha (Russian) (110) (1886), Western purslane (5, 156) (1913–1923), Western pusley (122) (1937)

Portulaca oleracea **L. var. *sativa* DC.** – See *Portulaca oleracea* L.

Portulaca parvula **Gray** – See *Portulaca halimoides* L.

Portulaca pilosa **L.** – Hairy portulaca (5, 97, 122) (1913–1937), Jump-up-and-kiss-me-quick (155) (1942), Kiss-me-quick [Kiss me quick] (50) (present), Shaggy garden purslane (109) (1949), Shaggy portulaca (155) (1942)

Portulaca **Tourn.** – See *Portulaca* L.

Portulaca umbraticola **H.B.K.** – Wing-pod purslane [Wingpod purslane] (50) (present)

Portuna floribunda **(Pursh) Nutt.** – See *Pieris floribunda* (Pursh) Benth. & Hook. f.

Potamogeton **(Tourn.) L.** – See *Potamogeton* L.

Potamogeton ×*faxonii* **Morong** [*illinoensis* × *nodosus*] – Faxon's pondweed (5) (1913)

Potamogeton ×*mysticus* **Morong** [*perfoliatus* × *pusillus*] – Mystic pondweed (5) (1913)

Potamogeton ×*spathuliformis* **(J. W. Robbins) Morong** – Spatulate-leaf pondweed [Spatulate-leaved pondweed] (5, 72) (1907–1913)

Potamogeton alpinus **Balbis** – Alpine pondweed (50) (present), Northern pondweed (5, 85, 131) (1899–1932)

Potamogeton amplexicaulis **Kar.** – See *Potamogeton perfoliatus* L.

Potamogeton amplifolius **Tuckern.** – Large-leaf pondweed [Largeleaf pondweed, Large-leaved pondweed] (5, 50, 93, 131, 155) (1899–present)

Potamogeton angustifolius **Berch. & Presl.** – See *Potamogeton illinoensis* Morong

Potamogeton confervoides **Reichb.** – Alga-like pondweed (5) (1913), Tuckerman's pondweed (50) (present)

Potamogeton crispus **L.** – Curly muckweed [Curly muck-weed] (5, 120, 156) (1913–1938), Curly pondweed (50, 155, 158) (1900–present), Muckweed [Muck-weed] (158) (1900), Pondweed [Pondweeds, Pond weed] (5, 156) (1913–1923), Water caltrop [Water caltrops] (158) (1900)

Potamogeton dimorphus **Raf.** – See *Potamogeton spirillus* Tuckerman

Potamogeton diversifolius **Barton** – See *Potamogeton spirillus* Tuck.

Potamogeton diversifolius **Raf.** – Pondweed [Pondweeds, Pond weed] (85) (1932), Water-thread pondweed [Waterthread pondweed] (3, 50) (1977–present), Furrow-leaf pondweed [Furrow-leaved pondweed] (187) (1818), Rafinesque's pondweed [Rafinesque pondweed] (5, 97, 120) (1913–1938)

Potamogeton epihydrus **Raf.** – Creek-grass [Creek grass] (5) (1913), Nuttall's pondweed (5, 72) (1907–1913), Pondweed [Pondweeds, Pond weed] (85) (1932), Ribbon-leaf pondweed [Ribbonleaf pondweed] (50, 155) (1942–present)

Potamogeton faxoni **Morong** – See *Potamogeton* ×*faxonii* Morong [*illinoensis* × *nodosus*]

Potamogeton foliosus **Raf.** – Leafy pondweed (3, 50, 72, 93, 97, 120, 131, 155) (1899–present)

Potamogeton foliosus **Raf. subsp.** *foliosus* – Leafy pondweed (50) (present)

Potamogeton friesii **Rupr.** – Fries' pondweed [Fries pondweed, Fries's pondweed] (5, 50, 72, 155) (1907–present)

Potamogeton gramineus **L.** – Grass pondweed [Grass pond-weed] (19) (1840), Variable pondweed (3) (1977), Variable-leaf pondweed [Variableleaf pondweed] (50, 155) (1942–present), possibly Swamp potamogeton (131) (1899)

Potamogeton heterophyllus **Schreb.** – See *Potamogeton illinoensis* Morong

Potamogeton hillii **Morong** – Hill's pondweed (5, 50, 131) (1899–present)

Potamogeton illinoensis **Morong** – Illinois pondweed (3, 50, 72, 155) (1942–present), Pondweed [Pondweeds, Pond weed] (85) (1932), Porter's pondweed [Porter pondweed] (155) (1942), Shining pondweed (5, 85, 97, 120, 156, 158) (1900–1938), Various-leaf pondweed [Various-leaved pondweed] (5, 93, 131) (1899–1936), Ziz's pondweed (5) (1913), possibly Corn-stalk weed [Cornstalk weed, Cornstalk-weed] (5, 156, 158) (1900–1923)

Potamogeton interruptus **Kitaibel** – See *Stuckenia vaginatus* (Turcz.) Holub

Potamogeton **L.** – Fishweed [Fish-weed] (1) (1932), Pondweed [Pondweeds, Pond weed] (1, 50, 93, 120, 122, 155, 156, 158, 184, 190) (~1759–present)

Potamogeton lateralis **Morong p.p.** – See *Potamogeton vaseyi* J. W. Robbins

Potamogeton lonchites **Tuckerm.** – See *Potamogeton nodosus* Poir.

Potamogeton longiligulatus **Fern.** – See *Potamogeton strictifolius* Benn.

Potamogeton lucens **auct. non L.** – See *Potamogeton illinoensis* Morong

Potamogeton marinus occidentalis **Robbins.** – See *Stuckenia filiformis* (Pers) Boerner subsp. *occidentalis* (J. W. Robbins) Haynes, D. H. Les, & M. Kral

Potamogeton mysticus **Morong** – See *Potamogeton* ×*mysticus* Morong [*perfoliatus* × *pusillus*]

Potamogeton natans **L.** – Batter-dock [Batter dock] (5, 156, 158) (1900–1923), Common floating pondweed (5, 72, 93, 158) (1900–1936), Common pondweed (156) (1923), Deil's spoons (5, 156, 158) (1900–1923), Fish-leaves (158) (1900), Flatterdock [Flatter-dock, Flatter dock] (158) (1900), Floating pondweed (50, 85, 156) (1923–present), Floating-leaf pondweed [Floating-leaved pondweed, Floatingleaf pondweed] (3, 155) (1942–1977), Pondweed [Pondweeds, Pond weed] (19) (1840), Tenchweed [Tench weed, Tench-weed] (5, 156, 158) (1900–1923)

Potamogeton nodosus **Poir.** – Long-leaf pondweed [Longleaf pondweed, Long-leaved pondweed] (3, 5, 50, 72, 93, 97, 131, 155) (1899–present)

Potamogeton nuttallii **Cham & Sch.** – See *Potamogeton epihydrus* Raf.

Potamogeton oakesianus **J. W. Robbins** – Oakes' pondweed (5, 50) (1913–present)

Potamogeton obtusifolius **Mert. & Koch** – Blunt-leaf pondweed [Bluntleaf pondweed] (3, 5, 50, 155) (1913–present)

Potamogeton palustris **Teesd.** – See *Potamogeton gramineus* L.

Potamogeton pectinatus **L.** – See *Stuckenia pectinatus* (L.) Boerner

Potamogeton perfoliatus **L.** – Clasping pondweed (72) (1907), Clasping-leaf pondweed [Clasping-leaved pondweed] (5, 50, 93, 156) (1913–present), Redhead-grass (156) (1923), Thoroughwort pondweed [Thorowort pondweed] (155) (1942)

Potamogeton perfoliatus **L. subsp.** *richardsonii* **(Benn.) Hultén** – See *Potamogeton richardsonii* (Benn.) Rydb.

Potamogeton perfoliatus **L. var.** *richardsonii* **Benn.** – See *Potamogeton richardsonii* (Benn.) Rydb.

Potamogeton perfoliatus richardsonii **Benn.** – See *Potamogeton richardsonii* (Benn.) Rydb.

Potamogeton praelongus **Wulfen** – White-stem pondweed [Whitestem pondweed, White stemmed pondweed] (3, 50, 72, 155) (1907–present)

Potamogeton pulcher **Tuckerm.** – Spotted pondweed (5, 50) (1913–present)

Potamogeton pusillus **L.** – Baby pondweed (155) (1942), Small pondweed (1, 50, 72, 93, 97, 120, 131) (1899–present)

Potamogeton pusillus **L. subsp.** *gemmiparus* **(J. W. Robbins) Haynes & C. B. Hellquist** – Small pondweed (50) (present), Thread-like pondweed (5) (1913)

Potamogeton pusillus **L. subsp.** *pusillus* – Baby pondweed (3) (1977), Small pondweed (50) (present)

Potamogeton pusillus **L. subsp.** *tenuissimus* **(Mert. & Koch) Haynes & C. B. Hellquist** – Baby pondweed (3) (1977), Small pondweed (50) (present)

Potamogeton pusillus **L. var.** *gemmiparus* **J. W. Robbins** – See *Potamogeton pusillus* L. subsp. *gemmiparus* (J. W. Robbins) Haynes & C. B. Hellquist

Potamogeton richardsonii **(Benn.) Rydb.** – Clasping-leaf potamogeton [Clasping-leaved potamogeton] (131) (1899), Red-head pondweed (3) (1977), Richardson's clasping pondweed (72) (1907), Richardson's pondweed (50) (present), Richardson's thorowort pondweed [Richardson thorowort pondweed] (155) (1942)

Potamogeton robbinsii **Oakes** – Robbins' pondweed [Robbins pondweed] (5, 50) (1913–present)

Potamogeton spathulaeformis **(Robbins) Morong.** – See *Potamogeton* ×*spathuliformis* (J. W. Robbins) Morong

Potamogeton spirillus **Tuck.** – Different-leaved pond-weed (187) (1818), Spiral pondweed (1, 50, 72, 85, 93, 97, 120) (1907–present)

Potamogeton strictifolius **Benn.** – Long-tongue pondweed [Longtongue pondweed] (155) (1942), Narrow-leaf pondweed [Narrowleaf pondweed] (50) (present)

Potamogeton vaginatus **Turcz.** – See *Stuckenia vaginatus* (Turcz.) Holub

Potamogeton varians **Morong** – See *Potamogeton* ×*spathuliformis* (J.W. Robbins) Morong

Potamogeton vaseyi **J. W. Robbins** – Vasey's pondweed (5, 50) (1913–present), possibly Opposite-leaf pondweed [Opposite-leaved pondweed] (5) (1913)

Potamogeton zosteraefolius **Schum.** – See *Potamogeton zosteriformis* Fern.

Potamogeton zosterifolius **Schum.** – See *Potamogeton zosteriformis* Fern.

Potamogeton zosteriformis **Fern.** – Eel-grass pondweed [Eel-grass pond-weed] (72, 85, 131, 156) (1894–1932), Flat-stem pondweed [Flatstem pondweed] (3, 50, 155) (1942–present), Grass-wrack [Grass wrack] (5, 156) (1913–1923)

Potentilla anglica **Laicharding** – Trailing tormetil (5) (1913), Wood cinquefoil (5) (1913)

Potentilla anserina **L.** – See *Argentina anserina* (L.) Rydb., Hoary cinquefoil (5, 156, 158) (1900)

Potentilla argentea **L.** – Silver cinquefoil (50, 138, 155) (1923–present), Silvery cinquefoil (3, 4, 5, 72, 156, 158) (1900–1986), Silvery five-finger (5) (1913)

Potentilla argentea **L. var.** *argentea* – Silver cinquefoil (50) (present)

Potentilla arguta **Pursh** – Glandular chinquefoil (63) (1899), Rough cinquefoil (82) (1930), Tall cinquefoil (3, 4, 50, 131) (1899–present), White cinquefoil [White cinquefoile] (82) (1930)

Potentilla arguta **Pursh subsp.** *arguta* – Five-finger [Fivefinger, Five finger] (40) (1928), Gĭ'tciöde'imīnīdji'bĭk (Chippewa, big heartberry root) (40) (1928), Glandular cinquefoil (5, 93) (1913–1936), Tall cinquefoil (5, 50, 72, 85, 93, 97, 127) (1907–present)

Potentilla biennis **Greene** – Biennial cinquefoil (50, 155) (1942–present)

Potentilla bimundorum **Soják** – Cut-leaf cinquefoil [Cut-leaved cinquefoil] (5) (1913)

Potentilla bipinnatifida **Dougl. ex Hook.** – Plains cinquefoil (5) (1913), Tansy cinquefoil (50) (present)

Potentilla canadensis **L.** – Barren-strawberry [Barren strawberry] (5, 156) (1913–1923), Cinquefoil [Cink-foil, Cinque-foil] (46, 48, 57, 92, 156) (1671–1923), Cinquefoil herb (92) (1876), Cinquefoil root (92) (1876), Common cinquefoil (5, 62, 138) (1912–1923), Common five-finger (19) (1840), Common wild cinquefoil (2) (1895), Fingerleaf [Finger leaf] (92) (1876), Five-finger [Fivefinger, Five finger] (2, 5, 62, 72, 92, 97, 156) (1876–1937), Potentilla (156) (1923), Running buttercups [Running buttercup] (5, 76, 156) (1896–1923) Oxford Co. ME, Sinkfield (5, 74, 156) (1893–1923) WV, no longer in use by 1923, Star flower [Starflower, Star-flower] (5, 156) (1913–1923), Wild strawberry [Wild strawberries] (5, 62) (1912–1913), possibly Dwarf five-finger (5) (1913)

Potentilla concinna **Richards** – Elegant cinquefoil (50, 131, 155) (1899–present)

Potentilla concinna **Richards. var.** *concinna* – Snowy cinquefoil (131) (1899) SD

Potentilla concinna **Richards. var.** *dissecta* **(S. Wats.) Boivin** – See *Potentilla saximontana* var. *dissecta* (S. Watson) Soják

Potentilla diversifolia **Lehm.** – Varileaf cinquefoil (50, 155) (1942–present)

Potentilla diversifolia **Lehm. var.** *diversifolia* – Blue-leaf cinquefoil [Blueleaf cinquefoil] (155) (1942), Varileaf cinquefoil (50) (present)

Potentilla effusa **Dougl.** – See *Potentilla hippiana* Lehm.

Potentilla emarginata **Pursh** – See *Potentilla nana* Willd. ex Schlecht.

Potentilla erecta – See *Potentilla erecta* (L.) Raeusch.

Potentilla erecta **(L.) Raeusch.** – Erect cinquefoil (50) (present), Tormentyll (179) (1526)

Potentilla fissa **Nutt.** – Big-flower cinquefoil [Bigflower cinquefoil] (50, 155) (1942–present)

Potentilla flabelliformis **Lehm.** – See *Potentilla gracilis* Dougl. ex Hook. var. *flabelliformis* (Lehm.) Nutt. ex Torr. & Gray

Potentilla glandulosa **Lindl.** – Gland cinquefoil (155) (1942), Glandular cinquefoil (131) (1899), Sticky cinquefoil (50) (present)

Potentilla glaucophylla **Lehm.** – See *Potentilla diversifolia* Lehm. var. *diversifolia*

Potentilla gracilis **Dougl.** – Nuttall's cinquefoil [Nuttall cinquefoil] (155) (1942), Slender cinquefoil (50, 131) (1899–present)

Potentilla gracilis **Dougl. ex Hook. var.** *fastigiata* **(Nutt.) S. Wats.** – Slender cinquefoil (50) (present)

Potentilla gracilis **Dougl. ex Hook. var.** *flabelliformis* **(Lehm.) Nutt. ex Torr. & Gray** – Fan-leaf cinquefoil [Fanleaf cinquefoil] (155) (1942), Slender cinquefoil (50) (Present)

Potentilla hippiana **Lehm.** – Branched cinquefoil (5) (1913), Cinquefoil [Cink-foil, Cinque-foil] (4) (1986), Horse cinquefoil (155) (1942), Saskatchewan cinquefoil (155) (1942), Silky cinquefoil (85) (1932), Woolly cinquefoil (5, 50, 93, 131) (1899–present)

Potentilla hippiana **Lehm. var.** *hippiana* – Summit cinquefoil (155) (1942), Woolly cinquefoil (50) (present)

Potentilla intermedia **L.** – Downy cinquefoil (5) (1913) MT

Potentilla **L.** – Barren-strawberry [Barren strawberry] (158) (1900), Cinquefoil [Cink-foil, Cinque-foil] (1, 2, 4, 7, 10, 50, 109, 138, 155, 156, 167, 184) (1793–present) five-leaved in French), Cowberry [Cow-berry, Cow berry] (1) (1932), Five-finger [Fivefinger, Five finger] (1, 2, 82, 93, 109) (1895–1949), Fivefinger-grass [Five-fingered grass] (190) (~1759), Marsh cinquefoil [Marsh cinque-foil] (1, 10, 158, 167) (1814–1932), Purple marshlocks [Purple marsh-locks] (1) (1932), Quinte-feuille (French) (8) (1785), Shrub cinquefoil (8) (1785), Star flower [Starflower, Star-flower] (76) (1896) Waverly MA

Potentilla leucocarpa **Rydb.** – See *Potentilla rivalis* Nutt. var. *millegrana* (Engelm. ex Lehm.) S. Wats.

Potentilla maculata **Pourret** – See *Potentilla neumanniana* Aschers.

Potentilla millegrana **Engelm.** – See *Potentilla rivalis* Nutt. var. *millegrana* (Engelm. ex Lehm.) S. Wats.

Potentilla monspeliensis **L.** – See *Potentilla norvegica* L. subsp. *monspeliensis* (L.) Aschers. & Graebn.

Potentilla nana **Willd. ex Schlecht.** – Arctic cinquefoil (5) (1913)

Potentilla neumanniana **Aschers.** – Northern cinquefoil (5) (1913)

Potentilla nicolletii **(S. Wats.) Sheldon** – See *Potentilla paradoxa* Nutt.

Potentilla nivea dissecta **Wats.** – See *Potentilla concinna* Richards. var. *concinna*

Potentilla nivea **L.** – Snow cinquefoil (50) (present), Snowy cinquefoil (5) (1913)

Potentilla norvegica **L.** – Barren-strawberry [Barren strawberry] (76) (1896) Hartford ME; Medford MA, Cinquefoil [Cink-foil, Cinquefoil] (19) (1840), Norwegian cinquefoil [Norway cinquefoil] (2, 4, 50, 155, 187) (1818–present), Strawberry-weed [Strawberryweed] (3) (1977)

Potentilla norvegica **L. subsp.** *hirsuta* **(Michx.) Hyl.** – See *Potentilla norvegica* L. subsp. *monspeliensis* (L.) Aschers. & Graebn.

Potentilla norvegica **L. subsp.** *monspeliensis* **(L.) Aschers. & Graebn.** – Barren-strawberry [Barren strawberry] (5, 156, 158) (1900–1923), Cinquefoil [Cink-foil, Cinque-foil] (40, 80, 82) (1913–1930), False strawberry (80) (1913) IA, Five-finger [Fivefinger, Five finger] (80, 82) (1913–1930), Hairy Norwegian cinquefoil (155) (1942), Montpelier cinquefoil (155) (1942), Norwegian cinquefoil [Norway cinquefoil] (50, 156) (1923–present), Rough cinquefoil (5, 62, 72, 93, 97, 131, 156, 158) (1899–1937), Tall cinquefoil (62) (1912), Three-leaf cinquefoil [Three-leaved cinquefoil] (156) (1923)

Potentilla norvegica – See *Potentilla norvegica* L.

Potentilla paradoxa **Nutt.** – Bushy cinquefoil (4, 5, 72, 85, 93, 131) (1899–1986), Nicollet's cinquefoil (5) (1913), Paradox cinquefoil (50) (present)

Potentilla pectinata **Raf.** – See *Potentilla pensylvanica* L. var. *litoralis* (Rydb.) Boivin

Potentilla pennsylvanica **L.** – See *Potentilla pensylvanica* L.

Potentilla pensylvanica **L.** – Cinquefoil [Cink-foil, Cinque-foil] (4) (1986), Pennsylvania cinquefoil (50, 155) (1942–present), Prairie cinquefoil (5, 72, 131) (1899–1913), Silvery prairie cinquefoil (93) (1936)

Potentilla pensylvanica **L. var.** *litoralis* **(Rydb.) Boivin** – Coast cinquefoil (5) (1913)

Potentilla pensylvanica **L. var.** *pensylvanica* – Pennsylvania cinquefoil (50) (present)

Potentilla pentandra **Engelm.** – See *Potentilla rivalis* Nutt. var. *pentandra* (Engelm.) S. Wats.

Potentilla plattensis **Nutt.** – Cinquefoil [Cink-foil, Cinque-foil] (4) (1986), Platte cinquefoil (155) (1942), Platte River cinquefoil (50) (present)

Potentilla propinqua **Rydb.** – See *Potentilla hippiana* Lehm. var. *hippiana*

Potentilla pulcherrima **Lehm.** – Beautiful cinquefoil (50) (present)

Potentilla pumila pumila **Poir.** – possibly *Potentilla canadensis* L.

Potentilla recta **L.** – Great cinquefoile (178) (1526), Rough-fruit cinquefoil [Rough fruited cinquefoil] (5) (1913), Strawberry-weed [Strawberryweed] (98) (1926), Sulfur cinquefoil [Sulphur cinquefoil] (3, 4, 50, 155) (1942–present), White cinquefoil [White cinquefoile] (178) (1526)

Potentilla reptans **L.** – Cinquefoil [Synkefoyle] (179) (1526), Creeping cinquefoil (92) (1876), Fiveleaf-grass [Five leaved grass, Fiue leued grasse] (92, 179) (1526–1876)

Potentilla rivalis **Nutt.** – Brook cinquefoil (3, 4, 50, 155) (1942–present)

Potentilla rivalis **Nutt. var.** *millegrana* **(Engelm. ex Lehm.) S. Wats.** – Diffuse cinquefoil (5, 93, 72, 131) (1899–1936)

Potentilla rivalis **Nutt. var.** *pentandra* **(Engelm.) S. Wats.** – Five-stamen cinquefoil [Five stamened cinquefoil] (5, 72, 93) (1907–1936)

Potentilla robbinsiana **Oakes ex Rydb.** – Robbins' cinquefoil (5) (1913)

Potentilla simplex **Michx.** – Common cinquefoil (50) (present), Decumbent five-finger (5) (1913), Old-field cinquefoil (3, 4) (1977–1986), Tormentile (46) (1671)

Potentilla tridentata **Aiton** – See *Sibbaldiopsis tridentata* (Aiton) Rydb.

Potentilla villosa **Pallas ex Pursh** – Hairy five-finger (19) (1840)

Poteridium annuum **(Nutt.) Spach.** – See *Sanguisorba annua* (Nutt. ex Hook.) Torr. & Gray

Poterium – See *Sanguisorba* L.

Poterium canadense **Benth. & Hook.** – possibly *Sanguisorba canadensis* L.

Poterium officinale – See *Sanguisorba officinalis* L.

Poterium sanguisorba **L.** – See *Sanguisorba minor* Scop. subsp. *muricata* (Spach) Nordborg

Poterium sitchense **S.Watson** – See *Sanguisorba stipulata* Raf.

Pothos foetidus **Michx.** – See *Symplocarpus foetidus* (L.) Salisb. ex Nutt.

Potomogeton – See *Potamogeton* L.

Pouteria campechiana **(Kunth) Baehni** – Canistel (109, 138) (1923–1949), Egg-fruit (109) (1949), Ti-es (109) (1949)

Pouteria sapota **(Jacq.) H. E. Moore & Stearn** – Marmalade-plum [Marmalade plum] (109) (1949), Sapota (109) (1949)

Prenanthes **(Vaill) L.** – See *Prenanthes* L.

Prenanthes alba **L.** – Cancerweed [Cancer weed, Cancer-weed] (5, 49, 156, 158) (1898–1923), Canker-root [Cankerroot, Canker root] (92) (1876), Cankerweed [Canker-weed, Canker weed] (92) (1876), Common white lettuce (2) (1895), Dado (40) (1928), Dado'cabodji'bĭk (Chippewa, milk root) (40) (1928), Dr. Witt's rattlesnake root (46) (1879) VA, Dr. Witt's snakeroot [Dr. Witts snake-root] (177) (1762), Gall-of-the-earth [Gall of the earth] (49) (1898), Joy-leaf [Joyleaf, Joy leaf] (5, 156) (1913–1923), Lion's-foot [Lion's foot, Lions' foot, Lyons fote] (5, 49, 61, 92, 156, 158) (1870–1923), Milkweed [Milk weed [Milk-weed] (5, 156) (1913–1923), Rattlesnake-root [Rattlesnake-root, Rattle-Snake-Root, Rattlesnakes' root, Rattlesnakeroot] (5, 46, 49, 72, 82, 85, 92, 131, 156, 158) (1876–1930), Rattlesnakeweed [Rattlesnake weed, Rattlesnake weede, Rattlesnakes' weed] (46) (1879), White canker-root (156) (1923), White cankerweed [White canker-weed] (5, 92, 158) (1876–1900), White lettuce (5, 19, 49, 82, 92, 156, 158) (1840–1930), White rattlesnake-root [White rattlesnakeroot] (3, 50, 155) (1942–present), White-flower ivy-leaf [White-flowered ivy-leaf] (187) (1818), White-flower wild lettuce [White-flowered wild lettuce] (187) (1818), Wild lettuce [Wild-lettuce, Wylde letuse] (5, 156) (1913–1923)

Prenanthes altissima **L.** – Birdbell [Bird-bell, Bird bell] (5, 75, 156) (1894–1923) NY, Joy-leaf [Joyleaf, Joy leaf] (5, 156) (1913–1923), Milkweed [Milk weed [Milk-weed] (5, 156) (1913–1923), Rattlesnake-root [Rattlesnake root, Rattle-Snake-Root, Rattlesnakes' root, Rattlesnakeroot] (106) (1930), Tall rattlesnake root (2) (1895), Tall white lettuce (5) (1913), White lettuce (2) (1895), Wild lettuce [Wild-lettuce, Wylde letuse] (5, 156) (1913–1923)

Prenanthes aspera **Michx.** – Cancerweed [Cancer weed, Cancer-weed] (157) (1929), Lion's-foot [Lion's foot, Lions' foot, Lyons fote] (157) (1929), Rattlesnake-root [Rattlesnake root, Rattle-Snake-Root, Rattlesnakes' root, Rattlesnakeroot] (5, 93, 157) (1900–1936), Rough rattlesnake-root [Rough rattlesnakeroot] (3, 50, 155) (1942–present), Rough white lettuce (5, 72, 131) (1899–1913), White cankerweed [White canker-weed] (157) (1929), White lettuce (157) (1929)

Prenanthes autumnalis **Walt.** – Dewitt's snakeroot [Dewitt snakeroot] (5, 156) (1913–1923), Slender rattlesnake root [Slender rattlesnakeroot] (5, 156) (1913–1923)

Prenanthes boottii **(DC.) Gray** – Boott's rattlesnake-root [Boott's rattlesnakeroot] (5) (1913)

Prenanthes crepidinea **Michx.** – Corymbed rattlesnake root (5) (1913)

Prenanthes cropidinea **Michx.** – See *Prenanthes crepidinea* Michx.

Prenanthes **L.** – Dewitt's snakeroot [Dewitt snakeroot] (7) (1828), Gall-of-the-earth [Gall of the earth] (7, 76) (1828–1896), Ivy-leaf (184) (1793), Lion's-foot [Lion's foot, Lions' foot, Lyons fote] (7) (1828), Milkweed [Milk weed, Milk-weed] (79) (1891) NH, Rattlesnakeroot [Rattlesnake root, Rattle-Snake-Root, Rattlesnakes' root, Rattlesnakeroot] (1, 2, 4, 50, 58, 155, 156, 158) (1895–present), Wild lettuce [Wild-lettuce, Wylde letuse] (184) (1793)

Prenanthes nana **(Bigelow) Torr.** – Low lion's-foot [Low lion's foot] (5) (1913), Low rattlesnake root (5) (1913)

Prenanthes racemosa **Michx.** – Purple rattlesnake root [Purple rattlesnakeroot] (50) (present)

Prenanthes racemosa **Michx. subsp.** *multiflora* **Cronq.** – Glaucous white lettuce (5, 72, 131) (1899–1913), Purple rattlesnake root [Purple rattlesnakeroot] (50) (present)

Prenanthes serpentaria **Pursh** – Cankerweed [Canker-weed, Canker weed] (5, 156) (1913–1923), Dr. Witt's snakeroot [Dr. Witts snakeroot] (187) (1818), Earthgall [Earth-gall, Earth gall, Erthe galle] (156) (1923), Gall-of-the-earth [Gall of the earth] (2, 5, 92, 156) (1876–1942), Lion's-foot [Lion's foot, Lions' foot, Lyons fote] (5, 92) (1876–1913), Rattlesnake-root [Rattlesnake root, Rattle-Snake-Root, Rattlesnakes' root, Rattlesnakeroot] (5, 156) (1913–1923), Snake-gentian [Snake gentian] (5, 156) (1913–1923), White lettuce (5, 156) (1913–1923)

Prenanthes trifoliolata **(Cass.) Fern.** – Gall-of-the-earth [Gall of the earth] (156) (1923), Tall rattlesnake root (5) (1913)

Prenanthes virgata **Michx.** – See *Prenanthes autumnalis* Walt.

Primula ×*polyantha* **P. Mill. (pro sp.)** [*veris* × *vulgaris*] – Polyanthus primrose (138) (1923)

Primula egalikensis **Hornem.** – See *Primula egaliksensis* Wormsk. ex Hornem.

Primula egaliksensis **Wormsk. ex Hornem.** – Greenland primrose (5) (1913)

Primula farinosa **L.** – See *Primula laurentiana* Fern.

Primula farinosa **L. var.** *americana* – See *Primula mistassinica* Michx.

Primula incana **M. E. Jones** – Primrose (4) (1986), Silvery primrose (50) (present)

Primula intercedens **Fernald** – See *Primula mistassinica* Michx.

Primula japonica **Gray** – Japanese primrose (138) (1923)

Primula **L.** – Cowslip [Cowslips, Cowslyp] (1) (1932), First-flower-of-the-spring [First flower of the spring] (10) (1818), Prime-vere (French) (10) (1818), Primrose (1, 10, 50, 138, 155, 156, 158) (1818–present)

Primula laurentiana **Fern.** – Birdeine (178) (1526), Bird's-eye [Birds eies] (178) (1526), Bird's-eye primrose [Bird's eye primrose, Birdseye primrose] (5, 72, 109, 138, 156) (1907–1949), Mealy primrose (5, 156) (1913–1923)

Primula mistassinica **Michx.** – Bird's-eye primrose [Bird's eye primrose, Birdseye primrose] (19) (1840), Dwarf Canadian primrose (5, 156) (1913–1923), Mistassini primrose (5) (1913)

Primula parryi **Gray** – Parry's primrose [Parry primrose] (138) (1923)

Primula polyantha – See *Primula* ×*polyantha* Mill. [*veris* × *vulgaris*]

Primula veris **L.** – Artetyke (179) (1526), Cowslip [Cowslips, Cowslyp] (109, 179) (1526–1949), Cowslip [Cowslips, two in a hose] (178) (1526), Cowslip primrose (92, 138) (1876–1923) England, Herb Peter (92) (1876), Herbe paralysy (179) (1526), Pagle (179) (1526), Polyanthus (92) (1876), Primrose (184) (1793)

Prinos glaber **L.** – See *Ilex glabra* (L.) Gray

Prinos **L.** – See *Ilex* L. (all US species)

Prinos verticillatus **L.** – See *Ilex verticillata* (L.) Gray

Prionopsis ciliata **Nutt.** – See *Grindelia papposa* Nesom & Suh

Prionopsis **Nutt.** – See *Grindelia* Willd. (all US species)

Proboscidea fragrans (**Lindl.**) **Decne.** – See *Proboscidea louisianica* (Mill.) Thell. subsp. *fragrans* (Lindl.) Bretting

Proboscidea jussieui **Keller** – See *Proboscidea louisianica* (Mill.) Thell.

Proboscidea louisianica (**Mill.**) **Thell. subsp.** *fragrans* (**Lindl.**) **Bretting** – Fragrant unicorn plant [Fragrant unicorn-plant] (97) (1937), Sweet unicorn plant [Sweet unicornplant] (138) (1923), Unicorn plant [Unicorn-plant, Unicornplant] (92, 103) (1870–1876)

Proboscidea louisianica (**Mill.**) **Thell. subsp.** *louisianica* – Ram's-horn [Ram's horn, Ram's horns] (50) (present)

Proboscidea louisianica (**P. Mill.**) **Thellung** – Common devil's-claws [Common devilsclaws] (155) (1942), Common unicorn plant [Common unicornplant, Common unicorn-plant] (2, 109, 138) (1895–1949), Cuckold's-horns [Cuckold's horns] (38) (1820), Devil's-claw [Devil's claw, Devil's claws, Devilsclaws] (1, 3, 4, 145, 156, 158) (1897–1986), Devil's-horns [Devil's horns] (156) (1923), Double-claw [Double claw] (5, 7, 92, 156, 158) (1828–1923), Elephant's-trunk [Elephant's trunk] (5, 156, 158) (1900–1923), Martinoe (5, 156, 158) (1900–1923), Martynia (92, 107, 156) (1876–1923), Mouse-bur (156, 158) (1900–1923), Pickled-rats [Pickled rats] (75) (1894) NY, possibly for appearance of pickled fruit, Proboscis flower [Proboscis-flower] (109, 156) (1923–1949), Ram's-horn [Ram's horn, Ram's horns] (50, 156) (1923–present), Toe-nails (156, 158) (1900–1923), Unicorn plant [Unicorn-plant, Unicornplant] (4, 5, 19, 38, 63, 72, 85, 92, 93, 97, 107, 122, 156, 158) (1820–1986)

Proboscidea **Schmidel** – Devil's-claw [Devil's claw, Devil's claws, Devilsclaws] (155) (1942)

Proboscidea **Schmidel (possibly)** – Unicorn plant [Unicorn-plant, Unicornplant] (1, 4, 50, 109) (1932–present)

Proserpinaca **L.** – Mermaid-weed [Mermaid weed] (1) (1932)

Proserpinaca palustris **L.** – Mermaid-weed [Mermaid weed] (5, 19, 63, 72, 97, 156) (1840–1937), Parrot-feather [Parrotfeather, Parrot's feather, Parrots-feather] (97) (1937) OK, Proserpinaca (174, 177) (1753–1762), Trixis (174, 177) (1753–1762)

Proserpinaca pectinata **Lam.** – Cut-leaf mermaid-weed [Cut-leaved mermaid-weed] (5) (1913)

Prosopis cinerascens **Gray** – See *Prosopis reptans* Benth. var. *cinerascens* (Gray) Burkart

Prosopis dulcis **Kunth.** – See *Prosopis laevigata* (Willd.) M. C. Johnst.

Prosopis glandulosa **Torr.** – Honey mesquite (4, 50, 155) (1942–present), Mesquit (76, 123) (1856–1896), Mesquite or Mesquite tree (3, 65, 103, 123, 125) (1856–1977), Mezquit (147) (1856), Mosqueit (103) (1870), Prairie mesquite (5, 97) (1913–1937)

Prosopis glandulosa **Torr. var.** *torreyana* (**L. Benson**) **M. C. Johnston** – Tornillo (106) (1930)

Prosopis juliflora (**Sw.**) **DC.** – Algaroba [Algarroba] (107, 158) (1900–1919), Algarola (Spanish) (76) (1896) AZ, Cashaw (158) (1900), Honey locust [Honeylocust, Honey-locust] (158) (1900), Honey mesquit [Honey-mesquit] (76, 158) (1896–1900) AZ, Honey mesquite (107) (1919), Honey-pod (158) (1900), July flower [July-flower] (158) (1900) Jamaica, Locust mesquite (158) (1900), Meskit (158) (1900), Mesquite (96, 158) (1891–1900), Mesquite or Mesquite tree (45, 50, 104, 107, 151, 153, 158) (1896–present), Mezquite (30) (1844), Musqueet (30) (1844), Screw bean [Screwbean, Screw-bean] (96, 107) (1891–1919)

Prosopis juliflora **DC.** – See *Prosopis juliflora* (Sw.) DC.

Prosopis **L.** – Ee'-yah (Pinal Leño Apache) (132) (1855), Mesquite or Mesquite tree (1, 106) (1930–1932), Mezquit (106) (1930)

Prosopis laevigata (**Willd.**) **M. C. Johnst.** – Algaroba [Algarroba] (107) (1919), Cashau (107) (1919), Guava (Spanish) (107) (1919), Pacai (Peru) (107) (1919), Paccay (Peru) (107) (1919)

Prosopis odorata – See *Prosopis glandulosa* Torr. var. *torreyana* (L. Benson) M. C. Johnston

Prosopis pubescens **Benth.** – Curly mesquite (76) (1896) NM, Curly mezquite (147) (1856), E-eesse (Cuchan Yuma) (132) (1855), Mesquite or Mesquite tree (106) (1930), Screw bean [Screwbean, Screwbean] (76, 103, 104, 106, 123, 132, 151, 153, 154) (1855–1930),

Screw mesquite (123) (1856), Screw-bean mesquite [Screw bean mesquite] (107) (1919), Screw-pod mesquit [Screw pod mesquit] (76, 107) (1896–1919), Tornilla (107) (1919), Tornillo (76, 103, 104, 106, 122, 124, 151) (1870–1937) NM, Mexico, Tornillo (Spanish) (123, 147, 153) (1852–1913)

Prosopis reptans **Benth. var.** *cinerascens* (**Gray**) **Burkart** – Screw bean [Screwbean, Screw-bean] (122, 124) (1937)

Protococcus nivalis [(**F. Bauer**) **C. A. Agardh**] – See *Chlamydomonas augustae Skuja*

Prunella grandiflora (**L.**) **Jacq.** – See Prunella grandiflora (L.) Scholler

Prunella **L.** – Bluecurls [Blue curls, Blue-curl, Blue-curls] (75) (1894), Self-heal [Self heal, Selfheal] (21, 38, 50, 155, 158) (1900–present)

Prunella laciniata (**L.**) **L.** – Cut-leaf selfheal [Cutleaf selfheal] (50), Stone comfrey (178) (1526)

Prunella vulgaris **L.** – All-heal [All heal] (5, 158) (1900–1913), Blue lucy (156) (1923), Bluecurls [Blue curls, Blue-curl, Blue-curls] (5, 156, 158) (1900–1923), Braunelle (158) (1900), Braun-heil (German) (158) (1900), Brownwort [Brown wort] (5, 157, 158) (1900–1929), Brunella (174, 177) (1753–1762), Carpenter's-herb [Carpenter's herb] (5, 156, 157, 158) (1900–1929), Carpenter's-square [Carpenter's square] (156) (1923), Carpenter's-weed [Carpenter weed, Carpenter-weed, Carpenter's weed] (1, 5, 73, 79, 80, 106) (1891–1932), Common healall (47) (1852), Common selfheal (41, 50, 155) (1770–present), Cure-all [Cure all, Cureall] (77) (1898) Western US, Dragonhead [Dragon-head, Dragon head, Dragon's head] (5, 75, 85, 156) (1894–1932), Heal-all [Healall] (1, 2, 5, 45, 57, 72, 82, 92, 93, 97, 106, 109, 114, 156, 158) (1876–1937), Heart-of-the-earth (5, 156, 158) (1900–1923), Heart's-ease [Heart's ease, Heartsease, Hearts' ease] (77) (1898) Cambridge MA, Hook-heal [Hook heal] (5, 92, 156, 158) (1876–1929), Hookweed [Hook weed, Hook-weed] (5, 92, 156, 157, 158) (1876–1923), Name'wûskons' (Chippewa) (40) (1928), Paquerette (French) (158) (1900), Pimpernel (158) (1900), Salf-heal (1) (1932), Self-heal [Self heal, Selfheal] (3, 4, 5, 10, 40, 48, 63, 80, 82, 97, 106 109, 124, 131, 156, 157, 158) (1818–1986), Sickle-heal (158) (1900), Sickleweed [Sickleweed, Sickle weed] (157, 158) (1900–1929), Sicklewort [Sickle wort, Sicklewort] (5, 92, 156, 158) (1876–1923), Slough-heal (158) (1900), Square-stem [Square stem, Squarestem] (156) (1923), Thimble-flower [Thimble flower] (5, 156, 158) (1900–1923), Wild sage (77) (1898) Paris ME

Prunella vulgaris **L. subsp.** *lanceolata* (**W. Bart.**) **Hultén** – Lance selfheal (50) (present)

Prunus (**Tourn.**) **L.** – See *Prunus* L.

Prunus alleghaniensis **Porter** – Allegheny plum (138) (1923), Allegheny sloe [Alleghany sloe] (5, 156) (1913–1923), Porter's plum (5) (1913)

Prunus allegheniensis (**sic**) – See *Prunus alleghaniensis* Porter

Prunus americana **Marsh.** – American plum (50, 82, 107, 137, 138, 155) (1919–present), August plum (107) (1919), Canadian plum [Canada plum] (46, 156) (1879), Common wild plum (2) (1895), Eastern wild plum (153) (1913) NM, Goose plum [Goose-plum] (5, 107, 156, 158) (1900–1923), Hog-plum [Hog plum, Hog's plum] (5, 74, 107, 156) (1893–1923) TX, Honesta (46) (1879), Horse plum [Horse-plum] (5, 156, 158) (1900–1923), Ikwe'mĭc (Chippewa) (40) (1928), Large yellow sweet plumb (8) (1785), Meadow plum (19) (1840), Native plum (5, 158) (1900–1913), Plum [Plomme, Plumb, Plumbs, Plums] or Plum tree [Plumb tree, Plum trees] (35, 46, 112, 114) (1806–1937), Plum-granite [Plum granite] (5, 156, 158) (1900–1923) no longer in use by 1923, Pomegranate (156) (1923) no longer in use by 1923, Prunier d'Amerique (French) (20) (1857), Prunier de Virginie (French) (8) (1785), Red plum (107) (1919), Sloe (107) (1919), Wild goose plum [Wild-goose plum, Wildgoose plum] (73) (1892), Wild plum or Wild plum tree (3, 4, 9, 22, 20, 37, 40, 47, 63, 72, 85, 95, 96, 101, 112, 113, 122, 130, 131, 137, 156) (1852–1986), Wild red plum (5, 93, 97, 137, 156, 158) (1900–1937), Wild yellow plum (5, 93, 97, 137, 156, 158) (1900–1937), Yellow plum (107) (1919)

Prunus amygdalus **Stokes var.** *dulcis* **Baillon** – possibly *Prunus dulcis*

(Mill.) D. A. Webber

***Prunus angustifolia* Marsh.** – Chichasaw plum (156) (1923), Chickasaw plum [Chicasaw plum, Chickasaw plumb] (1, 2, 3, 4, 5, 8, 50, 63, 72, 82, 93, 96, 97, 107, 109, 113, 122, 138, 155, 158, 164, 182) (1785–present), Kande (Omaha-Ponca) (37) (1919) Kande-hi (Plum tree), Kante (Dakota, plum) (37) (1919) Kante-hu (Plum tree), Kantsh (Winnebago) (37) (1919) Kantsh-hu (Plum tree), Niwaharit (Pawnee) (37) (1919), Osage plumb (35) (1806) William Clark, Prunier de Canada (French) (8) (1785), possibly Indian cherry [Indian-cherry] (107) (1919), possibly Meadow plum (19) (1840), possibly Mountain cherry (2, 74, 107) (1894–1919), possibly Red plum-peach [Redde plum peach] (181) (~1678), possibly Summer plum (19) (1840)

Prunus angustifolia* Marsh. var. *angustifolia – Big chickasaw plum (138, 155) (1923–1942)

***Prunus angustifolia* Marsh. var. *varians* W. Wight & Hedrick** – See *Prunus angustifolia* Marsh. var. *angustifolia*

***Prunus angustifolia* Marsh. var. *watsonii* (Sargent) Waugh** – Sand chickasaw plum (155) (1942), Sand plum (109, 137, 138) (1923–1949), Watson's plum (50) (present)

Prunus angustifolia varians – See *Prunus angustifolia* Marsh. var. *angustifolia*

***Prunus armeniaca* L.** – Abrecocke (178) (1526), Apricocke tree (178) (1526), Apricot (7, 19, 92, 106, 107) (1828–1930), Common apricot (109, 137) (1931–1949), Mischmisch (Persian) (110) (1886), Sing (Chinese) (110) (1886)

***Prunus avium* (L.) L.** – Bird cherry [Bird-cherry, Birdcherry, Birds cherries] (92, 107, 110, 178) (1526–1919), Black merry (5) (1913), Crab cherry (5) (1913), Gaskins (5, 92) (1876–1913), Gean (5, 107) (1913–1919), Hawkberry (5) (1913), Hedgeberry [Hedge berry] (92) (1876), Kerasaia (Modern Greek) (110) (1886), Kerasie (Albanian) (110) (1886), Mazard (5) (1913), Mazzard [Mazzards] (92, 107, 137, 138, 156) (1876–1931), Merry (5) (1913), Small bird cherry (19) (1840), Süsskirshbaum (German) (110) (1886), Sweet cherry (5, 92, 107, 109, 137, 156) (1876–1949), Wild cherry or Wild cherry tree [Wild cherry-tree] (5, 107) (1913–1919)

***Prunus capollin* Zucc.** – Wild cherry or Wild cherry tree [Wild cherry-tree] (149) (1904) NM

***Prunus caroliniana* (P. Mill.) Aiton** – American cherry-laurel (109) (1949), Carolina cherry-laurel (138) (1923), Carolina laurel cherry (2, 92) (1876–1895), Cherry-laurel [Cherry laurel] (74) (1893) Southern states, Evergreen (74) (1893) GA, Evergreen cherry (106) (1930), Laurel-cherry (106) (1930), Laurus Cerasus (183) (~1756), Laury-Mundy (106) (1930), Mock orange [Mock-orange, Mockorange] (74, 92, 106, 109) (1893–1949) Southern states, Wild orange [Wild-orange] or Wild orange tree (20, 74, 106, 109) (1857–1949) Southern states, Wild peach (74, 106, 122, 124) (1893–1937), Winter-laurel [Winter laurel] (7, 92) (1828–1876), possibly Almond cherry (20) (1857), possibly Evergreen wild cherry (106) (1930), possibly Laurier amande (Louisiana) (7) (1828)

***Prunus caroliniana* Aiton** – See *Prunus caroliniana* (Mill.) Aiton

***Prunus cerasifera* Ehrh.** – Cherry plum (107, 109) (1919–1949), Myrobalab plum (109) (1949), Myrobalan plum (137, 138) (1923–1931)

***Prunus cerasifera* var. *pissardii* (Carrière) Koehne** – See *Prunus pissardii* Carrière

***Prunus cerasus* L.** – Baumweischel (German) (110) (1886), Bluish Cherry [Blewish Cherrie] (178) (1526), Cherry [Cherries, Cherye] or Cherry tree [Cherry trees] (106, 107, 114) (1894–1930), Common English cherry [Common English cherrie] (178) (1526), Double-flower cherry [Double floured Cherrie] (178) (1526), Double-flower cherry bearing fruit [Double flowred Cherrie bearing fruit] (178) (1526), Egriot (5) (1913), Flanders cherry [Flaunders cherrie] (178) (1526), Garden cherry (19) (1840), Gascoine Cherrie (178) (1526), Grape cherry [Grape Cherrie] (178) (1526), Great black cherry [Great blacke cherrie] (178) (1526), Great hart cherry [Great hart cherrie] (178) (1526), Late ripe cherry [Late ripe cherrie] (178) (1526), Lesser black cherry [Lesser blacke cherrie] (178)

(1526), Lesser hart cherry [Lesser hart cherrie] (178) (1526), Morello (156) (1923), Morello cherry (1, 82) (1930–1932), Pie cherry (107) (1919), Red cherry or Red cherry tree (92) (1876), Richmond cherry (82) (1930) IA, Sauerkirschen (German) (110) (1886), Sour cherry (1, 5, 50, 107, 109, 110, 137, 138, 156) (1913–present), Sour French cherry [Sower French cherrie] (178) (1526), Spanish cherry [Spanish cherrie] (178) (1526), Visciolo (Italian) (110) (1886), Vyssine (Albanian) (110) (1886), Wechsel (German) (110) (1886)

***Prunus chicasa* Michx.** – possibly *Prunus angustifolia* Marsh.

***Prunus communis* [(L.) Arcang.]** – See *Prunus dulcis* (Mill.) D. A. Webber

***Prunus communis* Fritsch.** – possibly *Prunus dulcis* (Mill.) D. A. Webber

***Prunus demissa* (Nutt.) Walp.** – See *Prunus virginiana* L. var. *demissa* (Nutt.) Torr.

Prunus demissa melanocarpa – See *Padus virginiana* subsp. *melanocarpa* (A. Nelson) W. A. Weber

***Prunus domestica* L.** – Common plum (109, 110, 137, 138) (1886–1949), Cultivated plum (82) (1930), Damask plum [Damaske plomme] (179) (1526), Damasson (179) (1526), European plum (82, 107, 109) (1919–1949), French plums (55) (1911), Green gages (92) (1876), Muscle plum (178) (1526), Plum [Plomme, Plumb, Plumbs, Plums] or Plum tree [Plumb tree, Plum trees] (19, 92, 107, 178, 179, 182) (1526–1919), Prunes (55, 57, 92) (1876–1917), Prunum (55, 57) (1911–1917), Reine-claude (92) (1876), St. Catharine's prunes [Saint Catharine prunes] (92) (1876), Wild plum or Wild plum tree (41) (1770), Zwetchen (German) (110) (1886)

***Prunus domestica* L. var. *insititia* (L.) Fiori & Paoletti** – Bolays (179) (1526), Bullace (5, 107, 110) (1886–1919), Bullace plum (156) (1923), Corombile (Albanian) (110) (1886), Coromeleia (Modern Greek) (110) (1886), Damson (107) (1919), Haferschlehen (German) (110) (1886), Pflauenbaum (German) (110) (1886)

***Prunus domesticus* L.** – See *Prunus domestica* L.

***Prunus dulcis* (Mill.) D. A. Webber** – Almond or Almond tree (7, 59, 82, 106, 107, 110, 138, 165) (1526–1923), Amandalarios (107) (1919), Amugdalai (110) (1886), Amygdala amara (55, 57, 59) (1911–1917), Amygdalus (110) (1886), Bitter almond [Bytter almonde] (55, 57, 59, 92, 179) (1526–1911), Bullace (92) (1876), Greek nuts (92) (1876), Luz or lus (Hebrew) (110) (1886), Schaked (Hebrew) (110) (1886), possibly Amygdala dulcis (55, 57, 59) (1911–1917), possibly Sweet almond [Swete almond] (55, 57, 92, 179) (1526–1917)

***Prunus emarginata* (Dougl. ex Hook.) D. Dietr.** – Oregon cherry (107) (1919), Wild cherry or Wild cherry tree [Wild cherry-tree] (161) (1857)

***Prunus emarginata* (Dougl. ex Hook.) D. Dietr. var. *mollis* (Dougl. ex Hook.) Brewer** – Cerisier á feuilles molles (French) (20) (1857), Soft-leaf cherry [Soft-leaved cherry] (20) (1857), Wild cherry or Wild cherry tree [Wild cherry-tree] (20) (1857)

***Prunus emarginata* subsp. *mollis* (Douglas) A. E. Murray** – See *Prunus emarginata* (Douglas ex Hook.) D. Dietr. var. *mollis* (Douglas ex Hook.) W. H. Brewer

***Prunus emarginata* Walp.** – See *Prunus emarginata* (Dougl. ex Hook.) D. Dietr.

***Prunus eximia* Small** – See *Prunus serotina* Ehrh. var. *eximia* (Small) Little

***Prunus fasciculata* (Torr.) Gray** – Wild almond (74, 107) (1893–1919), Wild peach (107) (1919)

***Prunus fasciculata* Gray** – See *Prunus fasciculata* (Torr.) Gray

***Prunus fruticosa* Pallas** – Bush cherry (138) (1923), European dwarf cherry (109) (1949), Ground-cherry [Groundcherry, Ground cherry] (109) (1949)

***Prunus glandulosa* Thunb.** – Dwarf flowering plum (109) (1949), Prairie plum (100) (1850) TX

***Prunus gracilis* Engelm. & Gray** – Low plum (5, 97) (1913–1937), Oklahoma plum (3, 4, 50, 155) (1942–present)

***Prunus hortulana* Bailey** – Garden wild plum (5) (1913), Hog-plum

[Hog plum, Hog's plum] (76) (1896) Southwestern MO, Hortulan plum (50, 109 137, 138, 155) (1923–present), Wild goose plum [Wild-goose plum, Wildgoose plum] (3, 4, 5, 73, 97) (1892–1986)

***Prunus ilicifolia* (Nutt. ex Hook. & Arn.) D. Dietr.** – Cerisier á feuilles de houx (French) (20) (1857), Evergreen cherry (107) (1919), Holly-leaf cherry [Hollyleaf cherry, Holly-leaved cherry] (20, 109, 138) (1857–1949), Islay (74, 107, 109) (1893–1949) Southern CA and Western AZ, Mountain evergreen cherry (74) (1893) CA, Mountain-holly [Mountain holly] (107) (1919) CA, Oak-leaf cherry [Oak-leaved cherry] (76) (1896) CA, Spanish wild cherry (74) (1893), Wild cherry or Wild cherry tree [Wild cherry-tree] (107) (1919)

***Prunus ilicifolia* (Nutt. ex Hook. & Arn.) D. Dietr. subsp. *lyonii* (Eastw.) Raven** – Catalina cherry (109, 138) (1923–1949)

***Prunus ilicifolia* Walp.** – See *Prunus ilicifolia* (Nutt. ex Hook. & Arn.) D. Dietr.

***Prunus incisa* Thunb.** – See Cerasus × syodoi (Nakai) H. Ohba

***Prunus insititia* L.** – See *Prunus domestica* L. var. *insititia* (L.) Fiori & Paoletti

***Prunus* L.** – Agryote (179) (1526), Almond (158) (1900), Apricot (138, 155) (1923–1942), Cherry [Cherries, Cherye] or Cherry tree [Cherry trees] (1, 4, 7, 10, 63, 138, 148, 155, 158, 167, 179) (1526–1986), Cherry-laurel [Cherry laurel] (138) (1923), Chokecherry [Choke cherry, Choke-cherry, Choke cherries, Choke-cherries, Choak cherry] (93, 108, 153, 155) (1878–1942), Damacene (179) (1526), Flowering almond (112) (1937), Laurel-cherry (155) (1942), May Day tree (112, 63, 106) (1923–1937), Peach [Peaches] or Peach tree (4, 155, 158) (1900–1986), Plum [Plomme, Plumb, Plumbs, Plums] or Plum tree [Plumb tree, Plum trees] (1, 4, 7, 8, 10, 50, 63, 106, 138, 155, 158, 167, 184) (1785--present), Prunier (French) (8) (1785), Stone fruits [Stone-fruits] (109) (1949), Wild cherry or Wild cherry tree [Wild cherry-tree] (93, 148, 190) (~1759–1939), Wild plum or Wild plum tree (93, 190) (~1759–1936)

***Prunus lanata* Maxk. & Bush** – See *Prunus mexicana* S. Wats.

***Prunus laurocerasus* L.** – Cherry-laurel [Cherry laurel] (49, 57, 92, 107) (1876–1919), Common cherry-laurel (109) (1949), English cherry-laurel (138) (1923), Laurier cerise (French) (8) (1785), Laurocerasus (57) (1917)

***Prunus lusitanica* L.** – Portugal laurel [Portugal-laurel] (109) (1949)

***Prunus lyonii* Sarg.** – See *Prunus ilicifolia* (Nutt. ex Hook. & Arn.) D. Dietr. subsp. *lyonii* (Eastw.) Raven

***Prunus maackii* Rupr.** – See *Padus maackii (Rupr.) Kom.*

***Prunus mahaleb* L.** – Macanet grains (92) (1876), Mahaleb (3, 4, 5, 109) (1913–1986), Mahaleb cherry (137, 138, 156, 158) (1900–1931), Perfumed cherry (1, 4, 5, 156) (1913–1986), Saint Lucia wood (92) (1876), St. Lucie's cherry [St. Lucie cherry] (109, 137) (1931–1949), Weichselkirsche (German) (158) (1900), possibly Black plums (46) (1879), possibly Prunier maritime (French) (8) (1785), possibly Sand plum (5, 92, 156) (1876–1923), possibly Seaside plumb [Sea-side plumb] (8) (1785)

***Prunus maritima* Marsh. var. *gravesii* (Small) G. J. Anderson** – Graves' beach plum (5) (1913)

***Prunus maritima* Wang.** – possibly *Prunus maritima* Marsh.

***Prunus melanocarpa* (A. Nels.) Rydb.** – See *Prunus virginiana* L. var. *melanocarpa* (A. Nels.) Sarg.

***Prunus mexicana* S. Wats.** – Big-tree plum (3, 4) (1977–1986), Fulton's Mexican plum [Fulton Mexican plum] (155) (1942), Inch plum (155) (1942), Mexican plum (50, 122, 155) (1937–present), Polyandra Mexican plum (155) (1942), Wild plum or Wild plum tree (97, 124) (1937)

***Prunus mexicana* S. Wats. var. *flutonensis* (Sargent) Sargent** – See *Prunus mexicana* S. Wats.

***Prunus mexicana* S. Wats. var. *polyandra* (Sargent) Sargent** – See *Prunus mexicana* S. Wats.

***Prunus munsoniana* Wight & Hedr.** – Wild goose plum [Wild-goose plum, Wildgoose plum] (3, 4, 50, 109, 138, 155) (1923–present)

***Prunus nana* (Du Roi) Roemer** – See *Prunus virginiana* L.

***Prunus nana* DuRoi** – See *Prunus virginiana* L.

***Prunus nigra* Aiton** – Canadian plum [Canada plum] (3, 5, 137, 138, 156) (1913–1977), Horse plum [Horse-plum] (5, 156) (1913–1923), Pomegranate (5, 76) (1896–1913), Red plum (5) (1913), Wild plum or Wild plum tree (5) (1913), possibly Red cherry or Red cherry tree (20) (1857)

***Prunus padus* L.** – Bird cherry [Bird-cherry, Birdcherry, Birds cherries] (19, 82, 107) (1840–1930), Cluster cherry (92) (1876), European bird cherry (109, 137, 138) (1923–1949), European May Day tree (82) (1930) IA, Hagberry [Hag-berry] (92, 107) (1876–1919), Hoop ash (92) (1876), May Day tree (82) (1930)

***Prunus pensylvanica* L. f.** – Bird cherry [Bird-cherry, Birdcherry, Birds cherries] (3, 4, 5, 74, 107, 137, 156, 158) (1893–1986), Common wild bird cherry (135) (1910), Dogwood [Dog-wood, Dog wood] (5, 156) (1913–1923), Fire cherry (5, 76, 156, 158) (1896–1923) Franklin Co. ME, appering on newly burnt lands, Pigeon-cherry [Pigeon cherry] (5, 106, 137, 156, 158) (1900–1932), Pin cherry (2, 4, 50, 5, 82, 85, 107, 109, 131, 135, 137, 138, 155, 156, 158) (1895–present), Red cherry or Red cherry tree (5, 158) (1900–1913), Wild pin cherry (137) (1931), Wild red cherry (1, 2, 5, 63, 72, 82, 85, 92, 106, 107, 109, 130, 131, 137) (1895–1949)

Prunus pensylvanica* L. f. var. *pensylvanica – Bird cherry [Bird-cherry, Birdcherry, Birds cherries] (3, 4, 5, 47, 74, 107, 137, 156, 158) (1852–1986), Northern cherry (20) (1857), Red cherry or Red cherry tree (5, 20, 158) (1857–1913)

***Prunus persica* (L.) Batsch** – Amygdalus (52, 54) (1905–1919), Chinese wild peach (137, 138) (1923–1931), Flat peach (109) (1949), Melocoton (178) (1526), Melocoton duranzo (Spanish) (158) (1900), Melon peach (178) (1526), Nectarine (92, 165) (1768–1876), Nucipersica (110) (1587) nectarines, Peach [Peaches] or Peach tree (4, 5, 7, 19, 50, 52, 53, 54, 57, 58, 61, 72, 82, 92, 97, 106, 107, 109, 110, 125, 137, 138, 155, 156, 158, 165) (1633–present), Peche (179) (1526), Pêcher (French) (158) (1900), Persica (57) (1917), Pescanoce (Italian) (110) (1886) nectarines, Pfirsch (German) (158) (1900), Scheptata (Persian) (110) (1784), Tao (Japanese) (110) (1886)

***Prunus persica* (L.) Batsch var. *compressa* Bean** – See *Prunus persica* (L.) Batsch

***Prunus pissardii* Carrière** – Purple-leaf cherry [Purple leaf cherry] (112) (1937), Purple-leaf plum [Purpleleaf plum, Purple-leaved plum] (135, 137) (1910–1931)

***Prunus pumila* L.** – Beach plum (5, 76, 156, 158) (1896–1923) Aroostock Co. & Somerset Co. ME, Dwarf cherry (5, 72, 103, 107, 158) (1870–1919), Sand cherry [Sand cherry] (1, 2, 5, 50, 74, 82, 106, 107, 109, 113, 130, 135, 138, 155, 156, 158) (1890–present), Sand-hill plum (103) (1870), Western sand cherry (32) (1895)

***Prunus pumila* L. var. *besseyi* (Bailey) Gleason** – Aonyeyapi (Dakota) (37) (1919), Bessey's cherry [Bessey cherry] (5, 125, 138, 155) (1913–1942), Dwarf cherry (4) (1986), Kus apaaru kaaruts (Pawnee, cherry-sitting-hiding) (37) (1919), Nonpa tanga (Omaha-Ponca [big cherry] (37) (1919), Western sand cherry (1, 5, 50, 82, 85, 93, 109, 125, 131) (1913–present)

Prunus pumila* L. var. *pumila – Great Lakes sand cherry [Great Lakes sandcherry] (50) (present)

***Prunus pumila* L. var. *susquehanae* (hort. ex Willd.) Jaeger** – Appalachian cherry (5) (1913), Dwarf cherry (1) (1932), Sesquehana sand cherry [Sesquehana sandcherry] (50) (present)

***Prunus pygmaea* [Willd.]** – See *Prunus maritima* Marsh.

***Prunus reverchonii* Sargent** – See *Prunus rivularis* Scheele

***Prunus rivularis* Scheele** – Creek plum (4, 50, 107, 155) (1919–present), Hog-plum [Hog plum, Hog's plum] (4, 155) (1942–1986)

***Prunus serotina* Ehrh.** – Amerikanischer Ziersrauch (German) (158) (1900), Black cherry (3, 7, 50, 82, 92, 125, 131, 138, 155, 157) (1882–present), Black-choke (157, 158) (1900–1929), Cabinet cherry (156, 157, 158) (1900–1929), Capuli (Mexico) (107) (1919), Capulinos (Mexico) (107) (1919), Cerisier de Virginie (French)

(158) (1900), Chokecherry [Choke cherry, Choke-cherry, Choke cherries, Choke-cherries, Choak cherry] (156, 158) (1900–1923), Mountain black cherry (106) (1930), Prunus virginiana (57, 60) (1902–1917) This was the official name, but P. virginiana is the species usually called choke cherry, Rum cherry (71, 73, 107, 156, 157, 158) (1892–1898) Northeast US, Virginia prune [Virginian prune] (55) (1911), Whisky cherry [Whiskey cherry] (71, 156, 157, 158) (1898–1929), Wild black cherry (2, 4, 9, 59, 63, 71, 72, 82, 93, 95, 107, 109, 113, 114, 122, 156, 158) (1873–1986), Wild cherry or Wild cherry tree [Wild cherry-tree] (20, 52, 55, 57, 60, 65, 71, 96, 106, 156, 157, 158, 187) (1818–1931)

***Prunus serotina* Ehrh. var. *eximia* (Small) Little** – Escarpment cherry (122) (1937) TX

***Prunus serotina* Ehrh. var. *virens* (Woot. & Standl.) McVaugh** – Chisos wild cherry (122) (1937) TX

***Prunus serrulata* Lindl.** – Japanese flowering cherry (109) (1949), Oriental cherry (138) (1923)

***Prunus spinosa* L.** – Black thorn [Black-thorn] (92, 107, 109, 137, 138) (1876–1949), English sloe (19) (1840), Sloe (107, 109, 137, 179) (1526–1949), Sloe-tee blossoms [Sloe tee blossoms] (92) (1876), Slow shrub (41) (1770), Wild plum or Wild plum tree (92) (1876)

***Prunus subcordata* Benth.** – Pacific plum (107, 109) (1919–1949)

***Prunus subcordata* var. *kellogii* Lemmon** – Sisson plum (109) (1949)

***Prunus subhirtella* Miq.** – Higan cherry (138) (1923), Rosebud cherry (109) (1949)

***Prunus texana* F. G. Dietr.** – Nerango (124) (1937) TX, Sand plum (124) (1937) TX

***Prunus tomentosa* Thunb.** – Nanking cherry (50, 112, 138) (1923–present), Tomentose cherry (82) (1930)

***Prunus triloba* Lindl.** – Flowering almond (109) (1949), Flowering plum (135, 138) (1910–1923) MT

***Prunus umbellata* Ell.** – Sloe of the South (107) (1919)

***Prunus virens* (Woot. & Standl.) Shreve** – See *Prunus serotina* Ehrh. var. *virens* (Woot. & Standl.) McVaugh

***Prunus virginiana* L.** – A'sīsûwe'mǐnaga'wûnj (Chippewa) (40) (1928), Cabinet cherry (19) (1840), Čaŋpa (Lakota) (121) (1918?–1970?), Chokecherry [Choke cherry, Choke-cherry, Choke cherries, Choke-cherries, Choak cherry] (1, 3, 4, 9, 35, 40, 46, 47, 50, 57, 63, 72, 82, 92, 95, 103, 106, 107, 108, 109, 112, 113, 114, 121, 125, 126, 130, 131, 135, 137, 156, 157, 158, 187) (1806–present), Clustered black cherry (189) (1767), Common chokecherry (112, 137, 138, 155) (1923–1942), Gthoŋpa (Osage) (121) (1918?–1970?), Padus de Virginie (French) (8) (1785), Quussuckomineanug (46) (1879), Rum cherry (19, 92) (1840–1876), Virginia bird-cherry tree [Virginian bird-cherry-tree] (8) (1785), Virginia cherry tree (18) (1805), Wild black cherry (85, 92) (1876–1932), Wild cherry or Wild cherry tree [Wild cherry-tree] (12, 19, 20, 41, 48, 49, 53, 61, 92, 103, 157, 158, 187) (1770–1922), Red chokecherry [Red choke cherry] (85) (1932)

***Prunus virginiana* L. var. *demissa* (Nutt.) Torr.** – Chokecherry [Choke cherry, Choke-cherry, Choke cherries, Choke-cherries, Choak cherry] (22, 74, 101, 112, 113, 137) (1890–1937), Dwarf wild cherry (113, 114) (1890–1894), Malupwa (Crow) (101) (1905) MT, Rocky Mountain cherry (112) (1937), Schlascha (Flathead) (101) (1905) MT, Western chokecherry [Western choke cherry, Western chokecherry] (50, 82, 106, 137, 138, 155) (1923–present), Western wild cherry (72, 106, 131, 137) (1899–1931), Wild cherry or Wild cherry tree [Wild cherry-tree] (130, 137) (1895–1931)

***Prunus virginiana* L. var. *melanocarpa* (A. Nels.) Sargent** – Black chokecherry (50, 155) (1942–present), Chokecherry [Choke cherry, Choke-cherry, Choke cherries, Choke-cherries, Choak cherry] (85) (1932), Rocky Mountain wild cherry (5) (1913), Western chokecherry [Western choke cherry, Western choke-cherry] (5, 37, 93, 95) (1911–1936)

Prunus virginiana* L. var. *virginiana – Cabinet cherry (5) (1913), Chanpa (Dakota) (37) (1919), Chokecherry [Choke cherry, Choke-cherry, Choke cherries, Choke-cherries, Choak cherry] (5, 50, 37,

97) (1913–present), Eastern chokecherry [Eastern choke cherry] (93) (1936) Neb, Nahaapi nakaaruts (Pawnee, cherry tree) (37) (1919), Nonpa-zhinga (Omaha-Ponca, little cherry) (37) (1919), Rum cherry (5) (1913), Whisky cherry [Whiskey cherry] (5) (1913), Wild black cherry (5, 97) (1913–1937), Wild cherry or Wild cherry tree [Wild cherry-tree] (5) (1913)

Prunus virginica – See *Prunus virginiana* L.

***Prunus watsonii* Sargent** – See *Prunus angustifolia* Marsh. var. *watsonii* (Sarg.) Waugh

Prunus-cerasus virginiana – See *Prunus virginiana* L.

***Psamma arenaria* R. & S.** – See *Ammophila arenaria* (L.) Link

***Psathyrostachys juncea* (Fisch.) Nevski** – Russian wild rye [Russian wildrye] (3, 50) (1977–present)

***Psathyrostachys* Nevski** – Wild rye [Wild-rye, Wildrye] (50) (present)

***Psedera* Necker** – See *Hedera* L.

***Pseudocydonia sinensis* (Dum.-Cours.) Schneid.** – Chinese quince (109, 138) (1923–1949)

***Pseudofumaria lutea* (L.) Borkh.** – Yellow corydalis (138) (1923), Yellow fumiterre (178) (1526)

Pseudognaphalium canescens* (DC.) W. A. Weber subsp. *canescens – Wright's cudweed (50) (present)

Pseudognaphalium helleri* (Britt.) A. Anderb. subsp. *helleri – Heller's everlasting (5) (1913)

***Pseudognaphalium* Kirp.** – Cudweed [Cud-weed, Cud weed] (50) (present)

***Pseudognaphalium luteoalbum* (L.) Hilliard & Burtt** – Jersey livelong (92) (1876)

***Pseudognaphalium macounii* (Greene) Kartesz** – Balsamweed [Balsam weed, Balsam-weed] (5, 156) (1913–1923), Clammy everlasting (5, 156) (1913–1923), Everlasting (85, 156) (1923–1932), Kâsd'úta (Cherokee, simulating ashes) (102) (1886) from appearance of leaves, Macoun's cudweed (50) (present), Neglected life-everlasting (19) (1840), Sweet balsam (5, 156) (1913–1923), White everlasting (156) (1923), Winged cudweed [Winged cud-weed] (5, 156) (1913–1923)

Pseudognaphalium obtusifolium* (L.) Hilliard & Burtt subsp. *obtusifolium – Balsam (75) (1894), Balsamweed [Balsam weed, Balsam-weed] (5, 92, 156) (1876–1923), Cat's-foot [Cats foot, Cat's foot, Cat foot] (6) (1892), Chafeweed [Chafe-weed, Chafe weed] (5, 92) (1876–1913), Common everlasting (62, 156, 157) (1900–1923), Eternal flower (92) (1876), Featherweed [Feather weed, Featherweed] (5, 73, 156, 157) (1892–1923) Northern NY, seed heads used for bed filling, no longer in use by 1923, Field balsam (157) (1929), Fragrant cudweed (4, 155) (1942–1986), Fragrant everlasting (3, 4, 6, 62) (1892–1986), Fragrant life-everlasting [Fragrant life everlating] (5, 156) (1913–1923), Fussy-gussy [Fussy gussy] (5) (1913), Fuzzy-guzzy (73, 156) (1892–1923) Mansfiled OH, no longer in use by 1923, Immerschön Ruhkraut (German) (6) (1892), Immortelle (French) (6) (1892), Indian posy [Indian-posy, Indian posey] (5, 6, 49, 75, 76, 92) (1876–1913), Le Cotonnière (French) (6) (1892), Life-everlasting [Life everlasting] (6, 57, 73, 145, 157) (1892–1929), Life-of-man [Life of man, Life-o'-man] (5, 73) (1892–1913) Stratham NH, Live-forever [Liveforever, Live forever] (92) (1876), Moonshine (5, 75, 156, 157) (1894–1929) Dorset VT, Mouse-ear everlasting (157) (1929), None-so-pretty [None so pretty] (6) (1892), Old-field balsam [Old-field balsam] (5, 6, 49, 73, 92, 156, 157) (1892–1929), Poverty-weed [Povertyweed, Poverty weed] (5, 76, 92, 156, 157) (1896–1929) Paris ME, Rabbit-tobacco [Rabbit tobacco, Rabbittobacco] (5, 50, 75, 156, 157) (1894–present), Silver-leaf [Silver leaf, Silver-leaf] (6) (1892), Sweet balsam (5, 62, 92, 156, 157) (1876–1929), Sweet life-everlasting [Sweet life everlasting] (5) (1913), Sweet-scented life-everlasting [Sweet scented life everlasting] (19, 49, 92) (1840–1898), White balsam (5, 6, 61, 72, 92, 156, 157) (1870–1929)

***Pseudognaphalium stramineum* (Kunth) W. A. Weber** – Cotton-batting [Cotton batting] (4) (1986), Cotton-batting cudweed [Cotton-batting cudweed] (155) (1942), Cotton-batting plant [Cottonbatting plant] (50) (present)

Pseudognaphalium viscosum **(Kunth) W. A. Weber** – Clammy cudweed (4) (1986), Winged cudweed [Winged cud-weed] (50) (present)

Pseudolycopodiella caroliniana **(L.) Holub** – See *Lycopodiella caroliniana* (L.) Pichi Sermolli var. *caroliniana*

Pseudolysimachion longifolium **(L.) Opiz** – Blue speedwell (82) (1930) IA

Pseudopetalon glandulosum **[Raf.]** – See *Zanthoxylum clava-herculis* L.

Pseudophoenix sargentii **H. Wendl. ex Sarg.** – Sargent's palm [Sargent palm] (138) (1923)

Pseudoraphis spinescens **(R. Br.) Vickery** – Vetives (Louisiana) (67) (1890)

Pseudoroegneria **(Nevski) A. Löve** – Wheat grass [Wheat-grass, Wheatgrass] (50) (present)

Pseudoroegneria spicata **(Pursh) Á. Löve** – Wire bunch grass [Wire bunch-grass] (94, 118) (1898–1901)

Pseudoroegneria spicata **(Pursh) A. Löve subsp.** *inermis* **(Scribn. & J.G. Sm.) A. Löve** – Beardless blue-bunch wheat grass [Beardless bluebunch wheatgrass] (155) (1942), Beardless wheat grass (50) (present)

Pseudoroegneria spicata **(Pursh) A. Löve subsp.** *spicata* – Bearded blue-bunch wheat grass [Bearded bluebunch wheatgrass] (140, 155) (1942–1944), Blue bunch wheat grass [Bluebunch wheatgrass] (3, 50, 146, 185) (1936–present), Bunch grass [Bunchgrass, Bunch-grass] (163) (1852), Colorado bluestem [Colorado blue-stem, Colorado blue stem] (94) (1901), Vasey's bunch grass [Vasey's bunch-grass] (94) (1901), Western wheat grass [Western wheat-grass, Western wheatgrass] (56, 72, 94, 118) (1898–1907), Wild wheat grass [Wild wheat grass] (56) (1901)

Pseudosasa japonica **(Sieb. & Zucc. ex Steud.) Makino ex Nakai** – Arrow bamboo (138) (1923)

Pseudotsuga douglasii **Carr.** – See *Pseudotsuga menziesii* (Mirb.) Franco

Pseudotsuga douglasii glauca – See *Pseudotsuga menziesii* (Mirbel) Franco var. *glauca* (Beissn.) Franco

Pseudotsuga menziesii **(Mirb.) Franco** – Douglas fir [Douglas' fir] (20, 101, 108, 112, 123, 136, 138) (1857–1937), Douglas' spruce [Douglas spruce] (2, 108, 135, 136, 147, 153, 161) (1857–1930) MT, Douglas' spruce fir [Douglas spruce fir, Douglas's spruce fir] (14, 20) (1857–1882), Hemlock [Hemloc, Hemlocke] or Hemlock tree (147) (1856), Menzies' spruce (161) (1857), Menzies' spruce-fir [Menzies spruce fir] (20) (1857), Oregon pine (75, 147) (1856–1894), Red fir (101, 153) (1905–1913), Sapin de Douglas (French) (20) (1857), Sapin de Menzies (French) (20) (1857), White fir (153) (1913)

Pseudotsuga menziesii **(Mirbel) Franco var.** *glauca* **(Beissn.) Franco** – Blue Douglas fir [Blue Douglas-fir] (138) (1923)

Pseudotsuga menziesii **(Mirbel) Franco var.** *menziesii* – Douglas fir [Douglas' fir] (109, 149) (1904–1949), Oregon fir (149) (1904)

Pseudotsuga taxifolia **Britt.** – See *Pseudotsuga menziesii* (Mirbel) Franco var. *menziesii*

Psidium cattleianum **Sabine** – Strawberry guave (109, 138) (1923–1949)

Psidium guajava **L.** – Apple guava (107) (1919), Guajava or Guajavos (Peru & San Domingo) (110) (1886), Guava (92, 106, 109, 110, 138) (1876–1949), Guayabos (107) (1740), Guayva (92) (1876), Xalxocotl (Mexico) (110) (1886), Yellow guava (107) (1919)

Psidium **L.** – Guava (138) (1923)

Psidium pyriferum – See *Psidium guajava* L.

Psilocarya nitens **(Vahl) Wood** – See *Rhynchospora nitens* (Vahl) Gray

Psilocarya portoricensis **Britt.** – See *Rhynchospora nitens* (Vahl) Gray

Psilocarya scirpoides **Torr. var.** *grimesii* **Fern. & Grisc.** – See *Rhynchospora scirpoides* (Torr.) Gray

Psilostrophe **DC.** – Paper flower [Paperflower, Paper flowers] (1, 4, 155) (1932–1986), Psilostrophe (158) (1900)

Psilostrophe tagetina **(Nutt.) Greene** – Paper flower [Paperflower,

Paper flowers] (148) (1939), Psilostrophe (148) (1939), Woolly paper flower [Woolly paperflower] (50, 155) (1942–present)

Psilostrophe tagetina **(Nutt.) Greene var.** *cerifera* **(A. Nels.) B.L. Turner** – Paper flower [Paperflower, Paper flowers] (3) (1977), Plains psilostrophe (5, 97) (1913–1937), Woolly paper flower [Woolly paperflower] (50) (present)

Psophocarpus tetragonolobus **(L.) DC.** – Asparagus pea (109) (1949)

Psoralea argophylla **Pursh** – See *Pediomelum argophyllum* (Pursh) J. Grimes

Psoralea bituminosa **L.** – See *Bituminaria bituminosa* (L.) Stirt.

Psoralea collina **Rydb.** – See *Pediomelum argophyllum* (Pursh) J. Grimes

Psoralea cuspidata **Pursh** – See *Pediomelum cuspidatum* (Pursh) Rydb.

Psoralea digitata **Nutt.** – See *Pediomelum digitatum* (Nutt. ex Torr. & Gray) Isely

Psoralea eglandulosa **Elliott** – See *Orbexilum pedunculatum* (Mill.) Rydb.

Psoralea esculenta **Pursh** – See *Pediomelum esculentum* (Pursh) Rydb.

Psoralea floribunda **Nutt. ex Torr. & Gray** – See *Psoralidium tenuiflorum* (Pursh) Rydb.

Psoralea hypogaea **Nutt.** – See *Pediomelum hypogaeum* (Nutt. ex Torr. & Gray) Rydb. var. *hypogaeum*

Psoralea **L.** – See *Psoralidium* Rydb. (all US species assigned to other genera)

Psoralea linearifolia **Torr. & Gray** – See *Pediomelum linearifolium* (Torr. & Gray) J. Grimes

Psoralea onobrychis **Nutt.** – See *Orbexilum onobrychis* (Nutt.) Rydb.

Psoralea pedunculata **(Mill.) Vail** – See *Orbexilum pedunculatum* (Mill.) Rydb. var. *pedunculatum*

Psoralea psoralioides **(Walt.) Cory var.** *eglandulosa* **(Ell.) F. L. Freeman** – See *Orbexilum pedunculatum* (Mill.) Rydb. var. *pedunculatum*

Psoralea reverchonii **S. Wats.** – See *Pediomelum reverchonii* (S. Wats.) Rydb.

Psoralea tenuiflora **Pursh** – See *Psoralidium tenuiflorum* (Pursh) Rydb.

Psoralea tenuiflora **Pursh var.** *floribunda* **(Nutt.) Rydb.** – See *Psoralidium tenuiflorum* (Pursh) Rydb.

Psoralea tenuiflora **Pursh var.** *tenuiflora* – See *Psoralidium tenuiflorum* (Pursh) Rydb.

Psoralidium lanceolatum **(Pursh) Rydb.** – Lance-leaf psoralea [Lance-leaved psoralea] (5, 93, 97, 131) (1899–1937), Lemon scurf-pea [Lemon scurfpea, Lemon scurf pea] (4, 50, 98) (1923–present), Lemonweed [Lemon weed] (106) (1930), Shoe-string plant (85) (1932) SD, Tumbleweed [Tumble weed, Tumble-weed] (5, 93) (1913–1936)

Psoralidium **Rydb.** – Psoralea (158) (1900), Scurf-pea [Scurf pea, Scurfpea] (4, 50, 138) (1923–present)

Psoralidium tenuiflorum **(Pursh) Rydb.** – Few-flower psoralea [Few-flowered psoralea] (5, 72, 93, 97, 121, 131) (1899–1937), Many-flower psoralea [Many-flowered psoralea] (93, 97) (1936–1937), Psoralea (125, 148) (1930–1939), Scurvy-pea [Scurvy pea] (5, 122, 156) (1913–1937), Slim-flower scurf-pea [Slimflower scurfpea] (50) (present), Tičaničahu taŋka hu (Lakota, Large curlew plant) (121) (1918?–1970?), Tichanicha-hu (37) (1919), Wild alfalfa (3, 4, 98, 146) (1926–1986)

Psorothamnus spinosus **(Gray) Barneby** – Indigo bush [Indigobush, Indigo-bush] (106) (1930)

Psychotria **L.** – Psychotria (138) (1923)

Ptelea baldwinii **Torr. & Gray** – See *Ptelea trifoliata* L. subsp. *trifoliata* var. *trifoliata*

Ptelea crenulata **Greene** – California hop tree [California hop-tree] (106) (1930)

Ptelea **L.** – Boispuant (French, Louisiana Purchase) (7) (1828) Louisiana Purchase, Hop tree [Hop-tree, Hoptree] (1, 4, 50, 15, 82, 109, 138, 155, 158) (1895–present), Ptelea (8) (1785), Ptelea (French) (8) (1785), Shrubby-trefoil [Shrubby trefoil] (1, 82)

(1930–1932), Shrub-trefoil [Shrub trefoil] (13) (1849), Skunk bush [Skunkbush, Skunk-bush] (153) (1913), Wafer-ash [Wafer ash] (15) (1895), Water-ash [Water ash] (122) (1937), Wingseed [Wing seed, Wing-seed] (7) (1828)

Ptelea monticola **Greene** – See *Ptelea trifoliata* L. subsp. *polyadenia* (Greene) V. Bailey

Ptelea trifoliata **L.** – Aguebark [Ague bark, Ague-bark] (5, 92, 156, 157, 158) (1876–1929), Carolina shrub-trefoil (8) (1785), Caroliniana shrub-trefoil (8) (1785), Common hoptree (50, 137, 138, 155) (1923–present), Dreiblattrige Lederbaum [Driblattrige Lederbaum] (German) (6) (1892), Hop tree [Hop-tree, Hoptree] (3, 4, 6, 49, 53, 82, 92, 106, 107, 112, 137, 156) (1892–1986), Hopfenbaum (German) (158) (1900), Kleebaum (German) (158) (1900), Orme à trois feuilles (French) (8, 158) (1785–1900), Orme de Samaire a Trois Feuilles (French) (6) (1892), Penny tree [Penny-tree] (156) (1923), Pickawat anise (157) (1929), Pickaway (6) (1892), Pickaway anise [Pickaway-anise] (5, 92, 156, 158) (1876–1923), Prairie-grub [Prairie grub] (5, 92, 156, 158) (1876–1923), Ptelea (92, 174) (1753–1876), Ptelea à trois feuilles (French) (8) (1785), Quinine tree [Quinine-tree] (5, 106, 156, 157, 158) (1900–1930), Sang tree [Sang-tree] (56, 156, 158) (1900–1923), Shrubby-trefoil [Shrubby trefoil] (5, 6, 49, 53, 92, 106, 107, 156, 157, 158) (1892–1929), Skunk bush [Skunkbush, Skunk-bush] (156) (1923), Stinking ash (6, 92, 156, 157, 158) (1892–1929), Stinking prairie bush [Stinking prairiebush, Stinking prairie-bush] (92, 156, 158) (1876–1923), Stinking-ash [Stinking ash] (6, 92, 156, 157, 158) (1892–1929), Swamp-dogwood [Swamp dogwood] (5, 6, 49, 92, 156, 157, 158) (1892–1929), Three-leaf hoptree [Three-leaved hop tree, Three-leaved hop-tree, Three-leaved hoptree] (2, 5, 72, 97, 156, 157, 158) (1895–1929), Tree trefoil [Tree trefoil] (6) (1892), Wafer-ash [Wafer ash] (48, 156) (1882–1923), Wahoo [Waahoo, Waa-hoo, Wauhoo, Whahoo] (106) (1930), Water-ash [Water ash] (4, 5, 6, 47, 49, 52, 53, 57, 61, 65, 74, 92, 124, 137, 156, 157) (1852–1986), Wingseed [Wing seed, Wing-seed] (5, 6, 49, 53, 92, 156, 157, 158) (1892–1929)

Ptelea trifoliata **L. subsp.** *angustifolia* **(Benth.) V. Bailey var.** *angustifolia* **(Benth.) M. E. Jones** – Hop tree [Hop-tree, Hoptree] (112) (1937)

Ptelea trifoliata **L. subsp.** *polyadenia* **(Greene) V. Bailey** – Wafer-ash [Wafer ash] (124) (1937) TX

Ptelea trifoliata **L. subsp.** *trifoliata* **var.** *mollis* **Torr. & Gray** – Hop tree [Hop-tree, Hoptree] (112, 137) (1931–1937)

Ptelea trifoliata **L. subsp.** *trifoliata* **var.** *trifoliata* – Baldwin's hoptree [Baldwin hoptree] (155) (1942), Narrow-leaf wafer-ash [Narrow-leafed wafer ash] (124) (1937)

Pteridium aquilinum **(L.) Kuhn** – Bracken (4, 103, 107, 109, 138) (1871–1986), Brake (1, 4, 5, 72, 103, 107, 109, 131) (1871–1986), Brake fern (101, 148) (1905–1939), Braken (148) (1939), Braken fern (97) (1937), Common brake (2, 14, 97, 187) (1818–1937), Female fern [Female Ferne] (178) (1596), Fern [Ferne] (178, 179) (1526–1596), Hog brake (73, 79) (1891–1892) hogs like roots, Poor-man's-soap [Poor man's soap] (78) (1898) Alabama, willmake a lather with water, Western bracken fern [Western brackenfern] (50) (present)

Pteridium aquilinum **(L.) Kuhn var.** *latiusculum* **(Desv.) Underwood ex Heller** – Bracken fern [Brackenfern] (3) (1977), Common bracken (3) (1977), Eastern bracken (155) (1942), Western bracken fern [Western brackenfern] (50) (present)

Pteridium aquilinum **(L.) Kuhn var.** *pseudocaudatum* **(Clute) Heller** – Western bracken fern [Western brackenfern] (50) (present)

Pteridium aquilinum **(L.) Kuhn var.** *pubescens* **Underwood** – Hairy bracken fern [Hairy brackenfern] (50) (present), Western bracken fern [Western brackenfern] (155) (1942)

Pteridium aquilinus – See *Pteridium aquilinum* (L.) Kuhn

Pteridium **Gleditsch ex Scop.** – Bracken (4, 138, 155) (1923–1986), Bracken fern [Brackenfern] (50) (present), Brake (1) (1932)

Pteridium latiusculum **(Desv.) Hieron.** – See *Pteridium aquilinum* (L.)

Kuhn var. *latiusculum* (Desv.) Underwood ex Heller

Pteridium **Scop.** – See *Pteridium* Gleditsch ex Scop.

Pteris aquilina **L.** – See *Pteridium aquilinum* (L.) Kuhn

Pteris atropurpurea **(L.) Link.** – See *Pellaea atropurpurea* (L.) Link

Pteris cretica **L.** – Cretan brake (50, 138) (1923–present)

Pteris ensiformis **Burm. f.** – Sword brake (138) (1923)

Pteris **L.** – Brake (2, 109, 138, 184) (1793–1949), Brake fern (50) (present)

Pteris longifolia **L.** – Long-leaf brake [Longleaf brake] (50) (present)

Pteris multifida **Poir.** – Spider brake (50, 138) (1923–present)

Pteris serrulata **L.** – See *Pteris multifida* Poir.

Pteris tremula **R. Br.** – Australian brake (138) (1923)

Pterocarya **Kunth** – Wingnut (138) (1923)

Pterocarya stenoptera **C. DC.** – Chinese wingnut (138) (1923)

Pterocaulon **Ell.** – Blackroot [Black-root, Black root] (7) (1828), Hinih (Western Indians) (7) (1828)

Pterocaulon pycnostachyum **(Michx.) Ell.** – See *Pterocaulon virgatum* (L.) DC.

Pterocaulon virgatum **(L.) DC.** – Blackroot [Black-root, Black root] (10, 19, 57) (1818–1917)

Pterospora andromedea **Nutt.** – Albany beechdrops [Albany beech drops] (5, 7, 19, 92, 156, 158) (1828–1923), Crawley (61) (1870), Dragonroot [Dragon root, Dragon-root, Dragon's root] (7) (1828), False crawley (92, 156, 158) (1876–1923), Fever-root [Fever root, Feverroot] (7, 58) (1828–1869), Gall-of-the-earth [Gall of the earth] (92, 156, 158) (1898–1923), Giant bird's-nest [Giant bird's nest] (5, 93, 156, 158) (1900–1936), Pinedrops [Pine drops, Pine-drops] (1, 3, 4, 5, 85, 93, 95, 122, 131, 156, 158) (1899–1986), Pterospore paradoxe (French) (7) (1828), Scaly dragonclaw (7) (1828), Woodland pinedrops (50, 155) (1942–present)

Pterospora **Nutt.** – Giant bird's-nest [Giant bird's nest] (1) (1932), Pinedrops [Pine drops, Pine-drops] (50, 155, 158) (1900–present)

Ptilimnium capillaceum **(Michx.) Raf.** – Bolewort [Bole wort] (5, 156) (1913–1923), Bullwort [Bull wort, Bull-wort] (5, 156) (1913–1923), Herb William [herb-William] (5, 156) (1913–1923), Mock bishop's-weed [Mock bishop's weed, Mock bishop-weed, Mock Bishopweed] (5, 97, 156) (1913–1937), Wood nep [Wood-nep] (5, 156) (1913–1923)

Ptilimnium nuttallii **(DC.) Britton** – Laceflower [Lace flower, Laceflower] (50) (present), Mock bishop's-weed [Mock bishop's weed, Mock bishop-weed, Mock Bishopweed] (3, 4, 158) (1900–1986), Nuttall's mock bishop's-weed [Nuttall's mock bishop-weed, Nuttall's mock bishop's weed] (5, 97) (1913–1937)

Ptiloria pauciflora **(Torr.) Raf.** – See *Stephanomeria pauciflora* (Torr.) A. Nels.

Ptiloria **Raf.** – See *Stephanomeria* Nutt. (all US species)

Ptiloria ramosa **Rydb.** – See *Stephanomeria runcinata* Nutt.

Ptychosperma **Labill.** – Seaforthia palm (109) (1949)

Puccinellia angustata **(R. Br.) Rand & Redf.** – Arctic meadow grass (5) (1913), Narrow alkali grass [Narrow alkaligrass] (50) (present)

Puccinellia cusickii **Weath.** – See *Puccinellia nuttalliana* (J. A. Schultes) A. S. Hitchc.

Puccinellia distans **(Jacq.) Parl.** – Alkali grass [Alkali-grass, Alkaligrass] (140) (1944) CO, Clustered spear grass (66) (1903), Reflexed meadow grass (66) (1903), Sea meadow grass (5) (1913), Sea spur grass (92) (1876), Spreading meadow grass (5) (1913), Spreading spear grass [Spreading spear-grass] (94) (1901), Sweet grass [Sweet-grass, Sweetgrass] (5) (1913), Weeping alkali grass [Weeping alkaligrass] (50, 140, 155) (1942–present)

Puccinellia distans **(Jacq.) Parl. subsp.** *distans* – Weeping alkali grass [Weeping alkaligrass] (50) (present)

Puccinellia distans **(L.) Parl.** – See *Puccinellia distans* (Jacq.) Parl.

Puccinellia fasciculata **(Torr.) Bicknell** – Saltmarsh alkali grass [Saltmarsh alkaligrass] (50) (present), Torrey's meadow grass (5) (1913)

Puccinellia lemmonii **(Vasey) Scribn.** – Lemmon's speargrass

[Lemmon's spear-grass] (94) (1901)

Puccinellia maritima (**Huds.**) **Parl.** – Creeping sea meadow grass (66) (1903), Goose grass [Goosegrass, Goose-grass] (5, 45, 66) (1896–1913), Sea meadow grass (5, 92) (1876–1913), Sea spear grass [Sea spear-grass] (5, 66, 90, 94) (1885–1913), Seaside alkali grass [Seaside alkaligrass] (50) (present)

Puccinellia nuttalliana (**J. A. Schultes**) **A. S. Hitchc.** – Alkali grass [Alkali-grass, Alkaligrass] (3) (1977), Alkali mountain grass (141) (1899), Nuttall's alkali grass [Nuttall alkali grass, Nuttall alkaligrass, Nuttall's alkaligrass] (50, 146, 155) (1939–present), Slender meadow grass [Slender meadow-grass] (5) (1913)

Puccinellia **Parl.** – Alkali grass [Alkali-grass, Alkaligrass] (50) (present), Meadow grass [Meadow-grass, Medow Grasse] (1, 93) (1932–1936)

Pueraria **DC.** – Kudzu (50) (present), Kudzu vine [Kudzu-vine] (4) (1986), Kudzubean [Kudzu-bean] (155) (1942), Pueraria (138) (1923)

Pueraria lobata (**Willd.**) **Ohwi** – See *Pueraria montana* (Lour.) Merr. var. *lobata* (Willd.) Maesen & S. Almeida

Pueraria montana (**Lour.**) **Merr. var.** *lobata* (**Willd.**) **Maesen & S. Almeida** – Kudzu (50) (present), Kudzu vine [Kudzu-vine] (4, 109) (1949–1986), Kudzubean [Kudzu-bean] (138) (1923), Thunberg's kudzu-bean [Thunberg kudzubean] (155) (1942)

Pueraria thunbergiana **Benth.** – See *Pueraria montana* (Lour.) Merr. var. *lobata* (Willd.) Maesen & S. Almeida

Pulicaria dysenterica (**L.**) **Bernh.** – Great fleabane (178) (1526), Small fleabane (92) (1876)

Pulicaria **Gaertn.** – Policary (179) (1526)

Pulmonaria **L.** – Lungwort [Lung-wort] (7, 10, 109, 138) (1818–1949)

Pulmonaria officinalis **L.** – Blue lungwort (109) (1949), Common lungwort (138) (1923), Cowslips of Jerusalem (178) (1526), Jerusalem cowslip (92, 107) (1876–1919) OK, Jerusalem sage [Jerusalemsage] (92, 109) (1876–1949), Lungwort [Lung-wort] (19, 57, 61, 92, 107) (1840–1919), Spotted comfrey (92) (1876), Spotted lungwort (92) (1876)

Pulmonaria saccharata **Mill.** – Bethlehem lungwort (138) (1923), Bethlehem-sage (109) (1949)

Pulmonaria virginica [**L.**] – See *Mertensia virginica* (L.) Pers. ex Link

Pulsatilla hirsutissima (**Pursh**) **Britton** – See *Pulsatilla patens* (L.) Mill. subsp. *multifida* (Pritz.) Zamels

Pulsatilla **Mill.** – Blue-tulip [Bluetulip, Blue tulip] (1) (1932), Lion's-beard [Lion's beard, Lions' beard] (1) (1932), Pasque flower [Pasque-flower, Pasqueflower, Pasque floures] (1, 13, 50, 93, 158) (1849–present), Wild crocus (1) (1932) Madison WI

Pulsatilla occidentalis (**S. Wats.**) **Freyn** – Oregon anemone (155) (1942), Western pasque flower [Western pasqueflower] (155) (1942)

Pulsatilla patens (**L.**) **Mill.** – American pasqueflower [American pasque-flower] (50) (present), American pulsatilla (5) (1913), April-fools [April fools, April-fool] (5) (1913), Badger [Badgers] (5) (1913), Easter flower [Easter-flower, Easter flowers] (5) (1913), Gosling (5) (1913), Hartshorn plant [Hartshorn-plant] (5) (1913), Headache plant [Head-ache plant, Headache-plant] (5) (1913), Hokshi-chekpa wah'cha (Dakota, twin flower) (37) (1919), Mayflower [May flower, May-flower] (5) (1913), Pasque flower [Pasque-flower, Pasqueflower, Pasque floures] (5, 37, 85) (1913–1932), Prairie anemone (5) (1913), Prairie-smoke [Prairie smoke] (5) (1913), Rock-lily [Rock lily, Rock lilies] (5) (1913), Twin flower [Twin-flower, Twin-flower] (37) (1919), Wild crocus (5) (1913), Windflower [Wind flower, Wind-flower, Wind-floures, Winde-floures] (5, 93) (1913–1936)

Pulsatilla patens (**L.**) **Mill. subsp.** *multifida* (**Pritz.**) **Zamels** – Bastard anemones (180) (1633), possibly Coquelourdes (French) (180) (1633), possibly Coventry bells [Couentrie bels] (Cambridgeshire) (180) (1633), possibly Flaw floure (180) (1633), possibly Kneckenschell (Dutch) (180) (1633), possibly Lesser purple passe flower [Lesser purple Passe floure] (180) (1633), possibly Passe flower [Passe floure] (180) (1633), possibly Pulsatilla (180) (1633),

possibly Purple passe flower [Purple passe floure] (180) (1633), possibly Red Passe flower [Red Passe floure] (180) (1633), possibly White passe flower [White passe floure] (180) (1633), American pasqueflower [American pasque-flower] (138, 157, 158) (1900–1929), American pulsatilla (6, 49, 157, 158) (1892–1929), Apium risus (Laughing parsley) (86) (1878) old name, said to cause laughing and foolishness and convulsions by poisonous qualities, April-fools [April fools, April-fool] (74, 157, 158) (1893–1929) Rockford IL, possibly becuase it flowers around April 1 and often is snowed under, Badger [Badgers] (76) (1896) WI, Badgerweed [Badgerweed] (157, 158) (1900–1929), Crocus [Crocuses] (6, 74, 126, 127) (1892–1933), Crowfoot [Crow-foot, Crow foot, Crowfote, Crow's foot] (76) (1896), Cut-leaf anemone [Cutleaf anemone, Cut-leaved anemone] (50) (present), Easter flower [Easter-flower, Easter flowers] (157, 158) (1900–1929), Gogeda'djibûg (Chippewa) (40) (1928), Goslin weed (6) (1892), Gosling (74, 157, 158) (1893–1929) MN, Hartshorn plant [Hartshorn-plant] (6, 74, 157, 158) (1892–1929), Headache plant [Head-ache plant, Headache-plant] (74, 157, 158) (1893–1929), Lyall's anemone [Lyall anemone] (155) (1942), Mayflower [May flower, May-flower] (6, 157, 158) (1892–1929), Nuttall's pasqueflower [Nuttall's pasque-flower, Nuttall's pasque flower] (86, 157, 158) (1878–1929), Pasque flower [Pasque-flower, Pasqueflower, Pasque floures] (3, 4, 6, 40, 49, 63, 72, 82, 86, 106, 109, 126, 127, 131, 148, 157, 180) (1633–1986), Prairie anemone (157, 158) (1900–1929), Prairie crocus (106, 157, 158) (1900–1930), Prairie flower (6) (1892), Prairie-smoke [Prairie smoke] (74) (1893), Rock-lily [Rock lily, Rock lilies] (76) (1896) WI, Spreading anemone (138) (1923), Spreading pasqueflower (155) (1942), Wild crocus (76, 157, 158) (1896–1929), Wild pasqueflower [Wild pasque flower] (2) (1895), Windflower [Wind flower, Wind-flower, Wind-floures, Winde-floures] (76) (1896), Woolly-leaf anemone [Woolly-leaved anemone] (165) (1807)

Punctelia borreri (**Sm.**) **Krog** – Chan wiziye (Dakota) (37) (1830), Lichen (37) (1830)

Punica granatum **L.** – Carthaginian apple (92) (1876), Common pomegranate (138) (1923), Granatum (54, 57, 59, 60) (1902–1917), Grenadier (92) (1876), Pomegranate or Pomegranate tree (7, 19, 52, 57, 58, 59, 60, 92, 107, 109, 110, 178) (1526–1949), Pomgarnade (179) (1526), Punic-apple [Punic apple] (92) (1876), Wild pomegranate (92) (1876)

Punica **L.** – Pomegranate or Pomegranate tree (138) (1923), Sige (Albanian) (110) (1886)

Purshia **DC. ex Poir.** – Antelope-brush [Antelope brush] (138) (1923)

Purshia hispida [**Lehm.**] – See *Onosmodium virginianum* (L.) A. DC.

Purshia mexicana (**D. Don**) **Henrickson** – Cliff-rose [Cliff rose] (106) (1930), Quinine bush [Quinine-bush] (106) (1930)

Purshia stansburiana (**Torr.**) **Henrickson** – Alouseme (Mexican) (147) (1856), Cliff-rose [Cliff rose] (106) (1930), Quinine bush [Quinine-bush] (106) (1930)

Purshia tridentata (**Pursh**) **DC.** – Antelope-brush [Antelope brush] (106, 138) (1923–1930), Buckbrush [Buck brush, Buck-brush] (106) (1930) Northeast Oregon, Wormwood of the voyageurs (33) (1827)

Pycnanthemum albescens **Torr. & Gray ex Gray** – White mountain-mint [White mountain mint] (4) (1986), White-leaf mint [White leaf mint] (124) (1937), White-leaf mountain-mint [Whiteleaf mountain-mint, White-leaved mountain mint, White-leaved mountain-mint] (5, 50, 97) (1913–present)

Pycnanthemum clinopodioides **Torr. & Gray** – Basil mountain mint (5) (1913)

Pycnanthemum flexuosum (**Walt.**) **Britton, Sterns & Poggenb.** – Flax-leaf basil [Flax-leaved basil] (187) (1818), Flax-leaf brachystemum [Flax leaved brachystemum] (42) (1914), Hyssop mountain-mint [Hyssop mountain mint] (5) (1913), Mountain-mint [Mountain mint, Mountainmint] (82) (1930), Narrow-leaf mountain-mint [Narrowleaf mountainmint, Narrow-leaved mountain mint, Narrow-leaved mountain-mint] (72, 97, 106) (1907–1937), Virginia thyme [Virginian thyme] (19) (1840)

Pyrola maculata L.

Pycnanthemum incanum (**L.**) **Michx.** – Hoary basil (187) (1818), Horse-mint [Horsemint, Horse mint] (46) (1879), Mountain-mint [Mountain mint, Mountainmint] (10) (1818)

Pycnanthemum incanum (**L.**) **Michx. var.** *incanum* – Calamint [Calamynt] (5) (1913), Hoary mountain-mint [Hoary mountain mint] (5, 97) (1913–1937), Wild basil (5, 19) (1840–1913)

Pycnanthemum lanceolatum **Pursh** – See *Pycnanthemum virginianum* (L.) T. Dur. & B. D. Jackson ex B. L. Robins. & Fern.

Pycnanthemum **Michx.** – Basil (4) (1986), Horse-mint [Horsemint, Horse mint] (1, 93) (1932–1936), Mountain-basil [Mountain basil] (2, 4) (1895–1986), Mountain-mint [Mountain mint, Mountainmint] (1, 2, 7, 10, 50, 82, 93, 138, 155, 156, 158) (1818–present), Wild basil (7) (1828)

Pycnanthemum montanum **Michx.** – Mountain-mint [Mountain mint, Mountainmint] (57, 92) (1876–1917), Thin-leaf mountain-mint [Thin-leaved mountain mint] (5) (1913)

Pycnanthemum muticum (**Michx.**) **Pers.** – Calamint [Calamynt] (5) (1913), Short-tooth mountain-mint [Short-toothed mountain mint] (5) (1913), possibly Winter savory [Wintersaverie] (46) (1629)

Pycnanthemum pilosum **Nutt.** – See *Pycnanthemum verticillatum* (Michx.) Pers. var. *pilosum* (Nutt.) Cooperrider

Pycnanthemum pycnanthemoides (**Leavenworth**) **Fern. var.** *pycnanthemoides* – Calamint [Calamynt] (5) (1913), False mountain (19) (1840), Southern mountain mint (5) (1913)

Pycnanthemum setosum **Nutt.** – Awned mountain mint (5) (1913), Wild basil (5, 92) (1876–1913)

Pycnanthemum tenuifolium **Schrad.** – Narrow-leaf mountain-mint [Narrowleaf mountainmint, Narrow-leaved mountain mint, Narrow-leaved mountain-mint] (50) (present), Slender mountain-mint [Slender mountainmint] (138, 155) (1923–1942), Slender-leaf mountain mint [Slender-leaved mountain mint] (4) (1986), Virginia thyme [Virginian thyme] (156) (1913)

Pycnanthemum verticillatum (**Michx.**) **Pers.** – Whorled mountain-mint [Whorled mountainmint] (50) (present)

Pycnanthemum verticillatum (**Michx.**) **Pers. var.** *pilosum* (**Nutt.**) **Cooperrider** – Downy mint (82) (1930) IA, Hairy mountain-mint [Hairy mountain mint] (4, 5, 97) (1913–1986), Pycnanthemum (92) (1876), Whorled mountain-mint [Whorled mountainmint] (50) (present), Wild basil (49) (1898), Woods mountain-mint [Woods mountain mint] (3) (1977)

Pycnanthemum verticillatum (**Michx.**) **Pers. var.** *verticillatum* – Torrey's mountain-mint [Torrey's mountain mint] (5) (1913)

Pycnanthemum virginianum (**L.**) **T. Dur. & B. D. Jackson ex B. L. Robins. & Fern.** – Basil (5, 106) (1913–1930), Basil-pennyroyal [Basil pennyroyal] (156) (1923), Mountain-mint [Mountain mint, Mountainmint] (3, 40, 82, 85, 106, 156) (1923–1977), Mountain-thyme [Mountain thyme] (5, 156, 157) (1900–1929), Name'wûckons (Chippewa, little sturgeon plant) (40) (1928), Pennyroyal [Pennyroyal, Penny royal, Penniroyal] (5, 75) (1894–1913), Prairie hyssop (5, 92, 156, 157) (1876–1929), Virginia mountain-mint [Virginia mountain mint, Virginia mountainmint] (4, 5, 50, 72, 97, 121, 138, 155, 157) (1900–present), Virginia thyme [Virginian thyme] (5, 156, 157) (1913–1929), Waxpe čejaka (Lakota, leaf mint) (121) (1918?–1970?), Lance-leaf basil [Lance-leaved basil] (187) (1818), Narrow-leaf Virginia thyme [Narrow-leaf Virginian thyme, Narrow leaved Virginia thyme] (19, 92) (1840–1876), Winter savory [Wintersaverie] (46) (1629)

Pycnanthemum virginicum – possibly *Pycnanthemum virginianum* (L.) T. Dur. & B. D. Jackson ex B. L. Robins. & Fern.

Pycreus flavicomus (**Michx.**) **C. D. Adams** – See *Cyperus flavicomus* Michx.

Pyracantha angustifolia (**Franch.**) **Schneid.** – Narrow-leaf firethorn [Narrowleaf firethorn] (138) (1923)

Pyracantha coccinea **M. Roemer** – Christ's thorn [Christ-thorn] (5, 156) (1913–1923), Egyptian thorn (5) (1913), Evergreen thorn (5, 156) (1913–1923), Firethorn [Fire thorn] (5, 156) (1913–1923), Pyracanth (5) (1913), Scarlet firethorn (138) (1923)

Pyracantha crenulata (**D. Don**) **Roemer** – Nepal firethorn (138) (1923)

Pyracantha **M. Roemer** – Firethorn [Fire thorn] (138) (1923)

Pyrethrum carneum [**M. Bieb.**] – See *Tanacetum coccineum* (Willd.) Grierson

Pyrethrum coccineum (**Willd.**) **Vorosch.** – See *Tanacetum coccineum* (Willd.) Grierson

Pyrethrum **Medik.** – See *Tanacetum* L.

Pyrethrum parthenium **Smith** – See *Tanacetum parthenium* (L.) Schultz-Bip.

Pyrethrum **Sm.** – See *Chrysanthemum* L.

Pyrocoma (*sic*) **Hook.** – See *Pyrrocoma* Hook.

Pyrola (**Tourn.**) **L.** – See *Pyrola* L.

Pyrola americana **Sweet** – American pyrola (155) (1942), American wintergreen (50) (present), Canker-leaf [Canker leaf] (49) (1898), Canker-lettuce [Canker lettuce] (5, 53, 58, 92, 156) (1869–1923), Coffee leaf [Coffee-leaf] (156) (1923), Common wintergreen (43) (1820), Consumption-weed [Consumption weed] (5, 58, 92, 156, 158) (1869–1923), Copalm (156) (1923) no longer in use by 1923, Copperleaf [Copper-leaf, Copper leaf] (5, 158) (1900–1913), Dollarleaf [Dollar-leaf, Dollar leaf] (5, 92, 156, 158) (1876–1923), European pyrola (138, 155) (1923–1942), False wintergreen (5, 49, 53, 58, 61, 156, 158) (1869–1923), Holz mangolt (German) (46) (1879), Indian lettuce (5, 92, 156, 158) (1876–1923), Larger wintergreen (158) (1900), Lettuce-liverwort [Lettuce liverwort] (92) (1876), Liverwort lettuce (5, 156, 158) (1900–1923), Pear-leaf wintergreen [Pear leaf wintergreen, Pear leaved wintergreen, Pear-leaved wintergreen] (5, 19, 49, 92, 158) (1840–1913), Pirola (46) (1671), Pyrola (46, 178) (1596–1879), Pyrole (French) (158) (1900), Pyrole à feuilles rondes (French) (8) (1785), Rough-leaf wintergreen [Rough-leaved wintergreen] (156) (1923), Roundleaf (58) (1869), Round-leaf American wintergreen [Round-leaved American wintergreen] (5) (1913), Round-leaf pyrola [Roundleaf pyrola, Round leaved pyrola] (8, 92, 138) (1785–1923), Round-leaf wintergreen [Round-leaved wintergreen, Round-leaved winter-green] (4, 85, 131, 156, 158, 187) (1818–1986), Shin-leaf [Shin leaf, Shinleaf] (19, 49, 53, 92, 156) (1840–1923), Umbellated pyrola (5) (1913), Waldmangolt [Waltmangold] (German) (46, 158) (1879–1900), Wild lettuce [Wild-lettuce, Wylde letuse] (5, 7, 92, 156, 158) (1828–1923), Wild lily-of-the-valley [Wild lily of the valley] (3) (1977), Wintergreen [Winter greene, Winter-green] (46, 178) (1526–1879), Winter-grün (German) (46) (1879)

Pyrola aphylla **Sm.** – See *Pyrola picta* Sm.

Pyrola asarifolia **Michx.** – Alpine pyrola (155) (1942), Bog wintergreen (5, 85, 156) (1913–1932), Liver-leaf wintergreen [Liverleaf wintergreen, Liver-leafed wintergreen] (5, 50, 85, 156) (1913–present), Round-leaf wintergreen [Round-leaved wintergreen, Round-leaved winter-green] (3, 4) (1977–1986)

Pyrola chlorantha **Sw.** – False wintergreen (156) (1923), Green pyrola (155) (1942), Green-flower wintergreen [Greenflowered wintergreen, Green flowered wintergreen, Green-flowered wintergreen] (50, 95, 157) (1911–present), Greenish-flower wintergreen [Greenish-flowered wintergreen] (5, 131) (1899–1913), Sharp-petal wintergreen [Sharp-petaled wintergreen] (5) (1913), Shin-leaf [Shin leaf, Shinleaf] (5, 158) (1900–1913)

Pyrola dentata **Sm.** – See *Pyrola picta* Sm.

Pyrola elliptica **Nutt.** – Lesser wintergreen (156) (1923), Ninbegoskok (Chippewa) (105) (1932), Roundleaf (7) (1828), Shin-leaf [Shin leaf, Shinleaf] (2, 5, 63, 72, 85, 86, 95, 105, 131, 138, 156, 157, 158) (1878–1932) leaves used as "shin-plasters" for wounds of the shin and elsewhere, Wax-flower pyrola [Waxflower pyrola] (155) (1942), Wax-flower shinleaf [Waxflower shinleaf] (50) (present), White wintergreen [White winter-green] (19) (1840), Wild lily-of-the-valley [Wild lily of the valley] (3, 4, 5, 75, 157, 158) (1894–1986), Wintergreen [Winter greene, Winter-green] (86) (1878), Wood-lily [Wood lily] (156) (1923), Yaskobgedek (Chippewa) (105) (1932)

Pyrola **L.** – Pyrola (138, 155) (1923–1942), Pyrole (French) (8) (1785),

Shin-leaf [Shin leaf, Shinleaf] (2, 109, 156, 158) (1895–1949), Wintergreen [Winter greene, Winter-green] (1, 2, 4, 8, 10, 50, 93, 127, 158, 167, 184) (1793–present)

Pyrola maculata **L.** – See *Chimaphila maculata* (L.) Pursh

Pyrola minor **L.** – Lesser wintergreen (5) (1913), Shin-leaf [Shin leaf, Shinleaf] (5) (1913), Wood lily (5) (1913)

Pyrola oxypetala **Austin ex Gray** – See *Pyrola chlorantha* Sw.

Pyrola picta **Sm.** – Leafless pyrola (155) (1942), Tooth-leaf pyrola [Toothleaf pyrola] (155) (1942), White-vein wintergreen [Whiteveined wintergreen] (50) (present)

Pyrola rotundifolia **L.** – See *Pyrola americana* Sweet

Pyrola rotundifolia **L. var. *americana* (Sweet) Fern.** – See *Pyrola americana* Sweet

Pyrola secunda **L.** – See *Orthilia secunda* (L.) House

Pyrola uliginosa **Torr.** – See *Pyrola asarifolia* Michx.

Pyrola virens **Schweigg** – See *Pyrola chlorantha* Sw.

Pyrostegia venusta **(Ker-Gawl.) Miers** – Flaming trumpet (138) (1923)

Pyrrhopappus carolinianus **(Walt.) DC.** – Carolina desert-chicory (50) (present), Leafy-stem false dandelion (3, 157) (1929–1977), Leafy-stem false dandelion [Leafy-stemmed false dandelion] (5, 97) (1913–1937)

Pyrrhopappus **DC.** – Desert-chicory (50) (present), False dandelion (1, 2, 158) (1900–1986), Rough false dandelion (5, 97) (1913–1937)

Pyrrhopappus grandiflorus **(Nutt.) Nutt.** – Tuber false dandelion (3, 4) (1977–1986), Tuberous desert-chicory (50) (present)

Pyrrhopappus multicaulis **DC. var. *geiseri* (Shinners) Northington** – See *Pyrrhopappus pauciflorus* (D. Don) DC.

Pyrrhopappus pauciflorus **(D. Don) DC.** – Small-flower desert-chicory [Smallflower desert-chicory] (50) (present)

Pyrrhopappus rothrockii **Gray** – See *Pyrrhopappus pauciflorus* (D. Don) DC.

Pyrrocoma **Hook.** – Pyrocoma (158) (1900)

Pyrrocoma integrifolia **(Porter ex A. Gray) Greene** – Canby's aster [Canby aster] (155) (1942), Rush goldenweed (155) (1942), Whole-leaf goldenweed [Wholeleaf goldenweed] (155) (1942)

Pyrrocoma lanceolata **(Hook.) Greene var. *lanceolata*** – Lance-leaf goldenweed [Lanceleaf goldenweed] (50, 155) (1942–present)

Pyrrocoma uniflora **(Hook.) Greene var. *uniflora*** – Damiana goldenweed (155) (1942), Plantain goldenweed (155) (1942)

Pyrularia oleifera **(Muhl. ex Willd.) A. Gray** – American oil nut (19) (1840), Oil nut [Oilnut, Oil-nut] (2, 5, 7, 10, 107, 156) (1818–1919)

Pyrularia pubera **Michx.** – Buffalo nut [Buffalo-nut] (2, 5, 107, 156) (1895–1923), Elknut [Elk nut, Elk-nut] (5, 156) (1913–1923), Indian olive (182) (1791), Physic nut [Physic nuts, Physick Nut, Physicnut] (182) (1791), Rabbit-wood (156) (1923), Thunderwood [Thunder-wood] (156) (1923)

Pyrus **(Tourn.) L.** – See *Pyrus* L.

Pyrus americana **(Marsh.) DC.** – See *Sorbus americana* Marsh.

Pyrus arbutifolia **L.** – See *Photinia pyrifolia* (Lam.) Robertson & Phipps

Pyrus arbutifolia **L. f.** – See *Photinia pyrifolia* (Lam.) Robertson & Phipps

Pyrus arbutifolia **var. *melanocarpa* Hook.** – See *Photinia melanocarpa* (Michx.) Robertson & Phipps

Pyrus aucuparia **(L.) Ehrh.** – See *Sorbus aucuparia* L.

Pyrus aucuparia **Ehrh.** – See *Sorbus aucuparia* L.

Pyrus auricularis **Knoop** – See *Sorbopyrus auricularis* (Knoop) C. K. Schneid.

Pyrus baccata **L.** – See *Malus baccata* (L.) Borck.

Pyrus calleryana **Dcne.** – Callery pear (138) (1923)

Pyrus canadensis **(L.) Farw.** – Juneberry [June-berry, June berry] (187) (1818), Shad bush [Shadbush, Shad-bush] (92) (1876), Snowy medlar (187) (1818), Wild pear [Wylde pere] or Wild pear tree [Wild pear-tree] (187) (1818)

Pyrus caronaria – See *Malus coronaria* (L.) Mill. var. *coronaria*

Pyrus communis **L.** – Apios (Greek) (110) (1886), Birn (German) (110) (1886), Chokepear [Choke-pear, Choke pear] (5) (1913), Common pear (82, 137, 138) (1923–1930), Gruscha (Russian) (110) (1886), Hrusska (Bohemian) (110) (1886), Madaria (Basque) (110) (1886), Pauta (Armenian and Georgian) (110) (1886), Pear (1, 5, 19, 82, 92, 107, 109, 110) (1840–1949), Udarea (Basque) (110) (1886), Vatzkor (Hungarian) (110) (1886), Wild pear [Wylde pere] or Wild pear tree [Wild pear-tree] (92) (1876)

Pyrus coronaria **L.** – See *Malus coronaria* (L.) Mill. var. *coronaria*

Pyrus cydonia **L.** – See *Cydonia oblonga* Mill.

Pyrus fusca **Raf.** – See *Malus fusca* (Raf.) Schneid.

Pyrus intermedia **Ehrh** – See *Sorbus intermedia* (Ehrh.) Pers.

Pyrus ioensis **(Wood) Bailey** – See *Malus ioensis* (Wood) Britton var. *ioensis*

Pyrus ioensis **(Wood) Bailey var. *texana* (Rehder) Bailey** – See *Malus ioensis* (Wood) Britton var. *texana* Rehd.

Pyrus ioensis **Bailey** – See *Malus ioensis* (Wood) Britton var. *ioensis*

Pyrus japonica **Thunb.** – See *Chaenomeles japonica* (Thunb.) Lindl. ex Spach

Pyrus **L.** – Apple (10, 82, 256) (1818–1930), Crab apple [Crab-apple, Crabapple] (4) (1986), Crab tree [Crab-tree] (167) (1814), Pear (10, 82, 106, 109, 156, 158, 184) (1793–1949), Poirier (French) (8) (1785), Tame pere (179) (1526), Wild pear [Wylde pere] or Wild pear tree [Wild pear-tree] (179) (1526)

Pyrus melanocarpa **(Michx.) Willd.** – See *Photinia melanocarpa* (Michx.) Robertson & Phipps

Pyrus prunifolia **Willd.** – See *Malus prunifolia* (Willd.) Borkh.

Pyrus pyrifolia **(Burm. f.) Nakai** – Late pear (137, 138) (1923–1931)

Pyrus serotina **Rehd.** – See *Pyrus pyrifolia* (Burm. f.) Nakai

Pyrus torminalis **Ehrh.** – See *Torminaria torminalis* (L.) Dippel

Pyrus-malus cydonia – See *Cydonia oblonga* Mill.

Pyrus-malus fusea **Raf.** – See *Malus fusca* (Raf.) Schneid.

Pyrus-malus **L.** – possibly *Malus sylvestris* (L.) Mill.

Pyxidanthera barbulata **Michx.** – Flowering-moss [Flowering moss] (2, 5, 156) (1895–1923), Pine Barrens beauty [Pine-barren beauty, Pine-barrens beauty] (5, 156) (1913–1923), Pixy (2) (1895), Pyxie (5, 156) (1913–1923), Pyxie moss (73) (1892) NJ

Q

Quamasia hyacinthina (Raf.) Britton – See *Camassia scilloides* (Raf.) Cory

Quamoclit coccinea hederifolia – See *Ipomoea hederifolia* L.

Quamoclit Moench – See *Ipomoea* L.

Quamoclit pennata Bojer – See *Ipomoea quamoclit* L.

Quamoclit pinnata – See *Ipomoea quamoclit* L.

Quamoclit quamoclit (L.) Britton – See *Ipomoea quamoclit* L.

Quercus (Tourn.) L. – See *Quercus* L.

Quercus ×benderi Baenitz [*coccinea* × *rubra*] – Black oak [Blacke oak, Black-Oak, Black Oake] (5, 156) (1913–1923), Ink-ball oak (19) (1840), Red oak [Red-oak, Red oake] (5, 156) (1913–1923), Scarlet oak [Scarlet oake] (1, 2, 5, 12, 20, 19, 33, 58, 72, 82, 93, 95, 97, 109, 113, 135, 138, 156) (1820–1949), Spanish oak [Spanish Oake] (5, 156) (1913–1923)

Quercus ×heterophylla Michx. f. [*phellos* × *rubra*] – Bartram's oak [Bartram oak] (10, 20, 33, 97, 187) (1818–1937), Burrier's oak (19, 187) (1818–1840), Variable oak (138) (1923)

Quercus ×leana Nutt. [*imbricaria* × *velutina*] – Chêne de Lea (French) (20) (1857), Lea's oak (20) (1857)

Quercus ×pauciloba Rydb. [*gambelii* × *turbinella*] – Chêne ondule (French) (20) (1857), Fendler's oak [Fendler oak] (155) (1942), Plains shinnery (122) (1937) TX, Rocky Mountain oak (20) (1857), Rocky Mountain scrub oak (107) (1919), Wavy-leaf oak [Wavyleaf oak] (4, 155) (1942–1986)

Quercus acuminata (Michx.) Houba – See *Quercus muehlenbergii* Engelm.

Quercus acuminata (Michx.) Sarg. – See *Quercus muehlenbergii* Engelm.

Quercus agrifolia Née – California field oak (107) (1919), California live oak [Californian live oak] (138) (1923), Chêne à feuilles houx (French) (20) (1857), Encino (Spanish) (75) (1894) CA, Evergreen oak (75, 161) (1857–1894) CA, Field oak (106) (1930), Holly-leaf oak [Holly-leaved oak] (20) (1857), Scrub oak (75) (1894) CA

Quercus alba L. – Chêne blanc (French) (8) (1785), Common American white oak (8) (1785), Mangummenauk (Narraganset) (46) (1879), Mountain white oak (17) (1796), Stave oak (5, 156) (1913–1923), Stone oak (157, 158) (1900–1929), Tanner's oak (157) (1929), White oak [White-oak, White oake] or White oak tree (1, 3, 4, 5, 8, 9, 10, 17, 18, 20, 19, 33, 41, 46, 50, 52, 57, 58, 65, 72, 82, 92, 93, 95, 97, 107, 109, 112, 113, 122, 124, 130, 135, 138, 155, 156, 157, 158, 177, 181, 187, 190) (~1678–present), White oak bark (157) (1929)

Quercus alba minor – See *Quercus stellata* Wangenh.

Quercus alba palustris – See *Quercus bicolor* Willd

Quercus alba var. *minor* Marshall – See *Quercus stellata* Wangenh.

Quercus alba var. *palustris* J. B. Marshall – See *Quercus bicolor* Willd

Quercus aquatica (Lam.) Walter – See *Quercus nigra* L.

Quercus arizonica Sargent – Live oak [Live oake, Live-oak] (149, 153) (1904–1919)

Quercus arkansana Sargent – Arkansas oak (138) (1923)

Quercus banisteri [Michx.] – See *Quercus ilicifolia* Wangenh.

Quercus bicolor Willd – Chêne blanc de marais (French) (8) (1785), Minšminš (Chippewa) (105) (1932), Swamp oak (5, 105, 156) (1913–1932), Swamp white oak [Swamp white oake, Swamp white oke] (4, 5, 8, 20, 19, 33, 46, 50, 72, 93, 97, 109, 138, 155, 156) (1785–present), White swamp oak (1, 2) (1895–1932)

Quercus borealis maxima – See *Quercus rubra* L. var. *rubra*

Quercus borealis Michx.f. – See *Quercus rubra* L. var. *ambigua* (Gray) Fern.

Quercus borealis Michx. f. var. *maxima* (Marsh) Ashe – See *Quercus rubra* L. var. *rubra*

Quercus brayi Small – See *Quercus muehlenbergii* Engelm.

Quercus castanea – possibly *Quercus muehlenbergii* Engelm.

Quercus catesbaei Michx. – See *Quercus laevis* Walt.

Quercus cerris L. – Austrian turkey oak (138) (1923), Bitter oak (92) (1876), European turkey oak (138) (1923), Turkish oak (107) (1919)

Quercus chrysolepis Liebm. – California live oak [Californian live oak] (75) (1894) CA, Fulvous oak (161) (1857)

Quercus coccinea Muenchh. (possibly) – Scarlet oak [Scarlet oake] (187) (1818)

Quercus coccinea Wang. – See *Quercus ×benderi* Baenitz [*coccinea* × *rubra*]

Quercus coccinea Willd. And Pursh – possibly *Quercus coccinea* Muenchh.

Quercus confertiflora [Torr.] – possibly *Quercus hypoleucoides* A. Camus (current species depends on author)

Quercus discolor Ait. – See *Quercus velutina* Lam.

Quercus douglasii Hook. & Arn. – Blue oak (138) (1923), Chêne de Douglas (French) (20) (1857), Douglas' oak [Douglas's oak] (20) (1857), Mountain white oak (106) (1930)

Quercus drummondii Liebm. – See *Quercus margarettiae* (Ashe) Small

Quercus dumosa Nutt. – Small-leaf oak [Small-leaved oak] (20) (1857)

Quercus durandii Buckl. – See *Quercus sinuata* Walt. var. *sinuata*

Quercus ellipsoidalis E. J. Hill – Black oak [Blacke oak, Black-Oak, Black Oake] (82, 156) (1923–1930), Hill's oak (4, 5, 72, 156) (1907–1986), Northern pin oak (4, 50, 82, 138, 155) (1923–present), Yellow oak (82, 156) (1923–1930)

Quercus elongata Muhl. – See *Quercus falcata* Michx.

Quercus emoryi Torr. – Black oak [Blacke oak, Black-Oak, Black Oake] (149, 153) (1904–1919) NM, Emory's black oak (122) (1937) TX

Quercus falcata Michx. – Chêne noir à feuilles digitées (French) (8) (1785), Chêne rouge de montagne (French) (8) (1785), Downy black oak (19, 33) (1827–1840), Downy red oak [Downy-red oak] (187) (1818), Finger-leaf black oak [Finger-leaved black oak] (8) (1785), Red oak [Red-oak, Red oake] (5, 33, 156) (1827–1923), Southern red oak (138) (1923), Spanish oak [Spanish Oake] (2, 5, 10, 12, 20, 19, 33, 82, 93, 97, 109, 156, 164, 181, 187) (~1678–1949), Turkey oak (5, 156) (1913–1923), Upland red oak (8) (1785), Water oak (5, 93, 97, 156) (1913–1937)

Quercus fendleri Liebm. – See *Quercus ×pauciloba* Rydb. [*gambelii* × *turbinella*]

Quercus ferruginea [Michx. f.] – See *Quercus marilandica* Muench

Quercus fusiformis Small – Live oak [Live oake, Live-oak] (4) (1986), Plateau oak (50) (present)

Quercus gambelii Nutt. – Gambel's oak [Gambel oak] (4, 50, 155) (1942–present)

Quercus gambelii Nutt. var. *gambelii* – New Mexico shinnery [New Mexican shinnery] (122) (1937) TX, White oak [White-oak, White oake] or White oak tree (153) (1913) NM

Quercus garryana Dougl. ex Hook. – Chêne occidental (French) (20) (1857), Oregon oak (138) (1923), Western oak (20, 107) (1857–1919), White oak [White-oak, White oake] or White oak tree (35, 160) (1806–1860)

Quercus geminata Small – Dwarf willow-leaf oak [Dwarf Willow leaved Oak] (183) (~1756)

Quercus georgiana M. A. Curtis – Georgia oak (138) (1923)

Quercus gravesii Sudworth – Chisos red oak (122) (1937) TX

Quercus grisea Liebm. – Live oak [Live oake, Live-oak] (153) (1913) NM

Quercus grisea Liebm. – Mountain white oak (122) (1937) TX

44, 46, 92, 97) (1827–1937), Black oak [Blacke oak, Black-Oak, Black Oake] (8, 9, 18, 41, 113, 177, 181) (~1678–1910), Chêne noir (French) (8) (1785), Common Pennsylvania black oak [Common Pennsylvanian black oak] (8) (1785), Duck oak (5) (1913), Highland willow oak (189) (1767), Jack oak (106) (1930), Possum oak (5) (1913), Punk oak (5) (1913), Scroby's oak [Scroby oak] (18) (1805), Spotted oak (5) (1913), Swamp oak (12, 41) (1770–1821), Water oak (2, 5, 19, 20, 33, 65, 72, 97, 106, 109, 122, 124, 138, 156, 181, 187, 189) (~1678–1937)

Quercus nigra pumila **Marshall** – See *Quercus ilicifolia* Wangenh.

Quercus nigra **var.** *digitata* **Marshall** – See *Quercus falcata* Michx.

Quercus oblongifolia **Torr.** – Evergreen oak (107) (1919), Evergreen white oak (75) (1894), Live oak [Live oake, Live-oak] (75, 107, 149, 153) (1894–1919)

Quercus obtusiloba **Michx.** – See *Quercus stellata* Wangenh.

Quercus olivaeformis **Michx.** – See *Quercus macrocarpa* Michx. var. *macrocarpa*

Quercus oliviformis **Michx.** – See *Quercus macrocarpa* Michx. var. *macrocarpa*

Quercus pagoda **Raf.** – Elliot's oak (5) (1913)

Quercus pagodaefolia **(Ell.) Ashe** – See *Quercus pagoda* Raf.

Quercus pagodifolia **(Ell.) Ashe** – See *Quercus pagoda* Raf.

Quercus palustris **Muench.** – Pin oak (1, 3, 4, 5, 20, 19, 33, 50, 82, 109, 112, 135, 138, 155, 156, 187) (1827–present), Spanish oak [Spanish Oake] (82, 106) (1930), Swamp oak (1, 5, 12, 93, 97, 156) (1913–1937), Swamp Spanish oak (2, 5, 10, 33, 156) (1818–1923)

Quercus pedunculata **Ehrl.** – See *Quercus robur* L.

Quercus phellos **L.** – Laurel oak (156) (1923), Peach oak (5) (1913), Sand jack oak (5) (1913), Swamp oak (41) (1770), Willow oak [Willow oake] (2, 5, 10, 12, 14, 20, 19, 33, 65, 97, 107, 109, 138, 156, 177, 187) (1762–1949), Willow-leaf oak [Willow-leaved oak] (8, 34, 82, 122, 124) (1785–1937)

Quercus phellos latifolia – See *Quercus incana* Bartr.

Quercus phellos sempervirens – See *Quercus virginiana* Mill.

Quercus phellos **var.** *latifolia* **Marshall** – See *Quercus incana* Bartr.

Quercus phellos **var.** *sempervirens* **Marshall** – See *Quercus virginiana* Mill.

Quercus platanoides **(Lam.) Sudw.** – See *Quercus bicolor* Willd

Quercus prinoides **Willd.** – Chêne nain à feuilles chataignier (French) (8) (1785), Chinkapin [Chincapin] (5) (1913), Chinkapin oak (158) (1900), Chinquapin [Chinquepin] (10, 19) (1818–1840), Chinquapin oak [Chinquepin oak] (1, 2, 8, 18, 33, 156, 187) (1785–1932), Dwarf chestnut oak (2, 5, 8, 10, 33, 93, 97, 156, 187) (1785–1937), Dwarf chinkapin oak (4, 50, 155) (1942–present), Dwarf chinquapin oak (3, 138) (1923–1977), Dwarf oak [Dwarfe Oak] (29) (1869), Low yellow oak (113) (1890), Running white oak (5, 156) (1913–1923), Scrub chestnut oak (1, 5, 72, 93, 95, 97, 158) (1900–1937), Scrub oak (156) (1923), Small chestnut oak (20, 33, 122) (1827–1937)

Quercus prinos pumila – See *Quercus prinoides* Willd.

Quercus prinos **W.** – possibly *Quercus prinus* L.

Quercus prinus acuminata – See *Quercus muehlenbergii* Engelm.

Quercus prinus chinquapin – See *Quercus prinoides* Willd.

Quercus prinus discolor – See *Quercus bicolor* Willd

Quercus prinus humilis – See *Quercus prinoides* Willd.

Quercus prinus **L.** – Basket oak (109) (1949), Chêne à feuilles chataignier (French) (8) (1785), Chestnut oak [Chestnut-Oak, Chestnut Oake] (2, 19, 41, 107, 122, 138, 156, 177, 181, 189) (~1678–1937), Chestnut white oak (10, 33, 187) (1818–1826), Chestnut-leaf oak [Chestnut-leaved oak] (8) (1785), Graybark [Grey bark] possibly (46) (1649), Mountain oak (5, 19, 156) (1840–1923), Rock chestnut oak (5, 10, 20, 33, 97, 156, 187) (1818–1937), Rock oak (5, 19, 156) (1840–1923), Tan-bark oak [Tan bark oak, Tanbark oak] (5, 156) (1913–1923), White chestnut oak (5, 92, 156) (1876–1923), White oak [White-oak, White oake] or White oak tree (33) (1827), possibly Swamp chestnut oak (5, 19, 33, 156) (1827–1923), possibly Swamp oak (14, 19, 92) (1840–1882)

Quercus prinus **var.** *chincapin* **F. Michx.** – See *Quercus prinoides* Willd.

Quercus prinus **var.** *discolor* **F. Michx.** – See *Quercus bicolor* Willd

Quercus pumila **Walt.** – Running oak (33) (1827)

Quercus robur **L.** – Black oak [Blacke oak, Black-Oak, Black Oake] (107) (1919), British oak (55) (1911), Common European oak (20) (1857), English oak (93, 138) (1923–1936), European white oak (20) (1857), Oaken tree [Oken tree] (179) (1526), Truffle oak (107) (1919), possibly Spanish oak [Spanish Oake] (41) (1770)

Quercus robur pedunculata – See *Quercus robur* L.

Quercus robur **var.** *pedunculata* **Hook. f.** – See *Quercus robur* L.

Quercus rubra ambigua – See *Quercus rubra* L.

Quercus rubra **L.** – Black oak [Blacke oak, Black-Oak, Black Oake] (156, 158) (1900–1923), Butter oak (46) (1649), Buude-hi (37) (1919), Champion (156) (1923), Champion oak (14, 158) (1882), Chêne rouge à grande espèce (French) (8) (1785), Chêne rouge aquatique (French) (6) (1892), Common red oak (138) (1923), Gray oak [Grey oak] (156) (1923), Largest red oak (8) (1785), Nahatapahat (Pawnee, red tree) (37) (1919), Northern red oak (50) (present), Red oak [Red-oak, Red oake] (2, 5, 8, 10, 12, 14, 18, 20, 19, 33, 37, 40, 41, 46, 58, 61, 65, 72, 78, 82, 92, 93, 95, 97, 106, 112, 113, 122, 124, 135, 156, 158, 177, 181, 187) (1629–1937), Scarlet oak [Scarlet oake] (181) (~1678), Spanish oak [Spanish Oake] (78, 156, 158) (1898–1923) Southwest MO, Uta (Dakota) (37) (1919) Uta-hu (Oak tree), Water red oak (8) (1785), White oak with pointed notches (189) (1767), Willow oak [Willow oake] (189) (1767), Wi'sugi'mītīgo'mĭc (Chippewa, bitter oak) (40) (1928)

Quercus rubra **L. var.** *ambigua* **(Gray) Fern.** – Gray oak [Grey oak] (5, 19, 20, 33) (1827–1913), Northern red oak (138, 155) (1923–1942), Red oak [Red-oak, Red oake] (4, 109) (1949–1986)

Quercus rubra **L. var.** *rubra* – Eastern red oak (155) (1942), Northern red oak (50, 93) (1936–present), Red oak [Red-oak, Red oake] (3) (1977)

Quercus rubra nana – See *Quercus ilicifolia* Wangenh.

Quercus rubra ramosissima – See *Quercus rubra* L.

Quercus rubra **var.** *maxima* **Marshall** – See *Quercus rubra* L.

Quercus rubra **var.** *montana* **Marshall** – See *Quercus falcata* Michx.

Quercus rubra **var.** *nana* **Marshall** – See *Quercus ilicifolia* Wangenh.

Quercus shumardii **Buckl.** – Shumard's oak [Shumard oak] (50, 155) (1942–present), Shumard's red oak (3, 122, 124) (1937–1977)

Quercus shumardii **Buckl. var.** *schneckii* **(Britt.) Sargent** – Schneck's oak [Schneck oak] (5, 50, 72, 97) (1907–present)

Quercus sinuata – See *Quercus pumila* Walt.

Quercus sinuata **Walt.** – Scarlet oak [Scarlet oake] (182) (1791)

Quercus sinuata **Walt. var.** *breviloba* **(Torr.) C. H. Muller** – White oak shinnery (122, 124) (1937) TX

Quercus sinuata **Walt. var.** *sinuata* – Durand's white oak (122, 124) (1937)

Quercus stellata **Wangenh.** – Arkansas post oak (155) (1942), Barren white oak (8, 187) (1785–1818), Box white oak (2, 5, 156) (1895–1923), Brash oak (5, 156) (1913–1923), Brown-wood post oak [Brownwood post oak] (155) (1942), Chêne blanc de moyenne grandeur (French) (8) (1785), Iron oak (2, 5, 19, 72, 156, 187) (1818–1925), Post oak (1, 3, 4, 5, 18, 19, 20, 27, 33, 50, 65, 72, 82, 97, 109, 113, 124, 138, 155, 156, 164) (1804–present), Rough oak (2, 156) (1895–1923), Rough white oak (5, 156) (1913–1923), Turkey oak (5, 156) (1913–1923), Upland white oak (10, 33, 187) (1818–1826), White oak [White-oak, White oake] or White oak tree (5) (1913), White rough bark (46) (1649)

Quercus stellata **Wangenh. var.** *attenuata* **Sargent** – See *Quercus stellata* Wangenh.

Quercus stellata **Wangenh. var.** *parviloba* **Sargent** – See *Quercus stellata* Wangenh.

Quercus suber **L.** – Cork oak (20, 107, 138) (1857–1932), Cork or Cork tree [Cork-tree, Corktree] (92) (1876), Cork wood [Cork-wood, Corkwood] (92) (1876), Savanna bark (92) (1876)

Quercus texana **Buckl.** – Red oak [Red-oak, Red oake] (156) (1923), Spanish oak [Spanish Oake] (124) (1937) TX

351

Quercus tinctoria **Bart.** – See *Quercus velutina* Lam.

Quercus undulata **Torr.** – See *Quercus ×pauciloba* Rydb. [*gambelii × turbinella*]

Quercus utahensis – See *Quercus gambelii* Nutt. var. *gambelii*

Quercus velutina **Lam.** – Black bark (46) (1649), Black oak [Blacke oak, Black-Oak, Black Oake] (1, 2, 3, 4, 5, 14, 18, 19, 20, 33, 46, 50, 65, 78, 82, 92, 93, 95, 97, 109, 124, 138, 155, 156, 157, 158, 182, 187) (1629–present), Dyer's oak (5, 14, 92, 156, 157, 158, 187) (1818–1929), False red oak (19) (1840), Female oak (157, 158) (1900–1929), Gigantic black oak (182) (1791), Great black oak (182) (1791), Missouri black oak (155) (1942), Querceton (1) (1932), Querciton oak (46) (1879), Quercitron (2, 5, 58, 82, 92, 156, 157) (1869–1930), Quercitron oak (19, 158) (1840–1900), Scarlet oak (157) (1929), Spotted oak (5, 156, 157, 158) (1900–1929), Yellow oak (72) (1907), Yellow-bark oak [Yellow bark oak, Yellow-barked oak] (2, 5, 58, 82, 156, 157, 158) (1869–1930)

Quercus velutina **Lam. var.** *missouriensis* **Sargent** – See *Quercus velutina* Lam.

Quercus virens **Aiton** – See *Quercus virginiana* Mill.

Quercus virginiana **Mill.** – Chêne faule toujours vert (French) (8) (1785), Evergreen willow-leaf oak [Evergreen willow-leaved oak] (8) (1785), Live oak [Live oake, Live-oak] (2, 3, 5, 10, 14, 19, 20, 33, 92, 97, 106, 107, 124, 138, 156, 181, 182) (~1678–1977), Willow oak [Willow oake] (181) (~1678)

Quercus wislizeni **A. DC. var.** *frutescens* **Engelm.** – Desert oak (75) (1894) Southern CA

Quinaria **Raf.** – See *Parthenocissus* Planch.

Quincula lobata **(Torr.) Raf.** – Chinese lantern [Chineselantern] (3, 50) (1977–present), Plains chinese-lantern [Plains chineselantern] (155) (1942), Prostrate purple physalis (124) (1937), Purple ground-cherry [Purple ground cherry] (4) (1986), Purple-flower ground-cherry [Purple-flowered ground-cherry, Purple-flowered ground cherry (5, 97) (1913–1937)

Quincula **Raf.** – Chinese lantern [Chineselantern] (155) (1942), Quincula (50, 158) (1900–present)

Quisqualis indica **L.** – Rangoon-creeper (109, 138) (1923–1949)

Quercus virginiana Mill. [as *Quercus sempervirens*] with pileated woodpecker
(M. Catesby, 1754)

352

R

Racodium papyraceum **Pers.** – Paper sponk (92) (1876)

Radicula **Hill** – See *Rorippa* Scop.

Radicula hispida **(Desvar.) Britton** – See *Rorippa palustris* (L.) Bess. subsp. *hispida* (Desv.) Jonsell

Radicula nasturtium-aquaticum – See *Rorippa nasturtium-aquaticum* (L.) Hayek

Radicula obtusa **(Nutt.) Greene** – See *Rorippa teres* (Michx.) R. Stuckey

Radicula sessiflora **(Nutt.) Greene** – See *Rorippa sessiliflora* (Nutt.) A. S. Hitchc.

Radicula sinuata **(Nutt.) Greene** – See *Rorippa sinuata* (Nutt.) A. S. Hitchc.

Radicula sylvestris **(L.) Druce** – See *Rorippa palustris* (L.) Bess.

Radicula walteri **(Ell.) Greene** – See *Rorippa teres* (Michx.) R. Stuckey

Radiola linoides **Roth** – All-seed [All seed] (156) (1923)

Raimannia humifusa **(Nutt.) Rose** – See *Oenothera humifusa* Nutt.

Raimannia laciniata **(Hill) Rose** – See *Oenothera laciniata* Hill

Raimannia rhombipetala **(Nutt.) Rose** – See *Oenothera rhombipetala* Nutt. ex Torr. & Gray

Rajania cordata **L.** – Cockscomb-yam (138) (1923)

Rajania pleioneura **Griseb.** – See *Rajania cordata* L.

Ramalina leptocarpha **Tuck.** – Lace lichen (123) (1856)

Randia aculeata **L.** – Indigoberry [Indigo berry] (92) (1876)

Randia clusiifolia **(Jacq.) Chapman** – See *Casasia clusiifolia* (Jacq.) Urban

Randia latifolia – See *Randia aculeata* L.

Ranunculus **(Tourn) L.** – See *Ranunculus* L.

Ranunculus abortivus **L.** – Abortive-flower crowfoot [Abortive-flowered crow-foot] (187) (1818), Chicken-pepper [Chicken pepper] (156, 158) (1900–1923), Common buttercup (85) (1932), Crowfoot [Crow-foot, Crow foot, Crowfote, Crow's foot] (80) (1913) IA, Early wood buttercup (3, 4) (1977–1986), Kidney-leaf buttercup [Kidney-leaved buttercup] (126) (1933), Kidney-leaf crowfoot [Kidney-leaved crowfoot] (5, 62, 97, 127, 131, 156, 158) (1899–1937), Little-leaf buttercup [Littleleaf buttercup] (50, 155) (1942–present), Small buttercup (125) (1930), Small-flower crowfoot [Small-flowered crowfoot] (62, 63, 80, 156) (1899–1923), Smooth-leaf crowfoot [Smooth-leaved crowfoot] (5, 93) (1913–1936)

Ranunculus acris **L.** – Acrid buttercups (6) (1892), Acrid crowfoot (7) (1828), Bachelor's-button [Bachelor's button, Bachelor's buttons, Batchelor's buttons] (5, 76, 92) (1876–1913) Bethlehem PA, Biting crowfoot (156) (1923), Blister plant (5) (1913), Blister-flower [Blister flower] (156, 157, 158) (1900–1929), Blisterweed, Blisterweed (6, 7, 92, 157, 158) (1828–1929), Blisterwort [Blister wort, Blister-wort] (156) (1923), Burwort [Burr wort, Bur-wort] (6, 7, 92) (1828–1932), Buttercress [Butter cress, Butter-cress, Butter cresses] (5, 156, 157, 158) (1900–1929), Buttercup [Butter cup, Buttercups] (7, 19, 157, 158) (1828–1929), Butter-daisy [Butter daisy] (156, 157, 158) (1900–1929), Butter-flower [Butter flower] (156) (1923), Butter-rose [Butter rose] (5, 156) (1913–1923), Common buttercup (156) (1923), Crazy (157, 158) (1900–1929), Crowfoot [Crowfoot, Crow foot, Crowfote, Crow's foot] (19, 46) (1649–1840), Cuckoo-buds [Cuckoo buds] (157, 158) (1900–1929), Double yellow crowfoot [Double yellow crowfoote] (178) (1526), Field buttercup (157, 158) (1900–1929), Globe-amaranth [Globe amaranth] (92) (1876), Goldballs [Gold balls, Gold-balls] (156) (1923) no longer in use by 1923, Goldcup [Gold cup, Gold cups, Goldcups] (92) (1876), Goldenknops [Golden-knops] (157, 158) (1900–1929), Goldicup [Goldicups] (92, 157, 158) (1876–1929), Goldknops [Goldknops, Gold knops] (5, 157, 158) (1900–1929), Goldweed [Gold weed, Gold-weed] (156) (1923), Guilty-cup [Guilty cup] (157, 158) (1900–1929), Horse-gold [Horse gold] (5, 156, 157, 158) (1900–1929), Kingcup [King cup, King cups, Kingcups, King's cup, Kings' cup] (76, 157, 158) (1896–1929) ME, Mary-buds [Mary bud] (157, 158) (1900–1929) Shakespeare, Meadow buttercup [Meadow buttercups] (5, 157, 158) (1900–1929), Meadow-bloom [Meadow bloom, Meadowbloom] (6, 7) (1828–1932), Paigle (158) (1900), Pilewort [Pile-wort, Pile wort] (7) (1828), Queen's-button [Queens-button] (76) (1896) Sulphur Grove OH, Renoncule (French) (6, 158) (1892–1900), Renoncule acre (French) (7) (1828), Scharf Hahnenfuss (German) (6, 158) (1892–1900), Tall buttercup (3, 4, 6, 45, 50, 72, 138, 145, 155, 157, 158) (1892–present), Tall crowfoot (6, 63, 156) (1892–1923), Upright buttercups (6) (1892), Upright crowfoot (6) (1892), Yellow bachelor's-buttons [Yellow batchelor's button, Yellow bachelor's buttons] (158) (1900), Yellow cress (157, 158) (1900–1929), Yellow daisy (79) (1891) Northeast US, Yellow gowan [Yellow gowans] (5, 156, 157, 158) (1900–1929) Scotland, Yellow pileweed [Yellow pile-weed] (6) (1892), Yellow-caul (157, 158) (1900–1929), Yellows (7) (1828), Yellow-weed [Yellow weed] (7, 92) (1828–1876)

Ranunculus allegheniensis **Britt.** – Mountain crowfoot (5) (1913)

Ranunculus alleni **Robinson** – See *Ranunculus allenii* B. L. Rob.

Ranunculus allenii **B. L. Rob.** – Allen's buttercup (5, 50) (1913–present)

Ranunculus ambigens **S. Wats.** – Water plaintain spearwort (2) (1895)

Ranunculus aquatica – See *Ranunculus aquatilis* L.

Ranunculus aquatilis **(L.) var. capillaceous (Thuill.) DC.** – See *Ranunculus trichophyllus* Chaix var. *trichophyllus*

Ranunculus aquatilis **L.** – Common white water crowfoot [Common white water-crowfoot] (120) (1938), Water crowfoot (19, 92) (1840–1876), Water milfoil (156) (1923), White water crowfoot [White water-crowfoot] (156) (1923)

Ranunculus arvensis **L.** – Corn buttercup (50, 155) (1942–present), Corn crowfoot (5, 158) (1900–1913), Devil's-claw [Devil's claw, Devil's claws, Devilsclaws] (5, 156, 158) (1900–1923), Goldweed [Gold weed, Gold-weed] (5, 158) (1900–1913), Hellweed [Hellweed, Hell weed] (5, 156, 158) (1900–1923), Horse-gold [Horse gold] (5, 156, 158) (1900–1923) IA KS, Hungerweed [Hunger weed, Hunger-weed] (5, 92, 156, 158) (1876–1923), Starve-acre [Starve acre] (5, 156) (1913–1923)

Ranunculus auricomus **L.** – Gold thrum crowfoote double (178) (1526), Greenland buttercup (50) (present)

Ranunculus bulbosus **L.** – Biting crowfoot (156) (1923), Blister-flower [Blister flower] (5, 156) (1913–1923), Bulb buttercup (155) (1942), Bulbous buttercup (2, 3, 4, 5, 6, 93, 158) (1895–1986), Bulbous crowfoot [Bulbous crowfoote] (6, 45, 49, 63, 156, 178) (1526–1923), Buttercress [Butter cress, Butter-cress, Butter cresses] (156) (1923), Buttercup [Butter cup, Buttercups] (46, 49, 57, 92, 107, 156) (1876–1923), Butter-daisy [Butter daisy] (156) (1923), Butter-flower [Butter flower] (5, 6, 156) (1892–1913), Butter-rose [Butter rose] (156) (1923), Common bulbous crow-foot (187) (1818), Crowfoot [Crowfoot, Crow foot, Crowfote, Crow's foot] (46, 49, 57, 61) (1870–1917), Cuckoo-buds [Cuckoo buds] (5, 92) (1876–1913), Frogwort [Frog wort] (5, 92, 158) (1876–1913), Frostwort [Frost wort] (158) (1900), Gill-cup (158) (1900), Goldballs [Gold balls, Gold-balls] (156) (1923) no longer in use by 1923, Goldcup [Gold cup, Gold cups, Goldcups] (5, 6) (1892–1913), Golden knops (5) (1913), Goldweed [Gold weed, Gold-weed] (156) (1923), Gowan [Gowans] (5) (1913), Hog's-turnip [Hog's turnip] (158) (1900), King-cob [King cob] (46) (1879), Kingcup [King cup, King cups, Kingcups, King's cup, Kings' cup] (5, 6, 46, 92) (1879–1913), Knollinger Hahnenfuss

353

(German) (6) (1892), Meadow-bloom [Meadow bloom, Meadow-bloom] (92, 158) (1876–1900), Palewort [Pale-wort] (158) (1900), Pilewort [Pile-wort, Pile wort] (5, 92) (1876–1913), Pissabed (5, 158) (1900–1913), St. Anthony's rape (6, 156, 158) (1892–1923), St. Athony's turnip (5, 6, 50, 156, 158) (1892–present), Yellow gowan [Yellow gowans] (156) (1923), Yellow-weed [Yellow weed] (5) (1913)

***Ranunculus cardiophyllus* Hook.** – Heart-leaf buttercup [Heartleaf buttercup, Heart-leaved buttercup] (5, 50) (1913–present)

***Ranunculus circinatus* Sibth.** – See *Ranunculus longirostris* Godr.

***Ranunculus cymbalaria* Pursh** – Alkali buttercup (50) (present), Seaside buttercup (127) (1933), Seaside crowfoot [Sea side crowfoot] (2, 5, 63, 72, 85, 97, 131, 156) (1895–1937), Shore buttercup (3, 4, 155) (1942–1986)

***Ranunculus delphiniifolius* Torr.** – See *Ranunculus flabellaris* Raf.

***Ranunculus fascicularis* Muhl. ex Bigelow** – Bundle-root buttercup [Bundle-rooted buttercup] (5) (1913), Cowslip [Cowslips, Cowslyp] (5, 156, 158) (1900–1923), Dwarf buttercup (156, 158) (1900–1923), Early buttercup (3, 4, 5, 50, 97) (1913–present), Early crowfoot (82, 156) (1923–1930), Low buttercup (156, 158) (1900–1923), Tufted buttercup (5, 97, 138, 155, 156, 158) (1900–1937)

***Ranunculus ficaria* L.** – Bryght (179) (1526), Buttercup [Butter cup, Buttercups] (107) (1919), Celendyne (179) (1526), Crain (5, 156) (1913–1923), Ficaria (55) (1911), Figwort [Fig-wort, Figwoort] (156) (1923), Figwort buttercup (5) (1913), Golden guineas (5) (1913), Goldencup [Golden-cup, Golden cup] (5) (1913), Lesser celandine (5, 55, 107, 156) (1911–1923), Pilewort [Pile-wort, Pile wort] (5, 55) (1911–1913), Small celandine (107) (1919)

***Ranunculus filiformis* Michx.** – See *Ranunculus flammula* L. var. *filiformis* (Michx.) Hook.

***Ranunculus flabellaris* Raf.** – Thread-leaf buttercup [Threadleaf buttercup] (3, 4) (1977–1986), Water buttercup (127, 158) (1900–1933), Water crowfoot (85) (1932), Yellow water buttercup (50) (present), Yellow water crowfoot [Yellow water crow foot, Yellow water crowfoot] (2, 5, 63, 72, 93, 97, 131, 156, 158) (1895–1937)

***Ranunculus flammula* L.** – Creeping spearwort (5, 156) (1913–1923), Greater creeping spearwort (50) (present), Smaller spearwort (2, 82, 156) (1895–1930), Spearwort (4, 19, 92) (1840–1986), Spearwort buttercup (155) (1942), Spereworde (179) (1526)

***Ranunculus flammula* L. var. *filiformis* (Michx.) Hook.** – Creeping spearwort (2) (1895), Greater creeping spearwort (50) (present)

***Ranunculus glaberrimus* Hook.** – Sagebrush buttercup (50, 155) (1942–present)

***Ranunculus glaberrimus* Hook. var. *ellipticus* (Greene) Greene** – Elliptical buttercup (50) (present)

***Ranunculus gmelinii* DC.** – Gmelin's buttercup (50) (present), Pursh's buttercup (5) (1913), Small yellow buttercup (3, 4) (1977–1986)

***Ranunculus harveyi* (Gray) Britt.** – Harvey's buttercup (5) (1913)

***Ranunculus hederaceus* L.** – Ivy-leaf crowfoot [Ivy-leaved crowfoot] (5) (1913)

***Ranunculus hispidus* Michx.** – Bristly buttercup (3, 4, 50, 138, 155) (1923–present), Early buttercup (72) (1907), Hispid buttercup (5, 63, 97) (1899–1937), Hispid crow-foot (187) (1818), Marsh buttercup (4) (1986)

***Ranunculus hispidus* Michx. var. *nitidus* (Chapman) T. Duncan** – Common buttercup (82) (1930), Creeping buttercup (2, 80) (1895–1913), Early buttercup (158) (1900), Early crowfoot (156) (1923), Marsh buttercup (3, 5, 72, 85, 93, 158) (1900–1977), Northern buttercup (80, 97, 127) (1913–1937), Swamp buttercup (5, 80, 97, 131, 138, 155, 156, 158) (1899–1942)

***Ranunculus hyperboreus* Rottb.** – Arctic buttercup (5) (1913)

***Ranunculus inamoenus* Greene** – Graceful buttercup (50) (present)

***Ranunculus inamoenus* Greene var. *alpeophilus* (A. Nels.) L. Benson** – Graceful buttercup (50) (present)

***Ranunculus* L.** – Buttercup [Butter cup, Buttercups] (1, 2, 4, 13, 15, 50, 63, 93, 106, 109, 127, 138, 155, 156, 158) (1849–present), Crowfoot [Crow-foot, Crow foot, Crowfote, Crow's foot] (1, 2, 4, 10, 13, 15,

63, 93, 109, 155, 156, 158, 167, 184) (1793–1986), Cuckoo-buds [Cuckoo buds] (14) (1882), Goldcup [Gold cup, Gold cups, Gold-cups] (14) (1882), Kingcup [King cup, King cups, Kingcups, King's cup, Kings' cup] (14) (1882), Water crowfoot (93) (1936), White water crowfoot [White water-crowfoot] (1, 93) (1932–1936), Yellow gowan [Yellow gowans] (92) (1876)

***Ranunculus lapponicus* L.** – Lapland buttercup (5) (1913)

***Ranunculus laxicaulis* (Torr. & Gray) Darby** – Mississippi buttercup (50) (present), Water-plantain spearwort [Water plantain spearwort] (4, 156) (1923–1986)

***Ranunculus longirostris* Godr.** – Long-beak buttercup [Longbeak buttercup] (50, 155) (1942–present), Stiff water crowfoot (Stiff water-crowfoot) (2, 63, 156) (1895–1931), Stiff white water crowfoot (5) (1913), White water crowfoot [White water-crowfoot] (3, 4) (1977–1986)

***Ranunculus macounii* Britton** – Macoun's buttercup [Macoun's buttercups] (3, 4, 5, 50, 127, 131) (1899–present)

***Ranunculus macranthus* Scheele** – Large buttercup (122, 124) (1937)

***Ranunculus micranthus* Nutt.** – Rock buttercup (50) (present), Rock crowfoot [Rock crow foot] (5, 97) (1913–1937)

***Ranunculus multifidus* Pursh** – See *Ranunculus flabellaris* Raf.

***Ranunculus muricatus* L.** – Spiny-fruit crowfoot [Spiny-fruited crowfoot] (5) (1913)

***Ranunculus nivalis* L.** – Snow buttercup (5) (1913)

***Ranunculus oblongifolius* Ell.** – See *Ranunculus pusillus* Poir. var. *pusillus*

***Ranunculus ovalis* Raf.** – See *Ranunculus rhomboideus* Goldie

***Ranunculus parviflorus* L.** – Small-flower crowfoot [Small-flowered crowfoot] (5, 97) (1913–1937)

***Ranunculus parvulis* L. (sp?)** – possibly *Ranunculus sardous* Crantz.

***Ranunculus parvulus* L.** – See *Ranunculus sardous* Crantz.

***Ranunculus pedatifidus* J. E. Smith** – Northern buttercup (5) (1913), Rough-fruit crowfoot [Rough-fruited crow-foot] (5) (1913)

***Ranunculus pensylvanicus* L. f.** – Bristly buttercup (5, 93, 131) (1899–1936), Bristly crowfoot (3, 4, 5, 63, 72, 156) (1899–1986), Pennsylvania buttercup (50, 155) (1942–present)

***Ranunculus pusillus* Poir.** – Dwarf crowfoot (5) (1913), Low spearwort (5) (1913)

Ranunculus pusillus* Poir. var. *pusillus – Oblong-leaf spearwort [Oblong leaved spearwort] (5) (1913)

***Ranunculus pygmaeus* Wahlenb.** – Pygmy buttercup [Pigmy buttercup] (5) (1913)

***Ranunculus recurvatus* Poir.** – Blister plant (156) (1923), Blister-flower [Blister flower] (156) (1923), Blisterwort [Blister wort, Blister-wort] (50) (present), Hooked buttercup (3, 4, 155) (1942–1986), Hooked crowfoot (5, 63, 72, 93, 156) (1899–1936), Hook-style crowfoot [Hook styled crowfoot] (2) (1895), Rough crowfoot (5) (1913)

***Ranunculus repens* L.** – Buttercress [Butter cress, Butter-cress, Butter cresses] (156) (1923), Butter-daisy [Butter daisy] (5, 107, 156) (1913–1923), Butter-flower [Butter flower] (156) (1923), Butter-rose [Butter rose] (156) (1923), Creeping buttercup (5, 6, 50, 72, 138, 155, 156, 158) (1892–present), Creeping crowfoot [Creeping crow-foot] (6, 107, 187) (1818–1919), Crowfoot [Crow-foot, Crow foot, Crowfote, Crow's foot] (46) (1649), Cursed crowfoot (148) (1939) CO, Devil's-gut [Devil's gut, Devil's-guts, Devil's guts, Devil's-guts] (158) (1900), Double-flower creeping buttercup [Double-flowered creeping buttercup] (109) (1949), Garden ranunculus (2) (1895), Goldballs [Gold balls, Gold-balls] (5, 156) (1913–1923), Goldknops [Gold-knops, Gold knops] (5) (1913), Goldweed [Gold weed, Gold-weed] (156) (1923), Granny-threads (156, 158) (1900–1923), Hahnenfuss (German) (6) (1892), Hod-the-rake (156, 158) (1900–1923), Horse-gold [Horse gold] (5, 156) (1913–1923), Lantern-leaves (156, 158) (1900–1923), Meadow buttercup [Meadow buttercups] (158) (1900), Meg-many-feet (156, 158) (1900–1923), Ram's-claws [Ram's claws] (5, 156, 158) (1900–1923), Ranoncule (French) (6) (1892), Setsticker (158) (1900), Sitfast (5, 156, 158) (1900–1923), Spotted-leaf buttercup (5, 156, 158) (1900–1923),

Reseda luteola **L.**

Tether-toad (156, 158) (1900–1923), Yellow-gowan [Yellow gowan] (5, 107, 156) (1913–1923)

***Ranunculus repens* L. var. *pleniflorus* Fern.** – See *Ranunculus repens* L.

***Ranunculus reptans* L.** – See *Ranunculus flammula* L. var. *filiformis* (Michx.) Hook.

***Ranunculus rhomboideus* Goldie** – Dwarf buttercup (85) (1932), Labrador buttercup (50, 155) (1942–present), Prairie buttercup (3, 4) (1977–1986), Prairie crowfoot (5, 63, 65, 72, 93, 127, 131) (1899–1936)

***Ranunculus rivularis* Rydb.** – See *Ranunculus macounii* Britton

***Ranunculus sardous* Crantz. (possibly)** – Hairy buttercup (5, 50) (1913–present)

***Ranunculus sceleratus* L.** – Biting crowfoot (5, 156, 158) (1900–1923), Blister buttercup (155) (1942), Blisterwort [Blister wort, Blisterwort] (5, 156, 158) (1900–1923), Bristly buttercup (85) (1932), Celery crowfoot (19) (1840), Celery-leaf crowfoot [Celery-leaved crowfoot, Scelery-leaved Crow-foot] (5, 6, 93, 97, 125, 131, 158, 187) (1818–1937), Crowfoot [Crow-foot, Crow foot, Crowfote, Crow's foot] (179) (1526), Cursed buttercup (50) (present), Cursed crowfoot (3, 4, 5, 6, 63, 125, 156, 158) (1892–1986), Ditch buttercup (126, 127) (1933), Ditch crowfoot (5, 156) (1913–1923), Marsh crowfoot (5, 6, 156) (1892–1923), Ranoncule (French) (6) (1892), Scharf Hahnenfuss (German) (6) (1892), Water-celery [Water celery] (5, 156, 158) (1900–1923)

***Ranunculus sceleratus* L. var. *multifidus* Nutt.** – Cursed buttercup (50) (present)

Ranunculus sceleratus* L. var. *sceleratus – Cursed buttercup (50) (present)

***Ranunculus septentrionalis* Poir.** – See *Ranunculus hispidus* Michx. var. *nitidus* (Chapman) T. Duncan

***Ranunculus subrigidus* Drew** – See *Ranunculus longirostris* Godr.

Ranunculus trichophyllus* Chaix var. *trichophyllus – Circinate white water crowfoot (72) (1907), Common white water crowfoot [Common white water-crowfoot] (72) (1907), Green eelgrass [Green eel grass] (5) (1913), Pickerel weed [Pickerelweed, Pickerel-weed] (5) (1913), Thread-leaf crowfoot [Threadleaf crowfoot] (50) (present), Water crowfoot (131) (1899), Water milfoil (5) (1913), White water crowfoot [White water-crowfoot] (3, 5, 63, 85, 127) (1899–1977)

***Raphanistrum* (Tourn.) All.** – See *Raphanus* L.

***Raphanus* (Tourn.) L.** – See *Raphanus* L.

***Raphanus* L.** – Jointed charlock (1) (1932), Radish (1, 15, 50, 82, 138, 155, 156, 158) (1895–1942)

***Raphanus raphanistrum* L.** – Black mustard (5, 156) (1913–1923), Cadlock (5, 76) (1896–1913) Nova Scotia, Charlock (6, 19, 156) (1840–1923), Curlock (5) (1913), Jointed charlock (5, 6, 15, 80, 106, 107, 156) (1892–1930), Krautweed [Kraut-weed, Kraut weed] (5, 156) (1913–1923), Radish (106) (1930), Raifoot, Commune (French) (6) (1892), Rape (5) (1913), Runch (107) (1919), Shedlock (5) (1913), Warlock (5) (1913), White charlock (5) (1913), Wild mustard (5, 107) (1913–1919), Wild radish (5, 6, 15, 19, 50, 72, 80, 106, 107, 156) (1840–present), Wild rape [Wilde rapes] (5, 156) (1913–1923), Wilde Rettig (German) (6) (1892)

***Raphanus sativus* L.** – Biting radish (178) (1526), Black mustard (76) (1896), Black radish [Blacke radish] (178, 180) (1526–1633) John Gerarde, Cacanon (180) (1633), Common garden radish (92) (1876), Common radish (158) (1900), Cultivated radish (50) (present), Garden radish (5, 19, 72, 155, 158, 180) (1633–1942), Pear-fashion radish [Peare-fashion radish] (180) (1633), Rabone (158, 180) (1633–1900), Radish (4, 7, 82, 85, 92, 107, 109, 114, 138, 158, 180, 184) (1633–1986), Radus (Low Dutch) (180) (1633), Ranano (Spanish) (180) (1633), Raphano (Italian) (180) (1633), Rawbone (158) (1900), Raysshe (179) (1526), Reefort (158) (1900), Round radish (180) (1633), Round-root black radish [Round rooted blacke Radish] (178) (1526), Ruifort (French) (180) (1633), Rzedfew (Bohemian) (180) (1633), Small garden radish (180) (1633), Wild radish (3) (1977)

***Ratibida columnaris* (Sims) D. Don** – See *Ratibida columnifera* (Nutt.) Wood & Standl.

***Ratibida columnifera* (Nutt.) Wood & Standl.** – Ahawǐ akǎ'tǎ' (102) (1886), Brush (5, 76, 158) (1896–1913), Coneflower [Cone-flower, Cone flower] (38, 106) (1820–1930), Gray-head coneflower [Gray-headed coneflower, Gray-headed coneflower, Gray-headed coneflower] (122, 156) (1923–1937), Green coneflower [Green coneflower] (82) (1930), Long-head coneflower [Long headed cone flower, Long-headed cone-flower, Long-headed coneflower, Long-headed coneflower] (5, 72, 93, 122, 124, 127, 156, 158) (1900–1937), Prairie coneflower [Prairie cone-flower, Prairieconeflower] (3, 5, 82, 95, 97, 98, 131, 156) (1899–1977), Upright prairie coneflower [Upright prairieconeflower] (50, 155) (1942–present), Wah'cha-zi chikala (Dakota) (37) (1919)

***Ratibida pinnata* (Vent.) Barnh.** – Asaŋpi ijatke (Lakota) (121) (1918?–1970?), Bašta (Osage) (121) (1918?–1970?), Coneflower [Cone-flower, Cone flower] (85, 95, 114) (1894–1932), Gray-head coneflower [Gray-headed coneflower, Gray-headed coneflower, Gray-headed cone-flower] (5, 72, 93, 97, 131) (1899–1937), Gray-head prairie coneflower [Grayhead prairie coneflower] (3) (1977), Long-head coneflower [Long-headed coneflower] (121) (1970), Napošstaŋ (Lakota) (121) (1918?–1970?), Pinnate prairie coneflower (50) (present), Prairie coneflower [Prairie cone-flower, Prairieconeflower] (121) (1970), Wiŋawazi kutkaŋ (Lakota, burr root) (121) (1918?–1970?)

***Ratibida* Raf** – Coneflower [Cone-flower, Cone flower] (1, 50, 82, 93, 109, 158) (1900–present), Prairie coneflower [Prairie cone-flower, Prairieconeflower] (4, 50, 155) (1942–present)

***Ratibida tagetes* (James) Barnhart** – Green prairie coneflower (50) (present), Short-ray coneflower [Shortrayed cone flower, Short-rayed coneflower, Short-rayed cone-flower] (5, 97, 122, 124) (1913–1937), Short-ray prairie coneflower [Shortray prairie coneflower] (3, 4) (1977–1986)

***Ravenala madagascariensis* Sonnerat** – Travelers' tree [Travelers-tree] (50, 92) (1876–present) cup-like leaf bases hold water from which travelers are said to drink

***Rayjacksonia annua* (Rydb.) R. L. Hartman & M. A. Lane** – Viscid sideranthus (5, 93) (1913–1936), Viscid tansy-aster [Viscid tansyaster] (50) (present)

***Rayjacksonia phyllocephala* (DC.) R. L. Hartman & M. L. Lane** – Large-flower aplopappus [Large flowered aplopappus] (124) (1937)

***Razoumofskya pusilla* (Peck) Kuntze** – See *Arceuthobium pusillum* Peck

***Redfieldia flexuosa* (Thurb.) Vasey** – Blowout grass [Blow-out grass, Blowoutgrass] (3, 50, 111, 119, 140, 155) (1915–present), Redfield's grass (5, 94, 119) (1901–1938)

***Redfieldia* Vasey.** – Blowout grass [Blow-out grass, Blowoutgrass] (1, 50, 93, 155) (1932–present), Sand grass [Sand-grass, Sandgrass] (2) (1895)

***Reichardia picroides* (L.) Roth** – French scorzonera (107) (1919)

***Reimaria oligostachya* Munro in Benth.** – See *Reimarochloa oligostachya* Munro ex Benth.

***Reimarochloa oligostachya* Munro ex Benth.** – Creeping reimaria (94) (1901)

***Renealmia usneoides* L.** – See *Tillandsia usneoides* (L.) L.

***Reseda alba* L.** – Crambling rocket (180) (1633), Great crambling rocket (178) (1526), Pignocomon (180) (1633), White cut-leaf mignonette [White cut-leaved mignonette] (5) (1913), White upright mignonette (109) (1949)

***Reseda* L.** – Mignonette (50, 138, 155, 158) (1923–present)

***Reseda lutea* L.** – Crambling rocket (5, 156, 178) (1596–1923), Italian rocket (180) (1633), Mignonette (95, 157) (1911–1929), Reseda (4) (1986), Wild mignonette (4) (1986), Yellow cut-leaf mignonette [Yellow cut-leaved mignonette] (5) (1913), Yellow mignonette (50, 155, 156) (1923–present)

***Reseda luteola* L.** – Ash-of-Jerusalem (156) (1923), Dutch pink (5, 92, 156) (1876–1923), Dyer's mignonette (5, 156) (1913–1923), Dyer's rocket (5, 15, 72) (1895–1913), Dyer's weed [Dyers' weed, Dyer's-weed] (5, 15, 19, 92, 156) (1840–1923), Dyer's weld (156) (1923), Italian rocket (5, 156) (1913–1923), Luteolin (92) (1876), Weld (5, 92, 156) (1876–1923), Wild woad (5, 156) (1913–1923), Yellow rocket [Yellowrocket, Yellow-rocket] (5, 156) (1913–1923), Yellow-weed [Yellow weed] (15, 92, 156) (1895–1923)

Reseda odorata L. – Common mignonette (109, 138) (1923–1949), Mignonette (82, 92, 106, 114) (1894–1930), Mignonetter (19) (1840)

Retama monosperma (L.) Boiss. – Bridal-veil broom (138) (1923)

Reverchonia arenaria Gray – Sand reverchonia (50) (present)

Rhamnus alnifolia L'Her. – Alder buckthorn [Alder-buckthorn] (3, 4, 138, 155) (1923–1986), Alder-leaf buckthorn [Alderleaf buckthorn, Alder-leaved buckthorn] (5, 50, 82, 93, 156, 158) (1900–present), Buckthorn [Bucke thorne] (184) (1793), Dogwood [Dog-wood, Dog wood] (5, 156) (1913–1923), Dwarf alder (5, 19, 76, 156, 158) (1840–1923) Western US, Green alder (156) (1923), Low buckthorn (113) (1890)

Rhamnus californica Eschscholtz – See *Frangula californica* (Eschsch.) Gray

Rhamnus californica tomentella – See *Frangula californica* (Eschsch.) Gray subsp. *tomentella* (Benth.) Kartesz & Gandhi

Rhamnus caroliniana Walt. var. mollis Fren. – See *Frangula caroliniana* (Walt.) Gray

Rhamnus cathartica L. – Bourquepine (French) (6) (1892), Buckthorn [Bucke thorne] (5, 6, 7, 19, 57, 61, 58, 59, 82, 92, 112, 126, 135, 158, 178) (1526–1937), Cathartic buckthorn (20) (1857), Common buckthorn (3, 4, 50, 55, 106, 109, 138, 155, 156) (1923–present), Espina cerval (Spanish) (158) (1900), Hartshorn (6, 59) (pre-1066–1911), Hart's-thorn [Hart's thorn] (156, 158) (1900–1923), Hirschdorn (German) (158) (1900), Kreuzdorn (German) (6, 158) (1892–1900), Neprun purgatif (French) (158) (1900), Nerprun (French) (6) (1892), Purging berries (92) (1876), Purging buckthorn (6, 92, 156, 158) (1892–1923), Rain-berry thorn (156, 158) (1900–1923), Ramno catartico (Spanish) (158) (1900), Rhineberry [Rhine-berry] (156, 158) (1900–1923), Waythorn [Way-thorn] (6, 59, 92, 156, 158) (1892–1923), Wegdorn (German) (6) (1892)

Rhamnus crocea Nutt. – Buckthorn [Bucke thorne] (103) (1870), Redberry [Red-berry, Red berry] (106) (1930), Red-berry buckthorn [Red-berried buckthorn] (109) (1949), Squaw bush [Squawbush, Squaw-bush] (106) (1930) CA

Rhamnus croceus – See *Rhamnus crocea* Nutt.

Rhamnus dahurica – possibly *Rhamnus davurica* Pallas

Rhamnus davurica Pallas – Dahurian buckthorn (50, 138, 155) (1923–present)

Rhamnus davurica Pallas subsp. davurica – Dahurian buckthorn (50) (present)

Rhamnus frangula L. var. angustifolia Loud. – See *Frangula alnus* Mill.

Rhamnus L. – Buckthorn [Bucke thorne] (5, 6, 7, 19, 57, 61, 58, 59, 82, 92, 112, 126, 135, 158) (1818–1937)

Rhamnus lanceolata Pursh – Buckthorn [Bucke thorne] (85, 95, 113) (1890–1932), Lance-leaf buckthorn [Lanceleaf buckthorn, Lance-leaved buckthorn] (5, 50, 72, 82, 155) (1907–present), Narrow-leaf buckthorn [Narrow-leaved buckthorn] (2) (1895), Stinkberry (113) (1890) Neb

Rhamnus lanceolata Pursh subsp. glabrata (Gleason) Kartesz & Gandhi – Lance-leaf buckthorn [Lanceleaf buckthorn, Lance-leaved buckthorn] (4, 50) (1986–present)

Rhamnus lanceolatus Pursh (sic) – See *Rhamnus lanceolata* Pursh

Rhamnus purshiana DC. – See *Frangula purshiana* (DC.) Cooper

Rhamnus zizyphus L. – See *Ziziphus zizyphus* (L.) Karst.

Rhapidophyllum hystrix (Pursh) H. Wendl. & Drude ex Drude – Blue palmetto (2, 106) (1895–1930), Needle palm (50, 106, 138) (1923–present)

Rhaponticum repens (L.) Hidalgo – Russian centaurea (155) (1942), Russian knapweed (3, 4) (1977–1986), Turkestan thistle (3, 122) (1937–1977)

Rheum L. – Pie plant [Pieplant, Pie-plant] (1, 82) (1930–1932), Rewbarbe (Rhubarb) (179) (1526), Rhubarb (1, 4, 7, 14, 57, 92, 138, 155, 158, 184) (1793–1986)

Rheum rhabarbarum L. – Common rhubarb (138) (1923), French rhubarb (92) (1876), Garden rhubarb (50, 109, 155) (1942–present), Indländischer Rhabarber (German) (158) (1900), Pie plant [Pieplant, Pie-plant] (73, 82, 85, 92, 107, 109, 158) (1892–1949) Middle states and west, Pie rhubarb (19) (1840), Rhapontic (French) (158) (1900), Rhapontic rhubarb (158) (1900), Rhapontic root (92) (1876), Rhapontikrhabarber (German) (158) (1900), Rhubarb (4, 85, 107, 148) (1919–1986), Wine plant [Wine-plant] (77, 109) (1898–1949), Wine rhubarb (158) (1900)

Rhexia aristosa Britton – Awn-petal meadow-beauty [Awn-petaled meadow beauty] (5) (1913)

Rhexia ciliosa Michx. – See *Rhexia petiolata* Walt.

Rhexia L. – Deer-grass [Deergrass, Deer grass] (2) (1895), Meadow-beauty [Meadowbeauty, Meadow beauty] (1, 2, 4, 122, 138, 155, 158) (1895–1986)

Rhexia mariana L. – Maryland meadow-beauty [Maryland meadow-beauty, Maryland meadow beauty] (5, 97, 138, 156) (1913–1937), Soapwood [Soap-wood] (184) (1793)

Rhexia mariana L. var. interior (Pennell) Kral & Bostick – Maryland meadow-beauty [Maryland meadowbeauty, Maryland meadow beauty] (50) (present)

Rhexia mariana L. var. leiosperma Fer. & Grisc. – See *Rhexia mariana* L. var. *mariana*

Rhexia mariana L. var. mariana – Maryland meadow-beauty [Maryland meadowbeauty, Maryland meadow beauty] (122, 124) (1937)

Rhexia petiolata Walt. – Ciliate meadow beauty (5) (1913)

Rhexia stricta Pursh – See *Rhexia virginica* L.

Rhexia virginica L. – Common meadow-beauty [Common meadow-beauty] (122, 138) (1923–1937), Deer-grass [Deergrass, Deer grass] (5, 19, 86, 92, 156) (1840–1923), Handsome Harry (5, 76) (1896–1913) Eastern MA, Meadow-beauty [Meadowbeauty, Meadow beauty] (5, 19, 63, 72, 86, 92, 97, 124, 156) (1840–1937), Soapweed [Soap weed, Soap-weed] (181) (~1678), Soopwood (177) (1762)

Rhinanthus borealis Chabert subsp. kyrollae (Chabert) Pennell – See *Rhinanthus minor* L. subsp. *minor*

Rhinanthus crista-galli L. – See *Rhinanthus minor* L. subsp. *minor*

Rhinanthus kyrollae Chab. – See *Rhinanthus minor* L. subsp. *minor*

Rhinanthus L. – Little rattlepot (155) (1942), Mederacle (179) (1526), Rattlebox [Rattle box, Rattle-box] (1) (1932), Rattlepot (155) (1942), Yellow rattle (156) (1923–1932)

Rhinanthus minor L. subsp. minor – Cow-wheat [Cow wheat] (156) (1923), Money-grass [Money grass] (5, 156) (1913–1923) no longer in use by 1923, Penny-grass [Penny grass] (5, 92, 156) (1913–1923) no longer in use by 1923, Penny-rattle [Penny rattle] (5, 156) (1913–1923) no longer in use by 1923, Rattle (5) (1913), Rattle-bags [Rattle bags] (5) (1913), Rattlebox [Rattle box, Rattle-box] (5, 85, 156) (1913–1932), Yellow cock's-comb [Yellow cock's comb, Yellow coxscomb] (5, 19, 156) (1840–1923), Yellow rattle (5, 19, 92, 156) (1840–1923)

Rhipsalis baccifera (Soland. ex J. Mill.) Stearn – Mistletoe cactus (138) (1923), Mistletoe rhipsalis (155) (1942)

Rhipsalis cassutha – See *Rhipsalis baccifera* (Soland. ex J. Mill.) Stearn

Rhipsalis Gaertn. – Mistletoe cactus (14) (1882), Rhipsalis (155) (1942)

Rhizophora americana Nutt. – See *Rhizophora mangle* L.

Rhizophora L. – Mangrove or Mangrove tree (7) (1828)

Rhizophora mangle L. – American mangle (20) (1857), Mangrove or Mangrove tree (19, 20, 92) (1840–1876), Peekandel (174) (1753), Rhizophore d'Amerique (French) (20) (1857)

Rhizopus nigricans Ehrenb. – Black mould (56) (1901)

Rhizopus stolonifer (Ehrenb.) Vuill. – Mould (92) (1876)

Rhodiola rosea L. – Heal-all [Healall] (156) (1923), Roseroot [Rose root, Rose roote, Rose-root] (5, 109, 156, 178) (1526–1949), Rose-root stonecrop (50, 138, 155) (1923–present), Rose-scent root [Rose scented root] (156) (1923), Rosewort [Rose woort] (5, 92, 156, 178) (1526–1923), Rosy-flower stonecrop [Rosy-flowered stonecrop] (107) (1919), Snowdon's rose [Snowdon rose] (5, 156) (1913–1923)

Rhododendron albiflorum **Hook.** – Rocky Mountain rhododendron (138) (1923)

Rhododendron arborescens **(Pursh) Torr.** – Smooth azalea (5, 156) (1913–1923), Smooth honeysuckle (5) (1913), Sweet azalea (138) (1923), Tree azalea (5, 156) (1913–1923)

Rhododendron atlanticum **(Ashe) Rehd.** – Coast azalea (138) (1923)

Rhododendron calendulaceum **(Michx.) Torr.** – American upright honeysuckle (41) (1770), Fiery azalea (156) (1923), Flame azalea (5, 109, 138, 156) (1913–1949), Flame-colored azalea (156) (1923), Flaming pinkster (156) (1923), Honeysuckle [Honey suckle, Honeysuckle, Honisuckles] (177) (1762), Pinxterbloem (Swedish, Witsunday flower) (177) (1762), Yellow honeysuckle (5, 156) (1913–1923)

Rhododendron calendulaceum **Torr.** – See *Rhododendron calendulaceum* (Michx.) Torr.

Rhododendron canadense **(L.) Torr.** – False honeysuckle [False-honeysuckle] (19) (1840), Lambkill [Lamb-kill, Lamb kill] (5, 156) (1913–1923), May pink (156) (1923), Rhodora (5, 19, 109, 138, 156) (1840–1949)

Rhododendron canescens **(Michx.) G. Don** – See *Rhododendron canescens* (Michx.) Sweet

Rhododendron canescens **(Michx.) Sweet** – Gray downy rosebay [Grey downy rose bay] (42) (1814), Hoary azalea (5, 122, 124, 156) (1913–1937), Mountain azalea (5, 156) (1913–1923), Piedmont azalea (138) (1923)

Rhododendron carolinianum **Rehd.** – Carolina rhododendron (5, 138) (1913–1923)

Rhododendron catawbiense **Michx.** – Carolina rose-bay (156) (1923), Catawba rhododendron (5, 138) (1913–1923), Catawba rose-bay (156) (1923), Laurel (5, 156) (1913–1923), Mountain rose-bay [Mountain rose bay] (5, 109, 156) (1913–1949)

Rhododendron flammeum **(Michx.) Sarg.** – Flaming azalea (182) (1791)

Rhododendron japonicum **(Gray) Sur.** – Japanese azalea (138) (1923)

Rhododendron **L.** – Azalea (2, 106, 138) (1895–1930), Azalée (French) (8) (1785), Dwarf rose bay [Dwarf rose-bay] (8) (1785), Great laurel (156) (1923), Laurel (12, 75) (1821–1894), Mountain laurel [Mountain Lawrell] (7, 10, 167) (1814–1828), Rhododendron (1, 138) (1923–1932), Rhodora (138) (1923), Rose-bay [Rose bay, Rosebay] (2, 7, 42, 109, 184) (1793–1949), Springbloom [Spring-bloom, Spring bloom] (7) (1828), Swamp pink [Swamppink, Swamp-pink] (7) (1828), Swamp-honeysuckle [Swamp honeysuckle] (10, 156) (1818–1923), Upright honeysuckle [Upright honey-suckle] (8) (1785), Wild honeysuckle [Wild honey-suckle] (7) (1828)

Rhododendron lapponicum **(L.) Wahlenb.** – Lapland rhododendron (138) (1923), Lapland rose-bay [Lapland rose bay] (5, 107, 156) (1913–1923), Laurel (5, 156) (1913–1923)

Rhododendron macrophyllum **D. Don ex G. Don** – Coast rhododendron (138) (1923), Red laurel [Redlaurel] (35) (1806)

Rhododendron maximum **L.** – American rosebay (71) (1898), Bee laurel (5, 156) (1913–1923) no longer in use by 1923, Big laurel (71, 156) (1898–1923), Big-leaf laurel (5, 71, 156) (1898–1923), Coe plant (5) (1913), Cow plant [Cowplant] (71, 75, 156) (1898–1923) no longer in use by 1923, Deer laurel (5, 156) (1913–1923), Deer's-tongue [Deer's tongue, Deer tongue, Deer-tongue] (71) (1898), Dwarf rose bay [Dwarf rose-bay] (5, 20) (1857–1913), Great laurel (5, 57, 71, 156) (1898–1923), Great rosebay [Great rose-bay] (2, 156) (1895–1923), Horse laurel (5, 71, 75, 156) (1894–1923) PA, Laurel (18, 71) (1805–1898) PA, Mountain laurel [Mountain Lawrell] (5, 20, 71, 92, 156, 177) (1762–1923), Pennsylvania mountain laurel [Pennsylvanian mountain laurel] (8, 34) (1785–1834), Rhododendron (14, 71) (1882–1898), Rockrose of Pennsylvania [Rockrose of Pennsylvania] (189) (1767), Rose-bay [Rose bay, Rosebay] (5, 71, 156) (1898–1923), Rose-bay rhododendron [Rosebay rhododendron] (138) (1923), Spoon-hutch [Spoon hutch] (5, 71, 156)

(1898–1923) NH, no longer in use by 1923, Wild laurel (2, 156) (1895–1942), Wild rosebay [Wild rose bay] (5, 19, 92) (1840–1913)

Rhododendron minus **Michx.** – Piedmont rhododendron (138) (1923)

Rhododendron nudiflorum **Torr.** – See *Rhododendron periclymenoides* (Michx.) Shinners

Rhododendron occidentale **(Torr. & Gray ex Torr.) Gray var. *occidentale*** – Western azalea (138) (1923)

Rhododendron periclymenoides **(Michx.) Shinners** – Azalée à fleurs rouge (French) (8) (1785), Early honeysuckle (5) (1913), Election pink (5, 73, 79, 156) (1891–1923) NH, bloomed at election time, no longer in use by 1923, False honeysuckle [False-honeysuckle] (156) (1923), Honeysuckle [Honey suckle, Honey-suckle, Honisuckles] (73) (1892) MD, May apple [Mayapple, May-apple] (156) (1923), Mayflower [May flower, May-flower] (5, 41, 75, 156) (1770–1923), Naked red-flower rose-bay [Naked red flowered rose bay] (42) (1814), Pink azalea (5, 97, 156) (1913–1937), Pinkster (156) (1923), Pinkster flower [Pinxter flower, Pinxter-flower] (2, 5, 92, 109, 156) (1895–1949), Pinxterbloem (Swedish, Witsunday flower) (41) (1770), Purple azalea (2, 5, 97, 156) (1895–1937), Purple honeysuckle (5) (1913), Red-flower azalea [Red-flowered azalea] (8) (1785), River-pink [River pink] (5, 73, 156) (1892–1923) Cavendish VT, Spice flower [Spice-flower] (156) (1923), Swamp pink [Swamppink, Swamp-pink] (5, 73, 156) (1892–1923) Northeastern US, Swamp-apple [Swamp apple] (73, 92, 156) (1876–1923) Eastern MA, Swamp-cheeses [Swamp cheeses] (92, 156) (1876–1923), Swamp-honeysuckle [Swamp honeysuckle] (5, 156) (1913–1923), Wild honeysuckle [Wild honey-suckle] (5, 41, 75, 156, 187) (1770–1923) WV

Rhododendron vaseyi **Gray** – Pink-shell azalea [Pinkshell azalea] (138) (1923)

Rhododendron viscosum **(L.) Torr.** – Azalée visqueuse (French) (8) (1785), Blue-leaf acacia [Blueleaf acacia] (138) (1923), Cinnamon honeysuckle (75, 156) (1894–1923) WV, Clammy azalea (5, 156) (1913–1923), Clammy honeysuckle (5) (1913), June pink (77) (1898) NH, Meadow pink [Meadow-pink] (5, 92, 156) (1876–1923), Springbloom [Spring-bloom, Spring bloom] (92, 156) (1876–1923), Swamp azalea (8, 138) (1785–1923), Swamp pink [Swamppink, Swamp-pink] (5, 19, 73, 92, 156) (1840–1923) MA, Swamp-honeysuckle [Swamp honeysuckle] (5, 19, 75, 92) (1840–1876) MA, Upright honeysuckle [Upright honey-suckle] (189) (1767), White azalea (5, 97) (1913–1937), White honeysuckle [White honey-suckle] (5, 19, 75) (1840–1913) Alabama, White swamp honeysuckle (2, 109, 156) (1895–1949), White sweet azalea (8) (1785), Woodbine-flower Virginia cistus [Woodbine flowered Virginia cistus] (181) (~1678), possibly Azalea (92) (1876), possibly Azalée visqueuse des marais (French) (8) (1785), possibly Shining rose-bay [Shining rose bay] (42) (1814), possibly Wild honeysuckle [Wild honey-suckle] (92) (1876)

Rhododendron viscosum **Torr. var. *glaucum* Gray** – See *Rhododendron viscosum* (L.) Torr.

Rhododendrum maximum – See *Rhododendron maximum* L.

Rhodomyrtus **(DC.) Reichenb.** – Rose-myrtle [Rosemyrtle] (138) (1923)

Rhodomyrtus tomentosus **(Aiton) Hassk.** – Downy rosemyrtle (138) (1923)

Rhodora canadensis **L.** – See *Rhododendron canadense* (L.) Torr.

Rhodora **L.** – See *Rhododendron* L.

Rhodora **L'Her.** – See *Rhododendron* L.

Rhodotypos scandens **(Thunb.) Makino** – Jetbead (138) (1923), White kerria (112) (1937)

Rhodotypos **Siebold & Zucc.** – Jetbead (138) (1923)

Rhombolytrum albescens **(Vasey) Nash** – See *Tridens albescens* (Vasey) Woot. & Standl.

Rhus **(Tourn.) L.** – See *Rhus* L.

Rhus aromatica **Aiton** – Fragrant sumac [Fragrant sumach] (4, 6, 12, 49, 50, 52, 53, 54, 107, 155, 158) (1820–present), Pole-cat bush [Polecat bush] (4) (1986), Skunk bush [Skunkbush, Skunk-bush] (6)

(1892), Skunkbush [Skunk bush] (6) (1892), Squawberry [Squaw berry, Squaw-berry] (6) (1892), Stink bush [Stinkbush] (6) (1892), Sweet-scented sumac [Sweet-scented sumach] (6, 72, 156, 158) (1892–1923)

Rhus aromatica **Aiton var. *aromatica*** – Aromatic sumac [Aromatic sumach] (3) (1977), Fragrant sumac [Fragrant sumach] (5) (1913), Illinois fragrant sumac (155) (1942), Sweet-scented sumac [Sweet-scented sumach] (5, 65, 97) (1913–1937)

Rhus aromatica **Aiton var. *flabelliformis* Shinners** – See *Rhus trilobata* Nutt. var. *trilobata*

Rhus aromatica **Aiton var. *pilosissima* (Engelm.) Shinners** – Aromatic sumac [Aromatic sumach] (3) (1977)

Rhus aromatica **Aiton var. *serotina* (Greene) Rehd.** – Aromatic sumac [Aromatic sumach] (3) (1977), Fragrant sumac [Fragrant sumach] (50) (present), Late fragrant sumac (155) (1942)

Rhus canadensis **Marsh. var. *trilobata* (Nutt.) Gr.** – See *Rhus trilobata* Nutt.

Rhus cismontana **Greene** – See *Rhus glabra* L.

Rhus copallina **L.** – See *Rhus copallinum* L.

Rhus copallinum **L.** – Black sumac [Black shumack, Black sumach] (76, 93, 95, 156, 157) (1896–1936), Common sumac [Common sumach] (5, 156) (1913–1923), Downy sumac (145) (1897) KS, Dwarf black sumac (5) (1913), Dwarf sumac [Dwarf sumach] (3, 4, 15, 95, 106, 107, 113, 156, 157) (1890–1986), Flame-leaf sumac [Flame-leaf sumach] (50, 155) (1942–present), Gummi Copal (177) (1762), Lentiscus-leaf sumach [Lentiscus-leaved sumach] (8) (1785), Mastich tree (46) (1879), Mountain sumac [Mountain sumach] (5, 19, 92, 107, 156, 157) (1840–1929), Shining sumac (109, 138) (1923–1949), Smooth sumac [Smooth shumach, Smooth sumach] (5, 156) (1913–1923), Sumac [Sumach, Shumac, Sumack] (181) (~1678), Sumac copalme (French) (8) (1785), Upland sumac [Upland sumach] (5, 97, 156, 157) (1900–1937), Varnish sumac [Varnish sumach] (156) (1923), Wing-rib sumac [Wing-rib sumach] (19) (1840), possibly Quahiutl Patlahoac (Mexico) (177) (1762)

Rhus copallinum **L. var. *latifolia* Engl.** – Winged sumac (50) (present)

Rhus cotinoides **Nutt.** – possibly *Cotinus obovatus* Raf.

Rhus diversiloba **Torr. & Gray** – See *Toxicodendron diversilobum* (Torr. & Gray) Greene

Rhus glabra cismontana – See *Rhus glabra* L.

Rhus glabra **L.** – Čaŋzi (Lakota, yellow wood) (121) (1918?–1970?), Chan-zi (Dakota, yellow-wood) (37) (1919), Haz-ni-hu (Winnebago, water-fruit bush) (37) (1919), Indian salt (92) (1876), Makibûg (Chippewa) (40) (1928), Minbdi-hi (Omaha-Ponca) (37) (1919), Moŋbidse bakoŋ (Osage) (121) (1918?–1970?), Mountain sumac [Mountain sumach] (157, 158) (1900–1929), Nuppikt (Pawnee, sour top) (37) (1919), Pakwan-minš (Chippewa) (105) (1932), Pennsylvania sumac [Pennsylvania sumach] (5, 49, 53, 55, 156, 157, 158) (1898–1929), Red sumac (106) (1930), Scarlet sumac [Scarlet sumach] (5, 85, 93, 95, 106, 107, 156, 157, 158) (1900–1932), Senhalanac [Senhalenac] (5, 74, 156, 158) (1893–1923) Ferrisburgh VA name of Saranac River comes from this, Shoe-make [Shoe make] (5, 73, 158) (1892–1913), Shoemate (35) (1806), Sleek sumac [Sleek sumach] (5, 19, 156, 157, 158) (1840–1929), Smooth Pennsylvania sumac [Smooth Pennsylvanian sumach] (8) (1785), Smooth sumac [Smooth shumach, Smooth sumach] (3, 4, 5, 9, 15, 27, 37, 41, 49, 50, 52, 53, 72, 82, 92, 95, 105, 109, 113, 121, 130, 131, 138, 145, 156, 157, 158, 187) (1770–present), Smooth upland sumac (97) (1937), Smooth-leaf sumac [Smooth leaved sumach] (41) (1770), Staghorn sumac [Staghorn sumach, Stag-horn sumach, Stag's horn sumach, Stag-horn-shumach] (122) (1937), Sumac [Sumach, Shumac, Sumack] (22, 38, 40, 48, 55, 57, 58, 59, 61, 85) (1820–1932), Sumac glabre (French) (8) (1785), Sumac of East Texas (124) (1937), Upland sumac [Upland sumach] (49, 53, 58, 92, 93, 156, 157, 158) (1869–1936), Vinegar tree [Vinegar-tree] (5, 107, 156, 157, 158) (1900–1929), White sumac [White sumach, White shumack] (5, 76, 156, 157, 158) (1896–1929) Southwestern MO, Yellow sumac (138) (1923)

Rhus hirta **(L.) Sudworth** – American sumac (5) (1913), Bastard hemp [Bastard-hemp] (10) (1818), Common sumac [Common sumach] (15) (1895), Cut-leaf sumac (112) (1937), False hemp (19, 92) (1840–1876), Hairy sumac [Hairy sumach] (5, 156) (1913–1923), Moŋbidse xtsi (Osage, real sumac) (121) (1918?–1970?), Staghorn [Stag-horn, Stag's horn] (5, 92, 156) (1876–1923), Stag-horn sumac [Staghorn sumach, Stag-horn sumach, Stag's horn sumach, Stag-horn-shumach] (2, 8, 14, 15, 19, 34, 40, 46, 50, 72, 82, 107, 109, 121, 131, 135, 138, 156, 187) (1785–present), Velvet sumac [Velvet sumach] (5, 92, 156) (1876–1923), Vinegar plant (92) (1876), Vinegar tree [Vinegar-tree] (5, 156) (1913–1923), Virginia sumac [Virginia sumach, Virginian sumach] (5, 14, 34, 107, 156) (1834–1923)

Rhus integrifolia **(Nutt.) Benth. & Hook. f. ex Brewer & S. Wats.** – Lemonade-and-sugar tree [Lemonade and sugar tree] (76) (1896) San Diego, CA, Lemonade-berry (109) (1949), Lentisco (76) (1896) San Diego, CA, Mahogany sumac (106) (1930), Mountain-mahogany [Mountain mahogany, Mountainmahogany] (106) (1930) CA, Serrate-leaf stryphonia [Serrate leaved stryphonia] (20) (1857), Sourberry [Sour-berry, Sour berry] (109) (1949)

Rhus integrifolia **Benth. & Hook.** – See *Rhus integrifolia* (Nutt.) W. H. Brewer & S. Watson

Rhus **L.** – Poison oak [Poison-oak, Poisonoak] (13) (1849), Poison tree [Poison-tree] (13) (1849), Shoe-make [Shoe make] (35) (1806), Shoemate (35) (1806), Skunk cabbage [Skunk-cabbage, Skunkcabbage] (1) (1932), Sumac (French) (8) (1785), Sumac [Sumach, Shumac, Sumack] (1, 4, 7, 8, 10, 13, 14, 15, 10, 50, 82, 93, 106, 138, 155, 158, 190) (~1759–present), Wah'-hah-tūt-se (Hueco Pawnee) (132) (1855)

Rhus lanceolata **(Gray) Britt.** – Dwarf sumac [Dwarf sumach] (124) (1937) TX

Rhus laurina **Nutt.** – See *Malosma laurina* (Nutt.) Nutt. ex Abrams

Rhus michauxi – See *Rhus michauxii* Sarg.

Rhus michauxii **Sargent** – Michaux's poison sumac [Michaux poison sumac] (138) (1923)

Rhus microphylla **Engelm.** – Desert sumac (4) (1986), Little-leaf sumac [Littleleaf sumach] (50, 155) (1942–present), Shawnee-haw (106) (1930)

Rhus ovata **S. Wats.** – Lemonade-and-sugar tree [Lemonade and sugar tree] (76) (1896) San Diego, CA, Lentisco (76) (1896) San Diego, CA, Sugar bush (106, 109) (1930–1949)

Rhus quercifolia **[Steud.]** – See *Toxicodendron pubescens* Mill.

Rhus radicans **L.** – See *Toxicodendron radicans* (L.) Kuntze subsp. *radicans*

Rhus rydbergii **Small.** – See *Toxicodendron rydbergii* (Small ex Rydb.) Greene

Rhus **Tourn.** – See *Rhus* L.

Rhus toxicodendron **var. *radicans*** – See *Toxicodendron radicans* (L.) Kuntze

Rhus trilobata **Nutt.** – Canyon shrub (112) (1937) Neb, Ill-scented sumac [Ill-scented sumach] (109, 122, 156) (1923–1949), Lemita (149) (1904) NM, Lemonade sumac (138) (1923), Low sumac [Low sumach] (113, 130) (1890–1895), Red-fruit sumac [Red-fruited sumac] (157) (1929), Skunk bush [Skunkbush, Skunk-bush] (85, 106, 131, 155, 156) (1899–1942), Skunkbush [Skunk-bush] (85, 106, 131, 155, 156) (1899–1942), Skunk-bush sumac [Skunkbush sumac] (50, 155) (1942–present), Squaw bush [Squawbush, Squaw-bush] (106) (1930), Squawberry [Squaw berry, Squaw-berry] (106) (1930), Stink bush [Stinkbush] (112) (1937), Sweet sumac [Sweet sumach] (101) (1905), Three-leaf sumac [Three-leaved sumac, Three-leaved sumach] (149, 156) (1904–1923)

Rhus trilobata **Nutt. var. *trilobata*** – Aromatic sumac [Aromatic sumach] (3) (1977), Fetid sumac (93) (1936), Fragrant sumac [Fragrant sumach] (108) (1878), Ill-scented sumac [Ill-scented sumach] (5, 65, 97) (1913–1937), Lemita (153) (1913) NM, Skunk bush [Skunkbush, Skunk-bush] (5, 93) (1913–1936), Skunk-bush sumac [Skunkbush sumac] (50) (present), Stinking sumac (65) (1931) OK

Rhus typhina **L.** – See *Rhus hirta* (L.) Sudworth

Rhus typhina **L. var.** *laciniata* **Wood** – See *Rhus hirta* (L.) Sudworth

Rhus typhina **Torner.** – possibly *Rhus typhina* L.

Rhus typhinum – possibly *Rhus typhina* L.

Rhus vernix **L.** – See *Toxicodendron vernix* (L.) Kuntze

Rhus virens **Lindh.** – See *Rhus virens* Lindheimer ex Gray

Rhus virens **Lindheimer ex Gray** – Evergreen sumac (122, 124) (1937) TX, Green sumac (106) (1930), Kinnikinnick [Kinnikinik, Kinnikin-nick, Kinnikinic, Kinnikinnik] (106) (1930)

Rhus-toxicodendron – possibly *Toxicodendron toxicarium* (Salisb.) Gillis

Rhus-toxicodendron radicans – possibly *Toxicodendron radicans* (L.) Kuntze

Rhus-toxicodendron vernix – possibly *Toxicodendron vernix* (L.) Kun-tze

Rhynchosia americana **(Houst. ex P. Mill.) M. C. Metz** – One-leaf bean [Oneleaf bean] (122) (1937)

Rhynchosia americana **Mill.** – See *Rhynchosia americana* (Houst. ex Mill.) M. C. Metz

Rhynchosia difformis **(Ell.) DC.** – Twining dolicholus (5, 97) (1913–1937)

Rhynchosia latifolia **Nutt. ex Torr. & Gray** – Prairie dolicholus (97) (1937), Prairie rhynchosia (5) (1913), Prairie snoutbean (50) (present)

Rhynchosia **Lour.** – Rosary-bean [Rosarybean] (138) (1923)

Rhynchosia phaseoloides **(Sw.) DC.** – Rosary-bean [Rosarybean] (138) (1923)

Rhynchosia precatoria **DC.** – Mexican rosary-bean [Mexican rosary-bean] (138) (1923)

Rhynchosia reniformis **DC.** – Round-leaf rhynchosia [Round-leaved rhynchosia] (5) (1913)

Rhynchosia senna **Gillies ex Hook. var.** *texana* **(Torr. & Gray) M. C. Johnston** – One-leaf bean [One-leafed bean] (124) (1937) TX

Rhynchosia tomentosa **(L.) Hook. & Arn. var.** *tomentosa* – Erect rhynchosia (5) (1913)

Rhynchosida physocalyx **(Gray) Fryxell** – Buffpetal (50) (present)

Rhynchospora alba **(L.) Vahl** – White beaked-rush [White beaked rush] (5) (1913), White beak-rush [White beak rush] (66) (1903)

Rhynchospora capillacea **Torr.** – Beaked rush (85) (1932), Beakrush [Beak rush] (3) (1977), Capillary beaked-rush [Capillary beaked rush] (5) (1913), Needle beaksedge (50) (present), Small's beak-rush [Small's beaked rush, Small beak rush] (5, 66) (1903–1913)

Rhynchospora capitellata **(Michx.) Vahl** – Brownish beak-fern [Brownish beakfern] (50) (present)

Rhynchospora cephalantha **Gray** – Capitate beaked-rush [Capitate beaked rush] (5) (1913), Round-beak sedge [Round beak sedge] (66) (1903)

Rhynchospora colorata **(L.) H. Pfeiffer** – Dichonema (66) (1903), Narrow-leaf dichronema [Narrow-leaved dichronema] (5) (1913), White-top umbrella-grass [White-topped umbrella grass] (124) (1937)

Rhynchospora corniculata **(Lam.) A. Gray** – Beakrush [Beak rush] (156) (1923), Horned beakrush (155) (1942), Horned rush (5, 66, 156) (1903–1923), Short-bristle horned beak-sedge [Shortbristle horned beaksedge] (50) (Present)

Rhynchospora cymosa – See *Rhynchospora glomerata* (L.) Vahl

Rhynchospora fusca **(L.) Ait. f.** – Brown beaked-rush [Brown beaked rush] (5) (1913), Brown beak-rush [Brown beak rush] (66) (1903)

Rhynchospora globularis **(Chapman) Small** – See *Rhynchospora recognita* (Gale) Kral

Rhynchospora glomerata **(L.) Vahl** – Brown bog-rush (187) (1818), Clustered beaked rush (5) (1913), Clustered beaksedge (50) (present), Common beak rush (66) (1903), False bog rush (5, 156) (1913–1923), Grass-like beaked rush (5) (1913), Wrinkled beak-rush [Wrinkled beak rush] (66) (1903)

Rhynchospora gracilenta **Gray** – Slender beaked-rush [Slender beaked rush] (5, 19) (1840–1913), Slender beak-rush (66) (1903)

Rhynchospora harveyi **W. Boott** – Harvey's beaksedge (50) (present)

Rhynchospora inexpansa **(Michx.) Vahl** – Drooping beak rush (66) (1903), Nodding beakrush [Nodding beaked rush] (5) (1913)

Rhynchospora knieskernii **Carey** – Knieskern's beaked rush (5) (1913), Tufted beak-rush [Tufted beak rush] (66) (1903)

Rhynchospora latifolia **(Baldw. ex Ell.) Thomas** – Broad-leaf dichro-nema [Broad-leaved dichronema] (5) (1913)

Rhynchospora macrostachya **Torr. ex Gray** – Clustered rush (66) (1903), Horned rush (3) (1977), Tall horned beak-sedge [Tall horned beaksedge] (50) (present)

Rhynchospora nitens **(Vahl) Gray** – Short-beak bald-rush [Short-beaked bald rush] (5) (1913), Short-beak beaksedge [Shortbeak beaksedge] (50) (present)

Rhynchospora nivea **Boeckl.** – Showy whitetop (50) (Present)

Rhynchospora oligantha **A. Gray** – Few-flower beakrush [Few-flow-ered beaked rush] (5) (1913)

Rhynchospora pallida **M. A. Curtis** – Pale beaked rush (5) (1913)

Rhynchospora recognita **(Gale) Kral** – Globe beaksedge (50) (pres-ent)

Rhynchospora scirpoides **(Torr.) Gray** – Bald rush [Bald-rush] (66, 156) (1903–1923), Long-beak baldrush [Long-beaked bald rush] (5) (1913), Long-beak beaksedge [Longbeak beaksedge] (50) (present)

Rhynchospora torreyana **Gray** – Torrey's beak rush (66) (1903), Tor-rey's beaked rush (5) (1913)

Rhynchospora **Vahl** – Beaked rush (1, 156) (1923–1932), Beakrush [Beak rush] (155) (1942)

Ribes alpinum **L.** – Alpine currant (107, 109) (1919–1949), Mountain currant (109, 138) (1923–1949)

Ribes americanum **Mill.** – American black currant (50, 109 138, 155) (1923–present), Black currant [Black currants] (46, 107) (1649–1919), Blue currant [Blue current] (35) (1806), Chap-ta-haza (Da-kota, beaver berries) (37) (1919), Common black currant (22, 47) (1852–1893), Flowering currant (156) (1923), Groseiller de Pensyl-vanie à fruit noir (French) (8) (1785), Mik-min (Chippewa) (105) (1932), Pennsylvania black currant [Pennsylvanian black currants] (8) (1785), Pezi nuga (Omaha-Ponca, Male gooseberry) (37) (1919), Quinsy-berry [Quinsy berry] (5, 156) (1913–1923), Wild black cur-rant (2, 3, 4, 5, 9, 19, 37, 63, 72, 92, 93, 95, 105, 108, 112, 113, 130, 156) (1840–1986)

Ribes aureum **Pursh** – Buffalo currant [Buffalo currants] (2, 63, 72, 92, 93, 106, 107, 108, 131, 135, 149, 156, 158) (1878–1936), Clove cur-rant (73, 156, 158) (1892–1923), Crandall currant (2) (1895), Flow-ering currant (73, 112, 135, 156, 158) (1892–1937), Gadelier sau-vage (French) (89) (1820), Golden currant [Golden currants] (2, 50, 63, 82, 93, 107, 109, 113, 114, 130, 131, 135, 149, 155, 156, 158) (1890–present), Indian currant [Indian-currant, Indian currants] (35) (1806), Lewis and Clarke's currant (28) (1850), Missouri currant [Missouri currants] (2, 63, 82, 93, 103, 107, 108, 130, 156, 158) (1870–1936), Slender golden currant (112, 138) (1923–1937), Spice currant (156) (1923), Yellow currants (35) (1806)

Ribes aureum **Pursh var.** *villosum* **DC.** – Buffalo currant [Buffalo cur-rants] (3, 4, 5, 109) (1913–1986, Clove currant (5, 155) (1913–1942), Flowering currant (5) (1913), Golden currant [Golden cur-rants] (5, 50, 85, 122, 138) (1913–present), Missouri currant [Missouri currants] (5, 97, 109) (1913–1949)

Ribes bracteosum **Dougl. ex Hook.** – California black currant [Califor-nian black currant] (107) (1919)

Ribes cereum **Dougl.** – Resinous currant (108) (1878), Squaw currant (130) (1895), Wax currant (50, 138, 155) (1923–present), Western red currant (4) (1986), Wild red currant (113) (1890)

Ribes cereum **Dougl. var.** *cereum* – Sticky currant (155) (1942), Wax currant (50) (present)

Ribes cereum **Dougl. var.** *inebrians* **(Lindl.) C. L.Hitchc** – See *Ribes cereum* Dougl. var. *pedicellare* Brewer & S. Wats.

Ribes cereum **Dougl. var.** *pedicellare* **Brewer & S. Wats.** – Western red currant (3) (1977), Whisky currant (50) (present), White-flower currant [White-flowered currant] (5, 93) (1913–1936)

Ribes curvatum **Small** – Georgia gooseberry (138) (1923)

Ribes cynosbati **L.** – Dog bramble (5, 107, 156) (1913–1923), Dog-berry [Dog-berry, Dog berry] (3, 4, 5, 156, 158) (1900–1986), Eastern prickly gooseberry (50) (present), Gousailiers blans (46) (1879), Groseiller à fruit hérisssé (French) (8) (1785), Kauwe-šabu-min (Chippewa, prickly gooseberry) (105) (1932), Pasture gooseberry (138, 155, 156) (1923–1942), Prickly gooseberry (19, 47, 63, 82, 85, 105, 107, 113) (1840–1932), Prickly wild gooseberry (5, 156, 158) (1900–1923), Prickly-fruit gooseberry [Prickly-fruited gooseberry] (46) (1879), Prickly-fruit wild gooseberry [Prickly fruited wild goose-berry] (8) (1785), Smooth gooseberry (9) (1873), Smooth pasture gooseberry (155) (1942), Wild gooseberry (5, 65, 72, 97, 156, 158) (1900–1937)

Ribes cynosbati **L. var.** *inerme* (**Rehd.**) **Bailey** – See *Ribes cynosbati* L.

Ribes glandulosum **Grauer** – Fetid currant (2, 5, 107, 156) (1895–1923), Skunk currant (5, 73, 138, 156) (1892–1923) ME, from odor of fruit, Wabos'odji'bĭk (Chippewa, rabbit leaf) (40) (1928), Wild currant [Wild currants] (40) (1928)

Ribes gossularia – possibly *Ribes uva-crispa* L. var. *sativum* DC.

Ribes gracile **Michx.** – Common wild gooseberry (63, 95) (1899–1911), Gooseberry [Goose berry, Gooseberries] (22, 82) (1893–1930), Illinois gooseberry (76, 156) (1896–1923) KY, Missouri gooseberry (82, 130, 156) (1895–1930), Slender gooseberry (72, 156) (1907–1923), Slender-branch gooseberry [Slender-branched gooseberry] (107) (1919), Snow gooseberry (138) (1923), Šuns-šabu-min (Chippewa, smooth gooseberry) (105) (1932)

Ribes grossularia **L.** – See *Ribes uva-crispa* L. var. *sativum* DC.

Ribes hirtella – See *Ribes hirtellum* Michx.

Ribes hirtellum **Michx.** – Gooseberry [Goose berry, Gooseberries] (103) (1870), Hairy-stem gooseberry [Hairystem gooseberry] (50, 155) (1942–present), Low wild gooseberry (5) (1913), Purple gooseberry (46) (1879)

Ribes hudsonianum **Richards.** – Black currant [Black currants] (85) (1932), Hudson Bay currant (107) (1919), Northern black currant (5, 156) (1913–1923), Quinsy-berry [Quinsy berry] (5, 156) (1913–1923)

Ribes inebrians **Lindl.** – See *Ribes cereum* Dougl. var. *pedicellare* Brewer & S. Wats.

Ribes inerme **Rydb.** – Wine gooseberry (138) (1923)

Ribes irriguum – See *Ribes oxyacanthoides* L. subsp. *irriguum* (Dougl.) Sinnott

Ribes **L.** – Currant [Currants] (2, 4, 7, 10, 50, 82, 93, 106, 109, 138, 155, 156, 158, 184) (1793–present), Currant bush [Currant-bush] (8) (1785), Gooseberry [Goose berry, Gooseberries] (2, 4, 7, 10, 35, 82, 95, 106, 109, 138, 155, 156) (1828–1986), Groseiller (French) (8) (1785), Micidji'mĭnaga'wûnj (Chippewa, fuzzy fruit) (40) (1928), Samita (103) (1870) NM, Wild black currant (190) (~1759), Wild currant [Wild currants] (40, 101, 103) (1870–1928), Wild gooseberry (101) (1905)

Ribes lacustre (**Pers.**) **Poir.** – Lake gooseberry (2) (1895), Lowland gooseberry (130) (1895), Marsh currant (108) (1878), Prickly currant (50, 155) (1942–present), Swamp currant (3, 4, 85, 155) (1932–1986), Swamp gooseberry (2, 5, 19, 107, 130, 156) (1840–1923)

Ribes missouriense **Nutt.** – Haz-ponoponoh' (Winnebago, crunching fruit) (37) (1919), Illinois gooseberry (5) (1913), Missouri gooseberry (3, 4, 5, 50, 72, 85, 138, 155) (1907–present), Pezi (Omaha-Ponca) (37) (1919), Slender gooseberry (5) (1913), Wichagnashka (Dakota Teton) (37) (1919), Wichaknaska (Dakota Yankton) (37) (1919), Wild gooseberry (37) (1919), Wuchah'deshka (Dakota) (37) (1919)

Ribes nigrum **L.** – Black corrans [Blacke corrans] (178) (1526), Black currant [Black currants] (14, 19, 41, 46, 49, 92, 107, 110) (1770–1919), Black garden currant (156) (1923), Blackberry [Black-berry] (156) (1923), Currant tree [Currant-tree] (41) (1770), European black currant (109, 138) (1923–1949), Quinsy-berry [Quinsy berry] (92, 156) (1876–1923)

Ribes nigrum **var.** *pennsylvanicum* **Marshall** – See *Ribes americanum* Mill.

Ribes odoratum **Wendl. f.** – See *Ribes aureum* Pursh var. *villosum* DC.

Ribes oxyacanthoides **L.** – Canadian gooseberry [Canada gooseberry] (50, 155) (1942–present), Groseiller à feuilles d'aube-épine (French) (8) (1785), Hawthorn gooseberry (156, 158) (1900–1923), Mountain wild gooseberry (8) (1785), Northern gooseberry (72) (1907), Smooth gooseberry (19, 130, 156) (1840–1923), Smooth wild gooseberry (107, 158) (1900–1919)

Ribes oxyacanthoides **L. subsp.** *irriguum* (**Dougl.**) **Sinnott** – Mountain-stream gooseberry [Mountain stream gooseberry] (108) (1878)

Ribes oxyacanthoides **L. subsp.** *oxyacanthoides* – Cabo'mĭnaga'wûnj (Chippewa, smooth berry) (40) (1928), Gooseberry [Goose berry, Gooseberries] (40) (1928), Hawthorn (5) (1913), Northern gooseberry (5, 85) (1913–1932), Smooth gooseberry (5) (1913)

Ribes oxyacanthoides **L. subsp.** *setosum* (**Lindl.**) **Sinnott** – Bristly gooseberry (3, 4, 5, 85, 107) (1913–1986), Inland gooseberry (50) (present), Missouri gooseberry (107) (1919), Red-shoot gooseberry [Redshoot gooseberry] (155) (1942), Spiny gooseberry (130) (1895), Western wild gooseberry (95) (1911)

Ribes pinetorum **Greene** – Orange gooseberry (138) (1923)

Ribes recurvatum – See *Ribes nigrum* L.

Ribes rotundifolium **Michx.** – Eastern wild gooseberry (5) (1913), Round-leaf gooseberry [Roundleaf gooseberry] (107, 138) (1919–1923), Smooth gooseberry (5) (1913), Wild gooseberry (19) (1840)

Ribes rubrum **L.** – Castilles (French) (46, 110) (1879–1886), Common currant (109) (1949), Common red currant (47, 138) (1852–1923), Garden currant (85, 109) (1932–1949), Gardes (France) (110) (1886) possibly from gardis "rough, harsh, pungent, or sour", Garnetberry [Garnet-berry, Garnet berry] (92, 156) (1876–1923), Grades (France) (110) (1886), Gradilles (France) (110) (1886), Groseille d'outre mer (French) (46) (1879), Groseillier d'outremer (French "currant from beyond the seas") (46) (1879), Kastilez (Brittany) (110) (1886), Meertrübli (Soleure, Switzerland) (110) (1886), Northern red currant (109) (1949), Raisin de mare (Geneva, Switzerland) (110) (1886), Raisin tree [Raisin-tree, Raisintree] (46, 92, 156) (1876–1923), Red corrans (178) (1526), Red currans (46) (1671) deliberately introduced by English colonists by 1671, Red currant (14, 46, 49, 55, 63, 72, 92, 107, 110, 114) (1879–1922) often spelled as currans in historical documents, Red garden currant (5, 156) (1913–1923), Resp (Swedish) (110) (1886), Ribs (Danish) (110) (1886), Risp (Swedish) (110) (1886), Rissels (156) (1923), Rizzer-berry (156) (1923), Šabu-min (Chippewa) (105) (1932), White corrans (178) (1526), Wild coranies (46) (1617), Wild red currant (105) (1932), Wineberry [Wine berry, Wine-berry] (92, 156) (1876–1923)

Ribes sanguineum **Pursh** – Winter currant (138) (1923)

Ribes sativum **Syme** – See *Ribes rubrum* L.

Ribes setosum **Lindl.** – See *Ribes oxyacanthoides* L. subsp. *setosum* (Lindl.) Sinnott

Ribes speciosum **Pursh** – Fuchsia-flower gooseberry [Fuchsia-flowered gooseberry] (109) (1949)

Ribes triflorum **Willd.** – See *Ribes rotundifolium* Michx.

Ribes triste **Pallas** – American red currant (5, 155) (1913–1942), Cigagwa'tĭgon (Chippewa, skunk-like) (40) (1928), Red currant (40, 50, 85) (1928–present), Swamp currant (3, 4) (1977–1986), Swamp red currant (156) (1923)

Ribes uva-crispa **L.** – Garden gooseberry (72) (1907), Gooseberry [Goose berry, Gooseberries] (110) (1886), Smooth gooseberry (19) (1840)

Ribes uva-crispa **L. var.** *sativum* **DC.** – Berry tree [Berry-tree] (5, 156) (1913–1923), Carberry [Car-berry] (5, 156) (1913–1923), Cultivated gooseberry (82) (1930), Dayberry [Day-berry] (5, 156) (1913–1923), Diuers sorts of Gooseberries (178) (1526), European gooseberry (82, 156) (1923–1930), Fabes (5, 156) (1913–1923) no longer in use by 1923, Fayberry [Fay berry, Fay-berry] (5, 156) (1913–1923), Feaberry [Fea berry, Fea-berry] (5, 110, 156) (1886–1923), Garden gooseberry (156) (1923), Gaskins (156) (1923) no longer in use by 1923, Goggles (156) (1923) no longer in use by 1923, Gooseberry [Goose berry, Gooseberries] (92, 107, 110, 114) (1876–1919),

Groseille à maquereaux (French "mackerel currant") (110) (1886), Honey-blobs [Honey blobs] (5, 156, 157, 158) (1913–1929), Red gooseberry [Red gooseberries] (178) (1526), Teaberry [Tea-berry, Tea berry, Tea-berries] (5, 156) (1913–1923), Wineberry [Wine berry, Wine-berry] (5, 156) (1913–1923), possibly English gooseberry (19, 109) (1840–1949)

Ribes viscidulum **Berger** – See *Ribes cereum* Dougl. var. *cereum*

Ribes vulgare **Lam.** – See *Ribes rubrum* L.

Riccia fluitans **L.** – Forked stem (92) (1876), Forkstems (19) (1840)

Ricciocarpos natans **(L.) Corda** – Floating liverwort (19) (1840)

Richardia africana **[Kunth]** – See *Zantedeschia aethiopica* (L.) Spreng.

Richardia scabra **L.** – Mexican clover (74, 87, 106, 109) (1884–1949), Richardia (174) (1753), White ipecac (92) (1876)

Richardsonia scabra – See *Richardia scabra* L.

Ricinus communis **L.** – Agno casto (Portuguese) (110) (1886) usually refers to Vitex agnus castus, Bofareira (92) (1876), Castor (7) (1828), Castor bean [Castor-bean] (5, 21, 78, 85, 92, 97, 106, 109, 122, 124, 125, 148, 156) (1876–1949), Castor-oil plant [Castor]oil plant, Castor-oil-plant) (5, 10, 19, 85, 92, 107, 109, 110, 125, 156) (1818–1949), Common castor-bean (138) (1923), Figuero inferno (Portuguese) (110) (1886), Girasole (Italian) (110) (1886), Hand-of-God [Hand of God] (178) (1526), Lamourou (West Indies) (110) (1886), Man's-motherwort [Man's motherwort] (5, 156) (1913–1923), Mexican seed [Mexico seed] (5, 92) (1876–1913), Mexican weed [Mexico-weed] (156) (1923), Oil plant (5, 92) (1876–1913), Palma Christi (5, 10, 19, 92, 109, 110, 156) (1840–1949), Palmcristi (7) (1828), Steadfast (156) (1923), Stedfast (5) (1913), Wunderbaum (German) (110) (1886)

Ricinus **L.** – Castor bean [Castor-bean] (138) (1923), Castor-oil plant [Castor]oil plant, Castor-oil-plant) (156) (1923), Palma Christi (167) (1814)

Ridans alternifolius **(L.) Britton** – See *Verbesina alternifolia* (L.) Britton ex Kearney

Rivina humilis **L.** – Inkberry [Ink-berry, Ink berry] (97) (1937) OK, Pigeon-berry [Pigeon berry] (122, 124) (1937) TX, Rivina (138, 174) (1923–1949), Rouge plant [Rouge-plant] (109, 138) (1923–1949)

Rivina tinctaria **Ham. ex G. Don** – See *Rivina humilis* L.

Robertiella robertiana **(L.) Hanks.** – See *Geranium robertianum* L.

Robinia ×*holdtii* **Beissn.** [*neomexicana* × *pseudacacia*] – Holdt's locust [Holdt locust] (138) (1923)

Robinia hispida **L.** – Bristly acacia (5) (1913), Bristly locust or Bristly locust tree (2, 50, 82, 156, 158) (1895–present), Bristly rose-acacia [Bristly rose acacia] (92) (1876), Cacia rose (8) (1785), Honey locust [Honeylocust, Honey-locust] (5, 74, 156) (1893–1923), Moss locust [Moss-locust] (5, 92, 156, 158) (1876–1923), Mossy locust (3) (1977), Rose locust (19) (1840), Rose-acacia [Rose-acacia] (2, 5, 14, 19, 82, 92, 97, 109, 112, 138, 152, 156, 158) (1882–1949), Rose-acacia locust [Roseacacia locust] (155) (1942)

Robinia hispida **L. var. *hispida*** – Pallid locust (155) (1942)

Robinia hispida **L. var. *kelseyi* (Cowell ex Hutchinson) Isely** – Kelsey's locust [Kelsey locust] (138) (1923)

Robinia hispida **var. *nana* (Elliott) DC.** – Rose-colored robinia [Rose coloured robinia, Rose-coloured robinia] (8) (1785)

Robinia kelseyi – See *Robinia hispida* L. var. *kelseyi* (Cowell ex Hutchinson) Isely

Robinia **L.** – Black locust (93) (1936), Faux acacia (French) (8) (1785), Locust or Locust tree (1, 2, 4, 10, 50, 82, 155, 156, 158, 184) (1793–present)

Robinia montana **Bart.** – possibly *Robinia viscosa* Vent. (taxonomic status is unresolved (PL))

Robinia neo-mexicana – See *Robinia neomexicana* Gray

Robinia neomexicana **Gray** – Agarroba (153) (1913) NM, New Mexico black locust [New Mexican black locust] (149, 153) (1904–1919), New Mexico locust [New Mexican locust] (138) (1923)

Robinia neomexicana **Gray var. *neomexicana*** – Western locust (138) (1923)

Robinia neomexicana luxurians – See *Robinia neomexicana* Gray var. *neomexicana*

Robinia pallida **Ashe** – See *Robinia hispida* L. var. *hispida*

Robinia pseudacacia **L.** – See *Robinia pseudoacacia* L.

Robinia pseudoacacia **L.** – Acacia blanc (French) (8) (1785), Acacia with rose-coloured flowers (189) (1767), American locust (46, 187) (1818–1879), Bastard acacia (5, 157, 158) (1900–1929), Black locust (3, 4, 5, 6, 27, 44, 49, 50, 61, 65, 72, 82, 85, 92, 93, 97, 106, 109, 112, 114, 122, 124, 125, 135, 148, 155, 156, 157, 158) (1894–present), Common locust or Common locust tree (2, 6, 82, 138, 157, 158) (1892–1930), Falsche Acazie (German) (158) (1900), Falsche Acazie [Falsche Acacien] (German) (6, 158) (1892–1900), False acacia [False acasia] (2, 5, 6, 14, 19, 49, 63, 82, 93, 106, 107, 156, 157, 158, 187) (1818–1936), Faux acacia (French) (8) (1785), Fevier (French) (17) (1796), Green locust (5, 156) (1913–1923), Honey locust [Honeylocust, Honey-locust] (5, 157, 158) (1900–1929), Locus tree (181) (~1678), Locust or Locust tree (5, 8, 14, 19, 20, 41, 49, 92, 106, 107, 157, 158) (1785–1930), Locust tree of Virginia (189) (1767), North American locust tree (157, 158) (1900–1929), Pea-flower locust [Pea flower locust] (5, 157, 158) (1900–1929), Post locust (5, 156, 157, 158) (1900–1929), Red flowering locust (5) (1913), Robinier (French) (6, 158) (1892–1900), Silver-chain [Silver-chain] (5, 156, 157, 158) (1900–1929), Sweet locust (85) (1932) SD, Sweet-smelling locust (177) (1762), Treenail (6) (1892), White honey flower [White honey-flower] (156) (1923), White laburnum (157, 158) (1900–1929), White locust or White locust tree [White locust-tree] (5, 74, 106, 156, 157, 158, 187) (1818–1929), White-flower robinia [White flowering robinia] (8) (1785), Whya tree (157, 158) (1900–1929), Yellow locust (5, 6, 49, 74, 92, 106, 156, 157, 158) (1876–1930)

Robinia pseudo-acacia **L.** – See *Robinia pseudoacacia* L.

Robinia rosea **Ell.** – See *Robinia hispida* var. *nana* (Elliott) DC.

Robinia viscosa **Vent.** – Clammy locust or Clammy locust tree (2, 5, 19, 46, 92, 109, 138, 156) (1840–1949), Honey locust [Honeylocust, Honey-locust] (5, 156) (1913–1923), Red locust (5, 156) (1913–1923), Rose-acacia [Rose-acacia] (5, 156) (1913–1923), Rose-flower locust [Rose flowering locust] (5, 20) (1857–1913)

Roccella fuciformis **(L.) DC.** – Angola weed (92) (1876)

Roccella tinctoria **DC.** – Archil (92) (1876), Canary archil (92) (1876), Canary weed (92) (1876), Capeweed [Cape weed] (92) (1876), Chickenweed [Chicken weed, Chicken-weed] (92) (1876), Chimneyweed [Chimney weed] (92) (1876), Dyer's lichen [Dyers' lichen] (92) (1876), Lacmus (92) (1876), Litmus (49, 92) (1876–1879), Orchil (92) (1876), Orchilla weed (49, 92) (1876–1898), Tournesol (49) (1898), Turnesole (49) (1898)

Rollinia mucosa **(Jacq.) Baill.** – Sugar-apple [Sugar apple] (107) (1919)

Romneya coulteri **Harvey** – Coulter's canyon-poppy [Coulter canyon-poppy] (138) (1923), Matilija poppy [Matilija-poppy] (74, 109) (1893–1949)

Romneya **Harvey** – Canyon poppy (138) (1923)

Romneya trichocalyx **Eastw.** – Bridal canyon-poppy (138) (1923)

Roripa palustris **(L.) Bess.** – See *Rorippa palustris* (L.) Bess.

Roripa siniata **(Nutt.) A. S. Hitchc.** – See *Rorippa sinuata* (Nutt.) A.S. Hitchc.

Rorippa amphibia **(L.) Bess.** – Watercress [Water-cress, Water cress] (107) (1919)

Rorippa austriaca **(Crantz) Bess.** – Austrian fieldcress (4, 155) (1942–1986), Austrian yellowcress (50) (present)

Rorippa calycina **(Engelm.) Rydb.** – Persistent-sepal yellow-cress [Persistent sepal yellowcress] (50) (present)

Rorippa curvipes **Greene** – Blunt-leaf yellow cress [Blunt-leaved yellow cress, Blunt-leaf yellowcress, Bluntleaf yellowcress] (50) (present)

Rorippa microphylla **(Boenn. ex Reichenb.) Hyl. ex A. & D. Löve** – One-row yellow-cress [Onerow yellowcress] (50) (present)

Rorippa nasturtium-aquaticum **(L.) Hayek** – Berro (158) (1900), Brunnenkresse (German) (158) (1900), Carsous (158) (1900), Common watercress [Common water-cress] (157, 158) (1900–1929), Crashed (5) (1913), Cresson de fontaine (French) (158) (1900), Eker Teng-tongues (German) (158) (1900), Kars (158) (1900), Karse (158) (1900), Water-kers (158) (1900)

Rorippa obtusa (Nutt.) Britton – See *Rorippa teres* (Michx.) R. Stuckey

Rorippa palustris (L.) Bess – Yellow watercress [Yellow water-cress, Yellow water cress] (7, 92, 156, 157, 158) (1828–1929), Yellow woodcress [Yellow wood cress, Yellow wood-cress] (156, 157, 158) (1900–1929), Bell-ragges (157, 158) (1900–1929), Bog marsh cress [Bog marshcress] (155) (1942), Bog yellow cress (4, 50) (1986–present), Marsh watercress [Marsh water-cress, Marsh water cress] (92, 131, 157, 158) (1876–1929), Cresson jaune (French) (17) (1796), Marsh cress (2, 63, 72, 107, 156) (1895–1923)

Rorippa palustris (L.) Bess. subsp. *fernaldiana* (Butters & Abbe) Jonsell – Fernald's yellow-cress [Fernald's yellowcress] (50) (present)

Rorippa palustris (L.) Bess. subsp. *glabra* (Butters & Abbe) R. Stuckey – See *Rorippa palustris* (L.) Bess. subsp. *fernaldiana* (Butters & Abbe) Jonsell

Rorippa palustris (L.) Bess. subsp. *hispida* (Desv.) Jonsell – Hispid yellow-cress [Hispid yellow cress, Hispid yellowcress] (5, 50, 131) (1899–present)

Rorippa palustris (L.) Bess. subsp. *palustris* – Marsh cress (80) (1913), Marsh watercress [Marsh water-cress, Marsh water cress] (5, 85, 97) (1913–1937), Yellow watercress [Yellow water-cress, Yellow water cress] (5, 120) (1913–1938), Yellow woodcress [Yellow wood cress, Yellow wood-cress] (5) (1913)

Rorippa Scop. – Marsh cress (1) (1932), Yellow watercress [Yellow water-cress, Yellow water cress] (1, 93) (1932–1936), Yellowcress [Yellow cress, Yellow-cress] (4, 50) (1986–present)

Rorippa sessiliflora (Nutt.) A. S. Hitchc. – Sessile-flower cress [Sessile-flowered cress, Sessile-flowered cress] (5, 72, 97) (1907–1937) IA OK, Stalkless yellow-cress [Stalkless yellowcress] (50) (present), Yellowcress [Yellow cress, Yellow-cress] (3, 4, 145) (1897–1986)

Rorippa sinuata (Nutt.) A. S. Hitchc. – Creeping yellow cress [Creeping yellowcress] (3, 4) (1977–1986), Spreading yellow-cress [Spreading yellow cress] (3, 4, 5, 50, 72, 97, 131) (1899–present), Teng grass (35) (1806), Yellowcress [Yellow cress, Yellow-cress] (85, 145) (1897–1932)

Rorippa sphaerocarpa (Gray) Britt. – Round-fruit cress [Round-fruited cress] (5, 97) (1913–1937)

Rorippa sylvestris (L.) Bess. – Creeping yellow cress [Creeping yellowcress] (50) (present), Creeping yellow water cress (5) (1913), Woodcress [Wood-cress] (156) (1923), Yellowcress [Yellow cress, Yellow-cress] (5, 15, 156) (1895–1923), possibly Creeping water rocket (10) (1818)

Rorippa tenerrima Greene – Modoc yellowcress (50) (present)

Rorippa teres (Michx.) R. Stuckey – Blunt-leaf cress [Blunt leaved cress] (72) (1907), Blunt-leaf yellow cress [Blunt-leaved yellow cress, Blunt-leaf yellowcress, Bluntleaf yellowcress] (5, 97) (1913–1937), Obtuse fieldcress (155) (1942), Southern marsh yellow-cress [Southern marsh yellowcress] (50) (present), Walter's cress (97) (1937)

Rosa (Tourn.) L. – See *Rosa* L.

Rosa ×*alba* L. [*arvensis* × *gallica*] – White rose (19, 92, 178) (1526–1876)

Rosa ×*damascena* Mill. [*gallica* × *moschata*] – Attar of roses (57) (1917) source, Damask rose [Damaske rose] (19, 109, 138) (1840–1949)

Rosa ×*harisonii* Rivers [*foetida* × *spinosissima*] – Harison's yellow rose [Harisons yellow rose] (109) (1949) originated in garden of Rev Harison of New York City about 1830

Rosa acicularis bourgeauiana – See *Rosa acicularis* Lindl. subsp. *sayi* (Schwein.) W. H. Lewis

Rosa acicularis Lindl. – Prickly rose (5, 50, 85, 93, 131, 138, 155) (1899–present), Prickly wild rose (4) (1986), Say's rose (130) (1895)

Rosa acicularis Lindl. subsp. *sayi* (Schwein.) W. H. Lewis – Bourgeau prickly rose (155) (1942), Bourgeau rose (138) (1923), Prickly rose (72) (1907), Prickly wild rose (3) (1977)

Rosa adenosepala Woot. & Standl. – See *Rosa woodsii* Lindl. var. *woodsii*

Rosa arkansana Porter – Arkansas rose (72, 85, 138, 155) (1923–1942), Arkansas rose [Arkansa rose] (72) (1907), Bi'jikiwi'ginīg (Chippewa, cattle rose) (40) (1928), Prairie rose (50, 113, 130) (1890–present), Prairie wild rose (3, 4, 98) (1926–1986), Wild rose (40, 114, 127, 145) (1894–1933)

Rosa arkansana Porter var. *arkansana* – Prairie rose (50) (present)

Rosa arkansana Porter var. *suffulta* (Greene) Cockerell – Arkansas rose (5, 93) (1913–1936), Onzhinzhintka (Dakota) (37) (1919) Onzhinzhintka-hu (Rose bush), Pahatu (Pawnee, red) (37) (1919), Prairie rose (37, 50, 82) (1919–present), Sunshine rose (155) (1942), Swamp rose [Swamp-rose] (187) (1818), Wazhide (Omaha-Ponca) (37) (1919), Wild prairie rose (80) (1913), Wild rose (37, 80) (1913–1919)

Rosa blanda Aiton – Damask rose [Damaske rose] (46) (1617), Early white rose (108) (1878), Early wild rose (2, 5) (1895–1913), Meadow rose (5, 85, 93, 131, 138, 155, 158) (1899–1942), Pale rose (158) (1900), Pale wild rose (5) (1913), Prairie rose (47) (1852), Smooth rose (5, 50, 93, 130, 158) (1895–present), Smooth wild rose (3, 4, 72, 82, 127) (1907–1986), Swamp rose [Swamp-rose] (130) (1895) SD

Rosa blanda Aiton var. *blanda* – Smooth rose (50) (present)

Rosa bracteata Wendl. – Evergreen rose (5) (1913), Macartney's rose [Macartney rose] (109, 122, 138) (1923–1949) introduced to England from China by Lord Macartney about 1793

Rosa californica Cham. & Schlecht. – California wild rose (138) (1923)

Rosa canina L. – Bedeguar (5, 92) (1876–1913), Bird brier (5) (1913), Bramble brier (5) (1913), Brere rose (5) (1913), Brier rose (107) (1919), Canker blooms (Shakespeare) (5) (1913), Canker rose (5) (1913), Cat whin (5) (1913), Cynosbata (49) (1898), Dog brier [Dog-brier, Dog-brier] (107, 138) (1919–1923), Dog rose (5, 19, 49, 55, 57, 58, 92, 109, 156) (1840–1949), Dog thorn (5) (1913), Eglantine gall (92) (1876), Hedge-peak [Hedge peak] (5) (1913), Hep tree (92) (1876), Hip fruit (92) (1876), Hip rose (5) (1913), Hip tree [Hip-tree] (5, 49, 58, 92) (1869–1913), Hips (92) (1876), Horse bramble (5) (1913), Lawyers (5) (1913), Soldiers (5) (1913), Sweetbrier [Sweetbriar, Sweet briar, Sweet brier, Sweet bryar, Sweet bryer] (177) (1762), Wild brier (5, 58) (1869–1913), Wild rose (49) (1898)

Rosa carolina L. – Carolina rose (50, 155, 156) (1923–present), False eglantine (possibly) (46) (1649), Pasture rose (4) (1986), Swamp rose [Swamp-rose] (2, 5, 19, 86, 135, 156, 158) (1840–1923), Wild rose (5) (1913)

Rosa carolina L. var. *carolina* – Large-flower Carolina rose [Large-flower carolina rose] (155) (1942), Rehder's Carolina rose [Rehder Carolina rose] (155) (1942), Subserrulata rose (155) (1942)

Rosa carolina L. var. *grandiflora* (Baker) Rehd. – See *Rosa carolina* L. var. *carolina*

Rosa centifolia L. – Cabbage rose (55, 57, 92, 107, 109, 138) (1876–1949), Great Holand Rose (178) (1526), Great red rose (178) (1526), Hundred-leaf rose [Hundred leaf rose, Hundred-leaved rose] (19, 57, 92) (1840–1917), Pale rose (49, 57, 92) (1876–1917), Red Prouince rose (178) (1526)

Rosa chinensis Jacq. – Bengal rose (109) (1949), China rose (109) (1949), Chinese rose (138) (1923)

Rosa cinnamomea L. – Cinnamon rose (19, 82, 107, 109, 138, 178) (1526–1949), Double cinnamon rose (178) (1526), Kitchen rose (73) (1892) Boston MA, Primrose (76) (1896) Paris ME, Wild rose (103) (1870)

Rosa damascena Miller – See *Rosa* ×*damascena* Mill. [*gallica* × *moschata*]

Rosa eglanteria L. – Bedeguar (5) (1913), Common sweetbrier [Common Sweete brier] (178) (1526), Double sweetbrier [Double sweete brier] (178) (1526), Eglantere (158) (1900), Eglantine [Eglentyne] (19, 46, 63, 92, 107, 109, 156, 158, 179) (1526–1949) Shakespeare and Spenser, Eglantine rose (5, 92, 158) (1876–1913), Hip brier (5, 158) (1900–1913), Hip rose (5) (1913), Kitchen rose (5, 158) (1900–1913), Primrose (5) (1913), Sweet breer (158) (1900), Sweetbrier [Sweetbriar, Sweet briar, Sweet brier, Sweet bryar, Sweet bryer] (3, 5, 19, 46, 63, 72, 92, 107, 109, 138, 156, 158) (1671–1977), Sweetbrier rose [Sweetbrier rose] (50, 155) (1942–present), Wild brier (92) (1876)

Rosa fendleri Crépin – See *Rosa woodsii* Lindl. var. *woodsii*

Rosa foliolosa Nutt. – Leafy rose (4, 155) (1942–1986), White prairie rose (4, 50) (1986–present)

Rosa gallica L. – Common rose (19) (1840), French rose (19, 49, 58, 109, 138) (1840–1949), Provence rose (49, 55) (1911–1922), Provins rose (92) (1876), Red rose (49, 57, 58, 92, 178) (1526–1917)

Rosa gratissima – See *Rosa woodsii* Lindl. var. *gratissima* (Greene) Cole

Rosa gymnocarpa Nutt. – Bald-hip rose (138) (1923)

Rosa harisonii Rivers – See *Rosa ×harisonii* Rivers [*foetida* × *spinosissima*]

Rosa L. – Brere (179) (1526), Kenukatía-minš (Chippewa) (105) (1932), Ogĭni'mĭnaga'wûnj (Chippewa, rose berries) (40) (1928), Rose (1, 4, 7, 10, 35, 40, 50, 82, 83, 92, 106, 109, 138, 155, 156, 158, 167, 179, 184) (1526–present), Rose bush (108) (1878), Rosier (French) (8) (1785), Thorn (179) (1526), Wild rose (101, 105) (1905–1932)

Rosa laevigata Michx. – Cherokee rose (19, 106, 109, 122, 138, 156) (1840–1949), Jamaica buckthorn (156) (1923)

Rosa macdougali – See *Rosa nutkana* K. Presl var. *hispida* Fern.

Rosa macounii Greene – See *Rosa woodsii* Lindl. var. *woodsii*

Rosa minutifolia Engelm. – Parry's Mexican rose (76) (1896)

Rosa mohavensis – See *Rosa woodsii* Lindl. var. *glabrata* (Parish) Cole

Rosa moschata J. Herrm. – Musk rose (19, 109, 138) (1840–1949), possibly Double musk rose (178) (1526), possibly Single muske Rose (178) (1526), possibly Spanish musk rose [Spanish muske rose] (178) (1526)

Rosa multiflora cathayensis – See *Rosa multiflora* Thunb. ex Murray

Rosa multiflora Thunb. ex Murray – Cathay rose (138) (1923), Crimson rambler (82) (1930), Japanese rose [Japan rose] (4, 19, 138, 155) (1840–1986), Many-flower rose [Many-flowering rose] (135) (1910), Multiflora rose (4, 50) (1986–present), National rose (138) (1923)

Rosa multiflora var. *cathayensis* Rehder & E. H. Wilson) – See *Rosa multiflora* Thunb. ex Murray

Rosa nitida Willd. – Bristly rose (138) (1923), Northeastern rose (5) (1913), Shining rose (5) (1913), Wild rose (5) (1913)

Rosa nutkana – See *Rosa nutkana* K. Presl

Rosa nutkana hispida – See *Rosa nutkana* K. Presl var. *hispida* Fern.

Rosa nutkana K. Presl – Nutka rose (138) (1923)

Rosa nutkana K. Presl var. *hispida* Fern. – Bristly Nutka rose (138) (1923), Macdougal's rose [Macdougal rose] (138) (1923)

Rosa odorata (Andr.) Sweet – Tea rose (109, 138) (1923–1949) from odor

Rosa odorata Sweet. – See *Rosa odorata* (Andr.) Sweet

Rosa palustris Marsh. – Rosier des marais (French) (8) (1785), Small wild rose [Small wild-rose] (187) (1818), Swamp Pennsylvania rose [Swamp Pennsylvanian rose] (8) (1785), Swamp rose [Swamp-rose] (106, 109, 138) (1923–1949)

Rosa pimpinellifolia L. – See *Rosa spinosissima* L.

Rosa pinetorum Heller – Pinewoods rose (138) (1923)

Rosa pratincola Greene – See *Rosa arkansana* Porter var. *suffulta* (Greene) Cockerell

Rosa rubrifolia Vill. – Red-leaf rose [Redleaf rose] (138) (1923)

Rosa rugosa Thunb. – Japanese rose [Japan rose] (82, 135) (1910–1930), Mau (107) (1919), Rugosa rose (138) (1923), Turkestan rose (107) (1919)

Rosa sayi Schwein. – See *Rosa acicularis* Lindl. subsp. *sayi* (Schwein.) W.H. Lewis

Rosa setigera Michx. – Climbing prairie rose (3, 113) (1890–1977), Climbing rose (4, 5, 50, 72, 82, 93, 156) (1907–present), Climbing

wild rose (2) (1895), Michigan rose (5, 156) (1913–1923), Prairie queen rose (82) (1930), Prairie rose (4, 5, 93, 97, 109, 135, 138, 155, 156) (1910–1986), Prairie wild rose (2) (1895), Rose blush (5, 76) (1896–1913) Southwestern MO

Rosa setigera Michx. var. *tomentosa* Torr. & Gray – Fuzzy prairie rose (155) (1942)

Rosa spinosissima L. – Burnet rose (19, 107) (1840–1919), Pimpernel rose [Pimpernell rose] (178) (1526), Scotch rose (19, 109, 138) (1840–1949)

Rosa spithamea S. Wats. var. *sonomensis* (Greene) Jepson – Sonoma rose (138) (1923)

Rosa stellata Woot. – New Mexico rose [New Mexican rose] (138) (1923)

Rosa subserrulata Rydb. – See *Rosa carolina* L. var. *carolina*

Rosa suffulta Greene – See *Rosa arkansana* Porter var. *suffulta* (Greene) Cockerell

Rosa virginiana Mill. – Dwarf wild rose (5) (1913), Low rose (5, 97) (1913–1937) OK, Pasture rose (5, 97) (1913–1937) OK

Rosa wichuraiana Crépin – Wichurian rose (138) (1923)

Rosa woodsi fendleri – See *Rosa woodsii* Lindl. var. *woodsii*

Rosa woodsii Lindl. – Low rose (113, 130) (1890–1895), Western wild rose (3, 4, 127) (1933–1986), Woods' rose [Wood's rose, Woods rose, Wood rose] (5, 50, 72, 97, 131, 138, 155) (1899–present)

Rosa woodsii Lindl. var. *glabrata* (Parish) Cole – Mohave rose (138) (1923)

Rosa woodsii Lindl. var. *gratissima* (Greene) Cole – Sweetleaf rose (138) (1923)

Rosa woodsii Lindl. var. *woodsii* – Fendler's rose [Fendler rose] (130, 138) (1895–1923), Macoun's rose [Macoun rose] (138, 155) (1923–1942), Pecos rose (155) (1942), Tall rose (113) (1890), Woods' rose [Wood's rose, Woods rose, Wood rose] (50) (present)

Rosa xanthina Lindl. – Hugo rose (109) (1949), Hugonis rose (112, 138) (1923–1937), Korean rose (138) (1923)

Rosmarinus L. – Rosemary (109, 138) (1923–1949)

Rosmarinus officinalis L. – Old-man [Old man] (106) (1930), Rosemarie (178) (1526), Rosemary (19, 46, 55, 57, 58, 106, 107, 138, 179) (1526–1930)

Rotala L. – Rotala (50, 155, 158) (1900–present)

Rotala ramosior (L.) Koehne – Lowland rotala (50) (present), Rotala (72, 155) (1907–1942), Tooth-cup [Tooth cup, Tooth-cup] (3, 4, 5, 93, 97) (1913–1986)

Rottboellia dimidiata (L.) L. f. – See *Stenotaphrum secundatum* (Walt.) Kuntze

Rottboellia L. f. – Joint-tail [Jointtail] (155) (1942)

Rottlera tinctoria – See *Mallotus philippensis* (Lam.) Muell.-Arg.

Roubieva multifida (L.) Moq – See *Chenopodium multifidum* L.

Roystonea borinquena O. F. Cook – Palma real (106) (1930), Royal palm (106) (1930)

Roystonea elata (Bartr.) F. Harper – Cuban royal palm (109) (1949), Florida royal palm [Floridian royal palm] (109) (1949), Royal palm (138) (1923)

Roystonea elata F. Harper – See *Roystonea elata* (Bartr.) F. Harper

Roystonea O. F. Cook – Royal palm (138) (1923)

Roystonea regia O. F. Cook – See *Roystonea elata* (Bartr.) F. Harper

Rubacer parviflorum (Nutt.) Rydb. – See *Rubus parviflorus* Nutt.

Rubacer Rydb. – See *Rubus* L.

Rubia brownei Michx. – See *Galium hispidulum* Michx.

Rubia L. – Madder (7, 10) (1818–1828)

Rubia peregrina Walt. – See *Galium hispidulum* Michx.

Rubia tinctoria L. – Dyer's madder (49, 92) (1876–1898), Madder (19, 49, 57, 92, 109, 110, 179, 193) (1526–1949), Red madder (178) (1526), Rubia (57) (1917), Warence (179) (1526)

Rubigo alnea (Pers.) Link – Blight (92) (1876)

Rubus (Tourn.) L. – See *Rubus* L.

Rubus aboriginum Rydb. – Garden dewberry (50) (present)

Rubus allegheniensis Porter – Allegheny blackberry (50, 138, 155) (1923–present), Blackberry [Black-berry] (82, 93, 156) (1923–1936),

Cloudberry [Cloud berry, Cloud-berry, Clowde-berry] (156) (1923), Common blackberry (4) (1986), Finger-berry [Finger berry] (156) (1923), Mountain blackberry (5, 82, 97, 158) (1913–1937), Sow-teat blackberry (3) (1977), Tetéga-min (Chippewa) (105) (1932), Thimbleberry [Thimble berry, Thimble-berry] (156) (1923), Wild blackberry (62, 105) (1912–1932)

Rubus allegheniensis Porter var. *allegheniensis* – Blackberry [Blackberry] (72, 95, 157) (1900–1929)

Rubus andrewsianus **Blanch.** – Erect blackberry (82) (1930)

Rubus arcticus **L.** – See *Rubus ostryifolius* Rydb.

Rubus argutus **Link.** – See *Rubus ostryifolius* Rydb.

Rubus baileyanus **Britton** – Dewberry [Dew-berry, Dew berry] (82) (1930)

Rubus caesius **L.** – Dewberry [Dew-berry, Dew berry] (14) (1882)

Rubus canadensis **L.** – Bearberry [Bear berry, Bear-berry] (156) (1923), Creeping blackberry (49) (1898), Dewberry [Dew-berry, Dew berry] (2, 46, 58, 63, 92, 103, 105, 107) (1671–1932), Low blackberry [Low black berry] (2, 49, 53, 58, 107) (1869–1922), Millspaugh's blackberry (5, 72) (1907–1913), October-berry (156) (1923), Ronce de Canada (French) (8) (1785), Šingábi-min (Chippewa) (105) (1932), Smooth-stalk Canadian bramble [Smooth stalked Canadian bramble] (8) (1785), Thornless blackberry (2, 138) (1895–1923), Trailing blackberry (107) (1919)

Rubus canadensis var. *invisus* **Bailey** – See *Rubus invisus* (Bailey) Britt.

Rubus canadensis var. *roribaccus* **Bailey** – See *Rubus roribaccus* (Bailey) Rydb.

Rubus chamaemorus **L.** – Baked-apple berry [Baked-apple-berry] (5, 73, 156) (1892–1923) Grand Mana ID, Black-apple [Black apple] (73, 107) (1892–1919) NB, Grand Mana ID, Cloudberry [Cloud berry, Cloud-berry, Clowde-berry] (5, 7, 14, 46, 106, 107, 156) (1671–1930), Dwarf mulberry [Dwarfe Mulberries] (178) (1526), Heath mulberry (156) (1923), Knotberry [Knot-berry, Knot berry, Knotberries] (5, 6, 46, 92, 178) (1526–1913), Low mulberry (156) (1923), Molka (107) (1919), Mountain bramble (5, 156) (1913–1923), Mountain raspberry (5, 156) (1913–1923), Salmon-berry [Salmonberry, Salmon berry] (107) (1919), Yellow-berry [Yellow berry] (107) (1919)

Rubus coesius – See *Rubus caesius* L.

Rubus cuneifolius **Pursh** – Brierberry [Brier berry, Brier-berry] (5, 156) (1913–1923), Knee-high blackberry (5, 156) (1913–1923), Low blackberry [Low black berry] (5) (1913), Sand blackberry (2, 5, 76, 107, 138, 156) (1895–1923), Sand raspberry (72) (1907)

Rubus deliciosus **Torr.** – Boulder raspberry (4, 112, 138, 155) (1923–1986), Delicious raspberry (50) (present), Rocky Mountain flowering raspberry (135) (1910), Rocky Mountain raspberry (107) (1919), Thimbleberry [Thimble berry, Thimble-berry] (4) (1986)

Rubus ellipticus **Sm.** – Yellow Himalayan raspberry (138) (1923)

Rubus enslenii **Tratt.** – See *Rubus flagellaris* Willd.

Rubus flagellaris **Willd.** – Bailey's blackberry (5, 97) (1913–1937), Dewberry [Dew-berry, Dew berry] (3, 5, 62, 72, 97, 107, 156, 187) (1818–1977), Low running blackberry (5, 62) (1912–1913), Northern dewberry (4, 50, 135, 138, 155) (1910–present), Small-leaf blackberry [Small-leaved blackberry] (187) (1818), Southern dewberry [Southern dew berry] (2) (1895), Blackberry [Black-berry] (46, 52, 53, 59, 82, 92, 107, 113, 114) (1671–1930) IA, Cloudberry [Cloud berry, Cloud-berry, Clowde-berry] (92) (1876), Cloud-berry root [Cloud berry root] (92) (1876), Common blackberry (63, 96, 103) (1870–1899), Common blackberry bush [Common blackberry-bush] (186, 187) (1814–1818), Finger-berry [Finger berry] (74) (1893) Ann Arbor MI, Haarige Himbeere (186) (1814), Hairy American bramble (186) (1814), Rubus (59) (1911), Running blackberry (156, 186) (1814–1923), Sow-tit [Sow tit, Sow-tit] (74) (1893) CT NH, Standing blackberry (186) (1814), Thimbleberry [Thimble berry, Thimble-berry] (74) (1893)

Rubus frondosus **Bigelow** – Blackberry [Black-berry] (40) (1928), Leafy raspberry (19) (1840), Leafy-flower blackberry [Leafy-flowered blackberry] (5) (1913), Yankee blackberry (50, 155) (1942–present)

Rubus hancinianus **Bailey** – Windswept-prairie dewberry [Windswept prairie dewberry] (50) (present)

Rubus hispidus **L.** – American dewberry bush (8) (1785), Hispid blackberry (5) (1913), Ronce velue (French) (8) (1785), Running blackberry (107) (1919), Running swamp blackberry (2, 5) (1895–1913), Swamp blackberry (107) (1919), Swamp dewberry (138) (1923)

Rubus idaeus **L.** – American red raspberry (50) (present), Arnberry (158) (1900), European raspberry (107, 138, 158) (1900–1923), European red raspberry (1) (1932), Framboise (French) (107, 158) (1900–1919), Frambuesa (Spanish) (158) (1900), Garden raspberry (19) (1840), Hainberry (158) (1900), Hindberry [Hind-berries] (92, 158) (1876–1900), Raspberry (49, 53, 57) (1898–1922), Raspis bush (178) (1526), Red raspberry (155) (1942), Sanguesa (Spanish) (158) (1900), Sivven (158) (1900)

Rubus idaeus **L. subsp.** *sachalinensis* **(Levi.) Focke** – See *Rubus idaeus* L. subsp. *strigosus* (Michx.) Focke

Rubus idaeus **L. subsp.** *strigosus* **(Michx.) Focke** – Agthamungi (37) (1919), American raspberry (46) (1879), American red raspberry (1, 93, 155, 156, 158) (1900–1942), Aparu (Pawnee, berry) (37) (1919), Common red raspberry (138) (1923), Cultivated red raspberry (135) (1910), Flowering raspberry (47) (1852), Framboysses (46) (1879), Gray-leaf red raspberry [Grayleaf red raspberry] (50) (present), Mīs'kominaga'wûnj (Chippewa, having reddish berries) (40) (1928), Mountain red raspberry (85) (1932), Mulberry [Molberye] (5, 156) (1913–1923), Purple wild raspberry (5, 158) (1900–1913), Purple-cane raspberry [Purplecane raspberry] (138, 155) (1923–1942), Raspberry (92, 103, 114) (1870–1894), Red raspberry (4, 19, 40, 49, 58, 92, 101, 107, 113, 130, 131, 156) (1840–1986), Red-fruit raspberry [Red-fruited raspberry] (187) (1818), Rocky Mountain red raspberry (1) (1932), Sku-min (Chippewa) (105) (1932), Takanhecha (Dakota) (37) (1919) Takanhecha-hu (raspberry bush), Wild raspberry (37, 153) (1913–1919)

Rubus idaeus var. *melanolasius* **(Dieck) R. J. Davis** – See *Rubus idaeus* L. subsp. *strigosus* (Michx.) Focke

Rubus illecebrosus **Focke** – Strawberry raspberry (138) (1923)

Rubus invisus **(Bailey) Britt.** – Bartel parent (2) (1895), Ithaca dewberry (97) (1937)

Rubus invisus **Bailey** – See *Rubus invisus* (Bailey) Britt.

Rubus **L.** – Blackberry [Black-berry] (1, 4, 50, 106, 138, 155, 158, 181) (1814–present), Bramble (7, 8, 10, 82, 156, 184) (1785–1930), Cloudberry [Cloud berry, Cloud-berry, Clowde-berry] (1) (1932), Dewberry [Dew-berry, Dew berry] (4, 138, 155) (1923–1986), Flowering raspberry (1) (1932), Raspberry (1, 4, 106, 138, 155) (1923–1986), Raspberry bush (8) (1785), Ronce (French) (8) (1785), Salmonberry [Salmon berry] (1) (1932), Thimbleberry [Thimble berry, Thimble-berry] (1, 106) (1930–1932), Wild raspberry (93) (1936)

Rubus leucodermis **Dougl. ex Torr. & Gray** – White-bark raspberry [Whitebark raspberry] (138) (1923)

Rubus linkianus **Ser.** – Link blackberry (138) (1923)

Rubus millspaughii **Britton.** – See *Rubus canadensis* L.

Rubus mollior **Bailey** – Soft-leaf blackberry [Softleaf blackberry] (50) (present)

Rubus neglectus **Peck** – See *Rubus idaeus* L. subsp. *strigosus* (Michx.) Focke

Rubus nigricans **Rydb.** – See *Rubus setosus* Bigelow

Rubus nigrobaccus **Bailey** – See *Rubus allegheniensis* Porter var. *allegheniensis*

Rubus occidentalis **L.** – Agthamungi (37) (1919), American blackberry bush (41) (1770), American bramble (41) (1770), American raspberry (8, 12) (1785–1820), Aparu (Pawnee, berry) (37) (1919), Black raspberry [Black-raspberry] (1, 3, 4, 5, 9, 19, 40, 46, 47, 50, 63, 72, 82, 85, 93, 97, 107, 113, 130, 131, 156, 157, 158, 187) (1818–present), Blackberry [Black-berry] (5, 74, 157, 158) (1893–1929), Blackcap [Black cap, Black-cap] (1, 2, 5, 74, 93, 107, 156, 157, 158) (1893–1937), Blackcap raspberry (155) (1942), Common black raspberry (135) (1910), Common blackcap (138) (1923), Common raspberry (96) (1891), Hindberry [Hind-berries] (46) (1622), Kadem-sku-min

(Chippewa) (105) (1932), Oda'tagago'mĭnaga'wûnj (Chippewa) (40) (1928), Purple raspberry (5) (1913), Raspberry (114) (1894), Ronce d'Occident (8) (1785), Scotch caps (5) (1913), Takanhecha (Dakota) (37) (1919) Takanhecha-hu (raspberry bush), Thimbleberry [Thimble berry, Thimble-berry] (2, 5, 22, 19, 46, 92, 107, 156, 187) (1818–1923), Wild black raspberry (95, 105) (1911–1932), Wild purple raspberry (157, 158) (1900–1929), Wild raspberry (37, 106) (1919–1930)

Rubus odoratus L. – Canadian raspberry (5) (1913), Flowering raspberry (19, 47, 107, 138, 156) (1840–1923), Flowering-mulberry [Flowering mulberry] (46) (1879), Framboisier odorant de Virginie (French) (8) (1785), Mulberry [Molberye] (2, 5, 46, 73, 76, 156) (1879–1923), Purple-flower raspberry [Purple-flowered raspberry, Purple-flowering raspberry, Purple flowering raspberry] (2, 5, 82, 105, 156) (1895–1932), Rose-flower raspberry [Rose flowering raspberry, Rose-flowering raspberry] (5, 187) (1818–1913), Scotch caps (5, 73) (1892–1913) Hemmingford Quebec, Sweet-scented rubus (187) (1818), Thimbleberry [Thimble berry, Thimble-berry] (5, 74, 156) (1893–1923), Tut'kag-minan (Chippewa) (105) (1932), Virginia raspberry (5, 156) (1913–1923), Virginia rose-flower raspberry [Virginian rose-flowering raspberry] (8) (1785), Wild mulberry (19) (1840)

Rubus ostryifolius Rydb. – Arctic bramble (5, 107, 155) (1913–1942), Argutus (82) (1930) IA, Cloudberry [Cloud berry, Cloudberry, Clowde-berry] (5) (1913), Common blackberry (135) (1910), Crimson bramble (107) (1919), High-brush blackberry [Highbrush blackberry] (155) (1942), Tall blackberry (5) (1913), Thimbleberry [Thimble berry, Thimble-berry] (5) (1913)

Rubus parviflorus Nutt. – Flowering raspberry (106) (1930), Japanese raspberry (155) (1942), Salmonberry [Salmon berry, Salmon-berry] (5, 82, 85, 106, 130, 131, 158) (1895–1932), Thimbleberry [Thimble berry, Thimble-berry] (3, 4, 5, 50, 85, 106, 153, 158) (1900–present), White-flower raspberry [White flowering raspberry, White-flowering raspberry, White-flowered raspberry] (5, 138, 156, 158) (1913–1923)

Rubus pensilvanicus Poir. – Bramble (3) (1977), Pennsylvania blackberry (50) (present)

Rubus pergratus Blanch. – Upland blackberry (50) (present)

Rubus plicatifolius Blanch. – Plait-leaf dewberry [plaitleaf dewberry] (50) (present)

Rubus procumbens Muhl. – See *Rubus flagellaris* Willd.

Rubus pubescens Raf. – Creeping blackberry (4) (1986), Dwarf blackberry (4, 85) (1932–1986), Dwarf raspberry (3) (1977), Dwarf red blackberry (50, 155) (1942–present)

Rubus pubescens Raf. var. *pubescens* – Bogberry [Bog-berry] (156) (1923), Dewberry [Dew-berry, Dew berry] (5, 73) (1892–1913), Dwarf raspberry (2, 63, 72, 107, 131, 156) (1895–1907), Dwarf red blackberry (5, 50) (1913–present), Eyeberry [Eye-berry] (105) (1932), Mulberry [Molberye] (5, 73) (1892–1913) Washington Co ME, NB, Pigeon-berry [Pigeon berry] (5, 76, 156) (1896–1923) Western US, no longer in use by 1923, Plum bogberry [Plum bog berry] (5) (1913), Plumbog (73) (1892) Newfoundland, Running raspberry (5, 76, 156) (1896–1923) Oxford Co. ME, Skižgu-min (Chippewa, eyeberry) (105) (1932), Swamp raspberry (156) (1923), Swampberry [Swamp berry, Swamp-berry] (5, 73, 156) (1892–1923) Newfoundland

Rubus roribaccus (Bailey) Rydb. – Lucretia dewberry (2, 50) (1895–present)

Rubus rosaefolius Sm. – See *Rubus rosifolius* Sm.

Rubus rosifolius Sm. – Brier rose (92) (1876), Flowering bramble (92) (1876), Mauritius raspberry (107) (1919) Rose-leaf raspberry [Roseleaf raspberry] (138) (1923)

Rubus rubrisetus Rydb. – See *Rubus trivialis* Michx.

Rubus saxatilis L. – Brier herb (19, 92) (1840–1876), Rock blackberry (19, 92) (1840–1876), Roebuck-berry [Roebuck berry] (107) (1919), Stone berry (107) (1919)

Rubus setosus Bigelow – Bristly blackberry (5) (1913), Bristly raspberry (19) (1840)

Rubus spectabilis Pursh – Salmon-berry [Salmonberry, Salmon berry] (76, 103, 106, 107, 160, 161) (1857–1930)

Rubus strigosus Michx. – See *Rubus idaeus* L. subsp. *strigosus* (Michx.) Focke

Rubus triflorus Richards – See *Rubus pubescens* Raf. var. *pubescens*

Rubus trivialis Michx. – Blackberry [Black-berry] (46) (1879), Creeping blackberry (19, 92) (1840–1876), Dewberry [Dew-berry, Dew berry] (19, 124) (1840–1937), Low blackberry [Low black berry] (92) (1876), Low-bush blackberry [Low bush blackberry] (5, 49, 53, 107) (1898–1922), Red-bristle dewberry [Red-bristled dewberry] (97) (1937), Southern dewberry [Southern dew berry] (4, 5, 49, 50, 97, 138, 155) (1898–present), Southern low blackberry (2) (1895)

Rubus ulmifolius Schott – Elm-leaf blackberry [Elmleaf blackberry] (138) (1923)

Rubus ursinus Cham. & Schlecht. – Salmon-berry [Salmonberry, Salmon berry] (107) (1919), Western blackberry (107) (1919)

Rubus villosus Aiton – See *Rubus flagellaris* Willd.

Rubus villosus var. *humifusa* Torr. & Gray – See *Rubus baileyanus* Britton

Rubus villosus var. *montanus* Prter. – See *Rubus allegheniensis* Porter

Rubus vitifolius Cham. & Schlecht. – California dewberry (138) (1923)

Rudbeckia alismaefolia T. & G. – See *Rudbeckia grandiflora* (D. Don) J. F. Gmel. ex DC. var. *alismifolia* (Torr. & Gray) Cronq.

Rudbeckia amplexicaulis Vahl – See *Dracopis amplexicaulis* (Vahl.) Cass.

Rudbeckia angustifolia [L.] – See *Coreopsis angustifolia* L.

Rudbeckia bicolor Nutt. – Pinewoods coneflower (138) (1923), Two-color coneflower [Two-colored cone-flower] (97) (1937)

Rudbeckia brittonii Small – See *Rudbeckia hirta* L. var. *hirta*

Rudbeckia californica Gray – California coneflower (138) (1923), Coneflower [Cone-flower, Cone flower] (138) (1923)

Rudbeckia columnaris Nutt. – See *Ratibida columnifera* (Nutt.) Wood & Standl.

Rudbeckia columnaris Pursh – See *Ratibida columnifera* (Nutt.) Wood & Standl.

Rudbeckia fulgida Aiton – Ahawĭ akă'tă' (Cherokee, deer eye) (102) (1886), Brilliant coneflower [Brilliant cone-flower] (5, 86) (1878–1913), Coneflower [Cone-flower, Cone flower] (102) (1886), Orange coneflower [Orange cone-flower] (5, 138) (1913–1923)

Rudbeckia fulgida Aiton var. *speciosa* (Wenderoth) Perdue – Showy coneflower [Showy cone-flower] (5, 138) (1913–1923)

Rudbeckia fulgida Aiton var. *umbrosa* (C. L. Boynt. & Beadle) Cronq. – Woodland coneflower [Woodland cone-flower] (5) (1913)

Rudbeckia grandiflora (D. Don) J. F. Gmel. ex DC. – Large-flower coneflower [Large-flowered cone-flower] (5, 97, 122) (1913–1937), Rough coneflower (3, 4, 50) (1977–present)

Rudbeckia grandiflora (D. Don) J. F. Gmel. ex DC. var. *alismifolia* (Torr. & Gray) Cronq. – Clasping-leaf brown-eyed Susan [Clasping leaf brown-eyed-Susan] (97) (1937), Coneflower [Cone-flower, Cone flower] (97) (1937)

Rudbeckia grandiflora (Sweet) DC. – See *Rudbeckia grandiflora* (D. Don) J. F. Gmel. ex DC.

Rudbeckia hirta L. – Black-eyed Susan [Blackeyed Susan] (3, 4, 5, 50, 62, 63, 72, 73, 76, 80, 82, 85, 93, 95, 97, 105, 122, 127, 131, 138, 155, 156, 157, 158) (1892–present), Brown daisy [Brown-daisy] (5, 75, 156, 157, 158) (1894–1929) Concord MA, Brown-Betty [Brown Betty] (5, 75, 156, 158) (1900–1923) Passiac, NJ, no longer in use by 1923, Brown-eyed Susan [Browneyed Susan, Brown-eyed-Susan, Browneyedsusan] (5, 76, 156, 157, 158) (1896–1929), Bull's-eye daisy [Bull's eye daisy, Bullseye daisy] (156) (1923), Bull's-eyes [Bull's eyes, Bullseye, Bulls-eyes] (76) (1896) Paris ME, Coneflower [Cone-flower, Cone flower] (45, 80, 148) (1896–1939), Darkey-head [Darkey head] (5, 62) (1912–1913), English bull's-eye [English bull's eye, English bullseye] (5, 76, 157, 156, 158) (1896–1929) York Co. ME, Golden Jerusalem (5, 73, 156, 158) (1892–1923) NH, no longer in use by 1923, Ox-eye daisy [Oxeye daisy,

Rudbeckia hirta L. var. *hirta*   SCIENTIFIC NAMES INDEX

Oxeyedaisy, Ox-eyed daisy] (75, 76, 158) (1894–1900), Poorland daisy [Poor-land daisy] (5) (1913), Wézawab-gonik (Chippewa, yellow flower) (105) (1932), Yellow ox-eye daisy (5, 156) (1913–1923), Yellow-daisy [Yellow daisy, Yellow daisies] (5, 62, 73, 156, 157, 158) (1892–1929)

Rudbeckia hirta L. var. *hirta* – Britton's coneflower [Britton's cone flower] (5) (1913), California coneflower (5) (1913)

Rudbeckia hirta L. var. *pulcherrima* Farw. – Black-eyed Susan [Blackeyed Susan] (50, 109) (1949–present), Yellow-daisy [Yellow daisy, Yellow daisies] (109) (1949)

Rudbeckia L. – Coneflower [Cone-flower, Cone flower] (1, 2, 4, 50, 82, 93, 109, 138, 155, 156, 158) (1895–present), Dwarf sunflower [Dwarf sun-flower] (167) (1814), Goldenglow [Golden glow, Golden-glow] (1) (1932)

Rudbeckia laciniata L. – Conedisk [Cone disk, Cone-disk] (92, 57) (1876–1900), Cone-disk sunflower (156, 158) (1900–1923), Coneflower [Cone-flower, Cone flower] (40, 46, 57, 58, 82, 95, 157) (1869–1930), Cut-leaf coneflower [Cutleaf coneflower] (50, 138, 155) (1923–present), Gi' zĭso'bûgons' (Chippewa, sun, little leaf) (40) (1928), Gi'zûswe'bigwa'ĭs (Chippewa, it is scattering) (40) (1928), Goldenglow [Golden glow, Golden-glow] (3, 4, 5, 125, 148, 156, 157, 158) (1900–1986), Green-head coneflower [Green-headed cone-flower, Green-headed coneflower, Green-headed cone flower] (5, 62, 97, 131, 156, 157, 158) (1899–1937), Jagged-leaf rudbeckia [Jagged-leaved rudbeckia] (187) (1818), Sunflower [Sun-flower] (157) (1929), Tall coneflower [Tall cone-flower, Tall cone flower, Tall cone-flower] (5, 62, 72, 85, 92, 93, 97, 126, 127, 156, 157, 158) (1876–1937), Thimble-weed [Thimble weed, Thimble-weed] (5, 48, 57, 58, 92, 156, 157, 158) (1869–1929), Wild golden-glow [Wild golden glow] (127) (1933) ND

Rudbeckia laciniata L. var. *laciniata* – Cut-leaf coneflower [Cutleaf coneflower] (50) (present)

Rudbeckia maxima Nutt. – Great coneflower [Great cone-flower] (5, 97, 122, 124, 138) (1913–1937)

Rudbeckia occidentalis Nutt. – Western coneflower (148) (1939)

Rudbeckia pinnata Vent. – See *Ratibida pinnata* (Vent.) Barnh.

Rudbeckia purpurea L. – See *Echinacea purpurea* (L.) Moench

Rudbeckia serotina Nutt. – See *Rudbeckia hirta* L. var. *pulcherrima* Farw.

Rudbeckia speciosa Wenderoth – See *Rudbeckia fulgida* Aiton var. *speciosa* (Wenderoth) Perdue

Rudbeckia subtomentosa Pursh – Sweet coneflower [Sweet cone-flower] (3, 4, 5, 50, 72, 97, 109, 121, 122, 138, 155) (1907–present), Yellow-daisy [Yellow daisy, Yellow daisies] (82) (1930), Žahiu (Osage) (121) (1918?–1970?)

Rudbeckia triloba L. – Black-eyed Susan [Blackeyed Susan] (82) (1930) IA, Brown-eyed Susan [Browneyed Susan, Brown-eyed-Susan, Browneyedsusan] (3, 4, 5, 50, 63, 109, 138, 155, 156, 158) (1899–present), Coneflower [Cone-flower, Cone flower] (82) (1930), Thin-leaf coneflower [Thinleaf coneflower, Thin-leaved cone-flower] (5, 62, 72, 97, 122, 156, 158) (1892–1937), Three-lobe rudbeckia [Three-lobed rudbeckia] (156) (1923)

Rudbeckia umbrosa Boynton & Beadle – See *Rudbeckia fulgida* Aiton var. *umbrosa* (C. L. Boynt. & Beadle) Cronq.

Ruella tuberosa – See *Ruellia tuberosa* L.

Ruellia (Plumier) L. – See *Ruellia* L.

Ruellia brevifolia (Pohl) C. Ezcurra – Red-spray ruellia [Redspray ruellia] (138) (1923)

Ruellia caroliniensis (J. F. Gmel.) Steud. (possibly) – Roella (183) (~1756)

Ruellia caroliniensis (J. F. Gmel.) Steud. subsp. *caroliniensis* var. *caroliniensis* – Slender hairy ruellia (5, 122) (1913–1937)

Ruellia ciliosa Pursh – See *Ruellia humilis* Nutt.

Ruellia ciliosa Pursh var. *humilis* Britton – See *Ruellia humilis* Nutt.

Ruellia drummondiana (Nees) Gray – Wild blue petunia (124) (1937) TX

Ruellia drummondii (Nees) Gray – See *Ruellia drummondiana* (Nees) Gray

Ruellia humilis Nutt. – East Tennessee pinkroot [East Tennessee pink-root] (157) (1929), Fringe-leaf ruellia [Fringeleaf ruellia] (3, 4) (1977–1986), Fringe-leaf wild petunia [Fringeleaf wild petunia] (50) (present), Hairy ruellia (5, 72, 93, 97, 122, 124, 157) (1900–1937), Long-tube ruellia [Long-tubed ruellia] (5, 86, 93, 157) (1878–1936), Tennessee pinkroot (64) (1907), Wild petunia (156, 157) (1923–1929)

Ruellia L. – Ruellia (1, 138, 155) (1923–1942), Wild petunia (50, 93) (1936–present)

Ruellia nudiflora (Engelm. & Gray) Urban – Tall ruellia (124) (1937)

Ruellia parviflora (Nees) Britton – See *Ruellia caroliniensis* (J.F. Gmel.) Steud. subsp. *caroliniensis* var. *caroliniensis*

Ruellia pedunculata Torr. ex Gray – Stalked ruellia (5, 97, 122, 138) (1913–1937)

Ruellia strepens L. – Limestone ruellia (3, 4, 155) (1942–1986), Limestone wild petunia (50) (present), Ruel (19) (1840), Short-tube ruellia [Short-tubed ruellia] (5) (1913), Smooth ruellia (5, 72, 97, 122, 124) (1907–1937)

Ruellia tuberosa L. – Many-root [Many root] (92) (1876)

Rulac negundo – See *Acer negundo* L.

Rumex ×acutus L. [*crispus* × *obtusifolius*] – Common dock (187) (1818)

Rumex acetosa L. – Cock sorrel (5, 156) (1913–1923), Common sorrel [Common-sorrel] (92) (1876), English sorrel (5, 156) (1913–1923), Garden sorrel (19, 92, 109, 156) (1840–1949), Green sorrel (5, 156) (1913–1923), Greensauce [Green-sauce, Green sauce] (5) (1913), Meadow sorrel (5, 92, 156) (1876–1923) WV, Redshank [Red shank, Red-shank, Red shanks, Redshanks, Red-shanks] (5, 156) (1913–1923), Sharp dock (5, 156) (1913–1923), Sheep sorrel [Sheep-sorrel, Sheep's sorrel] (45) (1896), Sorrel [Sorell, Sorrell] (46, 49, 107, 179) (1526–1919), Sour dock (1, 5, 107, 156) (1913–1932), Sour-grass [Sourgrass, Sour grass] (5, 156) (1913–1923)

Rumex acetosella L. – Bitter dock (40) (1928), Common field sorrel (41) (1770), Common sheep sorrel (50) (present), Common sorrel [Common-sorrel] (157, 158) (1900–1929), Cow sorrel (5, 73, 156, 157, 158) (1892–1929) Miramichi NB, pronounced cow-serls, Field sorrel (5, 19, 62, 156, 157, 158) (1840–1929), Gentleman's sorrrel (5, 73, 156, 158) (1892–1923) Cambridge MA, Greensauce [Green-sauce, Green sauce] (156, 158) (1900–1923), Horse-sorrel [Horse sorrel] (5, 6, 62, 73, 75, 80, 156, 157, 158) (1898–1929), Mountain sorrel (5, 156, 157, 158) (1900–1929), Oza'widji'bĭk (Chippewa [yellow root) (40) (1928), Ranty-tanty (156, 158) (1900–1923), Red sorrel (5, 21, 62, 75, 93, 148, 156) (1893–1936), Red-top sorrel (156, 157, 158) (1900–1929), Redweed [Red-weed, Red weed] (5, 75, 156, 157, 158) (1900–1929) WV, Sheep sorrel [Sheep-sorrel] (1, 3, 4, 5, 19, 48, 56, 58, 61, 62, 72, 73, 80, 85, 92, 97, 106, 122, 125, 131, 145, 148, 155, 156, 157, 158) (1869–1986), Sorrel [Sorell, Sorrell] (12, 46, 106, 157) (1821–1930), Sorrel dock (93) (1936), Sour dock (5, 93, 95, 156, 158) (1900–1936), Sour-grass [Sourgrass, Sour grass] (5, 75, 156, 157, 158) (1894–1929) Sulphur Grove OH, Sourleaf [Sour-leaf, Sour leaf] (156) (1923), Sour-leek [Sour leak, Sour leek] (5, 156, 158) (1900–1923), Sourweed [Sour weed] (62) (1912), Toad sorrel [Toad's sorrel] (5, 73, 156, 158) (1892–1923) Stratham NH, Wood sorrel [Wood-sorrel, Woodsorrel] (5, 93, 156) (1913–1936)

Rumex acutus Sm. – See *Rumex ×acutus* L. [*crispus* × *obtusifolius*]

Rumex alpinus L. – Bastard rhubarb [Bastard rubarbe] (178) (1526), Monk's-rhubarb [Monk's rhubarb, Munks rubarbe] (92, 178) (1526–1876), Mountain-rhubarb [Mountain rhubarb] (92, 107) (1876–1919)

Rumex altissimus Wood – Dock [Docke] (21) (1893), Pale dock (3, 4, 5, 50, 145, 156) (1897–present), Peach-leaf dock [Peachleaf dock, Peach-leaved dock] (5, 80, 93, 122, 131, 156) (1899–1937), Smooth dock (80) (1913), Taku šašala hu iječeča (Lakota, smartweed-like plant) (121) (1918?–1970?), Tall dock (5, 93, 156) (1913–1936), Water dock (46, 121) (1879–1981)

Rumex aquaticus L. – See *Rumex orbiculatus* Gray

Rumex aquaticus L. var. *fenestratus* (Greene) Dorn – Sheep sorrel [Sheep-sorrel] (35) (1806), Western dock (3, 4, 5, 50, 72, 85, 155) (1907–present)

Rumex conglomeratus Murr. – Clustered dock (5) (1913), Smaller green dock (5) (1913)

Rumex crispus L. – Coffe-weed (156) (1923), Curled dock (1, 5, 6, 56, 62, 64, 69, 72, 77, 80, 92, 93, 97, 107, 125, 131, 145, 156, 157, 158, 187) (1818–1937), Curly dock (3, 4, 50, 58, 98, 155) (1869–present), Curly-leaf dock [Curly-leaved dock] (85, 122) (1932–1937), Dock [Docke] (19, 56) (1840–1901), Garden patience (6) (1892), Ginoje'wûkûn (Chippewa, pike plant) (40) (1928), Krauser Ampfer (German) (6) (1892), Narrow dock (5, 6, 64, 69, 77, 92, 93, 156, 157, 158) (1892–1936), Oza'widji'bĭk (Chippewa [yellow root]) (40) (1928), Patience Friseé (French) (6) (1892), Rumex (64) (1907), Sharp-point dock [Sharp-pointed dock] (46) (1671) accidentally introduced by 1671, Shiakipi (Dakota) (37) (1919), Sorrel [Sorell, Sorrell] (41) (1770), Sour dock (5, 37, 62, 64, 69, 80, 92, 156, 157, 158) (1876–1929), Yellow dock (5, 6, 40, 48, 49, 52, 53, 57, 58, 61, 62, 64, 69, 80, 92, 97, 156, 157, 158) (1869–1987)

Rumex divaricatus Thuillier – See *Rumex conglomeratus* Murr.

Rumex geyeri Trel. – See *Rumex paucifolius* Nutt.

Rumex hastatulus Baldw. – Dwarf dock (97) (1937), Engelmann's dock (122) (1937), Engelmann's sorrel (5) (1913), Heart-wing sorrel [Heartwing sorrel] (3, 4, 50, 155) (1942–present)

Rumex hymenosepalus Torr. – Canaigre (37, 57, 107, 109, 122, 124, 138, 155, 158) (1900–1955), Canaigre dock (50) (present), Kahts-pirakari or kahts-pilakari (Pawnee, medicine with many children) (37) (1919), Wild pie-plant (158) (1900), Wild rhubarb [Wild-rhubarb] (4, 109) (1949–1986)

Rumex L. – Dock [Docke] (1, 2, 4, 7, 10, 50, 93, 101, 103, 109, 138, 155, 156, 158, 167, 179, 184) (1526–present), Reed dock [Reed docke] (179) (1526), Sorrel [Sorell, Sorrell] (1, 2, 4, 93, 109, 138, 156, 190) (~1759–1986), Sour dock (101) (1905), Yerba colorado (103) (1870) AZ

Rumex longifolius DC. – Dooryard dock (50) (present), Yard dock (4) (1986)

Rumex maritimus L. – Golden dock (1, 3, 4, 5, 50, 72, 85, 93, 98, 131, 155, 156) (1899–present)

Rumex maritimus L. var. *fueginus* (Phil.) Dusen – See *Rumex maritimus* L.

Rumex mexicanus Meisn. – See *Rumex salicifolius* Weinm. var. *mexicanus* (Meisn.) A. S. Hitchc

Rumex obtusifolius L. – Bitter dock (3, 4, 5, 6, 50, 58, 62, 64, 69, 80, 93, 97, 122, 145, 155, 156, 157, 158) (1869–present), Bluntleaf dock [Blunt leaf dock, Blunt leaved dock, Blunt-leaved dock] (5, 6, 49, 58, 64, 69, 92, 156, 157, 158) (1869–1929), Broad-leaf dock [Broad-leaved dock] (5, 62, 64, 69, 72, 92, 93, 97, 156, 157, 158) (1872–1937), Butter dock [Butter-dock] (5, 64, 156, 157, 158) (1900–1929) leaves used for wrapping butter, Celery-seed [Celery seed] (5, 156, 157, 158) (1900–1929), Common dock (64, 69, 157, 158) (1900–1929), Fiddle dock (157) (1929), Grindwurz (German) (6) (1892), Poison dock (77) (1898) Sulphur Grove OH, Red-vein dock [Red veined dock, Red-veined dock] (80) (1913), Sour dock (77) (1898), Western dock (131) (1899), Wild patience (92) (1876)

Rumex occidentalis S. Wats. – See *Rumex aquaticus* L. var. *fenestratus* (Greene) Dorn

Rumex orbiculatus Gray – Great water dock [Great water-dock, Great-water dock] (3, 4, 49, 92) (1876–1986), Greater water dock (50) (present), Herba britannica (174) (1753), Pond dock (155) (1942), Water dock (19) (1840)

Rumex orbiculatus Gray var. *borealis* Rech. f. – Greater water dock (50) (present)

Rumex orbiculatus Gray var. *orbiculatus* – Greater water dock (50) (present)

Rumex pallidus Bigelow – Large-tubercle dock [Large-tubercled dock] (5) (1913), White dock (19, 156) (1840–1923)

Rumex patienca – See *Rumex patientia* L.

Rumex patientia L. – Garden dock (19) (1840), Garden patience (5, 92, 107, 156, 158) (1876–1923), Herb patience (107, 109) (1919–1949), Monk's-rhubarb [Monk's rhubarb, Munks rubarbe] (5, 107, 156, 158) (1900–1923), Passions (5, 92, 156, 158) (1876–1923) no longer in use by 1923, Patience (1, 19, 46, 92) (1671–1932) cultivated by English colonists by 1671, Patience dock (3, 4, 5, 50, 72, 97, 107, 138, 145, 155, 156, 158) (1897–present), Patientia (107) (1640), Spinach dock [Spinach-dock] (109) (1949)

Rumex paucifolius Nutt. – Mountain dock (101) (1905) MT

Rumex persicarioides L. – See *Rumex maritimus* L.

Rumex pulcher L. – Fiddle dock (5, 122, 156) (1913–1937)

Rumex salicifolius Weinm. – Narrow dock (35) (1806), Pale dock (131) (1899), White dock (2) (1895), Willow dock (50, 155) (1942–present), Willow-leaf dock [Willow leaved dock] (72) (1907)

Rumex salicifolius Weinm. var. *mexicanus* (Meisn.) A. S. Hitchc – Mexican dock (50, 155) (1942–present), Narrow-leaf dock [Narrowleaf dock, Narrow-leaved dock] (85) (1932), Pale dock (5, 93) (1913–1936), White dock (5, 93) (1913–1936), Willow-leaf dock [Willow-leaved dock] (3, 4, 5, 93) (1913–1986)

Rumex sanguineus L. – Bloodwort [Blood wort, Blood-wort] (5, 46, 107) (1671–1919), Bloody dock (5, 10) (1818–1913), Bloody-vein dock [Bloody-veined dock] (107) (1919), Olcott's root [Olcott root] (5, 19, 92) (1840–1913), Red-vein dock [Red veined dock, Red-veined dock] (5, 72) (1907–1913)

Rumex stenophyllus Ledeb. – Narrow-leaf dock [Narrowleaf dock, Narrow-leaved dock] (50) (present)

Rumex venosus Pursh – Pink-flower dock [Pink-flowered dock] (127) (1933), Showy dock (98) (1926), Sour dock (28, 98) (1850–1926), Sour greens (1) (1932), Veiny dock [Veined dock] (3, 5, 50, 93, 97, 131, 155) (1913–present), Wild begonia (1, 4, 98) (1926–1986), Wild hydrangea (1) (1932), Winged dock (5, 85, 93, 97) (1913–1937)

Rumex verticillata – See *Rumex verticillatus* L.

Rumex verticillatus L. – Swamp dock (2, 5, 50, 58, 72, 97, 122, 155, 156) (1869–present), Water dock (3, 4) (1977–1986)

Rumohra adiantiformis (G. Forst.) Ching – Leather fern [Leatherfern] (138) (1923)

Ruppia cirrhosa (Petag.) Grande – Ditch-grass [Ditch grass, Ditchgrass] (157) (1929), Spiral ditch-grass [Spiral ditchgrass] (50) (present), Tassel pondweed [Tassel-pond weed] (157) (1929), Tassel-pond weed (157) (1929), Western ruppia (5, 10, 85, 131) (1818–1932)

Ruppia L. – Ditch-grass [Ditch grass, Ditchgrass] (1, 158) (1900–1932), Widgeonweed (50, 155) (1942–present)

Ruppia maritima L. – Ditch-grass [Ditch grass, Ditchgrass] (3, 92, 97, 156, 158) (1900–1977), Sea teasel-grass (5) (1913), Sea-grass [Sea grass] (5, 156, 158) (1900–1923), Tassel pond-grass (158) (1900), Tassel pondweed [Tassel-pond weed] (5, 156, 158) (1900–1923), Tassel-grass [Tassel grass] (5, 156, 158) (1900–1923), Widgeon-grass [Widgeongrass, Widgeon grass] (50, 155, 156) (1923–present), Zherbes (156) (1923)

Ruppia occidentalis S. Wats. – See *Ruppia cirrhosa* (Petag.) Grande

Russelia equisetiformis Schlecht. & Cham. – Coral plant [Coral-plant] (109) (1949), Fountain plant [Fountain-plant] (109) (1949), Honduras coralblow (138) (1923)

Russelia Jacq. – Coralblow [Coral-blow] (109, 138) (1923–1949)

Russelia juncea – See *Russelia equisetiformis* Schlecht. & Cham.

Ruta graveolens L. – Common rue (7, 109, 138) (1828–1949), Countryman's-treacle [Countrymans' treacle, Country-man's treacle] (92, 156) (1898–1923), Garden rue (49, 53) (1898–1922), Herb-of-grace [Herb of grace, Herb-o'-grace] (14, 92, 107, 156) (1876–1923), Rew (46) (1671) cultivated by English colonists by 1671, Rue (14, 19, 53, 55, 57, 61, 92, 107, 156) (1840–1923), Rue vulgaire (French) (7) (1828), Ruta (57) (1917)

Ruta L. – Rue (109, 138) (1923–1949)

Rutosma texana Gray – See *Thamnosma texana* (Gray) Torr.

Rynchospora alba (L.) Vahl – See *Rhynchospora alba* (L.) Vahl

Rynchospora axillaris (Lam.) Britton – See *Rhynchospora cephalantha* Gray

Rynchospora cymosa Ell. – See *Rhynchospora glomerata* (L.) Vahl

Rynchospora fusca (L.) Ait. – See *Rhynchospora fusca* (L.) Ait. f.

Rynchospora glomerata (L.) Vahl – See *Rhynchospora glomerata* (L.) Vahl

Rynchospora gracilenta A. Gray – See *Rhynchospora gracilenta* Gray

Rynchospora inexpansa (Michx.) Vahl – See *Rhynchospora inexpansa* (Michx.) Vahl

Rynchospora knieskernii Carey – See *Rhynchospora knieskernii* Carey

Rynchospora oligantha A. Gray – See *Rhynchospora oligantha* A. Gray

Rynchospora pallida M.A. Curtis – See *Rhynchospora pallida* M. A. Curtis

Rynchospora smallii Britton – See *Rhynchospora capillacea* Torr.

Rynchospora torreyana A. Gray – See *Rhynchospora torreyana* Gray

Rynchospora Vahl – See *Rhynchospora* Vahl

Rhynchospora alba
(J. Kops, 1844)

S

Sabal Adans. – Latanier (7) (1828), Palmetto (2, 106, 138) (1895–1930), Palmetto palm (109) (1949), Sand palm (7) (1828), Small fan-palm (10) (1818), possibly Fan-palmetto (167) (1814)

Sabal deeringiana Small – See *Sabal minor* (Jacq.) Pers.

Sabal etonia Swingle ex Nash – Scrub palmetto (106, 138) (1923–1930)

Sabal exul – See *Sabal mexicana* Mart.

Sabal glabra Sarg., non Mill. – See *Sabal minor* (Jacq.) Pers.

Sabal mexicana Mart. – Texas palm (124) (1937) TX, Texas palmetto [Texan palmetto] (109, 122, 138) (1923–1949), Victoria palmetto (138) (1923)

Sabal minor (Jacq.) Pers. – Bluestem [Blue-stem, Blue stem] (106) (1930), Blue-stem palmetto [Bluestem palmetto] (138) (1923), Bush palmetto (109) (1949), Dwarf palmetto (2, 50, 97) (1895–present), Palmetto (122) (1937), Small palmetto (12) (1819)

Sabal palmetto (Walt.) Lodd. ex J. A. & J. H. Schultes – Blackburn's palmetto [Blackburn palmetto] (138) (1923), Cabbage palm (182) (1791), Cabbage palmetto (2, 106) (1895–1930), Cabbage tree (182) (1791), Common palmetto (109) (1949), Great cabbage palm (182) (1791), Hispaniolan palmetto (109) (1949), Palm tree [Palm trees] (92) (1876), Palmetto (92) (1876), Palmetto palm (107) (1919), Palmito tree (107) (1613)

Sabal texana Becc. – See *Sabal mexicana* Mart.

Sabal umbraculifera Mart. – See *Sabal palmetto* (Walt.) Lodd. ex J. A. & J. H. Schultes

Sabatia Adans. – American centaury (2, 5, 19, 156) (1840–1923), Marsh pink (158) (1900), Rose-gentian [Rosegentian, Rose gentian] (138, 155) (1923–1942)

Sabatia angularis (L.) Pursh – American centaury (57, 58, 92, 156, 158, 186) (1814–1923), American red centaury (158) (1900), Angular centaury (7, 49, 61) (1828–1898), Angular-stalk sabbatia [Angular-stalked sabbatia] (186) (1814), Bitter-bloom [Bitter bloom] (5, 7, 92, 156, 158) (1828–1923), Bitter-clover [Bitter clover] (5, 92, 156, 158) (1876–1923), Centaurée americaine (French) (158) (1900), Centaurée anguleuse (French) (7) (1828), Centaury (186, 187) (1814–1818), Centory (186) (1814), Centry (186, 187) (1814–1818), Eckige Chironie (German) (186) (1814), Eyebright [Eye-bright, Eye bright] (92) (1876), Pinkbloom [Pink bloom, Pink bloom] (5, 75, 156, 158) (1894–1923) WV, Red centaury (92) (1876), Rose-gentian [Rosegentian, Rose gentian] (156) (1923), Rose-pink [Rose pink] (3, 4, 5, 50, 7, 49, 92, 122, 124, 156, 158) (1876–present), Square-stem rose-gentian [Squarestem rosegentian] (155) (1942), Square-stem sabbatia [Square-stemmed sabbatia] (5, 97, 156, 158) (1900–1937), Texas star (77) (1898), Wild succory (7, 92) (1828–1876), possibly Angular-stem American centaury [Angular stemmed American centaury] (42) (1814)

Sabatia brachiata Ell. – Narrow-leaf sabbatia [Narrow-leaved sabbatia] (5) (1913)

Sabatia brevifolia Raf. – Branching sabbatia (5) (1913), Elliot's sabbatia (5) (1913), Quinine flower (5, 57) (1913–1917)

Sabatia calycina (Lam.) Heller – Coast sabbatia (5, 122) (1913–1937)

Sabatia campanulata (L.) Torr. – Bell-flower chironia [Bell flowered chironia] (42) (1814), Slender marsh pink (5, 156) (1913–1923)

Sabatia campestris Nutt. – American centaury (48) (1882) KS, Meadow pink [Meadow-pink] (156) (1923), Prairie gentian [Prairiegentian] (122) (1937), Prairie rose-gentian [Prairie rosegentian, Prairie rose gentian] (3, 4, 138, 155) (1923–1986), Prairie sabbatia (5, 97, 156) (1913–1937), Texas star (50, 156) (1923–present)

Sabatia chloroides Pursh – Chlora-like chironia [Chlora like chironia] (42) (1814), Many-flower chironia [Many flowered chironia] (42) (1814)

Sabatia difformis (L.) Druce – Felwort [Fellwort] (10) (1818), Lance-leaf sabbatia [Lance-leaved sabbatia] (5) (1913)

Sabatia dodecandra (L.) Britton, Sterns & Poggenb. – Large marsh pink (5) (1913), Marsh rose-gentian [Marsh rosegentian] (138) (1923)

Sabatia elliottii Steud. – See *Sabatia brevifolia* Raf.

Sabatia kennedyana Fern. – New England rose-gentian [New England rosegentian] (138) (1923)

Sabatia lanceolata Torr.& Gray. – See *Sabatia difformis* (L.) Druce

Sabatia paniculata (Michx.) Pursh – See *Sabatia brevifolia* Raf.

Sabatia paniculata Pursh – See *Sabatia brevifolia* Raf.

Sabatia stellaris Pursh – Marsh pink (5, 122, 156) (1913–1937), Rose-of-Plymouth (5, 156) (1913–1923), Sea pink [Sea-pink] (5, 156) (1913–1923)

Sabbatia angularis Pursh – See *Sabatia angularis* (L.) Pursh

Sabbatia campestris Nutt. – See *Sabatia campestris* Nutt.

Sabbatia elliottii Steud – See *Sabatia brevifolia* Raf.

Sabina monosperma (Engelm.) Rydb. – See *Juniperus monosperma* (Engelm.) Sarg.

Sabina pachyphlaea (Torr.) Antoine – See *Juniperus deppeana* Steud.

Sabina virginiana [Antoine] – See *Juniperus virginiana* L. var. *virginiana*

Saccharina longicruris (Bachelot de la Pylaie) Kuntze – Deb's apron strings (73) (1892) ME, Devil's-apron [Devil's apron] (73) (1892) Northeastern US, Devil's-apronstrings [Devil's apron strings] (73) (1892) NE coast

Saccharum alopecuroidum (L.) Nutt. – Plume grass [Plume-grass, Plumegrass] (5) (1913), Silver plume grass [Silver plume-grass, Silver plumegrass] (50, 119, 122) (1937–present), Spiral-awn plume grass [Spiral-awned plume-grass] (94) (1901), Woolly beard grass [Woolly beard-grass, Wooly beard-grass] (5, 66, 163) (1852–1913), Woolly bearded grass [Wooly bearded grass] (92) (1876)

Saccharum brevibarbe (Michx.) Pers. var. brevibarbe – Short-awn woolly-beard [Short-awned woolly beard] (66) (1903), Short-beard plume grass [Shortbeard plumegrass, Short-bearded plume-grass] (5, 50) (1913–present)

Saccharum brevibarbe (Michx.) Pers. var. contortum (Ell.) R. Webster – Beard grass [Beard-grass, Beardgrass] (163) (1852), Bent-awn plume grass [Bent awn plume grass] (122) (1937), Soft-beard plume grass [Softbeard plumegrass] (50) (present), Spiral-awn beard grass [Spiral-awned beard-grass] (5, 119) (1913–1938)

Saccharum contortum (Ell.) Nutt. – See *Saccharum brevibarbe* (Michx.) Pers. var. *contortum* (Ell.) R. Webster

Saccharum giganteum (Walt.) Pers. – Densely-flowered plume grass [Densely-flowered plume-grass] (56, 94) (1897–1901), Gamagrass [Gama-grass, Gama grass] (5) (1913), Plume grass [Plume-grass, Plumegrass] (5) (1913), Sesame grass [Sesame-grass] (5) (1913), Sugarcane plume (122) (1937) TX, Sugarcane plume grass [Sugarcane plumegrass] (50) (present)

Saccharum L. – Plume grass [Plume-grass, Plumegrass] (56, 155) (1901–1942), Sugarcane [Sugar cane, Sugar-cane] (7, 56) (1828–1901), Woolly beard (66) (1903)

Saccharum officinale – See *Saccharum officinarum* L.

Saccharum officinarum L. – Indian salt (92) (1876), Java sugar (7) (1828), Kan (Chinese) (110) (1886), Kan-chê (Chinese) (110) (200 BC), Kyum (Burmese) (110) (1886), Mia (Cochin-Chinese) (110) (1886), Ribbon cane (163) (1852), Saccharum (59) (1911), Sugarcane [Sugar cane, Sugar-cane] (10, 19, 45, 57, 59, 66, 67, 92, 94, 107, 109, 110, 138, 163) (1840–1949), Sugre rede (178, 179) (1526–1596), Supickerreidt (Dutch) (180) (1633), Tabu (Malay) (110) (1886)

369

Saccharum ravennae (**L.**) **L.** – Hardy pampas grass [Hardy pampas-grass] (163) (1852), Plume grass [Plume-grass, Plumegrass] (109) (1949), Ravenna grass [Ravennagrass, Ravenna-grass] (50, 109, 138, 155, 163) (1852–present), Woolly beard grass [Woolly beard-grass, Wooly beard-grass] (45, 163) (1852–1896)

Saccharum violaceum – See *Saccharum officinarum* L.

Sacciolepis striata (**L.**) **Nash** – American cupscale (50) (present), Gibbous panic grass [Gibbous panic-grass] (5, 94, 119, 163) (1852–1938)

Saciosa maritima **L.** – possibly *Scabiosa atropupurea* L.

Sagina apetala **Ard.** – Annual pearlwort [Annual pearl-wort] (19) (1840)

Sagina decumbens (**Ell.**) **Torr. & Gray** – Decumbent pearlwort (5, 97) (1913–1937), Trailing pearlwort (4, 50, 155) (1942–present), possibly Corn spurry [Corn spurrey, Corn-spurrey] (167) (1814)

Sagina **L.** – Pearlweed [Pearl-weed] (158) (1900), Pearlwort [Pearl-wort, Pearl wort] (1, 4, 50, 10, 13, 15, 46, 109, 138, 155, 156, 158) (1818–present)

Sagina nodosa (**L.**) **Fenzl** – Knotted pearlwort (5, 156) (1913–1923), Pearlweed [Pearl-weed] (156) (1923), Red sandwort [Red sandwort] (19) (1840), Spurrey (156) (1923)

Sagina pergula laricina **Huds.** – possibly *Sagina subulata* (Sw.) K. Presl

Sagina procumbens **L.** – Bird's-eye [Bird's eye, Bird's-eyes, Birds-eyes] (5, 156) (1913–1923), Breakstone (5, 156) (1913–1923), Creeping pearlwort (156) (1923), Make-beggar (156) (1923), Pearlwort [Pearl-wort, Pearl wort] (19, 92) (1840–1876), Poverty (5, 156) (1913–1923), Procumbent pearlwort (5) (1913)

Sagina saginoides (**L.**) **H. Karst.** – Arctic pearlwort (5) (1913), Field spurry (155) (1942), Pearl spurry (19) (1840), Pearlwort spurry [Pearl-wort spurrey] (187) (1818)

Sagina subulata (**Sw.**) **K. Presl** – Pearlwort [Pearl-wort, Pearl wort] (138) (1923)

Sagittaria acutifolia **Pursh** – See *Sagittaria graminea* Michx. subsp. *graminea*

Sagittaria ambigua **J. G. Sm.** – Arrowhead [Arrow-head, Arrow head] (3) (1977), Kansas arrowhead (50) (present), Kansas sagittaria (5, 97) (1913–1937)

Sagittaria brevirostra **Mack & Bush** – Short-beak arrowhead [Short-beak arrowhead, Short-beak arrow-head] (5, 50, 138, 155) (1913–present)

Sagittaria calycina **Engelm.** – Hooded arrowhead (50) (present)

Sagittaria calycina **Engelm.** var. *calycina* – Giant arrowhead (3, 138, 155) (1923–1977), Hooded arrowhead (50) (present), Large lophotocarpus (93, 97) (1936–1937), Small lophotocarpus (5, 97) (1913–1937)

Sagittaria calycina **Engelm.** var. *spongiosa* **Engelm.** – Large lophotocarpus (5, 120) (1913–1938), Lophotocarpus (131) (1899), Spatulate lophotocarpus (5) (1913), Spongy lophotocarpus (5) (1913)

Sagittaria cristata **Engelm.** – Crested arrowhead (50, 72) (1907–present), Crested sagittaria (5) (1913)

Sagittaria cuneata **Sheld.** – Arum-leaf arrowhead [Arumleaf arrow-head, Arum-leaved arrowhead] (5, 50, 72, 93, 97, 131) (1894–present), Duck-potato arrowhead [Duck potato arrowhead, Duckpotato arrowhead] (3, 155) (1942–1977), Swamp potato (101) (1905) MT, Wappatoo [Wapatoo, Wap-pa-to, or Wappato] (101) (1905) MT

Sagittaria eatonii **J. G. Smith** – See *Sagittaria graminea* Michx. var. *graminea*

Sagittaria engelmanniana **J. G. Sm.** – Arrowleaf [Arrow-leaf, Arrow leaf] (5) (1913), Engelmann's arrowhead [Engelmann arrowhead, Engelmann's arrow-head] (5, 50, 72, 155) (1893–present)

Sagittaria falcata **Pursh** – See *Sagittaria lancifolia* L. subsp. *media* (Micheli) Bogin

Sagittaria graminea **Michx.** – Arrowhead [Arrow-head, Arrow head] (85) (1932), Grass-leaf arrowhead [Grass-leaved arrowhead] (72) (1907), Grass-leaf sagittaria [Grass-leaved sagittaria] (5, 93, 97, 120, 131) (1899–1938), Grassy arrowhead (50, 155) (1942–present)

Sagittaria graminea **Michx.** var. *cristata* (**Engelm.**) **Bogin** – See *Sagittaria cristata* Engelm.

Sagittaria graminea **Michx.** var. *graminea* – Eaton's sagittaria (5) (1913), Grassy arrowhead (50) (present)

Sagittaria heterophylla **Pursh** – See *Sagittaria rigida* Pursh

Sagittaria **L.** – Arrowhead [Arrow-head, Arrow head] (1, 93, 109, 120, 138, 155, 156, 167, 184) (1793–1949), Arrowleaf [Arrow-leaf, Arrow leaf] (122) (1937), Duck-potato (109) (1949), Swamp potato (1, 10) (1818–1932), Swan (1) (1932)

Sagittaria lancifolia **L.** – Bull-tongue arrowhead [Bulltongue arrowhead] (50) (present)

Sagittaria lancifolia **L.** subsp. *lancifolia* – Acute-leaf arrowhead [Acute-leaved arrow-head] (187) (1818)

Sagittaria lancifolia **L.** subsp. *media* (**Micheli**) **Bogin** – Arrowleaf [Arrow-leaf, Arrow leaf] (124) (1937), Scythe-fruit sagittaria [Scythe-fruited sagittaria] (5) (1913)

Sagittaria lancifolia **L.** var. *media* **Micheli** – See *Sagittaria lancifolia* L. subsp. *media* (Micheli) Bogin

Sagittaria latifolia **Willd.** – American arrow-head (46) (1879) NY, Arrowhead [Arrow-head, Arrow head] (14, 40, 78, 92, 103, 107, 121, 156) (1871–1928), Arrowleaf [Arrow-leaf, Arrow leaf] (37, 75, 156) (1830–1923), Arrow-leaf arrowhead [Arrow-leaved Arrow-head] (187) (1818), Broad-leaf arrowhead [Broad-leaved arrow-head, Broad-leaved arrowhead] (5, 50, 72, 85, 93, 97, 120, 131, 156) (1899–present), Common arrowhead (3, 138, 155, 157) (1923–1977), Downy arrowhead (155) (1942), Hairy arrowleaf [Hairy arrow-leaf] (5) (1913), Katniss (41, 46) (1770–1879), Kirit (Pawnee, cricket) (37) (1830), Kits-kat (Pawnee, standing in water) (37) (1830), Long-barb arrowhead [Longbarb arrowhead] (3) (1977), Long-beak arrowhead [Long-beaked arrow-head, Longbeak arrowhead] (5, 50, 72, 97, 155) (1907–present), Muj'ota'bûk (Chippewa, moose leaf) (40) (1928), Narrowhead (19) (1840), Obtuse-leaf arrowhead [Obtuse-leaved arrow-head] (187) (1818), Pshitola (Dakota) (37) (1830), Pšitola hu (Lakota, bead+very+stem or plant) (121) (1918–1970), Sin (Omaha-Ponca) (37) (1830), Sinporo (Winnebago) (37) (1830), Sin-poro (Winnebago) (37) (1830), Sticky arrowhead (155) (1942), Swamp potato (103, 107) (1871–1919), Swan root (78) (1898) CA, Swan-potato [Swan potato] (103, 107) (1871–1919), Tule potato (157) (1929), Tule root (157) (1929), Wab-es-i-pinig (Chipewa) (103) (1871), Wappatoo [Wapatoo, Wap-pa-to, or Wappato] (35, 46, 157, 161) (1896–1929), Waterlily [Water lily, Water-lily, Water-lilies] (78) (1898) MO, Θiŋ (Osage) (121) (1918–1970), possibly Old-world arrowhead (109, 138) (1923–1949)

Sagittaria longiloba **Engelm. ex J. G. Sm.** – Long-barb arrowhead [Longbarb arrowhead] (50, 138, 155) (1923–present), Long-lobe arrowhead [Long-lobed arrow-head] (5, 93, 97) (1913–1937), Narrow-leaf arrowhead [Narrow-leaved arrow-head] (85) (1932)

Sagittaria longirostra (**Micheli**) **J. G. Sm.** – See *Sagittaria latifolia* Willd.

Sagittaria lorata (**Chapm.**) **Small** – See *Sagittaria subulata* (L.) Buch.

Sagittaria mohrii **J. G. Sm.** – See *Sagittaria platyphylla* (Engelm.) J. G. Smith

Sagittaria montevidensis **Schlect. & Cham. subsp.** *calycina* (**Engelm.**) **Bogin** – See *Sagittaria calycina* Engelm. var. *calycina*

Sagittaria obtusa **Muhl. ex Willd., non Thunb.** – See *Sagittaria latifolia* Willd.

Sagittaria platyphylla (**Engelm.**) **J. G. Smith** – Delta arrowhead (50, 155) (1942–present), Mohr's arrowhead [Mohrs arrowhead] (155) (1942), Ovate-leaf sagittaria [Ovate-leaved sagittaria] (5, 97) (1913–1937)

Sagittaria pubescens **Muhl. ex Nutt.** – See *Sagittaria latifolia* Willd.

Sagittaria rigida **Pursh** – Sessile-fruit arrowhead [Sessilefruit arrow-head, Sessile-fruited arrow-head, Sessile-fruited arrowhead] (5, 50, 72, 93, 97) (1907–present), Stiff arrowhead (138, 155) (1923–1942)

Sagittaria sagittifolia **Michx. and Muhl.** – possibly *Sagittaria latifolia* Willd.

Sagittaria subulata **(L.) Buch.** – Awl-leaf arrowhead (50, 138) (1923–present), Subulate sagittaria (5) (1913), Thong-leaf sagittaria [Thong-leaved sagittaria] (5) (1913)

Sagittaria subulata **(L.) Buch. var.** *natans* **(Michx.) J. G. Sm.** – See *Sagittaria subulata* (L.) Buch.

Sagittaria teres **S. Wats.** – Slender arrowhead (50) (present), Slender sagittaria (5) (1913)

Sagittaria variabilis **Engelm.** – See *Sagittaria latifolia* Willd.

Sagittaria viscosa **C. Mohr** – See *Sagittaria latifolia* Willd.

Sairocarpus coulterianus **(Benth. ex A. DC.) D. A. Sutton** – Chaparral snapdragon (138, 155) (1931–1942), Corn snapdragon (5, 155) (1913–1942), Orcutt's snapdragon [Orcutt snapdragon] (155) (1942), Nuttall's snapdragon [Nuttall snapdragon] (155) (1942)

Salicornia bigelovii **Torr.** – Bigelow's glasswort (5) (1913), Dwarf samphire (19) (1840), Glasswort [Glass-wort, Glassewoort] (122) (1937)

Salicornia herbacea **auct. non (L.) L.** – See *Salicornia maritima* Wolff & Jefferies

Salicornia **L.** – Glasswort [Glass-wort, Glassewoort] (1, 2, 10, 26, 41, 93, 155, 158) (1770–1942), Kelpwort [Kelp-wort] (7) (1828), Pickleweed (50) (present), Saltwort (158) (1900), Samphire (1, 2, 7, 93) (1828–1936)

Salicornia maritima **Wolff & Jefferies** – Berrelia (46) (1671), Chicken's-toes [Chicken toe, Chickens'-toes, Chickens' toes, Chicken's toes] (73) (1892) Kittery ME, Glasswort [Glass-wort, Glassewoort] (19, 46, 92, 95, 156, 157, 178) (1526–1929), Marsh samphire (5, 107, 156) (1913–1923), Saltwort [Salt wort, Salt woort] (92, 107, 178) (1526–1919), Samphire (19, 92) (1840–1876), Slender glasswort [Slender glass-wort] (131) (1899)

Salicornia perennis **Mill.** – See *Sarcocornia perennis* (Mill.) A. J. Scott

Salicornia rubra **A. Nels.** – Red swampfire (50) (present), Rocky Mountain glasswort [Rocky Mountain glasswort] (155) (1942), Saltwort [Salt wort, Salt woort] (3, 4) (1977–1986)

Salix ×*conifera* **Wangenh.** [*discolor* × *humilis*] – Cone-gall willow (19) (1840), Rose willow [Rose-willow] (19) (1840)

Salix ×*obtusata* **Fernald** [*myricoides* × *pyrifolia*] – Blunt-leaf willow [Blunt-leaved willow] (5) (1913)

Salix ×*pendulina* **Wenderoth** [*babylonica* × *fragilis*] – Niobe willow (109) (1949), Thurlow's weeping willow [Thurlow weeping willow] (109, 138, 155) (1923–1949), Wisconsin weeping willow (50, 109) (1949–present)

Salix ×*rubens* **Schrank** – Hybrid crack willow (50) (present)

Salix ×*waghornei* **Rydb.** [*arctica* × *glauca*] – Waghorne's willow (5) (1913)

Salix acutifolia – See *Salix arbusculoides* Anderss.

Salix adenophylla **Hook.** – See *Salix cordata* Michx.

Salix alba caerulea – See *Salix alba* L.

Salix alba calva – See *Salix alba* L.

Salix alba **L.** – Cane withy (158) (1900) SD, Common European willow (93, 158) (1900–1936), Common willow (5, 156) (1913–1923), Cricket-bat willow [Cricketbat willow] (138) (1923), Duck willow (5, 156, 158) (1900–1923), European willow (5, 49, 156) (1898–1913), Golden osier (72, 158) (1900–1907) IA, Golden willow (112, 138) (1923–1937), Huntingdon's willow [Huntingdon willow] (5, 156, 158) (1900–1923), Pyramidal white willow (138) (1923), Rose willow [Rose-willow] (178) (1526), White willow (3, 5, 49, 50, 52, 58, 72, 82, 85, 92, 107, 109, 138, 155, 156, 158, 187) (1818–present), Yellow willow (19, 135, 187) (1818–1977), Yellow-stem white willow [Yellowstem white willow] (4, 155) (1942–1986)

Salix alba **L. subsp.** *vitellina* **(L.) Arcang.** – See *Salix alba* L.

Salix alba **L. var.** *vitellina* **(L.) Stokes** – See *Salix alba* L.

Salix ambigua **Pursh, non Ehrh.** – See *Salix nigra* Marsh.

Salix amygdaloides **Anderss.** – Almond willow (113, 130) (1890–1895), Almond-leaf willow [Almond-leaved willow] (5, 156) (1913–1923), Black willow (5, 156) (1913–1923) often mistaken for Salix nigra, Peach-leaf willow [Peachleaf willow, Peach-leaved willow] (1, 3, 4, 5, 50, 65, 72, 82, 85, 91, 93, 95, 97, 138, 155,

156) (1907–present), White willow (130) (1895), Wide-leaf willow [Wide leaf willow] (35) (1806), Wright's peach-leaf willow [Wright peachleaf willow] (155) (1942)

Salix amygdaloides **Anderss. var.** *wrightii* **(Anderss.) Schneid.** – See *Salix amygdaloides* Anderss.

Salix anglorum **Cham.** – See *Salix phlebophylla* Anderss.

Salix arbusculoides **Anderss.** – Sharp-leaf willow [Sharpleaf willow] (138) (1923)

Salix arctica **Pallas** – Arctic willow (5) (1913), Ground willow (5) (1913)

Salix argophylla – See *Salix exigua* Nutt.

Salix argyrocarpa **Anderss.** – Labrador willow (138) (1923), Silver willow (1, 5) (1913–1932)

Salix aurita **L.** – Round-ear willow [Round-eared willow] (138) (1923)

Salix balsamifera **(Hook.) Barrett** – See *Salix pyrifolia* Anderss.

Salix barclayi **Anderss.** – Barclay's willow (5) (1913)

Salix bebbiana **Sargent** – Beak willow [Beak-willow] (138, 156) (1923), Beaked willow (1, 4, 5, 93, 138, 156) (1890–1986), Bebb's willow [Bebb willow] (5, 50, 72, 85, 131, 155) (1899–present), Livid willow (5) (1913), Long-beak willow [Long-beaked willow] (3) (1977), Smooth Bebb's willow [Smooth bebb willow] (155) (1942)

Salix bebbiana **Sargent var.** *perrostrata* **(Rydb.) Schneid.** – See *Salix bebbiana* Sarg.

Salix bebbii – See *Salix bebbiana* Sarg.

Salix blanda **Anderss.** – See *Salix* ×*pendulina* Wenderoth [*babylonica* × *fragilis*]

Salix brachycarpa **Nutt.** – Prostrate willow (20) (1857)

Salix candida **Flueggé ex Willd.** – Bog willow [Bog-willow] (85) (1932), Hoary willow (1, 3, 4, 5, 72, 93) (1907–1986), Sage willow [Sage-willow] (5, 85, 93, 155) (1913–1942), Sage-leaf willow [Sageleaf willow] (50) (present), Sage-leaf willow [Sageleaf willow] (2, 5, 50, 138) (1895–present), White willow (19) (1840)

Salix caprea **L.** – Goat willow (109, 138) (1923–1949), Sallow (109) (1949)

Salix caroliniana **Michx.** – Black willow (158) (1900), Carolina willow (3, 4) (1977–1986), Coastal plain willow (50) (present), Harbison's willow [Harbison willow] (155) (1942), Ward's coastal-plain willow [Ward coastalplain willow] (155) (1942), Ward's willow (5, 82, 97) (1913–1937)

Salix caudata **(Nutt.) Sudw.** – See *Salix lucida* Muhl. subsp. *caudata* (Nutt.) E. Murr.

Salix chlorolepis **Fernald** – Green-scale willow [Green-scaled willow] (5) (1913)

Salix cinerea **L.** – Gray willow [Grey willow] (138) (1923)

Salix cinerea **L. subsp.** *oleifolia* **(Sm.) Macreight** – Olive-leaf willow [Oliveleaf willow] (138) (1923)

Salix cinerea oleifolia – See *Salix cinerea* L. subsp. *oleifolia* (Sm.) Macreight

Salix columbiae **Nels & Macbr.** – possibly *Salix pyrifolia* Anderss.

Salix conifera **W.** – See *Salix* ×*conifera* Wangenh. [*discolor* × *humilis*]

Salix cordata **Michx.** – Furry willow (5, 131) (1899–1913)

Salix cordata **Muhl. var.** *vestita* **Anderss.** – See *Salix eriocephala* Michx.

Salix cordata vestita **Anders.** – See *Salix eriocephala* Michx.

Salix daphnoides **Vill.** – Daphne willow (138) (1923)

Salix desertorum **Richards** – See *Salix glauca* L. subsp. *glauca* var. *acutifolia* (Hook.) C. K. Schneid.

Salix discolor **Muhl.** – Apple-leaf willow [Apple-leaved willow] (85) (1932), Basket willow (19) (1840), Black willow (55) (1911), Bog willow [Bog-willow] (5, 19, 156, 158) (1840–1923), Geslings (158) (1900) England, catkins, Glaucous willow (5, 72, 82, 108, 130, 131, 156, 158) (1878–1930), Lamb's-tail [Lamb's tail, Lamb's tails] (156, 158) (1900–1923) England, catkins, Large pussy willow (3) (1977), Pawms (i.e. palms) (158) (1900) England, catkins, Pussy willow [Pussywillow, Pussy willows] (1, 4, 5, 82, 85, 106, 109, 138, 155, 156, 158) (1900–1986), Pussy-cats [Pussy cats] (156, 158) (1900–1923), Red-root willow [Red-rooted willow] (19, 187) (1818–1840),

Salix discolor Muhl. var. *overi* Ball   SCIENTIFIC NAMES INDEX

Salicis nigrae (55) (1911), Silver willow (5, 156, 158) (1900–1923), Sooty willow (19) (1840), Swamp willow [Swamp-willow] (5, 156, 158) (1900–1923)

Salix discolor Muhl. var. *overi* Ball – See *Salix discolor* Muhl.

Salix elaeagnos Scop. – Rosemary willow (138) (1923)

Salix elegantissima K. Koch – See *Salix ×pendulina* Wenderoth [*babylonica × fragilis*]

Salix eriocephala Michx. – Diamond willow (3, 4, 5, 9, 22, 78, 85, 113, 130, 155) (1873–1986), Heart-leaf willow [Heart-leaved willow] (1, 5, 19, 72, 93, 97, 108, 130, 131, 138, 155) (1840–1942), Missouri River willow (50) (present), Missouri willow (5, 72, 85, 97) (1907–1937), Red willow (130) (1895), Rose willow [Rose-willow] (19) (1840), Stiff-leaf willow [Stiff-leaved willow] (19, 187) (1818–1840)

Salix exigua Nutt. – Coyote willow (3, 4, 155) (1942–1986), Hinds' willow [Hinds willow] (155) (1942), Linear-leaf willow [Linear-leaved willow] (97) (1937), Narrow-leaf willow [Narrow leaf willow, Narrow-leaved willow] (35, 50, 101) (1806–present), Parish's willow [Parish' willow] (155) (1942), Sandbar willow [Sand bar willow, Sand-bar willow] (1, 4) (1932–1986), Saule à feuilles argentees (French) (20) (1857), Silver-leaf willow [Silverleaf willow, Silver-leaved willow] (20, 155) (1857–1942), Slender willow (5, 20, 93, 97) (1857–1937), Texas sandbar willow (155) (1942)

Salix exigua Nutt. subsp. *exigua* – See *Salix exigua* Nutt. (not recognized in US)

Salix exigua Nutt. subsp. *interior* (Rowlee) Cronq. – See *Salix interior* Rowlee

Salix exigua var. *sessilifolia* (Nutt.) Dorn – See *Salix sessilifolia* Nutt.

Salix fericea – See *Salix sericea* Marsh.

Salix fluviatilis Nutt. – See *Salix interior* Rowlee

Salix fragilis L. – Brittle willow (5, 72, 109, 138, 155, 156, 158) (1900–1942), Crack willow (3, 4, 5, 50, 85, 107, 109, 156, 158) (1900–present), Red-wood willow [Red wood willow, Redwood willow, Redwood-willow] (5, 156, 158) (1900–1923), Snap willow (5, 156, 158) (1900–1923), Stag's-head [Stag's head] (5, 156) (1913–1923), Varnished willow (5, 156, 158) (1900–1923)

Salix geyeriana Anderss. – Western pond willow (20) (1857)

Salix glauca L. – Northern willow (5) (1913)

Salix glauca L. subsp. *glauca* var. *acutifolia* (Hook.) C. K. Schneid. – Desert willow (5) (1913), Prairie willow (5) (1913)

Salix glauca L. subsp. *glauca* var. *villosa* (D. Don ex Hook.) Anderss. – Hairy willow (130) (1895)

Salix glauca villosa Anders. – See *Salix glauca* L. subsp. *glauca* var. *villosa* (D. Don ex Hook.) Anderss.

Salix glaucophylla Bebb. – See *Salix myricoides* Muhl. var. *myricoides*

Salix gooddingii Ball – Gooding's willow [Goodings willow] (50, 155) (1942–present)

Salix grisea Willd. – See *Salix sericea* Marsh.

Salix hastata L. – Halberd willow (138) (1923)

Salix herbacea L. – Dwarf willow (5) (1913), Herb-like willow (5) (1913), Pygmy willow (138) (1923)

Salix hindsiana Benth. – See *Salix exigua* Nutt.

Salix hindsiana Benth. var. *parishiana* (Rowlee) Ball – See *Salix exigua* Nutt.

Salix hookeriana Barratt ex Hook. – Hooker's willow (20) (1857), Piper willow (138) (1923)

Salix humilis Marsh. – Bush willow (5, 93, 156) (1913–1936), Dwarf prairie willow (3) (1977), Dwarf willow (8) (1785), Low willow (5, 156) (1913–1923), Prairie willow (4, 5, 50, 72, 82, 93, 97, 113, 130, 131, 138, 155, 156) (1890–present), Saule nain (French) (8) (1785)

Salix humilis Marsh. var. *humilis* – Prairie willow (50) (present)

Salix humilis Marsh. var. *tristis* (Aiton) Griggs – Cone-bearing willow (187) (1818), Dwarf gray willow (5, 72, 82, 156) (1907–1930), Dwarf pussy willow (138, 155) (1923–1942), Dwarf upland willow (156) (1923), Dwarf willow (46, 113, 156) (1879–1923), Gray willow [Grey willow] (156) (1923), Great medicine (46) (1879), King physic (46) (1879), Micco hoyenejau (Creek) (46) (1879), Mourning

willow (19) (1840), Prairie willow (50, 85) (1932–present), Pussy willow [Pussywillow, Pussy willows] (156) (1923), Shrub willow [Shrub-willow] (19) (1840), Speckled willow (19) (1840)

Salix incana – See *Salix elaeagnos* Scop.

Salix interior Rowlee – Coyote willow (3) (1977), Kokbenognik keya (Chippewa, willow for making baskets) (105) (1932), Longleaf willow [Longleaf willow, Long-leaved willow] (2, 5, 19, 108, 112, 138, 156, 158) (1840–1937), Narrow-leaf willow [Narrow leaf willow, Narrow-leaved willow] (5, 101, 130, 156, 158) (1895–1923), Osier willow [Osier-willow] (5, 156, 158) (1900–1923), Red willow (5, 155, 156, 158) (1900–1942), River willow (20, 155) (1857–1942), Riverbank willow [River-bank willow, River bank willow] (5, 93, 97, 156, 158) (1900–1937), Sandbar willow [Sand bar willow, Sand-bar willow] (1, 4, 5, 22, 47, 50, 65, 72, 82, 85, 93, 95, 97, 105, 112, 113, 130, 131, 155, 156, 158) (1852–present), Sasgob-minš (Chippewa) (105) (1932), Shrub willow [Shrub-willow] (5, 156, 158) (1900–1923), White willow (5, 156, 158) (1900–1923)

Salix interior Rowlee var. *angustissima* (Anderss.) Dayton – See *Salix exigua* Nutt.

Salix irrorata Anderss. – Blue-stem willow [Bluestem willow] (138) (1923)

Salix L. – Goslings (75) (1894) Frankin Centre PQ, Kitapato (Pawnee) (37) (1919), Osier (2, 109) (1895–1949), Ozi'sïgo'bimïc (Chippewa) (40) (1928), Pussy willow [Pussywillow, Pussy willows] (75) (1894), Ruhi (Winnebago) (37) (1919), Saff (158) (1900), Salghe (158) (1900), Sallow (158) (1900), Sally (158) (1900), Sauce (Spanish) (158) (1900), Saugh (158) (1900), Saule (French) (8, 158) (1785–1900), Sauz (Spanish) (158) (1900), Seel (158) (1900), Selly (158) (1900), Soafs (158) (1900), Thiuxe (Osage) (121) (1918?–1970?), Wah'pe-popa (Dakota) (37) (1919), Waxpepopa (Lakota, possibly meaning bursting leaf) (121) (1918?–1970?), Weide (German) (158) (1900), Widdy (158) (1900), Wiffs (158) (1900), Wilf (158) (1900), Willey (158) (1900), Willow [Wyloue] or Willow tree [Wyloue tree] (1, 4, 7, 8, 10, 40, 50, 82, 92, 93, 106, 108, 109, 114, 122, 138, 155, 156, 158, 167, 179, 184, 190) (1526–present), Willow-oak [Willow oak] (2) (1895), Withe (92) (1876), Withy (92, 158) (1876–1900), Wythy (158) (1900)

Salix lasiandra Benth. – See *Salix lucida* Muhl. subsp. *lasiandra* (Benth.) E. Murr.

Salix ligulifolia (Ball) Ball ex Schneid. – Strap-leaf willow [Strap-leaved willow] (85) (1932)

Salix ligulifolia Ball. – See *Salix ligulifolia* (Ball) Ball ex Schneid.

Salix ligustrina Michx. f. – See *Salix nigra* Marsh.

Salix linearifolia Rydb. – See *Salix exigua* Nutt.

Salix longifolia Muhl. – See *Salix interior* Rowlee

Salix longipes Shuttlew. var. *wardii* (Bebb) Schneid. – See *Salix caroliniana* Michx.

Salix longirostris Michx. – See *Salix humilis* Marsh. var. *tristis* (Aiton) Griggs

Salix lucida Muhl. – Glossy willow (5, 93, 95, 156) (1911–1936), Shining willow (1, 3, 4, 5, 19, 20, 50, 72, 82, 93, 113, 138, 155, 156) (1840–present)

Salix lucida Muhl. subsp. *caudata* (Nutt.) E. Murr. – Tail-leaf willow [Tailed-leaved willow] (85) (1932)

Salix lucida Muhl. subsp. *lasiandra* (Benth.) E. Murr. – Sweet willow (35) (1806)

Salix lutea Nutt. – Diamond willow (3) (1977), Saule jaune (French) (20) (1857), Western yellow willow (20) (1857), Yellow willow (1, 4, 50, 85, 155) (1932–present)

Salix maccalliana Rowlee – McCalla's willow (50) (present)

Salix mackenziana Barratt. – See *Salix prolixa* Anderss.

Salix mackenzieana (Hook.) Barratt ex Andersson – See *Salix prolixa* Anderss.

Salix macrocarpa [Nutt.] – See *Salix geyeriana* Anderss.

Salix macrostachya [Nutt.] – See *Salix sessilifolia* Nutt.

Salix matsudana Koidzumi – Hankow willow (138) (1923)

Salix melanopsis **Nutt.** – Dusky willow (20) (1857), Saule noirâtre (French) (20) (1857)

Salix miricoides **W.** – See *Salix myricoides* Muhl.

Salix missouriensis **Bebb** – See *Salix eriocephala* Michx.

Salix muhlenbergiana **W.** – See *Salix humilis* Marsh. var. *tristis* (Aiton) Griggs

Salix myricoides **Muhl.** – Gale leaf willow (19) (1840)

Salix myricoides **Muhl. var. *myricoides*** – Blue-leaf willow [Blueleaf willow] (138, 156) (1923), Broad-leaf willow [Broad-leaved willow] (5) (1913)

Salix myrsinifolia **Salisb.** – Myrtle willow (138) (1923)

Salix myrtilloides **L.** – See *Salix pedicellaris* Pursh

Salix nigra **Marsh.** – Black willow (1, 3, 4, 5, 9, 20, 19, 49, 50, 52, 53, 54, 58, 61, 65, 72, 80, 92, 93, 95, 97, 108, 112, 113, 131, 138, 149, 153, 155, 156, 157, 158) (1840–present), Brittle-joint willow [Brittle joint willow] (19) (1840), Champlain willow (20) (1857), Gulf black willow (155) (1942), Pussy willow [Pussywillow, Pussy willows] (5, 49, 53, 54, 92, 157, 158) (1876–1929), Puzzle willow (155) (1942), Rough American willow (8) (1785), Saule noir (French) (8) (1785), Scythe-leaf willow [Scythe-leaved willow] (5) (1913), Swamp willow [Swamp-willow] (5, 93, 156, 157, 158) (1900–1936), Texas black willow (155) (1942), Willow catkins (92) (1876)

Salix nigra **Marsh. var. *altissima* Sargent** – See *Salix nigra* Marsh.

Salix nigra **Marsh. var. *lindheimeri* Schneid.** – See *Salix nigra* Marsh.

Salix nivalis **Hook.** – Minute willow (20) (1857)

Salix obtusata **Fernald** – See *Salix ×obtusata* Fernald [*myricoides × pyrifolia*]

Salix pedicellaris **Pursh** – Bog willow [Bog-willow] (1, 4, 5, 50, 72, 131, 155, 156) (1899–present), Stem-berry willow [Stem-berried willow] (19) (1840), Whortle-berry willow [Whortleberry willow] (138, 155) (1923–1942)

Salix pellita **(Anderss.) Anderss. ex Schneid.** – Satiny willow (5) (1913)

Salix pellita **Anderss.** – See *Salix pellita* (Anderss.) Anderss. ex Schneid.

Salix pennata **Ball** – See *Salix planifolia* Pursh

Salix pentandra **L.** – Bay willow (109, 112) (1937–1949), Bay-leaf willow [Bay-leaved willow] (156) (1923), Laurel willow (50, 112, 138, 155) (1923–present), Laurel-leaf willow [Laurel-leaved willow] (3, 4, 85, 109, 135) (1910–1986), Long-leaf bay willow [Long-leaved bay willow] (20) (1857), Saule laurier (French) (20) (1857)

Salix petiolaris **Sm.** – Dark long-leaf willow [Dark long-leaved willow] (5) (1913), Meadow willow (3, 4, 50, 85) (1932–present), Slender willow (5, 72) (1907–1913)

Salix phlebophylla **Anderss.** – Brown's willow (5) (1913)

Salix piperi – See *Salix hookeriana* Barratt ex Hook.

Salix planifolia **Pursh** – Diamond-leaf willow [Diamondleaf willow] (50) (present), Feather-vein willow [Feathervein willow] (155) (1942), Mono planeleaf willow (155) (1942), Nelson's plane-leaf willow [Nelson planeleaf willow] (155) (1942), Park willow (155) (1942), Plane-leaf willow [Planeleaf willow] (4, 155) (1942–1986), Serviceberry willow (3, 4) (1977–1986)

Salix planifolia **Pursh var. *monica* (Bebb) Schneid.** – See *Salix planifolia* Pursh

Salix planifolia **Pursh var. *nelsonii* (Ball) Ball ex E. C. Sm.** – See *Salix planifolia* Pursh

Salix prolixa **Anderss.** – Diamond willow (1, 101) (1905–1932) younger stem form diamond-shaped excrescences about the "knots"

Salix pseudomonticola **C. R. Ball** – See *Salix planifolia* Pursh

Salix purpurea **L.** – Basket willow (85) (1932), Bitter purple willow (6) (1892), Bitter willow (5, 156) (1913–1923), Opurpurishe Weide (German) (6) (1892), Purple osier (109, 138) (1923–1949), Purple willow (5, 6, 85, 156) (1892–1932), Red willow (6) (1892), Rose willow [Rose-willow] (5, 58, 156) (1869–1923), Whipcord willow [Whipcord-willow] (5, 156) (1913–1923)

Salix pyrifolia **Anderss.** – Balsam willow (1, 5, 131, 138) (1899–1932)

Salix recurvata **Pursh** – See *Salix humilis* Marsh. var. *tristis* (Aiton) Griggs

Salix reticulata **L.** – Net-vein willow [Net-veined willow] (5) (1913)

Salix reticulata **L.** – Wrinkle-leaf willow [Wrinkled-leaf willow] (5, 156) (1913–1923)

Salix rigida **Muhl. var. *rigida*** – See *Salix eriocephala* Michx.

Salix rigida **Muhl. var. *watsonii* (Bebb) Cronq.** – See *Salix lutea* Nutt.

Salix rotundifolia **Trautv.** – Round-leaf willow [Round-leaved willow] (20) (1857)

Salix rubra **Richards., non Huds.** – See *Salix interior* Rowlee

Salix scouleriana **Barr.** – Blunt-leaf willow [Blunt-leaved willow] (20) (1857), Pond willow (20) (1857), Scouler's willow [Scouler willow] (50, 155) (1942–present), Western pussy willow (3, 4) (1977–1986), Yellow Scouler's willow [Yellow Scouler willow] (155) (1942), Yellow willow (130) (1895)

Salix scouleriana **Barratt ex Hook. var. *flavescens* (Nutt.) J. K. Henry** – See *Salix scouleriana* Barr.

Salix sericea **Marsh.** – Gray willow [Grey willow] (19) (1840), Pond willow (20) (1857), Saules à feuilles soyeuses (French) (8) (1785), Silky willow (5, 22, 72, 138) (1907–1923), Ozier (8) (1785), Silky-leaf willow [Silky leaved willow] (8) (1785)

Salix serissima **(Bailey) Fern.** – Autumn willow (1, 3, 4, 5, 50, 85, 138, 155) (1913–present)

Salix sessilifolia **Nutt.** – Long-spike willow [Long-spiked willow] (20) (1857), Soft-leaf willow [Soft-leaved willow] (20) (1857)

Salix sitchensis **Sanson ex Bong.** – Satin willow (138) (1923), Velvet willow (20) (1857)

Salix stagnalis **Nutt.** – See *Salix scouleriana* Barr.

Salix trista **Aiton** – See *Salix humilis* Marsh. var. *tristis* (Aiton) Griggs

Salix tristis **Aiton** – See *Salix humilis* Marsh. var. *tristis* (Aiton) Griggs

Salix uva-ursi **Pursh** – Bearberry willow (5, 138) (1913–1923)

Salix vestita **Pursh** – Diamond willow (135) (1910) MT, Hairy willow (5) (1913)

Salix viminalis **L.** – Ausier (5, 156) (1913–1923), Basket willow (5, 19, 92, 109, 156) (1840–1949), Common osier (5, 138, 156) (1913–1923), Osier willow [Osier-willow] (5, 109, 156) (1913–1949), Twigwithy (5, 156) (1913–1923), Velvet osier (5, 156) (1913–1923), White osier (5, 156) (1913–1923), Wilgers (5, 156) (1913–1923)

Salix vitellina **L. var. *aurea*** – See *Salix alba* L.

Salix waghornei **Rydb.** – See *Salix ×waghornei* Rydb. [*arctica × glauca*]

Salix wardii **Bebb.** – See *Salix caroliniana* Michx.

Salomonia biflora **(Walt.) Britton** – See *Polygonatum biflorum* (Walt.) Ell.

Salomonia commutata **(R. & S.) Britton** – See *Polygonatum biflorum* (Walt.) Ell. var. *commutatum* (J.A. & J.H. Schultes) Morong

Salpichroa origanifolia **(Lam.) Baill.** – Cock's-eggs [Cocks-eggs] (109, 138) (1923–1949)

Salpiglossis **K. Koch** – Salpiglossis (138) (1923) Greek for tube and tongue alluding to the form of the corolla and appearance of the style

Salpiglossis **Ruiz & Pavon** – See *Salpiglossis* K. Koch

Salpiglossis sinuata **Ruiz & Pavón** – Painted-tongue (109) (1949), Scalloped salpiglossis (138) (1923)

Salpingostylis coelestina **(Bartr.) Small** – See *Calydorea coelestina* (Bartr.) Goldblatt & Henrich

Salsola collina **Pallas** – Slender Russian thistle (50) (present), Tumbleweed [Tumble weed, Tumble-weed] (4) (1986)

Salsola kali **L.** – Barilla (182) (1791), Common Russian thistle [Common Russianthistle] (155) (1942), Common saltwort (156) (1923), Eestrige (158) (1900), Kelpwort [Kelp-wort] (5, 156, 158) (1900–1923), Prickly glasswort (5, 156, 158) (1900–1923), Prickly saltwort [Prickly salt wort] (92, 158) (1876–1900), Russian cactus (156) (1923), Russian thistle [Russianthistle] (5, 75, 156) (1894–1923), Salt-grape [Salt grape, Saltgrape] (5, 156, 158) (1900–1923), Saltwort [Salt wort, Salt woort] (5, 19, 72, 158, 187) (1818–1907), Sea-grape [Seagrape, Sea grape] (5, 92, 158, 178) (1596–1913), Sea-thrift [Sea thrift] (5, 156, 158) (1900–1923), Sowdwort (158) (1900), Sparrow's-dung (158) (1900), Tumbleweed [Tumble weed, Tumble-weed] (156) (1923)

Salsola kali L. subsp. _tragus_ (L.) Celak.

Salsola kali **L. subsp.** _tragus_ **(L.) Celak.** – See _Salsola tragus_ L.

Salsola **L.** – Barilla (7) (1828), Glasswort [Glass-wort, Glassewoort] (158) (1900), Russian thistle [Russianthistle] (1, 50, 155) (1932–present), Saltwort (1, 2, 10, 93, 158) (1818–1936)

Salsola pestifer **A. Nelson** – See _Salsola tragus_ L.

Salsola soda **L.** – Kali (174) (1753), Soda plant (92) (1876)

Salsola tragus **L.** – Prickly Russian thistle (50) (present), Russian cactus (4, 62, 75, 158) (1894–1913), Russian thistle [Russianthistle] (3, 4, 5, 21, 37, 50, 62, 72, 75, 80, 85, 93, 95, 97, 125, 126, 131, 145, 146, 157, 158) (1893–present), Tumbleweed [Tumble weed, Tumble-weed] (4) (1986)

Salvia **(Tourn.) L.** – See _Salvia_ L.

Salvia ×superba **Stapf** [_sylvestris × villicaulis_] – Blue sage (82) (1930) IA, Oriental sage (138) (1923)

Salvia aethiopis **L.** – Aethiopian mulleine (178) (1526), Aethiopis (178) (1526), Mediterranean sage (50) (present)

Salvia amabilis **[Kunth & Bouche]** – See _Salvia farinacea_ Benth.

Salvia apiana **Jepson** – Greasewood [Grease-wood] (75) (1894), White bee-sage (138) (1923), White sage (106) (1930)

Salvia argentea **L.** – Silver sage (138) (1923), White sage (92) (1876)

Salvia azurea grandiflora – See _Salvia azurea_ Michx. ex Lam. var. _grandiflora_ Benth.

Salvia azurea **Michx. ex Lam.** – Azure blue sage (50) (present), Azure sage (138, 155) (1923–1942), Blue sage (4) (1986), Giant blue sage (124) (1937) TX, Pitcher's sage [Pitchers sage, Pitcher sage] (4) (1986), Tall blue sage (182) (1791)

Salvia azurea **Michx. ex Lam. var.** _grandiflora_ **Benth.** – Great azure sage (138) (1923), Kansas sage (48) (1882), Pitcher's sage [Pitchers sage, Pitcher sage] (3, 5, 50, 72, 93, 95, 97, 155) (1907–present), Tall sage (5) (1913), Wild sage (48, 114) (1882–1894)

Salvia ballotaeflora **Benth.** – See _Salvia ballotiflora_ Benth.

Salvia ballotiflora **Benth.** – Majorano (75) (1894) TX & Mexico, Shrubby blue sage (124) (1937) TX

Salvia carduacea **Benth.** – Annual sage (106) (1930), Thistle sage (106, 109, 138) (1923–1949)

Salvia claytoni **Ell.** – See _Salvia verbenaca_ L.

Salvia coccinea **L.** – See _Salvia coccinea_ P.J. Buchoz ex Etlinger

Salvia coccinea **P.J. Buchoz ex Etlinger** – Texas sage (138) (1923)

Salvia coccinea **var.** _pseudococcinea_ **[(Jacq.) A. Gray]** – See _Salvia coccinea_ P.J. Buchoz ex Etlinger

Salvia columbariae **Benth.** – Annual sage (106) (1930), California chia (104) (1896), Chia (77, 106, 107) (1898–1930) CA, Wild sage (77) (1898) CA, Winter-oat [Winter oat] (77) (1898) CA

Salvia columbariaea **Benth.** – See _Salvia columbariae_ Benth.

Salvia farinacea **Benth.** – Loving sage (106) (1930), Mealy blue sage (124) (1937) TX, Mealy-cup sage [Mealycup sage] (138) (1923)

Salvia glutinosa **L.** – Jupiter's-distaff [Iupiters Distaffe] (178) (1526), Sticky sage (50) (present)

Salvia greggi – See _Salvia greggii_ Gray

Salvia greggii **Gray** – Autumn sage (138) (1923)

Salvia hispanica **L.** – Chia seed (92) (1876)

Salvia **L.** – Sage (1, 2, 4, 7, 10, 50, 82, 93, 106, 109, 138, 155, 156, 158, 184) (1793–present), Salvia (158) (1900)

Salvia lanceaefolia **Poir.** – See _Salvia reflexa_ Hornem.

Salvia lanceifolia **Poir.** – See _Salvia reflexa_ Hornem.

Salvia lanceolata **Willd.** – See _Salvia reflexa_ Hornem.

Salvia leucophylla **Greene** – Purple sage (106) (1930), Silver sage (106) (1930), White-leaf sage [White-leaved sage] (106) (1930)

Salvia lyrata **L.** – Cancerweed [Cancer weed, Cancer-weed] (3, 4, 5, 19, 92, 156) (1840–1986), Lyre-leaf sage [Lyre-leaved sage] (4, 5, 97, 124, 156) (1913–1986), Meadow sage (92) (1876), Wild sage (5, 19, 92) (1840–1913)

Salvia mellifera **Greene** – Ball sage (106) (1930), Black sage (106) (1930), Button sage (106) (1930)

Salvia nemorosa **L.** – European sage (85) (1932), Sage (4) (1986), Violet sage (138, 155) (1923–1942), Woodland sage (50, 155) (1942–present)

Salvia officinalis **L.** – Common garden sage (106) (1930), Curled sage (178) (1526), European sage (82) (1930) IA, Garden sage (49, 53, 58, 92, 138, 156) (1869–1923), Indian white sage (178) (1526), Pig sage (178) (1526), Sage (19, 46, 49, 53, 55, 57, 59, 61, 92, 107, 109) (1671–1949), Salvia (55, 107) (1911–1919) from ancient Latin, Sawge (179) (1526), Spotted sage (178) (1526), Winged white sage (178) (1526)

Salvia pitcheri **Torr. ex Benth.** – See _Salvia azurea_ Michx. ex Lam. var. _grandiflora_ Benth.

Salvia pratensis **L.** – Introduced sage (50) (present), Meadow sage (5, 138) (1913–1923), Salvia (82) (1930)

Salvia reflexa **Hornem.** – Blue sage (80) (1913), Lance-leaf sage [Lanceleaf sage, Lance-leaved sage] (3, 4, 5, 50, 72, 93, 97, 131, 155) (1899–present), Lance-leaf salvia [Lance-leaved salvia] (80) (1913), Rocky mountain sage (4) (1986), Wild blue sage (82) (1930), Wild sage (114, 145) (1894–1897)

Salvia sclara – possibly _Salvia sclarea_ L.

Salvia sclarea **L.** – Clammy sage (92) (1876), Clary [Clarey, Clarry] (5, 19, 46, 92, 107, 109, 156, 179) (1526–1949), Clear-eye (5, 156) (1913–1923), Common clary (138) (1923), Garden clary [Garden clarie] (178) (1526), See-bright [See bright] (5, 156) (1913–1923)

Salvia sonomensis **Greene** – Creeping sage (106) (1930)

Salvia splendens **Sellow ex Roemer & J. A. Schultes** – Scarlet sage (19, 82, 92, 109, 138) (1840–1949)

Salvia urticifolia **L.** – Nettle sage (19) (1840), Nettle-leaf sage [Nettle-leaved sage] (5) (1913), Wild sage (5) (1913), Christ's eye (92) (1876), Clear-eye (92) (1876), Eyeseed [Eye seed] (5, 156) (1913–1923), Vervain sage (5, 19, 138) (1840–1923), Wild clary [Wilde clarie] (5, 92, 156, 178) (1526–1923), Wild sage (5, 106) (1913–1930)

Salvia verbenacea **L.** – See _Salvia verbenaca_ L.

Salvia verbenica – See _Salvia verbenaca_ L.

Salvia verticillata **L.** – Lilac sage (138) (1923)

Salvia virgata **Hort.** – See _Salvia ×superba_ Stapf [_sylvestris × villicaulis_]

Salvinia **Adans.** – See _Salvinia_ Séguier

Salvinia auriculata **Aubl.** – Eared watermoss (50) (present)

Salvinia natans **(L.) All.** – Floating moss (5) (1913), Floating watermoss (50) (present), Salvinia (5) (1913)

Salvinia **Séguier** – Salvinia (109, 138) (1923–1949) for Antonido Maria Salvini, 1623–1729, professor in Florence Italy

Samanea saman **(Jacq.) Merr.** – Monkey pod [Monkey-pod] (109) (1949), Rain tree [Rain-tree] (107, 109) (1919–1949), Saman (107, 109) (1919–1949), Zaman (109) (1949), Zamang (107) (1919)

Samanea saman **Merr.** – See _Samanea saman_ (Jacq.) Merr.

Sambucus **(Tourn.) L.** – See _Sambucus_ L.

Sambucus caerulea **Raf.** – See _Sambucus nigra_ L. subsp. _cerulea_ (Raf.) R. Bolli

Sambucus callicarpa **Greene** – See _Sambucus racemosa_ L. var. _racemosa_

Sambucus canadensis **L.** – See _Sambucus nigra_ L. subsp. _canadensis_ (L.) R. Bolli

Sambucus cerulea **Raf.** – See _Sambucus nigra_ L. subsp. _cerulea_ (Raf.) R. Bolli

Sambucus coerulea **Raf.** – See _Sambucus nigra_ L. subsp. _cerulea_ (Raf.) R. Bolli

Sambucus ebulus **L.** – Blood elder (92) (1876), Danewort [Danewoort] (92, 107, 178) (1526–1919), Dwarf elder (107) (1919), Dwarf elderberry [Dwarf elder berries] (92) (1876), Ebulus (174, 178) (1523–1753), Walewort (92) (1876), Wallwort [Wall wort, Wallwoort] (92, 107, 178) (1526–1919), Walworde (179) (1526)

Sambucus glauca **Nutt.** – See _Sambucus nigra_ L. subsp. _cerulea_ (Raf.) R. Bolli

Sambucus **L.** – Elder [Eldre] or Elder tree (1, 2, 8, 10, 82, 93, 109, 112, 138, 155, 156, 158, 184) (1785–1949), Elderberry [Elder-berry, Elder berry] (4, 50) (1986–present), Sureau (French) (8) (1785)

Sambucus mexicana **K. Presl ex DC.** – See _Sambucus nigra_ L. subsp.

canadensis (L.) R. Bolli

Sambucus microbotrys Rydb. – See *Sambucus racemosa* L. var. *racemosa*

Sambucus nigra L. – Alderne (158) (1900), American black-berried elder (8) (1785), Black-berry elder [Black-berried elder] (158) (1900), Bone-tree (158) (1900), Boor tree [Boor-tree] (92, 158) (1876–1900), Bore tree [Bore-tree] (158) (1900), Bountry (92, 158) (1876–1900), Boutry (158) (1900), Bur tree [Bur-tree] (158) (1900), Common elder (55, 158) (1900–1911), Elderberry [Elder-berry, Elder berry] (107) (1919), Eldre (179) (1526), Ellan wood [Ellanwood] (92, 158) (1876–1900), Ellar (158) (1900), Ellarne (158) (1900), Ellen (158) (1900), Ellet (158) (1900), Ellhorn (92, 158) (1876–1900), Elnorne (158) (1900), Elren (158) (1900), European black elderberry (50) (present), European elder (82, 107, 109, 138, 155, 158) (1919–1949), Flieder (German) (158) (1900), German elder (158) (1900), Hilder (158) (1900), Hillerne (158) (1900), Hollunder (German) (158) (1900), Hylder (158) (1900), Iagged elder (Jagged elder) (178) (1526), Judas tree [Judas' tree, Judas-tree] (158) (1900), Parsley elder (158) (1900), Sahuco (Spanish) (158) (1900), Skaw (158) (1900), Sureau (French) (158) (1900), Sureau noir (French) (8) (1785), Whist-aller (158) (1900), Winlin-berry (158) (1900)

Sambucus nigra L. subsp. canadensis (L.) R. Bolli – American elder or American elder tree (5, 41, 49, 53, 72, 93, 97, 109, 122, 124, 138, 155, 156, 157, 158) (1770–1949), Bapoki hi (Osage, popping blackhaw plant) (121) (1970), Black elder (7) (1828), Black-berry elder [Black-berried elder] (19, 85, 156) (1840–1932), Bore tree [Bore-tree] (156) (1923), Bottery tree [Bottery-tree] (156) (1923) no longer in use by 1923, Canadian elderberry (107) (1919), Canadian red-berry elder [Canadian red-berried elder] (8) (1785), Canadische Hollunder (German) (6) (1892), Chaputa (Dakota) (37) (1919) Chaputa-hu (elder bush), Common elder (2, 5, 38, 47, 63, 82, 92, 106, 156, 157) (1852–1930), Common elderberry (4, 50) (1986–present), Elder [Eldre] or Elder tree (9, 49, 52, 53, 57, 58, 61, 95, 112, 113, 114, 125, 130, 148, 157, 158, 187, 190) (~1759–1939), Elder bush (6) (1892), Elder flowers [Elder-flowers] (92, 158) (1876–1900), Elder rob (92) (1876) juice of elderberries, Elderberry [Elder-berry, Elder berry] (3, 6, 22, 37, 105, 121, 125, 145, 156, 157) (1892–1977), Elder-blow [Elder-blows] (156, 158) (1900–1923), Florida elder (155) (1942), Mexican elder (153, 155) (1913–1942), Pipe tree [Pipe-tree] (190) (~1759), Pipigwe-minan (Chippewa) (105) (1932), Sambucus (57) (1917), Skirariu (Pawnee) (37) (1919), Sureau du Canada (French) (6, 8) (1785–1892), Sweet elder (5, 76, 92, 93, 109, 131, 156, 157, 158) (1896–1949), Tapiro (153) (1913) NM, Wagathahashka (Omaha-Ponca) (37) (1919) Wagathahashka-hi (elder bush)

Sambucus nigra L. subsp. cerulea (Raf.) R. Bolli – Blue elder (109) (1949), Blue elderberry (106, 122) (1930–1937), Blue-berry elder [Blueberry elder] (138) (1923), Elderberry [Elder-berry, Elder berry] (101) (1905)

Sambucus pubens leucocarpa – See *Sambucus racemosa* L. var. *racemosa*

Sambucus pubens Michx. – See *Sambucus racemosa* L. var. *racemosa*

Sambucus pubens Michx. var. arborescens Torr. & Gray – See *Sambucus racemosa* L. var. *racemosa*

Sambucus racemosa L. – Boor tree [Boor-tree] (5, 156) (1913–1923), Bore tree [Bore-tree] (5, 35, 156) (1806–1923) no longer in use by 1923, Boutry (5, 156) (1913–1923) no longer in use by 1923, Elder [Eldre] or Elder tree (106) (1930), European red elder (109, 138) (1923–1949), Mountain elder or Mountain elder tree [Mountaine elder tree] (5, 92, 156, 178) (1526–1923), Poison elder (5, 156) (1913–1923), Racemed elder (131) (1899), Red elder (2) (1895), Red elderberry [Red elder-berry] (156) (1923), Red-berry elder [Red-berried elder] (5, 19, 46, 63, 82, 92, 156) (1840–1923), Scarlet elder (156) (1923)

Sambucus racemosa L. subsp. pubens (Michx.) House – See *Sambucus racemosa* L. var. *racemosa*

Sambucus racemosa L. var. melanocarpa (Gray) McMinn

– Black-bead elder [Blackbead elder] (138) (1923)

Sambucus racemosa L. var. racemosa – Albino elder (138) (1923), American red elder (109) (1949), Bunchberry elder (155) (1942), Elder [Eldre] or Elder tree (112) (1937), Mountain elder or Mountain elder tree [Mountaine elder tree] (158) (1900), Pacific red elder (155) (1942), Poison elder (76, 158) (1896–1900) Oxford Co. ME, Red elder (158) (1900), Red elderberry [Red elder-berry] (50) (present), Red-berry elder [Red-berried elder] (4, 72, 85, 86, 130, 158) (1878–1986), Scarlet elder (138, 155) (1923–1942), Stinking elderberry (3) (1977), Tree elder (138) (1923), Tree scarlet elder (155) (1942), Yellow-berry elder [Yellow-berried elder] (85) (1932)

Sambucus simpsonii Rehd. ex Sargent – See *Sambucus nigra* L. subsp. *canadensis* (L.) R. Bolli

Samolus (Tourn.) L. – See *Samolus* L.

Samolus cuneatus Small – See *Samolus ebracteatus* Kunth subsp. *cuneatus* (Small) R. Knuth

Samolus ebracteatus Kunth – Lime-water brookweed [Limewater brookweed] (50) (present), Texas water-pimpernel [Texas water pimpernel] (97) (1937)

Samolus ebracteatus Kunth subsp. cuneatus (Small) R. Knuth – Limewater brookweed (50) (present), Water-pimpernel [Water pimpernel] (4) (1986)

Samolus L. – Brookweed [Brook-weed, Brook weed] (4, 50, 138) (1900–present), Water-pimpernel [Water pimpernel] (1, 2, 4, 156, 158) (1895–1923)

Samolus parviflorus Raf. – See *Samolus valerandi* L. subsp. *parviflorus* (Raf.) Hultén

Samolus valerandi L. – Brookweed [Brook-weed, Brook weed] (19, 92, 184) (1793–1876), Seaside brookweed (50) (present), Water-pimpernel [Water pimpernel] (19, 92) (1840–1876)

Samolus valerandi L. subsp. parviflorus (Raf.) Hultén – Brookweed [Brook-weed, Brook weed] (5, 10, 156) (1818–1923), Samolus (3) (1977), Samolus valerandi (50) (present), Water-pimpernel [Water pimpernel] (5, 10, 97, 156) (1818–1937)

Samolus valerandi var. americanus Gray. – See *Samolus valerandi* L.

Samolus valerandi var. floribundus Britton, Sterns & Poggenb. – See *Samolus valerandi* L.

Samuela carnerosana – See *Yucca faxoniana* (Trel.) Sarg.

Samuela faxoniana – See *Yucca faxoniana* (Trel.) Sarg.

Samuela Trel. – See *Yucca* L. (all US species)

Sanguinaria (Dill) L. – See *Sanguinaria* L.

Sanguinaria canadensis L. – Bloodroot [Blood-root, Blood root] (1, 2, 4, 5, 6, 13, 14, 15, 19, 37, 40, 41, 46, 47, 49, 50, 52, 53, 54, 55, 57, 58, 59, 60, 61, 63, 64, 65, 72, 82, 85, 92, 97, 105, 106, 109, 127, 131, 138, 155, 156, 157, 158, 177, 184, 186, 187) (1770–present), Bloodwort [Blood wort, Blood-wort] (7, 10, 184) (1793–1828), Blutkraut (German) (158) (1900), Blutwurzel (German) (6, 158) (1892–1900), Bolo-root (156) (1923), Canadisches Bludkraut (German) (186) (1814), Common bloodroot (7) (1828), Coonroot [Coonroot, Coon root] (64, 74, 157, 158) (1893–1929), Cornroot [Cornroot, Corn root] (156) (1923), Dragon's-blood [Dragon's blood] (46) (1649), Indian paint [Indian-paint] (6, 49, 53, 186, 187) (1818–1922), Minigathe makan wau (Omaha-Ponca, woman-seeking medicine) (37) (1919), Mĭs'kodji'bĭk (Chippewa, red root) (40) (1928), Musquaspene (46) (1879), Pauson (6, 7, 64, 92, 156, 158) (1828–1923) no longer in use by 1923, Peh'-hishuji (Winnebago [to make gourds red] (37) (1919), Puccoon (6, 10, 46, 49, 53, 74, 76, 155, 177, 181, 186, 187) (~1678–1942), Puccoon root [Puccoon-root] (5, 64, 74, 156, 158) (1893–1923), Purron root [Purron-root] (157) (1929), Puuson (186) (1825), Red Indian paint [Red Indian-paint] (64, 156, 157, 158) (1900–1929), Red paint root (92) (1876), Red puccoon (6, 7, 49, 53, 58, 64, 76, 92, 156, 157, 158) (1828–1929), Red turmeric (58) (1869), Redroot [Red-root, Red root] (6, 7, 49, 53, 58, 64, 76, 92, 157, 158, 186) (1825–present), Sanguinaire (French) (6, 158) (1892–1900), Sanguinaire du Canada (French) (7) (1828), Sanguinaria (52, 54, 55, 57, 59, 64) (1905–1917), Snakebite [Snake bite, Snake-bite] (64, 73, 156, 157, 158) (1892–1929), Sweet-slumber

(64, 76, 156, 157, 158) (1896–1929), Tetterwort (5, 6, 49, 53, 64, 156, 157, 158) (1892–1929), Turmeric (6, 7, 64, 156, 158) (1828–1923), White puccoon (64, 74, 158) (1893–1908) NY, White Virginia crowfoot [White Virginia crowfoote] (181) (~1678)

Sanguinaria L. – Bloodroot [Blood-root, Blood root] (50, 82, 93, 138, 155, 156, 190) (~1759–present), Puccoon (167) (1814)

Sanguisorba annua (**Nutt. ex Hook.**) **Torr. & Gray** – Annual burnet (122) (1937), Plains poteridium (5, 97) (1913–1937), Prairie burnet (4, 50, 155) (1942–present)

Sanguisorba canadensis L. – American burnet (138) (1923), American great burnet (5) (1913), Burnet saxifrage [Burnet-saxifrage] (19) (1840), Canadian burnet (2, 156) (1895–1923), possibly Wild burnet (2) (1895)

Sanguisorba L. – Burnet (1, 2, 4, 50, 138, 155, 156, 158) (1895–present), Great burnet (10) (1818), Salad burnet (1) (1932)

Sanguisorba minor **Scop.** – Pimpernelle (156) (1923), Small burnet (50, 138, 155) (1923–present)

Sanguisorba minor **Scop. subsp. *muricata*** (**Spach**) **Nordborg** – Bibernel (92) (1876), Bibernell (German) (158) (1900), Bilbernel (5) (1913), Bloodwort [Blood wort, Blood-wort] (5, 156, 157, 158) (1900–1929), Burnet (19, 45, 46, 107, 109, 157, 158, 178) (1526–1949), Burnet clover (129) (1894), Common burnet (157, 158) (1900–1929), Garden burnet (5, 156, 157, 158) (1900–1929), Pimpernelle (5) (1913), Pimprenelle (157, 158) (1900–1929), Salad burnet (5, 156, 157, 158) (1900–1929), Small bibernel (92, 157, 158) (1876–1929), Small burnet (50) (present), Toper's plant (5, 156, 157, 158) (1900–1929), Lesse saxifrage (179) (1526), Pimpinella (178) (1526)

Sanguisorba officinalis L. – Burnet (14) (1882), Great burnet (156, 158) (1900–1923)

Sanguisorba sanguisorba (**L.**) **Britton** – See *Sanguisorba minor* Scop. subsp. *muricata* (Spach) Nordborg

Sanicula bipinnatifida **Douglas ex Hook.** – Screw bean [Screwbean, Screw-bean] (15, 107, 156) (1895–1923)

Sanicula canadensis L. – Black snakeroot [Black snake-root, Black-snake root] (157, 158) (1900–1929), Bur snakeroot (40) (1928), Canadian sanicle [Canada sanicle] (3, 155) (1942–1977), Mûkûde'widji'bǐk (Chippewa, black root) (40) (1928), Short-style sanicle [Short-styled sanicle] (157) (1929), Short-style snakeroot [Short-styled snake root, Short styled snakeroot, Short-styled snakeroot, Short-styled snake-root] (5, 72, 93, 97, 122, 131, 157, 158) (1899–1937)

Sanicula canadensis L. var. *canadensis* – Canadian black snakeroot [Canadian blacksnakeroot] (50) (present)

Sanicula gregaria **Bickn.** – See *Sanicula odorata* (Raf.) K. M. Pryer & L. R. Phillippe

Sanicula L. – Black snakeroot [Black snake-root, Black-snake root] (2) (1895), Sanicle (1, 2, 10, 50, 155, 156, 158, 184) (1793–present), Snakeroot [Snake root, Snake-root] (1, 93, 158) (1900–1936)

Sanicula marilandica L. – American sanicle (157, 158) (1900–1929), Black sanicle (5, 92, 155, 157, 158) (1876–1942), Black snakeroot [Black snake-root, Black-snake root] (3, 5, 49, 58, 85, 92, 93, 97, 131, 156, 157, 158) (1869–1977), Maryland sanicle (50) (present), Pool root [Poolroot, Pool-root] (49, 156, 157, 158) (1900–1929), Sanicle (7, 19, 48, 49, 58, 61, 72, 156, 157, 157) (1828–1929)

Sanicula odorata (**Raf.**) **K. M. Pryer & L. R. Phillippe** – Cluster sanicle (3) (1977), Clustered black snakeroot [Clustered blacksnakeroot] (50) (present), Clustered snakeroot [Clustered snake root, Clustered snake-root] (5, 72, 93, 97) (1907–1937)

Sanicula trifoliata **Bicknell** – Large-fruit snakeroot [Large-fruited snake-root] (5, 72) (1907–1913)

Sansevieria hyacinthoides (**L.**) **Druce** – Bowstring-hemp [Bowstring hemp] (92) (1876), Caballine aloes (92) (1876), Horse aloes (92) (1876)

Sansevieria **Thunb.** – Bowstring-hemp [Bowstring hemp] (109) (1949)

Santalum L. – Saunders (92) (1876)

Santolina chamaecyparissus L. – Cypress herb (92) (1876),

Lavender-cotton [Lavendercotton, Lavender cotton] (46, 92, 109, 138) (1671–1949) cultivated by English colonists by 1671, Josselyn, Sea wormwood (178) (1526)

Santolina L. – Lavender-cotton [Lavendercotton, Lavender cotton] (138, 155, 158) (1900–1942)

Sanvitalia **Lam.** – Sanvitalia (138) (1923)

Sanvitalia procumbens **Lam.** – Common sanvitalia (138) (1923), Sanvitalia (92) (1876)

Sapindus L. – Soapberry [Soap berry] or Soapberry tree (4, 13, 50, 109, 138, 155, 156, 158, 167) (1814–present)

Sapindus marginatus **Willd.** – See *Sapindus saponaria* L. var. *saponaria*

Sapindus mukorossi **Gaertner** – See *Sapindus saponaria* L.

Sapindus saponaria L. – Chinese soapberry (138) (1923), Soapberry [Soap berry] or Soapberry tree (10, 12, 15, 92) (1818–1895), Southern soapberry (138) (1923)

Sapindus saponaria L. var. *drummondii* (**Hook. & Arn.**) **Bensons** – Chinaberry [China-berry, China berry] or Chinaberry tree (106) (1930), Drummond's soapberry (5, 97) (1913–1937), Indian soap plant [Indian soap-plant] (5, 156) (1913–1923), Soapberry [Soap berry] or Soapberry tree (1, 3, 4, 106, 121, 125, 153, 156) (1913–1986), Wanoŋpihi (Osage, necklace tree) (121) (1918?–1970?), Western soapberry [Western soap berry] (50, 124, 138, 155) (1923–present), Wild China or Wild China tree [Wild China-tree] (5, 65, 97, 106, 110, 124, 156) (1913–1937), Wild chinaberry tree (153) (1913)

Sapindus saponaria L. var. *saponaria* – Florida soap berry (20) (1857), Indian soap plant [Indian soap-plant] (92) (1876), Savonnier de la Floride (French) (20) (1857), Soapberry [Soap berry] or Soapberry tree (103, 149) (1870–1904), Soaproot [Soap-root, Soap root] (92) (1876), Soapwood [Soap-wood] (96) (1891) OK, Wild China or Wild China tree [Wild China-tree] (147, 164) (1854–1856)

Sapindus **Tourn.** – See *Sapindus* L.

Sapium aucuparium [**Willd.**] – See *Sapium glandulosum* (L.) Morong

Sapium glandulosum (**L.**) **Morong** – Yerba de la flecha (52) (1919)

Sapium **Jacq.** – Sapium (155) (1942)

Sapium **P. Br.** – See *Sapium* Jacq.

Sapium sebiferum **Roxb.** – See *Triadica sebifera* (L.) Small

Saponaria L. – Bouncing Bet [Bouncing-Bet, Bouncingbet] (1, 93) (1932–1936), Cow cockle [Cowcockle] (1, 93) (1932–1936), Cowherb (1, 158) (1900–1932), Soapwort [Soap-wort, Sope woort, Sope-wort] (1, 7, 10, 15, 50, 93, 109, 138, 155, 156, 158, 167, 184) (1793–present)

Saponaria ocymoides L. – Rock soapwort (138) (1923)

Saponaria officinalis L. – Boston pink (5, 64, 74, 156, 157, 158) (1893–1929) Poland ME, Bouncing Bess (156) (1923), Bouncing Bet [Bouncing-Bet, Bouncingbet] (1, 4, 50, 5, 19, 49, 62, 64, 80, 85, 92, 95, 97, 109, 114, 131, 138, 148, 155, 156, 157, 158, 187) (1818–present), Bruisewort [Bruise wort, Bruise-wort, Bruse-wort] (5, 64, 92, 156, 157, 158, 180, 187) (1633–1929), Burit (179) (1526), Buryt (157, 158) (1900–1929), Chimney pink [Chimney pinks] (5, 64, 74, 157, 158) (1893–1929), Common soapwort (64, 157, 158) (1900–1929), Crow-soap [Crow soap] (64, 156, 157, 158, 179) (1526–1929), Floptop [Flop-top] (156) (1923), Fuller's grass [Fullers grasse] (179) (1526), Fuller's herb [Fuller's-herb] (5, 49, 64, 92, 156, 157, 158) (1898–1929), Hedge-pink [Hedge pink] (5, 62, 64, 156, 157, 158) (1900–1929), Herbe phylyp (179) (1526), Lady-by-the-gate [Lady by the gate] (5, 64, 76, 156, 157, 158) (1896–1929), Latherwort (64, 156, 157, 158) (1900–1929), London pride [London-pride] (5, 64, 73, 156, 157, 158) (1892–1929) Salem MA, Mock gilliflower [Mock gillyflower] (5, 64, 156, 157, 158) (1900–1929), Monthly pink (76) (1896) Greene Co. MO, Official soapwort [Official soap-wort] (187) (1818), Old-maid's pink [Old maid pink, Old maid's pink] (5, 64, 73, 92, 157, 158) (1876–1929), Saponaria (57, 64, 178, 180) (1596–1917), Saponaria (Spanish) (158) (1900), Saponary (64, 157, 158, 179) (1526–1929), Savonnière (French) (157) (1929), Scourweed (156) (1923), Scourwort (64, 156,

158) (1900–1929), Seifenwurzel (German) (158) (1900), Sheep-weed [Sheep weed, Sheep-weed] (5, 64, 92, 156, 157, 158) (1876–1929), Soaproot [Soap-root, Soap root] (5, 49, 64, 92, 156, 157, 158) (1898–1929), Soapwort [Soap-wort, Sope woort, Sope-wort] (1, 4, 5, 10, 19, 49, 57, 62, 64, 72, 80, 85, 92, 131, 148, 156, 178, 180) (1526–1986) sap from some species will make lather, Soapwort gentian [Soapwort-gentian (5, 156) (1913–1923), Sweet Betty [Sweet Betties, Sweet Bettie] (5, 64, 76, 156, 157) (1896–1923) no longer in use by 1923, Waschwurzel (German) (158) (1900), Wild Sweet William [Wild Sweet-William] (5, 64, 156, 157, 158) (1900–1929), Wood phlox [Woods phlox] (5, 64, 73, 156, 157, 158) (1892–1929), World's-wonder [World's wonder] (5, 64, 76, 156, 157, 158) (1896–1929) Eastern MA

Saponaria vaccaria **L.** – See *Vaccaria hispanica* (Mill.) Rauschert

Sarcobatus **Nees** – Chico (1, 93) (1932–1936), Greasebush [Grease-bush, Grease bush] (108) (1878), Greasewood [Grease-wood] (1, 50, 93, 155, 158) (1900–present)

Sarcobatus vermiculatus **(Hook.) Torr.** – Black greasewood (155) (1942), Chico (148, 153) (1913–1939), Fleshy-leaf thorn [Fleshy-leaved thorn] (35) (1806), Greasebush [Grease-bush, Grease bush] (108) (1878), Greasewood [Grease-wood] (3, 4, 5, 50, 75, 85, 93, 101, 113, 130, 146, 148, 153) (1890–present), Pulpy-leaf thorn [Pulpy leaved thorn] (35) (1806)

Sarcocornia perennis **(P. Mill.) A. J. Scott** – Bush glasswort (122) (1937), Lead-grass [Lead grass] (77) (1898) Southold Long Island, from weight in salt-meadow hay, Leadweed [Lead weed] (77) (1898) Southold Long Island, from weight in salt-meadow hay, Woody glasswort (5) (1913)

Sarcodes sanguinea **Torr.** – Snow plant (75) (1894) CA

Sarcoscypha coccinea **(Jacq.) Boud.** – Scarlet-cup [Scarlet cup] (128) (1933) ND

Sarcostemma cynanchoides **Dcne.** – See *Funastrum cynanchoides* (Dcne.) Schlechter subsp. *cynanchoides*

Sargassum bacciferum **(Turner) Agardh** – See *Sargassum natans* (Linnaeus) Gaillon

Sargassum natans **(L.) Gaillon** – Gulfweed [Gulf weed] (41, 92, 181) (~1678–1876), Laver (92) (1876), Sargasso [Sargazo] (41, 174, 181) (~1678–1770), Sea-lentil [Sea lentil] (181) (~1678)

Sarothamnus vulgaris **Wimmer** – See *Cytisus scoparius* (L.) Link

Sarothra dummondii **Grevar. & Hook.** – See *Hypericum drummondii* (Grev. & Hook.) Torr. & Gray

Sarothra gentianoides **L.** – See *Hypericum gentianoides* (L.) Britton, Sterns & Poggenb.

Sarracenia ×catesbaei **Ell.** [*flava* × *purpurea*] – Catesby's pitcherplant [Catesby pitcherplant] (138) (1923)

Sarracenia alata **Wood** – Pitcherplant [Pitcher plant, Pitcher-plant] (124) (1937)

Sarracenia catesbaei – See *Sarracenia ×catesbaei* Ell. [*flava* × *purpurea*]

Sarracenia drummondii **Croom.** – See *Sarracenia leucophylla* Raf.

Sarracenia flava **L.** – Biscuits (5, 156) (1913–1923) no longer in use by 1923, Long-leaf side-saddle flower [Long leaved Sidesaddle Flower] (181) (~1678), Sarasena with a large Yellow Flower (183) (~1756), Side-saddle flower [Sidesaddle flower, Side saddle flower] (177) (1762), Trumpet [Trumpets] (5, 10, 15, 46, 156) (1818–1923), Trumpet flower [Trumpet-flower, Trumpet-flowers] (177, 181) (~1678–1762), Trumpet pitcherplant (138) (1923), Trumpet-leaf [Trumpet leaf, Trumpit Leaf] (5, 92, 156, 183) (~1756–1923), Watches (5, 156) (1913–1923), Water-cup [Watercup, Water cup] (5, 92, 156) (1876–1923), Yellow pitcher plant [Yellow pitcher-plant] (156) (1923), Yellow trumpetleaf [Yellow trumpet leaf] (2) (1895), Yellow trumpets (5, 156) (1913–1923), Eve's-cups [Eve's cup, Eve's cups] (92) (1876)

Sarracenia **L.** – Pitcherplant [Pitcher plant, Pitcher-plant] (15, 109, 138) (1895–1949), Side-saddle flower [Sidesaddle flower, Side saddle flower] (1, 2, 10, 13, 14, 15, 86, 167) (1814–1932) from flower shape

Sarracenia leucophylla **Raf.** – Drummond's pitcherplant [Drummond's pitcher plant, Drummond pitcherplant] (84, 86, 138) (1878–1923), Drummond's sidesaddle flower (84) (1880), Great trumpetleaf [Great trumpet leaf] (2) (1895), Trumpet [Trumpets] (15, 109) (1895–1949), Trumpet-leaf [Trumpet leaf, Trumpit Leaf] (15) (1895), Watches (15) (1895)

Sarracenia minor **Walt.** – Hooded pitcherplant (138) (1923)

Sarracenia psittacina **Michx.** – Parrot pitcher plant [Parrot pitcherplant] (2, 86, 138) (1878–1923), Parrot-head pitcher-plant [Parrot-headed pitcher-plant] (86) (1878)

Sarracenia purpurea **L.** – Adam's-cup [Adam's cup] (5, 73, 156) (1892–1923) Dudley MA, Common pitcherplant [Common pitcherplant] (109, 138) (1923–1949), Dumb-watch [Dumb watch, Dumb watches] (74, 156) (1893–1923) Cape May Co. NJ, Eve's-cups [Eve's cup, Eve's cups] (6) (1892), Fevercup [Fever cup, Fever-cup] (5, 74, 156) (1893–1923), Fly-catcher [Fly catcher] (6) (1892), Flytrap [Fly-trap, Fly trap] (5, 49, 52, 57, 92, 156) (1898–1923), Forefather's-cup [Forefather's cup, Forefathers' cup] (5, 74, 92, 156) (1876–1923) New England, Forefather's-pitcher [Forefather's pitcher] (5, 76) (1896–1913) ME, Foxglove [Fox glove, Foxglove, Foxgloves] (5, 73, 76, 156) (1892–1923) NH, Huntsman's-cup [Huntsman's cup, Huntsmans' cup] (5, 6, 13, 15, 49, 74, 92, 156) (1849–1923) New England, Indian cup [Indian-cup] (5, 156) (1913–1923), Indian pitcher (5, 73, 156) (1892–1923) NH, Indian teakettles (156) (1923), Meadow-cup [Meadow cup] (5, 76, 156) (1896–1923) ME, O'mûkiki'wida'sûn (Chippewa, frog leggings) (40) (1928), Pitcherplant [Pitcher plant, Pitcher-plant] (1, 2, 5, 6, 40, 47, 49, 52, 57, 63, 92, 156) (1852–1932), Saddle plant (92) (1876), Sarracenia (61) (1870), Side-saddle (19) (1840), Side-saddle flower [Sidesaddle flower, Side saddle flower] (5, 6, 15, 46, 49, 63, 92, 156, 187) (1818–1923), Side-saddle plant [Sidesaddle plant] (49, 52, 57, 92) (1876–1919), Skunk cabbage [Skunk-cabbage, Skunkcabbage] (5, 76, 156) (1896–1923) St. Paul MN, Smallpox plant [Small-pox plant (5, 92, 156) (1876–1923), St. Jacob's-dipper [St. Jacob's dipper] (156) (1923), Watches (5, 74, 156) (1893–1923) Atlantic City NJ, Water-cup [Watercup, Water cup] (6, 49, 52) (1892–1919), Whip-poorwill's-boots [Whippoorwill's boots, Whip-poor-will's boots] (5, 76, 156) (1896–1923) Philadelphia PA, no longer in use by 1923, Whippoorwill-shoes [Whipoorwill shoes, Whip-poor-will's shoe, Whip-poor-will shoe, Whip-poor-will shoes, Whippoorwill's shoes, Whip-poor-will's shoes] (5, 76, 156) (1896–1923) ME, no longer in use by 1923

Sarracenia purpurea **L. subsp.** *purpurea* **var.** *purpurea* – Hollow-leaf lavender [Hollow leave'd Lavender] (181) (~1678), Hollow-leaf sea lavender [Hollow-leaved sea lavender] (181) (~1678), Side-saddle flower [Sidesaddle flower, Side saddle flower] (181) (~1678)

Sarracenia purpurea **var.** *venosa* – See *Sarracenia purpurea* L. subsp. *purpurea* var. *purpurea*

Sarracenia rubra **Walt.** – Red-flower trumpet-leaf [Red-flowered trumpet leaf] (2, 86) (1878–1895), Sweet pitcher-plant [Sweet pitcherplant] (109, 138) (1923–1949)

Sarracenia sledgei **MacFarlane** – See *Sarracenia alata* Wood

Sassafras albidum **(Nutt.) Nees** – Adhotathny (46) (1879), Ague tree [Ague-tree] (5, 92, 156, 158) (1876–1923), American sassafras tree (14) (1882), Cinnamon wood [Cinnamon-wood] (5, 92, 156, 158) (1876–1923), Common sassafras (138, 155) (1923–1942), Fenchelholz (German) (158) (1900), Gombo sassafras (107) (1919), Laurier sassafras (French) (8) (1785), Menagwake-minš (Chippewa, fragrant root tree) (105) (1932), Panameholz (German) (158) (1900), Saloop (5, 92, 156, 158) (1876–1923), Sasaunckapamuck (Naraganset) (46) (1879), Sasfras (Spanish) (158) (1900), Sassafrack (156) (1923), Sassafras (French) (158) (1900), Sassafras [Sassaphras] or Sassafras tree [Sassafras-tree] (2, 5, 8, 18, 19, 20, 38, 41, 46, 53, 57, 58, 61, 72, 92, 97, 105, 106, 107, 109, 124, 156, 158, 177, 181, 182, 187, 189) (~1678–1949), Sassafras bark (92) (1876), Sassafras root (92) (1876), Sassafras wood (92) (1876), Sausfras (35) (1806), Saxefras (46) (1879), Saxifrax (92, 158) (1876–1900), Silky sassafras

(155) (1942), Smelling-stick [Smelling stick] (5, 156, 158) (1900–1923), White sassafras (3, 19) (1840–1977), Winauk (181) (~1678)

***Sassafras albidum* (Nutt.) Nees var. *molle* (Raf.) Fern.** – See *Sassafras albidum* (Nutt.) Nees

***Sassafras* Nees. & Eberm.** – Ague tree [Ague-tree] (1) (1932), Sassafras [Sassaphras] or Sassafras tree [Sassafras-tree] (1, 4, 50, 138, 155, 158) (1900–present)

***Sassafras officinale* Nees.** – See *Sassafras albidum* (Nutt.) Nees

Sassafras officinalis – See *Sassafras albidum* (Nutt.) Nees

***Sassafras sassafras* (L.) Kaarst.** – See *Sassafras albidum* (Nutt.) Nees

***Sassafras* Trew** – See *Sassafras* Nees. & Eberm.

***Sassafras variifolium* (Salisb.) Kuntze** – See *Sassafras albidum* (Nutt.) Nees

Satureia – See *Satureja* L.

Satureia rigida – See *Piloblephis rigida* (Bartr. ex Benth.) Raf.

Satureja acinos – See *Acinos arvensis* (Lam.) Dandy

***Satureja arkansana* (Nutt.) Briq.** – See *Clinopodium arkansanum* (Nutt.) House

***Satureja hortensis* L.** – Sauerey (179) (1526), Savory (5, 184) (1793–1913), Summer savory (19, 46, 49, 57, 58, 92, 106, 107, 109, 138, 156) (1671–1949) cultivated by English colonists by 1671

***Satureja* L.** – Savory (109, 138, 156) (1923–1949)

***Satureja montana* L.** – Winter savory [Winter Sauorie] (19, 92, 106, 107, 109, 138, 178) (1526–1949)

Satureja nepeta – See *Calamintha nepeta* (L.) Savi subsp. *nepeta*

***Satureja viminea* L.** – Pennyroyal tree (92) (1876)

***Satureja virginica* L.** – See *Pycnanthemum virginianum* (L.) T. Dur. & B. D. Jackson ex B. L. Robins. & Fern.

***Saururus cernuus* L.** – Breastweed [Breast weed, Breast-weed] (5, 19, 92, 106, 156, 158) (1840–1930), Common lizardtail (138, 155) (1923–1942), Lizard's-tail [Lizards' tail, Lizards-tail, Lizard's tail, Lizard-tail, Lizard tail, Lizardtail] (1, 4, 5, 7, 10, 19, 92, 97, 106, 120, 156, 158) (1818–1986), Nodding lizard's-tail (187) (1818), Swamp-lily [Swamp lily] (5, 106, 156) (1913–1930), Water-dragon [Water dragon] (3) (1977), Waterlily [Water lily, Water-lily, Water-lilies] (187) (1818)

***Saururus* L.** – Heart-leaf lizard's-tail [Heart leaved lizard's tail] (190) (~1759), Lizard's-tail [Lizards' tail, Lizards-tail, Lizard's tail, Lizard-tail, Lizard tail, Lizardtail] (1, 2, 109, 138, 155, 158, 167, 184) (1793–1929), Saururus (50, 93, 155, 158) (1900–present)

***Sauvagesia erecta* L.** – St. Martin's-wort [Saint Martin's wort] (92) (1876)

***Savastana nashii* Bicknell** – See *Hierochloe odorata* (L.) Beauv.

***Savastana odorata* (L.) Scribn.** – See *Hierochloe odorata* (L.) Beauv.

***Saxifraga* (Tourn.) L.** – See *Saxifraga* L.

***Saxifraga aizoides* L.** – Sengreen saxifrage (5) (1913), Sengren saxifrage (156) (1923), Yellow mountain saxifrage (5, 156) (1913–1923)

Saxifraga aizoon – See *Saxifraga paniculata* Mill. subsp. *neogaea* (Butters) D. Löve

Saxifraga caespitosa* L. subsp. *caespitosa – Tufted saxifrage (5) (1913)

***Saxifraga caroliniana* Gray** – Gray's saxifrage (5) (1913)

***Saxifraga cernua* L.** – Drooping bulbous saxifrage (5) (1913), Nodding bulbous saxifrage (5) (1913), Nodding saxifrage (4, 131) (1899–1986), Saxifrage (3, 85) (1932–1977)

***Saxifraga foliolosa* R. Br.** – Foliose saxifrage (5) (1913)

***Saxifraga forbesii* Vasey** – See *Saxifraga pensylvanica* L.

***Saxifraga hirculus* L.** – Yellow marsh saxifrage (156) (1923)

Saxifraga hirculus* L. subsp. *hirculus – Three-tooth saxifrage [Three toothed saxifrage] (5) (1913), Yellow marsh saxifrage (5) (1913)

***Saxifraga* L.** – Mayflower [May flower, May-flower] (76) (1896) Auburndale MA, Mountain saxifrage (1) (1932), Purple saxifrage (1) (1932), Saxifrage (1, 10, 109, 138, 155, 156, 158, 167, 184) (1793–1949), Spotted saxifrage (1) (1932), Stonebreak (92) (1876), Yellow saxifrage (1) (1932)

***Saxifraga mertensiana* Bong.** – Coconut [Cocoanuts] (74) (1893) Southern CA, bulbs

***Saxifraga michauxii* Britt.** – Michaux's saxifrage [Michaux saxifrage] (5, 138) (1913–1923)

***Saxifraga micranthidifolia* (Haw.) Steud.** – Lettuce saxifrage (5, 156) (1913–1923)

***Saxifraga nivalis* L.** – Clustered alpine saxifrage (5) (1913)

***Saxifraga occidentalis* S. Wats.** – Alberta saxifrage (50, 155) (1942–present)

***Saxifraga oppositifolia* L.** – Mountain saxifrage (1, 156) (1923–1932), Purple saxifrage (156) (1923), Twin-leaf saxifrage [Twinleaf saxifrage] (138) (1923)

Saxifraga oppositifolia* L. subsp. *oppositifolia – Mountain saxifrage (5) (1913), Purple saxifrage (5) (1913)

***Saxifraga paniculata* Mill. subsp. *neogaea* (Butters) D. Löve** – Aizoon saxifrage (138) (1923), Live-long saxifrage [Livelong saxifrage] (5, 156) (1913–1923)

Saxifraga peltata – See *Darmera peltata* (Torr. ex Benth.) Voss

***Saxifraga pensylvanica* L.** – Eastern swamp saxifrage (50) (present), King's-evilroot [Kings' evil root] (52) (1919), Pennsylvania saxifrage (5) (1913), Saxifrage (52) (1919), Scrofula bush (52) (1919), Swamp saxifrage (2, 5, 72, 107, 156) (1895–1923), Tall saxifrage (52, 187) (1818–1919), Water saxifrage (19) (1840)

***Saxifraga pensylvanica* L. subsp. *interior* Burns** – See *Saxifraga pensylvanica* L.

***Saxifraga rivularis* L.** – Alpine brook saxifrage (5, 156) (1913–1923)

***Saxifraga sarmentosa* L.** – See *Saxifraga stolonifera* Meerb.

Saxifraga stellaris – See *Saxifraga stellaris* L.

***Saxifraga stellaris* L.** – Kidneywort [Kidney-wort] (5, 156) (1913–1923), Star saxifrage (5) (1913), Starry saxifrage (5, 156) (1913–1923)

***Saxifraga stellaris* L. var. *comosa* Poir.** – See *Vaccaria hispanica* (Mill.) Rauschert

***Saxifraga stolonifera* Meerb.** – Beefsteak [Beef steak] (19) (1840), Beefsteak plant [Beefsteak-plant, Beefsteakplant] (92) (1876), Creeping saxifrage (19) (1840), Otaheite (76) (1896) Paris ME, Sailor plant (92) (1876), Strawberry saxifrage (138) (1923), Strawberry-geranium (109) (1949), Wandering-Jew [Wandering Jew] (92) (1876)

***Saxifraga texana* Buckl.** – Texas saxifrage [Texan saxifrage] (5, 50, 97) (1913–present)

***Saxifraga tridactylites* L.** – Rue nailwort [Rue Naile woort] (178) (1526), Rue-leaf saxifrage [Rueleaf saxifrage] (50) (present), Whitlow-grass [Whitlow grass, Whitlowgrass] (92) (1876)

***Saxifraga virginica* [Nutt.]** – possibly *Saxifraga virginiensis* Michx. (taxonomic status is unresolved (PL))

***Saxifraga virginiensis* Michx.** – Early saxifrage (2, 86, 156, 187) (1818–1923), Early white saxifrage (86) (1878), Everlasting (76, 156) (1896–1923) Lynn MA, Mayflower [May flower, May-flower] (73, 156) (1892–1923) Allston MA, Rock saxifrage (19, 156) (1840–1923), Sweet Wilson (5, 76, 156) (1896–1923) Abingdon MA, named by Mrs. Ward for Wilson Ward around 1850, Virginia saxifrage (138) (1923), possibly Spring saxifrage (156) (1923)

Saxifraga virginiensis* Michx. var. *virginiensis – Early saxifrage (5) (1913), Everlasting (5) (1913), Mayflower [May flower, May-flower] (5) (1913), Spring saxifrage (5) (1913)

***Scabiosa arvense* L.** – See *Knautia arvensis* (L.) Duby

***Scabiosa atropupurea* L.** – Mourning-bride [Mourning bride] (76, 92) (1876–1896) Sulphur Grove OH, Mourning-widow [Mourning widow] (76, 92) (1876–1896) Sulphur Grove OH, Sweet scabiosa (138) (1923), Sweet scabious [Sweet-scabious] (19, 82, 109) (1840–1949), Sweet scabish (92) (1876), possibly Scabious of the sea (178) (1526)

Scabiosa australis – See *Succisella inflexa* (Kluk) G. Beck

***Scabiosa* L.** – Mourning-bride [Mourning bride] (82, 109) (1930–1949), Scabiosa (138) (1923), Scabious [Scabius, Scabyous] (109) (1949)

***Scabiosa ochroleuca* L.** – Yellow scabiosa (138) (1923)

***Scabiosa stellata* L.** – Cat's-eye [Cats eye, Cats' eye, Cat's eye] (19, 92) (1840–1876), Spanish scabious (178) (1526), Star scabious (19, 92) (1840–1876)

Scabiosa succissa – See *Succisa pratensis* Moench

Scandix cerefolium L. – See *Anthriscus cerefolium* (L.) Hoffmann

Scandix pecten – See *Scandix pecten-veneris* L.

Scandix pecten-veneris L. – Adam's-needle [Adam's needle] (5, 156) (1913–1923), Beggar's-needles [Beggar's needles] (5, 156) (1913–1923), Crake-needles [Crake needles] (5) (1913), Crape-needle (156) (1923) no longer in use by 1923, Crow-needles [Crow-needle, Crow needles] (5, 156) (1913–1923) obsolete by 1923, Devil's-darn-ing-needle [Devil's darning needle] (5, 156) (1913–1923) no longer in use by 1923, Hedgehog [Hedge hog, Hedge hogs] (5, 156) (1913–1923) no longer in use by 1923, Lady's-comb [Lady's comb] (5, 156) (1913–1923) no longer in use by 1923, Needle-chervil [Needle chervil] (5, 156) (1913–1923) no longer in use by 1923, Pecten Veneris (178) (1526), Pink-nee-dle [Pink needle] (5, 156) (1913–1923), Poukenel (5, 156) (1913–1923) no longer in use by 1923, Pucker-needle [Pucker needle] (92) (1876), Scandix (107) (1919), Shepherd's-needle [Shepherds' nee-dle, Shepherd's needle, Shepherds'-needle] (5, 50, 92, 156) (1876–present), Venus'-comb [Venus' comb, Venus comb] (5, 92, 107, 156) (1876–1923), Wild chervil (107) (1919)

Schaefferia cuneifolia Gray – Capul (122) (1937) TX, Desert yaupon (122, 124) (1937) TX

Schedonnardus paniculatus (Nutt.) Trel. – Schedonnardus (5, 72, 158) (1900–1913), Slender-tail grass (66) (1903), Texas crab-grass [Texas crab grass, Texas crab-grass, Texan crab grass, Texan crabgrass, Texan crab-grass] (5, 56, 72, 94, 119, 134, 140) (1901–1944), Tumble grass [Tumble-grass, Tumblegrass] (3, 50, 122, 140, 155) (1937–present), Wild crabgrass [Wild crab grass] (111, 129, 152) (1894–1915), Wire grass [Wire-grass, Wiregrass] (5, 119) (1913–1938)

Schedonnardus Steud. – Tumble grass [Tumble-grass, Tumblegrass] (50, 155) (1942–present)

Schedonorus ×festucaceus (Link) Kartesz [*arundinaceus × praten-sis*] – Slender spiked fescue (66) (1903)

Scheuchzeria L. – Less-flowering-rush (167) (1814), Rannoch-rush [Rannochrush, Rannoch rush] (50) (present), Scheuchzeria (155) (1942)

Scheuchzeria palustris L. – Less flowering rush (19) (1840), Rannoch-rush [Rannochrush, Rannoch rush] (50) (present), Scheuchzeria (155) (1942)

Scheuchzeria palustris L. subsp. *americana* (Fern.) Hultén – Ran-noch-rush [Rannochrush, Rannoch rush] (50) (present)

Schinus L. – Pepper tree [Pepper-tree, Peppertree] (138) (1923)

Schinus molle L. – Australian pepper (107) (1919), California pep-per tree [California pepper-tree, California peppertree] (109, 138) (1923–1949), Molle (107) (1919), Pepper tree [Pepper-tree, Pepper-tree] (76, 106) (1896–1930) red berries are used as pepper substi-tute, Peruvian mastic tree [Peruvian mastic-tree] (109) (1949), Peru-vian mastich (92) (1876)

Schinus terebinthifolius Raddi – Brazilian peppertree [Brazilian pep-per-tree] (109, 138) (1923–1949), Christmas berry tree [Christmas-berry-tree] (109) (1949)

Schizachne Hack. – False melic [Falsemelic] (50) (present)

Schizachne purpurascens (Torr.) Swall. – False melic [Falsemelic] (3, 50, 140, 155) (1942–present), Purple oat [Purple oats] (5, 93) (1913–1936), Purple wild oat [Purple wild oats] (66, 90) (1885–1903), Wild oat grass [Wild oat-grass, Wild oats grass] (87, 90) (1884–1885)

Schizachyrium cirratum (Hack.) Woot. & Standl. – Texas beard grass [Texas beardgrass] (122) (1937)

Schizachyrium littorale (Nash) Bicknell – Sea-coast beard grass [Sea-coast beard-grass] (5, 163) (1852–1913), Shore little blustem (50) (present)

Schizachyrium maritimum (Chapman) Nash – Sand broom-sedge [Sand broom sedge] (94) (1901)

Schizachyrium Nees – Little bluestem [Little blue stem, Little blue-stem] (50) (present), Sage grass [Sage-grass] (152) (1912) NM

Schizachyrium sanguineum (Retz.) Alston var. *sanguineum* – Short-beard broom-sedge [Short-bearded broom sedge] (94) (1901)

Schizachyrium scoparium (Michx.) Nash – Blue-stem grass [Bluestem grass] (5) (1913), Broom grass [Broom-grass] (5) (1913), Broom-sedge [Broom sedge, Broomsedge] (5) (1913), Bunch grass [Bunch-grass, Bunch-grass] (5) (1913), Little bluestem [Little blue stem, Lit-tle blue-stem] (50) (present), Purple beard grass [Purple beard-grass] (187) (1818), Redstem [Red-stem] (5) (1913)

Schizachyrium scoparium (Michx.) Nash var. *divergens* (Hack.) Gould – Little bluestem [Little blue stem, Little blue-stem] (122) (1937)

Schizachyrium scoparium (Michx.) Nash var. *scoparium* – Beard grass [Beard-grass, Beardgrass] (45, 108) (1878–1896), Big blue-joint [Big blue joint] (75) (1894), Big bluestem [Big blue-stem Big blue stem] (75) (1894), Bluejoint [Blue-joint, Blue joint] (5, 45) (1896–1913), Broom beard grass [Broom beard-grass, Broom beardgrass, Broom bearded grass] (5, 42, 72, 99, 131) (1814–1923), Broom beard-sedge [Broom beard sedge] (62) (1912), Broom grass [Broom-grass] (19, 45, 66, 87, 90) (1840–1912), Broom-sedge [Broom sedge, Broomsedge] (45, 75, 128, 134, 163) (1852–1933), Bunch grass [Bunchgrass, Bunch-grass] (65, 75, 128) (1894–1931), Little bluestem [Little blue stem, Little blue-stem] (3, 11, 22, 50, 56, 65, 85, 93, 94, 98, 111, 115, 119, 124, 129, 134, 140, 144, 146, 155, 163) (1852–present), New Mexico bluestem [NewMexico bluestem] (155) (1942), Prairie beard grass [Prairie beardgrass] (140) (1944), Purple wood grass (66, 90) (1885–1903), Wood grass [Wood-grass] (87, 90) (1884–1885)

Schizachyrium tenerum Nees – Beardless broom sedge (94) (1901)

Schizaea pusilla Pursh – Curly grass (5, 11, 22) (1888–1913), Little curly-grass fern [Little curlygrass fern] (50) (present), New Jersey tea [New-Jersey-tea, New-Jersey tea] (86) (1878), One-sided fern (19) (1840)

Schizanthus pinnatus Ruiz & Pavón – Wing-leaf butterfly flower [Wingleaf butterfly flower] (138) (1923)

Schizanthus Ruiz & Pavón – Butterfly flower [Butterfly-flower, But-terflyflower] (109, 138) (1923–1949)

Schizococcus nissenanus (Merriam) Eastw. – See *Arctostaphylos nis-senana* Merriam

Schlumbergera Lem. – Crab cactus [Crabcactus] (138, 155) (1923–1942), Easter cactus [Eastercactus] (138) (1923)

Schlumbergera truncata (Haw.) Moran – Christmas cactus (109, 138) (1923–1949), Crab cactus [Crabcactus] (109) (1949)

Schmaltzia crenata (Mill.) Greene – See *Rhus aromatica* Aiton var. *ar-omatica*

Schmaltzia tribolata (Nutt.) Small. – See *Rhus trilobata* Nutt. var. *tri-lobata*

Schoenocaulon drummondii Gray – Green lily (122, 124) (1937)

Schoenolirion albiflorum (Raf.) R. R. Gates – White sunnybell (50) (present)

Schoenolirion croceum (Michx.) Wood – Yellow sunnybell (50) (pres-ent)

Schoenoplectus (Reichenb.) Palla – Bulrush [Bull rush, Bullrush, Bul-Rush, Bulrushes] (50) (present)

Schoenoplectus acutus (Muhl. ex Bigelow) A. & D. Löve var. *acutus* – Bulrush [Bull rush, Bullrush, Bul-Rush, Bulrushes] (35, 101, 152) (1806–1912), Great bulrush (121) (1918–1970), Hard-stem bulrush [Hardstem bulrush, Hardstem bulrush] (3, 50) (1977–present), Psa (Lakota) (121) (1918–1970), Tule bulrush (155) (1942), Θa udse-toŋga (Osage, large-based rush) (121) (1918–1970)

Schoenoplectus acutus (Muhl. ex Bigelow) A. & D. Löve var. *oc-cidentalis* (S. Wats.) S. G. Sm. – Tule (50) (present), Tule-grass (156) (1923), Viscid great bulrush (5) (1913), Western bulrush (139) (1944)

Schoenoplectus acutus (Muhl. ex Bigelow) Á. & D. Löve – Hard-stem bulrush [Hardstem bulrush, Hardstem bulrush] (50) (present)

Schoenoplectus americanus (Pers.) Volk. ex Schinz & R. Keller – American bulrush (139, 155) (1942–1944), Bulrush [Bull rush, Bull-rush, Bul-Rush, Bulrushes] (85) (1932), Chairmaker's bulrush (50) (present), Chairmaker's rush [Chairmakers rush, Chair-makers rush]

(156) (1923–1977), Sword-grass [Sword grass] (5, 156) (1913–1923), Three-side rush [Three-sided rush] (187) (1818), Three-square (5, 156) (1913–1923), Three-square rush (72) (1907)

Schoenoplectus californicus (C. A. Mey.) Palla – Giant bulrush (124) (1937), Tule (122) (1937)

Schoenoplectus deltarum (Schuyler) Soják – Delta bulrush [Delta bullrush] (50) (present)

Schoenoplectus etuberculatus (Steud.) Soják – Canby's bulrush (5, 50) (1913–present), Pole-rush [Pole rush] (5) (1913), Pool-rush [Pool rush] (5) (1913)

Schoenoplectus fluviatilis (Torr.) M. T. Strong – River bulrush (3, 50, 72, 155, 156) (1907–present), River club-rush [River club rush] (5, 129, 156) (1894–1923), River rush (66) (1903), Slough grass [Slough-grass, Sloughgrass] (129) (1894) SD

Schoenoplectus hallii (Gray) S. G. Sm. – Hall's bulrush [Halls bulrush] (50) (present)

Schoenoplectus heterochaetus (Chase) Soják – Pale great bulrush (5) (1913), Slender bulrush (3, 50, 155) (1942–present)

Schoenoplectus juncoides (Roxb.) Palla subsp. *purshianus* (Fern.) Soják – See *Schoenoplectus purshianus* (Fern.) M. T. Strong

Schoenoplectus maritimus (L.) Lye – Alkali bulrush (139, 155) (1942–1944), Cosmopolitan bulrush (50) (present), Fernald's bulrush (5) (1913), Prairie bulrush (5) (1913), Prairie-rush [Prairie rush] (3) (1977), Sea bulrush (66) (1903), Sea club-rush (129) (1894), Seaside bulrush (107) (1919), Slough grass [Slough-grass, Sloughgrass] (129) (1894) SD, Spurt-grass [Spurt grass] (92) (1876), Tuber bulrush (141) (1899) WY

Schoenoplectus mucronatus (L.) Palla – Bog bulrush (156) (1923)

Schoenoplectus novae-angliae (Britt.) M. T. Strong – New England bulrush (5, 50) (1913–present)

Schoenoplectus pungens (Vahl) Palla – Common threesquare (50) (present)

Schoenoplectus pungens (Vahl) Palla var. *pungens* – Chair-bottom rush (66) (1903), Chairmaker's rush [Chairmakers rush, Chair-makers rush] (129) (1894), Common threesqaure (50) (present), Sharp-point rush [Sharp pointed rush] (129) (1894)

Schoenoplectus purshianus (Fern.) M. T. Strong – Weak bulrush (155) (1942), Weak-stalk bulrush [Weakstalk bulrush] (50) (present), Weak-stalk club-rush [Weak-stalked club rush] (5) (1913), Weak-stem rush (66) (1903)

Schoenoplectus robustus (Pursh) M. T. Strong – Saltmarsh bulrush [Salt marsh bulrush] (5) (1913), Spurt-grass [Spurt grass] (5) (1913), Sturdy bulrush (50) (present)

Schoenoplectus rubiginosus (Beetle) Soják p.p. – See *Schoenoplectus acutus* (Muhl. ex Bigelow) A. & D. Löve var. *occidentalis* (S. Wats.) S. G. Sm.

Schoenoplectus saximontanus (Fern.) Raynal – Rocky Mountain bulrush [RockyMountain bulrush] (50, 155) (1942–present)

Schoenoplectus smithii (Gray) Soják – Smith's bulrush [Smiths bulrush] (50, 155) (1942–present)

Schoenoplectus subterminalis (Torr.) Soják – Floating clubrush [Floating club-rush] (66) (1903), Swaying bulrush (50) (present), Water club-rush [Water club rush] (5) (1913)

Schoenoplectus tabernaemontani (C. C. Gmel.) Palla – possibly Bass (158) (1900), possibly Bulrush [Bull rush, Bullrush, Bul-Rush, Bulrushes] (37, 66, 107, 158) (1830–1919), possibly Bumble (158) (1900), possibly Cat-tail [Cat's tail, Cats Taile, Cat's-tail, Cats tails] (103) (1871), possibly Club rush [Club-rush] (158) (1900), possibly Common bulrush (1, 14, 40, 139) (1882–1944), possibly Frail-rush [Frail rush] (158) (1900), possibly Great bulrush (72, 93, 138, 155, 156, 158) (1900–1942), possibly Panier-rush [Panier rush] (158) (1900), possibly Tall bulrush [Tall bull-rush] (187) (1818), possibly Teel [Teele] (14) (1882), possibly Tule (75, 101, 107, 156) (1894–1923), possibly Tulé (Spanish) (161) (1857), possibly Tule root (103) (1871)

Schoenoplectus tabernaemontani (K. C. Gmel.) Palla – American great bulrush (5) (1913), Ana'kun (Chippewa) (40) (1928), Bent

(156, 158) (1900–1923), Black rush [Black-rush] (5, 75, 156, 158) (1894–1923), Bolder (156, 158) (1900–1923), Boulder bast [Boulder-bast] (5, 156) (1913–1923), Giant bulrush (85) (1932), Lake rush (156) (1923), Mat rush [Mat-rush] (5, 156, 158) (1900–1923), Pole-rush [Pole rush] (156, 158) (1900–1923), Psa (Dakota) (37) (1830), Sa-hi (Omaha-Ponca) (37) (1830), Sistat (Pawnee) (37) (1830), Soft-stem bulrush [Softstem bulrush] (3, 50, 155) (1942–present), Spurt-grass [Spurt grass] (156, 158) (1900–1923), Taburnaemontanus bulrush (155) (1942)

Schoenoplectus torreyi (Olney) Palla – Torrey's bulrush [Torrey bulrush] (5, 50, 155) (1913–present), Torrey's rush [Torrey rush] (66) (1903)

Schoenus effusus Sw. – See *Cladium mariscus* (L.) Pohl subsp. *jamaicense* (Crantz) Kükenth.

Schoenus glomeratus L. – See *Rhynchospora glomerata* (L.) Vahl

Schoenus L. – Bog rush [Bogrush] (10, 50) (1818–present), Rush-grass [Rushgrass, Rush grass, Rush-grasse] (184) (1793)

Schoenus mariscoides M. – See *Cladium mariscoides* (Muhl.) Torr.

Schollera graminea – See *Heteranthera dubia* (Jacq.) MacM.

Schollera graminifolia Willd. – See *Heteranthera dubia* (Jacq.) MacM.

Schrankia angustata Torr. & Gray. – See *Mimosa microphylla* Dry.

Schrankia horridula (Michx.) Chapm. – See *Mimosa microphylla* Dry.

Schrankia microphylla (Dry.) J. F. Macbr. – See *Mimosa microphylla* Dry.

Schrankia nuttallii (DC.) Standl. – See *Mimosa nuttallii* (DC.) B.L. Turner

Schrankia occidentalis (W. & S.) Standl. – See *Mimosa rupertiana* B. L. Turner

Schrankia uncinata Willd. – See *Mimosa microphylla* Dry.

Schrophularia nodosa – See *Scrophularia nodosa* L.

Schubertia disticha Mirbel – See *Taxodium distichum* (L.) L. C. Rich.

Schwalbea americana L. – Chaffseed [Chaff-seed, Chaff seed] (5, 19, 156) (1840–1923)

Schwalbea L. – Chaffseed [Chaff-seed, Chaff seed] (2) (1895)

Scilla fraseri A. Gray – See *Camassia scilloides* (Raf.) Cory

Scilla hispanica Mill. – See *Hyacinthoides hispanica* (Mill.) Rothm.

Scilla L. – Squill [Squills] (109, 138) (1923–1949)

Scilla nonscripta Hoffmgg. & Link – See *Hyacinthoides nonscripta* (L.) Chouard ex Rothm.

Scilla nutans Sm. – See *Hyacinthoides nonscripta* (L.) Chouard ex Rothm.

Scilla siberica Haw. – Siberian squill (106, 138) (1923–1930)

Scirpus ×*peckii* Britt. [*atrocinctus* × *atrovirens* and × *pedicellatus*] – Peck's bulrush (5) (1913)

Scirpus americanus Pers. – See *Schoenoplectus americanus* (Pers.) Volk. ex Schinz & R. Keller

Scirpus atrocinctus Fern. – Black-girdle bulrush [Blackgirdle bulrush] (50) (present), Common bulrush (156) (1923), Dark-green bulrush [Darkgreen bulrush, Dark green bulrush] (3, 5, 72) (1907–1977), Green bulrush (50, 138, 139, 155) (1923–present)

Scirpus atrovirens Willd. var. *atrovirens* – See *Scirpus atrovirens* Willd.

Scirpus atrovirens Willd. var. *georgianus* (Harper) Fern. – See *Scirpus georgianus* Harper

Scirpus atrovirens Willd. var. *pallidus* Britt. – See *Scirpus pallidus* (Britt.) Fern.

Scirpus autumnalis L. – See *Fimbristylis autumnalis* (L.) Roemer & J.A. Schultes

Scirpus caespitosus L. var. *austriacus* (Pallas) Aschers. & Graebn. – See *Trichophorum caespitosum* (L.) Hartman

Scirpus californicus (C. A. Meyer) Britton – See *Schoenoplectus californicus* (C. A. Mey.) Palla

Scirpus campestris [Willd. ex Kunth] – See *Eleocharis palustris* (L.) Roemer & J. A. Schultes

Scirpus cernuus – See *Isolepis cernua* (Vahl) Roemer & J. A. Schultes

Scirpus coloradoensis Britt. – See *Eleocharis parvula* (Roem. & Schult.) Link ex Bluff, Nees & Schauer

       Scleropogon **Phil.**

Scirpus cyperinus **(L.) Kunth** – Brown cotton-grass (187) (1818), Cottongrass [Cotton-grass, Cotton grass] (156, 184) (1793–1923), Red cotton-grass [Red cotton grass] (19) (1840), Wool-grass [Wool grass, Woolgrass] (3, 50, 66, 72, 156) (1903–present), Wool-grass bulrush [Woolgrass bulrush] (155) (1942)

Scirpus divaricatus **Ell.** – Spreading bulrush (5, 50) (1913–present)

Scirpus eriophorum **Michx.** – See *Scirpus cyperinus* (L.) Kunth

Scirpus etuberculatus **(Steud.) Kuntze** – See *Schoenoplectus etuberculatus* (Steud.) Soják

Scirpus expansus **Fern.** – Meadow rush (129) (1894), Wood bulrush (5) (1913), Wood club-rush [Wood club rush, Wood clubrush] (5) (1913), Wood rush (19, 66) (1840–1903), Woodland bulrush (50) (present)

Scirpus fluviatilis **(Torr.) Gray** – See *Schoenoplectus fluviatilis* (Torr.) M. T. Strong

Scirpus fontinalis **Harper** – See *Scirpus lineatus* Michx.

Scirpus georgianus **Harper** – Dark-green bulrush [Darkgreen bulrush, Dark green bulrush] (3) (1977), Georgia bulrush (50) (present)

Scirpus glomeratus **L.** – See *Fimbristylis spathacea* Roth

Scirpus hallii **Gray** – Hall's bulrush [Halls bulrush] (3, 50, 139, 155) (1942–present), Hall's club rush (5, 72) (1907–1913), Hall's rush [Hall rush] (129) (1894)

Scirpus heterochaetus **Chase** – See *Schoenoplectus heterochaetus* (Chase) Soják

Scirpus hotarui **auct. non Ohwi** – See *Schoenoplectus purshianus* (Fern.) M. T. Strong

Scirpus koilolepis **(Steud.) Gl.** – See *Isolepis carinata* Hook. & Arn. ex Torr.

Scirpus **L.** – Bulrush [Bull rush, Bullrush, Bul-Rush, Bulrushes] (1, 50, 93, 109, 138, 139, 156) (1923–present), Club rush [Club-rush] (1, 92) (1876–1932), Club-grass (184) (1793), Rush [Rushes] (152, 155, 158) (1900–1942), Tule (1, 10, 93) (1818–1936)

Scirpus lacustris **L.** – See *Schoenoplectus lacustris* (L.) Palla

Scirpus lineatus **Michx.** – Chairmaker's rush [Chairmakers rush, Chairmakers rush] (120) (1938) OK, Drooping bulrush (50) (present), Porter's rush (66) (1903), Reddish bulrush (5, 72, 120) (1907–1938), Three-corner-grass [Three cornered grass] (129) (1894) SD

Scirpus maritimus **L. var.** *paludosus* **(A. NelScirpus) Kukenth.** – See *Schoenoplectus maritimus* (L.) Lye

Scirpus microcarpus **J. & K. Presl** – Panicled bulrush (50, 139, 155) (1942–present), Small-fruit bulrush [Small-fruited bulrush] (5) (1913)

Scirpus microcarpus **Presl. var.** *rubrotinctus* **(Fern.) M. E. Jones** – See *Scirpus microcarpus* J. & K. Presl

Scirpus mucronatus – See *Schoenoplectus mucronatus* (L.) Palla

Scirpus nanus **Spreng.** – See *Eleocharis quinqueflora* (F. X. Hartmann) Schwarz

Scirpus nevadensis **S. Wats.** – Nevada bulrush (50, 155) (1942–present)

Scirpus occidentalis **(S. Wats.) Chase** – See *Schoenoplectus acutus* (Muhl. ex Bigelow) A. & D. Löve var. *occidentalis* (S. Wats.) S. G. Sm.

Scirpus olneyi **Gray** – See *Fimbristylis annua* (All.) R. & S.

Scirpus pallidus **(Britt.) Fern.** – Bulrush [Bull rush, Bullrush, Bul-Rush, Bulrushes] (41) (1770), Cloaked bulrush (50) (present), Dark-green bulrush [Darkgreen bulrush, Dark green bulrush] (3) (1977), Pale bulrush (5, 139) (1913–1944)

Scirpus paludosus **A. Nelson** – See *Schoenoplectus maritimus* (L.) Lye

Scirpus pauciflorus **Lightf.** – See *Eleocharis quinqueflora* (F. X. Hartmann) Schwarz

Scirpus pendulus **Muhl.** – Rufous bulrush (50) (present)

Scirpus planifolius **Muhl., non Grimm** – See *Trichophorum planifolium* (Spreng.) Palla

Scirpus polyphyllus **Vahl** – Cluster-head rush (66) (1903), Leafy bulrush (5, 50) (1913–present)

Scirpus robustus **Pursh var.** *novae-angliae* **(Britt.) Beetle** – See *Schoenoplectus novae-angliae* (Britt.) M. T. Strong

Scirpus rubiginosus **Beetle p.p.** – See *Schoenoplectus acutus* (Muhl. ex Bigelow) A. & D. Löve var. *occidentalis* (S. Wats.) S. G. Sm.

Scirpus rufus **(Huds.) Schrad. var.** *neogaeus* **Fern.** – See *Blysmus rufus* (Huds.) Link

Scirpus saximontanus **Fern.** – See *Schoenoplectus saximontanus* (Fern.) Raynal

Scirpus smithi – See *Schoenoplectus smithii* (Gray) Soják

Scirpus spadiceus **auct. non L.** – See *Fimbristylis thermalis* S. Wats.

Scirpus subterminalis **Torr.** – See *Schoenoplectus subterminalis* (Torr.) Soják

Scirpus sylvaticus **L. p.p.** – See *Scirpus expansus* Fern.

Scirpus tenuis **W.** – See *Eleocharis tenuis* (Willd.) J. A. Schultes

Scirpus torreyi **Olney** – See *Schoenoplectus torreyi* (Olney) Palla

Scirpus validus **Vahl** – See *Schoenoplectus tabernaemontani* (K.C. Gmel.) Palla

Scleranthus annuus **L.** – Annual knawel (4, 155) (1942–1986), German knotgrass [German knot grass, German knot-gass] (5, 50, 92, 156, 158) (1876–present), German millet-grass [German millet grass] (92) (1876), Gnavelle (French) (158) (1900), Gravel chickweed (5, 19, 92, 156, 158) (1840–1923), Knawel (1, 5, 10, 92, 156, 158, 187) (1818–1932), Parsley breakstone (178) (1526), Parsley piert (5, 156) (1913–1923), Wilde Knauel (German) (158) (1900)

Scleranthus **L.** – German knotgrass [German knot grass, German knot-gass] (50, 187) (1818–present)

Scleranthus **L.** – Knawel (4, 13, 155, 158) (1900–1986)

Scleria **Berg.** – Nutrush [Nut rush] (1, 50) (1932–present), Razor-sedge [Razorsedge] (155) (1942), Whip-grass [Whip grass] (10, 167) (1814–1818)

Scleria ciliata **Michx.** – Fringed nutrush (50) (present), Fringed razor-sedge [Fringed razorsedge] (155) (1942), Hairy nut rush (5) (1913)

Scleria muehlenbergii **Steud.** – Muehlenberg's nutrush (50) (present)

Scleria oligantha **Michx.** – Few-flower nutrush [Few-flowered nut rush] (5, 66) (1903–1913), Little-head nutrush [Littlehead nutrush] (50) (present)

Scleria pauciflora **Muhl. ex Willd.** – Few-flower nutsedge [Fewflower nutsedge] (50) (present), Few-flower razor-sedge [Fewflower razor-sedge, Fewflower razorsedge] (3, 155) (1942–1977), Papillose nutrush [Papillose nut rush] (5) (1913)

Scleria pauciflora **Muhl. ex Willd. var.** *caroliniana* **(Willd.) Wood** – Carolina nutsedge (50) (present)

Scleria pauciflora **Muhl. ex Willd. var.** *pauciflora* – Few-flower nutsedge [Fewflower nutsedge] (50) (present)

Scleria reticularis **Michx.** – Netted nutrush (50) (present), Reticulated nut-rush [Reticulated nut rush] (5) (1913), Sessile nut-rush [Sessile nut rush] (66) (1903)

Scleria reticularis **Michx. var.** *pubescens* **Britt.** – See *Scleria muehlenbergii* Steud.

Scleria triglomerata **Michx.** – Tall nut-rush [Tall nut rush] (5, 72, 156) (1907–1923), Whip nut-rush [Whip nutrush] (50) (present), Whip razor-sedge [Whip razorsedge] (3, 19, 155) (1840–1977), Whip-grass [Whip grass] (5, 66, 92, 156) (1903–1923)

Scleria verticillata **Muhl. ex Willd.** – Dwarf nut rush (66) (1903), Low nutrush [Low nut rush] (5, 50) (1913–present)

Sclerocactus uncinatus **(Galeotti) N. P. Taylor var.** *wrightii* **(Engelm.) N. P. Taylor** – Fishhook cactus (138) (1923) AZ NM

Sclerochloa **Beauv.** – Hard grass [Hardgrass] (50, 155) (1942–present)

Sclerochloa dura **(L.) Beauv.** – Common bear grass [Common bear-grass] (50) (present), Hard grass [Hardgrass] (155) (1942)

Sclerolepis uniflora **(Walt.) Porter** – Golden thistle (92) (1876), Scleropis (5) (1913)

Scleropoa rigida **(L.) Griseb.** – See *Desmazeria rigida* (L.) Tutin

Scleropogon brevifolius **Phil.** – Burro grass [Burrograss, Burro-grass] (3, 50, 122, 155, 163) (1852–present), Needle grass [Needle-grass, Needlegrass] (152) (1912) NM

Scleropogon **Phil.** – Burro grass [Burrograss] (50) (present), False needle grass [False needle-grass] (152, 163) (1852–1912) NM

Sclerotinia tuberosa [(Hedw.) Fuckel] – See *Dumontinia tuberosa* (Bull.) L. M. Kohn

Sclerotium clavus DC. – Cockspur rye (92) (1876), Hornseed [Horn seed] (92) (1876), Mother-of-rye [Mother of rye] (92) (1876), Smut of rye (92) (1876)

Sclerotium clavus Dec. – See *Sclerotium clavus* DC.

Scolochloa festucacea (Willd.) Link – Common river grass [Common rivergrass] (14, 50) (1882–present), Fescue scolochloa (56, 72) (1901–1907), Prickle fescue (5) (1913), Prickly fescue (115) (1932), Spangletop [Spangle top, Spangle-top] (85, 93, 94) (1901–1936), Sprangle-top [Sprangletop, Sprangle top] (3, 50, 111) (1915–present)

Scolochloa Link – Prickly fescue (93) (1936), River grass [Rivergrass] (50, 155) (1942–present)

Scolopendrium vulgare Smith – possibly *Asplenium scolopendrium* L. var. *americanum* (Fern.) Kartesz & Gandhi

Scolymus hispanicus L. – Black oyster plant (107) (1919), Black salsify [Black-salsify] (107, 138) (1919–1923), Écorce noire (French) (110) (1886), Golden thistle (107, 109) (1919–1949), Leimonia (107) (322 BC) in American seed catalogs in 1870's, Scorzonera (110, 178) (1526–1886), Scorzonera (Spain) (107) (1570) Spanish oyster plant [Spanish oysterplant, Spanish oyster-plant] (107, 109, 138) (1919–1949), Spanish salsify (110) (1886), Viper's plant (110) (1886), Viper's-grass [Viper's grass, Vipers' grass] (92, 107) (1876–1919) said to be antidote for bite of adder

Scolymus L. – Golden thistle (92) (1876)

Scorzonera hispanica L. – See *Scolymus hispanicus* L.

Scorzonera L. – False salsify (4) (1986), Scorzonera (50) (present), Serpentroot (138, 155) (1923–1942), Winter-asparagus [Winter asparagus] (158) (1900)

Scorzonera laciniata L. – Cut-leaf vipergrass [Cutleaf vipergrass] (50) (present), Mediterranean serpentroot (155) (1942)

Scrophularia aquatica L. – See *Scrophularia umbrosa* Dumort.

Scrophularia L. – Figwort [Fig-wort, Figwoort] (1, 2, 4, 7, 10, 50, 82, 93, 155, 156, 158) (1818–present), Heal-all [Healall] (7) (1828), Holmes' weed [Holmes'-weed, Holmes weed, Holmesweed] (7) (1828)

Scrophularia lanceolata Pursh – Figwort [Fig-wort, Figwoort] (3, 82) (1930–1977), Hare figwort (5, 72, 93, 97) (1907–1937), Lance-leaf figwort [Lanceleaf figwort] (50, 155) (1942–present), Western figwort (5, 85, 97, 155) (1913–1942)

Scrophularia leporella Bicknell – See *Scrophularia lanceolata* Pursh

Scrophularia marilandica L. – American figwort (157, 158) (1900–1929), Carpenter's-square [Carpenter's square] (5, 50, 92, 156) (1876–present), Figwort [Fig-wort, Figwoort] (19, 61, 62, 63, 85, 92, 93, 106, 156, 184, 187) (1793–1936), Figwort herb (92) (1876), Hairy figwort (97) (1937), Heal-all [Healall] (92, 93, 131, 156) (1876–1936), Holmes' weed [Holmes'-weed, Holmes weed, Holmesweed] (92, 156, 157, 158) (1876–1929), Maryland figwort [Maryland fig-wort (3, 5, 72, 97, 131, 155, 157, 158) (1899–1977), Maryland heal-all (5) (1913), Maryland pilewort (5) (1913), Pilewort [Pile-wort, Pile wort] (62, 93, 156) (1912–1936), Scrofula plant [Scrofula-plant] (5, 92, 156) (1876–1923), Simpson's honey plant [Simpson honey plant] (80, 82, 106) (1913–1930), Squarestalk [Square-stalk, Square stalk] (92) (1876)

Scrophularia neglecta Rydb. ex Small – See *Scrophularia marilandica* L.

Scrophularia nodosa L. – Carpenter's-square [Carpenter's square] (6, 52, 58) (1869–1919), Figwort [Fig-wort, Figwoort] (6, 52, 57, 58, 178) (1526–1917), Figwort root (92) (1876), Heal-all [Healall] (6, 52, 58) (1869–1919), Holmes' weed [Holmes'-weed, Holmes weed, Holmesweed] (6) (1892), Kernelwort (92) (1876), Knotty-root figwort [Knotty rooted figwort] (92) (1876), Kropfwurz (German) (6) (1892), Scrofula plant [Scrofula-plant] (6, 52) (1869–1919), Scrophelnpflanze (German) (6) (1892), Scrophulaire (French) (6) (1892), Squarestalk [Square-stalk, Square stalk] (6, 58) (1869–1892)

Scrophularia nodosa var. *Americana* Michaux – See *Scrophularia nodosa* var. *marilandica* Gray.

Scrophularia nodosa var. *marilandica* Gray. – Carpenter's-square [Carpenter's square] (77) (1898) Southwestern MO

Scrophularia occidentalis (Rydb.) Bicknell – See *Scrophularia lanceolata* Pursh

Scrophularia umbrosa Dumort. – Bishop's-leaves [Bishop's leaves] (92, 107) (1876–1919), Brownwort [Brown wort] (107) (1919), Water betony (92) (1876), Water figwort (92) (1876), Water-betony (107) (1919)

Scutellaria (Rivin.) L. – See *Scutellaria* L.

Scutellaria brittonii Porter – Britton's skullcap [Brittons skullcap] (4, 5, 50, 155) (1913–present)

Scutellaria bushii Britt. – Bush's skullcap (5) (1913)

Scutellaria caroliniana Walt – See *Scutellaria ovata* Hill subsp. *ovata*

Scutellaria drummondii Benth. – Drummond's skullcap (4, 50, 97) (1937–present), Skullcap [Scull cap, Scullcap, Skull-cap, Skull cap] (124) (1937)

Scutellaria galericulata L. – Common skullcap [Common Skull-cap] (187) (1818), European skullcap (5, 157, 158) (1900–1929), Helmet flower [Helmet-flower] (46) (1879), Hooded skullcap (93) (1936), Hooded willow-herb [Hooded willow herb, Hooded willow herbe] (5, 92, 156, 157, 158, 178) (1526–1929), Marsh skullcap [Marsh skull-cap, Marsh skull cap] (3, 4, 5, 50, 72, 93, 131, 156, 157, 158) (1899–present), Skullcap [Scull cap, Scullcap, Skull-cap, Skull cap] (19, 46, 82) (1840–1879)

Scutellaria gracilis Nutt. – See *Scutellaria nervosa* Pursh

Scutellaria hyssopifolia L. – See *Scutellaria integrifolia* L.

Scutellaria incana Biehler – Downy skullcap [Downy skull cap] (5, 72) (1907–1913), Hoary skullcap (4) (1986)

Scutellaria integrifolia L. – Cacida (183) (~1756), Entire-leaf skullcap [Entire-leaved Skull-cap] (187) (1818), Hyssop skullcap (5) (1913), Hyssop-leaf skullcap [Hyssop-leaved Skull-cap] (187) (1818), Large-flower skullcap [Large-flowered skullcap] (5) (1913), Larger skullcap (5) (1913)

Scutellaria L. – Helmet flower [Helmet-flower] (158) (1900), Helmkraut (German) (158) (1900), Schildkraut (German) (158) (1900), Scutellaire (French) (158) (1900), Skullcap [Scull cap, Scullcap, Skull-cap, Skull cap] (1, 2, 4, 10, 50, 63, 82, 93, 109, 138, 155, 156, 158, 184) (1793–present)

Scutellaria lateriflora L. – American skullcap (157, 158) (1900–1929), Blue pimpernel (5, 6, 156, 157, 158) (1892–1929), Blue skullcap [Blue skull-cap, Blue scullcap] (3, 5, 50, 58, 85, 92, 93, 97, 156) (1869–present), Dhood wort (19) (1840), Gû'nïgwali'skï (Cherokee, it becomes discolored when bruised) (102) (1886) Red juice comes out of stem when bruised or chewed, Helmet flower [Helmet-flower] (92) (1876), Helmkraut (German) (6) (1892), Hooded willow-herb [Hooded willow herb, Hooded willow herbe] (92) (1876), Hoodwort [Hood-wort] (5, 6, 52, 58, 77, 92, 156, 157, 158) (1869–1929) Western US, Mad dog skullcap [Mad dog scull cap, Mad dog scullcap] (2, 6, 19, 63, 72, 75, 82) (1840–1930), Mad-dog [Mad dog] (5, 157) (1900–1929), Mad-dog skullcap [Mad-dog skull-cap, Mad-dog skull cap, Mad-dog scullcap] (93, 131, 156, 157, 158) (1899–1936), Mad-dog weed [Mad dog weed] (6, 92) (1876–1892), Madweed [Madweed] (5, 6, 49, 52, 53, 92, 156, 157, 158) (1892–1929), Scutellaire (French) (6) (1892), Scutellaria (54, 55, 57, 59) (1905–1917), Side-flower skullcap [Sideflowering skullcap, Side-flowering scull-cap, Side flowering scullcap, Side-flowering skullcap] (5, 92, 155, 158) (1876–1942), Skullcap [Scull cap, Scullcap, Skull-cap, Skull cap] (48, 49, 52, 53, 54, 55, 57, 58, 61, 92, 102, 157) (1869–1929), Virginia skullcap [Virginian skull cap] (6) (1892)

Scutellaria nervosa Pursh – Slender skullcap [Slender skull-cap] (187) (1818), Veined skullcap [Veined skull cap] (5, 72) (1907–1913)

Scutellaria ovata Hill – Egg-leaf skullcap [Eggleaf skullcap] (3, 4) (1977–1986), Heart-leaf skullcap [Heartleaf skullcap, Heart-leaved skull-cap, Heart-leaved skullcap, Heart leaved skull cap] (50) (present)

Scutellaria ovata **Hill subsp.** *ovata* – Heart-leaf skullcap [Heartleaf skullcap, Heart-leaved skull-cap, Heart-leaved skullcap, Heart leaved skull cap] (5, 72, 82, 97) (1907–1937)

Scutellaria ovata **Hill subsp.** *versicolor* **(Nutt.) Epling** – See *Scutellaria ovata* Hill subsp. *ovata*

Scutellaria parvula **Michx.** – Little skullcap (5) (1913), Small skullcap [Small skull cap] (4, 5, 50, 72, 82, 93, 97, 131, 155, 157) (1899–present)

Scutellaria parvula **Michx. subsp.** *parvula* – See *Scutellaria parvula* Michx. var. *parvula*

Scutellaria parvula **Michx. var.** *australis* **Fassett** – Small skullcap [Small skull cap] (50) (present), Southern small skullcap (3) (1977)

Scutellaria parvula **Michx. var.** *leonardii* **(Epl.) Fern.** – See *Scutellaria parvula* Michx. var. *missouriensis* (Torr.) Goodman & Lawson

Scutellaria parvula **Michx. var.** *missouriensis* **(Torr.) Goodman & Lawson** – Leonard's skullcap (50) (present), Leonard's small skullcap [Leonard small skullcap] (3) (1977)

Scutellaria parvula **Michx. var.** *parvula* – Small skullcap [Small skull cap] (3, 50) (1977–present)

Scutellaria pilosa **Michx.** – Hairy skullcap (5, 97) (1913–1937)

Scutellaria resinosa **Torr.** – Resinous skullcap (4, 5, 97, 155) (1913–1986), Sticky skullcap (50) (present)

Scutellaria saxatilis **Riddell** – Rock skullcap (5) (1913)

Scutellaria serrata **Andr.** – Showy skullcap (5) (1913)

Scutellaria wrightii **Gray** – Wright's skullcap (50, 86) (1878–present)

Sebastiania fruticosa **(Bartr.) Fern.** – See *Ditrysinia fruticosa* (W. Bartram) Govaerts & Frodin

Secale cereale **L.** – Cekela or zekhalea (Basque) (110) (1886), Centeno (French) (158) (1900), Centeno (Spanish) (180) (1633), Cereal rye (50) (present), Common rye (119, 163) (1852–1938), Cretan rye (66) (1903), Cultivated rye (56, 93, 163) (1852–1936), Ferrago (180) (1633), Mountain rye (94, 155) (1901–1942), Rez (Polish) (110) (1886), Rie (Rye) (14, 180) (1633–1882), Rig (Anglo-Saxon) (110) (1886), Roggen (German) (158) (1900), Rûgr (Scandinavian) (110) (1886), Rye (7, 56, 85, 92, 107, 109, 110, 122, 138, 140, 155, 158, 178, 179) (1526–1949), Rye grass [Rye-grass, Ryegrass] (92) (1876), Segal (Breton) (110) (1886), Segala (Italian) (180) (1633), Seigle (French) (158, 180) (1633–1900)

Secale **L.** – Rye (50, 138, 155, 158, 184) (1793–present)

Secale montanum **Guss.** – See *Secale cereale* L.

Secale villosum – See *Dasypyrum villosum* (L.) P. Candargy

Sechium edule **(Jacq.) Sw.** – Chayote (106, 107, 109, 110, 138) (1919–1949), Chayotl (Aztec) (110) (1886), Chayotli (Mexico) (107) (1919), Chocho (Jamaica) (106, 107, 110) (1886–1930), Choco [Choko] (107, 110) (1886–1919), Christophine (109) (1949)

Sechium edule **Sw.** – See *Sechium edule* (Jacq.) Sw.

Sechium **P. Browne** – Chayote (138) (1923)

Securigera securidaca **(L.) O. Deg. & Dorf.** – Hatchet vetch (178) (1526)

Sedum acre **L.** – Bird's-bread [Bird's bread] (5, 156) (1913–1923), Biting stonecrop [Biting stone crop] (5, 49, 57, 92, 156) (1898–1923), Common stonecrop (109) (1949), Creeping charlie [Creeping-charlie, Creeping charley] (5, 156) (1913–1923), Creeping Jack (5, 156) (1913–1923) no longer in use by 1923, English moss (57) (1917), Ginger [Gynger] (5, 156) (1913–1923) no longer in use by 1923, Gold-chain [Gold chain] (5, 156) (1913–1923), Golden moss (5, 156) (1913–1923), Golden-moss [Golden moss] (5, 156) (1913–1923), Goldmoss [Gold moss] (138, 156) (1923), Gold-moss stonecrop [Goldmoss stonecrop] (155) (1942), Illecebra (178) (1526), Jack-of-the-buttery [Jack of the buttery] (92) (1876), Kit-of-the-wall (156) (1923), Little houseleek [Little house leek] (5, 156) (1913–1923), Love-entangled [Love entangled, Love entangle, Love-entangle] (5, 73, 86, 156) (1878–1923) Northern Ohio, Mossy stonecrop (3, 5, 49, 156) (1898–1977), Mountain-moss [Mountain moss] (5, 156) (1913–1923), Pepper-crop [Pepper crop] (5, 156) (1913–1923), Poor-man's-pepper [Poor-man's pepper, Poor man's pepper] (5, 156) (1913–1923), Pricket (5, 156) (1913–1923) no longer in use by

1923, Prick-madam [Prick madam, Prick-madame] (5) (1913), Rock plant [Rock-plant] (5, 156) (1913–1923), Small houseleek [Small house leek, Small house-leek] (49, 92) (1876–1898), Stone crop (85) (1932), Stonecrop [Stone crop, Stone-crop] (85) (1932), Tangle-tail [Tangle tail] (5, 156) (1913–1923) no longer in use by 1923, Treasure-of-love (5, 76) (1896–1913) Boston MA, Wall-moss [Wall moss] (5, 156) (1913–1923), Wall-pepper [Wall pepper] (5, 92, 156, 178) (1526–1923), Wallwort [Wall wort, Wallwoort] (156) (1923)

Sedum aizoon **L.** – Aizoon stonecrop (138, 155) (1931–1942)

Sedum alboroseum – See *Hylotelephium erythrostictum* (Miq.) H. Ohba.

Sedum album **L.** – Prick-madam [Prick madam, Prick-madame] (92) (1876), Stonecrop [Stone crop, Stone-crop] (107) (1919), White stonecrop (92, 138, 155) (1876–1942), Worm-grass [Wormgrass, Worm grass] (92) (1876)

Sedum dasyphyllum **L.** – Leafy stonecrop (138, 155) (1931–1942)

Sedum hispanicum **L.** – Plume stonecrop (138, 155) (1931–1942), Spanish stonecrop (138, 155) (1931–1942)

Sedum hybridum **L.** – Evergreen stonecrop (155) (1942), Hybrid stonecrop (138) (1923)

Sedum kamtschaticum **Fisch. & C. A. Mey.** – Orange stonecrop (138, 155) (1931–1942)

Sedum **L.** – Live-forever [Liveforever, Live forever] (93) (1936), Orpine (1, 2, 109) (1895–1949), Stonecrop [Stone crop, Stone-crop] (1, 2, 4, 10, 50, 86, 93, 109, 138, 155, 156, 157, 158, 167) (1814–present)

Sedum lanceolatum **Torr.** – Narrow-petal stonecrop [Narrow-petaled stonecrop] (5, 93) (1913–1936), Spear-leaf stonecrop [Spearleaf stonecrop] (50) (present), Stonecrop [Stone crop, Stone-crop] (3) (1977), Western stonecrop [Western stone crop] (131) (1899), Worm-leaf sedum [Wormleaf sedum] (155) (1942), Yellow-flower stonecrop [Yellow-flowered stonecrop] (38) (1820)

Sedum lanceolatum **Torr. subsp.** *lanceolatum* – Spear-leaf stonecrop [Spearleaf stonecrop] (50) (present)

Sedum nevii **Gray** – Nevis' stone crop (86) (1878)

Sedum nuttallianum **Raf.** – Nuttall's stonecrop [Nuttall stonecrop] (5, 97, 155) (1913–1942), Stonecrop [Stone crop, Stone-crop] (3) (1977), Yellow stonecrop (50) (present)

Sedum oppositifolium – See *Sedum spurium* M. Bieb.

Sedum pulchellum **Michx.** – Beautiful sedum (2) (1895), Flowering-moss [Flowering moss] (5, 156, 158) (1900–1927), Mountain-moss [Mountain moss] (5, 156) (1913–1923), Rock-moss [Rock moss] (5, 76, 97, 156, 158) (1896–1937), Stonecrop [Stone crop, Stone-crop] (3, 48, 106) (1882–1977), Texas stonecrop (138, 155) (1923–1942), Widow's-cross [Widow's cross] (5, 50, 156, 158) (1900–present)

Sedum purpureum – See *Hylotelephium telephium* (L.) H. Ohba. subsp. *telephium*

Sedum reflexum **L.** – Creeping Jenny [Creeping Jennie, Creeping-Jennie, Creeping-jenny] (156) (1923), Crooked stonecrop (156) (1923), Crooked yellow stonecrop (5) (1913), Dwarf houseleek [Dwarf house-leek, Dwarf house leek] (5, 156) (1913–1923), Jenny stonecrop (138, 155) (1931–1942), Love-in-a-chain (156) (1923), Reflexed stonecrop (5) (1913), Yellow stonecrop (156) (1923)

Sedum rosea **Scop.** – See *Rhodiola rosea* L.

Sedum roseum **Scop. (*sic*)** – See *Rhodiola rosea* L.

Sedum sarmentosum **Bunge** – Stringy stonecrop (138, 155) (1923–1942)

Sedum sexangulare **L.** – Hexagon stonecrop (138, 155) (1923–1942)

Sedum smallii **(Britton) H. E. Ahles** – Red moss (74) (1893)

Sedum spectabile – See *Hylotelephium spectabile* (Boreau) H. Ohba.

Sedum spurium **M. Bieb.** – Two-row stonecrop (138) (1923)

Sedum stenopetalum **Pursh** – See *Sedum lanceolatum* Torr.

Sedum stoloniferum **Gmel.** – Running stonecrop (138, 155) (1931–1942)

Sedum telephinum **L.** – See *Hylotelephium telephium* (L.) H. Ohba. subsp. *telephium*

Sedum telephioides – See *Hylotelephium telephioides* (Michx.) H. Ohba.

Sedum telephium **L.** – See *Hylotelephium telephium* (L.) H. Ohba. subsp. *telephium*

Sedum ternatum **Michx.** – False ice plant (19) (1840), Iceland moss (156) (1923), Live-forever [Liveforever, Live forever] (2) (1895), Mountain stonecrop (138, 155) (1931–1942), Three-leaf sedum [Three-leaved sedum] (2) (1895), Three-leaf stonecrop [Three-leaved stonecrop, Three-leaved stone-crop] (156, 187) (1818–1923), Wild stonecrop (156) (1923)

Sedum texanum **J. G. Smith** – See *Lenophyllum texanum* (J.G. Sm.) Rose

Sedum triphyllum **(Haw.) S. F. Gray** – See *Hylotelephium telephium* (L.) H. Ohba. subsp. *telephium*

Selaginella apoda **(L.) Spring** – Creeping selaginella (5) (1913), Meadow spikemoss (50) (present), Moss selaginella (97) (1937), possibly Basket selaginella (109, 138) (1923–1949)

Selaginella apus **(L.) Spring.** – See *Selaginella apoda* (L.) Spring

Selaginella arenicola **Underwood subsp.** *riddellii* **(Van Eselt.) R. Tryon** – Common selaginella (122) (1937), Groundpine [Ground-pine, Ground pine] (124) (1937)

Selaginella **Beauv.** – Little clubmoss [Little club-moss] (1, 10, 19) (1818–1932), Selaginella (1, 138, 155, 158) (1900–1942) diminutive of Selago an ancient name of a lycopodium, Spike-moss [Spike-moss] (4, 50) (1986–present)

Selaginella densa **Rydb.** – Clubmoss [Club-moss, Club moss] (146) (1939) MT, Lesser spikemoss (50) (present), Selaginella (146) (1939), Small club-moss [Small clubmoss] (3) (1977)

Selaginella densa **Rydb. var.** *densa* – Lesser spikemoss (50) (present)

Selaginella flabellata **(L.) Spring** – Fan selaginella (138) (1923)

Selaginella lepidophylla **(Hook. & Grev.) Spring** – Flower-of-stone [Flower of stone] (50) (present), Resurrection plant [Resurrection-plant] (14, 92, 109, 124, 138) (1882–1949), Rose-of-Jericho [Rose of Jericho] (14) (1882)

Selaginella peruviana **(Milde) Hieron** – Peruvian spike moss [Peruvian spikemoss] (4, 50) (1986–present)

Selaginella riddellii **Van Eseltine** – See *Selaginella arenicola* Underwood subsp. *riddellii* (Van Eselt.) R. Tryon

Selaginella rupestris **(L.) Spring** – Christmas evergreen (5, 92, 158) (1876–1913), Dwarf club-moss (5, 158) (1900–1913), Evergreen (92) (1876), Festoon-pine [Festoon pine] (5, 19, 92, 158) (1840–1913), Northern selaginella (50) (present), Resurrection plant [Resurrectionplant] (5) (1913), Rock selaginella (5, 97, 131, 138, 155, 158) (1899–1942), Rock spike moss [Rock spikemoss] (4) (1986), Running clubmoss [Running club-moss] (187) (1818), Small Virginia wolf's-sclaw [Small Virginia wolfsclaw] (181) (~1678), Spring rock selagenilla (72) (1907)

Selaginella selaginoides **(L.) Beauv. ex Mart. & Schrank** – Club spike moss (50) (present), Clubmoss [Club-moss, Club moss] (46) (1879), Low selaginella (5) (1913), Mountain moss (5) (1913), Prickly club moss (5) (1913)

Selaginella selaginoides **(L.) Link.** – See *Selaginella selaginoides* (L.) Beauv. ex Mart. & Schrank

Selaginella uncinata **(Desv. ex Poir.) Spring** – Blue selaginella (138) (1923)

Selaginella underwoodii **Hieron.** – Underwood's spike-moss [Underwood's spikemoss] (4, 50) (1986–present)

Selenia aurea **Nutt.** – Golden selenia (3, 4, 50) (1977–present), Selenia (5, 97) (1913–1937)

Selenicereus **(Berger) Britt. & Rose** – Moon cereus (109) (1949) for moon-goddess cereus, Moonlight cactus [Moonlightcactus] (155) (1942), Snake cactus [Snakecactus] (155) (1942)

Selenicereus **Britt. & Rose** – See *Selenicereus* (Berger) Britt. & Rose

Selenicereus grandiflorus **(L.) Britt. & Rose** – Cactus (55) (1911), Cereus (60) (1902), Night-blooming cereus [Nightblooming cereus, Night blooming cereus] (52, 55, 57, 61, 92) (1870–1917), Queen-of-the-night [Queenofthenight, Queen of the night] (50, 138, 155) (1923–present), Vanilla cactus (92) (1876)

Selinocarpus diffusus **Gray** – Moonpod (155) (1942), Spreading moonpod (4, 50) (1986–present)

Selinocarpus **Gray** – Moonpod (4, 155) (1942–1986), Selinocarpus (158) (1900)

Selinum canadense **Michx.** – See *Conioselinum chinense* (L.) Britton, Sterns & Poggenb.

Sempervivum arboreum – See *Aeonium arboreum* (L.) Webb & Berthel.

Sempervivum **L.** – Houseleek [House leek] (109, 138, 155, 156) (1923–1949)

Sempervivum tectorum **L.** – Ayegreen [Aye-green] (156, 180) (1633–1923), Bullock's-eye [Bullocks eie, Bullock's eye] (92, 156) (1876–1923), Common houseleek (109) (1949), Great houseleek [Great houseleeke] (178) (1526), Healing-blade [Healing blade] (156) (1923), Hen-and-chickens [Hen and chickens] (73, 109, 155, 156) (1892–1949), Homewort (156) (1923), Houseleek [House leek] (19, 46, 58, 92, 156, 179) (1526–1923), Jobarde (179) (1526), Jojarbe (156) (1923), Jupiter's-beard [Jupiter's beard, Jupitersbeard, Jupiters-beard] (92, 156) (1898–1923), Jupiter's-eye [Jupiter's eye] (92) (1876), Old-man-and-woman (109) (1949), Poor Jan's leaf (156) (1923), Roof houseleek (138) (1923), Selfegrene (179) (1526), Sen-green (156) (1923), Thunder plant [Thunder-plant] (92, 156) (1898–1923), possibly Bullock's-eye [Bullocks eie, Bullock's eye] (180) (1633)

Senebiera **Poir.** – possibly *Coronopus* Zinn

Senebriera **DC.** – See *Coronopus* Zinn

Senecio **(Tourn.) L.** – See *Senecio* L.

Senecio antennariifolius **Britton** – See *Packera antennariifolia* (Britt.) W. A. Weber & A. Löve

Senecio atriapiculatus **Rydb.** – See *Senecio integerrimus* Nutt. var. *exaltatus* (Nutt.) Cronq.

Senecio aureus **L.** – See *Packera aurea* (L.) A. & D. Löve

Senecio aureus **L. var.** *aquilonius* **Fern.** – See *Packera aurea* (L.) A. & D. Löve

Senecio aureus **var.** *obvatus* – See *Packera obovata* (Muhl. ex Willd.) W. A. Weber & A. Löve

Senecio balsamitae **Muhl.** – See *Packera paupercula* (Michx.) A. & D. Löve

Senecio bicolor **(Willd.) Todaro subsp.** *cineraria* **(DC.) Chater** – Dusty-miller [Dustymiller, Dusty miller] (92, 109) (1876–1949), Silver cineraria (138) (1923)

Senecio columbianus **Greene** – See *Senecio integerrimus* Nutt. var. *exaltatus* (Nutt.) Cronq.

Senecio congestus **(R. Br.) DC.** – Marsh fleabane [Marsh flea bane] (50) (present), Marsh fleawort (5, 72, 156, 158) (1900–1923), Marsh groundsel (156, 158) (1900–1923), Marsh ragwort (131) (1899), Pale ragwort (5, 156, 158) (1900–1923), Swamp ragwort (3, 4) (1977–1986)

Senecio crassulus **Gray** – Thick-leaf groundsel [Thickleaf groundsel] (155) (1942), Thick-leaf ragwort [Thickleaf ragwort] (50) (present)

Senecio crawfordii **Britton** – See *Packera paupercula* (Michx.) A. & D. Löve

Senecio cruentus **DC.** – See *Pericallis cuneata* (L'Hér.) Bolle

Senecio densus **Greene** – See *Packera tridenticulata* (Rydb.) W. A. Weber & A. Löve

Senecio discoideus **(Hook) Britton** – See *Packera pauciflora* (Pursh) A. & D. Löve

Senecio douglasii **DC.** – See *Senecio flaccidus* Less. var. *douglasii* (DC.) B. L. Turner & T. M. Barkl.

Senecio douglasii **DC. var.** *longilobus* **(Benth.) L. Benson** – See *Senecio flaccidus* Less. var. *flaccidus*

Senecio elegans **L.** – Purple groundsel (138) (1923), Purple ragwort (109) (1949)

Senecio elongatus **Pursh** – See *Packera obovata* (Muhl. ex Willd.) W. A. Weber & A. Löve

Senecio eremophilus **Richards** – Desert groundsel (155) (1942), Desert ragwort (50) (present), Groundsel [Groundsell] (85) (1932), Mountain ragwort (131) (1899)

Senecio flaccidus Less. var. *douglasii* (DC.) B. L. Turner & T. M. Barkl. – Douglas' ragwort (131) (1899)

Senecio flaccidus Less. var. *flaccidus* – Thread-leaf groundsel [Thread-leaf groundsel] (155) (1942), Thread-leaf ragwort [Threadleaf ragwort] (50) (present)

Senecio frigidus Less. – See *Tephroseris atropurpurea* (Ledeb.) Holub

Senecio gaspensis Greenm. – See *Packera paupercula* (Michx.) A.& D. Löve

Senecio glabellus Poir. – See *Packera glabella* (Poir) C. Jeffrey

Senecio hieraciifolius L. – See *Erechtites hieraciifolia* (L.) Raf. ex DC. var. *hieraciifolia*

Senecio hydrophilus Nutt. – Water groundsel (155) (1942), Water ragwort (50) (present)

Senecio integerrimus Nutt. – Entire-leaf groundsel [Entireleaf groundsel, Entire-leaved groundsel] (5, 122, 131) (1899–1937), Groundsel [Groundsell] (148) (1939), Lambs-tongue groundsel [Lambstongue groundsel] (155) (1942), Lambs-tongue ragwort [Lambstongue ragwort] (50) (present)

Senecio integerrimus Nutt. var. *exaltatus* (Nutt.) Cronq. – Black-seed groundsel [Black-seeded groundsel] (72) (1907), Groundsel [Groundsell] (85) (1932)

Senecio integerrimus Nutt. var. *integerrimus* – Lambs-tongue ragwort [Lambstongue ragwort] (50) (present)

Senecio jacobea L. – Bunweed (92) (1876), Cankerweed [Canker-weed, Canker weed] (5, 156) (1913–1923), Fairy horse [Fairies' horse] (5, 156) (1913–1923), Felonweed [Felon weed, Felon-weed] (5, 156) (1913–1923), Kettle-dock [Kettle dock] (5, 156) (1913–1923), Ragweed [Rag-weed, Rag weed] (5, 156) (1913–1923), Ragwort [Ragwort] (92) (1876), Saracen's-compass [Saracen's compass] (5, 156) (1913–1923), St. James'-wort [Saint James' wort, Saint James wort] (5, 92) (1876–1913), Staggerweed [Stagger weed, Stagger-weed] (92) (1876), Staggerwort (156) (1923), Starwort [Star-wort, Star wort] (156) (1923), Staverwort (92, 156) (1898–1923), Stave-wort (5) (1913), Stinking-Alexander [Stinking Alexander] (156) (1923), Stinking-Willie [Stinking Willie] (92, 156) (1898–1923), Tansy [Tansey, Tansie] (156) (1923), Tansy ragwort [Tansy-ragwort] (5, 156) (1913–1923)

Senecio L. – Butterweed [Butter weed, Butter-weed] (106) (1930), Fireweed [Fire weed, Fire-weed] (7) (1828), Groundsel [Groundsell] (1, 2, 4, 7, 93, 106, 109, 138, 155, 156, 158, 162, 184) (1793–1986), Othonna (138, 155) (1923–1942), Ragwort [Rag-wort] (1, 10, 50, 93, 126, 127, 156, 167) (1814–present), Sky flower [Skyflower, Sky-flower] (167) (1814), Squaw-weed [Squawweed, Squaw-weed] (1, 93, 158) (1900–1936)

Senecio lobatus Pers. – See *Packera glabella* (Poir) C. Jeffrey

Senecio longilobus Benth. – See *Senecio flaccidus* Less. var. *flaccidus*

Senecio lugens Richards. – Black-tip groundsel [Black tipped groundsel] (131) (1899)

Senecio mikanioides Otto – See *Delairea odorata* Lem.

Senecio obovatus Muhl. – See *Packera obovata* (Muhl. ex Willd.) W. A. Weber & A. Löve

Senecio palustris (L.) Hook. – See *Senecio congestus* (R.Br.) DC.

Senecio pauperculus Michx. – See *Packera paupercula* (Michx.) A. & D. Löve

Senecio pseudoarnica Less. – Sea-beach senecio (5) (1913)

Senecio purshianus Nutt. – See *Packera cana* (Hook.) W. A. Weber & A. Löve

Senecio rapifolius Nutt. – Open-woods ragwort [Openwoods ragwort] (50) (present)

Senecio riddellii Torr. & Gray – Groundsel [Groundsell] (148) (1939), Riddell's groundsel [Riddell groundsel] (155) (1942), Riddell's ragwort [Riddell ragwort] (3, 4, 50, 98) (1926–present), Riddell's senecio (5, 93, 97) (1913–1937)

Senecio robbinsii Oakes ex Rusby – See *Packera schweinitziana* (Nutt.) W. A. Weber & A. Löve

Senecio scandens – See *Delairea odorata* Lem.

Senecio sonchifolia – See *Emilia sonchifolia* (L.) DC.

Senecio sonchifolius (L.) Moench – See *Emilia sonchifolia* (L.) DC.

Senecio spartioides Torr. & Gray – Broom groundsel (155) (1942), Broom-like ragwort [Broomlike ragwort] (50) (present), Broom-like senecio (5, 93, 122) (1913–1937)

Senecio sylvaticus L. – Wood groundsel (5) (1913)

Senecio tomentosus Michx. – See *Packera tomentosa* (Michx.) C. Jeffrey

Senecio viscosus L. – Fetid groundsel (5) (1913), Viscous groundsel (5) (1913)

Senecio vulgaris L. – Birdseed [Bird-seed, Bird seed] (5, 156, 158) (1900–1923), Chickenweed [Chicken weed, Chicken-weed] (5, 156, 158) (1900–1923) no longer in use by 1923, Chincone (156, 158) (1900–1923), Common groundsel (3, 5, 122, 131, 155, 156, 158, 187) (1818–1977), Fleawort [Fleawort, Flea wort] (92, 156, 158) (1876–1923), Grinsel (5, 156, 158) (1900–1923) no longer in use by 1923, Groundie-swallow [Groundie swallow] (92, 156, 158) (1898–1923), Groundsel [Groundsell] (4, 19, 46, 92, 158) (1649–1986) accidentally introduced at least by 1671, Grownswell (179) (1526), Jacobskraut (German) (158) (1900), Kreuzkraut (German) (158) (1900), Old-man-in-the-Spring (50) (present), Sencion (156, 158) (1900–1923), Senecon (Spanish) (158) (1900), Simson (5, 156, 158) (1900–1923), Swichen (158) (1900)

Senna alata (L.) Roxb. – Ring-worm bush [Ring worm bush] (92) (1876), Ring-worm cassia [Ringworm cassia] (109, 138) (1923–1949)

Senna alexandrina Mill. – Egyptian senna (19) (1840), False senna (19) (1840), Senna (57, 58, 61, 92) (1869–1917), Senna husks (92) (1876)

Senna artemisioides (Gaud. ex DC.) Randell – Wormwood senna (138) (1923)

Senna corymbosa (Lam.) Irwin & Barneby – Flowery senna (138) (1923)

Senna hirsuta (L.) Irwin & Barneby var. *hirsuta* – Woolly senna (138) (1923)

Senna ligustrina (L.) Irwin & Barneby – Flower-fence (177) (1762)

Senna lindheimeriana (Scheele) Irwin & Barneby – Lindheimer's cassia (124) (1937)

Senna marilandica (L.) Link – American senna (5, 7, 49, 53, 57, 92, 156, 157, 158, 186, 187) (1818–1929), Casse (186) (1814), Cassia (157, 186) (1814–1929), Cassie (186) (1814), Cassier (186) (1814), False acacia [False acasia] (42) (1814), Kasie (186) (1814), Kasien (186) (1814), Kassia (186) (1814), Kassien (186) (1814), Locust plant [Locust-plant] (7, 92, 156, 157, 158) (1828–1929), Marilandische Cassia (German) (7) (1828), Marilandische Cassie (German) (186) (1814), Maryland senna [Maryland-senna] (4, 50, 186) (1825–present), Medsger's wild senna (5, 97) (1913–1937), Senna (106) (1930) Southern states, Senna Americana (Official name of Materia Medica) (7) (1828), Senne' d'Amerique (French) (5) (1913), Ûnnagéi (Cherokee, black) (102) (1886) medicinal for disease of this name that was said to turn hands and eyesockets black, Wild senna [Wild-senna] (3, 5, 7, 19, 42, 49, 53, 62, 63, 72, 82, 92, 95, 97, 102, 109, 138, 145, 155, 156, 157, 158, 186, 187) (1814–1977)

Senna Mill. – Senna (50) (Present)

Senna obtusifolia (L.) Irwin & Barneby – Java-bean (50) (present)

Senna occidentalis (L.) Link – Coffee senna (5, 97, 122, 124) (1913–1937), Coffee weed [Coffee-weed] (5, 156) (1913–1923), Magdad coffee (5, 156) (1913–1923) no longer in use by 1923, Negro coffee (5) (1913), Negro-weed (156) (1923), Stinking-weed [Stinking-weed, Stinking weed] (107) (1919), Stypticweed [Styptic weed] (5, 92) (1876–1913)

Senna roemeriana (Scheele) Irwin & Barneby – Roemer's cassia (124) (1937), Two-leaf senna [Twoleaf senna, Two-leaved senna] (4, 50) (1986–present)

Senna septentrionalis (Viviani) Irwin & Barneby – Smooth senna (138) (1923)

Senna siamea (Lam.) Irwin & Barneby – Kassod tree [Kassod-tree] (109) (1949), Siamese senna (138) (1923)

Senna tora (L.) Roxb. – Coffee weed [Coffee-weed] (5, 156) (1913–1923), I-go-to-sleep [I go to sleep] (183) (~1756), Low senna (5, 63, 72, 97, 158) (1899–1937), Sickle senna (5, 7, 50, 92, 122, 124, 155, 158) (1828–present), Sicklepod [Sickle pod, Sickle-pod] (156) (1923)

Sequoia Endl. – Redwood [Red wood] (138) (1923), Sequoia (138) (1923) for Sequoyah, about 1770–1843, Cherokee from Georgia

Sequoia gigantea – See *Sequoiadendron giganteum* (Lindl.) Buchh.

Sequoia sempervirens (Lamb. ex D. Don) Endl. – Evergreen taxodium (20) (1857), Redwood [Red wood] (50, 109, 138, 147, 161) (1856–present), Redwood of California (14) (1882)

Sequoia sempervirens Endl. – See *Sequoia sempervirens* (Lamb. ex D. Don) Endl.

Sequoia wellingtonia Seem. – See *Sequoiadendron giganteum* (Lindl.) Buchh.

Sequoiadendron giganteum (Lindl.) Buchh. – California big tree [California big-tree] (109) (1949), Giant sequoia (50, 138) (1923–present), Mammoth tree (14, 161) (1857–1882), Mammoth Washington tree (147) (1856)

Serapias helleborine L. – See *Epipactis helleborine* (L.) Crantz

Serapis helleborine L. – See *Epipactis helleborine* (L.) Crantz

Serenoa Hook. f. – Saw palmetto (109, 138) (1923–1949)

Serenoa repens (Bartr.) Small – Cabbage tree (20) (1857), Dwarf prickly fan-leaf palmetto [Dwarf prickly fan-leaved palmetto] (182) (1791), Royal palmetto (7) (1828), Sabal (55, 57, 59) (1911–1917), Saw palmetto (2, 14, 49, 52, 53, 54, 55, 57, 59, 107, 138) (1895–1923), Small saw palmetto (106) (1930)

Serenoa serrulata Bentham and Hooker – See *Serenoa repens* (Bartr.) Small

Sericocarpus asteroides (L.) Britton, Sterns & Poggenb. – Fleabane [Flea-bane, Flea bane] (42) (1814), Plowman's-wort [Ploughman's wort, Plowmans'-wort, Plowmans'-wort, Plowmanwort] (184, 187) (1793–1818), White-top aster [White-topped aster] (156) (1923)

Sericocarpus linifolius (L.) Britton, Sterns & Poggenb. – Goldenrod aster [Golden-rod Aster] (187) (1818), Narrow-leaf white-top aster [Narrow-leaved white-topped aster] (5) (1913), White-top starwort [White-topped star-wort] (187) (1818), possibly Goldenrod starwort [Golden rod star wort] (42) (1814)

Sericocarpus tortifolius (Michx.) Nees – Rattlesnake-master [Rattlesnake master, Rattlesnake's master, Rattlesnakes' master, Rattlesnake's-master] (156) (1923), Rough white-top aster [Rough white-topped aster] (156) (1923), Silk-seed aster (156) (1923), White-tip aster [White-tipped aster] (156) (1923)

Serinia oppositifolia (Raf.) Kuntze – See *Krigia caespitosa* (Raf.) Chambers

Serinia Raf. – See *Krigia* Schreb.

Seriphidium tridentatum (Nutt.) W. A. Weber subsp. *wyomingense* (Beetle & Young) W. A. Weber – See *Artemisia tridentata* Nutt. subsp. *wyomingensis* Beetle & Young

Serratula glauca L. – See *Vernonia glauca* (L.) Willd.

Serratula L. – Saw-wort [Saw woort, Saw wort, Sawwort] (184) (1793)

Serratula noveboracensis L. – See *Vernonia noveboracensis* (L.) Michx.

Serratula spicata L. – See *Liatris spicata* (L.) Willd.

Serratula tinctoria L. – Saw-wort [Saw woort, Saw wort, Sawwort] (92, 178) (1526–1876), White saw-wort [White saw woort] (178) (1526)

Sesamum indicum DC. – See *Sesamum orientale* L.

Sesamum indicum L. – See *Sesamum orientale* L.

Sesamum L. – Benny (7) (1828), Giugiolena (Itlay) (7) (1828), Jugotine (French) (7) (1828), Vangle (Jamaica) (7) (1828), Zezehan (7) (1828)

Sesamum orientale L. – Bene-benni (19) (1840), Benne (49, 57, 92) (1876–1917), Oil plant (92) (1876), Oily grain (19) (1840), Sesame (49, 107, 110, 138) (1886–1923), Sesame leaves (92) (1876), Sesamum (57) (1917), Teel [Teele] (92) (1876), Tillseed [Tilseed] (92) (1876)

Sesban Adans. – See *Sesbania* Scop.

Sesbania exlatata (Raf.) Rydb. – See *Sesbania herbacea* (Mill.) McVaugh

Sesbania grandiflora (L.) Poir. – Vegetable humming-bird (107) (1919)

Sesbania grandiflora Poir. – See *Sesbania grandiflora* (L.) Poir.

Sesbania herbacea (P. Mill.) McVaugh – Bequilla (4) (1986), Big-pod sesbania [Bigpod sesbania] (50) (present), Colorado hemp (158) (1900), Hemp sesbania (155) (1942), Long-pod sesban [Long-podded sesban] (97) (1937)

Sesbania macrocarpa Muhl. – See *Sesbania herbacea* (Mill.) McVaugh

Sesbania punicea (Cav.) Benth. – Purple sesbania (138) (1923)

Sesbania Scop. – Pea tree [Pea-tree] (92) (1876)

Sesbania vesicaria Ell. – See *Glottidium vesicarium* (Jacq.) Harper

Seseli L. – Meadow saxifrage (10) (1818)

Seseli libanotis (L.) W. D. J. Koch – Black gentian (92) (1876), Herbe Franckincense (178) (1526), Moon-carrot [Mooncarrot] (50) (present)

Seseli triternatum – See *Lomatium triternatum* (Pursh) Coult. & Rose

Sesleria dactyloides Nutt. – See *Buchloe dactyloides* (Nutt.) Engelm.

Sesuvium L. – Sea-purslane [Sea purslane] (1, 2, 4, 15, 50, 158) (1895–present), Sesuvium (155) (1942)

Sesuvium maritimum (Walt.) Britton, Sterns & Poggenb. – Sea-purslane [Sea purslane] (5, 156) (1913–1923)

Sesuvium pentandrum Ell. – See *Sesuvium maritimum* (Walt.) Britton, Sterns & Poggenb.

Sesuvium portulacastrum (L.) L. – Sea-purslane [Sea purslane] (122) (1937) TX, Seaside purslane (107) (1919)

Sesuvium sessile Pers. – Western sea purslane (5, 97) (1913–1937)

Sesuvium verrucosum Raf. – Verrucose sea-purslane [Verrucose sea-purslane] (50) (present)

Setaria Beauv – Bristle grass [Bristlegrass] (50, 155) (1942–present), Foxtail [Fox tail, Fox-tail, Fox tails, Foxetaile, Fox-taile] (56) (1901), Foxtail grass [Fox tail grass, Fox-tail grass, Foxtail-grass] (1, 93) (1932–1936), Indian caustic barley [Indian causticke barley] (181) (~1678), Millet [Myllet] (155, 158) (1900–1942), Pigeon grass [Pigeon-grass, Pigeongrass, Pigeon's- grass, Pigeon's grass] (56, 155) (1901–1942)

Setaria corrugata (Ell.) J. A. Schultes – Rough foxtail (94) (1901)

Setaria faberi Herrm. – Chinese foxtail (3) (1977), Japanese bristle grass [Japanese bristlegrass] (50) (present)

Setaria geniculata (Lam.) Beauv. – See *Setaria parviflora* (Poir.) Kerguélen

Setaria germanica [(Mill.) P. Beauv.] – See *Setaria italica* (L.) Beauv.

Setaria glauca (L.) Beauv. – See *Pennisetum glaucum* (L.) R. Br.

Setaria grisebachii Fourn. – Grisebach's bristle grass [Grisebach bristle grass] (122) (1937)

Setaria italica (L.) Beauv. – Bengal grass (45, 66, 92, 107) (1896–1919), Cat-tail millet [Cattailmillet, Cat-tails millet] (5, 45) (1896–1913), Common millet (32, 45, 56, 119, 140) (1895–1944), Foxtail bristle grass [Foxtail bristlegrass] (50) (present), Foxtail millet (3, 68, 109, 119, 122, 140, 155) (1913–1977), German millet (5, 45, 56, 68, 87, 88, 90, 109, 119, 151, 156) (1884–1949), Golden millet (5, 45, 56, 151, 158) (1896–1931), Golden-wonder millet [Golden wonder millet] (56, 109, 119) (1901–1949), Hungarian grass (5, 45, 56, 66, 67, 87, 88, 90, 94, 109, 131, 158) (1884–1949), Hungarian millet (5, 56, 66, 68, 92, 119, 158) (1876–1938), Italian millet (5, 45, 56, 85, 87, 90, 92, 93, 94, 107, 110, 140, 151, 152, 158, 163) (1852–1944), Italian oatmeal [Italian oatemeale] (178) (1596), Japanese millet (107) (1919), Little crabgrass [Little crab-grass, Little crab grass] (94) (1901), Mammoth millet (45) (1896), Millet [Myllet] (11, 21, 56, 66, 129, 138) (1888–1923), Millet grass [Millet-grass] (92) (1876), Panyke (178, 179) (1526–1596), Turkestan millet (109, 119) (1938–1949)

Setaria italica (L.) Beauv. var. *stramineofructa* Bailey – See *Setaria italica* (L.) Beauv.

Setaria italica germanica [(Mill.) Schrad.] – See *Setaria italica* (L.) Beauv.

Setaria leucopila (Scribn. & Merr.) K. Schum. – Stream-bed bristle grass [Streambed bristlegrass] (50) (present)

Setaria lutescens (Weigel) F. T. Hubbard – See *Pennisetum glaucum* (L.) R. Br.

Setaria magna Griseb. – Giant bristle grass [Giant bristlegrass] (50, 122) (1937–present), Giant foxtail grass [Giant foxtail-grass] (5, 163) (1852–1913), Giant millet (56, 94) (1897–1901)

Setaria palmifolia (Koenig) Stapf – Palm grass [Palm-grass, Palm-grass] (109, 138) (1923–1949)

Setaria parviflora (Poir.) Kerguélen – Knotroot bristle grass [Knotroot bristlegrass] (3, 122, 155) (1937–1977), Marsh bristle grass [Marsh bristlegrass] (50) (present), Perennial foxtail (119) (1938), Perennial foxtail grass (5) (1913)

Setaria ramiseta (Scribn.) Pilger – Narrow-top panic [Narrow-topped panic] (94) (1901)

Setaria reverchonii (Vasey) Pilger – Reverchon's bristle grass [Reverchon's bristlegrass] (50) (present), Reverchon's panic (94) (1901)

Setaria setosa (Sw.) Beauv. – Bristle grass [Bristlegrass] (87) (1884), Foxtail [Fox tail, Fox-tail, Fox tails, Foxetaile, Fox-taile] (87) (1884)

Setaria verticillata (L.) Beauv. – Barbed foxtail grass (85) (1932)

Setaria verticillata (L.) Beauv. – Bristly foxtail [Bristly fox tail, Bristly fox-tail] (3, 5, 66, 80, 93, 94, 111, 129) (1903–1977), Brown foxtail (5) (1913), Bur bristle grass [Bur bristlegrass] (140) (1944), Foxtail grass [Fox tail grass, Fox-tail grass, Foxtail-grass] (5, 163) (1852–1913), Hooked bristle grass [Hooked bristlegrass] (50, 140, 155) (1942–present), Perennial foxtail (122) (1937), Rough bristle grass [Rough bristle-grass] (5) (1913), Whorled millet (56) (1901)

Setaria viridis (L.) Beauv. – Barn grass [Barngrass, Barn-grass] (78) (1898) ME, Bottle grass [Bottle-grass] (50, 56, 66, 90, 92, 129, 143) (1885–present), Green bottle grass [Green bottle-grass] (119) (1938), Green bristle grass [Green bristle-grass, Green bristlegrass] (50, 122, 140, 143, 155) (1936–present), Green foxtail [Green fox tail] (3, 11, 50, 56, 66, 80, 87, 90, 111, 115, 119, 129, 131, 134, 140, 143, 145) (1884–present), Green foxtail grass (92) (1876), Green pigeon (87) (1884), Green pigeon grass (88) (1885), Pigeon grass [Pigeon-grass, Pigeongrass, Pigeon's-grass, Pigeon's grass] (85, 50, 119, 129) (1894–present), Puss grass (129) (1894) SD, Wild millet (119) (1938)

Setaria viridis (L.) Beauv. var. *viridis* – Foxtail [Fox tail, Fox-tail, Fox tails, Foxetaile, Fox-taile] (152) (1912) NM, Green bottle grass [Green bottle-grass] (5) (1913), Green bristle grass [Green bristle-grass, Green bristlegrass] (50) (present), Green foxtail [Green fox tail] (93, 94) (1901–1936), Green foxtail grass (5) (1913), Pigeon grass [Pigeon-grass, Pigeongrass, Pigeon's- grass, Pigeon's grass] (5) (1913), Wild millet (5) (1913)

Setaria vulpiseta (Lam.) Roemer & J. A. Schultes – Branching foxtail (94) (1901), Plains bristle grass [Plains bristlegrass] (50, 122, 155) (1937–present)

Setiscapella cleistogama (Gray) Barnhart – See *Utricularia subulata* L.

Setiscapella subulata (L.) Barnhart – See *Utricularia subulata* L.

Seymeria macrophylla Nutt. – See *Dasistoma macrophylla* (Nutt.) Raf.

Seymeria Pursh – Afzelia (155, 158) (1900–1942), Mullein foxglove [Mullen foxglove] (93) (1936)

Seymeria tenuifolia Pursh – See *Seymeria cassioides* (J.F. Gmel.) Blake

Shepherdia argentea (Pursh) Nutt. – Argosier argenté (French) (20) (1857), Beef-suet tree [Beef suet tree] (5, 156, 158) (1900–1923) no longer in use by 1923, Bois à perdix (French, shrub for partridges) (41) (1770), Buffalo-berry [Buffalo berry, Buffaloberry] (3, 4, 5, 14, 22, 33, 37, 72, 75, 78, 85, 92, 93, 95, 101, 103, 107, 108, 109, 112, 113, 120, 131, 135, 153, 156, 158) (1827–1986), Buffalo-fat [Buffalo fat] (20) (1857), Buffalo-grease [Buffalo grease] (35) (1806) William Clark, Bullberry [Bull-berry, Bull berry] (5, 36, 101, 104, 108, 156, 158) (1830–1923) no longer in use by 1923, Grains de

boeuf (French) (28) (1850), Graisse du boeuf (French) (20, 89, 101) (1820–1905), Grise de buff (35) (1806) William Clark, Háŋse (Mandan) (35) (1806) Ås-sáy according to William Clark, Haz-shutz (Winnebago, red fruit) (37) (1919), Ingahawmp (Snakes) (101) (1905) MT, Laritsits (Pawnee) (37) (1919), Marish-isha (Crow) (101) (1905) MT, Mashtincha-puté (Dakota, rabbitnose) (37) (1919), Naaní'Is (Arkikara) (35) (1806), Rabbit-berry [Rabbitberry, Rabbit berry] (5, 10, 20, 35, 36, 92, 93, 156, 158) (1806–1936), Silver buffaloberry (50, 138, 155) (1923–present), Silver bush [Silverbush, Silverbush] (156) (1923), Silverberry [Silver berry, Silverberry] (82) (1930), Silverbush [Silver-bush] (156) (1923), Silverleaf [Silver leaf, Silver-leaf] (5, 156, 158) (1900–1923), Western shepherdia (20) (1857), Wild oleaster tree [Wild oleaster-tree] (5, 156, 158) (1900–1923), Wild olive [Wilde oliue] or Wild olive tree [Wild olive-tree] (5, 156, 158) (1900–1923), Zhon-hoje-wazhide (Omaha-Ponca) (37) (1919), Zhon-hoje-wazhide h'uta (Omaha-Ponca) (37) (1919)

Shepherdia canadensis Nutt. – Bearberry [Bear berry, Bear-berry] (156) (1923), Canadian buffaloberry [Canadian buffalo berry, Canadian buffalo-berry] (5, 85, 93, 131, 156, 158) (1899–1932), Canadian bullberry [Canadian bull berry] (108) (1878), Canadian sea-buckthorn (8) (1785), Canadian shepherdia (20) (1857), Low shepherdia (130) (1895), Rabbit-berry [Rabbitberry, Rabbit berry] (3, 4) (1977–1986), Rhamnoide de Canada (French) (8) (1785), Russet buffalo-berry [Russet buffaloberry] (50, 138, 155, 156) (1923–present), Sea buckthorn (19) (1840), Soapberry [Soap-berry] (104) (1896), Soopoo lalia (5) (1913), Wild oleaster tree [Wild oleaster-tree] (5, 156, 158) (1900–1923), Wild olive [Wilde oliue] or Wild olive tree [Wild olive-tree] (5, 156, 158) (1900–1923)

Shepherdia Nutt. – Buffalo-berry [Buffalo berry, Buffaloberry] (1, 50, 82, 93, 108, 138, 158) (1878–present)

Shepherdia Nutt. – Bullberry [Bull-berry, Bull berry] (1) (1932), Silver bush [Silver-bush, Silverbush] (7) (1828), Silverbush [Silver-bush] (7) (1828)

Sherardia arvensis L. – Blue field madder (5, 50, 156) (1913–present), Herb sherard (5, 156) (1913–1923), Spurwort [Spur-wort] (5, 156) (1913–1923)

Sherardia L. – Field madder (156) (1923), Sherardia (50) (Present)

Shinnersoseris rostrata (Gray) S. Tomb – Annual skeleton-weed (3) (1977), Annual lygodesmia (5, 93) (1913–1936), Beaked skeletonweed [Beaked skeletonweed] (50) (present)

Shinnersoseris S. Tomb – Beaked skeleton-weed [Beaked skeletonweed] (50) (present)

Shortia galacifolia Torr. & Gray – Oconee-bells (109, 138) (1923–1949)

Sibara Greene – Sibara (158) (1900), Winged rockcress (50) (present)

Sibara virginica (L.) Rollins – Podded Virginia Cress (181) (~1678), Rockcress [Rock-cress, Rock cress] (3, 4) (1977–1986), Virginia rockcress [Virginia rock cress, Virginia rock-cress] (5, 97) (1913–1937), Virginia winged rockcress (50) (present), Lady's-smock [Ladies' smock, Lady's smock, Ladiesmock, Ladies-smock] (184) (1793)

Sibbaldia procumbens L. – Sibbaldia (5) (1913)

Sibbaldiopsis Rydb. – Sibbaldiopsis (50) (Present)

Sibbaldiopsis tridentata (Aiton) Rydb. – Mountain cinquefoil (19) (1840), Shrubby five-fingers [Shrubby fivefingers] (50) (Present), Three-tooth cinquefoil [Three-toothed cinquefoil] (2, 3, 4, 5, 72, 156) (1907–1986), Wine-leaf cinquefoil [Wineleaf cinquefoil] (138, 155) (1923–1942)

Sicana odorifera (Vell.) Naud. – Casabanana (109, 138) (1923–1949), Curuba (109) (1949)

Sicyos angulata L. – See *Sicyos angulatus* L.

Sicyos angulatus L. – Bryony [Briony] (7) (1828), Bur cucumber [Burcucumber, Burcucumber, Burr cucumber] (3, 4, 82, 107, 131, 157, 158) (1899–1986), Cho-cho vine (86) (1878), Nimble-Kate [Nimble Kate] (5, 156, 157, 158) (1900–1929), One-seed bur-cucumber [Oneseed burr cucumber, One-seeded bur cucumber] (5, 50, 63,

72, 93, 97, 106, 122, 156, 157, 158) (1899–present), One-seed cucumber [One-seeded cucumber] (46, 92) (1876–1879), Single-seed cucumber [Single-seeded cucumber] (10, 19, 86, 92, 156) (1818–1923), Star-cucumber [Star cucumber] (5, 86, 156, 157, 158) (1878–1929), Wall bur-cucumber [Wall burcucumber] (155) (1942), Wild cucumber [Wild-cucumber, Wilde cucumbers] (5, 7, 76, 156, 157, 158) (1828–1929)

Sicyos **L.** – Bur cucumber [Bur-cucumber, Burcucumber, Burr cucumber] (1, 4, 50, 155) (1932–present), One-seed bur-cucumber [One-seed burr cucumber, One-seeded bur cucumber] (149) (1904), One-seed cucumber [One-seeded cucumber] (82, 158) (1900–1930), Single-seed cucumber [Single-seeded cucumber] (167) (1814), Star-cucumber [Star cucumber] (1, 2) (1895)

Sicyos **Michx.** – possibly *Momordica* L.

Sida abutilon **L.** – See *Abutilon theophrasti* Medik.

Sida elliottii **Torr & Gray.** – Elliot's sida (5) (1913)

Sida hederacea **Torr.** – See *Malvella leprosa* (Ortega) Krapov

Sida hermaphrodita **(L.) Rusby** – Virginia mallow (5) (1913)

Sida **L.** – Fan-petals [Fanpetals] (50) (present), Indian mallow [Indian-mallow, Indian mallows] (93, 158, 184) (1793–1936), Sida (155, 158) (1900–1942), Softy (7) (1828)

Sida **L. Kunth.** – See *Sida* L.

Sida spinosa **L.** – False mallow [False-mallow, Falsemallow, False mallows] (5, 92, 156) (1876–1923), Indian mallow [Indian-mallow, Indian mallows] (5, 92, 156) (1876–1923), Prickly fanpetals (50) (present), Prickly sida (3, 4, 62, 72, 97, 155, 156) (1907–1986), Princkly sida (5) (1913), Sida (80, 145) (1897–1932), Thistle mallow (62) (1912), Thorny Indian mallow (187) (1818), Wireweed [Wire weed, Wire-weed] (156) (1923)

Sida stipulata **Nutt.** – See *Sida acuta* Burm. f.

Sidalcea candida **Gray** – White prairie-mallow [White prairiemallow] (138) (1923)

Sidalcea **Gray** – Checker-bloom [Checkerbloom] (50) (present), Checker-mallow [Checkermallow] (155) (1942), Globemallow [Globe-mallow, Globe mallow] (158) (1900), Prairie mallow [Prairiemallow] (138) (1923)

Sidalcea malvaeflora **Gray** – See *Sidalcea malviflora* (DC.) Gray ex Benth.

Sidalcea malviflora **(DC.) Gray ex Benth.** – Checker-bloom [Checkerbloom] (106, 109, 138) (1923–1949), Wild hollyhock [Wild hollyhocks] (106) (1930)

Sidalcea neomexicana **Gray** – New Mexico checker-mallow [New-mexican checkermallow] (155) (1942), Salt spring checkerbloom (50) (present)

Sidalcea neomexicana **Gray subsp.** *neomexicana* – Salt spring checkerbloom (50) (present)

Sideranthus annuus **Rydb.** – See *Rayjacksonia annua* (Rydb.) R.L. Hartman & M. A. Lane

Sideranthus cotula **Small** – See *Machaeranthera pinnatifida* (Hook.) Shinners subsp. *pinnatifida*

Sideranthus glaberrimus **Rydb.** – See *Machaeranthera pinnatifida* (Hook.) Shinners subsp. *pinnatifida*

Sideranthus grindelioides **(Nutt.) Britton** – See *Machaeranthera grindelioides* (Nutt.) Shinners var. *grindelioides*

Sideranthus spinulosus **(Nutt.) Sweet** – See *Machaeranthera pinnatifida* (Hook.) Shinners subsp. *pinnatifida*

Sideritis romana **L.** – Simple-beak ironwort [Simple-beaked iron-wor (5) (1913)

Sideroxylon celastrinum **(Kunth) T. D. Pennington** – Ironwood [Iron wood, Iron-wood] (124) (1937) TX, Narrow-leaf bumelia [Narrow-leaved bumelia] (20) (1857), Sapotillier à feuilles drites (French) (20) (1857)

Sideroxylon decandrum **L.** – See *Sideroxylon lycioides* L.

Sideroxylon foetidissimum **Jacq. subsp.** *foetidissimum* – Foetid bumelia (20) (1857), Sapotillier tres fetide (French) (20) (1857)

Sideroxylon **L.** – Buckthorn [Bucke thorne] (1, 153, 158) (1900–1932) NM, Bully (50) (present), Bumelia (155) (1942), Ironwood [Iron wood, Iron-wood] (7) (1828), Jungle-plum [Jungleplum] (155) (1942), Sideroxylon (158) (1900), Turlbay (7) (1828)

Sideroxylon lanuginosum **Michx.** – Arizona buckthorn (106) (1930), Black haw [Black-haw, Blackhaw] (5, 156) (1913–1923), Elastic gum (65) (1931) OK, False buckthorn (107, 156) (1919–1923), Gum elastic (5) (1913), Gum-elastic (106, 156) (1923–1930), Shittim-wood [Shittimwood, Shittim wood] (5, 106) (1913–1930), Woolly buckthorn (5, 97, 122) (1913–1937), Woolly-bucket bumelia [Woollybucket bumelia] (155) (1942), Woolly-leaf bumelia [Wooly leaved bumelia] (20) (1857)

Sideroxylon lanuginosum **Michx. subsp.** *oblongifolium* **(Nutt.) T. D. Pennington** – Gum bully (50) (present), Oblong-leaf bumelia [Oblong-leaved bumelia] (20) (1857), Woolly buckthorn (3, 4) (1977–1986)

Sideroxylon lycioides **L.** – Bumelia (5) (1913), Bumelia-ironwood (156) (1923), Carolina buckthorn (5, 156) (1913–1923), Chittam wood [Chittam-wood, Chittem wood, Chittim wood, Chittim-wood] (5) (1913), Coma (Mexican) (5, 106, 156) (1913–1930), Ironwood [Iron wood, Iron-wood] (5, 20, 106) (1857–1930), Milkwood [Milk wood] (20) (1857), Mock orange [Mock-orange, Mockorange] (5, 156) (1913–1923), Sapotillier à feuilles de lieier (French) (20) (1857), Smooth-leaf bumelia [Smooth leaved bumelia] (20) (1857), Southern buckthorn (2, 5, 106, 122, 156) (1895–1930)

Sideroxylon reclinatum **Michx. subsp.** *reclinatum* – Western buckthorn (107) (1919)

Sideroxylon tenax **L.** – Sapotillier tenace (French) (20) (1857), Silky-leaf bumelia [Silky-leaved bumelia] (20) (1857)

Sieversia ciliata **(Pursh) G. Don** – See *Geum triflorum* Pursh var. *ciliatum* (Pursh) Fassett

Sieversia ciliata **(Pursh) Rydb.** – See *Geum triflorum* Pursh var. *ciliatum* (Pursh) Fassett

Sieversia radiata **(Michx.) G. Don** – Spiceroot [Spice root] (7) (1828)

Sieversia **Willd.** – See *Geum* L.

Silene acaulis **L.** – Cushion pink (5, 109, 156) (1913–1949), Moss campion (1, 5, 15, 85, 92, 109, 131, 138, 156) (1895–1949), Moss pink [Moss-pink] (5, 76, 156) (1896–1923) Paris ME

Silene alba **Muhl.** – See *Silene nivea* (Nutt.) Muhl. ex Otth

Silene antirrhina **L.** – Sleepy campion (2, 15, 95) (1895–1936), Sleepy catchfly (1, 4, 5, 62, 72, 85, 93, 97, 122, 127, 131, 155, 156) (1899–1986), Sleepy silene (50, 155) (1942–present), Snapdragon catchfly (15, 156, 187) (1818–1895), Tarry cockle (62) (1912)

Silene armeria **L.** – Bunch pink (156) (1923), Dwarf French pink [Dwarf French pinks] (5, 74, 156) (1893–1923), Garden catchfly (5, 19, 156) (1840–1923), Limewort (156) (1923), Limewort catchfly (5, 92) (1876–1913), Mice pink (5, 76, 156) (1896–1923) Hennepin IL, no longer in use by 1923, Mock sweet william [Mock sweet-william] (5, 74, 156) (1893–1923) Southern IN, None-so-pretty [None so pretty] (5, 73, 156) (1892–1923) Hatfield MA, Old-maid's pink [Old maid pink, Old maid's pink] (5, 74, 156) (1893–1923) Canada and Western MA, Pretty-Nancy [Pretty Nancy] (5, 73, 156) (1892–1923) Franklin Center Quebec, no longer in use by 1923, Sweet Susan (5, 73, 79, 156) (1891–1923) Northeastern US, no longer in use by 1923, Sweet William [Sweetwilliam, Sweet-william] (5) (1913), Sweet William catchfly (109, 138, 156) (1923–1949), Wax plant [Wax-plant, Waxplant] (5, 73, 156) (1892–1923) Mansfield OH, no longer in use by 1923

Silene borealis **Bigel.** – possibly *Stellaria borealis* Bigelow subsp. *borealis*

Silene californica **Dur.** – California Indian pink (109) (1949), Indian pink (76) (1896) CA

Silene caroliniana **subsp.** *pensylvanica* **(Michx.) Clausen** – Drooping catchfly (138) (1923), Peat pink [Peatpink] (138) (1923), Pennsylvania campion [Pennsylvanian campion] (2) (1895), Pennsylvania catchfly (156, 187) (1818–1923), Pink catchfly [Pink catch-fly] (19) (1840), Wild pink (2, 15, 156, 187) (1818–1923)

Silene caroliniana **Walt.** – Indian pink (76) (1896), Wild pink (5, 109) (1913–1949)

Silene coeli-rosa (L.) Godr. – Rose-of-heaven [Rose of heaven] (109, 138) (1923–1949)

Silene conica L. – Cone-fruit catch-fly (19) (1840), Corn catchfly (5, 156) (1913–1923), Striate catchfly (5) (1913)

Silene cserei Baumg. – Balkan catchfly (50) (present), Smooth catchfly (4) (1986)

Silene cucubalus Wibel – See *Silene vulgaris* (Moench) Garcke

Silene dichotoma Ehrh. – Catchfly [Catch fly] (80) (1913), Dichotoma silene (50) (present), Forked catchfly (4, 5, 19, 93) (1840–1986), Forked silene (155) (1942)

Silene dioica (L.) Clairville – Adder's-flower [Adder's flower] (156) (1923) no longer in use by 1923, Bachelor's-button [Bachelor's button, Bachelor's buttons, Batchelor's buttons] (156) (1923), Devil's flower (156) (1923) no longer in use by 1923, Morning campion (109, 156) (1923–1949), Poor Robin [Poor-robin] (156) (1923), Red bird's-eye [Red-bird's-eye] (156) (1923) no longer in use by 1923, Red campion (109, 138, 156) (1876–1949), Red lychnis (15) (1895), Red Robin [Red-Robin] (156) (1923) no longer in use by 1923, Robins (156) (1923) no longer in use by 1923, Soldiers (156) (1923) no longer in use by 1923, White campion [White campions] (15) (1895), White soapwort (92, 156) (1876–1923)

Silene drummondii Hook. var. *drummondii* – Drummond's campion [Drummond campion] (50, 155) (1942–present), Drummond's pink (5, 131) (1899–1913)

Silene gallica L. – English catchfly (5) (1913), Small-flower catchfly [Small-flowered catchfly] (5) (1913)

Silene inflata Sm. – See *Silene vulgaris* (Moench) Garcke

Silene involucrata (Cham. & Schlecht.) Bocquet subsp. *involucrata* – Arctic lychnis (5) (1913)

Silene L. – Campion (1, 4, 10, 13, 15, 93, 109, 138, 156) (1818–1986), Catchfly [Catch fly] (1, 4, 10, 13, 15, 50, 93, 109, 138, 156, 158, 167, 184) (1793–present) insects often caught in sticky exudate, Limewort (86) (1878) beacuse many species exude sticky substance like bird lime, Silene (155) (1942), Spattling poppy [Spatling poppy, Spatling Poppie] (178) (1526), Wild pink (10) (1818–1828)

Silene laciniata Cav. – Mexican campion (138) (1923), Wild pink (74) (1893) Santa Barbara CA

Silene latifolia (Mill.) Britton & Rendle – See *Silene vulgaris* (Moench) Garcke

Silene latifolia Poir. – Bladder campion (50) (present), Cowbell silene (155) (1942)

Silene latifolia Poir. subsp. *alba* (Mill.) Greuter & Burdet – Bull-rattle [Bull-rattle] (5, 156, 158) (1900–1923) no longer in use by 1923, Cowbell silene (155) (1942), Cow-rattle [Cow rattle, Cow-rattle] (5, 156, 158) (1900–1923) no longer in use by 1923, Cuckoo-flower [Cuckooflower, Cuckoo flower] (5, 156) (1913–1923), Double field campion (178) (1526), Evening campion (109, 138, 155, 156) (1923–1949), Evening lychnis (5, 15, 156) (1895–1923), Evening-blooming lychnis (158) (1900), Peat pink [Peatpink] (138) (1923), Ragged-robin [Ragged robin] (158) (1900), Snake flower [Snakeflower, Snake-flower] (5, 156, 158) (1900–1923) no longer in use by 1923, Thunder flower [Thunder-flower] (5, 156, 158) (1900–1923) no longer in use by 1923, White bachelor's-buttons [White bachelor's buttons] (156, 158) (1900–1923), White campion [White campions] (4, 5, 15, 62, 80, 85, 95, 109, 131, 156, 158) (1895–1986), White champion (72) (1907), White cockle (4, 62, 80) (1912–1986), White cuckoo flower [White cuckoo-flower] (158) (1900), White-robin [White robin] (5, 156, 158) (1900–1923) no longer in use by 1923, Wild cuckoo flower [Wild cuckoo-flower] (158) (1900)

Silene menziesii Hook. – Menzies' campion (50) (present), Menzies' pink (5) (1913), Menzies' silene [Menzies silene] (155) (1942)

Silene menziesii Hook. subsp. *menziesii* var. *menziesii* – Menzies' campion (50) (present), Nottingham catchfly (5, 156) (1913–1923)

Silene nivea (Nutt.) Muhl. ex Otth – Evening campion (50) (present), Snowy campion (3, 4, 5, 138, 156, 158) (1900–1986), Snowy silene (155) (1942), Western campion (85) (1932), Western white campion (5, 72, 158) (1900–1913), White campion [White campions] (93, 156) (1923–1936)

Silene noctiflora L. – Gentleman's-hats [Gentleman's hats] (73) (1892) Gilsum NH, Night-blooming catchfly (1, 5, 97) (1913–1937), Night-flowered catchfly (19) (1840), Night-flowering catchfly (4, 62, 72, 80, 85, 93, 95, 127, 131, 156) (1899–1986), Night-flowering silene [Nightflowering silene] (50, 155) (1942–present), Sticky cockle (4, 62) (1912–1986)

Silene nutans L. – Dover catchfly (5, 156) (1913–1923), Nodding catchfly (5, 156) (1913–1923), Nottingham catchfly (5, 156) (1913–1923)

Silene obovata Porsild – See *Silene menziesii* Hook. subsp. *menziesii* var. *menziesii*

Silene pendula L. – Drooping catchfly (138) (1923)

Silene pennsylvanica Michx. – See *Silene caroliniana* Walter subsp. *pensylvanica* (Michx.) Clausen

Silene pratensis (Raf.) Godr. & Gren. – See *Silene latifolia* Poir. subsp. *alba* (Mill.) Greuter & Burdet

Silene regia Sims. – Piskies (156, 158) (1900–1923), Pixie (156, 158) (1900–1923), Royal campion (2) (1895), Royal catchfly (3, 4, 5, 15, 50, 97, 156, 158) (1895–present), Royal silene (155) (1942), Splendid catchfly (156) (1923), Wild pink (5, 76, 156, 158) (1896–1923)

Silene rotundifolia Nutt. – Round-leaf catchfly [Round-leaved catchfly] (5, 15, 156) (1895–1923)

Silene stellata (L.) Aiton f. – King's cure-all [King's-cure-all] (156) (1923), Snakeroot [Snake root, Snake-root] (156) (1923), Starry campion (2, 4, 5, 15, 65, 86, 93, 95, 97, 109, 114, 131, 138, 156) (1878–1986), Starry catchfly (86) (1878), Starry champion (72, 85) (1907–1932), Starry silene (155) (1942), Thermon (156) (1923), Thermon snakeroot [Thermon snake root] (5) (1913), Widow's-frill [Widowsfrill] (50) (present), possibly Campion (184) (1793), possibly Four-leaf campion [Four-leaved campion, Four leaved campion] (42, 187) (1814–1818)

Silene suecica (Lodd.) Greuter & Burdet – Arctic campion (109, 138) (1923–1949), Red alpine campion (5) (1913)

Silene uralensis (Rupr.) Bocquet subsp. *uralensis* – Nodding lychnis (5) (1913)

Silene virginica L. – Catchfly [Catch fly] (15, 92) (1876–1895), Crimson catchfly (187) (1818), Early-flowering red lychnis [Early flowering Red Lychnis] (183) (~1756), Firepink [Fire pink] (2, 5, 15, 92, 97, 109, 138, 156) (1895–1949), Indian pink (5, 156) (1913–1923), Pink catchfly [Pink catch-fly] (92) (1876), Tall catchfly (187) (1818), Virginia campion [Virginian campion] (2) (1895), Virginia catchfly [Virginian catchfly] (86) (1878), Wild pink (23, 92) (1810–1876)

Silene vulgaris (Moench) Garcke – Behen (5, 156) (1913–1923) no longer in use by 1923, Bird's-eggs [Bird's eggs] (5, 156) (1913–1923) no longer in use by 1923, Bladder campion (5, 15, 92, 93, 107, 109, 156) (1876–1936), Bladder champion (45) (1896), Bladder silene (155) (1942), Bullrattle [Bull-rattle] (5, 156) (1913–1923) no longer in use by 1923, Campion pink (7, 92) (1828–1876), Coe bell (5) (1913), Cowbell [Cow-bell] (156) (1923) no longer in use by 1923, Cowbell silene (155) (1942), Cow-paps (156) (1923) no longer in use by 1923, Devil's-rattlebox [Devil's rattle box, Devil's rattle-box] (5, 76, 156) (1896–1923) Stockbridge MA, no longer in use by 1923, Frothy poppy (5, 156) (1913–1923) no longer in use by 1923, Knap-bottle [Knap bottle] (5, 156) (1913–1923) no longer in use by 1923, Maiden's-tears [Maiden's tears] (5, 76, 156) (1876–1923) Orono ME, Rattle-bags [Rattle bags] (5, 156) (1913–1923) no longer in use by 1923, Rattlebox [Rattle box, Rattle-box] (74) (1893) Berkshire Co. MA, Scarlet Virginia catchfly (181) (~1678), Sea pink [Sea-pink] (5, 7, 92, 156) (1828–1923) no longer in use by 1923, Snappers (5, 73, 156) (1892–1923) no longer in use by 1923, Spattling (156) (1923) no longer in use by 1923, Spattling poppy [Spatling poppy, Spatling Poppie] (5, 92) (1876–1913), White Ben (5, 156) (1913–1923) no longer in use by 1923

Silphium asperrimum Hook. – See *Silphium radula* Nutt.

Silphium asteriscum L. – Rough-leaf rosinweed [Rough-leaved rosin-weed] (50) (present), Starry rosinweed [Starry rosin-weed, Starry rosin weed] (5, 97) (1913–1937)

Silphium compositum var. *reniforme* (Raf. ex Nutt.) Torr. & Gray – Cup plant [Cup-plant] (50) (present), Kidney-leaf silphium [Kidney-leaved silphium] (5) (1913)

Silphium gatesii C. Mohr – See *Silphium radula* Nutt.

Silphium integrifolium Michx. – Entire-leaf rosinweed [Entire-leaved rosin-weed] (93, 97) (1936–1937), Entire-leaf rosinwood [Entire-leaved rosin wood] (5, 72) (1907–1913), Rosinweed [Rosin-weed, Rosin weed] (82) (1930), Whole-leaf rosinweed [Wholeleaf rosin-weed] (3, 50, 155) (1942–present)

Silphium integrifolium Michx. var. *integrifolium* – Whole-leaf rosin-weed [Wholeleaf rosinweed] (50) (present)

Silphium integrifolium Michx. var. *laeve* Torr. & Gray – Kidney-leaf silphium [Kidney-leaved silphium] (5) (1913), Showy rosinweed (3) (1977), Whole-leaf rosinweed [Wholeleaf rosinweed] (50) (present)

Silphium L. – Compass plant [Compass-plant, Compassplant] (1, 93) (1932–1936), Cup plant [Cup-plant] (1, 93) (1932–1936), False sun-flower [False sun-flower] (167) (1814), Mit-le-go-mish-ai-e-buck-ish-in-a-guack (Monominie) (23) (1810), Prairie dock (1) (1932), Rosin plant [Rosin-plant] (2, 147) (1856–1895), Rosinweed [Rosin-weed, Rosin weed] (1, 4, 50, 57, 63, 82, 93, 109, 138, 155, 156) (1840-present), Turpentine sunflower (7) (1828)

Silphium laciniatum L. – Chanshilshila (Dakota Teton) (37) (1919), Chanshinshinla (Dakota) (37) (1919), Compass plant [Compass-plant, Compassplant] (3, 4, 5, 14, 37, 47, 50, 58, 63, 72, 82, 86, 93, 95, 97, 109, 131, 138, 155, 156, 157, 158) (1852–present), Compass-weed [Compass weed] (92, 122) (1876–1937), Gum plant [Gum-plant, Gum-plant] (156) (1923), Gumweed [Gum weed] (37) (1919), Kahts-tawas (Pawnee, rough medicine) (37) (1919), Makan-tanga (Omaha-Ponca, big medicine or root) (37) (1919), Nakisokiits (Paw-nee, pine water) (37) (1919), Nakisu-kiitsu (Pawnee, pine water) (37) (1919), Pilotweed [Pilot-weed, Pilot weed] (5, 37, 92, 156, 157, 158) (1876–1929), Polar plant [Polar-plant] (5, 14, 92, 156, 157, 158) (1882–1929), Rosinweed [Rosin-weed, Rosin weed] (2, 5, 14, 37, 47, 58, 82, 156, 157) (1852–1930), Shokanwa-hu (Winnebago, gum plant) (37) (1919), Turpentine plant [Turpentine-plant] (156) (1923), Turpentine-weed [Turpentine weed] (5, 156) (1913–1923), Zha-pa (Omaha-Ponca, bitter weed) (37) (1919)

Silphium perfoliatum L. – Akûn'damo (Chippewa, watcher or spy) (40) (1928), Anglestem [Angle stem] (37) (1919), Compass plant [Compass-plant, Compassplant] (85) (1932) SD, Cup plant [Cup-plant] (3, 4, 5, 37, 40, 47, 49, 50, 58, 62, 63, 72, 82, 92, 93, 97, 106, 109, 127, 131, 156, 158) (1852–present), Cup rosinweed (138, 155) (1923–1942), Indian cup [Indian-cup] (5, 62, 93, 109, 156, 158) (1900–1949), Indian cup plant (49, 61, 92) (1870–1898), Ragged-cup [Ragged cup] (5, 19, 49, 92, 156, 158) (1840–1923) TX, Rake-ni-ozhu (Winnebago, weed that holds water) (37) (1919), Rake-paraparatsh (Winnebago, square weed) (37) (1919), Rosinweed [Rosin-weed, Rosin weed] (85, 95, 106, 158) (1900–1932), Square-stem [Square stem, Squarestem] (37) (1919), Zha tanga (Omaha-Ponca, big weed) (37) (1919), Zha-baho-hi (Omaha-Ponca, weed with angled stem) (37) (1919)

Silphium radula Nutt. – Rough-stem rosinweed [Roughstem rosin-weed] (50) (present)

Silphium speciosum Nutt. – See *Silphium integrifolium* Michx. var. *laeve* Torr. & Gray

Silphium terebinthinaceum Jacq. – Compass plant [Compass-plant, Compassplant] (156) (1923), Dock rosinweed (138) (1923), Gum plant [Gumplant, Gum-plant] (156) (1923), Prairie burdock (5, 92, 156) (1876–1923), Prairie dock (2, 5, 72, 122, 156) (1895–1937), Rosin plant [Rosin-plant] (5, 156) (1913–1923), Rosinweed [Rosin-weed, Rosin weed] (156) (1923), Turpentine sunflower (156) (1923)

Silphium terebinthinaceum L. – possibly *Silphium terebinthinaceum* Jacq.

Silphium ternifolium Michx. – possibly *Silphium trifoliatum* L.

Silphium trifoliatum L. – Prairie dock (2) (1895), Three-leaf rosin-weed [Three-leaved rosin-weed] (156) (1923), Whorled rosinweed [Whorled rosin weed] (5, 72) (1907–1913)

Silybum Adans. – Milk thistle [Milk-thistle] (109, 158) (1900–1949)

Silybum marianum (L.) Gaertn. – Blessed milk-thistle [Blessed milk-thistle] (50, 155) (1949–present), Blessed thistle (46, 50, 109) (1649–present), Chardon Marie (French) (158) (1900), Frauendistel (German) (158) (1900), Holy thistle [Holy thystle] (107, 109, 156, 158) (1900–1949), Lady's-milk [Lady's milk] (156, 158) (1900–1923), Lady's-thistle [Lady's thistle] (156, 158) (1900–1923), Mary thistle (52, 92) (1876–1919), Milk thistle [Milk-thistle] (5, 42, 52, 107, 156, 158) (1814–1923), Our Lady's thistle (158) (1900), St. Mary's thistle [St. Marys thistle] (52, 54, 109) (1905–1949), Steck-körner (German) (158) (1900), Virgin Mary's-thistle [Virgin Mary's thistle] (156, 158) (1900–1923)

Silybum marianum Gaertn. – See *Silybum marianum* (L.) Gaertn.

Simarouba Aubl. – Bitterwood [Bitter-wood, Bitter wood] (15) (1895), St. Mary's thistle [St. Marys thistle] (109) (1949)

Simaruba excelsa – See *Picrasma excelsa* (Sw.) Planch.

Simmondsia californica Nutt. – See *Simmondsia chinensis* (Link) C.K. Schneid.

Simmondsia chinensis (Link) C. K. Schneid. – Bitterwood [Bitter-wood, Bitter wood] (92) (1876), Jajoba (107) (1919), Pignut [Pig-nut, Pig nut] (78) (1898) AZ, Quassia (92) (1876)

Sinapis alba L. – California yellow mustard (109) (1949), Caucasian yellow mustard (109) (1949), Charlock (5, 157, 158) (1900–1929), Dutch yellow mustard (109) (1949), English yellow mustard (109) (1949), Gelber Senf (German) (158) (1900), Jajoba (107) (1919), Kedlock (5, 92, 157, 158) (1876–1929), Mostaza blanco (Span-ish) (158) (1900), Moustarde blanc (French) (6) (1892), Moutarde blanche (French) (158) (1900), Pignut [Pig-nut, Pig nut] (78) (1898), Senvie (5) (1913), Senvre (158) (1900), Weisser Senf (German) (6, 158) (1892–1900), White London mustard (109) (1949), White mus-tard (3, 4, 5, 6, 15, 50, 52, 53, 57, 58, 59, 69, 72, 85, 92, 93, 107, 109, 131, 138, 155, 156, 157, 158) (1869–present), Yellow mustard (6, 53, 69, 92, 157) (1876–1929), Yellow-seed mustard (19) (1840)

Sinapis arvensis L. – Bastard rocket (5, 157) (1900–1929), California rape (109) (1949), Chadlock [Chadlocke] (5, 157, 180) (1633–1929), Charlock (3, 4, 5, 14, 15, 14, 41, 85, 92, 97, 107, 109, 155, 180) (1170–1986), Charlock mustard (50) (present), Corn kale [Corn-kale] (5, 157) (1900–1929), Corn mustard (5, 92, 157) (1876–1929), Crowdweed [Crowd-weed, Crowd weed] (5, 74) (1893–1913) WV, Curlock (5) (1913), English charlock (145) (1897) KS, Field kale [Field-kale] (5, 157) (1900–1929), Field mustard (107) (1919), Ked-lock (5) (1913), Kerlock (5) (1913), Krautweed [Kraut-weed, Kraut weed] (5, 74, 157) (1893–1929), Mustard weld (14) (1882), Runch (157) (1929), Runchweed [Runch-weed, Runch weed] (5) (1913), Warlock (157) (1929), Watercress [Water-cress, Water cress] (5) (1913), Wild mustard (5, 41, 92, 97, 157) (1770–1937), Wild radish (92) (1876), Yellow-flower [Yellow flower] (5, 157) (1913–1929), possibly Lampsana (180) (1633), possibly Water chadlocke (180) (1633), possibly Wild rape [Wilde rapes] (180) (1633), possibly Wild turnip [Wilde turneps] (180) (1633)

Sinapis L. – Charlock (1, 93) (1932–1936), Mustard [Mustards] (1, 7, 50, 93, 158, 184) (1793–present)

Sinapis nigra L. – See *Brassica nigra* (L.) W. D. J. Koch

Sinocalamus latiflorus (Munro) McClure – Hemp bamboo (138) (1923)

Siphonychia Torr. & Gray – See *Paronychia* Mill. (all US species)

Sison canadense [L.] – See *Cryptotaenia canadensis* (L.) DC.

Sisymbrium (Tourn.) L. – See *Sisymbrium* L.

Sisymbrium alliaria Scop. – See *Alliaria petiolata* (Bieb.) Cavara & Grande

Sisymbrium altissimum L. – Jim Hill mustard (156) (1923), Sauce-alone [Sauce alone] (107) (1919), Tall sisymbrium (5, 72, 97) (1907–1937), Tall tumble-mustard [Tall tumblemustard] (50) (present),

Tumble-mustard [Tumble mustard, Tumblemustard] (155) (1942), Tumbling mustard (4, 62, 63, 80, 98, 131, 156) (1899–1986)

Sisymbrium canescens **Nutt.** – See *Descurainia pinnata* (Walter) Britton subsp. *pinnata*

Sisymbrium incisum **Engelm.** – See *Descurainia incana* (Bernh. ex Fisch. & C. A. Mey.) Dorn subsp. *incisa* (Engelm.) Kartesz & Gandhi

Sisymbrium irio **L.** – London rocket (4, 50) (1986–present)

Sisymbrium **L.** – Hedge mustard [Hedgemustard, Hedge-mustard] (4, 13, 15, 50, 156) (1849–present), London rocket (4, 50) (1986–present), Mustard [Mustards] (63) (1899), True water-cress [True water cress] (93) (1936), Tumble-mustard [Tumble mustard, Tumblemustard] (1, 93) (1932–1936), Watercress [Water-cress, Water cress] (10, 184) (1793–1818), Water-radish [Water radish] (10) (1818)

Sisymbrium loeselii **L.** – Small tumbleweed mustard (50) (present), Tall hedge-mustard [Tall hedge mustard] (3, 4) (1977–1986)

Sisymbrium nasturtium-aquaticum **L.** – See *Rorippa nasturtium-aquaticum* (L.) Hayek

Sisymbrium officinale **(L.) Scop** – Bank cress (107, 157, 158) (1919–1929), Bankweed [Bank-weed] (156) (1923), California cress (156) (1923), California mustard (76, 157, 158) (1896–1929) Rumford ME, Crambling rocket (107) (1919), English water cress (92) (1876), Eresimo (Spanish) (158) (1900), Erysimum (French) (158) (1900), Hederich (German) (158) (1900), Hedge mustard [Hedge-mustard, Hedge-mustard] (3, 4, 5, 7, 13, 15, 49, 50, 62, 63, 72, 76, 80, 85, 92, 97, 107, 131, 145, 156, 157, 158) (1828–present), Hedge-weed [Hedge weed, Hedge-weed] (5, 156, 158) (1900–1923), Herbe aux chantres (French) (158) (1900), Lucifer-matches (157, 158) (1900–1929), Officinale hedge-mustard (187) (1818), Tansy-mustard [Tansy mustard, Tansymustard] (122) (1937), Tortelle (French) (158) (1900), Vélar (French) (158) (1900), Wilder Senf (German) (158) (1900)

Sisymbrium officinale **Scop.** – See *Sisymbrium officinale* (L.) Scop

Sisymbrium sophia **L.** – See *Descurainia sophia* (L.) Webb ex Prantl

Sisymbrium thalianum **Gay.** – See *Arabidopsis thaliana* (L.) Britton

Sisymbrium vulgare **Pers.** – possibly *Rorippa palustris* (L.) Bess. (taxonomic status is unresolved (PL))

Sisyrinchium albidum **Raf.** – Spear-like blue-eyed grass (5) (1913), White blue-eyed-grass [White blue-eyed grass] (5, 50) (1913–present)

Sisyrinchium anceps **Gay.** – See *Sisyrinchium angustifolium* Mill.

Sisyrinchium angustifolium **Mill.** – Bernuda blue-eyed-grass [Bernuda blue-eyedgrass] (155) (1942), Blue-eyed Mary [Blue eyed Mary, Blue eyed Marys] (5, 156, 157, 158) (1900–1929), Blue-eyed-grass [Blue-eyed grass] (3, 19, 46, 65, 85, 156, 157) (1840–1977), Blue-eyed-lily [Blue-eyed lily, Blue-eyed lilly] (5, 156, 157, 158) (1900–1929), Blue-grass [Blue grass, Bluegrass] (5, 75, 156, 158) (1894–1923) Concord MA, Common blue-eyed-grass [Common blue eyed grass] (72, 138, 155, 157) (1923–1942), Forget-me-not [Forget me not, For-get-me-not, For-get-me-nots, Forgetmenot] (78) (1898) Hartford ME, Grassflower [Grass-flower, Grass flower] (5, 75, 156, 157, 158) (1894–1929) Concord MA, children, Narrow-leaf blue-eyed grass [Narrowleaf blue-eyed grass] (50) (present), Northern blue-eyed grass [Northern blue eyed grass] (72) (1907), Pepper-grass [Peppergrass, Pepper grass] (5, 156) (1913–1923), Pigroot [Pig-root] (5, 156, 157, 158) (1900–1929), Pointed blue-eyed grass (5, 15, 93, 97, 158) (1895–1937), Rush lily (156, 157, 158) (1900–1929), Satin-lily [Satin lily] (156) (1923), Star-eyed grass (5, 75, 156, 157, 158) (1894–1929) Concord MA, children, Stout blue-eyed grass (5, 97) (1913–1937), Two-edge blue-eyed grass [Two-edged blue-eyed grass] (187) (1818)

Sisyrinchium apiculatum **Bickn.** – See *Sisyrinchium atlanticum* Bicknell

Sisyrinchium arenicola **Bicknell** – See *Sisyrinchium fuscatum* Bickn.

Sisyrinchium asheianum **Bickn.** – See *Sisyrinchium albidum* Raf.

Sisyrinchium atlanticum **Bicknell** – Eastern blue-eyed grass (5, 50) (1913–present), Pepper-grass [Peppergrass, Pepper grass] (5) (1913)

Sisyrinchium bellum **S. Wats.** – Western blue-eyed-grass (138) (1923)

Sisyrinchium bermudiana – See *Sisyrinchium angustifolium* Mill.

Sisyrinchium campestre **Bickn.** – Prairie blue-eyed grass (5, 50, 93, 97) (1913–present), White-eyed-grass [White-eyed grass] (3, 85) (1932–1977)

Sisyrinchium campestre **Bickn. var. *campestre*** – White-eyed-grass [White-eyed grass] (3) (1977)

Sisyrinchium chilense **Hook.** – Sword-leaf blue-eyed grass [Swordleaf blue-eyed grass] (50) (present)

Sisyrinchium demissum **Greene** – Stiff blue-eye grass (50) (present)

Sisyrinchium ensigerum **Bickn.** – See *Sisyrinchium chilense* Hook.

Sisyrinchium fuscatum **Bickn.** – Coastal blue-eyed grass (50) (present), Sand blue-eyed grass (5) (1913)

Sisyrinchium graminioides **Bicknell** – See *Sisyrinchium angustifolium* Mill.

Sisyrinchium incrustatum **Bickn.** – See *Sisyrinchium fuscatum* Bickn.

Sisyrinchium **L.** – Blue-eyed-grass [Blue-eyed grass] (1, 50, 92, 93, 109, 122, 124, 138, 156, 158) (1900–present), Lily-grass [Lily grass] (7, 10) (1818–1828), Satin-flower (109) (1949), Scurvy-grass [Scurvy grass] (7) (1828)

Sisyrinchium langloisii **Greene** – Roadside blue-eyed grass (50) (present), Texas blue-eyed grass [Texas blue-eyedgrass] (155) (1942), Variable blue-eyed grass (97) (1937)

Sisyrinchium montanum **Greene** – Strict blue-eyed grass (50) (present)

Sisyrinchium montanum **Greene var. *montanum*** – Strict blue-eyed grass (5, 50) (1913–present)

Sisyrinchium mucronatum **Michx.** – Michaux's blue-eyed grass (5) (1913), Needle-tip blue-eyed grass [Needletip blue-eyed grass] (50) (present), Sword-leaf blue-eyed grass [Swordleaf blue-eyed grass] (187) (1818)

Sisyrinchium scabrellum **Bickn.** – See *Sisyrinchium albidum* Raf.

Sisyrinchium septentrionale **Bickn.** – Blue-eyed-grass [Blue-eyed grass] (85) (1932)

Sisyrinchium strictum **Bickn.** – See *Sisyrinchium montanum* Greene var. *montanum*

Sisyrinchium varians **Bickn.** – See *Sisyrinchium langloisii* Greene

Sitanion elymoides **Raf.** – See *Elymus elymoides* (Raf.) Swezey subsp. *elymoides*

Sitanion glaber **J. G. Smith** – See *Elymus elymoides* (Raf.) Swezey

Sitanion hanseni **(Scribn.) J. G. Sm.** – See *Elymus ×hansenii* Scribn. [*glaucus × elymoides or multisetus*]

Sitanion hystrix **(Nutt.) J. G. Am. var. *hystrix*** – See *Elymus elymoides* (Raf.) Swezey

Sitanion hystrix **(Nutt.) J. G. Sm.** – See *Elymus elymoides* (Raf.) Swezey subsp. *elymoides*

Sitanion hystrix **(Nutt.) J. G. Sm. var. *brevifolium* (J. G. Sm.) C. L. Hitchc.** – See *Elymus elymoides* (Raf.) Swezey subsp. *brevifolius* (J. G. Sm.) Barkworth

Sitanion **Raf.** – See *Elymus* L.

Sitilias caroliniana **(Walt.) Raf.** – See *Pyrrhopappus carolinianus* (Walt.) DC.

Sitilias grandiflora **(Nutt.) Greene** – See *Pyrrhopappus grandiflorus* (Nutt.) Nutt.

Sitilias **Raf.** – See *Pyrrhopappus* DC.

Sium **(Tourn.) L.** – See *Sium* L.

Sium carsoni **Durand** – See *Sium carsonii* Dur. ex Gray

Sium carsonii **Dur. ex Gray** – Carson's water parsnip (5) (1913)

Sium **L.** – Water-parsnip [Water parsnip, Waterparsnip, Water parsnep, Water-parsnep] (1, 2, 4, 7, 10, 50, 155, 158, 184) (1793–present)

Sium nodiflorum **[L.]** – possibly *Apium nodiflorum* (L.) Lag.

Sium suave **Walt.** – American water-parsnip [American water parsnip] (157, 158) (1900–1929), Hemlock [Hemloc, Hemlocke] (156) (1923), Hemlock water parsnip (72, 131, 157) (1899–1907), Hemlock-parsley [Hemlockparsley, Hemlock-spruce] (5, 50, 155) (1913–present), Jažopi hu (Lakota, whistle stem) (121) (1918?–1970?),

Water-parsley [Water parsley] (156) (1923), Water-parsnip [Water parsnip, Waterparsnip, Water parsnep, Water-parsnep] (3, 4, 46, 48, 85, 95, 21, 126, 133, 148, 157, 190) (~1759–1986), Wild parsnip [Wild-parsnip, Wilde parsnep] (157, 158) (1900–1929)

***Smallanthus uvedalius* (L.) Mackenzie ex Small** – Bear's-foot [Bear's foot, Bearsfoot] (4, 49, 52, 53, 54, 57, 158) (1898–1986), Hairy leafcup (50) (present), Large-flower leafcup [Large-flowered leaf-cup] (5, 97, 158) (1900–1937), Leafcup [Leaf-cup, Leaf cup] (52, 53, 92, 156) (1876–1923), Polymnia (54) (1905), Uvedalia (53, 158) (1900–1922), Yellow bear's-foot [Yellow bears-foot] (5, 156, 158) (1900–1923), Yellow leaf-cup [Yellow leafcup] (5, 19, 52, 54, 72, 155, 158) (1840–1942), Yellow-flower leaf-cup [Yellow-flowered leaf-cup] (156) (1923)

***Smilacina bifolia* [(L.) Desf.]** – See *Maianthemum dilatatum* (Wood) A. Nels. & J. F. Macbr.

***Smilacina racemosa* (L.) Desf.** – See *Maianthemum racemosum* (L.) Link subsp. *racemosum*

***Smilacina sessilifolia* Nutt. ex Baker** – See *Maianthemum stellatum* (L.) Link

***Smilacina stellata* Desf.** – See *Maianthemum stellatum* (L.) Link

***Smilacina trifolia* Desf.** – See *Maianthemum trifolium* (L.) Sloboda

***Smilax bona-nox* L.** – Bamboo vine (78) (1898) TX, Bristly greenbrier [Bristly greenbriar] (5, 97) (1913–1937), Carolina prickly-leaf smilax [Carolinian prickly leaved smilax] (8) (1785), Catbrier [Cat briar, Cat-brier] (117, 156) (1908–1923), Fiddle-shaped greenbrier (5) (1913), Fringed greenbrier [Fringed green-briar] (156) (1923), Greenbrier [Green brier, Greenbriar, Green briar, Green bryar] (3, 117, 156) (1908–1977), Salsepareille à feuilles ciliées (French) (8) (1785), Saw greenbrier (50, 155) (1942–present), Stretchberry [Stretch berry, Stretch-berry] (78, 156) (1898–1923) TX

***Smilax caduca* [L.]** – See *Smilax rotundifolia* L.

***Smilax caduca* Willd. and Pursh** – See *Smilax rotundifolia* L.

***Smilax domingensis* Willd** – See *Smilax smallii* Morong

***Smilax ecirrata* (Engelm. ex Kunth) S. Wats.** – Carrion-flower [Carrionflower, Carrion flower] (156) (1923), Greenbrier [Green brier, Greenbriar, Green briar, Green bryar] (3) (1977), Upright carrion flower [Upright carrionflower] (50) (present), Upright smilax (5, 72, 97) (1907–1937)

***Smilax glauca* Walt.** – Bamboo brier [Bamboo-brier] (92) (1876), Cat greenbrier (50, 155) (1942–present), False sarsaparilla (156) (1923), Glaucous-leaf greenbrier [Glaucous-leaved greenbrier] (5, 93, 97) (1913–1937), Ivy-leaf rough bindweed [Ivy leaved rough bindweed] (8) (1785), Mecapatli (177) (1762), Mechoacan (181) (~1678), Oschbe (46) (1879), Salsepareille de Virginie (French) (8) (1785), Sarsaparilla (5, 8, 46, 187) (1785–1913), Sawbrier [Saw-brier, Saw brier] (156, 157) (1923–1929), Saxifarilla (46) (1879), Virginia sarsaparill (92) (1876), Zarzaparilla (46) (1879)

***Smilax herbacea* L.** – American Jacob's-ladder [American Jacob's ladder] (158) (1900), Bohea tea (19) (1840), Carrion-flower [Carrionflower, Carrion flower] (3, 72, 85, 97, 109, 156, 157, 158) (1900–1977), Carrion-flower greenbrier [Carrionflower greenbrier] (155) (1942), Field yam-root (156) (1923), Herbaceous carrion-flower (93) (1936), Jacob's flower (5, 14, 22, 40) (1882–1913), Jacob's-ladder [Jacob's ladder, Jacobs-ladder] (19, 30, 92) (1830–1876), Long-peduncle smilax [Long-peduncled smilax] (187) (1818), Ma'kodji'bĭk (Chippewa, bear root) (40) (1928), Smooth carrion flower [Smooth carrionflower] (50) (present), Stinking rough bindweed [Stinking rough bind-weed] (187) (1818), Tall carrion flower [Tall carrion-flower] (156) (1923), Toshunk ah'unshke (Winnebago, otter armlet) (37) (1830)

Smilax herbacea* L. var. *herbacea – possibly *Smilax herbacea* L.

***Smilax herbacea* L. var. *lasioneuron* (Small) Rydb.** – See *Smilax lasioneura* Hook.

***Smilax herbacea* L. var. *pulverulenta* (Michx.) Gray** – See *Smilax pulverulenta* Michx.

***Smilax hispida* Muhl.** – See *Smilax tamnoides* L.

***Smilax illinoensis* Mangaly** – Illinois greenbrier (50) (present), Squine (French) (17) (1796)

***Smilax* L.** – Carrion-flower [Carrionflower, Carrion flower] (1) (1932), Catbrier [Cat briar, Cat-brier] (1, 92, 93) (1876–1936), China brier (2) (1895), Greenbrier [Green brier, Greenbriar, Green briar, Green bryar] (1, 8, 12, 50, 93, 106, 109, 122, 138, 155, 156) (1785–present), Rough bindweed (8, 10) (1785–1818), Salsepareille (French) (8) (1785), Sarsaparilla (7, 57, 158) (1828–1917), Smilax (1, 10, 14, 93) (1818–1936)

***Smilax lasioneura* Hook.** – Blue Ridge carrionflower [Blueridge carrionflower, Blue Ridge carrionflower] (50) (present), Carrion-flower [Carrionflower, Carrion flower] (3) (1977), Smilax (85) (1932)

***Smilax laurifolia* L.** – Bamboo vine (5) (1913), Bay-leaf rough bindweed [Bay leaved rough bindweed] (8) (1785), Green thorn (41) (1770), Laurel greenbrier (50, 138) (1923–present), Laurel-leaf greenbrier [Laurel-leaved greenbrier] (5) (1913), Laurel-leaf smilax [Laurel-leafed smilax] (124) (1937), Salsepareille à feuilles de laurier (French) (8) (1785)

***Smilax megacarpa* Morong p.p.** – See *Smilax laurifolia* L.

***Smilax peduncularis* [Muhl. Ex Willd.]** – See *Smilax herbacea* L.

***Smilax peduncularis* Willd. and Pursh** – See *Smilax herbacea* L.

***Smilax pseudo-china* L.** – See *Smilax pseudochina* L.

***Smilax pseudochina* L.** – American chinaroot [American china root] (5, 49, 92) (1876–1913), Bamboo vine (50) (present), Bastard china (8) (1785), Bastard china root (92) (1876), Bull brier [Bull-brier] (5, 156) (1913–1923), China brier (2, 49) (1895–1898), China root of Mexico (49) (1898), Chinese smilax (124) (1937) TX, Chyna roots (46) (1879), False chinaroot [False china root, False china-root] (5, 49, 156) (1913–1923), False sarsaparilla (156) (1923), Halberd-leaf smilax [Halberd-leaved smilax] (5) (1913), Long-stalk greenbrier [Long-stalked greenbriar, Long-stalked greenbrier] (5, 72, 97) (1907–1937), Salsepareille à racines rouges (French) (8) (1785), Sarsaparilla (5) (1913), Tsinaw (181) (~1678), possibly Smilax with red berries (189) (1767)

***Smilax pulverulenta* Michx.** – Carrion-flower [Carrionflower, Carrion flower] (3) (1977), Downy carrion-flower [Downy carrionflower] (50) (present)

***Smilax pumila* Walt.** – Sarsaparilla vine (50) (present)

***Smilax rotundifolia* L.** – Bamboo brier [Bamboo-brier] (5, 156) (1913–1923), Biscuit plant (75) (1894) Allston MA, children eat tendrils and new leaves, Biscuitleaves [Biscuit leaves, Biscuit-leaves] (5, 73, 156) (1892–1923) Allston MA, children eat tendrils and new leaves, Bread-and-butter (5, 73, 156) (1892–1923) Cape Ann MA, young leaves are eaten by children, Brier (92) (1876), Bull brier [Bull-brier] (109) (1949), Bull-grip (156) (1923), Canadian round-leaf smilax [Canadian round leaved smilax] (8) (1785), Catbrier [Cat briar, Cat-brier] (156) (1923), Common greenbrier [Common green brier, Common green-brier] (2, 130) (1895), Deciduous rough bindweed [Deciduous rough bind-weed] (187) (1818), Devil's hop-vine [Devil's hop vine] (5, 156) (1913–1923), Dog brier [Dogbrier, Dog-brier] (78) (1898) MA, Greenbrier [Green brier, Greenbriar, Green briar, Green bryar] (5, 19, 72, 92, 97, 107, 156, 187) (1818–1937), Horsebrier [Horse-brier, Horse brier, Horse briar] (5, 19, 44, 75, 109, 156) (1894–1949), Hunger-root (156) (1923), Hungry vine [Hungry-vine] (5, 156) (1913–1923) no longer in use by 1923, Round-leaf greenbrier [Roundleaf greenbrier] (50) (present), Round-leaf smilax [Round-leaved smilax] (187) (1818), Salsepareille à feuilles rondes (French) (8) (1785), Salsepareille qui perd ses feuilles (French) (8) (1785), Three-nerve rough bindweed [Three-nerved rough bindweed] (8) (1785), Wait-a-bit (5, 73, 156) (1892–1923)

***Smilax rotundifolia* L. var. *crenulata* Small & Heller** – See *Smilax rotundifolia* L.

***Smilax rotundifolia* Willd. and Pursh** – See *Smilax rotundifolia* L.

***Smilax sarsaparilla* L.** – See *Smilax glauca* Walt.

***Smilax smallii* Morong** – Jackson vine [Jackson-vine] (156) (1923), Lance-leaf greenbrier [Lance-leaved greenbrier] (5, 50) (1913–present), Red-berry Virginia smilax [Red berried Virginian smilax] (8)

(1785), Salsepareille lancéolée (French) (8) (1785), Southern smilax (156) (1923)

***Smilax tamnifolia* Michx.** – See *Smilax pseudochina* L.

***Smilax tamnoides* L.** – Bamboo greenbrier (155) (1942), Bristly greenbrier [Bristly greenbriar] (3, 50, 138, 155) (1923–present), Bristly sarsaparilla (5) (1913), Bryony-leaf rough-bindweed [Bryony leaved rough bindweed] (8) (1785), Greenbrier [Green brier, Greenbriar, Green briar, Green bryar] (9, 35, 85, 113, 130) (1806–1932), Hispid greenbrier [Hispid greenbriar] (5, 35, 72, 93, 97) (1806–1937), Salsepareille à feuilles de tamnus (French) (8) (1785), Smilax with bryony leaves (189) (1767), Thorny greenbriar (93) (1936)

***Smilax walteri* Pursh.** – Coral greenbrier [Coral green-brier, Coral green-briar] (50, 138, 156) (1923–present), False sarsaparilla (156) (1923), Red-berry bamboo [Red-berried bamboo] (5, 156) (1913–1923), Sarsaparilla (5) (1913), Walter's greenbrier (5) (1913)

***Smyrnium aureum* L.** – See *Thaspium trifoliatum* var. *aureum* (Nutt.) Britton

***Soja max* (L.) Piper** – See *Glycine max* (L.) Merr.

***Solandra* Sw.** – Chalice vine [Chalice-vine] (109, 138) (1923–1949)

***Solanum americanum* Mill.** – Black nightshade [Black night-shade] (3) (1977), Deadly nightshade (187) (1818)

***Solanum angustifolium* Mill.** – Horned nightshade (155) (1942)

***Solanum capsicastrum* Link ex Schauer** – False Jerusalem cherry [False Jerusalem-cherry] (109, 138) (1923–1949)

***Solanum carolinense* L.** – Apple-of-Sodom [Apple of Sodom] (5, 156, 157, 158) (1900–1929), Bull nettle [Bull-nettle] (5, 49, 52, 53, 62, 75, 77, 156, 157, 158) (1898–1929), Carolina horsenettle [Carolina horse nettle] (4, 50) (1986–present), Horsenettle [Horse nettle] (1, 3, 5, 19, 49, 52, 53, 56, 57, 62, 63, 70, 72, 80, 85, 92, 95, 97, 122, 145, 156, 157, 158, 187) (1818–1977), Ivrepeba (181) (~1678), Jatropha (52) (1919), Juripeba (181) (~1678), Radical (75) (1894) WV, Radical-weed [Radical weed] (5, 156, 157, 158) (1900–1929), Sand briar [Sand-briar, Sand brier] (5, 49, 53, 62, 75, 156) (1898–1923), Thornapple [Thorn apple, Thornapple, Thorn apples, Thorne Apple] (156) (1923), Threadsaf (49) (1898), Thread-soft [Tread soft, Treadsoft] (49, 53, 62) (1898–1922), Tread-softly [Treadsoftly, Tread softly] (5, 156) (1913–1923)

Solanum carolinense* L. var. *carolinense – Carolina horsenettle [Carolina horse nettle] (50) (present)

***Solanum citrullifolium* A. Br.** – Melon-leaf nightshade [Melon-leaved nightshade] (4, 5) (1913–1986), Watermelon nightshade (50, 155) (1942–present)

***Solanum cornutum* Lam.** – See *Solanum angustifolium* Mill.

***Solanum dimidiatum* Raf.** – Purple nightshade (122) (1937), Purple-flower nightshade [Purple flowered nightshade] (124) (1937), Torrey's nightshade [Torrey nightshade] (5, 72, 97, 155) (1907–1942), Torrey's solanum (86) (1878), Western horse-nettle [Western horsenettle] (4, 50) (1986–present)

***Solanum dulcamara* L.** – Amara-dulcis [Amara dulcis] (158, 178) (1599–1900), Bitter nightshade (155, 156) (1923–1942), Bittersüss (German) (6, 158) (1892–1900), Bittersweet [Bitter sweet, Bitter-sweet] (1, 3, 4, 5, 6, 14, 19, 49, 52, 53, 55, 57, 61, 62, 71, 92, 93, 156, 158, 187) (1818–1986), Blue bindweed (5, 156, 158) (1900–1923), Climbing nightshade (4, 5, 50, 62, 93, 97, 156, 158) (1900–present), Dogwood [Dog-wood, Dog wood] (5, 156) (1913–1923), Douce-Amere (French) (6) (1892), Dulcamara (53, 55, 57, 187) (1818–1917), Dulcamara (Spanish) (158) (1900), Dwale (158) (1900), European bittersweet [European bitter-sweet] (109) (1949), Fellen (156) (1923), Felonwort [Fellenwort] (5, 92, 156, 158) (1876–1923), Fever-twig [Fever-twig] (71, 158) (1898–1900), Gloria (Spanish) (158) (1900), Hindischkraut (German) (158) (1900), Morelle grimpante (French) (158) (1900), Morrel (158) (1900), Nightshade [Night-shade, Night shade, Nyght shade] (72, 158) (1900–1907), Nightshade vine (71, 92) (1876–1898), Poison flower [Poison-flower] (156, 158) (1900–1923), Poison-berry [Poison berry] (156, 158) (1900–1923), Pushion-berry (158) (1900), Scarlet-berry [Scarlet berry] (49, 53, 92, 156, 158) (1876–1923), Skaw-coo (158)

(1900), Snakeberry [Snake berry, Snake-berry] (156, 158) (1900–1923), Staff vine [Staff-vine] (71) (1898), Terrididdle (158) (1900), Tether-devil [Tether devil] (158) (1900), Tetonwort (71) (1898), Violet-bloom [Violet bloom] (6, 49, 53, 92, 158) (1892–1922), Wolf-grape [Wolf grape] (92, 158) (1876–1900), Wood nightshade (77, 178) (1526–1898), Woody nightshade [Woody night-shade] (6, 19, 49, 52, 53, 57, 71, 92, 156, 158, 187) (1818–1923)

***Solanum elaeagnifolium* Cav.** – Bull nettle [Bull-nettle] (150) (1894), Horsenettle [Horse nettle] (150) (1894), Prickly nightshade (145) (1897), Purple nightshade (156) (1923), Silver-leaf nightshade [Silverleaf nightshade, Silver-leaved nightshade] (3, 4, 5, 50, 97, 122, 124, 155, 156, 158) (1900–present), Trompillo (150, 158) (1894–1900) NM, Trompillos (Mexico) (5, 107) (1913–1919), White horse-nettle [White horse nettle] (156) (1923)

Solanum esculentum – See *Solanum melongena* L.

***Solanum fendleri* Gray ex Torr.** – Native potato (103) (1870), Potato [Potatoes] (103) (1870)

***Solanum heterodoxum* Dunal (possibly)** – Melon-leaf nightshade [Melon-leaved nightshade] (72) (1907)

***Solanum interius* Rydb.** – Deadly nightshade (50) (present), Inland nightshade (155) (1942), Plains black nightshade (4) (1986)

***Solanum jamesii* Torr.** – Wild potato [Wild potatoe, Wild potatoes, Wild-potato] (1) (1932)

***Solanum* L.** – Bittersweet [Bitter sweet, Bitter-sweet] (1, 93) (1932–1936), Buffalo bur [Buffalo-bur, Buffalo burr] (1) (1932), Horsenettle [Horse nettle] (1, 93) (1932–1936), Love-apple [Love apple] (1) (1932), Nightshade [Night-shade, Night shade, Nyght shade] (1, 4, 10, 50, 92, 109, 138, 148, 155, 156, 184) (1793–present), Potato [Potatoes] (1, 93, 158) (1900–1936), Tomato [Tomatoes] (109, 138, 155, 156, 158) (1900–1949)

Solanum lycopersicon – See *Solanum lycopersicum* L.

***Solanum lycopersicum* L.** – Garden tomato (50) (present), Love-apple [Love apple] (19, 92) (1840–1876), Tomato [Tomatoes] (19, 92) (1840–1876)

***Solanum lycopersicum* L. var. *cerasiforme* (Dunal) Spooner, J. Anderson & R. K. Jansen** – Cherry tomato [Cherry tomatoes] (122) (1937) TX, Wild cherry tomato (124) (1937) TX

Solanum lycopersicum* L. var. *lycopersicum – Aethiopian apple (180) (1633), Amorous apples (107) (1588), Apples-of-love [Apples of loue] (180) (1633), Cherry tomato [Cherry tomatoes] (5) (1913), Common tomato (155) (1942), Garden tomato (50) (present), Glaucium (180) (1633), Gold-apple [Gold apple] (107) (1919), Golden apples (180) (1633), Jerusalem apple (107) (1835), Jew's-ear [Jew's ear, Jews' ear] (5, 156, 158) (1900–1923), Love-apple [Love apple] (5, 14, 85, 107, 110, 156, 158) (1882–1923), Paradise-apple [Paradise apple] (158) (1900), Poma Amoris (180) (1633), Poma Peruviana (107) (1588), Pomi del Peru (107) (1919), Pomi d'oro (107) (1554), Pomme d'amour [Pommes d'amour] (French, love apple) (107, 158, 180) (1586–1900), Pomo dei Mori (Italian, Morocco apple) (158) (1900), Red apples-of-love [Red apples of loue] (178) (1526), Tamate (158) (1900) Spanish America, Tomates (107) (1604), Tomati (Mexican and Nahua natives) (107) (1919), Tomatl (107) (1651), Tomato [Tomatoes] (5, 14, 57, 95, 107, 110, 114, 138, 156, 158) (1882–1923), Yellowish apples-of-love [Yellowish apples of loue] (178) (1526)

***Solanum mammosum* L.** – Turkey-berry [Turkey berry] (92) (1876)

***Solanum melongena* L.** – Apples of love (46, 107) (1879–1919), Aubergine (110, 156) (1886–1923), Becengenes (46) (1879), Bedengiam (110) (16th century), Belingela (107) (1658), Berengenas (107) (1919), Brinjal (156) (1923), Common eggplant (138) (1923), Egg-apple [Egg apple] (92, 156) (1876–1923), Eggplant [Egg-plant, Egg plant] (19, 82, 85, 92, 107, 156) (1840–1932), Garden egg (156) (1923), Guinea squash (156) (1923), Jew's-apple [Jew's apple] (107, 156) (1919–1923), Mad-apple [Mad apples, Mad-apples] (107, 156, 178) (1526–1923), Melanzana (Italy) (110) (16th century), Raging-apples [Raging apples] (178) (1526), Yellow mad-apple [Yellow mad apples] (178) (1526)

Solanum nigrum – See *Solanum ptychanthum* Dunal

Solanum nigrum (**auct. non L.**) – See *Solanum ptychanthum* Dunal

Solanum nigrum **L.** – Black nightshade [Black night-shade] (2, 5, 62, 71, 72, 80, 92, 93, 107, 124, 125, 126, 131, 138, 155, 156, 157, 158) (1895–1936), Bonewort [Bone wort] (77) (1898) Western US, Common nightshade [Common night shade, Common night-shade] (2, 71, 80, 85, 92, 95, 107, 156, 157, 158) (1895–1937), Deadly nightshade (5, 19, 62, 71, 92, 93, 97, 124, 156) (1840–1937), Duscle (5, 156, 157, 158) (1900–1929), Garden huckleberry (156) (1923), Garden nightshade (5, 71, 92, 93, 125, 156, 157, 158) (1876–1936), Hound's-berry [Hound's berry] (5, 156, 157, 158) (1900–1929), Morelle (French) (158) (1900), Morelle [Morel] (156) (1923) no longer in use by 1923, Nightshade [Night-shade, Night shade, Nyght shade] (63, 71, 122, 145, 148) (1897–1937), Petty morel [Pettymorel, Petty-morel, Petty-morrel, Pettymorrel, Petty morrell, Petymorell] (5, 156, 157, 158, 179) (1526–1929), Schwartzer Nachtschatten (German) (158) (1900), Small morel (157) (1929), Stubbleberry (80, 157) (1929–1930), Wonder-berry [Wonder berry] (126, 156) (1923–1933)

Solanum physalifolium **Rusby** – Hairy nightshade (3) (1977), Hoe nightshade (50) (present), Viscid nightshade (4) (1986)

Solanum pimpinellifolium **Jusl.** – Currant tomato (138) (1923)

Solanum pseudocapsicum **L.** – Bastard Ginnie Pepper (178) (1526), Jerusalem cherry [Jerusalem-cherry] (19, 92, 109, 138) (1840–1949), Tree nightshade (92) (1876)

Solanum pseudo-capsicum **L.** – See *Solanum pseudocapsicum* L.

Solanum ptychanthum **Dunal** – Black nightshade [Black night-shade] (4) (1986), Lesse morell (179) (1526), Nightshade [Night-shade, Night shade, Nyght shade] (179) (1526), Nightshade with the white flower (46) (1671), West Indian nightshade (50) (present)

Solanum rostratum **Dunal** – Beaked nightshade (5, 131, 156, 158) (1899–1923), Buffalo bur [Buffalo-bur, Buffalo burr] (3, 4, 5, 56, 62, 70, 75, 80, 85, 93, 95, 97, 114, 122, 125, 156, 158) (1894–1986), Buffalo-bur nightshade [Buffalobur nightshade] (50, 155) (1942–present), Kansas thistle (4, 77) (1898–1986), Potato-bug plant [Potato bug plant] (62) (1912) original host of Colorado potato beetle, Prickly nightshade (5, 62, 125, 156) (1912–1931), Prickly-potato [Prickly potato] (5, 62, 156) (1912–1923), Sand bur [Sand-bur, Sand burr, Sand bur] (5, 63, 72, 93, 156, 158) (1899–1936), Texas nettle (62, 145, 156) (1897–1923), Texas thistle (131) (1899), Yellow nightshade (156) (1923)

Solanum sarrachoides **Sendtner** – See *Solanum physalifolium* Rusby

Solanum seaforthianum **Andr.** – Brazilian nightshade (138) (1923)

Solanum sisymbrifolium **Lam.** – Viscid nightshade (5) (1913)

Solanum triflorum **Nutt.** – Čaŋxlóǧaŋ škiškita (Lakota, rough weed) (121) (1918?–1970?), Cut-leaf nightshade [Cut-leaved nightshade] (3, 4, 5, 50, 72, 85, 93, 97, 121, 126, 131, 148, 155, 156) (1899–present), Spreading nightshade (71, 145, 157) (1897–1929), Wild potato [Wild potatoe, Wild potatoes, Wild-potato] (71, 156) (1898–1923)

Solanum triquetrum **Cav.** – Potato-jasmine [Potato jasmine] (77) (1898) Waco TX, Vine nightshade (122, 124) (1937) TX

Solanum tuberosum **L.** – Aquinas (107) (1919), Bastard potatoes (178) (1526), Batatas (107) (1919), English batata (Brazil) (110) (1886), Irish potato (156) (1923), Openawk (110) (1886), Papas (Chile, Peru) (107) (1919), Pape (46) (1879), Potato [Potatoes] (19, 107, 109, 110, 138, 156) (1840–1949), Round potato (156) (1923), Virginia potato [Virginian potato] (110) (1585), White potato (156) (1923)

Solanum villosum **Mill.** – See *Solanum physalifolium* Rusby

Solanum wallacei (**Gray**) **Parish** – Catalina nightshade (138) (1923)

Solanum wendlandii **Hook. f.** – Costa Rican nightshade [Costa Rica nightshade] (138) (1923)

Solanum xanti **Gray** – Purple nightshade (138) (1923)

Soleirolia soleirolii (**Req.**) **Dandy** – Baby's-tears [Babys-tears] (109) (1949)

Solidago altissima **L.** – See *Solidago canadensis* L. var. *scabra* Torr. & Gray

Solidago arguta **Aiton** – Cut-leaf goldenrod [Cutleaf goldenrod, Cut-leaved golden-rod, Cut-leaved goldenrod] (5, 131, 122) (1899–1937), Sharp-notch goldenrod [Sharp-notched golden-rod] (19, 187) (1818–1840)

Solidago arguta **var.** *boottii* (**Hook.**) **Palmer & Steyermark** – Boott's goldenrod [Boott's golden-rod, Boott goldenrod] (5, 97, 122, 138) (1913–1937)

Solidago axillaris **Pursh** – See *Solidago caesia* L. var. *caesia*

Solidago bicolor **L.** – Belly-ache weed [Belly-ache-weed, Bellyache weed] (5, 76, 156) (1896–1923) Paris ME, Cream-colored goldenrod (106) (1930), Pale goldenrod [Pale golden-rod] (5, 156) (1913–1923), Silver-rod (156) (1923), Silverweed [Silver weed, Silver-weed] (5, 75, 76, 156) (1896–1923) ME NY, White goldenrod [White golden-rod] (5, 19, 106, 138, 156) (1840–1930), White-flower goldenrod [White-flowered golden-rod] (187) (1818)

Solidago boottii **Hook.** – See *Solidago arguta* Aiton var. *boottii* (Hook.) Palmer & Steyerm.

Solidago caesia **L.** – Blue-stem goldenrod [Blue-stem golden-rod, Blue-stemmed golden-rod, Blue-stemmed goldenrod] (5, 19, 72, 97, 156) (1840–1937), Slender goldenrod [Slender goldenrod] (156) (1923), Woodland goldenrod [Woodland golden-rod] (5, 156) (1913–1923), Wreath goldenrod [Wreath golden-rod] (5, 138, 156) (1913–1923)

Solidago caesia **L. var.** *curtisii* (**Torr. & Gray**) **Wood** – Curtis' goldenrod [Curtis' golden-rod] (5) (1913), Furry goldenrod (138) (1923), Mountain goldenrod [Mountain golden-rod] (5) (1913)

Solidago caesia **var.** *caesia* **L.** – Axil goldenrod [Axil golden-rod] (19) (1840)

Solidago canadensis **L.** – Canadian goldenrod [Canadian golden-rod, Canada goldenrod, Canada golden-rod] (4, 5, 19, 50, 62, 72, 80, 82, 85, 95, 97, 122, 127, 131, 138, 155, 156, 158) (1840–present), Double goldenrod [Double golden-rod] (158) (1900), Goldenrod [Golden-rod, Golden rod] (56, 80, 145) (1897–1901), Gulden-rod (177) (1762), High goldenrod [High golden-rod] (158) (1900), Rock goldenrod [Rock golden-rod] (5, 156) (1913–1923), Three-nerve goldenrod [Three nerved goldenrod, Three-nerved golden-rod] (187) (1818), Yellow-weed [Yellow weed] (76, 156, 158) (1896–1923)

Solidago canadensis **L. var.** *canadensis* – Canadian goldenrod [Canadian golden-rod, Canada goldenrod, Canada golden-rod] (3, 50) (1977–present)

Solidago canadensis **L. var.** *gilvocanescens* **Rydb.** – Canadian goldenrod [Canadian golden-rod, Canada goldenrod, Canada golden-rod] (3) (1977), Short-hair goldenrod [Shorthair goldenrod] (50) (present)

Solidago canadensis **L. var.** *hargeri* **Fern.** – Canadian goldenrod [Canadian golden-rod, Canada goldenrod, Canada golden-rod] (3) (1977), Harger's goldenrod (50) (present)

Solidago canadensis **L. var.** *salibrosa* (**Piper**) **M. E. Jones** – Canadian goldenrod [Canadian golden-rod, Canada goldenrod, Canada golden-rod] (3) (1977), Creek goldenrod (155) (1942), Salibrosa goldenrod (50) (present)

Solidago canadensis **L. var.** *scabra* **Torr. & Gray** – A'djidamo'wano (Chippewa, squirrel tail) (40) (1928), Canadian goldenrod [Canadian golden-rod, Canada goldenrod, Canada golden-rod] (3, 50) (1977–present), Common goldenrod [Common golden rod] (58) (1869), Double goldenrod [Double golden-rod] (5, 156) (1913–1923), Goldenrod [Golden-rod, Golden rod] (40) (1928), Great goldenrod [Great golden-rod] (19, 187) (1818–1840), High goldenrod [High golden-rod] (5) (1913), Tall goldenrod [Tall golden-rod] (5, 97, 122, 138, 155, 156) (1913–1942), Tallest goldenrod [Tallest golden-rod] (187) (1818), Variable goldenrod [Variable golden-rod] (19) (1840), Yellow-weed [Yellow weed] (5, 156) (1913–1923)

Solidago ciliaris **W.** – See *Solidago juncea* Aiton

Solidago concinna **A. Nelson** – See *Solidago missouriensis* Nutt.

Solidago curtsii **Torr. & Gray** – See *Solidago caesia* L. var. *curtisii* (Torr. & Gray) Wood

Solidago cutleri **Fern.** – Cutler's alpine goldenrod [Cutler's alpine golden-rod] (5) (1913)

Solidago elliottii **Torr. & Gray.** – See *Solidago latissimifolia* Mill.

Solidago elliptica **Aiton** – See *Solidago latissimifolia* Mill.

Solidago elliptica **W.** – See *Solidago latissimifolia* Mill.

Solidago elongata **Nutt.** – See *Solidago canadensis* L. var. *salebrosa* (Piper) M. E. Jones

Solidago erecta **Pursh** – Scepter goldenrod (138) (1923), Slender goldenrod [Slender goldenrod] (5, 72, 131) (1899–1913)

Solidago fistulosa **Mill.** – Pine Barren goldenrod [Pine Barren goldenrod] (5) (1913)

Solidago flexicaulis **L.** – A'djidamo'wano (Chippewa, squirrel tail) (40) (1928), Broad-leaf goldenrod [Broadleaf goldenrod, Broad-leaf golden-rod] (3, 4, 5, 19, 82, 85, 131, 138) (1840–1986), Wave-stem goldenrod [Waved-stemmed golden-rod] (187) (1818), Zigzag goldenrod [Zig-zag goldenrod, Zig-zag golden-rod] (5, 19, 50, 72, 155) (1840–present)

Solidago gattengeri **Chapman** – Gattinger's goldenrod [Gattinger's goldenrod] (5, 72) (1907–1913)

Solidago gigantea **Aiton** – Giant goldenrod [Giant golden-rod] (19, 50, 72, 138, 155) (1840–present), Goldenrod [Golden-rod, Golden rod] (80, 145) (1897–1913), Large goldenrod [Large golden-rod] (187) (1818), Late goldenrod [Late goldenrod] (3, 4, 5, 72, 82, 93, 95, 97, 122, 131) (1899–1986), November goldenrod (138, 155) (1923–1942), Smooth goldenrod [Smooth golden-rod] (19, 80) (1840–1913), Tall smooth goldenrod [Tall smooth golden-rod] (127) (1933)

Solidago gigantea **Aiton var.** *leiophylla* **Fern.** – See *Solidago gigantea* Aiton

Solidago gillmani **(Gray) Steele** – See *Solidago simplex* var. *gillmanii* (Gray) Ringius

Solidago glaberrima **Martens** – See *Solidago missouriensis* Nutt. var. *fasciculata* Holz.

Solidago glomerata **Michx.** – Cluster goldenrod (138) (1923)

Solidago graminifolia **(L.) Salisb.** – See *Euthamia graminifolia* (L.) Nutt. var. *graminifolia*

Solidago graminifolia **(L.) Salisb. var.** *graminifolia* – See *Euthamia graminifolia* (L.) Nutt. var. *graminifolia*

Solidago graminifolia **(L.) Salisb. var.** *gymnospermoides* **(Greene) Croat** – See *Euthamia gymnospermoides* Greene

Solidago gymnospermoides **(Greene) Fern.** – See *Euthamia gymnospermoides* Greene

Solidago hispida **Muhl.** – See *Solidago nemoralis* Aiton

Solidago juncea **Aiton** – A'djidamo'wano (Chippewa, squirrel tail) (40) (1928), Early goldenrod [Early goldenrod] (5, 106, 156) (1913–1930), Fringed goldenrod [Fringed golden-rod] (19) (1840), Plume goldenrod [Plume golden-rod] (5, 156) (1913–1923), Pyramid goldenrod [Pyramid golden-rod] (5, 156) (1913–1923), Rough-stalk goldenrod [Rough-stalk golden-rod] (19) (1840), Sharp-tooth goldenrod [Sharp-toothed golden-rod, Sharp-toothed goldenrod] (5, 156) (1913–1923), Yellowtop [Yellow-top, Yellow top, Yellowtops, Yellow-tops] (5, 156) (1913–1923)

Solidago **L.** – Common goldenrod [Common golden rod] (92) (1876), Flower-of-gold [Flower of gold] (76) (1896) CA, Gi'zĭso'mûki'ki (Chippewa, sun medicine) (40) (1928), Goldenrod [Golden-rod, Golden rod] (1, 2, 4, 10, 14, 21, 37, 40, 50, 63, 82, 93, 98, 106, 109, 114, 138, 155, 156, 158, 167, 184, 190) (~1759–present), Pyramid goldenrod [Pyramid golden-rod] (75) (1894), Yellowtop [Yellow-top, Yellow top, Yellowtops, Yellow-tops] (73, 76) (1892–1896), Yellow-weed [Yellow weed] (75) (1894), Zha-sage-zi (Omaha-Ponca, hard yellow weed) (37) (1919)

Solidago lanceolata **L.** – See *Euthamia graminifolia* (L.) Nutt.

Solidago latifolia **L.** – See *Solidago flexicaulis* L.

Solidago latissimifolia **Mill.** – Elliott's goldenrod [Elliott's golden-rod] (5) (1913), Oval-leaf goldenrod [Oval-leaf golden-rod] (19) (1840)

Solidago limonifolia **Pers.** – See *Solidago sempervirens* var. *mexicana* (L.) Fern.

Solidago lindheimeriana **Scheele** – See *Solidago petiolaris* Aiton var. *angusta* (Torr. & Gray) Gray

Solidago macrophylla **Pursh** – Large-leaf goldenrod [Largeleaf goldenrod, Large-leaved golden-rod] (5, 122) (1913–1937)

Solidago mexicana **L.** – See *Solidago sempervirens* var. *mexicana* (L.) Fern.

Solidago microphylla **Engelm.** – See *Solidago ulmifolia* Muhl. ex Willd.

Solidago minor **(Michx.) Fern.** – See *Euthamia tenuifolia* (Pursh) Nutt. var. *tenuifolia*

Solidago missouriensis **Nutt.** – Goldenrod [Golden-rod, Golden rod] (148) (1939), Missouri goldenrod [Missouri golden-rod] (3, 50, 72, 82, 85, 95, 97, 127, 131, 155) (1899–present), Prairie goldenrod (3, 4, 98) (1926–1986)

Solidago missouriensis **Nutt. var.** *fasciculata* **Holz.** – Missouri goldenrod [Missouri golden-rod] (5, 50, 93, 97, 122) (1913–present)

Solidago mollis **Bartl.** – Goldenrod [Golden-rod, Golden rod] (148) (1939), Ground goldenrod [Ground golden-rod] (5, 93, 156) (1913–1936), Soft goldenrod (3, 98) (1926–1977), Velvety goldenrod [Velvety golden-rod] (5, 50, 72, 93, 95, 97, 122, 156) (1907–present)

Solidago mollis **Bartl. var.** *mollis* – Velvety goldenrod [Velvety golden-rod] (50) (present)

Solidago monticola **Torr. & Gray.** – See *Solidago caesia* L. var. *curtisii* (Torr. & Gray) Wood

Solidago multiradiata **Aiton** – Northern goldenrod [Northern golden-rod] (5) (1913)

Solidago nemoralis **Aiton** – Dwarf goldenrod [Dwarf golden-rod] (5, 93, 122, 156, 158) (1900–1937), Dyer's weed [Dyers' weed, Dyer's-weed] (5, 131, 156, 158) (1899–1923) Dyer's-weed goldenrod [Dyersweed goldenrod] (155) (1942), Field goldenrod [Field golden-rod] (5, 62, 72, 93, 131, 156, 158) (1899–1936), Gray goldenrod [Gray golden-rod] (3, 5, 50, 82, 93, 97, 127, 156, 158) (1900–present), Hairy goldenrod [Hairy golden-rod] (5, 72, 93, 97, 155) (1907–1942), Low goldenrod (156) (1923), Old-field goldenrod [Oldfield goldenrod] (138) (1923), Woolly goldenrod [Woolly golden-rod] (19) (1840)

Solidago nemoralis **Aiton var.** *longipetiolata* **(Mackenzie & Bush) Palmer & Steyermark** – Dwarf goldenrod [Dwarf golden-rod] (85) (1932), Gray goldenrod [Gray golden-rod] (50) (present)

Solidago nitida **T. & G.** – See *Oligoneuron nitidum* (Torr. & Gray) Small

Solidago occidentalis **(Nutt.) Torr. & Gray** – See *Euthamia occidentalis* Nutt.

Solidago odora **Aiton** – Anise-scented goldenrod [Anise-scented golden-rod] (5, 97, 156) (1913–1937), Blue mountain tea (5, 49, 52, 156) (1898–1923), Fragrant goldenrod [Fragrant golden-rod] (138, 187) (1818–1923), Fragrant-leaf goldenrod [Fragrant-leaved goldenrod] (49, 52) (1898–1919), Goldenrod [Golden-rod, Golden rod] (57) (1917), Sweet goldenrod [Sweet golden-rod] (5, 7, 49, 52, 104, 107, 122, 156) (1828–1937), Sweet-scented goldenrod [Sweet-scented golden-rod, Sweet scented goldenrod] (19, 49, 52, 58, 92) (1840–1919), True goldenrod [True golden-rod] (5, 156) (1913–1923), Wormweed [Worm weed, Worm-weed] (92) (1876)

Solidago ohioensis **Riddell.** – See *Oligoneuron ohioense* (Frank ex Riddell) G. N. Jones

Solidago pallida **(Porter) Rydb.** – See *Solidago speciosa* Nutt. var. *pallida* Porter

Solidago patula **Muhl. ex Willd.** – Rough-leaf goldenrod [Roughleaf goldenrod] (5, 72, 122, 138) (1907–1937), Spread goldenrod [Spread golden-rod] (19) (1840), Spreading goldenrod [Spreading golden-rod] (5) (1913), Spreading-branch goldenrod [Spreading-branched golden-rod] (187) (1818)

Solidago petiolaris **Aiton** – Downy goldenrod [Downy golden-rod] (3) (1977), Downy ragged goldenrod [Downy ragged golden-rod] (5, 50, 97, 122) (1913–present), Late goldenrod [Late goldenrod] (19) (1840)

Solidago petiolaris **Aiton var.** *angusta* **(Torr. & Gray) Gray** – Downy goldenrod [Downy golden-rod] (4) (1986), Downy ragged goldenrod [Downy ragged golden-rod] (50) (present), Lindheimer's goldenrod

[Lindheimer's golden-rod, Lindheimer goldenrod] (5, 97, 122, 155) (1913–1942), Ward's goldenrod [Ward goldenrod] (155) (1942)

***Solidago procera* Aiton** – See *Solidago canadensis* L. var. *scabra* Torr. & Gray

***Solidago ptarmicoides* (Nees) Boivin** – See *Oligoneuron album* (Nutt.) Nesom

Solidago pubens – See *Solidago caesia* L. var. *curtisii* (Torr. & Gray) Wood

***Solidago puberula* Nutt.** – Downy goldenrod [Downy golden-rod] (5) (1913), Minaret goldenrod [Minaret golden-rod] (5) (1913)

***Solidago pulcherrima* A. Nels.** – See *Solidago nemoralis* Aiton var. *longipetiolata* (Mackenzie & Bush) Palmer & Steyermark

***Solidago radula* Nutt.** – Western rough goldenrod [Western rough golden-rod] (5, 50, 97, 122, 131) (1899–present)

***Solidago randii* (Porter) Britton** – See *Solidago simplex* Kunth subsp. *randii* (Porter) Ringius var. *racemosa* (Greene) Ringius

***Solidago riddellii* Frank.** – See *Oligoneuron riddellii* (Frank ex Riddell) Rydb.

***Solidago rigida* L.** – See *Oligoneuron rigidum* (L.) Small var. *rigidum*

Solidago rigida* L. var. *rigida – See *Oligoneuron rigidum* (L.) Small var. *rigidum*

***Solidago rigidiuscula* (Torr. & Gray) Porter** – See *Solidago speciosa* Nutt. var. *rigidiuscula* Torr. & Gray

***Solidago rugosa* Mill.** – Bitterweed [Bitter weed, Bitter-weed] (5, 156) (1913–1923), Blue mountain tea (156) (1923), Dyer's weed [Dyers' weed, Dyer's-weed] (5, 156) (1913–1923), Pyramid goldenrod [Pyramid golden-rod] (5, 156) (1913–1923), Rough goldenrod [Rough golden-rod] (156) (1923), Tall hairy goldenrod [Tall hairy golden-rod] (5, 72, 106, 122, 156) (1907–1937), Wrinkled goldenrod [Wrinkled golden-rod] (19, 138) (1840–1923), possibly Wrinkle-leaf goldenrod [Wrinkled-leaved goldenrod] (5, 97, 187) (1818–1937)

***Solidago rugosa* Mill. subsp. *aspera* (Aiton) Cronq.** – Drummond's goldenrod [Drummond's golden-rod] (5) (1913), Rough goldenrod [Rough golden-rod] (19, 187) (1818–1840)

Solidago rugosa* Mill. subsp. *rugosa* var. *rugosa – Harsh goldenrod [Harsh golden-rod] (19) (1840), Scabrous-leaf goldenrod [Scabrous-leaved golden-rod] (187) (1818)

***Solidago rugosa* Willd.** – possibly *Solidago rugosa* Mill.

***Solidago rupestris* Raf.** – Rock goldenrod [Rock golden-rod] (72, 131) (1899–1907)

***Solidago scabra* Muhl. ex Willd., non Muhl.** – See *Solidago rugosa* Mill. subsp. *rugosa* var. *rugosa*

***Solidago sciaphila* Steele** – Shadowy goldenrod [Shadowy golden-rod] (5) (1913)

***Solidago sempervirens* L.** – Beach goldenrod [Beach golden-rod] (5, 156) (1913–1923), Narrow-leaf goldenrod [Narrowleaf goldenrod, Narrow-leaf golden-rod, Narrow-leaved goldenrod, Narrow-leaved golden-rod] (19) (1840), Saltmarsh goldenrod [Salt-marsh golden-rod, Salt-marsh goldenrod] (5, 156) (1913–1923), Seaside goldenrod [Sea-side golden-rod, Seaside golden-rod, Sea-side goldenrod] (5, 138, 156) (1913–1923), Twig goldenrod [Twig golden-rod] (19) (1840)

***Solidago sempervirens* var. *mexicana* (L.) Fern.** – Seaside goldenrod [Sea-side golden-rod, Seaside golden-rod, Sea-side goldenrod) (46) (1879)

***Solidago serotina* Aiton** – See *Solidago gigantea* Aiton

***Solidago serotina gigantea* Gray.** – See *Solidago gigantea* Aiton

***Solidago serotina* var. *gigantea* (Aiton) A. Gray** – See *Solidago gigantea* Aiton

***Solidago shortii* Torr. & Gray** – Short's goldenrod [Short's golden-rod] (5) (1913)

***Solidago simplex* Kunth subsp. *randii* (Porter) Ringius var. *racemosa* (Greene) Ringius** – Rand's goldenrod [Rand's golden-rod] (5) (1913), Riverbank goldenrod [River-bank golden-rod] (5) (1913)

***Solidago simplex* var. *gillmanii* (Gray) Ringius** – Gillman's goldenrod [Gillman's golden-rod] (5) (1913)

***Solidago sparciflora* Gray** – See *Solidago velutina* DC.

***Solidago speciosa* Nutt** – Noble goldenrod [Noble golden-rod] (5, 155, 156) (1913–1942), Showy goldenrod [Showy golden-rod] (5, 50, 72, 82, 97, 156) (1907–present), Showy-wand goldenrod [Showywand goldenrod] (3, 4) (1977–1986)

***Solidago speciosa* Nutt. var. *angustata* Torr. & Gray** – See *Solidago speciosa* Nutt. var. *rigidiuscula* Torr. & Gray

***Solidago speciosa* Nutt. var. *pallida* Porter** – Goldenrod [Golden-rod, Golden rod] (85) (1932), Pale-leaf goldenrod [Paleleaf goldenrod] (138, 155) (1923–1942), Showy goldenrod [Showy golden-rod] (50) (Present)

***Solidago speciosa* Nutt. var. *rigidiuscula* Torr. & Gray** – Narrow-leaf showy goldenrod [Narrow-leaved showy goldenrod] (82) (1930), O'zawa'bigwûn (Chippewa, yellow flower) (40) (1928), Showy goldenrod [Showy golden-rod] (50) (Present), Showy-wand goldenrod [Showywand goldenrod] (155) (1942), Slender showy goldenrod [Slender showy golden-rod] (5, 72, 97, 122, 131) (1899–1937)

***Solidago speciosa* var. *erecta* (Pursh) MacM.** – See *Solidago erecta* Pursh

***Solidago spectabilis* (D.C. Eat.) Gray** – Nevada goldenrod (138) (1923)

***Solidago sphacelata* Raf.** – False goldenrod [False golden-rod] (5, 156) (1913–1923)

***Solidago squamosa* Nutt. ex Hook.** – See *Solidago squarrosa* Muhl.

***Solidago squarrosa* Muhl.** – Big goldenrod (156) (1923), Large-flower goldenrod [Large-flowered goldenrod] (156) (1923), Stout ragged goldenrod [Stout ragged golden-rod] (5) (1913)

***Solidago stricta* Aiton** – Wand-like goldenrod [Wand-like golden-rod] (5) (1913), Willow-leaf goldenrod [Willow-leaf golden-rod] (5, 19) (1840–1913)

***Solidago tenuifolia* Pursh** – See *Euthamia tenuifolia* (Pursh) Nutt. var. *tenuifolia*

***Solidago tortifolia* Ell.** – Twisted-leaf goldenrod [Twisted-leaf golden-rod] (5, 97) (1913–1937), Twist-leaf goldenrod [Twistleaf golden-rod] (122) (1937)

***Solidago trinervata* Greene** – See *Solidago velutina* DC.

***Solidago uliginosa* Nutt.** – Bog goldenrod [Bog goldenrod] (5, 72) (1907–1913), Swamp goldenrod [Swamp golden-rod] (5, 138) (1913–1923)

Solidago uliginosa* Nutt. var. *uliginosa – Few-ray goldenrod [Few-rayed golden-rod] (5) (1913), Pyramid goldenrod [Pyramid golden-rod] (5, 156) (1913–1923), Swamp goldenrod [Swamp golden-rod] (5, 156) (1913–1923)

***Solidago ulmifolia* Muhl. ex Willd.** – Elm goldenrod [Elm golden-rod] (19) (1840), Elm-leaf goldenrod [Elmleaf goldenrod, Elm-leaved golden-rod, Elm-leaved goldenrod] (3, 4, 5, 50, 72, 82, 86, 97, 122, 187) (1818–present)

Solidago ulmifolia* Muhl. ex Willd. var. *ulmifolia – Elm-leaf goldenrod [Elmleaf goldenrod, Elm-leaved golden-rod, Elm-leaved goldenrod] (50) (present)

***Solidago uniligulata* (DC.) Porter** – See *Solidago uliginosa* Nutt. var. *uliginosa*

***Solidago velutina* DC.** – Arizona goldenrod (155) (1942), Three-nerve goldenrod [Three nerved goldenrod, Three-nerved golden-rod] (3, 4, 50, 155) (1942–present)

***Solidago viminea* [Aiton]** – See *Solidago sempervirens* L.

Solidago virgaurea – See *Solidago virgaurea* L.

***Solidago virgaurea* L.** – Common goldenrod [Common golden rod] (41) (1770), European goldenrod [European golden-rod] (19, 92, 138) (1840–1923)

***Solidago wardii* Britton** – See *Solidago petiolaris* Aiton var. *angusta* (Torr. & Gray) Gray

***Sollya fusiformis* Briq.** – See *Sollya heterophylla* Lindl.

***Sollya heterophylla* Lindl.** – Australian bluebell-creeper [Australian bluebell creeper] (109, 138) (1923–1949)

***Sollya* Lindl.** – Bluebell creeper [Bluebell-creeper] (138) (1923)

***Sonchus* (Tourn.) L.** – See *Sonchus* L.

Sonchus arvensis L. – Corn sow-thistle [Corn sow thistle] (5, 19, 122, 157, 158) (1840–1937), Dindle (5, 157, 158) (1900–1929) no longer in use by 1929, Field sowthistle [Field sow thistle, Field sow-thistle] (3, 4, 50, 82, 155, 157) (1900–present), Goutweed [Gout-weed, Gout weed] (157) (1929), Gutweed [Gut-weed] (5, 158) (1900–1913), Milk thistle [Milk-thistle] (157, 158) (1900–1929), Perennial sow-thistle [Perennial sow thistle] (62, 80, 82, 106) (1912–1930), Rose-may (158) (1900), Sow thistle [Sow-thistle, Sowthistle] (85) (1932), Swine sow-thistle (157) (1929), Swine thistle (5, 158) (1900–1913), Tree sow-thistle [Tree sow thistle] (5, 157, 158) (1900–1929)

Sonchus arvensis L. subsp. *uliginosus* (Bieb.) Nyman – Moist sow thistle [Moist sowthistle] (50) (present)

Sonchus asper (L.) Hill – Lion's-heart [Lion's heart, Lionsheart, Ly-onsheart] (29) (1869), Prickly sow-thistle [Prickly sowthistle] (4, 98, 155) (1926–1986), Sharp-fringe sow-thistle [Sharp-fringed sow-thistle] (5) (1913), Sow thistle [Sow-thistle, Sowthistle] (80, 82, 95, 122, 145, 157) (1897–1937), Spiny sow-thistle [Spiny sow thistle, Spiny sowthistle] (3, 5, 50, 62, 72, 82, 85, 93, 131) (1899–present), Spiny-leaf sow-thistle [Spiny-leaved sow-thistle] (156) (1923)

Sonchus asper Vill. – See *Sonchus asper* (L.) Hill

Sonchus canadensis [L.] – possibly *Lactuca canadensis* L.

Sonchus floridanus Willd. – See *Lactuca floridana* (L.) Gaertn.

Sonchus L. – Sow thistle [Sow-thistle, Sowthistle] (1, 4, 10, 50, 93, 106, 155, 157, 158, 184) (1793–present)

Sonchus oleraceus L. – Annual sow-thistle [Annual sow thistle] (5, 72, 80, 122, 156, 157, 158) (1900–1937), Common sow thistle [Common sowthistle, Common sow-thistle] (3, 4, 50, 19, 62, 80, 82, 155, 157, 158, 187) (1818–present), Dashel (157, 158) (1900–1929), Gänsedistel (German) (158) (1900), Gänsekopf (German) (186) (1814), Hare's colewort (5, 156, 157, 158) (1900–1929), Hare's lettuce (5, 62, 156, 157, 158) (1900–1929) IN, old English name, Hare's thistle (5, 156, 157, 158) (1900–1929), Hare's-palace [Hare's palace] (62, 157, 158) (1900–1929) IN, old English name, Laiteron (French) (158) (1900), Mild thistle (157) (1929), Milk this-tle [Milk-thistle] (5, 76, 156, 158) (1896–1923), Milkweed [Milk weed [Milk-weed] (5, 156, 157, 158) (1900–1929), Milky-dickles [Milky dickles] (157, 158) (1900–1929), Milky-tassel [Milky-tas-sels, Milk tassel] (5, 156, 157, 158) (1900–1929), Saudistel (Ger-man) (158) (1900), Sow thistle [Sow-thistle, Sowthistle] (46, 92, 93, 107, 157, 158) (1671–1936) accidentally introduced by 1671, Sow-dindle (157, 158) (1900–1929), Sow-dingle (157, 158) (1900–1929), St. Mary's-seed (157, 158) (1900–1929), Swinies (5, 156, 157, 158) (1900–1929), Yellow-flower sow-thistle [Yellow-flowered sow-this-tle] (187) (1818)

Sonchus uliginosus Bieb. – See *Sonchus arvensis* L. subsp. *uliginosus* (Bieb.) Nyman

Sophia Adans. – See *Descurainia* Webb & Berth.

Sophia hartwegiana (Fourn.) Greene – See *Descurainia incana* (Bernh. ex Fisch. & C. A. Mey.) Dorn subsp. *procera* (Greene) Kartesz & Gandhi

Sophia incisa (Engelm.) Greene – See *Descurainia incana* (Bernh. ex Fisch. & C. A. Mey.) Dorn subsp. *incisa* (Engelm.) Kartesz & Gandhi

Sophia pinnata (Walt.) Howell – See *Descurainia pinnata* (Walt.) Brit-ton subsp. *brachycarpa* (Richards.) Detling

Sophia sophia (L.) Britton – See *Descurainia sophia* (L.) Webb ex Prantl

Sophora affinis Torr. & Gray – Bearberry [Bear berry, Bear-berry] (124) (1937) TX, Eve's-necklace [Eve's necklace] (97) (1937) OK, Pink sophora (122) (1937) TX

Sophora alba Michx. – See *Baptisia alba* (L.) Vent.

Sophora japonica L. – Chinese scholar tree [Chinese scholartree, Chi-nese scholartree] (109, 138) (1923–1949), Japanese pagoda-tree (109) (1949), Pagoda tree [Pagoda-tree] (156) (1923) IA

Sophora L. – Necklace-pod [Necklacepod] (50) (present), Sophora (138, 155, 158) (1923–1942)

Sophora nuttalliana B. L. Turner – Silky sophora (5, 50, 93, 97, 122, 124, 125, 131, 148, 155, 157) (1899–present), White loco (4) (1986)

Sophora secundiflora (Ortega) Lag. ex DC. – Coral bean [Coralbean] (106, 153) (1913–1930), Frijolillo (Spanish) (104, 106, 107, 122) (1896–1937), Mescal-bean [Mescal bean, Mescalbean] (109, 122, 124, 138) (1923–1949)

Sophora secundiflora Lag. – See *Sophora secundiflora* (Ortega) Lag. ex DC.

Sophronanthe pilosa (Michx.) Small. – See *Gratiola pilosa* Michx.

Sorbaria (Ser. ex DC.) A. Braun – False spiraea [False-spiraea] (109, 138) (1923–1949), Sorbaria (82) (1930)

Sorbaria A. Br. – See *Sorbaria* (Ser. ex DC.) A. Braun

Sorbaria arborea Schneid. – Tree spiraea (138) (1923)

Sorbaria lindleyana [Maxim.] – See *Sorbaria sorbifolia* (L.) A. Braun

Sorbaria sorbifolia (L.) A. Braun – Lindley's false spiraea [Lindley false-spiraea] (138) (1923), Sorbaria (82, 112) (1930–1937), Sorb-leaf schizonotus [Sorb-leaved schizonotus] (5) (1913), Starry fasle spiraea (138) (1923), Ural false spiraea [Ural false-spiraea] (138) (1923)

Sorbaria sorbifolia var. *stellipila* Maxim. – See *Sorbaria sorbifolia* (L.) A. Braun

Sorbus americana Marsh. – American mountain-ash [American moun-tain ash] (2, 5, 6, 82, 135, 138) (1892–1930), American rown tree (5) (1913), American service tree (5, 6, 8) (1785–1913), Dogberry [Dog-berry, Dog berry] (5, 156) (1913–1923) no longer in use by 1929, Eastern mountain ash (85) (1932), Elder-leaf mountain-ash [Elder-leaved mountain ash, Elder leaved-mountain ash] (5, 156) (1913–1923), Elder-leaf sumach [Elder-leaved sumach] (156) (1923) no longer in use by 1929, Indian mozemize (5, 74) (1893–1913) Fer-risburgh VT, Life-of-man [Life of man, Life-o'-man] (5) (1913), Missey-moosey [Missey moosey] (5, 73, 156) (1892–1923) NH, no longer in use by 1923, Moose misse (74) (1893), Moose missy (5) (1913), Mountain ash [Mountain-ash, Mountainash] (47, 156) (1852–1923), Quickbeam [Quick-beam] (46) (1671), Round tree (5, 73, 92) (1876–1913) NB, from rowan tree, Roundwood [Round-wood, Round wood] (5, 92, 156) (1876–1923), Rowan tree [Rowan-tree] (92, 156) (1898–1923), Rowan-wood (156) (1923), Service tree [Servicetree, Seruice tree] (92) (1876), Sorbier d'Amérique (French) (8, 20) (1785–1857), Sorbis (French) (6) (1892), Vogelbeeren (Ger-man) (6) (1892), Wild ash (46) (1671), Wine tree (5) (1913), Witch-wood [Witch-wood, Witch wood] (5, 73) (1892–1913) NH, said to ward off witches

Sorbus aucuparia Gaertn. – possibly *Sorbus aucuparia* L.

Sorbus aucuparia L. – European mountain ash (82, 135, 137, 138) (1910–1931), Mountain ash [Mountain-ash, Mountainash] (41, 49, 107, 112) (1770–1937), Quickbeam [Quick-beam] (107) (1919), Quicken tree (178) (1526), Rowan tree [Rowan-tree] (107) (1919), possibly Sorb tree (41) (1770)

Sorbus decora (Sargent) Schneid. – Showy mountain-ash (138) (1923)

Sorbus L. – Mountain ash [Mountain-ash, Mountainash] (1, 4, 8, 7, 10, 138, 156, 158) (1828–1986), Quickbeam [Quick-beam] (8) (1785), Service tree [Servicetree, Seruice tree] (7, 8) (1785–1828), Sorbier (French) (8) (1785)

Sorbus sambucifolia (Cham. & Schlecht.) M. Roemer – Elder-leaf mountain-ash [Elder-leaved mountain ash, Elder leaved-mountain ash] (2) (1895), Elder-leaf rowan tree [Elder-leaved rowan tree] (2) (1895), Mountain ash [Mountain-ash, Mountainash] (130, 137) (1895–1931), Western mountain-ash [Western mountain ash] (131, 135, 137) (1899–1931)

Sorbus scopulina Greene – American rowan tree (5) (1913), Greene's mountain ash, Greenes mountainash (50, 155) (1942–present), Moun-tain ash [Mountain-ash, Mountainash] (4, 153) (1913–1986), Western mountain-ash [Western mountain ash] (3, 5, 85) (1913–1977)

Sorghastrum elliottii (C. Mohr) Nash – Long-bristle Indian grass [Long-bristled Indian-grass, Long-bristled Indian grass] (5, 163) (1852–1913), Slender Indian grass [Slender indiangrass] (50) (pres-ent)

Sorghastrum Nash – Goldstem [Gold stem] (93) (1936) Neb, Indian grass [Indian-grass, Indiangrass] (1, 50, 93, 155) (1932–present)

397

Sorghastrum nutans (L.) Nash – Beard grass [Beard-grass, Beardgrass] (19, 92) (1840–1876), Bushy bluestem [Bushy blue-stem, Bushy blue stem] (5, 11, 56, 99, 119, 129, 131) (1888–1938), Fringed bear grass [Fringed bear-grass] (187) (1818), Indian beard grass [Indian beard-grass] (56) (1901), Indian grass [Indian-grass, Indiangrass] (3, 5, 45, 50, 56, 66, 72, 85, 87, 92, 94, 115, 119, 122, 131, 134, 140, 144, 163) (1852–present), Indian reed (163) (1852), Wild oat grass [Wild oat-grass, Wild oats grass] (5, 21) (1893–1913), Wood grass [Wood-grass] (5, 45, 66, 87, 92) (1884–1913), Yellow Indian grass [Yellow Indiangrass] (140, 155) (1942–1944)

Sorghastrum secundum (Ell.) Nash – Banner sorghum (94) (1901), Wild oat [Wild oats] (163) (1852)

Sorghum almum Parodi – Columbus grass (50) (present)

Sorghum bicolor (L.) Moench – African millet (19) (1840), Black millet (67) (1890), Broom (184) (1793), Chicken corn [Chicken-corn, Chickencorn] (56) (1901) IA, Chinese sugarcane [Chinese sugar-cane, Chinese sugar cane] (56) (1901) IA, Egyptian rice-corn (56) (1901) IA, Feterita (109, 119) (1938–1949), Guinea corn [Guinea-corn] (56, 92) (1876–1901), Imphee (56, 92) (1876–1901), Indian millet (56) (1901), Johnson grass [Johnson-grass, Johnsongrass] (75) (1894) Neb, Kaffir corn [Kafir corn, Kafir-corn] (56) (1901), Kao-liang (Chinese "tall millet or great millet" (110) (1886), Melega (Millanois, Lombardy) (180) (1633), Millet [Myllet] (56) (1901) IA, Small maize (92) (1876), Sorgho (Italy) (180) (1633), Sorghum (50, 56, 67) (1890–present), Sweet sorghum (110) (1886), Tree millet (110) (1886), Turkey hirsse [Turkie hirsse] (180) (1633), Turkey mill (180) (1633), Turkey millet [Turky millet] (180) (1633)

Sorghum bicolor (L.) Moench subsp. *bicolor* – African millet (87) (1884), Black millet (158) (1900), Broomcorn [Broom-corn, Broom corn] (14, 56, 66, 87, 92, 107, 109, 119, 155, 158) (1882–1949), Broom-corn grass [Broom corn grass] (92) (1876), Brown durra (155) (1942), Chinese sugarcane [Chinese sugar-cane, Chinese sugar cane] (66, 87, 158) (1884–1903), Chocolate corn (87) (1884), Coffee corn (19, 92) (1840–1876), Common sorghum (110) (1886), Doura (158) (1900), Doura corn (87) (1884), Dourra (Modern Egypt) (110) (1886), Durra (107, 119, 155, 158) (1900–1942), Egyptian corn (107) (1919), Grain sorghum (50) (present), Guinea corn [Guinea-corn] (14, 66, 87, 184) (1793–1903), Imphee (158) (1900), Indian millet (19, 66, 87, 92, 158) (1840–1903), Jerusalem corn (119) (1938) OK, Kaffir [Kafir] (109, 119, 155) (1938–1949), Kaffir corn [Kafir corn, Kafir-corn] (107, 119, 151) (1896–1938), Millo maize (151) (1896), Milo (119) (1938), Milo maize (119) (1938) NM, Negro corn (92, 107) (1876–1919), Pampas-rice [Pampas rice] (87, 107) (1884–1919), Pearl millet [Pearlmillet] (158) (1900), Rice-corn [Rice corn] (107) (1919), Shallu (109, 155) (1942–1949), Small maize (66) (1903) Barbary, Sorgho (66, 92, 109, 155) (1903–1949), Sorgho sucre (66) (1903), Sorghum (92, 107, 109, 117, 119, 138, 155, 158, 163, 178) (1526–1949), Sorghum sugar cane (87) (1884), Sugar sorghum (67, 109) (1890–1949), Sugarcane [Sugar cane, Sugar-cane] (56, 109) (1901–1949), Sweet sorghum (109) (1949), Tennessee rice (107) (1919), Turkey millet [Turkie millet] (178) (1596)

Sorghum bicolor (L.) Moench subsp. *drummondii* (Nees ex Steud.) de Wet & Harlan – Chicken corn [Chicken-corn, Chickencorn] (109, 155) (1942–1949), Sudan grass [Sudan-grass, Sudangrass] (50, 109, 119, 138) (1923–present)

Sorghum bicolor (L.) Moench var. *sudanense* (Piper) A. S. Hitchc. – See *Sorghum bicolor* (L.) Moench subsp. *drummondii* (Nees ex Steud.) de Wet & Harlan

Sorghum halepense (L.) Pers. – Aleppo grass [Aleppo-grass] (109) (1949), Arabian millet grass (88) (1885), Arabian millett (45, 87) (1884–1896), Australian grass (158) (1900), Chinese sugarcane [Chinese sugar-cane, Chinese sugar cane] (45) (1896), Cuba grass (5, 45, 87, 158) (1885–1913), Doura (45) (1896), Durra (45) (1896), Egyptian grass [Egyptian-grass] (45, 158) (1896–1900), Egyptian millet (5, 45, 158) (1896–1913), Egyptian rice-corn (45)

(1896), Evergreen millet (5, 87, 88) (1884–1913), False Guinea grass (87) (1884), Great millet (45) (1896), Green Valley grass (45) (1896), Guinea corn [Guinea-corn] (45) (1896), Guinea grass [Guineagrass, Guinea-grass] (45, 88, 158) (1885–1900), Imphee (45) (1896), Indian millet (45) (1896), Johnson grass [Johnson-grass, Johnsongrass] (5, 45, 50, 56, 72, 80, 85, 87, 88, 94, 109, 111, 119, 122, 129, 138, 140, 152, 155, 158, 163) (1852–present), Maiden cane [Maidencane, Maiden-cane] (5, 158) (1900–1913), Means' grass [Means-grass, Means grass] (45, 87, 88, 109, 158) (1885–1949) Southern states, introduced by Gov. Means of SC in 1835, Millet seed (92) (1876), Moroccan millet [Morocco millet] (158) (1900), St. Mary's grass [Saint Mary's grass] (5, 45) (1896–1913), Syrian grass (5, 45) (1896–1913)

Sorghum L. – See *Sorghum* Moench

Sorghum miliaceum [(Roxb.) Snowden] – See *Sorghum halepense* (L.) Pers.

Sorghum Moench – Broom grass [Broom-grass] (10) (1818), Broomcorn [Broom-corn, Broom corn] (7) (1828), Cane [Canes] (78) (1898) OH, Indian millet (7) (1828), Sorghum (50, 155, 158) (1900–present) from East Indian vernacular name, Sugar cane (78) (1898) OH

Sorghum nigrum [Roem. & Schult.] – See *Sorghum bicolor* (L.) Moench

Sorghum saccharatum – See *Sorghum bicolor* (L.) Moench subsp. *bicolor*

Sorghum vulgare Pers. – See *Sorghum bicolor* (L.) Moench subsp. *bicolor*

Sorghum vulgare Pers. var. *caffrorum* Hubbard & Rehd. – See *Sorghum bicolor* (L.) Moench subsp. *bicolor*

Sorghum vulgare Pers. var. *caudatus* Bailey – See *Sorghum bicolor* (L.) Moench

Sorghum vulgare Pers. var. *durra* (Forsk.) Hubbard & Rehd. – See *Sorghum bicolor* (L.) Moench subsp. *bicolor*

Sorghum vulgare Pers. var. *roxburghii* Haines – See *Sorghum bicolor* (L.) Moench subsp. *bicolor*

Sorghum vulgare Pers. var. *saccharatum* (L.) Boerl. – See *Sorghum bicolor* (L.) Moench subsp. *bicolor*

Sorghum vulgare Pers. var. *technicum* (Koern.) Jáv. – See *Sorghum bicolor* (L.) Moench subsp. *bicolor*

Sorghum vulgare var. *caudatum* (Hack.) A. F. Hill – See *Sorghum bicolor* (L.) Moench

Sparaxis fragrans (Jacq.) Ker-Gawl. subsp. *grandiflora* (D. Delar.) Goldbl. – Big wandflower (138) (1923)

Sparaxis grandiflora – See *Sparaxis fragrans* (Jacq.) Ker-Gawl. subsp. *grandiflora* (D. Delar.) Goldbl.

Sparaxis Ker-Gawl. – Wand flower [Wand-flower, Wandflower] (109, 138) (1923–1949)

Sparganium (Tourn.) L. – See *Sparganium* L.

Sparganium acaule (Beeby) Rydb. – See *Sparganium angustifolium* Michx.

Sparganium americanum Nutt. – American bur-reed [American burreed] (50, 155) (1942–present), Lake bur-reed (19) (1840), Nuttall's bur-reed (5, 120) (1913–1938)

Sparganium androcladum (Engelm.) Morong – Branched bur-reed (50) (present), Branching bur-reed (5, 72) (1907–1913), Shining-fruit bur-reed [Shining fruited bur-reed] (5) (1913)

Sparganium angustifolium Michx. – Floating bur-reed (19) (1840), Many-stalk bur-reed [Many-stalked bur-reed] (5) (1913), Narrowleaf bur-reed [Narrowleaf burreed, Narrowleaf bur-reed, Narrow-leaved bur-reed] (5, 50, 155) (1913–present), Stemless bur-reed (5, 10) (1818–1913)

Sparganium chlorocarpum Rydb. – See *Sparganium erectum* L. subsp. *stoloniferum* (Graebn.) Hara

Sparganium diversifolium Graebn. – See *Sparganium emersum* Rehmann

Sparganium emersum Rehmann – Various-leaf bur-reed [Various-leaved bur-reed] (5) (1913)

Sparganium erectum **L.** – Bur-reed [Burr reed, Burr-reed, Bur-reed, Burreed, Burre-Reed] (19, 92, 187) (1818–1876), Burweed [Bur weed, Bur-weed, Burr weed, Burrweed, Burr-weed] (184) (1793), Simple-stem bur-reed [Simplestem bur-reed] (50) (present)

Sparganium erectum **L. subsp.** *stoloniferum* **(Graebn.) Hara** – Black-weed [Black weed] (156) (1923), Bur-reed [Burr reed, Burr-reed, Bur-reed, Burreed, Burre-Reed] (3, 156) (1923–1977), Burweed [Bur weed, Bur-weed, Burr weed, Burrweed, Burr-weed] (156) (1923), Green-fruit bur-reed [Green-fruited bur-reed] (5) (1913), Simple-stem bur-reed [Simplestem bur-reed, Simple-stemmed bur-reed] (5, 50, 72) (1907–present), Smaller bur-reed [Smaller bur reed] (2) (1895)

Sparganium eurycarpum **Engelm. ex Gray** – Broad-fruit bur-reed [Broad fruited bur-reed, Broad-fruited bur-reed] (5, 50, 93, 131) (1899–present), Bur-reed [Burr reed, Burr-reed, Bur-reed, Burreed, Burre-Reed] (85, 129) (1894–1932), Common bur-reed (72) (1907), Giant bur-reed [Giant burreed] (155) (1942), Great bur-reed (3) (1977)

Sparganium fluctuans **(Morong) B. L. Robins.** – Floating bur-reed (5, 50) (1913–present)

Sparganium hyperboreum **Laest.** – Northern bur-reed (5, 50) (1913–present)

Sparganium **L.** – Bede-sedge (158) (1900), Bede-segg (158) (1900), Bede-seggin (158) (1900), Broad-fruit bur-reed [Broad fruited bur-reed, Broad-fruited bur-reed] (93) (1936), Bur-flag (158) (1900), Bur-reed [Burr reed, Burr-reed, Bur-reed, Burreed, Burre-Reed] (1, 50, 155, 158, 167, 180) (1633–present), Butomus (180) (1633), Knop-sedge (158) (1900), Levers (158) (1900), Reed-grass [Reedgrass, Reed grass] (158) (1900), Sparganio (Italian) (180) (1633)

Sparganium lucidum **Fernald & Eames** – See *Sparganium androcladum* (Engelm.) Morong

Sparganium minimum **Fries.** – See *Sparganium natans* L.

Sparganium multipedunculatum **(Morong) Rydb.** – See *Sparganium angustifolium* Michx.

Sparganium natans **L.** – Small bur-reed (5, 50) (1913–present), Smallest bur-reed [Smallest bur reed] (2) (1895)

Sparganium ramosum **Sw.** – See *Sparganium erectum* L.

Sparganium simplex **Huds.** – See *Sparganium erectum* L. subsp. *stoloniferum* (Graebn.) Hara

Spartina alterniflora **Lois. var.** *glabra* **(Muhl.) Fern.** – See *Spartina alterniflora* Loisel.

Spartina alterniflora **Loisel.** – Creek-sedge [Creek sedge] (94) (1901), Rough marsh grass (66) (1903), Saltmarsh grass [Salt marsh-grass] (163) (1852), Smooth cordgrass (122) (1937), Smooth marsh grass (66) (1903), Thatch (94) (1901)

Spartina cynosuroides **(L.) Roth** – Big cordgrass (122) (1937), Bog cord grass [Bog cordgrass] (50) (present), Cord grass [Cord-grass, Cordgrass] (11, 129) (1888–1894), Creek stuff (5) (1913), Creek thatch (5) (1913), Fall marsh grass (87) (1884), Freshwater cord grass [Fresh-water cord-grass, Fresh-water cord-grass, Freshwater cord-grass] (45, 56, 66, 87, 90, 94) (1884–1912), Many-spike salt grass [Many-spiked salt-grass] (19) (1840), Marsh grass [Marshgrass, Marsh-grass] (21) (1893), Salt reed grass [Salt reed-grass] (45, 66, 88, 94, 163) (1852–1903), Slough grass [Slough-grass, Sloughgrass] (22, 56, 144) (1893–1901), Tall marsh grass [Tall marsh-grass] (66, 72, 90) (1885–1907)

Spartina cynosuroides **(L.) Roth var.** *polystachya* **(Michx.) Beal ex Fern.** – See *Spartina cynosuroides* (L.) Roth

Spartina glabra – See *Spartina alterniflora* Loisel.

Spartina gracilis **Trin.** – Alkali cordgrass (3, 50, 146, 155) (1939–present), Cord grass [Cord-grass, Cordgrass] (93) (1936), Inland cord grass (5) (1913), Little cord grass (111, 129) (1894–1915), Marsh grass [Marshgrass, Marsh-grass] (85, 90) (1885–1932), Slender cord grass (5) (1913), Western cord grass [Western cord-grass] (94) (1901)

Spartina juncea **Willd.** – See *Spartina patens* (Ait.) Muhl.

Spartina maritima **(M. A. Curtis) Fern.** – Cord grass [Cord-grass, Cordgrass] (92) (1876), Creek thatch (5) (1913), Creek-sedge [Creek sedge] (5) (1913), Low creek-stuff [Low creek stuff] (5) (1913), Marsh grass [Marshgrass, Marsh-grass] (92) (1876), Saltmarsh grass [Salt marsh grass] (5, 45, 66, 90, 92) (1876–1913), Small cord grass [Small cordgrass] (50) (present), Smooth marsh grass (5, 90) (1885–1913), Spart grass (5) (1913), Twin-spike grass [Twin spike grass] (5) (1913)

Spartina michauxiana **Hitchc.** – See *Spartina pectinata* Bosc ex Link

Spartina patens **(Ait.) Muhl.** – Fox grass [Fox-grass] (5, 94) (1901–1913), Marsh grass [Marshgrass, Marsh-grass] (87, 88) (1884–1885), Marshahy cord grass [Marshahy cordgrass] (155) (1942), Rush grass [Rush-grass] (88) (1885), Rush salt grass [Rush salt-grass] (5, 19, 45, 66, 87, 90, 92) (1840–1913), Salt grass [Saltgrass, Salt-grass] (87, 88, 90) (1884–1885), Saltmarsh grass [Salt marsh grass] (5) (1913), Salt-meadow cord grass [Salt meadow cord-grass] (50) (present), Salt-meadow grass [Salt meadow grass, Salt meadow-grass] (5) (1913), Three-fork grass (5) (1913), White-rush [White rush] (5) (1913)

Spartina patens **(Ait.) Muhl. var.** *juncea* **(Michx.) A. S. Hitchc.** – See *Spartina pectinata* Bosc ex Link

Spartina pectinata **Bosc ex Link** – Bull grass [Bull-grass, Bull grass] (5, 119) (1913–1938), Cord grass [Cord-grass, Cordgrass] (119) (1938), Fall marsh grass (99) (1923), Freshwater cord grass [Fresh-water cord-grass, Fresh-water cord-grass, Freshwater cord-grass] (5) (1913), Prairie cord-grass [Prairie cordgrass] (3, 50, 122, 140, 155) (1937–present), Rush salt grass [Rush salt-grass] (163) (1852), Salt-meadow cord grass [Saltmeadow cordgrass] (122) (1937), Sidu-hi (Omaha-Ponca) (37) (1830), Slough grass [Slough-grass, Slough-grass] (37, 65, 111, 115, 119, 163) (1830–1938), Tall marsh grass [Tall marsh-grass] (5, 119, 163) (1852–1938), Upland creek stuff (5) (1913)

Spartina polystachya **Willd.** – See *Spartina cynosuroides* (L.) Roth

Spartina **Schreber** – Cord grass [Cord-grass, Cordgrass] (45, 50, 155) (1896–present), Marsh grass [Marshgrass, Marsh-grass] (1, 7, 10, 45, 66, 93) (1818–1936), Slough grass [Slough-grass, Sloughgrass] (93) (1936) Neb

Spartina spartinae **(Trin.) Merr. ex A. S. Hitchc.** – Rush-like spartina (94) (1901)

Spartina stricta **(Ait.) Roth** – See *Spartina maritima* (M. A. Curtis) Fern.

Spartina stricta maritima **(Walt.) Scribn.** – See *Spartina alterniflora* Loisel.

Spartium junceum **L.** – Spanish broom (19, 92, 109, 156) (1526–1949), Weaver's-broom [Weavers-broom, Weavers broom] (109, 138) (1923–1949)

Spartium **L.** – Weaver's-broom [Weavers-broom, Weavers broom] (138) (1923)

Spathyema foetida **(L.) Raf.** – See *Symplocarpus foetidus* (L.) Salisb. ex Nutt.

Spathyema **Raf.** – See *Symplocarpus* Salisb. ex Nutt.

Specularia biflora **(Ruiz and Pavon) F. & M.** – See *Triodanis perfoliata* (L.) Nieuwl. var. *biflora* (Ruiz & Pavón) Bradley

Specularia **Heister** – See *Triodanis* Raf. ex Greene

Specularia holzingeri **(McVaugh) Fern.** – See *Triodanis holzingeri* McVaugh

Specularia leptocarpa **(Nutt.) Gray** – See *Triodanis leptocarpa* (Nutt.) Nieuwl.

Specularia perfoliata **(L.) DC.** – See *Triodanis perfoliata* (L.) Nieuwl. var. *perfoliata*

Specularia speculum-veneris **(L.) Tanfani** – See *Legousia speculum-veneris* (L.) Fisch. ex A. DC.

Spergula arvensis **L.** – Ackerspergel (German) (158) (1900), Bed sandwort [Bedsandwort] (76) (1896) Western US, Beggarweed [Beggar weed, Beggar-weed] (158) (1900), Corn spurry [Corn spurrey, Corn-spurrey] (1, 3, 4, 5, 19, 50, 85, 107, 110, 155, 156, 158, 187) (1840–present), Cowquake [Cow-quake, Cow quake] (5, 156, 158) (1900–1923) no longer in use by 1923, Devil's-gut [Devil's gut, Devil's-guts, Devil's guts, Devil's-guts] (76, 158) (1896–1900) Paris ME, Erba renaiola (Italian, fom rena "sand" (110) (1886), Espargata

(Portuguese) (110) (1886), Esparicllas (Spanish) (110) (1886), Farmer's-ruin (158) (1900), Frank spurry [Franke spurrie] (178) (1526), Fryle (Swedish) (110) (1886), Giant spurrey (129) (1894) SD, Girr or Kirr (Danish) (110) (1886), Humb or hum (Danish) (110) (1886), Knutt (Swedish) (110) (1886), Nägde (Swedish) (110) (1886), Pick-purse [Pick-purse, Pick purse] (5, 156, 158) (1900–1923) no longer in use by 1923, Pine-cheat [Pine cheat] (5, 156, 158) (1900–1923) no longer in use by 1923, Pineweed [Pine-weed, Pine weed] (79) (1891), Poverty-weed [Povertyweed, Poverty weed] (5, 156) (1913–1923), Sandweed [Sand weed, Sand-weed] (5, 92, 156, 158) (1876–1923) no longer in use by 1923, Skorff (Swedish) (110) (1886), Spargoule (French) (110) (1886), Spark (German) (110) (1886), Spergola (Italian) (110) (1886), Spergula (110) (1886), Spergule (French) (158) (1900), Spurry [Spurrey] (1, 5, 92, 109, 118, 131, 138, 156, 158) (1876–1949), Tare [Tares] (92) (1876), Toadflax [Toad flax, Toad-flax] (107, 156) (1919–1923), Toritsa (Russian) (110) (1886), Yarr (5, 156, 158) (1900–1923) no longer in use by 1923

Spergula L. – Spurrey (10, 156) (1818–1923), Spurry [Spurrey] (10, 15, 138, 155, 156, 158) (1818–1942)

Spergula maxima (**Weihe ex Boenn.**) – See *Spergula arvensis* L.

Spergula nodosa L. – See *Sagina nodosa* (L.) Fenzl

Spergula saginoides L. – See *Sagina saginoides* (L.) H. Karst.

Spergula sativa **Boenn.** – See *Spergula arvensis* L.

Spergularia (**Pers.**) **J. & K. Presl** – Chickweed [Chick-weed, Chick weed] (93, 158, 165) (1768–1936), Purple sandwort (156) (1923), Sand spurry [Sandspurry, Sand-spurrey, Sand spurrey] (50, 155) (1942–present), Spurrey sandwort (13) (1849), Starwort [Star-wort, Star wort] (158) (1900), Three-valve sandwort [Three-valved sandwort] (13) (1849)

Spergularia alata **Wiegand** – See *Spergularia salina* J. & K. Presl

Spergularia canadensis (**Pers.**) **G. Don** – Northern sand spurry [Northern sand spurrey] (156) (1923), Red sandwort [Red sand-wort] (156) (1923), Sand spurry [Sandspurry, Sand-spurrey, Sand spurrey] (1) (1932)

Spergularia canadensis (**Pers.**) **G. Don var. canadensis** – Bed sandwort [Bedsandwort] (5) (1913), Northern sand spurry [Northern sand spurrey] (5) (1913)

Spergularia leiosperma (**Kindb.**) **F. Schmidt** – See *Spergularia salina* J. & K. Presl

Spergularia marina (**L.**) **Griseb.** – See *Spergularia salina* J. & K. Presl

Spergularia rubra (**L.**) **J. & K. Presl** – Bed sandwort [Bedsandwort] (5) (1913), Field sandwort (42) (1814), Purple sandwort (5, 156) (1913–1923), Red sandwort [Red sand-wort] (19, 42, 49, 156) (1814–1923), Salt sand-spurry [Salt sandspurry] (50) (present), Sand spurry [Sandspurry, Sand-spurrey, Sand spurrey] (5, 49, 156) (1898–1923), Spurrey sandwort (49) (1898)

Spergularia rubra **var. campestris Gray** – See *Spergularia rubra* (L.) J. & K. Presl

Spergularia salina **J. & K. Presl** – Northern sand spurry [Northern sand spurrey] (156) (1923), Red sandwort [Red sand-wort] (156, 158) (1900–1923), Salt sand spurry [Salt sandspurry] (50) (present), Salt-marsh sand spurry [Salt marsh sand spurrey, Saltmarsh sand-spurry] (4, 5, 155, 156) (1913–1986), Sea-bed sandwort [Sea bed sandwort] (5) (1913), Sea-side sandwort [Sea side sandwort, Seaside sandwort] (5, 156) (1913–1923)

Spergulastrum lanuginosum **Ell.** – See *Arenaria lanuginosa* (Michx.) Rohrb.

Spermacoce glabra **Michx.** – Buttonweed [Button-weed, Button weed] (3) (1977), Smooth buttonplant (155) (1942), Smooth buttonweed [Smooth button-weed] (4, 5, 97, 122, 156) (1913–1986), Smooth false buttonweed (50) (present)

Spermacoce **L.** – Buttonweed [Button-weed, Button weed] (1, 4, 158) (1900–1986), False buttonweed (50) (present)

Spermolepis divaricata (**Walt.**) **Britton** – Forked scale-seed (4) (1986), Forked spermolepis (3) (1977), Rough-fruit scaleseed [Roughfruit scaleseed] (50) (present), Rough-fruit spermolepis [Rough-fruited spermolepis] (5, 97) (1913–1937)

Spermolepis echinata (**Nutt. ex DC.**) **Heller** – Bristly scaleseed (50) (present), Bristly-fruit spermolepis [Bristly-fruited spermolepis] (5, 97) (1913–1937), Smallage (46, 92) (1671–1876)

Spermolepis echinatus (**Nutt.**) **Heller** – See *Spermolepis echinata* (Nutt. ex DC.) Heller

Spermolepis inermis (**Nutt. ex DC.**) **Mathias & Constance** – Red River scale-seed [Red River scaleseed] (50) (present), Spreading spermolepis (3, 5, 97) (1913–1977)

Spermolepis **Raf.** – Scale-seed [Scaleseed] (4, 50) (1986–present)

Sphaeralcea angusta (**Gray**) **Fern.** – See *Malvastrum hispidum* (Pursh) Hochr.

Sphaeralcea angustifolia (**Cav.**) **G. Don** – Brick globemallow (138) (1923), Cheeseweed [Cheese weed] (76) (1896), Fendler's globemallow [Fendler's globemallow] (50) (present), Rusty globe-mallow [Rusty globemallow] (50) (present), Sharp-fruit globe-mallow [Sharp-fruited globe mallow] (5, 97) (1913–1937), Yerba del negro (Spanish) (150) (1894) NM

Sphaeralcea bonariensis (**Cav.**) **Griseb.** – Brick globemallow (138) (1923), False red mallow (85) (1932) IA

Sphaeralcea cisplatina **A.St.-Hil.** – See *Sphaeralcea bonariensis* (Cav.) Griseb.

Sphaeralcea coccinea (**Nutt.**) **Rydb.** – Red false mallow (3, 4) (1977–1986), Scarlet globe-mallow [Scarlet globemallow] (50, 155) (1942–present)

Sphaeralcea coccinea (**Nutt.**) **Rydb. subsp. coccinea** – Cowboy's delight (98) (1926) Neb, False mallow [False-mallow, Falsemallow, False mallows] (127, 157) (1900–1933), Heyoka ta pezhuta (Dakota, medicine of the heyoka) (37) (1919), Moss-rose [Moss rose] (5, 76, 156, 157) (1896–1929) Burnside SD, Prairie mallow [Prairiemallow] (5, 156) (1913–1923), Red false mallow (5, 37, 97, 156) (1913–1937), Red mallow (95, 127, 131, 157) (1899–1933), Scarlet malva (98) (1926)

Sphaeralcea cuspidata **Torr.** – See *Sphaeralcea angustifolia* (Cav.) G. Don

Sphaeralcea emoryi **Torr. ex Gray** – Cheeseweed [Cheese weed] (76) (1896) CA, Comarona (Spanish) (76) (1896) CA

Sphaeralcea emoryi **Torr. ex Gray var. nevadensis** (**Kearney**) **Kearney** – See *Sphaeralcea angustifolia* (Cav.) G. Don

Sphaeralcea fendleri **Gray** – Globemallow [Globe-mallow, Globe mallow] (156) (1923)

Sphaeralcea remota – possibly *Iliamna rivularis* (Dougl. ex Hook.) Greene var. *rivularis*

Sphaeralcea rivularis (**Dougl. ex Hook.**) **Torr.** – See *Iliamna rivularis* (Dougl. ex Hook.) Greene

Sphaeralcea **St. Hill.** – Globemallow [Globe-mallow, Globe mallow] (4, 50, 109, 138, 155, 158) (1900–present), Globepea (155) (1942)

Sphaerophysa **DC.** – Alkali swainsonpea (50) (present), Globepea (155) (1942)

Sphaerophysa salsula (**Pallas**) **DC.** – Alkali swainsonpea (50) (present), Locoweed [Loco weed, Loco-weed] (131) (1899), Salt globepea [Salt globepea] (155) (1942)

Sphagnum gracile **Michx.** – See *Sphagnum capillifolium* (Ehrh.) Hedw.

Sphagnum **L.** – Asa'kûmĭg (Chippewa) (40) (1928), Sphagnum (40, 50) (1928–present)

Sphagnum obtusifolium **Ehrh.** – See Sphagnum palustre L.

Sphagnum palustre **L.** – Bog moss [Bog-moss] (107, 184) (1793–1919), Peat moss [Peet moss] (19) (1840), Sphagnum (107) (1919)

Sphagnum vulgare **Michx.** – See Sphagnum palustre L.

Sphedamnocarpus **Planch. ex Benth. & Hook. f.** – Wild hopseed [Wilde hop seed, Wilde hop-seed] (181) (~1678)

Sphenopholis ×*pallens* (**Biehler**) **Scribn.** [*obtusata* × *pensylvanica*] – Eaton's grass [Eaton's-grass] (111) (1915), Tall Eaton's grass (5) (1913)

Sphenopholis intermedia (**Rydb.**) **Rydb.** – Prairie wedge grass [Prairie wedgegrass] (3, 4) (1977–1986), Slender wedgescale (50, 155) (1942–present)

Sphenopholis nitida (**Biehler**) **Scribn.** – Eaton's grass [Eaton's-grass]

Spiraea latifolia **Borkh.**

(56, 94, 129) (1894–1901), Pennsylvania eatonia [Pennsylvanian eatonia] (56, 66, 72) (1901–1907), Slender Eaton's grass (5) (1913), Slender sphenopolis (163) (1852), Slender wedgescale (50) (present)

Sphenopholis obtusata **(Michx.) Scribn.** – Blunt hair grass (42) (1814), Blunt-scale eatonia [Blunt scaled eatonia] (56, 72) (1901–1907), Blunt-scale grass [Blunt scaled grass] (134, 140) (1932–1944), Blunt-scale sphenopholis [Blunt-scaled sphenopholis] (119) (1938), Early bunch grass [Early bunchgrass, Early bunch-grass] (5, 56, 94, 111, 119, 129, 140) (1894–1944), Obtuse-flower hair grass [Obtuse-flowered hair-grass] (187) (1818), Prairie bunch grass [Prairie bunch-grass] (129) (1894), Prairie grass [Prairie-grass] (5, 11, 75, 144) (1888–1913), Prairie sphenopholis (134) (1932), Prairie wedge grass [Prairie wedgegrass] (122) (1937), Prairie wedgescale (50, 140, 155) (1942–present), Truncated koeleria (66) (1903)

Sphenopholis obtusata **(Michx.) Scribn. var. *major* (Torr.) Erdman** – See *Sphenopholis intermedia* (Rydb.) Rydb.

Sphenopholis obtusata **(Michx.) Scribn. var. *obtusata*** – Prairie wedgescale (50) (present)

Sphenopholis pallens **(Spreng.) Scribn.** – See *Sphenopholis ×pallens* (Biehler) Scribn. [*obtusata × pensylvanica*]

Sphenopholis pensylvanica **(L.) A. S. Hitchc.** – Marsh false oat (5) (1913), Marsh oat grass [Marsh oat-grass] (5, 66, 94) (1901–1913), Marsh wedgescale (50) (present), Pennsylvania oat grass (42) (1814)

Sphenopholis **Scribn.** – Bunch grass [Bunchgrass, Bunch-grass] (93) (1936), Wedgescale (50, 155) (1942–present)

Sphenopolis nitida **(Spreng.) Scribn.** – See *Sphenopholis nitida* (Biehler) Scribn.

Sphenopolis robusta **(Vasey) Heller** – See *Sphenopholis intermedia* (Rydb.) Rydb.

Spiesia lamberti **(Pursh) Kuntze** – See *Oxytropis lambertii* Pursh

Spiesia viscida **(Nutt.) Kuntze** – See *Oxytropis borealis* DC. var. *viscida* (Nutt.) Welsh

Spigelia anthelmia **L.** – Pinkroot [Pink root] (2, 138, 156) (1895–1923)

Spigelia **L.** – Indian pink (92, 186) (1814–1876), Pinkroot [Pink root] (2, 138, 156) (1895–1923), Worm-grass [Wormgrass, Worm grass] (2) (1895)

Spigelia marilandica **(L.) L.** – American wormroot (64) (1907), Carolina pinkroot [Carolina pink root, Carolina pink-root] (5, 6, 10, 49, 53, 55, 57, 64, 92, 156, 184, 186) (1793–1923), Indian pink (5, 6, 55, 64, 92, 97, 122, 124, 156) (1876–1937), Maryland pink (49, 52, 53, 54, 64) (1905–1922), Maryland pinkroot [Maryland pink root] (6) (1892), Maryland scarlet lonicera (8) (1785), Mikaa (Osage) (6) (1892), Nordamerikanischer Spigelie (German) (6, 186) (1814–1892), Perennial worm grass (6) (1892), Pinkroot [Pink root] (5, 6, 14, 19, 49, 53, 55, 57, 58, 59, 60, 64, 92, 138, 156) (1840–1923), Snakeroot [Snake root, Snake-root] (6) (1892), Spigelia (53, 54, 55, 59, 64) (1905–1922), Spigélia de Maryland (French) (6) (1892), Spigelia du Maryland (French) (8) (1785), Starbloom [Star-bloom, Star bloom] (5, 6, 64, 92, 156) (1892–1923), Unsteetle (6, 186) (1814–1892), Unsteetle (Cherokee) (6) (1892), Worm-grass [Wormgrass, Worm grass] (5, 6, 14, 49, 53, 64, 186) (1814–1923), Wormweed [Worm weed, Worm-weed] (64, 156) (1908–1923)

Spilanthes **Jacq.** – Spilanthes (5, 97) (1913–1937)

Spilanthes repens **(Walt.) Michx.** – See *Acmella oppositifolia* (Lam.) R. K. Jansen var. *repens* (Walt.) R. K. Jansen

Spilanthes repens **Michx.** – See *Acmella oppositifolia* (Lam.) R. K. Jansen var. *repens* (Walt.) R. K. Jansen

Spiloma melaleuca – See *Spiloma melaleucum* Ach.

Spiloma melaleucum **Ach.** – Efflorescent lichen (19) (1840)

Spinacia **L.** – Spinach (109, 138) (1923–1949), Spinage (7) (1828), Spynache (179) (1526)

Spinacia oleracea **L.** – Common spinach (138) (1923), Ebanach (Arabic) (110) (1886), Meadowsweet [Meadow-sweet, Meadow sweet] (82, 85) (1930–1932), Prickly-seed spinach [Prickly-seeded spinach] (109) (1949), Spinach (19, 92, 107, 110, 184) (1793–1919), Spinage (109) (1949)

Spiraea **(Tourn.) L.** – See *Spiraea* L.

Spiraea ×pyramidata **Greene** [*betulifolia × douglasii*] – Pyramid spiraea (138) (1923), Queen-of-the-meadow [Queen of the meadow] (74, 156) (1893–1923)

Spiraea ×vanhouttei **(Briot) Carr.** [*cantoniensis × trilobata*] – Vanhoutte's spiraea [Vanhoutte spiraea] (112) (1937)

Spiraea alba **Du Roi** – Garland spiraea (112) (1937), Meadow spiraea (138) (1923), Meadowsweet [Meadow-sweet, Meadow sweet] (3, 109) (1949–1977), Mountain ash [Mountain-ash, Mountainash] (4) (1986), Narrow-leaf meadowsweet [Narrowleaf meadowsweet, arrow-leaved meadow sweet] (5, 155) (1913–1942), White meadowsweet (50) (present)

Spiraea alba **Du Roi var. *latifolia* (Aiton) Dippel** – American meadowsweet [American meadow sweet] (5) (1913), Meadowsweet [Meadow-sweet, Meadow sweet] (109, 156) (1923–1949), Pink meadow spiraea (138) (1923), Quaker lady [Quaker ladies, Quaker-ladies] (5) (1913), Queen-of-the-meadow [Queen of the meadow] (5) (1913), Queen-of-the-prairie [Queen of the prairie] (2, 63, 92) (1876–1895), Spice hardhack [Spice hard-hack] (5) (1913)

Spiraea aruncus **L.** – See *Aruncus dioicus* (Walt.) Fern. var. *vulgaris* (Maxim.) Hara

Spiraea betulifolia **Pallas** – Birch-leaf meadowsweet [Birchleaf meadowsweet] (155) (1942), White spiraea (50) (present), Wild spiraea (4) (1986)

Spiraea betulifolia **Pallas var. *corymbosa* (Raf.) Maxim.** – Birch-leaf meadowsweet [Birch-leaved meadow sweet] (5) (1913), Corymbed spiraea (5) (1913), Meadowsweet [Meadow-sweet, Meadow sweet] (85) (1932)

Spiraea betulifolia **Pallas var. *lucida* (Dougl. ex Greene) C. L. Hitchc.** – Carolina rose-leaf spiraea [Carolinian rose-leaved spiraea] (8) (1785), Corymbed spiraea (131) (1899), Mountain meadowsweet (3) (1977), Shiny-leaf spiraea [Shinyleaf spiraea] (50, 155) (1942–present)

Spiraea chamaedryfolia **L.** – Elm-leaf spiraea [Elmleaf spiraea] (138) (1923), Germander spiraea (138) (1923)

Spiraea chamaedryfolia **L. var. *ulmifolia* (Scop.) Maxim.** – Birch-leaf meadowsweet [Birch-leaved meadow sweet] (155) (1942), Elm-leaf spiraea [Elmleaf spiraea] (138) (1923)

Spiraea corymbosa **Raf.** – See *Spiraea betulifolia* Pallas var. *corymbosa* (Raf.) Maxim.

Spiraea densiflora **Nutt.** – See *Spiraea splendens* Baumann ex K. Koch var. *splendens*

Spiraea douglasi – See *Spiraea douglasii* Hook.

Spiraea douglasii **Hook.** – Douglas' meadowsweet [Douglas meadow sweet] (135) (1910), Douglas' spiraea [Douglas spiraea] (138) (1923), Fortune's spiraea [Fortune spiraea] (138) (1923)

Spiraea douglasii **Hook. var. *menziesii* (Hook.) K. Presl** – Menzies' spiraea [Menzies spiraea] (138) (1923), Ninebark [Nine bark, Ninebark] (8, 19, 184, 187) (1785–1840)

Spiraea fortunei – See *Spiraea japonica* L. f. var. *fortunei* (Planch.) Rehd.

Spiraea hypericifolia **L.** – Canadian spiraea (8) (1785), John's-wort hardhack [John's-wort hard-hack] (19) (1840), May-wreath [May wreath] (92) (1876), Mille-pertuis (French) (8) (1785)

Spiraea japonica **L. f.** – Japanese spiraea (5, 138) (1913–1923), Meadowsweet [Meadow-sweet, Meadow sweet] (1, 4, 156, 167, 184) (1793–1986)

Spiraea japonica **L. f. var. *fortunei* (Planch.) Rehd.** – Canadian spiraea (8) (1785), Fortune's spiraea [Fortune spiraea] (138) (1923)

Spiraea **L.** – American meadowsweet [American meadow sweet] (5) (1913), Meadowsweet [Meadow-sweet, Meadow sweet] (1, 4, 82, 85, 156, 167) (1814–1986), Spice hardhack [Spice hard-hack] (73) (1892) Bonny River NB, Spiraea [Spirea] (8, 50, 109, 112, 138) (1785–present)

Spiraea latifolia **(Aiton) Borkh.** – See *Spiraea alba* Du Roi var. *latifolia* (Aiton) Dippel

Spiraea latifolia **Borkh.** – See *Spiraea alba* Du Roi var. *latifolia* (Aiton) Dippel

Spiraea lucida Dougl.

Spiraea lucida Dougl. – See *Spiraea betulifolia* Pallas var. *lucida* (Dougl. ex Greene) C. L. Hitchc.

Spiraea menziesi – See *Spiraea douglasii* Hook. var. *menziesii* (Hook.) K. Presl

Spiraea opulifolia L. – See *Physocarpus opulifolius* (L.) Maxim. var. *opulifolius*

Spiraea prunifolia Sieb. & Zucc. – Bridalwreath [Bridal-wreath, Bridal wreath] (109, 135, 138) (1910–1949), Double bridalwreath [Double bridal wreath] (112) (1937)

Spiraea prunifolia Sieb. & Zucc. var. plena Schneid. – See *Spiraea prunifolia* Sieb. & Zucc.

Spiraea pyramidata – See *Spiraea* ×*pyramidata* Greene [*betulifolia* × *douglasii*]

Spiraea salicifolia L. – American meadowsweet [American meadow sweet] (72) (1907), Bridewort [Bride wort, Bride-wort] (156) (1923), Demágene-minš (Chippewa, Pipestem wood) (105) (1932), Hardhack [Hard-hack] (156) (1923), Meadowsweet [Meadow-sweet, Meadow sweet] (19, 82, 105, 156) (1840–1932), Meadwort [Mead-wort] (156) (1923), Mock willow (156) (1923), Quaker lady [Quaker ladies, Quaker-ladies] (156) (1923), Queen-of-the-meadow [Queen of the meadow] (74, 156) (1893–1923) NY, Spice (156) (1923) no longer in use by 1923, Spiraea [Spirea] (156) (1923), Willow hard-hack (19) (1840), Willow-leaf meadowsweet [Willow-leaved meadow-sweet, Willow-leaved meadowsweet] (130, 131) (1895–1899), Willow-leaf spiraea [Willowleaf spiraea] (138) (1923), possibly Common meadowsweet (2, 63) (1895–1899)

Spiraea salicolia L. – possibly *Spiraea salicifolia* L.

Spiraea splendens Baumann ex K. Koch var. splendens – Meadowsweet [Meadow-sweet, Meadow sweet] (85) (1932)

Spiraea stipulata L. – possibly *Porteranthus stipulatus* (Muhl. ex Willd.) Britt.

Spiraea thunbergi – See *Spiraea thunbergii* Sieb. ex Blume

Spiraea thunbergii Sieb. ex Blume – Horseweed [Horse-weed, Horse weed] (92) (1876), Thunberg's spiraea [Thunberg spiraea] (138) (1923)

Spiraea tomentosa L. – Hardhack [Hard-hack] (2, 5, 48, 49, 57, 58, 92, 109, 138, 156) (1869–1949), Hoary-leaf Virginia mock syringa [Hoary leaved Virginia mock syringa] (181) (~1678), Horseweed [Horse-weed, Horse weed] (92) (1876), Meadowsweet [Meadow-sweet, Meadow sweet] (5, 19, 49, 58, 92, 156) (1840–1923), Poorman's-soap [Poor man's soap] (5, 156) (1913–1923), Purple hardhack [Purple hard-hack] (19, 76, 156) (1840–1923), Rosy bush [Rosey bush, Rosy-bush] (5, 92, 156) (1876–1923), Scarlet-flower Philadelphia spiraea [Scarlet flowered Philadelphian spiraea] (8) (1785), Silverleaf [Silver leaf, Silver-leaf] (5, 49, 92, 156) (1898–1923), Silverweed [Silver weed, Silver-weed] (5, 92, 156) (1876–1923), Spiraea tomenteux (French) (8) (1785), Spiraea tomenteux à fleurs blanches (French) (8) (1785), Steeple bush (2, 5, 19, 48, 49, 58, 92, 109, 156) (1840–1923), Whitecap [White-cap, White cap] (5, 49, 92, 156) (1876–1923), Whiteleaf [White leaf, White-leaf] (49, 92) (1876–1898), Whiteweed [White weed, White-weed] (156) (1923)

Spiraea trilobata L. – Three-lobe spiraea [Threelobe spiraea] (138) (1923)

Spiraea ulmaria L. – See *Filipendula ulmaria* (L.) Maxim. subsp. *ulmaria*

Spiraea vanhouttei – See *Spiraea* ×*vanhouttei* (Briot) Carr. [*cantoniensis* × *trilobata*]

Spiraea virginiana Britt. – Virginia spiraea (138) (1923)

Spiranthes beckii Lindl. – See *Spiranthes lacera* (Raf.) Raf. var. *gracilis* (Bigelow) Luer

Spiranthes cernua (L.) L. C. Rich. – Drooping lady's-tresses [Drooping ladies' tresses] (5) (1913), Drooping-flower lady's-traces [Drooping-flowered ladies' traces] (86) (1878), Hen's-toes [Hens' toes] (78) (1898) ME, Lady's-tresses [Ladies' tresses, Ladies tresses, Ladies'-tresses] (3, 85, 98) (1926–1977), Nodding lady's-tresses [Nodding ladies' tresses, Nodding ladiestresses, Nodding ladies'-tresses, Nodding ladies-tresses] (5, 19, 50, 72, 93, 97, 109, 122, 138,

156) (1840–present), Screw-auger [Screw auger] (5, 75, 156) (1894–1923) Nova Scotia, Wild tuberose [Wild tube-rose, Wild tube rose] (5, 156) (1913–1923)

Spiranthes diluvialis Sheviak – Diluvim ladies'-tresses (50) (present)

Spiranthes lacera (Raf.) Raf. – Northern slender lady's-tresses [Northern slender ladies' tresses] (50) (present), Slender lady's-tresses [Slender ladies' tresses, Slender ladies-tresses, Slender ladiestresses, Slender ladies'-tresses] (3) (1977)

Spiranthes lacera (Raf.) Raf. var. gracilis (Bigelow) Luer – Corkscrew plant (5, 156) (1913–1923), Little lady's-tresses [Little ladies' tresses, Little ladiestresses, Little ladies'-tresses] (5, 122) (1913–1937), Northern slender lady's-tresses [Northern slender ladies' tresses] (50) (present), Slender lady's-tresses [Slender ladies' tresses, Slender ladies-tresses, Slender ladiestresses, Slender ladies'-tresses] (5, 72, 122, 138, 156) (1907–1937), Twisted-stalk [Twisted-stalk, Twisted stalk] (5, 75, 156) (1894–1923) WV

Spiranthes lacera (Raf.) Raf. var. lacera – Northern slender lady's-tresses [Northern slender ladies' tresses] (50) (present)

Spiranthes longilabris Lindl. – Short-leaf lady's-tresses [Short-leaf ladies-tresses] (138) (1923)

Spiranthes lucida (H. H. Eat.) Ames – Shining ladies'-tresses [Shining ladies' tresses] (50) (Present), Wide-leaf lady's-tresses [Wide-leaved ladies' tresses] (5) (1913)

Spiranthes magnicamporum Sheviak – Great Plains lady's-tresses [Great Plains ladies'-tresses] (50) (present)

Spiranthes ochroleuca (Rydb.) Rydb. – Yellow nodding lady's-tresses [Yellow nodding ladies'-tresses] (50) (present)

Spiranthes ovalis Lindl. – October lady's-tresses [October ladies' tresses] (50) (present)

Spiranthes ovalis Lindl. var. ovalis – October lady's-tresses [October ladies' tresses] (50) (present), Small-flower lady's-tresses [Small-flowered ladies' tresses] (5) (1913)

Spiranthes praecox (Walt.) S. Wats. – Grass-leaf lady's-tresses [Grass-leaf ladiestresses, Grass-leaved ladies' tresses] (5, 122) (1913–1937), Green-vein lady's-tresses [Greenvein ladies' tresses] (50) (present)

Spiranthes Rich. – Lady's-dresses [Ladies' dresses] (75) (1894), Lady's-traces [Ladies' traces] (75) (1894), Lady's-tresses [Ladies' tresses [Ladies tresses, Ladies'-tresses] (1, 50, 75, 93, 109, 138, 156) (1923–present), Orchis (124) (1937), Spiral orchid (75) (1894)

Spiranthes romanzoffiana Cham. – Hooded lady's-tresses [Hooded ladies' tresses] (3, 50, 93) (1936–present), Lady's-tresses [Ladies' tresses, Ladies tresses, Ladies'-tresses] (127) (1933)

Spiranthes stricta Rydb. – See *Spiranthes romanzoffiana* Cham.

Spiranthes torta (Thunb.) Garay & H. R. Sweet – Lady's-tresses [Ladies' tresses, Ladies tresses, Ladies'-tresses] (187) (1818), Spiral neottia (187) (1818), Summer lady's-tresses [Summer ladies' tresses] (19) (1840)

Spiranthes tuberosa Raf. – Little lady's-tresses [Little ladies' tresses, Little ladiestresses, Little ladies'-tresses] (3, 5, 50) (1913–present)

Spiranthes vernalis Engelm. & Gray – Linear-leaf lady's-tresses [Linear-leaved ladies' tresses, Linear-leaved ladies'-tresses] (5, 97) (1913–1937), Spring lady's-tresses [Spring ladies' tresses, Spring ladies'-tresses] (50) (present), Twisted lady's-tresses [Twisted ladies'-tresses] (3) (1977)

Spirodela polyrhiza (L.) Schleid. – Common duckmeat (50) (present), Duckmeat [Duck-meat, Duck-meat, Ducke meate, Ducks' meat, Ducks' meat, Duck'smeat, Duck's-meat] (3, 156) (1923–1977), Duckweed (156) (1923), Giant duckweed (50) (present), Great duckwood (72) (1907), Greater duckweed (5, 93, 97, 120) (1913–1938), Larger duckweed (156) (1923), Water flaxseed (19) (1840)

Spirodela Scheilen – Duckmeat [Duck-meat, Duck-meat, Ducke meate, Duck's meat, Ducks' meat, Duck'smeat, Duck's-meat] (50) (present), Large duckweed (93) (1936), Larger duckweed (1) (1932)

Spirogyra Link In C. G. Nees – Frog slime (78) (1898) NH, Frog spawn (73) (1892) Parts of NB, Frog spit (73) (1892)

Splachnum ampullaceum Hedw. – Small capsule dung moss (50) (present), Umbrella moss (19) (1840)

Spondias cytherea **Sonn.** – See *Spondias dulcis* Parkinson

Spondias dulcis **Forster** – See *Spondias dulcis* Parkinson

Spondias dulcis **Parkinson** – Ambarella (109) (1949), Evi or hevi (Polynesia) (110) (1886), Otaheite apple [Otaheite-apple] (92, 109) (1876–1949), Tahiti apple (110) (1886)

Spondias **L.** – Acaja (174) (1753)

Spondias mombin **L.** – Hog-plum [Hog plum, Hog's plum] (107, 109) (1919–1949), Ibamerara (174) (1753), Spondias (174) (1753), Yellow mombin (109) (1949)

Spondias purpurea **L.** – Hog-plum [Hog plum, Hog's plum] (107) (1919), Red mombin (109) (1949), Spanish plum [Spanish-plum] (107, 109) (1919–1949)

Sporobolus airoides **(Torr.) Torr.** – Alkali dropseed (116, 140) (1944–1958), Alkali grass [Alkali-grass, Alkaligrass] (129) (1894) SD, Alkali sacaton (3, 50, 119, 122, 140, 146, 155) (1937–present), Bunch grass [Bunchgrass, Bunch-grass] (116, 129, 149, 151, 152) (1894–1958), Finetop [Fine-top, Fine top] (144) (1899), Fine-top grass [Fine top grass] (151) (1896), Fine-top salt grass [Fine-top salt-grass] (5, 94) (1901–1913), Hair grass [Hairgrass, Hair-grass] (93, 94) (1901–1936), Hair-grass dropseed (5) (1913), Rush grass [Rush-grass] (5, 85) (1913–1932), Salt grass [Saltgrass, Salt-grass] (5, 87, 119, 151) (1885–1938)

Sporobolus angustus **Buckley** – See *Sporobolus indicus* (L.) R. Br. var. *indicus*

Sporobolus asper **(Michx.) Kunth var.** *asper* – See *Sporobolus compositus* (Poir.) Merr.

Sporobolus asper **(Michx.) Kunth var.** *clandestinus* **(Bichler) Shinners** – See *Sporobolus clandestinus* (Biehler) A. S. Hitchc.

Sporobolus asper **(Michx.) Kunth var.** *hookeri* **(Trin.) Vasey** – See *Sporobolus compositus* (Poir.) Merr. var. *compositus*

Sporobolus asper **(Michx.) Kunth var.** *pilosus* **(Vasey) Hitchc.** – See *Sporobolus compositus* (Poir.) Merr. var. *drummondii* (Trin.) Kartesz & Gandhi

Sporobolus asper **(Michx.) Kunth.** – See *Sporobolus compositus* (Poir.) Merr. var. *compositus*

Sporobolus asperifolius **(Nees & Meyen) Thurber** – See *Muhlenbergia asperifolia* (Nees & Meyen ex Trin.) Parodi

Sporobolus berterianus **(Trin.) A. S. Hitchc. & Chase** – See *Sporobolus indicus* (L.) R. Br. var. *indicus*

Sporobolus buckleyi **Vasey** – Buckley's rush grass [Buckley's rush-grass] (94) (1901), Crawly grass (78) (1898) TX, Tickle grass [Ticklegrass, Tickle-grass] (78) (1898) TX

Sporobolus canovirens **Nash** – See *Sporobolus clandestinus* (Biehler) A. S. Hitchc.

Sporobolus clandestinus **(Biehler) A. S. Hitchc.** – Gray-green rush grass [Grey-green rush grass] (5) (1913), Hidden dropseed (155) (1942), Long-leaf rush grass [Long-leaved rush-grass, Long leaved rush grass] (56, 99) (1901–1923), Long-leaf sporobolus [Long-leafed sporobolus] (94) (1901), Prairie grass [Prairie-grass] (5) (1913), Rough dropseed (3, 50) (1977–present), Rough rush grass [Rough rush-grass] (5, 119) (1913–1938)

Sporobolus compositus **(Poir.) Merr.** – Composite dropseed (50) (present), Rough dropseed (3) (1977), Rough-leaf vilfa [Rough-leaved vilfa] (66) (1903), Rush grass [Rush-grass] (66) (1903)

Sporobolus compositus **(Poir.) Merr. var.** *compositus* – Composite dropseed (50) (present), Dropseed [Drop-seed, Drop seed] (116) (1958), Long-leaf rush grass [Long-leaved rush-grass, Long-leaved rushgrass, Long-leaved rush grass] (5, 93, 116, 134, 140, 155, 163) (1852–1958), Prairie dropseed (115, 116, 134, 140) (1932–1958), Prairie grass [Prairie-grass] (5, 94) (1901–1913), Rough dropseed (3) (1977), Rough-seed dropseed [Rough-seeded dropseed] (99) (1923), Tall dropseed (116, 140, 155) (1942–1958)

Sporobolus compositus **(Poir.) Merr. var.** *drummondii* **(Trin.) Kartesz & Gandhi** – Drummond's dropseed (50) (present), Drummond's rush grass (5) (1913), Hairy rush grass (5) (1913), Meadow tall dropseed (155) (1942)

Sporobolus compressus **(Torr.) Kunth.** – See *Muhlenbergia torreyana*

Sporobolus (J. A. Schultes) A. S. Hitchc.

Sporobolus confusus **(Fourn.) Vasey** – See *Muhlenbergia minutissima* (Steud.) Swall.

Sporobolus contractus **Hitchc.** – Spike dropseed (50) (present)

Sporobolus coromandelianus **(Retz.) Kunth** – Madagascar dropseed (50) (present), Pointed dropseed [Pointed drop-seed] (119) (1938), Pointed dropseed grass [Pointed dropseed-grass] (5, 163) (1852–1913), Whorled dropseed (3, 155) (1942–1977)

Sporobolus cryptandrus **(Torr.) Gray** – Dropseed grass [Drop seed grass, Drop-seed grass] (56, 144, 145) (1897–1901), Large-panicle vilfa [Large-panicled vilfa] (66) (1903), Prairie grass [Prairie-grass] (5, 111, 119, 129) (1894–1938), Sand dropseed [Sand drop-seed] (3, 50, 93, 99, 115, 116, 119, 122, 134, 140, 155) (1923–present), Sand rush grass [Sand rushgrass, Sand rush-grass] (56, 94, 134, 140) (1901–1944)

Sporobolus cryptandrus **(Torr.) Gray var.** *strictus* **Scribn.** – See *Sporobolus contractus* Hitchc.

Sporobolus cuspidatus **Wood.** – See *Muhlenbergia cuspidata* (Torr. ex Hook.) Rydb.

Sporobolus domingensis **(Trin.) Kunth** – West Indian rush grass [West Indian rush-grass] (94) (1901)

Sporobolus drummondii **(Trin.) Vasey** – See *Sporobolus compositus* (Poir.) Merr. var. *drummondii* (Trin.) Kartesz & Gandhi

Sporobolus ejuncidus **Nash** – See *Sporobolus junceus* (Beauv.) Kunth

Sporobolus filiformis **(Thurb.) Scribn.** – See *Muhlenbergia filiformis* (Thurb. ex S. Wats.) Rydb.

Sporobolus flexuosus **(Thurb. ex Vasey) Rydb.** – Mesa dropseed (3, 50, 122, 155) (1937–present)

Sporobolus giganteus **Nash** – Giant dropseed (3, 50, 155) (1942–present)

Sporobolus heterolepis **(Gray) Gray** – Bunch grass [Bunchgrass, Bunch-grass] (5, 119, 129) (1894–1938), Iowa bunch grass (56) (1901), Northern dropseed [Northern drop-seed] (5, 93, 115, 116, 119, 134) (1913–1958), Prairie dropseed (3, 116, 155) (1942–present), Strong-scented sporobolus (56, 94) (1897–1901), Strong-scented vilfa (66) (1903), Wire grass [Wire-grass, Wiregrass] (111, 129) (1894–1915)

Sporobolus indicus **(L.) R. Br.** – Liendrilla (45) (1896)

Sporobolus indicus **(L.) R. Br.** – Smut grass [Smut-grass] (87, 94) (1884–1901)

Sporobolus indicus **(L.) R. Br. var.** *indicus* – Blackseed [Black seed] (5) (1913), Dense rush grass (5) (1913), Indian bent grass [Indian bent-grass] (165) (1768), Rat-tail smutgrass [Rattail smutgrass] (155) (1942), Smut grass [Smut-grass] (5, 119, 163) (1852–1938), Swamp grass (5) (1913), Sweet grass [Sweet-grass, Sweetgrass] (5) (1913)

Sporobolus jonesii **Vasey** – See *Muhlenbergia jonesii* (Vasey) Hitchc.

Sporobolus junceus **(Beauv.) Kunth** – Pineywoods dropseed (50, 155) (1942-present), Purple dropseed grass [Purple dropseed-grass] (5, 163) (1852–1913), Rush grass [Rush-grass] (5, 94) (1901–1913), Rush-like dropseed [Rush-like drop seed] (66) (1903), Wire grass [Wire-grass, Wiregrass] (5) (1913)

Sporobolus longifolius **(Torr.) Wood** – See *Sporobolus clandestinus* (Biehler) A. S. Hitchc.

Sporobolus nealleyi **Vasey** – Nealley's dropseed [Neally dropseed] (122) (1937), Nealley's dropseed grass (152) (1912), Nealley's rush grass [Nealley's rush-grass] (94) (1901)

Sporobolus neglectus **Nash** – Dropseed [Drop-seed, Drop seed] (80) (1913), Poverty grass [Poverty-grass, Povertygrass] (3) (1977), Puff-sheath dropseed [Puffsheath dropseed] (50, 155) (1942–present), Rush grass [Rush-grass] (80) (1913), Small rush grass [Small rush-grass] (5, 56, 80, 93, 111, 119, 163) (1852–1938)

Sporobolus pilosus **Vasey** – See *Sporobolus compositus* (Poir.) Merr. var. *drummondii* (Trin.) Kartesz & Gandhi

Sporobolus pyramidatus **(Lam.) Hitchc.** – See *Sporobolus coromandelianus* (Retz.) Kunth

Sporobolus **R. Br.** – Dropseed [Drop-seed, Drop seed] (1, 50, 93)

(1932–present), Dropseed grass [Drop seed grass, Drop-seed grass, Drop-seed-grass] (45, 66, 152) (1896–1912), Rush grass [Rush-grass] (1, 93) (1932–1936)

Sporobolus serotinus **Gray** – See *Muhlenbergia uniflora* (Muhl.) Fern.

Sporobolus simplex **Scribn.** – See *Muhlenbergia filiformis* (Thurb. ex S. Wats.) Rydb.

Sporobolus tenacissimus **Beauv.** – See *Sporobolus indicus* (L.) R. Br.

Sporobolus texanus **Vasey** – Texas dropseed [Texas drop-seed] (3, 50, 94, 119, 155, 163) (1852–present)

Sporobolus thurberi **Scribn.** – See *Muhlenbergia thurberi* (Scribn.) Rydb.

Sporobolus torreyanus **(Schultes) Nash** – See *Muhlenbergia torreyana* (J.A. Schultes) A. S. Hitchc.

Sporobolus uniflorus **Muhl.** – See *Muhlenbergia uniflora* (Muhl.) Fern.

Sporobolus vaginaeflorus **(Torr.) Wood** var. *vaginiflorus* – See *Sporobolus vaginiflorus* (Torr. ex Gray) Wood var. *vaginiflorus*

Sporobolus vaginaeflorus **Vasey** – See *Sporobolus vaginiflorus* (Torr. ex Gray) Wood

Sporobolus vaginiflorus **(Torr. ex Gray) Wood** – Dropseed [Drop-seed, Drop seed] (80) (1913), Dropseed grass [Drop seed grass, Drop-seed grass, Drop-seed-grass] (145) (1897), Hidden-flower vilfa [Hidden flowered vilfa] (66) (1903), Poverty dropseed (50, 155) (1942–present), Prairie grass [Prairie-grass] (11) (1888), Rush grass [Rush-grass] (80) (1913), Sheathed rush grass [Sheathed rush-grass] (5, 56, 80, 93, 99) (1901–1936), Southern poverty grass [Southern poverty-grass] (5, 94, 111, 129) (1894–1915), Wire grass [Wire-grass, Wire-grass] (145) (1897) KS

Sporobolus vaginiflorus **(Torr. ex Gray) Wood** var. *ozarkanus* **(Fern.) Shinners** – Ozark dropseed (50) (present)

Sporobolus vaginiflorus **(Torr. ex Gray) Wood** var. *vaginiflorus* – Poverty dropseed (50) (present), Poverty grass [Poverty-grass, Pov-ertygrass] (3) (1977), Southern poverty grass [Southern poverty-grass] (163) (1852)

Sporobolus vaginiflorus **(Torr.) Wood** var. *neglectus* **(Nash) Scribn.** – See *Sporobolus neglectus* Nash

Sporobolus virginicus **(L.) Kunth** – Seashore dropseed (50) (present), Sea-shore rush grass [Sea-shore rush-grass] (5, 99, 163) (1852–1923), Seaside rush grass [Seaside rush-grass] (94) (1901), Virginia bent grass [Virginian bent grass] (165) (1768)

Sporobolus wrightii **Munro ex Scribn.** – Bunch grass [Bunchgrass, Bunch-grass] (163) (1852), Sacaton [Saccaton, Saccatone] (45, 94, 122, 149, 152, 163) (1852–1937) NM TX

Sporobolus wrightii **Munro ex Scribn.** – Zacate grass (Spanish) (45) (1896), Zacaton (Spanish) (45) (1896) "great grass" also used for other species

Sporobolus wrightii **Scribn.** – See *Sporobolus wrightii* Munro ex Scribn.

Stachy lanata – See *Stachys germanica* L.

Stachys **(Tourn.) L.** – See *Stachys* L.

Stachys affinis **Bunge** – Chorogi (138) (1923)

Stachys agraria – See *Stachys crenata* Raf.

Stachys ajugoides **Benth.** – White hedge-nettle [White hedge nettle] (106) (1930)

Stachys ambigua **(Gray) Britton** – See *Stachys tenuifolia* Willd.

Stachys arenicola **Britton** – See *Stachys pilosa* Nutt. var. *arenicola* (Britton) G. Mulligan & D. Munro

Stachys arvensis **L.** – Corn woundwort (5, 156) (1913–1923), Field woundwort (5, 156) (1913–1923)

Stachys aspera **Michx.** – Base-horehound [Base hoarhound, Base-hoar-hound] (5) (1913), Hedge nettle [Hedgenettle, Hedge-nettle] (114, 187) (1818–1894), Rough hedge nettle (5, 62, 72, 93, 131, 157) (1899–1936), Rough woundwort [Rough wound-wort] (5, 62, 157) (1912–1929), Stachys (157) (1929)

Stachys aspera **Michx.** var. *tenuiflora* **Hitchc.** – See *Stachys aspera* Michx.

Stachys asperrima **Rydb.** – See *Stachys pilosa* Nutt. var. *pilosa*

Stachys atlantica **Britton** – See *Stachys hyssopifolia* Michx.

Stachys betonica **Benth.** – See *Stachys officinalis* (L.) Trev.

Stachys borealis **Rydb.** – See *Stachys pilosa* Nutt. var. *pilosa*

Stachys byzantina **K. Koch ex Scheele** – All-heal [All heal] (107, 156) (1919–1923), Lamb's-ears [Lambs-ears] (109) (1949)

Stachys cordata **Riddell.** – See *Stachys nuttallii* Shuttlw. ex Benth.

Stachys crenata **Raf.** – Mint (106) (1930)

Stachys drummondii **Benth.** – Downy woundwort (5) (1913), Pink-mint [Pinkmint] (124) (1937) TX

Stachys germanica **L.** – Downy woundwort (5) (1913), Hedge net-tle [Hedgenettle, Hedge-nettle] (1, 2, 93) (1895–1936), Mouse-ear [Mouse ear, Mouse ears, Mouse's ear, Mows eare] (5) (1913), Woolly betony (138) (1923)

Stachys glabra **Riddell** – See *Stachys tenuifolia* Willd.

Stachys grandiflora **(Willd.) Benth.** – Big betony (138) (1923)

Stachys homotricha **(Fern.) Rydb.** – See *Stachys pilosa* Nutt. var. *pilosa*

Stachys hyssopifolia **Michx.** – Coast hedge nettle (5) (1913), Hyssop hedge-nettle [Hyssop hedge nettle] (5) (1913)

Stachys **L.** – Betony (109, 138, 155) (1923–1949), Broad-tooth hedge-nettle [Broad-toothed hedge nettle] (5) (1913), Épiaire (French) (158) (1900), Hedge nettle [Hedgenettle, Hedge-nettle] (4, 10, 50, 63, 106, 156, 158) (1818–present), Rattlesnake-tail [Rattle snake tail] (183) (~1756), Woundwort [Wound-wort] (10, 106, 158, 184) (1793–1930), Yerba de la feridura (Spanish) (158) (1900), Ziest (German) (158) (1900)

Stachys latidens **Small ex Britt.** – Broad-tooth hedge-nettle [Broad-toothed hedge nettle] (5) (1913)

Stachys nuttallii **Shuttlw. ex Benth.** – Common betony (138) (1923), Light-green hedge nettle (5) (1913), Nuttall's hedge-nettle [Nuttall's hedge nettle] (5) (1913), Sage-like hedge-nettle [Sage-like hedge nettle] (5) (1913)

Stachys officinalis **(L.) Trev.** – Bethony (179) (1526), Betonica (57) (1917), Betonie with white flowers (178) (1526), Betony (5) (1913), Bishop's-wort [Bishop's wort, Bishopswort] (5) (1913), Common betony (138) (1923), Herb Christopher [Herb-Christopher] (5) (1913), Lamb's-ears [Lambs-ears] (109) (1949), Wild hop [Wild hops] (5) (1913), Wood betony [Wood-betony, Woodbetony] (5, 92) (1876–1913)

Stachys palustris **L.** – All-heal [All heal] (107, 156) (1919–1923), Ande'gobûg (Chippewa, crow leaf) (40) (1928), Clown's all-heal [Claownes All-heale] (5, 178) (1526–1913), Clown's woundwort (5, 156) (1913–1923), Clown's-heal [Clown heal, Clown's heal] (5, 92, 156) (1876–1923), Cockhead [Cock head] (5) (1913), Com-mon hedge nettle (62) (1912), Deadnettle [Dead-nettle, Dead nettle] (5, 156) (1913–1923), Hedge nettle [Hedgenettle, Hedge-nettle] (5, 40, 72, 82, 85, 92, 93, 127, 131, 156) (1899–1936), Marsh wound-wort (5, 93, 156) (1913–1936), Rough-weed [Rough weed] (5, 62, 156) (1912–1923), Slender hedge-nettle [Slender hedge nettle] (82) (1930), Woundwort [Wound-wort] (82, 107, 156) (1919–1930)

Stachys palustris **L.** var. *phaneropoda* **Weatherby** – See *Stachys pilosa* Nutt. var. *pilosa*

Stachys palustris **L.** var. *pilosa* **(Nutt.) Fern.** – See *Stachys pilosa* Nutt. var. *pilosa*

Stachys palustris **L.** var. *puberula* **Jennings** – See *Stachys pilosa* Nutt. var. *pilosa*

Stachys pilosa **Nutt.** – Hairy hedge-nettle [Hairy hedgenettle] (50) (present)

Stachys pilosa **Nutt.** var. *arenicola* **(Britton) G. Mulligan & D. Munro** – Corn woundwort (5, 156) (1913–1923), Hairy hedge-nettle [Hairy hedgenettle] (50) (present), Sand hedge-nettle [Sand hedge nettle] (5) (1913)

Stachys pilosa **Nutt.** var. *pilosa* – Coast hedge nettle (5) (1913), Hairy hedge-nettle [Hairy hedgenettle] (50) (present), Hedge nettle [Hedgenettle, Hedge-nettle] (3, 4) (1977–1986), Hyssop hedge-nettle [Hyssop hedge nettle] (5) (1913), Marsh betony (4) (1986), Pink-mint [Pinkmint] (124) (1937)

Stachys salvioides **Small.** – See *Stachys nuttallii* Shuttlw. ex Benth.

Stachys tenuifolia **Willd.** – Big betony (138) (1923), Dense-flower hedge-nettle [Dense-flowered hedge nettle] (5, 72) (1907–1913), Hyssop hedge-nettle [Hyssop hedge nettle] (156) (1923), Slender-leaf betony [Slenderleaf betony] (3, 4, 155) (1942–1986), Smooth hedge-nettle [Smooth hedge nettle, Smooth hedgenettle] (5, 50, 72, 93, 97) (1907–present), Thin-leaf betony [Thinleaf betony] (4) (1986)

Stanleya bipinnata – See *Stanleya pinnata* (Pursh) Britt. var. *bipinnata* (Greene) Rollins

Stanleya integrifolia **James ex Torr.** – See *Stanleya pinnata* (Pursh) Britton var. *integrifolia* (James ex Torr.) Rollins

Stanleya **Nutt.** – Desert prince's-plume [Desert princesplume] (50, 155) (1942–present)

Stanleya pinnata **(Pursh) Britt.** var. *bipinnata* **(Greene) Rollins** – Prince's-plum [Princesplum] (148) (1939)

Stanleya pinnata **(Pursh) Britton** – Golden prince's-plume [Golden princesplume] (50) (present), Prince's-plume [Prince's plume, Princesplume] (4) (1986), Stanleya (5, 131) (1899–1913)

Stanleya pinnata **(Pursh) Britton** var. *integrifolia* **(James ex Torr.) Rollins** – Desert prince's-plume [Desert princesplume] (50) (present), Prince's-plume [Prince's plume, Princesplume] (1, 3, 4, 50, 85, 106) (1930–present), Whole-leaf desert prince's-plume [Wholeleaf desert princesplume] (155) (1942)

Stanleya pinnata **(Pursh) Britton** var. *pinnata* – Prince's-plume [Prince's plume, Princesplume] (3) (1977)

Stanleya pinnata **(Pursh) Britton** var. *typica* **Rollins** – See *Stanleya pinnata* (Pursh) Britton var. *pinnata*

Stapelia **L.** – Blue elderberry (106) (1930), Carrion-flower [Carrion-flower, Carrion flower] (109, 155) (1942–1949)

Staphylea bolanderi **Gray** – Bladder nut [Bladder-nut, Bladdernut] ot Bladder nut tree (8) (1785), Bolander's bladdernut [Bolander bladdernut] (138) (1923)

Staphylea **L.** – Bladder nut [Bladder-nut, Bladdernut] ot Bladder nut tree (4, 13, 15, 50, 93, 109, 138, 158) (1849–present), Nez-coupé (French) (8) (1785)

Staphylea trifolia **L.** – American bladdernut [American bladder-nut, American bladder nut] (2, 4, 50, 5, 65, 72, 97, 107, 109, 138, 155, 156) (1895–present), Bladder nut [Bladder-nut, Bladdernut] ot Bladder nut tree (58, 61, 82, 92, 95, 177, 184, 187) (1793–1930), Nez-coupé à feuilles ternée (French) (8) (1785), Three-leaf bladder nut [Three leaved bladder nut] (190) (~1759), Three-leaf bladdernut tree [Three-leaved bladder-nut-tree] (8) (1785)

Statice – See *Limonium* Mill.

Statice caroliniana – See *Limonium carolinianum* (Walt.) Britt.

Statice carolinianus – See *Limonium carolinianum* (Walt.) Britt.

Steinchisma hians **(Ell.) Nash** – Gaping grass (50) (present), Gaping panic grass (5) (1913)

Steironema ciliatum **(L.) Raf.** – See *Lysimachia ciliata* L.

Steironema hybridum **(Michx.) Ref.** – See *Lysimachia hybrida* Michx.

Steironema intermedium **Kearney** – See *Lysimachia tonsa* (Wood) Wood ex Pax & R. Knuth

Steironema laevigatum **T. J. Howell** – See *Lysimachia lanceolata* Walt.

Steironema lanceolatum **(Walt.) Gray** – See *Lysimachia lanceolata* Walt.

Steironema lanceolatum **(Walt.) Gray** var. *hybridum* **(Michx.) Gray** – See *Lysimachia lanceolata* Walt.

Steironema pumilum **Greene** – See *Lysimachia ciliata* L.

Steironema quadriflorum **(Sims.) A. S. Hitchc.** – See *Lysimachia quadrifolia* L.

Steironema radicans **(Hook.) Gray** – See *Lysimachia radicans* Hook.

Steironema radicans **Gray.** – See *Lysimachia radicans* Hook.

Steironema **Raf.** – See *Lysimachia* L.

Stellaria alsine **Grimm** – Bog starwort [Bog-starwort] (5, 19, 187) (1818–1913), Bog stitchwort (5, 156, 187) (1818–1923), Fountain chickweed (187) (1818), Marsh chickweed (5, 156) (1913–1923), Marsh stitchwort (5, 156) (1913–1923), Swamp stitchwort [Swamp stichwort] (5, 156) (1913–1923)

Stellaria aquatica **(L.) Scop.** – See *Myosoton aquaticum* (L.) Moench

Stellaria borealis **Bigelow** – Northern starwort (50) (1942–present), Speedwell chickweed (46) (1671)

Stellaria borealis **Bigelow** subsp. *borealis* – Northern stitchwort (5, 131) (1899–1913)

Stellaria borealis **Bigelow** var. *simcoei* **(T. J. Howell) Fern.** – See *Stellaria calycantha* (Ledeb.) Bong.

Stellaria calycantha **(Ledeb.) Bong.** – Northern starwort (155) (1942–present), Northern stitchwort (4) (1986)

Stellaria corei **Shinners** – Tennessee chickweed (5) (1913)

Stellaria crassifolia **Ehrh.** – Fleshy starwort (50) (present), Fleshy stitchwort (4, 122) (1937–1986)

Stellaria crassifolia **Ehrh.** var. *crassifolia* – Fleshy starwort (50) (present), Fleshy stitchwort (5) (1913)

Stellaria edwardsii **R. Br.** var. *arctica* **(Schischkin) Hultén** – See *Stellaria longipes* Goldie subsp. *longipes*

Stellaria fontinalis **(Short & Peter) B. L. Robins.** – Water stitchwort (5) (1913)

Stellaria graminea **L.** – Common switchwort (3) (1977), Goosebill [Goosbyll] (179) (1526), Grass-like starwort [Grasslike starwort] (50) (present), Lesser starwort (5) (1913), Lesser stitchwort (5) (1913), Long-leaf starwort [Longleaf starwort, Long-leaved starwort, Long-leaved star wort] (187) (1818), Long-leaf stitchwort [Long-leaved stitchwort, Long-leaved stitch wort] (187) (1818)

Stellaria holostea **L.** – Adder's-meat [Adder's meat] (5, 156) (1913–1923) no longer in use by 1923, All-bone [Allbone, All bones, All-bones] (5, 156, 180) (1633–1923), Easter bell [Easter-bell, Easter-bell, Easter bells, Easterbells] (5, 109, 138, 156) (1923–1949), Greater starwort (5, 156) (1913–1923), Greater stichwort (5, 156) (1913–1923), Lady's-lint [Lady's lint] (5, 156) (1913–1923) no longer in use by 1923, Piskies (5, 156) (1913–1923) no longer in use by 1923, Pixie (5) (1913) no longer in use by 1923, Snake flower [Snakeflower, Snake-flower] (5, 156) (1913–1923) no longer in use by 1923, Snake-grass [Snake grass, Snakegrass] (5, 156) (1913–1923) no longer in use by 1923, Snapjack [Snap jack, Snap-jack] (5, 156) (1913–1923) no longer in use by 1923, Snappers (5, 156) (1913–1923) no longer in use by 1923, Star flower [Starflower, Star-flower] (5, 156) (1913–1923) no longer in use by 1923, Stychewort [Styche wort] (179) (1526), Thunder flower [Thunder-flower] (5, 156) (1913–1923) no longer in use by 1923, White bird's-eye [White bird's eye] (5) (1913), White-bird [White bird] (156) (1923)

Stellaria hultenii **Boivin** – See *Stellaria longipes* Goldie subsp. *longipes*

Stellaria humifusa **Rottb.** – Low chickweed (5) (1913)

Stellaria **L.** – Chickweed [Chick-weed, Chick weed] (1, 4, 13, 15, 156, 167) (1814–1986), Starwort [Star-wort, Star wort] (1, 13, 50, 15, 155, 156) (1849–present), Stitchwort [Stitch wort] (4, 10, 19) (1818–1986)

Stellaria lanceolata **(Michx.) Torr.** – Blind starwort (19) (1840)

Stellaria laxmannii **Fisch.** – See *Stellaria longipes* Goldie subsp. *longipes*

Stellaria longifolia **Muhl. ex Willd.** – Long-leaf starwort [Longleaf starwort, Long-leaved starwort, Long-leaved star wort] (50) (present), Long-leaf stitchwort [Long-leaved stitchwort, Long-leaved stitch wort] (3, 4, 156) (1923–1986), Stitchwort [Stitch wort] (46) (1671)

Stellaria longifolia **Muhl. ex Willd.** var. *laeta* **(Richards.) S. Wats.** – See *Stellaria longipes* Goldie subsp. *longipes*

Stellaria longifolia **Muhl. ex Willd.** var. *longifolia* – Long-leaf stitchwort [Long-leaved stitchwort, Long-leaved stitch wort] (5, 72, 131) (1899–1913), Long-stalk starwort [Longstalk starwort] (50) (present), Stitchwort [Stitch wort] (93) (1936)

Stellaria longipes **Goldie** – Long-stalk stitchwort [Long-stalked stitchwort] (4, 5) (1913–1986)

Stellaria longipes **Goldie** subsp. *longipes* – Cheekweed [Cheek weed] (46) (1671), Chickweed [Chick-weed, Chick weed] (1, 4, 13, 15, 156, 167) (1814–1986), Grass-leaf stitchwort [Grass-leaved stitch-wort] (187) (1818), Long-stalk starwort [Longstalk starwort] (50, 155) (1942–present), Meadow-star [Meadow star] (92) (1876), Stitchwort [Stitch wort] (46) (1671)

***Stellaria longipes* Goldie var. *subvestita* (Greene) Polunin** – See *Stellaria longipes* Goldie subsp. *longipes*

***Stellaria media* (L.) Cyr.** – See *Stellaria media* (L.) Vill.

***Stellaria media* (L.) Vill.** – Adder's-mouth [Adder mouth, Adder's mouth (92) (1876), Chickenweed [Chicken weed, Chicken-weed] (156) (1923) no longer in use by 1923, Chickweed [Chick-weed, Chick weed] (19, 40, 49, 57, 80, 92, 106, 107, 122, 155) (1840–1942), Common chickweed (3, 4, 50, 15, 156, 187) (1818–present), Satin-flower [Satin flower] (92, 156) (1898–1923), Star chickweed (49) (1898), Starwort [Star-wort, Star wort] (107, 156) (1919–1923), Stellaria (57) (1917), Stichwort (92) (1876), Stitchwort [Stitch wort] (92, 107) (1876–1919), Tongue-grass [Tongue grass] (156) (1923) no longer in use by 1923, White bird's-eye [White bird's eye] (156) (1923) no longer in use by 1923, Wi'nibĭdja'bibaga'no (Chippewa, toothplant) (40) (1928), Winterweed [Winter weed, Winter-weed] (156) (1923)

Stellaria media* (L.) Vill. subsp. *media – Chickenweed [Chicken weed, Chicken-weed] (5, 157, 158) (1900–1929), Chickweed [Chick-weed, Chick weed] (7, 42, 85, 95, 131) (1814–1932), Common chickweed (5, 62, 72, 93, 97, 157, 158, 165) (1768–1937), Satin flower [Satin-flower] (157, 158) (1900–1929), Satin-flower [Satin flower] (157, 158) (1900–1929), Tongue-grass [Tongue grass] (157, 158) (1900–1929), White bird's-eye [White bird's eye] (5) (1913), White-bird [White bird] (157, 158) (1900–1929), Winterweed [Winter weed, Wnter-weed] (5, 157, 158) (1900–1929)

***Stellaria nodosa* Scop.** – See *Sagina nodosa* (L.) Fenzl

***Stellaria palmeri* (Rydb.) Tidestrom** – See *Stellaria longipes* Goldie subsp. *longipes*

***Stellaria palustris* (Murr.) Retz.** – Glaucous starwort [Glaucous star wort] (5) (1913), Great chickweed (15, 156) (1895–1923), Meadow-star [Meadow star] (92) (1876), Stitchwort [Stitch wort] (92) (1876)

***Stellaria pubera* Michx.** – Great chickweed (5, 158) (1900–1913), Great starwort (155) (1942), Oval-leaf starwort [Oval-leaved star wort] (187) (1818), Star chickweed (5, 50, 156, 158) (1900–present)

***Stellaria uliginosa* Sr.** – See *Stellaria alsine* Grimm

***Stenanthium gramineum* (Ker-Gawl.) Morong** – Death camas [Death-camas, Death camass] (156) (1923), Eastern featherbells (50) (present), Grass-leaf stenanthium [Grass-leaved stenanthium] (5) (1913), Hog-potato [Hog potato, Hog's potato, Hog-potatoe, Hog's potato] (156) (1923)

***Stenanthium gramineum* (Ker-Gawl.) Morong var. *robustum* (S. Wats.) Fern.** – Eastern featherbells (50) (present), Featherfleece [Feather-fleece] (109, 138) (1923–1949), Stout stenanthium (5) (1913)

***Stenocereus thurberi* (Engelm.) Buxbaum** – Pitahaya (Mexicans) (103, 107) (1870–1919), Pitahya dulce (104) (1896), Thurber's cactus (103) (1870)

***Stenolobium* D. Don** – See *Tecoma* Juss.

***Stenolobium stans* Seem.** – See *Tecoma stans* (L.) Juss. ex Kunth

***Stenophyllus capillaris* (L.) Britton** – See *Bulbostylis capillaris* (L.) Kunth ex C. B. Clarke subsp. *capillaris*

***Stenophyllus* Raf.** – See *Bulbostylis* Kunth

***Stenosiphon linifolium* (Nutt.) Britton** – See *Stenosiphon linifolius* (Nutt. ex James) Heynh.

***Stenosiphon linifolius* (Nutt. ex James) Heynh.** – False gaura (50) (present), Flax-leaf stenosiphon [Flax-leaved stenosiphon] (5, 97) (1913–1937), Giant gaura (124) (1937) TX, Narrow-leaf stenotus [Narrow-leaved stenotus] (5) (1913), October beauty (86) (1878) name suggested by Thomas Meehan, Stenosiphon (3, 4, 50, 86, 158) (1878–present)

***Stenosiphon linifolius* (Nutt.) Britton** – See *Stenosiphon linifolius* (Nutt. ex James) Heynh.

***Stenosiphon* Spach** – Stenosiphon (50, 158) (1900–present)

***Stenosiphon virgatus* Spach** – See *Stenosiphon linifolius* (Nutt. ex James) Heynh.

***Stenotaphrum secundatum* (Walt.) Kuntze** – Mission grass [Mission-grass] (94) (1901), Shore grass [Shore-grass] (163) (1852), St. Augustine grass [St. Augustine's grass] (109, 122, 138, 163) (1852–1949)

***Stenotus acaulis* (Nutt.) Nutt.** – Tufted goldenweed (155) (1942)

Stenotus acaulis* (Nutt.) Nutt. var. *acaulis – Stemless goldenweed (155) (1942)

***Stenotus armerioides* Nutt.** – Thrift mock goldenweed (50) (present)

Stenotus armerioides* Nutt. var. *armerioides – Thrift mock goldenweed (50) (present)

***Stenotus* Nutt.** – Stenotus (158) (1900), Mock goldenweed (50) (present)

***Stephanandra incisa* (Thunb.) Zabel** – Cut-leaf stephanandra [Cutleaf stephanandra] (138) (1923), Yeddo stephanandra (138) (1923)

***Stephanandra* Sieb. & Zucc.** – Stephanadra (138) (1923)

Stephanomeria minor* (Hook.) Nutt. var. *minor – Narrow-leaf wire-lettuce [Narrowleaf wirelettuce] (50) (present)

***Stephanomeria* Nutt.** – Ptiloria (158) (1900), Skeleton-weed [Skeleton weed, Skeletonweed] (4) (1986), Skeleton-weed [Skeletonweed] (4) (1986), Wire-lettuce [Wirelettuce, Wire lettuce] (4, 50, 155) (1942–present)

***Stephanomeria pauciflora* (Torr.) A. Nels.** – Brown-plume ptiloria [Brown-plumed ptiloria] (5, 93, 97) (1913–1937), Brown-plume wire-lettuce [Brownplume wirelettuce] (50) (present), Wire-lettuce [Wirelettuce, Wire lettuce] (3) (1977)

***Stephanomeria runcinata* Nutt.** – Desert wire-lettuce [Desert wirelettuce] (50, 155) (1942–present), White-plume ptiloria [White-plumed ptiloria] (5, 93) (1913–1936)

***Sterculia* L.** – Bottletree [Bottle-tree] (138) (1923), Chinese parasol tree [Chinese parasoltree, Chinese parasol-tree] (138) (1923), Stewartia (8, 138) (1785–1923), Stewartia (French) (8) (1785)

***Sternbergia lutea* (L.) Ker-Gawl. ex Spreng.** – False daffodil [False-daffodil] (138) (1923)

***Stewartia malacodendron* L.** – Malacodendron (174, 177) (1753–1762), Round-fruit stewartia [Round-fruited stewartia] (5) (1913), Stewartia (174, 177) (1753–1762), Stewartia de Virginie (French) (8) (1785), Virginia stewartia [Virginian stewartia] (8, 138) (1785–1923)

***Stewartia ovata* (Cav.) Weatherby** – Angled-fruit stewartia [Angled-fruited stewartia] (5) (1913), Mountain stewartia (5, 138) (1913–1923)

***Stewartia pentagyna* L'Her.** – See *Stewartia ovata* (Cav.) Weatherby

***Sticta pulmonaria* (L.) Biroli** – Hazel crottles (92) (1876)

***Sticta pulmonaria* (L.) Schaer.** – See *Lobaria pulmonaria* (L.) Hoffm.

***Stigmaphyllon* A. Juss.** – Amazon-vine [Amazonvine] (50, 138) (1923–present)

***Stillingia* Garden ex L.** – Privet-leaf stillingia [Privet-leaved stillingia] (20) (1857), Queen's-root [Queens' root, Queen's root Queen root, Queen-root] (1, 156) (1923–1932), Stillingia (155, 158) (1900–1942), Toothleaf (50) (present)

***Stillingia sebifera* [(L.) Michx.]** – See *Triadica sebifera* (L.) Small

***Stillingia sylvatica* Garden ex L.** – Cock-up-hat [Cockup-hat] (6, 7, 92, 158) (1828–1900), Marcory (6, 7, 92, 158) (1828–1900), Nettle-potato [Nettle potato, Nettle potatoe] (5, 64, 156, 158) (1900–1923), Queen-of-the-lights [Queen of the lights] (75) (1894) GA, corruption of Queen's delight, Queen's-delight [Queens' delight, Queen's delight] (3, 4, 5, 6, 7, 49, 50, 53, 54, 55, 57, 58, 64, 75, 92, 97, 122, 156, 158) (1869–present), Queen's-delight stillingia [Queensdelight stillingia] (155) (1942), Queen's-root [Queens' root, Queen's root Queen root, Queen-root] (5, 6, 49, 52, 53, 57, 58, 60, 64, 92, 156, 158) (1869–1923), Silverleaf [Silver leaf, Silver-leaf] (49, 53, 58, 64, 92, 156, 158) (1869–1923), Stillingia (52, 54, 55, 57, 59, 61, 64, 92) (1870–1917), Stillingie (French) (6, 158) (1892–1900), Stillingie (German) (6, 158) (1892–1900), Yawroot [Yaw root, Yaw-root] (5, 6, 7, 49, 53, 55, 58, 92, 156, 158) (1828–1923)

***Stipa avenacea* Walt.** – See *Piptochaetium avenaceum* (L.) Parodi

Stipa bloomeri **Boland.** – See *Achnatherum ×bloomeri* (Boland.) Barkworth [*hymenoides × occidentale*]

Stipa canadensis **Poir.** – See *Piptatherum canadense* (Poir) Barkworth

Stipa columbiana **Macoun** – See *Achnatherum lemmonii* (Vasey) Barkworth

Stipa comata **Trin. & Rupr.** – See *Hesperostipa comata* (Trin. & Rupr.) Barkworth subsp. *comata*

Stipa coronata **Thurber** – See *Achnatherum coronatum* (Thurb.) Barkworth

Stipa eminens – See *Achnatherum eminens* (Cav.) Barkworth

Stipa fimbriata – See *Piptochaetium fimbriatum* (Kunth) A.S. Hitchc.

Stipa lettermani **Vasey** – See *Achnatherum lettermanii* (Vasey) Barkworth

Stipa leucotricha **Trin. & Rupr.** – See *Nassella leucotricha* (Trin. & Rupr.) Pohl

Stipa macounii **Scribn.** – See *Piptatherum canadense* (Poir) Barkworth

Stipa neesiana **Trin. & Rupr.** – See *Nassella neesiana* (Trin. & Rupr.) Barkworth

Stipa neomexicana **(Thurb.) Scribn.** – See *Hesperostipa neomexicana* (Thurb. ex Coult.) Barkworth

Stipa neo-mexicana **(Thurb.) Scribn.** – See *Hesperostipa neomexicana* (Thurb. ex Coult.) Barkworth

Stipa occidentalis **Thurb. ex S. Wats.** – See *Achnatherum occidentale* (Thurb. ex S. Wats.) Barkworth subsp. *occidentale*

Stipa occidentalis **Thurb. ex Walts var. minor (Vasey)** – See *Achnatherum occidentale* (Thurb. ex S. Wats.) Barkworth subsp. *occidentale*

Stipa oregonensis **Scribn.** – See *Achnatherum occidentale* (Thurb. ex S. Watson) Barkworth

Stipa parishii **Vasey** – See *Achnatherum parishii* (Vasey) Barkworth var. *parishii*

Stipa pringlei **Scribn.** – See *Piptochaetium pringlei* (Beal) Parodi

Stipa richardsonii **Link** – See *Achnatherum richardsonii* (Link) Barkworth

Stipa robusta **Scribn.** – See *Achnatherum robustum* (Vasey) Barkworth

Stipa spartea **Trin.** – See *Hesperostipa spartea* (Trin.) Barkworth

Stipa spartea **Trin. var. curtiseta A. S. Hitchc.** – See *Hesperostipa comata* (Trin. & Rupr.) Barkworth

Stipa speciosa **Trin. & Rupr.** – See *Achnatherum speciosum* (Trin. & Rupr.) Barkworth

Stipa tenuissima **Trin.** – See *Nassella tenuissima* (Trin.) Barkworth

Stipa vaseyi **Scribn.** – See *Achnatherum robustum* (Vasey) Barkworth

Stipa viridula **Trin.** – See *Nassella viridula* (Trin.) Barkworth

Stizolobium – See *Mucuna* Adans.

Stizolobium deeringianum – See *Mucuna pruriens* (L.) DC. var. *utilis* (Wallich ex Wight) Baker ex Burck

Stizolobium hassjoo **Piper & Tracy** – See *Mucuna pruriens* (L.) DC. var. *utilis* (Wallich ex Wight) Baker ex Burck

Stokesia laevis – See *Stokesia laevis* (Hill) Greene

Stokesia laevis **(Hill) Greene** – Blue stokesia (86) (1878), Stokes' aster [Stokes aster] (86, 109) (1878–1949), Stokesia (138) (1923)

Stokesia **L'Hér.** – Stokes' aster [Stokes aster] (109) (1949), Stokesia (138) (1923) for Johnathan Stokes, 1755–1831, English botanist with no connection to flower

Stomoisia cornuta **(Michx.) Raf.** – See *Utricularia cornuta* Michx.

Stomoisia juncea **(Vahl.) Barnhart** – See *Utricularia juncea* Vahl

Stomoisia virgulata **Barnhart** – See *Utricularia juncea* Vahl

Streptanthus hyacinthoides **Hook.** – Smooth jewel-flower [Smooth jewelflower] (50) (present), Velvet flower [Velvet-flower] (97) (1937)

Streptanthus maculatus **Nutt. subsp. obtusifolius (Hook.) Rollins** – Arkansas cabbage (19) (1840), Bottletree [Bottle-tree] (138) (1923)

Streptanthus **Nutt.** – Twist flower [Twist-flower, Twistflower] (4, 155) (1942–1986)

Streptopus amplexifolius **(L.) DC.** – Clasping-leaf twistedstalk [Clasping-leaved twisted stalk, Clasping-leaved twisted-stalk, Clasingleaf twistedstalk] (5, 97, 155) (1913–1942), Clasp-leaf twistedstalk [Claspleaf twistedstalk] (50) (present), Liverberry [Liver-berry, Liver berry] (5, 75) (1894–1913) ME, from said medicinal properties of cathartic fruit, Twisted-stalk [Twistedstalk, Twisted stalk] (85, 156) (1923–1932), White mandarin (3) (1977)

Streptopus amplexifolius **(L.) DC. var. amplexifolius** – Laurus alexandrina (174) (1753)

Streptopus distortus **Michx.** – See *Streptopus amplexifolius* (L.) DC.

Streptopus lanceolatus **(Ait.) Reveal var. roseus (Michx.) Reveal** – Agwĭn'gûsibûg (Chippewa, ground squirrel leaf) (40) (1928), Jacob's-ladder [Jacob's ladder, Jacobs-ladder] (78) (1898) ME, Liverberry [Liver-berry, Liver berry] (5, 75) (1894–1913) ME, from said medicinal properties of cathartic fruit, Rose bellwort [Rose bell wort] (19) (1840), Rosy twisted-stalk [Rosy twistedstalk] (138) (1923), Scootberry [Scoot berries] (79) (1891) NH, Sessile-leaf twisted-stalk [Sessile-leaved twisted stalk] (5) (1913), Solomon's-seal [Solomon's seal, Solomon seal, Solomon's seal, Solomons-seal, S'alomon's seal, Salamons seale] (78) (1898) Western US, Twisted-stalk [Twistedstalk, Twisted stalk] (40, 50, 156) (1923–present)

Streptopus lanuginosus **Michx.** – See *Disporum lanuginosum* (Michx.) Nichols

Streptopus **Michx.** – See *Uvularia* L.

Streptopus roseus **Michx.** – See *Streptopus lanceolatus* (Ait.) Reveal var. *roseus* (Michx.) Reveal

Strobus americanus – possibly *Pinus strobus* L.

Strobus weymouthiana **Opiz.** – See *Pinus strobus* L.

Strophostyles **Ell.** – Fuzzybean (50) (present), Wild bean [Wild-bean, Wildbean, Wild beans] (1, 4, 82, 155, 158) (1900–1986)

Strophostyles helvola **(L.) Britton** – See *Strophostyles helvula* (L.) Ell.

Strophostyles helvola **(L.) Ell.** – See *Strophostyles helvula* (L.) Ell.

Strophostyles helvula **(L.) Ell.** – Makatomnič̣a (Lakota, ground bean) (121) (1918?–1970?), Trailing fuzzybean (50) (present), Trailing wild bean [Trailing wildbean] (5, 82, 93, 97, 121, 131, 155) (1899–1937), Trailing wild rose (72) (1907) IA, Wild bean [Wild-bean, Wildbean, Wild beans] (3, 80, 95, 145) (1897–1977)

Strophostyles leiosperma **(Torr. & Gray) Piper** – Omnica hu (Lakota) (121) (1918?–1970?), Slick-seed bean (4) (1986), Slick-seed fuzzybean [Slickseed fuzzybean] (50) (present), Small wild bean [Small wildbean] (5, 72, 82, 93, 97, 131, 155) (1899–1937), Smooth-seed wild bean [Smoothseed wild bean] (3) (1977), Wild bean [Wildbean, Wildbean, Wild beans] (85, 95, 121, 145) (1897–1932)

Strophostyles pauciflora **(Benth.) S. Wats.** – See *Strophostyles leiosperma* (Torr. & Gray) Piper

Strophostyles umbellata **(Muhl.) Britton** – Pink wild bean (5, 97) (1913–1937)

Struthiopteris pennsylvanica **W.** – See *Matteuccia struthiopteris* (L.) Todaro

Strychnos **L.** – Ordeal root (92) (1876)

Strychnos spinosa **Lam.** – Natal orange [Natal-orange] (109) (1949)

Stuckenia **Boerner** – Pondweed [Pondweeds, Pond weed] (50) (present)

Stuckenia filiformis **(Pers) Boerner** – Fine-leaf pondweed [Fineleaf pondweed] (50) (present)

Stuckenia filiformis **(Pers) Boerner subsp. alpinus (Blytt) Haynes, D. H. Les, & M. Kral** – Fine-leaf pondweed [Fineleaf pondweed] (50) (present)

Stuckenia filiformis **(Pers) Boerner subsp. filiformis** – Filiform pondweed (5) (1913), Fine-leaf pondweed [Fineleaf pondweed] (50) (present), Western pondweed (85) (1932)

Stuckenia filiformis **(Pers) Boerner subsp. occidentalis (J. W. Robbins) Haynes, D. H. Les, & M. Kral** – Inland pondweed (5, 85) (1913–1932), Western fine-leaf pondweed [Western fineleaf pondweed] (50) (present), Western pondweed (131) (1899)

Stuckenia pectinatus **(L.) Boerner** – Duck-grass (156) (1923), Duck-moss (156) (1923), Fennel-leaf pondweed [Fennel-leaved pondweed, Fennel-leaved pond-weed, Fennelleaf pondweed] (5, 72, 93, 97, 120, 131, 155, 156, 158) (1899–1942), Pondgrass [Pondgrass] (5, 156, 158) (1900–1923), Potato-moss (156) (1923), Sago pondweed [Sago pond-weed] (3, 50, 85, 156) (1923–present)

Stuckenia vaginatus (**Turcz.**) **Holub** – Interrupted pondweed (5) (1913), Sheathed pondweed (50, 155) (1942–present)

Stylisma aquatica (**Walt.**) **Chapman** – Water breweria (5) (1913)

Stylisma humistrata (**Walt.**) **Chapman** – Southern breweria (5) (1913)

Stylisma pickeringii (**Torr. ex M. A. Curtis**) **Gray** – Patterson's dawn-flower (50) (present), Pickering's breweria (5, 97) (1913–1937)

Stylisma pickeringii (**Torr. ex M. A. Curtis**) **Gray var.** *pattersonii* (**Fern. & Schub.**) **Myint** – Patterson's dawnflower (50) (present), Pickering's breweria (72) (1907)

Stylomecon heterophylla (**Benth.**) **G. Taylor** – Flame-poppy [Flame-poppy] (138) (1923)

Stylophorum diphyllum (**Michx.**) **Nutt.** – Celandine poppy (2, 5, 13, 15, 92, 109, 138, 156) (1849–1949), Yellow poppy (5, 156) (1913–1923)

Stylophorum diphyllum **Nutt.** – See *Stylophorum diphyllum* (Michx.) Nutt.

Stylosanthes biflora (**L.**) **B.S.P. var.** *hispidissima* (**Michx.**) **Pollard & Ball** – See *Stylosanthes biflora* (L.) Britton, Sterns & Poggenb.

Stylosanthes biflora (**L.**) **Britton, Sterns & Poggenb.** – Afterbirth-weed (158) (1900), Decumbent pencil flower (5) (1913), Hispid sty-losanthes (187) (1818), Pencil flower [Pencil-flower] (3, 4, 5, 19, 57, 92, 97, 158) (1840–1986), Sidebeak pencil-flower [Sidebeak pencil-flower] (50) (Present), Yellow clover (174, 177) (1753–1762)

Stylosanthes elatior **Schwartz.** – See *Stylosanthes biflora* (L.) Britton, Sterns & Poggenb.

Stylosanthes riparia **Kearney** – See *Stylosanthes biflora* (L.) Britton, Sterns & Poggenb.

Styphonia serrata – See *Rhus integrifolia* (Nutt.) W. H. Brewer & S. Watson

Styrandra **Raf.** – See *Maianthemum* G. H. Weber ex Wiggers

Styrax americana **Lam.** – See *Styrax americanus* Lam.

Styrax americanus **Lam.** – American snowball (156) (1923), Ameri-can snowbell (138) (1923), American snowdrop tree (122) (1937) TX, Carolina storax tree [Carolinian storax tree] (8) (1785), Downy storax (5, 122) (1913–1937), Large silver bell tree (124) (1937) TX, Smooth storax (5, 97, 156) (1913–1937), Spring-orange [Spring or-ange] (5, 92, 156) (1876–1923), Syrax d'Amérique (French) (8) (1785)

Styrax glabrum **Lam.** – possibly *Styrax americanus* Lam.

Styrax grandifolius **Aiton** – American snowball (156) (1923), Large-leaf storax [Large-leaved storax] (5) (1913), Mock orange [Mock-orange, Mockorange] (156) (1923)

Styrax japonica – See *Styrax japonicus* Sieb. & Zucc.

Styrax japonicus **Sieb. & Zucc.** – Japanese snowbell (138) (1923)

Styrax **L.** – Snowbell (109, 138) (1923–1949), Spring-orange [Spring orange] (7) (1828), Storax or Storax tree [Storax trees] (2, 8, 10, 109, 167) (1785–1949), Styrax (French) (8) (1785)

Styrax platanifolius **Engelm. ex Torr.** – Sycamore-leaf storax [Syca-moreleaf storax] (122) (1937)

Styrax pulverulentus **Michx.** – See *Styrax americanus* Lam.

Suaeda americana (**Pers.**) **Fern.** – See *Suaeda calceoliformis* (Hook.) Moq.

Suaeda calceoliformis (**Hook.**) **Moq.** – American seepweed (155) (1942), Pursh's seepweed [Pursh seepweed] (50, 155) (1942–pres-ent), Sea blite [Sea-blite] (107) (1919), Sea goosefoot (156) (1923), Tall sea-blite (156) (1923), Western blite [Western blight] (131) (1899), Western sea blite [Western sea-blite] (5, 93) (1913–1936), Western seepweed (155) (1942)

Suaeda **Forsch. ex Scop** – See *Suaeda* Forsk. ex J.F. Gmel.

Suaeda **Forsk. ex J. F. Gmel.** – Alkali seepweed (155) (1942), Blite (158) (1900), Sea-blite [Sea blite] (1, 2, 158) (1895–1932), Seep-weed (4, 50, 155) (1942–present)

Suaeda fruticosa – See *Suaeda moquinii* (Torr.) Greene

Suaeda linearis (**Ell.**) **Moq.** – Sea goosefoot (5) (1913), Seepweed (122) (1937) TX, Tall sea-blite (5, 97) (1913–1937)

Suaeda linearis **Moq.** – See *Suaeda linearis* (Ell.) Moq.

Suaeda maritima (**L.**) **Dumort.** – Frog-grass [Frog grass, Frog grasse, Frogge-grasse] (178) (1526), Little glasswort [Little glasswoort] (178) (1526), Sea pig-weed (19) (1840)

Suaeda maritima (**L.**) **Dumort. subsp.** *maritima* – Annual sea blite (5) (1913), Low sea blite (5) (1913)

Suaeda maritima **Dum.** – See *Suaeda maritima* (L.) Dumort.

Suaeda minutiflora **S. Wats.** – See *Suaeda calceoliformis* (Hook.) Moq.

Suaeda moquinii (**Torr.**) **Greene** – Alkali seepweed (155) (1942), Bush seepweed (155) (1942), Mohave sea-blite [Mohave seablite] (50) (present), Seepweed (4) (1986), Torrey's seepweed [Torrey seep-weed] (155) (1942), Western blite [Western blight] (108) (1878)

Suaeda nigra **J. F. Macbr.** – See *Suaeda moquinii* (Torr.) Greene

Suaeda occidentalis (**S. Wats.**) **S. Wats.** – See *Suaeda calceoliformis* (Hook.) Moq.

Suaeda ramosissima (**Standl.**) **I. M. Johnston** – See *Suaeda moqui-nii* (Torr.) Greene

Suaeda suffrutescens **S. Wats.** – Desert seepweed (3, 4, 50, 155) (1942–present)

Suaeda torreyana **S. Wats.** – See *Suaeda moquinii* (Torr.) Greene

Subularia aquatica **L.** – Awlwort [Awl wort] (13, 15, 19, 92, 156) (1840–1923), Water awlwort (5) (1913)

Subularia **L.** – Awlwort [Awl wort] (13, 15) (1849–1895) from subula (awl)

Succisa australis (**Wulf.**) **Reichenb.** – See *Succisella inflexa* (Kluk) G. Beck

Succisa pratensis **Moench** – Devil's-bit [Devil's bit, Devilbit] (50) (present), Devil's-bit herb [Devil's bit herb] (92) (1876), Devil's-bit root [Devil's bit root] (92) (1876), Devil's-bite [Deuylles bytte] (179) (1526), Pincushion [Pincushions, Pin-cushion, Pin cushions] (76) (1896) Sulphur Grove OH, Scabious [Scabius, Scabyous] (92) (1876), Wood scabious (92) (1876)

Succisella inflexa (**Kluk**) **G. Beck** – Pincushion flower (5, 156) (1913–1923), Southern scabious (5) (1913)

Suckleya **Gray** – Remcope (179) (1526), Suckleya (50, 155, 158) (1900–present)

Suckleya suckleyana (**Torr.**) **Rydb.** – Poison suckleya (4, 50, 155) (1942–present), Suckleya (148) (1939)

Sullivantia sullivantii (**Torr. & Gray**) **Britton** – Sullivantia (5, 72) (1907–1913)

Svida amomum (**Mill.**) **Small** – See *Cornus amomum* Mill.

Svida femina (**Mill.**) **Rydb.** – See *Cornus foemina* Mill.

Svida **Opiz.** – See *Cornus* L.

Svida stolonifera (**Michx.**) **Rydb.** – See *Cornus sericea* L. subsp. *seri-cea*

Sweitenia mahogani **Jacq.** – See *Swietenia mahagoni* (L.) Jacq.

Swertia caroliniensis (**Walt.**) **Kuntze** – See *Frasera caroliniensis* Walt.

Swertia difformis **L.** – See *Sabatia difformis* (L.) Druce

Swertia **L.** – Green gentian (4) (1986)

Swietenia **Jacq.** – Mahogany or Mahogany tree (138) (1923)

Swietenia mahagoni (**L.**) **Jacq.** – Mahogany or Mahogany tree (7, 15, 20) (1828–1895), Mahogony (19, 109) (1840–1949) from native American name, West Indian mahogany (138) (1923)

Swietenia mahagoni **L.** – See *Swietenia mahagoni* (L.) Jacq.

Syagrus **C. Martius** – Arikury-palm [Arikurypalm] (155) (1942)

Syagrus romanzoffiana (**Cham.**) **Glassman** – Datil palm (138) (1923), Pindo palm (138) (1923)

Symphoria **J.** – possibly *Symphoricarpos* Duham.

Symphoria racemosa **Michx.** – See *Symphoricarpos albus* (L.) Blake var. *albus*

Symphoria **Raf.** – possibly *Symphoricarpos* Duham.

Symphoricarpos albus (**L.**) **Blake** – Airelle blanche (French) (8) (1785), Common snowberry (50) (present), Dwarf common snow-berry (155) (1942), Maïn'gamûna'tïg (Chippewa, wolf wood) (40) (1928), Pennsylvania white whortleberry [Pennsylvanian white whortle-berry] (8) (1785), Waxberry [Wax-berry, Wax berry] (40, 109) (1928–1949), White coralberry (4) (1986)

Symphoricarpos albus (**L.**) **Blake var.** *albus* – Bluewood [Blue-wood]

(38) (1820), Buckbrush [Buck brush, Buck-brush] (106) (1930), Common snowberry (138) (1923), Eggplant [Egg-plant, Egg plant] (5, 158) (1900–1913), Peter's-wort [Peter's wort] (19) (1840), Snowdrop-berry [Snow-drop-berry, Snowdrop berry] (5, 157, 158) (1900–1929), Waxberry [Wax-berry, Wax berry] (5, 75, 106, 157, 158) (1894–1930)

Symphoricarpos albus (L.) Blake var. *laevigatus* (Fern.) Blake – Canterbury (156) (1923) no longer in use by 1923, Coralberry [Coralberry, Coral berry] (37, 72, 93, 95, 97, 125, 131, 158) (1899–1936), Eggplant [Egg-plant, Egg plant] (156) (1923), Garden snowberry (138) (1923), Snowberry [Snow berry, Snow-berry] (82, 156) (1923–1930), Snowdrop-berry [Snow-drop-berry, Snowdrop berry] (156) (1923) no longer in use by 1923, Waxberry [Wax-berry, Wax berry] (156) (1923)

Symphoricarpos albus (L.) Blake var. *pauciflorus* (J.W. Robbins) S.F. Blake – Dwarf snowberry (138) (1923), Low snowberry (95, 131) (1899–1911), Snowberry [Snow berry, Snow-berry] (3, 40, 109, 130) (1895–1949)

Symphoricarpos Duham. – Buckbrush [Buck brush, Buck-brush] (112) (1937), Common snowberry (50, 155) (1942–present), Coralberry [Coral-berry, Coral berry] (1, 4, 82, 93, 112) (1930–1986), Honeysuckle [Honey suckle, Honey-suckle, Honisuckles] (35) (1806), Indian currant [Indian-currant, Indian currants] (82) (1930), Snowberry [Snow berry, Snow-berry] (1, 4, 50, 82, 108, 138, 146, 155, 156, 158, 160, 161) (1857–present), Stagberry [Stag-berry] (1) (1932), Wolfberry [Wolf berry, Wolf-berry] (1, 4) (1932–1986), possibly Badgerbrush [Badger-brush] (156) (1923), possibly Bluewood [Blue-wood] (7) (1828), possibly Raccoon-berry [Raccoon berry, Raccoonberry] (7) (1828)

Symphoricarpos Juss. – possibly *Symphoricarpos* Duham.

Symphoricarpos mollis Nutt. – Spreading snowberry (138) (1923)

Symphoricarpos occidentalis Hook. – Buckbrush [Buck brush, Buckbrush] (5, 9, 37, 98, 101, 106, 113, 114, 127, 130, 156, 158) (1873–1933), Coralberry [Coral-berry, Coral berry] (4, 50, 80, 82, 106, 109, 121, 122, 124, 156) (1923–present), Indian currant [Indiancurrant, Indian currants] (112) (1937), Juneberry [June-berry, June berry] (101, 156) (1905–1923), Partridge-berry [Partridgeberry, Partridge berry] (156) (1923), Quailberry [Quail-berry] (156) (1923), Snowberry [Snow berry, Snow-berry] (108) (1878), Stagberry [Stagberry] (156) (1923), Western snowberry (3, 4, 50, 98, 138, 155) (1923–present), Wolfberry [Wolf berry, Wolf-berry] (2, 4, 5, 9, 37, 63, 72, 75, 82, 92, 93, 95, 106, 108, 109, 113, 127, 130, 131, 156, 157, 158) (1873–1986)

Symphoricarpos orbiculatus Moench – Indian currant [Indian-currant, Indian currants] (2, 8, 63, 80, 92, 106, 109, 113, 114, 130, 156, 158) (1785–1949), Indian currant snowberry [Indiancurrant snowberry] (155) (1942), Palmer's snowberry (4, 50) (1986–present), Red snowberry (156) (1923), Red waxberry (156) (1923), St. Peter's-wort [St. Peter's wort, Saint Peters wort] (8) (1785), Sympharicarpos (French) (8) (1785), ŽoᴎΘi žiᴎga (Osage, little yellow-wood plant) (121) (1918?–1970?)

Symphoricarpos oreophilus Gray – Mountain snowberry (138) (1923)

Symphoricarpos pauciflorus (Robbins) Britton – See *Symphoricarpos albus* (L.) Blake var. *pauciflorus* (J. W. Robbins) S. F. Blake

Symphoricarpos racemosus var. *laevigatous* Fern. – See *Symphoricarpos albus* (L.) Blake var. *laevigatus* (Fern.) Blake

Symphoricarpos symphoricarpos (L.) MacMill. – Buckbrush [Buck brush, Buck-brush] (5, 9, 37, 98, 101, 106, 113, 114, 127, 130, 156, 158) (1894–1986), Coralberry [Coral-berry, Coral berry] (2, 63, 92, 108, 112, 138) (1878–1937), Inshtogah'te-hi (Omaha-Ponca, eye-lotion plant (37) (1919), Snapberry [Snap berry, Snap-berry] (5, 156, 157, 158) (1900–1929), Snowdrop-berry [Snow-drop-berry, Snowdrop berry] (156) (1923), Turkey-berry [Turkey-berry] (5, 156, 157, 158) (1900–1929), Zuzecha-ta-wote sapsapa (Dakota, black snake food) (37) (1919)

Symphoricarpos vulgaris Michx. – See *Symphoricarpos orbiculatus* Moench

Symphoricarpus – See *Symphoricarpos* Duham.

Symphoricarpus racemosus Michx. – See *Symphoricarpos albus* (L.) Blake var. *albus*

Symphyotrichum ×*amethystinum* (Nutt.) Nesom [*ericoides* × *novae-angliae*] – Amethyst aster (5, 72, 93, 138, 155) (1907–1942)

Symphyotrichum ×*longulum* (Sheldon) Nesom [*boreale* × *puniceum*] – Bog aster (85) (1932)

Symphyotrichum anomalum (Engelm.) Nesom – Many-ray aster [Many ray aster, Manyray aster, Many-rayed aster] (3, 4, 5, 50, 97) (1913–present)

Symphyotrichum ascendens (Lindl.) Nesom – Western aster (5, 50) (1913–present)

Symphyotrichum boreale (Torr. & Gray) A. & D. Löve – Northern bog aster (50) (present), Rush aster (85) (1932)

Symphyotrichum chilense (Nees) Nesom var. *chilense* – Pacific aster (155) (1942)

Symphyotrichum ciliatum (Ledeb.) Nesom – Hankow aster (155) (1942), Rayless alkali aster (50) (present), Rayless aster (3, 4, 5, 85, 93, 95) (1911–1986)

Symphyotrichum ciliolatum (Lindl.) A. & D. Löve – Lindley's aster [Lindley aster] (5, 50, 82, 131, 155) (1899–present)

Symphyotrichum concolor (L.) Nesom – Eastern silvery aster (5) (1913), Lilac-flower aster [Lilac-flowered aster] (5) (1913), Soft-leaf aster [Soft-leaved aster] (187) (1818)

Symphyotrichum cordifolium (L.) Nesom – Arrowleaf [Arrow-leaf, Arrow leaf] (106) (1930), Arrow-leaf aster [Arrow-leaved aster] (3, 4, 5, 72, 82, 93, 97, 106, 131) (1899–1986), Beeweed [Bee weed, Bee-weed] (5, 156, 158) (1900–1923), Blue wood-aster [Blue wood aster] (62, 95, 109, 138) (1911–1949), Common blue aster (93) (1936), Common blue wood aster (5, 50, 72, 82, 97, 156) (1907–present), Heart-leaf aster [Heartleaf aster, Heart-leaved aster] (62, 82, 155, 156, 187) (1818–1942), Heart-leaf starwort [Heart leaved star wort] (42) (1814), Starwort [Star-wort, Star wort] (58) (1869), Tongue (5, 76, 156, 158) (1896–1923) S. Berwick ME, Wood aster (127) (1933)

Symphyotrichum depauperatum (Fern.) Nesom – Serpentine aster (5, 156) (1913–1923)

Symphyotrichum divaricatum (Nutt.) Nesom – Salt-marsh aster [Salt-marsh aster] (4) (1986), Slim aster (5, 97) (1913–1937), Southern annual salt-marsh aster [Southern annual saltmarsh aster] (50) (present)

Symphyotrichum drummondii (Lindl.) Nesom – Drummond's aster [Drummond aster] (50) (present)

Symphyotrichum drummondii (Lindl.) Nesom var. *drummondii* – Drummond's aster [Drummond aster] (3, 4, 5, 50, 72, 82, 93, 97, 122, 155) (1907–present)

Symphyotrichum dumosum (L.) Nesom var. *dumosum* – Bushy aster (5, 72, 97, 131, 155, 156) (1899–1937), Rice-button aster [Rice button aster, Ricebutton aster] (5, 122, 156) (1913–1937)

Symphyotrichum eatonii (Gray) Nesom – Eaton's aster [Eatons aster] (4, 50, 97, 155) (1937–present), Oregon aster (155) (1942)

Symphyotrichum ericoides (L.) Nesom – White heath aster (50) (present)

Symphyotrichum ericoides (L.) Nesom var. *ericoides* – Button aster (156) (1923), Dense-flower aster [Dense-flowered aster] (5, 72, 82, 93, 97, 131) (1899–1937), Dense-flower wreath aster [Dense-flowered wreath-aster] (158) (1900), Dog-fennel [Dog fennel, Dog's fennel, Dog's fennel] (5, 156, 158) (1900–1923), Fallflower [Fall flower, Fall-flower] (5, 156, 158) (1900–1923), Farewell-summer [Farewell summer] (5, 156) (1913–1923), Fringe-leaf aster [Fringed-leaved aster] (187) (1818), Frost aster (82, 106) (1930), Frost-blow (156) (1923), Frostweed [Frost weed, Frost-weed] (5, 156) (1913–1923), Frostweed aster [Frost-weed aster] (156) (1923), Heath aster (109, 138, 155) (1923–1949), Heath-leaf aster [Heath-leaved aster] (187) (1818), Heath-like aster (82, 156) (1923–1930), Many-flower aster [Manyflowered aster, Many-flowered aster] (80, 187) (1818–1913), Mare's-tail [Marestail, Mare's tail, Mare's-tails] (5, 156, 158)

(1900–1923) no longer in use by 1923, Michaelmas daisy [Michaelmas daisies] (5, 156, 158) (1900–1923), Scrub bush [Scrub-bush] (5, 156, 158) (1900–1923), Steelweed [Steel weed, Steel-weed] (5, 62, 156) (1912–1923), White aster (3, 4, 80, 85, 98, 106) (1913–1986), White heath aster [White heath-aster] (5, 50, 62, 72, 82, 156, 158) (1900–present), White prairie aster (85, 127) (1932–1933), White wreath aster [White wreath-aster] (156, 158) (1900–1923), White-rosemary [White rosemary] (5, 156, 158) (1900–1923), Wreath aster (138) (1923)

Symphyotrichum ericoides (**L.**) **Nesom var.** *pansum* (**Blake**) **Nesom** – Many-flower aster [Manyflowered aster, Many-flowered aster] (50) (present)

Symphyotrichum ericoides (**L.**) **Nesom var.** *prostratum* (**Kuntze**) **Nesom** – Ciliate-leaf aster [Ciliate-leaved aster] (72) (1907), White heath aster (50) (present)

Symphyotrichum falcatum (**Lindl.**) **Nesom** – White prairie aster (50) (present)

Symphyotrichum falcatum (**Lindl.**) **Nesom var.** *commutatum* (**Torr. & Gray**) **Nesom** – White prairie aster (5, 50, 131, 122) (1899–present)

Symphyotrichum falcatum (**Lindl.**) **Nesom var.** *falcatum* – White prairie aster (50) (present)

Symphyotrichum fendleri (**Gray**) **Nesom** – Fendler's aster [Fendler aster] (3, 4, 5, 50, 93, 97, 122) (1913–present)

Symphyotrichum foliaceum (**DC.**) **Nesom** – Alpine leafy-bract aster [Alpine leafybract aster] (50) (present)

Symphyotrichum foliaceum (**DC.**) **Nesom var.** *apricum* (**Gray**) **Nesom** – Alpine leafy-bract aster [Alpine leafybract aster] (155) (1942)

Symphyotrichum foliaceum (**DC.**) **Nesom var.** *canbyi* (**Gray**) **Nesom** – Burke's leafy-bract aster [Burke leafybract aster] (50) (present), Canby's aster [Canby aster] (50) (present), Large-bract aster [Large-bracted aster] (5, 93) (1913–1936)

Symphyotrichum foliaceum (**DC.**) **Nesom var.** *foliaceum* – Leafy-bract aster [Leafybract aster, Leafy-bracted aster] (5, 155) (1913–1942)

Symphyotrichum foliaceum (**DC.**) **Nesom var.** *parryi* (**D. C. Eat.**) **Nesom** – Tall leaf-bract aster [Tall leafbract aster] (155) (1942)

Symphyotrichum frondosum (**Nutt.**) **Nesom** – Leafy aster (155) (1942)

Symphyotrichum grandiflorum (**L.**) **Nesom** – Great aster (138, 155) (1931–1942), Large-flower aster [Large-flowered aster] (5) (1913)

Symphyotrichum greatae (**Parish**) **G. L. Nesom** – San Gabriel aster [SanGabriel aster] (155) (1942)

Symphyotrichum laeve (**L.**) **A. & D. Löve var.** *concinnum* (**Willd.**) **Nesom** – Narrow-leaf smooth aster [Narrow-leaved smooth aster] (5, 72) (1907–1913)

Symphyotrichum laeve (**L.**) **A. & D. Löve var.** *geyeri* (**Gray**) **Nesom** – Geyer's aster (50) (present)

Symphyotrichum laeve (**L.**) **A. & D. Löve var.** *laeve* – Blue aster (82, 85) (1930–1932), Smooth aster (5, 72, 82, 93, 95, 97, 122, 131, 138, 155) (1899–1937), Smooth blue aster (3, 4, 50, 127) (1933–present)

Symphyotrichum laeve (**L.**) **A.& D. Löve var.** *purpuratum* (**Nees**) **Nesom** – Southern smooth aster (5) (1913)

Symphyotrichum lanceolatum (**Willd.**) **Nesom** – White panicle aster (50) (present)

Symphyotrichum lanceolatum (**Willd.**) **Nesom subsp.** *hesperium* (**Gray**) **Nesom** – Lilac aster (85) (1932) SD, Paniced aster (3, 4) (1977–1986), Siskiyou aster (155) (1942), White panicle aster (50) (present)

Symphyotrichum lanceolatum (**Willd.**) **Nesom subsp.** *lanceolatum* – Panicled aster (3, 4, 5, 42, 72, 82, 131, 155, 156, 187) (1814–1986), Tall white aster (5, 82, 93, 127, 156) (1913–1936), White aster (85) (1932), White panicle aster (50) (present)

Symphyotrichum lateriflorum (**L.**) **A. & D. Löve** – Calico aster (50) (present), Devioweed [Devio-weed] (75) (1894) WV, Fareweel summer (75) (1894) WV, Nail-rod [Nail rod] (5, 75, 156) (1894–1923) WV, Old Virginia stickweed [Old Virginia stick-weed] (75, 158) (1894–1900) WV, Old-field sweet (75) (1894) WV, White devil

(75) (1894) WV, Wireweed [Wire weed, Wire-weed] (75) (1894) WV, possibly Drooping aster (187) (1818), possibly Red-flower aster [Red-flowered aster] (187) (1818), possibly Small-flower aster [Small-flowered aster] (187) (1818), possibly Small-flower starwort [Small flowered star wort] (42) (1814), possibly White starwort [White star wort] (42) (1814)

Symphyotrichum lateriflorum (**L.**) **A.& D. Löve var.** *lateriflorum* – Calico aster (50, 85, 155, 156) (1923–present), Farewell-summer [Farewell summer] (5, 156) (1913–1923), Frost flower [Frost flower, Frost-flower] (106, 156) (1923–1930), Hairy-stem aster [Hairy stemmed aster] (5, 72, 156) (1907–1923), Old Virginia (5, 156) (1913–1923), Old-field sweet (5, 158) (1900–1913), Old-field wheat [Old field wheat] (156) (1923), Rosemary (156) (1923), Side-flower goldenrod [Side-flowered golden-rod] (19) (1840), Small white aster (5, 72, 97, 122, 155) (1907–1942), Starved aster (5, 72, 82, 122, 131, 156) (1899–1937), Stickseed [Stick seed, Stick-seed] (5) (1913), Stickweed [Stick-weed, Stick weed] (156) (1923), White field aster (106) (1930), White-devil [White devil] (5, 156, 158) (1900–1923), Wireweed [Wire weed, Wire-weed] (158) (1900), Wiseweed [Wiseweed] (5, 156) (1913–1923)

Symphyotrichum lowrieanum (**Porter**) **Nesom** – Beeweed [Bee weed, Bee-weed] (5, 75) (1894–1913) WV, Blue-devil [Blue devil, Blue devils, Blue-devils] (5, 75) (1894–1913) WV, Fall aster (5) (1913), Lowrie's aster [Lowrie aster] (5, 72, 155) (1907–1942), Stickweed [Stick-weed, Stick weed] (75) (1894)

Symphyotrichum **Nees** – Aster (50) (present)

Symphyotrichum novae-angliae (**L.**) **G. L.Nesom** – Farewell-summer [Farewell summer] (156) (1923), Hardy aster (76) (1896), Last-rose-of-summer (156) (1923), Michaelmas daisy [Michaelmas daisies] (76, 158) (1896–1900), New England aster [NewEngland aster] (3, 4, 5, 50, 62, 72, 82, 85, 93, 97, 109, 127, 131, 138, 155, 156, 158) (1899–present), New England starwort [New England star wort] (42) (1814), Rosy New England aster (138, 155) (1931–1942), Spurious aster (187) (1818), Spurious star wort (42) (1814), Wini'sīkĕns (Chippewa, dirty, little) (40) (1928)

Symphyotrichum novi-belgii (**L.**) **Nesom var.** *novi-belgii* – Flank starwort [Flanke starwoort] (178) (1526), Glaucous starwort [Glaucous star wort] (42) (1814), Green starwort [Green star wort] (42) (1814), Long-leaf aster [Longleaf aster, Long-leaved aster] (5, 48, 72, 82, 93, 138, 155) (1907–1942), New Holland starwort [New Holland star wort] (42) (1814), New York aster (5, 72, 82, 109, 138, 155, 156) (1907–1949)

Symphyotrichum novi-belgii (**L.**) **Nesom var.** *villicaule* (**Gray**) **J. Labrecque & L. Brouillet** – Lake St. John's-aster [Lake St. John aster] (155) (1942), Northeastern aster (5) (1913)

Symphyotrichum oblongifolium (**Nutt.**) **Nesom** – Aromatic aster (3, 4, 5, 50, 72, 82, 93, 97, 122, 131, 155) (1899–present), Blue prairie aster (127) (1933) ND, Kumlien aster (155) (1942), Oblong-leaf aster [Oblong-leaved aster] (82) (1930), Prairie aster (85) (1932)

Symphyotrichum ontarione (**Wiegand**) **Nesom** – Bottom-land aster [Bottomland aster] (50) (present), Missouri aster (4, 5) (1913–1986), Ontario aster (155) (1942), possibly Small aster (187) (1818)

Symphyotrichum oolentangiense (**Riddell**) **Nesom** – Sky-blue aster [Skyblue aster] (50) (Present)

Symphyotrichum oolentangiense (**Riddell**) **Nesom var.** *oolentangiense* – Azure aster (4) (1986), Blue aster (106) (1930), Blue-devil [Blue devil, Blue devils, Blue-devils] (156) (1923), Sky-blue aster [Skyblue aster] (5, 50, 72, 82, 93, 95, 97, 122, 156) (1907–present), Stickweed [Stick-weed, Stick weed] (156) (1923)

Symphyotrichum parviceps (**Burgess**) **Nesom** – Small white aster (4) (1986), Small-head aster [Small-headed aster] (5, 50) (1913–present)

Symphyotrichum patens (**Aiton**) **G. L. Nesom var.** *patens* – Large purple aster (156) (1923), Late purple aster (5, 50, 72, 97, 156) (1907–present), Purple daisy (5, 156) (1913–1923), Showy blue aster (82) (1930), Sky-drop aster [Skydrop aster] (138, 155) (1923–1942), Spreading aster (86, 187) (1818–1878), possibly Stem-clasping aster

[Stem clasping aster] (42) (1814)

Symphyotrichum phlogifolium (**Muhl. ex Willd.) Nesom** – Phlox-leaf aster [Phlox-leaved aster] (187) (1818), Thin-leaf purple aster [Thin-leaved purple aster] (5, 72) (1907–1913)

Symphyotrichum pilosum (**Willd.) Nesom** – Hairy white old-field aster [Hairy white oldfield aster] (50) (present)

Symphyotrichum pilosum (**Willd.) Nesom** var. *pilosum* – Hairy white old-field aster [Hairy white oldfield aster] (50) (present), Hairy-stem aster [Hairy stemmed aster] (72) (1907)

Symphyotrichum pilosum (**Willd.) Nesom** var. *pringlei* (**Gray) Nesom** – Faxon's aster (5) (1913), Pringle's aster (5) (1913)

Symphyotrichum porteri (**Gray) Nesom** – Porter's aster [Porters aster] (155) (1942)

Symphyotrichum potosinum (**A. Gray) G. L. Nesom** – Willow aster (5, 62, 72, 82, 85, 93, 97, 131, 156) (1899–1936)

Symphyotrichum praealtum (**Poir.) Nesom** – Willow-leaf aster [Willowleaf aster, Willow-leaved aster] (50) (present)

Symphyotrichum praealtum (**Poir.) Nesom** var. *nebraskense* (**Britton) Nesom** – Nebraska aster (5, 50, 93) (1913–present)

Symphyotrichum praealtum (**Poir.) Nesom** var. *praealtum* – Willow-leaf aster [Willowleaf aster, Willow-leaved aster] (3, 4, 50, 80, 82, 155, 187) (1818–present)

Symphyotrichum prenanthoides (**Muhl. ex Willd.) Nesom** – Crooked-stem aster (5, 72, 82, 156) (1907–1930), Swamp aster (156) (1923)

Symphyotrichum priceae (**Britt.) Nesom** – Miss Price's aster (5) (1913)

Symphyotrichum puniceum (**L.) A. & D. Löve** var. *puniceum* – Bog aster (4) (1986), Cocash (5, 49, 156, 158) (1898–1923) no longer in use by 1923, Cocash root (92) (1876), Cold-water root [Cold water root] (92) (1876), Early purple aster (5, 156, 158) (1900–1923), Meadow scabish [Meadow-scabish] (5, 49, 92, 156, 158) (1898–1923) no longer in use by 1923, Mountain aster (85) (1932), Purple-stem aster [Purple stemmed aster, Purple-stemmed aster, Purplestem aster] (5, 50, 72, 93, 106, 156, 158) (1900–present), Red-stalk aster [Red stalked aster, Red-stalked aster] (5, 49, 92, 156, 158, 187) (1818–1923), Red-stem aster [Red-stemmed aster] (93) (1936), Rough-stem aster [Rough-stemmed aster] (156) (1923), Squaw-weed [Squawweed, Squaw-weed] (49, 92, 156, 158) (1876–1923), Star flower [Starflower, Star-flower] (92) (1876), Swamp aster (3, 4, 138, 155, 156) (1923–1986), Swamp-weed [Swamp-weed] (156) (1923), Swanweed [Swan weed, Swanweed] (5, 92, 156, 158) (1876–1923), Winǐ'sǐkĕns (Chippewa, dirty, little) (40) (1928)

Symphyotrichum retroflexum (**Lindl. ex DC.) Nesom** – Curtis' aster [Curtis aster] (138, 155) (1931–1942)

Symphyotrichum sericeum (**Vent.) Nesom** – Silky aster (3, 4, 72, 85, 122, 155) (1907–1986), Western silky aster (5, 93, 131) (1899–1936), Western silver aster (50) (present), Western silvery aster (5, 97) (1913–1937)

Symphyotrichum shortii (**Lindl.) Nesom** – Georgia aster (138, 155) (1931–1942), Short's aster (5, 72) (1907–1913)

Symphyotrichum spathulatum (**Lindl.) Nesom** var. *spathulatum* – Fremont's aster [Fremont aster] (155) (1942), Western aster (155) (1942)

Symphyotrichum subulatum (**Michx.) Nesom** – Annual salt-marsh aster [Annual saltmarsh aster] (5, 155) (1913–1942), Flax-leaf starwort [Flax-leaved star wort] (19) (1840), Sea aster (19) (1840)

Symphyotrichum tenuifolium (**L.) Nesom** – Perennial salt-marsh aster (5) (1913), Saline aster (155) (1942)

Symphyotrichum tradescantii (**L.) Nesom** – Blue camomile [Blue chamomile] (92, 156) (1898–1923), Blue daisy [Blue daisies] (156) (1923), Michaelmas daisy [Michaelmas daisies] (5, 72, 82, 92, 138) (1876–1930), Tradescant's aster [Tradescant aster] (5, 82, 155) (1913–1942)

Symphyotrichum turbinellum (**Lindl.) Nesom** – Prairie aster (4, 5, 97, 138, 155) (1923–1986), Smooth violet prairie aster (50) (present)

Symphyotrichum undulatum (**L.) Nesom** – Wave aster (138, 155) (1931–1942), Wave-leaf starwort [Wave leaved star wort] (42) (1814), Wave-stem aster [Waved-stemmed aster] (187) (1818), Wavy-leaf aster [Wavy-leaved aster] (5, 97) (1913–1937)

Symphyotrichum urophyllum (**Lindl.) Nesom** – Arrow aster (138, 155) (1923–1942), White arrow-leaf aster [White arrowleaf aster] (50) (present)

Symphyotrichum walteri (**Alexander) Nesom** – Walter's aster [Walter aster] (155) (1942)

Symphytum (**Tourn.) L.** – See *Symphytum* L.

Symphytum asperimum **Donn.** – See *Symphytum asperum* Lepechin

Symphytum asperrimum **Donn.** – See *Symphytum asperum* Lepechin

Symphytum asperum **Lepechin** – Bugloss [Buglos, Buglosse] (77) (1898) Paris ME, Prickly comfrey (106, 109, 138) (1923–1949), Rough comfrey (5) (1913)

Symphytum **L.** – Comfrey (1, 109, 138, 155, 156, 158) (1900–1949)

Symphytum officinale **L.** – Ass's-ear [Ass-ear] (64, 156) (1908–1923), Backwort [Back wort] (5, 64, 156) (1907–1923), Blackwort [Black wort] (5, 64, 156) (1907–1923), Boneset (5, 107, 156) (1913–1923), Bruiseroot [Bruise root] (5, 64, 156) (1907–1923), Comfrey (5, 19, 46, 49, 52, 53, 57, 58, 64, 92, 107) (1649–1922), Comfrey with the white flowers [Compherie with the white flower] (46) (1671) accidentally introduced by 1671, Common comfrey (109, 138, 156) (1923–1949), Consound (5, 156) (1913–1923), Great comfrey (178) (1526), Gum plant [Gumplant, Gum-plant] (5, 64, 156) (1907–1923) no longer in use by 1923, Healing herb [Healing-herb] (5, 64, 92, 156) (1876–1923), Knitback [Knit-back Knit back] (5, 64, 92, 156) (1876–1923), Knobby comfrey [Knobbie comfrey] (178) (1526), More consould (179) (1526), Slippery root [Slippery-root] (64, 156) (1908–1923), Symphytum (57, 64) (1908–1917)

Symplocarpus foetidus (**L.) Salisb. ex Nutt.** – Bearweed [Bear weed] (86) (1878), Beerenwortel (German) (186) (1814), Björnblad (Swedish, bear's leaf) (41) (1770), Björnrötter (Swedish, bear's root) (41) (1770), Bonsenkraut (German) (186) (1814), Byorn-blad (Bear's leaf) (186) (1814), Byorn-retter (Bear's foot) (186) (1814), Clump-foot cabbage [Clumpfoot cabbage] (5) (1913), Collard [Collards] (5, 64, 156) (1908–1923), Cow-collard (186) (1814), Dracontium (64) (1908), Ellebore (186) (1814), Fetid hellebone (64) (1908), Fetid hellebore (156) (1923), Fetid pothos (23) (1810), Foetid hellebore (6) (1892), Hellebore (186) (1814), Irish cabbage (186) (1814), Itchweed [Itch-weed, Itch weed, Ich weed] (186) (1814), Meadow cabbage (5, 6, 53, 64, 92, 156) (1876–1923), Pockweed (64) (1908), Poke (186) (1814), Pokeweed [Poke-weed, Poke-weed] (156) (1923), Pole-cat collard [Polecat-collard] (186) (1814), Pole-cat root [Polecat root] (41) (1770), Pole-cat weed [Pole cat weed, Polecat weed, Polecat-weed] (5, 6, 41, 53, 64, 92, 156, 186, 187) (1770–1923), Polk weed (5, 73) (1892–1913) Brookline MA, Pothos fetide (French) (6) (1892), Skunk cabbage [Skunk-cabbage [Skunk-cabbage (5, 6, 14, 41, 46, 50, 53, 57, 58, 61, 64, 72, 86, 92, 106, 138, 156, 186, 187) (1770–present), Skunkweed [Skunk-weed, Skunk weed] (5, 6, 42, 53, 86, 92, 156, 177, 186, 187) (1762–1923), Stinkende Drachenwurzel (German) (6) (1892), Stinkende Zehrwurtz (German) (186) (1814), Stinking poke (64, 92, 156) (1876–1923), Stinking pothos (186) (1814), Swamp-cabbage [Swamp cabbage] (5, 64, 92, 156, 186) (1825–1923), Symplocarpus (57) (1917)

Symplocarpus foetidus **Salisb.** – See *Symplocarpus foetidus* (L.) Salisb. ex Nutt.

Symplocarpus **Salisb. ex Nutt.** – Collard [Collards] (92) (1876), Midas' ears (1) (1932), Skunk cabbage [Skunk-cabbage [Skunkcabbage (50, 138, 156) (1923–present)

Symplocos **Jacq.** – Hopéa (8) (1785), Sweetleaf [Sweet-leaf, Sweet leaf] (109, 138, 156) (1923–1949)

Symplocos paniculata (**Thunb.) Miq.** – Asiatic sweetleaf (138) (1923), Sapphire-berry (109, 156) (1923–1949)

Symplocos paniculata **Wall.** – See *Symplocos paniculata* (Thunb.) Miq.

Symplocos tinctoria (**L.) L'Her.** – Common sweetleaf (50, 138) (1923–present), Dye-leaves [Dye leaves] (5, 75, 156) (1894–1923) Banner Elk NC, Florida laurel (5, 156) (1913–1923), Hopéa des teinturiers (French) (8) (1785), Horse-sugar [Horse sugar] (2, 7, 93, 156, 183) (~1756–1936), Sweetleaf [Sweet-leaf, Sweet leaf] (2, 5, 7, 20, 19, 92, 156) (1828–1923), Yellowleaf [Yellow leaf] (10) (1818), Yellow-wood [Yellowwood, Yellow wood] (5, 156) (1913–1923)

Symplocos tinctoria **L'Her.** – See *Symplocos tinctoria* (L.) L'Her.

Synandra hispidula **(Michx.) Britton** – Rue-anemone [Rue anemone] (1, 93) (1932–1936), Synandra (5) (1913)

Syndesmon **Hoffmgg.** – See *Thalictrum* L.

Syndesmon thalictroides **(L.) Hoffmg.** – See *Thalictrum thalictroides* (L.) Eames & Boivin

Syngonanthus flavidulus **(Michx.) Ruhl.** – Yellow hatpins (50) (present), possibly Yellow pipewort (5, 10) (1818–1913)

Synosma **Raf.** – See *Hasteola* Raf.

Synosma suaveolens **(L.) Raf.** – See *Hasteola suaveolens* (L.) Pojark.

Syntherisma filiformis **(L.) Nash** – See *Digitaria filiformis* (L.) Koel.

Syntherisma ischaemum **(Schred.) Nash** – See *Digitaria ischaemum* (Schreb.) Schreb. ex Muhl.

Syntherisma linearis **(Krock.) Nash** – See *Digitaria ischaemum* (Schreb.) Schreb. ex Muhl.

Syntherisma marginata **(Link) Nash** – See *Digitaria ciliaris* (Retz.) Koel.

Syntherisma sanguinalis **(L.) Dulac** – See *Digitaria sanguinalis* (L.) Scop.

Syntherisma villosa **Walt.** – See *Digitaria villosa* (Walt.) Pers.

Syntherisma **Walt** – See *Digitaria* Haller

Synthyris bullii **(Eat.) Heller** – See *Besseya bullii* (Eat.) Rydb.

Synthyris rubra **(Dougl. ex Hook.) Benth.** – See *Besseya rubra* (Dougl. ex Hook.) Rydb.

Synthyris rubra **Benth** – See *Lunellia rubra* (Douglas ex Hook.) Nieuwl.

Syringa **×persica L. [*afghanica* × *laciniata*]** – Persian lilac (19, 82, 92, 109, 112, 135, 138) (1840–1949)

Syringa amurensis **var. *japonica* Franch & Star.** – See *Syringa reticulata* (Blume) H. Hara subsp. *reticulata*

Syringa japonica **Decne.** – See *Syringa reticulata* (Blume) H. Hara subsp. *reticulata*

Syringa josikaea **Jacq. f. ex Reichenb.** – Hungarian lilac (109, 112, 138) (1923–1949), Juliana lilac (138) (1923)

Syringa **L.** – Chinese tree (112) (1937), Lilac (1, 82, 109, 112, 138, 156) (1923–1949)

Syringa pekinensis – See *Syringa reticulata* subsp. *pekinensis* (Rupr.) P. S. Green & M. C. Chang

Syringa persica **L.** – See *Syringa* ×*persica* L. [*afghanica* × *laciniata*]

Syringa reticulata **(Blume) H. Hara subsp. *reticulata*** – Japanese lilac (82) (1930), Japanese tree lilac (138) (1923)

Syringa reticulata **(Blume) Hara subsp. *amurensis* (Rupr.) P. S. Greene & M. C. Chang** – Manchurian lilac (138) (1923)

Syringa reticulata **subsp. *pekinensis* (Rupr.) P. S. Green & M. C. Chang** – Peking lilac (138) (1923)

Syringa villosa **Vahl** – Fragrant lilac (112) (1937), Late lilac (138) (1923)

Syringa vulgaris **L.** – Blue pipe [Blew pipe] (5, 178) (1526–1913), Blue-ash [Blue ash] (5, 156) (1913–1923), Common lilac (82, 109, 112, 138, 156) (1923–1949), Common purple lilac (112) (1937), Common white lilac (112) (1937), Laylock (156) (1923) no longer in use by 1923, Lelache (156) (1923), Persian elder (156) (1923), Persian jasmine (156) (1923), Pipe tree [Pipe-tree] (5, 92, 156) (1876–1923), Pipe-privets [Pipe privets] (5, 156) (1913–1923), Prince's-feather [Prince's feather, Princes-feather, Princesfeather] (156) (1923), Purple lilac (135) (1910), Roman willow (5, 156) (1913–1923), Spanish ash (156) (1923), White ash (156) (1923), White lilac (92, 135) (1876–1910), possibly Lilac (5, 7, 19, 63, 85, 97, 114, 184) (1793–1937), possibly Lilaca (92) (1876)

Syzygium cumini **(L.) Skeels** – Jambolan (109) (1949), Jambolan-plum (109, 138) (1923–1949)

Syzygium **Gaertn.** – See *Syzygium* P. Br. ex Gaertn.

Syzygium jambos **(L.) Alston** – Malabar plum [Malabar-plum] (138) (1923), Malaccaschambu [Malacca-schambu] (Malabar) (110) (1886), Rose-apple [Rose apple] (109, 110) (1886–1949)

Syzygium jambos **Alston** – See *Syzygium jambos* (L.) Alston

Syzygium malaccense **(L.) Merr. & Perry** – Malay apple (110) (1886)

Syzygium **P. Br. ex Gaertn.** – Rose-apple [Rose apple] (109) (1949)

T

Tabebuia heterophylla **(DC.) Britt.** – Roble blanco (Spanish) (109) (1949)

Tabernaemontana coronaria – See *Tabernaemontana divaricata* (L.) R. Br. ex Roemer & J. A. Schultes

Tabernaemontana divaricata **(L.) R. Br. ex Roemer & J. A. Schultes** – Calvel de la India (109) (1949), Crape-jasmine (109, 138) (1923–1949)

Taenidia **(Torr. & Gray) Drude** – Taenidia (50, 155) (1942–present)

Taenidia integerrima **(L.) Drude** – Golden alexanders (5, 156) (1913–1923), Yellow pimpernel (4, 5, 50, 72, 85, 97, 156) (1907–present), Yellow taenidia (3, 155) (1942–1977)

Taenidia montana **(Mackenzie) Cronq.** – Mountain pimpernel (156) (1923), Virginia mountian pimpernel (5) (1913)

Tagetes erecta **L.** – African marygold (19, 109) (1840–1949), Aztec marigold (109, 138) (1923–1949), Big marigold (109) (1949), Great African marigold (178) (1526), Great double Affrican Marigold (178) (1526)

Tagetes **L.** – Marigold [Marigolds, Mary gold, Marygold] (109, 138) (1923–1949)

Tagetes patula **L.** – French marigold [French marygold] (19, 109, 138) (1840–1949), Lesser African marigold [Lesser Affrican marigold] (178) (1526), Single French marigold (178) (1526), Striped marigold (138) (1923)

Tagetes signata – See *Tagetes patula* L.

Talinum **Adans.** – Fameflower [Fame flower, Fame-flower] (1, 4, 50, 155) (1932–present), Flameflower [Flame flower, Flame-flower] (93, 109) (1936–1949), Rock-pink [Rock pink] (158) (1900), Rock-pink fameflower [Rockpink fameflower] (155) (1942)

Talinum aurantiacum **Engelm.** – Flameflower [Flame flower, Flame-flower] (122) (1937), Orange fameflower (50, 155) (1942–present), Yellow flame flower [Yellow flameflower] (124) (1937)

Talinum calycinum **Engelm.** – Fameflower [Fame flower, Fame-flower] (3, 4) (1977–1986), Large-flower fameflower [Largeflower fameflower] (50) (present), Large-flower talinum [Large-flowered talinum] (5, 93, 97) (1913–1937), Pink flameflower [Pink flame flower] (124) (1937), Rock-pink [Rock pink] (4, 5, 76, 156, 158) (1896–1986)

Talinum menziesii **Hook.** – See *Calandrinia ciliata* (Ruiz & Pav.) DC.

Talinum paniculatum **(Jacq.) Gaertn.** – Pink babysbreath [Pink baby breath] (122, 124) (1937) TX

Talinum parviflorum **Nutt.** – Dwarf flameflower [Dwarf flame flower] (122, 124) (1937), Prairie fameflower (3, 4, 155) (1942–1986), Small-flower talinum [Small-flowered talinum] (5, 93, 97) (1913–1937), Sunbright (50) (present)

Talinum rugospermum **Holzinger** – Prairie fameflower (50) (present), Prairie talinum (5) (1913), Wrinkle-seed fameflower [Wrinkleseed fameflower] (155) (1942)

Talinum teretofolium **Pursh** – See *Phemeranthus teretifolius* (Pursh) Raf.

Tamarindus indica **L.** – Balam-pulli (174) (1753), Black tamarind (92) (1876), Tamarind (7, 57, 107, 109, 138) (1828–1949), Tamarindo (109) (1949)

Tamarindus **L.** – Tamarind (138) (1923)

Tamarix africana **Poir.** – African tamarix (138) (1923)

Tamarix aphylla **(L.) H. Karst.** – Aethl (122) (1937) TX, Aethyl (124) (1937) TX, Athel tamarisk (109) (1949), Atlee galls (92) (1876) abnormal parasitic growth on this species, Evergreen tamarix (124) (1937) TX

Tamarix aphylla **Karst** – See *Tamarix aphylla* (L.) H. Karst.

Tamarix articulata **Vahl** – See *Tamarix aphylla* (L.) H. Karst.

Tamarix chinensis **Lour.** – Asiatic tamarisk (82) (1930), Chinese tamarix (109, 138) (1923–1949), Five-stamen tamarisk [Fivestamen tamarisk] or Fivestamen tamarix (50, 138, 155) (1923–present), Juniper tamarix (138) (1923)

Tamarix gallica **L.** – Arabian manna (92) (1876), False manna (92) (1876), French tamarisk (82, 109, 135) (1910–1949), French tamarix (138) (1923), Italian tamarisk [Italian tamariske] (178) (1526), Manna plant [Manna-plant] (107) (1919), Salt-cedar [Salt cedar, Saltcedar] (106, 122, 124, 153) (1913–1937), Tamaryte (178, 179) (1526–1596), Taray (Spanish) (107) (1919)

Tamarix juniperina – See *Tamarix chinensis* Lour.

Tamarix **L.** – Salt-cedar [Salt cedar, Saltcedar] (4, 122) (1937–1986)

Tamarix **L.** – Tamarisk [Tamarix] (1, 15, 50, 109, 112, 138, 155, 158) (1895–present)

Tamarix odessana – See *Tamarix ramosissima* Ledeb.

Tamarix orientalis – See *Tamarix aphylla* (L.) H. Karst.

Tamarix parviflora **DC.** – Four-stamen tamarisk [Fourstamen tamarisk] or Four-stamen tamarix [Fourstamen tamarix] (138, 155) (1923–1942), Salt cedar (3, 4) (1977–1986), Small-flower tamarisk [Small-flower tamarisk] (50, 155) (1942–present)

Tamarix pentandra **Pallas** – See *Tamarix chinensis* Lour.

Tamarix ramosissima **Ledeb.** – Odessa tamarix (138) (1923), Salt-cedar [Salt cedar, Saltcedar] (3, 4, 50) (1977–present)

Tamarix tetrandra **auct. non Pallas** – See *Tamarix parviflora* DC.

Tanacetum balsamita – See *Balsamita major* Desf.

Tanacetum bipinnatum **(L.) Schultz-Bip. subsp. *huronense* (Nutt.) Breitung** – Huron tansy (138) (1923), Lake Huron tansy (5) (1913)

Tanacetum coccineum **(Willd.) Grierson** – Insect flowers (57) (1917), Persian insect powder (92) (1876)

Tanacetum crispum – See *Tanacetum vulgare* L.

Tanacetum huronense **Nutt.** – See *Tanacetum bipinnatum* (L.) Schultz-Bip. subsp. *huronense* (Nutt.) Breitung

Tanacetum **L.** – Tansy [Tansey, Tansie] (1, 4, 10, 50, 109, 138, 155, 156, 158) (1818–present)

Tanacetum **L.** – Feverfew [Fever few, fever-few] (10) (1818)

Tanacetum parthenium **(L.) Schultz-Bip.** – Bertram (158) (1900), Bridal-roses [Bridal roses] (75) (1894), Camphor geranium (75) (1894) Western MA, Common feverfew (5, 156) (1913–1923), Double feverfew [Double feuerfew] (75, 178) (1526–1894) Western MA, Featherfew [Feather few, Feather-few, Fetherfew] (5, 19, 46, 49, 76, 92, 156, 158) (1671–1923), Febrifuge plant (92, 158) (1876–1900), Fetter-foe (158) (1900), Feverfew [Fever few, fever-few] (4, 49, 50, 57, 58, 61, 76, 92, 109, 138, 158) (1869–present), Feverfew chrysanthemum (155) (1942), Feverfew-camomile [Feverfew-chamomile] (138) (1923), Golden-feather [Golden feather] (109) (1949), Matricaire (French) (158) (1900), Matricaria Parthenium (58) (1869), Mutterkraut (German) (158) (1900), Parthenium (57) (1917), Pellitory (5, 156, 158) (1900–1923), Sweet feverfew [Sweete feuerfew] (178) (1526), Whitewort (158) (1900), Wild camomile [Wild cammomile, Wild chamomile, Wild camomille] (5, 58, 156, 158) (1869–1923)

Tanacetum vulgare **L.** – Bitter-buttons [Bitter buttons] (5, 69, 156, 158) (1900–1923), Chrysanthemum (82) (1930) IA, Common tansy [Common tansey] (3, 4, 50, 63, 109, 138, 155, 156) (1899–present), Crisp tansy [Crispe tansie] (178) (1526), Curled tansy [Curled Tansie] (178) (1526), Double tansy (92, 158) (1876–1900), English cost (158) (1900), Giant daisy [Giant-daisy, Giantdaisy] (138, 155) (1923–1942), Ginger plant [Ginger-plant] (5, 69, 156, 158) (1900–1923), Herbe aux vers (French) (158) (1900), High daisy (109) (1949), High-daisy [High daisy] (109) (1949), Hindheal [Hind-heal, Hindheel] (92, 156, 158) (1876–1923), O'ckinigi'kweäni'bĭc (Chippewa, young woman's leaf) (40) (1928), Parsley-fern [Parsley fern] (69, 158) (1900–1904), Rainfarn (German) (6, 158) (1892–1900),

Tanacetum vulgare L. var. crispum DC.

Scented-fern [Scented fern] (69) (1904), Tanaceto (Spanish) (158) (1900), Tanaisie (French) (6, 158) (1892–1900), Tansy [Tansey, Tansie] (5, 6, 7, 19, 40, 41, 46, 49, 53, 57, 58, 61, 62, 72, 80, 85, 92, 93, 97, 107, 131, 158, 179, 184, 187) (1526–1937), Wurmkraut (German) (158) (1900)

Tanacetum vulgare L. var. crispum DC. – See *Tanacetum vulgare* L.

Taraxacum (Haller) Ludw. – See *Taraxacum* G. H. Weber ex Wiggers

Taraxacum dens-leonis Desf. – See *Taraxacum officinale* G. H. Weber ex Wiggers subsp. *officinale*

Taraxacum G. H. Weber ex Wiggers – Dandelion (1, 4, 50, 82, 109, 138, 155, 156) (1923–present)

Taraxacum laevigatum (Willd.) DC. – Red-seed dandelion [Red-seeded dandelion] (5, 72, 80, 82, 85, 93, 95, 97, 127, 156) (1907–1937), Red-seed-lettuce [Red-seeded-lettuce] (3, 4) (1977–1986), Rock dandelion (50) (present), Smooth dandelion (155) (1942)

Taraxacum officinale G. H. Weber ex Wiggers – Aphaka (177, 180) (1633–1762), Aphake (107) (1919), Arnica (5, 157, 158) (1900–1929), Blow-ball [Blowball] (5, 62, 64, 69, 156, 157, 158) (1900–1929), Cankerwort (5, 62, 64, 69, 156, 157, 158) (1900–1929), Caput monach (180) (1633), Clock (64) (1907), Common dandelion (4, 7, 50, 63, 80, 82, 95, 109, 127, 155, 156) (1828–present), Couronne de moine (French) (158) (1900), Dado'cabodji'bïk (Chippewa, milk root) (40) (1928), Dandelion (3, 5, 10, 19, 37, 41, 52, 53, 57, 59, 62, 64, 69, 72, 80, 85, 93, 97, 106, 107, 114, 131, 138, 145, 157, 158, 180, 184, 187) (1633–1977), Dens leonis (177, 180) (1633–1762), Dent de lion (French) (158) (1900), Dent de lyon (French) (180) (1633), Diente de leon (Spanish) (158) (1900) MA, Dindle (157, 158) (1900–1929), Doonhead (64) (1907), Doon-head-clock (69, 157, 158) (1900–1929), Fortune-teller (64, 69, 156, 157, 158) (1900–1929), Grunsel (156, 157, 158) (1900–1929), Hawkbit [Hawk bit] (41) (1770), Horse gowan [Horse-gowan] (64, 69, 156, 157, 158) (1900–1929), Irish daisy (5, 64, 69, 156, 157, 158) (1900–1929), Lion's-tooth [Lion's tooth, Lions' tooth] (5, 82, 157, 158) (1900–1930), Löwenzahn (German) (158) (1900), Milk gowan (156, 157) (1923–1929), Milk witch gowan (5) (1913), Monk's-head [Monk's head] (5, 156, 157, 158) (1900–1929), One-o'clock (64, 69, 156, 157, 158) (1900–1929), Papencruitz (Low Dutch) (180) (1633), Peasant's-clock [Peasant's clock] (62) (1912) IN, Old English name, Pfaffenröhrchen (German) (158) (1900), Pisseabed (180) (1633), Pissenlit (French) (158) (1900), Pissenlit commun (French) (7) (1828), Pissenlit en couronne de prestre (French) (180) (1633), Priest's-crown [Priest's crown] (5, 156, 157, 158) (1900–1929), Puffball [Puff-ball, Puff ball, Puffballs, Puff balls] (5, 7, 92, 156, 157, 158) (1828–1929), Witch gowan (156, 157, 158) (1900–1929), Yellow gowan [Yellow gowans] (5, 64, 69, 156, 157, 158) (1900–1929), possibly Knotty-root dandelion [Knottie rooted Dandelion] (180) (1633)

Taraxacum officinale G. H. Weber ex Wiggers subsp. officinale – Common dandelion (50, 55) (1911–present), Dandelion (6, 46, 47, 58, 61, 92) (1671–1892), Dent de lion (French) (6) (1892), Löwenzahn (German) (6) (1892), Pfaffen-Rohrlein (German) (6) (1892), Pissabed (6, 7) (1828–1892), Pissenlit commune (French) (6) (1892), Priest's-crown [Priest's crown] (92) (1876), Puffball [Puff-ball, Puff ball, Puffballs, Puff balls] (6) (1892), Swine's-snout [Swine snout] (92) (1876), Wild endive (92) (1876)

Taraxacum officinale G. H. Weber ex Wiggers subsp. vulgare (Lam.) Schinz & R. Keller – Dende lyon (190) (~1759), Dens leon (59) (1488), Mountain dandelion (5) (1913)

Taraxacum officinalis – See *Taraxacum officinale* G. H. Weber ex Wiggers

Taraxacum palustre (Lyons) Symons – Marsh dandelion (19, 92) (1840–1876)

Taraxacum taraxacum L. – See *Taraxacum officinale* G. H. Weber ex Wiggers

Taxodium ascendens Brongn. – Pond cypress [Pondcypress] (5, 50, 109, 138) (1913–present)

Taxodium distichum (L.) L. C. Rich. – American bald cypress (2) (1895), Bald cypress [Baldcypress] (5, 20, 46, 50, 65, 97, 109) (1857–present), Black cypress (Georgia & Carolinas) (20) (1857), Black cypress wood (92) (1876), Black swamp cypress (5, 20) (1857–1913), Common baldcypress (138) (1923), Cypre (Louisiana) (20) (1857), Cyprès (French) (20) (1857), Cyprès à feuilles d'Acacia (French) (8) (1785), Cypress of America (189) (1767), Cypress or Cypress tree [Cypress-tree, Cypresse tree] (7, 65) (1828–1931), Cyprus (12) (1819), Deciduous cypress (14) (1882), Red swamp cypress (5) (1913), Sabino tree (5) (1913), Southern cypress (2, 122, 124) (1895–1937), Virginia cypress (92) (1876), Virginia deciduous cypress tree [Virginian deciduous cypress-tree] (8) (1785), Virginia swamp cypress (5) (1913), White cypress (20) (1857), White swamp cypress (5) (1913), American cypress (189) (1767)

Taxodium distichum (L.) L. C. Rich. var. imbricarium (Nutt.) Croom – See *Taxodium ascendens* Brongn.

Taxodium L. C. Rich. – Bald cypress [Baldcypress] (138) (1923)

Taxodium mucronatum Ten. – Montezuma bald cypress [Montezuma baldcypress] (138) (1923)

Taxodium sempervirens – See *Sequoia sempervirens* (Lamb. ex D. Don) Endl.

Taxus (Tourn.) L. – See *Taxus* L.

Taxus baccata L. – Chinwood [Chin wood] (92) (1876), English yew (50, 109, 138) (1923–present), Ewe (178, 179) (1526–1596), Globeberry [Globe berry, Globe berries] (92) (1876), Ground hemlock (10, 29) (1818–1869), Yew or Yew tree (49, 92, 107, 135) (1876–1919)

Taxus brevifolia Nutt. – Ground hemlock (101) (1905), If occidental (French) (20) (1857), Pacific yew (138) (1923), Western yew (20, 109, 161) (1857–1949), Yew or Yew tree (161) (1857)

Taxus canadensis Willd. – American yew (2, 72, 92) (1876–1907), Canadian yew [Canada yew] or Canadian yew tree [Canadian yew-tree] (5, 8, 50, 138) (1785–present), Creeping hemlock (5, 75) (1894–1913), Dwarf yew (5, 92) (1876–1913), Ground hemlock (2, 19, 92, 109) (1840–1949), If (French) (5, 8) (1785–1913), Juniper or Juniper tree [Juniper-tree] (79) (1891) NH, Ne'bagandag' (Chippewa, it is one-sided) (40) (1928), Shinwood [Shin-wood, Shin wood] (5, 92) (1876–1913), Yew or Yew tree (19, 40, 147) (1840–1928)

Taxus cuspidata Sieb. & Zucc. – Japanese yew (109, 112, 136, 138) (1923–1949)

Taxus L. – Chinwood [Chin wood] (7) (1828), If (French) (8) (1785), Yew or Yew tree (1, 7, 8, 109, 50, 138, 167) (1785–present)

Taxus occidentalis – See *Taxus brevifolia* Nutt.

Tecoma capensis (Thunb.) Lindl. – Cape-honeysuckle (109, 138) (1923–1949)

Tecoma Juss. – Crossvine [Cross vine, Cross-vine] (7) (1828), Tecomaria (138) (1923), Trumpet bush [Trumpetbush] (138, 155) (1923–1942), Trumpet flower [Trumpet-flower, Trumpet-flowers] (1, 2, 7, 158) (1828–1932), Trumpet-creeper [Trumpet creeper, Trumpet-creeper] (1) (1932)

Tecoma radicans Juss. – See *Campsis radicans* (L.) Seem. ex Bureau

Tecoma stans (L.) Juss. ex Kunth – Florida trumpetbush (138) (1923), Hardy Florida trumpetbush (138) (1923), Yellowbell [Yellow-bell, Yellow bell, Yellow bells, Yellow-bells, Yellowbells] (109) (1949)

Tecoma stans angustata – See *Tecoma stans* (L.) Juss. ex Kunth

Tectaria Cav. (possibly) – Male fern [Malefern, Male-fern, Male ferne] (7, 10) (1818–1828), possibly Shield fern [Shield-fern] (2) (1895), possibly Sweetbrake (7) (1828)

Telanthera bettzickiana – See *Alternanthera bettzichiana* (Regel) Voss

Telesonix jamesii (Torr.) Raf. – James' boykinia [James boykinia] (155) (1942), James' saxifrage (4) (1986), James' telesonix (50) (present)

Telesonix Raf. – Brookfoam (50) (present)

Tephroseris atropurpurea (Ledeb.) Holub – Arctic senecio (5) (1913)

Tephrosia hispidula (Michx.) Pers. – Few-flower goat's rue [Few-flowered goat's rue] (5, 97) (1913–1937)

Tephrosia hispidula Pers. – See *Tephrosia hispidula* (Michx.) Pers.

Tephrosia leucosericea (Rydb.) Cory – See *Tephrosia virginiana* (L.) Pers

Tephrosia lindheimeri **Gray** – She string (124) (1937)

Tephrosia **Pers.** – Catgut [Cat gut, Cat-gut] (7) (1828), Devil's-shoe-string [Devil's shoe-string, Devil's shoe string, Devil's-shoestrings, Devil's shoe-strings, Devil's shoestrings, Devil's shoe strings] (7) (1828), Hoary pea [Hoarypea, hoary-pea] (50, 156) (1923–present), Suckehihaw (Osage) (7) (1828), Tephrosia (155) (1942), Turkey-pea [Turkey pea] (7) (1828)

Tephrosia purpurea **(L.) Pers.** – Indigo (92) (1876)

Tephrosia spicata **(Walt.) Torr. & Gray** – Loose-flower goat's-rue [Loose-flowered goat's rue] (5) (1913)

Tephrosia spicata **Torr. & Gray.** – See *Tephrosia spicata* (Walt.) Torr. & Gray

Tephrosia virginiana **(L.) Pers** – Catgut [Cat gut, Cat-gut] (2, 4, 5, 49, 63, 92, 102, 156, 158) (1886–1986) from long wiry roots, Cat-gut weed [Catgut weed] (157) (1929), Devil's-shoestring [Devil's shoe-string, Devil's shoe string, Devil's-shoestrings, Devil's shoe-strings, Devil's shoestrings, Devil's shoe strings] (5, 49, 92, 102, 156, 157, 158) (1876–1929), Distai'yĭ (Cherokee, the roots are tough) (102) (1886), Erebinthus (177) (1762), Goat's rice (157) (1929), Goat's-rue [Goatsrue, Goat's rue, Goats-rue] (2, 4, 5, 19, 49, 63, 72, 92, 97, 102, 156, 157, 158, 187) (1818–1986), Hoary pea [Hoarypea, hoary-pea] (5, 49, 86, 92, 156, 157, 158) (1878–1929), Pastel-pea [Pastel pea] (124) (1937) TX, Rabbit-pea [Rabbit pea] (5, 156, 157, 158) (1900–1929), Tephrosia (3) (1977), Téphrosie (French) (158) (1900), Turkey peak (157) (1929), Turkey-pea [Turkey pea] (5, 49, 86, 102, 156, 158) (1878–1923) Southern US, Virginia goat's-rue [Virginian goat's rue] (86) (1878), Virginia tephrosia (50, 155) (1942–present), Wild pea (76) (1896), Wild sweetpea [Wild sweet pea] (5, 85, 156, 157, 158) (1900–1932)

Terminalia catappa **L.** – Badamier de Malabar (20) (1857), Indian almond [Indian-almond] (20, 107, 109, 138) (1857–1949), Myrobalan (109) (1949), Tropical-almond (109) (1949)

Tetradium **Lour.** – Evodia (138) (1923)

Tetragonanthus deflexus **(J. E. Smith) Kuntze** – See *Halenia deflexa* (Sm.) Griseb.

Tetragonia expansa **Murray** – See *Tetragonia tetragonioides* (Pallas) Kuntze

Tetragonia **L.** – New Zealand spinach [New-Zealand-spinach] (138) (1923)

Tetragonia tetragonioides **(Pallas) Kuntze** – New Zealand spinach [New-Zealand-spinach] (15, 50, 92, 107, 109, 110, 138) (1895–present) brought by Capt. Cook from New Zealand and used like spinach greens

Tetragonotheca helianthoides **L.** – Melon-apple flower [Mellon-appel flower] (7, 177) (1762–1828), Tetragonotheca (5) (1913)

Tetragonotheca **L.** – Yellow coneflower (122) (1937) TX

Tetraneuris acaulis **(Pursh) Greene** – Butte marigold (127) (1933) ND, Stemless four-nerve daisy (50) (present), Stemless tetraneuris (5, 97) (1913–1937)

Tetraneuris acaulis **(Pursh) Greene var. *acaulis*** – Northern stemless actinea (155) (1942), Sagebrush stemless acaulis (1, 138, 155, 158) (1900–1942), Stemless acaulis (124) (1937) TX, Stemless actinea (155) (1942), Stemless bitterweed (122) (1937) TX, Stemless four-nerve daisy (50) (present), Stemless hymenoxys (3, 4) (1977–1986), Stemless picradenia (131) (1899)

Tetraneuris acaulis **(Pursh) Greene var. *arizonica* (Greene) Parker** – Arizona stemless actinea (155) (1942)

Tetraneuris acaulis **var. *caespitosa* A. Nelson** – Woolly stemless actinea (155) (1942)

Tetraneuris grandiflora **(Torr. & Gray ex Gray) Parker** – Gray-lock actinea [Graylock actinea] (155) (1942)

Tetraneuris **Greene** – Four-nerve daisy (50) (present)

Tetraneuris herbacea **Greene** – Actinella (156) (1923), Early marigold (156) (1923), Eastern tetraneuris (5) (1913), Ontario actinea (155) (1942), Spring marigols (156) (1923)

Tetraneuris lanigera **Daniels** – See *Tetraneuris acaulis* (Pursh) Greene var. *caespitosa* A. Nelson

Tetraneuris linearifolia **(Hook.) Greene** – Fine-leaf four-nerve daisy [Fineleaf fournerved daisy] (50) (present), Fine-leaf tetraneuris [Fine-leaved tetraneuris] (5, 97) (1913–1937)

Tetraneuris linearifolia **(Hook.) Greene var. *linearifolia*** – Fine-leaf actinea [Fineleaf actinea] (155) (1942), Fine-leaf bitterweed [Fineleaf bitterweed] (122) (1937), Fine-leaf four-nerve daisy [Fineleaf fournerved daisy] (50) (present)

Tetraneuris scaposa **(DC.) Greene** – Stemmed actinea (124) (1937), Stemmed bitterweed (122) (1937)

Tetraneuris scaposa **(DC.) Greene var. *scaposa*** – Narrow-leaf tetraneuris [Narrow-leaved tetraneuris] (5) (1913), Stemmy four-nerve daisy [Stemmy fournerved daisy] (50) (present)

Tetraneuris septentrionalis **Rydb.** – See *Tetraneuris acaulis* (Pursh) Greene var. *acaulis*

Tetraneuris stenophylla **Rydb.** – See *Tetraneuris scaposa* (DC.) Greene var. *scaposa*

Tetranthera californica **Hook. & Arn.** – See *Umbellularia californica* (Hook. & Arn.) Nutt. var. *californica*

Tetranthera geniculata **(Walter) Nees** – See *Litsea aestivalis* (L.) Fern.

Tetrapanax papyriferus **(Hook.) K. Koch** – Rice-paper plant (109, 138) (1923–1949)

Tetrapanax papyriferus **Koch** – See *Tetrapanax papyriferus* (Hook.) K. Koch

Teucrium **(Tourn.) L.** – See *Teucrium* L.

Teucrium botrys **L.** – Cut-leaf annual germander [Cut-leaved annual germander] (5) (1913)

Teucrium canadense **L.** – American germander (4, 5, 62, 80, 82, 93, 95, 138, 155, 156, 158) (1900–1942), American wood-sage [American wood sage, American woodsage] (97, 158) (1900–1937), Betony (77) (1898) Western US, Canadian germander [Canada germander] (50) (present), Germander (19, 57, 80, 82, 92, 106, 131, 184) (1793–1930), Groundpine [Ground-pine, Ground pine] (5, 158) (1900–1913), Head-betony [Head betony] (77) (1898) Western US, Iagged germander (Jagged germander) (178) (1526), Teucrium (57) (1917), Water germander (46) (1649), Wild germander (48) (1882), Wood betony [Wood-betony, Woodbetony] (77) (1898) Western US, Wood germander (124) (1937), Wood-sage [Wood sage] (4, 5, 19, 48, 62, 72, 80, 82, 85, 92, 93, 95, 106, 114, 131, 156) (1840–1986), possibly Nettle-leaf germander [Nettle-leaved germander] (187) (1818)

Teucrium canadense **L. var. *canadense*** – Narrow-leaf germander [Narrow-leaved germander] (5, 97) (1913–1937)

Teucrium canadense **L. var. *occidentale* (Gray) McClintock & Epling** – Germander (127, 158) (1900–1933), Hairy germander (5, 72, 93, 97, 131, 155) (1899–1942), Western germander (50, 82) (1930–present)

Teucrium cubense **Jacq.** – Coast germander (124) (1937) TX

Teucrium fruticans **L.** – Tree germander (138) (1923)

Teucrium **L.** – Germander (1, 2, 4, 7, 10, 50, 82, 109, 138, 155, 156) (1818–present), Wood-sage [Wood sage] (1, 4, 167) (1814–1986)

Teucrium laciniatum **Torr.** – Cut-leaf germander [Cutleaf germander, Cut-leaved germander] (3, 4, 6, 97) (1892–1986), Lacy germander (50) (present), Prairie germander (124) (present)

Teucrium littorale **Bickn.** – See *Teucrium canadense* L. var. *canadense*

Teucrium occidentale **Gray** – See *Teucrium canadense* L. var. *occidentale* (Gray) McClintock & Epling

Teucrium scorodonia **L.** – Ambrose (156) (1923), Eupatory (179) (1526), Garlic sage (92, 156) (1898–1923), Germander sage (156) (1923), Hyndhele (179) (1526), Mountain sage [Mountain-sage] (156) (1923), Rock-mint [Rock mint] (156) (1923), Wild sawge [Wylde sawge] (179) (1526), Wood germander (5, 107) (1913–1919), Wood sage (92, 107, 156) (1898–1923)

Thalesia fasciculata **(Nutt.) Britton** – See *Orobanche fasciculata* Nutt.

Thalesia uniflora **(L.) Britton** – See *Orobanche uniflora* L.

Thalia dealbata **Fraser ex Roscoe** – Powdered thalia (138) (1923), Powdery alligator-flag (50) (present), Powdery thalia (5, 97, 120, 122, 124) (1913–1938)

Thalia **L.** – Thalia (138) (1923) for Johann Thalius, German naturalist of the 16th Century

Thalictrum **(Tourn.) L.** – See *Thalictrum* L.

Thalictrum alpinum **L.** – Arctic meadow rue (5) (1913), Dwarf meadow rue (5) (1913)

Thalictrum anemonoides **Michx.** – See *Thalictrum thalictroides* (L.) Eames & Boivin

Thalictrum aquilegifolium **L.** – Columbine meadowrue (138) (1923)

Thalictrum caulophylloides **Small.** – See *Thalictrum coriaceum* (Britt.) Small

Thalictrum clavatum **DC.** – Mountain meadowrue [Mountain meadow rue] (5) (1913), Slender meadow rue (5) (1913)

Thalictrum confine **Fern.** – See *Thalictrum venulosum* Trel.

Thalictrum coriaceum **(Britt.) Small** – Cohosh meadow rue (5) (1913), Thick-leaf meadow rue [Thick-leaved meadow rue] (5) (1913)

Thalictrum dasycarpum **Fisch. & Avé-Lall.** – Meadow rue [Meadow-rue, Meadowrue] (37, 82) (1919–1930), Nisude-hi (Omaha-Ponca, flute-plant) (37) (1926), Purple meadow rue [Purple meadow-rue, Purple meadowrue] (3, 4, 50, 138, 155) (1923–present), Purplish meadow rue [Purplish meadow-rue] (5, 93, 97) (1913–1937), Ska-diks or skariks (Pawnee) (37) (1919), Skariks (Pawnee) (37) (1919), Tall meadow-rue [Tall meadow rue, Tall meadowrue] (5, 85, 93, 127) (1913–1936), Wazimna (Dakota, pine smell) (37) (1919)

Thalictrum dioicum **L.** – Dioecous meadow-rue (187) (1818), Early meadow-rue [Early meadow rue, Early meadowrue] (2, 5, 50, 63, 72, 82, 85, 86, 127, 131, 138, 155, 156, 158) (1878–present), Feathered columbine (5, 156, 158) (1900–1923), Meadow rue [Meadow-rue, Meadowrue] (19, 92) (1840–1876), Poor-man's-rhubarb [Poor-man's rhubarb, Poor man's rhubarb] (5, 92, 156, 158) (1876–1923), Quicksilver-weed (3, 4, 5, 73, 4, 158) (1894–1986) Penobscot Co, ME, Shining-grass [Shining grass] (5, 158) (1900–1913)

Thalictrum hultenii **Boivin** – Little rhubarb [Little Rubarbe] (178) (1526), Low meadowrue (138) (1923), Purple meadow rue [Purple meadow-rue, Purple meadowrue] (187) (1818)

Thalictrum **L.** – Anemonella (138, 155) (1923–1942), Maid-of-the-mist [Maid of the mist] (1) (1932), Meadow rue [Meadow-rue, Meadow-rue] (1, 2, 4, 7, 10, 13, 15, 41, 50, 63, 82, 93, 109, 127, 138, 155, 156, 158, 167) (1770–present), Rue-anemone [Rue anemone] (1, 13, 93, 109, 156, 158) (1849–1949), Rue-weed (184) (1793)

Thalictrum nigromontanum **Boivin** – Black Hills meadow-rue (50) (present)

Thalictrum occidentale **Gray** – Western meadow rue (131) (1899)

Thalictrum pubescens **Pursh** – Celandine (5, 76, 156) (1896–1923) Oxford Co. ME, Fall meadow rue (5) (1913), Feather columbine (156) (1923), King-of-the-meadow [King of the meadow] (79) (1891) Northeast US, Musketweed [Musket weed] (5) (1913), Musquash-weed [Musquash weed] (5, 76, 156) (1896–1923) Oxford Co. ME, Polygamous meadow rue [Polygamous meadow-rue] (187) (1818), Quicksilver-weed (156) (1923), Rattlesnake-bite [Rattlesnake bite] (5, 156) (1913–1923), Shining-grass [Shining grass] (156) (1923), Silverweed [Silver weed, Silver-weed] (5, 76, 156) (1896–1923) Oxford Co. ME, Tall meadow-rue [Tall meadow rue, Tall meadow-rue] (2, 63, 72, 138, 156) (1895–1923)

Thalictrum purpurascens **L.** – Purple meadow rue [Purple meadow-rue, Purple meadowrue] (63) (1899)

Thalictrum revolutum **DC.** – Rough-leaf meadow rue [Rough-leaved meadow-rue] (187) (1818), Waxy meadow rue (5) (1913)

Thalictrum thalictroides **(L.) Eames & Boivin** – Anemone (76) (1896) Sulphur Grove OH, Anemone rue (49) (1898), Anemonella (138, 155) (1923–1942), Mayflower [May flower, May-flower] (5, 74, 156) (1893–1923) Eastern MA, Meadow rue [Meadow-rue, Meadowrue] (102) (1886), Rue-anemone [Rue anemone] (3, 4, 5, 19, 49, 50, 63, 72, 76, 97, 156) (1840–present), Ûtsatĭ uwadsĭska (Cherokee, fish scales) (102) (1886) from shape of leaves, Windflower [Wind flower, Wind-flower, Wind-floures, Winde-floures] (5, 156) (1913–1923), Windflower meadow rue [Wind flower meadow rue, Wind-flower meadow-rue] (86) (1878)

Thalictrum venulosum **Trel.** – Critical meadowrue (155) (1942), Early meadow-rue [Early meadow rue, Early meadowrue] (3, 4) (1977–1986), Veiny meadow-rue [Veiny meadow rue, Veiny meadowrue] (5, 50, 131, 155) (1899–present)

Thamnosma texana **(Gray) Torr.** – Rue-of-the-mountains [Rue of the mountains] (50) (present), Texas desert-rue [Texas desertrue] (155) (1942)

Thamnosma **Torr. & Frem.** – Desert rue [Desertrue] (50, 155) (1942–present), Dutchman's-breeches [Dutchman's breeches, Dutchmans' breeches, Dutch-mans' breeches, Dutchmans-breeches] (4) (1986)

Thapsia trifoliata **(sic)** – See *Thaspium trifoliatum* (L.) Gray

Thaspium aureum **(L.) Nutt.** – See *Thaspium trifoliatum* (L.) Gray var. *aureum* Britt.

Thaspium barbinode **(Michx.) Nutt.** – Bûsidji'bĭkûgûk (Chippewa, plump root) (40) (1928), Hairy-joint meadow-parsnip [Hairy-jointed meadow parsnip, Hairy-jointed meadow-parsnip] (5, 50, 72, 97) (1907–present), Meadow-parsnip [Meadow parsnip, Meadowparsnip] (4, 40, 85, 95) (1911–1986)

Thaspium barbinode **(Michx.) Nutt. var. angustifolium Coult. & Rose** – See *Thaspium barbinode* (Michx.) Nutt.

Thaspium **Nutt.** – Meadow-parsnip [Meadow parsnip, Meadowparsnip] (1, 4, 50, 156, 158) (1900–present), Round-heart [Round heart, Roundheart] (7) (1828), Thaspium (155) (1942)

Thaspium pinnatifidum **(Buckl.) Gray** – Cut-leaf meadow parsley [Cut-leaved meadow parsley] (5) (1913)

Thaspium trifoliatum **(L.) Britton** – See *Thaspium trifoliatum* (L.) Gray

Thaspium trifoliatum **(L.) Gray** – Purple Alexanders (158) (1900), Purple meadow-parsnip [Purple meadow parsnip, Purple meadow-parsnip] (5, 50, 158) (1900–present), Round-heart [Round heart, Roundheart] (158) (1900), Round-heart plant [Round heart-plant] (92) (1876), Three-leaf thaspium [Three-leaved thaspium] (3) (1977)

Thaspium trifoliatum **(L.) Gray var. aureum Britt.** – Alexanders [Alexander] (19, 92) (1840–1876), Golden alexanders (8) (1785), Golden meadow-parsnip [Golden meadow parsnip] (8) (1785), Golden Pastinake (German) (8) (1785), Meadow-parsnip [Meadow parsnip, Meadowparsnip] (8, 156) (1785–1923), Purple Alexanders (156) (1923), Purple meadow-parsnip [Purple meadow parsnip, Purple meadowparsnip] (156) (1923), Round-heart [Round heart, Roundheart] (8, 156) (1785–1923)

Thea **L.** – See *Camellia* L.

Thelesperma ambiguum **Gray** – Colorado greenthread (50, 155) (1942–present)

Thelesperma filifolium **(Hook.) Gray** – Greenthread (4) (1986), Stiff greenthread (50) (present)

Thelesperma filifolium **(Hook.) Gray var. filifolium** – Fine-leaf thelesperma [Fine-leaved thelesperma] (5, 97) (1913–1937), Nippleweed [Nipple weed, Nipple-weed] (93) (1936) Neb, Stiff greenthread (50) (present), Tall thelesperma (124) (1937)

Thelesperma filifolium **(Hook.) Gray var. intermedium (Rydb.) Shinners** – Greenthread (3) (1977), Stiff greenthread (50) (present), Stiff thelesperma (5) (1913)

Thelesperma gracile **(Torr.) Gray** – See *Thelesperma megapotamicum* (Spreng.) Kuntze

Thelesperma intermedium **Rydb.** – See *Thelesperma filifolium* (Hook.) Gray var. *intermedium* (Rydb.) Shinners

Thelesperma **Less.** – Greenthread (50, 155) (1942–present), Thelesperma (158) (1900)

Thelesperma megapotamicum **(Spreng.) Kuntze** – Greenthread (98) (1926), Hopi tea greenthread (50) (present), Nippleweed [Nipple weed, Nipple-weed] (98) (1942) Neb, Rayless thelesperma (5, 93, 97) (1913–1937)

Thelesperma subnudum **Gray var. marginatum (Rydb.) T. E. Melchert ex Cronq.** – Navaho tea (50) (1977–1986)

Thelesperma trifidum **(Poir.) Britton** – See *Thelesperma filifolium* (Hook.) Gray var. *filifolium*

Thelocactus setispinus (Engelm.) E. F. Anderson − Twisted rib (109) (1949)

Thelypodiopsis elegans (M. E. Jones) Rydb. − Wild cabbage (106) (1930) Grand Junction CO

Thelypodium Endl. − Thelepodium (158) (1900), Thelypody (50, 155) (1942–present)

Thelypodium integrifolium (Nutt.) Endl. ex Walp. − Entire-leaf thelypodium [Entire-leaved thelypodium] (5, 72) (1907–1913), Entire-leaf thelypody [Entireleaved thelypody] (50) (present)

Thelypodium integrifolium (Nutt.) Endl. ex Walp. subsp. *integrifolium* − Entire-leaf thelypody [Entireleaved thelypody] (50) (present)

Thelypodium wrightii Gray − Wright's thelypody [Wright thelopody] (50, 155) (1942–present)

Thelypteris dentata (Forsk.) E. St. John − Downy wood fern [Downy woodfern] (138) (1923)

Thelypteris hexagonoptera (Michx.) Weath. − See *Phegopteris hexagonoptera* (Michx.) Fee

Thelypteris nevadensis (Baker) Clute ex Morton − Sierra Nevada shield fern [Sierra Nevada shield-fern] (86) (1878)

Thelypteris noveboracensis (L.) Nieuwl. − Bear's-paw [Bear's paw] (78) (1898) Plattsburg NY, New York fern [New-York-fern] (5, 109, 122, 138) (1913–1949)

Thelypteris palustris Schott − Eastern marsh fern [Eastern marshfern] (50) (present), Marsh fern [Marshfern] (46, 3) (1879–1977), Snuffbox fern (19) (1840)

Thelypteris palustris Schott var. *pubescens* (Lawson) Fern. − Eastern marsh fern [Eastern marshfern] (4, 50) (1986–present), Female fern [Female Ferne] (158) (1900), Fragrant meadow fern [Fragrant meadow-fern] (158) (1900), Marsh fern [Marshfern] (5, 109, 138, 155, 158) (1913–1949), Marsh shield fern [Marsh shieldfern, Marsh shield-fern] (5, 97, 122) (1913–1937), Meadow fern (158) (1900), Quill fern (5, 158) (1900–1913), Shield fern (72) (1907), Swamp fern (5, 158) (1900–1913), Wood fern [Woodfern] (5) (1913)

Thelypteris phegopteris (L.) Slosson − See *Phegopteris connectilis* (Michx.) Watt

Thelypteris Schmidel − Beech fern (4) (1986), Maiden fern (50) (present), possibly Beech fern (1) (1932)

Thelypteris simulata (Davenport) Nieuwl. − Bog fern (50) (present), Dodge's shield fern [Dodge's shield-fern] (5) (1913)

Thelypteris Slosson − possibly *Thelypteris* Schmidel

Theobroma cacao L. − Cacao (107, 109, 110, 138) (1886–1949), Cacao beans (92) (1876), Cacao butter (92) (1876) the fixed oil, Cacautl (Mexico) (107) (1919), Chocolate (92) (1876), Chocolate nuts (92) (1876), Cocoa (107) (1919)

Thermopsis mollis (Michx.) M. A. Curtis − Allegheny thermopsis [Allegheny thermopsis] (5) (1913), Bush pea (5, 156) (1913–1923), False lupine (156) (1923), Soft thermopsis (138) (1923), Yellow pea [Yellow-pea] (156) (1923)

Thermopsis mollis Curtis − See *Thermopsis mollis* (Michx.) M. A. Curtis

Thermopsis R. Br. ex Aiton f. − Buckbean [Buck bean, Buck-bean] (4) (1986), False lupine (158) (1900), Golden-banner [Goldenbanner] (50) (present), Prairie bean [Prairie-bean] (93) (1936), Thermopsis (138, 155) (1923–1942), Yellow pea [Yellow-pea] (93) (1936), Yellow-bean (148) (1939) CO

Thermopsis rhombifolia (Nutt. ex Pursh) Nutt. ex Richards. − Bush pea (5) (1913), False lupine (5, 37, 126) (1913–1933), Golden pea (3) (1977), Prairie buckbean (4) (1986), Prairie golden pea (98) (1926), Prairie thermopsis (5, 50, 131, 93, 155) (1899–present), Yellow pea [Yellow-pea] (4, 5) (1913–1986), Yellow wild pea (85) (1932) SD

Thermopsis rhombifolia (Nutt.) Richards − See *Thermopsis rhombifolia* (Nutt. ex Pursh) Nutt. ex Richards.

Thermopsis rhombifolius Nutt. ex Richards var. *rhombifolia* − See *Thermopsis rhombifolia* (Nutt. ex Pursh) Nutt. ex Richards.

Thermopsis villosa (Walt.) Fern. & Schub. − Carolina thermopsis (138) (1923), Hairy wild indigo (5, 97) (1913–1937)

Therofon aconitifolium (Nutt.) Millsp. − See *Boykinia aconitifolia* Nutt.

Thesium corymbosulum Michx. − possibly *Comandra umbellata* (L.) Nutt.

Thesium linophyllon L. − Bastard toadflax [Bastard toad flax, Bastard toad-flax] (92) (1876), Flaxleaf (50) (present)

Thesium umbellatum L. − See *Comandra umbellata* (L.) Nutt.

Thespesia populnea (L.) Soland. ex Correa − Portia tree [Portia-tree, Portiatree] (109, 138) (1923–1949)

Thespesia populnea Soland. − See *Thespesia populnea* (L.) Soland. ex Correa

Thevetia neriifolia − See *Thevetia peruviana* (Pers.) K. Schum.

Thevetia peruviana (Pers.) K. Schum. − Yellow oleander (109) (1949), Yellow-oleander (138) (1923)

Thevetia peruviana Schum. − See *Thevetia peruviana* (Pers.) K. Schum.

Thinopyrum A. Löve − Wheat grass [Wheat-grass, Wheatgrass] (50) (present)

Thinopyrum intermedium (Host) Barkworth & D. R. Dewey − Bearded wheat grass (129) (1894), Blue grass [Bluegrass, Bluegrass] (75) (1894) Neb, Bluejoint [Blue-joint, Blue joint] (45, 87, 88) (1884–1896), Bluestem [Blue-stem, Blue stem] (45, 67, 87, 88) (1885–1896), Colorado blue grass (75) (1894), Colorado bluestem [Colorado blue-stem, Colorado blue stem] (144) (1899), Intermediate wheatgrass (3, 50) (1977–present), Intermedium wheatgrass (97) (1937), Pond grass (75) (1894) Neb, Slough grass [Sloughgrass, Sloughgrass] (75) (1894) Neb, Stiff-hair wheat grass [Stiff-hair wheatgrass] (155) (1942), Wheat grass [Wheat-grass, Wheatgrass] (11, 22, 75) (1888–1894)

Thinopyrum ponticum (Podp.) Z.-W. Liu & R.-C. Wang − Rush wheat grass [Rush wheatgrass] (50) (present), Tall wheat grass [Tall wheatgrass] (3, 155) (1942–1977)

Thinopyrum pycnanthum (Godr.) Barkworth − Coast wheat grass (5) (1913), Tick quack grass (50) (present)

Thlaspi arvense L. − Bastard cress (5, 158) (1900–1913), Dish mustard (5, 156, 158) (1900–1923), False cress (156) (1923), Fanweed [Fan-weed] (156) (1923), Field cress (85) (1932) SD, Field pennycress [Field penny cress, Field penny-cress] (4, 5, 50, 63, 72, 80, 97, 155, 156, 158) (1899–present), Field peppergrass [Field pepper-grass, Field pepper grass] (131) (1899) SD, Frenchweed [French weed, French weed] (5, 126, 156) (1913–1933), Jim Hill weed (156) (1923), Mithridate mustard (46, 156, 158) (1879–1923), Pennycress [Penny cress, Penny-cress] (3, 19, 80, 92, 107) (1840–1977), Stinkweed [Stink-weed, Stink weed] (80) (1913), Treaclewort [Treacle wort, Treacle-wort] (5, 156, 158) (1900–1923), possibly Dish Mustard (180) (1633)

Thlaspi bursa-pastoris L. − See *Capsella bursa-pastoris* (L.) Medik.

Thlaspi campestre [L.] − See *Lepidium campestre* (L.) Aiton f.

Thlaspi L. − Pennycress [Penny cress, Penny-cress] (1, 4, 93) (1932–1986), Shepherd's purse (10) (1818), Wild sweet alyssum (1) (1932)

Thlaspi perfoliatum L. − See *Microthlaspi perfoliatum* (L.) F. K. Mey.

Thrinax floridana − See *Thrinax radiata* Lodd. ex J. A. & J. H. Schultes

Thrinax keyensis − See *Thrinax morrisii* H. Wendl.

Thrinax L. f. − See *Thrinax* Sw. (Greek for fan for leaves)

Thrinax microcarpa − See *Thrinax morrisii* H. Wendl.

Thrinax morrisi − See *Thrinax morrisii* H. Wendl.

Thrinax morrisii H. Wendl. − Brittle thatch palm (138) (1923), Key thatch palm (138) (1923), Morris thatch palm (138) (1923)

Thrinax parviflora − See *Thrinax radiata* Lodd. ex J. A. & J. H. Schultes

Thrinax radiata Lodd. ex J. A. & J. H. Schultes − Florida thatch palm (138) (1923), Jamaica thatch palm (138) (1923)

Thrinax Sw. − Peaberry palm (109) (1949), Thatch palm (138) (1923)

Thuja gigantea Nutt. − See *Thuja plicata* Donn ex D. Don

Thuja L. − Arborvitae or Arborvitae tree [Arbor vita, Arbor vitae, Arborvita] (1, 8, 50, 10, 14, 109, 138, 167) (1785–present), Arbre de vie (French) (8) (1785), Tree-of-life [Tree of life] (8) (1785), White cedar (1) (1932)

Thuja occidentalis douglasii aurea − See *Thuja occidentalis* L.

Thuja occidentalis L. − American arbor-vitae [American arbor vitae, American arborvitae] (2, 8, 107, 109, 112, 136, 138) (1785–1949),

American sweet-scented arborvitae [American sweet-scented arbor vitae] (8) (1785), Arborvitae or Arborvitae tree [Arbor vita, Arbor vitae, Arborvita] (5, 6, 7, 20, 49, 50, 52, 53, 54, 57, 61, 92, 136, 174, 177, 178, 184) (1596–present), Canadian arbor-vitae (46) (1879), Cedar or Cedar tree (75) (1894) ME, Cédre blanc (French) (19, 40, 41) (1770–1928), Common arborvitae (135) (1910), Douglas' golden arborvitae [Douglas golden arborvitae] (136) (1930), False white cedar (5, 49, 53, 92) (1876–1922), Feather-leaf cedar (5, 19) (1840–1913), Gi'jikan'dûg (Chippewa, cedar-like) (40) (1928), Hackmatack [Hack-matack, Hacmatack] (6) (1892), Hvita cedern (Swedish) (41) (1770), Lebesbaum (German) (6) (1892), Occidental arborvitae [Occidental arbor vitae] (41) (1770), Striped-leaf arborvitae [Striped leaved arbor vitae] (8) (1785), Thuia du Canada (French) (6) (1892), Thuja (6, 57, 60) (1892–1917), Thuya de Canada (French) (8) (1785), Thuya d'Occident (French) (8) (1785), Tree-of-life [Tree of life] (6, 49, 53, 178) (1596–1922), Western arborvitae [Western arbor vitae] (6) (1892), White cedar (2, 7, 52, 54, 75, 107) (1828–1919), Yellow cedar (49, 53) (1922)

Thuja odorata **Marshall** – See *Thuja occidentalis* L.

Thuja plicata **Donn ex D. Don** – Arborvitae or Arborvitae tree [Arbor vita, Arbor vitae, Arborvita] (5, 6, 10, 35, 38, 40, 41) (1806–1928), Cedar or Cedar tree (101) (1905) MT, Giant arborvitae [Giant arborvitae] (103, 109, 138) (1871–1949), Gigantic arborvitae [Gigantic arbor vitae] (20) (1857), Great arborvitae [Great arbor vitae] (161) (1857), Nee's arborvitae [Nee's arbor vitae] (20) (1857), Straight cypress (35) (1806), Thuia gigantesque (French) (20) (1857), Western arborvitae [Western arbor vitae] (161) (1857), Western red cedar (50) (present), White cedar (35, 101) (1806–1905), White cedar of California (14) (1882)

Thunbergia alata **Bojer ex Sims** – Black-eyed clockvine (138) (1923), Black-eyed Susan [Blackeyed Susan] (109) (1949), Thunbergia (92) (1876)

Thunbergia fragrans **Roxb.** – Sweet clockvine (138) (1923)

Thunbergia grandiflora **Roxb.** – Bengal clockvine (138) (1923)

Thunbergia laurifolia **Lindl.** – Laurel clockvine (138) (1923)

Thunbergia **Retz.** – Clockvine [Clock-vine] (109, 138) (1923–1949)

Thuya – See *Thuja* L.

Thuya gigantea – See *Thuja plicata* Donn ex D. Don

Thuya odorata – See *Thuja occidentalis* L.

Thuya variegata – See *Thuja occidentalis* L.

Thymelaea passerina **(L.) Coss. & Germ.** – Mezereon (50) (present)

Thymophylla acerosa **(DC.) Strother** – Prick-leaf dogweed [Prickleaf dogweed] (155) (1942), Prickly dogweed (50) (present)

Thymophylla aurea **(Gray) Greene ex Britt.** – Many-awn prickly-leaf [Manyawn pricklyleaf] (50) (present)

Thymophylla aurea **(Gray) Greene ex Britton var.** *aurea* – Many-awn prickly-leaf [Manyawn pricklyleaf] (50) (present), Thyme-leaf [Thymeleaf] (5, 122) (1913–1937)

Thymophylla **Lag.** – Tiny-Tim [Tiny Tim] (1) (1932)

Thymus **L.** – Thyme (106, 109, 138, 184) (1793–1949)

Thymus praecox **Opiz subsp.** *arcticus* **(Dur.) Jalas** – Brotherwort (5) (1913), possibly Ground thyme (7) (1828), possibly Thyme (10) (1818)

Thymus vulgaris **L.** – Common thyme (92, 109, 138) (1876–1949), Garden thyme (92) (1876), Hard time (178) (1526), Mother time (178) (1526), Thyme (19, 49, 57, 58, 92, 107) (1840–1919), Time (46, 178) (1526–1671) deliberately introduced by colonists by 1671

Thysanocarpus curvipes **Hook.** – Lacepod [Lace pod] (76) (1896) CA

Tiarella cordifolia **L.** – Allegheny foamflower (138) (1923), Coolwort (5, 156) (1913–1923), False miterwort [False mitrewort, False mitre wort] (5, 92, 156) (1876–1923), Foamflower [Foam flower] (5, 156) (1913–1923), Gem fruit [Gem-fruit] (5, 19, 92, 156) (1840–1923), Mitrewort [Mitre-wort, Mitre wort] (19, 92) (1840–1876), Nancy-over-the-ground (74) (1893) MA, Paasemung (Algic tribes) (7) (1828), Rough-leaf [Rough leaf] (29) (1869), White coolwort [White cool wort] (5, 74, 156) (1893–1923) NY

Tiarella **L.** – False miterwort [False mitrewort, False mitre wort] (1, 2, 109) (1895–1949), Foamflower [Foam flower] (138) (1923)

Tibouchina **Aubl.** – Glorybush (138) (1923)

Tidestromia lanuginosa **(Nutt.) Standl.** – Cladothrix (5, 97) (1913–1937), Woolly tidestromia (3, 50, 155) (1942–present)

Tidestromia **Standl.** – Cladothrix (158) (1900), Honeysweet [Honeysweet, Honey sweet] (50) (present), Tidestromia (155) (1942)

Tila americana **(Tourn.) L.** – See *Tilia americana* L.

Tilia **(Tourn.) L.** – See *Tilia* L.

Tilia ×europaea **L.** – Teil tree [Teil-tree] (178) (1526)

Tilia ×vulgaris **Hayne** [*cordata × platyphyllos*] – Common linden (138) (1923), European basswood (112) (1937), European linden (106, 109, 112) (1930–1949), German basswood (112) (1937), Linden flowers (92) (1876), Locust bloom (92) (1876), Teyl tree (92) (1876), Til tree [Til-tree] (92) (1876)

Tilia americana **L.** – American basswood (50, 109) (1949–present), American black lime (8) (1785), American lime or American lime tree [American lime-tree] (20, 157, 158) (1857–1929), American linden or American linden tree (3, 5, 8, 85, 93, 95, 97, 109, 112, 131, 138, 155, 156, 157, 158) (1785–1977), American lin-tree (157, 158) (1900–1929), Bass tree [Bass-tree] (156) (1923), Basswood [Bass wood, Bass-wood] (4, 5, 9, 20, 35, 40, 72, 82, 85, 49, 93, 97, 105, 106, 112, 113, 114, 121, 130, 131, 135, 156, 157, 158) (1806–1986), Basswood lime tree (57) (1917), Bast tree [Bast-tree] (5, 92, 157, 158) (1876–1929), Bee tree [Bee-tree] (5, 156, 157, 158) (1900–1929), Black lime tree [Black lime-tree] (5, 156, 157, 158) (1900–1929), Bois blanc (French, white wood) (41) (1770), Daddy-nut [Daddy-nuts] or Daddy-nut tree (156, 157, 158) (1900–1929), Hinde-hi (Omaha-Ponca) (37) (1919), Hinshke (Winnebago) (37) (1919), Hinta-chan (Dakota) (37) (1919), Hiṇdse (Osage) (121) (1918?–1970?), Hiṇta (Lakota) (121) (1918?–1970?), Lime or Lime tree [Lime-tree, Limetree] (121) (1918?–1970?), Lin tree (5, 76) (1896–1913) Sulphur Grove OH, Linden or Linden tree [Linden-tree] (4, 41, 46, 49, 57, 65, 82, 106, 112, 121, 135) (1649–1986), Line tree (46) (1671), Linn [Lynn] or Linn tree [Linn-tree] (35, 49, 156) (1806–1923), Linnwood (156) (1923), Monkey-nut tree [Monkey nut tree, Monkey-nut-tree] (5, 156, 157, 158) (1900–1929), Red basswood (157, 158) (1900–1929), Southern linn (5, 156) (1913–1923), Spoonwood [Spoon wood [Spoon-wood] (5, 156) (1913–1923), Tilleul d'Amérique (French) (8) (1785), Whistlewood [Whistle wood, Whistle-wood] (5, 156, 157, 158) (1900–1929), White lin [White linn] (156) (1923), White lind (5, 157, 158) (1900–1929), Whitewood [White wood, White-wood] (5, 49, 76, 92, 106, 156, 157, 158) (1896–1929), Wickup [Wickop] (156, 157, 158) (1900–1929), Wigobi-minŝ (Chippewa) (105) (1932), Wigub'imïj (Chippewa) (40) (1928), Yellow basswood (156, 157, 158) (1900–1929)

Tilia americana **L. var.** *americana* – Basswood [Bass wood, Basswood] (19, 92, 187) (1818–1876), Blue Ridge basswood [Blueridge basswood] (155) (1942), Blue Ridge linden [Blueridge linden] (155) (1942), Gray linden (138) (1923), Linden or Linden tree [Linden-tree] (19, 92, 187) (1818–1876), Quebec linden (155) (1942), Spoonwood [Spoon wood, Spoon-wood] (187) (1818), Wuckopy (92) (1876)

Tilia americana **L. var.** *caroliniana* **(P. Mill.) Castigl.** – Basswood of the Southeastern United States (124) (1937), Carolina basswood (109) (1949), Carolina oblique-leaf lime tree [Carolinian oblique-leaved lime-tree] (8) (1785), Crop-ear bass wood (19) (1840), Downy lime tree (20) (1857), Southern basswood [Southern bass wood] (5) (1913), Southern white wood (5) (1913), Tilleul de la Louisiane (French) (8) (1785)

Tilia americana **L. var.** *heterophylla* **(Vent.) Loud.** – Bee tree [Bee-tree] (5, 156) (1913–1923), Bee-tree linden [Beetree linden] (138) (1923), Cottonwood [Cotton wood, Cotton-wood] or Cottonwood tree [Cotton wood tree] (156) (1923), Large-leaf linden [Large-leaved linden] (20) (1857), Lime or Lime tree [Lime-tree, Limetree] (19, 92, 187) (1818–1876), Linden or Linden tree [Linden-tree] (5, 156) (1913–1923), Linn-wahoo (156) (1923), Michaux's basswood

[Michaux's bass wood] (5) (1913), Silver-leaf poplar [Silver-leaved poplar] (156) (1923), Teil tree [Teil-tree] (156) (1923), Tile tree [Tile-tree] (156) (1923), Tilleul heterophylle (French) (20) (1857), Wahoo [Waahoo, Wa-a-hoo, Wauhoo, Whahoo] (156) (1923), White basswood [White bass wood] (5, 156) (1913–1923), White lin [White linn] (156) (1923)

Tilia caroliniana **Mill.** – See *Tilia americana* L. var. *caroliniana* (Mill.) Castigl.

Tilia cordata **Mill.** – Little-leaf European linden [Littleleaf European linden] (138) (1923), Small-leaf linden [Small-leaved linden] (109) (1949)

Tilia euchlora **K. Koch** – Crimean linden (109, 138) (1923–1949)

Tilia europaea **L.** – See *Tilia ×vulgaris* Hayne [*cordata × platyphyllos*]

Tilia glabra **Vent.** – See *Tilia americana* L. var. *americana*

Tilia grandifolia **[Ehrh.]** – See *Tilia platyphyllos* Scop.

Tilia heterophylla **Vent.** – See *Tilia americana* L. var. *heterophylla* (Vent.) Loud.

Tilia **L.** – Basswood [Bass wood, Bass-wood] (1, 2, 4, 7, 13, 15, 50, 107, 109, 122, 124, 155) (1895–present), Bee tree [Bee-tree] (2) (1895), Daddy-nut [Daddy-nuts] or Daddy-nut tree (74) (1893) Madison WI, Lime or Lime tree [Lime-tree, Limetree] (8, 10, 13, 15, 107, 109, 158, 167) (1785–1949), Linden or Linden tree [Linden-tree] (1, 2, 4, 7, 8, 10, 13, 15, 92, 93, 109, 122, 138, 155, 158) (1785–1986), Linn [Lynn] or Linn tree [Linn-tree] (124) (1937), Spoonwood [Spoon wood [Spoon-wood] (7) (1828), Sucumug (Mohegans) (7) (1828), Sucuy (Algic tribes) (7) (1828), Sugumuck (Mohegans) (7) (1828), Tilleul (French) (8) (1785), Whitewood [White wood, White-wood] (7, 107) (1828–1919), Wuckopy (Algic tribes) (7) (1828)

Tilia michauxii **Nutt.** – See *Tilia americana* L. var. *heterophylla* (Vent.) Loud.

Tilia neglecta **Spach** – See *Tilia americana* L. var. *americana*

Tilia petiolaris **DC.** – Lime or Lime tree [Lime-tree, Limetree] (106) (1930), Silver linden (109, 138) (1923–1949), Weeping linden (138) (1923), Weeping white linden (109) (1949), White linden (109) (1949)

Tilia platyphyllos **Scop.** – Big-leaf European linden [Bigleaf European linden] (138) (1923), Large-leaf lime [Large-leaved lime] (109) (1949), Lime or Lime tree [Lime-tree, Limetree] (34) (1834)

Tilia pubescens **Aiton** – See *Tilia americana* L. var. *caroliniana* (Mill.) Castigl.

Tilia tomentosa **Moench** – See *Tilia petiolaris* DC.

Tilia venulosa **Sargent** – See *Tilia americana* L. var. *americana*

Tilia vulgaris – See *Tilia ×vulgaris* Hayne [*cordata × platyphyllos*]

Tillaea ascendens **Ea.** – See *Crassula aquatica* (L.) Schoenl.

Tillaeastrum aquaticum **(L.) Britton** – See *Crassula aquatica* (L.) Schoenl.

Tillandsia baileya **Rose** – See *Tillandsia baileyi* Rose ex Small

Tillandsia baileyi **Rose ex Small** – Bailey's ballmoss [Bailey ball moss] (122, 124) (1937) TX

Tillandsia bartramii **Ell.** – See *Tillandsia bartramii* Elliott

Tillandsia bartramii **Elliott** – Tillandsia tea-grass (183) (1756)

Tillandsia **L.** – Airplant [Air-plant] (50) (present), Long moss (10, 167) (1814–1818), Tillandsia (8, 138) (1785–1923) for Elias Tillands, 1640–1603, Sweden, made catalogue of the plants of Abo Finland in 1673, Tillandsia (French) (8) (1785)

Tillandsia recurvata **(L.) L.** – Small ball moss (122, 124) (1937)

Tillandsia recurvata **L.** – See *Tillandsia recurvata* (L.) L.

Tillandsia usneoides **(L.) L.** – American moss (14) (1882), Black moss (2, 5, 92) (1876–1913), Carolina tillandsia [Carolinian tillandsia] (8) (1785), Florida moss (5, 156) (1913–1923), Gray moss (156) (1923), Hanging moss (5, 156) (1913–1923), Long moss (2, 5, 92, 156, 182) (1791–1923), Longbeard [Long beard] (5, 156) (1913–1923), New Orleans moss (12, 14) (1821–1882), Old-man's-beard [Old man's beard] (Jamaica) (14) (1882), Southern moss (156) (1923), Spanish beard (18) (1805), Spanish moss [Spanish-moss] (5, 7, 92, 109, 122) (1828–1949), Tillandsia de Caroline (French) (8) (1785), Tree-beard [Tree beard] (5, 92, 156) (1876–1923), Vegetable hair (5, 92, 156) (1876–1923)

Tillandsia utriculata – See *Tillandsia utriculata* L.

Tillandsia utriculata **L.** – Spreading airplant (50) (present), Wild pine (19) (1840)

Tiniaria cilinodis **(Michx.) Small.** – See *Polygonum cilinode* Michx.

Tiniaria convolvulus **(L.) Webb & Moq.** – See *Polygonum convolvulus* L.

Tiniaria cristata **(Engelm. & Gray) Small.** – See *Polygonum scandens* L. var. *cristatum* (Engelm. & Gray) Gleason

Tiniaria dumetorum **(L.) Opiz** – See *Polygonum scandens* L. var. *dumetorum* (L.) Gleason

Tiniaria scandens **(L.) Small** – See *Polygonum scandens* L. var. *scandens*

Tiniaria **Webb & Moq.** – See *Polygonum* L. (all US species)

Tipularia discolor **(Pursh) Nutt.** – Crane-fly orchis [Cranefly orchis] (5, 122, 156) (1913–1937), Tallow root [Tallow-root] (5, 156) (1913–1923)

Tissa **Adans.** – See *Spergularia* (Pers.) J.& K. Presl

Tissa marina **(L.) Britton** – See *Spergularia salina* J.& K. Presl

Tissa rubra **(L.) Britton** – See *Spergularia rubra* (L.) J.& K. Presl

Tithymalopsis arundelana **(Bartlett) Small.** – See *Euphorbia ipecacuanhae* L.

Tithymalopsis corollata **(L.) Kl. & Garcke.** – See *Euphorbia corollata* L.

Tithymalopsis ipecacuanhae **(L.) Small.** – See *Euphorbia ipecacuanhae* L.

Tithymalopsis **Kl. & Garcke.** – See *Euphorbia* L.

Tithymalopsis marilandica – See *Euphorbia corollata* L.

Tithymalus arkansanus **(Engelm. & Gray) Klotzsch & Garcke** – See *Euphorbia spathulata* Lam

Tithymalus commutatus **(Engelm.) Kl. & Garcke** – See *Euphorbia commutata* Engelm.

Tithymalus cyparissias **(L.) Hill.** – See *Euphorbia cyparissias* L.

Tithymalus darlingtonii **(Gray) Small.** – See *Euphorbia purpurea* (Raf.) Fern.

Tithymalus helioscopia **(L.) Hill.** – See *Euphorbia helioscopia* L.

Tithymalus lathyris **(L.) Hill.** – See *Euphorbia lathyris* L.

Tithymalus lucidus **(Waldst. & Kit.) Kl. & Garcke** – See *Euphorbia lucida* Waldst. & Kit.

Tithymalus missouriensis **(J. B. S. Norton) Small** – See *Euphorbia spathulata* Lam

Tithymalus obtusatus **(Pursh) Klotzsch & Garcke** – See *Euphorbia spathulata* Lam

Tithymalus peplus **(L.) Hill.** – See *Euphorbia peplus* L.

Tithymalus platyphyllos **(L.) Hill.** – See *Euphorbia platyphyllos* L.

Tithymalus robustus **(Engelm.) Small** – See *Euphorbia brachycera* Engelm.

Tofieldia glabra **Nutt.** – Smooth tofieldia (50) (present)

Tofieldia glutinosa **(Michx.) Pers. subsp. *glutinosa*** – False asphodel (5) (1913), Glutinous triantha (5) (1913), Sticky tofieldia (50) (present)

Tofieldia glutinosa **Willd.** – possibly *Triantha glutinosa* (Michx.) Baker

Tofieldia **Huds.** – False asphodel (2) (1895), Scottish asphodel (1) (1932), Tofieldia (50) (present)

Tofieldia pusilla **(Michx.) Pers.** – Scotch false asphodel (50) (present)

Tofieldia racemosa **(Walt.) Britton, Sterns & Poggenb.** – Coastal false asphodel (50) (present), False asphodel (5) (1913), Viscid tofieldia (5) (1913)

Tolmiea menziesii **(Pursh) Torr. & Gray** – Piggy-back plant (109) (1949), Thousand-mothers [Thousand mothers] (109) (1949), Youth-on-age (109) (1949)

Tolmiea menziesii **Torr. & Gray** – See *Tolmiea menziesii* (Pursh) Torr. & Gray

Torenia fournieri **Linden ex E. Fourn.** – Blue torenia (138) (1923)

Torenia **L.** – Torenia (138) (1923)

Torilis **Adans.** – Hedge-parsley [Hedge parsley, Hedgeparsley] (1, 4, 50) (1932–present)

Torilis anthriscus **(L.) Gmel.** – See *Torilis japonica* (Houtt.) DC.

Torilis arvensis (**Huds.) Link** – Erect hedge-parsley (5, 97, 122, 156) (1913–1937), Scabby-head [Scabby head] (5, 156) (1913–1923), Spreading hedge-parsley [Spreading hedgeparsley] (50) (present)

Torilis arvensis (**Huds.) Link subsp.** *arvensis* – Spreading hedge-parsley [Spreading hedgeparsley] (50) (present)

Torilis japonica (**Houtt.) DC.** – Bur beakchervil (155) (1942), Hedge-parsley [Hedge parsley, Hedgeparsley] (4) (1986), Hemlock-chervil [Hemlock chervil] (5, 156) (1900–1923), Rough chervil (5, 156) (1913–1923), Rough cicely (5, 156) (1913–1923)

Torilis nodosa (**L.) Gaertn.** – Knotted hedge-parsley (5, 97, 122) (1913–1937)

Torresia odorata (**L.) Hitchc.** – See *Hierochloe odorata* (L.) Beauv.

Torreya **Arn.** – Torreya (138) (1923) For John Torrey, 1796–1873, American botanist

Torreya california – See *Torreya californica* Torr.

Torreya californica **Torr.** – California nutmeg [California-nutmeg] or California nutmeg tree (19, 78, 92, 138, 161) (1840–1898), Nutmeg tree (75) (1894), Nutmeg tree (of California) (147) (1856), Stinking nutmeg (14) (1882)

Torreya myristica **Hook.** – See *Torreya californica* Torr.

Torreya taxifolia **Arnot.** – Florida nutmeg (50) (present), Florida torreya (138) (1923), Florida yew tree (19) (1840), Torreya à feuilles d'If (French) (20) (1857), Yew-leaf torrya [Yew-leaved torrya] (20) (1857)

Torreyochloa pallida (**Torr.) Church var.** *pallida* – Pale false manna grass [Pale false mannagrass] (50) (present), Pale manna grass [Pale manna-grass] (5, 66, 90, 92, 94) (1885–1913)

Torreyochloa pallida (**Torr.) Church var.** *pauciflora* (**J. Presl) J. I. Davis** – Weak manna grass [Weak mannagrass] (140) (1944)

Tovara **Adans.** – See *Polygonum* L. (all US species)

Tovara virginiana (**L.) Raf.** – See *Polygonum virginianum* L.

Tovaria virginica – possibly *Polygonum virginianum* L.

Townsendia exscapa (**Richards.) Porter** – Low townsendia (5) (1913), Silky Townsend flower (86) (1878), Silky townsendia (5) (1913), Stemless Townsend daisy (50) (present), Stemless townsendia (155) (1942)

Townsendia grandiflora **Nutt.** – Large-flower Townsend daisy [Large-flower Townsend daisy] (50) (present), Large-flower townsendia [Large-flowered townsendia] (5, 97) (1913–1937)

Townsendia **Hook.** – Easter daisy (4) (1986), Townsend daisy (50) (present), Townsendia (93, 155, 158) (1900–1942)

Townsendia hookeri **Beaman** – Hooker's townsend daisy (50) (present)

Townsendia texensis **Larsen** – Texas Townsend daisy (50) (present)

Toxicodendron (**Tourn.) Mill.** – See *Toxicodendron* Mill

Toxicodendron diversilobum (**Torr. & Gray) Greene** – California poison sumac (71) (1898), Poison ivy (71) (1898), Poison oak [Poison-oak, Poisonoak] (15, 71, 76, 106, 161) (1857–1930), Yeara (71, 76) (1896–1898) CA, Yeard (15) (1895)

Toxicodendron **Mill** – Poison ivy (1, 4, 93) (1932–1986), Poison oak [Poison-oak, Poisonoak] (1, 4, 50) (1932–present), Poison sumac [Poison sumach, Poison shumach] (1) (1932), Poison tree [Poison-tree] (8) (1785)

Toxicodendron pubescens **Mill.** – Atlantic poison oak (50) (present), Poison oak [Poison-oak, Poisonoak] (8, 156) (1785–1923)

Toxicodendron quercifolium (**Michx.) Greene** – See *Toxicodendron toxicarium* (Salisb.) Gillis

Toxicodendron radicans (**L.) Kuntze** – Black mercury vine [Black mercury-vine] (5) (1913), Climbing ivy (5) (1913), Climbing poison ivy (85, 93) (1932–1936), Climbing sumac (5) (1913), Climbing sumach (19, 92) (1840–1876) KS, Eastern poison ivy (50) (present), Markry (5) (1913), Markweed [Mark weed, Mark-weed] (5) (1913), Picry [Pickry] (5) (1913), Poison ivy (4, 5, 19, 41, 92, 108, 122, 125) (1770–1986), Poison vine [Poison-vine] (8, 92) (1785–1876), Three-leaf ivy [Three-leaved ivy] (5) (1913), Trailing sumac [Trailing sumach] (5) (1913)

Toxicodendron radicans (**L.) Kuntze subsp.** *negundo* (**Greene) Gillis** – Eastern poison ivy (50) (present), Poison ivy (3) (1977)

Toxicodendron radicans (**L.) Kuntze subsp.** *pubens* (**Engelm.) Gillis** (**Scheele) Gillis** – Common poison ivy [Common poisonivy] (155) (1942), Eastern poison ivy (50) (present), Poison ivy (3, 181) (~1678–1977)

Toxicodendron radicans (**L.) Kuntze subsp.** *radicans* – Arbre à la puce grimpant (French) (8) (1785), Black mercury (71, 158) (1898–1900) ME, Black mercyrt (157) (1929), Climath (157, 158) (1900–1929), Climbing ivy (157, 158) (1900–1929), Climbing sumac (157, 158) (1900–1929), Dogwood [Dog-wood, Dog wood] (48) (1882) KS, Giftbaum (German) (158) (1900), Giftsumach (German) (158) (1900), Markery (158) (1900), Markry (71) (1898), Markweed [Mark weed, Mark-weed] (71, 157, 158) (1898–1929) ME, Mercury (5, 71) (1898–1913), Picry [Pickry] (71, 157, 158) (1898–1929), Poison ivy (41, 46, 62, 71, 72, 95, 131, 157, 158) (1770–1929), Poison oak [Poison-oak, Poisonoak] (14, 62, 71, 131, 157, 158, 177) (1762–1929), Poison vine [Poison-vine] (8, 38, 62, 71, 92, 157, 158, 187) (1785–1929), Poisonweed [Poysonweed] (181) (~1678), Sumach vénéneux (French) (158) (1900), Three-leaf ivy [Three-leaved ivy] (71, 157, 158) (1898–1929), Trailing sumac [Trailing sumach] (157, 158) (1900–1929), Twining sumac [Twining sumach] (41) (1770), Zumaque venenoso (Spanish) (158) (1900)

Toxicodendron radicans (**L.) Kuntze subsp.** *verrucosum* (**Scheele) Gillis** – Eastern poison ivy (50) (present), Poison ivy (3, 97) (1937–1977)

Toxicodendron rydbergii (**Small ex Rydb.) Greene** – Poison ivy (3, 4, 5, 85, 93, 126, 148) (1932–1986), Poison oak [Poison-oak, Poisonoak] (153) (1913), Poison sumac [Poison sumach, Poison shumach] (48, 148) (1882–1939), Western poison ivy [Western poisonivy] (50, 95, 155) (1911–present)

Toxicodendron toxicarium (**Salisb.) Gillis** – Arbre à la puce (French) (8) (1785), Arbre a poison (French) (6) (1892), Atlantic poison ivy (50) (present), Black mercury (73) (1892) Harmony ME, Black mercury vine [Black mercury-vine] (156) (1923), Climath (156) (1923), Climbing ivy (156) (1923), Climbing sumac (156) (1923), Eastern poison ivy (4) (1986), Giftsumach (German) (6) (1892), H'thiwathe-hi (Omaha-Ponca, plant that makes sore) (37) (1919), Markry (3, 73, 76, 156) (1892–1977), Markweed [Mark weed, Mark-weed] (73, 156) (1892–1923), Mercury (6, 73, 76, 156) (1892–1923), Picry [Pickry] (76, 156) (1896–1923) Hartford ME, Poison ash (19) (1840), Poison ivy (2, 3, 6, 9, 13, 15, 19, 47, 49, 52, 53, 54, 57, 72, 80, 82, 102, 113, 122, 130, 145, 156) (1840–1977), Poison oak [Poison-oak, Poisonoak] (2, 5, 6, 8, 13, 14, 15, 37, 48, 49, 52, 53, 54, 57, 61, 92, 97, 130, 145, 156) (1849–1937), Poison sumac [Poyson sumack] (190) (~1759), Poison vine [Poison-vine] (6, 13, 49, 53, 76, 92) (1849–1922), Rhus tox (54) (1905), Sumac veneneux (French) (6) (1892), Three-leaf ivy [Three-leaved ivy] (6, 156) (1892–1923), Trailing sumac [Trailing sumach] (92, 156) (1898–1923)

Toxicodendron vernix (**L.) Kuntze** – Bow-wood [Bow wood] (5) (1913), Dogwood [Dog-wood, Dog wood] (71) (1898) MA, Mijimniguns (Chippewa) (105) (1932), Poison ash (5, 6, 8, 47, 71, 76, 92, 156) (1785–1923) VT, Poison dogwood (2, 5, 6, 13, 15, 71, 92, 156) (1849–1923), Poison elder (2, 5, 6, 13, 15, 19, 71, 74, 92, 156) (1840–1923) Alabama, Poison oak [Poison-oak, Poisonoak] (71, 92, 105, 122, 124, 156) (1876–1937), Poison sumac [Poison sumach, Poison shumach] (2, 5, 6, 13, 15, 19, 46, 50, 71, 92, 105, 156, 187) (1818–present), Poison swamp sumac (71) (1898), Poison tree [Poison-tree] (5, 6, 13, 71, 156) (1849–1923), Poisonous elder (187) (1818), Poisonous sumac (41, 62) (1770–1912), Poisonwood [Poison wood, Poison-wood] or Poison-wood tree (5, 6, 46, 71, 92) (1876–1913), Sumac vernis (French) (8) (1785), Swamp sumac [Swamp sumach, Swamp shumach] (5, 6, 41, 71, 92, 156, 187) (1770–1923), Swamp-dogwood [Swamp dogwood (5, 6, 156) (1892–1923), Thunderwood [Thunder-wood] (71, 156) (1898–1923), Varnish tree (8) (1785)

Toxicodendrum pinnatum **Miller** – possibly *Metopium toxiferum* (L.) Krug & Urban

Toxicoscordion gramineum **Rydb.** – See *Zigadenus venenosus* S. Wats. var. *gramineus* (Rydb.) Walsh ex M. E. Peck

Toxicoscordion nuttallii **(A. Gray) Rydb.** – See *Zigadenus nuttallii* (Gray) S. Wats.

Toxicoscordion **Rydb.** – See *Zigadenus* Michx. (all US species)

Toxylon aurantiacum **Raf.** – See *Maclura pomifera* (Raf.) Schneid.

Toxylon pomiferum **Raf.** – See *Maclura pomifera* (Raf.) Schneid.

Tracaulon arifolium **(L.) Raf.** – See *Polygonum arifolium* L.

Tracaulon **Raf.** – See *Polygonum* L. (all US species)

Tracaulon sagittatum **(L.) Small** – See *Polygonum sagittatum* L.

Trachelospermum difforme **(Walt.) Gray** – Climbing dogbane [Climbing dog's-bane, Climing dogs bane] (97, 156) (1923–1937), Trachelospermum (5) (1913)

Trachelospermum difforme **Gray.** – See *Trachelospermum difforme* (Walt.) Gray

Trachelospermum jasminoides **(Lindl.) Lem.** – Confederate-jasmine (138) (1923), Star-jasmine [Starjasmine] (109) (1949)

Trachelospermum jasminoides **Lem.** – See *Trachelospermum jasminoides* (Lindl.) Lem.

Trachelospermum **Lem.** – Star-jasmine [Starjasmine] (138) (1923)

Trachypogon spicatus **(L.) Kuntze** – Crinkle awn (122) (1937) TX

Trachyspermum copticum **(L.) Link** – Ajava seed (92) (1876), Akasgia (92) (1876), Bishop's-weed [Bishop's weed, Bishop weed] (92) (1876), Ordeal poison of Africa (92) (1876)

Tradescantia bracteata **Small ex Britt.** – Bracted spiderwort (138, 155) (1923–1942), Long-bract spiderwort [Long-bracted spiderwort] (5, 10, 14, 50, 93) (1840–present), Spiderwort (3, 85, 98, 127) (1926–1977), Tintabloom (German for ink plant) (98) (1926) Neb

Tradescantia congesta **(Moench) D. Don** – See *Tradescantia virginiana* L.

Tradescantia crassifolia **Cav.** – Inch plant (73) (1892) MA, Jacob's-ladder [Jacob's ladder, Jacobs-ladder] (73, 78) (1892–1898), Joint plant (73) (1892) Cambridge MA, Mother-of-thousands (75) (1894) Boston MA, Wandering-Jew [Wandering Jew] (73, 78) (1892–1898)

Tradescantia fluminensis **Vell.** – Wandering-Jew [Wandering Jew] (109, 138) (1923–1949)

Tradescantia gigantea **Rose** – Spiderwort (117) (1908)

Tradescantia hirsutiflora **Bush** – Pilose spiderwort (97) (1937)

Tradescantia **L.** – Indian paint [Indian-paint] (78) (1898) Mineral Point WI, juice said to irritate skin and make it red, Spiderflower [Spider flower, Spider-flower] (7) (1828), Spiderwort (1, 50, 93, 109, 122, 124, 138, 155, 156, 158, 167) (1814–present) wrongly thought to be cure for spider bites or because juice is stringy and viscid like spider webs

Tradescantia montana **Shuttlw.** – See *Tradescantia subaspera* Ker-Gawl. var. *montana* (Shuttlw. ex Britt.) E. S. Anderson & Woods.

Tradescantia occidentalis **(Brit.) Smyth** – Prairie spiderwort (3, 50, 155) (1942–present), Spiderwort (85) (1932), Western spiderwort (5, 93, 97) (1913–1937)

Tradescantia occidentalis **(Britt.) Smyth var.** *occidentalis* – Prairie spiderwort (50) (present)

Tradescantia ohiensis **Raf.** – Bluejacket (50) (present), Čaŋxloǧaŋ paŋpaŋla (Lakota, soft weed) (121) (1918?–1970?), Ohio spiderwort (121) (1918–1970), Reflexed spiderwort (5, 72, 97) (1907–1937)

Tradescantia pilosa **Lehm.** – See *Tradescantia subaspera* Ker-Gawl. var. *subaspera*

Tradescantia reflexa **Raf.** – See *Tradescantia ohiensis* Raf.

Tradescantia subaspera **Ker-Gawl. var.** *montana* **(Shuttlw. ex Britt.) E. S. Anderson & Woods.** – Mountain spiderwort (5) (1913), Zigzag spiderwort (50) (present)

Tradescantia subaspera **Ker-Gawl. var.** *subaspera* – Zigzag spiderwort (5, 50) (1913–present)

Tradescantia subaspera **Ker-Gawl. var.** *typica* **E. S. Anderson & Woods.** – See *Tradescantia subaspera* Ker-Gawl. var. *subaspera*

Tradescantia tharpii **E. S. Anderson & Woods.** – Tharp's spiderwort [Tharp spiderwort] (3, 50) (1977–present)

Tradescantia virginiana **L.** – Common spiderwort (109) (1949), Ephemerine de Virginie (French) (86) (1878) because flowers remain open only one day, Short-stemmed spiderwort (5, 72, 97) (1907–1937), Snake-grass [Snake grass, Snakegrass] (156) (1923), Soon-fading spiderwort of Virginia [Soone-fading spiderwort of Virginia] (180) (1633), Spider flower [Spiderflower [Spider-flower (92) (1876), Spider-lily [Spider lily] (5, 75, 156) (1894–1923), Spiderwort (5, 19, 37, 72, 86, 92, 97, 156) (1840–1937), Star flower [Starflower, Star-flower] (86) (1878), Star-of-Bethlehem [Star of Bethlehem, Starre of Bethlem, Stars of Bethlehem] (86) (1878), Tradescantia (174, 177) (1753–1762), Tradescant's spiderwort [Tradescants spiderwort] (180) (1633), Tradescant's Virgiania spiderwort [Tradescants Virgianian spiderwort] (180) (1633), Trinity (5, 37, 156) (1913–1919), Trinity violet (156) (1923), Virginia spiderwort (50, 138) (1923–present), Widow's-tears [Widow's tears] (156) (1923)

Tradescantia zebrina **hort. ex Bosse** – Wandering-Jew [Wandering Jew] (109) (1949), Wandering-jew zebrina (138) (1923)

Tragia betonicifolia **Nutt.** – Betony-leaf noseburn [Betonyleaf noseburn] (50) (present), Catnep tragia (97, 156) (1923–1937), Noseburn (4) (1986), Stinging nettle (78) (1898) Western MO

Tragia cordata **Michx.** – Heart-leaf noseburn [Heartleaf noseburn] (50) (present), Twining large-fruit tragia [Twining large-fruited tragia] (5) (1913)

Tragia **L.** – Noseburn (4, 50, 155) (1942–present), Tragia (158) (1900)

Tragia macrocarpa **Willd.** – See *Tragia cordata* Michx.

Tragia nepetaefolia **Cavar.** – See *Tragia betonicifolia* Nutt.

Tragia ramosa **Torr.** – Branched noseburn (50) (present), Branching tragia (5, 97) (1913–1937), Noseburn (4) (1986)

Tragia urens **L.** – Eastern tragis (5) (1913)

Tragopogon **(Tourn.) L.** – See *Tragopogon* L.

Tragopogon dubius **Scop.** – Goat's-beard [Goat's beard, Goats-beard, Goatsbeard] (3, 4, 98) (1926–1986), Western salsify (4) (1986), Yellow salsify (50) (present)

Tragopogon **L.** – Goat's-beard [Goat's beard, Goats-beard, Goatsbeard] (4, 50, 109) (1949–present), Oyster plant [Oyster-plant, Oysterplant] (1) (1932), Oyster-root [Oyster root] (7) (1828), Salsify (1, 4, 155, 158) (1900–1986)

Tragopogon major **Jacq.** – See *Tragopogon dubius* Scop.

Tragopogon porrifolium **L.** – See *Tragopogon porrifolius* L.

Tragopogon porrifolius **L.** – Goatbeard [Goat beard] (19) (1840), Goat's-beard [Goat's beard, Goats-beard, Goatsbeard] (19, 92, 184) (1526–1939), Jerusalem star [Jerusalem-star] (5, 92, 156, 158) (1876–1923), Nap-at-noon (5, 75, 156, 158) (1894–1923), Oyster plant [Oyster-plant, Oysterplant] (5, 63, 72, 95, 97, 107, 109, 155, 158) (1899–1949), Oyster-root [Oyster root] (5, 92, 156, 158) (1876–1923), Purple goat's-beard [Purple goat's beard [Purple goates beard] (5, 156, 158, 178, 181) (1526–1923), Purple salsify (85) (1932), Salsafy (19, 92, 158) (1840–1900), Salsify (3, 4, 5, 50, 95, 97, 107, 109, 110, 156, 158) (1886–present), Vegetable-oyster [Vegetable oyster] (4, 5, 19, 92, 107, 109, 138, 156, 158) (1840–1986), Vegetable-oyster salsify (155) (1942)

Tragopogon pratensis **L.** – Goat's-beard [Goat's beard, Goats-beard, Goatsbeard] (63, 107, 146, 156, 178) (1526–1939), Go-to-bed-at-noon [Go to bed at noone] (5, 156, 158, 178) (1526–1923), Jack-by-the-hedge [Iacke by the hedge] (158) (1900), Jack-go-to-bed-at-noon (50) (present), Joseph's flower (5, 156, 158) (1900–1923), Meadow salsify (4, 5, 131, 155, 156, 158) (1876–1900), Noon-day flower [Noon day flower, Noon-day-flower] (92, 158) (1876–1900), Noon-flower [Noon flower, Noon-flower] (5, 92, 156, 158) (1876–1923), Noontide [Noon tide, Noon-tide] (5, 92, 156, 158) (1876–1923), Oyster plant [Oyster-plant, Oysterplant] (146) (1939), Salsify (146) (1939), Shepherd's-clock (158) (1900), Star-of-Jerusalem [Star of Jerusalem] (5, 92, 156, 158) (1876–1923), Vegetable-oyster [Vegetable oyster] (158) (1900), Wild salsify (93) (1936), Yellow goat's-beard [Yellow goats'-beard, Yellow goats-beard, Yellow goat's beard] (5, 72, 93, 95, 156, 158) (1900–1936), Yellow salsify (85) (1932)

Tragopogon virginicum L. – See *Krigia biflora* (Walt.) Blake

Tragopogon virginicus L. – See *Krigia biflora* (Walt.) Blake

Tragus berteronianus **J. A. Schultes** – Prickle grass [Prickle-grass, Pricklegrass] (163) (1852), Western prickle grass [Western prickle-grass] (94) (1901)

Tragus racemosus **(L.) All.** – Burdock grass (5) (1913), Prickle grass [Prickle-grass, Pricklegrass] (5) (1913), Stalked bur grass [Stalked burr grass] (50) (present)

Trametes hispida **Bagl.** – Trametes (128) (1933)

Trapa bispinosa – See *Trapa natans* L.

Trapa **L.** – Water caltrop [Water caltrops] (156) (1923), Water-chestnut [Waterchestnut, Water chestnut] (138) (1923)

Trapa natans **L.** – Buffalo nut [Buffalo-nut] (156) (1923), Jesuit's-nut [Jesuit nut, Jesuits-nut, Jesuits' nuts] (92, 107, 109) (1876–1949), Jesuit's-waternut [Jesuit's water-nut] (156) (1923), Ling (107) (1919), Saligot (107) (1919), Sanghara-nut (156) (1923), Singhara-nut (138) (1923), Swimming water nut (5) (1913), Trapa nut (107) (1919), Water caltrop [Water caltrops] (5, 107, 109, 156) (1913–1949), Water-chestnut [Waterchestnut, Water chestnut] (107, 109, 138) (1919–1949), Water-nut [Water-nuts, Waternuts] (92, 156) (1876–1923)

Trautvetteria caroliniensis **(Walt.) Vail** – False bugbane (5, 156) (1913–1923)

Trautvetteria **F. & M.** – False bugbane (2, 156) (1895–1942)

Tremella **L.** – See *Tremella* Pers.

Tremella nostoc **L.** – Will-o'the-wisp (92) (1876)

Tremella **Pers.** – Tree-jelly [Treejelly] (7) (1828), Witch's-butter [Witch's butter] (50) (present)

Triadenum fraseri **(Spach) Gleason** – Fraser's marsh St. John's-wort [Fraser's marsh St. Johnswort] (50) (present)

Triadenum **Raf.** – Marsh St. John's-wort [Marsh St. John's wort, Marsh St. Johnswort] (1, 50, 93) (1932–present), Triadenum (158) (1900)

Triadenum virginicum **(L.) Raf.** – Marsh St. John's-wort [Marsh St. John's wort, Marsh St. Johnswort] (3, 4, 5, 72) (1907–1986), St Peter's-wort [St Peter's wort] (46) (1671)

Triadenum walteri **(J. G. Gmel.) Gleason** – Larger marsh St. John's-wort [Larger marsh St. John's wort] (5) (1913)

Triadica sebifera **(L.) Small** – Chinese tallow or Chinese tallow tree [Chinese tallowtree, Chinese tallow-tree] (50, 109, 138) (1923–present), Kuei-xu (46) (1879) China, Pippal yank (46) (1879) India, Stillingier port-suif (French) (20) (1857), Tallow tree [Tallow-tree] (10, 14, 20, 46, 92) (1818–1882)

Triantha glutinosa **(Michx.) Baker** – False asphodel (156) (1923), Sticky tofieldia (50) (present)

Trianthema portulacastrum **L.** – Desert horse-purslane [Desert horse-purslane] (50) (present), Horse-purslane [Horse purslane] (4) (1986)

Tribulus **L.** – Bur nut [Bur-nut] (1, 174) (1753–1932), Caltrop [Caltrops] (1, 13, 14, 15, 93, 158) (1849–1932), Puncture vine [Puncture-vine, Puncturevine] (50) (present)

Tribulus terrestris **L.** – Automobile-weed (156) (1923), Bur nut [Bur-nut] (85, 156) (1923–1932), Caltrop [Caltrops] (80, 156, 178) (1526–1923), Earth caltrops (177) (1762), Goat's head [Goat head] (4) (1986), Ground bur-nut [Ground bur nut, Ground burnut] (5, 72, 97, 156) (1907–1937), Ground-burnut [Ground but nut, Ground bur-nut] (5, 72, 97, 156) (1907–1937), Land caltrop [Land caltrops] (5, 107, 156, 158, 174) (1753–1923), Puncture vine [Puncture-vine, Puncturevine] (3, 4, 50, 93, 122, 148, 155, 156, 174) (1753–present), Punctureweed [Puncture-weed] (156) (1923), Sandbur [Sand bur, Sand-bur] (156) (1923), Texas but (156) (1923)

Tribulus trijugatus **Nutt.** – See *Kallstroemia maxima* (L.) Hook. & Arn.

Tricachne (sic) insularis **(L.) Nees** – See *Digitaria insularis* (L.) Mez ex Ekman

Tricachne californica **(Benth.) Chase (sic)** – See *Digitaria californica* (Benth.) Henr.

Tricera **Willd.** – possibly *Pachysandra* Michx.

Trichachne californica **(Benth.) Chase** – See *Digitaria californica* (Benth.) Henr.

Trichachne insularis **(L.) Nees** – See *Digitaria insularis* (L.) Mez ex Ekman

Trichilia hirta **L.** – White bitterwood (138) (1923)

Trichloris pluriflora **Fourn.** – See *Chloris pluriflora* (Fourn.) W. D. Clayton

Trichodium **L.** – See *Agrostis* L.

Trichodium laxiflorum **Ell.** – possibly *Agrostis scabra* Willd.

Tricholaena rosea **Nees** – See *Melinis repens* (Willd.) Zizka

Trichomanes boschianum **Sturm.** – Appalachian bristle fern (50) (present), Bristle fern (5) (1913), Filmy-fern (5) (1913)

Trichophorum alpinum **(L.) Pers.** – Alpine bulrush (50) (present), Alpine cotton-grass [Alpine cotton grass] (5) (1913), Cottongrass [Cotton-grass, Cotton grass] (66) (1903)

Trichophorum caespitosum **(L.) Hartman** – Deer-grass [Deergrass, Deer grass] (46) (1879), Deer's-hair [Deer's hair, Deer hair] (5, 46, 156) (1879–1923), Scaly club-rush (66) (1903), Scaly rush (19) (1840), Tufted bulrush (50, 139) (1944–present), Tufted club-rush [Tufted club rush] (5) (1913)

Trichophorum clintonii **(Gray) S. G. Sm.** – Clinton's bulrush (50) (present), Clinton's club rush (5) (1913)

Trichophorum cyperinum – See *Scirpus cyperinus* (L.) Kunth

Trichophorum **Pers.** – Alpine cotton grass (1) (1932)

Trichophorum planifolium **(Spreng.) Palla** – Bashful bulrush (50) (present), Flat club-rush (66) (1903), Wood club-rush [Wood club rush, Wood clubrush] (5) (1913)

Trichosanthes anguina **L.** – Bur cucumber [Bur-cucumber, Burcucumber, Burr cucumber] (107) (1919)

Trichostema brachiatum **L.** – Blue-gentian [Blue gentian] (19) (1840), False pennyroyal [Falsepennyroyal] (19, 63) (1840–1899), Fluxweed [Flux weed, Flux-weed] (75) (1894)

Trichostema dichotomum **L.** – Bastard pennyroyal (2, 5, 106) (1895–1930), Bluecurls [Blue curls, Blue-curl, Blue-curls] (5, 19, 92, 106, 124, 158) (1840–1937), Common bluecurls [Common blue-curls, Common blue curls] (2) (1895), False pennyroyal [Falsepennyroyal] (156) (1923), Forked blue-curls [Forked bluecurls] (50) (present)

Trichostema **L.** – Bluecurls [Blue curls, Blue-curl, Blue-curls] (2, 4, 50, 138, 155, 158) (1894–present), Hair-stamen (167) (1900)

Trichostema lanatum **Benth.** – Romero (138) (1923)

Trichostema lanceolatum **Benth.** – Bluecurls [Blue curls, Blue-curl, Blue-curls] (106) (1930), Camphorweed [Camphor-weed, Camphor weed] (156) (1923), False pennyroyal [Falsepennyroyal] (156) (1923), Fleaweed [Flea-weed] (156) (1923), Turpentine (156) (1923), Vinegar weed [Vinegar-weed] (156) (1923)

Trichostema lineare **Nutt.** – See *Trichostema setaceum* Houtt.

Trichostema setaceum **Houtt.** – Narrow-leaf blue-curls [Narrow-leaved blue curls] (5) (1913)

Trichostomum **Bruch** – Trichostomum moss (50) (present)

Tricuspis cornuta – See *Triplasis americana* P. Beauv.

Tricuspis purpurea **Gray** – See *Triplasis purpurea* (Walt.) Chapman

Tricuspis sesleroides **[Torr.]** – See *Tridens flavus* (L.) A.S. Hitchc.

Tricyrtis hirta **(Thunb.) Hook.** – Hairy toadlily (138) (1923), Toad-lily [Toadlily, Toad lily] (109) (1949)

Tricyrtis hirta **Hook.** – See *Tricyrtis hirta* (Thunb.) Hook.

Tricyrtis **Wallich** – Toad-lily [Toadlily, Toad lily] (138) (1923)

Tridens albescens **(Vasey) Woot. & Standl.** – White prairie grass (5) (1913), White tridens (3, 50) (1977–present), Whitetop [White top, White-top] (94) (1901)

Tridens elongatus **(Buckley) Nash** – See *Tridens muticus* (Torr.) Nash var. *elongatus* (Buckl.) Shinners

Tridens flavus **(L.) A. S. Hitchc.** – Fall redtop [Fall red-top] (99) (1923), Purple-top [Purpletop] (3, 144) (1977–1899), Purple-top tridens [Purpletop tridens] (50) (present), Redtop [Red-top, Red top] (19, 187) (1818–1840), Tall redtop [Tall red top, Tall red-top] (5, 56, 87) (1884–1913), Tall red-top grass [Tall red top grass] (21, 66, 72) (1893–1903)

Tridens flavus **(L.) A. S. Hitchc. var. flavus** – False redtop [False red-top, False red top] (134) (1932), Purple-top [Purpletop] (119, 122,

Trifolium pratense L.

134, 155, 163) (1852–1942), Purple-top tridens [Purpletop tridens] (50) (present), Tall redtop [Tall red top, Tall red-top] (119, 163) (1852–1938)

Tridens muticus (**Torr.**) **Nash** – Slim tridens (3, 50) (1977–present), Wiry triodia (94) (1901)

Tridens muticus (**Torr.**) **Nash var.** *elongatus* (**Buckl.**) **Shinners** – Long-panicle three-tooth grass [Long-panicled three-toothed grass] (5) (1913), Long-panicle triodia [Long-panicled triodia] (119, 140) (1938–1944), Rough triodia (122, 140, 155) (1937–1944), Slim tridens (50) (present)

Tridens muticus (**Torr.**) **Nash var.** *muticus* – Slender triodia (94) (1901), Slim triodia (122) (1937)

Tridens pilosus (**Buckl.**) **Hitchc.** – See *Erioneuron pilosum* (Buckl.) Nash

Tridens **Roemer & J. A. Schultes** – Tridens (50) (present)

Tridens strictus (**Nutt.**) **Nash** – Long-spike tridens [Longspike tridens] (50) (present), Long-spike triodia [Longspike triodia] (155) (1942), Narrow three-tooth grass [Narrow three-toothed grass] (5, 99, 119) (1913–1938), Spiked triodia (94) (1901)

Trientalis americana **Pursh** – See *Trientalis borealis* Raf. subsp. *borealis*

Trientalis borealis **Raf. subsp.** *borealis* – American chickweed wintergreen (2) (1895), American starflower (138) (1923), Chick wintergreen (19, 92) (1840–1876), Chickweed wintergreen (5, 156, 179) (1526–1923), Hare trefle (179) (1526), May star [May-star] (75, 156) (1894–1923) NY, Snake flower [Snakeflower, Snake-flower] (156) (1923), Star anemone (73, 75) (1892–1894) MA, Star chickweed (156) (1923), Star flower [Starflower, Star-flower] (2, 5) (1895–1913), Star-of-Bethlehem [Star of Bethlehem, Starre of Bethlem, Stars of Bethlehem] (73, 75, 77) (1892–1898), Threeleaf-grass [Three leaved grass, Thre leued grasse] (179) (1526), Trefle (187) (1818)

Trientalis **L.** – Chickweed [Chick-weed, Chick weed] (50, 167) (1814–present), Chickweed wintergreen (2, 156) (1895–1942), Star flower [Starflower, Star-flower] (1, 50, 138) (1923–present), Wintergreen [Winter greene, Winter-green] (50, 167) (1814–present)

Trifolium (**Tourn.**) **L.** – See *Trifolium* L.

Trifolium agrarium **L.** – See *Trifolium aureum* Pollich

Trifolium alexandrinum **L.** – Alexandrine clover (110) (1886), Berseem (109) (1949), Egyptian clover (109) (1949) Clark

Trifolium arvense **L.** – Bottle-grass [Bottle grass] (5, 76, 156, 158) (1896–1923) MA, no longer in use by 1923, Calf clover [Calf-clover] (5, 76, 156, 158) (1896–1923) Southold Long Island, no longer in use by 1923, Dogs-and-cats [Dogs and cats] (5, 156, 158) (1913–1923) no longer in use by 1923, Field clover (19, 158) (1840–1900), Hare-foot clover [Hare's-foot clover, Hare's foot clover] (5, 156) (1913–1923), Hare's-foot [Hares foot, Hares foote, Hairs foot] (92, 158, 178, 187) (1526–1900), Lagopus (174, 177, 178) (1526–1762), Old-field clover [Old field clover] (5, 156, 158) (1900–1923), Poverty-grass [Poverty grass] (5, 156, 158) (1900–1923), Pussies (5, 76, 156, 158) (1896–1923) no longer in use by 1923, Pussy clover [Pussy-clover] (5, 156, 158) (1900–1923), Pussy-cats [Pussy cats] (5, 76, 156, 158) (1896–1923) no longer in use by 1923, Rabbit-foot clover [Rabbitfoot clover] (3, 4, 5, 50, 82, 155, 156, 158) (1900–present), Rabbit's-foot [Rabbit foot, Rabbits' foot, Rabbitfoot] (5, 92) (1876–1913), Stone clover [Stone-clover] (5, 72, 92, 156, 158) (1876–1923), Watch clover (158) (1900), Welch clover (92) (1876)

Trifolium aureum **Pollich** – Gullkulla (Swedish) (46) (1879), Hop clover [Hop-clover] (5, 46, 80, 156) (1879–1923), Hop trefoil [Hop-trefoil] (156) (1923), Jordhumble (Swedish) (46) (1879), Large hop-trefoil (46, 80) (1879–1913), Skogshumble (Swedish) (46) (1879), Yellow clover (5, 63, 72, 80, 156) (1899–1923), Yellow hop clover [Yellow hop-clover] (82, 156) (1923–1930)

Trifolium beckwithii **Brewer ex S. Wats.** – Beckwith's clover [Beckwith clover] (4, 5, 50, 129, 131, 155) (1894–present)

Trifolium biflorum **L.** – See *Stylosanthes biflora* (L.) Britton, Sterns & Poggenb.

Trifolium campestre **Schreber.** – Dwarf hop clover [Dwarf hop-clover] (156) (1923), Field clover (50) (present), Hop clover [Hop-clover] (19, 82, 85, 106) (1840–1932), Low hop clover [Low hop-clover] (4, 5, 63, 80, 97, 122, 131, 155, 156) (1899–1986), Perennial clover (174, 177) (1753–1762), Plains clover (3) (1977), Small hop clover [Small hop-clover] (72) (1907), Smaller hop clover (5) (1913), Smaller hop trefoil (5) (1913), White clover (109) (1949), Yellow clover (19, 80) (1840–1913)

Trifolium carolinianum **Michx.** – Carolina clover (2, 3, 4, 5, 50, 97, 122, 155) (1895–present)

Trifolium dubium **Sibth.** – Least hop clover [Least hop-clover] (5, 122) (1913–1937), Least hop trefoil [Least hop-trefoil] (5, 158) (1900–1913), Shamrock (5) (1913), Small hop clover [Small hop-clover] (3, 4) (1977–1986), Suckling clover (50, 155) (1942–present), True shamrock (158) (1900), Wild trefoil (5, 158) (1900–1913), Yellow clover (158) (1900), Yellow suckling (5) (1913), Yellow trefoil (5, 158) (1900–1913)

Trifolium elegans **Savi** – See *Trifolium hybridum* L.

Trifolium erectum **Walt.** – See *Rhynchosia tomentosa* (L.) Hook. & Arn. var. *tomentosa*

Trifolium fragiferum **L.** – Strawberry clover (4, 50, 109, 155) (1942–present), Strawberry-head clover [Strawberry-headed clover] (3) (1977)

Trifolium hybridum **L.** – Alsatian clover (5, 93, 156, 158) (1900–1936), Alsike (129, 158) (1894–1900), Alsike clover (3, 4, 5, 45, 50, 68, 76, 82, 85, 93, 106, 109, 110, 129, 138, 155, 156, 158) (1894–present), Honey clover [Honey-clover] (156) (1923), Hybrid clover (106, 156) (1923–1930), Showy clover (155) (1942), Swedish clover (5, 66, 95, 106, 156, 158) (1900–1930)

Trifolium incarnatum **L.** – Carnation clover [Carnation-clover] (5, 93, 156, 158) (1900–1936), Crimson clover (3, 4, 5, 45, 50, 63, 66, 68, 72, 82, 85, 93, 95, 97, 106, 109, 114, 138, 146, 155, 156) (1894–present), Farouch (French) (110) (1886), Farradje (French, Roussillon) (110) (1886), Farratage (French, Languedoc) (110) (1886), Fé (Catalan) (110) (1886), Fench (Catalan) (110) (1886), Feroutgé (French, Gascony) (110) (1886), French clover (5, 45, 93, 158) (1896–1936), German clover [Germaine Clauer] (68) (1913) Ottawa, Great hare's-foot [Great Hares foote] (178) (1526), Italian clover (5, 45, 68, 110, 156, 158) (1886–1923), Napoleons (5, 156, 158) (1900–1923), Scarlet clover (68) (1913) Ottawa, Trafoglio (Italian) (110) (1886)

Trifolium involucratum **Lam.** – possibly *Trifolium willdenovii* Spreng.

Trifolium **L.** – Clover (1, 4, 7, 35, 45, 50, 63, 82, 93, 138, 155, 156, 158) (1896–present), Star flower [Starflower, Star-flower] (177, 178) (1526–1762), Trefoil (1, 10, 45, 92, 156, 158) (1818–1932), White clover (106) (1930)

Trifolium longipes **Nutt. subsp.** *reflexum* (**A. Nels.**) **J. Gillett** – Rydberg's clover [Rydberg clover] (146) (1939)

Trifolium macrocephalum (**Pursh**) **Poir.** – Large-head clover [Large-headed clover] (76) (1896)

Trifolium medium **L.** – See *Trifolium pratense* L.

Trifolium megacephalum **Nutt.** – See *Trifolium macrocephalum* (Pursh) Poir.

Trifolium melilotus **var.** *caeruleum* **L.** – See *Trigonella caerulea* (L.) Ser.

Trifolium officinale **L.** – See *Melilotus officinalis* (L.) Lam.

Trifolium pratense **L.** – Ackerklee (German) (6) (1892), Beebread [Bee-bread] (157, 158) (1900–1929), Bristol three-leaf grass [Bristoll Three leafed grasse] (178) (1526), Broad-leaf clover [Broadleaved clover] (5, 45, 156, 157, 158) (1896–1929), Cleaver-grass [Cleaver grass] (92) (1876) archaic, Common clover (45) (1896), Common red clover (6) (1892), Cow clover [Cow-clover] (5, 109, 157, 158) (1900–1929), Cow-grass [Cow grass] (5, 45, 66, 68, 92, 156, 158) (1896–1923) Ottawa, no longer in use by 1923, Early red clover (45) (1896), Giant clover (5, 45, 158) (1896–1913), Honeysuckle clover [Honey-suckle clover] (5, 156, 157, 158) (1876–1929) England, Knap (5, 157, 158) (1900–1929), Mail-grass (158) (1900),

Trifolium procumbens L.   SCIENTIFIC NAMES INDEX

Mammoth clover [Mamoth clover] (5, 45, 138, 156, 158) (1896–1923), Marl-grass [Marl grass] (5, 92, 156, 157, 158) (1876–1929), Meadow clover (5, 93, 157, 158) (1900–1936), Pea-vine clover [Pea vine clover] (5, 45, 156, 158) (1900–1923), Perennial clover (66) (1903), Plyvens (157, 158) (1900–1929), Purple clover (5, 110, 157, 158) (1886–1929), Purplewort [Purple-wort, Purple woort] (156) (1923), Real sweet clover (73) (1892), Red clover (3, 4, 5, 6, 19, 45, 49, 50, 52, 53, 58, 61, 63, 66, 68, 72, 82. 85, 92, 93, 95, 97, 106, 107, 109, 114, 122, 129, 131, 138, 155, 156, 157, 158, 187) (1818–present), Rother Futterklee (German) (158) (1900), Rother Wiesen-klee (German) (158) (1900), Soukie clover (157, 158) (1900–1929), Suckles (5, 156, 157, 158) (1900–1929), Sugar-plum [Sugar plum, Sugar-plums, Sugar plums] (5, 156) (1913–1923), Threeleaf-grass [Three leaved grass, Thre leued grasse] (92) (1876), Trefle (French) (6) (1892), Zigzag clover [Zig zag clover, Zig-zag clover] (5, 66, 68, 109, 155, 156, 158) (1900–1949)

Trifolium procumbens L. – See *Trifolium campestre* Schreber.

Trifolium reflexum L. – Baffaloe clover (187) (1818), Black three-leaf grass [Blacke three leafed grasse] (178) (1526), Buffalo clover [Buffalo-clover] (3, 4, 5, 47, 50, 63, 72, 82, 85, 92, 93, 97, 122, 155, 156, 158) (1852–present)

Trifolium repens L. – Dutch clover (5, 45, 68, 156, 157, 158) (1896–1929), Dutch white clover (122, 124) (1937), Four-leaf-grass [Fower leafed grasse] (178) (1526), Honey-stalks [Honey stalks] (5, 156, 157, 158) (1900–1929), Honeysuckle [Honey suckle, Honey-suckle, Honisuckles] (76) (1896) Oxford Co. ME, Honeysuckle clover [Honey-suckle clover] (5, 156, 158) (1900–1923) no longer in use by 1923, Ladino clover (4) (1986), Lamb's-suck-lings [Lamb's sucklings, Lamb-sucklings] (5, 156, 157, 158) (1900–1929), Purple-grass [Purple grass] (5, 157, 158) (1900–1929), Purplewort [Purple-wort, Purple woort] (5, 157, 158, 178) (1526–1929), Quillet (157, 158) (1900–1929), Shamrock (5, 92, 156) (1876–1923), Sheep's-gowan [Sheep's gowan] (5, 156, 157, 158) (1900–1929), Suckling (157, 158) (1900–1929), Trefle blanc (French) (6) (1892), White clover (3, 4, 5, 6, 19, 41, 45, 50, 57, 63, 68, 72, 82, 85, 92, 93, 95, 97, 106, 107, 114, 129, 131, 138, 155, 156, 157, 158, 187) (1770–present), White honeysuckle [White honey-suckle] (157, 158) (1900–1929), White shamrock (92, 157, 158) (1876–1929), White trefoil (5, 93, 156, 157, 158) (1900–1936), Wiesen Klee (German) (6) (1892)

Trifolium resupinatum L. – Persian clover (4) (1986), Reversed clover (3, 50) (1977–present), Strawberry clover (138) (1923)

Trifolium rydbergii – See *Trifolium longipes* Nutt. subsp. *reflexum* (A. Nels.) J. Gillett

Trifolium simplicifolium Walt. – See *Rhynchosia reniformis* DC.

Trifolium stoloniferum Muhl. ex Eat. – Buffalo clover [Buffalo-clover] (7, 19) (1828–1840), Running buffalo clover (2, 3, 4, 5, 50, 72, 85, 93, 97, 131, 158) (1895–present)

Trifolium virginicum Small ex Small & Vail – Prostrate mountain clover (5) (1913)

Trifolium willdenovii Spreng. (possibly) – Cow clover [Cow-clover] (106) (1930), possibly Trefoil (107) (1919)

Triglochin L. – Arrowgrass [Arrow grass, Arrow-grass] (1, 50, 92, 148, 158, 167) (1814–present), Arrow-head-grass [Arrow-headed grass] (10, 41) (1770–1818), Goose-grass [Goosegrass] (148) (1939) CO, Podgrass (155) (1942), Sour-grass [Sourgrass, Sour grass] (148) (1939) CO

Triglochin maritimum L. – Arrowgrass [Arrow grass, Arrow-grass] (3, 19, 49, 92, 126, 138, 156) (1840–1977), Marsh arrowgrass [Marsh arrow-grass] (156) (1923), Seaside arrowgrass [Seaside arrow grass, Seaside arrow-grass, Sea-side arrow grass] (5, 50, 66, 72, 93, 131, 156) (1899–present), Shore podgrass (155) (1942), Spike-grass [Spike grass, Spiked-grass, Spiked grass] (5, 92, 156) (1876–1923), Tall arrow-grass [Tall arrow grass] (66) (1903)

Triglochin palustre L. – Arrow podgrass (155) (1942), Marsh arrowgrass [Marsh arrow-grass] (5, 50, 66, 85, 93, 131) (1899–present)

Triglochin striata R. & P. – See *Triglochin striatum* Ruiz & Pavón

Triglochin striatum Ruiz & Pavón – Three-rib arrowgrass [Threerib arrowgrass, Three-ribbed arrow-grass] (5, 50) (1913–present)

Trigonella caerulea (L.) Ser. – Blue melilot (41) (1770), Kraut curd-herb (Switzerland) (107) (1919)

Trigonella caerulea Ser. – See *Trigonella caerulea* (L.) Ser.

Trigonella corniculata (L.) L. – Assyrian Clauer (178) (1770)

Trigonella faenum-graecum L. – Fenugreek [Fenegreke] (19, 57, 92, 107, 109, 110, 129, 179) (1526–1949), Foenugreek seed (92) (1876), Foenum graecum (57) (1917), Helbeh (107) (1919), Tailis (Greek, ancient) (110) (1886), Trigonel (110) (1886)

Trilisa odoratissima (Walt.) Cass. – See *Carphephorus odoratissimus* (J. F. Gmel.) Herbert

Trilisa odoratissima Cass. – See *Carphephorus odoratissimus* (J. F. Gmel.) Herbert

Trilisa paniculata (Walt.) Cass. – See *Carphephorus paniculatus* (J. F. Gmel.) Herbert

Trillium catesbaei Elliott – Rose trillium (138) (1923)

Trillium cernuum L. – Benjamins [Benjamin] (156) (1923), Bethroot [Beth-root, Beth root] (7) (1828), Broad-leaf bethroot [Broadleaf bethroot] (7) (1828), Coughroot [Cough-root, Cough root] (5, 92, 156, 158) (1876–1923), Drooping three-leaf nightshade [Drooping three-leaved nightshade] (187) (1818), Drooping trillium (156) (1923), Ground lily (5, 7, 156, 158) (1828–1923), Indian balm (7) (1828), Indian shamrock (7) (1828), Jew's-harp [Jews harp] (7) (1828), Jew's-harp plant [Jews' harp plant, Jewsharp plant, Jew's-harp plant] (5, 156, 158) (1900–1923) no longer in use by 1923, Lamb's-quarters [Lambs' quarter, Lamb's quarters, Lamb's-quarters, Lambsquarter, Lambsquarters] (158) (1900), Mochar newachar (Indians of Missouri) (7) (1828), Nodding trillium (3, 138, 155, 156) (1923–1977, Nodding wakerobin [Nodding wake-robin, Nodding wake robin] (5, 72, 127, 156, 158) (1907–1933), Nodding white trillium (2) (1895), Pariswort [Paris wort] (7) (1828), Rattlesnake-root [Rattlesnake root, Rattle-Snake-Root, Rattlesnakes' root, Rattlesnakeroot] (5, 7, 156, 158) (1828–1923), Snakebite [Snake bite, Snake-bite] (5, 92, 156, 158) (1876–1923) no longer in use by 1923, Triole dilatee (French) (7) (1828), Truelove [True love] (7) (1828), Wakerobin [Wake robin, Wake-robin] (7) (1828), Whippoorwill flower [Whippoor-will flower] (50) (present), White Benjamin (5, 158) (1900–1913)

Trillium chloropetalum var. giganteum (Hook. & Arn.) Munz – California trillium (138) (1923)

Trillium declinatum (A. Gray) Gleason – See *Trillium flexipes* Raf.

Trillium declinatum Raf. – See *Trillium catesbaei* Elliott

Trillium erectum L. – Bathflower [Bath flower, Bath-flower (5, 64) (1908–1913), Bathroot [Bath-root, Bath root] (64, 156) (1908–1923), Benjamins [Benjamin] (73, 79) (1891–1892), Bethflower [Beth-flower] (5) (1913), Bethroot [Beth-root, Beth root] (5, 52, 64, 92, 156) (1876–1923), Birthroot [Birth-root, Birth root] (2, 6, 49, 57, 64, 75, 79, 92, 156) (1869–1923), Birthwort [Birth wort, Birth-wort] (64) (1908), Bumblebee root [Bumble bee root, Bumblebee-root] (5, 6, 64, 73, 156) (1874–1923) New England, no longer in use by 1923, Daffy-down-dilly [Daffy down dilly] (5, 64, 75) (1894–1913) Bradford VT, Death-root (156) (1923), Dishcloth [Dish cloth] (64, 73) (1892–1908) Franklin Center Quebec, Dog flower [Dog-flower] (156) (1923), False wakerobin [False wake robin] (19) (1840), Four-leaf nightshade [Four-leaved nightshade] (46) (1671), Ground lily (6, 49, 92) (1876–1892), Herb Paris (156) (1923), Herb true love (46) (1671), Herba paris (46) (1671), Ill-scented trillium (64, 156) (1908–1923), Ill-scented wake robin (5, 64, 72) (1893–1908), Indian balm (6, 49, 64, 92) (1876–1908), Indian shamrock (6, 64, 92) (1876–1908), Jew's-harp plant [Jews' harp plant, Jewsharp plant, Jew's-harp plant] (92) (1876), Lamb's-quarters [Lambs' quarter, Lamb's quarters, Lamb's-quarters, Lambsquarter, Lambsquarters] (5, 49, 92, 156) (1876–1923), Nodding wakerobin [Nodding wake-robin, Nodding wake robin] (19) (1840), Nosebleed [Nose-bleed, Nose bleed, Nose bleede (5,

424

6, 64, 75, 156) (1892–1923), Oneberry [One-berry, One berry] (46) (1671), Orange blossom [Orange blossoms] (5, 64, 75, 156) (1894–1923) no longer in use by 1923, Purple trillium (2, 64, 138, 155, 156) (1895–1942), Purple wakerobin [Purple wake robin] (5, 6, 64) (1874–1913), Rattlesnake-root [Rattlesnake root, Rattle-Snake-Root, Rattlesnakes' root, Rattlesnakeroot] (6, 92) (1876–1892), Red Benjamin [Red Benjamins] (5, 64, 78, 156) (1898–1923) ME, Red trillium (5, 64, 50, 156) (1908–present), Red wakerobin [Red wake robin, Red wake-robin] (5, 64, 156) (1908–1923), Shamrock (5, 156) (1913–1923), Snakebite [Snake bite, Snake-bite] (92) (1876), Squaw flower [Squawflower] (5, 64, 75) (1894–1913) Ferrisburgh VT, Squawroot [Squaw-root, Squaw root] (64, 73, 79, 156) (1891–1923) NH, Stinking-Benjamins [Stinking Benjamins] (73) (1892) NB, Stinking-dishcloth [Stinking dish-cloth] (73) (1892) Franklin Center PQ, Stinking-Willie [Stinking Willie] (156) (1923), Three-leaf nightshade [Three-leaved nightshade] (6) (1892), Trillium (57, 64) (1908–1917), Trillium (French) (6) (1892), Trillium (German) (6) (1892), Truelove [True love] (5, 64, 102, 156) (1886–1923), Wakerobin [Wake robin, Wake-robin] (6, 49, 57, 92, 156) (1876–1923), Wild peony (78) (1898) ME, Wild piny (78) (1898) ME, Wood-lily [Wood lily] (64) (1908)

***Trillium erectum* L. var. *flavum* Torr.** – See *Trillium erectum* L.

***Trillium erythrocarpum* Michx.** – See *Trillium undulatum* Willd.

***Trillium flexipes* Raf.** – Drooping wakerobin [Drooping wake robin] (5) (1913), Nodding wakerobin [Nodding wake-robin, Nodding wake robin] (50) (present), Shy trillium (155) (1942), Wakerobin [Wake robin, Wake-robin] (85) (1932) SD

***Trillium grandiflorum* (Michx.) Salisb.** – Bathflower [Bath flower, Bath-flower (5, 75) (1894–1913) Franklin Center Quebec, corruption of beth flower, which is corruption of birth flower, Buttermilk lily [Buttermilk-lily] (156) (1923), Easter flower [Easter-flower, Easter flowers] (156) (1923), Great white trillium (156) (1923), Great-flower white trillium [Great-flowered white trillium] (2) (1895), Ground lily (156) (1923), Inĭ'nĭwĭn'dĭbĭge'gûn (Chippewa) (40) (1928), Large-flower wakerobin [Large flowered wake robin, Large-flowered wake-robin] (5, 72, 156) (1907–1923), Moose flower [Moose-flower, Moose flowers] (156) (1923), Snow trillium (50, 138, 156) (1923–present), Trinity lily (5, 73, 156) (1892–1923) Wisconsin, Wakerobin [Wake robin, Wake-robin] (40) (1928), White lily [White lilies] (5, 73) (1892–1913), Wood lily (156) (1923)

***Trillium grandiflorum* Salisb.** – See *Trillium grandiflorum* (Michx.) Salisb.

***Trillium* L.** – American herb Paris (10) (1818), Benjamins [Benjamin] (73) (1892), Birthroot [Birth-root, Birth root] (1, 106, 158) (1900–1930), Moose flower [Moose-flower, Moose flowers] (75) (1894) NY, Pariswort [Paris wort] (92) (1876), Trillium (50, 106, 138, 155) (1923–present), Truelove of Canada [True-love of Canada] (167) (1814), Wakerobin [Wake robin, Wake-robin] (1, 93, 106, 109, 155, 156, 158) (1900–1949)

***Trillium nivale* Riddell** – Dwarf trillium (138, 155, 156) (1923–1942), Dwarf white trillium (3, 85) (1932–1977), Dwarf white wakerobin [Dwarf white wake-robin, Dwarf white wake robin] (2, 5, 50, 157, 158) (1895–present), Early trillium (156) (1923), Early wake-robin [Early wake robin] (5, 72, 93, 157, 158) (1900–1936), Showy wake-robin [Showy wake robin] (5) (1913), Snowy trillium (156) (1923)

***Trillium ovatum* Pursh** – Pacific trillium (138) (1923)

***Trillium pendulum* W.** – See *Trillium erectum* L.

***Trillium petiolatum* Pursh** – Idaho trillium (138) (1923)

***Trillium pusillum* Michx.** – Dwarf wakerobin [Dwarf wake robin] (19, 50) (1840–present)

***Trillium recurvatum* Beck** – Bloody-butcher [Bloody butcher, Bloody-butchers, Bloody butchers] (50, 156) (1923–present), Cowslip [Cowslips, Cowslyp] (78) (1898) IN, Jack-in-the-pulpit [Jack in the pulpit, Jackinthepulpit] (78) (1898) IL, Prairie trillium (138) (1923), Prairie wakerobin [Prairie wake robin] (5, 72) (1907–1913),

possibly Beefsteak plant [Beefsteak-plant, Beefsteakplant] (156) (1923), possibly Bloody-noses [Bloody noses] (156) (1923), possibly Nosebleed [Nose-bleed, Nose bleed, Nose bleede] (156) (1923), possibly Red trillium (156) (1923)

Trillium reflexum – possibly *Trillium recurvatum* Beck

***Trillium rhomboideum* Michx.** – See *Trillium erectum* L.

Trillium sessile californicum – See *Trillium chloropetalum* var. *giganteum* (Hook. & Arn.) Munz

***Trillium sessile* L.** – Beefsteak [Beef steak] (156) (1840), Beefsteak plant [Beefsteak-plant, Beefsteakplant] (156) (1923), Bethflower [Beth-flower] (48) (1882) KS, Bethroot [Beth-root, Beth root] (58) (1869), Birthroot [Birth-root, Birth root] (58) (1869), Bloody-butcher [Bloody butcher, Bloody-butchers, Bloody butchers] (156) (1923), Ground lily (58) (1869), Jew's-harp [Jews harp] (58) (1869), Nosebleed [Nose-bleed, Nose bleed, Nose bleede (156) (1923), Red trillium (156) (1923), Sessile-flower red wake-robin [Sessile-flowered red wake robin] (158) (1900), Sessile-flower wake-robin [Sessile-flowered wake robin] (5, 72) (1907–1913) IA, Three-leaf nightshade [Three-leaved nightshade] (5, 156) (1913–1923), Toad trillium (138, 155) (1923–1942), Toad-shade [Toadshade] (3, 50) (1977–present), Trefoil Herb Paris (181) (~1678)

***Trillium undulatum* Willd.** – Bathroot [Bath-root, Bath root] (29) (1869), Benjamins [Benjamin] (73, 156) (1892–1923), Painted trillium (2, 138, 156) (1895–1923), Painted-lady [Painted lady] (156) (1923), Sarah (75, 156) (1894–1923), Smiling wakerobin [Smiling wake-robin, Smiling wake robin] (19, 156) (1840–1923), White Benjamin (78) (1898), Wild pepper (156) (1923)

***Trillium viride* Beck** – Green trillium (155) (1942), Green wakerobin [Green wake robin, Green wake-robin] (5, 97) (1913–1937), Wood wakerobin [Wood wake-robin] (50) (present)

***Trillium viridescens* Nutt.** – Tape-tip wake-robin [Tapertip wakerobin] (50) (present), Wakerobin [Wake robin, Wake-robin] (97) (1937)

***Triodanis holzingeri* McVaugh** – Holzinger's Venus' looking-glass (50) (present)

***Triodanis lamprosperma* McVaugh** – Prairie Venus' looking-glass (50) (present)

***Triodanis leptocarpa* (Nutt.) Nieuwl.** – Slim-pod Venus' looking-glass [Slimpod Venus' looking-glass] (50) (present), Western Venus' looking-glass [Western Venus looking glass] (5, 93, 97, 122) (1913–1937)

***Triodanis perfoliata* (L.) Nieuwl.** – Clasping bellflower (19) (1840), Clasping Venus' looking-glass (50) (present)

***Triodanis perfoliata* (L.) Nieuwl. var. *biflora* (Ruiz & Pavón) Bradley** – Perfoliate bellflower [Perfoliate bell flower] (42) (1814), Small Venus' looking-glass [Small Venus' looking glass, Small Venus looking glass, Small Venuslookingglass] (5, 97, 122, 124, 155) (1913–1942)

Triodanis perfoliata* (L.) Nieuwl. var. *perfoliata – Clasping bellflower (5, 62, 156) (1912–1923), Clasping Venus' looking-glass (50, 155) (1942–present), Venus'-looking-glass [Venus' looking glass, Venus looking glass, Venus's looking glass, Venus lookingglass, Venuslookingglass] (5, 62, 63, 72, 93, 95, 97, 122, 124, 131, 156, 157) (1899–1937)

***Triodanis* Raf. ex Greene** – Venus'-looking-glass [Venus' looking glass, Venus looking glass, Venus's looking glass, Venus looking-glass, Venuslookingglass] (1, 2, 4, 50, 93, 138, 155, 156) (1923–present)

***Triodia albescens* (Munro) Vasey** – See *Tridens albescens* (Vasey) Woot. & Standl.

***Triodia cuprea* Jacq.** – See *Tridens flavus* (L.) A. S. Hitchc.

***Triodia elongata* (Buckl.) Scribn.** – See *Tridens muticus* (Torr.) Nash var. *elongatus* (Buckl.) Shinners

***Triodia flava* (L.) Smyth** – See *Tridens flavus* (L.) A. S. Hitchc. var. *flavus*

***Triodia grandiflora* Vasey** – See *Erioneuron avenaceum* (Kunth) Tateoka

Triodia mutica (Torr.) Scribn. – See *Tridens muticus* (Torr.) Nash var. *muticus*

Triodia pilosa (Buckl.) Merr. – See *Erioneuron pilosum* (Buckl.) Nash

Triodia pulchella H.B.K. – See *Dasyochloa pulchella* (Kunth) Willd. ex Rydb.

Triodia purpurea Hack. – See *Triplasis purpurea* (Walt.) Chapman

Triodia seslerioides – See *Tridens flavus* (L.) A.S. Hitchc.

Triodia stricta (Nutt.) Benth. (sic) – See *Tridens strictus* (Nutt.) Nash

Triodia stricta (Nutt.) Vasey – See *Tridens strictus* (Nutt.) Nash

Triodia trinerviglumis Benth. ex Vasey – See *Tridens muticus* (Torr.) Nash

Triosteum angustifolium L. – Horse-gentian [Horse gentian, Horse-gentian] (3) (1977), Narrow-leaf horse-gentian [Narrowleaf horse-gentian [Narrow-leaved horse-gentian [Narrow-leaved horse gentian] (5, 72, 155, 156) (1907–1942), Tinker's-weed [Tinker's weed, Tinker weed] (181) (~1678), Yellow horse-gentian [Yellow horse gentian] (5, 72, 156) (1907–1923), Yellow-flower horse-gentian [Yellow-flowered horse-gentian] (4) (1986), Yellow-fruit horse-gentian [Yellowfruit horse-gentian] (50) (present)

Triosteum aurantiacum Bickn. – Red-fruit horse-gentian [Red-fruited horse-gentian] (72) (present), Scarlet-fruit horse-gentian [Scarlet-fruited horse-gentian] (97) (1937) OK, Orange horse-gentian [Orange horse gentian, Orange horsegentian] (155, 156) (1923–1944), Orange-fruit horse-gentian [Orangefruit horse-gentian] (50) (present)

Triosteum aurantiacum Bickn. var. *aurantiacum* – Orange horse-gentian [Orange horse gentian, Orange horsegentian] (3) (1986), Orange-flower horse-gentian [Orange-flowered horse gentian] (4) (1986), Orange-fruit horse-gentian [Orangefruit horse-gentian] (50) (present), Scarlet-fruit horse-gentian [Scarlet-fruited horse-gentian] (5) (1913)

Triosteum aurantiacum Bickn. var. *illinoense* (Wiegand) Palmer & Steyermark – Illinois horse-gentian (50) (present)

Triosteum L. – Breittblättriger Dreistein (German) (186) (1814), Feverroot [Fever root, Feverroot] (158) (1900), Feverwort [Fever wort, Fever-wort] (2, 4, 10, 156) (1818–1986), Horse-gentian [Horse gentian, Horsegentian] (1, 2, 4, 50, 138, 155) (1895–present)

Triosteum perfoliatum L. – Bastard ipecac (6, 49, 57, 58, 157, 158) (1869–1929), Bastard ipecacuanha (186) (1814), Cinque (6, 177, 186) (1762–1892), Common horse-gentian [Common horsegentian] (138, 155) (1923–1942), Dr. Tinker's weed (6, 49, 58) (1869–1892), Dreistein (German) (6) (1892), False ipecac (6) (1892), False ipecacuanha (186) (1814), Fever-root [Fever root, Feverroot] (5, 6, 7, 19, 57, 58, 92, 107, 156, 158, 177, 184, 186, 187) (1793–1923), Feverwort [Fever wort, Fever-wort] (5, 6, 48, 49, 50, 63, 92, 97, 155, 156, 158, 186) (1825–present), Genson (5, 156, 158) (1900–1923) no longer in use by 1923, Gentian (186) (1814), Horse-gentian [Horse gentian, Horsegentian] (3, 4, 5, 6, 49, 58, 63, 72, 92, 93, 95, 105, 156, 157, 158) (1892–1986), Horse-ginseng [Horse ginseng] (5, 6, 7, 19, 92, 156, 158) (1828–1923), Ipecac (7) (1828), Moninswan (Chippewa) (105) (1932), Perfoliate fever-root (186, 187) (1814–1818), Red-flower fever-root [Red flowered fever-root, Red-flowered fever-root] (186, 187) (1814–1818), Sweet-bitter [Sweet bitter] (6) (1892), Tinkar's-root (158) (1900), Tinker's-weed [Tinker's weed, Tinker weed] (5, 6, 7, 92, 156, 157, 158) (1828–1929), Trioste (French) (6) (1892), White gentian (5, 92, 156, 158) (1876–1923), White ginseng (6, 7, 158) (1828–1900), Wild coffee [Wild-coffee] (5, 6, 7, 19, 49, 92, 107, 156, 157, 158, 186) (1825–1929), Wild ipecac (5, 6, 49, 76, 92, 156, 158) (1892–1923) Western US, Wood ipecac (5, 156, 158) (1900–1923)

Triphasia trifolia (Burm. f.) P. Wilson – Limeberry [Lime-berry] (109) (1949)

Triphasia trifolia P. Wils. – See *Triphasia trifolia* (Burm. f.) P. Wilson

Triphora Nutt. – Nodding-cap [Nodding cap] (1) (1932), Nodding-caps [Noddingcaps, Nodding cap] (1, 50) (1932–present)

Triphora trianthophora (Sw.) Rydb. – Nodding pogonia (3, 72, 156) (1907–1977), Three-bird orchis (19) (1840), Three-birds [Three-birds, Three birds] (5, 50, 156) (1913–present)

Triphora trianthophora (Sw.) Rydb. subsp. *trianthophora* – Pendant arethusa (42) (1814)

Triplasis americana P. Beauv. – Horned sand grass (66) (1903)

Triplasis Beauv. – Purple sand grass [Purple sand-grass, Purple sand-grass] (93) (1936), Sand grass [Sand-grass, Sandgrass] (1, 50, 155) (1932–present)

Triplasis purpurea (Walt.) Chapman – Plant-acid [Plant acid] (5) (1913), Purple sand grass [Purple sand-grass, Purple sandgrass] (50, 94, 155) (1901–present), Sand grass [Sand-grass, Sandgrass] (3, 56, 66, 72, 87, 92, 93, 111, 163) (1852–1977)

Tripleurospermum maritima (L.) W. D. J. Koch subsp. *maritima* – Arctic camomile [Arctic chamomile] (5, 93, 156) (1913–1936), False mayweed (50) (present), Wild camomile [Wild cammomile, Wild chamomile, Wild camomille] (3, 4) (1977–1986)

Tripleurospermum perforata (Merat) M. Lainz – Arctic camomile [Arctic chamomile] (156) (1923), Corn mayweed (5, 156) (1913–1923), Great sea starwort [Great sea star woort] (155) (1942), Lesser sea starwort [Lesser sea Star woort] (178) (1526), Scentless camomile [Scentless chamomile] (5, 93, 156) (1913–1936) Neb, Scentless false camomile [Scentless false chamomile, Scentless false-chamomile] (109, 138) (1923–1949), Scentless false mayweed (50) (present), Scentless mayweed (155) (1942)

Tripleurospermum Schultz-Bip. – Mayweed [May-weed, May weed] (50) (present)

Tripolium pannonicum (Jacq.) Dobrocz. – Tripoli aster (155) (1942)

Tripsacum dactyloides (L.) L. – Buffalo grass [Buffalo-grass, Buffalo-grass] (5, 14, 107) (1882–1919), Bull grass [Bull-grass, Bull grass] (5, 119) (1913–1938), Eastern gama grass [Eastern gamagrass, Eastern gama-grass] (50, 155, 163) (1852–present), Gamagrass [Gamagrass, Gama grass] (2, 45, 46, 66, 67, 72, 87, 88, 92, 94, 111, 119, 144) (1884–1938), Sesame grass [Sesame-grass] (2, 5, 14, 45, 66, 87, 92, 119) (1876–1938), Slough grass [Slough-grass, Sloughgrass] (5, 19, 21) (1840–1913)

Tripsacum L. – Bull grass [Bull-grass, Bull grass] (93) (1936), Gamagrass [Gama-grass, Gama grass] (3, 45, 50, 93, 155) (1896–present), Sesame grass [Sesame-grass] (1, 93) (1932–1936) Neb

Tripterocalyx Hook. ex Standl. – Sandpuffs [Sand puffs, Sand-puffs] (1, 4, 50, 85) (1932–present)

Tripterocalyx micranthus (Torr.) Hook – Pink abronia (5, 93) (1876–1923), Sandpuffs [Sand puffs, Sand-puffs] (4) (1986), Small-flower sand-verbena [Smallflower sandverbena] (50) (present)

Trisetum canescens Buckl. – Nodding oat grass [Nodding oat-grass] (94) (1901), Silvery oat grass [Silvery oat-grass] (94) (1901)

Trisetum flavescens (L.) Beauv. – Golden oat grass [Golden oat-grass] (5, 45, 68) (1896–1913), Tall oat grass [Tall oatgrass, Tall oat-grass] (5) (1913), Three-awn oat grass [Three-awned oat-grass] (10) (1818), Yellow false oat (5, 68) (1913), Yellow oat [Yellow oats] (3, 45) (1896–1977), Yellow oat grass [Yellow oat-grass, Yellow oat-grass] (5, 45, 50, 56, 66, 68, 92) (1876–present), Golden oats (67) (1890)

Trisetum interruptum Buckl. – Prairie false oat (50) (present), Prairie trisetum (155) (1942), Slender oat grass [Slender oat-grass] (94) (1901)

Trisetum melicoides (Michx.) Vasey ex Scribn. – Dupontia grass (66) (1903), Graphephorum (5) (1913), Melic-like hair grass [Melic like hair grass] (42) (1814), Purple false oat (50) (present)

Trisetum molle – See *Trisetum spicatum* (L.) Richter

Trisetum montanum Vasey – See *Trisetum spicatum* (L.) Richter

Trisetum palustre (Michx.) Torr. – See *Sphenopholis pensylvanica* (L.) A. S. Hitchc.

Trisetum pennsylvanicum (L.) Beauv. – See *Sphenopholis pensylvanica* (L.) A. S. Hitchc.

Trisetum pensylvanicum (L.) Beauv. ex Roemer & J. A. Schultes – See *Sphenopholis pensylvanica* (L.) A. S. Hitchc.

Trisetum Pers. – False oat [False oats] (1, 93, 152) (1932–1936), Oat grass [Oatgrass, Oat-grass] (50) (present), Trisetum (155) (1942)

Trisetum pratense Pers. – See *Trisetum flavescens* (L.) Beauv.

Trisetum pubescens **Roem & Schultz** – See *Helictotrichon pubescens* (Huds.) Bess. ex Pilger

Trisetum spicatum **(L.) Richter** – Downy oat grass [Downy oatgrass] (5, 94) (1901–1913), Downy persoon (66) (1903), Narrow false oat (5) (1913), Rocky Mountain oat grass [Rocky Mountain oat-grass] (94) (1901), Rocky Mountain trisetum [Rocky-Mountain trisetum] (155) (1942), Spike trisetum (3, 50, 140, 155) (1942–present)

Trisetum subspicatum **(L.) Beauv.** – See *Trisetum spicatum* (L.) Richter

Trisetum wolfii **Vasey** – Beardless false oat (94) (1901), Wolf's false oat (94) (1901) Bedford Mass

Tristagma uniflorum **(Lindl.) Traub** – Spring star-flower (109) (1949)

Tristania **R. Br.** – See *Spartina* Schreber

Triteleia grandiflora **Lindl. var. *grandiflora*** – California hyacinth [Californian hyacinth] (107) (1919), Large-flower California hyacinth [Large-flowered California hyacinth] (86) (1878)

Triteleia ixioides **(Ait. f.) Greene** – Pretty-face [Pretty face] (109) (1949)

Triteleia ixioides **Greene** – See *Triteleia ixioides* (Ait. f.) Greene

Triteleia laxa **Benth.** – Grass-nut (109) (1949), Triplet lily [Triplet-lily] (109) (1949)

Triticum aestivum **L.** – Bearded wheat (158, 180) (1633–1900), Bled ou Fourment (French) (180) (1633), Bright wheat (180) (1633) John Gerarde, Common wheat (50, 109, 119) (1938–present), Corn [Corne] (180) (1633), Cultivated wheat (56) (1901), Double-ear wheat [Double eared Wheat] (180) (1633), Flat wheat (180) (1633), Flaxen wheat (180) (1633), Grano (Italian) (180) (1633), Red wheat (180) (1633), Spring wheat (66) (1903), Summer wheat (158) (1900), Terwe (Dutch) (180) (1633), Unbearded wheat (158) (1900), Wheat (21, 45, 56, 85, 94, 138, 140, 155, 158, 163) (1852–1932), Winter wheat (19, 66, 158) (1840–1903)

Triticum arvensis – See *Elymus repens* (L.) Gould

Triticum compositum – See *Triticum turgidum* L.

Triticum dicoccum **Schrank** – See *Triticum turgidum* L.

Triticum hybernum **L.** – See *Triticum aestivum* L.

Triticum **L.** – Corn (in England) (45) (1896), Wheat (7, 45, 50, 66, 93, 155, 158) (1828–present), Wheat grass [Wheat-grass, Wheatgrass] (92) (1876)

Triticum repens **L.** – See *Elymus repens* (L.) Gould

Triticum sativum – See *Triticum aestivum* L.

Triticum spelta **L.** – Ador (180) (1633), Adoreum (180) (1633), Alga (Millanois) (180) (1633), Biada (Tuscan) (180) (1633), Espeautre (French) (180) (1633), Farra (Italian) (180) (1633), Pirra (Italian) (180) (1633), Sinkel (German) (180) (1633), Spelt (56, 66, 67, 92, 107, 109) (1890–1949), Spelt corne (180) (1633), Spelt grass (92) (1876), Spelt wheat (66) (1903), Spelte (low Dutch) (180) (1633), Speltz (93, 109) (1936–1949), Speltz (German) (180) (1633)

Triticum turgidum **L.** – Egyptian wheat (19, 66, 67) (1840–1903), Emmer (107, 109) (1919–1949), English wheat (67, 109) (1890–1949), German wheat (107) (1919), Mediterranean wheat (109) (1949), Poulard wheat (109) (1949), Two-grain wheat [Two-grained wheat] (107) (1919)

Triticum vulgare **Vill.** – See *Triticum aestivum* L.

Tritoma uvaria **[Ker-Gawl.]** – See *Kniphofia uvaria* (L.) Oken

Trollius europaeus **L.** – Common globeflower (138) (1923), European globeflower (2) (1895), Globe crowfoot (92) (1876), Globeflower [Globe-flower, Globe flower] (109) (1949)

Trollius **L.** – Globeflower [Globe-flower, Globe flower] (138, 156) (1923)

Trollius laxus **Salisb.** – American globeflower (5) (1913), Cresses of India (180) (1633), Globeflower [Globe-flower, Globe flower] (19, 92) (1840–1876), Spreading globeflower [Spreading globe-flower] (156) (1923), Wild globe flower [Wild globeflower] (2) (1895)

Tropaeolum **L.** – Nasturtium (15, 82, 109, 138) (1895–1949) of gardeners

Tropaeolum majus **L.** – Common nasturtium (138) (1923), Garden nasturtium (82, 109, 138) (1923–1949), Indian cress [Indian cresses] (7, 19, 92, 107, 138) (1828–1923), Nasturtium (7, 19, 92) (1828–1876), Tall nasturtium (107) (1919)

Trophis americana **L.** – See *Trophis racemosa* (L.) Urban

Trophis racemosa **(L.) Urban** – Ramoon tree (107) (1919)

Troximon glaucum parviflorum **Gray** – See *Agoseris glauca* (Pursh) Raf. var. *laciniata* (D.C. Eat.) Smiley

Troximon glaucum **Pursh** – See *Agoseris glauca* (Pursh) Raf. var. *glauca*

Troximon parviflorum **Nutt.** – See *Agoseris parviflora* (Nutt.) Greene

Tryphane rubella **(Wahlenb.) Reichenb.** – See *Minuartia rubella* (Wahlenb.) Hiern.

Tsuga **(Endl.) Carr.** – See *Tsuga* Carr

Tsuga canadensis **(L.) Carr.** – Abies (53) (1922), Black Hills spruce (136) (1930) SD, Canadian hemlock [Canada hemlock] (109, 112, 136, 138) (1923–1949), Canadian pitch [Canada pitch] (57, 92) (1876–1917) source, Canadische Edeltanne (German) (6) (1892), Common hemlock (109) (1949), Eastern hemlock (50) (present), Ewe tree (46) (1609), Gaga'mimĭc (Chippewa) (40) (1928), Hemlock [Hemloc, Hemlocke] or Hemlock tree (2, 6, 19, 49, 53, 58, 61, 108, 136, 161) (1840–1930), Hemlock bark (92) (1876), Hemlock fir (6) (1892), Hemlock gum (92) (1876), Hemlock pine (5, 40) (1913–1928), Hemlock pitch (57, 92) (1876–1917), Hemlock spruce [Hemlock-spruce] (6, 8, 10, 20, 46, 52, 53, 54, 55, 57, 58, 92, 182, 187) (1791–1922), Hemlock spruce fir [Hemlok spruce-firr] or Hemlock spruce fir-tree (8, 14, 20) (1785–1882), Iffs (46) (1879), North American hemlock-spruce [North American hemlock spruce] (57) (1917), Perusse (French Canada) (20) (1857), Pix canadensis (57) (1917) source, Spruce pine (5) (1913), Weeping spruce (92) (1876), Yfs (46) (1879), Sargent's weeping hemlock (109) (1949), possibly Sapinette à feuilles d'if (French) (8) (1785), possibly Silver fir (138) (1923)

Tsuga canadensis **Carr. var. *pendula* Beissn.** – See *Tsuga canadensis* (L.) Carr.

Tsuga caroliniana **Engelm.** – Carolina hemlock (5, 50, 109, 138) (1913–present), Southern hemlock (5) (1913)

Tsuga **Carr** – Hemlock [Hemloc, Hemlocke] or Hemlock tree (1, 50, 109, 138) (1923–present)

Tsuga heterophylla **(Raf.) Sarg.** – Western hemlock (109, 138) (1923–1949)

Tsuga mertensiana **(Bong.) Carr.** – Mountain hemlock (109, 138) (1923–1949), Williamson's spruce (161) (1857)

Tuber griseum **Borch ex Pers.** – Black truffle (92) (1876)

Tuber **P. Micheli ex F. H. Wigg. (possibly)** – Truffle [Truffles] (7) (1828), possibly Tuckaho [Tuckaho, Tuckahoe] (7) (1828)

Tucahus **Raf.** – See *Pachyma* Fr.

Tuckermannia maritima **Nutt.** – See *Coreopsis maritima* (Nutt.) Hook.f.

Tuctoria greenei **(Vasey) J. Reeder** – Chico grass (94) (1901)

Tulipa acuminata **Vahl.** – See *Tulipa gesneriana* L.

Tulipa clusiana **DC.** – Lady tulip (109) (1949)

Tulipa gesneriana **L.** – Common tulip (19, 138) (1840–1923), Dalmation cap (178) (1596), Didier's tulip (50) (present), Tulip (92) (1876), Turkish tulip (109) (1949)

Tulipa **L.** – Case lale (180) (1633), Dalmation cap (180) (1633), Tulip (7, 50, 109, 138) (1828–present) from oriental word for turban, Turban (180) (1633), Turfan (180) (1633), Turk's-cap [Turk's cap, Turkscap] (180) (1633)

Tulipa sylvestris **L.** – Florentine tulip (138) (1923), Wild tulip (5, 50) (1913–present)

Tullia pycnanthemoides **Leavenw.** – See *Pycnanthemum pycnanthemoides* (Leavenworth) Fern. var. *pycnanthemoides*

Tulotis **Raf.** – See *Habenaria* Willd.

Tumion taxifolium **(Arn.) Greene** – See *Torreya taxifolia* Arnot.

Tunica saxifraga **Scop.** – See *Petrorhagia saxifraga* (L.) Link

Tunica **Scop.** – See *Petrorhagia* (Ser.) Link (all US species)

Turbina corymbosa (L.) **Raf.** – White campanilla (106) (1930)

Turnera aphrodisiaca **Ward** – See *Turnera diffusa* Willd. ex J.A. Schultes

Turnera diffusa **Willd. ex J. A. Schultes** – Damiana (50, 52, 54, 55, 57, 60) (1902–present), Turnera (57) (1917)

Turnera microphylla **Desvar.** – See *Turnera diffusa* Willd. ex J.A. Schultes

Turnera ulmifolia **L.** – British tobacco (187) (1818), Helianthemoides (1, 10, 13) (1818–1932), Ramgoat dashalong (50) (present)

Turritis glabra **L.** – See *Arabis glabra* (L.) Bernh.

Turritis **L.** – See *Arabis* L.

Tussilago farfara **L.** – Ass's-foot [Ass's foot] (5, 156) (1913–1923), British tobacco (92) (1876), Bull's-foot [Bull's foot, Bulls-foot, Bullsfoot] (5, 58, 92, 156) (1869–1923), Butterbur [Butter bur, Butter-bur] (5, 156) (1913–1923), Clayweed [Clay-weed] (5, 156) (1913–1923), Cleats [Cleets] (5, 156) (1913–1923) no longer in use by 1923, Colt herb [Colt-herb] (5, 156) (1913–1923), Coltsfoot [Colt's foot, Colt's-foot, Colt foot] (5, 14, 19, 49, 53, 55, 57, 58, 92, 156) (1840–1923), Common coltsfoot (138) (1923), Coughwort (5, 156) (1913–1923), Dove-dock [Dove dock] (5) (1913), Dummyweed [Dummy weed] (5, 156) (1913–1923) no longer in use by 1923, Foalfoot [Foal foot, Foal-foot, Foles foot] (5, 92, 156) (1876–1923), Ginger [Gynger] (5, 156) (1913–1923), Ginger root (75) (1894) MN, Hoofs (5, 156) (1913–1923) no longer in use by 1923, Horsefoot [Horse foot, Horse-foot] (5, 156) (1913–1923), Horse-hoof [Horse hoof, Horse-hoof] (5, 92, 156) (1876–1923), Sowfoot [Sow-foot, Sow foot] (5, 156) (1913–1923)

Tussilago frigida **W.** – See *Petasites fragrans* C.Presl

Tussilago **L.** – Butterbur [Butter bur, Butter-bur] (10) (1818), Coltsfoot [Colt's foot, Colt's-foot, Colt foot] (1, 10, 138, 167) (1814–1932)

Tussilago petasites **L.** – See *Petasites hybridus* (L.) G. Gaertn., B. Mey. & Scherb.

Typha angustifolia **L.** – Lesser reed-mace (5, 10, 14, 34) (1840–1882), Narrow-leaf cat-tail [Narrowleaf cattail, Narrow-leafed cat-tail, Narrow-leaved cats'-tail, Narrow-leaved cat-tail, Narrow-leaved cattail] (3, 50, 85, 93, 97, 124, 138, 155, 156, 187) (1818–present), Small bulrush [Small bull-rush] (107) (1919)

Typha domingensis **Pers.** – Southern cat-tail [Southern cattail] (50) (present)

Typha **L.** – Bechords (180) (1633), Cat-tail [Cat's tail, Cats Taile, Cat's-tail, Cats tails] (1, 7, 10, 50, 14, 93, 138, 148, 155, 158, 167, 180) (1633–present), Cat-tail reed [Cattail reed] (122) (1937), Donsen (180) (1633), Lischdoden (Dutch) (180) (1633), Marteau masses (French) (180) (1633), Mezza forda (180) (1633), Reed-mace [Reed-mace, Reed mace] (7, 158, 180) (1633–1900)

Typha latifolia **L.** – Apûk'we (Chippewa) (40) (1928), Blackamoor (5, 156, 157, 158) (1900–1929), Blackcap [Black cap, Black-cap] (5, 156, 157, 158) (1900–1929), Broad-leaf cat-tail [Broad-leaved cattail] (5, 50, 72, 93, 97, 120, 131, 156, 157, 158) (1907–present), Broad-leaf reed-mace [Broad-leaved reed-mace] (41) (1770), Bull-segg (5, 156, 158) (1900–1923), Bulrush [Bull rush, Bullrush, Bul-Rush, Bulrushes] (5, 107, 156, 157, 158) (1900–1929), Candlewick [Candle-wick] (5, 14, 156, 157, 158) (1882–1929), Cat-o'-nine-tails (5, 92, 156, 158) (1876–1923), Cat-tail [Cat's tail, Cats Taile, Cat's-tail, Cats tails] (5, 19, 21, 40, 41, 46, 49, 85, 92, 101, 107, 121, 156, 157, 158, 184, 187) (1671–1970), Cat-tail rush [Cattail rush] (49) (1898), Common cat-tail [Common cattail] (3, 35, 109, 138, 155, 156, 157, 158) (1806–1977), Cooper's flag (35) (1806), Cooper's reed (187) (1818), Cossack asparagus (107) (1919), Dunche-down (158) (1900), Flag (27, 35) (1806–1811), Flag-tule (157) (1929), Flax-tail [Flax tail, Flax-tail] (5, 156, 157, 158) (1900–1929), Great reed-mace (5, 41, 156, 157, 158) (1770–1929), Haŋtkaŋ or hiŋtkan (Lakota, hair, fur, or fuzz scraped off) (121) (1918–1970?), Hawa-hawa (Pawnee) (37) (1830), Kirit-tacharush (Pawnee, eye-itch) (37) (1830) flying down causing eye irritation, Ksho-hin (Winnebago, prairie chicken feather) (37) (1830), Mace-reed (14) (1882), Marsh-beetle [Marsh beetle] (5, 92, 156, 157, 158) (1876–1929), Marsh-pestle [Marsh-pistle] (5, 92, 156, 157, 158) (1876–1929), Mik-ethestsedse (Osage, possibly meaning, long raccoon rush) (121) (1918–1970), Reed-mace [Reedmace, Reed mace] (2, 27, 49, 92, 107, 187) (1811–1919), Reree (158) (1900), Wahab' igaskonthe (Omaha-Ponca, similar to corn) (19, 37) (1830–1840) name refers to floral spikes appearing when corn is ripe, Wakethe (Osage) (121) (1918–1970), Water-torch [Water torch] (5, 92, 156, 157, 158) (1876–1929), Wide-leaf cat-tail [Wide-leafed cat-tail (124) (1937), Wihuta hu (Lakota, tent bottom plant) (121) (1918–1970), Wihuta-hu (Dakota, bottom of tipi plant) (37) (1830)

Typha palustris – See *Typha latifolia* L.

U

Ulex europaeus **L.** – Common gorse (138) (1923), Fringepod [Fringe pod] (19, 106) (1840–1930), Furze (5, 19, 106, 156) (1840–1930), Gorse (5, 106, 156) (1913–1930), Prickly broom (5, 156) (1913–1923), Thistle [Thystle] (156) (1923), Thorn broom [Thorn-broom] (5, 156) (1913–1923), Ulim (5) (1913), Whin (5, 156) (1913–1923)

Ulex **L.** – Furse (45, 109) (1896–1949), Gorse (45, 138) (1896–1923)

Ulmaria rubra **Hill** – See *Filipendula rubra* (Hill.) Robinson

Ulmus alata **Michx.** – Cork elm (5, 158) (1900–1913), Small elm (3) (1977), Wahoo [Waahoo, Wa-a-hoo, Wauhoo, Whahoo] (1, 2, 5, 19, 20, 82, 92, 97, 109, 156, 158) (1840–1949), Water elm [Water-elm] (5, 156, 158) (1900–1923), White elm (38, 130) (1820–1895), Winged elm (1, 2, 4, 5, 50, 82, 97, 106, 109, 122, 124, 138, 155, 156, 158) (1895–present), Witch elm (5, 156) (1913–1923)

Ulmus americana **L.** – American elm (1, 3, 4, 5, 14, 37, 41, 46, 50, 82, 85, 97, 108, 109, 112, 122, 124, 138, 153, 155, 156, 157, 158) (1770–present), American rough-leaf elm tree [American rough leaved elm-tree] (8) (1785), American white elm (93) (1936), Bois dur (French) (8) (1785), Common elm (157, 158) (1900–1929), Elm or elm tree (19, 35, 12, 101, 164) (1806–1905), Ezhon zhon (Omaha-Ponca) (37) (1919), Ezhon zhon ska (White elm) (Omaha-Ponca) (37) (1919), Feather elm (124) (1937) TX, Orme d'Amérique (French) (8) (1785), Pe (Dakota) (37) (1919) Pe cha (Elm wood) pe ikcheka (Common elm), Red elm (78) (1898) Southwest MO, Rock elm (5, 113, 156, 157, 158) (1890–1929), Small-leaf elm [Small-leaved elm] (38) (1820), Swamp elm (5, 113, 156, 157, 158) (1890–1929), Taitsako taka (Pawnee, white elm) (37) (1919), Water elm [Water-elm] (5, 93, 109, 113, 130, 156, 157, 158) (1890–1929), White elm (1, 2, 5, 9, 20, 19, 37, 65, 72, 78, 85, 92, 95, 97, 101, 105, 108, 109, 112, 113, 130, 131, 157, 158) (1840–1949)

Ulmus carpinifolia **auct. non Ruppius ex G. Suckow** – See *Ulmus procera* Salisb.

Ulmus crassifolia **Nutt.** – Cedar elm (122, 124) (1937)

Ulmus fulva **Michx** – See *Ulmus rubra* Muhl.

Ulmus glabra **Huds.** – Common elm (55) (1911), Common European elm (20) (1857), English elm (82, 93, 107, 109, 112, 135, 138, 156) (1910–1949), Scotch elm (109, 138) (1923–1949), Wych elm (82, 92, 109) (1876–1949)

Ulmus japonica – possibly *Ulmus parvifolia* Jacq.

Ulmus **L.** – British tea (92) (1876), Elm or elm tree (1, 4, 8, 10, 50, 82, 93, 106, 109, 138, 158) (1785–present), Orme (French) (8) (1785), Whin (187) (1818–1949)

Ulmus minor – See *Ulmus procera* Salisb.

Ulmus montana **With.** – See *Ulmus glabra* Huds.

Ulmus parvifolia **Jacq.** – Chinese elm (82, 109, 138) (1923–1949), possibly Japanese elm (112) (1937)

Ulmus procera **Salisb.** – Lock elm (138) (1923), Smooth-leaf elm [Smoothleaf elm, Smooth-leaved elm] (109, 138) (1923–1949)

Ulmus pubsecens **Walt.** – See *Ulmus rubra* Muhl.

Ulmus pumila **L.** – Chinese elm (93, 112) (1936–1937), Dwarf Asiatic elm (138) (1923), Dwarf elm (109) (1949), Siberian elm (3, 4, 50, 109, 155) (1942–present)

Ulmus rubra **Muhl.** – American elm (157) (1929), Elm bark (157) (1929), Elm or elm tree (157) (1929), Ezhon zhide (Omaha-Ponca, red elm) (37) (1919), Ezhon zhide gthigthide (Omaha-Ponca, slippery red elm) (37) (1919), Gawa'komĭc (Chippewa) (40) (1919), Indian elm (5, 92, 156, 157, 158) (1876–1929), Moose elm (5, 20, 93, 156, 157, 158) (1857–1929), Orme fauve (French) (158) (1900), Orme gras (Upper Louisiana) (20) (1857), Pe tutuntunpa (Dakota Teton) (37) (1919), Pe tututupa (Dakota) (37) (1919), Red elm (1, 5, 7, 9, 19, 20, 37, 58, 72, 82, 85, 92, 93, 95, 107, 109, 112, 113, 130, 156, 157, 158) (1828–1949), Rock elm (5, 156, 157, 158)

(1900–1929), Salve bark (59) (1787), Slippery elm (1, 2, 3, 4, 5, 7, 19, 20, 34, 35, 37, 40, 49, 50, 53, 55, 57, 58, 59, 72, 78, 82, 85, 92, 93, 95, 97, 107, 109, 112, 113, 122, 124, 130, 131, 138, 155, 156, 157, 158) (1834–present), Sweet elm (5, 7, 92, 156, 157, 158) (1828–1929), Taitsako pahat (Pawnee, red elm) (37) (1919), Waki-dikidik (Winnebago) (37) (1919), White elm (78) (1898) Southwest MO

Ulmus serotina **Sarg.** – Red elm (5, 97) (1913–1937), September elm (97, 138) (1923–1937)

Ulmus thomasii **Sarg.** – Cliff elm (5, 156, 157, 158) (1900–1929), Cork elm (1, 5, 72, 82, 85, 93, 95, 109, 135, 156, 157, 158) (1900–1949), Corky white elm (2, 5, 156, 157, 158) (1895–1929), Ezhon zhon zi (Omaha-Ponca, yellow elm) (37) (1919), Hickory elm (5, 156, 157, 158) (1900–1929), Orme à grappe (French) (20) (1857), Pe itazipa (Dakota, bow elm) (37) (1919), Racemed elm (158) (1900), Racemed white elm (5, 156) (1913–1923), Rock elm (1, 3, 4, 5, 37, 50, 82, 85, 93, 95, 109, 130, 138, 155, 156, 157, 158) (1895–present), Swamp elm (5, 158) (1900–1913), Thomas's elm (20) (1857), Wahoo [Waahoo, Wa-a-hoo, Wauhoo, Whahoo] (5, 156, 158) (1900–1923)

Ulva **L.** – Sea-lettuce [Sea lettuce] (7) (1828)

Umbellularia **(Nees) Nutt.** – California laurel [California-laurel] (138) (1923)

Umbellularia californica **(Hook. & Arn.) Nutt.** – Balm-of-heaven [Balm of heaven] (14, 107, 154) (1857–1919), Bay lauerel (106) (1930), Bay tree [Bay-tree] (54, 106) (1905–1930), Cajeput or Cajeput tree [Cajeput-tree] (14, 75, 107) (1882–1919), California bay or California bay tree [Californian bay tree] (20, 109, 138) (1857–1949), California laurel [California-laurel] (14, 54, 57, 75, 106, 109, 138, 154, 161) (1857–1949), California olive [Californian olive] (75, 107) (1894–1919), California sassafras [Californian sassafras] (14) (1882), California umbellularia [Californian umbellularia] (20) (1857), Drimophylle pauciflore (20, 107) (1857–1919), Mexican buckeye (4) (1986), Mountain laurel [Mountain Lawrell] (107) (1919), Myrtle (106) (1930) OR, Pepperwood [Pepper-wood, Pepper wood] (77, 106) (1898–1930), Pepperwood tree (54) (1905), Sassafras laurel (107) (1919), Spice brush [Spice-brush] (54) (1905), Spice bush [Spice-bush, Spicebush] (14, 107, 154) (1857–1882), Spice tree [Spice-tree] (54) (1905)

Umbellularia californica **(Hook. & Arn.) Nutt. var. *californica*** – Mountain laurel [Mountain Lawrell] (54, 154) (1857–1905)

Umbellularia californica **Nutt.** – See *Umbellularia californica* (Hook. & Arn.) Nutt.

Umbellularia **Nutt.** – See *Umbellularia* (Nees) Nutt.

Umbilicaria **Hoffm.** – Rock tripe (92) (1876)

Umbilicaria muehlenbergii **(Ach.) Tuck.** – Rock tripe (107) (1919)

Umbilicaria vellea **(L.) Ach.** – Rock tripe (107) (1919)

Unamia **Greene** – See *Oligoneuron* Small (all US species)

Ungnadia speciosa **Endl.** – Mexican buckeye (15, 109, 122, 124) (1895–1949), New Mexico buckeye (153) (1913) NM, Spanish buckeye (109) (1949), Texas buckeye [Texan buckeye] (109) (1949)

Unifolium **Adans.** – See *Maianthemum* G. H. Weber ex Wiggers

Unifolium canadense **(Desf.) Greene** – See *Maianthemum canadense* Desf.

Uniola gracilis **Michx.** – See *Chasmanthium laxum* (L.) H. O.Yates

Uniola **L.** – Sea-oats [Sea oats, Seaoats] (50) (present), Spike grass [Spike-grass, Spikegrass] (1, 66) (1903–1932), Uniola L. (138, 155) (1923–1942)

Uniola laxa **(L.) B.S.P.** – See *Chasmanthium laxum* (L.) Yates

Uniola longifolia **Scribn.** – See *Chasmanthium sessiliflorum* (Poir.) Yates

Uniola maritima **Michx.** – See *Uniola paniculata* L.

Uniola paniculata **L.** – Beach grass [Beachgrass, Beach-grass] (5, 163) (1852–1913), Sea-oats [Sea oats, Seaoats] (5, 45, 50, 88, 109, 122) (1881–present), Seaside oats [Sea-side oat] (5, 94, 163, 177) (1762–1901), Spike grass [Spike-grass, Spikegrass] (5, 19, 66, 184) (1793–1912)

Uniola sessiliflora **Poir.** – See *Chasmanthium sessiliflorum* (Poir.) Yates

Uniola spicata **L.** – See *Distichlis spicata* (L.) Greene

Unisema deltifolia **Raf.** – See *Pontederia cordata* L.

Urania speciosa – See *Ravenala madagascariensis* Sonnerat

Urceolaria panyrga **Ach.** – Pitcher-shield lichen (19) (1840)

Uredo candida **(Pers. ex J. F. Gmel.) Pers.** – White rust (19) (1840)

Uredo linearis **Lam (possibly)** – Yellow grain-rust (19) (1840)

Uredo rosae-centifoliae **Pers.** – Rose rust (19) (1840)

Uredo segetum **Pers.** – possibly *Erysibe vera* Wallroth

Urnula craterium **(Schwein.) Fr.** – Black urn (128) (1933) ND

Urochloa ciliatissima **(Buckl.) R. Webster** – Fringed signal grass [Fringed signalgrass] (50) (present), India-wheat (94) (1901)

Urochloa fasciculata **(Sw.) R. Webster** – Brown-top millet [Brown top millet] (122) (1937) TX, Brown-top panicum [Browntop panicum] (155) (1942), Brown-top signal grass [Browntop signalgrass] (50) (present)

Urochloa maxima **(Jacq.) R. Webster** – Guinea grass [Guineagrass, Guinea-grass] (7, 56, 87, 92, 109, 110, 122, 163) (1828–1949)

Urochloa mutica **(Forsk.) T. Q. Nguyen** – Para grass [Para-grass] (45, 50, 87, 109, 122, 138, 163) (1852–present), Scotch grass (92) (1876)

Urochloa platyphylla **(Munro ex C. Wright) R. D. Webster** – Flat-leaf panic-grass [Flat-leaved panic-grass] (94) (1901)

Urochloa reptans **(L.) Stapf** – Jamaica crab grass [Jamaica crab-grass] (94) (1901), Low panic grass [Low panic-grass] (94) (1901)

Urochloa texana **(Buckl.) R. Webster** – Austin grass (118) (1898) TX, Colorado bottom grass (118) (1898) TX, Colorado grass [Colorado-grass] (56, 109, 119, 163) (1852–1949), Concho grass (118) (1898) TX, Congho grass (163) (1852), Green River grass (87) (1884), Texas millet (45, 87, 88, 94, 109, 118, 122, 163) (1852–1949), Texas panic grass (45) (1896), Texas panicum (3, 119, 155) (1938–1977), Texas signal grass [Texas signalgrass] (50) (present)

Urostachys selago **(L.) Herter ex Nessel** – See *Huperzia selago* (L.) Bernh. ex Mart. & Schrank var. *selago*

Urtica canadensis **L.** – See *Laportea canadensis* (L.) Weddell

Urtica chamaedryoides **Pursh** – Heart-leaf nettle [Heartleaf nettle] (50) (present), Low spring nettle (122) (1937), Weak nettle (2, 4, 97) (1895–1986)

Urtica dioica **L.** – Big-sting nettle [Bigsting nettle] (155) (1942), Brennessel [Brenn-Nessel] (German) (158) (1900), Common nettle (14, 19, 61, 92, 157, 158, 187) (1818–1929), Great nettle (5, 58, 93, 156) (1869–1936), Great stinging nettle (49, 92) (1876–1898), Greater nettle (157, 158) (1900–1929), Naughty-man's-playing (157, 158) (1900–1929), Nettle (22, 49, 52, 53, 57, 92, 107) (1893–1922), Ortie brulante (French) (158) (1900), Ortigo (French) (158) (1900), Scaddie (157, 158) (1900–1929), Stinging nettle (4, 5, 46, 49, 50, 53, 57, 58, 72, 92, 93, 95, 156, 157, 158) (1671–present), Tenging nettle (157, 158) (1900–1929)

Urtica dioica **L. subsp. *gracilis* (Aiton) Seland.** – Bepadji' ckanakīz'ĭt Ma'zana'tīg (Chippewa, prickly nettle) (40) (1928), California nettle (50) (present), Čaŋičaxpe hu (Lakota, woody whip) (121) (1918?–1970?), Great nettle (19) (1840), Hadoga (Osage) (121) (1918?–1970?), Hanuga-hi (Omaha-Ponca) (37) (1919), Lyall's nettle [Lyall nettle] (155) (1942), Manazhiha-hi (Omaha-Ponca) (37) (1919), Nettle (40, 80, 82, 85, 101, 145, 148, 160) (1860–1939), Shanpi (Sioux) (101) (1905) MT, Slender nettle (5, 62, 72, 93, 95, 131) (1899–1936), Slim nettle (155) (1942), Stinging nettle (3, 80, 101, 121, 155) (1905–1977), Tall nettle (62, 85, 155) (1912–1942), Tall wild nettle (5, 58, 93, 158) (1869–1936), Wicaro nakum (Sioux) (101) (1905) MT, Wood nettle (174) (1753)

Urtica dioica **L. var. *procera* (Muhl. ex Willd.) Weddell** – See *Urtica dioica* L. subsp. *gracilis* (Aiton) Seland.

Urtica gracilenta **Greene** – Tall nettle (122) (1937)

Urtica gracilis **Aiton** – See *Urtica dioica* L. subsp. *gracilis* (Aiton) Seland.

Urtica **L.** – Nas-sãn (Monominie) (23) (1810), Nettle (1, 4, 7, 10, 50, 82, 93, 155, 158, 167, 179, 184) (1526–present)

Urtica lyallii **S. Wats.** – See *Urtica dioica* L. subsp. *gracilis* (Aiton) Seland.

Urtica procera **W.** – See *Urtica dioica* L. subsp. *gracilis* (Aiton) Seland.

Urtica pumila – See *Pilea pumila* (L.) Gray var. *pumila*

Urtica urens **L.** – Brennessel [Brenn-Nessel] (German) (6) (1892), Burning nettle (5, 156) (1913–1923), Dwarf nettle (5, 6, 92, 156) (1876–1923), Dwarf stinger (19, 92) (1840–1876), Horned bladderwort (19, 92, 187) (1818–1876), L'Ortie (French) (6) (1892), Small nettle (5, 156) (1913–1923), Small stinging nettle (58) (1869), Stinging nettle (5, 6, 156) (1892–1923)

Urtica viridis **Rydb.** – See *Urtica dioica* L. subsp. *gracilis* (Aiton) Seland.

Urticastrum divaricatum **(L.) Kuntze** – See *Laportea canadensis* (L.) Weddell

Urticastrum **Fabr.** – See *Laportea* Gaud.

Usnea barbata **(L.) F. H. Wigg. var. *xanthopoga* Mull. Arg.** – See *Usnea xanthopoga* Nyl.

Usnea barbata **(L.) Weber ex F. H. Wigg.** – Chan wiziye (Dakota) (37) (1830), Lichen (37) (1830)

Usnea **Dill. ex Adans.** – Whisker moss (73) (1892) Mansfield OH

Usnea florida **(L.) F. H. Wigg.** – Long-beard moss [Long-bearded moss] (100) (1850) TX

Usnea hirta **(L.) F. H. Wigg.** – Death-head moss [Death head moss] (92) (1876)

Usnea xanthopoga **Nyl.** – Bearded lichen (50) (present)

Ustilago avenae **(Pers.) Rostr.** – Oat smut (157) (1929)

Ustilago carbo **Tulasne** – possibly *Erysibe vera* Wallroth

Ustilago maydis **(DC.) Corda** – Corn ergot [Corn-ergot] (48, 52) (1882–1919), Corn smut (37, 57, 157) (1830–1917), Devil's-snuff-box [Devil's snuff box] (73) (1892) Chestertown MD, Ergot of corn (92) (1876), Smut of corn (92) (1876), Wahaba hthi (Omaha-Ponca, corn sores or blisters) (37) (1830)

Utricularia ceratophylla **Michx.** – See *Utricularia inflata* Walt.

Utricularia cornuta **Michx.** – Horned bladderwort (5, 156) (1913–1923), Leafless bladderwort [Leafless bladder-wort] (19) (1840)

Utricularia fibrosa **Walt.** – See *Utricularia gibba* L.

Utricularia geminiscapa **Benj.** – Hidden-fruit bladderwort [Hidden-fruited bladderwort] (5) (1913), Hooded milfoil (5) (1913), Horned milfoil (5) (1913)

Utricularia gibba **L.** – Bladderwort (3) (1977), Cone-spur bladderwort [Conespur bladderwort] (4) (1986), Fibrous bladderwort (5, 122) (1913–1937), Hump-back bladderwort (124) (1937), Humped bladderwort (5, 50, 97) (1913–present), Little bladderwort (40) (1928), Swollen bladderwort (5) (1913), Swollen-spur bladderwort [Swollenspurred bladderwort] (122) (1937), Two-flower bladderwort [Two-flowered bladderwort] (5, 72, 97, 122, 156) (1907–1937), possibly Water-milfoil [Water milfoil, Water mill-foil, Watermillfoil] (184) (1793)

Utricularia inflata **Walt.** – Hooded milfoil (19) (1840), Large swollen bladderwort (5) (1913)

Utricularia intermedia **Hayne** – Flat-leaf bladderwort [Flatleaf bladderwort, Flat-leaved bladderwort] (5, 50, 72) (1907–present)

Utricularia juncea **Vahl** – Fairy-wand bladderwort (5) (1913), Rush bladderwort (5) (1913)

Utricularia **L.** – Bladderwort (1, 2, 4, 10, 26, 50, 93, 138, 156, 158) (1826–present)

Utricularia macrorhiza **Le Conte** – Bladder-snout (156, 158) (1900–1923), Bladderwort (3, 19, 85, 92) (1840–1977), Common bladderwort (4, 50, 156, 158) (1900–present), Great bladderwort (93) (1936), Greater bladderwort [Greater bladder-wort] (5, 63, 72, 95, 97, 131, 156, 158) (1899–1937), Hooded milfoil (92) (1876), Hooded water-milfoil [Hooded water milfoil] (92, 181)

(~1678–1876), Popweed [Pop weed, Pop-weed] (5, 156, 158) (1900–1923)

***Utricularia minor* L.** – Bladderwort (3) (1977), Lesser bladderwort (4, 5, 50, 72, 93) (1907–present), Little bladderwort (95) (1911)

***Utricularia obtusa* Sw.** – See *Utricularia gibba* L.

***Utricularia pumila* Walt.** – See *Utricularia gibba* L.

***Utricularia purpurea* Walt.** – Closed bladderwort (95) (1911), Hooded milfoil (5, 156) (1913–1923), Horned milfoil (5, 156) (1913–1923), Purple bladderwort (5, 156) (1913–1923)

***Utricularia radiata* Small.** – Small swollen bladderwort (5) (1913), Swollen bladderwort (122) (1937) TX

***Utricularia resupinata* B. D. Greene ex Bigelow** – Reclined bladderwort (5) (1913)

***Utricularia subulata* L.** – Closed bladderwort (5) (1913), Cockle [Cockel, Cokyll] (5) (1913), Pin bladderwort (5) (1913), Purple bladderwort (4) (1986), Reclined bladderwort (76, 156) (1896–1923), Tiny bladderwort (5, 178) (1526–1913), Zigzag baldderwort (5) (1913)

***Utricularia vulgaris* L.** – See *Utricularia macrorhiza* Le Conte

***Utricularia vulgaris* L. subsp. *macrorhiza* (Le Conte) Clausen** – See *Utricularia macrorhiza* Le Conte

***Uvaria* L.** – See *Asimina* Adans.

***Uvaria triloba* [(L.) Torr. & A. Gray]** – See *Asimina triloba* (L.) Dunal

***Uva-ursi uva-ursi* (L.) Britton** – See *Arctostaphylos uva-ursi* (L.) Spreng.

***Uvularia grandiflora* Smith.** – Bellwort [Bell-wort] (85) (1932), Big merrybells (138, 155) (1923–1942), Cornflower [Corn-flower, Corn flower] (156) (1923), Large bellwort (127, 156) (1923–1933), Large-flower bellwort [Large-flowered bellwort] (5, 50, 72, 97) (1907–present), Straw lily [Straw-lily, Straw lilies] (156) (1923), Straw-flower [Straw-flower] (156) (1923), Wood daffodil (156) (1923)

***Uvularia* L.** – Bellwort [Bell-wort] (1, 7, 109, 158, 184) (1793–1949), Liverberry [Liver-berry, Liver berry] (158) (1900), Merrybells [Merry bells] (138, 155, 156) (1923–1942), Twisted-stalk [Twisted-stalk, Twisted stalk] (1, 109, 138, 155, 158) (1900–1949), Wild oat [Wild oats] (158) (1900), possibly Smaller bellwort (1) (1932)

***Uvularia perfoliata* L.** – Bellwort [Bell-wort] (19, 49, 92, 107) (1840–1919), Fragrant bellwort (156) (1923), Greater & Lesser thorough leafed yellow Salomons Seale of America (181) (~1678), Mealy bellwort (5, 49, 156) (1898–1923), Mohawk weed (5, 92, 156) (1913–1923) no longer in use by 1923, Perfoliate bellwort [Perfoliate bell-wort (5, 187) (1818–1913), Perfoliated bellwort (72) (1907), Petiolate bellwort (50) (present), Solomon's-seal [Solomon's seal, Solomon seal, Solomon's seal, Solomons-seal, S'alomon's seal, Salamons seale] (46) (1879), Strawbell [Straw bell, Strawbells, Straw-bells] (5) (1913), Strawflower [Straw-flower] (156) (1923), Wild oat [Wild oats] (5) (1913), Wood merry-bells [Wood merrybells] (138, 156) (1923)

***Uvularia puberula* Michx.** – Mountain bellwort (50) (present)

***Uvularia sessilifolia* L.** – Bellwort [Bell-wort] (107) (1919), Cluster-like Solomon's-Seal of America [Cluster like Salomons Seale of America] (181) (~1678), Cornflower [Corn-flower, Corn flower] (78) (1898) ME, Lily convallie [Lilly convallie] (46) (1671), Little merry-bells [Little merrybells] (138, 155) (1923–1942), Sessile-leaf bellflower [Sessile-leaved bell-flower] (158) (1900), Sessile-leaf bellwort [Sessileleaf bellwort, Sessile-leaved bellwort, Sessile-leaved bell-wort] (48, 50, 72, 86) (1878–present) IA, Small bellflower [Small bell-flower] (158) (1900), Small bellwort (3, 127) (1933–1977), Smaller bellwort (85) (1932), Straw lily [Straw-lily, Straw lilies] (75, 158) (1894–1900) CT, Strawbell [Straw bell, Strawbells, Straw-bells] (156) (1923), Strawflower [Straw-flower] (156) (1923), Wild oat [Wild oats] (72, 73, 78, 156) (1892–1923)

Uvularia sessilifolia L.
(G. Cooke, 1827)

V

Vaccaria hispanica (**Mill.**) **Rauschert** – China cockle (157) (1929), Cockle [Cockel, Cokyll] (5, 76, 156, 157, 158) (1896–1929), Cow basil [Cow basill] (178) (1526), Cow cockle [Cowcockle] (1, 4, 85, 148) (1932–1986), Cow herb [Cow-herb, Cowherb] (1, 3, 4, 5, 19, 72, 80, 92, 95, 109, 156, 157, 158) (1840–1986), Cow soapwort (50, 138, 155) (1923–present), Cow-basil [Cow basil, Cow-Basill, Cow basill] (5, 156, 157, 158, 178, 180) (1526–1929), Cow-herd (131) (1899), Field soapwort (19, 156, 157, 158) (1840–1929), Red bearberry [Red bear-berry] (5, 93) (1913–1936), Rockberry [Rock-berry, Rock berry] (1, 158) (1900–1932), Spring cockle (157) (1929)

Vaccaria **Medik.** – See *Saponaria* L.

Vaccaria **von Wolf** – Soapwort [Soap-wort, Sope woort, Sope-wort] (50) (present)

Vaccaria vulgaris **Host.** – See *Vaccaria hispanica* (Mill.) Rauschert

Vaccinium album **L.** – See *Symphoricarpos albus* (L.) Blake

Vaccinium angustifolium **Aiton** – Blueberry [Blueberries, Blue berries, Blue berry] (40) (1928), Dwarf blueberry (5) (1913), Low black blueberry (5, 72) (1907–1913), Low-bush blueberry [Low bush blueberry, Lowbush blueberry] (5, 109) (1913–1949), Mĭn'aga'wûnj (Chippewa) (40) (1928), Strawberry huckleberry [Strawberry-huckleberry, Strawberry huckleberries, Strawberry-huckleberries] (5) (1913), Sugar blueberry (5) (1913)

Vaccinium arboreum **Marsh.** – Big blue huckleberry (50) (present), Farkleberry [Farkle-berry] (2, 5, 7, 19, 50, 92, 106, 155, 156, 158) (1828–present), Gooseberry [Goose berry, Gooseberries] (5, 156, 158) (1900–1923), Low-bush blueberry [Low bush blueberry, Low-bush blueberry] (5) (1913), Missouri farkleberry (155) (1942), Sparkleberry [Sparkle-berry] (3, 4, 5, 106, 156, 158) (1900–1986), Spoonwood [Spoon wood, Spoon-wood] (97) (1937), Tree huckleberry (5, 65, 97, 106, 124, 156, 158) (1900–1937), Tree whortleberry (8, 20) (1785–1857), Winter huckleberry (106, 156) (1923–1930), Winter whortleberry [Winter whortle-berry] (8) (1785)

Vaccinium caesariense **Mackenzie** – New Jersey blueberry (5) (1913)

Vaccinium caespitosum **Michx.** – Dwarf bilberry (5, 107, 156) (1913–1923)

Vaccinium canadense **Kalm.** – See *Vaccinium myrtilloides* Michx.

Vaccinium corymbosum **L.** – Airelle à fleurs en corymbe (French) (8) (1785), Big blue huckleberry (156) (1923), Blue bilberry (19, 156) (1840–1923), Cluster-flower vaccinium [Cluster-flowered vaccinium] (8) (1785), Common swamp blueberry (2) (1895), Giant whortleberry (19, 92, 156) (1840–1923), Great whortleberry (5) (1913), High blueberry [High blue-berry] (107, 156) (1919–1923), High whortleberry (156) (1923), High-bush blueberry [Highbush blueberry] (5, 106, 109, 138, 156) (1923–1949), Seedy dewberry (5) (1913), Swamp blueberry (5, 107, 109, 156) (1913–1949), Tall blueberry (5, 46) (1879–1913)

Vaccinium dumosa – See *Gaylussacia dumosa* (Andr.) Torr. & Gray

Vaccinium dumosum **Andrews** – See *Gaylussacia dumosa* (Andr.) Torr. & Gray

Vaccinium elliottii **Chapman** – Elliott's black blueberry (5) (1913)

Vaccinium erythrocarpum **Michx.** – Dingleberry (138, 156) (1923), Southern mountain cranberry (5, 156, 174) (1753–1923)

Vaccinium frondosum **L.** – See *Gaylussacia frondosa* (L.) Torr. & Gray

Vaccinium fuscatum **Aiton** – Black blueberry (5, 156) (1913–1923), High black blueberry (156) (1923)

Vaccinium hirsutum **Buckl.** – Bear huckleberry [Bear-huckleberry] (75) (1894) NC

Vaccinium hispidulum **Michx.** – possibly *Gaultheria hispidula* (L.) Muhl. ex Bigelow

Vaccinium **L.** – Airelle (French) (8) (1785), Airelle à fleurs en corymbe (French) (73) (1892), American cranberry (1, 7, 41, 73) (1770–1932), Bilberry [Bill berry] (1, 41, 73) (1770–1932), Blueberry [Blueberries, Blue berries, Blue berry] (1, 4, 50, 105, 106, 138, 155, 156) (1923–present), Bluets [Bluet] (73) (1892) New Brunswick, French Canadians, Buckberry [Buck-berry] (1) (1932), Cranberry [Cran berry] (1, 10, 156, 167) (1814–1932), Deerberry [Deer-berry, Deer berry] (1, 3, 4, 5, 27, 109, 156, 158) (1900–1986), Farkleberry [Farkle-berry] (1) (1932), Ground-hurts (73) (1892) Newfoundland, any low species, Huckleberry (1, 7, 10, 41, 158) (1770–1932), Mountain cranberry (1) (1932), Sparkleberry [Sparkle-berry] (1) (1932), Squaw huckleberry (1) (1932), Swedish cranberry (1) (1932), Tree huckleberry (1) (1932), Whortleberry [Whortle-berry] (1, 7, 8, 10, 73, 92, 158, 167) (1814–1932), Wisigak (Chippewa, bitter ash) (105) (1932)

Vaccinium ligustrinum [**L.**] – See *Arsenococcus ligustrinus* (L.) Small

Vaccinium macrocapum – See *Vaccinium macrocarpon* Aiton

Vaccinium macrocarpon **Aiton** – American cranberry (2, 5, 46, 47, 86, 109, 156, 158) (1852–1949), Ampimecan (Chippeways) (7) (1828), A'nibimĭn (Chippewa) (40) (1928), Atoca (7) (1828), Atopa (Canada) (7) (1828), Bankberry (72, 105) (1899–1932) Fortune Bay Newfoundland, Bearberry [Bear berry, Bear-berry] (5, 7, 73, 156) (1828–1923) Fortune Bay Newfoundland, Canneberge d'Amerique (French) (7) (1828), Common cranberry (7) (1828), Cranberry [Cran berry] (2, 14, 19, 40, 43, 47, 86, 92, 103, 106, 107, 109) (1820–1949), Craneberry [Crane-berry, Crane berry, Cranesberry] (7, 19) (1828–1840), Fen grape (92) (1876), Fenberry [Fen berry] (5, 92, 156) (1876–1923), Finberry [Finberries] (86, 92) (1876–1884), Large cranberry (2, 5, 7, 109, 156) (1828–1949), Marrish whorts (86) (1884), Marsh cranberry (5, 46, 73, 156) (1879–1923), Mossberry [Moss-berry, Moss berry] (7, 92, 107) (1828–1919), Pollom (7) (1828), Sasemineash (1, 7, 10, 41, 46, 73, 107, 158, 190) (~1759–1932), Soolabich (107) (1919), Sourberry [Sour-berry, Sour berry] (2, 7, 109) (1828–1949), Swamp redberry (7, 87) (1828–1884)

Vaccinium melanocarpum (**C. Mohr**) **C. Mohr ex Kearney** – See *Vaccinium stamineum* L.

Vaccinium membranaceum **Dougl.** – Big whortleberry (138, 155) (1923–1942), Huckleberry (35, 85, 101) (1806–1923), Mountain huckleberry (3, 4) (1977–1986), Thin-leaf huckleberry [Thinleaf huckleberry, Thin-leaved huckleberry] (5, 50) (1913–present)

Vaccinium myrsinites **Lam.** – Evergreen blueberry (156) (1923)

Vaccinium myrtilloides **Michx.** – Black whortleberry [Black whortle-berry] (131) (1899), Blueberry [Blueberries, Blue berries, Blue berry] (156) (1923), Canadian blueberry [Canada blueberry] (5, 138) (1913–1923), Sour-top (156) (1923), Sour-top blueberry (106, 107) (1919–1930), Velvet-leaf blueberry (106, 107, 156) (1919–1930)

Vaccinium myrtillus **L.** – Bilberry [Bill berry] (14, 107) (1882–1919), Black whortleberry [Black whortle-berry] (92) (1876), Blackberry [Black-berry] (14, 178) (1526–1882), Blaeberry (107) (1919), Bleaberry (92) (1876), Dyeberry [Dye berry] (92) (1876), European whortleberry (138) (1923), Huckleberry (92, 103) (1870–1876), Hurtleberry [Hurtleberye] (14) (1882), Whinberry [Whin berry] (107) (1919), Whortleberry [Whortle-berry] (107) (1919), Wineberry [Wine berry, Wine-berry] (92) (1876)

Vaccinium myrtillus **L. var.** *oreophilum* (**Rydb.**) **Dorn** – Huckleberry (153) (1913) NM

Vaccinium myrtillus microphyllum **Hook.** – See *Vaccinium scoparium* Leiberg

Vaccinium neglectum (**Small Fern.** – See *Vaccinium stamineum* L.

Vaccinium nigrum (**Wood.**) **Britton** – See *Vaccinium angustifolium* Aiton

Vaccinium opulus pimina (**Steud.**) **Michx.** – possibly *Vaccinium oxycoccos* L.

Vaccinium oreophilum [**Rydb.**] – See *Vaccinium myrtillus* L. var. *oreophilum* (Rydb.) Dorn

Vaccinium ovalifolium **J. E. Smith** – Blueberry [Blueberries, Blue berries, Blue berry] (106) (1930), Oval-leaf bilberry [Oval-leaved bilberry] (5) (1913), Tall bilberry (5) (1913)

Vaccinium ovatum **Pursh** – Box blueberry (138) (1923), California huckleberry (77) (1898) CA, Shallun (35) (1806)

Vaccinium oxycoccos **L.** – Bogberry [Bog berry] (5) (1913), Bogwort [Bog wort] (5) (1913), Box blueberry (107) (1919), California huckleberry (5) (1913), Cramberry [Cram berry] (5, 156) (1913–1923), Cranberry [Cran berry] (5, 107) (1913–1919), Craneberry [Crane-berry, Crane berry, Cranesberry] (5, 92, 156) (1876–1923), Crawberry [Craw-berry, Craw berry] (5, 156) (1913–1923), Croneberry [Crone-berry, Crone berry] (5, 156) (1913–1923), Crowberry [Crow-berry, Crow berry] (5, 156) (1913–1923), Dwarf whorleberry (5) (1913), European cranberry (5, 92, 109, 156) (1876–1949), Fenberry [Fen berry] (5) (1913), Low craneberry (19, 92) (1840–1876), Marsh cranberry (73, 156) (1892–1923) NB, Marshberry [Marshberry, Marsh berry] (5, 73, 156) (1892–1923) Newfoundland, Marshwort [Marsh wort] (5, 92) (1876–1913), Moorberry [Moor-berry, Moor berry] (5, 92, 107, 156) (1876–1923), Mossberry [Moss-berry, Moss berry] (5, 107, 156) (1913–1923), Moss-melons [Moss melons] (5, 92) (1876–1913), Moss-millions [Moss millions] (5) (1913), Small cranberry (2, 5, 109, 138, 156) (1895–1949), Sourberry [Sourberry, Sour berry] (5, 92, 156) (1876–1923), Sowberry [Sow berry, Sow-berry] (5, 92, 156, 158) (1876–1923) no longer in use by 1923, Swamp redberry (5, 92, 138, 156) (1876–1923), Tall cranberry (46, 174) (1753–1879), Wuchipoquameneash (46) (1879)

Vaccinium pallidum **Aiton** – Airelle de Pensylvanie (French) (8) (1785), Attitaash (New England Indians) (107) (1919), Black whortleberry [Black whortle-berry] (19) (1840), Black-blue whortleberry (19) (1840), Blue huckleberry (5, 63, 97) (1899–1913), Blue Ridge blueberry [Blueridge blueberry] (50, 138, 155) (1923–present), Blueberry [Blueberries, Blue berries, Blue berry] (103) (1870), Common huckleberry (47) (1852), Dryland blueberry (109, 138, 156) (1923–1949), Dwarf blueberry (46, 86, 106, 156) (1878–1930), Dwarf early blueberry (2) (1895), Early blueberry (107, 156) (1919–1923), Early sweet blueberry (106) (1930), Green-bark blueberry (46) (1879), Hartleberry [Hartleberries] (46) (1617), Hillside blueberry (4) (1986), Huckleberry (65) (1931), Late low blueberry (156) (1923), Low blueberry (5, 46, 92, 107) (1876–1919), Low pale blueberry (2, 156) (1895–1923), Low sweet blueberry (107, 156) (1919–1923), Low-bush blueberry [Low bush blueberry, Lowbush blueberry] (106, 138) (1923–1930), Mountain blueberry (5, 158) (1900–1913), Myrtle-leaf cranberry [Myrtle leaved cranberry] (8) (1785), Myrtle-leaf vaccinium [Myrtle leaved vaccinium] (8) (1785), Pale blueberry (5, 158) (1900–1913), Strawberry huckleberry [Strawberry-huckleberry, Strawberry huckleberries, Strawberry-huckleberries] (75) (1894) Weymouth MA, Sugar huckleberry (3) (1977), Sweet juniper-berry (156) (1923)

Vaccinium resinosum – See *Gaylussacia baccata* (Wang.) K. Koch

Vaccinium reticulatum **Sm.** – Ohelo (138) (1923)

Vaccinium scoparium **Leiberg** – Bilberry [Bill berry] (131) (1899), Buckberry [Buck-berry] (92, 97) (1876–1937), Grouse whortleberry (50, 155) (1942–present), Grouseberry [Grouse-berry, Grouse berry] (1, 3, 4, 85) (1932–1986), Small-leaf whortleberry [Small-leaved whortleberry] (130) (1895), Whortleberry [Whortle-berry] (35, 131) (1806–1899)

Vaccinium stamineum **L.** – Airelle à étamines longues (French) (8) (1785), Blaeberry (187) (1818), Buckberry [Buck-berry] (5, 97, 156, 158) (1900–1937), Common deerberry (155) (1942), Dangleberry [Dangle-berry] (5, 92, 156, 158) (1898–1923), Deerberry [Deerberry, Deer berry] (1, 2, 3, 4, 5, 19, 46, 50, 65, 92, 97, 107, 109, 138, 156, 158) (1879–present), Georgia farkleberry (155) (1942), Gooseberry [Goose berry, Gooseberries] (5, 156, 158, 177) (1762–1923), Long-leaf vaccinium [Long-leaved vaccinium] (8) (1785), Racomens (181) (~1678), Rawcomenes (46) (1879) natives on James

River, Raxcomens (5) (1913), Southern deerberry (155) (1942), Southern gooseberry (156) (1923), Squaw huckleberry (2, 5, 92, 103, 107, 156, 158) (1870–1923), Squaw whortleberry (5, 19, 158) (1840–1913), Squawberry [Squaw berry, Squaw-berry] (5, 92, 158) (1876–1913)

Vaccinium stamineum **L. var.** *neglectum* (**Small**) **Deam** – See *Vaccinium stamineum* L.

Vaccinium tenellum **Aiton** – Bog bilberry (174, 177) (1753–1762), Dwarf whorleberry (19) (1840), Small black blueberry (5) (1913)

Vaccinium trilobium **Marsh.** – See *Vaccinium oxycoccos* L.

Vaccinium uliginosum **L.** – Bilberry [Bill berry] (73) (1892), Blaeberry (5, 156) (1913–1923) no longer in use by 1923, Blueberry [Blueberries, Blue berries, Blue berry] (106) (1930), Bog bilberry (5, 107, 156) (1913–1923), Bog blueberry [Bog blue-berry] (5, 156) (1913–1923), Bog whortle-berry [Bog whortleberry] (5, 156) (1913–1923), Bullberry [Bull-berry, Bull berry] (156) (1923), Great bilberry (5) (1913), Moorberry [Moor-berry, Moor berry] (107) (1919), Whortleberry [Whortle-berry] (14) (1882)

Vaccinium vacillans **Kalm ex Torr.** – See *Vaccinium fuscatum* Aiton

Vaccinium virgatum **Aiton** – Rabbit-eye blueberry [Rabbiteye blueberry] (122, 138) (1923–1937), Red huckleberry (107) (1919), Red whortleberry (138) (1923), Small-flower blueberry [Smallflower blueberry] (50) (present), Southern black huckleberry (5, 97) (1913–1937)

Vaccinium vitis idaea – See *Vaccinium vitis-idaea* L.

Vaccinium vitisidaea – See *Vaccinium vitis-idaea* L.

Vaccinium vitis-idaea **L.** – Bilberry [Bill berry] (19, 92) (1840–1876), Blueberry [Blueberries, Blue berries, Blue berry] (106) (1930), Cowberry [Cow-berry, Cow berry] (5, 14, 19, 92, 107, 109, 138, 156, 178) (1526–1949), Cranberry [Cran berry] (107) (1919), Flowering boxberry [Flowering box-berry] (156) (1923), Foxberry [Fox berry, Fox-berry] (107, 156) (1919–1923) no longer in use by 1923, Lignonberry [Lignon-berry] (156) (1923), Lingberry [Ling-berry, Ling berry] (5, 156) (1913–1923), Lingenberry [Lingen-berry] (156) (1923), Mountain cranberry (5, 156) (1913–1923), Red bilberry (5, 92, 156) (1898–1923), Red whortleberry (5, 156) (1913–1923), Rock cranberry (5, 73, 156) (1892–1923) NB, Windberry [Windberry, Wind berry] (5, 156, 178) (1526–1923), Wineberry [Wine berry, Wine-berry] (5, 156) (1913–1923), Wi-sa-gu-mina (Cree) (107) (1919), possibly Clusterberry [Cluster berries] (5) (1913), possibly Flowering box (5) (1913), possibly Rawcomes (187) (1818), possibly Red lingon (41) (1770)

Vaccinium vitis-idaea **L. subsp.** *minus* (**Lodd.**) **Hultén** – Mountain cranberry (109, 138) (1923–1949)

Vaccinium vitisidaea minor – See *Vaccinium vitis-idaea* L. subsp. *minus* (Lodd.) Hultén

Vagnera **Adans.** – See *Maianthemum* G.H. Weber ex Wiggers

Vagnera racemosa (**L.**) **Morong.** – See *Maianthemum racemosum* (L.) Link subsp. *racemosum*

Vagnera stellata (**L.**) **Morong.** – See *Maianthemum stellatum* (L.) Link

Vagnera trifolia (**L.**) **Morong.** – See *Maianthemum trifolium* (L.) Sloboda

Vahlodea atropurpurea (**Wahlenb.**) **Fries ex Hartman** – Mountain hair grass [Mountain hair-grass] (5, 50, 94) (1901–present), Purple alpine hair grass (66) (1903)

Valeriana (**Tourn.**) **L.** – See *Valeriana* L.

Valeriana acutiloba **Rydb.** – Sharp-leaf valerian [Sharpleaf valerian] (50, 155) (1942–present)

Valeriana acutiloba var. acutiloba **Rydb.** – Sharp-leaf valerian [Sharpleaf valerian] (50) (Present)

Valeriana dioica **L.** – American speedwell (50, 95, 155) (1911–present), American wild valerian (158) (1900), Marsh valerian (50, 155) (1942–present), Northern valerian (5) (1913), Swamp valerian (92) (1876)

Valeriana dioica **L. var.** *sylvatica* **S. Wats.** – Wood valerian (131) (1899)

Valeriana edulis **Nutt.** – Edible valerian (63, 72, 155, 156, 158) (1899–1942), Kooyah (28, 76, 103) (1850–1896) Northwest Indians, Oregon tobacco (5, 156, 158) (1900–1923), Quee (Snake) (101) (1905), Queeah (Snake) (101) (1905) MT, Racine de tabac (French) (101, 103) (1870–1905), Swamp valerian (177) (1762), Tobacco-root [Tobacco root] (5, 28, 50, 76, 101, 103, 107, 131, 156, 158) (1850–present), Valerian (107) (1919), Wild valerian (103) (1870)

Valeriana **L.** – Tobacco-root [Tobacco root] (1) (1932), Valerian (1, 4, 10, 50, 109, 138, 155, 156, 158) (1818–present)

Valeriana locusta **L.** – See *Valerianella locusta* (L.) Lat.

Valeriana officinalis **L.** – All-heal [All heal] (5, 92, 156) (1876–1923), Cat valerian [Cat's valerian] (5, 156) (1913–1923), Common valerian (5, 109, 138, 156) (1913–1949), Cut-heal (5, 156) (1913–1923), Garden heliotrope [Garden-heliotrope] (5, 76, 109, 156) (1896–1949), Garden valerian (5, 156) (1913–1923), German valerian (92) (1876), Great wild valerian (5, 49, 53, 92, 156) (1898–1923), Hardy heliotrope (5, 76, 156) (1896–1923), Setewale (156) (1923) no longer in use by 1923, Setwall (5, 92, 156) (1876–1923) no longer in use by 1923, St George's herb (5, 156) (1913–1923), Summer heliotrope (5, 76, 156) (1896–1923), Valerian (49, 52, 53, 55, 57, 58, 59, 60, 61, 92) (1869–1922), Valerian root (92) (1876), Valeriana (57, 59, 60) (1902–1917), Vandal root [Vandal-root] (5, 92, 156) (1876–1923), Wild valerian (92) (1876)

Valeriana pauciflora **Michx.** – American valerian (7) (1828), American wild valerian (5, 156) (1913–1923), Large-flower valerian [Large-flowered valerian] (5, 156) (1913–1923)

Valeriana sylvatica **Banks.** – See *Valeriana dioica* L. var. *sylvatica* S. Wats.

Valeriana texana **Steyermark** – Texas valerian (122) (1937)

Valeriana uliginosa **(Torr. & Gray) Rydb.** – American wild valerian (5) (1913), Marsh valerian (5, 138, 156) (1913–1923), Swamp valerian (5, 156) (1913–1923)

Valerianella **(Tourn.) Hill** – See *Valerianella* Mill.

Valerianella amarella **(Lindheimer ex Engelm.) Krok** – Corn salad [Corn-salad, Cornsalad, Corn sallad, Corne Sallad, Corne sallade] (124) (1937), Hairy corn salad [Hairy cornsalad] (50) (present)

Valerianella amarella **Krok** – See *Valerianella amarella* (Lindheimer ex Engelm.) Krok

Valerianella chenopodiifolia **(Pursh) DC.** – Goose-foot corn salad (5, 72) (1907–1913), Lamb's-lettuce [Lamb's lettuce, Lamb lettuce] (19) (1840)

Valerianella locusta **(L.) Lat.** – Corn salad [Corn-salad, Cornsalad, Corn sallad, Corne Sallad, Corne sallade] (107, 109, 110, 138) (1886–1949), European corn salad (5, 156) (1913–1923), Fetticus (5, 156) (1913–1923), Lamb's-lettuce [Lamb's lettuce, Lamb lettuce] (5, 156, 107, 110) (1886–1923), Milk-grass [Milk grass] (5, 156) (1913–1923), White pot herb [White pot-herb] (5, 156) (1913–1923), Wild valerian (178) (1526)

Valerianella longiflora **(Torr. & Gray) Walp.** – Long-flower corn salad [Long-flowered corn salad] (5, 97) (1913–1937)

Valerianella **Mill.** – Corn salad [Corn-salad, Cornsalad, Corn sallad, Corne Sallad, Corne sallade] (1, 4, 50, 155, 156, 158) (1900–present), Lamb's-lettuce [Lamb's lettuce, Lamb lettuce] (1, 4, 158) (1900–1986)

Valerianella nuttallii **(Torr. & Gray) Walp.** – Nuttall's corn salad (97) (1937)

Valerianella olitoria **L.** – See *Valerianella locusta* (L.) Lat.

Valerianella radiata **(L.) Dufr.** – Beaked corn salad [Beaked cornsalad] (5, 50, 97, 122, 156, 158) (1900–present), Corn salad [Corn-salad, Cornsalad, Corn sallad, Corne Sallad, Corne sallade] (1, 3, 4, 7, 19, 92, 159, 178) (1526–1986), Lamb's-lettuce [Lamb's lettuce, Lamb lettuce] (1, 4, 5, 7, 92, 156, 158, 187) (1818–1986), Narrow-cell corn salad [Narrow-celled corn salad] (5, 97) (1913–1937), Narrow-leaf corn salad [Narrowleaf corn salad] (122) (1937), Wild lamb's-lettuce [Wild lamb lettuce] (19) (1840), Woods' corn salad [Wood's corn salad, Woods cornsalad] (5, 122, 155) (1913–1942)

Valerianella stenocarpa **(Engelm.) Krok.** – See *Valerianella radiata* (L.) Dufr.

Valerianella woodsiana **(Torr. & Gray) Walp.** – See *Valerianella radiata* (L.) Dufr.

Validallium **Small.** – See Allium L.

Vallisneria americana **Michx.** – American eel-grass [American eel-grass] (50) (present), American wild celery [American wildcelery] (155) (1942), Celery-grass (156) (1923), Eel-grass [Eel grass, Eel-grass] (5, 72, 92, 122, 131, 156, 158) (1899–1937), Spiral wild celery [Spiral wildcelery] (155) (1942), Spring plant [Spring-plant] (158) (1900) Australia, Tape-grass [Tape grass, Tapegrass] (3, 5, 19, 92, 120, 131, 156, 158, 187) (1818–1977), Water-celery [Water celery] (5, 156, 158) (1900–1923) Chesapeake Bay, Wild celery [Wildcelery] (5, 85, 138, 156) (1913–1932), possibly American vallisneria (187) (1818), possibly Channelweed [Channel-weed] (187) (1818), possibly Duck-grass (187) (1818)

Vallisneria **L.** – Eel-grass [Eel grass, Eelgrass] (2, 50, 109, 158) (1895–present), Tape-grass [Tape grass, Tapegrass] (2, 109, 158) (1895–1949), Wild celery [Wildcelery] (109, 155) (1942–1949)

Vallisneria spiralis **L.** – See *Vallisneria americana* Michx.

Vallisneria spiralis **L. var. *americana*** – See *Vallisneria americana* Michx.

Vancouveria hexandra **(Hook.) C. Morren & Decne. (possibly)** – Bitter-blain [Bitter blain] (93) (1936)

Vandellia diffusa – See *Lindernia diffusa* (L.) Wettst.

Vanilla aromatica **Sw.** – See *Vanilla mexicana* Mill.

Vanilla fragrans **Ames** – See *Vanilla planifolia* B.D. Jackson

Vanilla **Juss.** – See *Vanilla* Mill.

Vanilla mexicana **Mill.** – South American vanilla (138) (1923), Vanilla (107) (1919)

Vanilla **Mill.** – Vanilla (138) (1923) original Spanish name meaning "little sheath or pod"

Vanilla planifolia **Andr.** – See *Vanilla planifolia* B.D. Jackson

Vanilla planifolia **B.D. Jackson** – Common vanilla (109) (1949), Mexican vanilla (138) (1923), Vanilla (107) (1919)

Venidium fastuosum **(Jacq.) Stapf** – Monarch-of-the-Veldt (109) (1949)

Venidium **Less.** – Namaqualand daisy (109) (1949)

Veratrum **(Tourn.) L.** – See *Veratrum* L.

Veratrum album **L.** – Branch eliber (75) (1894), Dock (Swedish, dolls) (41) (1770), Dockor (Swedish, dolls) (41) (1770), Dockrötter (Swedish, dolls) (41) (1770), European hellebore (60) (1902), Itch-weed [Itch-weed, Itch weed, Ich weed] (41) (1770), White false hellebore (50) (present), White hellebore [White heelebore, White hellbore, White hellibore] (41, 52, 53, 55, 64, 92) (1770–1922), White veratrum (49, 52, 53) (1898–1922), Wild hellebore (41) (1770)

Veratrum californicum **Dur. var. *californicum*** – False hellebore [False-hellebore] (148) (1939)

Veratrum eschscholtzianum **(J. A. & J. H. Schultes) Rydb. ex Heller** – See *Veratrum viride* Ait.

Veratrum intermedium **Chapman** – See *Melanthium woodii* (J.W. Robbins ex Wood) Bodkin

Veratrum **L.** – False hellebore [False-hellebore] (1, 50, 109, 138, 156) (1923–present), Green-and-white hellebore [Green and whitte hellebore] (10) (1818), Skunk cabbage [Skunk-cabbage, Skunkcabbage] (1) (1932), White hellebore [White heelebore, White hellbore, White hellibore] (1, 167) (1814–1932)

Veratrum luteum **L.** – See *Chamaelirium luteum* (L.) A. Gray

Veratrum parviflorum **Michx.** – See *Melanthium parviflorum* (Michx.) S. Wats.

Veratrum viride **Ait.** – American false hellebore [American falsehellebore, American false-hellebore] (71, 139, 155) (1898–1944), American hellebore (49, 52, 53, 54, 55, 59, 60, 92) (1876–1922), American white hellebore (2, 7, 156) (1895–1923), Bear corn (5, 6, 64, 71, 156) (1874–1923), Big hellebore (5, 64) (1908–1913), Bugbane [Bugbane, Bug bane] (64, 71, 156) (1898–1923), Bugwort (64) (1908), Crow-poison [Crow poison, Crowpoison] (6, 71) (1892–1898),

434

Devil's-bite [Devil's bite, Devilsbite] (5, 64, 71, 92, 156) (1876–1923), Duck retten (5) (1913), Earthgall [Earth-gall, Earth gall, Erthe galle] (5, 7, 64, 71, 92, 156) (1828–1923), False hellebore [False-hellebore] (5, 6, 64, 71, 156) (1892–1923), Green false hellebore (50) (present), Green hellebore (49, 53, 55, 57, 64, 92, 156) (1876–1922), Green veratrum (49, 64) (1898–1908), Green-flowered hellebore (187) (1818), Grüner Germer (German) (6) (1892), Indian poke [Indianpoke] (2, 7, 53, 59, 64, 71, 78, 92, 107, 156) (1828–1922) ME, Itchweed [Itch-weed, Itch weed, Ich weed] (5, 6, 7, 19, 49, 59, 64, 71, 92, 156) (1828–1923), Meadow poke (6, 19, 71) (1818–1898), Pepper root [Pepper-root] (156) (1923), Pokeroot [Poke root, Poke-root] (5, 59, 60, 71, 75, 156) (1894–1923) Franconia NH, Poor Annie (5) (1913), Rattlesnake-weed [Rattlesnake weed, Rattlesnake weede, Rattlesnakes' weed] (156) (1923) no longer in use by 1923, Swamp hellebore (5, 49, 53, 59, 64, 71, 92, 156) (1876–1923), Swamp poke (187) (1818), Tickleweed [Tickle-weed, Tickle weed] (64, 92, 156) (1876–1923), True veratrum (64) (1908), White hellebore [White heelebore, White hellbore, White hellibore] (19, 46, 71, 107) (1840–1919), possibly American veratrum (55) (1911), possibly Dackretter (7) (1828), possibly Devil's-bit [Devil's bit, Devilbit] (7) (1828), possibly Duckretter [Duck retter] (71, 64, 92) (1876–1908), possibly Hellebore (7, 23) (1810–1828), possibly Indian uncus (71) (1898), possibly Puppet root (6, 7, 71) (1828–1898), possibly Wolf's-bane [Wolfbane, Wolf bane, Wolf's bane, Wolfsbane, Wolfs-bane] (7, 71) (1828–1898)

Veratrum viridum – possibly *Veratrum viride* Ait.

***Verbascum* (Tourn.) L.** – See *Verbascum* L.

***Verbascum blattaria* L.** – Cretan mullein [Cretan-mullein] (174) (1753), Moth mullein [Moth mullen] (3, 4, 5, 19, 45, 50, 62, 63, 72, 92, 97, 122, 124, 155, 156, 158, 178) (1526–present), Mullin with the white flower (46) (1671) accidentally introduced by 1671, Purple moth mulleine (180) (1633), Sleek mullein (19) (1840), Slippery mullein (77) (1898) Southold Long Island

***Verbascum* L.** – Black mullein [Blacke mulleine] (180) (1633), Mullein [Mullen, Mulleine] (1, 4, 10, 47, 50, 63, 85, 93, 95, 109, 122, 124, 131, 138, 155, 156, 158) (1818–present), White moth mullein (190) (~1759), Yellow moth mullen [Yellow moth mulleine] (178, 187, 190) (1526–1818)

***Verbascum lychnitis* L.** – Female mullein [Female mulleine] (178) (1526), White mullein [White mulleine] (156) (1923)

***Verbascum nigrum* L.** – Black mullein [Blacke mulleine] (92, 138) (1876–1923), White mullein [White mulleine] (174) (1753)

***Verbascum phlomoides* L.** – Clasping-leaf mullen [Clasping-leaved mullen] (5) (1913)

***Verbascum phoeniceum* L.** – Purple mullein (109, 138) (1923–1949)

***Verbascum thapsus* L.** – Aaron's-flannel [Aaron's flannel] (5, 158) (1900–1913), Adam's-flannel [Adam's flannel] (5, 14, 69, 156) (1882–1923), Adam's-rod [Adam's rod] (5, 14) (1882–1913), Blanket-leaf [Blanket leaf] (5, 69, 156, 158) (1900–1923), Bouillon blanc [Bouillon-blanc] (French) (6, 158) (1892–1900), Bullock's lungwort [Bullock's-lungwort, Bullock lungwort] (5, 14, 69, 92, 156, 158) (1876–1923), Candlewick [Candle-wick] (5, 69, 158) (1900–1913), Candle-wick mullein (156) (1923), Clown's lungwort [Clown's-lungwort] (69, 158) (1900–1904), Common mullein (3, 4, 6, 45, 50, 63, 109, 145, 156, 158) (1892–present), Cow's-lungwort [Cow's lungwort] (5, 6, 69, 156, 158) (1892–1923) no longer in use by 1923, Feltwort (5, 69, 156, 158) (1900–1923), Flannel flower (92) (1876), Flannel mullein (155) (1942), Flannel plant [Flannel-plant] (6, 156) (1892–1923), Flannel-leaf [Flannel leaf] (5, 69, 156, 158) (1900–1923), Gordoloba (Spanish) (158) (1900), Great mullein (174) (1753), Great mullen (5, 14, 34, 41, 69, 72, 93, 97, 157, 158) (1834–1937), Great white mullein (41) (1770), Hag taper (14, 156) (1882–1923) no longer in use by 1923, Hare herde (14, 156) (1882–1923), Hare's-beard [Hare's beard, Hares beard] (5, 69, 92, 156, 158) (1876–1923), Hedge-taper [Hedge-tapers, Hedge taper] (5, 69, 156, 157, 158) (1900–1929), High-taper [High taper] (5, 6, 14, 92, 158) (1882–1913), Hig-taper [Hig taper] (5, 158) (1900–1913),

Himmelbrand (German) (158) (1900), Hog-taper (158) (1900), Hygtaper (179) (1526), Ice-leaf [Ice leaf] (5, 69, 156, 158) (1900–1923), Indian tobacco [Indian-tobacco] (41) (1770), Jacob's-staff [Jacob's staff] (5, 69, 156, 158) (1900–1923), Jupiter's-staff [Jupiter's staff] (5, 69, 158) (1900–1913), Königskerze (German) (6, 158) (1892–1900), Lady's-foxglove [Lady's foxglove] (69, 158) (1900–1904), Lucernaria (156, 178) (1526–1923), Molène (French) (6, 158) (1892–1900), Moleyne (179) (1526), Mullein [Mullen, Mulleine] (6, 7, 19, 48, 49, 52, 53, 57, 58, 60, 61, 69, 80, 114, 157, 178) (1526–1929), Mullein dock [Mullen dock] (5, 69, 158, 174) (1753–1913), Old-man's-flannel [Old-man's flannel, Old man's flannel] (5, 69, 157, 158) (1899–1932), Peter's-staff [Peter's staff] (5, 69, 158) (1900–1913), Red moth mullein [Red Moth Mulleine] (69) (1904), Shepherd's-club [Shepherds' club, Shepherd's club] (5, 14, 69, 92, 158) (1882–1913), Torches (5, 69, 156, 158) (1900–1923) no longer in use by 1923, Torchwort (69, 158) (1900–1904), Velvet plant [Velvet-plant, Velvetplant] (5, 62, 69, 92, 156, 158) (1876–1923), Velvet-dock [Velvet dock] (5, 69, 156, 158) (1900–1923), Velvetleaf [Velvet leaf, Velvet-leaf] (45) (1896), White mullein [White mulleine] (46) (1649), Wild tobacco [Wild-tobacco, Wildtobacco] (41) (1770), Wollkraut (German) (6, 158) (1892–1900), Woolen [Woolen] (92, 158) (1876–1900)

***Verbena ambrosifolia* Rydb.** – See *Glandularia bipinnatifida* (Nutt.) Nutt. var. *bipinnatifida*

***Verbena angustifolia* Michx.** – See *Verbena simplex* Lehm.

***Verbena bipinnatifida* Nutt.** – See *Glandularia bipinnatifida* (Nutt.) Nutt. var. *bipinnatifida*

***Verbena bracteata* Lag. & Rodr.** – Bracted vervain (3, 82, 85, 127) (1930–1977), Large-bract vervain [Large-bracted vervain] (5, 72, 93, 97, 131, 1564, 138, 155) (1899–1937), Prostrate vervain (4, 5, 48, 80, 82, 93, 156) (1882–1986), Spreading verbena (145) (1897)

***Verbena bracteosa* Michx.** – See *Verbena bracteata* Lag. & Rodr.

***Verbena canadensis* (L.) Britton** – See *Glandularia canadensis* (L.) Nutt.

***Verbena canadensis* Britton** – See *Glandularia canadensis* (L.) Nutt.

***Verbena ciliata* Benth.** – See *Glandularia bipinnatifida* (Nutt.) Nutt. var. *bipinnatifida*

***Verbena halei* Small** – Slender vervain (97) (1937), Texas vervain (3, 50) (1977–present)

***Verbena hastata* L.** – American blue vervain (57, 157, 158) (1900–1929), American vervain (5, 156, 157, 158) (1900–1929), Blue verbena (155) (1942), Blue vervain (3, 4, 46, 58, 62, 63, 72, 80, 82, 85, 93, 97, 106, 122, 127, 131, 138, 156, 157, 158) (1869–1986), Chanhaloga pezhuta (Dakota) (37) (42), Clown's all-heal of New England [Clowne's all-heal of New England] (46) (1671), Common vervain (49, 53, 156, 157, 158) (1900–1929), False vervain (5, 93, 156, 157, 158) (1900–1936), Ironweed [Iron weed, Iron weed] (5, 75, 156, 158) (1900–1923), Pezhe makan (Omaha-Ponca) (37) (1919), Pinnate vervain (72) (1907), Purvane [Purvain] (5, 92, 156, 157, 158) (1876–1929), Simpler's-joy [Simpler's joy, Simplers joy, Simplers' joy] (7, 19, 49, 53, 58, 62, 92, 156, 157, 158) (1828–1929), Swamp verbena (50) (present), Tall vervain (187) (1818), Traveler's-joy [Traveler's joy, Traveller's joy, Traveller's-joy, Travellers Ioy] (92) (1876), Vervain (19, 40, 49, 53, 80, 92) (1840–1928), Wild hyssop (5, 7, 49, 53, 62, 92, 156, 157, 158) (1828–1929), Wild verbena (37) (1919), Wild vervain (157) (1929)

Verbena hastata* L. var. *hastata – Common verbain (37) (1919), Swamp verbena (50) (present)

***Verbena hastata* L. var. *scabra* Moldenke** – Swamp verbena (50) (present)

***Verbena hastata pinnatifida* (Lam.) Britton** – See *Verbena hastata* L.

***Verbena* L.** – Common vervain (80) (1913), Purvane [Purvain] (7) (1828), Verbena (1, 93, 138, 155, 158) (1900–1942), Vervain (1, 2, 4, 7, 10, 14, 50, 63, 82, 93, 106, 156, 158, 167) (1814–present) from Celtic ferfaen referring to cleansing power

***Verbena officinalis* L.** – Berbine (5) (1913), Blue vervain (156) (1923), Common vervain (41) (1770), Enchanter's herb [Enchanters' herb]

(92) (1876), Enchanter's plant (5, 156) (1913–1923), European vervain (5, 62, 97, 122, 156) (1912–1937), Herb grace [Herb-grace] (5, 156) (1913–1923), Herb-of-the-cross (5, 50, 62, 156) (1912–present), Holy herb (5, 62, 92) (1876–1913), Holy plant (156) (1923), Juno's-tears [Juno's tears] (5, 92, 156) (1876–1923) no longer in use by 1923, Pigeon-grass [Pigeon grass, Pigeongrass, Pigeon's- grass, Pigeon's grass] (5, 92, 156) (1876–1923) no longer in use by 1923, Pigeon-weed [Pigeonweed, Pigeon weed] (92) (1876), Simpler's-joy [Simpler's joy, Simplers joy, Simplers' joy] (5, 156) (1913–1923)

Verbena peruviana **Britton** – See *Glandularia peruviana* (L.) Druce

Verbena pinnatifida **Lam.** – See *Verbena hastata* L.

Verbena plicata **Greene** – Fan-leaf vervain [Fanleaf vervain] (4, 50) (1986–present)

Verbena pumila **Rydb.** – See *Glandularia pumila* (Rydb.) Umber

Verbena rigida **Spreng.** – Bastard vervain (187) (1818), Tuber verbena (138) (1923)

Verbena simplex **Lehm.** – Bur vine (77) (1898) Southwest MO, Narrow-leaf verbena [Narrow-leaved verbena] (3, 4) (1977–1986), Narrow-leaf vervain [Narrowleaf vervain [Narrow-leaved vervain] (5, 50, 62, 82, 93, 97) (1912–present), Pygmy vervain [Pigmy vervain] (19) (1840), White vervain (174) (1753)

Verbena spuria – See *Verbena stricta* Vent.

Verbena stricta **Vent.** – Blue vervain (92, 145) (1876–1897), Bur vine (77) (1898) Southwest MO, Common vervain (93, 95) (1911–1936), Feverweed [Fever weed, Fever-weed] (73, 156, 158) (1892–1923) Peoria IL, thought to be specific for fever and ague, Hoary verbena (50) (present), Hoary vervain (3, 4, 5, 62, 63, 72, 80, 82, 85, 97, 106, 131, 156, 158) (1899–1986), Mullein-leaf vervain [Mullein-leaved vervain [Mullenleaf vervain [Mullen-leaved vervain] (5, 93, 122, 156, 158) (1900–1937), Thimbleweed [Thimble weed, Thimbleweed] (77) (1898), Vervine (92) (1876), Wild verbena (114) (1894), Woolly verbena (155) (1942)

Verbena triphylla – See *Aloysia triphylla* (L'Hér.) Britt.

Verbena urticaefolia **L.** – See *Verbena urticifolia* L.

Verbena urticifolia **L.** – Actinomeris (174) (1753), Bur vine (77) (1898) Southwest MO, Nettle-leaf vervain [Nettle leaf vervain, Nettle leaved vervain, Nettle-leaved vervain] (3, 4, 5, 19, 48, 80, 92, 93, 95, 156, 157, 158) (1840–1986), White verbena (155) (1942), White vervain (2, 5, 50, 57, 58, 62, 63, 72, 80, 82, 92, 93, 95, 97, 114, 122, 131, 156, 157, 158) (1869–present), White-flower vervain [White-flowered vervain] (46) (1879), Wild verbena (174) (1753)

Verbena urticifolia **L. var.** *leiocarpa* **Perry & Fern.** – White vervain (50) (present)

Verbena urticifolia **L. var.** *urticifolia* – White vervain (50) (present)

Verbena venosa – See *Verbena rigida* Spreng.

Verbena wrightii **Gray** – See *Glandularia bipinnatifida* (Nutt.) Nutt. var. *bipinnatifida*

Verbesina alba **L.** – See *Eclipta prostrata* (L.) L.

Verbesina alternifolia **(L.) Britton ex Kearney** – Actinomeris (62, 72, 158) (1900–1907), Golden honey plant [Golden honey-plant] (106, 156) (1923–1930), Golden ironweed (156) (1923), Ironweed [Iron weed, Iron weed] (4, 80) (1913–1986), Riverweed [River-weed, River weed] (156) (1923), Winged ironweed [Winged iron-weed] (5, 62, 156) (1912–1923), Wingstem [Wing-stem] (4, 5, 50, 75, 82, 93, 97, 156, 158) (1894–present), Yellow ironweed [Yellow iron-weed] (5, 62, 82) (1912–1930), Yellow starwort of Virginia with a filmy stalk (174, 177) (1753–1762)

Verbesina coreopsis **Michx.** – Squarrose actinomeris (86) (1878), Stickweed [Stick-weed, Stick weed] (75, 158) (1894–1900)

Verbesina encelioides **(Cav.) Benth. & Hook. f. ex Gray** – Dogweed [Dog weed] (145) (1897) KS, Golden crownbeard [Golden crownbeard] (50, 155, 156) (1923–present), Skunk-daisy [Skunk daisy] (156) (1923), Sore-eye (106) (1930), Yellowtop [Yellow-top, Yellow top, Yellowtops, Yellow-tops] (106, 122, 124) (1930–1937)

Verbesina encelioides **(Cav.) Benth. & Hook. f. ex Gray subsp.** *exauriculata* **(Robins. & Greenm.) J. R. Coleman** – Golden crownbeard

[Golden crown-beard] (4, 5, 50, 97) (1986–present), Paper flower [Paperflower, Paper flowers] (122) (1937)

Verbesina exauriculata **(Robins. & Greenm.) Cockerell** – See *Verbesina encelioides* (Cav.) Benth. & Hook. f. ex Gray subsp. *exauriculata* (Robins. & Greenm.) J. R. Coleman

Verbesina helianthoides **Michx.** – Diabetes-weed [Diabetes weed] (156) (1923), Gravelweed [Gravel-weed, Gravel weed] (48, 50, 52, 53, 156) (1882–present), Gravelweed crownbeard (155) (1942), Sunflower crownbeard [Sunflower crown-beard, Sunflower-crownbeard] (97, 122, 124, 156, 158) (1900–1937)

Verbesina **L.** – Crownbeard [Crown beard] (1, 2, 4, 50, 93, 106, 155, 158) (1895–present), Ironweed [Iron weed, Iron weed] (82) (1930), Wingstem [Wing-stem] (4) (1986)

Verbesina micröptera **DC.** – Mesquite crownbeard [Mesquite crownbeard] (124) (1937) TX, Texas crownbeard (Texas crown-beard) (122, 124) (1937) TX

Verbesina occidentalis **(L.) Walt.** – Small yellow crownbeard (5, 97) (1913–1937), possibly Crownbeard [Crown beard] (19) (1840)

Verbesina occidentalis **Walt.** – See *Verbesina occidentalis* (L.) Walt.

Verbesina siegesbeckia **Michx.** – possibly *Verbesina occidentalis* (L.) Walt.

Verbesina texana **Buckl.** – See *Verbesina micröptera* DC.

Verbesina virginica **L.** – Crownbeard [Crown beard] (49) (1898), Frostweed [Frost weed, Frost-weed] (4) (1986), Gravelweed [Gravelweed, Gravel weed] (49) (1898), Herbe a 3 quarts (French, Louisiana) (7) (1828) Lousiana Purchase, Small white crownbeard (5, 97) (1913–1937), Virginia crownbeard [Virginia crown-beard] (122, 124) (1937) TX, White crownbeard [White crown-beard] (50, 156) (1923–present)

Verbesina virginica **L. var.** *virginica* – Small white crownbeard (5) (1913), Tung-oil tree [Tung-oil-tree, Tungoiltree] (174, 177) (1753–1762), Virginia crownbeard [Virginia crown-beard] (5, 97) (1913–1937)

Vernicia fordii **(Hemsl.) Airy Shaw** – China wood-oil tree [China wood-oil-tree] (109) (1949), Ironweed [Iron weed, Iron weed] (97) (1937), Tung-oil tree [Tung-oil-tree, Tungoiltree] (109, 138, 155) (1923–1949)

Vernonia altissima **Nutt.** – See *Vernonia gigantea* (Walt.) Trel. subsp. *gigantea*

Vernonia angustifolia **Michx.** – Ironweed [Iron weed, Iron weed] (92) (1876)

Vernonia arkansana **DC.** – Arkansas ironweed (50) (present), Bur ironweed (138, 155) (1923–1942), Great ironweed [Great iron-weed] (5, 97, 122) (1913–1937), Ironweed [Iron weed, Iron weed] (145) (1897)

Vernonia baldwinii **Torr.** – Baldwin's ironweed (50) (present), Common ironweed (124) (1937), Ironweed [Iron weed, Iron weed] (80, 92) (1876–1913), Western ironweed [Western iron weed, Western iron-weed] (4, 95) (1911–1986)

Vernonia baldwinii **Torr. subsp.** *interior* **(Small) Faust** – Interior ironweed (50) (present)

Vernonia corymbosa **Schwein.** – See *Vernonia fasciculata* Michx. subsp. *corymbosa* (Schwein. ex Keating) S. B. Jones

Vernonia crinita **Raf.** – See *Vernonia arkansana* DC.

Vernonia fasciculata **Michx.** – Common ironweed (80) (1913), Ironweed [Iron weed, Iron weed] (47, 48, 58, 82, 114, 127) (1869–1930), Prairie ironweed (50) (present), Western ironweed [Western iron weed, Western iron-weed] (5, 62, 72, 80, 93, 95, 97, 106, 131, 138, 155) (1899–1937)

Vernonia fasciculata **Michx. subsp.** *corymbosa* **(Schwein. ex Keating) S. B. Jones** – Prairie ironweed (50) (present), Western ironweed [Western iron weed, Western iron-weed] (85) (1932)

Vernonia fasciculata **Michx. subsp.** *fasciculata* – Prairie ironweed (50) (present) *Vernonia gigantea* **(Walt.) Trel. subsp.** *gigantea* – Tall ironweed [Tall iron-weed] (5, 97, 138) (1913–1937)

Vernonia gigantea **(Walter) Trel. ex Branner & Coville** – Giant ironweed (50) (present), Tall ironweed [Tall iron-weed] (62) (1912)

Vernonia glauca (**L.**) **Britton** – possibly *Vernonia glauca* (L.) Willd.

Vernonia glauca (**L.**) **Willd.** – New York ironweed [New York ironweed] (5, 97, 174, 177) (1753–1937), possibly Broad-leaf ironweed [Broad-leaved ironweed] (5) (1913)

Vernonia lettermanii **Engelm.** – See *Vernonia lettermannii* Engelm. ex Gray

Vernonia lettermannii **Engelm. ex Gray** – Letterman's ironweed [Letterman's iron-weed] (97) (1937)

Vernonia lindheimeri **Engelm. & Gray** – Lindheimer's ironweed (124) (1937)

Vernonia marginata (**Torr.**) **Raf.** – James' ironweed [James' ironweed] (5, 97) (1913–1937), Narrow-leaf ironweed [Narrow-leaved ironweed] (93) (1936), Plains ironweed (3, 4, 50) (1977–present)

Vernonia maxima **Small** – See *Vernonia gigantea* (Walt.) Trel. ex Branner & Coville

Vernonia missurica **Raf.** – Drummond's ironweed [Drummond's ironweed] (5) (1913), Missouri ironweed (50, 82) (1930–present)

Vernonia noveboracensis (**L.**) **Michx.** – Alpine speedwell (1, 93) (1932–1936), Common ironweed (2, 138) (1895–1923), Eastern ironweed [Eastern iron-weed] (62) (1912), Flat-top [Flat top] (19, 72, 86, 156) (1840–1923), Ironweed [Iron weed, Iron weed] (86, 156) (1878–1923)

Vernonia noveboracensis **Willd.** – See *Vernonia noveboracensis* (L.) Michx.

Vernonia praealta – See *Vernonia noveboracensis* (L.) Michx.

Vernonia **Schreber** – Ironweed [Iron weed, Iron weed] (1, 2, 7, 50, 63, 82, 93, 106, 109, 138, 155, 156, 158) (1828–present)

Veronica (**Tourn.**) **L.** – See *Veronica* L.

Veronica agrestis **L.** – Chickweed with leaves like germander [Chickweede with leaues like germander] (178) (1526), Field speedwell (3, 4, 5, 19, 155, 158) (1840–1986), Garden speedwell (5, 156, 158) (1900–1923), Germander-chickweed [Germander chickweed] (5, 156, 158) (1900–1923), Green-field speedwell [Green field speedwell] (50) (present), Neckweed [Neck-weed] (19) (1840), Winterweed [Winter weed, Wnter-weed] (5, 156, 158) (1900–1923)

Veronica alpina – See *Veronica wormskjoldii* Roemer & J.A. Schultes

Veronica americana **Schwein. ex Benth.** – American brooklime (5, 82, 93, 131, 156, 158) (1899–1936), American speedwell (50, 95, 155) (1911–present), Bluebell [Blue-bell, Blue bell, Blue bells, Blue-bells] (75, 156, 158) (1894–1923) Fort Fairfield ME, Brooklime [Brook-lime, Brook lime] (3, 4, 46, 48) (1629–1986), Wall-link [Wallink] (75, 156) (1894–1923) WV

Veronica anagallis-aquatica **L.** – Blue-flower pimpernel [Blew-flowered pimpernel] (46) (1671), Brook pimpernel (19) (1671), Long-leaf brooklime [Long-leaved brooklime] (19, 177) (1762–1840), Speedwell (85) (1932), Water pimpernel (5, 156, 158) (1900–1923), Water speedwell (3, 4, 5, 50, 63, 72, 82, 93, 95, 97, 107, 122, 131, 155, 156, 158) (1899–present)

Veronica arvensis **L.** – Common speedwell (85) (1932), Corn speedwell (3, 4, 5, 50, 63, 72, 82, 97, 122, 156) (1899–present), Wall speedwell (19, 97) (1840–1937), Water pimpernel (177) (1762), Water speedwell (177) (1762)

Veronica austriaca **L. subsp.** *teucrium* (**L.**) **D. A. Webb** – Hungarian speedwell (138) (1923)

Veronica beccabunga **L.** – Beccabunga (92) (1876), Brooklime [Brook-lime, Brook lime] (19, 92, 107) (1840–1919), European brooklime (156) (1923), Mouth-smart [Mouth smart] (92) (1876), Neckweed [Neck-weed] (7, 92) (1828–1876), Veronique aquatique (French) (7) (1828), Water pimpernel (107) (1919), Water purslane [Water purslain, Water-purslane, Waterpurslane]] (7, 92) (1828–1876), Water speedwell (7) (1828)

Veronica biloba **L.** – Bird's-eye [Bird's eye, Bird's-eyes, Birds-eyes] (5, 156) (1913–1923), Two-lobe speedwell [Twolobe speedwell] (50) (present)

Veronica chamaedrys **L.** – Angel's-eye [Angel's eye, Angel-eye] (5,

156) (1913–1923), Base vervain (5, 156) (1913–1923), Bird's-eye [Bird's eye, Bird's-eyes, Birds-eyes] (5, 156) (1913–1923), Bird's-eye speedwell [Birdeye speedwell] (158) (1900), Blue-eye [Blue eye, Blue eyes) (5, 156) (1913–1923), Cat's-eye [Cats eye, Cats' eye, Cat's eye] (5, 156) (1913–1923), Eyebright [Eye-bright, Eye bright] (5, 156) (1913–1923), Forget-me-not [Forget me not, For-get-me-not, For-get-me-nots, Forgetmenot] (5, 156) (1913–1923), Germander speedwell (5, 109, 156) (1913–1949), God's-eye [God's eye] (5, 156) (1913–1923)

Veronica comosa **Richter var.** *glandulosa* (**Farw.**) **Boivin** – See *Veronica anagallis-aquatica* L.

Veronica hederaefolia **L.** – See *Veronica hederifolia* L.

Veronica hederifolia **L.** – Ivy chickweed (5, 156, 158) (1900–1923), Ivy henbit [Iuie hen bit] (178) (1526), Ivy speedwell (5, 19) (1840–1913), Ivy-leaf speedwell [Ivyleaf speedwell, Ivy-leaved speedwell] (3, 4, 5, 50, 155, 156, 158) (1900–present), Morgeline (5, 158) (1900–1913), Mother-of-wheat [Mother of wheat] (5, 156, 158) (1900–1923), Small henbit (5, 156, 158) (1900–1923), Winterweed [Winter weed, Winter-weed] (5, 92, 156, 158) (1876–1923)

Veronica **L.** – Brooklime [Brook-lime, Brook lime] (1, 77, 93, 158) (1898–1936), Speedwell (1, 4, 10, 26, 50, 63, 77, 82, 93, 106, 109, 138, 155, 156, 158, 184) (1793–present)

Veronica marilandica **L.** – See *Polypremum procumbens* L.

Veronica officinalis **L.** – Common gypsyweed (50) (present), Common speedwell (2, 3, 4, 5, 62, 131, 156, 158) (1895–1986), Drug speedwell (155) (1942), Fluellin (5, 92, 156, 158) (1876–1923), Gipsy-weed [Gypsy weed, Gipsy weed, Gypsy-weed, Gypsyweed (5, 75, 156) (1894–1923) WV, Ground hele [Ground-hele, Ground heel] (5, 75, 92, 156, 158) (1876–1923), Llewellyn (158) (1900), Male speedwell (177) (1762), Paul's betony [Pauls' betony] (5, 156, 158) (1900–1923), Speedwell (19, 49, 57, 58, 92) (1840–1917), Upland speedwell (5, 156) (1913–1923), Virginia speedwell (92) (1876), Winterweed [Winter weed, Winter-weed] (187) (1818)

Veronica officinalis **L. var.** *tournefortii* (**Vill.**) **Reichenb.** – Bird's-eye [Bird's eye, Bird's-eyes, Birds-eyes] (5, 156) (1913–1923), Byzantine speedwell (5, 156) (1913–1923), Cat's-eye [Cats eye, Cats' eye, Cat's eye] (5, 156) (1913–1923), Tournefort's speedwell (5) (1913)

Veronica peregrina **L.** – Neckweed [Neck-weed] (2, 5, 50, 62, 80, 82, 131, 145, 156, 158) (1897–present), Purslane speedwell (2, 4, 5, 19, 62, 72, 80, 92, 93, 97, 122, 155, 156, 158) (1840–1986), Speedwell (80, 82, 107) (1919–1930)

Veronica peregrina **L. subsp.** *xalapensis* (**Kunth**) **Pennell** – Hairy purslane speedwell (50) (present), Purslane speedwell (3, 95) (1911–1977)

Veronica persica **Poir.** – Bird's-eye speedwell [Birdeye speedwell] (3, 4, 50) (1977–present)

Veronica polita **Fries** – Gray field speedwell (50) (present), Wayside speedwell (155) (1942)

Veronica scutella **L.** – See *Veronica scutellata* L.

Veronica scutellata **L.** – Marsh speedwell (3, 4, 5, 155, 156) (1913–1986), Narrow-leaf marsh speedwell [Narrow-leaved marsh speedwell] (46) (1879), Skullcap speedwell [Skull-cap speedwell] (5, 19, 50, 72, 156) (1840–present)

Veronica serpyllifolia **L.** – Ehrenpreis (158) (1900), Grundheil (German) (158) (1900), Heil-aller-Schaden (German) (158) (1900), Male fluellin (178) (1526), Paul's betony [Pauls' betony] (5, 19, 156) (1840–1923), Smooth speedwell (19) (1840), Stah-up-unga-weg (German) (158) (1900), Thyme-leaf speedwell [Thymeleaf speedwell, Thyme-leaved speedwell] (3, 4, 5, 50, 62, 72, 155, 156) (1907–present), Upland speedwell (158) (1900), Veroniken (German) (158) (1900), Véronique mâle (French) (158) (1900), Wundkraut (German) (158) (1900)

Veronica serpyllifolia **L. subsp.** *serpyllifolia* – Thyme-leaf speedwell [Thymeleaf speedwell, Thyme-leaved speedwell] (50) (present)

Veronica spicata **L.** – Spike speedwell (138) (1923)

Veronica spuria **L.** – Bastard speedwell (138) (1923)

Veronica teucrium – See *Veronica austriaca* L. subsp. *teucrium* (L.)

D. A. Webb

Veronica tournefortii **Gmelin.** – See *Veronica officinalis* L. var. *tournefortii* (Vill.) Reichenb.

Veronica triphyllos **L.** – Finger speedwell (50) (present)

Veronica virginica **L.** – See *Veronicastrum virginicum* (L.) Farw.

Veronica wormskjoldii **Roemer & J. A. Schultes** – Alpine speedwell (138) (1923), Wormskiold's speedwell (5) (1913)

Veronica xalapensis **Kunth** – See *Veronica peregrina* L. subsp. *xalapensis* (Kunth) Pennell

Veronicastrum **Heister ex Fabr.** – Beaumont's root [Beaumont root] (5, 7, 49, 53, 61, 92, 157, 158) (1828–1923), Culver's root [Culver's-root, Culvers-root, Culvert root] (158) (1900), Veronicastrum (50) (present)

Veronicastrum virginicum (**L.**) **Farw.** – Beaumont's root [Beaumont root] (5, 64, 92, 156, 157, 158) (1876–1923) no longer in use by 1923, Blackroot [Black-root, Black root] (5, 6, 7, 48, 49, 53, 61, 64, 77, 92, 93, 156, 157, 158) (1828–1936), Bowman's root [Bowman's-root, Bowman root, Bowmanroot] (5, 7, 49, 53, 64, 92, 93, 156, 157, 158, 178) (1526–1936), Brinton's root [Brinton root, Brinton-root] (5, 7, 19, 49, 53, 64, 92, 156, 157, 158) (1828–1929), Culver's physic [Culver's-physic, Culvers-physic, Culversphysic] (5, 6, 19, 48, 49, 53, 57, 92, 156, 157, 158) (1840–1929), Culver's root [Culver's-root, Culvers-root, Culvert root] (1, 2, 3, 4, 5, 6, 7, 40, 47, 49, 50, 52, 53, 54, 55, 57, 59, 63, 64, 72, 82, 92, 93, 106, 109, 131, 138, 155, 57, 158) (1828–present), Herbe à quartre feuilles (Four-leaved grass)(French) (17) (1796), High veronica (6) (1892), Hini (Missouri & Osage) (6, 7, 56, 92, 157, 158) (1828–1929), Leptandra (53, 55, 57, 59) (1911–1922), Leptandre rouge (French) (7) (1828), Oxadaddy (5, 92, 157, 158) (1876–1929), Oxadoddy (5, 92, 157, 158) (1876–1929), Physic root (7, 49, 64, 92) (1828–1907), Purple leptandra (7, 92) (1828–1876), Quintel (6) (1892), Quital (157) (1929), Quitel (55, 57, 59) (1911–1917), Quitel (Delaware) (5, 7, 56, 92) (1828–1913), Tall speedwell [Tall speed-well] (5, 6, 49, 53, 64, 92, 156, 157, 158) (1876–1929), Tall veronica (19, 49, 64, 157, 158) (1840–1929), Veronica (49) (1898), Veronique de Virginie (French) (6) (1892), Virginischer Ehrenpreis (German) (6) (1892), Whorlywort [Whorly wort, Whorly-wort] (6, 7, 49, 64, 92, 156, 157, 158) (1828–1929), Wi'sûgidji'bĭk (Chippewa, bitter root) (40) (1928)

Verpa bohemica (**Krombh.**) **J. Schröt.** – Ribbed verpa (128) (1933)

Vesiculina purpurea (**Walt.**) **Raf.** – See *Utricularia purpurea* Walt.

Vesiculina **Raf.** – See *Utricularia* L.

Vetiveria zizanioides (**L.**) **Nash** – Cuscus (92) (1876), Iwarancuse (92) (1876), Khas-khas (163) (1852), Khuskhus [Khus-khus, Khus khus] (92, 109, 163) (1852–1949), Kus kus (92) (1876), Vetiver (109, 122, 163) (1852–1949)

Viburnum acerifolium **L.** – Anib' (Chippewa) (40) (1928), Arrow-wood [Arrow wood] (40) (1928), Dockmackie (19, 92, 109, 156) (1840–1949), Dockmakie (5) (1913), Guelder-maple [Guelder maple] (92) (1876), Maple guelder-rose [Maple guelder rose] (19, 92) (1840–1876), Maple-leaf arrow-wood [Maple-leaved arrow-wood, Maple-leaf arrowwood, Mapleleaf arrowwood] (5, 122, 156) (1913–1937), Maple-leaf guelder-rose [Maple-leaf guelder rose, Maple-leaf guelder rose] (5, 156) (1913–1923), Maple-leaf viburnum [Mapleleaf viburnum, Maple-leaved viburnum] (8, 138) (1785–1923), Squashberry [Squash-berry, Squash berry] (5, 76, 156) (1896–1923), Viorne à feuilles d'érable (French) (8) (1785)

Viburnum alnifolium **Marsh.** – See *Viburnum lantanoides* Michx.

Viburnum americanum **L.** – possibly *Viburnum opulus* L. var. *americanum* Aiton

Viburnum bracteatum **Rehd.** – Bracted viburnum (138) (1923)

Viburnum buddleifolium **C. Wright** – Woolly viburnum [Wooly viburnum] (138) (1923)

Viburnum bushii **Ashe** – See *Viburnum prunifolium* L.

Viburnum cassinoides **L.** – See *Viburnum nudum* L. var. *cassinoides* (L.) Torr. & Gray

Viburnum dentatum **L.** – Arrow-wood [Arrow wood] (2, 5, 7, 46, 92,

109, 112, 138, 156) (1828–1949), Mealy tree [Mealy-tree] (5, 7, 92, 156) (1828–1923), Smale elderne (46) (1879), Tily (Indians) (7) (1828), Tooth-leaf arrow-wood [Tooth-leaved arrow wood] (8) (1785), Tooth-leaf viburnum [Toothed-leaved viburnum] (8, 177) (1762–1785), Viorne à feuilles dentées (French) (8) (1785), Withe rod [Withe-rod] (5, 156, 174) (1753–1923), Withewood [Withe wood, Withe-wood] (5, 76, 156) (1896–1923) S. Berwick ME

Viburnum dentatum **L.** var. *dentatum* – Downy arrow-wood [Downy arrowwood] (156) (1923), Downy viburnum (138) (1923), Downy-leaf arrow-wood [Downy-leaved arrow-wood] (5, 63, 72) (1899–1913), Roughish arrow-wood [Roughish arrow wood] (5) (1913)

Viburnum dentatum **L.** var. *venosum* (**Britt.**) **Gleason** – Veiny arrow-wood [veiny arrow wood] (5) (1913), Veiny viburnum (138) (1923)

Viburnum dilatatum **Thunb.** – Linden viburnum (138) (1923)

Viburnum edule (**Michx.**) **Raf.** – Few-flower cranberry tree [Few-flowered cranberry tree, Few-flowered cranberr-tree] (5, 158) (1900–1923), Highland cranberry (40) (1928), Mooseberry [Moose-berry, Moose berry] (4) (1986), Mooseberry viburnum (155) (1942), Pimbina (156) (1923), Squashberry [Squash-berry, Squash berry] (3, 4, 50, 156, 158) (1900–present), Tooth-leaf arrow-wood [Tooth-leaved arrow wood] (187) (1818)

Viburnum ellipticum **Hook.** – Arrow-wood [Arrow wood] (19) (1840), Oregon viburnum (138) (1923)

Viburnum **L.** – Arrow-wood [Arrow wood] (1, 2, 4, 38, 82, 93, 156) (1820–1986), Black haw [Black-haw, Blackhaw] (158) (1900), Cranberry bush (1) (1932), Cranberry tree (1) (1932), Laurestinus (82) (1930) IA, Pliant meally (8) (1785), Snowball [Snow ball, Snowballs, Snow-balls] (1) (1932), Viburnum (4, 50, 138, 155, 158) (1900–present), Viorne (French) (8) (1785), Wayfaring tree [Wayfaring tree, Way faring tree, Wayfaringtree, Wayfaring-tree] (8) (1785)

Viburnum lantana **L.** – European wayfaring tree (156) (1923), Lantana (112) (1937), Lithy tree (92) (1876), Wayfaring man's tree (156) (1923), Wayfaring tree [Way-faring tree, Way faring tree, Wayfaringtree, Wayfaring-tree] (4, 5, 50, 92, 109, 112, 138, 155, 158, 179) (1793–present)

Viburnum lantanoides **Michx.** – American wayfaring tree [American wayfaring tree, American wayfaring-tree] (5, 109, 156) (1913–1949), Devil's-shoestring [Devil's shoe-string, Devil's shoe string, Devil's-shoestrings, Devil's shoe-strings, Devil's shoestrings, Devil's shoe strings] (156) (1923), Dogberry [Dog-berry, Dog berry] (5, 156) (1913–1923), Dog-hobble [Dog hobble] (156) (1923), Dogwood [Dog-wood, Dog wood] (5, 76, 156) (1896–1923) Bath ME, Hobble bush [Hobblebush, Hobble-bush] (2, 5, 19, 29, 75, 92, 109, 138, 156) (1811–1949) branches often take root at ends, Maple-leaf mealy tree [Maple-leaved mealy-tree] (5, 35, 37, 57) (1806–1917), Moose bush [Moose-bush] (5, 75, 76, 156) (1894–1923), Mooseberry [Moose-berry, Moose berry] (5, 75, 76, 156) (1894–1923), Moosewood [Moose-wood, Moose wood] (73, 156) (1892–1923), Shin hoble (29) (1869), Tanglefoot [Tangle foot] (5, 75, 156, 174) (1753–1923), Tangle-legs [Tangle legs] (5, 19, 156, 174) (1753–1923), Triptoe [Trip-toe, Trip toe] (5, 75, 156) (1894–1923) Franconia NH, Viorne à feuilles d'aune (French) (8) (1785), Wild hydrangea (156) (1923), Witch hobble [Witch-hobble] (5, 156) (1913–1923) NH, Witch-hopple [Witch hopple] (5, 79, 156) (1891–1923)

Viburnum lentago **L.** – Akiwasas (Pawnee, naming names) (37) (1919), Black haw [Black-haw, Blackhaw] (5, 35, 37, 57, 156, 158) (1806–1923) Meriwether Lewis, Black thorn [Black-thorn] (5, 92, 156, 158) (1876–1923), Canadian viburnum (8) (1785), Mna (Dakota) (37) (1919) Mna-hu (black haw bush), Nanny bush [Nanny-bush, Nannybush] (5, 92, 156, 158) (1876–1923) no longer in use by 1923, Nannyberry [Nanny-berry, Nanny berry] (3, 4, 5, 37, 50, 53, 92, 93, 95, 107, 109, 112, 138, 156, 158) (1876–present), Nannyberry viburnum (155) (1942), Nanny-plum [Nanny plum] (5, 156, 158) (1900–1923) no longer in use by 1923, Nanshaman (Omaha-Ponca) (37) (1919), Sheepberry [Sheep berry, Sheep-berry] (2, 4, 5, 19, 53, 72, 82, 92, 95, 105, 107, 109, 113, 130, 156, 158) (1840–1986),

Sheepberry bark [Sheep berry bark] (92) (1876), Sweet viburnum (2, 5, 63, 92, 107, 131, 156, 158) (1895–1923), Sweetberry [Sweet berry, Sweet-berry] (5, 93, 156, 158) (1900–1936), Tea plant [Tea-plant] (5, 76, 156, 158) (1896–1923) Madison WI, no longer in use by 1923, Teta-minan (Chippewa) (105) (1932), Viorne à manchettes (French) (8) (1785), Wayfarer's tree (53) (1922), Wild raisin (5, 75, 107, 156, 158) (1900–1923) Penobscot Co. ME, Wuwu (Winnebago) (37) (1919)

Viburnum molle **Michx** – Black-alder [Black alder] (156) (1923), Kentucky viburnum (138) (1923), Poison-haw (156) (1923), Soft arrow-wood (156) (1923), Soft-leaf arrow-wood [Soft-leaved arrow-wood] (5, 82) (1913–1930)

Viburnum nudum **L.** – Bilberry [Bill berry] (5, 73, 156) (1892–1923), Black-alder [Black alder] (156) (1923), Larger with-rod [Larger withe rod] (5) (1913), Naked viburnum (107) (1919), Naked with-rod [Naked withe rod] (5, 122, 156) (1913–1937), Naked-cyme mealy-tree [Naked-cymed mealy-tree] (53) (1922), Nannyberry [Nanny-berry, Nanny berry] (5, 75, 156, 187) (1818–1923), Possum-berry [Possum berry] (75, 106) (1894–1930), Posum-haw [Possum haw, Possumhaw] (5, 156) (1913–1923), Shawnee-haw [Shawnee haw] (5, 156) (1913–1923), Smooth withe-rod (109, 138) (1923–1949), Swamp viburnum (8) (1785), Tinus-leaf viburnum [Tinus leaved viburnum] (8) (1785), Viorne nue (French) (8) (1785), Withe rod [Withe-rod] (107) (1919), Withewood [Withe wood, Withe-wood] (73) (1892)

Viburnum nudum **L. var.** *cassinoides* **(L.) Torr. & Gray** – Appalachian tea (5, 156) (1913–1923), False Paraguay tea (5, 156) (1913–1923), Teaberry [Tea-berry, Tea berry, Tea-berries] (156) (1923), Wild raisin (156) (1923), Withe rod [Withe-rod] (2, 5, 109, 112, 138, 156) (1895–1949) NH

Viburnum opulus **L.** – Cherry wood [Cherry-wood] (5, 156, 158) (1900–1923) no longer in use by 1923, Cramp bark [Cramp-bark] or Cramp-bark tree (5, 49, 52, 53, 54, 57, 58, 59, 92, 156, 158) (1869–1923), Cranberry bush (47) (1852), Cranberry tree (2, 63, 72, 107, 130, 131, 156, 158) (1895–1923), Dog rowan tree [Dog-rowan tree] (5, 156, 158) (1900–1923) no longer in use by 1923, Dog-elder [Dog elder] (156) (1923) no longer in use by 1923, Elder rose (178) (1526), European cranberry bush [European cranberrybush, European cranberry-bush] (50, 109 138) (1923–present), European cranberry viburnum (155) (1942), Gadrise (5, 156, 158) (1900–1923) no longer in use by 1923, Gaiter tree [Gaiter-tree] (5, 156, 158) (1900–1923) no longer in use by 1923, Gatten or Gatten tree [Gatten-tree] (5, 156, 158) (1900–1923), Grouseberry [Grouse-berry, Grouse berry] (156) (1923) no longer in use by 1923, Guelder-rose [Guelder rose] (19, 107, 178) (1596–1919), Gueldres-rose (158) (1900), High cranberry (49, 52, 53, 54, 58, 59, 61, 92, 156) (1869–1923), High cranberry bark (92) (1876), High-bush cranberry [Highbush cranberry] (3, 4, 35, 37, 52, 57, 73, 112, 156, 158) (1806–1986), Love-roses [Love roses, Love rose] (5, 156, 158) (1900–1923) no longer in use by 1923, Marshelder [Marsh elder, Marsh-elder] (5, 156, 158) (1900–1923), May-rose [May rose] (5, 156, 158) (1900–1923) no longer in use by 1923, Nepin-minan (Chippewa for summer berry) (35, 37) (1806–1919), Nipi minan (Cree) (107) (1919), Obier (French) (158) (1900), Ople tree [Ople-tree] (156) (1923) no longer in use by 1923, Pembina (37, 107) (1919), Pimbina (156) (1923), Pincushion tree [Pincushion-tree (5, 156, 158) (1900–1923) no longer in use by 1923, Red elder (5, 156, 158) (1900–1923), Rose-elder [Rose elder] (5, 92, 156, 158) (1876–1923), Snowball [Snow ball, Snowballs, Snow-balls] (5, 19, 135, 156, 158) (1840–1923), Snowball bush [Snowball-bush] (158) (1900), Snowball tree (107) (1919), Squaw bush [Squawbush, Squaw-bush] (5, 92, 156, 158) (1876–1923) no longer in use by 1923, Wasserhollder (German) (158) (1900), Wasserschwelke (German) (158) (1900), Water-elder [Water elder] (156, 158) (1900–1923), White dogwood [White dog-wood] (5, 156, 158) (1900–1923) England, White elder (5, 158) (1900–1913), Whitten tree [Whitten-tree] (5, 92, 107, 156, 158) (1876–1923) no longer in use by 1923, Wild guelder-rose [Wild guelder rose] (5, 63, 156, 158)

(1899–1923), Witch hobble [Witch-hobble] (5, 156, 158) (1900–1923) no longer in use by 1923, Witch-hopple [Witch hopple] (5, 156, 158) (1900–1923) no longer in use by 1923, Withewood [Withe wood, Withe-wood] (174) (1753), Wuchipoquameneash (Narragansett) (107) (1919)

Viburnum opulus **L. var.** *americanum* **Aiton** – American cranberry (50, 138, 155) (1923–present), Cranberry bush (105, 106, 109) (1930–1949), Mountain viburnum (8) (1785), Pimina des Canadiens (French) (8) (1785), Viorne des Canada (French) (8) (1785), Withe rod [Withe-rod] (174) (1753), possibly High-bush cranberry [High-bush cranberry] (4, 106) (1930–1986), possibly Nipinminan (Chippewa) (105) (1932), possibly Pembina (105) (1932)

Viburnum opulus **L. var.** *opulus* – Black haw [Black-haw, Blackhaw] (124) (1937), Guelder-rose [Guelder rose] (92, 109) (1876–1949), Snowball [Snow ball, Snowballs, Snow-balls] (92, 109) (1876–1949)

Viburnum pauciflorum **Pylaie** – See *Viburnum edule* (Michx.) Raf.

Viburnum plicatum **Thunb.** – Double-file viburnum [Doublefile viburnum] (138) (1923), Japanese snowball (109) (1949)

Viburnum prunifolium **L.** – Black haw [Black-haw, Blackhaw] (3, 4, 5, 8, 19, 48, 49, 50, 52, 53, 54, 57, 58, 59, 60, 61, 63, 72, 82, 92, 97, 106, 107, 109, 121, 138, 56, 158, 177, 181) (~1678–present), Blackhaw viburnum [Blackhaw viburnum] (155) (1942), Bo (Osage) (121) (1918?–1970?), Boots (158) (1900), Nannyberry [Nanny-berry, Nanny berry] (156, 158) (1900–1923), Plum-leaf mealy tree [Plumb-leaved mealy-tree] (187) (1818), Sheepberry [Sheep berry, Sheep-berry] (156, 158) (1900–1923), Sloe (5, 19, 49, 53, 58, 92, 156, 158) (1840–1923), Sloe-leaf viburnum [Sloe-leaved viburnum] (49, 53) (1898–1922), Stag bush [Stag-bush] (5, 49, 53, 54, 156, 158) (1898–1923), Sweet haw (4) (1986), Viorne à feuilles de prunier (French) (8) (1785)

Viburnum pubescens **Pursh** – See *Viburnum dentatum* L. var. *dentatum*

Viburnum rafinesquianum **Schult.** – Downy arrow-wood [Downy arrowwood] (3, 4, 50) (1977–present), Rafinesque's viburnum [Rafinesque viburnum] (155) (1942)

Viburnum rafinesquianum **Schultes var.** *affine* **(Bush ex Schneid.) House** – Southern viburnum (50) (present)

Viburnum roseum – See *Viburnum opulus* L. var. *opulus*

Viburnum rufidulum **Raf.** – Rusty blackhaw (50) (present), Rusty blackhaw viburnum (155) (1924), Southern black haw [Southern black-haw, Southern blackhaw] (3, 4, 8, 65, 97, 156) (1785–1986), Southern haw (5) (1913)

Viburnum scabrellum **(Torr. & Gray) Chapman** – See Viburnum dentatum L. var. dentatum

Viburnum setigerum **Hance** – Tea viburnum (138) (1923)

Viburnum sieboldii **Miq.** – American vetch (4, 5, 50, 72, 93, 95, 97, 131, 155, 156, 158, 187) (1818–present), Siebold's viburnum [Siebold viburnum] (138) (1923)

Viburnum tinus **L.** – Laurestinus (109, 138) (1923–1949)

Viburnum triloba – See *Viburnum opulus* L. var. *americanum* Aiton

Viburnum trilobum **Marsh** – See *Viburnum opulus* L. var. *americanum* Aiton

Viburnum venosum **Britton** – See *Viburnum dentatum* L. var. *venosum* (Britt.) Gleason

Vicia americana **Muhl. ex Willd.** – Buffalo-pea [Buffalo pea, Buffalo peas] (5, 76, 93, 156, 158) (1896–1936), Pea vine [Peavine, Pea-vine] (156) (1923), Pea-vine clover [Pea vine clover] (5) (1913), Purple vetch (5, 82, 156, 158) (1900–1923), Wild pea (101, 156) (1905–1923), Wild sweetpea [Wild sweet pea] (156) (1923), Wild vetch (127) (1933)

Vicia americana **Muhl. ex Willd. subsp.** *americana* – American vetch (3, 50) (1977–present), Bit-leaf American vetch [Bitleaf American vetch] (155) (1942), California vetch (155) (1942), Greek beans [Greeke beanes] (5, 107) (1913–1919), Oregon American vetch (155) (1942), Wild tare (178) (1526)

Vicia americana **Muhl. ex Willd. subsp.** *minor* **(Hook.) C. R. Gunn**

439

– American vetch (3) (1977), Club-leaf vetch [Clubleaf vetch] (155) (1942), Mat vetch (50) (present), Narrow-leaf American vetch [Narrow-leaved American vetch] (5, 72, 93, 97) (1907–1937), Narrow-leaf vetch [Narrowleaf vetch, Narrow-leaved vetch] (85, 131) (1899–1932), Stiff-leaf vetch [Stiffleaf vetch] (155) (1942), Trellis-leaf vetch [Trellisleaf vetch] (155) (1942), Wild vetch (114) (1894)

***Vicia americana* Muhl. ex Willd. var. *linearis* (Nutt.) S. Wats.** – See *Vicia americana* Muhl. ex Willd. subsp. *minor* (Hook.) C. R. Gunn

***Vicia americana* Muhl. ex Willd. var. *truncata* (Nutt.) Brewer** – See *Vicia americana* Muhl. ex Willd. subsp. *americana*

***Vicia angustifolia* L.** – See *Vicia sativa* L. subsp. *nigra* (L.) Ehrh.

***Vicia benghalensis* L.** – Purple vetch (109) (1949)

***Vicia californica* Greene** – See *Vicia americana* Muhl. ex Willd. subsp. *americana*

***Vicia californica* Greene var. *madrensis* Jepson** – See *Vicia americana* Muhl. ex Willd. subsp. *americana*

***Vicia caroliniana* Walt.** – Altsa'sti (Cherokee, wreath for the head) (102) (1886), Carolina vetch (5, 72, 97) (1907–1937), Pale vetch (5) (1913), Wood vetch (3) (1977)

***Vicia cracca* L.** – Aracus (110) (1886), Bird vetch [Bird-vetch] (4, 5, 50, 155, 156) (1923–present), Blue vetch (5, 156, 158) (1900–1923), Canadian pea [Canada pea] (5, 76, 156, 158) (1896–1923) Paris ME, Cat-pea [Cat-peas, Cat pea] (5, 156, 158) (1900–1923), Cow vetch [Cow-vetch] (72, 138, 155, 156, 158) (1900–1942), Crow vetch (155) (1942), Tine-grass [Tine grass] (5, 156, 158) (1900–1923), Tufted vetch (3, 5, 19, 107, 158) (1840–1977)

***Vicia dasycarpa* Ten.** – See *Vicia villosa* Roth subsp. *varia* (Host) Corb.

***Vicia dissitifolia* (Nutt.) Rydb.** – See *Vicia americana* Muhl. ex Willd. subsp. *minor* (Hook.) C. R. Gunn

***Vicia exigua* Torr. & Gray** – See *Vicia ludoviciana* Nutt. subsp. *ludoviciana*

***Vicia faba* L.** – Baba (Baque) (110) (1886), Beane [Beane] (110) (1886), Big bean (7, 179) (1526–1828), Broad bean [Broadbean] (107, 109, 110, 138, 155) (1886–1949), Creeping vetch (7) (1828), English bean (107) (1919), European bean (107, 109) (1919–1949), Feve commune (French) (7, 68) (1828–1913), Feverolles (7, 34, 92, 107) (1828–1919), Garden bean [Garden beans] (19, 46) (1671–1840), Horse bean [Horse-bean, Horsebean] (7, 68, 92, 107) (1828–1919), Sweet bean [Sweet-bean] (7) (1828), Windsor bean (7, 19, 107) (1828–1919)

***Vicia hirsuta* (L.) Gray** – Creeping vetch (19) (1840), Hairy tare (5, 19, 107) (1840–1919), Hairy vetch (5, 93, 156) (1913–1936), Strangle tare [Strangle-tare] (5, 156) (1913–1923), Tare [Tares] (156) (1923), Tare vetch [Tare-vetch] (5, 156) (1913–1923), Tine tare (5) (1913), Tineweed [Tine weed, Tine-weed] (5, 156) (1913–1923)

***Vicia* L.** – Tare [Tares] (2, 45, 156, 158) (1895–1923), Vetch (1, 2, 4, 10, 45, 50, 106, 109, 138, 155, 156, 158) (1818–present) from Vik of ancient European languages, Wild pea (1) (1932)

***Vicia leavenworthia* T. & G.** – See *Vicia ludoviciana* Nutt. subsp. *leavenworthii* (Torr. & Gray) Lassetter & Gunn.

***Vicia linearis* (Nutt.) Greene** – See *Vicia americana* Muhl. ex Willd. subsp. *minor* (Hook.) C. R. Gunn

***Vicia ludociciana* Nutt.** – Deer-pea vetch [Deer pea vetch] (4) (1986), Louisiana vetch (3, 5, 50, 97, 155) (1913–present)

***Vicia ludoviciana* Nutt. subsp. *leavenworthii* (Torr. & Gray) Lassetter & Gunn.** – Leavenworth's vetch (72) (1907)

Vicia ludoviciana* Nutt. subsp. *ludoviciana – Louisiana vetch (50) (present), Slim vetch (155) (1942), Texas vetch (97, 155) (1937–1942), White vetch (155) (1942)

***Vicia micrantha* Nutt.** – See *Vicia minutiflora* F. G. Dietr.

***Vicia minutiflora* F. G. Dietr.** – Reverchon's vetch (97) (1937), Small-flower vetch [Small-flowered vetch] (5, 97) (1913–1937)

***Vicia narbonensis* L.** – Narbonne vetch (107, 109) (1919–1949)

***Vicia producta* Rydb.** – See *Vicia ludoviciana* Nutt. subsp. *ludoviciana*

***Vicia reverchonii* S. Wats.** – See *Vicia minutiflora* F. G. Dietr.

***Vicia sativa* L.** – Common tare (5, 156, 158) (1900–1923), Common

vetch (4, 5, 68, 72, 80, 85, 109, 110, 138, 155, 158) (1886–1986), Fitch (92) (1876), Garden vetch (50) (present), Pebble vetch [Pebble-vetch] (5, 156, 158) (1900–1923), Spring vetch (3, 5, 68, 82, 109, 156, 158) (1900–1977), Tare [Tares] (14, 19, 68, 92, 107, 109, 110, 131) (1840–1949), Vetch (14, 92, 131) (1876–1899), White vetch (107) (1919), Wood pea (92) (1876), Wood vetch (92) (1876)

***Vicia sativa* L. subsp. *nigra* (L.) Ehrh.** – Narrow-leaf vetch [Narrowleaf vetch, Narrow-leaved vetch] (109, 155) (1942–1949), Smaller common vetch (5, 72) (1907–1913), Summer vetch (155) (1942)

***Vicia sepium* L.** – Bush vetch (5, 107) (1913–1919), Crow peas [Crowpeas] (5, 156) (1913–1923), Wild tare (5, 156) (1913–1923)

***Vicia sparsifolia* Nutt.** – See *Vicia americana* Muhl. ex Willd. subsp. *minor* (Hook.) C. R. Gunn

***Vicia tetrasperma* (L.) Moench** – Lentil tare (5, 156) (1913–1923), Slender vetch (5) (1913), Smooth tare (5) (1913)

***Vicia texana* (Torr. & Gray) Small** – See *Vicia ludoviciana* Nutt. subsp. *ludoviciana*

***Vicia trifida* Rydb.** – See *Vicia americana* Muhl. ex Willd. subsp. *minor* (Hook.) C. R. Gunn

***Vicia villosa* Roth** – Cow vetch [Cow-vetch] (85) (1932) SD, Hairy vetch (3, 4, 68, 82, 93, 95, 97, 109, 118, 138, 155) (1898–1986), Large Russian vetch (107) (1919), Winter vetch (50, 68, 82, 97, 109, 156) (1913–present), Woolly-pod vetch [Woollypod vetch] (4) (1986)

***Vicia villosa* Roth subsp. *varia* (Host) Corb.** – Smooth vetch (155) (1942), Winter vetch (50) (present), Woolly-pod vetch [Woollypod vetch] (3, 155) (1942–1977)

Vicia villosa* Roth subsp. *villosa – Diverse-leaf kidney bean [Diverse-leaved kidney-bean] (47) (1852), Winter vetch (50) (present)

***Vicia villosa* Roth var. *glabrescens* W. D. J. Koch** – See *Vicia villosa* Roth subsp. *varia* (Host) Corb.

***Vigna angularis* (Willd.) Ohwi & Ohashi** – Adzuki bean (109, 138) (1923–1949), Black gram (110) (1886)

***Vigna luteola* (Jacq.) Benth.** – Múng (5) (1913)

***Vigna luteola* Benth.** – See *Vigna luteola* (Jacq.) Benth.

***Vigna mungo* (L.) Hepper** – Black gram (109) (1949), Black-eyed bean (138) (1923), Green gram (110) (1886), Múng (110) (1886), Mung bean (107) (1919), Urd (109) (1949)

***Vigna* Savi** – Cow pea [Cow-pea, Cowpea] (50, 82, 138, 156) (1923–present)

***Vigna sinensis* (L.) Endl.** – Black-eyed bean (5, 156) (1913–1923), China bean (5) (1913), Chowley (5) (1913), Common cowpea (109) (1949), Cow pea [Cow-pea, Cowpea] (5, 82, 106, 109, 156) (1913–1949), Kidney bean [Kidney-bean] (156) (1923), Lady-pea (156) (1923), Towcok (5) (1913), Whippoorwill pea [Whip-poor-will pea] (156) (1923)

***Vigna unguiculata* (L.) Walp.** – Calavances (107) (1919), Lady-pea (5) (1913), Round-seed dolichos [Round seeded dolichos] (155) (1942)

***Viguiera* Kunth** – Goldeneye [Golden eye, Golden-eye] (4, 50, 155) (1942–present), Viquiera (158) (1900)

***Viguiera stenoloba* Blake** – Resin bush [Resinbush] (4, 50) (1986–present), Skeleton-leaf goldeneye [Skeletonleaf goldeneye] (155) (1942)

***Vilfa aspera* [P. Beauv.]** – See *Sporobolus compositus* (Poir.) Merr.

Vilfa vaginaeflora – See *Sporobolus vaginiflorus* (Torr. ex Gray) Wood

***Vilfa vaginiflora* Torr. ex A. Gray** – See *Sporobolus vaginiflorus* (Torr. ex Gray) Wood

***Villarsia aquatica* Gmel.** – See *Nymphoides aquatica* (J.F. Gmel.) Kuntze

***Vinca herbacea* Waldst. & Kit.** – Herbaceous periwinkle (50, 138) (1923–present)

***Vinca* L.** – Myrtle (1) (1932), Periwinkle (1, 4, 50, 109, 138, 155, 158) (1900–present) from ancient Latin name 'pervinca'

***Vinca major* L.** – Big-leaf periwinkle [Bigleaf periwinkle] (138) (1923), Death's flower (92) (1876), Hundredeyes [Hundred eyes, Hundred-eyes] (92) (1876), Large periwinkle (92) (1876), Periwinkle (92, 122) (1876–1937)

***Vinca minor* L.** – Blue myrtle (62, 156) (1912–1923), Common periwinkle (3, 50, 109, 138, 155) (1923–present), Great periwinkle [Great peruinkle] (174) (1753), Hundredeyes [Hundred eyes, Hundred-eyes] (156, 158) (1900–1923), Joy-of-the-ground (156) (1923), Kleines Sinngrün (German) (158) (1900), Myrtle (5, 73, 77, 158) (1892–1913), Pennywinkle (158) (1900), Penny-winkler (158) (1900), Periwinkle (5, 7, 19, 92, 124, 156, 158, 184) (1793–1937), Peruinkle (178) (1526), Pervenche petite (French) (158) (1900), Perwynke (179) (1526), Purple periwinkle [Purple peruinkle] (178) (1526), Running-myrtle [Running myrtle] (5, 109, 156, 158) (1900–1949), Small periwinkle (4, 5, 92, 156, 158) (1876–1986), Wintergreen [Winter greene, Winter-green] (77, 156) (1898–1923) Sulphur Grove OH

***Vincetoxicum gonocarpos* Walt.** – See *Matelea gonocarpos* (Walt.) Shinners

***Vincetoxicum hirsutum* (Michx.) Britton** – See *Matelea carolinensis* (Jacq.) Woods.

***Vincetoxicum nigrum* (L.) Moench** – See *Cynanchum louiseae* Kartesz & Gandhi

***Vincetoxicum obliquum* (Jacq.) Britton** – See *Matelea obliqua* (Jacq.) Woods.

***Vincetoxicum shortii* (A. Gray) Britton** – See *Matelea obliqua* (Jacq.) Woods.

***Vincetoxicum suberosum* (L.) Britton** – See *Matelea gonocarpos* (Walt.) Shinners

***Viola* (Tourn.) L.** – See *Viola* L.

***Viola* ×*primulifolia* L. [*lanceolata* × *macloskeyi*]** – Primrose violet (124) (1937), Primrose-leaf violet [Primrose-leaved violet] (2, 5, 72, 97, 156) (1895–1937), Sweet white violet (156) (1923)

***Viola adunca* J. E. Sm.** – Hook violet (5, 8, 155) (1913–1942), Hookspur violet [Hookspur violet, Hook-spurred violet] (4, 50) (1986–present), Small blue violet (3) (1977)

Viola adunca* J. E. Sm. var. *adunca – Sand violet (5, 85) (1913–1932)

***Viola affinis* Le Conte** – Bayou violet (155) (1942), Biloxi violet (155) (1942), Jacksonville violet (155) (1942), Le Conte's violet [LeConte violet] (5, 155) (1913–1942), Missouri violet (3, 5, 97, 155) (1913–1977), Sand violet (50) (present)

***Viola arvensis* Murray** – European field pansy (5, 50) (1913–present), Field violet (5, 156) (1913–1923), Wild pansy (3, 156) (1923–1977)

***Viola bicolor* Pursh** – Field pansy (5, 50, 93, 97) (1913–present), Field violet (155) (1942), Iberian violet (155) (1942), Johnny-jump-up [Johhnyjumpup, Johnny-jump-ups] (3, 4, 155) (1942–1986), Wild pansy (4, 156) (1923–1986)

***Viola blanda* Willd.** – Common white violet (156) (1923), Smooth violet (19) (1840), Sweet white violet (2, 5, 72, 97, 109, 131, 138, 156) (1895–1949)

***Viola brittoniana* Pollard** – Coast violet (5) (1913)

***Viola brittoniana* Pollard var. *pectinata* (Bickn.) Alexander** – Cut-leaf violet [Cut-leaved violet] (5) (1913)

***Viola canadensis* L.** – American sweet violet (5, 156, 158) (1900–1923), Canadian violet [Canada violet] (2, 5, 41, 72, 85, 93, 131, 138, 155, 156, 158) (1770–1942), Canadian white violet (50) (present), Hens (74, 156, 158) (1893–1923), June flower [June-flower] (156, 158) (1900–1923)

***Viola canadensis* L. var. *rugulosa* (Greene) A. S. Hitchc.** – Canadian violet [Canada violet] (3) (1977), Cheyenne violet (155) (1942), Creeping-root violet [Creepingroot violet] (50) (present), Rydberg's violet (5) (1913), Tall white violet (4) (1986), Wild white violet (127) (1933)

***Viola canina* L.** – American dog violet (174, 177) (1753–1762), Dog violet (2) (1895)

***Viola canina* Walter** – See *Viola walteri* House

***Viola conspersa* Reichenb.** – American dog violet (3, 5, 156) (1913–1977), Blue marsh violet (174, 177) (1753–1762), Early blue violet (5, 156) (1913–1923)

***Viola cucullata* Aiton** – Blue marsh violet (138) (1923), Common blue violet (19, 86, 156) (1840–1923), Early violet (156) (1923), Fighting-cocks [Fighting cocks] (76, 156) (1896–1923), Hairy pointed

violet (76) (1896) New Brunswick, Hooded blue violet (156) (1923), Hood-leaf violet (73) (1892), Hookers (156) (1923), Johnny-jump-up [Johhnyjumpup, Johnny-jump-ups] (74, 156) (1893–1923), Long-stem purple violet [Long-stemmed purple violet, Long-stemmed purple violet] (156) (1923), Marsh blue violet (5, 72, 93, 109) (1907–1949), Meadow violet (131, 156) (1899–1923), Roosters (74, 156) (1893–1923) NY, Thin-leaf wood violet [Thin-leaved wood violet] (72) (1907), Wild violet (114) (1894)

***Viola debilis* Michx.** – possibly *Viola canina* L.

***Viola emarginata* (Nutt.) Le Conte** – See *Viola sagittata* Aiton

***Viola esculenta* Ell.** – See *Viola palmata* L.

***Viola fimbriatula* J. E. Smith** – See *Viola sagittata* Aiton var. *ovata* (Nutt.) Torr. & Gray

***Viola hastata* Michx.** – Halberd violet [Halbert violet] (19) (1840), Halberd-leaf violet [Halberd-leaved violet] (2, 5, 156) (1895–1923), Halberd-leaf yellow violet [Halberdleaf yellow violet] (50) (present), Spear-leaf violet [Spear-leaved violet] (5) (1913), Spear-leaf yellow violet [Spear-leaved yellow violet] (156) (1923)

***Viola hirsutula* Brainerd** – Hairy violet (5) (1913), Southern wood violet (5) (1913)

***Viola kitaibeliana* [J. A. Schultes]** – See *Viola bicolor* Pursh

***Viola kitaibeliana* J. A. Schultes var. *rafinesquei* Fern.** – See *Viola bicolor* Pursh

***Viola* L.** – Heart's-ease [Heart's ease, Heartsease, Hearts' ease] (1, 82) (1930–1932), Pansy [Pansie, Pansey] (1, 13) (1849–1932), Violet (1, 4, 7, 10, 13, 15, 50, 82, 92, 109, 138, 155, 158) (1818–present)

***Viola labradorica* Schrank.** – Alpine violet (5) (1913)

***Viola lanceolata* L.** – Blue violet (124) (1937), Bog white violet (50) (present), Lance-leaf violet [Lanceleaf violet, Lance-leaved violet] (2, 5, 72, 93, 122, 138, 155, 156) (1895–1942), Water violet (5, 93, 156) (1913–1936)

***Viola langloisii* Greene** – See *Viola affinis* Le Conte

***Viola lovelliana* Brainerd** – Lovell's violet [Lovell violet] (50, 97, 155) (1937–present)

***Viola macloskeyi* Lloyd** – Big-leaf white violet [Bigleaf white violet] (155) (1942), Large-leaf white violet [Large-leaved white violet] (5) (1913), Macloskey's violet [Macloskey violet] (155) (1942), Northern white violet (5) (1913), Pallid violet (155) (1942), Small white violet (50) (present), Wild white violet (4) (1986)

***Viola missouriensis* Greene** – See *Viola affinis* Le Conte

***Viola nephrophylla* Greene** – Blue prairie violet (4) (1986), Blue violet (82, 127) (1930–1933), Bog violet (85) (1932) SD, Butterfly violet (122, 138, 155) (1923–1942), Common blue violet (5, 72, 82, 97) (1907–1937), Fighting-cocks [Fighting cocks] (5) (1913), Hooded blue violet (5, 93) (1913–1936), Kansas violet (155) (1942), Long-stem purple violet [Long-stemmed purple violet, Long-stemmed purple violet] (5) (1913), Meadow blue violet (85) (1932), Meadow violet (3, 5, 93, 97, 98) (1913–1977), Northern bog violet (4, 5, 50) (1913–present), Wanderer violet (155) (1942), Western blue violet (5) (1913)

***Viola novae-angliae* House.** – New England blue violet (5, 50) (1913–present)

***Viola nuttallii* Pursh** – Nuttall's violet [Nuttall violet] (4, 5, 50, 93, 127, 131, 155) (1899–present), Prairie yellow violet (85) (1932), Yellow prairie violet (3, 4, 5, 98, 156) (1913–1986)

***Viola odorata* L.** – English violet (5, 55) (1911–1922), Florist's violet [Florists violet] (109) (1949), Garden violet (109) (1949), March violet (5) (1913), Sweet violet (5, 15, 19, 49, 55, 92, 109, 138) (1840–1949), Sweet-scented violet (49) (1898), Violet (55, 107) (1911–1919)

***Viola ovata* –** See *Viola sagittata* Aiton var. *ovata* (Nutt.) Torr. & Gray

***Viola pallens* (Banks.) Brainerd** – See *Viola macloskeyi* Lloyd

***Viola palmata* L.** – Blue violet (85) (1932), Chicken-fighters [Chicken fighters] (5, 76, 156) (1896–1923) Newton NC, among children who play games with the flowers, Common blue violet (2) (1895), Early blue violet (5, 50, 72, 93, 156) (1907–present), Hand-leaf violet (5, 19, 156) (1840–1923), Johnny-jump-up [Johhnyjumpup,

Johnny-jump-ups] (5, 156) (1913–1923), Palm violet (122, 138) (1923–1937), Palmate violet (155) (1942), Roosters (5, 74) (1893–1923) Ferrisburgh VT, Salad violet (155) (1942), Stone's violet [Stones violet] (155) (1942), Three-lobe violet [Three-lobed violet] (5, 97) (1913–1937), Trilobe violet (155) (1942), Violet (107) (1919), Wild okra (107) (1919), Witmer Stone's violet (5) (1913), Wood violet (4) (1986)

Viola palmata **var. cucullata Gray** – See *Viola cucullata* Aiton

Viola palustris **L.** – Marsh violet (5, 50, 92, 109, 131, 155, 156) (1899–present), Northern marsh violet (4) (1986)

Viola papilionacea **Pursh** – See *Viola nephrophylla* Greene

Viola papilionacea **Pursh var.** *priceana* **(Pollard) Alexander** – See *Viola sororia* Willd.

Viola pectinata **Bicknell** – See *Viola brittoniana* Pollard var. *pectinata* (Bickn.) Alexander

Viola pedata **L.** – American pansy (156, 158) (1900–1923), Bird's-foot violet [Bird foot violet, Birdfoot violet, Bird-foot violet, Birdsfoot violet, Bird's foot violet] (2, 4, 5, 49, 50, 72, 82, 86, 92, 97, 109, 122, 124, 131, 155, 156, 158) (1876–present), Blue violet (48, 49, 92) (1876–1898), Crowfoot violet [Crow-foot violet] (5, 73, 156, 158) (1892–1923) New England, Horse violet [Horse-violet] (5, 73, 158) (1892–1913) New England, Horseshoe violet [Horse shoe violet] (5, 73, 74, 158) (1898–1913) MA, Johnny-jump-up [Johhnyjumpup, Johnny-jump-ups] (156, 158) (1900–1923), Lavender violet (156) (1923), Lilac bird-foot violet [Lilac birdsfoot violet] (138, 155) (1923–1942), Little pansy (156) (1923), Pansy [Pansie, Pansey] (5, 74) (1893–1913) Peoria IL, Pansy violet (3, 156) (1923–1977), Sand violet (5, 74, 156, 158) (1893–1923) CT, Small jagged-leaf Virginia pansy [Small jagged leaved Virginia pansy] (181) (~1678), Snake violet [Snake-violet] (5, 74, 156, 158) (1893–1923) Swansea & Boston, MA, Velvet violet (156) (1923), Velvets (5, 158) (1900–1913), Wild pansy (124) (1937), Wood violet (5, 156, 158) (1900–1923)

Viola pedata **L. var.** *lineariloba* **DC.** – See *Viola pedata* L.

Viola pedata lineariloba – See *Viola pedata* L.

Viola pedatifida **G. Don** – Larkspur violet (4, 5, 93, 138, 156) (1923–1986), Prairie blue violet (85) (1932), Prairie violet (4, 5, 50, 72, 93, 97, 127, 131, 155, 156) (1899–present)

Viola pedunculata **Torr. & Gray** – Yellow pansy violet (138) (1923)

Viola pratincola **Greene** – See *Viola nephrophylla* Greene

Viola priceana **Pollard** – See *Viola sororia* Willd.

Viola pubescens **Aiton** – Downy violet (155) (1942), Downy yellow violet (3, 4, 5, 50, 85, 138, 156) (1913–present), Downy-leaf violet [Downy-leaved violet] (2) (1895), Hairy yellow violet (5, 72, 131) (1899–1913), Smooth yellow violet (4) (1986), Stemmed yellow violet (156) (1923), Yellow violet (19, 46, 127) (1840–1933)

Viola pubescens **Aiton var.** *pubescens* – Smooth yellow violet (93) (1936), Smoothish yellow violet (5, 97) (1913–1937), Wool-pod violet [Woolpod violet] (155) (1942), Yellow violet (85) (1932)

Viola rafinesquei **Greene** – See *Viola bicolor* Pursh

Viola renifolia **Gray** – Kidney-leaf violet [Kidneyleaf violet, Kidney-leaved violet] (3, 4, 5, 155)) (1913–1986), White violet (50) (present)

Viola retusa **Greene** – See *Viola nephrophylla* Greene

Viola rosacea **Brainerd** – See *Viola affinis* Le Conte

Viola rostrata **Pursh** – Beaked violet (19, 92, 156) (1840–1923), Canker violet (92, 156) (1898–1923), Long-spur violet [Long-spurred violet] (2, 5, 109, 156) (1895–1949)

Viola rotundifolia **Michx.** – Early yellow violet (156) (1923), Round-leaf violet [Roundleaf violet] (2, 5, 138) (1895–1923), Round-leaf yellow violet [Round-leaved yellow violet] (156) (1923), Stemless yellow violet (156) (1923), Yellow violet (5) (1913)

Viola rugulosa **Greene** – See *Viola canadensis* L. var. *rugulosa* (Greene) A. S. Hitchc.

Viola sagittata **Aiton** – Arrow-head violet [Arrow-head violet] (4) (1986), Arrow-leaf violet [Arrowleaf violet, Arrow leaf violet] (50, 3, 5, 72, 86, 97, 124, 138, 155, 156) (1878–present), Early blue violet (5, 156) (1913–1923), Sand violet (5, 156) (1913–1923), Spade-leaf violet (5, 73) (1892–1913) Franklin MA, Triangle-leaf violet [Triangleleaf violet, Triangle-leaved violet] (5, 97, 155) (1913–1942)

Viola sagittata **Aiton var.** *ovata* **(Nutt.) Torr. & Gray** – Fringed violet (5, 156) (1913–1923), Ovate-leaf violet [Ovate-leaved violet] (5, 156) (1913–1923), Rattlesnake violet [Rattle snake violet, Rattlesnake violet, Rattlesnakes' violet, Rattlesnake's violet] (5, 92, 156) (1876–1923)

Viola selkirkii **Pursh ex Goldie** – Great spurred violet (3, 4, 5, 156) (1913–1986), Selkirk's violet [Selkirk violet] (2, 5, 50, 138) (1895–present), Wilderness violet (155) (1942)

Viola septemloba **Le Conte** – Southern coast violet (5) (1913)

Viola sororia **Willd.** – Beech-woods violet [Beechwoods violet] (155) (1942), Broad-leaf wood violet [Broad-leaved wood violet] (5) (1913), Confederate violet (109) (1949), Downy blue violet (3, 4) (1977–1986), Northern blue violet (5, 109, 138) (1913–1949), Ontario violet (155) (1942), Price's violet [Price violet] (138, 155) (1923–1942), Sister violet (155) (1942), Woolly blue violet (5, 93, 97) (1913–1937)

Viola striata **Aiton** – Cat's-faces (158) (1900), Cream violet (138, 156) (1923), Pale violet (2, 5, 156) (1895–1923), Striped violet (5, 19, 156) (1840–1923) Blue Ridge VA obsolete by 1923

Viola subvestita **Greene** – See *Viola adunca* Sm. var. *adunca*

Viola tricolor **L.** – Battlefield flower [Battle-field flower] (74, 158) (1893–1900) Gordonsville, VA, often found on old Civil War battlefields, Biddy's-eyes (158) (1900), Common pansy (138) (1923), Cupid's-delight [Cupid's delight] (73, 158) (1892–1900) Salem MA, Dreifaltigkeitskraut (German) (158) (1900), Fancy (158) (1900), Field pansy (6) (1892), Flamy (158) (1900), Freisamkraut (German) (6, 158) (1892–1900), Garden violet (19, 158) (1840–1900), Gardengate (158) (1900), Heart's-ease [Heart's ease, Heartsease, Hearts' ease] (5, 6, 15, 19, 57, 92, 97, 109, 158) (1840–1949), Heart's-pansy (158) (1900), Herb Trinity [Herb-Trinity] (158) (1900), Ie-länger-ie-lieber (German) (158) (1900), Johnnies (73) (1892) Mansfield OH, Johnny-jumper [Johnny jumper] (92, 158) (1876–1900), Johnny-jump-up [Johhnyjumpup, Johnny-jump-ups] (50, 73, 74, 158) (1892–present), Kisses (158) (1900), Kiss-me (158) (1900), Lady's-delight [Lady's delight] (5, 73, 158) (1892–1913) MA, Love-in-idleness (158) (1900) Shakespeare, Monkey face [Monkey's-face, Monkey faces] (158) (1900), None-so-pretty [None so pretty] (76, 158) (1896–1900) Abington MA, Pansy [Pansie, Pansey] (5, 6, 15, 19, 57, 72, 92, 97, 109, 158) (1893–1949), Pensee (French) (6) (1892), Pensée sauage (French) (158) (1900), Steifmutterchen-Kraut (German) (6) (1892), Stepmother (92, 158) (1876–1900), Stiefmütterchen (German) (158) (1900), Three-color violet [Three-colored violet] (6) (1892), Trinitaria (Spanish) (158) (1900), Trinity violet (6, 158) (1892–1900), Wild pansy (6, 155) (1892–1900)

Viola tricolor **L. var.** *hortensis* **DC.** – See *Viola tricolor* L.

Viola triloba **Schwein.** – See *Viola palmata* L.

Viola vallicola **A. Nels.** – Sagebrush violet (50, 146) (1939–present)

Viola viarum **Pollard** – Ozark violet (155) (1942), Plains violet (5) (1913), Two-flower violet [Twoflower violet] (50) (present)

Viola walteri **House** – Prostrate blue violet (5) (1913), Walter's violet [Walter violet] (138) (1923)

Viorna addisonii **(Britton) Small.** – See *Clematis addisonii* Britt.

Viorna bigelovii – See *Clematis bigelovii* Torr.

Viorna crispa **(L.) Small.** – See *Clematis crispa* L.

Viorna douglasii **Cockerell** – See *Clematis hirsutissima* Pursh

Viorna fremontii **(S. Wats.) Heller** – See *Clematis fremontii* S. Wats.

Viorna glaucophylla **Small** – See *Clematis glaucophylla* Small

Viorna ovata **(Pursh) Small.** – See *Clematis ochroleuca* Aiton

Viorna pitcheri **(Torr. & Gray) Britton** – See *Clematis pitcheri* Torr. & Gray var. *pitcheri*

Viorna **Reichnb.** – See *Clematis* L.

Viorna scottii **(Porter) Rydb.** – See *Clematis hirsutissima* Pursh var. *scottii* (Porter) Erickson

Viorna versicolor **Small.** – See *Clematis versicolor* Small ex Rydb.

Viorna viorna **(L.) Small.** – See *Clematis viorna* L.

Virgilia lutea **Michx.** – See *Cladrastis kentukea* (Dum.-Cours.) Rudd .

Viscum album **L.** – Bird lime (92) (1876), European mistletoe (50, 138) (1923–present), Mistletoe [Misseltoe, Misletoe, Misleto] (7, 10, 41, 52, 54, 55) (1770–1919)

Viscum flavescens **Pursh** – See *Phoradendron leucarpum* (Raf.) Reveal & M. C. Johnston

Viscum **L.** – Gui (French) (8) (1785), Mistletoe [Misseltoe, Misletoe, Misleto] (8, 50, 167) (1785–present)

Viscum rubrum – See *Phoradendron rubrum* (L.) Griseb.

Viscum verticillatum – See *Cissus verticillata* (L.) Nicolson & C. E. Jarvis

Vitex agnus-castus **L.** – Agnus castus (92) (1876), Alhuzama (106) (1930), Chaste tree [Chaste-tree, Chastetree] (7, 82, 92, 109, 158, 178) (1596–1949), Common chaste tree (4) (1986), Hemp tree [Hemp-tree] (82, 109, 158) (1930–1949), Lilac chaste tree [Lilac chaste-tree, Lilac chastetree] (50, 138, 155) (1923–present), Mexican lavender (106, 124) (1930–1937), Monk's pepper tree [Monks pepper-tree] (109, 158) (1900–1949), Tree-of-chastity [Tree of chastity] (92) (1876), Vigne (French) (158) (1900), Weinrebe (German) (158) (1900), Weinstock (German) (138) (1923)

Vitex **L.** – Chaste tree [Chaste-tree, Chastetree] (50, 82, 138) (1923–present)

Vitex negundo incisa – See *Vitex negundo* L. var. *negundo*

Vitex negundo **L.** – Chaste tree [Chaste-tree, Chastetree] (182) (1791), Negundo chaste tree [Negundo chaste-tree] (138) (1923)

Vitex negundo **L. var. *negundo*** – Cut-leaf chaste-tree [Cutleaf chaste-tree] (138) (1923), Japanese vitex (124) (1937)

Vitex negundo **var. *heterophylla* (Franch.) Rehder** – Chaste tree [Chaste-tree, Chastetree] (82) (1930), Hemp tree [Hemp-tree] (82) (1930) IA

Vitis **(Tourn.) L.** – See *Vitis* L.

Vitis ×*champinii* **Planch.** [*mustangensis* × *rupestris*] – Champin's grape [Champin grape] (138) (1923)

Vitis ×*doaniana* **Munson ex Viala** [*acerifolia* × *mustangensis*] – Doan grape (138) (1923)

Vitis acerifolia **Raf.** – Bush grape (3, 4) (1977–1986), Long's grape [Longs grape] (138, 155) (1923–1942), Maple-leaf grape [Mapleleaf grape] (7, 50) (1828–present)

Vitis aestivalis **Michx.** – Blue grape (5, 107, 156) (1913–1923), Blue-leaf grape [Blueleaf grape] (138) (1923), Blur grape (97) (1937), Bunch grape (15, 107) (1895–1919), Chicken grape [Chicken-grape] (46) (1879), Pigeon grape (3, 4, 15, 107, 109, 156) (1895–1986), Summer grape (2, 5, 15, 19, 27, 35, 46, 50, 72, 95, 97, 107, 109, 113, 138, 155, 156, 158) (1879–present), Winter grape [Winter-grape] (5, 156) (1913–1923)

Vitis aestivalis **Michx. var. *aestivalis*** – Fig-leaf grape [Figleaf grape] (155) (1942), Red-shank grape [Redshank grape] (155) (1942), Summer grape (50) (present)

Vitis aestivalis **Michx. var. *bicolor* Deam** – Summer grape (50) (present)

Vitis aestivalis **Michx. var. *cinerea* Engelm.** – See *Vitis cinerea* (Engelm.) Millard var. *cinerea*

Vitis aestivalis **Michx. var. *lincecumii* (Buckl.) Munson** – Lincecum's grape (124) (1937), Pine-wood grape (15, 107) (1895–1919), Pine-woods grape (138) (1923), Post-oak grape [Post oak grape] (15, 107, 109) (1895–1949), Turkey grape (15, 107) (1895–1919)

Vitis aestivalis **Michx. var. *linsecomii* Munson** – See *Vitis aestivalis* Michx. var. *lincecumii* (Buckl.) Munson

Vitis amara **Raf.** – possibly *Vitis rotundifolia* Michx.

Vitis arizonica **Engelm.** – Canyon grape (15, 107, 138) (1895–1923), Wild grape (153) (1913)

Vitis berlandieri **Planch.** – See *Vitis cinerea* (Engelm.) Millard var. *helleri* (Bailey) M. O. Moore

Vitis bicolor **LeConte** – See *Vitis aestivalis* Michx.

Vitis blanda **Raf.** – possibly *Vitis labrusca* L.

Vitis californica **Benth.** – California grape (138) (1923), Wild grape

(103) (1870)

Vitis candicans **Engelm.** – Mustang (122) (1937) TX, Mustang grape (15, 124, 138) (1895–1937) TX

Vitis candicans **Engelm. var. *coriacea* Bailey** – See *Vitis shuttleworthii* House

Vitis canina **Raf.** – possibly *Vitis labrusca* L.

Vitis caribaea **DC.** – See *Vitis tiliifolia* Humb. & Bonpl. ex Roem. & Schult.

Vitis champini – See *Vitis* ×*champinii* Planch. [*mustangensis* × *rupestris*]

Vitis cinerea **(Engelm.) Millard** – Ashy grape (5) (1913), Bunch grape (156) (1923), Can wíyape (Dakota Teton, tree-twiner) (37) (1919), Downy grape (2, 5, 72, 97, 122, 156) (1895–1937), Gray-bark grape [Graybark grape] (3, 50) (1977–present), Hapsintsh (Winnebago) (37) (1919), Hastanhanka (Dakota) (37) (1919), Kisúts (Pawnee) (37) (1919), Sweet winter grape (15, 138, 155, 156) (1895–1942), Wild grape (37) (1919)

Vitis cinerea **(Engelm.) Millard var. *baileyana* (Munson) Comeaux** – Possum grape (15) (1895)

Vitis cinerea **(Engelm.) Millard var. *cinerea*** – Fall grape (177) (1762), Hazi (Omaha-Ponca) (37) (1919) Hazi-hi (grape vine)

Vitis cinerea **(Engelm.) Millard var. *helleri* (Bailey) M. O. Moore** – Fall grape (15) (1895), Mountain grape (15) (1895), Spanish grape (15) (1895), Winter grape [Winter-grape] (15, 138) (1895–1923)

Vitis cordifolia **Michx.** – See *Vitis vulpina* L.

Vitis doaniana – See *Vitis* ×*doaniana* Munson ex Viala [*acerifolia* × *mustangensis*]

Vitis girdiana **Munson.** – Valley grape (15, 138) (1895–1923)

Vitis **L.** – Grape (1, 4, 50, 106, 109, 138, 155, 158) (1900–present), Grape vine (13, 15) (1849–1895), Šiwi-min (Chippewa) (105) (1932), Šu-min (Chippewa) (105) (1932), Vigne (French) (8) (1785), Vine (10, 15, 109) (1818–1949), Wild grape (93, 105, 112) (1932–1937), possibly Bullace grape [Bullace-grape] (1) (1932), possibly Muscadine grape (1) (1932)

Vitis labrusca **L.** – Fox grape [Foxgrape] (7, 15, 46, 107, 109, 138) (1828–1949), Northern fox grape (2, 5, 72, 156) (1895–1923), Northern grape (156) (1923), Northern plum grape (5) (1913), Plum grape [Plumb grape] (7, 19, 156) (1828–1923), Raccoon grape (156) (1923), Skunk grape (15, 107) (1895–1919), Swamp grape (156) (1923), Vigne sauvage (French) (8) (1785), Wild American vine (8) (1785), Wild vine (5, 156) (1913–1923), possibly Bland's grape [Blands' grape, Bland grape] (7) (1828), possibly Bull grape (7) (1828), possibly Bullet grape (7) (1828), possibly Dog grape [Dogs grape] (7) (1828), possibly Elkton grape (7) (1828), possibly Frost grape (7) (1828), possibly Tough grape (7) (1828), possibly Variable grape (7) (1828)

Vitis laciniosa **Raf.** – possibly *Vitis vinifera* L.

Vitis latifolia **Raf.** – possibly *Vitis labrusca* L.

Vitis lincecumi – See *Vitis aestivalis* Michx. var. *lincecumii* (Buckl.) Munson

Vitis lincecumii **Buckl.** – See *Vitis aestivalis* Michx. var. *lincecumii* (Buckl.) Munson

Vitis longi (Vitis longii **Prince)** – See *Vitis acerifolia* Raf.

Vitis luteola **Raf.** – possibly *Vitis labrusca* L.

Vitis monticola **Buckl.** – Mountain grape (106, 107) (1919–1930), Sweet mountain grape (15, 138) (1895–1923)

Vitis munsoniana **Simpson.** – See *Vitis rotundifolia* Michx. var. *munsoniana* (Simpson ex Munson) M. O. Moore

Vitis obliqua **Raf.** – See *Cissus erosa* Rich.

Vitis odoratissima **Donn.** – See *Vitis riparia* Michx.

Vitis palmata **Vahl** – Cat grape (15, 138. 156) (1895–1923), Catbird grape (156) (1923), Missouri grape (5, 72, 122) (1907–1937), Palmate grape (7) (1828), Red grape (15, 156) (1895–1923)

Vitis poiretia **Raf.** – See *Vitis vulpina* L.

Vitis riparia **Michx.** – Early wild grape (9, 113) (1873–1890), Frost grape (82, 107, 109) (1919–1949), June grape (15) (1895), June riverbank grape (155) (1942), Odoriferous grape (19) (1840),

Orwisburg grape (7) (1828), Quicksand riverbank grape (155) (1942), River grape (2, 7) (1828–1932), River-bank grape [River-bank grape, River bank grape] (3, 4, 50, 107, 155) (1919–present), Riverside frost grape [River-side frost-grape] (47) (1852), Sweet-scented grape [Sweet scented grape] (7) (1828), Vigne des battures (French) (168) (1803)

Vitis riparia **Michx. var.** *praecox* **Engelm. ex Bailey** – See *Vitis riparia* Michx.

Vitis riparia **Michx. var.** *syrticola* **(Fern. & Wiegand) Fern.** – See *Vitis riparia* Michx.

Vitis rotundifolia **Michx.** – Bull grape (15) (1895), Bullac grape (5) (1913), Bullace (2, 107) (1895–1919), Bullace grape [Bullace-grape] (15, 156) (1895–1923), Bullit grape (15) (1895), Muscadine (2, 15, 97, 107, 109, 156) (1895–1949), Muscadine grape (122, 124, 138, 168) (1803–1937), Scuppernong [Scupernong] (107, 156) (1919–1923), Scuppernong grape (2) (1895), Southern fox grape (2, 5, 15, 97, 107, 156) (1895–1937), possibly Bitter grape (7) (1828)

Vitis rotundifolia **Michx. var.** *munsoniana* **(Simpson ex Munson) M. O. Moore** – Bird grape (15) (1895), Ever-bearing grape [Ever-bearing grape] (15) (1895), Mustang grape (15) (1895)

Vitis rufotomentosa **Small** – See *Vitis aestivalis* Michx. var. *aestivalis*

Vitis rupestris **Scheele** – Bush grape (15, 107) (1895–1919), Mountain grape (5, 15, 107, 122) (1895–1937), Rock grape (15, 107) (1895–1919), Sand grape (2, 3, 4, 5, 15, 50, 74, 82, 97, 107, 138, 155, 156) (1893–present), Sand-beach grape (156) (1923), Sugar grape (2, 5, 15, 74, 82, 97, 107, 156) (1893–1937)

Vitis shuttleworthii **House** – Calloosa grape (15) (1895), Leather-leaf grape [Leatherleaf grape] (15) (1895)

Vitis smalliana **Bailey** – See *Vitis aestivalis* Michx. var. *aestivalis*

Vitis taurina **Walt.** – possibly *Vitis labrusca* L.

Vitis tiliifolia **Humb. & Bonpl. ex Roem. & Schult.** – Caribean grape (107) (1919)

Vitis vinifera **L.** – European grape (107, 138) (1919–1923), Grape of history (109, 178) (1526–1949), Raisin [Raisins] (57, 92) (1876–1917), Uva passa (57) (1917), Vine (14, 92, 110) (1876–1886), Wine grape (107, 109) (1919–1949), possibly Canadian parsley-leaf vine [Canadian parsley-leaved vine] (8) (1785), possibly Vigne à feuilles laciniées (French) (8) (1785)

Vitis vulpina **L.** – Bull grape (5, 74, 156, 158) (1893–1923) Alabama, Bullet grape (7) (1828), Chicken grape [Chicken-grape] (2, 7, 15, 73, 95, 107, 156, 158) (1828–1923), Early wild grape (95, 130) (1895–1911), Fox grape [Foxgrape] (5, 7, 8, 74, 156, 158) (1894–1923), Foxberry [Fox berry, Fox-berry] (92) (1876), Frost grape (2, 5, 7, 15, 19, 50, 72, 82, 92, 95, 97, 107, 108, 113, 122, 138, 155, 156, 158) (1828–present), Hapsintsh (Winnebago) (37) (1919), Hastanhanka (Dakota) (37) (1919), Hazi (Omaha-Ponca) (37) (1919), Jo'mĭnaga'wûnj (Chippewa) (40) (1928), Kisúts (Pawnee) (37)

(1919), Muscadine grape (7, 158) (1828–1900), Ozaha (46) (1879), Possum grape (5, 156, 158) (1828–1923), Raccoon grape (15) (1895), Raisin sauvage (French) (89) (1820), River-bank grape [Riverbank grape, River bank grape] (15, 138, 142, 156) (1895–1923), Riverside grape [River-side grape] (5, 72, 131, 156, 158) (1899–1923), Scupernong (7) (1828), Sour winter grape (156) (1923), Sweet-scented grape [Sweet scented grape] (5, 72, 97, 158) (1900–1937), Vigne de renard (French) (8) (1785), Wild grape (37, 82, 85, 92, 101) (1876–1932), Winter grape [Winter-grape] (3, 4, 5, 15, 27, 76, 107, 108, 109, 156, 158, 168) (1803–1986), Yânû Unihye stĭ (Cherokee) (102) (1886)

Vitis vulpina **L. var.** *praecox* **Bailey** – See *Vitis riparia* Michx.

Vitis vulpina **L. var.** *syrticola* **Fern. & Wiegand** – See *Vitis riparia* Michx.

Vitis-idaea **(Tourn.) Moench** – See *Vaccinium* L.

Vitis-idaea vitis idaea **(L.) Britton** – possibly *Vaccinium vitis-idaea* L.

Vleckia nepetoides **(L.) Raf.** – See *Agastache nepetoides* (L.) Kuntze

Volkameria inermis – See *Clerodendrum inerme* (L.) Gaertn.

Vulpia elliotea **(Raf.) Fern.** – See *Vulpia sciurea* (Nutt.) Henr.

Vulpia **K. C. Gmel.** – Fescue (50) (present)

Vulpia microstachys **(Nutt.) Munro var.** *microstachys* – Small fescue grass (87) (1884), Small-top fescue [Small-topped fescue] (94) (1901), Western fescue (87) (1884)

Vulpia myuros **(L.) K. C. Gmel.** – Capon's-tail grass [Capon's tail grass] (5, 92) (1876–1913), Foxtail fescue (122, 155) (1937–1942), Hairy-flower festuca [Hairy-flowered festuca] (187) (1818), Mousetail [Mousetail, Mouse-tail, Mousetaile] (5) (1913), Mouse-tail grass [Mouse tail gass] (92) (1876), Rat-tail fescue [Rat's-tail fescue, Rat's-tail fescue] (50, 94) (1901–present), Rat-tail fescue grass [Rat-tail fescue, Rat's tail fescue grass] (3, 5, 155) (1913–1977)

Vulpia octoflora **(Walt.) Rydb.** – Six-weeks fescue [Six weeks fescue, Sixweeks fescue] (50) (Present)

Vulpia octoflora **(Walt.) Rydb. var.** *glauca* **(Nutt.) Fern.** – Six-weeks fescue [Six weeks fescue, Sixweeks fescue] (50) (present), Slender fescue (56) (1901), Small fescue grass (66, 90) (1885–1903)

Vulpia octoflora **(Walt.) Rydb. var.** *hirtella* **(Piper) Henr.** – Hairy six-weeks fescue [Hairy sixweeks fescue] (155) (1942), Six-weeks fescue [Sixweeks fescue] (50) (present)

Vulpia octoflora **(Walt.) Rydb. var.** *octoflora* – Fescue grass [Fescue-grass] (85) (1932), Six-weeks fescue [Six weeks fescue, Sixweeks fescue] (3, 50, 119, 122, 140, 155) (1937–present), Slender fescue grass [Slender fescue-grass] (5, 56, 72, 94, 111, 119, 163) (1852–1938)

Vulpia sciurea **(Nutt.) Henr.** – Southern fescue grass [Southern fescue-grass (5, 119, 163) (1852–1938), Squirrel fescue (5, 119) (1913–1938)

Vulpia sciurea **(Nutt.) Henr.** – Squirrel-tail fescue [Squirreltail fescue] (50) (present)

W

Wahlenbergia marginata **(Thunb.) A. DC.** – Gentian rockbell (138) (1923)

Wahlenbergia **Schrad. ex Roth** – Grassy bells, Rockbell [Rock-bells] (138) (1923), Tufty bells (109) (1949)

Waldsteinia doniana **Tratt.** – See *Waldsteinia fragarioides* (Michx.) Tratt. subsp. *doniana* (Tratt.) Teppner

Waldsteinia fragarioides **(Michx.) Tratt.** – Barren-strawberry [Barren strawberry] (1, 2, 5, 109, 138, 156) (1895–1949), Dry strawberry (5, 156) (1913–1923)

Waldsteinia fragarioides **(Michx.) Tratt. subsp.** *doniana* **(Tratt.) Teppner** – Southern dry strawberry (5) (1913)

Waldsteinia fragarioides **Tratt.** – See *Waldsteinia fragarioides* (Michx.) Tratt.

Waldsteinia **Willd.** – Barren-strawberry [Barren strawberry] (156) (1923)

Waltheria **L.** – Giant hyssop [Gianthyssop] (2) (1895)

Warnera **Mill.** – possibly *Hydrastis* L.

Washingtonia divaricata **Britton** – See *Osmorhiza berteroi* DC.

Washingtonia filifera **(L. Linden) H. Wendl.** – California Washington palm (138) (1923)

Washingtonia **H. Wendl.** – Washington palm (109, 138) (1923–1949) for George Washington

Washingtonia longistylis **(Torr.) Britton** – See *Osmorhiza longistylis* (Torr.) DC.

Washingtonia obtusa **Coult. & Rose** – See *Osmorhiza depauperata* Phil.

Washingtonia **Raf.** – See *Osmorhiza* Raf.

Washingtonia robusta **H. Wendl.** – Mexican Washington palm (138) (1923)

Watsonia iridifolia **[Ker Gawl]** – See *Watsonia meriana (L.) Mill.*

Watsonia meriana **(L.) Mill.** – Iris-leaf bugle-lily [Irisleaf buglelily] (138) (1923)

Watsonia **Mill.** – Bugle-lily [Buglelily] (138) (1923)

Weigela floribunda **(Sieb. & Zucc.) K. Koch** – Crimson weigela (138) (1923)

Weigela rosea **[Lindl.]** – possibly *Diervilla florida* (Bunge) Siebold & Zucc.

Weigela **Thunb.** – Weigela (138) (1923)

Wellingtonia gigantea – See *Sequoiadendron giganteum* (Lindl.) Buchh.

Windsoria sesleroides **Michx.** – See *Tridens flavus* (L.) A.S. Hitchc.

Wislizenia **Engelm.** – Jackass clover (106) (1930) so named by C.I. Graham who once lost a team of jackasses in a field of these plants

Wislizenia refracta **Engelm.** – Golden clover (106) (1930), Jackass clover (106) (1930), Spectacle plant (124) (1937) TX, Spectacle-pod [Spectacle pod] (122) (1937) TX, Stinkweed [Stink-weed, Stink weed] (106) (1930), Wild stocks (124) (1937)

Wisteria floribunda **(Willd.) DC.** – Japanese wisteria (109, 138) (1923–1949), Long-cluster wisteria [Longcluster wisteria] (138) (1923)

Wisteria floribunda **DC.** – See *Wisteria floribunda* (Willd.) DC.

Wisteria frutescens **(L.) Poir.** – American wisteria (2, 5, 138) (1895–1923), Carolina shrubby kidney-bean [Carolinian shrubby kidney bean] (8, 106) (1785–1930), Glycine (2, 138) (1895–1923), Glycine ligneuse (French) (8) (1785), Japanese wisteria (174) (1753), Kentucky wisteria (138) (1923), Kidney-bean tree [Kidney bean tree] (5, 106, 156) (1913–1930), Long-cluster wisteria [Longcluster wisteria] (5, 97) (1913–1937), Virgin's-bower [Virgins-bower, Virgin's bower, Virgin bower] (5, 106, 156) (1913–1930), Wisteria [Wistaria] (85, 92, 156) (1876–1932), Woody wisteria (5) (1913), possibly Carolina kidney-bean tree [Carolina kidney bean tree] (10, 12) (1818–1820)

Wisteria frutescens **Poir.** – See *Wisteria frutescens* (L.) Poir.

Wisteria macrostachya **Nutt. ex Torr. & A. Gray** – See *Wisteria frutescens* (L.) Poir.

Wisteria macrostachys – possibly *Wisteria frutescens* (L.) Poir.

Wisteria multijuga **Van Houtte** – See *Wisteria floribunda* (Willd.) DC.

Wisteria **Nutt.** – Wisteria [Wistaria] (138) (1923) for Caspar Wistar, 1761–1818, professor of anatomy in the Univ.of Penn.

Wisteria sinensis **(Sims) DC.** – Chinese wisteria (109, 138) (1923–1949), Fugi (106) (1930), Glycine (92) (1876), Wisteria [Wistaria] (92, 112) (1876–1937)

Wisteria sinensis **Sweet** – See *Wisteria sinensis* (Sims) DC.

Wisteria speciosa **Nutt.** – possibly *Wisteria frutescens* (L.) Poir.

Wolffia borealis **(Engelm. ex Hegelm.) Landolt ex Landolt & Wildi** – Northern watermeal (50) (present)

Wolffia brasiliensis **Weddell** – Brazilian watermeal (50) (present), Dotted wolffia (5) (1913), Pointed duckweed (5) (1913), Punctate wolffia (72) (1907), Watermeal [Water-meal] (156) (1923)

Wolffia columbiana **Karst.** – Columbia wolffia (5, 72, 97, 120) (1907–1938), Columbian watermeal (50) (present)

Wolffia floridana **(J. D. Sm.) J. D. Sm. ex Hegelm.** – See *Wolffiella gladiata* (Hegelm.) Hegelm.

Wolffia **Horkel ex Schleid.** – Duckmeat [Duck-meat, Duck-meat, Ducke meate, Duck's meat, Ducks' meat, Duck'smeat, Duck's-meat] (158) (1900), Watermeal [Water-meal] (50) (present), Wolffia (93, 158) (1900–1936) for N.M. von Wolff, Polish naturalist

Wolffia punctata **Griseb.** – See *Wolffia brasiliensis* Weddell

Wolffiella gladiata **(Hegelm.) Hegelm.** – Florida mudmidget (50) (present), Florida wolffiella (5) (1913)

Woodsia alpina **(Bolton) S. F. Gray** – Alpine woodsia (5, 50) (1913–present), Flower-cup fern (5, 19, 92) (1840–1913), Northern woodsia (5) (1913)

Woodsia alpina **(Bolton) S. F. Gray var.** *bellii* **Lawson** – See *Woodsia alpina* (Bolton) S. F. Gray

Woodsia glabella **R. Br. ex Richards.** – Smooth woodsia (5, 50) (1913–present)

Woodsia ilvensis **(L.) R. Br.** – Fragrant woodsia (3) (1977), Oblong woodsia (5) (1913), Ray's woodsia (5) (1913), Rusty woodsia (4, 50, 72, 109, 138, 155) (1907–present)

Woodsia mexicana **Fee** – Mexican woodsia (155) (1942)

Woodsia neomexicana **Windham** – New Mexico cliff fern (50) (present)

Woodsia obtusa **(Spreng.) Torr.** – Blunt-lobe cliff fern [Bluntlobe cliff fern] (50) (present), Blunt-lobe fern [Blunt-lobed fern] (97) (1937), Blunt-lobe woodsia [Blunt-lobed woodsia] (3, 4, 72, 109) (1907–1986), Common woodsia (86, 109, 138, 155) (1878–1949), Rock polypody (86) (1878)

Woodsia obtusa **Torr.** – See *Woodsia obtusa* (Spreng.) Torr.

Woodsia oregana **D.C. Eat.** – Oregon cliff fern (50) (present), Oregon woodsia (3, 4, 5, 19, 97, 131, 155) (1840–1986)

Woodsia oregana **D.C. Eat. subsp.** *cathcartiana* **(B. L. Robins.) Windham** – Oregon cliff fern (50) (present)

Woodsia **R. Br.** – Cliff fern (50) (present), Flower-sup fern (158) (1900), Woodsia (4, 138, 155) (1923–1986) for Joseph Woods, 1776–1864, English botanist and rose expert

Woodsia scopulina **D.C. Eaton** – Rocky Mountain woodsia (3, 50, 109, 131, 138) (1899–present)

Woodwardia angustifolia **Smith** – See *Woodwardia areolata* (L.) T. Moore

Woodwardia areolata (**L.**) **T. Moore** – Chain fern [Chainfern, Chain-fern] (138) (1923), Kidney fern (19) (1840), Netted chain fern [Netted chain-fern] (86) (1878), Net-vein chain fern [Net-veined chain-fern] (5) (1913)

Woodwardia chamissoi – See *Woodwardia fimbriata* Sm.

Woodwardia fimbriata **Sm.** – Giant chain fern [Giant chainfern] (138) (1923)

Woodwardia radicans (**L.**) **J. Sm.** – European chain fern [European chainfern] (138) (1923), Root-leaf blechnum [Root-leaved blechnum] (19) (1840)

Woodwardia **Sm.** – Chain fern [Chainfern, Chain-fern] (2, 4, 5, 50, 78, 109, 138, 155, 158) (1895–present)

Woodwardia virginica (**L.**) **Sm.** – Blachnum (92) (1876), Common chain fern [Common chain-fern] (86) (1878), Virginia chain fern [Virginia chainfern] (5, 50) (1913–present), Virginian blechnum (19, 138) (1840–1923)

Woodwardia virginica **Willd.** – See *Woodwardia virginica* (L.) Sm.

Wyethia arizonica **Gray** – Arizona wyethia [Arizonian wyethia] (86) (1878)

Wyethia helianthoides **Nutt.** – White sunflower (101) (1905) MT

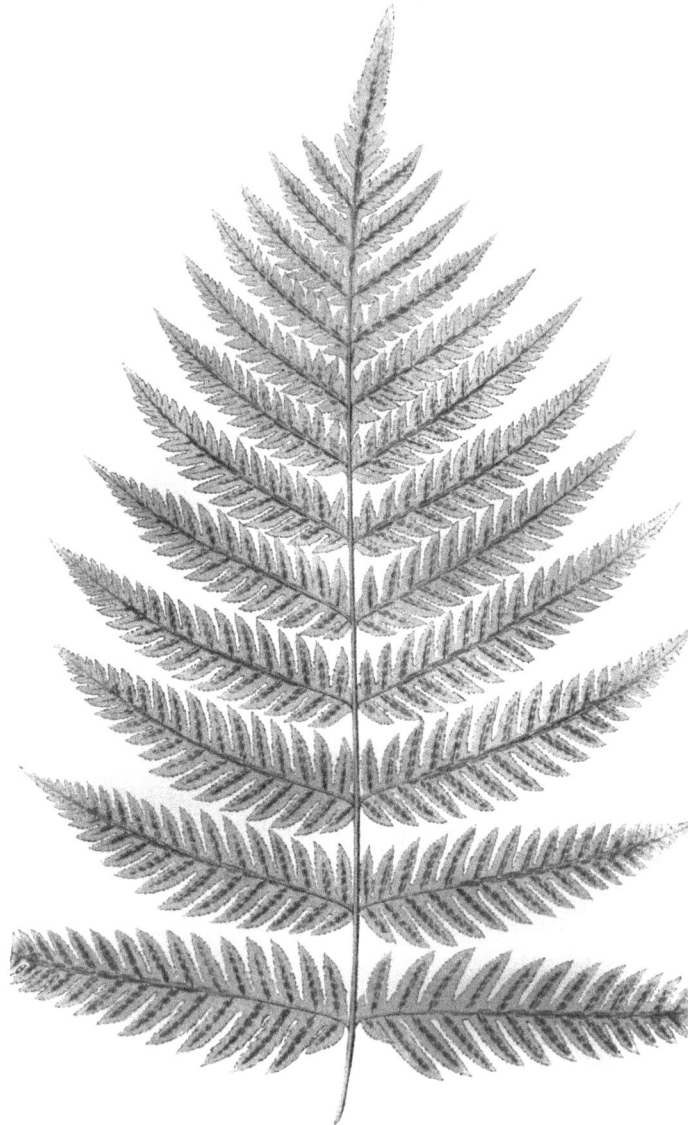

Woodwardia radicans (L.) Sm.
(E.J. Lowe, 1839)

X

Xanthisma DC. – Eriocarpum (158) (1900)

Xanthisma texanum DC. – Sleepy daisy (122, 124) (1937) TX, Star-of-Texas (109, 155) (1942–1949)

Xanthisma texanum DC. subsp. *drummondii* (**Torr. & Gray**) **Semple** – Drummond's sleepy-daisy [Drummond's sleepydaisy] (50) (present), Sleepy-daisy [Sleepy daisy] (3, 97) (1937–1977)

Xanthium (**Tourn.**) **L.** – See *Xanthium* L.

Xanthium americanum **Walt.** – See *Xanthium strumarium* L. var. *glabratum* (DC.) Cronq.

Xanthium canadense **Mill.** – See *Xanthium strumarium* L. var. *canadense* (Mill.) Torr. & Gray

Xanthium cenchroides **Millsp. & Sherff** – See *Xanthium strumarium* L. var. *canadense* (Mill.) Torr. & Gray

Xanthium commune **Britton** – See *Xanthium strumarium* L. var. *canadense* (Mill.) Torr. & Gray

Xanthium curvescens **Millsp. & Sherff** – See *Xanthium strumarium* L. var. *glabratum* (DC.) Cronq.

Xanthium echinatum **Murray** – See *Xanthium strumarium* L. var. *canadense* (Mill.) Torr. & Gray

Xanthium glabratum (**DC.**) **Britton** – See *Xanthium strumarium* L. var. *glabratum* (DC.) Cronq.

Xanthium glanduliferum **Greene** – See *Xanthium strumarium* L. var. *canadense* (Mill.) Torr. & Gray

Xanthium inflexum **Mackenzie & Bush** – See *Xanthium strumarium* L. var. *glabratum* (DC.) Cronq.

Xanthium italicum **Moretti** – See *Xanthium strumarium* L. var. *canadense* (Mill.) Torr. & Gray

Xanthium **L.** – Bur thistle [Bur-thistle, Burr thistle, Burthistle] (7) (1828), Burweed [Bur weed, Bur-weed, Burr weed, Burrweed, Burr-weed] (7) (1828), Clotbur [Clot-bur, Clotburr, Clote-bur, Clot Burre] (1, 2, 7, 10, 156, 158) (1818–1923), Cocklebur [Cockle bur, Cockle-bur, Cockle-burr, Cockle burr, Cockleburr] (1, 2, 4, 50, 93, 125, 155, 158) (1895–present)

Xanthium macrocarpum **var.** *glabratum* **DC.** – See *Xanthium strumarium* L. var. *glabratum* (DC.) Cronq.

Xanthium orientale **L.** – See *Xanthium strumarium* L. var. *glabratum* (DC.) Cronq.

Xanthium pensylvanicum **Wallr.** – See *Xanthium strumarium* L. var. *canadense* (Mill.) Torr. & Gray

Xanthium speciosum **Kearney** – See *Xanthium strumarium* L. var. *canadense* (Mill.) Torr. & Gray

Xanthium spinosum **L.** – American cocklebur (50) (present), Burweed [Bur weed, Bur-weed, Burr weed, Burrweed, Burr-weed] (14, 46, 62, 92, 156) (1878–1923), Clotbur [Clot-bur, Clotburr, Clote-bur, Clot Burre] (52, 148) (1919–1939), Clotweed [Clot-weed, Clott-weed] (156) (1923), Cocklebur [Cockle bur, Cockle-bur, Cockle-burr, Cockle burr, Cockleburr] (5, 52, 156, 158) (1900–1923), Dagger cocklebur [Dagger cockle-bur] (5, 62, 70, 156) (1895–1923), Prickly clotbur [Prickly clott-bur] (19) (1840), Spiny burweed [Spiny burweed] (5, 158) (1900–1913), Spiny clotbur [Spiny clot-bur] (5, 49, 53, 57, 80, 97, 156) (1898–1937), Spiny clotweed (5, 158) (1900–1913), Spiny cocklebur (3, 4, 50, 62, 70, 155, 158) (1895–present), Spring clotbur (158) (1900), Thorny burweed (5) (1913), Thorny clotbur [Thorny clot-bur] (5, 156, 158) (1900–1923)

Xanthium strumarium **L.** – Broad burweed [Broad bur-weed] (53) (1922), Broad cocklebur (1900) (158), Bur thistle [Bur-thistle, Burr thistle, Burthistle] (92, 158) (1876–1900), Burdock (34) (1834), Burweed [Bur weed, Bur-weed, Burr weed, Burrweed, Burr-weed] (58, 107, 158) (1869–1919), Buttonbur [Button-bur, Button bur] (158) (1900), Canadian cocklebur [Canada cocklebur] (50) (present), Clotebur [Clote-bur] (178) (1526), Clotweed [Clot-weed, Clott-weed] (184, 187) (1793–1818), Cocklebur [Cockle bur, Cockle-bur, Cockle-burr, Cockle burr, Cockleburr] (3, 4, 57, 58, 145, 187) (1818–1986), Common cocklebur [Common cockle-bur] (158) (1900), Cucklebur [Cuckle bur] (35) (1806), Cuckold burs (12) (1821), Dike-but (158) (1900), Ditchbur [Ditch-bur] (158) (1900), Kropfklette (German) (158) (1900), Lampourde (French) (12) (1821), Lesser burdock [Lesser burrdock] (158, 187) (1818–1900), Lesser clotbur [Lesser clot-bur] (46, 174) (1671–1753), Louse-bur (158) (1900), Petit glouteron (French) (158) (1900), Rough cocklebur [Rough cockleburr] (50) (present), Sea burdock (19, 92, 158) (1840–1900), Sheepbur [Sheep burr, Sheep-bur] (92, 158) (1876–1900), Small burdock (158) (1900), Spitzklette (German) (158) (1900), Strumarium (57) (1917), Beach clotbur (5, 72) (1907–1913)

Xanthium strumarium **L. var.** *canadense* (**Mill.**) **Torr. & Gray** – American cocklebur (5, 62, 72, 93, 97, 131, 158) (1899–1937), Beach cocklebur (93, 155) (1936–1942), Burweed [Bur weed, Bur-weed, Burr weed, Burrweed, Burr-weed] (156) (1923), Buttonbur [Button-bur, Button bur] (156) (1923), Cadio (150) (1894) NM, Canadian bur (158) (1900), Clotbur [Clot-bur, Clotburr, Clote-bur, Clot Burre] (5, 150, 156) (1894–1923), Cocklebur [Cockle bur, Cockle-bur, Cockle-burr, Cockle burr, Cockleburr] (5, 21, 63, 80, 85, 95, 97, 106, 145, 148, 150) (1893–1939), Common cocklebur [Common cockle-bur] (93, 95, 156) (1911–1936), Cucklebur [Cuckle bur] (76) (1896) Sulphur Grove OH, Glandular clotbur (5, 95) (1911–1913), Glandular cocklebur (93) (1936), Great clotbur (5, 97) (1913–1937), Great cocklebur (93) (1936) Neb, Hedgehog burweed [Hedge-hog-bur-weed] (62, 158) (1900–1912), Italian cocklebur (155) (1942), Lesser burdock [Lesser burrdock] (156) (1923), Pennsylvania clotbur (5, 97) (1913–1937), Sea cocklebur (158) (1900), Sea cucklebur (158) (1900), Sheepbur [Sheep burr, Sheep-bur] (156) (1923), Small burdock (156) (1923), Small cocklebur (85) (1932), Twinberry [Twin-berry, Twin berry] (177) (1762)

Xanthium strumarium **L. var.** *glabratum* (**DC.**) **Cronq.** – Burweed [Bur weed, Bur-weed, Burr weed, Burrweed, Burr-weed] (72) (1907), Buttonbur [Button-bur, Button bur] (5) (1913), Clotbur [Clot-bur, Clotburr, Clote-bur, Clot Burre] (5, 62) (1912–1913), Cocklebur [Cockle bur, Cockle-bur, Cockle-burr, Cockle burr, Cockleburr] (1, 2, 7, 156, 158) (1828–1923), Common cocklebur [Common cockle-bur] (62) (1912), Lesser burdock [Lesser burrdock] (5) (1913), Missouri clotbur (5) (1913), Oriental cocklebur (155) (1942), Rough cocklebur [Rough cockleburr] (50) (present), Sheepbur [Sheep burr, Sheep-bur] (5) (1913), Small burdock (5) (1913)

Xanthium strumarium **L. var.** *pensylvanicum* (**Wallr.**) **M. E. Peck** – See *Xanthium strumarium* L. var. *canadense* (Mill.) Torr. & Gray

Xanthocyparis nootkatensis (**D. Don**) **Farjon & D. K. Harder** – Nootka cypress (20, 161) (1857)

Xanthorhiza **Marsh.** – Shrub yellow-root [Shrub yellowroot, Shrub yellow root, Shrubb yellow root] (138, 186) (1814–1923), possibly Parsley-leaf yellow root [Parsley-leaved yellow root, Parsley-leaved yellow-root] (8, 10, 13, 15, 138, 155) (1785–1942), possibly Yellowroot [Yellow root, Yellow-root] (8, 10, 13, 15, 138, 155) (1785–1942)

Xanthorhiza simplicissima **Marsh.** – American shrub yellow-root [American shrub yellow root] (49) (1898), Parsley yellow-root (49) (1898), Parsley-leaf yellow root [Parsley-leaved yellow root, Parsley-leaved yellow-root] (1, 5, 49) (1898–1932), Sellerieblättrige Gelbwurz (German) (49) (1898), Shrub yellow-root [Shrub yellowroot, Shrub yellow root, Shrubb yellow root] (2, 5, 8, 49, 76, 92, 109) (1785–1949), Southern yellowroot [Southern yellow root] (49) (1898), Yellowroot [Yellow root, Yellow-root] (14, 49, 57, 58, 92,

156, 186) (1814–1923), Yellow-wort [Yellow wort] (7, 49, 92, 138) (1876–1930), Zanthorhize à feuilles de perfil (French) (8) (1785)

Xanthoriza simplicissima **Marsh.** – See *Xanthorhiza simplicissima* Marsh.

Xanthorrhiza apiifolia **Marsh.** – See *Xanthorhiza simplicissima* Marsh.

Xanthosoma sagittifolium **(L.) Schott** – Arrow-leaf spoonflower [Arrow-leaved spoonflower] (86) (1878), Cocushaw (46) (1879)

Xanthoxalis brittoniae **Small** – See *Oxalis stricta* L.

Xanthoxalis bushii **Small** – See *Oxalis stricta* L.

Xanthoxalis corniculata **(L.) Small** – See *Oxalis corniculata* L.

Xanthoxalis cymosa **(Small) Small** – See *Oxalis stricta* L.

Xanthoxalis florida **(Salisb.) Moldenke** – See *Oxalis stricta* L.

Xanthoxalis interior **Small** – See *Oxalis stricta* L.

Xanthoxalis priceae **Small** – See *Oxalis priceae* Small subsp. *priceae*

Xanthoxalis rufa **Small.** – See *Oxalis stricta* L.

Xanthoxalis **Small.** – See *Oxalis* L.

Xanthoxalis stricta **(L.) Small** – See *Oxalis stricta* L.

Xanthoxylon fraxineum – See *Zanthoxylum americanum* Mill.

Xanthoxylum americanum **Mill.** – See *Zanthoxylum americanum* Mill.

Xanthoxylum carolianum – See *Zanthoxylum clava-herculis* L.

Xanthoxylum Clava-Herculis **L.** – See *Zanthoxylum clava-herculis* L.

Xanthoxylum clava-Herculis **Lam.** – See *Zanthoxylum clava-herculis* L.

Xanthoxylum fraxinifolium **Marsh.** – See *Zanthoxylum americanum* Mill.

Xeniatrum umbellulatum **(Michx.) Small** – See *Clintonia umbellulata* (Michx.) Morong

Xerophyllum asphodeloides **(L.) Nutt.** – Eastern turkeybeard (50) (present), Turkey-beard [Turkeysbeard, Turkey beard] (5, 78, 138, 156) (1898–1923)

Xerophyllum douglasii **S. Watson** – See *Xerophyllum tenax* (Pursh) Nutt.

Xerophyllum **Michx.** – Turkey-beard [Turkeysbeard, Turkey beard] (109, 138) (1923–1949)

Xerophyllum tenax **(Pursh) Nutt.** – Bear-grass [Bear grass, Bear's grass, Bears' grass] (35, 101, 138) (1806–1923), Common bear grass [Common beargrass] (50) (present), Quipquip [Quip quip] (33) (1827)

Ximenia americana **L.** – Mountain-plum [Mountain plum] (20) (1857), Tallowwood (155) (1942), Ximenie Americaine (French) (20, 183) (~1756–1857)

Ximenia **Plum.** – Colorado desert aster (155) (1942), Hog-plum [Hog plum, Hog's plum] (15) (1895), Mountain-plum [Mountain plum] (15) (1895), Wild lime or Wild lime tree [Wild lime-tree] (15) (1895)

Xolisma ferruginea **[(Walter) A. Heller]** – See *Lyonia ferruginea* (Walt.) Nutt.

Xolisma ligustrina **(L.) Britton** – See *Lyonia ligustrina* (L.) DC. var. *ligustrina*

Xylococcus bicolor **Nutt.** – Mission manzanita (155) (1942)

Xylophacos **Rydb.** – See *Astragalus* L. (all US species) ()

Xylorhiza cognata **(Hall) T. J. Wats.** – Colorado desert aster (155) (1942), Parry's aster [Parry aster] (5) (1913)

Xylorhiza glabriuscula **Nutt.** – Alkali aster (155) (1942), Common woody aster (155) (1942), Smooth woody-aster [Smooth woodyaster] (50) (present)

Xylorhiza glabriuscula **Nutt. var.** *glabriuscula* – Parry's aster [Parry aster] (155) (1942)

Xylorhiza **Nutt.** – Woody aster [Woodyaster] (50) (present), Xylorrhiza (158) (1900)

Xylorhiza orcuttii **(Vasey & Rose) Greene** – Mohave aster (8, 13) (1785–1849), Orcutt's aster [Orcutt aster] (155) (1942)

Xylorhiza tortifolia **(Torr. & Gray) Greene var.** *tortifolia* – Mohave aster (155) (1942)

Xylosteon **Adans.** – See *Lonicera* L.

Xylosteon solonis **Eaton** – See *Lonicera villosa* (Michx.) J. A. Schultes var. *solonis* (Eat.) Fern.

Xyris caroliniana **Walt.** – Carolina yellow-eyed grass (5, 50) (1913–present), Common yellow-eyed grass (66) (1903), Slender yellow-eyed grass (5, 97) (1913–1937), Twisted yellow-eyed grass (5) (1913), Yellow flowering-rush [Yellow flowering rush] (5, 19, 156) (1840–1923), Yellow-eyed-grass [Yellow-eyed grass, Yellow eyed grass] (19, 92, 156) (1840–1923)

Xyris caroliniana **Walt. var.** *olneyi* **Wood** – See *Xyris smalliana* Nash

Xyris elata **Chapman** – See *Xyris jupicai* L.C. Rich.

Xyris fimbriata **Ell.** – Fringed yellow-eyed grass (5, 50, 124) (1913–present)

Xyris flexuosa **Muhl.** – See *Xyris caroliniana* Walt.

Xyris indica **L.** – See *Xyris torta* Sm.

Xyris jupicai **L.C. Rich.** – Richard's yellow-eyed grass [Richard's yelloweyed grass] (50) (present), Southern yellow-eyed grass (5) (1913), Tall yellow-eyed grass (5) (1913)

Xyris **L.** – Eye-grass [Eyegrass] (7, 10) (1818–1828), Headgrass (7) (1828), Yellow-eyed-grass [Yellow-eyed grass, Yellow eyed grass] (1, 50) (1932–present)

Xyris montana **H. Ries.** – Northern yellow-eyed grass (5, 50) (1913–present)

Xyris pallescens **(C. Mohr) Small** – See *Xyris caroliniana* Walt.

Xyris smalliana **Nash** – Congdon's yellow-eyed grass (5) (1913), Small's yellow-eyed grass [Small's yelloweyed grass] (50) (present)

Xyris smalliana **Nash var.** *olneyi* **(Wood) Gleason** – See *Xyris smalliana* Nash

Xyris torta **Sm.** – Katjiletti-pullu (174, 177) (1753–1762), Ranmotha (177) (1762), Yellow-eyed-grass [Yellow-eyed grass, Yellow eyed grass] (66) (1903)

Xyrophyllum setifolium **Michx.** – See *Xerophyllum asphodeloides* (L.) Nutt.

Y

Yucca aloifolia **L.** – Aloe yucca (50) (present), Aloe-leaf yucca [Aloe-leafed yucca] (124) (1937), Spanish bayonet [Spanish-bayonet] (2, 109) (1895–1949), Spanish dagger [Spanish-dagger, Spanish daggers] (75, 92, 138) (1876–1923)

Yucca angustissima **Engelm. ex Trel.** – Narrow-leaf yucca [Narrowleaf yucca] (50) (present)

Yucca arborescens **(Torr.) Trel.** – See *Yucca brevifolia* Engelm.

Yucca arkansana **Trel.** – Arkansas yucca (50, 124, 155) (1937–present)

Yucca baccata **Torr.** – Banana (103) (1871), Banana yucca (50, 138) (1923–present), Datil (153) (1913) NM, Datil yucca (155) (1942), Hosh-kawn (5) (1913), Mexican banana (158) (1900), Soap plant [Soap-plant] (158) (1900), Spanish bayonet [Spanish-bayonet] (5, 103, 107, 158) (1871–1919), Spanish dagger [Spanish-dagger, Spanish daggers] (5) (1913)

Yucca brevifolia **Engelm.** – Joshua yucca (138) (1923), Joshua-tree (109) (1949)

Yucca elata **(Engelm.) Engelm.** – Amole (149, 153) (1904–1913) NM, La palmilla (149, 153) (1904–1913) NM, Soapweed [Soap weed, Soap-weed] (149, 153) (1904–1913)

Yucca faxoniana **(Trel.) Sarg.** – Mexican date yucca (138) (1923), Texas date yucca (138) (1923)

Yucca filamentosa concava – See *Yucca filamentosa* L.

Yucca filamentosa **L.** – Adam's-needle [Adam's needle] (2, 50, 107, 109, 158) (1900–present), Adam's-needle yucca [Adamsneedle yucca] (155) (1942), Adam's-needle-and-thread [Adam's needle and thread] (78, 158) (1898–1900), Bear-grass [Bear grass, Bear's grass, Bears' grass] (5, 7, 92, 156, 158) (1828–1923), Bear-thread [Bear's thread, Bear's-thread] (5, 7, 19, 156, 158) (1828–1923), Cedar-apple [Cedar apple, Cedar-apples, Cedar apples] (100) (1850) the fruit, Common bear-grass [Common bear grass] (2) (1895), Common yucca (138) (1923), Curve-leaf yucca [Curveleaf yucca] (138, 155) (1923–1942), Eve's-darning-needle [Eve's darning needle, Eve's darning-needle] (5, 73, 156, 158) (1892–1923) Fort Worth TX, Eve's-thread [Eve's thread] (158) (1900), Needle palm (107) (1919), Our Lord's candle [Our Lords candle] (156) (1923), Silk aloes (7) (1828), Silk-grass [Silk grass, Silke grass] (5, 92, 156, 158, 177) (1526–1923), Spanish bayonet [Spanish-bayonet] (156) (1923), Spanish dagger [Spanish-dagger, Spanish daggers] (156) (1923), Spoon-leaf yucca [Spoon-leaf yucca] (138, 155) (1923–1942), Thread-and-needle (5, 19, 73) (1840–1913), Weak-leaf yucca [Weakleaf yucca] (138, 155) (1923–1942), White camas [White camass] (3) (1977), Yucca (156) (1923)

Yucca filamentosa **L. var.** *concava* **(Haw.) Baker** – See *Yucca filamentosa* L.

Yucca filamentosa **Pursh.** – See *Yucca filamentosa* L.

Yucca flaccida **Haw.** – See *Yucca filamentosa* L.

Yucca glauca **Nutt.** – Adam's-needle [Adam's needle] (5, 93) (1913–1936), Ammole (28) (1850), Amole (156) (1923), Bear-grass [Bear grass, Bear's grass, Bears' grass] (5, 72, 93, 97, 153, 156) (1907–1937), Chakida-kahtsu (Pawnee) (35, 37) (1806–1830), Dagger weed [Dagger weed] (37) (1830), Duwaduwa-hi (Omaha-Ponca) (37) (1830), Hupestola (Lakota, pointed stem) (121) (1918–1970), Hupestula (Dakota) (37) (1830), Palmillo (5, 156) (1913–1923), Small soapweed (155) (1942), Soap plant [Soap-plant] (28) (1850), Soapweed [Soap weed, Soap-weed] (5, 85, 93, 97, 109, 125, 156) (1913–1949), Soapweed yucca (50, 138) (1923–present), Spanish bayonet [Spanish-bayonet] (37, 85, 156) (1830–1932), Yucca (3, 121, 124, 125, 127) (1918–1977)

Yucca glauca **Nutt. var.** *glauca* – Adam's-needle [Adam's needle] (38, 108) (1820–1878), Grass-cactus [Grass cactus] (101) (1905), Soapweed [Soap weed, Soap-weed] (75, 101) (1894–1905), Soapweed yucca (50) (present)

Yucca gloriosa **L.** – Adam's-needle [Adam's needle] (92, 182) (1791–1876), Dagger-flower plant [Dagger flower plant] (92) (1876), Lord's candlestick (78) (1898) CA, Mound-lily yucca [Moundlily yucca] (50, 138) (1923–present), Palmetto royal (7, 182) (1791–1828), Roman-candle [Roman candle] (78) (1898) CA, Spanish dagger [Spanish-dagger, Spanish daggers] (109) (1949), Yucca [Iucca] (178) (1596)

Yucca harrimaniae **Trel.** – Harriman's yucca [Harriman yucca] (155) (1942), Spanish bayonet [Spanish-bayonet] (50) (present)

Yucca harrimaniae **Trel. var.** *neomexicana* **(Woot. & Standl.) Reveal** – New Mexico Spanish bayonet (50) (present), New Mexico yucca [NewMexican yucca] (155) (1942)

Yucca **L.** – Adam's-needle [Adam's needle] (10, 158, 167) (1814–1900), Bear-grass [Bear grass, Bear's grass, Bears' grass] (2) (1895), Date yucca (138) (1923), Grass-cactus [Grass cactus] (1, 93) (1932–1936), Palma (122) (1937) TX, Soaproot [Soap-root, Soap root] (1) (1932), Soapweed [Soap weed, Soap-weed] (1, 93, 148) (1932–1939), Spanish bayonet [Spanish-bayonet] (1, 2, 93, 156) (1895–1936), Yucca (1, 50, 138, 148, 155) (1923–present)

Yucca louisiana **Trel.** – See *Yucca louisianensis* Trel.

Yucca louisianensis **Trel.** – Early yucca (122, 124) (1937) TX

Yucca macrocarpa **(Torr.) Coville** – See *Yucca torreyi* Shafer

Yucca neomexicana **Woot. & Standl.** – See *Yucca harrimaniae* Trel. var. *neomexicana* (Woot. & Standl.) Reveal

Yucca recurvifolia **Salisb.** – See *Yucca filamentosa* L.

Yucca rupicola **Scheele** – Texas yucca (50) (present), Twisted-leaf yucca [Twistedleaf yucca] (122, 124) (1937)

Yucca smalliana **Fern.** – See *Yucca filamentosa* L.

Yucca torreyi **Shafer** – La palma (149, 153) (1904–1913) NM, Spanish bayonet [Spanish-bayonet] (149, 153) (1904–1913) NM, Spanish dagger [Spanish-dagger, Spanish daggers] (149, 153) (1904–1913) NM, Western dagger (124) (1937) TX

Yucca treculeana **Carr.** – Spanish bayonet [Spanish-bayonet] (138) (1923), Spanish dagger [Spanish-dagger, Spanish daggers] (122, 124) (1937) TX

Yucca whipplei **Torr.** – Our Lord's candle [Our Lords candle] (109) (1949)

Yucca whipplei **Torr. var.** *whipplei* – Chaparral yucca (138) (1923), Grass-leaf sotol [Grassleaf sotol] (138) (1923)

Z

Zamia floridana [A. DC.] – See *Zamia pumila* L. subsp. *pumila*

Zamia integrifolia Ait. – See *Zamia pumila* L.

Zamia integrifolia L. f. – See *Zamia pumila* L.

Zamia integrifolium – See *Zamia pumila* L.

Zamia pumila L. – Coontie (2, 50) (1895–present), Florida arrowroot (92) (1876), Sago cycad (107) (1919), St. John's coontie [St. Johns coontie] (138) (1923), possibly Sugarpine (7) (1828), possibly Tuckaho [Tuckaho, Tuckahoe] (10) (1818)

Zamia pumila L. subsp. pumila – Coontie (138) (1923)

Zannichellia (Mich) L. – See *Zannichellia* L.

Zannichellia intermedia Torr. – See *Zannichellia palustris* L.

Zannichellia L. – Horned pondweed (1, 50, 85, 156) (1923–present), Poolmat (155) (1942), Triple-head pondweed [Triple-headed pond weed] (167) (1814), Zannichellia [Zanichellia] (158) (1900)

Zannichellia palustris L. – Common poolmat (155) (1942), False pondweed [False pond-weed] (19) (1840), Horned pondweed (3, 50, 97, 120) (1937–present), Water-grass [Water grass] (93) (1936) Neb, Zannichellia [Zanichellia] (131) (1899), Zennichellia (72) (1907) for J. H. Zannichelli, Italian botanist, d. 1729

Zantedeschia aethiopica (L.) Spreng. – Calla (109) (1949) this is calla or calla lily of florists, Calla lily (5, 50, 92) (1876–present), Common calla (138) (1923), Egyptian lily (19) (1840), Negro arum (19) (1840)

Zantedeschia albomaculata (Hook.) Baill. – Spotted calla (109, 138) (1923–1949)

Zantedeschia albo-maculata Baill. – See *Zantedeschia albomaculata* (Hook.) Baill.

Zantedeschia Spreng. – Calla (138) (1923)

Zanthium canadense Mill. – See *Xanthium strumarium* L. var. *canadense* (Mill.) Torr. & Gray

Zanthorhiza apiifolia L'Her. – See *Xanthorhiza simplicissima* Marsh.

Zanthorhiza L. – See *Xanthorhiza* Marsh.

Zanthorhiza simplicissima Marsh. – See *Xanthorhiza simplicissima* Marsh.

Zanthoxylum (Catesby) L. – See *Zanthoxylum* L.

Zanthoxylum americanum Mill. – Agawak-minš (Chippewa, prickly tree) (105) (1932), Angelica tree [Angelica-tree] (5, 6, 49, 157, 158) (1892–1929), Ash-leaf toothache tree [Ash-leaved tooth-ach tree] (8) (1785), Clavalier (French) (158) (1900), Common prickly-ash [Common prickly ash] (50, 137, 138, 155) (1923–present), Fagara (French) (8) (1785), Frêne Épineux (French) (6, 8, 158) (1785–1900), Gawa'komĭc (Chippewa) (37) (1919), Hakusits (Pawnee, thorn) (37) (1919), Hantola (6) (1892), Hercules pricklyash (158) (1900), Northern prickly ash (2, 6, 49, 53, 55, 57, 82, 156, 157) (1892–1930), Pellitory (6, 7, 58) (1828–1892), Pellitory bark (92, 156, 157, 158, 184) (1793–1936), Prickly yellow-wood [Prickly yellowwood, Prickly yellow wood] (7, 156) (1828–1923), Prickly-ash [Prickly ash, Pricklyash] (1, 3, 4, 5, 9, 15, 19, 27, 35, 37, 40, 48, 49, 52, 54, 55, 58, 59, 60, 61, 65, 72, 85, 92, 93, 95, 97, 105, 109, 113, 130, 131, 157, 158, 184) (1793–1986), Shrubby prickly-ash [Shrubby prickly ash] (7) (1828), Suterberry [Suter-berry] (5, 6, 7, 49, 156, 157, 158) (1828–1929), Sutterberry bark (92) (1876), Toothache bark (92) (1876), Toothache bush [Toothache-bush, Toothe-ache bush] (7, 19, 49, 58, 92, 157, 158) (1828–1929), Toothache tree [Toothache-tree] (2, 4, 5, 6, 14, 15, 49, 92, 97, 137, 156, 157, 158) (1876–1986), West Indian yellow-wood (156) (1923), Xanthoxyle frene (French) (7) (1828), Xanthoxylum (54) (1905), Yellow (7) (1828), Yellow-wood [Yellowwood, Yellow wood] (6, 49, 156, 157, 158) (1892–1929), Zahnweholz (German) (6, 158) (1892–1900), Zahnwehrinde (German) (158) (1900)

Zanthoxylum clava-herculis L. – Angelica tree [Angelica-tree] (49, 156) (1898–1923), Carolina prickly-ash [Carolina prickly ash] (20) (1857), Clavalier de la Caroline (French) (20) (1857), Colima (158) (1900), Hercules pricklyash (155) (1942), Hercules'-club [Hercules' club, Hercules club, Herculesclub] (5, 14, 93, 124, 138, 156, 158, 181) (~1678–1936), Pepperwood [Pepper-wood, Pepper wood] (5, 15, 97, 156, 158) (1895–1937), Prickly yellow-wood [Prickly yellowwood, Prickly yellow wood] (5, 92, 156, 177, 189) (1762–1923), Prickly-ash [Prickly ash, Pricklyash] (12, 93, 106, 122, 124) (1821–1937), Sea-ash [Sea ash] (5, 15, 92, 156, 158) (1876–1923), Southern prickly-ash [Southern prickly ash] (2, 5, 8, 49, 53, 57, 58, 92, 97, 156, 158) (1785–1937), Suterberry [Suter-berry] (49) (1898), Toothache tree [Toothache-tree] (106) (1930), Wild orange [Wild-orange] or Wild orange tree (5, 15, 156, 158, 189) (1767–1923), Xanthoxylon tree (177) (1762), Yellow hercules (92, 158) (1876–1900), Yellow prickly-ash [Yellow prickly ash] (5, 156, 158) (1900–1923), Yellow-wood [Yellowwood, Yellow wood] (92, 158) (1876–1900)

Zanthoxylum fagara (L.) Sargent – Bastard iron wood (15, 20) (1857–1895), Clavalier aite (French) (20) (1857), Colima (106, 122, 124) (1930–1937)

Zanthoxylum flavum Vahl – Satinwood [Satin wood] (15) (1895)

Zanthoxylum floridanum Nutt. – See *Zanthoxylum fagara* (L.) Sarg.

Zanthoxylum fraxinifolium Marsh. – See *Zanthoxylum americanum* Mill.

Zanthoxylum fraxinifolium Walt – See *Zanthoxylum clava-herculis* L.

Zanthoxylum hirsutum Buckl. – Texas Hercules'-club [Texas Hercules' club] (50) (present)

Zanthoxylum juglandifolium Willd. – See *Zanthoxylum martinicense* (Lam.) DC.

Zanthoxylum L. – Frêne Épineux (French) (8) (1785), Prickly-ash [Prickly ash, Pricklyash] (1, 4, 10, 13, 15, 47, 50, 82, 93, 138, 155) (1818–present), Toothache tree [Tooth ache tree, Tooth-ache tree] (8, 10, 13) (1785–1849), Fagara (French) (8) (1785)

Zanthoxylum martinicense (Lam.) DC. – Walnut-leaf yellow-wood [Walnut-leaved yellow-wood] (20) (1857)

Zapania nodiflora Michx. – See *Phyla nodiflora* (L.) Greene

Zauschneria C. Presl – See *Epilobium* L. (all US species) ()

Zauschneria californica Presl. – See *Epilobium canum* (Greene) Raven subsp. *angustifolium* (Keck) Raven

Zea L. – Corn (45, 50) (1896–present), Indian corn [Indian-corn] (45, 155, 158, 163, 167) (1814–1942), Maize [Maiz, Mays] (45, 155, 158, 163) (1852–1942), Teosinte (138) (1923)

Zea mays L. – Barbary corn (Provence) (110) (1886), Blé de Turquie (French "Turkish wheat") (110) (1886) possibly from resemblance of ear to beards of Turkish men rather than to place of origin, Bled (46) (1879), Cintli (Mexico) (110) (1886) goddess Cinteutl was similar to Greek goddess Ceres, Corn (21, 50, 68, 92, 107, 182) (1791–present), Corn of Asia [Corne of Asia] (180) (1633), Egyptian corn (Turkey) (110) (1886), E'-tahl (Kioway) (132) (1855), Field corn (119) (1938), Guinea corn [Guinea-corn] (110) (1886), Guinea wheat (107, 158) (1586–1900), Hah-wib' (Chemehuevi Shoshonee) (132) (1855), Hŭn-i-bist (Comanche Shoshonee) (132) (1855), Hŭs'-quim (Delaware) (132) (1855), Indian corn [Indian-corn] (7, 10, 37, 40, 41, 56, 57, 66, 68, 87, 92, 94, 103, 106, 109, 110, 117, 119, 121, 138, 155, 158, 182, 184) (1791–1949), Indian millet (178) (1596), Indian wheat (Italy) (107) (1645), India-wheat (14, 18, 19, 37) (1805–1919), Jagong (92) (1876), Mahiz (Haiti) (107) (1919), Mais (180) (1633), Mais (French) (158) (1900), Mais (German) (158) (1900), Maize [Maiz, Mays] (10, 66, 67, 68, 92, 106, 107, 109, 110, 119, 121, 138, 155, 158, 180) (1492–1970) from aboriginal name, Maizim (107) (1493), Maizum (180) (1633), Manda'mĭn (Chippewa) (14, 37, 38, 40) (1820–1928), Mealies (158) (1900)

450

Australia, S. Africa, Mexican corn (56) (1901), Mi'-we (Zuñi) (132) (1855), Nikiís (Pawnee) (37) (1830), Ofizy (46) (1879), Oo-oon (Pima) (132) (1855), Ou'-in (Pima) (132) (1855), Pagatowr (Virginians) (180) (1633), Pa'-ho-with-lim (Cahuillo Shoshonee) (132) (1855), Roman corn (Lorraine and Vosges) (110) (1886), Sara (Inca) (107) (1919), Sicilian corn (Tuscany) (110) (1886), Sugar corn (109, 119) (1938–1949), Sweet corn (109, 114, 119) (1894–1949), Syrian dourra (Egypt) (110) (1886), Tan'-chi (Choctaw) (132) (1855), Tar-mi' (Shawnee) (132) (1855), Ter-di-cha (Diegeño Yuma) (132) (1855), Tĕr-ditch (Cuchan Yuma) (132) (1855), Ter-dítz (Mohave Yuma) (132) (1855), Turkey corn [Turkey-corn, Turkie Corne, Turky Corne] (158, 180) (1633–1900), Turkey wheat [Turky wheat] (158, 180) (1633–1900) archaic, Turkish corn [Turkish korn] (92, 107) (1876–1919), Ubatim (Brazil) (107) (1550), Wagmeza (Dakota Teton) (37) (1830), Wagmeza (Lakota) (121) (1918–1970), Wahába (Omaha-Ponca) (37) (1830), Wamnáheza (Dakota) (37) (1830), Wǎ-tò-jǎ (Oto) (38) (1820), Watoηϴi (Osage) (121) (1918–1970), Wǎt-tǎn-zé (Omaha) (38) (1820), Welschkorn (Germany) (107, 110) (1552), Wheat of Barbary (107) (1919), Wheat of Guinea (107) (1919), Wheat of Rome (107) (1919), Wheat of Spain (107) (1919), Wheat of Turkey (107) (1919), Ya'chi (Kiwomi Keres) (132) (1855), Ya'-o-ni (Kiwomi Keres) (132) (1855), Zaburso (Brazil) (107) (1550)

Zea mays L. subsp. *mays* – Dent corn (109, 119) (1938–1949), Flint corn (109, 119) (1938–1949), Pinsigallo (Argentina) (110) (1886), Pod corn (119) (1938), Pop corn (109, 119) (1938–1949), Rath-ripe corn (181) (~1678), Yankee corn (109, 119) (1938–1949)

Zea mays L. var. *everta* **Bailey** – See *Zea mays* L. subsp. *mays*

Zea mays L. var. *indentata* **Bailey** – See *Zea mays* L. subsp. *mays*

Zea mays L. var. *rugosa* **Bonaf.** – See *Zea mays* L.

Zea mays L. var. *tunicata* **St. Hil.** – See *Zea mays* L. subsp. *mays*

***Zea mays tunicata* St.-Hil.** – See *Zea mays* L. subsp. *mays*

Zea mexicana **(Schrad.) Kuntze** – Mexican teosinte (68) (1890) NM, Teosinte (56, 67, 101, 109, 138, 163) (1852–1949)

***Zebrina pendula* Schnizl.** – See *Tradescantia zebrina* hort. ex Bosse

Zelkova serrata **(Thunb.) Makino** – Saw-leaf zelkova [Sawleaf zelkova] (138) (1923)

***Zelkova* Spach** – Zelkova (138) (1923)

Zeltnera exaltata **(Griseb.) G. Mans.** – Mealy bush [Mealybush] (138, 181) (~1678–1923)

Zeltnera muehlenbergii **(Griseb.) G. Mans.** – Conchalagua (75) (1894) CA

Zenobia cassinefolia **(Vent.) Pollard** – See *Zenobia pulverulenta* (Bartr. ex Willd.) Pollard

***Zenobia* D. Don** – Zenobia (138) (1923)

Zenobia pulverulenta **(W. Bartram ex Willd.) Pollard** – Dusty zenobia (138) (1923), Mealy bush [Mealybush] (7, 92) (1828–1876), Zelkova (181) (~1678)

Zephyranthes atamasca **(L.) Herbert** – Atamasco lily [Atamasco-lily] (2, 5, 107, 109, 138, 156) (1895–1949), Atamosco (181) (~1678), Fairy lily (5, 156) (1913–1923), Stagger grass [Stagger-grass] (5, 156) (1913–1923), Swamp lily [Swamp-lily] (5, 156) (1913–1923)

***Zephyranthes atamasco* Herbert** – See *Zephyranthes atamasca* (L.) Herbert

Zephyranthes candida **(Lindl.) Herbert** – Autumn zephyr-lily [Autumn zephyrlily] (138) (1923)

***Zephyranthes* Herbert** – Fairy lily (156) (1923), Zephyr-lily [Zephyr-lily] (109, 138) (1923–1949)

***Zephyranthes longifolia* Hemsl.** – Copper zephyr-lily [Copper zephyrlily] (50, 155) (1942–present), Plains rain-lily [Plains rain lily] (122) (1937) TX

***Zephyranthes rosea* Lindl.** – Pink zephyr-lily [Pink zephyrlily] (138) (1923)

***Zephyranthes texana* Herb.** – See *Habranthus tubispathus* (L'Hér.) Traub

***Zigadenus elegans* Pursh** – Alkali-grass [Alkali-grass] (75, 157, 158) (1894–1929) MN, Death camas [Deathcamas, Death camass] (157)

(1929), Glaucous zygadenus (72, 133) (1903–1907), Mountain death camas [Mountain deathcamas, Mountain deathcamass] (50, 155) (1942–present), Swamp camas [Swampcamas] (133) (1903)

Zigadenus elegans* Pursh subsp. *elegans – Glaucous anticlea (5, 97) (1913–1937), Mountain death camas [Mountain deathcamas, Mountain deathcamass] (50) (present), White camas [White camass] (85) (1932)

***Zigadenus elegans* Pursh subsp. *glaucus* (Nutt.) Hultén** – Camas [Camass, Kamas, Kmass] (126) (1933)

***Zigadenus glaberrimus* Michx.** – Large-flower zygadenus [Large-flowered zygadenus] (5) (1913), Zigadene (19) (1840)

***Zigadenus gramineus* Rydb.** – See *Zigadenus venenosus* S. Wats. var. *gramineus* (Rydb.) Walsh ex M. E. Peck

***Zigadenus leimanthoides* Gray** – Pine Barren deathcamas [Pinebarren deathcamas] (50) (present), Pine Barren oceanus (5) (1913)

***Zigadenus* Michx.** – Soap plant [Soap-plant] (158) (1900), Death camas [Deathcamas, Death camass] (1, 50, 93, 155) (1932–present), Poison camas (1, 93) (1932–1936)

***Zigadenus muscitoxicus* (Walt.) Regel** – See *Amianthium muscitoxicum* (Walt.) Gray

***Zigadenus nuttallii* (Gray) S. Wats.** – Death camas [Deathcamas, Death camass] (3) (1977), Nuttall's camas [Nuttall's camass] (5, 93, 97) (1913–1937), Nuttall's death-camas [Nuttall deathcamas, Nuttall's deathcamas] (50, 155) (1942–present)

***Zigadenus venenosus* S. Wats.** – Death camas [Deathcamas, Death camass] (101) (1905), Meadow death-camas [Meadow deathcamas] (50, 155) (1942–present)

***Zigadenus venenosus* S. Wats. var. *gramineus* (Rydb.) Walsh ex M. E. Peck** – Alkali-grass [Alkali-grass] (148) (1939) CO, Camas [Camass, Kamas, Kmass] (148) (1939), Death camas [Deathcamas, Death camass] (3, 5, 85, 93, 133, 146, 148, 157, 158) (1903–1977), Grassy deathcamas (50, 155) (1942–present), Hog-potata [Hog potata] (158) (1900), Hog-potato [Hog potato, Hog's potato, Hog-potatoe, Hog's potato] (5, 158) (1900–1913), Mystery-grass [Mystery grass] (133) (1903) ND, Poison camas (85) (1932), Poison onion (148) (1939) CO, Poisonous zygadenus (158) (1900), Poison-sage [Poison sage] (148) (1939) CO, Sego lily [Segolily] (133) (1903) ND, Swamp camas [Swampcamas] (148) (1939), Wild leek [Wild leekes] (133) (1903) ND, Wild onion (133) (1903)

***Zingiber* Adans.** – See *Zingiber* Mill. (from ancient Sanskrit)

Zingiber cassumunar – See *Zingiber purpureum* Roscoe

Zingiber cassumuniar – See *Zingiber purpureum* Roscoe

***Zingiber* Mill.** – Ginger [Gynger] (138) (1923)

***Zingiber officinale* Roscoe** – Black ginger (92) (1876), Common ginger (109, 138) (1923–1949), Gingembre (French) (180) (1633), Ginger [Gynger] (92, 107, 178, 179) (1526–1919), Gingiber (180) (1633)

Zingiber officinalis – See *Zingiber officinale* Roscoe

***Zingiber purpureum* Roscoe** – Bengal root (92) (1876), Cassumuniar (92) (1876)

***Zinnia acerosa* (DC.) Gray** – Wild zinnia (153) (1913)

***Zinnia elegans* Jacq.** – See *Zinnia violacea* Cav.

***Zinnia grandiflora* Nutt.** – Bengal root (138) (1923), Prairie zinnia (5, 97, 122, 124) (1913–1937), Rocky Mountain zinnia [RockyMountain zinnia] (3, 4, 50, 155) (1942–present)

***Zinnia* L.** – Alexanders [Alexander] (92) (1876), Zinnia (50, 82, 138, 158) (1900–present) for Johann Gottfried Zinn, 1727–1759, professor of medicine at Gorttingen

***Zinnia pumila* A. Gray** – See *Zinnia acerosa* (DC.) Gray

***Zinnia violacea* Cav.** – Blood marigold (92) (1876), Bloody marigold [Bloody marygold] (19) (1840), Common zinnia (138) (1923), Oldmaid's pink [Old maid pink, Old maid's pink] (76) (1896) Sulphur Grove OH, Youth-and-old-age [Youth and old age] (73, 109) (1892–1949) Mansfield OH, Zinnia (82, 92) (1876–1930)

***Zizania aquatica* L.** – Annual wild rice [Annual wildrice] (155) (1942), Canadian rice [Canada rice] (5, 14, 157, 158) (1882–1929), Elymus (177) (1762), Folle avoine (French) (41, 66) (1770–1903),

Indian rice (2, 43, 46, 66, 67, 87, 88, 92, 107, 111, 129, 131, 157, 158, 187) (1818–1929), Katniss (46) (1879), Man-om-in (Chipewa) (103) (1871), Nattourne (46) (1879), Northern wild rice [Northern wildrice] (138) (1923), Pshu (Sioux) (103) (1871), Psin (Dakota) (5, 37) (1830–1919), Reed [Rede, Reeds] (94, 157, 158) (1900–1929), Sin (Winnebago) (37) (1830), Sinwaninda (Omaha-Ponca) (37) (1830), Tuscarora rice (67, 187) (1818–1890), Water oats (2, 66, 87, 92, 131, 157, 158) (1844–1929), Water rice (5, 157, 158) (1900–1929), Water tare grass [Water taregrass] (41) (1770), Wild oat [Wild oats] (107) (1821), Wild-oats (177) (1762), possibly Monomonie (11, 19, 23, 37, 41, 43) (1810–1919) may refer to any grain, possibly Wild rice [Wildrice] (5, 23, 45, 56, 66, 85, 87, 88, 94, 103, 107, 131, 157, 158) (1810–1932)

Zizania aquatica L. var. *angustifolia* A. S. Hitchc. – See *Zizania palustris* L. var. *palustris*

Zizania aquatica L. var. *interior* Fassett – See *Zizania palustris* L. var. *interior* (Fassett) Dore

Zizania fluitans – See *Luziola fluitans* (Michx.) Terrell & H. Rob.

Zizania L. – American rice (10) (1818), Indian rice (1, 45, 66, 93, 158) (1896–1936), Water oats (1, 45) (1896–1932), Wild rice [Wildrice] (3, 7, 45, 50, 93, 109, 138, 155, 158, 167) (1814–present)

Zizania miliacea Michx. – See *Zizaniopsis miliacea* (Michx.) Doell & Aschers.

Zizania palustris L. – Common wild rice [Common wildrice] (138) (1923), Mano'mǐn (Chippewa) (7, 40) (1828–1928), Northern wild rice [Northern wildrice] (50) (present), Wild rice [Wildrice] (40) (1928)

Zizania palustris L. var. *interior* (Fassett) Dore – Annual wild rice [Annual wildrice] (122) (1937), Northern wild rice [Northern wildrice] (50) (present)

Zizania palustris L. var. *palustris* – Northern wild rice [Northern wildrice] (50, 155) (1942–present)

Zizania texana A. S. Hitchc. – Texas wild rice (122) (1937)

Zizaniopsis miliacea (Michx.) Doell & Aschers. – Giant cut grass [Giant cutgrass] (50) (present), Indian rice (45) (1896), Marsh millet (163) (1852), Prolific rice (66) (1903), Southern wild rice [Southern wildrice] (119, 122) (1913–1937), Water-millet [Water millet] (94, 119, 163) (1852–1938), Wild rice [Wildrice] (45) (1896), Zizaniopsis (5, 119) (1913–1938)

Zizia aptera (Gray) Fern. – Alexanders [Alexander] (19) (1840), Heartleaf alexanders [Heart-leaved alexanders] (5, 72, 131) (1899–1913), Meadow zizia (50) (present), Meadow-parsnip [Meadow parsnip, Meadowparsnip] (3, 85) (1932–1977)

Zizia aurea (L.) W. D. J. Koch – Early meadow-parsnip [Early meadow parsnip] (5, 156, 158) (1900–1923), Golden alexanders (3, 5, 156, 158) (1900–1977), Golden meadow-parsnip [Golden meadow parsnip] (5, 72, 93, 95, 97, 122, 131, 156, 158) (1899–1937), Golden zizia (50, 155) (1942–present), Meadow-parsnip [Meadow parsnip, Meadowparsnip] (19, 92) (1840–1876), Wild parsley [Wildparsley] (5, 92, 156, 158) (1876–1923)

Zizia bebbii (Coult. & Rose) Britton – See *Zizia trifoliata* (Michx.) Fern.

Zizia cordata (Walt.) DC. – See *Zizia aptera* (Gray) Fern.

Zizia trifoliata (Michx.) Fern. – Alexanders [Alexander] (5) (1913), Bebb's zizia (5) (1913), Golden alexanders (5, 156) (1913–1923), Meadow alexanders (50, 155) (1942–present)

Zizia W. D. J. Koch – Alexanders [Alexander] (1, 93, 158) (1900–1936), Golden alexanders (4) (1986), Meadow-parsnip [Meadow parsnip, Meadowparsnip] (1, 93) (1932–1936), Zizia (50, 155, 158) (1900–present)

Ziziphus jujuba Lam. – See *Ziziphus zizyphus* (L.) Karst.

Ziziphus obtusifolia (Hook. ex Torr. & Gray) Gray – Lotibush (158) (1900), Texas buckthorn (106) (1930)

Ziziphus obtusifolia (Hook. ex Torr. & Gray) Gray var. *obtusifolia* – Indian jujube [India jujube] (106) (1930), Lote (122, 124) (1937)

Ziziphus parryi Torr. – Lotophagi (76) (1896) San Diego Co. CA, Lotus tree [Lotus-tree] (76) (1896) San Diego Co. CA

Ziziphus sativa Gaertn. – See *Ziziphus zizyphus* (L.) Karst.

Ziziphus zizyphus (L.) Karst. – Chinese date (107) (1919), Common jujube (109, 110, 138) (1886–1949), Indian jujube [India jujube] (110) (1886), Jujube (76, 92, 107, 110, 158) (1876–1919), Large jujube (106, 112) (1930–1937), Masson (Mauritius) (110) (1886)

Zizyphus Mill – Jujube (13, 50, 109, 138, 155, 158) (1849–present), Lotibush (13) (1849), Lotus tree [Lotus-tree] (13) (1849), Supple-Jack [Supplejack, Supple jack, Supple jacks] (10) (1818)

Zizyphus sativa – See *Ziziphus zizyphus* (L.) Karst.

Zoisia japonica Steud. – See *Zoysia japonica* Steud.

Zoisia matrella Merr. – See *Zoysia matrella* (L.) Merr.

Zoisia tenuifolia Willd. – See *Zoysia tenuifolia* Willd. ex Thiele

Zornia bracteata (Walt.) Gmel. – Rabbit-ears [Rabbit ears] (124) (1937) TX, Zornia (5) (1913)

Zostera marina L. – Barnacle grass [Barnacle-grass] (5, 156) (1913–1923), Bellware [Bell ware] (5, 156) (1913–1923), Drew (5, 156) (1913–1923), Eel-grass [Eel grass, Eelgrass] (107, 156) (1913–1919), Grassweed [Grass-weed] (5, 10, 19, 156) (1818–1840), Grass-wrack [Grass wrack] (5, 107, 156) (1913–1919), Sea eelgrass [Sea eel grass] (19) (1840), Sea oar (177) (1762), Sea wrack [Seawrack, Sea-wrack] (5, 50, 156) (1913–present), Sea-grass [Sea grass] (5, 107, 156) (1913–1919), Sweet-grass [Sweet grass, Sweetgrass] (5, 156) (1913–1923), Tiresome weed (5, 73, 156) (1894–1923) Little Egg Harbor NJ, from obstruction it offers to the oars of boats, Turtle-grass [Turtle grass] (5, 92, 156) (1876–1923), Widgeongrass [Widgeongrass, Widgeon grass] (5, 156) (1913–1923), Wrack [Wracks] (5) (1913)

Zostera pacifica L. – See *Zostera marina* L.

Zosterella Small. – See *Heteranthera* Ruiz. & Pavon.

Zoysia japonica Steud. – Japanese lawn grass [Japanese lawn-grass, Japanese lawngrass] (109, 138) (1923–1949), Korean lawn grass [Korean lawn-grass] (109) (1949)

Zoysia matrella (L.) Merr. – Korean lawn grass [Korean lawn-grass] (94) (1901), Manila grass [Manila-grass] (109, 138) (1923–1949)

Zoysia pungens Willd. – See *Zoysia matrella* (L.) Merr.

Zoysia tenuifolia Willd. ex Thiele – Korean velvet grass [Korean velvet-grass] (109) (1949), Mascarene grass [Mascarene-grass] (109, 138, 163) (1852–1949), Velvet grass [Velvet-grass] (163) (1852)

Zygadenus chloranthus [Richardson] – possibly *Zigadenus elegans* Pursh subsp. *elegans*

Zygadenus elegans Pursh. – See *Zigadenus elegans* Pursh

Zygadenus intermedius [Rydb.] – See *Zigadenus venenosus* S. Wats. var. *gramineus* (Rydb.) Walsh ex M.E. Peck

Zygadenus nuttallii – See *Zigadenus nuttallii* (Gray) S. Wats.

Zygadenus venenosus S. Wats. – See *Zigadenus venenosus* S. Wats. var. *gramineus* (Rydb.) Walsh ex M. E. Peck

Zygadenus venenosus Wats. var. *gramineus* (Rydb.) Walsh – See *Zigadenus venenosus* S. Wats. var. *gramineus* (Rydb.) Walsh ex M. E. Peck

Zygophyllidium hexagonum (Nutt.) Small. – See *Euphorbia hexagona* Nutt. ex Spreng.

PL. 2.

MAIS.

Zea mays L.
(P. Naudin, 1865)

The University of Nebraska–Lincoln does not discriminate
based on gender, age, disability, race, color,
religion, marital status, veteran's status,
national or ethnic origin,
or sexual orientation.